New STANDARD TWENTY FIRST CENTURY DICTIONARY

URDU TO ENGLISH

Over 50,000 Words, Phrases and Proverbs
Used in Spoken and Literary Urdu with
Copious Graphic Illustrations

Compiled by
Prof. Bashir Ahmad Qureshi

With a foreword by
Prof. Gopi Chand Narang

Revised and enlarged by
Dr. Abdul Haq

NEW STANDARD TWENTY FIRST CENTURY DICTIONARY
Urdu to English

Compiled by
Prof. Bashir Ahmad Qureshi

With a foreword by
Prof. Gopi Chand Narang

Revised and enlarged by
Dr. Abdul Haq

FOREWORD

BY

Prof. Gopi Chand Narang
Head, Dept. of Urdu
&
Dean, Faculty of Humanities and Languages
Jamia Millia Islamia

The publication of the Standard Twentieth Century Dictionary : Urdu-English, compiled by Mr. Bashir Ahmad Qureshi will be welcomed by Urdu speakers and students in India. This dictionary is different from other dictionaries in the sense that it contains modern English renderings of over 50,000 phrases and words used in the present-day literary Urdu. This is perhaps the first dictionary which has appeared with illustrations. It is hoped that with the ensuing editions these will be further improved.

The art of lexicography as it is practised in some of the developed languages of the western and eastern hemisphere is a challenging one, and some excellent models have been produced in English, French, Russian, German, Japanese and other languages. The Urdu lexicography has to take many strides to catch up with the standards set by scholars of these languages. It should be recalled that the European orientalists like John Gilchrist, John Shakespeare, Duncan Forbes, S.W. Fallon and John Platts did some excellent work in the field of Urdu-English lexicography. Of these Forbes' and Fallon's work laid a sound foundation for John Platts' excellent comprehensive Dictionary of Urdu, Classical Hindi and English. A lot of lexical work went in the preparation of this dictionary, and so much care was taken to explore the Sanskritic, Prakritic, Arabo-Persian and Turkish sources of Urdu and Hindustani words, that later this monumental work became a rich source-material for scholars working on the etymological sources of the lexical terms. The next landmark was achieved by Baba-e-Urdu, Maulvi Abdul Haq, who inspired some of the leading scholars of the day like the late Dr. Abdus Sattar Siddiqui and the late Dr. Abid Husain to assist him in the preparation of the Standard English – Urdu Dictionary for which the Concise Oxford English-English Dictionary served as the model. This work, though it needs revision and updating, is still in vogue.

The present Standard Twentieth Century Dictionary gives the semantic equivalents extensively. It lists substantives and verbals separately and also discusses proverbs and idioms. The calligraphy is in *nastaliq* to ensure its extensive use. Though the phonological table does not follow the phonetic detail exhaustively, still it is fairly representative. There has been a shift in the pronunciation of words where 'h' is preceded or followed by a short vowel like

بہر مہر مُہر ، احترام احتشام ، زحمت رحمت ، - سہرا چہرہ ، یہ وہ ، بہنا سہنا

The pronunciation obviously involves lowering and fronting of short vowels like *zer, zabar and pesh* when preceding or following the 'h' sound. The compiler has done his best to indicate the current pronunciation of the Urdu words with the help of an elaborate system of transliteration.

The efforts of Mr. M.M. Khan, (Mr. India), proprietor, Educational Publishing House, Delhi, who is bringing out this Dictionary for the benefit of Urdu students and readers in this country, are commendable. I hope the Dictionary will serve the purpose for which it is being brought out.

(Prof.) Gopi Chand Narang

Jamia Millia Islamia
December 13, 1980

FOREWORD

By
Prof. Gopi Chand Narang
Head, Dept. of Urdu

[Faculty] of Humanities and Languages
Jamia Millia Islamia

The publication of the Standard Twentieth Century Dictionary: Urdu-English compiled by Mr. Bashir Ahmad Qureshi will be welcomed by Urdu speakers and students of India. This dictionary differs from other dictionaries in the sense that it contains modern English renderings of over 50,000 phrases and words used in the present-day literary Urdu. This is perhaps the first dictionary which has appeared with illustrations. It is hoped that with the coming editions there will be further improved.

The art of lexicography as it is practised in some of the developed languages of the western and eastern hemisphere is a challenging one and some excellent models have been produced in English, French, Russian, German, Japanese and other languages. The Urdu lexicography has to take many strides to catch up with the standards set by scholars of these languages. It should be recalled that the European orientalists like John Gilchrist, John Shakespeare, Duncan Forbes, S. W. Fallon and John Platts did some excellent work in the field of Urdu-English lexicography. Gilchrist, Forbes and Fallon's work laid a sound foundation for John Platts' excellent comprehensive Dictionary of Urdu, Classical Hindi and English. A lot of lexical work went in the preparation of this dictionary and so much care was taken to explore the Sanskrit, Prakrit, Arabic, Persian and Turkish sources of Urdu and Hindustani words, that later this monumental work became a rich source material for scholars working on the etymological sources of the Urdu language. The same tradition was followed by Baba-e-Urdu, Moulvi Abdul Haq who inspired some of the leading scholars of the time like the late Dr. Abdus Sattar Siddiqui and the late Dr. Abid Hussain to assist him in the preparation of the Standard English-Urdu Dictionary for which the Concise Oxford English Dictionary served as the model. This work though it needs revision and updating is still invaluable.

The present Standard Twentieth Century Dictionary gives the semantic equivalents in English of the substantives and verbs separately and also discusses proverbs and idioms. The calligraphy is in nastaliq as [illegible]. Though the phonological table does not follow the phonetic [illegible] exhaustively, still it is fairly representative. There has been a shift in the pronunciation of words where 'h' is preceded or followed by a short vowel like

[illegible] The pronunciation [illegible] like [illegible] when preceding or following the 'h' sound. The compiler has tried his best to indicate the correct pronunciation of the Urdu words with the help of [illegible] transliteration.

The efforts of Mr. M. M. Khan (M/s. [illegible] Educational Publishing House, Delhi) who is bringing out this Dictionary for the benefit of Urdu students and readers in this country are commendable. I hope this Dictionary will serve the purpose for which it is intended [illegible].

Jamia Millia Islamia — Prof. Gopi Chand Narang
December 15, [illegible]

FOREWORD

BY

Dr. S.M. Abdullah, M.A.,D. Litt.

General Secretary, West Pakistan Urdu Academy; Chairman, Department of Urdu Encyclopaedia, University of the Punjab; Formerly Principal and Head of the Deparment of Urdu, University Oriental College, Lahore.

The present Standard Urdu-English Dictionary compiled by Prof. Bashir Ahmad Qureshi is decidedly an advance on the previous lexicographical works of this nature. The author has already won fame and distinction by producing an equally valuable English-Urdu Dictionary which is perhaps; the best practical reference book in its own field.

In the present dictionary, the author has taken great pains to indicate accent. He has also endeavoured to guide the reader in exact pronunciation. For instance, we find highly accurate transliteration of some extremely difficult phonetic complexities, rendered intelligible to an ordinary reader—especially thc foreign reader—by means of a well-thought-out system. Some such words as احترام and احتراز are often difficult to be pronounced correctly by a foreign learner because in the original language (*i.e.*, Arabic), the first *alif* is مکسور whereas in Urdu, in spite of its being مکسور it is pronounced somewhat differently, with the result that in the interest of accuracy the author had to transliterate these, as *eh tiram* and *ehtiraz,* instead of *ihtiram* and *ihtiraz* which do not correspond with the spoken form.

Similarly, we have the Persian word شہر which is neither شَہر nor شِہر but midway between the two forms—and it was extremely difficult for the compiler to reproduce it in its pure accuracy except as *shaih'r*. This secms to be correct because, the common transliteration *shehr* too is not in correspondence with the spoken form.

These instances would amply indicate the intricacies of the problems facing the author of this dictionary.

Prof. Bashir Ahmad Qureshi has incorporated quite a large number of new words drawn form English and other foreign languages. These words now form a part of the Urdu language and deserve a place in such a compilation. The number of such words is larger in this dictionary than in any other compilation of the same nature.

In my opinion, the present work is a great achievement and will be found extremely helpful in spreading the Urdu language in the English-speaking countries. It would also be of great help to all those, in Pakistan as well as abroad, who are called upon to undertake the work of translation from Urdu into English.

West Pakistan Urdu Academy, S. M. Abdullah
Lahore.

PREFACE

The cultural - cum - national language of the Islamic State of Pakistan has long deserved a much less shabby lexicographic treatment than a mere-reprint of Platts' outdated dictionary (issued recently) or a plethora of publications based on it. This is the *raison d'etre* of Kitabistan's 20th-Century Standard Urdu-English Dictionary now being offered to the public.

This is a dictionary with a difference in that it makes a truly linguistic approach to Urdu lexicography. It comprises well over half a lakh words, phrases and proverbs one most frequently comes across in one's contact with people or literature today. These are explained in various nuances and their modern English renderings are set out in all accuracy. All this makes the present compilation profitable for the common reader, illuminating for the foreign learner and indispensable for the student who is called upon to translate passages into English as an essential part of the examinatons.

The transliteration system adopted for indicating the pronunciation of Urdu words in this dictionary is based on principles which are by and larg accepted by modern Orientalists. It has the added advantage of being akin to the Roman Urdu script used for army education in this sub-continent over the past few generations.

A special feature of this work is the indication of accent in the pronunciation of Urdu words. This is not just an innovation. The attempt was first made by Dr. Fallon and his talented team, in New Hindustani-English Dictionary but has been overlooked by compilers ever since, resulting in ludicrous phonetic errors by foreign speakers of the language. The present work which owes a lot to that epoch-making lexicon as well as to *Farhang-i-Asafiyyah* and *Nur-ul-Lughat,* revives the unique feature in addition to presenting many new ones.

Preference in vocabulary, idiom and pronunciation in this compilation is given mainly to the Western dialect of Urdu which is cognate with the various regional languages of the sub-continent.

A word about etymological notes on various entries in this dictionary. For headwords of Arabic origin, the Urdu form closest to the Arabic root is given as being more serviceable and revealing to the ordinary student of Urdu than the Arabic root itself. English derivatives are not traced further beyond, save when of special interest. Other languages of origin are indicated at relevant places. Where, however, the derivation is not given, the word must be considered to be purely Urdu in origin.

The unprecedented reception accorded to this compilation has now encouraged the publisher to bring out this edition on photo blocks with the Urdu entries in *nasta'liq* script rather than *naskh* type. That should serve to make it still more presentable.

Bashir A 'Qureshi'

ABBREVIATIONS

Following abbreviations have been used in this book :

A	Arabic	Math	mathematics
ABB.	abbreviation	N.	noun
&	and	nurs.	nursery
arch.	archaic	OCC.	occasionally
CAUS.	causative	ONO.	onomatopoeic
col.	colloquial	OPP.	opposite
COZJ.	conjunction	**P**	Persian
CONT.	contraction	PH.	phrase
CORR.	corruption	PL.	plural
deprec.	deprecatory	**Por.**	Portuguese
derog.	derogatory	pr.	pronounced
dial.	dialect	PREC	preceding
dim.	diminutive	PREF.	prefix
E	English	PRON.	pronoun
euph.	euphemism	PROV.	proverb
F.	feminine	**R**	Russian
fig.	figurative	rare.	rare(ly)
FOL.	following	**S**	Sanskrit
G	Greek	SING.	singular
H	Hebrew	SUF.	suffix
H.	Hindu	**T.**	Turkish/Tartar
I.	intransitive	T.	transitive
IMP.	imperative	usu.	usual(ly),
INT.	interjection	V.	verb
iron.	ironical	W.	women's
joc.	jocose	★	**which please look up**
lit.	literary	∽	derived from
M.	masculine		

PRONUNCIATION & TRANSLITERATION

Pronunciation has been indicated by the following transliteration symbols :

Vowels

	a	ٹ	*ṭ*	ش	*sh*	ں	*ṅ*
ِ	*i*	ث	*s*	ص	*s*	و	*v*
و	*ū*	ج	*j*	ض	*z*	ہ	*h*
آ	*ā*	چ	*ch*	ط	*t*	ء	*'*
اے	*e*	ح	*h*	ظ	*z*	ی	
آے	*ai*	خ	*kh*	ع	*'*	ھ (یعنی ہائے مخلوط التلفظ)	*h*
ای	*ī*	د	*d*	غ	*gh*		
او	*o*	ڈ	*ḍ*	ف	*f*		
اُو	*oo*	ذ	*z*	ق	*q*		
اَو	*au*	ر	*r*	ک	*k*		
Consonants :		ڑ	*ṛ*	گ	*g*		
ب	*b*	ز	*z*	ل	*l*		
پ	*p*	ژ	*zh*	م	*m*		
ت	*t*	س	*s*	ن	*n*		

Accent :
The minute sign (') is placed immediately after every stressed syllable to denote accent.

NOTE : **The various letters have been given their Urdu (as distinct from Arabic) sound values.**

STANDARD 21st CENTURY DICTIONARY

URDU INTO ENGLISH

ا a'lif VOWEL. first letter of Urdu alphabet (equivalent to English a) initially used as carrier for another alif or mad, as ا , آ ā , for zabar, as اَ a , for zer, as اِ i ; for pesh as اُ ū medially and finally used to indicate ā ◐ (in jummal reckoning) 1 ; one.

آ ā VOWEL (called a'lif-e mamdoo'dah) represents ā V.I. (IMP. of آنا V.I. ★)

۲آ ā INT. sound uttered for modulating voice in vocal music or recitation آآ ā'ā INT.

آب ab N.M. (rare) water N.F. polish lustre or water (of gems) temper (of steel) edge or sharpness (of sword, etc.) splendour ; elegence dignity ; honour آب آب کرنا ā'b ā'b kar'nā V.T put to shame آب آب ہونا a'b ab ho'nā V.I. blush be thoroughly ashamed آبِ آتشیں āb-e ā'tash rang, آبِ آتش رنگ āb-e ātashīn' N.M. wine آب آمد تیمم برخاست āb ā'mad tayam'mūm barkhāst' PH. lesser things make room for greater ones آب آجانا āb ā jā'nā V.T. shine get polished آبِ آہن تاب āb-e ā'han tāb N.M. water in which steel is tempered آبِ آئینہ āb-e ā'i'nah N.F., آب اترنا ā'b ūtar'nā V.T. lose lustre or polish ; fade lose honour آبِ ارغوانی āb-e arghavā'nī N.M. (fig.) wine آبِ استادہ āb-e istā'dah N.M. still water stagnant waters آبِ بقا āb-e baqā' N.M. nectar water of life آبِ احمر ā-be ah mar N.M. (fig.) wine آبِ انگور āb-e angoor' N.M. wine آبِ انفعال āb-e infe'āl' N.M. sweat caused by shame, bashfulness or remorse آبِ باراں āb-e bā'rān N.M rain-water آبِ بستہ āb-e bas'tah N.M. (lit.) ice, frozen water آب بگڑنا a'b bigar'na V.I. loose lustre be disgraced آب پاش āb-pāsh N.M. (rare) watering can آب پاشی āb-pā'shī (arch.) N.F. irrigation آب پاشی کرنا āb-pā'shī kar'na V.T. water irrigate (land) کی آب پاشی ہونا kī āb-pā'shī ho'nā V.I. be watered : be irrigated آب تاب āb tāb' N.F. (col.) splendour lustre آبِ تلخ āb-e tal'kh N.M. (fig.) tears wine آبِ جاری āb-e jā'rī N.M. running water rivulet آبجو āb'-joo N.F streamlet , runnel آب جوش āb-josh N.M. (arch.) soup آب چڑھانا ab charhā'na V.T. burnish polish آبِ چشم āb-e chash'm N.M. tears آبِ حرام āb-e harām N.M. wine ; liquor آبِ حسرت āb-e has'rat N.M. wistfulness remorse آبِ حیات āb-e hayāt' ; آبِ حیواں āb-e hai'vāh (ped. -hā'yavān') N.M. name of a fabulous spring water of life ; water of immortality ; nectar آبِ خاصہ āb-e khās'sah N.M. (arch.) drinking water set apart for royalty, etc. آب خانہ āb-khā'nah N.M water repository آبِ خجالت āb-e khijā'lat N.F sweat caused by shame, bashfulness or remorse آبخورہ āb'khorah N.M. earthenware cup آبخورے بھرنا āb'khore bhar'na V.T fill earthenware cups with cold drink as an offering , make an offering of cold drinks آب خیز āb'-khez N.M. & ADJ. (land) with high water-table آبدار āb'dār N.M. butler one in c. arge of drinking water ADJ. lustrous , polished ; burnished (of gem) of high water ; lustrous well-tempered (steel) sharp (sword) آبدار خانہ āb'dār khā'nah N.M. repository of drinking water cellar آب و دانہ āb dā'nah N.M (col.) job employment means of subsistance lot destiny آبدست āb'-dast N.M. water for washing anus and hands after evacuation laving water آبدست لینا āb'-dast le'nā V.I. wash one's anus , lave آبِ دنداں āb-e dan'dān N.M lustre or polish of teeth آب دہن *āb-e dahan'* N.M. saliva آبدیدہ *āb-dī'dah* ADJ. tearful ADV in tears ; weeping آبدیدہ ہونا *āb-dī'dah ho'nā* V.I. be in tears ; shed tears , have tears in the eyes آبدیدہ کرنا *āb-dīdah kar'nā* V.T bring tears to (someone's) eyes ; cause (someone) to weep آب دینا *āb de'nā* V.I. temper (steel) burnish polish آب رحمت *āb-e raih'mat* N.M. (fig.) rain; much-needed rain salvation ; deliverance ; divine mercy آبریز *āb-rez'* N.F spoon for pouring water into inkpot place where water falls آب رواں *āb-e ravā'n* N.M. running water (arch.) lawn ; fine muslin آب زر *āb-e zar'* N.M gold water , liquid gold آب زر سے لکھنے کے قابل *āb-e zar' se likh'ne ke qā'bil* PH. golden آب زلال *āb-e zulāl'* N.M. pure clear water آب زمزم *āb-e zam' zam* N M water of the sacred Meccan well, Zam Zam آبزن *āb'-zan* N.M medicinal bath آبزن کرنا *āb'-zan kar'nā* V.T give (someone) medicinal bath آب شور *āb-e shor'* N.M. salt water sea water آب عشرت *āb-e 'ish'rat* N.M. (fig.) wine آبکش *āb -kash* N.M. (arch.) water-carrier drawer of water آب کوثر *āb-e kau'sar* N.M. water of the heavenly river, Kausar ; nectar ; water of life آبگزر *āb-guzar'* N.M (rare) watercourse آب گرم *āb-e gar'm* N.M. hot water warm water آب گلگوں *āb-e gulgoon'* N.M. (fig.) red wine آب گوشت *āb-e gosh't* N.M (rare) soup gravy آبگوں *āb'-goon* ADJ azure burnished آبگیر *āb-gīr'* N.M. (arch.) reservoir آبگیں *āb'-gīn* ADJ. (of eyes) watery , tearful آب مقطر *āb-e-muqat'tar* N.M. distilled water آب ندامت *āb-e nadā'mat* N.M. sweat caused by shame or remorse آب ندیدہ موزہ کشیدہ *āb na-dī'dah mau'zah kashī'dah* PH. too scrupulous over-cautious آب نقرہ *āb-i-nuq'rah* N.M. quicksilver , mercury آب نے *āb-nai'* N.F. bowl pipe of hookah آب و تاب *āb-o tāb* , (col. آب تاب *āb tāb'*) N.F splendour lustre آب و خور *ā'b-o-khūr* N.M. food and drink آب وخور حرام ہونا *ā'b-o-khūr harām' ho'nā* V.I. be greatly worried be too preoccupied آب و دانہ *āb-o dā'nah* (col. آب دانہ *āb dā'nah*) N.M. job means of subsistence lot آب و دانہ اٹھنا *āb-o-dā'nah uṭh'na* V.I. (of means livelihood) end be transferred (from a place) be about to die آب و دانے کا زور *āb-o dā'ne kā zor'* PH. fate , drift of circumstances آب و دانے کا زور ہونا *āb-o-dā'ne kā zor ho'nā* V.I. be driven by fate or by means of livelihood آب و رنگ *āb-o-rang* N.M. lustre, freshness or vitality (of face, etc.) آب و گل *āb-o-gil'* N.M. nature (of man, etc.) human body matter (rare) mud slush آب و ہوا *āb-o-havā'* N.F. climate آب و ہوا بدلنا (یا تبدیل کرنا) *āb-o-havā' badal'nā* (or *tabdīl' kar'nā*) V.I. have a change of climate go to a health resort آب و ہوا راس (یا موافق) (نہ) آنا *āb-o-havā' rās'* (or *mo'ā'-fiq*) (*na*) *ā'nā* V.I (of climate) (not) to agree آبی *ā'bī* ADJ. آبیاری *āb-yā'rī* N.F. watering ; irrigation آبیاری کرنا *āb-yā rī kar'nā* V.T. water , irrigate [P]

آبا *ābā'* N.M. PL. ancestors ; forefathers آباؤ اجداد *ābā''-o-ajdād'* N.M. PL. ancestors family lineage ; ancestry آبائے شہر *ābā'-e shah'r* N.M. city fathers آبائے علوی *ābā'e' ūl'vī* N.M PL (fig.) seven planets ; planets of the solar system آبائی *ābā''ī* ADJ. paternal ancestral hereditary [A ~ SING. اب father]

آباد *ābād'* ADJ. populated (area) cultivated (land) thriving, prosperous happy SUF borough ; colony , town آبادکار *ābād'-kār* N.M. settler ; colonizer pioneer colonialist cultivator ; one cultivating uncommanded land آبادکاری *ābād-kā'rī* N F colonization settlement , rehabilitation نظام آبادکاری *nizā'm-e ābād'kā'rī* N.M. colonialism colonial system آباد رہنا *ābād' raih'nā* V.I. continue to prosper ; thrive آباد کرنا *ābād kar'nā* V.T. settle ; colonize make (place) habitable populate bring uncommanded land under the plough گھر آباد کرنا *ghar ābād' kar'nā* V.T. get married marry آباد ہونا *ābād' ho'nā* V.I. prosper be colonized live happily with husband آبادانی *ābādā'nī* N.F. (arch.) being inhabited prosperity آبادی *ābā'dī* N.F. population inhabitants (of an area) habitation prosperity آبادیات *ābādiyyāt* N.F. demography آبادیاتی *ābādiyyā'tī* ADJ. demographic [P]

آبرو *āb'roo* N.F. honour prestige character fame آبرو اتارنا (یا بگاڑنا یا لینا) *āb'-roo ūtār'nā* (or *bigār'nā* or *le'nā*) disgrace ; defame ; dishonour rape ; ravish ; violate the chastity (of) آبرو بچانا *āb'roo bachā'nā* V.T. & I. safeguard (one's or someone's) honour آبرو بخشنا *āb'roo bakhsh'nā* V T. confer honour (on) honour آبرو خاک میں ملانا *āb'roo khāk men milā'nā* V.T. disgrace defame ;

slander ruin (someone's) character آبرو خاک میں ملنا *āb'roo khak meṅ mil'nā* V.I. be disgraced have one's character ruined آبرو بڑھنا *āb'roo baṛh'nā* V.I. (of someone) have greater honour : gain more honour آبرو بنانا *āb'roo banā'na* V.I. build up (one's) prestige earn a good name for (oneself) آبرو پر حرف آنا *ab'roo par ḥar'f ā'na,* آبرو میں بٹا لگنا *āb'roo meṅ baṭ'ṭa lag'nā* V.I. be disgraced آبرو رکھنا *āb'roo rakh'na* V.I. have honour; enjoy reputation آبرو ریزی *āb'roo re'zī* N.F. disgrace humiliation slander ; calumny rape آبرو ریزی کرنا *āb'roo re'zī kar'na* V.T. disgrace humiliate slander rape آبرو کا لاگو ہونا *āb'roo kā lā'goo ho'nā* V.I. try to ruin (someone's) character آبرو کھونا *ab'roo kho'nā* V.I. lose one's reputation آبرو کے پیچھے پڑنا *āb'roo ke pīchhe par'na* V.T. try to ruin (someone's) character آبرو جگ میں رہے تو بادشاہی جانیے *āb'roo jag meṅ ra'he to bādshā'hī jā'niye* PROV. one has everything if one's honour is retrieved آبرومند *ābroomand'* ADJ. respectable آبرومندانہ *ābrooman-dā'nah* ADJ. honourable ADV. honourably آبرومندی *ābrooman'dī* N.F. honour respectability [P ~ آب water + رو face]

آبپاشی *āb-pā'shī* N.F., آبیاری *āb-yā'rī* N.F. [see under آب N.M. ★]

آبدوز *āb'doz'* N.F., ADJ. submarine آبدوز کشتی *āb-doz' kash'tī* N.F. submarine [P ~ آب + دوختن stitch ; pierce]

آبستنی *ābas'tanī* ADJ. (lit.) pregnant (with) [P]

آبشار *āb-shār'* N.F. (ped. M.) waterfall ; cataract ; cascade [P ~ آب + شار]

آبکاری *āb-kā'rī* N.F. excise excise duty distillery محکمۂ آبکاری *maiḥ'kama-e āb-kā'rī* N.M. Excise department [P ~ آب + کاری]

آبگینہ *āb'gī'nah* N.M. glass crystal goblet winecup ; winebowl ; wineglass [P ~ آب + گینہ]

آبلہ *āb'lah* N.M. blister آبلہ پا *āb'la pa* ADJ. having blisters on the feet (fig.) tired ; exhausted آبلہ پائی *ā'bla pa''ī* N.F. (fig.) fatigue ; exhaustion آبلہ رو *āb'la roo* ADJ. & N.M. pock-marked (person) آبلہ روئی *āb'la roo''ī* N.F. being pock-marked [P]

آبنا *āb-nā'* N.F straits آبنائے باسفورس *āb-nā''-e basfo'ras* N.F. Bosphrus Straits [P آب + نائے pipe]

آبنوس *ābnoos'* N.M. ebony آبنوس کا کندہ *ābnoos' ka kun'dah* N.F. (joc.) fat dark person آبنوسی *ābnoo'sī* ADJ. ebony ; made of ebony black [P]

آبی *ā'bī* ADJ. aquatic ; water marine moist light blue bread made from meal kneaded in water in place of milk ; bun آبی برج *ā'bī būr'j* N.M. PL. Cancer, Scorpio and Pisces as three signs of zodiac supposed to be watery in nature آبی حرف *ā'bī ḥar'f* N.F. letter(s) ذ ر ج ش ک ق ظ س supposed to be watery in nature [P ~ آب]

آبیانہ *ābyā'na* N.M. water cess ; charges for supply of irrigational water [~ P]

آپ *āp* PRON. (polite for) you self selves yourself آپ آپ *āp āp* N.M. sycophancy آپ آپ کرنا *ā'p ā'p kar'na* V.I. flatter ; fawn upon آپ آئے بھاگ آئے *ā'p ā''e bhā'g ā''e* PH. most welcome you bring us good fortune آپ اپنے پاؤں پر کلہاڑی مارنا *ā'p apne pā''oṅ par kūlhā'ṛī mār'nā,* آپ اپنی قبر کھودنا *ā'p apni qab'r khod'nā* PROV. dig one's own grave آپ اچھے جہان اچھا *āp' achchhe jahān' ach'chha,* آپ بھلے تو جگ بھلا *āp' bhā'le to jag' bha'la* PROV. good mind good find آپ بھاتی *āp' bhā'tī* ADV. (rare) according to one's own pleasure آپ بیتی *āp' bī'tī* autobiography story of one's own suffering آپ جانیں آپ کا کام (جانے) *āp' ja'neṅ āp' ka kam' (jā'ne)* PH you do as you like that's none of my business آپ خورادے آپ مرادے *āp' khūrā'de āp' mūrā'de* PH. (W. dial.) selfish (person) (one) posing to be happy despite poverty آپ ڈال ڈال میں پات پات *ap ḍal' ḍal' mai'ṅ pat' pat* PH. I am more than a match for you in cleverness آپ ڈوبے تو جگ ڈوبا *ap ḍoo'be to jag' ḍoo'ba,* آپ زندہ جہان زندہ آپ مردہ جہان مردہ *āp' zin'dah jahān' zin'dah āp' mūr'dah jahān' mūr'dah,* آپ موئے تو جگ موا *āp' mū'e to jag mū'a* PROV. death's day is doomsday آپ سے *āp' se* PH. from you of you ADV. by itself ; by oneself آپ سے آپ *āp' se āp* ADV. by itself of its own accord voluntarily spontaneously unsolicited alone آپ سے اپے ہونا *āp' se a'be ho'nā* PH. be debased آپ سے گزر جانا *āp se gū'zar jā'na* V.I. renounce oneself (of someone) be no longer of use to anyone آپ کا بایاں قدم لیجیے *āp ka bā'yaṅ qa'dam lī'jiye* PH (iron.) he is a pastmaster in fraudulence آپ کاج مہا کاج *āp' kaj ma'hā kaj* PROV. self-done is well done آپ کا کیا بگڑتا ہے *āp' ka kyā' bigaṛ'ta hai* PH. you don't stand to lose آپ کا پاس (یا ملاحظہ یا منہ) ہے *āp' ka pās' (or mūla'ḥaza or mūṅh) hai* PH. it is only for your sake ; it is just out of respect (or regard) for you

آپ کا (اپنا) گھر ہے *ap'. ka (ap'na) ghar' hai* PH. feel yourself at perfect ease in my house آپ کو *ap' ko* PRON. oneself to you آپ کو آسماں پر کھینچنا *ap' ko asman par khenkh'na* V.I. give oneself airs; put on airs آپ کو بھول جانا *ap' ko bhool' ja'na* V.I. forget one's humble beginnings آپ کو پانا *ap' ko pa'na* V.T. make a correct appraisal of oneself آپ کو دور کھینچنا *ap' ko door' khench'na* V.T. keep oneself aloof (from someone) through pride, (etc.) آپ کو ڈبونا *ap' ko dabo'na* V.T. ruin oneself آپ کو کھونا (یا کھو آنا) *ap ko kho'na* (or *kho a'na* lose oneself (in) (fig.) become oblivious of oneself آپ کھائے بلی کو بتائے *ap' kha''e bil'li ko bata''e* PH. lay own blame at another's door; shift blame to escape censure آپ کے ہاں (یا یہاں) *ap' ke han* (or *ya'han*) ADV. at your place in your milieu آپ میاں صوبیدار گھر میں بیوی جھونکے بھاڑ *ap' miyan soo'bedar, ghar men bi'vi jhon'ke bhar* PROV. one putting on airs with penury prevailing at home آپ میاں منگتا (یا ننگے) باہر کھڑے درویش *ap' miyan mang'ta* (or *nan'ge*) *ba'har kha're darvesh'* PROV. what help can a penurious person render the needy آپ ہارے بلی کو مارے *ap ha're bil'li ko ma're* PH. a bad workman quarrel with his tools making a scapegoat of someone آپ ہی آپ *ap' hi ap'* ADV. all alone all by oneself by itself spontaneously آپ ہی کی جوتیوں کا صدقہ ہے *ap' hi ki joo'tiyon ka sad'qah hai* PH. it is all due to you (or your training, etc.) thanks to you آپ ہی مارے آپ ہی چلائے *ap' hi ma're ap hi chilla''e* PROV. culprit pretending innocence آپی *a'pi* PRON. (also آپی آپ *a'pi ap'*) by himself (etc.) [آپ + ہی]

¹ آپا *a'pa* N.F. elder sister آٹے کی آپا *a'te ki a'pa* N.F. simple woman simpleton

² آپا *a'pa* N.M. self one's senses; self-control آپا دھاپی *a'pa dha'pi* N.F. selfish scramble آپا سنبھالنا *a'pa sanbhal'na* V.I. come to (one's) senses آپے سے باہر ہونا *a'pe se ba'har ho'na* V.I. be beside oneself (with rage); fly into a passion be in ecstacy آپے میں آنا *a'pe men a'na* V.I. come to one's senses آپے میں ہونا *a'pe men ho'na* V.I. be in one's senses.

آپس *a'pas* N.F. mutuality (used only as :) آپسداری *a'pas da'ri* N.F. brotherhood relations آپس کا *a'pas ka* ADJ. mutual internal آپس کا معاملہ *a'pas ka mu'amalah* PH. (our) private affair; (our) internal affair آپس میں *a'pas men* ADV mutually privately between ourselves between friends together آپس میں رہنا *a pas men raih na* V.I. live together (peacefully, etc.) آپسی *a'pasi* ADJ. (rare) mutual [آپ ~]

آپی *a pi* PRON. (CONT. of آپ ہی) (see under PRON. ★)

آتش *a'tash* (pop. *a'tish*) N.F. fire; conflagration anger; rage; passion firebrand آتش افزارہ *atash-afza'rah* N.M. (arch.) rocket آتش افروز *atash-afroz'* ADJ. kindling seditious N.M. fuel incendiary mischief-monger آتش افگن *atash-af'gan*, آتش انداز *atash-andaz'* ADJ. fire-spitting N.M. spitfire آتش انگیز *atash-angez'* ADJ. incendiary stirring up fire seditious آتشبار *atash-bar'* ADJ. raining fire fiery N.M. (arch.), musket tinder-box آتشباز *a'tash-baz* N.M. fireworks exhibitor or manufacturer; pyrotechnist آتشبازی *atash-ba'zi* N.F. fireworks; pyrotechnics آتش بیان *a'tash-bayan'* ADJ. fiery (speaker) آتش بیانی *a'tash-ba ya'ni* N.F. being a fiery speaker آتش بے دود *a'tash-e be-dood'* N.F. (fig.) wine sun rage آتش پارہ *atash-pa'rah* N.M. spark (fig.) beauty (fig.) provoker of quarrels ADJ. quarrelsome آتش پرست *atash-parast'* N.M. fireworshipper; Guebre; Magus; Zoroastrian آتش پرستی *atash-paras'ti* N.F. fireworship آتش پیکار *a'tash-pai kar* N.M. creature of fiery region sun آتش پیما *a'tash-paima'* N.M. pyrometer آتش تر *a'tash-e tar'* N.F. (fig.) wine lips of a pretty woman آتش چرخ *a'tash-e charkh'* N.F. (rare) aurora آتش خاموش *atash-e khamosh'* V.T. extinguished fire (fig.) dormant passion آتش خانہ *atash-kha'nah* N.M. (arch.) fire temple fireplace powder-magazine آتش خو *a'tash-khoo* ADJ. fiery آتش خوار *atash-khar* N.M. fire-eater red-legged partridge آتشدان *atash-dan'* N.M. fireplace hearth آتش رخ *a'tash-rukh* ADJ. rosy-cheeked آتش ریز *a'tash-rez'* ADJ. fire-spitting incendiary quarrel-inciting آتش زبان *a'tash-zaban'* ADJ. fiery (speaker) آتشزدگی *a'tash-za'dagi* N.F. fire; conflagration آتش زدہ *a'tash-zadah* ADJ. burnt out gutted آتش زن *a'tash-zan'* N.M. one committing arson (arch.) touchwood آتشزنی *a'tash-za'ni* N.F arson آتش زیر پا *a'tash ze'r-e pa'* ADJ. restless آتش سیال *a'tash-e sayyal'* N.F (fig.) wine آتش شوق

آتشِ اشتیاق ā'tash-e-shauq' (or ishtiyāq') N.F. strong desire (to meet, etc.) passion آتش طبع ā'tash-tab'' ADJ. hot-tempered ; irascible passionate آتش فشاں ā'tash-fishāñ' ADJ fire-spitting N M (also آتش فشاں پہاڑ ā'tash-fishāñ' pahār') volcano آتش فشانی ā'tash-fishā'nī N.F. raining fire being a firebrand آتش کا پرکالہ ā'tash kā par kā'lah N.M. beauty ; beautiful woman too clever person آتشکدہ ā'tash-kadah N M. fire-temple (fig.) very hot place ADJ scorching gruelling آتشگیر ā'tash-gīr ADJ combustible N.M (arch.) pair of tongs آتشگیر مادہ ā'tash-gīr mād'dah N.M. combustible matter آتش مزاج ā'tash-mizāj' ADJ. fiery ill-tempered آتش مزاجی ā'tash-mizā'jī N.F. irascibility آتشناک ātash-nāk' ADJ fiery آتشناکی ātash-nā'kī N.F. being fiery آتش نفس ātash-e-nafs' N.F. (fig.) lust آتش نمرود ātash-e namrood' N.F Nimrod's pyre (lighted in bid to burn Abraham) آتش نوا ā'tash-navā ADJ. fiery (speaker, singer etc.) آتش نوائی ā'tash-navā''ī N.F being a fiery speaker (etc.) آتشی ā'tashī ADJ. of fire fiery hot irascible burning (glass) آتشی شیشہ ā'tashī shī'shah N.M. convex lens ; burning glass آتشی عینک ā'tashī'ai'nak N.M. (arch.) convex lens set in ring آتشیں ātashīñ' ADJ. of or like fire incendiary آتشیں اسلحہ ā'tashīñ as'lehah (ped. آتشی اسلحہ ā'tashī as'lehah N.M. PL. firearms آتشیں خو ātashīñ khoo' ADJ. passionate irascible [P]

آتشک āt'shak (ped. ā'tashak) N.F. syphilis آتشکیا āt'shakyā N.F. (col.) syphilitic [P ~ آتش]

آتما āt'mā N.F. (H. dial.) soul life [S]

آتو ā'too,, آتون ātoon' N.F (arch.) female teacher ; governess [T].

آٹا ā'ṭā N.M flour ; meal آٹا کرنا ā'ṭā kar'nā V.T reduce to powder ; pulverize مفلسی میں آٹا گیلا ہونا muf'lisī meñ ā'ṭā gī'lā ho'nā PH. be in trouble be despondent آٹے دال کا بھاؤ بتانا ā'ṭe dāl kā bhā''o batā'nā V.T take to task آٹے دال کا بھاؤ معلوم ہو جانا ā'ṭe dāl kā bhā''o ma'loom' ho jā'nā V.I. get into hot water آٹے دال کی فکر ā'ṭe dāl' kī fik'r PH. worry for bare necessities of life آٹے کا کارخانہ ā'ṭe kā kārkhā'na N.M flour mill آٹے کی آپا āt'e kī ā'pā N.M. (see under آپا N.F.★) ā'ṭe kī bil'lī N.F. apparent and not real danger آٹے میں نمک (یا نون) ā'ṭe meñ na'mak (or noon) PH just a pinch very little stuff آٹے میں نمک کے برابر ā'ṭe meñ na'mak ke barā'bar ADJ & ADV little not much

آٹم پاٹم ā'ṭam pā'ṭam ADV scattered all over

آٹھ āṭh N. & ADJ eight آٹھ آٹھ آنسو رونا ā'ṭh āṭh añ'soo ro'nā V.I. shed a flood of tears ; weep bitterly آٹھ آٹھ آنسو رلانا ā'ṭh āṭh añsoo rūlā'nā V.I. cause to weep bitterly آٹھ اٹھارہ اٹھائیس āṭh aṭṭhā'rah aṭṭhā''īs PH. eighth, eighteenth, twenty-eighth (as 'inauspicious' dates of the month) آٹھ بار نو تہوار āṭh bār' nau tehvār' PROV. too frequent revelry آٹھ پہر āṭh paihar' آٹھوں پہر ā'ṭhoñ paihar' ADV. day and night all the time ; constantly all the twenty-four hours آٹھ (یا آٹھوں) پہر سولی پر رہنا ā'ṭh (or ā'ṭhoñ paihar' soo'lī par raih'nā V.I. be in constant trouble , suffer unmitigated trouble آٹھ کونیا āṭh ko'niyā ADJ. (col.) octagonal آٹھ کھمبا āṭh khambā N.M. (arch.) eight-pillared canopy آٹھ گھنٹے کا دن āṭh ghañ'ṭe kā din PH. eight hour working day آٹھ ماسا āṭh mā'sā اٹھوانسا aṭhvāñ'sā ADJ. (child) born after eight months ; premature child field continually ploughed for eight months for sugar-cane آٹھواں āṭh'vāñ ADJ. eight آٹھوں کا میلہ āṭhoñ kā me'lah N.M. (dial.) post-'Holi' festival ; Lucknow festival celebrated on eighth day after 'Holi' آٹھ (یا آٹھوں) گانٹھ کمیت (یا کمید) āṭh (or ā'ṭhoñ) gāñṭh kūmait' (or kūmaid') PH. horse with all the eight leg-joints strong (fig.) shrewd veteran.

آثار[1] āsār' N.M. PL. signs ; symptoms tokens traces footprints vestiges remains relics effects ; impressions bases Traditions of the Holy Prophet breadth of wall آثار الصنادید āsā'r-us-sanādīd' N.F PL. relics of the ancients آثار بد āsā'r-e-bad N.M. PL. ominous signs آثار قدیمہ āsā'r-e qadī'mah آثار عتیقہ āsā'r-e 'atī'qah N.M. PL. archaeological finds محکمہ آثار قدیمہ maih'kama-e āsā'r-e qadī'mah N.M. archaeology department آثار قیامت āsā'r-e qiyā'mat N.M. PL. signs of the Day of Judgment; signs of the doomsday's approach آثار متحجرہ āsā'r-mutahaj'jarah N.M PL fossils آثار نیک āsā'r-e-nek' N.M. PL. good omens [A ~ SING. اثر]

آثار[2] āsār' N.M PL (ped.) seers [P ~ SING اسیر]

آثام āsām' N.M (PL of اثم N.M ★)

آثم *ā'sīm* N.M. sinner ADJ. sinful (person) [A ~ اثم]

آج *āj* N.M. & ADV. today this day آج برس کے پھر نہ برسوں گا *āj' ba'ras ke phir na bar'soonga* PH. (about heavy downpour) It shall rain with full force tonight آج تک *āj'-tak* ADV. till now yet آج تڑکے (یا سویرے) *āj' taṛ'ke* (or *save're*) ADV. early this morning آج سے *āj' se* PH. from today henceforth hence آج کا کام کل پر ڈالنا (یا چھوڑنا یا اٹھا رکھنا) *āj' ka kām kal' par ḍal'na* (er *chhoṛ'na* or *ūṭha rakh'na*) V.I. shirk work put of work procrastinate آج کدھر کا چاند نکلا *āj kidhar' ka chānd' nik'lā* PH. wonderful, how did you care to call after such a long time ? آج کس کا منہ دیکھا (تھا) *āj kis' ka mūṅh de'kha* (*tha*) PH. what an inauspicious person did you (etc.) come across this morning ? آج کریگا کل پائیگا *āj ka're ga kal pā''e ga* PROV. as you sow so shall you reap آجکل (یا آج کل) *āj'kal* ADV. these days N.M. nowadays modern times present-day world آج کل بارہ برس کی بٹیا بر مانگے *āj'kal ba'rah ba'ras kī biṭ'ya bar māṅ'ge* PROV. (col.) even quite young girls are sexy these days آج کل کرنا *āj'kal kar'na* V.I. procrastinate آج کل میں *āj'kal meṅ* ADV. in a day or two آج کی آج کے ساتھ کل کی کل کے ساتھ *āj' kī āj' ke sāth kal kī kal' ke sāth'* PROV. think of today, and tomorrow will take care of itself آج کیا جاتی دنیا دیکھی تھی *āj' kya jā'tī dūn'ya de'khī thī* PH. did the thought of death make you on me after such a long absence ? آج کے تھپے آج ہی نہیں جلتے *āj' ke thūpe āj' hī na'hīṅ jal'te* PROV. everything takes its own time آج مرے (یا موئے) کل دوسرا دن *āj' ma're* (or *mū'e*) *kal doos'ra din* PROV. the dead are soon forgotten آج میری منگنی کل میرا بیاہ، ٹوٹ گئی منگنی رہ گیا بیاہ *āj me'rī maṅg'nī kal' me'ra biyah', ṭooṭ' ga''ī maṅg'nī raih' ga'ya bīyah'* PROV. there is many a slip between the cup and the lip آج ہو کہ کل (ہو کے رہے گا) *āj ho ke kal'* (*ho' ke ra'he ga*) PH. today or tomorrow (happen it must) ; inevitable even though late آج ہے سو کل نہیں *āj' hai so kal' nahīṅ* PROV. do not leave till tomorrow what you can do today

آجانا *ā'jā'na* V.I. (see under آنا V.I. ★)

آچھیں *a'chhīṅ* N.F. sound of sneezing آچھیں کرنا *āchhīṅ' kar'na* V.I. sneeze [ONO.]

آخ تھو *ākh thoo'* N.F. sound of hawking INT. pooh tush آخ تھو کرنا *ākh' thoo kar'nā* V.I. hawk detest [ONO.]

آختہ *ākh'tah* ADJ. castrated emasculate آختہ کرنا *ākh'ta kar'na* V.T. emasculate آختہ ہونا *ākh'ta ho'nā* V.I. be emasculated

آخر *a'khir* ADV. at last ; at length in the end ultimately ADJ. last later final ultimate N.M. end conclusion termination آخر الامر *a'khir-ūl-am'r* CONJ. & ADV. eventually ; ultimately after all at last ; at length آخر الزمان *a'khir-ūz-zaman'* ADJ. last ; final آخر بین *a'khir-bīn* ADJ. far sighted (person) آخر دم *a'khir dam* ADV. ultimately ; at the last moment آخرش *a'khirash* CONJ. & ADV. at last ; at length after all آخر شب *a'khir-e shab* ADV. in the early hours of the morning آخر کار *a'khir-e kar*, (col. *a'khir kar*) ADV. & CONJ. at last ; at length eventually ; ultimately after all آخر کرنا *a'khir kar'na* V.T. bring to an end ; آخر وقت (میں) *a'khir vaqt* (*meṅ*) ADV. at the eleventh hour آخر ہونا *a'khir ho'na* V.I. end be pushed to the extremity آخری *a'khirī* (col. *akh'rī*) ADJ. last ultimate extreme آخری چہار شنبہ *a khirī* (or *ākh'rī*) *chahar' sham'bah* N.M. last Wednesday of 'Safar' when the Holy Prophet recovered from final illness (popularly supposed to be a day of rest) ; Last Wednesday آخری دیدار *a'khirī dīdār'* N.M. last glimpse آخری فیصلہ *a'khirī fai'salah* N.M. final decision آخری وقت *a'khirī vaqt'* N.M. closing time (of) (fig.) eleventh hour last breadth (fig.) closing years of life آخریں *a'khirīṅ* ADJ. last latest آخریں دم *a'khirīṅ dam'* N.M. last gasp ADV. last of all at the last moment [A]

آخرت *a'khirat* N.F. next world life after death ; the Hereafter doomsday اپنی آخرت بگاڑنا (یا سنوارنا) *ap'nī a'khirat bigaṛ'na* (or *saṅvar'na*) V.I. do an evil (or good) deed so as to mar (or make) one's future life [A ~ آخر]

آخور *akhor'* N.F. (arch.) stable (fig.) worthless stuff (fig.) sweepings آخور کی بھرتی *ākhor' kī bhar'tī* N.F. worthless stuff sweepings [P]

آخوند *ākhūnd'* ; آخون *ākhūn'* N.M. (arch.) teacher instructor teaching, recitation of the Holy Quran [T]

آداب *ādāb'* N.M. PL. greetings ; compliments salutation rules or etiquette (of) good manners mores INT. good-morning (etc.) good-bye آداب بجا لانا *adab' ba-ja la'na*, آداب عرض کرنا *adab' 'arz kar'na* V.T. pay one's respects (to) greet ; wish آداب عرض *adab' 'ar'z* N.M. greetings regards good morning (etc.) آداب محفل *adab-e-mahfil* N.M. PL. etiquette آداب والقاب *ada'b-o-alqab'* N.M. PL. courtesy title (in letters, etc.) آداب وتسلیمات *ada'b-o taslimat'* N.M. PL. compliments ; wishes; regards [A ~ SING. ادب]

آدرش *adarsh'* N.M. (dial.) ideal آدرشی *adarshi* ADJ. ideal idealistic [S]

آدم *a'dam* N.M. Adam human being آدم ثانی *a'dam-e sa'ni* N.M. (appellation of) Noah آدم خاکی *a'dam-e-kha'ki* N.M. mortal human being آدم خور *a'dam khor* ADJ. man-eating , cannibalistic N.M. man-eater ; cannibal آدم زاد *a'dam zad* N.M. human being (as distinct from supernatural being) آدم نہ آدم زاد *a'dam na a'dam zad'* INT. (wilderness with) not a trace of man [A]

آدمی *ad'mi* (ped. *a'dami*) N.M. man person ; human being individual (W. dial.) husband ; man servant man follower ; retainer intelligent person brave man ordinary human being human race ; mankind (11) folk (12) public ADJ. grown-up ; adult آدمی آدمی انتر کوئی ہیرا کوئی کنکر *ad'mi ad'mi an'tar ko'i hi'ra ko'i kan'kar* PROV. no two persons are alike among men some are jewels, some are pebbles آدمی بنانا *ad'mi bana'na* V.I. teach manners humanize civilize discipline آدمی اناج کا کیڑا ہے *ad'mi an'aj ka ki'ra hai* PH. man lives by bread alone ; cereal are must for mankind آدمی بن جانا *ad'mi ban ja'na* V.I. learn good manners have sense of responsibility come to one's senses آدمی پیچھے *ad'mi pichhe* ADJ. per head one by one severally آدمی چہرے سے پہچانا جاتا ہے *ad'mi cheh're se paihcha'na ja'ta hai* PROV. the face is the index of the mind آدمی صحبت سے پہچانا جاتا ہے *ad'mi sohbat se paihcha'na ja'ta hai* PROV. a man is known by the company he keeps آدمی (یا آدمیوں) کا جنگل *ad'mi* (or *ad'miyon*) *ka jan'gal* N.M. thickly populated place آدمی کے لباس میں آنا *ad'mi ke libas' men a'na* V.I. appear in human form ; assume human visage آدمی کچھ کھو کر ہی سیکھتا ہے *ad'mi kuchh kho' kar hi sikh'ta hai* PROV man learns by his mistakes آدمی نے آخر تو کچا ہی دودھ پیا ہے *ad'mi ne a'khir to kach'cha hi doodh piya hai* PROV. to err is human بڑے آدمی *ba're ad'mi* N.M. PL. gentry big guns classes مشینی آدمی *mashi'ni ad'mi* N.M. robot automaton آدمیت *a'dmiy'yat* N.F. good sense human nature good manners ; civility ; courtesy fellow-feeling ; commiseration magnanimity humanity (age of) discernment آدمیت آنا *adamiy'yat a'na*, آدمیت پکڑنا *adamiy'yat pakar'na* V.I. become civilized learn courtesy or civility come to one's senses reach the age of discernment (دنیا سے) آدمیت اٹھ جانا (*dun'ya se*) *adamiy'yat uth ja'na* V.I. (of world, etc.) become inhumane ; be a very bad world to live in آدمیت میں آنا *adamiy'yat men a'na* V.I. see reason آدمیت سے گزرنا (یا گزر جانا) *adamiy yat se guzar'na* (or *gu'zar ja'na*) V.I. behave improperly act inhumanly آدمیت سکھانا (یا سکھلانا) *adamiy'yat sikha'na* (or *sikhla'na*) V.T. civilize render humane polish teach politeness or good manners bring (someone) to his senses آدمیت کرنا (یا سے کام لینا) *adamiy'yat kar na* (or *se kam' le'na*) V.I. behave nicely

آدھ *adh* ADJ. half (hour, seer etc.) ایک آدھ *ek adh* (see under ایک ★)

آدھا *a'dha* ADJ. (F. آدھی *a'dhi*) half آدھا آدھا *a'dha a'dha* divided into equal parts half-and-half ; fifty-fifty آدھا تیتر آدھا بٹیر *a'dha ti'tar a'dha bater* PH. neither fish nor flesh nor good red herring worthless or ludicrous jumble آدھا ساجھا *a'dha sa'jha* N.M. equal share آدھا (یا آدھی) سیسی *a'dha* (or *a'dhi*) *si'si* N.F. (W. dial.) hemicrania آدھا کرنا *a'dha kar'na* halve divide into two parts bisect آدھا نام *a'dha nam* N.M. not full name آدھا ہونا *a'dha ho'na* be reduced to skin and bone ; become lean ; grow lank decrease in size آدھوں آدھ *a'dhon adh* ADV. half and half ; fifty fifty آدھی بات سننا *a'dhi bat sun'na* V.I. not to hear in full (rush to implement) without hearing full instructions آدھی چھوڑ ساری کو جائے (یا دھائے) آدھی رہے نہ ساری پائے *a'dhi chhor sa'ri ko ja''e* (or arch. *dha''e*) *a'dhi rahe' na sa'ri pa''e* PROV. catch at the shadow and lose the substance ; grasp all, lose all آدھی درجن *a'dhi dar'jan* ADJ. & N.F. half a dozen آدھی رات ادھر آدھی رات ادھر *a'dhi rat idhar a'dhi rat udhar'* ADV. & N.M. (at) about mid-night آدھی رات کو جمائی آئے شام ہی سے منہ پھلائے *a'dhi rat ko jama''i a''e sham' hi se munh* phūlā''e PROV. count the chickens before they are hatched آدھے پیٹ ā'dhe peṭ ADV. hungry not having eaten to the fill آدھے راستے ā'dhe ras'te meṅ ADV. midway آدھے سے کچھ زیادہ (یا کم) ā'dhe se kuchh ziyā'dah (or kam') PH. a little more (or less) than half

آدینہ ādī'nah N.M. (rare) Friday [P]

آڈٹ ā'diṭ N.M., آڈٹنگ ā'diṭing N.F. audit آڈیٹر ā'diṭar N.M. auditor [E]

آذر ā'zar N.M. (lit.) fire ninth month of Persian calendar (corresponding to December [P]

آذوقہ (or آذوقہ) ā'zūqah N.M. (same as آزوقہ N.M. ★)

آر[1] ār N.F. awl

آر[2] ār N.M. this side (of river, etc.) کے آر کرنا ke ār' kar'nā V.T. transfix

آر[3] ār N.F. (arch.) shame bashfulness [~A COR.]

آرا ā'rā (ped. ār'rah) N.M. frame-saw آرا چلانا (کھینچنا) ā'rā chalā'nā (or kheṅchnā) V.T. saw آرے سر پر چلنا ā're sir par chal'nā V.I. be tortured be tormented آرہ کش ār'rā kash N.M. sawyer

آرا[2] ārā' N.F. (PL. of رائے N.F. ★)

آرا[3] ārā SUF. adorning embellishing gracing آرائی ārā''ī SUF. decorating setting up

آراستگی ārās'tagī N.F. decoration adornment arrangement preparation آراستہ ārās'tah آراستہ پیراستہ ārā'sta pairās'tah ADJ. adorned ; decorated ; bedecked arranged equipped prepared [P ~ آراستن]

آرام ārām' N.M. cure rest respite repose comfort convenience relief ease health آرام پانا ārām pā'nā V.I. be at ease get all sorts of comfort آرام پائی ārām'-pā''ī N.F. (W. dial.) (arch) a kind of high-heeled wide-toed shoe آرام جاں ārā'm-e jāṅ, آرام دل ārā'm-e dil', دل آرام dil ārām' N.M. sweetheart ; beloved آرام چین ārām' chain N.M. peace of mind rest آرام حرام (یا تلخ) کرنا ārām ḥarām' (or tal'kh) kar'nā V.T. & I. make life hell for ; give hell to have no rest آرام داں ārām'-dāṅ N.M. basket for betel leaves ; betel-basket small domed betel-box آرام پہنچانا (یا دینا) ārām' pahuṅchā'nā (or de'nā) V.T. give relief allay give comfort give rest put at ease آرام سے ārām' se ADV. gently carefully softly. آرام طلب ārām'-ta'lab, آرام پسند ārām'-pasand' ADJ. slothful lazy ; idle indolent N.M. indolent person lotus-eater آرام طلبی ārām'-ta'labī, آرام پسندی ārām'-pasan'dī N.F. indolence slothfulness آرام کا اسباب ārām' kā asbāb N.M. (rare) furniture آرام کرسی ārām-kur'sī N.F. easy chair آرام کرنا ārām' kar'nā respectful or ironical آرام فرمانا ārām' farmā'nā V.I. rest ; take rest recline go to bed sleep آرام کی روکھی ہزار نعمت ہے ārām' kī roo'khī hazār' ne''mat hai PROV. a little in quiet is the best of all diet آرام گاہ ārām'-gah N.F. (also آخری آرام گاہ ā'khirī ārām-gah) grave ; tomb ; mausoleum (rare) rest house (rare) bed chamber کو آرام ہو جانا ko ārām' ho' jā'nā V.I. (of someone) have more peace be relieved آرامیدہ ārāmī'dah ADJ. (lit.) reposing at ease at rest

آرائش ārā''ish N.F. decoration adornment bedecking orderly arrangement (of shop-window) dressing آرائشی ārā''ishī ADJ. decorative [P ~ آراستن]

آر پار ār' pār ADJ. pierced through across from one end to the other

آرتی ār'tī N.F. Hindu religious rite comprising offering, etc. to idol ; idol-worship [S]

آرٹ ārṭ N.M. art آرٹسٹ ār'ṭisṭ N.M. artist artiste آرٹسٹک ārṭis'ṭik ADJ. artistic [E]

آرٹیکل ār'ṭikal N.M. article [E]

آر جار ār'-jār N.F. coming and going ; constant movement of people both ways

آرچ بشپ ārch'-bi'shap N.M. archbishop [E]

آرد ārd N.M. (ped.) flour ; meal [P]

آرڈر ār'ḍar N.M. order آرڈر بک ār'ḍar būk N.F. order book آرڈر بک کرانا ār'ḍar būk karā'nā V.I. book an order آرڈر دینا ār'ḍar de'nā V.T. place an order (with) [E]

آرزو ār'zoo N.F. wish ; desire ; longing inclination solicitude yearning love presumption faith request want (10) hope (11) trust (12) expectation آرزو بر آنا ār'zoo bar ā'nā V.I. (of desire) be fulfilled

آرزو خاک میں مل جانا *ar'zoo khāk' meṅ mil jā'nā* V.I. be frustrated have the hope shattered آرزو دل کی دل میں رہنا *ar'zoo dil' kī dil' meṅ raih'nā* V.I. not to have one's hope fulfilled آرزو کا خون ہونا *ar'zoo ka khoon' ho'nā* V.I. be greatly disappointed آرزو کرنا *ar'zoo kar'nā* V.I. desire long for yearn آرزومند *ar'zoo-mand* ADJ. wishing ; desirous importunate eager aspiring intent (on) concerned آرزومندی *ar'zoo-man'dī* N.F. eagerness desire yearning wistfulness. concern [P]

آرسی *ār'sī* N.F. small mirror set in ring worn on thumb ; mirrored thumb-ring mirror : looking-glass آرسی مصحف *ar'sī mus'haf* N.F. wedding rite comprising new couple's mutual introduction آرسی مصحف دکھانا (یا دکھلانا) *ar'sī mus'haf dikhā'nā* (or *dikhlā'nā*) V.T seat bride and groom beside or opposite each other under improvised canopy or sheet with a looking-glass and a copy of the Holy Quran between the couple

آروغ *arogh'* N.M. (rare) belching ; eructation [P]

آری *a'rī* N.F. small saw [DIM. of آرا]

آرے *a're* INT. (lit.) yes ; yea آرے بلے کرنا *a re ba'le kar'na* V.I. (arch.) procrastinate [P]

آریہ *ar'yah*, آریا *ar'ya* N.M. & ADJ. Aryan member of modern reformist but fanatical Hindu sect آریہ سماج *ar'yah samāj'* N.F. name of this sect ; *Arya Samaj* آریائی *aryā''ī* ADJ. Aryan [S noble]

آڑ *āṛ* N.F. cover shelter protection subterfuge pretence ambush (کی) آڑ لینا (*kī*) *āṛ le'nā* V.I. take cover or shelter (behind) آڑ میں *āṛ' meṅ* ADV. behind (lying) in ambush under cover (of) under the pretence (of)

آڑا *ā'ṛā* ADJ. (F. آڑی *ā'ṛī*) frilled (trousers) inclined ; bent athwart awry diagonal ; transverse cross oblique crooked آڑا ترچھا ہونا *ā'ṛa tir'chha ho'nā* V.I. be enraged (کے) آڑے آنا (*ke*) *ā'ṛe ā'nā* V.I. stand (someone) in good stead in time of need protect : shield آڑے ہاتھوں لینا *ā'ṛe ha'thoṅ le'nā* V.T chide ; scold ; upbraid run down

آڑا گوڑا *ā'ṛā go'ṛā* N.M. refuse ; sweepings آڑا گوڑی *ā'ṛā go'ṛī* N.F. name of a trick in wrestling

آڑو *ā'roo* N.M. peach چکئی (یا چپٹا) آڑو *chakai''ī* (or *chapṭā*) *ā'roo* N.M. flat peach

آڑھت *ā'ṛhat*, N.F. commission agency sale by commission brokerage ; commission آڑھتی *āṛhtī*, (pop. آڑھتیا *āṛh'tiyā*) N.M. commission agent broker correspondent ; agent

آزاد *āzād'* ADJ. independent free liberated at large scot-free uncontrolled N.M. a class of mendicants who regard themselves as above religious precept and practice hermit freeman free thinker آزادرو *āzād'-rau*, آزادہ رو *āzā'da-rau* ADJ. bold unbigoted liberal; liberal-minded N.M. libertine free thinker آزاد طبع *āzād'-tab''*, آزاد منش *āzād'-manish'* ADJ. & N.M. undaunted person liberal-minded ; liberal libertine آزاد کا سونٹا *āzād' kā son'ṭā* ADJ. (W. dial.) saucy آزاد کرانا *āzād' karā'nā* V.T. liberate (person, territory, etc.) آزاد کرنا *āzād' kar'nā* V.T. liberate free discharge آزاد ہونا *āzād' ho'nā* V.I. be free (to) be set a liberty be independent win independence آزادانہ *āzadā'nah* ADJ. free ; independent ADV. freely unfettered ; unhindered freely expressed آزادانہ رائے *āzadā'na rā''e*, N.F. free opinion ; independent view آزادگی *āzā' dagī* N.F. (arch.) freedom ; liberty آزادی *āzā'dī* N.F. freedom ; liberty liberation independence (rare) discharge (from prison, etc.) manumission enfranchisement آزادی خواہ *āzā'dī-khāh* ADJ. freedom-loving N.M. freedom-fighter [P]

آزار *āzār'* N.M. malady malaise woe SUF. annoying آزاردہ *āzār'-deh* ADJ. annoying , irksome ; teasing آزاردہی *āzār'-dehī'* torment bitterness ; irksomeness آزار دینا *āzār' de'nā* V.I torment annoy gall آزاری *āzā'rī* SUF. tormenting annoying galling [P]

آزردہ *āzūr'dah* ADJ. annoyed dejected dissatisfied troubled distressed uneasy gloomy glum آزردہ دل *āzūr'da-dil*, آزردہ خاطر *āzūr'da-khā'tir* ADJ. dejected troubled in mind displeased annoyed gloomy sorrowful despondent آزردہ دلی *āzūr'da-di'lī*, آزردہ خاطری *āzūr'da khā' tirī* N.F. displeasure annoyance sadness ; dejection آزردہ کرنا *āzūr'dah kar'nā* V.I. displease annoy afflict trouble آزردہ ہونا *āzūr'dah ho'nā* V.I. be displeased be annoyed be sad ; be dejected آزردگی *āzūr'dagī* N.F. displeasure annoyance sadness ; dejection trouble ; distress [P ~ آزردن]

آزمانا *āzmā nā* V.T. test ; prove try experiment scrutinize [~ P آزمودن try]

آزمائش *āzmā''ish* N.F. trial test examination proof آزمائش و خطا *āzmā''ish-o khatā* N.F. trial and error [P ~ PREC.]

آزمودہ *āzmoo'dah* tried tested experienced آزمودہ را آزمودن جہل است *āzmoo'da rā āzmoo'dan jah'l ast* PROV. it would be absurd to try again what has already proved a failure آزمودہ کار *āzmoo'da kār* ADJ. experienced skilled ; practised veteran N.M. veteran [P ~ PREC.]

آزوقہ (or آزوقہ or آزقہ or آذوقہ) *āzoo'qah* N.M. (arch.) bare sustenance meagre pittance [P]

آس *ās* N.F. Hope expectation prop supporting voice in vocal concerts *ā's aulād' vā'lā* N.M. & ADJ. (one) blessed with children آس پرائی وہ تکے جو جیتے ہی مرجائے *ās parā''ī voh take jo jī'te hī mar jā''* PROV. suspense is worse than death آس پوری ہونا *ās poo'rī ho'nā* V.I. have one's hope fulfilled آس توڑنا *ās toṛ'nā* V.T. disappoint آس باندھنا (یا رکھنا یا لگنا) *ās bāndh'nā* (or *rakh'nā* or *lāg'nā*) V.I. cherish hope آس بندھانا *ās bandhā'nā* V.T. raise hope آس ٹوٹنا (یا جاتی رہنا) *ās ṭooṭ'nā* (or *jātī raih'nā*) V.I. (of hope) shatter آس دینا *ās de'nā* V.T. raise hope solace sing as a supporting voice *ā'sā* (col.) ADJ. hopeful آسا جیئے نراسا مرے *ā'sa ji'ye nirā'sā ma're* PROV. but for hope, the heart would break

آسا *asā'* SUF. like [P]

آسان *āsān'* ADJ. easy simple convenient آسان کرنا *āsā'n kar'nā* V.I. simplify make easy remove difficulties آسانی *āsā'nī* N.F. ease simplicity convenience آسانی سے *āsā'nī se* ADV. easily ; without much difficulty [P]

آسائش *āsā''ish* N.F. comfort facility ease calm repose ; rest tran-quillity (life of) luxury [P ~ آسودن rest]

آس پاس *ās' pās* ADV. near , nearby in the neighbourhood (of) کہیں آس پاس *ka'hīn ās' pās* ADV. somewhere near here

آستان *ās'tān*, آستان *āstān'*, آستانہ *āstā'nah* N.M. (fig.) shrine ; mausoleum (lit.) threshold (of saint, superior, etc.) abode ; residence آستان بوس *ās'tān bos'* N.M. devotee آستان بوسی *ās'tān bo'sī* N.F. humble visit paying one's homage [P]

آستے *ās'te* ADV. (col.) gently , softly slowly [P. ~ آہستہ COR.]

آستین *āstīn'* (occ. آستان, آستین *ās'tīn*) N.F. sleeve cuff آستین پکڑنا *āstīn' pakaṛ'nā* V.T. kick up a row button-hole (someone) آستین جھاڑنا *āstīn jhāṛ'nā* V.I. give away everything renounce the world آستین کا سانپ *āstīn' kā sāṅp'* N.M. hidden enemy ; snake in the grass آستین میں سانپ پالنا *āstīn' meṅ sāṅp, pāl'nā* V.T. maintain someone who is bound to betray one later آستین چڑھانا *āstīneh chaṛhā'nā* V.I. tuck up one's sleeves (fig.) get ready to fight [P]

آسرا *ās'rā* N.M. support ; stay ; prop help hope trust refuge ; shelter means of subsistence آسرا بنانا *ās'rā banā'nā* V.T depend (on) آسرا تکنا (یا ڈھونڈنا یا لگانا) *ās'ra tak'nā* (or *ḍhoonḍ'nā* or *lagā'nā*) V.T. look (up to someone) for help or support seek protection (of) آسرا ٹوٹنا (یا ٹوٹ جانا) *ā'srā ṭooṭ'nā* (or *ṭooṭ jā'nā*) V.I. lose hope despair ; despond آسرا دینا *ās'rā de'nā* V.I. reassure give heart ; rouse hope encourage help succour آسرا کرنا *ās'rā kar'nā* V.T. rely ; depend count upon recline against آسرا کرنا *ās'rā ho'nā* V.I. be the prop (of) be the support (of) بے آسرا *be-ās'rā* ADJ. helpless

آسمان *āsmān'* (occ. آسمان *ās'mān*) N.M. sky , the heavens ; firmament celestial order great height Heaven آسمان پر اڑنا *āsmān' par ūṛ'nā* V.I. fly high (fig.) be very proud آسمان پر چڑھانا *āsmān' par chaṛhā'nā* V.T. flatter wheedle give fulsome praise آسمان پر چڑھا کر اتارنا *āsmān' par chaṛhā kar ūtār'nā* V.T. debase (someone) after showing respect to him آسمان پر تھوکا منہ پر آئے *āsmān' par thoo'kā mūṅh par a''e* PROV he that blows in the sky shall fill his own eye آسمان پر دماغ (یا مزاج) ہونا *āsmān' par dimāgh'* (or *mizāj'*) *ho'nā* V.I.

be vain ; be very proud gave oneself airs ; put on airs آسمان پھٹنا (یا ٹوٹ پڑنا) *āsmān' phaṭ'nā* (or *ṭooṭ par'nā*) V.I. be overwhelmed with trouble آسمان تاکنا (یا جھانکنا) *āsmān' tāk'nā* (or *jhāṅk'nā*) V.I. - wax strong (of fowl) be caproned آسمان جاہ *ās'mān jāh'* ADJ. (used as title) of exalted rank with sky-rocketing fame آسمان زمین ایک کر دینا *āsmān' zamīn' ek' kar de'nā* V.T. leave no stone unturned آسمان سر پر اٹھا لینا *āsmān' sir par uṭhā' le'nā* V.I. raise a hue and cry آسمان سے آگ برسنا *āsmān' se āg' baras'nā* V.I. (of weather) be very hot آسمان سے اترنا *āsmān' se ūtar'nā* V.I. (iron.) be of rare quality آسمان سے باتیں کرنا *āsmān' se bā'teṅ kar'nā* V.I. (of structure) be very high آسمان سے تارے اتارنا *āsmān se tā're ūtār'nā* V.T. (fig.) achieve the impossible آسمان سے گرا کھجور میں اٹکا *āsmān' se gi'rā khajoor' meṅ aṭ'kā* PROV. out of the frying pan into the fire آسمان سے گرنا *āsmān' se gir'nā* V.I. fall from the sky come as a windfall آسمان کھا گیا یا زمین *āsmān' khā' gayā' yā zmīn'* INT. (fig.) where has it vanished ? آسمان کی خبر لانا *āsmān' kī khabar lā'nā* V.I. rocket sky-high آسمان کی سیر کرنا *āsmān' kī sair' kar'nā* V.I. fall into an ecstasy آسمان کے تارے توڑنا *āsmān' ke tā're toṛ'nā* V.I. be very artful achieve the impossible آسمان گیری *āsmān'-gī'rī* N.F. cloth fastened to ceiling canopy awning inside room آسمان میں تھگلی لگانا *āsmān meṅ thig'lī lagā nā* V.I. be too clever آسمانی *ās'mānī* ADJ. celestial heavenly ; divine unexpected azure N.F. (slang) hemp ; hashish آسمانی بلا گرنا *āsmā'nī balā' gir'nā* V.I. be suddenly overtaken by misfortunes ; have a bolt from the blue آسمانی پلانا *āsmā'nī pilā'nā* V.I. make intoxicated with hemp portion آسمانی تیر *āsmā'nī tīr* N.M. (fig.) useless act آسمانی زبان *āsmā'nī zabān'* N.F. heavenly language آسمانی فرمانی *āsmā'nī farmā'nī* N.F. act of God ; heavenly decree آسمانی کتاب *āsmā'nī kitāb* N.F. revealed book ; scriptures آسمانی گولہ *āsmā'nī go'lah* N.F. (fig.) bolt from the blue hailstorm hitting standing crop [P]

آسن *ā'san* N.M. posture in coiture (rare) inner part of thigh آسن تلے آنا *ā san ta'le ā'nā* V.I. come under control آسن جمانا *ā'san jamā'nā* V.I. sit on the hams sit firmly آسن لگانا *ā'san lagā'nā* V.I. (arch.) stage a sit-down strike آسن مارنا *ā'san mār'nā* V.I. squat sit in one posture

آسودہ *āsoo'dah* ADJ. well-off ; well-to-do affluent rich ; opulent calm ; composed at ease living a life of luxury آسودہ حال *āsoo'dah ḥāl* ADJ. well-off ; well-to-do affluent cool ; composed ; unruffled ; serene آسودگان *āsoo'dagān'* N.M. PL. the affluent those at ease those lying in peace آسودگانِ خاک *āsoo'dagā'n-e-khāk'* N.M. PL. the dead, those lying buried آسودگی *āsoo'dagī* N.F. comfort prosperity ; good circumstances rest [P ~ آسودن rest]

آسیا *ā'siyā* N.F. (rare) mill ; grinding mil [P]

آسیہ *ā'siyah* ADJ. dejected N.M. this as the name of Pharaoh's wife who brought up Moses [P]

آسیب *āseb'* N.M. evil spirit (fig.) harm ; disaster (fig.) misfortune *āseb ūtār'nā* (or *door' kar'nā*) V.T. exorcise ; cast on an evil spirit آسیب زدہ *āseb' za'dah* ADJ. possessed haunted آسیب سر پر کھیلنا *āseb' sir par khel'nā* V.I. (of possessed person) dance in ecstasy آسیب ہونا *āseb' ho'na* V.I. be possessed آسیبی *āse'bī* ADJ. (col.) possessed haunted [P]

آسیمہ *āsī'mah* AFF. surprised astounded bewildered سر آسیمہ *sar āsī'mah*, آسیمہ سر *āsī'ma sar* ADJ. confounded ; confused bewildered [P]

آش *āsh* N.M., soup ; water آش پکانا *āsh pakā'nā* V.I. make a soup (fig.) contrive something against another ; plot (against) آشِ جو *āsh-e jau'* N.M. barley water [P]

آشا *ā'shā* N.F. (dial.) hope expectation desire ; longing [S]

آشام *āshām'* SUF. drinking ; quaffing one who drinks آشامی *āshā'mī* SUF. drinking ; quaffing [P ~ آشامیدن]

آشتی *āsh'tī* N.F. peace accord harmony reconciliation rapprochement detente صلح و آشتی *sūlḥ-o āshtī* N.F. peace and harmony [P]

آشرم *ash'ram* N.M. (dial.) Hindu hermitage [S]

آشفتہ *āshūf'tah* ADJ. perplexed confused afflicted ; distressed raving آشفتہ حال *āshūf'ta-ḥāl* ADJ. afflicted ; distressed perplexed آشفتہ خاطر *āshūf'tā-khā'tir*, آشفتہ دل *āshūf'-ta-dil* ADJ. troubled in mind uneasy آشفتہ خاطری *āshūf.'ta-khā'tirī*, آشفتہ دلی *āshūf'ta-dilī* N.F. uneasiness of mind آشفتہ دماغ *āshūf'ta-dimāgh'*, آشفتہ سر

ashuf'ta-sar ADJ. mentally deranged ; of unsound mind آشفتہ دماغ ashuf'ta-dimā'ghī, آشفتہ سری ashuf'ta-sarī N.F. unsoundness of mind آشفتہ طبع ashuf'ta-tab', آشفتہ مزاج ashuf'ta-mizaj' ADJ. distracted afflicted in mind آشفتہ طبعی ashuf'ta-tab''ī, آشفتہ مزاجی ashuf'ta-miza'jī N.F. destraction ; mental derangement آشفتگی ashuf'tagī N.F. perturbation disorder misery uneasiness raving derangement [P ~ آشفتن]

آشکارا ashkā'ra (lit. ashkar') ADJ. visible evident ; obvious disclosed known apparent clear آشکارا کرنا ashka'ra kar'nā V.T disclose ; divulge آشکارا ہونا ashka'ra ho'nā V.I. transpire come to light be disclosed [P]

آشنا ashna' N.M. acquaintance comrade friend paramour SUF. knowing deciphering known (by) آشنا ہونا ashna' ho'nā V.I. become friendly become intimate be conversant (with) (of animal) become tame or domesticated حرف آشنا harf-ashna' N.M. beginner ; abecedarian صورت آشنا soo'rat-ashna' N.M. knowing or known by sight only آشنائی ashnā''ī N.F. acquaintance friendship fellowship intimacy illicit relations آشنائی کرنا ashnā''ī kar'na associate be intimate know ; develop illicit relations with become paramour (of) آشنایانہ ashnāyā'nah ADJ. friendly ADV. in a friendly manner [P]

آشوب ashob' N.M. uproar ; disturbance ; tumult ill-luck tempest redness and swelling of eyes SUF. social satire ; satire on disturbed condition (of city, etc.) disturber آشوب چشم ashobʹ-e chash'm N.M. conjunctivities آشوب روزگار ashoʹb-e rozgar N.M. world-wide tumult beloved آشوب گاہ ashob'-gah N.F. tumultous place آشوب محشر asho'b-e maih'shar N.M. (fig.) great tumult unprecedented hue and cry شہر آشوب shaihr-ashob' N.M. satire on country or city's disturbed state of affairs [P]

آشیانہ ashiyā'nah (lit. آشیاں ashiyan') N.M. nest (fig.) abode ; residence آشیاں اٹھانا ashiyan ūtha'na V.T. abandon one's residence آشیاں بنانا (یا باندھنا) ashiyan bana'na (or bandh'na) V.T. & I. build (one's) nest have (one's) house (somewhere) take up abode

آشیانہ

آشیرباد ashīr'bad, اشیرباد ashīrbad N.F. (dial.) blessing ; benediction آشیرباد دینا ashīr'-

bād de'nā V.T. bless [S]

آصف a'saf N.M. name of Solomon's minister any able minister [A ~ H]

آغا a'gha N.M. (arch.) (title of respect for) chieftain (title for) elder brother (as courtesy title) respected ; venerable [P]

آغاز aghaz' N.M. beginning start آغاز کرنا aghaz' kar'na V.T. begin ; start open ; launch آغاز ہونا aghaz' ho'na V.I. be begun ; be started be opened ; be launched حرف آغاز harf-e aghaz' N.M. foreword prefatory note preliminary talk or discourse beginning نقطۂ آغاز nuqta-e aghaz' N.M. start-point

آغشتہ aghash'tah ADJ. & SUF. (blood) stained covered (with) [P ~ آغشتن]

آغوش aghosh' N.F. (rare M.) embrace lap bosom clasp آغوش گرم کرنا aghosh' gar'm kar'na V.T. embrace (of sweetheart) yield (to) آغوش لحد میں سونا agho'sh-e laihd meṅ so'na V.I. enjoy eternal rest آغوش میں آجانا aghosh' meṅ a' jana V.T. (of beloved) embrace آغوش میں لینا aghosh' meṅ le'na V.T. (of lover) embrace [P]

آغوں a'ghoṅ N.F. new-born infant's cry [ONO.]

آفات afat' N.F. PL. calamities catastrophes disasters dangers ; risks آفاتِ ارضی وسماوی afa't-e arzī'-o-samā'vī N.F. PL. unforeseen calamities all types of trouble acts of God [A ~ SING. آفت]

آفاق afaq' N.M. horizons آفاق گیر afa q'-gīr, آفاقی afa'qī ADJ. universal worldwide catholic ; oecumenical آفاقیت afaqīy'yat N.F. universality catholicity wide appeal (of) [A ~ SING. افق]

آفت a'fat N.F. (PL. آفات afat') calamity catastrophe disaster evil misfortune mishap wretchedness unhappiness difficulty ; hardship آفت آنا (یا پڑنا) a'fat a'na (or par'na) V.I. (of misfortune) befall (of ill) happen آفت اٹھانا afat ūtha'na V.I. raise hue and cry cause a tumult labour under affliction suffer or bear pain, etc. آفت برپا کرنا a'fat bar-pa' kar'na آفت توڑنا a'fat tor'na, آفت ڈھانا a'fat dha'na V.T. raise a tumult آفتِ جان a'fat-e jan' N.F. troublesome person (fig.) mischievous beloved آفت جھیلنا a'fat jhel'na V.I. suffer a calamity undergo trouble آفت خیز

آفت خیز *a' fat-khez* ADJ. tumultous calamitous آفت رسیدہ *a'fat-rasī' dah*, آفت زدہ *a'fat-za dah* ADJ oppressed by adversity, run down by misfortune miserable unlucky آفت کا پرکالہ *a'fat kā par kā'lah* ADJ. very naughty N.M. mischievous fellow astute person (fig.) beloved آفت کا مارا *a'fat ka mā'ra* N.M. & ADJ. afflicted (person) آفت کی پڑیا (یا پوٹ) *a'fat kī pur ya* (or *poṭ*) N.F & ADJ. naughty (person) mischievous (person) آفت مچانا *a'fat machā'nā* V.I. raise a hue and cry create much trouble make much noise آفت مول لینا *ā'fat mol' le'nā* V.I. invite trouble آفت میں پڑنا *ā'fat meṅ par'na* آفت میں پھنسنا *a'fat meṅ phaṅs'nā* V.I be overtaken by calamity or disaster [A]

آفتاب *āftāb'* N.M. sun آفتاب آمد دلیل آفتاب *āftā'b ā'mad dalī'l-e āftab* PROV it is an obvious truth آفتاب اقبال چمکنا *āftā'b-e iqbāl' cha'maknā* V.I. have (one's) star in the ascendant آفتاب اقبال غروب ہونا *āftā'be- iqbāl' ghuroob' ho'nā* V.I meet one's downfall آفتاب بیں *āftāb'-bīn* N.M. helioscope آفتاب طلوع ہونا *āftāb' tūloo'' ho'nā* V.I. (of sun) rise آفتاب غروب ہونا *āftāb' ghuroob' ho'nā* V.I. (of sun) set آفتاب پرست *āftāb' parast'* N.M. sun-worshipper Zoroastrian, Magus آفتاب سوا نیزے پر آنا *āftāb' sa'vā ne'ze par ā'nā* V.I. (of sun) draw close to earth on doomsday (fig.) be very hot آفتاب شام *āfta'b-e shām'* N.M. setting sun (fig.) very old person آفتاب عالمتاب *āfta'b-e 'ā lam-tāb'* N.M the sun illuminating the world آفتاب گیر *āftāb'-gīr* N.F. (arch.) umbrella parasol sunshade آفتاب لب بام *āfta'b-e lab-e bām'* N.M. setting sun very old person something decaying fast آفتاب نصف النہار پر پہنچنا *āftāb' nisf-ūn-nahār' par pahūṅch'nā* V.I. be midday (fig.) be at the zenith (of); be at the apogee of one's career, etc. آفتابی *āftā'bī* ADJ. solar bright N.F. a kind of fireworks آفتابی غسل *āftā'bī ghusl* N.M. sunbath [P]

آفتابہ *āftā'bah*, (arch.) col. آفتاوہ *āftā'va* N.M. spouted jug ewer [P]

آفتابہ

آفرید گار *āfrīd'gar* N.M. Creator آفریدہ *āfrī'dah* SUF. created N.M creature human being [P ~ آفریدن]

آفریں *af' rīn*, آفرین *āfrīn* INT well-done, brave N.F. praise ovation, acclamation applause SUF maker, creator آفریں کہنا *āfrīn' kaih'nā* V.I. applaud commend compliment praise جہاں آفریں *jahān' āfrīn'* N.M. (God as) (Creator of the world) جان آفریں *jan āf'rīn* N.M. (God as) Creator of soul) آفرینش *āfrī'nish* N.F creator: genesis آفرینندہ *āfrinin' dah* N.M creator maker the Supreme Being [P ~ آفریدن]

آفس *ā'fis* N M office [E]

آفندی *āfin'dī* N.M. (rare) esquire Mr [T]

آقا *ā'qā* N.M. employer lord master owner آقا و مولا *āqā'-o-mau'lā* N.M. master Lord; God [P]

آک *āk* N.M. swallow-wort آک کی بڑھیا *āk' kī būṛk'yā* N.F. swallow-wort down

آک

آکا *ā'kā* N.M. (arch.) title for) elder brother [P]

آکاس *ākās'*, آکاش *ākash'* N.M. (rare) sky, the heavens; firmament آکاش بانی *ākāsh' bā'nī* N F (dial.) All Indlia Radio, A.I.R. آکاس بیل *ākās bel* N.F dodder, air-creeper [S]

آکسیجن *āk sījan* N.F oxygen [E]

آگ *āg* N.F. fire conflagration blaze flame wrath jealousy آگ برسانا *āg barsā'nā* V.I. (of sun) be very hot bomb bombard; fire a volley, open a hot fire آگ برسنا *āg ba'rasnā* V.I be very hot, rain fire be parched up (of bullets, shells or bombs) be fired in plenty آگ بن جانا *āg' ban jā'nā* V.I. be consumed with rage آگ بن دھواں کہاں *āg' bin dhoo'' āṅ ka'hāṅ'* PROV. no smoke without fire آگ بوٹ *āg' boṭ* N.M. (arch). steamer; steamship آگ بھبوکا (یا بولا یا بگولا) ہونا *āg bhabhoo'kā* (or *baboo'lā* or *bagoo'lā*) *ho'nā* V.I. fly into a passion be mad with fury or rage آگ بجھانا *āg bujhā'nā* آگ بھڑکانا *āg bhaṛkānā* V.I. fan the flames provoke, incite آگ بھڑک اٹھنا *āg bhaṛak ūth'nā* V.I. (of fire) rage آگ بھی نہ لگاؤں *āg' bhī na lagā''ooṅ* INT (W. dial.) to Hell with it آگ پانی (یا پھونس) کا بیر *āg pā'nī* (or *phooṅs*) *ka bair'* PH. sworn enmity inherent antagonism آگ پانی کا سنجوگ *āg pā'nī kā sañjog'* PH union of the opposites آگ پانی کا کھیل *āg pā'nī kā khel'* PH machine worked by steam anything unpredictable or out of control owing to the interplay of elements in it (یا چھڑکنا) آگ پر تیل ڈالنا *āg par tel' ḍāl'nā* (or *chhiṛ'rik'nā*) PH. stir the fire incite further آگ پڑنا *āg' paṛ'nā* V.I. be very hot آگ پڑ جانا *āg' paṛ jā'nā* V.I. have a burning sensation (of bad blood) be created between be infuriated آگ پھانکنا *āg phāṅk'nā* V.I. feel a burning sensation be lashed into fury be jealous exaggerate آگ پھونکنا *āg phooṅk'nā* set on fire stir the fire provok ; incense آگ تاپنا *āg tāp'nā* V.I. warm oneself up before the fire آگ تلووں سے لگنا *āg tal'voṅ se lag'nā* V.I. be incensed آگ ٹھنڈی کرنا *āg ṭhaṅ'ḍī kar'nā* V.I. cool down passions pacify extinguish fire آگ جانے لہار جانے دھونکنے والے کی بلا جانے *āg' jā'ne lūhār' jā'ne dhauṅk'ne vā'le kī balā jā'ne* PROV. why should the agent worry آگ جگانا *āg' jagā'nā* V.T. stir up fire create a longing for آگ جلانا *āg jalā'nā* V.T. light or kindle fire آگ جھاڑنا *āg' jhāṛ'nā* V.T. brush ashes from embers strike fire (یا گاڑنا) آگ دبانا *āg dabā'nā* (or *gāṛ'nā*) V.T. & I. cover embers with ashes quell revolt (etc.) control anger (etc.) آگ دکھانا *āg dikhā'nā* V.T. set fire (to) heat آگ ڈھونا *āg ḍho'nā* V.T. brush ashes from embers آگ دینا *āg de'nā* V.I. set fire to (H. dial.) burn (a corpse) آگ روشن کرنا *āg rau'shan kar'nā* V.T. & I. light or kindle fire آگ سرد ہونا *āg' sard' ho'nā* V.I. (of fire) be extinguished ; be put out (of passions) cool down (of trouble) be quelled آگ سلگانا *āg sū'lgānā* V.T. set on fire burn fire in hearth foment trouble create disturbance آگ سُلگنا *āg sū'lagnā* V.I. (of fire) be kindled (of trouble) be fomented آگ سے پانی ہو جانا *āg se pā'nī ho jā'nā* PH. lose the heat of passion ; cool down recover from a violent fit of temper آگ کا باغ *āg kā bāgh'* PH. Nimrod's fire fireworks (fig.) goldsmith's crucible آگ کا پتلا *āg' kā pūt'lā* N.M. agile and diligent man astute person fiery being آگ کا جلا آگ ہی سے اچھا ہوتا ہے *āg' kā ja'lā āg' hī se ach'chhā ho'tā hai,* آگ کو آگ ہی مارتی ہے *āg ko āg' hī mār'tī hai* PROV. like cures likes ; diamond cuts diamond measure for measure ; tit for tat آگ کا پتنگا *āg kā pataṅ' gā* N.M. spark of fire ; particle of fire آگ کرنا *āg' kar'nā* kindle fire ; ignite make exceedingly warm enrage ; inflame آگ کو دامن سے ڈھانکنا *āg ko dā'man se ḍhaṅk'nā* V.T. & I. try unsuccessfully to hide a secret آگ کھائے گا انگارے ہگے گا *āg'khā''e gā aṅgā're ha' ge gā* INT. like cause like effect آگ کھائے منہ نہ جلے ادھار کھائے پیٹ جلے *āg' khā''e mūṅh na ja'le ūdhār' khā''e peṭ ja'le* PROV. borrowing is the mother of trouble آگ کہنے سے منہ نہیں جلتا *āg' kaih'ne se mūṅh nahīṅ' jal'tā* V.T. mere lip-service is ineffectual آگ لگا کر پانی کو (یا لیے) دوڑنا *āg lagā' kar pā'nī ko* (or *le*) *dauṛ'nā* PH. pretend to quell trouble after stirring it up آگ لگا کے تماشا دیکھنا *āg' lagā ke tamā'shā dekh'nā* PH enjoy stirring up trouble fiddle while Rome burns آگ لگانا *āg' lagā'nā* V.T. burn foment trouble ; stir up disunion provoke ; inflame lavish ; dissipate disdain kindle a passion (for) آگ لگاؤ *āg' lagā'oo* N.M. mischief-monger rabble-rouser ; firebrand آگ لگنا *āg' lag'nā* V.I. burn catch fire be inflamed ; be incensed burn with envy or rage آگ لگے *āg' la'ge* INT. (W. dial.) to Hell with it آگ لگے پر کنواں کھودنا *āg' la'ge par kūṅ''āṅ khod'nā* PH. lock the stable door after the steed is stolen آگ لینے کو آئی گھر والی بن بیٹھی *āg le'ne ko ā''ī ghar vā'lī ban bai'ṭhī* PROV. trespasser laying claim to ownership آگ لینے کو جائیں پیمبری مل جائے *āg' le'ne ko jā'' eṅ payam'barī mil jā''e* PROV. have a windfall آگ میں پانی ڈالنا *āg' meṅ pā'nī ḍāl'nā* extinguish fire slake thirst satiate hunger put down disturbance ; appease tumult آگ میں جھونکنا *āg' meṅ jhoṅk'nā* V.T. burn to ashes fling into fire squander dissipate آگ میں کودنا (یا گرنا) *āg' meṅ kood'nā* (or *gir'nā*) V.I. court trouble brave a danger آگ میں لوٹنا *āg' meṅ loṭ'nā* V.I. be afflicted with sorrow be consumed with jealously آگ نکالنا *āg nikāl'nā* V.T. strike fire آگ ہونا *āg' ho'nā* be set on fire become exceedingly hot be incensed be very hot-tempered

آگا *ā'gā* N.M forepart ; forelegs facade front (of house) front (of turban) visage prow van advance-guard avant-garde آگا بھاری ہونا *ā'gā bhā'rī ho'nā* V.T. be in the family way ; be big with child ; be pregnant آگا پیچھا *ā'gā pī'chhā* N.M. front and rear antecedents consequences آگا پیچھا دیکھنا (یا سوچنا) *ā'gā pī'chhā dekh'nā* (or *soch'nā*) V.T. & I. look before and after consider the prose and cons. آگا پیچھا کرنا *āgā pī'chhā kar'nā* hesitate, waver demur آگا تاگا لینا a'ga ta'ga le'na V.T look minutely have suspicions (about) pry into others' affairs آگا سنبھالنا a'ga sanbhal'na, آگا لینا a'ga le'na V.I. advance take the lead

آگاہ a'gah ADJ. aware informed; acquainted with warned; intelligent, shrewd SUF (also آگہ a'gah') aware آگاہ دل a'gah'-dil ADJ. mindful conscious clever shrewd; sagacious آگاہ کرنا a'gah' kar'na V.I. warn acquaint (with) inform آگاہ ہونا a'gah' ho'na V.T. know come to know take the warning آگاہی a'ga'hi, آگہی a'gahi N.F. knowledge information insight vigilance warning [P]

آگے a'ge ADV before in front (of) opposite face to face in advance ahead hereafter in future next in time or place (10) beyond (11) further on آگے آگے a'ge a'ge ADV. ahead future آگے آنا a'ge a'na V.I. appear advance; come forward come near fare challenge intervene lie between come about take place (10) befall آگے بڑھنا a'ge barh' na V.I proceed press forward improve go forth to meet or welcome a visitor outdo surpass defy; oppose act as a guide آگے پیچھے a'ge pichhe ADV. in a row in a series one after another in front and in the rear; fore and aft by and by close on the heels (of) confusedly sooner or later آگے خدا کا نام a'ge khuda' ka nam' PH. nothing after that آگے دوڑ پیچھے چھوڑ a'ge daur pichhe chhor try to run before learning to walk the farther we go the more we fall behind آگے دھر لینا a'ge dhar le'na V.T. get before make (someone) go before bring forward آگے دیکھنا a'ge dekh'na V.T. be vigilent; be cautious look to the future آگے ڈالنا a'ge dal'na V.T throw or place before آگے رکھنا a'ge rakh'na V.T. lay or set before exhibit present آگے سے a'ge se ADV. in future prior (to) ere beforehand in anticipation (of) previously آگے قدم بڑھانا (یا رکھنا) a'ge qa'dam barha'na) V.T. step forward آگے کا قدم پیچھے پڑنا a'ge ka qa'dam pichhe par'na V.I. be too confused to take the right-step be too unlucky to register any success آگے کرنا a'ge kar'na V.T. push forward present, offer expose exhibit آگے کو کان ہونا a'ge ko kan' ho'na V.I. be warned promise not to repeat the mistake etc. آگے لانا a'ge la'na V.T bring forward آگے نکل جانا a'ge ni'kal ja'na V.I advance pass آگے نہ a'ge na ho'na V.I. not to come forward stay behind the scene not to defy آگے ہونا a'ge ho'na V.I. act as a leader take the lead proceed be bold; be saucy oppose defy آگے ہی a'ge hi ADV already [~ آگا]

آگ گیا ag' gaya N.F (H. dial.) leave; permission order; command [S]

آگیں a'gin' SUF. -ful

آل[1] al N.F. progeny, family or followers (of a great person) آل اولاد al' aulad' N.F. children; offspring; progeny descendants house; race; family; kindered; dynasty آل سلطانی al-e sulta'ni N.F. royal family آل عبا al-e 'aba' N.M. the Holy Prophet, Hazrat Fatima, Hazrat Ali, Imam Hasan and Imam Husain [A]

آل[2] al N.F. long pumpkin green stalk of onion a tree yielding a dye; 'morinda citrifolia' moisture

آلا a'la, آلھا a'lha N.M. name of a legendary mediaeval Hindu hero his exploits against Muslims ballad traveller's tale boring tale آلا گانا a'la ga'na V.I. tell traveller's tales indulge in selfpraise [S]

آلا ala N.M. wet; moist (arch.) niche in wally (only in) آلا دے نوالہ a'la de niva'la PROV. upstart unable to adjust herself (etc.) to new surroundings

آلا بالا a'la ba'la N.M. dilly-dallying; prevarication آلا بالا (یا آلے بالے) بتانا a'la ba'la (or a'le ba'le) bata'na V.T. prevaricate; dilly-dally shilly-shally; hum and haw

آلات alat' N.M. PL. instruments implements tools weapons آلات حرب ala't-e harb' N.M. PL. weapons of war آلات کشاورزی ala't-e kashavar'zi N.M. PL. agricultural implements [A ~ sing. آلہ]

آلام alam' (N.M. (PL. of الم N.M. ★)

آلان alan' N.F. chain for elephant]

آلائش ala'ish N.F. filth [P ~ آلودن]

آلپین al'pin N.M pin (port.)

آلت *ā'lat* N.F. penis [P ~ A]
آلتی پالتی *āl'tī pāl'tī* N.F. cross-legged posture آلتی پالتی مارنا *āl'tī pāl'tī mār'na*, آلتی پالتی مار دے بیٹھنا *ālti pāl'tī mā'rie baiṭh'nā* V.I. sit cross-legged
آلتی پالتی مار کر بیٹھنے والا
آل جنجال *āl jin'jāl'* N.M. bad dream ; horrible visions
آلس *ā'las*, آلکس *āl'kas* N.F. lethargy laziness ; indoience آلسی *āl'sī*, آلکسی *āl'kasī* N.F. lethargy laziness ; indolence ; ADJ. & N.M. lazy (person) آلسیا *āl'siyā*, آلکسیا *āl'kasiyā* lazy (person)
آلن *ā'lan* N.M. pinch of wheat or gram meal put in potherb
آلنگ *ālang'* N.F. heat (of mare, etc.) آلنگ پر آنا (یا ہونا) *alang' par ā'nā* (or *ho'nā*) V.I. (of mare) be on heat
آلو *ā'loo* N.M. potato آلو بخارا *ā'loo bū*k*h*ā'*ārā* N.M. plum آلوچہ *āloo'-chah* N.M. damson [P]
آلوبخارا
آلودہ *āloo'dah* ADJ. polluted soiled SUF. (also آلود *ālood'*) mixed with) polluted آلودگی *āloo'dagī* N.F. pollution being soiled [P ~ آلودن]
آلہ *ā'lah* N.M. (PL. آلات *ālāt'*) tool implement. instrument weapon آلۂ تناسل *ā'la-e tanāsūl* N.M. penis ; male reproductive organ *a la-e kār'* N.M. tool ; cat's-paw آلہ کار بننا *ā'la-e kar' ban'na* V.I. become the tool (of) [A]
آم *ām* N.M. mango آم بوؤ آم کھاؤ املی بوؤ املی کھاؤ *ām bo''o ām' khā''o im lī bo''o im'lī khā''o* PROV. as you sow so shall you reap آم ٹپکنا *ām' ṭapak' na* (of mellow mangoes) drop from trees آم کھانے سے کام یا پیڑ گننے سے (مطلب) *ām' khā'ne se kām' yā per' gin'ne se (mat'lab)* PROV. I would have the fruit, not the basket آم کھائیے پال کے خربوزے کھائیے ڈال کے *ām' khā''iye pāl ke kharboo'ze khā''iye ḍāl ke* PH. best to eat mangoes when they are artificially mellowed but melons when freshly plucked آم کے آم گٹھلیوں کے دام *ām' ke ām' gūṭh'liyon ke dām'* PROV. kill two birds with one stone آم میں بور آنا *ām' men maur' ā'nā* V.I. (of mango trees) blossom پال کا (آم) *pal' kā (ām)* N.M. mango ripened in straw ڈال کا آم *ḍāl' kā ām* N.M. mango ripening on tree
آماج *āmaj'*, آماجگاہ *āmaj'-gah* N.F. target shelter [P]

آمادہ *āmā'dah* ADJ. & SUF. ready ; prepared آمادگی *āmā'dagī* N.F readiness inclination [P]
آماس *āmas'* N.M. swelling ; inflammation [P]
آمد *ā'mad* N.F. arrival, advent income inspiration ; poetic inspiration آمد آمد *ā'mad ā'mad* N.F. approach expected arrival آمدم برسر مطلب *ā'madam bar sar-e mat'lab* PH. coming to the point I revert to the topic آمد و خرچ *ā'mad-o kharch'* N.F. income and expenditure آمد و رفت *ā'mad-o raft'* آمد و شد *ā'mad-o shūd* traffic ingress and egress آمدن *ā'madan* N.M. coming N.F. (usu. *ām'dan*) income آمدن بہ ارادت رفتن بہ اجازت *ā'madan ba irā'dat raf'tan ba ijā'zat* PH. etiquette demands that one must stay till allowed to leave آمدنی *ām'danī* (ped. *ā'madanī*) N.F. income receipts revenue profit [P]
آمر *ā'mir* N.M. dictator آمرانہ *āmirā'nah* ADJ. dictatorial آمرانہ نظام *āmirā'na nizām* N.M. dictatorship *amirā'na nizām'* N.M. dictatorship آمریت *āmiriy'yat* N.F. dictatorship [A ~ آمر]
آمرزش *āmūr'zish* N.F. forgiveness ; pardon salvation آمرزگار *amūrz'gar* ADJ (God as) Forgiver ; Saviour [P ~ آمرزیدن]
آمریت *amiriy'yat* N.F. (see under آمر N.M. ★)
آملہ *ām'lah*, آنولہ *āṅv'lah* N.M. myrobalan آملہ (یا آنولہ) سار گندھک *āmlah* (or *āṅv'lah*) *sar gan'dhak* N.F. purified sulpher آملے کا کھایا بزرگ کا فرمایا پیچھے معلوم ہوتا ہے *ām'le kā khā'yā buzurg' kā farmā'yā pī'chhe ma'loom' ho'tā hai* PROV. good things, though unpalatable at first, prove their utility in the end
آمنا سامنا *ām'nā sām'nā* N.M. confrontation, confronting آمنے سامنے *ām'ne sām'ne* ADV. face to face opposite each other 'vis-a-vis'
آمنا وصدقنا *ā'mannā va sad'daqnā* PH. too true sure ; doubtless we believe in and testify to the truth okay آمنا وصدقنا کہنا *ā'mannā va sad' daqnā kaih'nā* V.T. bear (someone) out okay [A ~ ایمان + تصدیق]
آموختہ *āmokh tah* N.M. (arch.) previous lesson ADJ. & SUF. learnt taught [P ~ آموختن]
آموز *āmoz'* SUF. learning teaching آموزش *āmo'zish* N.F. (lit.) instruction آموزش گاہ *āmo' zish-*

gah N.F. (rare) school [P ~ آموختن]

آمیختہ āmekh'tah ADJ. & SUF mixed N.M. admixture P ~ آمیختن]

آمیز āmez' SUF. mixing کم آمیز kam āmez' ADJ. leading a comparatively secluded life unsociable آمیزش āme' zish N.F. adulteration mixture ; admixture association intercourse ; temperament [P ~ آمیختن]

آمین āmīn' N.F. & INT. amen آمین کہنا āmīn' kaih'nā V.I. say amen to [A ~ H]

آن¹ ān N.F. (PL. آنات ānāt') instant ; moment time آناً فاناً ā'nan fa'nan, آن کی آن میں ān' kī ān' meṅ, آنِ واحد میں ān-e vā'hid meṅ ADV. instantly ; immediately ; in a moment ; in a jiffy [A]

آن² ān N.F. behaviour grace affectation pride dignity modesty آن بان ān' bān N.F. pomp and show splendour آن بان سے رہنا ān' bān se raih'nā V.I. live elegently آن توڑنا ān' toṛnā V.I. humble (someone's) pride (rare) back out of (one's) words bring shame (to)

آں āṅ PRON. (rare) that آنحضرت āṅ-haz'rat sal'lallā'ho 'alai'he va sal'am N.M. the Holy Prophet ; He (peace be on him !) آنکہ āṅ'keh CONJ. that [P]

آنا ā'nā V.T. come reach ; arrive approach pass appear happen be possible آ ā INT. sound uttered for modulating the time in recitation or vocal music (usu. آ آ ā'ā) call to domestic fowl, etc. IMP. come آ بلا گلے پڑ نہیں پڑتی تو بھی پڑ ā' balā ga'le paṛ' na'hīṅ paṛtī to' bhī paṛ PROV. (allusion to) inviting trouble آ بننا ā' ban'nā V.T. befall be involved in trouble آ بوا لڑیں لڑے ā' boo''ā laṛ'eṅ, la're hamā'rī balā (allusion to) shrewish temper آ بے لانڈے جا بے لانڈے ā' be lam'de jā' be lam'de kar'nā V.I. prevaricate waste time over trifles آ بیل مجھے مار ā' bail mū'jhe mār' PROV. inviting trouble it is more painful to do nothing than to do something آ پڑنا ā' paṛ'nā befall (to) come come to live (with) occur ; happen assault آ پکڑنا ā' pakaṛ'nā seize overtake آ پہنچنا ā' pahūṅch'nā V.I. arrive draw near آ پھنسنا ā' phaṅs'nā V.I. get caught be duped آ جانا ā' jā'nā V.I. come آ دھمکنا ā dhā'maknā, آ دڑنا ā' daṭ'nā V.I. come suddenly come uninvited آ رہنا ā' raih'nā V.I. come to put up with fall down آ لگنا ā' lag'nā V.T. hit reach (of disease) affect (of boat) touch the shore, etc. آ لینا ā' le'nā V.T. overtake آ ملنا ā' mil'nā V.T. meet join آتا ā'tā N.M. dues known ; learnt, PR. P. coming آتا جاتا ā'tā jā'tā N.M. & ADJ. passer-by casual caller آتا ہو تو ہاتھ سے نہ دیجے، جاتا ہو تو غم نہ کیجے ā' tā ho to hāth se na dī'je, jā'tā ho to ghamī na kī'je PROV refuse not what comes your way, crave not what is evanescent آتی ہے ہاتھی کے پیر، جاتی ہے چیونٹی کے پیر ā'tī hai hā'thī ke pair, jā'tī hai chiyoṅ'ṭī ke pair PROV. agues (etc.) come on horseback, but go away on foot آتے آتے ā'te ā'te ADV. by and by ; slowly ; gradually on the way while coming till (someone's) arrival آنا جانا ā'nā jā'nā N.M. visits and return visits social contacts آئی ā''ī N.F. the inevitable misfortune doom calamity death آئی نہیں ٹلتی ā''ī na'hīṅ ṭal'tī PROV. the inevitable must happen; what will be, will be آئی بلا کو سر سے ٹالنا ā''ī balā' (ko) sir se ṭal'nā PH. avoid getting into trouble dodge آئی گئی ہو جانا ā''ī ga''ī ho' jā'nā V.I. come to end be forgotten ; be a thing of the past آئیں بی عاقلہ سب کاموں میں داخلہ ā''īṅ bī 'āqelah sab' kā'moṅ meṅ dā'khilah PROV. (W. dial.) here comes the meddlesome woman آناً فاناً ā'nan fa'nan ADV. (see under آن N.F. ★)

آنا کانی ā'nā kā'nī N.F. arrogance purposeful neglect dodging آنا کانی دینا (یا کرنا) ā'nā kā'nī de nā (or kar'nā) V.T. dodge ; prevaricate (A ~ آنا I)

آنت ānt N.F. intestine gut entrails ; bowels آنت اترنا ānt' ū'tarnā V.I. suffer from hernia ; have a rupture آنتیں الٹ جانا āṅ'teṅ ū'lat jā'nā V.I. vomit feel sick ; filled or overcome with nausea آنتیں قل ھو اللہ پڑھ رہی ہیں āṅ'teṅ qūl hūval'lah paṛh ra'hī haiṅ PH. I feel very hungry آنتوں کے بل کھلنا āṅ'toṅ ke bal' khul'nā PH. eat to one's fill after starvation آنتیں سوکھنا āṅ'teṅ sookh'nā PH. feel very hungry آنتیں منہ کو آنا āṅ'teṅ mūṅh ko ā'nā PH. be distressed be greatly worried feel suffocated الٹی آنتیں گلے پڑنا ūl'ṭī āṅ'te ga'leṅ paṛ'nā V.I. be involved in trouble catch a tartar

آنٹ āṅṭ N.F. purity test (of bullion) ; acid-test knot enmity malice آنٹ لگانا āṅṭ lagā'nā V.I. test purity of bullion knot breed enmity (towards) bear one) malice آنٹ سانٹ āṅṭ' sāṅṭ N.F.

plot reconciliation unlawful aliance
آنٹی *an'tī* N.F. aunt ; aunty [E]
آنٹی *an'tī* N.F. knot a kind of wrestling trick آنٹی بتانا *an'tī batā'na* V.T cause adversary to trip over
آنچ *anch* N.F blaze flame fire heat warmt' fervour loss trouble آنچ آنا *anch ā'na* (or *pahūnch'na*) PH. suffer a loss be in hot water ایک آنچ کی کسر رہ جانا *ek' anch kī ka'sar raih' jā'na* PH. fail at the critical moment fail despite hope سانچ کو آنچ نہیں *sanch' ko anch' na'hīn* PROV truth has nothing to fear
آنچل *an'chal* N.M. corner of stole (etc.) آنچل پلو *an'chal' pal'loo* N.M. embroidered border (of shawl) آنچل ڈالنا *an'chal' dāl'na* V.T veil (face, etc.) (H. dial.) marry آنچل میں گرہ دینا *an'chal men gi'reh de'na* V.T. use a memory tag (for errands, etc.)
اندو *an'doo* N.M. chain or rope for elephant's feet chain worn big wrestler as trophy
آندھی *an'dhī* N.F. dust storm strong wind storm آندھی اٹھنا (یا چلنا) *an'dhī uṭh'na* (or *chal'na*) V.I. (of dust storm) blow آندھی کی طرح آنا *an dhī kī tar'ḥ ā'na* PH. come suddenly like a storm آندھی کی طرح آنا بگولے کی طرح جانا *an'dhī kī tar'ḥ ā'na, bagoo'le kī tar'ḥ jā'na* V.I. leave as abruptly as someone (or something) had come آندھی کے آم *an'dhī ke am'* N.M. (fig.) windfall something going very cheap ; that which goes abegging
آنڈ، آنڈھ *and, andh* N.M. (dial.) testicle آنڈے بانڈے *an'de ban'de* N.M PL. a children's game. saunter آنڈے بانڈے کھانا (یا کھیلنا) *an'de ban'de khā'na* (or *khel'na*) V.I. saunter ; have a stroll
آنریری *an'rerī* ADJ. honourary [E]
آنسو *an'soo* N.M. tear آنسو آنا *an'soo ā'na,* آنسو باہر آنا *an'soo bā'har ā'na* weep have tears in the eyes ; have one's eyes filled with tears (of tears) gush forth in the eyes آنسو پونچھنا *an'soo ponchh'na* V.T. wipe (someone's or one's) tears comfort ; soothe console ; solace آنسو پی جانا *an'soo pī' ja'na* suppress (one's) tears control one's feelings آنسو ٹپکنا *an'soo ṭa'pakna* V.I. weep ; shed tears آنسو پھوٹ بہنا *an'soo phoot baih'na,* آنسوؤں سے منہ دھونا *an'sū'on se mūnh dho'na,* آنسوؤں کی جھڑی لگنا *an'sū'on kī jha'ṛī lag'na,* آنسوؤں کا تار بندھنا *an'sū'on kā tar' bandh'na* V.I. weep bitterly ; burst into tears
آنسہ *ā'nsah* N.F (courtesy title) Miss Mlle. mademoiselle [A ~ انس]
آنکڑا *an'k'ṛa* N.M. hook barb shepherd's staff ; crook
آنکس *an'kas* N.M. goad for elephant آنکس مارنا *an'kas mar'na* V.T goad (fig.) bring under control
آنکنا *ank'na* V.T. appraise evaluate weigh or measure for evaluation آنک *ank* N.F. appraisal evaluation weigh or measure for evaluation
آنکھ *ankh* N.F. eye آنکھ آنا *ankh ā'na* V.T. & I. have a sore eye fall in love (with) آنکھ آشوب کرنا *ankh ashob' kar'na* V.I. have a sore eye آنکھ اٹھا کر بھی نہ دیکھنا *ankh uṭhā' kar bhī na dekh'na* V.T. disregard displeased feel ashamed آنکھ اٹھا کر دیکھنا *ankh uṭhā', kar dekh'na* V.T. look at attend. to آنکھ اٹھنا *ankh uṭh'na* V.I. look at آنکھ اوجھل پہاڑ اوجھل *ankh o'jhal pahāṛ' o'jhal* PROV out of sight, out of mind آنکھ اونچی (یا برابر) نہ کرنا (یا نہ ہونا) *ankh ooṅ'chī* (or *barā' bar*) *na kar'na* (or *ho'na*) V.I not to look (someone) in the face (through shame or respect) آنکھ بچا جانا *ankh bachā jā'na* V.I. (fig.) evade : dodge ; avoid آنکھ بچا کے نکل جانا *ankh bachā' ke nikal' jā'na* V.I. slink away آنکھ بچی مال پرایا (یا یاروں کا) *ankh bachī mal parā'ya* (or *yā'roṅ kā*) PROV. eye withdrawn, property gone آنکھ (یا آنکھیں) بنانا *ankh* (or *an'kheṅ*) *banā'na* V.I. perform ophthalmic operation (on) replace someone's injured eye with an artificial one آنکھ (یا آنکھیں) بند کرنا *ankh* (or *an'kheṅ*) *band' kar'na* V. shut one's eyes sleep die آنکھ (یا آنکھیں) بند کئے چلے جانا *ankh* (or *an'kheṅ*) *band' ki'ye chā'le jā'na* V.I. move ahead without fear walk forth blindfoldedly move uncautiously آنکھ بھر کے (یا کر) دیکھنا *ankh bhar ke* (or *kar*) *dekh'na* V.T. look to the heart's fill آنکھ بہہ جانا *ankh baih' jā'na* V. become blind ; lose one's eyesight آنکھ بیٹھنا *ankh baiṭh'na* V.I. become blind (of eyeball) sag آنکھ (یا آنکھیں) پتھرانا *ankh* (or *ankh'eṅ*) *path'rā'na* V.I. be about to breathe one's last have glossy or glazed eyes آنکھ پر تنکا رکھنا *ankh par tin'kā rakh'na* V.T. & I. place a straw on pulsating eye (as supposed cure for it) آنکھ پر چڑھنا *ankh par chaṛh'na* PH. have a special liking for آنکھ پہچاننا *ankh paihchān'na* V.I. guess the intention (of) آنکھ پھڑکنا *ankh phaṛak'na* PH. have a premonitron (owing to pulsation in the eye)

آنکھ پھوٹنا *ānkh phoot'nā* V.I. lose one's eyesight; become blind آنکھ پھوٹی پڑ گئی *ānkh' phoo'ṭī pīr' ga'ī* PROV. better, the eye out than constant pain آنکھ پھوڑنا *ānkh phor'nā* V.T. hit (someone) in the eye make (someone) blind آنکھ (یا آنکھیں) پھیر لینا *ānkh* (or *ān'khen*) *pher' le'nā* V.T. turn away one's eye (from) withdraw one's favour (from) evade آنکھ پھیلا کر دیکھنا *ānkh phailā' kar dekh' nā* V.I. look carefully all over the place آنکھ پیدا کرنا *ānkh pai'dā kar'nā* V.T. develop keen appreciation have an eye (for) آنکھ (یا آنکھیں) تر ہونا *ānkh* (or *ān-khen tar' ho'nā* V.I. weep آنکھ ٹھنڈی کرنا *ānkh thān'dī kar'nā* V.T. & I. console ; solace please oneself (by the sight of) آنکھ ٹیڑھی کرنا *ānkh' te'ṛhī kar'nā* V.I. scowl ; glower آنکھ جھپکنا *ānkh jhа'paknā* V.I. wink nap be dazed آنکھ جھپکنے کی دیر نہ ہوئی کہ *ānkh jha'pakne kī .der na' hū'ī kah,* آنکھ جھپکتے میں *ānkh jhapak'te meṅ* ADV. in the stwinkling of an eye آنکھ (یا آنکھیں) جھکنا *ānkh* (or *ān'khen*) *jhuk'nā* V.I. have downcast eyes (owing to shame) آنکھ (یا آنکھیں) چرانا *ānkh* (or *ān' khen*) *churā'nā* PH. evade, dodge avoid آنکھ چڑھانا *ānkh charhā'nā* V.I. become angry آنکھ چڑھنا *ānkh charh'nā* V.I. have heavy eyes have eyes turned up while dying be drunk آنکھ چمکنا *ānkh chamkā'nā* V.T. & I. flash one's eyes آنکھ (یا آنکھیں) دکھانا *ānkh* (or *ān'khen*) *dikhā'nā* get the sight tested stare defiantly frighten آنکھ دبنا *ānkh dab'nā* V.I. yield admit being defeated آنکھ (یا آنکھیں) دکھنے آنا *ānkh* (or *ān'-khen*) *dukh'ne ā'nā* V.I. have sore eye(s) ; suffer from ophthalmia آنکھ دوڑانا *ānkh daurā'nā* V.I. look around آنکھ دھوئی دھائی *ānkh dho'ī dhā'ī* PH. unabashed unashamed آنکھ ڈالنا *ānkh' ḍāl'nā* V.T. look at cast an evil eye (on) آنکھ (یا آنکھیں) ڈبڈبا آنا *ānkh* (or *ān'khen*) *ḍūbḍūbā' ā'nā* V.I. (of eyes) be moistened with tears آنکھ (یا آنکھیں) روشن کرنا *ānkh* (or *ān'khen*) *rau'shan kar'nā* PH. delight (by appearance) آنکھ رکھنا *ānkh rakh'nā* V.T. & I. (lit.) cherish hope choose as one's target (etc.) آنکھ (یا آنکھیں) روشن ہونا *ānkh* (or *ān'khen*) *rau'shan ho'nā* PH. be delighted on meeting someone (met.) have children آنکھ سامنے کرنا *āṅ'kh sām'ne kar'nā* V.T. look at attend to آنکھ (یا آنکھیں) سرخ ہونا *ānkh* (or *ānkhen*) *sūrkh ho'nā* V.T. have redness in the eyes آنکھ سے آنکھ ملانا *ānkh se ānkh' milā'nā* V.T. look (someone) in the face claim equal status with challenge ; defy respond amorous glances آنکھ سے دیکھ کے *ānkh' se dekh' ke* ADV. knowingly with open eye آنکھ سے سلام لینا *ānkh se salām' le'nā* V.I. just wink at someone in return for greetings be too proud to return greetings save thus آنکھ سیدھی (سے) ہونا *ānkh* (*se*) *ānkh sī'dhī ho'nā* V.T. look on (someone) with favour آنکھ سے گرانا *ānkh se girā'nā* V.T debase withdraw آنکھ سے گرنا *ānkh se gir'nā* V.I. be debased آنکھ (یا آنکھیں) سینکنا *ānkh*, (or *ān'khen*) *senk'nā* V.I. feast the eyes on make eyes at ; cast amorous glances on آنکھ کا پانی ڈھلنا (یا مرنا) *ānkh kā pā'nī ḍhal'nā* (or *mar'nā*) PH. lose modesty ; lose all sense of shame have no courtesy left no longer have regard (for) آنکھ کا پردہ *ānkh' kā par'dah* N.M. modesty retina conjunctiva آنکھ کا تارا *ānkh kā tā'rā* ADJ. (one's) darling ; apple of (one's) eye آنکھ کا تل *ānkh kā til'* N.M. pupil of the eye آنکھ کا جالا *ānkh kā chā'lā* N.M. conjunctiva آنکھ کا ڈھلکا *ānkh kā-ḍhal'kā* N.M. a disease causing one to run at the eyes آنکھ کا ڈھیلا *ānkh kā ḍhe'lā* N.M. eyeball آنکھ کا غبار *ānkh kā ghūbār'* N.M. dimness of sight آنکھ کا لحاظ *ānkh kā-lihāz'* N.M. modesty آنکھ کا کھلنا *ānkh' khul'nā* V.I. get up ; rouse from sleep be born become aware (of) learn the truth about آنکھ (یا آنکھیں) کھلی کی کھلی رہ جانا *ānkh* (or *ān'khen*) *khu'lī kī khu'lī raih jā'nā* V.I. be wonderstruck آنکھ کھولنا *ānkh. khol'nā* V.T. open (someone's) eyes acquaint آنکھ (یا آنکھیں) کھول کر دیکھنا *ānkh* (or *ān'khen*) *khol' kar dekh'nā* V.T. look carefully examine directly آنکھ کی پتلی *ānkh kī put'lī* N.F. pupil of the eye pet آنکھ کی سیل *ānkh kī sīl'* N.F. modesty regard courtesy آنکھ کی کیچڑ *ānkh kī ki'chaṛ* N.F. discharge collecting in eye corners آنکھ کے ڈورے *ānkh ke ḍo're* N.M. PL. reddened veins in eye (as sign of drunkenness or sleeplessness) آنکھ (یا آنکھوں) کے آگے (یا سامنے) *ānkh* (or *ān'khon*) *ke ā'ge* (or *sām'ne*) ADV. under (someone's) nose آنکھ (یا آنکھیں) لجانا *ānkh lijā'nā* V.I. feel ashamed آنکھ لڑانا *ānkh* (or *ān'khen*) *ā'ge larā'nā* V.T. cast amorous glances آنکھ لڑنا *ānkh laṛ'nā* V.I. meet the eye exchange amorous glances آنکھ لگانا *ānkh lagā'nā* V.I. sleep doze off fall in love with make love to آنکھ لگنا *ānkh' lag'nā* V.I. fall in love (with) fall asleep آنکھ لگی *ānkh la'gī* N.F. mistress ; keep unwedded wife (of) آنکھ مارنا ānkh mar nā V.I. wink at drop a hint thus make eyes (at) آنکھ مچ جانا ānkh mich jā'nā V.I. (arch.) of eyes) close die آنکھ مچانا ānkh michā'nā V.T. wink at آنکھ مچولی ānkh michau'lī N.F. be-peep ; blindman's buff ; hide-and-seek tag آنکھ مچولی کھیلنا ānkh michau'lī khel'nā V.I. play hide-and-seek (with) آنکھ ملانا ānkh milā'nā V.T. exchange glances آنکھ (یا آنکھیں) مندنا ānkh (or ān'khen) mūnd'nā V.I. (of eyes) be closed sleep die آنکھ موند کے ānkh moond' ke ADV. with eyes shut ; blindly inconsiderately آنکھ (یا آنکھیں) موندنا ānkh (or ān'-khen) moond'nā V.I. shut the eyes die آنکھ میلی کرنا ānkh mai'lī kar'nā PH. frown ; glower ; scowl آنکھ میں پانی نہ ہونا ānkh men pā'nī na ho'nā V.I. be shamefaced be immodest آنکھ میں پھلی آنا ānkh men phūl'lī ā'nā V.I. have a white speck in the eye become blind آنکھ میں موتی کوٹ کوٹ کر بھرے ہونا ānkh men mo'tī kooṭ' kooṭ' kar bha're ho'nā V.I. (of someone's eyes) be exquisitely beautiful آنکھ میں نیل کی سلائی پھیرنا ānkh men nīl kī salā''ī' pher'nā V.T. blind (someone) by drawing indigo-tainted needle in his eyes ; blind آنکھ ناک سے درست ہونا ānkh' nāk se dūrūst' ho'nā V.I. have all the organs intact be unblemished آنکھ نم کرنا ānkh nam' kar'nā V.I. weep آنکھ نم ہونا ānkh nam' ho'nā V.I. (of eyes) be tearful آنکھ نہ اٹھانا ānkh na ūthā'nā V.T. & I. not to look at (through) shame or being busy آنکھ نہ ٹھہرنا ānkh na ṭhai'harnā V.I. be dazed (by the brightness of) ; be dazzled ; be dazed آنکھ نہ ناک بنو چاند سی ānkh' na nāk', ban'no chānd'sī PROV. (iron. for ugly woman) what a beauty ! آنکھ (یا آنکھیں) نیچی ہونا ānkh (or ān'khen) nī'chī ho'nā V.I. feel ashamed be heavily obliged (to) آنکھ والا ānkh vā'la N.M. & ADJ. (one) blessed with sight (one) able to appreciate آنکھ ہونا ānkh ho'nā V.T. & I. be blessed with sight love (someone) choose (someone) as one's target آنکھوں (ہی) آنکھوں میں ān'khon (hī) ān'khon men ADV. in a jiffy winkingly آنکھوں پر بٹھانا ān'khon par biṭhā'nā V.T. treat with respect or love hold dear آنکھوں پر پٹی باندھنا ān'khon par paṭ'ṭī bāndh'nā V.T. ignore connive at آنکھ پر (یا پہ) پردہ پڑنا ān'khon par (or pa) par'dah par'nā PH. be misled be deceived آنکھوں پر پلکوں کا بوجھ نہیں ہوتا ān'khon par pal'kon kā-bojh' nahīn ho'tā PROV. own things are never burdensome آنکھوں پر ٹھیکری رکھ لینا ān'khon par ṭhik'rī rakh le'nā PH. be blind to all behave in an unfriendly manner lose all sense of shame آنکھوں پر چربی چڑھنا ān'khon par char'bī charh'nā PH. be arrogant lose all sense of shame refuse to own or acknowledge friends آنکھوں پر چڑھنا ān'khon par charh'nā V.I. be liked (by) آنکھوں پر دیوار اٹھانا ān'khon par dīvār' ūṭhā'nā V.I. deny evident facts سر آنکھوں پر رکھنا sir ān'khon par rakh'nā PH. treat with respect or love hold dear آنکھوں پر ہاتھ رکھ لینا ān'khon par hāth' rakh le'nā V.I. (fig.) feel abashed آنکھوں تلے اندھیرا آنا ān'khon ta'le āndhe'rā ā'nā V.I. feel giddy be struck with consternation آنکھوں تلے پھرنا ān'khon ta'le phir'nā V.I. be ever in sight become large آنکھوں دیکھا مانا کانوں سنا نہ مانا ān'khon de'khā mā'nā, kā'non sū'nā na mā'nā, آنکھوں دیکھ بھٹ پڑا مجھے کانوں سننے دے ān'khon dekh bhaṭ parā, mū'jh- ...a'non sūn'ne de PROV. seeing is believing one eye-witness is better than hearsay آنکھوں دیکھی بات ān'khon de'khī bāt N.F. first-hand knowledge آنکھوں دیکھی مکھی نہیں نگلی جاتی ān'khon de'khī mak'khī na'hīn nig'lī jā'tī PROV. nobody will willingly swallow poison آنکھوں سکھ کلیجے ٹھنڈک ān'khon sūkh kale'je ṭhan-dak PH. by all means ; with pleasure آنکھوں سے (یا کے) اندھے نام نین سکھ ān'khon se (or ke) an'dhe nām' nain' sūkh PROV. black bloke called Mr. White ; be the victim of an irony of fate آنکھوں سے اوجھل ہو جانا ān'khon se o'jhal ho jā'nā V.I. go out of sight سر آنکھوں سے بجا لانا sir ān'khon se ba'jā lā'nā PH. obey willingly and cheerfully آنکھوں سے تلوے سہلانا ān'khon se tal've saihlā'nā V.T. & I. show love or respect (by rubbing eyelashes against sole of another's foot) آنکھوں سے گر (یا اتر) جانا ān'khon se gir (or ū'tar) jā'nā PH. lose favour (with) be no longer in the good books (of) آنکھوں سے لگانا ān'khon se lagā'nā V.T. treat (something) reverently by touching it with the eyes آنکھوں سے معذور ہونا ān'khon se ma'zoor' ho'nā V.I. be blind آنکھوں سے موہنی پیدا کرنا ān'khon se mo'hinī pai'dā kar'nā V.I. reflect love in one's eyes آنکھوں سے نیل ڈھلنا ān'khon se nīl dhal'nā V.I. be on the verge of death آنکھوں کا اندھا گانٹھ کا پورا ān'khon kā an'dhā gānṭh kā poo'rā PH. silly nevertheless careful of his pocket آنکھوں کا تیل نکالنا ān'khon kā tel nikāl'nā V.I. burn the midnight oil put a great strain on one's eyes by minute needlework, (etc.) آنکھوں کا کاجل چرانا *an'khon ka ka' jal chura'na* PH. be an expert thief be too clever آنکھوں کا نور *an'khon ka noor'* N.M. sight (one's) son one's progeny آنکھوں کی ٹھنڈک *an'khon ki than'dak* N.F. person who is (one's) heart's delight ابھی آنکھوں کی سوئیاں نکالنی باقی ہیں *a'bhi an'khon ki soo'iyan nikal'ni ba'qi hain* PROV. the critical moment is yet to come you can't be sure of the result so soon آنکھوں کے آگے اندھیرا آنا *an'khon ke a'ge andhe'ra a'na* V.I. feel giddy آنکھوں کے آگے تارے چٹکنا (یا چھٹنا) *an'khon ke a'ge ta're chatak'na* (or *chhutna*), آنکھوں کے آگے چاندنا ہونا *ankhon ke a'ge chand'na ho'na* V.I. have specks before eyes آنکھوں کے آگے ناک سوجھے کیا خاک *an'khon ke a'ge nak soojhe kya khak* PROV. one can hardly see one's own faults آنکھوں کے بل چل کر آنا (یا جانا) (سر) (sir) *an'khon ke bal chal' kar a'na* (or *ja'na*) V.I. come (or go) respectfully آنکھوں کے گڑھے *an'khon ke ga'rhe* N.M. PL. space round inner corners of eyes آنکھوں میں آنسو ڈبڈبا آنا *an'khon men an soo dubduba' a'na* V.I. (of tears) gush forth; well up in the eyes آنکھوں میں آنکھیں ڈالنا *an'khon men an'khen dal'na* V.T. exchange glances with look (someone) in the face آنکھوں میں پھرنا (یا بسنا) *an'khon men phir'na* (or *bas na*) PH. be greatly liked obsess; be ever present in one's mind آنکھوں میں پی جانا *an'khon men pi ja'na* V.T. & I. stare lovingly (at) refrain from reproof آنکھوں میں تکلے چبھونا *an'khon men tak'le chubho'na* V.T. torture آنکھوں میں تیل لگانا *an'khon men tel laga'na* V.T. trump up an excuse آنکھوں میں ٹھنڈک پڑنا *an'khon men than'dak par'na* V.I. be delighted آنکھوں میں جان آنا *an'khon men jan' a'na* V.I. be on the verge of death (of eyes) have rest آنکھوں میں جچنا *an'khon men jach'na*, آنکھوں میں جگہ کرنا *an'khon men ja'gah kar'na* V.I. be liked آنکھوں میں چربی چھانا *an'khon men char'bi chha'na* V.I. (of eyesight) weaken become proud lose all discretion آنکھوں میں چکاچوند آنا *an'khon men cha'ka chaund a'na* V.I. be dazed آنکھوں میں حلقے پڑ جانا *an'khon men hal'qe par ja'na* V.I. have sunken eyes آنکھوں میں تولنا *a'khon men tol'na* V.I. adjudge mentally آنکھوں میں خار ہونا *an'khon men khar' ho'na* PH. be ugly be an enemy be an eyesore آنکھوں میں خاک (یا دھول) ڈالنا (یا جھونکنا) *an'khon men khak'* (or *dhool'*) *dal'na* (or *jhonk'na*) PH. throw dust in (someone's) eyes cheat palm off one's wares (on)

آنکھوں میں خون اتر آنا *an'khon men khoon' u'tar a'na* V.I. fly into passion have bloodshot eyes آنکھوں میں دم ہونا *an'khon men dam' ho'na* V.I. be on the verge of death آنکھوں میں دنیا تاریک (یا اندھیر) ہونا *an'khon men dun'ya tarik'* (or *andher'*) *ho'na* V.I be greatly shocked آنکھوں میں رات کاٹنا *an'khon men rat kat na* PH. have a sleepless night آنکھوں میں سرسوں پھولنا *an'khon men sar'son phool'na* PH. see yellow on all sides آنکھوں میں سمانا (یا کھبنا) *an'khon men sama'na* (or *khub na*) V.I. be greatly liked آنکھوں میں رسیلا پن ہونا *an'khon men rasila' pan ho'na* V.I. have lovely eyes آنکھوں میں سفیدی چھانا *an'kon men sife'di chha'na* V.I. lose one's sight; become blind آنکھوں میں کھائے جانا *an'khon men kha''e ja'na* V.T. stare with menacing eyes آنکھوں میں کھٹکنا *an'khon men khatak'na* V.I. be the object of jealousy or enmity آنکھوں میں مرچیں بھرنا *an'khon men mir'chen bhar'na* V.T. not to let sleep آنکھوں میں موہنی ہونا *an'khon men mo'hini ho'na* V.I. have charming eyes آنکھیں الٹ جانا *an'khen u'lat ja'na* V.I. be on verge of death; have pupils upturned as sign of imminent death آنکھیں بچھانا *an'khen bichha'na*, آنکھیں فرش راہ کرنا *an'khen farshe-rah' kar'na* V.T. redcarpet show great respect (to) آنکھیں بند کیے *an'khen band ki'ye* ADV. blindly unmindful of the consequences آنکھیں بدل لینا *an'khen ba'dal le na* V.I. be fickle; be inconstant withdraw one's favour (from) آنکھیں بند کرنا *an'khen band kar'na* V.I. close one's eyes for contemplation sleep die آنکھیں بنوانا *an'khen banva'na* V.I. get eyes operated upon get an artificial eye آنکھیں پٹم ہو جانا *an'khen pat'tam ho ja'na* V.I. go blind آنکھیں پھٹنا *an khen phat'na* V.I. have a splitting headache be wonderstruck آنکھیں پھٹی کی پھٹی رہ جانا *an khen pha'ti ki pha'ti raih ja'na* V.I. be wonderstruck آنکھیں پھاڑ پھاڑ کر دیکھنا *an'khen phar' phar'kar dekh'na* PH. strain one's eyes gaze with wonder cast amorous glances آنکھیں پھوٹنا *an'khen phoot'na* V.I. become blind آنکھیں پھوٹ جانا *an'khen phoot' ja'na* V.I. get blind آنکھیں پونچھنا *an'khen ponch'na* V.I. wipe off one's tears console; comfort آنکھیں پھر جانا *an'khen phir' ja'na* V.I. (of one's condition) become precarious آنکھیں پھیر لینا *an'khen pher' le'na* V.T. withdraw one's favour (from) آنکھیں پھیرے طوطے کی سی باتیں کرے مینا کی سی *an'khen phe're to'te ki si, ba'ten ka're mai'na ki si* PROV. fair without, foul within

آنکھیں ترس جانا *ān'kheṅ ta'ras jā nā* v.i. yearn long enough (for the sight of someone) آنکھیں ٹھنڈی کرنا *āṅ kheṅ thanḍī kar'nā* v.i. be comforted (by the sight of) آنکھیں چار کرنا *ān'kheṅ chār kar'nā* v.t. face, come face to face with آنکھیں چار ہونا *āṅ'kheṅ chār' ho'nā* v.i. come across fall in love آنکھیں چرانا *āṅ'kheṅ chūrā'na* v.i. evade آنکھیں چھت سے لگنا *ān'kheṅ chhat' se lag'nā* ph. be on one's death-bed آنکھیں دکھانا *āṅ'kheṅ dikhā'na* v.t. glower get eyesight tested (by) آنکھیں دیکھنا *āṅ'kheṅ dekh'nā* v.t. test the eyesight (of) inculcate the habits (of) be influenced by the company (of) آنکھ سفید ہو جانا *āṅ'kheṅ sifed' ho jā'nā* ph. become blind (in expectation, etc.) آنکھیں گاڑنا *āṅ'kheṅ gāṛ'na* v.t stare fixedly (at) آنکھیں لال (پیلی) کرنا *āṅ'kheṅ lāl (pī'lī) kar'nā* v.i. show sings of anger آنکھیں مٹکانا *āṅ'kheṅ maṭkā'na* v.i. look with blandishment آنکھیں ملنا *āṅ'kheṅ mal'nā* v.i. rub one's eyes (to remove effects of sleep) آنکھیں نکالنا *āṅ'kheṅ nikāl'na* v.t. gouge out the eye scowl; glower آنکھیں نیلی پیلی کرنا *āṅ'kheṅ nī'lī pī'lī kar'nā* ph be enraged آنکھیں ہوئیں چار دل میں آیا پیار، آنکھیں ہوئیں اوٹ دل میں آیا کھوٹ *āṅ'kheṅ hū''iṅ chār' dil meṅ ā'ya payār', āṅ'kheṅ hū''īṅ oṭ dil meṅ ā'ya khoṭ'* prov. out of sight out of mind

آنگن *āṅ'gan* n.m. (dial. آنگنا *āṅg'nā*) courtyard, yard

آنند *ānand'* n.m. (dial.) delight luxury [S]

آنو *āṅ''o, ā''oṅ* n.f. mucous discharged in tenesmus; mucous

آنول *āṅ'val* n.f. afterbirth, secundiness: uterine discharge with foetus on delivery آنول نال *āṅ'val nāl* n.f new-born infant's navel-string, umbilical cord آنول جانول *āṅ'val' jhāṅ'val* n.m pl twins آنول گٹا *āṅ'val gaṭ'ṭa* n.m. dried myrobalan myrobalan fallen from tree [~ fol]

آنولہ *āṅv'lah* n.m. (same as آملہ ★)

آنہ *ā'nah* n.m. anna; a former coin equivalent to one-sixteeenth of a rupee one-sixteenth share (in something) آنے پائی کا حساب *ā'ne pā''ī kā ḥisāb'* n.m. full account adv to the penny

آنی جانی *ā'nī jā'nī* adj. transitory evanescent mortal [~ آنا]

آوا *āva* n.m. kiln آوے کا آوا ہی بگڑا ہوا ہے *ā ve kā ā'va hī big'ṛa hū''a hai* prov they are chips of the same block it is rotten from top to bottom

آوا جاوا *ā'vā jā'vā* n.m., آوا جائی *ā vā jā''ī* n.f uncalled for errands needless exchange of visits scamper [~ جانا - آنا]

آوارہ *āvā rah* n.m. & adj. tramp; vagabond debauchee profligate dissolute آوارہ گرد *āvā'ra-gar'd* n.m. & adj. tramp, vagabond profligate dissolute debauchee آوارہ گردی *āvā'ra gar'dī* n.f. vagrancy profligacy آوارہ مزاج *āvā ra-mizāj'* adj. dissolute unprincipled; unscrupulous irresponsible آوارہ مزاجی *āvā'ra-mizā'jī* n.f. irresponsibility being unprincipled profligacy آوارہ وطن *āvā'ra-vatan'* n.m. & adj. alien; (one) away from one's homeland آوارگی *āvā'ragī* (col. *āvār'gī*) n.f profligacy vagrancy irresponsibility lack of principles; being unscrupulous [P]

آواز *āvāz'* n.f sound voice اونچی (یا بلند) آواز *oonchī (or būland') āvāz'* n.f loud voice آواز اٹھانا *āvāz' ūṭhā'na* v.i. raise a voice (against). protest raise one's voice آواز بدل جانا *āvā' ba'dal jā'na*, آواز بگڑ جانا *āvāz' bi'gaṛ jā'na*, آواز بھاری ہونا *āvāz' bhā'rī ho'nā*, آواز بھرانا *āvāz' bharrā-nā* v.i. become hoarse آواز بیٹھنا *āvāz' baiṭh'nā* v.i. lose voice آواز بلند کرنا *āvāz' būland' kar'nā* v.i lift up one's voice register protest, raise one's voice (against); آوازِ پا *āvā'z-e pā* n.f footfall آواز پر *āvāz' par* adv. at the beck and call (of) guided just by the sound آوازِ جرس *āvāz-e jaras* n.f call for departure آواز دینا *āvāz de'nā* v.t call out آوازِ سگاں کم نکند رزقِ گدا را *āvā'z-e sa'gāṅ kam' na-kūnad' riz'q-e gadā' rā* ph. malicious endeavours of adversaries hardly affect a sincere person's lot آواز سے آواز ملانا *āvāz' se āvāz' milā'na* v.t bring in concord with; be armonious آواز سے آواز ملنا *āvāz se āvāz' mil'na* v.i. be concordant; be harmonious آوازِ صور *āvā'z-e soor'* n.f. sound of resurrection trumpet clarion-call آوازِ غیب *āvā'z-e ghaib'* n.f mysterious voice; voice from heaven آواز کا اتار چڑھاؤ *āvāz' kā ūtār' chaṛhā''o* n.m. rise and fall of the voice آواز کا پاٹ *āvāz' ka pāṭ* n.m. range of voice آواز میں رعشہ ہونا *āvāz meṅ ra''shah ho'nā* v.i. have a tremulous voice آواز کرنا *āvāz' kar'nā* v.i call aloud آواز کھل جانا *āvāz khūl' jā'na* v.i. recover voice آواز گونجنا *āvāz goonj'na* v.i. echo, resound have a stentorian voice آواز لگانا *āvāz lagā'nā* V.I. (of beggar) cry out (of pedlar) cry out one's wares (of vocalist) raise his voice (of birds) sing ; chirp آواز میں پتی لگنا *āvāz' meṅ pat'tī lag'nā* V.I. (of vocalist's voice) not to to be clear آواز میں چھریاں (یا کٹاریاں) بھری ہونا *āvāz' meṅ chhūr'yāṅ* (or *kaṭā'riyāṅ*) *bharī ho'nā'* V.I. have a very sarcastic tone آواز میں لوچ ہونا *āvāz' meṅ loch' ho'nā* V.I. have an appealing voice آواز میں نمک ہونا *āvāz' meṅ na'mak ho'nā* PH. have a pathetic tone آوازہ *āvā'zah* N.M. report fame ; reputation slander آوازہ بلند ہونا *āvā'zah būland' ho'nā* V.I. (of something's fame) spread آوازہ (آوازے) کسنا *āvā'zah* (or *avā'ze*) *kas'nā* V.T. taunt yell out shanderous remarks [P]

آوازہ *āvā'zah* N.M. (see under آواز ★)

آواگون *ā'vā gav'an* N.M. (dial.) metempsychosis; transmigration of soul [S coming and going]

آور *ā'var* SUF cause of something that brings آورد *āvard* N.F. (in versification) art ; lack of normal flow ADJ. artificial ; lacking natural flow SUF. result of ; brought about by ; aftermath of آوردہ *āvar'dah* ADJ. (amount) brought forward N.M. protege aftermath (of) [P ~ آوردن bring]

آویختہ *āvekh'tah* SUF. hanging ; suspended attached [P ~ آویختن]

آویز *āvez'* SUF. hanging attracting آویزاں *āve'zāṅ* ADJ. hanging ; suspended ; pendant attached آویزاں کرنا *āve'zāṅ kar'nā* V.T. hang; suspend attach آویزہ *āve'zah* N.M. ear-ring [P ~ PREC.]

آویزش *āve'zish* N.F. enmity differences [P ~ PREC.]

آہ *āh* N.F. sigh cry of pain ; moan INT alas , ah ; ah ah; dear ; dear me ; oh dear آہ (آہیں) بھرنا *āh'* (or *ā'heṅ*) *bhar'nā*, آہ کرنا *āh' kar'nā* V.I. sigh ; lament cry with pain آہ پڑنا *āh par'nā* V.T suffer retribution for oppression ; be overtaken by Nemesis آہِ جاںکاہ *ā'h-e jāṅ'kāh'* N.F. heart-reading sigh آہِ جگرسوز *ā'h-e ji'gar-soz'* N.F. burning sigh آہِ رسا *ā'h-e rasā'* N.F. sigh evoking response ; effective sigh آہِ سرد *ā'h-e sard'* N.F. deep sigh آہِ سرد کھینچنا *ā'h-e sard' khench'nā* V.I. heave a deep sigh آہ کرنا یا کھینچنا *āh' kar'nā* (or *khench'nā*) V.I. sigh moan آہ لینا *āh' le'nā* V I oppress ; tyrannize invite Nemesis ; deserve retribution آہِ نیم شب *ā'h-e nīm' shab*, آہِ نیم شبی *ā'h-e nīm sha'bī* N.F. midnight lamentation midnight prayer آہ و بکا *ā'h-o-būkā'*, آہ و زاری *ā'h-o-zā'rī*, آہ و فغاں *ā'h-o-fighān* N.F groans wailing lamentation [P]

آہا *ā'hā*, اہاہا *ah'hā* INT (expressing delight or wonder) oh wonderful

آہٹ *ā'haṭ* N.F. footfall آہٹ پانا *ā'haṭ pā'nā* V.I. hear the footfall (of) get an inkling (of), آہٹ لیتے رہنا *ā'haṭ le'te raih'nā* PH. be on the alert ; be vigilant

آہستہ *āhis'tah* ADV. slowly softly ; tenderly leisurely ADJ. slow slack tardy soft آہستہ آہستہ *āhis'tah āhis'tah* ADV. slowly gradually by degrees آہستہ رو *āhis'ta rau'* ADJ. slowpaced آہستگی *āhis'tagī* N.F. slowness tardiness delay mildness softness [P]

آہن *ā'han* N.M. (ped.) iron مردِ آہن *mar'd-e ā'han* N.M. strong man آہنگر *ā'han-gar* N.M. blacksmith ; smith آہنگری *ā'han-garī* N.F. blacksmith's trade آہنی *ā'hanī* ADJ. iron ferric strong hard آہنی سلاخ *ā'hanī salākh'* N.F. steel bar آہنی سیف *ā'hanī sef* N.M. iron safe آہنیں *ā'hanīṅ* ADJ. like iron strong hard عزمِ آہنیں *azm-e ā'hanīṅ*, آہنی عزم *ā'hanī 'azm* N.M. firm resolve ; unshakable resolution [P]

آہنگ *āhang'* N.M. sound music melody harmony purpose ; intention way ; mode time ; occasion [P]

آہو *ā'hoo* N.M. deer ; antelope آہو چشم *ā'hoo chashm* ADJ. gazelle-eyed آہوئے حرم *ahoo'-e haram'* N.M. (fig.) inaccessible beloved antelope of the sanctuary آہوئے فلک *āhoo'-e falak'* N.M. (fig.) sun [P]

آئنہ *ā'inah* N.M. (ABB. of آئینہ N.M. ★)

آؤ *ā''o* N.M. coming used only in :) آؤ بھگت *ā''o bha'gat* N.F. warm welcome , courteous reception آؤ دیکھا نہ تاؤ *ā''o de'khā na tā''o* PH. in great hurry indiscriminately [~ آنا]

آئندہ *ā'in'dah* ADJ. next future coming ensuing subsequent ADV. in future again ; afterwards آئندہ اختیار بدستِ مختار *ā'indah ikhtiyā'r ba-das't-e mukhtār'* PH. you have my word of advice ; now it is up to you to accept or reject it آیند *ā'ind'* N.M. comer (only in: آیند و روند N.M. passer(s)-by

آئی *a''ī* N.F. & V.I. (see under آنا ★)

آئی سی ایس *a''ī sī ais'* N.M. (arch.) Indian Civil Service ; I.C.S. Civilian [E]

آئین *a'in'* N.M. constitution (arch.) law (arch.) regulation manners آئین بندی *a'īn ban'dī* N.F. public decorations illuminations آئینِ دادرسی *a'ī'n-e dād'-ra'sī* N.M. trial procedure way of justice آئینِ تحریری *a'ī'n-e tahrī'rī*, تحریری آئین *taihrī'ri a'ī'n* N.M. written constitution آئینِ غیر تحریری *a'ī'n-e ghair tahrī'rī* غیر نوشتہ آئین *ghair navish'tah a'ī'n* N.M. unwritten constitution آئینِ کہن *a''īn-e kohan'* N.M. old order former constitution آئین نامہ *a'īn' na'mah* N.M. constitution (arch.) manual of rules and regulations آئینِ نو (یا نوی) *a''īn-e nau* (or *navī'*) N.M. new constitution new order آئینی *a'ī'nī* ADJ. constitutional [P]

آئیں بائیں شائیں *a''eṅ ba''eṅ sha''eṅ* N.F. irrelevant talk silly talk of discomfited person آئیں بائیں شائیں کرنا *a''eṅ ba''eṅ sha''eṅ kar'na* V.I. talk irrelevantly talk in a silly manner

آئینہ *a'ī'nah* N.M. mirror ; looking-glass آئینہ اندھا ہو جانا *a'ī'nah an' dha ho ja'na* V.I. (of mirror) blind ; lose its polish آئینۂ باطن *a'ī'na-e ba' tin* N.M. (fig.) purity of heart ; heart ; clarity of conscience آئینہ بنانا *a'ī'nah bana'na* V.T. manufacture a mirror perplex آئینۂ حلب (یا حلبی) *a''īna-e ha'lab* (or *ha'labī*) N.M. quality mirror (arch.) such a one made in Aleppo آئینہ خانہ *a'ī'na kha'nah* N.M. mirrored chamber آئینہ دار *a'īna-dar* ADJ. reflecting or echoing (views, etc. of) N.M. (arch.) one holding a mirror (to) آئینہ دکھانا *a'ī'nah dikha'na* V.T. hold a mirror (to) show the pros and cons (of) آئینہ رخ (یا رو) *a'ī'na-rūkh'* (or *roo'*) ADJ. fair ; blonde آئینہ ساز *a'ī'na-saz'*, آئینہ گر *a'ī'na-gar* N.M. mirror manufacturer glazier آئینہ سامنے سے نہ ہٹنا *a'īnah sam'ne se na hat'na* V.I. pay constant attention to one's make-up آئینۂ سکندر (یا سکندری) *a'ī'na-e sikan'dar* (or *sikan'darī*) N.M. (arch.) polished steel mirror stated to have been installed by Alexander to detect movement of enemy ships (lit.) magic mirror آئینہ سیما *a'ī'na-sīma* ADJ. very beautiful respondent آئینہ کر دینا *a'ī'nah kar de'na* V.T. cause to glisten (fig.) clarify; make absolutely clear آئینۂ مجوف *a'ī'na-e mūjav'vaf*, مجوف آئینہ *mūjav' vaf a'ī'nah* N.M. concave mirror آئینۂ محدب *a'īna-e mohad'dab* محدب آئینہ *mohad'dab a'ī'nah* N.M. convex mirror آئینے میں بال *a'ī'ne meṅ bal* N.M. crack in the mirror آئینے میں بال آنا *a'ī'ne meṅ bal a'na* V.I. (of mirror) be cracked آئینہ میں منہ دیکھو *a'ī'ne meṅ mūṅh de'kho* PH. don't give yourself airs [P]

آیا *a'ya* N.F. nurse lady's maid آیا گری *a ya-garī* N.F. midwifery

آیا[2] *a'ya* CONJ. whether if whether or not [P]

آیا[3] *a'ya* V.I. (P.T. of آنا V.I. ★)

آیت *a'yat* N.F. آیہ *a'yah* N.M. (N.F. PL. آیات *a'yat'*) (Quranic) verse sign (of God) mark آیت الکرسی *a'yat-ūl kūr'sī* N.F. the Throne Verse ; verse 2 : 255 of the Holy Quran describing God's authority آیتِ کریمہ *a'yat-e karī'mah* N.F. the Penitential Verse ; Verse 21:87 of the Holy Quran repeated as a penitential formula

اب *ab* ADV. now presently; just now اب بھی *ab, bhī* ADV. even now till now ; to the present time ; to this moment yet ; still اب پچھتائے کیا ہوت جب چڑیاں چگ گئیں کھیت *ab pachh'ta'e kya hot jab chir'yaṅ chūg' ga''īṅ khet'* PROV. it is no use crying over spilt milk اب تب کرنا *ab' tab kar'na* V.I. evade ; dodge اب تب ہونا *ab' tab ho'na* V.I. be on the point of death اب تک *ab' tak* (arch. اب تلک *ab' talak*) ADV. till now ; yet ; still hitherto اب رنگ لائی گلہری *ab' rang la''ī gilaih'rī* PH. (exclamation about mischievous person) now does he show his true colours اب سے *ab' se* ADV. henceforth, henceforward ; from now on ; in future اب کا *ab' ka* ADJ. of the present time the next ; the following اب کی *ab' kī* اب کی بار *ab' kī bar'* CONJ. & ADV. this time this once اب کی بات اب کے ساتھ جب کی بات جب کے ساتھ *ab' kī bat' ab' ke sath, jab' kī bat' jab' ke sath* PROV. changed circumstances call for a changed idiom اب کے *ab' ke* CONJ. & ADV. this time اب کے بچے تو سب گھر رچے *ab' ke ba'che to sab' ghar ra'che* PROV. saved once's saved for ever اب نہ تب *ab'na tab'* ADV. never in no case ; under no circumstances اب کے برس *ab'ke ba'ras* ADV. this year

اب[2] *ab* N.M. (PL. *aba'*) (ped.) variant of ابو *abo'o* N.M. ★) father ابوی *a'bavī* ADJ. partiarchal paternal [A]

ابا *iba* N.M. refusal ; denial detestation ابا کرنا *iba' kar'na* V.I. detest

ابا *ab'ba* N.M. daddy ; papa; pop ابا جان *ab'ba jan'*, ابا جی *ab'ba ji* N.M. respectable father INT. dear daddy ; dear papa

ابابیل *aba'bil* N.M. swallow ; martin N.M. PL. flock or swarm (of birds, etc.) [~SING. ابالہ swarm]

اباحت *iba'hat* N.F. leave ; permission liberty ; licence [A]

ابالنا *ubal'na* V.T. boil ابال *ubal'* N.M. boiling ; ebullition rage ; fury ; fit of passion ابال آنا / اٹھنا *ubal' a'na* (or *uth'na*) V.I. start boiling have a fit of passion have a sudden but transitory longing (for) or aversion (to) ابالا سبالا *uba'la suba'la* ADJ. (of dish) badly cooked merely boiled tasteless ; vapid ابلی دال ملنا *uba'li dal mil'na* V.I. have tasteless food [~ ابلنا CAUS]

ابتدا *ibtida'* N.F. commencement beginning origin ابتدا کرنا *ibtida kar'na* V.T. begin make a beginning take the initiative ابتدا ہونا *ibtida' ho'na* V.I. be begun ابتدا میں *ibtida' men* ADV. in the beginning : at first ; originally ابتدائی *ibtida''i* ADJ. preliminary initial primary ابتدائی تعلیم *ibtida''i ta'lim'* N.F. primary education ابتدائی حروف *ibtida''i huroof'* N.M. PL. initials initial forms of letters opening words ابتدائی طبی امداد *ibtida''i tib'bi imdad'* N.F. first-aid ابتدائی مدرسہ *ibtida''i mad'rasah* N.M. primary school ابتدائی مدارس *ibtidai mada'ris* N.M. PL. primary schools [A]

ابتداع *ibtida''* N.M. innovation [A ~ بدعت]

ابتذال *ibtizal'* N.M. triteness meanness vileness contempt [A ~ بذل]

ابتر *ab'tar* ADJ. spoiled ; spoilt vitiated ruined destitute miserable confused disorderly (rare) issueless ابتر کرنا *ab'tar kar'na* V.T. spoil vitiate upset ruin ابتر ہونا *ab'tar ho'na* V.I. be ruined be spoilt be thrown into disorder ابتری *ab'tari* N.F. disorder mismanagement confusion ruin [~A بتر curtail]

ابتسام *ibtisam'* N.M. (ped.) smile cheerfulness تبسم *tabas'sum'* N.M.★ [A]

ابتلا *ibtila* N.M. misfortune ; stroke of ill-luck temptation trial [A ~ بلا]

ابتہاج *ibtehaj'* N.M. happiness cheerfulness gaiety hilarity [A ~ بہجت]

ابٹنا *ubat'na* (col. بٹنا *bu't'na*, ابٹن *ub'tan*) N.M. cosmetic unguent mixture of perfumes oil, flour etc. for rubbing the body with ابٹنا ملنا *ubat'na mal'na* V.I. rub (body) with it ; apply unguent (to body)

ابجد *ab'jad* N.F. Arabic alphabet according to Hebrew order of letters alphabet ABC ; rudiments (properly called جمل *jum'mal*) mode of reckoning numbers by the letters of the alphabet. (Following is the value attached to each letter according to this system of reckoning :

ا 1	ب 2	ج 3	د 4	ہ 5	و 6	ز 7	ح 8	ط 9	ی 10
ک 20	ل 30	م 40	ن 50	س 60	ع 70	ف 80	ص 90		
ق 100	ر 200	ش 300	ت 400	ث 500	خ 600	ذ 700	ض 800	ظ 900	غ 1,000

Any letter not included above has the same numerical value as the one written like it in this table.) ابجد خواں *ab'jad khan* N.M. one who is beginning to learn his alphabet ; abecedarian beginner ; novice ; tyro [A]

ابحار *abhar'*, ابحر *ab'hur* N.M. (PL. of بحر N.M. ★)

ابخرہ *ab'khirah* N.M. PL. vapours steam evaporation exhalations fumes [A ~ SING. بخار]

ابخل *ab'khal* ADJ. & N.M. very miserly (person) [A ~ بخل]

ابد *a'bad* N.M. eternity ; time without end ابدالآباد *a'bad-ul-abad'* ADJ. eternity of eternities ; time without end ابدالآباد تک *a'bad-ul-abad' tak* ADV. forever ; forever and ever ابداً *a'badan'* ADJ. forever ; eternally ابدی *a'badi* ADJ. eternal ; everlasting perpetual endless ابدیت *abadiy'yat* N.F. eternity ; everlastingness perpetuity endlessness [A]

ابداع *ibda''* N.M. innovation [A ~ بدعت]

ابدال *abdal'* N.M. PL. an order of saints saints devotees ; religious persons [A ~ SING. بدل or بدیل]

ابدال ibdal' N.M. (gram.) substitution of one letter for another ; substitution [A ~ بدل]

ابدان abdān' N.M. (PL. of بدن N.M. ★)

ابدی a'badī ADJ. ابدیت abadiy'yat N.F. (see under ابد N.M. ★)

ابر abr N.M. cloud (ابر بہار یا بہاراں یا بہاری abr-e bahār' (or bahā'rān or bahā'rī (rare ابر بہمن ab'r-e baih'-man) N.M. spring clouds ابر باراں abr-e-ba'rān, ابر تر abr-e tar' N.M. rain cloud(s) ابر تنک abr-e tūnūk' N.M. light cloud ابر چھانا abr chha'na V.I: be cloudy (of clouds) be overcast ; overshadow ابر دار abr-dār' cloudy ابر دریا بار abr-e dar'ya-bār' N.M. saturated clouds ; rain-bearing clouds (fig.) generous person ابر رحمت abr-e raih'mat ابر کرم abr-e karam N.M. much needed cloud God's grace ابر سیاہ abr-e siyah N.M. dark cloud ابر غلیظ abr-e ghalīz N.M. thick cloud(s) ابر کھلنا abr khūl'na V.I. (of clouds) be dispersed (of sky) become clear ابر گھر آنا abr ghir ā'na V.I. (of cloud) be overcast ابر مردہ abr-e mūr'dah N.M. sponge ابر نیساں abr-e nai'sān N.M. spring cloud(s) (this as) rain-bearing cloud [P]

ابرا ab'ra, ابرہ abrah N.M. outer fold of a double garment ; outer fold ابرا اور استر ab'ra aur as'tar N.M. outer fold and lining [P]

ابرار abrār' N.M. holy men [A ~ SING.]

ابراہیم ibrahīm' (occ. براہیم barahīm' among Christians ابرہام abrahām') N.M. Abraham · گلزار ابراہیم gūlza'r-e ibrahīm' N M. pyre metamorphosed into garden [A ~ H]

ابرام ibram' N.M. pressing necessity solicitude persistence [A]

ابرص ab'ras ADJ. leprous (one) suffering from leucoderma [A ~ برص]

ابرک ab'rak (Arabicised as ابرق ab'raq) N.M. mica ; talc

ابرو ab'roo N.F. eyebrow (ابرو پر (یا میں) بل آنا (یا پڑنا) ab'roo par (or meh) bal' ā'na (or par'nā) V.I. knit the brow ; frow ; scowl ; glower ابرو پر میل نہ آنا ab'roo par mail' na ā'na V.I. not take something ill ابرو تاننا ab'roo tān'na VT. & I. knit the brow ; frown ; scowl , glower. ابروئے فلک abroo'-e falak' N.M. (fig.) crescent [P]

ابری ab'rī N.F. marble paper [P]

ابریشم abre'sham, N.M. raw-silk silk cocoon ابریشمی abre'shamī ADJ. silk ; silken [A ~ P]

ابریق ibrīq' N.M. ewer spouted waterpot [A]

ابسنا ū'basnā (rare بسنا būs'nā) V.I. become stale rot ابسانا ūbsā'na V.T. cause to rot

ابصار absār' N.M. (PL. of بصر N.F. ★)

ابطال abtāl' N.M. (PL of بطل N.M. ★)

ابطال ibtāl' N.M. refutation falsification باطل ba'til ADJ. ★ [A ~ بطلان N.M.]

ابعاد ab'ād' N.F. PL. dimensions extremeties ابعاد ثلاثہ ab'ā'd-e salā'sah N.M. PL. the three dimensions, viz., length, breadth, and depth (or thickness) [A ~ SING. بعد]

ابعد ab''ad ADJ. SUP (ped.) farthest , most distant ; remotest [A ~ SUP بعید]

ابکا ub'ka N.M. slip knot round neck of vessel for drawing water.

ابکار abkār' N.F. (ped.) (PL. of بکر bik'r) virgins (PL. of بکرہ būk'rah) mornings [A]

ابکائی ūbka''ī N.F. act of vomiting nausea sickness ابکائی آنا ūbka''i ā'na, ابکنا ū'bakna V.I. vomit ; disgorge expel ; cast out

ابل i'bil N.M. PL. camels [A]

ابلاغ iblāgh' N.M. communication اظہار و ابلاغ izhā'ro iblāgh' N.M. expression and communication [A ~ بلوغ]

ابلق ab'laq ADJ. piebald ; mottled blank and white N.M. piebald horse ابلق ایام ab'laq-e ayyam' N.M. nights and days ; motley time [A]

ابلقا ab'laqa N.M. a species of cuckoo

ابلنا ū'balnā V.I boil swell flow over rise well up ابل آنا ū'bul ā'na V.I. boil over overflow ابل پڑنا ū'bal par'na V I. boil over over flow swell ابالنا ūbāl'na V T ★

ابلہ ab'lah N.M. PL. بلہ būlh) simpleton · ADJ simple stupid ; gullible bashful ابلہ فریب ab'la fareb' ADJ. sly ; wily knave impostor huckster ابلہی ab'lahī N.F. foolishness ; folly stupidity ; gullibility [A]

ابلیس iblīs' N.M. (PL. ابالیس abālīs'. ابالسہ aba'lisah)

devil Satan mischievous person [A ~ بلس] frustrated person]

ابن ibn, بن bin N.M. (PL. ابنا abnā') son child ابن آدم ib'n-e ā'dam N.M. man mankind (dial.) Son of Man ; Jesus ابن الامیر ib'n-ul-amīr ADJ. high-born ; of noble birth or blood ابن السبیل ib'n-us sabil' N.M. traveller ابن الغرض ib'n-ul-gha'raz N.M. selfish person ابن مریم ib'n-e mar'yam N.M. Mary's son ; Jesus ابن الوقت ib'n-ul-vaq't N.M. time server abnā' N.M. PL. sons people ابنائے جنس abnā'-e-jins N.M. PL. persons (of same quality and rank) ; companions equals ابنائے جہاں abnā'-e jahān', ابنائے دہر abnā'-e dah'r (or daih'r), ابنائے روزگار abnā''-e roz-gār' ابنائے زمانہ abnā'-e zamā'nah N.M. PL. people humanity ; mankind contemporaries [A]

ابو aboo', اب ab N.M. (PL. آبا ābā) father PREF. (ABB. boo) father having ; evincing possessor of ; owner of connected (with) distinguished (by) ابوالبشر abūl-bashar' N.M. father of humanity ; Adam ابوبکر aboo'bak'r N.M. appellation of first orthodox Caliph ; Abu Bakr ابوتراب aboo' tūrāb', بوتراب boo-tūrab' N.M. Dusty (as appellation of fourth Orthodox Caliph) ابوجہل aboo' jah'l N.M. (or jaih'l) Father of Ignorance (as appellation of one of the earliest antagonists of Islam) ; Abu Jahl ابوہریرہ aboo' hūrai'rah N.M. Kitten-owner (as appellation of one of the Companions of the Holy Prophet) ; Abu Hurairah ابوی a bavī ADJ. (see under ابے N.M ★) [A]

ابواب abvāb' N.M. (PL. of باب N.M. ★)

ابھارنا ubhār'nā V.T. (see under ابھرنا V.I. ★)

ابھاگن abhā'gin ADJ. & N.F. unfortunate (woman) [بھاگ ~]

ابہام ibhām' N.M. ambiguity thumb [A]

ابھرنا u'bharnā V.I. rise . grow gain in prominenee ; become prominent come to the forefront ; come into the lime light become salient achieve fame ; become prominent ابھارنا ubhār'nā V.T. rise up ; lift unload induce ; persuade incite excite give prominence cause to be salient

ابھی a'bhī ADV. now just now ; right now even now already in a short while this very moment ; immediately ; instantly till now [ہی - اب ~]

ابی ib'bī N.F. toss-stroke (at tip-cat) ابی دبی کرنا ib'bī dūb'bī kar'nā V.I. play tipcat

ابے a'be INT. you rascal sirrah , siree ابے تبے کرنا a'be ta'be kar nā V.I. address disrespectfully

ابیات abyāt' N.M. PL. of بیت N.F. ★)

ابیانا ūbyā'nā V. I. get sick (of) get tired (of) be or get fell up (with) ابیاہٹ ūbyā'-hat N.F. irksomeness ; weariness

ابیر abīr' N M. (rustic for عبیر N.M. ★)

ابیض ab'yaz ADJ. white snow-white milk-white more or most splendid بحر ابیض bah'r-e ab'yaz N.M. White Sea [A ~ بیض]

ابیقوری abīqoor'rī N.M. & ADJ. epicurean ابیقوریت abīqooriy'yat N.F. epicureanism [E ~ G]

ابیل دبیل abail' dabail' ADJ. & N.M. weakling subservient

اپارنا ūpār'nā V.T. uproot cause to blister اپار ūpar' N.F. blistering (of skin) اپار کرنا ūpar' kar'nā V.I. (of skin) blister [~ اپڑنا CAUS.]

اپاہج apā'haj ADJ. crippled lazy ; indolent N.M. cripple indolent person

اپج ū'paj N.F. new idea flight of fancy wit (lit.) produce ; yield اپجنا ū'pajnā V.I. spring up , grow sprout ; germinate (of idea) rise in mind

اپدیش ūpdesh' N M. (dial.) sermon اپدیش کرنا (یا دینا) ūpdesh' kar'nā (or de'nā) V.T. preach اپدیشک ūpde'shak N.M. (dial.) preacher [S]

اپریل aprail' N.M. April اپریل فول aprail' fool N.M. All Fools' Day April Fool [E]

اپڑنا u'parnā V.I. give a good impression be well-printed (of skin) blister

اپسرا ap'sarā N.F. (dial.) gay girl ; prostitute; courtesan (H. myth.) dancer at Indra's court (H. myth.) nymph [S]

اپلا ūp'lā N.M. dung-cake اپلے تھاپنا (یا پاتھنا) ūp'le thāp'nā (or dial. pāth'nā) V.I. prepare dung-cake

اپلیکیشن ap'līkashan N.F. application [E]

اپنا ap'nā PRON. one's own personal ; individual appropriate exclusive N.M. relation , relative , kith and kin. اپنا آپا ap'nā ā'pā N.M.

one's self ; oneself اپنا اپنا *ap'nā ap'nā* ADJ. respective personal individual اپنا اپنا ہے پرایا پرایا *ap'nā ap'nā hai, parā'yā parā'yā* PROV. close sits my shirt but closer my skin ; blood is thicker than water اپنا الّو سیدھا کرنا *ap'nā ul'loo sī'dhā kar'nā* PH. wheedle someone grind one's own axe ; look to one's own interests اپنا الّو کہیں نہیں گیا *ap'nā ul'loo ka'hīn na'hīn ga'yā* PROV. I stand in no way to lose اپنا بنا لینا *ap'nā banā' le nā* V.I. win (someone) over اپنا بیگانہ (یا پرایا) *ap'nā begā'nah* (or *parā'yā*) N.M. all and sundry friend and foe related and unrelated persons اپنا پوت پرایا ڈھینگرا *ap'nā poot parā'yā ḍhīngra* PROV. every man thinks his own geese swans اپنا پیٹ تو کتا بھی پالتا ہے *ap'nā peṭ to kut'tā bhī pāl'tā hai* PROV. it is not manly on one's part to look just to self-interest اپنا پیسہ کھوٹا تو پرکھنے والے کا کیا قصور *ap'nā pai'sā khoṭā to parakh'ne vā'le kā kya qusoor'* PROV. if your money is bad, the assayer is not to blame اپنا پیٹ پہلے ڈھانپو دوسرے کو ننگا پیچھے کہنا *ap'nā peṭ paih'le ḍhānpo doos're ko nanga pī'chhe kaih'nā* V.I. those who live in glass houses should not throw stones at others اپنا توشہ اپنا بھروسہ *ap'nā to'shah ap'nā bharo'sah,* اپنا توشہ اپنے ساتھ *ap'nā to'shah ap'ne sā'th* PROV. every tub must stand on its bottom اپنا ٹھکانا کرنا *ap'nā ṭhikā'na kar'nā* V.I. shift for oneself arrange separate residence for oneself اپنا حساب کرنا *ap'nā hisāb' kar'nā* V.I. settle one's account (with) اپنا رستہ لینا *ap'nā ras'tah le'nā* V.I. wend one's way not to meddle with other, affairs اپنا رکھ پرایا چکھ *ap'nā rakh parā'ya chakh* PROV. save one's own and spend another's اپنا رونا رونا *ap'nā ro'nā ro'nā* V.I. air one's grievance talk of one's woes اپنا سا منہ لے کر رہ جانا *ap'nā sa mūnh le kar raih' jā'nā* V.I. hang down (or hide) one's head in shame اپنا سبیتا کرنا *ap'nā sube'ta kar'nā* V.I. fend for oneself اپنا سر پیٹ لینا *ap'nā sir' pīṭ le'nā* V.I. curse oneself اپنا سر کھانا *ap'nā sir' khā'nā* V.I. (iron.) do what one wills not to pester others اپنا سوجھتا کرنا *ap'nā soojh'ta kar'nā* V.I. fend for oneself اپنا عیب بھی ہنر معلوم ہوتا ہے *ap'nā 'aib bhī hunar ma'loom' ho'tā hai* PH. one's own vice seems a virtue اپنا کام دوسرے پر نہ ڈالو *ap'nā kām doos're par na ḍā'lo* PH. if you want a thing done well, do it yourself اپنا کرنا *ap'nā kar'nā* V.T. make (someone or something) one's own attach (someone) to oneself embezzle اپنا کیا پانا (یا بھگتنا) *ap'nā ki'yā pā'nā* (or *bhug'gatnā*) V.T. suffer the consequence of one's misdeeds face the music اپنا گھر بھرنا *ap'nā ghar' bhar'nā* V.I. aggrandize oneself use one's position to one's personal advantage اپنا گھر دور سے سوجھتا (یا نظر) آتا ہے *ap'nā ghar' door' se soojh'tā* (or *na'zar*) *ā'tā hai* PH. one seizes on one's personal advantage اپنا لہو پینا *ap'nā lā'hoo pī'nā* V.I. suffer oneself اپنا منہ دھو رکھو *ap'nā mūnh dho ra(k)'kho* PH. don't you hanker after it you do not deserve it اپنا منہ دیکھو *ap'nā mūnh de'kho* PH. you do not deserve it اپنا نام بدل ڈالنا *ap'nā nām' ba'dal ḍāl'nā* V.I. change one's name put one's honour at stake for something اپنی آگ میں آپ جلنا *ap'nī āg' men āp' jal'nā* V.I. vent one's rage on oneself اپنی اپنی بولی بولنا *ap'nī ap'nī bo'lī bol'na* V.I. (of each) press one's claim simultaneously اپنی اپنی پڑنا *ap'nī ap'nī paṛ'nā* V.I. look out each for oneself اپنی اپنی ڈفلی اپنا اپنا راگ *ap'nī ap'nī ḍaf'lī ap'nā ap'nā rāg* PROV. everyone has his own fad اپنی ایڑی دیکھو *ap'nī e'ṛī de'kho* PH. do not cast a malignant look اپنی بات پر اڑ جانا *ap'nī bāt par aṛ' jā'nā* V.I. take a firm stand اپنی پیٹھ دکھائی نہیں دیتی *ap'nī pīṭh dikhā''ī na'hīn de'tī* PH. none can see the beam in one's own eye اپنی ران کھولیے آپ ہی لاجوں مریے *ap'nī rān' kho'liye āp' hī lājon mar'ye* PROV. wash your dirty linen in public and be put to shame اپنی راہ لگنا (یا لینا) *ap'nī rāh' lag'nā* (or *le'nā*) V.I. not to meddle with others affairs اپنی کھال میں مست رہنا *ap'nī khāl men mast' raih'nā* V.I. be happy despite poverty اپنی کہی نہ اور کی سنی *ap'nī kahī' na aur kī sū'nī* PH. without ever getting a chance to express one's feelings اپنی گانا *ap'nī gā'nā* V.I. talk big اپنی گرہ سے کیا جاتا ہے *ap'nī gi'reh se kyā jā'tā hai* PH. I do not stand to lose اپنی گڑیا سنوار دینا *ap'nī guṛ'yā sanvār' de'nā* V.I. settle enough dower on one's daughter اپنی گلی میں کتا بھی شیر ہوتا ہے *ap'nī ga'lī men kut'tā bhī sher' ho'tā hai* PROV. even cowards are bold at their own post ; every dog is valient at his own door every cock is proud of his own dunghill اپنی گوں کا یار *ap'nī gaun' kā yār'* PH. selfish friend اپنی ناک کٹی تو کٹی پرائی بدشگونی تو ہو گئی *ap'nī nāk ka'ṭī to ka'ṭī, parā''ī bad shagoo'nī to ho' ga'ī* PROV. never mind if the nose is cut, at least the face has been spited اپنی نیند سونا اپنی نیند اٹھنا *ap'nī nīnd so'nā ap'nī nīnd uṭh'nā* V.I. lead a carefree life be subservient to none اپنے آپ *ap'ne āp* ADV. by itself (etc.) اپنے پاؤں پر کھڑے ہونا *ap'ne pa''on par khaṛe ho'nā* V.I. stand on one's feet achieve self sufficiency اپنے اپنے وقت پر ہر چیز اچھی لگتی ہے *ap'ne ap'ne vaq't par har chī'z' achchhī lag'tī hai* PROV. everything is good in its season اپنے پاؤں آپ کلہاڑی مارنا *ap'ne pā''on āp kul'hā'ṛī mār'nā* PH. dig one's own grave اپنے تئیں *ap'ne ta'in* PH. (arch.) oneself اپنے حساب (یا حسابوں) *ap'ne ḥisāb'* (or *ḥisābon*) ADV. according to oneself اپنے حق میں کانٹے بونا *ap'ne ḥaq meṅ kāṅ'ṭe bo'nā* V.I. cause one's own ruin اپنے ڈھب کا *ap'ne ḍhab ka* PH. (person, etc.) after one's heart the type needed اپنے سائے سے بھی ڈرنا *ap'ne sāi'e se bhī ḍar'nā* V.I. be very cowardly اپنے کام سے کام رکھنا *ap'ne kām se kām rakh'nā* V.I. mind one's own business اپنے کیے پر پچھتانا *ap'ne ki'ye par pachhtā'nā* V.I. regret one's actions اپنے کیے کا کیا علاج *ap'ne kī'ye kā kya 'ilāj'* PH. there is no remedy for one's own misdeeds اپنے کیے کی سزا بھگتنا *ap'ne kī'ye kī sazā' bhu'gatnā* (or *pā'nā*) V.I. face the music اپنے گریبان میں منہ ڈالنا (یا ڈال کر دیکھنا) *ap'ne girebān' meṅ muṅh ḍāl'nā* (or *ḍāl kar dekh'nā*) V.I. undertake honest self-criticism اپنے منہ میاں مٹھو *ap'ne muṅh mi'yāṅ mit'thoo* PH. self-praise is no recommendation اپنے منہ میاں مٹھو بننا *ap'ne muṅh miyāṅ mithoo ban'nā* V.I. be one's own trumpeter; indulge in self-praise اپنے منہ پر طمانچہ مارنا *ap'ne muṅh par tamāṅchah mār'nā* V.I. chastise oneself اپنے ہی تن کا پھوڑا ستاتا ہے *ap'ne hī tan' kā pho'ṛā satā'tātā hai* V.I. one is betrayed only by friends *apnā'nā* V.T. adopt make (something or someone) one's own اپنایت *apnā'yat* N.F. kinship family relation

اپنشد *u'panishad* N.M. philosophical portion of Hindu scriptures [S]

اپھرنا *a'pharnā* V.I. swell out gormandize be satisfied with food be full grow strong boast be puffed up with pride become very rich; have one's head turned with affluence N.M. (*aphra'*) flatulence ADJ. (*aph'ra*) swollen elated satisfied اپھر جانا *a'phar jā'nā* V.I. be overloaded be elated be satiated اپھرانا *aphrā'nā* V.T. stuff gorge feed (someone) so that his belly swells out give (money, etc.) to the utmost extent of someone's desire

اپھننا *uphan'nā* V.I. froth; foam; effer vesce boil over (fig.) make a wry face [~ پھپھن]

اپی *ūp'pī* ADJ. (of sword, etc.) burnished whetted

اپیل *apīl'* N.F. (dial. M.) appeal اپیل داخل کرنا *apīl' dā'khil kar'nā* V.T. & O. file an appeal اپیل کرنا *apīl' kar'nā* V.T. file an appeal اپیل منظور کرنا *apīl' manzoor' kar'nā* V.I. allow an appeal اپیل خاص *apīl' khās'* N.F. special appeal اپیل سرسری *apīl' sar'sarī* N.F. summary appeal اپیل عام *apīl' 'ām* N.F. regular appeal اپیل متخالف *apīl' mūtakhā'lif* N.F. cross appeal [E]

ات *at* N.F. extreme ات کا *at kā* ADV. extreme ات گت *at' gat* ADV. very much

اتا *atā'* N.M. father chief اتابک *atā bik* N.M. (arch.) Turkish chief prince's tutor Premier اتاترک *atā'-tūrk'* N.M. Turkey's father (as appellation of Mustafa Kamal, the builder of Post-Caliphate Turkey [T]

اِتّا *it'tā* ADJ. (col. for اتنا *it'nā*) this much; that much a اتّا سا *it'tā sā* ADJ. & ADV. this much a little; woe bit [~ اتنا]

اتا پتا *a'tā pa'tā* N.M. whereabouts details اتا پتا بتانا *a'tā pa'tā batā'nā* V.I. give details about tell the whereabouts (of)

آتارنا *ūtār'nā*, آتار دینا *ūtār' de'nā* V.T. cause to alight or dismount unload (cargo, etc.) land lower; bring down take down tear off cut off disgrace resent enthrall (11) expel. (12) make a recompense (13) shave off (14) remove (15) free from (16) take off (clothes) (17) cast off (18) make away (19) uncock (gun) (20) let down (21) lay (in grave) (22) produce (23) distil آتار *ūtār'* N.M. descent slope ebb-tide fall decrease reduction in price alms آتار چڑھاؤ *ūtār' chaṛhā''o* N.M. ebb and flow rise and fall fluctuation ups and downs: vicissitudes (of life) loss and gain plot آتار جانا *ūtār jā'nā* V.T. gulp down آتار دینا *ūtār' de'nā* V.T. (pull down) take off dishonour; disgrace آتار لینا *ūtār' le'nā* V.T. copy take down insert آتارا *ūtā'ra* N.M. slope running into river, etc.); wharf halting place cast off clothes offering (moved a certain number of times from head or foot of someone to appease or exorcise evil spirit) آتارا کرنا *ūtā'ra kar'nā* V.T. take down dismount آتارا اتارنا *ūtā'ra ūtār'nā* V.I. dispossess evil spirit thus; exorcise آتارن *ūtā'ran* N.M. cast off clothes آتارو *ūtā'roo* ADJ. sloping bent upon اتارو ہونا *ūta'roo ho'nā* V.I. descend be bent upon اُتارنا *ūtar'na* V.I. ★

اتاشی *atā'shī*, اتاچی *atāchī* N.M. attache اتاچی کیس *atā'chī kes'* N.M. attache case

پریس اتاشی *pares' atā'shī* N.M. Press attache [E]

اتالیق *atā'līq'* N.M. tutor ; coach ; structor precepter mentor

اتالیقی *atāli'qi* N.F. private tuition ; coaching preceptorship [T~ اتا father]

اتاؤلا *ūtā''olā* ADJ. precipate impatient hasty اتاؤلا سو باؤلا *ūtā''olā sobā''olā* PROV haste make waste اتاولی *ūtā''oli* N.F. precipitation impatient haste ADJ. impatiently hasty

اتائی *atā''ī* N.M. & ADJ. (same as عطائی N.M. ★)

اتباع *atbā'* N.M. PL. followers ; following اتباع *i'ttibā'* N.M. following ; toeing the line obedience [A ~ تبع]

اتحاد *itt'ehād'* N.M. unification unity union united front alliance amity friendship treaty اتحادِ ثلاثہ *itteḥā'd-e salā'sah* V.I (arch.) Triple Alliance. اتحادی *itteḥa'dī* N.M. (arch.) Allied Powers ; Allies ADJ. ally [A ~ وحدت]

اُتّر *ūt'tar* N.M. north ADJ. northern [S]

اترانا *itra'nā* V.I. strut give oneself airs behave boastfully act coquettishly

اترایا *itrā'ya* ADJ. boastful conceited ; arrogant coquettish

اترائی *ūtra'ī* N.F. اترتا *ūtarta* ADJ. (see under اترنا V.I. ★)

اترسوں *atar'soṅ* N.M. & ADJ. day after tomorrow day before yesterday

اترنا *ū'tarnā*, اتر جانا *ū'tar jā'nā* V.I. alight ; get down land disembark lodge; put up ebb wane cross fall off fade be born (11) reach (12) decrease ; abate (13) fall in value or dignity (14) be freed from debt (15) become insipid (16) flatter (17) be disgraced (18) grow old (19) become pale (20) grow thin (21) be pulled down (22) die (23) fall upon (24) change (25) come down ; descend (26) be revealed اتر پڑنا *ū'tar paṛ'na* V.I. settle alight get down lodge اترا *ūt'ra* اترا ہوا *ūt'ra hū'a* ADJ. fallen dismissed descended weakened waned ebbed alighted اترا شحنہ مردک نام *ūt'ra shaiḥ'na mar'dak nām* PROV. no power, no respect ; out of place, out of grace اترائی *ūtra'ī* N.F. coming-down ; descent come-down ferriage اترتا *ūtar'tā* ADJ. & ADV. waning (moon) ebbing (tide) descending decreasing اترتا ہوا *ū'tarta hū'a* ADJ. worse meagre of lower quality *ūt'ran* N.F. cast off clothes

اترنگ *ūtrang'* N.F. top piece of door-case

اتروانا *ūtarvānā* V.T. cause to alight cause be taken off ; get doffed [~ اترنا CAUS.]

اتصاف *ittisāf'* N.M. description praise qualification [A ~ وصف]

اتصال *ittisāl'* N.M. junction being adjacent [A ~ وصل]

اتفاق *ittifāq'* N.M. agreement concord ; harmony coincidence amity alliance unity ; union consent chance; opportunity event ; accident equality (11) probability اتفاق بننا *ittifāq' ban'na* V.I turn out well harmonize اتفاق پڑنا *ittifaq par'nā* V.I. occur ; come to pass ; happen اتفاق حسنہ *ittifā'q-e ha'sanah* N.M. favourable opportunity lucky chance good fortune ; stroke of good luck اتفاق رائے *ittifā'q-e rā''e* N.M. unanimity consensus concurrence اتفاق رائے سے *ittifā'q-e rā''e se* ADV. unanimously اتفاق رائے ہونا *ittifā'q-e rā''e ho'na* V.I. have consensus of opinion (of concensus of opinion) be اتفاق رکھنا *ittifāq' rakh'na* V.I. live in harmony be on terms of intimacy اتفاق سے *ittifāq' se* by chance ; accidentally fortuitously together ; conjointly in conjunction (with) اتفاق کرنا *ittifāq' kar'na* V.T. unite agree (with or to) conspire form a friendship اتفاق ہونا *ittifāq' ho'nā* V.I. happen be agreed harmonize grow intimate اتفاقاً *ittifā'qan* ADV. accidentally ; by chance occasionally اتفاقات *ittifāqat'* N.M. chances events accidents occurrences اتفاقاتِ حسنہ *ittifāqā't-e ha'sanah* N.M. PL. unexpected terms of good fortune agreeable accidents اتفاقاتِ زمانہ *ittifāqā't-e zamā'nah* N.M. PL. vicissitudes of fortune اتفاقی *ittifā'qī* ADJ. accidental ; chance ; fortuitous incidental contingent (expenditure) casual (leave) agreed ; unanimous اتفاقیہ *ittifāqiy'yah* ADJ. chance ; accidental casual contingent

ADV. by chance ; casually [A ~ وفق]

اتقا *ittiqa'* N.M. piety abstinence shunning [A ~ وقایت]

اتقیا *atqiya'* N.M. PL. the pious ADJ. pious devout righteous ; virtuous [A ~ SING. تقی]

اتکا *ittika* N.M. reclining (against) dependence ; reliance [A تکیہ]

اتکہ *it'kah* (or *at'-*) N.M. husband of one's foster-mother or midwife [T]

اتلاف *itlaf'* N.M. loss destruction ruin decay [A ~ تلف]

اتم *ut'tam* ADJ. best highest excellent اتم کھیتی مدھم بیوپار نکھد چاکری بھیک ندار *ut'tam khe'ti mad'dham biyopar, nikhad' cha'karī bhīk na-dār'* PROV. of means of livelihood agriculture is excellent business mediocre, service the lowest and begging the worst

atām' ADJ. (more or) most perfect utmost extreme بدرجۂ اتم *ba-dar'ja-e atam'* (ped. *da'raja-*) PH. extremely to the utmost [A ~ تام SUP.]

اتمام *itmām'* N.M. completion accomplishment perfection اتمام حجت *itmā'm-e huj'jat* N.M. final bed fulfilment of a condition [A ~]

اتنا *it'na* ADJ. (F. اتنی *it'nī*) as much as this so much thus far اتنی سی بات *it'nī sī bat* N.F. a minor point ; just that much اتنی سی جان گز بھر کی زبان *it'nī sī jan' gaz' bhar kī zabān'* PH. too saucy for one's years اتنے سے اتنا ہونا *it'ne se it'nā ho'na* V.I. from poverty to pelf ; from mite to million اتنے *it'ne* ADJ. so many اتنے کی بڑھیا نہیں جتنے کا لہنگا پھٹ گیا *it'ne kī buṛh'ya na'hīn jit'ne ka laihh'ga phaṭ ga'ya* PROV. cheap things cost more to maintain than to buy it is easier to build a new house than to patch an old one اتنے میں *it'ne meh* ADV. meanwhile ; in the meantime upon this ; at this اتنا *ut'na* ADJ. (F. اتنی *ut'nī*) as much as that ; so much ; that much that far اتنا ہی *ut'na hī* ADJ. exactly that much اتنے *ut'ne* ADV. as many as that ; so many

اتو *ut'too* N.M. (arch.) embroidering or plaiting plaiting ; puckering ; marking plaits ; pleat اتو بنانا (یا کرنا) *ut'too bana'na* (or *kar'nā*) V.T. (arch.) embroider (arch.) pleat (fig.) beat blue (fig.) vilify (fig.) make a fool of اتوکش *ut'too-kash*, اتوساز *ut'too-saz*, اتوگر *ut'too-gar* N.M. plaiter embroiderer اتو ہونا *ut'too ho'nā* V.I. be disgraced be scandalized [CORR. of P pr. *u'too*]

اتوار *itvar'* N.M. Sunday

اتہام *ittehām'* N.M. imputation charge ; accusation suspicions slander censure اتہام بے جا *itteha'm-e be-jā'*, بے جا اتہام *be-jā' ittehām'* N.M. false accusation uncalled-for slander [A ~ تہمت]

اتھاہ *athāh'* ADJ. abysmal ; bottomless unfathomable deep unfordable [~ NEG. + تھاہ]

اتھلا *uth'lā* ADJ. shallow (fig.) unable to keep a secret

اتھلنا *u'thalnā* V.I. turn topsy-turvy ; upset turn over اتھلنا پتھلنا *u'thalna pu'thalna* V.T. upset ; turn topsy-turvy اتھلانا *uthla'na* V.T. turn topsy-turvy upset اتھل پتھل *u'thal pu'thal* ADJ. upset ; topsy-turvy اتھل پتھل کرنا *u'thal pu'thal kar'na* V.T. turn topsy-turvy ; upset اتھل پتھل ہونا *u'thal pu'thal ho'na* V.I. be topsy-turvy be upset

اٹاٹٹ *a'ṭa ṭuṭ'* ADV. (full) to the brim [~ اٹنا]

اٹاچی *aṭa'chī* N.M. same as اتاشی N.M

اٹاری *aṭa'rī* N.F. upper room ; garret penthouse

اٹالا *aṭa'la* N.M. lumber goods chattels stock mass, heap commodities ; provisions اٹالا کرنا *aṭa'la kar'na* V.T. heap mass اٹالا لادنا *aṭa'la lad'na* V.T overload

اٹانا *aṭa'na* V.T. fill fit [~ اٹنا CAUS.]

اٹاوہ *aṭa-vah* N M name of an Indian town اٹاوے کا کاریگر *aṭa've ka ka'rigar* N.M. (fig.) bragging workman who does not turn out to be very skilled at his trade

اٹپٹانا *aṭpaṭa'na* V.I. talk nonsense waver linger اٹپٹ بولنا *aṭ'paṭ bol'na* V.I. speak incoherently talk nonsense

اٹ سٹ *aṭ' saṭ* N.F. cleverness ; ingenuity plot ; intrigue اٹ سٹ لڑانا *aṭ saṭ laṛa'na* V.T. plot اٹ سٹ لڑی ہونا *aṭ' saṭ la'ṛī ho'na* have inspired have an equation (with)

اٹکانا *aṭka'na* V T. stop hinder impede restrain cause to falter postpone

اٹکاؤ *aṭka'o* N.M. postponement hurdle ;

hindrance restraint detention [اٹکنا CAUS].

اٹکل *aṭ'kal* N.F. guess ; conjecture supposition presumption opinion rough estimate اٹکل باز *aṭ'kal bāz* ADJ. conjecturer اٹکل پچو *aṭ'kal-pach'choo* N.M. wild guess ; random guess ; mere conjecture ADJ. uncertain conjectural ADV. at random اٹکل سے *aṭ'kal se* ADV. approximately ; by conjecture اٹکل سے کام لینا *aṭ'kal se kām le'nā* V.I. guess ; hazard a guess

اٹک مٹک *a'ṭak ma'ṭak* N.F. coquetry

اٹکنا *aṭak'nā* V.I hesitate stick rest falter be entangled be dependant (on) اٹکانا *aṭ'kānā* V.T ★

اٹکن بٹکن *aṭ'kan baṭ'kan*, اٹکن مٹکن *aṭ'kan maṭ'kan* N.F. (formula for) children's game comprising self-prepared make-believe feast

اٹکھیلی *aṭkhe'lī* N. (USU. PL.) gambol playfulness blandishment coquetry اٹکھیلیاں سوجھنا *aṭkhe'liyāṅ soojh'nā* V.I. be in a playful mood اٹکھیلیاں کرنا *aṭkhe'liyāṅ kar'nā* V.I. be conquetish

اٹل *aṭal'* ADJ. inexorable inevitable permanent unchanging firm ; determined ; resolved [~ NEG. + ٹل]

اٹلس *aiṭ'las* N.F. atlas [E]

اٹم *a'ṭam* N.M. heap

اٹنا *aṭ'nā*, اٹ جانا *aṭ' ja'nā* V.I. be filled to the brim

اٹنگا *ūṭaṅ'gā* ADJ. (F. اٹنگی *ūṭaṅ'gī*) teddy (trousers) ; high drainpipe (trousers) shrivelled ; badly shaped

اٹنگن *ūṭaṅ'gan* N.M. a species of nettle

اٹوانٹی کھٹوانٹی اٹوائی کھٹوائی *aṭvāṅ'ṭī khaṭvāṅ'ṭī*, *aṭvā'ṭī khaṭvā'ṭī* N F. state of women who takes to her bed in grief or trouble or feigned illness اٹوائی کھٹوائی لے کر پڑ رہنا *aṭvā'ṭī khaṭvā'ṭī li'ye par' raih'nā* PH. be confined to bed thus feign illness in protest

اٹوٹ *aṭooṭ'* ADJ. inviolate unbreakable indestructible integral اٹوٹ انگ *aṭooṭ' ang* PL. (dial.) integral part [NEG. ا + ٹوٹ]

اٹھ *aṭh* SUF eight اٹھ پہری (یا پہریا) *aṭh paih'ri* (or *paih'riyā*) N.M. & ADJ. (one) with round-the-clock duty

اٹھا *aṭ'ṭhā* N.M. (at cards) eight [~ اٹھ]

اٹھا بیٹھی *ūṭ'ṭhā bai'ṭhī* N.F. (see under اٹھنا V.I. ★)

اٹھارہ *a(ṭ)ṭhā'rah* N M. & ADJ. eighteen اٹھارواں *a(ṭ)ṭhā'ravāṅ* ADJ. eighteenth

اٹھاسی *a(ṭ)ṭhā'sī* N.M. & ADJ. eighty-eight اٹھاسیواں *a(ṭ)ṭhā'sīvāṅ* ADJ. eighty-eighth

اٹھان *ūṭhān'* N.F. (see under اٹھانا V.T. ★)

اٹھانا *ūṭhā'nā* N.T. lift take up hoist erect take (an oath on) take away pack up produce invent awake (11) excite (12) bear ; suffer ; endure (13) carry (14) gain (15) incur (loss) (16) expend (17) remove ; drive (18) nullify (19) abolish (20) put aside (21) steal (22) eject (23) breed ; bring up (24) raise or rear (wall) (25) effect اٹھا دینا *ūṭhā'-de'nā* V.T. exterminate erase abolish do away with اٹھا رکھنا *ūṭhā' rakh'nā* V.T. assume (responsibility) ; take (responsibility) upon oneself put off (till tomorrow , etc.) spare اٹھا لینا *ūṭhā' le'na* V.T. take up, pick up clear undertake اٹھا لے جانا *ūṭhā' le ja'nā* V.T. take away kidnap abduct walk off with اٹھان *ūṭhān'* N.F. (dial. M.) upbringing growth rise ; ascent elevation opening sexual desire development of breasts اٹھاؤ *ūṭhā''oo* ADJ. portable mobile ; moveable اٹھاؤ چولھا *ūṭhā''oo choo'lhā* N.M. portable stove rolling stone اٹھائی گیرا *ūṭhā''ī-gī'rā* N.M. petty thief ; pilferer ; larcener larcenist [~ اٹھنا CAUS.]

اٹھانوے *a(ṭ)ṭhān've* N.M. & ADJ. ninety-eight اٹھانویں *a(ṭ)ṭhān'vevāṅ* ADJ. ninety-eighth

اٹھاؤ *ūṭhā''oo* N.M. (see under اٹھانا V.T. ★)

اٹھاون *a(ṭ)ṭhā'van* N.M. & ADJ. fifty-eight اٹھاونواں *a(ṭ)ṭhā'vanvāṅ* ADJ. fifty-eighth

اٹھائیس *a(ṭ)ṭhā''īs* N.M. & ADJ. twenty-eighth اٹھائیسواں *a(ṭ)ṭhā''īsvāṅ* ADJ. twenty-eighth

اٹھائی گیرا *ūṭhā''ī gī'rā* N.M. (see under اٹھانا ★)

اٹھ *ūṭh* V.I., اٹھتا *ūṭ(ṭ)hā* ADJ., اٹھلا *aṭh'lā* ADV. (see under اٹھنا V.I. ★)

اٹھتر *aṭhat'tar* N.M. & ADJ. seventy-eight اٹھترواں *aṭhat'tarvāṅ* ADJ. seventy-eighth

اٹھلانا *aṭhlā'nā* V.I. struct walk coquettishly walk indifferently

اٹھلو *ūṭh al'loo* N.M. tramp ; one who has no fixed dwelling rolling stone ADJ unreliable or untrustworthy (person)

اٹھنا *ūṭh'nā* V.I get up rise stand proceed leave come on be ready be brought up let bear ; endure ; suffer (11) (of pain) be ; be experienced (12) (of money) be spent (on something) (13) end ; come to an end (14) be obtained (15) be raised be reared اٹھنا بیٹھنا *ūṭh'nā baiṭh'nā* N M manners, etc. ; etiquette V.I. be frequently getting up and sitting down visit associate *ūṭh-baiṭh*, اٹھا بیٹھی *ūṭ'ṭhā-bai'ṭhī*, اٹھا بیٹھک *ūṭ'ṭhā bai'ṭhak* N.F. frequently rising up and sitting down restlessness fidgeting اٹھ بیٹھ لگانا *ūṭh baiṭh lagā'nā* V.I. frequently rise up and sit down be restless اٹھ بیٹھنا *ūṭh baiṭh-ā* V.I. sit up get up ; wake up get well revive اٹھ جانا *ūṭh'jā'nā* V.I. come to an end be abolished die disappear go away اٹھ چلنا *ūṭh' chal'nā* V.I. depart اٹھ کھڑا ہونا *ūṭh khā'ṛā ho'nā* V.I. rise up suddenly wake up recover اٹھا *ū(ṭ')ṭhā'* ADJ. (F. اٹھی *ū(ṭ')ṭhī'*) risen اٹھی پیٹھ آٹھویں دن *ūṭ'ṭhī paiṭh' āṭh'veṅ din* ADV. prestige once lost is not easy to regain اٹھتا *ūṭh'tā* ADJ. (F. اٹھتی *ūṭh'tī*) rising ascending budding flourishing languishing fading اٹھتا جوبن *ūṭh'tā jo'ban* N.M. swelling of breasts bloom of woman's youth اٹھتی جوانی *ūṭh'tī javā'nī* N.F. prime of life blooming youth اٹھتے *ūṭh''te* ADV. rising اٹھتے ہی ٹانگ ٹوٹی *ūṭh'te hī ṭāṅg ṭoo'ṭī* PH. misfortune overtaking right at the outset اٹھتے جوتی بیٹھتے لات *ūṭh te joo'tī baiṭh'te lā't* PH. (W. dial.) frequent disgrace harsh treatment اٹھتے بیٹھتے *ūṭh'te baiṭh'te* ADV. easily by degrees in a leisurely manner slowly quickly at odd intervals

اٹھنگن *aṭhan'gan* N.M. prop ; support used for preventing something from rolling

اٹھنی *aṭhan'nī* N.F. (arch) eight-anna bit half-rupee [~ آٹھ + آنہ]

اٹھوارا *aṭh'vā'rā* N M. eight-day period : week

اٹھوانا *ūṭhvā'nā* V.T cause to be lifted cause to be removed cause to be abolished [~ اٹھنا CAUS.]

اٹی *aṭ'ṭī* N.F. (same as انٹی *aṅ'ṭī* N.F. ★)

اٹیرنا *aṭer'nā* V.T. wind (thread) train (a horse) اٹیرن *aṭer'an* N.M winder reel ADV. very lean اٹیرن کر دینا *aṭe'ran kar de'nā* V.T. reduce (someone) to a skeleton

اٹیرن

اٹیک *aṭek'* ADJ. without a prop [~ ٹیکنا]

اثاث البیت *asā's-ul-bait'* N.M. household furniture [A ~ fol. بیت house]

اثاثہ *asā'sah* N.M. property wealth goods or chattles [A]

اثبات *isbāt'* N.M. recognition proof confirmation ; affirmation ascertaining verification establishing being positive اثبات جرم *isbā't-e jūrm'* N.M. conviction اثبات حقیقت *isbā't-e haqqiy'yat* N.M. proof of right [A ~ ثبت]

اثر *a'sar* N.M. mark sign token impression effect trace influence operation issue consequence (11) action (12) virtue or effect (of medicine) ; efficacy (13) Tradition of the Holy Prophet اثر انداز *a'sar-andāz'* ADJ. influential effective اثر انداز ہونا *a'sar-andāz' ho'nā* V.I. have effect (on) اثر پذیر ہونا *a'sar pazīr' ho'nā* V.I. take effect be efficacious اثر رکھنا *a'sar rakh'nā* V.I. be effective اثر کرنا *a'sar kar'nā* V.T. operate effect touch influence اثر و رسوخ *a'sar rūsookh'* اثر و نفوذ *a'sar-o nufooz'* N.M. influence اثر ہونا *a'sar ho'nā* V.I. have effect be influenced [A]

اثقال *asqāl'* N.M. (PL. of ثقل N.F. ★), اثقل *as'qal* ADJ. (ped.) heaviest ; very heavy [A ~ ثقل]

اثم *ism* N.M. (PL. آثام *āsām'*) sins (rare) crime

اثمار *asmār'* N.M. PL. fruits results [A ~ SING. ثمرہ or ثمر]

اثنا *asnā'* N.M. middle ; interval ; interim period ; meantime اثنائے حال میں *asnā'-e hāl' meṅ* ADV. during ; in the midst of a certain state or condition اثنائے راہ میں *asnā'-e-rāh' meṅ* ADV. on the road whilst travelling اثنائے گفتگو میں *asnā'-e g̣ft-o-goo' meṅ* ADV. in the course of the talk اس اثنا میں *is asnā' meṅ* دریں اثنا *dar'īn ansā'* CONJ. & ADV. at this ; upon this n. the interval meanwhile ; in the meantime [A]

اثنا عشر *is'nā 'ashar'*, اثنا عشرہ *is'nā 'a'sharah* N.& ADJ. (rare) twelve اثنا عشرہ *is'nā 'ashar* ...

is'nā 'ashar N.M. PL. the twelve Shi'ite Imams اثنا عشری *is'nā 'a'sharī* N.M & ADJ. twelver ; Shi'ite believing in twelve Imams [A ~ اثنا two عشر ten]

اثیرا *asīr* ADJ. high lofty [A]

اثیر *asīr'* N.M. ether [A ~ G]

اجابت *ijā'bat* N.F. grant ; acceptance consent, compliance answering ouph.) motion ; stool اجابت (کھل کر) ہونا *ijā'bat (khal' kar) ho'nā* V.I. have a good motion [A ~ جواب]

اجارہ *ijā'rah* N.M. monopoly contract lease اجارہ دار *ijā'ra-dār'* N.M. monopolist lease-holder اجارہ داری *ijā'ra-dā'rī* N.F. monopoly اجارہ دینا *ijā'rah de'nā* V.T. give monopoly اجارہ کرنا *ijā'rah kar'nā* V.T. engage be accountable for اجارہ لینا *ijā'rah le'nā* V.T. take monopoly (lease a monopoly (etc.) اجارہ نامہ *ijā'ra-nā'mah*, اجارے کا پٹہ *ijā're kā paṭ'ṭā* N.M. deed of lease (etc.) اجارے دینا *ijā're de'nā* V.T. give on contract [A]

اجاڑنا *ujāṛ'nā* V.T. uproot pull down lay waste plunder ; ravage depopulate ruin اجاڑ *ujāṛ'* ADJ. ruined demolished deserted waste depopulated desolate N.M. desert wilderness ; waste ; wasteland devastation, ruin اجاڑو *ujā'roo* N.M. wastrel ; spendthrift ; prodigal ADJ squandering ; prodigal اجڑنا *u'jaṛnā* V.I. ★

اجازت *ijā'zat* N.F. permission ; leave sanction licence consent اجازت چاہنا *ijā'zat chāh'nā* V.T. take leave of seek permission اجازت خواہ *ijā'zat khāh* N.M. one asking permission اجازت دینا *ijā'zat de'nā* V.T. permit ; allow authorize empower اجازت ملنا *ijā'zat mil'nā* V.I. get permission get a licence [A]

اجاگر *ujā'gar* ADJ. manifest bright ; luminous conspicuous اجاگر کرنا *ujā'gar kar'nā* V.T show off or up make conspicuous اجاگر ہونا *ujā'gar ho'nā* V.I. be or become conspicuous

اجالا *ujā'lā* (dial. [illegible] *ujyā'lā*) N.M. sunshine daybreak ; dawn light (fig.) glory (of اجالا ہونا *ujā'lā ho'nā* V.I. dawn ; (of day) break be light be lighted ; be lit up اجالے کا تارا *ujā'le kā tā'rā* N.M. Morning Star ; Venus اجالنا *ujāl'nā* V.T. burnish polish brighten cleanse

اجان *ujān'* ADV. (rare) upstream

اجانب *ajā'nib* N.M. (PL. of اجنبی ADJ. & N.M. ★)

اجبار *ijbār'* N.M. compulsion ; constraint force repression [A ~ جبر]

اجتبا *ijtibā'* N.M. choice ; selection [A]

اجتماع *ijtimā''* N.M. gathering ; concourse meeting assemblage congregation combination conjunction co-existence community society اجتماع ضدین *ijtimā''-e ziddain'* N.M co-existence or combination of opposites اجتماع کرنا *ijtimā'' kar'nā* V.I. gather ; combine ; league hold a meeting convene روح الاجتماع *roo'h-ul ijtimā''* N.F. spirit of society 'espirit de corps' اجتماعی *ijtimā''ī* ADJ. social collective community congregational اجتماعی تحفظ *ijtimā''ī taḥaf'fuz* N.M. collective security اجتماعی ترقی *ijtimā''ī taraq'qī* N F. community development اجتماعی جد وجہد *ijtimā''ī jid'd-o jah'd* N.M. collective effort اجتماعی منصوبہ *ijtimā''ī mansoo'bah* N.M. community project [A ~ جمع]

اجتناب *ijtinab'* N.M. keeping aloof ; shunning abstinence abstination اجتناب کرنا *ijtinab' kar'nā* V.T. shun ; keep aloof (from) [A ~ جانب]

اجتہاد *ijtehād'* N.M. exercise of judgment exertion earnest effort interpretation of Islamic law , authoritative interpretation اجتہادی *ijtehā'dī* ADJ. interpretative اجتہادی مسئلہ *ijtehā'dī mas''alah* N.M. interpretation of law-point

اجداد *ajdād'* N.M. PL. ancestors ; forefather [A ~ SING. جد]

اجڈ *ujaḍ'* ADJ. rude ; unmannerly idiotic ignorant inconsiderable N.M. ill mannered fellow errant blockhead lout idiot اجڈ گنوار *ujaḍ' gaṅvār'* N.M. unmannerly boor

اجر *aj'r* N.M. reward ; recompense remuneration اجر دینا *aj'r de'nā* V.T remunerate recompense ; reward [A]

اجرا *ijrā'* N.M. enforcement issue execution service circulation اجرا کرنا *ijrā' kar'nā* V T execute (decree) issue set on foot اجرائے ڈگری ijrā-e ḍig'rī N.M. execution of a decree [A ~ جاری]

اجرام ajrām' N.M. PL. bodies اجرام فلکی ajrā'm-e-fa'lakī N.M. PL. heavenly bodies [A ~ SING. جرم jirm]

اجرت ij'rat N.F wages remuneration [A ~ اجر]

اجڑا ūj'ṛā ADJ (see under اجڑنا V.I ★)

اجڑنا ū'jaṛnā V.I. be ruined become desolate be demolished be ravaged be plundered be deprived of inhabitants ; be deserted be spent die be violated اجڑا ūj'ṛā ADJ. ruined desolate depopulated deserted اجڑا دیار ūj'ṛā diyār' N.M. wasteland اجڑا گھر ūj'ṛā ghar N.M. house lying in ruins (fig.) ruined family اجڑا پجڑا ūj'ṛā pūj'ṛā ADJ. (F. اجڑی پجڑی ūj'ṛī pūj'ṛī) in ruins ; desolate اجڑوانا ūjaṛvā'nā V.T. cause to be laid waste cause to be ruined

اجزا ajzā' N.M. PL. parts ; portions members ingredients constituents elements parts اجزائے ترکیبی ajzā-e tarkī'bī N.M. PL. constituents [A ~ SING. جزو]

اجساد ajsād' N.M. (PL. of جسد N M. ★)

اجسام ajsām' N.M. (PL. of جسم N.M. ★)

اجگر aj'gar N.M. boa constrictor dragon

اجل a'jal N.F. death hour of death term of life stated time destiny اجل رسیدہ a'jal-rasī'dah ADJ. overtaken by fate doomed اجل سر پر کھیلنا a'jal sir par khel'nā V.I. (of death) loom large اجل گرفتہ a'jal-girif'tah ADJ. doomed in the jaws of death [A]

اجلّ ajal' ADJ. (more or) most glorious [A ~ جلیل SUP.]

اجلا ūj'lā ADJ. (F. اجلی ūj'lī) white clean clear luminous ; radiant splendid lovely اجلا آدمی ūj'lā ād'mī N.M. (fig.) respectable man اجلا اجلا ūj'lā ūj'lā ADJ. quite white quite clean اجلاپن ūj'lā pan N.M. whiteness cleanliness lustre intelligence اجلنا ūjal'nā V.I. (of jewellery) be polished اجالنا ūjāl'nā, اجلوانا ūjalvā'nā V.T get (jewellery) polished

اجلاس ijlās N.M. sitting session bench (of court) meeting اجلاس فرما ijlās' farmā' ADJ. & ADV. presiding in session اجلاس کامل ijlā's-e kā'mil N.M. full bench (of law-court) اجلاس کرنا ijlās' kar'nā V.I. be in session preside sit in court خصوصی اجلاس khusoo'sī ijlās' N.M. extraordinary meeting سالانہ اجلاس salā'nah ijlās' N.M. annual meeting کھلا عام اجلاس khūl'lā 'ām' ijlās' N.M. open general session عمومی اجلاس 'ūmoo'mī ijlās' N.M. general meeting [A ~ جلسہ]

اجلاف ajlāf' N.M. PL. scum of society the vulgar ignoble people [A ~ SING. جلف jilf]

اجلال ijlāl' N.M. exaltation glorification اجلال و احترام ijlā'l-o eḥtirām' N.M. respect and glorification نزول اجلال nūzoo'l-e ijlāl' N.M. arrival (of important personage) نزول اجلال فرمانا nūzoo'l-e ijlāl farmā'nā V.T. (of important personage) arrive ; come [A ~ جلال]

اجلہ ajil'lah N.M. (PL. of جلیل ADJ. ★)

اجماع ijmā'' N.M. consensus اجماع امت ijmā''-e ūm'mat N.M. consensus of Muslim opinion اجماعی ijmā''ī ADJ. based on consensus [A ~ جمع]

اجمال ijmāl' gist ; abstract ; epitome ; summary abridgment synopsis (arch.) joint possession تفصیل اس اجمال کی یہ ہے tafsīl' is ijmāl' kī yeh hai PH. a detailed account of the points is (that) اجمالی ijmā'lī ADJ. brief abridged (rare) joint ; undivided اجمالی خاندان ijmāl'lī khāndān' N.M. (arch.) joint family [A]

اجمل aj'mal ADJ. more or most beautiful lovely [A ~ جمیل SUP.]

اجمعین ajma'īn' PL. all together whole [A ~ SING. اجمع ~ جمع]

اجمود ajmood' N.M. parsley

اجناس ajnās' N.F. PL. commodities crops cereals goods genuses [A ~ SING جنس ~ G]

اجنبی aj'anbī (ped. اجنب aj'nab) N.M. (PL. اجانب ajā'nib) stranger foreigner ; alien ADJ. strange foreign new to a place unfamiliar اجنبیت ajnabiyat N.F. unfamiliarity strangeness cold attitude ; lack of warmth [A]

اجوائن ajvā''in N.F. a species of dill dill-seed اجوائن خراسانی ajvā''in khūrāsānī N.F back henbane seed

اجورہ | *ajoo'rah* N.M. (ped.) reward wages remuneration [A ~ اجر]

اجہل | *aj'hal* ADJ. most ignorant ignoramus dunce [A ~ جاہل SUP.]

اجھینا | *ūjhe'nā* N.M. dung cakes or firewood arranged in hearth before setting fire to it

اجی | *a'jī* INT. (for calling attention) Hallo I say Sir اجی جانے بھی دیجیے | *a'jī jā'ne bhī dī'jiye* PH. don't you tell me leave it alone [~ جی + اے]

اجیالا | *ūjyā'lā* ADJ. (same as اجالا N.M. ★)

اجیٹن | *aj'ītan* N.M. adjutant [~ E CORR.)

اجیر | *ajīr'* N.M. employee [A ~ اجر]

اجیرن | *ajī'ran* ADJ. vexatious wearisome burdensome opperessive distasteful اجیرن کر دینا | *ajī'ran kar de'nā* V.T. make things difficult for اجیرن ہو جانا | *ajī'ran ho jā'nā* V.I. grow burdensome become vexatious be distasteful be sickening

اچاپت | *ūchā'pat* N.F. things (esp. provisions) bought on credit اچاپت اٹھانا | *ūchā'pat ūṭhā'nā* V.I. give (provisions, etc.) on credit اچاپت لانا | *ūchā pat lā'nā* V.I. bring (provisions, etc.) on credit

اچاٹ | *ūchāṭ'* ADJ. disgusted ; dissatisfied tired dull bored اچاٹ ہو جانا | *ūchāṭ' ho jā'nā* V.I. grow veary be bored become disgusted

اچار | *āchār'* N.M. pickles اچار ڈالنا | *achār' ḍāl'nā* V.T. pickle preserve (fig.) cause to vegetate اچار نکالنا | *achār' nikāl'nā* V.I. crush

اچانک | *achā'nak* ADJ. (dial. اچانچک | *achān'chak*) all of a sudden ; all at once unawares by chance unknowing

اچپلا | *ach'palā* ADJ. playful ; sprightly restless اچپلاہٹ | *achpalā'haṭ* N.F. playfulness ; sprightliness restlessness

اچٹنا | *ūchaṭnā* V.T. be separated (as plaster from wall) rebound (as sword striking obliquely) be disheartened be displeased be sick of اچٹتا ہوا | *ū'chaṭtā hū'ā* ADJ. cursory careless اچٹتی ہوئی نظر | *ū'chaṭī hū'ī na'zar* N.F. cursory glance اچٹانا | *ūchṭā'nā* V.T disgust cause to turn away from

اچرج | *achar'j* (dial. *a'charaj*) ADJ. strange surprising uncommon ; out of the way

اچرنا | *ū'charnā* V.I. (rare) be uttered be spoken be pronounced

اچکا | *ūchak'kā* N.M. pilferer pickpocket swindler bad character knave اچکاپن *ūchak'kā pan* N.M. pilfering swindling ; fraud knavery

اچکن | *ach'kan* N.M. tight long coat with full-buttons in front, achkan

اچکنا | *ū'chaknā* V.T. & I. rise on tiptoe jump swoop down carry away understand ; guess اچک کر *ū'chak kar* ADV. rising on tiptoe leaping up اچک لینا | *ū'chak le'nā* V.T. swoop down carry away guess correctly slip out (of) reach اچک لینا | *ū'chak le'nā* V.I. swoop down

اچنبھا | *acham'bhā* N.M. wonder marvel astonishment ADJ. wonderful prodigious strange uncommon اچنبھا ہونا | *acham'bhā ho'nā* V.I. be astonished اچنبھے کا | *acham'bhe kā* ADJ. astonishing ; marvellous اچنبھے کی بات *acham'bhe kī bāt* N.F. strange affair اچنبھے میں آنا (یا ہونا) | *acham'bhe meṅ ā'nā* (or *ho'nā*) V.I. be lost in amazement be perplexed be astonished be bewildered

اچھا | *ach'chhā* ADJ. (F. اچھی | *ach'chhī*) good excellent sound pleasing ; agreeable appropriate serviceable ; useful righteous ; virtuous healthy pure correct (11) genuine (12) lucky (13) cheap (14) productive (soil) (15) lovely (16) delicious ; wholesome (17) noble (18) benevolent (19) clever ; skilful ADV. well granted nicely admirably INT. yes well ; very well exactly very good no matter never mind well done fine all right too true اچھا خاصا | *ach'chhā khā'sā* ADJ. & ADV. quite well not bad اچھا رہنا | *ach'chhā raih'nā* V.I. fare well اچھا کرنا | *ach'chhā kar'nā* V.T. cure do good do right اچھا کہنا | *ach'chhā kaih'nā* V.T. say yes call good speak well (of) اچھا لگنا | *ach'chhā lag'nā* V.I. be pleasing afford pleasure be agreeable look nice fit well enjoy relish benefit

اچھا ہونا | *ach'chhā ho'nā* V.I. recover, be cured be in sound health (اچھی طرح (سے | *ach'chhī tar'h (se)* ADV. well carefully duly suitably thoroughly ; fully plentifully satisfactorily اچھی کہی | *ach'chhī ka'hī* INT. (iron.) well said what next strange ; how strange too true اچھے | *ach'chhe* N.M. PL. the good betters patrons ancestors ; forefathers upper classes men of birth, position, literary merit, etc. اچھے | اچھے | *ach'chhe ach'chhe* N.M. PL. persons quite high up in life اچھے اچھوں کو | *ach'chhe ach'hoń ko.* N.M. your betters men who count اچھے دن | *ach'chhe din* N.M. PL. better days اچھے سے اچھا | *ach'chhe se ach'chhā* ADJ. best of all اچھائی | *ach'chhā''ī* N.F. good virtue good point good features

اچھالا *ūchhā'lā* N.M. (of water) gush, spurt or sport [~ اچھلنا]

اچھال چھکا | *ūchhal' chhak'kā* N.F. strumpet wanton who exposer her bosom

اچھالنا | *ūch'hchāl'nā* V.T. throw up toss ; fling up make known ; make famous bring to disgrace ; scandalize (of child) vomit (milk) سونا اچھالتے چلے جاؤ | *so'nā ūchhal'te cha'le jā''o* PH. (there was such security of life and property then that) you could go about lossing gold on the road [~ اچھلنا CAUS.]

اچھائی | *achchhā''ī* N.F. (see under اچھا ADJ. ★)

اچھتانا پچھتانا | *achhtā'nā pachhtā'nā* V.T. (col.) repent repine

اچھلنا | *ū'chhalnā* V.I. leap ; bound issue gush forth ; spurt out fly out rejoice be full of glee be puffed up with pride be in high spirits ; be wild with rage اچھل پڑنا | *ū'chhal par'nā* V.I. leap up with joy spring break into a passion be frightened اچھلتے پھرنا | *ūchhalte phir'nā* V.I. feel elated be in high spirits be puffed up with pride اچھل کود | *ū'chhal kood'* N.F. leaping and jumping ; hopping and skipping frolicking revelry

اچھو | *ūch'chhoo* N.M. suffocation choking اچھو ہونا | *ūch'chhoo ho'nā* V.I. have a catch or frog in the throat be suffocated (in the act of swallowing) ; get choked

اچھوانی | *achhvā'nī* N.F. caudle

اچھوت | *achhoot'* N.M. & ADJ. (H. dial.) untouchable [~ NEG. چھوت]

اچھوتا | *achhoo'tā* ADJ. untouched by hand unused new unique remarkable اچھوتی | *achhoo'tī* N.F virgin (dial.) such Shi'ite devotee ADJ. untouched, by hand unique untouched by death اچھوتی کوکھ | *achhoo'tī kookh* N.F. woman whose offspring are all alive

احاد | *ahād'* N.M. PL. units ; any figure between 1 and 9 Traditions transmitted by only one narrator in each link of chain [A ~ SING. احد]

احادیث | *ahādīs'* N.F. PL. Traditions of the Holy Prophet (rare) news [A ~ SING. حدیث]

احاطہ | *ehā'tah* N.M. enclosure compound; close premises precincts boundry circuit area ; territory احاطہ کرنا *ehā'tah kar'nā* V.T. enclose surround fence limit confine [A ~ حائط wall]

احباب | *ahbab*, احبا | *ahibbā'* N.M. PL. friends lovers dear ones [A ~ SING. حبیب]

احبار | *ahbār'* N.M. PL. Jewish priests [A ~ SING. حبر *hibr*]

احتباس | *ehtibās'* N.M. stoppage restraint (rare) imprisonment [A ~ حبس]

احتجاب | *ehtijāb'* N.M. (ped.) seclusion retreat [A ~ حجاب]

احتجاج | *ehtijāj'* N.M. protest بصد احتجاج *ba-sad' ehtijāj* PH. after great protest زیر احتجاج *zer-i ehtijāj'* PH. under protest صدائے احتجاج *sadā'-e-ehtijāj* N.F. voice of protest صدائے احتجاج بلند کرنا *sadā'-e ehtijāj būland kar'nā* PH. raise a voice of protest [A ~ حجت]

احتراز | *ehtirāz'* N.M. abstension ; refraining from abstinence for bearance avoidance evasion guarding against احتراز کرنا *ehtirāz' kar'nā* V.I. abstain (from avoid refrain (from) [A]

احتراق | *ehtirāq'* N.M. combustion burning ; conflagration scorching heat [A]

احترام | *ihtirām'* N.M. honour respect adoration ; veneration [A ~ حرمت]

احتساب | *ehtisāb'* N.M. check evaluation restraint reckoning making up accounts police administration [~ حساب]

احتشام | *ehtishām'* N.M. pomp magnificance

parade retinue [A ~ حشم]

احتظاظ *ehtizaz'* N.M. (lit.) enjoyment [A ~ حظ]

احتکار *ehtikar'* N.M. hoarding [A]

احتلام *ehtilām'* N.M. wet dream ; nocturnal pollution Bright's disease [A ~ حلم *hulm*]

احتمال *ehtimāl'* N.M. apprehension conjecture likelihood doubt supposition probability presumption احتمالی *ehtimā'lī* ADJ. conjectural probable likely hypothetical doubtful ماضی احتمالی *mā'zī ehtimā'lī* N.F. (gram.) hypothetical past tense [A ~ حمل]

احتیاج *ehtiyāj'* N.F. want need indigence necessity emergency احتیاجات *ehtiyājāt'* N.F. PL. wants requisites necessities [A ~ حاجت]

احتیاط *ehtiyāt'* N.F. caution circumspection care foresight scrupulousness heed احتیاط سے *ehtiyat' se* carefully cautiously احتیاط برتنا *ehtiyāt ba'ratnā* V.I. be cautious ; act cautiously احتیاط کرنا (یا رکھنا) *ehtiyāt' kar'nā* (or *rakh'nā*) V.I. attend be careful take precautionary measures watch guard against احتیاطاً *ehtiyāt'tan* ADV. as a precautionary measure prudently احتیاطی *ehtiyā'tī* ADJ. precautionary احتیاطی تدابیر *ehtiyāt'tī tadābīr'* N.M. PL. precautionary measures ; precautions [A]

احد *a'had* N.M. one unity God احدیت *ahadiy'yat* N.F. unity oneness ; being individual harmony alliance ذات احدیت *zā't-e ahady'yat* N.F. God as unity احدی *ah'dī* N.M (ped. *a'hadī*) (one of) a body of soldiers in the reign of Akbar somewhat of the nature of pensioners sluggard idler ; undolent fellow ; busy person [A ~ احد]

احداث *ehdās'* N.M. (ped.) invention novelty [A ~ حدیث]

احرار *ahrār'* (or *aih-*) N.M. PL. free-born persons liberals the noble generous persons ingenuous persons [A ~ SING. حر *hūr*]

احراق *ehrāq'* N.M. burning setting on fire [A]

احرام *ehrām'* N.M. pilgrim robe ; shroud-like garment comprising two white unstiched sheets worn by Muslims during pilgrimage to Mecca interdicting all worldly enjoyments احرام باندھنا *ehrām' bandh'nā* V.I. don pilgrim robe make a vow of pilgrimage preparatory to entrance into Mecca جامۂ احرام *jā'mā-e ehrām'* N.M. pilgrim robe [A]

احزاب *ahzāb'* N.M. PL. parties N.F. the Holy Prophet's defensive war against the onslaught of allied clans [A ~ حزب]

احزان *ahzān'* N.M. (PL. of حزن N.M. ★)

احساس *ehsās'* N.M. sense feeling sensitiveness perception احساس دلانا *ehsās' dilā'nā* V.T. cause to feel احساس کرنا *ehsās' kar'nā* V.I. have a feeling احساس ہونا *ehsās' ho'nā* V.I. feel [A ~ حس]

احسان *ehsān'* N.M. favour ; kindness good office obligation احسان (کا بدلہ) اتارنا *ehsān' (kā bad'lah) ūtār'nā* V.T. do (someone) a good turn in return for his favour احسان اٹھانا *ehsān'-ūthā'nā* V.I. come under (someone's) obligation owe a debt of gratitude (to) احسان جتانا *ehsān' jatā'nā* V.T. speak or boast of favours conferred احسان دھرنا (یا رکھنا) *ehsān' dhar'nā* (or *rakh'nā* V.T. place under an obligation احسان فراموش *ehsān'-farāmosh'* ADJ. thankless ; ungrateful احسان فراموشی *ehsān'-farāmo'shī* N.F. thanklessness ; ungratefulness ; ingratitude احسان کرنا *ehsān' kar'nā* V.T. oblige ; favour ; do a favour to احسان لینا *ehsān' le'nā* V.T. be under obligation be indebted احسان ماننا *ehsān' mān'nā* V.I. feel thankful (to) ; feel obliged (to) احسان مند *ehsān'-mand'* ADJ. thankful ; grateful obliged ; under obligation (to) ; indebted (to) احسان مندانہ *ehsān-mandā'nah* ADJ. grateful (attitude, etc.) احسانمندی *ehsān'-man'dī* N.F. thankfulness ; gratitude indebtedness [A ~ حسن]

احسن *ah'san* (or *aih'-*) ADJ. best better perferable more or most lovely excellent بطریق احسن *ba-tarī'q-e aih'sān* ADV. in an excellent manner ; nicely احسنت *aihsan't, ahsan'ta* INT. bravo ; well-done احسنت کہنا *aihsan't kaih'nā* V.I. buck up say well-done [A ~ PREC.]

احشا *ahshā* N.M. PL. bowels ; intestines (rare) contents of thorax (like heart, liver lungs) [A ~ SING. حشا]

احصا *ehsā'* N.M. calculus counting ; enumerating narrating comprehension [A]

احصان | *eḥsān'* N.M. chastity ; sexual restraint (rare) besieging ; investing ; circumscribing [A ~ حصن]

احضار | *eḥzār'* N.M. attendance appearance summons summoning احضار بالجبر *eḥzā'r bil jabr'* forced attendance [A ~ حضور]

احفاد | *aḥfād'* N.M. PL. grandchildren [A ~ حفيد]

احق *aḥaq'* ADJ. (more or) most proper (more or) most deserving [A ~ حق SUP.]

احقاق | *eḥqāq'* N.M. demonstration of truth (of doctrine etc.) proving due administration (of justice, etc.) احقاق حق | *eḥqā'q-e ḥaq* N.M. establishing the truth (of) proof of truth [A ~ حق]

احقر | *aḥ'qar* (or *aiḥ'-*) ADJ. (more or) most contemptible meanest lowest N.M. (USU. *aiḥ'qar*) (as self-humiliating expression used out of courtesy for other's) I your most humble servant [A ~ حقير SUP.]

احکام | *aḥkām'* (or *aiḥ-*) N.M. (PL. of حکم *ḥukm* N.M. ★) احکام | *eḥkām'* N.M. strengthening ; reinforcement احکم | *aḥ'kam* ADJ. very strong firmer most stable [A ~ حکم]

احلام | *aḥlām'* N.M. PL. dreams [A ~ SING. حلم *ḥulm*]

احمد | *aḥ'mad* (col. *aiḥ'mad*) ADJ. (more or) most commendable N.M. the Holy Prophet Ahmad this as a male name احمد کی پگڑی محمود کے سر *aiḥ'mad kī pag'ṛī maiḥmood' ke sir* PROV. rob Peter to pay Paul احمد کی داڑھی بڑی یا محمود کی *aiḥ'mad kī da'ṛhī baṛī ya maiḥmood' kī* PROV. quibbling احمدی | *aiḥ'madī* ADJ. of Ahmad N.M. (also احمدیہ | *aiḥmadiy'yah*) (member of) a new Muslim Messianic sect name of an old gold coin [A ~ حمد praise]

احمر | *aḥ'mar* ADJ. red بحر احمر | *baḥ'r-e aḥ'mar* N.M. Red Sea [A]

احمق *aiḥ'maq* (ped. *aḥ'maq*) ADJ. (PL. حمقا *ḥumaqā'*) very foolish silly ; stupid thick-skulled N.M. fool dunce blockhead idiot moron احمق بنانا | *aiḥ'maq banā'na* V.T. befool gull ; dupe cheat احمق الذی | *aiḥ'maq-ul-lazī* N.M. (PL. احمق الذین | *aiḥ'-maq-ul-lazīn'*) arrant fool احمق بنانا | *aiḥ'maq banā'nā* V.T. befool gull ; dupe pull (someone's) leg(یا پینا) احمق پن | *aiḥ'maq pan* (or *pa'nā*) N.M. folly stupidity idiocy احمقانہ *aiḥ-maqānah* ADJ. silly foolish idiotic احمقی *aiḥ'maqī* N.F folly stupidity idiocy [A ~ حماقت]

احناف | *aḥnāf'* N.M. PL. Hanafites ; followers of the juridical school of Imam Abu Hanifah of second century of the Hegira era [A ~ حنیف ~ ابوحنیفہ]

احوال *aḥval'* (col. *aiḥval'*) N.M. SING. report of state or condition N.M. PL. affairs ; circumstances ; incidents ; events احوال بتانا (یا سنانا یا کہنا) *aḥval' batā'nā* (or *sūnā'nā* or *kaih'nā*) report (someone's) condition (to) give an account (of) tell the story (of) احوال پرسان *aḥval'-pūr'sāṅ* ADV. enquiring after (someone's) health, (etc.) N.M. & ADJ. solicitous (person) احوال پرسی | *aḥval' pūr'sī* N.F. inquiry (after) solicitude (for) احوال پرسی کرنا | *aḥ'val pūr'sī kar'na* inquire (after) show solicitude (for) ; be solicitous (for) [A ~ SING. حال]

احول *aḥ'val* ADJ. (ped.) squint-eyed [A]

احیا[1] *ehyā* N.M PL. the living living things [A ~ SING. حی *hay*]

احیا[2] *ehyā* N.M. giving life preserving revival ; resuscitation quickening احیا الموات | *el yā-ūl-mavāt'* revival ; resuscitation (fig.) bringing wasteland under plough احیائے علوم وفنون | *ehyā-e' 'ūloo'm(-o-f ūnoon')* Renaissance ; Renascence [A ~ حی *hay*]

احیاناً *aḥyā'nan* ADV. occasionally now and then from time to time sometimes [A ~ SING. حین]

اخ *akh* (rare اخو | *akhoo'*) N.M. (PL. اخوان *ikhvan'* اخوہ | *ikh'vah*) brother [A]

اخا *akh'kha*, اخاہ | *akhkhāh'* INT. (expressing surprise) ha ; O ; oh oh no well

اخبار *akhbār'* N.M. newspaper اخبارات *akhbarāt'* N.M. PL. newspapers daily Press اخبار فروش | *akhbār firosh'* N.M. newsagent ; newsboy ; newsman اخبار نویس *akhbār'-navīs'* N.M. journalist working journalist newspaper editor (arch.) intelligence man اخبار نویسی | *akhbār'-navī'sī* N.F. journalism profession of working journalist اخباری | *akhbā'rī* ADJ. Press اخباری فلم *akhba'rī fil'm* N.M. (or F.) news reel اخباری کانفرنس

-akhbā'rī kan'farans N.F. Press conference [A ~ SING. اخبر]

اخبث akh'bas ADJ. (more or) most impure very mean [A ~ خبیث SUP.]

اخت ukht N.F. (PL. اخوات akhavāt') sister congenial thing [A]

اختتام ikhtitām' N.M. end termination conclusion completion coming to an end قریب الاختتام qarīb'-ul-ikhtitām' ADV. approaching the end ; almost ending almost at the end of one's tether [A ~ ختم]

اختر akh'tar N.M. star luck omen nature اختر شماری akh'tar-shūmā'rī N.F. (spending) wakeful night(s) اختر شناس akh'tar shinās' N.M. (rare) astronomer astrologer اختر شناسی akhtar shinā'sī N.F. (rare) astronomy astrology بد اختر bad' akh-tar ADJ. & N.M. ill-natured (person) ; malicious person cursed (person) نیک اختر ne'k akh'tar ADJ. & N.M. good-natured (person) (of) lovable personality اختری akh'tarī ADJ. stellar N.F. (as a female name) Stella [P]

اختراع ikhtirā'' (col. نئی اختراع na''ī ikhtirā'') N.M. contrivance contraption something devised invention innovation novelty lie اختراع کرنا ikhtirā'' kar'nā V.T. contrive invent devise concoct a (lie) [A]

اختر بختر akh'tar bakh'tar N.M. (col.) bag and baggage

اختصار ikhtisār' N.M. bravity abridgement ; curtailment contraction summary precis synopsis compendium اختصار کرنا ikhtisār' kar'na V.T. summarize abridge curtail reduce اختصار کے ساتھ ikhtisar' ke sath ADV. briefly اختصار نویس ikhtisār navīs' N.M. (arch.) same as مختصر نویس N.M., اختصار نویسی ikhtisār' navī'sī N.F. (arch.) same as مختصر نویسی N.F. (see under مختصر ADJ. ★) [A]

اختصاص ikhtisās' N.M. specialization appropriation [A ~ خاص]

اختفا ikhtifā' N.M. concealment going into concealment اختفا کرنا ikhtifā kar'na V.T. hide ; conceal cover [A ~ خفی]

اختلاج ikhtilāj' N.M. palpitation اختلاج قلب ikhtilā'j-e qal'b N.M. palpitation of the heart [A ~ خلجان]

اختلاط ikhtilāt' N.M. intercourse promiscuity intimacy amalgamation friendship ; amity concord ; unison [A ~ خلط]

اختلاف ikhtilāf' N.M. difference dissimilarity disparity divergence dissensions ; strife misunderstanding opposition disagreement dissent distinction اختلاف رائے ikhtilāf-e rā''e N.M. dissent difference of opinion اختلاف کرنا ikhtilāf' kar'nā V.I. hold a different view (from) beg to differ (from) اختلاف ہونا ikhtilāf' ho'nā V.T. differ (from) اختلافی ikhtilā'fī ADJ. non-agreed divergent اختلافی امور ikhtilā'fī umoor' N.M. PL. points of difference ; differences اختلافی مسائل ikhtilā'fī masā''il N.M. PL. points of difference اختلافی نوٹ ikhtilā'fī noṭ' N.M. note of dissent [A]

اختلال ikhtilāl' N.M. disorder obstruction; hindrance interruption penury . want [A ~ خلل]

اختو بختو akh'to bakh'to N.F. stock names for two shrewish marionettes in puppet show [~ اختری ~ P اختر COR.]

اختیار ikhtiyār' N.M. (PL. اختیارات ikhtiyārāt') power authority command discretion control choice option اختیار دینا ikhtiyār' de'nā, اختیار سے باہر ہونا ikhtiyār se bā'har ho'nā V.I. be out of control lie beyond one's power or jurisdiction اختیار کرنا ikhtiyār' kar'nā V.I. adopt choose elect اختیار ملنا ikhtiyār' mil'nā V.I. be invested with power اختیار میں ہونا ikhtiyār men ho'nā V.I. be subject to the authority (of) اختیاری ikhtiyā'rī ADJ. optional elective voluntacy in one's power at one's disposal [A ~ خیر]

اخذ akh'z N.M. exaction seizure adoption inference اخذ کرنا akhz kar'nā V.I. take seize assume adopt get the hang (of) infer ; conclude اخذ و جبر akh'z-o jab'r N.M. extortion نتیجہ اخذ کرنا nat'ijah akhz' kar'nā V.T. & I. infer [A]

اخراج ikhrāj' N.M. expulsion ; eviction dislodgment evacuation extraction discharge rejection [A ~ خرج]

اخراجات akhrājāt' N.M. expenses charges disbursement costs (A ~ خرج double PL.]

اخروٹ akhroṭ' N.M. walnut.

اخروی ukh'ravī ADJ. pertaining to afterlife ; of hereafter [A ~ اخریٰ]

اخص **akhas'** ADJ. more particular most special [A ~ خاص SUP.]

اخضر **akh'zar** ADJ. green [A ~ خضر]

اخفا **ikhfa'** N.M. hiding concealment اخفا کرنا **ikhfa' kar'na** V.T. cover hide conceal render oneself invisible اخفائے جرم **ikhfa-e jur'm** N.M. concealment of an offence [A ~ خفی]

اخفش **akh'fash** ADJ. dim-sighted ; weak-sighted having small eyes N.M. name of a famous Arabic grammarian بز اخفش **bz'z-e akh'fash** N.M. brainless fellow [A]

اخگر **akh'gar** N.M. ember live ashes [P]

اخلاص **ikhlas'** N.M. sincerity. loyalty attachment اخلاص بڑھانا **ikhlas' barha'na** V.I. have increased intimacy اخلاص جوڑنا **ikhlas' jor'na** V.T. breed intimacy ; contract friendship اخلاص رکھنا (یا کرنا) **ikhlas' rakhna** (or **kar'na**) V.I. entertain love (for) have regard (for) be friendly (with) be sincere (to) اخلاص مند **ikhlas'-mand** ADJ. sincere intimate اخلاص مندی **ikhlas-man'di** N.F. sincerity love. friendliness [A ~ خلص]

اخلاط **akhlat'** N.M. PL. (bodily) humours اخلاط اربعہ **akhla't-e ar'ba'ah** N.M. PL. all the four humours, *viz.*, blood, phlegm, choler (yellow bile) and melancholy (black bile) [A ~ SING. خلط **khilt**]

اخلاف **akhlaf'** N.M. PL. progeny ; offspring [A ~ SING. خلف]

اخلاق **akhlaq'** N.M. PL. manners ; disposition virtues morality ethics (also علم الاخلاق **'il'm-ul akhlaq'**) اخلاق سے آدمی بنتا ہے **akhlaq' se ad'mi ban'ta hai** PROV. manners maketh the man اخلاق سے اخلاق بڑھتا ہے **akhlaq' se akhlaq' barh'ta hai** PROV. love begets love; kindness begets kindness اخلاقی **akhla qi** ADJ. moral ethical غیر اخلاقی **ghair akhla'qi** ADJ. immoral اخلاقیات **akhlaqiyyat'** N.M. ethics [A ~ SING. خلق **khulq**]

اخوان **ikhvan'** N.M. brothers اخوان زماں **ikhva'n-e zaman** N.M. contemporaries اخوان الشیاطین **ikhva'n-ush-shayatin'** devils ; wicked people اخوان الصفا **ikhvan-us-safa'** N.M. Brethren of Purity ; (members of) a secret society of Abbasid intellectuals رسائل اخوان الصفا **rasa''il-o ikhva'n-us-safa'** N.M. the Encyclopaedia of the Brethren of Purity [A ~ SING. اخ]

اخوت **ukhuv'vat** N.F. brotherhood fraternity brotherly relations [A ~ PREC.]

اخوند **akhund'** (rare اخون **akhun'**) N.M. (arch.) teacher [P]

اخیار **akhyar'** N.M. virtuous persons [A ~ SING. خیر]

اخیافی **akhya'fi** ADJ. uterine (brother, etc.) [A]

اخیر **akhir'** ADJ. last ; final conclusive N.M. end ; conclusion completion [A]

ادا **ada'** N.F. payment execution accomplishment performance discharge ادا کرنا **ada' kar'na** V.T. pay repay defray execute perform discharge accomplish do justice to ادا ہونا **ada' ho'na** V.I. be payed be done ; be performed be discharged be expressed or uttered intelligibly حق ادا ہونا **haq' ada' ho'na** V.T. pay the dues do full justice to ادائگی **ada''igi** (arch. ادائی **ada''i**) N F. payment repayment [A]

ادا ² **ada'** N.F. (also PL.) blandishment ; coquetry grace expression handsomeness embellishment elegance ; graceful manners اداشناس **ada'-shinas'**, ادافہم **ada'-faih'm** one who readily takes a hint one who understands another ADJ. tactful اداشناسی **ada'-shina'si'** ادا فہمی **ada'-faih'mi** N.F. readiness to understand tactfulness ; tact اداکار **ada-kar** N.M. actor N.F. (col. اداکارہ **ada' ka'rah**) actress اداکارانہ **ada'-kara'nah** ADJ. histrionic اداکاری **ada-ka'ri** N F. acting ; action stage-craft histrionics [P]

ادات **adat'** N.M. (PL. ادوات **adavat'**) (gram.) particle (logic) cupola instrument; tool [A]

ادارت **ida'rat** N.F. editorship ادارتی **ida'rati** ADJ. editorial [A ~ دور]

ادارہ **ida'rah** N.M. institution organization establishment administration office department [A doublet of PREC.]

اداریہ **idariy'yah** N.M. editorial ; leader ; leading article اداریہ نویس **idariy'yah nav'si** N.M. leader-writer [A ~ ادارت]

اداس **udas'** ADJ. sad melancholy lonely bleak depressed ; dejected اداس ہونا **udas' ho'na** V.I. be depressed be cheerless ; be dejected feel lonely اداسی **uda'si** N.M. depression ; sadness loneliness bleakness (اداسی چھانا (یا برسنا **uda'si chha'na** (or **ba'** rasnā) V.I be clouded with sorrow become dull be gloomy

اداسا ūdāsa N.M. (slang) (beggar's) bagga اداسا کسنا ūdā'sā kas'nā V.T. & I. (slang) pack up

ادام adā'm INT. may perpetuate ; may give permanence (usu. in) ادام اللہ برکاتہم (یا فیوضہم) adā'm-allā'h-o barakā't-i him (or fuyoo'z-i him) INT. may God perpetuate (for us) their bounties ادام اللہ adā'mahūllāh' INT. may God perpetuate him ; may God preserve him [A ~ دوام]

ادانی adā'nī N.M. PL. mean persons [A ~ SING. ادنیٰ]

اداہٹ ūdā'haṭ, اوداہٹ ooda'haṭ N.F. purpleness lividness (of lips) from fear, etc. [اودا ~]

ادائگی adā'egī N.F. (see under ادا N.F.

ادب a'dab N.M. literature decorum respect courtesy ; civility ; politeness etiquette ; manners formality ادب آموز a'dab āmoz' ADJ. that teaches literature or politeness ادب سکھانا a'dab sikhā'nā V.T. teach good manners train ادب سے a'dab se ADV. respectfully ; reverentially politely ادب عالیہ a'dab-e 'ā'liyah N.M. sublime pieces (or genres) of literature ادب کرنا a'dab kar'nā V.I. behave politely esteem venerate show respect ادب لطیف a'dab-e latīf' N.M. 'belles-lettres' [A]

ادبا ūdabā' N.M. men of letters ; 'litterateurs writers of other than fact ; prose writers شعراؤادبا shī''arā-o-ūdabā' N.M. PL. poets and prose writers [A ~ SING. ادیب]

ادبار idbār' N.M. downfall ; fall ill-luck ; misfortune mishap affliction (ped.) turning back ادبار آنا idbār' ā'nā V.I. fall on evil days be oppressed by calamity [A ~ دبر]

ادبدا کر adbadā' kar, ادبدا کے adbadā' ke ADV. out of stubbornness mischievously just for the fun of it

ادخال idkhāl' N.M. shoving insertion entry [A ~ دخول]

ادراج idrāj' N.M. gradation doing L, gradual process ادراج وتسہیل idrā'j-o tamhīl' N.M. gradual process gradation [A ~ درجہ]

ادرار idrār' N.M. flowing (of urine, etc.) freely [A ~ درّ]

ادراک idrāk' N.M. perception comprehension sagacity [A ~ درک]

ادرک ad'rak N.F. (undried) ginger ادرک کا لچھا adrak kā lach'chhā N.M. ginger cut into the form of a tape

ادریس idrīs' N.M. name of a prophet Enoch

ادڑا گدڑا ūd'ṛā gūd'ṛā, اوڑ گدڑ ū'daṛ gū'daṛ N.M.PL. rags cast off clothes. [گودڑ ~]

ادعا idde'ā' N.M. pressing right or claim pretension [A ~ دعویٰ]

ادعیہ ad''iyah N.M. PL. prayers benedictions ادعیۂ ماثورہ ad''iya-e māsoo'rah N.F. PL. prayers reported from the Holy Prophet [~ A SING. دعا]

ادغام idghām' N.M. duplication of a letter by tashdīd contraction of one letter into another [A]

ادق adaq' ADJ. very difficult profound abstruse [A ~ دقیق SUP.]

ادگدرا adgad'ra ADJ. half-ripe

ادل بدل a'dal ba'dal N.M. alteration commutation exchange barter ADJ. 'mutatis mutandis'; 'vice versa' ادلے کا بدلہ ad'le kā bad'lah N.M. tit for tat ادل بدل کرنا a'dal ba'dal kar'na V.T. interchange commute barter transform shift [A ~ بدل COR.]

ادلہ adil'lah N.M. PL. arguments proofs introductions [A ~ SING. دلیل]

ادنیٰ ad'na ADJ. ordinary small trifling inferior lowly wretched mean; base scanty petty mediocre (11) vulgar (12) meek (13) (rare.) nearest ; nearer N.M. (ped. PL. ادانی ada'nī) commoner persons of no consequence the humbler classes; commonalty ادنیٰ ادنیٰ لوگ ad'nā ad'nā log N.M. PL. quite mean people ادنیٰ و اعلیٰ ad'nā-o a'lā N.M. the high and the low the high-born and the base-born ; the noble and the ignoble the prince and the peasant [A]

ادوار advār' N.M. PL. periods ages epochs ; eras [A ~ SING. دور]

ادوائن advā''in N.F. bedstring ; string at the foot of bed for tightening it ادوائن کھینچنا advā''in khench'na V.T. tighten the bed string

ادویہ ad'viyah (col. ادویات adviyāt') N.F. PL. medicines ; drugs علم الادویہ 'il'm-ul-adviyah N.M. pharmacology ادویاتی adviyāt'ī ADJ. medicinal ; pharmaceutical ; [A ~ SING. دوا]

ادھ adh PREF. half ادھ بنا adh-ba'nā ADJ. half-formed unfinished ادھ پکا adh pa(k)'kā ADJ. unripe immature half-cooked parboiled ادھ جلا adh-ja'lā ADJ. half-burnt ادھ کچا adh-kach'chā halfripe immature unripe ادھ کچرا adhkach'rā ADJ. half-dressed (food) half-ripe ادھ کہا adh-ka'hā ADJ. half-spoken half-expressed not fully articulated ادھ کھلا adh-khi'lā ADJ. half-bloomed (flowers) ادھ کھلا adh-khi'lā ADJ. half-open ajar ادھ گدرا adh-gad'rā ADJ. half-ripe immature ادھ موا adh-mu'ā ADJ. half-dead ; as good as dead ; almost dead [~ آدھا]

ادھا ad'dhā N.M. half-bottle half a bottle [~ PREC.]

ادھار ūdhār' N.M. loan debt credit ADJ. lent loaned out ; advanced borrowed ADV on credit ادھار دیجیے دشمن کیجیے ūdhār dī'jiye dūsh'man kī'jiye PROV. lend and lose a friend ادھار دینا ūdhār' de'nā V.T. lend give on credit advance (a loan) ادھار کھانا ūdhār' khā'nā V.I live on credit ادھار لینا ūdhar le'nā V.T borrow buy on credit (par) ادھار کھائے بیٹھنا ūdhār' khā''e baiṭh'nā PH. treat (someone) as one's mortal foe treat (something) as antagonistic be bent upon (doing) ادھار محبت کی قینچی ہے ūdhār' mahab'bat kī qain'chī hai PROV. he that lends, his friends lose him ادھار کھانے سے بھوکا پڑا رہنا اچھا ہے ūdhār' khā'ne se bhoo'kā parā' raih'nā ach'chhā hai PROV. better go to bed supperless than rise in debt ادھار کی کیا ماں مری ہے ūdhār' kī kyā man' ma'rī hai PROV. if you have no hard cash, why can't you borrow ? نو نقد نہ تیرہ ادھار nau naqd'na te'rah ūdhār' PROV. a bird in hand is worth two in the bush

ادھر ū'dhar ADV. in that place on that side thither; in that direction ادھر سے ū'dhar se ADV. from that side or place from that direction thence ادھر کو ū'dhar ko ADV. to that side thither ; in that direction

ادھر i'dhar ADV. on this side hither . to this place here this way ادھر ادھر i'dhar u'dhar ADV. up and down here and there right and left around ادھر ادھر کی باتیں i'dhar u'dhar kī ba'teṅ N.M. divers points general talk irrelevent talk ادھر سے ادھر ہونا i'dhar se ū'dhar ho'nā V.I. be lost be gone be made away with be turned upside down ادھر سے ادھر کر دینا i'dhar se ū'dhar kar de'nā V.T. disarrange turn topsy-turvy ادھر کنواں ادھر کھائی i'dhar koo''āṅ ū'dhar khā''ī PROV. between the devil and the deep sea ; between two fires ادھر کی ادھر لگانا i'dhar kī ū'dhar lagā'nā V.I. carry tales ادھر کی دنیا ادھر ہو جانا i'dhar kī dūn'yā ū'dhar ho jā'nā V.I. turn topsyturvy undergo a revolutionary change چاہے ادھر کی دنیا ادھر ہو جائے chā'he i'dhar kī dūn'yā ū'dh'ar ho jā''e PH. come what may ادھر کے رہے نہ ادھر کے i'dar ke ra'he na ū'dhar ke PH. we (etc.) are outcastes for both sides ; we etc.) have been rejected by both the parties ادھر یا ادھر i'dhar yā ū'dhar ADV. at a critical moment. ادھر یا ادھر ہونا i'dhar yā ū'dhar ho'nā V.I. (of dispute, life, etc.) come to a decisive stage

ادھر adhar' ADV. (arch.) in between ادھر میں adhar' meṅ ADV. (hanging) in between between heaven and earth mid-way, half-way in the centre

ادھڑنا ūdhar'nā V.I. open at the seams be peeled off be unrolled be ripped open be undone کھال ادھڑنا khāl ū'dhaṛ'nā V.I. have a good hiding ادھڑا ūdhṛā ADJ. opened at seams unrolled

ادھلنا ū'dhal'nā, ادھل جانا ūdhal jā'nā V.I. be spoilt (of woman) become loose be beside oneself (with some passion)

ادھم¹ ūd'dham N.M. (same as ادھم N.M. ★)

ادھم² ad'ham (lit.) N.M. bay ADJ. dark ; bay [A]

ادھن a'dhan N.M. water heated to boil or poach something ; boiling water

ادھنا adhan'nā N.M., ادھنی adhan'nī N.F. half anna an old coin [~ آنہ + آدھ]

ادھواڑ adhvār' ADJ. & N.F. mediocre (quality) [~ آدھا]

ادھورا adhoo'rā ADJ. (F. ادھوری adhoo'rī) incomplete half-done half-prepared half-dressed half-baked imperfect [~ آدھا]

ادھوڑی adhau'rī N.F. hide ; thick coarse leather tanned hide coarse animal skin ادھوڑی تاننا adhau'rī tān'nā V I eat to one's fill

ادھی ad'dhī N.F. old coin equivalent to half a 'damri'; 512th part of rupee half a piece of cloth lawn ادھی ادھی پر جان دینا ad'dhī ad'dhī par jān' de'na PH. be niggardly ادھی ادھی کا حساب ad'dhī ad'dhī ka hisāb' N.M. full account ADV. to the penny ادھی کی ہنڈیا بھی ٹھونک بجا کر لیتے ہیں ad'dhī kī hand'yā bhī ṭhonk' bajā' kar le'te hain PROV. no one buys a stuff without fully testing it [~ آدھا]

ادھیانا adhyā'nā V.T. (col.) halve [~ آدھا]

ادھیراج adhirāj' N.M. (dial.) chief ruler مہاراج ادھیراج mahārāj' adhirāj' N.M. (dial.) the great ruler the emperor [S]

ادھیڑ adheṛ' ADJ. middle-aged (person) middling (age) ادھیڑ عمر کا adheṛ' 'ūm'r kā ADJ. middle-aged [~ آدھا]

ادھیڑنا ūdheṛ'nā V.T. open at seams unroll; unfold untwist peel off dismantle (roof, etc.) کھال ادھیڑنا khal ūdheṛ'nā V.T. give a good hiding ادھیڑ ūdheṛ N.F. opening at the seams untwisting peeling off dismantling ادھیڑ بن ūdheṛ' būn N.F. anxious thought perplexity dilemma; deliberation embarrassment reflection; meditation

ادھیلا adhe'lā, دھیلا dhe'lā N.M. half-pice; an old coin ادھیلی adhe'lī, دھیلی dhe'lī N.F. half-rupee ادھیلا نہ دے ادھیلی دے adhe'lā na de adhe'lī de PROV. penny wise and pound foolish

ادیان adyān' N.M. (PL. of دین dīn N.M. ★)

ادیب adīb' N.M. (PL. ادبا ūdabā') writer 'littérateur' [A ~ ادب]

ادیم adīm' N.M. (lit.) skin tanned leather surface (of earth, sky) [A]

اڈا ad'dā, ad'dah N.M. stand stop station (air)port worker's seat (criminal's) den rendezvous perch pigeon-stand embroidery frame اڈے چڑھانا (یا پر لگانا) ad'de charhā'nā (or par lagā'nā) V.T. seduce prevail upon

اڈو اڈو ūd'do, اڈو اڈو ūd'do ūd'do N.F. loose woman اڈو اڈو کرنا ūd'do ūd'do ho'nā V.I. be scandalized become the talk of the town

اڈول adol' ADJ. firm steady [~ NEG. ا + ڈولنا]

اڈیٹر adī'ṭar N.M. (same as ایڈیٹر N.M. ★)

اڈیشن adī'shan N.M. (same as ایڈیشن N.M. ★)

اڈیشنل adish'nal ADJ. (same as ایڈیشنل ADJ. ★)

اڈوانس advāns' N.M. same as ایڈوانس N.M. ★)

اذان azān' N.F. Muslim summon to prayers; call to prayers اذان دینا (یا کہنا) azān' de'nā (or kaih'nā) V.I. give the call for prayers [A ~ اذن]

اذبک ūz'būk (usu. ازبک) N.M. Name of a Tartar tribe (arch.) fool [T]

اذعان iz'ān' N.M. obedience submission trust; confidence belief [A]

اذکار azkār' N.M. PL. rehearsal of prayers eulogy of God recitals commemoration اذکار izkār' N.M. refreshing someone's memory [A ~ ذکر zikr)

اذکیا azkiyā' N.M. (PL. of ذکی za'kī ADJ. ★)

اذل azal' ADJ. most despicable; very contemptible; basest [A ~ ذلیل SUP.]

اذن izn N.M. leave; permission consent (of contracting parties as in marriage) اذن عام izn-e 'ām' N.M. general permission free or unrestricted admission [A]

اذن ū'zūn N.M. (PL. آذان āzān') ear [A]

اذہان azhān N.M. PL. (of ذہن N.M. ★)

اذیت aziy'yat N.F. oppression; torment trouble suffering woe; sorrow; distress hurt annoyance اذیت دینا aziy'yat de'nā V.T. harm hurt harass trouble torment اذیت اٹھانا (یا برداشت کرنا) aziyat ūṭhā'nā (or bardāsht' kar'nā) V.I. suffer [A]

ار[2] ar N.F., ارا arā N.M. spoke (of wheel)

ار ar CONJ. (rare) if; granting that [P ~ اگر ABB.]

ارابہ arā'bah N.M. (arch.) gun carriage wagon [P]

اراٹا arrā'ṭa N.M. loud dull prolonged sound (as from gun-fire or collapse of building) moan gasp in stubborn child's wailing [ONO.]

ارادت irā'dat N.F. devotion faith; belief [A doublet of FOL.]

ارادہ irā'dah N.M. intention desire mind bent fancy design; plan ارادہ کرنا irā'dah kar'nā V.I. intend mean devise design ; plan ارادۃً irā'datan ADV. on purpose ; purposely ; intentionally deliberately ارادی irā'dī ADJ. intentional deliberate [A]

اراروٹ a'rāroṭ N.M. arrawroot [E]

اراذل arā'zil N.M. PL. the vulgar the ignoble Tom, Dick and Harry [A ~ SING. ارذل]

اراضی arā'zī N.F. (PL. اراضیات araziyat') lands fields ; agricultural lands اراضی دار arā'zī dār N.M. landholder اراضی خالصہ ārā'zī-e khā'lisah N.F. Crown land ; State land افتادہ اراضی fiā'dah arā'zī, پڑتی اراضی paṛ'ti arā'zī N.F. fallow, desolate or barren lands نو برار (یا نو برآمد) اراضی nau bar-ār' (or nau bar-ā'mad) arā'zī N.F. alluvial soil [A ~ SING. ارض]

اراکین arākīn' N.M. PL. members (rare) pillars ; columns اراکین دولت (یا سلطنت) arākīn-e dau'lat (or saltanat) N.M. PL. pillars of State ; grandees

ارب arab N.M. thousand million (U.S.) billion ارب پتی a'rab pa'tī N.M. & ADJ. billionaire

ارباب arbāb' N.M. PL. owners lords proprietors officers members N.M. (SING.) landlord ; chief ارباب بست وکشاد arbā'b-e bas't-o-kushād' ارباب حل وعقد arbā'b ḥall-o-'aq'd N.M. PL. authorities ارباب بصیرت arbā'b-e basī'rat N.M. PL. the prudent ; the sagacious ارباب جاہ arbā'b-e jāh' N.M. PL. men of rank or position ارباب دانش arbā'b-e dā' nish, ارباب فہم arbā'b-e faih'm ارباب فہم ودانش arbāb-e faih'm-o-dā'nish N.M. PL. intelligentsia intellectuals ارباب سخن arbāb-e sūkhan N.M. PL. poets the eloquent linguists ارباب شرع arbā'b-e shar'' N.M. PL. jurists (arch.) law officers ارباب معانی arbā'b-e ma'ā'nī N.M. PL. spiritual persons ارباب نشاط arbā'b-e nashāt' N.M. PL. dancing girls dancers, singers and musicians the gay world ارباب ہمت arbā'b-e him'mat N.M. PL. men of spirit men of lofty aspirations

اربڑانا arbaṛa'na V.I. (same as ہڑبڑانا V.I. ★)

اربع ar'ba', اربعہ arba'ah' ADJ. Four اربع عناصر arba' 'anā'sir N.M. PL. elements ; the four elements, (viz., earth, water, air and fire) اربعہ متناسبہ arba'a-e mū'tanā'sibah (col. اربعہ ar'ba'ah) N.M. ratio (of three known and one unknown quantity) اربعہ لگانا ar'bā'ah lagā'nā V.I. find out the unknown quantity through known ratios (fig.) hazard a guess حدود اربعہ hūdoo'd-e arba'ah N.M. (seeunder ★) [A]

اربعین arba'īn ADJ. forty N.M. collection of any forty Traditions of the Holy Prophet (by) forty-day period of (religious or other) confinement fortiethday funeral rite [A ~ اربع]

ارتباط irtibāt' N.M. alliance inter course friendship familiarity affinity [A ~ ربط]

ارتجال irtijāl' N.M. extemporisation ارتجالاً irtijalan ADV. extempore ; impromptu ارتجالاً کہنا irtijā'lan kaih'nā V.I. extemporize (verse) [A]

ارتحال irtiḥāl' N.M. death ; demise ; expiration departure journeying [A ~ رحلت]

ارتداد irtidād' N.M. apostacy ; rejection of one's faith refraction recantation فتنۂ ارتداد fitnā-e irtidād' N.M. the revolt of apostates (in early Islam) [A ~ رد]

ارتسام irtisām' N.M. mark design painting [A ~ رسم]

ارتعاش irte'āsh' N.M. vibration shaking tremor [A ~ رعشہ]

ارتفاع irtifā'' N.M. elevation height ascent eminence rise grandeur dignity exaltation [A ~ ارفع]

ارتقا irtiqā' N.M. evolution ارتقا پذیر irtiqā' pazīr' ADJ. evolutionary ارتقا پذیری irtiqā' pazī'rī N.F. being subject no evolution ارتقائی irtiqā''ī ADJ. evolutionary [A]

ارتکاب irtikāb' N.M. commission (of offence) perpetration (of crime undertaking (of enterprise) ارتکاب جرم irtikā'b-e jūrm' N.M. perpetration of crime ارتکاب کرنا irtikāb' kar'nā V.T. commit (crime) undertake a venture or enterprise [A]

ارتھی arthī N.F. (dial.) bier (of a Hindu) [S]

ارث irs N.M. inheritence ; heritage legacy [A]

ارجاع irjā' N.M. (arch.) reference recourse suit [A ~ رجوع]

ارجمند arj'mand ADJ. noble honourable worthy happy beloved fortunate [P ~ ارج worth + مند]

ارجنٹ ar'jant ADJ. urgent [E]

ارحام arham' N.M. PL. wombs matrices ذوی الارحام zavil' arham' N.M. PL. maternal relations [A ~ SING. رحم]

ارحم ar'ham ADJ most merciful ; most compassionate ارحم الراحمین arhamur-rahimin' N.M. (God as) the Most Merciful [A ~ رحیم SUP.]

ارخا ir'kha N.M. slackening loosening [A]

ارد ūrd N.M. (same as اڑد ūrd N.M. ★)

اردا بیگنی ūr'dā be'ganī N F. armed female follower in royal harem ; seraglio Amazon [~T]

ارد گرد ir'd gir'd ADV. around round about on all sides

اردلی ar'dalī N.M. orderly [E]

اردو ūr'doo N.M. Urdu ; name of one of Pakistan's national languages horde (arch.) army (arch.) bivouac (arch.) camp ; encampment ; cantonment اردو بازار ūr'doo bazār' N.M. (arch.) camp market market of Urdu books اردوئے معلّیٰ ūrdoo'-e mo'a'llā N.M. (arch.) royal army royal encampment اردوئے معلّیٰ کی زبان ūrdoo'-e mo'al'lā kī zabān' N.F. (arch.) Urdu court language [T]

اردی بہشت ūr'dī bihisht', اردی ūr'dī N.M. spring month of Persian calender (corresponding to April)

ارذل ar'zal ADJ. (PL. اراذل ara'zil) base mean most despicable [A ~ رذیل SUP.]

ارز arz N.M. cost value reverence ; respect ; honour quantity [P]

ارزاق arzāq' N.M. (PL. of رزق N.M. ★)

ارزاں ar'zān ADJ. cheap inexpensive low-priced ارزانی arzā'nī N.F. cheapness low price abundance of provisions ارزانی کرنا arzā'nī kar'nā V.T. present give away ; give gratuitously ارزانی ہونا arz'nī ho'nā V I. be conferred be cheap (of cheapness) prevail [P ~ ارز]

ارژنگ arzhang' N.M. picture-gallery of the painter Mani collection of Mani's pictures album [P]

ارسال irsal' N.M. remittence despatch ارسال کرنا irsal' kar'na V.T. remit despatch send [A]

ارسطاطالیس arastātālīs' ارسطو aras'too N.M. Aristotle ارسطاطالیسی arastātālī'sī ADJ. Aristolelian [A ~ G]

ارسلان arsalān N M. (rare) lion [T]

ارشاد irshād' N.M. words something said order ; behest ; command guidance showing the path of righteousness ارشاد کرنا یا فرمانا irshād' kar'nā (or farmā'nā) (of superior) say desire command ordain dictate desire direct ; guide [A ~ رشد]

ارشد ar'shad ADJ. well-guided most honest [A ~ رشید SUP.]

ارشمیدس arshamī'das N.M. Archimedes اصول ارشمیدس usoo'l-e arshamī'das N.M Archimedean principle (either about working of lever or about relation of weight of immersed object and water displaced by it [A ~ G]

ارض ar'z N.F. earth world land country ارض و سما ar'z-o-samā' N.M. PL. heaven and earth whole universe طبقات الارض tabaqā'tūl-arz' N M. PL. geological strata علم طبقات الارض 'ilm-e tabaqā't-ūl-arz' N.M. geology ارضی ar'zī ADJ. earthly ; terrestrial mundane جنت ارضی ar'zī jan'nat, ارضی جنت jan'nat-e ar'zī N.F. earthly paradise حور ارضی hoo'r-e ar'zī N.F. exquisite beauty ارضی و سماوی ar'zī-o-samā'vī ADJ. terrestrial and celestial ; earthly and heavenly ارضیات arziyyāt' N.F. geology ارضیاتی arziyyā'tī ADJ. geological ارضیاتی جائزہ arziyya'tī ja''izah N.M. geological survey [A]

ارغن arghan, ارغنون arghanoon N.M. organ [A ~ G]

ارغنون

ارغوان arghavān' N.M. purple colour name of a plant bearing purple flowers and fruit ارغوانی arghavā'nī ADJ. purple violet crimson [P]

ارفع ar'fa' ADJ. most elevated pre-eminent [A ~ رفیع SUP.]

ارقام irqam' N.M. (ped.) writing putting down in black and white ارقام کرنا irqam kar'nā V.T. pen ; write ارقام ہونا irqam' ho'nā V.I. be penned ; be written arqam N.M. PL. figures ; numbers items [A ~ SING. رقم]

ارکان arkan' N.M. PL. members pillars ; columns props components, ingredients basic principles ; fundamentals tenets ارکان اسلام arkā'n-e islām', ارکان دین arkā'n-e dīn' N.M. PL. fundamentals of faith ارکان دولت (یا سلطنت) arkā'n-e dau'lat (or sal'tanat) N.M. pillars of state ; grandees [A ~ SING. رکن]

ارگجا ar'gajā N.M. a perfume made of rose, sandalwood, musk, etc.

ارل arl N.M. earl [E]

ارم i'ram N.M. ancient Arabia's Aad sovereign, Shaddad's garden built to rival paradise earthly paradise [A]

ارمان armān' (poet. ارماں ar'māṅ) N.M. desire ; longing yearning wistfulness ارمان پورا (یا پورے) کرنا armān' poo'rā (or poo're) kar'nā, ارمان نکالنا armān' nikāl'nā V.T. & I. gratify one's ambition ارمان رہ جانا armān' raih' jānā V.I. be disappointed in one's wish or hope ارمان نکلنا armān' nikal'nā V.I. have one's wishes fulfilled ارمان ہونا armān' ho'nā V.I. wish aspire long for [P]

ارمغان ar'mug͟hāṅ, ar'mag͟han N.M. gift, present rarity ; curiosity [P]

ارنا ar'nā, ارنا بھینسا ar'nā bhaiṅsā N.M. (F. ارنی ar'nī) wild buffalo

ارنڈ arand' N.M., ارنڈی araṅ'ḍī N.F. 'recinus communis' ; castor-oil plant ارنڈ خربوزہ arand' k͟harboo'zah 'carica papaya' ارنڈی کا تیل araṅ'ḍī kā tel' N.M. castor-oil ارنڈی کی جڑ araṅ'ḍī kī jaṛ' N.F. (fig.) flimsy stuff weak thing

ارنی a'rinī V.T. manifest Thyself to me ; (as words of Moses' prayer to God at Mount Sinai) ارنی گو a'rinī go N.M. (fig.) presumptive person ارنی گوے طور a'rinī go'-e toor' N.M. Moses [A]

ارواح arvāḥ' N.F. PL. souls spirits [A ~ SING. روح]

اروی ar'vī N.F. arum

ارہ ar'rah N.M. (same as آرہ N.M. ★) [P]

ارہر ar'har N.F. a kind of pulse ; 'arhar'

ارے a're INT. for calling men's attention with love or contempt) O ; ho ; hello (expressive of surprise) O no ; oh no ; dear اری a'rī INT. (for calling woman's attention with love or contempt) hello ; ho (expressive of surprise) O no ; oh no ; dear

اریب ūreb' ADJ. frilled (trousers) slanting ; sloping deceptive ; crafty ; crooked اریب پاجامہ ūreb' pājā'mah N.M. frilled trousers

اریب arīb' ADJ. wise [A]

اڑ aṛ N.F. (see under اڑنا aṛ'nā V.I. ★)

اڑاڑادھم aṛā'ṛā dham' ADV. (come down) pat ; (fall) flat [ONO.]

اڑاس aṛās' N.F. narrowness اڑاس کی جگہ aṛās' kī ja'gah N.F. narrow space [~ اڑنا aṛnā V.I.]

اڑان ūṛān' N.F. (see under اڑنا ūṛ'nā' V.I. ★) اڑن گھائی ūṛan' ghā''ī N.F. trick ; ruse ; feint deception evasion ; shuffling اڑن گھائی بتانا ūṛan' ghā''ī batā'nā V.I. misleed dupe evade ; shuffle

اڑانا ūṛā'nā V.T. fly ; cause to fly waste ; squander fritter away spend lavishly allure eat away pilfer copy ; plagiarize give currency to (story, etc.) pull (someone's) leg (11) enjoy (12) sing (a tune) (13) remove (14) elope with (15) guess (16) cut off (head) اڑا پڑا دینا ūṛā' puṛā' de'nā V.T. spend lavishly ; squander بے پر کی اڑانا be par' kī ūṛā'na V.T. & O. give currency to baseless stories اڑاؤ ūṛā''oo N.M. spendthrift ; squanderer ; prodigal ; ADJ. prodigal ; extravagant [~ اڑنا ūṛ'nā CAUS.]

اڑانا aṛā'nā V.T. cause to stand or stop cause to check motion fasten something to another ram ; plug ; thurst پرائے پھٹے میں ٹانگ اڑانا parā''e phaṭ'e meṅ ṭāṅg' aṛā'nā PROV. poke one's nose into other people's affairs ; meddle with other things [~ اڑنا aṛ'nā CAUS.]

اڑبڑ aṛ'baṛ N.M. nonsense ; meaningless words ADJ. nonsense irregular ; rough uneven craggy اڑبڑ بکنا aṛ' baṛ' bak'nā V.I. talk nonsense talk wildly talk idly

اڑبنگا arbaṅ'gā ADJ bent rough ; rugged not straight ; crooked N.M. obstacle

اڑپ جھڑپ a'ṛap jha'ṛap N.M. tiff scuffle struggle

اڑتالیس aṛtā'līs N.M. & ADJ. forty-eight اڑتالیسواں aṛtā'līsvāṅ ADJ. forty-eighth

اڑتلا aṛ'talā N.M. excuse shelter ; refuge defence اڑتلا لینا aṛ'talā le'nā V.T. & I. put up an excuse take shelter

اڑتیس aṛtīs' N.M. & ADJ. thirty-eight اڑتیسواں aṛtīs'vāṅ ADJ. thirty-eighth

اڑچ arich', اڑینچ araiṅch' N.F. malice enmity اڑچ (یا اڑینچ) رکھنا arich (or araiṅch) rakh'nā V.I. bear malice (towards)

اڑد ūrd, (ped. اُرد ūrd) N.M. a kind of vetch ; vetchling اڑد پر سفیدی ūrd par sife'di PH. a wee bit (not) a bit

اڑسٹھ ar'saṭh N.M. & ADJ. sixty-eight اڑسٹھواں ar'saṭhvāṅ ADJ. sixty-eighth

اڑسنا ū'rasnā, اڑس لینا ū'ras le'nā V.T. tuck up

اڑم a'ram N.M. heap

اڑنا ūr'nā V.I. fly soar move very fast be worn out fade evaporate explode spread get lost (of head) be cut off (11) be removed (12) be cast to the winds (13) be blown away (14) feel out of sorts (15) vanish (16) (of words, print, etc.) fail to give impression (17) disappear (18) (of story) get round (19) (of luxury, joke, etc.) be indulged in (20) (of tune) be sung (21) feel elated اڑان ūran' N.F. flight (arch.) kind of curtain on coach, etc. اڑان ہونا ūran' ho'nā V.I. be sick of (place) be disgusted ; be bored اڑچلنا ūr' chal'-na V.I. walk with a stately step strut be conceited اڑفاختہ ūr' fākhtah N.F. (fig.) gull ; simple person اڑکے جانا ūr ke ja'nā V.I. go by chance get shelter اڑکے لگنا ūr' ke lag'na V.I. (of infection) catch ; spread اڑکے ملنا ūr ke mil'na V.I meet on one's own meet with pleasure اڑن ū'ran ADJ. flying raging اڑن چھو ہو جانا ū'ran chhoo' ho jā'na V.I. disappear ; vanish run away sneak away اڑن طشتری ū'ran tash'tarī N.F. flying saucer اڑن کھٹولا ū'ran khaṭo'la N.M. (legendary) flying car اڑن گھائی بتانا ū'ran ghā''ī batā'nā V.I. deceive ; dupe ; gull اڑتی اڑتی طاق پر بیٹھی ū'rī ū'rī tāq' par bai'ṭhī PROV. the report gradually spread ; the scandal spread soon enough it became talk of the town

اڑنا ar'nā V.I. stop come to a standstill refuse to budge oppose be obstinate be wayward put up an excuse اڑ ar N.F. stubbornness ; obduracy dispute contention heaviness (of stomach) اڑاوقت a'ṛā vaqt' N.M. difficulty hard times اڑبیٹھنا ar baiṭh'nā V.I. be stubborn importune اڑپیچ ar pech' N.F. obstacle اڑجانا ar ja'na V.I. stick to (one's) guns lay a stake upon اڑی a'ṛī N.F. trick stubbornness obstacle اڑیل ar'yal ADJ. obstinate wayward; headstrong اڑیمار a'ṛī-mār ADJ. & N.M. trickster اڑے (یا ٹھڑے) وقت a'ṛe (thū're) vaq't ADV. in times of difficulty اڑتا ūr'tā ADJ. (F. اڑتی ūr'tī) flying اڑتی تول ūr'tī tol اڑتی ہوئی ūr'tī hū'ī ADJ. weighing less ; under weighed اڑتی چڑیا پہچاننا ūr'tī chir'ya paihchan'nā, اڑتی چڑیا کے پر گننا ūr'tī chir'ya ke par' gin'na V.I. be shrewd know a crook at sight اڑتی (سی) خبر ūr'tī (sī) khabar N.F. rumour hearsay

اڑنگا araṅ'ga N.M. hitch ; hindrance ; prop tripping اڑنگا لگانا (یا مارنا) aranga lagā nā (or mar'nā) اڑنگے پر چڑھانا araṅ'ge par chaṛhā'nā V.T. trip (someone)

اڑنگ بڑنگ araṅg' baraṅg N.M. (children's game called) catch-the-thief name of players in it nonsense اڑنگ بڑنگ بکنا araṅg' baraṅg' bak'nā V.I. talk nonsense

اڑواڑ arvār' N.F. prop (under falling roof, etc.)

اڑوس پڑوس aros paros' N.M. neighbourhood ; vicinity ADV. nearby hereabout

اڑھانا ūrhā'na V.T. (see under اوڑھنا V.I. ★)

اڑھائی arhā''ī ADJ. two-and-a-half half-past two اڑھائی چاول الگ گلانا arhā''ī chā'val alag' galā'na V.I. (always) hold a different opinion اڑھائی دن کا جھونپڑا arhā''ī din kā jhonp'ṛā N.M. (fig.) transitory thing flimsy structure اڑھائی چلو لہو پی جانا arhā''ī chul'loo la'hoo pī jā'na V.I. (threaten to) suck the blood of اڑھیا arhay'yā N.M. two-and-a-half seer weight or measure two-and-a-half times multiplication table

از az PREP. (ped.) from than by of with ازاں azāṅ' ADV. thence ازاں جملہ azāṅ'-jūm'lah ADV. of those out of that total or sum ازبر az bar' ADJ. memorized well learnt ازبر کرنا az bar kar'na V.T. memorize ; learn by heart ; learn by rote ازبر ہونا az bar' ho'nā V.I. be memorized ازبس az bas' ADV. much adequately ازبسکہ az bas-keh CONJ. since however ; nevertheless ; notwithstanding much ازجانب az jā'nib ADV. on the part of on behalf of for from ازحد az ḥad' ADV. boundless, infinite indefinite surprising ADV. very much extremely infinitely beyond description ازخود az khūd' ADV. of one's own record voluntarily by self 'suo moto' ازخود رفتہ az khud' raf'tah' ازخویش رفتہ az khesh' raf'tah ADJ. absent-minded distracted not in one's sense ازراہ az rā'h-e ADJ. by the way of ; 'apropos' ازروئے az roo''e ADV. by virtue of ; by reason of under ازسرتاپا az sar tā pā' ADV from head to foot from top to toe perfectly wholly ازسرِنو az sar-e nau' ADV. afresh ; anew 'de novo' ازغیب az ghaib' ADJ. providential; God-sent ADV. providentially مردے ازغیب بروں آید وکارے بکند mar'de az ghaib' biroon' ā'yad-o kā're bi-kunad PH 'deus ex-machina' God will send someone to help [P]

ازار izār' N F. trousers drawers ازاربند izār-band' N.M trouser-string ازاربندی رشتہ (یا تعلق) izār'-ban'dī rish'tah (or ta'al'luq) N M. relation on wife's side ; petticoat interest ازار میں ڈال کر پہن لینا izār' meṅ ḍal' kar pai'han le'nā V.T. (fig.) be devoid of all sense of shame be saucy

ازالہ izā'lah N.M nullification revocation abolition removal amends compensation ازالۂ بکر izā'la-e bikr' N M. (causing) loss of virginity ازالۂ حیثیت عرفی izā'la-e haisiy'yat-e 'ur'fī N M. defamation slander [A ~ زائل]

ازبک ūz'baik (or ūz'bak) N.M. (same as ازبک ★) Uzbek [T]

ازدحام izdehām' (P. COR. اژدہام izhdehām') N.M. crowd ; throng milling crowd mob rabble [A]

ازدواج izdivāj' N M. marriage, matrimony espousal nuptials تعددِ ازدواج ta'ad'd'ud-e izdivāj' N.M bigamy polygamy ازدواجی izdivā'jī ADJ. marital ازدواجی حیثیت izdivā'jī haisiy'yat N.F. marital status [A ~ زوج]

ازدیاد izdiyād' N.M. increase enlargement augmentation escalation [A ~ زیادہ]

ازرق az'raq ADJ. blue azure ازرق چشم az'raq chash'm ADJ. blue-eyed [A ~ زرق]

ازکیا azkiyā' N.M. PL. pious people [A ~ SING. زکی]

ازل a'zal N.F. beginning eternity source origin روزِ ازل ro'z-e a'zal N.M. the beginning ; the first day ازل سے ابد تک a'zal se a'bad tak ADV. from beginning to end forever ازلی a'zalī ADJ. eternal perpetual unending ازلیت azaliy'yat N.F. eternal existence [A]

ازمنہ az'minah N.M. PL. times eras ; epochs periods stages ازمنۂ ثلاثہ az'mina-e salā'-sah N.M. the three times, (viz., present, past and future) [A ~ SING. زمانہ]

ازواج azvāj' N.F. wives spouses couples ازواجِ مطہرات azvāj'-e mutah'harāt' N.F. PL. Holy Wives (as referring to the spouses of the Holy Prophet) [A ~ زوج]

اژدہا azhdahā' N.M dragon winged serpent cockatrice; basilisk boa constrictor python اژدہے کے منہ میں ہاتھ دینا azh'dahe ke mūṅh meṅ hāth' de'nā V.I. court trouble [P]

اژدر azh'dar N.M. (lit.) dragon [P]

اژدہام izhdehām' N M. (same as ازدحام ★) [P ~ A]

اس is ADJ. demonstrative this اس اثنا میں is asnā' meṅ' ADV. meanwhile ; in the meantime اس برتے پر تتا پانی is' bir'te pa tat'tā pā'nī PROV. a hope of success despite this inefficiency اس کان سنی اس کان اڑا دی is' kān sū'nī ūs kān ūṛā'dī PH. forgotten as soon as heard ; in at one ear, out at the other اس کو میرا (یا سات) سلام is ko me'rā (or sāt) salām' PH. to Hell with it اس ہاتھ لے اس ہاتھ دے is hāth' le ūs hāth' de PH. open the purse and then open thy sack tit for tat Namesis comes soon اسے چھپاؤ اسے نکالو i'se chhūpā''o ū'se nikā'lo PH. they are exactly alike اسے وہاں ماریے جہاں پانی نہ ملے i'se va'hāṅ mā'riye ja'hāṅ pā'nī na mi'le PH you should not show him any mercy give him no quarter اس تک is' tak (arch. اس تلک is' ta'lak) ADV. to this extent ; so much اس دم is' dam ADV. now right now forthwith immediately اس پر is' par CONJ. for this reason hence at this اس پر بھی is' par bhī CONJ. moreover notwithstanding even at this اس طرح سے is' tar'h se ADV. in this way ; thus اس قدر is' qadar ADV. as this this much so many to this extent اس لیے is' li'ye, اس واسطے is' vās'te CONJ. hence ; therefore

اس ūs (demonstrative) that PRON. him her it اس پر ūs' par ADV. upon that ; at that thereafter upon which اس دم ūs' dam ADV. then there and then اس وقت ūs' vaq't ADV. at that time on that occasion at which moment اس میں ūs' meṅ ADV. meanwhile ; in the meantime in that in him (or her or it)

اساتذہ *asā'tizah* N.M. PL. teachers school-masters [A ~ SING. استاذ ~ P استاد]

اسارا *ūsā'ra* N.M. shed ramshackle structure

اساڑھ *asāṛh'* N.M. fourth solar month of Hindu calendar (corresponding to June-July)

اساڑھی *asā'ṛhī* N.F. 'rabi' crop [S]

اساطیر *asāṭīr'* N.M. PL. myths اساطیر الاولین *asāṭīr-ul-avvalīn'* N.F. PL legends of an ancient people myths [A ~ SING. اسطورہ]

اساطین *asāṭīn'* N.M. PL. pillars [A ~ SING, اسطوانہ]

اسافل *asā'fil* N.M. PL. the mean the vulgar [A ~ SING. اسفل]

اسالیب *asālīb'* N.M. PL. styles modes ; manners ; ways اسالیب بیان *asālīb-e bayān'* N.M. PL. modes of expression [A ~ SING. اسلوب]

اساس *asās'* N F. foundation base plinth basis اساسی *asā'sī* ADJ. basic ; fundamental [A]

اسامی *asā'mī* N.F. (col. آسامی *āsā'mī*)' post tenant , cultivator debtor customer permanent loser (at gambling, etc.) N.M. PL. (rare) names شکمی اسامی *shi'kamī asā'mī* N.M. such tenant موروثی اسامی *mauroo'sī asā'mī* N.M. hereditary tenant دخیل کار اسامی *dakhīl-kar asā'mī* N.M. occupancy tenant [A double PL. of اسما ~ SING. اسم]

اسانا *ūsā'na* V.T. winnow

اسانید *asānīd'* N.F. (double PL. of سند N.F. ★)

اساوری *asā'varī* N.F. name of a musical mode

اسب *asb* N.M. (same as اسپ N.M. ★)

اسباب *asbāb'* N.M. luggage ; baggage equipage goods and chattles furniture property ; effects provisions N.M PL. reasons causes motives اسباب خانہ داری *asbā'b-e khā'na dā'rī* N.M. household effects اسباب سفر *asb'b-e sa'far* N.M. travelling requisites [A ~ SING. سبب]

اسبوع *ūsboo'* N.M. (lit.) week [A ~ سبع]

اسباط *asbāt* N.M. PL. Jewish tribes ; the Tribes grandchildren ; progeny ; off-spring [A ~ SING. سبط]

اسپ *asp*, (rare اسب *asb*) N M. (lit.) horse (at chess) knight [P]

اسپات *ispāt'* N.M (rare) steel (Por.)

اسپتال *aspatāl'*, ہسپتال *haspatāl* N.M. hospital [E]

اسپغول *aspaghol'* N.M. fleawort-seed [P]

اسپنج *ispañj'*, سپنج *sapañj'*, اسفنج *isfañj* N.M. sponge [E]

اسپند *ispand'*, سپند *sipand'* N.M. wild rue ; (a seed burnt as incense or charm) [P]

استاد *ūstād'* (ped استاذ *ūstāz'*) N.M. (PL. اساتذہ *asā'tizah* F. استانی *ūstā'nī*) teacher instructor ; tutor professor preceptor mentor skilful man clever person ingenious person dance or music master decrepit wrestler serving as coach ; wrestling coach استادی *ūstā'dī* N F. teacher's job or office masterly skill cleverness trick ; finesse ADJ. masterly finished [P]

استادہ *istā'dah* ADJ. standing erect raised rampant استادگی *istā'dagī* N.F. creetion standing waiting raising constancy resistance [P]

استانی *ūstā'nī* N.F. lady teacher ; mistress [~ P استاد F.]

استبداد *istibdād'* N.M. despotism tyranny استبداد پسند *istibdād' pasand'* استبدادی *istibdā'dī* ADJ. despotic (powers) [A]

استبرا *istibrā'* N.M. use of toilet paper (or clod, etc.) [A ~ بری]

استبرق *istib'raq* N.M. silk cloth (esp.) green-satin [A]

استتار *istitār'* N M. hiding ; concealment secrecy [A ~ ستر]

استثقال *istisqāl'* N.M. (ped.) heaviness [A ~ ثقل]

استثنا *istisnā'* N.M. expection distinction qualification of a statement with the PH. 'In-sha-Allah' (or God-willing) (name of fifth book of Taurah) ; Deutronomy [A]

استجابت *istijā'bat* N.F. acceptance (of prayer, request, application, etc.) [A ~ جواب]

استجازہ *istijā'zah* N.F. (ped.) taking leave seeking permission [A ~ اجابت]

استحاضہ *isteḥā'zah* N.M. prolonged morbid mensturation [A ~ حیض]

استحالہ *isteḥā'lah* N.M. change [A ~ حالت]

استحباب *isteḥbāb'* N.M. making friendship supererogation [A ~ حب]

استحسان *isteḥsān'* N.M. lenient interpretation (as a principle of jurisprudence) approval praise [A ~ حسن]

استحصال *isteḥsāl* N.M exploitation extortion acquisition gain ; profit استحصال بالجبر *isteḥsāl' -bil-jab'r* N.M. extortion unlawful exaction wrongful aequisition expropriation [A ~ حصول]

استحضار *isteḥzār'* N.M. sending for ; summoning [A ~ حضور]

استحقار *isteḥqār'* N.M. scorn ; disdain ; holding in contempt vilification [A ~ حقارت]

استحقاق *isteḥqāq'* N.M. claim right title merit privilege [A ~ حق]

استحکام *isteḥkām'* N.M reinforcement stability solidarily strength support rectification ; corroboration confirmation [A ~ محکم]

استحلاف *isteḥlāf'* N.M. causing to swear ; administration of oath [A ~ حلف]

استخارہ *istikhā'rah* N.M. judgment from omens augury prayer for dream serving as augury [A ~ خیر]

استخراج *istikhrāj'* N.M. deduction deductive logic removal deportation ; extradition refusal expulsion taking out ; ejection [A ~ خارج]

استخفاف *istikhfāf* N.M. slight disdain vilification contemptuous treatment [A ~ خفت]

استخلاص *istikhlās* N.M. liberation freedom استخلاص وطن *istikhlās-e vatan'* N.M. liberation of homeland [A ~ خلاص]

استخوان *ūstūkhān'* N.M. bone (rare) stone (of fruits) [P]

استدامت *istidā'mat* N.F. constancy firmness diligence assiduity

استدراج *istidrāj'* N.M. escalation raising bringing close to deception ; fraud deception by a pagan showing a marvel [A ~ درجہ]

استدراک *istidrāk'* N.M. clarification qualification overtaking حرف استدراک *harf-e istidrāk'* N.M. clarifying particle , qualifying conjunction (*viz.* لیکن) [A ~ درک]

استدعا *istid'ā'* N.F. request ; prayer entreaty petition solicitation supplication [A ~ دعا]

استدلال *istidlāl'* N.M arguing argument proof reason ratiocination استدلال کرنا *istidlāl' kar'nā* V.I. argue reply insist [A ~ دعا]

استر *as'tar* N.M. lining mule استرکاری *as'tar-kā'ri* N.F. coating plastering استرکاری کرنا *as'tar-kā'rī kar'nā* V.T. plaster [P]

استرا *ūs'tara* (ped. استرہ *ūstūrah*) N.M. razor [P ~ ستردن]

استراحت *istirā'ḥat* N.F. sleep siesta rest ; repose relief quietness ; peace [A ~ راحت]

استرخا *istirkhā'* N.M. flabbiness ; flaccidity [A ~ رخا]

استرداد *istirdād'* N.M. veto revocation ; repeal ; setting aside reversal حق استرداد *ḥaq'q-e istirdād'* N.M. right to veto حق استرداد استعمال کرنا *ḥaq'qe istirdād' iste'māl' kar'nā* V.I. veto [A ~ رد]

استرضا *istirzā'* N.M. bid to please willingness assent [A ~ رضا]

استری *is'tarī* N.F. iron (dial.) woman استری کرنا *is'tarī kar'nā* V.T. iron

استسقا *istisqā'* N.M. dropsy [A ~ سقایت]

استشہاد *istishhād'* N.M. (lit.) citing of witnesses production of evidence (from [A ~ شہادت]

استصواب *istisvāb'* N.M. plebescite referendum reference commendation seeking advice ; taking counsel استصواب رائے (عامہ) *istisvā'b-e rā''e ('ām'mah)* N.M. plebescite referendum استصواب کرنا *istisvāb' kar'nā* V.I. hold plebescite hold referendum refer seek advice or counsel [A ~ صواب]

استطاعت *istitā''at* N.F. capacity power potentiality wherewithal [A ~ طاعت]

استعاذہ *iste'ā'zah* N.M. seeking God's protection doing this through repetition of formula *a'oo'z-o billāh'* [A ~ عوذ]

استعارہ *iste'ā'rah* N.M. metaphor استعارے کی زبان *iste'ā're kī zabān'* N.M. metaphorical language ; figurative expression [A ~ عاریت]

استعانت | iste'a'nat N.F. (lit.) seeking of help soliciting of aid succour relief [A ~ عون]

استعجال | iste'jāl' N.M precipitation hastening (a crisis, etc) [A ~ عجلت]

استعداد | iste'dād' N.F. qualification skill capability capacity aptitude proficiency ability talent means [A]

استعفا | iste''fā N.M. resignation (from an office) asking pardon استعفا دینا | iste''fā de'nā V.I. resign استعفا منظور کرنا | iste''fā manzoor' kar'nā V.T. accept resignation (of) [A ~ عفو]

استعفاف | iste'fāf' N.M. abstention from evil [A ~ عفت]

استعلا | iste'lā' N.M. supremacy bid to achieve supremacy [A ~ علو]

استعمار | iste'mār' N.M. colonization colonial power استعمار پسند | iste'mār' pasand', استعماری iste'mā'rī ADJ. colonial استعماری طاقتیں | iste'mā'rī ta'qaten N.F. PL. colonial powers [A ~ عمران]

استعمال | iste'māl' N.M. use empolyment application usage استعمال کرنا | iste'māl kar'nā V.T. use apply طریق (یا ترکیب) استعمال tarīq'-e (or tarkīb-e) iste'māl' N.M. way of use ; method of use استعمالی | iste'mālī ADJ. of use employed customary practical [A ~ عمل]

استغاثہ | istighā'sah N.M. complaint ; suit plaint استغاثہ دائر کرنا | istighā'sah dā''ir kar'nā V.T. & I. file a suit [A ~ غوث]

استغراب | istighrāb' N.M. (lit.) amazement ; wonder surprise great admiration [A ~ غرابت]

استغراق | istighrāq' N.M. engrossment ; absorption [~ غرق]

استغفار | istighfār' N.M. asking forgiveness from God through repetition of formula astaghfirūllāh' craving mercy begging pardon استغفار کرنا | (istighfār' kar'nā) beg pardon of God implore ask for mercy استغفراللہ | astagh'firūllāh INT. I entreat forgiveness of God God forbid far be it from me (to) [A ~ غفران]

استغنا | istighnā' N.M. content ability to dispense with carelessness [A ~ غنا]

استفادہ | istifā'dah N.M. seeking profit benefiting attainment gain استفادہ کرنا istifā'dah kar'nā V.I profit (by) benefit (from) [A ~ فائدہ]

استفاضہ | istifā'zah N.M. benefit [A ~ فیض]

استفتا | istiftā N.M. seeking advice on a point of religious law seeking someone's opinion استفتا کرنا | istiftā' kar'nā V.T. seek such advice (from) [A ~ فتویٰ]

استفراغ | istifrāgh' N.M. vomiting [A ~ فراغت]

استفسار | istifsār N M. query inquiry seeking of information reference استفسار کرنا istifsār kar'nā V.T. refer make a reference to call for information question [A ~ تفسیر]

استفہام | istifhām' N M. interrogation question inquiry investigation حرف استفہام harf-e istifhām' N.M. interrogative particle (or pronoun) علامت استفہام | 'alā'mat-e istifhām' N.M. mark or sign of interrogation ; questionmark ; query استفہامیہ | istifhāmiy'yah ADJ. interrogative جملہ استفہامیہ | jūm'l-e istifhāmiy'yah N.M. interrogative sentence [A ~ فہم]

استقامت | istiqā'mat N.F. firmness stability constancy steadfastness rectitude ; uprightness [A ~ قیام]

استقبال | istiqbāl' N.M. reception welcome (to) future futurity future tense استقبال کرنا | istiqbāl' kar'nā V.T. advance to meet a person receive (a person) welcome (a visitor) [A ~ قبل]

استقرا | istiqrā' N M. induction inductive logic استقرائی | istiqrā''ī ADJ. inductive [A ~ قرأت]

استقرار | istiqrār' N.M. declaration ; confirmation taking place ; consummation istiqrār'-e haqqiy'yat N.M. declaration of title استقرار حمل | istiqrā'r-e ham'l N.M. becoming pregnant ; pregnancy [A ~ قرار]

استقصا | istiqsā' N.M. reaching the limits (of) research deep probe استقصا کرنا | istiqsā' kar'nā V.T. look deep into (a matter) [A ~ اقصیٰ]

استقلال | istiqlāl' N.M. perseverance fortitude constancy steadiness firmness resolution independence ; freedom جشن استقلال | jash'n-e istiqlāl' N.M. independence day [A]

استکانت | istikā'nat N.F. humility [A ~ مسکین]

استکبار | istikbār' N M. (lit.) pride ; conceit ; haughtiness vainglory presumption [A ~ کبر]

استکراہ | istikrāh' N.M. repugnance abhorrence dislike demur duress جبر و استکراہ | jab'r-o-istikrāh' N.M. constraint duress بجبر و استکراہ | ba-jab'r-o-istikrāh' ADV. under duress unwillingly [A ~ کراہت]

استکشاف *istikshaf* N.M. exhibitionism bid to expose disclosure revelation manifestation [A ~ کشف]

استکمال *istikmal'* N.M. (lit.) accomplishment perfection [A ~ کمال]

استلام *is'tilam* N.M. kissing (the Black Stone) at the Holy Ka'aba [A]

استلذاذ *istilzaz'* N.M. enjoyment [A ~ لذت]

استلزام *istilzam'* N.M. (lit.) necessitating being necessary [A ~ لازم]

استماع *istima'* N.M. hearing listening audition hearsay; rumour indirect evidence listening to music [A ~ سماعت]

استمالت *istima'lat* N.F. persuasion wheedling ; coaxing ; cajoling leaning towards someone [A ~ میل]

استمداد *istimdad'* N.M aid-seeking asking for help استمداد کرنا *istimdad' kar'na* V.I. seek aid ask for help [A ~ مدد]

استمرار *istimrar'* N.M. continuance perpetuity repetition استمرار دار *istimrar'-dar* N.M. permanent tenure-holder استمراری *istimra'ri* ADJ. perpetual permanent ; uninterrupted lasting (gram.) continuous (tense) استمراری پٹہ *istimra'ri pat'tah* N.M. perpetual lease بندوبست استمراری *band-o-bast'(-e) istimra'ri* N.M. permanent settlement ماضی استمراری *ma'zi(-e) istimra'ri* N.F. past continuous tense [A ~ مرور]

استمزاج *istimzaj'* N.M. (lit.) sounding the disposition or inclination (of) [A ~ مزاج]

استناد *istinad'* N.M. referring to (something or someone) as authority [A ~ مسند]

استنباط *istimbat'* N.M. deduction conclusion استنباط کرنا *istimbat' kar'na* V.I. deduce conclude ; draw the conclusion (from) [A]

استنجا *istinja'*, (col. *istan'ja*) N.M. cleaning after a natural evacuation or pissing ; laving استنجا کرنا *istan'ja kar'na* V.T. lave [A ~ نجات]

استنکار *istinkar'* N.M. (lit.) disowning ; refusing to acknowledge [A ~ انکار]

استنکاف *istinkaf'* N.M. disparagement [A]

استنشاق *istinshaq'* N.M (lit.) washing the nostrils snuffing up odours etc. [A ~ نشق]

استوا *istiva'* N.M. evenness parallelism parity خط استوا *khat't-e istiva'* equator equinoctical line استوائی *istiva''i* ADJ. equatorial استوائی خطہ *istiva''i khit'tah* N.M. equatorial region [A ~ ساوی]

استوار *ustuvar'* ADJ. strong secure mighty ; vigorous sturdy compact; secure steady stable ; firm bold resolute استواری *ustuva''ri* N.F strength force; vigour firmness steadiness constancy boldness determination [P]

استھان *asthan'* N.M. idolators' temple without any idol in it ; shrine abode place [S]

استھائی *astha''i* N.F. first line of song

استہزا *istehza'* N.M. ridicule mockery derison scoff jeer joke rebuke [A]

استہلاک *istehlak'* N.M. (lit.) squandering (money) [A ~ ہلاک]

استیصال *istisal'* N.M. eradication uprooting pulling down ; demolishing extirpation destruction devastation [A ~ اصل]

استیعاب *isti'ab'* N.M. (lit.) taking hold of the whole بالاستیعاب *bil-isti'ab'* ADV. wholly ; completely [A]

استیفا *istifa'* N M. taking one's rights in full [A ~ فی]

استیلا *istila'* N.M. supremacy predominence overlordship hegemony conquest capture [A ~ ولایت]

استیناس *istinas'* N.M. (lit.) fellowship ; familiarly intimacy [A ~ انس]

استیناف *istinaf* N.M. (lit.) starting anew taking initiative appeal [A]

اسٹابری *istab'ri* N.F. strawberry [~ E CORR.]

اسٹاف *istaf'*, سٹاف *sataf'* N M. staff [E]

اسٹامپ *istamp'* (dial. اسٹام *istam'*, اشٹام *ishtam'*) N.M. non-judicial stamped paper اسٹامپ عدالتی *istamp' 'ada'lati* N.M. judicial stamp ; court-fee stamp اسٹام فروش *istam firosh'* N M. stamp vendor [E]

اسٹیٹ *istet'* N F. estate state [E]

اسٹیج *istej'*, سٹیج *satej'* N.M. (dial. F.) stage stagecrafts dais [E]

اسٹوپ | *istop'* N.M. stove primus stove [~E stove CORR.]

اسٹور | *istor'* N.M. same as سٹور N.M. ★)

اسٹیشن | *iste'shan*, سٹیشن *sate'shan* N.M. station railway station [E]

اسٹیشنری | *istesh'narī* (same as سٹیشنری N.F. ★)

اسٹیمر | *istī'mar* N.M. (same as سٹیمر N.M. ★)

اسحار | *ashār'* N.F. (PL. of سحر *sahar'* N.F. ★)

اسحاق | *ishāq* N.M. Isaac [A~H]

a'sad N.M. lion Leo ; the fith sign of the Zodiac اسداللہ | *a'sadullāh'* N.M. Lion of God (as the appellation of the fourth orthodox Caliph, Hazrat Ali) [A]

اسرار | *isrār'* N.M. mystery hiding ; concealment اسرار | *asrār'* N.M. (SING.) mystery N.M. PL. secrets اسرار الٰہی | *asrā'r-e ilā'hī* N.M PL. divine secrets اسرار و رموز | *asrā'r-o rumooz'* N.M. PL. secrets and symbols [A~SING. اسر]

اسراف | *isrāf* N.M. extravagance ; prodigality abuse (of wealth) ; waste [A]

اسرافیل | *isrāfīl'* سرافیل *sarāfīl* N.M. name of the angel who will sound the trumpet on the day of resurrection [A~H]

اسرائیل | *isrā''īl* N.M. Israel (as a appellation of the Prophet Jacob) (so-called State of) Israel بنی اسرائیل، بنو اسرائیل *ba'noo isrā''īl*, *ba'nī isrā''īl'* N.M. PL. Israelites ; Jews اسرائیلی *isrā'ī'lī* N.M. Jew ADJ. Israelite ; Jewish [A~H]

اسسٹنٹ | *asistant* N.M. & ADJ. assistant [E]

اسطوخودوس | *istukhuddoos'* N.M. name of a medicinal herb [A]

اسطرلاب | *us'turlab* (or *as'-*) N.M. (same as اصطرلاب ★)

اسعد | *as''ad* ADJ. very lucky extremely happy [A~ سعید SUP.]

اسف | *as'f* N.M. sorrow regret [A]

اسفار[1] | *asfar'* N.M. (PL. of سفر *sa'far* N.M. ★)

اسفار[2] | *asfar'* N.M. (lit.) books volumes ; tomes rolls scrolls [A~SING. سفر *sifr*]

اسفل | *asāfil* (A) adj. (plu. of اسفل *asfal*) Most mean; very mean (fellows). [A]

اسفنج | *isfanj* N.M. (same as سپنج | *ispanj*. ★)

اسقاط | *isqāt'*, اسقاط حمل | *isqā't-e ham'l* N.M. abortion. miscarriage [A~ سقوط]

اسقام | *asqām'* N.M. (PL. of سقم N.M. ★)

اسقف | *us'quf* N.M. bishop [A~G]

اسکات | *iskāt'* N.M. rendering speechless calming down [A~ سکوت]

اسکندر | *iskan'dar* N.M. same as سکندر N.M. ★)

اسکوائر | *isko'ā'yar* N.M. ESQUIRE' Esq.); [E]

اسکول | *iskool'* N.M. (same as سکول N.M. ★)

اسکیمو | *iskī'mo* N.M. Eskimo [E]

اسلاف | *aslāf'* N.M. PL. ancestors ; forefathers ; progenitors ancients ننگ اسلاف *nang-e aslāf'* N.M infamous descendant (polite style for oneself) I [A~ سلف]

اسلام | *islām'* N.M. Islam (i.e. Submission to God as the sole religion preeched by all the Prophet of God and as finally presented by the Holy Prophet, the only true religion اسلام لانا (یا قبول کرنا) | *islām' lā'nā* (or *qubool kar'nā*) V.I. be converted to Islam ; adopt Islamic faith اسلامی | *islāmī* N.M. Islamic Muslim

اسلامیات | *islāmiyyāt'* N.M. Islamic studies Islamics [A]

اسلحہ | *as'lehah* N.M. PL. arms armour اسلحہ خانہ *asleha-khānah* N.M. arsenal ; armoury [A~SING. سلاح]

اسلوب | *usloob'* N.M. (PL. اسالیب | *asālīb'*) style mode method way ; manner form ; shape arrangement خوش اسلوب *khush-usloob'* ADJ. elegant methodical well-regulated ; well arranged [A]

اسم | *ism* N.M. (PL. اسما | *asmā'*) name appellation denomination (gram.) noun اسم استفہام | *is'm-e istifhām'* N.M. interrogative pronoun اسم اشارہ | *is'm-e ishārah* N.M. demonstrative adjective اسم اعظم | *is'm-e a''zam* N.M. Almighty's name the Ineffable Word (cherished for incantation) اسم بامسمّٰی *ism' bā mūsam'mā* N.M. one actually possessing the attribute implicit in his or her name اسم تفضیل *ism-e tafzīl'* N.M. adjective of superlative (or comparative) degree اسم تنکیر *ism-e tankīr'*, اسم نکرہ *ism-e na'kirah* N.M. indefinite noun اسم جامد *ism-e jāmid* N.M. primitive noun اسم جلالی *ism-e jalā'lī* N.M. the illustrious name of God اسم جنس *ism-e jins'* N.M. generic noun appellative اسم حالیہ *ism-e ḥāliy'yah* N.M. present participle اسم صفت *ism-e sifat'* N.M. adjective اسم ضمیر *ism-e zamīr'* N.M. personal pronoun اسم فاعل *ism-e fā''il* N.M. subject اسم فرضی *ism-e far'zī* N.M. fictitious name assumed name اسم کلی *ism-e kūl'lī* N.M. generic noun اسم معرفہ *ism-e-ma''rifah* N.M. proper noun اسم مفعول *ism-e maf'ool'* N.M. passive participle اسم موصول *ism-e mausool'* N.M. relative pronoun اسم نویسی *ism-e navī'sī* N.F. writing out the list of witnesses cataloguing اسم وار *ism-vār'* ADJ. name-wise اسما *asmā'* N.M. PL. names appellations denominations nouns اسماءالرجال *asmā'' ūr-rijāl'* N.M. cyclopedia of narrators Traditions branch of knowledge judging merits or otherwise of Tradition-narrators dictionary of national biography اسمائے حسنیٰ (یا عظمیٰ) *asmā'-e ḥūs'na* (or *ūz'mā*) N.M. PL. the Beautiful (or Great) Names ; ninety-nine epithets of God [A]

اسمار *asmār'* N.M. PL. nightly talks nocturnal stories [A ~ SING. سمر *sa'mar*]

اسماع *asmā''* N.M. PL. (lit.) ears [A ~ SING. سمع]

اسماعیل *ismā'īl'* N.M. Ishmael (as the name of Abraham's elder son) Isma'il (as the name of a seventh and last Imam of a Shi'ite sect called after him) اسماعیلی *ismā'ī'lī* ADJ. descended from Ishmael pertaining to Isma'ili sect N.M. Isma'ili ; member of his sect اسماعیلیہ *ismā'īliy'yah* N.M. Isma'ilis ; the Sevener Shi'ites ; the Seveners [A ~ H]

اسمبلی *asaim'balī* N.F. Assembly Hall ; Assembly Chambers [E]

اسناد *asnād* N.F. (dial. M.) (PL. of سند *sa'nad* N.F. ★)

اسنان *asnān'* N.M. PL. (lit.) teeth [A ~ SING. سن *sin*]

اسوار *asvār'* N.M. (col.) (same as سوار N.M. ★

اسوانسی *asvāṅ'si* N.F. a lineal land measure

اسوج *asooj'* N.M. seventh month of Hindu calender (corresponding to September-October [S]

اسود *as'vad* ADJ. black N.M. (PL. سود *sood*, سودان *soodān'*) Negro اسود و احمر *as'vad-o-aiḥ'mar* N.M. (members of) the black and the white races بحر اسود *baiḥ'r-e as'vad* N.M. the black Sea [A]

اسہال *ishāl'* N.M. diarrhoea flux اسہال دموی *ishā'l-e da'mavī* N.M. bloody flux ; haematic discharage [A ~ سہل]

اسہل *as'hal* ADJ. very easy [A ~ سہل SUP.]

اسوہ *ūs'vah* N.M. example ; pattern ; ideal اسوۂ حسنہ *ūs'va-e ḥa'sanah* N.M. the ideal of good good example (of the Holy Prophet [A]

اسی *i'sī* ADJ. its own PRON. this very اسی دن کو پالا تھا *i'sī din ko pā'lā thā* PH. did I bring you up for this reward ? [~ اس *is* + ی]

اسی *ū'sī* ADJ. its own PRON. that very [~ اس *ūs* + ی]

اسی *as'sī* N.M. & ADJ. Eighty اسیواں *as'sīvāṅ* ADJ. eightieth اسی کی آمدنی چوراسی کا خرچ *as'sī kī ām'danī, chaura'sī kā kharch'* PROV. live at the rate of six scores to the hundred اسی برس کی عمر نام میاں معصوم *as'sī ba'ras kī 'ūmr' nām miyāṅ ma'soom'* PROV. person feigning ignorance

اسیاف *asyāf'*, اسیف *as'yūf* N.F. (PL. of سیف *saif* N.F. ★)

اسیر *asīr'* N.M. prisoner captive اسیر آب و گل *asī'r-e ā'b-o-gil'* attached to one's native land bound by mundane things اسیر سلطانی *asī'r-e sūltā'nī* N.M. prisoner of State اسیری *asī'rī* N.F. imprisonment confinement ; incarceration captivity [A]

اسیس *asīs'* N.F. (dial.) blessing ; benediction [S]

اسیسر *ase'sar* N.M. assessor [E]

اشارات *ishārāt'* N.M. (PL. of اشارہ N.M. ★)

اشارت *ishārat'* N.F. insinuation hint [A ~ doublet of FOL.]

اشارہ *ishā'rah* N.M. (PL. اشارات *ishārāt'*) hint suggestion indication gesticulation gesture wink sign token note clue (11) symbol اشارہ کرنا *ishā'rah kar'nā* V.T.

signal beckon hint suggest indicate اشارے پر چلنا *ishā're par chal'nā* V.I. be at the beck and call (of) be under control (of) عقلمند کو اشارہ کافی ہے *aql'mand ko ishā'rah kā'fī hai* PROV. a word may suffice to a wise person اشاراتی *ishārā'tī* ADJ. symbolic اشاری *ishā'rī* ADJ. symbolic index (card) اشاریہ *ishāriy'yah* N.M. index اشاریہ مرتب کرنا *ishāriy'yah murat'tab kar'nā* V.T. compile an index (of) [A]

اشاعت *ishā''at* N.F. publication propagation dissemination circulation, spread ; difusion edition (*nā'*) *qā'bil-e ishā''at* ADJ. (not) suitable for publication [A ~]

اشاعرہ *ashā''irah* N.M. (PL. of N.M. ★)

اشباح *ashbāh'* N.M. (lit.) Bodies objects [A ~ SING.]

اشباہ *ashbāh'* N.M. (PL. of شبہ *shib'h* N.F ★)

اشباع *ish'ā''* N.M. elongation of vowel sound اشباعی *ishbā''ī* ADJ. elongated (short-vowel) ضمّہ (یا فتحہ یا کسرہ) اشباعی *zam'ma* (or *fat'ha* or *kas'ra*)-*e ishbā''ī* N.M. elongated *u* (or *a* or *i*)

اشتباہ *ishtibāh'* N.M. ambiguity doubt suspicion uncertainty hesitation distress اشتباہی *ishtibā'hī* ADJ. doubtful scrupulous [A ~ شبہ]

اشتداد *ishtidād'* N.M. strengthening increasing in violence [A ~ شدت]

اشتر *ūsh'tūr* N.M. (same as *sh'ı'tūr* N.M. ★)

اشترا *ishtirā'* N.M. purchase selling trade ; commerce [A ~ شری]

اشتراک *ishtirāk'* N.M. partnership society company co-operation collaboration (rare) subscription (to periodical) بدل اشتراک *ba'dal-e ishtirāk'* N.M. (rare) subscription (to periodical) اشتراکی *ishtirā'kī* N.M. socialist ADJ. socialist socialistic اشتراکیت *ishtirākiy'yat* N.F. socialism [A ~ شرکت]

اشتعال *ishte'āl'* N.M. provocation instigation incitement اشتعال دینا (یا دلانا) *ishte'āl' de'nā* (or *dilā'nā*) V.T. provoke ; incite ; instigate اشتعال طبع *ishte'āl-e tab''* N.M. provocation اشتعالک *ishte'ā'lak* N.F. instigation incitement اشتعالک دینا *ishte'ā'lak de'nā* V.T instigate incite [A ~ شعلہ]

اشتغال *ishtighāl'* N.M. occupation avocation trade engagement [A ~ شغل]

اشتقاق *ishtiqāq'* N.M. Derivation علم الاشتقاق *il'm-ul-ishtiqāq'* N.M. etymology [A ~ شق]

اشتمال *ishtemāl'* N.M. (land) consolidation comprising ; containing اشتمال اراضی *ishtemā'l-e arā'zī* N.M. land consolidation ; consolidation of landholdings اشتمال بے جا *ishtimā'l-e be' jā'* N.M. misjoinder اشتمال دعویٰ *ishtimā'l-e da''vā* N.M. joinder of causes of action اشتمالی *ishtim'lī* ADJ. & N.M. Communist ; Communistic اشتمالیت *ishtimāliy'yat* N F. Communism [A ~ شامل]

اشتہا *ishtehā'* N.F. appetite hunger (rare) urge [A]

اشتہار *ishteh.r'* N.M. (PL. اشتہارات *ishtehārāt'*) advertisement bill ; poster handbill notification, notice publicity currency placard (arch.) renown ; celebrity اشتہارات آویزاں (یا چسپاں) کرنا *ishtehar' āve'zāh* (or *chas'-(pān) kar'nā*, اشتہار لگانا *ishtehar' laga'nā* V.T put up (or affix) a poster اشتہار دینا *ishtehār' de'nā* V.T. advertise اشتہار کرنا *ishtehar' kar'nā* V.T. (arch.) notify ; publish اشتہاری *ishtehā'rī* ADJ. proclaimed popularized through advertisement اشتہاری مجرم *ishtehā'rī mūj'rim* N.M. proclaimed offender one who has decamped [A ~ شہرت]

اشتیاق *ishtiyāq'* N.M. liking ; fondness wish ; longing yearning ; hankering bent ; desire [A ~ شوق]

اشٹمی *ash'ṭamī* N.F. eight day (of Hindu month) [I]

اشجار *ashjār'* N.M. (PL of شجر N.M. ★)

اشجع *ash'ja'* ADJ. Braver or bravest (more or) most valiant [A ~ شجاع SUP.]

اشخاص *ashkhās'* N M (PL of شخص N.M. ★)

اشد *ashad'* ADJ more or most vehement urgent extreme severe excessive violent اشد ضرورت *ashad' zaroo'rat* N.F. urgency اشد ضروری *ashad' zaroo'rī* ADJ. very important urgent [A ~ شدید SUP.]

اشر *ashar'* ADJ. (more or) most wicked ; more or most vicious اشر الناس *ashar'r-ūn-nās'* N.M. the most wicked of men اشرار *ashrār'* N.M. PL. the wicked criminals malicious persons [A ~ شر]

اشراف *ashraf'* N.M. PL. nice people the high-born aristocracy N.M. (SING.) gentleman اشرف وجس کے پاس اشرفی *ashraf' voh jis ke pas ash'rafi* PROV. money often makes the man اشرافی *ashrā'fī* ADJ. oligarchical اشرافیہ *ashrāfiy'yah* N.M. oligarchy [A ~ SING. اشریف]

اشراق *ishrāq'* N.M. dawn daybreak radiance ; brilliancy Platonic idealism as interpreted by Muslim mystics ; Muslim Platonic mysticism نماز اشراق *namā'z-e ishrāq'* N.F. mid-morning prayer اشراقی *ishrā'qī* ADJ. Platonist follower of Platonic mysticism oriental ; eastern having the splendour of the East Saracen اشراقیین *ishrāiqi'yīn'* N.M. PL. Platonists Muslim Platonic mystics [A ~ شرق]

اشرف *ash'raf* ADJ. noblest ,most distinguished اشرف المخلوقات *ash'raf-ul makhlooqāt'* N.M. man (as the most eminent of created beings) mankind اشرف الناس *ashraf-ūn nās'* N.M. the noblest of men [A ~ شریف SUP.]

اشرفی *ash'rafī* F. (old use) gold coin equivalent to about sterling ; gold mohur ; gold coin worth 16 rupees ; guinea (usu. گل اشرفی *gul ash'rafī*) marigold اشرفیاں لٹیں کوئلوں پر مہر *ash'rafiyān lū'ṭen ko''ilon par moh'r* PROV. penny wise pound foolish [A ~ PREC.]

اشعار *ash'ār'* N.M. (PL. of شعر *she'r* N.M. ★)

اشعری *ash''arī* ADJ. & N.M. PL. اشاعرہ *ashā''irah* Ash'arite اشعریہ *ash'ariy'yah* N.M. orthodox school of scholastic philosophy in Islam ; Ash'arite [A ~ founder's name]

اشعاع *ish'ā''* N.M. directing the rays اشعاعی *ish'ā'ī* ADJ. radiological اشعاعی علاج *ish'ā''ī 'ilāj'* N.M. radio-theraphy اشعاعیات *ish'aiyyat* N.F. radiology اشعہ *ashe' 'ah* N.F. PL. beams ; rays of light [A ~ شعاع]

اشغال *ashghal'* N.M. (PL. of شغل N.M. ★)

اشغلہ *ushghūlah*, اشقلہ *ash'qūlah* N.M. scandal mischievous lie

اشفاق *ashfāq'* N.M. PL. compassions favours اشفاق *ishfāq'* N.M. favouring fearing [A ~ PREC.]

اشقیا *ashqiyā'* N.M. (PL. of شقی N.M. ★)

اشک *ash'k* N.M. tear اشک افشاں *ashkh'-ofshān*, اشک فشاں *ashk-fishāṅ'*, اشکبار *ashk'-bār* ADJ. shedding tears ; weeping mourning اشک افشانی *ashk-afshā'nī*, اشک فشانی *ashk-fishā'nī* اشکباری *ashk'-bārī* N.M. weeping ; shedding tears mourning اشک افشاں (یا فشاں یا بار) کرنا *ashk-ofshāṅ'* (or *fishāṅ'* or *bār'*) *kar'na* V.T. cause to weep bring tears down in someone's) eyes cause to mourn اشک افشاں (یا فشاں یا بار) ہونا *ashk-ofshāṅ'* (or *fishāṅ*, or *bār'*) *ho'na* V.I. weep ; shed tears mourn اشک رواں *ashk-e ravāṅ'* N.F. flowing tears اشک شوئی *ashk-sho''ī* N.F. comforting ; soothing consolation superficial consolation اشک شوئی کرنا *ashk-sho''ī kar'na* V.T. solace give superficial consolation (to) سیل اشک *sail-e ashk'* N.M. flood of tears [P]

اشکال *ishkāl'* N.M. PL. of شکل N.F. ★) اشکال *ishkāl'* N.M. (PL اشکالات *ishkālāt'*) ambiguity difficulty complication [A]

اشلک لگانا *ash'lak lagā'na* V.T. (arch,) accuse falsely ; bring false charge against [~ T. اشلق *ishlaq* accusation]

اشلوک *ashlok'*, شلوک *shalok'* N.M. Hindu religious verse couplet (of it) [S]

اشمام *ishmām'* N.M. (lit.) diffusion, of scent ; shedding of perfume [A ~ شمیم]

اشنان *ashnān'* N.M. (dial.) bath bathing fair [S]

اشہاد *ashhād'* N.M. PL. witnesses deponents علیٰ رؤوس الاشہاد *'alā rū'oo's-il-oshhad'* ADV. openly before eye-witnesses اشہاد *ishhād'* N.M. bringing forward testimony ; leading of evidence [A ~ (a) شہادت (b) شہید]

اشہب *ash'hab* ADJ. grey ; ash-coloured ; dun N.M. dun horse [A]

اشہد *ash'had-o* V.I. I bear witness اشہدان لاالہ الا اللہ *ash'had-o aṅ lā' ilā'ha il'lallā'h(-o)* PH. (opening words of a portion of the Muslim creed) I bear witness that there is no god but one God [A ~ شہادت]

اشیا *ash'yā* N.F. (PL. of شے N.F. ★)

اشیر باد *ashīr'bad* N.F. (dial.) (same as آشیرباد *ashīr'-bād* N.F. ★)

اصابت *isā'bat* N.F. hitting the nail on the head correctness maturity (of opinion, etc.) اصابت رائے *isā'bat-e ra'e* N.F. maturity of judgment or opinion

اصاغر *asā'ghir* N.M. PL. the small fry the lower classes [A ~ SING. اصغر]

اصالت *asā'lat* N.F. determination ; tenacity of purpose integrity genuineness being the real person اصالۃً asa'latan ADV in person ; 'in propria persona' originally primarily [A ~ اصل]

اصح asah' ADJ. (more or) most authentic اصح الکتب asah'h-ūl-kū'tūb N.M. the most authentic book

اصحاب ashāb' N.M. PL. Companions (of the Holy Prophet) comrades friends preceptors disciples nobles ; peers possessors of ; those having those pertaining to اصحاب الفیل ashā'b-ūl-fīl', اصحاب فیل ashā'b-e fīl' N.M. PL. the army with elephants ; the pre-Islamic Abyssinian invaders of Mecca اصحاب کہف ashā'b-e kah'f N.M. PL. Catacomb Comrades [A ~ SING. صاحب or صحابی]

اصدار isdār' N.M. proceeding appearance production issue [A ~ صدور]

اصرار isrār' N.M. obduracy persistance constancy [A]

اصطباغ istibāgh' N.M. baptism اصطباغ دینا istibāgh de'nā V.T. baptise اصطباغ لینا istibāgh le'na V.I. be baptised

اصطبل as'tabal N.M. stable [A ~ L]

اصطرلاب (or اسطرلاب) ūs'tarlāb' (or as'-) N.M. astrolable ; [A ~ G]

اصطفا istifā' N.M. choice ; selection [A ~ صفا]

اصطلاح istilāh' N.F. term ; technical term slang expression conventional phraseology اصطلاحات istilāhāt' N.F. PL. terms ; technical terms slang expressions وضع اصطلاحات vaz''-e istilāhāt' N.M. coining of technical terms اصطلاحی istilā'hī ADJ. technical conventional secondary اصطلاحی معنی istilā'hī ma''na (or -nī) N.M. technical sense conventional meaning [A ~ صلح]

اصغر as'ghar ADJ. little tiny younger or youngest smaller or smallest N.M. (PL. اصاغر asā'ghir) younger or youngest son, etc. this as male name a person of no importance اصغری asgharī N.F. (false feminine used as female name) younger or youngest daughter, etc. [A ~ صغیر SUP.]

اصفر as'far ADJ. yellow saffron-coloured ; of the colour of mustard-flower [A]

اصفیا asfiya N.M. (PL. of صفی N.M. ★)

اصل as'l N.F. original principal ; principal sum stock-in-trade root essence ; quintessence cause ; root-cause spring, source base ; foundation plinth basis (11) truth ; reality (12) lineage (13) pedigree ADJ. essentially vital fundamental ; basic substantive positive important principal chief legitimate real ; true (11) actual (12) factual اصل اصول asl-e ūsool' اصل الاصول asl-ūl-ūsool' N.M. fundamental principal اصل السوس asl-ūsoos' N.F. liquorice root اصل خیر سے asl' khair se ADV. (W. dial.) safely اصل مع سود asl ma' sood' principal with interest اصل و فرع as'l-o-far'' N.M. root and branch cause and effect اصل نسل asl' nas'l N.F. (col.) lineage اصل نفع as'l naf'' N.M. net profit اصلا as'lā اصلاً as'lan ADV. never at any time at all ; in the least altogether اصلی as'lī ADJ. true ; real genuine authentic pure ; unadulterated original natural basic ; fundamental actual ; factual اصلیت asliy'yat N.F truth ; reality basic facts (about) origin genuineness purity authenticity originality [A]

اصلاح islāh' N.F. (PL. اصلاحات islāhāt') reform reformation correction (of pupil's exercise) writing pattern (written by teacher for pupil) (rare) haircut (rare) timming of (beard) اصلاح بنانا islāh' banā'na V.T. trim (beard) اصلاح پذیر islāh'-pazīr ADJ. docile amenable اصلاح دینا (یا کرنا) islāh' de'na (or kar'nā) V.T. correct rectify amend improve revise reform اصلاح مذہب islā'h-e maz'hab N.F. Reformation ; the Protestant Reformation اصلاح نسل islā'h-e nas'l N.F. eugenics اصلاح ہر وقت ممکن ہے islāh' har' vaq't mūm'kin hai PROV. it is never too late to mend اصلاحات islāhāt' N.F. PL. reforms اصلاحات نافذ کرنا islāhāt' na'fiz kar'nā V.T. impliment reforms تحریک اصلاح taihrī'k-e-islāh' N.F. Reformation [A ~ صلح]

اصلی as'lī ADJ. اصلیت asliy'yat N.F. (see under اصل N.F. ★)

اصم asam' ADJ. deaf (math.) surd مقدار اصم miqdā'r-e asam' N.F. (PL. مقادیر اصم maqādīr-e asam') surd [A ~ صم]

اصناف asnāf' N.F. PL. genres sexes species اصناف سخن asnā'f-e sū'khan N.F. PL. genres of literature [A ~ SING. صنف]

اصنام *asnām'* N.M. (PL. of صنم N.M. ★)
اصوات *asvāt'* N.F. (PL. of صوت N.F. ★)
اصول *ūsool* N.M. principle N.M. PL. fundamentals causes principles principles of Muslim jurisprudence dogmas manners اصول متعارفہ *ūsool-e mūta'ā'rafah* N.M. PL. axioms اصول موضوعہ *ūsool'l-e mauzoo''ah* N.M. PL. (math.) postulates اصول وفروع *ūsoo'l-o-fūroo'* N.F. PL. causes and effects creed and law (of faith) according to Shi'ite sect [A ~ SING. اصل]
اصیل *asīl* ADJ. pedigreed of good extraction high-born ; noble genteel pure ; unmixed اصیل گھوڑے کو چابک کی ضرورت نہیں *asīl' gho'ṛe ko chā'būk kī ḥā'jat na'hīṅ* PROV a good horse should be seldom spurred [A ~ اصل]
اضافت *izā'fat* N.F. genitive case mutual construction (of two nouns) ; construct phrase appendage ; adjunct reference کسرۂ اضافت *kas'ra-e-izā'fat* N.M. sign of construct phrase [A doublet of FOL.]
اضافہ *izā'fah* N.M. enhancement addition enlargement excess surplus اضافی *izā'fī* ADJ. relative comparative additional supplementary surplus [A]
اضافیت *izā'fiy'yat* نظریۂ اضافیت *nazariy'ya-e izā'fiy'yat* N.F. (theory of relativity اضافی *izāfī* ADJ. (see under اضافہ N.M. ★) [A ~ PREC.]
اضحوکہ *ūzhoo'kah* N.M. laughing-stock اضحوکۂ روزگار *ūzhoo'ka-e roz-gār'* N.M. butt of ridicule [A ~ ضحک]
اضحی *azḥa* N.M. PL. sacrifices ; sacrificial animals victims عید الاضحی *'īd-ul-azḥā* N.F. the sacrificial Eid ; Eid-ul-Azha [A ~ SING. اضحیہ *uzḥiy'yah*]
اضداد *azdād* N.F. PL. opposites words each of which conveys two opposite meanings [A ~ ضد]
اضطراب *iztirab'* N.M. impatience restlessness ; uneasiness anxiety agitation anguish vexation disturbance; commotion اضطرابی *iztirā'bī* N.F. agitated uneasy اضطرابی کیفیت (یا حالت) *iztirā'bī kaifiy'yat* (or *ḥa'lat*) uneasiness restlessness [A]
اضطرار *iztirar'* N.M. constraint force ; coercion restraint agitation violence perturbation اضطراری *iztirā'rī* ADJ. involuntary uncontrolled اضطراری حالت یا کیفیت *iztirā'rī ḥa'lat* (or *kaifiy'yat*) N.F. compulsion involuntary state [A]
اضعاف *az'āf'* N.M. PL. double things twofold things multiples *zoo az'ā'f-e aqal'* N.M. lowest common multiple LCM اضعاف مضاعفہ *az'ā'f-e muzā'afah* N.M. PL. manifold things [A ~ SING. ضعف *ze'f*]
اضعف *az''af* ADJ. most (or more) feeble decrepit [A ~ ضعیف SUP.]
اضغاث احلام *azghā's-e aḥlām* N.M. PL. meaningless nightmares disturbed dreams [A]
اضلاع *azlā'* N.F. administrative district ; districts parts ribs sides (of figuce) [A ~ SING. ضلع]
اضلال *izlāl'* N.M. leading astray [A ~ ضلال]
اضمار *izmar'* N.M. use of a pronoun اضمار قبل الذکر *izmar' qab'l-uz-zik'r* N.M. use of a pronoun before mentioning its antecedent ; pronoun preceding own antecedent [A ~ ضمیر]
اضمحلال *izmeḥlal'* N.M. weakness depression طبیعت پر اضمحلال طاری ہونا *tabī''at par izmeḥlal' ta'rī ho'na* V.I. feel very much run down be enervated [A]
اضیاف *azyāf'* N.M. (PL. of ضیف N.M. ★)
اطاعت *iṭā''at* N.F. obedience reverence worship اطاعت شعار (یا گزار) *iṭā'at shi''ar'* (or *gūzār*) ADJ. obedient اطاعت شعاری (یا گزاری) *iṭā'at shi'ā'rī* (or *gūzā'rī*) N.F. obedience اطاعت کرنا *iṭā''at kar'nā* V.T. obey pay homage (to) worship [A]
اطاق *ūṭaq'* N.M. (rare) room اطاقی *ūṭāqī* ADJ. (rare) pertaining to room rooming اطاقی جوڑا *ūṭā'qī jo'ṛa* N.M. rooming couple
اطال *aṭal'* INT. may elongate اطال اللہ عمرہٗ *aṭa'l-allā'ho ūm'rahoo* INT. may God grant him a long life [A ~ طول]
اطالیہ *iṭā'liyah* N.F. Italy اطالوی *iṭā'lavī* ADJ. Italian [E ~ It.]
اطبّا *aṭibbā'* N.M. PL. physicians practitioners of indigenous system of medicine [A ~ SING. طبیب]
اطراف *aṭrāf'* N.F. PL. directions side extremities suburbs environs outpost boundaries اطراف واکناف *aṭrā'f-o-aknaf'* N.M. PL. surroundings all sides اطراف شہر *aṭrā'f-e shaih'r* N.F. environs of city or town suburbs [A ~ SING طرف]

اطریفل itrī'fal N.F. a kind of medicated pudding [A ~ S تریپھلا]
اطعمہ at''imah N.M. (PL. of طعام N.M. ★)
اطفا itfā' N.M. extinction (of fire) [A]
اطفال atfāl' N.M. PL. children babies issues بازیچۂ اطفال bāzī'cha-e atfāl' N.M. child's play [A ~ SING. طفل]
اطلاع ittilā' N.F. information intimation comunication intelligence report notice notification اطلاع حاضری ittilā''e ha'zirī N.F. joining report اطلاع دینا یا کرنا ittilā'' de'nā (or kar'nā) inform apprise acquaint report give notice communicate اطلاع نامہ ittilā''-na'mah N.M. written notice اطلاع یابی ittilā''-yā'bī getting information receipt or acknowledgment of notice, etc. اطلاعاً ittilā''-an ADV. by way of notification for information اطلاعاً عرض ہے ittilā''an 'arz' hai PH. submitted for information [A ~ طلوع]
اطلاق itlāq' N.M. application (lit.) setting at liberty اطلاق رکھنا itlāq' rakh'nā V.I. be applicable (to) اطلاق کرنا itlāq' kar'nā V.T. apply (to) use (a word or phrase) in a particular sense اطلاق ہونا itlāq' ho'nā V.I. be apt be applicable علی الاطلاق 'alal itlāq' ADJ. absolute ADV. absolutely حاکم علی الاطلاق ha'kim(-e) 'alal itlāq' N.M. (God as) the Absolute Ruler [A]
اطلس at'las N.M. satin اطلسی at'lasī ADJ. satin [A]
اطمینان itmīnān' N.M. satisfaction calmness ; composure complacency confidence respite pledge surety اطمینان خاطر یا قلب itmīnā'n-e kha'tir (or qalb') N.M. satisfaction of mind اطمینان کرنا itmīnān' karnā V.T. & I. satisfy (someone or oneself) اطمینان کے لائق itmīnān' ke lā''iq ADJ. trustworthy ; reliable [A]
اطناب itnāb' N.M. verbosity profuseness (of speech) [A]
اطناب atnāb' N.F. (PL. of طناب N.F. ★)
اطوار atvār' N.M. PL. conduct ; behaviour ways ; manners deportment characteristics practices customs خوش اطوار khush-atvār' ADJ. well-mannered affable polite ; courteous [A ~ SING. طور]
اطہار athar' ADJ. & N.M. PL. unpolluted chaste (persons) non-menstrual periods [A ~ SING. (a) طاہر (b) طہر]
اطہر at'har ADJ. (more or) most pure [A ~ طاہر SUP.]
اظلال azlāl' N.M. (PL. of ظل N.M. ★)
اظلم az'lam ADJ. darkest (more or) most cruel] [A ~ ظلم or ظلمت SUP.]
اظہار izhār N.M. expression ; expressing disclosure examination or deposition of a witness testimony display proclamation اظہار حلفی izhā'r-e ha'lfī N.M. deposition اظہار دینا izhār' de'nā V.I. bear testimony attest depose اظہار کرنا izhār' kar'nā express unfold announce assert اظہار لینا izhār' le'nā V.T. examine (witness) put (someone) in the witness-box اظہار نویس izhār'-navīs' N.M. deposition writer اظہار و ابلاغ izhā'r-o iblāgh N.M. expressing and conveying of meaning ; communication [A ~ ظہور]
اظہر az'har ADJ. evident ; obvious clear plain اظہر من الشمس az'har min-ash-shams' ADJ. crystal clear ; quite manifest
اعادہ e'ā'dah N.M repetition revision review renewal اعادہ کرنا e'ā'dah kar'nā V.T. repeat revise [A ~ عود]
اعادی a'ādī N.M. PL. foes ; enemies [A ~ PL. of عدو]
اعاظم a'ā'zim ADJ. & N.M. (PL. of اعظم ADJ. ★)
اعالی a'ā'lī ADJ. & N.M. (PL. of اعلیٰ ADJ. ★)
اعانت e'ā'nat N.F. help ; assistance support abetment ; facilitation ; extension of facility اعانتِ جرم e'ā'nat-e jurm' N.F. abetment of crime امداد و اعانت imdā'd-o-e'ā'nat N.F. help succour [A ~ عون]
اعتبار e'tibār N.M. credence confidence ; faith credit esteem (lit.) taking a lesson from accordance کے اعتبار سے ke e'tibār' se PH. according to اعتبار آنا e'tibār' ā'nā V.T. believe اعتبار اٹھ جانا e'tibār' uṭh' ja'nā V.T. lose credit اعتبار کرنا e'tibār' kar'nā V.T. believe trust give credit (to) have faith (in) ; repose confidence (in) depend (upon) اعتبار کھونا e'tibār' kho'nā V.T. lose credit lose reputation با اعتبار ba-e'tibār' ADJ. reliable ; trustworthy creditable بنظر اعتبار دیکھنا ba-na'zar-e e'tibār dekh'nā V.T. take a lesson from (some event) ; draw a moral for oneself (from something)

اعتباری *e'tibari* ADJ. reliable, trustworthy creditable [A]

اعتدا *e,tidā'* N.F. tyrannizing cruelty [A]

اعتدال *e'tidāl'* N.M. moderation temperance evenness balance اعتدال پر رہنا *e'tidāl par raih'nā* V.I. be temperate observe the golden mean [A ~ عدل]

اعتذار *e'tizār'* N.M. apology excuse [A ~ عذر]

اعتراض *e'tirāz'* N.M. objection fault-finding criticism observation taking exception protest resistance animadversion اعتراض (پیش) کرنا *e'tirāz (pesh) kar'nā* V.I. take exception (to) raise an objection cavil at call in question protest disapprove اعتراض رفع کرنا *e'tirāz' raf'' kar'nā* V.I. remove the cause of an objection redress the grievance (of) اعتراض ضابطہ *e'terā'ze zā'bitah* N.M. technical objection [A ~ عرض]

اعتراف *e'tirāf'* N.M. admission confession avowal recognition *e'tirāf' kar'nā* V.I. confess; admit own, acknowledge اعتراف گناہ *e'tirā'f-e gūnāh'* N.M. confession of one's sin [A ~ عرفان]

اعتزاز *e'tizāz'* N.M. eminence respectability [A ~ عزت]

اعتزال *e'tizāl'* N.M. dissent secession withdrawal Rationalism (as a school of Muslim scholastic philosophy) [A ~ اعزل]

اعتصام *e'tisām'* N.M. holding fast catching hold (of) refraining from اعتصام بحبل اللہ *e'tisām be-ḥablillāh'* N.M. holding fast to the covenant with God [A ~ عصمت]

اعتقاد *e'tiqād'* N.F. belief faith credence reliance (in) اعتقاد رکھنا *e'tiqād' rakh'nā* V.I. believe (in) have faith (in) repose confidence (in) اعتقاد دلانا *e'tiqād' lā'nā* V.I. believe (in) become a convert (to) اعتقاد ہونا *e'tiqād' ho'nā* V.T. & I. have faith (in) believe اعتقادی *e'tiqā'dī* ADJ. (matters, etc.) pertaining to belief [A ~ عقیدہ]

اعتکاف *e'tikāf'* N.M. retirement (to mosque) for continued prayer اعتکاف کرنا *e'tikāf' kar'nā* V.I. retire thus [A]

اعتلا *e'tilā'* N.M. (lit.) rise raise increase [A ~ علو]

اعتماد *e'timād'* N.M. faith confidence trust reliance اعتماد رکھنا (یا کرنا) *e'timād' rakh'nā (or kar'nā)* V.T. repose confidence in depend upon [A]

اعتنا *e'tinā'* N.F. care solicitude exertion; labour; taking pains اعتنا کے قابل *e'tinā' ke qā'bil*, درخور اعتنا *dar' khūr-e e'tinā'* ADJ. worthy of attention [A]

اعجاز *e'jāz'* N.M. miracle marvel wonder اعجاز مسیحا (ئی) *e'jā'z-e masīḥā'('ī)* N.M. Messiah's miracle (fig.) wonderful cure [A ~ عجز]

اعجمی *a''jamī* N.M. non-Arab, عجمی *'a'jamī* N.M. (see under عجم N.M. ★)

اعجوبہ *o'joo'bah* N.M. wonder [A ~ عجب *'ajab*]

اعدا *a'dā'* N.M. (PL. of عدو N.M. ★)

اعداد *a'dād'* N.M. PL. numbers اعداد متباینہ *a'dā'd-e mūtaba' yinah* N.M. PL. (math.) prime numbers اعداد متوافقہ *a'dā'd-i-mū' tavā'-fiqah* N.M. PL. (math.) composite numbers اعداد متداخلہ *a'dā'd-e mūtadā'khilah* N.M. PL. (math.) concordant numbers اعداد و شمار *a'dā'd-o-shumār'* N.M. PL. statistics facts and figures [A ~ SING. عدد]

اعراب *e'rāb'* N.M. vowel points cases (of nouns, etc.) [A]

اعرابی *a'rābī* N.M. (PL. اعراب *a'rāb'*) Bedouin; Arabian nomad [A]

اعراض *e'rāz'* N.M. shunning shrinking from eschewing اعراض کرنا *e'rāz' kar'nā* shun shrink from eschew decline [A ~ عرض]

اعراض *a'rāz'* N.F. (PL. of عرض *'araz* N.F. ★)

اعراف *a'rāf'* (col. *ai'-*) N.M. place between Heaven and Hell Purgatory [A]

اعرج *a''raj* ADJ. (lit.) lame [A]

اعزاز *e'zāz'* N.M. (PL. اعزازات *e'zāzāt'*) esteem award title; title of honour (conferred by government, etc.) exaltation extolling اعزازی *e'zā'zī* ADJ. honorary اعزازیہ *e'zāziy'yah* N.M. honorarium reception [A ~ عزت]

اعزہ *a'iz'zah* N.M. PL. relations, relatives اعزہ و اقارب *a'iz'za-o-aqā'rib* N.M. PL. kith and kin; near and distant relations [A ~ SING. عزیز]

اعشار *a'shār'* N.M. PL. pieces torn or broken pieces (of) tens [A ~ عشر]

اعشاریہ *a'shāriy'yah* N.M. decimal decimal point اعشاری *a'shā'rī* (or *ai'-*) ADJ.

decimal اعشاری سکہ a'shā'rī sik'kah N.M. decimal coin اعشاری نظام a'shā'rī nizām' N.M. decimal system [A ~ عشر]

اعصاب a'sāb' N.M. PL. nerves muscles اعصابی a'sā'bī ADJ. nervous اعصابی جنگ a'sā'bī jang' N.F. war of nerves [A ~ SING. عصب]

اعصار e'sār' N.M. extracting the juice (of) crushing اعصار a'sār' N.M. PL. times ages eras [A ~ عصر]

اعضا a'zā' N.M. PL. organs limbs اعضائے رئیسہ a'zā-e ra'ī'sah N.M. PL. chief organs of the body (viz., heart, brain, liver, testicles) اعضا شکنی a'zā' shi'kanī N.F. fatigue pain in limbs (owing to feverishness, etc.) [A ~ SING. عضو]

اعطا e'tā' N.M. bestowal grant [A ~ عطا]

اعظم a''zam ADJ. & N.M. (PL. اعاظم a'ā'zim) greatest (person, etc.) the great عاد اعظم 'add-e a''zam N.M. highest common factor ; H.C.F. قائد اعظم qā''id-e a''zam N.M. the Great Leader (as title of the Founder of Pakistan) ; the Quaid-i-Azam مغل اعظم mū'ghal-e a''zam N.M. the Great Moghul (as appellation of the Moghul emperor of India, Akbar) [A ~ عظیم SUP.]

اعلا e'lā' N.M. upholding elevation اعلائے کلمۃ الحق e'lā'-e kalimat-ūlhaq' N.M. upholding the truth [A ~ علو]

اعلام a'lām' N.M. (PL. of علم 'alam N.M. ★)

اعلام e'lām' N.M. (lit.) notification announcement اعلامیہ e'lāmiy'yah N.M. Press Note handout proclamation [A ~ علم 'ilm]

اعلان e'lān' N.M. notification announcement pronouncement [A]

اعلیٰ a'la ADJ. & N.M. (PL. اعالی a'ā'lī) topmost first-rate principal superior higher elevated most dignified (person) supreme being God [A ~ علو]

اعم a'am' ADJ. very common most (or more) common [A ~ عام SUP.]

اعماق a'māq' N.M. (PL. of عمق N.M. ★)

اعمال a'māl' N.M. actions acts behaviour ; conduct اعمالنامہ a'mālnā'mah N.M. record of (someone's) doings record of (someone's) misdeeds [A ~ SING. عمل]

اعمام a'mām' N.M. PL. uncles [A ~ اعم]

اعمیٰ a''ma ADJ. blind [A]

اعوان a'vān' N.M. name of a Rajput clan its members N.M. P.L. helpers [A ~ SING. اعون]

اعیان a'yān' N.M. PL. eyes dignatories اعیان دولت (یا سلطنت) a'yā'n-e dau'lat (or sal'tanat) N.M. PL. dignatories of State [A ~ SING. عین]

اغتنام ightinām' N.M. capture as booty; seizing pillaging [A ~ غنیمت]

اغذیہ agh'ziya'h N.M. (PL. of غذا N.F. ★)

اغراض aghrāz' N.M. (PL. of غرض gharaz N.F. ★)

اغراق ighrāq' N.M. exaggeration hyperbole [A ~ غرق]

اغلاط aghlāt N.M. PL. mistakes errors [SING. غلط A ~ غلطی]

اغلاق ighlāq' N.M. abstruseness [A]

اغلال aghlāl' N.M. PL. yokes chains [A ~ SING. غل ghūl]

اغلام ighlām' N.M. sodomy ; paederasty [A ~ غلام boy]

اغلب agh'lab ADV. probably very likely ADJ. probable quite possible [A ~ SUP.]

اغل بغل a'ghal ba'ghal ADJ. on either side right and left [~ P بغل]

اغلف agh'laf ADJ. uncircumcized [A ~ غلاف]

اغماض ighmāz' N.M. overlooking ; neglect connivance اغماض برتنا (یا روا رکھنا یا کرنا) ighmāz' ba'ratnā (or ravā' rakh'na (or kar'na) V.I. overlook connive (at) [A]

اغنیا aghniya' N.M. PL. the upper classes rich people [A ~ SING. غنی]

اغوا ighva' N.M. abduction (rare) seduction ; enticement ; leading astray اغوا کرنا ighva kar'na V.T. abduct (rare) seduce ; lead astray [A ~ غوی]

اغیار aghyar' N.M. PL. strangers unfamiliar persons rivals opponents [A ~ SING. غیر]

اف ūf INT. ah ; oh no alas fie ; for shame اف رے ūf' re INT. ah ; oh no اف تک نہ کرنا ūf' tak na kar'na V.I. not even to raise one's little finger not even to utter a faint cry اف کرنا ūf' kar'na V.I. sigh utter a cry of pain mourn burn ; consume ; destroy اف ہو جانا ūf' ho jā'na V.I. be burnt ; be consumed ; be destroyed [A]

افادہ **ifā'dah** N.M. (PL. افادات ifādāt) benefit imparting benefit note meaning use ; utility (rare) welfare افادی ifā'dī ADJ. & N.M. utilitarian افادیت ifādiy'yat N.F. utilitarianism [A ~ فائدہ]

افاضل **afā'zil** N.M. (PL. of ADJ. & N.M. ★)

افاغنہ **afā'ghinah** N.M. PL. the Afghans [A ~ P SING. افغان]

افاقہ **ifā'qah** N.M. relief convalescence recovery افاقہ ہونا ifā'qah ho'nā (of illness) be relieved ; lessen ; abate (of patient) feel relief

افتا **iftā'** N.M. give legal opinion give judicial verdict [A فتوی]

افتاد **ūftād'** N.F. calamity misfortune mishap bent (of mind) افتاد پڑنا ūftad' par'nā V.I. have the misfortune (to) (of calamity) befall (of temperament) be so formed (of someone's nature) be such افتاد طبع uftā'd-e tab'' N.F. (someone's) bent of mind ; (someone's) formation of nature افتادہ ūftā'dah ADJ. fallen miserable worthless fallow (land) افتادگی ūftā'dagī N.F. fall helplessness weakness disability inability [P افتادن ~ fall]

افتاں **ūf'tān** ADJ. tumbling افتاں و خیزاں ūf tān(-o-) khe'zān ADV. with great difficulty ; with much ado [P ~ PREC.]

افتتاح **iftitāh'** N.M. inauguration opening ceremony ; inaugural ceremony or function opening افتتاحی iftitā'hī ADJ. inaugural opening افتتاحیہ iftitāhiy'yah ADJ. inaugural (function N.M. leading article ; leader ; editorial [A ~ فتح]

افتخار **iftikhar** N.M. honour pride موجب افتخار و مسرت ہونا moo'jib-e iftikhā'r-o-masar'rat ho'nā V.I. be the cause of pride and delight (for) [A ~ فخر]

افترا **iftirā'** N.F. imputation malicious accusation scandle slander deception افترا پرداز iftirā-pardāz' ADJ. & N.M. slanderer scandalmongerer mischievous (fellow) افترا پردازی iftirā'-pardā'zī N.F. scandal mongering mischief-making [A]

افتراق **iftirāq** N.M. separation parting [A ~ فرق]

افتضاح **iftizāh'** N.M. disgrace opprobrium [A ~ فضیحت]

افتیموں **af-tīmoon'** N.F. air-creeper ; dodder [A]

افراتفری **af'ra-taf'rī** N.F. افراتفری کا عالم af'rā-taf'rī kā 'ā'lam PH. hurly-burly ; hurry-scurry ; confusion disorder disturbance turmoil wild commotion consternation افراتفری پھیلنا af'rā-taf'rī phail'nā V.I. (of everything) be in disorder be in a confused state [~ A افراط و تفریط CORR.]

افراد **afrād'** N.M. PL. individuals persons ; people singular members [A ~ SING. فرد]

افراد **ifrād'** N.M. (lit.) doing something in retirement from society separation performance of just the major pilgrimage during one visit [A ~ PREC.]

افراز **afrāz'** SUF. elevating ; lifting exalting commanding افرازی afra'zī SUF. elevation exaltation [P ~ افراختن elevate]

افراط **ifrāt'** N.F. excess abundance exuberance surplus ; upper limit or extremity (of something) افراط آبادی ifrā't-e ābā'dī overpopulation افراط زر ifrā't-e zar' N.M. inflation افراط و تفریط ifrāt-o-tafrīt N.M. going to the extremes A ~ فرط]

افرنگ **afrang** (rare) افرنج afranj' N.M. PL. Westerners westernized persons N.M. the Christian West ; christendam (same as فرنگ N.M. ★)

افروختہ **afrokh'tah** ADJ. kindled lighted afire inflamed [P ~ FOL.]

افروز **afroz'** SUF. igniting enlightening آتش افروز ā'tash-afroz' N.M. kindling fire mischief-making افروزی afrozī SUF. lighting kindling [P ~ افروختن burn]

افزا **afzā'** SUF. adding increasing ; augmenting افزائش afzā''ish N.F. increase ; augmentation افزائش نسل afz''ish e nas'l N.F. breeding; reproduction افزائندہ afzā'in'dah ADJ. increasing ; augmenting enhancing N.M. that increases ; that augments ; that enhances [P ~ افزودن increase]

افزود **afzood'** N.M. increase enlargement greatness plenty SUF. additional; augmented more exeessive superfluous ; redundant [P ~ PREC.]

افزوں **afzoon'** SUF. increasing ; augmenting ADJ. larger more numerous diverse aggregate manifold افزوں ہونا afzoon' ho'nā V.I. increase augment enlarge rise in price افزونی afzoo'nī N.F. increase augmentation plenty rise (in price) [P ~ PREC.]

افساں afsāṅ N.F. (same as افشاں N.F. ★)

افسانہ afsā'nah, فسانہ fasā'nah N.M. short story concocted story fiction افسانہ خواں afsā'na-khāṅ, افسانہ گو afsā'na-go N.M. fabulist ; romance or story teller افسانہ نگار afsā'na-nigār', افسانہ نویس afsā'na navīsī' N.M. short-story writer افسانہ نگاری afsā'na-nigā'rī, افسانہ نویسی afsā'na-navī'sī N.F. short-story writing مختصر افسانہ mūkhtasar-afsā-nah N.M. short-story طویل مختصر افسانہ tavīl' mūkh'-tasar-afsā'nah N.M. long short-story [P]

افسر af'sar N.M. officer افسر اعلیٰ af'sar a''la N.M. superior officer chief authority افسر بالادست af sar-e ba'la das't N.M. superior officer افسر مال afsar(-e) mal N.M. Revenue Assistant افسری af'sarī N.F. being an officer officer's rank or cadre [E]

افسر af'sar N.M. crown [P]

افسردہ afsūr'dah ADJ. dejected spiritless melancholy bleak frigid benumbed ; deprived of sensation withered extinguished ; extinct افسردہ خاطر afsūr'da-khā'tir, افسردہ دل afsūr'da-dil ADJ. disheartened downcast افسردگی afsūr'dagī N.M. dejection melancholy ; depression bleakness extinction (rare) frozenness [P ~ افسردن]

افسنتین afsañtīn' N.F. wormwood ; absinth [A ~ G]

افسوس afsos' N.M. sorrow woe distress trouble ; affliction remorse ; repentance INT. (also ہائے افسوس ha''e afsos') alas ah dear ; dear dear افسوس کرنا afsos'kar'na V.I. deplore regret moan ; bewail ; lament grieve ; sorrow ; pity mourn [P]

افسوں afsooṅ' N.M. charm ; enchantment incantation magic ; sorcery افسوں چلنا afsooṅ' chal'na V.I. be successful in charming افسوں کرنا afsooṅ' kar'na V.I. enchant use spells or charms conjure exercise افسوں گر afsooṅ-gar N.M. magician conjurer wizard seer [P]

افشا ifshā' N.M. divulging disclosure افشائے راز ifshā'-e raz' N.M. disclosure of a secret [A ~ افشا]

افشاں af'shāṅ N.F. tinsel strips for bedecking face, hair, etc. SUF. sprinkling ; dispersing ; diffusing ; spreading strewing strewn sprinkled diffused افشاں چننا af shāṅ chūn'na V.T. sprinkle tinsel strips افشانی afshā'nī SUP. strewing diffusing scattering ADJ. sprinkled with gold dust [P ~ افشاندن strewing]

افشردہ afshūr'dah N.M. juice squash SUF. crushed pressed ; squeezed out filtered ; strained افشردۂ انگور afshūr'dā-e angoor N.M. (fig.) wine [P ~ افشردن strain]

افصح af'saḥ ADJ. eloquent (more or) most eloquent [A ~ فصیح SUP.]

افضال afzāl' N.M. PL. favours excellences [A ~ SING. فضل]

افضال ifzāl' N.M. (rare) doing goor causing to excel or exceed leaving a balance [A ~ PREC.]

افضل af'zal ADJ. & N.M. (PL. افاضل afā'zil) excellent supreme most prominent (person) افضل المرسلین af'zal-ūl-mūrsalīn' N.M. (the Holy Propet as) the most distinguished of the prophets افضلیت afzaliy'yat N.F. supremacy excellence [A ~ PREC.]

افطار iftār' N.M. (col. افطاری iftā'rī N.F.) breaking a fast breakfast light breakfast افطار کرنا iftār'karnā V.T. break a fast [A]

افعال af'āl' N.M. PL. acts ; actions deeds conduct functioning افعال الادویہ af'al-ūl-ad'viyah N.F. pharmacology افعال الاعضا af'al-ūl-a'zā' N.F. physiology [A ~ SING. فعل]

افعی af''ī (ped. af''ā) N.M. asp ; adder ; viper ; serpent [A]

افغاں afghān' فغاں fighān' (or fū-) N.M. wail clamour complaint [P]

افغان afghān' or (af'ghan) N.M. Pathan a native of Afghanistan [P]

افق ū'fūq N.M. (PL. آفاق āfāq') horizon ūf'qī N.M. (ped. ū'fūqī) ADJ. horizontal [A]

افکار ūfkār' N.F. ideas thoughts ; thinking notions meditation cars ; worries poetical works writings philosophical system ; philosophy [A ~ SING. فکر]

افگار afgār', فگار figār' ADJ. wounded ; lacerated SUF. wounding ; lacerating [P]

افگن af'gan, فگن figan' SUF. overthrowing ; flinging hurling ejecting افگندہ دیا افگندہ ADJ. & SUF. thrown fallen prostrate افگندگی afgan'dagī, فگندگی figan'dagī N.F. flinging hurling throwing down casting away downtrodden state [P ~ افگندن]

افلاس *iflas'* N.M. poverty ; penury ; indigence want [A]

افلاطون *aflātoon'*, فلاطون *falātoon'* N.M. Plato boaster ; braggart افلاطون کا سالا *aflātoon' kā sā'lā* PH. (col.) conceited person بڑا آیا کہیں سے افلاطون کا سالا *ba'ṛā ā'yā ka'hīṅ se aflātoon' kā sā'lā* PH. what a conceited person ! افلاطونی *aflātoo'nī* ADJ. Platonic نو فلاطونیت *nau-falātooniy'yat* N.F. neo-Platonism [A ~ G]

افلاک *aflak'* N.M. PL. heavenly spheres, spheres the heavens ; sky ; firmament starry host Heaven [A ~ SING. فلک]

افواج *af'vāj'* N.F. PL. armies armed forces hosts crowds legion افواج قاہرہ *afvā'j-e qā'hirah* N.F. victorious army armed forces بحری افواج *baiḥ'rī afvāj'* N.F. PL. Navy بری افواج *bar'rī afvāj'* N.F PL. Army ; land forces فضائی (یا ہوائی) افواج *fazā''i* (or *hava''ī*) *afvāj'* N.F. PL. Air Force [A ~ SING. فوج]

اُف، اُفوہ *uf'fo*, *uf'foh* INT. (expressive of surprise or regret) oh [ONO.]

افواہ *afvāh'* N.F. rumour hearsay gossip town-talk افواہ (یا افواہیں) اڑانا (یا پھیلانا) *afvāh* (or *afvā'heṅ*) *uṛā'nā* (or *phailā'nā*) V.T. spread rumour(s) ; bruit abroad افواہ (یا افواہیں) اڑنا (یا پھیلنا) *afvāh'* (or *afvā'heṅ*) *uṛ'nā* (or *phail'nā*) V.I. be rumoured (of rumour) be spread [~ A SING. فوہ *fooh* or فم *fam* mouth]

افہام *ifhām'* N.M. causing (someone) to understand ; driving home to افہام و تفہیم *ifhā'm-o-tafhīm'* N.M. mutual understanding talks ; negotiations conciliation rapprochement [A ~ فہم CAUS.]

افیم *afīm'* افیون *afyoon'* N.F. opium افیم (یا افیون) کا گھولا *afīm'* (or *afyoon'*) *kā gho'lā* N.M. dilute opium افیم (یا افیون) کی چسکی *afīm'* (or *afyoon'*) *kī chus'kī* N.F. a sip of opium افیمچی *afīm'chī*, افیمی *afī'mī*, افیونی *afyoo'nī* N.M. opium-eater افیمن *afī'man* N.F opium eater [~ FOLL.]

افیون *afyoon'* N.F. (same as افیم N.F ★) افیونی *afyoo'nī* N.M. same as افیمی (see under افیم N.F ★) [A]

اقارب *aqā'rib* N.M PL relatives, relations kindred عزیز و اقارب *azī'z-o aqā'rib* N.M. PL. kith and kin ; kindred near and dear ones [A ~ اقرب ~ قریب SUP.]

اقالیم *aqālīm'* N.F. (PL. of اقلیم N.F. ★)

اقامت *iqā'mat* N.F. stay sojourn dwelling اقامت اختیار کرنا *iqā'mat ikhtiyār' kar'nā* V.I. stay dwell اقامت گاہ *iqā'mat-gāh* N.F. dwelling ; lodging ; abode (rare) hostel [A ~ قیام]

اقانیم *aqānīm'* N.M. PL. bases اقانیم ثلاثہ *aqānī'me salā'sah* N.M. PL. (dial) Trinity [A ~ SING. اقنوم]

اقبال *iqbāl'* N.M. prosperity luck ; fortune confession acknowledgment name of philosopher-poet who gave people vision of Pakistan ; Iqbal اقبال دعوی *iqbāl-e da''vā* N.M. confession of guilt ; 'cognovit' acknowledgment of a claim اقبال سکندری *iqbāl-i-sikan'darī* N.M. (fig.) extremely good fortune اقبال کرنا *iqbāl' kar'nā* admit confess (guilt) اقبال مند *iqbāl-mand* ADJ. fortunate well-off thriving prosperous اقبالی *iqbā'lī* ADJ. confessional N.M. confessor اقبالیات *iqbāliyyāt'* N.M. books on the poet-philosopher Iqbal Iqbal bibliography [A ~ قبل]

اقتباس *iqtibās'* N.M. excerpt ; extract quotation derivation (of bene. etc.) [A]

اقتدا *iqtidā'* N.F. following (person, action or example) accepting the leadership (of) کی اقتدا میں *kī iqtidā' meṅ*, under the leadership of [A ~ قیادت]

اقتدار *iqtidār'* N.M. power sway authority influence eminence ; dignity اقتدار اعلی *iqtidār-e a''lā* N.M. supreme authority [A ~ قدیر]

اقتران *iqtirān'* N.M. closeness ; getting close together [A ~ قرین]

اقتصاد *iqtisād'* N.M. economy (rare) moderation علم الاقتصاد *ilm-ul-iqtisād'* N.M. (rare) political economy , economics اقتصادی *iqtisā'dī* ADJ. economic اقتصادیات *iqtisādiyyāt'* N.F. economics ; political economy [A ~ قصد]

اقتضا *iqtizā'* N.M. exigency expediency need ; necessity demand ; requisition اقتضائے مصلحت *iqtizā'-e maslahat* N.F expediency حالات کا اقتضا *hālāt kā iqtizā'* N.M. exigency of situation [A]

اقدار *aqdār'* N.F. PL. values اخلاقی اقدار *akhlā'qī-aqdār'* N.F. PL. moral values روحانی اقدار

rooha'ni aqdar' N.F. PL. spiritual values مادی اقدار mad'di aqdar' N.F. PL. material(istic) values [A ~ SING. قدر qadr]

اقدام aqdam' N.M. PL. of قدم N.M. ★)

اقدام iqdam' N.M. initiative courage ; valour going forward attempt intent اقدام قتل iqda'm-e qat'l N.M. murderous assault اقدام کرنا iqdam' kar'na V.I. take the initiative attempt take steps (to) [A ~ قدم]

اقدس aq'das ADJ. (more or) most holy very sacred ذات اقدس za't-e aq'das N.F. sacred personality [A ~ قدس SUP.]

اقرار iqrar' N.M. promise assent admission contract declaration اقرار کرنا iqrar' kar'na V.I. promise ; confess admit accept assent agree اقرار نامہ iqrar'-na'mah N.M. agreement contract written bond indenture assurance declaration compact ; covenant pact ; treaty اقرار صالح iqra'r-e sa'leh N.M. solemn declaration اقرار نامہ ثالثی iqrar-na mah sa'lisi N.M. arbitration agreement اقراری iqra'ri ADJ. confessing confessional N.M. confessor [A ~ اقرار]

اقران aqran' N.M. PL. peers [A ~ SING. قرن qirn]

اقرب aq'rab ADJ. (more or) most near N.M. (PL. اقارب aqa'rib) relative ; relation [A ~ قریب SUP.]

اقربا aqriba' N.M. PL. relations ; relatives kindred ; kith and kin allies [A ~ SING. قریب]

اقساط aqsat' N.F. PL. instalments parts بالاقساط bil-aqsat' ADV. by instalment

اقسام aqsam' N.F. PL. kinds sets various kinds very sorts جملہ اقسام jum'la aqsam' N.M. all types [A ~ SING. قسم qism]

اقسام aqsam' N.M. PL. oaths [A ~ SING. قسم qasam]

اقصیٰ aq'sa ADJ. most (or more) distant; farthest مسجد اقصیٰ mas'jid-e aq'sa' N.F. Dome of the Rock [A]

اقطار aqtar' N.M. PL. regions ; zones diameters [A ~ SING. قطر]

اقطاع iqta'' N.M. PL. tracts ; pieces of land [A ~ SING. قطعہ]

اقطاع iqta'' N.M. (PL. اقطاعات iqta'at') feudal grant ; fief اقطاعیت iqt''iy'pat N.F. feudalism [A ~ قطعہ]

اقل aqal' ADJ. least بدرجۂ اقل ba-da'raja-e aqal' minimum اقلاً aqal'lan ADV. (rare) at least اقلیت aqalliy'yat N.F. minority اقلیتی aqalliy'yati ADJ. minority اقلیتی فرقہ aqalliy'yati fir'qah N.M. minority community [A ~ قلیل SUP.]

اقلف aq'laf ADJ. & N.M. uncircumcized (person) [A]

اقلیدس uqli'das N.M. Euclid geometry [A ~ G]

اقلیم iqlim' N.F. (PL. اقالیم aqalim') country zone clime ہفت اقلیم haft iqlim' N.M. the whole world [A ~ G]

اقنوم uqnoom N.M. (PL. اقانیم aqanim') basis (dial.) one of the Trinity [A]

اقوا iqva' N.M. rhyming with unidentical vowel sound(s) use of imperfect rhyme [A]

اقوال aqval' N.M. PL. sayings ; saws ; maxim words precepts اقوال و اعمال aqva'l-o a'mal' N.M. PL. precepts and practices [A ~ SING. قول]

اقوام aqvam' N.M. PL. nations races castes اقوام متحدہ aqva'm-e mut'tahidah, ادارۂ اقوام متحدہ ida'ra-e aqva'm-e mut'tahidah N.F. United Nations (Organization) ; U.N.(O.) اقوام مغرب aqva'm-e magh'rib N.F. PL. Western nations ; the West [A ~ SING. قوم]

اک ik ADJ. one اک بار ik bar' ADV. once اکبارگی ik-bar'gi ADV. suddenly ; all at once اکتارا ikta'ra N.M. single-stringed harp اک تالا ik-ta'la N.M. name of a tune on 'tabla' اک جا ik-ja' ADV. together at one place اک دم ik dam' ADV. suddenly immediately ; in a jiffy اک رخی ik-ru'khi ADJ. one-sided اک رخی تصویر ik-ru'khi tasvir N.F. onesided picture profile silhouette اک گونہ ik-goo'nah ADV. sort of a little ; somewhat اک لڑا ik-la'ra N.M. single-stringed (necklace) [~ ایک CONTR.]

اکا ik ka N.M. ace (in cards) a kind of old-fashioned carriage ADJ. one single unique اکا دکا ik'ka duk'ka ADJ. desultory one or two just a few [~ ایک]

اکابر aka'bir N.M. nobles high-ups ; big guns ADJ. greatest اکابر و اصاغر aka'bir-o asa'ghir N.M. rich and poor ; great and small [A ~ SING. اکبر]

اکادشی ikad'shi N.F. (rare) eleventh day of Hindu months [S]

اکادمی | akād'mī, اکیڈمی | akai'ḍimī N.F. academy [E ~ G]

اکاذیب | akā'zib' N.M. PL. lies ; untruths ; travesties of truth [A ~ کذاب SING. کذب]

اکارت | akā'rat ADJ. vain ; unavailing unprofitable ineffectual ; fruitless useless worthless unserviceable اکارت جانا | akā'rat jā'nā V.I. be of no avail be in vain be useless be profitless go (to) waste come to naught

اکاسرہ | akā'sirah N M. chosroes (as title of ancient Persian kings) [A ~ SING. کسریٰ ~ P خسرو]

اکاسی | ikā'sī ADJ. & N.M. eighty-one اکاسیواں ikā'sīvāñ ADJ. eighty-first

اکال | akāl' N.M. (dial.) timeless ; eternal (as God's attribute) اکالی | akā'lī N.M. (member of) a religious order of Sikhs [S]

اکانوے | ikān've, اکیانوے | ikyān've ADJ. & N.M. ninety-one اکیانویواں | ikān'vevāñ ADJ. ninety first

اکاون | ikā'van, اکیاون | ikyā'van ADJ. & N.M. fifty-one اکاونواں | ikā'vanvāñ ADJ. fifty-first

اکاؤنٹ | ikā''ūnṭ N.M. account اکاؤنٹنٹ | ikā''ūnṭanṭ N.M. accountant اکاؤنٹنٹ جنرل | ikā''ūnṭanṭ-jan'ral N.M. Accountant-General ; A.G. اکاؤنٹنسی ikā''ūnṭansī N.F. accountancy [E]

اکائی | ikā''ī N.F. unit digit one any digit from zero to nine unity [~ ایک]

اکبر | ak'bar ADJ. greatest greater N.M. (PL. اکابر | akā'bir) appellation of the Great Mogul a male Muslim name اکبری | ak'barī N.F female Muslim name (old use) guinea ADJ of Emperor Akbar اکبری نورتن | ak'barī nau-ra'-tan N.M. nine gems (i.e., nine famous courtiers) of Akbar

اکت | u'kat' N.F. strange thing اکت کی لینا | ū'kat kī le'nā V.T. say strange things

اکتالیس | ikta'līs ADJ. & N.M. forty-one اکتالیسواں ikta'līsvāñ forty-first

اکتانا | ūkta'nā V.I. be bored be disgusted be tired of ; be weary be browned off اکتاہٹ | ūkta'haṭ N.F. boredom disgust

اکتساب | iktisāb' N.M. gaining (skill) with effort attainment earning اکتسابی iktisā'bī ADJ. gained with effort result of effort not inherent lacking natural flow [A ~ کسب]

اکتشاف | iktishāf' N.M. discovery unearthing [A ~ کشف]

اکتفا | iktifā' N.F. content sufficiency اکتفا کرنا iktifā' kar'nā V.I. be content (with) [A ~ کافی]

اکتوبر | aktoo'bar N.M. October [E]

اکتیس | ikat'tīs (rare iktīs') ADJ. & N.M. (thirty-one اکتیسواں | ikattīs'vāñ ADJ. thirty-fir

اکٹا | ūk'ṭa ADJ. (F. اکٹی | ūk'ṭī) mean fellow

اکٹنا | ū'kaṭnā V.T. & I. revile worn out (secret, etc. from someone) dig up

اکٹھا | ikaṭ'ṭhā, اکٹھا | ikhaṭ'ṭā ADJ (F. اکٹھی | ikaṭ'ṭhī ikhaṭ'ṭī) tied up united collected اکٹھا کرنا | ikaṭ'ṭhā kar'nā V.T. gather اکٹھے | ikaṭ'ṭhe' ikhaṭ'ṭe ADV. together in bulk

اکثر | ak'sar ADJ. most much ; very many frequent ADV. frequently ; usually ; often mostly ; generally chiefly اکثر اوقات ak'sar auqāt' ADV. mostly often ordinarily usually اکثریت | aksariy'yat N.F. majority [A ~ of کثیر SUP.]

اکرا | ak'ra N.M. vetch growing under spring crop uncleaned crop

اکرام | ikrām' N.M. veneration deference respect ; esteem honouring [A ~ کرم]

اکراہ | ikrāh' N.M. duress dislike ; disgust abhorrence [A ~ کراہت]

اکرم | ak'ram ADJ. most munificent most gracious ; most benevolent [A ~ کریم SUP

اکڑ | a'kaṛ N.F. pride vanity ; conceit ; haughtiness stiffness ; rigidity ; firmness اکڑباز a'kaṛ-bāz' N.M. proud ; haughty ; vain affected person fop اکڑبازی | a'kaṛ-bā'zī, اکڑفوں a'kaṛ fooñ N.F. pride vanity affectations اکڑنا | a'kaṛnā V.I. give oneself airs be proud look defiantly at be ready to pick a quarrel stiffen be cramped

اکڑوں | ūk'ṛooñ ADJ. squatting ; on the hams اکڑوں بیٹھنا | ūk'ṛooñ baiṭh'nā V.I. squat ; sit on the hams

اکسانا | ūksā'nā V.T. excite , incite ; instigate provoke ; fan a flame urge encourage lift ; stir up (flame, wick, etc. اکساہٹ | ūksā'haṭ N.F. instigation inducement

اکسائز | iksā'iz N M. excise [E]

اکسٹھ | ik'saṭh ADJ. & N.M. sixty-one اکسٹھواں | ik'saṭhvāñ ADJ. sixty-first

اکسنا ūkas'nā V.I. raise oneself be stirred wriggle out come out

اکسیر iksīr' N.F. elixir sovereign remedy, penacea alchemy اکسیر گر iksīr'-gar N.M. alchemist [A]

اکفا ikfā' N.M. a kind of false rhyme its use [A]

اکل کھرا akal khū̄rā ADJ. selfish jealous unsociable unmannerly

اکل و شرب ak'l-o-sharb' N.M. eating and drinking victuals [A]

اکلوتا iklau'tā ADJ. (F. اکلوتی iklau'tī) the only (child) sole ; solitary

اکلیل iklīl' N.M. crown [A]

اکمل ak'mal ADJ. perfect supreme [A ~ کامل SUP.]

اکناف aknāf' N.M. borders environs [A ~ SING. کنف]

اکنوں ak'nooṅ ADV. (lit.) now ; at present ; presently [P]

اکونا ikau'nā ADJ. unmixed ; picked (grain)

اکھاڑا akhā'ṛā N.M. arena ; lists court اندر کا اکھاڑا in'dar ka akhā'ṛā N.M. Indra's court place with a bevy of beauties اکھاڑے میں اترنا akhā're meṅ ū'tarnā V.I. enter the lists

اکھاڑنا ūkhāṛ'nā V.T. uproot pull out dislocate demolish destroy ; ruin

اکھاڑ ūkhāṛ' N.F. uprooting ruinous trick اکھاڑ پچھاڑ ūkhāṛ pichhāṛ N.F. uprooting bungling pell-mell

اکہتر ikhat'tar ADJ. & N.M. seventy-one اکہترواں ikhat'tarvaṅ ADJ. seventy-first

اکہرا ikaih'rā ADJ. (F. اکہری ikaih'rī) single-folded one-sided lean gaunt [~ ایک]

اکھٹا ikhaṭṭā ADJ. (same as اکٹھا A)

اکھرنا akharnā V.T. (of something) offend

اکھڑ ak'khaṛ ADJ. uncouth ; uncivilised ; unmannerly rough ; rude boorish obstinate quarrelsome recalcitrant N.M. lout ; boor churlish person اکھڑپن ak'khaṛ-pan N.M. obstinacy rudeness ; roughness ; churlishness

اکھڑنا ū'khaṛnā V.I. be uprooted be displaced be torn asunder be pulled out go off the track اکھڑوانا ukhaṛvā'nā V.T. cause to uproot have pulled out

اکھلی ūkh'lī N.F. (same as اوکھلی N.F. ★)

اکھنڈ akhaṅḍ' ADJ. (rare) undivided pre-partition [S]

اکھو مکھو akkho mak'kho N.F. (Nurs.) formula recited by woman while stroking infant face while it stares at lamp hoax

اکیاسی ikyā'sī, ADJ. & N.M. (same as اکاسی ikā's ADJ. & N.M. ★)

اکیانوے ikyān've ADJ. & N.M. (same as اکانوے ADJ. & N.M. ★)

اکیاون ikyā'van ADJ. & N.M. (same as اکاون ikā'van ADJ. & N.M. ★)

اکید akīd' ADJ. sure (reminder, etc.) [A]

اکیس ik'kīs ADJ. & N.M. twenty-one اکیسواں ik'kisvāṅ ADJ. twenty-first

اکیلا ake'lā ADJ. (F. اکیلی ake'lī) lonely ; solitary alone ; single peerless ; unique [~ ایک]

اگاڑی agā'ṛī N.F. forelegs ropes with which horse's forelegs are tied front fore part ADV. forward ahead ; further on in front اگاڑی پچھاڑی لگانا agā'ṛī pichhā'ṛī lagā'nā V.T. tie together fore and hind legs of a horse اگاڑی مارنا agā'ṛī mār'nā V.T. attack in the front attack the vanguard defeat enemy forces

اگال ūgāl' N.M. spittle something spit out after chewing اگالدان ūgāl'dān' N.M. spittoon اگالنا ūgālnā V.T. spit out spew, spue

اگانا ūgā'nā V.T. grow (crop) ; raise [~ اگنا CAUS.]

اگاہنا ūgāh'nā V. realize (debt) collect gather اگاہی ūgā'hī N.F. realisation (of debt) by instalments collection (of rent, etc.) proceeds receipts

اگر ¹ a'gar N.M. aloe اگردان a'gar-dān' N.M. censer اگر کی بتی a'gar (kī) bat'tī N.F. aloe stick

اگر ² a'gar CONJ. if ; in case اگرچہ a'gar-cheh CONJ. although ; though ; even if ; even though ;

اگر مگر a'gar ma'gar N.F. hesitation excuses ifs and buts [P]

اگڑ بگڑ a'gaṛ-ba'gaṛ, اگرم بگرم ag'ram bag'ram N.F. mess ; disorder ; pell-mell nonsense trash odds and ends

اگر دھتا a'gaṛ dhat'tā ADJ. tall very large; hefty

اگڑدھوں دھوں | *a'gar dhauñ dhauñ'* ADJ. plump ; fleshy ; corpulent
اگست | *agast'* N.M. August [F]
اگلا | *ag'la* ADJ. (F. اگلی | *aglī*) next past previous ; former future first ; foremost اگلا جنم | *ag'la ja'nam* N.M. (rare) former existence future existence اگلا پچھلا | *ag'la pichh'la* ADJ. (F. اگلی پچھلی | *ag'lī pichh'lī*) whole; the whole lot past and present
اگلنا | *ū'galna* V.T. spit out vomit , spew ; spue disclose (secret, money, etc.)
اگن | *a'gan* PREF. fire اگن بوٹ | *a'gan-boṭ* N.M. steamer [آگ ~]
اگنا | *ūg'na* V.I. grow rise sprout; spring up germinate
اگولا | *agau'la*, گولا | *gau'la*, اکھولا | *akhau'la* N.M. top-shoot of sugar-cane
اگھاڑنا | *ūghar'na* V.T. undress expose reveal betray (someone's secret) اگھاڑا | *ūgha'ṛa* ADJ. apparent bare undressed
اگھن | *a'ghan* N.M. eighth month of Hindu calendar corresponding to November-December [S]
ال | *al* PREF. (lit.) the الامان | *al-amān'* INT. God preserve us ; God help us dear ; dear dear الآن | *al-an'* ADV. (lit.) now ; at present ; presently الحاج | *al-ḥaj'* N.M. one who has performed the Haj ; pilgrim الحاصل | *al-ḥa'sil* ADV. in short ; briefly PH. the long and short of it is الحال | *al-ḥal* ADV. (lit.) now ; at present at this moment ; just now الحذر | *al-ḥazar'* INT. God forbid ; God preserve us الحفیظ | *al-ḥafīz'* INT. Heaven defend us ; God preserve us dear ; dear dear الامان والحفیظ | *al-amān-o-al-ḥafīz'* INT. God help us الحق | *al-ḥaq'* ADV. (lit.) really ; indeed ; in truth الحمد للہ | *al-ḥam'd-o-lillāh'* INT. God be praised السلام علیکم | *as-salā'm-o 'alai'kūm* PH. (salutation) peace be on you ; safety attend you good morning, (etc.) العبد | *al-'ab'd* N.M. (in application) yours obediently العطش *al-'atash'* (lit.) INT. I feel thirsty ; water N.F. thirst العظمۃ للہ | *al-'a'zamat-o lillāh* INT. (lit.) God is great, all else comes to naught الغرض | *al-gharaz* ADV. in short ; briefly on the whole الغیاث *al-ghayas'* INT. (lit.) help, help do me justice ; justice القصہ | *al-qis'sah* ADV. briefly ; in short PH. to cut the long story short القط | *al'-qat* ADJ. stopped ; ended القط کرنا | *al'-qat kar'na* N.M. bring to an end المضاعف | *al-mūza''af* ADJ. double twofold الوداع | *al-vadā''* (col. *al-vidā''*) N.M. farewell INT. good-bye ; adieu farewell الوداع کہنا | *al-vadā'' kaih'na* V.T. bid adieu [A]
الا | *il'lā* ADV. or else ; otherwise if not except ; save الا ماشاءاللہ | *il'lā māsh'allah'* PH. save what God wills except as a remote possibility rarely [A ~ ان if لا not]
الا بلا | *alā' balā'* N.F. worthless and unwanted stuff cheap snacks undesirable results
الاپ | *alāp'* N.F. (music) modulation prelude to singing الاپنا | *alāp'na* V.T. & I. modulate sing as prelude
الار | *ūlār'* ADJ. (of cart) heavily laden at the back liable to be upset
الارم | *alā'ram* N.M. alarm [E]
الاسٹک | *elās'ṭik* N.M. & ADJ. elastic (cord, etc.)
الائچی | *ilā''ichī* N.M. cardamom الائچی دانہ *ilā''chī-dā nah* N.M. sugar-coated cardamom دانہ الائچی | *dāna(-e-)ilā''ichī* N.F. cardamom seed [P]
الاؤ | *alā''o* N.M. bonfire large fire
الاؤنس | *ilā''ūns* N.M. allowance [E]
الاہنا | *ūlāh'na* N.M. (same as اولاہنا *ūlah'na* N.M. ★)
الانگنا | *ūlāng'na* V.T. jump over (something) ; jump across ; move astride
الباب | *albāb'* N.M. wisdom ; intelligence hearts [A ~ SING. لب]
البتہ | *albat'tah* ADV. of course surely ; certainly positively ; decidedly [A]
البرز | *albūrz'* N.M. name of a Persian mountain [P]
البم | *ail'bam* N.M. album [A]
البیلا | *albe'la* ADJ. (F. البیلی | *albe'lī*) foppish cute playful ; wanton lively ; gay care-free coquetish lovely N.M. fop ; beau ; dandy ; coxcomb belle cute (girl) coquet البیلا پن | *albe'lā-pan* N.M. beauty ; elegance ; loveliness playfulness . gaiety ; frolic coquetry

الپاکا | alpā'kā N.M. alpaka [E ~ Sp.]

التباس | iltibās' N.M. confusion (of meaning) vagueness similarity resemblance [A ~ لباس]

التتمش iltūt'mish (CORR. التمش al'tamash) N.M. advance-guard name of a king [T]

التجا | iltijā' N.F. entreaty ; supplication petition ; prayer التجا کرنا | iltijā' kar'nā V.I. beg ; request ; beseech ; entreat [A]

التزام | iltizām' N.M. taking upon oneself being necessary making concomitant [A ~ لازم]

التفات | iltifāt' N.M. regard ; attention courtesy inclination friendship ; amity respect consideration التفات کرنا | iltifāt kar'nā V.I. show regard (for) ; have respect (for) [A]

التماس | iltimās N.F. request ; entreaty prayer ; petition supplication التماس کرنا iltimās' kar'nā V. request ; implore ; beseech supplicate submit [A]

التمش | al'tamash N.M. (same as التتمش | N.M. ★)

التنی al'tanī N.F. rope round elephant's neck providing stirrups for driver

التوا | iltivā' N.M. postponement ; defering delay adjournment stay cessation التوائے جنگ | iltivā'-e jang' N.M. cease-fire ; truce ; cessation of hostilities [A]

التیام | iltiyām' N.M. healing (of wound) [A]

الٹ ū'laṭ N.M. inversion reverse overturning ; upsetting ADJ. opposite contrary reverse obverse الٹ پڑنا | ū'laṭ paṛ'nā V.I. change side or direction change side to attack الٹ پلٹ ہونا | ū'laṭ pa'laṭ ho'nā V. be upside down be topsy-turvy be in a mess الٹ پھیر | ū'laṭ pher' N.M. deception ; trickery embarrassment perplexity الٹ کے کروٹ نہ لینا ū'laṭ ke kar'vaṭ na le'nā V.T. forget altogether pay no head drop from (one's mind الٹ کے کہنا ū'laṭ ke kaih'na V.I say in reply repeat

الٹا ūl'ṭā ADJ. (F. الٹی | ul'ṭī) inverted , topsy-turvy opposite perverse ADV. in the contrary , on the other hand الٹا بھاگنا ul'ṭā bhāg'na V.I. flee run away الٹا پلٹا ūl'ṭā pūl'ṭā ADJ. confused jumbled upside down inverted topsy-turvy الٹا پھیر آنا ūl'ṭā phir ā'nā V.I. retrace one's steps turn back on | الٹا توا | ūl'ṭā ta vā N.M. inverted hot plate ; convex hot plate ADJ. (fig.) jet black الٹا جواب | ūl'ṭā javāb' N.M. impertinent reply crooked reply retort rejoinder الٹا چور کوتوال کو ڈانٹے ūl'ṭā chor kotvāl' ko dān'te PROV. criminal chiding the judge الٹا سمجھنا | ūl'ṭā sa'majhnā V.I. misunderstand ; misapprehend misconstrue

الٹانا ūlṭā'nā V T. turn upside down ; overturn , overset upset pervert ; thwart reverse convert modify الٹانا پلٹانا | ūlṭā'na pūlṭā'nā V.T. mix up shake up modify الٹنا | ūlṭa'nā (AMPH.) الٹ دینا | ū'laṭ de'nā overturn ; tilt upset turn over refute cancel counteract turn over empty overthrow

الٹی | ūlṭī ADJ. (F. of الٹا | ADJ. ★) N.F. vomit الٹی آنا ūl'ṭī ā'nā V.I. vomit feel sick , feel nausea الٹی پٹی پڑھانا | ūl'ṭī paṭ'ṭī paṛhā'nā V.T. mislead poison the mind الٹی تسبیح پھیرنا | ūl'ṭī tasbīh' pher'nā V.I. invoke a curse by counting one's beads backwards الٹی ریت | ūl'ṭī rīt' N.F. strange way الٹی سمجھ | ūl ṭī sa'majh N.F. perversion erroneous view الٹی سیدھی سنانا | ūl'ṭī sīdhī-sūnā'nā V.I. insult abuse scold الٹی کرنا ūl'ṭī kar'nā V. vomit ; spew الٹی کھوپڑی | ūl'ṭī khop'ṛī PH. crooked mind stupidity الٹی ہوا | ūl'ṭī havā' N.F. contrary wind (fig.) strange trends الٹے پاؤں پھرنا | ūl'ṭe pā''on phir'nā V.I. retrace one's steps go back immediately

الٹی میٹم al'ṭī me'ṭam N.M. ultimatum [E]

الجبرا | aljab'rā N.M. algebra [E ~ A الجبر و المقابلہ]

الجھنا ū'lajhnā V.T. quarrel ; be involved (in quarrel or difficulty) ; fall foul (of) prevent ; hinder be entangled be confused feel uneasy جی الجھنا | jī ulajh'na V.I. feel uneasy ; be disturbed الجھانا | uljhā'na V.T. ravel entangle ; complicate involve ; embroil entwine entrap ; ensnare confuse mislead ; deceive embarrass confuse الجھا ūl'jhā N.M. tangle الجھا پڑ جانا | ūl'jhā paṛ jā'nā V.I (of thread) be tangled الجھا چھڑانا | ūl'jhā chhūṛā'na V.I. disentangle الجھاؤ | uljhā''o, N.M. الجھن | ūl'jhan

N.F. complex entanglement ; intricacy complication complexity ; confusion derangement difficulty embarrassment الجھ پڑنا ū'lajh paṛ'nā V.T. fall foul (of) الجھ جانا ū'lajh jā'nā V.I. be entangled be delayed be detained الجھیڑا ūljhe'ṛā N.M. difficulty ; quarrel ; broil entanglement ; intricacy

الحاح ilhāh' N.M. beseeching [A]

الحاد ilhād' N.M. atheism ; disbelief heresy [A]

الحاق ilhāq' N.M. annexation joining together contiguity [A]

الحان ilhān N.M. modulation ; recitation الحان alhān' N.M. (PL. of [A ~ لحن]

الخ ilākh' ADV. to the end of it 'et cetera' [A ~ الی آخرہ ABB.]

الزام ilzām' N.M. accusation ; charge allegation imputation blame الزام لگانا ilzām' lagā'nā V.T. accuse ; charge blame [A]

الست ala'st PH. aint I N.M. (day of) creation [A ~ + لیس]

السنہ al'sinah N.F. languages tongues السنۂ شرقیہ al'sina-e-sharqiy'yah N.F. PL. Oriental languages [A ~ SING. لسان]

السی al'sī N.F. linseed

السی

السیٹ alseṭ N.F. obstruction fraud ; deception difference ; quarrel procrastination dilly-dallying السیٹیا alse'ṭiyā N.M. deceiver quarrelsome person

الش ū'lūsh N.M. leavings (of food, dish, etc.) الش کرنا ū'lūsh kar'nā V.I. eat a little from) [T]

الغارفی algha'reh ADV. & ADJ. very much [~ T]

الغوزہ alghho'zah N.M. flageolet ; oboe

الطاف altāf' N.M. PL. [A ~ SING. لطف]

الف لیلہ alf' lai'lah N.F. the Arabian Nights [A الف alf thousand لیلہ lai'lah night]

الف a'lif ADJ. N.M. name of first letters of Urdu alphabet ADJ. one alone straight stark الف بے a'lif be' N.F. alphabet abc ; rudiments الف ہونا a'lif ho'nā V.I. (of horse) rear be naked [A]

الفاظ alfāz' N.M. PL. words terms [A ~ SING. لفظ]

الفت ūl'fat N.M. attachment ; affection friendship ; intimacy love الفت کا بندہ ūl'fat kā ban'dah N.M. sincere and loving friend one held in thrall by love الفت کرنا ūl'fat kar'nā V.T. make love (to) be intimate (with) [A]

الفتہ alaf'tah, آلفتہ āl-f'tah N.M. outsider, alien [~ P]

الفی al'fī N.F. long sleaveless shirt open at sides

القا ilqā' N.M. inspiration revelation [A]

القاب alqāb' N.M. honorific form of address in letters N.M. PL. (ped.) epithets القاب وآداب alqāb-o ādāb' N.M. PL. forms of address [A ~ SING. لقب]

الکلی al'kali N.F. alkali [E ~ A]

الگ alag ADJ. separate alone aloof distinct apart detached ; loose asunder الگ الگ alag' alag' ADV. separately severally individually one by one ; apart الگ تھلگ alag' thalag' ADJ. solitary alone apart ; unconnected disjointed الگ رہنا alag' raih'nā V. live alone live apart refrain from, shun الگ کرنا alag' kar'nā V.T. separate set apart part divide remove unravel dispose of dismiss ; discharge, sack

الگنی al'gani N.F. washline ; clothes-line ; line

الگنی

اللٹپ alalṭap' ADV. at random الجھپ alaljhap' ADJ. fickle unreliable slovenly

اللذی نہ اللذی il'lallazī na il'lallazī N.M. vacillating undecided [~ A الذی CORR.]

اللہ al'lāh, allāh' N.M. Allah ; God اللہ اکبر al'lāh-o ak'bar God is great اللہ اللہ al'la al'lāh INT. my goodness good God ; good gracious wonderful اللہ اللہ خیر سلا al'la al'lā khair sal'lā PH. thank God it is all over that was the end to it اللہ اللہ کرکے al'la al'lāh kar ke ADV with great difficulty after a long time اللہ آمین کا al'la āmīn' kā PH. (of child) the only, solitary begotten through prayers اللہ بخشے al'lāh bakh'she PH. God bless his soul اللہ بیلی al'lāh belī, اللہ نگہبان al'lāh nigehbān', PH. good bye God be with you اللہ رے al'lāh re INT. good God اللہ کا نام لینا al'lāh ka nām' le'nā V.I. take the name of God ; fear God اللہ لوگ al'lāh log N.M. simpleton اللہ مارا al'lāh ma'ra N.M. & ADJ. wretch unfortunate (person) اللہ میاں al'lah miyāń' N.M. God اللہ والا al'lāh vā'la N.M. pious person simpleton [A]

الّے تلّے alal'le talal'le N.M. PL. extravagance prodigality profligacy الّے تلّے اڑانا alal'le tala'le ūṛānā V.I. squander live like a lord indulge in sensual pleasures

الم a'lam N.M. affliction ; pain, torment ; grief ; anguish ; agony المناک alamnak' ADJ. painful ; grievous ; المناکی alamna'kī N.F. agony painfulness المیہ alamiy'yah N.M. tragedy ADJ. tragic [A]

الماری almārī N.F. cupboard ; almirah [Sp. ~ A]

الماس almās' N.M. diamond الماس تراش almās' tarāsh' N.M. diamond cutter diamond dust ADJ. diamond-cut الماسی almā'sī ADJ. diamond-cut [A]

الم غلم al'lam ghal'lam N.M. nonsense ; idle talk pell-mell trash الم غلم بکنا al'lam ghal'lam bak'nā V.I. talk nonsense

الم نشرح a-lam' nash'rah, الم نشر alam nash'r (ped.) ADJ. divulged الم نشر کرنا alam' nash'r kar'nā V.T. divulge scandalize [A ~ ا + نشرح + لم]

الّو ul'loo N.M. owl fool ; idiot greenhorn الّو بنانا ul'loo banā'nā V.T. dupe ; befool ; make a fool (of) اپنا الّو سیدھا کرنا ap'nā ūl'loo sī'dhā kar'nā V.I. aggrandize oneself الّو پھانسنا ūl'loo phāns'nā V.T. dupe a greenhorn الّن ūl'lan N.F. female owl silly woman

الواح alvāḥ' N.M. PL. tablets [A ~ SING. لوح]

الوان alvān' N.M. PL. colours ; hues sorts ; kinds الوانِ نعمت alvā'n-e- ne''mat N.M. various good dishes [A ~ SING. لون]

الول کلول کرنا alol' N.F frolic ; gambol ; caper alol' kalol'kar'nā V.I. gambol ; frolic ; caper

الوہیت ūloohiy'yat N.F. divinity ; godhead ; [A ~ الہ]

الٰہ elāh' N.M. (PL. آلہہ ā'lihah) god ; deity [A]

الہام ilhām' N.M. revelation inspiration [A]

الھڑ al'lhaṛ ADJ. (of young women or youth) lithe ; lissome sexy undisciplined unsophisticated

الہنا ulah'nā, اُلاہنا ūlāh'nā N.M. taunt complaint الہنا دینا ūlāh'nā de'nā V.T. taunt reproach complain

الٰہی il'ā'hī N.M. my God ADJ. divine heavenly INT O God سنِ الٰہی san'n-e ilā'hī N.M. era introduced by Akbar in 1556 A.C.

الٰہیات ilāhiyyat' N.F. metaphysics الٰہیاتی ilāhiyyā'tī ADJ. metaphysical [A ~ الٰہ]

الیاس ilyas' N.M. Elias [A ~ H]

الیکشن ilaik'shan N.M election [E]

الیم alīm ADJ excurciating ; agonizing [A ~ الم]

ام im PREF. this امسال im-sāl ADV. this year ; in the current year امشب im-shab ADV. tonight [P doublet of ایں]

ام ūm N.F. mother source rootcause ام الامراض ūm'm-ūl-amrāz' N.F. catarrh ; cold ; bronchitis ام الخبائث ūm'm ūl-khabā''is N.F. liquor (as mother of evils) ام الصبیان ūm'm-ūs-sibyān' N.F. epilepsy (in children) ام القریٰ ām'm-ūl-qūrā' N.F. Mecca, the city of cities ; the heart of Islam ام الکتاب ūm'm-ūl-kitāb' N.F. the Holy Quran its basic teachings [A]

اما am'mā CONJ. (ped.) but ; however امابعد am'mā ba''d CONJ. (ped.) and then ; after that [A]

امارت imārat N.F. authority command office of governor riches opulence [A ~ امیر]

امارہ ammā'rah ADJ. wayward domineering imperious [A ~ امر]

اماکن amā'kin N.M. PL. house ; habitations places [A ~ SING. مکان]

امالہ imā'lah N.M. change of vowel sound a to e [A ~ میل]

امام | *imām'* N.M. PL. leader chief large bead in rosary امام باڑہ *imām' bā'rah* N.M. Muharram functions' sanctuary امام ضامن | *imām' zā'min* N.M. guardian saint Imam Kazim امام ضامن کا روپیہ | *imām zā'min kā rūpa'yah* N.M. rupee tied to arm as offerty to guardian-saint امامت | *imā'mat* N.F. leadership guidance امامیہ | *imāmiy'yah* N.M. Shiites ADJ Shi'ite [A]

اماں | *am'māṅ* N.F. mother ; mummy [doublet of ماں]

اماں | *a'māṅ* (rare اماں *am'māṅ*) INT. hallo [~ ارے + میاں]

امان | *amān'* N.F. protection ; quarter safety security immunity mercy ; grace [A ~ امن]

امانت | *amā'nat* N.F. entrusted thing or person ; trust charge deposit security integrity trustworthiness امانت دار *amā'nat-dār* N.M. trustee guardian ADJ. honest faithful امانت داری *amā'nat-dā'rī* N.F. integrity trustworthiness fidelity امانت رکھنا | *amā'nat rakh'nā* V.T. entrust deposit امانت میں خیانت (کرنا) *amā'nat meṅ khiyā'nat (kar'nā)* N.F. & V.I. (be guilty of the) breach of trust امانی *amā'nī* ADJ. official work done other than through contract [A]

اماوس | *amā'vas* N.F. (rare) lunar month's last night [S]

امبر | *am'bar* N.M. (dial.) sky clouds sheet ; covering [S]

امبیا | *ambiyā* N.F. small unripe mango [~ آم DIM.]

امپائر | *ampā''ar* N.M. umpire [E]

امت | *a'mat, 'a'mat* N.F. slave-girl (of) [A]

امت | *ūm'mat* N.F. (PL. امم | *ūmam'*) disciples ; followers ; adherents nation brethren in faith [A]

امتثال | *imtisāl'* N.M. obedience ; compliance ; execution امتثال امر | *imtisā'l-e am'r* N.M. compliance with orders ; carrying out of orders [A]

امتحان | *imteḥān'* N.M. examination ; test experiment trial امتحان دینا | *imteḥān' de'nā* V.I. sit for an examination ; take the test امتحان پاس کرنا *imteḥān pās kar'nā* V.I. pass the examination امتحان لینا (یا کرنا) *imteḥān lenā* (or *kar'nā*) test; examine try experiment [A ~ محنت]

امتداد | *imtidād'* N.M. prolongation passage (of time) امتداد زمانہ | *imtidād-e zamānah* N.M. passage of time [A ~ مدت]

امتزاج | *imtizāj'* N.M. mixture mingling , commingling کیمیائی امتزاج *kimyā''ī imtizāj'* N.M. chemical mixture [A ~ مزاج]

امتلا | *imtilā'* N.M. sickness ; nausea [A]

امتناع | *imtinā''* N.M. prohibition restraint stay ; injunction امتناعی | *imtinā''ī* ADJ. prohibitive حکم امتناعی *ḥūkm-e imtinā''ī* injunction stay order [A ~ منع]

امتنان | *imtinān'* N.M. gratitude [A ~ منت]

امتی | *ūm'matī* N.M. follower of a faith Muslim [A ~ امت]

امتیاز | *imtiyāz'* N.M. discrimination distinction نشان امتیاز *nishān-e imtiyāz'* N.M. order of distinction امتیاز کرنا | *imtiyāz' kar'nā* V.T. distinguish discriminate امتیاز عطا کرنا | *imtiyāz' 'atā kar'nā* V.T. decorate امتیازی | *imtiyā'zī* ADJ. distinctive distinguished special preferential امتیازی اوصاف | *imtiyā'zī ausāf'* N.M. PL. distinctive features امتیازی حقوق | *imtiyā'zī ḥūqooq'* N.M. PL. preferential rights ; privileges concessions امتیازی سلوک *imtiyā'zī sūlook'* N.M. preferential treatment [A+]

امٹ | *amiṭ'* ADJ. indelible [~ NEG. ا + مٹ]

امثال | *amsāl'* N.M. PL. proverbs maxims sayings ; adages fables examples امثلہ *am'silah* N.F. PL. examples ; instances [A ~ SING. مثال]

ام جانا | *am' jā'nā* V.I. be exhausted be benumbed

امجد | *am'jad* N.M. most glorious [A ~ ماجد SUP.]

امچور | *am-choor* N.M. sun-dried mango parings (used as seasoning) powder of these [~ آم + چورا powder]

امداد | *imdād'* N.F. aid ; subsidy relief support succour help ; assistance امداد باہمی | *imdā'd-e bā'-hamī* N.F. co-operation *imdād' kar'nā* V. help assist succur subsidy give relief مالی امداد *ma'lī imdād'* N.F. financial aid grant-in-aid aid امدادی *imdā'dī* ADJ. reserve subsidiary co-operative [A ~ مدد]

امڈنا | *ūmaḍ'nā* V.I. (same as اُمنڈنا V.I. ★)

امر | *am'r* N.M. order ; command ; behest ; matter affair business Point thing imperative mood تنقیح طلب امر *tanqīḥ' ta'lab am'r* N.M. point for determination ; issue ; point at issue امر و نہی *am'r-o nah'y* N.M. command(s) and prohibition(s) (gram.) imperative and prohibitive tenses [A]

امر *amar'* ADJ. (rare) immortal امربیل *amar' bel* N.F. aircreeper ; dodder [~ NEG. ا + مرنا]

پیڑ پر امربیل

امرا *ūmarā'* N.M. PL. the rich ; affluent people lords ; nobles grandees [A ~ SING امیر]

امراض *amrāz'* N.M. PL. diseases ; ailments maladies [A ~ SING. مرض]

امرت *am'rit* N.M. (rare) water of life ; nectar [S]

امرتی *am'ritī* N.F. a kind of sweetmeat

امرد *am'rad* N.M. (PL. مرد *mūrd*) beardless lad Ganymede minion ; catamite امرد پرست *am'rad parast'* N.M. sodomite ; homosexual ; paederast امرد پرستی *am'rad paras'tī* N.F. sodomy ; homosexuality ; paederasty [A]

امرس *am'-ras* N.M. thickened mango juice [~ آم + رس]

امرود *amrood'* N.M. guava [P]

امروز *im-roz'* ADV. today the times امروز و فردا *im-ro'z-o far'dā* N.M. the times prevarication امروز و فردا کرنا *imro'z-o far'dā kar'nā* V.I. prevaricate [P]

امرود

امریاں *amriy'yañ* N.F. (SING. declined as PL.) mango grove

امزجہ *am'zijah* N.M. PL. temperaments ; disposition (bodily) humours their combinations [A ~ SING. مزاج]

امس *ū'mas* N.F. sultriness ; stuffiness ; closeness (of weather)

امساک *imsāk'* N.M. (sexual) retention parsimony ; miserliness امساک باراں *imsāk'-e bā'rāñ* N.M. drought [A]

امصار *amsār'* N.M. PL. cities ; town garrison towns ; cantonments [A ~ SING. مصر]

امعا *am'ā'* N.F. PL. bowels get [A]

امعان *im'ān'* N.M. depth of vision امعان نظر سے دیکھنا *im'ā'n-e na'zar se dekh'nā* V.T look (into something) carefully [A]

امکا ڈھمکا *am'kā dham'kā*, امک ڈھمک N.M. Tom, Dick and Harry nobody

امکان *imkān'* N.M. possibility potentiality contingent existence امکانی *imkā'nī* ADJ. possible potential contingent [A]

امل ۱ *a'mal* N.M. (PL. آمال *āmāl'*) hope expectation desire ; wish [A]

امل ۲ *a'mal* N.M. intoxication addiction to drugs عملی *am'li* N.M. drug-addict

املا *imlā'* N.M. dictation orthography taking dictation املا نویس *imlā'- navīs* N.M. one who takes dictation [A]

املاک *amlāk'* N.F. property possessions estate املاک غیر منقولہ *amlā'k-e ghair' manqoo lah* N.F. immovable property ; real estate املاک منقولہ *amlā'k-e manqoo'lah* N.F. movable property

املتاس *a'maltās* N.M. tubular plant used as purgative ; 'cassia fistula'

املتاس

ملغم *amal'gham* N.M. amalgam amalgamation [~ E]

املی *im'lī* N.F. tamarind

امم *ūmam'* N.F. PL. nations races followers of various faiths as distinct groups [A ~ SING. امت]

امن *am'n* N.M. peace tranquillity security ; safety امن چین *am'n chain* N.M. peace tranquillity comfort امن و امان *am'n-o amān'* N.M. peace order [A]

امنڈنا *ūmand'nā*, اُمڈنا *ū'madnā* V.I. gush forth swell (of tears) fall (of clouds) overcast

امنگ *ūmang'* N.F. longing yearning passion ambition

اموا *am'vā* N.M. (dial. or endearingly) mango [~ آم]

اموات *amvāt* N.F. PL. deaths persons dead [A ~ SING. موت]

امواج *amvāj'* N.F. PL. waves billows ; surges [A ~ SING. موج]

اموال *amvāl'* N.M. PL. goods ; chattels property [A ~ SING. مال]

امور *ūmoor'* N.M. PL. matters affairs things business actions orders ; commands امور حوالہ *ūmoo'r-e havā'lah* N.M. terms of reference امور ملکی *ūmoo'r-e mūl'kī* N.M. political affairs ; affairs of the State [A ~ SING. امر]

امہات *ummahat'* N.F. PL. mothers امہات المومنین *ummahā'l-ul-mominīn'* N.F. PL. wives of the Holy Prophet (as mothers of the faithful) امہات سفلی *ūmmahā't-e sif'lī* N.F. PL. the four elements امہات علوی *ūmmahā't-e 'ul'vī* N.F. PL. spirits souls [A ~ SING. ام *ūm*]

امی *ammī* N.F. mummy ; mom [~ اماں DIM.]

امی *ūm'mī* ADJ. illiterate unlettered [A ~ ام *ūm*]

امی جمی سے *a'mī ja'mī se* ADJ. (W. dial.) safely

امید *ummīd* (COL. *umed'*) N.F. hope ; expectation trust anticipation pregnancy امید رکھنا *ummīd' rakh'na* V.I. hope expect anticipate trust امید سے ہونا *ummid' se ho'nā* V.I. be pregnant ; be in the family way امیدوار *ummīd'-vār* N.M. candidate ADJ. hopeful expectant امیدوار ہونا *ummīd'-vār ho'nā* V.I. be a candidate ; be an applicant (for a post) hope expect امیدواری *ummīd'-vā'rī* N.F. candidature hopefulness ; expectation ; dependence ; apprenticeship ; candidature [P]

امیر *amīr'* N.M. (PL. امرا *ūmara*) rich person ruler governor prince commander امیر الامرا *amī'r-ul-ūmarā'* N.M. doyen of the nobles Prime Minister امیر البحر *amī'r-ul-bah'r* N.M. admiral امیرزادہ *amīr'-za'dah* N.M. prince son of wealthy man ; scion of wealthy family امیر المومنین *amī'r-ul-mominīn'* N.M. Commander of the Faithful (as title of caliph) امیرانہ *amīrā'nah* ADJ. princely ; lordly of the rich امیری *amī'rī* N.F. wealth ; riches affluence ; opulence [A]

امین *amīn'* ADJ. trustworthy faithful N.M. trustee guardian minor (revenue or attachment) official custodian امینی *amīnī* custody guardianship [A ~ امانت]

ان *an* PREF. (used for negation) un- ; in- ; non- ان بن *ān'-ban* N.F. discord ; disagreement ان پڑھ *an-park'* ADJ. illiterate unlettered uneducated ان دیکھا *an-de'khā*, ADJ. (F. ان دیکھی *an-dekhi*) unique unseen ان تھک *ān-thak'* ADJ. untiring diligent انجان *an-jān'* ADJ. ignorant unacquainted stranger انجان بننا *an-jān' ban'na* V. feign ignorance ; be ignorant انجانا *an-jā'nā*, ADJ. (F. ان جانی *an-ja'nī*) unknown unacquainted unique ان گنت *an-gin't*, *an-gi'nat* (col. ان گن *an-gin'*) ADJ. countless ; innumerable انمل *an-mil'* ADJ. ill-assorted انمول *an-mol'* ADJ. precious priceless ; invaluable

ان *in* PRON. these , (polite PL. for single person) he, she ان دنوں *in di'noṅ* ADV. these days ; now-a-days ; at present

ان *ūn* PRON those (polite PL. for single person) he ; she ان دنوں *ūn di'noṅ* ADV. then ; in those days ; at that time

انا *a'na* N.F. ego self PRON. (ped.) I انا پرست *a'na parast'* ADJ. selfish egotistical N.M. egoist انانیت *ananiy'yat* N.F. ★ [A]

انا *an'nā* N.F. wet-nurse

انابت *inā'bat* N.F. repentance ; penitence انابت الی اللہ *inābat ilallāh'* PH. return to God through penitence [A]

انابیب *anābīb'* N.F. PL. tubes ; ducts ; canals انابیب شعری *anābī'b-e sha''rī* N.F. capillary tubes tiny ducts uniting veins and arteries [A ~ SING. انبوب]

اناپ شناپ *anāp' shanāp'* ADJ. nonsense ; silly اناپ شناپ بکنا *anāp' shanāp bak'na* V.I. talk nonsense

اناث *inās'* N.F. PL. women female [A ~ SING. انثیٰ]

اناج *anāj'* N.M. grain ; cereals

اناجیل *anājīl'* N.F. PL. the, New Testament ; gospel [A ~ SING. انجیل ~ H]

انار *anār'* N.M. pomegranate a kind of fireworks اناردانہ *anār'-dā'nah* N.M. dried pomegranate-seeds انارکلی *anār' kalī* N.F. pomegranate blossom [P]

انارکی *ānar'kī* N.F. anarchy انارکسٹ *anār'-kist* N.M. anarchist [E]

اناڑی *anā'rī* ADJ. unskilled unskilful ; inapt inexperienced green artless ; clumsy N.M. novice ; tyro blockhead sloven bungler اناڑی پن *anā'rī-pan* N.M. slovenliness clumsiness lack of skill

اناسی *ūnā'sī* ADJ. & N.M. seventy-nine اناسیواں *ūnā'sīvan* ADJ. seventy-ninth

انام *anām'* N.M. mankind creatures [A]

انامل *anā'mil* N.F. PL. fingers finger tips [A ~ SING. انملہ]

انانیت *ananiy'yat* N.F. egotism conceit self-praise egoism [A ~ انا]
انبار *ambar'* N.M. heap ; pile collection stack store انبار لگنا *ambar' lag'na* V.I. be piled up انبار لگانا *ambar lagā'nā* V.T. pile up [P]
انبساط *imbisāt'* N.M. cheerfulness merriment ; mirth joy ; delight [A ~ بسط]
انبوہ *amboh'* N.M. crowd ; throng mob multitude concourse abundance ; great quality [P]
انبہ *am'bah* N.M. (ped.) mango [P]
انبیا *ambiyā'* N.M. PL. Prophets [A ~ SING. نبی]
انت *ant* (dial.) N.M. end ADV. in the end [S]
انتالیس *ūntā'lis* ADJ. & N.M. thirty-nine انتالیسواں *ūntā'lisvān* ADJ. thirty-ninth
انتباہ *intibāh'* N.M. warning caution [A]
انتخاب *intikhāb'* N.M. selection choice extract ; excerpt انتخاب کرنا *intikhāb' kar'nā* V.T. elect select ; choose extract pick up compile edit [A]
انتداب *intidāb'* N.M. mandate انتدابی *intidā'bi* ADJ. mandatory [A]
انتر *an'tar* (dial) N.M. distance dissimilarity ADJ. different
انترا *an'tarā* N.M. second line onward of song
انتڑی *ant'ri* N.F. intestines entrails ; bowels انتڑی کا بل کھولنا *ant'ri kā bal' khol'nā* V. eat to the fill انتڑیاں جلنا *ant'riyan jal'nā*, انتڑیوں کا قل ہواللہ پڑھنا *ant'riyon kā qul hūval'lāh parh'nā*, انتڑیوں میں آگ لگنا *ant'riyon men āg' lag'nā* V.I. be very hungry [~ آنت DIM.]
انتساب *intisāb'* N.M. delication connection [A ~ نسبت]
انتشار *intishar* N.M. confusion ; anxiety broadcasting erection [A ~ نشر]
انتظار *intizār'* N.M. waiting anxiously (for) expectation انتظار دیکھنا *intizār' dekh'nā* V.I. be on the look out (for) انتظار کرنا *intizār' kar'rā* V.T. await ; wait (for) expect to look out for anticipate انتظار کش *intizār' kash'* ADJ. awaiting ; waiting looking out (for) expecting anticipating زحمت کش انتظار *zaih'mat-kash-e intizār'* ADJ. awaiting anxiously زحمت کش انتظار ہونا *zaih'mat-kash-e intizār' ho'nā* V.I. await anxiously [A ~ نظر]
انتظام *intizām'* N.M. arrangement management administration regulation ; order organization method انتظام خانگی *intizā'm-e khā'nagi* (or col. *-ngi*) N.M. domestic management private arrangement انتظام رکھنا *intizām' rakh'nā* V.I. maintain order and discipline manage انتظام کرنا *intizām' kar'nā* V.I. manage arrange regulate انتظامی *intizā'mī* ADJ. administrative انتظامیہ *intizāmiy'yah* N.F. executive administration [A ~ نظم]
انتفاع *intifā''* N.M. derivation of benefit ; profiting (by) [A ~ نفع]
انتقال *intiqāl'* N.M. death transfer alienation transmission conduction travelling ; departure migration movement transportation conveyance (11) (also انتقال پذیری *intiqāl' pazī'rī* N.F.) mobility انتقال اراضی *intiqāl'-e arā'zī* N.M. transfer of land ; alienation انتقال جائداد *intiqā'l-e jā''edād'* N.M. transfer of property انتقال حقیقت *intiqā'l-e haqq'y'yat* N.M. transfer of rights انتقال دائمی *intiqā'l-e dā''imī* N.M. permanent alienation انتقال رہن *intiqā'l-e reh'n* N.M. transfer of mortgage انتقال کرنا *intiqāl' kar'nā* V.T. & I. die ; pass away transfer carry out the mutation انتقال کنندہ *intiqāl' kunin'dah* N.M. deceased alienator انتقال نامہ *intiqāl'nā'mah* N.M. deed of transfer [A ~ نقل]
انتقام *intiqām'* N.M. revenge , vengeance reprisal retaliation انتقام لینا *intiqām' le'na* V.T. avenge take revenge retaliate ; hit back [A]
انتہا *inteha'* N.F. extreme utmost limit ; extremity completion end ; close ; finish انتہا کا *inteha kā* ADJ. extreme ; utmost perfect ; consummate [A ~ نہایت]
انتیس *ūn'tis* (dial. *ūnal'tis*) ADJ. & N.M. twenty-nine انتیسواں *ūn'tisvān* ADJ. twenty-ninth
انٹا *an'ṭā* N.M. large ball of opium billiard ball large pill marble any ball-like thing انٹا غفیل ہونا *an'ṭā ghafīl' ho'nā* V.I. be under effect of opium be unconscious انٹا گھر *an'ṭa-ghar* N.M. billiard room
انٹرویو *in'ṭar viyoo* N.M. interview انٹرویو کرنا (یا لینا) *inṭarviyoo kar'nā* (or *le'nā*) V.T. interview [E]
انٹ سنٹ *anṭ' sanṭ'* ADJ. irrelevant ADV. at random
انٹی *anṭī* *aṭ'ṭī* N.F. thread reel wound round spindle ; spindle skein any small bundle handful (in wrestling) a leg-trick

(انٹی دینا یا لگانا) *an'ṭī de'nā* (or *lagā'nā*) V.T. trip (someone) up use the leg-trick

انٹرنس *'intarain's* N.M. entrance ; matriculation examination [E]

انٹرنیشنل *in'ṭarnaishnal* ADJ international [E]

انثیٰ *un'sā* N.F. (PL. اناث *inās'*) (lit.) woman female [A]

انجاح *injāh'* N.M. fulfilment [A ~ نجاح]

انجام *anjām'* N.M. result consequence issue accomplishment end conclusion انجام بخیر ہونا *anjām' ba-khair' ho'nā* V.I. have a good ending انجام پانا *anjām' pā'nā* V.I. be brought to an end (or a close) be performed انجام دینا *anjām' de'nā* V.T. accomplish; complete bring to an end manage comply with discharge انجام سوچنا *anjām' soch'nā* V.I. have an eye on the end provide against be prudent be far-sighted انجام کار *anjā'm-e kār'* ADV. at last ; in the end ; at length eventually ; ultimately [P]

انجبار *anjabār'* N.M. (drug obtained from) a kind of creeper [P]

انجذاب *injizāb'* N.M. absorption diffusion [A ~ جذب]

انجر پنجر *an'jar pan'jar* N.M. limbs joints skeleton انجر پنجر ڈھیلے ہونا *an'jar pan'jar ḍhī'le ho'nā* V.I. weakening of limbs (through fatigue, etc.)

انجم *an'jum* N.M. PL. stars [A ~ نجم]

انجماد *injimād'* N.M. freezing congealing ; curdling condensation [A ~ جمود]

انجمن *an'juman* N.F. association society union meeting assembly انجمن اتحاد مزدوراں *an'juman-e ittehād-e mazdoo'rān'*, مزدور انجمن *mazdoor' an'juman* N.F. labour union ; workers' union انجمن ہائے امداد باہمی *anjuman-hā'-e imdād-e ba-hamī* N.F. PL. co-operative societies

انجن *an'jan* N.M. antimony collyrium

انجن *in'jan* N.M. engine locomotive any motive force [E]

ریل کا انجن

انجیر *anjīr'* N.M. fig [P]

انجیل *injīl'* N.F. (PL. اناجیل *anājīl'*) New Testament, Gospel [A ~ H]

انجیر

انجینیر *injī'niyar* N.M. engineer انجینیری *injī'narī* N.F. engineering [E]

انچ (trade spelling انچہ) *inch* N.M. inch [E]

انچاس *unchās'* (dial. ننچاس *ananchās'*) ADJ. & N.M forty-nine انچاسواں *unchās'vān* ADJ. forty-ninth

انچے انچے رہنا *an'che an'che raih'nā* V.I. keep the distance

انحراف *inhirāf'* N.M. deflection deviation refraction declination turning away (from) swerving repudiation evasion انحراف کرنا *inhirāf' kar'nā* V.I. deviate deflect decline turn against repudiate recant rebel disobey evade [A ~ حرف]

انحصار *inhisār'* N.M. reliance ; dependence encirclement [A ~ حصر]

انحطاط *inhitāt'* N.M. decline degradation detrioration fall [A]

ان داتا *an'dā'tā* N.M. sustainer master

انداز *andāz'* N.M. blandishment way ; manner ; method style measure SUF. throwing firing ; shooting arranging [P]

اندازہ *andā'zah* N.M. estimate guess measurement weight evaluation conjecture forecast اندازۂ ذہانت *andā'za-e zihā'nat* N.M. intelligence quotient ; I. Q. اندازۂ ذہانت کرنا *andā'za-e zihā'nat kar'nā* V.T. determine the I.Q. (of) اندازۂ فصل *andā'za-e fasl* N.M. crop forecast اندازہ کرنا *andā'zah kar'nā* (or *lagā'nā*) V.I. make a rough estimate guess conjecture weigh measure evaluate اندازاً *andā'zan* ADJ. (col.) roughly approximately [P]

اندام *andām'* N.M. body figure اندام نہانی *andā'm-e nehā'nī* N.F. female private parts [P]

اندر *an'dar* PREP. within inside ADV. inward اندر خانے *an'dar-khā'ne* ADV. covertly اندر سے *an'dar se* ADV. from within from inside internally inwardly اندر کرنا *an'dar kar'nā* V. (esp.) put behind the bars drive in bring in [~P]

اندر *in'dar* (ped. *ind'ra*) Indra ; Hindu god of rain (counterpart of Greek Zeus) اندر کا اکھاڑہ *in'dar kā akhā'ṛā* N.M. Indra's court place with bevy of beauties [S]

اندراج **indiraj** N.M. entry insertion record اندراج کرنا indiraj' kar'na V.T. make an entry of place on record insert [A ~ درج]

اندرائن کا پھل indara''in ka phal' N.M. wild gourd ; colocynth (fig.) surly or malicious person

اندرسا and'rasa N.M. rice pastry

اندرون an'daroon', اندرون andaroon' ADJ. within ; interior ; inside اندرون خانہ andaroo'n-e kha'nah N.M. women-folk ; female members of family ; wife and children inner apartments [P]

اندک an'dak ADJ. & ADV. a little slight little wee-bit [P]

اندمال andimal' N.M. healing (of wound) recovery [A]

اندوختہ andokh'tah N.M. savings SUF. set apart saved gained [P ~ اندوختن]

اندوز andoz' SUF. acquiring gaining receiving hoarding اندوزی ando'zi SUF. acquisition gaining hoarding [P ~ PREC.]

اندوہ andoh' N.M. sorrow grief غم و اندوہ gham-e andoh' N.M. affliction ; misery اندوہناک andoh'nak ADJ. sad ; sorrowful full of grief اندوہگین andoh'-gin ADJ. aggrieved afflicted miserable ; wretched afflicted sad ; sorrowful grievous heart-rending [P]

اندھا andha, ADJ. (F. اندھی an'dhi) blind careless ; heedless thoughtless ; undiscerning ; indiscreet N.M. blind man اندھا بانٹے ریوڑیاں اپنوں ہی کو دے an'dha bante re'varyan, ap'non hi ko de PROV. mother's bowel yearns towards her own child اندھاپن an'dha-pan N.M. blindness obscurity folly indiscretion اندھا خرچ an'dha kharch' N.M. lavish expenditure اندھا دھند andha' dhund' ADV. [illegible]criminate excessive careless [illegible] blindly indiscriminately desperately اندھا دھند لٹانا andha' dhund' luta'na V.T. squander spend lavishly اندھا کرنا an'dha kar'na V.T. blind befool ; dupe defraud ; deceive throw dust in (someone's) eyes enamour cause to dote اندھا کنواں an'dha kun''an N.M. dry well اندھا ہونا an'dha ho'na V.T. become blind ; lose one's sight go astray behave rashly ; act desperately

اندھیارا andhya'ra N.M. darkness اندھیاری andhyari N.F. blinkers

اندھیر andher' N.M. misrule mess bungling oppression ; violence ; tyranny disorder ; tumult inequity ; injustice outrage اندھیر مچانا andher' macha'na V.T. do wrong (to) oppress ; tyrannise (over) outrage اندھیر کھاتہ andher' kha'ta N.M. mess bungling mismanagement embezzlement.

اندھیرا andhe'ra N.M. darkness dusk gloom obscurity ADJ. (F. اندھیری andhe'ri) dark dusky gloomy obscure اندھیرا کرنا andhe'ra kar'na V.T. darken ; put out light(s) obscure overcast اندھیرا گھپ andhe'ra ghup' N.M. utter darkness اندھیرے گھر کا اجالا andhe're ghar' ka uja'la N.M. the only son very dear child اندھیرے منہ andhe're munh ADV. in the early hours of the morning اندھیری کوٹھڑی andhe'ri koth'ri N.F. dark room dark cell black-hole

اندیش andesh' SUF. thinking ; considering meditating minded intentioned اندیشی ande'shi SUF. thinking meditating [P ~ FOLL.]

اندیشہ ande'shah N.M. anxiety , concern dread ; fear suspicion thought , deliberation reflection ; meditation اندیشہ کرنا ande'shah kar'na V. feel anxiety or concern (for) ; be anxious (about) apprehensive (of); fear reflect اندیشناک andesh'-nak ADJ. fearful ; dreadful sad thoughtful ; meditative [P]

انڈا an'da N.M. egg انڈا دینا an'da de'na V.I. lay an egg انڈا گندہ ہونا an'da gan'da ho'na V. (of egg) go bad ; become addled انڈوں پر آنا an'don par ana V.T. (be about to) start laying eggs انڈے بچے an'de bach'che N.M. (fig.) kiddies ; children انڈے بچے دینا an'de bach'che de'na V.I. procreate multiply انڈے سینا an'de se'na V. sit on eggs ; hatch eggs ; brood lead a retired life

انڈیلنا undel'na V.T. pour out empty discharge

انزال in'zal' N.M. seminal discharge [A ~ نزول]

انس in's N.M. man mankind humanity [A]

انس un's N.M. attachment fellowship friendship ; amity love ; affection [A]

انساب *ansāb'* N.M. PL. genealogy generations families races علم الانساب *'ilm'-ul-ansāb'* N.M. branch of history dealing with genealogies [A ~ SING. نسب]

انسان *insān'* (poet. also انساں *insāṅ'*) N.M. man human being mankind ; humanity انسان بنانا *insān' banā'nā* V.T. civilize educate polish humanize انسان ہی تو ہے *insān' hī to hai'* PH. but human ; man is fallible ; one is liable to err انسانی *insān'nī* ADJ. human انسانیت *insāniyyat'* N.F. anthropology انسانیات *insāniy'yat'* N.F. humanity civility affability ; human kindness politeness human nature mankind [A ~ انس]

انسب *an'sab* ADJ. most suitable of very noble descent [A ~ نسب]

انسپکٹر *inspik'tar* N.M. inspector انسپکٹر جنرل *inspik'tar jan'ral* N.M. Inspector-General [E]

انسٹھ *un'saṭh* ADJ. & N.M. fifty-nine انسٹھواں *un'saṭh'-vāṅ* ADJ. fifty-ninth

انسداد *insidād'* N.M. end ; termination prevention , check bar ; hindrance , obstacle management arrangement انسدادی *insidā'dī* ADJ preventive انسدادی تدابیر *insidā'dī tadābīr'* N.M PL. preventive measures [A ~ سد wall]

انشا *inshā'* N.F. composition style diction writing انشاپرداز *inshā' pardāz'* N.M. writer master of prose beletrist انشاپردازانہ *inshā'-pardāzā'nah* ADJ. elegant (diction) ADV. (writing) elegently انشاپردازی *inshā'-pardā'zī* N.F. writing composition authorship elegance of composition letter-writing belles-lettres انشائیہ *inshā'iy'yah* N.M. essay (also ADJ.) (sentence) expressing uncertainty, order, wish, etc. [A]

انشاءاللہ تعالیٰ *in-shā'-allāh (ta'ā'lā)* PH. God (Almighty) willing [A ~ ان if + شاء wished]

انشراح *inshirāḥ'* N.M. laying open making clear manifestation lack of prejudice انشراح صدر سے *inshirā'ḥ-e sad'r se* PH. with an open mind without prejudice [A ~ شرح]

انشورنس *insho'rans* N.M. insurance [E]

انصار *ansār'* N.M. PL. Medinite compansions (of the Holy Prophet) ; 'Ansars' helpers ; friends انصاری *ansā'rī* ADJ. scion of 'Ansar'; 'Ansari' weaver [A ~ SING. ناصر]

انصاف *insāf'* N.M. justice ; equity fairplay impartiality division into halves ; bisection انصاف چاہنا *insāf' chāh'nā* V.T. seek justice demand fairplay seek redress انصاف کرنا *insāf' kar'nā* V.T. do justice be impartial انصاف کا خون کرنا *insāf' kā khoon' kar'nā* V.T. be unjust be partial be prejudiced tyrannize misrule [A ~ نصف]

انصرام *insirām'* N.M. management (of estate or business) administration accomplishment performance conclusion ; completion [A]

انضباط *inzibāt'* N.M. discipline regulating restraint , self-control انضباط اوقات *inzibā't-e auqāt'* N.M. schedule ; time-table [A ~ ضبط]

انطباع *intibā'* N.M. impression being printed [A ~ طباعت]

انطباق *intibāq'* N.M aptness (of example) [A ~ مطابق]

انعام *in'ām'* N.M. prize reward favour grant gift ; present gratuity tip انعام واکرام *in'ām-o-ikrām'* N.M. bestowal largesse انعام دینا *in'ām de'nā* V.T. award a prize reward ; give a reward tip انعام تقسیم کرنا *in'ām taqsīm' kar'nā* V. give away prizes ; distribute prizes انعامی *in'ā'mī* ADJ. prize ; presentable انعامی رقم *in'ā'mī raq'm* N.F. honorarium gratuity قومی انعامی بانڈ *qau'mī in'ā'mī baunḍ* N.M. national prizebond [A ~ نعمت]

انعام *an'ām'* N.M. PL. cattle [A]

انعطاف *in'itāf'* N.M. refraction [A ~ عطف]

انعقاد *in'iqād'* N.M. holding taking place celebration [A ~ عقد]

انعکاس *in'ikās'* N.M. reflection inversion being reflected [A ~ عکس]

انفاس *anfās'* N.M. PL. breaths [A ~ SING. نفس *nafas'*]

انفرادی *infirā'dī* ADJ. individual solitary; lonely انفرادی مشاہدہ *infirā'dī mushā'hadah* N.M. individual observation case work *infirādiy'yat* N.F. individuality [A ~ نفس]

انفس *an'fus* N.M. PL. souls people [A ~ SING. نفس *naf's*]

انفصال *infisāl'* N.M. separation decision settlement انفصال مقدمہ *infisā'l-e muqad'-*

damah N.M. decision of case [A ~ فصل]

انفعال infe'al' N.M. shame modesty bashfulness contrition reactions passivity عرق انفعال a'raq-e infe'al' N.M perspiration caused by shame [A ~ فعل]

انفکاک infikak' N.M. redemption dislocation انفکاک رہن infika'k-e reh'n N.M. redemption of mortgage [A ~ فک]

انفلوئنزا in'flooain'za N.M. influenza [E]

انقباض inqibaz N.M. dullness ; heaviness contraction detention ; restraint [A ~ قبض]

انقسام inqisam' N.M. distribution apportionment division partition [A]

انقضا inqiza' N.M. expiry (of term) lapse ; end (of period) termination completion extinction [A ~ قضا]

انقطاع inqita'' N.M. separation discontinuance being cut or broken amputation [A ~ قطع]

انقلاب inqilab' N.M. (PL. انقلابات inqilabat') revolution change ; alteration vicissitudes [A ~ قلب]

انقیاد inqiyad' N.M. (lit.) submission obedience subjection compliance [A ~ قیادت]

انکار inkar' N.M. refusal ; declining denial; disvowal contradiction negation انکار کرنا inkar' kar'na V.I. refuse ; decline deny ; disown disallow [A ~]

انکسار inkisar' N.M. (col. انکساری inkisa'ri N.F.) humility meekness modesty [A ~ کسر]

انکشاف inkishaf' N.M. disclosure ; revelation exposition discovery [A ~ کشف]

انکم in'kam N.F. income انکم ٹیکس in'kam-taks N.M. income-tax [E]

انکھڑیاں ankh'riyan N.F. PL. eyes [~ انکھیں DIM. used endearingly]

انگ ang N.M. body limb organ breasts style (in music) انگ انگ پھڑکنا ang' ang phar'akna V.I. have youthful exuberance انگ لگنا ang' lag'na V.I. (of food) go to strengthen the body

انگارا anga'ra N.M. live coal embers ; ADJ. red hot انگاروں پر لوٹنا anga'ron par lot'na V.I. be on thorns be agitated burn with envy or rage انگارے برسنا anga're barasna V.I. be excessively hot

انگبین ang'bin, an'gabin N.M. (lit.) honey [P]

انگرکھا ang'rakha N.M. narrow-sleeved 'achkan' like coat with double fold on one breast and single fold on the other

انگریز angrez' N.M. Englishman Briton Anglicized person انگریز پرست angrez'-parast' N.M. & ADJ. Anglophile (one loving English way and manners انگریز پرستی angrez'-paras'ti N.F. love for English ways and manners انگریزی angre'zi N.F. English language ADJ. English [E ~ F Anglaise]

انگڑ کھنگڑ an'gar khan'gar N.M. variety of old stuff

انگڑائی angra''i N.F. yawn oscitation انگڑائی لینا angra''i le'na V.I. yawn ; oscitate stretch the limbs

انگشت angusht' N.F. finger انگشت حیرت در دہاں angush't-e hai'rat dar dahan' PH. aghast agape انگشت شہادت angush't-e shaha'dat N.F. forefinger انگشتانہ angushta'nah N.M. thimble انگشتری angush'tari N.F. ring [P]

انگشتانہ

انگل un'gal N.M. finger finger's breadth (as measure) [doublet of FOLL.]

انگلی ung'li N.F. finger انگلی دھرنا ung'li dhar'na, انگلی رکھنا ung li rakh'na V.T. criticize cavil (at) find fault (with) take into possession ; bring under control pick and choose انگلی نہ لگانا ung'li na laga'na V.T. not to touch at all show complete indifference انگلیاں اٹھنا ung'liyan uth'na V.I. be ridiculed achieve notoriety انگلیاں چٹخانا ung'liyan chatkha'na V.T. snap the fingers انگلیاں نچانا ung'liyan nacha'na V.T. twiddle ; twirl fiddle with fingers انگلیوں پر نچانا ung'liyon par nacha'na V.T. make a fool of wheedle (someone) into following (one's) whims

انگنائی angna''i N.F. yard; courtyard [~ انگن DIM.]

انگوٹھا angoo'tha N.M. thumb (also پاؤں کا انگوٹھا pa''n ka angoo'tha) great toe انگوٹھا چوسنا angootha choos'na V.T. suck the thumb انگوٹھا چومنا angootha choom'na V.T. show great love for انگوٹھا دکھانا angootha dikha'na V.T. refuse outright mock ; jeer irritate challenge use an obscene symbol

انگوٹھی *angoo'ṭhī* N.F. ring شادی کی انگوٹھی *shā'dī kī angoo'ṭhī* N.F. wedding ring

انگوچھا *ango'chhā* N.M. towel-cum-topless bathing sheet used by the poorer among Hindus ; towel ; kerchief

انگور *angoor'* N.M. grapes granulation (of healing wound) scab (of sore) انگوری سرکہ *angoo'rī sir'kah* N.M. vinegar انگوری شراب *angoo'rī sharāb'* N.F. wine

انگیا *ang'yā* N.F. bodice brassiers (The old style *angyā* was much different from the modern brassiers. It looked like a full-length half-sleeved bodice show in the picture) [~ انگ]

انگیٹھی *angī'ṭhī* N.F. stove grate brazier

انگیخت *angekht'* N.F. instigation [P انگیختن ~]

انگیز *angez'* SUF. exciting ; rousing raising causing instigating انگیزی *ange'zī* SUF. exciting ; rousing [P PREC.]

انگیزنا *angez'nā* V.I. bear ; endure ; brook

اناس *anannās* N.M. pineapple ; ananas [Peruv.]

انوار *anvār'* N.M. PL. light brightness lustre [A ~ SING. نور]

انواع *anvā''* N.F. PL. species kinds ; sorts; varieties انواع واقسام *anvā''-o-aqsām'* N.F. all sorts ; various kinds ; large variety [A ~ SING. نوع]

انوپ *anoop'* ADJ. (dial.) peerless ; incomparable [S]

انوٹ *an'vaṭ* N.F. grace blandishment belled ring for great toe

انور *an'var* ADJ. splendid resplendent very brilliant [A ~ نور]

انوکھا *ano'khā*, ADJ. (F. انوکھی *ano'khī*) curious singular extraordinary ; rare unusual

انہار *anhār'* N.F. PL. canals [A ~ SING. نہر]

انہتر *unhat tar* ADJ. & N.M. sixty-nine انہترواں *unhat'tar-vāṅ* ADJ. sixty-ninth

انہدام *inhidām'* N.M. demolition [A ~ ہدم]

انہزام *inhizām'* N.M. sustaining defeat [A ~ ہزم]

انہماک *inhimāk'* N.M. absorption concentration [A]

انہوریاں *anho'riyāṅ* N.F. PL. prickly heat

انہیں *i'nheṅ*, انہیں *u'nheṅ* PRON. them

انی *a'nī* N.F. point (of spear) prow (of boat) انی چلنا *a'nī chal'nā* V.I. thurst (in fencing)

انیائے *annayā''e* N.M. (dial.) injustice [S ~ NEG. نیائے +]

انیس *anīs'* N.M. companion friend [A ~ انس *ūns*]

انیس *ūn'nīs* N.M. & ADJ. nineteen انیس بیس کا فرق ہونا *ūn'nīs bīs' (kā far'q ho'nā)* PH. (be) slightly different ; (be) almost equal انیس نہیں *ūn'nīs na'hīṅ* PH. (is) in no way inferior انیس ہونا *ūn'nīs ho'nā* V.I. be inferior (to) انیسواں *ūnnīs'vāṅ* ADJ. nineteenth

انیسون *anīsoon'* N.M. (rare) anise aniseed [A ~ G]

انیلا *anī'lā* ADJ. (F. انیلی *anī'lī*) gull ; dupe انیلاپن *anī'lā-pan* N.M. gullibility

او *o* INT. O ; oh

اواخر *avā'khir* N.M. end (as PL.) final portions [A ~ SING. آخر]

اوازہ توازہ *avā'zah tavā'zah* N.M. taunt ; jeer invends [~ P آوازہ CORR.]

اوامر *avā'mir* N.M. PL. orders commands matter affairs [A ~ SING. امر]

اوائل *avā''il* N.M. beginning ; commencement (as PL.) early portions, etc. اوائل عمر *avā''il-e 'um'r* N.F. childhood early age [A ~ SING. اول]

اوائی *avā''ī* N.F. (correct but rare spelling of (ہوائی) rumour [~ آواز CORR.]

اوباش *aubāsh'* N.M. vagabond dissolute ; debauchee ; rake ; voluptuary ; libertine ; profligate ADJ. licentious ; dissolute ; profligate اوباشانہ *aubāshā'nah* ADJ. rakish depraved اوباشی *aubā'shī* N.F. debauchery ; dissipation ; dissoluteness; rakishness depravity [A ~ وبش *vabsh* mean]

اوپچی *op'chī* N.M. & ADJ. armed (person) mail-clad (person)

اوپر *oo'par* ADV. up on ; at upon over above high aloft اوپر آنا *oo'par ā'nā* V.I. come up rise ascend اوپر اوپر *oo'par oo'par* ADV. over and above one's head secretly ; covertly اوپر اوپر سے *oo'par oo'par se* ADV. superficially just for a show اوپر اوپر کا *oo'par oo'par kā* ADJ. best cream of اوپر تلے

oo'par ta'le ADV. one after another ; in succession ; continuously in a row اوپر تلے کے بچے *oo'par ta'le-ke bach'che* N.M. children born in (quick) succession اوپر سے *oo'par se* ADV. from above overhead in addition (to) over and above اوپر کی آمدنی *oo'par kī ām'danī* N.M. bribe ; unlawful gratification اوپر والا *oo'par vā'lā* N.M. God (W. dial.) crescent اوپر والیاں *oo'par vā'liyāṅ* N.F. PL. maids, maidservants spirits ; residents of upper storey (W. dial.) fairies (W. dial.) evil spirits اوپر والے *oo'par vā'le* N.M. residents of upper storey officers stars ; heavenly bodies strangers ; other persons servants اوپر ہی اوپر *oo'par hī oo'par* ADV. secretly ; covertly اوپر کا کام *oo'par kā kām'* N.M. odd jobs ; miscellaneous work ; general duty اوپری *oo'prī* ADJ. unknown superficial specious N.M. stranger

اوت *oot* issueless dunce crack اوت نپوتا *oot' na-poo'tā* ADJ. & N.M. issueless (person)

اوتاد *autād'* N.M. a category of saints comprising only four at any time in the world [A]

اوتار *autār'* (ped. *avtār'*) N.M. (dial.) deity incarnate (according to Hindus) [S]

اوٹ *oṭ* N.F. shelter cover screen ; curtain veil mask hiding ; concealment اوٹ کرنا *oṭ' kar'nā* V.I. hide ; conceal cover screen shield اوٹ ہونا *oṭ' ho'nā* V.I. be concealed ; be hidden be behind cover اوٹل *oṭal'* ADJ. lost to view behind cover

اوٹ پٹانگ *ooṭ' paṭāṅg'* ADJ. nonsense absurd ; silly ridiculous

اوٹنا *oṭ'nā* V.T. gin (cotton) اوٹنی *oṭ'nī* N.F. ginning machine

اوج *auj* N.M. zenith acme apex apogee summit top highest point [A]

اوجھ *ojh* N.M. guts ; tripe اوجھڑی *ojh'ṛī* N.F. tripe

اوجھا *o'jhā* ADJ. wizard اوجھائی *o'jhā''ī* N.F wizardy

اوجھل *o'jhal* ADJ. hidden ; concealed invincible out of sight اوجھل کرنا *o'jhal kar'nā* V.T. screen conceal ; hide اوجھل ہونا *o'jhal ho'nā* V.I. hide ; be concealed be screened become invisble آنکھ اوجھل پہاڑ اوجھل *āṅkh' o'jhal pahāṛ' o'jhal* PROV. out of sight out of mind

اوچھا *o'chhā* ADJ. (F. اوچھی *o'chhī*) mean ; contemptible ; low-bred fickle ; capricious petty ; trivial awry grazing light amiss اوچھا پن *o'chhā-pan* N.M. shallowness meanness اوچھا وار *o'chhā vār* N.M. attack going amiss grazing stroke اوچھا ہاتھ *o'chhā hāth'* N.M. light grip grazing stroke اوچھا ہونا *o'chhā ho'nā* V.I. be shallow be mean be capricious

اوچھن پوچھن *o'chhan po'chhan* N.M. crumbs food left over

اود بلاؤ *oo'd-blā''o* N.M. otter

اودا *oo'dā* ADJ. (F. اودی *oo'dī*) purple violet اداہٹ *ū'dā'haṭ* N.F. being of purple colour

اودھم *oo'dham*, اُدھم *ud'dham* N.M. noise uproor ; tumult turmoil ; perturbation disturbance اودھم مچانا *oo'dham machā'nā* N.M. make a noise kick up a row create disturbance

اور *aur* CONJ. and also ADJ. more not this different else اور ایک *aur' ek* ADJ. another different one more اور سنو *aur' sū'no* INTJ. just listen ridiculous how strange اور کیا *aur' kyā* ADV. what else indeed besides this اور نہیں تو *aur' na'hīṅ to* ADV. why not ? if not, then otherwise اور ہی *aur' hī* quite different quite changed اور *or* N.F. (dial.) side direction climax (of) اور نہ چھور *or na chhor* PH. endless

اوراد *aurād'* N.M. PL. daily round of prayer-formula [A ~ SING. ورد]

اوراق *aurāq'* N.M. PL. leaves (of book) leaves (of tree) [A ~ SING. ورق]

اورما *or'mā* N.M. hemming اورما کرنا *or'mā kar'nā* V.T. & I. hem

اورنگ *aurang'* N.M. throne اورنگ زیب *aurang-zeb'* N.M. adorner of throne this as appellation of a Mughal Emperor (adorner of the throne) اورنگ زیبی پھوڑا *aurang-ze'bī pho'ṛā* N.M. carbuncle اورنگ شاہی *aurań'g-e shā'hī* N.M. imperial throne [P]

اوریئنٹل *oryań'ṭal* ADJ. oriental [E]

اوڑا *o'ṛā* N.M. dearth (of)

اوڑھنا *oṛh'nā* V.T. cover (body) with sheet dress (oneself) in a sheet اوڑھنا بچھونا *oṛh'nā bichhau'nā* N.M. coverlet ; covering and bedding (fig.) sole interest solitary or total possession اوڑھنی *oṛh'nī* N.F. stole (usu. cotton) shawl

اوزار *auzār'* N.M. instrument ; tools implements apparatus weapon [A]

اوزان *auzān'* N.M. PL. weights measures (in versification metres [A ~ SING. وزن]

اوس *os* N.F. dew (پڑنا (پر) اوس پڑنا *(par) os' par'nā* V.I. despair ; feel disappointed ; (of wet blanket) be thrown over

اوسان *ausān'* N.M. self-possession ; presence of mind ; senses اوسان خطا ہونا *ausān' kha'tā ho'nā*, اوسان کھونا *ausān' kho'nā* V.I. lose one's senses ; lose presence of mind be stupefied ; be stunned be non-plussed اوسان قائم رکھنا *ausān' qā''im rakh'nā* V.I. not to lose presence of mind not to be perturbed

اوسر *au'sar* ADJ. barren ; unproductive unreproductive ; barren

اوسط *au'sat* ADJ. & N.M. (PL. اواسط *avāsit*) average mean medium ; middling middle اوسط آمدنی *au'sat ām'danī* N.F. average income اوسط تنخواہ *au'sat tankhvāh* N.F. average pay اوسط نکالنا *au'sat nikāl'nā* V.T. strike an averge شرق اوسط *shar'q-e au'sat* (or usu.) though incorrectly مشرق وسطیٰ *mash'riq-e vus'tā*) N.M. Middle East [A ~ وسط]

اوشدھالیہ *aushad-dhā'liyah* N.M. (dial.) dispensary ; drug-shop [S]

اوصاف *ausāf'* N.M. PL. attributes characteristics qualities ; properties praises manners morals ; virtues properties اوصاف حمیدہ *aūsā'f-e hamī'dah* N.M. commendable attributes ; noble qualities [A ~ SING. وصف]

اوصیا *ausiyā'* N.M. PL. (ped.) (of will) executors; administrators [A ~ SING. وصی]

اوضاع *auzā'* N.M. PL. ways اوضاع و اطوار *auzā''-o atvār'* N.M. PL. habits traits of character [A ~ SING. وضع]

اوقات *auqāt'* N.M. PL. times ; hours schedule N.F. status ; position ; standing اوقات بسری *auqāt' ba'-sarī* N.F. whiling away one's time means of livelihood اوقات بسری کرنا *auqāt' ba'-sarī kar'nā* V. subsist exist ; eke out one's existence pass one's time اوقات تلخ ہونا *auqāt' tal'kh ho'nā* V.I. have a bad time lead a miserable life تلخیٔ اوقات *tal'khi-e auqāt'* N.F. misery bitterness of conditions اوقات ضائع کرنا *auqāt' zā''e' kar'nā* V.T. waste time تضییع اوقات *tazyi''-e' auqāt'* N.F. waste of time [A ~ SING. وقت]

اوقاف *auqāf'* N.M. PL. endowments charitable endowments trusts properties held in trust (also محکمہ اوقاف *maih'kama-e auqāf*) the Auqaf department [A ~ SING. وقف]

اوک *ok* N.F. palm of hand contracted to hold drinking water

اوک چوک *ook'chook'* N.F. oversight error; error and omission ; E. & O. slip

اوکنا *ok'nā* V.I. feel sick vomit

اوکھ *ookh*, اِکھ *īkh* N.F. (dial. M.) thin sugarcane (as standing crop)

اوکھلی *okh'lī* N.F. large wooden mortar

اوکھلی

اوگرا *og'rā* ADJ. (of stew etc.) unseasoned with butter oil, etc.

اوگن *au'gūn* N.M. (dial.) bad quality [S ~ گن *gūn*]

اوگھٹ *au'ghat* ADJ. rugged impassable

اوگی *au'gī* N.F. embroidered upper of shoe

اوگی

اول *av'val* ADJ first foremost best excellent ADV. at first ; in the first place in the beginning N.M. (PL. اوائل *avā'il*) first part earlier part commencement beginning اول خویش بعد درویش *av'val khesh' ba'd darvesh'* PROV. charity begins at home اول درجے کا *av'val dar'je kā* ADJ. first-class ; first-rate class posh top اول دن سے *av'val din' se* ADV. from the very first day from the very beginning ; right from the start اول رہنا *av'val raih'nā* V.I. stand first ; obtain the first position top the list اولاً *av'valan* ADV. at first in the first place initially اول و آخر *av'lval-o ākhir* ADJ. the first and the last N.M. God اولیت *avvaliy'-yat* N.F. priority pre-eminence superiority excellence اولین *av'valīn* ADJ. first premiers former ancients past original اولین و آخرین *āv'valīn-o ākhirīn* ADJ. the first and the last [~ A اول]

اولا *olā* N.M. hail اولا ہو جانا *o lā ho jā'nā* V. become very cold

اولا مولا *au'lā mau'lā* ADJ. good-for-nothing N.M. simpleton

اولاد *aulād'* N.F. PL. chidren decendants offspring ; progeny اولادِ اناث *aulā'd-e inās'* N.F. PL. daughters اولادِ ذکور *aul'd-e zūkoor'* N.F. PL. sons حلال کی اولاد *halāl' kī a'ūlād'* N.F PL. legitimate children well-behaved progeny ناخلف اولاد *nā-kha'laf aulād'* N.F. PL. unmannerly or good-for-nothing progeny [A ~ SING. ولد]

اولتی *aul'tī* N.F. lower edge of roof

اول جلول *ool'-jalool'* ADJ stupid unmannerly awkward ; clumsy slovenly untidy

اولتی

اول فول *aul'-faul* N.M. nonsense اول فول بکنا *aul' faul bak'nā* V.I. talk nonsense

اولما *ol'mā* N.M. boiled mince meat اولما کرنا *ol'mā kar'nā* V.T. mince meat beat severely [~T لوٹ CORR.]

اولیٰ *oo'lā* ADJ. better best preferable chief ; main ; major [A ~ اول]

اولمپک *ulim'pik* ADJ. Olympic اولمپک کھیل (یا مقابلے) *ulim'pik khel* (or *muqābale*) N.M. PL. Olympic [E ~ G]

اولو *ūloo'*, اولی *ūlī'* PREF. possessed of having ; possessing owners of اولوالابصار *ūlūl'-absār'* N.M. PL. discerning ; wise اولوالامر *ūlūl'-am'r* N.M. PL. chose in authority اولوالالباب *ūlūl'-albāb'* N.M. PL. wise men ; person of understanding اولوالعزم *ūlūl'-az'm* ADJ. enterprising ; venturesome ; adventurous ambitious aspiring resolute اولوالعزمی *ūlūl'-'az'mī* N.F. resolution determination ambition enterprise اولوالعلم *ūlūl'-'il'm* N.M. PL. learned people savants sages [A]

اولو اولو *au'loo au'loo* ADJ. awkward ; strange giving a strange feeling (on being worn)

اولیا *auliyā'* N.M. PL. saints ; holy men (ped.) associates ; companions [A ~ SING. ولی]

اولیت *avvaliy'yat* N.F. اولین *av'valīn* ADJ. (see under اول ADJ. ★)

اوم *om* N.M. (Hindu name for) God [S]

اون *oon* N.F. wool اونی *oo'nī* ADJ. ★

اونٹ *ooṅṭ* N.M. camel اونٹ دیکھیے کس کل (یا کروٹ) بیٹھے *ooṅṭ de'khiye kis kal* (or *kar'vat*) *baiṭhe* PROV. let us see how the wind blows اونٹ رے اونٹ تیری کونسی کل سیدھی *ooṅṭ re ooṅṭ' te'rī kaun'sī kal sī'dhī* PROV. it is rotten all over

اونٹنی اونٹ

اونٹ کٹارا *ooṅṭ kaṭā'rā* N.M. a kind of thistle eaten by camels اونٹ کے منہ میں زیرہ *ooṅṭ' ke mūṅh men zī'rah* PROV. a giant will starve on what surfeits a draft اونٹنی *ooṅṭ'nī* N.F. dromedary she-camel

اوٹانا *auṅṭā'nā* V.T. boil اوٹنا *auṅṭ'nā* V.I. seethe bubble over boil

اونٹنی *ooṅṭ'nī* N.F. (see under اونٹ N.M. ★)

اونچا *ooṅ'chā* ADJ. (F. اونچی *ooṅ'chī*) high lofty elevated tall precipitous ; steep senior اونچا (یا بڑا) بول بولنا *ooṅ'chā* (or *baṛā*) *bol bol'nā* PH. brag اونچا سننا *ooṅ'chā sūn'nā* V.I. be hard of hearing ; be deaf ہاتھ اونچا ہونا *hāth ooṅ'chā ho'nā* V.T. have the upper hand be munificent اونچی دکان پھیکا پکوان *ooṅ'chī dūkān' phī'kā pakvān* PROV. great cry little wool اونچے بول کا منہ نیچا *ooṅ che bol' kā mūṅh' nī'chā* PROV. "pride goeth before a fall اونچائی *ooṅ'chā''ī* N.F. height ; altitude elevation loftiness tallness steepness اونچ نیچ *ooṅ'ch nīch'* N.F. inequality difference in social status vicissitudes ; ups and down high and low

اوندھا *auṅ'dhā* ADJ. (F. اوندھی *auṅ'dhī*) prove upside down ; inverted topsy-turvy perverted اوندھا لیٹنا *auṅ dhā leṭ'nā* V.I. lie face downward اوندھی کھوپڑی *auṅ'dhī khop'ṛī* ADJ. (fig.) stubbornness perversion

اونس *auṅs* N.M ounce ; oz. [E]

اونگنا *ooṅg'nā* V.T. grease the axle (esp. of ox-driven carriage) with tallow-coated jute

اونگھ *ooṅgh* N.F. dozing drowsiness sleepiness nod doze اونگھنا *ooṅgh'nā* V.I. feel drowsy doze off

اونہہ *ooṅh* INT. oh well

اوں ہوں *ooṅ'-hooṅ* INT. no ; never

اونی *oonī* ADJ. woollen اونی دھاگا (یا دھاگہ) *oo'nī dhāgā* (or *dhā'gah*) worsted knitting wool woollen yarn [~ اون]

اونی ادنی *oo'nī oo'nī* ADJ. idling ; wasting one's time

اونے پونے *au'ne pau'ne* ADV. more or less irrespective of loss or profit at a loss at the price offered at cut price

اوورسیر *o'var-sī''ar* N.M. overseer [E]

اوورکوٹ *o'var-koṭ'* N.M. overcoat [E]

اوورکوٹ

اوہام *auhām'* N.M. PL. superstitions apprehensions fear [A ~ SING. وہم]

oh INT. who cares never mind

اوہو *o'ho* INT. ho, hey

اوئی *oo''ī*, اوئی اللہ *oo''ī al'lah* INT. (W. dial.) Heaven forbid oh ;

اوير سوير *aver' saver'* ADV at all hours early or late

اہالی *ahā'lī* N.M. PL. residents of a place ; people ; inhibitants citizens اہالی موالی *ahā'lī mavālī* (ped. اہالی و موالی *ahā'lī-omavā'lī*) N.M. PL. dependents retinue [A ~ PL. of اہل]

اہانت *ihā'nat* N.F. affront ; insult slight slander contempt ; scorn اہانت کرنا *ihā'nat kar'nā* V. insult ; slight defame ; slander [A]

اہا ہا *ahā'-hā* INT. (expressing surprise, pleasure or pain) oh ; ah

اہتدا *ehtidā'* N.M. guidance [A ~ ہدایت]

اہتزاز *ehtizāz'* N.M. blowing (of wind), vibration rejoicing [A]

اہتمام *ehtimām* N.M. arrangement effort management administration supervision vigilance care [A]

اہرام *ahrām'* (or *aih-*) N.M. PL. pyramids pyramids (of Egypt) [A ~ ہرم]

اہر تہر *a'hir ta'hir* N.F. restlessness during approach of death ; pangs of death uneasiness

اہرمن *ah'raman* (or *aih-*) N.M. Zoroastrian god of darkness devil ; Satan [P]

اہرن *aih'ran* N.M. anvil

اہل *ai'hl* (ped. *ahl'*) N.M. fit capable worthy suitable deserving N.M. members of a family inhabitants citizens people followers master ; owners اہل اجتہاد *aih'l-e ejtihād'* N.M. PL. qualified jurists (of Islam) اہل اللہ *ahl-ūllāh'* N.M. PH. saints pious people اہل باطن *aih'l-e bā'tin* N.M. PL. saints pious people اہل بیت (اطہار) *aih'l-e bait'* (-*e athar'*) N.M. PL. members of the Holy Prophet's family comprising Hazrat Fatima, Hazrat Ali and their children (according to the Shi'ites) اہل التسنن *aih'l-e tasann'ūn* N.M. PL. Sunnis اہل تشیع *aih'l-e tash ay'yo'* N.M. PL. Shi'ites اہل تفسیر *aih'l-e tafsīr'* N.M. exegetical experts اہل حرفہ *aih'l-e hir'fah* N.M PL. workmen artificers ; artisans tradesmen اہل خانہ *aih'l-e khā'nah* N.M. members of the household ; owner N.F. wife N.M. PL family اہل خرد *aih'l-e khirad'* N.M. PL sages ; wise people اہل دل *aih'l-e dil'* N.M. PL. saints ; pious people اہل دنیا *aih'l-e dūn'yā* N.M. PL. worldly people laymen اہل دولت *aih'l-e dau'lat* N.M. PL. the rich the upper classes اہل ذوق *aih'l-e zauq'* N.M. PL. connoisseurs اہل زبان *aih'l-e zabān'* N.M. people whose mother tongue a particular language اہل زمین *aih'l-e zamīn'* (or *zīn'*) N.M. PL. inhabitants of the earth people of this world اہل زہد *aih'l-e zoh'd* N.M. PL. pious people ascetics اہل سخن *aih'l-e sakhūn'*) N.M. PL. poets eloquent persons litterateurs اہل سنت (والجماعت) *aih'l-e sūn'nat* (*val-jamā''at* N.M. PL. Sunnis اہل سیف *aih'l-e saif'* N.M. PL. swordsmen soldiers combatants اہل شرع *aih'l-e shar''* N.M. PL. observers of Islamic laws اہل صفا *aih'l-e safā'* N.M. PL. the pure in heart saints اہل صنعت *aih'l-e san''at* N.M. PL. workmen artisans tradesmen اہل طریقت *aih'l-e tarī'qat* N.M. PL. (first-stage) mystic اہل ظرف *aih'l-e zar'f* ADJ. magnanimous great اہل عرفان *aih'l-e 'irfān'* (or *'irfān*) N.M. PL. mystics people having a real understanding of the ways of God اہل عقل *aih'l-e 'aq'l* N.M. PL. wise men sagacious persons اہل علم *aih'l-e 'il'm* N.M. PL. the learned erudite persons scholars savants intellectuals intelligentsia اہل غرض *aih'l-e gha'raz* N.M. PL. interested persons selfish persons vested interests اہل فرنگ *aih'l-e farang'* N.M. PL. Europeans Westerners اہل فن *aih'l-e fan* N.M. PL. artists artistes اہل فکر *aih'l-e fik'r* N.M. PL. thinkers philosophers intellectuals intelligentsia اہل قبلہ *aih'l-e qib'lah* N.M. PL. Muslims اہل قلم *aih'l-e qa'lam* (or *-lam'*) N.M. PL. men of letters اہلکار *aihl-kār'* minor official public servant اہل کتاب *aih'l-e kitāb'* N.M. PL. people of the book (*i.e.*, Jews, Christians and Sabians) اہل کرم *aih'l-e ka'ram* N.M. PL. charitable people ; generous persons liberal people اہل کسب *aih'l-e kas'b* N.M. PL. tradesmen اہل مجلس *aih'l-e maj'lis* N.M. PL. participants of a meeting members of a society اہلمد *aih'l-mad* N.M. minor court official office in charge اہل معرفت *aih'l-e ma''rifat* N.M. PL. people with an intimate knowing knowledge of God saints اہل مقدمہ *aih'l-e mūqad'damah* N.M. PL. parties to a suit اہل منصب *aih'l-e man'sab* N.M. PL. officers dignitaries اہل نظر *aih'l-e nazar* discerning people far sighted persons worshippers (of beauty) اہل نفاق *aih'l-e nifāq'* N.M. PL. hypocrites اہل ورع *aih'l-e var''* N.M. PL. holy ; godly pious people ascetics اہل وعیال *aih'l-o 'ayāl'* N.M. PL. family اہل ہنر *aih'l-e hū'nar* (or *nar'*) N.M. PL. artisans skilled worker

اہلاً و سہلاً مرحبا *ah'lan va-sah'lan mar'habā* INT

welcome اہلیت *aihliy'yat* N.F. worth capability aptitude skill possession اہلیہ *aihliy'yah* N.F. wife [A]

اہلے گہلے *aih'le gaih'le* ADV. coquetishly اہلے گہلے پھرنا *aih'le gaih'le phir'nā* V.I. move about coquetishly

اہم *aham'* ADJ. most important urgent pressing grave significant momentous ; stupendous اہم امور *aham' ūmoor'* N.M. PL. important affairs ; matters of import اہمیت *ahammīy'yat* (COL. *aih'miyat*) N.F. importance gravity significance [A]

اہنسا *ahin'sā* N.F. (dial.) non-violence 'ahimsa

اہیر *ahīr* N.M. cowherd this as a caste

ائتلاف *e'tilāf'* N.M. amity friendship association connection alliance unity [A ~ الفت]

ائمہ *a'im'mah* N.M. PL. leaders religious leaders [A ~ SING. امام]

اے *ai* VOCATIVE PARTICLE oh O اے کاش *ai kāsh'* INT. would to God ! O, how I wish اے ہے *ai hai* INT. O

ایاز *ayāz'* N.M. name of the first Muslim Governor of Lahore who was originally a trusted slave of Mahmud of Ghazna محمود و ایاز *maihmoo'd'o ayāz* N.M. PL. loving pair ایاز قدر خود بشناس *ayāz' qad'r-e khūd bi-shinās* PROV. know thy worth, man one should not forget one's humble beginnings [T]

ایاغ *ayāgh* N.M. wine-cup ; wine glass [T]

ایال *ayāl* N.F mane [P]

ایالت *iyā'lat* N.F. governorship government sway ; domination [A]

ایام *ayyām'* N.M. PL. days time period duration menstural period (rare) wars ; battles engagements ایام بیض *ayyā'm-e bīz'* N.M. PL. thirteenth, fourteenth and fifteenth nights of a lunar month (as the brightest nights) ایام سے ہونا *ayyām' se ho'nā* V.I. menstruate have the menses ایام مستی *ayyā'm-e mas'tī* N.M. PL. heat period [A ~ SING. یوم]

ایامی *ayā'mā* N.M. (or F.) (PL. of ایم ★)

ایبک *ai'bak* (rare *i-*) N.M slave messenger appellations of two famous Muslim kings (one ruling India, the other Egypt) [T]

ایتام *aitām* N.M. PL. orphans [A ~ SING. یتیم]

ایٹم *ai'ṭam* N.M. atom ایٹم بم *aiṭam bam* N.M. atom bomb [E]

ایثار *īsār'* N.M. selflessness [A]

ایجاب *ījāb'* N.M. assent proposal (by one of the parties to a bargain) positiveness ایجاب و قبول *ījā'b-o qabool'* N.M. proposal and consent (in matrimonial negotiations) ایجابی *ījā'bī* ADJ. positive affirmative ایجابیت *ījabiy'yat* N.F. positivism [A]

ایجاد *ījād'* N.M. invention contrivance contraption (lit.) creation ایجاد کرنا *ījād' kar'nā* V.T. invent devise originate creat ایجاد ہونا *ījād' ho'nā* V.I. be created [A ~ وجود]

ایجاز *ījāz'* N.M. brevity [A]

ایجنٹ *e'janṭ* N.M. agent ایجنسی *e'jansī* N.F. agency [E]

ایجنڈا *ejan'ḍā* N.M. agenda [E]

ایجوکیشن *ai'jookeshan* N.F education

ایچ پیچ *ech' pech*, (col. اینچ پینچ *ench' pench*) N.M. complication fraud ; deceit crooked ways ایچ پیچ کی باتیں *ech' pech kī ba'teṅ* N.F. crookedness double dealings ایچ پیچ نہ جاننا *ech' pech na jān'nā* V.I be straightforward have straight dealings

ایڈریس *aiḍ'ras* N.F address [E]

ایڈوانس *aiḍvāns* اڈوانس *aḍvāns* N.M. advance [E]

ایڈوکیٹ *aiḍ'vokeṭ* N.M. advocate [E]

ایڈہاک *aiḍ hāk'* ADV 'ad hoc' [E]

ایڈیٹر *ai'ḍiṭar*, اڈیٹر *aḍī'ṭar* N.M. editor *aiḍīṭo'riyal* N.M. & ADJ. editorial [E]

ایڈیشن *aiḍī'shan*, اڈیشن *aḍī'shan* N.M. edition [E]

ایڈیشنل *aiḍīsh'nal*, اڈیشنل *aḍish'nal* ADJ. additional [E]

ایڈی کانگ *a'ḍī kāng* N.M. aide-de camp [E ~ F]

ایذا *īzā'* N.F. affliction pain trouble distress vexation ; annoyance oppression ایذا دینا *īzā de'nā* V.T. afflict injure hurt pain annoy ; vex ایذارساں *īzā'-rasāṅ'* ADJ. vexatious troublesome annoying oppressing ایذارسانی *īzā'-rasā'nī* N.F. causing harm ; doing injury [A ~ اذیت]

ایرا پھیری *e'rā phe'rī* N.F. fraud shady deal (rare) exchange

ایراد *īrād'* N.M. (PL. ایرادات *īrādāt'*) objection [A ~ ورود]

ایرا غیرا نتھو خیرا *ai'rā ghai'rā (nat'thoo khairā)* N.M. Tom, Dick and Harry the scum of society

ایران *īrān'* N.M. Persia ; Iran ایرانی *īrā'nī* ADJ. & N.M. Persian ; Iranian [P]

ایڑ *eṛ* N.F. spur ایڑ لگانا *eṛ lagā'nā* V.T. spur ; urge (a horse) [~ FOLL.]

ایڑی *e'ṛī* N.F. heal ایڑی چوٹی کا زور لگانا *eṛī cho'ṭī kā zor lagā'nā* PH. strain every nerve ایڑی دیکھو *e'ṛī de'kho* PH. may the evil eye have no effect ایڑی سے چوٹی تک *e'ṛī se cho'ṭī tak* PH. from head to foot ; from top to toe (or bottom ایڑیاں رگڑنا *e'riyāṅ ra'garnā* V.I. (fig.) be in straitened circumstances ; pass through hard times be helpless

ایزاد *īzād'* N.M. addition (of) ایزاد کرنا *īzād' kar'nā* V.I. add [pseuda A ~ زیادہ]

ایزد *e'zad* N.M. God ایزدی *e'zadī* ADJ. divine ; heavenly [P]

ایسا *ai'sā* ADJ. (F. ایسی *ai'sī*) such like like this resembling ایسا ویسا *ai'sā vai'sā* ADJ. (F. ایسی ویسی *ai'sī vai'sī*) inferior indecent ; smutty so-so ایسی تیسی *ai'sī tai'sī* (vulg.) PH. to hell with ایسی تیسی کرنا *ai'sī tai'sī kar'nā* V.T. do one's worst ایسے میں *ai'se meṅ* ADV. at this juncture in these circumstances ایسے ہی *ai'se hī'* ADV. so to speak ; accidently ; casually ; by the way ADJ. so-so INT. why ; how

ایسٹر *īs'ṭar* N.M. Easter [E]

ایسوسی ایشن *aiso'sīe'shan* N.F. association [E]

ایشور *īsh'var* N.M. (Hindu word for) God [S]

ایشیا *e'shiyā* N.M. Asia ایشیائی *eshiyā''ī* ADJ. Asiatic ; Asian PREF. Asio- [E]

ایصال *īsāl'* N.M. conveying conduction ایصال ثواب *īsā'l-e savāb'* N.M. conveying reward of virtuous deed or rite ایصال حرارت *īsā'l-e harā'rat* N.M. conduction of heat [A ~ وصل]

ایضاً *aizan* ADV. ditto [A]

ایطا *īṭā'* N.M. repetition of rhyme [A]

ایفا *īfā'* N.F. fulfilment observance return execution ایفائے ڈگری *īfā'-e ḍig'rī* N.F. satisfaction ایفائے عہد *īfā'-e 'ah'd* (or-*'aih'd*) N.M. fulfilment of promise ; honouring one's word [A ~ وفا]

ایقان *īqān'* N.M. knowing for a fact certainty faith [A ~ یقین]

ایک *ek* ADJ. one only single sole a certain one singular unique ایک آدھ *ek' ādh* ADJ. some just a few N.M. a half ایک آدھ بار *e'k ādh bār* PH. once or twice ایک (ہی) آدھ جگہ *ek' (hī) ādh ja'gah* PH. (just) at one place ایک انڈا وہ بھی گندا *ek' anḍā voh' bhī gan'dā* PROV. but one egg and that addled ; the only child turning out to be good-for-nothing ایک بار *ek' bār* ADV. once at one time once upon a time all suddenly ایکبارگی *ek-bār'gī* ADV. suddenly ; all of a sudden all at once simultaneously ایک پیٹ کے *ek' peṭ ke* ADJ. uterine (brother or sister) ایک تال *ek tāl'* N.M. harmony unison ; concord ایک جان *ek jān'* ADJ. of one mind intimate well-mixed ایک دل *ek' dil* ADJ. unanimous of one mind of one accord ایک دل ہو کر *ek' dil ho kar* ADV. like one man solidly, unanimously ایک دم (سے) *ek dam' (se)* ADV. instantly ; immediately forthwith ایک زبان ہونا *ek zabān' ho'nā* V.I. be of one accord be unanimous سدا ایک سے دن نہ رہنا *sa'dā ek' se din na raih'nā* PH. (of fortune) have vicissitudes ایک کی دس سنانا *ek kī das' sunā'nā* V.I. to retaliate much more sharply ایک ماں باپ کے *ek' māṅ' bāp ke* ADJ. (of children) born of the same parents ایک مشت *ek mush't* ADJ. lump sum entire ADV. entirely ; in lump sum ایک نہ ایک *ek' na ek* ADJ. one or the other ایک ہی *ek' hī* ADJ. only one ; solitary unique ADV. very ; extremely

ایکا *e'kā* N.M. unity alliance pact friendship unity of interest

ایکا ایکی *e'kā e'kī* ADV. all of a sudden suddenly unexpectedly [~ P یکایک CORR.]

ایکٹ *aik'ṭ* N.M. act (of law) act (of drama) ایکٹر *aic'ṭar* N.M. actor ایکٹرس *aik'-ṭares* N.F. actress ایکٹنگ N.F. acting ; action [E]

ایکسٹرا *aik'ṭsrā* ADJ. extra N.F. extra girl ; extra [E]

ایکسرے *aik's re* N.F. X-ray ایکسرے کرنا *aik's re kar'nā* V.T. X-ray [E]

ایکھ *īkh* N.F. (same as اوکھ N.F. ★)

ایلچی *el'chī* N.M. envoy ; ambassador . emissary [T]

ایلوا *el'vā* N.M. aloe

ایلوپیتھی *ailopaithī* N.F. allopathy [E]

ایلومینیم *ailominiyam* المونیم *ailmo-niyam* N.M. aluminium [E]

ایم *ay'yim* N.M. widowed person ایامی *ayā'mā* N.M. PL. widowed persons [A]

ایما *īmā'* N.M. sign hint suggestion ; instance intention assent کے ایما پر *ke īmā par* PH. at the instance or suggestion of [A]

ایمان *īmān'* N.M. faith ; religion belief creed confidence trustworthiness integrity ایمان بیچنا *īmān bech'nā* V.I. betray one's faith (or truth) ایمان دار *īmān'-dār* ADJ. faithful honest ; upright ; conscientious trustworthy true loyal ایمانداری *īmān'-dā'rī* N.F. faith faithfulness constancy integrity ; honesty ; uprightness trustworthiness conscientiousness ایمان سے *īmān' se* INT. & ADV. by God ایمان سے کہنا *īmān' se kaih'nā* V.I. depose ایمان لانا *īmān' lā'nā* V.I. believe accept a faith ; enter the fold of a religion ایمان میں خلل آنا *īmān' meṅ kha'lal ā'nā* V.I. prove faithless fall pray to temptation [A ~ امن]

ایمبولینس *aim'boolans*, ایمبولنس *aim'-boolans* N.F. ambulance [E]

ایمن *e'man* ADJ. most happy auspicious [P ~ A امن]

2 ایمن *e'man* N.M. name of a musical mode [S]

3 ایمن *ai'man* N.M. right-hand ADJ. right ; right hand وادیٔ ایمن *vā'dī-e ai'man* N.F. Sinai Valley lying to the right of the mountain where Moses had a glimpse of God [A ~ یمین]

امونیا *aimo'niyā* N.F. ammonia امونیم *aimo'nīyam* N.M. ammonium [E]

ایں *aiṅ* INT. (expressing surprise) oh; O

ایں *īṅ* ADJ. (only in combinations) this ایں جانب *īṅ'jā'nib* PRON. I ; we

اینٹ *īṅṭ* N.F. brick ingot any bricklike thing اینٹ کی چنائی *īṅṭ' kī chunā''ī* N.F. brickwork اینٹ سے اینٹ بجانا *īṅṭ' se īṅṭ bajā'nā* V. destroy demolish work havoc with اینٹ کا جواب پتھر سے دینا *īṅṭ' kā javāb' pat'thar se de'nā* V.T. give blow for blow give tit for tat rataliate sharply اپنی ڈیڑھ اینٹ کی مسجد الگ بنانا *ap'nī ḍeṛh' īṅṭ kī mas'jid alag' banā'nā* V.I. (fig.) recede show schismatic tendencies

اینٹھن *aiṅ'ṭhan* N.F. convulsion contortion gripe colic arrogance obstinacy اینٹھنا *aiṅṭh'nā* V.I. strut , swagger be offended contort tighten stiffen

اینچا تانی *eṅ'chā tā'nī*, کھینچا تانی *kheṅ'chā tā'nī* N.F. struggle tension

ایندھن *īṅ'dhan* N.M. fuel firewood

اینڈ *aīṅḍ* ADJ. unfinished اینڈ ہونا *aīṅḍ ho'nā* V.I. be unfinished

اینڈنا *aīṅḍ'nā* V.T. strut ; swagger walk affectedly اینڈ کر *aīṅḍ kar* ADV. with a swaggering gait

اینڈوا *īṅd'vā* N.M. اینڈوی *īṅdvī* N.F. circular pod for supporting weight on head

اینڈی بینڈی *aiṅ'ḍī baiṅ'ḍī* ADJ. (of talk) silly nonsense rude crooked اینڈی بینڈی سنانا *aiṅ'ḍī baiṅ'ḍī sunā'nā* V.T. abuse ; call names ; swear (at) talk rudely

ایوان *aivān'* (Arabicized as *īvān'*) N.M. (PL. ایوانات *īvānāt'*) palace court hall; gallery House ایوان بالا (یا زیریں) *aivā'n-e bā'lā* (or *zeriṅ*) Upper (or Lower) House (of Legislature [P]

ایوب *ay'yoob'* N.M. Job صبر ایوب (یا ایوبی) *sab'r-e ayyoob'* (or *ayyoo'bī*) PH. Job's patience (fig.) great patience (fig.) forbearance [A ~ H]

ایہام *īhām'* N.M. 'double-entendre' ambiguity [A ~ وہم]

ب

ب *be* second letter of Urdu alphabet (equivalent to English *b*) (in 'jummal'). 2 ; two

با *bi* PREF. (usu. before Arabic article as PR. *bil* or *bi*+consonant following (ال) by with from in into on for towards near according to (11) I swear by (12) be ransom for بابی انت و امی *bi-abī' an'ta va um'mī* PH. my parents be ransom for; non are dearer to me than even my kith and kin بالاتفاق *bil-it'tifāq'* ADV. unanimously with one voice with a concensus of opinion بالاجمال *bil-ijmāl'* ADV. briefly ; in brief ; in short بالارادہ *bil-irā'dah* ADV. deliberately ; intentionally purposely ; on purpose voluntarily بالتخصیص *bit-takhsīs'* ADV. specially particularly بالتصریح *bit-tasrīh'* ADV. explicitly specifically . expressly distinctly in detail ; at length بالتفصیل bil-tafsīl' ADV. at length in detail ; detailed بالجبر bil-jab'r ADV. forcibly violent under duress ADJ. forced بالجملہ bil-jum'lah ADV. on the whole ; altogether in a word ; in short ; briefly بجنسہٖ bi-jin'si-hī ADJ. identical the same ADV. exactly ; precisely بالخیر bil-khair' ADV. well happily in a good manner ADJ. good welcome propitious (iron.) unlawful; illegitimate unwelcome بالضرور biz-zaroor' ADV. necessarily inevitably certainly definitely بالعکس bil-'ak's ADV. on the other hand on the contrary ; contrariwise بالعموم bil-'umoom' ADV. generally commonly universally بعینہٖ bi-'ai'nihī ADV. exactly precisely ADJ. the same بالفرض bil-far'z ADV. supposing granted ; granting that ; admitting for the sake of argument hypothetically speaking بالفعل bil-fe''l ADV. now ; at present in fact ; actually ADJ. active real بالکل bil'-kul ADV. entirely ; wholly ; completely ADJ. all بالکل ٹھیک bil'-kul ṭhīk PH. all right بالکلیہ bil kulliy'yah ADV. as a general principle باللہ bil-lāh' ADV. by God بالمشافہ bil-mushā' fahah' ADV. face to face ; 'vis-a-vis' بالمقابل bil-muqā'bil N.M. adversary ADV.. opposite facing بالمقابلہ bil-muqā'-balah ADV. as compared (to) ; in comparison (with) [A]

ب bi PREF. (used for emphasis before certain Persian tenses) do [P]

ب ba PREF. (used before nouns) (joined to the next letter or written as بہ) with by for from to up to into in on upon بافراط ba-ifrāt' ADV. in abundance ADJ. abundant plenty بپا ba-pā' ADV. on foot ; afoot going on ; being held ; proceeding بتدریج ba-tadrīj' ADV. gradually ; by degrees بتصریحات ذیل ba-tasrīhā't-e zail' ADV. with (the following) remarks بجواب ba-javāb'(-e) ADV. in reply (to) ; in response (to) inspired بحساب ba-hisāb'(-e) ADV. at the rate (of) in the proportion (of) according (to) in the name (of) ; debited to the account (of) بحق ba-haq'q(-e) ADV. in favour of in the matter of ; in the case of on account of بحکم ba-huk'm (-e) ADV. under the orders (of) by command (of) by authority (of) بخلاف ba-khilāf', برخلاف bar khilāf' ADV. contrary (to) in opposition (to) بخوبی ba-khoo'bī ADV. well nicely ; in a good manner thoroughly with grace ; gracefully بخوشی ba-khū'shī ADV. with pleasure ; gladly cheerfully by all means as you like it بخیر ba-khair' ADV. in safety in peace well ADJ. (in salutation) good night, etc.) بدرجہ ba-da' rajah (-e) ADV. in a degree بدرجۂ اقل ba-da'raja-e aqal ADV. at least بدرجۂ اولیٰ bada'raja-e oo'lā ADV. in the first place بدستور ba-dastoor' ADV. as usual in the usual manner unchanged بدقت ba-diq'qat ADV. with difficulty بدقت تمام ba-diq'qat-e tamām' ADV. with great difficulty بدل ba-dil', بدل و جان ba-dil-o-jān' ADV. with all one's heart ; from the core of one's heart not just outwardly کی بدولت kī ba-dau'lat ADV. through by means of by dint of بدون ba-doon' PREP. except ; save without lacking ; wanting for want (of) بزور ba-zor' ADV. perforce by force ; orcibly ; under duress بسبب ba-sabab' ADV. because (of) ; by reason (of) on account (of) بسر و چشم ba-sa'r-o chash'm ADV. by all means most whillingly بسلسلہ ba-sil'silah(-e) ADV. in continuation (of) as a sequel to بشدت ba-shid'dat ADV. fully ; in full measure forcefully severely very much بشرطیکہ ba-shar'te-keh ADV. if in case on condition that provided that ; with the proviso that بصد ba-sad' ADV. with much بصورت ba-soo'rat(-e) ADV. by way (of) in case (of) ; in the event (of) in the manner (of) بصورت خلاف ورزی ba-soo'rat-e khilāf'-var'zī in case of breach (of) بصیغہ ba-sī'ghah(-e) ADV. the department (of) on the (civil, etc.) side بضد ہونا ba-zid' ho'nā V.I. stubbornly insist بطرز ba-tar'z ADV. in the manner (of) in the form (of) بطور ba-taur' (-e) ADV. as in the capacity (of) after the manner (of) بطور خود ba-tau'r-e khud ADV. of one's own accord voluntarily in one's own way on one's own account بظاہر ba-zā'hir ADV. apparently outwardly ostensibly بعوض ba-'ivaz' in exchange (for) in place (of) in lieu (of) ; instead (of) بعون ba-'aun'(-e) ADV. by the help (of) ; with the assistance (of) بعینہٖ bi'ai'nihī ADV. exactly بغیر ba-ghair' ADV. without except ; save lacking ; wanting بقدر ba-qa'dar (or ba-qad'r(-e) ADV. to the extent (of) by the power (of) according (to) in the measure (of) بقول ba-qual'(-e) ADV. according (to) on the authority (of) in the words (of) بکار ba-kār'(-e) ADJ. useful ; serviceable PREP. for on behalf (of) بکار سرکار ba-kā'r-e sarkār' PH. on official duty state service بکار دولت پاکستان ba-kā'r-e dau'lat-e pā'kistān PH. on

State service بکثرت ba-kas'rat ADJ. plentiful ; abundant ADV. in abundance بمجرد ba-mūjar'rad ADV. instantly immediately forthwith بمرتبہ ba-mar'tabah ADV. to some extent ; in a degree to the extent (of) بمقتضائے ba-mūqtazā'-e ADV. in consequence of owing to because of for reasons of بمنزلہ ba-man'zilah ADV. in the place (of); instead (of) of the status (of) بموجب ba-moo'jib ADV. by reason (of) in pursuance (of) in accordance (with); according (to) ; in conformity (with) as per by under بنام ba-nām' ADV. in the name (of) to بہ نسبت ba-nis'bat ADV. in comparison (with) ; compared (to) than بوجہ ba-vaj'h ADV. for ; because (of) ; by reason (of) ; owing (to) بہ یک کرشمہ دو کار ba yak' kirish'mah do kār' PH. kill two birds with one stone [P]

با bā PREP. by ; with possessing ; having با اصول bā-ūsool' ADJ. principled (man) of principles با اصولی bā-ūsoo'lī N.F. acting on one's principles being principled با اینکہ bā-īn'-keh, با آنکہ bā-āṅ'-keh ADV. notwithstanding that ; in spite of that despite that بااثر ba-a'sar ADJ. influential effectual efficacious بااختیار ba-ikhtiyār ADJ. in authority ; weilding power powerful authorized بااخلاص bā-ikhlās' ADJ. sincere ; cordial باادب bā-adab' ADJ. respectful polite ; well-mannered INT. (also) باادب باملاحظہ ہوشیار ba-adab' bā-mūlā'ḥazah hoshyār') Gentleman please rise in your seats (His Majesty, etc. arrives) باندازہ bā-andā'zah ADJ. & ADV. moderate(ly) proportionate(ly) according to measure باایمان bā īmān' ADJ. honest pious religious faithful باایں ہمہ bā-īn'-hamah' ADV. in spite of all that ; despite all that باتدبیر bā-tadbīr' ADJ. wise discreet ; prudent resourceful باتمیز bā-tamīz' ADJ. civilized ; cultured polite ; courteous ; civil sensible ; wise باحیا bā ḥayā' ADJ. modest bashful باخبر bā-kha'bar ADJ. well-informed ; well-posted not stupid باخدا bā-khūdā' ADJ. godly religious pious باشعور bā-shū'oor' ADJ. well-mannered wise ; intelligent shrewd ; sagacious باضابطہ bā-zā'bitah ADV. formal official ; in accordance with law (etc.) بافراغت bā farā'ghat ADJ. (man) of means ADV. leisurely in a satisfactory manner باقاعدہ bā-qā''idah ADJ. regular formal ; official procedural in accordance with law (etc.) باقرینہ bā-qarī'nah ADJ. well-arranged بامروت bā-mūrūv'vat ADJ. obliging generous kind humane بامزہ bā-ma'zah ADJ. tasteful delicious کے باوجود ke bā vūjood' PREP. in spite of ; despite باوجودیکہ bā-vūjoo'de-keh ADV. although notwithstanding ; in spite of the fact that ; despite the fact that باوردی bā-var'dī ADJ. in uniform liveried کے باوصف ke bā-vas'f PREP. notwithstanding in spite of ; despite باوضع bā-vaz'' ADJ. sticking to habits snobbish civilized ; cultured civil ; polite true ; loyal ; faithful باوضو bā-vū'zoo ADJ. having performed the ablutions

باب bāb N.M. chapter door ; gate topic; head subject ; affair ; kind اس باب میں is bāb meṅ PH. with regard to this ; in this matter [A]

بابا bā'bā N.M. old man grandfather father (CORR. of) baby بابا آدم کے زمانے کا bā'ba ā'dam ke zamā'ne kā ADJ. old ; ancient antiquated outdated ; outmoded باباجان bābā jān N.M. dear grandfather dear daddy pop بابا لوگ bā'ba log N.M.SING. or PL. (CORR. of) baby mendicant(s) [P]

بابت bā'bat PREP. usu. used as PH. کی بابت kī bā'bat PREP. as regards regarding ; about [~A باب]

بابر bā'būr N.M. lion (as appellation of an Indo-Pakistan Moghul ruler) [T]

بابل bā'būl N.M. father

بابل bā'bil N.M. Babylon ; (Bib.) Babel [A]

بابو bā'boo (endearingly or respectfully بابوجی bā'boo-jī N.M. clerk father ; daddy lord Mr.

بابونہ bāboo'nah N.M. camomile ; wild ivy [P]

بابی bā'bī N.M. (also بابیت bā-biy'yat) name of a heresy of Islam Babi faith follower of this heresy [~ founder's appellation باب A]

باپ bāp N.M. father باپ بنانا bāp' banā'nā V.T. regard (someone) as one's father cajole wheedle باپ تک پہنچنا (یا جانا) bāp' tak pahūṅch'na (or jā'nā) PH. go to the extent of abusing (someone's) father باپ دادا bāp' dā'dā N.M. forefather ; ancestors ; progenitors باپ رے bāp' re, باپ رے باپ bāp' re bāp INT. (expressing surprise ; fear, etc.) dear, dear dear ; dear me help mercy باپ کا نوکر bāp' kā nau'kar N.M. (met.) humble servant باپ مارے کا بیر bāp' *ma're ka bair'* PH. family feud ; longstanding enmity باپ دادا *bap da'da* N.M. forefathers ; ancestors elders باپ دادا کا نام روشن کرنا *bap da'da ka nam raushan kar'na* V.T. & I. bring credit to one's ancestors be a source of pride to one's family (iron.) bring a bad name to one's family باپو *ba'poo* N.M. (dial.) father

بات *bat* N.F. matter affair subject ; topic issue ; question word saying speech ; discourse ; talk news gossip story ; tale ; account point ; particular (11) proposal ; proposition (12) substance (13) taunt (14) advice (15) occurrence ; happening بات بات میں *bat' bat' men* ADV. every time ; on every occasion in every particular بات بدلنا *bat ba'dalna* V.I. back out of one's word بات بڑھانا *bat barha'na* V.T. prolong a dispute بات بگاڑنا *bat bigar'na* V.T. ruin one's credit mar (someone's) plan bring disgrace بات بنانا *bat bana'na* V.I. tell tales concoct a story کی بات بننا *ki bat ban'na* V.I. prosper ; flourish succeed بات نہ پچنا *bat' na pach'na* V.I. be unable to keep a secret بات پکڑنا *bat pa'karna* V.T. carp at ; cavil at بات پکی کرنا *bat pak'ki kar'na* V.I. have (something) confirmed confirm contract سے بات پوچھنا *se bat poochh'na* V.T. ask question inquire from کی بات پوچھنا *ki bat poochh'na* V.T. inquire after (someone's) health or welfare express concern for welcome show due respect to بات پھیرنا *bat pher'na* V.I. change the topic equivocate ; prevaricate بات پھیلانا *bat phaila'na* V.T. give currency to a report ; spread a rumour بات پھیلنا *bat phail'na* V.I become the talk of the town be talked about ; be bruited about or abroad بات پی جانا *bat pi' ja'na* V.I. put up with an insult ; pocket an insult bear without demur hide a secret بات پیدا کرنا *bat pai'da kar'na* V.I. attain excellence create something new put up an excuse بات ٹالنا *bat tal'na* V.I. evade or dodge (an issue or insult) put off بات ٹھنڈی پڑنا *bat than'di par'na* V.I. be shelved ; be put in cold storage بات ٹھنڈی پڑنے دینا *bat than'di par'ne de'na* V.T. allow the matter to cool down بات ٹھہرنا *bat thai'harna* V.I. be engaged be settled بات ٹھہرانا *bat thaihra'na* V.I. make a settlement arrive at a decision betroth کی بات جانا *ki bat' ja'na* V.I. be disgraced ; lose one's credit بات جمانا *bat jama'na* V.T bring someone) round to one's viewpoint بات چبا جانا *bat chaba' ja'na* V.I. swallow one's word بات چلانا *bat chala'na* V.T. cut the ice initiate (a subject) in discussion بات چیت *bat' chit* N.F. chat gossip talk ; conversation negotiations , parleys بات چیت کرنا *bat' chit kar'na* V.I. chat gossip talk converse have negotiations ; have parleys بات دہرانا *bat dohra'na* V.T. repeat recapitulate کی بات رہنا (یا رہ جانا) *ki bat' raih'na* (or *raih ja'na*) V.I. have the upper hand prevail succeed بات کا بتنگڑ بنانا *bat ka batan'gar bana'na* V.I. exagerate awfully ; make mountains out of molehills بات کا پکا (یا پورا یا سچا) *bat ka pak ka* (or *poo'ra* or *sach'cha*) ADJ. true to one's word; as good as as one's word بات کاٹنا *bat' kat'na* V.T. cut in بات کا سر پیر نہ ہونا *bat ka sir' pair na ho'na* V.I. (of words, etc.) be irrelevant be baseless ; be unfounded be illogical بات کان پڑنا *bat kan' par'na* V.I. hear ; learn بات کرتے پتھر مارنا *bat' kar'te pat'thar mar'na* V. talk rudely give a curt reply بات کو کھٹائی میں ڈالنا *bat ko khata''i men dal'na* V.T. defer ; postpone ; procrastinate put in cold-storage ; shelve بات کھلنا *bat' khul'na* V.I. (of secret) be out ; be laid bare بات کھونا (یا کھو دینا) *bat kho'na* (or *kho de'na*) V.I. lose credit ; injure (one's) prestige بات کھولنا *bat khol'na* V.T. have a straight talk reveal or disclose (a secret) بات کہی پرائی ہوئی *bat' ka'hi para''i hu'i* PROV. a word spoken is an arrow let fly بات کیے پھول جھڑنا *bat' ki'ye phool' jhar'na* V.I. be eloquent be soft-spoken بات گھڑنا *bat' ghar'na* V.T. fabricate forge ; trump up (excuse, story, etc.) بات لاکھ کی کرنی خاک کی *bat lakh' ki, karni khak' ki* PROV. roaring clouds seldom rain بات ماننا *bat' man'na* V.I. obey accept a suggestion بات میں سے بات نکلنا *bat' men se bat' nikal'na* V.T. bring out fresh point(s) بات میں سے بات نکالنا *bat' men se bat nikal'na* V.I. (of fresh points) emerge from talk بات میں فی نکالنا *bat men fi' nikal'na* V.T. cavil at pick holes in an argument (etc.) باتوں میں آنا *ba'ton men a'na* V.I. be taken in ; be gulled ; be duped باتوں میں اڑانا *ba'ton men ura'na* V.T. talk (someone) out of his wits ridicule ; hold to ridicule باتوں میں بہلانا *ba'ton men baihla'na* V.T. delude with fair words باتوں میں لگانا *ba'ton men laga'na* V.T. engage (someone) in conversation divert (someone's) attention باتیں سنانا *ba'ten suna'na* V.I. talk repeat one's story relate one's adventure abuse ; revil reprove ; reproach باتیں سننا *ba'ten sun'na* V.I. listen lend ears eaves drop put up with unpleasant remarks have to listen to reproof باتونی *batoo'nī* ADJ. & N.M. talkative or garrulous (person) باتونی پن *batoo'nī pan* N.F. talkativeness ; garrulity

باٹ[1] *bāṭ* N.M. weight باٹ اور ترازو *bāṭ aur tarā'zoo* N.M. weights and scales

باٹ[2] *bāṭ* N.F. path

باج *bāj* N.M. tribute (rare) tax باج گزار *bāj-gūzār'* ADJ. N.M. one who pays tribute ; tax-payer ADJ. feudatory ; tributary [P]

باجا *bā'jā* N.M. musical instrument باجا گاجا *bā'jā gā'jā* N.M music musical instrument

باجرا *bāj'rā* N.M. millet (rare) drizzle باجرا برسنا *bāj'rā ba' rasnā* V.I. drizzle باجرے کی سی بارش *bāj're kī sī bā'rish* V.T drizzle

باجنا *bāj'nā* V.T. (dial.) (of musical instrument, etc.) sound

باجی *bā'jī* N.F sister ; elder sister [T]

باچھ *bāchh* N.F. corner of the mouth assessment of share of tax or subscription باچھ ڈالنا *bāchh ḍāl'nā* V.I. levy tax , raise by subscription باچھیں آنا *bā'chheṅ ā'nā* V.I. have an inflamation at the corners of the mouth باچھیں کھلنا (یا کھل جانا) *bā'chheṅ khil'nā* (or *khil jā'nā*) V.I. laugh ; laugh loudly smile burst with joy be satisfied be overjoyed

باختر *bākh'tar* N.M. west Bactria [P]

باختہ *bākh'tah* SUF. played beaten (at play lost (by gambling) having lost ; deprived of [P ~ باختن]

باد *bād* N.F wind breeze air بادبان *bād-bān'* poet(also بادباں *bād'-bāṅ*) N.M. sail بادپا *bād-pā'* ADJ. fast , swift N.M. courser بادپیما *bād-paimā'* ADJ. fast ; swift N.M. aerometer courser idle talker one who builds castles in the air بادتند *bād-e tūn'd* N.F. windstorm tempestuous gale بادرفتار *bād-raftār'* ADJ. swift N.M. courser بادرنگ *bād-rang'* (CORR. as باد رنگ *bā''o barang'*) N.M. a cucumber-like drug root بادسموم *bād-e samoom'* N.F. simoom بادسنج *bād'-sanj* N.M. air guage one who builds castles in the air بادشرط *bād-e shūr't* N.F. favourable wind ; fair wind بادصبا *bād-e sabā'* N.F. the zephyr morning breeze بادفرنگ *bād-e farang'* N.F. syphilis بادفروش *bād-firosh'* N.M. flatterer ; sycophant بادفروشی *bād-firo'shī* N F. sycophancy بادکش *bād kash* N.M. ventilator exhaust fan بادگرد *bād-gard*, گرد باد *gird'-bād* N.M. whirlwind بادمخالف *bād-e mūkhā'lif* N.F. contrary wind بادمراد *bād-e mūrād'* N.F. fair wind بادموافق *bād-e mo''ā'fiq* N.M. favourable wind ; fair wind بادنما *bād-nūmā'* N.M. weathercock ; vane [P]

بادام *badām'* N.M. almond بادامی *badā'mī* ADJ. almond almond shaped light brown ; nut-brown بادامی آنکھ *badā'mī aṅ'kheṅ* N.F. PL. almond-shaped eyes

بادشاہ *bādshāh'* (also پادشاہ *pādshāh'*) N.M. king ; sovereign ruler magnate highest name (in) بادشاہ زادہ *bād'shāh-zā'dah* N.M. (arch.) prince بادشاہ زادی *bād'shāhzā'dī* N.F (arch.) princess , sister or wife of a prince بادشاہ گر *bad shāh-gar* ADJ. & N.M. king-maker بادشاہت *bādshā'hat* N.F. kingship sovereignty realm ; kingdom ; empire بادشاہی *bādshā'hī* N.F. reign ; rule ; sovereignty kingship realm , kingdom empire ADJ royal regal ; imperial [P]

بادل *bā'dal* N.M. cloud بادل آنا *bā'dal ā'nā* V I. be cloudy بادل چھانا *bā'dal chhā'nā* V.I. be cloudy ; be overcast with clouds بادل گرجنا *bā'dal ga'raj'nā* V. I. (of clouds) thunder [P]

بادلا *bād'lā* بادلہ *bād'lah* N.M. brocade gold or silver thread

بادنجان *bā'datjān* N.M. brinjal [P]

بادہ *bā'dah* N.M. liquor , wine , spirits ; strong drinks ; drink بادہ پرست *bā'da-parast'* ADJ. & N.M. drunkard ; toper بادہ پرستی *bā'da-paras'tī* N.F. intemperance ; fondness for liquor بادہ کش *bā'da-kash'* ADJ. & N.M. one who drinks , wine-addict بادہ کشی *bā'da-kashī* N.F. intemperance ; fondness for drinks بادہ نوش *bā'da nosh'* ADJ. wine-addict ; one who drinks بادہ نوشی *bā'da-noshī* N.F. fondness for drinks [P]

بادی[1] *bā'dī* ADJ. beginning first ; بادی النظر میں *bā'dī-ūn-na'zar meṅ* (ped. *bā'din-na'zar meṅ*) ADV 'prima facie'; at first sight

بادی[2] *bā'dī* ADJ. flatulent ; windy rheumatic بادی بدن *bā'dī ba'dan* N.M. corpulence; bloated body [P ~ باد]

بادیان *badiyān'*, بادیاں *bā'diyāṅ* N.F. anise aniseed [P]

بادیہ[1] *bā'diyah* N.M. desert wilderness ; waste ; wasteland بادیہ پیما *bā'diya paimā'* ADJ. wanderer ; tramp desert-traveller بادیہ پیمائی *bā'diyā-paimā''ī* N.F. desert travel tramp [A]

بادیہ[2] *bā'diyah* N.M. bowl [P]

باڈی[1] *bā'ḍī* N.M. body [E]

باڈی[2] *bā'ḍī* bodice ; brassiers [~E bodice CORR.] باڈی گارڈ *bā'ḍī- gār'd* N.M. body guard [E]

بار[1] *vār* N.M. turn time chance ; occasion ; opportunity (dial.) day of the week بار بار *bār' bār* ADV. repeatedly ; again and again ; time and again بارہا *bār'-hā* ADV often ; frequently times out of number [P]

بار[2] *bār* N.M. burden ; load liability heaviness leave ; permission ; admission court sitting of a sovereign to give audience ; audience produce ; fruit onus (of proof) بارآور *bār-ā'var* ADJ. bearing fruit fructuous باربردار *bār-bardār* ADJ. (beast) of burden N.M. porter ; carrier باربرداری *bār-bardā'rī* N.F. transport freight beasts of burden بارِ ثبوت *bā'r-e sūboot'* N.M. onus of proof ; burden of proof بارِ خاطر *bā'r-e khā'tir* ADJ. unpleasant disagreeable offensive بارخانہ *bār-khā'nah* N.M. godown بارِ خدا(یا) *bār-e khūdā(yā)* INT. Great God ; Lord God باردار *bār'-dār* ADJ. (of tree) burdened with fruit pregnant fortunate باردانہ *bār-dā'nah* N.M. gunny bags (etc. in which provisions are kept) ; packages provisions forage بارِ عام *bār-e 'ām'* N.M. public audience بار کرنا *bār-kar'nā* V.T. load بارکش *bār'kash* N.M. cart or animal for carrying loads ; load-carrier بارگاہ *bār'-gāh* N.F. palace court place of audience بارگیر *bār'gīr* N.M. pack animal rider or cavalier not owning the horse he rides باروَر *bār'-var* ADJ. fruitful successful fortunate laden with fruit بار ہونا *bār'-ho'nā* V.I. be laden be an obstacle or burden باریاب *bār-yāb* ADJ. & ADV. admitted at court or into company ; granted audience باریابی *bār-yā'bī* N.F. admittance at court ; audience [P]

بارا *bā'rā* N.M. lifting of irrigation water in bucket from well with a lever; lever-lift irrigation bucket used for the purpose person turning the bucket song sung on the occasion

بارات *barāt'*, برات *barāt'* N.F. marriage proccession

باراں *bā'rāṅ* N.M. rain ADJ. raining بارانی (زمین) *barā'nī (zamīn')* ADJ. & N.M. rain-irrigated (land) relating to or depending on rain

بارایٹ لا *bār-aiṭ-lā'* PH. Bar(rister)-at-Law [E]

باربد *bār'bad* N.M. name of a legendary Persian musician [P]

بارجا *bār'jā*, بارجہ *bār'jah* N.M. inside balcony

بارد *bā'rid* ADJ. (F. & PL. باردہ *bā'ridah*) ADJ. cold frigid [A]

بارز *bā'riz* ADJ. apparent manifest [A]

بارش *bā'rish* N.F. rain showers plenty windfall [P ~ باریدن]

بارک اللہ *bā'rak-allāh* INT. God bless you ; may you prosper [A ~ اللہ + برکت]

بارگ *bā'rag* N.F. (usu. as PL.) barracks [~E CORR.]

بارود *bārood'* (col. بارُوت *bāroot'*) N.F. gunpowder بارود خانہ *bārood-khā'nah* N.M. powder magazine gunpowder factory [~T]

بارہ[1] *bā'rah* ADJ. twelve بارہ امام *bā'rah imām'* N.M. the twelve 'Imams' (religious leaders) of the Shi'ite sect (viz., Hazrat 'Ali, Imam Hasan, Iman Husain, Imam Zain-ul Abidin, Imam Baqar, Imam Ja'far Sadiq Imam Musa Kazim, Imam Riza, Imam Naqi, Imam Taqi, Imam Hasan 'Askari, Imam Mahdi) بارہ باٹ ہونا *bā'rah bāṭ ho'nā* V.I. be scattered be torn by internal dissensions confused nonplussed بارہ برس کے بعد گھورے کے بھی دن پھرتے ہیں *bā'rah ba'ras ke ba'd ghoo're ke bhi din phir'te hain* PROV. adversity is followed by prosperity بارہ برس دلی میں رہے اور بھاڑ جھونکا *bā'rah ba'ras dellī men ra'he aur bhāṛ jhoṅ'kā* PROV. a boor who has failed to accept the civilising influences of society ; arrant fool بارہ پتھر باہر *bā'rah pat'thar bā'har* N.M. outside the city limits بارہ دری *bā'ra-da'rī* N.F. (usu. square) summer house with a dozen-doorway pavilion بارہ سنگھا *bā'ra-siṅ'ghā* N.M. stag بارہ ماسہ *bā'ra-mā'sah* N.M. calendar (as a genre of Hindi and Panjabi poetry describing woman's pangs of separation through various months of the year) بارہ وفات *bā'rah vafāt'* N.F. Rabi-ul-Avval 12 (as the Holy Prophet's) death anniversary (and now mostly as his Nativity day) بارہواں *bār'havāṅ* ADJ. twelfth

بارہ دری

بارہ[2] *bā'rah* ADV. (same as بارے ★)

باری[1] *bā'rī* N.M. the Creator باری تعالےٰ *bā'ri ta'ā'lā* N.M. the Elevated Creator ; God [A]

باری[2] *bā'rī* N.F. time ; turn باری کا بخار *bā'rī kā bukhār'* N.M. باری تپ *bā'rī kī tap* N.F. intermittent fever باری باری *bā'rī bā'rī* ADV.

in turn ; each in due course [~P [بارا]
باریک bārīk' ADJ. fine thin minute slender delicate threadlike subtle nice باریک بات bārīk'-bat' N.F subtle point باریک بیں bārīk' bīṅ ADJ. shrewd sagacious penetrating باریک بینی bārīk'-bī'nī N.F. shrewdness subtlety hair-splitting باریکی bārīkī N.F. fineness thinness delicacy, subtlety discernment (میں) باریکیاں نکالنا (meṅ) bārī'kiyāṅ nikāl'na V.I. pick holes (in); find fault (with) split hairs
بارے bā're' بارہ bā'rah ADV. at last, a length کے بارے میں ke bā're meṅ ADV with regard to, in respect of regarding concerning about [P]
بالے bā're ADV at last at leng h [P ~ [بارا]

باڑ bāṛ N.F. hedge fence edge (of weapon or tool) باڑ لگانا (یا باندھنا) bāṛ lagā'na (or bāndh'na) fence put a hedge round
باڑا bā'ṛā, باڑہ bā'rah N.M. enclosure pen, fold
باڑھ bāṛh' N.F volley باڑھ مارنا bāṛh' mār'na V.I fire a volley
باز[1] bāz N.M hawk falcon بازدار bāz'-dār N.M. falconer one in charge of someone's hawks [~A [بازی]
باز[2] bāz SUF. agent actor, doer player [P]
باز[3] bāz PREF. re- aga back باز آنا bāz' ā'nā V.I. abandon ; lea off turn back (from) ; obstain (from) efuse decline بازپرس bāz'-purs' N.F. explanation called scrutiny interrogation, inquiry calling to account بازپسیں bāz'pasīṅ' ADJ. last بازحراست bāz-ḥirā'sat N.F remand to custody بازدید bāz' dīd N.F return visit باز رکھنا bāz' rakh'na V T prevent ; prohibit dissuade restrain ; hold back hinder repress disallow debar باز رہنا bāz raih'nā V.I. desist, refrain, obstain forbear shun leave off, cease بازگشت bāz -gasht N.F return retreat relapse resumption (also صدائے بازگشت sadā'-e bāz'-gasht') echo بازیابی bāz-yā'bī N.F recovery بازیافت bāz-yāft' N.F. recovery resumption (of alienated land) [P]
بازار bāzār' N.M. bazaar market بازار گرم ہونا bāzār' gar'm ho'nā V.I. (of thing) be in great demand (of trade) thrive, be brisk be in vogue, be the order of the day, be rampant بازار لگانا bāzār' lagā'nā V I establish a market display one's wares gather people (round oneself) بازار مندا (یا سرد) ہونا bāzār' manda (or sar'd) ho'nā V.I. be in the little demand (of trade) be dull چور بازار chor bāzār' N.M. blackmarket چور بازاری chor bāzā'rī N.F. blackmarket, blackmarketing چور بازاری کرنے والا chor bāzārī kar'ne vā'la N.M. blackmarketeer کھلا بازار khu'la bāzār N.M. open market بازاری bāzārī ADJ. vulgar inferior relating to the market indecent lax in morals uncultured incredible (report, etc.) بازاری آدمی bāzā'rī ād'mī N M vulgar person ; uncultured person low common person بازاری عورت bāzā'rī 'au'rat N.F prostitute harlot ; whore ; street-walker, woman on the street بازاری گپ bāzā rī gap N.F. incredible report hearsay rumour بازاری نرخ bāzā'rī nir'kh بازار کا بھاؤ bāzār' kā bhā''o N.M market rate [P]
بازو bā zoo I. arm wing (of bird) side frame (of door) side of bedstead flank (of army) accompanist, accompanyist (of 'marsia' or dirge-singer) companion supporter associate بازوبند bā'zoo-band N.M. armlet bracelet بازو پھڑکنا bā'zoo phaṛak'na V.I. have an augury of meeting some friend بازو ٹوٹنا bā'zoo ṭooṭ'nā V I. lose one's supporter (through death, etc.) بازو دینا bā'zoo de'nā V aid, assist, help support, lend a helping hand بازو دعویٰ bā'zoo da''vā N.M suit for the restitution of conjugal rights [P]
بازی bā'zī N.F. sport, game, play wager bet ; stake بازی بدنا bā'zī bad'nā V.I bet ; lay a wager بازی جیتنا (یا مار جانا) bā'zī jīt'nā (or mār jā'nā) V I win come out victorious excel بازی دینا bā'zī de'nā V.T. beat win (a game) checkmate بازی کھانا (یا ہارنا) bā'zī khā'na (or hār'nā) V.T lose be defeated بازیگاہ bā'zī-gah N.F. theatre circus playground stadium بازیگر bā'zī-gar N.M. acrobat rope-dancer juggler, conjurer magician; sorcecer بازیگرنی bā'zī-garnī N.F female acrobat acrobat's wife sorceress بازیگری bā'zī-ga'rī N.F rope-dancing jugglery legerdemain بازی لگانا bā'zī lagā'nā V.I. wager lay a wager stake, lay at stake بازی لے جانا bā'zī le jā'nā V.I. win excel بازیچہ bāzī'chah N.M. toy plaything fun fr

bazī'cha-e atfāl' N.M. child's play [P]

باس *bās* N.F. smell, adour sent unpleasant odour N.M. (dial.) abode, dwelling

باسٹھ *bā'saṭh* ADJ. & N.M. sixty-two باسٹھواں *bā'saṭhvāṅ* ADJ. sixty-second

باسط *bā'sit* N.M. Giver of prosperity (as an attribute of God) [A ~ بسط]

باسمتی *bās'matī* N.M. basmati ; a superior kind of rice

باسلیق *bāsalīq'* N.F 'vena basilica', the great vein in the arm [A ~ G]

باسن *bā'san* N.M. vessel ; utensil

باسی *bā'sī* ADJ. stale overnight N.M. (dial.) dweller, inhabitant باسی بچے نہ کتا کھائے *bā'sī ba'che na kūt'tā khā''e* PROV not to lay by a penny باسی عید *bā'sī 'īd* N.F stale Eid, day(s) after it باسی کرنا *bā'sī kar'na* V.T. make stale باسی کڑھی میں ابال (آنا) *bā'sī ka'ṛhī meṅ ūbāl' (ā'nā)* PH wish to be young in old age storm after event باسی منہ *bā'sī mūnh* ADV before breakfast

باش *bāsh* SUF. staying, living being INT (ped.) stop ; stay باشی SUF stay being existence [P ~ بودن be]

باشندہ *bāshin'dah* N.M. citizen resident ; inhabitant [P ~ PREC.]

باشہ *bā'shah* N.M falcon ; hawk ; sparrowhalk

باصرہ *bā'sirah* N.M sight [A ~ بصر]

باطل *bā'til* ADJ spurious false null and void futile, ineffectual fictitious unsound باطل سمجھنا (یا جاننا) *bā'til sa'majhnā* (or *jān'nā*) V I. regard as false باطل کرنا *bātil kar'nā* V.T nullify rescind, cancel abolish vitiate revoke falsify [A]

باطن *bā'tin* N M. heart mind innermost part inside باطنی *bā'tinī* ADV internal intrinsic hidden concealed, latent esoteric Carmathian (sect of the Shi'ites) باطنی فرقہ *bā'tinī fir'qah* N.M. Carmathian sect [A ~ بطن]

باعث *bā''is* N.M cause reason condition ground basis origin (rare) instigator [A]

باغ *bāgh* N.M garden orchard grove دل باغ باغ ہونا (یا ہو جانا) *(dil) bāgh' bāgh ho nā* (or *ho jā'nā*) PH rejoice greatly be overjoyed سبز باغ *sab'z bāgh* N M (fig.) deceitful promises vain hopes سبز باغ دکھانا *sab'z bāgh dikhā nā* V T (fig.) raise vain hopes excite desire and expectation by deceitful promises باغ معلق

bāgh-e-ma'l'laq N.M. braging gardens باغ و بہار *bāgh-o-bahar* N.M. garden in spring ; spring garden ADJ. beautiful (scene) delectable (personality) باغبان *bāgh-bān'* N.M. gardener vagetable grower باغبانی *bāgh-bā'nī* N.F. gardening ; horticulture vegetable growing باغات *bāghāt'* N.M. PL. gardens orchards باغاتی *bāghā'tī* ADJ. pertaining to gardens horticultural باغیچہ *baghī'chah* (rare باغچہ *bāgh'chāh*) N M. grove orchard kitchen garden [P]

باغی *bā'ghī* N.M. rebel insurgent traitor mutineer [~ بغاوت]

باف *bāf* SUF weaver woven کناری باف *kinā'rī-bāf'* N.M. lace weaver زری باف *za'rī bāf* N.M. gold-lace weaver [P ~ FOLL.]

بافت *bāft* texture web. بافتگی *bāf'tagī* N.F. weaving knitting بافتہ *bāf'tah* ADJ. woven knitted N.M. tissue بافندہ *bāfindah* N.M. weaver [P ~ بافتن weave]

باقر *bā'qir* N.M. rich scholar ADJ. possessing great learning and wealth [A]

باقرخانی *bā'qir-khā'nī* N.F. a kind of crisp fragile bread

باقرخانی

باقلا *bā'qilā* N M a kind of bean, a potherb [A ~ بقل]

باقی *bā'qī* ADJ. remaining outstanding existing alive perpetual N.M. balance remainder surplus arrears باقی حساب *bā'qī hisāb'* N.M balance of an account باقی دار *bā'qī-dār'* N.M. owing a balance debtor defaulter باقی رہنا *bā'qī raih'nā* V I. be left remain (unpaid) have a balance باقیماندہ (or باقی ماندہ) *bā'qī-māṅ'dah* N.M remainder residue ADJ remaining residuary باقی نکالنا *bā'qī nikāl'nā* V T subtract find the difference between two numbers strike a balance باقیات *bāqiyāt'* N.M PL. arrears balance remnants باقیات صالحات *bāqiyā't-e-sālehāt* N F PL. the good that one does memory of one's good deeds [A ~ بقا]

باک *bāk* N.M fear terror harm [P]

باکرہ *bā kirah* N F virgin [A ~ بکر *bikr*]

باکھ *bākh* N.M udder باکھڑی *bākh'ṛī*, باکھلی *bākh'lī* N.F. cow or buffalo when she has given milk for five months or so باکھل *bā'khal* N.M enclosure ; courtyard enclosed by several horse cattle-sheds, etc

باگ bāg N.F. rein bridle باگ اٹھانا bāg ūṭhā'na V.I. start on horseback give the rein set at full gallop باگ ڈور bāg'-ḍor N.F. rein halter (fig.) control کسی کے ہاتھ میں باگ ڈور ہونا ki'sī ke hath' meṅ bāg'-ḍor ho'nā V.I. (fig.) exercise control over باگ ڈھیلی کرنا bāg ḍhī'lī kar'nā V.T. give free reins (to) leave (someone) free in his evil ways باگ لینا bāg' le'nā V.I. take the rein pull up باگ موڑنا bāg' moṛ'na V.T. turn the reins change the direction (of horse, conversation, etc.) باگ ہاتھ سے چھوٹنا bāg' hath' se chhooṭ'nā V.I. lose control miss opportunity

باگا bā'gā N.M. (dial.) apparel bridegrooms garment

باگڑ بلا bāg'aṛ bil'lā N.M. wild cat (nurs.) for scaring child) tom-cat (fig.) chubby child.

باگھ bāgh N.M. tiger

باگیسری bāges'rī N.F. name of musical mode [S]

بل bil PREF. see under بِ★ [A PREP. بِ + DEFINITE ARTICLE ال]

۱ بال bal N.M. (ped.) heart mind condition ; state [A]

۲ بال bal N.M. wing, pinion بال و پر نکالنا ba'l-par nikāl'nā V.I. be fledged learn to fly oppose betray malicious designs [P]

۳ بال bal N.M. hair crack (in glass or china) N.F. ear (of corn) بال آنا bal'āl'na V.I. (of glass or china) be cracked have hair (on chin or face) بال اتارنا bal ūtār'na V.T. shave off cut the hair بال بال bal bal' ADV. altogether completely بال بال بچنا bal bal' bach'na PH. escape by a hair's bredth ; have a narrow escape بال بال بندھنا bal bal' bandh'na V.I. be inextricably entangled بال باندھا غلام bal bań'dha ghūlām' N.M. very obedient servant ; one held in thrall بال باندھنا bal bandh'na V.T. set the hair braid بال بچے bal' bach'che N.M. (one's) children one's family بال برابر فرق نہ ہونا bal' bara'bar far'q na ho'nā V.I. be identical ; have no difference at all بال بکھرنا bal' bi'kharnā V.I. have dishevelled hair بال بنانا bal' banā'na V.T. do the hair, dress the hair کا بال بیکا نہ ہونا ka bal' bī'kā na ho'nā PH. not to receive the slightest injury, escape unharmed بال پکنا bal' pak'na V.I. (of corn) ripen (of hair) grey بال توڑ bal'-toṛ N.M. & ADJ. (boil) caused by breaking of hair بال تراش bal'-tarāsh' N.M. hair dresser بال جھڑنا bal' jhaṛ'na V.I (of hair) fall off, (of baldness) approach بالچھڑ bal'-chhaṛ N.M. spikenard, hyacinth بال دار bal'-dar ADJ. cracked (glass or china) بال رکھنا bal' rakh'na V.I. allow the hair to grow wear (long, short, etc.) hair بال سفید ہونا bal sifed' ho'nā V.I. grey. grow grey age remain no longer young become elderly بال کمانی bal-kamā'nī N.F. hairspring (of watch) بال کھڑے ہونا bal khaṛe ho'nā V.I. (of hair) stand on end بال کی کھال نکالنا (یا کھینچنا) bal kī khal nikal'na (or khench'na V.T split hairs be hyporcritical بال لینا bal' le'nā V. shave one's private parts بال والا bal'vā'lā ADJ. hairy بالوں کا برش ba'loṅ ka būrsh' N.M. hair-brush بالوں کا تیل bā'loṅ kā tel' N.M. hair oil بالوں کی کثرت bā'loṅ kī kas'rat N.F. hairiness بالوں کی کمی ba'loṅ kī ka'mī N.F. thinness of hair

۴ بال bāl (used as بال بچے bal bach'che) N.M. (PL.) children بال ہٹ bal' haṭ N.F. obstinacy (of child) childish obstinacy

۱ بالا bā'lā N.M. adolescent mere boy, stripling large ear-ring grainsprout ADJ. new young بالا بھولا ba'lā bho'lā ADJ. childlike بالے بھولے ba'le bhole N.M. PL. children, tiny tots بالا پن ba'lā-pan N.M. childhood infancy adolescence لڑکا بالا lar'kā ba'lā N.M. a mere lad a slip of a boy لڑکے بالے lar'ke ba'le N.M. PL boys lads and lasses

۲ بالا bā'lā PREP. above on upon ADJ. high, lofty exalted foregoing, aforesaid ; above-mentioned SUF. super. N.M. top upper part stature ; height بالا بالا bā'la bā'la, بالا ہی بالا bā'la hī ba'la ADV. by underhand means over and above the head (of) secretly ; privately بالا بتانا ba'la batā'na V.T. dodge ; give an evasive reply بالا بند bā'la band N.M. broach for turban بالا پوش ba'la posh N.M. overcoat coverlet, coverlid cover bed cover بالا خانہ ba'lā-khā'nah N.M. upper room, antic upper storey brothel بالا دست ba'lā-dast' ADJ. superior high having the upper hand بالا دستی ba'la-das'tī N.F. superiority hegemony بالا نشین ba'la-nashīn' ADJ. occupying the chief seat بالا و پست bā'lā-o-past' N.M. high and low heaven and earth [P]

بالائی balā'ī ADJ. over and above external unusual, extraordinary superficial illegal (gratification, income etc.) N.F (euphemism for ملائی) cream بالائی آمدنی balā'ī ām'danī, بالائی یافت balā'ī yaft' N.F. perquisites bribe ; illegal gratification received بالائی اخراجات bala'i akhraiat' N.M. overhead expenses [P ~ PREC.]

بالٹی bal'ṭi N.F. pail bucket

بالچھڑ bal'chhar N.F. spikenard ; hyacinth

بالش ba'lish N.F. pillow cushion [P]

بالشت balish't N.F. span بالشت بھر balisht' bhar ADJ. (of the length of) a span بالشتیا balish'tiya N.M. dwarf ; pigmy ; midget [P]

بالشت

بالشویک bal'shavik ADJ. & N.M. bolshevik [R]

بالغ ba'ligh ADJ. of age ; major having attained puberty having reached the age of maturity N.M. adult بالغ رائے دہی (کا حق) ba'ligh ra''e-de'hi (ka haq') N.F. (M.) adult franchise بالغ ہونا ba'ligh ho'na V.I. attain majority ; come of age [A]

بالک ba'lak N.M. child ; infant بالکا bal'ka N.M (dial.) Hindu sadhu's disciple

بالم ba'lam N.M. lover (usu. woman's) sweetheart husband ADJ. young youngish ; boyish large and superior

بالنگو balan'goo N.M. a kind of citron تخم بالنگو tukhm-e-balan'goo N.M. its seed used in a cold drink [P]

بالو ba'loo N.F. sand بالو کی بھیت ba'loo ki bhit N.F. well of sand (fig.) anything frail

بالوشاہی ba'loo-sha'hi N.F. a kind of sweetment ; disc pastry

بالوشاہی

بالی ba'li N.F. small girl ; mere slip of a girl ear-ring ; spike (of corn) ADJ. very young بالی عمر ba'li 'umar' بالی عمریا ba'li 'umar'ya N.F. young age (esp. of girls, sweethearts, etc.) [~ بال]

بالیدہ bali'dah ADJ. grown up increased enhanced بالیدگی bali'dagi N.F. growth increase expansion lush vegetation [P ~ بالیدن]

بالین ba'lin N.M. pillow cushion the head of a bed [P]

بام[1] bam N.M. housetop roof terrace لب بام lab-e bam N.F. (& ADV.) (on) the edge of the roof

بام[2] bam, بانب banb, بام مچھلی bam machh'li, N.F. eel [S]

بامداد bam dad N.M dawn morning بامداداں bamda'dan ADV. early in the morning at dawn [P]

بامن ba'man N.M. بامنی bam'ni N.F. (see under برہمن N.M. ★)

بامنی bam'ni N.F. a kind of lizard disease shedding eyelashes yellow stamens of lotus moonplant

بان[1] ban N.M. rush string (for plaiting bedstead, etc.) bloody track of wounded animal (dial.) arrow (Hindu myth.) rocket

بان[2] ban N.M. a tree yielding benzoin [A]

بان[3] ban SUF. driver guardian keeper [P]

بانا ba'na N.M. woof ; weft staff with balls fixed at ends and used as weapon ; balled staff its use as military weapon (arch.) distinct uniform (arch.) guise

بنات banat' N.F. broadcloth

بنابی ban'bi N.F. (snake's) hole

بانٹ banṭ N.F. division distribution share (rus.) feed بانٹنا banṭ'na V.T. divide distribute apportion share dispose of

بانجھ banjh ADJ. sterile barren بانجھ پن banjh-pan N.M. sterility

بانچنا banch'na V.I. decipher (letters) make out read carefully ignore overlook

باندھنا bandh'na V.T. bind pack the pack fasten chain fetter ; shackle shut construct ; build (bridge) embank (11) plan ; design (12) seize (13) bind in marriage (14) set (15) settle (16) form (17) compose (18) versify (an idea) (19) pitch (20) set (21) take (aim.) (22) charm ; captivate (23) pair (24) liken (25) put on (armour) (26) take upon oneself

باندی ban'di N F. handmaid maid باندی تھی سو بیوی ہوئی، بیوی تھی سو باندی ہوئی ban'di thi so bi'vi hu''i bi'vi thi so ban'di hu''i PROV. victim of vicissitudes of fortune

بانڈ band N.M. bond انعامی بانڈ in'am band N.M. prize bond [E]

بانڈا ban'da ADJ. & N.M. (person) with crooked legs tailless (bird or reptile)

بانس bans N.M. bamboo ten-foot-long measure بانس پر چڑھانا bans' par charha'na V.T. (fig.) praise (an unworthy man) بانسوں اچھلنا (یا کودنا) ban'son u'chhalna (or kood'na) V.I. (fig.) be overjoyed بانسی ban'si ADJ. bamboo ; of bamboo

بانسا *bañ'sā* N.M. bridge of the nose بانسا پھر جانا *bañ'sā phır' jā'nā* V.I. approach of death (denoted by the turning of the bridge of the nose)

بانسری *bañs'rī* (rus. بانسلی *bāns' lī*) N.F. pipe ; flute reed ; fife [~ بانس]

بانک *bañk* N.F. anklet dagger-play type of dagger used in it ; curved dagger piece of wood protecting a wheel fault ; offence ; wickedness

بانکا *bañ'kā* N.M. fop ; beau ; coxcomb snobbish bully (esp. of Lucknow) ADJ. curved crooked ; cunning spirited بانکپن *bāñk'-pan* N.M. cuteness smartness foppishness ; gaiety ; wantonness بانکی *bañ'kī* ADJ. & N.F. cute (woman)

بانگ *bāñg* N.F. crowing (of) cock) ; crow cry ; shout (usu. بانگِ اذان *bāñ'g-e azān'*) call to prayer بانگِ درا *bāñ'g-e darā'* N.F. sound of bell (as signal for start of caravan) بانگ دینا *bāñg' de'nā* V.I. crow [P]

بانگر *bāñgar* N.M. & ADJ. upland ; highland

بانگڑو *bāñg'roo* churlish stupid ignorant N.M. boor highlander

بانگی *bāñ'gī* N.F. sample

بانو *bā'no* (ped. *bā'noo*) N.F. lady princess SUF. (used with female names) woman [P]

بانوے *bān've* ADJ. & N.M. ninety-two بانوے واں *bān'vevāñ* ADJ. ninety-second

بانہہ *bāñh* N.F. arm sleeve support supporter surety ; guarantee بانہہ پکڑنا *bāñh' pa'kaṛnā* V.T. succour support defend come to the aid of بانہہ ٹوٹنا *bāñh' ṭooṭ'nā* V.I. have a broken arm lose one's prop ; support or friend بانہہ دینا *bāñh' de'nā* V.T. help ; aid succour بانہہ گہنا *bāñh gaih'nā* V.T. (rare) support ; come to the aid of ;

بانی *bā'nī* N.M. founder ; author originator builder cause of (trouble, etc.) بانیِ فساد *bā'nī-e fasād'* N.M. mischief-monger one stirring up trouble [A ~ بنا]

بانی *bā'nī* N.F. words sounds tale nature bad habits

باوا *bā'vā* N.M. father grandfather (nurs.) doll (someone's) superior consummate knave باوا آدم *bā'vā ā'dam* N.M. Adam باوا آدم نرالا ہونا کا *kā bā'vā ā'dam nirā'lā ho'nā* V.T. (fig.) (of person) being curious (of situation) being strange باوا کا *bā'vā kā* ADJ. (iron.) own ; personal inherited

باور *bā'var* N.M. credibility faith ; belief trust ADJ. credible trustworthy true باور کرنا *bā'var kar'nā* V.T. trust believe to be true باور ہونا (یا آنا) *bā'var ho'nā* (or *ā'nā*) V.I. be believed

باورچی *bāvar'chī* N.M. cook باورچی خانہ *bāvar'chī-khā'nah* N.M. kitchen باورچی گری *bāvar'chī ga'rī* N.F. culinary art

باون *bāvan* ADJ. & N.M. fifty-two باون تولہ پاؤ رتی *bā'van to'le pā''o rat'tī* ADJ. exactly ; precisely باون گز کا *bā'van gaz kā* ADJ. tall mischievous لنکا میں جو ہے سو باون گز کا *lañ'kā meñ jo' hai so bā'van gaz kā* PROV. everyone here outdoes the others in mischief (or oddity) باونواں *bā'vanvāñ* ADJ. fifty second

باہ *bāh* N.F. lust virility قوتِ باہ *qūv'vat-e bāh* N.F. virility [A]

باہر *bā'hir* (col. *bā'har*) N.M. & ADV. out outside away abroad beyond external exceeding باہر باہر *bā'hir bā'hir* ADV. outside at a distance INT. keep away باہر جانا *bā'hir jā'nā* V.I. go out go abroad go overseas باہر کا *bāhir kā* N.M. outsider foreigner ADJ. outer external باہر کرنا *bā'hir kar'nā,* باہر نکالنا *bā'hir nikāl'nā* V.T. turn out ; expel oust ; erect exclude dismiss ; omit strike out باہر بھیجنا *bā'hir bhej'nā* V.I. send out expire send overseas باہر لے جانا *bā'hir le jā'nā* V.T. take out (of) export take abroad کہنے سے باہر ہونا *kaih'ne se bā'hir ho'nā* disobey refuse to listen be out of control باہری *bā'hirī* ADJ. exterior [A]

باہم *bā'-ham* ADV. together jointly mutually reciprocally باہم دگر *bā'ham-di'gar* ADJ. mutual reciprocal ADV. together mutually reciprocally باہمی *bā'-hamī* ADJ. mutual reciprocal [P ~ با + ہم]

باہمن *bāh'man,* بامن *bā'man* N.M. (col.) brahmin باہمنی *bāh'manī,* بامنی *bām'nī* N.F. (col.) brahmin woman [~ برہمن CORR.]

باہنا *bāh'nā* V.T. till (land) open wide (mouth) show (teeth)

بائبل *bā''ibal* N.M. Bible [E]

بائع *bā''e* N.M. seller [A ~ بیع]

باؤ *bā''o* N.F. wind flatulence rheumatism باؤ برنگ *bā''o barañg'* N.M. a cucumber-like drug-root 'embelia ribes' باؤ سرنا (یا آنا) *bā''o*

sar'nā (or *ā'nā*) v.i. pass wind ; fart باؤ گولا *ba''o go'lā* n.m. flatulence (esp. in women) ; hysteria

باوڑی *bā''oṛī* n.f. (also بیجو باوڑی *be'jo bā''oṛī*) children's game played on small field by lifting potsherds in toes filed for it

باؤلا *bā''olā* (dial. باوڑا *bā''oṛā*) adj. rabid mad insane ; crazy باؤلا پن *bā''olā pan* n.m. craziness باؤلا کتا *bā''olā kut'tā* n.m. rabid dog باؤلی *bā''olī* (dial. باوڑی *bā''oṛī*) n.f. crazy woma adj. crazy

باؤلی *bā''olī* n.f. deep well with steps, etc. leading to water-level

باؤنی *bā''onī* n.f. seed time sowing [~ بونا *bo'nā*]

بائی *bā''ī* n.f. madam (as title for dancing girl) 'mother bawd ; old abbess ; la bonne (dial.) lady ; dame (dial.) flatus (dial.) fart rheumatic pain

بائیس *bā''īs* adj. & n.m. twenty-two بائیسواں *bā''īsvāṅ* adj. twenty-second

بایاں *bā'yāṅ* adj. left junior bass n.m. left had بایاں پاؤں پوجنا *bā'yāṅ pā''oṅ pooj'nā* بایاں قدم لینا *bā'yāṅ qa'dam le'nā* v.t. bow to someone's superior cunning بائیں ہاتھ سے رکھوا لینا *bā''eṅ hāth se rakhvā' le'nā* v.t. extort ; get by force بائیں ہاتھ کا کرتب (یا کھیل) *bā''eṅ hāth kā kar'tab* (or *khel*) ph. easy job (for someone)

باید و شاید *bā'yad-o shā'yad* adj. meet and proper ; as it should be rare [P بایستن + شائستن ~]

بب *bib* n.m. bib [E]

ببر، شیر ببر، ببر شیر *ba'bar*, *she'r-e ba'bar*, *ba'bar sher* n.m. lion [P PRON. *ba'būr* or *ba'būr*]

ببرا *bab'rā* n.m. blue piebald pigeon

ببری *bab'rī* n.f. lock of cropped hair hanging on woman's forehead

ببوا *ba'bū'ā* n.m. boy boy's (clay) effigy as plaything [~ بابو].

ببول *babool'* n.f. acacia ببول کا کانٹا *babool' kā kāṅ'ṭā* n.m. acacia ببول کے پیڑ بونا *babool' ke peṛ' bo'nā* v.i. (fig.) do something evil.

ببولا *baboo'lā*, بگولا *bagool'lā* n.m. whirlwind

ببی *bab'bī*, پپی *pap'pī* n.f. (nurs.) kiss کھٹی (ببی) *khaṭ'ṭī* (*bab'bī*) n.f. (nurs.) first kiss مٹھی (ببی) *miṭ'ṭhī* (*bab'bī*) n.f. (nurs.) second kiss

ببیانہ *bibyā'nah* n.m. & adj. ladies stuff [~ P بی بی]

بپتا *bip'tā* n.f. misfortune adversity distress ; woe calamity اپنی بپتا کہنا (یا سنانا) *ap'nī bip'tā kaih'nā* (or *sunā'nā*) v.t. relate one's tale of woe بپتا پڑنا *bib'tā par'nā* v.i. (of misfortune) befall

بپتسمہ *baptis'mah* n.m. baptism [G]

بپھرنا *bi'pharnā* v.i. fall into passion be enraged be out of control defy revolt show obstinacy

بت *but* n.m. idol image statue mistress ; beloved lovely person adj. stupefied stunned dumbfounded بت بنا کھڑا ہونا *but' ba'nā khā'ṛā ho'nā* v.i. be struck dumb ; be dumbfounded بت پرست *but'-parast'* adj. & n.m. worshipper of images ; idolater بت پرستی *but paras'tī* n.f. idolatry ; idol-worship بت تراش *but-tarāsh'* n.m. carver of idols sculptor ; statuary بت تراشی *but-tarā'shī* n.f. sculpture statuary بتخانہ *but-khā'nah* n.m. idol-temple place with a bevy of beauties بت شکن *but-shi'kan* adj & n.m. iconoclast ; image-breaker بتکدہ *but-ka'dah* n.m. idol-temple (rare) pagoda [P ~ S Buddha]

بتا *but'tā* بتولا *bato'lā* n.m. delusion cajolery fraud ; trick ; evasion (usu. in) بتا (یا بتولا) دینا (یا بتانا) *but'tā* (or *batolā*) *de'nā* (or *batā'nā*) v.t. deceive ; defraud dupe overreach evade ; dodge بتے (یا بتولے) میں آنا *but'te* (or *bato'le*) *meṅ ā'nā* v.i. be duped

بتاسا *batā'sā*, بتاشا *batāshā* n.m. puffed sugar drop a kind of small fire-work bubble

بتانا *bitā'nā* v.t. pass or spend (time) [~ بیتنا caus.]

بتانا² *batā'nā* n.m. iron ring used as measure for bangles

بتانا *batā'nā* v.t. tell explain indicate point out ; show acquaint describe instruct make sexy signs in dancing etc.

بتلانا *batlā'nā* v.t. tell explain talk ; converse point out ; show explain teach ; instruct [~ بات]

بتر *ba'tar* adj. worse [P ~ بدتر]

بترا *but'rā* adj. having a dull blade

بتکڑ *batak'kar* adj. garrulous [~ بات]

بتنگڑ *batan'gaṛ* n.m. accurate (usu. in) بات کا بتنگڑ بنانا *bāt kā batan'gaṛ banā'nā* v.t. exaggerate unduly [~ بات]

بتورا *bataurā* n.m. dung-cake heap

بتول *batool* N.F. chaste woman who is God's true devotee (as title of Hazrat Fatimah) virgin [A]
بتولا *bato'lā* N.M. (same as بتا ★)
بتی *bat'ti* N.F. wick candle any sort of lamp electric light any stick like thing suppository plug (for wound, etc.) بتی جلانا *bat'tī jalā'nā* V.T. light a candle (or lamp, etc.) switch on a light بتی چڑھانا *bat'tī charhā'nā* V.T. raise wick (of lamp) بتی دکھانا *bat'tī dikhā'nā* V.T. show a light بتی دینا *bat'tī de'nā* V.T. plug (wound with gauze, etc.) سو (وغیرہ) بتی کی طاقت *sau* (etc.) *bat'tī kī tā'qat* N.F. 100 (etc.) candle-power بتی گل کرنا *bat'tī gul' kar'nā* V.T. put out a lamp (etc.) ; switch off the light
بتھوا *bath'vā* N.M. a kind of potherb; 'chenopodium album'
بتولا *bato'lā* N.M. (same as بتا N.M. ★)
بتولن *bato'lan* N.F. deceitful woman loquacious woman [~ بات]
بتی *battī* N.F. wick light ; lamp
بتیس *bat'tīs* ADJ. & N.M. thirty-two بتیسواں *bat'tīsvāṅ* ADJ. thirty-second بتیس دانتوں میں زبان (ہونا) *bat'tīs dāṅ'toṅ meṅ zabān' (ho'nā)* PROV. (be) surrounded by enemies
بتیسہ *batī'sah* (col. پتیسا *patī'sā*) N.M. a kind of crisp sweetmeat ; crisp candy
بتیسی *battī'sī* N.F. set of teeth any collection comprising thirty-two units بتیسی دکھانا *battī'sī dikhā'nā* V.T. grin laugh mockingly (or in a silly manner) بتیسی بجنا *battī'sī baj'nā* V.I. (of teeth) clatter (with cold)
بٹ *baṭ* N.F. path portion (also باٹ *bāṭ*) measure of weight fold (on fat body) any fold shiny part of tripe banyan بٹمار *baṭ-mār'* N.M. highwayman footpad
بٹا *baṭ'ṭā*, بٹہ *baṭ'ṭah* N.M. measure of weight brickbat piece of stone pestle discount juggler's casket blemish stigma بٹا لگانا *baṭ'ṭā lagā'nā* V.T. reduce the value stigmatize بٹا لگنا *baṭ'ṭā lag'nā* V.I. have (value) reduced be sold at discount be stigmatized ; be defamed بٹہ کھاتہ *baṭ'ṭah-khā'tah* N.M. irrecoverable balances ; bad debts account بٹے باز *baṭ'ṭe-bāz'* ADJ. artful ; crafty; fraudulent N.M. swindler ; sharper (old use) juggler بٹے پر *baṭ'ṭe par* ADV. at a discount
بٹانا *baṭānā* V.T. get divided divert (attention, etc.) بٹائی *baṭā''ī* N.F. division of crop between cultivator and landlord wages for twisting ropes
بٹن *ba'ṭan* N.M. button [E]
بٹنا *baṭ'nā* V.T. be divided (of attention) be diverted form by twisting N.M. instrument with which ropes are twisted
بٹنا *būṭ'nā* N.M. same as N.M. or N.M. ★)
بٹو *biṭṭo* N.F. (same as بٹیا ★)
بٹوا *baṭ'vā* N.M. purse ; wallet بٹوا سا *baṭ'vā sā* ADJ. (F. بٹوی سی *baṭ'vā sī*) small but lovely compact
بٹوارا *baṭvā'rā* N.M. partition ; division of (each) person's share of) joint property بٹوارا کرنا *baṭvā'rā kar'nā* V.T. partition بٹوار *baṭvār'* N.M. toll collector tax gatherer who collects in kind [~ بانٹنا ~ بٹنا]
بٹوانا *baṭvā'nā* V.T. cause to twist get (something) partitioned [~ بٹنا CAUS.]
بٹورنا *baṭor'nā* V.I. amass (wealth) by fraudulent means
بٹھانا *biṭhā'nā*, بٹھا دینا *biṭhā' de'nā* V.T. seat instal (on throne) impress plant set fix cause to sit down persuade (election candidate) to withdraw cause (child) to pass stools send (child to school) for first time (11) not to send (married girl) to in-laws بٹھا رکھنا *biṭhā' rakh'nā* V.T. keep seated keep waiting refuse to send married daughter to her home keep daughter's marriage in abeyance for long
بٹیا *biṭ'yā*, بٹو *biṭṭo* N.F. daughter INT. my little daughter [~ بیٹی DIM.]
بٹیر *baṭer'* N.F. quail
بجا *ba-jā* ADJ. correct right ; proper opportune suitable ; fit in the proper place ADV. properly precisely بجا آوری *ba-jā' ā'varī* N.M. execution (of orders) compliance (with wish) بجا (ارشاد) فرمانا *ba-jā' (irshād') farmā'nā* V.I. (said of a superior) speak aright بجا لانا *ba-jā' lā'nā* V.I. obey comply with ; obey put into effect ; implement ; execute accomplish ; perform [P ~ بہ in + جا place]
بجا *būj'jā*, بجنا *b j'nā* N.F. (crude form of) sanitary towel plug (to stop flux from (hole)
بجار *bijār'* N.M. bull (fig.) lusty fellow
بجالا *bijā'lā* ADJ. full of seed [~ بیج]

بجانا *baja'na* V.T. play upon (musical instrument) beat (drum) blow (whistle) (vulg.) be active agent in sex relation [~ بجنا *baj'na*]

کی بجائے *kī ba-jā''e*, کے بجائے *ke ba-jā''e* ADV. in place of instead of ; in lieu of [~P بہ + جا]

بجٹ *ba'jaṭ* N.M. budget [E]

بجر *baj'jar, ba'jar* N.M. hard heavy stone thunderbolt ADJ. unwieldy immovable

بجرا *baj'ra* N.M. yacht flat-bottomed boat

بجر بٹو *ba'jar baṭ'ṭoo* N.M. juggler's wooden ball toy a kind of black seed for making necklace

بجری *bāj'rī* N.F. gravel small hailstone

بجز *ba-jūz* PREP. except ; save ; with the exception (of) withoht [P ~ بہ + جز]

بجلی *bij'lī* N.F. electricity (electric) current lightning thunderbolt kernel of mango stone ear-ring ADJ. active ; smart very swift (بجلی چمکنا (یا کوندنا یا لپکنا) *bij'lī cha'makna* (or *kaund'na* or *la'pakna* or *launkna*) V.I. (of lightning) flash بجلی پڑنا یا گرنا *bij'lī paṛ'na* (or *gir'na*) V.I. (of lightning) strike (fig.) blast (fig.) (of evil) befall بجلی کی تلوار *bij'lī kī talvār'* N.M. sharp-edged sword بجلی کڑکنا *bij'lī ka'rakna* V.I. thunder بجلی کی کڑک *bij'lī kī ka'ṛak* N.F., بجلی کا کڑکا *bij'lī ka kaṛ'ka* N.M. thunderclap

بجنا *baj'na* V.I. sound be sounded (of musical instrument) be played (of bell) be rung (of teeth) clatter (of clock) strike , chime strike so as to produce sound (vulg.) be poked for sexual act بجوانا *bajvā'na* V.T. cause to sound cause (musical instrument) to be played (vulg.) be passive agent in sex relation

بجنا *bujnā* N.M. (sameas بجا *būjjā* N.M. ★)

بجو *bij'joo* N.M. badger hyena (fig.) tiny-faced or small-eyed person

بجوری *bijau'rī* N.F. small knobbed lid (for pitcher, etc.)

بجوگ *bijog'* N.M. separation of lovers [S]

بجھارت *bujhā'rat* بجھول *būjhav'val* N.F. riddle [~ بوجھنا]

بجھنا *bujh'na* V.I. be quenched be put out ; he extinguished (of spirits) be dumped ; be depressed بجھانا *bujhā'na* V.T. extinguish ; put out quench slake (lime) temper (steel) depress smother (anger) explain cause to comprehend bring round pose (a riddle) [~ بجھنا CAUS.]

بچا *būch'cha*, بوچا *boo'cha* ADJ. (F. بچی *būch'chī*, بوچی *boo'chī*) ear-cropt (fig.) usu. نکٹی بچی *nak'ṭī būch'chī*) with no jewellery in ears (fig.) shameless (woman)

بچار *bichār'* N.M. (usu. as سوچ بچار *soch bichār'*) reflection worry ; care بچارنا *bichār'na* V.I. & I. (dial.) think ; ponder

بچارا *bichā'ra* ADJ. (F. بچاری *bichā'rī*) same بیچارہ (see under بے)

بچالی *bichā'lī* N.F. straw for horse's bed

بچپن *bach'pan*, بچپنا *bach'pana* N.M. in fancy childhood بچپنے کی باتیں *bach'pane kī bā'ten* N.M. PL. childhood's memories childish ways

بچت *ba'chat* N.F. (see under بچنا V.I. ★)

بچگان *bach'chagan* N.M. PL. (rare) children little ones بچگانہ *bach'chaganah* (col. *bachgā'nah*) ADJ. of or for children childish [P ~ SING. بچہ]

بچن *ba'chan* N.M. (dial.) pledge ; word of honour [S]

بچنا *bach'na* V.T. escape (from) ; save oneself dodge ; evade ; avoid be spared recover survive (of money) remain unspent (of material) remain unused ; prove to be spare بچا کھچا *ba'cha khū'cha* ADJ. N.M. remainder ; residue ADJ. remaining left over (after use or exploitation) بچانا *bachā'na* V.T. protect save spare preserve defend ; guard help secure put aside بچاؤ *bachā''o* N.M. rescue defence protection preservation security escape بچاؤ کی صورت نکالنا *bachā''o kī soo'rat nikāl'na* V.I. contrive escape بچت *ba'chat* N.F. savings profit بچو *ba'cho* INT. look out ; watch

بچو *bach'choo*, بچو جی *bach'choo jī* INT. sonny (as a term of endearment for own son) sonny (as term of contempt for foe بچونگڑا *bachoong'ṛa* N.M. (term of endearment for) child brat [~P بچہ]

بچولی *bicho'lī*, بچولیا *bichol'ya* N.M. player participating in match on both sides mediator arbitrator agent pimp ; pander [~ بیچ]

بچہ *bach'chah* N.M. child baby infant young person young (of an animal) ADJ. green inexperienced innocent

بچہ بازی bach'cha-bā'zī N.F pederasty بچہ دان، زہدانی bach'cha-dān' (or dā'nī) N.M. womb ; uterus بچے بھرانا bach che- bhara'nā V.T. (of birds) feed the young بچوں کا کھیل bach chon kā khel' N.M. entertainment for children children's play (fig.) mere child's play بچہ کشی bach'cha-kushī N.F. infanticide بچوں کا لشکر bach'chon ka lash'kar N.M. large number of children بچہ کچا bach'chah kach'cha N.M. (PL بچے کچے bach'che kach'che) mere child [P]

بچھڑا bachh'ra N.M. calf بچھڑا کھونٹے کے بل پر ناچتا ہے bachh'ra khoon'te ke bal' par nach'tā hai PROV every dog is valiant at his own door بچھیا bachh'ya N.F. ★]

بچھڑنا bi'chhaṛnā V.I. be separated (from) go astray get lost

بچھنا bichh'nā V.I. be spread lie flat humble oneself (before) (of mangoes, etc.) be helped ; lie in heap بچھا جانا bi'chhā jā'nā V.I. be extremely polite بچھانا bichhā'nā V.T. spread extend lay

بچھوانا bichhvā'nā V.T. cause to spread

بچھو bich'choo N.M. scorpion

بچھوا bichh'va N.M. iron claw a kind of dagger ring for toe

بچھونا bichhau'nā N.M. bedding ; bedspread [~ بچھنا]

بچھیا bachh'yā N.F. female calf بچھڑا bachh'ra N.M. ★]

بچھیرا bachhe'ra N.M. colt بچھیری bachhe'rī N.F. foal ; filly

بچی bach'chī N.F girl female child [~ P بچہ]

بحال ba-ḥal' ADJ. reinstated restored in normal state or condition unaltered upheld refreshed flourishing again بحال رکھنا ba-ḥal' rakh'nā V.T. maintain 'status quo' uphold a decision maintain in the same condition keep (something) as it was INT. as you were بحال کرنا ba-ḥal' kar'nā V.T. reinstate restor re-establish issue orders for maintenance of 'status quo' refresh بحال ہونا ba-ḥal' ho'nā V.I be reinstated return to a former state or condition begin to flourish again be refreshed بحالی ba-ḥa'lī N.F. 'status quo' ; 'status quo ante' reinstatement restoration maintenance rehabilitation return to former state or condition prosperity recovery ; recuperation بحالی اراضی ba-ḥa'lī-e ara'zī N.F land reclamation [~ P ~ A حال]

بحث baiḥ's (ped. baḥ's) N.F discussion debate controversy question ; issue argument ; dispute ; alteration بحثا بحثی baiḥ'sa baiḥ'sī N.F. prolonged argument بحثنا baiḥs'na V.T. argue ; dispute بحث کرنا baiḥ's kar'nā V.T. discuss raise a question debate dispute ; argue [A]

بحر baiḥ'r (ped. baḥ'r) N.M. (PL. ابحار abḥār' ab'ḥur, بحور buḥoor') sea ; ocean N.F. (PL. بحور buḥoor) metre بحر کھلنا baiḥ'r khul'nā V.T. (of memory, intellect, etc.) improve بحر اوقیانوس (یا ظلمات) baiḥ'r-e oqiyānoos' (or arch. zulumāt', arch. col. zulmāt') N.M. Atlantic Ocean بحر منجمد شمالی baiḥ'r-e mun'jamid-e) shimā'lī N.M. Arctic Ocean بحر منجمد جنوبی baiḥ'r-e mun'jamid-e) janoo'bī N.M. Antarctic بحر ہند baiḥ'r-e hind' N.M. Indian Ocean بحری baiḥ'rī (ped. baḥ-) ADJ. sea of the sea marine nautical maritime naval بحریہ baiḥriy'yah (ped. baḥ-) N.M. navy پاکستانی بحریہ pakistā'nī baiḥriy'yah N.M. Pakistan Navy بحیرہ boḥai'rah N.M. ★ [A]

بحران boḥran' N.M. crisis, critical moment turning point of disease (etc.) abnormal condition بحرانی boḥrā'nī ADJ. critical abnormal بحرانی کیفیت boḥrā'nī kaifiy'yat' N.F. crisis abnormal condition [A]

بحور bāḥoor' N.M. PL. seas ; oceans ; N.F metres [A ~ SING. بحر.]

بحیرہ buḥai'rah N.M. sea large lake بحیرہ اسود boḥai'ra(-e) as'vad N.M. Black Sea بحیرہ روم boḥai'ra(-e) room' N.M. Mediterranean بحیرہ قلزم boḥai'ra(-e) qul'zum N.M. Red Sea بحیرہ خضر boḥai'ra(-e) kha'zar N.M Caspian Sea [A ~ بحر dim.]

بخار bukhār' N M. fever ague steam ; vapour grief ; anguish worry ; anxiety rage ; anger grudge ; animosity بخار آنا bukhār' ā'nā V.I. have fever ; run a temperature ; be feverish بخار دل میں رکھنا bukhār' dil' men rakh'nā V.I. bear a grudge ; harbour animosity دل کا بخار نکالنا dil' kā bukhār' nikal'nā V.I. vent (one's) rage , give (someone) hell air (one's) grievances بخارات bukhārāt' N.M PL. steam fume vapours [A]

بخاری bukhā'rī N.F. high-up niche used as granary fireplace in wall (also صحیح بخاری saḥīḥ' bukhā'rī) name of a famous collection of Traditions ADJ of Bukhara (in Central Asia) [A ~ T]

بخت bukh't N.M. lot fate portion luck ; good fortune prosperity بخت آزمائی bakh't-āzmā''ī N.F. trying one's luck venture hazard بخت آزمائی کرنا bakh't-āzmā''ī kar'nā V.I. try one's luck بخت آور bakht-ā'var ADJ. lucky ; fortunate بخت جلنا bakht jal'nā V.I. (fig) be in bad luck fall on evil days سیہ بخت siyah'-bakht, سیاہ بخت siyāh'-bakht, تیرہ بخت tī'ra-bakht N.M. unlucky ; unfortunate سیہ بختی siyah'-bakh'tī, سیاہ بختی siyāh'-bakh'tī, تیرہ بختی tī'ra-bakh'tī N.F. adversity misfortune بخت خفتہ bakh't-e khūf'tah N M. bad luck ; misfortune adversity خفتہ بخت khūf'ta-bakh't ADJ. unlucky ; unfortunate بختیار bakht'-yār ADJ. (rare) fortunate ; lucky [P]

بختی būkh'tī N.F. dromedary [P]

بختے bakh'te N.M. PL. parched and shelled gram

بخرہ bakh'rah N.M. share portion despatched share (of invited but unattending guests) [P]

بخش bakh'sh SUF. forgiving imparting ; bestowing N.M. share ; lot portion بخش دینا bakh'sh de'nā V.T. forgiving grew ; bestow بخشش bakh'shish N.F. salvation forgiveness ; pardon generosity; beneficence gift ; boon (ped. for col. بخشیش bakhshīsh') tip بخشنا bakhsh'nā V.T. forgive ; pardon absolve excuse give ; grant ; bestow reward بخشندہ bakhshin'dah ADJ. pardoner giver ; bestower بخشوانا bakhshvā'nā V.T. obtain pardon cause to give بخشی bakh'shī N.M. (arch.) bursar paymaster C-in-C ; Commander-in-Chief بخشی الممالک bakh'shī-ūl-mamā'lik (arch.) C-in-C Paymaster-General بخشی خانہ bakh'shī-khā'nah N.M. (arch.) Military Accounts Office بخشی گری bakh'shī-ga'rī N.F. Office of Paymaster-General [P]

بخل būkh'l N.M. miserliness ; stinginess ; niggardliness ; parsimony greed ; avarice بخیل bakhīl' N.M. miser ADJ. miserly ; stingy ; niggardly بخیلی bakhī'lī N F. miserliness ; stinginess ; niggardliness ; parsimony [A]

بخیہ bakh'yah N.M. stitching stitches basting tacks بخیہ لگانا bakh'yah lagā'nā V T. stitch baste tack بخیے ادھیڑنا bakh'ye ūdher'nā V.T. unsew ; open at stitches (fig.) expose (someone) [P]

بد[1] bad ADJ. bad wicked , evil malicious mischievous , naughty clever N.M. (col.) pig بد اچھا بدنام برا bad ach'chhā bad'nām' bū'rā PROV. give a dog a bad name and hang him بداختر bad-akh'tar ADJ. unlucky ; unfortunate ill-starred بداخلاق bad-akhlāq' ADJ. immoral rude ; coarse ill-mannered بداخلاقی bad-akhlā'qī N.F. immorality rudeness بداسلوب bad-ūsloob' ADJ. in elegant ill-behaved ill-shaped بداصل bad-as'l ADJ. base-born mean بداطوار bad-atvār' ADJ. ill-mannered vulgar of evil ways ; immoral بداعتقاد bad-e'tiqād' ADJ. faithless ; lacking in faith or belief of wavering faith unorthodox بدافعال bad-af'āl' ADJ. (rare) wicked immoral بدآموز bad-āmoz' ADJ. (one who counsel evil بدآموزی bad-āmozī N.F. evil counsels بدانتظام bad-intizām' ADJ. bungling mismanaged بدانتظامی bad-intizā'mī N.F mismanagement maladministration bungling بدانجام bad-añjam' ADJ. having a bad end بداندیش bad-añdesh' ADJ. inimical malicious ; malevolent بداندیشانہ bad-añdeshā'nah ADJ. malicious malignant بداندیشی bad-añde'shi N.F. ill-will ; malice ; malevolence malignity بدباطن bad-bā'tin ADJ. evil minded malicious بدباطنی bad-bā'tinī N.F. evil-mindedness ;malic بدبخت bad-bakht' ADJ. wretched unlucky; unforrtunate evil-minded ; malicious; malicious; malignant بدبختی bad-bakh'tī N.F. ill-luck ; misfortune adversity wretchedness misery بدبو bad-boo' N.F. bad adour stink; stench بدبودار bad-boo dār ADJ. odorous stinking بدبیں bad-bīñ' ADJ. malicious inimical بدبینی bad-bī'nī N.F. malevolence بدپرہیز bad-parhez' ADJ. over-indulging (in food, etc.) contravening of dietary rules or instructions بدپرہیزی bad-parhe'zī N.F. such over indulgence such contravention بدتر bad -tar (ped. bad'-tar) ADJ. worse inferior بدچلن bad-cha'lan (or bad'-) ADJ. immoral debauched بدحال bad-hal' ADJ. in bad circumstance ; in evil plight fallen on evil days بدحواس bad-havas' ADJ. nervous confused struck with consternation unnerved ; one whose nerves are on the edge ; jittery بدحواسی bad-havā'sī N.F. nervousness mistake made through it ; ludicrity بدخصلت bad-khas'lat, بدخصال bad-khisal' ADJ. evil ill-disposed ; ill-natured بدخصلتی bad-khas'latī N.F. evil disposition بدخط bad-khat' ADJ. (one who writes a bad hand بدخطی bad-khat'tī N.F. scrawl , bad hand بدخلق bad-khul'q ADJ. rude vulgar بدخلقی

bad-khul'qi N.M. rudeness بدخو **bad-khoo'** ADJ. evil-minded malicious rude بدخوئی **bad-khoo''i** N.M.. malice ; evil disposition rudeness بدخوابی **bad-kha'bi** N.F. insomnia ; sleeplessness بدخواہ **bad-khah'** ADJ. malicious ; malevolent malignant inimical N.M. evil-wisher enemy بدخواہی **bad-kha'hi** N.F. enmity ; animosity malevolence بددعا **bad-do'a'** N.F. curse ; malediction ; imprecation بددل **bad-dil'** ADJ. frustrated disgusted disheartened hopeless بددلی **bad-di'li** disgust frustration بددماغ **bad-dimagh'** ADJ. haughty ; prude peevish ; fretful rude بددماغی **bad-dima'ghi** N.F. pride ; vanity preevishness rudeness بددیانت **bad-diya'nat** ADJ. dishonest unreliable faithless بددیانتی **bad-diya'-nati** N F. dishonesty بدذات **baz-zat'** (or ped. **bad-zat'**) ADJ. low-born ; of bad disposition ; base ; ill-bred ; unprincipled vicious ; evil-minded wicked base ; low-born بدذاتی **bad-za'ti** N.F. wickedness vileness meanness بدذائقہ **bad'-za''iqah** ADJ. unpalatable بدراہ **bad-rah'** ADJ. wicked sinful evil debauched بدرکاب **bad-rikab'** ADJ. (of horse) difficult to ride بدرنگ **bad-rang'** ADJ. discoloured dull ; faded بدرو **bad-roo'** ADJ. ugly ; ungainly بدروئی **bad-roo''i** N.F. ugliness بدزبان **bad-zaban'** ADJ. abusive; reviling; foulmouthed بدزبانی **bad-zab'ni** N.F. abusive language ; abuse بدزیب **bad-zeb'** ADJ. ungraceful ugly بدزیبی **bad-ze'bi** N.F. ill grace ; bad grace بدساعت **bad-sa''at** N.F. unhappy moment unfortunate occasion بدسرشت **bad-sirisht'** ADJ. ill-natured بدسگال **bad-sigal'** ADJ. malicious ; malovolent ; malignant بدسلوکی **bad-sulook'i** N.F. maltreatment misbehaviour بدسیرت **bad-si'rat** ADJ. ill-natured evil unmannerly rude بدسیرتی **bad-si'rati** N.F. maliciousness rudeness بدشکل **bad-shak'l** ADJ. ugly ; unbeautiful ; ungainly بدشکلی **bad-shak'li** N.F. ugliness بدشگونی **bad-shugoo'ni** N.F. ill omen inauspiciousness بدصورت **bad-soo'rat** ADJ. ugly ; ungainly بدصورتی **bad-soo'rati** N.F. ugliness ungainliness بدطینت **bad-ti'nat** ADJ. malicious ; malevolent ; evil-minded بدطینتی **bad-ti'nati** N.F. malice بدظن **bad-zan'** ADJ. suspicious distrustful بدظنی **bad-zan ni** N.F. distrust suspicion بدعہد **bad-'aih'd** ADJ. false ; faithless ; treacherous disloyal untrue to one's word بدعہدی **bad-aih'di** N.F. breach of promise backing out of one's words faithlessness treachery

بدفعلی **bad-fe''li** N.F. criminal assault unnatural offence بدکار **bad-kar'** ADJ. sinful (sexually) immoral بدکردار **bad-kirdar'** ADJ. sinful wicked ; evil بدکردار شخص **bad-kirdar' shakh's** N.F. bad character evil person بدگمان **bad-guman'** ADJ. suspicious ; distrustful disbelieving بدگمانی **bad-guma'ni** N.F. suspicion ; distrust بدگو **bad-go'** ADJ. foulmouthed N.M. slanderer ; calumniator بدگوئی **bad-go'i** N.F. abuse ; slander ; calumny بدگوہر **bad-gau'har** ADJ. (lit.) evil بدلحاظ **bad-lihaz'** ADJ. rude disrespectful impudent بدلحاظی **bad-liha'zi** N.F. rudeness impudence بدلگام **bad-lagam'** ADJ. foul-mouthed rude (of horse) hard-mouthed ; wayward بدلگامی **bad-laga'mi** N.F. rudeness waywardness بدمزاج **bad-mizaj'** ADJ. peevish ; fretful proud ; haughty بدمزاجی **bad-miza'ji** N.F. peevishness pride ; vanity بدمزگی **bad-maz'gi** (ped. **bad-ma'zagi**) N.F. bad taste unpleasantness between friend tiff بدمزہ **bad-ma'zah** ADJ. unpalatable having a bad taste tasteless ; vapid ; insipid بدمست **bad-mast'** ADJ. deed-drunk inebriated ; sottish ; tippled (fig.) lustful (fig.) drunk (with power) بدمعاش **bad-ma'ash'** ADJ. immoral ; of an evil profession roguish N.M. bad character blackguard rascal بدمعاملہ **bad-mo'ma'alah** ADJ. dishonest ; fraudulent untrue to one's word unfair in dealings بدمعاملگی **bad-mo'a'malagi** N.F. unfair dealing dishonesty بدنام **bad-nam'** ADJ. notorious ; disreputable ; infamous ; ignominous defamed vilified ; slandered بدنام کرنا **bad-nam' kar'na** V.T. defame ; asperse ; slander ; vilify بدنامی **bad-nami** N.F. notoriety desrepute infamy ignominy dishonour ; disgrace بدنسل **bad-nas'l** ADJ. of low breed of low origin بدنصیب **bad-nasib'** ADJ. unlucky ; unfortunate miserable ; wretched بدنصیبی **bad-nasi'bi** N.F. ill-luck ; misfortune misery بدنما **bad-numa'** ADJ. awkward ; clumsy ungraceful ; inelegant unbecoming بدنمائی **bad-numa''i** N.F. awkwardness ; clumsiness ungracefulness inelegence بدنہاد **bad-nihad'** ADJ. ill-intentioned ill-natured ; evil ; malice بدنہادی **bad-niha'di** N.F. evil disposition بدنیت **bad- niy'yat** ADJ. greedy ; avaricious ill-intentioned ; ill-disposed malicious ; malevolent dishonest بدنیتی **bad- niy'yati** N.F. ill-will malice ; evil intention dishonesty greed ; avarice بدوضع **bad-vaz''** ADJ. ugly ungainly clumsy ; awkward unmannerly

بدوضعی *bad-vaz''ī* N.F. ugliness evil disposition unmannerliness dishonesty evil ways بدہضمی *bad-haz'mī* N.F. indigestion ; dyspepsia بدہیئت *bad-hai'at* ADJ. ugly inelegent ; ungraceful awkward ; clumsy بدیمن *bad-yūm'n* ADJ. (lit.) ill-omened unpropitious بدیمنی *bad-yūm'nī* N.F. (lit.) ill-luck بدی *ba'dī* N.F. vice evil wickedness mischief بدی پر اترنا *ba'dī bar ū'tarnā* V.I. be bent upon mischief بدی کرنا *ba'dī kar'nā* V.T. do harm (to someone) [P]

²بد *bad'* N.F. bubo [S]

بداہت *badā'hat* N.F. extemporization [A]

بدائع *badā''e'* ADJ. wonders rarities curios rhetorical devices [A ~ SING. بدیعہ بدیع ~]

بدبدانا *būdbūdā'nā*, بدبدر کرنا *bū'dar bū'dar kar'nā* V.I. mumble mutter grumble

بدر *bad'r* N.M. moon بدر کامل *bad'r-e kā'mil* full moon (fig.) exquisitely beautiful person [A]

بدر *ba-dar'* ADV. out ; outside SUF. banished from بدر کرنا *ba-dar' kar'nā* V. extern banish extradite expatriate دربدر *dar' ba-dar'* ADJ. from door to door forced to lead a tram's life دربدر خاک بسر ہونا *dar' ba-dar' khāk' ba-sar' ho'nā* PH. be forced to lead a tramp's life move from door to door without success fall on evil days شہربدر *shaih'r ba-dar'* ADJ. banished from city ; expelled from town ملک بدر *mūl'k ba-dar'* ADJ. exiled ; banished extradited [P ~ بہ + در door]

بدررو *ba'dar-rau* (ped. *ba-dar'-rau*) N.F. sewer [F]

بدرقہ *bad'raqah* N.M. escort convoy drug moderating effect of others in a recipe; moderating drug [A]

بدرہ *badrah* N.M. (arch.) purse purse containing a thousand rupees

بدعت *bid''at* N.F. innovation in religion schism heresy any innovation بدعتی *bid''atī* N.M. innovator in religion one creating schism heretic innovator [A]

بدکنا *bi'daknā* V.I. shy . start be scared take flight بدکانا *bidkā'nā* V.T. cause to shy . startle scare . frighten estrange

بدل *ba'dal* N.M. substitute alternative noun in apposition بدل جانا *ba'dal jā'nā* V.I. change back out بدل دینا *ba'dal de'nā* V.T. change بدل لینا *ba'dal le'nā* V.I. exchange (something with) بدل اشتراک *ba'dal-ishtirāk'* N.M. (ped.) subscription (of periodical)

بدلنا *ba'dalnā* V.T. change alter shift move vary بدلی *badlī* N.F. transfer change of guards بدلانا *badlā'na* V.T. cause to change alter exchange بدلائی *badlā''ī* N.F. exchange commission barter [A ~ PREC.]

بدلہ *bad'lah* N.M. exchange ; lieu ; compensation revenge retaliation exchange ; return ادلے کا بدلہ *ad'le kā bad'lah* PH. tit for tat بدلہ دینا *bad'lah de'nā* V.T. requite ; reward compensate ; indemnify بدلہ لینا *bad'lah le'nā* V.T take revenge ; wreak vengeance on ; avenge [~ PREC.]

بدلی *bad'lī* N.F. small cloud [~ بادل DIM.]

بدن *ba'dan* N.M. body physique بدن ٹوٹنا *ba'dan toot'nā* V.I. suffer racking pains in the body feel feverish بدن پھیلنا *ba'dan phail'nā* V.I. have boils all over the body بدن پھیکا ہونا *ba'dan phī'kā ho'nā* V.I. feel feverish be running a temperature بدن چرانا *ba'dan chūrā'nā* V.I. feel abashed (بدن کے) رونگٹے کھڑے ہونا (*ba dan ke*) *rauṅg'ṭe khaṛe ho'nā* V.I. have the hair stand on the end (owing to extreme fear or cold) feel intense cold be terror-striken بدنی *ba'danī* ADJ. bodily ; corporal corporeal [A]

بدنا *bad'nā* شرط بدنا *shart bad'nā* V.T. & I. bet ; wager بدا ہونا *ba'dā ho'nā* V.I. be preordained بدا بدی *ba'dā ba'dī* N.F. emulation ; contention ADV. trying to excel , outbidding

¹بدو *bad'doo* N.M. & ADJ. (one) who has a bad name

²بدو *bad'doo* N.M Bedouin [~ foll ; CORR.]

بدوی *ba'davī* ADJ. & Bedouin desert , of desert N.M. the desert [A ~ بادیہ]

بدھ *būdh* N.M the Buddha Buddhist(s) wisdom ; commonsense consciousness Wednesday (the planet) Mercury بدھ مت *būdh mat* N.M. Buddhism بدھو *būd'dhoo* N.M. simpleton arrant fool بدھ بدھ کے گٹے *būdh' būdh ke gaṭ'ṭe* N.M. P.L. small potsherds tossed and caught in opposite side of hand in children's game [~ S]

بدھائی *badhā''ī* N.F. (dial.) congratulation

بدھنا *badh'nā* N.M. earthen jar for Persian wheel spouted earthen jug

بدھی *bad'dhī* N.F. garland mark left on body by a hit
بدھیا *badh'yā* N.M. castrated animal bullock بدھیا کرنا *badhyā kar'nā* V.T. castrate
بدیا *bid'deyā*, ودیا *vid'deyā* N.F. (dial.) knowledge ; skill کرتے کی بدیا *kar'te kī bid'deya* PROV. skill comes with practice [S]
بدیس *bades'* N.M. foreign land ; alien country ADV. abroad بدیسی *bade'sī* ADJ. foreign ; alien N.M. foreigner [~دیس]
بدیع *badī'* ADJ. wonderful novel N.M. (PL. بدائع *badā''e'*) rhetorical device also علم بدیع *'il'm-e badī'* science dealing with rhetorical devices ; rhetoric بدیع الجمال *badī''-ul-jamāl'* N.M. paragon of beauty ADJ. exquisitely beautiful [A]
بدیہہ *badī'hah* ADJ. appropriate apt extempore ; impromptu بدیہہ گوئی *badī'ha-go'ī* N.F. extemporization بدیہی *badī'hī* ADJ. self-evident axiomatic plain unpremeditated. بدیہیات *badīhiyyāt'* N.F. PL. axioms ; self-evident truths [A ~ بداہت]
بڈھا *bud'dhā* ADJ. aged old elderly N.M. old man father بڈھا پھونس *būd'dhā phoons'* ADJ. & N.M. decrepit old man بڈھی *būd'dhī* ADJ. (arch.) old
بذل *baz'l* N.M. munificence [A]

بذلہ *baz'lāh* N.M. witticism ; joke wit بذلہ سنج *baz la-sanj'* ADJ. witty (person) بذلہ سنجی *baz'la-san'jī* N.F. wittiess [A]
بر ۱ *bar* N.M. land land mass بر اعظم *bar're-ā''zam* N.M. continent بری *bār'rī* ADJ. ★ بریہ *barriy'yah* N.M. (see under بری *bar'rī* ADJ. ★) [A]
بر ۲ *bar* N.M. body lap ; flank [P]

بر ۳ *bar* N.M. groom ; bridegroom husband width (of cloth)
بر ۴ *bar* PREF. on upon at above out SUF: bearer ; carrier N.F. bosom ; breast heart body fruit بر آنا *bar ā'nā* V.I. (of hope) be fulfilled برپا *bar-pā'* ADV. afoot ; on foot in progress برپا کرنا *bar-pā' kar'nā* V.T. establish set on foot convene برپا ہونا *bar-pā' ho'nā* V.I. happen ; take place befall be established be convened be in progress برتر *bar'-tar* ADJ. higher suprerior eminent excellent supreme برتری *bar'-tarī* N.F. supremacy superiority excellence برجستہ *bar-jas'tah* ADJ. apt apposite extempore ; impromptu برحق *bar-haq'* ADJ. right justifiable inevitable incontrovertable کے برخلاف *ke bar-khilāf'*, کے برعکس *ke bar-ak's* ADV. on the contrary as against برزبان تسبیح و در دل گاؤ خر *bar zabān' tasbī'h-o dar dil' ga''o khar'* PROV. be a wolf in sheep's skin برطرف *bar taraf* ADJ. sacked ; dismissed ; discharged aside apart separated برطرف کرنا *bar-ta'raf kar'nā* V.I. sack ; dismiss ; discharge برطرف ہونا *bar-ta'raf ho'nā* V. be sacked ; be dismissed; be discharged برطرفی *bar-tar'fī* (ped. *-ta'rafī*) N.F. dismiss ; discharge برقرار *bar-qarār'* ADJ. continuing as before extant firm established برلانا *bar lā'nā* V.T. fulfil grant برمحل *bar-mahal'*, برموقع *bar-mau'qa'*, بروقت *bar-vaq't* ADJ. apt ; apposite opportune ; in the nick of time برملا *bar-malā* ADV. openly publicly [P]
بر *bir* N.F. virtue obedience ADJ. (rare) obedient [A]
بر *būr* N.M. nap, N.F. vagina

برا *bū'rā* N.M. bad person ill-wisher accused ADJ. (F. بری *bū'rī*) bad worthless faulty defective mischievous ill-mannered ugly ungraceful برا بننا *bū'rā ban'nā* V.I. be deemed an enemy be accused be condemned برا بھلا *bū'rā bha'lā* ADJ. indifferent tolerable ; passable of all sorts assorted good or bad N.M. abuse reproach ; admonition only برا بھلا کہنا *bū'rā bha'lā kaih'nā* V.T. abuse ; revile admonish ; reproach give (someone) hell برا حال *bū'rā hal* N.M. straitened circumstances. pitiable condition برا حال کرنا *bū'rā hal kar'nā* V.T. maltreat reduce to pitiable condition badger chaff ; annoy ruin ; reduce to straitened circumstances برا کام *bū'rā kām* N.M. evil deed sexual intercourse برا لکھا *bū'rā lik'khā* N.M. bad luck برا لگنا *bū'rā lag'nā* V.I. be unpleasant ; be disagreeable برا ماننا *bū'ra mān'nā* V.I. take offence ; feel offended ; take as an affront be displeased ; take (something) ill براوقت *bū'ra vaq't* N.M. evil days ; hard times برے حالوں جینا *bū're ha'loṅ jī'nā* V.I. fall on evil days بروں کی جان کو رونا *bū'roṅ kī jān' ko ro'nā* PH. complain of tyranny complain of wrong step taken by elders برے وقت کا کوئی ساتھی نہیں *bū're vaq't kā ko''ī sā'thī na'hīṅ* PROV. none helps in adversity برائی

būrā''ī N.F. ★

برا *bar'ra* N.M. (dial.) (same as بڑا *ba'ṛa* N.M.★)

برابر *barā'bar* ADJ. equal ; equivalent even ; level uniform plain smooth straight like alike on a par (with) exact accurate opposite regular continuous ADV. equally abreast uniformly evenly smoothly straight similarly exactly near over against beside opposite regularly continuously برابر برابر *barā'bar barā'bar* (col. برا برابر *ba'rā-barā'bar*) ADJ. half equal ADV. side by side abreast continuously regularly برابر کا *barā'bar kā* ADJ. equal match grown-up برابر کا بیٹا *barā'bar kā be'ṭā* N.M. grown-up son برابر کرنا *barā'bar kar'nā* V.T. squander level up smooth match adjust divide equally assimilate do continuously do unhesitatingly برابر کی ٹکر کا *barā'bar kī ṭak'kar kā* ADJ. equal on a par (with) match برابر ہو جانا *barā'bar ho jā'nā* V.I. become equal be on a par (with) be full to the brim become level be balanced be spent ; be squandered برابر ہونا *barā'bar ho'nā* V.I. be equal fit be on a par (with) overtake come abreast (of) suit be spent be squandered end ; come to an end برابری *barā'barī* N.F. equality parity par emulation competition contest برابری کرنا *barā'barī kar'nā* V.T. try to equal emulate vie (with) match contest resist

برات[1] *barāt'*, بارات *bārāt'* N.F. marriage procession (fig.) crowd ; concourse برات چڑھنا *barāt' chaṛh'nā* V.I. (of marriage procession) set out for bride's house *barā'tī* N.M. wedding-guest (fig.) participant of a procession

برات[2] *barāt'* (ped. براءت *barā''at*) N.F. lot (ped.) cheque برات عاشقاں بر شاخ آہو *barāt-e 'ā'shiqāṅ bar shākh'-e ā'hoo* PROV. lovers are penniless true love goes unrewarded شب برات *shab-barāt'*, شب براءت *shab-e barā''at*, لیلۃ البراءت *lai lat-ul barā''at* N.F. (see under شب N.F. ★) [~A براءت]

براجمان *birāj'mān* ADV. (dial.) sitting (on throne, etc.) براجمان ہونا *birāj'mān ho'nā* V.I. (dial.) sit ; be seated ; grace

برادر *birā'dar* N.M. brother cousin (distant) relation برادر اخیافی *birā'dar-e akhyā'fī* N.M. half-brother (*i.e.* one born of same mother but different father) برادر حقیقی *birā'dar-e ḥaqīqī* N.M. brother ; own brother برادر رضائی *birā'dar-e rizā''ī* N.M. foster brother برادر زادہ *birā'dar-zā'dah* N.M. nephew ; brother's son برادر علاتی *birā'dar-e 'alā'tī* N.M. step-brother ; brother descended from same father but different mother برادر کش *birā'dar-kūsh* ADJ. & N.M. fratricide برادر کشی *birā'dar-kū'shī* N.F. fractricide برادر نسبتی *birā'dar-e nis'batī* N.M. brother-in-law ; wife's brother or sister's husband برادرانہ *birā'dar'nah* ADJ. brotherly ; fraternal ADV. fraternally برادری *birā'darī* N.F. outer family circle kith and kin brotherhood ; fraternity group ; coterie [P]

برادہ *būrā'dah* N.M. filings sawdust powder [P]

براڈ کاسٹ *brādkāsṭ* N.M. broadcast براڈ کاسٹنگ *brād'kāsṭing* N F. broadcasting [E]

براز *barāz'* N.M. faeces ; stool ; motion بول و براز *baul-o barāz'* N.M. excrement of bowels and bladder [A]

براز *birāz'* N.M. single combat challenge to it [A ~ براز]

برافروختہ *bar-afrokh'tah* ADJ. (of person) enraged ; in a fit of passion (of fire, etc.) enkindled [P ~ بر + افروختن]

براق *būrāq'* N.M. lightning horse (*i.e.* the quadruped on whose back the Holy Prophet journeyed during Ascension [A]

براق *būrrāq'* (ped. *barrāq'*) ADJ. shining سفید براق *sifed' būrrāq'* ADJ. very white milk white [A برق]

برآمد *bar-ā'mad* N.F. (PL. برآمدات *bar-āmadāt'*) export land thrown up by a river recovery recovered property coming up coming out exit برآمدہ *bar-ā'madah* ADJ. exported recovered thrown up by river [P ~ بر out + آمدہ come]

برآمدہ *barām'dah* N.M verandah برآمدے میں *barām'de meṅ* ADV. on the verandah [Pg ~ L or Pg ~ P]

بران *būr'rāṅ* ADJ. of sword, etc.) cutting , sharp [P]

برانا *barrā'nā* V.I. talk in one's sleep rave (in delirium)

برانا *bar'ānā* V.I. (of hope) come true prove more than a match (for) [~ P بر + آمدن]

برانچ *baranch'* N.F. branch [E]

برانڈی *baran'dī* N.F. brandy [E]

برانگیختہ *bar-angekh'tah* ADJ. roused ; awakened stirred up excited erect enraged برانگیختہ کرنا *bar-angekh'tah kar'na* V. rouse stir up incite enrage برانگیختہ ہونا *bar angekh'tah ho'nā* V.I. rouse stir up be incited be enraged ; fall into a fit of passion [P ~ بر + انگیختن]

براہمہ *bara'himah* N.M. PL. Brahmins [A ~ S SING.]

براہین *barahīn'* N.M. (PL. of برہان N.F. ★)

براءت *bara''at* (preferably to be written as برائت) N.F. acquittal [A ~ بری]

برائی *bura''ī* N.F. badness evil vice mischief wickedness harm ; wrong adverse comments سے برائی کرنا *se bura''ī kar'nā* V.T. harm ; do wrong to برائی پر کمر باندھنا *burā''ī par ka'mar bāndh'nā* PH. be bent upon, mischief پیٹھ پیچھے (کسی کی) برائی کرنا *pīṭh' pī'chhe (ki'sī kī) burā''ī kar'nā* PH. backbite (someone) [~ برا ADJ. ★]

برائے *barā''e* ADV. for on account of ; owing to ; by reason of for the sake of in order to ; with a view to ; to the end that برائے بیت *barā''e bait'* ADV. nominally ; cursorily just a little not enough برائے خدا *barā''e khudā'* ADV. for God's sake برائے نام *barā''e nām'* ADV. nominally ; cursorily just a little not enough [P]

برایا *barā'yā* N.F. (ped.) creation ; creatures people [A ~ SING. بریہ]

برباد *bar-bād'* ADJ. ruined ; destroyed ; laid waste wasted squandered flung to the winds برباد کرنا *bar-bād' kar'na* V.T. destroy ; ravage waste ; squander fling to the winds برباد ہونا *bar-bād' ho'nā* V.I. be ruined ; be destroyed be wasted ; be squandered be flung to the winds بربادی *bar-bā'dī* N.F. ruin destruction ravage waste loss [P ~ بر on + باد wind]

بربرانا *burburā'nā* V.T. (same as برکنا ★)

بربریت *barbariy'yat* N.F. barbarity [A ~ بربر Berber]

بربط *bar'bat* N.M. a kind of harp ; duckharp [~ بط]

برت *bar't* N.M. fast as kept by Hindus [S]

برتا *bir'tā* N.M. power courage ability support برتے پر اچھلنا *birte par uchhalnā* V.I. pride oneself on the support (of) کس برتے پر تتا پانی *kis bir'te pa tat'tā pā'nī* PROV. why this vain show ?

برتن *bar'tan* N.M. vessel ; utensil

برتنا *ba'ratnā* V.T. use put to use treat try know by experience برتانا *bartā'nā* V.T. dish out cause to use برتاؤ *bartā''o* N.M. treatment behaviour conduct practice intimacy usage سے برتاؤ کرنا *se bartā''o kar'nā* V.I. treat ; behave (towards)

برتھ کنٹرول *barth kantrol'* N.M. birth control [E]

برج بھاشا *birj' bhā sha,* برج بھاکا *birj' bhā ka* N.F. mediaeval dialect spoken in eastern U.P. in India in the area now called Mathura then known as 'birj' or cowshed of Krishna

برج *būr'j* N.M. (PL. بروج *būrooj*) tower turret bastion sign of the zodiac برجی *būr'jī'* N.F. turret [~ A]

برجس *bir'jis* N.F. breeches [E]

برجیس *birjīs'* N.M. Jupiter [P]

برچھا *bar'chhā* N.M. spear lance javelin برچھی *bar'chhī* N.F. small spear dart برچھیت *barchhait* N.M. lancer

برخاست *barkhāst'* N F. sacked dismissed discharged removed (of court) rising up (of meeting) adjourned برخاست کرنا *barkhāst' kar'nā* V.T. dismiss discharge remove from office (of meeting break up (of court) rise for the day (of Assembly) adjorn برخاست ہونا *barkhāst' ho'nā* V.I. be saked be dismissed be discharged rise for the day break up adjourn برخاستگی *barkhās'tagī* N.F. dismissal discharge recall removal breaking-up dissolution adjournment [P]

برخوردار *barkhūrdār'* N.M. (euph. for) son lad ADJ. enjoying long life and prosperity [P]

برد[1] *būrd* SUF. requisition borne taking away N.F. checkmate owing to loss of all pieces save king [P ~ بردن]

برد[2] *būrd* N.F. striped shawl بردیمانی *būrd-e yamā'nī* N.F. striped Yemen shawl [A]

بردار *bar-dār'* SUF. carrier bearer برداری *bardārī* SUF. carrying transport [P ~ POLL.]

برداشت *bar-dāsht'* N.F. endurance patience tolerance resignation برداشت کرنا *bar dāsht' kar'nā* V.T. brook ; bear ; endure ; tolerate برداشت ہونا *bar-dāsht' ho'nā* V.I. be tolerable be endured ; be brooked برداشتہ *bardāsh'tah* affixed raised removed برداشتہ خاطر ہونا *bardāsh'ta-khā'tir ho'nā* V.I. be disgusted be frustrated [P ~ بر up + داشتن have]

بردبار *bürdbār'* ADJ. forbearing ; enduring tolerant patient meek بردباری *bürd-ba'rī* N.F. forbearance ; endurance patience toleration ; bearing of a burden [P]

بردہ *bar'dah* N.M. (arch.) slave woman abducted or person kidnapped for being sold as slave بردہ فروش *bar'da-firosh'* N.M. (arch.) slave dealer trafficker in women and children بردہ فروشی *bar'da-firo'shī* N.F. (arch.) slave trade trafficking in women and children

برزخ *bar'zakh* N.M. partition purgatory [A]

برزن *bar'zan* N. street quarter (of town) [P]

برس *ba'ras* N.M. year برس دن کے دن *ba'ras din' ke din* PH. at this annual festival برسی *bar'sī* N.F. death anniversary (rare) any annual commemoration

برسات *barsāt'* N.F. rainy season ; the rains برساتی *barsā'tī* N.F. raincoat ; makintosh open-sided room on top of house patio ADJ. of rainy season flooded by rains [~ برسنا]

برسرکار *bar sar-e kār* ADJ. employed engaged in business [P ~ بر + سر + کار]

برسنا *ba'rasnā* V.I. rain (fig.) pour a torrent of invective on برس پڑنا *ba'ras par'nā* V.I. begin to rain (fig.) give (someone) a piece of one's mind برسانا *barsā'nā* V.T. cause to rain shower down pour down winnow

برش *bür'rish* N.F. cutting ; sharpness [P]

برش *bürsh* N.M. brush [E]

برشگال *barshagāl'* N.M. rainy season ; the rains

برص *ba'ras* N.M. leucoderma [A]

برطانیہ *bartā'niyah* N.M. Britain برطانوی *bartān'vī* ADJ. British [A ~ E]

برف *bar'f* N.F. or F. ice snow ADJ. ice-cold snow white برف پوش *bar'f posh'* ADJ. snowcapped برف پڑنا *bar'f par'nā* V.I. snow برف ہونا *bar'f ho'nā* V.I. (of thing) become ice-cold be benumbed برفانی *barfā'nī* ADJ. very cold ice ; icy snowcapped [P]

برفی *bar'fī* N.F. white toffee [~ PREC.]

برق *bar'q* N.F. electricity lightning (arch.) firing برقاب *barq-āb'* N.F. hydroelectricity برقابی *barq-ā'bī* ADJ. hydro-electric برق انداز *bar'q-andāz'* N.M. musketeer sentinel برق پیما *bar'q-paimā'* N.M. electrometer برق زدہ *bar'q-za'dah* ADJ. struck with lightning برق گیر *bar'q-gīr'* N.M. conductor برق نما *bar'q-nūmā'* N.M. electroscope برقی *bar'qī* ADJ. electric ; electrical برقی رو *bar'qī rau* N.F. current ; electric current برقی شعاع *bar'qī sho'ā'* N.F. flashlight برقی علاج *barqī 'ilāj'* N.M. electropathy برقی موت *bar'qī maut* N.F. electrocution برقی قوت *bar'qī qūv'vat* N.F. electricity برقی توانائی *barqī tuvānā'ī* N.F. electric energy برقی لیمپ *bar'qī laimp* N.M. electric lamp برقی مقناطیس *bar'qī maq'nātīs* N.M. electromagnet برقی موٹر *bar'qī mo'ṭar* N.M. electric-motor برقانا *barqā'nā* V.I. electrify برقیات *barqiyyāt'* N.F. electrology electricity برقیہ *barqiy'yah* N.M. electron [A]

برقع *(or* برقعہ *bür'qa'* N.M gowned veil ; 'burqa' (rare) veil برقع پوش *bür'qa' posh'* ADJ. & N.F. veiled (woman) [A]

برکت *bar'kat* (ped. *ba'rakat*) N.F. (PL. برکات *barakāt*) auspiciousness good fortune blessing abundance prosperity (euphanism for) nothing ; nil ; nought برکت دینا *bar'kat de'nā* V. (of God) bring good fortune (of God) vouchsafe abundance (dial. bless [A]

برکنا *bü'raknā,* برُبرانا *bürbürā'na* V.T. add a pinch

برکھا *bar'khā* N.F. rain برکھا رت *bar'khā rūt* N.F. rainy season ; the rains [~ S]

برگ *barg* N.M. leaf petal provisions for journey برگ و بار *bārg-o-bār'* N.M. leaves and fruit (of tree) provisions property برگ و نوا *bar'g-o navā* PH. provisions گلبرگ *gūl-bar'g* N.M. petal ; rose-petal

برگد *bar'gad* N.M. banyan

برگزیدہ *bar-güzī'dah* ADJ. chosen elite elect saintly برگزیدگی *bar-güzī'dagī* N.F. saintliness being respected [P ~ بر up + گزیدن choose]

برگستوان *bargūstūvān'* N.M. armour (for horse or rider) [P]

برگشتگی *bar-gash'tagī* N.F. disgust renunciation revolt برگشتہ *bar-gash'tah* ADJ. disgusted (person) rebel [P ~ بر + گشتن]

برما *bar'mā* N.M. drill auger gimlet برمانا *barmā'nā* V.T. drill (fig.) pierce

برمونہی *būr-moon'hī* N.F. ugly person eye-sore forbidding countenance cat ADJ. foul nasty [~ برا + مونہہ]

برن *ba'ran* N.M. (rare) figure face looks [S]

برنا *barnā'* N.M. youth ADJ. young برنائی *barnā''ī* N.F. youth ; youthfulness [P]

برنج *biriṅj'* N.M. rice brass برنجی *biriṅ'jī* ADJ. brass ; brazen N.F. small nail [P]

بروا *bar'vā* N.F. name of a musical mode

بروا *bir'vā* N.M. plant sapling ہونہار بروا کے چکنے چکنے پات *hon'hār bir'vā ke chik'ne chik'ne pāt'* PROV. a precocious child shows the man inside him

بروج *būrooj'* N.M. (PL. of برج *būr'j* N.M. ★)

برودت *būroo'dat* N.F. coolness coldness chilliness [A]

بروگ *birog'* N.M. separation بروگی *biro'gī* N.M. separted lover بروگن *biro'gan* N.F. separated beloved grass-widow

برومند *baroo'mand'* ADJ. lucky ; fortunate prosperous ; thriving [P]

بروں *biroon'* ADV. out ; outside externally [P ~ بیروں CONTR.]

برہ *bar'rah* N.M. kid lamb also *bar'ra-e fa'lak*) Aries [P]

برہ *bi'rah* برہا *bir'hā* N. separation of lovers (rare) song describing pangs of separation برہا کی ماری *bi'rah kī mā'rī*, برہن *bir'han* N.F. woman separate from her beloved

برہا *bar'hā* N.M. channel for passage of water from well to field ; aqueduct

برہان *būrhān'* N.F. (PL. براہین *barāhīn'*) argument cause ; reason proof manifestation [A]

برہم *bar'-ham* ADJ. annoyed ; upset displeased ; angry in a mess disordered ; troubled درہم برہم *dar'-ham bar'-ham* ADV. topsy-turvy upset ; in a mess confused jumbled troubled برہمی *bar'-hamī* N.F. annoyance ; vexation anger ; displeasure confusion ; upsetting anarchy [P ~ بر + ہم]

برہما *barah'ma* N.M. supreme Hindu deity Brahma برہم *barahm'* PREF. of Brahma

برہم چاری *brahm-chārī* N.M. (dial.) celibate [S]

برہمن *barah'man* (or in P construction *bar'haman*) N.M. Hindu priest high caste of Hindus ; Brahmin [S]

برہنگی *baraih'nagī* N.F. nakedness nudity bareness obscenity shamelessness برہنہ *baraih'-nah* (rare *bar'hanah*) ADJ. naked nude bare obscene shameless [P]

برہی *bir'hī*, ADJ. (of bread) inlaid with minced meat, etc. and fried برہی روٹی *bir'hī ro'ṭī* N.F. such bread ; salt pie

بروٹھا *baroṭhā* N.M. vestibute

بری [1] *ba'rī* N.F. groom's wedding gifts to bride

بری [2] *ba'rī* ADJ. acquitted released exonerated free ; absolved بری الذمہ *bariy'y-ūz-zim'mah* ADJ. free from blame free from obligation absolved of responsibility unaccountable ; not responsible بریت *bariy'yat* N.F. acquittal release exoneration [A]

بری *bar'rī* ADJ. land ; of land بریہ *barrīy'yah* N.M. land force [A ~ برا]

بریاں *bir'yāṅ* ADJ. parched grilled broiled roast ; roasted بریانی *biryā'nī* N.F. multi-coloured) rice cooked in soup ; sophisticated variety of 'pulao' [P برشتن roast]

بریت *bariy'yat* (rare بریہ *bariy'yah*) N.F. (PL. برایا *barā'yā*) creation ; creature (see also under بری [2] *ba'rī* ADJ. ★) [A]

برید *barīd'* N.M. (ped.) messenger runner courier postman برید فلک *barī'd-e fa'lak* N.M. (fig.) Saturn [A]

بریں *barīṅ'* ADJ. high ; lofty sublime ADV. at this ; thereupon then [P بر + ایں]

بریشم *bare'sham* N.M. (CONTR. ~ ابریشم ★)

بڑ [1] *baṛ* N.M. banyan

بڑ [2] *baṛ* N.F. brag ; boast ; boastful talk tall story بڑبولا *baṛ-bo'lā* N.M. braggart ADJ. boastful ; bragging بڑبولا پن *baṛ-bo'lā pan* N.M. boastfulness ; bragging بڑ ہانکنا *baṛ hāṅkna*, *baṛ' lagā'nā* V.I. boast ; brag

بڑا [1] *ba'ṛā* (dial. بڑا *baṛ'rā*) N.M. (usu. as PL.) pulse-pie دہی بڑے *da'hī ba'ṛe* N.M. PL. pulse-pics served in curds

۲ بڑا *ba'ṛa* ADJ. (F. بڑی *baṛī*) old elder eldest large; big huge senior superior chief supreme rich respectable noble grand بڑا بول آگے آتا ہے *ba'ṛa bol ā'ge ā'tā hai* PROV. pride goeth before a fall vain boasts are liable to be exposed بڑا بول بولنا *ba'ṛa bol bol'na* V.I. boast; brag بڑا تیر مارنا *ba'ṛa tīr' mār'na* PH. (iron.) achieve a lot accomplish nothing بڑا دن *ba'ṛa din* N.M. (dial.) Christmas long day ADV. much daytime left بڑا دیدہ ہونا *ba'ṛa di'dah ho'nā* PH. be saucy بڑا صاحب *ba'ṛa sāhb* N.N. (col.) 'burra sa'b'; big boss بڑا کوئی *ba'ṛa ko''ī* ADJ. (iron.) clever skilful wicked; sly بڑا گھر *ba'ṛa ghar* N.M. spacious house (fig.) rich or noble family (iron.) gaol بڑے گھر کی سیر کرانا *ba're ghar' kī sair' karā'na* PH. jail; send to gaol; put behind bars بڑا گھرانا *ba'ṛa gharā'na* N.M. rich or noble family بڑا نام کرنا *ba ṛā nām' kar'na* PH. fame بڑے بول کا سر نیچا *ba're bol' kā sir' nī'chā* PROV. pride goeth before a fall بڑی *ba'ṛī*, بی بی *ba'ṛī bī''* N.F. grandma (title of respect for) old woman بڑے *ba're* also N.M. PL. big people big bosses the Big (one) elder بڑے میاں *bu're mi'yān* N.M. (title of respect for) old man بڑے میاں سو بڑے میاں چھوٹے میاں سبحان اللہ *ba're mi'yān so ba're mi'yān chho'ṭe mi'yān subḥā'n-allāh* PROV. the senior was just bad, the junior is much worse بڑائی *baṛā''ī* N.F. greatness magnanimity superiority excellence bulk hugeness boast; vaunt praise exaltation exaggeration بڑائی کرنا *baṛā''ī kar'na* V.I. brag; boast; vaunt parise; extol exaggerate

بڑبڑ *baṛ'baṛ* N.F. chatter; prate بڑبڑ کرنا *baṛ'baṛ kar'na* V.I. prate; chatter بڑبڑ لگا رکھنا *baṛ'baṛ lagā' rakh'na* V.I. prate; chatter rant بڑبڑیا *baṛ baṛiy'ya* N.M. chatterbox

بڑبڑ *buṛ'buṛ* N.F. murmur grumbling بڑبڑانا *burburā'na* V.I. mutter murmur grumble

بڑھبس *būṛbhas* N.F. youthful lust in old age بڑھبس لگنا *būṛbahas lag'na* V.I feel such lust بڑھاپا *būṛhapā* N.M. old age senility [~ بوڑھا]

بڑھنا *baṛhnā* V.I. advance moveforward rise swell grow increase stretch expand exceed surpass thrive; prosper rise (in social position) (of kite) fly higher (of lamp) be put out (of shop) be closed (of dining-table) be cleared be surplus (of profit) be yielded بڑھ کے *baṛh ke* ADV. out (do) forward exceeding limits in behaviour or talk بڑھ بڑھ کے بولنا *baṛh baṛh' ke bol'nā* V.I. brag; vaunt بڑھوتری *baṛho'tarī* N.F. gain profit surplus prosperity increment advancement increase; enhancement بڑھانا *baṛhā'nā* V.I. advance; put forward augment; increase enlarge expand extend; lengthen aggrandize amplify promote; elevate praise; eulogise exalt clear (dining-table) put out (lamp) close (shop) fly (kite) higher take off; change دودھ بڑھانا *doodh' baṛhā'nā* PH. wean بڑھاؤ *baṛ'hā''o* N.M. projection swell بڑھتی *baṛh'tī* ADJ. increasing; enhancing growing rising more than usual N.F. excess surplus بڑھیا *baṛh'yā* ADJ. superior quality; of good quality class posh

بڑھئی *baṛhā''ī* N.M. carpenter

بڑھیا *būṛh'yā* N.F. old woman (rus.) mother hag بڑھیل *birhail* N.F. hag [~ بوڑھا]

بڑی *baṛī* N.F. (PL. بڑیاں *baṛ'yāṅ*) sundried pulse-dough for stewing

بز *būz* N.F. goat بز اخفش *bu'z-e akh'fash* N.M. dunce بز کوہی *bū'z-e ko'hī* N.M. mountain goat

بزدل *būz dil'* ADJ. & N.M. chickenhearted (person); coward dastardly (person) بزدلی *būz-di'lī* N.F. cowardice; dastardliness [P]

بزاز *bazzāz'* (col. *bazāz'*) N.M. draper; cloth-merchant بزازا *bazā'zā* N.M. (slang) cloth-market بزازی *bazā'zī* N.F. (slang) drapery [A]

بزرگ *būzūr'g* ADJ. aged venerable great noble N.M. old man (one's) elder saint religious preceptor (usu. PL.) ancestors gentleman بزرگ منش *būzūr'g-ma'nish* ADJ. magnanimous بزرگوار *būzūrg-vār'* N.M. saint (one's) elder gentleman *būzūr'gī* N.F. greatness grandeur eminence old age [P]

بزم *baz'm* N.F. association meeting company social gathering

بزن *bi-zan'* IMP. strike slay behead charge بزن کرنا *bi-zan' kar'nā* V.T. strike slay behead put to the sword charge [P ب + زن ~]

بس *bas* ADJ. enough, sufficient plenty abundant ADV. in short and so INT. halt; stop enough; no more بس بس *bas' bas* INT. no thank you, no more of it stop, stay halt بس حد ہو گئی *bas had' ho ga'i* PH. stop, this is the limit بس دیکھ لیا *bas dekh' liyā* PH. you have (or it has) been exposed بس کرنا *bas' kar'nā* V.I. stop ; cease end ; close finish ازبسکہ *az bas'-keh* ADV. whereas although بسا اوقات *basā auqāt'* ADV. many a time often ; generally ; very frequently mostly ; generally [P]

بس *bas* N.M. control power authority sway ; influence ; control بس چلنا *bas' chal'nā* V.I. have power (over) avail (against) بس میں *bas' men* under control ; under one's thumb بس میں آنا *bas' men ā'na*, بس میں پڑنا *bas' men par'nā* V.T. fall into the clutches (of) ; come under the control (of) بس میں رکھنا *bas' men rakh'nā* V.T. keep (someone) under control بس میں کرنا *bas' men kar'nā* V.T. overpower control subdue ; subjugate [E]

بس۳ *bas* N.F. omnibus بس پکڑنا *bas pa'karna* V.I. catch the bus بس میں سوار ہونا *bas men savār' ho'nā* V.T. get into the bus [E]

بس *bis* N.M. venom بس اگلنا *bis ū'galna* V.I. spit venom say spiteful things بس بونا *bis' bo'nā* V.I. create trouble بس بھرا *bis' bha'ra* ADJ. (usu. F. form) venomous malicious ; spiteful virulent بس کی پڑیا *bis' kī pur'ya*, بس کی گانٹھ *bis' kī ganth'* N.F. malicious or spiteful person devil mischief-monger

بساتی *bisā'tī* N.M. (correct but little used spelling of بساطی N.M. ★)

بسارا *bisā'ra* N.M. seed loaned out on condition of double payment after crop [~ FOLL.]

بسارنا *bisār'nā* V.T. (see under بسرنا ★)

بساط *bisāt'* N.F. capacity ; capability chess-board اس کی بساط کیا *ūs kī bisāt' kyā* PH. what can he do ? ; he has no power بساط الٹنا *kī bisāt' ū'latna* PH. end (someone's) power ; spell (someone's) ruin be upset ; come to an end [A]

بساطی *bisā'tī* N.M. (more correctly but rarely spelt as بساتی) pedlar ; huckster

بساطی

بسالت *basā'lat* N.F. bravery , courage [A]

بسان *ba-sā'n-e* ADV. like ; in the manner of [P ~ بہ + سان like]

بسانا *basā'na* V.T. from (into a State) build (city) colonize (land or country) bring under plough settle (someone somewhere) (of man) get married have sex relations (with wife) cause (something) to be sented [~ بسنا CAUS.]

بساند *basand'*, بسانده *basāndh'* N.F. smell ; stink ; fetidness

بست *bas't* N.M. thing (only in) چیز بست *chīz' bast* N.F. things ; articles

بست و کشاد *bas't-o kushād'* N.F. control of affair ارباب بست و کشاد *arbā'b-e bas't-o-kūshād* N.M. PL. those at the helm of affairs [P ~ بستن bind + کشادن open]

بستان *būstān'*, بوستان *bos'tān* N.M. garden orchard [P]

بستر *bis'tar* (col. بسترا *bis'tarā*) N.M. bedding بستر (یا بسترا) بچھانا (لگانا یا کرنا) *bis tar* (or *bis'tara*) *bichhā'na* (or *lagā'nā* or *kar'nā*) V.I. do the bedding بستر بند *bis'tar band* N.M. hold all بستر (یا بسترا) باندھنا (یا گول کرنا) *bis'tar* (or *bis'tara*) *bāndh'nā* (or *gol' kar'nā*) V.I. roll the bedding (fig.) quit ; leave for good [P]

بستگی *bas'tagī* N.F. lack of gaiety constipation ; costiveness congelation ; congealment [FOLL. P ~]

بستنی *bas'tanī* N.F. covering for cage case for musical instruments [P ~ بستن bind]

بستہ *bas'tah* N.M satchel bundle bufcase ADJ. frozen ; congealed tied ; bound بستہ بردار *bas'ta-bardār'* N.M. recordcarrier ; servant carrying (boss's) papers [P ~ PREC.]

بستی *bas'tī* N.F. any peopled place ; village ; town ; city بستی بسانا *bas'tī basā'na* V.I. colonize a place have a new settlement [~]

بسر *ba-sār* (ped. *ba-sar'*) ADV. passed ; come to a close ; spent readily بسر کرنا *ba'-sar kar'nā* V.T. pass ; spend بسر ہونا *ba'-sar ho'nā* V.I, pass ; spend ; come to a close بسر و چشم *ba-sa'r-e chash'm* ADV. readily by all means

بسرنا *bi'sar'nā*, بسر جانا *bi'sar jā'nā* V.T. & I. forget be forgotten ; slip out of memory بسارنا *bisar'nā* V.T. forget بھولی بسری *bhoolī bis'rī* ADJ. long-forgotten بسرانا *bisrā'nā* V.T. put of mind cause to forget

بسط *bas't* N.M. expansion ; detail (used only in) شرح و بسط *shar'h-o beas't* N.M. detailed exposition [A]

بسکھپرا *biskhap'ra* N.M. at kind of somewhat large venomous lizard name of a grass-like drug ; polypody [~ بس +]

بسم اللہ *bis'm-illā h* ADV. in the name of God INT. watch it ; mind it ; don't fall down welcome ; hail N.F. beginning ; commencement opening (ceremony) child's first lesson on first admission to school بسم اللہ الرحمٰن الرحیم *bis'm-illā'h-ir-rahmā'n-ir-ahīm'* PH. (formula preceding all but one chapters of the Holy Quran ; In the name of the most Merciful, most Bountiful God بسم اللہ کرنا *bis'm-illah kar'nā* V.I. begin (at table) be the first to start eating commence بسم اللہ کے گنبد میں بیٹھنا *bis'm-illāh ke gum'bad meṅ baiṭh'nā* PH. be complacent ; be selfsatisfied act like a simpleton [A ~ ب + اسم + اللہ]

بسمل *bismil* N.M. & ADJ. victim ; sacrificial animal chagrined (lover) wounded (victim) بسمل کرنا *bis'mil kar'nā* V.T. immolate wound lover's heart) [A ~ PREC.]

بسنا *bas'nā* V.I. settle inhabit dwell ; reside ; abide live in husband's home have sex relations with him (also میں بسنا *meṅ bas'nā*) be scented with

بسنت *basaṅt'* N.F. early spring festival of Hindus name of a musical mode بسنت پھولنا *basaṅt' phool'nā* V.I. (of mustard flowers) blossom in early spring grow pale ; have a yellowish colour آنکھوں میں بسنت پھولنا *āṅ'khoṅ meṅ basaṅt' phool'nā* PH. be dazzled بسنتی *basaṅ'tī* ADJ. yellow

بسورنا *bisoor'nā* V.I. sob prepare to weep put on a crying face

بسولا *baso'lā* N.M. axe بسولی *baso'lī* N.F. brick-axe

بسولی

بسوہ *bis'vah* N.M. land measure (equivalent to one-twentieth of 'bigah') بسوہ دار *bis'va-dār* N.M. shareholder in coparcenary village بیس ریا بسوے (سو) *bīs* (or *sau*) *bis've* ADJ. surely ; certainly بسوانسی *bisvaṅ'sī* N.F. one-twentieth of 'bisvah'

بسیار *bisyār'* ADJ. (lit.) much many very plenty ; abundant [P]

بسیرا *base'rā* N.M. roost; perch a night's lodging abode roosting بسیرا کرنا (یا لینا) *base'rā kar'nā* (or *le'nā*) V.I. roost بسیرے کا وقت *base're kā vaq't* N.M. roosting time [~ بسنا]

بسیط *basīt'* ADJ. simple primary unmixed expansive [A ~ بسط]

بشارت *bishā'rat* (col. *būshā-*) N.F. good news ; glad tidings divine inspiration بشارت دینا *bishā'rat de'nā* V.T. convey good news ; give glad tidings [A]

بشاش *bashshāsh'* ADJ. hilarious ; cheerful ; in good spirits بشاشت *bashā'shat* N.F. cheerfulness ; gaiety [A]

بشر *ba'shar* N.M. human being ; man بشری *ba'sharī* ADJ. human بشریت *basharīy'yat* N.F. human nature human weaknesses frailties of flesh and blood [A]

بشرہ *bush'rah* (ped. *ba'sharah*) N.M. face ; countenance visage physiognomy [A]

بشنو *bishnoo'*, وشنو *vish'noo* N.M. Vishnu ; Preserver (as one of Hindu Trinity [S]

بشیر *bashīr'* ADJ. harbinger of glad tidings (dail.) evangelist [A ~ بشارت]

بصارت *basā'rat* N.F. sight ; eyesight vision محروم بصارت *mahroo'm-e basā'rat*, بصارت سے محروم *basā'rat se maihroom'* ADJ. blind [A ~ بصر]

بصائر *basā''ir* N.M. (PL. of بصیرت N.F. ★)

بصر *ba'sar* N.F. (PL. *absār'*) sight vision eye بے بصر *be-ba'sar* ADJ. blind unperceiving ; lacking foresight [A]

بصرہ *bas'rah* N.M. name of an Iraqi port-town بصری *bas'rī* (rare *bis'rī*) ADJ. of Basra

بصیر *basīr'* ADJ. Omniscient (as an attribute of God) wise prudent [A ~ بصر]

بصیرت *basī'rat* N F. sight insight discernment prudence [A ~ PREC.]

بضاعت *bizā''at* N.F. stock-in-trade merchandise capital بے بضاعت *be'biz''at* ADJ. poor ; penniless incapable of anything [A]

بط *bat* N.F. duck goose swan بطے *ba't-e mai'* N.F. (duck-shaped) goblet [A]

بطحا *bat'hā* N.M. a name for Mecca وادی بطحا *vādī-e bat'hā* (ped. *vā'dī bathā*) N.M. the vale of Mecca [A]

بطخ *bat'takh* N.F. duck duckling [P]

بطریق *bitrīq'* N.M. bishop crusading General [A ~ G]

بطل *bat'l* N.M. (PL. ابطال *abtāl*) hero [A]

بطلان *būtlān'* N.M. refutation abolition [A باطل]

بطلیموس *bat'lmoos* N.M. Ptolmey بطلیموسی *bat'lmoosī* ADJ. Ptolemaic (system) [A ~ G]

بطن *bat'n* N.M. (PL: بطون *būtoon'*) belly ; abdomen womb inside (of anything) mind کے بطن سے *ke bat'n se* ADV. borne by ; born of بطون *būtoon'* N.M. PL. bellies interior parts wombs minds [A]

بعث *ba''s* N.M. resurrection بعثت *be''sat* N.F. Annunciation (of the Holy Prophet)

apostleship [A]

بعد ba'd ADV. after; afterwards subsequently later SINCE PREF. post بعد از آں ba''d az-āń' ADV. afterwards after that بعد از جنگ ba''d az jang' ADJ. post-war ADV. after the war کے بعد سے ke ba''d se ADV. ever since بعد از خرابی بسیار ba''d az kharā bī-e bisyār' PH. with great difficulty having had to eat the humble pie بعد از سلام واضح ہو ba''d az salām vā'zeḥ ho PH. (arch.) (formula used as opening line of letter; after salutation be it known بعد از مرگ واویلا ba''d az marg' vā-vai'lā PROV. crying over spilt milk بعد الموت ba''d-al-maut' ADV after death 'post mortem' بعدہ ba''do-hoo ADV after that [A]

بعد bo''d N.M. distance ; remoteness ; difference بعد المشرقین bo''d-ūl-mashriqain' N.M. radical difference بعد المشرقین ہونا میں men bo''d-ūl mashriqain' ho'nā PH. (be) poles asunder [A]

بعض ba''z ADJ. some a few certain [A]

بعید ba''īd' ADJ. distant ; far remote بعید از عقل ba''ī'd az 'aq'l ADJ. improbable not rational بعید از قیاس ba''ī'd az qiyās' ADJ. inconceivable improbable [A ~ بعد]

بغاوت bag̠hā'vat N.F. revolt ; rebellion mutiny disobedience defiance recalcitrance [A]

بغتۃً bag̠h'tatan ADV. suddenly ; all of a sudden [A]

بغچہ būg̠h'chah (ped. بقچہ būq'chah) N.M. bundle ; small bundle tied in a piece of cloth [~T]

بغدا būg̠h'dā N.M. heavy chopping knife ; cleaver

قصائی کے ہاتھ میں بغدہ

بغض būg̠h'z N.M. spite malice grudge, hatred animosity للّٰہی بغض būg̠h'z lillā'hī unreasonable hostility [A]

بغل ba'g̠hal N.F. armpit side بغل کا چور ba'g̠hal kā chor' PH. favourite turned enemy بغل گرم کرنا ba'g̠hal gar'm kar'nā V.T. embrace (lover or behaved) condescend to have sexual relations بغل گند ba'g̠hal-gand' N.F. stinking armpits بغلگیر ہونا ba'g̠hal-gīr ho'nā V.T. hug embrace (for salutation) بغل میں دبانا ba'g̠hal meń dabā'nā V.T conceal (something) under armpit (fig.) carry (something) off deceitfully بغل میں لینا ba'g̠hal meń le'nā V. hug embrace be taller than (someone)

بغلگیر ہونے والے

بغلیں بجانا bag̠h'leń bajā'nā V.I. be overjoyed be happy over (someone's) downfall mock (someone) بغلیں جھانکنا bag̠h'leń jhāńk'nā V.I. feel ashamed ; hang one's head in shame ; look from side to side in discomfiture be non-plussed look blank or foolish لڑکا بغل میں ڈھنڈورا شہر میں lar'kā ba'g̠hal meń ḍhańdo'rā shaih'r meń PH. much ado about nothing بغلی bag̠h'lī ADJ. of armpit side (room) ; ante (chamber) بغلی تکیہ N.F beggar's sack trick in wrestling bag̠h'lī tak'yah N.M. long, pillow for sides بغلی گھونسا bag̠h'lī ghoon'sā, بغلی دشمن bag̠h'lī dūsh'man N.M enemy in disguise, hidden enemy ; friend turned foe [P]

بغلول bag̠hlol' N.M. simpleton dullard ; dunce حاجی بغلول hā'jī bag̠hlol' N.M. respectable-looking fool

بغی bag̠h'y N.F. transgression disobedience [A]

بفا ba'fā N.F. scurf ; dandruff

بقا baqā' N.F life existence continuance permanence بقائے دوام baqā'-e davām N.F. everlastingness immortality بقائے اصلح baqā'-e as'lah N.F. survival of the fittest [A]

بقال baqqāl' N.M. grocer greengrocer petty shopkeeper [A ~ بقل]

بقایا baqā'yā N.M. dues arrears remainder balance [A ~ SING. بقیہ - بقا]

بقچہ būq'chah N.M. (same as بغچہ N.M. ★)

بقرعید ba'qar īd' N.F. sacrificial festival ; Muslim festival of Zilhij 10 in commemoration of Abraham's sacrifice [~A بقر cows + عید 'Beiram']

بقراط būqrāt N.M Hippocrates [A ~ G]

بقعہ būq''ah N.M. distinct patch (of land) ; prominent spot بقعہ نور bāq''a noor' N.M. dazzling light luminous spot [A]

بقل baq'l, بقلہ baq'lah N.F. (ped.) vegetable potherb بقلۃ الحمقا baqlat-ūl-hamqā' N F purslane [A]

بقیع baqī'', جنت البقیع jan'nat-ūl-baqī'' N.M. the sacred Madina graveyard [A]

بقیہ baqiy'yah N.M. remainder arrears dues balance بقیۃ السیف baqiy'yat-us-saif' ADJ survivors of war, etc [A ~ بقا]

بکا būkā N.F. weeping wailing lamentation آہ و بکا ā'h-o būkā' N.F lamentation moaning [A]

بکارت **baka'rat** N.F. virginity ; maidenhood ازالۂ بکارت **izā'la-e baka'rat** N.M. (woman's) first sexual intercourse [A]

بکاؤ **bika'oo** ADJ. on sale ; for sale saleable venal

بکاول **bika'val** (or **vūl**) N.M. head cook , chef butler steward [A]

بکاؤلی **baka''olī** (or **baka'valī**) coveted legendary flower legendary princess who is the heroine of a well-known romantic tale 'Gul Bakavali' گل بکاؤلی **gul baka''olī** N.M this lagendary flower

بکائن **baka''in** N.M. a kind of tree ; 'melia sempe virens'

بک بک **bak'-bak**, بک جھک **bak'-jhak**, بک بک جھک جھک **bak'-bak jhak-jhak** N.F. chatter ; babble ; gabble prattle بک بک کرنا **bak'-bak kar'nā** V.I. talk idly; prate babble ; gabble

بکبکا **bak'ba'ka** ADJ. (dial.) vapid ; insipid

بکتر **bak'tar** N.M. armour cuirass بکتر بند **bak'tar-band** ADJ. armoured (vehicle, or soldier) بکتر پوش **bak'tar-posh** ADJ. clad in armour N.M. cuirassier زرہ بکتر **zi'reh bak'tar** N.M. (soldier's) defence equipment (زرہ بکتر لگانا (یا باندھنا **zi'reh bak'tar lagā'nā** (or) **bāndh'nā** V.I. put on armour [P]

بکٹا **bük'ṭā** N.M. handful clawing بکٹا بھرنا **bük'ṭā bhar'nā** V.T. claw

بکر **bik'r** N.F. virginity , maidenhood [A]

بکرا **bak'rā** N.M he-goat بکری **bak'rī** N.F. goat she-goat

بکری **bik'rī** N.F. sale [~ بکنا **bik'nā**]

بکس **bak's** (col. بکسا **bak'sā**) N.M. box [E]

بکسنا **bi'kasnā** V.I. blossom wither

بکسوا **baksoo''ā** N.M. buckle [~ E buckle [سوا

بکل **bük'kal** N.M. upturn (of stole, shawl, etc.) (بکل لگانا (یا مارنا **bük'kal lagā'nā** (or **mār'nā**) upturn (stole, etc.)

بکم **bük'm** ADJ. dumb ; mute (only in Quranic PH.) صم بکم **sūm'mūn bük'mun** deaf and dumb unaffected [A ~ SING. ابکم

بکنا **bak'nā** V.I. talk idly prate prattle bable , gabble بکواس **bakvās'** N.F. ★

بکنا **bik'nā** V.I. be sold be disposed of بکوانا **bikvā'nā** V.T. cause to be sold ; get disposed of بکوائی **bikvā''ī** N.F. salesman's commission

بکواس **bak'vās** N.F. idle talk chatter prattle damn lie silly stuff incredible yarn loquacity ; garrulity talkativeness بکواسی **bakvā'sī** N.M idle talker chatterbox lier ADJ. talkative [~ بکنا **bik'nā**]

بکھرنا **bi'kharnā** V.I. be scattered be dispersed (of hair) be dishevelled بکھیرنا **bakhe'r'nā** V.T scatter sow disperse

بکھیڑا **bakhe'ṛā** N.M. dispute ; quarrel fix awkward or difficult situation vexatious point difficulty trouble complication contention (usu. undesirable means بکھیڑا چکانا **bakhe'ṛā chük'ānā** V.T. settle a dispute , stop a quarrel بکھیڑا ڈالنا **bakhe'ṛā ḍāl'nā** V.T. create a difficulty raise a dispute complicate matters بکھیڑیا **bakhe'ṛiyā** ADJ quarrelsome contentious troublesome difficult (person) N.M brawler mischiefmonger

بکی **bak'kī** ADJ. talkative N.M chatterbox prater braggart lier [~ بکنا **bak'nā**]

بگاڑ **bigāṛ'** N.M. بگاڑنا **bigāṛ'nā** V.T (see under V.I. ★)

بگٹٹ **bag'-ṭuṭ** ADV. at full gallop , very fast [باگ + ٹوٹنا ~]

بگر **ba'gar** N.M. (flour of) rice بگر کا آٹا **ba'gar kā ā'ṭā** N.M. rice-meal بگر کی روٹی **ba'gar kī ro'ṭī** N.F. rice-meal bread

بگڑنا **bi'gaṛnā** V.I. go out of order be out of gear be damaged be impaired be disfigured become debauched or vicious lose modesty be enraged rebel ; revolt deteriorate be spoilt , be spoiled بگڑ بیٹھنا **bi'gaṛ baiṭhnā** V.I be displeased ; take offence بگاڑ **bigāṛ'** N.M. unpleasantness estrangement discord quarrel enmity bad blood deterioration harm damage میں بگاڑ ڈالنا **men bigāṛ' ḍāl'nā** V.I. cause unpleasantness sow seeds of discord create bad-blood , create misunderstanding بگاڑنا **bigāṛ'nā** V.T. mar spoil bungle damage injure ruin disfigure سے بگاڑنا **se bigāṛ'nā** V.T. displease بگاڑو **bigā'ṛoo** N.M one who spoils a show etc. clumsy or ill-intentioned worker

بگل **bi'gal** N.M bugle [~ E CORR.]

بگلا **bag'lā** N.M. crane , heron ADJ. very white بگلا بھگت **bag'lā bha'gat** N.M. hypocrite

بگویا **bago'yā** N.M. (W. dial.) evil-speaking lampoon [CORR. of. بدگوئیاں ~ P + گوئی]

بگولا bāgoo'la N.M. whirlwind آگ بگولا ہونا āg bagoo'lā ho'nā V.I. be enraged ; fly into a passion
بگھارنا baghār'na V. season with freed condiments ; season ; بگھار baghār' N.M. seasoning fried condiments for seasoning
بگھی bag'ghī N.F. buggy light carriage gig horsefly
بگھیلا baghe'la N.M. young tiger name of a Rajput tribe
بل bal N.M. strength ; vigour might power twist contortion convulsion wrinkle coil بل بوتا bal boo'tā N.M. strength might بل پڑنا bal' parnā V.I. have convulsive pain be curved be twisted bal'-dār ADJ. twisted coiled curved crooked بل دینا bal' de'nā V.T. twist entwine coil curl بل کھانا bal' khā'nā V.I. be twisted be entwined be curled fret and fume بل نکالنا bal nikāl'na V.T. straighten (coil) set right punish بل نکلنا (یا کھلنا) bal ni'kalnā (or khul'nā) V.I. be uncoiled straighten out be set right بل بے bal' be INT. (iron.) bravo how unreasonable
بل bil N.M. hole burrow (fig.) hideout
۲بل bil N.M. bill draft legislation ; Bill draft بل بنانا bil' banā'nā V.I. draw a bill بل جاری کرنا bil' jā'rī kar'nā V.T. issue a draft draw a bill بل دینا (یا ادا کرنا) bil de'nā (or adā' kar'nā) V.T. pay the bill foot the bill [E]
بلا bil'la N.M. bat
بلا bil'la N.M. cat tom cat badge
بلا balā' N.F. calamity misfortune distress evil fiend undesirable consort awful or terrible thing trial ADJ. terrible ; dreadful awful ; enormous بلا اپنے سر لینا balā' ap'ne sir le'nā, بلا مول لینا balā' mol' le'nā V.I. nvite trouble get involved in trouble بلا بدتر balā' bad'tar N.F. rubbish worthless stuff unhygienic eatables بلا ٹلنا balā' ṭal'na V.I be relieved of trouble میری بلا جانے me'rī balā' jā'ne PH. who cares ? it is no concern of mine (etc.) بلا زدہ balā'.za'dah ADJ. in the grip of calamity ; struck with misfortune بلا سے balā' se PH. who cares ? بلا کا balā' kā ADJ. extreme intense ; severe excessive بلاکش balā-kash ADJ. afflicted industrious بلا گرداں balā'-gar'dān ADJ. (person) offering himself as a sacrifice for others بلانوش balā-nosh' ADJ. toper glutton بلائے بے درماں balā'-e be- darmān N.F. great calamity unmanageable person بلائیں لینا balā''en le'nā V.T. express extreme affection and concern (for) offer oneself as sacrifice (for) ; pass one's hands over another's head in token of drawing all his calamities on oneself [A]
بلا bi-lā' N.M. without un- بلا اکراہ bi-lā' ikrāh' ADV. voluntarily ; without compulsion بلا تامل bi-lā' tā'am'mul ADV. without hesitation ; unhesitatingly instantaneously ; recklessly ; rashly بلا تحاشا bi-lā taḥā'shā, بے تحاشا be taḥā'shā ADV. rashly ; recklessly headlong excessively بلا تردد bi-lā trad'dud ADV. without hesitation ; without ; rluctance ; unhesitatingly بلا تصنع bi-lā' tasan'no' ADJ. & ADV. unembelished spontaneous(ly) frank(ly) بلا تکلف bi-lā' takal'luf ADV. without hesitation ; unhesitatingly without form...y بلا توقف bi-lā' tavaq'quf ADV. without delay ; without loss of time speedily بلا شک bi-lā' shak', بلا ریب bi-lā'raib' ADV. without doubt or suspicion; doubtlessly ; undoubtedly unquestionably بلا شرط bi-lā' shar't ADJ. & ADV. unconditional(ly) absolute-(ly) بلا ناغہ bi-lā' nā'ghah ADV. daily regularly constantly without intermission بلا واسطہ bi-lā' vās'tah (or ped. -vā'sitah) direct directly بلا وجہ bi-lā 'vaj'h ADV. without any rhyme or reason [A ~ ب with + لا not]
بلاد bilād' N.M. PL. towns ; cities N.M. SING. country [A ~ SING. بلد]
بلاغ balāgh' N.M. communication conveying [A]
بلاغت balā'ghat N.F. rhetoric eloquence [A ~ PREC.] 
بلاق būlāq' N.M. septum-ring septum
بلانا būlā'na V.T. eall summon invite convene اجلاس بلانا ijlās' būlā'nā summon or convene a meeting بلا لانا būlā' lā'na V.T. fetch (someone)
بلاوا būlā'vā N.M. invitation بلاوا بھیجنا būlā'vā bhej'-nā V.T. send out invitation (to)
بلاؤ bilā'o N.M. wild cat tom-cat [~ بلا bil'lā]
بلب balb' N.M. bulb [E]
بلبل būl'būl N F. (or M.) (ped. PL. بلابل balā'bil) nightingale بلبل چشم būl'būl-chash'm N.M. a kind of chequered

cloth [~ A]

بلبلا *bul'bulā* N.M. bubble

بلبلانا *balbalā'nā* V.I. (of camel) cry (of camel) be in heat

بلبلانا *bilbilā'nā* V.I. sob blubber feel uneasy ; be restless complain from pain or grief بلبلا اٹھنا *bilbilā' uṭh'nā* V.I. cry from torturous pain

بلٹنا *bi'latnā* V.I. get lost insist childishly بلٹانا *bilṭā'nā* V.T. ruin cause to get lost

بلٹی *bilṭī* N.F. consignment bill of lading receipt for railway consignment [Et. dubious ; prob. E ~ CORR. of B.L.T. PR. *bee-el-tee'* ABB. of bill of lading by train]

بلد *ba'lad*, بلدہ *bal'dah* N.M. city town settlement region بلاد *bilād'*, بلدان *buldān'* N.M. PL. cities ; towns country بلدیہ *baldiy'yah* N.F. municipality ; municipal committee urban area with local self-government بلدیات *baldiyyāt'* N.F. PL. municipalities ; local bodies بلدیاتی *baldiyyā'tī* ADJ. local body ; municipal بلدیاتی ادارہ *baldiyyā'tī idā'rah* N.M. municipal body بلدیاتی نظام *baldiyyā'tī nizām'* N.M. system of local self-government municipal system [A]

بلمیٹر *bal'lamtair* N.M. (iron. CORR. of) volunteer [E]

بلسان *balasān'* N.M. balsam

بلسنا *bilas'nā* V.I. enjoy ; derive pleasure from

بلغا *bulaghā'* N.M. PL. eloquent persons [A ~ SING. بلیغ]

بلغم *bal'gham* N.M. one of the four humours phlegm بلغمی *bal'ghamī* ADJ. phlegmatic generating phlegm sluggish بلغمی مزاج *bal'ghamī mizāj'* N.M. & ADJ. (of) sluggish temperament [A ~ G]

بلقیس *bilqīs'* N.F. the Sabaean queen converted by Solomon

بلکنا *bi'laknā* V.I. weep bitterly cry persistently be uneasy or restless demand by crying consistently wail *bilkā'nā* V.T. let child weep bitterly

بلکہ *bal'keh* CONJ. rather on the contrary; on the other hand

بلکیا *bal'kiyā*, ولکیا *val'kiyā* N.M. silly boy چل بے بلکیے کہیں کے *chal' be bal'kiye ka'hīn ke* PH. (lovingly) begone you silly lad !

بلم *bal'lam* N.M. lance ; spear sceptre staff of authority بلم بردار *bal'lam bardār'* N.M. lancer one carrying the staff of authority before its owner ; sceptrecarrier

بلم *ba'lam*, بلما *bal'mā* N.M. lover paramour husband (as beloved) [~ بالا]

بلند *buland'* ADJ. loud high lofty tall raised ; elevated exalted sublime بلند آواز *bulan'd-āvāz'* ADJ. loud-voiced Stentorian loud بلند پایہ *buland'-pā'yah* ADJ. exalted high-ranking بلند آہنگ *bulan'd-āhang'* ADJ. loud high-sounding بلند پرواز *buland'-parvāz'* ADJ. sublime ambitious soaring high بلند پروازی *buland'-parvā'zī* N.F. high thinking soaring ambition high flight sublimity بلند حوصلہ *buland hau'salah* (col. *ḥaus'lah*) ADJ. ambitious ; aspiring magnanimous N.M. highstepper بلند حوصلگی *buland haus'lagī* (ped. *hau'salagī*) N.F. magnanimity ambition بلند کرنا *buland kar'nā* V.T. raise ; lift elevate exalt بلند مرتبہ *buland'-mar'tabah*, بلند رتبہ *buland'-rut'bah* ADJ. high-ranking بلند رتبہ لوگ *buland'-rut'bah log* N.M. PL. the elite (of the the city, etc.) بلند نظر *buland'-nazar* ADJ. ambitious noble-minded بلند ہمت *buland'-him'mat* ADJ. ambitious ; aspiring magnanimous بلند ہمتی *buland'-him'matī* N.F. ambition of magnanimity بلند ہونا *buland' ho'nā* V.I. ascend be above (something) *bulan'dī* N.F. height elevation loftiness stature exaltation [P]

بلوہ *bal'vah* N.M. riot tumult disturbance بلوائی *balvā'ī* N.M. rioter ADJ. riotous [~ A بلویٰ]

بلوانا *bulvā'nā* V.T. send for summon invite [~ بلانا ~ بولنا CAUS.]

بلور *billaur'* (ped. *balloor'* N.M. crystal glass ADJ. transparent bright بلوری *billau'rī*, بلوریں *billau'rīn* ADJ. crystal ; glass transparent bright [P]

بلوط *baloot'* (ped. *balloot'*) N.M. (also شاہ بلوط *shāh' baloot'*) oak chestnut tree acorn [A]

بلوط

بلوغ *buloogh'*, N.M. بلوغت *buloo'ghat* N.F. maturity ; majority puberty coming of age [A]

بلوں بلوں *bi'loon bi'loon* N.M. hue and cry (esp. over some trouble esp. hunger) want ; scarcity

بلونا *bilo'nā* V.T. churn بلونی *bilo'nī*, N.F. churning pot

بلونت *balvant'* ADJ. (dial.) brave N.M. hero [S]

بلہاری *baliha'ri* ADV. term of affection) offering oneself as sacrifice to protect (child or beloved)

بلّی *bal'li* N.F. prop long wooden post long thick bamboo (for rowing or steering boats) بلیمار *bal'li-mar* N.M. boatman بلیماراں *bal li-maran'* N.M. name of a well-known Delhi street (originally known as Boatmen's street)

بلّی *bil'li* N.F. cat female cat bolt latch بلی الانگھنا *bil'li ulang'na* PH. (of cat) cross someone's way (fig.) be upset بلی کو چھیچھڑوں کے خواب *bil'li ko chhichh'ron ke khab* PH. wishful thinking بلی کے بھاگوں چھینکا ٹوٹنا *bil'li ke bha'gon chhin'ka toot'na* PH. be a godsend (to someone) بلی لوٹن *bil'li lo tan* N.F. spikenard ; hyacinth [F. ~ بلا *bil'la*]

بلیات *baliyyat'* N.F. (PL. of بلیہ N.F. ★)

بلید *balid'* ADJ. & N.M. thick-skulled ; dunce ; duffer [A]

بلیڈ *baled'* N.M. blade : razor blade [E]

بلیرڈ *bil'yard* N.M. billiards [E]

بلیغ *baligh'* ADJ. (PL. بلغا *bulagha'*) eloquent (person or style) [A ~ بلاغت]

بلیک *balaik'* ADJ. & N.M. black blackmarket *balaik a''ut* N.M. black out بلیک بورڈ *balaik' bo'rd* N.M. blackboard بلیک مارکیٹ *balaik markit* N.F. black-market بلیک مارکیٹیا *balaik' markitya* N.M. black-marketeer بلیک میل *balaik'mal* N.M. blackmail بلیک میلر *balaik me'lar* N.M. black mailer [E]

بلینڈا *balen'da* N.M. بلینڈی *balen'di* N.F. long bamboo ; ridge pole (fig.) tall person

بلیلہ *bale'lah* N.F. 'bellaric myrobalan'

بلیہ *baliy'yah* N.F. (PL. بلیات *baliyyat'*) calamity misfortune fiend [A ~ بلا]

بم¹ *bam* N.F. shaft (of carriage for yoking horse) uproar بم چخ *bam'-chakh* N.F. uproar ; clamour بم چخ مچانا *bam'chakh macha'na* V.I. clamour [P]

بم *bam'* N.F. bass ; deep tone زیر و بم *zi'r-o-bam'* N.F. base and soprano N.M. PL. ups and downs ; vicissitudes [P]

بم *bam* N.M. bomb بمباری *bam-ba'ri* N.F. bombing بمباری کرنا *bam-ba'ri kar'na* V.T. bomb [E]

بمبا *bam'ba* N.M. hand-pump tap fountain ; source (of river) ; waterhead pill-box [~E pump]

بن *ban* N.M. wood ; forest ; jungle بن باس *ban bas'* N.M. banishment ; ostracism ; exile بن بلاؤ *ban bila'o* N.M. wild cat بن مانس *ban-ma'nas* N.M. guerilla ; chimpanzee

بن *bun* N.F. root [P]

بن¹ *bin* N.M. son [A ABB. of ابن used between two names]

بن² *bin*, بنا *bina* ADV. without ; except ; unless بن آئی مرنا *bin a''i mar'na* V.I. die a sudden death be ruined for no cause بن جانے *bin ja'ne* ADV. unknowingly ; unwittingly بن داموں غلام *bin da'mon ghulam'* N.M. one under heavy obligation devoted person one held in thrall بن مانگے موتی ملیں اور مانگے ملے نہ بھیک *bin man'ge mo'ti mi'len our man'ge mi'le'na bhik'* PROV. fortune has its vicissitudes بن بلایا مہمان *bin bula'ya mehman'* PH. uninvited guest بن بلائے خدا کے ہاں بھی نہیں جاتے *bin bula''e khuda' ke han bhi na'hin ja'te* PROV. to a wedding (or christening) go not without an invitation بن روئے ماں بھی بچے کو دودھ نہیں دیتی *bin ro''e man bhi (bach'che ko) doodh na'hin de'ti* PROV. a closed mouth catches no flies ; nothing venture, nothing gain

بنا *ba'na* (rus. بنّا *ban'na* or بنڑا *ban'ra*) N.M. (F. بنی *ba'ni*, *ban'ni* بنڑی *ban'ri*) groom ; bridegroom

بنا *bina'* N.F. (PL. ابنیہ *ab'niyah*) foundation basis root cause motive origin edifice structure بنا بر آں *bina' bar-an'*, بنا بریں *bina' bar-in'* ADV. therefore owing to this because of it بنا کرنا *bina' kar'na* V. begin start ; commence بنا رکھنا *bina' rakh'na* V.T. lay the foundation (of) give rise to [A]

بنا بنایا *ba'na bana'ya* ADJ. completed finished manufatured readymade بنا بنایا کھیل بگاڑنا *ba'na bana'ya khel' bigar'na* V.T. upset the (or someone's) apple-cart [~ بننا + بنانا]

بنات *banat'* N.F. PL. daughters girls بنات النعش *bana't-un-na''sh* N.F. constellations of the Greater and the Lesser Bear [A ~ SING. بنت]

بنا ٹھنا *ba'na tha'na* (F. بنی ٹھنی *ba'ni tha'ni*) ADJ. foppish chic .. welladorned

بنادر *bana'dir* N.M. PL. بندرگاہیں *bandarga'hen* N.F. PL. ports ; harbours [P ~ SING. بندر]

بنارس *bana'ras* N.M. name of an Indian city well-known for its Hindu shrines بنارسی ٹھگ *banar'si thag* N.M. respectable looking swindler or 'thug' بنارسی کپڑا *banar'si kap'ra* N.M. brocade بنارسی لنگڑا *banar'si lang'ra* N.M. a kind of good quality mango صبح بنارس *sub'h-e bana'ras* N.M exquisite Benaras morning when lovely bodies bathing in the river present a sight to see

بناسپتی **banās'patī** N.F. vegetable (oil) بناسپتی گھی banās'patī ghī vegetable 'ghee' 'vanaspati'

بناگوش **būnā-gosh'** N.M. lobe of the car [P]

بنانا **banā'nā** V.T. make prepare form shape manufacture invent repair mend fabricate invent versify ; compose (verse) acquire dress (food) pluck (fowl) mock ; pull (some one's) leg [~ بننا CAUS.]

بناوٹ **banā'vaṭ** N.F. make build embellishment form figure shape formation show ; display affectation deceit ; fraudulent behaviour artfulness texture knitting weaving بناوٹی banā'vaṭī ADJ. artificial fabricated fake [PREC.]

بناوٹ **būnā'vaṭ** N.F. texture [~ بننا bun'na]

بناؤ **banā''o** N.M. harmony concord reconciliation make-up بناؤ سنگھار (سنگار) کرنا banā''o singār (or singhār') kar'nā V.T. do (one's) make-up [~ بننا ban'nā]

بنت **bin t** N.F. daughter girl بنت العنب bin't-ul-'i'nab N.F. (fig.) wine [A]

بنٹا **ban'ṭā** N.M. large utensil marble (for playing)

بنتی **bin'tī** N.F. (dial.) entreaty [S]

بنج **ba'naj** N.M. (dial.) business trade ; commerce transaction بنج بیوپار ba'naj bepār N.M. business profession بنجارا banjā'rā N.M. huckster pedlar (arch.) grain-merchant بنجارن banjā'ran N.F. pedlar's wife

بنجر **ban'jar** ADJ. barren fallow N.F. barren land ; wasteland land lying fallow بنجر جدید ban'jar' jadīd' N.F. land lying fallow for four years past بنجر خارج الجمع banjar khā'rij-uj-jam'' N.F. fallow land exempt from revenue بنجر قدیم ban'jar qadīm N.F. land lying fallow at new settlement

بنچ **bainch** N.M. (or F.) bench [E]

بند **band** N.M. embankment 'bund' , dam ; dyke knot joint knuckle (lit.) band ; belt (lit.) imprisonment ; captivity (lit.) fetters fastening stanza ADJ. closed ; shut tied · bound fastened ceased still stopped prevented checked barred confidential SUF. binder -er بند باندھنا band' bāndh'nā V.T. throw a dyke ; build a dam check inundation by building a dam بند بند band' band ADJ. depressed ; dejected ADV. all over (the body) ; in every joint N.M. every joint بند بند ٹوٹنا band band' ṭooṭ'nā V.T. feel pain in every joint (or all over the body) be dead tired بند بند جدا کرنا band band' jū'dā kar'nā V.T. hack into pieces unscrew all parts بند ڈھیلے کر دینا band ḍhī'le kar de'nā V.T. tire out بند پانی band' pā'nī N.M. stagnant water بند سوال band' so'āl (col. -savāl') N.M. confidential query بند کرنا band' kar'nā V.T. close ; shut put in (costs, etc.) lock up imprison ; put behind bars fasten stop prevent cease ; discontinue wind up ; finish (show, etc.) بند گوبھی band' go'bhī N.F. cabbage بند ہونا band' ho'nā V.I be closed ; be shut be over ; be finished ; come to an end be abolished cease stop for the time being بند ہیضہ band' hai'zah N.M. choleraic diarrhoea [P]

بند² **band** N.M. bun [E]

بندا **būn'dā** N.M. ear-drop pendant earring

بندر **ban'dar** N.M. harbour port port-town maritime city

بندر² **ban'dar** N.M. monkey بندریا ban'daryā N.F. female monkey

بندش **ban'dish** N.F. prohibition act of binding phrase style composition elegance of diction (old use) plot (old use) artifice بندش باندھنا ban'dish bāndh'nā V.I. use a phrase (old use) plot ; contrive [P]

بندکی **būnd'kī** N.F. tiny drop spot light shower بندکیاں پڑنا būndkiyāṅ paṛnā V.I. have drizzle بندکی دار būnd'kī dār ADJ. (of cloth, etc.) spotted [~ بند DIM.]

بندگان **bandagān'** N.M. PL. slaves servants (God's creatures بندگان عالی bandagā'n-e 'ā'lī N.M. Chief Feudatory (as tittle for the Nizam) [P ~ SING. بندہ]

بندگی **ban'dagī** N.F. worship service servility servitude (dial.) salutation بندگی بجا لانا ban'dagī ba-jā' lā'nā V.I. (old use) serve pay one's respects (to) بندگی بیچارگی ban'dagī be-chā'ragī PH. there is little to choose between service and servitude [P ~ بندہ]

بندوبست ban'd-o-bast' N.M arrangement management system (revenue) settlement بندوبست استمراری ban'd-o-bast-e istimrā'rī N.M. permanent settlement چند روزہ بندوبست chand ro'zah ban'd-o-bast N.M. temporary settlement [P].

بندوق bandooq' N.F. gun rifle (old use) musket بندوق بھرنا bandooq' bhar'nā V.I. load a gun بندوق چلانا bandooq' chalā'nā V.I. fire a gun fire shoot (at) بندوق چھتیانا bandooq' chhatyā'nā V.I. put gun to the shoulder ; whip it out بندوقچی ban'dooq'chī N.M.. musketeer [T]

بندہ ban'dah N.M. I slave , bondsman obedient person بندہ بشر ہے ban'dah ba'shar hai PROV. to err is human بندہ پرور ban'da-par'var. بندہ نواز ban'da-navāz' ADJ. patron benefactor (respectful or iron ; mode of address) boss ; cherisher of this slave of yours بندہ پروری ban'da-par'varī' بندہ نوازی ban'da-navā'zī N F. kindness munificence بندہ درگاہ ban'da-e dargāh' N M devoted servant most humble servant بندہ زادہ ban'da-zā'dah N.M. one's son (when introducing or referring him to one's superior

بندھنا bandh'nā V.I be tied stand committed be arrested fall into a trap بندھائی bandhā''ī N.F. remuneration for binding بندھن bandhan N.M. relationship tie بندھن ہار ban'dhan har, بندھن وار bandhanvar N.M. garland hung at someone's door by gardener on ceremonial occasion بندھوانا bandhvā'nā V.T. implicate accuse cause to be bound بندھی مٹھی لاکھ برابر ban'dhī muṭ'ṭhī lākh' barā'bar PROV. unity is strength

بندھنا bindh'nā V.I. probe ; drive a hole in be probed ; be strung بندھ جانا bindh' jā'nā V.I. (of pearl, etc.) be bored or strung be aptly used بندھ گیا سو موتی bindh' ga'yā so mo'tī PROV. whatever is done is well-done whatever word is used is aptly used

بندھنیا būndhan'yā N.M. mixture of parched coriander-seed, etc.

بندی ban'dī N.F. (rare) prisoner بندی خانہ ban'dī khā'nah N.M. prison ; gaol [P ~ بندہ]

بندی bin'dī N.F. (dial.) zero ; cypher saffron speck (or crystal spangle for forehead)

بنڈل ban'dal N.M. bundle [E]

بنڈی ban'ḍī N.F. quilted waistcoat

بنڑا ban'ṛā N.M., بنڑی ban'ṛī N.F. (see under بنّا N.M ★)

بنسلوچن bansalochan N.F. bamboo-sugar [بانس ~]

بنسی ban'sī N.F. pipe ; flute fishing rod [بانس ~]

بنفشہ banaf'shah N.F. & M. violet

بنک baink (or bank) N.M. bank (for monetary transaction) بنکاری bankā'rī N.F. banking بنک بیلنس bank' bai'lans N.M. bank balance [E]

بنکارنا ban'kār'nā V.I. make noise ; be noisy

بنگالی bangā'lī N.F. Bengali (language) Bengali (citizen) ADJ. of Bengal

بنگلہ bang'lah N.M. bungalow a kind of betel-leaf N.F. Bengali language

بنگو ban'goo N.M. بنگی ban'gī N.F. humming top

بننا ban'nā V.I. be made be constructed be built be manufatured be prepared be mended be cooked be achieved have affected manners pose بنا رہنا ba'nā raih'nā V.I. be unaltered last long prosper ; thrive remain in good state بنوانا banvā'nā V.T. cause to be made get built or constructed cause to prepared have repaired have mended بنوائی ban'vā''ī N.F. remuneration for making, mending, etc. completion ; manufacture

بننا būn'nā V.T. weave knit بنوانا būnvā'nā V.T. get woven get knitted (of chair) have (it) caned بنوانا būnvā'nā V.T. cause to be knitted have woven get caused بنوائی būnvā''ī N.F. remuneration for caning (chair), weaving or knitting weaving, knitting or caning

بنوٹ binnauṭ' N.F. club-fight fencing with cudgels, etc. بنوٹ کا ہاتھ binnauṭ' kā hāth' N.M. (& V.I.) use a trick of this game

بنو ba'noo N.M. PL. (same as بنی N.M. PL. ★) [A]

بنولا binau'lā N.M. cottonseed

بنی¹ ba'nī, ban'nī N.F. (~ بنا N.M. ★)

بنی² ba'nī (rare) بنو ba'noo) N.M. PL. children (of) ; tribe (of) sons (of) بنی آدم ba'nī ā'dam N.M. mankind ; human beings بنی اسرائیل ba'nī is'rā'īl N.M. Jews ; children of Israel ; Israelites [A ~ SING. ابن]

بنیا **ban'ya** N.M. petty-shopkeeper petty-minded person miser usurer [~ بنج]
بنیاد **būn'yad'** N.F. foundation foundation-stone groundwork basis بنیاد ڈالنا *būnyad' dal'na* V.T. begin introduce set the fashion بنیاد رکھنا *būnyad' rakh'na* V.T. found lay the foundation (of) lay the foundation-stone بنیادی *būnya'di* ADJ basic ; fundamental بنیادی جمہوریت *būnya'di jūmhooriy'yat* N.F Basic Democracy ; B.D. system [P]
بنیان **būnyan'** N.F. structure بنیان مرصوص *būnya'n-i marsoos'* N.M. reinforced structure strong group
بنیان **banyan'** N.F. (dial. M.) vest
بنیٹی **bane'ṭi**, بنیٹھی *bane'ṭhi* N.F. whirling torch, rod lighted at both ends and used as weapon, etc.
بو **boo** (P) N.F. smell ; odour stink scent بو آنا *boo' a'na* V.I. stink ; smell بو پانا *boo' pa'na* V.I. (of dog) scent know ; guess بو دار *boo'-dar'* ADJ. stinking adorous
بو **boo** N.M. father possesser of endowed with having -er بوتراب *boo' tūrab'* N.M. title of Hazrat Ali بو علی سینا *boo' 'a'li si'na* N.M. Avicenna بوالعجبی *būl-'a'jabi* N.F. wonder marvel folly strange thing بوالفضول *būl-fuzool'* N.M. prattler unmannerly person بوالہوس *būl-havas'* N.M. lustful person ; slave of passions one false in love ADJ. lustful false avaricious بوالہوسی *būl-ha'vasi* N.F. lust pretension of love avarice بوقلموں *boo-qa'lmooñ* ADJ. variegated marvellous بوقلمونی *boo-qalamoo'ni* N.F. colourfulness variety [A]
بوا **boo''a** N.F sister paternal aunt (woman's title of respect for) older female friend
بواسیر **bavasir'** N.F. piles خونی بواسیر *khoo'ni bava'sir* N.F. haemorrhoids [A]
بوانا **būva'na** V.T. (rus.) cause to be sown get covered بوائی *būva''i* (dial. بوار *būvar'*) N.F. seed-time sowing [~ بونا *bo na*]
بواعث **bava''is** N.M. PL. reasons ; causes [A ~ SING. باعث]
بوائی **biva''i** N.F. chilblain kibe بوائی پھٹنا *biva''i phaṭ'na* V.I. have chilblains ; suffer from kibes جس کے نہ پھٹے بوائی وہ کیا جانے پیڑ پرائی *jis ke na pha'ṭe biva''i voh' kya ja'ne pir' para''i* PROV one who has not suffered cannot understand the suffering of others
بوبک **boo'bak** N.M. simpleton aged jester, fool

بوبو **bo'bo** N.F. elder sister old governess
بوتا **boo'ta** N.M. strength ; might ; power بل بوتا *bal boo'ta* N.M. strength ; might , power
بوتام **botam'** N.M. (old use) button [~ E. CORR.]
بوتل **bo'tal** N.F. bottle liquor bottleful of ; as much as a bottle will contain بوتل میں بھرنا *bo tal meñ bhar'na* V.T. bottle [E]
بوتہ **boo'tah** N.M. (rare) crucible [E]
بوتہ **bo'tah**, بوتا *bo'ta* N.M. young camel [P]
بوتیمار **boo'timar** N M. heron [P]
بوٹ **booṭ**, بونٹ *booñṭ* N.M. green gram
بوٹ **booṭ** N.M. shoe bootie ladies' sandal فل بوٹ *ful' booṭ* N.M. boot [E]
بوٹا **boo'ṭa** N.M. plant sapling floral pattern (on something) بوٹا سا قد *boo'ṭa sa qad'* ADJ. small but well proportioned stature بوٹے کاڑھنا *booṭe kaṛh'na* V.I. embroider work floral patterns بوٹے دار *boo'ṭe-dar* ADJ. embroidered
بوٹی **bo'ṭi** N.F. joint slice of meat for serving at table بوٹی اتار لینا *bo'ṭi ūtar' le'na* V bite off (piece of flesh) بوٹی بوٹی پھڑکنا *bo'ṭi bo'ṭi pha'rakana* V.I. be naughty; be full of mischief بوٹیاں اڑانا *bo'ṭiyañ ūṛa'na* V.I. give a good hiding beat black and blue بوٹیاں توڑنا (یا کاٹنا یا نوچنا) *bo'ṭiyañ toṛ'na* (or *kaṭ'na* or *noch'na*) V.I. press hard demand with constant taunt give corporal punishment بوٹیاں کتوں سے نچوانا *bo'ṭiyañ kūt'toñ se nūchva'na* PH. (threat to) bring torturous death
بوٹی **boo'ṭi** N.F. herb or root used as drug Indian hemp [~ بوٹا DIM.]
بوجھ **bojh** N.M. load burden encumbrance debt obligation responsibility بوجھ (سر سے) اتارنا *bojh (sir' se) ūtar'na* V.T put down the load or burden discharge the obligation throw off the encumbrance pay off the debt relieve (someone) of responsibility بوجھ (سر پر) اٹھانا *bojh (sir pr) ūṭha'na* V.I bear lift up the burden carry the load undertake the responsibility be under an obligation بوجھ سر پر ہونا *bojh sir' par ho'na* V.I. be under an obligation بوجھل *bo'jhal* ADJ.
بوجھنا **boojh'na** V.T. guess make out بوجھ *boojh* N.F. (rare) understanding سمجھ بوجھ

sa'majh-boojh, سوجھ بوجھ *soojh'-boojh* N.F. commonsense understanding sagacity بوجھ بجھول *boojh būjhav'val* N.F. solving the riddles بوجھ بجھکڑ *boojh b jhak'kar* N.M. wiseacre ; sententious fool بوجھ پڑنا *boojh' par'nā* V.I. (rus.) appear : seem

بوچا *boo'chā* ADJ (F. بوچی *boo'chī*) same as *būch'cha* ADJ. ★)

بوچڑ *boo'char* N.M butcher beefvendor [E]

بوچھاڑ *bauchhar'* N F. driving rain ; wind and rain heavy shower spray drift abundance volley (of questions, etc.) windiall بوچھاڑ پڑنا *bauchhar' par'nā* V.I. face heavy shower کی بوچھاڑ ہونا *kī bauchhar' ho'nā* V.I. face severe (criticism) face volley (of questions) have a windfall (of) کی بوچھاڑ کرنا *kī bauchhar' kar'nā* V. squander ; spend lavishly give in abundance talk incessantly بوچھاڑی *bauchhā'rī* N.F. sunshade

بود *bood* N.F. existence V.I. was بود و باش *bood-o-bash'* N.F. residence existence (some one's) society بود *ba'vad* V.I is proves to be [P ~ بودن be]

بودا *bo'dā* ADJ. (F. بودی *bo'dī*) weak ; feeble timid ; faint-hearted foolish بودا کرنا *bo'da kar'nā* V.T. weaken enervate [P]

بودلا *bod'la* N.M. simpleton name of a mendicant fraternity ADJ. simple ; gullible *bod'lī* N.F. tomboy member of this fraternity ADJ. simple ; gullible

بودم بے دال *boo'dam be dāl'* (joc.) fool [P ~ بوم owl = بودم — د I was] بور کے لڈو

بور *boor* N.F. chaff ; husk sawdust *boor' ke lad'doo* N.M. a kind of sweetmeat deceit ; specious thing false hope بور کے لڈو کھائے تو پچھتائے نہ کھائے تو پچھتائے *boor' ke lad'doo khā''e to' pachhtā''e na khā''e to' pachhtā''e* PROV. attractive but unpalatable ; something whose charm wears away soon

بورا *boo'rā* N.M. powdered sugar sawdust

بورا *bo'rā* N.M., بوری *bo'rī* N.F. gunny bag sack

بورانی *boorā'nī* N.F. roasted brinjal served in curds [P]

بورڈ *bor'd* N.M. board بورڈنگ *bor'ding* N.M. boarding house [E]

بوری *bau'rī* N.F parched barley

بوری *bo'rī* N.F. gunny bag

بوریا *bo'riyā* N.M. palm-leaf mat بوریا بندھنا *bo'riyā badh'nā* N.M. (one's) belongings بوریا بندھنا اٹھانا *bo'riyā bad'nā ūṭhā'nā* V.I. quit make a move بوریا بستر اٹھانا *bo'riyā bis'tar ūṭhā'nā* V.I. quit make a move [P]

بوڑھا *boo'rhā* N.M. old man ADJ. (F. بوڑھی *boo'rhī*) old ; aged elderly بوڑھا بابا *boo'rha bā'ba* N.M. old man بوڑھا بالا برابر *boo'rha ba'la barā'bar* PROV. an old man is twice a child بوڑھا چونچلا *boo'rha chochla,* بوڑھی گھوڑی لال لگام *boo'rhī gho'rī lāl' lagām'* PH. youthful blandishments in old age بوڑھا ہونا *boo'rha ho'nā* V.I. grow old or aged

بوڑی *boo'rī* N.F. spike at end of staff point of spear

بوزہ *boo'zah'* N.M. beer بوزہ گر *boo'za-gar* ADJ. brewer بوزہ خانہ *boo'za-khā'nah* N.M. brewery beer shop pub [P]

بوزنہ *booz'nah.* بوزینہ *boozī'nah* N.M monkey [P]

بوستاں *bos'tan,* بستان *būs'tan* orchard name of a Persian classic [P]

بوسہ *bo'sah* N.M. kiss بوسہ بازی *bo'sa-bā'zī* N.F. fondling ; kissing ; dalliance بوس *bos* SUF kissing touching (as فلک بوس *fa'lak-bos* N.M. ski-high بوس و کنار *bo's-o kinār'* fondling ; kisses and caresses ; kissing and hugging [P] –

بوسیدہ *bosī'dah* ADJ. decayed decaying rotten بوسیدگی *bosī'dagī* N.F. decay rot [P]

بوغمہ *bogh'mah* N.M. rags ; tatters worthless stuff ADJ. ugly [T]

بوق *booq* N.M. bugle ; clarion [A]

بوکھلانا *baukh'lānā* V.I. be unnerved be confused lose one's presence of mind بوکھلاہٹ *baukhlā'hat* N.F. nervousness confusion jitters بوکھل *bāū'khal* N.M. & ADJ. nervous (person)

بوگی *bo'gī* N F. bogie [E]

بول *baul* N M. urine [A]

بول *bol* N.M. words of a song utterance ; speech ; words syllable fame میٹھا بول *mī'ṭhā bol* N.M. soft words ; sweet words میٹھا بول بولنا *mī'ṭhā bol bol'nā* V.I. say sweet words بول اٹھنا *bol' ūṭh'na* V.I. speak out exclaim بول بالا *bol' bā'la* N.M. success ; prosperity بول بالا ہونا *bol ba'la ho'nā* V.I. achieve fame thrive ; prosper چین بول جانا *chīn' bol ja'na* V.I. lose one's patience بول چال bol'-chal' N.F. talk conversation dialogue dialect بول چال ہونا bol'-chal' ho'na V.I. be on speaking terms [~ بولنا]

بولانا baula'na, بولا جانا baulā' jā'na V.I. lose one's wits ; lose one's presence of mind have the jitters

بولنا bol'na V.I. speak say talk utter tell call pronounce sound bid chirp be reconciled rave (of peacock, etc.) scream بولنا چالنا bol'na chal'na V.I. talk converse

بولی bo'lī N.F. dialect speech ; language chirping song taunt bid auction بولی دینا bo'lī de'nā V.I. bid at an auction bo'lī ṭho'lī N.F. taunts ; jeers بولی مارنا bo'lī mār'na V.T. taunt ; jeer بولیاں بولنا bo'liyan bol'na V. babble speak in (different) dialects or languages chirp ; song بولیاں سننا bo'liyan sūn'na V.I. hear taunts [~ PREC.]

بوم boom N.M. (lit.) owl land [P]

بونا bau'na N.M. بونی bau'nī N.F. dwarf ; pygmy ; midget ADJ. dwarfish

بونا bo'na V.T. sow cultivate plant (of stallion) cover بوائی buvā''ī N.F. (seeunder V.T. ★)

بوند boond N.F. raindrop drop بوند بوند boond' boond ADV. drop by drop بوندا باندی boon'dā bān'dī N.F. drizzle بوند بھر boond' bhar ADJ. just a drop ; just a little بوندیں ٹپکنا boon'deh ṭa'pakna V.I. drip ; trickle بوند بوند کر کے تالاب بھرتا ہے boond' boond kar ke talāb' bhar'tā hai PROV. small additions regularly made become large accretions

بوندی boon'dī N.F. a kind of sweetmeat ; gram drops [P ~ PREC. DIM.]

بونڈی boon'ḍī N.F. the germ of a plant after the flower is shed

بونس bo'nas N.M. bonus بونس واوچر bo'nas vā''ūchar N.M. bonus voucher [E]

بونگا baun'ga N.M. garrulous fool ADJ. stupid awkward بونگی baun'gī N.F. such woman nonsensical talk

بوہرا boh'rah N.M. member of an Ismaili sect (old use) (member of) a class of village money-lenders

بوہنی boh'nī N.F. first sale for ready money in the morning ; handsel ; hausel

بوئیا bo''iya N.M. small basket for spinning cotton

بوسیا bave'siyā, ببیسیا babe'siya N.M. confirmed catamote in advanced age one suffering from piles (fig.) chatterbox

بہ beh ADJ. (rare) well ; good بہتر beh'tar ADJ. better superior بہتری beh'tarī N.F. welfare betterment improvement good بہترین behtarīn' ADJ. best [P]

بہ beh N.M. hole pricked in woman's ear or nose for holding jewellery

بھابر bhā'bar N.M. a kind of plant yielding fibre for bed strings

بھابی bhā'bī N.F. (same as بھاوج N.F. ★)

بہا bahā' N.M. (lit.) value price rate خون بہا khoon-bahā' N.M. (see under خون N.M. ★)

بھابی bhā'bī N.F. sister-in-law ; brother's wife

بھاپ bhāp N.F. steam vapour exhalation بھاپ نکلنا bhāp' ni'kalna V.I. emission of steam or vapour

بھات bhāt' N.M. boiled rice dower given to bride by her maternal uncle دال بھات dāl-bhāt' N.M. daily bread ; bread and butter

بھاٹ bhāṭ N.M. (dial.) bard ; minstrel

بھاٹا bhā'ṭa N.M. ebb-tide جوار بھاٹا javār' bhā'ṭa N.M ebb and flow

بھاجی bhā'jī N.F. (dial.) vegetable dish guest's share

بہادر bahā'dūr ADJ. brave bold courageous valiant honourable N.M. hero ; champion بہادری bahā'dūrī N.F. bravery boldness courage valour [P]

بھادوں bhā'don N.M. fifth month of Hindu calendar (corresponding to August-September) بھادوں کی بھرن bhā'don kī bha'ran N.F. heavy August rains (inundating dried-up ponds) بھادوں کا جھالا bhā'don kā jhā'la N.M. بھادوں کے ڈونگرے bhā'don ke dong're N.M. PL. light August showers

بہار bahār' N.F. spring verdure prime (of life) ; bloom (of youth) beauty elegance flourishing state pleasure ; enjoyment بہار پر آنا bahār' par ā'nā V.I. blossom. flourish بہاریں لوٹنا bahā'reh looṭ'na V.I. enjoy revel in lead a life of pleasure بہارستان bahā'ristān' N.M. springfield بہاری bahā'rī ADJ. vernal [P]

بھار bhār N.M. man-load of crop

بھارکس bhār'kas N.M. cart strap binding draught animal to carriage shafts [~ P بارکش weight-pulling CORR.]

بھارت bhā'rat N.M. (Hindu name for post-partition India بھارت ورش bhā'rat var'sh N.M. (ancient Hindu name for) India [S]

بہارنا bohar'na V.T. sweep dust tidy up

بہارن boha'ran N.F. sweepings بہارو boha'roo, بہاری boha'ri (usu. جھاڑو بہارو jha'roo boha'roo N.F. broom جھاڑو بہارو کرنا jha'roo boha'roo kar'na V.T. sweep dust

بھاری bha'ri ADJ. heavy weighty fat large ; big voluminous great loud hard ; difficult cumbersome sluggish (11) strong (12) costly (13) valuable (14) important (15) ominous بھاری بھرکم bha'ri bhar'kam ADJ. grave fat plump heavy بھاری پتھر چوم کر چھوڑ دینا bha'ri pat'thar choom kar chhor' de'na V.I. withdraw from a difficult under taking بھاری لگنا bha'ri lag'na V.I. appear to be heavy find difficult or tiresome بھاری ہونا bha'ri ho'na V.I. be heavy be fat be cumbersome ominous be sluggish

بھاڑ bhar N.M. fire-place for parching grain oven furnace wages of sin بھاڑ جھونکنا bhar' jhonk'na V.I. make a fire of faggot for parching grain be unable to equip oneself for a means of livelihood بھاڑ کھانا bhar' kha'na V.I. be a pimp live on the wages of sin run a brothel بھاڑ میں جھونکنا bhar' men jhonk'na V.T. squander ; cast to the dogs

بھاڑا bha'ra N.M. fare freight hire bha'ra kar'na V.I. hire settle the fare بھاڑے کا ٹٹو bha're ka tat'too N.M. hired pony hireling drugaddict thing in need of constant repairs

بھاشا bha'sha, بھاکھا bha'kha N.F. (rare) dialect vernacular language speech [S]

بہاگ bihag' N.M. name of a musical mode [S]

بھاگ bhag' N.M. lot fate ; destiny fortune ; good luck ; honour بھاگ پھوٹنا bhag' phoot'na V.I. be unfortunate ; be very unlucky بھاگ جاگنا bhag' jag'na, بھاگ کھلنا bhag' khul'na, بھاگ لگنا bhag' lag'na V.I. be fortunate; be in luck become rich be honoured ; be exalted بھاگوان bhag'van' ADJ. lucky ; fortunate wealthy munificent

بھاگ bhag V.I. (see under بھاگنا V.I. ★)

بھاگڑ bha'gar N.F. stampede flight from immediate danger defeat بھاگڑ مچنا bha'gar mach'na V.I. be a stampede [~ FOLL.]

بھاگنا bhag'na V.I. run run away escape بھاگ جانا bhag' ja'na V.I. escape run away flee abscond elope بھاگم بھاگ bha'gam bhag' ADV. hurriedly swiftly بھاگ اٹھنا bhag' uth'na V.I. run away ; take to heels

بھال bhal N.F. spike point (of arrow, or bayonet, etc.) blade (of spear, lance, etc.) search دیکھ بھال dekh'-bhal' N.F. search supervision reconnaissance دیکھ بھال کرنا dekh-bhal kar'na V.T. look reconnoitre

بھالا bha'la N.M. spear ; lance

بھالو bha'loo N.M.

بھانا bha'na V.I. turn out to be likeable please ; be pleasing be agreeable (to) be acceptable (to)

بہانا baha'na V.T. spill shed (blood) cause to flow set afloat or adrift squander spend lavishly روپیہ پانی کی طرح بہانا rupa'yah pa'ni ki tar'h baha'na V.I. squander money spend lavishly

بھانپنا bhanp'na V.I. guess make out know ; perceive surmise divine see through بھانپ جانا bhanp' ja'na, بھانپ لینا bhanp' le'na V.I. guess

بھانت بھانت کا bhant' bhant ka ADJ. diverse of various kinds assorted ill-assorted

بھانج bhanj N.F. discount in getting change

بھانجا bhan'ja N.M. sister's son ; nephew بھانجی bhan'ji N.F. sister's daughter ; nice

بھانجی bhun'ji N.F. obstruction putting a spoke in another's wheel ; marring someone's plans tale-bearing backbiting بھانجی خور bhan'ji-khor, بھانجی مار bhan'ji-mar ADJ. mar-plot; one who tries to put a spoke in another's wheel بھانجی مارنا bhan'ji mar'na V.I. tell tales to mar (someone's plans) put a spoke in someone's wheels

بھانڈ bhand N.M. buffoon street actor jester mimic blab disreputable person بھانڈ بھگتیے bhand' bhag'tiye N.M. PL. buffoons street actors riff-raff

بھانڈ

بھانڈا bhan'da N.M. earthen vessel (fig.) secret بھانڈا (چوراہے میں) پھوٹنا bhan'da (chaura'he men) phoot'na V.I. be found out (in public) lose one's character (of secret) be divulged be publicly disgraced بھانڈا (چوراہے میں) پھوڑنا bhan'da (chaura'he men) phor'na V.T. divulge (some-

(one's) secret disgrace publicly

بھان متی bhan'-mati N.M. juggler ; magician بھان متی کا کنبہ bhan'-mati ka kun'bah PH. ill-assorted things ill-matched things or persons unholy alliance کہیں کی اینٹ کہیں کا روڑا بھان متی نے کنبہ جوڑا ka'hin ki int' ka'hin ka ro'ra bhan'-mati ne kun'bah jo'ra PROV. ill-assorted group unholy alliance

بہانہ baha'nah N.M. excuse plea, pretext pretence feint ; ruse evasion بہانہ جو baha'na-joo ADJ. (person) seeking an excuse بہانہ جوئی baha'na-joo'i N.F. (putting up) false excuses بہانہ ڈھونڈنا baha'nah dhoond'na, بہانہ کرنا baha'nah kar'na V.I. put up a lame excuse ; evade ; dodge come out with an excuse بہانہ ساز baha'na-saz ADJ. (person) who puts up lame excuses بہانہ سازی baha'na-sa'zi N.F. (putting up) false excuses [P]

بہائم baha''im N M. PL. animals ; quadrupeds bruits [A ~ SING. بہیمہ]

بھاؤ bha''o N.M. rate market price gesticulation (in dancing) بھاؤ اترنا (یا گرنا یا گھٹنا) bha''o u'tarna (or gir'na or ghat'na) N.F. fall in price (of price) fall بھاؤ بتانا bha''o bata'na V.T. give the rate gesticulate (in dancing) بھاؤ چڑھنا (یا تیز ہونا) bha''o charh'na (or tez' ho'na) rise in price (of price) rise or soar بھاؤ چکانا bha''o chuka'na V.I. settle the rate(s)

بہاؤ baha''o N.M. flux flow gliding along direction of current [~ بہنا]

بھاوج bha'vaj, بھابی bha'bi N.F. brother's wife ; sister-in-law

بہائی baha''i N.M. (member of) a heretic sect of Islam which has tried to set itself as a separate religion [~ founder's name بہا ~ A]

بھائی bha''i N.M. brother kinsman friend companion ; comrade ally بھائی بھائی bha''i bha''i N.M. PL. friends allies comrades بھائی بند bha''i band N.M. PL. kindered ; kinsmen ; kith and kin relations brethren fraternity بھائی بندی bha''i bandi, بھائی چارا bha''i cha'ra N.M. friendship fraternity

بھائیں بھائیں bha''en bha''en N.F. calf's cry بھائیں بھائیں کرنا bha''en bha''en kar'na V.I. (of house) be deserted (of place) be desolate

بھبک bha'bak N.F. sudden burst (of flame) بھبکا bhab'ka N.M. effusion (of stench) offensive vapour blast (from furnace) alembic still mug ; tankard بھبکنا bha'bakna V.I. burst into flame (of flame) burst catch fire fly into a rage

بھبکی bhab'ki N.F. threat ; menace گیدڑ بھبکی gi'dar bhab'ki N.F. (usu. PL.) bullying empty threat بھبکی دینا bhab'ki de'na V.T. bully threaten گیدڑ بھبکیوں میں آنا gi'dar bhab'kiyon men a'na V.T. feel jittery before a bully

بھبوت bhaboot' N.M. cow-dung ; ashes بھبوت رمانا (یا لگانا یا ملنا) bhaboot' rama'na (or laga'na or mal'na) become a (Hindu) saint by besmearing body with ashes [S]

بہبود beh-bood' N.F. welfare well-being good betterment benefit : utility بہبود خلائق beh-bood-e khala''iq N.F. public welfare public utility [P ~ بہ + بودن]

بھبوکا bhaboo'ka N.M. blaze flame ADJ. ablaze hot glowing furious lovely [~ بھبک]

بھپارا bhapa'ra N.M. steam vapour steam-bath بھپارا دینا bhapa'ra de'na V.T. give a steam bath (to)

بھپاڑا bhapa'ra N.M. fraud ; deceit

بہت ba'hot' (dial. bahut') ADJ. many much most copious excessive enough ; sufficient plentiful ; abundant ADV. much very much largely excessively enormously exceedingly intenesely بہت اچھا ba'hot ach'cha ADV. all right ; OK very well very good accepted ; agreed ; granted بہت ٹھیک ba'hot thik' ADV. all right quite true too true بہت خوب ba'hot khoob' ADV. well-said well-done all right ; okay ; OK بہت سا ba'hot sa ADJ. a great deal quite a lot much plentiful ; abundant بہت رات گئے ba'hot rat ga'e ADV. quite late in the evening in the early hours of the morning

بھتا bhat'ta N.M. allowance emoluments in addition to salary (arch.) travelling allowance ; T.A.

بہتات bohtat', (dial. bahutat') N.F. abundance ; plenty excess

بہتان bohtan' N.M. slander ; calumny aspersion false accusation imputation بہتان باندھنا (یا دھرنا یا لگانا) bohtan' bandh'na (or dhar'na or laga'na) V.T. bring a false accusation against slander ; calumniate

بہتر bahat'tar ADJ. & N.M. seventy-two بہترواں bahat'tarvan ADJ. seventy-second

بہتر beh'tar ADJ. (see under ADJ. ★)

بھتنا *bhut'nā* N.M. imp ; goblin ghost demon ugly person بھتنا بنا ہونا *bhut'nā ba'nā ho'nā* V.I. be so untidy or besmeared as to look like a demon بھتنی *bhut'nī* N.F. female demon old hag ugly woman بھتنے کی چڈی *bhut'ne kī chad'dhī* N.F. a kind of boys' game

بھتی *bhat'tī* N.F. funeral feast بھتی کھانا *bhat'tī khā'nā* PH. (also fig.) see (someone) dead بہتے پانی میں ہاتھ دھونا *baih te pā'nī men hath dho'nā* PH. make hay while the sun shines

بھتیجا *bhatī'jā* N.M. brother's son ; nephew بھتیجی *bhatī'jī* N.F. brother's daughter ; niece

بہتیرا *baihte'rā, bahote'rā* ADJ. many much ADV. enough ; sufficient quite sufficient a great deal much ; most

بھٹ *bhaṭ* N.M. den ; lair pit hole hovel glowing plaster of fire-place بھٹ پڑے وہ سونا جس سے ٹوٹیں کان *bhaṭ pa're voh so'nā jis se ṭoo'ṭeh kān'* PROV. to hell with the treasure that brings harm

بھٹا *bhuṭ'ṭā* N.M. cob ; corn-cob بھٹا سا (سر) اڑانا *bhuṭ'ṭā sā (sir) uṛā'nā* PH. cut (head) off clean with one stroke بھٹے کی گلی *bhuṭ'ṭe kī gullī* N.F. ear of corn without grain

بھٹا *bhaṭ'ṭa*, بھٹہ *bhaṭ'ṭah* N.M. kiln

بھٹکانا *bhaṭkā'nā* V.I. mislead lead astray cause to wander deceive بھٹکنا *bhaṭak'nā* V.I. go astray lose one's way miss the right path roam about بھٹکا (یا بھٹکتا) پھرنا *bhaṭ'kā (or bha'ṭaktā phir'nā)* V.I. lose (one's way room about (in search of)

بھٹ کٹیا *bhaṭ kaṭay'yā* N.F. a kind of wild prickly plant

بھٹنی *bhiṭ'nī* N.F. pap ; teat

بھٹئی *bhaṭai''ī* N.F. fawning ; sycophancy [بھاٹ]

بھٹی *bhaṭ'ṭī* N.M. furnace (washerman's) cauldron still name of an Indo-Pakistan class بھٹی چڑھانا *bhaṭ'ṭī chaṛhā'nā* V.T. boil clothes in cauldron light fire in furnace

بھٹیارا *bhaṭyā'ra* N.M. innkeeper cook working at an inn, etc. بھٹیار خانہ *bhaṭ'yar'-khā'nah* N.M. (fig.) home with frequent brawls slum mean restaurant بھٹیاری *bhaṭyā'rī* N.F. female innkeeper inn-keeper's wife female cook at an inn

بہجت *bah'jat* (or *baih-*) N.F. joy ; happiness delight beauty ; grace [A]

بھج *bhuj*, بھچ *bhach* N.M. & ADJ. lout(ish) flat and dark

بھجن *bha'jan* N.M. (dial.) hymn [S]

بھجنگ *bhujang*, بھجنگا *bhujan'gā* N.M. king crow ADV (of person, etc.) jet (black)

بھجوانا *bhijvā'nā* V.T. send cause to be sent [~ بھیجنا CAUS.]

بھجیا *bhuj'yā* N.F. fried vegetable dish [~ بھوننا]

بھچنا *bhich'nā*, بھچ جانا *bhich jā'nā* V.I. be squeezed be compressed be sitting in a very tight place

بھد *bhad* N.F. disgrace thud بھد سے گرنا *bhad' se gir'nā* V.I. fall with a thud کی بھد نکلنا (یا اڑنا) *kī bhad ni'kalnā (or uṛ'nā)* V.I. (of someome) be disgraced بھد بھد *bhad bhad* N.F. footfall (of duck or fat person)

بھدا *bhad'dā*, ADJ. (F. بھدی *bhad'dī*) ugly awkwardness ; clumsiness

بھداکا *bhadā'ka* N.M. dull heavy sound (of fall) ; thud

بہدانہ *beh-dā'nah*, بہیدانہ *be'hī-dā'nah* N.M. (see under بہی N.F. ★)

بھدرا *bhad'ra* N.M. shaving off top hair (in Hindu mourning) [S]

بھدرک *bhad'rak* N.F. elegance ; grace constancy

بھدوار *bhadvār'* N.F. land prepared for sugar-cane cultivation

بہر *baih'r*, از بہر *az baih'r-e* PREP. (lit.) for ; on account of ; for the sake of [P]

بہر *ba-har'* PREP. (lit.) in every to every بہرحال *ba-har' hāl'* ADV. anyhow ; in any case ; at any rate بہرطور *ba-har taur'* بہرصورت *ba-har' soor'rat*, بہرکیف *ba-har' kaif* ADV. by all means somehow or other at all events ; in any case ; at any rate ; anyhow

بھر *bhar'* AFF. full all whole up to as far as as much as a , one (as سیر بھر *ser' bhar* a seer) بھرپانا *bhar' pā'nā* V.I. be paid in full be fed up with بھرپائی *bhar-pā''ī* N.F. receipt in full بھرپور *bhar-poor'* ADJ. full complete brimful بھرپیٹ *bhar peṭ'* ADV. to one's fill بھرمار *bhar mar'* N.F. plenty ; abundance excess کی بھرمار کرنا *kī bhar-mār' kar'na* V.T. do or give in abundance کی بھرمار ہونا *kī bhar-mar' ho'nā* V.I. be in abundance be in full strength دن بھر *din, bhar* ADV. the whole day ; all the day long عمر بھر *'ūm'r bhar* ADV. during the whole (of one's) life ; all (one's)

lifetime مقدور بھر *madoor' bhar* ADV. to the best of one's ability or power to the utmost
بھرا *bhar'rā* N.M. (also PL.) deceit incitement ; instigation بھرا دینا *bhar'rā de'nā* V.T. deceive incite instigate بھرے میں آنا *bhur're meṅ ā'nā*, بھروں میں آنا *bhar'roṅ meṅ ā'nā* V.I. be deceived
بھرا *bhūr'rā* ADV. jet (black)

بہرا *baih'rā* ADJ. & N.M. (F. بہری *baih'rī*) deaf (person) hard of hearing
بہرام *baihrām'* N.M. Mars a Persian name بہرام گور *baihrām' gor* N.M. name of an ancient Persian King fond of zebra-hunting
بھرانا *bhara'nā* V.T. cause to be filled (of bird) feed its young get (animal) covered بھرائی *bharā''ī* N.F. filling stuffing watering getting covered remuneration for these [~ بھرنا CAUS.]
بھرانا *bharrā'nā* V.I. be husky become hoarse
بھربھرا *bhūr'bhū'rā* ADJ. (F. بھربھری *bhūr' bhūrī*) crisp (of soil) somewhat sandy بھربھرانا *bhūrbhurā'nā* V.T. sprinkle (salt, sugar, etc.)
بھربھراہٹ *bhūrbhūrahaṭ* N.F. crispness
بھربھنڈ *bhar bhand'* ADV. upset, topsy-turvy

بھرت *bha'rat* N.M. copper, lead and zinc alloy [~ بھرنا]
بھرتا *bhūr'tā* N.M. mash ; fried vegetables mashed in curds بھرتا نکالنا (یا کر دینا) *bhūr'ta nikāl'nā* (or *kar de'nā*) V.T. make a mash of beat to a pulp give a good hiding
بھرتی *bhar'tī* N.F. recruiting ; enrolment ; enlistment stuffing ; insertion of inferior stuff filling completion بھرتی کرنا *bhar'tī kar'nā* V.T. recruit ; enlist ; enrol بھرتی کا مال *bhar'tī kā māl'* N.M. inferior stuff mixture [~ بھرنا]
بھرشٹ *bharish't* ADV. (dial.) polluted بھرشٹ کرنا *bharish't kar'nā* V.I. pollute [S]
بھرکس *bhūr'kas* N.M. husk ; chaff chips ; splinters بھرکس نکالنا *bhūr'kas ni'kal'nā* V.I. be severely beaten (مار مار کر) بھرکس نکالنا (*mār' mār kar*) *bhūr'kas nikāl'nā* V.T. beat black and blue
بھرم *bha'ram* N.M. credit ; trust prestige secret بھرم جانا (یا کھلنا) *bha'ram jā'nā* (or *khul'nā*) V.I. be exposed lose one's credit بھرم گنوانا *bha'ram ganvā'nā* V.I. lose one's prestige بھرمانا *bharmā'nā* V.T. tempt deceive mislead

بھرن *bha'ran* N F. heavy Bhadon shower بھرن پڑنا (یا برسنا) *bha'ran pa'ṛnā* (or *ba'rasnā*) V.T. fall in heavy shower [~ FOLL.]
بھرنا *bhar'nā* V.T & I. fill load be filled (of wound) heal pay indemnity irrigate pollute be polluted besmear be besmeared pay realise suffer tolerate (of body) grow fat grow or make rich (of fare) be crowded بھرآنا *bhar'ā'na* V.I. (of wound) heal (of heart) be filled with pity بھرا پرا *bha'ra pū'ra* ADJ. happy (home) بھرا گھر *bha'ra ghar'* N.M. happy or well-equipped home بھر دینا *bhar de'nā* V.T. fill besmear make good (loss) give presents or settle dower profusely بھر نظر دیکھنا *bhar' na'zar dekh'nā* V.T. glance fully بھر نیند سونا *bhar' nīnd' so'nā* V.I. have a sound sleep بھری برسات *bha'rī barsāt'* N.F. heavy rains بھری جوانی *bha'rī javā'nī* N.F. prime of life ; blooming youth بھری جوانی مانجھا ڈھیلا *bha'rī javā'nī māṅ'jha dhī'la* PH. one lazy in youth بھری گود خالی ہونا *bha'rī god' khā'lī ho'nā* V.I. become issueless on child's death بھرا لتھڑا *bha'rā lith'ṛa* ADJ. besmeared bedraggled بھری مجلس (یا محفل) میں *bha'rī maj'lis* (or *maih'fil*) *meṅ* ADV. publicly ; in every body's presence بھرا بیٹھا ہونا *bha'rā bai'ṭhā ho'nā* V.I. be greatly enraged be on the point of weeping بھرنا بھرنا *bhar'nā bhar'nā* V.I. pay debts incurred hy others support someone unwillingly بھرے کو بھرنا *bha're ko bhar'nā* V.T. bestow more on someone who is already rich
بہروپ *baihroop* N.M. disguise actor's make-up mimicry بہروپ بھرنا *baihroop' bhar'nā* V.I. disguise oneself mimic بہروپیا *baihroop'piyā* N.M. street histrion character actor expert in changing one's guise
بھروسا *bharo'sā*, بھروسہ *bharo'sah* N.M. confidence ; faith trust reliability assurance بھروسا کرنا *bharo'sā kar'nā* V.I. trust rely on

بہرہ *baih'rah* N.M. share ; portion lot destiny fortune بہرہ مند *baih'ra-mand'* بہرہ ور *baih'ra-var*, بہرہ یاب *baih'rayāb'* ADJ. lucky ; fortunate prosperity بہرہ مندی *baih'ra-man'dī*, بہرہ یابی *baih'ra yā'bī* N.F. happiness prosperity [P]
بہری *baih'rī* N.F. female hawk ; falcon ADJ. (see under بہرا ADJ. ★)
بھڑ *bhiṛ* N.F. wasp ; hornet بھڑوں کا چھتا *bhi'roṅ kā chhat'tā* N.M. hornets' nest بھڑوں کے چھتے میں ہاتھ ڈالنا

bhi'ron ke chhat'te men hath' ḍal'na, بھڑوں کے چھتے کو چھیڑنا *bhi'ron ke chhat'te ko chher'na* PH. stir up a hornet's nest سوتی بھڑوں کو جگانا *so'tī bhi'ron ko jaga'na* PH. rouse a sleeping monster

بھڑاس *bhaṛas'* N.F. grudge ; resentment rage ; animosity ; spleen دل کی بھڑاس نکالنا *dil' kī bhaṛas' nikāl'na* V.I. vent one's spleen (on)

بھڑانا *bhiṛa'na* V.T. bring into collision bring into clash embroil set up one against the other [~ بھڑنا CAUS.]

بھڑبھڑ *bhar' bhaṛ* N.F. crackling (of fuel) بھڑبھڑ کرنا *bhar' bhaṛ kar'na* V.I. (of fuel) crackle burn fiercely

بھڑبھڑانا *bhar bhaṛa'na* V.T. play on or beat 'tabla'

بھڑبھونجا *bharbhoon'ja* N.M. بھڑبھونجن *bharbhoon'jan* N.F. one whose trade is parch grain

بھڑک *bha'ṛak* N.F. sheen lustre glitter blaze ; refulgence flash ostentation rage ; fury shying (of horse) nervousness jitters بھڑکدار *bha'ṛak-dār'* ADJ. refulgent gorgeous tawdry فوق البھڑک *fau'q-ul bha'ṛak* ADJ. refulgent or gorgeous (dress) بھڑکیلا *bha'ṛ-ki'la* ADJ. (F. بھڑکیلی *bhaṛkī'lī*) gorgeous ; splendid refulgent tawdry [~ FOLL.]

بھڑکنا *bharak'na* V.I. flare up be enraged ; fly into passion startle (of horse) shy

بھڑکانا *bhaṛka'na* V.T. kindle inflame incite ; instigate scare startle

بھڑنا *bhiṛ'na* V.I. collide clash fight (of door) be shut (of opposed armies) fall upon

بھڑوا *bhaṛ'va* (dial. بھڑمل *bhaṛ'mal*) N.M. pimp ; pander ; procurer shameless man

بھڑولنا *bhaṛol'na* V.T. betray (someone's secret)

بھڑی دینا *bha'ṛī de'na* V I. train pigeons badger

بھڑیری *bhaṛe'rī* N.F. pile (of utensils) placed one above the other

بھس *bhus* N.M. husk bran chaff straw gram chaff, etc. (for asses) بھس کرنا *bhus' kar'na* V.T. stuff with chaff (fig.) fill with stupidity بھس میں چنگی (یا چنگاری) ڈال بی جمالو دور کھڑی *bhus men chingī (or chingari) ḍal' bī jama'lo door' kha'ṛī* PROV. mischief-monger washes his hands of the crime after instigating it بھسکو *bhusa'koo* N.M. snatch ... [illegible]

بھسم *bha'sam* N.F. ashes ; cinders بھسم کرنا *bha'sam kar'na* V.T. reduce to ashes ; burn out destroy بھسم ہونا *bha'sam ho'na* V.I. be reduced to ashes ; be burnt be destroyed writhe (in rage)

بہشت *behisht'* N.F. paradise ; heaven بہشت کی ہوا *behisht' kī havā'* N.F. cool refreshing breeze بہشتی *behishtī* ADJ. blessed celestial N.M. water-carrier

بھک *bhak* N.F. blast ; sound of explosion roaring (of fire) puffing (of steam-engines etc.) بھک بھک کرنا *bhak bhak kar'na* V.I. puff chug بھک سے اڑجانا *bhak se uṛ' ja'na* V.I. blast explode be cut clean off fly off بھک سے اڑجانے والا مادہ *bhak' se uṛ' ja'ne va'la mad'dah* N.M. combustible material explosion

بھکاری *bhika'rī* N.M. (F بھکارن *bhika'ran*) beggar mendicant [~ بھیک]

بہکانا *baihka'na* V.T. seduce allure mislead ; lead astray cause to err tempt بہکا لے جانا *baihka' le ja'na* V.T. elope kidnap carry off lure away بہکاوا *baihka'va* N.M. delusion trick misleading بہکاوے میں آنا *baihka've men a'na* V.I. be deluded (by) be taken in (by) fall into the snare (of) be tempted (by) [~ بہکنا CAUS.]

بھکشا *bhik'sha* N.F. (dial.) alms [S]

بھکشو *bhik'shoo* N.M. Buddhist mendicant ; Buddhist priest [S ~ PREC.]

بھکوسنا *bhakos'na* V.T. eat greedily devour

بھک منگا *bhik' man'ga* beggar pauper [~ بھیک + مانگنا]

بہکنا *bai'hakna,* بہک جانا *bai'hak ja'na* V.I. be deluded go astray ; be misled talk in a state of intoxication بہکی بہکی باتیں کرنا *baih'kī baih'kī ba'ten kar'na* V.I. talk as if drunk talk nonsense

بھکوا *bhak'va* ADJ. (F. بھکوی *bhak'vī*) fool

بھگانا *bhaga'na* V.T. put to rout ; put to flight ; defeat gallop (a horse) away drive off cause to flee or escape بھگا لے جانا *bhaga' le ja'na* V.T. elope kidnap to run away with ; carry away drive off

بھگت *bha'gat* N.M. (dial.) devotee rogue

بھگتیا *bhag'tiya* N.M. street-dancer

بھگتنا *bhug'gatna* V.I. bear with patience suffer experience pay the penalty settle with be requited (for) appear (at a court-hearing) بھگتان *bhugtan'* N.M. payment adjustment full settlement disposal (of customers, etc.) بھگتانا *bhugta'na* V.T. dispose of pay adjust settle do; execute

بھگدڑ *bhag'dar'* N.F. stampede; sudden wild commotion; flight due to panic

بھگندر *bhagan'dar'* N.M. fistula in rectum

بھگوان *bhagvan'* N.M. (dial.) God بھگوت *bhag'vat*, بھگونت *bhag'vant'* ADJ. (dial.) Divine بھگوت گیتا *bhag'vat gi'ta* N.F. Divine Song (name of a Hindus scripture) [S]

بھگوڑا *bhagau'ra*, (dial. بھگو *bhag'goo*, بھگیلا *bhage'la*) ADJ. & N.M. (F. بھگوڑی *bhagau'ri*) deserter run away; fugitive

بھگونا *bhigo'na*, بھگو دینا *bhigo' de'na* V.T. wet moisten soak drench بھگو بھگو کے مارنا *bhigo' bhigo' ke mar'na* V.T. put to great shame taunt with apparent suavity indulge mock praise [~ بھیگنا CAUS.]

بھلا *bha'la* ADJ. (F. بھلی *bha'li*) nice excellent good virtuous gentle; noble humane; courteous pleasing; agreeable delectable ADJ. & N.M. good virtue favour بھلا چنگا *bha'la chan'ga* ADJ. in good health; hale and hearty; healthy بھلا سا نام ہے *bha'la sa nam' hai* PH. what d'ye call it بھلا لگنا *bha'la lag'na* V.I. look agreeable be attractive بھلا آدمی *bha'la ad'mi*, بھلا مانس *bha'la ma'nus* (or *ma'nas*) N.M. gentleman nice person respectable person بھلا چاہنا *bha'la chah'na* V.T. wish (someone) well بھلا کرنا *bha'la kar'na* V.I. do good do a favour بھلا ہونا *bha'la ho'na* V.I. be good be well that بھلی کرنا *bha'li kar'na* V.I. (iron.) treat unfairly بھلی ہونا *bha'li ho'na* V.I. (iron.) get a rough tdeal بھلے آئے *bha'le a''e* PH. (iron.) you turned up well on time بھلے دن *bha'le din* PL. good old times better days بھلے کو *bha'le ko* CONJ. it was a happy coincidence it is well that بھلائی *bhala''i* N.F. good virtue welfare prosperity beneficence kindness; gain; benefit بھلائی کرنا *bhala''i kar'na* V.T. do good show kindness

بھلانا *bhula'na*, بھلا دینا *bhula' de'na* V.T. forget; cause to forget

بہلانا *baihla'na* V. divert amuse; entertain cheer coax; cajole بہلاوا *baihla'va* N.M. entertainment; amusement cajolery false hope بہلاوے دینا *baihla've de'na* V.T. raise false hopes (in mind)

بھلاوا *bhula'va* N.M. guile; deception بھلاوا دینا *bhula'va de'na* V.T. beguile; deceive play a truck; use a ruse

بلک بلک *bha'lak cha'lak* ADV. (weep) bitterly

بھلکڑ *bhulak'kar* ADJ. very forgetful; oblivious thoughtless; careless; negligent remiss [~ بھولنا]

بھلمنساہٹ *bhal'mansa'hat*, بھلمنسی *bhalman'si* N.F. nobility civility; politeness nice treatment [~ بھلا + مانس]

بہلنا *bai'halna*, بہل جانا *bai'hal ja'na* V.I. be diverted be amused; be entertained

بہلول *baihlol'* (ped. *bahlool'*) N.M. cynic joker simpleman (also بہلول دانا *baih'lol-e da'na*) name of a cynical saint [A]

بہلی *baih'li*, بہل *baih'l* N.F. light two wheeled ox carriage

بہلہ *baih'lah* N.M. falconer's leather glove

بھلاواں *bhula'van* N.M. 'semi-carpus anacurdium'; nut used by washerman for marking clothes

بہم *ba-ham'* ADV. together بہم پہنچانا *ba-ham' pahuncha'na* V.T. procure provide supply convey bring about بہم پہنچنا *ba-ham' pahunch'na* V.I. be procured be provided supplied be acquired come to hand

بہمدگر *ba-ham'di'gar* ADJ. mutual reciprocal ADV. together بہم رسانی *ba-ham' rasa'ni* supply provision [P ~ بہ + ہم]

بہمن *baih'man* N.M. eleventh month of Persian calendar (corresponding to February)

بہن *bai'han* (dial. *ba'han, ba'hin*) N.F. sister female cousin بہنا *baih'na* N.F. (dial.) sister dear sister بہناپا *baih'napa* N.M. sisterly affection or kindness friendship between girls or women بہناپا جوڑنا (یا کرنا) *baihna'pa jor'na* (or *kar'na*) V.T. (of girls) become (mutual) friends

بہنا *baih'na* V.I. flow float drift (of liquid) run (of sore) run (of solid) melt; dissolve بہہ جانا *baih ja'na* V.I. (of liquid) run; run out (of solid) melt away

بھنانا *bhuna'na*, بھنوانا *bhunva'na* V.T. get (small change for cause to be fried or parched

بھنائی *bhuna''i*, بھنوائی *bhunva''i* N.F. discount on giving change remuneration for parching

بھنانا *bhinna'na* V.I. (of ears) have a ringing sound (also بھنا اٹھنا *bhinna' uth'na*) be

annoyed react, sharply
بھنبیری *bhanbī'rī* N.F. a humming insect constantly dancing on water بھنبیری سا دوڑتا پھرنا *bhanbī'rī sā daur'tā phir'nā* V.I (of child) run swiftly
بھنبھنانا *bhinbhinā'na* V.I. buzz hum *bhin bhin*, بھنبھناہٹ *bhinbhinā'hat* N.F. buzz hum buzzing humming
بھنبھوڑنا *bhanbhor'nā* V.T. (of beast) gnaw ; devour by gnawing mangle
بھنڈار *bhandār'*, بھنڈارا *bhandā'rā* N.M. free meals public mess at shrives, etc. almshouse meal store serving free meals belly
بھنڈارا لگنا *bhandā'rā lag'nā* V.I. (of mess) be run
بھنڈارا کھلنا *bhandā'rā khul'nā* V.I. (of belly) be ripped open بھنڈاری *bhandā'rī* N.M. steward keeper or persons in charge of free mess
بھنڈی *bhin'dī* N.F. lady's finger
بھنکنا *bhi'nak'nā*, بھنک رہا ہونا *bhi'nak' rahā ho'nā* V.I. (of flies) buzz swarm around
بھنک *bhi'nak* N.F. buzz hum rumour something in the air کان میں بھنک پڑنا *kān meṅ bhi'nak par'nā* V.T. get wind (of) [~ FREC.]
بھنگ *bhang* N.F. hemp ; cannabis plant yielding it بھنگڑ *bhan'gar* N.M. hemp-addict silly braggart rumour-monger irresponsible talker بھنگڑ خانہ *bhan'gar-khānah* N.M. hemp pub noisy place with idlers lolling around بھنگڑ خانے کی گپ *bhan'gar-khā'ne kī gap* PH. silly rumour
بھنگا *bhun'ga* N.M. a kind of winged monsoon insect
بھنگڑا *bhang'ra* N.M. name of a Pakistani folk dance ; Pakistani jig a kind of herb
بھنگی *bhangī* N M. sweeper scavenger a sikh caste بھنگیوں کی توپ *bhangiyon kī top* N.F. Kim's Gum
بہنگی *baihn'gī* N.F. thick bamboo stick with slings at ends for carrying load on shoulder
بھننا *bhun'nā* V.I. be roasted (of rupee, etc.) be converted into small change
بھنوانا *baunvā'na* V.T. cause to be fried (cause to) get small change (same as *bhunā'na* V.T. ★)
بھنور *bhan'var* N.M. whirlpool eddy, vortex (fig.) grief misfortune بھنور جال *bhan'var jāl* N.M. worldy its temptations worldy cares بھنور میں پڑنا (یا پھنسنا) *bhan'var men par'nā* (or *phans'nā*) V.I. be afflicted suffer from vicissitudes of fortune be caught up in an eddy
بہنوئی *baihno''ī* N.M. brother-in-law ; sister's husband [~ بہن]
بہنی *boh'nī* N.F. (same as بوہنی *boh'nī* ★)
بہنیلی *bahne'lī* N.F. adopted sister girl's female friend بہنیلا *baihne'la* N.M. sisterly affection ; friendship between girls [~ بہن]
بہو *ba'hoo* N.F. daughter-in-law bride wife بڑی بہو *ba'rī ba'hoo* N.F. senior wife elder son's wife چھوٹی بہو *chho'ṭī ba'hoo* N.F. junior wife younger son's wife بہو بیٹیاں *ba'hoo be'ṭiyaṅ* N.F. PL. respectable woman chaste homely women
بہوار *behvar'* N.M. (also کاربہوار *kār' behvār'*) N.M. (rus.) business بہوار کی بات *behvar' kī bāt'* PL. fair deal straight talk
بھوپالی *bhoopā'lī* N.F. name of a musical mode
بھوبھل *bhoo'bhal* N.F. hot ashes ; embers
بھوپوں بھوپوں *bhoo'poon bhoo'poon* N.F. hoot (of car) [ONO.]
بھوت *bhoot* N.M. (F. بھتنی *bhut'nī*) demon fiend ; ghost apparition, evil spirit goblin ugly figure (fig.) rage بھوت اتارنا *bhoot' utār'na* V.T. exorcize بھوت اترنا *bhoot' u'tarna* V.I. بھوت چڑھنا (یا سوار ہونا) *bhoot' charh'nā* (or *savār' ho'nā*) V.T. (of evil spirit) possess be obsessed ; be possessed be distracted with rage be intoxicated act like a devil بھوت پریت *bhoot' paret'* N.M. ghosts and fiends بھوت ہونا *bhoot' ho'nā* V.I. be very untidy look shabby act like a devil بھوت بن کر (یا ہو کر) لپٹنا *bhoot' ban kar* (or *ho kar*) *lipatnā* V.T. possess (someone like a devil) distress annoy bore, obsess بھوتنی *bhoot'nī* N.F. (same as بھتنی *bhut'nī* N.F. ★)
بھوج پتر *bhoj' pal'tar* N.M. Indian papyrus leaf bark of a birch-like tree for writing on
بھوجن *bho'jan* N.M. (dial.) meals ; victuals, food [S]
بھوچکا *bhauchak'kā* ADV. (same as بھوچکا ADJ. ★)
بھور *bhor* N.F. (rare) dawn, early morning ; daybreak ; break of day

بھورا *bho'ra* ADJ. (F. بھوری *bhoori*) buff (paper, etc.) auburn (hair) brownish
بھوڑا *baho'ra*, بھوڑے کا کھانا *baho're ka kha'na* N.M. meals sent to groom's house along with bridal procession
بھوسا *bhoo'sa* N.M. chaff srraw بھوسی *bhoosi* N.F. husk bran
بھوسڑا *bhos'ra* N.M. vagina بھوسڑی *bhos'ri* N.F. dim) vagina (derog.) woman
بھوک *bhook* N.F. hunger appetite need; want desire keenness lust بھوک لگنا *bhook' lag'na* V.I feel hungry بھوک پیاس مارنا *bhook' pyas' mar'na* V.T. repress one's appetite mortify oneself بھوک مارنا *bhook' mar'na* V.I. lose appetite be no longer hungry N.M lose of appetite بھوکوں مرنا *bhook'koṅ mar'na* V I. starve to death بھوکوں مارنا *bhoo'koṅ mar'na* V.I famish ; die of hunger be hard up بھوک ہڑتال *bhook' hartal* N.F. hunger-strike بھوکا *bhoo'ka* ADJ. (F. بھوکی *bhooki'*) huugry starving famished desirous needy
بھوگنا *bhog'na* V I. suffer endure

بھول *bhool* N.F forgetfulness ; oblivion oversight mistake , fault oversight lapse omission بھول بھلیاں *bhool bhulay yaṅ* N.F. maze labyrinth baffling matters بھول چوک لینی دینی *bhool' chook' le'ni de'ni* PH. errors and omissions excepted ; E. & O.M. بھول چوک معاف *bhool' chook mo'af* PH. oversight overlooked بھول کے بھی نہیں *bhool' ke bhi na'hiṅ*, بھولے سے بھی نہیں *bhoo'le se bhi na'hiṅ* PH. never, under no circumstances . (not) even by mistake [~ بھولنا]
بھولا *bho'la* ADJ. (F بھولی) simple artless, guileless inexperienced innocent childlike بھولا بھالا *bho'la bha'la* ADJ. innocent, guileless بھولاپن *bho'la-pan*, بھولپن *bhol-pan* N.M. being childlike inexperience artlessness childlike innocence guileless beauty بھولی باتیں *bho'li ba'teṅ* N.F. PL. innocent prattle comments lacking shrewdness بھولی بھولی باتیں *bho'li bho'li ba'teṅ* N.F. PL. innocent prattle
بھولنا *bhool na* V.T. forget , become oblivious miss err stray be deluded , be deceived be misled go astray estray
بھولا بسرا *bhoo'la bis ra* ADJ. (F. بھولی بسری *bhoo'li bis'ri*) forgotten (matter, story caller, etc.) بھولا بھٹکا *bhoo'la bhat'ka* ADJ. (F بھولی بھٹکی *bhoo'li bhat'ki*) stray traveller etc. بھولی صورت *bho'li soo'rat* N.F. innocent looks
بھومی *bhoo'mi* N.F. (dial.) land . place (usu. in) جنم بھومی *ja'nam bhoo'mi* N.F. birthplace native land [S]
بھوں *bhauṅ* N.F. eyebrow بھوؤں کا گلہ آنکھ کے سامنے *bha'voṅ ka gi'lah aṅkh' ke sam'ne* PROV. complain against someone before his friends بھویں تاننا (یا چڑھانا) *bha'veṅ tan'na* (or *charha'na*) V.I. knit the brow become angry
بھون *bha'van* N.M. (dial.) house ; building [S]
بھونپو *bhoṅpoo* N.M. horn (of car, etc.) hooter
بھونچال *bhauṅchal'* N.M. earthquake ; earth tremor ; quake [چلنا ~ بھوں]
بھونچکا *bhauṅ'chak'ka* بھوچکا *bhau'chak'ka* ADV. aghast; astonished flabbergasted بھوچکا رہ جانا *bhauṅ'chak'ka raih ja'na* V I. be struck aghast be flabbergasted
بھوندو *bhoṅ'doo* N.M. simpleton , booby , noodle, greenhorn
بھونڈا *bhoṅ'da* ADJ. (F. بھونڈی *bhoṅ'di*) awkward ugly ungainly deformed unlucky بھونڈاپن *bhoṅ'da-pan* N.M. ugliness awkwardness
بھونرا *bhauṅ'ra* (or *bhauṅra*) N.M. moth-like insect black beetle cellar بھونری *bhauṅ'ri*, *bhaṅv'ri* N.F. female black beetle patch of hair growing in a distinct circle
بھونکنا *bhauṅk'na* V.I. bark talk foolishly بھونکانا *bhauṅka'na* V.T. cause to bark
بھونکنا *bhoṅkna* V.T. thrust ; drive in چھرا بھونکنا *chhura bhoṅk'na* V.T. stab
بھوننا *bhoon'na* V.T. roast parch fry burn torment بھون ڈالنا *bhoon dal'na* V.T. burn torment بھون کھانا *bhoon' kha'na* V.T. roast and eat squander
بھئی *bha'i* (mode of address) dear friend look [~ ABB. بھائی]
بہی *ba'hi* N.F. day-book old type accounts book sown at end بہی کھاتہ *ba'hi kha'ta* N.M. daybook and ledger accounts بہی پر چڑھانا *ba'hi par charha'na* V.T. enter in day-book
بہی *be'hi* N.F. quince بہی دانہ *be'hi-da'nah*, بہدانہ *beh-da'nah* N.M quince-seed (used as drug) [P]
بہی خواہ *behi-khah*, ADJ well-wisher بہی خواہی *be'hi-kha'hi* N.F. good wishes being a well-wisher [P ~ بہ]
بھی *bhi* ADV. also , too even as well as well as likewise moreover

بھیا *bhay'yā* N.M. (usu. with PL. V.) brother elder brother (term of endearment) dear brothe. (mode of address) dear friend [~ بھائی]

بھیانک *bhayā'nak* ADJ. terrible ; dreadful ; frightful ; formidable dismal desolate

بھیت *bhīt* N.F. wall embankment vestige of dilapidated house

بھیتر *bhī'tar* ADV indoors inside within

بھیجا *bhe'jā* N.M. brain grey matter (animal's) brain (used as food) بھیجا کھانا *bhe'ja khā'nā* PH. bother tire out with questions

بھیجنا *bhej'nā* V.T. send despatch remit transmit grant ; bestow

بھید *bhed* N.M. secret mystery point بھید پانا *bhed pā'nā* V.I. discover a secret solve a mystery بھید دینا *bhed' de'nā* V.T. divulge a secret give a clue بھید رکھنا *bhed' rakh'nā* V.I. keep a secret بھید کھولنا *bhed khol'nā* V.I. divulge a secret betray a confidence بھید لینا *bhed le'nā* V.I. find out a secret spy ; pry into worm oneself into another's confidence بھیدی *bhe'dī* N.M. person in the know of a secret confidant گھر کا بھیدی لنکا ڈھائے *ghar' kā bhe'dī lań'kā ḍhā''e* PROV. betrayers turn victories into defeats

بہیر *bahīr* N.F. camp followers baggage of army lines near army camp where soldiers, families live بہیر بنگا *bahīr' būn'ga* N.M. rabble of camp followers 'impedimenta' of an army

بھیروں *bhai'roń* N.M. one of the major modes of classical Indo-Pakistan music connected with early winter بھیروی *bhair'vī*, بھیرویں *bhaira'viń* N.F. name of an early morning musical mode

بھیڑ *bhīṛ* N.F. crowd , throng ; press , multitude mob ; concourse بھیڑ بھاڑ *bhīṛ' bhāṛ*, بھیڑ بھڑکا *bhīṛ bharak'ka* N.M. crowd ; rush بھیڑ لگنا *bhīṛ' lag'nā* V.I. (of people) gather in large numbers بھیڑ لگانا *bhīṛ lagā'nā* V.T. collect concourse ; gather people (round oneself)

بھیڑ *bheṛ* N.F. sheep ewe بھیڑ چال *bheṛ' chāl* بھیڑیا چسال *bhe'ṛya chāl* N.F. mob mentality following a custom blindly craze بھیڑ کا گوشت *bheṛ' kā gosht* N.M. mutton بھیڑا *bheṛā* N.M. ram

بہیڑا *baheṛa* N.M. beleric myrobalan

بھیڑیا *bhe'ṛiya* N.M. wolf بھیڑیا چال *bhe'ṛiy.* (see under بھیڑ *bheṛ*)

بھیس *bhes* N.M. guise , disguise garb feigned appearance assumed likeness بھیس بدلنا *bhes' ba'dal'nā* V.I. disguise oneself change the guise

بھیک *bhīk* N.F. alms charity بھیک کا ٹھیکرا *bhīk' kā ṭhīk'ṛā* N.M. beggar's bowl بھیک مانگنا *bhīk' mang'na* V.T. beg beg alms

بھیگنا *bhīg'nā*, بھیگ جانا *bhīg' jā nā* V.I. get wet become moist be drenched (of whiskers) grow (of night) be advanced بھیگی بلی *bhī'gī billī* PH. wolf in sheep's clothing بھیگی بلی بتانا *bhī'gī billī batā'nā* PH. prevericate shun ; work thus

بھیل *bhīl* N.M. name of an aboriginal tribe of the Indo-Pakistan sub-contident

بھیلی *bhe'lī* N.F. گڑ کی بھیلی *gūṛ' kī bhe'lī* N.F. lump of raw sugar

بھینا *bhaī'nā* N.F. VOC. (dial.) sister [~ بہن]

بھینٹ *bheṅṭ'* N.F. sacrifice (کی) بھینٹ چڑھانا (*kī*) *bheṅṭ' chaṛhā'nā* v . sacrifice for (کی) بھینٹ چڑھنا (*kī*) *bheṅṭ chaṛh'nā* V.I. be sacrificed for

بھینچنا *bhīnch'nā* V.I press squeeze بھنچنا *bhinchnā* V.I. be pressed be squeezed

بھینس *bhaiṅs* N.F. (female) buffalo ; water buffalo بھینسا *bhaiṅ'sā* N.M. (male) buffalo water buffalo بھینس کے آگے بین بجانا *bhaiṅs' ke ā'ge bīn bajā'nā* PH. caste (one's) pearls before swine

بھینگا *bhaiṅ'gā* ADJ. & N.M. بھینگی *bhaiṅ'gī*, squint-eyed (person)

بھینگاپن *bhaiṅ'gā-pan* N.M. squint

بھینی *bhī'nī*, بھینی بھینی *bhī'nī bhī'nī* ADJ. mild (scent)

بی *bī* AFFIX. (somewhat respectful title for women used as PREF. or SUF. with their names) Mrs. Miss N.F. lady بڑی بی *ba'ṛī bī* N.F. old woman grandmother senior woman in the house چھوٹی بی *chhoṭī bī* N.F. young Miss little woman بی بی *bī'bī* N.F. lady respectable woman housewife , mistress of the house AFFIX (respectable title for woman used as PREF. or SUF. with names) Mrs. Miss

بے[1] *be* VOC. PAR. (familiarly or contemptuously used for men and male children) O ; oh PRON. you

بے[2] *be* PREF. not without lacking in ; un ; il- , dis- ; un- , -less بے آب *be-āb'* ADJ. waterless lustreless dull lacklustre بے آب و گیاہ *be ā'b-o-gayāh'* ADJ. barren desolate بے آبرو *be-āb'-roo* ADJ shameless disreputable ignoble ignominious

بے آبروئی be-āb-roo''ī N.F. disgrace dishonour بے اتفاقی be-ittifa'qī N.F. discord lack of unity want of harmony بے اثر be-a'sar ADJ. unaffective ineffectual inefficacious powerless having no voice lacking force not producing the desired effect بے احتیاط be-ehtiyat' ADJ. careless ; negligent ; reckless indiscreet ; imprudent intemperate not caring for health بے احتیاطی be-ehtiyā'tī N.F. carelessness negligence incautiousness imprudence indiscretion intemperance indifference to hygienic rules or dietary regulations بے اختیار be-ikhtiyār' ADJ. helpless having no control powerless ; wielding no authority having no choice faced with no alternative ADV. involuntarily بے اختیاری be-ikhtiya'rī N.F. helplessness powerlessness lack of choice ADJ. involuntary بے ادب be-a'dab ADJ. disrespectful insubordinate rude impudent insolent unmannerly بے ادبی be-a'dabī N.F. disrespectful rudeness impudence insubordination unmannerliness بے آرام be-ārām' ADJ. uncomfortable بے آرامی be-ārā'mī N.F. lack of comfort restlessness uneasiness بے اصل be-as'l ADJ. unfounded groundless baseless بے اعتبار be-e'tibār' ADJ. unreliable untrustworthy of no credit بے اعتباری be-e'tibā'rī N.F. untrustworthiness mistrust ; distrust discredit بے اعتدال be-e'tidāl' ADJ. immoderate intemperate بے اعتدالی be-e'tidālī N.F. immoderation intemperance بے اعتقاد be-e'tiqād' ADJ. disbelieving lacking faith incredulous بے اعتقادی be-e'tiqadī disbelief lack of faith بے التفاتی be-iltifa'tī N.F. disregard ; want of regard unconcern ; indifference inattention inconsiderateness بے امتیاز be-imtiyaz' ADV. without discrimination بے انتظامی be-intiza'mī N.F. mismanagement bungling بے انتہا be-inteha' ADJ. extreme unlimited ; endless ; boundless infinite ADV. extremely infinitely بے اندازہ be-andā'zah ADJ. countless numberless ADV. extremely infinitely بے انصاف be-insaf' ADJ. unjust, iniquitous unfair بے انصافی بے اولاد be-aulād' ADJ. childless ; issueless بے ایمان be-īmān' dishonest ; lacking integrity unprincipled having no conscience faithless ; infidel بے ایمانی کرنا be-īmā'nī kar'nā V.I. act dishonestly cheat misappropriate embezzle . defalcate play false ; betray بیباق be-bāq' ADJ. clear (account) paid up or off having no arrears بیباق کرنا be-baq' kar'nā clear pay up بیباق ہونا be-bāq' ho'nā V.I. be cleared ; paid settled be paid up or off بیباقی be-bā'qī N.F. settlement (of account) repayment quittance بیباک be-bāk' ADJ. bold fearless daring بیباکی be-bā'kī N.F. boldness fearlessness temerity بے بال و پر be-bā'l-o par ADJ. helpless powerless having no resourcess unplumed unfledged بے بدل be-badal' ADJ. incomparable matchless unique inimitable بے برگ و بار be bar'g-o bār' ADJ. (of tree) bare ; desiccated بے بس be-bas' ADJ. helpless powerless weak having no authority بے بسی be-ba'sī N.F. helplessness powerlessness debility weakness بے بنیاد be būnyād' ADJ. unfounded groundless basseless بے بہا be-bahā' ADJ. invaluable very precious of inestimable value بے بہرہ be-baih'rah ADJ. unfortunate unsuccessful deprived (of) lacking بے پایاں be- pā'yāh ADJ. unfathomed abysmal baseless ; unfounded بے پردگی be-par'dagī N.F. going about unveiled unveiling being open to view exposure of residents to neighbours' view بے پردہ be-par'dah ADJ. nnveiled going about unveiled (of house) exposing its residents to neighbours' view بے پروا be-parvā' ADJ. careless ; heedless negligent inconsiderate unconcerned ; indifferent above want ; content بے پروایانہ be-parvā'yā'nah ADV. & ADJ. indifferent(ly) ; unconcerned(ly) careless(ly) contented(ly) بے پروائی be-parvā''ī N.F carelessness negligence indifference بے پیر be-pīr' ADJ. unskilful cruel merciless بیتاب be-tāb' ADJ. impatient restless fidgety anxious ; keen بیتابانہ be-tābā'nah ADJ. & ADV. impatient(ly) restless(ly) anxious(ly) keen(ly) بیتابی be-tā'bī N.F. impatience restlessness keenness ; anxiety بے تاثیر be-tasīr' ADJ. (of drug, etc.) useless ; inefficacious بے تال be-tāl ADJ. out of tune بے تامل be-ta'am'mul ADV. pat unhesitatingly ; without hesitation without deliberation ADJ. prompt بے تحاشا be-tahā'shā ADV. excessively ; extremely rashly ; recklessly headlong بے تدبیر be-tadbīr' ADJ. imprudent indiscreet resourceless بے تدبیری be-tadbī'rī N.F. imprudence indiscretion resourcelessness بے تعلق be ta'al'lūq ADJ unconnected ; unrelated unconcerned ; indifferent بے تعلقی be-ta'al'lūqī N.F. being unconnected or unrelated indifferent بے تقصیر be-taqsīs' ADJ. innocent ; blameless guiltless ; not guilty innocent ADV. without one's fault ; through no fault of his بے تکلف be-takal'lūf ADJ. frank informal unceremonious (of friends) fast ; close ; intimate ADV. frankly ; openly intimately بے تکلفانہ be-takal'lūfā'nah ADV. & ADJ. frank(ly) intimate(ly) بے تکلفی be-takal'lūfī N.F. frankness informality بے تمیز be-tamīz ADJ. uncivil unmannerly ; mannerless silly بے توجہ be-tavaj'joh ADJ. inattentive inadvertent بے توجہی be-tavaj'johī N.F. inattentiveness ; lack of attention inadvertance indifference بے ٹھکانا be-ṭhikā'nā ADJ. (of talk) meaningless (of person) seldom found at home uncertain بے ثبات be-sabāt' ADJ. impermanent unstable transitory passing inconstant بے ثباتی be-saba'tī N.F. impermanence instability transitoriness بے ثمر be-sa'mar ADJ. fruitless unfruitful ; infructuous vain ; unsuccessful بے ثمری be-sa'marī N.F. fruitlessness vanity ; futility failure بے جا be-jā' ADJ. improper illtimed unreasonable out of place ; misplaced wrong بے جا ہونا be-jā' ho'nā V.I. be improper be ill-timed impropriety بے جان be-jān' ADJ. lifeless dead inanimate listless بے جرم be-jūr'm ADJ. innocent ; faultless بے جوڑ be-joṛ' ADJ. unmatched ; unsuitable inharmonious discordant بیچارہ be-chā'rah ADJ. (F. بیچاری be-chā'rī) (col. بچارہ bichārā M. بچاری F. bichārī) poor unfortunate miserable بے چراغ be-chirāgh' ADJ. (of home) childless (rare) (of place) dark ; unlighted بے چون وچرا be-choo'n-o-chirā' ADV. & ADJ. unhesitating(ly) without demur unquestioning(ly) بے چین be-chain' ADJ. restless uneasy worried ; anxious بے چینی be-chai'nī N.F. uneasiness restlessness anxiety ; worry بے حال be-ḥal' ADJ. out of sorts ; out of condition indisposed weary ; tired miserable on the verge of death بے حالی be-ḥa'lī N.F. miserable plight بے حجاب be-ḥijāb' ADJ. unveiled immodest unreserved بے حجابانہ be-ḥijab'nah ADV. unveiled immodestly unreservedly بے حجابی be-ḥijā'bī N.F. going about unveiled immodesty بے حد be-ḥadd' ADJ. boundless ; endless ADV. extremely excessively infinitely بے حرکت be-ḥa'rakat ADJ. motionless still immobile بے حرمت be-ḥūr'mat ADJ. disgraced molested without any sense of prestige بے حرمتی be-ḥūr'matī N.F. disgrace molestation بے حس be-ḥis' ADJ. unconscious senseless بے حساب be-ḥisāb' ADJ. excessive unlimited countless innumerable بے حوصلہ be-ḥau'salah ADJ. weak dispirited ; spiritless having no guts بے حوصلگی be-ḥau'salagī N.F. weakness lack of guts want of enterprise unenterprising ; unadventurous بے حیا be-ḥayā' ADJ. shameless immodest impudent ; bare-faced ; brazen-faced بے حیائی be-ḥayā''ī N.F. shamelessness immodesty impudence بے خار be-khār' ADJ. without thorns beardless minion بے خانماں be-khā'n-o-māṅ ADJ. homeless destitute driven from home بے خبر be-khā'bar ADJ. unknowing ignorant stupid careless ; negligent uninformed ; not well-posted بے خبری be-khā'barī N.F. ignorance stupidity بے خطا be-khatā' ADJ. innocent guiltless blameless (rare) infallible بے خطر be-khā'tar ADJ. safe undaunted بے خواب be-khāb' ADJ. sleepless restless ; uneasy بے خوابی be-khā'bī N.F. sleeplessness insomnia restlessness بے خود be-khūd' ADJ. transported ; enraptured ; in ecstasy intoxicated ; inebriate unconscious beside oneself (with) unegoistic ; selfless بیخودی be-khū'dī N.F. ecstasy ; rapture inebriety unconsciousness forgetfulness of ego ; selflessness بیداد be-dād' N.F. injustice ; iniquity tyranny ; oppression بیداد گر be-dād'-gar بیداد پیشہ be-dād'-pe'shah ADJ. unjust ; iniquitous tyrannous ; tyrannical بے داغ be-dāgh ADJ. spotless immaculate unblemished innocent بے دال کا بودم b-dāl' kā boo'dam PH. (same as بودم بے دال PH.★) بے دام be-dām', بے درم be-di'ram ADJ. & ADV. got without incurring any expense بندۂ بے دام (یا بے درم) ban'da-e be-dām' (or be-di'ram) devoted servant slave got free بے دانش be-dānish ADJ. foolish short-sighted imprudent بیدانشی be-dā'nishī N.F. folly imprudence بیدانہ be-dā'nah ADJ. seedless بیدخل be-dakh'l ADJ. evicted ; ejected بیدخلی be-dakh'lī N.F. eviction ; ejectment بیدرد be-dard' ADJ. cruel ; merciless ruthless بیدردانہ be-dardā'nah ADV. & ADJ. merciless(ly) ; ruthlessly بے دردی be-dar'dī N.F. mercilessness ; cruelty بے درماں be-darmāṅ ADJ. incurable بلائے بے درماں balā'-e be dar'māṅ N.F. unavoidable calamity درد بے درماں

dar'd-e be-darmān' N.M. incurable ailment بیدرنگ *be-darang'* ADV. at once ; without delay unhesitatingly بیدریغ *be-daregh'* ADJ. unstinted ungrudging ADV. ungrudgingly blindly rashly بے دست و پا *b-das't-o-pā'* ADJ. crippled helpless resourceless powerless بے دست و پائی *be-das't-o pā''ī* N.F. being crippled helplessness lack of resources powerlessness بیدل *be-dil'* ADJ. sad ; dejected dispirited disgruntled chagrined loving ; devoted N.M. devotee lover بیدلی *be-di'lī* N.F. dejection dissatisfaction chagrin lack of hope devotion; love بیدم *be-dam'* ADJ. breathless lifeless fatigued ; dead tired بیدماغ *be-dimāgh'* ADJ. irritable impatient senseless indifferent بیدماغی *be-dimā'ghī* N.F. irritability indifference بے دوا *be-davā'* ADJ. incurable بیدھڑک (or بے دھڑک) *be-dha'rak* ADV. rashly readily fearlessly without fear or hesitation bold; fearless ; dauntless ; undaunted بے دین *be-dīn'* ADJ. faithless ; irreligious dishonest unreliable بے دینی *be-dī'nī* N.F. lack of faith; irreligiousness dishonesty بے ڈول *be-daul'* ADJ. ugly ; ungainly shapeless ; unshapely disproportionate awkward بیڈھب *be-dhab'* ADJ. awkward ugly unmannerly بے ذوق *be-zauq'* ADJ. unappreciative , lacking taste (for fine arts) tasteless ; insipid ; without relish بے ذوقی *be-zau'qī* N.F. lack of taste , inappreciation tastelessness inspidity بے راہ *be-rāh'* ADJ. wrong , erring walking in sinful ways ; debauched ; dissolute not on the right path بے راہ روی *be-rāh'-ravī* N F. debauchery not being on the right path بے ربط *be-rab't* ADJ. irregular ; contrary disjointed , unconnected incongruous delirious بے ربطی *be-rab'tī* N.F being disjointed incongruity بے رحم *be-raih'm* ADJ. cruel merciless ; ruthless tyrannous ; tyrannical بیرحمی *be-raih'mī* N.F. cruelty tyranny بے روک ٹوک *be-rok' tok* ADV. without let or hindrance ; unhindered بے ریا *be-riyā'* ADJ. sincere ; candid guileless unpretentious not showy بے ریائی *be-riyā''ī* N.F sincerity ; candour unpretentiousness lack of show بے ریش *be-rīsh'* ADJ. beardless N M. minion بے ریشہ *be-re'shah* ADJ. fibreless , without fibre بیزار *be-zār* ADJ. disgusted (with) , sick (of) ; fed up (with) chagrined بیزاری *be-zā'rī* N.F disgust chagrin بے زبان *be-zabān'* ADJ. dumb ; mute speechless quiet ; taciturn helpless N.M. brute بے زبانی *be-zabā'nī* N.F. dumbness muteness speechlessness taciturnity helplessness بے زر *be-zar'* ADJ. poor ; destitute having no wherewithal ; moneyless بے زری *be-za'rī* N.F. poverty want بے زن و فرزند *be-za'n-o-farzand'* ADJ. widower bachelor ; unmarried بے زور *be-zor'* ADJ. weak powerless بے زیب و زینت *be-ze'b-o zī'nat* ADJ. inelegant unadorned بیساختہ *be-sākh'tah* ADJ. artless natural spontaneous ; unpremeditated ADV. artlessly extempore ; impromptu unpremeditatedly بیساختگی *be-sākh'tagī* بے ساختہ پن *be-sākh'ta-pan* N.M. artlessness unstudied or natural behaviour unpremeditated ; spontaniety بے سبب *be-sabab'* ADJ. without rhyme or reason unfounded بے سخن *be-sū'khan* ADJ. quiet taciturn بے سرا *be-sū'rā* ADJ. out of tune unmusical بے سر و پا *be-sa'r-o-pā* ADJ. absurd ; baseless without head or tail ; unreliable ; untrustworthy بے سر و سامان *be-sa'r-o-sāmān'* ADJ. without means unprovided unequipped ; not fully equipped ; lacking necessary equipment بے سر و سامانی *be-sa'r-o-sāmā'nī* N.F. poverty lack of means helplessness بے سلیقہ *be-salī'qah* ADJ. impolite ; unmannerly clumsy ; awkwaed unaccomplished unskilful unmethodical بے سلیقگی *be-salī'qagī* N.F. lack of manners want of accomplishments unskilfulness lack of method awkwardness ; clumsiness بے شرم *be-shar'm* ADJ. shameless immodest immoral impudent بے شرمی *be-shar'mī* N.F. shamelessness immodesty immorality impudence بے شعور *b-sho'oor'* ADJ. unmannerly stupid ignorant بے شعوری *be-sho'oo'rī* N.F. unmannerliness stupidity ignorance بے شک و شبہ *be-shak'k-o-shūb'h* ADV. certainly ; undoubtedly ; doubtless(ly) بے شمار *be-shumār'* ADJ. innumerable ; numberless ; countless numerous بے صبر *be-sab'r* (col. بے صبرا *be-sab'rā*) ADJ. impatient restless anxious بے صبری *be-sab'rī* N.F. impatience restlessness anxiety بے ضابطہ *be-zā'bitah* ADJ. irregular unlawful unmethodical بے ضابطگی *be zā'bitagī* (col. *be-zāb'tagī*) N.F. irregularity unlawfulness بے طاقت *be-tā'qat* ADJ. weak enervated powerless بے طاقتی *be-tā'qatī* N.F. weakress powerlessness بے طرح *be-ta'h, be-ta'rah* (col.) ADV. excessively ; exceedinly inextrically ADJ. (of 'ghazal') not to the set pattern بے طور *be-taur'* ADV. excessively ; exceedingly inextrically بے عزت be'iz'zat ADJ disgraceful disgraced without any sense of honour بے عزتی be-'iz'zatī N.F. disgrace بے عقل be-'aq'l ADJ. unwise stupid بے عقلی be-'aq'lī N F. folly stupidity بے علت be-'il'lat ADJ causeless بے عیب be-'aib' ADJ. faultless unblemished بے غرض be-gha'raz ADJ selfless disinterested unselfish ; having no axe to grind بے غرضانہ be-gharazā'nah ADV & ADJ. unselfishly selflessly بے غرضی be-gha'razī N F unselfishness selflessness بے غل وغش be-ghil'l-o ghish ADJ. pure unadulterated plain ; straightforward بے غم be-gham' ADJ happy knowing no grief بے غور و فکر be-ghau'r-o fik'r ADV unpremeditated(ly) thoughtless(ly) بے غیرت be-ghai'rat ADJ. shameless immodest wanton N.M cuckold بے غیرتی be ghai'ratī N.F. shamelessness immodesty wantonness cuckoldry بے فائدہ be fā''idah ADJ. useless ; in vain of no consequence unprofitable silly. absurd ill-timed بے فکر be-fikr' (col. بے فکرا be-fik'rā) ADJ. free from care or anxiety thoughtless, unreflecting inconsiderate contented بے فکری be-fik'rī N.F. freedom from care or anxiety contentedness unconcern thoughtlessness بے فیض be-faiz' ADJ. & N.M. miserly ungenerous بے قابو be-qā'boo ADJ. wayward ncontrolled ; uncontrollable out of one's reach بیقاعدگی be-qā''idagī N.F. irregularity disarrangement بیقاعدہ be-qā''idah ADJ. irregular unlawful ungrammatical not properly arranged بے قدر be-qad'r ADJ. worthless ; unimportant not in demand ungrateful ; thankless بے قدری be-qad'rī N.F. worthlessness disesteem ingratitude بیقرار be-qarār' ADJ. uneasy ; restless impatient anxious perturbed بیقراری be-qarā'rī N.F. restlessness impatience anxiety perturbation بے قصور be-qūsoor' ADJ. faultless not guilty innocent بے قصوری be-qūsoo'rī N.F. faultlessness innocence بے قیاس be-qiyās' ADJ. immense unlimited inconceivable بیکار be-kār' ADJ. unemployed ; jobless idle worthless ; unserviceable useless silly ; absurd unprofitable بیکار کرنا he-kār' kar'nā V.T. render, useless make unserviceable throw out of job بیکاری b-kā'rī N.F. unemployment idleness worthlessness absurdity بیکراں be-karāh' ADJ. boundless, shoreless immense enormous بیکس be'-kas ADJ. helpless, lonely forlorn destitute بیکسانہ be-kasā'nah ADV. & ADJ. helpless(ly) alone بیکسی be'-kasī N.F. helplessness loneliness destitution بے کفن be-ka'fan ADJ. unshrouded بے کل be-kal' ADJ restless uneasy disturbed بے کلی be-ka'lī N.F. restlessness ; uneasiness بے کم و کاست be-kam-o-kās't ADV. & ADJ. exact(ly) ; accurate(ly) without any omission بے کھٹکے be-khaṭ'ke ADV. unhesitatingly undauntedly doubtlessly بے گماں be-gūmān' ADJ. doubtless without the least suspicion بیگناہ be-gūnāh' ADJ. blameless guiltless sinless innocent بے لحاظ be-lihaz' ADJ. impertinent inconsiderate بے لطف be-lūt'f ADJ. tasteless insipid dull unpleasant بے لطفی be-lūt'fī N.F. tastelessness dullness insipidness unpleasantness بے لگام be-lāgām' ADJ. unbridled wayward uncontrollable بے مایہ be-mā'yah ADJ. poor ; indigent resourceless mean ; low بے مائگی be-mā''igī (or ped. be-mā'yagī N.F. poverty ; indigence resourcelessness meanness بیمثل be-mis'l ADJ. incomparable matchless ; unparalleled ; peerless ; unequalled unique بے محابا be-moḥā'bā ADV. undauntedly ; fearlessly unhesitatingly ADJ. fearless ; undaunted بے محل be-mahal' ADJ. improper ill-timed out of place بے مروت be-mūrūv'vat ADJ. unkind ungrateful inhuman impolite بے مروتی be-mūrūv'vatī N.F. unkindness ingratitude incivility بے مزگی be maz'gī (ped. ma'zagī) N.F. tastelessness insipidity unpleasantness بے مزہ be-ma'zah ADJ. tasteless insipid unpleasant بے معنی be-ma''nā (or be-ma''nī) ADJ. meaningless silly ; foolish absurd useless ; vain بے مقدور be-maqdoor' ADJ. powerless resourceless weak poor بے مقدوری be-maqdoo'rī N.F. powerlessness proverty lack of resources بے منت be-min'nat ADJ. without incurring obligation بے موسم be-mau'sim ADJ. (col. M. بے موسما be-maus'mā, F. بے موسمی be-maus'mī) unseasonable ; out of season بے موقع be-mau'qa' (ped. بے موقعی be mau'qe'ī) ADJ. improper ; inopportune ill-timed ; untimely out of place inapt بے موقع محل be-mau'qa' mahal' ADJ. & ADV. inopportune ill-timed بیمہر be-meh'r ADJ. unkind ; cruel unfaithful بیمہری be-meh'rī N.F. unkindness ; cruelty unfaithfulness بے نام و نشان be-nā'm-o nishān' ADJ. unknown unidentified insignificant issueless wiped out بینامی be-nā'mī ADJ. (of sale, etc.) in another's name بے نصیب be-nasīb' ADJ. unfortunate cursed بے نصیبی be-nas'bī N.F. misfortune ; ill-luck بینظیر be-nazīr ADJ. incomparable matchless ; unparalleled ; unequalled ; peerless unique بے نمک be-na'mak ADJ. insipid unattractive saltless بے نمکی be-na'makī N.F. insipidity unattractiveness being without salt بے ننگ و نام be-nań'g-o-nām, بے ننگ و ناموس be-nań'g-o- nāmoos' ADJ, characterless notorious without sense of honour بے نوا be-navā' ADJ. poor ; indigent ; destitute بے نور be-noor' ADJ. without light ; dark (of eyes) blind بے نیاز be-niyāz ADJ. without want independent ; free carefree unconcerned indifferent بے نیازی be-niyā'zī N.F. indifference independence بے نیل مرام be-nai'l-e marām' ADV. unsuccessful بے وجہ be-vaj'h ADJ. causeless without rhyme or reason بے وزن be-vaz'n ADJ. not weighty ; insignificant worthless بے وطن be-va'tan ADJ. homeless away from homeland بے وطنی be-va'tanī N.F. homelessness بیوفا be-vafā' ADJ. faithless ungrateful treacherous ; perfidious بیوفائی be-vafā''ī N.F faithlessness ingratitude treachery perfidy بے وقار be-vaqār' ADJ. undignified disreputable بے وقری be-vaq'rī N.F. blow to prestige بے وقت be-vaq't ADJ. & ADV. out of season untimely ill-timed بے وقت کی راگنی گانا be-vaq't kī rāg'nī gā'nā, بے وقت کی شہنائی بجانا be-vaq't kī shaihnā''ī bājā'nā PH. do (or say) something at a time when nobody is prepared to appreciate if ; do ill-timed (things) بیوقوف be-vūqoof' ADJ. silly ; foolish ; stupid gullible unwise ignorant بیوقوف بنانا be-vūqoof' banā'nā (or simply بنانا banā'nā) V.T. ridicule make a fool (of) ; make fun (of) بیوقوفی be-vūqoo'fī N.F. foolishness ; stupidity want of understanding lack of wisdom ignorance بے ہمت be-him'mat ADJ. unambitious ; unaspiring unadventurous ; unenterprizing cowardly ; pusillanimous lazy ; slothful ; indolent بے ہمتا be-hamtā' ADJ. unique peerless incomparable بے ہنر be-hū'nar ADJ. unskilful unskilled unaccomplished بے ہنگام be-hańgām' ADJ. untimely بے ہنگم be-hań'gam ADJ. unwieldly egregions بیہودگی be-hoo'dagī N.F. absurdity folly breach of etiquette frivolity obscenity بیہودہ be-hoo'dah ADJ. absurd foolish unmannerly obscene frivolous ADV. foolishly idly بیہودہ گو be-hoo'da-go ADJ. one who talks nonsense foul-mouthed person بیہودہ گوئی be-hoo'da-go''ī N.F. talking nonsense idle talk بیہوش be-hosh' ADJ. unconscious senseless in a fit careless ; inattentive بیہوشی be-ho'shī unconsciousness senselessness carelessness [~P]

بیا ba'yā (dial. bay'yā) N.M. weaver-bird

بیابان bayābān' (lit. بیاباں bayā'bāń) N.M. desert ; wilderness اجاڑ بیابان ūjāṛ bayābān' N.M.. wasteland بیا اور اس کا گھر بیابان گرد, bayā'bāń gard, بیابان نورد bayā'bāń navard' N.M. wanderer one traversing deserts بیابانی bayābā'nī ADJ. desert ; of the desert wild N.M. wanderer [P ~ آب + ب]

بیاج bayāj' N.M. (dial.) interest [S]

بیاسی bayā'sī ADJ. & N.M. eighty-two بیاسیواں bayā'sīvāń ADJ. eighty-second

بیاض bayāz' N.F. commonplace-book N.M. whiteness [A]

بیالیس bayā'līs ADJ. & N.M. forty-two بیالیسواں bayā'līsvāń ADJ. forty-second

بیام bayām' (rare بویام boyām') N.M. earthen jar

بیان bayān' (lit also -ān) N.M. statement ; declaration account ; description narration explanation (also علم بیان 'il'm-e bayān') branch of rhetoric dealing with metaphorical use of language بیان بدلنا bayān' ba'dalnā V. go back upon one's statement ; prevaricate بیان دینا bayān' de'nā V.I. (in law-court) make a statement ; declare بیان کرنا bayan kar'nā V.T. state relate ; narrate ; recount describe بیانیہ bayāniy'yah ADJ. & N.M. narrative [A]

بیانا bayā'nā V. (of animals) bring forth young

بیاہ biyāh' (or byāh') N.M. marriage ; wedding ; wedlock بیاہ رچانا biyāh' rachā'nā V.I. celebrate a marriage بیاہ کرنا biyāh' kar'nā V.T. & I. marry be married بیاہ لانا biyāh lā'nā V.T. bring home (the bride) بیاہا biyā'hā, ADJ. (F. بیاہی biyā'hī) married بیاہتا biyāh'tā N.F. married woman ADJ. duly married (wife) بیاہنا biyāh'nā V.T. marry give away in marriage بن بیاہا bin-biyā'hā ADJ. unmarried ; bachelor بن بیاہی bin biyā'hī ADJ. unmarried (girl) ; virgin spinster

بی بی bībī N.F. lady title of respect (also as بی بی جی bī'bī jī) Mrs. ; Miss

بیتی bait'lī ADJ. unfortunate (woman)

بیپار **bepar'** N.M. بیپاری **bepa'ri** N.M. (same as بیوپار N.M. ★ بیوپاری N.M. ★)

بیت **bait** N.F. distich ; couplet N.M. house ; abode cell بیت اللہ **bai't-ullah'** N.M. the Holy Ka'bah (as the House of Allah) بیت الحرام **bai't-ul-haram'** N.M. the Holy Ka'bah (as the Sacred House) بیت الحزن **bai't-ul huz'n** (or **ha'zan**) N.M. house in which Jacob bewailed Joseph's separation cell of sorrow بیت الخلا **bait-ul-khala'** N.M. latrine ; lavatory ; privy بیت العتیق **bait-ul-'atiq'** N.M. the Holy Ka'bah (as the most Ancient House) بیت العنکبوت **bait-ul-'ankaboot'** N.M. (rare) spider's web (met.) something very frail بیت الغزل **bai't-ul-gha'zal** N.M. best verse (of ode, etc.) بیت اللحم **bai't-ul-lah'm** N.M. Bethlehem ; birthplace of Jesus بیت المال **bai't-ul-mal'** N.M. public exchequer ; treasury بیت المعمور **bai't-ul-ma'moor'** N.M. the Inhabited House ; prototype of the Holy Ka'bah in heaven بیت المقدس **bai't-ul-muqad'-das** (or **bai't-ul-maq'dis**) القدس **al-qud's** N.M. the Dome of the Rock بیت بازی **bait'-bazi** N.F. verse-recitation contest , a contest in which each opposed team has to recite a couplet beginning with the last letter of the couplet recited by the adversaries [A]

بیت **bet** N.M. cane [~ P بید CORR.]

بیتال **baital'** N.M. ghost ; goblin ; fiend بیتال پچیسی **baital' pachchi'si** N.M. title of a book comprising twenty-five tales narrated by a ghost [S]

بیتنا **bit'na** V.I. befall happen (of life) pass ; elapse (of time) elapse become a thing of the past

بیٹ **bit** N.F. droppings (of a bird)

بیٹ **bait** N.M. bat [E]

بیٹا **be'ta** N.M. son boy (endearingly to either sex) my child بیٹا بنانا **be'ta bana'na,** بیٹا گود لینا **be'ta god' le'na** V.I. adopt a son بیٹا بیٹی **be'ta be'ti** N.M. PL. (someone's) children بیٹے والا (یا والے) **be'te va'la** (or **va'le**) N.M. groom's father (or relations)

بیٹھک **bai'thak** N.F. (unpretentious) drawing room a kind of exercise in which one alternately squats and rises posture بیٹھک دینا **baithak de'na** V.I. convene of spiritual assembly held to the accompaniment of dance and music (esp. as practised by women) [~ FOLL.]

بیٹھنا **baith'na,** بیٹھ جانا **baith ja'na** V.I. sit sit down perch subside (of heart) sink (of house, etc.) collapse (of boiled rice) become a hash settle down (at bottom بیٹھ کر نکلنا **baith kar ni'kalna** V.I. (of moon) rise late on the 15th night of each lunar month بیٹھواں **baith'van** ADJ. flat flat-bottomed low بیٹھے بٹھائے **bai'the bitha''e,** بیٹھے بٹھلائے **bai'the bith'la''e,** بیٹھے بیٹھے **bai'the bai'the** ADV. suddenly ; all of a sudden abruptly unexpectedly unjustly easily بیٹھے رہنا **bai'the raih'na** V.I. stay on reside permanently (of woman) stay at parents' home بیٹھواں **baith'van** ADJ.

بیٹی **be'ti** N.F. daughter (endearingly) my child بیٹی دینا **be'ti de'na** V.T. give away one's daughter in marriage بیٹی والا (یا والے) **be'ti va'la** (or **va'le**) N.M. bride's father (or relations) [F ~ بیٹا]

بیج **bij** N.M. seed source ; origin بیج بونا **bij' bo'na,** بیج ڈالنا **bij dal'na** V.I. sow (fig.) engender ; sow the seed (of) (fig.) be the cause of بیج دار **bij'-dar,** بیجیلا **bijila** ADJ. seedy full of seeds بیج مار کرنا **bij'-mar kar'na** V.T. destroy the whole family (of) annihilate

بیجو **be'jo** N.F. goal in children's game called باوڑی N.F. ★

بیچ **bich** N.M. middle centre mid , midst interlude interval interstice distance difference ADV. in ; into between ; among during ; (in the) meantime بیچ بچاؤ **bich bicha''o** N.M. ediation settlement intervention بیچ بچاؤ کرنا (یا کر دینا) **bich' bicha''o kar'na** (or **kar de'na**) V.T. mediate; settle intervene بیچ کا **bich' ka** ADJ. interval central medium average بیچ کی انگلی **bich' ki ung'li** N.F. middle finger بیچ میں پڑنا **bich' men par'na** V.T. intervene arbitrate; mediate stand surety (for) بیچوں بیچ **bi'chon bich** ADV. right in the middle keeping clear of the sides or edges centrally

بیچا **bi'cha** N.M. (nurs.) bogey]

بیچارا **becha'rah** ADJ. (see under بے)

بیچک **bi'chak** N.M. invoice

بیچنا **bech'na** V.T. sell ; vend dispose of transfer by sale بیچنے کے لائق **bech'ne ke la''iq** ADJ. saleable not worth retaining بیچ کھانا **bech' kha'na** V.T. sell away and squander proceeds بیچنے والا **bech'ne va'la** N.M. seller ; vendor

بیخ **bekh** N.F. root origin foundation بیخ کنی **bekh'-ka'ni** N.F extirpation extermination eradication annihilation بیخکنی کرنا bekh'-ka'nī kar'nā v.t. uproot ; extirpate exterminate eradicate annihilate [P]

بید baid n.m. (dial.) same as وید vaid n.m. ★

بید[1] bed n.m. cane willow بیدباف bed'-bāf n.m (old use) cane-weaver basket maker بید کی طرح کانپنا bed' kī tar'h kāṅp'nā v.i. tremble with fear shiver in one's shoes بید مارنا bed' mār'nā v.t. cane flog بیدِ مجنوں be'd-e. maj'nooṅ n.m. a species of willow بیدمشک bed'-mūshk n.m. musk willow its essence [P]

بید[2] bed n.m. (same as) وید ved n.m. ★)

بیدار bedār' adj. awake ; wakeful watchful ; vigilant alert بیدار بخت bedār'-bakh't adj. lucky ; fortunate بیدار مغز bedār'-magh'z adj. wise intelligent shrewd بیداری bedā'rī n.f. wakefulness vigilance alertness

بیدھا bī'dhā adj. & n.m. person under influence of magic

بیر bīr' ویر vīr n.m. (dial.) hero brother adj. brave بیرتا bīr'tā n.m. (dial.) bravery ; gallantry [S]

بیر bair n.m. enmity ; animus ; animosity ; hostility malice ; ill-will ; grudge میں بیر پڑنا men bair' par'nā v.i. be bad blood between بیر باندھنا (یا کرنا یا رکھنا) bair bāndh'nā (or kar'nā or rakh'nā) v.t. hate bear malice ; harbour a grudge against بیر لینا (یا نکالنا) bair le'nā (or nikāl'nā) v.t. take revenge ; retaliate avenge بیری bai'rī n.m., (f. بیرن bai'ran) enemy adj. hostile malevolent

بیرا ber n.m. jujube ; a kind of berry

بیرا[2] bai'rā n.m. bear ; table servant ; boy [~ Anglo-Pakistani [E bearer corr.]

بیرا bai'rā n.m. tenon-like piece driven in wall to hold door frame in place

بیراج bei'rāj' n.m. barrage [E]

بیراگ bairāg' n.m. (dial.) renunciation of worldly pleasures; asceticism بیراگ لینا bairag' le'nā v.i. renounce worldly pleasures بیراگی bairā'gī n.m. (f. بیراگن bairā'gan) (dial.) Hindu recluse ascetic cross-shaped stick

بیر بہوٹی bīr ba'hūṭī n.f. scarlet fly

بیرسٹر bairis' (ait la') n.m. barrister-at-law

بیرق bai'raq n.m. pennon ; pennant ; flag on spear standard ; banner ; ensign [P]

بیرن bai'ran n.f. & adj. (see under بیر bair n.m. ★)

بیرن bī'ran n.m. (dial.) brother [~S بیر bīr]

بیرنگ berang' (or bai'rang) adj. (of letter, etc.) postage unpaid ; bearing (postage) n.m. pl. ball bearing [E]

بیرومیٹر bai'romīṭar n.m. barometer [E]

بیرزہ bero'zah (col. بروزہ biro'zah) n.m rosin گندہ بروزہ gan'dah biro'zah n.m. resin [P]

بیروں be'rooṅ برون biroon' prep. out outside adv. outside بیرونجات beroon'jāt n.m. suburbs (old use) overseas بیرونجاتی beroonjā'tī adj suburban rural outside n.m (old use) rustic بیرونی beroo'nī adj. external outer outside

بیری bai'rī n.m. (see under بیر bair n.m ★)

بیری be'rī n.m. (see under بیر ber n.m. ★)

بیڑا be'ṛā n.m fleet large boat raft (کا) بیڑا پار کرنا (kā) be'ṛā pār kar'nā (or lagā'nā) v.t. bring success (to) relieve from remove difficulties (of) (rare) ferry across (کا) بیڑا پار ہونا (kā) be'ṛā pār' ho'nā v.i achieve success ; gain one's object tide over a difficulty (of boat, etc.) arrive at the destination

بیڑا bī'ṛā n.m. prepared betel-leaf folded in triangular shape ; triangular fold of betel-leaf (کا) بیڑا اٹھانا (kā) bī'ṛā ūṭhā'nā v.i. pick or take up the gauntlent undertake (to do something) (rare) accent a folded betel-leaf

بیڑا

بیڑی be'ṛī n.f (usu. pl.) shackles ; fetters irons ; chain irons for animals' feet boat boat-like bamboo basket for watering fields ; watering-basket بیڑیاں پڑنا be'riyān par'nā v.i. be shackled ; be chained be put in irons بیڑیاں ڈالنا beriyān ḍalnā v.t. shackle ; fetter put in irons بیڑیاں کاٹنا be'riyān kaṭ'nā v.t unfetter ; take off the chains set free ; liberate

بیڑی bī'ṛī n.f a kind of inferior cigarette tobacco rolled in cheap leaves ; 'bidi'

بیز bez suf. sifting diffusing dispersing

بیزی be'zī suf. sifting diffusing dispersing [P ~ بیختن]

بیزار *bezār'* ADJ. disgusted displaced annoyed bored **بیزار کرنا** *bezār' kar'nā* V.T. disgust annoy bore **بیزار ہونا** *bezār' ho'nā* V.I. be disgusted be annoyed be bored **بیزاری** *bezā'rī* N.F. disgust displeasure annoyance [P]

بیس *bīs* ADJ. & N.M. twenty **بیسواں** *bīs'vāñ* ADJ. twentieth **بیسوں** *bī'soñ*, **بیسیوں** *bī'siyoñ* ADJ. many ; many a ; scores of numerous **بیسی** *bī'sī* N.F score a collection of twenty **بیسی گھیسی** *bī'sī ghī'sī* N.F. (woman) looking old while yet in her twenties . teen-ager looking old too soon

بیساکھ *baisakh'* N.M. second month of Hindu calendar (corresponding to April-May) **بیساکھی** *baisā'khī* N.F. (esp. Sikh) fair held on the first day of Baisakh (usu PL.) crutch

بیستون *be-sūtoon'* N M name of a Persian mountain which lagendary lover Farhad had to dig out a milk-canal to win the hand of Shirin [P]

بیسن *be'san* N.M. gram-flour **بیسنی روٹی** *be'sanī ro'ṭī* N.F bread with condiments and gram-flour in it ; salt pan-cake

بیسوا *bes'vā* N.F. prostitute . whore ; harlot loose woman

بیسواں *bīs'vāñ* ADJ., **بیسوں** *bī'soñ* ADJ., *bī'siyoñ* ADJ., **بیسی** *bī'sī* N.F. (see under ADJ. & N.M. ★)

بیش *besh* ADJ. more better superior excellent high (priced, etc.) *be'sh az besh'* (ped. **بیش از پیش** *be'sh az pesh'*) ADJ. more than ever evermore great deal of **بیش بہا** *besn bahā'*, **بیش قیمت** *besh-qī'mat* ADJ. costly ; expensive precious **بیشتر** *besh'tar* ADJ. most major ; chief ADV. mostly often **بیشی** *be'shī* N.F. increase ; emancement addition surplus excess

بیشہ *be'shah* N.M. wood ; forest ; jungle wilderness [P]

بیضا *baizā'* ADJ. white bright ; luminous incandescent refulgent **ید بیضا** *ya'd-e baizā'* N.M. the refulgent hand (as one of the miracles of Moses) [A ~ بیاض]

بیضہ *bai'zah* N.M. egg (usu. PL.) testicle *baiz* N.M. PL. (ped.) eggs **بیضوی** *bai'zavī* ADJ. oval [A ~ بیاض]

بیطار *bai'tār* N.M. veterinary surgeon (old. use) farrier **بیطاری** *baitā'rī* N.F. veterinary science profession of a veterinary surgeon [A]

بیع *bai'* N.F. sale deal **بیع کرنا** *bai' kar'nā* V.T. sell ; transfer by sale **بیع نامہ** *bai'-nā'mah* N M sale-deed **بیع وشری** *bai''-o sharā'* N.F. sale and purchase business transaction [A]

بیعانہ *bai'ā'nah* N.M. earnest money **بیعانہ دینا** *bai'ā'nah de'nā* V.T. give earnest money ; give money in advance agree to sell **بیعانہ لینا** *bai'ā'nah le'nā* V.T. reserve earnest money agree to sell [A ~ PREC.]

بیعت *bai''at* N.F. ritual for accepting (to become) a disciple oath of allegiance (to a saint, etc.) homage ; fealty **(کی) بیعت کرنا (یا ہونا)** *(kī) bai''at kar'nā* (or *ho'nā*) V.T take the oath of allegiance (to saint, etc) ; become (his disciple **بیعت لینا** *bai''at le'nā* V.I. administer an oath of allegiance accept (someone) as a disciple

بیک *ba-yak'* ADV with one **یک بیک** *yak' ba-yak'* ADV. suddenly ; all of a sudden **بیک کرشمہ دوکار** *ba-yak' kirish'ma dū kār'* PROV. kill two birds with one stone

بیکا *bī'kā* ADJ. awry (usu. in) **بال بیکا نہ ہونا** *bāl bī'kā na ho'nā* PH. escape unhurt be out of harm's way

بیگ *baig* N.M. bag [E]

بیگ *beg* N.M. (Mughal title of respect corresponding to) Lord ; master ; boss SUF (part of a Mughal Muslim name) [T]

بیگار *begār'* N.F. forced labour ; duress **بیگار پکڑنا** *begār pakaṛnā* V.T. cause to work under duress press (someone) into one's service **بیگار ٹالنا** *begār' ṭāl'nā* V.I. work carelessly ; work in a perfunctory manner not to have one's heart in the work **بیگاری** *begā'rī* N.M. impressed or forced labourer ; one working under duress one working carelessly or in a perfunctory manner

بیگانہ *begā'nah* N.M. unrelated person stranger unfriendly person ADJ. not related (one) outside a group unfriendly callous strange ; queer **بیگانہ خو** *begā'na-khoo'* ADJ. unfriendly callous hard-hearted ; adamant **بیگانہ وار** *begā'na-var* ADV & ADJ. like a stranger callous(ly) in an unfriendly manner indifferent(ly) **بیگانہ وضع** *begā'na vaz''* ADJ. queerly dressed strange-mannered **بیگانگی** *begā'nagī* N.F. not being related or aquainted strangeness shyness unfriendliness

بیگم *be'gam* (ped. *be'gūm*) N.F. wife part of female Muslim names (as title of respect lady بیگم صاحبہ *be'gam sa'ḥibah* (col. بیگم صاحب *be'gam sab*) N.F. mistress of the house lady صاحب اور بیگم *sa'ḥib aur begam* (col. *sab-*) Mr. & Mrs. master and mistress of the house بیگمی *be'gamī* N.M. & ADJ. a superior quality of (rice) a superior quality of (betel-leaf [T]

بیگھہ *bī'gha* N.M. land-measure equivalent to 120 feet square or four kanals

بیل[1] *bel* N.M. spade mattock shovel بیلچہ *bel'chah* N.M. spade hoe بیلدار *bel'-dar* N.M. assistant to gardener digger labourer in a construction work [P]

بیل[2] *bel* N.F. creeping plant ; creeper climber offsprings embroidery lace tip (given to singers, dancing girls etc.) ; charity-tip a kind of crustaceous fruit بیل بوٹا *bel' boo'ṭa* N.M. shrubbery ; shrubs and creepers بیل بوٹے *bel' boo'ṭe* N.M. embroidery floral design بیلدار *bel' dar* ADJ. embroidered engraved with floral designs بیل منڈھے چڑھنا *bel'-man'ḍhe chaṛh'na* PH. (of something) succeed ; thrive

بیل *bail* N.M. ox ; bullock blockhead ; fool بیل گاڑی *bail-ga'ṛī* N.F. bullockcart

بیلا *be'la* N.M. a kind of jasmine shrubbery or forest along river bank; riparian shrubbery a fiddle-like musical instrument charity (esp. one given on wedding) بیلا بٹنا *be'la baṭ'na* V.I. (of charity) be given بیلا بردار *be'la-bardar'* N.M. person entrusted with the task of distributing charitable money ; charity ;-bursar ; dispenser

بیلن *be'lan* N.M. rolling-pin roller cane-crusher cylinder بیلنا *bel'na* N.M. rolling-pin cane-crusher cylinder V.T. roll (flour) into flat cake crush (cane) [~FOLL.]

بیلنا *bel'na* V.T. roll crush (cane, etc.)

بیلون *bailoon'* N.M. balloon [E]

بیلی *be'lī* N.M. guardian ; helper ; protector friend ; companion ; comrade اللہ بیلی *allah' be'lī* (or *al-*) PH. good-bye ; farewell ; adieu God take care (of)

بیم *bīm* N.M. fear ; terror danger ; dread [P]

بیمار *bīmar* ADJ. sick ; ill ; ailing unwell ; indisposed N.M. patient sick person (fig.) unrequited lover بیمار پرسی *bīmar'-pur'sī* N.F. visit to a patient inquiry after (someone's) health بیمار پرسی کرنا *bīmar'-pur'sī kar'na* V.T. visit a patient inquire after (someone's) health بیمار خانہ *bīmar'-kha'nah* N.M. (old use) hospital infirmary بیماردار *bīmar'-dar'* N.M. (ped.) (sick person's) attendant ; nurse بیمارداری *bīmar-da'rī* N.F. (ped.) nursing بیمار کی رات پہاڑ برابر *bīmar' kī rat' pahaṛ' bara'bar* PROV. hard times are prolonged times بیماری *bīma'rī* N.F. disease sickness ; illness ; ailment indisposition بیماریٔ دل *bīma'rī-e dil* N.M. love (rare) heart trouble [P]

بیمہ *bīmah* N.M. insurance ; assurance زندگی کا بیمہ *zin'dagī ka bīmah*, بیمۂ زندگی *bī'ma-e zin'dagī*, بیمہ جان *bī'ma-e jan'* (arch.) N.M. life insurance ; life assurance ; policy on life آتش زنی (یا آگ) کا بیمہ *a'tash-za'nī* (or *ag'*) *ka bī'mah* N.M. fire insurance (کا) بیمہ کرنا (*ka*) *bī'mah kar'na* V.I. insure (someone or something) (کا) بیمہ کرانا (*ka*) *bī'mah kara'na* V.T. insure (something or oneself) ; get insured بیمہ کی قسط *bī'mah kī qist* (or *bīme-*) N.F. premium insurance premium [~P بیم]

بین *bīn* SUF. seeing seer scope sighted بینی *bī'nī* SUF. seeing [P ~ دیدن see]

بین *bīn* N.F. dried gourd flute ; snake charmer's flute ولایتی بین *vila'yatī bīn* N.F. bag-pipe

بین *bain* bag-pipe (usu. PL.) wailing (over the dead) ; lamentation

بین *bain* PREF. inter PREF. between بین الاقوامی *bain-ul-aqva'mī* ADJ. international بین الملی *bain-ul-mil'lī* ADJ. intra-Islamic بین بین *bain' bain* ADJ. middling ADV. between ; betwixt بین الجامعاتی *bain-ul jami'a'tī* ADJ. inter-university بین السطور *bain-us-sutoor'* N.M. distance between two consecutive lines ADV. between the lines بین صوبائی *bain'-sooba''ī* ADJ. inter-provincial بین کلیاتی *bain-kullīya'tī* ADJ. inter-collegiate بین المملکتی *bain-ul-mam'lakatī* (ped. بین الممالکی *bain-ul-mama'likī*) ADJ. inter-dominion international [A]

بیّن *bay'yin* ADJ. obvious ; evident clear lucid cogent (reason) apparent بیّنہ *bay'yinah* N.F. cogent argument obvious truth ADJ. cogent categorical evident; obvious بیّنات *bayyinat'* N.M. PL. cogent arguments categorical proofs obvious truths ADJ. cogent categorical obvious [A]

بینا *bīna'* ADJ. having eye-sight ; not blind discerning wise بینا کرنا *bīna' kar'na* V.I. give eyesight (to) restore eyesight confer discernment (on) بینا ہونا *bīna' ho'na* V.I. not to be blind ; have (one's) eyesight intact بینائی *bīna''ī* N.F. sight ; eye sight ; vision [P ~ دیدن see]

بینامی *bena'mī* N.F. & ADJ. dummy (sale); (sale of property) apparently in name of other than real buyer
بیندھنا *bindh'nā* V.I. bore perforate say piercing words (to)
بینڈ *baind'* N.M. band (of outdoor music players) [E]
بینڈا *bain'ḍā* N.M. latch ADJ. (F. بینڈی *bain'ḍī*) awry uncouth
بینڈی *bīnḍī* N.F. braided hair skein (of thread, etc.) twist (of fibres)
بینڈیا *bīn'ḍiyā* N.M. extra draught animal used as support
بینش *bī'nish* N.F. eye-sight discernment [P ~ دیدن to see]
بینگن *bain'gan* N.M. brinjal egg-plant تھالی کا بینگن *thā'lī kā bain'gan* PH. unreliable; untrustworthy (person); trimming his sails according to the prevailing wind fickle capricious
بینا *bīn'nā* V.T. glean
بیں ہتھا *bain' hat'thā* ADJ. & N.M. left-handed (person) [~بایاں + ہاتھ]
بینی *bī'nī* N.F. nose guard of sword upturned side of binding reinforcing strip of wood fixed to door-board, etc. بینی بریدہ *bī'nī būrī'dah* ADJ. nose-clipt (person)
بیوپار *be'opār'* (col. *baipār'*) N.M. business; trade بیوپاری *be'opā'rī*, (col. بپاری *baipā'rī*) N.M. dealer; businessman, trader; merchant
بیوت *buyoot'* N.M. PL. houses N.M. & (PL. بیوتات *buyotāt'* palace household expenditure [A ~ SING. بیت]
بیورا *bayo'rā* N.M. detailed account day-book; journal بیورے دار *bayo're-vār* ADJ. detailed ADV. in detail
بیونتنا *biyoṅt'nā* V.T. cut off (cloth) according to measurements بیونت *biyoṅt'* N.M. cutting (of cloth); according to measurements cut slashing (of expenditure)
بیوہ *be'vah* N.F. widow بیوگان *be'vagāṅ* N.F. PL. widows بیوگی *be'vagī* N.F. widowhood [P]
بیوہار *bayohār'* N.M. custom transaction بیوہار کی بات *bayohār' kī bāt'* N.F. something fair
بیوی *bī'vī* N.F. wife mistress of the house lady chaste woman free woman Hazrat Fatimah بیوی کا غلام *bī'vī kā ghulām'* N.M. henpecked (husband); uxorious person بیوی کی صحنک (یا نیاز) *bī'vī kī saiḥ'nak* (or *niyāz*) N.F., بیوی کا دانہ (یا کونڈا) *bī'vī kā dā'nah* (or *kooṅ'ḍā*) N.M. sacred feast to commemorate Hazrat Fatimah
بیہڑ *baihaṛ* N.M. uncultivated and uneven land (usu. near river bank)
بیہودہ *behoo'dah* ADJ. silly; stupid; foolish; nonsensical; absurd vain; fruitless impolite foul obscene; sweetly immoral بیہودہ باتیں *behoo'dah bā'teṅ* N.F. PL. nonsense obscene talk indecent language immoral pursuits بیہودہ گو *behoo'da-go* N.M. foul-mouthed fellow بیہودہ گوئی *behoo'da-go''ī* N.F. idle talk nonsense obscene talk بیہودگی *behoo'dagī* N.F. nonsense absurdity silly behaviour
بیئر *bī'ar* N.F. beer [E]

پ

پ *pe* third letter of Urdu alphabet (equivalent to English *p*) (also called *Bā'-e Fā'risī*) (in jummal reckoning equivalent to ب; hence) 2
پا¹ *pā* N M. fifth note of national gamut; fa
پا² SUF. (denoting abstract quality) footed continuing; lasting [P]
پا³ *pā* N.M. foot leg root; stem *pā-andāz'*, فرش پا انداز *far'sh-e pā-andāz'* N.M. doormat پا بدست دگرے دست بدست دگرے *pā ba'-das'te di'gare das't ba-das't-e di'gare* PH. under duress not having free hand پا بہ رکاب *pā ba-rikāb'*, پا در رکاب *pā dar rikāb'* ADV. ready to move پا بہ زنجیر *pā-bazanjīr*, پا بجولاں *pā ba-joo'lāṅ* ADJ in chains; fattered پابند *pā-band'* N.F. & ADJ. in bound; committed habituated restrained detained, imprisoned checked controlled subservient پابند رہنا *pā-band' raih'nā* V.I. stick; adhere follow; conform stand committed پابند کرنا *pā-band' kar'nā* V.T. check bind down restrain پابند ہونا *pā-band' ho'nā* V.I. be bound down stand committed پابندی *pā-ban'dī* N.F. restraint; restriction detention check; control subservience commitment پابوس *pā-bos'* ADJ. adoring worshipping flattering; licking (someone's) feet N.M. (rare) worship پابوسی *pā-bo'sī* N.F. salutation adoration worship sycophancy; licking someone's hoofs پابوسی کرنا *pā-bo'sī kar'nā* V.I. revere adore worship پاپوش *pā posh'* N.F. (arch.) shoe پاپوش پر مارنا

pa-posh' par mar'na V.T. spurn پاپیادہ *pā-piyā'dah* ADJ. on foot walking پاتابہ *pā-tā'bah*, پیتاوہ *paitā'vah* N.M. inner sole پاجامہ *pā-jā'mah* N.M. trousers پاخانہ *pā-khā'nah* N.M. latrine ; lavatory ; privy stools ; excrement of bowels پازیب *pā-zeb'* N.F. anklet پاشکستہ *pā-shikas'tah* ADJ. dead tired resourceless پاشویہ *pā-sho'yah* N.M. fomentation of the feet laving of the feet پالغز *pā lagh'z* slip wrong step 'faux pas' پامال *pā-māl'*, پائمال *pā'e-māl'* ADJ. trampled downtrodden laid low ruined devastated پامالی *pā-mā'lī*, پائمالی *pā'e-mā'lī* N.F. trampling ruin devastation پامردی *pā-mar'di* N.F. bravery ; valour پایاب *pā-yāb'* ADJ. shallow ; fordable

پاپ *pāp* N.M. (dial.) sin vice پاپ کٹنا *pāp' kaṭ'nā* PH. (of dispute) be settled (of trouble) end پاپی *pā'pī* N.M. (dial) sinner [S]

پاپا *pāpā* N.M. papa ; pop ; father Pope پاپائے روم *pāpā'-e rom'* N.M. the Pope [E]

پاپا *pa'pā* N.M. rusk

پاپڑ *pā'par* N.M. thin saltish cake dried layer (of mango-juice) ADJ. very thin dry ; parched پاپڑ بیلنا *pā'par bel'nā* V.I. roll out these cakes (fig.) undergo much suffering (fig) turn to one thing after another in a bid to do something or earn one's livelihood

پاپڑا *pāp'ṛā* N.M. fruit of 'butia frondesa' used as a drug پاپڑا کھار *pāp'ṛā khār* N.F. its askes used as seasoning

پات *pāt* N.M. leaf metal plate ornament for upper part of ear , earplate [doublet of پتہ]

پاتال *pātāl'* N.M. (dial.) Hades ; hell ; (according to Hindus) lowest region of world infested by fiends and serpents [S]

پاتھنا *pāth'nā* V.T. get dung cakes ready for drying up mould (bricks)

پاٹ *pāṭ* N.M. breadth (of river, etc.) milestone depth (of voice) پاٹ دار *pāṭ'-dār* ADJ. (of voice) deep ; sonorous پاٹنا *pāṭ'nā* V.T. fill up (pity, stream, etc.) roof cover plaster spread loose earth over shut pile ; overstock give in abundance

پاجی *pājī* ADJ. mean ; base silly پاجی پن *pā'jī-pan* N.M. meanness stupidity [P]

پاچھنا *pāchh'nā* V.T. incise make an incision (for extracting blood from body or opium from poppy, پاچھ *pāchh* N.M. incision

پاد *pād* N.M. (vulg.) fart پادنا *pād'nā* V.I. fart ; pass wind (fig.) pass a silly remark (fig.) show the white weather

پاداش *padāsh'* N.M. punishment retaliation penalty requital کی پاداش میں *kī padāsh meṅ* PH. as a penalty for [P]

پادری *pād'rī* N.M. clergyman minister of the church [Pg.]

پادشاہ *pād'shah* N.M., پادشاہت *pādshā'hat* N.F. پادشاہی *pādshā'hī* N.F. (same as بادشاہ N.M. بادشاہت N.F. بادشاہی N.F. (see under بادشاہ N.M. ★)

پادنا *pād'nā* V.I. (see under پاد)

پار *par* N.M. opposite bank opposite shore other side termination (of life) successful end ADV. across over on the other side to the other side through beyond ADJ. past ; last پار اتارنا *pār'utar'nā* V.T. ferry over take across پار اترنا *par' u'tarnā* V.I. cross get or move across get through gain one's end die ; pass away پار کرنا *pār' kar'nā* V.I. ferry over get across finish transfix پار لگانا *pār' lagā'nā* V.T. ferry over bring success ; make successful kill squander پار لگنا *pār lag'nā* V.I. be ferried over succeed finish be squandered ; go waste

پارٹی *pār'ṭī* N.F. party پارٹی باز *pār'ṭī-bāz* ADJ. & N.M. factious (person) (one) guided by party spirit پارٹی بازی *pār'ṭī-bā'zī* N.F. party spirit factiousness [E]

پارچہ *pār'chah* N M. (ped.) cloth piece of cloth dress ; garment piece ; fragment پارچہ فروش *pār'cha firosh'* N.M. (ped.) draper پارچہ فروشی *pār'cha-firo'shī* N.F. (ped.) drapery

پارس *pā'ras* N.M. philosopher's stone

پارس *pār's* N.M. Persia ; Iran پارسی N.M. & F. ★

پارسا *pārsā'* ADJ. chaste abstemious ; virtuous holy pious پارسائی *parsā''ī* N.F. chastity abstinence virtue piety [P]

پارسال *pār'sāl* ADV. last year [P ~ پار + سال]

پارسل *pār'sal* N.M. parcel پارسل بھیجنا (یا کرنا) *pār'sal bhej'nā* (or *kar'nā*) V.T. send a parcel by post [E]

پارسی *pār'sī* N.M. (F. same as occ. پارسن *pār'san*) Parsi N.F. Persian language ; Persian [P]

پارلیمان *pār'limān* N.F. Parliament پارلیمانی *pārli-mā'nī* ADJ. Parliamentary پارلیمانی نظام *pārli-mā'nī nizām'* N.M. Parliamentary system (of government) [~E POLL.]

پارلیمینٹ *pār'limaṅt* N.M. Parliament پارلیمنٹری *pār'limaṅ'ṭarī* ADJ. Parliamentary [E]

پارہ [1] (or پارا) *pā'ra* N.M. mercury ; quick silver

پارہ [2] *pā'rah* N.M. piece scrap slice fragment پارہ پارہ کرنا *pā'ra pā'rah kar'nā* V.T. tear to pieces [P]

پارینہ *pārī'nah* ADJ. outdated outmoded دفتر پارینہ *daftar-e pārī'nah* N.M. (fig.) outmoded stuff [P ~ پار]

پاڑ *pāṛ* N.F. scaffold scaffolding hole made by burglar پاڑ باندھنا *pāṛ' bāṅdh'nā* V.I. scaffold پاڑ کھولنا *pāṛ' khol'nā* V.T. dismantle the scaffolding

پاڑا *pā'ṛā*, N.M. (also پاڑھا *pā'ṛhā*, col. پہڑا *pah'ṛā*) a species of deer hamlet boundary of field پاڑے کاٹنا *pā're kāṭ'nā* V.I. harrow (paddy-field, etc.)

پاژند *pāzhand'* N.F. exegesis of Zoroastrian scriptures ژند و پاژند *zhaṅ'd-o-pāzhand'* N.M. Zoroastsian scriptures with their exegesis [P]

پاس [1] *pās* ADV. near ; close about alongside up to at hand nearby ; close by with پاس آنا *pās' ā'nā* V.I. come near ; draw closer to come up to ; approach پاس بٹھانا *pās biṭhā'nā* V.T. seat close (to) accept as apprentice (to) teach manners پاس بیٹھنا *pās' baiṭh'nā* V.I. sit near be a constant companion of be apprenticed to learn manners from پاس بیٹھنے والا *pās' baiṭh'ne vāl'ā* N.M. constant companion ; companion disciple (of) apprenticed (to) پاس پاس *pās' pās* ADV. close by next to each other next-door to each other roundabout thereabouts پاس پڑوس *pās' paṛos'* N.M. neigebourhood vicinity پاس نہ پھٹکنا *pās' na phaṭ'aknā* V.I. not to come near not to call (on) پاس نہ پھٹک سکنا *pās' na phaṭ'ak sak'nā* V.I. dare not approach کے پاس *ke pās'* PREP. with کے پاس ہونا *ke pās' ho'nā* V.T. hay

پاس [2] *pās* N.M. regard ; consideration deference watch three-hour period پاسبان *pās-bān'* N.M. watchman sentinel ; guard protector ; guardian پاسبانی *pās-bā'nī* N.F. watch guard protection , guardiansihp پاس خاطر *pā's-e khā'tir* N.M. out of regard; in consideration بپاس خاطر *ba-pā's-e khā'tir* PH. out of regard for پاسدار *pās'dār'* ADJ. partial to N.M. partisan پاسداری *pās-dā'rī* N.F. partiality favouritism favour regard ; consideration کا پاس کرنا *kā pās' kar'nā* V.T. show regard for be partial to favour take sides (with) [P]

پاس [3] *pās* N.M. pass success in examination ADJ. passed successful approved پاس دینا *pās de'nā* V.T. issue a pass پاس کرنا *pās kar'nā* V.T. & I. get through (examination) declare successful (in examination) پاس ہونا *pās ho'nā* V.I. get through be approved; be passed ; pass master [E]

پاسا *pā'sā* N.M. (same as پانسہ *pāṅ'sah* N.M. ★)

پاستان *pās'tāṅ*, باستان *bās'tāṅ* ADJ. ancient ; old [P]

پاسخ *pā'sukh* N.M. reply [P]

پاسنا *pās'nā* V.T. fondle animal's teats urging her to yield milk

پاسنگ *pā-sang'* N.M. make-weight ; some thing placed in one scale to balance the other insignificant portion [P ~ پا + سنگ]

پاسی *pā'sī* N.M. fowler name of a low caste of Hindus crude net ; meshed container for bundle of hay

پاش *pāsh* SUF. sprinkling shedding scattering پاشی *pā'shī* SUF. sprinkling shedding scattering [P ~ پاشیدن]

پاش پاش *pāsh' pāsh* ADJ. shattered broken to pieces shivered پاش پاش کرنا *pāsh' pāsh kar'nā* V.T. shatter break to pieces shiver پاش پاش ہونا *pāsh' pāsh ho'nā* V.I. be broken to pieces shiver [P]

پاشا *pā'shā* N.M. (Turkish title) lord governor boss general [T]

پاشنہ *pāsh'nah* heal [P]

پاک *pāk* ADJ. pure undefiled spotless ; immaculate chaste holy ; sacred free innocent (ABB. for) Pakistani N.M. (ABB. for) Pakistan پاکباز *pāk-bāz'* ADJ. pure undefiled chaste پاکبازی *pāk-bā'zī* N.F. chastity virtue پاک خصلت *pāk-khaslat* ADJ. chaste well disposited پاکدامن *pāk-dā'man* ADJ. virtuous modest chaste پاکدامنی *pāk-dā'manī* N.F. chastity; modesting virtue innocence پاک سیرت *pāk-sī'rat* ADJ. virtuous angelic پاک صاف *pāk' sāf* ADJ. clear pure undefiled ; unpolluted spotless ; immaculate پاک صورت *pāk'-soorat* ADJ. pretty ; lovely پاک کرنا *pāk kar'nā* V.T. clean cleanse purify wash settle or square pay off in full پاک محبت *pāk maḥabbat* N.F. Platonic love پاک ہونا *pāk ho'nā* V.I. be clean be pure be purified (of account) be settled have current menses over پاکی *pā'kī* N.F. cleanliness chastity shaving of the pubes پاکی لینا *pākī le'nā* V.T. shave pubes ; shave underparts پاکیزہ *pākī'zah* ADJ. clean neat; tidy pure chaste پاکیزگی *pākī'zagī* N.F. cleanliness neatness ; tidiness purity chastity [P]

پاکستان *pākistān'* N.M. name of the fifth largest State of the present-day world ; Pakistan پاکستانی *pākista'nī* ADJ. Pakistan ; Pakistani N.M. Pakistani (national) [acronym comprising names of its constituents + P ستان together meaning 'holy land']

پاکھا *pa'khā* N.M. wing (of building)

پاکھر *pa'khar* N.M. caparison armour for horse or elephant (rare) tarpaulin

پاکھنڈ *pākhand'* N.M. fraud hypocricy mischief پاکھنڈی *pākhan'ḍī* N.M. & ADJ. fraudulent (person) hypocrite mischief-monger

پاگل *pā'gal* ADJ. mad ; insane foolish stupid idiotic beside oneself (with) N.M. madman ; lunatic fool idiot پاگل پن *pāgal pan* N.M. madness ; insanity stupidity ; foolishness پاگل خانہ *pā'gal-khā'nah* N.M. lunatic asylum ; bedlam ; mental hospital ; mad-house پاگل ہونا *pā'gal ho'nā* V.I. be mad پاگل ہو جانا *pā'gal ho jā'nā* V.I. go mad be mad after

پاگنا *pāg'na* V.T. sugar-coat

پال *pāl* N.F. straw in which raw mangoes, etc. are placed for mellowing پال کا آم *pāl' kā ām* N.M. straw mellowed mango-strew پال کا پکا *pāl' kā pak'kā* ADJ. mellowed (fruit) پال لگانا *pāl lagā'nā* V.T. straw-ripen (fruit) [~ پالنا rear]

پالا *pā'lā* N.M. frost ; hoarfrost separating line in kabaddi field 'kabaddi' half-field; part of it under charge of one team dealings encounter ; contact (with undesirable, etc. persons) پالا پڑنا *pā'lā par'nā* V.I. be covered with frost come under the sway (of wicked person) encounter پالا مارنا *pā'lā mār'nā* V.I. win (in 'kabaddi') succeed

پالان *pālān'* N.M. packsaddle [P]

پالتو *pāl'too* ADJ. pet [~ پالنا rear]

پالٹ *pā'lat* N.M. hit at feet as trick in clubbing

پالش *pā'lish* N.M. polish shol blackening پالش کرنا *po'lish kar'nā* V.T. shine or blacken shoes [E]

پالک *pā'lak* N.F. spinach (also پالک کا ساگ *pā'lak kā sāg'*) this as potherb

پالکی *pā'l'kī* N.F. palanquin ; litter

پالنہار *pā'lan hār'* N.M. (God as) Sustainer ; Nourisher ; Cherisher

پالنا *pā'lnā* V.T. bring up rear cherish sustain N.M. a cradle پالنا پوسنا *pāl'nā pos'nā* V.I. bring up rear

پالیز *pāl'ez*, فالیز *fālez'* N.F. melon field [P]

پالہنگ *pā'lahang* N.M. bridle tether [P]

پالی *pā'lī* N.F. quail-fight quail-fight arena Pali (language)

پالیسی *pā'lisī* N.F. policy [E]

پام *pām* N.F. gold or silk lace protacting string along lace

پام *pām* N.M. any species of palm cocoanut palm date-palm [E]

پان *pān* N.M. betel-leaf starch used by weavers piece of leather on top of heel پاندان *pān'-dān* N.M. betel-box پاندان کا خرچ *pān'-dān kā kharch'* N.M. wife's pocket-tmoney پان کھلائی *pān-khilā''ī* N.F. betel-leaf presentation (as betrothal ceremony or wedding fun) پان بنانا (یا لگانا) *pān banā'nā* (or *lagā'nā*) V.T. coat betel-leaf with lime, catechu, etc. ; prepare betel-leaf

پانا *pā'nā* V.T. get obtain find پا جانا *pā' jā'nā* V.T. see the point get the hang of , understand guess ; get پایا جانا *pā'yā jā'nā* V.I. be found feel ashamed پا لینا *pā' le'nā* V.T. receive understand guess see the point

پانچ *pānch* ADJ. five very clever پانچ سات *pānch' sat* پان سات *pān' sāt* N.M. a flew (also سات پانچ *sāt' pānch*) dodging پانچواں *pānch'vān* ADJ. fifth پانچواں کالم *pānch'vān ka'lam* N.M. fifth column پانچوں *pānchon* ADJ. all five پانچوں انگلیاں برابر نہیں ہوتیں *pān'chon ūng'liyān barā'bar na'hīn ho'tīn* PROV. all are not alike all are not equally bad (or good) پانچوں انگلیاں پانچوں چراغ *pān'chon ūngliān pān'chon chirāgh'* PH. very accomplished (young lady) پانچوں (انگلیاں) گھی میں ہونا *pān'chon (ūng'liān) ghī meṅ ho'nā* enjoy to heart's content be all in all (somewhere) پانچوں عیب شرعی *pāñ'chon 'aib shar''ī* N.M. deadly sins ; the five prohibited sins, viz., lying, stealing, drinking, fornication and gambling (پانچویں سواروں میں (ہونا *pāñch'veñ savā'roñ meñ (ho'nā)* PROV. (be a) self-imposed comrade of heroes پانسو *pāñ'sau* ADJ. five hundred

پانڈا *pāñḍā* (usu. پانڈے جی *pāñḍe jī*) N.M. (dial.) Brahman title a learned man ; scholar ; village school master

پانڈو *pāñ'ḍoo* N.F. chalky soil

پانس *pāñs* N.M. alluvium manure dung-hill پانس ڈالنا *pāñs ḍāl'nā* V.T. manure

پانسہ *pāñ'sah*, پانسا *pāñ'sā* N.M. dice پانسہ پھینکنا *pāñ'sah pheñk'nā* V.T. throw the dice; پانسہ الٹا پڑنا *pāñ'sah ul'ṭā par'nā* V.I. loose be unlucky (in throw) پانسہ پڑنا *pāñ'sah par'nā* V.I. win be lucky (in throw) پانسہ پلٹنا *pāñ'sah pa'laṭnā* N.M. turn of the tide V.I. (fig.) (of tide) turn

پانوں (or پانو *pā''oñ* N.M. (same as پاؤں★)

پانی *pā'nī* N.M. water rain tears sweat flood polish ; burnish ; lustre plating modesty chastity gust ; courage ADJ. watery very dilute thin or dense پانی آنا *pā'nī ā'nā* V.I. rain suffer from cataract suffer from the whites (or) leucorrhoea have water be floody پانی اترنا *pā'nī u'tarnā* V.T. & I. (of water-level) fall suffer from cataract پانی باندھنا *pā'nī bāñdh'nā* V.T. build dam or dyke round پانی بہنا *pā'nī baih'nā* (of water) flow پانی بھرنا *pā'nī bhar'nā* V.T draw water be or become subservient to منہ میں پانی بھر آنا *muñh' meñ pā'nī bhar ā'nā* V.I. (of mouth) water be avid پانی بند کرنا *pā'nī band kar'nā* V.T. put a stop to flow of water stop water-supply (to) پانی بہانا *pā'nī bahā'nā* V.T. pour or spill water (of eyes) shed tears ; weep bitterly پانی پانی کرنا *pā'nī pā'nī kar'nā* V.T. put (someone) to shame پانی پانی ہونا *pā'nī pā'nī ho'nā* V.I. be overwhelmed with shame be drenched پانی پڑنا *pā'nī par'nā* V.I. rain (of wound, etc.) suppurate پانی پھر جانا *pā'nī phir jā'nā* V.I. be in or regain good health ; be radiant with health (of achievement, etc.) go to waste be undone پانی پھیر دینا *pā'nī pher de'nā* V.T. undo end ruin ; destroy guild ; plate give radiant health (پانی پی پی کر کوسنا (یا کوسنے دینا *pā'nī pī pī kar kos'nā* (or *kos'ne de'nā*) PH. heap curses upon پانی پینا *pā'nī pī'nā* V.I. drink water پانی تارا ہونا *pā'nī tā'rā ho'nā* PH. (of water-level in well) by very deep پانی توڑنا *pā'nī toṛ'nā* V.T. decrease or pilfer water-supply پانی چرانا *pā'nī chu̲rā'nā* V.T. & I. (of wound) suppurate pilfer irrigation water پانی چڑھنا *pā'nī charh'nā* V.I. (of waterlevel) rise (of river) be in spate پانی چھوڑنا *pā'nī chhoṛ'nā* V.T. discharge (water, etc.) پانی دکھانا *pā'nī dikhā'nā* V.T. take animal to the watering place cause it to drink پانی چوانا *pā'nī cho'ā'nā* V.T. let water fall drop by drop پانی دینا *pā'nī de'nā* V.T. water ; irrigate give water (to) پانی ڈھلنا *pā'nī ḍhal'nā* V.I. loose radiance lose shame پانی سا پتلا *pā'nī sā pat'lā* ADJ. watery (of milk) adulterated پانی سر سے اونچا ہونا *pā'nī sir se ooñ'chā ho'nā* V.T. (usu fig.) be in deep waters پانی سمونا *pā'nī samo'nā* V.I. mix hot water in cold one پانی کا بلبلہ *pā'nī kā bul'bulah* N.M. bubble (fig.) unstable thing پانی کاٹنا *pā'nī kāṭ'nā* V.I. turn off the water into another channel breast the waves پانی کے مول *pā'nī ke mol'* PH. very cheap پانی کرنا *pā'nī kar'nā* V.I. stop flow be stagnant پانی کی چادر *pā'nī kī chā'dar* N.F. sheet of water پانی لگنا *pā'nī lag'nā* V.I. (of water of some place) agree with ; improve (someone's) health پانی مرنا *pā'nī mar'nā* V.I. (of water) seep (in wall, etc.) be a weak point (in) be put to shame پانی میں آگ لگانا *pā'nī meñ āg' lagā'nā* V.I. sow seeds of dissension do a miracle ; work wonders پانی میں بجھانا *pā'nī meñ bujhā'nā* V.T. temper (steel, etc.) پانی نہ مانگنا *pā'nī na māñg'nā* V.I. die all of a sudden be killed with a single stroke پانی ہارنا *pā'nī hār'nā* V.I. (in quial-fight) lose (one etc.) round (in a total of ten)

پائپ *pā''ip* N.M. pipe [E]

پائندہ *pā'in'dah* ADJ. durable ; lasting everlasting پائندہ باد *pā''in'da-bād'* INT. long live ; 'viva la' [P]

پاؤ *pā''o* N.M. quarter seer fourth part ; quarter پاؤ بھر *pā''o bhar*, پاؤ سیر *pā''o ser* ADJ. quarter seer پاؤ روٹی *pā''o ro'ṭī*, نان پاؤ *nān' pā''o* N.M., ڈبل روٹی *ḍa'bal ro'ṭī* N.F. bread ; loaf of bread پاؤلی *pā''ulī* N.F. quarter-rupee (arch.) four anna bit

پاؤں (or پانو or پانوں *pā''oñ* N.M. foot step foothold leg pedestal basis root standing guts ; courage firmness پاؤں اترنا *pā''oñ u'tarnā* V.I. (of ankle, etc.) dislocated (of foot) be sprained پاؤں اٹھانا *pā''oñ uṭhā'nā* V.I. step forward ; move ahead پاؤں اٹھا کے چلنا *pā''oñ uṭhā' ke chal'nā* V.I. walk at a swift pace

پاؤں اڑانا pā''oṅ ara'nā V.T. meddle ; interfere پاؤں اکھڑنا pā''oṅ ukhaṛ'na V.T. lose ground lose footing be routed ; take to flight be pushed back be carried off one's feet پاؤں باہر نکلنا (یا نکالنا) pā''oṅ ba'hir nikal'nā (or nikāl'nā) V.I. transgress limits پاؤں بچلنا pā''oṅ bi'chalnā V I. slip lose firmness yield fall a prey to temptation پاؤں بڑھانا pā''oṅ baṛhā'nā V.I. step forward move faster transgress limits پاؤں بھاری ہونا pā''oṅ bhā'rī ho'nā V.I. be pregnant ; be in the family way be tired پاؤں بیچ میں ہونا pā''on bich' meṅ ho'nā V.I. be mediating be responsible پاؤں پاؤں چلنا pā''oṅ pā''oṅ chal'nā V.I. (of baby) walk without support پاؤں پر پاؤں رکھنا pā''oṅ par pā''oṅ rakh'nā V I. sit cross-legged lounge lead on easy life پاؤں پر پاؤں گرنا pā''oṅ par pā''oṅ gir'nā, پاؤں پڑنا pā''oṅ paṛ'nā, پاؤں پکڑنا pā''oṅ pa'karnā V.T. fall at the feet of implore ; entreat ; beseach اپنے پاؤں پر آپ کلہاڑی مارنا ap'ne pā''oṅ par āp' kulhā'ṛī mār'nā PH. mar one's own career , spoil one's own chances پاؤں پسارنا pā''oṅ pasār'nā V.I, stretch one's legs be obstinate ; show stubbornness die پاؤں پکڑنا pā''oṅ pa'karnā V.T. (also) prevent from moving ahead پاؤں پھٹنا pā''oṅ phaṭ'nā V.I. have chilblains پاؤں پھسلنا pā''oṅ phi'salnā slip err yield fall a prey to temptation پاؤں پھولنا pā''oṅ phool'nā V.T. be unnerved پاؤں پھونک پھونک کر رکھنا pā''on phoonk phoonk kar rakh'nā V.I. tread softly be cautious or circumspect پاؤں پھیلا کر سو رہنا pā''oṅ phailā' kar so' raih'nā V.I. sleep with the legs stretched out be perfectly happy and contend پاؤں پیٹنا pā''oṅ pīṭ'nā V.I. beat one's heals پاؤں پیچھے ہٹنا pā''oṅ pī-chhe haṭ'nā V.I. loose heart beat retreat پاؤں تلے ملنا pā''oṅ ta'le mal'nā V.T. trample under foot پاؤں تلے سے زمین نکل جانا pā''oṅ ta'le se zamīn' ni'kal jā'nā V.I. stagger be stunned feel the ground slipping from under one's feet پاؤں ٹکنا (یا جمنا) pā''oṅ ṭik'nā (or jam'nā) V.I. be serene not to be beside oneself پاؤں جمانا (یا گاڑنا) pā''oṅ jamā'nā (or gāṛ'nā) V.I. plant (one's) feet firmly ; get a firm footing پاؤں جھننانا pā''oṅ jhunnā'nā V.I. be on pins and needles پاؤں چھلنی ہو جانا pā''oṅ chhal'nī ho jā'nā V.I. (of feet) be blistered be dead tired ; be fatigued پاؤں دابنا (یا چپی کرنا) pā''oṅ dāb'nā (or chap'pī kar'nā) V.T. press (someones) feet by way of message پاؤں دھرنا (یا رکھنا) pā''oṅ dhar'nā (or rakh'nā) V.I. set foot on enter; step in begin (enterprise, etc) ; get پاؤں دھو (یا دھو دھو) کر پینا pā''oṅ dho' (or dho dho') kar pī'na V.I. wash (someone's) feet revere پاؤں ڈگمگانا pā''oṅ dagmagā'nā V.I. feel shaby fall a prey to temptation پاؤں رگڑنا pā''oṅ ra'gaṛnā V.I. make fruitless efforts have a very uneasy time implore پاؤں رہ جانا pā''oṅ raih' jā'nā V.I. be exhausted ; be fatigued پاؤں زمین پر نہ رکھنا pā''oṅ zamīn' par na rakh'nā V.I. be overjoyed be very haughty پاؤں زمین پر نہ پڑنا (یا ٹکنا) pā''oṅ zamīn' par na paṛ'nā (or ṭik'nā) V.I. be overjoyed be haughty be very naughty fidget پاؤں سر پر رکھ کر بھاگنا pā''oṅ sir par rakh' kar bhag'nā PH. flee ; run away پاؤں سو جانا pā''oṅ so' jā'nā V.I. (of foot) be benumbed پاؤں سو سو من کے ہو جانا pā''oṅ sau' sau man ke ho jā'nā V.I. be very much fatigued پاؤں سے لگی سر میں بجھی pā''oṅ se la'gī sir meṅ bū'jhī PH. flare up be greatly upset be greatly hurt پاؤں کی انگلی pā''oṅ kī ung'lī N.F. toe پاؤں کا انگوٹھا pā''oṅ ka angoo'ṭhā N.M. big toe ; great toe پاؤں گور (یا قبر) میں لٹکائے بیٹھنا pā''oṅ gor (or qa'bar) meṅ laṭkā''e baiṭh'nā V. be very old ; have one foot in the grave پاؤں گھسنا pā''oṅ ghis'nā V.I. run useless errands پاؤں میں چکر ہونا pā''oṅ meṅ chak'kar ho'nā V.I. be ever on the move پاؤں میں مہندی لگنا pā''oṅ meṅ maihn'dī lag'na V.I. have the feet coated with henna paste be unable to set foot on ground not be in position to move پاؤں نکالنا pā''oṅ nikāl'nā V.I. be coming up transgress ; exceed limits step out of withdraw from دبے پاؤں آنا da'be pā''oṅ ā'nā trend softly come unperceived

پائی pā''ī N.F. pie ; a small Pakistani coin no longer current

پاہونا pāhoo'nā N.M. پاہونی pāhoo'nī N.F. (usu. PL.) song(s) sung at bride's departure for her new home

پاہی pā'hī N.M. temporary tenant ADJ. temporary (tenancy)

پائے pā''e N.M. (PL. of پایہ N.M. ★)

پائے تخت pā''e takh't N.M. (same as پایۂ تخت ★)

پائجامہ pā'e-jā'mah N.M. (old spelling of پاجامہ N.M. ★)

پائدار pā'e-dār ADJ. durable wearing well permanent پائداری pā''e-dā'rī N.F. durability permanence firmness long wear [P ~ پا + داشتن]

پائدان pā''e-dān' N.M. running board footboard doormat [~ P پا + دان]

پائے رفتن نہ جائے ماندن pā''e raf'tan na jā''e man'dan PROV. utter helplessness [P]

پاۓ کوب pā'e-kob' ADJ. dancing پاۓ کوبی pā'e-kobī N.F. dance [F ~ پا + کوبیدن]

پائمال pā'e māl (same as پامال★)

پائنچہ pā''incha N.F. one of the legs of a pair trousers [~P پا]

پائیں pā''iṅ ADJ. & ADV. back-side ; back lower under beneath پائیں باغ pā''iṅ-bāgh N.M. backside garden kitchen garden [P]

پائنتی pā''īntī N.F. foot of the bed

پایاں pā'yāṅ N.F. end conclusion extreme extremity پایانِ کار pāyān-e kār' ADV. at last ; at length ; ultimately [P]

پایل pā'yal ADJ. (child) born with feet first N.F. jingled anklet

پایہ pā'yah N.M. leg foot pedestal support base step rank ; status پایۂ تخت pā'ya-e takh't, پاۓ تخت pā''e-takh't capital seat or headquarters of government پایۂ ثبوت کو پہنچنا pā'ya-e sūboot ko pahūṅch'nā V.T. be proved ; be established beyond doubt [P]

پبلشر pab'lishar N.M. publisher پبلیکیشن pub'līkayshan N.F. publication [E]

پبلک pab'lik N.F public [E]

پپڑانا papṛā na V.I. become crusty پپڑ pa'paṛ N.M. plaster coming off the wall پپڑا pap'ṛa N.M. (F. پپڑی papṛī) crust ; scab a kind of sweetmeat پپڑیاں جم جانا pap'ṛiyāṅ jam jā'nā V.I. (of lips) get parched پپڑیا pap'riyā ADJ. layered پپڑیا کتھا pap'riyā kat'thā N.M. white catechu

پپوٹا papo'tā N.M. eyelid

پپولنا papol'nā V.T. munch , masticate

پپیتا papī'tā N.M. papaw fruit

پپیہا papī'hā (dial. پپیہا papay'yā) N.M. crested cuckoo with yellow eyes and patches of white on its black coat children's whistle made of leaves or mango-stone

پت pit N.M. bile gall chlorophyll پت ڈالنا pit ḍāl'nā V.I. vomit bilious stuff

پت جھڑ pat'-jhaṛ N.M autumn , fall پت جھڑ ہونا pat'-jhaṛ ho'nā V.I. lose leaves in autumn (fig.) decay (from old age) [~ پتا + جھڑنا]

پتا pi'tā N.M. (dial.) father sire

پتر pat'tar N.M. leaf sheet metal plated metal ; gilt پتری pat'rī N.F. brace

پتل pat'tal N.F. (dial.) leaf trenchar

پتلا pat'lā, ADJ (F. پتلی pat'lī) thin lean fine sharp watery straitened پتلا حال pat'lā ḥāl' N.M. sad plight ; straitened circumstances پتلا دبلا pat'lā dub'lā ADJ. lean delicate پتلا کرنا pat'la kar'nā V.I. dilute sharpen make slim ; reduce پتلا ہو جانا pat'la ho jā'nā V.I. slim become watery

پتلا pūt'lā N.M. puppet effigy statue عقل کا پتلا 'aq'l kā pūt'lā ADJ. clever ; skilful foolish ; stupid خاک کا پتلا khāk' kā pūt'lā N.M. human body human being

پتلون patloon' N.F. slacks ; Western type of trousers [~E pantaloon]

پتلی pūt'lī N.F. pupil (of the eye) puppet cute woman ; spruce little lady frog (of horse's hoof) پتلیوں کا تماشا pūt'liyoṅ ka tamā'shā N.M. puppet show پتلیاں پھر جانا pūt'liyāṅ phir' jā'nā V.I. (of eyes) turn at the approach of death ; be on the verge or point of death

پتنگ patang' N.M. flying kite ; kite پتنگ اڑانا patang' ūṛā'nā V.I. fly a kite ; پتنگ باز patang'-bāz N.M. kite-flier پتنگ بازی patang'-ba'zī PH. of kite-flying پتنگ کٹ جانا patang' kaṭ' jā'nā V.I. (of kite) have its string snapped and drift away

پتنگا patan'gā N M. moth (rare) spark پتنگے لگنا patan'ge lag'nā V.I. (fig.) be incensed ; be annoyed

پتوار patvār' N.M. rudder helm

پتہ pa'tah N M. address whereabouts clue sign , symptom پتہ بتانا patah batā'nā, پتہ دینا pa'tah de'nā V.T. give one's address give a clue direct پتہ لگانا pa'tah lagā'nā V.T. locate ; trace search out , out discover get a clue پتہ لگنا pa'tah lag'nā, پتہ چلنا pa'tah chal'nā, پتہ ملنا patah mil'nā V.I. know be known پتے کی کہنا pa'te kī kaih'nā V.I. expose (someone) tell the truth (about (something) make a point مجھے پتہ نہیں mū'jhe pa'tah nahīṅ PH. I do not know who knows پتہ ہونا patah ho'nā V I. know be known پتے کی بات pa'te kī bāt N.F. fact of the matter the truth the point

پتہ pat'tah پتا pat'ta N.M. leaf card (in game of cards) an ear ornament پتہ پتہ pat'ta pat'tah N.M. every leaf پتہ توڑ کر بھاگنا pat'tah toṛ' kar bhāg'nā V.I run away make oneself scarce پتہ کاٹنا pat'tah kāṭ'nā V.I. sack destine death پتہ کھڑکا بندہ سرکا pat'tah khaṛ'kā ban'dah sar'kā PH. (used of a cowardly person) flitting at the stirring of a leaf پتوں والی pat'toṅ valī N.F. (W. dial.) radish

پتہ pit'tah N.M. gall bladder anger ; pasion guts پتہ مارنا pit'tah mār'nā V.I. work hard control one's passion پتہ مرنا *pit'tah mar'nā* V.I. be appeased پتہ پانی ہونا *pit'tah pā'nī ho'nā* V.I. have the blue funks be appeased have no aspirations

پتھر *pat'thar* N.M. stone anything hard ADJ. hard heavy inflexible difficult callous cruel hailstone پتھر برسنا *pat'thar ba'ras'nā* V.I. hail پتھر بن جانا *pat'thar ban jā'nā* V.I. pertrify become as hard as stone grow callous پتھر پانی ہونا *pat'thar pā'nī ho'nā* V.I. (of stone) melt (of tyrant) give way to compassion پتھر پڑنا *pat thar par'nā* V.T. & I. hail be cursed پتھر (پھینک) مارنا *pat'thar (phenk') mār'nā* V.I. (fig.) give curt reply say (something) rashly پتھر تلے سے ہاتھ نکلنا *pat'thar ta'le se hāth ni'kalnā* V.I. get rid of trouble or tyrant پتھر تلے کا ہاتھ *pat'thar ta'le ka hā'th* PH. straitened circumstances پتھر چاٹنا *pat'thar chāt'nā* V.I. be sharpened on whetstone پتھر چھاتی پر رکھنا *pat'thar chhā'tī par rakh'nā* V.I. be patient ; suffer without grouse پتھر ڈھونا *pat'thar dho'nā* V.T. & I. carrry stones work hard پتھر سے سر مارنا (یا پھوڑنا) *pat'thar se sir' mār'nā* (or *phor'nā*) PH. try to drive something home to unreceptive person پتھر کا چھاپا *pat'thar kā chhapa* N.M. lighography lithograph پتھر کی لکیر *pat'thar kī lakīr'* ADJ. unchangeable ; unalterable inexorable پتھر مارنا (یا پھینکنا یا برسانا) *pat'thar mār'nā* (or *phenk'nā* or *barsā'nā*) V.T. pelt stones ; aim stone(s) at پتھر کو موم کرنا *pat'thar ko mom' kar'nā* V.T. persuade cruel person to show mercy

پتھرانا *pathrā'nā* V.I. (of eyes) become glassy become blind be petrified پتھراؤ *pathrā''o* N.M. stoning ; lapidation پتھراؤ کرنا *pathrā''o kar'nā* V.I. pelt stones ; lapidate throw brickbats پتھری *path'rī* N.F. stone in the bladder ; calculus grit پتھریلا *pathrī'lā* ADJ. (F. پتھریلی *pathrī'lī*) stony rocky gritty

پتھیر *pather'* N.M. place for moulding bricks پتھیرا *pathe'rā* N.M. brick-moulder

پتی *pa'tī* N.M. (dial.) husband پتنی *pat'nī* N.F. (dial.) wife

پتی *pat'tī* N.F. petal small leaf thin metal plate hemp leaves share ; portion پتی دار *pat'tī-dār* N.M. shareholder

پتیانا *patyā'nā* V.T. care (for)

پتیلا *patī'lā* N.M. large saucepan ; small cauldron پتیلی *patī'lī* N.F. saucepan

پٹ *paṭ* N.M. (of door) flap ; leaf ; valve fold single width (of cloth) screen a kind of coarse cloth sound of falling or beating ADJ. prone ; prostrate upside down ; overturned ADV. pat ; promptly پٹ بند کرنا *paṭ band' kar'nā*, پٹ بھیڑنا *paṭ bher'nā* V. close the door ; shut the door پٹ کھولنا *paṭ khol'nā* V. open the door unveil uncover open

پٹا *paṭā*, پٹہ *pa'ṭah* N.M. cudgel-play foil wooden scimitar cudgel پٹا ہلانا *pa'ṭā hilā'nā* پٹا بازی N.M. *pa'ṭa bā'zī* N.F. clubbing ; false fencing پٹے باز *pa'ṭe-bāz*, پٹہ باز *pa'ṭa-bāz*, پٹیت *paṭait* N.M. cudgel player ; club-man

پٹا پٹ *paṭā'-paṭ* ADV. constant tapping sound (of raindrops, falling fruits, beating, etc.)

پٹاخا *paṭā'kha* N.M. cracker ; squib frolicsome beloved

پٹارا *piṭā'rā* N.M. (wicker-work or palm-leaf) basket پٹاری *piṭā'rī* N.F. betel-basket clothes basket basket (of juggler or snake charmer)

پٹاخ *paṭākh* N.M. sharp report ; burst pat thump

پٹاک *paṭāk'* N.F. sound of falling fruit

پٹخنا *pa'ṭakhnā* V.T. (same as پٹکنا V.T. ★)

پٹخنی *pa'ṭkhanī* N.F. same as پٹکنی N.F. (see under V.T. ★)

پٹرول *paṭrol''* N.M. petrol [E]

پٹڑا *paṭra* N.M. washerman's plank harrow plank for bathing corpse low wooden seat damage پٹڑا کر دینا *paṭ'ra kar de'nā* V.T. damage ruin پٹڑا ہو جانا *paṭ'ra ho ja'nā* V.I. be damaged be ruined دھوبی پٹڑا *dho'bī-paṭ'ra* N.M. name of a wrestling trick دھوبی پٹڑا مارنا *dho'bī-paṭ'ra mār'nā* V.T. throw adversary supine over one's shoulders

پٹڑی *paṭ'rī* N.F. rail track path ; root thigh پٹڑی جمانا *paṭrī jamā'nā* V.I. sit firmly on horseback [~ PREC.]

پٹس *piṭ'ṭas* N.F. beating wailing پٹس پڑنا *pi'ṭas paṛ'nā* be beaten wail

پٹ سن *paṭ san*, سن *san* N.F. jute ; gold fibre

پٹکا *paṭ'kā* N.M. turban girdle mortar layer (between rows of bricks) پٹکا باندھنا *paṭ'ka bāndhnā* V. wear a turban pat a girdle (round the waist) gird up the loins ; resolve firmly prevent

پٹکنا *pa'ṭaknā*, پٹخنا *paṭakhnā*, پٹک (یا پٹخ) دینا *pa'ṭak* (or *pa'ṭakh*) *de'nā* dash against throw down violently crack burst پٹکنی *paṭkanī*, پٹخنی *paṭkhanī* پٹکی *paṭ'kī* پٹخی *paṭ'khī* N.F. throw sharp blow fall پٹکنی (یا پٹخنی) دینا *paṭ'kanī* (or *paṭ'khanī*) *de'nā* V.T. dash against on the ground with violence ; throw down violently پٹکنی (یا پٹخنی) کھانا *paṭ'kanī* (or *paṭ'khanī*) *khā'nā* V.I. be dashed against ; fall down with a thump

پٹکی *pūṭ'kī* N.F. destruction curse پٹکی پڑے *pūṭ'kī pa'ṛe* PH. ruin seize (it) ; may it come to naught

پٹم *pa'ṭam* ADJ. closed [~ پٹنا *paṭ'nā*] پٹن *paṭ'ṭan* N.M. ferry wharf

پٹنا *piṭ'nā* V.I. be beaten ; get a beating N.M. mallet ; wooden hammer used for pounding پٹو *piṭ'too* N.M. one who often gets beaten

پٹوانا *piṭvā'nā* V.T. cause to be beaten

پٹنا *paṭ'nā* V.I. be roofed (of pits, etc.) be filled (of roof) be plastered (of land) be watered (of price) be settled (of account) be squared be in abundance پٹوانا *paṭvā'nā* V.T. get filled or plastered get roofed get (land) watered

پٹو *paṭ'too* N.M. a kind of coarse woollen cloth

پٹوا *paṭ'vā* N.M. braid maker

پٹواری *paṭvā'rī* N.M. lowest revenue official village registrar ; patwari پٹوار *paṭvār'* N.F. patwari's job

پٹہ *paṭ'tah*, پٹا *paṭ'ṭā* N.M. collar (for dog) girth (for house) lease lease deed (usu. PL.) locks (of bobbed hair) پٹا اتارنا *paṭ'ṭā ūtār'nā* V.T. unite (dog, etc.) sock پٹا تڑانا *paṭ'ṭā tuṛā'nā* V.T. break loose break the collar پٹے دار *paṭ'ṭe-dār* N.M. lessee ; lease-holder lessee

پٹھ *puṭh* N.F. animal's hip joint (as food)

پٹھا *puṭ'ṭhā* N.M. muscle tendon sinew young deciple (esp. of wrestler) young person پٹھے *paṭ'ṭhe* N.M. PL. bobbed hair

پٹھا *puṭ'ṭhā* N.M. rump buttock withers پٹھے پر ہاتھ نہ رکھنے دینا *puṭ'ṭhe par hāth na rakh'ne de'nā* PH. be restive ; be inaccessible (of one's withers) be unwrung

پٹھان *paṭhān'* N.M. (Pushtu speaking) people of former N.W.F.P. of Pakistan

پٹھو *piṭ'ṭhoo* N.M. stooge campfollower (old use) playmate (in children's game)

پٹھی *piṭhī* N.F washed pulse ground when still wet

پٹھیا *paṭh'yā* N.F. young hen young female buffalo young woman [~ پٹھا]

پٹی *paṭ'ṭī* N.F. bandage strip (of cloth) side of the bed (writing) tablet calligraphy lesson parted hair row ; line a kind of crisp sweetmeat coaxing ; cajoling reduction trickery tutoring (of witness) پٹی باندھنا *paṭ'ṭī bāndh'nā* V.T dress ; bandage blindfold پٹی پڑھانا ... پٹی دینا *paṭ'ṭī de'nā* V.T. deceive ; cheat پٹی پڑھانا *paṭ'ṭī paṛhā'nā* V.T. seduce counsel evil tutor (witness) پٹیاں جمانا *paṭ'ṭiyāṅ jamā'nā* V.T. comb hair down to the temples پٹی کرنا *paṭ'ṭī kar'nā* V.T. dress bandage

پٹیل *paṭel'* N.M. village headman

پٹیلنا *paṭīl'nā* V.T. cheat ; diddle ; swindle beat sell at fantastically low price

پٹیلوں *paṭī'lcoṅ* N.M. cry of partridge

پٹین *pūṭīn* N.F pudding putty [E]

پجاری *pūjā'rī* N.M. (dial.) Hindu priest devotee lover پجارن *pūjāran* N.F (dial.) Hindu priestess female devotee devoted woman [~ پوجنا]

پجنا *pūjnā* V.I. be worshipped ; be adored [of پوجنا]

پچ *pach* N.M. point of prestige partisanship defence PREF. (ABB. of پانچ five

پچ کرنا *pach kar'nā* V.T. support take the side (of) پچ آ پڑنا *pach'ā paṛ'nā* V.I. become a point of prestige call for defence

پچارا *pachā'rā* N.M. thin coarting of clay, lime, etc. wiping with wet cloth whitewashing brush

پچاس *pach'chās'*, *pachās* ADJ. & N.M. fifty پچاسواں *pach'chās'vāṅ*, *pachās'vāṅ* ADJ. fiftieth

پچاسی *pachchā'sī*, *pachā'sī* ADJ. eighty five پچاسیواں *pachchā'sīvāṅ* ADJ. eighty-fifth

پچانا *pachā'nā* V.T. digest ; assimilate keep secret پچاؤ *pachā''o* N.M. digestion , assimilation maintenance of secrecy (about)

پچانوے *pachchān've*, *pachān've* ADJ. & N.M. ninety-five پچانویں *pachchān'vevāṅ* ADJ. ninety-fifth

پچپچانا *pichpichā'nā* V.I. be clammy become damp be flaccid پچپچا *pich'pichā* ADJ. clammy damp ; moist flaccid

پچپن *pach'pan* ADJ. & N.M. fifty-five پچپنواں *pach'panvāṅ* ADJ. fifty-fifth

پچر *pach'char* N.F. piece stuffed in crevice wedge obstacle پچر اڑانا (یا لگانا یا ٹھونکنا) *pach'char aṛā'nā* (or *lagā'nā* or *thoṅk'nā*) V.T. insert a piece (in crevice) drive a wedge (in)

پچر مارنا *pach'char mār'nā* V.I. put up obstacles

پچرنگا *pach-raṅ'gā* ADJ. five-coloured multicoloured [پانچ + رنگ ~]

پچکارنا *pūchkār'nā* V.T caress kiss from a distance cajole appease call for fondling پچکا *puch'kā* پچکاری *puchkā'rī* N.F. caress kiss from a distance

پچکاری *pichkā'rī* N.F. syringe squirt douche injection inoculation enema پچکاری مارنا *pichkā'rī mār'nā* V. discharge liquid from a syringe, quirt, etc.

پنچ کلیان *pach-kalyāṅ'* ADJ. animal with white patches on hooves and forehead

hybrid low-caste ایرے غیرے پچکلیاں ai're ghai're pach-kalyāṅ N.M. PL. riff-raff ; scum of society
پچکنا pī'chaknā V.I. be squeezed ; be pressed together پچکانا pichkā'nā V.T. squeeze ; press
پچلڑی pach-la'ṛī ADJ. five-stringed (neclace etc.) [~ پانچ + لڑی]
پچ میل pach-mel' ADJ. assorted lowbred [~ پانچ + میل]
پچنا pachnā V.I. be digested ; be assimilated be kept secret بات پچنا bāt' pach'nā V.I. maintain secrecy about something
پچھاڑنا pichhāṛ'nā V.T. prostrate , throw down on the back defeat (in a wrestling bout) overcome پچھاڑ pichhāṛ' N.F. prostration defeat پچھاڑ(یں) کھانا pachhā'ṛ(eṅ) khā'nā V.I. be prostrated suffer reverses [~ پیچھا]
پچھاڑی pichhā'ṛī N.F rear rope for tying horse's hind legs heel ropes ADV. behind . in the rear پچھاڑی مارنا pichhā'ṛī mār'nā V.I. (of horse) kick with hind legs attack in the rear پچھاوا pichhā'vā N.M. hind part of brassiers [~ پیچھا]
پچھتانا pachhtā'nā, پچتانا pachtā'nā V.I. rue regret repent پچھتاوا، پچتاوا pachhtā'vā, pachtā'vā N.M. sorrow ; grief regret compunction
پچھتر pachhat'tar ADJ. & N.M. seventy-five پچھتروان pachhat'tarvāṅ ADJ. seventy-fifth
پچھڑنا pichhaṛ'nā, پچھڑ جانا pi'chhaṛ jā'nā V.I. fall down lag behind be overthrown (in wrestling bout) be defeated suffer a reverse [~ پیچھا]
پچھلا pichh'lā ADJ. (F. پچھلی pichhlī) latter last back hindmost late succeeding earlier preceding پچھلا پہر pichh'lā paih'r last quarter (of night, etc.) old age پچھلی رات pichh'lī rāt' N.F. early hours of the morning last night پچھلے پاؤں پھرنا (یا پھر آنا) pichh'le pā''oṅ phir'nā (or phir ā'nā) V.I. return immediately refrace one's steps immediately [~ پیچھا]
پچھل پائی pi'chhal pā''ī N.F. witch [~ پیچھا + پاؤں]
پچھم pach'chham (dial. chhim) N.M. west پچھمی pach'chhamī ADJ. west ; western پچھمی پاکستان pachchimi pā'kistān N.M. (dial.) West Pakistan پچھوا pachh'vā N.F. ★)
پچھنا pachh'nā N.M. scarification scarificator
پچھوا pachh'vā, (col. پچھوائی pachh'vā''ī) N.F. West wind (as being rain-bearing and useful for agriculture , Westerly
پچھواڑا pichhvā'ṛā N.M. backyard rear [~ پیچھا]
پچھوانا pūchhvā'nā V.T. making inquiries through [~ پوچھنا CAUS.]
پچھوت pichhoot' N.M. late crop back of a house ADJ. (rus.) last [~ پیچھا]
پچھوڑنا pichhoṛ'nā V.T. winnow پچھوڑ pichhor پچھوڑن pichho'ṛan N.F. chaff flying off during (or got from) winnowing , winnowing chaff [~ پیچھا]
پچھیت pichchhet N.F. back wall compound in rear of house [~ پیچھا]
پچی pach'chī ADJ. firmly joined firm crushed ; bruised پچی کاری pach'chī-kā'rī N.F mosaic work ; tessallation پچی کاری کا pach'chī-ka'rī kā ADJ. tessalate پچی کرنا pach'chī kar'na V T. join fix squeeze crush , bruise پچی ہونا pach'chī ho'nā V.I. be glued together be wedged (in) be jammed be squeezed be deeply attached (to)
پچیس pach'chīs ADJ. & N.M. twenty-five پچیسواں pachchīs'vāṅ ADJ. twentyfifth پچیسی pachchī'sī N.F. collection comprising twenty-five game of chance played with cowries
پچیت pichait' N M. & ADJ. veteran wrestler (wrestlers) expert in tricks of game
پچیتی pichaitī N.F. wrestling bout art of wrestling wrestling tricks
پخ pakh' N.F. hindrance condition objection dispute wrangle پخ کرنا pakh' kar'nā V.I. raise objection ; take a strong exception پخ لگانا pakh lagā'nā V.I. lay down the condition پخیا pakh'yā N.M. wrangler untakeable person
پخال pakhāl N.M. (same as پکھال N.M. ★)
پختری pūkh'tarī پخترڑی pūkhtaṛī N.F. fried bread bread pilfered by cook (usu. PL.) unearned daily bread [~ P پختن cook]
پخت وپز pūkh't-o pūz N.F. hatching (of plot, etc.) private discussion finalized arrangement [L ~ پختن cook]
پختہ pūkh'tah ADJ. mature (mind) firm (resolve) baked (bread) cooked (food) dressed (meat) standard (weight or measure) ripe strong solid پختہ کار pūkh'ta-kār' ADJ. experienced veteran پختہ کاری pūkh'ta-kā'rī N.F. experience solid workmanship پختہ کرنا pūkh'tah kar'nā V.I. rainforce make firm make definite پختہ ہونا pūkh'tah ho'nā V.I. be strong be firm

be definite پختگی *pukh'tagī* N.F. ripeness maturity development strength ; firmness [P]

پدا *piddā* N.M. brown robin

پدر *pi'dar* N.M. father پدر سوختہ *pi'dar-sokh'tah* ADJ. rogue ; scoundral ; blackguard پدر کشی *pi'dar kush'ī* N.F. patricide پدرم سلطان بود *pi'daram sultān' bood* PROV. brag ; boastful talk unsuccessful idler's boast about his noble ancestry پدرانہ *pidarā'nah* ADJ. fatherly ; paternal *pidari* ADJ. paternal patriarchal [P]

پدڑی *pid'rī* N.F. tomtit ; titmouse

پدم *pa'dam* ADJ. one thousand billion N.M. (dial.) lotus

پدمنی *pad'manī* N.F. paragon of feminine beauty and virtue exquisitely beautiful lady [S]

پدو *pad'doo* پدوڑا *padau'rā* N.M. one addicted to farting coward ; dastardly person

پدیدار *padidār'* ADJ. apparent ADV. in sight [P]

پڈنگ *pu'ding* N.F. pudding [E]

پذیر (or پزیر) *pazīr'* SUF. able ; ible susceptible to liable to endowed with admitting (of) taking پذیرائی (or پزیرائی) *pazīrā''ī* N.F. welcome reception ovation acceptance پذیری (or پزیری) *pazī'rī* SUF. capacity for acceptance of ability ; ibility [P]

پر *par* PREP. at on upon above at the point of by for through after CONJ. yet still ; but still how ever ; nevertheless but

پر *par* N.M. feather pinion ; wing پرافشاں *par'-afshāñ'* ADJ. fluttering the wings perturbed پرافشانی *par-afshā'nī* N.F. flutter پرباندھنا *par' bandh'nā* V.T. bind (bird's) wings render unable to fly or act پر پرزے نکالنا *par pūr'ze nikāl'nā* V.I. come up پر تولنا *par tol'nā* V.I. get ready to fly plan to run away پر پرزوں سے درست ہونا *par' pūr'zoñ se dūrūst' ho'nā* V.I. be fully equipped پر ٹوٹنا *par' ṭooṭ'nā*, پر جلنا *par' jal'nā* PH. not to have access (to) become powerless پر جھاڑنا *par' jhaṛ'nā*, پر گرانا *par' girā'na* V.I. moult; shed feathers پردار *par'-dār* ADJ. winged پرشکستہ *par'-shikas'tah* ADJ. disabled afflicted پرشکستگی *par' shikas'tagī* N.F. disability affliction پر قینچ کرنا *par' qaiñch kar'nā*, پر لینا *par' le'nā* V.T. pinion disable پر کا قلم *par' kā qa'lam* N.M. quill-pen پر کا کوا بنا دینا *par' ka kav'va banā' de'nā* PH. make a mountain out of a mole-hill پر کٹی اڑانا *par' kaṭī ūṛā'nā* PH. پر لگنا *par lag'nā* PL. be fledged come up become decorous پر نہ مارنا *par' na mār'nā* V.I. not to be able to approach پر نکالنا *par' nikāl'nā*, پر و بال نکالنا *par'-o bāl' nikāl'na* V. grow up be fledged grow new feathers

پر *pūr* ADJ. full of abounding in -ing -ous -ful پرپیچ *pūr-pech'* ADJ. intricate winding ; serpentine abstruse پرتکلف *pūr-takal'luf* ADJ. (of feast sumptuous formal ceremonious ; standing on ceremony پرخطر *pūr-kha'tar* ADJ. dagerous risky ; hazardous پردرد *pūr-dard'* ADJ. painful doleful ; dolorous tragic pathetic پرسوز *pūr-soz'* ADJ. pathetic tragic doleful ; dolerous پرفریب *pūr-fareb'* ADJ. treacherous fraudulent پرکینہ *pūr-kī'nah* ADJ. spiteful پرملال *pūr-malāl* ADJ. sad ; sorrowful پرنور *pūr-noor'* ADJ. luminous refulgent holy

پرا *pa'rā* N.M. rank ; file ; troops herd (of animals) swarm (of birds) wing (of army) پرے باندھنا (یا جمانا) *pa're bāndh'nā* (or *jamā'nā*) V.T. draw up in battle array

پراپیگنڈا *parā'pegan'ḍā* N.M. propaganda [E]

پرات *parāt'* N.F. flour-kneading basin

پراٹھا *parā'ṭha* N.M. fried bread ; pie-crust

پراسپیکٹس *praspaik'tus* N.M. prospectus [E]

پرارتھنا *parār'thanā* N.F. (dial.) prayer request [S]

پراکرت *parāk'rit* N.F. one of the ancient Sanskrit dialects

پراگندہ *paragan'dah* ADJ. dispersed scattered disturbed ; distracted پراگندگی *paragan'dagī* N.F. dispersion disturbance being dishevelled [P ~ پراگندن]

پرال *pūrāl'* (or *paral*) پرالی *pūrā'lī* (or *parā'lī*) N.M. paddy stems used as loose matting

پرامیسری نوٹ *parāmes'arī noṭ* N.M. promissory note ; IOU

پران *purān'* N.M. part of Hindu scriptures [S]

پران *parān'* N.M. (dial) soul [S]

پرانا *purā'nā* ADJ. (F. پرانی *purānī*) old ancient antiquated outdated outmoved worn out experienced . veteran پرانا گھاگ *purā'nā ghāg* ADJ. crafty old-timer پرانے لوگ *pūrā'ne log* N.M. elderly persons

.ancient people

پراویڈنٹ فنڈ *parāvidant fund* N M. provident fund [E]

پرائمری *parā'aimary* ADJ. primary [E]

پرائم منسٹر *parā''im minis'ṭar* N.M. Prime Minister [E]

پرائیویٹ *parā''ivaṭ* ADJ. private [E]

پرایا *parā'yā* ADJ. (F. پرائی *parā''ī*) not one's own another's N.M. person not related one stranger اپنے پرائے ،اپنا پرایا *ap'nā parā'yā*, *ap'ne parā''e* N.M. own and other people پرایا دھن *parā'yā dhan*, پرایا مال *parā'yā māl* N.M. other person's property (fig.) daughter(s) ; girls پرائی آگ میں پڑنا (یا کودنا) *parā''ī āg' meṅ paṛ'nā* (or *kood'nā*) PH. take a risk for others sake پرائے شگون کے لیے اپنی ناک کٹوانا *parā''e shūgoon' ke li'ye ap'nī nāk' kaṭ'vā'nā* PROV. cut off one's nose to spite one's face پرائے بس میں *parā''e bas meṅ* PH. under another's control

پربال *par-bāl'* N.F a depilatory eye-disease causing crooked hair to grow again on eyelashes

پربت *par'bat* N.M. (dial) mountain ; hill [S]

پربھو *para'bhoo* N.M. (dial.) God [S]

پرپرار *par' parār* ADV. year before last [~P پار]

پرپوتا *par-po'tā* N.M. paternal great-grandson پرپوتی *par'po'tī* N.F. great-grand-daughter [~S remote ; another+ پوتا]

پرتلا *par'talā* N.M. sword-belt cress-belt

پرتو *par'tau* N.M. reflection short view splendour influence پرتو پڑنا *par'tau paṛ'nā* V.I. come under the influence of [P]

پرتوا *par'tavā* N.M. (col. for پرتو N.M. ★)

پرجا *par'jā* (ped. *pra'jā*) N F. (dial.) subjects راجا پرجا *rā'jā par'jā* N.M. PL. the rulers and the ruled

پرچ *pir'ch* N.F. saucer, پرچ پیالی *pir'ch payā'lī* N.F. cup and saucer

پرچار *parchār'* N.M. (dial.) preaching propaganda propagation پرچار کرنا *parchār' kar'nā* V.T. (dial.) preach propagate publicize

پرچانا *parchā'nā* V.T. make (child, etc.) familiar with one appease (child) cajole ; coax console

پرچک *pūr'chak* N F. mild instigation support

پرچم *par'cham* N.M. flag banner ensign پرچم اڑانا (یا لہرانا یا بلند کرنا) *par'cham ūṛā'nā* (or *laihrā'nā* or *būland' kar'nā*) V.I. hoist a flag [P]

پرچنا *pa'rachnā* V.I be coaxed ; be cajoled be satisfied be consoled appeased become familiar (with)

پرچول *parchol'* N.F. scrutiny inquiry ; probe

پرچون *parchoon'* N.M. grocery retail پرچونیا *parchoo'niyā* N.M. grocer retailer

پرچہ *par'chah* N.M. question-paper answer book ; script scrap of paper slip ; chit periodical first information report (with police) ; F.I.R. پرچہ چاک کرنا *par'chah chāk' kar'nā* V.I. record a first information report ; prepare an F.I.R. پرچہ دینا *par'chah de'nā* V.T. answer question paper . distribute question-paper report to the police پرچہ سزا *par'cha-e sazā'* N.M. conviction slip پرچہ نویس *par'cha-navīs'* N.M. repoter report writer spy پرچہ نویسی *par'cha navī'sī* N.F. reporting espionage

پرچھا *par'chha* N.M. reel for winding thread ; reel

پرچھاواں *parchhā'vāṅ* N.M. influence possession or obsession by evil spirit (rare) shadow پرچھاواں پڑنا *parchhāṅ'vāṅ paṛ'nā* V. possession by evil spirit

پرچھائیں *parchhā''īṅ* N.F. shadow reflection پرچھائیں سے بھی بھاگنا *parchhā''īṅ se bhī bhāg'nā* PH. fly from the influence (of)

پرچھتی *parchhat'tī* N.F. subsidiary root thatch, etc. on leaky housetop

پرچی *par'chi* N.F. slip of paper ballot coupon [~ پرچہ]

پرخاش *pūrkhash'* N.F. quarrel conflict tiff wrangle پرخاش جو *pūrkhāsh'-joo* ADJ. quarrelsome [P]

پرخچے *parakh'che* N.M. PL. pieces ; bits پرخچے اڑانا *parach'che uṛa'nā* V. tear to pieces thrash ; give a good hiding

پرداد *par-dā'dā* N.M. (paternal) gerat-grand father پردادی *par-dā'dī* N.F. (paternal grea grandmother [~S remote ; another+ دادا]

پرداخت *pardakh't* N.F. care ; patronage accomplishment [P]

پرداز *pardaz'* SUF. -er ; -or initiator one who does or accomplishes something N.F. beginning adornment decoration پرداز کرنا (یا ڈالنا) *pardaz' kar'nā* (or *ḍalnā*) V.T. begin adorn پردازی *pardā'zī* SUF. doing beginning adorning decoration -ing [P ~ پرداختن]

پردہ *par'dah* N.M. veil going about veil women's stay indoors privacy curtain screen cover secrecy drum (of ear) pretext (11) key (of musical instrument) musical note پردہ اٹھانا *par'dah uṭhā'nā* V.T. lift or raise the curtain reveal ; expose raise the veil discard the veil ; go about barefaced پردہ پڑنا *pur'dah paṛ'nā* V.I. be covered ; be concealed عقل پر پردہ پڑنا *'aq'l par par'dah paṛ'nā* PH. lose commonsense پردہ پوش *par'da-posh'* N.M. & ADJ. veiled woman one who connives at the faults of others پردہ پوشی *par'da-po'shī* N.F. keeping a secret connivance پردہ چھوڑنا *par'dah chhoṛ'nā* V T. discard veil hang a curtain keep secret پردہ دار *par'da-dār'* N M. & ADJ veiled (woman) one who does not let out a secret پردہ داری *par'da-dā'rī* N.F being veiled ; going about in a veil keeping secret ; secretiveness پردہ در *par'da dar* N.M. & ADJ. betrayer of secrets (one) who rends veils پردہ دری *par'da-da'rī* N.F. betrayal of secrets rending the veil پردہ ڈالنا *par'dah ḍāl'nā* V.T. draw the curtain hang a curtain keep a secret connive at پردہ رکھنا *par'dah rakh'nā* V.T. hide things (from) conceal ; not to reveal ; not to give out پردہ رہ جانا *par'dah raih jā'nā* PH. not to be exposed پردہ غیب *par'da-e ghaib'* N.M. the invisible hand of Heaven the inscrutable ways of nature پردہ فاش کرنا *par'dah fāsh' kar'nā* V.T. expose betray پردہ کرنا *par'dah kar'nā* V.I. go about in a veil stay indoors not to come before hide oneself پردہ کرانا *par'dah karā'nā* V.T. cause to stay indoors cause to go about in a veil پردے بٹھانا *par'de biṭhā'na* V.T. cause growing up girl to take up the veil

پردھان *pardhān'* N M. (dial.) president chief or leader (esp. of any evil groups)

پردیس *pardes* N.M. foreign soil ; alien country پردیسی *parde'sī* N.M. foreigner ; stranger [پر far + دیس country]

پرزہ *pūr'zah* N.M. part (of machine) (PL.) works (of clock, etc.) scrap (of paper) bit piece پرزے اڑانا *pūr'ze uṛā'na* V.T. hack to piece tear to bits پرزہ پرزہ کرنا *pūr'za pūr'zah kar'nā* V.T. hack to pieces tear to bits پرزہ پرزہ ہونا *pūr'za pūr'zah ho'nā* V. be hacked to pieces be torn to bits (of machinery) have parts dispersed چلتا پرزہ *chal'ta pūr'zah* N.M. (same for F.) cunning person resourceful person [P]

پرس *par's* N.M. purse ; ladies' handbag [E]

پرس *pūr's* SUF. one who inquires پرسی *pūr'sī* SUF. inquiring ; inquiry [P ~ پرسیدن]

پرسا *pūr'sā* N.M. condolence visit for this purpose پرسا دینا *pūr'sa de'nā* V.I. condole call at (someone) to condole

پرسان *pūrsān'* N.M & SUF. one who inquires حال پرسان *ḥāl pūr'sān* (col. پرسان حال *pūrsa'n-e ḥāl'*) inquiring after someone's health ; solicitous about someone [P ~ پرستن]

پرست *parast'* SUF. worshipper devotee پرستی *paras'tī* SUF. worship devotion [P]

پرستار *parastār'* N.F. worshipper devotee پرستارزادہ *parastār'-za dah* N.M. son of a free father and a slave-girl پرستاری *parasta'rī* N.M. worship devotion service [P ~ PREC.]

پرستان *paristān'* N.M. fairyland wonderland [P ~ پری + ستان]

پرستش *paras'tish* N.F. worship devotion excessive love or greed (for) پرستش گاہ *paras'tish gah* N.F. place of worship [P ~ پرستن]

پرسش *pūr'sish* N.F. inquiry questioning chastisement [~ پرسیدن]

پرسوت کا بخار *parsoot' kā būkhār'* N.M. puerperal fever

پرسوں *par'soṅ* ADV. the day before yesterday the day after tomorrow

پرسیاوشان *parsiyā''oshāṅ* N.M. name of a medicinal herb ; 'pteris lamulata' ; maidenhair

پرکار *parkār'* N.M. compasses ; pair of compasses

پرکار *pūrkar'* ADJ. clever پرکاری *pūrka'rī* N.F. cleverness [P ~ پر + کار]

پرکالہ *parkā'lah* N.M. spark *parkā'-la-e ā'tash* N.M. (usu. fig.) spark آفت کا پرکالہ *ā'fat ka parkā'lah* ADJ. very clever naughty [P]

پرکھ *pa'rakh* N.F. test scrutiny جانچ پرکھ *jāṅch' pa'rakh* N.F. scrutiny test پرکھنا *pa'rakh'na* V.T. try test scrutinize

پرکے *par'ke* ADV. last year [~ پار P]

پرگنہ *par'ganah* N.M. (old adminstrative) subdivision ; tehsil پرگنہ دار *par'ganadār'* N.M. chief executive of 'par'ganah'

پرلا *par'la* (col. *pal'lā*) ADJ (F پرلی *par'lī* col. *pal'lī*) next oppsite distant of the other side ADV. on the other side for beyond ; for away ; a long way off ; in the distance next door opposite پرلے درجے کا *par'le dar'je ka*, پرلے سرے کا *par'le si're ka* ADV. extremely excessively ; exceedingly thoroughly ; utterly ADJ. arrant egregious extreme پرلی طرف *par'li ta'raf* ADV. on the other side next opposite

پرلوک *parlok'* N.M. (dial.) the next world پرلوک سدھارنا *parlok' sidhar'na* V.I. (dial.) die [S]

پرماتما *parmat'ma* N.M. (dial.) (Hindu name for) God (as the supreme spirit)

پرمٹ *par'mit* N.M. permit [E]

پرمل *par'mal* N.M. (name of) a low-quality rice parched rice, barley, maize, etc.

پرمیشور *parmesh'var* N.M. (dial.) (Hindu name for) God (as chief god) [S]

پرنالہ *parna'lah* N.M. gargoyle drain ; drain-pipe conduit; drain پرنالی *parna'li* N.F. small drain; small drainpipe

پرنانا *par-na'na* N.M. maternal great-grandfather پرنانی *par-na'ni* N.F. maternal great-grandmother [~ S پر remote ; another + نانا]

پرنٹر *parin'tar* N.M. printer [E]

پرند *parand'* N.F. fine quality printed silk

پرندہ *parin'dah* (rare lit. پرند *parind*) N.M. bird پرندہ پر نہیں مار سکتا *parin'dah par na'hin mar sak'ta* PH. none dare approach

پرنسپل *parin'sipal* N.M. (or F.) Principal Principle [E]

پرنیاں *par'niyan* N.M. a kind of fine painted Chinese silk dress made of it [P]

پروا *parva'* N.F. care concern ; solicitude worry ; anxiety ; fear inclination ; affection want ; desire

پروا *pur'va* N.F. east wind (as foreboding rain) ; easterly breeze [~ پورب]

پرواز *parvaz'* N.F. flight SUF. flying soaring پروازی *parva'zi* SUF. flying soaring [P]

پروان چڑھنا *parvan' charh'na* V.I. (of child) grow up thrive ; prosper (of hope) be realised become perfect پروان چڑھانا *parvan' charha'na* V.T. cause to grow up make prosperous make perfect cause to be achieved

پروانہ *parva'nah* N.M. moth (fig.) lover ; self-immolating love pass permit licence command warrant پروانۂ تلاشی *parva'na-e tala'shi* N.M. search warrant پروانۂ راہداری *parva'na-e rah-da'ri* N.M. pass permit safe conduct ; passport پروانۂ گرفتاری *parva'na-e girifta'ri* N.M. warant of arrest پروانہ وار فدا ہونا *parva'nah var fida ho'na*, پروانہ ہونا *parva'nah ho'na* V.I. be an ardent lover پروانجات *parva'najat* N.M. PL. passes permits پروانگی *parva'nagi* N.F. (rare) permission [P]

پروایا *parva'ya* N.M. piece of wood, brick, etc. placed under bed to raise it

پروتا *parota* N.M. food gift to menials at ceremonies

پروٹسٹنٹ *parautastant* N.M. Protestant [E]

پرور *par'var* SUF. nourisher ; cherisher ; protector پروری *par'vari* SUF. nourishing protecting بندہ پرور *ban'da par'var* my lord (iron.) patron بندہ پروری *banda'par'vari* N.F. patronage [P ~ پروردن]

پروردگار *parvardigar'* N.M. providence ; cherisher (as epithet of God) [P ~ پروردن]

پروردہ *parvar'dah* N.M. domestic servant brought up in master's house from infancy slave ADJ. reared brought up nourished patronized [P پروردن]

پرورش *par'varish* N.F. nourishment sustenance protection patronage rearing ; fostering upbringing پرورش پانا *par'varish pa'na* V.I. be brought up be fostered ; be nourished پرورش کرنا *par'varish kar'na* V.I. bring up ; rear nourish ; foster support patronise [P ~ پروردن]

پروفیسر *parofai'sar* N.M. Professor پروفیسری *parofai'sari* N.F. professorship [E]

پروگرام *parogaram'* N.M. programme [E]

پرونا *piro'na* V.T. thread (needle) pass (thread through eye of needle) string (pearls, flowers, etc.) prepare (garland)

پرونوٹ *paronot'* N.M. promissory note ; IOU [E]

پروہت *paro'hit* N.M. (dial.) family priest [S]

پروین *parvin'* (lit. also پرویں *par'vin*) N.M. Pleiades ; Pleiads a female Muslim name [P]

پرہیز *parhez'* N.M. prevention forbearance abstinence temperance abstention keeping aloof evasion regimen پرہیز سب سے اچھا نسخہ ہے *parhez' sab se achha nus'khah hai* PROV. prevention is better than cure پرہیز کرنا *parhez' kar'nā* V.T. abstain (from) avoid keep aloof (from) be on guard (against) be under regimen پرہیزی *parhe'zī* ADJ. (of food) etc. prescribed for one under regimen پرہیزی کھانا *parhe'zī khā'nā* N.M. diet prescribed for one under regimen [P]

پری *pa'rī* N.F. fairy ; peri graceful lady ; exquisitely beautiful woman ; beauty PREF. fairy angelic پری پیکر *pa'rī-pai'kar*, پری چہرہ *pa'rī-cheh'rah*, پری رخسار *pa'rī-rukh'sār'* پری رو *pa'rī-roo* N.M. & ADJ. fairy-faced angelic (beauty) very graceful (woman) پری زاد *pa'rī-zād* N.M. & ADJ. exquisitely beautiful (woman) fairy-born superhuman پری کا سایہ ہونا *pa'ri kā sā'yah ho'nā* V.I. be possessed by a fairy پری وش *pa'rī-vash* N.M. & ADJ. fairylike very graceful (person) lovely (woman) پری شیشے میں اتارنا *pa'rī shī'she meṅ ūtār'nā* PH. coax, cajole or wheedle the beloved پریوں کا اکھاڑہ *par'yoṅ kā akhā'ṛā* N.M. assembly of beauties [P]

پرے N.M. (PL. of پرا N.M. ★)

پرے ² *pa're* ADV. away on the other side further off at a distance beyond yonder پرے پرے *pa're pa're*, پرے رہنا *pa're raih'nā* V.I. keep away not to keep aloof پرے پرے رہنا *pa're pa're raih'nā* V.I. not to mix with others ; not to be a sociable type

پریت *parīt'* N.F. (dial.) love beloved پریتم *parī'tam* N.M. (dial.) love beloved [S]

پریت *paret'* N.M. evil spirit (usu. as) بھوت پریت *bhoot' pa'ret* N.M. ghost and evil spirit

پریدہ *parī'dah* AFFIX. flown پریدگی *parī'dagī* AFFIX. flying away ; flitting [P]

پریڈ *pareḍ* (col. *pareṭ'*) N.F. parade [E]

پریزیڈنٹ *pare'zīḍanṭ* N.M. President [E]

پریس *pares'* N.M. press the Press [E]

پریشان *pireshān''* (lit. also پریشاں *pire'shān*) ADJ. perplexed ; confused disturbed troubled (in mind) dishevelled (hair) embarrassed distracted ; deranged miserable dispersed loose (leaves] harassed پریشاں حال *pire'shān-hāl* ADJ. embarrassed miserable پریشاں خاطر *pire'shān-khā'tir*, پریشان دل *pire'shān-dil* trouble in mind پریشان کرنا *pire'shān kar'nā* V.T. embarrass hare confuse ; perple perturb dishevel (hair) scalter cast to the winds پریشاں گوئی *pire'shān-go''ī* N.F. confused talk پریشاں نظر *pire'shān-na'zar* ADJ. & N.M. purposeless distracted پریشاں نظری *pire'shān-na'zarī* N.F. lack of purpose distraction پریشان ہونا *pireshān' ho'nā* V. be perplexed ; be confused distressed feel embarrassed پریشانی *piresha'nī* N.F. perplexity confusion embarrassment perturbation misery scattering

پریم *parem'* N.M. (dial.) love پریمی *pare'mī* N.M. lover [S]

پریوی کونسل *parī'vī kauṅ'sal* N.F. final British court of appeal [E]

پڑا *pa'ṛa* ADJ. prostrate پڑا پانا *pa'ṛa pa'nā* V.I. find (something) lying find (it on high-way, etc.) get for nothing پڑا پڑ *pa'ṛa paṛ'* ADV. (beat) with incessant strokes پڑا رہنا *pa'ṛa raih'nā* V.I. remain unused be idly all along [~ پڑنا]

پڑا *pū'ṛā* N.F. large packet ; parcel ; package

پڑاؤ *paṛā''o* N.M. camping ground encampment camp halting-place ; halt پڑاؤ ڈالنا *paṛā''o ḍāl'nā* V.I. encamp [~ پڑنا]

پڑتا *paṛ'ta* N.M. share ; portion dividend contribution revenue rate [~ پڑنا]

پڑتال *paṛtāl* N.F. scrutiny checking ; check audit re-appraisal جانچ پڑتال *jāṅch' paṛtāl'* N.F. scrutiny پڑتال کرنا *paṛtāl' kar'nā* V.T. scrutinize check audit reappraise

پڑنا *paṛ'nā* V. lie down rest ; repose fall ; drop down befall hang about (or around) concern ; worry پڑ جانا *paṛ jā'nā* V.I. lie down ; fall flat پڑے پڑے *pa're pa'ṛe* ADV. while lying down while in bed idly اسے کیا پڑی ہے *ū'se kyā pa'ṛī hai* PH. why should (he, etc.) ?

پڑوس *paṛos'* N.M. neighbourhood vicinity پڑوسی *paṛo'sī* N.M. neighbour پڑوسن *paṛo'san* N.F. female nighbour

پڑھن *pa'ṛhin* N.F. mullet

پڑھنا *paṛh'nā* V.T. & I. learn to read read decipher repeat recite پڑھا لکھا *paṛh'ā lik'khā*, ADJ. (F. پڑھی لکھی *paṛ'hī lik'khī*) educated learned literate پڑھا پڑا جن *paṛ'hā hū''ā jin* PH. intractable person پڑھے نہ لکھے نام محمد فاضل *pa'ṛhe nā lik'khe nām moham'mad fā'zil* PROV. brag of knowledge without education پڑھیں فارسی بیچیں تیل *paṛ'hen fār'sī be'chen tel'* PROV. educated but unfortunate پڑھانا *paṛhā'nā* V.T. make literate teach instruct teach (bird) to talk tutor (witness) mislead incite پڑھائی *parkā''ī* N.F. literacy education teaching tuition پڑھنت *parhant'* N.F. charm ; magical incantation پڑھوانا *pārkvā'na* V.T. cause to be read have (something) read out get educated

پڑیا *pūr'yā* N.F. small packet does of medicine ; powder [~ پڑا *pūṛā*]

پزاوہ *pazā'vah* N.M. kiln [P]

پزشک *pizish'k* N.M. (rare) doctor [P]

پژمردہ *pazhmūr'dah* ADJ. dejected blighted pallid withered decayed bleak پژمردگی *pazhmūr'dagī* N.F. dejection blight pallor being withered decay bleakness [P]

پس *pas* CONJ. then therefore so hence ADV. after behind پس انداز کرنا *pas-andāz' kar'nā* N.M. save by and by پسپا *pas-pā'* ADJ. driven back ; repulsed پسپا کرنا *pas-pā' kar'nā* V.T. drive back rout; repulse پسپا ہونا *pas-pā' ho'nā* V.I. retreat be routed پس پشت *pa's-e pūsh't* ADV. behind one's back in one's absence پس پشت ڈالنا *pa's-e pūsh't ḍāl'nā* V. postpone ; put off neglect ; ignore پس خوردہ *pas-khūr'dah* N.M. food left over on the table crumbs پسماندہ *pas-mān'dah* ADJ. backward remaining behind surplus survivor پسماندگان *pas-mān'dagān'* N.M. PL. survivors پس منظر *pas-man'zar* N.M. background پس وپیش *pas-o pesh'* N.M. hesitation ; reluctance indecision ; doubt shilly-shallying vacillation پس وپیش کرنا *pas-o pesh' kar'nā* V.I. hesitate ; show reluctance shilly-shally vacillate [P]

پسارنا *pasār'nā* V.T. stretch spread extend display پسارا *pasā'ra* N.M. spread extension (mangoes, etc.) spread out

پسانا *pisā'nā*, پسوانا *pisvā'nā* V.T. cause to grind [~ پیسنا CAUS.]

پسانا *pasā'nā* V.T. pour off water in which (rice, etc,) has been boiled پساؤ *pasā''o* water in which something has been boiled

پسائی *pisā''ī*, پسوائی *pisvā''ī* N.F. remuneration for grinding [~ پیسنا]

پست *past* ADJ. low mean vile inferior lowbrow پست خیال *pas't-khayāl'* ADJ. having low ideas N.M. low idea پست فطرت *pas't-fit'rat* ADJ. base ; mean N.F. vile nature پست قامت *pas't-qā'mat* پست قد *past qad'* ADJ. of small size dwarfish N.M. dwarf short stature پست کرنا *pas't kar'na* V.T. lower پست بلند *pas't-o būland'* N.M. ups and downs , vicissitudes پست ہمت *pas t-him'mat* ADJ. spiritless unambitious cowardly N.F. low spirits پست ہمتی *pas't-him'matī* N.F. low spirits cowardice پست ہونا *pas't ho'nā* V.I. be low be short statured be humiliated duck پستی *pas'tī* N.F. lowness inferiority humility lowland [P]

پستان *pistān'* N.M. pap ; teat ; nipple ; breasts

پستول *pistaul'* N.M. pistol revolver [E]

پستہ *pis'tah* N.M. pistachio nut پستئی *pistai''ī* ADJ. pea-green (colour) [P]

پسر *pi'sar* N.M. son boy پسر نوح *pi'sar-e nooh'* PH. (Noah's son as example of) vicious progeny of the virtuous [P]

پسرنا *pa'sarnā* V.I. (of child) insist unduly or behave obstinately be spread out be distended

پسرہٹا *pasār hattā* N.M. grocery market [~ پنساری + ہاٹ]

پسلی *pas'lī* N.F. rib infantile tuberculosis پسلی پھڑکنا *pas'lī pha'raknā*, پسلی پھڑک اٹھنا *pas'lī pha'rak ūṭh'nā* PH. (quivering sensation in the ribs as) sign of absent friends impending visit know without physical communication be restless owing to beloved's absence پسلی کا درد (یا دکھ یا عارضہ) *pas'lī kā dard* (or *dūkh* or *'ārizah*) N.M. pleurisy پسلیاں توڑنا *pas'līyān tor'nā* V.T. give a good hiding (cause to laugh) to excess

پسنا *pis'nā* V.I. be ground be pulverized be crushed be ruined [~ پیسنا]

پسند *pasand'*, پسندیدگی *pasandī dagī* N.F. choice approval approbation liking discretion پسندیدہ *pasandī'dah* ADJ. choice ; chosen favourite approved desirable pleasing ; delectable [P]

پسندا *pasandā* N.M. slice of slashed meat such roasted slice as food [~ P PREC.]

پسنہاری *pi'sanhārī* N.F. corngrinder ; woman grinding corn. etc. for livelihood [~ پیسنا]

پسو *piss'oo* N.M. flea

★ پسوانا *pisvā'nā* V.T. same as پسانا *pisā'nā* V.T.

★ پسوائی *pisvā''ī* N.F. پسائی *pisā''ī* N.F.

پسوجنا *pasooj'nā* V.T. baste tack پسوج *pasooj'* N.F. basting

پسیجنا *pasīj'nā* V.I. show compassion (of heart) melt with pity become oversaturated owing to humidity (of limb-ends)

be wet with sweet

پسینہ **pasi'nah** N.M. sweat ; perspiration پسینہ پسینہ ہونا **pasi'nah pasi'nah ho'nā** V. be covered with sweat (owing to boil or heat) perspire profusely (owing to shame) پسینے میں ڈوبنا (یا نہا جانا) **pasi'ne meṅ ḍoob'na** (or **naha' jā'nā**) V.T. be drenched in sweat ; perspire profusely

پشت **push't** N.F. back backbone generation ancestry descent support prop پشت بہ پشت **push't ba push't** پشت در پشت **push't dar push't** ADV. generation after generation پشت پر رہنا (یا ہونا) **push't par raih'na** (or **ho'na**) V.I. back up ; support ; be at the back (of) پشت پناہ **push't-panāh'**, پشت و پناہ **push't-o panāh** N.F. patron support refuge ; ally پشت دکھانا **push't dikhana** V.I. flee set out on a journey پشت دینا **push't de'nā** V.T. flee ; turn tail back out پشتیبان **push'tī-bān** N.M. helper support پشتیبانی **pushtī-ba'nī** N.F. help support succor پشتینی **pushtī'nī** ADJ. hereditary [P]

پشتارہ **pushtā'rah** N.M. bundle load [~P پشت]

پشتک **push'tak** N.F. (horse's) kick with hind legs children's game in which one bends with palms resting on his knee and others jump over his back پشتک دینا **push'tak de'na** V.I. (of horse) kick with hind legs [~P پشت]

پشتو **pash'to** (dial. **push'to** or پختو **pakh'to**) N.F. the language of the 'Pathans'

پشتہ **push'tah** N.M. embankment ; 'bund' dyke dam buttress prop back of a binding پشتہ بندی **push'ta-bań'dī** N.F. embankment [P ~ پشت]

پشم **pashm** N.F. wool fur hairgrowth around private parts پشم پر مارنا **pash'm par mār'na** V.I. (indecent) care not a fig. بر پشم قلندر **bar pash'm-e qalań'dar** PH. (indecent) I do not care a fig for it پشمینہ **pashmī'nah** N.M. a kind of costly woollen cloth [P]

پشواز **pishvāz'** N.F. dancing girls' long gown with ample folds ; dancing dress [~P پیش]

پشہ **pash'shah** N.M. mosquito gnat [P]

پشی **pashī'** (mers.) N.M. urine INT. urinate

پشیمان **pishe'mān'**, پشیماں **pishemań'** ADJ. remorseful disgraced put to shame

پشیمانی **pishemā'nī** N.F. remorse shame lumility [P]

پطرس **pit'ras** N.M. Peter 'non-deplume' of a great Urdu humorist [L]

پکا **pak'kā** ADJ. (F. پکی **pak'kī**) ripe ; mellow (of meal) baked of (meat, etc.) cooked ; dressed (of bricks) burnt (of building) firm ; strong (of road) metalled (of colour) fast experienced shrewd ; cunning instructed ; tutored fearless resolute authentic valid sound true settled ; finalized permanent پکا پکایا ملنا **pak'kā pakā'yā mil'nā** PH. get without toil or trouble پکا پوڑھا **pak'kā poo'ṛhā** ADJ. (F. پکی پوڑھی **pak'kī poo'ṛhī**) settled ; finalized پکا پھوڑا **pak'kā pho'ṛā** N.M. suppurated boil person on the verge پکا پیسا **pak'kā pī'sā** ADJ. (F. پکی پیسی **pak'kī pī'sī**) shrewd well-tutored of bursting from anger or grievance پکا کرنا **pak'kā kar'na** V.T. reinforce ensure confirm corroborate ; attest پکا ہونا **pak'kā ho'nā** V.I. be confirmed be made permanent be reinforced be established be settled ; be finalized [~ پکنا]

پکارنا **pukār'nā** V.T. shout ; call ; cry ; bawl exclaim complain پکارے گلے **pukā're ga'le** ADV. loudly پکار **pukār'** N.F. complaint call cry shout bawl

پکانا **pakā'na** V.T. (of food) cook ; dress ; bake (of bricks) burn پکائی **pakā''ī**, **pakvā''ī** N.F. remuneration for cooking, etc.

پکٹنگ **pik'ṭing** N.F. picketing [E]

پکچر **pik'char** N.F. cinematograph film ; film picture [E]

پکڑنا **pa'karna**, پکڑ لینا **pa'kaṛ le'na** V.T. seize catch hold of handle overtake detect (error) pick holes in arrest ; apprehend catch ; capture پکڑ **pakaṛ** N.F. hold grasp grip ; clutch punishment پکڑنا **pakṛā'nā**, پکڑوانا **pakarvā'nā**, پکڑا دینا **pakṛā' de'nā** V.T. cause to be arrested make over ; hand over ; deliver پکڑ دھکڑ **pa'kaṛ dha'kaṛ** N.F. round-up (of bad characters, etc.) ; arrests پکڑ لانا **pa'kaṛ lā'nā** V.T. arrest fetch

پکنا **pak'nā** V.I. be cooked, dressed or baked ripen ; mellow (of hair) grey (of boil, etc.) suppurate become an expert پکوان **pakvān'** N.M. cookies fried foodstuffs prepared from gram-flour, etc. اونچی دکان پھیکا پکوان **ooń'chī dūkān' phī'ka pakvān'** PROV. great show without real worth پکوانا **pakvā'na** V.T. cause to cook or be cooked پکوائی **pakvā'ī**, پکائی **pakā''ī** N.F. remuneration for cooking

پکوڑا **pakau'ṛā** N.M. fried saltish gramflour paste; fried gram drop ; saltish pastry پکوڑا سی ناک

pakau'ṛā sī nāk N.F. thick large nose پکوڑی *pakau'ṛī* N.F. (usu. PL.) such small bits served in curds
پکھال *pakhāl'*, پکھال *pakhāl'* N.F. water-hide
پکھاوج *pakhā'vaj* N.M. a kind of drum ; timbrel پکھاوجی *pakhā'vajī* N.M. accompanist drummer
پکھراج *pūkhrāj'* N.M. topaz
پکھوا *pakh'vā* N.M. lap (of one's mother)
پکھیرو *pakhe'roo* N M bird پنکھ پکھیرو *pu... pakhe'roo* N.M. PL. winged creatures
پگ *pag* N.M. (rare) foot پگڈنڈی *pag-ḍan'ḍī* N F path ; footpath by path; pathway
پگانا *pugā'nā* V T & I. (cause to) end (game)
پگاہ *pagāh* N.F. dawn ; morning [P]
پگڑی *pag'ṛī* N.F. turban black-transaction gratification پگڑی اتارنا (یا اچھالنا) *pag'ṛī ūtār'nā* (or *ūchhāl'nā*) V.T. disgrace in public scandalize پگڑی باندھنا *pag'ṛī bāndh'na* V.T. & I. wear a turban tie a turban round (someone's) head in token of some qaalification, etc. پگڑی بندھنا *pag'ṛī bandh'nā* V.I be honoured thus N.M. investiture admission to a degree پگڑی بدلنا *pag'ṛī ba'dalnā* V.T. interchange turbans (in token of intimacy) پگڑی پیروں پر رکھنا *pag'ṛī pai'roṅ par rakh'nā* V.T. place one's turban at another's feet for apology پگڑی سنبھالنا (یا تھامنا) *pag'ṛī sanbhāl'nā* (or *thām'nā*) PH. try to maintain one's honour پگڑی والا *pag'ṛī vā'la* N.M. turbaned person (arch.) doctor لال پگڑی والا *lāl pag'ṛī vā'lā* N.M. policeman
پگلا *pag'lā* ADJ. & N.M. (F. پگلی *pag'lī*) silly (person) ; fool mad
پگھلنا *pighal'nā* V.I. melt be smelted fuse dissolve softed be mollified
پگھلانا *pighlā'nā* V.T. melt smelt fuse dissolve soften پگھلاؤ *pighlā'o* N.M. melting
پگیا *pag'yā* N.F. (dim.) small turban [~ پگڑی]
پل *pal* N.M. (old use) time measure about a second moment پل بھر میں *pal' bhar meṅ* ADV in a moment ; in a jiffy پل کی پل *pal' kī pal* ADV for a while
پل *pul* N.M. bridge causeway ; causey پل باندھنا *pūl bāndh'nā* V.T. bridge thow a bridge across ; build a bridge across exaggerate (in praise) پل صراط *pul-sirāt'* N.F. extremely narrow bridge ; providing the only approach to paradise , paradise pathway
پالا *pa'lā* N.M. ladle پلی *pa'li* N.F. ★
پلا *pal'lā* N.M. pan , scale ; one side of balance border (of cloth) ; side leaf, shutter or fold (of food) distance help ; support (arch.) three-maund weight load carried on head or back پلا بھاری ہونا *pal'lā bhā'rī ho'nā* V.I. have greater chances of success have stronger allies be heavier پلا پاک ہونا *pal'lā pāk' ho'nā* V.I. be settled be rid of پلا پکڑنا *pal'lā pa'karnā* V.T. fall back on (for support, help. etc.) پلا چھڑانا *pal'lā chhūṛā'na* V.T. get rid of (of woman) get a divorce (from) پلے باندھنا *pal'le bāndh'na* V.T. not to forget , remember (derogatory) marry someone (to) give away in marriage پلے پڑنا *pal'le paṛ'nā* V.T. be allotted (to) be married (to) پلے کچھ نہ پڑنا *pal'le kuchh na paṛ'nā* V.I not to get the hang of ; fail to understand anything پلے کچھ ہونا *pal'le ho'nā* V.I. be wealthy پلے کچھ نہ ہونا *pal'le kuchh na ho'nā*, پلے ٹکا نہ ہونا *pal'le ṭa'kā na ho'nā* V.I. be poor ; be without means ; have no money پلے دار *pal'le-dār'* N.M. porter porter in grain market
پلا *pil'lā* N.M. pup ; puppy whelp حرامی پلا *harā'mī pil'lā* ADJ. bastard
پلا پلایا ، پلی پلائی *pa'lā palā'yā*, *pa'lī palā''ī* ADJ. (see under پلنا V I. ★)
پلاٹ *palāṭ'* N.M. plot [E]
پلاس[1] *palās'* N.M. pliers [E]
پلاس[2] *palās'* N.M. hessian jute matting
پلاس[3] *palās'* N.M. (tree called) 'butia frondesa پلاس پاپڑا *palās' pāp'ṛā* N.M its seeds (used as drug)
پلاسنا *palās'nā* V.T smooth edges (of shoes, etc.)
پلاسٹک *palās'ṭik* N.M. plastic [E]
پلانا *pilā'nā* V.T. cause to drink give a drink suckle take animal to water add (molten metal to) soak in , saturate with run (weapon) through speak (to someone) against پلائی *pilā''ī* N.F. wet-nurse . foster-mother suckling wages [~ پینا CAUS]
پلاؤ *pulā''o* (ped. *palā'o*) N.M. rice cooked in meat soup ; 'palau' [P]
پلپلا *pilpila* ADJ. (F. پلپلی *pilpilī*) flabby , flaccid weak , feeble soft پلپلانا *pilpila na*

v.i. soften پلپلاہٹ *pilpilā'hat* N F: flabbiness softness

pūlpūlā'nā v.t. chew without (using) teeth پلپلانا پلپلا *pūl'pūla* ADJ flabby ; flaccid soft

pal'ṭā N.M., پلٹانا *palṭā'nā* v.t. (see under پلٹنا v.i. ★)

پلٹا *pal'ṭā* N.M. reverse retreat turn stroke (of ill-luck) , vicissitude lucky stroke change retaliation ladle for turning pancakes, etc. پلٹا دینا *pal'ṭā de'nā* v.t. turn reverse hurl back upturn , tilt پلٹا کھانا *pal'ṭā khā'nā* v. tilt turn over turn upside down change (for the better or the worse) پلٹانا *palṭā'nā* v.t. turn over convert return پلٹا دینا *pal'ṭā de'nā* v.t. return give back پلٹا لینا *pal'ṭā le'nā* v.t. take back پلٹی *pal'ṭī* N.F. somersault پلٹیاں کھانا *pal'ṭiyāṅ khā'nā* v.i. whirl round [~ پلٹنا]

پلٹس *pūl'ṭas* N.F. poultice [E]

پلٹن *pal'ṭan* N.F. regiment [E ~ *platoon*]

پلٹنا *pa'laṭnā* v.t. & i. return retreat rebound suffer reverse turn over (of fortune) cause reverse

پلڑا *pal'rā* N.M. pan ; scale ; one side of balance پلڑا بھاری ہونا *pal'rā bhā'rī ho'nā* v.t. have the upper hand پلڑا برابر ہونا *pal'rā barā'bar ho'nā* (of scales) be even

پلستر *palas'tar* N.M. plaster [E]

پلک *pa'lak* N.F. (PL. پلکیں *pal'keṅ*) eyelash پلک پٹیا *pa'lak paṭ'yā* N.M. blink person پلک جھپکنا *pa'lak jha'paknā* v.t. wink blink پلک جھپکتے میں *pa'lak jha'pakte (meṅ)* ADV. in the twinkling of an eye ; in a moment in an instant , in a jiffy پلک سے پلک نہ لگنا *pa'lak se pa'lak nā lag'nā* v t. not to have a wink of sleep ; have a sleepless night پلکوں سے زمین جھاڑنا *pal'koṅ se zamīn' jhāṛ'nā* show great respect extend warm welcome serve with full devotion پلکوں سے نمک اٹھانا (یا چننا) *pal'koṅ se na'mak uṭhā'nā* (or *chun'nā*) v.i undertake arduous task

پلکا *pil'kā* N.M. mottled pigeon

پلنا *pil'nā*, پل پڑنا *pil' paṛ'nā* v.t. assalut ; attack rush press be trodden be bruised jostle ; push , press

پلنا *pal'nā* v.i be brought up be reared be nourished be bloated thrive ; prosper پلا پلایا *pa'lā palā'yā* ADJ (F. پلی پلائی *pa'lī palā''ī*) grown up carefully nurtured

پلندا *pūlan'dā* N.M. parcel ; package pile bundle

پلنگ *pa'lang* N.M. couch bedstead پلنگ پوش *pa lang-posh* N.M. bedspread coverlet; counterpane پلنگ توڑ *pa'lang-toṛ* N.M. idler one given to sleeping too long good-for-nothing fellow پلنگ نشین چور *pa'lang tīn' chor* N.M. Greater and Lesser Bear پلنگ کو لات مار کر کھڑا ہونا *pa'lang ko lāt' mār kar khā'ṛā ho'nā* v.i. recover after serious illness have a safe delivery پلنگڑی *pa'langṛī* N.F. cot

پلو *pal'loo* N.M. (of cloth) border , hem پلودار *pal'loo-dār'* ADJ. having an expensive border N.M. fringe-maker

پلوانا *pilvā'nā* v.t. cause to be crushed cause to serve (water, etc.) for drink

پلوٹھا *palo'ṭhā* پلوٹھی کا *palo'ṭhī kā* N.M & ADJ (same as پہلوٹا N.M. & ADJ. ★)

پلی *pa'lī* N.F. ladle for measuring out liquids from canister, drum, etc. پلی پلی جوڑنا *pa'lī pa'lī joṛ'nā* v.t. lay by gradually ; save little by little

پلیا *pūl'yā* N.F. small bridge culvert [~ پل DIM.]

پلیتا *palī'tā*, فلیتہ *falī'tā* N.M. wick ignited wick for fireworks (arch.) match (of gun) پلیتا چاٹ جانا *palī'tā chāṭ jā'nā* v.t. flash in pan پلیتا دینا *palī'tā de'nā* v.t. ignite (gun-powder, etc.) instigate

پلیتھن *pale'than* N.M. dry flour used for faciliating the rolling of bread پلیتھن نکالنا *pale'than nikāl'nā* PH. give a good hiding

پلیٹ فارم *paleṭ'fā'ram* N.M. dais platform platform ticket [E]

پلیڈر *palī'dar* N.M pleader ; lawyer ; counsel [E]

پمپ *pamp* N.M. pump [E]

پمفلٹ *pamf'laṭ* N.M. pamphlet [E]

پلید *palīd'* ADJ. unclean defiled , polluted evil spirit, etc. پلیدی *palī'dī* N.M. uncleanliness pollution [P]

پن[1] *pan*, پنا *pana* SUF (denoting the abstract quality) -ness -ity -hood

پن[2] *pan* PREF. (ABB. for پانی) water (ABB. for پانچ) five (ABB. for پان) betel-leaf

پن[3] *pin* N.F pin hairpin [E]

پن *pun* N.M. (dial.) charity ; alms [S]

پنا *pa'na* SUF. (same as پن SUF. ★)

پنا *pa'na* N.M. width ; breadth ; span [~P پہنا]

پنا *pan'na* N.M. emerald upper (of shoe) sheet (of metal) tinsel (gold or silver) leaf sweetened tamarind water

پنا *pinna* N.M. lump of oil-cake, etc. anything rolled into a ball ; roll real *panana* V.T. fondle (animal's) udders in preparation for milking

پناہ *panah'* N.F. protection refuge shelter asylum پناہ دینا *panah' de'na* V.T. protect harbour give shelter پناہ گاہ *panah'-gah* N.F. shelter asylum refuge پناہ گزین *panah'-guzin'* (or ~-*zin*) پناہ گیر *panah'-gir* N.M. refugee پناہ لینا *panah' le'na* V.T. seek protection take shelter ; take cover take refuge پناہ مانگنا *panah' mang'na* V.T. avoid ; shun seek riddance (from) seek protection (of) take refuge (with) [P]

پن بجلی *pan bij'li* N.F. hydroelectricity ; hydel power [بجلی + پانی]

پنبہ *pam'bah* N.M. (lit.) cotton پنبہ دانہ *pam'ba-da'nah* N.M. (ped.) cottonseed پنبہ دوز *pam'ba-doz* N.M. cotton carder پنبہ بگوش *pam'bah-ba-gosh'*, پنبہ در گوش *pam'ba-dar gosh'* ADJ. feigning deafness deaf پنبہ دہن *pam'ba-da'han* ADJ. (lit.) quiet ; taciturn [P]

پنپنا *pa'napna* V.T. flourish ; thrive ; prosper (of plant) take root ; grow recover revive gain in strength fatten

پنتھ *panth* N.M. (dial.) (esp. Sikh) relgious order path ایک پنتھ دو کاج *ek' panth do' kaj'* PROV. kill two with one stone پنتھی *pan'thi* N.M. (dial.) follower of (a religious leader or order) [S]

پنج *panj* ADJ. five (arch.) five-year-old (horse) (arch.) in cards or dice cinq ; cinque ; five پنجاب *panjab'* N.M. the Punjab (a former province of West Pakistan as the land of five rivers) پنجابی *panja'bi* N.M. inhabitant of the Panjab ; Punjabi N.F. Punjabi (language) ADJ. of or from the Punjab پنجالی *panja'li* N.F. five-pronged rake locking yoke (for a team of oxen) پنجتن *panj'-tan*, پنجتن پاک *panj'-tan pak'* N.M. the Holy Prophet, Hazrat Ali, Hazrat Fatimah, Imam Hasan and Imam Hussain (as the 'five holy persons' esp. revered by Shi'ites) پنج روزہ *panj-ro'zah* ADJ. of five days short-lived (as human life) نوبت پنج روزہ *nau'bat-e panj-ro'zah* N.F. short span of life short tenure of office, etc. پنج سالہ *panj-sa'lah* ADJ. five-year (plan, etc.) quinquennial ; five-yearly پنج شاخہ *panj shakh'ah* N.M. metallic hand with fingers ivory hand to scratch the back with five pronged chandelier پنجشنبہ *panj-sham'bah* N.M. Thursday پنجگانہ نماز *panj-ga'nah namaz'*, نماز پنجگانہ *nama'z-e panj-ga'nah* N.F. five daily prayers پنج عیب شرعی *panj 'aib shar'i* PH. same as پانچوں عیب شرعی PH. ★ پنج گوشہ *panj-go'shah* ADJ. pentangular five-cornered N.M. pentagon

پنجاہ *panjah'* ADJ. & N.M. (ped.) fifty

پنجر *pan jar* N.M. skeleton ribs انجر پنجر ڈھیلا ہونا *an'jar pan'jar dhi'la ho'na* V.I. be aching all over the body; owing to severe jolts پنجر ہونا *pan'jar ho'na* V.I. become very lean; be reduced to a skeleton

پنجرا *pinj'ra*, پنجرہ *pinj'rah* N.M. cage trap

پنجم *panjum* ADJ. & ADV. fifth(ly) N.F. fifth class (in school) پنجمیں *pan'jumin* ADV. fifthly [P ~ پنج]

پنجنی *pinj'ni* N.M. a bow used for cleaning and beating cotton

پنجہ *pan'jah* N.M. open hand (of one hand) all fingers (of one foot) all toes toe claw grasp ; clasp (in cards) five (of dice) cast of five impression of open hand rays پنجۂ آفتاب *pan'ja-e aftab'* N.M. (lit.) rays of the sun پنجۂ مریم *pan'ja-e mar'yam* N.M. a kind of fragrant grass پنجہ پھیرنا *pan'jah pher'na* V.T. twist (adversary's) hand by interlocking fingers پنجہ کرنا (یا لڑانا) *pan'jah kar'na* (or *lara'na*) V.T. interlock fingers (with someone) in a bid to twist his hand پنجہ کش *pan'ja-kash* N.M. instrument for exercising fingers in interlocking one practised in interlocking fingers پنجہ مارنا *pan'jah mar'na* V.T. pounce upon claw پنجوں کے بل چلنا *pan'jon ke bal chal'na* V.I. tiptoe ; walk on tiptoe پنجے جمانا (یا گاڑنا) *pan'je jama'na* (or *gar'na*) V.T. sit formly stabilize one's position claw پنجے جھاڑ کر پیچھے پڑ جانا *pan'je jhar' kar pi'chhe par' ja'na* PH. harass press hard take to task severely ; carpet

پنجیرا *panji'ra* N.M. tinman

پنجیری *panji'ri* N.F. sweet fried flour this with a total of five ingredien.

used as caudle

پنچ *pach* N.M. arbiter; member of 'panchayat' ADJ. (dial.) five پنچایت *pancha'yat* N.F. rural council; council of village elders (rural) court of arbitration (usu. comprising five members) پنچایت کرنا (یا جوڑنا) *pancha'yat kar'na* (or *jor'na*) V.T. convene the 'panchayat' پنچایت بیٹھنا *pancha'yat baith'na* V.I. (of such council) sit پنچایت نامہ *pancha'yat na'mah* N.M. award of such court of arbitration پنچ شیلا *panch shi'la* N.M. the so-called five principles of peace سرپنچ *sar-panch* N.M. Panchayat Chairman chief ringleader

پن چکی *panchak'ki* N.F. watermill [~ پانی + چکی]

پنچم *pan'cham* N.M. shrill musical note; soprano; treble [S ~ پنج]

پنچمی *pan'chami* N.F. fifth day of the lunar month [S ~ پنج]

پنچھالا *punchhala*, پنچھلا *punchh'la* N.M. tail of (paper) kite one who shadows another; one who dogs another's steps

پنچھی *pan'chhi* N.M. bird

پند *pand* N.F. advice; counsel پند و موعظت *pan'd-o mau''izat*, پند و نصیحت *pand-o nasi'hat* N.M. advice; counsel armonition

پندار *pindar'* N.M. pride; arrogance; conceit thinking

پندرہ *pand'rah* ADJ. & N.M. fifteen پندھواڑہ *pan'darhva'rah* N.M. fortnight پندرھواں *pandrhavan* ADJ. fifteenth

پنڈ *pind* N.M. body person (rare save in PH.) پنڈ چھڑانا *pind chhura'na* V.T. get rid of; escape avoid پنڈ چھوٹنا *pind chhoot'na* V.I. be rid of

پنڈا *pin'da* N.M. body; person (rare save in) پنڈا پھیکا ہونا *pind'da phi'ka ho'na* PH. feel feverish

پنڈال *pindal'* N.M. canopy under which meeting is held

پنڈت *pan'dit* N.M. one versed in Hindu religious lore Brahman teacher pandit

پنڈتائی *pandita''i* N.F. pundit's status پنڈتانی *pandta'ni* N.F. pundit's wife, etc. [S]

پنڈلی *pind'li* N.F. shin, calf پنڈلی کی نلی *pind'li ki na'li* N.F. shin bone

پنڈول *pindol'* N.F. fuller's earth

پنس *pi'nas* N.F. (same as پینس N.F. ★)

پنس *pains'* N.M. pence; penny [E]

پنساری *pansa'ri* N.M. (F. پنسارن *pansa'ran*) grocer پنسار ہٹا *pansar'hat'ta* N.M grocery market

پنساری

پنسال *pansal'* N.M. water-guage (in canals, etc.) level پنسال نویس *pansal'navis'* record-keeper of water flow [~ پانی]

پنسل *pin'sal* N.F. pencil [E]

پنسلین *pain'salin* N.M. penicillin [E]

پنسیری *panse'ri* N.F. five-seer weight [~ پانچ + سیر]

پنشن *pin'shan* N.F. pension پنشن پانا *pin'shan pa'na* V.I. retire on a pension پنشن یافتہ *pin'shan-yaf'tah* N.M. & ADJ. pensioner [~E]

پنکھ *pankh* N.M. feather; wing; pinion

پنکھا *pank'kha* N.M. fan پنکھا لگنا *pank'kha lag'na* V.I. (of fan) be installed پنکھا جھلنا *pank'kha jhal'na* V.T. move a fan; fan پنکھیا *pankh'ya* N.F. small fan N.M. a category of mendicants fanning everyone

پنکھڑی *pankh'ri* N.F. petal [~ پنکھ DIM.]

پنک *pi'nak* N.F. (same as N.F. پینک ★)

پنگوڑا *pingoo'ra* N.M. cradle

پنگھٹ *pan'-ghat* N.M. quay for drawing water community well [~ پانی + گھاٹ]

پننا *pin'na*, پینا *pin'na* V.T. card (cotton) carpet پنوانا *pinva'na* V.T. have (cotton) carded cause to be abused

پننا *pun'na* V.T. heap foul names on; slander

پنواڑی *panva'ri* N.M. betel-seller betel-leaf garden [~ پان]

پنہارا *panha'ra* N.M. (F. پنہاری *panha'ri*) water-carrier; person supplying water in non-leathern containers

پنہاں *pin'han* ADJ. hidden; concealed secret

پنہتر بگڑنا *punhat'tar bi'garna* V.I. be out of wits (owing to heat, etc.)

پنی *pan'ni* N.F. shining upper (of shoe) thatch tinsel brass leaf.

پنی *pin'ni* N.F. rice-flour roll as sweetmeat

پنیر **panīr'** N.M. cheese

پنیر **pan'yar** N.M. spaniel ; cocker-spaniel

پنیری **panī'rī** N.F. seeding ; a young flowering plant پنیری جمانا (یا لگانا) *panī'rī jamā'nā* (or *lagā'nā*) V.I. sow seedlings

پو **pau** N.F. dawn (in dice) ace پو بارہ (ہونا) *pau bā'rah (ho'nā)* N.F. (cast) the ace and the twelve in dice (fig.) (achieve) success پو پھٹنا *pau phaṭ'nā* V.I. dawn

پوا **pav'vā** N.M. quarter seer quarter bottle quarter [~ پاؤ]

پوائی **pavā''ī** N.F. single foot (of shoe, etc.)

پوپ **pop'** N.M. Pope [L]

پوپلا **pop'lā** ADJ. (F. پوپلی *poplī*) toothless soft-spoken

پوپنی **pop'nī** N.F. child's bugle

پوت **poot** N.M. son پوت کے پاؤں پالنے میں نظر آجاتے ہیں *poot' ke pā''oṅ pāl'ne meṅ na'zar ā jā'te haiṅ* PROV coming events cast their shadows before; child is the father of man

پوتا **po'tā** N.M. (paternal) grandson (see under پوتنا V.T. ★) پوتی *po'tī* N.F. (paternal) grand-daughter

پوتڑا **pot'ṛā** N.M. clout پوتڑوں کے امیر (یا رئیس) *pot'ṛoṅ ke amīr'* (or *ra'īs'*) N.M. born with a silver spoon in the mouth

پوتنا **pot'nā** V.T. plaster ; besmear پوتا *po'tā* N.M. whitewashing brush پوتا پھیرنا *po'tā pher'nā* V.T. whitewash

پوتھی **po'thī** N.F. clove (of garlic) (dial.) book

پوٹ **poṭ** N.F. inner margin bundle گناہوں کی پوٹ *gūnā'hoṅ kī poṭ'* PH. condemned sin ner ; reprobate

پوٹا **po'ṭā**, پوٹہ *po'ṭah* N.M. (of bird) crop ; craw gizzard stomatch ; capacity status fledgeling young child پوٹا تر ہونا *po'ṭā tar ho'nā* PH. (fig.) be fully satisfied be wealthy

پوٹلی **poṭ'lī** N.F. powder, etc. tied in cloth

پوجنا **pooj'nā** V.T. worship adore ; idolize پوجا *poo'jā* N.F. (dial.) worship پوجا پاٹ *poo'jā pāṭ* N.F. Hindu worship

پوچ' **poch** ADJ. nonsense ; absurd worthless ; trifling mean ; base ہیچ پوچ *hech'-poch'* N.M. silly stuff پوچ گو *poch'-go* ADJ. prater ; blabber writer producing worthless stuff silly versifier پوچ گوئی *poch'-go''ī* N.F. prating blabbing silly versification worthless stuff [P]

پوچ' **poch** ADJ. poached (egg) پوچ کرنا *poch kar'nā* V.T. poach (egg) [E]

پوچھنا **poochh'nā** V.T. ask question inquire interrogate inquire (after) honour value care for ; show solicitude for help invite پوچھ پاچھ *poochh' pāchh*, پوچھ تاچھ *poochh' tāchh*, پوچھ گچھ *poochh' gachh* N.F. interrogation inquiry

پود **pod** N.M. woof ; welf تار و پود *tā'r-o-pod'* N.F. warf and woof [P]

پود **paud** N.F. seedling sapling offspring igeneration نئی پود *na''ī paud* N.F. younger generaton ; new generation [~FOLL. DIM.]

پودا **pau'dā** N.M. sapling پودا لگانا *pau'dā lagā'nā* V.I. plant a sapling

پودنا **pod'nā**, پودنہ *pod'nah* N.M. a kind of very small yellowish bird hopping about in grass and building a dowed nest therein midget

پودینہ **poodī'nah** N.M. mint پودینے کا ست *poodī'ne kā sat* N.M. peppermint [P]

پوڈر **pau'ḍar** n.M. powder [E]

پور **por** N.F., پورا *po'rā* N.M., پوری *po'rī* N.F. phalange ; phalanx

پور **poor** N.M. rare son [P]

پورا **poo'rā** ADJ. (F. پوری *poo'rī*) full ; complete whole ; entire firm ripe skilled (in) sufficient (for) پورا اترنا *poo'rā ū'tarnā* V.I. come up to the mark succeed پورا پڑنا *poo'rā paṛ'nā* V.T. suffice پورا کرنا *poo'rā kar'nā* V.T. fulfil accomplish carry out fill complete reimburse indemnify پورا ہونا *poo'rā ho'nā* V.I. be fulfilled be accomplished suffice die come to an end be compensated پوری بات *poo'rī bāt* N.F. the whole matter full facts complete proposition پوری نہ پڑنا *poo'rī na paṛ'nā* PH. be unable to make the two ends meet be insufficient پورے دنوں سے ہونا *poo're di'noṅ se ho'nā* V.I. (of woman) be about to deliver

پورب **poo'rab** N.M. east orient پوربو *poor'bo* ADJ. (dial) east ; eastern پوربو پاکستان *poor'bo pā'kistān* N.M. East Pakistan پوربی *poor'bī* ADJ. eastern oriental N.F. eastern dialect of Urdu name of a musical mode timed for late afternoon پوربیا poor'biyā N.M. inhabitant of eastern U.P.

پورم پور poo'ram poor' ADJ. full brimful [~ پورا]

پورنماشی poo'rn-mā'shi N.F. (dial.) night of full moon [S]

پوری po'rī N.F. (see under پور por N.F. ★)

پوری poo'rī N.F. thin pan-cake

پوڑا poo'ṛā, (dial. پوا poo''ā) N.M. fried cookie

پوز[1] poz N.M. muzzle, mouth of horse پوزبند poz'-band N.M. muzzle

پوز[2] poz N.M. posture before camera ; pose [E]

پوزش po'zish N.F. apology پوزش پذیر po'zish-pazīr' ADJ. forgiving [P]

پوس poos N.M. tenth month Hindu calendar (corresponding to January-February)

پوست pos't N.M. crust ; shell skin rind bark poppy poppyhead used as drug پوست کن pos't-kan N.M. skinner ; flayer پوست post-kan'dah ADJ. full bring hidden facts to light ADV unreservedly پوست کھینچنا post khench'nā V.T. flay ; skin پوستی pos'tī N.M. poppyhead addict (fig.) indolent person

پوستین pos.tīn N.F. fur coat leathern coat پوستین دوز pos'tīn doz N.M. furrier maker of leathern garments [P ~ پوست]

پوسٹ آفس pos'ṭ-ā'fis N.M. post office پوسٹ ماسٹر posṭ-mās'ṭar N.M. post-master پوسٹ ماسٹر جنرل posṭ-mā:'ṭar jan'ral N.M Post-master General · P.M.G. پوسٹ مین posṭ-main N.M. postman [E]

پوسٹ مارٹم posṭ-mār'ṭam N.M post morten examination ; autopsy [E ~ L]

پوسنا pos nā (usu. as پالنا پوسنا pal'na pos'nā) V T bring up ; rear nourish , foster

پوش posh SUF. wearing covering [P]

پوشاک poshāk' N.F. clothes dress garments , attire livery accoutrement ; equipment پوشش po'shish N.F clothes dress garments , raiment livery accoutrement upholstery [P ~ پوشیدن]

پوشیدہ poshī'dah ADJ. secret hidden concealed covered underhand ulterior پوشیدگی poshī'dagi N.F secrecy concealment [P ~ پوشیدن]

پوش پوش posh posh', پوش posh پوس po'ıs INT (by donkey-drivers, etc) watch make room please [~ P]

پوکھر po khar N.M. pool name of a fencing or cudgeling trick

پول[1] pol N.M land measure equivalent to fifty yards ; pole Pole ; Polish national [E]

پول[2] pol N.M. hollowness (ڈھول کا) پول کھلنا (dhol kā) pol' khul'nā PH. (of hollowness) be exposed [~ FOLL.]

پولا po'lā ADJ. (F. پولی polī) hollow empty soft ; spongy

پولا poo'lā N.M. bottle of grass or hay پولے تلے گزران کرنا poo'le ta'le gūzrān kar'nā PH be miserably off

پولو po'lo N.F polo [E]

پولیٹیکل poli'ṭikal ADJ. political [E]

پولیس pū'lıs (or polīs') N.F. police پولیس چوکی polīs chau'kī N.F. police post [E]

پون paun, پونا pau nā ADJ. (F. پونی pau'nī) three-quarters N.M. quarter to one

پَوَن pa'van N.F. mild wind autumn wind winnowing wind

پونجی poon'jī N F. capital principal stock wealth wherewithal

پونچا paun'chā ADJ five-and-a half (times table)

پونچھ poonchh N.F. tail

پونچھنا ponchh'nā V.T wipe clean dust پونچھ پانچھ کے ponchh pānchh ke ADV. having wiped having cleaned having dusted

پونڈ paund N.M. pound ; £ pound ; lb [E]

پونڈا paun'dā N.M. thick variety of sugarcane

پونگا pongā N.M. any hollow tube phalange پونگی pon gī N.F. flute juggler's flute serpant-catcher's pipe

پونی poo'nī N.F cotton roll for spinning

پونیا po'nıyā ADJ. (of paper, cloth, etc.) of sub-standard size

پویہ po'yah ADJ. amble canter پویہ چلنا po yah chal'nā V.I amble canter [~ P پویاں]

پہ pa, pe CONJ. but ; yet , still PROP. on at [~ پر ABB.]

پھاپھا کٹنی phā'-phā kuṭ'nī N.F. hag procuress tale-bearer mischievous woman

پھاٹک phā'ṭak N M gate barrier

پہاڑ **pahar'** N.M. mountain range of mountains ADJ. (also پہاڑ سا **pahar sa**) huge difficult arduous burdensome tiring ; tiresome long and tedius terrible (پہاڑ ٹوٹنا (یا گرنا یا ٹوٹ پڑنا) **pahar' toot'na** (or **gir'na** or **toot par'na**) V.I. be overhelmed (with troubles) پہاڑ سی رات **pahar' si rat** PH. terribly long and tedious night (of separation, etc.) پہاڑ ڈھانا **pahar dha'na** PH. subject (to tyranny), پہاڑ سے ٹکر لینا **pahar' se tak'kar le'na** PH. be pitted against a strong adversary ; face heavy odds پہاڑ کاٹنا **pahar kat'na** V. do the impossible پہاڑ کا دامن **pahar' ka da'man**, دامن کوہ **da'man-e koh'** N.M. foot of the mountain پہاڑی **paha'ri** N.F hill hill-lock mount name of a musical mode hill-man ; mountaineer ADJ. hilly mountainous پہاڑی کوا **paha'ri kav'va** N.M. a jackdaw

پہاڑا **paha'ra** N.M. multiplication table پہاڑے یاد کرنا **paha're yad kar'na** V.I learn one's tables

پھاڑنا **phar'na** V.I. tear rend rip split cleave mangle پھاڑ کھانا **phar'khana** V.T. tear to pieces mangle gnaw

پھاگ **phag** N.M. (dial.) Hindu festival of 'Holi' coloured water thrown during it its revelry لنگوٹی میں پھاگ کھیلنا **lango'ti men phag' khel'na** PH. (derog.) be happy despite poverty

پھاگن **pha'gun** N.M. twelfth month of Hindu calendar (corresponding to February March)

پھال **phal** N.F., پھل **phal** N.M. ploughshare

پھانا **pha'na**, فانہ **fa'nah** wedge any bit driven into a crevice to fill it up

پھاندنا **phand'na** V.I. leap jump spring پھاند **phand** N.F. leap jump spring (پھاند لگانا (یا مارنا) **phand laga'na** (or **mar'na**) V.I. leap

پھاندی **phan'di** N.F. bundle of sugar-cane

پھانس **phans** N.F. splinter پھانس چبھ جانا **phans' chubh ja'na** V.I. have a splinter driven (into) [~ پھنسنا]

پھانسنا **phans'na** V. involve ensnare catch entrap

پھانسی **phan'si** N.F. hanging till death capital punishment strangulation execution noose look پھانسی پانا **phan'si pa'na**, پھانسی چڑھنا **phan'si charh'na**, پھانسی لگنا **phan'si lag'na** V.I mount the scaffold be hanged till death پھانسی دینا **phan'si de'na** V.T. hang till death execute پھانسی کی ٹکٹکی **phan'si ki tik'tiki** N.F crossbar for hanging noose [پھانسنا~]

پھانسی

پھانک **phank** N.F. (see under پھانکنا V.T. ★)

پھانکڑ **phan'kar**, پھانکڑا **phank'ra** ADJ. robust ; lusty bold

پھانکنا **phank'na** V. chuck (powder, etc.) into the mouth from the palm of the hand پھانک **phank** N.F. flake slice piece mouthful (of) پھانکی **phanki** N.F. mouthful (of) (rare) slice or flake (or fruit)

پھاوڑا **pha''ora** N.M. mattock shovel spade پھاوڑا سے دانت **pha''ora se dant'** N.M. very long teeth پھاوڑی **pha''ori** N.F. shovel dung-rake mendicant's crutch gymnastic staff (for 'dand')

پھاہا **pha'ha**, پھایا **pha'ya** N.M. pledget lint scented cotton flock پھاہا رکھنا **phaha rakh'na** V.T. put a pledget on soothe console

پھبتی **phab'ti** N.F. witty remark fun verbal carricature (پھبتی اڑانا (یا کہنا) **phab'ti ura'na** (or **kaih'na**) V.I. make fun of come out with a verbal caricature پھبتی سوجھنا **phab'ti soojh'na** V.I. (of verbal caricature or funny resemblance strike [~ FOLL.]

پھبکنا **pha'bakna**, پھپکنا **pha'pakna** V.I. (of plants) grow, flourish (of seed) shoot forth fatten thrive پھبک **pha'bak**, پھپک **pha'pak** N.F. growth flourishing of plants, etc.)

پھبنا **phab'na** V.T. suit sit well on be desirable پھبن **pha'ban** N.F. grace

پھپھا **phup'pha** N.M. (same as پھوپھا N.M. ★) پھپھی **phup'phi** N.F. (same as پھوپھی N.F. see under پھوپھا N.M. ★) پھپھیا ساس **phup'pha sas** N.F. father-in-law's sister پھپھیا سسر **phup'pha su'sar** N.M. her husband

پھپھڑ **phaphat** N.F. noise noisy stubbornness پھپھڑ مچانا **phap'phat macha'na** V.I. make noise noisily insist پھپھڑ دلالے **phap'phar dala'le** N.M. PL. specious sympathy

پھپھس **phap'phas** ADJ. very fat ; plump

پھپکارنا **phapkar'na** V.I. (of snake or steamengine) hiss

پھپھولا **phapho'la** N.M. blister puffed up part پھپھولے پھوٹنا **phapho'le phoot'na** V.I. (of blister) burst جلے دل کے پھپھولے پھوڑنا **ja'le dil ke phapho'le phor'na** PH. take revenge for grudge rail at appease one's wrath by castigating with harsh or sarcastic words

پھپھوندی *phaphoondi* N.F. mould ; mildew پھپھوندنا *phaphoond'na* V.I. become mouldy be mildewed

پھپھیرا *phuphe'ra*, ADJ. (F. پھپھیری *phuphe'ri*) related through ; paternal aunt

پھٹا *phaṭ'ta* N.M. board (obsolete save in) پرائے پھٹے میں پاؤں دینا *para''e phaṭ'ṭe men pa''on de'na*, پرائے پھٹے میں ٹانگ اڑانا *para''e phaṭ'ṭe men ṭang aṛa'na* PH. meddle with unnecessarily ; put one's finger in another's pie ; poke one's nose in other people's affairs

پھٹکارنا *phiṭkarna* V.I. reproach revile cry shame on curse پھٹکار *phiṭ'kar* N.F. reproach curse ; malediction پھٹ پھٹ *phiṭ phiṭ* N.F. opprobrium پھٹے منہ *phi'ṭe mūnh* INT. shame پھٹکارنا *phiṭkar'na* V.T. strike (with whip) beat (of hair) flap for drying پھٹکار *phiṭkar'* N.F. sound (of whip) sound of beating (person, laundry, etc.)

پھٹکا نہ کھانا *phaṭka na kha'na* PH. die on the spot [~ پھٹکنا]

پھٹکری *phiṭ'kari* or *phaṭ'kari* N.F. alum

پھٹکل *phuṭ'kal* ADJ. miscellaneous odd ; sundry retail

پھٹکنا *phaṭak'na* V.T. winnow sift separate (usu. NEG.) pay a flying visit ; come near پھٹکن *phaṭkan* N.F. husk ; chaff siftings

پھٹنا *phaṭ'na* V.I. burst crack break up disperse (of clouds) scatter (of milk) become sour wear off be torn become tattered be estranged have chilblains پھٹا پرانا *pha'ṭa pūra'na* N.M. cast-off clothes rags ADJ. worn off tattered پھٹ پڑنا *phaṭ' paṛna* V.I. burst swell come out with grievances become excessively fat دل پھٹنا *dil phaṭ'na* PH. be estranged کلیجہ پھٹنا *kale'jah phaṭ'na* PH. be grievously shocked پھٹا پڑنا *pha'ṭa paṛ'na* V.I. (of beauty, youth, etc.) be out of control پھٹ سے *phaṭ se* ADV. immediately ; without hesitation پھٹے حالوں *pha'ṭe ḥa'lon* ADV. in miserable condition پھٹے پھٹے دیدے *pha'ṭe pha'ṭe di'de* N.M. PL. large eyes آنکھیں پھٹی کی پھٹی رہ جانا *āṅ'khen pha'ṭi ki pha'ṭi raih ja'na* PH. be stunned be astonished look aghast

پھٹکی *phaṭ'ki* N.F. fowler's net. etc.

پھٹکی *phuṭki* N.F. tailor bird spot badly prepared curds undissolved portion of soluble stuff stain

پہچاننا *paihchan'na* V.T. recognise identify comprehend discriminate پہچان *paihchan'* N.F. acquaintance recognition discernment sign ; distinction

پھدکنا *phū'dakna* V.I. (of small birds or children) hop dance about in token of delight پھدکی *phūd'ki* N.F. a sparrow-like bird; hopper hop پھدکیاں مارنا *phūdki'yan mar'na* V.I. hop around (with joy, etc.)

پھر *phūr* N.F. sound of small bird suddenly taking wing ; whir ; whiz پھر سے اڑ جانا *phūr' se ūṛ ja'na* V.I. take wing suddenly

پھر *phir* ADV. & CONJ. then again afterwards ; later ; later on some other time پھر آنا *phir' a'na* V.I. come again return come some other time ; come later to have visited پھر بھی *phir' bhi'* ADV. yet ; still even then; notwithstanding ; nevertheless ; nonetheless پھر جانا *phir' ja'na* V.I. back out (of one's words) retract ; recant ; revoke revolt go again have visited پھر سے *phir' se* ADV. again ; anew ; afresh

پہر *paih'r* N.M. (arch.) watch eighth part of a day ; three-hour period پہر دن چڑھنا *paih'r din chaṛhe* ADV. long after sunrise پہر رات گئے *paih'r rat' ga''e* ADV. late in the evening

پہرا *paih'ra* N.M. watch guard ; time ; season پہرا بٹھانا *paih'ra biṭha'na* V.T. place a guard over impose restrictions ; curl پہرا دینا *paih'ra de'na* V.I. keep a watch (over) wait till late in the night [~ PREC.]

پھرا *phar'ra* N.M. thin sewed strip (of beam)

پھرانا *phira'na* V.T. turn ; to wheel ; cause to go round take out for a stroll show round ; take round on sight seeing پھراؤ *phira''oo* ADJ. (of goods sold) returnable

پھرپھندی *pharphan'di* N.M. swindler ADJ. artful; tricky

پھرتی *phūr'ti* N.F. agility ; alacrity alterness promptness ; readiness پھرتی سے *phūr'ti se* ADV. quickly; briskly پھرتی کرنا (یا دکھانا) *phūr'ti kar'na* (or *dikha'na*) پھرتی سے کام لینا *phūr'ti se kam le'na* V.I. be quick ; hurry up act briskly پھرتیلا *phūrti'la* ADJ. (F. پھرتیلی *phūrti'li*) smart quick ; active alert nimble agile

پھرکی *phir ki* N.F. shuttle ; anything turning on an axis whirligig small top ; top's taper used as separate plaything

پھرنا *phir'na* V.I. walk about stroll ; take a stroll turn ; whirl ; wheel return travel ; wander evacuate (bowels) back out (of one's words) ; retract ; recant change be coated or besmeared with real سر پھرنا *sir' phir'na* PH. go mad منہ پھرنا *mūnh' phir'na* PH. become satiated پھرتا *phir'tā* ADJ. (rare) return (fare, etc.) پھرتا رہنا *phir'tā raih'na* V.I. walk about wander go about in search

پھریرا *phare'rā* N.M. flag ; standard ; banner

پھریری *phūre'rī* N.F. shudder shiver scented flock of cotton پھریری آنا *phūre'rī ā'na* V.I. shudder shiver have the hair standing on end پھریری لینا *phūre'rī le'na* V.I. shudder shiver

پھڑ *phaṛ* N.M. gambling den پھڑیا *phaṛ'yā* N.M keeper of gambling den cheat huckster

پھڑپھڑانا *phaṛphaṛā'nā* V.I. (of wings, flag, etc) flutter move with convulsive motion be impatient پھڑپھڑاہٹ *phaṛphaṛā'haṭ* N.F. flutter agitation impatience

پھڑکنا *pha'ṛaknā* V.I. twitch throb; palpitate writhe flutter , display vibrate involuntarily appreciate greatly be moved be dying for , pine ; languish

پھڑک *pha'ṛak* N.F. flutter throb , palpitation , vibration involuntary restlessness پھڑک پھڑک کر *pha'ṛak pha'ṛak kar* ADV. with great difficulty پھڑک اٹھنا (یا جانا) *pha'ṛak ūṭh'nā* (or *jā'nā*) be moved ; be greatly appreciated be affected by love پھڑکانا *phaṛ'kānā* V.T twitch cause to throb flutter ; display move effect ; be greatly appreciated پھڑکن کا *phaṛ'kan kā* ADJ. (of child) cherished

پھڑیا *phuṛ'yā* N.F small boil ; small sore

پھس *phus* N.F. low hiss whisper پھس پھس میرے کان میں گھس *phūs' phūs me're kān' meṅ ghus'* PH. (said to child given to whispering in people's ears) you whisperer

پھس *phis* INT (used to put unsuccessful child to) shame

پھسپھسا *phūs'phusā* ADJ. (F. پھسپھسی *phus'phūsī*) flabby , spongy insipid ; vapid weak ; feeble

پھسڈی *phisad'dī* ADJ. (OPP.) loser laggard late tail of (class, etc.)

پھسر پھسر *phu'sar phu'sar*, کھسر پھسر *khū'sar phū'sar* N.F. whispering

پھسکڑا *phasak'ṛā* N.M sprawling پھسکڑا مار کر بیٹھنا *phasak'ṛā mār kar baiṭh'na* V.I. (usu. of women) sprawl

پھسکنا *pha'saknā* V.I. be squeezed ; be pressed slip become loose at seams, etc.

پھسلانا *phislā'na* V.T. cause to slip cause to skid cause to slide cause to err [~ پھسلنا *phi'salnā* CAUS.]

پھسلانا *phūslā'na* V.T. entice ; seduce coax ; cajole ; wheedle amuse *phūslā'va* N.M. cajolery seduction: enticement پھسلاوا دینا *phūslā'va de'nā* V.T. cajole entice ; seduce

پھسلنا *phi'salnā* V.I. slip skid slide err incline towards پھسلن *phis'lan* N.F. slippery ground error ; slip پھسلواں *phisalvāṅ* ADJ. slippery

پھک پھک *phak' phak* N.F intermittent gush (of air, etc.)

پھکڑ *phak'kaṛ* N.M. indecent talk mutual abuse پھکڑ باز *phak'kaṛ-bāz* N.M. indecent prater one indulging in obscene language

پھکڑی *phak'ṛī* N.F. disgrace پھکڑی کرنا *phak'ṛī kar'nā* V.I. disgrace slandar bring bad name (to someone)

پھکنا *phūk'na* N.M. bladder child's balloon V.I. (also پھنکنا *phūnk'nā*) be blown up into a flame be very hot (of body) be running high temperature

پھکنی *phūk'nī* N.F. blow-pipe

پھکیتی *phike'tī* N.F. clubbing ; cudgelling (as an art) lancing fencing پھکیتی کا ہاتھ پھینکنا *phike'tī ka hāth phenk'nā* N.F. use a fencing, lancing or cudgelling trick پھکیت *phiket* N.M. fencer club-fighter

پہل *pai'hal* N.F. initiative precedence beginning ; commencement cotton flock cotton pad پہل کرنا *pai'hal kar'nā* V.I. take the initiative ; take the lead precede begin ; start ; commence

پھل *phal* N.M. fruit yield ; produce ; harvest benefit ; profit reward result ; effect ; outcome child , progeny (of knife, etc.) blade ploughshare پھل آنا (یا لگنا) *phal' ā'nā* (or *lag'nā*) V.I. bear fruit پھل پانا (یا ملنا) *phal' pā'nā* (or *mil'nā*) V.I. reap the reward (of) پھل کھانا *phal khā'nā* V.T. eat fruit get the reward of پھل کھانا آسان نہیں *phal' khā'nā āsān' na'hīṅ* PROV. profits do not come without toils پھل دار *phal'-dār* ADJ. fruit bearing (tree) fruitful , profitable پھل لانا (یا دینا) *phal' lā'nā* (or *de nā*) V.T. bear fruit succeed reap the reward of bear child پھل نیا کرنا *phal na'yā kar'nā* V.I. eat a fruit for the first time in the season

پہلا *paih'lā* ADJ. (F. پہلی *pah'lī*) first premier primary; preliminary prior chief; main original old ancient پہلے *paih'le* ADV. at first; in the beginning originally پہلے پہل *paih'le paihal'* ADV. at first; in the beginning پہلے ہی سے *paih'le hī se* ADV. from the very start پہلی بار *paih'lī bār* ADV. (for the) first time

پھلا *pha'lā* SUF. bladed edged دو پھلا *do-pha'lā* ADJ. two-bladed double-edged [~ پھل]

پھلّا *phūl'lā* N.M. parched swollen rice cataract [~ پھولنا]

پھلانا *phūlā'nā* V.T. swell inflate; distend fatten give airs (to); puff up by flattery [~ پھولنا CAUS.]

پھلانگنا *phalāng'nā* V.I. jump; across leap across پھلانگ *phalāng'* N.F. stride leap

پھلروا *phūlar'vā* N.M. small flower پھلروا سا بچہ *phūlar'vā sā bach'chah* PH. sweet child; lovely infant

پھلجھڑی *phūl'-jhaṛī* N.F. small fountainlike firework; scintillating stick; coruscant stick scintillating smile joke; witticism report aimed at stirring up quarrels پھلجھڑیاں چھوڑنا *phūl'-jhaṛ'yāṅ chhoṛ'nā* PH. display such sticks indulge in witticisms smile thus spread quarrel-stirring reports

پھلکا *phūl'kā* N.M. light puffed-up bread

پھلکاری *phūlkā'rī* N.F. tissued flower on cloth cloth with floral embroidery

پھلنا *phal'nā* V.I. bear fruit have issue have blisters prosper; flourish; thrive پھلنا پھولنا *phal'nā phool'nā* V.I. prosper; flourish; thrive

پہلو *paih'loo* N.M. side rib flank (of army) wing (of building) lap viewpoint way out method interpretation (پہلو بچانا (یا دینا *paih'loo bachā'nā* (or *de'nā*) V.I. keep aloof avoid evade پہلو پر *paih'loo par* ADV. aside پہلو تہی *paih'loo te'hī* N.F. evasion پہلو تہی کرنا *paih'loo-te'hī kar'nā* V.I. evade; dodge withdraw پہلو دار *paih'loo-dār* ADJ. (of figure) with protruding corners (of chair) armed (of words or talk) allusive پہلو دبانا *paih'loo dabā'nā* V.I. press one's side press (enemy's) flank overpower conceal (something) پہلو گرم (یا آباد) کرنا *paih'loo gar'm* (or *ābād'*) *kar'nā* V.T. & I. give (someone) the pleasure of one's company sit in lap (of) sit beside پہلو مارنا *paih'loo mār'nā* V.T. emulate پہلو میں *paih'loo meṅ* ADV. by the side (of); beside in the lap (of) next (to) پہلو میں بیٹھنا *paih'loo meṅ baiṭh'nā* V.I. be in the company of sit beside sit in the lap of پہلو نکالنا *paih'loo nikal'nā* V.I. be an occasion (for) [P]

پھلواڑی *phūlvā'ṛī* (dial. پھلواڑی *phūlvā'ṛī*) N.F. small garden پھل پھلواڑی *phal' phūlvā'ṛī* N.F. various kind of fruits, greens, etc. [~ پھل]

پہلوان *paihlavān'* N.M. wrestler stout and sturdy person athlete champion پہلوانی *paihlavā'nī* N.F. wrestling physical exercise championship

پہلوٹھا *paihlo'ṭā*, پہلونٹا *paihlon'ṭā*, پلوٹھا *paloṭhā*, پہلونٹی کا *paihlon'ṭī kā*, پلوٹھی کا *palo'ṭhī kā* ADJ. first born N.M. eldest child

پھلی *pha'lī* N.F. pod (of leguminous plant) loop

پھلی *phūl'lī* N.F. flower-like ornament worn in nose or ear white speck in eye (nurs.) baby's penis

پہلے *paih'le* ADV. پہلے پہل *paih'le paihal'* ADV. (see under پہلا ADJ. ★)

پھلیانا *phalyā'nā* V.I. (col.) bear fruit

پھلیل *phūlel'* N.M. perfumed oil عطر پھلیل *'it'r phūlel'* N.M. scent and perfumed oil

پھن *phan* N.M. hood (of snake) پھن اٹھانا *phan uṭhā'nā* V.I. (of snake) distend or spread the hood پھنپھنانا *phanphanā'nā* (of snake) spread the hood and hiss (of or like snake) spring up suddenly move about briskly

پہن *paihan'* N.M., پہناور *paihnā'var* N.F. expensive extensive wide [P]

پہنانا *paihnā'nā* V.T. clothe, to dress cause to wear put on (meaning; sense, etc.)

پہناوا *pahnā'vā* N.M. dress garments style of dress

پہنائی *pahnā'ī* (ped. پہنا *paih'nā* N.F. expanse width; breadth [P ~ پہن]

پہنچنا *pahuṅchnā* V.I. reach; arrive come (up to) achieve; attain befall; happen (to) understand; get the hang (of) have access (to) influence پہنچ *pa'huṅch* N.F. access reach influence capacity understanding پہنچانا *pahuṅchā'nā*

V.T. cause to arrive cause to send supply convey inflict bring ; cause پہنچا ہوا *pa'huncha hū''a* ADJ. (F. پہنچی ہوئی *pa'hunchi hū''ī*) God's chosen ; saintly (person) secretly in league with adversary پہنچوانا *pahunchva'na* V.T. cause to arrive cause to be sent cause to be conveyed

پہنچا *pa'huncha* N.M. wrist

پہنچی *pa'hunchi* N.F. bracelet پہنچی

پھندا *phan'da* N.M. noose snare grasp; clutches ; stranglehold entanglement knot پھندا پڑنا (یا لگنا) *phan'da par'na* (or *lag'na*) V. be entangled be strangled be noosed be knotted پھندا لگانا *phan'da laga'na* V.T. entangle ensnare knot پھندے میں آنا یا پڑنا یا پھنسنا *phan'de men a'na* (or *par'na* or *phans'na*) V.I. be trapped fall into a trap get into trouble ; get into hot water پھندے میں پھانسنا *phande men phans'na* V.T. entrap ensnare put into trouble

پھندنا *phund'na* N.M. tassel

پھنسنا *phans'na* V.I. be arrested ; be held be ensnared be caught stick get involved ; be entangled get into hot water پھنسانا *phansa'na*, پھنسوانا *phansva'na* V.T. cause to be held or arrested entrap ; ensnare cause to be ensnared or entrapped

پھنسی *phun'si* N.F. pustule pimple

پھنکا *phan'ka* N.M. mouthful (of) پھنکا لگانا (یا مارنا) *phan'ka laga'na* (or *mar'na*) V.I. make a mouthful (of)

پھنکارنا *phunkar'na* V.I. (of snake) hiss پھنکار *phunkar'* N.F. hiss ; hissing

پھنکنا *phun'kna* V.I. (same as پھکنا V.I. ★)

پھنکوانا *phunkva'na* V.T. cause to be blown have (something) set ablaze [~ پھونکنا CAUS.]

پھنکوانا *phinkva'na* V.I. (see under پھینکنا V.T ★)

پھنگا *phan'ga* N.M. grasshopper

پھنگی *phun'gi* N.F. sprout

پھننگ *phu'nang* N.F. top (of tree) پھنگ

پھنی *phun'ni* پھنیا *phan'ya* N.F. (nurs.) child's penis

پھوار *pho'ar'*, پھوہار *phohar'* N.F. drizzle fine drops of rair پھوار پڑنا *pho'ar' par'na* V.I. drizzle

پھوپھا *phoo'pha* N.M. paternal uncle پھوپھی *phoo'phi* N.F. paternal aunt

پھوٹ *phoot*, پھونٹ *phoont* N.F. vapid melon

پھوٹنا *phoot'na* V.I. burst split be broken ; be shattered bud ; sprout ; shoot up (of boil) burst (of tears) flow (of luck) become adverse (of earthenware) break (of head or eye) be smashed پھوٹ N.F. discord split ; schism breakage ٹوٹ پھوٹ *toot' phoot* N.F. breakage wear and tear پھوٹ پڑنا *phoot' par'na* V.I. (of dissention) arise (of split) occur پھوٹ ڈالنا *phoot' dal'na* V.T. sow seeds of discord or dissention cause a split پھوٹ پھٹک *phoot' pha'tak* N.F. discord پھوٹ بہنا *phoot' baih'na* V.I. (of boil) burst (of tears) fall پھوٹ پھوٹ کر رونا *phoot' phoot kar ro'na* V.I. burst into tears پھوٹی کوڑی پاس نہ ہونا *phoo'ti kau'ri pas' na ho'na* PH. be quite penniless پھوٹا منہ *phoo'ta munh* N.M. tongue of ill-disposed person پھوٹ کر نکلنا *phoot kar ni'kalna* V.I. erupt (of unjust acquisition) afflict acquirer with leprosy پھوٹی قسمت یا تقدیر *phoo'ti qismat* (or *taqdīr'*) N.F. ill-luck ; misfortune

پھوڑا *phoo'ra* N.M. boil abscess inflammation پھوڑا پھنسی *pho'ra phun'si* N.M. boils and eruptions

پھوڑنا *phor'na* V.T. break cause to burst shatter split سر پھوڑنا *sir phor'na* V.I. break the head try unsuccessfully to convince (a fool or tyrant) بھانڈا پھوڑنا *bhan'da phor'na* V.T. (see under بھانڈا N.M. ★)

پھوس *phoos*, پھونس *phoons* N.M. hay thatch ADJ. decrepit (old man) بڈھا پھونس *buddha phoons* N.M. decrepit old man

پھوسڑا *phoos'ra*, پھونسڑا *phoons'ra* N.M. rag ravel (fig.) child ; brat

پھوک *phok* N.M. residue left after extraction of juice (fig.) worthless stuff; dross

pho'ka (F. پھوکی *pho'ki*) ADJ. hollow light soft (soil) mere پھوکٹ *pho'kat* N.F. worthless stuff anything obtained gratis پھوکٹ میں *pho'kat men* ADV. gratis

پھول *phool'* N.M. flower blossom (dial.) (PL.) charred bones (of cremated corpse) charred part of wick any light thing پھول آنا *phool' a'na* V.I. blossom have the first menses پھول پان *phool'-pan* N.M. slender body good and evil پھول پتی *phool'-pat'ti* N.F. riband knot rosette ; cockade پھول جھڑنا پھول توڑنا *phool' tor'na* V.I. pluck flowers *phool' jhar'na* V.I. (of decayed flowers) fall منہ سے پھول جھڑنا *mūnh se phool' jhar'na* PH. speak sofrly or swiftly speak with a rhetorical flourish of style پھول چڑھانا *phool' charhā'na* V.T. place a wreath (on tomb, etc.) پھول چننا *phool' chūn'nā* V.T. pluck flowers glean charred bones پھول سے *phool' sā* ADJ. delicate like a flower پھول کترنا *phool' ka'tarnā* V.I. trim the wick پھول کھلنا *phool' khil'nā* V.I. bloom ; blossom ; flower پھول کی چھڑی بھی نہ لگانا *phool' kī chha'rī bhī na lagā'nā* PH. not to beat at all پھول گوبھی *phool' go'bhī* N.F. cauliflower پھولوں میں تلنا *phoo'loṅ meṅ tūl'nā* V. be very delicate lead life of luxury پھول والا *phool' vā'lā* N.M. flower vender پھول والوں کی سیر *phool' vā'loṅ kī sair'* N.F. annual festival near Delhi (introduced by later Moghuls) پھولوں کی چھڑی *phoo'loṅ kī chha'rī* N.F. garlanded wand (used in post-marital cermony پھولوں کی چادر *phoo'loṅ kī chā'dar* N.F. large interwoven garland ; wreath پھولوں کی سیج *phoo'loṅ kī sej* N.F. bed with a layer of flowers on it ; bed of roses پھولوں کا گہنا *phoo'loṅ kā gaih'nā* N.F. elaborate wedding garlands

پھولنا *phool'nā*, پھول جانا *phool' jā'nā* V.I. swell bloat fatten be inflated exult; be pleased flourish ; prosper ; thrive

پھولا *phoo'lā*, پھلا *phūl'la* N.M. white speck in the eye پھولا پھرنا *phoolā phir'nā* V.I. be overjoyed be puffed up پھولا پھلا *phoo'lā phā'lā* ADJ. grown-up developed prosperous blooming پھولا نہ سمانا *phoo'lā na samā'nā* V.T. be unable to contain oneself (for joy)

پھوں *phooṅ'* N.F. hiss (of snake) sniff; snort (of cat, etc.) brag pride ; conceit پھوں پھاں کرنا *phooṅ' phāṅ' kar'nā* V.I. brag; boast; swagger take the airs پھوں پھوں کرنا *phooṅ' phooṅ kar'nā* V.I. sniff snort boast ; swagger take the airs

پھونس *phooṅs* N.M. (same as پھوس N.M. ★)

پھونکنا *phooṅk'nā* V.T. puff blow blast set on. squander breathe ; exhale charm پھونک *phooṅk'* N.F. puff blow exhalation charm پھونک دینا *phooṅk' de'nā* V.T. burn down blow up squander whisper mislead incite ; instigate blow (bugle, etc.) پھونک ڈالنا *phooṅk' dāl'nā* V.T. burn down charm پھونک پھونک کر قدم رکھنا *phooṅk' phooṅk' kar qa'dam rakh'nā* V.I. act cautiously be very scrupulous پھونک مارنا *phooṅk mār'nā* V. puff blow sniff (candle, etc.) ; put out charm پھونک نکل جانا *phooṅk' ni'kal jā'nā* V.I. breathe one's last

پھوہڑ *phoo'har* ADJ. slovenly (woman) ; sluttish; slatternly N.F. sloven ; slut slattern پھوہڑپن *phoo'har-pan* N.M. slovenliness ; sluttishness ; slatterness

پھوہار، پھوار *phohār'*, *pho'ār'* N.F. drizzle پھوہار پڑنا *phohār' par'nā* V.I. drizzle

پھوئی *phoo''ī* N.F. mildew butter oil scum drizzle fine drop پھوئی پھوئی *phoo''ī phoo''ī*, پھوئیوں پھوئیوں *phoo''iyoṅ phoo''iyoṅ* ADV. (of rain) in fine drops little by little

پھویا *pho'yā* N.M. scented cotton flock (soaked) cotton nipple (for feeding infants week person

پہیا *pa'hiyā*, پہیہ *pa'hiyah* N.M. wheel

پھیپھڑا *phephṛā* N.M. lung

پھیٹا *phai'ṭā* N.M. (same as N.M. پھینٹا N.M. ★)

پھیٹنا *phaiṭ'nā* V.T. (same as پھینٹنا V.T. ★)

پھیر *pher* N.M. wrong notion dubious course thing of doubtful value crookedness stroke of ill (luck) dilemma catastrophe drastic change ; revolution loss (ofan amount) error (of judgment or discernment) curve ; bend ; turning circuitousness distance difference discrepency پھیر دینا *pher' de'nā* V.T. turn (something) return restore refund ; reimburse پھیر پڑنا *pher' par'nā* V.I. be a discrepency (of) پھیر لانا *pher'lā'nā* V.T. bring back پھیر لینا *pher' le'nā* V.T. take back (of expected baby) delay delivery پھیر میں آنا (یا پڑنا) *pher' meṅ ā'nā* (or *par'nā*) V.I. be involved in difficulties follow a course of doubtful benefit harbour wrong notions be misled پھیر میں ڈالنا *pher' meṅ dāl'nā* V.T. mislead face (someone) with a dilemma [~ پھرنا]

پھیرا *phe'rā* N.M. visit ; call pilgrimage perambulation circumambulation (round bride or beggar) پھیرا پھیری *phe'rā phe'rī* N.F. (frequent) interchange [~ پھرنا]

پھیرنا *pher'nā* V.T. return refund; reimburse turn over ; to return reverse change shift besmear with (print, etc.) break ; break in (a horse) [~ پھرنا CAUS.]

پھیری *phe'rī* N.F. hawking pedlar's پھیری لگانا *phe'rī lagā'nā* V.T. & I. hawk ; peddle پھیری والا *phe'rī vā'lā* N.M. pedlar ; hawker ہیرا پھیری *he'rā phe'rī* ہیرا پھیری *he'rā phe'rī* N.F fraud shady deal ہیرا پھیری کرنا (or ایرا (یا ہیرا) پھیری کرنا) e'ra (or he'ra) phe'rī kar'nā V.I. deceive practise fraud (on) [~ پھرنا]

پھیرے phe're N.M. PL. (dial.) marriage (according to Hindu rites) ; circumambulation of groom and bride round bonfire to solemnize marriage (according to Hindu rites) پھیرے ڈالنا (یا لینا) phe're ḍāl'nā (or le'nā) V.T. solemnize marriage according to Hindu ritual [~ پھرنا]

پھیکا phī'kā, ADJ. (F. پھیکی phī'kī) tasteless ; insipid ; vapid with little sugar (or salt) pale ; sallow dull faint ; light dull off colour ashamed ; feeling humiliated پھیکا پڑنا phī'kā paṛ'nā V.I. fade ; become faint be ashamed

پھیلنا phail'nā V.I. expand spread grow luxuriantly become public be scattered be diffused پھیلانا phailā'nā V.T. expand spread distend stretch propagate ; publish ; diffuse increase ; multiply extend open out پھیلاؤ phailā''o N.M. growth development diversity expense ; expansion extent breadth spread prolixity profuseness profundity expense پھیلاوٹ phailā'vaṭ N.F. expense ; expansion extent prolixity profuseness profundity

پہیلی pahe'lī N.F. enigma ; riddle ; puzzle پہیلی بوجھنا pahe'lī boojh'nā V.I. answer a riddle پہیلی (یا پہیلیاں) بجھوانا pahe'lī (or pahe'liyān) bujhvā'nā V.T. riddle (someone)

پھین phain N.M foam scum

پھینٹا phain'ṭā, پھینٹنا phainṭ'nā N.F. small turban

پھینٹنا phainṭ'nā, پھیٹنا phaiṭ'nā V.T. beat (the egg) beat ; thrash

پھینٹی phain'ṭī N.F. skein (of thread)

پھینکنا phenk'nā, پھینک دینا phenk' de'nā V.I. throw fling hurl cast throw away spill waste squander ignore

پھینی phe'nī N.F. thin bread-like concentric strings ; vermicilli bread

پئی pa''ī N.F. suitcase picking (of cotton, etc.) پئی کو جانا pa''ī ko jā'nā V.I. go out for picking

پی pī N.M. (same as پیا N.M. ★

پے pai N.M. foot footstep pursuit پے pa''e, درپے dar pa''e ADV. in the footstep of in pursuit of PREP. after پیاپے payā' pai, پے بہ پے pai' ba pai' پے درپے pai' dar pai' ADV. one after another repeatedly incessantly consecutively on end ; in a row کے درپے ہونا ke dar pai' ho'nā V.T. be after pursue vigorously importune [P]

پیا pi'yā, pī N.M. (woman's) beloved ; sweetheart lover husband (joc.) acronoym for Pakistan International Airlines (P.I.A.)

پیادہ payā'dah N.M. (at chess) pawn foot-soldiers one who goes about on foot jay-walker (also پیادۂ محاصل payā'da-e maḥā'sil) bailiff پیادہ پا payā'da-pā' ADJ. on foot پیادہ رو payā'da-rau' N.M. pavement ; side-walk پیادہ گزر payā'da gūzar N.F. zebra crossing [P]

پیار piyār' N.M. love affection friendship attachment kiss پیار آنا piyār ā'nā V.T. feel a love for پیار دینا piyār' de'nā V.I. fondle ; caress pay regards (to) pay compliments (to) پیار کرنا piyār' kar'nā V.I. love fondle ; caress kiss پیارا piyā'rā ADJ. (F. پیاری piyā'rī) dear beloved favourite sweet charming delightful pleasing ; delectable N.M.. sweetheart friend relative dear one پیاروں پیٹی piyā'roṅ pī'ṭī N.F one with near and dear ones dead

پیاز piyāz' N.F. onion پیاز کا گنٹھا piyāz' kā gan'ṭhā N.M. پیاز کی گنٹھی piyāz' kī gan'ṭhī N.F. onion bulb پیازی piyā'zī ADJ. pink [P]

پیاس piyās' N.F. thirst strong desire ; longing (for) پیاس بجھانا piyās' bujhā'nā V.I. slake or quench thirst satisfy desire (for) ; satiate پیاس لگنا piyās' lag'nā V be or feel thirsty پیاسا piyā'sā ADJ. & N.M. (F. پیاسی piyā'sī) thirsty (person) desirous (of) ; thirsting (for) ; longing (for) پیاسا مرنا (یا مر رہا ہونا) piyā'sā mar'nā (or mar' ra'hā ho'nā) V.I. be dying of thirst be very thirsty پیاس مرجانا piyās' mar' jā'nā V.I. (of thirst) have its sense lost owing to extremity of need be no longer thirsty

پیال payāl, پیالی payā'lī N.F. dry stalks of rice or grain ; straw ; dried grass ; fruit

پیالہ payā'lah N.F. goblet bowl cup beggar's bowl (of mendicants) third-day funeral rite (musket) firepan (fencers') assembly (fencers') feast پیالہ بھر payā'lah bhar ADJ. cupful of پیالہ بھر جانا payā'lah bhar' jā'na V.I. (of the cup of one's life)

be full; die fill the cup پیالہ پینا payā'lah pī'nā v.i. drink drink the cup (of) become the disciple (of mendicant, etc.) پیالہ دینا payā'lah de'nā v.t. offer (someone) a drink ہم پیالہ (و) ہم نوالہ ham payā'lah(-o) ham nivā'lah n.m. (usu. pl.) boon companion bosom friend پیالی payā'lī n.f. cup پرچ پیالی pir'ch payā'lī n.f. cup and saucer

پیام payām' n.m. message errand communication پیامبر payam -bar, پیمبر payam'-bar n.m. messenger apostle ; prophet پیمبری payam'barī n.f. apostleship; prophethood پیامی payami n.m. messenger

پیانو piyā'no n.m. piano [E]

پیاؤ piyā''o n.m. free wayside stall or tub for drinking water [~ پینا]

پیپ pīp n.f. pus ; matter ; discharge ; purulence پیپ پڑنا pīp' par'nā v.i. fester become mattery suppurate

پیپا pī'pā n.m. cask barrel canister

پیپرمنٹ pe'parmint n.m. peppermint [E]

پیپرویٹ pepar-vet n.m. paperweight [E]

پیپل pī'pal n.m. a sacred Hindu tree; peepul, 'feans religiosa a drug called long pepper پپلی pī'plī peepul fruit پیپلا pīp'lā n.f. point of sword پیپلامول (یا موڑ) pīp'lā mool (or maor) n.m. long-pepper root

پیت pīt n.f. love ; affection پیت کی ریت نرالی pīt' kī rīt nirā'lī prov. strange are the ways of love پیتم pītam n.m. woman's sweetheart ; lover beloved husband

پیتادہ paitā'vah n.m. (col.) same as پاتا (see under پا[3])

پینترا paint'rā, پیترا pait'rā n.m. wrestler's preparatory poses pre-fight flourish (of cudgel, etc.) trick tactics ; strategy stand ; stance پینترا بدلنا paint'rā ba'dalnā v.i. change one's tactics change the stance change one's stand

پیتل pī'tal n.m. brass

پیتم pī'tam n.m. (see under پیت n.m. ★)

پیٹ pet n.m. abdomen , belley , stomach ovary ; womb ; uterous pregnancy interior of anything , bowels cavity capacity hunger mundane needs livelihood side ; team پیٹ اپھرنا pet a'pharnā v.i. suffer from flatulence be puffed up with pride be pregnant پیٹ باندھنا pet bāndh'nā v.i. not to eat stint oneself of food پیٹ بری بلا ہے pet bu'rī balā' hai prov. we are driven by our physical needs پیٹ بجانا pet bajā'nā v.i. be overjoyed پیٹ بڑھنا pet' barh'nā v.i. became fat be gluttonous be greedy پیٹ بڑھانا pet barhā'nā v.t. become gluttonous پیٹ بھر pet' bhar adv. bellyful پیٹ بھرنا pet bhar'nā v.t. & i. eat ; fill the stomach be satisfied پیٹ بولنا pet' bol'nā v.i. (of stomach) rumble پیٹ بھاری ہونا pet bhā'rī ho'nā v.i. suffer from indigestion ; have heaviness in the stomach پیٹ بھرے کی باتیں کرنا pet bha're kī bā'teṅ kar'nā v.i. have a rich person's view-point پیٹ پالنا pet' pāl'nā v.t. maintain or support (family, etc.) live from hand to mouth اپنا ہی پیٹ پالنا ap'nā hī pet' pāl'nā v.i. be selfish پیٹ پر پتھر باندھنا pet par pat'thar bāndh'nā v.i. starve (oneself) lead a life of austerity پیٹ پانی ہونا pet pā'nī hona v.i. have watery motions پیٹ پکڑ کر بھاگنا pet' pa'kar kar bhāg'nā v.i. be greatly shocked run nervously پیٹ پیٹنا pet' pīt'nā v.i. be impatient with hunger پیٹ پیٹھ سے لگنا pet pīth' se lag'nā be very lean be very hungry پیٹ ٹھنڈا رہنا pet than'dā raih'nā v.i. have the children alive پیٹ پھولنا pet phool'nā v.i. suffer from flatulence have the belly swollen (of dead body) start rolling be pregnant پیٹ پھٹنا pet phatna v.i. (of belly) burst be jealous laugh to excess پیٹ چپاتی ہو جانا pet chapā'tī ho jā'nā v.i. be very hungry پیٹ چلنا (یا جاری ہونا) pet' chal'nā (or jā'rī ho'nā) v.i. suffer from diarrhoes پیٹ چوٹی pet-cha'tī adj. pregnant woman whose belly does not swell پیٹ دکھانا pet dikhā'nā v.t. beg for food; undergo an examination by midwife پیٹ ڈالنا (یا گرانا) pet' dāl'nā (or girā'nā) v.i. have an abortion پیٹ رہنا (یا رہ جانا) pet' raih'nā (or raih jā'nā) v.i. become pregnant پیٹ سب رکھتے ہیں pet' sab' rakh'te haiṅ prov. no food, no service ; no supper, no song ; money makes the mare go پیٹ سب کچھ سکھا لیتا ہے pet' sab' kuchh sikhā' letā hai prov. the belly teaches all arts ; stomach is the greatest schoolmaster پیٹ سے pet se adj. pregnant ; in the family way پیٹ سے ہونا pet' se ho'nā v.i. be pregnant ; be in the family way پیٹ سے پاؤں باہر نکالنا pet se pāo'ṅ bā'har nikāl'nā v.i. transgress ; go beyond bounds show one's claws پیٹ کا بچہ pet' kā bach'chah n.m. own child get unborn child پیٹ کا پانی ہلنا pet kā pā'nī hil'nā v.i. have no jolts (in carriage, etc.) پیٹ کاٹ کے *peṭ' kāṭ ke* ADV. starving oneself ; at great personal deprivation پیٹ کاٹنا *peṭ' kāṭ'nā* V.I. starve oneself ; pinch one's belly deprive (someone) of livelihood ; kick in the stomach پیٹ کا کتا *peṭ kā kut'tā* ADJ. greedy gluttenous پیٹ کا ہلکا *peṭ' kā hal'kā* ADJ. unable to keep a secret پیٹ کی آگ *peṭ' kī āg'* N.F. maternal affection ; hunger پیٹ کی آگ بجھانا *peṭ' kī āg bujhā'nā* V.I. eat something keep the wolf from the door پیٹ (کی) کھرچن (یا پوچھن) *peṭ (kī) khur'-chan* (or *poń'chhan*) N.F. (woman's) last child پیٹ گرنا *peṭ' gir'nā* V.I. have a miscarriage; have an abortion پیٹ مارنا *peṭ' mār'nā* V.I. eat less پیٹ میں آنت نہ منہ میں دانت *peṭ' meṅ āṅt' nah muṅh meṅ dāṅt'* ADJ. old and decrepit پیٹ میں انگارے بھرنا *peṭ' meṅ angā're bhar'nā* V.T. amass wealth by unfair means پیٹ میں بل پڑ پڑ جانا *peṭ' meṅ bal' paṛ paṛ jā'nā* V.I. laugh excessively پیٹ میں پاؤں ہونا *peṭ' meṅ pā''oṅ ho'nā* V.I. be too clever پیٹ میں داڑھی ہونا *peṭ' meṅ dā'ṛhī ho'nā* V.I. be a precocious child پیٹ میں سانس نہ سمانا *peṭ' meṅ sāṅs' na samā'nā* V.I. be jittery ; have the blue funks پیٹ ہے یا بے ایمان کی قبر *peṭ' hai yā be-īmān' kī qa'bar,* پیٹ ہے یا خواجہ خضر کی زنبیل *peṭ' hai yā khā'ja khiz'r kī zambīl'* PROV. he is a glutton پیٹ میں چوہے دوڑنا *peṭ' meṅ choo'he dauṛ'nā* V.I. be very hungry پیٹ میں بیٹھنا *peṭ' meṅ baiṭh'nā* V.T. warm oneself into another's secret پیٹ والی *peṭ' vā'lī* N.F. pregnant پیٹو *pe'ṭoo* N.M. glutton ADJ. gluttonous

پیٹا *pe'ṭā* N.M. span circumference river channel curve in stretched thing string (of kite while flying) کے پیٹے میں *ke pe'ṭe meṅ* ADJ. about so many years' old

پیٹنا *pīṭ'nā* V. thrash ; beat strike dash punish tread thresh mourn ; lament curse پیٹ پیٹ کر *pīṭ' pīṭ kar* ADV. with great difficulty after a severe beating by dashing پیٹا *pī'ṭā* ADJ. cursed ; cussed پٹک پیا *piṭ'ṭak pay'yā* N.M. general mourning melee,

پیٹنٹ *pe'ṭanṭ* ADJ. patent [E]

پیٹھ *pīṭh* N.F. back backbone loins back part support پیٹھ پر کا *pī'ṭh par kā* ADJ. younger (child) پیٹھ پر ہاتھ پھیرنا *pīṭh par hāth pher'nā* V.I. pat on the back; encourage پیٹھ پر ہونا *pīṭh' par ho'nā* V.I. be at the back (of) پیٹھ پھیرنا *pīṭh pher'nā* V.I. turn one's back on depart ; withdraw flee پیٹھ پیچھے *pīṭh' pī'chhe* ADV. behind (someone's) back ; in (someone's) absence پیٹھ پیچھے کہنا *pīṭh pī'chhe kaih'nā* V.I. backbite ; talk against (someone) behind his back پیٹھ ٹھونکنا (یا ٹھوکنا) *pīṭh' ṭhoṅk'nā* (or *ṭhok'nā*) V.I. encourage ; embolden buck up پیٹھ دکھانا *pīṭh dikhā'nā* V.I. depart turn tail پیٹھ چارپائی سے لگ جانا *pīṭh' chārpā''ī se lag jā'nā* V.I. become very weak owing to illness پیٹھ دینا *pīṭh' de'nā* V.I. depart shrink from flee پیٹھ لگنا *pīṭh' lag'nā* V.I. fall flat supinely have a sore back be defeated in wrestling پیٹھ لگانا *pīṭh' lagā'nā* V.I. be thrown down in wrestling پیٹھ نہ لگنا *pīṭh' na lag'nā* V.I. be impatient

پیٹھا *pe'ṭhā* N.M. ash gourd ; sweet gourd

پیٹھنا *paiṭh'nā* V.T. sit seep through گھس پیٹھ کر *ghus' paiṭh kar* ADV. squeezing in پیٹھ *paiṭh* N.F. influences weekly market fair

پیٹی *pe'ṭī* N.F. belt box iron safe پیٹی اتارنا *pe'ṭī utār'nā* V.T. sack or suspend (constable, etc.) پیٹی اترنا *pe'ṭī utar'nā* V.T. (of constable be) sacked

پیجامہ *pai-jāmah* N.M. (same as پاجامہ *pā-ja'mah* N.M. ★)

پیچ *pī'ch* N.F. water strained from boiled rice, rice-water ; rice gruel

پیچ *pech* N.M. screw tricks (in wrestling) tactic ; strategem turn twist entanglement (of kites) turn of turban complication deceit ; fraud پیچ پڑنا *pech' paṛ'nā* V.I. become intricate occur as an obstacle (of kites) be entangled پیچ باندھنا *pech' bāndh'nā* V.T. grapple in wrestling tie a turban پیچ چلنا *pech' chal'nā* V.I. resort to (new) strategem پیچ دینا *pech' de'nā* V.T. screw twist deceive circumvent پیچدار *pech'-dār* ADJ. twisted coiled ; spiral winding complicated intricate ambiguous پیچ چھٹنا *pech' chhuṭ'nā* V.I. (of kites) be disentangled پیچ در پیچ *pech' dar pech'* ADV. coil within coil complicated ; intricate entangled complex پیچ چلنا *pech' chal'nā* V.I. play a trick پیچ ڈالنا *pech' ḍāl'nā* V.I. put obstacles ; make matters complicated entangle kite's string (with another) پیچ کرنا *pech' kar'nā* V.I. seize in wrestling entangle deceive پیچ کش *pech'-kash* N.M. screw-driver پیچ و تاب کھانا *pe'ch o tāb' khā'nā* V.I. fret and fume پیچ کھلنا *pech' khul'nā* V.I. be disentangled be untwisted be unscrewed of (mystery) be unravelled پیچ کھولنا *pech khol'-nā* V.T unscrew untwist unravel solve پیچ کھیلنا *pech khel'na* V.T. play a trick (on) پیچ لڑانا V.T. entangle kite's string (with that of another) پیچ و تاب *pe'ch-o-tab'* N.M. annoyance ; vexation restlessness writhing پیچ و خم *pe'ch-o-kham*, پیچاک *pechak'* N.M. bends and curves of path twists and turns (of tresses) intricacy difficulty [~P]

پیچش *pe'chish* N.F. dysentery ; gripes [P ~ پیچیدن]

پیچک *pe'chak* N.F. reel (of thread) [~P]

پیچوان *pechvan'* ADJ. hookah with long flexible pipe [~P]

پیچھا *pi'chha* N.M. rear back hind part absence pursuit following support پیچھا بھاری (یا قوی) ہونا *pi'chha bha'ri* (or *qa'vi ho'na* V.I. have parental or other support have a large following be liable to face trouble later be pitted against a reinforced enemy پیچھا چھڑانا *pi'chha chhura'na* V.T. get rid (of) shake (someone) off escape (from) پیچھا چھوٹنا *pichha chhoot'na* V.I. be rid (of) escape (from) پیچھا چھوڑنا *pi'chha chhor'na* V.T. let alone cease give up پیچھا کرنا *pi'chha kar'na* V.I. pursue give the chase shadow press ; importune of gune ase bet on or back (a horse) پیچھا لینا V.T. pursue pester importune (of gun) recoil پیچھا نہ چھوڑنا *pi'chha na chhor'na* V.T. continue to shadow or harass or pursue or follow ; harass force one's company on importune پیچھے *pi'chhe* ADV. behind at the back in the rear ; astern in the absence (of) after the death (of) for the sake (of) as a result (of) پیچھے آنا *pi'chhe ana* V.I. be late follow ensue پیچھے پڑنا *pi'chhe par'na* V.T. importune pester pursue doggedly run after; dance attendance (on) put heart and soul (in work) پیچھے پھرنا *pi'chhe phir'na* V.T. run after pursue follow return پیچھے پیچھے *pi'chhe pi'chhe* ADV. behind shadowing backward ; back پیچھے پیچھے رہنا *pi'chhe pi'chhe raih'na* V.T & I. be shy not to come in the limelight follow show respect to پیچھے ڈالنا *pichhe dal'na* V.I. outstrip ; leave behind lay by ; save ignore cause to follow ; set on ; urge (horse, etc.) after cause to harass پیچھے رہنا *pi'chhe raih'na* V.I. lag behind keep back پیچھے لگنا *pi'chhe lag'na* V.T. pursue follow doggedly پیچھے لگا دینا *pi'chhe laga' de'na* V.T set on cause to shadow cause to harass cause to importune پیچھے ہو لینا *pi'chhe ho le'na* V.T follow become a disciple of pursue

پیچیدہ *pechi'dah* ADJ. twisted , coiled complicated ; intricate difficult پیچیدہ معاملہ *pechi'dah mo'a'malah* N.M. difficult case intricate problem tricky question پیچیدگی *pechi'dagi* N.F. complication; intricacy difficulty ; abstruseness [P ~ پیچیدن]

پیخال *pai'khal'* N.F. droppings (of bird)

پیخانہ *paikha'nah* N.M. (same as پاخانہ N.M. ★)

پیدا *pai'da* ADJ. born created brought into being for existence gained produced manufactured (lit.) clear ; manifest obvious ; evident N.F. income produce gain پیدا آور *pai'da-a'var* ADJ. gainful productive غیر پیدا آور *ghair paida-a'var* ADJ. unproductive unprofitable پیدا کرنا *pai'da kar'na* V. give birth to create bring into being (or existence) hatch produce manufacture find ; obtain ; procure earn gain pose (question) ; lead to (objection) پیدا ہونا *pai'da ho'na* V.I. be born be created come into being (or existence) be produced be earned (of question, etc.) arise ; crop up (of idea, etc.) strike ; spring up پیداوار *pai'davar* (col. پیداواری *pai'davari*) N.F. produce (of land) fruit out-turn income پیدائش *paida''ish* N.F. birth creation Genesis (as first part of the Torah) engendring پیدائشی *paida'ishi* ADJ inherent ; innate natural born (blind, etc.) پیدائشی حق *paida''ishi haq* N.M. birth-right پیدائی *paida''i* N.F. manifestation [P]

پیدل *pai'dal* ADV. on foot ADJ. foot پیدل فوج *pai'dal fauj* N.F. foot soldiers ; infantry

پیڈل *pai'dal* N.M. pedal [E]

پیر[1] *pir*, پیر کا دن *pir ka din* N.M. Monday [~P]

پیر[2] *pir* N.M. (PL. also پیراں *pi'ran*) spiritual guide saint (lit.) old man پیر تسمہ پا *pi'r-e tas'ma-pa* N.M. Sinbad's lanky captor difficult to get rid of پیر بھائی *pir bha''i* N.M fellow-disciple پیر پکڑنا (یا بنانا) *pir' pa'karna* (or *bana'na*) V.I. adopt spiritual (guide) پیر زادہ *pir-za'dah* N.M. saint's son ; saint's progeny پیر زال *pir'-e zal'* N.F (lit.) old woman hag پیر شو بیاموز *pir' shau ba-yamoz'* PROV live and learn پیرِ طریقت pīr-e-tarī'qat N.M. spiritual guide پیرِ فرتوت pī'r-e-fartoot' N.M. decrepit old man پیرِ کنعاں pī'r-e-kan'āṅ' N.M. old man of Kanaan; (the prophet) Jacob پیر مرد pīr'-mar'd N.M. old man پیرِ مغاں pī'r-e-mughāṅ' N.M. tavern-keeper (fig.) spiritual guide پیرِ نابالغ pī'r-e nā-bā'ligh N.M. old fool پیری pī'rī N.F. (lit.) old age (also پیری مریدی pī'rī murī'di) spiritual guidance as profession پیری مریدی کرنا pī'rī murī'dī kar'na V.I. become professional guide پیراں نمی پرند مریداں می پرانند pirāṅ na-mī parand' murī'dān mī parā'nand PROV. sycophants turn their patrons' head پیرانہ pīrā'nah ADJ. old elderly growing old پیرانہ سال pīrā'na-sal ADJ. old پیرانہ سالی pīra-na-sa'lī پیرانہ سری pīrā'na-sa'rī N.F. old age [P]

پیر pair N.M. (usu. except in Luck. dial.) foot footprint پیر کا نشان pair' ka nishān' N.M. footprint پیر بھاری ہونا pair bhā'rī ho'na V.I. be pregnant پیروں میں مہندی لگنا pai'roṅ meṅ maihṅ'dī lag'na V.I. come out with a lame exuse

پیرا[1] pai'ra, پیراگراف, N.M. paragraph [E]

پیرا[2] pai'ra N.M. superstitious sign of (some-one's) arrival

پیرا[3] pai'ra SUF. decorating manifesting پیرائی paira''ī N.F. decoration manifestation [P ~ پیراستن]

پیراستہ pairas'tah ADJ. decorated; adorned trimmed پیراستگی pairas'tagī N.F. decoration (ped.) trimming [P ~ PREC.]

پیراک pairak' N.M. swimmer پیراکی pairā'kī N.F. swimming پیراکو paira''oo ADJ. (of water) too deep to ford (of water) deep enough to swim able to swim پیرائی paira''ī N.F. remuneration for swimming

پیرائی pera''ī N.M. drum maker singer

پیراموں pe'rāmooṅ ADV. around about [P]

پیراہن pairā'han, پیراہن pai'rahan, N.M. shirt dress کاغذی پیراہن kā'ghazī pai'ra han N.M. plaintiff's dress mortal coil پیراہن کاغذی ہونا pairā'han kā'ghazī ho'na V.I. be a plaintiff be mortal [P]

پیرایہ pairā'yah N.M. manner; style behaviour پیرایۂ بیان pairā'ya-e bayān' N.M. style way of exposition [P]

پیروڈی pai'rodī N.F. parody [E]

پیرو pai'rau' N.M. disciple follower پیروکار pai'-rau-kār' N.M. follower pleader; litigant s agent in law-suit پیروکاری pai-rau-kā'rī N.F. pleading (of law-suit) پیروی pai'ravī N.F. devotion following pleading (of law -suit)

پیرول pairol' N.M. parole [E]

پیڑ pīṛ N.F. (dial.) pain پرائی پیڑ parā''ī pīṛ N.F. other person's trouble

پیڑ peṛ N.M. tree sapling پیڑ لگانا peṛ lagā'na V.I. plant sapling(s)

پیڑ paiṛ N.F. footprints track

پیڑو pe'ṛoo N.M. pelvis

پیڑا pe'ṛa N.M. dough ball a kind of sweetmeat made of evaporated milk

پیڑھی pī'ṛhī N.F. low old-fashioned chair; low stool generation پیڑھی در پیڑھی pī'ṛhī dar pī'ṛhī ADV. generation after generation; for successive generations پیڑھا pī'ṛha N.M. low old-fashioned chair

پیزار paizar' N.F. shoe ہماری پیزار سے hamā'rī paizar' se INT. my foot who cares پیزار پر مارنا paizar' par mārna V.I. spurn condemn پیزار دکھانا paizar' dikhāna V.T. slight show no regard for [P ~ پا]

پیسہ pai'sah N.M. hundredth (or formerly sixty-fourth) part of a rupee; copper money wealth; riches پیسہ اڑانا pai'sah ūṛā'nā V.I. squander spent lavishly embazzle; defalcate پیسہ بنانا pai'sah banā'na V.T. earn; make money پیسہ ٹھیکری کرنا pai'sah ṭhī'k'rī kar'nā V.I. spend lavishly پیسے والا pai'se vā'la ADJ. rich; wealthy moneyed پیسے کا کھیل pai'se ka khel PH. matter of money privilege of wealth

پیسنا pīs nā, پیس ڈالنا pīs' ḍal'na V.T. grind; pulverize gnash (teeth) bruise crush ruin

پیش pesh N.M. vowel point represented as o or u front fore past former state PREP. before in front of PREF. fore far ahead پیش آنا pesh' ā'na V.I. happen; occur; come to pass behave; treat پیش از مرگ واویلا pesh az mar'g vā-vai'la (or col. ve'la) PROV. cry before one is hurt; call a surgeon before one is wounded پیش ازیں pe'sh az-īṅ' ADV. formerly before that پیش امام pe'sh-imām' پیش بند pesh'-band' N.M. apron harness belt pass over horses breast پیش بندی pesh-bań'di N.F. foresighted پیش بیں pesh-bīn' ADJ. wise prudent; far-sighted; circumspect پیش بینی pesh-'

bi'nī N.F. foresight ; prudence پیش پا افتادہ pe'sh-e pā if'tā'dah ADV. not far to seek easily struck (idea) self-evident (truth) quite ordinary trite پیشتر pesh'-tar ADV. formerly before sooner than ; prior to ; earlier than پیش جانا pesh' jā'nā V.I. (only NEG. & INTER.) have effect پیش خدمت pesh'-khid'mat N.M. servant پیش خیمہ pesh'-khe'mah (ped. khai-) N.M. prelude (rare) tent, etc. sent in advance پیش دالان pesh-dālān' N.M. vestibule پیش دستی pesh-das'tī N.F. initiative transgression پیش دستی کرنا pesh'-das'tī kar'nā V.T. take the initiative exceed the limits پیشرو pesh'-rau' N.M. forerunner leader in football ; hockey, etc.) forward دایاں پیشرو bāy'āṅ pesh'-rau N.M. left forward دایاں پیشرو dā'yaṅ pesh'-rau N.M. right forward وسطی پیشرو vas'tī pesh'-rau N.M. centre forward پیشروی pesh'-ra'vī N.F. preceding advance leadership پیش قبض pesh'-qab'z dagger پیش قدمی pesh-qa'damī (col. pesh'qad'mī) N.F. attack forward step forward initiative پیش قدمی کرنا pesh'-qa'damī kar'nā V.T. attack push forward take, the initiative پیش کار pesh'-kar N.M. a minor court official ; reader producer (of film, etc.) agent پیش کرنا pesh' kar'nā V.T. present ; submit ; put up پیشکش pesh'-kash N.F. offer artistic presentation پیش کنندہ pesh-kanin'dah N.M. one who presents ; producer پیش گاہ pesh'-gāh N.F. court پیش گوئی pesh-go''ī پیشین گوئی peshīn'-go''ī N.F. prediction prophecy forecast پیشگوئی کرنا pesh-go''ī kar'nā V.T. predict prophecy foretell پیش لفظ pesh-laf'z N.M. foreword پیش نظر pe'sh-e na'zar ADJ. & ADV. in view in sight کے پیش نظر ke pe'sh-e na'zar ADV. owing to in view of پیشنہاد pesh'-nihād N.M. presentation tender [P]

پیشاب peshāb' N.M. urine ; piss پیشاب بند ہونا peshāb' band' ho'nā V.I. be unable to pass urine پیشاب خطا ہونا peshāb' khatā' ho'nā V.T. have very great fear ; urinate (for fear) پیشاب کرنا peshāb' kar'nā V.I. make water ; urinate ; pass urine spurn پیشاب بھی نہ کرنا peshāb' bhī na kar'nā V.I. have no regard for ; despise [P ~ پیش + آب]

پیشانی peshā'nī N.F. forehead ; brow fate title top portion of printed paper left blank پیشانی پر بل آنا (یا لانا یا پڑنا) peshā'nī par bal' ā'na (or lā'na or paṛ'nā) V.I. frown ; scowl view with dislike پیشانی رگڑنا peshā'nī ra'gaṛnā V.I. supplicate ; humbly implore

پیش بندی pesh ban'dī N.F. پیشتر pesh'tar ADV. پیشرو pesh'rau پیش قدمی peshqa'damī N.F. پیشکار peshkar' N.M. پیشکش pesh'kash N.F. پیشگوئی pesh go''ī N.F. (see under پیش N.M. ★)

پیشگی pesh'gī N.F. earnest money ; an advance earnest money ADJ. advance ADV. in anticipation پیشگی ادائگی pesh'gī adā''igī N.F. advance payment [P ~ پیش]

پیشوا pesh'vā N.F. leader guide chief priest (old use Mahratta minister's title پیشوائی peshvā''ī N.F. leadership guidance reception ; going out to receive (someone) پیشوائی کرنا peshvā''ī kar'nā V.T. welcome going out to receive [P ~ پیش]

پیشہ peshah N.M. profession ; calling ; trade SUF. practising پیشہ ور pesha-var N.M. artisan, workman ; tradesman انجمن پیشہ وراں an'jūman-e pe'sha-va'rāṅ N.F. trade union [P]

پیشی pe'shī N.F. court hearing ; hearing date of hearing trial presence کچی پیشی kach'chī pe'shī N.F. preliminary hearing [P ~ پیش]

پیشین pe'shīn ADJ. (lit.) ancient former N.F (also نماز پیشین namā'z-e pe'shīn early afternoon prayers پیشین گوئی peshīn go''ī (same as پیشگوئی N.F. ★ which see under پیشی ★) [P ~ پیش]

پیغارہ paighā'rah N.M. (lit.) taunt پیغارہ جو paighā'ra-jo ADJ. (lit.) taunting [P]

پیغام paighām' N.M. message communication پیغام بر paighām'-bar N.M. messenger envoy emissary پیغمبر paigham -bar N.M. prophet apostle messenger of God پیغمبری paigham'-barī N.F. apostleship prophethood office of God's messenger [P]

پیک paik N.M. messenger courier [P]

پیک کرنا paik' kar'nā V.T. pack پیکنگ pai'king N.F. packing پیکٹ pai'kit N.M. packet [E]

پیک pīk N.F. betel-leaf spittle پیکدان pīk' dān N.M. spittoon [P]

پیکار paikār N.F. war battle fight برسر پیکار bar sar-e paikār' ADV. fighting pitted against [P]

پیکان paikān' (lit. also پیکاں paikaṅ') N.M. arrowhead blade (of any pointed missible)

پیکر pai'kar N.M. embodiment (of) body [P]

پیل pīl, فیل fīl N.M. (lit.) elephant (col. فیلا fī'la) bishop (at chess) پیلبان pīl'bān فیلبان fīl'-bān N.M. 'mahout'; elephant-keeper پیل پا pīl'-pa N.F. elephantiasis پیل پایہ pīl-pā'yah pillar ; column پیلتن pīl'-tan ADJ. gigantic ; huge پیل مرغ pīl'-murgh N.M. turkey fowl [P]

پیلا pī'lā ADJ. (F. پیلی pī'lī) yellow pale sallow jaundiced پیلاپن pīl'a-pan N.M.

yellowness paleness sallowness

پیلنا *pel'nā* V.T. shove ; push ; crush (seed in oil mill, etc.) extract oil from oilseed do (the physical exercise called) 'danr'

پیلو *pī'loo* N.M. 'salvadora persica' its fruit name of a musical mode

پیلہ *pī'lah* N.M. cocoon کرم پیلہ *kir'm-pī'lah* N.M. chrysalis silkworm [P]

پیما *paimā'* SUF. meter travelling traversing پیمائی *paimā'ī* SUF. measuring travelling ; traversing [P ~ پیمودن]

پیمان *paimān'* (lit also پیماں *pai'mān*) N.M. promise assurance پیمان باندھنا *paimān' bāndh'nā* V.I. hold out a promise give word of honour (to) [P]

پیمانہ *paimā'nah* N.M. measure cup (of wine) [P]

پیمائش *paimā''ish* N.F. measurement survey پیمائش بندوبست *paimā''ish ban'd-o bast'* N.F. revenue survey [P ~ پیمودن]

پیمبر *payam'bar* N.M. (see under پیام N.M. ★)

پینک *pai'mak* N.F. gold or silver lace gold or silver string

پیں پیں *pīn* N.F. buzz squeak پیں بولنا *pīn bol'nā* V.I. eat the humble pie [ONO.]

پینا *pī'nā*, پی لینا *pī' le'nā* V.T. drink quaff gulp down smoke absorb suppress one's (wrath, etc.) smoke پی جانا *pī' jā'nā* V.T. drink quaff suppress (one's wrath) refrain from retort, etc. pocket (insult, etc.)

پان اسلامزم *pai'n-islā'mizm* N.M. pan-Islamism پین اسلامک *pai'n-islā'mik* ADJ. pan-Islamic [E]

پینتالیس *paintā'līs* ADJ. & N.M. forty-five پینتالیسواں *paintā'līsvāṅ* ADJ. forty-fifth

پینتیس *pain'tīs* ADJ. & N.M. thirty-five پینتیسواں *pain tīsvāṅ* (ADJ.) thirty-fifth

پینٹھ *painṭh* N.F. weekly village market ; mart پینٹھ لگانا *painṭh lagā'nā* V.I. (of such market) be held

پینجنی *painj'nī* N.F. strip with tiny bells for pigeons' feet support for axle-tree

پینچ *painch* N.F. tail (of peacock)

پیندا *pen'dā* N.M. پیندی *pen'dī* N.F. bottom of vessel, etc. پیندے کا ہلکا *pen'de kā hal'kā* ADJ. unreliable ; untrustworthy

پینڈی *pin'dī* N.F. fried sweet ball this as tonic or candle

پینس *pī'nis* (col. پینس *pī'nas*), فینس *fī'nas* N.F. palanquin ; litter

پینسٹھ *pain'saṭh* ADJ. & N.M. sixty-five پینسٹھواں *pain'saṭhvāṅ* ADJ. sixty-fifth

پینک *pī'nak*, پنک *pi'nak* N.F. drowsiness (caused by opium)

پینکی *pī'nakī* N.M. one drowsy from opium-eating

پینگ *pīng* N.F. (dial. M.) motion of swing (rare) swing پینگ بڑھنا *pīng' baṛh'nā* V.I. be swung with force grow more intimate پینگ چڑھانا (بڑھانا) *pīng' chaṛhā'nā* (or *baṛhā'nā*) V.T. take the swing high up (usu. pl.) develop intimacy (with)

پینی *pai'nī* N.F. penny [E]

پیوست *paivas't* ADJ. sticking pasted joined; linked transfixed پیوستگی *paivas'tagī* N.F. connection link adhesion attachment پیوستہ *paivas'tah* ADJ. always ; ever contiguous in separable sticking ; pasted linked [P ~ پیوستن]

پیوند *paivand'* N.M. patch graft ; engraft (usu. unmatched) connection پیوند لگانا *paivand' lagā'nā* V.T. patch graft پیوندی *paivan'dī* ADJ. grafted ; ungrafted N.M. engrafted tree's fruit پیوندی مونچھیں *paivan'dī moon'chhen* N.F. PL. moustaches joining the beard [P ~ پیوستن]

پیہ *pīh* N.F. tallow [P]

پیہر *pī'har* N.M. (woman's) father's house

پیہم *pai'-ham* ADV. one after another ; in a series ; in a row [P ~ پا + ہم]

پیہو *pī'hoo*, پیہو پیہو *pī'hoo pī'hoo* N.F. crested cuckoo's cry

ت

ت *te* fourth letter of Urdu alphabet having no equivalent in English ; sound represented as *t* (in jummal reckoning) 400

ت *ti* PREF. three [~ تین CONT.]

تا[1] *tā* INT. (nurs.) I am seeing you Eureka behold

تا[2] *tā* ADV. & PREP. to ; up to until ; as far as as long as CONJ. since while in order that ; to the end that ; so that

تا زیست **tā ba-zist'**, تا بحیات **tā ba-hayāt'** ADV. till تا بکجا **tā ba-kujā'** ADV. how long how far whither تا بکے **tā ba-kai'** ADV. how much how many till when تا چند **tā chand'** ADV. how long how many how much? تا حال **tā hal'** ADV. till now yet ; hitherto تا زندگی **tā zin'dagī**, تا زیست **tā zist'** ADV. till death ADJ. life-long تا کہ **ta-keh** CONJ. so that ; to the end that تا ہم **tā'-ham** CONJ. yet; still nevertheless nonetheless تا ہنوز **tā-hūnooz'** CONJ. yet still ADV. till more [P]

تاب **tab** N.F. power endurance light refulgence heat convulsion twist curl radiation SUF. shining; luminous illuminating تاب لانا **tab' la'na** V.I. endure ; suffer patiently تاب نہ لانا **tab' na la'na** V.I. be unable to endure be powerless تاب طاقت **tāb-o-tā'qat**, تاب و تواں **tā'b-o-tūvāń** N.F. endurance capacity strength تاباں **tā'bāń** ADJ. refulgent glittering splendid تابانی **tabā'nī** N.F. refulgence ; brilliance splendour تاب تلی **tab' til'lī**. (CORR. تاپ تلی **tap til'lī**) N.F. enlargement of the spleen ; splenic fever ; splenitis تابدار **tāb'-dar** ADJ. luminous ; refulgent warm curly تابناک **tāb'nak** ADJ. brilliant refulgent [P ~ تابیدن]

تابڑ توڑ **tā'baṛ-toṛ'** ADJ. successive ; repeated ADV. repeated ; one after another

تابستان **tā'bistān** N.M. summer تابستانی **tabistā'nī** ADJ summer [P]

تابش **tā'bish** N.F. refulgence ; brilliance splendour heat grief [P ~ تابیدن]

تابع **tā'be'** ADJ. subordinate obedient N.M. follower doublet used as adjunct تابعدار **tā'be'-dār** ADJ. (col.) obedient N.M. (col.) loyal , servant تابعداری **tā'be'-dā'rī** N.F. loyalty allegiance obedience تابع مہمل **tā'be'-e moh'mal** N.M. meaningless adjunct [A]

تابعی **tā'be'ī** N.M. (PL. تابعین **tābe'īn'**) successors to the Holy Prophet's companions [A ~ PREC.]

تابندہ **tābin'dah** ADJ. bright ; luminous refulgent تابندگی **tabin'dagī** N.F brightness [P ~ تابیدن]

تابوت **tāboot'** N.M. coffin bier [A]

تابوت

تاپ **tap'** N.M. fever تاپ تلی **tap' til'lī**. (col. for تاب تلی **tāp' til'lī**) N.F. (see under تاپ N.F.★)

تاپنا **tāp'na** V.T. warm oneself at or over (fire)

تاتار **ta'tar'** N.M. Tartary تاتاری **tata'rī** N.M. & ADJ. Tartar [T]

تا تا تھئی **tā' tā thai''ī** N.F. words used for beating time with dance, drum, etc. time signal dance or music measure [ONO]

تاثر **ta'as'sūr** N.M. impression تاثرات **ta'as'sūrāt'** N.M. PL. impressions تاثر پیدا کرنا **tā'as'ur pai'dā kar'nā**, تاثر دینا **ta'as'sūr de'nā** V.T. give or create the impression تاثر لینا **tā'as'ūr le'nā** V.I. form the impression [A ~ اثر]

تاثیر **tāsīr'** N.F. effect efficacy [A ~ اثر]

تاج **tāj'** N.M. crown ; diadem sovereign authority , the crown (cock's) comb ; crest تاجپوشی **tāj-po'shī** N.F. coronation تاجدار **tāj'-dār**, تاجور **tāj'-var** N.M. sovereign تاجداری **tāj-dā'rī**, تاجوری **tāj'-va'rī** N.F. sovereignty ; kingship تاج محل **tāj'mahal'** N.M. the Taj [A]

تاجر **tā'jir** N.M. merchant businessman trader [A ~ تجارت]

تاجیک **tājīk'**, تاجک **tā'jik** SUF. inhabitant of Tajkistan in Russia (arch.) trader (arch.) one born in Arabia but bred in a Persian or Turkish speaking country [T]

تاخت **tākh't** N.F. invasion ; inroad; incursion attack , assault plunder ; ravage تاخت و تاراج کرنا **tākh't-o tā'rāj kar'na** V.T. invade plunder ; ravage ransack devastate [P]

تاخر **tā'akh'khūr** N.M. being late delay ; postponement [A ~ آخر]

تاخیر **tā'khīr'** N.F. delay procrastination تاخیر سے **tā'khīr' se** ADV. late تاخیر کرنا **tā'khīr' kar'na** V.T. be late put off ; postpone procrastinate [A ~ آخر]

تادیب **tadīb'** N.F. chastisement ; admonition; correction discipline teaching manners تادیب کرنا **tadīb' kar'na** V.T chastise ; admonish discipline [A ~ ادب]

تار **tār** N.M. telegram wire thread string steel wire warp chord elongated drop of sticky substance oily speck floating on liquid way ; manner تار باندھنا **tār' bāndh'na** V.T. repeat interruptedly send out a spate (of) , overwhelm or deluge (with) تار برقی **tār bar'qī** N.M. (arch.) telegram تار بندھنا **tār' bandh'na** V.I. be deluged (with) تار تار **tār' tār** ADJ. tattered torn to pieces تار تار کرنا **tār' tār kar'na** V.T. tear to pieces تار ٹوٹنا **tār' ṭooṭ'na** V.I. (of series, etc.) be broken be interrupted تار عنکبوت **tā'r-e 'ankaboot'** N.M. cobweb تارکش **tār'-kash** N.M. wiredrawer تارکشی **tār'-ka'shī** N.F. kind of embroidery done by pulling out woof wiredrawing تارگھر **tār'-ghar**

N.M. telegraph office تار و پود *ta'r-o pod'* N.M. warp and woof texture structure existence تار و پود بکھیرنا *tār'-o-pod' bakher'na* [P]

تار۲ *tar* ADJ. black تیرہ و تار *ti'ra-o-tar'* ADJ. quite dark [P]

تارا *tā'ra* N.M. star apple (of the eye) تارا ٹوٹنا *tā'ra ṭooṭ'na* V.I. (of star) shoot تارا ہو جانا *tā'ra ho jā'na* V.I look tiny owing to great distance تارے نظر آنا *tā're nazar ā'na*, تارے دکھائی دینا *tā're dikha''ī de'na* N.F. be stunned with blow be perplexed تارے توڑنا (یا اتارنا) *tā're toṛ'na* (or *ūtar'na*) V.T. do the impossible be very tricky ; be too clever تارے چھٹنا *tā're chhaṭ'na* V.I. (of sky) be or become clear تارے دکھانا *tā're dikha'na* V.T. bring out (as a sixth-day ritual after delivery) تارے گننا *tā're gin'na* V.I. have no sleep ; pass a sleepless night دمدار تارا *dūm'-dar tā'ra* N.M. comet

تاراج *taraj'* N.M. ravage ; plunder spoliation devastation تاراج کرنا *taraj' kar'na* V.T ransack ; ravage , plunder despoil devastate تاراج ہونا *taraj' ho'na* V.I. be ravaged ; be ransacked [P]

تارپیڈو *tar'pīdo* N.M. torpido [E]

تارپین *tar'pīn* N.M. turpentine تارپین کا تیل *tar'pīn ka tel'* N.M. turpentine oil [E]

تارک *tā'rik* N.M. relinquisher abstainer one who foregoes confirmed bachelor ADJ. relinquishing abstemious abstaining تارک الدنیا *ta'rik-ūd-dūn'ya* N M. hermit recluse ADJ. leading the life of a recluse تارکہ *tā'rikah* N.F. spinster [~A ترک]

تارک *tā'rak* N.M. bead ; crown ; pate helmet [P]

تارکول *tārkol*, کولتار *kol'tar* N.M. tar [~E tar + coal]

تاریخ *tarīkh'* N.F. date history annals; chronicle date (of hearing) ; hearing (usu. verse) anagram recording year of some occurrence ; chronogram تاریخ ٹھہرانا *tarīkh' ṭhaihra'na* V.T. fix date (of marriage, etc.) تاریخ ٹھہرنا *tarīkh' ṭhai'harna* V.T. (of such date) be fixed تاریخ چڑھانا *tarīkh' charha'na* V.I. date تاریخ دینا *tarīkh' de'na* V.T. give the date of next hearing تاریخ کہنا *tarīkh' kaih'na* V.I. compose a chronogram تاریخ مقررہ *tarī'kh-e mūqar'rarah* N.F. fixed date day of appointment تاریخ وقوع *tarī'kh-e vūqoo'* N.F. date of occurrence تاریخ وار *tarīkh'-var* ADV. datewise [A]

تاریک *tarīk'* ADJ. dark obscure تاریکی *tarī'kī* N.F. darkness obscurity تاریکی چھا جانا *tarī'kī chha' ja'na* V.I. (of darkness) spread all over تاریکی کرنا *tarī'kī kar'na* V T. darken switch off or put out the lights [P]

تاڑ *tāṛ* N.M. a kind of palm ; toddy-palm تاڑی *ta'ṛī* N.F. toddy

تاڑنا *taṛ'na* V.T. stare mark out with evil intentions ogle make out تاڑ جانا *taṛ ja'na* V I. make out guess ; conjecture understand ; perceive apprehend تاڑ *taṛ* N.F. stare evil-intentioned look perception تاڑباز *taṛ'-bāz* (dial. تاڑو *ta'ṛoo*, تاڑیا *ta'ṛiya*) ADJ. quick of apprehension

تاڑی *ta'ṛī* N.F. (see under تاڑ N.M. ★)

تازہ *tā'zah* ADJ. (F. same ; col. F. تازی *ta'zī*) latest recent new fresh not stale not gone bad تازہ بتازہ *ta'za ba-ta'zah* ADJ. fresh latest new ; brand new up-to-date not stale freshly blooming تازہ دم *tā'za-dam* ADJ. fresh ready untired تازہ دم ہونا *ta'za-dam ho'na* V.I. be refreshed be in good spirits be untired تازہ کرنا *ta'zah kar'na* V.I revive or refresh (memory) change (hookah) water تازہ وارد *tā'za-vā'rid* N. new-comer تازہ ہونا *ta'zah ho'na* V.T. (of memory, etc.) ; be revived; be refreshed تازگی *ta'zagī* N.F. freshness [P]

تازی۱ *ta'zī* N.M. & ADJ. Arab (horse or dog) reputed for swiftness of its speed تازی کتا *tā'zī kut'ta* N.M. greyhound [P]

تازی۲ *ta'zī* ADJ. (see under تازہ ★)

تازیانہ *taziya'nah* N.M. whip ; scourage تازیانہ لگانا (یا مارنا) *taziya'nah laga'na* (or *mar'na*) V. whip ; flog ; scourage ; castigate

تاسف *ta'as'sūf* N.M. regret remorse grief ; affliction pity ; commiseration *ta'as'sūf kar'na* V.T. & I. regret grieve pity [A ~ اسف]

تاسیس *tasīs'* N.F. foundation ; establishment تاسیس کرنا *tasīs' kar'na* V.T. set up ; establish ; found یوم تاسیس *yaum-e tasīs'* N.M. foundation day [A ~ اساس]

تاش *tāsh* N.M. playing cards ; cards (arch.) gold foil (arch.) tissue brocade

تاشہ *tā'shah* N.M. semi-spherical drum [P]

تافتہ *taf'tah* N.M. taffeta ADJ. glossy cream horse or pigeon [P ~ تافتن]

تاک tak N.F. vine [P]

تاکنا tak'na V.T. stare at peep ogle aim ambush ; lie in wait for تاک tak N.F. keep look-out aim waiting for opportunity ogle تاک جھانک tak' jhank N.F. ogling peeping peeping about تاک رکھنا tak' rakh'na V.T. have an eye on تاک میں رہنا tak' men raih'na V.T. be on the look out for lie in wait for تاک لگانا tak' laga'na V.T. stare ogle. ambush تاک کر مارنا tak' kar mar'na V.T. take (a good) aim at

تاکید taki̇d' N.F. stress ; emphasis urging pressure تاکید کرنا taki̇d' kar'na V.T. stress ; emphasize ; enjoin press ; urge insist (on) enjoin تاکیداً taki̇'dan ADV. as a reminder strictly emphatically peremptorily تاکیدی taki̇'di ADJ. urgent emphatic peremptory [A]

تاگا ta'ga N.M. (same as دھاگا N.M. ★)

تال[1] tal N.M. lake pool

تال[2] tal N.F. musical measure rhythmic beat (of hands) تال دینا tal' de'na V.I. beat time in music تال بتال ہونا tal' be-tal' ho'na, تال سے بتال ہونا tal' se be-tal' ho'na V.I, be out of tune تال میل tal' mel N.F. accord agreement hamono تال میل کھانا tal' mel kha'na

تالا ta'la N.M. lock تالا لگانا ta'la laga'na V.T. lock put padlock on تالا کنجی ta'la kun'ji N.M. lock and key تالے کی کنجی ta'le ki kun'ji N.M. key (to lock) key (to) تالی ta'li N.F. ★ تالابندی ta'la-ban'di N.F. lock-out.

تالاب talab' N.M. pond ; pool water reservoir [~ تال + P آب]

تالف ta'al'luf N.M. (ped.) intimacy friendship [A ~]

تالم ta'al'lum N.M. grief torment [A ~ الم]

تالمکھانہ talmukhkha'nah N.M. lotus seed (used as drug)

تال میل tal mel N.M. admixture impact

تالو ta'loo N.M. palate uvula an equestrian disease تالو اٹھانا ta'loo utha'na V.T. raise (infant's) uvula تالو سے زبان نہ لگنا ta'loo se zaban' na lag'na V.I. talk incessantly ; chatter تالو لٹکنا ta'loo la'takna V.I. (of uvula) fall

تالی ta'li N.F. clapping (col.) key تالیاں ta'liyan N.F. PL. applause ; plandit تالی (یا تالیاں) بجانا (یا پیٹنا) ta'li (or ta'liyan) baja'na (or pit'na) V.T. & I. clap applaud ; clap

تالیاں بجنا (یا پٹنا) ta liyan baj'na (or pit'na) V.I. be applauded be ridiculed with clapping تالی ایک ہاتھ سے نہیں بجتی ta'li ek' hath' se na'hin baj'ti, تالی دونوں ہاتھوں سے بجتی ہے ta'li do'non ha'thon se baj'ti hai PROV. it makes two to make a quarrel

تالیف tali̇f' N.F. compilation consolation winning over تالیف قلب tali̇'f-e qal'b, تالیف قلوب tali̇'f-e quloob' N.F. winning over تالیف کرنا tali̇f' kar'na V.T. compile [A ~ الفت]

تام tam, تامہ tam'mah ADJ. full ; complete entire ; whole [A ~ تمام]

تام چینی tam chi̇ni N.F. enamel ware ; enamelled iron vessels

تام جھام tam' jham, تامجان tam'jan N.M. airy palanquin

تامل ta'am'mul N.M. hesitation hitch delay disinclination careful thought deliberation meditation تامل کرنا ta'am'mul kar'na V.I. hesitate delay consider deliberate meditate [A ~ امل]

تاملوٹ tam'lot, تاملیٹ tam'lat N.M. tumbler any drinking vessel [~ E CORR.]

تان tan N.F. (in music) keynote tune palanquin's steel bracing تان (یا تانیں) اڑانا tan (or ta'nen) ura'na V.I. sing strike up tune(s) تان بھرنا (یا لینا یا مارنا) tan bhar'na (or le'na or mar'na) V.I. sing repeat (tune) تان توڑنا tan' tor'na V.T. wind up a tune end talk (with) finally come out with the basic point (at) تان سین tan'-sen N.M. title of a famous singer great musician

تانا ta'na N.M. wrap تانا بانا ta'na ba'na N.M. wrap and woof [~ تاننا]

تانبا tan'ba N.M. copper تانبا سا آسمان ہونا tan'ba sa asman' ho'na V.T. (of sky) be clear and hot تانبے کا تار نہ ہونا tan'be ka tar' na ho'na PH. be penniless ; be destitute

تانت tant N.F. gut catgut chord (of guitar, etc.) تانت سا tant sa ADJ. very lean

تانتی tan'ti N.F. line or row (of) (dial.) weaver (fig.) children.

تانتا tan'ta N.M. long line mobile crowd flux تانتا بندھنا (یا بندھ جانا یا لگ جانا) tan'ta bandh'na (or bandh' ja'na or lag' ja'na) V.I. (of people) be a flux

تانسنا tans'na V.T. maltreat be unkind to menace

تانگہ tan'gah, تانگا tan'ga N.M. tonga ; dog cart

تاننا *tan'na* V.T. stretch extend expand pull tight (over) knit (the eyebrow) tighten be at full length brandish **تان کر** *tan' kar* ADJ. having stretched with full force

تانے تشنے *tā'ne tash'ne*, **طعنے تشنے** *ta''ne..tish'ne* N.M. PL. (col.) taunts [A ~ طعن و تشنیع N.F. ★]

تانیث *tānis'* N.F. feminine gender being a female

تاوان *tāvān'* N.M. damages compensation indemnity mulct penalty reparation **تاوان دینا** *tāvān' de'nā* V.T. make amends pay a penalty **تاوان لگانا** *tāvān' lagā'nā* V.T. fine amerce penalize

تاویل *tāvīl'* N.F. interpretation elucidation reinterpretation interpret with ulterior motives **تاویل کرنا** *tāvīl' kar'nā* V.T. interpret elucidate reinterpret interpret with ulterior motives [A]

تاہل *ta'ah'hūl* N.M. marriage become a family man [A ~ اہل]

تائب *tā''ib* N.M. penitent one who is remorseful [A ~ توبہ]

تاؤ *tā''o* N.M. heat rage ; passion twist curl **تاؤ آنا** *tā''o ā'nā* V.I. fly into a passion ; be enraged accept a challenge ; pick up the gauntlet **تاؤ بگڑنا** *tā''o bi'garna* V.I. loose the opportunity be spoiled in cooking **تاؤ بھاؤ** *tā''o bhā''o* ADV. very little **تاؤ پر تاؤ آنا** *tā''o par tā''o ā'nā* V.I. heat curl (moustache) **تاؤ کھانا** *tā''o khā'nā*, **تاؤ میں آنا** *tā''o meṉ ā'na* V.I. be enraged ; be angry fly into a passion

تاؤ[2] *tā''o* N.M. (dial.) uncle ; father's elder brother [~ تایا]

تاؤلا *tā''olā* ADJ. & N.M. hasty (person)

تائید *tā'īd'* N.F. support corroboration aid ; assistance seconding ; sponsoring being seconded ; being sponsored **تائید کردہ** *tā'īd'-kar'dah* ADJ. seconded by ; sponsored by **تائید کرنا** *tā'īd' kar'nā* V.T. support corroborate confirm second sponsor **تائید کلام** *tā'ī'd-e kalām'* N.F. support of statement [A ~ ید]

تایا *tā'yā* N.M. uncle ; father's elder brother **تائی** *tā''ī* N.F. wife of father's elder brother

تب *tab* ADV. then ; at that time ; afterwards **تب بھی** *tab' bhī* ADV. & CONJ. yet ; still ; even then notwithstanding ; nevertheless ; nonetheless **تب تک** *tab' tak* ADV. & CONJ. till then up to that time **تب تو** *tab' to* ADV. & CONJ. then in that case ; in that instance **تب سے** *tab' se* ADV. & CONJ. since then thereafter ; thence **تب ہی** *tab' hī*, **تبھی** *ta'bhī* ADV. at that very moment ; exactly then for that very reason **تب ہی تو** *tab' hī to*, **تبھی تو** *ta'bhī to* ADV. for that very reason ; owing to the very fact **تب ہی سے** *tab' hī se*, **تبھی سے** *ta'bhī se* ADV. thence; thenceforth from that very moment

تب[2] *tab* N.F. (rare) (same as تپ N.F. ★) **تب و تاب** *ta'b-o-tāb'* N.F. guts heat labour [P]

تبادل *tabā'dūl* N.M. (ped.) exchange [A ~ بدلہ]

تبادلہ *tabād lah* (pseudo-ped. *tabā'dūlah*) N.M. transfer exchange **تبادلہ خیالات کرنا** *tabād'la-e khayālāt' kar'nā* V.T. exchange views have a chat [~ A تبادل]

تبار *tabār'* N.M. family dynasty [A]

تبارہ *tibā'rah* ADV. third time thrice [~ت+P بار]

تبارک *tabā'rak* ADJ. (of God) hallowed; glorified **تبارک و تعالیٰ** *tabā'rak(a)-va-ta'ālā* INT. hallowed and magnified (be His name) [A ~ برکت]

تباسی *tibā'sī* ADJ. three days' stale

تباشیر *tabāshīr'* N.F. medical sugar found between bamboo joints

تباہ *tabāh'* ADJ. ruined destroyed wasted spoiled wretched **تباہ کرنا** *tabāh' kar'nā* V.T. waste squander ruin **تباہ ہونا** *tabāh' ho'nā* V.I. be wasted be squandered be ruined **تباہ حال** *tabāh'-hāl* ADJ. ruined reduced to straits poverty striken miserable **تباہی** *tabā'hī* N.F. ruin destruction perdition wreck misery **تباہی آنا** *tabā'hī ā'nā* V.I. be ruined be wrecked **تباہی کا مارا** *tabā'hī kā mā'rā* ADJ. wretched afflicted ruined **تباہی لانا** *tabā'hī lā'nā* V.T. ruin destroy [P]

تباین *tabā'yūn* N.M. difference [A ~ بین *bain*]

تبخالہ *tab-khā'lah* N.M. eruptions on mouth corners (as aftermath) of fever [P ~ تب+خال]

تبختر *tabakh'tur* N.M. swagger [A]

تبخیر *tabkhīr'* N.F. evaporation vaporisation heart burn low fever temperature [A ~ بخار]

تبدل *tabad'dūl* N.M. (lit.) change ; alteration (usu. in) **تغیر و تبدل** *taghay'yūr-o tabad'dūl* PH.

changes reshuffling [A ~ بدل]
تبدیل *tabdīl'* N.F. change ; alteration modification تبدیل شدہ *tabdīl' shu'dah* ADJ. changed transferred تبدیل آب و ہوا *tabdī'l-e a'b-o havā'* N.F. change of climate تبدیل کرنا *tabdīl kar'nā* V.T. transfer change; alter تبدیل ہونا *tabdīl' ho'nā* V.I. be transferred change ; alter تبدیل ہیئت کرنا *tabdī'l-e hai''at kar'nā* V.T. disguise change the aspect metamorphose [A ~ بدل]
تبدیلی *tabdī'lī* N.F. transfer changing alteration تبدیلی کرنا *tabdī'lī kar'nā* V.T. transfer change ; alter تبدیلی ہونا *tabdī'lī ho'nā* V.I. be transferred be changed ; be altered [~ A تبدیل]
تبذیر *tabzīr'* N.F. extravagance [A ~ بذر]
تبر *ta'bar* N.M. hatchet axe تبرزن *ta'bar-zan* N.M. wood-cutter [P]
تبرا *tabar'rā* N.M. curse malediction expression of disapproval abuse; abusive language ; fulmination ; invective تبرا بھیجنا (یا کرنا) *tabar'rā bhej'nā* (or *kar'nā*) V.T. express disapproval curse fulminate inveigh تبرائی *ta'bar'rā''ī* N.M. member of a seat expressing disapproval of (or fulminating) against first orthodox Caliphs [A ~ براءت]
تبرج *ta'bar'ruj* N.M. (of woman) make a show of her make-up, etc. ; move about enticingly [A]
تبرک *tabar'ruk* N.M. left over food or other gift from a saint or shine gift benediction تبرکاً *tabar'rukan* ADV. as a gift ; as a present for receiving benediction تبرکات *tabar'rukāt'* N.M. PL. such gifts relics [A ~ برکت]
تبرید *tab'rīd* N.F. cooling dose taken after purgative (fig.) cooling down [A ~ برودت]
تبسم *tabas'sum* N.M. smile تبسم کرنا *tabas'sum kar'nā* V.I. smile [A]
تبصرہ *tab'sirah* N.M. review criticism [A ~ بصر]
تبع *tab'ʻ* N.M. follower تبع تابعین *tab''-e tābi'īn'* N.M. follower of the successors to the Holy Prophet's Companions (usu. as the third link in chain of tradition narrators) [A]
تبلیغ *tablīgh'* N.F. preaching missionary work proselytism spread or propagation (of views) تبلیغ و اشاعت *tablī'gh-o ishā''at* N.F. propagation (of faith, view, etc.) [A ~ بلاغ]
تپ *tap* (rare تب *tab*) N.F. fever تپ اتارنا *tap' utār'nā* V.T. reduce temperature ; cure of fever تپ اترنا *tap' u'tarnā* V.I. be cured of fever تپ چڑھنا *tap' charh'nā* V.T. have fever تپ دق *ta'p-e diq* N.F. consumption ; pulmonary tuberculosis تپ زرد *ta'p-e zard'* N.F. yellow fever تپ کا موت جانا *tap kā moot' jā'nā* V.I. having after-fever eruption on corners of mouth تپ لرزہ *ta'p-e lar'zah* N.F. malaria ague تپ محرقہ *ta'p-e moh'riqah* N.F. typhoid تپ نوبت *ta'p-e nau'bat* N.F. (ped.) intermittent fever [P]
تپاک *tapāk'* N.M. ardour ; warmth ; zeal cordiality regard ; esteem [P]
تپاں *tapāñ* ADJ. agitated restless ; uneasy hot [P]
تپانا *tapā'nā* V.T. heat cause to glow test (metal) [~ تپنا CAUS.]
تپائی *tipā''ī* N.F. trivet tripod teapoy ; small table low stool (dial.) [تے three +P]
تپڑ *tap'par* N.M. (dial) matting mat seat
تپسیا *tapas'siyā* N.F. (dial.) prayer [S]
تپش (or طپش) *ta'pish* N.F. heat ardour uneasiness grief [P]
تپنا *tap'nā* V.I. become hot glow burn with grief
تپنچہ (or طپنچہ) *tapañchah* N.M. pistol revolver [P]
تپیدہ *tapī'dah* ADJ. glowing restless [P ~ تپیدن]
تتا *tat'tā* ADJ. (rare) hot warm ; tepid
تتبع *tatab'boʻ* N.M. following toeing the line following in (someone's) footsteps تتبع کرنا *tatab'boʻ kar'nā* V.T. following toe the line fellow in (someone's) footsteps
تتر بتر *tit'tar bit'tar* ADJ. dispersed scattered ; lying here and there تتر بتر ہونا *tit'tar bit'tar ho'nā* V.T. be dispersed be scattered
تتق *tu'tuq* N.M. (lit.) tent its curtains تتق نیلی *tu'tuq-e nī'lī* N.M. the heavens ; sky [P]
تتلانا *tutlā'nā* V.I. lisp
تتلی *tit'lī*, تیتری *tīt'rī* N.F. butterfly sportive beauty ; painted doll
تتمبا *titam'bā* N.M. (W. dial) fix dispute
تتمہ *tatim'mah* N.M. supplement appendix post-script [A ~ تمام]
تتو تھمبو کرنا *tat'too tham'boo kar'nā* V.T. delay console

تہرڑا *tateh'ra* N.M. تہرڑی *tateh'ri* N.F water-heater

تلیا *talay'ya* N.F. red and yellow wasp ADJ. clever sharp pungent

تثلیث *tas'lis* N.F. Trinity ; triple godhead of Pauline Christianity trine ; aspect of two planets 120 apart division into three [A ~ ثلاثہ]

تثنیہ *tas'niyah* N.M. dual form ; dual [A ~ اثنین]

تج *taj* N.F. (bark of) bay-tree cinnamon cassia

تجاذب *taja'zub* N.M. attraction gravitation [A ~ جذب]

تجار *tujjar'* N.M. merchants ; traders business community ملک التجار *ma'lik-ut-tujjar'* N.M. business magnate ; tycoon [A ~ SING. تاجر]

تجارب *taja'rib* N.M. PL. experiences experiments [A ~ SING. تجربہ]

تجارت *tija'rat* N.F. trade ; commerce traffic business تجارت کرنا *tija'rat kar'na* V.T. deal (in) trade ; traffic business تجارت گاہ *tija'rat-gah* N.F. market business centre تجارتی *tija'rati* ADJ. commercial mercantile business تجارتی ادارہ *tija'rati ida'rah* N.M. business firm commercial firm تجارتی خطوط پر *tija'rati khutoot' par* ADV. on business lines تجارت خارجہ *tija'rat-e kha'rijah* N.F. foreign trade [A]

تجاوز *taja'vuz* N.M. transgression deviation exceeding (one's limits, etc.) تجاوز کرنا *taja'vuz kar'na* V.I. transgress deviate exceed (one's limits) [A]

تجاہل *taja'hul* N.M. feigned ignorance indifference ; apathy تجاہل عارفانہ *taja'hul-e 'arifa'nah* N.M. feigned ignorance [A ~ جہالت]

تجدد *tajad'dud* N.M. freshness novelty [A]

تجدید *tajdid'* N.F. renewal revival [A ~ جدید]

تجربہ *taj'ribah* N.M. experience experiment تجربہ کار *taj'riba-kar'* (or. -be) ADJ. experienced skilful ; expert conversant (with) veteran تجربہ کاری *taj'riba-ka'ri* N.F. experience practical knowledge ; know-how being conversant with تجربہ کرنا *taj-ribah kar'na* V.T. experience experiment try تلخ تجربہ *tal'kh taj'ribah* N.M. bitter experience تجربات *taj'ribat'* N.M. PL. experiences wide experience experiments تجرباتی *tajriba'ti* ADJ. experimental [A]

تجرد *tajar'rud* N.M. celibacy unmarried state (ped.) solitude [A]

تجرید *taj'rid'* N.F. abstraction solitude separation restriction to single meaning (as figure of speech) تجریدی *tajri'di* ADJ. abstract (art, idea, etc) تجریدی مصوری *tajri'di musav'viri* N.F. abstract art [A]

تجزیہ *taj'ziyah* N.M. (rare تجزی *tajaz'zi* N.F.) analysis نفسیاتی تجزیہ *naf'siyya'ti taj'ziyah* N.M. psychological analysis تجزیاتی *tajziya'ti* ADJ. analytical [A ~ جزو]

تجسس *tajas'sus* N.M. curiosity inquisitiveness ; prying inquiry ; diligent ; search تجسس کرنا *tajas'sus kar'na* V.T. explore be inquisition ; pry into show curiosity [A ~ جاسوس]

تجسم *tajas'sum* N.M. incarnation ; embodiment [A ~ جسم]

تجلی *tajal'li* (pseudo ped. تجلیٰ *tajal'la*) N.F. manifestation brilliance ; refulgence splendour تجلی بخش *tajal'li bakh'sh*, تجلی ریز *tajal'li-rez* ADJ. refulgent splendid making (oneself) manifest [A ~ جلوہ]

تجلید *tajlid'* N.F. flaying binding (of book) [A ~ جلد]

تجمل *tajam'mul* N.M. magnificence pomp and show decoration adornment [A ~ جمال]

تجنا *taj'na* V.T. renounce abandon

تجنیس *tajnis'* N.F. alliteration pun equivocation use of similarly spelt or sounded words (as a literary device) تجنیس تام *tajni's-e tam'* N.F. (use of) heteronyms تجنیس خطی *tajni's-e khat'ti* N.F. (use of) pair of words written alike but with different vowel-points تجنیس زائد *taj'ni's-e za''id* N.F. (use of) two words which are alike otherwise but one of which has an extra letter تجنیس قلب *taj'ni's-e qal'b* N.F. (use of) pair of words spelt in exactly the opposite ways تجنیس مرکب *tajni's-e murak'kab* N.F. (use of) pair of words one of which forms part of another تجنیس ناقص *tajni's-e na'qis* N.F. (use of) pair of words whose initial letters only are different تجنیس مزدوج *tajni's-e muz'davj* N.F. (use of) pair of synonymous words one of which is simple and other compound [A ~ جنس]

تجوید *tajvid'* N.F. phonetics declamation recitation of the Holy Quran [A ~ جید]

تجویز *taj'viz'* N.F. suggestion proposal motion plan ; scheme prescription (of medicines) consideration تجویز کرنا *tajviz' kar'nā* V.I. suggest propose move plan write out a prescription ; prescribe تجویز ہونا *tajvīz' ho'nā* V.I. be proposed be moved be planned (of medicine) be prescribed زیر تجویز *ze'r-e tajvīz'* ADV. proposed under consideration

تجھ **tūjh** PRON. you thee تجھ کو *tūj'he,* تجھے *tūjh, ko,* تجکو *tūj'ko* PRON. (accusative) you thee تجھ کو پرائی کیا پڑی اپنی نبیڑ تو *tūjh' ko parā''ī kyā pa'ṛī ap'nī naber' too* PROV. mind your own business ; do not poke your nose into the affairs of others physician cure thyself تجھی *tū'jhī* PRON. you alone ; thee alone

تجہیز **tajhīz'** N.F. taking out of funeral procession تجہیز و تکفین *tajhī'z-o tak'fīn'* N.F. obsequies ; funeral rites and ceremonies [A ~ جہاز]

تحائف **tahā''if** N.M. (PL. of تحفہ ★)

تحت **tah't** (or *taih't*) N.M. subjection subordination charge ; control ADV. subordinate (to) under control (of) below beneath inferior (to) PREF. infra under تحت الثریٰ *tah't-ūs-sarā'* N.F. nether regions ADV. deep down in earth تحت الشعور *tah't-ash-shū'oor'* N.M. subconscious (mind) Id تحت اللفظ *tah't-ūl-laf'z* ADJ. (of translation) literal (of its printing) interlinear (of verse) recitation (without singing) تحت اللفظ پڑھنا *tah't-ūl-laf'z parh'nā* V.T. recite (without) singing تحت میں آنا *taih't men ā'nā* V.I. come under the control (of) تحتانی *tahtā'nī* ADJ. (letter of alphabet) having dots underneath ; downdotted [A]

تحجر **tahaj'jūr** N.M. fossilization [A ~ حجر]

تحدی **tahad'dī** N.F. challenge [A]

تحدیث **tahdīs'** N.F. narration ; recounting [A ~ حدیث]

تحدید **tah'dīd** N.F. restriction limitation [A ~ حد]

تحذیر **tah'zīr'** N.F. threatening cautioning [A ~ حذر]

تحریر **tahrīr'** N.F. (act of) writing (piece of) writing manuscript composition document undertaking manumission line like stain (of antimony) (old use) Euclid's elements تحریراً *tahrī'ran* ADV. (rare) in writing ; written تحریر اقلیدس *tahrī'r-e uqlī'dis* N.F. Euclid's elements بین السطور تحریر *bain-ūs-sūtoor tahrī'r* N.F. writing between the lines تحریر ظہری *tahrī'r-e zah'rī* N.F. endorsement writing on the back تحریر کرنا *tahrīr' kar'nā* V.T. write ; reduce to writing put in black and white give in writing compile compose record (rare) free (slave) تحریر ہونا *tahrīr' ho'nā* V.I. be written be recorded تحریری *tahrī'rī* ADJ. documentary in writing ; written [A]

تحریص **tahrīs'** N.F. temptation instigation [A ~ حرص]

تحریض **tahrīz'** N.F. incitement [A]

تحریف **tahrīf** N.F. distortion (of meaning) tampering (with text) [A ~ حرف]

تحریک **taihrīk'** (or *taih-*) N.F. movements agitation motion incitement urging encouragement تحریک چلانا *tahrīk chalā'nā* V.T. launch a movement تحریک کرنا *tahrīk' kar'nā* V.T. urge move incite تحریک پیش کرنا *tahrīk' pesh kar'nā* V.I. put forth or bring forward or move a motion تحریک پیش ہونا *tahrīk' pesh ho'nā* V.I. (of motion) be moved تحریک منظور کرنا *tahrīk' manzoor' kar'nā* V.T. adopt a resolution ; accept a motion تحریک منظور ہونا *tahrīk' manzoor' ho'nā* V.I. (of motion) be carried [A ~ حرکت]

تحریم **tahrīm'** N.F. glorification ; honour prohibition assumption of a pilgrim's garb تحریمہ *tahrī'mah* ADJ. forbidding other things than prayer [A ~ حرمت]

تحسین **tahsīn'** (or *taih-*) N.F. appreciation approbation acclamation تحسین کرنا *tahsīn' kar'nā* V.T. praise approve appreciate applaud acclaim [A ~ حسن]

تحشیہ **tahshiyah** N.M. annotation [A ~ حاشیہ]

تحصیل **tahsīl'** N.F. administrative division in district its headquarters (revenue) collection acquisition attainment learning تحصیل حاصل *tahsī'l-e hā'sil* N.F. superfluous attempt تحصیلدار *tahsīl'-dār* N.M. Tehsildar ; revenue and administrative official incharge of tehsil تحصیلداری *tahsīl'-dārī* N.F. office of Tehsildar تحصیلات *tahsīlāt'* N.F. PL. (old use) collections acquisitions education تحصیل کرنا *tahsīl' kar'na* V.T. acquire receive education collect (revenue) تحصیل مالگذاری *tahsi'l-e māl-gūzā'rī* N.F. revenue collection of revenue [A ~ حصول]

تحفظ **tahaf'fūz** N.M. safeguard preservation conservation تحفظات *tahaf'fūzāt'* N.M. PL. safeguards تحفظ اثمار *tahaf'fūz-e asmār'* N.M. fruit preservation تحفظ اراضی *tahaf'fūze arā'zī* N.M. soil conservation تحفظ شکار و اشجار *tahaf'fūze* *shikā'r-o ashjār'* N.M. preservation of fauna and flora [A ~ حفاظت]

تحفہ *toh'fah* N.M. gift : present rarity تحائف *tahā''if,* تحف *to'haf* N.M. PL. gifts ; presents rarities curious [A]

تحقق *tahaq'qūq* N.M. ascertainment [A ~ حقیقت]

تحقیر *tahqīr'* N.F. contempt ; scorn ; disdain [A ~ حقارت]

تحقیق *tahqīq'* (or *taih-*) N.F. research inquiry investigation ascertainment verification ADV. verily ; truly indeed

تحقیقی *tahqī'qī* ADJ. research verified authentic تحقیقات *tahqīqāt'* N.F. investigation inquiry research [A ~ حقیقت]

تحکم *tahak'kūm* N.M. imperiousness domination تحکم جتانا *tahak'kūm jatā'nā* V.T. act imperiously تحکم پسند(انہ) *tahakk'ūm-pasand(ā'nah)* ADJ. & ADV. imperious [A ~ حکومت]

تحکیم *tahkīm'* N.F. arbitration

تحلیف *tahlīf* N.F. administration of oath [A ~ حلف]

تحلیل *tahlīl'* N.F. analysis dissolving legalization تحلیل کرنا *tahlīl kar'nā* V.T. dissolve assimilate analyse تحلیل نفسی *tahlīl-e naf'sī* N.F. psychological analysis تحلیل ہونا *tahlīl ho'nā* V.I. be dissolved تحلیلی *tahlī'lī* ADJ. analytical تحلیل نفسیات *tahlī'lī-o nafsiyyāt'* N.F. psycho-analysis [A ~ حل]

تحمل *taham'mūl* N.M. toleration ; forbearance patience ; endurance تحمل کرنا *taham'mūl kar'nā* V.T. forbear tolerate; bear endure [A ~ حمل]

تحمید *tahmīd'* N.F. praise of God [A ~ حمد]

تحویل *tahvīl'* N.F. (Math.) reduction passage of heavenly body (from one sign of zodiac to another) trust ; charge custody تحویل میں دینا *tahvīl' men de'nā* V.T. pluck in custody of تحویل میں لینا *tahvīl' men le'nā* V.T. take custody of take hold of تحویل تصرف *tahvī'l-e tasar'rūf* N.M. (arch.) misappropriation ; embezzlement ; defalcation تحویلدار *tahvīl'-dār* N.M. (old use) trustee treasurer [A ~ حوالہ]

تحیر *tahay'yūr* N.M. wonder astonishment amazement [A ~ حیرت]

تحیہ *tahiy'yah* N.M. (PL. تحیات *tahiyyāt'*) salutation [A]

تخالف *takhā'lūf* N.M. mutual opposition ; contention [A ~ خلاف]

تخت *takh't* N.M. throne wooden bed تخت بخت *takh't bakh't* N.M. (as blessing) throne and fortune wedlock and wealth تخت پر بٹھانا *takh't par biṭhā'nā* V.T. be enthroned become a king تخت چھوڑنا *takh't-chhoṛ'nā* V.I. abdicate تخت رواں *takh't-e ravān'* N.M. mobile throne flying sedan تخت سلیمان *takh't-e sulaimān'* N.M. flying sedan of Solomon تخت سے اتارنا *takh't se utār'nā* V.T. dethrone تخت طاؤس *takh't-e tā'oos'* N.M. the Peacock Throne تخت کی رات *takh't kī rāt* N.F. wedding night تخت گاہ *takh't-gāh* N.M. capital seat of government تخت نشین ہونا *takh't-nashīn' ho'nā* V.I. ascend the throne assume royal powers تخت نشینی *takh't-nashī'nī* N.F accession to the throne coronation تخت یا تختہ *takh't yā takh'tah* PROV do or die reign or ruin [P]

تختہ *takh'tah* N.M. plank ; a board sign sign-board (ships) deck drawbridge (flower) bed تختہ الٹنا *takh'tah ū'laṭnā* V.T. overthrow (government) ruin , destroy تختہ برقی *takh'ta-e bar'qī* N.M. switch-board تختہ بندی *takh'ta ban'dī* N.F. arrangement of flowers bed wainscot تختہ بندی کرنا *takh'ta bandī kar'nā* V.T. arrange flower beds plank تختہ پل *takh'ta pūl* N.M. drawbridge تختہ تابوت *takh'ta-e tāboot'* N.M. bier hearse تختہ سیاہ *takh'tah siyāh'* N.M. blackboard تختہ مشق *takh'ta-e mash'q* N.M. tablet victim تختہ نرد *takh'ta-e nar'd* N.M. backgammon تختہ ہو جانا *takh'tah ho jā'nā* V.T. (of body) become stiff تختی *takh'tī* N.F. tablet small board [P]

تخرجہ *takh'rijah* N.M. chronogram-writing ; recording of date in chronogram form [A ~ خرج]

تخریب *takhrīb'* N.F. destruction subversion تخریبی *takhrī'bī* ADJ. destructive تخریبی کارروائیاں *takhrī'bī karravā''iyāṅ* N.F. sabotage [A ~ خراب]

تخشع *takhash'shoʻ* N.M. (lit.) humility [A ~ خشوع]

تخصیص *takhsīs'* N.F. specialization peculiarity ; singularity [A ~ خاص]

تخفیف *takh'fīf'* N.F. retrenchment reduction ; decrease alleviation ; mitigation cut curtailment remission commutation تخفیف قیمت *takhfīf-e-qīmat* N.F. devaluation pricecut ; reduction in price تخفیف کرنا *takh'fīf kar'nā* V.T. retrench decrease , reduce curtail mitigate

alleviate تخفیف میں لانا takhfif' men lā'na v.t. retrench (person) abolish (post) [A ~ تخفیف]
تخلص takhal'lus n.m. (poet's) pen-name 'nom de plume' (rare) deviation (in ode from introduction to theme) [A]
تخلف takhal'luf n.m. being left behind going back on one's words [A ~ خلف]
تخلیہ takh'liyah n.m. privacy private meeting [A ~ خلا]
تخم tukh'm n.m. seed (fig.) origin تخم بالنگو (یا بالنگا) tukh'm-e bālan'goo (or bālañ'gā) n.m. mountain-balm seed ; a kind of seed saturated to form part of cold drink تخم بد tukh'm-e bad', تخم حرام tukh'm-e ḥarām' adj. bastard تخم تاثیر صحبت کا اثر tukh'm tāsīr' soh'bat kā a'sar prov. heredity and environment go to make the man تخم ریحاں tukh'm-e raihan' n.m. purslane تخم ریزی tukh'm-re'zī n.f. sowing ; broadcasting تخم کتاں tukh'm-e-katān' n.m. linseed [P]
تخمہ tukh'mah n.m. gastro-enteritis [A]
تخمیر takhmīr' n.f. fermentation ; leavening [A ~ خمیر]
تخمین takhmīn' n.m. estimate guess zan'n-o takhmīn' n.m. mere guess guess fork conjecture تخمیناً takhmī'nan adj. about ; approximately تخمینہ takhmī'nah n.m. guess ; conjecture evaluation appraisal [A]
تخویف takhvīf' n.f. intimidation تخویف مجرمانہ takhvī'f-e mūjrimā'nah n.f. criminal intimidation [A ~ خوف]
تخیل takhay'yul n.m. imagination ; fancy idea ; thought of imagery suspicion تخیلات takhayyulāt' n.m. pl. idea ; thoughts flights of fancy [A ~ خیال]
تدارک tadā'ruk n.m. amends remedy reparation precaution safeguards redress readiness تدارک کرنا tadā'rūk kar'na v.t. remedy redress provide against safeguard be prepared for تدارک ہونا tadā'-rūk ho'nā v.i. be remedied be redressed [A]
تدبر tadab'bur n.m. statesmanship prudence deliberation غور و تدبر ghau'r-o-tadab'būr n.m. careful thought [A]
تدبیر tadbīr' n.f. (pl. تدابیر tadābīr') policy device ; contrivance advice ; council arrangement course of action ; way out plan تدبیر سلطنت tadbī'r-e sal'ṭanat n.f. (arch.) management of state affairs ; politics تدبیر منزل tadbī'r-e man'zil n.f. domestic economy تدبیر فاسد tadbī'r-e fā sid v.t. plot vicious plan [A]
تدرو tadar'v n.m. cock pheasant [P]
تدریج tadrīj' n.f. gradation regular step (rare) scale بتدریج ba-tadrīj' adv. gradually ; by degrees ; step by step [A ~ درجہ]
تدریس tadrīs' n.f. instruction teaching lectures (on) تدریسی tadrī'sī adj. teaching ; instructional [A ~ درس]
تدفین tadfīn' n.f. burial ; interment [A ~ دفن]
تدقیق tadqīq' n.f. close or minute study going into minutia (rare) pulverization [A ~ دقیق]
تدوین tadvīn' n.f. compilation editing [A ~ دیوان]
تدین taday'yun n.m. religiousness prudery [P ~ دین]
تذبذب tazab'zūb n.m. vacillation wavering suspense
تذکار tazkār' n.m. account narrative [A ~ ذکر]
تذکرہ taz'kirah n.m. mention memoir biography collection of biographical notes (on poets, etc.) [A ~ ذکر]
تذکیر tazkīr' n.f. admonition helping to recall refreshing the memory [A ~ ذکر]
تذلل tazal'lul n.m. humiliation ; humiliating oneself [A ~ ذلت]
تذلیل tazlīl' n.f. humiliation degradation abasement تذلیل کرنا tazlīl' kar'nā v.t. abase تذلیل ہونا tazlīl' ho'nā v.t. be abased [A ~ ذلت]
تر¹ tar adj. wet, moist ; damp saturated fresh refreshed green ; lush ; juicy
تربتر tar' ba-tar' adj. shaked drenched quite wet (of food) rich with much butter oil in it تردامن tar-dā'man adj. sinful guilty immoral تردامنی tar-dā'manī n.f. sinfulness guilt immorality ترکرنا tar' kar'nā v.t. soak saturate ترلقمہ tar' lūq'mah, ترمال tar' māl, ترنوالہ tar nivā'lah n.m. morsel of rich food (fig.) good catch adj. easy work godsend تر و تازہ ta'r-o ta'zah adj. fresh and mellow تری ta'rī n.f. moisture wetness ocean hydrosphere [P]
تر² tar suf. (indicating comparative degree) more ; greater ; -er [P]
تراب tūrāb' n.m. earth dust soil ابوتراب a'boo tūrāb' n.m. (see under ابو n.m. ★) ترابی tūrā'bī adj. earthen [A]

تراجم tarā'jim N.M. translation translated books renderings [A ~ SING. ترجمہ]

ترارا tarāra N.M. (of horse) leap: gallop ترارا بھرنا tarā'rā bhar'nā ترارا بھرتے ہوئے جانا tarā're bhar'te hū''e jā'nā V.I. gallop run away

ترازو tarā'zoo N.F. balance ; pair of scales ترازو ہو جانا tarā'zoo ho ja'nā V.I. (of arrow) transfix and lie evenly balanced [P]

تراسی tirā'sī ADJ. & N.M. eighty-three ترا سیواں tirā'sīvāṅ ADJ. eighty-third

تراش tarāsh' N.F. (of clothes, hair, etc.) cut style ; fashion SUF. cutting carver

تراش خراش tarāsh'-kharāsh' N.F. cut ; style ; fashion elegance بت تراش būt'-tarā'sh N.M. image-carver ; sculptor سنگ تراش sang'-tarā'sh N.F. sculptor stone-cutter سنگ تراشی saing'-tarā'shī N.F. sculpture carving of stones [P ~ تراشیدن]

تراشنا tarāsh'nā V.T. cut carve shave slice shape تراشہ tarā'shah N.M. (of newspaper etc.) cutting ; clipping [~ P PREC.]

تراضی tarā'zee N.F. mutual agreement conciliation [A ~ راضی]

ترانا ti'rānā V.T. let float [~ تیرنا CAUS.]

ترانوے tirān've ADJ. & N.M. ninety-three ترانویں tirān'vevāṅ ADJ. ninety-third

ترانہ tarā'nah N.M. song anthem قومی ترانہ qau'mī tarā'nah N.M. national anthem [P]

تراوش tarā'vish N.F. dripping [P ~ تراویدن]

تراویح tarāvīḥ' N.F. special night prayers in 'ramazan' [A ~ SING. ترویح]

ترّاہ ترّاہ مچنا tirāh' tirāh' mach'nā V.T. be a hue and cry

تراہا tirahā N.M. junction of three roads trifurcation [ت + P راہ]

ترائی tarā''ī N.F. land lying along river course most land strip of land at foot of kill

تربت tūr'bat N.F. grave tomb sepulchre

ترب tū'rūb N.F. radish [P]

ترب ta'rab N.M. supporting string in guiter, etc.

تربوز tarbooz' N.M. water-melon

تر بھر ہونا tir' bhir ho'nā V.I. be enraged

تربیت tar'biyat N.F. training bringing up; breeding ; rearing instruction تربیت پذیر tar'biyat-pazīr' ADJ. tractable amenable docile تربیت دینا (یا کرنا) tar'biyat de'nā (or kar'nā) bring up ; rear ; bread instruct [A]

ترپال tirpāl' N.M. tarpaulin [E]

ترپائی tūrpā''ī, ترپن tur'pan N.F. (see under ترپنا V.T. ★)

ترپن tari'pan ADJ. & N.M. (same as ترپن ADJ. & N.M. ★)

ترپنا tū'rapnā V.T. hem stitch to conceal first seams ترپائی turpā''ī N.F. such stitches hem neat stiches stitching ترپن tūrpan N.F. neat stitches

ترپولیا taripauliyā N.M. set of three adjacent gates for easier access

ترپھلا tir'phlā N.M. powder of three myrobalans (used as drug) [~ تر (=تین) + پھل]

ترت tūr't ADV. soon quickly immediately straight ; direct ترت پھرت turt'-phurt' N.F. quickness ; promptness ADJ. active agile nemble

ترترا tūr'tūra, ترتریا tūrturay'yā ADJ. active ; agile facile

ترتیب tar'tīb' N.F. arrangement order formation deployment compilation classification composing assorting ترتیب تہجی tartī'b-e tahaj'jī N.F. alphabetical order ترتیب دینا tar'tīb de'nā V.T. arrange assort put in order compose classify compile set up; establish ترتیب سے tar'tīb' se, ترتیب وار tartīb'-vār ADV. in proper order methodically regularly [A ~ رتبہ]

ترتیل tartīl' N.F. clear and distinct recitation (esp. of Holy Quran) [A]

ترجمان tarjūmān' N.M. interpreter turgoman [A ~ ترجمہ]

ترجمہ tar'jamah N.M. translation rendering (rare) life-sketch ترجمہ کرنا tar'jamah kar'nā V.T. translate ; render into ترجمہ ہونا tar'jamah ho'nā V.I. be translated لفظی ترجمہ laf'zī tar'jamah N.M. literal translation بین السطور ترجمہ bai'n-ūs-sūtoor' tar'jamah N.F. interlinear translation با محاورہ ترجمہ bā-moḥā'varah tar'jamah N.M. idiomatic translation ; idiomatic rendering [A]

ترجیح tar'jīḥ N.F. preference priority ; precedence ترجیح دینا tar'jīḥ' de'nā V.I. prefer give preference give priority or precedence ترجیح ملنا tar'jīḥ' mil'nā V.I. be given preference be given priority or precedence ترجیحی tarjī'ḥī ADJ. preferential ترجیحی سلوک tarjī'ḥī sulook' N.M. preferential treatment [A ~ رجحان]

ترجیع *tarjī''* N.F. repetition of formula 'in'na lillah' at news of someone's death return of heavenly body to previous position (of singer or bird) lapse into earlier tune ; remodulation return ترجیع بند *tarjī''-band'* N.M. stanzas with same refrain [A ~ رجوع]

ترچھا *tir'chhā* ADJ. (F. ترچھی *tir'chhī*) slanting awry ; oblique crosswise ; crossways askance ترچھا دیکھنا *tir'chhā dekh'nā* V.I. squint ; look askance ترچھی نظر (یا نگاہ) سے دیکھنا *tir'chhī na'zar* (or *nigah'*) *se dekh'nā* V.I. frown ; scowl ; glower ترچھی نظر (یا نگاہ) *tir'chhī na'zar* (or *nigāh'*) N.F. ogle leer

ترحم *tarah'hum* N.M. mercy kindness pity ; compassion نظر ترحم ڈالنا (یا سے دیکھنا) *na'zar-e tarah'hum dāl'nā* (or *se dekh'nā*) V.T. have pity (on) show mercy (to) be compassionate [A ~ رحم]

ترخیم *tarkhīm'* N.F. (gram.) apocope curtailment [A]

تردد *tarad'dud* N.M. hesitation wavering; vacillation suspense anxiety ; worry delay [A ~ رد]

تردید *tardīd'* N.F. contradiction ; refutation; repudiation rebuttal venial تردید کرنا *tardīd' kar'nā* V.T. contradict ; confute ; refute ; repudiate relent deny تردید ہونا *tardīd' ho'nā* V.I. be contradicted be rebutted be denied [A ~ رد]

ترسنا *ta'rassnā* V.I. desire anxiously long for ترس *ta'ras* N.M. pity ; compassion mercy ترس آنا (یا کھانا) *ta'ras ānā* (or *khā'nā*) V.I. pity give way to compassion ترسا ترسا کر دینا *tarsā' tarsā' kar de'nā* V.T. tantalize dole out insufficient amounts ترسانا *tarsā'nā* V. tantalize cause to long for

ترسا *tarsā'* N.M. monk magus ; fire-worshipper christian SUF. terrifying threatening ; menacing [P]

ترس *ta'ras* N.M. fear terror cowardice timidity ترساں *tar'sāṅ* ADJ. fearful ; afraid timid ترسناک *ta'rasnāk* ADJ. terrifying ; horrible (rare) terrified

ترسٹھ *tarisath* ADJ. & N.M. (same as تریسٹھ ADJ. & N.M. ★)

ترسول *tarisool'* N.M. trident [S]

ترسوں *tar son*, اترسوں *atar'soṅ* N.M. & ADV. second day after tomorrow or before yesterday

ترسیل *tar'sīl'* N.F. despatch transmission remittance شعبۂ ترسیل *sho''ba-e tarsīl'* N.M. despatch section [A]

ترش *tur'sh* ADJ. sour acrid cross ; crabbed acrid ; surly ترش رو *tursh'roo* ADJ. peevish cross ; crabbed surly; acrid ترشروئی *tur sh-roo''ī* N.F. peevishness surliness ترش مزاج *tur'sh-mizāj'* ADJ. peevish cross ; crabbed surly ; acrid ترش مزاجی *tur'sh-mizā'jī* N.M. peevishness surliness ترشانا *turshā'nā*, ترشا جانا *turshā' jā'nā* V.I. turn sour acidulate ترشہ *tur'shah* N.M. acid ترشی *tur'shī* N.F. sourness acidity [P]

ترشح *tarash'shoh* N.M. drizzle sprinkling ترشح کرنا *tarash'shoh kar'nā* V.T. sprinkle water over ترشح ہونا *tarash'shoh ho'nā* V.I. drizzle [A]

ترشنا *ta'rashnā* be cut be clipped [~ تراشنا]

ترشہ *tur'shah*, ترشی *tur'shī* N.F. (see under ترش ADJ. ★)

ترصد *taras'sud* N.M. (lit.) ambush hope expectation [A ~ رصد]

ترصیع *tarsī''* N.F. setting (jewels) ; studding with (jewels) adornment ; bedecking setting out one phrase against another in corresponding rhymes composing (lovely poem) [A]

ترغیب *targhīb'* N.F. inducement incitement persuasion temptation reduction ترغیب دینا *targhīb' de'nā* V.T. induce incite persuade tempt seduce ; ترغیب وتحریص *targhī'b-o tahrīs'* N.F. temptation ترغیب وتحریض *targhī'b-o-tahrīz'* N.F. inducement [A ~ رغبت]

ترقی *taraq'qī* N.F. progress ; advancement improvement development promotion preferment proficiency increase ; enhancement ترقی دینا *taraq'qī de'nā* V.T. develop promote give or allow increment ترقی پانا (یا ملنا یا حاصل کرنا) *taraq'qī pā'nā* (or *mil'nā* or *hā'sil kar'nā*) V.I. develop be promoted get increment ترقی کرنا *taraq'qī kar'nā* V.I. advance ; develop [A]

ترقیم *tarqīm'* N.F. writing out figures [A ~ رقم]

ترک *tur'k* N.M. Turk (fig.) sweetheart ; beloved ترکتاز *turk-tāz* N.F. plunder spoliage depredation inroad ; incursion [T]

ترک *tar'k* N.M. giving up quitting relinguishing abdication desertion breaking (a habit) forsaking dropping (mission) desisting ترک کرنا *tar'k kar'nā* quit relinquish ; forsake desist from leave out ; drop ; suit ترکِ وطن *tar'k-e va'tan* N.M. emigration ترکِ وطن کرنا *tar'k-e va'tan kar'nā* V.I. emigrate go into exile [A]

ترکاری *tarkā'rī* N.F. vegetable , green (esculent) vegetables [P ~ تر]

ترکتاز *tūrk'tāz* N.F. see under ترک *tūr'k* N.M. ★)

ترکش *tar'-kash* (ped. *tīr* -) N.M. quiver [P ~ تیر + کش]

ترکمان *tūr'kamān* N.M. Turcoman Turkoman [P]

ترکم ترکا *tar'kam tar'kā* N.M. estrangement [A ~ ترک]

ترکہ *tar'kah* N.M. legacy bequest estate (of deceased person inheritance ترکہ بلا وصیت *tar kah bi-lā vasiy'yat* N.M. intestate property [A ~ ترک]

ترکی *tūr'kī* N.M. Turkish (language) (also ترکیہ *tūrkiy'yah*) Turkey bravery ADJ. Turkish ترکی بہ ترکی جواب *tūr'kī ba tūr'kī javāb' de'nā* V.T. pay in the same coin ; give tit for tat ترکی تمام ہونا *tūr'kī tamām' ho'nā* V.I. be all over (with) have courage spent up [T]

ترکیب *tarkīb'* N.F. (PL. تراکیب *tarākīb'*) analysis composition mixture structure construction formation mode method ; plan ترکیب بتانا *tarkīb' batā'nā* N.F. suggest plan or way ترکیب بند *tarkīb' band'* N.M. stanza ending with couplet ترکیب دینا *tarkīb' de'nā* V.T. compose prepare (mixture) ; mix join form ترکیب سے چلنا *tarkīb' se chal'nā* V.I. work methodically ترکیب کرنا *tarkīb' kar'nā* V.T. analyse devise ; plan ; scheme کسی ترکیب سے *ki'sī tarkīb' se* ADV. somehow or other by hook or by crook ترکیبی *tarkī bī* ADJ. component ; constituent composed عناصر ترکیبی *'anā'sir-e tarkī'bī* N.M. PL. component parts; constituents elements going into the forma-

ترمرا *tir'mirā* N.M. (floating) speck ocular speck or spectrum (caused by virtigo, etc.)

ترمیم *tarmīm'* N.F. amendment modification change improvements ترمیم شدہ *(ta)rmīm'-shū'dah* ADJ. amended modified changed improved (میں) ترمیم کرنا *(meṅ) tarmīm' kar'nā* V.T. amend modify ; change improve (میں) ترمیم ہونا *(meṅ) tarmīm' ho'nā* V.I. be amended be modified be changed be improved [A ~ رمّت]

ترنج *tūranj'* N.M. grape-fruit citron embroidered pattern like betel-leaf ترنجبین *tūranj'bīn* N.M. Persian manna ; lime juice cordial prepared in honey [P]

ترنگ *tarang'* N.F. caprice ; whim fancy inebriation whizz tinkle rattle ترنگی *tarañ'gī* ADJ. capricious whimsical ترنگا *tirañ'gā* ADJ. tricoloured [~ ت + رنگ]

ترنم *taran'nūm* N.M. singing modulation ترنم سے *taran'nūm se* ADV. singing (and not just reciting [A]

ترویج *tarvīj'* N.F. currency circulation popularization ترویج دینا *tarvīj' de'nā* V.T. give currency on position ترویج پانا *tarvīj' pā'nā* V.T. become current come into vogue [A ~ رواج]

ترئی *tūrai''ī* N.F. kind of cucumber (also *tūr'ī*) trumpet ترئی کا پھول *tūrai''ī ka phool'* V.T. beedy eyes

تری *ta'rī* N.F. (see under تر ★)

تریا *tir'yā* N.F. (ped & dial. *tri'ya*) woman تریا چرتر (تریا چلتر) *tir'yā charit'r* (or *chalit'tar*) N.M. (usu. PL.) women's wiles or guiles; female cunning تریاہٹ *tir'yā'-haṭ* N.F. female obstinacy [S]

تریاق *tir'yāq'* N.M. antidote (usu. تریاک *tiryāk'* opium تریاکی *tiryā'kī* N.M. opium eater ADJ. addict [A ~ P]

ترپن *tire'pan* ADJ. & N.M. fifty-three ترپنواں *tire'panvān* fifty-third

تریڑا *tare'ṛā* N.M. spurt (of usu. hot water) ; get fomentation with spurt (of hot water) تریڑا دینا *tare'ṛā de'nā* V.T. foment with a spurt (of hot water)

تریز *tarīz'* N.F. gusset ; transverse piece in shirt, etc. [P]

تریسٹھ *tire'saṭh*, ترسٹھ *tiri'saṭh* ADJ. sixty-three تریسٹھواں *tire'saṭh'vāṅ* ADJ. sixty-third

ترین *tarīn'*, ترِیں *tarīṅ'* SUF. (denoting superlative degree) most ; greatest ; est [P]

تڑ *taṛ* N.F. sound of slapping, etc. ; whack تڑ تڑ *taṛ' taṛ* N.F. crack ADV. quickly تڑ سے *taṛ' se* ADV. with a whack تڑاتڑ *ta'ṛātaṛ'* ADV with continuous whacks

تڑاق *taṛāq'*, تڑاک *taṛāk* N.M whack crack crash تڑاق پڑاق *taṛāq' paṛāq*, تڑاک پڑاک *taṛāk' paṛāk'* ADV. insolently boldly arrogantly naughtily تڑاق سے *taṛāq' se* ADV. with a whack with a crash quickly pat

تڑاقا *taṛāqā*, تڑاکا *taṛa'kā* N.M. whack crack crash snap smack sound of smoking hookah drought starvation *taṛa'qā bīt'nā* V.I. have to starve (تڑاقے کا (کی *taṛa'qe kā* (or *kī*), (تڑاکے کا (کی *taṛa'ke kā* (or *kī*) ADJ. bitter (cold) scorching (heat) severe intense unhearable

تڑانا *tūṛa'nā*, تڑوانا *tūṛvā'nā* V. break ; break loose from change (money) [~ توڑنا CAUS.]

تڑپنا *ta'ṛapnā* V.I. be uneasy ; be restless roll or toss about restlessly write ; wriggle flutte flounce be doing for thirst (after) ; be anxious or eager (for) suffer for unrequited love تڑپ *ta'ṛap* N.F. restlessness uneasiness great eagerness (for) suffering in unrequited love passion (for) pain lossing flash fury تڑپانا *taṛpā'nā* V.T. make uneasy made restless cause to flutter cause to suffer from unrequited love تڑپڑ *taṛ' paṛ* تڑتڑ *taṛ taṛ* ADV. (reply) quickly (reply) with audacity

تڑخنا *ta'ṛakhnā*, تڑقنا *ta'ṛaqnā* V.I. crack split snap burst [ONO.]

تڑکا *taṛ'kā*, نور کا تڑکا *noor' kā taṛ'kā* N.M. dawn ; day break تڑکے *taṛ'ke*, نور کے تڑکے *noor' ke taṛke* ADV. at dawn ; at daybreak ; in the early morning تڑکا ہونا *taṛ'kā ho'nā* V.I. (of day) break be rained be beaten suffer from vertigo

تڑی *ta'ṛī* N.F. beating deceit loss

تزک *tū'zūk* (col. *tūz'k*) N.M. pomp and show diary memoirs تزک و احتشام *tūz'k-o eḥti-shām'* N.M. pomp and show [T]

تزکیہ *taz'kiyah* N.M. purification ; catharsis تزکیۂ نفس *taz'kiyae naf's* N.M. purification of mind [A ~ زکا]

تزلزل *tazal'zūl* N.M. earthquake commotion trepidation (at death, etc.) [A ~ زلزلہ]

تزویج *tazvīj'* N.F. marrying ; taking a wife coupling [A ~ زوج]

تزویر *taz'vīr'* N.F. bamboozling ; fraud deception دام تزویر *dām-e tazvīr'* N.M. fraudulent trap [A ~ زور]

تزیین *tazyīn'*, تزئین *taz'īn'* N.F. make-up decoration ornament [A ~ زینت]

تس *tis'* PRON. تس پر *tis' par* ADV. تس پر بھی *tis' par bhī* PH. (same as اس پر، اس پر بھی see under اس is ADJ. ★)

تسالہ *tisalah* ADJ. three-year-old triennial [ث + P سال]

تسامح *tasā'moḥ* N.M. pardon ; forgiveness ; indulgence connivance mistake تسامحات *tasāmoḥāt'* N.M. PL. mistakes [A ~ سماحت]

تساہل *tasā'hūl* N.M. carelessness negligence laziness ; tardiness تساہل کرنا *tasā'hūl kar'nā* V.I. show carelessness neglect be lazy be tardy

تسبیح *tasbīḥ'* N.F. rosary chaplet glorification of God sanctification of God (by saying 'Subhan Allah') (تسبیح پڑھنا (یا پھیرنا *tasbīḥ' paṛh'nā* (or *pher'nā*) V.T. tell ones beads [A]

تسخیر *taskhīr'* N.F. control subjugation capture captivation control over some (evil) spirit spiritualism تسخیر قلوب *taskhī'r-e-qūloob'* N.F. winning over of people captivation of hearts [A]

تسطیر *tastīr'* N.F. writing ; scribbling [A ~ سطر]

تسکین *taskīn'* (lit. also تسکین *tas'kīn*) N.F. consolation, comfort ; soothing appeasement ; pacification mitigation assuaging rest tranquillity تسکین بخش *taskīn'-bakh'sh* ADJ. soothing allaying consolatory تسکین دینا *taskīn' de'nā* V.T. soothe console; solace ; comfort ; appease calm ; tranquilllize تسکین ہونا *task'īn' ho'nā* V.I. be soothed be consoled ; be solaced be appeased , be pacified [A ~ سکون]

تسلا *tas'lā* N.M. trough

تسلسل *tasal'sūl* N.M. continuity sequence association (of ideas) [A ~ سلسلہ]

تسلط *tasal'lūt* N.M. sway ; domination [A]

تسلی *tasal'lī* N.F. satisfaction consolation comfort ; solace assurance reassurance تسلی بخش *tasal'lī-bakh'sh* ADJ. satisfactory consolatory , comforting assuring reassuring تسلی دینا *tasal'lī de'nā* V.T. comfort ; console ; solace assure کی تسلی کرنا *kī tasal'lī kar'nā* V.T satisfy تسلی ہونا *tasal'lī ho'nā* V.I. be comforted be consoled be assured (کی) تسلی ہونا (*kī*) *tasal'lī ho'nā* V.I. be satisfied [A]

تسلیم *taslīm'* N.F salutation greetings compliments acceptance , admission conceding ; granting entrusting surrender تسلیمات *taslīmat'* N.F. PL. salutations INT. good-morning (etc.) تسلیمات بجالانا *taslīmat' ba'ja lā'nā* V.T. great pay one's respects make obeisance take leave (*of*) ; bid adieu تسلیم کرنا *taslīm' kar'nā* V.T. confer admit concede ; grant salute pay homage surrender تسلیم ورضا *tasli'm-o-riza* N.F. surrender to another's (particularly God's) will تسلیم ہونا *taslim' ho'na* V.I. be resigned ; be committed ; surrender [A ~ سلام]

تسمہ *tas'mah* N.M. thong (shoe) lace تسمہ لگا نہ رکھنا *tas'mah la'ga na rakh'na* V.T. sever all relations تسمہ پا *tas'ma-pa* ADJ. having lanky legs [P]

تسمیہ *tas'miyah* N.M. christening ; naming taking God's name saying 'bismillah' [A ~ اسم]

تسنن *tasan'nun* N.M. following 'Sunnah' profess being 'Sunni' اہلِ تسنن *ah'l-e tasan'nun* N.M. PL. the Sunnis [A ~ سنت]

تسنیم *tasnim'* N.M. name of a heavenly fountain or stream [A]

تسو *tas'soo* N.M. one-and-a-half inch measure

تسوید *tasvid'* N.F. writing drafting blackening [A ~ سوید]

تسویہ *tas'viyah* N.M. setting right adjustment putting in order ; arrangement [A ~ مساوات]

تسہیل *tashil'* N.F. facilitation making easy [A ~ سہل]

تشابہ *tasha'boh* N.M. likeness resemblance similitude [A ~ شبیہہ]

تشاکل *tasha'kul* N.M. mutual resemblance [A ~ شکل]

تشبیب *tashbib'* N.F. introductory part of ode ; amatory preface [A ~ شباب]

تشبیہ *tashbih'* N.F. simile comparison likening تشبیہ دینا *tashbih' de'na* V.T. liken compare use a simile [A ~ تشبیہ]

تشت *tasht* N.M. تشتری N.F. (less usual spelling of طشتری طشت) (see under طشت N.M. ★)

تشتت *tashat'tut* N.M. disunity افتراق و تشتت *iftira'qo tashat'tut* N.M. schism and disunity [A ~ شتی]

تشخص *tashakh'khus* N.M. identity identification [A ~ شخص]

تشخیص *tashkhis'* N.F. diagnosis ascertainment evaluation assessment ; appraisal تشخیص جمعبندی *tashkhis' jam'-ban'di* N.F. annual revenue assessment تشخیص کرنا *tashkhis' kar'na* V.T. diagnose evaluate assess ; appraise تشخیص گاہ *tashkhis'-gah* N.F. clinic [A ~ شخص]

تشدد *tashad'dud* N.M. violence third degree methods تشدد برتنا *tashad'dud ba'ratna* V.T. resort to violence [A ~ شدت]

تشدید *tashdid'* N.F. doubling a letter orthographical sign used for it [A ~ شدت]

تشرع *tasharro'* N.M. acting on tenets of faith [A ~ شرع]

تشریح *tashrih'* N.F. anatomy explanation; exposition ; elucidation ; commentary ; exegisis تشریحات *tashrihat'* N.F. PL. detailed comments تشریح الابدان *tashri'h-ul-abdan'* N.M. anatomy تشریح کرنا *tashrih' kar'na* V.T. explain elucidate give details تشریحی *tashrihi* ADJ. anatomical detailed explanatory تشریحی یادداشت *tashri'hi yad-dasht'* N.F. explanatory memorandum [A ~ شرح]

تشریف *tashrif'* N.F. exaltation (arch) investiture with robes تشریف ارزانی فرمانا *tashrif' arza'ni farma'na* V.T. be pleased to take a seat honour with (one's) presence تشریف رکھنا *tash'rif' rakh'na* V.I. take a seat be pleased to sit down تشریف لانا *tashrif' la'na* V.I. come تشریف لے جانا *tashrif' le ja'na* V.I. go ; go away , leave ; depart [A ~ شرف]

تشفی *tashaf'fi* N.F. consolation satisfaction reassurance تشفی کرنا *tashaf'fi kar'na* V.T. satisfy [A ~ شفا]

تشکک *tashak'kuk* N.M. doubt ; suspicion scepticism [A ~ شک]

تشکیک *tashkik'* N.F. raising doubts ; causing suspicion making sceptical [A ~ شک]

تشکل *tashak'kul* N.M. taking shape morphology [A ~ شکل]

تشکیل *tashkil* N.F. formation setting up organisation [A ~ شکل]

تشنج *tashan'nuj* N.M. cramps convulsion spasm [A]

تشنہ *tish'nah* (ped. *tash'-*) ADJ. thirsty eager تشنہ کام *tish'na-kam'* ADJ. thirsty unsuccessful unlucky ; with unrequieted love تشنہ لب *tish'na-lab* ADJ. thirsty with parched lips unsuccessful unlucky eager with unrequieted love تشنہ لبی *tish'na-labi'* N.F. thirst having parched lips eagerness failure to achieve object تشنگی *tish'nagi* (ped.) *tash-*) N.F. thirst ; desire ; longing ; temptation [P]

تشنیع *tashni''* N.F. reproach طعن و تشنیع *ta''n-o tashni''* N.F. taunts and reproach [A ~ شناعت]

تشویش *tashvish'* N.F. anxiety worry disquietude [A]

تشہد *tashah'hud'* N.M. avowing faith by reciting the formula called 'kalima-e shahadat' [A ~ شہادت]

تشہیر *tashhīr'* N.F. public exposure (rare) publication (rare) publicity **تشہیر کرنا** *tash'hīr' kar'nā* V.T. expose publicity **تشہیر ہونا** *tashhīr' ho'nā* V.I. be exposed publicly [A ~ شہرت]

تشیع *tashay'yo'* N.M. profession of shite faith grouping [A ~ شیعہ]

تصادم *tasā'dūm* N.F. collision clash ; conflict. [A ~ صدمہ]

تصانیف *tasānīf'* N.F. (PL. of تصنیف ★)

تصاویر *tasāvīr'* N.F. (PL. of تصویر ★)

تصحیح *tasḥīḥ'* N.F. correction ; rectification amendment proof-reading **تصحیح کرنا** *tashīḥ' kar'nā* V.T. correct ; rectify amend read proofs **تصحیح ہونا** *tashīḥ' ho'nā* V.T. be corrected ; be rectified be amended (of proofs) be read [A ~ صحیح]

تصدق *tasad'dūq* N.M. giving alms charity sacrifice **تصدق کرنا** *tasad'dūq kar'nā* V.T. sacrifice give charity **تصدق ہونا** *tasad'dūd ho'nā* V.T. be sacrificed be given away in charity [A ~ صدقہ]

تصدیعہ *tasdī''ah* N.M., **تصدیع** *tasdī''* N.F. annoyance ; vexation trouble ; inconvenience worry (rare) headache **تصدیعہ اٹھانا** *tasdī''ah uṭhā'nā* V.T. take trouble be put to inconverence worry (over) be vexed ; be annoyed [A]

تصدیق *tasdīq'* N.F. verification certification ; attestation affirmation authentication countersignature (logic) premise ; premiss **تصدیق شدہ** *tasdīq'-shŭ'dah'* ADJ. verified ; certified attested ; authenticated affirmed countesigned **تصدیق کرنا** *tasdīq' kar'nā* V.T. verify ; certify attest confirm affirm authenticate countersign **تصدیق نامہ** *tasdīq'-nā'mah* N.M. certificate testimonial **تصدیق ہونا** *tasdīq' ho'nā* V.I. be verified be certified **تصدیقی دستخط** *tasdī'qī dast'-khat* N.M. countersignature [A ~ صدق]

تصرف *tasar'rūf* N.M. possession use expenditure disposal extravagance change tampering with Urduization (etc. of foreign word) taking back **اپنے تصرف میں لانا** *ap'ne tasar'rūf meṅ la'nā* V.T. put to one's own use **تصرف بیجا** *tasat'rūf e be'jā* N.M. misappropriation ; embezzlement ; defalcation **تصرفات** *tasarrūfat'* N.M. PL. sum-total of expenses (unauthorized) changes **تصرفی** *tarsar'rūfī* N.F. ADJ. (food) for servants (OPP. خاصہ) [A ~ صرف]

تصریح *tasrīḥ'* N.F. clarification elucidation explanation **تصریح کرنا** *tasrīḥ' kar'nā* V.T. clarify elucidate [A ~ صراحت]

تصریف *tasrīf'* N.F. conjugation declension inflection conversion change from one state to another [A ~ صرف]

تصغیر *tasghīr'* N.F. diminutive form **اسم تصغیر** *is'm-e tasghīr'* N.M. diminutive (form of) noun [A ~ صغر]

تصفیہ *tas'fiyah* N.M. decision settlement disposal reconciliation rapprochement purification ; (of mind) purgation purity **تصفیہ کرانا** *tas fiyah karā'nā* V.T. cause to be reconciled **تصفیہ کرنا** *tas'fiyah kar'nā* V.T. decide settle reconcile ; **تصفیہ ہونا** *tasfiyah' ho'nā* V.I. be settled be decided [A ~ صفا]

تصلیب *taslīb* N.F. crucifixion [A ~ صلیب]

تصنع *tasan'no'* N.M. hypocrisy artificiality [A ~ صنع]

تصنیف *tasnīf'* N.F. writing compilation book literary (or other) work **تصنیف کرنا** *tasnīf' kar'nā* V.T. write (book etc.) compile compose **تصنیف ہونا** *tasnīf' ho'nā* V.I. (of book) be written be composed **حق تصنیف** *ḥaq'q-e tasnīf'* N.M. copyright **تصنیفات** *tasnīfāt'*, **تصانیف** *tasānīf'* N.F. PL. books works writings [A]

تصور *tasav'vūr* N.M. idea conception fancy ; imagination contemplation reflection apprehension (logic) term **تصور کرنا** *tasav'vūr kar'na* V.I. imagine ; fancy picture to oneself ; think ; believe consider **تصور ہونا** *tasav'vūr ho'nā* V.I. be thought be considered ; be believed [A ~ صورت]

تصوف *tasav'vūf* N.M. mysticism Sufism [A ~ صوف]

تصویر *tasvīr'* N.F. photograph ; photo picture painting portrait image likeness **تصویر بن جانا** *tasvīr' ban ja'na* V.I. be struck dumb ; be dumb founded **تصویر خانہ** *tasvīr'-khā'nah* N.M. picture gallery **تصویر کا دوسرا رخ** *tasvīr' ka doos'rā rukh* PH. the other side of picture **تصویر کھینچنا** *tasvīr' khench'nā* V.T. take a snap draw a picture paint a picture portray **عکسی تصویر** *'ak'sī tasvīr'* N.F. (arch.) photograph ; photo [A ~ صورت]

تضاد *tazād'* N.M. contradiction contrast inconsistency [A ~ ضد]

تضحیک *tazḥīk'* N.F. ridicule derision mocking **تضحیک کرنا (یا کا نشانہ بنانا)** *tazḥīk'* *kar'nā* (or *kā nīshā'nah ban'ā'nā*) V.T. ridicule expose to ridicule deride mock [A ~ مضحکہ]

تضرع *tazar'ro'* N.M. humility supplication lamentation [A]

تضمین *tazmin'* N.F. citation of anchor poet's live or couplet on one's verse تضمین کرنا *tazmīn' kar'nā* V.T. site another line in one's verse [A ~ ضمن]

تضییع *tazyī''* تضیع *taz'ī''* N.F. waste spoiling تضییع اوقات *tazyī''-e auqāt'* N.F. waste of time idling ; lounging [A ~ ضائع]

تطابق *tatā būq* N.M. conformity concurrence congruity [A ~ طبق]

تطاول *tatā'vāl* N.M. high-handedness دست تطاول دراز کرنا *das't-e tatā'vāl darāz kar'nā* PH. show high-handedness (towards someone)

تطبیق *tatbīq'* N.F likening comparison تطبیق دینا *tatbīq' de'nā* V.T. make exactly alike compare [~ A طبق]

تطہیر *tathīr'* N.F. purification purgation [A ~ طہارت]

تظلم *taza'lum* N.M. complaint (against) injustice endurance (rare) cutting down (someone's) rights ; usurpation (mistakenly) oppression دست تظلم دراز کرنا *das't-e tazal'lum darāz' kar'nā* V.T. complain or pray against oppression (mistakenly) show high-handedness [A ~ ظلم]

تعارض *tā'ā'rūz* N.M. inconsistency confrontation contention [A ~ عرض]

تعارف *tā'ā'rūf* N.M. introduction presentation (at court or in society) preface تعارف کرنا *tā'ā'rūf karā'nā* V.T. introduce (someone) to تعارف پیدا کرنا *ta'ā'rūf pai'dā kar'nā* V.T. get to know (someone) [A ~ عرف]

تعاقب *ta'ā'qūb* N.M. chase pursuit ; تعاقب کرنا *ta'ā'qūb kar'nā* V.T. chose pursue [A ~ عقب]

تعالی *ta'ā'lā* ADJ. most high , exalted تعالی اللہ *ta'āl-allah'* INT. God be exalted how lovely [A ~ علو]

تعاون *ta'ā'vūn* N.M. co-operation mutual help (سے) تعاون کرنا *(se) tā'ā'vūn kar'nā* V.T. co-operate (with)

تعب *ta''ab* N.M. fatigue exertion [A]

تعبیر *ta'bir'* N.F. interpretation (of dream) explanation putting up (new) construction (on words) تعبیر گو *ta'bir'-go'* N.M. interpreter of dreams [A ~ عبارت]

تعبیہ *ta''biyah* N.M. concealment plastering accoutrement make-up ; getting ready

تعجب *ta'aj'jūb* N.M. surprise astonishment amazement admiration (پر) تعجب کرنا *(par) ta'aj'jūb kar'nā* (کو) تعجب ہونا *(ko) ta'aj'jūb ho'nā* V.I. be surprised wonder admire be amazed [A ~ عجیب]

تعجیل *ta'jīl'* N.F. haste ; hurry quickness; agility expedition despatch تعجیل کرنا *ta'jīl' kar'nā* V.I. hurry ; expedite act with despatch تعجیلی *ta'jī'lī* ADJ. express (letter, telegram, etc.) تعجیلی تقسیم *ta'jī'lī taqsīm'* N.M. express delivery تعجیل کار شیاطین بود *ta'jīlt ka'r-e shayā'tīn ba'vad* PROV. fruit of haste is repentence [A ~ عجلت]

تعداد *ta'dād'* N.F. number strength تعداد بتانا *ta'dād' baṭā'nā* V.T. give or tell the number of [A ~ عدد]

تعدد *ta'ad'dūd* N.M. frequency being more than one being numerous ; large number تعدد ازدواج (یا ازوج) *ta'ad'dūd-e izdivāj'* (or *azvāj*) N.M. polygamy simultaneously having more than one wife [A ~ عدد]

تعدی *ta'ad'dī* N.F. cruelty oppression tyranny (rare) transgression [A ~ عدوان]

تعدیل *ta'dīl'* N.F. making balances equalisation adjustment proper functioning correct performance تعدیل ارکان *ta'dī'l-e arkan'* N.F. (in prayers) correct performance of various postures [A ~ عدل]

تعرض *ta'ar'rūz* N.M. opposition hindrance getting in the way سے تعرض (نہ) کرنا *se ta'ar'rūz (na) kar'nā* V.T. (not) to stand in the way of [A ~ عرض]

تعریب *ta'rīb'* N.F. Arabicization [A]

تعریض *ta'rīz'* N.F. hint veiled reference sly hit [A ~ عرض]

تعریف *ta'rīf'* N.F. praise ; admiration ; commendation definition (polite form used for) name definition ; making (noun) definite use of definite article (before noun) تعریف کرنا *ta'rīf' kar'nā* praise admire تعریف کرتے منہ سوکھنا *ta'rīf kar'te mūnh' sookh'na* تعریفوں کے پل باندھنا *ta'rī'fon ke pūl bāndh'na* V.T. lavish praise ; praise very highly آپ کی تعریف *āp kī ta'rīf'* PH. may I know your (or the other person's) name [A ~ معرفہ]

تعزیت *ta''ziyat* N.F. condolence تعزیت کرنا *ta''ziyat kar'nā* V.T. condole تعزیت نامہ *ta''ziyat na'mah* N.M. letter of condolence

تعزیر *ta'zīr'* N.F. punishment ; penalty penalization تعزیری *ta'zī'rī* ADJ. punitive penal تعزیری پولیس *ta'zī'rī pūlis'* N.F. punitive police تعزیری قوانین *ta'zī'rī qavānīn'* N.M. penal laws تعزیری کارروائی *ta'zī'rī kar-ravā'ī* N.F. punitive action or measure تعزیر و عقوبت *ta'zī'r-o 'ūqoo'bat* V.I. تعزیرات پاکستان *ta'zīra't-e pākistan'* N.F. Pakistan Penal Code [A]

تعزیہ *ta''ziyah* N.M. Imam Hussain's sarcophagus ; commemorative model of Imam Hussain's tomb carried by Shi'tes in procession during 'Muharram' Shi'te commemorative funeral procession تعزیہ اٹھانا *ta'' ziyah ūthā'na* V.I. carry 'taziyah' in procession تعزیہ ٹھنڈا کرنا *ta'' ziyah thān'da kar'na* V.T. immerse or bury 'ta'ziyah' تعزیہ دار *ta'' ziya-dār* N.M. 'ta'ziyah' maker 'Muharram' mourner تعزیہ داری *ta'' ziya-da'rī* N.F. 'Muharam' mourning [A ~ عزا]

تعشق *ta'ash'shūq* N.M. love [A ~ عشق]

تعصب *ta'as'sūb* N.M. prejudice bigotry [A ~ عصبیت]

تعطل *ta'at'ūl* N.M. deadlock suspension (of activity, service, etc.) [A]

تعطیل *ta'tīl'* N.F. holiday vacation تعطیل منانا (یا کرنا) *ta'tīl' manā'na* (or *kar'na*) V.I. have a holiday enjoy one's vacation تعطیل ہونا *ta'tīl' ho'na* V.I. be a holiday (of work) be suspended [A]

تعظیم *ta'zīm'* N.F. honour respect reverence obeisance (کی) تعظیم بجا لانا (*kī*) *ta'zīm' ba-jā' lā'na* V.T. show respect make obeisance (کی) تعظیم کرنا (*kī*) *ta'zīm' kar'na* V.T. honour ; respect [A ~ عظمت]

تعفن *ta'af'fūn* N.M. bad smell offensive adour stink stench fastidness [A ~ عفونت]

تعلق *ta'al'lūq* N.M. connection concern pertinence ; relevance ; relevancy bearing relation belonging relationship (سے) تعلق توڑنا یا قطع کرنا (*se*) *ta'ūl'lūq tor'na* (or *qat'' kar'na*) V.T. sever relations (with) ; snap ties (with) (سے) تعلق رکھنا (*se*) *ta'al'lūq rakh'na* V.T. be concerned with have connection with appertain to ناجائز تعلق *nā-ja''iz ta'al'lūq* N.M. illegitimate relation [A ~ علاقہ]

تعلقہ *ta'al'lūqah* N.M. estate administrative division of district تعلقہ دار *ta'al'lūqa-dār'* N.M landlord ; owner of estate [A ~ علاقہ]

تعلم *ta'al'lūm* N.M. learning ; being a student [A ~ علم]

تعلی *ta'all'ī* N.F. brag ; boast arrogance ; conceit تعلی کرنا *ta'al'lī kar'na* تعلی کی لینا *ta'al'lī kī le'na* V.T. boast ; brag [A ~ علو]

تعلیل *ta'līl'* N.F. vowel-change causation تعلیلات *ta'līlāt'* N.F. PL. vowel-changes [A ~ علت]

تعلیم *ta'līm'* N.F. education teaching ; instruction تعلیم پانا (یا لینا یا حاصل کرنا) *ta'līm' pa'na* (or *le'na* or *ha'sil kar'na*) V.I. receive instruction ; study (under) be educated تعلیم دینا *ta'līm' de'na* (arch.) تعلیم کرنا *tā'līm' kar'na* V.T. teach ; instruct educate [A ~ علم]

تعمق *ta'am'mūq* N.M. deepness getting to the bottom (of something) probe [A ~ عمق]

تعمیر *ta'mīr'* N.F. building structure ; construction تعمیر کرنا *ta'mīr' kar'na* V.T. build ; construct ; raise or rear (a structure) تعمیر ہونا *ta'mīr' ho'na* V.I. be built تعمیر و تخریب *ta'mī'r-o takhrīb'* N.F. construction and destruction تعمیری *ta'mī'rī* ADJ. constructive تعمیری تنقید *ta'mī'rī tanqīd'* N.F. constructive criticsim [A ~ عمق]

تعمیل *ta'mīl'* N.F. compliance carrying out execution (of contract order, etc) obedience تعمیل حکم کرنا *ta'mī'l-e hūk'm kar'na* V.I. carry out an order تعمیل شدہ *tā'mīl'-shū'dah* ADJ. complied with execute (contract, order etc.) کی تعمیل میں *kī ta'mīl' meṅ* ADV. in compliance with ; in conformity with [A ~ عمل]

تعمیم *ta'mīm'* N.F. popularization making or becoming common universalization [A ~ عام]

تعمیہ *ta''miyah* N.M. concealment enigmatic chronogram [A ~ اعمیٰ]

تعوذ *ta'av'vūz* N.M. seeking refuge in God from devil (by saying 'a'ooz-o billah') [A ~ اعوذ]

تعہد *ta'ah'hūd* N.M. promise assurance agreement [A ~ عہد]

تعویذ *ta'vīz* N.M. amulet charm talisman upper part of grave ; (usu.) sculpture sarcophagus تعویذ پہننا *ta'vīz' paihnā'na* V.I. wear a charm or talisman [A ~ عوذ]

تعویق *ta'vīq'* N.F. delay procrastination [A]

تعیش *ta'ay'yūsh* N.M. luxury pleasant life debauchery [A ~ عیش]

تعین *ta'ay'yūn* N M. fixation ; determination appointment posting تعینات *ta'ayyunat'* ADJ. (col.) appointed تعیناتی *ta'ayyūnā'tī* N.F. (col.) appointment posting [A]

تعیین ta'yin' N.F. fixation determination [A]

تغار taghar' N.M. mason's lime-pit heap of mud, masonry, etc. تغاری tagha'ri N.F. trough [P]

تغافل taghā ful N.M. indifference inadvertance unmindfulness neglect ; negligence تغافل شعار tagha'ful shi'ar', تغافل کیش tagha'ful kesh ADJ. indifferent unmindful [A ~ غفلت]

تغذیہ tagh'ziyah N.M. nutrition feeding nourishment [A ~ غذا]

تغزل taghaz'zul amatory poetry composisition of ode love element in poetry ecstasy of love [A ~ غزل]

تغلب taghal'lub N.M. domination [A ~ غلبہ]

تغلیط taghlit' N.F. contradiction proving to be wrong putting in the wrong [A ~ غلط]

تغیر taghay'yur N.M. change alteration mutation تغیر و تبدل taghay'yur-o tabad'dul N.M. changes alterations upheaval mutations تغیر کرنا taghāy'yur kar'nā V.T. change alter entering mutations تغیر ہونا taghay'yur ho'nā V.I. be changed be altered تغیرات taghayyurat' N.M. change alterations تغیرات ہر سالہ taghayyura'l-e har sa'lah N.F. annual record of rural mutations [A ~ تغیر]

تغییر taghyir' N.F. change تغییر حال taghyi'r-e hal', تغییر رنگ taghyi'r-e rang' N.F. change of state [A ~ تغیر]

تف taf N.M. vapour steam [P]

تف tuf N.M. curse (rare) spittle INT. shame ; fie تف ہے اس پر tuf' hai us' par PH. shame curse be on him (etc.) [~ P تفو]

تفاخر tafa'khur N.M. boast ; vaunt vainglory [A ~ فخر]

تفاسیر tafasir' N.F. PL. commentaries ; exegetical works or writings [A ~ SING. تفسیر]

تفاصیل tafasil', تفصیلات tafsilat' N.F. PL. details [A ~ تفصیل]

تفاوت tafa'vut N.M. difference disparity diversity [A ~ فوت]

تفاؤل tafa''ul N.M. augury taking good omen [A ~ فال]

تفتہ taf'tah (rare) ADJ. parched N.M. (fig.) lover

تفتیش taftish' N.F. investigation inquiry research تفتیش جرائم tafti'sh-e jara''im N.F. criminal investigation تحقیق و تفتیش tahqi'q-o taftish N.F. research [A]

تفحص tafah'hus N.M. search research [A]

تفرج tafar'ruj N.M. recreation تفرج گاہ tafar'ruj-gah N.F. place of recreation [A]

تفرقہ taf'riqah N.M. dissension sabism division discord separation differences تفرقہ انداز (یا پرداز) taf'riqa anda'z' (or pardaz') N.M. one sowing seeds of dissension disruptionist تفرقہ اندازی (یا پردازی) taf'riqa anda'zi (or parda'zi) N.F. sowing of dissention disruption تفرقہ ڈالنا taf'riqah da'lna V.T. disrupt create dissension ; sow seeds of discord [A ~ فرق]

تفرنج tafar'nuj N.M. (rare) Westernization [A ~ E Frank]

تفریح tafrih' N.F. (PL. تفریحات tafrihat') entertainment amusement diversion fun jest stroll recess ; mid-morning break

تفریحاً tafri'han, ADV. by way of amusement jestingly for fun تفریح طبع tafri'h-e tab'' N.F. cheerfulness ; hilarity amusement تفریح کرنا tafrih' kar'nā V.T. refresh oneself take a stroll amuse oneself [A ~ فرحت]

تفریس tafris' N.F. Persianization [A ~ P]

تفریط tafrit' N.F. minimizing lower extremity [A ~ فرط]

تفریق tafriq' N.F. subtraction differentiation split-up تفریق ڈالنا tafriq' dal'nā V.I create dissention disrupt تفریق کرنا tafr'q kar'nā V.T. subtract differentiate [A ~ فرق]

تفسیر tafsir' N.F. exegesis of the Holy Quran, Quranic exegesis exegetical writing commentary [A]

تفصیل taf'sil' N.F. detail particulars تفصیل بیان کرنا taf'sil' bay'an kar'na, تفصیل کرنا taf'si kar'na V. detail ; give details ; explain in full تفصیل وار tafsil'-var ADJ. in detail ; detailed بالتفصیل bil tafsil' ADV. itemwise in detail at length بتفصیل ذیل ba-tafsi'l-e zail' ADV. as follows ; as under تفصیلی tafsi'li N.M. detailed تفصیلات tafsilat' N.F. PL. details particulars [A ~ فصل]

تفضیل tafzial' N.M. comparison excellence pre-eminence اسم تفضیل is'm-e tafzil' N.M adjective of comparative or superlative degree تفضیل بعض tafzi'l-e ba''z N.F. comparative degree (of adjectives) تفضیل کل tafzi'l-e kul' N.F. superlative degree (of adjectives) تفضیل نفسی tafzi'l-e naf'sī N.F. positive degree (of adjectives) [A ~ فضل]

تفقد tafaq'qūd N.M. kindness تفقد کرنا tafaq'qūd kar'nā V.T. show kindness (to) [A ~ فقدان]

تفقہ tafaq'qoh N.M. discrimination knowledge being conversant with Muslim jurisprudence [A ~ فقہ]

تفکر tafak'kur N.M. thoughtfulness reflection cogitation meditation [A ~ فکر]

تفنگ tafang' N.F. musket gun [P ~ توپ]

تفنن tafan'nūn N.M. diversion pastime amusement ; entertainment تفنن طبع tafan'nūn-e-tab'' N.M. diversion of mind amusement [A ~ فن]

تفوق tafav'vūq N.M. superiority precedence (پر) تفوق حاصل ہونا (par) tafav'vūq hāsil ho'nā V.I. have precedence over [A ~ فوق]

تفویض tafvīz' N.F. entrusting delegation (of rights etc.) giving (woman) away in marriage without dowry تفویض اختیارات tafvī'z-e ikhtiyārāt' N.M. PL. delegation of powers [A]

تفہم tafah'hūm N.F. understanding ; getting to know [A ~ فہم]

تفہیم tafhīm' N.F. teaching , instructions causing to understand تفہیمات tafhīmāt' N.F. PL. explanation elucidation aids to understanding [A ~]

تقابل taqābūl N.M. encounter comparison [A ~ فہم]

تقارب taqārīb' N.F. (PL. of تقریب N.F. ★)

تقاریر taqārīr' N.F. (PL. of تقریر N.F. ★)

تقاضا taqā'zā N.M. dun importunity demand urgency تقاضائے سن (یا عمر) taqāzā'-e-sin (or 'ūm'r) ADV. demands or age, etc. تقاضائے شدید taqāzā'-e shadīd' N.M. strong pressure ; great stress تقاضائے وقت taqāzā'-e-vaq't N.M. call of times تقاضا کرنا taqā'zā kar'nā V.T. urge press importune dun تقاضائی taqāzā'ī N.M. dun [A ~ تقاضی CORR.]

تقاطر taqā'tūr N.M. distillation falling in drops drizzle [A ~ قطرہ]

تقاطع taqā'to' N.M. intersection [A ~ قطع]

تقاوی taqā'vī N.F. "taccavi ; pecuniary advance to peasantry for capital expenditure [A]

تقاویم taqāvīm' N.F. PL. calendars almanacs [A ~ SING. تقویم]

تقدس taqad'dūs N.M. sanctity holiness تقدس مآب taqad'dūs-ma'āb' ADJ. holy ; sacred N.M. (as title) His Holiness [A ~ قدس]

تقبیل taqbīl' N.F. (lit.) kissing [A]

تقدم taqad'dūm N.M. priority precedence (in time, order or rank) advance ; moving forward [A ~ قدم]

تقدیر taqdīr' N.F. luck fate fortune destiny lot predestination ; luck divine decree (rare) estimate تقدیر آزمانا taqdīr'āzmā'nā V.I. try one's luck تقدیر بگڑنا taqdīr' bi'garnā V.I. fall on evil days come under an evil star تقدیر پھرنا (یا پلٹنا) taqdīr' phirnā (or pa'latnā) V.I. have change in circumstances تقدیر پھوٹنا (یا پھوٹ جانا یا سو جانا) taqdīr' phooṭ'nā (or phooṭ jānā or so jā'nā) V.I. face hard time come under an unlucky star fall on evil days تقدیر جاگنا (یا لڑنا) taqdīr' jāg'nā (or lar'nā) V.I. have luck ; have a stroke of good fortune prosper ; thrive ; flourish تقدیر کا کھیل taqdīr' kā khel' N.M. stroke of (good or bad) luck تقدیر کا پلٹا taqdīr' ka palt'a N.M. (good or bad) change of fortune تقدیر کا لکھا (یا بدا) taqdīr kā lik'kha (or ba'dā) N.M. lot ; fate divine decree writing on the wall تقدیر کا ہیٹا taqdīr' kā he'ṭa N.M. unlucky bloke ; unfortunate person تقدیر کے آگے تدبیر نہیں چلتی taqdīr' ke ā'ge tadbīr' na'hīn chal'tī PROV. there is no cure for bad luck ; none can withstand what is decreed by heaven [A ~ قدر]

تقدیس taqdīs' N.F. sanctity sanctification glorification [A ~ قدس]

تقدیم taqdīm' N.F. presentation precedence [A ~]

تقرب taqar'rūb N.M. nearness ; proximity access; approach تقرب حاصل کرنا taqar'rūb hāsil kar'nā V.T. have access obtain proximity [A ~ قرب]

تقرر taqar'rūr N.M. appointment nomination پروانۂ تقرر parva'na-e taqar'rūr N.M. letter of appointment تقرری taqar'rūrī N.F. (col.) appointment [A ~ قرار]

تقریب taqrīb' N.F. (PL. تقاریب taqārīb' تقریبات taqrībāt') function ceremony festival occasion تقریباً taqrī'ban ADV. about nearly approximately round about [A ~ قرب]

تقریر taqrīr' N.F. (PL. تقاریر taqārīr') speech oration discourse address talk lecture (rare) comment تقریر کرنا taqrīr' kar'nā make or deliver a speech ; speak lecture address ; give an address give a discourse give a talk تقریری taqrī'rī ADJ. verbal ; oral declamation (contest, etc.) [A]

تقریظ taqrīz' N.F. (critical) appreciation favourable review [A]

تقسیم taq'sīm' N.F. division partition distribution apportionment. circulation تقسیم کار taqsīm-e kār' N.F. division of work تقسیم کرنا taqsīm' kar'nā V.T. divide distribute apportion partition share (between) تقسیم مرکب taqsī'm-e murak'kab N.F. compound division تقسیم مفرد taqsī'm-e muf'rad N.F. simple division تقسیم مکمل taqsī'm-e mūkam'mal N.F. division without remainder, exact division تقسیم نامہ taqsīm nā'mah N.M. partition deed تقسیم ہونا taqsīm' ho'nā V.I. be divide be shared be partitioned be distributed be apoortioned [A ~ قسمت]

تقصیر taqsīr' N.F. mistake ; error omission shortcoming , defect fault sin crime ; guilt ; [A ~ قصور]

تقطیر taqtīr' N.F. distilatlion falling drop by drop تقطیر البول taqtī'r ūl-baul' N.M. painful discarge of urine in drops [A ~ قطرہ]

تقطیع taqtī'' N.F. scanning size (of book, paper, etc.) [A ~ قطع]

تقلید taqlīd' N.F. conformation ; conformity; being a conformist following in the footsteps (of) emulation تقلید کرنا taqlīd' kar'nā V.T. conform follow emulate تقلیدی taqlī'dī ADJ. conformist [A ~ قلادہ]

تقلیل taqlīl' N.F. minimising diminution . diminishing تقلیل افادہ taqlīl-e ifā'dah N.F. diminishing utility تقلیل حاصل taqlīl-e hā'sil N.F. diminishing returns

تقویٰ taq vā N.F. fear of God piety abstinence ; abstemiousness اہل تقویٰ ah'l-i taq'vā (or aih'.) N.M. pious persons God-fearing persons abstemious persons [A ~ وقابت]

تقویت taq'viyat N.F. strength strengthening support تقویت دینا taq'viyat de'na V.T. strengthen back up [A ~ قوت]

تقویم taqvīm' N.F. (PL. تقاویم taqāvīm') almanac calendar تقویم پارینہ taqvī'm-e parī'nah, N.F. past year's almanac (fig.) worthless things ; outdated or outmoded stuff

تقویمی taqvī'mī ADJ. calendar تقویمی سال taqvī'mī sal N.M. calendar year [A]

تقی ta'qī ADJ. pious devout abstemious

تقیید taqay'yūd N.M. condition; proviso restriction [A ~ قید]

تقیہ taqiy'yah N.M. permissibled subterfuge [A ~ وقابت]

تک tak PREP. till until to up to towards as far as ; so far as

تک tuk N.F. (fig.) relevance ; sense ; justification (rare) ryhme تک بندی tūk'-bandī N.F. insipid versification تک میں تک ملانا tūk' meṅ tūk' milā'na V.T. agree (with) ; play second fiddle (to) بے تکا be-tū'kā N.M. unreliable person outward or difficult ADJ. without rhyme or reason ; unjustified meaningless irrelevant بے تکی be-tūkī N.F. bosh ; nonsense ADJ. nonsensical irrelevant بے تکی ہانکنا be-tūkī hank'nā V.I. talk nonsense

تکا tik'kā, تکہ tik'kah N.M. bit or piece of flash grilled piece of flesh تکا بوٹی کرنا tik'kā bo'ṭī kar'nā V.T. tear to pieces hack mangle pull to pieces

تکا tūk'kā N.M. grainless cob pointless missible mere conjecture . guess لگا تو تیر نہیں تو تکا la'ga to tīr' na'hīṅ to tūk'kā PROV. a dart wide of the mark is no better than a straw

تکاسل takā'sūl N.M. laziness ; indolence . carelessness [A ~ کسل]

تکالیف takālīf' N.F. (PL. of تکلیف N.F. ★)

تکان takān' N.F. fatigue; tiredness تکان اتارنا (یا دور کرنا) takān ūtār'nā (or door', kar'nā) V.T. & I. give or take some rest تکان چڑھنا takān' chaṛh'na, V.I. b tired be fatigued [doublet of تھکن ~]

تکان takān' N.F. shaking jerk تکان دینا takān de'nā V.T. jerk [P]

تکبر takab'bur N.M. pride; conceit; haughtiness arrogance egotism insolence (rare) loftiness [A ~ کبر]

تکبیر takbīr' N.F. praise of God repetition the words 'Allah-o Akbar' takbir' announcement of initiation of congregational prayers تکبیر اولےٰ takbī'r-e oo'lā N.F. initial 'takbir' تکبیر کہنا takbīr' kaih'nā V.T. announce initiation of congregational prayers repeat the words 'Allah-o Akbar' (پر) تکبیر پڑھنا (par) takbīr' paṛh'nā V.T. (begin to) slaughter animal in Muslim way [A ~ تکبیر]

ٹخ ٹخ
تک تک *tik' tik* N.F. & INT. (same as *ṭakh' ṭakh* N.F. & INT. ★)
تکثیر *taksīr'* N.F. increase ; augmentation ; multiplication تکثیرِ افادہ *taksī'r-e ifā'dah* N.F. increasing utility تکثیرِ حاصل *taksī'r-e ḥā'sil* N.F. increasing returns [A ~ کثرت]
تکثیف *taksīf'* N.F. condensation density [A ~ کثیف]
تکدر *takad'dūr* N.M. turbidity disquietude unpleasantness misunderstanding [A ~ کدورت]
تکذیب *takzīb'* N.F. contradiction falsification تکذیب کرنا *takzīb' kar'nā* V.T. falsify contradict [A ~ کذب]
تکرار *takrār'* N.M. tautology repetition argument altercation contention میں تکرار ہونا *meṅ takrār' ho'nā* V.I. argue ; quarrel تکرار کرنا *takrār' kar'nā* V.T. quarrel ; argue repeat تکراری *takrā'rī* ADJ. contentious querulous [A ~ کر]
تکریم *takrīm'* N.F. respect honour reverence تکریم کرنا *takrīm' kar'nā* V.I. show respect تکریم ہونا *takrīm' ho'nā* V.I. be shown respect [A ~ کرم]
تکڑا *tak'ṛā* ADJ. (F. تکڑی *tak'ṛī*) stout well-built
تکسر *takas'sūr* N.M. (math.) carrying figures (rare) being shattered [A ~ کسر]
تکسیر *taksīr'* N.F. (math.) carrying figures shattering [A ~ کسر]
تکفل *takaf'fūl* N.M. support ; maintenance [A ~ کفالت]
تکفیر *takfīr'* N.F. infidelity charge excommunication [A ~ کفر]
تکفین *takfīn'* N.F. shrouding تکفین کرنا *takfīn' kar'nā* V.T. shroud [A ~ کفن]
تکل *tūk'kal* N.F. diamond shaped paper kite
تکلا *tak'lā* N.M. spindle تکلے کے سے بل نکالنا *tak'le ke se bal nikāl'nā* V.T. bring (someone) to his senses ; put (someone) to rights سوکھ کر تکلا ہونا *sookh' kar tak'lā ho'nā* V.I. grow the very lean peak and pine
تکلف *takal'lūf* N.M. formality ceremony inconvenience ; trouble ; pains lavish expenditure تکلف برطرف *takal'lūf bar ta'raf* ADV. ceremony aside ; frankly speaking ; to be frank تکلف برتنا (یا کرنا) *takal'lūf ba'ratnā* (or *kar'nā*) V.I. stand on ceremony take pains be ceremonious بے تکلف *be-takūl'lūf* ADJ. unceremonious plain frank forthright informal (of friend) free تکلفات *takullūfat'* N.M. PL. ceremonies formalities رسمی تکلفات *ras'mī takallūfāt'* N.M. PL. formalities specious cordiality مجلسی تکلفات *maj'lisī takallūfāt'* N.M. PL. etiquette social ceremony [A]
تکلم *takal'lūm* N.M. speech , speaking conversation [A ~ کلام]
تکلیف *taklīf'* N.F. trouble ; inconvenience difficulty ; hardship suffering torment ; affliction (rare) responsibility تکلیف اٹھانا *taklīf' ūṭhā'nā* V.I. suffer be put to inconvenience undergo hardship تکلیف دینا *taklīf' de'nā* V.T. trouble put to or cause inconvenience vex ; annoy تکلیف کرنا *taklīf' kar'nā*, V.I. take the trouble تکلیفِ مالایطاق *taklī'f-e mā'-lā yūṭāq'* N.F. unbearable trouble staggering or overwhelming responsibility [A]
تکملہ *tak'milah* N.M. appendix [A ~ کمال]
تکمہ *tūk'mah* N.M. button-hole loop ; eyelet گھنڈی تکمہ *ghūn'ḍī tūk'mah* N.M. cord knob and eyelet (as outmoded button and button-hole
تکمیل *takmīl'* N.F. completion implementation ; execution authentication consumation conclusion termination تکمیلِ تمسک *takmī'l-e tamas'sūk* N.F. execution of bond تکمیلِ رہن *takmī'l-e rah'n* (col. *reh'n*) N.F. termination of mortgage تکمیل کرنا *takmīl' kar'nā* (پایۂ) تکمیل کو پہنچانا *(pā'ya-e) takmīl' ko puhūnchā'nā* V.T. complete authenticate execute ; implement (پایۂ) تکمیل کو پہنچنا *(pā'yā-e) takmīl' ko pahūnch'nā*, تکمیل ہونا *takmīl' ho'nā* V.I. be complete conclude terminate be executed ; be implemented [A ~ کمال]
تکنا *tak'nā* V.T. & I. look at gaze stare at ogle expect (کی) راہ تکنا *(kī) rāh' tak'nā* V.T. wait for ; look out (for) پرایا ہاتھ تکنا *parā'ya hāth tak'nā* V.T. depend upon (someone) ; be parasitical تکی لگانا *tak'kī lagā'nā* V.I. stare ogle
تکنیک *taknīk'* N.F. technique تکنیکی *taknī'kī* ADJ. technique technical [~ E]
تکون *ti-kon'* N.F. triangle تکونا *ti-ko'nā*, تکونیا *ti-ko'niyā* ADJ. three-cornered ; triangular [~ کونا + تین]
تکوین *takvīn'* N.F. creation bringing Genesis [A ~ کون]
تکیہ *tak'yah* N.M. pillow bolster reliance support prop hermitage (پر) تکیہ کرنا *(par) tak'yah kar'nā* V.T. depend (on) ; rely

(upon) تکیہ کلام tak'ya-e kalām' N.M. expletive تکیہ نشین tak'ya nashīn' N.M. hermit recluse saint تکینی takī'nī' N.F. small pillow [A]

تگ tag N.F. (only in compounds) running تگ و پو ta'g-ā-po, تگ و تاز ta'g-o-tāz' N.F. running about search endeavour gallop تگ و دو ta'g-o-dau' N.F. running about endeavour [P]

تگڈم tigaḍ'ḍam N.M. clique of three ; cliques entanglement of (strings of) three kites

تگرگ tāgarg' N.M. (lit.) hailstone [P]

تگنا tig'nā, ADJ. (F. تگنی tig'nī) threefold triple triplicate ; thrice تگنی کا ناچ نچانا tig'nī kā nāch' nachvā'nā PH. dance (somoene) to one's tune harass [~ اگنا + تین]

تگی tig'gī N.F. a three (in cards) [~ تین]

تل til' N.M. sesame-seed ; sesamum pupil of eye small particle mole تل برابر til' barā'bar ADJ. very little تل چاولی til' chā'valī N.F. rice mixture ADJ. grizzled تل چٹا til-chaṭ'ṭā N.M. cockroach تل چٹانا til' chaṭā'nā V.I. (as wedding rite) cause to become hen-pecked تل دھرنے کی جگہ نہ ہونا til' dhar'ne kī ja'gah na ho'nā V.I. (of place) be overcrowded ; be filled to capacity تل بھگا til'-bhug'gā N.M. crushed sesamum sweetmeat تل شکری til'-shak'rī, تل کٹ til'-kūṭ, تل تل til'-til ADV. little by little ان تلوں میں تیل نہیں in ti'loṅ meṅ tel' na'hīṅ INT. you can't hope to have your way with so-and-so تلوا til'vā N.M. sweet sesamum rolls [P]

تل tal PREF. low down تل نظرا tal-naz'ra ADJ. & N.M. (W. dial.) sly person avoiding looking others in the face [~ تلے]

تلا ta'lā N.M. sole (of shoe) coating clump (of) shoes bottom ground flour تلا دینا ta'lā de'nā V.T. coat bottom of (saucepan) with fuller's earth, etc.

تلا til'lā N.M. drawn gold gold lace تلا سازی til'lā-sā'zī N.F. gold-lace making

تلادان ti'llā dan N.M. (dial.) alms equal to distributor's weight [~ تولنا + تلنا]

تلازم talā'zum N.M. being mutually necessary تلازمہ talā'zumah N.M. (in speech, etc.) mechanical use of words relating to one idea [A ~ لزوم]

تلاش talāsh' N.F. search quest تلاش کرنا talāsh' kar'nā V.T. search for ; seek تلاش معاش talā'sh-e ma'āsh' N.F. search for employment ; job-hunting تلاشی talā'shī N.F. search کی تلاشی لینا kī talā'shī le'nā V.T. search جامہ تلاشی jā'ma-talā'shī N.F. searching (someone's) persons خانہ تلاشی khā'na talā'shī N.F. searching (someone's) house [P]

تلاطم talā'ṭum N.M. storm dashing ; buffeting (of billows) [A ~ لطمہ]

تلافی talā'fī N.F. making amends recompense ; compensation reparation تلافی کرنا talā'fī kar'nā V.T. compensate make amends تلافی ہونا talā'fī ho'nā V.I. be recompensed تلافی مافات talā'fī-e mā-fāt' PH. letting bygones be bygones [A]

تلامذہ talā'mizah تلامیذ talāmīz' N.M. (PL. of تلمیذ N.M. ★)

تلانا tūlā'nā V.T. (see under تلنا tūl'nā V.I. ★)

تلاؤ talā''o N.M. pool pond lake [~ تال]

تلاوت tilā'vat N.F. (of the Holy Quran) reading recitation [A]

تلبیس talbīs N.F. impersonation disguise deception counterfeiting (currency) [A ~ لباس]

تلبیہ tal'biyah N.M. (during 'Haj') saying 'labbaik......' ; assurance of being at God's beck and call

تلپٹ tal'paṭ ADJ. topsy-turvy ruined wasted lost [~ تل tal]

تلچھٹ tal'chhaṭ N.F. sediment [~ تل tal]

تلچھنا ta'lchhnā V.I. feel uneasy be restless toss (from pain, etc.) تلچھو ملچھو کرنا tal'chhoo mal'chhoo kar'nā, تلچھوں ملچھوں کرنا tal'chhooṅ mal'chooṅ kar'nā V.I. be fidgety

تلخ tal'kh ADJ. bitter pungent unpalatable acrid ; acrimonious تلخ آب talkh-āb' تلخابہ talkh-ā'bah N.M. bitter water wine bitterness تلخ حقیقت tal'kh haqī'qat N.F. unpalatable truth تلخ کام talkh-kām' ADJ. frustrated (person) تلخ کامی talkh-ka'mī N.M. frustration تلخ گو talkh-go, تلخ نوا tal'kh-navā' ADJ. person saying bitter things ; uttering unplatable truths تلخ گوئی tal'kh-go''ī, تلخ نوائی talkh-navā''ī N.F. utterance of unpalatable truths تلخ مزاج tal'kh-mizāj'' ADJ. surly تلخ مزاجی tal'kh-mizājī N.F. surliness تلخ و ترش tal'kh-o-tūr'sh N.M. vicissitudes of life ADJ. sour and bitter تلخ ترش شیریں tal'kh tūr'sh shī'rīn N.F. (fig.) various aspects of life تلخی tal'khī N.F. bitterness acidity pungency acrimony unpleasantness ; bad blood [P]

تلخیص **talkhīs'** N.F. abridgment تلخیص کرنا talkhīs' ka'rnā V.T. abridge [A]

تلذذ **talaz'zūz** N.M. enjoyment; deriving pleasure [A ~ لذت]

تلسی **tūl'sī** N.F. sweet basil

تلطف **talat'tūf** N.M. kindness favour از رہِ تلطف az ra'h-e tala'tūf ADV kindly; graciously تلطف کرنا talat'tūf karnā V.T. do favour show kindness [A ~ لطف]

تلف **ta'laf** N.M. destruction; ruin loss waste تلف کرنا ta'laf kar'nā V.T. destroy; ruin waste; squander lose تلف ہونا ta'laf ho'nā V.I. be destroyed be ruined be wasted, be squandered [A]

تلفظ **talaf'fūz** N.M. pronunciation کا تلفظ ہونا kā talaf'fūz ho'nā V.I (of word) be pronounced [A ~ لفظ]

تلقین **talqīn'** N.F. persuasion religious instruction (esp. at death-bed) pronouncing the creed to urge dying person to repeat it [A]

تلک **ta'lak** ADV (arch. or col. form of تک ADV. ★)

تلک **ti'lak** N.M. (dial.) colour-mark placed by Hindus on brow تلک دھاری ti'lak-dhārī N.M. one daily besmearing brow with 'tilak' تلک لگانا ti'lak lagā'nā V.T besmear (one's brow) with 'tilak'

تلی **talal'lī** (dial تلتلی tūl'tūlī) N.F. jet, spurt تلی باندھنا tulal'li bāndh'nā V.T. direct a jet تلی بندھنا tūlal'lī bandhnā V.I. spurt out

تلمذ **talam'mūz** N.M. being or becoming a pupil studentship سے شرفِ تلمذ ہونا se sha'raf-e talam'mūz ho'nā V.T. be a pupil of [A ~ تلمیذ]

تلملانا **talmala nā** V.I. be impatient be restless; feel uneasy fret تلملاہٹ talmalā'hat تلملی tal'malī N.F. uneasiness fretting

تلمیح **talmīh'** N.F. (PL. تلمیحات talmīhāt') allusion [A ~ لمحہ]

تلمیذ **talmīz'** N.M. (PL تلامذہ talā'mızah or تلامیذ talāmīz') pupil student [A]

تلنا **tal'nā** V fry roast تلوانا talvā'nā V.T have (something) fried

تلنا **tūl'nā** V.I. (see under تولنا V.T. ★)

تلنگا **tilan'gā** N.M. (during British occupation of the sub-continent) native soldier in Western uniform (owing to original batches' training in Telingana) Telegu-speaking person

تلنگی **tilangī'** N.F. Telegu

تلوا **tal'vā**, تلا **talā'** N.M. sole (of foot) تلوا کھجانا tal'vā khūjā'nā V.I. (of sole) itch have a foreboding of travel تلوا نہ لگنا tal'va na lag'nā V.I. be restless, be impatient تلووں سے آگ لگنا tāl'voṅ se āg' lag'nā V.I. be in a rage تلووں سے لگنا سر میں جا کے بجھنا tal'voṅ se lag'nā sir' meṅ jā ke būjh'nā V.T be greatly hurt تلووں سے ملنا tol'voṅ se mal'nā V.I. trample تلووں سے آنکھیں ملنا tal'voṅ se āṅ'kheṅ mal'na V.T. evince humility be meek تلوے چاٹنا (یا سہلانا) tal've chāṭ'nā (or saihlā'nā) V.T. fawn on flatter coax cajole; today تلوے چھلنی ہونا tal've chhal'nī ho'nā V.I. have a tiresome journey have run about a lot have endeavoured much تلوے سے لگنا tal've se lag'nā V.I. follow meekly

تلوار **talwār** N.F. sword sabre scimitar تلوار چلانا talvār' chālā'nā V.T. strike with a sword put to the sword N.M. fencing تلوار چلنا talvār' chal'nā V I. be fighting with swords N.M. sword-fight تلوار کا دھنی talvār' kā dha'nī N.M. good swordsman تلوار سونتنا talvār' soṅt'nā, تلوار کھینچنا talvār' kheṅch'nā V.I. draw the sword, unsheathe the sword تلوار کا گھاؤ talvār' kā ghā''o N.M. sword-cut; sword-wound تلوار میان (یا نیام) میں کرنا talvār' miyān' (or neyām') meṅ kar'nā V.I. sheathe the sword تلواروں کی چھاؤں میں talvā roṅ kī chā''oṅ meṅ PH well-guarded; under shadow of swords ننگی تلوار لیے nāṅ'gī talvār' lī'ye ADV with a drawn sword تلوریا tal'varyā N.M. swordman

تلوانسا **tilvāṅ'sā** تلونڈا tilauṅḍā, تلونسا tilauṅ'sa ADJ. (of lamp) aslant (to bring oil nearer wick)

تلون **tulav'vūn** N.M. fickleness capriciousness تلون طبع talav'vūn-e tab'' N.M. capriciousness fickle-mindedness تلون مزاج talav'vūn mizāj' ADJ. capricious whimsical fickle-minded تلون مزاجی talav'vūn mızājī N.F capriciousness fickle-mindedness [A ~ لون]

تلی **til'lī** N.F. spleen milt this as food

تلے **ta'le** ADV. on the groundfloor down under, below beneath کے تلے ke ta'le ADV. at the bottom of at the foot of تلے اوپر ta'le oo'par ADV. one upon the other تلے اوپر کے ta'le oo'par ke ADJ. (of children) born in succession تلے اوپر کی اولاد ta'le oo'par kī aulād' N.F. children born in succession تلے پڑنا ta'le par' nā V.I. sleep on the floor

تلے دانی **ta'le dā'nī** N.F. needle-pouch, housewife

تلیٹی **talai''tī**, تلیٹھی talat''thī N.F submontane region

تیلیر **til'yar** N.M. starling

تم **tum** PRON. (nominative) you

تماثل **tamā'sul** N.M. similarity ; likeness ; resemblance [A ~ مثل]

تمادی **tamād'dī** N.F. (lit.) passage (of time) duration تمادیٔ ایام **tamad'dī-e ayyām'** N.F. passage of time [A ~ مدت]

تمارض **tamā'ruz** N M. valetudenarism malingering

تمازت **tamā'zat** N.F. heat ; intense heat [A]

تماشہ تماشہ **tama'sha** تماشہ **tama'shah** N.M. show entertainment spectacle fun sport oddity film show business تماشائی **tamā'shā'ī** N.M. onlooker spectator تماش بین **tamash'bīn** N. rake ; libertine ; debauchee تماش بینی **tamashbī'nī** N.F. licentiousness ; debauchery تماشا دیکھنا **tamā-sha dekh'na** V.I. witness a show enjoy other's misfortune تماشا کرنا **tamāsha kar'na** V.T. put on a show stage a play jeer ; jest ; make fun (of) (rare) see , view تماشا کرنے والا **tama'sha kar'ne vala** N.M. showman exhibitor actor one who makes sport funny person تماشے کی بات **tama'she ki bat'** N.F. funny thing تماشگاہ **tamash'-gah'** N.F. show place theatre [A ~ تماشی CORR.]

تمام **tamam'** ADJ. entire , whole total complete full N.M. end ; conclusion تمامتر (or تمام تر) **tamam'-tar** ADJ. most all entire تمام شد **tamam' shud** PH. its all over ; its done with تمام کرنا **tamam' kar'na** V.T. complete conclude کا کام تمام کرنا **ka kam tamam' kar'na** V.T. kill ; murder تمام ہونا **tamam' ho'na** V.I. be finished ; be concluded ; come to an end be completed; be over کا کام تمام ہونا **ka kam tamam' ho'na** V.I. be dead تمام وکمال **tama'm-o-kamal'** ADV. thoroughly wholly ; entirely fully ; completely totally تمامی **tama'mī** N.F. completion conclusion N.M. a variety of brocade [A]

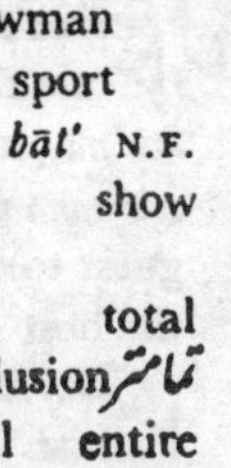

تمباکو **tamba'koo** N.M. tobacco [Sp. ~ Haiti red Indian word]

تمت **tam'mat** ADJ. finis [A ~ تمام]

تمتع **tamat'to'** N.M. utilization gain performance of minor pilgrimage along with the major one [A ~ متاع]

تمتمانا **tam'tama na** V.I. glow flush (of face) redden ; be enraged sparkle flash تمتماہٹ **tam'tama'hat** N.F. glow reddening (of face) sparkling

تمثال **tamsal'** N.F. stature portrait likeness [A ~ مثل]

تمثیل **tamsīl'** N.F. drama ; play allegory parable apologue instance example resemblance similitude تمثیل پیش کرنا **tamsīl' pesh kar'na** V.T. put on a play adduce an example تمثیل لانا **tamsīl' la'na** V.T. adduce an example تمثیلاً **tamsī'lan** ADV. for instance ; for example allegorically ; as a parable [A ~ مثل]

تمجید **tamjīd'** N.F. glorification (of God) [A ~ مجد]

تمدن **tamad'dūn** N.M. civilisation urbanization

تمرد **tamar'rūd** N.M. disobedience insolence transgression ; exceeding the limits haughtiness ; concert (rare) tyranny [A]

تمسخر **tamas'khur** N.M. joke ; jest fun ; buffoonery [A]

تمسک **tamas'sūk** N.M. (monetary or legal) bond promissory note (rare) clinging (to) ; sticking fast [A]

تمغہ **tamghah** N.M. medal (arch.) royal charter (arch.) official stamp, etc. on merchandise (arch.) polltax [P]

تمکنت **tam'kanat** N.F. gravity power pomp grandeur haughtiness [A]

تمکین **tam'kin** N.F. dignity gravity [A ~ doublet of PREC.]

تملق **tamal'lūq** N.M. flattery [A]

تملیک **tamlik'** N.F. possession settlement of property [A ~ املاک]

تمندار **tū'man-dar** N.M. centurion chief (among certain Baluch tribes) [T+ تمن 100 soldiers+P دار]

تمنا **taman'na** N.F. wish desire longing تمنا (ظاہر) کرنا **taman'na (za'hir) kar'na** V.T. wish desire ; express a desire for

تموج **tamav'vaj** N.M. billowing (of waves) commotion [A ~ موج]

تموز **tamooz** (rare **tammooz'**) N.M. name of a summer month intense heat [A]

تمول **tamav'vūl** N.M. riches ; wealth wealthiness [A ~ مال]

تمہارا **tumha'ra** PRON. your yours [~ تم]

تمہید **tamhīd'** N.F. introduction ; preface preamble ; prolegomena preliminary discourse preparation opening ; beginning تمہید اٹھانا tamhīd' ūṭhā'nā N.F. introduce a subject broach or introduce a topic begin ; initiate تمہیدیں باندھنا tamhī'deṅ bandh'nā V.I. make vain suppositions make false promises try to introduce subtly make advances تمہیدی tamhī'dī ADJ. introductory preliminary [A ~ مہد]

تمہی tūm'hī, تمہیں tūmhīṅ PRON. you you ; yourself [~ تم]

تمہیں tūm'heṅ PRON. you ; to you [~ تم]

تمیز tamīz' N.F. manners etiquette sense judgment direction distinction تمیزدار tamīz'-dār ADJ. well-mannered discreat judicious تمیز کرنا tamīz' kar'nā V.I. be mannerly distinguish بدتمیز bad-tamīz' (ped. بے تمیز be-tamīz') ADJ. unmannerly [A ~ FOLL. CORR.]

تمییز tamyīz' N.F. distinction qualification category حرف تمییز harf-e tamyīz' N.M. qualifying word adverb [A]

تن tan N.M. body person تن آساں tan-āsān' ADJ. lazy ; indolent تن آسانی tan-āsā'nī N.F. laziness ; indolence تناور tan-ā'var ADJ. large sturdy تن بدن پھونکنا tan' ba'dan phoonk'nā V.T. consume the body تن بدن میں آگ لگنا tan' ba'dan meṅ āg' lag'nā V.I. fly into a passion ; be enraged grow very jealous تن پرور tan'-par'var ADJ. selfish self-indulgent indolent تن پروری tan-par'varī N.F. selfishness self-indulgence indolence تن تنہا ta'n-e tanhā' ADJ. all alone all by one self تندرست tan'dūrūst' ADJ. healthy hale and hearty تندرست کرنا tan-dūrūst' kar'nā V.T. cure تندرست ہونا tan'dūrūst' ho'nā V.T. recover recoup health تندرستی tan'dūrūs'tī N.F. health recovery تندرستی ہزار نعمت ہے tan'dūrūs'tī hazār ne''mat hai PROV. health is better than wealth تندہی (or تن دہی) tan'dehī' N.F. devotion diligence تن ڈھانکنا tan' ḍhāṅk'nā V.I. have clothes go about in ordinary clothes تنزیب tan'-zeb N.M. a kind of muslin a kind of waistcoat تن من tan' man' N.M. body and soul تن من دھن tan' man' dhan' N.M. body, soul and wealth all one's resources تن من دھن سے tan' man' dhan' se ADV. with full devotion تن من سے tan' man' se ADV. with all one's heart and soul تن من مارنا tan' man' mār'na V.T. suppress one's feelings work with devotion تن من وارنا tan' man vār'nā V.I. be ready to lay down one's life تن و توش ta'no-tosh' N.M. strong body تنومند tan-oo mand' ADJ. sturdy [P]

تننا tan'nā V.I. (same as تنتا V.I. ★)

تنازع tanā'zo' N.M. struggle dispute contention تنازع للبقا tanā'-zo' lilbaqā' N.M. struggle for existence تنازعہ tanā'zo'ah N.M. (col. quarrel ; dispute [A ~ نزاع]

تناسب tanā'sūb N.M. proportion تناسب اعضا tanā'sūb-e a'zā' N.M. due proportion of the limbs تناسب مرکب tanā sūb-e mūrak'kab N.M. compound proportion تناسب مفرد tanā'sūb-e mūf'rad N.M. simple proportion تناسب منقلب tanā'sūb-e mūn'qalib N.M. inverse proportion [A ~ نسبت]

تناسخ tanā'sukh N.M. metempsychosis ; transmigration of soul (rare) transformation [A]

تناسل tanā'sūl N.M. reproduction ; procreation آلۂ تناسل ā'la-e tanā'sūl N.M. genitals penis [A ~ نسل]

تنافر tanā'fur N.F. putting together words hard to pronounce mutual aversion repugnance [A ~ نفرت]

تناقض tanā'qūz N.M. incompatibility discrepancy [A ~ نقض]

تناول tanā'vūl N.M. eating (rare) extending one's hand to grip تناول کرنا (یا فرمانا) tanā'vūl kar'nā (or farm'nā) V.T. eat ماحضر تناول کرنا mā-ha'-zar tanā'vūl kar'nā V.T. (humble request to guest to) eat whatever is made available by the host ; partake of feast [A]

تنبا tam'ba (col. for تنبان tambān') N.M. loose trousers [P ~]

تنبو tam'boo N.M. tent

تنبورا tamboo'rā, طنبورہ tamboo'rah N.M. tambourine

تنبولن

تنبول tambol' N.M. cash wedding-gift (rare) betel-leaf تنبول پڑنا tambol' par'na V.I. (of cash wedding-gifts) be collected

تنبولی tambo'lī N.M. betel-leaf vendor

تنبولن tambo'lan N.F. woman vending betel-leaf seller

تنبہ tanab'boh N.M. awakening taking the warning [A ~ FOLL.]

تنبیہ tambīh' N.F. warning reproof admonition reprimand (ped.) awakening ; arousing تنبیہ کرنا tambīh' kar'nā warn admonish reprimand تنبیہ ہونا tambīh' ho'nā V.I. realise be warned [A]

تن پھن کرنا tūn' phūn kar'nā V.T. say angry things be haughty

تنت کا وقت *tant' kā vaq't* N.M right moment

تنتر *tan'tar* تنتر منتر *tan'tar man'tar* N.M (dial.) charm ; enchantment

تن تنی *tun'tunī* N.M a kind of guitar

تنخواہ *tankhāh'* N.M. pay ; assignment salary wages pay تنخواہ دار *tankhā'-dār* N.M. paid (servant) one of the salaried class [P ~ تن + خواستن]

تند *tund* ADJ. fierce furious violent rough severe rapid swift ; fast تند خو *tund-khoo'* ADJ. fierce ; furious irascible surly تند رفتار *tund-raftār'* ADJ. fleet-footed rapid تند زبان *tund-zabān'* ADJ. foul-mouthed sharp-tongued تند مزاج *tund'-mizāj* ADJ. fierce ; furious hot-heated irascible surly باد تند *bā'd-e-tund'*, تند باد *tund'-bād* N.F tempest storm strong wind تندی *tun'dī* N.F. fierceness ferocity fury violence swiftness sharpness severity force [P]

تندور *tandoor'* N.M. (col for تنور N.M. ★)

تندیل *tundail* N.M. & ADJ pot-bellied (person) [~ توند]

تنزل *tanaz'zul* N.M. decline decay demotion ; degradation تنزل ہونا *tanaz'zul ho'nā* V.I. decline be demoted be degraded [A ~ نزول]

تنزیل *tanzil'* N.F. revelation (of the Holy Quran) [A ~ نزول]

تنزیہ *tanzīh'* N.F. purification purigation keeping (someone) away from sins [A ~ نزہت]

تنسیخ *tan'sikh* N.F. repeal abrogation quashing cancellation revocation annulment [A ~ نسخ]

تنصیب *tansib'* N.F. installation [A ~ نصب]

تنصیف *tansif'* N.M. bisection [A ~ نصف]

تنظیم *tanzīm'* N.F. organisation , party organisation ; setting in order discipline regimentation arrangement (rare) threading (pearls) (rare) versification [A ~ نظم]

تنعم *tana''ūm* N.M easy life life of luxury prosperity [A ~ نعمت]

تنغض *tanagh'ghuz* N.M disgust [A]

تنفر *tanaf'fūr* N.M disgust dislike aversion [A ~ نفرت]

تنفس *tanaf'fūs* N.M. breathing ; respiration آلاتِ تنفس *ālāt-e tanaf'fus* N.M. respiratory organs نظامِ تنفس *nizā'm-e tanaf'fūs* N.M. respiratory system تنفسی *tanaf'fūsī* ADJ. respiratory [A ~ نفس *nafas*]

تنقیح *tanqīh'* N.F. issue (in law-suit) point of issue search ; inquiry clearance of doubt decision ; determination ; settlement تنقیحات *tanqīhāt* N.M. PL. issue (in law-suit) تنقیح طلب *tanqīh'-ta'lab* ADJ. (point) at issue (point) to be determined ; decided or settled تنقیح کرنا *tanqīh' kar'nā* V.T. determine or settle issue in a law-suit تنقیح قائم کرنا *tanqīh' qā''im kar'nā*, تنقیح نکالنا *tanqīh nikal'nā*) V.T. frame or draw up [A]

تنقید *tanqīd'* N.F. criticism review critical appreciation fault-finding animadversion کو ہدف تنقید بنانا *ko ha'daf-e tanqīd' banā'nā* V.T. criticize slate [A ~ نقد]

تنقیص *tan'qīs'* N.F. fault-finding adverse criticism (rare) curtailment [A ~ نقص]

تنقیہ *tan'qiyah* N.M. purgation purge [A ~ نقی]

تنک *tunūk* ADJ. (lit.) slight having little thin weak short lacking largeness تنک ظرف *tun'nūk-zar'f* ADJ. mean تنک مزاج *tunūk-mizāj* ADJ. short tempered ; peevish ; irritable [P]

تنکا *tin'kā* N.M. straw blade (of grass) dried stalk تنکا اتارنا اور چھپر رکھ دینا *tin'kā utār'nā aur chhap'par rakh' de'nā* PH. put under great obligation for a small favour تنکا اتارنے کا احسان ماننا *tin'kā utār'ne kā ehsān mān'nā* PH. be oblidged for a small favour تنکا بھی نہ توڑ سکنا *tin'kā bhī na toṛ sak'nā* V.T. extremely lazy be very indolent تنکا دانتوں میں لینا *tin'kā dāṅ'toṅ meṅ le'nā* V.T. admit defeat ; throw up the sponge ask for mercy تنکا نہ رہنا *tin'kā na raih'nā* V.I. be divested of everything تنکا ہو جانا *tin'kā ho jā'nā* V.I. become thin and lean ; be emaciated تنکے چننا *tin'ke chūn'nā* V.I. be intoxicated ; go mad ; become insane be intoxicated ; be dead drunk تنکے چنوانا *tin'ke chūnvā'nā* V.T. drive made make insane تنکے کا پہاڑ *tin'ke kā pahāṛ' banā'nā* PH. make mountains out of molehills تنکے کا سہارا لینا *tin'ke kā sahā'ra le'nā* V.I. catch at straw تنکے کی اوٹ پہاڑ *tink'e kī oṭ pahāṛ'* PH. just a shadow of lurking calamity even small timely more highly effective

تنکنا *ti'naknā* V.T. flare up react sharply be uneasy flutter ruffle

تنکیر *tankīr'* N.F. being or making a common noun be unwary [A ~ نکرہ]

تنگ *tang* ADJ. narrow tight strait too small scanty contracted compressed straitened bored ; fed up poor distressed N.M. lap sack ; bag girth تنگ آنا *tang' ānā* V.I. be fed up (with) be utterly sick (of) ; have one's patience exhausted تنگ حال *tang'-hāl'* ADJ. in straitened circumstances تنگ حالی *tang'hā'lī* N.F. poverty want تنگ دست *tang'-das't* ADJ. poor ; penniless destitute stingy ; miserly تنگ دستی *tang'-das'tī* N.F. poverty ; want destitution تنگ دل *tang'-dil'* ADJ. mean miserly ; niggardly narrow-minded تنگدلی *tang'-di'lī* N.F. meanness niggardliness narrow-mindedness تنگ دہن *tang'-da'han* ADJ. small-mouthed (as sign of beauty) تنگ ظرف *tang'-zar'f* ADJ. (less approved form of (تنک ظرف) mean تنگ کرنا *tang' kar'nā* V.T. tease ; harass vex ; pester badger narrow down tighten contract ; compress تنگ وقت *tang'-vaq't* N.M. eleventh hour short notice تنگ ہونا *tang' ho'nā* V.I. be penniless be badly off squeezed be in a difficulty ہاتھ تنگ ہونا *hāth tang' ho'nā* V.I. be penniless ; be in straits تنگنائے *tang'-nā''e* N.F. strait ; narrow place or passage تنگی *tan'gī* N.F. narrowness tightnests trouble ; difficulty hardship poverty ; want تنگی ترشی *tan'gī tūr'shī* N.F. want ; poverty trouble difficulty ; hardship تنگی ترشی سے بسر ہونا *tan'gī tur'shī se ba-sar' ho'nā* V.I. live from hand to mouth eke out (one's) existence تنگی دینا *tan'gī de'nā* V.T. make life hard (for) تنگی ہونا *tan'gī ho'na* V.I. lead a miserable life be in trouble be in property [P]

تننا (or تنا) *tan'nā* V.I. be stretched be pulled tight stand erect or up-right sit straight react sharply defy stiffen (one's) attitude

تنور *tanoor'* (col. تندور *tandoor'* ped. *tannoor'*) N.M. stove oven تنور جھونکنا *tanoor' jhoṅk'nā* V.I. heat an oven light a stove eat ; (fig.) fill the belly [A]

تنوع *tanav'vo'* N.M. variety diversity [A ~ نوع]

تنومند *tanoo'mand* ADJ. well-built stout robust تنومندی *tanoo'mandī* N.F. robustness [P ~ تن]

تنویر *tanvīr'* N.F. refulgence rays of light

تنوین *tanvīn* N.F. nunation ; doubled short vowel at end of word read as the particular single vowel + ن written with an extra الف save when the final letter is or 'ta'-e tanis'' [A ~ نون]

تنہ *ta'nah* تنا *ta'nā* N.M. trunk ; stem stalk [P ~ تن]

تنہا *tanhā'* ADJ. alone lonely solitary single ADV. single-handed تنہائی *tanhā''ī* N.F. loneliness solitude [P]

تنی *ta'nī* N.F. clothes-line string share تنی میں گانٹھ دینا *ta'nī meṅ gāṅṭh' de'nā* V.T. (dial). tie knot as memory aid betroth تنیا *tan'-yā* N.M. drawers comprising strip of cloth held by string [~ تاننا]

تو *to* (dial. *tau*) ADJ. then in that case at that time therefore ; hence moreover in short N.F. (also تو تو *to' to'*) cry to call dog تو بھی *to' bhī* CONJ. still ; yet ; even then nevertheless ; nonetheless

تو *too* PRON. thou تو بھی رانی میں بھی رانی ، کون بھرے گا پانی *too' bhī rā'nī meṅ bhī rā'nī kaun bhare gā pā'nī* PROV. all are generals, none a soldier تو سہی *to sa'hī* PH. (if it is so) then I will see to it تو تڑاق کرنا *too taṛāq' kar'nā* V.T. talk rudely or discourteously quarrel brawl تو تکار *too takār'*, تو تو میں میں *too' too maiṅ' maiṅ* N.F. rude talk brawl تو تو میں میں ہونا *too'-too maiṅ' maiṅ ho'nā* V.I. have a loud argument ; brawl

توا *ta'vā* N.M. hot plate griddle ; crock for hookah top copper plate at bottom of water-heater leaden base in well for cooling water (slang) gramophone disc ADJ. jet black ; very dark (person) الٹا توا *ūl'ṭā ta'vā* N.M. convex or inverted hot plate ADJ. jet black ; very dark person توے کا ہنسنا *ta've kā haṅs'-nā* V.I. soot corruscation under hot plate (as good omen)

تواب *tawāb'* N.M. (attribute of God as) Acceptor of Repentence penitant [A ~ توبہ]

توابع *tavā'be'* N.M. PL. adjuncts followers [~ SING. تابع]

تواتر *tavā'tur* N.M. succession ; continuity being unbroken series (in tradition) having numerous chains of narrators [A]

توارد *tavā'rūd* N.M. sameness of theme in verses of two or more poets [A ~ ورود]

تواریخ *tavārīkh'* N.F. (arch). history [A ~ SING. تاریخ]

توازن *tavā'zūn* N.M. balance counter-balance توازن اقتدار *tavā zūn-e iqtidār'* N.M.

balance of power [A ~ وزن]

تواضع *tavā'zo'* N.F. entertainment hospitality (rare) humility (rare) politeness تواضع سے کام لینا *tavā'zo' se kam' le'nā* V.T. be polite show humility تواضع کرنا *tavā'zo' kar'nā* V.T entertain show hospitality تواضع ہونا *tavā'zo' ho'nā* V.I. be entertained [A ~ وضع]

توافق *tava'fūq* N.M. agreement concord harmony [A ~ موافق]

توالد *tava'lūd* N.M. procreation [A ~ ولد]

توام *tau''am* ADJ. twin [A]

توانا *tūvā'nā* ADJ. strong robust powerful توانائی *tūvānā''ī* N.F. energy strength ; power [P ~ توانستن can]

توبڑا *tob'rā* N.M. nose-bag (of horse)

توبہ *tau'bah* N.M. repentence penitence adjuration ; renunciation ; giving up conversion ; reiteration of faith توبۃ النصوح *tau'bā't ūn-nasooh'* N.F. true repentence توبہ تلا *tau'bah til'lah* N.F. repentence hue and cry توبہ تلا کرنا *tau'bah til'lah kar'nā* V.T. repent beg pardon raise a hue and cry توبہ توڑنا *tau'bah toṛ'nā* V.T. violate one's faith perjure توبہ توبہ *tau'bah tau'bah* INT. good gracious heaven forbid ; never again توبہ توبہ کر کے کہنا *tau'bah tau'bah kar ke kaih'nā* V.T. utter some unpalatable truth in all humility توبہ تنسوحا *tau'bah tansoo'hā* N.M. (CORR. of توبۃ النصوح N.F. ★) توبہ شکن *tau'bā-shi'kan* ADJ. perjurer توبہ شکنی *tau'ba-shi'-kani* N.F. perjury توبہ کرانا *tau'bah kara'nā* V.T. cause (someone) to repent make (someone) penitent توبہ کرنا *tau'bah kar'nā* V.I. repent renounce (sin, etc.) توبہ گاہ *tau'ba gāh'* N.F. penitentiary [A]

توبیخ *taubīkh'* N.F. reproach ; opprobrium ; obloquy زجر و توبیخ *zaj'r-o-taubīkh'* N.F. rebuke and reproach [A]

توپ *top* N.F. gun ; cannon (fig.) corpulent person توپچی *top'chī* N.M. gunner ; artillery man ; cannoneer ; bombardier توپ چلانا (یا داغنا) *top chala'nā* (or *dagh'nā*) V.T. fire a gun or cannon cannonade توپ چلنا (یا دغنا) *top chal'nā* (or *dagh'nā*) V.I. (of gun) be fired *top-khā'nah* N.M. arsenal battery artillery توپ دم کرنا *top'-dam kar'nā*, توپ سے اڑانا *top se uṛā'nā*, توپ کے منہ اڑانا *top' ke mūṅh ūṛā'nā* V.T blow off with a cannon [A]

توت *toot*, شہتوت *shaih'toot* (ped. *shah-*) N.M. mulberry توتڑی *toot'ṛī* N.F. smaller mulberry [P]

توتا *to'ta* (usu. but wrongly spelt طوطا) N.M. parrot brat ; infant with sweet prattle cock (of matchlock) توتا پالنا *to tā pāl'nā* V.I. keep a parrot as a pet aggravate disease by concealing it توتا چشم *to'tā chash'm* ADJ. treacherous توتے کی سی آنکھیں پھیرنا *to'te kī sī āṅ'kheṅ pher'nā*, توتے کی طرح دیدے بدلنا *to'te kī tar'h dī'de ba'dalnā* V.I. withdraw the affections from ; prove faithless to ہاتھوں کے توتے اڑنا *hā'thoṅ ke to'te ūṛ'nā* V. be taken aback be nonplussed ; be confounded

توتلا *tot'lā* ADJ. (F. توتلی *tot'lī*) lisping (child)

توتو *to to'* (also تو *to'*) INT. & N.F. cry to call dog

توتی *too'tī* N.F. (rare but same as طوطی N.F. ★)

توتیا *too'tiyā* N.M. blue vitriol collirium [P]

توتے باندھنا *too'te bāndh'nā* توتے (یا توتیے) جوڑنا *to'te* (or *too'tiye*) *joṛ'na'* V.T. slander ; scandalize [CORR. of A توطئہ]

توثیق *tausīq'* N.F. confirmation verification ratification ; corroboration توثیق کرنا *tausīq' kar'nā* V.T. confirm verify ratify ; corroborate bear (someone) out [A ~ وثاق]

توجہ *tavaj'joh* N.M. attention care regard inclination ; tendency kindness ; favour consideration توجہ طلب *tavaj'joh ta'lab* ADJ. worth noting ; requiring attention calling for consideration کی توجہ مبذول کرانا *kī tavaj'joh mabzool' karā'nā* PH. call, draw or invite (someone's) attention [A ~ وجہ]

توجیہ *taujīh'* N.F. excuse explanation notification causation ; tracing (something) to its cause descriptive roll توجیہ کرنا *taujīh' kar'nā* V.T. explain away give as the reason (of) [A ~ وجہ]

توحش *tavah'hush* N.M. shying unsociability [A ~ وحش]

توحید *tauhīd'* N.F unity of God monotheism ; belief in God's unity oneness [A ~ واحد]

تودہ *to'dah* N.M. mound heap تودۂ خاک *to'da-e khāk'* N.M. heap of dust (fig.) dead human body ; corpse [P]

تورات *taurāt'*, توریت *tauret'* N.F. the Taurah, Pentateuch

تورع *tavar'ro'* N.F piety [A ~ ورع]

تورہ *to'rah* N.M. (arch.) Jhenghiz Khan's constitution custom honour pride ostentation prudery blandishment sweetmeats on platters mutually exchanged by groom and bride's families توڑہ بندی to'ra-bań'dī N.F such exchange تورے پیٹی to're pe'tī N.F. bragging woman تورے دار to're-dār' N.M. respectable families receiving gifts from royal feasts تورے والی to're va'lī N.F prudish woman [T]

توریا to'rīya N.M. rapeseed

توریت tauret' N.F (same as تورات N.F ★)

توریہ tau'rıyah N.M concealment of real feeling this as literary device [A]

توڑا to'ṛa N.M. shortage piece of string a kind of ornamental chain for neck (arch.) purse containing one thousand pounds, etc) (arch.) match (of musket) توڑے دار بندوق to're-dār bańdooq' N.F matchlock ; musket

توڑنا toṛ'nā V.T break sunder pluck tear ; rend break into discontinue , stop win over (from opposite side) plough sever (ties) decrease remove (math.) reduce دم توڑنا dum toṛ'nā V.I. die ; pass away مفت کی روٹیاں توڑنا mŭf't kī ro'ṭiyāń toṛ'nā V.I. go on the bum ; sponge on others live without earning own livelihood توڑ toṛ N.M. remedy counteraction counter-measure defence (against trick, etc.) توڑ پھوڑ toṛ' phoṛ N.F. destruction subversion توڑ دینا toṛ' de'nā V.T. break spoil disrupt end destroy توڑ ڈالنا toṛ' ḍāl'nā V.T. break destroy pull down توڑ کرنا toṛ' kar'nā V.T. counteract retaliate توڑ لینا toṛ' le'nā V.T. pluck (flowers) gather fruit win over (members of opposite party, etc.) توڑا مروڑی to'ṛa maro'ṛī N.F. (vul.) bursts and twists توڑ جوڑ toṛ' joṛ جوڑ توڑ joṛ' toṛ N.M. PL. tricks plottings

توزع tavaz'zo' N.M. be scattered be dispersed [A]

توزیع tauzī'' N.F. rent roll descriptive roll statement [A ~ PREC.]

توس tos N.M. toasted slice of bread [E ~ toast CORR.]

توسط tavas'sŭṭ N.M. good offices کے توسط سے ke tavas'sŭt se PH. through ; through the good offices of [A ~ وسط]

توسل tavas'sŭl N.M. means mediation good offices (uses of sacred beings) کے توسل سے ke tavas'sŭl se PH. through [A ~ وسیلہ]

توسن tau'san N.M. steed war-horse unbroken horse توسن طبع tau'san-e tab'' N.M. nature ability [P]

توسیع tausī'' N.F. extension enlargement prolongation [A ~ وسعت]

توش tosh N.M. energy (only in) تن و توش tan-o tosh' N.M. physique robust body [P]

توشک to'shak N.F. mattress توشک خانہ to'shak-khā'nah N.M. quiet store or factory [P]

توشہ toshah N.M. provisions for a journey, provision supplies توشۂ آخرت to'sha-e ā'khirat, عاقبت کا توشہ 'a'qibat kā toshah N.M. provision for hereafter ; virtuous deeds توشہ خانہ to'sha-khānah N.M. wardrobe ; clothing store توشہ دان، توشدان to'sha-dān, tosh'-dān N.M. tiffin carrier cartridge box [P]

توصیف tausīf' N.F. praise eulogy commendation [A ~ وصف]

توضیح tauẓīḥ' N.F. clarification explanation elucidation (math.) corollary توضیحات tauẓīhāt' N.F. PL. clarifications elucidations corollaries [A ~ واضح]

توطئہ tau'te'ah N.M. plot ; scheme slander preliminary remarks repetition of rhyme [A]

توغل tavagh'ghŭl N.M. skill through long practice ; experience [A]

توفیر taufīr' N.F increase excess and surplus [A ~ وافر]

توفیق taufīq' N.F. divine help or guidance favourable turn of circumstances [A ~ موافق]

توقع tavaq'qo'' N.F. expectation hope trust ; reliance توقع اٹھ جانا tavaq'qo' ŭṭh' jā'nā V.I. (of hope) end توقع رکھنا (یا کرنا) tavaq'qū rakh'nā (or kar'nā) V.I. expect hope trust [A ~ وقوع]

توقف tavaq'qŭf N.M. delay heritation stay respite suspension توقف کرنا tavaq'qŭf kar'nā V.I. delay hesitate wait stay be suspended [A ~ وقوف]

توقیر tauqīr' N F. veneration honour [A ~ وقر]

توقیع tauqī'' N.F. royal charter [A ~ وقوع]

توکل tavak'kŭl N.M. trust in God توکل کرنا (یا پر بیٹھنا) tavak'kŭl kar'nā (or par baiṭh'nā) V.I. trust in God علی التوکل a'lat-tavak'kŭl (col. alat-tavak'kŭl) PH. at random [A ~ وکالت]

تولا to'lā, تولہ to'lah N.M. 12 'masha' weight

تولا taval'la N.M. love affection , attachment تولائی tavallā''ī N.M. Shi'ite who does not say tabar'ra [A ~ تولی CORR.]

تولّد *taval'lūd* N.M. birth nativity تولد ہونا *taval'lūd ho'nā* V.I. be born [A ~ ولد]

تولنا *tol'nā* V.T. weigh estimate worth, etc. (of) تول *tol* N.M. weight process of weighing

تولیت *tau'liyat* N.F. trusteeship governorship supervision [A ~ ولی]

تولید *taulīd'* N.F. reproduction generation ضبط تولید *zab't-e taulīd'* N.F. birth control ; contraception family planning مادۂ تولید *mād'da-e taulīd'* N.M. semen [A ~ ولد]

تولیہ *tau'liyah* N.M. towel

تومڑی *to'mṛī* N.F. hollow gourd a kind of firework projection on crocodile's nose [~ تونبا]

تومنا *toom'nā* V.T. card (cotton or wool) with finger (before combing)

توئنا *too'nā* توجانا *too' jā'nā* V.I. animal abort mis-carry

تونبا *toṅ'ba* N.M. hollow gourd bowl made of it guitar made of it ; gourd-guitar *toṅ'bī* N.F. fresh gourd small gourd-guitar

تونْد *toṅd* N.F. pot-belly تُندل *toṅ'dal*, تُندیل *toṅdail* ADJ pot-bellied

تونسنا *tauṅs'nā* V.I. feel very thirsty owing to heat

تونگر *tūvaṅ'gar* ADJ. well-to-do rich ; wealthy opulent تونگری *tūvaṅ'garī* N.F. wealth ; riches opulence [P ~ توان]

توہّم *tavah'hūm* N.M. halucination fancy superstition [A ~ وہم]

توہین *tauhīn'* N.F. insult disgrace contempt defamation ; libel توہینِ عدالت *tauhī'n-e 'adālat* N.F. contempt of court توہین کرنا *tauhīn' kar'nā* V.T. insult defame disgrace [A ~ وہن]

توئی *too''ī* N.F. a kind of embroidery

تہ *taih* N. F. (usu. spelt as تہہ *taih*) except in construct phrases layer ; stratum crease fold surface bottom ADJ. under beneath below تہِ آب *taih-e āb'* ADV under water تہا تہی رکھنا *te'hā tehī rakh'nā* V.I. keep (clothes, etc.) intact تہ بازاری *taih-bazā'rī* N.F. ground rent (for use of street area of self-built stall, etc.) ; cess levied from shopless vendors تہ بہ تہ *taih' be taih'* ADV. in layers fold on fold piled one over another تہ بہ تہ کرنا *taih, ba taih' kar'nā* V.T. fold ; pile one over another تہ بچھانا *taih' bichā'nā* V.T. put a layer (of) تہ بند *taih-band'*, تہمد *taih'mad* N.F. sheet use as garment for lower part of body ; leg-sheet تہ پیچ *taih pech* N.M. strip of cloth worn under turban تہِ تیغ کرنا *taih-e tegh' kar'nā* V.T. put to sword murder massacre تہ جمانا *taih jamā'nā* V.T. place layer upon layer تہ خانہ *taih'-khā'nah* N.M. basement cellar تہ دار *taih-dār'* ADJ. plaited with a bottom or base تہِ دل سے *taih'-e dil' se* ADJ. sincerely cordially from the bottom of one's heart تہ دیگی *taik-de'gī* N.F. pot scrapings تہ دینا *taih' de'nā* V.T. add slightly tinge کا ذکر تہ کر رکھنا *kā ẓik'r taih kar rakh'nā* PH. leave aside تہ کرنا *taih kar'nā* V.T. fold (cloth, etc.) roll (bed, etc.) تہ کو پہنچنا *taih' ko pahuṅch'nā* V.T. find out discover get to the bottom (of) تہ نشین ہونا *taih-nashīn' ho'nā* V.T. settle down as sediment تہ و بالا *tai''h-o bā'lā* ADJ. upset ; topsy-turvy upside down overthrown undone destroyed ; ruined تہ و بالا کرنا *tai''h-o-bālā kar'nā* V.T. upset overthrow ruin windo destroy ; ruin [P]

تھاپنا *thāp'nā* V.T. pat beat daub roll dung-cakes for drying up

تھاپ *thāp* N.F. thump beat (of dream) *thā'pa* N.M. mark of palm daub on wall paw-mark تھاپی *thā'pī* N.F. pat its sound bat beater implement for beating clay

تھال *thāl* N.M. tray (rare) platter (rare) salver تھالا *thā'la* N.M. pit for planting sapling trench round tree trunk for watering base ; bottom buttocks تھالی *thā'lī* N.F. dish flat dish (rare) platter (rare) salver تھالی اچھالو تو سر پہ گرے *thā'lī uchhā'lo to sir' par gi're* PH. be a milling crowd تھالی کا بینگن *thā'lī ka baiṅ'gan* N.M. time-server ; turncoat capricious person

تھامنا *thām'nā* V.T. hold hold in hands pull up (horse) prop from falling down conceal (stolen goods) for another retain stop arrest progress, etc. (of) set on foot accept (earnest money, etc.) (12) hear support , maintain (14) detain (15) recline (on)

تہامی *tehā'mī* N.M. & ADJ. (holy prophet as resident of Hedjaz

تہاں *ta'hāṅ* ADJ. thither ; there only in PH. جہاں تہاں *ja'hāṅ ta'hāṅ* ADV. all over ; everywhere

تھان *thān* N.M. piece of (cloth) ; (cloth lace, etc. in) roll of standard measure stall (for livestock, esp. horses) stable تھان کا ٹرّا *thān' ka ṭar'rā* PH. naughty at home but shy outside

تھانگ *thang* N.F. hide-out (of thieves, etc.) track of thieves تھانگ لگانا *thang' laga'na* V.T. trace thieves or stolen property تھانگی *than'gi* N.M. one in league with thieves their chief detective

تھانہ *tha'nah* N.M. police station تھانہ بٹھانا *tha'nah bitha'na* V.T. post ; police تھانیدار *tha'ne-dar* N.M. station house officer ; S. H. O. Police Sub-Inspector ; چھوٹا تھانیدار *chho'ta tha'ne-dar*

تھاہ *thah* N.F. bottom (of sea, etc.) end ; limit ; object تھاہ پانا *thah pa'na* V.I. get to the bottom (of)

تہائی *tiha''i* ADJ. one-third [~ تین]

تھپڑ *thap'par* N.M. slap cuff boy buffet rebuff تھپڑ لگانا (یا مارنا) *thap'par laga'na* (or *mar'na*) V.T. slap rebuff تھپڑ کھانا (یا پڑنا) *thap'par kha'na* (or *par'na*, V.I. be slapped be rebuffed

تھپکنا *tha'pakna* V.T. pat lull to sleep pacify encourage instrigate تھپکی *thap'ki* N.F. pat تھپک تھپک کر سلانا *thap'ak tha'pak kar sula'na* V.T. pat to induce sleep تھپکی دینا *thap'ki de'na* V.T encourage ; buck up instigate

تھپنا *thup'na* V.I. be daubed be imputed [~ تھوپنا]

تھپیڑا *thape'ra* N.M. buffet (of bellow) gust or blast (of wind)

تہتر *tehat'tar* ADJ. & N.M. seventy-three تہترواں *tehat'tarvan* ADJ. seventy-third

تھتکارنا *thutkar'na* V.I. pooh pooh, scorn exorcise emit sound of spitting for either purpose تھتکار *thutkar'* N.F. sound of spitting تھتکاری *thutka'ri* N.F. (dial) harridan ; vixen تھتکاریاں *thutka'riyan* N.F. PL. (dial.) slippers fetters تھتھانا *thutha'na* V.T. pout منہ تھتھانا *munh' thutha'na* PH. pout one's lips

تہجد *tahaj''jud* N.M. supererogatory prayers in early hours of morning [A]

تہجی *tahaj'ji* N.F. orthography spelling حروف تہجی *huroof-e tahaj'ji* N.M. alphabet ; letters of the alphabet [A ~ ہجا]

تھکتھکانا *thuk' thuka''na* V.T. hate ; despise express dislike by emmitting spitting sound emit such sound for driving away evil [doublet of تھتکارنا]

تہدید *tahdid'* (or *taih-*) N.F. holding a threat ; threatening threat menace [A]

تہدیہ *tah'diyah* (or *taih'*) N.M. presentation present [A ~ ہدیہ]

تہذیب *tahzib'* (or *taih-*) N.F. civilization etiquette manners politeness ; courtesy polish ; refinement instruction ; education discipline culture (rare) priming (rare) editing تہذیب اخلاق *tahzi'b-e akhlaq'* N.F. instruction in manners moral edification تہذیب یافتہ *tahzib'-yaf'tah* ADJ. cultured ; polished polite ; courteous [A]

تہرا *teh'ra* ADJ. (F. تہری *teh'ri*) triple ; three-fold [~ تین]

تھرانا *tharra'na* V.I. tremble ; shudder shake; quiver quake تھرتھرانا *thar'thara'na* V.I. vibrate shake shiver quake تھرتھراہٹ *thar'thara'hat*, تھرتھری *thar'thari* N.F. vibration shivering quivering trembling tremor awe fear

تھرکنا *thi'rakna* V.I. walk with dalliance belly-dance dance with sexy gestures

تہری *tah'ri*, طاہری *ta'hiri* N.F. rice cooked in left over stew, etc.

تھڑا *tha'ra* N.M. (dial.) shopkeeper's seat

تھڑنا *thur'na* V.I. decrease result in shortage تھڑی *thuri* N.F. shortage INT. fie ; shame تھڑی تھڑی ہونا *thu'ri thu'ri ho'na* V.I. be reproached by all تھڑدلا *thur-di'la* ADJ. mean

تہس نہس *tai'has nai'has* ADJ. ruined ; destroyed ; ransacked تہس نہس کرنا *tai'has nai''has kar'na* V.T. ruin ; destroy تہس نہس ہونا *tai''has nai'has ho'na* V.I. be ruined; be destroyed

تھکا فضیحتی *thuk'ka fazi'hati* N.F. taunts disgrace

تھکنا *thak'na* V.I. tire ; be tired be fatigued be exhausted fag away be fed up تھکا *tha'ka* ADJ. tired ; fatigued exhausted ; fagged تھکا اونٹ سرائے کو تکتا ہے *tha'ka oont' sara''e ko tak'ta hai* PROV. to seek solace one turns homeward تھکا بیل *tha'ka bail* N.M. sluggard vateran outliving his utility تھکا ماندہ *tha'ka man'dah* ADJ. tired ; worn-out تھکن *tha'kan*, تھکاوٹ *thaka'vat*, تکان *takan'* N.F. tiredness fag ; fatigue ; exhaustion weeking تھکانا *thaka'na* V.T. tire ; fatigue weary ; fag harass

تھگلی *thig'li*, تھیگلی *theg'li* N.F. patch تھگلی لگانا *thig'li laga'na* V.T. put up a patch آسمان میں تھگلی لگانا *asman' men thig'li laga'na* V.I. be much too clever ; be very mischievous

تھل *thal* N.M. land desert wharf تھل بیڑا *thal' be'ra* N.M wharf trace (of)

تھل بیڑا لگنا **thal be'ṛa lag'nā** V.I. achieve aim تھل بیڑا معلوم ہونا **thal' berā ma'loom ho'nā** V.I know (one's bearings تھل تھل کرنا **thal' thal kar'nā** V I be flabby

تہلکہ **tah'lūkah** (col. **tai'halkā**) N.M. panic stir (rare) death ; perdition (ped.) mortal being تہلکہ مچانا **tah'lūkah machā'nā** V.T. create a stir cause a panic [A ~ ہلاک]

تہلیل **tahlil'** N.M. declaration of God's unity by pronouncing 'la ilaha illallah, [A]

تھم **tham** N.M. pillar column post ; prop plantain stem

تہمت **toh'mat** N.F. imputation , aspersion calumny , تہمت کی جگہ **toh'mat kī ja'gah** N.F. house or place of ill-repute تہمت باندھنا (یا دھرنا یا لگانا) **toh'mat bāndhnā** (or **dhar'nā** or **lagā'nā**) V.T. slander , calumniate تہمتی **toh'matī** ADJ. slandering (person) N.M. slanderer ; calumniator [A]

تہمتن **teh'm-tan** ADJ. stout; strongly built (person)

تہمد **taih'mad** N.F./M. same as تہبند N.F./M. (see under تہ ★)

تھمنا **tham'nā** V.T. stop , come to stop case تھامنا **thamā'nā** V.T. cause to hold give stop

تھن **than** N.M. udder , teat , dug ; pap

تہنیت **tah'niyat** (or **taiht'**) N.F. congratulation greetings good wishes [A]

تھو **thoo**, تھو تھو **thoo' thoo** N.F. sound of spitting hatred [ONO]

تھوا **thoo'' a** N.M. heap of clay

تہوار **taihvār'**, تیوہار **te'ohār'** N.M. festival festive occasion

تھوبڑا **thob'ṛa** N M. (joc. or iron) mouth , snout

تھوپنا **thop'nā** V.T. daub plaster impute الزام (وغیرہ) کسی کے سر تھوپنا **ilzām** (etc.) **ki'sī ke sir' thop'nā** V.T. by the blame at someone's door

تھوتھ **thoth** N.F. snout hollowness cavity

تھوتھا **thothā** N.M. ADJ. hollow vain nonsensical N.M. blunt or pointless missile (blue) vitriol تھوتھا چنا باجے گھنا **tho'thā cha'nā bāje gha'nā** PROV. empty vessels make much noise ; barking dogs seldom bite

تھوتھنی **thoth'nī** N.F. animal's pointed mouth (joc. or iron.) human face ; mouth

تہور **tahav'vūr** N.M. rashness intrepidity temerity [A]

تھور **thoor'** N.F. (dial.) salinity

تھورنا **thoor'nā** V.T. beat devour تھور تھار کر **thoor thār kar**

تھوڑا **tho'ṛā** ADJ. (F. تھوڑی **tho'ṛī**) less a little a few meagre scanty تھوڑا تھوڑا **tho'ṛā tho'ṛā** ADV. little by little تھوڑا بہت **tho'ṛā ba'hūt** ADJ. a little whatever is easily possible ADV. more or less ; somewhat تھوڑا کرنا **tho'ṛā kar'nā** V.T. decrease; reduce; lessen تھوڑا ہونا **tho'ṛā ho'nā** V.I. be decrease ; be reduced · be in short supply تھوڑے دنوں سے **tho'ṛe di'non se** ADV. of late تھوڑے سے تھوڑا **tho'ṛe se tho'ṛā** ADJ. very little , the least ; the minimum possible

تھوک **thook** N.M. (see under تھوکنا V.T & I. ★)

تھوک **thok** N.M. wholesale تھوک فروش **thok'-firosh'** N.M. wholesaler

تھوکنا **thook'nā** V.T. & I. spit spit at , despise reproach تھوک **thook** N.M. spittle تھوک دینا **thook' de'nā** V.T. cool down (one's anger) renounce in disgust تھوک کر چاٹنا **thook' kar chāṭ'nā** V.I. withdraw one's gift go back on one's word تھوک لگانا **thook' lagā'nā** V.T. (vul.) humiliate defeat play a trick on

تھولی **thoo'lī** N.F. sweet porridge

تھونی **thoo'nī** N.F. prop

تھوہر **tho'har** N.M. cactus

تھئی **thai''ī** N.F. pile (of loaves) heap of clothes)

تھئی تھئی **tha''ī tha''ī** N.F. timing beat in music or dance dance and music

تھیئٹر **thi'e'ṭar** N.M. theatre ; playhouse ; show place [E]

تئیں **ta''īn** (arch.) for (with genitive)

تہی **tehī'** ADJ. empty void vain تہی دست **tehī'-dast'** ADJ. poor ; indigent empty-handed تہی دماغ **tehī'-dimāgh'** ADJ. foolish ignorant (سے) پہلو تہی کرنا **(se) paih'loo-tehī' kar'nā** V.T. dodge ; evade ; abstain (from) [P ~ تہ]

تھیلا **thai'lā** N.M. briefcase haversack bag تھیلا کر دینا **thai'la kar de'nā** V.T. beat mercilessly تھیلی **thai'lī** N.F. purse pouch

تھیوری **theyoo'rī** N.M. theory [E]

تہیہ *tahiy yah* N.M. resolve ; determination arrangements (for) preparations تہیہ کرنا *tahiy'yah kar'nā* V.I. resolve make preparations (for) [A]

تیار (rare طیار) *tayyār'* ADJ. ready set to prepared (of fruit) ripe (of work) complete fat ; plump (of wrestler) in full vigour trained تیار کرنا *tayyār' kar'nā* V.T. make or get ready prepare (for) complete train fatten ripen تیار ہونا *tayyār' ho'nā* V.I. be ready be prepared (for) be complete be fattened be in full vigour ripe تیاری *tayyā'rī* N.F. readiness preparation final touches fatness

تیاگنا *tayag'nā* renounce ; abandon تیاگ *tayag'* N.M. renunciation تیاگی *tayā'gī* N.M. (dial.) ascetic ; recluse ; hermit [S]

تیپچی *tep'chī* N.F. basting ; tack ADJ. flimsy short-lived (marriage, etc.)

تیتر *tī'tar* N.M. partridge بن تیتر *ban-tī'tar* N.M. sandgrouse تیتری *tī't'rī*, (تتری *tit'rī*) N.F. female partridge (also تتلی *tit'lī*) butterfly

تی تی *tī' tī* INT. cry to rally domestic fowl ; call to hens

تیجا *tī'jā* N.M. (dial.) funeral rites on third day after death [doublet of تیسرا]

تیج پات *tej'-pāt* N.M. leaf of lawas cassica (used as spice)

تیر *tīr* N.M. arrow dart (rare) (also تیر ماہ *tīr'-māh*) fourth month of Persian calendar تیر انداز *tī'r-andāz'*, تیر زن *tīr'-zan* N.M. archer ; Bowman تیراندازی *tī'r-andā'zī*, تیرزنی *tīr'-za'nī* N.F. archery تیر بہدف *tīr'-ba ha'daf* ADJ. efficacious hitting the nail on the head تیر پھینکنا (یا چلانا) *tīr' phenk'nā* (or *chalā'nā*) V.T. shoot an arrow ; do something wonderful (تیر) ترازو ہونا (*tīr*) *tarā'zoo ho'nā* V.T. (of arrow) transfix body and stay there تیر سا لگنا *tīr sā lag'nā* V.T. cut to the quick تیر فلک *tī'r-e fa'lak* N.M. (planet) mercury تیر کرنا *tīr' kar'nā* V.T. pilfer cause to end or disappear swiftly pass (life days, etc.) تیر کوے تیر *tīr' kav've tīr'* PH. take flight تیر مارنا *tīr' mār'nā* V.T. shoot an arrow accomplish something extraordinary [P]

تیرا *te'rā* PRON. they thine

تیراک *tairāk'* N.M. & ADJ تیراکی *tairā'kī* N.F. (see under تیرنا V.I. ★)

تیرنا *tair'nā* swim float تیراک *tairāk'* N.M. swimmer تیراک ہی ڈوبتا ہے *tairāk' hī doob'tā hai* PROV. pride goeth before a fall even skilled people are likely to suffer through carelessness تیرانا *tairā'nā*, ترانا *tirā'nā* V.T. cause to swim ; set afloat

تیرتھ *tī'rath* N.F. Hindu pilgrimage centre تیرتھ یاترا *tī'rath yāt'rā* N.F. (dial.) pilgrimage [S]

تیرہ *te'rah* ADJ. & N.M. thirteen تیرہ تیزی *te'rah te'zī* تیراں تیزی *te'rāṅ te'zī* N.M. first thirteen days of Safar regarded as inauspicious owing to the Holy Prophet's illness تیرھواں *ter'havāṅ* ADJ. thirteenth

تیرہ *tī'rah* ADJ. dark ; gloomy تیرہ بخت *tī'ra-bakh't*, تیرہ روز *tī'ra roz* تیرہ روزگار *tī'ra roz-gār'* ADJ. unlucky ; unfortunate تیرہ بختی *tī'ra-bakh'tī*, تیرہ روزی *tī'ra-ro'zī* N.F. ill-luck ; misfortune تیرگی *tīragī* N.F. darkness obscurity [P]

تیز *tez* ADJ. swift sharp pointed keen pungent caustic strong violent clever (of price) up ; high ; soaring whetted تیز پرواز *tez-parvāz'* ADJ. swift in flight تیز دستی *tez-das'tī* N.F cleverness تیزرو (یا رفتار) *tez'-rau* (or *-raftār*) ADJ. fast swift fleet-footed تیزروی (یا رفتاری) *tez'-ra'vī* (or *raftā'rī*) N.F. speed ; swiftness تیز طبع *tez-tab'* ADJ. shrewd shewish quarrelsome تیز فہم *tezfaih'm* ADJ. intelligent sharp-witted تیز فہمی *tez-faih'mī* N.F. quickness of apprehension ; intelligence ; acumen ; acuteness ; aptness تیز کرنا *tez' kar'nā* V.T. sharpen what speed up make clever or skilled تیز گام *tez-gām'* ADJ. swift تیز گامی *tez-gā'mī* N.F. swiftness تیز نگاہ *tez-nigāh'* ADJ. sharp-sighted sharp-witted تیز ہونا *tez' ho'nā* V.I. be speeded up be sharpened be whetted become skilled or clever be enraged ; fly into passion تیزی *te'zī'* N.F. swiftness speed sharpness acrimony violence [P]

تیزاب *tezāb'* N.M. acid 'aqua fortis' [P ~ تیز + آب]

تیس *tīs* ADJ. & N.M. thirty تیسواں *tīs'vāṅ* ADJ. thirtieth (مہینے کے) تیسوں دن (*mahī'ne ke*) *tī'soṅ din* PH. throughout the month everyday تیس مار خان *tīs' mār khān'* N.M. lucky sluggard (iron.) brave guy

تیسا *tai'sā* N.M. such person ADJ. such ; like that ADV. in that manner ایسے (یا جیسے) کو تیسا *ai'se* (or *jai'se*) *ko tai'sā* PH. tit of tat

تیسرا *tīs'rā* ADJ. third تیسرا آنکھوں میں ٹھیکرا *tīs'ra āṅkhoṅ meṅ thīk'ra* PROV. intruder (esp. loving couple's affairs) تیسرے *tīs're* ADV. thirdly

تیشہ *te'shah* N.M. axe ; adze [P]

تیغ **tegh** N.F. sword تیغ بکف *tegh' ba-kaf'* ADJ. & ADV. sword in hand bent upon killing تیغ زن *tegh'-zan* N.M. swordsman تیغ زنی *tegh'za'ni* N.F. swordsmanship fencing [P]

تیغہ **teghah**, تیغا *tegha* N.M. short broad scimitar تیغا کرنا *te'ghah, kar'na* V.T. close (doorway, arch, etc.) with bricks [P ~ PREC.]

تیقن **tayaq'qun** N.M. certainty ascertainment [A ~ یقین]

تیکھا **ti'kha** ADJ. pointed sharp graceful curt تیکھاپن *tikha-pan* N.M. sharpness curtness grace

تیل **tel** N.M. oil تیل چڑھانا *tel' charha'na* V.T. anoint bride and groom an wedding ritual تیل ڈالنا (یا لگانا) *tel' dal'na* (or *laga na* V.T. anoint rub oil مٹی کا تیل *mit'ti ka tel* N.M. kerosine oil ; gasolene تیل دیکھو تیل کی دھار دیکھو *tel' de'kho tel' ki dhar' de'kho* PROV. see which way wind blows

تیلی **te'li** N.M. oilman oil crustier تیلی تنبولی *te'li tanbo'li* N.M. low classes تیلی کا تیل جلے مشعلچی کی جان جلے *te'li ka tel' ja'le mash''alchi ki jan'* (etc.) *ja le* PH. be over-solicitous for something تیلڑی *tel'ri* N.F. small oil pot تیلن *te'lan* N.F. wife of teli تیلیا *te'liya* ADJ. oily greasy (of colour) dark

تیمار دار **ti'mar-dar** N.M. person attending a patient N.F. nurse تیمارداری *timar'-da'ri* N.F. attending a patient nursing [P]

تیمم **tayam'mum** N.M. dry ablutions [A]

تیمن **tayam'mun** N.M. blessing benediction auspiciousness [A ~ یمن]

تین **tin** ADJ. three تین تیرہ *tin' ter'ah* dispersed scattered تین تیرہ کرنا *ti'n-te'rah kar'na* PH. scatter cast to the winds disperse تین تیرہ ہونا *tin'-te'rah ho'na* PH. disperse تین پانچ *tin'-panch'* quarrel contention تین پانچ کرنا *tin'-panch' kar'na* PH. quarrel contend (پر) تین حرف *(par) tin har'f* ADJ. curse (on)

تینتالیس **tenta'lis** ADJ. & N.M. forty three تینتالیسواں *tanta'lisvan* ADJ. forty-third

تینتیس **ten'tis** ADJ. & N.M. thirty-three تینتیسواں *ten'tisvan* ADJ. thirty-third

تیندو **ten'doo** N.M. a kind of tree whose leaves are used in 'bidi' manufacture ; tendu its leaf or flower

تیندوا **ten'du'a** leopard like animal legendary forcious sea animal small melon-like fruit for animals

تیور **te'var** N.M. visage countenance expression on face (glowering) look تیور بدلنا (یا پھیرنا) *te'var ba'dal'na* (or *pher'na*) V.I. change countenance glower ; scowl change attitude (to) تیور بگڑنا (یا پھرنا) *te'var bi'gar-na* (or *phir'na*) V.I. glower ; scowl with hold affection تیوری *te'ori* N.F. frown scowl تیوری میں بل ڈالنا *te'o'ri men bal dal'na*, تیوری چڑھانا *te'o'ri charha'na* V.T. frown ; scowl knit the brow show displeasures

تیورانا **te'ora'na** V.T. faint be giddy stagger

تیوہار **te'ohar'** N.M. (same as تہوار N.M. ★)

تیہا **te'ha** N.M. anger passion pride

تیئیس **te''is** ADJ. & N.M. twenty three تیئیسواں *te''isvan* ADJ. twenty-third

ٹ

ٹ **te** (also called ta-e Hindi) fifth letter of Urdu alphabet (equivalent to English word represented as) (in jummal variant for ت and equivalent to) 200

ٹاپ **tap** N.F. (horse's) hoof (horse's) tramp of hoof ٹاپدار *tap'-dar* ADJ. (person) with disproportionately thick head (something) tapering backwards

ٹاپا **ta'pa** N.M. hen-coop bamboo frame for catching fish muslin-covered cradle-cover a kind of boat sugar-cane field

ٹاپنا **tap'na** V.I. leap over (wall etc.) (of horse, etc.) paw beat time with feet try unsuccessfully feel-happy be impatient; be restless ; be fidgety wait impatiently search in vain ٹاپا ٹوئی کرنا *ta'pa to'i kar'na* V.T. search impatiently repair leaking roofs etc. (of house)

ٹاپو **tap'oo** N.M. island islet

ٹاٹ **tat** N.M. Hessian sackcloth seat at shoes counter green gram ٹاٹ الٹنا *tat' u'latna* V.I. (of business) close (or be closed) down become bankrupt ٹاٹ باف *tat'-baf* N.M. shoe-embroiderer ٹاٹ بافی *tat'-ba'fi* N.M. shoe-embroidery ; embroidery of shoe uppers with gold, etc. thread ٹاٹ بافی جوتا *tat' ba'fi joo'ta* N.M. embroidered shoe

ٹاراٹوک **ta'ra tok** ADV. (weighing) exactly ADJ. exact

ٹافی **ta'fi** N.F. toffee [E]

ٹال *ṭal* N.F. firewood shop stack ; rick bell for animal's neck ٹالی *ṭa'lī* N.F. such small bell

ٹالنا *ṭal'na* V.T. shilly-shally ; dilly-dally ; put off dodge ; evade prevaricate put up lame excuses get rid of thus send away ٹال مٹول *ṭal' maṭol'* N.F. shilly-shallying ; dilly-dallying ; putting off dodging ; evasion prevarication ٹال مٹول کرنا *ṭal' maṭol' kar'na* V.I. delay shill-shally ; dilly-dally ; put off dodge ; evade ٹالا *ṭa'la* ٹالا بالا *ṭa'la ba'la* N.M. shilly-shallying putting off evasion ٹالا بالا بتانا *ṭa'la ba'la baṭa'na* V.T. dodge ; evade make excuses put off ; delay

ٹامک ٹوئیے مارنا *ṭa'mak ṭo''iye mar'na* V.I. fumble or grope (in the dark) hazard a guess follow mere conjecture

ٹانٹ *ṭanṭ* N.F. skull ; crown ; pate ٹانٹ کھجانا (یا کھجلانا) *ṭanṭ khuja'na* (or *khujla'na* V.T. (vul.) invite trouble scratch one's head ٹانٹ گنجی ہونا *ṭanṭ gan'jī ho'na* V.I. (vul.) have a shoe beating grow bald

ٹانٹا *ṭan'ṭa*, ٹانٹھا *ṭan'ṭha* ADJ. strong ; stout

ٹانڈ *ṭanḍ* N.F. inside gallery (used as storeroom etc.) scaffolding

ٹانڈا *ṭan'ḍa* N.M. (arch.) merchandize family bag and baggage ; caravan ٹانڈا لادنا *ṭan'ḍa lad'na* V.I. pack up ; be ready to leave

ٹانک *ṭank* N.F. quarter 'tola'

ٹانک *ṭa'nik* N.F. tonic [E]

ٹانکنا *ṭank'na* V.T. tack sew ; stitch put on; join to cobble solder annex add submit (petition, etc.) write down ٹانکا *ṭanka* N.M. stitch patch solder (rainwater) reservoir ٹانکا (یا ٹانکے) ادھڑنا *ṭan'ka* (or *ṭan'ke* *u'dharna* V.I. open out at stitches (of character) be exposed ٹانکا (یا ٹانکے) ادھیڑنا *ṭan ka* (or *ṭan'ke*) *udher'na* V.T. unstich expose ٹانکا بھرنا *ṭan'ka bhar'na* V.T. sew stitch ٹانکا ٹوٹنا (یا کھلنا) *ṭan'ka. ṭooṭ'na* (or *khul'na*) V.T. be unstitched open out a stiches be exposed ٹانکا لگانا *ṭan'ka laga'na* V.T. tack sew stitch solder ٹانکی *ṭan'ki* N.F. square piece cut out of whole melon to examine quality a kind of venereal ulcer notch chisel ٹانکی لگنا *ṭan'kī lag'na* V.I. (of melon) be examined thus

ٹانگ *ṭang'* N.F. leg ٹانگ اٹھانا *ṭang' uṭha'na* V.I. raise the leg ٹانگ اڑانا *ṭang' aṛa'na* V.T. meddle; pop one's nose in others' affairs ٹانگ برابر *ṭang' bara'bar* ADJ. (of child) small ٹانگ تلے سے نکالنا *ṭang' ta'le se nikal'na* ٹانگ کی راہ نکالنا *ṭang' kī rah nikal'na* V.T. (vul.) subdue persuade to yield ٹانگ تلے سے نکلنا *ṭang' ta'le se ni'kalna*, ٹانگ کی راہ نکلنا *ṭang kī rah' ni''kalna* V.I. submit yield ٹانگ توڑنا *ṭang' toṛ'na* V.T. dabble (in) render ineffective write shoddy (verse, etc.) break the leg ٹانگ ٹوٹنا *ṭang ṭooṭ'na* (of leg) be broken (of verse, etc.) be shoddy ٹانگ سے ٹانگ باندھ کر بٹھانا *ṭang' se ṭang bandh' kar biṭhana* V.T. not to allow to leave or move seat (someone) (beside one ٹانگ لینا *ṭang' le'na* V.T, (of dog) seize (someone's leg) to bite stop with force ٹانگیں اٹھانا *ṭan'gen uṭha'na* V T. raise (one's, etc.) legs (vul.) copulate yield ٹانگیں رہ جانا *ṭan'gen raih' jana* V.I. be too tired to walk any further

ٹانگنا *ṭang'na*, ٹانگ دینا *ṭang' de'na*, ٹانگ لینا *ṭang le'na* hang up implicate

ٹائپ *ṭa''ip* N.M. type kind ٹائپ رائٹر *ṭa''ip-ra''iṭar* N.M. typewriter ٹائپسٹ *ṭa''ipist* N.F. typist [E]

ٹائٹل *ṭa''iṭal* N.M. title [E]

ٹائر *ṭa'yar* N.M. tyre [E]

ٹائم *ṭa''im* (CORR. *ṭaim*) N.M. time ٹائم پیس *ṭa''im pees* N.F. alarm clock ٹائم ٹیبل *ṭa''im ṭa'bul* N.M. time-table ; schedule [E]

ٹاؤن *ṭa''un* N.F. town ٹاؤن کمیٹی *ṭa''un kame'ṭī* N.F. town committee ٹاؤن ہال *ṭa''un hal'* N.M Town Hall [E]

ٹائی *ṭa''ī* N.F. necktie [~E]

ٹائیں ٹائیں فش *ṭa''in ṭa''in fish'* PH. flop bluff that has been called ; mere brag

ٹب *ṭab* N.M. tub [E]

ٹبا *ṭib'ba* N.M (rare) sand dune

ٹپ *ṭap* N.M. tonga shade ; tonga bonnet

ٹپا *ṭap'pa* N.M. name of a (musical) mode range (of bullet, etc.) distance tack (dial.) post office small administrative sub-division ٹپا بھرنا (یا ڈالنا یا مارنا) *ṭap'pa bhar'na* (or *ḍal'na* or *mar'na*) V.I tack advance unmethodically ٹپا کھانا *ṭap'pa kha'na* V.T. (of ball, bullet, etc.) rebound

ٹپٹپانا *ṭapṭapa'na* V.I. trickle patter ٹپ ٹپ *ṭap' ṭap* N.F. patter (of raindrops) trickle (of tears) ٹپ ٹپ گرنا *ṭap' ṭap gir'na* V.I. (of rain) patter (of tears) trickle

ٹپس *ṭip'pas* N.F. access connection contrivance (old use) foundation ٹپس (لڑانا (یا لگانا یا جمانا) *ṭip'pas laṛā'nā* (or *lagā'nā* or *jamā'nā*) V.I. seek access (to) contrive to profit from (arch.) lay foundation

ٹپکنا *ṭa'paknā* V.I. drip trickle leak (of fruit) drop ٹپک پڑنا *ṭa'pak paṛ'nā* V.T. leak drip drop ٹپکا *ṭap'kā* N.M. continuous leaking (of roof, etc.) continuous dripping fall of mellow fruit mango ripening on tree ٹپکا پڑنا *ṭap'kā paṛ'nā* V.I. be too evident ٹپکا ٹپکی *ṭap'kā ṭap'kī* N.F. trickling dropping of ripe fruit one after another deaths one after the other ٹپکا لگنا *ṭap'kā lag'nā* V.I. become leaky (of ripe mangoes) drop continuously from tree ٹپکانا *ṭapkā'nā* V.T. cause to drip; cause to trickle cause to drop ٹپکاؤ *ṭapkā'o* N.M. dripping ٹپکی *ṭap'kī* N.F. coquetry ٹپکی پڑنا *ṭap'kī paṛ'nā* V.I. be conquetish

ٹٹ پونجیا *ṭaṭ-pooṅ'jiyā* ADJ. petty trader having small capital [~ ٹاٹ + پونجی]

ٹٹر *ṭaṭ'ṭar* N.M. large screen serving as door

ٹٹروں ٹوں *ṭuṭ'rooṅ ṭooṅ'* N.M. (dove's) coo ADJ. all alone; forlorn

ٹٹری *ṭaṭ'rī* N.F. (usu. bald) pate ٹٹری گنجی ہو جانا *ṭaṭ'rī gaṅ'ji ho jā'nā* V.I. have a good (shoe) beating

ٹٹکارنا *ṭiṭkār'nā* (ٹٹخارنا *ṭiṭkhār'nā*) V.T. clack tongue to urge animal on ٹٹکاری *ṭiṭkā'rī* N.F. clack of tongue to urge animal on

ٹٹو *ṭaṭ'too* N.M. (F. ٹٹوانی *ṭaṭvā'nī*) pony undersized horse (F. mare) بھاڑے کا ٹٹو *bhā'ṛe kā ṭaṭ'too* ADJ hired pony mercenary; hireling

ٹٹولنا *ṭaṭol'nā* V.T. grope search or examine by feeling; feel ٹٹول *ṭaṭol'* N.F. groping feeling search sounding

ٹٹی *ṭaṭ'ṭī* N.F. thatched screen matted shutter light (wooden, etc.) framework latrine; privy ٹٹی جانا *ṭaṭ'ṭī jā'nā* V.I. answer call of nature ٹٹی کی آڑ میں (یا اوٹ) میں شکار کھیلنا *ṭaṭ'ṭī kī āṛ'* (or *oṭ'*) *meṅ shikār' khel'nā* V.I. adopt underhand means ٹٹی لگانا *ṭaṭ'ṭī lagā'nā* V.I. fence screen

ٹٹیری *ṭaṭī'rī* N.F. sandpiper child's plaything emitting sound کہیں ٹٹیری سے آسمان تھمے گا *ka'hiṅ ṭaṭī'rī se āsmān tha'me-gā* PROV. wherefore this brag

ٹچا *ṭuch'chā* N.M. rake scoundrel; blackguard ADJ. mean worthless

ٹکھٹکھا سا *ṭikh'khā sā* ADV. (of opened eyes) fully

ٹخ ٹخ *ṭikh' ṭikh*, ٹک ٹک *ṭik' ṭik* N.F. & INT. call to horse, bullock etc. to go on; go, go

ٹخنہ *ṭakh'nah*, ٹخنا *ṭakhnā* N.M. ankle

ٹڈا *ṭid'dā* N.F. grasshopper; cicala; cigala; cicada

ٹڈی *ṭid'dī* N.F. locust ٹڈی دل *ṭid'dī dal* N.M. locust swarm

ٹر *ṭar* N.F. croak (of frog) chatter silly talk fare held on day next to Eid; post-Eid fare ٹرا *ṭar'rā* ADJ. garrulous naughty ٹرٹر *ṭar'-ṭar* N.F. chatter silly talk ٹرٹر کرنا *ṭar'-ṭar kar'nā* V.I. croak chatter; talk rudely ٹرا *ṭar'rā* ADJ. chattering talkative; garrulous quarrelsome proud

ٹرام *ṭarām'*, ٹریم *ṭaraim'* N.F. tram [E]

ٹرانا *ṭarrā'nā*, V.T. chatter; murmur; talk rudely

ٹرانسپورٹ *ṭarāns'porṭ* N.F. transport [E]

ٹرپھس *ṭir'phis* N.F. impudence sullenness

ٹرخانا *ṭarkhā'nā*, ٹرکانا *ṭarkā'nā* V.I. work carelessly or perfunctorily prevaricate ٹرخل *ṭar'khal*; ٹرخو *ṭarkho* N.F. silly woman hag

ٹرنک *ṭarank'* N.M. steel trunk; box [E]

ٹریڈ *ṭared'* N.M. trade ٹریڈ مارک *ṭared' mārk* N.M. trade mark [E]

ٹریڈل *ṭare'ḍal* N.F. treadle printing press [E]

ٹریژری *ṭare'zha rī* N.F. treasury [E]

ٹریفک *ṭarai'fik* N.F. traffic [E]

ٹرین *ṭaren'* N.F. railway train ٹرین کرنا *ṭaren, kar'nā* V.T. train ٹرین ہونا *ṭaren' ho'nā* V.I. be trained *ṭarend'* ADJ. trained having a teacher's diploma ٹریننگ *ṭare'ning* N.F. training [E]

ٹسر *ṭa'sar* N.F. tussore; tusser; tussur

ٹسر مسر *ṭa'sar ma'sar* N.F. shilly-shallying; putting off prevarication hesitation

ٹس سے مس نہ ہونا *ṭas' se mas' na ho'nā* V.I not to be moved at all not to change

ٹسکنا *ṭa'saknā* V.I. move go away

ٹسکنا *ṭū'saknā* V.I. sob cry

ٹسوے *ṭi'sve* N.M. crocodile tears ٹسوے بہانا *ṭis've bahā'nā* V.I. shed corcodile tears

ٹفن *ṭi'fan* N.M. tiffin [Anglo-Pakistani **E**]

ٹک *ṭuk* (obs.) ADV. for a while; for a moment; a little while ADJ. a little ٹک جیا تو کیا جیا *ṭuk ji'yā to kyā jiyā* PH. a little rest brings no relief

ٹکا *ṭa'kā* N.M. old coin worth 1/32 rupee (fig.) pelf ٹکا پاس نہ ہونا *ṭa'kā pās' na ho'nā* V.I. be penniless have no money ٹکے کا آدمی *ṭa'ke kā ā'damī* N.M. mean person ٹکے کی اوقات *ṭa'ke kī auqāt* N.F. low status ٹکے گز کی چال چلنا *ṭa'ke gaz' kī chāl' chal'nā* V.I. lead a simple life ٹکا سا جواب دینا *ṭa'kā sā javāb' de'nā* V.T. refuse pointblank

ٹکانا *ṭikā'nā* V.T. lodge (someone) fix (someone) up lay on beat ; give (slap, etc.) ٹکاؤ *ṭikā''o* N.M. stability ; firmness

ٹکٹ *ṭi'kaṭ* N.M. ticket (postage) stamp judicial stamp label ٹکٹ چسپاں کرنا *ṭi'kaṭ chas'pāṅ kar'nā* V.I. affix stamps (to) ; stamp ٹکٹ گھر *ṭi'kaṭ-ghar* N.M. booking office [**E**]

ٹک ٹک *ṭik'ṭik* N.F. tick ; sound of clock, watch, etc. [**E**]

ٹکٹکی *ṭik'ṭikī* N.M. stare steadfast to gaze tripod which criminals are tied for being flogged ٹکٹکی باندھنا (یا لگانا) *ṭik-ṭikī bāndh'nā* (or *lagā'nā*) V.I. stare (at) regard with a fixed look ٹکٹکی سے باندھنا *ṭik'ṭikī se bāndh'nā* V.T. tie to the tripod for flogging

ٹکر *ṭak'kar* N.F. butt collision antagonism revalry encounter competition کی ٹکر کا *kī ṭak'kar kā* ADJ. match for ٹکر کھانا *ṭak'kar khā'nā* V. stumble bump against collate with vie (with) ٹکر لڑانا *ṭak'kar laṛā'nā* V.T. butt ٹکر لگانا *ṭak'kar lagā'nā* V.T. dash against collide with ٹکر لگنا *ṭak'kar lag'nā* V.I. be injured in collision knock against ٹکر مارنا *ṭak'kar mār'nā* V.I. but strive ; endeavour say (one's) prayers perfunctorily or too quickly برابر کی ٹکر کا *barā'bar kī ṭak'kar kā* ADJ. equally matched ; equally good پہاڑ سے ٹکر لینا *pahāṛ se ṭak'kar le'nā* V.I. fight against heavy odds [~ FOLL.]

ٹکرانا *ṭakrā'nā* V.I. clash bring into collision clang butt ٹکراؤ *ṭakrā''o* N.M. clash

ٹکر ٹکر دیکھنا *ṭū'kar ṭū'kar dekh'nā* V.T. look wistfully look eagerly give (someone) a surprised look gaze despondently ٹکر ٹکر (یا ٹک ٹک) دیدم دم نہ کشیدم *ṭū'kar ṭū'kar* (or *ṭuk' ṭuk*) *dī'dam dam na kashī'dam* PH. looked wistfully without daring to speak

ٹکڑ *ṭik'kaṛ* N.M. thick hard cake

ٹکڑا *ṭuk'ṛā* N.M. piece portion fraction bit slice morsel livelihood excerpt ٹکڑ گدا *ṭuk'ar gadā'* N.M. beggar ٹکڑا مانگنا *ṭuk'ṛā māng'nā* V.I. beg alms چاند کا ٹکڑا *chānd kā ṭuk'ṛā* ADJ. exquisitely beautiful person ; a charming creature ٹکڑوں پر پڑنا *ṭuk'roṅ par paṛ'nā* V.T. be dependent (on) ٹکڑے ٹکڑے *ṭuk're ṭuk're* ADV. disjointed piecemeal in pieces ٹکڑے ٹکڑے کرنا *ṭuk're ṭuk're kar'nā* V.I. cleave hack to pieces ٹکڑے کرنا *ṭuk're kar'nā* V.T. divide share cut into pieces ٹکڑی *ṭuk'ṛī* N.F. detachment group ; company flock (of pigeons) piece (of glass or mirror) ٹکڑ *ṭuk'kaṛ* N.M. hard overbaked bread

ٹکسال *ṭaksāl'* N.F. mint ٹکسال باہر *ṭaksāl' bā'har* ADJ. base ; spurious ; counterfeit unidiomatic (words) unchaste language ٹکسال چڑھنا *ṭaksāl' chaṛh'nā* V.T. bear the mint stamp be judged for its worrh be perfect be rude ٹکسالی *ṭaksā'lī* ADJ. of mint minted pure ; chaste ٹکسالی زبان *ṭaksā'lī zabān'* N.F. idiomatic language chaste phraseology ٹکسالیہ *ṭaksā'liyah* N.M. mintmaster

ٹکلی *ṭik'lī* N.F. wafer small bread pendent for forehead

ٹکنا *ṭik'nā* V.I. rest tarry stay put up

ٹکنا *ṭak'nā*, ٹنکنا *ṭank'nā* V.I. be tacked (of file) have points sharpened

ٹکوا *ṭak'vā* N.M. chopper chopping-wheel

ٹکور *ṭakor* N.F. fomentation sound of drum ٹکور کرنا *ṭakor' kar'nā* V.I. foment

ٹکورا *ṭako'rā* N.M. beat of drum

ٹکیائی *ṭakyā''ī*, ٹکھیائی *ṭakhyā''ī* N.F. low-class harlot [~ ٹکا]

ٹکیا *ṭik'yā* ٹکیہ *ṭik'yah* N.F. tablet (of medicine) cake (of soap) wafer small bread

ٹلٹلانا *ṭilṭilā'nā* V.I. have loose bowels

ٹلکنا *ṭū'laknā* V.I. move with feeble steps (fig.) die

ٹل *tal* N.F. tale talk, boast ٹلیں مارنا *tal'len mār'na* V.I. boast ; brag

ٹلم *til'lam* ADJ. nonsense silly

ٹلنا *tal'nā*, ٹل جانا *tal' jā'na* V.I. get out of the way withdraw vanish flinch . shrink from ٹلانا *talā'na* V.T. get rid of dodge ; evade prevaricate

ٹم ٹم *tam'-tam* N.F. tandem [~ E CORR.]

ٹماخ *timākh*, ٹماک *timāk'* N.M. (dial.) female vanity tawdriness [~ A داغ CORR.]

ٹمپریچر *tampre'char* N.M. temperature [E]

ٹمٹمانا *timtima'nā* V.I. (of light) (of star) twinkle (of life) flicker ; be at the last gasp ٹمٹماہٹ *timtimā'hat* N.F. flicker . glimmer twinkle

ٹن *tan* N.M. pride sense of dignity

ٹن *tan* N.M. ton [E]

ٹنا *ta'nā*, ٹراں *ta'rañ* N.M. clitoris

ٹن ٹن *tan tan'* N.F. ring (of bell) chime (of clock)

ٹنٹا *tañ'ta* N.M. quarrel brawl ; wrangle trouble ٹنٹے باز *tañ'te-baz* N.M. brawler

ٹنچ *tūnch* ADJ. very little ٹنچ لڑانا *tūnch laṛa'na* V.I. start from scratch win by slow degrees

ٹنڈ *tūnd* N.M. stump of arm stump of tree

ٹنڈا *tūñ'dā* ADJ. (F. ٹنڈی *tūñ'dī*) handless having chopped hands

ٹنڈا *tiñ'da* N.M. (usu. PL. as ٹنڈے *tiñ'de*) a well-known vegetable

ٹنڈر *taiñ'dar* N.M. tender [E]

ٹنڈرا *tūnd'ra* N.M. the Tundras [E]

ٹنڈوار *taṅdvār* N.F. peg in wall of room with which to tie a sheet to serve as ceiling

ٹنکارنا *tankār'na* V.T. pull (string) to test tautness tap (crockery, etc.) to see if it is tracked

ٹنگارنا *tangar'na* V.T. eat little by little

ٹنگڑی *tang'rī* N.F. (leg) ٹنگڑی پراڑانا *tang'ri par aṛā'na* V.T. trip (adversary) [~ ٹانگ *tang*]

ٹنگنا *tang'na* V.T. be hung N.M. clothes-line [~ ٹانگنا]

ٹوپی *to'pī* N.F. cap hat hood gun-cap ٹوپی اچھالنا *to'pī uchhāl'na* V.T. jump with joy disgrace (someone) publicity slander ٹوپی دار بندوق *to'pī-dār bandooq'* N.F. match-lock ٹوپ *top* N.M. hat hood helmet thimble کنٹوپ *kan-top'* N.M. cap that can be drawn down to cover ears ٹوپا *to'pa* N.M. tack quilted cap

ٹوٹا *to'ta* N.M. (arch. or dial.) loss . damage candle-end ٹوٹا اٹھانا (یا سہنا) *to'tā ūthā'na* (or *saih'na*) V.I. incur loss ٹوٹا بھرنا (یا دینا) *to'tā bhar'na* (or *de'na*) V.T. indemnify make reparations ٹوٹا پڑنا *to'tā par'na* V.I. incur loss

ٹوٹرو *tot'roo* N.M. a kind of small turtle-dove ADJ. fool ٹوٹرو سا *tot'roo sā* ADJ. lovely ; solitary ; forlorn foolish

ٹوٹکا *tot'kā* N.M. charm . spell quack remedy ٹوٹکے ہائی *tot'ke-hā''ī* N.F. & ADJ. (woman) resorting to spells . witch

ٹوٹنا *toot'nā* V.I. break; be broken: be smashed be fractured be cut off . be separated dissociate rush upon sally forth (of body) be feverish fall down befall (of ablution) stand in need of renewal (of price) be slashed come down be plucked (13) snap ٹوٹ *toot* N.F. breach coolness (in friendship) ٹوٹ پھوٹ *toot'-phoot* N.F. breakage wear and tear fracture ٹوٹ جانا *toot jā'na* V.I. break ; be broken snap be smashed ٹوٹ (ٹوٹ) کر برسنا *toot' (toot) kar ba'rasna* V.I rain cats and dogs ٹوٹ پڑنا *toot' par'na* V.T. rush (upon) fall avidly upon ٹوٹا *too'tā* ADJ broken ٹوٹا پھوٹا *too'tā phoo'tā* ADJ. in a state of bad repair damaged broken to pieces demolished

ٹوڈی [1] *to'dī* N.M. toady [E]

ٹوڈی [2] *to'dī* میاں کی ٹوڈی *mi'yāñ kī to'dī* N.F. name of a musical mode

ٹورا *to'rā* N.M. (in tip-cat) hit

ٹورنامنٹ *toor'nāmant* N.M tournament [E]

ٹوری *to'rī* N.M. tory [E]

ٹوکرا *tok'ra* N.M. basket ٹوکری *tok'rī* N.F small basket ٹوکری ڈھونا *tok'rī dho'na* V.I engage in very low kind of labour

ٹوکنا *tok'na* V.T. check prevent challenge object cavil ٹوک *tok* N.F. check challenge cavilling influence of an evil eye ٹوک ٹاک *tok'-tāk* N.F. objections

ٹول *tol* N.M. toll [E]

ٹول *ṭavil'* N.F. twill [E]

ٹولہ *ṭo'lah,* ٹولا *ṭolā* N.M. band clique quarter of town inhabited by one trade ; a large pebble ٹولی *ṭo'lī* N.F. band clique small group

ٹوم چھلا *ṭoom' chhal'la* N.M. petty ornament trinkets

ٹونا *ṭo'nā* N.M. charm witchcraft ٹونا کرنا *ṭo'nā kar'nā* V.T. cast evil spell ٹونے باز *ṭo'ne-bāz* N.M. enchanter ; charmer ٹونہائی *ṭon'hā'ī* N.F. & ADJ. (woman) resorting to spells ; witch

ٹونٹی *ṭoṅ'ṭī* N.F. spout sugar-cane root left in earth for regrowth ٹونٹی والا لوٹا *ṭoṅ'ṭī-vā'lā lo'ṭa* N.M. ewer

ٹونڈی *ṭooṅ'ḍī* ٹنڈی *ṭuṅ'ḍī* N.F. navel thicker end (of carrot, radish, etc.)

ٹونگنا *ṭong'nā* V.T. (same as ٹھونگنا V.T. ★)

ٹوہنا *ṭoh'nā* V.T. feel search grope sound be on the lookout (for) ٹوہ *ṭoh* N.F. search spying watching secretly tracing ٹوہ لگانا *ṭoh' lagā'nā* V.T. watch secretly trace be on the look-out (for)

ٹھاٹر *ṭhā'ṭar* N.M. lattice such framework for illuminations dove-cote

ٹھاٹھ *ṭhāṭh,* ٹھاٹ *ṭhāṭ* N.M. (usu. PL.) splendour pomp and show dignity decoration elegance equipage bamboo frame for thatching name of a fencing trick (pigeon's) joyful flutter ٹھاٹ باندھنا *ṭhāṭh bāndh'nā* V.I. prepare frame for thatch (of fencers stand at ready سب ٹھاٹ پڑا رہ جانا *sab ṭhāṭh' pa'ṛā raih jā'nā* V.I. (of dying person) quit all belongings ٹھاٹھ بدلنا *ṭhāṭh' ba'dalnā* V.I. change posture in fencing بڑے ٹھاٹ باٹ سے *ba'ṛe ṭhāṭh bāṭ se,* ٹھاٹھ کے ساتھ *ṭhāṭh' ke sāth'* ADV. with great pomp and show elegently

ٹھارا *ṭhā'ṛa,* ٹھاڈا *ṭhā'ḍa* ADJ. stout standing

ٹھاکر *ṭhā'kūr* N.M. (dial.) Hindu diety idol chief landlord ; village chief ٹھاکر دوارہ *ṭhā'kūr-davā'rah* N.M. idol temple

ٹھال *ṭhāl* N.F. idleness unemployment ٹھالا *ṭhā'lā* ADJ. idle jobless

ٹھانسنا *ṭhāṅs'nā* V.I. (doublet of ٹھونسنا used as letter's adjunct) thurst

ٹھاننا *ṭhān'nā* V.T. resolve ; be intent upon جی (یا دل) میں ٹھاننا *jī* (or *dil*) *meṅ ṭhān'nā* V.I. set one's heart on

ٹھائیں ٹھائیں *ṭhā''eṅ ṭhā''eṅ* N.F. reports of shot-gun etc. ٹھائیں ٹھائیں ہونا *ṭhā''eṅ ṭhā''eṅ ho'nā* V.I. (of shotguns) be fired ٹھائیں ٹھائیں کرنا *ṭhā''eṅ ṭhā 'eṅ kar'nā* V.I. quarrel ; brawl clash [ONO.]

ٹھپہ *ṭhap'pah,* ٹھپا *ṭhap'pa* N.M. pattern mould die stamp impress (distinctive) mark ٹھپا لگانا *ṭhap'pa lagā'nā* V.T. stamp mark

ٹھٹ *ṭhaṭ* N.M. throng ; crowd ٹھٹ کے ٹھٹ *ṭhaṭ' ke ṭhaṭ'* N.M. PL. milling crowd ٹھٹ کے ٹھٹ لگے ہونا *ṭhaṭ' ke ṭhaṭ la'ge ho'nā* V.I. (of crowd) be ; gather

ٹھٹھا *ṭhaṭ'ṭhā* N.M. laughter jest ridicule ٹھٹھا کرنا *ṭhaṭ'ṭha kar'nā* V.I. jest ridicule deride ٹھٹھا لگانا (یا مارنا) *ṭhaṭ'ṭha lagā'nā,* (or *mār'nā*) V.I. burst with laughter ٹھٹھے باز *ṭhaṭ' ṭhe-bāz* ADJ. facetious N.M. jester humorous person witty person ٹھٹھے بازی *ṭhaṭ' ṭhe-bāzī* N.F. jest fun ridicule ; derision wit ٹھٹھے میں اڑانا *ṭhaṭ' ṭhe meṅ ūṛā'nā* V.T. ridicule ; deride make fun (of)

ٹھٹھرنا *ṭhi'ṭhar'nā* V.I. benumbed shiver with (old) feel (very cold) be nipped ٹھٹھرانا *ṭhiṭhrā'nā* benumb chill nip

ٹھٹکنا *ṭhi'ṭhaknā,* ٹھٹک کر رہ جانا *ṭhi'ṭhak kar raih' jā'nā* V.I. draw back in amazement shrink (from) come to sudden stop for fear, etc.

ٹھٹھول *ṭhaṭhol'* N.F. ridicule , derision jesting ; fun N.M. jester witty person

ٹھٹھیرا *ṭhaṭhe'rā* N.M. brazier maker of hardware vessels seller of hardware vessels maize stalk

ٹھڈا *ṭhad'da* N.M. main stick of kite (which is crossed by کانپ N.F. ★)

ٹھڈا *ṭhūḍ'da* N.M. a kick ; kicking with the boot

ٹھڈی *ṭhūḍ'dī* N.F. (usu. PL.) unslit parched grain (same as ٹھوڑی N.F. ★) ٹھڈی پکڑنا *ṭhūḍ'dī pa'kar'nā* V.T. flatter curry favour with

ٹھر *ṭhir* N.F. chill

ٹھرا *ṭhar'rā* N.M. cheap wine a cheap kind of shoe main string of brassiere bad unbaked brick

ٹھس *ṭhas* ADJ. solid crammed heavy lazy obstinate ; mulish N.M. short weight or measure cracked (common vessel)

ٹھس *ṭhūs* ADJ. dull-headed ; stupid (of coin) not jingling heavy stolid

ٹھسا *thas'sa* N.M. clegance affected gait

ٹھساٹھس *tha'sa thas* ADV. (filled) to capacity

ٹھسک *tha'sak* N.F. ٹھسکا *thas'ka* N.M. low sound of coughing ٹھسکنا *thasak'na* V.T. tap earthenware vessel to see if it is cracked

ٹھسنا *thus'na* V.I. be stuffed be filled with capacity ٹھسوانا *thusva'na* V.T. get stuffed get filled (to capacity)

ٹھک ٹھک *thak' thak* N.F. repeated hammer knock boring work quarrel tiff brawl

ٹھکانا *thika'na* N.M. residence ; place; whereabouts address destination limit end decency ; suitability reasonableness trust ; reliance ٹھکانا ڈھونڈنا *thika'na dhoond'na* V.I. look for residence hunt for job look for match (for marriageable young woman) ٹھکانا کرنا *thika'na kar'na* V.I. find a room (for oneself) take asylum (in) ٹھکانے چکانا *thika'ne chuka'na* V.I. pay off meanials, dues on death of one of family ٹھکانے کا آدمی *thika'ne ka ad'mi* N.M. suitable person ٹھکانے کی بات *thika'ne ki bat* N.F. reasonable point ٹھکانے لگانا *thika'ne laga'na* V.T. kill ; assassinate marry off dispose of squander ; waste spend in right manner help achieve objective ; cause to succeed ٹھکانے لگنا *thika'ne lag'na* V.I. be killed be married off be disposed of be squandered be spent in right manner (of endeavour, etc.) succeed بے ٹھکانا *be-thika'na* ADJ. homeless unreliable inconsistent uncertain

ٹھکرانا *thukra'na*, ٹھکرا دینا *thukra' de'na* V.T. spurn kick ; trample upon [~ ٹھوکر]

ٹھکرانی *thakura'ni* N.F. (dial.) village chief's wife [~ ٹھاکر]

ٹھکنا *thuk'na* V.I. be beaten be defeated (of nail) be hammered (into) incur loss (of an amount) be gaoled [~ ٹھونکنا]

ٹھگ *thag* N.M. thug ; cut throat robber footpad swindler ٹھگ بازی *thag-ba'zi*. (rare ٹھگ بدیا *thag bid'diya*) N.F. swindling ; cheating thuggee ٹھگی *tha'gi*, ٹھگائی *thaga'i* N.F. swindling ; cheating thuggee ٹھگنا *thag'na*, ٹھگ لینا *thag' le'na*, ٹھگی کرنا *tha'gi kar'na* V.T. swindle ; cheat rob ٹھگنی *thagni* N.F. woman swindler female thug

ٹہل *taih'l* N.F. (dial.) drudgery : service

ٹہلنا *tai'halna* V.I. stroll , take a stroll walk slowly ٹہلانا *taihla'na* V.T. take out for a stroll walk (horse) get rid of

ٹھلیا *thil'ya* N.M. small pitcher

ٹھمری *thum'ri* N.F. light classical song music to which it is set

ٹھمکنا *thu'mak'na* V.I. strut amorously ; move coquetishly ; walk with dalliance ٹھمک *thum'mak* (rare *thum'mak*) N.F. coquetish strut or gait ٹھمک ٹھمک کر *thu'mak thum'ak kar* ADV. with a coquetish gait ٹھمک چال *thum'ak chal* N.F. graceful carriage coquetish gait

ٹھمکی *thum'ki* N.F. jerk given to string to keep kite flying ٹھمکی دینا (یا لگانا) *thum'ki de'na* (or *laga'na*) V. give a jerk (to kite string [PREC.]

ٹہنا *taih'na* N.M. bough

ٹھناکا *thana'ka*, ٹھن ٹھن *than' than'* N.F. jingle chime clang ٹھن ٹھن گوپال *than' than gopal'* N.M. blockhead nought ADJ. worthless

ٹھننا *than'na* V.I. occur a clash (between) be pitted against be resolved be fixed (in mind) میں ٹھن جانا *men than' ja'na* V.I. (of clash) occur between

ٹھنٹھ *thunth* N.M. stump leafless branch amputated hand

ٹھنڈ *thand* N.F. cold chill ٹھنڈا *than'da* ADJ. (F. ٹھنڈی *than'di*) cool cold frozen cold-blooded ; level-headed extinguished pacified ; appeased patient ; enduring impotent frigid having a slump ٹھنڈا کرنا *than'da kar'na* V.T. cool down extinguish appease kill ; murder ٹھنڈا پڑ جانا *than'da par ja'na* V.I. be appeased become cold lose lustre be defeated ٹھنڈا ہونا (یا ہو جانا) *than'da ho'na* (or *ho ja'na*) V.I. become cold die be extinguished have a slump کلیجہ ٹھنڈا ہونا *kale'ja than'da ho'na* V.I. have the satisfaction of revenge ٹھنڈی آگ *than'di ag* N.F. dormant love ٹھنڈی سانس *than'di sans* N.F. ٹھنڈا سانس *than'da sans* N.M. sigh ٹھنڈی گرمیاں *than'di gar'miyan* N.F. PL. outward love unsuccessful coquetry ٹھنڈے ٹھنڈے *than'de than'de* ADV. early in the day ; while it is yet cool ٹھنڈی (یا ٹھنڈا) سانس بھرنا *than'di* (or *than'da sans bhar'na*) V.I. heave a sigh in despair ٹھنڈے دل *than'de dil se* ADV. impassionately cool-headedly

ٹھنڈائی *thanda''i* N.F. hemp beverage fresh cooling sherbet (of almonds and cucumber-seed)

ٹھنڈک *than'dak* N.F. coolness chill comfort satisfaction کلیجے کی ٹھنڈک *kale'je ki than'dak* N.F. satisfaction of having revenge (also آنکھوں کی ٹھنڈک *ankhon ki than'dak*) loved child (of) ٹھنڈک پڑنا ṭhan'ḍak paṛ'na v.i. be cooled have satisfaction of revenge succeed in endeavour ٹھنڈی ṭhanḍī n.f. smallpox (col.) cold

ٹھنکنا ṭha'nakna v.i. (of a coin) ring ٹھنکانا ṭhankā-nā v.t. ring (a coin)

ٹھنکنا ṭhi'nakna v.i. whine coaxingly whimper

ٹھنگنا ṭhing'nā adj. (f. ٹھنگنی ṭhing'nī) dwarfish n.m. dwarf midget

ٹھنگیرنا ṭhunger'na v.t. eat (something) grain by grain ٹھنگیر ṭhunger' n.f. process of eating thus for idling away time (doublet of ٹھونگنا]

ٹھنی ṭaih'nī n.f. branch bough twig spray

ٹھوٹ ṭhoṭ, ٹھوٹھ ṭhoṭh adj. unlettered ; illiterate thick-skulled

ٹھور ṭhaur n.m. abode assigned place trace ٹھور بے ٹھور ṭhaur' be ṭhaur adj. & adv. everywhere (at an) inopportune (moment) ٹھور ٹھکانا ṭhaur' ṭhi'kāna n.m. abode assigned place trace ٹھور ٹھکانا نہ ہونا ṭhaur' ṭhikā'nā na ho'nā v.i. be homeless be untraceable have no assigned place

ٹھوڑی ṭho'ṛī n.f. (col. ٹھوڈی ṭhuḍ'ḍī) chin ٹھوڑی پکڑنا ṭho'ṛī pa'karnā v.i. cajole or appease (by touching someone's chin) flatter thus ٹھوڑی تارا ṭho'ṛī ta'ra n.m. mole (or artificial mark) on chin

ٹھوس ṭhos adj. solid compact heavy (load) cogen (argument) real ; not superficial (knowledge)

ٹھوکنا ṭhok'na v.t. (same as ٹھونکنا v.t. ★) ٹھوک بجا کے ṭhok' bajā' ke adv. after close examination ; having scrutinized

ٹھوکا ṭaho'ka n.m. nudge push with hand or feet ٹھوکے دینا ṭaho'ke de'na n.m. pl. nudge jerk to rouse or call attention ٹھوکنا ṭahok'nā v.t. nudge good

ٹھوکر ṭho'kar n.f. stumble kick mistake wrong step misfortune toe (of shoe) artificial waterfall ; cascade ٹھوکر کھانا ṭho'kar khā'nā v.i. trip stumble make a mistake go off the track ٹھوکر لگنا ṭho'kar lag'na v.i. stumble (over) collide (with) have a misfortune learn a lesson ٹھوکر لگانا (یا مارنا) ṭho'kar lagā'nā (or mār'nā) v.t. spurn kick strike against ٹھوکریں کھانا (یا کھاتے پھرنا) ṭho'karen khā'nā (or khā'te phir'nā) v.t. suffer reverses have hard time

ٹھوں ٹھاں ṭhoon ṭhān n.f. sound of coughing

ٹھونسنا ṭhons'nā v.t. thurst shove in stuff fill to capacity impose ; foist ٹھونس ٹھانس ṭhons' ṭhāns' n.f. thrusting

ٹھونکنا ṭhonk'nā, ٹھوکنا ṭhok'nā v.t. drive in (nail, etc.) hammer shove (in) beat thump pit tap ٹھونک دینا ṭhonk' de'nā v.t. drive in (nail, etc.) hammer پیٹھ ٹھونکنا pīṭh ṭhonk'nā v.t. encourage ; buck up

ٹھونگا ṭhon'gā, ٹھونگ ṭhong n.m. beak ; bill beak stroke ٹھونگے مارنا ṭhon'ge mār'nā v.t. strike with beak ٹھونگنا ṭhong'nā v.t. (of bird) eat put into mouth little by little

ٹھہرانا ṭhaihrā'nā, ٹھیرانا ṭhairā'nā v.t. stop cause to stop stay settle conclude ṭhai'harnā, ٹھیرنا ṭhair'nā v.i. stay stop put up (with) cease wait delay take a stand (against) be proposed be settled be at rest ; be no longer perturbed be proved be regarded ; be cousidered ٹھہراؤ ṭhaihrā''o, ٹھیراؤ ṭhairā''o n.m. stillness serenity permanence

ٹھیٹ ṭheṭ, ٹھیٹھ ṭheṭh adj. idiomatic chaste (language) mere ; pure and simple ; thorough

ٹھی ٹھی ṭhī' ṭhī n.f. (sound of) giggling

ٹھیس ṭhes n.f. knock blow shock ٹھیس لگانا ṭhes lagā'na v.t. knock shock ٹھیس لگنا ṭhes lag'nā v.i. be knocked be shocked be pained (in the heart) ; be grieved (at heart)

ٹھیک ṭhīk adj. right ; correct exact regular proper ; meet and accurate definite suit ; certain true suitable reliable ; dependable adv. ll right right exactly ٹھیک ٹھاک ṭhīk' a'na v.t. ṭhīk' ṭhāk adj. right correct adv. all right okay ; O.K. quite correct ٹھیک ٹھیک ṭhīk' ṭhīk adv. really exactly ٹھیک کرنا ṭhīk' kar'nā v.t. correct ; put tight adjust set (someone) right bring (someone) senses beat اس کا کیا ٹھیک ūs kā kyā' ṭhīk' ph. (col.) how can you depend upon him you can't be sure of him

ٹھیکہ ṭhe'kah, ٹھیکا ṭhe'kā n.m. contract to job-work liquor shop ; wineshop prop rest drum to beat time beating time with drum as accompanist ٹھیکہ بجانا ṭhe'kah bajā'nā v.i. beat time with drum as accompanist ٹھیکے لینا ṭhe'ke le'nā v.t. take out contract monopolize submit a tender ٹھیکے پر ṭhe'ke par adv. on contract ; on contract basis ٹھیکیدار

ṭhe'ke-dār N.M. contractor liquor vendor monopolist

ٹھیکرا ṭhīk'ra N.M. potsherd through (for dog's food) روزی کا ٹھیکرا ro'zī kā ṭhīk'ra N.M. means by which one lives ; means of livelihood

ٹھیکری ṭhīk'rī N.F. small potsherd

ٹھیکیدار ṭhe'ke-dār N.M. (see under ٹھیکہ N.M. ★)

ٹھیکی ṭhe'kī N.F. bag load ٹھیکی لگانا ṭhe'kī lagā'nā V.T. fill bag with grain ٹھیکی لینا ṭhe'kī le'nā V.I. unburden oneself take the load off oneself take a support

ٹھیلا ṭhe'la N.M. trolly car pulled or pushed by men

ٹھیلنا ṭhel'nā V.T. push roll propel (rare.) nudge

ٹھینگا ṭhīn'ga N.M. thumb small club (vul.) penis ٹھینگا باجنا ṭhīn'ga bāj'nā V.I (of quarrel) take place ٹھینگا دکھانا ṭhīn'ga dikhā'nā V.T. refuse turn down tease pay no regard to

ٹیاں ṭoy'yān, ٹوئیاں ṭo''iyān ADJ. wee-bit dwarfish N.M. a kind of small parrot

ٹی اے ṭee'-e N.M. travelling allowance , T.A. [E]

ٹی بی ṭī'-bī N.F. tuberculosis T.B [E]

ٹی پارٹی ṭī'-pār'ṭī (col. ṭī-pā'ṭī) tea party [E]

ٹیپ ṭep N.M. tape ٹیپ ریکارڈر ṭep' rikār'ḍar N.M. tap-recorder ٹیپ (ریکارڈ) کرنا ṭep (rikār'd) kar'nā V.T. tape-record [E]

ٹیپ ṭīp N.F. shrill note best (of the verses) refrain cement streak along brick borders (in wall) ; grouting ٹیپ ٹاپ ṭīp-ṭāp N.F. adornment outward show ٹیپ کا ṭīp' kā ADJ. choicest or best (hemistic or couplet of poem) ٹیپ کرنا ṭīp' kar'nā V.T. grout

ٹیٹک منجھا ṭī'ṭak man'jhā difficulty embarrassment broken cot

ٹی ٹی ṭī'-ṭī N.M. train ticket examiner ; T.T.E. [E]

ٹیچر ṭī'char N.M. teacher [E]

ٹیرنا ṭīr'na, ٹیر کر دینا ṭīr' kar de'na V.T. spend (night, life,etc.)

ٹیروا ṭer'vā N.M. water-pipe of hookah

ٹیڑھا ṭe'ṛhā, ADJ. (F. ٹیڑھی ṭe'ṛhī) crooked bent awry uneven difficult, person ; difficult to tackle ٹیڑھ ṭeṛh N.F. (same as ٹیڑھاپن N.M. ★) ٹیڑھا بانکا ṭe'ṛhā bān'kā ADJ. beau ; fop ; coxcomb ٹیڑھا میڑھا ṭe'ṛhā me'ṛhā ADJ. crooked zig zag irregular ٹیڑھاپن ṭe'ṛhā pan N.M. ṭeṛh N.F. crookedness ٹیڑھا کرنا ṭe'ṛhā kar'nā V.T. slant bend ; tip ٹیڑھا ہونا ṭe'ṛhā ho'nā V.I. slant ٹیڑھی انگلی کے بغیر گھی نہیں نکلتا ṭe'ṛhī ūnglī ke ba-ghair' ghī na'hīn ni'kaltā PROV. crooked persons call for harsh treatment ٹیڑھی آنکھ سے دیکھنا ṭe'ṛhī āṅkh se dekh'nā V.T. cast angry looks look with evil intentions ٹیڑھی کھیر ṭe'ṛhī khīr' N.F. difficult task

ٹیس ṭīs N.F. shooting pain (in book-binding) single stitch through all formes ٹیس اٹھنا ṭīs' ūṭh'nā V.T. have shooting pain ٹیس مارنا ṭīs' mār'nā V.T. (in book-binding) give single stitch

ٹیسو ṭī'soo N.M. 'butia froudesa' flower

ٹیک ṭek N.F. prop support (dial.) promise ; vow ٹیکنا ṭek'nā V.T. put prop

ٹیکرا ṭīk'ra N.M. (sand) dune hillock knoll

ٹیکس ṭaik's N.M. tax [E]

ٹیکسٹ بک ṭaiksṭ'-būk N.F. text-book [E]

ٹیکسی ṭaik'sī N.F. taxi [E]

ٹیکنا ṭek'nā V.T. rest (something on) ṭek N.F. rest prop ٹیکن ṭe'kan N.F. prop

ٹیکہ ṭī'kah, ٹیکا ṭī'kā N.M. injection inoculation vaccination stain blot a kind of ornament for forehead ٹیکہ لگانا ṭī'kah lagā'nā V.T. inject inoculate vaccinate (dial.) stain کلنک کا ٹیکہ لگانا kalank' kā ṭī'kā lagā'nā V.I. be stigmatized

ٹیکنیکل ṭaiknī'kal ADJ. technical [E]

ٹی کوزی ṭī ko'zī N.F. tea cosy [E]

ٹیلہ ṭī'lah, ٹیلا ṭī'lā N.M. knoll hillock

ٹیلر ṭe'lar, ٹیلر ماسٹر ṭe'lar mas'ṭar N.M. tailor [E]

ٹیلیفون ṭai'lifon N.M. telephone [E]

ٹیلیگرام ṭai'li-garām N.F. telegram [E]

ٹیلیویژن ṭailī-vī'zhan N.F. television [E]

ٹیم ṭaim N.M. time [~ E CORR.]

ٹیم *ṭem* N.F. snuff (of candle, etc.)

ٹیم *ṭim* N.F. team ٹیم ورک *tīm'-vark* N.M. teamwork [E]

ٹیم ٹام *ṭīm' ṭām* N.F. outward show decoration [E]

ٹین *ṭin* N.M. tin canister [E]

ٹینٹ *ṭeṅṭ* N.M. speck in eye cotton pod

ٹینٹ *ṭaiṅṭ* N.M. tent ٹینٹ لگانا *ṭaiṅṭ lagā'nā* V.T. pitch a tent [E]

ٹینٹوا *ṭeṅṭ'vā* N.M. wind-pipe throat ٹینٹوا دبانا دبوچنا *ṭeṅṭ'vā dabā'nā* (or *daboch'nā*) V.T. strangle ; strangulate ; throttle force to do something ; constrain bring pressure to bear upon

ٹیں ٹیں *ṭeṅ' ṭeṅ* (dial. *ṭaiṅ' ṭaiṅ*) N.F. & INT. (parrot's cry prate ٹیں ٹیں کرنا *ṭeṅ' ṭeṅ kar'nā* V.I. (of parrot) cry prate

ٹینس *ṭai'nis* N.F. tennis [E]

ٹینک *ṭaiṅk* N.M. tank [E]

ٹینی *ṭe'nī* N.M. small hybrid species of hens ADJ. (hen) of this species tiny dwarfish

ٹیوا *ṭe'vā* N.M. (dial.) horoscope guess

ٹیوب *ṭyoob'* N.F. fluorescent tube thin pipe [E]

ث *se* sixth letters of Urdu alphabet ; (it is a definite proof of the Arabic origin of word containing ;) it (it is doubled to replace ل whenever Arabic definite article heads it) (in jummal reckoning) 500

ثابت *sā'bit* ADJ. (col. *sā'būt*) whole ; unbroken uninjured ; unharmed undamaged proved ; prove established firm stationary N.M. PL. ثوابت *savā'bit* star (OPP. سیارہ N.M. planet) ثابت قدم *sā'bit-qa'dam* ADJ. steadfast firm constant persevering resolute unswerving ثابت قدمی *sā'bit-qa'damī*, ثابت کرنا *sā'bit kar'nā* V.T. prove ; establish ثابت ہونا *sā'bit ho'nā* V.I. be proved ; be established [A ~ ثبوت]

ثاقب *sā'qib* ADJ. glittering glistening; shining brightly شہاب ثاقب *shehā'b-e sā'qib* N.M. glittering meteor [A]

ثالث *sā'lis* N.M. arbitrator mediator arbiter third person impartial person non-partisan ثالث بالخیر *sā'lis bil-khair'* N.M. impartial person bastard (child) ثالث حصری *sā'lis-e ḥas'rī* N.M. mutually acceptable arbitrator ثالث نامہ *sā'lis nā'mah* (col. ثالثی نامہ *sāl'sī nā'mah* N.M. arbitration award ثالثہ *sā'lisah* N.F. arbitress ثالثی *sā'lisī* (col. *sāl'sī*) N.F. arbitration mediation ثالثاً *sā'lisan* ADV. thirdly ; in the third place ثالوث *sāloos* N.M. (dial.) Trinity [A ~ ثلثہ]

ثامن *sā'min* ADJ. eighth ثامناً *sā'minan* ADV. eighthly [A ~ ثمانیہ]

ثانوی *sā'navī* ADJ. (see under ثانی ADJ. ★)

ثانی *sā'nī* ADJ. second peer ; equal match ثانوی *sa'navī* ADJ. secondary اعلیٰ ثانوی *ā''lā sā'navī* Higher Secondary ثانوی تعلیمی بورڈ *sā'navī ta'līmī bor'd* N.M. Board of Secondary Education (اعلیٰ) ثانوی تعلیم *(ā''lā) sā'navī ta'līm'* N.F. (Higher) Secondary Education (اعلیٰ) ثانوی مدارس *(ā'lā) sā'navī madā'ris* N.M. PL. (Higher) Secondary Schools ثانیاً *sā'niyan* ADV. secondly ; in the second place ثانیہ *sā'niyah* N.M. second moment [A ~ اثنین]

ثبات *sabāt'* N.M. permanence endurance stability firmness constancy resolution ; resolve [A ~ FOLL.]

ثبت *sabt* N.M. affixing (signature or stamp) put or impress (seal) ثبت کرنا *sab't kar'nā* V.T. affix inscribe put impress enter ; put down give permanence to make lasting ثبت ہونا *sab't ho'nā* V.T. be affixed be inscribed be put ; be impressed be made lasting [A]

ثبوت *sūboot'* N.M. proof testimony evidence probate بدیہی ثبوت *badī'hī sūboot'* ثبوت بادی النظر *sūboo't-e bā'din-nazar'* N.M. obvious proof ; 'prima facie' proof تائیدی ثبوت *tā'ī'dī sūboot'* N.M. corroborative evidence تحریری ثبوت *tahrī'rī sūboot'* N.M. documentary evidence تردیدی ثبوت *tardī'dī sūboot'* N.M. rebutting evidence ثبوت صریحی *sūboo't-e sariḥ'*, (col. صریحی ثبوت *sarī'ḥī sūboot'*) N.M. direct proof ضمنی ثبوت *zim'nī sūboot'* N.M. collateral evidence قرائنی ثبوت *qarā''nī sūboot'* N.M. circumstantial evidence قطعی ثبوت *qat''ī sūboot'* N.M. conclusive proof لسانی ثبوت *lisā'nī sūboot'* N.M. verbal evidence بار ثبوت *bā'r-e sūboot'* N.M. onus of proof [A]

ثخذ *sakh'khaz* N.M. seventh set of *abjad* order of letters [A ~ H]

ثروت *sar'vat* N.F. riches : wealth affluence opulence ثروتمند *sar'vat-mand* ADJ. rich wealthy opulent affluent ثروتمندی *sar'vat-mandi* N.F. riches opulence , affluence [A]

ثریٰ *sara'* N.M. earth soil تحت الثریٰ *tah't-ūs-sara'* N.F. nether regions very low position [A]

ثریا *sūray'ya* N.M. the Pleiades ; the Pliads ثریاجاه *sūray'ya-jāh* ADJ. exalted اوج ثریا *au'-je sūray'ya* N.M. very exalted status [A]

ثعلب مصری *sa''lab mis'rī* N.F salep pulverized 'orchis' root [A]

ثغور *sūghoor'* N.M. PL. borderland , marches [A ~ SING ثغر]

ثقافت *saqā'fat* N.F. culture ثقافتی *saqā'fatī* (ped. ثقافی *saqā'fī*) ADJ. cultural ثقافتی میلہ *saqā'fatī me'lah* N.M. cultural show ثقافتی سرگرمیاں *saqā'fatī sar-gar'-miyān* N.F. PL. cultural activities [A]

ثقالت *saqā'lat* N.F. heaviness turgidity (of word, etc.) bombast [A ~ ثقل]

ثقاہت *siqā'hat* N.F. trustworthiness reliability authoritativeness serenity [A ~ ثقہ]

ثقل *siq'l* N.M. (PL. اثقال *asqāl*) gravity indigestion ; heaviness in stomach sluggishness of liver hardness (of hearing) load burden turgidity [A]

ثقلین *saqalain'* N.M. mankind and spirits the world and hereafter [A ~ PREC.]

ثقہ *si'qah* N.M. (PL. ثقات *siqāt'*) authoritative (person or statement) reliable trustworthy [A]

ثقیل *saqīl'* (of word) difficult turgid bombastic (of food) rich indigestible (of stomach) heavy burdensome [A ~ ثقل]

ثلاثی *sūlā'sī* ADJ. & N.M. triliteral (root) ثلاثی مجرد *sūlā'sī-e mūjar'rad* N.M. pure triliteral ثلاثی مزید فیہ *sūlā'sī mazīd'fīh* N.M. triliteral root with additions

ثلث *sūls* ADJ. one-third N.M. name of a calligraphic style , offshoot of 'naskh' with decorative flourishes in inscriptions

ثمار *simār'* N.M. (PL. of ثمر ★)

ثمانیہ *sa'mā'niyah* ADJ. (lit.) eight [A]

ثمر *sa'mar* ثمرہ *sam'rah* (ped. *sa'marah*) N.M. (PL. also ثمار *simār'*) fruit produce offspring reward result ; outcome ثمرور *sa'mar var* ADJ. fruitful successful ثمردار *sa'mar-dār'* ADJ. fruit-bearing (tree) fruitful (endeavour) ثمرات *samarāt'* N.M. PL. fruits [A]

ثمن *sa'man* N.M. price cost value ثمین *samīn'* ADJ. valuable costly ; expensive [A]

ثنا *sanā'* N.F. praise eulogy encomium ثناخواں *sanā'khān* ثناگر *sanā'gar* ثناگستر *sanā'-gūs'tar* N.M. one who praise ; eulogist encomiast ثناخوانی *sanā'-khā'nī* ثناگری *sanā'-ga'rī*, ثناگستری *sanā'-gūs'tarī* N.F. praise praising eulogizing

ثواب *savāb'* N.M. reward (of virtue) (also ثواب کا کام *savāb' kā kām*) virtuous deed [A]

ثوابت *savābit* N.M. PL. stars (OPP. سیارے planets) [A ~ SING. ثابت]

ثور *saur* N.M. (a sign of Zodiac called Taurus (lit.) bull (also غار ثور *ghā'r-e saur'*) Saur Cave ; name of cave in which the Holy Prophet sojourned during his exodus to Medina [A]

ج

ج *jīm* seventh letter of Urdu alphabet (equivalent to English *j*) in jummal reckoning) 3

جا *ja* (rare or in construction جائے *jā''e*) N.F. (lit.) place space ; room seat جابجا *jā' ba'jā* ADV. everywhere here and there ; hither and thither جا بےجا *ja be-jā'* جاوبےجا *jā'-obe-jā* at all times in or out of place right or wrong جاضرور *jā-zūroor'*, جائے ضرور *jā'-e zūroor'* N.M. latrine ; privy lavatory جانشین *jānashīn'* (or-*shin*) ADJ. & N.M. F. successor deputy viceroy ; vice-gerent lieutenant جانشینی *jā-nashī'nī* N.F. succession vicegerency ; lieutenancy جانماز *ja-namāz'* N.F. prayer-mat , prayer carpet جائے اعتراض *jā'-e e'tirāz'* N.F. room objection جائے پناہ *jā'-e panāh'* N.F. refuge ; asylum shelter [P]

جابر *jā'bir* ADJ. despotic tyrannical strong N.M. despot tyrant [A ~ جبر]

جاپ *jāp* N.M. (dial.) muttering of prayers counting (of beads) [~ جپنا]

جاپا *jā'pa* N M. delivery , accouchement

جات *jāt* N.F. (dial.) caste high caste جات پات *jāt'-pāt* N.F (dial.) caste Hindu caste system [~S]

جاترا *jāt'ra* N.F. جاتری *jāt'rī* N.M. (same as یاترا *yāt'ra* N.F. یاتری *yāt'rī* N.M.) (see under یاترا N.F. ★) [S]

جاتی *jā'tī* N.F. (dial.) community ; communal group (dial.) caste Hindu community [S]

جاٹ *jāṭ* N.M. (F. جاٹنی *jāṭ'nī*) name of an agriculturist caste

جاٹھ *jāṭh* N.M. roller (of oil or sugar mill)

جاجم *jā'jam* N.M. printed linen carpet [T]

جادو *jā'doo* N.M. magic wizardry ; sorcery; necromancy conjuring charm ; spell enchantment جادو برحق کرنے والا کافر *jā'doo bar-haq' kar'ne-vā'la kā'fir* PROV. magic is a fact, its practice is however banned جادو جگانا *jā'doo jagā'na* V.T. test the effectiveness of magic charm جادو چلنا (یا ہونا) *jā'doo chal'nā* (or *ho'nā*) V.I. be charmed be under a spell succeed in bringing round جادو کا کھیل *jā'doo kā khel'* N.M. conjuring trick conjuring جادو کرنا (یا چلانا یا ڈالنا) *jā'doo kar'nā* (or *chalā'nā* or *ḍāl'nā*) V.T. charm ; enchant test a spell جادوگر *jā'doo-gar* N.M. magician a sorcerer conjurer جادوگرنی *jā'doo-gar'nī* N.F. witch sorceress جادوگری *jā'doo-ga'rī* N.F. magic wizardry ; sorcery ; necromancy charm ; enchantment [P]

جادہ *jā'dah* (ped. *jād'dah*) N.M. road centre of road paved or metalled portion (of road)

جاذب *jā'zib* ADJ. attractive; alluring absorbent N.M. blotter ; blotting-paper جاذبہ *jā'zibah* N.F. (power of) absorption (power of) gravitation [A ~ جذب]

جار¹ *jār* N.M. (PL. جیران *jīrān'*) (lit.) neighbour [A]

جار² *jār* ADJ. that gives 'zer' (ِ) to words ; that puts in genitive or dative case ; ADJ. drawing giving 'kasrah' thus حرف جر *har'f-e jar'* حرف جار *harf'-e jār* N.M. preposition (PL. حروف جارہ *hurooʻf-e jār'rah*) [A ~ جر]

جارجٹ *jār'jaṭ* N.F. georgette [E]

جارحانہ *jāriḥā'nah* ADJ. offensive aggressive جارحیت *jāriḥiy'yat* N.F. aggression جارحیت پسند *jāriḥiy'yat pasand'* ADJ. agressive جارحیت پسندی *jāriḥiy'yat pasandi* N.F. aggression aggressive policy [A]

جاروب *jārob'* N.F. (ped.) broom besom brush جاروب کش *jāroob'kash* N.M. sweeper scavenger جاروب کشی *jāroob'-ka'shī* N.F. sweeping [P ~ جا + روب]

جاری *jā'rī* ADJ. current (of law) in force prevalent continuing flowing جاری رکھنا *jā'rī rakh'nā* V.T. continue carry on maintain جاری رہنا *jā'rī raih'nā* V.I. continue be in force remain in force جاری کرنا *jā'rī kar'nā* V.T. issue start ; begin institute ; set on foot give currency enforce cause to flow جاری ہونا *jā'rī ho'nā* V.I. issue get going be current be in force be all the vogue flow [A]

جاریہ *jā'riyah* N.F. slave-girl ; maid [A]

جاڑا *jāṛa* N.M. winter cold ague جاڑا پڑنا *jā'ṛa paṛ'nā* V.I. be cold of winter come have ague جاڑا لگنا *jā'ṛa lag'nā* V.I. feel cold

جازم *jā'zim* ADJ. rendering final letter quiescent [A ~ جزم]

جاسوس *jāsoos'* N.M. spy detective جاسوسی *jāsoo'sī* N.F. spying ; espionage detective's work جاسوسی کرنا *jāsoo'sī kar'nā* V.T. act as a spy ; carry on espionage work as detective [A ~ تجسس]

جاکٹ *jā'kaṭ* jacket [E]

جاکڑ *jā'kaṛ* N.M. conditional purchase

جاکھن *jā'khan* N.M. wooden foundation of brickwork in well

جاگنا *jāg'nā* V.I. get up from sleep wake rouse be vigilant جاگ اٹھنا (یا پڑنا) *jāg' uṭh'nā* (or *paṛ'nā*) V.I. wake up get up from bed جاگ جانا *jāg' jā'nā* V.T. be up (from bed) (of many people) wake up جاگتا *jāg'ta* ADJ. awake vigilant جیتا جاگتا *jī'ta jāg'ta* ADJ. alive

جاگیر *jāgīr'* N.F. estate fief ; feud land revenue grant جاگیر دوام *jāgī'r-e davām'* N.F. estate perpetually rent-free جاگیردار *jāgīr'-dār* N.M. estate owner feudatory grantee جاگیرداری *jāgīr'dā'rī* N.F. fedudalism جاگیردارانہ نظام *jāgīr'-dārā'nah nizām'* N.M. feudal system جاگیر سیر *jāgīr'-sīr* N.F. such charitable grant [P ~ جا]

جال *jā'l* N.M. net snare trawl trap fraud جال بچھانا (یا پھیلانا) *jāl bichhā'nā* (or *phailā'nā*) V.T. spread a net trawl ; trawl a net set a trap جال پھینکنا *jāl phenk'nā*, V.I. trawl جال ڈالنا *jāl ḍāl'nā* V.T. spread a net trawl lay a snare set a trap جال میں پھانسنا (یا پھنسانا) *jāl' men phans'na* (or *phansa'na*) V.T entrap dupe جال میں پھنسنا *jal' men phans'na* V I be entrapped be duped

جالا *ja'la* N.M cobweb gossamer pellicle, web-eye [~PREC.]

جالوت *jaloot'* N.M. Goliath [A~H]

جالی *ja'li* N.F net network wire-netting grate lattice; trellis work lace caul integument (of foetus) thick coating (of mango-stone) جالی پڑنا *ja'li par'na*, V. hardening (of mango-stone) جالی کاڑھنا *ja'li karh'na* V.I. embroider stitch work جالی لوٹ *ja'li lot* N.M. bobbinet [~PREC.]

جالینوس *ja'linoos* N. Galen [A~G]

جام[1] *jam* N.M. jam [E]

جام[2] N.M. (lit.) cup : bowl goblet ; wine cup جام جم *ja'm-e jam*, جام جہاں نما *ja'm-e jahan-numa'* N.M. Jamshid's wine-cup ; goblet of the mythical Persian king in which he could view the whole world any wonderful possession جام چڑھانا *jam' charha'na* V.T quaff the wine جام صحت پینا *ja'm-e seh'hat pi'na* V.T drink a toast , drink to the health of [P]

جامد *ja'mid* ADJ. unprogressive ; static inorganic inanimate (of noun) concrete اسم جامد *is'm-e ja'mid* N.M. concrete noun [A~جمود]

جامدانی *jamda'ni* N.F. muslin with patterns woven into it leather or wooden box جامہ دان *ja'ma-dan* N.M. such box wardrobe [P~ جامہ + دان]

جامع *ja'me'* ADJ. comprehensive principal (mosque) N.M. (ped). principal mosque جامع کمالات *ja'm'-e kamalat* ADJ. & N.M. all-round (scholar) ; all-rounder جامع مسجد *ja'me' mas'jid* N.F. principal mosque of locality جامعیت *jame'iy'yat* N.F. comprehensiveness [A~جمع]

جامعہ *ja'me'ah* N.M. university (ped) society [A~جمع]

جامن *ja'man* N.F. rennet any coagulator 'jambolana' ADJ. mauve جامنی *ja'mani* ADJ. mauve

جامہ *ja'mah* N.M. (lit.) garment (arch.) frilled gown جامہ تلاشی *ja'ma-tala'shi* N.F. searching the person جامہ زیب *ja'ma-zeb* ADJ. graceful ; (one) on whom every dress fits well جامہ زیبی *ja'ma-ze'bi* N.F. grace ; being one of whom every dress fits well جامے سے باہر ہونا *ja'me se ba'har ho'na* V I. be unable to restrain oneself with anger جامے میں پھولا نہ سمانا *ja'me men phoo'la na sama'na* V.T. be overjoyed [P]

جان *jan'* (lit also *jan*) N.F life soul ; spirit essence vigour ; energy sweetheart , beloved ; love ; lady-love darling جان آنا (یا آجانا) *jan ana* (or *a ja'na*) V I be refreshed ; regain strength recoup health جان آفریں *jan afrin'* N M. Creator ; جانباز *jan-baz'* ADJ. intrepid daring , venturesome جانبازی *jan-bazi* N.F. spirit of sacrifice جان بچانا *jan, bacha'na* V.I. save one's skin (کام) سے جان بچانا (*kam*) *se jan' bacha'na* V.T shirk work جان بچی لاکھوں پائے (خیر سے بدھو گھر کو آئے) *jan' ba'chi lakhon pa''e* (*khair se bud'dhoo ghar' ko a''e*) save life save a million جان بحق (تسلیم) ہونا *jan ba'haq* (*taslim'*) *ho'na* V T die ; expire ; give up the ghost جان بخشی *jan-bakh'shi* (or *jan-*) N.F. sparing life ; forgiveness , pardon granting of life جانبر (نہ) ہونا *jan' bar* (*na*) *ho'na* V.I (not) to survive جاں بلب (ہونا) *jan' ba-lab'* (*ho'na*) ADJ. (& V.I.) be dying ; be at the point of death جان بھاری ہونا *jan' bha'ri ho'na* V I. grow weary of life جان پر بننا *jan' par ban'na* V I. be in danger of one's life جان پر کھیلنا *jan par khel'na*, V.I. jeopardize one's very existence lay down one's life جان پڑنا *jan' par'na* V.I. be revived become graceful being to thrive (پر) جان تصدق کرنا (*par*) *jan tasad'duq kar'na* V.T sacrifice one's life (for) جان توڑ کر لڑنا *jan' tor' kar lar'na* V.I. fight desperately جان جوکھوں کا کام *jan' jo'khon ka kam* N.M. hazardous task جان جوکھوں میں ڈالنا *jan' jo'khon men dal'na* V.I. hazard one's life; jeopardize one's existence جان چرانا *jan' chura'na* V T shirk shrink from جان چھڑانا *jan' chhura'na* V.T. get rid of , escape جان چھڑکنا *jan' chhi'rakna* V.T. be deeply devoted (to) ; be ready to sacrifice one's life (for) جاندار *jan'dar* N.M. animal ADJ. animate active vigorous جان دوبھر ہونا *jan doo'bhar ho'na* V.I be heavy of one's life جان دینا *jan' de'na* V.T. die پر جان دینا *par jan' de'na* V T. die for sacrifice one's life for be deeply in love with جانسپار *jan-sipar'* ADJ. devoted (of lover or servant) ready to lay down his life for mistress or master جانسپاری *jan-sipari* N.F devotion readiness to lay down (one's) life جانستاں *jan-sitan'* ADJ. killing (work) cruel (person) جانستانی *jan-sita'ni* N.F. cruelty callousness etc. سوختہ جاں *sokh'ta-jan'* (or *jan'*) ADJ. afflicated tormented جاں سوز *jan-soz'* ADJ. tormenting ; soul-racking جان سے جانا *jan se ja'na* V.I. die جان سے مارنا *jan' se mar'na* V.T. kill ; murder جان سے ہاتھ دھونا *jan' se hath' dho'na* V.I. despair of (one's) life جانفزا *jan fiza'* ADJ. animating invigorating ; bracing refreshing جانفزائی *jan-fiza''i* N.F. invigorating nature جانفشاں *jan' fishan'*

ADJ. devoted ready to lay down one's life very diligent جانفشانی jān-fishā'nī N F devotion readiness to lay down one s life diligence جان کا جنجال jān' kā jan'jāl, وبال جان vabā'l-e jān' N.M. problematick person (or thing) جان کا صدقہ مال jān' kā sad'qa māl' PROV save life save a million (کی) جان کا لاگو ہونا kī jān kā lā'goo ho'nā V T. pursue one to death جان لیوا jān-le'vā ADJ fatal , mortal deadly lethal جانکاہ jān-kah' ADJ. sad ; pathetic heart-rending calling for diligence جانکاہی jān-kāhī N F sadness deligence کسی پر جان دینا ki'sī par jān' de'nā V T be deep in love with (کی) جان کو آنا (kī) jān ko ā'nā V.T take (someone) to task vex جانکنی (کی حالت) jān'-kanī (kī ḥā'lat) N.F agonies of death agony anguish (بروں کی) جان کو رونا (bur'ron kī) jān' ko ro'nā V.I wish (oneself) dead جان کھانا jān' khā'nā V.T. vex , annoy plague جان کھپانا (یا مارنا) jān' khapā'nā (or mār'nā) V.I. work very hard ; work diligently جان کی امان jān' kī amān' N,F indulgence pardon ; forgiveness quarter جان کی امان پاؤں jān' kī amān' pā'ooṅ PH. crave your indulgence جان کے برابر رکھنا jān' ke barā'bar rakh'nā V.T. regard (someone) no less dear than one's life جان کے لالے پڑنا jān' ke lā'le par'nā V.I. on the point of death despair of life جان گداز jān-gūdāz', جانگسل jān-gūsil' ADJ. killing baneful jān' lara'nā V.I. jeopardize one's life lay down جان لینا jān' le'nā V.T. kill deprive (someone) of his life جان میں جان آنا jān' meṅ jān' ā'nā be comforted be revived be no longer jittery feel no longer worried جانثار jāṅ-nisār' ADJ. devoted جانثاری jāṅ' nisā'rī N.F. devotion جان من jā'n-e man PH. my darling be jān' ADJ. lifeless ; dead inanimate weak enervated listless insipid [P]

جانا jā'nā V.I. (PAST T. ga'yā irregularly formed) go pass , set out depart disappear be lost be stolen be wasted be no more جانے (بھی) دو jā'ne (bhī) do PL. never mind forget and forgive leave it off let (me, etc.) go no more of this silly stuff I can't stomach the lie جانے دینا jā'ne de'nā V.T. let go forgive ; pardon

جاناں jā'nāṅ N.M. beloved , sweetheart [P ~ SING جان]

جانب jā'nib N.F. (PL. جوانب javā' nib) side ; direction جانب jā'nib-e, کی جانب kī jā'nib ADV towords اینجانب īṅ -jā'nib PROV. (arch.) I ADV (lit.) this side جانبدار jā'nib-dār ADJ. partial biased N.M. supporter, partisan جانبداری jā'nib-dā'rī N.F. partiality جانبین jānaibain' N.M. both the parties جانبین سے jānaibaiṅ se ADV from both sides mutually reciprocally [A]

جانچنا jāṅch'nā evaluate appraise assess test ; try survey جانچ jāṅch N.M. evaluation assessment appraisal test ; trial survey جانچ پرکھ jāṅch pa'rakh N.F. scrutiny

جانگلو jāṅg'loo ADJ. wild ; undomesticated savage uncultured [P ~ جنگل]

جانگھ jāṅgh N.F. thigh

جانگیہ jāṅ'giyah (usu but less correct form of) جانگیا jāṅ'ghiyā) N.M. underwater drawers panties wrestlers breeches [~ جانگھ loins]

جانماز jā-namāz' N.F. prayer-carpet ; prayer-mat [P ~ نماز + جا]

جاننا jān'nā V.T. known be aware of think ; believe ; deem , hold conceive fancy own ; recognize understand ; apprehend perceive جان jān N.F knowledge awareness belief idea جانا بوجھا jā'nā boo'jhā ADJ. well frequented not unknown جانا پہچانا jā'nā paihchā'nā ADJ. well-known جان پڑنا jān' par'nā V.T. appear جان بوجھ کر (یا کے) jān' boojh' kar (or ke) ADV. on purpose ; purposely knowingly ; knowing full well intentionally جان پہچان jān paihchan' N.F. acquaintance جان کر انجان بننا jān' kar aṅ-jān' ban'nā V.T. pretend ignorance جان لینا jān' le'nā V. apprehend ; perceive جان نہ پہچان jān' na pehchān' PH. no acquaintance

جانور jān'var N.M. animal fool ADJ. stupid ; foolish uncultured [P ~ جان + ور]

جانی jā'nī ADJ. vital mortal ; sanguine hearty , cordial N.M. beloved sweetheart darling جانی دشمن jā'nī dūsh'man N.M. mortal enemy ; sanguine foe [P ~ جان]

جاوتری jāvat'rī N.F. nutmeg bark ; mace

جاودان jā'vidāṅ, جاودانی jāvidā'nī جاوید jāved' (or jāvid') ADJ. everlasting ; eternal ; perpetual [P]

جاہ jāh N.F. status ; rank station in life dignity ; grandeur جاہ و جلال jā'h-o jalāl' جاہ و حشم jā'h-o ḥa'sham N.M. rank and dignity grandeur ; magnificence splendour جاہ و منصب jā'h-o man'sab N.M rank and position [P]

جاہل jā'hil, (PL. جہلا johalā ; جہال johhāl') ADJ. ignorant unlettered ; illiterate uncouth uncivilized uncultured [A ~ جہالت]

جائداد jā'e-dād' (rare جاداد jā-dad') N.F. property estate real estate آبائی جائداد abā'ī *ja'e-dād'* N.F. ancestral property ; inherited property زرعی جائداد *zar'ī ja''e-dād* N.F. agricultural property ; landed property غیر منقولہ جائداد *ghair manqoo'lah ja'e-dād'* جائداد غیر منقولہ *ja'e-dād' ghair manqoo'lah* N.F. immovable property متروکہ جائداد *matroo'kah ja'e-dād'* N.F. evacuee property متنازعہ جائداد *mūtanā' za'ah ja'e-dād'* N.F. disputed property جائداد مرہونہ *ja'e-dā'd-e marhoo'nah* N.F. mortgaged property مشترکہ جائداد *mushta'rakah ja'e-dād'* N.F. joint property جائداد معافی *ja'e-dā'd-e mo'ā'fī* N.F. rent-free property جائداد معافی دوام *ja'e-dā'd-e mo'ā'fī-e davām'* N.F. permanent land grant مقروقہ جائداد *maqroo'qah ja'e-dād'* N.F. attached property ; sequestered property مکسوبہ جائداد *maksoo'bah ja'e-dād'* N.F. self-acquired property مکفولہ جائداد *makfoo'lah ja'e-dād'* N.F. hypothecated property جائداد منقولہ *ja'edād-manqoo'lah* N.F. movable property موروثی جائداد *mauroo'sī ja'e-dād'* N.F. ancestral property ; inherited property [P ~ جا]

جائز *ja''iz* ADJ. permissible lawful ; legal right ; proper just justified جائز رکھنا *ja''iz rakh'na* V.T. permit ; allow justify ; legalise جائز قرار دینا *ja''iz qarar' de'na* V.T. uphold permit ; allow ناجائز *na-ja''iz* ADJ. not permissible wrong unjust unlawful ناجائز طور سے *na-ja''iz taur' se* ADV. wrongly unjustly unlawfully [A ~ جواز]

جائزہ *ja''izah* N.M. checking review examination survey exploration (of possibility) جائزہ لینا *ja''izah le'na* V.T. check review survey examine explore [A ~ PREC.]

جائفل *ja''ifal* (rare جائے پھل *ja''e phal*) N.M. nutmeg [A ~ S]

جب *jab* ADV. & CONJ. when at the time ; if ; in case then جب تک *jab' tak* ADV. & CONJ. till ; until as long as ; so long as while ; whilst till then جب سے *jab' se* ADV. & CONJ. since جب کبھی *jab' ka'bhī* ADV. & CONJ. whenever everytime that جبھی *ja'bhī* ADV. & CONJ. at that very time therefore ; hence جبھی تو *ja'bhī to* ADV. & CONJ. therefore ; hence on that account ; for that very reason

جبار *jabbar'* ADJ. mighty N.M. Omnipotent (as an attributive of God) [P ~ FOLL.]

جبر *jab'r* N.M. force ; might compulsion oppression ; coercion constraint (ped.) joining (broken bone, etc.) reduction of fractions to integrals جبر کرنا *jab'r kar'na* V.T. oppress ; use force ; coerce compel , constrain جبر و تعدی *jab'r-o ta'ad'dī* N.M. oppression ; coercion cruelty ; tyranny جبر و مقابلہ *jab'r-o mūqā'balah* N.M. algebra جبراً *jab'ran*, بالجبر *bil-jab'r* by force ; forcibly violently جبراً و قہراً *jab'ran va qah'ran* ADV. willy-nilly زنا بالجبر *zinā' bil-jab'r* N.M. rape جبری *jab'rī* ADJ. force under constraint involuntary compulsory جبری بھرتی *jab'rī bhar'tī* N.F. conscription [A]

جبروت *jabroot'* N.F. majesty magnificence omnipotent heaven (as sphere of God's omnipotence) [A ~ جبر]

جبریل *jibrīl'*, جبرئیل *jib'rā'īl*, جبرائیل *jibra'il'* N.M. Gabriel ; Archangel [A ~ H]

جبڑا *jab'ṛā* N.M. jaw

جبل *jab'bal* N.M. (PL. جبال *jibāl'*) hill mountain جبل الطارق *jā'bal-ūt-ṭā'riq* N.M. Gibralter جبل رحمت *ja'bal-e rah'mat* Mercy ; name of a hill near Mecca [A]

جبلت *jibil'lat* N.M. instinct nature ; natural disposition جبلی *jibil'lī* ADJ. N.M. instinctive innal natural [A]

جبن *jūb'n* N.M. cowardice ; dastardliness

جبہ *jūb'bah* N.M. gown robe toga جبہ و دستار *jūb'ba-o-dastār'* N.M. PL. gown and turban (fig.) religiousness incorporate

جبہہ *jab'hah* N.M. forehead ; brow جبہہ سا *jab'ha-sā* ADJ. (one) humbling, oneself to beseach جبہہ سائی *jabha-sā''ī* N.F. beseeching humbly , fawing on humiliating (oneself) [A]

جبین *jabīn'* (or *īn'*) N.F. forehead ; brow جبین نیاز *jabī'n-e nayāz'* N.M. (lowering of) forehead in humility

جپنا *jap'nā* V.T. (dial.) tell one's leads repeat God's name جپ جی *jap' jī* N.F. (dial.) Sikh prayer book رام رام جپنا پرایا مال اپنا *rām' nam jap'nā parā'yā māl' ap'nā* PROV. saint abroad, devil at home

جتانا *jatā'nā*, جتلانا *jatlā'nā* V.T. remind someone after his failure admonish point out caution ; warn

جتانا *jitā'nā*, جتوانا *jitvā'nā* V.T. cause to win or conquer [~ جیتنا CAUS.]

جتن *ja'tan*, (ped. *jat'n*) N.M. (usu PL.) effort ; endeavour exertion ; striving trick ; contrivance ہزار (یا بڑے) جتن کرنا *hazār'* (or *ba'ṛe*) *jat'an kar'nā* PH. leave no stone unturned

جتنا *jit'nā*, جتنی *jit'nī* ADV. & CONJ. , as much , as many as much as the more (etc.) ...the جتنا چھانو اتنا ہی کرکرا *jit'na chhā'no ūt'na hī kir'*

kira PROV. the more you sift (something) the worse you will find it جتنا چھوٹا اتنا کھوٹا *jit'na chho'ta ūt'na kho'ta,* جتنا اوپر اتنا نیچے *jit'nā oo'par ūt'nā ni'che* PROV. small or dwarfish but naughty جتنا گڑ ڈالو گے اتنا میٹھا ہوگا *jit'na gūṛ ḍā'loge ūt'na mi'ṭha ho'ga* PROV. the deeper the well the warmer the water جتنی چادر دیکھیے اتنے پاؤں پھیلائیے *jit'nī chādar de'khiye ūt'ne pā''ñ phailā''iye* PROV. cut your coat according to your cloth جتنے دم اتنے غم *jit'ne dam ūt'ne gham* PROV. life is a series of sorrows جتنی دولت اتنی مصیبت *jit'nī dau'laṭ ūt'nī mūsī'bat* PROV. the more the wealth the greater the worry جتنی دیگ اتنی کھرچن *jit'nī deg ūt'nī hī khūr'chan* PROV. spend less get less ; جتنے منہ اتنی باتیں *jit'ne mūñh ūt'nī bā'ten* PROV. opinions are ever diverse everyone hazards a different guess

جتنا *jūt'na* V.I. (of animal) be yoked (of land) be ploughed جتاؤ *jūtā''oo* ADJ. arable ; culturable جتائی *jūtā''ī* N.F. tilling ; ploughing ; bringing under the plough tillage *jūtvā'nā* V.I. cause to till get (land) tilled cause to be yoked [~ جوتنا]

جتھہ *jat'thah,* جتھا *jat'thā* (occ. *ja'thā*) N.M. party ; gang mob strength unity جتھا بند *jat'thā bandh'nā* V.I. unite

جتیانا *jūtyā'nā* V.T. give a shoe-beating [~ جوتا]

جتی ستی *ja'tī sa'ti* ADJ. (dial.) celibate [S]

جٹ *jūṭ* N.F. pair equal ; peer

جٹا *ja'ṭā* N.F. (dial.) matted hair جٹادھاری *ja'ṭā dhā'rī* N.M. (dial.) Hindu mendicant with matted hair

جٹنا *jūṭ'nā* V.T. set to (a task) earnestly toil grapple fight ; close with join be joined to copulate be matted

جٹھانی *jiṭhā'nī* N.F. wife of husband's elder brother [~ جیٹھ]

جثہ *jūs'sah* N.M. body corporeal figure عظیم الجثہ *'azi'm-ūl jūs'sah* ADJ. huge [A]

جج *jaj* N.M. judge ججی *ja'jī* N.F. courts [E]

ججمان *jajmān',* ججمانی *jajma'nī* N.F. superior ; person entitled to menial's services

جچا *jach'chā* N.M. lying in woman [~P زچہ CORR.]

جچنا *jach'nā* V.I. suit fit well be tested ; be tried be appraised be estimable کی نظروں میں جچنا *kī naz'roñ meñ jach'nā* V.I. be approved by look presentable to

جحیم *jahīm'* N.M. Hell [A]

جد *jad* N.M. (PL. اجداد *ajdād'*) grandfather ; ancestor ; glory (of God) felicity جدی *jad'dī* ADJ. ancestral جدہ *jad'dah* N.F. grandmother; granny [A]

جد *jid* N.F. effort ; endeavour seriousness ; earnestness جدوجہد *jid'do-jah'd* (or *joh'd*) N.F. effort ; endeavour toil ; labour جدوجہد کرنا *jid'd-o jah'd kar'nā* V.T. make an effort ; endeavour strive [A]

جدا *jū'dā* ADJ. separate distinct different disparate discrete peculiar aside apart asunder جدا جدا *jū'dā jū'dā* ADV. separately severally distinctly one by one جدا کرنا *jū'dā kar'nā* V.T. separate detach disunite disengage جداگانہ *jū'dā-gā'nah* ADV. & ADJ. separately جدا ہونا *jū'dā ho'nā* V.I. be separated جدائی *jūdā''e* N.F. separation absence differences [P]

جدال *jidāl'* N.M. contest dispute altercation fight ; affray جدال وقتال *jidā'l-o qitāl'* N.M. contest ; fighting contention affray fight [A ~ جدل]

جداول *jadā'vil* N.M. (PL. of جدول N.F. ★)

جدت *jid'dat.* N.M. innovation originality freshness new point *jid'dat pasand* ADJ. & N.M. (one) fond of new ways (of life, etc.) (one) fond of new twins of speech جدت پسندی *jid'dat pasañ'dī* N.F. such fondness جدید *jadīd'* ★ [A]

جدل *ja'dal* fight contention جنگ وجدل *jan'g-o ja'dal* N.M. fight encounter contention جدلی *jada'lī* N.M. dialectician ADJ. dialectical جدلی مادیت *ja'dalī māddiy'yat* N.F. dialectics *jadaliy'yat* N.F. dialectics [A]

جدوار *jadvar'* N.M. zedoary

جدول *jad'val* (PL. جداول *jadā'vil*) N.F. (usu. double) marginal line tabulated information ; table ; schedule (rare) streamlet جدول بندی *jad'val-bañ'dī* N.F. tabulation جدولی *jad'valī* ADJ. marked with straight lines جدولی پیمانہ *jad'valī paimā'nah* N.M. schedule scale [A]

جدھر *ji'dhar* ADV. where whither wherever there جدھر تدھر *ji'dhar ti'dhar* ADV. (arch.) everywhere wherever جدھر رب ادھر سب *ji'dhar rab' ū'dhar sab'* PROV. he who has God on his side has everything

جدی *jad'y* (col. *ja'dī*) N.M. capricorn خط جدی *khat'-t-e jad'y* N.M. tropic of Capricorn [A]

جدید *jadīd* ADJ. new ; fresh modern [A ~ جدت]

جذام *jūzām'* N.M. leprosy **جذامی** *jūza'mī* N.M. leper ADJ. leperous [A]

جذب *jaz'b* N.M. attraction absorption **جذب کرنا** *jaz'b kar'nā* V.T. attract absorb imbibe **جذب ہونا** *jaz'b ho'nā* V.I. be absorbed ; be soaked **جذب مقناطیسی** *jaz'b-e maqnātī'sī* N.M. magnetic attraction [A]

جذبات *jazabāt'* N.M. PL. **جذباتی** *jazabā'tī* ADJ. **جذباتیت** *jazabā- tiy'yat* N.F. (see under **جذبہ** N.M. ★)

جذبہ *jaz'bah* (ped. *ja'zabah*) (PL. **جذبات** *jazabāt'*) N.M. feeling strong desire ; passion emotion sentiment **جذباتی** *jazbā'tī* (ped. *jazabā'tī*) ADJ. emotional ; sentimental **جذباتیت** *jazbatiy'yat* N.F. emotionalism [A ~ **جذب**]

جذر *jaz'r* N.M. square root ; figure multiplied by itself root (of any power) **جذر سالم** *jaz'r-e sā'lim* N.M. root of integer **جذر الکعب** *jaz'r-ul ka''b* N.M. third root **جذر مربع** *jaz'r-e mūrab'ba'* N.M. fourth root **جذر مکسر** *jaz'r-e mūkas'sar* N.M. root of fraction [A]

جر *jar* N.M. dragging ; drawing genitive case 'kasrah' at end of word **حرف جر** *har'f-e jar'* **حرف جار** *har'fe jār* N.M. preposition **جر ثقیل** *jar'r-i saqīl* N.M. mechanics [A]

جراب *jūrāb'* (ped. *jūrrāb'*) N.M. sock stocking hose [P]

جرأت *jūr''at* N.F. courage ; boldness ; daring valour ; bravery temerity audacity **جرأت کرنا** *jūr''at kar'nā* V.T. dare have the courage have the audacity (to) **جری** *ja'rī* ADJ. ★[A]

جراثیم *jarā'sīm* N.M. PL. bacteria [A ~ SING. **جرثومہ**]

جراح *jarrāh'* N.M. surgeon **جراحی** *jarrā'hī* N.F. surgery **عمل جراحی** *'a'mal-e jarrā'hī* N.M: surgical operation ; operation [A ~ FOLL.]

جراحت *jirā'hat* N.F. wound sore [A]

جرار *jarrār'* ADJ. (of army) very large ; huge [A]

جرائد *jarā''id* N.M. PL. newspapers ; dailies [A ~ **جریدہ**]

جرائم *jarā''im* N.M. crimes sins **ارتکاب جرائم** *irtikā'be jarā''im* N.M. committing of crimes crime incidence **جرائم خفیفہ** *jarā''im-e khafīfah* N.M. PL. petty offences **سنگین جرائم** *sangīn' jarā''im* N.M. PL. sérious crimes ; felony **رفتار جرائم** *raftār'-e jarā''im* N.F. crime incidence [SING **جرم**]

جرثومہ *jūrsoo'mah* N.M. (PL. **جراثیم** *jarāsīm'*) bacterium **جرثومیات** *jūrsoomiyyat'* ADJ. bacteriology **جرثومہ دان** *jūrsoo'mā-dān* N.M. bacteriologist **جرثومیاتی** *jursoomiyyā'tī* N.M. bacteriological [A]

جرح *jar'h* (col. *jir'h*) N.M. wound sore cross-examination criticism **جرح کرنا** *jar'h kar'nā* V.T. cross-examine **جرح و تعدیل** *jarh-o ta'dīl* N.F. critical examination [A]

جرس *ja'ras* N.M. bell [A]

جرعہ *jūr''ah* N.M. draught sip gulp drop **جرعہ کش** *jar''a-kash* N.M. drinker toper [P]

جرگہ *jir'gah* (rare *jar'gah*) N.M. tribal jury ; jirgah **جرگے کے سپرد کرنا** *jir'gah ke sipūrd' kar'nā* V.T. refer (case) to jirgah [P]

جرم *jir'm* N.M. (PL. **اجرام** *ajrām'*) body (esp. of inanimate object) **جرم فلکی** *jir'm-e fa'lakī* N.M. heavenly body [A]

جرم *jūr'm* N.M. (PL. **جرائم** *jara''im*) crime; criminal act offensive guilt transgression fault **اثبات جرم** *isbā't-e jūr'm* N.M. proving of guilt **ارتکاب جرم** *irtikā'b-e jūr'm* N.M. commitment of offence **اقبال جرم** *iqba'l-e jūr'm* N.M. confession of guilt **اقدام جرم** *iqdā'm-e jūr'm* N.M. attempt to commit offence **بے جرم** *be-jūr'm* ADJ. innocent ; guiltness **ثبوت جرم** *sūboo't-e jūr'm* N.M. proof of guilt **جرم خلاف وضع فطری** *jūr'm e khilā'f-e vaz'e fit'rī* N.M. unnatural offence **جرم خفیف** *jūr'm-e khafīf* N.M. petty offence ; minor offence **جرم سے منکر ہو جانا** *jūr'm se mūn'kir ho jā'nā* V.T. plead not guilty **جرم شدید** *jūr'm-e shadīd'* N.M. grevious offence **جرم عظیم** *jūr'm-e 'azīm'* N.M. capital crime **جرم قابل دست اندازی (پولیس)** *jūr'm qā'bil-e das't andā'zī (pūlees')* N.M. cognizable offence **قابل ضمانت جرم** *qā'bil-e zamā'nat jūr'm* N.M. bailable offence **جرم کا مرتکب ہونا** *jūr'm kā mūr'takib ho'nā* V.I. commit an offence **واجب القتل جرم** *vā'jibul-qat'l jūr'm* N.M. offence punishable with death **جرمیات** *jūrmiyyat'* N.M. criminology **ماہر جرمیات** *ma'hir-e jurmiyyat'* N.M. criminologist [A]

جرمانہ *jūrmā'nah* N.M. fine penalty **جرمانہ دینا** *jūrmā'nah de'nā* V.T. pay a fine pay a penalty **جرمانہ کرنا** *jūrmā'nah kar'na* V.T. fine **جرمانہ معاف کرنا** *jūrmā'nah mo'āf kar'nā* V.I. remit fine [~ PREC. A]

جرنل *jar'nal* N.M. journal ; periodical **جرنلزم** *jar'nalizm* N.M. journalism **جرنلسٹ** *jar'nalist* N.M. journalist [E]

جروا *jūr'vā* N.F. (derog.) wife [~ **جورو**]

جری *ja'rī* ADJ. courageous ; bold valiant brave interpid [A ~ **جرأت**]

جری *jū'rī* N.M. rinderpest

جریان *jarayān'* N.M. (col. *jiryān'* Bright's disease glest flux circulation [A ~ **جاری**]

جریب *jarīb'* N.F. sixty-yard land-measure chain for measuring that much (arch.) stick staff جریب کرنا (یا ڈالنا) *jarīb kar'nā* (or *ḍāl'nā*) V.T. measure land by chain جریب کش *jarīb'-kash* N.M. land measure جریب کشی *jarīb-'kashī* N.F. measurement of land [A ~ P گزی]

جریدہ *jarī'dah* ADJ. N.M. (PL. جرائد *jarā'id*) periodical ; daily newspaper ADJ. lonely ; solitary alone ; unattended [A]

جڑ *jaṛ* N.F. root stern basis origin root-cause جڑ (سے) اکھاڑنا *jaṛ (se) ūkhaṛ'nā* V.T. uproot extirpate جڑ پکڑنا *jaṛ pa'kaṛnā* V.I. take root be firmly rooted جڑ (یا جڑیں) کاٹنا *jaṛ* (or *ja'ṛeṅ*) *kaṭ'nā* V.T. strike at the root (of) destroy root and branch جڑیلا *jaṛī'la* ADJ. (F. جڑیلی *jaṛī'lī*) having hardened roots

جڑاول *jaṛā'val* N.F. warm clothes ; winter apparel; woollies [~ جاڑا]

جڑنا *jaṛ'nā* V.T. frame stud ; set (jewels) strike ; lay on (blow) stick on affix جڑانا *jaṛā'nā*, جڑوانا *jaṛvā'nā* V.T. have (picture, etc.) framed have (jewels) studded cause to be set with jewels جڑاؤ *jaṛā''oo* ADJ. studded set with stones جڑائی *jaṛā''ī* N.F. setting (of jewels) remuneration for it جڑیا *jaṛ'yā* N.M jeweller enameller paederast

جڑنا *jūṛ'nā* V.T. join ; be joined unite be mended (of money) be saved be obtained ; come to hand جڑائی *jūṛā''ī* N.F joining mending remuneration for it جڑواں *jūṛ'vāṅ* ADJ. twin جڑواں بچے *jūṛ'vāṅ bach'che* N.M. PL. twins جڑوانا *jurvā'nā* V.T. cause to join ; cause to unite get (something) mended

جڑی *ja'ṛī* N.F. root of medical herb جڑی بوٹی *ja'ṛī boo'ṭī* N.F. medicinal herbs

جز *jūz*, بجز *ba-jūz'* ADV. except ; save ; excepting ; with the exception of besides [P]

جز *jūz*, جزو *jūz'v* N.M. (PL. اجزا *ajzā'*) part ; portion ingredient folded forms (of book) جزو بدن ہونا *jūz'v-e ba'dan ho'nā* V.I. be assimilated; be digested جز بندی *jūz-bań'dī* N.F. binding (of book) with forms separated stitched جزدان *jūz-dān'* N.M. case for one's copy of the Holy Quran portfolio satchel جزرس *jūz-ras'* ADJ. frugal niggardly, جزرسی *jūz-ra'sī* N F. frugality niggardliness جزائے ضربی *jū'z-e zar'bī* N.M. (PL. اجزائے ضربی *ajzā''e zar'bī*) factor جز وقتی *jūz-vaq'tī* ADJ. (of service) part-time جزو کل *jū'z-o kūl'*, جزو و کل *jūz'v-o-kūl* ADV. wholly ; entirely ; totally from top to bottom ADJ. whole ; entire جزو لا یتجزیٰ *jūz'v-e la yatajaz'za* N.M. indivisible particle ; atom جزو لا ینفک *jūz'v-e lā yanfak'* N.M. inseparable part جزئی *jūz''ī*, جزوی *jū'zavī* (col. *jūz'vī*) ADJ. partial جزئیات *jūz'iyyāt'* N.F. details ; minor details [A]

جزا *jazā'* N.F. reward ; requital blessing compensation retribution جزاک اللہ *jazā'-kallāh'* INT. (PL. جزاکم اللہ *jazā'kūm ūllāh'*) God bless you [A]

جزائر *jazā''ir* N.M. islands ; isles [A ~ SING. جزیرہ]

جز بز *jiz'-biz* ADJ. offended ; displeased ; annoyed ; vexed جز بز ہونا *jiz'-biz ho'nā* V.T. take the offence ; be offended be displeased be annoyed ; be vexed

جزر *jaz'r* N.M. ebb-tide ; the reflux of the sea جزر و مد *jaz'r-o mad'*, مد و جزر *mad'd-o jaz'r* N.M. ebb and flow of tide [A]

جزع *ja'za'* N.F. impatience جزع و فزع *ja'za'-o fa'za* N.F. crying ; bewailing mourning [A]

جزم *jaz'm* N.M. diacritical mark making letter quiescent determination ; resolve ; firmness عزم بالجزم *'az m-bil-jaz'm* N.M. firm resolve settled purpose [A]

جزیرہ *jazī'rah* N.M. island ; isle جزیرہ نما *jazī'ra-nūmā'* N.M. peninsula [A]

جزیہ *jiz'yah* N.M. poll tax ; capitation-tax levied for exemption from military duty [A ~ جزا]

جس *jas* N.M. (dial.) reputation (W. dial.) merit ; virtue ہمارے نمک ہی میں جس نہیں *hamā're na'mak hī meṅ jas nahīṅ'* PH. our salt has no virtue our solicitude evokes no response

جس *jis* PRON. who which whom what that جس پر *jis' par* ADV. at which whereupon ; whereat جس تس *jis tis* PRON. (arch.) whoever whatever someone or the other جس تن لاگے سو تن جانے *jis' tan lā'ge so tan jā'ne*, جس کے نہ پھٹی بوائی وہ کیا جانے پیر پرائی *jis ke na pha'ṭī bavā''ī voh kyā jā'ne pīṛ parā''ī* PROV. nobody can fully realize the other's pain جس جس *jis' jis* PROV. whichever each of which جس جگہ *jis-ja'gah* ADV. where wherever جس دم *jis'-dam* ADV. when while ; whilst as soon as ; no sooner than جس طرح *jis' ta'rah* (ped. *jis' tar'h*) ADV. as just as جس طرف *jis' ta'raf* ADV. wherever in the direction that جس قدر *jis' qad'r* (or *jis' qa'dar*) ADV. as much as to the extent that جس کا *jis kā* PRON. (F. جس کی *jis kī*) whose ; of whom جس کسی کا *jis' ki'sī kā* ADV. of whomsoever جس کسی کو *jis' ki'sī ko* ADV. (to) whomsoever جس نے بیٹی دی اس نے کیا نہ رکھا *jis ne be'ṭī dī ūs ne kyā' rak'khā* PROV. let none malign the bride's poverty-striken father for giving no dower جس وقت *jis' vaq't* ADV. when جس وقت بھی *jis' vaq't bhī* ADV. whenever جس کا کام اسی کو ساجے اور کرے تو ٹھینگا باجے *jis' kā kām' ūsī ko sa'je (aur' ka're to thīn'ga ba'je)* PROV. every man to his trade جس کا کھائے اسی کا گائے *jis' kā khā''e ūs' kā ga''e* PROV. every man praises the bridge he passes over جس کو رکھے سائیاں اسے مار سکے نہ کوئی *jis' ko rak'khe sāi''yāṅ ū'se mār sa'ke na ko''ī* PROV. he whom God protects none call kill جس کے ہاتھ ڈوئی اس کا سب کوئی *jis ke hath do''ī ūs' kā sab ko''ī* PROV. everyone is a friend to him who gives generously جس کی لاٹھی اس کی بھینس *jis' kī lā'ṭhī ūs' kī bhaiṅs* PROV. might is right جس ہانڈی میں کھائیں اسی میں چھید کریں *jis' hāṅ'ḍī meṅ khā''eṅ ū'sī meṅ chhed' kar'reṅ* PROV. ungrateful person is foe to own benefactors جسے پیا چاہے وہی سہاگن *ji'se pi'yā chā'he vohī sohā'gan* PROV. fancy passes beauty

جسارت *jasā'rat* N.F. presumption intrepidity; temerity boldness audacity [A]

جسامت *jasā'mat* N.F. bulk dimension [A ~ جسم]

جست[1] *jas't* N.F. leap ; bound جست بھرنا (یا لگانا) *jas't bhar'nā (or lagā'nā)* V.I leap ; bound [P ~ جستن *jas'tan*]

جست[2] *jas't* N.M. zinc جستی *jas'tī* ADJ. zinc (of steel) made rust-proof with a thing coating of zinc

جستجو *just-joo'* N.F. search quest جستجو کرنا *justūjoo' kar'nā* V.T. search جستجو ہونا *justūjoo' ho'nā* V.I. searched [P ~ جست + جو ~ جستن *jūs'tan*]

جستہ جستہ *jas'ta jas'tah* ADV. from here and there ; desultorily

جسد *ja'sad* N.M. (PL. اجساد *ajsād*) body [A]

جسم *jism* N.M. (PL. اجسام *ajsām*,) body جسم جمادی *jis'm-e jamā'dī* N.M. inorganic body جسم حیوانی *jis'm-e ḥayavā'nī* N.M. animal body جسم نباتاتی *jis'm-e nabā'tī* N.M. vegetable body جسمانی *jismā'nī*, (rare. جسمی *jis'mī*) ADJ. bodily physical ; corporal carporeal material carnal جسمانی سزا *jismā'nī sazā'* N.F. corporal punishment جسمانی صحت *jismā'nī seḥ'hat* N.F. physical fitness جسمانی ورزش *jismā'nī var'zish* N.F. physical exercise جسمانیت *jismāniy'yat*, جسمیت *jismiy'yat* N.F. materiality [A]

جسیم *jasīm'* ADJ. fat ; bulky ; corpulent [A ~ PREC.]

جشن *jash'n* N.M. festival festivity rejoicings jubilee جشن الماسی *jash'n-e almā'sī* N.M. Diamond Jubilee جشن زریں (یا طلائی) *jashn-e zar'rīṅ (or tilā''ī)* N.M. Golden Jubilee جشن سیمیں (یا نقرئی) *jash'n-e sī'mīṅ (or naq'ra'ī)* N.M. Silver Jubilee جشن منانا *jash'n manā'na* V.T. celebrate a festival [P]

جعد *ja'd* N.M. curl ; curly lock [A]

جعل *ja'l* N.M. forgery fabrication جعلساز *ja'l-saz'* N.M. forgerer جعلسازی *ja'lsa'zī* N.M. forgery [A]

جعلی *ja''lī* ADJ. forged counterfeit spurious جعلی دستاویز *ja'lī dastavez'* N.F. forged document جعلی سکہ *ja''lī sik'kah* N.F. base coin counterfeit coin [A ~ PREC.]

جعفری *ja' farī* N.F. lattice ; trellis a kind of yellow flower [P]

جغادری *jagha'darī' جگادری jūgā'darī* ADJ. veteran seasoned huge

جغرافیہ *jūghrā'fiyah* N.M. geography جغرافیائی *jūghra-fiyā''ī* (ped. جغرافی *jūghrā'fī*) ADJ. geographical [A ~ G]

جفا *jafā'* N.F. oppression ; violence ; injury injustice جفا پیشہ *jafā'-peshah*, جفا جو *jafā'-joo*, جفا شعار *jafā'-she'ār'* جفا کار *jafā'-kār'* جفا کیش *jafā'-kesh* جفا گستر *jafā'-gūs'tar* ADJ. cruel oppressive unjust jilting beloved جفاکاری *jafā'-kā'rī* N.F. cruelty ; oppression ; tyranny unrequited love جفاکش *jafā'-kash* ADJ. hard-working ; diligent جفاکشی *ja'fā ka'shī* N.F. diligence جفا کفا *jafā' kafā'* N.F. hardship hard times trials and tribulations [A]

جفت *jūf't* ADJ. even (number) mated (with) ; coupled (with) N.M. pair of shoes

جفتہ *jūf'tah* N.M. fold crease wrinkle crack threads running together spot ADJ. bent wrinkled جفتے پڑنا *juf'te paṛ'nā* be threadbare have unwanted creases have (honour) blemished جفتی *jūf'tī* N.F. pairing or mating (of animals) جفتی کھانا *jūf'tī khā'nā* V.I. (of animals) pair ; copulate [P]

جفر *jaf'r* N.M. occult science of numbers and letters ; numerology cum-literology [A]

جکڑنا *ja'karnā* V.I. bind ; fasten ; tie pinion stiffen ; become rigid bring under control join together جکڑ بند *ja'kar-band'* ADJ. fight bound strung ; taut جکڑ جانا *ja'kar ja'na* V.T. be bound stiffen ; become rigid be joined together

جگ[1] *jag* N.M. (dial.) world universe others people ; masses ; public جگ بیتی *jag-bī'ti* N.F. things concerning other people : tales or deeds of other people جگ ہنسائی *jag-hańsā''ī* N.F. public ridicule

جگ[2] *jag* N.M. jug [E]

جگ *jūg* N.M. (dial.) epoch of the various ages of the world according to Hindus

جگ جگ *jūg' jūg* ADV. forever and ever eternally always جگ جگ جیو *jūg' jūg jī'yo* INT. live forever جگا جگا کر رکھنا *jūgā' jūgā' kar rakh'na* جگا کے رکھنا *jūga ke rakh'na* V.T. save little by little keep carefully

جگادری *jūgad'rī* ADJ. (same as جغادری ADJ. ★)

جگالی *jūga'lī* N.F. cud rumination جگالی کرنا *jūga'lī kar'na* (rus. جگالنا *jūgal'na* V.I. chew the cud ; ruminate

جگان *jūgan'* N.M. laundry ; bundle of washed clothes

جگانا *jaga'na* V.T. waken rouse from sleep make conscious of test efficacy of (magic) light ; kindle [~ جاگنا CAUS.]

جگانا *jūga'na* V.T. keep with care (only in)

جگت *ja'gat* N.F. rim of well N.M. (dial.) world universe جگت استاد *ja'gat-ūstād'*, جگت گرو *ja'gat-gū'roo* N.M. renowned teacher skilled craftsman [S]

جگت *jū'gat*, ضلع جگت *zi'la jū'gat* N.F. wit witticism joke pun trick coaxing enticing جگت باز *jū'gat-baz*, جگتی *jūg'tī*, جگتیا *jūgat'ya* N.M. witty person quibbler punster clever ; skilful cunning جگت بازی *jūgat ba'zī* N.F. witticism quibble pun جگت بولنا *jū'gat bol'na* V.I. pun quibble indulge in witticism جگت لگانا (یا ملانا) *jū'gat laga'na* (or *mīla'na*) V.T. coax intrigue entice جگت رنگ *jū'gat-rang* N.M. witty person quibbler punster

جگجگا *jag' jaga* N.M. brass tinsel thin ornamental brass plate

جگجگی *jig'jigī* N.F. sycophancy

جگر *ji'gar* N.M. liver (fig.) soul-heart (fig.) courage (fig.) endurance جگرا *jig'ra* N.M. (col.) courage endurance جگر بند *ji'gar-band* N.M. son child جگر چاک (یا خون) ہونا *ji'gar chak'* (or *khoon'*) *ho'na* V.I. suffer a lot جگر خراش *ji'gar-kharash'*, جگر دوز *ji'gar-doz* ADJ. pathetic; heart-rending جگر خون کرنا *ji'gar khoon' kar'na* V.T. & I. take great pains torment جگر سوختہ *ji'gar sokh'tah* ADJ. deep in love جگر سوز *ji'gar-soz'* ADJ. tormenting جگر سوزی *ji'gar-so'zī* N.F. suffering pains جگر فگار *ji'gar-figār'* ADJ. heart-broken heart-rending جگر کا ٹکڑا *ji'gar ka ṭūk'ra* N.M. son child darling جگر کاوی *ji'gar kā'vī* N.F. hard labour suffering جگر گوشہ *ji'gar go'shah*, لخت جگر *lakh't-e ji'gar* N.M. (fig.) son child darling جگری *jig'rī* (ped. *ji'garī*) ADJ. intimate (friend) hepatic [P]

جگمگانا *jagmagā'nā* V.I. glitter shine burn ; brightly جگمگ *jag'mag*, جگمگ جگمگ *jag'mag jag'mag* ADJ. & ADV. shining ; glittering جگمگ جگمگ کرنا *jag'mag* (*jag'mag*) *kar'nā* V.I. glisten glittle dazzle shine brightly

جگمگا *jag'magā* ADJ. illuminated glittering dazzling جگمگاہٹ *jagmagā'haṭ* N.F. dazzle sheen glitter ; brightness

جگنو *jūg'noo* N.F. firefly ; glow-worm (also جگنی *jug'nī*) thin diamond-cut locket (worn in string tied to neck)

جگہ *ja'gah* N.F. place room post vacancy occasion جگہ جگہ *ja'gah ja'gah* ADV. everywhere جگہ چھوڑنا *ja'gah chhoṛ'nā* V.I. leave a blank leave a post or place make room for جگہ دینا *ja'gah de'nā* V.T. make room for fix up (in some job) provide (someone) a place

جل[1] *jūl* N.M. trick fraud , deceit ; cheating circumvention جل باز *jūl'-baz* N.M. cheat knave جل دینا *jūl'-de'nā*, جل کھیلنا *jūl khel'na* V.T. cheat defraud dupe جل میں آنا *jūl' men ā'na* V.I. be tricked ; be cheated ; be defrauded be deceived be duped

جل[2] *jūl* N.F. horse-cloth housing

جل *jal* N.M. (rare) water جل بانک *jal'-bāṅk* N.F. (arch.) dagger-play in water ; marine dagger-play جل پان *jal-pān* N.M. (rare.) light repast جل پری *jal' pa'rī* N.F. mermaid جل ترنگ *jal'-tarang'* N.M. trough bowls or glasses partly filled with water and beaten with sticks to produce music ; musical bowls جل تھل *jal' thal'* N.M. marsh ; swamp ; bog water and land جل تھل ایک ہونا *jal' thal' ek' ho'na* V.I. rain abundantly جل توری *jal'-to'rī* N.M. (Hindu euphemism for) fish جل مانس *jal mā'nūs* N.M. merman

جل *jal'la* ADV. glorified ADJ. glorious جل شانہ *jal'la shā'nohoo*, جل جلالہ *jal'la jala'lohoo* PH. God is glorious [A ~ جلال]

جلا *jilā'* N.F. brightness sheen ; lustre polish burnish nickel plating clearness جلادار *jilā-dar'* ADJ. bright glittering ; glistening nickel polish جلا دینا *jilā' de'nā* V.T. polish burnish purify جلا کار *jilā' kar'* N.M. polisher nickel plater burnisher [A]

جلاب *julab'* (ped. *jūllab'*) N.M. purgative julep جلاب دینا *jūlāb' de'na* V.T. administer a purgative جلاب لگنا *jūlab' lag'na* V.I. have motions (owing to purgative or fear) جلاب لینا *jūlāb' le'na* V.I. take a purgative [A ~ P گلاب]

جلاپا *jalā'pa* N.M. jealous spite [~ جلنا]

جلاجل *jalā'-jil* N.M. PL. anklets [A]

جلاد *jallād'* N.M. executioner ADJ. cruel , tyrannous جلادِ فلک *jal lā'd-e fa'lak* N.M. Mars جلادی *jallā'dī* N.F. cruelty ; tyranny [A ~ جلد]

جلادت *jalā'dat* N.F. tyranny endurance [A]

جلال *jalāl* N.M. majesty grandeur glory awe-inspiring qualities holy person's wrath جلالی *jalā'lī* ADJ. majestic glorious awe-inspiring wrathful invoking God's awe-inspiring attributes جلالت *jalā'lat* N.F. majesty dignity جلالۃ الملک *jalā'lat-ul ma'lik* N.M. His Majesty [A]

جلانا *jilā'na*, جلا دینا *jila' de'na* V.T. quicken (the dead) revive give a new lease of life

جلانا *jalā'na* V.T. (see under جلنا V.I. ★)

جلاوطن *jalā'-va'tan* ADJ. exile ; banished person جلاوطن کرنا *jalā'-va'tan kar'na* V.T. exile ; banish جلاوطن ہونا *jalā'-va'tan ho'na* V.I. be exiled; be banished جلاوطنی *jalā'-vat'nī* (ped. *va'tanī*) ADJ. exile ; banishment جلاوطنی کی زندگی گزارنا (یا بسر کرنا) *jalā-vat'nī kī zin'dagī gūzar'na* (or *basar' kar'na*) V.I. live in exile lead the life of an exile [P ~ A]

جلاہا *jūlā'ha* N.M. (F. جلاہی *jūlā'hī*) (same as جولاہا N.M. ★)

جلب *jal'b* N.M. getting ; darvation ; acquisition جلبِ منفعت *jal'b-e man'fa'at* N.M. deriving benefit [A]

جِلد *jil'd* N.F. skin binding (of book) volume copy جلد باندھنا *jil'd bandh'na* V.T. bind (a book) جلدساز *jil'd-saz* (arch. جلدبند *jil'd-band*, جلد گر *jil'd-gar*) N.M. book-binder جلدسازی *jil'd-sa'zī* (or arch. جلدبندی *jil'd-ban'dī*, جلدگری *jil'd ga'rī*) N.F. bookbinding جلدی *jil'dī* ADJ. skin جلدی امراض *jil'dī amraz'* N.M. PL. skin diseases [A]

جلد *jal'd* ADV. soon quickly , swiftly at once جلد باز *jal'd-baz* ADJ. hasty rash impetuous جلد بازانہ *jal'd-baza'nah* ADJ. hasty precipitate ; expeditions ADV. hurriedly ; hastily expeditiously rashly ; impetuously جلد بازی *jal'd ba'zī* N.F. haste expedition جلدی *jal'dī* N.F. hurry ; haste quickness , swiftness celerity جلدی سے *jal'dī se* ADV. quickly ; swiftly at once speedily جلدی کرنا *jal'dī kar'na* V.I. hurry up make haste hasten expedite [A]

جلسہ *jal'sah* N.M. public meeting meeting gathering get together (in prayer) final sitting جلسہ کرنا *jal'sah kar'na* V.I. hold a meeting جلسہ ہونا *jal'sah ho'na* V.I. (of meeting) be held [A ~ جلوس]

جلق *ja'laq* N.M. masturbation ; self-abuse ; self-relief جلق لگانا *ja'laq laga'na* V.I. masturbate

جلنا *jal'na* V.I. burn be kindled be enraged feel jealous be inflamed with love, etc. جلن *ja'lan* N.F. burning ; sensation inflammation heart burn heart-burning jealously sense of frustration جل اٹھنا *jal' uṭh'na* V.I. (or fire) break out جل جانا *jal' ja'na* V.T. be burnt ; be consumed be cut to the quick become jealous جل مرنا *jal' mar'na* V.I. be burnt to death جلا *ja'la* ADJ. (F. *jalī*) burnt enraged جلا بھنا *ja'la bhu'na* ADJ. scorched enraged جلے پاؤں کی بلی *ja'le pa''on kī bil'lī* PH. uneasy roving جلے پر نون چھڑکنا *ja'le par noon chhiṛak'na* V.I add insult to injury جلی کٹی سنانا *ja'lī ka'ṭī sūna'na* V.T. say things bitter and stinging جلانا *jala'na* V.T. burn light ; kindle inflame make jealous cut to the quick جلا دینا (یا ڈالنا) *jala' de'na* (or *ḍal'na*) V.T. burn down consume جلوانا *jalva'na* V.T. cause to burn cause to be burnt

جلندھر *jalan'dhar*, جلندر *jalan'dar* N.M. dropsy [~ S جل water]

جلف *ja'laf* N M. (PL. اجلاف *ajlaf'*) mean person [A]

جلو *jilau* retinue equipage bridle کے جلو میں *ke jilau meṅ* ADV. in company (of) ahead (of) in front of جلوخانہ *jilau'-kha'nah* N.M. porch ; vestibule open space opposite palace gate جلودار *jilau'-dār* N.M. member of the royal retinue companion royal servant [P]

جلوت *jal'vat* N.F. public place crowd multitude جلوت میں *jal'vat meṅ* ADV. in public جلوت و خلوت *jal'vat-o-khal'vat* N.F. (one's) public and private life جلوت و خلوت میں *jal'vat-o-khal'vat meṅ* ADV. in public and private [A]

جلوس *jūloos'* N.M. procession accession to throne ; accession (rare) sitting [A]

جلوہ *jal'vah* N.M. manifestation splendid sight bridal display appearance (of sweetheart, etc.) lustre ; effulgence جلوہ گاہ *jal'va gah* N.F. place of manifestation place of display nuptial throne جلوہ گر *jal'va-gar* ADJ. manifest present ; in sight جلوہ گر ہونا *jal'va-gar ho'na* V.I. come make (oneself) manifest جلوہ گری *jal'va-ga'rī* N.F. manifestation splendid appearance جلوۂ طور *jal'va-e toor'* N.M. manifestation of God to Moses at the Sinai Mountain [A]

جلی *ja'lī* ADJ. salient conspicuous evident (of type, etc.) bold (of handwriting) plain and large خط جلی khat' t-e ja'lī N.M large plain handwriting جلی حروف ja'lī ḥ'roof', N.M. & PL. bold letters or type جلی قلم jal'lī qa'lam N.M. & ADV. (in) bold letters (or type) ; type or bold letters ذکر جلی zik'r-e ja'lī N.M. invoking God's name loudly [A]

جلیبی jale'bī N.F. fried coil kind of sweetmeat

جلیس jalīs' (also ہم جلیس ham-jalīs') N.M. (PL. جلسا jū'lasā') comrade ; companion [A ~ جلوس]

جلیل jalīl' ADJ. (PL. اجلہ ajil'lah) great illustrious glorious جلیل القدر jalī'l-ūl-qad'r ADJ. illustrious glorious one of the elite of society [A ~ جلال]

جم jam, جمشید jamshed' (or shīd') N.M. name of mythical Persian king جمجاہ jam-jah' ADJ. glorious like Jamshed [P]

جمادات jamādāt N.M. minerals inorganic matter [A ~ جماد]

جمادی الاخریٰ jūmā'd-al ūkh'ra, جمادی الثانیہ jūmā'd-as sā'niah (col. جمادی الاخر jamā'diy-ūl-ākhir, جمادی الثانی jamā'diy-ūs-sā'nī) N.M. sixth month of Hijri calendar جمادی الاولیٰ jūmā-d-al-oo'lā (col. جمادی الاول jamā'diy-ūl-av'val) N.M. fifth month of Hijri calendar [A ~ جماد]

جمازہ jammā'zah N.M. she-camel dromedary [A]

جماع jimā' N.M. sexual intercourse ; copulation ; coition جماع کرنا jimā'' kar'nā V.T. copulate (with woman) [A ~ جمع]

جماعت jamā''at N.F. party body ; organization association ; society class congregation congregational prayers جماعت بندی jamā' at-ban'dī N.F. classification جماعت وکلا jamā''at-e vūkalā' N.F. bar association جماعت وار jamā''at-var ADJ. class-wise جماعت سے کرامت ہے jamā''at se karā'mat hai PROV. union is strength جماعہ دار jamā''ah-dār N.M. (ped. for جمعدار N.M. ★) [A ~ جمع]

جماگی jumā'gī N.F. weak-end pocket money [P ~ A جمعہ]

جمال jamāl' N.M. beauty prettiness loveliness elegence grace جمالی jamā'lī ADJ. manifesting divine mercy and beneficence merciful love inspired N.M. a kind of muskmelon

جمال گوٹہ jamāl' go'ṭah, جمال گوٹا jamāl' go'ṭā N.M. a kind of purgative nut drug prepared from it

جمانا jamā'nā V.T. freeze congeal ; coagulate curdle impress hit (blow, etc.) fix , affix جماؤ jamā''o N.M. freeze congealment , coagulation cohesion consolidation crowd جماوٹ jamā'vaṭ N.F. freezing congealment fitting [~ جمنا CAUS.]

جماہی jamā'hī, جمائی jemā''ī N.F. yawn gape جماہی لینا jamā'hī le'nā V.I. yawn gape

جم جم jam' jam ADV. (dial.) forever and ever جم ہی جم jam' hī jam PH. (euph) nothing never

جمخانہ jim-khā'nah N.M. gymkhana [E game + P خانہ]

جمشید jamshed' or jamshīd' N.M. (same as جم N.M. ★)

جمع jam'' (col. ja'ma') N.F. addition plural total ; sum-total receipts deposits collection ; accumulation state revenue جمعبندی jam'' ban''dī N.F. revenue ; settlement settlement record جمع جتھا ja'ma'' ja'thā N.F. savings جمع (و) خرچ jam''(-o-)khar'ch N.M. receipts and disbursements debit and credit cash account جمع کرنا jam'' kar'nā V.I. add up total amass collect bring together deposit جمع نویس jam''-navīs' N.M. (arch.) accountant جمع ہونا jam'' ho'nā V.I. be added total be collected ; be gathered together come together be deposited amass

جمعدار jam''-dār' (ped. جماعہ دار jamā''ah-dār') N.M. minor army ; official sweeper [P ~ جماعہ]

جمعہ jūm''ah (ped. jū'mo'ah) N.M. Friday جمعہ جمعہ آٹھ دن (کی پیدائش) jūm''a jūm''ah āṭh' din (kī paidā''sh) PROV. (existence of) very few days جمعرات jū'me'rāt (ped. jū'm'a-rāt') N.F. Thursday [A ~ جمع]

جمعیت jam'iy'yat N.F. organisation league gathering peace ; transquillity satisfaction جمعیت اقوام jam'iy'yat-e aqvām' N.F. league of Nations جمعیت خاطر jam'iy'yat-e khā'tir N.F. peace of mind [A ~ جمع]

جم غفیر jam'm-e ghafīr' N.M. milling crowd [~A]

جمگھٹا jam'ghaṭā, جمگھٹ jam'ghaṭ N.M. crowd

جمل ja'mal N.M. camel dromedary [A]

جمل jū'mal N.M. (PL. of جملہ N.M. ★)

جمل jūm'mal N.M. system of reckoning according to 'abjad' order in which every succeeding letter has been assigned an ascending values [A]

جملہ jūm'lah N.M. (PL. جمل jū'mal) sentence clause all the whole ADJ. entire whole جملہ معترضہ jūm'la-e mo''tarīzah N.M. parenthetical clause or sentence (something said) by the way ; by the by witty interpolation فی الجملہ fil-jūm'lah ADV. on the whole *min-jŭm'lah* ADV. out of (these) of all (these [A]

جمن *ja'man* N.F. (Persianized form of جمنا N.F. ★)

جمنا¹ *jam'nā* (ped. *ja'mūnā*), جمن *jaman* N.F. the Jamuna (a northern India river sacred to Hindus) گنگ و جمن *gań'g-o ja'man* N.M. PL. the Ganges and the Jamuna گنگا جمنی *gań'ga-jam'nī* of variegated hue with gold fillings on silver

جمنا² *jam'nā* V.I. freeze congeal ; coagulate curdle stick be firmly established have a firm hold consolidate take a firm stand

جمناسٹک *jimnas ṭik* N.M. gymnastics [E]

جمود *jŭmood'* N.M. inertness listlessness inactivity state of suspended animation lack of vitality lack of progress پر جمود (کی حالت) طاری ہونا *par jumood' (kī ḥā'lat) ṭā'rī ho'nā* V.I. be inactive [A]

جمہور *jŭmhoor'* (col. *jam'hoor'*) (PL. جماہیر *jamā'hīr*) masses people جمہوری *jŭmhoo'rī* ADJ. democratic of the masses جمہوریت *jŭmhooriy'yat* N.F. democracy republic ; democratic State بنیادی جمہوریت *bŭnyā'dī jŭmhooriy'yat* N.F. Basic Democracy controlled democracy guided democracy [A]

جمیع *jamī'* ADJ. all whole [~ جمع]

جمیل *jamīl'* ADJ. (F. or PL. جمیلہ *jamī'lah*) beautiful pretty comely sweet lovely elegant graceful [A ~ جمال]

جن *jin'* N.M. (PL. جنات *jinnat'* or lit. جنہ *jin'nah*) spirit ; ginius ; jinnee headstrong person one with extraordinary capacity for work جن اتارنا *jin' ŭtar'nā* V.T. exorcize جن چڑھانا *jin' chaṛh'nā* be possessed fly into passion جنات *jinnat'* N.M. PL. genii جناتی *jinna'tī* ADJ. supernatural of genii difficult (word or style) bad (hand) [A]

جنا *ja'nā* N.M. (rare) (F. جنی *ja'nī* person ADJ. begotten [~ جننا]

جناب *janab'* N.M. Mr. the honourable N.F. (rare) brink (royal, etc.) court جناب اقدس *jan'ab-e aq'das* INT. your honour جناب عالی *janā'b-e 'ā'lī* INT. respected sir ; your honour عالیجناب *'ā'lī janab'* ADV. the respected ; the honourable جناب من *janab-e man* INT. my dear sir [A]

جنابت *janā'bat* N.F. pollution (resulting from coition) غسل جنابت *ghŭs'l-e janā'bat* N.M. post-coition bath [A]

جنایت *jinā'yat* N.F. sin crime [A]

جناح *jinah'* N.M. wing ; pinion wing of army ذوالجناح *zŭl janāh'* N.M. (see under ذو PREF. [A]

جنازہ *janā'zah* N.M. funeral bier corpse funeral prayers جنازہ اٹھانا *janā'zah ŭṭhā'nā* V.T. take out funeral procession جنازہ پڑھنا *janā'zah paṛh'nā* V.T. say funeral prayers ; perform funeral rites نماز جنازہ *namā'z-e janā'zah* N.F. funeral prayers غائبانہ (نماز) جنازہ *ghā'ibā'nah (namā'z-e) janā'zah* N.F. funeral prayers in absentia (کا) جنازہ نکالنا *(ka) janā'zah ni'kalnā* V.I. (of funeral procession) be taken out (of person) die (of plan, endeavour) come to naught [A]

جنانا *janā'nā* V.T. (of midwife) assist in delivery جنائی *janā''ī* N.F. midwife [~ جننا CAUS.]

جنبان *jŭm'bāń* ADJ. shaking vibrating trempulous جنبانی *jumbā'nī* SUF. initiating [P ~ جنبیدن]

جنبش *jum'bish* N.F. movement ; motion gesture turn جنبش دینا *jŭm'bish de'nā* V.T. move shake [P ~ جنبیدن]

جنبہ *jam'bah* N.F. (rare) side ; part جنبہ داری *jam'bādā'rī* N.F. partiality جنبہ (داری) کرنا *jam'bah (dārī) kar'nā* V.T. show partiality ; be partial to [A]

جنت *jan'nat'* N.F. (PL. جنات *jannāt'*) paradise ; heaven (lit.) garden (fig.) bliss جنت نگاہ *jan'nat-e nigāh'* N.F. something wonderful to look at delectable sight جنتی *jan'natī* ADJ. heavenly blessed N.M. blessed person [A]

جنتا *jan'tā* N.M. (dial.) people ; masses ; public [S]

جنتر *jan'tar* N.M. (dial.) charm still machine (also جنتری *jan'tarī*) perforated steel plate for drawing wire جنتر منتر *jan'tar man'tar* N.M. (dial.) charm magic observatory [S]

جنتری *jan'tarī* N.M. almanac perforated steel plate for drawing wire [S ~ PREC.]

جنٹلمین *jan'ṭal-main* N.M. gentleman جنٹلمینی *jan'ṭal mai'nī* N.F. foppishness [E]

جنجال *jańjal'*, جان کا جنجال *jān kā jańjāl'* N.M. encumbrance difficult embrassment heavy work large family جنجال میں پڑنا (یا پھنسنا) *jańjal' meń paṛ'nā* (or *phańs'nā*) V.I. be beset with difficulties have too many encumbrances have very heavy work have to support a large family جنجالی *jańja'lī* N.M. quarrelsome or troublesome person

جند بیدستر *jŭn'd-e bedas'tar* N.M. otter's dried testics (used as drug) [P]

جنڈی jinda'rī N.F. (W. dial.) life جنڈی اجڑا (یا پٹیا) jind'rī ūj'ṛa (or pī'ṭā) ADJ. (W. dial.) dead cuss'd [P ~ جان DIM]

جنرل jain'ral N.M. General ADJ. general جنرل پوسٹ آفس jain'ral post' ā'fis N.M. G.P.O. General Post Office جنرل نالج jain'ral nālij general, knowledge جنرل ہیڈکوارٹر jain'ral haiḍ' ko'ār'ṭar N.M. General Headquarters ; G.H.Q. [E]

جنس jin's N.F. (logic) genus sex kind (opp of cash) cereals thing ; material ; stuff category (gram.) gender ادنیٰ جنس ad'nā jin's N.F. inferior stuff. etc. اعلیٰ جنس a''lā jin's N.F. superior stuff ; quality stuff (etc.) جنس قوی jin's-e qa'vī N.F. the sterner sex جنس کثیف jin's-e kasīf N.F. (joc.) the ungainly sex جنس لطیف jin's-e latīf' N.F. the fair sex جنس وار jin's-vār ADV. quality-wise N.M. revenue (etc.) schedule of taxable produce (imports, etc.) ابنائے جنس abnā'-e jin's N.M. fellow human beings بجنسہٖ bi-jin'sehī ADV. exactly as it is in every particular the whole of it جنسی jin'sī ADJ. sexual sex جنسی بھوک jin'sī bhook' N.F. appetite جنسی کشش jin'sī ka'shish N.F. sex appeal ہم جنسی ham-jin'sī N.F. homogeneity similarity homosexuality ADV. homosexual جنسیات jinsiyyāt' N.F. sex; science of sex; sexology جنسیت jinsīy'yat N.F (gram.) gender sex لاجنسی lā-jin'sī ADJ. asexual N.F. asexuality ہم جنسیت ham jinsiy'yat N.F. homosexuality. [A ~ G]

جنکشن jank'shan N.M. junction railway junction [E]

جنگ jang N.F. war battle fight conflict جنگ آزما jang āz'mā N.M. & ADJ. soldier جنگ آزمودہ jang-āzmoo'dah ADJ. & N. M. veteran war-veteran جنگجو jang'-joo' ADJ. quarrelsome, contentious N.M. soldier جنگ دیدہ jang'-dī'dah ADJ. war جنگ زرگری jang-e zar'-garī N.F. collusive fight جنگ کرنا jang' kar'nā V.T. wage war ; make war fight quarrel جنگ و جدل jang-o-jadal N.F. armed clash battle fighting melee brawl conflict جنگ ہونا jang ho'nā V.I. (of war) be بعد از جنگ ba''d az jang ADJ postwar ADV. after the battle قبل از جنگ qab'l az jang' ADJ. prewar ADV. before the battle جنگی jan'gī ADJ. martial military war warlike huge ; large, big جنگی بیڑا jan'gī be'rā N.M. fleet, armada Navy جنگی پرنالہ jan'gī parnā'lah N.M drain with a gargoyle جنگی جہاز jan'gī jahāz' N.M man-of-war جنگی فوج jan'gī fauj N.F. war-levy combatant force [P]

جنگل jan'gal N.M. jungle ; wood ; forest جنگل میں منگل jan'gal meṅ man'gal N.M. facilities of urban life in backward area illuminations, etc. in a deserted place colonization, etc. of desert area جنگل میں منگل ہونا jan'gal meṅ man'gal ho'nā V.I. be on the spree be decorated (etc.) be colonized be urbanized جنگل میں مور ناچا کس نے دیکھا jan'gal meṅ mor' nā'chā kis' ne de'khā PROV. wasting one's sweetness in the desert air [P]

جنگلہ jang'lah, جنگلا jang'lā railing fence enclosure sheet, etc. with a gold lace جنگلا لگانا jang'lā lagā'nā V.T. enclosure fence build a rail fence around جنگلی jang'lī ADJ. wild savage boorish جنگلی بلی jang'lī bil'lī N.M. wild cat جنگلی پیاز jang'lī payāz' N.M. squill جنگلی سور jang'lī sū''ar N.M. boar (fig.) stout ungainly bully جنگلی کوا jang'lī kav'vā N M. raven

جنم ja'nam N.M. (dial.) birth life cycle of existence جنم اشٹمی N.M. (dial.) ja'nam ash'-ṭamī N.F. (dial.) Hindu festival of Krishna's birthday جنم بھومی ja'nam bhoo'mī, جنم استھان ja'nam asthān' N.M. (dial.) birth-place native country ; motherland جنم پتری ja'nam pat'rī N.F. (dial.) horoscope جنم جلا ja'nam ja'lā, ADJ. (F. جنم جلی ja'nam ja'lī) cursed ; cussed unfortunate little جنم جنم ja'nam ja'nam ADV. always جنم دن ja'nam din N.M. (dial.) birthday جنم روگی ja'nam ro'gī ADJ. unfortunate valetudinarian جنم مرن کا ja'nam ma'ran kā ADJ. life-long جنم نہ دیکھا بوریا سپنے آئی کھاٹ ja'nam nā de'khā bo'rīyā sūp'ne ā''i khāṭ PROV. destitute person emulating the rich جنم لینا ja'nam le'nā V.I. be born come into existence جنم کا ja'nam kā ADJ. inherent inborn lifelong جنم کے اندھے نام نین سکھ ja'nam ke an'dhe nām nain sukh PROV. a disabled person calling himself Samson

جنوانا janvā'nā V.T. (same as جنانا V.T. ★)

جنوائی jan'-vā''ī son in law گھر جنوائی ghar' jan'vā''ī N.M. man putting up with in-laws

جنوب janoob' N.M. south (rape) south wind جنوبی janoo'bī ADJ. southern نصف کرہ جنوبی nis'f kūra-e janoo'bī N.M. Southern Hemisphere [A]

جنوری jan'varī N.M. January [E]

جنون jūnoon' N.M. madness, lunacy ; insanity fit for frenzy ; passion, fury zeal جنون آنا jūnoon ā'nā V.I. be enraged جنون چڑھنا jūnoon' chaṛh'nā V.T. fly into passion be furious have a fit of frenzy go mad have a zeal (for) جنون ہونا jūnoon' ho'nā V.I. be mad have a zeal (for) جنونی jūnoo'nī ADJ. & N.M mad insane rash ; impulsive zealous : zealot

جنّہ jin'nah N.M. PL. genii [A ~ SING. جن]

جنہیں jin'heṅ PROV. whom whomsoever

جنیا jan'ya N.F. darling [~ P جان]

جنین janin' N.M. embryo ; foetus [A]

جنیئو jane''oo N.M. (dial.) sacred thread worn by Hindus جنیئو کا ہاتھ jane''oo kā hath' N.M. slauting stroke (in fancing, etc.)

جو jo PROV. who what which that CONJ. if ; in case جو جو jo' jo' PROV. whoever whatever whichever جو چیز jo' chīz, جو کچھ jo' kuchh PROV. whatever whichever جو کوئی jo' ko''ī PROV. whoever whatever (thing) whichever جو ہو سو ہو jo ho' so ho' PH. come what may ; no matter what the consequences جو بولے سو گھی کو جائے jo bo'le so ghī' ko jā''e PROV. whoever ventures a suggestion should come جو پھل چکھا نہیں وہی میٹھا jo phal' chak 'khā nahīṅ' vo'hī mīthā PROV. forbidden fruit tastes sweet جو چڑھے گا سو گرے گا jo cha'ṛhegā so gi'regā PROV. pride goeth before a fall جو سحری کھائے سو روزہ رکھے jo sa'ḥarī khā''e so ro'zah rak'khe PROV. he must suffer pain who has stood to gain جو گرجتے ہیں برستے نہیں jo ga'rajte haiṅ ba'raste nahīṅ' PROV. barking dogs seldom bite جو ہانڈی میں ہوگا وہی نکلے گا jo hāṅ'ḍī meṅ ho'gā vo'hī nik'legā PROV. nothing comes out of a sack but what is put in it

جو jau N.M. barley garlic capsule stitch one-third of an inch ADJ. (also جو بھر jau' bhar a little small جو کوب jau-kob' ADJ. powder thick grain جو کوب کرنا jau-kob kar'nā V.T. powder to thick grain جویں javīṅ' ADJ. barley نانِ جویں nā'n-e javīṅ' N.M. brown bread poor livelihood [P]

جو jav, جوِّ بسیط jav'v-e basīt' N.F. (lit.) space ; region beyond atmosphere

جو[1] joo (in const. جوئے joo''e), جوئبار joo''e-bār N.M. brook ; stream جوئے شیر لانا joo''e shīr' lānā V.I. do a Herculean task ; accomplish the impossible [P]

جو[2] joo SUF. seeking ; seeker [P]

جوا[1] joo''ā N.M. gambling ; playing with dice any game of chance with stake جوا کھیلنا joo''ā khel'nā V.I. gamble جواری jo'ā'rī N.M gambler جواری ڈھنڈاری jo'ā'rī ḍhūṅḍā'rī N.M. (usu. PL.) gambler walking in evil ways جوئے باز joo''e-bāz' N.M. gambler جوئے خانہ joo''e-khā'nah N.M. gambling den

جوا[2] joo''ā N.M. yoke کا جوا اتارنا kā joo'ā ūtār'nā V.I. unyoke be freed

جوا

جواب javāb' N.M. answer ; reply defence match; parallel dismissal ; discharge ; sack refusal جوابِ باصواب jqvā'b-e bā-savāb' N.M. proper answer جوابِ جاہلاں باشد خموشی javā'b-e ja'hilāṅ bā'shad khamo'shī PROV. reticence is the safest reply to a fool (or uncultured person) جوابِ دعویٰ javā'b-e dā''vā (col. javāb' dā''vā) N.M. answer to plaint جواب دِہ javāb'-deh ADJ. answerable ; accountable N.M. respondent جواب دِہی javāb'-de'hī liability ; responsibility defence (in law suit, etc.) جواب دِہی کرنا javāb' de'hī kar'nā V.I. defend (in law) be held responsible explain ; account for جواب دِہی سے بری کرنا javāb' de'hi se ba'rī kar'nā V.T. no longer to hold responsible ; exonerate جواب دینا یا دے دینا javāb' de'nā (or de' de'nā) V.T. & I. answer ; reply explain ; account for sack ; dismiss discharge refuse جواب سوال javāb' so'āl' N.M. questions and answers argument ; dialogue جوابِ صاف javāb-e sāf, صاف جواب sāf' 'javāb' N.M. جواب طلب javāb' ta'lab ADJ. reply paid (letter etc.) (matters) calling for an explanation جواب طلب کرنا javāb' ta'lab kar'nā V.I. ask (or call) for an explanation جواب طلبی javāb'ta'labī N.F. explanation calling (someone's) explanation کی جواب طلبی کرنا kī javāb' ta'labī kar'nā V.T. call (someone's) explanation قطعی جواب qat''ī javāb' N.M. definite reply categorical No جواب ملنا javāb' mil'nā V.I. get a reply be asked ; be dismissed ; be discharged be refused (something) جواب ہونا javāb' ho'nā V.I. be sacked be refused جوابی javā'bī ADJ. post paid (letter, etc.) retaliatory counterpart N.M. chorus in elegiac recitation counterpart (arch.) respondent

جواد javād' ADJ. generous ; munificent N.M. Bountiful (as one of God's attributes) [A ~ جود]

جوّاد javvād' ADJ. munificent [A ~ جود]

جوار[1] javār' N.F. corn, millet

جوار[2] javār' N.M. flood-tied جوار بھاٹا javār'-bhā'ṭā N.M. ebb and flow of the tide

جوار[3] javār' (col. jivār') N M. vicinity ; neighbourhood ; area [~ A جواری]

جوارح *java'reh* N.M. PL. limbs اعضا و جوارح *a-za'-o-java'reh* N.M. PL. body limbs and organs [A]

جوارش *java'rish* N.F. digestive medicine جوارش جالینوس *java'rish-e jālīnoos* N.M. digestive medicine named after Galen [A]

جواری *jo'a''rī* N.M. (see under جوا ★)

جواری *java'rī* N.F. cross-string over bridge of stringed musical instrument

جواز *javaz'* N.M. justification legality; lawfulness propriety [A]

جواکھار *ja'va khar'* N.M. salt obtained from burnt barley; barley-salt

جوالا *java'la* V.T. wheat adulterated with barley [~ جَو *jau*]

جوالا مکھی *jo'a'la-mukhī* N.F. (dial.) volcano [S ~ جوالا flame]

جوالہ *javvā'lah* ADJ. spinning fast-revolving شعلۂ جوالہ *sho''la-e javvā'lah* N.M. spinning flame (fig.) blazing beauty (fig.) evasive sweetheart [A ~ جولان]

جوان *javan'* N.M. youth young man ordinary soldier; jawan ADJ. (lit. also جواں *javān*) adult grown up young جواں بخت *javān bakht* ADJ. fortunate; having bright prospects جواں سال *javān'-sal'* ADJ. youthful جواں مرد *javān' mar'd* N.F. man of marriageable age جوانمرد *javān mar'd* ADJ. brave; bold; courageous heroic generous; magnanimous N.M. hero brave man fine young fellow gallant نوجوان *nau-javan'* ADJ. young N.M. young man; youth جوانمردی *javān-mar'dī* N.F. bravery; courage gallantry generosity; magnanimity جوانمرگ *javān'-mar'g*, جوانا مرگ *java'na mar'g* ADJ. dead in the prime of life cursed (owing to debauchery or high-handedness) جواں موت *javan' maut* N.F. untimely death; death in the prime of life نوخیز جوان *nau-khez' java n* N.M. teenager جوانی *java'nī* N.F. ★ [P]

جوانب *java'nib* N M. PL. vicinity environs part (of the country); area اطراف و جوانب *atrā'f-o java'nib* N.M. PL. vicinity; neighbour parts; quarter; area sides [A ~ SING جانب]

جوانی *java'nī* N.F. youth, season of youth manhood adolescence puberty اٹھتی جوانی *uth'tī javā'nī* N.F. flower of youth freshness of youth جوانی چڑھنا *java'nī charh'nā* V.T. be adolescent attain puberty be full of youthful lust attain youthful vigour جوانی دیوانی *javā'nī divā'nī* PH youth is blind impulsive youth جوانی ڈھلنا *java'nī ḍhal'na* V T. become old cross the threshold of youth lose youthful vigour جوش جوانی *jo'sh e javā'nī* N.M. exuberance of youth ardour of youth [P ~ جوان]

جواہر *java'hir*, جواہرات *javāhirāt'* N.M. PL. jewelry; jewellery essences; quintessence جواہر خانہ *java'hir khā'nah* N.M. jewelry vault جواہر نگار *java'hir-nigār'* ADJ. studded with jewels ornamented زر و جواہر *zar-o java'hir* N.M. jewelry; jewellery wealth [A ~ SING جوہر ~ P گوہر]

جوبلی *jūb'lī* (or *job'lī*) jubilee ڈائمنڈ (یا سلور یا گولڈن) جوبلی *ḍā'yamanḍ* (or *silver* or *golden*) *jubilee* [E]

جوبن *jo'ban* N M. female beauty bloom of (female) youth well-developed breasts puberty جوبن ابھرنا *jo'ban u'bharnā* V.I. (of breasts) swell جوبن پر آنا *jo'ban par a'nā* V.I. reach the age of puberty bloom جوبن پھٹ پڑنا *jo'ban phaṭ par'nā* V.I. (of woman's youth bloom) (of breasts) swell جوبن ڈھلنا *jo'ban ḍhal'na* V.I. (of woman's (youth) begin to decay جوبن لٹنا *jo'ban lūṭ'nā* V.I. be ravished جوبن کی بہاریں لوٹنا *jo'ban kī bahā-reṅ looṭ'nā* V I. ravish جوبن کی ماتی *jo'ban kī ma'tī* N.F. woman in bloom of youth

جوت *jot* N.F. light lustre wares in shop string which pans of scale are tied cultivation tilling cultivated land land rent paid by tiller strap fastening yoke, etc. to ox's neck جوت جگانا *jot jaga'na* V.I. kindle the light (of)

جوت *joot* N.M. shoe جوت پڑنا (یا لگنا) *joot' par'na* (or *lag'na*) have a shoe-beating be punished have rebuff suffer the loss (of) جوت چلنا *joot chal'nā* V.I. fight it out to settle mutual differences [~ FOLL.]

جوتا *joo'tā* N.M shoe pair of shoes جوتا اٹھانا *joo tā uṭhā'nā* V.T. & I. serve devotedly defy pilfer shoes جوتا اچھلنا (یا چلنا) *joo'tā u'chhal-nā* (or *chal'nā*) V.I. have a boorish fight جوتا برسنا *joo'tā ba'rasnā* V.I. have a shoe-beating be hailed with shoes fight with shoes جوتا لگنا *joot'a lag'nā* V.T. & I. (of shoes) pinch feel ashamed incur a loss جوتا مارنا *joo'tā mar'nā* V.T. give (someone) a shoe beating administer a sharp rebuff put to shame by kind treatment جوتی *joo'tī* N.F. ★

جوتش *jo'tish*, جیوتش *jyo'tish* N.M. astrology جوتشی *jot'shī*, جیوتشی *jyo'tishī* N.M. astrologer [S]

جوتنا *jot'na* V.T. till; plough yoke force (someone) to do something

جوتی *joo'tī* N.F shoe pair of shoes sandals slippers جوتی پر جوتی چڑھنا *joo'tī par joo'tī charh'na*

v.i. be an omen of impending travel جوتی (کی نوک) پر مارنا joo'tī (kī nok') par mar'na v.t. not to care a damn spurn جوتی پر رکھ کر روٹی دینا joo'tī par rakh' kar ro'ṭī de'na v.i. feed humiliatingly جوتی (یا جوت) پیزار joo'tī (or joot') paizar' n.f. quarrel at a low level constant tiffs جوتی پیزار ہونا joo'tī paizar' ho'na v.i. have a quarrel at a low level جوتی چھپائی joo'tī chhūpa''ī n.f. money extracted by bride's sisters from groom by concealing his shoes on wedding day جوتی چور joo'tī-chor n.m. shoe lifter adj. mean of no consequence جوتی خور joo'tī kho'r(a) adj. given to having a shoe beating جوتیاں اٹھانا joo'tiyan ūṭha'na v.t serve with devotion جوتیاں چٹخاتے پھرنا joo'tiyan cha kha'te phir'na v.i. loaf walk about be jobless جوتیاں سیدھی کرنا joo'tiyan sī'dhī kar'na v.t. serve with devotion جوتیاں گانٹھنا joo'tiyan ganth'na v.i. mend shoes جوتیاں کھانا joo'tiyan kha'na v.i. have shoe-beating be taunted be humiliated جوتیاں مارنا joo'tiyan mar'na v.t. give a shoe-beating taunt humiliate جوتیوں میں دال بٹنا joo'tiyon men dal baṭ'na have a domestic quarrel [~ جوتا]

جوٹ joṭ n.m. pair (of oxen) under one yoke adj. match ; equal [~ جوتا]

جود jood' n.m. generosity ; munificence liberality جود و سخاوت joo''d-o sakha(vat) n.f. generosity [A]

جوجو joo' joo' n.m. (dial.) bogey

جوجھنا joojh'na v.i. fight , take up arms against جوجھ مرنا joojh' mar'na v.i. die fighting

جودت jau'dat n.f. sharp intellect keen apprehension جودت طبع jau'dat-e tab'' n.f. quick-wittedness ingenuity

جودی joo'dī n.f. hilltop in Ararat range where Noah's Arch came to rest in Deluge [A ~ H]

جور jaur n.m. tyranny ; oppresion high handedness جور و ستم jaur-o si'tam, ظلم و جور zūl'mo jaur n.m. oppression and tyranny [A]

جورو jo'roo n.f. wife جورو کا بھائی jo'roo ka bha''ī n.m. wife's brother ; brother-in-law ساری خدائی ایک طرف جورو کا بھائی ایک طرف sa'rī khuda''ī ek ta'raf jo roo ka bha''ī ek ta'raf prov. one would listen to the wife's brother rather than the whole world جورو خصم jo'roo khas'm n.m. fol. man and wife جورو کا غلام (یا مزدور) jo'roo ka ghūlam (or mūzdoor') n m. hen-pecked husband uxorious husband جورو نہ جاتا اللہ میاں سے ناتا jo'roo na ja'ta al'lah mi'yan se na'ta ph. one living in single-blessedness

جوڑ joṛ n.m. join joint connecting link seam patch connection combination addition total spelling match pair comrade ; companion جوڑ بٹھانا joṛ' biṭha'na v.i. dovetail fit in a joint جوڑ توڑ joṛ' toṛ n.m. (usu. pl.) intrigue , conspiracy contrivance جوڑ توڑ کرنا joṛ' toṛ kar'na v. intrigue ; conspire contrive جوڑ جوڑ joṛ' joṛ n.m. all joints every joint of the body جوڑ دینا joṛ' de'na v. join ; connect link set unite جوڑ لگانا joṛ' laga'na v.i. fit in a joint patch solder add ; sum up calculate [~ جوڑنا]

جوڑا jo'ṛa n.m. couple pair pair of shoes suit of clothes suits in bridal dowery match counterpart other member of pair ; partner بھاری جوڑا bha'rī jo'ṛa n.m. costly (bridal) suit جوڑا بڑھانا jo'ṛa baṛha'na v.i. take off the suit [~ جوڑنا]

جوڑا joo'ṛa n.m. back-knot (of hair) hand-knot crest (of hoopoe nightingale, etc.) hollow pad used as rest for pitcher etc.

جوڑنا joṛ'na v.t. joint connect set (love) affix annex unite add ; total calculate patch ; mend solder match pair , mate ; lay aside (money) ; lay by . save collect harness yoke invent (plot, etc.) put (blame bring forth accusations

جوڑی jo'ṛī n.f. couple pair peer ; equal match counterpart other member of pair ; partner pair of shoes double-value door pair of tambourines pair of cymbals pair of dumbles جوڑی دار jo'ṛī-dar n.m. comrade ; companion colleague [~ جوڑنا]

جوڑی joo'ṛī n.f. ague [~ جاڑا]

جوز jauz n.m. nut (also جوز خراسانی jau'z-e khūrasa'nī) walnut جوز بوا jauz bo''a, جوز بویا jauz boya n.m. nutmeg [A]

جوزا jauza' n.m. the Gemini ; the Twins (as a sign of the Zodiac) [A]

جوش josh n.m. zeal ardour enthusiasm excitement fervour passion ebullition ; boiling effervescence exuberance جوشاں jo'shan adj. & adv. ebullient boiling ; bubling up excited جوش آنا josh' a'na v.i. boil flow over effervesce swell with anger have zeal ; be fervid be enthusiastic be excited جوشاندہ joshan'dah n.m. decoction جوش جوانی josh-e java'nī n.m. ardour of youth جوش خون jo'sh-e khoon' (or khooh) n.m. plethora paternal affection جوش دلانا josh' dila'na v.t. enrage instigate جوش دینا josh de'na v.t.

boil جوش زن *josh'-zan* ADJ. boiling in a fit of passion fervid جوشش *jo'shish* N.F. exuberance fervour enthusiasm جوش کھانا *josh' kha'na* V.I. boil up effervesce over flow ; swell chase fly into a rage be excited frenzid جوش مارنا *josh' mar'na* V.I. boil chafe be frenzied (of blood) have a sudden spurt of affection جوش و خروش *jo'sh-o-kharosh'* N.M. excitement enthusiasm fervour [P ~ A]

جوشن *jau'shan* N.M. coat-of-mail armour cuirass armlet [P]

جوع *joo'* N.M. hunger ; appetite جوع الارض *joo''-ul-ar'z* N.F. love for territorial aggrandizement جوع البقر *joo' ul-ba'qar*, جوع الکلب *joo''-ul-kal'b* N.F. gluttony N.M. glutton ADJ. gluttonous; voracious [A]

جوف *jauf* N.M. cavity hollow interior belly spear wound in belly [A]

جوق *jauq* (ped. *jooq*) N.M. crowd (rare) swarm (of birds) جوق جوق *jauq' jauq'*, جوق در جوق *jauq dar jauq'* ADV. in large numbers [P]

جوکوب *jau-kob'* ADJ. see under [~ جو *jau* ★]

جوکھم *jo'kham* N.F. (same as جوکھوں N.F. ★)

جوکھوں *jo'khon*, جوکھم *jo'kham* N.F. danger jeopardy risk ; hazard suffering tribulation جوکھوں اٹھانا *jo'khon utha'na* V.I. undertake hazardous work jeopardise life or limb under tribulations جوکھوں کا کام *jo'khon ka kam'* N.M. hazardous task dangerous undertaking جوکھوں میں ڈالنا *jo'khon men dal'na* V.I. risk endanger ; jeopardize cause to suffer جوکھوں میں پڑنا *jo'khon men par'na* N.M. run a risk be endangered jeopardize life or limb undergo tribulations

جوگ *jog* N.M. (dial) the Yoga (dial.) asceticism (dial.) meditation lucky union lucky moment ADJ. suitable ; befitting جوگ سادھنا (یا لینا) *jog' sadh'na* (or *le'na*) V.I. (dial) become an ascetic lead the life of an ascetic quit lay life جوگن *jo'gan* N.F. female Hindu ascetic sorceress witch جوگنی *jog'ni* N.F. witch sorceress جوگی *jo'gi* N.M. Hindu ascetic sorcerer ; magician جوگی کس کے میت *jo'gi kis' ke mit* PROV. ascetics are friend to none جوگیا *jo'giya* N.M. reddish name of a musical mode a kind of pigeon ADJ. reddish [S]

جوگا *jo'ga* ADJ. (rare) fit ; suitable آپ جوگا *ap' jo'ga* PH. suitable for you

جولاں *jo'lan* (or *joo'lan*) N.M. fetters ; shackles irons ; chains پابجولاں (or پا بہ جولاں) *pa ba-jolan* or *pa-ba-joo'lan* ADJ. chained ; fettered ; shackled [P]

جولان *jaulan* (ped. *javalan'*) N.M. coursing ; wandering springing جولانگاہ *jau'lan-gah'* N.F. race-course parade ground [A]

جولانی *jaula'ni* (ped. *javala'ni*) N.F. strength of body or mind ; acumen ; fleetness ; quickness ; swiftness [P ~ A PREC.]

جولاہا *jaula'ha*, جلاہا *jula'ha* N.M. (F. جولاہی *jaula'hi* جلاہی *jula'hi*) weaver جولاہے کی مسخری ماں بہن کے ساتھ *jaula'he ki mas'khari man' bai'han ke sath'* PROV. mean person ridicules own friends

جولائی *jula''i* N.M. July [E]

جون *joon* N.M. June [E]

جون ۲ *joon* N.F. (dial.) cycle of birth جون بدلنا *joon' ba'dalna* V.I. undergo a change change from one cycle to another

جوں ۱ *joon* N.F. louse something very small جوں مونہا *joon' mooh'ha* ADJ. weak-looking but mischievous جوئیں پڑنا *joo'en par'na* V.I. become lousy

جوں ۲ *joon* ADV. (arch.) like ; as ; such as جوں توں کرکے *joon' toon' kar' ke* ADV. somehow ; somehow or other with much difficulty جوں جوں *joon' joon* ADV. as long as as far as جوں کا توں *joon' ka toon'* ADV. as it was unchanged جوں ہی *joon' hi* ADV. as soon as ; no sooner than the very moment immediately as

جونا *joo'na* N.M. improvized grass rope small rush bundle for dish-washing ADJ. (arch.) old

جون پور کا قاضی *jaun' poor ka qa'zi* N.M. (fig.) fool

جونسا *jaun'sa* ADJ. whoever whichever

جونک *jonk* N.F. leech پتھر کو جونک نہیں لگتی *pat'thar ko jonk' na'hin lag'ti* PROV. hard hearts never melt جونک لگانا *jonk' laga'na* V.T. apply leeches جونک ہو کے لپٹنا *jonk' ho ke li'patna* V.T. not to get away (from) pester

جونی *joo'ni* N.F. string etc. of balance

جوہر *jau'har* N.M. jewel ; jem pearl essence ; quintessence substance merit ; worth skill sharpness intellect talent جوہر دار *jau'har dar* ADJ. (of sword) sharp جوہر دکھانا *jau'har dikha'na* V.T. show one's mettle ; display one's sterling qualities جوہر فرد *jau'har-e far'd* N.M. indivisible atom (fig.) unmatched personality جوہر قابل *jau'har-e qa'bil* N.M. talented person جوہر کھلنا *jau'har khul'na* V.I. (of talent) be known shine اہل جوہر ah'l-e jau'har N.M. talented persons جوہری jau'harī N.M. jeweller [A ~ P گوہر]

جوہر[2] jau'har N.M. (dial.) Rajput custom of killing family before going out for (desperate fight) battle

جوہڑ joh'r N.M. pond ; pool of dirty water

جوہی joo'hī N.F. wild jessamine (or jasmine)

جوئندہ join'dah, جویا jo'ya, جویاں jo'yāñ N. & ADJ. seeker scarching جوئندہ یابندہ jo'in'dah yābin'dah PROV. seek and thou shalt find

جویں javīñ' (see under جو jau★)

جہات jehat' N.F. PL. directions [A ~ SING. جہت]

جہاد jehād' N.M. (religious) war supreme effort [A ~ جہد]

جھابا jhā'ba N.M. leathern oil container leathern table-cloth straw plate

جھاری jhā'rī N.F. long-necked ewer

جھابڑ جھلا jhā'bar jhal'la N.M. ungainly person جھابڑ جھلا سا jhā'bar jhal'lā sa ADJ. ugly loose lazy

جھاڑ jhāṛ N.M. chandlier a kind of firework brake ; bramble (small) thorny tree volley (of abuses, etc.) جھاڑ باندھنا jhāṛ bāndh'na V.I. utter a volley of abuses جھاڑ جھنکاڑ jhāṛ jhankār' N.M. (usu. PL.) brambles ; (small thorny trees جھاڑ کا کانٹا jhāṛ ka kān'ta N.M. (fig.) whom it is difficult to get rid of جھاڑ ہو کر لپٹنا jhāṛ ho kar lipaṭ'na V.T. stick pesteringly to

جھاڑا jhā'ṛa N.M. charm ; incantation [~ جھاڑنا]

جھاڑن jhā'ṛan N.M. (see under جھاڑنا V.T. ★)

جھاڑنا jhāṛ'nā V.T. dust sweep brush clean knock off shake off beat (bushes) moult repeat spells or charms (over) exorcise جھاڑنا پھونکنا jhāṛ'na phoonk'na V.T. exorcise repeat spells or charms (over) جھاڑ پھونک jhāṛ'-phoonk N.F. locus pocus exorcising charm ; incantation جھاڑ پونچھ jhāṛ'-ponch N.F. dusting tidying up

جھاڑو jhā'ṛoo N.F. broom brush جھاڑو بہارو jhā'ṛoo bohā'roo N.M. broom dusting جھاڑو بہارو کرنا jhā'ṛoo bohā'roo kar na V.T. sweep dust جھاڑو پھیر جانا jhā'ṛoo phir jā'na V.T. be made a clean sweep of have everything lost lose one's all ; be ruined جھاڑو پھیرنا (یا پھیر دینا) jhā'ṛoo pher'nā (or pher' de'nā) V.T. make a clean sweep of undo ; ruin جھاڑو دینا jhā'ṛoo de'na V.T. sweep جھاڑو بہارو ملنا jhā'ṛoo bohā'roo mil'nā V.T. be swept be dusted جھاڑن jhā'ṛan N.M. duster [~ PREC]

جھاڑی jhā'ṛī N.F. bush , shrub ; a thicket bramble

جہاز jāhaz' (ped. jehāz') N.M. ship ; boat ; vessel aeroplane (rare) dowry جہاز کا جہاز jahaz' ka jahaz' ADJ. huge جہاز کا کوا jahaz' ka kav'va N.M. (fig.) one who has to return again again to the same place for a living جہاز کو لنگر کرنا jahaz' ko lan'gar kar'na V.I. anchor a ship جہازی jahā'zī ADJ. naval nautical huge N.M. sailor جہازی کتا jahā'zī kut'ta N.M. greyhound [A]

جھاگ jhag N.M. foam froth scum effervescense جھاگ آنا jhāg ā'nā V.I. effervesce جھاگ لانا jhag' lā'na V.I. foam with rage

جہال johhāl' N.M. ignoramuses fools [A ~ SING. جاہل]

جھال jhal N.F. hot taste (of chillies, etc.) left in mouth pungency large basket soldering artificial cascade in canals

جھالا jhā'la N.M. short local shower earrings comprising pearl rings

جہالت jahā'lat N.F. ignorance imperfect knowlege illiteracy fooly [A]

جھالر jhā'lar N.F. fringe frill جھالردار jhā'lar-dār ADJ. fringed frilled

جھالرا jhāl'rā N.M. well of solid masonry ; well cascade

جھالنا jhāl'na V.T. season pickles solder cool (in saltpetre solution, etc)

جھام jhā'm N.M. large hoe used in sinking wells

جھامر jhā'mar N.M. whetstone for spindles, etc. جھامر jhā'mar جھومر jhoo'mar N.F. illusion

جہان jahāñ' N.M. (lit, also جہاں jahāñ) world جہاں آرا jahāñ' ā'rā ADJ. world adorning جہاں آفریں jahāñ'-āfrīñ' N.M. God (as creator of the world) ; creator جہانباں jahāñ'-bāñ N. & ADJ. sovereign ; ruler world administrator جہانبانی jahāñ'-bānī N.F. sovereignty world administration جہاں بیں jahāñ'-bīn N. & ADJ. traveller well travelled (person) eye جہاں پناہ jahāñ'-panāh' N.M. His (or Her) Majesty protector of the world INT. Your Majesty جہاندار jahāñ'-dār N.M. sovereign rule of the world جہانداری jahāñ'-dārī

N.F. sovereignty minion world-rule جہاندیدہ jahān'-dī'dah widely travelled experienced seasoned veteran جہاندیدہ بسیار گوید دروغ jahān'-dī'dah bisyār' go'yad darogh PROV. travellers tell false tales جہانسوز jahān'-soz' ADJ. world-inflamming جہاں گرد jahān'-gar'd N.M. tourist traveller globe-trotter جہاں گردی jahān'-gar'dī N.F. globe trotting جہانگیر jahān'gīr' ADJ. world conquering N.M. world conqueror appellation of a Moghul emperor Jehangir جہانگیری jahān'-gī'rī N.F. world conquest ; world domination ADJ. of a relating to emperor Jehangir جہاں نما jahān'-nūmā' ADJ. world mirror جہانی jahā'nī ADJ. pertaining to the world آنجہانی āṅjahā'nī ADJ. with (non-Muslim names) the late [P]

جہاں jahāṅ ADV. where in which place while since جہاں تک jahāṅ tak ADV. as far as, so far as جہاں تک (اس) کا تعلق ہے ja'hāṅ tak (is)' kā ta'al'lūq hai PH. as far as this is concerned جہاں جہاں ja'hāṅ ja'hāṅ, جہاں کہیں ja'hāṅ ka'hīṅ ADV. wherever; wheresoever جہاں سے ja'hāṅ se ADV. whence ; from where جہاں کا تہاں ja'hāṅ kā ta'hāṅ ADV. as it was in the very place, in the same place as before

جھانپ jhāṅp N.F. coarse mat (used as door, screen, etc.) mat or plank resting on beam, etc. to form ceiling

جھانپو jhāṅ'po N.F king crow loose woman

جھانٹ jhāṅṭ N.F pubic hair ; pubes

جھانجن jhāṅ'jan, جانجھن jāṅ'jhan N.F. anklet with small bells

جھانجھ jhāṅjh N.F. heat (of anger) impatience cymbals

جھانسا jhāṅ'sā N.M. wheedling trick cheating ; deception جھانسا دینا jhāṅ'sā de'nā V.T. wheedle trick cheat deceive ; defraud جھانسے میں آنا jhāṅ'se meṅ ā'nā V.I. be wheedled be tricked be cheated deceived جھانسیا jhāṅ'siyā N.M. cheat fraud

جھانکنا jhāṅk'nā V.I. peep look out of window, etc. cast sly looks look furtively جھانک آنا jhāṅk ā'nā V.T. pay a short visit to جھانک jhāṅk' N.F. peeping تاک جھانک tāk' jhāṅk, جھانکا جھانکی jhāṅ'kā jhoṅ'kī N.F peeping sly looks ogling جھانکی jhāṅ'kī N.F. (dial.) isolated scene of play tableau ; tableau vivant

جھانواں jhāṅ'vāṅ N.M pumice-stone ; pumice

جھانورا jhāṅ'o'rā ADJ (F. جھانوری jhāṅ''orī) tawny

جھانولی jhāṅ''olī, جھاولی jhā''olī N.F. ogle sly look short view جھانولی دکھانا jhāṅ''olī dikhā'nā V.T. ogle for a short while

جھاؤ jhā''oo N.M. a riverine plant from whose twigs baskets are made

جھائیاں jhā''iyāṅ N.M. PL. sk discoloration (of face) ; dark spots (on face)

جھائیں جھائیں jhā''īṅ jhā''īṅ N.F. quarrel ; argument

جھائیں جھپا jhā''īṅ jhap'pā N.M. shortlived coquetish blandishment trick deceit

جھائیں مائیں jhā''īṅ mā''īṅ N.F. a children's game ; round-and-round we go cawing like the noisy crow

جھبا jhab'bā N.M. tuft tassel

جھبرا jhab'rā, ADJ. (F. جھبری jhab'rī) shaggy (dog)

جھپ jhap N.F. swiftness (only in following) جھپا جھپ jha'pā jhap, جھپ جھپ jhap' jhap ADV. hurriedly جھپ سے jhap se ADJ. in a jiffy جھپاک سے jhapāk se ADV. swiftly ; with a lightning speed

جھپانا jhipā'nā, جھنپانا jhiṅpā'nā V.T. cause to feel abashed [~ جھینپنا CAUS.]

جھپٹنا jha'paṭnā V.T. pounce swoop leap; spring fly (at) attack suddenly snatch away جھپٹ jha'paṭ N.F. جھپٹا jhapaṭ'ṭā N.M. pounce swoop onrush ; onset leap ; bound جھپٹا مارنا jhapaṭ'ṭā mār'nā V.T. pounce swoop leap ; spring make a rush snatch away جھپٹ لینا jha'paṭ le'nā V.T. snatch away pounce upon swoop (of speeding vehicle) crush جھپٹ (یا جھپٹے) میں آنا jha'paṭ (or jhapaṭ'ṭe) meṅ ā'nā V.I. be run down (by) جھپیٹ jhapeṭ' N.F. onrush of speeding vehicle

جھپکنا jha'paknā, جھپکانا jhapkā'nā, پلک جھپکنا palak jha'paknā V.T wink (eye) blink (eye doze off move eyelids coquetishly, fearfully or bashfully جھپک jha'pak N.F. coquetish movement of eyelids modesty جھپکی jhap'kī N.F drowsiness short view جھپکی لینا jhap'kī le'nā V.I doze off

جہت je'hat N.F. (pl. جہات jehāt') direction side reason ; cause اس جہت سے is' je'hat se, بدیں جہت badīṅ' je'hat CONJ. owing to ; because of for this reason شش جہت shash' je'hat N.F. & ADJ. (in) all the six directions

جھٹ jhaṭ, جھٹ پٹ jhaṭ' paṭ, جھٹ سے jhaṭ' se ADV quickly ; swiftly hastily, hurriedly instantaneously in a jiffy

جھٹالنا *jhuṭāl'nā* V.T. eat a little (usu. out) of a large dish [~ جھوٹا]

جھٹپٹا *jhuṭ'puṭā* N.M. twilight ; gloaming

جھٹکنا *jha'taknā* V.I. jerk twitch shake pull violently جھٹکا *jhaṭ'kā* N.M. jerk twitch shake quake violent pull shock (dial.) non-Muslim way of slaughtering animals

جھٹل *jhuṭ'ṭal* ADJ. feigned ; pretended mock [~ جھوٹ]

جھٹلانا *jhuṭlā'nā* V.T. belie ; give the lie to falsify [~ جھوٹ]

جھٹیل *jhuṭail'* N.F. leavings ADJ. promiscuous (woman) [~ جھوٹا]

جھجر *jhaj'jar* N.M. earthen flask long necked pitcher جھجری *jhaj'rī* N.F. small earthen flask

جھجکنا *jhi'jaknā* V.I. boggle start with ; fight ; start or boggle ; shrink ; recoil hesitate ; demur have a stage-fright جھجک *jhi jak* N.F. shyness hesitation demur stage-fright

جہد *jah'd* or *joh'd* N.F. strenuous effort endeavour exertion جہد البقا *jah'd lil-baqā'* N.F. struggle for existence [A]

جھڈو *jhuḍ'ḍoo* ADJ. cuckold lacking sense of honour

جہر *jah'r* N.M. loud voice ; audible voice بالجہر *bil-jah'r* ADV. loudly audibly [A]

جھر *jhir* N.F., جھراٹا *jhirā'ṭā* N.M. sound made in tearing cloth [ONO.]

جھرجھرا *jhir'jhrā* ADJ. flimsy (cloth)

جھرجھری *jhur'jhurī* N.F. shiveringfit shiver; shake جھرجھری لینا *jhur' jhu'rī le'nā* V.I. shiver shake

جھرکٹ *jhur'kaṭ* ADJ. (of tree) with lopped branches withered drooping

جھرمٹ *jhur'maṭ* N.M. crowd; multitude (esp. women's) circle hiding the face by throwing stole across it جھرمٹ مارنا *jhur'maṭ mar'na* V.T. (of women) circle round conceal body with stole

جھرنا *jhar'nā* V.I. trickle ooze N.M. cascade sheet of water oozing through perforations in an inclined plane cullender ; colander

جھرنا

جھروکا *jharo'kā*, جھروکہ *jharo'kah* N.M. casement window ventilator

جھری *jhur'rī* N.F. (usu. PL.) wrinkle پر جھریاں پڑنا *par jhurriyāṅ paṛ'nā* V.I. be wrinkled be wizened,

جھری *jhi'rī* N.F. chink slit

جھڑ *jhaṛ* N.F. bolt (of lock) (also جھڑی *jha'ṛī*) continuous downpour جھڑبیری *jhaṛ' be'rī* N.F. jujube ; wild berry

جھڑپ *jha'ṛap* N.F. quarrel brawl skirmish passage-at-arms

جھڑجھڑانا *jhaṛ jhaṛā'nā* V.T. shake ruddy give (someone) good shaking [~ جھاڑنا]

جھڑکنا *jhi'ṛaknā* V.T. scold ; chide snap at , browbeat جھڑکی *jhiṛ'kī* N.F. scolding browbeating rebuff

جھڑنا *jhaṛ'nā* V.T. drop (of leaves, hair, etc.) fall off (of feathers) be shed ; be moulted discharge semen ejaculate جھڑیل *jhaṛ'yal* ADJ. nonsensical

جھڑوس *jhaṛoos* N.M. cuckold

جھڑی *jha'ṛī*, جھڑ *jhaṛ* N.F. continuous downpour جھڑی لگنا *jha'ṛī lag'nā* V.I. rain continuously

جھک *jhak* N.F. nonsense silly talk vain endeavour جھک مارنا *jhak' mar'nā* V.I. talk nonsense make vain effort eat humble pie agree to adopt the rejected course جھک جھک *jhak' jhak* جھکندن *jhakan'dan* N.F. dispute quarrel wrangle جھک جھوری *jhak' jho'rī* N.F. dalliance جھکی *jhak'ki* ADJ. talkative nonsensical

جھکانا *jhikā'nā* V.T. cause to cry harass [~ جھکنا CAUS.]

جھکڑ *jhak'kaṛ* N.M. intermittent blasts squall hurricane storm

جھکور *jhakor'* N.F. waft (of wind etc.) oss

جھکنا *jhuk'nā* V.I. bend bow incline dip submit ; yield stoop show respect to جھک کر سلام کرنا *jhuk' kar salām' kar'nā* V.I. make obeisance salute respectfully (dial.) dip shock جھکانا *jhukā'nā* V.T. bring (someone) down on his knees cause to stoop hang down (head) in shame , etc. bend bow incline جھکاؤ *jhukā''o* N.M. inclination flexibility predilection

جھکولا *jhako'lā* N.M. waft (of wind, etc.)

جھگڑنا *jha'gaṛnā* V.T. quarrel have an argument with ; contend , argue dispute , wrangle brawl جھگڑا *jhag'ṛā* N.M. quarrel dispute argument ; contention squabble brawl wrangle جھگڑا اٹھانا *jhag'ṛā uṭhā'nā* V.I. raise a quarrel dispute جھگڑا کرنا *jhag'ṛā kar'nā* V.I. quarrel wrangle, brawl جھگڑالو *jhagṛā lū* ADJ. quarrelsome ; contentious N.M. disputer brawler

جہل *jah'l* N.M. ignorance stupidity جہل مرکب *jah'l-e mūrak'kab* N.M. false pretensions to knowledge gross ignorance [A]

جہلا *johalā'* N.M. the ignoramuses fools [A ~ SING. جاہل]

جھلانا *jhallā'nā* V.I. fly into passion fret and fume جھل *jhal* N.F. passions heat جھل بجھانا (یا مٹانا) *jhal bujhā'nā* (or *miṭā'nā*) V.T cool (someone's) passions جھلا *jhal'lā* N.M. large basket ADJ. (F. جھلی *jhal'lī*) sultry angry جھل ہائی *jhal hā''ī* N.F. ADJ. lustful woman

جھولانا *jhūlā'nā* V.T. rock in cradle swing [~ CAUS.]

جھلجھلانا *jhaljhalā'nā* V.I. glisten ; glitter ache throb feel pungency have a burning sensation (owing to chillies etc.) جھلجھلاہٹ *jhaljhalā'haṭ* N.F. glisten ; glitter pungency burning sensation

جھلسنا *jhū'lasnā*, جھلسانا *jhūlsā'nā*, جھلس دینا *jhū'las de'nā* V.T. burn scorch singe جھلسنا *jhulas'nā* جھلس جانا *jhū'las jā'nā* V.I. be burnt be scorched be singed

جھلکنا *jha'laknā* V.I. shine flash twinkle appear ; be apparent جھلک *jha'lak* N.F. glimpse reflection refulgence جھلکی *jhal'kī* N.F. (usu. pl.) glimpse

جھلملانا *jhilmilā'nā* V.I. twinkle flicker glimmer undulate (as the flame of a candle or water) جھلمل *jhil'mil* N.M. twinkle جھلمل کرنا *jhil'mil kar'nā* V. to sparkle ; to flash ; to twinkle جھلملی *jhil'milī* N.F. shutter ; Venetian blind

جھلنا *jhal'nā* V.T. move (fan) force flies, etc. to keep away be soldered جھلوانا *jhalvā'nā* V.T. cause to move (fan) cause to be soldered

جھلنگا *jhilan'gā* N.M. worn-out bed rush strings' fabric taken out of bed intact ADJ. week lean

جھلی *jhil'lī* N.F. pellicle ; thin skin membrane parchment

جھمجھمانا *jhamjhamā'nā* V.I. glitter جھما جھم *jha'mā-jham* N.F. glitter of clothes, gold lace, etc.

جھمکا *jhūm'kā* N.M. earring with bell-shaped pendant سات سہیلیوں کا جھمکا *sāt' sahe'liyoṅ kā jhūm'kā* N.M. the Pleiades ; the Pleiads

جھمکڑا *jhamak'ṛā* N.M. coquetish beauty ravishing charm

جھمیلا *jhame'lā*, جھنجھٹ *jhañ'jhaṭ* N.M. bother trouble complication fuss ; ado confusion جھمیلیا *jhame'liyā*, جھنجھٹیا *jhañ'jhaṭyā* ADJ. quarrelsome ; contentious

جھنجھلانا *jhūṅjhlā'nā*, جھنجھلا اٹھنا *jhūṅjhlā' uṭh'nā* V.I. fret and fume be irritated جھنجھلا کر *jhūṅjh'lā kar* ADV. peevishly جھنجھلاہٹ *jhūṅjhlā'haṭ* N.F. irritation peevishness

جھنجھنانا *jhañjhanā'nā* V.I. jingle ; tinkle rattle جھنجھناہٹ *jhañjhanā'haṭ* N.F. jingle tinkle rattle

جھنجھنا *jhūn jhūnā* N.M. rattle

جھنجھنی *jhūn' jhunī* N.F. tingling ; pins and needless جھنجھنیاں *jhūnjhūnyāṅ* N.F. PL. fetters

جھنجی *jhañ'jī* ADJ. (shell) broken at top جھنجی کوڑی *jhañ'jī kau'ṛī* N.F. such shell (fig.) sou ; mite

جھنجھوڑنا *jhañjhoṛ'nā* V.T. shake to rouse shake rudely جھنجھوڑی *jhañjho'ṛī* N.F. such shaking

جھنڈ *jhūnḍ* N.M. clump or cluster (of trees) swarm (of birds) جھنڈ کے جھنڈ *jhūnḍ ke jhūnḍ* N.M. swarms (of birds)

جھنڈا *jhañ'ḍā* N.M. flag banner standard جھنڈا گاڑنا *jhañ'ḍā gāṛ'nā* V.I. vanquish; conquer جھنڈا لہرانا *jhañ'ḍā lahrā'nā* V.I. hoist a flag جھنڈے پر چڑھانا *jhañ'ḍe par chaṛhā'nā* V. publicize scandalize جھنڈی *jhañ'ḍī* N.F. flag ; small flag

جھنڈولا *jhanḍoo'lā* ADJ. baby with yet untonsured head

جھنک *jha'nak* N.F. jingle (esp of tinkling anklets) [doublet of FOLL.]

جھنکار *jhankār'* N.F. jingle tinkle chinking scream (of peacock)

جھنکاڑ *jhañ'kāṛ* N.M. leafless tree

جہنم *jahan'nam* N.F. hell جہنمی *jahan'namī* ADJ. infernal hellish doomed cursed cussed [A]

جھوت *jhot* N.F. narrow lane between two walls with their drains opening on to it

جھوٹ *jhooṭ'* N.M. lie, falsehood untruth fabrication prevarication جھوٹ باندھنا *jhooṭ bāndh'nā* V.T. slander ; calumniate جھوٹ بنانا *jhooṭ' banā'nā* V.I. invent a lie جھوٹ بولنا *jhooṭ bol'nā* V.I. lie ; tell a lie جھوٹ جاننا *jhooṭ'. jān'nā* V. disbelieve جھوٹ سچ *jhooṭ' sach* N.M. fabrication garbled version of facts جھوٹ سچ لگانا *jhooṭ' sach lagā'nā* V.T. slander calumniate misrepresent جھوٹ کا پتلا *jhooṭ ka put'la* ADJ embodiment of falsehood brazenfaced liar جھوٹ کے پاؤں نہیں ہوتے *jhooṭ ke pā''oṅ na'hīṅ ho'te* PROV. falsehood has no legs to stand upon جھوٹ کی پوٹ *jhooṭ' kī poṭ'* ADJ egregious lie جھوٹ موٹ *jhooṭ' mooṭ* ADV. all lies ; for nothing at all in jest ; jestingly جھوٹوں نہ پوچھنا *jhoo'ṭoṅ nā poochh'nā* V.I not even to show outward cordiality جھوٹے منہ *jhho'ṭe mūṅh* ADV. with unwashed face (usu. NEG.) outwardly ; just in formal way جھوٹا *jhoo'ṭā* N.M. liar ADJ. untrue fabricated imitation (work) spurious ; base unwashed (dish, etc.) (of served food) no longer untouched (of henna) badly daubed or fading of tinsel (and not of pure gold or silver) unwashed (face, mouth) جھوٹا پڑنا *jhoo'ṭā par'nā* V.I. be proved false جھوٹا کام *jhoo'ṭā kām* N.M. tinsel (etc.) embroidery جھوٹا مصالحہ *jhoo'ṭā masā'lah* N.M. tinsel, etc. used in embroidery جھوٹوں کا بادشاہ *jhoo'ṭoṅ ka bādshāh'* N.M. arch-liar جھوٹی *jhooṭī* N.F. liar ADJ. false untrue جھوٹی خبر *jhoo'ṭī khabar* N.F. a false report : a rumour جھوٹی قسم *jhoo'ṭī qa'sam* N.F. perjury

جھوٹا *jho'ṭā*, جھونٹا *jhoṅ'ṭā* N.M. (F. جھوٹی *jho'ṭī* جھونٹی *jhoṅ'ṭī*) young (one of) buffalo

جھوجھرا *jhojhrā* ADJ. (F. جھوجھری *jhojhrī*) vessel with cracked sound

جھوڑ *jhaur* N.F. quarrel

جہول *jahool* ADJ. very silly N.M. ignoramus [A ~ جہل]

جھول *jhol* N.M. bagginess ; pucker rumple farrow ; brood gilt ; plating جھول ڈالنا *jhol' dāl'nā* V.T. make baggy pucker rumple جھول نکالنا *jhol' nikāl'nā* V.T. remove rumple ; remove crease brood farrow

جھول *jhool* N.F. housing

جھولا *jho'lā* N.M. knapsack ; haversack palsy blight ADJ. loose ; not tight baggy

جھول بولے *jhaul bau'le* ADV. at daybreak

جھولنا *jhool'nā* V.I. swing away to and fro oscillate N.M. cradle جھولا *jhoo'lā* N.M. a swing ; the swinging rope ; a cradle

جھولی *jho'lī* N.F. bag ; sack pouch

جھومر *jhoo'mar* N.M. forehead jewellery a dance number with dancing girls in a circle

جھومنا *jhoom'nā* V.I. swing rock rock and roll sway to and fro stagger walk with a staggering step be in an ecstatic mood be enraptured, be overjoyed جھوم جھوم (یا جھام) کر *jhoom jhoom* (or *jhām*) *kar* ADV. enjoyingly in an ecstacy

جھونا *jho'na* ADJ. flimsy N.M. flimsy cloth superior quality betelnut V.T. & I. work (mill) to grind begin whine ; lament strike with (staff, etc.)

جھونپڑا *jhoṅp'ṛā* N.M. جھونپڑی *jhoṅp'ṛī* N.F. cottage ; hut

جھونٹا *jhoṅ'ṭā* N.M. motion (of swing) back (or top) knot of hair (same as جھوٹا *jho'ṭā* N.M. ★) جھونٹم جھانٹا *jhooṅ'ṭam jhaṅ'ṭā* N.M. & ADV. pulling each other's hair

جھنجال *jhooṅ'jal* N.F. vexation rage جھنجال اتارنا *jhooṅ'jhal ūtār'nā* V.T. vent one's spleen on) take revenge (from)

جھونک *jhoṅk* N.F. sleep, (etc. as effect of drug) lowering of scale جھونک مارنا *jhoṅk mar'nā* V.T. force down one scale of balance by unfair means

جھونکا *jhoṅ'kā* N.M. gust (of wind) blast puff doze جھونکے آنا *jhoṅ'ke ā'nā* V.I. (of wind) blow intermittently feel drowsy

جھونکنا *jhoṅk'nā*, جھونک دینا *jhoṅk' de'nā* V.T. caste (in oven) feed (oven) with fuel set fire to throw (dust) waste over useless venture cause to perish in vain

جھیرا *jhe'rā* N.M. well which is choked or fallen in

جہیر الصوت *jahīr'-ūs-saut'*, آلۂ جہیر الصوت *ā'lā-e jahī'r-ūs-saut'* N.M. loudspeaker

جہیز *jahez'* N.M. dowry ; bride's portion [P ~ A جہیز]

جھیکنا *jhīk'nā*, جھینکنا *jhīṅk'nā* V.I. complain whine N.M. complaint ; grievance whining

جھیل *jhīl* N.F. lake pool (in music) 'piano' ; 'pianissimo'

جھیلنا *jhel'nā* V.I. suffer ; undergo bear ; endure (dial.) ford جھیلنی *jhel'nī* N.F. support (tucked up in hair) for ear ornaments supporting jerk (in delivery)

جھینپنا *jheṅp'nā*, جھیپنا *jhep'nā* V.I. feel abashed be ashamed جھینپ *jheṅp*, جھیپ *jhep* N.F. shyness bashfulness shame modesty

جھینگا *jhīṅ'gā* N.M. prawn ; shrimp

جھینگر *jhīṅ'gar* N.M. cricket جھینگر چاٹنا (یا لگنا) *jhīṅ'gar chāṭ'nā* (or *lag'nā*) V.I. (of cloth) be moth-eaten

جئی *ja''ī* N.F. oats

جی[1] **ji** N.M. polite form of address sir madam miss INT (also) ہاں جی ، ہاں جی **han' ji** yes

جی[2] **ji** N.M. heart mind soul ; spirit life living being health courage temperament جی آنا (یا آجانا) **ji a'na** (or **a ja'na**) V.I. fall in love (with) جی اچٹنا (یا اکتانا) **ji u'chaṭna** (or **ukta'na**) V.I. be bored be browned off be disgusted be sick (of) جی اداس ہونا **ji udas' ho'na** V.I. be sad be gloomy جی باغ باغ ہونا **ji bagh bagh ho'na** V.I. be highly pleased جی بجھ جانا **ji bujh' ja'na** V.I. be sad be downcast جی برا کرنا **ji bu'ra kar'na** V.T. (of talk) displease ; offend جی بکھرا جانا **ji' bikh'ra ja'na** V.I. feel sick at جی بھاری کرنا **ji bha'ri kar'na** V.I. be gloomy ; be dejected جی بھر آنا **ji bhar a'na** V.I. be deeply moved جی بھر کے **ji' bhar' ke** ADV. to heart's covent جی بھر بھرانا **ji' bhar bhara'na** V.I. feel the temptation جی بھرنا (یا بھر جانا) **ji' bhar'na** (or **bhar' ja'na**) V.I. be fed up جی بڑھانا **ji' barha'na** V.T. buck up encourage جی بہلانا **ji baihla'na** V.T. divert the mind (of) amuse oneself جی بہلنا **ji bai'halna** V.I. be amused get used to جی بیٹھنا (یا بیٹھا جانا) **ji baith'na** (or **bai'tha ja'na**) V.I. (of heart) sink be dismayed be shocked جی پر کھیلنا (یا کھیل جانا) **ji' par khel'na** (or **khel ja'na** V.I. risk one's life ; جی ترسنا **ji' ta'rasna** V.I. yearn without hope جی ٹوٹنا (یا ٹوٹ جانا) **ji' ṭooṭ'na** (or **ṭooṭ ja'na**) V.I. feel frustrated thoroughly disgusted be grieved جی ٹھنڈا کرنا **ji' ṭhan'ḍa kar'na** V.I. have a desire fulfilled avenge جی ٹھنڈا ہونا **ji ṭhan'ḍa ho'na** V.I. have a desire fulfilled be avenged جی جان سے فدا (یا قربان) ہونا **ji jan' se fida'** (or **qurban'**) **ho'na** V.I. be devoted heart and soul (to) be ready to lay down one's life (for) جی جلانا **ji jala'na** V.T. hurt ; grieve vex ; annoy جی جلنا **ji' jal'na** V.I. be hurt ; be grieved be vexed ; be annoyed جی چاہنا **ji' chah'na** V.I. desire ; long for yearn جی چرانا **ji' chura'na** V.I. shirk (work) جی چھوٹنا **ji' chhooṭ'na** V.I. be discouraged be disheartened جی چھوڑنا **ji' chhoṛ'na** V.I. be disheartened throw up the sponge جی دار **ji-dar'** ADJ. courageous ; bold جی ڈوبنا **ji' ḍoob'na** V.I. (of heart) sink جی ڈھیا جانا **ji' ḍha'ya ja'na** جی رکنا **ji' ruk'na** V.I. hesitate , demur جی جمار رکھنا **ji' rakh'na** V.I. console جی سے اتر جانا **ji' se u'tar ja'na** V.T. lose favour (with) جی سنسنانا **ji' sansana'na** V.I. feel enervated fear جی سے جانا (یا گزرنا) **ji' se ja'na** (or **gu'zarna**) V.I. die ; lose one's life جی کڑا کرنا **ji' (ka'ṛa) kar'na** V.I. dare ; muster courage جی کھپانا **ji khapa'na** V.T. worry (over) work assiduously جی کھٹا میٹھا ہونا **ji' khaṭ'a miṭ'ṭha ho'na** V.I. be tempted جی کھٹا ہونا **ji khaṭ'ṭa ho'na**, on desires ; restrain one's passions جی کی جی میں رہنا (یا رہ جانا) **ji' ki ji' meṅ raih'na** (or **raih ja'na**) V.I. have one's desire unfulfilled be unable to express one's desire جی گھبرانا **ji' ghabra'na** V.I. feel uneasy ; be restless be unnerved جی لبھانا **ji' lubha'na** V.T. wheedle ; coax amuse be liked by جی لگانا **ji' laga'na** V.I. do (something) attentively (get used to) evince interest fall in love (with) جی لگنا **ji' lag'na** V.I. get used (to) be at home (in) evince interest (in) fall in love (with) جی للچانا **ji' lalcha'na** V.T. have temptation (for) جی مارنا **ji' mar'na** V.T. mortify one's soul keep a check on desires ; restrain one's passions جی مرنا **ji mar'na** V.I. (of soul, desires, etc.) be mortified جی متلانا **ji' matla'na** V.I. feel sick (at) ; feel nausea جی ملنا **ji mil'na** V.I. feel friendship (for) جی میں آنا **ji' meṅ a'na** V.I. occur (to one) , have an idea جی میں بیٹھنا **ji' meṅ baiṭh'na** V.I. be impressed on the mind جی میں رکھنا **ji' meṅ rakh'na** V.T. keep to oneself ; not to disclose harbour (grudge, etc.) جی میں گھر کرنا **ji' meṅ ghar' kar'na** V.I. be agreeable have the heart fixed upon جی ہارنا **ji' har'na** V. be depressed; be spiritless be discouraged جی ہٹنا (یا ہٹ جانا) **ji' haṭ'na** (or **haṭ ja'na**) be disgusted be fed up جی ہٹانا **ji haṭa'na** V.T. turn away one's affection (from) جی ہی جی میں **ji' hi ji meṅ** ADV. in one's mind ; at heart

جیا **ji'ya**, جیوڑا **jiyoo'ṛa** N.M. heart [~PREC. DIM.]

جے **jai** N.F. (dial.) victory جے کی **ki jai'** V.T. (dial.) long live جیکارا **jaika'ra** N.M. (dial.) shout of 'long live...' جیکارے بھرنا **jaika're bhar'na** V.T. (dial.) shot 'long live...' [S]

جیب **jeb** (ped. **jaib**) N.F. pocket (lit.) collar (of garment) (lit.) bosom جیب تراش **jeb'-tarash'** N.M. pick-pocket جیب تراشی **jeb'-tara'shi** N.F. picking of people's pockets جیب تراشی کرنا **jeb'-tara'shi kar'na** V.T. pick-pocket جیب خاص **je'b e khas'** N.M. privy purse جیب خرچ **jeb'-khar'ch** N.M. pocket money جیب کترا **jeb'- kat'ra** N.M. pickpocket جیب کترنا **jeb - ka'tarna** V.I. pick (someone's) pocket جیب گھڑی **jeb'-gha'ṛi** N.F. pocket watch [A]

جیبھ **jib** جیبھ **jibh** N.F. (rare) tongue جیبھ نکالنا **jibh nikal'na** V.I. (of dog, etc.) pant feel very thirsty

جیتا **ji'ta** ADJ. (see under جینا V.I. ★)

جیتنا **jit'na** V.T. win beat (at game) ; be victorious overcome ; conquer جیت **jit** N.F victory success جیت لینا **jit' le'na** V.T. win ;

annex (trophy, etc.) جیت ہونا *jīt' ho'nā* V.I. gain a victory attain success جیتی مانا نہ ہاری مانا *jī'tī mān'nā na hā'rī man'nā* V.I. show intransigence

جیٹھ *jeṭh* N.M. brother-in-law; husband's elder brother third month of Hindu calendar (corresponding to May-June) جیٹھانی *jeṭhā'nī* N.F. sister-in-law; wife of husband's elder brother

جیجا *jī'jā* N.M. (dial.) brother-in-law; sister's husband جیجی *jī'jī* N.F. (dial.) sister teat; nipple

جے جیونتی *jai'jaivah'tī* N.F. name of a musical mode

جیحوں *je'hoon* (ped. *jaihoon'*) N.M. Oxus [P]

جید *jay'yid* ADJ. good; excellent [A]

جیسا *jai'sā*, جیسی *jai'si* جیسے *jai'se* ADV. like in the manner of such as according as جیسا دیس ویسا بھیس *jai'sā des vai'sā bhes* PROV. when in Rome do as the Roman; do جیسا راجہ ویسی پرجا *jai'sā rā'jah vai'sī par'jā* PROV. as is the king so is the court جیسا کروگے ویسا بھروگے *jai'sā ka'roge vai'sā bha'roge* جیسی کرنی ویسی بھرنی *jai'si kar'nī vai'sī bhar'nī* PROV. as you sow so shall you reap جیسے تیسے *jai'se tai'se* ADV. somehow or other by hook or by crook جیسے چاہو *jai'se chā'ho* ADV. as you please; do what you will it is all up to you جیسے کا تیسا *jai'se kā tai'sā* ADV. the self-same unaltered untouched جیسے کو تیسا *jai'se ko tai'sā* PROV. tit for tat; measure for measure جیسی روح ویسے فرشتے *jai'sī rooh' vai'se firish'te* PROV. like priest like parish (or people)

جیش *jaish* N.M. (PL. جیوش *jūyoosh'*) army detachment [A]

جیغہ *jī'ghah* N.M. gold ornament worn over turban (fig.) feather (in cap) [T]

جیفہ *jī'fah* N.M. carcass; carcase [A]

جیل *jel*, جیل خانہ *jel'-khā'nah* N.M. jail; gaol; prison جیل بھیجنا *jel' bhej'nā* V.T. send to gaol جیل جانا *jel' jā'nā* V.I. be gaoled جیلر *je'lar*, داروغہ جیل *dāro'gha-e jel'* N.M. jailor; jail warden [E]

جیلی *jī'lī* N.F. rake

جیلی *jai'lī* N.F. jelly; a sweet dish [E]

جین *jain* N.M. founder of follower of Hindu heresy worshipping twenty-four tiraths or saints as superior to Hindu pantheon ADV. (usu. جینی *jai'nī*) Jain cult or its follower جین مت *jain'mat* N.M. Jainism [S]

جینا *jī'nā* V.I. live; exist be alive N.M. life existence جی اٹھنا *jī' uṭh'nā* V.I. come to life; quicken turn away one's affections be disgusted جی پڑنا *jī' paṛ'nā* V.I. come to life (of embryo) show signs of life جیتا *jī'tā* ADJ. (F. جیتی *jī'tī*) alive; living جیتا جاگتا *jī'ta jāg'ta* (F. جیتی جاگتی *jī'tī jāg'tī*) ADJ. alive; living that has come alive real substantial جیتے جی *jī'te jī* ADV. in the life-time (of) جیتی مکھی نگلنا *jī'tī mak'khī ni'galnā* V.I. invite trouble entangle oneself جینے کے لالے پڑنا *jī'ne ke lā'le paṛ'nā* V.I. be in danger of life

جیو *jiyoo'* N. & INT. (arch.) (same as جی ★) جیو ہتیا *jiyoo'hat'tiyā*, جیو ہنسا *jiyoo'han'sā* N.F. destruction of life

جیوائی *jīvā''ī* N.F. rent-free land land assigned dependents, etc. as subsistence

جیوتش *jiyotish'* N.F. same as جوتش N.F. ★)

جیوٹ *jī'vaṭ* ADJ. & N.M. courageous; bold [~ جی]

جیوری *jiyoo'rī* N.F. jury [E]

جیوش *jūyoosh'* N.M. PL. armies detachments [A ~ SING. جیش]

جیومیٹری *jūmaiṭ'rī* geometry [E ~ G]

جیون *jī'van* N.M. (dial.) life جیون مرن *jī'van ma'ran* N.M. life and death

چ *che* (also called *jī'm-e fā'risī*) eighth letter of Urdu alphabet (not used in classical Arabic (in jummal reckoning regarded as equivalent to ج) three

چابک *chā'bŭk* N.M. whip ADJ. (lit.) skilful active agile چابکدست *chā'bŭk-das't* ADJ. skilful; dextrous چابکدستی *chāb'ŭk'-das'tī* N.F. skill dexterity چابک سوار *chā'bŭk-savār'* N.M. expert rider jockey horse-breaker چابک مارنا *chā'bŭk mār'nā* V.T. whip چابکی *chāb'ŭkī* N.F. agility celerity; alertness [P]

چابنا *chāb'nā* V.T. crunch graw chew [doublet, of چبانا]

چابی *chā'bī* N.F. key

چاپ *chāp* N.F. sound (of footsteps) قدموں کی چاپ *qad'moṅ kī chāp* N.F. footfall

چاپٹ chā'pat N.F. bran ; husk

چاپڑ chā'par N.F. hard soil

چاپلوس chāplous' ADJ. & N.M. flatterer sycophant چاپلوسی chāploo'sī N.F. flattery ; sycophancy fawning چاپلوسی کرنا chāploo'sī kar'nā V.T. flatter ; fawn (on) [P]

چاتر chā'tur ADJ. (same as چتر ADJ. ★)

چاٹنا chāt'nā V.T. lick ; lap taste چاٹ chāt N.F. spicy-sweet mixture of fruit, gram, etc., spicy-sweet dish ; fruit salad relish ; taste craving habit چاٹ پڑنا یا لگنا chāt par'nā (or lag'nā) V.T. acquire a taste (for) crave (for) چاٹ جانا یا لینا chāt jā'nā (or le'nā) V.T. lick up ; lap consume

چاٹی chā'tī N.F. churning vessel churn

چاچا chā'chā N.M. (dial.) younger brother of father ; uncle چاچی chā'chī N.F. wife of father's younger brother ; aunt [doublet of چچا]

چادر chā'dar N.F. sheet coverlet veil waterfall پھولوں کی چادر phoo'lon kī chā'dar N.F. wreath sheetlike wreath لوہے کی چادر lo'he kī chā'dar N.F. steel sheet C.I. sheet ; corrugated iron sheet چادر اتارنا chā'dar utār'nā V.T. tear off the veil insult a woman thus in public چادر اوڑھنا chā'dar orh'nā V.I. put on a veil cover oneself with a sheet چادر بچھانا chā'dar bichhā'nā V.I. spread a sheet lay the cloth چادر تان کر سونا chā'dar tān kar so'nā V.I. enjoy a care-free sleep lead an easy life چادر چڑھانا chā'dar charhā'nā V.T. place a wreath on (tomb etc.) چادر دیکھ کر پاؤں پھیلانا chā'dar dekh' kar pā''n phailā'nā V.I. live within one's means چادر ڈالنا chā'dar dāl'nā V.T. (dial.) marry (a widow) چادر ہے تھوڑی پیر پسارے بہت chā'dar hai tho'rī pair pasā're ba hūt PROV. living beyond one's means چادر ہلانا chā'dar hilā'nā V.I. throw up the sponge [P]

چار chār ADJ. four چار آدمی chār' ādmī' N.M. arbitrators a few persons public آنکھیں چار ہونا āṅ'kheṅ chār' ho'nā V.I. come face to face (with) see each other چار آئینہ chār ā'ī'nah (or ā''ī-) N.M. plate armour چار ابرو کا صفایا ہونا chār ab'roo kā safā'yā ho'nā N.M. shaving off of head, eyebrows, moustaches and beard being clean-shaven casting orthodoxy to the winds چار باغ chār'-bāgh N.M. stole with embroidered corners چار بالش chār-bā'lish N.M. (arch.) large cushion sofa ; large cushioned seat چار بند chār' band' N.M. limb joints (چار پانچ لانا (یا کرنا chār' pānch' lā'nā (or kar'nā) V.I dodge trump up excuses چار پائی chār-pā''ī N.F. cot ; bed ; bedstead چار پائی پر پڑنا chār-pā''ī par par'nā V.I. fall ill ; go to bed چار پائی سے پیٹھ لگ جانا chār-pā''ī se pīth' lag jā'nā V.I. be bed-ridden (of patient) grow very week (through prolonged illness) have bed-sore چار پایہ chār-pā'yah N.M. quadruped ; چار پیسے chār pai'se N.M. PL. (also) some money چار تار chār'-tār N.M. four ornaments or dresses چار تال chār'-tāl N.M. a kind of tambourine note چار جامہ chār'-jā'mah N.M. treeless saddle ; cloth saddle چار چالے chār' chā'le N.M. four parties thrown to room and his relations by bride's family چار چاند لگنا chār' chānd' lag'nā V.I. have increase in dignity (of beauty be enhanced چار چشم chār' chash'm ADJ. untrustworthy ; faithless treacherous چار خانہ chār' khā'nah N.M. & ADJ. chequered (cloth) ; check چار دانگ chār'-dāng N.M. the four quarters (of the globe) all over چار دانگ عالم میں chār'-dāng-e 'ālam meṅ ADV. all over the world چار دن کی چاندنی chār' din kī chānd'nī N.F. transitory glory passing phase (of something desirable) چار دن کی چاندنی اور پھر اندھیری رات ہے chār' din kī chānd'nī aur phir' andhe'rī rāt hai PROV. to every spring there is an autumn چار دیواری chār-divā'rī N.F. enclosure boundary wall (city) wall چار دیواری کرنا chār divā'rī kar'nā V.T. put up an enclosure round چار زانو بیٹھنا chār' zā'noo baith'nā V.I. sit cross-legged squat چار (یا چہار) شنبہ chār (or chahār') sham'bah N.M. Wednesday چار (یا چہار) عنصر chār' (or chahār') 'ūn'sar N.M. PL. the four elements (viz. earth, air, fire and water) چار کھونٹ chār' khooṅt' N.M. the four quarters چار گوشہ chār go'shah ADJ. quadrangle چار گنا chār gu'nā ADJ. fourfold چاروں chā'roṅ ADJ. all the four چاروں شانے چت کرنا (یا گرنا) chā'roṅ shā'ne chit kar'nā (or gir'nā) V.I. fall at full length on the back sprawl supinely چاروں مغز chā'roṅ magh'z N.M. PL. the various cucumber and melon-seeds used together for medicinal purposes چار یار chār'-yār N.M. the orthodox caliphs [P doublet of چہار]

چارج chār'j N.M. charge چارج دینا یا لینا chār'j de'nā (or le'nā) V.I. assume (or give) charge (of something to someone) [E]

چار (و) ناچار chār (-o) nā-chār' ADV. inevitably whilly milly [P]

چارہ[1] chā'rah, چارا chā'ra N.M. fodder bait چارہ ڈالنا chā'rah dāl'nā V.T. give fodder (to) چارہ لگانا chā'rah lagā'nā V.T. bait (a hook)

چارہ[2] chā'rah N.M. remedy help expedient resource cure چارہ جوئی chā'ra-jo''ī (or joo''ī) N.F. seeking remedy قانونی چارہ جوئی کرنا qānoo'nī chā'ra jo''ī kar'nā V.I. seek legal remedy file a suit چارہ سازی chā'ra sā'zī, چارہ گری chā'ra-ga'rī N.F. preparing a remedy remedying ; curing [P]

چاشت chāsht' N.M. breakfast time , mid-morning [P]

چاشنی chāsh'nī N.F. viscous state of a syrup freshly prepared syrup taste ; relish admixture (of) sweet and sour in taste چاشنی دار chāsh'nī-dār ADJ. tasty sweet and sour چاشنی گیر chāsh'nī-gīr N.M. chef ; head cook [P]

چاق chāq ADJ. alert (usu. as) چاق (و) چوبند chāq(-o) chāuband' ADJ. nimble alert healthy in good health smart [T]

چاقو chā'qoo (vul. chak'koo) N.M. knife pen-knife چاقو کا پھل chā'qoo kā phal N.M. blade of knife چاقو کا دستہ chā'qoo kā das'tah N.M. handle of knife [P]

چاک[1] chāk N.M. rent slit cut fissure ADJ. torn lacerated چاک چاک chāk' chak ADV. torn (with grief) چاک کرنا chāk kar'nā V.T. tear rend slit چاک گریباں chā'k-e gire'-bān N.M. collar slit گریباں چاک gire'bān-chāk ADJ. mad afflicted sad [P]

چاک[2] chāk N.M. potter's wheel sugar-making vessel pulley for

چاک[3] chāk N.M. chalk [E]

چاکر chā'kar N.M. (derog.) servant under-servant نوکر چاکر nau'kar chā'kar N.M. PL. servants چاکری chāk'rī N.F. service menial employment servitude [P]

چاکسو chāk'soo N.M. name of an ophthalmic medicine used for its astringent effect

چاکلیٹ chāk'let N.F. chocolate [E]

چاکی chā'kī N.F. name of trick in fencing, clubbing, etc.

چال chāl N.F. gait ; carriage motion movement ; pace (of horse) (in chess, etc.) move trick strategem tactic method device custom چال چلن chāl' cha'lan N.M. character conduct چال چلنا chāl' chal'nā V.I. play a ruse on deceive (at chess, etc) make a move adopt a method use a strategem walk with the gait (of) چال ڈھال chāl' ḍhāl N.F. gait pace (of horse) manner ; mode ; style کی چال میں آنا kī chāl' meṅ ā'nā V.I. fall into the trap (of) be cheated چالباز chāl'-bāz چالیا chā'liya ADJ. & N.M trickster tricky person [~ چلنا]

چالا chā'lā N.M. bride's first departure to groom's house [doublet of PREC.]

چالاک chā'lak' ADJ. clever astute cunning ; artful چالاکی chālā'kī N.F. cleverness astuteness craftiness ; cunning چالاکی کرنا chālā'kī kar'nā V.T. over-reach [P]

چالان chālan' N.M. challan : registering a criminal case or forwarding it to magistrate for trial invoice bank 'challan'; remittance

چالیس chālīs' ADJ. & N.M. forty چالیسا chālī'sā N.M. forty-year-old person champion who has trounced forty persons in various bouts چالیسواں chālis'vāṅ ADJ. fortieth N.M. funeral rites on fortieth day after the death (of someone)

چام chām N.M. hide skin leather چام کے دام چلانا chām ke dām' chalā'nā V.I. stretch one's transient authority to the utmost [~ چمڑا]

چانپ[1] chāṅp N.F. chop fried (mutton, etc.) chop [~ E CORR.]

چانپ[2] chāṅp N.F. part of gun connecting barrel with stock ; lock (of gun) (arch.) arrow چانپ چڑھانا chāṅp chaṛhā'nā V.I. cock a gun

چانپا chāṅ'pā N.F. (in book-binding) leaf etc. pasted with a folded forme dough

چانٹا chāṅ'ṭā N.M. slap ; cuff چانٹا لگانا (یا رسید کرنا) chāṅ'ṭā lagā'nā (or pseudo-ped rasīd' kar'nā) V.I. slap ; cuff

چاند chāṅd N.M. moon new moon lunar month white spot on animal's forehead target N.F. crown ; pate چاند پر تھوکا اپنے ہی منہ پر آتا ہے chāṅd' par thoo'kā ap'ne hī mūṅh par ā'tā hai PROV. bid to malign a noble character is self-condemnatory چاند تارا chāṅd'-tā'rā V.I. چاند چڑھنا chāṅd'-chaṛh'nā V.I. (of new moon) appear (of moon) rise چاند رات chāṅd'-rāt N.F. night of the new moon; first night of lunar month چاند سا مکھڑا chāṅd' sā mūkh'ṛā N.M. & ADJ. bright lovely (face) چاند کا ٹکڑا chāṅd kā ṭūk'ṛā N.M. & ADJ very lovely (figure) چاند کو گرہن لگنا chāṅd ko garai'han lag'nā V.I. (of moon) eclipse چاند گہن (یا گرہن) chāṅd' gai'han (or garai'han) N.M. lunar eclipse چاند ماری chāṅd'-mā'rī N.F. target practice rifle range چاند ماری کرنا chāṅd'mā'rī kar'nā V.I. practice firing at a target خالی کا چاند khā'lī ka chāṅd' N.M. appearance of eleventh Hijri month's moon (so called because the month has no festival falling in it) چاند ہونا chāṅd ho'nā V.I. (of new moon) be sighted appear عید کا چاند ہو جانا 'īd' kā chāṅd ho jā'nā V.I. be seen very rarely . appear at long interv... چاند نہ چاہیے بندا chāṅd' nā chā'he bāṅ'dā PR...

a handsome face needs no paints چاندنا chand'na N.M. (rare & arch.) light چاندنی chand'ni N.F. moonlight moonbeams cloth spread over a carpet a kind of flower چاندنی چٹکنا (یا چھٹکنا) chand'ni cha'taknā (or chha'taknā) V.I. (of moonlight) spread چاندنی کھلنا chand'ni khil'nā V.I. (of moonlight) spread چاندنی رات chand'ni rat' N.F. moonlit night

چاندی chan'di N.F. silver wealth gain ; profit ashes چاندی کا ورق chan'di ka va'raq N.M. silver leaf چاندی کر دینا chan'di kar de'na V.I. burn down to ashes چاندی ہونا (یا ہو جانا) chan'di ho'nā (or ho ja'na) V.I. make good money be burnt down to ashes

چانسلر chans'lar N.M. chancellor [E]

چاول cha'val, (vulg. چانول chan'val) N.M. rice rice-dish one-eighth of 'ratti'

چاہ[1] chah N.M. well pit چاہ بابل cha'h-e ba'bil N.M. the Babylonian pit (where Haroot and Maroot were hung by the heels as penalty for their love for Venus) ; the (Oriental) Tartarus چاہ ذقن cha'h-e zaqan, چاہ زنخدان cha'h-e zanakh'dan N.M. dimple of the chin چاہ کن را چاہ در پیش chah'-kan ra chah' dar pesh' PROV. he who digs a well for others often falls into it چاہ نخشب cha'h-e nakh'shab N.M. Muqanna's well with artificial moon at its bottom marvel of magic چاہی cha'hi ADJ. well-irrigated (land) [P]

چاہ[2] chah N.F. love fondness longing want ; need wish چاہت chahat N.F. want; need fondness love چاہو cha'ho CONJ. (do what) you will either...or [~ FOLL.]

چاہنا chah'na V.T. like love ask for want ; need desire require pray ; request order aim چاہیے cha'hiye AUX. V. should ; ought must have to ADV. die right چاہے cha'he CONJ. no matter what چاہے... چاہے cha'he...cha'he CONJ. either......or چاہے جتنا cha'he jit'nā ADV. howsoever much ; however great چاہے جو cha'he jo ADV. whoever whatever whatever چاہیتا chahe'ta N.M. (F. چاہیتی chahe'ti) sweetheart ; beloved ADJ. favourite

چاؤ cha''o N.M. eagerness keenness longing gusto چاؤ چوچلا cha''o choch'la N.M. (usu. PL.) fondling dalliance eagerness

چاؤش cha''ush N.M. herald door-keeper ; janitor [T]

چاوں چاوں cha''oon cha''oon N.F. (same as چائیں چائیں N.F. ★)

چائے cha''e N.F. tea چائے پوچی cha''e po'chi N.F. (arch.) (same as چائے دانی N.F. ★) cha''e-da'ni N.F. [P ~ Chinese]

چائیں چائیں cha''in cha''in چاوں چاوں cha''oon cha''oon N.F. fuss ; ado

چبانا chaba'na V.T. chew masticate gnaw crunch champ bite چبا چبا کے بات کرنا chaba' chaba' ke bat' kar'na V.I. mince one's words speak affectedly چبنی ہڈی chab'ni had'di N.F. cartilage ; gristle چبوانا chabva'na V.T. cause to chew ; cause to masticate ناک چنے چبوانا nak' chane chabva'na V.T. set a very difficult task harass set hard row to hoe put (someone) in hot water

چبڑ چبڑ cha'bar cha'bar N.F. chatter silly talk [ONO.]

چبکنا cha'bakna V.I. (of wound) throb be painful thus چبک cha'bak N.F. painful throb (of wound)

چبلا chabil'la ADJ. childish (disposition) چبلاپن chibilla-pan N.M. childishness

چبوترا chaboot'ra' چبوترہ chaboot'rah N.M. platform dais terrace

چبھنا chubh'na V.I. be pricked be pierced be thrust be goaded pinch ; be disagreeable feel pinpricks چبھتی chubh'ti ADJ. & N.F. stinging ; pinpricks چبھتی کہنا chubh'ti kaih'na V.I. say stinging things چبھن chu'bhan' N.F. prick ; pricking pinch ; pinching pinching pain pinpricks چبھونا chubho'na V.T. prick pierce thrust (into) sting goad

چبینا chabi'na N.M. parched grain, etc. for munching [~ چبانا]

چپ chap ADJ. left (side) چپ راست chap-rast INT. (as drill caution) left right چپ و راست chap-o rast N.M. & ADV. right and left all directions [P]

چپ chup N.F. silence quietness stillness INT. silence ; quiet mum is the word don't talk nonsense ; shut up چپ چاپ chup chap ADV. silently quietly sneakingly with muffled sound ADJ. quite ; silent reticent چپ چپ chup' chup, چپ گپ chup' g p ADJ. reticent secretive چپ چپاتے chup' chupa'te, چپکے چپکے chup'ke chup'ke ADV. secretly stealthily sneakingly quietly چپ رہنا chup' raih'na, چپ (یا چپکی) سادھنا chup' (or chup'ki) sadh'na V.I. keep mum keep quiet ; remain silent give no reply چپ کرانا chup' kara'na V.T. silence pacify ; appease amuse (weeping child) چپ کرنا chup' kar'na V.I. (of weeping child) be amused be appeased keep quiet stop talking چپ کی داد خدا دیتا ہے chup' ki dad khuda' de'ta hai PROV. patience hath a reward چپ لگنا chup' lag'na V.T. be struck dumb lose power of speech چپ ہونا *chup' ho'na* V.T. keep mum ; keep quiet be silent make no reply

چپا *chap'pa*, چپہ *chap'pah* N.M. hand breadth very little space چپّا چپّا *chap'pa chap'pa* N.M. every inch of ground ; every nook and corner چپّا چپّا چھان مارنا *chap'pā chap'pa chhan mar'nā* V.T. look all over the place ; search every nook and corner

چپانا *chapā'nā* V.I. humiliate cause to feel shame cause to smart [CAUS ~ چپنا]

چپاتی *chapā'tī* N.F thin cake of unleavened dough: chupatty

چپاول *chapā'val* N.F depredation assault by a detachment [P]

چپت *cha pat* N.M. slap cuff box rebuff کے منہ پر چپت *ke mūnh par cha'pat* PL. (esp.) rebuff کے چپت لگانا (یا جڑنا) *ke cha'pat lagā'nā* (or *jaṛ'nā*) V.T. slap rebuff

چپٹا *chap'ṭa* ADJ. (F چپٹی *chap'ṭī*) flat flattened compressed N.M. flat-nosed person

چپٹنا *chi'paṭna* V T cling (to) stick (to) adhere (to) be joined (to) embrace

چپٹانا *chipṭa'na* V.T glue stick join fasten patch embrace

چپٹی *chap'ṭī* ADJ. flat flattened compressed N.F flat-nosed woman female homosexuality چپٹی کھیلنا *chap'ṭī khel'na* V.T & I. (of woman) practise homosexuality

چپچپانا *chipchipā'nā* V. be sticky be glutinous be adhesive چپچپا *chip'chipa* ADJ. sticky glutinous adhesive چپچپاہٹ *chipchipā'haṭ* N.F stickiness glutinousness adhesiveness

چپراس *chapras'* N.F. peons' breast-plate peon's office چپراسی *chaprā'sī* N.M. peon orderly

چپڑ چپڑ *cha'par cha'par* N.F. sound of lapping undesireable sound made in eating jabbar ADV. in an unmannerly fashion چپڑ خندی *cha'par-khan'dī* N.M. loose woman چپڑ غٹو کر کے *cha'par ghaṭ'ṭoo kar ke* PH. having involved in trouble چپڑ قناتیا *cha'par-qanā'tiyā* ADJ. & N.M. mean (person) sycophant

چپڑا *chap'ra* N.M. blear-eyed one with constant discharge from eyes

چپڑا *chip'ṛa* ADJ. & N.F. purified (sealing-wax)

چپڑنا *chū'par na* V.T. besmear (bread with butter (one's bread) anoint lubricate oil grease چپڑی *chup'rī* ADJ. buttered oiled greasy (usu. چکنی چپڑی *chik'nī chup'rī*) plausible cajoling said with a facile tongue

چپڑی روٹی *chup'rī ro'ṭī* N.F buttered bread ; besmeared bread چپڑی اور دو دو *chup'rī aur do' do* PROV you cannot eat your cake and have it too

چپقلش *chapqūlash* (col *chap'qalish*) N.F had blood row ; alteration struggle ; strife ☆ (old use) sword fight [T]

چپک *chippak* چپخ *chip'pakh* N.F goatsucker

چپکنا *chi'pakna* V.I. stick be pasted be affixed adhere be compressed ; be flattened ; be flat چپکانا *chipkā'na* V.T. stick paste affix cause to adhere compress flatten

چپکن *chap'kan* N.F. a kind of 'angrakha now forming part of peon's livery [P]

چپل *chap'pal*, چپلی *chap'lī* N.F. sandle slipper

چپنا *chap'na* V.I. smart feel humiliated

چپنی *chap'nī* N.F. lid (for pot or pitcher) knee-cap چپنی بھر پانی میں ڈوب مرو *chap'nī bhar pa'nī men doob ma'ro* INT. shame ; fie ; die of shame

چپو *chap'poo* N.M. oar ; paddle چپو چلانا *chapp'oo chalā'na* V.I. row, paddle ; oar ; propel with oars

چپوٹا *chapo'ṭa* N M. slap cuff

چپوٹی *chapo'ṭī* N.F tattered turban worn-out cap caved-in hat

چپی *chap'pī* N.F. massage, kneading (of limbs) چپی کرنا *chapp'pī kar'na* V.T. knead (someone's limbs (fig.) coax ; cajole (fig.) serve

چپی *chip'pī* N.F. (same as چپنی N.F ★)

چپیٹ *chapet'* N.F. slap blow shock sudden loss

چت *chit* N.F. mind memory thought idea ADJ. supine ADV lying on the back چت پر چڑھنا *chit' par chaṛh'na* V T & I. take possession of (someone's) mind be remembered by ride, etc. on the back of چت چور *chit'-chor* ADJ. heartenticing N.M. darling beloved sweetheart چت کرنا *chit kar'na* V.T (in wrestling defeat ; throw (someone) on his back overcome overpower discomfit چت لیٹنا *chit' leṭ na* V.I. lie on one's back

چتا *chi'ta* N F pyre ; funeral pile

چتر *chat'r* N.M. umbrella parasol garden umbrella

چتر **chit'r** چترا **chit'rā** N.M. (dial.) picture painting چتراکار **chit'rā-kār** N.M. (dial.) artist painter [S]

چتر **cha'tur** چاتر **chā'tur** ADJ. & N.M. clever trickster cunning چترائی **chaturā''ī** N.F. cleverness cunning

چتکبرا **chitkab'rā** ADJ. (F. چتکبری **chitkab'rī**), **chit'lā** (F. چتلی **chit'lī**) spotted speckled

چتون **chit'van** N.F. countenance ; visage sight ; look ; glance aspect . appearance looks چتون چڑھانا **chit'van charhā'nā** V.I. frown ; scowl ; glower تیکھی چتون **tī'khī chit'van** N.F. frown ; scowl ; glower چتون پرمیل نہ لانا **chit'van par mail' (na) lā'nā** V.I. (not) to be displeased (not) to show signs of displeasure

چتھاڑنا **chithār'nā** V.T. tatter tear to pieces debase . put to shame چتھاڑ **chithār'** N.F. humiliation ; abasement [~ چیتھڑا]

چتھل **chut'thal** N.M. (W. dial.) court fool ; jester چتھل بازی **chut'thal-bā'zī** N.F. acting the fool joking , jesting

چتلی **chit'lī** N.F. spot stain scar چتلی پڑھانا **chit'lī parhā'nā** V.I. become spotted ripen be fully baked چتلی دار **chit'lī-dār** ADJ. spotted ; speckled stained scarred

چتیرا **chite'rā** N.M. metalware engraver

چٹ **chit** N.F. slip . scrap of paper note scribbled on a slip introductory (etc.) letter chit [Anglo-Pakistani ~ چٹھی]

چٹ **chat**, چٹ پٹ **chat' pat** ADV. quickly instantly without delay چٹ پٹ ہونا **chat' pat ho'nā** V.I. die instantaneously ; die in no time چٹ منگنی پٹ بیاہ **chat' mang'nī pat biyāh'** PH. instantaneous implementation ADV. in a jiffy ; instantaneously چٹ کر جانا **chat' kar jā'nā** V.T. eat up devour ; consume lick the platter clean

چٹا **chit'tā** ADJ. (F. چٹی **chit'tī**) white (only in) گورا چٹا **go'rā chit'tā** ADJ. white fair

چٹاخ **chatākh** N.F. sound of cracking sound of beating spot spot caused by beating چٹاخ پٹاخ **chatākh' patākh'** ADV. pat saucily without hesitation at once in quick succession N.F. sound of crack smack

چٹاخا **chatā'khā**, چٹاکا **chatā'kā** N.M. crack explosion smack force (of) abundance (of)

چٹان **chatān'** N.F. rock rocky ground a large block of stone

چٹانا **chatā'nā** V.T. cause to lick [~ چاٹنا CAUS.]

چٹائی **chatā''ī** N.F. mat ; rush or palm mat

چٹپٹا **chat'patā** ADJ. (F. چٹپٹی **chat'patī**) savoury tasty

چٹ چٹ **chat' chat**, چٹاچٹ **cha'tā chat** N.F. repeated cracks (of finger's) crack crackle چٹ چٹ بلائیں لینا **chat chat' balā''eṅ le'nā** V.T. overwhelm (child) with kisses

چٹخارا **chitkhā'rā** . (dial. چٹکا **chat'kā**) N.M. relish zest taste smack cluck چٹخارے بھرنا (یا لینا) **chatkhā're bhar'nā (or le'nā)** V.I. cluck or smack tongue in craving or appreciation

چٹک مٹک **cha'tak ma'tak** N.F. wanton gait coquetry blandishment چٹک مٹک سے چلنا **cha'tak ma'tak se chal'nā** V.I. walk with a coquetish gait

چٹکلا **chut'kulā** N.M. joke humour wit witticism pleasantry cheap but efficacious remedy mischief چٹکلا چھوڑنا **chut'kula chhor'nā** V.I. jest let off a squib

چٹخنا **cha'takhnā**, چٹکنا **cha'taknā** V.I. bloom open out split crack crackle speak rudely چٹخ (یا چٹک) جانا **cha'takh (or cha'tak) jā'na** V.I. crack split چٹخانا **chatkhā'na**, چٹکانا **chatkā'nā** V.T. crackle crack snap (fingers) split

چٹخنی **chat'khanī** چٹکنی **chat'kanī** N.F. bolt (of door etc.)

چٹکی **chut'kī** N.F. pinch pinch (of) little bit snap (of fingers) twist the hammer of a gun چٹکی بجانا **chut'kī bajā'nā** V.I. snap the fingers چٹکی بجاتے میں **chut'kī bajā'te meṅ** ADV. at once ; in a moment ; in a trice ; in a jiffy چٹکی بھر **chut'kī bhar** ADJ. a pinch of ; a little چٹکی بھرنا (یا لینا) **chut'kī bhar'nā (or le'nā)** V.T. pinch nip (usu. چٹکیاں لینا **chut'kiyāṅ le'nā**) make restless چٹکیوں میں اڑانا **chut'kiyoṅ meṅ ūrā'nā** V.T. ridicule put (someone) off with a joke show no regard (for)

چٹکیلا **chatkī'lā** ADJ. (F. چٹکیلی **chatkī'lī**) (of colour gaudy (of taste) sharp more than usual unpleasantly excessive رنگیلا چٹکیلا **rangī'la chatkī'la** N.M. (euphemism for) parched gram

چٹلا **chut'lā** N.M. (also چوٹی **cho'tī**) hair plaited at back ; pigtail tassel plaited into it

چٹنی **chat'nī** N.F sauce chutney any highly seasoned paste چٹنی بنانا **chat'nī banā'nā**, چٹنی کر ڈالنا **chat'nī kar dāl'na** V.T. eat up hurriedly grind very fine beat black and blue چٹنی ہو جانا **chat'nī ho jā'na** V.I. (of dish) be finished too soon [~ چاٹنا]

چٹوانا **chatvā'nā** V.T. cause to lick [~ چاٹنا CAUS.]

چٹورا **chaṭo'ra** N.M. gourmet ; epicure gourmand . glutton one given to eating every now and then چٹورپن **chaṭor'-pan** N.M. epicurean tastes gluttony one wasting one's money on eating delicacies every now and then

چٹھا **chaṭ'ṭha** N.M. skin spot (indicating diseased condiction)

چٹھا **chiṭ'ṭha** N.M. pay roll pay wages account book inventory کچا چٹھا **kach'cha chiṭ'ṭha** N.M. unsavoury details account of misdeeds کا کچا چٹھا کھولنا **ka kach'cha chiṭ'ṭha kho'lna** V.T. expose (someone)

چٹھی **chiṭ'ṭhi** N.F. letter note chit bill; draft certificate چٹھی ڈالنا **chiṭ'ṭhi ḍal'na** V.I. post a letter چٹھی رساں **chiṭ'ṭhi rasan** N.M. (hybrid compound) postman چٹھیاں بانٹنا **chiṭ'ṭhiyan banṭ'na** V.T. deliver letters ; deliver mail

چٹی **chaṭ'ṭi** N.F. fine . damages چٹی بھرنا **chaṭ'ṭi bhar'na** V.I. indemnify pay damage

چٹی **chiṭ'ṭi** ADJ. (see under چٹا ADJ. ★)

چٹیا **chuṭ'ya** N.M. hair plaited at back worn by the male Hindu

چٹیانا **chuṭya'na**, چٹیلنا **chuṭel'na** V.T. bite wound ; bruise

چٹے بٹے **chaṭ'ṭe baṭ'ṭe** N.M. PL. balls, etc. used in juggler's tricks چٹے بٹے لڑانا **chaṭ'ṭe baṭ'ṭe laṛa'na** V.T. (of juggler) play conjuring tricks ; juggle ایک ہی تھیلی کے چٹے بٹے **ek' hi thai'li ke chaṭ'ṭe baṭ'ṭe** PH. birds of the same feather ; chips of the old block

چٹیکن **chaṭe'kan** N.F. slap ; rap

چٹیل **chaṭ'yal** ADJ. treeless (tract) desolate (land) level (ground)

چیجی **chij ji** N.F. same as چیزی N.F. (see under چیز N.F. ★)

چچا **cha'cha** N.M. father's (younger) brother uncle چچا بنا کر چھوڑنا **cha'cha bana kar chhoṛ'na** V.T. penalize set (someone) right چچازاد بھائی (یا بہن) **cha'chazad bha''i** (or **baihan**) N.M. cousin paternal uncle's son (or daughter)

چچانا **chucha'na**, چچھانا **chuchha'na** چچیانا **chuchya'na** V.I. (of fruit) be bursting as though about to exude be oozy drip (of cheeks) be rosy ; flush

چچڑی **chich'ri**, چچڑی **chich'ri** N.F. tick

چچوڑنا **chachoṛ'na** V.T. chew and suck (bones)

چچی **cha'chi** N.F. wife of father's younger brother; aunt [~ چچا]

چچیرا **chache'ra** ADJ. related on the side of one's paternal uncle [~ چچا]

چخ **chakh** N.F. quarrel brawl چخا چخی **cha'kha cha'khi**, چخ چخ **chakh' chakh** N.F. chatter quarrel dispute wrangling brawl (میں) چخ چلنا **(men) chakh' chal'na** V.T. (of quarrel) take place (between) چخیا **chakh ya** N.M. prattler : chatterer

چخے **cha'khe** INT. be off ; begone ; avaunt

چدانا **chuda'na** V.I. (of female) have sexual intercourse چداس **chudas'** N.F. female's desire for it ; heat ; sexual urge [CAUS. ~ چودنا]

چدریا **chad'dar** N.M. (vulg. for چادر N.F. ★)

چدر **chadar'ya** N.F. small coverlet small shawl [~ P چادر DIM.]

چڈا **chaḍ'ḍa**, چڈھا **chaḍ'ḍha** N.M. groin (also چڈا گل خیرو **chaḍ'ḍa gul-khai'roo**) buffon ; fool

چڈھی **chaḍ'ḍhi** N.F. riding on (someone's) back چڈھی چڑھنا (یا توڑنا) **chaḍ'ḍhi charh'na** (or **toṛ'na**) V.T. ride on the back چڈھی چڑھانا **chaḍ'ḍhi charha'na** V.T. carry (someone) on the back چڈھی دینا **chaḍ'ḍhi de'na** V.T. carry thus be the minion to [PREC.]

چر **char** N.F. چرانا **charra'ṭa** N.M. sound made in tearing cloth

چراغ **chara'gh** (ped. **chiragh'**) N.M. lamp ; light چراغ بجھانا **charagh' baṛha'na**, چراغ بڑھانا **charagh' bujha'na**, چراغ ٹھنڈا کرنا **charagh' ṭhan'ḍa kar'na**, چراغ گل کرنا **charagh gul kar'na** V.I. put out a light extinguish a lamp چراغ پا ہونا **charagh' pa ho'na** V.I. be angry چراغ تلے اندھیرا **charagh' ta'le andhe'ra** PROV. darkness prevails at the lamp's base چراغ جلنا **charagh' jal'na**, چراغ روشن ہونا **charagh' rau'shan ho'na** V.I. (of lamp) be lighted چراغ جلانا **charagh' jala'na** V.T. light a lamp dispel darkness چراغدان **charagh'-dan** N.M. lamp-stand چراغ دکھانا **charagh' dikha'na** V.T. show a light چراغ سحر(ی) **chara'gh e sa'har(i)** ADJ. approaching the end of life چراغ سے پھول جھڑنا **charagh' se phool' jhaṛ'na**, چراغ کا ہنسنا **charagh' ka hans'na** V.I. leaking of oil from lamp (as good omen) چراغ میں بتی پڑنا **charagh' men bat'ti paṛ'na** V.I. (of might) approaching چراغ سے چراغ جلتا ہے **charagh' se charagh jal'ta hai** PROV. one lamp serves to light others چراغ لے کر ڈھونڈنا **charagh' le kar dhoonḍ'na** V.T. search for (something) thoroughly گھی کے چراغ جلنا **ghi ke charagh' jal'na** V. make great pomp and show be overjoyed بے چراغ **be charagh'** ADJ. dark ; unlit deserted home laoking male issue چراغاں **chara'ghan** N.M. illuminations چراغی **chara'ghi** N.F. offerings for light at shrine چراغی دینا (یا چڑھانا) **chara'ghi de'na** (or **charha'na**) V.T. make such offering

چراگاہ **charāgāh'** N.F. meadow pasture grazing ground [P ~ گاہ + چرانا]

چرانا **charānā'** V.T graze ; pasture make a fool (of)

چرانا **chūrā'na** V.T. steal pilfer : filch embezzle ; defalcate turn away (eyes from) آنکھ چرانا **āṅkh chūrā'nā** V.T. turn away the eyes (from) ; dodge ; evade

چرانڈ **chirāṅd'** N.F. smell of burning leather, hair, etc.

چرائتا **chira''tā**, چرائتہ **chira''etah** N.M. a species of gentian ; gentian

چرائی **chira''ī** N.F. (see under چرنا **chir'nā** V.I. ★)

چرائی **chara''ī** N.F. (see under چرنا **char'nā** V.I. ★)

چرب **char'b** ADJ. fat , greasy ; oily (of food) rich facile چرب زبان **charb-zabān'** ADJ. glib facile plausible (person) چرب زبانی **char'b-zabā'nī** N.F. facile tongue , glibness plausibility [P]

چربانک **charbaṅk'**, چرباک **charbāk'** ADJ. clever saucy

چربہ **char'bah** N.M. tracing copy duplicate copy for printing چربہ اتارنا **char'bah ūtār'na** V. make a tracing copy prepare a duplicate [P]

چربی **char'bī** N.F. fat suet tallow چربی دار **char'bī-dar** ADJ. fat ; fatty greasy [P]

چرپرانا **charparā'nā** V.I. (of wound) smart چرپرا **char'parā** ADJ. pungent acrid چرپراہٹ **charpara'haṭ** N.F. acridity

چرتر **charit'r** N.M. (usu. PL.) trick تریا چرتر **tir'ya chasit'r** N.M. (usu. PL.) women's wiles [S]

چرچ **char'ch** N.M. church [E]

چرچا **char'chā** N.M. publicize spread reports (about) چرچا ہونا **char'cha ho'nā** V.I. be talked about be discussed become the talk of the town be publicized get a lot of publicity

چرچرانا **charcharā'nā** V.I. be hot ; be pungent smart chatter ; prate چرچرا **char'charā** ADJ. (F. چرچری **char'charī**) hot , pungent چرچراہٹ **charcharā'haṭ** N.F. creaking (of shoes or bed) crackling pain

چرخ **char'kh** N.M. sky ; the heavens sphere wheel potter's wheel lathe pulley wheel for pressing woollen shawls circular motion چرخ اخضر **char'kh-e akhzar** N.M. ethereal sphere چرخ اطلس **char'kh-e at'las** N.M. heaven , crystaline sphere چرخ بریں **char'kh-e barīn'** N.M. high heaven چرخ چڑھانا **char'kh charhā'nā** V.T. turn on a lethe چرخ کھانا **char'kh khā'nā** V.I. turn round whirl rotate revolve چرخ ہنڈولا **char'kh haṅdo'lā** N.M. merry-go-round [P]

چرخ چوں **char'rakh choon** N.F. sound of spinning wheel [ONO.]

چرخہ **char'khah** N.M. spinning wheel (rare) skeleton ADJ. lean run.down decrepit چرخہ کاتنا **charkhah kāt'na** V.I. spin; draw thread from cotton on a spinning wheel چرخہ پونی **char'khah poo'nī** N.M. spinning wheel and its concomitants woman's responsibility ; feminine accomplishments چرخہ ہو جانا **char'khah ho jā'nā** V.I. grow old be enervated چرخی **char'khī** N.F. small spinning wheel gin reel a kind of fire-works ; catherine-wheel چرخی فانوس **char'khī fānoos'** N.M. revolving lamp projecting pictures on shade [~ P چرخ]

چرس **cha'ras** N.F. hemp extract ; cannabis resin ; marijuana ; pot large leathern bucket چرسی **char'sī** N.M. one addicted to hemp-extract smoking ; pot addict

چرسا **char'sa** N.M. large leathern bucket ; irrigation bucket hide skin چرسا بھر **char'sā bhar** ADJ. (of land) as little as can be irrigated with a bucket

چرغہ **char'ghah** N.M. (dial.) roast fowl

چرغلینہ **charghilnah** ADJ. squint-eyed mean

چرک **chirk** N.M. (rare.) filth dirt چرکیں **chir'kīn** N.M. non-de-plume of an Urdu poet filthy [P]

چرکا **charkā** N.M. slight wound چرکا لگانا (یا دینا) **char'kā lagā'nā** (or **de'nā**) V.T. wound

چرکٹا **char'kaṭā** N.M. one who feeds elephant low fellow [~ کاٹنا + چارہ]

چرکنا **chi'rakna** V.I. have scanty stools

چرکنا **chū'rakna** V.I. (derog.) speak out

چرم **char'm** N.M. (ped.) leather skin hide چرمی **char'mī** ADJ. leather : leathern [P]

چرمر **chūr' mūr** N.M. pounded ; pulverized

چرمرانا **chirmirā'na** V.I. smart چرمراہٹ **chirmirā'haṭ** N.F smart ; prickly sensation

چرن **cha'ran** N.M. (dial.) foot چرن چھونا (یا لینا) **cha'ran chhoo'nā** (or **le'nā**) V.T. (dial.) touch the feet (of) [S]

چرنا **chir'na** V.I. be torn be cleft be slit be sawed چروانا **chirva na** V.T cause to be torn cause to be sawed چرائی، چروائی **chirā''ī, chirvā'ī** N.F. remuneration for sawing

چرنا **char'na** V.T. graze چروانا **charvā'na** V.T. cause

to graze

چرندہ charın'dah (rare.) چرند charind N.M. grazing animal, quadruped چرند و پرند charın'd(o) parınd' N.M beasts and birds ; beasts of earth and birds of air [P]

چرواہا charvā'hā N.M. shepherd herdsmen چرواہی charvā'hī N.F. shepherdess remuneration for pasturage

چرونجی chiron'jī N.F. pickle berry

چری cha'rī N.F. unripe corn cut for fodder

چڑ chir N.F. pet aversion (someone's) mocking name nickname vexation banter چڑ نکالنا chir' nikal'nā V.T. banter vex mock invents a mocking name (for)

چڑ chur N.F. vulva چڑمرانی chur marā'nī N.F. & ADJ. (as swear-word) food.

چڑا chi'ṛā N.M. cock-sparrow.

چڑانا chiṛā'nā V.T. vex mock offend make grimaces

چڑ چڑ chaṛ' chaṛ, چڑبڑ chaṛ' baṛ N.F. silly talk ; prattle sputter sizzle crackle

چڑچڑ chiṛ' chiṛ N.F. sizzle sputter

چڑچڑا chiṛ' chiṛā ADJ. peevish ; cross ; fretful ; irritable چڑچڑاپن chiṛ'-chiṛā-pan N.M. peevishness, fretfulness irritability

چڑنا chiṛ'nā V.I. be irritated be vexed ; fret and fume

چڑھانا chaṛhā'nā V.T. raise lift cause to ascend cause to mount put into include enter quaff ; gulp fix affix dye (with colour) string (bow) brace (drum) make an offering increase (16) augment چڑھا جانا chaṛhā' jā'nā V.T. gulp down چڑھاؤ chaṛhā''o N.M. ascent rise (of river, prices etc.) increase inundation اتار چڑھاؤ ūtār' chaṛhā''o N.M. ascent and discent rise and fall ebb and flow چڑھاوا chaṛhā'vā N.M. offering, oblation چڑھائی chaṛhā''ī N.F. ascent invasion ; inroad ; incursion

چڑھنا chaṛh'nā V.I. get on the back of, mount ascend climb rise embark be offered (at shrine; etc.) be used as a covering cover چڑھتا chaṛh'tā ADJ. (F. چڑھتی chaṛh'tī) rising soaring increasing چڑھتی جوانی chaṛh'tī javā'nī N.F. bloom of youth ; prime of youth چڑھیت chaṛhait N.M. paederast

چڑیا chiṛ'ya N.F. sparrow ; hen-sparrow (dial.) bird چڑیا گھر chiṛ'yā-ghar N.M. the zoo سونے کی چڑیا son'e kī chiṛ'ya N.F. highly valued prize rich bag

چڑیل chūṛail N.F. witch (dial.) ghost of woman dying during pregnancy bag vixen shrew slut slattern

چڑیمار chi'ṛī-mār N.M. fowler ; birdcatcher [~ چڑیا + مارنا]

چسانا chūsā'nā V.T. cause to sip suckle [CAUS. ~ چوسنا]

چسپاں chas'pāṅ ADJ. affixed pasted stuck, sticking applicable apt چسپاں کرنا chas'pāṅ kar'nā V.T. affix paste ; apply use aptly چسپاں ہونا chas'pāṅ ho'nā V.I. be affixed be pasted be applicable be to the point [P ~ چسپیدن]

چسپیدگی chaspī'dagī N.F. adhesion [P ~ چسپیدن]

چست chūst ADJ. active agile smart alert brisk چست (و) چالاک chūst(o) chālāk' ADJ. active and alert clever چستی chūs'tī N.F. alertness smartness nimbleness [P]

چسک cha'sak N.F. (see under چسکنا V.I. ★)

چسکا chas'kā N.M. taste (for) relish habit (of) fondness (for) چسکا پڑنا chas'ka par'na V.I. acquire a taste (for) develop a fondness for

چسکنا cha'saknā V.I. throb have mild pain چسک chasak N.F. throbbing pain mild sensation (of pain)

چسکی chūskī N.F. sip draught چسکی لگانا chūs kī lagā'nā V.T. sip have a draught (of)

چسنا chūsnā V.I. be sucked be sipped be enervated grow lean [~ چوسنا]

چسنی chūs'nī, چوسنی choos'nī N.F (child's soother [~ چوسنا]

چشتی chish'tī N.M. name of Muslim mystical school its follower appellation of its founder

چشم chash'm N.F. eye (lit.) hope ; expectation چشم بد دور chash'm-e bad door' INT. God preserve you from evil eyes well-done wonderful کے لیے چشم براہ ہونا ke lī'ye chash'm ba-rah' ho'na V.I. look forward keenly to چشم بیمار chash'm-e bīmār' N.M. languid eye (as attribute of beauty) (fig.) beloved ; sweetheart چشم پوشی chash'm-po'shī N.F. connivance ; overlooking forgiving, pardoning چشم پوشی کرنا chash'm po'shī kar'nā V.T. connive (at) overlook excuse ; pardon چشم زدن chash'm za'dan N.F. wink ; blinking winking چشم زدن میں chash'm za'dan meṅ ADV. in an instant ; instantaneously ; in a trice ; in a jiffy چشم نمائی chash'm nūmā''ī N.F. reproof ; reprimand scolding threat چشم نمائی کرنا chash'm nūmā''ī kar'na V.T. reprove ; reprimand scold threaten چشم وچراغ *chash'm-o-charāgh'* (or-*chi*-) N.M. scion (of a family) darling آہو چشم *ā'hoo-chash'm* ADJ. gazelle-eyed ; (as attribute of beloved) beloved ; sweetheart [P]

چشمک *chash'mak* N.F. misunderstanding bad blood (between) flash wink [P ~ PREC.]

چشمہ *chash'mah* N.M. fountain ; spring spectacles ; glasses goggles (also سرچشمہ *sar-chash'mah*) source [P]

چغتائی *chaghatā''ī* (col. *chughtā''ī*) N.F. (descended from) Jhengiz's son [T]

چغد *chū'ghad* N.M. a small kind of owl ; screech-owl (fig.) fool

چغل *chugh'l* N.M (usu. چغل خور *chugh'l-khor'*) bearer ; a backbiter ; tell-tale ; tale-bearer pebble placed in hookah bowl to prevent tobacco from falling down چغل خور *chugh'l-kho'r* N.M. back-biter . tell-tale ; tale-bearer چغل خوری *chugh'l-kho'rī* N.F. back-biting ; tale-bearing چغلی *chugh'lī* N.F. back-biting ; tale-bearing چغلی کھانا *chugh'lī khā'na* V.T. backbite [P]

چغہ *chū'ghah*, چوغہ *cho'ghah* N.M. cloak ; gown

چفتی *chaf'tī* N.F. flat ruler footrule ; ruler [E]

چق *chiq* (col. چک *chik*) N.F. folding bamboo, screen ; hanging screen transparent screen [T]

چقماق *chaqmāq'* N.M. flint [T]

چقندر *chūqan'dar* N.M. beet ; sugar-beet ; beet-root

چک *chik* N.F (same as چق *chiq* N.F. ★)

چک *chūk* N.F. back-ache ; pain in the loins

چک *chik* N.M. (same as چیک N.M. ★)

چک *chak* N.M. landed estate tenure holding Hindu butcher curdling چک بندی *chak-bandī* N.F. delimitation of estate

چکا *chak'kā* (dial. ٹھکا *thak'kā*) N.M. rectangular heap (of masonry, etc.) for counting or measuring mass of curdled stuff ADJ. curdled congealed چکا باندھنا (یا لگانا) *chak'kā bāndh'na* (or *lagā'nā*) V.T. make such a heap for measuring or counting

چکاچک *cha'kā chak'* چک چک *chak chak* N.F. sound of rapid cuts (with sword) ADJ. fried in lot of butter چک چک لونڈے *chak' chak laun'de* N.M. PL. well-buttered morsels

چکاچوند *cha'kā-chaund'* N.F. glare effulgence daze

چقندر

چک

چکارا *chikā'ra* N.M. a kind of antelope ; ravine deer two-stringed guitar ; small fiddle

چکاری *chikā'rī* N.F. hunting knife

چکان *chakān'* SUF. dripping [P ~ چکیدن]

چکانا *chūkā'na* V.T. settle (dispute) pay (price) in full pay off (debt) ; repay adjust or clear (account) wangle چکائی *chūkā''ī* N.F. settlement ; adjustment ; wages for settlement ; omission ; an unintentional error

چکاوک *chakā'vak* N.M. settle (price) lark [P]

چک پھیری *chak-phe'rī* N.F. moving about in a circle roaming چک پھیریاں لینا *chak-phe'-riyāṅ le'na* V.I. move about in a circle roam about a aimlessly

چکٹنا *cha'katna* V.I. bite

چکتی *chak'tī* N.F. fatty tail of sheet round. metal plate round leather piece tablet

چکٹنا *chi'kaṭnā* V.I. become greasy be clammy become untidy چکٹ *chik'kaṭ* ADJ. greasy untidy dirty میلا چکٹ *mai'lā chik'kaṭ* ADJ. greasy untidy

چکر *chak'kar* N.M. circumference circuit arbet circle circular concise detour visit fix ; difficulty misfortune confusion giddiness ; vertigo round about disc discuss wheel whirl fraud چکر آنا *chak'kar ānā* V.I. become giddy ; faint چکرانا *chakrā'nā* V.I. be confused be perplexed be bewildered lose one's bearings چکر دینا *chak'kar de'nā* V.I. turn round and round lounge (a horse) defraud چکر کاٹنا (یا لگانا) *chak kar kāṭ'na* (or *lagā'nā*) visit again and again ; pay repeared visits move in a circle چکر کھانا *chak'kar khā'na* V.I. turn round and round whirl rotate revolve make a detour چکر میں آنا *chak'kar meṅ ānā* V.I. be duped be non-plussed be involved in trouble be entangled چکر میں ڈالنا *chak'kar meṅ ḍāl'nā* V.T confuse perplex lead astray involve in trouble

چکرمکر *cha'kar ma'kar* N.F. fraud ; hoax

چکری *chak'rī* N.F. pulley [~ چکر]

چکڑی *chik'ṛī* N.F. comb-wood

چکلا *chak'la*, چکلہ *chak'lah* N.M. brothel red-light area, depraved street (wooden) platter for rolling bread ADJ. (usu. چوڑا چکلا *chau'ṛā chak'la*) wide ; broad circular stodgy

چکلی *chak'lī* N.F. piece of stone for grinding

condiments pulley (of well)

چکمہ **chak'mah**, چکما **chak'mā** N.M. trick fraudulent temptation چکمہ دینا **chak'mah de'nā** V.T. cheat ; defraud play a trick (on) offer fraudulent temptation چکمہ کھانا **chak'mah kha'nā** V.I. be cheated ; be deceived ; be duped fall a prey to fraudulent temptation

چکن **chikan** N.F. embroidered muslin چکن دوز **chikan-doz** N.M. embroiderer چکن دوزی **chikan-dozī** N.F. embroidery (as a profession)

چکنا **chik'nā**, ADJ. (F. چکنی **chik'nī**) oily ; greasy fatty sleek glossy ; polished varnished facile unfaithful چکنا چپڑا **chik'nā chūp'ṛā** ADJ. well-groomed چکنا گھڑا **chik'nā gha'ṛā** N.M. shameless person چکنی چپڑی باتیں کرنا **se chik'nī chūp'ṛī bā'teṅ kar'nā** V.I. flatter coax ; cajole ; wheedle چکنی سپاری **chik'nī sūpā'rī**, چکنی **chik'nī** N.F. milksaturated betel-nut چکنی مٹی **chik'nī maṭ'ṭī** N.F. clay ; clayey soil چکناہٹ **chikna'hat** N.F. oiliness fat content sleekness gloss ; polish ; varnish چکنائی **chiknā''ī** N.F. oil grease fat butter oiliness

چکنا **chūk'nā** V.I. (of price, issue, disputed) be settled (of debt) be repayed AUX. V. be over be a matter of the past finish (doing)

چکنا چور **chak'nā-choor** ADJ. smashed ; broken to pieces ; smashed to smithereens dead tired ; exhausted (with fatigue) چکنا چور کرنا **chak'nā-choor kar'nā** V.T. smash ; break to pieces exhaust (with fatigue) چکنا چور ہونا **chak'nā choor ho'nā** V.I. be smashed ; be broken ; to pieces be exhausted (with fatigue) ; be dead tired

چکوا **chakvā** N.M. (F. چکوی **chak'vī**) ruddygoose ; sheldrake

چکوتا **chūkau'tā** N.M. settlement on stipulated terms bargain fixed rate [~ چکنا **chūk'nā**]

چکوترا **chakot'rā** N.M. pomelo grapefruit shaddock

چکور **chakor'** N.M. red-legged partridge (fig.) loving woman Phoebe's lover

چکھنا **chakh'nā**, کا مزہ چکھنا **kā ma'zah chakh'nā** V.T. taste relish experience (hardship) suffer ; undergo punishment (for mistake etc.) چکھانا **chakhā'nā**, کا مزہ چکھانا **kā ma'zah chakhā'nā** V.T. cause to taste cause to experience (hardship) cause to suffer inflict punishment (for crime, etc.) چکھوتیاں **chakhau'tiyāṅ** N.F. PL choice dishes چکھوتیاں کرنا **chakhau'tiyāṅ kar'nā** V.I eat choice dishes چکھی **chak'khī** N.F. relish (for)

چکوی **chak'vī** N.F. (see under چکوا N.M. ★)

چکی **chak'kī** N.F. mill handmill چکی پیسنا (یا جھونا) **chak'kī pīs'nā** (or dial. **jho'nā**) V.T. work a mill ; grind (corn, etc. (in a mill ; undergo hardship do routine work undergo penal servitude چکی کا پاٹ **chak'kī kā pāṭ'** N.M. millstone چکی کی مشقت **chak'kī kī mashaq'qat** N.F. grinding of millstone as part of penal servitude

چکی پکی **chūk'kī pūk'kī** ADV. (nurs) finished

چکیدہ **chakī'dah** ADJ. dripped [P ~ چکیدن]

چگنا **chūg'nā** V.T. peck چگانا **chūgā'nā** V.T. cause to peck چگی **chūg'gī** ADJ. (of beard) thin ; scanty

چگونہ **chigoo'nah** ADV. (lit.) how in what manner of what kind چگونگی **chigoo'nagī** N.F. (lit.) nature details ; circumstances style ; manner [~ چہ + گونہ]

چل بچل **chal' bi'chal** N.F. disorder panic ADJ. out of order ; out of joint rickety out of place ; misfit

چل **chūl** N.F. itch sudden desere sexual urge ; heat چلچلانا **chūlchūlānā** V.I. itch

چلا **chillā** N.F. fried leavened bread embroidered end of turban (same as چلہ N.M. ★)

چلبلا، چلبلانا **chūlbū'lānā** V.I. be restless , fidget چلبلا **chūl'būlā** ADJ. (F. چلبلی **chūlbūlī**) sportive ; gay coquettish fidgety active چلبلاپن **chūl'būlā-pan**, چلبلاہٹ **chūlbūlā'haṭ** N.F. sportiveness ; gaiety cognetry restlessness

چلتہ **chil'tah** N.M. coat of mail armour [P]

چلچلانا **chilchilā'nā** V.I. (of sun) be very hot چلچلاتی دھوپ **chilchilā'tī dhoop** N.F. blazing sun ; scorching heat

چلغوزہ **chilgho'zah** N.M. pine-nut [P]

چلم **chi'lam** N.F. hookah bowl . fire bowl in hookah چلم بھرنا **chi'lam bhar'nā** V.I. fill hookah-bowl (with tobacco and live-coal) چلمیں بھرنا **chil'meṅ bhar'nā** V.I. serve as a menial (of debauchee) be reduced to penury ; become one's erstwhile concubine's servant [~ P]

چلمچی **chi'lamchī** N.F. handwashing basin wash stand wash basin [T]

چلمن **chil'man** N.M. (arch. or lit.) folding bamboo screen ; hanging screen

چلنا **chal'nā** V.I. go on foot walk go travel move sail flow blow be in demand be in force have influence proceed ; go ahead چل **chal** INT. be off ; begone ; avaunt ; away (with you) go away ; make yourself scarce چل بسنا **chal' bas'nā** V.T. die ; expire ; pass away چل پڑنا **chal' paṛ'nā** V.T. start leave became a going concert چل پھر **chal' phir** N.F. gait way of moving چل چلاؤ **chal-chal''ao** N.M., چلا چلی **cha'lā-cha'lī** last gasps ; approach of death life's transitoriness چل دینا **chal' de'nā** V.T. leave ; start decamp (with) چل جانا **chal' jā'nā** V.I. (of quarrel) arise quarrel (of mind) become eccentric دماغ چل جانا **dimāgh' chal jā'nā** V.I. become insane ; go mad ہلچل **hal'chal** N.F. commotion disturbance چلانا **chalā'nā** V.T. help (someone) walk drive ; propel cause help or force to move stir impel help walk fire (gun, etc.) enforce issue spread ; give currency (to) advance money (on interest) carry on run (business, shop, etc.) چلاؤ **chalā''oo** ADJ. stop-gap or make shift (arrangement) temporary ; transitory shaky ; unstable second rate چلتا **chal'tā**, ADJ. (F. چلتی **chal'tī**) passable ; current thriving ; flourishing in great demand چلتا پرزہ **chal'tā pūr'zah** N.M. (or F.) very clever person intriguer having winning ways چلتی دکان **chal'tī dūkān'** N.F. shop with thriving business ; one with brisk trade چلتا رکھنا **chal'ta rakh'nā** V.T. keep (something) going چلتا رہنا **chal'ta raih'nā** V.I. keep on walking or moving چلتا کرنا **chal'tā kar'nā** V.T. send away kill cause to disappear چلتے پھرتے نظر آؤ **chal'te phir'te na'zar ā''o** PH. چلن **cha'lan** N.M. character behaviour custom currency (of corn, etc.) چلوانا **chalvānā** V.T. make (someone) walk help (someone) conduct

چلانا **chillā'nā** V.T. shriek scream exclaim cry out ; bawl cry ; complain چلاہٹ **chillā'hat** N.F. shriek ; scream

چلہ ۱ **chil'lah** N.M. any forty-day period forty-day seclusion for mystic communion (usu. PL. **chil'lā**) forty-day post-delivery confinement چلہ کرنا یا کھینچنا **chil'lah kar'nā** (or **khainch'nā**) V.I. retire (for forty days) into mystic seclusion [P ~ چہل]

چلہ ۲ **chil'lah**, چلا **chil'lā** N.M. string (of bow) (arch.) gold lace for turban border چلہ باندھنا **chil'lah bāndh'nā** V.I. (dial.) make a vow (by tying thread to tomb) چلہ چڑھانا **chil'lah chaṛhā'nā** V.T. string (a bow)

چلو **chūl'loo** N.M. palm contracted to serve as bowl ; hollowed palm چلو بھر **chūl'loo bhar** ADJ. handful of (a liquid) چلو بھر پانی میں ڈوب مرنا **chūl'loo bhar pā'nī meṅ ḍoob' mar'nā** V.I. be put to great shame چلو سے پانی پینا **chūl'loo se pā'nī pī'nā** V.T. drink water out of one's hand چلو میں الو ہونا **chūl'loo meṅ ūl'loo ho'nā** V.I. be intoxicated with a mouthful

چلو **chalau'**, چلاؤ **chalā''o** N.M. boiled rice [P]

چلیپا **chalī'pā** N.F. cross crucifix ; anything crooked or bent [P]

چمار **chamār'** N.M. currier tanner shoemaker cobbler worker in leather (regarded by Hindus as low-caste person) چماری **chamā'rī** N.F. wife of chamar [~ چمڑا]

چمپا **cham'pā**, چنپا **chan'pā** N.F. shrub with small golden and fragrant flowers; champak champak buds or flowers چمپا کلی **cham'pā ka'lī** N.F. champak bud champak necklace ; necklace shaped like champak buds چمپئی **champā''ī** ADJ. champakcoloured yellow golden

چمپت ہونا **cham'pat ho'nā** V.T. to decamp (with) run away scamper disappear

چمٹا **chim'ṭā** N.M. pair of tongs [~ FOLL.]

چمٹنا **chi'maṭnā** V.T. embrace stick (to) ; cling (to) adhere be pasted ; be offered چمٹانا **chimṭā'nā** V.T. cause to adhere, fix or paste embrace

چمٹی **chim'ṭī** N.F. pincers forceps [~ PREC.]

چمچ **cham'mach** N.M. (COL.) ladle spoon dessert spoon [~ چمچہ]

چمچچڑ **chamchich'chaṛ** چمچوڑ **chamchoṛ'** N.M. one sticking like a leech

چمچہ **cham'chah** N.M. spoon ladle (dial.) stooge (dial.) sycophant چمچہ بھر **cham'chah bhar** ADJ. spoonful ہردیگی چمچہ **hardegī cham'chah** ADJ. sponger چمچی **cham'chī** N.F. teaspoon dessert spoon

چم خم **cham' kham** N.M. glamour lovely contours

چمرخ **cham'rakh** N.F. leather support for spindle ADJ. lean ; gaunt ; haggard

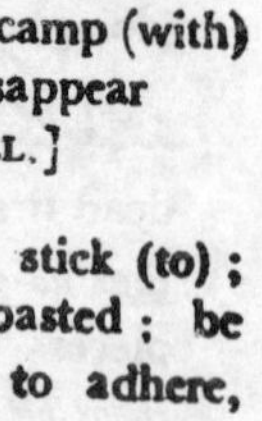

چمرس **cham'ras** N.F. wound caused by pinching shoes [~ FOLL]

چمڑا **cham'ṛā** N.M. leather skin hide چمڑی **cham'ṛī** N.F. skin چمڑی ادھیڑنا یا کھینچنا **cham'ṛī** ūdher'nā (or khench'nā) V.T. beat severely ; give a good hiding skin ; flay

چمک cha'mak N.F. (see under چمکنا ★)

چمکارنا chūmkār'nā V.T. caress make a kissing sound to appease [~ چومنا]

چمکنا cha'maknā V.I. shine ; glitter ; glisten be polished sparkle ; coruscate come up ; be lively fly into a passion (of business) flourish ; prosper چمکانا chamkānā V.T. polish burnish brighten cause to glitter cause to prosper or thrive make lively put (someone) on his mettle چمک cha'mak N.F. brilliance shean glitter ; glisten چمکارا chamkā'ra N.M. glare چمکدار cha'mak-dār ADJ. (col.) brilliant shinning glittering ; glistening چمک دمک cha'mak da'mak N.F. splendour brilliance shean ; glitter ; glisten چمکو chamak'ko N.F. wanton چمکی cham'ki N.F. spangle tinsel چمکیلا chamkī'lā ADJ. bright shining glittering brilliant

چمگادڑ chamga'daṛ N.F. bat flying fox

چمن cha'man N.M. flower garden flower bed چمن بندی کرنا chama'n bah'dī kar'nā V.T. lay out a garden چمن زار chaman-zār, چمنستان cha'manistān N.M. garden (fig.) lovely place [P]

چموٹا chamo'ṭā N M. strop ADJ. fool چموٹی chamo'ṭī N.F. leather pad to protect leg from being bruished by shackles

چمورانی chūmmo rā'nī N.F. a kind of game like hop, skip and jump

چنا chā'nā N.M. gram لوہے کے چنے lo'he ke cha'ne N.M. PL. very difficult task difficulty لوہے کے چنے چبوانا lo'he ke cha'ne chabvā'nā V.T. set a very difficult task cause great trouble

چنامنا chūn'nā mūn'nā ADJ. (F. چنی منی chīn'nī mūn'nī) ADJ. (nurs.) wee-bit

چننا chūn'nā V.T. glean pick; choose select; gather crimp or plait (cloth)

چنار chanār' N.M. poplar ; a tree with sparkling leaves resembling human hand [P]

چناں و چنیں chūnāh' (-o) chūnih' N.F. evasion subterfuge چناں وچنیں کرنا chūnāh(-o) chūnih kar'nā V.T. cavil (at) ; pick holes (in) dilly-dally evade procrastinate [P]

چنانچہ chūnāh'cheh ADV. hence ; therefore so accordingly for example ; for instance [P ~ چناں + چہ]

چناؤ chunā''o N.M. election selection, nomination چناوٹ chūnā'vaṭ V I crimping gathering plating چنائی chūnā''ī N.F. laying up (of bricks) building up (of wall) remuneration for it [چننا]

چنبر cham'bar N M. disc hoop any thing circular cover for hookah bowl چنبریں chambarīh ADJ. disc-like ; round [P]

چنبیلی chambelī N.F. jasmine ; jessamine

چنپا cham'pā N.F. same as چمپا N.F. ★)

چنبیلی

چنٹ chūn'naṭ N.F. plait crimping

چنتا chin'tā N.F. (dial). worry ; anxiety [~ S]

چنچل chan'chal ADJ wanton sportive ; playful

چنچنانا chinchinā'nā V.I. be nettled ; be stung fret and fume چنچنا chin'chinā ADJ. peevish ; fretful چنچنے chin'chine N.M. PL. ascarides

چند chand ADJ. some a few many ; many a ADJ. how many how much ; how often how long چند بار chand' bār ADV. on some occassions چند روزہ chand ro'zah ADJ. short-lived ; ephemeral temporary ; transitory ہر چند har'chand ADV. though ; although notwithstanding [P]

چندا chah'dā (dial. چندا chah'dar, چندرما chah'dar-ma) N.M. moon چندر مکھی chah'dar-m'ū'khī N.M. moon flower ADJ. lovely like Phoebe چندا ماموں chah'dā mā'mooh N M. (nurs.) moon ; uncle moon

چنداں chah'dāh ADJ. (lit.) so much as much as ; as many as not much however much چنداں مضایقہ نہیں chah'dāh mīzāya'qah nahih' PH. doesn't matter ; it matters little ; don't you worry چنداں کہ chahdāh' keh CONJ. insomuch that in so far as چندری chānd'rī N.F. (same as چنری N.F. ★)

چندرانا chandrā'nā V.I. ask (someone) after pretending own ignorance

چندن chan'dan N.M. sandalwood tree yielding it (rare) moon چندن ہار chah'dan-hār N.M. spangled necklace

چندوا chānd'vā N.M. crown (of cap; veil, etc.) (rare) awning [~ چاند]

چندہ chah'dah N.M. subscription donation contribution چندہ دینا chah'dah de'nā V.T. subscribe to donate چندہ کرنا chah'dah kar'nā V.T. raise a subscription

چندھا chūh'dhā ADJ. blear-eyed purblind چندھیانا chūndhiyā'nā V.I. be dezzled

چندی chin'di N.F. rag fragment • چندی چندی کرنا chin'di chin'di kar'nā V.T. shred ہندی کی چندی کرنا hih'di kī chin'dī kar'nā V.T. split hairs

چندے chah'de ADJ. some a little a few a while for a short while ADV sometime ; for sometime [P ~ چند]

چنڈیا **chand'ya** N.F. crown ; pate [~ چاند]

چنڈال **chandal'** N.M. miscreant wretch (dial.) low-caste ADJ. base-life چنڈال چوکڑی **chandal' chauk'ri** N.F. miscreant group

چنڈو **chan'doo** N.M. opium extract smoked earthen pipe ; smoking-opium چنڈو باز **chan'doo baz** N.M. opium-smoker چنڈو پینا **chan'doo pi'na** V.T. smoke opium چنڈو خانہ **chan'doo kha'nah** N.M. opium-smoker's den چنڈو خانے کی گپ **chan'doo kha'ne ki gap** N.F. brag

چنڈول **chandol'** N.M. crested lark (arch.) sedan children's play-thing comprising earthen pots

چنڈی **chan'di** N.F. corn

چنری **chun'ri**, چندری **chund'ri**, چنریا **chunar'ya**, N.F. (usu. coloured) scarf or stole

چنکنا **cha'nakna** V.I. (of seed) burst out of husk

چنگ **chang** N.M. harp ; lute claw kite with cymbals چنگ نواز **chang'-navaz'** N.M. harpist چنگ نوازی **chang' nava'zi** N.F. playing on a harp

چنگا **chan'ga** ADJ. (rare save in) بھلا چنگا **bha'la chan'ga** PH. hale and hearty safe and sound

چنگاری **chinga'ri** N.F. spark چنگاری ڈالنا **chinga'ri dal'na** V.T. throw a spark (into) (fig.) sow discard

چنگھاڑنا **chinghar'na** V.I. (of elephant) trumpet چنگھاڑ **chinghar'** N.F. trumpeting (of elephant) ♦

چنگل **chan'gul** (col. **chun'gal**), چنگال **changal'** claw talon grip grasp [P]

چنگی **chun'gi** N.F. octroi octroi post local duty (arch.) grain cess ; cess levied on grain trade and realized in kind چنگی محرر **chun'gi mohar'rir** N.M. octroi clerk

چنگیر **changer'** N.F. straw tray (or basket) for bread (rare) flower pot

چننا **chun'na** V.T. glean pick choose ; select crimp (cloth) lay bricks arrange ; put in order چنوانا **chunva'na** V.T. cause to pick and choose cause to select cause to be put in order cause to be selected cause to crimp (cloth) cause bricks to be layed cause to lay bricks چنوائی **chun'va''i** N.F. cost of laying bricks rate of payment for it

چنور **chan'var** N.M. fly whisk

چنیا **chun'ya** ADJ. small tiny چنیا بطخ **chun'ya bal'takh** N.F. duck چنیا بیگم **chun'ya be'gam** (or-**gam**) N.F. opium چنیا سا **chun'ya sa** ADV. wee-bit

چنیں **chunin'** ADV. thus ; like this ; in this manner [P ~ چوں + ایں]

چو **cho'** ہمچو **ham'-cho** ADV. like [P ~ ہم + چو]

چو **chau** PREF. four چوبائی **chauba''i** N.F. wind blowing from all sides چوبارہ **chauba'rah** N.M. room on upper storey (usu. with four doors or windows) single-room (for tenant) چوبچہ **chaubach'chah** N.M. (CORR. of چہ بچہ **chah-bach'chah**) cistern large tub pit چوبغلا **chau-baghla** N.M. (arch.) gusset sleeveless jacket چوبندی **chau-ban'di** N.F. full set of new shoes for horse چوپایہ **chau-pa'yah** N.M. quadruped ; animal beast چوپٹ **chau'pat** (open) on all sides in a mess ruined inefficient چوپٹ کرنا **chau'pat kar'na** V.T. make a mess of چوپڑ **chau'par** N.F. dice board dice (game) چوپہلو **chaupaih'loo** ADJ. four-sided ; quadrangular چوپہیہ **chauopa'hiya** N.F. & ADJ. four-wheel (cart) چوپھیر **chau-pher'** ADV. all around on all sides چوتارا **chau-ta'ra** N.M. four stringed guitar چوتالا **chau-ta'la** N.M. name of a musical mode played on tambourine چوتہی **chau'-tehi** N.F. four-folded bedsheet چوراہہ **chau-ra'hah**, چوراہا **chau-ra'ha** N.M. crossing ; crossroads; junction of four roads چورس **chau'ras** ADJ. rectilinear level چوکنا **chaukan'na** ADJ. watchful ; vigilant alert circumspect چوکنا ہونا **chaukan'na ho'na** V.I. be on the alert be vigilant چوکور **chaukor'** ADJ. N.F. quadrilateral four-sided figure چوکھٹ **chau'khat** N.F. door sill ; sill door posts چوکھٹا **chau'khata** N.M. picture frame چوگرد **chau-gir'd** ADV. all around چوکھونٹا **chau-khoon'ta** ADJ. four-cornered چوگنا **chau'-guna** ADJ. four-fold ; quadruple four-times چوگوشہ **chau-go'shah**, چوگوشیہ **chau-go'-shiyah** ADJ. four-cornered چولڑا **chau-la'ra** ADJ. four stringed necklace) چوماسہ **chau-ma'sah**, چوماسا **chau-ma'sa** N.M. the four months of the rainy season چومکھ **chau-mukh** (col. **makh**) N.M. four-wicked lamp چومکھا **chau-mukha**, چومکھی **chau-mukhi** ADJ four-faced ; four-headed N.M. F. single handed fight against all چومکھی لڑنا **chau-mu'khi lar'na** V.I. fight single handed on all sides چومنزلہ **chau-man'zilah** ADJ. چومحلہ **chaumaih'lah** ADJ. (arch.) four-storeyed چومیخا **chau-me'kha** N.M. cross on which criminate limbs are tied to four pegs ; a kind of pillory چومیخا کرنا **chau-me'kha kar'na** V.T. pillory ; put on such cross چوہٹہ **chau-hat'tah**, چوہٹا **chau-hat'ta** N.M. crossroads market place with four shops چوہرا **chauh'ra** four-fold

چووا **chav'va** N.M. set of four (at cards) four

چوالیس **chavā'lis** ADJ. & N.M. forty-four چالیسواں **chavālis'vāṅ** ADJ. forty-fourth

چوانا **cho'ā'nā** V.T. drip ; cause to drip [~ چونا **choo'nā** CAUS.]

چوب **chob** N F. wood timber staff , mace pole (of tent) drumstick stick redness (of eye) owing to hurt چوبدار **chob'-dār** N.M. herald ; mace-bearer usher چوب کاری **chob'-kā'rī** N.F. embroidery چوبی **cho'bī**, چوبیں **cho'bīṅ** ADJ. wooden ; wood

چوبا **cho'bā**, چوبھا **cho'bhā** N.M. boiled rice with cloying butter oil and sugar (as wedding feast) iron peg post

چوبے **chau'be** N.M. Hindu priest (esp. one learned in the four Vedas)

چوبیس **chaubīs'** ADJ. & N.M. twenty-four چوبیسواں **chaubīs'vāṅ** ADJ. twentyfourth

چوپال **chaupāl'** N.F. village pavilion ; rural club

چوپان **chaupān'** N.M. (lit.) shepherd cowherd چوپانی **chaupā'nī** N F. tending sheep in cattle shepherd's profession

چوپٹ **chau'paṭ** ADJ. (see under چو chau ★)

چوپڑ **chaupar** N.F. (see under چو chau ★)

چوت **choot** N.F. (vul.) vulva چوتیا **choo'tiyā**) ADJ. & N.M. fool; foolish (person) چوتیاپا **chootiyā'pā** چوتیاپن **choo'tiyā-pan** N.M. silliness ; ineptitude چوتیا شہید **chootiyā shahīd'** man suffering from consequences of excessive indulgence in sexual act

چوتڑ **choo'taṛ** N.M. buttocks ; bum چوتڑ دکھانا **choo'taṛ dikhā'nā** V.T. (vul.) take to one's sheets ; show the clean pair of heels, run away shame facedly چوتڑوں پر کھانا **choo'taṛoṅ par khā'nā** V.I. be spanked thus

چوتھ **chauth** ADJ. (old use) one fourth of produced levied as tax court fee levied from winning party [~ FOLL.]

چوتھا **chau'thā** ADJ. (F. چوتھی **chau'thī**) fourth چوتھائی **chauthā'ī** ADJ. fourth (part) ; one-fourth [~ چار]

چوتھی **chau'thī** N.F. brides first visit to parents house after marriage چوتھی چالا **chau'thī-chā'lā** N.M. feast on the occasion چوتھی کھیلنا **chau'thī khel'nā** V.I. bandy on this occasion fruits, vegetables, etc. sent by groom's people ; (of groom) throw fruit, etc. thus [~ PREC.]

چونتیس **chauṅ'tīs** ADJ. & N.M. thirty-four چونتیسواں **chauṅtīs'vāṅ** ADJ. thirty-fourth

چوٹ **choṭ** N.F. hurt bruise blow stroke lose damage ; injury shock taunt rival ; peer ; equal misfortune چوٹ آنا **choṭ' ā'nā** V.I. be hurt ; hurt oneself چوٹ پھیٹ **choṭ' phaṭ** N.F. hurt ; blow injury چوٹ کرنا **choṭ' kar'nā** V.T. taunt attack hurt چوٹ کھانا **choṭ' khā'nā** V.I. be hurt ; hurt oneself suffer loss (of) چوٹ لگنا **choṭ lag'nā** V.I. be hurt ; hurt oneself

چوٹا **choṭ'ṭā** N.M. (F. چوٹی **choṭ'ṭī**) pilferer ; petty thief چوٹی بلی جلیبیوں کی رکھوالی **choṭ'ṭī bil'lī jale'biyoṅ kī rakhvā'lī** PROV. set a thief to catch a thief [~ چور]

چوٹا **cho'ṭā** N.M. top knot or back knot of hair top-lock (worn by Hindu male)

چوٹی **cho'ṭī** N.F. peak summit ; top peak plaiteu hair ; pigtail pony tail riband for holding pigtail ; pigtail braid top lock worn by Hindu made چوٹی دار **cho'ṭī-dār** ADJ. with a pyramidical top ; (filled) to the top چوٹی کا **cho'ṭī kā** ADJ. class top excellent ; pre-eminent to excel ; to be unrivalled چوٹی کا آدمی **cho'ṭī kā ād'mī** PH. topmost man (in some field چوٹی کے لوگ **cho'ṭī ke log** N M. PL. important people ; VIP's the elite چوٹی کرنا **cho'ṭī kar'nā** V.T. plait or braid the hair

چوچلا **choch'lā**, چونچلا **chonch'lā** N.M. (usu. PL.) blandishment ; coquetry airs ; affectation fondling coquetish demands چوچل ہائی **cho'chal ha''ī** ADJ. coquetish

چوچی **choo'chī** N.F. teat ; nipple ; dug ; breast

چودہ **chau'dah** ADJ. & N.M. fourteen چودھواں **chau'dh'vāṅ** ADJ. fourteenth

چودنا **chod'nā** V.T. (vul.) have sexual intercourse (with woman) ; fuck ; F—K

چودھری **chaudh'rī** N.M. village headman title for landlord title of Rajputs boss ; chief چودھراہٹ **chaudhrā'yat** N.F. headman's office chieftainship being a landlord being a boss

چور **chor** N.M. burglar thief ; pilferer (fig) misgiving (fig.) fear ; lurking fear ADJ. clever ; sly چور اچکا **chor ūchak'kā** N.M. bad character one without lawful means of livelihood چور بازار **chor' bazār'** N.M. black market (rare) second-hand stuff market چور بازاری **chor' bazā'rī** N.F. black-marketing چور بازاریا **chor bāzā'riyā** N.M black marketteer چور بدن **chor badan** N.M. stout body whose fatness is not visible چور تھانگ **chor'-thāng** N.M. receiver of stolen goods چور پڑنا **chor' paṛ'nā** breaking into a house ; thieving ; stealing چور پہرہ **chor'-paih'rā** N.M. the advanced guard of an army چور اور چتر **chor aur cha'tar (or-tar)** N.M. crafty thief crafty person thief who is also the judge چورچکار chor'-cha'kar N.M. thieves and the like ; thief, etc. burglar چورخانہ chor'-kha'nah N.M. secret drawer چوردروازہ chor'-darvā'zah N.M. back door trap-door چورزمین chor'-zamīn N.F. quicksand bog ; quagmire چور سے کہے چوری کر ساہ سے کہے تیرا گھر لٹا chor' se ka'he cho'rī kar sadh' se ka'he te'rā ghar lu'ṭā PROV. (person) playing a double game چور کا بھائی گرہ کٹ (یا گٹھ کترا) chor' kā bhā''ī gi'reh-kaṭ (or gaṭh-kat'rā) PROV. birds of a feather flock together chips of the old block چور کی داڑھی میں تنکا chor kī dā'ṛhī meṅ tin'kā PROV. a guilty conscience needs no accuser چور کے پیر کہاں chor' ke pair' ka'hān چور کے گھر میں مور پڑنا chor' ke ghar' meṅ mor' paṛ'nā be outwitted چورمحل chor'-mahal N.M. concubine's apartments N.F keep concubine ; mistress چورمنڈلی chor'-mand'lī N.F. band of thieves children's game in which a pebble hidden in rubbish is to be discovered دل میں چور ہونا (یا بیٹھنا) dil meṅ chor' ho'nā (or baiṭh'nā) V.I. have a lurking fear چورہٹیا chor' haṭ'yā N.M. pawn-shop owner shopkeeper buying ware from thieves چوری cho'rī N.F. ★

چور choor ADJ. powdered ; powder pulverized smashed intoxicated toped exhausted (with fatigue) چورچور choor' choor' ADJ smashed ; broken to pieces چور چور ہونا choor' choor' ho'nā V.I. be smashed ; be broken to pieces نشے میں چور (ہونا) na'she meṅ choor' (ho'nā) V.I be dead drunk ; be steeped in liquor

چورا choo'rā N.M. powder bruised (cereal) filings anything crushed چورا کرنا choo'rā kar'nā V.T. powder crush break to bits

چوراسی chaura'sī ADJ. & N.M. eighty-four چوراسیواں chaurā'sīvāṅ ADJ. eighty-fourth

چورانوے chauran've ADJ. & N.M. ninety-four چورانویاں chauran'veṅāṅ ADJ. ninety-fourth

چورسی chaur'sī N.F. scraper

چورما choor'mā N.M. (dial.) crumbled bread rolled in sugar and butter oil

چورن choo'ran N.M. digestive powder ; aromatic powder

چوری choo'rī N.F. crumbled bread rolled in sugar and butter oil ; mashed bread

چوری chaurī N.F. horse-hair fly-whisk (same as چونری chaun'rī N.F. ★)

چوری cho'rī N.F. stealth theft burglary چوری چوری cho'rī cho'rī ADV. stealth secretly ; clandestinely چوری کا مال cho'rī kā māl N.M. stolen goods چوری کرنا cho'rī kar'nā V.T. steal pilfer burgle چوری لگانا cho'rī lagā'nā V.T. accuse (someone) of theft [~ چور]

چوڑا chau'ṛā ADJ. (F. چوڑی chau'ṛī) broad wide expansive extensive چوڑا چکلا chau'ṛā chak'lā ADJ. extensive , well-built abroad expansive چوڑان chauṛān', چوڑائی chauṛā''ī N.F. breadth width extension expense

چوڑا choo'ṛā N.M. set of bangles ADJ. wet drenched untidy

چوڑی choo'ṛī N.F. bangles pucker; crumple چوڑی دار choo'ṛī-dār ADJ. crumpled چوڑیدار پاجامہ choo'ṛī-dār pā-jāmah N.M. tight trousers crumpled at ends when worn چوڑیاں پہننا choo'ṛiyāṅ pai'hannā V.I. wear bangles become effeminate lack manly qualities (of widow) remarry چوڑیاں ٹھنڈی کرنا choo'ṛiyāṅ ṭhan'ḍī kar'nā V.T. (of freshly widowed woman) break her bangles کیا چوڑیاں ٹوٹ جائیں گی kyā choo'ṛiyāṅ ṭooṭ jā''eṅ gī PH. (said tauntingly to woman shirking work) will your bangles break ?

چوزہ choo'zah N.M. chicken fledgeling young bird (vul.) young woman چوزہ باز choo'za -bāz' N.F. woman with young paramour

چونسٹھ chauṅ'saṭh چَونسٹھ chau'saṭh ADJ. & N.M. sixty-four چونسٹھواں chauṅ'saṭhvāṅ ADJ. sixty-fourth

چوسر chau'sar N.M. dice

چوسنا choos'nā V.I. suck imbibe absorb چوسنی choos'nī N.F. (same as چسنی N.F. ★)

چوغہ cho'ghah N.M. same as چغہ N.M. ★)

چوک chook N.F. oversight omission mistake a kind of sour green بھول چوک معاف bhool' chook' mo'āf' PH. error and omission excepted [~ چوکنا]

چوک chauk N.M. square crossing ; cross roads market

چوکا chauk'kā N.M. (in cards) four aggregate of four in cricket four runs four front teeth (dial.) Hindu dining room (in multiplication tables) four times

چوکر cho'kar N.M. husk ; bran

چوکڑی chau'kaṛī N.F. spring , leap ; bound (old use) four horsed vehicle چوکڑی بھرنا chau'kaṛī bhar'nā V.I. leap ; bound ; spring چوکڑی بھولنا chau'kaṛī bhool'nā V.I. (fig.) be confounded be struck with terror

چوکس chau'kas ADJ. alert watchful ; vigilent cautions; circumspect چوکس رہنا chau'kas raih'nā V.I. be on one's guard (against) be watchful , be vigilant be cautious چوکسی chau'kasī N.F. alertness watchfulness ; vigilance carefulness ; cautiousness چوکسی کرنا chau'kasī kar'nā be on the alert keep watch over ; be vigilant be cautious

چوکنا ***ch*ook'nā** V.I. overlook miss omit make a mistake (چوک ***ch*ook** N.F. ★)

چوکھٹ ***ch*aukhaṭ** N.F. چوکھٹا ***ch*aukhaṭa** N.M. (see under چو ***ch*au** PREF. ★)

چوکی ***ch*au'kī** N.F. low wooden seat stool chair watch ; guard out post police post octroi post band (of singers) singing by this band a kind of ornament چوکیدار ***ch*au'kī-dār** N.M. watchman guard چوکیداری ***ch*auki-dā'rī** N.F. watch and ward watchman's job watchman's pay چوکی دینا (یا بھرنا) ***ch*aukī de'nā** (or **bhar'nā**) V.I. (of singers' band, birds, etc.) sing

چوگا ***ch*o'gā** N.M. food چوگا بدلنا ***ch*o'ga ba'dalnā** (of bird) feed its young (of bird's) bill [~ چگنا]

چوگان ***ch*augān'** N.M. polo polo-stick expansive ground چوگان باز ***ch*augān'-bāz** N.M. polo-player چوگان گاہ ***ch*augān'-gāh** N.M. polo-ground [P]

چول ***ch*ool** N.F. tenon dovetail ; part of joiner's work which fits into another end (of axle tree) dovetail (of door etc.) tenon (for mortise) چولیں ڈھیلی ہو جانا ***ch*oo'len ḍhī'lī ho jā'nā** V.T. (of joints) become loose (of badly constitution) become weak

چولا ***ch*o'lā** N.M. cloak (fig.) human body چولا بدلنا ***ch*o'lā ba'dalnā** V.I. (of soul) transmigrate undergo metamorphoses

چولائی ***ch*aula''ī** N.F. a species of potherb

چولھا ***ch*oo'lha** N.M. stove oven a hearth fire place

چولی ***ch*o'lī** N.F. (women's) small jacket body of gown etc. bodice small betel-case (میں) چولی دامن کا ساتھ ہونا **(meṅ) *ch*o'lī dā'man kā sāth' ho'nā** V.I. be indissolubly linked (with) good terms ; be the sine 'qua non' (of)

چومنا ***ch*oom'nā** V.T. kiss چوما ***ch*oo'mā** N.M. kiss چوما چاٹی ***ch*oo'ma *ch*ā'ṭī** N.F. fondling and caressing ; billing and cooing چوما چاٹی کرنا ***ch*oo'ma *ch*ā'ṭī kar'nā** V.I. fondle ; caress ; bill and coo

چون ***ch*av'van** ADJ. & N.M. fifty four چونواں ***ch*av'van-vān** ADJ. fifty-fourth

چوں ***ch*ooṅ** N.F. complaint squeak creak sound of farting چوں چوں ***ch*ooṅ *ch*ooṅ** N.F. chirp ; warbling squak creak چوں نہ کرنا ***ch*ooṅ nā kar'nā** V.I. not to make the slightest noise complain in the least ; not to grumble

چوں ***ch*ooṅ** PRON. INTERROG. (rare) why چوں (و) چرا ***ch*oo'n-o *ch*irā'** N.F. grumble complaint why and wherefore چوں وچرا کرنا ***ch*oo'n-o-*ch*ārā' kar'nā** V.I. grumble dispute [P]

چون ***ch*oon** N.M. lime fillings dust (of)

چونا ***ch*oo'nā** V.I. leak ooze drop menstruate (of fruit) drop after ripening N.M. lime nativity song چونا گچ ***ch*oo'nā gach** N.M. lime used as mortar چونا لگانا ***ch*oo'nā lagā'nā** V.I. dupe ; deceive ; defraud defame discomfit چونے کی بھٹی ***ch*oo'ne kī bhaṭ'ṭī** N.M. lime kiln

چونپ ***ch*auṅp** N.F. gold nail driven in tooth stubbornness passion ; fondness

چونتیس ***ch*auṅ'tīs** ADJ. & N.M. thirty four چونتیسواں ***ch*auṅ't.svāṅ** ADJ. thirty-fourth

چونچ ***ch*oṅch** N.F. beak ; bill (fig.) point (of) چونچ سنبھالو ***ch*oṅch' sambhā'lo** INT. hold your tongue

چونچال ***ch*auṅchal'** ADJ. active

چونڈا ***ch*ooṅ'dā** N.M. (of hair) top knot back knot چونڈا دھوپ میں سفید کرنا ***ch*ooṅ'ḍa dhoop meṅ sifed nā kar'nā** V.I. (of woman) not to be unexperienced چونڈے پر ڈولا اچھلنا ***ch*ooṅ'de par ḍo'lā ū'chhal'nā** V.I. find the husband taking a second wife

چونری ***ch*auṅ'rī**, چوری ***ch*au'rī**, N.F. (usu. horse-hair) fly whisk

چونسٹھ ***ch*auṅ'saṭh** ADJ. & N.M. sixty-four چونسٹھواں ***ch*auṅ'saṭhvāṅ** ADJ. sixty-fourth

چونکنا ***ch*auṅk'nā** V.T. start ; be startled to be ogle ; be roused be alarmed چونک اٹھنا ***ch*auṅk ūṭh'nā**, چونک پڑنا ***ch*auṅk paṛ'nā** V. start; be startled be roused be alarmed چونکانا ***ch*auṅkā'nā** V.T. startle rouse alarm چونکیل ***ch*auṅkail** ADJ. shy ; nervous

چونکہ ***ch*ooṅ-keh** ADV. as ; because ; since [P ~ چوں + کہ]

چونگا ***ch*oṅ'ga**, چونگے باز ***ch*oṅ'ge-bāz** N.M. toady ; sycophant (also چونگلا ***ch*oṅg'la**) scroll-case hollow bamboo or cylindrical tin piece used as such

چونی ***ch*oo'nī** N.M. coarse-grained gram-flour coarse food

چونی ***ch*avan'nī** N.F. an old coin ; four-anna bit [~ چار + آنہ]

چوہا ***ch*oo'hā** N.M. (F. چوہیا ***ch*oo'hiya**) mouse rat چوہے دان ***ch*oo'he-dān** rat trap چوہے دنتی ***ch*oo'he-dan'tī** N.F. bracelet with file's like projections

چوہتر *chauhat'tar* ADJ. & N.M. seventy-four چوہتر واں *chauhat'tarvāṅ* ADJ. seventy-fourth

چوہڑا *chooh'ṛā* N.M. sweeper چوہڑا چمار *chooh'ṛā chamār'* ADJ. low-caste

چوہیا *choo'hiyā* N.F. female mouse female rat چوہیا سے دانت *choo'hiyā se da'nt* N.F. small teeth [~ چوہا]

چہ[1] *chah* N.M. well چہ بچہ *chah'bach'chah* N.M. pit near well [P doublet of چاہ]

چہ[2] *chah* SUF. (denoting demunitive form) cule ; let [P]

چہ *che* PRON. INTERROG. what چہ خوش *chekhush* INT. (iron.) wonderful چہ معنی دارد *che mu''nī* (or-na) *dā'rad'* یعنی چہ *ya'nī che* PH. what does all this mean چہ میگوئیاں *che'me go''iyāṅ* N.F. PL. chat rumours gossip چہ نسبت خاک را با عالم پاک *che' nis'bat khāk rā bā 'ā'lam-e pāk'* PROV. so low bears no comparison to high

چھ *chhai* ADJ. & N.M six چھٹا *chha'ṭā* ADJ. ★

چہا *cha'hā* N.F. snipe

چھابا *chhā'bā* N.M., چھابڑی *chhāb'ṛī* N.F. hawker's basket, flat wicker basket ; چھابے والا *chhā'be vā'lā*, چھابڑی والا *chhāb'ṛī vā'lā* N.M. hawker ; huckster

چھاپنا *chhāp'nā* V.T. print (book etc.) publish ; bring out stamp impress چھاپ *chhāp* N.F. print ; impression seal stamp

چھاپا *chhā'pā*, چھاپہ *chhā'pah* raid edition print; impression seal stamp چھاپہ مارنا *chhā'pā mār'nā* V.T. raid organize a raid پتھر کا چھاپا *pat'thar kā chhā'pā* N.M. lithography چھاپے خانہ *chhā'pe khā'nah* N.F. press ; printing press چھپائی *chhapā''ī* N.F. printing impression, addition cost of printing

چھاتا *chhā'tā* N.M. umbrella parasol sunshade چھاتم چھاتا *chhātam chhā'tā* N.F. interlocking of two kites in the air

چھاتی *chhā'tī* N.F. chest ; breast ; bosom (fig.) courage ; bravery ; (fig.) heart (usu. PL.) breasts ; teats چھاتی بھر آنا *chhā'tī bhar ā'nā* V.I. be deeply moved چھاتی پر پتھر رکھنا (یا دھرنا) *chhā'tī par pat'thar rakh'nā* (or *dhar'nā*) V.I. suffer quitely چھاتی پر سانپ لوٹنا *chhā'tī par sāṅp' loṭ'nā* V.I. burn with jealousy چھاتی پر مونگ (یا کودوں) دلنا *chhā'tī par moong* (or *ko'doṅ*) *dal'nā* V.T. do something in (someone's) presence to vex him, challenge (someone's) honour thus چھاتی پک جانا *chhā'tī pak jā'nā* V.I. (of breasts) be inflamed (fig.) be deeply grieved have no relief in sorrow چھاتی پکڑ کر رہ جانا *chhā'tī pa'kaṛ kar raih' jā'nā* V.I. be struck with consternation چھاتی پھٹنا *chhā'tī phaṭ'nā* V.I. (of heart) burst with grief ; be deeply grieved چھاتی پیٹنا *chhā'tī pīṭ'nā* V.I. beat the breast in grief lament چھاتی سے لگانا *chhā'tī se lagā'nā* V.T embrace console thus give (someone) a sense of belonging چھاتی نکال کر چلنا *chhā'tī nikāl' kar chal'nā* V.I. strut ; swagger چھاتی کا ابھار *chhā'tī kā ubhār'* N.M. curves of breast swelling of breast puberty

چھاج *chhāj* N.M winnowing fan

چھاچھ *chhāchh* N.M. beaten curds, dilute curds دودھ کا جلا چھاچھ کو پھونک پھونک کر پیتا ہے *doodh' kā ja'lā chhāchh' bhī phoonk phoonk' kar pī'tā hai* PROV a burnt child dreads fire

چہار *chahār'* ADJ., N.M. & PREF. four چہار دہ *chahār'-dah* ADJ. fourteen چہار شنبہ *chahār'-sham'bah* N.M. Wednesday چہارم *chahā'rum* ADJ. fourth [P]

چھاکٹا *chhāk'ṭā* N.M. arrant knave

چھاگل *chhā'gal* N.F. spouted leathern bottle kind of ornament for feet

چھال *chhāl* N.F. rind ; bark peel skin چھال اتارنا *chhāl utār'nā* V.T. bark peel pare

چھالا *chhā'lā* N.M. blister pustule

چھالیا *chhā'liyā* N.F. betel-nut

چھان[1] *chhān* N.F. husk chaff چھان بین *chhān bīn'*, چھان پھٹک *chhān pha'ṭak* N.F. sifting scrutiny examination investigation [~ چھاننا]

چھان[2] *chhān* N.F. (see under چھانا ★)

چھانا *chhā'nā* V.I. loom overspread ; overcast become overpowerful چھا جانا *chhā' jā'nā* V.I. overspread ; overcast become overpowerful ; overpower چھان *chhān* N.F. (building with) thatched roof

چھانٹنا *chhāṅṭ'nā* V.I. prune trim cut ; clip choose ; select glean sort out abridge cut (cloth) display (knowledge superiority, etc.) with facile tongue چھانٹ *chhāṅṭ* N.F. siftings extraction refuse چھانٹ لینا *chhāṅṭ le'nā* V.T. choose ; select sort out glean N.F. siftings cuttings clippings scrapings refuse چھانٹی *chhāṅ'ṭī* N.F. retrenchment چھانٹی کرنا *chhāṅ'ṭī kar'nā* V.T. retrench چھانٹی ہونا *chhāṅ'ṭī ho'nā* be retrenched چھاننا *chhān'nā* V.T. sift strain filter چھان مارنا (یا ڈالنا) *chhān' mār'nā* (or *ḍāl'nā*) V.T search for explore چھان *chhān* N.F. ★

چھاندا **chhān'dā** N.M. share money

چھانڈنا **chhānḍ'nā** V.I. spew ; vomit

چھاؤں **chhā''oṅ** N.F. shade

چھاؤنی **chhā''onī** N.F. cantonment ; camp ; encampment thatching چھاؤنی چھانا chhā''onī chhā'nā V.I. be encamped be thatched چھاؤنی ڈالنا chhā'onī ḍāl'nā V.T. encamped set up a garrison town [~ چھانا]

چھایا **chhā'yā** N.F. shadow illusion

چھب **chhab** N.F. grace charm gracefulness on wearing something چھب تختی chhab-takh'tī N.F. woman's breasts چھبیلا chhabī'lā ADJ. (F. چھبیلی chhabī'lī) comely graceful چھیل چھبیلا chhail' chhabī'lā N.M. foppish

چھبیس **chhab'bīs** ADJ. & N.M. twenty-six چھبیسواں chhbbis'vāṅ ADJ. twenty-sixth

چھپ چھپ **chhap chhap** N.F. (of) water splashing (water) on face

چھپائی **chhapā''ī** N.F. (see under چھپنا chhap'nā V.I. ★)

چھپٹی **chhap'ṭī** N.F. wood splinter [~ P چفتی CORR.]

چھپر **chhap'par** N.M. thatched roof patio hut ; cot ; cottage چھپر چھانا chhap'par chha'nā V.I. thatch a hut چھپر پھاڑ کر دینا chhap'par phār' kar de'nā V.T bestow wealth in an unexpected manner ; enrich miraculously چھپر پھاڑ کر ملنا chhap'-par phaṛ kar mil'nā PH. get wealth from unexpected quarters ; enrich miraculously (احسان) کا چھپر سر پر رکھنا (ehsān' kā) chhap'par sir par rakh'nā V.T. do a great favour expect many thanks for small favour

چھپر کھٹ **chha'par-khaṭ** N.F. canopy ; canopied bed [+ PREC. + کھاٹ]

چھپکا **chhap'kā** N.M. splash (of water) splashing face with water small net for catching pigeons a kind of ornament for forehead ; brow pendant

چھپکلی **chhip'kalī**, (dial chhūp'kalī) N.F. lizard

چھپن **chhap'pan** ADJ. & N.M. fifty-six چھپنواں chhap'panvāṅ ADJ. fifty-sixth

چھپنا **chhūp'nā**, (dial. chhip'nā) V. hide , be hidden ; be concealed go into hiding go underground disappear lurk go about in a veil observe purdah (from) (of sun) set , go down in the west چھپا chhūpā ADJ. hidden ; concealed unknown undiscovered چھپا رستم chhū'pā rus'tam N.M. unknown genious

چھپانا chhūpā'nā V.T. hide , conceal give asylum (to) چھپاؤ chhūpā''o secrecy concealment

چھپنا **chhap'nā** V.I. be printed be published چھپانا chhapā'nā, چھپوانا chhapvā'nā V.T. cause to print چھپائی chhapā''ī, (rare چھپوائی chhapvā''ī) N.F printing printing charges

چھت **chhat** N.F. roof ceiling house top چھت پر (سے) chhat' par (se) ADV. (from) on the house-top چھت گیری chhat'gī'rī N.F. ceiling cloth

چھتا **chhat'tā**, چھتہ chhat'tah N.M. beehive; honeycomb hive covered (portion of) lane

چھتر **chhat'r** N.M. large umbrella sunshade canopy asylum چھتری chhat'rī N.F. umbrella parasol sun-shade canopy small (dome over) shrine bulbous perch (for pigeons)

بارش کی ب. کبوتروں کی چھتری

چھتیانا **chhatyā'nā** V.T. aim (gun) at

چھتیس **chhat'tīs** ADJ. & N.M. thirty-six چھتیسواں chhat'tīsvāṅ ADJ. thirty-sixth چھتیسا chhattī'sā ADJ. (F. چھتیسی chhattī'sī) artful · crafty one with affected modesty چھتیسا پن chhattī'sā-pan N.M. craftiness ; cunning

چھٹ **chhūṭ** PREF. (denoting smallness) small ; petty چھٹ بھیا chhūṭ bhay'yā N.M. (derog.) petty shopkeeper low-born person

چھٹا **chhaṭ'ā** ADJ. (F. چھٹی chha'ṭī) sixth چھٹے چھماہے chha ṭe chhai-mā'he ADV. occasionally ; now and then ; long intervals [~ چھ]

چھٹا ہوا **chha'ṭā hu''ā** ADJ. arrant (knave etc.)

چھٹانک **chhaṭāṅk'** N.F. sixteenth part of a seer ; weight equivalent to about two ounces

چھٹائی **chhūṭā'ī** N.F. smallness ; littleness inferiority pettiness چھٹپن chhū'ṭ'pan, چھٹپنا chhūṭ'panā N.M. childhood infancy tender age [~ چھوٹا]

چھٹکارا **chhūtkā'rā** N.M. rescue ; escape deliverance freedom ; liberation ; release exemption exoneration exculpation چھٹکارا پانا (یا حاصل کرنا) chhūtkā'rā pā'nā (or ḥā'sil kar'nā) V.I. be rescued be freed be released be exempted be exonerated چھٹکارا دلانا chhūṭkā'rā dilā'nā V.T. rescue free release exempt exonerate [~ چھوٹنا]

چھٹکنا **chhiṭak'nā** V.I. (of moonlight, etc.) be diffused ; (of moon) shine چاندنی چھٹکنا chānd'nī chhi'ṭaknā V.I. (of moonlight) be diffused

چھٹنا **chhaṭ'nā** V.I. (of clouds) disperse (of well) be desilted (of body) become lean be pruned be sacked be selected , be picked out

چھٹنا *chhūṭ'nā* V.I. freed ; be liberate be acquitted ; be discharged ; be let off be abandoned escape ; slip (from) (of gun) (or bullet) be fired (of tram, etc.) be set in motion (of colour) wash off ; come off be discarded be left out ; be omitted

چھٹی *chhaṭī'* N.F. sixth lunar day ; birth ritual performed on sixth day of delivery ADJ. (see under چھٹا ADJ. ★) چھٹی کا دودھ یاد آنا *chha'ṭī kā doodh' yad' ā'nā* PROV. be in great trouble live to rue the former comforts

چھٹی *chhūṭ'ṭī* N.F. holiday vacation leave furlough release ; discharge dismissal death liberation acquittal

چھجا *chhaj'jā* N.M. balcony gallery eaves protective projection cow catcher

چھجنا *chhij'nā* V.I. (of warp and woof) become loose

چہچہانا *chaihchahā'nā* V.I. chirp چہچہا *chaih'chaha* N.M. chirping

چوہچہانا *chohchahā'nā* V.I. be coquetish be bright red چوہچہا *choh'chohā* ADJ. coquetish red ; reddened

چھچھڑا *chhichhṛā* N.M. (same as چھیچھڑا N.M. ★)

چھچھلنا *chhi'chhalnā* V.I. fly past with just a touch graze چھچھلا *chhich'la* ADJ. (of water) shallow (of vessel) not deep چھچھلتی ہوئی *chhi'chhaltī hū''ī* ADJ. cursory (glance, etc.)

چھچھورا *chhichho'ra,* (or *chhoo'*) childish ; puerile shallow but showy چھچھوراپن *chhichho'rā-pan* N.M. childishness ; puerility shallowness

چھچھوندر *chhachhoon'dar* N.F. mole ; musk-rat ; kind of (fire-work) squib

چھدا *chhūd'dā* N.M. blame obligation چھدا اتارنا *chhūd'dā ūtār'nā* V.T. do something perfunctorily just to escape blame چھدا رکھنا *chhūd'da rakh'nā* V.T. blame

چھدام *chhadām'* N.F. (arch.) one-fourth of a pice (fig.) sou

چھدرا *chhid'rā* ADJ. (F. چھدری *chhid'rī*) sparse ; not dense چھدرا کر چلنا *chhidrā kar chal'nā* V.I. stride چھدرانا *chhidrā'nā* V.I. be sparse

چھیدنا *chhid'nā* V.T. be pierced be wounded [~ چھیدنا]

چھرا *chhū'rā* N.F. dagger ; large knife چھرا گھونپنا *chhū'rā ghoṅp'nā* (or *bhoṅk'nā*) V.T. stab

چھرا *chhar'rā* N.M. small shot minute pebble in tiny bell

چہرہ *cheh'rah* N.M. face ; countenance ; visage mask obverse facade چہرہ اترنا *cheh'rah ū'tarnā* V.I. be downcast چہرہ تمتمانا *cheh'rah tamtamā'nā* V.I. (of face) become ruddy چہرے پر مردنی (یا پژمردگی) چھانا *cheh're par mūr'dānī* (or *pazhmūr'dagī*) *chhā'nā* V.I. be downcast be run down چہرے پر ہوائیاں اڑنا *cheh're par havā''iyāṅ ūṛ'nā* V.I. feel jittery ; have the blue funks چہرہ شاہی *cheh'ra(-e) shā'hī* N.M. rupee ADJ. (coin or note) with king's effigy چہرہ مہرہ *cheh'rah moh'rā*, چہرہ بشرہ *cheh'rah būsh'rah* N.M. features physiognomy قلمی چہرہ *qa'lamī cheh'rah* N.M. sketch ; pen portrait [P]

چھری *chhū'rī* N.F. table-knife ; knife چھری پھرنا *chhū'rī phir'nā* V.I. be slaughtered be slain چھری پھیرنا *chhū'rī pher'nā* slay slaughter چھری تلے دم لینا *chhū'rī ta'le dam' le'nā* V. to be patient under difficult circumstances چھری سے کاٹنا *chhū'rī se kaṭ'nā* N.M. cut curved چھری مارنا *chhū'rī mār'nā* V.T. stab میٹھی چھری *mī'ṭhī chhurī* N.F. treacherous person ; false friend

چھریرا *chhare'rā* ADJ. (of body) lean چھریرے بدن کا *chhare're ba'dan kā* ADJ. lean ; lank

چھیڑ *chhaṛ* N.F. thin long bamboo pole (of spear ; etc.) fishing rod spikenard

چھڑا *chha'ṛā* ADJ. unmarried alone single چھڑا چھانٹ (یا چھٹانک) *chha'ṛa chhāṅṭ* (or *chhaṭāṅk*) N.M. unmarried person grass widower

چھڑانا *chhuṛa'nā* چھڑوانا *chhūṛvā'nā* V.T. cause to liberate cause to be set free rescue

چھڑکنا *chhi'ṛaknā* V.T. sprinkle جان چھڑکنا *jān' chhi'ṛaknā* V.I. be ready to lay down one's life (for) چھڑکوانا *chiṛakvā'nā* V.T. cause to be sprinkled چھڑکاؤ *chhiṛkā''o* N.M. sprinkling (of place) with water

چھڑنا *chhaṛ'nā* V.T. husk (paddy) beat (grain) to separate it from husk N.M. paddy husking چھڑوانا *chhaṛvā'nā* V.T. get husked

چھڑنا *chhiṛ'nā* V.I. (of war, etc.) break out (of topic) be broached (of talk, discussion, etc.) open (of music or instrument) begin to be played or sung

چھڑی *chha'ṛī* N.F. walking stick ; rod ; cane ; wand ; switch thorn used as pen (saint's) ensign or banner ADJ. (see under چھڑا *chha'ṛā* ADJ. ★)

چھڑیا *chhaṛ'yā* N.F. narrow passage

چھکا *chhak'kā* N.M. (in cricket stroke) sixer (at duce) throw of six (at cards) six racket چھکا پنجا کرنا *chhak'ka pan'ja kar'nā* V.T. deceive ; play tricks چھکے چھڑانا *chhak'ke chhuṛā'nā* V.T. perplex چھکے چھوٹ جانا *chhak'ke chhooṭ jā'nā*

V.I. (fig. from a dice) tricked ; be at one's wits end

چھکا *chaih'kā* N.M. pavement (of roof, courtyard etc.)

چھکار *chaihkār'* N.F. chirp warble singing (of bird)

چھکڑا *chhak'ṛa* N.M. yan cart bullock cart چھکڑی *chhik'ṛī* N.F. throw of six (in d ce)

چھکنا *chai'haknā* V.I. chirp warble whistle

چھل *chhal* N.M. delusion fraud deception چھل اور مایا *chhal' aur mā'yā* N.F. deception and delution چھل بٹے *chhal' baṭ'te* N.M. deception چھل بل *chhal' bal* N.F. fraud pomp and show tawdriness چھلیا *chhal'ya* N.M. fraudulent person ; cheat

چہل *chohal* N.F. fun pleasantry quips and cranks چہل کرنا *chohal kar'nā* V.I. make merry indulge in pleasantries

چہل *che'hal* ADJ. forty چہل چراغ *che'hal chirāgh* N.M. forty-pronged chandelier چہل قدمی *che'hal-qa'damī* N.F. walk stroll چہل قدمی کرنا *che'hal qa'damī kar'nā* V.I. take a stroll چہل کاف *che'hal-kāf* N.M. name of a verse prayer with each couplet beginning with the letter 'kaf'

چہلا *chaih'la* N.M. slime puddle splinter چہلا نکالنا *chaih'la nikal'nā* V.T. split up into pieces چہلے کی بھینس *chaih'le kī bhains* PH. (fig.) lazy lout

چھلا *chhal'lā* N.M. ring equally wide all over ; ring kutcha wall with baked brick lining on the outside چھلے دار *chhal'le-dar'* ADJ. ringed curled

چھلانگ *chhalāng'* N.F. leap ; spring jump bound چھلانگ لگانا (یا مارنا) *chhalāng' lagā'na* (or *mār'na*) V.I. leap ; spring jump bound

چھلاوا *chhalā'vā* N.M. will-o'-the-wisp ; 'ignis fatnus'

چھل پلانا *chhal pilā'na* V.T. give a drink of water (to travellers, etc.)

چہل پہل *chai'hal pai'hal* N.F. hustle bustle mirth at d merriment

چھلکا *chhil'ka* N.M. skin peal shell crust scale husk ; bark ; rind scab چھلکا اتارنا *chhil'ka ūtār'nā* V.T. skin peel husk ; bark چھلکنا *chha'laknā* V.I. over flow be spilt چھلکتا ہوا *chha'laktā (hū''ā)* ADJ. full to the brim ; brimful

چھلکنا *chha'laknā* V.I. spill (of urine) be passed involuntarily چھلکانا *chhal'kāna* V.T. cause to spill

چہلم *cheh'lum* ADJ. funeral rite performed fortieth day of death ; day mourning [P ~ چہل]

چھلنا[1] *chhal'na* V.T. cheat ; deceive ; defraud overreach

چھلنا[2] *chhal'nā* N.M. strainer چھلنی *chhal'nī* N.F. sieve strainer چھلنی ہونا *chhal'nī ho'nā* V.I. be full of holes ; be fully perforated ; be pieried be bruised

چھلنا *chhil'nā* V.I. be scratched be bruised be scraped

چھم چھم *chham chham* N.F. tingle (of small bells) jingle of ornaments patter of rain ADV. pattering with a jingle چھم چھم برسنا *chham' chham' ba'rasnā* V I. patter

چھم چھما *chham'chhama* N.F. joke strange fact

چھن بھر میں *chhin bhar men* ADV. in a trice ; in a jiffy

چھن *chhan*, (*chhān*) N F. sizzle a drop inkle of of small bells jingle of coin چھن چھن *chhan' chhan*, چھن چھناہٹ *chhan chhanā'haṭ* N.F. tinkle of small bells jingle of coins چھناک *chhanāk'* N.F. jingle of a drop چھناکا *chhanā'kā* N.M. tinkle of small bells coming of dancing girl (rare) jingle of coin

چھنال *chhanāl'* N.F. loose woman prostitute; whore ; harlot چھنال پن *chhanal'-pan* N.M. lewdness prostitution whoredom ; harlotry

چھنٹائی *chhanta''ī* N.F. sifting sorting cleaning remuneration for' sifting [~ چھانٹنا]

چھند *chhand* N.M. fraud plagiarism

چھنگا *chhan'gā* N.F. person with six fingers. [~ چھ + انگلی]

چھنگلیا *chhun'galya* N.F. the little finger

چھن من *chhun' mun*, چھنن منن *chhū'nan mū'nan* N.M. sizzle

چھننا *chhan'nā* V.I. be strained be sifted be (riddled with bullets) چھننی *chhan'nī* N.F. strainer چھنوانا *chhan-vā na* V.T. cause to sifted cause to strain خاک چھنوانا *khak chhanvā'nā* V.T. force to wander [~ چھاننا]

چھننا *chhin'nā* V.I. be snatched be wrested be deprived چھنوانا *chhinvā'nā* V.T. cause to be snatched cause to wrest cause to be deprived

چھو *chhoo* N.F. sound of sniffing puffing after incantation چھوا چھو *chhoo''ā-chhoo'* N F sound of breath while beating clothes on slab چھو منتر *chhoo' man'tar* N.M charm ; incantation اڑ چھو ہونا *ū'ran chhoo ho'nā* V.I. disappear suddenly , vanish (like a ghost)

چھوارا **chho'a'rā** N.M. (same as چھوہارا **chho'hā'a** N.M. ★)

چھوانا **chho''a'na** V.T. touch cause to touch [~ چھونا]

چھوپنا **chhop'nā** V.I. make wall surface even with mud fill holes with mud چھوپا **chho'pā** N.M. mud used for the purpose

چھوت **chhoot** N.F. infection contamination (dial.) touch of member of low caste; physical contact with such person چھوت والی بیماری *chhoot' vā'lī bī'mārī* N.F. infectious disease چھوت لگنا *chhoot lag'na* V.I. (of disease) be infectious (dial.) be contaminated wit touch

چھوٹ **chhooṭ** N.F. discount remission) of revenue radiance (of gem) off-hand tip to dancer or other entertainer [~ چھوٹنا]

چھوٹا **chho'ṭa** ADJ. (F. چھوٹی **chho'ṭī**) little; small younger; junior; minor low; mean; base; vile trifling چھوٹا منہ بڑی بات *chho'ṭa muṅh ba'ṛī bāt'* PROV. brag; boastful words; big words out of a small mouth چھوٹی بات *chho'ṭī bāt* N.F. trifling affair; matter of no consequence چھوٹائی *chhoṭa''ī*, چھٹائی *chhuṭa''ī* N.F. smallness; littleness

چھوٹنا **chhooṭ'nā** V.T. be released be acquitted be let off be freed; be liberated be abandoned be sacked be separated break away chains (of train) start (of firework) be let off; explode (of fountain) flow; spurt (12) (of stain) be removed [~ چھوڑنا]

چھوچھک **chhoo' chhak** N.F. childbirth ceremony at woman's visit to her parents

چھوچھو **chhoo' chhoo** N.F. (nurs.) dry nurse urine

چھوڑنا **chhoṛ'nā** V.T. give up quit leave; desert abdicate; resign abstain from let off release pardon; forgive emit to discharge fire (gun or bullet) separate divorce remit give discount

چھوکرا **chhok'rā** N.M. lad; boy servant چھوکری **chhok'rī** N.F. lass; girl wench maid-servant

چھولداری **chhol'-dārī** N.F. small tent (for menials etc.)

چھونا **chhoo'nā** V. touch feel meddle with; temper with broach (topic, etc.) چھوئی موئی *chhoo''ī moo''ī* N.F. name of a sensitive plant touch-me-not anything frail ADJ. touchy; testy

چھہتر **chhehat'tar** ADJ. & N.M. seventy-six چھہترواں **chhehat'tarvāṅ** ADJ. sixty-sixth

چھی چھی **chhī' chhī** N.F. (nurs.) bowel INT dirty leave it

چھیاسٹھ **chhiyā'saṭh** ADJ. & N.M. sixty-six چھیاسٹھواں **chhiyāsaṭhvāṅ** ADJ sixty-sixth

چھوہارا **chhohā'rā**, چھوارا **chho'a'ra** N.M. dry date

چھیا **chūh'ya**, چوہیا **chooh'ya** N.F. female mouse [~ چوہا F]

چھیاسی **chhiyā'sī** ADJ. & N.M eighty-six چھیاسیواں **chhiyāsivāṅ** ADJ. eighty-sixth

چھیالیس **chhiyā'līs** ADJ. forty-six چھیالیسواں **chhiyalīs'-vāṅ** ADJ. forty-sixth

چھیانوے **chhiyān've** ADJ. & N.M ninety-six چھیانواں **chhiyān'vevāṅ** ADJ. ninety-sixth

چھیپ **chhīp** N.F. skin spot (as disease) stain fishing rod rod with a rag at one end for flying pigeons (of animal) butting with horns چھیپی **chhī'pī** N.M. cloth printer rod with rag at one end for flying pigeons

چہیتا **chahe'ta**, چاہیتا **chāhe'lā** ADJ. (F. چہیتی **chahe'lī**, چاہیتی **chāhe'lī**) favourite pet N.M. darling [~ چاہنا]

چھیجنا **chhīj'nā** V.I. decrease; decay pine away چھیج **chhīj** N.F. decrease diminution decay; waste

چھیے جانا **chhe jā'na** V.I of puncture in ear-lobe) open out at bottom

چھیچھڑا **chhīchh'ṛā**, چھچھڑا **chhichh'ṛa** N.M. (usu. PL.) skinny part of flesh; part of flesh unfiit for human consumption بلی کو چھیچھڑوں کے خواب *bil'lī ko chhīchh'ṛoṅ ke khāb* PROV. needy person indulging in wishful thinking

چھید **chhed** N.M. prick hole bore opening orifice چھیدنا **chhed'na** V.T. perforate pierce bore penetrate transfix

چھیڑ **chheṛ** N.F. molestation harassment irritation; vexation fun; pleasantry چھیڑ چھاڑ **chheṛ' chhāṛ**, چھیڑ خانی **chheṛ'-khā'nī** N.F. vexing provocation fun, pleasantry joke; jest

چھیڑنا **chheṛ'nā** V.T molest; harass make fun of vex; irritate commence stir up play on (musical instrument) start song or musical note) broach (topic) open (talk)

چھیلا **chhailā**, چھیل چھبیلا **chhail chhabī'la** N.M. fop; dandy; beau; coxcomb a kind of sweet-smelling herb ADJ. foppish

چھیلنا **chhīl'nā** V.T. skin peel bark scrape scratch erase چھیلن **chhī'lan** N.F. parings peelings scrapings scratch

چھینٹ **chhīnt** N.F. chintz spray of water tiny drop of (usu. filthy) liquid چھینٹا **chhīn'ṭā** N.M. sprinkling scattering splash light rain tiny ball of smoking opium fraud ; deception چھینٹا مارنا (یا دینا) **chhīn'ṭā mār'nā** (or **de'nā**) V.T. sprinkle ; scatter ; broadcast deceive

چھینکنا **chhīnk'nā**, چھینک مارنا **chhīnk' mār'nā** V.I. sneeze چھینک **chhīṅk** N.F. sneeze

چھینکا **chhīn'kā** N.M. muzzle (for animal) network for hanging pots in

چھیننا **chhīn'nā**, چھین لینا **chhīn' le'nā** V.T. snatch ; wrench deprive (someone) of grab usurp چھینا جھپٹی **chhī'nā jhap'ṭī**, چھین جھپٹ **chhīn' jha'paṭ** N.F. mutual bid to grab scramble

چھینی **chhai'nī** (dial. **chhe'nī**) N.F. chisel

چیاں **chiy'yāṅ** N.M. tamarind stone چیاں سی **chiy'yāṅ sī** ADJ. (of eyes) very small ; tiny

چیپ **chep** N.M. stickness ; viscosity sticky juice

چیپڑ **chī'paṛ** N.M. (usu. PL.) rheum in (inside corner of) eye

چیپی **che'pī**, چپی **chip'pī** N.F. slip (for pasting) on

چیت **chait** (dial. **chet**) N.M. first month of Hindu calendar (corresponding to March-April)

چیتا **chītā** N.M. leopard ; panther

چیتل **chī'tal** N.M. oxis, spotted deer a large kind of spotted snake leopard ; panther ADJ. spotted ; speckled

چیتنا **chet'nā** V.I. (dial.) rouse ; awaken remember

چیتھڑا **chīth'ṛā** N.M. (usu. PL.) rag ; tatter frayed piece of cloth small worthless thing چیتھڑے لگانا **chīth'ṛe lagā'nā** V.I. be in rags go about in tatters چیتھڑے لگنا **chīth'ṛe lag'nā** V.I. be reduced to penury چیتھڑے ہونا **chīth'ṛe ho'nā** V.I. be tattered ; become wragged be torn to bits ; be torn or to pieces

چیٹک **chai'ṭak** N.F. passion (for something)

چیچڑی **chīch'ṛī** N.F. (same as چچڑی N.F. ★)

چیچک **che'chak** N.F. small-pox چیچک رو **che'chak-roo** ADJ. pock-marked

چیخ **chīkh** N.F. cry scream shriek screech چیخ مارنا **chīkh' mār'nā** V.I. cry out shriek scream screach

چیدہ **chī'dah**, چیدہ چیدہ **chī'dah chī'dah** ADJ. selected elect چیدہ (چیدہ) لوگ **chī'dah (chī'dah) log** N.M. PL. the elite [P ~ چیدن pick]

چیرنا **chīr'nā** V.T. saw cleave split rend tear slit perform a surgical operation incise چیر **chīr** N.F. rent tear cut slit چیر آنا **chīr' ā'nā** V.I. have a scratch or slit چیر پھاڑ **chīr' phāṛ** N.F. dissection surgical operation چیر پھاڑ کرنا **chīr'-phāṛ kar'nā** V.T. perform a surgical operation

چیرا **chī'rā** N.M. incision cut slit particoloured turban چیرا باندھنا **chī'rā bāṅ'dh'nā** V.T & I. tie such a turban go about with such a turban چیرا دینا **chī'rā de'nā** V.T. make an incision

چیرا **che'rā** N.M. slave servant چیری **che'rī** N.F. slave girl maid-servant

چیئرمین **che''armain** N.M. chairman چیئرمینی **che'armai'nī** N.F. chairmanship [E]

چیرہ دست **chī'ra-dast'** ADJ. high-handed oppressive.; tyrannical چیرہ دستی **chī'ra-das'tī** N.F. highhandedness [P]

چیڑ **chīṛ** N.M. pine

چیز **chīz** N.F. thing commodity a kind of musical mode ornament چیز بست **chīz'-bast** N.F. goods ; chattels bag and baggage چیزے **chī'ze** ADV. somewhat ; a little چیزی **chī'zī**, جیجی **chij'jī** N.F. (nurs.) sweet ; sweetmeat

چیستان **chīs'tān** N.F. enigma ; puzzle ; riddle

چیف **chīf** N.M. & ADJ. chief چیف جسٹس **chīf' jas'tis** N.M. Chief Justice چیف کورٹ **chīf kor'ṭ** N.F. Chief Court چیفس کالج **chīf's kā'lij** N.M. Chief's lege [E]

چیکٹ **chī'kaṭ** N.F. mixture of oil and dust ADJ. oily ; greasy

چیل **chīl'** N.F. a bird of prey ; kite چیل انڈا چھوڑتی ہے **chīl an'ḍā chhoṛ'tī hai** PH. it is extremely hot چیل جھپٹا **chīl' jhapaṭ'ṭā** N.F. children's game in which blind-folded boy tries to pounce upon playmates snatching چیل کی طرح منڈلانا **chīl' kī tar'h mandlā'nā** PH. hover about restlessly چیل کے گھونسلے میں ماس کہاں **chīl' ke ghoṅs'le meṅ mās' kahāṅ'** PROV. prodigals have no wherewithal

چیلا **che'lā** N.M. چیلی **che'lī** N.F. disciple ; follower devotee pupil servant, etc. brought up in the house چیلے چانٹے **che'le chāṅ'ṭe** N.M. devotees disciples ; followers camp-followers

چیلک **chī'lak** N.F. mark put across disliked word, etc.

چیلنج **chai'lanj** N.M. challenge چیلنج دینا یا کرنا **chai'lanj de'na** (or **kar'na**) V.T. challange چیلنج قبول کرنا **chai'lanj qabool' kar'na** V.I. accept challenge [E]

چین[1] **chain** N.M. comfort ease test ; repose peace ; tranquillity چین کرنا **chain' kar'na** V.I. be at ease enjoy comforts راوی چین لکھتا ہے **ra'vi chain' likh'ta hai** PH. (formula at end of legendary tales) peace reigns henceforth

چین[2] **chain** N.M. chain [E]

چیں[1] **chīn'** N.F. wrinkle frown چیں بجبیں ہونا **chīn' ba-jabīn ho'na** V.I. frown ; scowl ; glower knit the brow [P]

چیں[2] **chīn'** N.F. cry squeak chirp چیں بلانا **chīn' būlā'na** V.T. make (someone) cry out reduce to straits چیں بولنا **chīn' bol'na** V.I. utter a cry of helplessness چیں چپڑ کرنا **chīn' cha'par kar'na** V.I. wrangle چیں چیں کرنا **chīn chīn' kar'na** V.I. chirp murmur ; grumble chatter چیں ماننا **chīn' mān'na** V.I. admit defeat

چینا **chī'na** N.M. a kind of corn چینا گوند **chī'na gond** N.M. gum arabic چینا بادام **chī'na badām'** N.M. (dial.) ground nut

چینٹ **chīnt'** N.F. bruise

چینچ **chainch** N.F. small corn for birds

چینچلا **chainch'la** N.M. fledgling skein of thread

چینگی پوٹے **cheṅ'gi po'ṭe** N.M. PL. sparrow's fledglings

چیند **chend** N.F. fraud

چینی **chī'nī** N.F. sugar Chinese language N.M. Chinese ADJ. Chinese چینی پرند **chī'nī parand** N.F. (arch.) soft Chinese

چیولی **che'o'lī** N.M. taffeta

چیونٹا **chyoon'ṭa** N.M. large ant چیونٹے کے پر لگنا **chyoon'ṭe ko par lag'na** V.I. be at death's door چیونٹے کی گرہ پیٹ میں ہونا **chyoon'ṭe ki gi'reh peṭ' meṅ ho'na** PH. be in the habit of eating sparingly چیونٹی **chyoon'ṭī** N.F. ant چیونٹیاں لگنا **chyoon'ṭiyaṅ lag'na** V.I. (of skin) become sensitive owing to heat

چیونٹی **chyoon'ṭī** N.F. (see under چیونٹا N.M. ★)

ح

ح **he** N.F. ninth letter of Urdu alphabet (also called **ha'-e huṭ'ṭi** or **ha-e moh'malah**) (used only in words of Arabic derivation) (in jummal reckoning) eight

حاتم **ha'tim** N.M. name of a pre-Islamic Arab chieftain of 'Tai' tribe and famous for his generosity generous person liberal person ; munificent person حاتم کی قبر پر لات مارنا **ha'tim ki qab'r par lāt' mār'na** PH. (iron.) be very generous

حاجب **ha'jib** N.M. doorkeeper , janitor chamberlain Lord Chamberlain [A ~ حجاب]

حاجت **ha'jat** (PL. حاجات **hājāt'**) N.F. need ; want requirement ; necessity poverty wish prayer ; supplication call of nature حاجت روائی **ha'jat-ravā'ī** N.F. حاجت براری **ha'jat-bar-ā'rī** supply of want fulfilment of wish or desire حاجت رفع کرنا **ha'jat raf'' kar'na** V.I. answer the call of nature supply (someone's) need حاجت روا کرنا **ha'jat ra'va kar'na** V.T. grant (someone's) wish supply (someone's) need قضائے حاجت **qazā'-e ha'jat** N.F answering the call of nature حاجتمند **ha'jat-mand** ADJ. poor ; indigent needy

حاجتی **ha'jatī** N.F bed pan [A]

حاجز **ha'jiz** N.M. obstacle barrier screen ADJ. hindering intervening [A]

حاجی **ha'ji** (rare حاج **haj** ped. الحاج **al-haj**) N.M. one who has performed the pilgrimage to Mecca; 'haji' pilgrim حاجی الحرمین **ha'j-il-haramain'** N.M. pilgrim who has been to both Mecca and Medina [P ~ A حاج CORR.]

حادث **ha'dis** ADJ. created (OPP. eternal) new ; fresh incipient [A]

حادثہ **ha'disah** N.M. (PL. حادثات **ha'disāt** حوادث **havā'dis**) accident adventure misfortune calamity [A ~ PREC.]

حادہ **had'dah** ADJ. acute contracted زاویہ حادہ **za'viya-e had'dah** N.M. acute angle

حاذق **ha'ziq** ADJ. expert skilful طبیب حاذق **tabīb-e ha'ziq**, حکیم حاذق **hakī'm-e ha'ziq** N.M. expert physician

حار **har** ADJ. (with PL. حارہ **har'rah**) hot [A ~ حرارت]

حارج **ha'rij** N.M. hindrance ; obstruction ADJ. hindering [A ~ حرج]

حاسد **ha'sid** ADJ. jealous N.M. jealous person [A ~ حسد]

حاسہ **has'sah** N.F. (PL. حواس **havās'**) sense [A ~ حس]

حاشا **ha'sha** INT. God forbid ADV. (rare) besides حاشا وکلا **ha'sha va-kal'la** INT. God forbid no ; never ; not at all حاشاک اللہ **hashāk allāh'** INT God preserve you from it God forbid [A]

حاشیہ **ha'shiyah** N.M. marginal note ; note margin border ; hem حاشیہ بردار **ha'shiyah-bar-dar'** N.M. fellow-traveller lackey menial

حاشیہ چڑھانا *ha'shiyah chaṛha'na* V.T. add marginal notes ; make addition make comments embellish an account حاشیہ چھوڑنا *ha'shiyah chhoṛ'na* V.I. leave a margin حاشیہ دار *ha'shiya-dar'* ADJ. bordered حاشیہ کا گواہ *ha'shiyah ka gavah'* N.M. witness to the execution of a deed ; marginal witness حاشیہ نشین *ha'shiya-nashin'* N.M. fellow-traveller companion lackey [A]

حاصل *ha'sil* N.M. produce ; product crop gain ; profit revenue ; tax ; duty collection result ; inference consequence الحاصل *al-ha'sil* CONJ. (see under ال★) حاصل بازاری *ha'sil-bazari* N.M. market cess حاصل تفریق *ha'sil-e tafriq'* N.M. (Math.) remainder ; balance حاصل جمع *ha'sil-e jam''* N.M. (Math.) total حاصل تقسیم *ha'sil-e taqsim'* N.M. (Math.) quotient حاصل ضرب *ha'sil-e zar'b* N.M. (multiplication) product حاصل کرنا *ha'sil kar'na* V.T. obtain ; get gain learn حاصل کلام *ha'sil-e kalam'* N.M. gist resume the points made حاصل ہونا *ha'sil ho'na* V.I. be had ; be obtained accrue come to hand حاصل نہ حصول *ha'sil na husool'* PH. ungainful putsuit silly (talk etc.) [A ~ حصول]

حاضر *ha'zir* ADJ. present in attendance ready willing ; agreeable at hand (gram.) the second person حاضر باش *ha'zir-bash* ADJ. regular in attendance ; attending regularly حاضر باشی *ha'zir-ba'shi* N.F. regularity in attendance حاضر جواب *ha'zir-javab'* ADJ. ready-witted quick at repartee حاضر جوابی *ha'zir-java'bi* N.F. repartee readiness in reply حاضر رہنا *ha'zir raih'na* V.I. be present کی خدمت میں حاضر رہنا *ki khid'mat meh ha'zir raih'na* V.I. wait on حاضر ضامن *ha'zir za'min* N.M. surety for (someone's) personal appearance in-law-court one offering bail for (someone) حاضر ضامنی *ha'zir zam'ni* N.F. such bail or surety حاضر کرنا *ha'zir kar'na* V.T. produce (someone) present ; lay before summon make ready حاضر (و) ناظر *ha'zir(-o-) na'zir* ADJ. (of God) omnipresent and omniscient خدا کو حاضر (و) ناظر مان کے *khuda' ko ha'zir (-o-) na'zir man'ke* ADV. believing God to be Omnipresent and Omniscient proving one's 'bona fides' حاضر ہونا *ha'zir ho'na* V.I. attend be present be at hand be ready be at the service of غیر حاضر *ghair'-ha'zir* ADJ. absent ; away not present missing حاضرات *hazirat'* N.F. invocation of spirits exorcizing authority over spirits necromancy حاضرات کرنا *hazirat' kar'na* V.I. invoke spirits exorcise حاضراتی *hazira'ti* N.M. necromancer exorciser حاضری *ha'ziri* (col. *ha'zri*) N.F. attendance presence appearance (in court) roll-call muster-roll Western style breakfast offering of victuals sacred funeral dinner in commemoration of Imam Husain's martyrdom حاضری دینا *ha'ziri de'na* V.I. attend حاضری کھانا *ha'ziri kha'na* V.I. have Western-style breakfast partake of this sacred meal حاضری لینا *ha'ziri le'na* V.T. call the roll ; call out the names (of) چھوٹا حاضری *cho'ta haz'ri* (ped. چھوٹی حاضری *chho'ti ha'ziri*) N.F. bed tea حاضرین *hazirin'* N.M. PL. audience INT. gentlemen حاضرین جلسہ *haziri'n-e jal'sah* N.M. PL. audience this meeting [A ~ حضور]

حافظ *ha'fiz* N.M. one who knows the Holy Quran by heart ; Koran-conner preserver protector ; guardian ; a governor (God as) protector ; preserver blind man pen-name of a Persian poet of the Timurid period celebrated for his mystical-erotic poetry حافظ حقیقی *ha'fiz-e haqi'qi* N.M. (God as) true protector [A ~ حفظ]

حافظہ *ha'fizah* N.M. memory retentive memory حافظہ تیز (یا کند) ہونا *ha'fizah tez'* (or *kund'*) *ho'na* V.I. have a good (or bad) memory [A ~ حفظ]

حاکم *ha'kim* N.M. ruler official ; officer commander chief ; boss حاکم اعلیٰ *ha'kim-e a''la*, حاکم بالا *ha'kim-e ba'la* N.M. higher authority the supreme authority حاکم دیوانی *ha'kim-e diva'ni* N.M. officer of the civil court civil authority حاکم ضلع *ha'kim e zil''* N.M. Deputy Commissioner Deputy Collector حاکم علی الاطلاق *ha'kim 'alal-itlaq'* N.M. (God as) Omnipotent حاکم فوجداری *ha'kim-e fauj da'ri* N.M. judge president over a criminal court حاکم مطلق *ha'kim-e mut'laq* N.M. despot one wielding absolute power (God as) Omnipotent *ha'kim-e vaq't* N.M. the ruler of the day ; the present ruler حاکمانہ *hakima'nah* ADJ. authoritative ADV. like an officer حاکمی *ha'kimi* N.F. (col.) authority being an officer حاکمیت *hakimiy yat* N.F. sovereignty authority حاکمیت اعلیٰ *hakimiy yat-e a'la* N.F. ultimate authority true sovereignty [A ~ حکم]

حال *hal* N.M. condition ; state situation circumstances details ; particulars rapture ; ecstasy (gram.) present tense ; the present حال آنا (یا کھیلنا) *hal a'na* (or *khel'na*) V.I. be enraptured ; be thrown into ecstasy حالانکہ *ha'-lan-keh* ADV. though ; although ; even though despite the fact that حال پرساں *hal' pur'san* (col. پرسان حال *pursa'n-e hal'*) ADJ. those inquiring after solicitous حال پتلا ہونا *hal pat'la ho'na* V.I. be in a miserable condition حال پرسی *hal'-pur'si* N.M. enquiring after (someone's) health solicitude حال سے بے حال ہونا *hal' se be-hal' ho'na* V.I. have (one's) condition aggravated go from bad to worse بُرا حال *ba'ra hal* N.M. bad condition evil days بُرے حالوں *ba're ha'loṅ* ADV. fallen on evil days in tatters بہرحال *ba-har' hal'* ADV. in any case ; at any rate however ; nevertheless ; nonetheless تباہ حال *tabah'-hal*, تبہ حال *tabah'-hal* شکستہ حال *shikas'ta-hal* ADJ. in bad circumstances ; passing through hard times ; fallen on evil days ruined (person) خوشحال *khush-hal'* ADJ. well-to do rich ; wealthy prosperous صورت حال *soo'rat-e hal'* N.F. state of affairs فی الحال *fil-hal'* ADV. now ; at present at the moment مقتضائے حال *muqtaza'-e hal'* N.M. exigency of the situation حال و قال *ha'l-o qal'* N.M. state ; condition real and apparent condition [A]

حالا *ha'la* CONJ. yet [P ~ A حال]

حالات *halat'* N.M. PL. details ; particulars conditions circumstances صورت حالات *soo'rat-e halat'* N.F. state of affairs حالات کا تقاضا *halat' ka taqa'za* N.M. exigency of the circumstances [A ~ FOLL.]

حالت *ha'lat* N.F. (PL. حالات *halat'*) state of affairs حالت غیر ہونا *ha'lat ghair' ho'na* V.I. be in the throes of death be in a miserable condition حالت نزع *ha'lat-e naz'* N.F. the throes of death the last gasps بری حالت *bu'ri ha'lat* N.F. miserable condition bad circumstances aggravated state [A ~ حال]

حامد *ha'mid* N.M. one who praises God panegyrist [A ~ حمد]

حامض *ha'miz* ADJ. sour ; acid sharp ; pungent [A]

حامل *ha'mil* N.M. bearer (of something) حامل رقعہ ہذا *ha'mil-e ruq''ah (ha'za)* PH. the bearer of this note [A ~ حمل]

حاملہ *ha'milah* N.F. pregnant (rare) bearer (of something) حاملہ کرنا *ha'milah kar'na* V.T. make pregnant حاملہ ہونا *ha'milah ho'na* V. conceive ; be or become pregnant ; be in the family way [A ~ حمل]

حامی *ha'mi* N.M. supporter ally helper (rare) protector (usu. ہامی *ha'mi*) assurance yes حامی (یا ہامی) بھرنا *hami* (or *ha'mi*) *bhar'na* V.I. say yes agree ; consent assure acknowledge [A]

حانث *ha'nis* N.M. (lit.) perjurer [A]

حاوی *ha'vi* ADJ. skilled ; expert comprehending comprehensive controlling

حائضہ *ha''izah*, حائض *ha''iz* N.F. & ADJ. menturating (woman) [A ~ حیض]

حائل *ha''il* ADJ. intervening hindering standing in the way disturbing حائل کرنا *ha''il kar'na* V.T. raise (wall) between حائل ہونا *ha''il ho'na* V.T. intervene come in the way interrupt disturb stand (as a wall) between separate

حب *hub* N.F love affection حب الوطنی *hub'b-ul-va'tani*, حب وطن *hub'b-e-va'tan* N.F. patriotism حب ذات *hub'b-e-zat'*, حب نفس *hub'b-e naf's* N.M. egotism selfishness حب و بغض *hub'b-o-bugh'z* N.M. love and hatred عمل حب *'a'mal-e hub* N.M. love charm [A]

حب *hab* N.F. (PL. حبوب *huboob'*) pill (rare) grain (rare) seed حب الملوک *hab'b-ul-mulook'* N.M. croton seed [A]

حباب *habab'* N.M. bubble حباب آسا *haba'b asa'* ADJ. like a bubble flimsy short-lived حباب اٹھنا *habab' uth'na* V. to bubble [A]

حبذا *hab'baza* INT. (rare) buck up bravo ; well done

حبس *hab's* N.M. imprisonment ; confinement retention ; withholding inability to pass (urine, etc.) close or sultry weather حبس البول *hab's-ul-baul* N.M. strangury حبس بے جا *hab's-e be' ja'* N.M. wrongful confinement حبس دم *hab's-e dam'* N.M. holding the breath suffocation حبس دوام *hab's-e davam'* N.M. life-term ; life imprisonment حبس دوام (بعبور دریائے شور) *hab's-e davam' (ba-'uboo'r-e darya'-e shor)* N.M. transportation for life حبسیات *habsiyyat'* N.M. (esp.) verse composed during imprisonment ; gaol musings [A]

حبشی *ha'bashi* N.M African (rare) Abyssinian Negro ; nigger one of the black races tawny (person) حبش *ha'bash*, حبشہ *ha'bashah* N.M. Abyssinia ; Ethiopia [A]

حبل *hab'l* N.F. rope cord حبل المتین *hab'l-ul matin'* N.F. strong rope حبل الورید *hab'l-ul varid'* N.F. jugular vein ;

حبوب *huboob'* N.M. PL. pills (rare) grains (rare) seeds [A ~ SING. حب *hab*]

حبہ *hab'bah* N.M. grain (fig.) little amount حبہ بھر *hab'bah bhar* ADV. a little [A doublet of حب *hab*]

حبیب *habib'* N.M. friend favourite beloved حبیب خدا *habi'b-e khuda'* N.M. the Holy Prophet (as the friend of God)

حتی *hat'ta* PREF. as far as to ; up to till حتی الامکان *hat'tal-imkan'*, حتی الوسع *hat'tal-vas'*, حتی المقدور *hat'tal-maqdoor'* ADV. to one's utmost ; to the best of one's ability ; as far as lies in one's power حتی کہ *hat'ta keh* CONJ. till ; until to the extent of so that

حتمی *hat'mī* ADJ. definite categorical final sure ; certain [A]
حتّی *hit'tī* N.M. & ADJ. Hittite
حج *haj* N.M. seasonal pilgrimage to Mecca Hajj pilgrimage حج اصغر *haj'j-e as'ghar* N.F. non-seasonal pilgrimage to Mecca ; 'umra' حج اکبر *haj'j-e ak'bar* N.M. seasonal pilgrimage to Mecca with ritual falling on Friday pilgrimage performed after the conquest of Mecca امیر الحج *amī'r-ul-haj* N.M. pilgrim caravan chief leader of pilgrim congregation [A]
حجاب *hijāb* (PL. حجب *hu'jūb*) N.M. curtain veil modesty lack of familiarity; lack of intimacy حجاب اٹھانا *hijāb' ūṭhā'nā* V.I. lift the veil . breed familiarity create intimacy deprive of sense of shame حجاب اٹھنا (یا جاتا رہنا) *hijab' ūṭh'nā* (or *jā'tā raih'nā*) V.I. (or veil) be removed become familiar, have intimacy lose sense of shame حجاب چشمی *hijab'-chash'mī* N.F. ogling ; casting sheep's eye حجاب کرنا *hijab'-kar'nā* V.I. veil (oneself) conceal one's face (from) blush ; be abashed [A]
حجاج *hujjāj'* N.M. PL. pilgrims [A ~ SING. حاجی or حاج]
حجام *hajjām'* N.M. (see under حجامت N.F ★)
حجامت *hijā'mat* (col. *hajā'mat*) N.F. hair cut shave tonsure phlebotomy حجامت بنانا *hajā'mat banā'nā* V.T. shave cut the hair tonsure despoil defraud حجامت ہونا *hajā'mat ho'nā* V.I. have a shave or haircut be defrauded of money حجام *hajjām'* N.M. barber hair dresser phlebotomist حجامی *hajjāmī* N.F. barber's trade phlebotomist's trade [A]
حجب *hu'jūb* N.M. (PL. of حجاب N.M ★)
حجت *huj'jat* N.F (PL. rare حجج *hi'jaj*) argument , reason proof objection excuse ; pretext altercation dispute حجت کرنا *huj jat kar'nā* V. reason ; argue object ; raise an objection cavil taunt حجت لانا *huj'jat la'nā* V.T. object adduce an argument حجتی *huj'jatī* ADJ. quarrelsome [A]
حجر *ha'jar* N.M. (PL حجار *hijār'*, احجار *ahjār'*) stone pebble rock حجر اسود *ha'jar-e as'vad* N.M. black stone of the Ka'aba [A]
حجرہ *huj'rah* N.M. chamber closet cell small room in mosque, etc for residence [A]
حجلہ *haj'loh* (ped. حجلہ *ha'jalah*) N.M. bridal chamber canopied bed حجلۂ عروسی *haj'la-e 'aroo'sī* N.M. bridal chamber [A]
حجم *haj'm* N.M. volume ; thickness (of book) [A
حد *had* N.F. (PL. حدود *hudood'*) limit ; boundary ; extremity margin extent (Islamic law) restrictive or penal ordinance penalty for transgressing it definition ADV. to the utmost degree extremely at least حد اقل *had-d e aqal'* N.F. minimum حد اکثر *had'd-e ak'sar* N.F. maximum حد باندھنا *had' bandh'nā* V.T. delimit define حد بست *had'-bas't* N.M. delimitation (of lands) boundary settlement حد بندی *had'-bañ'dī* N.F. delimitation boundary حد بلوغ *had'd-e būloogh'* N.F. majority ; age of puberty حد بلوغ کو پہنچنا *had'd-e būloogh' ko pahūñch'nā* V.I. attain majority حد سے بڑھنا *had' se barh'nā* V.I. transgress exceed one's powers go beyond limits حد سے زیادہ *had se ziya'dah* ADV. very much extremely حد شکنی *had'-shi'kanī* N.F encroachment transgression حد کرنا *had' kar'nā* V.T. & I. act in a strange manner do one's utmost exceed limits push (something) to extremity حد لگانا (یا قائم کرنا) *had' lagā'nā* (or *qa''im kar'nā*) V.T. (Islamic law penalize for transgressing limits حد متوسط *had'd-e mūtavas'sat* N. medium حد محدود *had'd-e mahdood'* N.M. limited leasehold حد ہونا *had' ho'nā* V.I. exceed bounds be very surprising از حد *az had*, بیحد *be had* ADV. extremely ; excessively [A]
حدت *hid'dat* N.F. pungency sharpness acuteness virulence [A]
حدی *hūdā'* N.F. (correct but ped. pronunciation of حدی *hū'dī* ★)
حداثت *hadā'sat* N.F. freshness prime (of life)
حداد *haddād'* N.M. ironmonger smith [A ~ حدید]
حدائق *hadā''iq* N.M. PL. of حدیقہ N.M. ★)
حدث *ha'das* N.M. farting, or answering call of nature, etc. necessitating fresh ablutions [A]
حدوث *hūdoos'* N.M newness , freshness novelty [A]
حدود *hūdood'* N.F (dial M.) limits boundaries , confines , limits definitions (Islamic law) restrictive or penal ordinances حدود اربعہ *hūdoo'd-e-ar'ba'ah* N.F. (dial. M.) the four boundaries حدود شرعیہ *hūdoo'd-e shar'iy'yah* N.F. (dial. M.) restrictive or penal ordinances of Islam penalties for transgressing these [A ~ حد PL.]

حدیث **ḥadīs'** N.M. (PL. احادیث *aḥādīs'*) tradition of the Holy Prophet ; tradition narrative (rare) news ADJ. new ; fresh [A]

حدید **ḥadīd'** N.M. iron [A]

حدیقه **ḥadī'qah** N.M. (PL. حدائق *ḥada''iq*) walled garden

حذاقت **ḥizāqat** N.F. skill ; expertness [A ~ حاذق]

حذر **ḥa'zar** N.M. prudence abstinence caution fear [A]

حذف **ḥaz'f** N.M. omission dropping out apocope elision حذف کرنا *ḥaz'f kar'nā* V.I. mit drop [A]

حر **ḥur** ADJ. (PL. احرار *aḥrār'*) free (rare) noble [A]

حرارت **ḥarā'rat** N.F. heat warmth slight fever ; temperature zeal , fervour حرارت غریزی *ḥarā'rat-e gharī'zī* N.F. natural heat (of the body) حرارت ہونا *ḥarā'rat ho'nā* V.I. feel feverish

حراره **ḥarā'rah** N.M. calory fury حراره لانا (لینا) *ḥarā'rah lā'nā* (or *le'nā*) V.I. fly into passion [A]

حراست **ḥirā'sat** N.F. (police) custody ; arrest (rare) watch ; guard حراست میں لینا *ḥirā'sat meṅ le'nā* V.I. (of police, etc.) take into custody ; arrest

حراف **ḥarrāf'** ADJ. (F. حرافه *ḥarrā'fah*) cunning ; tricky facile [A ~ حرف]

حرام **ḥarām'** ADJ. unlawful ; forbidden ; prohibited sacred N.M. unlawful act حرام خور *ḥarām'-khor* N.M. & ADJ. corrupt (person) shirker حرامزاده *ḥarām'-za'dah* حرامی *ḥarā'mī* N.M. & ADJ. (F. حرامزادی *ḥarām-zā'dī*) bastard ; illegitimate child ; one born out of wedlock (swear word) bastard (swear word) scoundrel ; rascal حرامزدگی *ḥarām'-za'dagī* (col. *ḥarām'-zad'gī*) N.F. villainy , rascality (rare) illegitimacy حرام کاری *ḥarām-kā'rī* N.F. unlawful sexual relations ; adultery ; fornication حرام کھانا *ḥarām' khā'nā* V.I. be corrupt , accept bribe get money by unlawful means مال حرام *mā'l-e ḥarām'*, حرام کا مال *ḥarām' kā māl'* N.M. ill-gotten wealth مال حرام بود بجائے حرام رفت *mā'l-e ḥarām' bood' ba-jā'-e ḥarām' raft'* PROV. ill-got, ill-spent مسجد حرام *mas'jid-e ḥarām'* N.M. the Holy Ka'aba (and its precincts) حرام مغز *ḥarām' magh'z* N.M. cerebellum spinal marrow حرام موت *ḥarām' maut'* N.F. suicide wasteful sacrifice حرامی *ḥarā'mī* (same as حرامزاده N.M. & ADJ. ★)

حرب **ḥar'b** N.F. battle war حربه *ḥar'bah* N.M. weapon ruse ; trick حربی *ḥar'bī* ADJ. warlike combatant tactical strategic pertaining to logistics [A]

حربا **hirba'** N.F. chamelion [A]

حربه **ḥar'bah** N.M. (see under حرب ★)

حرج **ḥa'raj** N.M. (usu. ہرج *har'j*) harm ; obstacle حرج (یا ہرج) مرج *ḥa'raj* (or *harj'*) *mar'j* N.M. harm damage row ; altercation [A]

حرز **ḥir'z** N.M. charm ; amulet ; talisman (rare) fortification حرز جاں بنانا *ḥir'z-e jāṅ' banā'nā* V.T. regard as the most prized object hold very dear [A]

حرص **ḥir's** N.F. greed avidity حرصی *ḥir'sī* N.M & ADJ. (col.) greedy (person) prurient salacious [A]

حرف **ḥar'f** N.M. (PL. حروف *ḥaroof'*) letter of the alphabet ; letert (gram.) particle speech ; talk short note blame , censure - obloquy ; stigma opprobrium (rare) brink حرف آشنا *ḥar'f-āshnā'* N.M. one able to read a little حرف آنا *ḥar'f ā'nā* V.I. be blamed be stigmatised be disgraced حرف اٹھانا *ḥar'f ūṭhā'nā* V.I. learn the letters of the alphabet decipher find legible read حرف بحرف *ḥar'f ba-ḥar'f* ADJ. literal complete ADV. literally ; word of word ; verbatim exactly completely حرف بٹھانا (یا جمانا) *ḥar'f biṭhā'nā* (or *jamā'nā*) V. compose (type) حرف بنانا *ḥar'f banā'nā* V.T. cast letters correct someone's wiiting indite حرف پکڑنا *ḥar'f pa'karnā* V.T. criticize حرف پہچاننا *ḥarf paihchān'nā* V.I. learn the alphabet حرف تردید *ḥar'f-e tardīd'* N.M. disjunctive conjunction حرف تشبیه *ḥar'f-e tashbīh'* N.M. adverb of similitude حرف تعریف *ḥar'f-e ta'rīf'* N.M. definite article حرف تنکیر *ḥar'f e tankīr'* N.M. indefinite article حرف جار *ḥar'f-e jār'*, حرف جر *ḥar'f-e jar'* N.M. (PL. حروف جاره *ḥūroo'f-e jār'rah* حروف جر *ḥūroo'f-e jār*) preposition حرف رکھنا *ḥar'f rakh'nā* V.T. blame stigmatize حرف شرط *ḥar'f-e shar't* N.M. conditional conjunction حرف صحیح *ḥar'f-e saḥīḥ* N.M. (PL. حروف صحیحه *ḥūroo'f-e saḥī'ḥah*) consonant حرف علت *ḥar'f-e 'il'lat* N.M. (pl. حروف علت *ḥūroo'f-e 'il'lat*) vowel حرف گیری *ḥar'f-gī'rī* N.M. objection criticism cavilling ; carping حرف لانا *ḥar'f lā'nā* V.I. blame blemish carp and cavil حرف ندا *ḥar'f-e ni'dā* N.M. interjection حرفاً حرفاً *ḥar'fan ḥar'fan* ADV. (of lesson, etc.) letter by letter ; syllable by syllable حرفی *ḥar'fī* ADJ. literal pertaining to letters [A]

حرفت **ḥir'fat** N.F. trade ; profession craft skill cunning حرفت باز *ḥir'fat-bāz* (col. حرفتی *ḥir'fatī*) N.M. cunning صنعت و حرفت *san''at o ḥir'fat*

N.F. industry industrialization [A]

حرفہ *hir'fah* N.M trade craft اہل حرفہ *ah'l-e hir'fah* (col. *ahl'-*) N.M artisans craftsmen workmen نشان حرفہ *nisha'n-e hir'fah* N.M. (arch.) trade mark [A doublet of PREC.]

حرکت *har'kat* (ped. حَرَکَت *ha'rakat*) N.F motion, movement action gesture posture (gram.) short vowel misdemeanour mischief travel حرکت دوری (یا دوریہ) *ha'rakat-e dau'rī* (or *dauriy'yah*) N.F rotation حرکت دینا *ha'rakat de'nā* V.T move set in motion (gram.) put a vowel-point over حرکت کرنا *ha'rakat kar'nā* V.I move, make a move do (something) improper do as mischief حرکات *harakāt'* N.F. PL. motions; movements actions (gram.) vowel-points حرکات وسکنات *harakā't-o sakanāt'* N.F. ([illegible] M.) gestures postures movements [A]

حرم *ha'ram* N.M. the sanctuary of Mecca; the Ka'aba close sanctuary 'women's apartment harem seraglio wife حرم سرا *ha'ram-sarā'* N.F harem, seraglio حرمین شریفین *ha'ramain-e sharīfain* N.M. PL. the two as sanctuaries of Mecca and Medina [A]

حرماں *hir'mān* حرمان *hirman'* N.M. dismay, disappointment, despondence dejection deprivation حرماں نصیب *hir'mān-nasīb'* ADJ. & N.M. unfortunate dismayed (person) [A ~ محروم]

حرمت *hur'mat* N.F. dignity, honour, esteem sanctity unlawfulness حرمت والا *hur'mat-vā'lā* ADJ. venerable sacred prohibited [A ~ حرام]

حرمل *har'mal* N.M wild rue [A]

حروف *huroof'* N.M. letters of (the alphabet) حروف تہجی *huroo'f-e-tahaj'jī* حروف الہجا *huroo'ful-hijā'* N.M. PL. letters of the alphabet [A ~ SING. حرف]

حریت *hurriy'yat* (or *hur'riyat*) N.F. freedom; liberty emancipation, enfranchisement [A ~ حر]

حریر *harīr'* N.M. silk silk-cloth حریری *harīrī* ADJ. silk silken soft sleek fine [A]

حریرہ *harī'rah* N.M. a kind of caudle; batter-caudle

حریص *harīs'* ADJ. greedy covetous gluttonous (rare) avid [A ~ حرص]

حریف *harīf'* N.M. & ADJ. opponent adversary rival equal; peer colleague (one) able to stand [A]

حریم *harīm* (N.M PL حرم *hūrūm*) boundry the Ka'aba sanctuary house. residence outer walls of the house (rare) wife [A]

حزب *hiz'b* (PL. احزاب *ahzāb'*) N.M party group (rare) army, force حزب اختلاف *hiz'b-e-ikhtilāf'* N.M. the Opposition opposition party حزب اقتدار *hiz'b-e iqtidār'* N.M. party in power Government party, Treasury Benches [A]

حزم *haz'm* N.M vigilance carefulness, watchfulness حزم واحتیاط *haz'm-o ihtiyāt'* N.M vigilance and carefulness, cautiousness [A]

حزن *hūz'n*, (or *ha'zan*) (or *ha'zin*) N.M. sorrow, grief affliction حزیں *hazīn* ADJ. sorrowful sad grieved; afflicted melancholy [A]

حس *his* N.F (PL. حواس *havās'*) sense; sensation حس باطنی *his's-e bā'tinī* N.F perception حس ظاہری *his's-e zā'hirī* N.F sensation حس مشترک *his's-e mush'tarak* N.F (rare or ped.) common sense [A]

حساب *hisāb* N.M arithmetic (col.) mathematics account rate counting; reckoning calculation, computation حساب بیباق کرنا *hisāb' be-bāq' kar'nā* V.T. pay off debts settle or clear an account; be quits حساب پاک کرنا *hisāb' pāk kar'nā* V.T. settle or clear account end murder حساب پاک ہونا *hisāb' pāk ho'nā* V.I. be quits (of accounts) be settled or clear be honest حساب جو جو بخشش سو سو *hisāb' jau' jau bakhshish' sau' sau* PROV. munificance apart account must be clear حساب جوڑنا *hisāb jor'nā* V.T. add up; total calculate; compute حساب دان *hisāb'-dān* N.M. mathematician accountant حساب دوستاں در دل *hisāb-e dos'tān dar dil'* PROV. friend do not keep an account of presents exchanged mutually حساب دینا *hisāb' de'nā* V.T. render an account حساب رکھنا *hisāb rakh'nā* V.I. keep account maintain an account حساب کتاب *hisāb' kitāb'* N.M. accounts حساب کرنا *hisāb' kar'nā* V.I. calculate: compute settle an account حساب کی کتاب *hisāb kī bāt* PL. matter pertaining to an account reasonable stand حساب لگانا *hisāb' lagā'nā* V.T. estimate calculate حساب لینا *hisāb' le'nā* V.T. take an account (from) حساب میں رکھنا (یا لینا) *hisāb' meṅ rakh'nā* (or *le'nā*) V.I. consider take into account حساب نویس *hisāb'-navīs* N.M. ledger writer اپنے حسابوں *ap'ne hisā'boṅ* ADV. according to me (etc.) حسابی *hisā'bī* ADJ. pertaining to accounts arithmetical reasonable N.M. mathematician one strict in matters of account [A]

حساس *hassās'* ADJ. sensitive emotional [A ~ حس]

حسام *ḥusām* N.F. sword [A]

حسب *ha'sab* N.M. lineage pedigree nobility حسب و نسب *ha'sab-(o) na'sab* N.M. N.M. lineage pedigree nobility [A]

حسب *has'b* N.M accordance حسب *ḥas'b-e* ADV. & PREF according to in conformity with حسب ارشاد *has'b-e irshād'*, حسب الحکم *ḥas'b-ūl-ḥūk'm*, حسب ہدایت *hasb-hidā'yat* ADV. as desired ; as ordered in compliance with orders, instructions, etc. حسب حال *ḥas'b-e ḥāl'* ADV. as demanded by the exigency of the situation حسب دلخواہ *ḥas'b-e dil-khāh'* ADV. after one's own heart حسب ذیل *ḥas'b-e zail'* ADV. the following ; as follows ; حسب ضابطہ *ḥas'b-e zā'bitah*, حسب قاعدہ *ḥas'b-e qā''idah* ADV. in accordance with the procedure ADJ. procedural حسب قانون *ḥas'b-e qānoon'* ADV. legally ; according to law حسب معمول *ḥas'b-e ma''mool* ADV. as usual حسب موقع *ḥasb-e mau'qe'*, حسب موقعہ *ḥasb-e mau'qah* ADV. as the case may demand ; according to the need of the occasion [A]

حسد *ḥa'sad* N.F. jealousy malice حسد رکھنا (یا کرنا) *ḥa'sad rakh'nā* (or *kar'nā*) V.I. be jealous bear malice [A]

حسرت *ḥas'rat* N.F. regret wistfulness longing pining حسرت آلود *ḥas'rat-ālood'*, حسرت آلودہ *has'rat-āloo'dah*, حسرت زدہ *ḥas'rat za'dah* ADJ. sad ; sorrowful ; full of sorrow grief-stricken ; overwhelmed with grief wistful ; pining حسرت بھری *ḥas'rat bha'rī* ADJ. (of looks) longing wistful pining [A]

حسن *ḥūs'n* N.F. beauty prettiness ; comeliness handsomeness grace ; gracefulness elegance the beautiful a beauty حسن اتفاق *ḥūs'n-e ittifāq'* N.M. lucky chance good fortune ; stroke of luck حسن اخلاق *ḥūs'n-e akhlāq'* N.M. manners ; good manners etiquette politeness ; courtesy حسن انتظام *ḥūs'n-e intizām'* N.M. good discipline ; good management managerial efficiency حسن تدبیر *ḥūs'n-e tadbīr'* N.M. sound policy حسن تعلیل *ḥūs'n-e ta'līl'* N.F. ascribing to a different cause حسن صبیح *ḥūsn-e sabīḥ'* N.M. blondness blond, blonde حسن طلب *ḥūs'n-e ta'lab* N.M. nice way of asking حسن ظن *ḥūs'n-e zan'* N.M. good opinion favourable view حسن عمل *ḥūs'n-e 'amal* N.M. good deeds walking in the ways of God حسن مطلع *ḥūs'n-e mat'la'* N.M. second couplet of the ode حسن مطلق *ḥūs'n-e mūt'laq* N.M. (God as) the Absolute Beauty حسن مقید *ḥūs'n-e muqay'yad* N.M. mortal beauty حسن ملیح *ḥūs'n-e malīḥ'* N.M. the coloured beauty مقابلہ حسن *muqā'balā-e ḥūs'n* N.M. beauty contest ; beauty competition [A]

حسن *ha'san* ADJ. good N.M. name of the second Shi'ite Imam حسنہ *ha'sanah* ADJ. good حسنات *hasanāt'* N.F. PL. good actions ; virtuous deeds virtues [A ~ SING. حسنہ]

حسود *ḥasood'* ADJ. jealous grudging N.M. jealous person [A ~ حسد]

حسین *ḥasīn'* حسین *ḥasīn* ADJ. handsome, pretty ; beautiful comely graceful حسینہ *ḥasī'nah* N.F. beautiful woman ; a beauty حسینہ عالم *ḥasī'na-e 'ā'lam* N.F. Miss universe [A ~ حسن *ḥūs'n*]

حسین *ḥusain'ī* N.M. name of the second Shi'ite Imam martyred at Kerbala

حشر *ḥash'r* N.M. resurrection ; doomsday wailing ; lamentation tumult hue and cry حشر برپا (یا بپا) کرنا *ḥash'r bar-pā'* (or *ba-pā'*) *kar'nā* V.T. weep and wail aloud cause a tumult یوم الحشر *yau'm-ūl-ḥash'r* N.M. the day of resurrection ; the Doomsday حشری باغی *ḥash'rī bā'ghī* N.M. (col.) traitor for following the rabble [A]

حشرات *ḥasharāt'* N.M. PL. حشرات الارض *ḥasharā't-ūl-ar'z* N.M. PL. insects (esp. as seen creeping after rains) the scum of society too many and unprovided-for children [A]

حشفہ *ḥash'fah* N.M. 'glans penis'; head of penis [A]

حشم *ḥa'sham* N.M. PL. retinue, train (of servants) equipage خدم وحشم *kha'dam-o ḥa'sham* N.M. PL. equipage [A ~ SING. حشمت]

حشمت *ḥash'mat* N.F. pomp dignity riches ; wealth [A]

حشو *ḥash'v* N.M. padding stuffing حشو وزوائد *ḥash'v-o zavā''d* N.M. padding [A]

حشیش *ḥashīsh'* N.M. dry hemp leaves ; حشیشین *ḥashīshiyyīn'* N.M. PL. Assassins ; fanatic followers of the Middle Ages Shi'ite leader Hasan bin Sabah [A]

حصار *ḥisār* N.M. fort ; fortress ; castle, fortification rampart enclosure حصار باندھنا *ḥisār' bāndh'nā* V.I. set up an enclosure بالا حصار *ba'la-ḥisār'* N.M. citadel [A]

حصر *ḥas'r* N.M. reliance counting ; reckoning taking (of something) into account [A]

حصص *ḥi'sas* N.M. shares stocks parts portions [A ~ حصہ]

حصن *ḥis'n* N.M. fort ; fortress ; castle fortification حصن حصین *ḥis'n-e ḥasīn'* N.M. impregnable fortress name of a prayer book [A]

حصول *ḥusool'* N.M. acquisition achievement, attainment

حصہ *his'sah* N.M. (PL. also حصص *hi'sas*) part portion share lot حصہ دار *his'sa-dar*, *his'se-dar* N.M. partner shareholder حصہ داری *his'sa da'ri*, *his'se-da'ri* N.F. partnership sharing حصہ رسدی *his'sah-rasadi* N.F. proprortionate share حصہ لینا *his'sah le'na* V.T. participate ; take part in receive (one's) share حصے (بخرے) کرنا *his'se (bakhre) kar'na* V.I. apportion distribute share (something) between or among [A]

حضر *ha'zar* N.M. sojourn (as opposed to travel) (rare.) settled (as opposed to nomadic) state

حضرت *haz'rat* N.M. (PL. حضرات *hazarat'*) title preceding name of saint, etc. (rare) court mischievous person scoundrel حضرت ظل سبحانی *haz'rat zil'l-e subha'ni* N.M. (the king as) the shadow of God ; His Majesty بڑے حضرت *ba're haz'rat* N.M. arrant knave ; consummate rascal حضرات *hazarat'* N.M. PL. title preceding names of saints, poets, etc. gentlemen INT Gentlemen

حضور *hazoor'* INT. sir Your Honour (etc.) N.M. presence (of superior) court کے حضور (میں) *ke huzoor (men)* before (a superior) حضور پر نور *hazoo'r-e pur-noor'* N.M. his illustratious Honour (etc.) حضور والا *hazoo'r-e va'la*, حضور اقدس *hazoo'r-e aq'das* N.M. His Honour (etc.) INT. you; Your Honour (etc.) حضوری *hazoo'ri* N.F presence N.M. attendant [A]

حضیض *hazi'z'* N.M. depth low-lying ground [A]

حطیم *hatim'* N.M. western wall near Ka'aba a year-old plant ADJ. broken [A]

حظ *haz* N.M. pleasure delight lot ; portion حظ اٹھانا *haz utha'na* V.I. enjoy derive pleaure حظ نفسانی *haz'z-e nafsa'ni* N.M. sensual pleasure حظ و کرب *haz'z-o kar'b* N.M. pleasure and pain [A]

حفاظ *haffaz'* N.M. (PL. of حافظ *ha'fiz* N.M. ★)

حفاظت *hifa'zat* N.F. safety ; security custody defend protection preservation حفاظت کرنا *hifa'zat kar'na* V. protect defend preserve [A doublet of FOLL.]

حفظ *hifz* N.M. memorization ; learning by heart ; learning by rote defence protection preservation حفظ کرنا *hifz kar'na* V.T. commit to memory ; learn by heart ; learn by rote حفظ ما تقدم (کے طور پر) *hif'z-e ma' taqad'dam (ke taur' par)* N.M. (as) a precautionary measure حفظ مراتب *hif'z-e mara'tib* N.M. observing the etiquette paying due regard to the status of each حفظ نظر *hifz-e na'zar* PH. (W. dial.) May escape influence of evil eye [A]

حفیظ *hafiz'* N.M. (God as) Guardian protector [A ~ حفظ]

حق *haq* ADJ. & N.M. God truth right equity ; justice lot ; share claim due remuneration حق ادا کرنا *haq' ada' kar'na* V.T. give (someone) his due do justice (to) ;do full justice (to) حق آسائش *haq' q-e asai''ish* N.M. right of convenience حق العباد *haq'q-ul-'ibad'* N. rights of human beings حق اللہ *haq'q-ullah'* N.M. rights of God حق ارجاع نالش *haq' q-e-irja'-e na'lish* N.M right of appeal حق بجانب *haq' ba-ja'nib* ADJ. justified حق بحق دار رسید *haq ba-haq-dar' rasid'* PROV. everyone gets his due حق پرست *haq-paras't* ADJ. & N.M. pious (person) true believer godly (person) حق پرستی *haq para'sti* N.F. true faith godliness حق تصنیف *haq'q e tasn f'* N.M. copyright حق تعالیٰ *haq ta'a'la* N.M. the Most High God ; the Great God حق تلفی *haq ta'lafi* N.F. usurpation حق تلفی کرنا *haq ta'lafi kar'na* V.T. usurp the rights (of) encroach (upon) حق پہنچنا *haq' pahunch'na* V.I. have the right to حق ثابت کرنا *haq' sa'bit kar'na* V.I. prove one's claim حق جتانا *haq jata'na* V.T. press one's right or claim حق جوئی *taqq joo''i* N.F. search for truth pursuit of truth حق حین حیاتی *haq'q-e hin haya'ti* N.M. life interest حق خود ارادیت *haq'q e khud iradiy'yat* N.M right of self-determination حقدار *haq-dar'* ADJ. deserv g (person) rightful having a right or cla (to) حق دبانا (یا مارنا) *haq daba'na* (or *mar'na*) V.T usurp (someone's) right deprive (someone) of his due حق رائے دہی *haq'q-e ra''e dehi'* N.M. right to vote حق رسی *haq'-ra'si* N.F. redress relief justice حق رسی کرنا *haq' ra'si kar'na*. V.T. do full justice to حق شفعہ *haq'q-e sh f''ah* N.M. right of pre-emption حق شناس *haq-shinas'* ADJ. godly righteous pious giving everyone his due dutiful appreciative حق شناسی *haq-shina'si* N.F. godly righteousness justice ; doing even-hand d justice dutifulness appreciation حق مالکانہ *haq'q-e malika'nah* N.M. (PL. حقوق مالکانہ *huqoo'q-e malika'nah*) proprietary rights کے حق میں *ke haq men* PREP. for in the interests of حق نمک ادا کرنا *haq: na'mak ada' kar'na* V.I. do one's duty creditably make a sacrifice for one's master حقا *haq'qa* ADV. truly ; verily By God حقانی *haqqa'ni* ADJ. godly حقانیت *haqqaniy'yat* (col. *haqqa'niyat*) N.F. truth ; veracity godliness righteousness [A]

حقارت *hiqa'rat* N.F. contempt ; scorn ; disdain hatred حقارت کرنا *hiqa'rat kar'na*, حقارت کی نظر سے دیکھنا *hiqarat ki na'zar se dekh'na* V.T. despise , look down upon disdain [A]

حقائق *haqā''iq* N.M. truths facts [A ~ SING. حقیقت]

حقنہ *hūq'nah* N.M. enema ; clyster حقنہ کرنا *hūq'nah kar'nā* V.T. clyster [A]

حقوق *hūqooq'* N.M. rights , dues ; privileges duties remuneration حقوق ادا کرنا *hūqooq' adā' kar'nā* V.I. give (someone) his dues do (something) nicely حقوقِ زوجیت *hūqooq'q-e zaujiy'yat* N.M. PL. conjugal rights بنیادی حقوق *bunyā'dī hūqooq'* N.M. PL. fundamental rights [A ~ SING. حق]

حقہ *hūq'qah* N.M. hookah ; hubble bubble (rare) casket (rare) fraud ; trick حقہ باز *hūq'qa-bāz* N.M. trickster impostor juggler (joc.) hookah-addict حقہ بردار *hūq'qa-bardar'* N.M. servant carrying master's hookah حقہ پانی بند کرنا *hūq'qah pā'nī band' kar'nā* V.T boycott excommunicate حقہ تازہ کرنا *hūq'qah tā'zah kar'nā* V.I. change water in 'hookah' bowl ; wash 'hookah' pipes, etc. [A]

حقیت *haqqiy'yat* N.F. ownership proprietary right فردِ حقیت *far'd haqqiy'yat* N.F proprietary statement [A ~ حق]

حقیر *haqīr'* ADJ. abject vile contemptible despicable mean ; base petty حقیر جاننا *haqīr' jān'nā* V.T. despise ; look down upon disdain regard as petty [~ حقارت]

حقیقت *haqīqat* N.F. fact ; fact of the matter ; reality condition ; state account truth veracity حقیقت پسند *haqī'qat-pasand'* N.M. realist ADJ. realistic حقیقت پسندانہ *haqī'qat pasandā'nah* ADJ. realistic ADV. realistically حقیقت پسندی *haqī'qat-pasan'dī* N.F. realism realistic attitude حقیقۃً *haqī'qatan* ADJ. in fact; in truth; in reality really حقیقی *haqī'qī* ADJ. real actual factual own sanguine حقیقی بھائی *haqī'qi thā''ī* N.M. brother حقیقی بہن *haqī'qī bai'han* N.F sister حقیقی رشتہ *haqī'qī rish'tah* N.M. full blood [A]

حک *hak* N.M. erasure deletion cutting gem, etc. حک کرنا *hak kar'nā* V.T. erase delete حک و اصلاح *hak'k-o islāh'* N.F. deletion and correction حک و اضافہ *hak'k-o izā'fah* N.M. deletion and addition حک و ترمیم *hak'k-o tarmīm'* N.F. deletion and amendment [A]

حکام *hukkā n'* N.M. officers authorities commanders rulers [A ~ SING. حاکم]

حکایت *hikā'yat* N.F. tale story fable detail narrative report حکایات *hikāyāt'* N.F. PL. tales fables stories [A]

حکم *hūk'm* N.M. order ; command decree ordinance decision ; verdict precept jurisdiction authority prediction حکماً *hūk'man* ADV by or under orders حکمِ امتناعی *hūk'm-e imtinā''ī* N.M. injunction ; prohibitory order حکم بجا لانا *hūk'm ba-jā' lā'nā* V.I. obey carry out the order (of) حکم بردار *hūk'm-bardār'* ADJ. mandatory obedient حکم برداری *hūk'm-bardā'rī* N.F. mandate obedience حکم جاری کرنا *hūk'm ja'ri kar'nā* V.T. issue an order حکم جاری ہونا *hūk m jā'rī ho'nā* V.I. (of order) be issued حکمِ حاکم مرگِ مفاجات *hūk'm-e ha'kim mar'g-e mūfājāt'* PROV. what cannot be cured must be endured حکم چلانا *hūk'm chalā'nā* V.I rule , to govern exercise authority control ; keep under the thumb حکم دینا *hūk'm de'nā* V.T. order ; issue an order pass an order حکمران *hūk'm-rā'nī* N.M. sovereign , ruler حکمرانی *hūkm-rā'nī* N.F. power rule reign sway control حکم سنانا *hūk'm sūnā'nā* V.I. announce the judgement give the verdict , give the decision سزا کا حکم سنانا *sazā' kā hūk'm sūnā'nā* V.T. convict حکمِ ضبطی *hūk'm-e zab'tī* N.M. forfeiture orders حکمِ ظہری *kūk'm-e zah'rī* N.M. endorsement (on petition, etc.) حکم عدولی کرنا *hūk'm 'ūdoo'lī kar'nā,* حکم کرنا *hūk'm kar'nā* V.T. & I. infringe an order , violate impugn قطعی حکم *qa't''ī hūk'm* آخری حکم *ā'khirī hūk'm* N.M. final order categorical imperative حکم کرنا *hūk'm kar'nā* V.T order command decree , give the verdict حکم لگانا *hūk'm lagā'nā* V.I. predict حکمِ ناطق *hūk'm-e nā'tiq* N.M. peremptory order حکم نامہ *hūk'm-nā'mah* N.M. decree written orders judgment حکمی *hūk'mī* ADJ. (of remedy) efficacious infallible sure , certain [A]

حکم *ha'kam* N.M. arbitrator , mediator umpire ; referee [A]

حکما *hukamā'* N.M. philosophers sages physicians [A ~ SING. حکیم]

حکمت *hik'mat* N.F. wisdom philosophy medical practice policy skill device trick raison d'etre science علم و حکمت *'ilm-o hik'mat* N.F. arts and science حکمتِ عملی *hik'mat-e 'a'malī* N.M. policy tactics strategem device practical skill 'savoir-faire' skill in management حکمتی *hik'matī* ADJ. (col.) artful ; ingenious clever [A]

حکومت *hūkoo'mat* N.F. government sovereignty rule power control authority sway dominion حکومت جتانا *hūkoo'mat jatā'nā* V.I. assert one's authority جمہوری حکومت *jūmhoo'rī hūkoo'mat* N.F. democracy ; republic , government of the people ; government of the people for the people by the people شخصی حکومت *shakh'sī hūkoo'mat* N.F. one man rule despotism dictatorship monarchy حکومت کرنا *hūkoo'mat kar'nā* V.I. govern reign rule exercise authority hold sway (over) [A ~ حکم ḥuk'm]

حکیم **ḥakīm'** N.M physician ; doctor philosopher sage ; savant حکیم فرزانہ *ḥakī'm-e farzā'nah* N.M. philosopher sage حکیم مطلق *ḥakī'm-e mut'laq* N.M. (God as) the Supreme Sage نیم حکیم *nīm' ḥakīm'* N.M. quack; charlatan حکیمانہ *ḥakīmā'nah* ADJ. philosophical physician-like sage-like حکیمی *ḥakī'mī* N.F. medical practice philosophy [A ~ حکمت]

حل **ḥal** N.M. solution liquefaction dilution untying ; loosening doing (a sum) حل کرنا *ḥal' kar'nā* V.T. solve liquefy dilute loosen حل وعقد *ḥal'l-o 'aq'd* N.M. control authority management ; administration ارباب حل وعقد *arbāb-e ḥal'l-o-'aq'd* N.M. PL. the authorities حل ہونا *ḥal ho'nā* V.I. be solved be dissolved be diluted be resolved [A]

حلال **ḥalāl'** ADJ legitimate lawful having religious sanction righteousness (of animal) slaughtered in the prescribed Islamic way حلال خور *ḥalāl'-khor* N.M. sweeper ; scavenger one with lawful earnings one who earns by the sweat of one's brow حلال خوری *ḥalāl-kho'rī* N.F. woman scavenger ; sweepress lawful arning by the sweat of one's brow حلال کرنا *ḥalāl kar'nā* V.I. slaughter (animal) in the prescribed way punish severely give a good hiding do real service in return for (money, etc.) make lawful [A ~ PREC.]

حلاج **ḥallāj'** N.M. carder appellation of a martyred Muslim mystic of the Middle Ages [A]

حلالہ **ḥalā'lah** N.F. woman re-marrying first husband after being divorced by second one حلالہ کرنا *ḥalā'lah kar'nā* V.T. marry (divorced woman) temporarily with the intention of making her re-marriage to first husband lawful [A ~ حلال]

حلاوت **ḥalā'vat** N.F. sweetness suavity [A]

حلت **ḥil'lat** N.F. lawfulness legality [A ~ حلال]

حلجان **ḥaljān'** N.M. feast given by wife with money collected from groom's family حلجان کرنا *ḥaljān' kar'nā* V.I. throw such party

حلف **ḥa'laf** N.F. oath حلفاً *ḥa'lafan* ADV. on oath حلف اٹھانا *ḥa'laf uṭhā'nā* V.I. swear take an oath حلف دروغی *ḥa'laf-daro'ghī* N.F. false swearing perjury حلف دینا *ḥa'laf de'nā* V.T. administer an oath حلف نامہ *ḥa'laf-nā'mah* N.M. affidavit declaration on oath [A]

حلق **ḥal'q** N.M. throat حلق میں پھنسنا *ḥal'q meṅ phaṅs'nā* V.I. have a catch in the throat حلق میں نوالہ پھنسنا *ḥal'q meṅ nivā'lah phaṅs'nā* V.T. (of morsel) choke the throat (of dear friend, etc.) be remembered while eating something good *ḥal'qī* ADJ. gutteral (sound, letter, etc. [A]

حلقوم **ḥul'qoom** N.M. throat [A]

حلقہ **ḥal'qah** N.M. circle gathering ; assembly ward knocker buttonhole circuit loop link (کے گرد) حلقہ باندھنا *(ke gir'd) ḥal'quh bāndh'nā* V.I. form a circle (round) حلقہ بگوش *ḥal'qa ba-gosh'* N.M. devoted friend slave حلقہ بگوشی *ḥal'qah-ba-go'shī* N.F. slavery devotion [A]

حلم **ḥil'm** N.M. toleration ; tolerance affability serenity suavity [A]

حلہ **ḥul'lah** N.M. (PL. *ḥu'lal*) garment (in paradise) [A]

حلوا **ḥal'vā** N.M. batter pudding حلوا خوردن روئے باید *ḥal'vā khūr'dan rā roo''e bā'yad* PROV. success calls for skill حلوا سمجھنا *ḥal'vā sa'majhnā* V.T. regard (something) as very easy حلوائے بے دود *ḥalvā''-e be-dood'* N.M. fruit mellowing on tree anything soft and sleek effiminate boy beardless youth حلوے مانڈے سے کام رکھنا *ḥal've māṅ'ḍe se kām (rakh'nā)* PH. be interested only in personal gain حلوائی *ḥalvā''ī* N.M. confectioner ; sweetmeat-seller حلوائی کی دوکان اور دادا جی کی (دیا کا) فاتحہ *ḥalvā''ī kī dūkān' aur dā'dā jī kī (dial.. kā) fā'teḥah* PROV. cocks make free with horse's corn [same as A حلاوت ~ حلوی]

حلول **ḥulool'** N.M. transmigration ; slighting of divine spirit (on someone) penertration [A ~ حل]

حلیف **ḥalīf'** N.M. ally sworn friend [A ~ حلف]

حلیم **ḥalīm'** N.M. cereals cocked in meat ADJ. mild suave affable tolerant serene [A ~ حلم *ḥil'm*]

حلیہ **ḥul'yah** N.M. features figure description of (someone's) features حلیہ بگاڑنا *ḥul'yah bigaṛ'nā* V.T. disfigure offer a harsh treatment [A]

حمار **ḥimār'** N.M. (PL. حمیر *ḥamīr*, حمر *ḥu'mur*) ass jackass [A]

حماقت **ḥamāqat** N.F. folly stupidity ineptitude [A]

حمال **ḥammāl'** N.M. porter [A ~ حمل]

حمام **ḥammām'** N.M. bagnio ; Turkish bath bath water-heater حمام کرنا *ḥammām' kar'nā* V.T. take a hot bath حمام کی لنگی *ḥammām' kī lūn'gī* N.F. common property cheap thing placed out for common use حمام میں سب ننگے *ḥammām' meṅ sab naṅ'ge* PROV. a general weakness ; an evil in which most people indulge حمامی *ḥammā'mī* N.M. bath keeper bath-attendant masseur masseuse [A]

حمامہ *ḥamā'mah* N.F. dove pigeon [A]

حمائل *ḥamā''il* N.F. pocket edition of the Holy Quran sword belt ; cross-belt a kind of necklace حمائل کرنا *ḥamā''il kar'nā* V.T. sling across the shoulders hang round the neck بازو گلے میں حمائل کرنا *bā'zoo gale meṅ ḥama''l kar'nā* V.T throw one's arms round (someone's) neck [A]

حمایت *ḥimā'yat* N.F. defence protection support patronage حمایت کرنا *ḥimā'yat kar'nā* V.T. defend protect support back patronise حمایتی *ḥimā'yatī* N.M. defender protector patron supporter partisan ally حمایتی کا ٹٹو *ḥimā'yatī kā ṭaṭ'ṭoo* N.M. (iron.) weakling relying on outside support [A]

حمد *ḥam'd* N.F. praise (of God) حمد کرنا *ḥam'd kar'nā* V.T. praise (God)

حمق *ḥum'q* N.M. folly stupidity ineptitude [A doublet of حماقت]

حمل *ḥam'l* N.M. pregnancy burden ; load conveyance ; transportation اسقاط حمل *isqā't-e ḥam'l* abortion ; miscarriage حمل ساقط ہونا *ḥam l sā'qiṭ ho'nā* V.I. have an abortion حمل سے ہونا *ḥam'l se ho'nā* V. conceive ; be pregnant be in the family way حمل ونقل *ḥam'l-o-naq'l* N.M. transportation ذرائع حمل ونقل *zarā'e'-e ḥam'l-o-naq'l* N.M. PL. transportation means of transportation ; conveyance [A]

حمل *ḥa'mal* N.M. name of a sign of Zodiac ; Aries برج حمل *būr'j ḥa'mal* N.M. Aries [A]

حملہ *ḥam'lah* N.M. attack , assault invasion charge ; onset ; onslaught حملہ آور *ḥam'la-ā'var* N.M. invader assailant attacker حملہ آور ہونا *ḥam'la-ā'var ho'nā* V.T. attack ; assail invade charge حملہ کرنا *ḥam'lah kar'nā* V.T. attack ; assault ; invade charge storm sally forth [A ~ حمل]

حمیت *ḥamiy'yat* N.M. concern for what one is honour bound to defend sense of honour [A doublet of حمایت]

حمید *ḥamīd'* ADJ. (F. حمیدہ *ḥamī'dah*) laudable; praiseworthy اوصاف حمیدہ | اخلاق حمیدہ *akhlā'q-e ḥamī'dah, ausā'f-e ḥamī'dah* N.M. praiseworthy qualities ; laudable traits of character [A ~ حمد]

حنا *ḥinā'* (PED. *ḥinnā'*) N.F. myrtle ; privet , henna privet powdered myrtle leaves (used as dye) حنابندی *ḥinā'-bah'dī* N.F dying (hands and feet) with henna this as wedding custom حنائی *ḥinā''ī* ADJ. henna coloured ; light-red حنائی کاغذ *ḥinā''ī kāghaz* N.M. light-red paper [A]

حنان *ḥannān'* ADJ. N.M. (God as) Merciful ADJ. merciful ; clement [A]

حنبلی *ḥam'balī* N.M. & ADJ. (PL. حنابلہ *ḥanā'bilah*) Hanbilite [A]

حنجرہ *ḥah'jarah* N.M. gullet throat [A]

حنظل *ḥin'zal* N.M. wild gourd [A]

حنفی *ḥa'nafī* N.M. & ADJ. (PL. احناف *aḥnāf'*) Hanafite [A ~ ابو حنیفہ founder]

حنوط *ḥanoot'* N.M mummification embalming (the dead body [A]

حنیف *ḥanīf'* N.M. follower of Abraham one breaking with all others to worship God [A]

حوا *ḥav'va* N.F. Eve حوا زادیاں *ḥav'va zā'diyāṅ* N F. PL. Eve's daughters حوا کی بیٹی *ḥav'va kī be'ṭī* N.F woman [A]

حوادث *ḥavā'dis* N.M. accidents occurrences misfortunes حوادث زمانہ *ḥavā'dis-e zamā'nah* حوادث زندگی *ḥavā'dis-e ziṅ'dagī* N.F PL. vicissitudes of life (or fortune) [A ~ SING. حادثہ]

حواری *ḥavā'rī* N.M. partisan companion apostle ; one of Christ's) apostles N.M. PL. (rare) stunted venomous adders [A]

حواس *ḥavās'* N.M. PL. senses حواس باختہ (ہونا) *ḥavās'-bākh'tah* (hona) ADJ. (be) out of one's senses be flurried حواس ٹھکانے (یا قائم) ہونا *ḥavās' ṭhikā'ne* (or *qā''im*) *ho'nā* V.I. have one's senses about ; be all there حواس ٹھکانے لگنا *ḥavās' ṭhikā'ne lag'nā* V.I. come to one's senses حواس خمسہ *ḥavās's-e kham'sah* N.M. PL. five senses (viz. sight, hearing, taste, smell and touch) [A ~ حاسہ]

حواشی *ḥavā'shī* N.M. notes ; marginal notes [A ~ SING. حاشیہ]

حواصل *ḥava'sil* N.M. a pelican-like bird [~ A]

حوالات *ḥavālāt'* N.F. lock-up [A ~ SING. حوالہ]

حوالدار *ḥavāl'-dār* N.M. sergeant ; havildar حوالدار میجر *ḥavāl-dār-me'jor* N.M. sergeant major ; havildar-major [A ~ حوالہ]

حوالہ *ḥavā'lah* N.M reference quotation care ; custody frame of reference حوالہ دینا *ḥavā'lah de'nā* V.I. give a reference quote or an authority حوالے کرنا *ḥavā'le kar'nā* V.T. make over , hand over consign surrender [A]

حوالی *ḥavā'lī* (PED. *ḥavālai*) N.F. environs ADV.

around حوالی موالی *ḥavā'lī mavā'lī* N.M. companions attendants neighbours [~A]

حوائج *ḥavā''ij* N.M. PL. needs ; necessities wants حوائج ضروریہ *ḥavā''ij zarooriyah* N.M. PL. call of nature [A ~ SING. حاجت]

حوت *hoot* N.F. fish (sign of the zodiac) Pisces [A]

حور *ḥoor* N.F. hourie ; black-eyed heavenly nymph an exquisite beauty حور شمائل *ḥoor'-shamā''il* ADJ. exquisitely beautiful (beloved, etc. [A ~ SING. حورا *ḥaurā'*]

حوصلہ *ḥau'salah* N.M. guts courage ; spirit ambition gizzard حوصلہ مند *ḥau'sala-mand* ADJ. courageous ambitious حوصلے دیکھنا *ḥau'sale dekh'nā* V.I. know how puny-hearted (someone) is حوصلہ نکالنا *ḥau'salah nikal'nā* V.I. gratify one's desires to the full عالی حوصلہ *a'lī-ḥau'salah* ADJ. ambitious magnanimous [A]

حوض *ḥauz* N.M. reservoir tank pond cistern space inside margin of book text [A]

حونق *ḥavan'naq* N.M. fool stupid person ; silly guy dunce

حویلی *have'lī* N.F. mansion ; spacious house

حی *hay* ADJ. alive animate ; living immortal حی و قیوم *ḥay'y-o qayyoom'* N.M. immortal [A]

حیا *ḥayā'* N.F. modesty shyness bashfulness shame حیادار *ḥayā'-dār* ADJ. modest shy retiring bashful shame-faced حیادار اپنی حیاسے ڈرا بے حیا سمجھا مجھ سے ڈرا *ḥayā'-dār ap'nī ḥayā' se ḍar'ā be'-ḥayā sam' jhā m-jh' se ḍar'ā* PROV. brazen-faced person ill construes manners and modesty بے حیا *be'-ḥayā* ADJ. immodest shameless brazen-faced بے حیائی *be-ḥayā''ī* N.F. immodesty shamelessness بے حیائی سے کام لینا *behaya' i se kām' le'nā* V.I. brazen it out [A]

حیات *ḥayāt'* N.F. life existence حیات تازہ *ḥayā't-e tā'zah* N.F. new base of life حیات مستعار *ḥayā't-e mūsta'ar'* N.F. frailty of life ; mortal life [A]

حیاتین *ḥayatīn'* N.M. vitamin حیاتین اب ج *ḥayātīn alif be jim......* N.M. Vitamin A,B,C.......[A ~ PREC.]

حیث *ḥais* ADV. since where من حیث *min ḥais'* ADV from the point of view of من حیث المجموع *min ḥais-il majmoo'* PH. on the hole by and large [A]

حیثیت *ḥaisiy yat* N.F. status ; rank prestige standing wealth ability ; capacity

حیثیت عرفی *ḥaisiy yat-e 'ūr'fī* N.F. character prestige reputation ازالہ حیثیت عرفی *iza'la-e ḥaisiy'yat-e 'ūr'fī* N.F. libel ; defamation [A ~ PREC.]

حیدر *ḥai'dar* N.M. lion short-statured person appellation of the fourth Orthodox Caliph [A]

حیران *ḥairān'* ADJ. perplexed at one's wit's end confused bewildered astonished surprized حیران کرنا *ḥairan kar'nā* V.T. perplex ; amuse confuse astonish surprise حیران و سرگرداں *ḥairā'n-o sar gar'dāṅ'* ADJ. bewildered distracted حیران ہونا *ḥairān ho'nā* V.I. be perplexed ; be amazed be confused be astonished be surprised be bewildered [~A CORR. of *ḥayarān* ~ FOLL.]

حیرت *ḥairat* N.F wonder ; astonishment amazement perplexity ; confusion surprise حیرت افزا *ḥai'rat-afzā'* ADJ. astonishing حیرت زدہ *ḥai'rat-za'dah* ADJ. aghast amazed wonder struck حیرت زدہ ہونا *ḥai'rat-za'dah raih jā'nā* V.T. be struck with amazement حیرت ہونا *ḥai'rat ho'nā* V.I. be amazed حیرتی *ḥai'ratī* N.M. one struck with amazement [A]

حیز *ḥay'yiz* N.M. place bounds (of something) [A]

حیص بیص *ḥais' bais* N.F. dilemma suspense hesitation confusion حیص بیص میں گزرنا *ḥais' bais meṅ gūzar'nā* V.I. (of time) be wasted in confusion [A]

حیض *ḥaiz* N.F. menses ; menstural course ; turns حیض کا لتہ *ḥaiz kā lat'tah* N.M. sanitary towel sordid thing ولد الحیض *va'lad-ūl ḥaiz'* N.M. wicked person ; miscreant bastard [A]

حیطہ *ḥai'tah*, (or *ḥi'tah*) N.M. bounds (of) حیطۂ تحریر میں لانا *ḥaita-e tahrīr meṅ lā'nā* V.T. put in black and white [A]

حیف *ḥaif* INT. ah ; alas fie ; for shame N.M. shame صد حیف *sad ḥaif* INT. for shame [A]

حیلہ *ḥī'lah* N.M. (PL. حیل *ḥiyal'*) trick ; ruse excuse means prevarication fraud حیلہ باز *ḥī'la-bāz*, حیلہ ساز *ḥī'lā-saz*, حیلہ گر *ḥī'la-gar* ADJ. artful cunning ; shy حیلہ حوالہ *ḥī'lah ḥavā'lah* N.M. evasion prevarication pretense حیلہ کرنا *ḥī'lah kar'nā* V.I. employ a ruse practise deceit put up a lame excuse adopt some means حیلے حوالے کرنا *ḥī'le ḥavā'le kar'na* V.T. & I. dodge ; evade prevaricate حیلے رزق بہانے موت *ḥī'le riz'q bahā'ne maut'* PROV. livelihood has some means and death has some cause حیل *ḥiyal'* N.M. PL tricks excuses means [A].

حین **hin** N.M. time duration (تا) حین حیات (tā) hi'n-e hayat' ADV. during the life-time of ; lifelong ; lifetime [A]

حیوان **haivān'** (ped. hayavān') N.M. animal ; beast ; brute animals object ; living being blockhead ; dunce cruel person ; callous person ; beastly person حیوانِ مطلق haivā'n-e mut'laq N.M. animal arrant fool حیوانِ ناطق haivā'n-e nā'tiq N.M. man ; human being ; rational animal حیوانی haivā'nī, (ped. hayavā'nī) ADJ. animal beastly ; brutish حیوانیت haivāniy'yat N.F. beastliness brutality shamelessness ; indecency ; animal nature ; beastly nature [A ~ حیات]

خ

خ **khe** (called khā'-e mo''jamah or khā'-e manqoo'tah) tenth letter of Urdu alphabet (equivalent to guttural Scottish (ch) (in jummal reckoning) 600

خاتم **khā'tam** (occ. khā'tim) N.F. ring seal stamp with subscription in letter, etc. خاتم النبیین khā'tam un-nabiy'yīn' N.M. (appellation of the Holy Prophet) seal of prophets ; last among prophets ; the final messenger of God خاتم سلیمان khā'tam-e sulaimān' N.F. Solomon's signet-ring controlling power [A ~ ختم]

خاتم **khā'tim** ADJ. final finishing ; ending ; concluding N.M. one who brings (something) to a close (rare) ring (rare) seal [A ~ ختم]

خاتمہ **khā'timah** N.M. end conclusion finish epilogue consequence sequal خاتمہ بالخیر khā'timah bil-khair' N.M. happy ending ; happy conclusion death in circumstances conducive to redemption خاتمہ ہونا khā'timah ho'nā V.I. end ; come to an end ; come to close finish cease to be die ; pass away [A ~ PREC.]

خاتون **khātoon'** N.F. (PL. خواتین khavātīn') lady the first lady of (the state, etc.) خاتونِ جنت khātoo'n-e jannat (appellation of Hazrat Fatimah) خاتونِ پاکستان khātoo'n-e pā'kistān N.F. the first lady of Pakistan [P ~ T]

خادم **khā'dim** N.M. (PL. خدام khuddām', خدم khā'dam) servant attendant خادمہ khā'dimah N.F. maid-servant lady's attendant [A ~ خدمت]

خار **khar** N.M. thorn ; bramble thistle pike barb spur (on cock's leg) jealousy ; grudge خارپشت khār'-push't N.M. hedgehog ; porcupine خاردار khār-dār ADJ. (of wire) barbed thorny difficult خارزار khār'-zār N.M. thicket of thorns خار کھانا khār. khā'nā V.I. feel jealous harbour grudge خاروخس khā'r-o khas N.M. rubbish ; litter refuse [P]

خارا **khā'rā**, سنگِ خارا sang-e khā'rā N.M. marble granite any hard stone خاراشگاف khā'rā-shigāf' ADJ. stone-splitting very strong and sharp خاراشگافی khā'rā-shigā'fī N.F. arduous task [P]

خارج **khā'rij** ADJ. external outer outside extraneous rejected excluded expelled externed struck off irrelevant خارج از بحث khā'rij az baih's ADJ. irrelevant ; out of the question ; beside the point خارج از عقل khā'rij az 'aq'l ADJ. absurd ; meaningless foolish ; silly contrary to reason incredible unbelievable خارج قسمت khā'rij-e qis'mat N.M. quotient خارج کرنا khā'rij kar'nā V.T. strike off the rolls ; expel exclude (of petition) be dismissed خارج ہونا khā'rij ho'nā V.T. be struck off the rolls be expelled be excluded (of petition) be dismissed خارجہ khārijah N.F. external affairs ; foreign affairs ADJ. outside ; outer ; external foreign , extaneous خارجہ حکمت عملی khā'rijah hik'mat-e 'a'malī N.F. foreign policy امور خارجہ ūmoor-e khā'rijah N.M. external affairs, foreign affairs محکمۂ خارجہ maih'kama-e khā'rijah, دفتر خارجہ daf'tar-e khā'rijah N.M. Foreign Department ; Foreign Office , Ministry of External Affairs وزیر خارجہ vazī'r-e khā'rijah N.M. Minister of External Affairs ; Foreign Minister خارجی khā'rijī N.M. foreign ; external extraneous N.M. PL. خوارج khavā'rij) (one of) a sect dissenting from Hazrat Ali ; Kharijite dissenter schismatic [A]

خارش **khā'rish** N.F. itch scabies mange خارشت kharisht' N.F. (rare) scabies mangy خارشی khā'rishī, خارشتی kharish'tī ADJ. mangy scab [P ~ خاریدن]

خارق عادت **khā'riq-e 'ā'dat** N.M. (PL. خوارق عادت khavā'riq-e 'ā'dat) marvel miracle supernatural event ADJ. supernatural surpassing reason and experience [A ~ خرق tear]

خازن **khā'zin** N.M. treasurer cashier financial secretary [A ~ خزانہ]

خاستائی **khastā''ī** N.M. hybrid pigeon noted for swiftness of speed dove-pigeon ADJ. fawn,

fawn coloured

خاسر **kha**sir N.M one incurring loss [A ~ خسران]

خاشاک **khāshāk** N.M. sweepings rubbish, litter خس وخاشاک **khas-o khashāk'** N.M. rubbish; litter trash, insignificant things [P]

خاص **khās** ADJ. special particular peculiar private personal specific select; selected N.M. (PL. خواص **khavās'**) persons of rank خاص بردار **khās'-bar-dār'** N.M. arms carrier خاص چیز **khās' chīz'** N.F. specialty خاصدان **khās-dān'** N.M. betel dish with lid خاصکر **khās' kar** ADV. especially particularly, inparticular خاص وعام **khās'(s)o 'ām'** N.M. general public the high and the low: people belonging to all strata of society خاصا **kha'sā** ADJ. good fair indifferent ADV. quite خاصگی **khās agī** N.F. slave girl living as master's concubine good thing specialty N.M. attendant courtier خاصہ **khās'sah** N.M. PL. خواص **khavās'**) traits of character distinctive qualities peculiarities dinner dainty food coarse flimsy lines steed ADJ better ADV especially particularly خاصیت **khāsiy'yat** N.F. (PL. خواص **khavās'**) quality peculiarity virtue (of medicine) [A]

خاطر **kha'tir** N.F. heart, mind consideration sake, behalf, account خاطر جمع رکھنا **kha'tır jam'' rakk'nā** V I. rest assured be calm and collected set one's mind at ease خاطرخواہ **kha'tir-khah** ADV. satisfactory, to one's entire satisfaction as one desires خاطرداری **kha'tir-dā'rī** N.F. reception welcome hospitality entertainment regard; consideration خاطرداری کرنا **kha'tir-dā'rī kar'nā** V.T. welcome; extend hearty welcome (to) show hospitality (to) entertain خاطر میں نہ لانا **kha'tir men na la'nā** V.T. pay no regard to care a hang for خاطرنشان رکھنا **kha'tir-nishān' rakh'nā** V.I. (dial.) rest assured جمعیت خاطر **jam'iy'yat-e kha'tır** N.F. peace tranquillity sati faction content [A]

خاطف **kha'tif** ADJ. pouncing falling like lightning [A]

خاطی **kha'tī** N.M. wrongdoer [A ~ خطا]

خاقان **khaqan** N.M. emperor (as title of Mongol rulers) خاقانی **khaqā'nī** ADJ. attached to Emperor [P ~ T]

خاک **khāk** N.F dust earth territory, land nought, nothing ruin خاک اڑانا **khāk' uṛa'nā** N.F. roam about wander aimlessly raise dust defame slander, calumniate خاک اڑنا **khāk' uṛ'nā** V I (of dust) be raised خاک انداز **khāk'-andāz** N M dustbin خاک بسر **khāk'-ba-sar'** ADJ. & ADV in a miserable state دربدر خاک بسر **dar ba-dar' khāk' ba-sar** PH up rooted jobless; without any means of livelihood خاک پھانکنا **khāk' phāṅk'nā** V.I wander aimlessly roam about خاک چھاننا **khāk chhān'na** V I wander aimlessly search hard خاکدان **khāk'-dān** N.M dustbin (fig.) world خاک دھول **khāk'-dhool** N.F. dust nothing خاک ڈالنا **khāk' ḍāl'nā** V.T conceal an ugly affair not to wash dirty linen in public give up all thought of خاکروب **khāk-rob'** N.M sweeper خاکسار **khāk-sār'** ADJ. lowly; humble PRON (out of courtesy) I N.M. (member of) brown shirt political party carrying spades; Khaksar خاکساری **khak-sā'rī** N.F. humility خاک شفا **khā'k-e shifā'** N.F sacred tablet of Kerbela earth خاک کا پتلا **khāk' kā pūt'la** N.M human being, dust خاک لے ڈالنا **khāk le ḍāl'nā** V.I. pay frequent visits (to the house of) خاک کرنا (یا میں ملانا) **khāk' kar'nā** (or **men milā'nā**) V.T. ruin; destroy bring to nought reduce to a miserable state cause death defame خاکم بدہن **khākam ba-da'han** INT. (when saying something obviously bad or profane) God forbid خاک میں ملنا **khāk' men mil'nā** V.I die perish be ruined be reduced to a reasonable state خاک ہو جانا **khāk' ho jā'nā** V T be ruined; come to nought die, perish خاکی **khākī** N'M. & ADJ. ★ [P]

خاکستر **khākis'tar** N.F. ashes calx خاکستر ہونا **khākis'tar ho'nā** V.T. be reduced to ashes خاکستری **khākis'tarī** ADJ ash coloured; ashen N.M ashen colour [P]

خاکسی **khāk'sī** N.F bramble, blackberry seed [P]

خاکنائے **khāk'-nā'e** N.F isthmus [P ~ خاک + نائے]

خاکہ **kha'kah** N.M. outline outline map sketch tracing rough plan draft outline خاکہ اتارنا **khā'kah ūtār'nā** V.T. trace خاکہ کھینچنا **khākah 'khench'na** V.T. make a rough plan of prepare a draft plan خاکہ اڑانا **khā'kah ūṛa'nā** V.T. ridicule; make fun (of) defame slander, calumniate [P]

خاکی **khā'kī** ADJ. earthly earthy, terrestrial mundane buff brown, khaki خاکی انڈا **khā'kī aṅ'ḍa** N.M. wind egg (fig.) bastard خاکی وردی **khā'kī var'dī** N.F khaki (uniform) [P ~ خاک]

خاگینہ **khāgī'nah** N.M. salty egg dish salty omelette [P]

خال¹ khal N.M. mole (on skin) a kind of pigeon (rare) maternal uncle خال خال khal' khal ADJ. rare here and there little sparse خط و خال khat't-o khal', خد و خال khad'd-o-khal' N.M. PL. features [P]

خال² khal N.M. (rare) maternal uncle [A]

خالص kha'lis ADJ. pure unadulterated genuine real خالصہ kha'lisah ADJ. (col. khal'sa) (appellation for) Sikh (old use) Crown land خالصے لگانا khalse laga'na V.T. confiscate ; declare ; forefeit ruin ; waste خالصے لگنا khal'se lag'na V.I. be forefeited ; be confiscated be ruined ; be wasted ; go to waste V.T. squander [A ~ خلوص]

خالق khaliq N.M. (God as) Creator [A ~ خلق]

خالو kha'loo N.M. husband of mother's sister [A ~ خال²]

خالہ kha'lah N.F. mother's sister , maternal aunt, aunt ; aunty خالہ جی کا گھر kha'lah ji ka ghar' PH. easy affair خالہ چاندنی کا کنبہ kha'lah chand'ni ka kun'bah PH. family (or group) of fools خالہ زاد بھائی (یا بہن) kha'la-zad bha'i (or baihan) N.M. (F.) cousin

خالی kha'li ADJ. empty vacant ; unoccupied blank ; unfilled free ; exempt mere useless ; aim N.M. (col.) Islamic month Zul-qa'dah خالی کا چاند kha'li ka chand' N.M Zul-qa'dah خالی کرنا kha'li kar'na V.T. empty vacate evacuate خالی ہاتھ kha'li hath ADJ. empty-handed poor ; penniless خالی خولی kha'li khoo'li ADJ. & ADV. mere(ly) خالی جانا kha'li ja'na V.I. fail to hit target خالی دینا kha'li de'na V.T. parry [A ~ خلو]

خام kham ADJ. raw unripe unbaked crude green ; unexperienced ; immature crude unperfect vain خام خیالی kham khaya'li N.F. vain thought misgiving خام کو کام سکھا لیتا ہے kham' ko kam' sikha' le'ta hai PROV. experience is the best teacher خامی kha'mi N.F. error ; mistake flaw ; defect inexperience immaturity [P ~ PREC]

خاموش khamosh' ADJ. silent reticent taciturn خاموشی khamo'shi N.F. silence taciturnity reticence [A]

خامہ kha'mah N.M. pen خامہ فرسا kha'ma farsa' N.M. one who indites خامہ فرسائی kha'ma farsa''i N.M. inditing ; writing [P]

خان khan N.M. chief ; prince ; lord title used before or after Pathan names خان خاناں khan'-kha'nan (ped kha'n-e-kha'nan) N.M. chief peer doyen of the nobility Prime Minister [P ~ T]

خاندان khan'dan N.M. family household dynasty house lineage خاندانی khanda'ni ADJ. of noble descent ancestral hereditary pedigreed [P]

خانساماں khan-sa'man N.M. butler cook (also kha'n-e saman') the Royal Steward ; Lord Chamberlain [P ~ سامان + خان]

خانساماں

خانقاہ khan'qah N.M. convent monastry shrine [P]

خانگی kha'nagi ADJ. & N.M. (see under خانہ N.M ★)

خانم kha'num (col. kha'nam) N.F. wife title of wife) Mrs. lady (rare) princess [P ~ خان]

خانماں khanuman' N.M. home household furniture , one's belongings خانماں برباد kha'numan-barbad', خانماں خراب kha'numan-kharab' ADJ. ruined unfortunate miserable [P ~ خانہ]

خانوادہ khanva'dah N.M. family household dynasty lineage line (of saints, etc.) [P ~ FOLL.]

خانہ kha'nah N.M. house dwelling ; residence room ; chamber compartment shelf pigeon-hole drawer column خانہ آبادی kha'na-aba'di N.F marriage setting up one's house شادی خانہ آبادی sha'di kha'na-aba'di N.F. propitious marriage خانہ بدوش kha'na-ba-dosh' ADJ. nomadic homeless N.M. nomad gipsy tramp homeless person خانہ بدوشی kha'na-ba-do'shi N.F. travel wandering aimlessly roving namadic life خانہ برانداز kha'na-bar andaz' N.M. spendthrift ; prodigal خانہ بربادی kha'na-barba'di N.F. ruin end of family life خانہ پری kha'na-pu'ri N.F. filling in the column (of form, etc.) perfunctory work خانہ پری کے لیے kha'na-pu'ri ke li'ye ADV. for filling up the form perfunctorily خانہ تلاشی kha'na-tala'shi N.F house search خانہ جنگی kha'na-jan'gi N.F. civil war خانہ خدا kha'na-e khuda' N.M. the Holy Ka'aba mosque any temple خانہ خراب kha'na-kharab' ADJ. ruined miserable N.M. wretch ; miserable person خانہ خرابی kha'na-khara'bi N.F. ruin; destruction misery خانہ داری kha'na-da'ri N.F. house-keeping household management ; domestic economy امور خانہ داری سے واقف ہونا umoo'r-e kha'na-da'ri se va'qif ho'na V.T. be well-up in house-keeping خانہ داماد kha'na-damad' N.M. man living with in-laws خانہ دوست kha'na-dos't ADJ. stay-at home (person) خانہ زاد kha'na-zad' N.M. child of (one's) slave devoted person خانہ ساز kha'na-sāz' ADJ. home-made rough خانہ شماری kha'na-shŭmā'rī N.F. house-count census خانہ نشین khā'na-nashīn' (or-shīn) ADJ. retired (person) (one) leading a life retirement idle خانگی khā'nagī ADJ. domestic private N.F. (usu. khān'gī) loose women ; streetwalker ; unlicenced prostitute صاحب خانہ sā'ḥib-e khā'nah N.M. master of the house کتبخانہ kŭ'tŭb-khā'nah N.M. library bookstall [P]

خاور khā'var N.M. the east خاوری khā'varī ADJ. eastern N.M. one hailing from East Persia [P]

خاوند khā'vind (ped. khā'vand) N.M. husband [P]

خائف khā''if ADJ. frightened ; terrified fearful timid afraid [A]

خائن khā''in N.M. (one) guilty of embezzlement cheat treacherous [A]

خایہ khā'yah N.M. testicle خایہ بردار khā'ya-bar'dār N.M. sycophant ; toady [P]

خباثت khabā'sat, (خبث khŭb's) N.M. wickedness ; depravity (rare) impurity خبث نفس khŭb's-e naf's N.M. malignity wickdness خبیث khabīs' ADJ. & N.M. ★

خبر kha'bar N.F. news ; piece of news information; word; intelligence advice tidings awareness rumour ; report خبر اڑانا kha'bar ŭṛa'nā V.I. spread a rumour خبر اڑنا kha'bar ŭṛ'nā V.I. be rumoured be bruited خبر پہنچانا kha'bar pahŭnchā'nā V.T. send word (to) ; information (to) خبر پوچھنا kha'bar poochh'nā V.T. ask after خبردار kha'bar-dār ADJ. warned watchful cautions on guard careful ; vigilant acquainted ; aware alert خبردار کرنا kha'bar-dār kar'nā V.T. to warn ; forewarn put someone on (his) guard ; alert caution خبرداری kha'bar-dā'rī N.F. vigilance care ; custody awareness خبردہندہ kha'bar-dehin'dah N.M. informer one who warns خبر دینا (یا کرنا) kha'bar de'nā (or kar'nā) V.T. inform ; give information (to) acquaint خبررساں kha'bar-rasāṅ' ADJ. news ; information N.M. a messenger ; one who gives information خبررساں ادارہ kha'bar-rasāṅ' idā'rah N.M. news agency خبر رکھنا kha'bar rakh'nā V.I. be wide awake be well informed to be acquainted with ; be aware (of) keep in touch with خبر گرم ہونا kha'bar gar'm ho'nā V.I. be rumoured be bruited خبرگیری kha'bar-gī'rī N.F. attention ; care looking after management espionage خبرگیری کرنا kha'bar-gī'rī kar'nā V.T. take care (of) ; look after خبر لگانا kha'bar lagā'nā V.T. trace out fish for information خبر لینا kha'bar le'nā V.I. look after manage ask after ; inquire after help ; support come to the aid or rescue خبر ہونا kha'bar ho'nā V.I. be informed be aware of ; have knowledge of بے خبر be-kha'bar ADJ. unaware ignorant ; uninformed careless regardless senseless بے خبری be-kha'barī N.F. ignorance lack of information unawareness senseless [A]

خبط khab't N.M. fad craze silliness insanity خبطی khab'tī N.M. & ADJ. faddist crazy insane (person) silly (person) [A]

خبیث khabīs' ADJ. wicked evil wretched malignant (rare) foul : filthy ; impure [A ~ خبث]

خبیر khabīr' N.M. & ADJ. Omniscient well informed ; well-posted [A ~ خبر]

ختکا khŭt'ka N.M. pestle (for pounding hemp) club ; cudgel

ختم khat'm ADJ. ended ; finished done terminated N.M. recitation of the whole of the Holy Quran end conclusion seal ختم المرسلین khat'm ŭl-mŭrsalīn' N.M. (the Holy Prophet as) God's last messenger or the seal of Prophet's ختم کرنا khat'm kar'nā V. end ; finish conclude terminate ruin kill ختم ہونا khat'm ho'nā V.I. end ; come to an end : be finished die ; pass away [A]

ختن khŭ'tan N.M. name of a Central Asian area famous for musk [P ~ T]

ختنہ khat'nah N.F. circumcision ختنہ کرنا khat'nah kar'nā V.T. circumcise ختنہ ہونا khat'nah ho'nā V.I. be circumcized [A]

خٹا khŭṭṭā N.M. testicle

خجالا khaja'lā N.M. & ADJ. foolish (person)

خجالت khaja'lat N.M. (see under خجل ADJ. ★)

خجستہ khŭjas'tah ADJ. auspicious fortunate خجستہ اختر khŭjas'ta akh'tar ADJ. fortunate ; having one's star in the ascendant [P]

خجل kha'jil ADJ. ashamed penitant خجل کرنا kha'jil kar'nā V.T. put (someone) to shame خجالت khajā'lat N.F. shame sense of shame repentance [A]

خچر khach'char N.M. mule

خد *khad* N.M. cheek خد وخال *khad'd-o khal'* N.M. features [A]

خدا *khūdā'* N.M. God SUP. owner ; master خداپرست *khūdā'-paras't* ADJ. godly ; pious faithful خداترس *khūdā'-tar's* ADJ. God-fearing خداجانے *khuda' jā'ne* CONJ. God knows who knows خدا(ئے)تعالیٰ *khūdā' (-e) ta'ā'la* N.M. the Most High God خداکرے *khūdā' ka're,* خداچاہے *khūdā' chā'he* ADV. God willing INT. may God خداحافظ *khūdā'-hā'fiz* INT. good-bye ; farewell خدا خدا کرکے *khūdā'-khūdā' kar' ke* ADV. with great difficulty کفر ٹوٹا خدا خدا کرکے *k f'r too'tā khūdā' khūdā' kar ke* PROV. success has come after all though with great difficulty خدا خدا کرنا *khūdā' khūdā' kar'nā* V.T. take the name of God fear God and refrain from telling lies, etc. خداداد *khūdā'-dād'* ADJ. God-given خدا دیتا ہے تو چھپر پھاڑ کر دیتا ہے *khūdā' de'tā hai to chhap'par phar' kar de'tā hai* PROV. a gift of God will make its way through stone walls خدارا *khūdā'-rā* ADV. for God's sake . for Heaven's sake خدارسیدہ *khūdā'-rasī'dah* ADJ. Godly pious ; virtuous خدا (سلامت) رکھے *khūdā' (salā'mat) rak'khe* INT. May protect you (etc.) , may you (etc.) live long خدا سمجھے *khūdā' sam'jhe* INT. May God punish him (etc.) curse on him (etc.) خدا سے لو لگانا *khūdā' se lau' lagā'nā* be devoted to God be in the throes of death خدا شکر خورے کو شکر ہی دیتا ہے *khūdā sha'kar-kho're ko sha'kar hī de'tā hai* PROV. he that eats good meal shall have a good meal خداشناس *khūdā'-shinās'* ADJ. & N.M. Godly; pious (person) God-knowing person خداشناسی *khūdā' shinā'sī* N.F. Godliness ; piety knowledge of God خدا غارت کرے *khūdā' ghā'rat ka're* CONJ. to hell with خدا کا دیا *khūdā' kā di'yā* N.M. God's gift خدا کا کارخانہ *khūdā' kā kar-khā'nah* N.M. the world ; world affairs خدا کا گھر *khūdā' ka ghar'* N.M. the Holy Ka'aba mosque any temple خدا کا نام *khūdā kā nam'* N.M. God's name nothing خدا کا نام لو *khūda ka nam' lo* INT. fear God and refrain from cruelty or telling lies etc. خدا کو مان *khūdā' ko man'* INT. for God's sake refrain from doing it or thinking like that خدا کی پناہ *khūdā kī panāh* INT. God forbid خدا کی چوری نہیں تو بندے کی کیا چوری *khūdā' kī cho'rī nahin to bande kī kyā cho'rī* PROV. why fear people when you need not fear God خدا کی دین *khūdā' kī den'* N.F. God خدا کی سنوار *khūdā kī sanvār'* N.F. may God teach you sense خدا کی لاٹھی بے آواز ہے *khūdā kī la'thī be-āvāz' hai,* خدا کی لاٹھی میں آواز نہیں *khūdā kī la'thī men āvāz' nahin'* PROV. the long arm of the Almighty makes no sound when it strikes خدا کی مار *khūdā' kī mār'* N.F. & INT. God's curse (on) خدا کے پاس (یا گھر) جانا *khūdā' ke pās' (or ghar') jā'nā* V.I. die خدا کے گھر سے پھرنا *khūdā' ke ghar se phir'nā* V.T survive after great difficulty خدا گنجے کو ناخن نہ دے *khūdā' gan'je ko nā'khūn na de* PROV. a great fortune in the hands of a fool is a great misfortune خدا لگتی کہنا *khūdā' lag'tī kaih'nā* V.I. say what is right and just speak the truth خدانخواستہ *khūdā' na-khās'tah* INT. God forbid خدا واسطے کا بیر *khūdā' vās'te kā bair* خدا واسطے کی دشمنی *khūdā vās'te kī dush'manī* PH. purposeless enmity خدایگان *khūdā''egān* N.M. overlord خدائے مجازی *khūdā'-e majā'zī* N.M. husband خدایا *khūdā'yā* INT. O God dear ; dear dear خدا یاد آنا *khūdā' yād' ā'nā* V.I. be impressed by a marvel be in a pitiable state خدائی *khūdā''ī* N.F. ★ [P]

خدام *khūddām'* N.M. PL. servants [A ~ SING. خادم]

خداوند *khūdā'vand* N.M. lord master خداوند نعمت *khūdāvan'd-e ne''mat* INT. & N.M. (as title or form of address) beneficent master ; lord of bounty خداوندی *khūdāvan'dī* N.F. providence sovereignty [P ~ خدا]

خدائی *khūdā''ī* N.F. people masses world Godhead ; divinity providence ADJ. divine خدائی خوار *khūdā''ī-khār* N.M. & ADJ. wretched (person) shameless person vagabond tramp خدائی کا *khūdā''ī kā* ADJ. arrant egregious خدائی کرنا *khūdā''ī kar'nā* V.T. rule with absolute power claim to be divine [P ~ خدا]

خدشہ *khad'shah* N.M. (PL. خدشات *khadashāt'*) fear . apprehension doubt ; misgiving danger alarm anxiety ; worry [A]

خدم *kha'dam* N.M. PL. servants خدم وحشم *kha'dam-o ha'sham* N.M. PL. equipage [A ~ SING. خادم]

خدمت *khid'mat* N.F. service use , function duty job ; office presence attendance خدمت کرنا *khid'mat kar'nā* V.T. serve attend (on) خدمتگار *khid'mat gar'* N.M servant attendant ; table servant ; a butler خدمتگاری *khid'mat-gā'rī* N.F. service attendance خدمت گزار *khid'mat-gūzār'* N.M. & ADJ. servant devoted خدمت گزاری *khid'mat-gūzā'rī* N.F. service (کی) خدمت میں *(kī) khid'mat men* ADV. in the service before ; in front of خدمتی *khid'matī* N.M. servant. attendant [A]

خدنگ *khadang'* N.M. arrow white poplar (whose wood goes into the making of arrows) [P]

خدیو *khadīv'* (rare. خدیوی *khūdai'vī*) N.M. (as title of Egyptian rulers under Ottoman Caliphate) Prince [P]

خذ ماصفا ودع ماکدر *khuz' mā safa va da' mā kadir* PROV be an eclectic accept the good points and reject the bad ones [A]

خر *khar* N.M. donkey ; ass (fig.) ass ; fool PREF large خرِ دجال *kha'r-e dajjāl'* N.M. the ass of Antichrist profaw خردماغ *khar-dimagh'* ADJ. pig-headed stupid خردماغی *khar-dimā'ghī* N.F. pig headedness stupidity خرمستی *khar-mas'tī* N.F. horse lay خر وار *khar var'* N.M. ass load مشتے نمونہ از خروارے *mush'te namoo'na-e az khar-vā're* PH. sample a little would let you judge the whole [P]

خراب *kharāb'* ADJ. bad wretched miserable poor depraved corrupt obscene spoiled defiled ruined dilapidated deserted خستہ خراب *khas'ta kharāb'* ADJ. spoiled wretched ; miserable ruined tired ; fatigued خراب کرنا *kharāb' kar'na* V.T spoil mar corrupt ; vitiate seduce ; lead astray ravish ruin populate desolate ; lay waste خرابی *khara'bī* N.F defect flaw evil : ill ; badness ; depravity mischief misery ruin , destruction , desolation [A]

خرابات *kharābāt'* N.F. pub , tavern : bar : alehouse brothel ; depravity street خراباتی *kharābā'tī* N.M. drunkard , toper debauchee; rake [A ~ SING. FOLL.]

خرابہ *khara'bah* N.M. ruins ; place lying in ruins [A ~ خراب]

خراٹا *kharra'ṭā* N.M. snoring خراٹے لینا *kharra'ṭe le'nā* V.I. snore [ONO.]

خراج *kharāj'* N.M. tribute (rare) revenue homage خراجِ تحسین (یا عقیدت) ادا کرنا *kharā'j-e-tahsīn (or 'aqī'dat) adā' kar'nā* V.T. pay homage (to) [A]

خراد *kharād* (ped. *kharrād'*) N.M lathe خراد چڑھنا *kharād' chaṛh'nā* V.I. be turned ; be cut on the lathe (of words, etc.) become polished or refined become cultured learn manners خرادنا *kharād'nā* خراد پر چڑھانا *kharād' par chaṛhā'na* V.T. turn خرادی *khara'dī* N.M. turner [A]

خرادی مرادی *khura'dī murā'dī* N.M. & ADJ. selfish (person)

خراس *kharās'* N.M. ox-driven flour-mill [P ~ خر + آسیا]

خراسان *khurāsān* N.M. East Persia name of a Persian musical mode [P]

خراش *kharāsh'* N.F. scratch خراش آنا *kharāsh' ā'na* V.I. have a scratch ; be scratch خراش تک نہ آنا *kharāsh' tak na ā'nā* V.I. escape unhurt [P ~ خراشیدن]

خرافات *khurāfāt'* N.F. silly talk nonsense obscenity myth mythology خرافات بکنا *khurāfāt' bak'nā* V.I. talk nonsense use abusive language ; utter filthy language [A]

خرام *khirām'* (col. *kharām'*) N.F. pace gait walking ; walk خوش خرام *khūsh khirām'* ADJ. (one) walking elegantly , with a graceful gait خراماں خراماں *khirā'māṅ khirā'māṅ* ADV. with graceful gait walking slowly [P ~ خرامیدن]

خرانٹ *khurānṭ'* ADJ. crafty wily ; sly experienced

خربوزہ *kharboo'zah* خربزہ *khar'bāzah*, خرپزہ *khar'pizah* N.M. melon ; muskmelon خربوزے کو دیکھ کر خربوزہ رنگ پکڑتا ہے *kharboo'ze ko dekh kar kharboo'zah rang pakar'tā hai* PH. sickness is catching company makes the man

خرج *khar'j* N.M. (rare) expenditure دخل و خرج *dakh'l-o kharj* N.M. income and expenditure [A]

خرجین *khurjīn'*, خورجین *khoorjīn'*, (cor.) خرجی *khur'jī* N.F. pack saddle خرچ *khar'ch* N.M. expenditure ; expense spending disbursement allowance خرچ اٹھانا *khar'ch uṭhā'nā* V.I incur expenditure bear expenses of خرچ اٹھنا *khar'ch uṭh'nā* V.I. be spent خرچ اخراجات *khar'ch akhrājāt'* N.M expenditure ; expenses lavish expenditure خرچ خانہ داری *khar'ch kha'na-dā'rī* N.M. household expenses خرچ دینا *khar'ch de'nā* V.T. advance (someone) money for expenses give (someone) an allowance خرچ ہونا *khar'ch ho'nā* V.I. be spent خرچ کرنا *khar'ch kar'nā* V.T. & I. spend use ; put to use متفرق خرچ *mutafar'raq khar'ch* N.M. contingencies ; contingent expenditure خرچنا *khar'chnā* V.T. spend use بالائی خرچ *bālā'ī khar'ch* N.M. overhead expenditure additional expenses جیب خرچ *jeb'-khar'ch* (ped *jaib'-*) N.M. pocket money روزانہ (یا روزمرہ) خرچ *rozā'nah* (or *rozmar'rah*) *khar'ch* N.M. daily expenses current expenditure خرچہ *khar'chah* N.M. costs of law-suits costs ; expenses خرچہ دلانا *khar'chah dilā'nā* V.T. (of law court) award costs مع خرچہ *ma'-khar'chah*, خرچے سمیت *khar'che samet'* ADV. with costs خرچی *khar'chī* N.F. prostitute's remuneration wages of sin خرچیلا *kharchī'la* ADJ. prodigal [A ~ PREC. CORR.]

خرچنگ *khar-chang* N.M crab [P خر چنگ]

خرخر **khur'khur** N.F. purr (of cat ONO.)

خرخشہ **khar'-khashah** N.M. silly dispute ; causeless wrangle fear ; danger premonition ; doubt ; misgiving [P]

خرد **khi'rad** N.M. wisdom intellect intelligence shrewdness ; sagacity خردمند **khi'rad mand'** ADJ. wise intelligent shrewd ; sagacious خردمندی **khi'rad-man'di** N.F. wisdom intelligence sagacity [P]

خرد **khur'd** (commonly misspelt خورد **khur'd**) ADJ. small little minute young PREF. micro young خردبین **khur'd-bin'** N.F. microscope خردبینی **khur'd-bi'ni** ADJ. microscopic خردسال **khur'd-sal'** ADJ. young ; of tender age خردسالی **khur'd-sa'li** N.F. tender age [P]

خرداد **khardad'** N.M. third month of Persian calendar corresponding to June

خردل **khar'dal** N.M. mustard-seed [P]

خردہ **khur'dah** N.M. small change pedlar's small wares fragment point flaw weakness ; weak point خردہ فروش **khur'da-firosh'** N.M. pedler ; hawker ; huckster خردہ گیری **khur'da-gi'ri** N.F. carping ; cavilling خردہ گیری کرنا **khur'da-gi'ri kar'na** V.T. carp at [P]

خرطوم **khartoom** N.M. (elephant's) trunk [A]

خرسند **khursand'** (usu. misspelt خورسند ADJ. glad ; happy ; delighted [P]

خرفہ **khur'fah** N.M. parslain [P]

خرق عادت **khir'q-e 'a'dat** N.M. (PL. خوارق عادت **khava'riq-e 'a'dat**) miracle supernatural event [A ~ خرق + عادت]

خرقہ **khir'qah** N.M. patched garment this as saintly dress ; sartorial symbol of saintliness (in saintly hierarchy) vicegerency or succession خرقہ پوش **khir'qa-posh** N.M. mendicant saint خرقہ وسجادہ **khir'qa-o-sajja'dah** N.M. patched garment and prayer mat symbols of saintliness [A]

خرقہ پوش

خرگاہ **khar gah'** N.M. large tent pavilion [P ~ خر + گہ]

خرگوش **khar-gosh'** N.M. rabbit hare [P ~ خر + گوش]

خرم **khur'ram** ADJ. glad ; happy ; merry ; cheerful خوش وخرم **khush-o-khur'ram** ADJ. happy and cheerful خرمی **khur'rami** N.F. happiness ; mirth cheerfulness [P]

خرما **khur'ma** N.M. (fruit called) date date-like sweetmeat [P]

خرمہرہ **khar-moh'rah** N.M. cowries ; cowry [P ~ خر + مہرہ]

خروج **khurooj'** N.M. flux ejection cosming revolt ; rebellion [A]

خروش **kharosh'** N.M. noise calmour ; tumult [P]

خرید **kharid'** N.F. purchase price ; cast خرید وفروخت **khari'd-o-farokh't.** N.F. trade ; commerce buyin and selling business transaction خرید کے بھاؤ (یا مول) **'kharid' ke bha''o (or mol)** ADV. at cost price قیمتِ خرید **qi'mat-e kharid'** N.F. cost price خریدار **kharidar'** N.M. buyer ; purchaser customer خریداری **kharida'ri** N.F. buying purchase business turnover custom ; demand خریدنا **kharid'na** V.T. buy purchase خرید کردہ **kharid'-kar'dah** ADJ. purchased N.M. purchase [P خریدن]

خریطہ **kharī'tah** N.M. purse ; wallet (rare) map ; chart خریطی **kharī'ti** N.F. case for needles, etc. ; housewife [A]

خریف **kharif'** N.M. autumn ; fall autumnal crops فصلِ خریف **fas'l-e kharif'** N.F. autumn crops خریفی **kharifi'** ADJ. autumal [A]

خزاں **khazan**, (col. **khizan**) autumn ; fall (fig.) decay خزاں دیدہ، خزاں رسیدہ **khazan'-di'dah, khazan'-rasi'dah** ADJ. decaying خزاں ناآشنا **khazan'-na ashna'** ADJ. still young ever-blooming (پر) خزاں آنا **(par) khazan a'na** V.I. lose beauty of beauty (wither) [P]

خزانچی **khazanchi** N.M. (see under ★خزانہ)

خزانہ **khizanah**, (col. **khaza'nah**) N.M. (PL. خزائن **khaza''in**) treasure treasury magazine tank ; reservoir battery accumulator برقی خزانہ **bar'qi khiza'nah** electric cell accumulator خزانۂ عامرہ **khiza'na-e 'a'mirah** N.M. state exchequer government treasury خزانچی **khazan'chi** (col. **khizan'chi**) N.M. cashier treasurer financial secretary [A]

خزف **kha'zif** N.F. potsherd pottery ; earthenware cheap stuff [A]

خزینہ **khazi'nah** N.M. treasury, treasure-house store ; godown [A doublet of خزانہ]

خس **khas** N.F. sweet-scented grass hay rubbish خس پوش **khas-posh'** ADJ. thatched covered with scented grass خس کی ٹٹی **khas' ki tat'ti** N.M. screen of sweet scented grass ; hay-screen خس وخاشاک **kha's-o-khashak'** N.M. rubbish sweepings [P]

خسارہ **khasa'rah** N.M. loss damage خسارہ اٹھانا (یا برداشت کرنا) **khasa'ra utha'na (or bardash't kar'na)** V.I. sustain or incur a loss [P]

خست **khis'sat** N.F. meanness niggardliness stinginess ; parsimony خست کرنا **khis'sat kar'na** V.I. be stingy , be niggardly [A]

خستہ **khas'tah** ADJ. crisp bruised wounded tired , fatigued distressed afflicted خستہ حال **khas'ta-hal** ADJ. afflicted distressed N.M. miserable creature wretch خستگی **khas'tagi** N.F. crispiness wound sore sickness fatigue ; exhaustion [P]

خسر **khu'sar** (ped. **khusur**) N.M. father-in-law [P]

خسراں **khusran'** N.M loss [A doublet of خسارہ N.M. ★]

خسرو **khus'rau** N.M. Chosroes king خسروانہ **khusruva'nah** ADJ. & ADV. imperial royal , regal kingly ; princely خسروی **khus'ravi** ADJ. imperial royal ; regal kingly ; princely [P]

خسرہ **khas'rah** N.F. list of village fields in a village (correctly کھسرہ **khas'rah**) measles [P]

خسوف **khasoof'** N.M. lunar eclipse [A]

خسیس **khasis** ADJ. mean niggardly stingy , parsimonious [A ~ خست]

خشت **khish't** N.F. brick tile خشت اول **khish't-e av'val** N.F foundation-stone خشتی **khish'ti** ADJ. brick tiled [P]

خشخاش **khashkhash'** N.M (also خشخاش کا دانہ **khashkhash' ka da'nah**) poppy seed this is as unit of weight خشخاش کے دانے کے برابر **khashkhash' ke da'ne ke bara'bar** ADV. very little خشخاشی **khashkha'shi** خشخشی **khash'khashi** ADJ. close cropped (beard) [P]

خشخشی **khash'khashi** ADJ. (see under خشخاش N.M. ★)

خشک **khush'k** ADJ. dry dehydrated withered cold , not cordial خشک سالی **khush'k-sa'li** N.F. drought خشک کرنا **khush'k kar'na** V.T. dry dehydrate خشک ہونا **khush'k ho'na** V.I. be dried be dehydrated be parched خشکہ **khush'kah** N.M. boiled rice خشکہ کھاؤ (پنیر کے ساتھ) **khush'kah kha''o, (panir' ke sath)** PH. cherish no vain hopes خشکی **khush'ki** N.F. land flour for besmearing rolled dough dryness cynicism peevishness [P]

خشم **khash'm** N.M. anger rage fury خشم آلود **khash'm-alood'**, خشم آگیں **khash'm-agin'**, خشمگیں **khash'm-gin**, خشمناک **khash'm-nak** ADJ. angry enraged , wrathful irate [P]

خشوع **khushoo''** N.M. humility fear [A]

خشونت **khushoo'nat** N.F harshness severity fierceness callousness cruelty hardness roughness [A]

خشیت **khash'yat** N.F. fear dread خشیت الٰہی **khash'yat-e ila'hi** N.F. fear of God [A]

خصال **khisal'** N.M. PL. (see under خصلت N.F. ★)

خصائص **khasa''is** N.M. PL. peculiarities [A ~ SING خاصیت]

خصلت **khas'lat** N.F. good quality ; quality, trait of character خصال **khisal'** N.M. PL. qualities ; traits of character good qualities خوش خصال **khush-khisal'** ADJ. (one) having delectable qualities [A]

خصم [1] **khas'm** N.M. enemy antagonist [A]

خصم [2] **khas'm** N.M. husband خصم پیٹی **khas'm-pi'ti** N.F. (dial.) widow خصموں جلی **khas'mon ja'li** N.F. (dial.) one who has not had a good treatment at the hands of her husband ; disillusioned wife

خصوص **khusoos'** N.M being particular بالخصوص **bil-khusoos'** ADV particularly ; especially **khusoo'san** ADV. particularly , especially [A ~ خاص]

خصوصیت **khusoosiy'yat** (col **khusoo'siyat**) N.F peculiarity distinctive feature distinction خصوصیات **khusoosiyyat'** N.F. PL peculiarities distincitive features خصوصی **khusoo si** ADJ. special peculiar particular secret personal private اشاعت خصوصی **isha''at-e khusoo'si** N.F. special issue (of periodical [A]

خصومت **khusoo'mat** N.F enmity strife contention bad blood (between) [A ~ خصیم]

خصی **khas'si** (ped. **kha'si**) N.M eunuch gelding ADJ. castrated (animal) non-protruding gargoyle خصی کرنا **khas'si kar'na** V.T castrate خصیہ **khus'yah** N.M. testicle خصیتین **khusayatain'** N.M. PL. testes ; testicles [A]

خضاب **khizab'** N.M. hair dye hair tincture خضاب کرنا **khizab' kar'na** V.T. dye (the hair) apply hair-dye (to)

خضر **kha'zir** or **khaz'r** (col. **khiz'r** (or **khi'zar**) N.M. Khizr , name of a prophet immortalized by the fountain of life guide leader خضر راہ **khaz'r-e rah'** N.M. the guide [A]

خضرا **khazra'** ADJ. green گنبد خضرا **gum'bad-e khazra** N.M the Holy Prophet's mausoleum ; the Green Dome [A ~ خضر]

خضوع *khuzoo'* N.M. humility خشوع وخضوع *khushoo''-o khuzoo''* N.M. fear of God and humility [A]

خط *khat* N.M. (PL. خطوط *khutoot'*) letter ; epistle note writing handwriting script line streak beard sign of its growth خط آزادی *khat't-e aza'di* N.M. manumission charter خط آنا *khat' a'na* V.I. (of lad) begin to grow beard خط استوا *khat'te istiva'* N.M Equator خط بنانا *khat bana'na* V.T. shave trim the beard خط بنوانا *khat banva'na* V.T. get a shave get the beard trimmed خط جدی *kha't-e jad'y* N.M. tropic of capricorn خط جلی *khat't-e ja'li* N.M bold hand-writing ; bold hand bold script خط سرطان *khat't-e sartan'* N.M. tropic of cancer خط شکست *khat t-e shikas't*, خط شکستہ *khat't-e shikas'tah* N.M. running hand خط عمود *khat t-e 'amood'* N.M. perpendicular (line) خط کش *khat'-kash* N.M. ruler خط کھینچنا *khat khench'na* V. to draw a line خط متوازی *khat't-e mutava'zi* N.M. parallel line خط مستدیر *khat't-e mustadir'* N.M. circular line خط مستقیم *khat't e mustaqim'* N.M. stright line خط منحنی *khat't-e mun'hani* N.M. curved line خط نستعلیق *khat't-e nasta'liq'* N.M. plain round Persian writing ; 'Nastaliq' خط نسخ *khat't-e nas'kh* N.M. usual form of Arabic script ; 'Naskh' خط وخال *khat't-o khal'*, خد وخال *khad'd-o khal'* N.M. features خط وکتابت *khat't-o-kita'bat* (col. خط کتابت *khat kita'bat*) N.F. correspondence [A]

خطا[1] *khata'* N.F. error ; mistake fault miss ; failure slip ; oversight خطاکار *khata'-kar'*, خطاوار *khata'-var'* ADJ. guilty N.M. miscreant culprit خطا کرنا *khata' kar'na* V.T. err ; commit error ; make a mistake miss hit wide of the mark اوسان خطا کرنا *ausan' khata' kar'na* V.T. confuse confound خطا ہونا *khata' ho'na* V.I. be missed ; be wide of the mark اوسان خطا ہونا *ausan' khata' ho'na* V.I. be confused be confounded [A]

خطا[2] *khata'* N.M. Cathay

خطاب *khitab'* N.M. title speech ; address ; lecture خطاب دینا *khitab' de'na* V.T. award title خطاب کرنا *khitab' kar'na* V.T. deliver a lecture address accost خطابت *khita'bat* N.F. oratory ; oration declamation rhetoric eloquence [A]

خطاط *khattat'* N.M. calligraphist خطاطی *khatta'ti* N.F. calligraphy [A ~ خط]

خطائی *khata''i* ADJ. pertaining to Cathay N.F. (also نان خطائی *nan-e khata''i*) small crisp cake [T]

خطبہ *khut'bah* N.M. sermon oration discourse prologue , introduction ; foreword خطبہ پڑھنا *khut'bah parh'na* V I. give a sermon کے نام کا خطبہ پڑھنا *ke nam ka khut'bah parh'na* V I. reiterate (ruler's) name in sermon خطبہ دینا *khut'bah de'na* V.I. give a sermon address (a gathering) [A ~ خطاب]

خطر *kha'tar* N.M. risk ; hazard danger , peril jeopardy thought خطرناک *kha'tar-nak*, پرخطر *pur' kha'tar* ADJ risky ; hazardous rightful dangerous ; perilous [A]

خطرہ *khat'rah* N.M. (PL. خطرات *khatarat'*) danger peril risk ; hazard خطرہ مول لینا *khat'rah mol le'na* V.I. run a risk jeopardize one's life venture خطرے میں ڈالنا *khat're men dal'na* V.T. endanger ; perilize risk jeopardize [A ~ PREC.]

خطوط *khutoot'* N.M. (PL. of خط N.M. ★)

خطمی *khat'mi* N.F. marsh-mallow ریشہ خطمی *re'sha-e khat'mi* N.M. marsh-mallow fibre (used as medicine)

خطہ *khit'tah* N.M. (PL. خطط *khi'tat*) region [A]

خطیب *khatib'* N.M. orator ; public speaker preacher [A ~ خطبہ]

خطیر *khatir'* ADJ. much ; large زرخطیر *za'r-e khatir'* N.M. large sum [A]

خفا[1] *khifa'* N.F. concealment secrecy خفائی *khifa''i* N.M. & ADJ. obscure (person) [A]

خفا[2] *kha'fa* ADJ. displeased offended angry ; enraged خفا کرنا *kha'fa kar'na* V.T. offend ; incense infuriate خفا ہونا *kha'fa ho'na* V.I. be offended ; be incensed be infuriated خفگی *kha'fagi* (col. *khaf'gi*) N.F. displeasure anger ; indignation

خفاش *khaffash'* N.M. bat [A]

خفگی *kha'fagi* N.F. (see under خفا★)

خفت *khif'fat* N.F. slight ; affront disgrace , indignity ; humilitation lightness خفت آمیز *khif'fat-amez'* ADJ. slighting disgraceful خفت اٹھانا *khif'fat utha'na* V.I. be slighted be disgraced (کو) خفت ہونا *(ko) khif'fat ho'na* V.I. be slighted be disgraced خفیف *khafif'* ★ [A]

خفتان *khaftan'* N.M. underwear for coat of mail [P]

خفتہ *khuf'tah* ADJ. sleeping خفتن *khuf'tan* N.M (rare) sleep night (prayers) [P]

خفقان *khafaqan'* N.M. palpitation melancholy hysteria [A]

خفگی ***kh**af'gī* (ped. ***kh**a'fagī*) N.F. (see under خفا ***kh**a'fa* ADJ. ★)

خفی ***kh**a'fī* ADJ. hidden ; concealed imperceptible small (type, handwriting, etc.) not loud ; whispering ذکرِ خفی *zik'r-e **kh**a'fī* S.M. low invocation of God's name [A ~ خفا ***kh**ifa'* N.M.]

خفیف ***kh**afīf'* ADJ. light slight ordinary insignificant petty ; trivial minor ; little ; small mean disgraced خفیف ہونا ***kh**afīf' ho'nā* V.I. be slighted be put to shame be disgraced ضربِ خفیف *za'rb-e **kh**afīf'* N.M. simple hurt ; minor injury [A]

خفیفہ ***kh**afī'fah* N.F. minor case ; small cause minor capacity ADJ. small minor ; little insignificant light عدالتِ خفیفہ *'adā'lat-e **kh**afī'fah* N.F. small cause court [A ~ PREC.]

خفیہ ***kh**ūf'yah* ADJ. secret hidden ; concealed disguised خفیہ پولیس ***kh**ūf'yah pūlīs'* N.F. Criminal Investigation Department ; C.I.D. Criminal Investigation Agency ; C.I.A. Federal Bureau of Investigation , F.B.I. Intelligence Department خفیہ کارروائی ***kh**ūf'yah kārravā''ī* N.F. secrecy secret action private enquiry [A ~ خفا ***kh**ifa'* N.M.]

خلا ***kh**al'a* N.M. space vacuum hollowness lacuna خلا ملا ***kh**a'la malā'* N.M. intimacy : close relations frequent intercourse ADJ. partly filled خلائی ***kh**alā''ī* ADJ. space ; pertaining to space خلائی جہاز ***kh**alā''ī jahā'z* N.M. spaceship ; spacecraft خلائی دور ***kh**alā''ī daur* N.M. space age خلائی سفر ***kh**alā''ī sa'far* N.M. space travel [A]

خلاب[1] ***kh**allāb'* N.M. mud ; mire [P]

خلاب[2] ***kh**allāb'* N.M. & ADJ. (one) who wheedles [A]

خلاص ***kh**alās'* N.M. (lit.) liberation (lit.) redemption ; deliverance ADJ. (col.) empty (vul.) discharged ; having ejaculated خلاص ہونا ***kh**alās' ho'nā* V.I. (vul.) ejaculated [A]

خلاصہ ***kh**ūlā'sah* N.M. note ; notes (on) summary ; precis ; gist abstract ; abridgement inference ; moral conclusion moral (of fable) extract essence quintessence خلاصہ کرنا ***kh**ūlā'sah kar'nā* V.T. summarize make a precis of خلاصہ لکھنا ***kh**ūlā'sah likh'nā* V.T. write notes on [A]

خلاصی ***kh**alā'sī* N.F. freedom release exemption redemption N.M. coolie ; cooly minor trolly-driver tent-pitcher minor member of ship's crew ; sailor خلاصی پانا ***kh**alā'sī pā'nā* V.T. be set free ; be liberated ; be released be exempted خلاصی ہونا ***kh**alā'sī ho'nā* V.I. be released be allowed to go away [~ A PREC.]

خلاف ***kh**ilāf'* N.M. (rare) enmity ; opposition ADJ. opposed contrary خلاف ***kh**ilā'f-e*, کے (بر) خلاف *ke (bar) **kh**ilāf'* PREP. & ADV. against contrary to opposite versus ; VS. خلاف بیانی ***kh**ilāf'-bayā'nī* N.F. misrepresentation ; misrepresentative خلافِ حکم ***kh**ilā'f-e hūk'm* ADV. contrary to orders خلافِ دستور ***kh**ilā'f-e-dastoor'*, خلافِ ضابطہ ***kh**ilā'f-e zā'bitah*, خلافِ قاعدہ ***kh**ilā'f-e qā''idah* ADJ. irregular ; contrary to the rules خلاف سمجھنا ***kh**ilāf' sa'majhnā* V.T. regard as one's opponent think otherwise خلافِ شرع ***kh**ilā'f-e shar''* ADJ. contrary to religion ; against the tenets of faith lacking religious sanction illegal ; unlawful ADV unlawfully against the tenets of faith خلافِ طبع ***kh**ilā'f-e-tab''* ADJ. disgusting against (someone's) will revolting خلافِ عقل ***kh**ilā'f-e aq'l* ADJ. absurd contrary to reason خلافِ قیاس ***kh**ilā'f-e qiyās'* ADJ. improbable inconceivable , incredible anomalous not analogous absurd کے خلاف کہنا *ke **kh**ilāf' kaih'nā* V.T. say (something) against (someone) oppose خلافِ مرضی ***kh**ilā'f-e mar'zī* ADJ. involuntary ADV. involuntarily against the wishes (of) خلاف ورزی ***kh**ilāf'-var'zī* N.F. violation (of law etc.) کی خلاف ورزی کرنا *kī **kh**ilāf'-var'zī kar'nā* V.T. violate (law, etc.) oppose احکام (یا حکم) کی خلاف ورزی کرنا *ahkām'* (or *hūk'm*) *kī **kh**ilāf' var'zī kar'nā* V.T. disobey خلافِ وضعِ فطری ***kh**ilā'f-e vaz''-e fit'rī* ADJ. unnatural (offence) فعلِ خلافِ وضعِ فطری *fe''l-e **kh**ilā'f-e vaz''-e fit'rī* N.M. unnatural offence homosexuality کے خلاف ہونا *ke **kh**ilāf' ho'nā* V.T. oppose be opposed to [A]

خلافت ***kh**ilā'fat* N.F. Caliphate خلافتِ راشدہ ***kh**ilā'fat-e rā'shidah* N.M. Orthodox Caliphate خلیفہ ***kh**alī'fah* N.M. ★ [A]

خلاق ***kh**allāq'* N.M. (God as) the Creator خلاقِ عالم ***kh**allā'q-e 'ā'lam* N.M. the Creator خلاقی ***kh**allā'qī* N.F. divinity being the Creator [A ~ خالق]

خلال ***kh**ilāl* (col. ***kh**alāl*) N.M. tooth-pick خلال کرنا ***kh**ilāl' kar'nā* V.T. pick one's teeth [A]

خلائق ***kh**alā''iq* N.F. PL. people creation , creatures مقبولِ خلائق *maqboo'l-e **kh**alā''iq* ADJ. universally disliked [A]

خلجان ***kh**aljan* (ped. ***kh**a'lajān'*) N.M. anxiety , worry grave misgivings [A]

خلخال ***kh**alkhāl'* N.M. anklet hemmed with tiny jingling bells [A]

خلخلا ***kh**al'**kh**ala* ADJ. loose flatty

خلد ***kh**ul'd* N.M. paradise خلد آشیاں ***kh**ul'd-a'shiyañ* ADJ. the late with his abode in heaven خلد بریں ***kh**ul'd-e barīn'* N.M. the heaven above [A]

خلش ***kh**a'lish* N.F. prick (of the conscience) worry ; anxiety pain [P ~ خلیدن]

خلط ***kh**il't* N.F. (PL. اخلاط *akhlāt'*) humour ; one of the four humours, viz., blood, phlegm, choler, melancholy [A]

خلط ***kh**al't* N.F. mixture ; medley confusion خلط ملط ***kh**al't mal't* ADJ. intermixed jumbled in a state of confusion خلط ملط کرنا ***kh**al't mal't kar'na* V.T. confuse jumble

خلطہ ***kh**al'tah* N.M. long old-fashioned shirt

خلع ***kh**ul'* N.M. divorce obtained on wife's initiative [A]

خلع ***kh**al'* N.M. taking off separation removal [A]

خلعت ***kh**il''at* N.M. dress ; robe of honour this as princely award or investiture خلعت پہنانا (یا دینا یا عطا کرنا) ***kh**il''at paihnā'nā* (or *de'nā* or *'atā' kar'nā*) invest (someone) with a robe of honour [A]

خلف ***kh**a'laf* N.M heir successor son descendants ADJ. dutiful خلف الرشید ***kh**a'laf-ur-rashīd'* خلف الصدق ***kh**a'laf-us-sid'q* N.M worthy son ناخلف *nā **kh**a'laf* ADJ. undutiful

خلفا ***kh**ulafā'* N.M. PL. Caliphs successors spiritual successors خلفائے راشدین ***kh**ulafā'-e rāshidīn'* N.M. PL. the Orthodox Caliphate the four Orthodox Caliphs [A ~ SING. خلیفہ]

خلق ***kh**ul'q* N.M manners nature politeness , civility , amiability ; affability خوش خلق ***kh**ush-**kh**ul'q* ADJ. affable , amiable خوش خلقی ***kh**ush-**kh**ul'qī* N.F politeness ; courtesy good manners affability ; amiability کج خلق *kaj-**kh**ul'q*, بدخلق *bad-**kh**ul'q* ADJ. ill-mannered uncivil , impolite , discourteous کج خلقی *kaj-**kh**ul'qī*, بدخلقی *bad-**kh**ul'qī* N.F ill manners incivility [A]

خلق ***kh**al'q* N.F. (PL. خلائق ***kh**alā''iq*) people mankind N.M. creation [A]

خلقت ***kh**al'qat* N.F. (PL خلائق ***kh**alā''iq*) people crowd [A ~ PREC.]

خلقت ***kh**il'qat* N.F. creation birth nature عجیب الخلقت *'ajī'b-ul-**kh**il'qat* ADJ. & N.M. freak ; monster prodigy strange (person خلقی ***kh**il'qī* ADJ. inherent natural [A]

خلل ***kh**a'lal* N.M. disorder disturbance derangement unsoundness defect , flaw interference interruption hindrance emnity خلل آنا (یا پڑنا) ***kh**a'lal ā'na* (or *par'na*) V.I. be disturbed be disordered be upset be deranged خلل انداز ***kh**a'lal-andāz* N.M. & ADJ. interfering meddlesome interruptory خلل انداز ہونا ***kh**a'lal-andāz' ho'nā* V.T. interfere ; interrupt disturb خلل پذیر ***kh**a'lal-pazīr'* ADJ. upset troubled disordered خلل دماغ ***kh**a'lal-e dimāgh'* N.M. derangement madness , lunacy خلل ڈالنا ***kh**a'lal dāl'nā* V.I. upset disturbs interfere [A]

خلو ***kh**ulūv'* N.M. emptiness ; vacuity freedom from worry خلو ذہن ***kh**ulūv'v-e zeh'n* N.M. concentration [A]

خلوت ***kh**al'vat* N.F privacy closet private conference sexual intercourse خلوت خانہ ***kh**al'vat-**kh**ā'nah* N.M. خلوت گاہ ***kh**al'vat-gāh'* N.M. closet place of retirement خلوت گزیں ***kh**al'vat-guzīn*, خلوت نشین ***kh**al'vat-nashīn'* ADJ. & N.M. recluse hermit (one) sitting in solitude (one) leading a life of retirement سے خلوت کرنا *se **kh**al'vat kar'nā* V.T. have sexual intercourse with (woman) [A ~ خلا]

خلود ***kh**ulood'* N.M. eternity immortality remaining for ever [A]

خلوص ***kh**uloos'* N.M. sincerity candour warmth of affection purity خلوص نیت ***kh**uloo's-e niy'yat* N.M. sincerity of intention ADJ. ★ [A]

خلیا ساس ***kh**al'yā sās* N.F mother-in-law's sister [~ A خالہ + ساس]

خلیج ***kh**alīj'* N.F gulf ; bay chasm yawning gulf (of) کے مابین خلیج حائل ہونا *ke mā-bain' **kh**alīj' hā''il ho'nā* V.I. have great differences have a yawning gulf between [A]

خلیرا ***kh**ale'rā* ADJ. related through one's maternal aunt خلیرا بھائی (یا بہن) ***kh**ale'rā bhā''ī* (or *bai'han*) N.M (F.) son of one's maternal aunt; cousin (or daughter) [~ A خالہ]

خلیطی ***kh**alī'tī*, خلیتی ***kh**alī'tī* N.F. needle case housewife [~ A خریطہ CORR.]

خلیفہ ***kh**alī'fah* N.M. (PL. خلفا ***kh**u'lafa*) Caliph spiritual successor (euphemism for) barber [A ~ خلف]

خلیق ***kh**alīq'* ADJ courteous ; polite ; civil suave amiable ; affable [A ~ خلق ***kh**ul'q*]

خلیل ***kh**alīl'* N.M. friend (also خلیل اللہ ***kh**alī'l-ullah'*) N.M (Abraham's appellation as) God's friend [A]

خلیہ **khali'yah** N.M. (PL. خلیات khaliyyāt') cell of organism [A]

خم **kham** N.M. curl ; ringlet curve bend twist noose ; loop ADJ. twisted crooked bent خم ٹھوکنا (یا ٹھونکنا) **kham ṭhok'nā** (or **ṭhoṅk'nā**) N.M. strike hands against opposite arms as challenge before wrestling N.M. such challenge خم ٹھونک کر سامنے آنا **kham ṭhoṅk' kar sām'ne ā nā** V.T. challenge be ready to give a fight خمِ چوگان **kha'm-e chaugāṅ'** N.M. polo-stick خمدار **kham-dār'** ADJ. curled twisted bent curved crooked خم دینا **kham de'nā** V.T. curl twist bend خم و چم **kha'm-o chum'** N.M. coquetry enticing movement

خم **khum** N.M. pitcher large jar خمخانہ **khum-khā'nah**, خمکدہ **khum'-ka'dah** N.M. tavern ; pub ; bar خم پر خم چڑھانا **khum' par khum chaṛh'ānā** خم کے خم لنڈھانا **khum ke khum' luṅḍhā'na** V.I. drink to excess

خمار **khumār'** N.M. hang-over intoxication خمار آلود(ہ) **khumār'-āloo'd(ah)** ADJ. deeply drunk ; intoxicated ; inebriate showing sign of hang-over [A ~ خمر]

خمار **khimār'** (PL. **khu'mur**) N.M. shawl , stole [A]

خمار **khammār'** N.M. vintner wine merchant tavern-keeper [A ~ خمر]

خمر **khamr** N.M. wine liquor [A]

خمرا **khumrā'** N.M. name of mendicant fraternity its male member خماری **khum'rī** N.F. its female member

خمس **khums** ADJ. fifth ; one fifth [A ~ FOLL.]

خمسہ **kham'sah** N.M. series of five epics, etc. by same poet ; pentalogy [A]

خموش **khamosh'** ADJ., خموشی **khamo'shī** N.F. (ABB. of خاموش and خاموشی (see under ADJ. ★)

خمول **khumool'** N.M. oblivion گوشۂ خمول میں پڑا **go'shā-e khumool' meṅ pa'ṛā** PH. forgotten [A]

خمیازہ **khamyā'zah** N.M. penalty retribution; Nemesis gape ; yawn خمیازہ اٹھانا (یا بھگتنا) **khamyā'zah uṭhā'nā** (or **bhu'gatnā**) V.I. suffer for one's mistake, etc. face retribution face the music خمیازہ کھینچنا **khamyā'zah khench'nā** V.I. gape ; yawn suffer punishment for (one's) wrongdoings ; face the music [P]

خمیدہ **khamī'dah** ADJ. bent crooked خمیدگی **khamī'dagī** N.F. crookedness [P ~ خمیدن]

خمیر **khamīr** N.M. leaven ; yeast ferment nature خمیر اٹھانا **khamīr' uṭhā'nā** V.T. ferment خمیر اٹھنا **khamīr' uṭh'nā** V.I. be leavened be fermented become sour (owing to fermentation) خمیر بگڑنا **khamīr' bi'gaṛnā** V.I. suffer a change for the worse خمیرہ **khamī'rah** N.M. scented hookah tobacco leavened and solidified medicinal syrup خمیری **khamī'rī** ADJ. leavened خمیری روٹی **khamī'rī ro'ṭī** N.F. leavened bread [A]

خنا **khan'nā** N.M. nonsense

خنا **khūn'nā** N.M. silly person خنا بہکنا **khūn'nā baihak'nā** V.I. vaunt become proud rave خنی **khūn'nī** N.F. silly woman shrew

خنازیر **khanāzīr'** N.F. scrofula N.M. PL. pigs hogs [A]

خناس **khannās** N.M. devil slanderer , calumniator deserter devilish person [A]

خناق **khū'nāq** N.M. quinsy [A]

خنثیٰ **khūn'sā** N.M. eunuch hermaphrodite [A]

خنجر **khan'jar** N.M. dagger خنجری **khan'jarī** (col کھنجری **khan'jarī**) N.F. small jingled tambourine a kind of printed silk stripe in it [A]

خنخنانا **khūnkhūnā'nā** V.I. speak through the nose ; snuffle

خنداں **khan'dāṅ** ADJ. (see under خندہ N.M ★)

خندق **khan'daq** N.M. ditch moat [A ~ P]

خندہ **khan'dah** ADJ. N.M. laugh laughter ; PREF merry ; cheerful laughter خندہ آور **khan'da-ā'var** ADJ. provoking , laughter laughable خندہ پیشانی **khan'da-peshā'nī**, خندہ رو **khan'da-roo'** ADJ. merry ; cheeful of smiling contenance خندہ روئی **khan'da-roo''ī** N.F. cheerfulness gaiety خنداں **khan'dāṅ** ADJ. laughing merry cheerful خندہ زن **khan'da-zan** ADJ. laughing deriding ; ridiculing خندی **khan'dī** N.F. silly laughing wench loose woman [P]

خنزیر **khinzīr'** N.M. (PL. خنازیر **khanāzīr'**) pig , hog (fig.) something forbidden [A]

خنک **khū'nuk** ADJ. cold cool lucky ; fortunate خنکی **khūn'kī** N.F. cold ; coldness coolness chill [P]

خنگ **khiṅg** N.M. white steed silvery steed [P]

خنیا **khūn'yā** N.F. song singing , vocal music خنیاگر **khūn'yā-gar** N.M. songster خنیاگرِ فلک **khūnyā-gar-e fa'lak** N.M. the planet Venus [P]

خو **khoo** N.F. nature disposition habit manners خوبو **khoo' boo** N.F. habit characteristics behaviour خو پڑنا **khoo' par'na** V.I. get into or form a habit become an addict خو چھوڑنا **khoo' chhor'nā** V.I. break or give up a habit خو ڈالنا **khoo ḍal'nā** V.T. & I. get into or form a habit habituate خو پذیر **khoo' pazīr'**, خوگر **khoo'-gar**, خوگرفتہ **khoo'-girif'tah** ADJ. accustomed habituated addicted amenable ; tractable ; decile [P]

خواب **khāb'** N.M. sleep dream vision خواب آلود(ہ) **khāb-āloo'd(ah)** ADJ. drowsy ; sleepy خواب آور **khā'b-ā'var** ADJ. soporific hypnotic خواب آور گولیاں **khāb-ā'var go'liyāṅ** N.F. PL. sleeping pills خواب پریشان **khā'b-e pirī'shāṅ**, **khā'b-e āsh f tah** N.F dreadful dream خواب خرگوش **khā'b-e khargosh'** N.F. deep sleep carelessness خواب خرگوش میں پڑے رہنا **khā'b-e khargosh' meṅ pa're raih'nā** V.I. obvious of one's interests come to grief owing to vanity or overweening pride خواب دیکھنا **khāb' dekh'nā** V.I. dream a dream ; have a dream have a vision کے خواب دیکھنا **ke khāb' dekh'nā** V.I. entertain vain hopes of خواب کی باتیں (کرنا) **khāb' kī bāt'eṅ (kar'nā)** N.M. PL. (V.I.) baseless things (building) castles in the air خوابگاہ **khāb'-gāh** N F. bedroom dormitory خواب گراں **khā'b-e girāṅ** N.M. sound sleep ; deep sleep گراں خوابی **girāṅ khā'bī** N.F. (being in) deep sleep گراں خواب **girāṅ-khāb'** ADJ. absorbed in deep sleep خواب وخیال **khāb-o khayāl'** N.M. delusion vision fantasy ; phantasy خوابیدہ **khābī'dah** ADJ. sleeping ; asleep dormant inactive oblivious of one's interests [A]

خواتین **khavātīn'** N.F. (PL. of خاتون N.F. ★)

خواجہ **khā'jah** N.M. (PL. خواجگان **khājagān**) (title of respect) master ; lord rich person tycoon ; business magnate خواجہ تاش **khā'jā-tāsh** N.M. slaves of the same master in relation to one another ; slave colleagues disciples of the same teacher, etc. in mutual relationship خواجہ خضر **khā'jah khā'zir** (see under خضر N.M. ★) خواجہ سرا **khā'ja sarā'** N.M. eunuch emasculate person put in charge of a seraglio خواجگی **khā'jagī** N.F. being rich being a master overlordship [P]

خوار **khār** ADJ. poor friendless miserable , wretched ignoble disgraced thrown on the streets SUF. eating accepting خواری **khā'rī** N.F. misery friendlessness abjectness disgrace [P]

خوارج **khavā'rāj** N.M. (PL. of خارجی N.M. ★)

خوارق **khavā'rīq** N.M marvels miracles supernatural happenings [A ~ SING. خارقہ ~ خارق]

خواست **khās't** AFFIX wish ; desire خواستہ **khās'tah** ADJ. wished for desired [P ~ خواستن]

خواستگار **khās't-gār** N.M. suitor candidate aspirant petitioner خواستگاری **khāst'-gā'rī** N.F. being a suitor candidature desire aspiration petition [P]

خواص **khavās'** N.F. slave girl N.M. PL. (of خاصیت qualities peculiarities virtues (of medicine) N.M. PL. (of خاص gentry the elite favourites خواصی **khavā'sī** N.M. service hind seat on elephant's back [A]

خوان **khān** N.M. tray خوان پوش **khān-posh'** N.M. tray cover خوانچہ **khān'chah** N.M. hawkers tray خوانچہ فروش **khān'cha-firosh'** N.M. hawker ; pedler خوانچہ لگانا **khān'chah lagā'nā** V.I. peddle eatables [P]

خواندہ **khāṅ'dah** ADJ & N.M. (PL. خواندگان **khāṅ'dagān** literate persons ناخواندہ **nā-khāṅ'dah** ADJ. & N.M. (PL. ناخواندگان **nā-khāṅ'dagan**) illiterate persons خواندگی **khānd'gī** (ped. **khāṅ'dagī**) N.F. literacy خوانندہ **khānindah**, (PL. خوانندگان **khāniṅ'dagān'**) reader [P ~ خواندن]

خوانین **khavānīn'** N.M. (PL. of خان N.M. ★)

خواہ **khāh** SUF. desirous of wishing for demanding CONJ. either ; whether خواہ ... خواہ **khāh......khāh** CONJ. either......or خواہ نہ ...... نہ **khāh nā...nā** CONJ. neither...nor خاطر خواہ **khā'tir khāh** ADJ. satisfactory ADV. to one's heart's content enough satisfactorily خواہ مخواہ **khāh'-ma-khāh'**, (rare) خواہ نخواہ **khāh' nā-khāh'**, خواہ نخواہی **khā'hī na-khā'hī** ADV. definitely ; positively ; at all events willy-nilly ; willing or not willing without rhyme or reason ADJ. baseless , unfounded unauthorized self-imposed self-styled خواہاں **khā'hāṅ** ADJ. desirous of seeking ; looking (for) [P ~ خواستن wish]

خواہر **khā'har** N.F. (PL. خواہران **khā'haran**) sister [P]

خواہش **khā'hish** N.F. (PL. خواہشات **khāhishāt'**) wish request prayer demand desire will خواہش رکھنا (یا کرنا) **khā'hish rakh'nā** (or **kar'nā**) V.I. wish desire express a desire (for) خواہشمند **khā'hish-mand** ADJ. & N M. desirous [P ~ S خواہ]

خواہی نخواہی *kha'hi na-kha'hi* ADV. same as (see under خواہ SUF. ★)

خوب *khoob* ADJ. good well lovely ; pretty ; beautiful pleasant amiable ; affable N.M. sweetheart beauty ; beautiful person خوبرو *khoob'-roo* خوبصورت *khoob'-soo'rat* ADJ. comely ; lovely handsome ; pretty ; beautiful خوبصورتی *khoob-soo'rati* خوبروئی *khoob'-roo''i* N.F. comeliness ; loveliness ; prettiness ; beauty خوباں *khoo'bañ* N.M. sweethearts beauties ; fair ones خوب تر *khoob'-tar* ADJ. better superior خوب ترین *khoob'-tarin'* ADJ. best excellent خوبی *khoo'bi* N.F. quality excellence elegance virtue (of medicine) بخوبی *ba-khoobi* ADV. well nicely easily with a swing [P]

خوبانی *khooba'ni* N.F. apricot [P]

خوب کلاں *khoob' kalañ'* N.M. blackberry seed [P]

خوبی *khoo'bi* N.F. (see under خوب ★)

خوجہ *kho'jah* N.M. (one of) a caste of petty traders (one of) a caste of Shi'ite businessmen (rare) eunuch

خوخیانا *khaukhiana* V.I. be enraged (of monkey) emit bullying sound

خود *khod* N.M. helmet آہنی خود *a'hani khod* N.F. steel helmet [P]

خود *khud* N. (one's) self PREF. self خودآرا *khud-ara'* ADJ. & N.M. self-adorning (person) خودآرائی *khud-ara''i* N.F. self-adornment fop dandy foppishness خود بخود *khud' ba-khud* ADV. voluntarily ; of one's own accord automatically خود بدولت *khud-ba-dau'lat* N.M. yourself INT. you your majesty خودبین *khud-bin'* ADJ. vain ; proud ; arrogant presumptuous self-conceited N.M. introvert egotist خودبینی *khud-bi'ni* N.F. pride ; vanity arrogance ; self-conceit introversion egotism خودپرست *khud-paras't* ADJ. selfish self-conceited narcissite egoistical N.M. egoist خودپرستی *khud-paras'ti* N.F. selfishness self-conceit egoism narcissism خودپسند *khud-pas'and'* ADJ. self-complacent vain ; proud self-conceited having a superiority complex egotistical N.M. egotist خوددار *khud-dar'* ADJ. self-respecting having self-restraint patient خودداری *khud-da'ri* self-respect selfrestraint patience خودرائے *khud-ra''e* ADJ. wayward ; headstrong opinionated wilful ; self-willed خودرائی *khud-ra''i* N.F. selfwill being headstrong waywardness از خود رفتہ *az khud-raf'tah* ADJ. dead drunk senseless ; unconscious mad از خود رفتگی *az khud-raf'tagi* N.F. drunkenness intoxication senselessness madness خودرو *khud'-ro* (col. *-rau'*) ADJ. wild (plant; etc.) خودستا *khud-sita'* ADJ. egotist خودستائی *khud-sita''i* N.F. self-praise egotism خودسر *khud-sar'* ADJ. wilful wayward; headstrong stubborn arrogant خودسری *khud-sa'ri* N.F. wilfulness waywardness stubbornness arrogance خودغرض *khud-gha'raz* ADJ. selfish ulterior motives خودغرضی *khud-gha'razi* (col. *ghar'zi*) N.F. selfishness ulterior motives خودفراموش *khud-faramosh'* ADJ. unmindful of oneself selfless enraptured خودفراموشی *khud-faramo'shi* N.F. rapture ; ecstasy being unmindful of onself خودکار *khud-kar'* ADJ. automatic self-propelled N.M. automation خودکاری *khud-ka'ri* N.F. automation خودکام *khud-kam'* ADJ. selfish خودکامی *khud-ka'mi* N.F. selfishness خودکاشت *khud-kash't* N.F. cultivation (managed) by landlord himself ADJ. owner-cultivated (field) خودکردہ *khud-kar'dah* ADJ. one's own doing self-invited خودکردہ را علاجے نیست *khud-kar'dah ra 'ila'je nes't* PROV. now face the music ; you (etc.) have dug your own grave خودکشی N.F. suicide خودکشی کرنا *khud-ku'shi kar'na* V.I. commit suicide خودکفیل *khud-kafil* ADJ. self-sufficient self-supporting خودمختار ADJ. independent self-governing free to decide self-willed خودمختاری *khud-mukhta'ri* N.F. independence self government freedom to decide self-will خودنما *khud-numa* ADJ. ostentatious proud vain ; self-conceited bragging ; boastful خودنمائی *khud-numa''i* N.F. self-conceit ostentation pride ; vanity خودی *khu'di* N.F. self ; ego self-conciousness (arch.) vanity ; pride بےخودی *be-khu'di* N.F. rapture ecstasy ; transport madness senselessness selflessness [P]

خور *khor*, خوار *khar* SUF. eating drinking accepting [P ~ خوردن]

خور *khur* N.F. eating خوردونوش *khur-o-nosh'* N.F. food and drink [P ~ خوردن]

خوراک *khoorak'* (ped. *khu-*), خورش *khu'rish* N.F food diet dose [P ~ خوردن]

خورد برد *khur'd-bur'd* N.F. embezzlement defalcation ; peculation making away with squandering خورد برد کرنا *khur'd-bur'd kar'na* V.I. misappropriate ; embezzle ; defalcate make away with squander خورد برد ہونا *khur'd-bur'd ho'na* V.I. be misappropriated be embezzled be squander [P ~ خوردن eat + بردن take away]

خوردنی **khūr'danī** ADJ. edible ; eatable اشیائے خوردنی **ash yā''e khūrd'nī** N.F. PL. eatables ; edible stuff [P ~ خوردن]

خورسند **khūrsand'** ADJ. pleased happy ; delighted خورسندی **khūrsan'dī** N.F. joy ; happiness ; pleasure ; delight [P]

خورش **khū'rish** N.F. (lit.) (same as خوراک N.F. ★) [P ~ خوردن]

خورشید **khūrshīd'** N.M. sun [P]

خوش **khūsh** ADJ. happy ; glad pleased gay ; merry ; cheerful good healthy ; wholesome fair ; beautiful pleasant sweet خوشا **khūshā'** INT. lucky how happy خوشامد **khūsh-ā'mad** N.F. flattery sycophancy toadying coaxing ; wheedling خوشامد کرنا **khūsh-ā'mad kar'nā** V.I. flatter toady fawn on coax ; cajole ; wheedle خوشامدی **khūsh-ā'madī** N.M. & ADJ. flatterer sycophant toady خوش آمدید **khūsh-āmaded'** INT. welcome ovation reception خوش آمدید کہنا **khūsh-āmaded' kaih'nā** V.I. welcome hold a reception in honour of خوش آنا **khūsh ā'nā** V.I. be liked turn out to be pleasant خوش آواز **khūsh-āvāz'** ADJ. melodious ; sweet-voiced خوش آوازی **khūsh-āvā'zī** N.F. melodiousness خوش آئند **khūsh-ā''ind** ADJ. pleasing agreeable holding bright prospects ; bright خوش اسلوب **khūsh-ūsloob'** ADJ. elegant snave خوش اسلوبی **khūsh ūsloo'bī** N.F. elegance ; grace nicety snavity خوش اطوار **khūsh-atvār'** ADJ. mannerly well-bred خوش الحان **khūsh-ilhān'** ADJ. melodious , sweet voiced خوش الحانی **khūsh-ilhā'nī** N.F. melodiousness خوش اندام **khūsh-andām'** ADJ. lovely ; pretty attractive having a charming figure خوش باش **khūsh-bāsh** ADJ. merry cheerful quite at ease ; comfortable ; living comfortably خوشبو **khūsh-boo'** N.F. fragrance perfume scent ; scented odour aroma (usu. خوشبودار **khūsh-boo-dār'** ADJ. fragrant sweet-smelling perfumed scented aromatic خوش بیان **khūsh-bayān'** ADJ. (of speaker) eloquent convincing perspicuous facile خوش بیانی **khūsh-bayā'nī** N.F. eloquence facile tongue felicity of phrase خوش پوش **khūsh-posh'**, خوش پوشاک **khūsh-poshāk'** ADJ. well-dressed foppish خوشحال **khūsh-hāl'** ADJ. rich well-to-do prosperous happy well-settled خوشحالی **khūsh-hālī** N.F. prosperity خوشخبری **khūsh-kha'barī** N.F. good news ; happy news ; glad tidings خوش خرام **khūsh-khirām'** ADJ. having a graceful gait ; with elegant movements خوش خصال **khūsh-khisāl'** ADJ. mannerly well-bred خوش خط **khūsh-khat'** ADJ. & N.M. one writing in a beautiful hand ; (one) having a good hand writing written in a beautiful hand خوش خطی **khūsh-khat'tī** (or col. **khūsh-kha'tī**) N.F. good hand writing calligraphy خوش خلق **khūsh-khūl'q** ADJ. courteous ; civil , polite affable ; amiable خوش خلقی **khūsh-khūl'qī** N.F. civility ; politeness ; courtesy affability ; amiability خوش خوراک **khūsh-khoorāk'** ADJ. (col. خوش خورا **khūsh-kho'rā**) ADJ. fond of rich food خوش خوراکی **khūsh-khoora'kī** N.F. fondness for rich food خوش خیال **khūsh-khayāl'** ADJ. poet (or writer) with freshness of ideas خوش خیالی **khūsh-khayā'lī** N.F. freshness of ideas خوشدامن **khūsh-dā'man** N.F. mother-in-law خوشدل **khūsh dil'** ADJ. happy cheerful well-disposed without spite خوشدلی **khūsh-di'lī** N.F. happiness cheerfulness lack of spite خوش ذائقہ **khūsh-zā''eqah** ADJ dainty palatable tasteful ; pleasing to the taste خوش رفتار **khūsh-raftār'** ADJ. with graceful movements خوش رفتاری **khūsh-raftā'rī** N.F. graceful movements خوش رنگ **khūsh-rang'** ADJ. bright-coloured with lovely hours خوش رنگی **khūsh-ran'gī** N.F. lovely hues (of) خوش رو **khūsh-roo'** ADJ. pretty ; beautiful ; handsome , lovely charming خوش روئی **khūsh-roo''ī** N.F. beauty ; loveliness خوش رہنا **khūsh-raih'nā** be happy live happily خوش زبان **khūsh-zabān'** ADJ. eloquent facile خوش زبانی **khūsh-zabā'nī** N.F. eloquence facile tongue خوش سلیقہ **khūsh-salī'qah** ADJ. & N.M. with good managerial qualities ; good manager خوش سلیقگی **khūsh-salī'qagī** N.F. good managerial qualities خوش طالع **khūsh-tā'le** ADJ. lucky ; fortunate with one's star in the ascendant خوش طبع **khūsh-tab''** ADJ. jocular , jocase cheerful having a good disposition خوش طبعی **khūsh-tab''ī** N.F. cheerfulness good disposition pleasantry خوش طینت **khūsh-tī'nat** ADJ. good-natured خوش طینتی **khūsh-tī'natī** N.F. good nature خوش فعلی **khūsh-fe''lī** N.F. pleasantry خوش فکر **khūsh-fik'r** ADJ. freshness of ideas خوش فکری **khūsh-fik'rī** N.F. freshness of ideas خوش فہم **khūsh-faih'm** (ped. fah'm). sensible optimistical vainly hopeful خوش فہمی **khūsh-faih'mī** (ped. fah-) N.F. good sense optimism vain hopes خوش قسمت **khūsh-qis'mat** ADJ. lucky , fortunate خوش قسمتی **khūsh-qis'matī** N.F. luck ; good fortune ; stroke of good luck خوش قسمتی سے **khūsh-qis'matī se** ADV. luckily خوش کرنا **khūsh' kar'nā** V.T. please ; delight amuse gratify خوش گپیاں **khūsh-gap'piyāṅ** N.F. gossip pleasant خوش گزران **khūsh-gūzarān'** ADJ. & N.M. living in ease and comfort leading a comfortable life خوش گلو khūsh-gūloo' ADJ. sweet-voiced, melodious خوش گلوئی khūsh-gūloo''ī N.F melodiousness خوشگو khūsh-go ADJ & N.M. eloquent facile خوشگوئی khūsh-go''ī N.F. eloquence facile tongue felicity of phrase خوشگوار khūsh-gūvār ADJ. pleasant wholesome agreeable bracing tasteful خوشگواری khūsh-gūvā'rī N.F pleasantness خوش باش khūsh-libās' ADJ. well-dressed foppish خوش لباسی khūsh-libā'sī N.F. being well-dressed dandyism خوش نصیب khūsh-nasīb' ADJ. lucky fortunate خوش نصیبی khūsh-nasī'bī N.F. luck; good fortune خوش نصیبی کی بات ہونا khūsh-nasī'bī kī bāt ho'nā V.I be fortunate that خوشنما khūsh-nūmā' ADJ. beautiful (thing) lovely or charming (sight) splendial خوشنمائی khūsh-nūmā''ī N.F. beauty charm splendour خوش نوا khūsh-navā' ADJ. melodious, sweet-voiced (poet) reciting well good (poet) خوش نوائی khūsh-navā''ī N.F. melodiousness sweet recitation خوشنود khūshnood' ADJ happy pleased خوشنودی khūshnoo'dī N.F happiness pleasure خوشنویس khūsh-navīs N.M. a calligraphist ADJ. (one) writing a good hand خوشنویسی khūsh-navī'sī N.F calligraphy خوش وخرم khūsh-o-khur'ram ADJ. happy cheerful leading a comfortable life خوش وقتی khūsh-vaq'tī N.F happiness خوش ہونا khūsh' ho'nā V.I. rejoice enjoy be glad be pleased be happy; be delighted خوشی khū'shī N.F ★ [P]

خوشہ kho'shah N.M. bunch (of grapes, etc.) ear (of corn) spike (of plant) خوشہ چین kho'sha-chīn N.M. gleaner dependent (someone) for literary inspiration, writer taking his ideas from another (euphemism for) plagiarist inspired (by) dependent (on) خوشہ چینی kho'sha-chī'nī N.F. gleaning drawing inspiration (from) plagiarism dependence [P]

خوشی khū'shī N.F. pleasure; delight; happiness; gladness joy, mirth rejoicings festivity cheerfulness willingness خوشی خوشی khū'shī khū'shī, خوشی سے khū'shī se ADV. happily; gladly joyously with pleasure willingly; voluntarily cheerfully خوشی کرنا یا منانا khū'shī kar'nā (or manā'nā) V.I. be pleased be delighted enjoy rejoice hold festivities خوشی میں آنا khū'shī men ā'nā V.I. be pleased, be delighted اپنی خوشی سے a'pnī khūshī se ADV. willingly, voluntarily [P ~ خوش]

خوض khauz N.M. plunged (rare save in) غور وخوض ghau r-o khauz' N.M. careful consideration deep thought meditation [A]

خوف khauf N.M. fear dread, terror apprehension doubt, misgiving خوف دلانا khauf dilā'nā V.T frighten; terrify threaten, menace خوفزدہ khauf'-za'dah ADJ. afraid, frightened terrified; terror-stricken imperilled خوفزدہ کرنا khauf'-za'dah kar'nā frighten terrorize خوفزدہ ہونا khauf'-za'dah ho na, خوف کرنا khauf' kar'nā, خوف کھانا khauf' khā'nā V.T fear be afraid be terrified خوفناک khauf'-nāk' ADJ. terrifying frightful; dreadful terrifying terrific great (calamity, etc.) horrid, horrible [P]

خوک khook N.M. pig; hog; swine; boar [P]

خوگر khoo-gar ADJ. habituated, accustomed inured addict [P ~ خو + گر]

خوگیر khoo-gīr' N.M. pack-saddle saddle lining pad, stuffing خوگیر کی بھرتی khoo-gīr kī bhar'tī N.F. stuffing (of saddle) padding (fig.) worthless stuff [P خوی perspiration]

خول khol N.M. case cover sheath خول چڑھانا khol charhā'nā V.T. encase cover sheathe

خولنجان kholañ'jān (or khoo-) N.M. galingale [A ~ Gr.]

خون khoon N.M. blood murder man slaughter; homicide slaughter killing خوناب khooñ-nāb, خونابہ khooñ-nā'bah N.M. tears of blood blood خونابہ فشاں khooñ-nā'ba-fishāñ ADJ. shedding tears (etc.) of blood خونابہ فشانی khooñ-nā'ba-fishā'nī N.F. shedding tears of blood killing خون آشام khooñ āshām' ADJ. tyrannous ferocious خون آشامی khooñ āshāmī' N.M. ferocity tyranny خون آلود(ہ) khoon-ālood(ah) ADJ. blood-stained خونبار khooñ-bār' ADJ. shedding tears of blood خونبہا khooñ-bahā' N.M. ransom; blood-money خون بہانا khooñ bahā'nā V.T. shed blood, kill; murder خون پانی ایک کرنا khoon' pā'nī ek' kar'nā V.T. work very hard leave no stone unturned خون پینا khoon' pī'nā V.T. suck blood murder inflict great suffering on vex; harass; pester خون تھوکنا khoon' thook'nā V.I. spit blood work oneself to death have a great shock خونچکاں khooñ-chakāñ ADJ. bleeding. blood-dripping خون خرابہ khooñ' kharā'bah N.M. bloody fight killing خونخوار khooñ-khār' ADJ. blood-thirsty murderous ferocious N.M. ferocious person beast of prey خونخواری khooñ-khā'rī N.F. being blood-thirsty ferocity خونریز khooñ'-rez' ADJ. bloody; sanguinary خونریزی khooñ-re'zī N.F. bloodshed; carnage; massacre خون سفید ہونا khoon' sifed' ho'nā V.I. be callous be apathetic خوم خون khoo'nam

khoon, خونا خون **kh**oo'nā **kh**ooṅ ADJ. much wounded besmeared with blood خون کا پیاسا **kh**oon' kā pyā'sā ADJ. blood-thirsty N.M. bitter enemy خون کا دباؤ **kh**oon' kā dabā''o N.M. blood pressure خون کا دباؤ زیادہ (یا کم) ہونا **kh**oon' kā dabā''o ziyā'dah (or kam') ho'nā V.I. have high (or low) blood pressure خون کا دورہ **kh**oon' kā dau'rah N.M. circulation of blood خون کرنا **kh**oon' kar'nā V.T. kill ; murder assassinate ruin shatter (hopes) خون ہونا **kh**oon' ho'nā V.T. be killed ; be murdered be assassinated be ruined (of hopes) be shattered خونی **kh**oo'nī N.M. murderer; assassin ADJ. blood (relation) bitter (foe) خونیں **kh**o'onīṅ ADJ. bloody blood stained pitiable [P]

خوید **kh**avīd N.F. wheat or barley when still green; green wheat stalks

خویش **kh**esh N.M. (PL. خویشاں **kh**e'shāṅ) close relation (someone's) in-law kinsman (pl.) family ; people خویش و اقربا (یا اقارب) **kh**e'sh-o-aqribā' (or aqā'rib) N.M. PL. kith relations; relation kith and kin ; kinsmen [P]

خیابان **kh**ayābān' خیابان **kh**ayā'bāṅ N.M. flower-bed garden walk , walk road [P]

خیار **kh**iyār' N.M. cucumber [P] خیارین **kh**iyārain' N.M. PL. the two varieties of cucumber تخم خیارین tukh'm-e **kh**iyārain' N.M. PL. seeds of cucumber varieties [A]

خیاط **kh**ayyāt' N.M tailor , seamster [A ~ خیط thread]

خیال **kh**ayāl' N.M. (PL. خیالات **kh**ayālāt') thought notion idea conception fancy ; imagination vision coneeth care ; concern regard opinion ; consideration image name of a musical mode خیال آرائی **kh**ayā'l-arā''ī N.F. conceits (in poetry) خیال باطل **kh**ayā'l-e bā'til N.M. wrong idea ; false notion misconception خیال باندھنا **kh**ayāl' bāndh'nā V.T. form an idea imagine versify an idea خیال بندی **kh**ayāl'-bañ'dī N.F use of poetical images train of thoughts خیال پڑنا (یا چڑھنا) **kh**ayāl' paṛ'nā (or par chaṛh'nā) V I occur ; come to mind ; be recalled get the hang of ; get the point ; understand خیال چھوڑنا **kh**ayāl' chhoṛ'nā V.T. give up the idea (of) ; relinquish all thought (of) خیال خام **kh**ayā'l-e **kh**ām' N.M. silly idea wrong notion خیال رکھنا **kh**ayāl'-rakh'nā V.T. remember , bear in mind خیال رہنا **kh**ayāl' raih'nā V.I. be kept in mind خیال فاسد **kh**ayāl'-e fā'sid N.M. wrong idea , false notion خیال کرنا **kh**ayāl' kar'nā V.T & I. image ; to fancy think ; to consider care (for) ; show concern (for) ; be solicitous (about) have regard (for) خیال لاطائل **kh**ayā'l-e la-tā''il N.M. absurd idea خیال میں نہ لانا **kh**ayāl' meṅ na lā'nā V. pay no attention (to) have no regard (for) خیال نہ رہنا **kh**ayāl' na raih'nā V.T. forget all (about) خیال نہ کرنا **kh**ayāl' na kar'nā V.T take no notice of ; pay no attention (to) خیالات **kh**ayālāt' N.M. ideas ; thoughts fancies ; imaginations خیالی **kh**ayā'lī ADJ. imaginary visionary fanciful ; fantastical خیالی پلاؤ **kh**ayā'lī pulā''o N.M. imaginary castles in the air ; vain speculation خیالی پلاؤ پکانا **kh**ayā'lī pulā''o pakā'nā V.I. build castles in the air ; indulge in vain speculation [A]

خیام **kh**iyām' N.M. (PL. of خیمہ ★)

خیام **kh**ayyām' N.M. tent-maker [A ~ خیمہ]

خیانت **kh**iyā'nat N.F. embezzlement , defalcation breach of trust perfidy خیانت کرنا **kh**iyā'nat kar'nā V.I. embezzle be guilty of breach of trust خیانت مجرمانہ **kh**iyā'nat-e mujrimā'nah N.F. criminal breach of trust [A]

خیر **kh**air' N F. good , goodness virtue health , happiness safety welfare ADV all right ; very well ADJ. good best PREF. well خیر اندیش **kh**air-andesh' ADJ. well-wisher خیر اندیشی **kh**air-ande'shī N.F. well-wishing friendship solicitude خیر باد **kh**air-bād' INT. good-bye , farewell , adieu N.F. well-wishing farewell, adieu خیر باد کہنا **kh**air'bād' kaih'nā V.T. bid farewell ; say good-bye خیر خواہ **kh**air'-**kh**āh ADJ. well wisher خیر خبر **kh**air' **kh**a'bar N.F news good news news about the health (of) خیر خواہی **kh**air-**kh**ā'hī N.F. well-wishing friendship solicitude خیر سلا **kh**air' sal'lā N.F. (ped. خیر و صلاح **kh**air-o salāh') (someone's) welfare خیر گزرنا **kh**air' gu'zarnā V.I. escape unhurt ; survive an accident خیر مانگنا **kh**air' māṅg'nā, خیر منانا **kh**air' manā'nā V.T & I. pray for the safety (of) pray for (someone's) welfare خیر محض **kh**ai'r-e mah'z ADJ. very pious N.F. categorical good خیر مقدم **kh**air maq'dam N.M. welcome ovation خیر مقدم کرنا **kh**air-maq'dam kar'nā V.T. welcome give a warm reception (to) receive cordially خیر و عافیت **kh**ai'r-o 'āfiyat N.F. well-being health and prosperity خیر (تو) ہے **kh**air' (to) hai' INT. what is the matter with you are you all right? are you all there خیریت **kh**airiy'yat N.F ★ [A]

خیرات **kh**airāt' N.F alms , charity خیرات خانہ **kh**air'āt-**kh**ā'nah N.M. alms-house ; poor-house خیراتی **kh**airā'tī ADJ. charitable free خیراتی شفاخانہ **kh**airā'tī shifa-**kh**ā'nah N.M. charitable dispensary.

or hospital free dispensary or hospital [A ~ PREC.]

خیرہ ***khi'rah*** ADJ. dazzled dazed immodest shameless proud ; vain خیرگی ***khiragi*** N.F. dazzle daze immodesty shamelessness pride ; vanity [P]

خیرو ***khi'roo*** N.M. a kind of blue flower [P]

خیریت ***khairiy'yat*** N.F happiness health and happiness ; good health welfare safety [~A. خیر]

خیز ***khez*** N.F leap , bound , rising SUF. rising getting up leaping galloping causing . giving rise to خیزاں ***khe'zan*** ADJ. rising اُفتاں و خیزاں ***uf'tan-o khezan*** ADV. now rising ; now falling with great difficulty much fatigued willy nilly خیزش ***khe'zish*** N.F. (sexual) erection concupiscence خیزی ***khe'zi*** SUF. rising rousing [P خاستن rise]

خیسانده ***khesan'dah*** N.M. infusion [P]

خیل ***khail*** N.M horses host ; multitude horde [A]

خیلا ***khe'la*** N.M. & ADJ. silly (person خیلاپن ***khe'la-pan*** N.M. silliness

خیمہ ***khai'mah*** (col. ***khe'mah***) N.M. (PL. خیام ***khiyam***) tent pavilion خیمہ دوز ***khai'ma-doz'*** N.M. tent-maker خیمہ زن ***khai'ma'-zan*** ADJ. tent-pitcher encamping (army, etc.) خیمہ زن ہونا ***khai'ma-zan ho'na*** V.I. encamp خیمہ گاہ ***khai'ma-gah*** N.F. camp encampment camping ground [A]

د

د ***dal*** eleventh letter of Urdu alphabet (also called ***da'l-e moh'malah***) (in jummal reckoning) 4

داب ***dab*** N.M. manner ; customs ; ways condition ; state pump and show magnificence fear ; terror (usu. as رعب داب ***ro''b dab***) awe-inspiring authority [A]

دابنا ***dab'na*** V.T. press press down squeeze massage bury . inter usurp with hold ; keep back داب ***dab*** N.F. impression (in printing) ; single impression withholding pressure control ; authority داب بچھانا ***dab' bicha'na*** V.T give full impression (in printing) exercise authority over ; bring under control داب بیٹھنا (یا رکھنا یا لینا) ***dab baith'na*** (or ***rakh'na*** or ***le'na***) V.T usurp , seize take illegal possession embezzle press conceal keep back; withhold refuse to return داب چوک جانا ***dab' chook' ja'na*** V.I. (of paper) be unturned at corner, etc. and fail to receive impression (in printing) داب دینا ***dab' de'na*** V.T. bury ; inter

داتا ***da'ta*** N.M. God one who gives away generously one liberal in alms-giving داتا گنج بخش ***da'ta ganj' bakh'sh*** N.M. treasure-bestower (as appellation of Lahore saint) [~ دینا]

داتن ***da'tan*** N.F. tooth brush twig used as such [~ دانت]

داخل ***da'khil*** ADJ. admitted ; enrolled registered filed inserted ; included inner arriving ; entering داخل خارج ***da'khil-kha'rij*** N.M. registration of transfer of property mutation داخل دفتر ***da'khil daf'tar*** ADJ. filed shelved ; put in cold storage داخل دفتر کرنا ***da'khil daf'tar kar'na*** V.T. file put in cold storage داخل دفتر ہونا ***da''khil daf'tar ho'na*** V.I. be filed be shelved داخل کرنا ***da'khil kar'na*** V.T admit; enrol to enter ; include ; insert deposit file place داخل ہونا ***da'khil ho'na*** V.I. be admitted ; be enrolled arrive enter be inserted; be included be deposited be registered; be filed داخلہ ***da'khilah*** N.M. admission ; admittance entrance (also فیس داخلہ ***fees da'khilah***) admission fee (also امور داخلہ ***umoo'r-e da'khilah***) Home Affairs , Interior داخلی ***da'khili*** ADJ. internal ; inner , not extraneous of Home Affairs ; Interior PREF. in- داخلی گروہ ***dakhili garoh'*** N.M. in-group داخلی موضع ***da'khili mau'za'*** N.M. subsidiary village [A ~ دخل]

داد[1] ***dad*** N.M. ringworm ; herpes

داد[2] ***dad*** N.M. praise ; appreciation , compliments justice ; equity appeal complaint revenge law داد پانا ***dad' pa'na*** V.I. be praised obtain justice داد چاہنا ***dad' chah'na*** V. seek redress ; demand justice wish for compliments داد خواہ ***dad'-khah*** N.M. plaintiff complainant داد خواہی ***dad-kha'hi*** N.F. suit for redress petition for justice seeking redress داد دہی ***dad'-dehi*** N.F. administration of justice داد دینا ***dad' de'na*** V.T. praise ; pay compliments; give due appreciation do justice make reparation redress دادرس ***dad'-ras*** N.M. judge دادرسی ***dad'-ra'si*** N.F. justice redress of grievances دادرسی کرنا ***dad' ra'si kar'na*** V.T. redress the grievance (of) دادرسی ہونا ***dad'-ra'si ho'na*** V.I. (of someone) have justice داد شجاعت دینا ***da'd-e shaja''at de'na*** V.I. display great valour داد فریاد ***dad' faryad'*** N.F. cry for justice petition for seeking redress داد فریاد کرنا *dad' faryād' kar'nā* V.I. cry for justice seek redress raise a hue and cry داد کو پہنچنا *dad' ko pahūt'ch'nā* V.T. come to the aid (of) dispense justice redress the grievance of دادگر *dād'-gar* N.M. judge ; administrator of justice دادگستر *dād'-gūs'tar* ADJ. just N.M. judge دادگستری *dād'-gūs'tarī* N.F. administration of justice داد لینا *dād' le'nā* V.I. be complimented (on) get praise (for) get an avation be appreciated داد ملنا *dād' mil'nā* V.I. be complimented get an ovation داد نہ فریاد *dad nā faryād'* N.F. high-handedness injustice ; tyranny داد و دہش *dā'd-o dehish'* N.F. charity; bounty liberality beneficence ; munificence داد و ستد *dā'd-o sitad'* N.F. monetary transaction settlement of accounts business deal [P ~ دادن give]

داوا *dā'dā* N.M. paternal grandfather ; grandfather ; gaffer old man (dial.) precocious child (dial.) bad character ; hooligan ; miscreant ; tough دادی *da'dī* N.F. paternal grand-mother ; grandmother ; granny old woman

دادر *da dar* N.M. toad

دادرا *dād'rā* N.M. name of a staccato musical mode with quick tempo

دادس *dā'das* N.F. mother-in-law's mother-in-law; consort's paternal grandmother دادسرا *dā'dasra* N.M. father-in-law's father ; consort's paternal grandfather [~ ساس or سسر + دادا]

دار ۱ *dar* N.F. gibbet ; cross دار پر کھینچنا (یا چڑھانا) *dar' par khench'nā* (or *charhā'na*) V.T. impale gibbet دارکش *dar'-kash* N.M. hangman ; executioner [P]

دار ۲ *dar* SUF. having owner of holder -er N.F. holding ; keeping (used only in PH.) دار و گیر *da'r-o-gir'* N.F. ہنگامۂ دار و گیر *hanga'ma-e dār'-o gīr'* N.M. tumult melee indiscriminate arrests دار (و) مدار *da'r (-o-) ma-dār'* N.M. dependence: reliance پر دار و مدار ہونا *par da'r-o ma-dār' ho'nā* V.I. (of something) depend (on the existence, etc.) (of something else) ; depend [P ~ داشتن have]

دار ۳ *dar* N.M. house ; dwelling ; abode ; habitation place ; centre دارالآخرت *da'r-ūl-ā'khirat*, دارالآخرہ *da'r-ūl-ākhirah* N.M. the next world دارالاقامہ *dā'r-ūl-iqā'mah* N.M. (rare) boarding house ; hotel lodge ; house admitting paying guests دارالامان *da'r-ul-amān'* N.M. house of peace and safety friendly country دارالامرا *da'r-ūl-u'mara* N.M. House of Lords دارالبقا *da'r-ul-baqā'* N.M. the eternal abode; the heavenly home the next world; Hereafter دارالجزا *da'r-ūl-jazā'* N.M. the next world ; the heavenly home place of reward place of retribution دارالحرب *da'r-ūl-har'b* N.M. enemy territory non-Muslim country دارالحکومت *dā'r-ūl hukoo'mat* N.M. capital government headquarters دارالخلافہ *dā'r-ūl-khilafa* N.M. seat of the Caliphate; Caliph's headquarters دارالسلطنت *dā'r-ūs-sal'tanat* N.M. capital ; government headquarters دارالشفا *dā'r-ūsh-shifa'* N.M. (ped.) hospital دارالضرب *dā'r-ūz-zar'b* N.M. (rare) mint دارالعلوم *dā'r-ūl-'ūloom'* N.M. seat of learning college of orthodox Islamic learning دارالعمل *dā'r-ūl-'a'mal* N.M. the place of action ; this world دارالفنا *dār-ūl-fanā'* N.M. the abode of mortals دارالمکافات *dā'r-ūl-mukāfāt'* N.M. this world the place of retribution دارالنعیم *dār-ūn-na'īm'* N.M. the place of blessings paradise ; heaven [A]

دارا *dā'rā* N.M. possessor Darius [P ~ داشتن have, possess]

دارابی *dara'bī* N.F. gun rigging

داربست *dār'bast* N.F. scaffolding frame for creeper

دارچینی *dār-chī'nī* N.F. cinnamon [P]

دارو *da'roo* N.F. cure ; remedy drug ; medicine (col.) liquor دوا دارو *dava' dā'roo* N.F. medicine (medical) treatment داروئے درماں *daroo'-e darmāh'* (col. دارو درمن *dā'roo dar'man*) N.F. (medical) treatment [P]

داروغہ *dāro'ghah* N.M. inspector (official) in charge (of) (also داروغہ جی *dāro'ghah jī*) sub-inspector of police ; S.I. ; Station House Officer ; S.H.O. داروغۂ آبکاری *dāro'gha-e abka'rī* N.M. excise inspector داروغۂ پولیس *dāro'gha-e pūlīs'* N.M. sub-inspector of police; S.I. داروغۂ توپ خانہ *dāro'gha-e top-khā'nah* N.M. (old use) official in charge of artillery or arsenal keeper داروغۂ جنگلات *dāro'gha-e jangalāt'* N.M. ranger ; forest ranger داروغۂ جیل *dāro'gha-e jel* N.M. superintendent of jail; warden داروغۂ صفائی *dāro'gha-e safā'ī* N.M. sanitary inspector داروغہ فارم *dāro'ghah far'm* N.M. farm supervisor داروغہ گھاٹ *dāro'ghah ghāṭ* N.M. ferry collector داروغۂ محصولات *dāro'gha-e mahsoolāt'* N.M. tax inspector داروغگی *dāro'ghagī* N.F. office of 'darogha' ; supervisor's job [P]

داری *dā'rī* N.F. woman enslaved in battle loose woman

دارین *darain'* N.M. this the world and the hereafter [A ~ دار dual]

داڑھ *dāṛh* (dial. ڈاڑھ *ḍāṛh*) N.F. grinder داڑھ بھی گرم نہ ہونا *dāṛh bhī gar'm na ho'nā* V.I. have very little to eat داڑھا *dā'ṛhā* (dial. ڈاڑھا *ḍā'ṛhā*) N.M. (joc large beard corner-stones

داڑھی dāṛ'hī (dial. داڑھی dā'ṛhī) N.F. beard داڑھی پیٹ میں ہونا dā'ṛhī peṭ' meṅ ho'nā V.I. (of child) be precocious داڑھی پیشاب سے منڈوانا dā'ṛhī peshāb' se muṅḍvā'nā disgrace, eat the humble pie داڑھی چھوڑنا (یا رکھنا) dā'ṛhī chhoṛ'nā (or rakh'nā) V.I. grow a beard داڑھی مونڈنا dā'ṛhī mooṅḍ'nā V.I. shave off one's beard

داس dās N.M. (dial.) servant داسی dā'sī N.F. (dial.) maid servant female devotee [S]

داسا dā'sā N.M. wall-plate

داستان dāstān', داستان dās'tān N.F. legend ; romance late ; fable story داستان گو dās'tān-go' N.M. story-teller professional (orally) relating legends or tales داستان گوئی dās'tān-go''ī N.F storytelling profession of relating legends or tales [P]

داشت dāsh't SUF. keeping care (of) یادداشت yād-dāsh't N.F memory note memorandum داشتہ dāsh'tah N.F. mistress ; concubine SUF. kept , maintained [P ~ داشتن have]

داعی dā''ī (الداعی ad-dā''ī) N.M. (PL. داعیان dā'iyān' دعاۃ do'āt') preacher one making a call (for some cause) one who invites داعی (یا الداعی) الی الخیر dā''ī (or ad-dā''ī) ilal-khair' N.M. one who makes a call for a noble cause ; one who invites towards virtue [A ~ دعوت]

داعیہ dā''īyah N.M. desire ; wish motive arrogant claim USU. دم داعیہ dam-dā''iyah) guts [A ~ PREC.]

داغ dāgh N.M. mark spot blemish stigma scar burn loss ; injury shock calamity داغ اٹھانا dāgh uṭhā'nā V.I. suffer a reverse of fortune داغ بیل dāgh-'bel' N.F. spade (for laying mark out a road ; road demarcation (کی) داغ بیل ڈالنا (kī) dāgh'-bel' ḍāl'nā V.T. begin ; start ; initiate lay the foundation (of) داغدار dāgh'-dār ADJ. blemished sullied spotted stained burnt ; scarred soiled داغدار کرنا dāgh'-dār' kar'nā V.T. sully داغدار ہونا dāgh'-dār' ho'nā V.I. be sullied داغ دینا dāgh'-de'nā V.T. brand grieve die and cause grief (to) داغ کھانا dāgh'-khā'nā V.I. suffer the shock (of) be greatly grieved داغ لگانا dkgh'-lagā'nā V.I. sully ; stigmatize; blacken the name (of) grieve داغ لگنا dāgh'-lag'nā V.I. be sullied be branded ; be stigmatised be grieved by the death (of) داغی dā'ghī ADJ. damaged ; soiled ; spoiled [P]

داغنا dāgh'nā V.T. brand fire (gun, etc.) [1. ~ prec ; 2. ONO.]

دافع dā'fe' ADJ. driving away repelling curative curing [A ~ دفع]

داکھ dākh N.F. grapes a species of small sour grapes

دال ۱ dāl N.F. name of the letter دال فے عین ہونا dāl fe 'ain' ho'nā V.I. go away ; make oneself scarce

دال ۲ dāl N.F. split pulse vetch scale ; crust granulation yellow spot on fledglings beak concentrated rays دال باہی روٹی dāl bā'hī ro'ṭī N.F. fired pancake with a layer of pulse in it دال بندھنا dāl' bandh'nā V.I. (of wound) granulate دال چپو ہونا dāl' chap'poo ho'nā V.T. grapple with each other (of kite strings) become entangled دال دلیا dāl' dal'yā N.M. coarse fare ; poor food whatever is readily available for eating دال روٹی dāl' ro'ṭī N.F. humble food poor sustenance bare existence (کی) دال گلنا (kī) dāl' gal'nā V.I. (of someone's cause) prosper make headway دال میں کچھ کالا ہونا dāl' meṅ (kuchh) kā'lā ho'nā V.I. smell a rat (کی) دال نہ گلنا (kī) dāl' na gal'nā V.I. fail to make headway ابھی تو (منہ کی) دال بھی نہیں جھڑی a'bhī to (muṅh kī) dāl' bhī na'hīṅ jhaṛ'ī PH. he is as yet a fledgling

دال ۳ dāl ADJ. proof (of) indicative (of) ; expressive (of) denoting ; signifying پر دال ہونا par dāl ho'nā V.T. be proof (of) be indicative (of) denote ; signify دلیل

دالان dālān' N.M. varandah hall [P]

دام ۱ dām N.M. net snare trap کے دام میں لانا ke dām' meṅ ā'nā V.I. come under the spell (of) be duped (by) be seduced (by) be ensnared (by) (کو) دام میں لانا (ko) dām' meṅ lā'nā V.T. ensnare entrap dupe [P]

دام ۲ dām' N M. price cost value money; wherewithal a small coin now out of use; son دام بھرنا dām' bhar'nā V.I. pay the penalty (of) indemnify دام پٹ جانا dām paṭ' jā'nā V.I. (of price) be settled دام چکانا dām chukā'nā V.I. settle price or rate دام دینا dām' de'nā V. to pay the price دام کھرے ہونا dām' khā're kar'nā V.I. sell off (something) and receive the money دامے درمے قدمے سخنے dā'me di'rame qa'dame sukhā'ne ADV. all types of (help) [P]

دام ۳ dā'ma INT. (F. دامت dā'mat) may it last for ever ; may it be prepetuated دام اقبالہٗ dā'ma iqbā'lohoo INT. may his star continue to be in the ascendent دامت دولتہٗ dā'mat dau'latohoo INT. may his sovereignty (or prosperity) perpetuate دام ظلہٗ dā'ma zil lohoo INT. may his protection last for me

دائم ملکہ *dā'ma mūl'kohoo* INT may his sovereignty last [A]

داماد *damad* N.M. son-in-law [P]

دامان *da'mān*, دامن *dā'man* N.M. skirt (of garment) foot (of hill) part of river always under water edge SUF. skirted having دامن اٹھا کر چلنا *dā'man ūṭhā' kar chal'na* V.I. walk carefully act cautiously دامن پکڑنا *da'man pakaṛ'nā* V.T. cling (to) with hold come under the protection (of) complain (against) (کے) دامن پر فرشتے نماز پڑھیں *(ke) dā'man par firish'te namāz' pa'ṛhen* PH. very pious دامن پھیلانا *da'man phaila'na* V.I. beg implore; beseech دامن چھڑانا *dā'man chhūṛā'nā* V.T. & I. shake off get rid (of) دامن گیر *dā'man-gīr* ADJ. plaintiff accuser dependent دامنگیر *dā'man-gīr ho'nā* V.T. accuse complain (against) cling (to) (of anxiety) continue to recur دامنی *dā'mānī* SUF. being skirted having N.F. saddle cloth housings shawl ; stole [P]

1 دان *dān*, دان *dān* SUF. knowing understanding case container ; receptacle pot ; vase

2 دان *dān* N.M. (dial.) alms ; charity gift دان پن *dān' pūn* N.M. (dial.) alms ; charity [S cognate of دینا]

دانا *da'nā* ADJ. wise shrewd sagacious دانا (و) بینا *dānā'(-o) bī'nā* ADJ. wise (of God) All-knowing and All-seeing دانائے راز *dānā'-e raz'* N.M. & ADJ. (one) knowing the secret (of) دانائی *dānā''ī* N.F. wisdom sagacity shrewdness [P]

دانت *dānt* N.M. tooth tusk dent cog tooth (of saw or comb) دانت اکھاڑنا *dānt' ukhāṛ'nā* V.I. extract tooth (of someone) دانت بٹھانا *dānt' biṭhā'nā* V.T. cause to collapse دانت بیٹھنا *dānt' baiṭh'nā* V.I. collapse دانت (سے دانت) بجنا *dānt' (se dānt') baj'nā* V.I. shrive with cold دانت بنانا *dānt' banā'nā* V.I. make a denture set artificial teeth دانت بنانے والا *dānt banā'ne vā'lā* N.M. dentist دانت پیسنا (یا چبانا یا کٹکٹانا یا کچکچانا) *dānt' pīs'nā* (or *chabā'nā* or *kiṭkiṭā'nā* or *kichkichā'nā*) V.I. gnash one's teeth in anger دانت توڑ ڈالنا *dānt toṛ ḍāl'nā* V.T. break (someone's) teeth defeat دانت ٹوٹ جانا *dānt ṭooṭ jā'nā* V.I. (of tooth) break be defeated ; suffer a reverse دانت دیکھنا *dānt dekh'nā* V.I. judge animal's age by looking at its set of teeth ; look (animal) in the teeth پر دانت رکھنا (یا ہونا) *par dānt' rakh'nā* (or *ho'nā*) V.I. cherish desire for ; try to get دانت سلسلانا *dānt' salsalā'nā* V.I. (of tooth) ache دانت کاٹی روٹی (کھانا) *dānt kā'ṭī ro'ṭī* (*khā'nā*) V.I. have very cordial relations with دانت کرکرے ہونا *dānt kir'kire ho'nā* V.I. (of tooth) be set on edge دانت کریدنا *dānt kūred'nā* V.I. pick one's teeth دانت کڑکڑانا *dānt karkaṛā'nā* V.I. grind the teeth (in sleep) دانت کھٹے کرنا *dānt khaṭ'ṭe kar'nā* V.I. frustrate defeat ; discomfit دانت مارنا *dānt mār'nā* V.T bite دانت نکالنا *dānt nikāl'nā* V.I. grin laugh cut teeth fray دانت نکلنا *dānt ni'kalnā* V.I. cut teeth دانتوں پر ہونا *dān'toṅ par ho'nā* V.I. (of child) be cutting one's teeth دانتوں میں انگلی دینا (یا دبانا) *dān'toṅ meṅ ūṅg'lī de'nā* (or *dabā'nā*), دانت تلے انگلی دینا (یا دبانا) *dānt ta'le ūṅg'lī de'nā* (or *dabā'nā*), دانتوں میں تنکا لینا *dān'toṅ meṅ tin'kā le'nā* V.I. express one's helplessness دانتا *dāṅ'tā* N.M. tooth (of saw or comb) cog (of wheel) دانتا کلکل *dāṅ'tā kil'kil* N.F. constant quarrels continued tiffs

دانتن *dāṅ'tan* N.F. (same as داتن N.F. ★)

دانتوا *dānt'vā* N.M. dicky

داند *dānd* N.F. (dial.) high-handedness mischievous movements

دانست *dānis't* N.F. view , opinion understanding دانستہ *dānis'tah* ADV knowingly purposely; on purpose deliberately دیدہ و دانستہ *dī'da-o dānis'tah* ADV. deliberately intentionally; purposely; on purpose نادانستہ *nā-dānis'tah* ADV. unwittingly [P ~ دانستن]

دانش *dā'nish* N.F. understanding sagacity (rare) knowledge دانشکدہ *dā'nish-ka'dah* N.M. (rare) college دانشگاہ *dā'nish'-gāh'* N.F. (rare) university دانشمند *dā'nish-mand'* ADJ. wise sagacious دانشمندی *dān'ish-man'dī* N.F. wisdom sagacity دانشور *dān'ish-var* N.M. intellectual [P ~ دانستن]

دانگ *dāng* N.F. quarter drachm direction چار دانگ *chār-dāng(-e)* N.M. PL. all the four directions (of) شش دانگ *sha sh'dāng'(-e)* all the six sides or directions (of) [P]

دانو *dān''o* N.M. (same as داؤں N.M. ★)

دانہ *dā'nah* (col. *dā'nā*) N.M. grain ; corn seed feed bread pimple pustule pock دانہ بدلی کرنا *dā'na bad'lī kar'nā* V.I. bill an coo دانہ بندی *dā'na-bandī* N.F. preliminary revenue assessment (of crops) دانہ پانی *dā'na pā'nī* N.M. victuals lot ; fortune دانہ دار *dā'na-dār* ADJ. granulated crystalline دانہ دنکا *dā'nah dūn'ka* N.M. grain (as birds food) [P]

داوا *dā'vā* N.M. (dial.) husband of one's wet nurse

داور *dā'var* N.M. God ; God of Justice ; the Just God just sovereign [P]

داہنا *dāhinā,* داہنا *daih'nā,* دایاں *dā'yān* ADJ. right (hand) داہنے *dā'hine* ADV. on the right hand side to the right

دائر *dā''ir* ADJ. (of law-suit) filed ; instituted circling ; whirling دائر کرنا *dā'ir kar'nā* V.T. institute (a case) ; file (a law-suit) دائر ہونا *dā''ir ho'nā* V.I. (of law-suit) be filed [A ~ دور]

دائرہ *dā''irah* N.M. circle orbit large tambourine [A ~ دور]

دائم *dā''im* ADJ. eternal perpetual permanent ; lasting continual ceaseless ADV. always ever permanently دائم الحبس *dā''im-ūl-ḥab's* ADJ. imprisoned for life دائم المرض *dā''im-ūl-ma'raz* ADJ. sickly N.M. valetudinarian دائمی *da''imī* ADJ. continual ; lasting permanent ; lasting continual perpetual eternal [A ~ دوام]

دائن *da''in* N.M. debtor [A ~ دین *dain*]

داؤد *dā'ood* N.M. David مزامیر داؤد *mazāmī r-e da'ood* N.M. PL. psalms of David ; the psalms داؤدی *da'oo'dī* ADJ. pertaining to David (use گل داؤدی *gūl-e da'oo'dī*) chrysanthemum [A ~ H]

داؤں *dā''n,* داو *dāñ''o* N.M. (wrestling) trick grasp move (in game) throw (of dice) strategem ambush ; ambuscade turn ; chance داؤں پر چڑھنا *dā''oñ par chaṛh'nā* V.I. be entraped be overpowered by adversary داؤں پر رکھنا *dā''oñ par rakh'nā* V.T. stake ; put at stake ; hazard داؤں پڑنا *dā''oñ paṛ'nā* V.I have a good throw (of dice) داؤں پھینکنا *dā''oñ phenk'nā* V.I. throw the dice داؤں پیچ *dā''oñ pech'* N.M. (usu. PL.) (wrestling) tricks داؤں دینا *dā''oñ de'nā* V.T. give (someone) his turn trick; take in داؤں کرنا *dā''oñ kar'nā* V.I. trick ; deceive use (wrestling) trick داؤں کھیلنا *dā''oñ khel'nā* V.T. play a trick (upon) employ a strategem (against) داؤں لگانا *dā''oñ lagā'nā* V.I. throw the dice put at stake lie in wait ambush ; ambuscade wait for one's chance داؤں لگنا *dā''oñ lag'nā* V. get a chance or opportunity داؤں گھات *dā''oñ ghāt'* N.M. tricks strategem ambush ; ambuscade داؤں میں آنا *da''oñ meñ ā'nā* V.I. be taken in ; be deceived (by) be ambushed (by)

دائی *dā''ī* N.F. (col. for دایہ *dā'yah*) midwife دائی جنائی *dā''ī janā''ī* N.F. midwife دائی سے پیٹ چھپانا *dā''ī se peṭ chhūpā'nā* V.I. try to conceal from one who is in the know of things دائی کھلائی *dā''ī khilā''ī* N.F. governess baby-sitter دائی گیری *dā''ī-gī'rī* N.F. (col.) midwifery [or ~ P دایہ CORR.]

دایاں *dā'yāñ* ADJ. (same as داہنا ADJ. ★)

دائیں *dā''eñ* ADV. to the right ; on the right hand side دائیں بائیں *dā''eñ bā''eñ* ADV. right and left

دایہ *dā'yah* N.F. midwife child's nurse ; dry nurse ; governess ; baby-sitter wet nurse دایہ گری *dā'ya-garī* N.F. midwifery [P]

دب *dūb* N.M. (rare) bear دب اصغر *dūb'b-e as'ghar* N.M. the (constellation) Little Bear دب اکبر *dūb'b-e ak'bar* N.M. the (constellation) Great Bear [A]

دبا *dab'bā* N.M. twig (for replantation) [~ دبنا]

دبانا *dabā'nā* V.T. press down squeeze curb crush ; subdue check ; restrain usury bury ; inter suppress hush up دبا دینا *dabā' de'nā* V.T. bury ; inter suppress hush up press down دبا لینا *dabā' le'nā* V.T. usurp seize encroach upon overawe control ; keep under the thumb overcome curb suppress [~ دبنا CAUS.]

دباغت *dibā'ghat* N.F. tanning currying (leather) دباغ *dabbāgh* N.M. tanner currier [A]

دباؤ *dabā''o* N.M. pressure constraint influence awe دباؤ ڈالنا *dabā''o ḍāl'nā* V.I. press down influence ; bring pressure to bear upon دباؤ ماننا *dabā''o mān'nā,* دباؤ میں آنا *dabā''o meñ ā'nā* V.I. yield to the pressure of [~ دبانا]

دبدبہ *dab'dabah* N.M. awe state majesty [P]

دبدھا *dūb'dhā,* دگدا *dūg'dā* N.M. dilemma demur suspense ; uncertainty hesitation اسی دبدھے میں ہونا *i'sī dūb'dhe meñ ho'nā* V.I. be on the horns of a dilemma دبدھا کرنا *dūb'dhā kar'nā* V.I. doubt ; have misgivings hesitate

دبر *du'būr* N.F. anus posterior bottom ; bum [A]

دبڑو گھسڑو *dab'roo ghus roo* N.M shy (person) nervous (person) coward ly) [~ دبنا + گھسنا]

دبستان *dabis'tān* (or *dabistān'*) N.M. sch [P ~ A دب]

دبکانا *dabkā'nā* V.T. reprove ; rebuke snub (arch.) hide ; conceal دبکنا *da'baknā* V.I. crouch shrink from fear squeez lie in a ambush دبک کر بیٹھنا *da'bak kar baiṭh'nā* V.I. crouch دبک جانا *dabak jā'nā* V.I. be overawed crouch

دبلا *dub'lā* ADJ. (F. دبلی *dub'lī*) lean lank thin gaunt weak دبلا پتلا

dūb'la pat'la ADJ. (F. دبلی پتلی dūb'li pat'li) lean lank thin, gaunt weak دبلا پن dūb'la pan N.F leanness thinness weakness

دبنا dab'na V.I. be pressed down be squeezed. be compressed be suppressed; be quelled restrained be defeated, be overcome; bow down crouch yield be mortified be buried be hard-pressed دب جانا dab' ja'na V.I yield be mortified be suppressed; be quelled be buried (under debris, etc.) دب مرنا dab' mar'na V.I. be crushed to death; be hard-pressed دبو دبو کرنا dab'boo dab'boo kar'na V.I. create a hush-hush atmosphere دبی آگ کریدنا da'bī ag kūred'na V.T. try to stir up (old feud) again دبی زبان سے da'bī zaban' se ADV. in a low voice (say something) timorously دبے پاؤں da'be pa''oṅ ADV. treaking softly; sneakingly دبیل dabail' ADJ. mortified N.M. weakling subordinate

دبنگ dabang' ADJ. (F. دبنگی dabaṅ'gī) stout bulky fat and ugly N.M. bully courageous (person)

دبوچنا daboch'na V.T. seize hold down pounce upon catch آ دبوچنا a daboch'na, جا دبوچنا ja daboch'na V.T. pounce upon hold down دبوچ لینا daboch' le'na V.T. seize clutch catch hold down

دبی dūb'bī N.F. balancing (at tip-cat)

دبیر dabīr' N.M. (arch. or lit.) secretary writer دبیر فلک dabī'r-e fa'lak N.M (the planet) Mercury [A]

دبیز dabīz' ADJ. (of paper, etc.) thick

دبیل dabail' ADJ. & N.M. (see under دبنا V.I. ★)

دپٹ da'paṭ N.F. browbeating swift movement دپٹنا dapaṭ'na V.T. walk quickly browbeat دپٹانا dapṭa'na V.T. cause to move quickly

دت dūt INT. be off; away, begone, avaunt دتکارنا dūtkar'na V.T. (same as دھتکارنا V.T. ★)

دتھونا dithau'na N.M. rag on child's forehead to prevent influence of evil eye

دجال dajjal' N.M. antichrist great deceiver [A ~ دجل]

دجل daj'l N.M. deception: fraud دجل و فریب daj'l-o fareb' N.M. fraud fraudulence [A]

دجلہ dij'lah (col. daj-) N.M. Tigris [A]

دجی dūja' N.M. dark of night dark night بدر الدجیٰ bad'r-ūd-dūja' N.M. full moon in the dark of night luminary [A]

دخان dūkkan' N.M. smoke (rare) steam دخانی dukha'nī ADJ steam (ship, etc.) دخانی جہاز dukha'nī jahaz' N.M. steamer دخانی کل dukha'nī kal N.F. steam engine [A]

دخت dūkh't N.F. (see under دختر N.F ★)

دختر dūkh'tar N.F. daughter girl دخت dūkh't N.F. (ABB. of دختر) daughter girl دخت رز dūkh't-e raz', دختر رز dūkh'tar-e raz' N.F wine [P]

دخل dakh'l N.M. interference, possession meddling access, admission skill knowledge دخل انداز dakh'l-andaz' ADJ meddle-interfering دخل اندازی dakh'l-anda'zī N.F interference meddling دخل بیجا dakh'l-e be-ja' دخل ناجائز dakh'l-e na-ja''iz N.M. trespass unlawful possession interference meddling دخل بالجبر dakh'l bil-jab'r N.M. forcible possession دخل پانا dakh'l pa'na V.I. have access gain admission obtain possession دخل در معقولات dakh'l dar ma'qoolat' N.M. meddling; uncalled for interference دخل در معقولات کرنا dakh'l dar ma'qoolat' kar'na V.T. meddle (with) poke one's nose into others affairs دخل دینا dakh'l de'na V.T. interfere possession دخل نامہ dakh'l-namah N.M. writ of possession document giving right of occupancy دخل یاب ہونا dakhl-yab' ho'na V.I. enter get rights (over) obtain possession دخل یابی dakh'l-ya'bī N.F. entry right (to) obtaining possession [A]

دخمہ dakh'mah N.M. Zoroastrian graveyard [P]

دخول dūkhool' N.M. penetration shoving in entry [A ~ doublet of دخل]

دخیل dakhīl' ADJ. having influence (with or over) occupying; possessing admitted interfering adopted (word) دخیل کار dakhīl' kar N.M. occupancy tenant دخیل کاری dakhīl'-ka'rī N.F. hereditory occupancy (of agrarion land) دخیل ہونا dakhīl' ho'na V.T. & I. interfere meddle کے مزاج میں (بہت) دخیل ہونا ke mizaj' meṅ (bahūt') dakhīl' ho'na V.I. have (great) influence (with or over) [A ~ دخل]

دد dad N.M. beast of prey [P]

ددا da'da N.F. governess

دودھار dūdhar', دودھیل dūdhīl' ADJ. milch (animal) animal giving much milk [~ دودھ]

دودھڑ dūd'dhaṛ N.M. double gain دودھڑ لگنا (یا ہونا) dūd'dhaṛ lag'na (or ho'na) V.I. have one's cake and eat it too

دودھی *dūd'dhī* N.F. teat : pap a herb with milky sap

ددھیال *dadhyāl'* N.F. father's family (of someone) [دادا ~]

دد یا خسر *dad'yā khus'r* N.M. spouses paternal grand father دد یا ساس *dad'yā sās* spouses paternal grandmother [~ دادا]

در۱ *dar* N.M. door gate PREF. in into about درآمد *dar-ā'mad* N.F. (PL. درآمدات *dar-āmadāt'*) import درآمد برآمد *dar-ā'mad barā'mad* N.F. (PL. درآمدات و برآمدات *dar-āmadā't-o bar-āmdāt'*) import and export درآنا *dar ā'nā* V.T. enter ; force entry into penetrate succeed درانداز *dar-andāz'* ADJ. & N.M. slanderer backbiter دراندازی *dar andā'zī* N.F. slander backbiting درباب *dar-bāb'*, دربارہ *dar-bā'rah* PROP. about ADV. with regard to دربان *dar-bān'* N.M. doorkeeper ; gatekeeper jointer دربدر *dar' ba-dar'* ADV. leading a miserable life from door to door ; from pillar to post ; driven from one place to another دربدر پھرنا *dar' ba-dar' phir'nā* V.I. go from door to door be driven from pillar to post lead a tramp's life دربدر خاک بسر *dar' ba-dar' khāk' ba-sar'* PH. miserable leaving a miserable life disgraced دربندی *dar-ban'dī* N.F. lock-out درپردہ *dar-par'dah* ADV. by underhand means secretly privately کے درپے ہونا *ke dar-pai' ho'nā* V.T. be after pursue be in search of press درپے آزار ہونا *dar pa-e āzār' ho'nā* V.I. harass درپے جان ہونا *dar pa''e jān' ho'nā* V.I. be deadly enemy (of) be intend on killing (someone) درپیش *darpesh'* ADV. facing ; confronting placed before ; under consideration under trial before ; in front (of) placed before درپیش ہونا *dar pesh ho'nā* V.I. face ; confront happen ; occur befall be under trial be under consideration درحقیقت *dar haqī'qat* ADV. in fact ; as a matter of fact undoubtedly CONJ. the fact of the matter is درخواست *darkhās't* N.F. application petition request درخواست دینا *darkhās't de'nā* V.I. apply ; submit an application petition ; file a petition درخواست دہندہ (یا کنندہ یا گزار) *darkhās't-dehindah'* (or *kunin'dah* or *guzār'*) N.M. applicant petitioner درخواست کرنا *darkhāst kar'nā* V.I. request implore apply درخور *dar'-khur* ADJ. fit for worth درخور اعتنا *dar'-khur-e e'tina* ADJ. worthy of attention ; worth notice درکار *dar-kār'* ADJ. of use; useful wanted(ly) ; needed(ly) درکار نہ ہونا *dar-kar' na ho'nā* V.I. be of (no) use to ; be (not) wanted by درکنار *dar-kanār'* ADV. apart what to say of درگزر *dar'-gu'zar* N.F. pardon connivance درگزر ہونا *dar'-gū'zar kar'nā* V.I. forgive ; pardon overlook connive (at) درگزر کرنا *dar'-gū'zarna* V.T. give up quit give up as lost hope کے درمیان *ke dar-mayān'* ADV. between among in the centre (of) amidst ; midst ; in the midst of درمیانہ *darmayā'nah* ADJ. central middle middling so so درمیانہ درجہ *darmayā'nah dar'jah* (ped. *-dara'jah*) N.M. inter. class (railway compartment, etc.) درمیانی *darmayā'nī* ADJ. central middle middling so so mean (of two qualities) در و دیوار *da'r-o divār'* N.M. every nook and corner دریں چہ شک *dar-īn' che shak'* INT. undoubtedly too true why not [P]

در۲ *dar* N.M. rate درلگانا *dar lagā'nā* V.T. charge at the rate of

در۳ *dar* SUF. tearing piercing دری *da'rī* SUF. tearing piercing [P ~ دریدن]

دُر۱ *dur'* INT. be off fie upon you دُر دُر (پھٹ پھٹ) *dur' dur* (*phiṭ' phiṭ*) N.F. cries of shame دُر دُر (پھٹ پھٹ) کرنا *dur dur* (*phiṭ' phiṭ*) *kar'nā* V.T. drive away ignominiously دُر دُر ہونا *dur' dur ho'nā* V.I. be driven away ignominiously

دُر۲ *dur* (rare *dur'rah*) N.M. (PL. دُرر *du'rar*) pearl دُرافشاں *dur-afshāṅ'* ADJ. eloquent دُرافشاں ہونا *dur-afshāṅ ho'nā* V.I. speak eloquently دُرافشانی *dur-afshā'nī* N.F. eloquence utterance دُرِ شہوار *dur'r-e shah-vār'* (or *du'r-e*) N.M. large pearl of the first water ; pearl worthy of kings دُرِ مکنون *dur'r-e maknoon'* (or *du'r-e*) N.M. hidden pearl pearl of the first water دُرِ ناسفتہ *dur'r-e nā-s f'tah* (or *du'r-e*) N.M. unbored pearl virgin دُرِ نجف *du'r-e na'jaf* (or *du'r-e*) N.M. precious Najaf stone for beads دُرِ یتیم *dur'r-e yatīm'* (or *du'r-e*) دُرِ یکتا *dur'r-e yak-ta'* (or *du'r-e*) N.M. matchless pearl [A]

درا *darā'* N.F. bell caravan bell بانگ درا *bāṅ'g-e darā'* N.F. ringing of caravan bell call for march [P

دُرّاج *dur'rāj* N.M. partridge [A]

دراڑ *darāṛ'* N.F. creak ; crack ; fissure ; rent

دراز *darāz'* ADJ. & AFFIX. tall high long extended outstretched spread out sprawling درازدست *darāz'-dast* ADJ. high-handed ; oppressive tyrannical درازدستی *darāz'-das'tī* N.F. high-handedness ; oppression ; tyranny درازقد، درازقامت *darāz'-qa'mat, darāz'-qad* ADJ. tall of high stature درازکرنا *darāz' kar'nā* V.T. prolong ; lengthen stretch sprawl درازگوش *darāz'-gosh* N.M. (rare) hare ADJ. long-eared درازہونا *darāz' ho'nā* V.I. lie down take rest lie with legs sprawling زباں دراز zabāń'-darāz' ADJ. impudent; pert ; saucy زباں درازی zabāń-darā'zī N.F. impudence; sauciness درازی darā'zī N.F. height tallness length extension stretching [P]

دراز daraz' N.M. drawers ; underwear panties drawers (of table, etc.) [E]

دراک darrak' ADJ. sagacacious keen-witted [A ~ درک]

درانتی darāń'tī N.F. sickle ہتھوڑا اور درانتی hathauṛā aur darāń'tī N.M. PL. hammer and sickle N.M. these as symbol of Communism

دراہم darā'him N.M. (PL. of درہم dirham N.M. ★)

درایت darā'yat N.F. understanding; knowledge higher criticism [A]

دربار darbār' N.M. (royal or saintly) court (royal or saintly) audience ; lover shrine mausoleum prominent citizen's gathering to meat bureaucrat دربار خاص darbā'r-e khās' N.M. private audience meeting of ruler's privy council دربارداری darbār'-dā'rī N.F. attendance at royal court courtly manners sycophancy دربارداری کرنا darbār'-dā'rī kar'nā V.T. dance attendance upon دربار عام darbā'r-e 'ām' N.M. General audience ; public audience دربار کرنا یا لگانا darbār' kar'nā (or lagā'nā) V.I. hold a court دربار لگنا darbār' lag'nā V.I. (of court) be held (of people) gather at saints shrine, etc. درباری darbā'rī N.M. courtier one entitled to a seat in bureaucrats' gathering ADJ. courtly (of idiom or language) chaste · polished court [P]

درت dū'rat N.F. name of a musical mode (as opposed to بلمپت bilam'pat N.F.)

درج dūr'j N.M. casket [A]

درج dar'j N.M. entry ; writing ; recording درج کرنا dar'j kar'nā V.T. write ; enter ; record ; register insert include نام درج کرنا nām' dar'j kar'nā V.I. enrol enlist admit درج ہونا dar'j ho'nā V.I. be entered in a book ; be record ; be registered ; be written be inserted be included [A]

درجن dar'jan N.F. dozen [E]

درجہ dar'jah (ped. da'rajah) N.M. (PL. درجات darajāt') degree angle ; degree of a circle mark point stage class ; grade compartment plight rank; status درجہ بدرجہ dar'ja ba-dar'jah' ADV. gradually , by degrees step by step according to one's status درجہ بڑھانا dar'jah baṛhā'nā V.T. upgrade honour درجہ گھٹانا dar'jah ghaṭā'na V.T. degrade disgrace [A]

درخت darakh't N.M. tree درخت لگانا darakh't lagā'nā V.I. plant a sapling [P]

درخشاں darakh'shāń ADJ. shining ; luminous resplendent brilliant درخشانی darakhshā'nī N.F. brilliance splendour [P ~ درخشیدن]

درخشندہ darakhshiń'dah ADJ. shining glittering splendid درخشندگی darakhshiń'dagī N.F brightness ; refulgence splendour [P ~ درخشیدن]

درخواست dar-khās't N.F (see under در N.M. & SUF. ★)

درخور dar'-khūr ADJ (see under در ★)

درد dar'd N.M. pain ; ache affliction grief pity commiseration درد آلود dar'd-alood', درد آمیز dar'd āmez ADJ. painful grieved touching ·pathetic درد آمیزی dar'd āme'zī N F. pitiableness درد سر dar'd-e sar' N.M. headache vexation درد شکم dar'd-e shi'kam N.M. colic pain stomach trouble درد کرنا dar'd kar'nā. V.T. pain ache feel compassion for درد گردہ dar'd-e gūr'dah N.M. kidney pain; renal colic درد مند dar'd-mańd ADJ. sympathetic compassionate دردمندی dar'd-mań'dī N.F. sympathy; compassion دردناک dar'd-nāk' ADJ. sad touching ; pitiable heart-rending دردناکی dar'd-nā'kī N.F. sadness pitiableness درد ہونا dar'd ho'nā V. pain ; ache بیدرد be-dar'd ADJ. hard-hearted callous pitiless; cruel بیدردی be'-dar'dī N.F. callousness cruelty ADJ. (col.) cruel (beloved) [P]

درد dūr'd N.F. sediment ; dregs درد تہ جام dūr'd-e teh-e jām' N.F. lees [P]

دردرا dar'darā ADJ. coarsely ground

درز dar'z N.F. crack creak ; fissure

درزی dar'zī N.M. tailor ; seamster dress-maker درزن dar'zan N.F. seamstress ; sempstress dress-maker tailor's wife [P]

درس dar's N.M. lesson lecture درس دینا dar's de'nā V. teach instruct give a lesson or lecture درسگاہ dar's-gāh N M. educational institution school college alma-mater درس لینا dar's le'nā V.I. learn take a lesson درسی dar'sī ADJ. instructional educational [A]

درس da'ras (or da'rs) N.M. (dial.) look , view sight درس دکھانا da'ras dikhā'nā V.T condescend to appear (before) [S]

درست *dūrūst'* ADJ. correct true right fit ; proper safe sound good ; well repaired rectified set right inperfect order درست کرنا *dūrūst' kar'nā* V.T. correct rectify set right put in order mend ; repair adjust درست ہونا *dūrūst' ho'nā* V.I. be set right be corrected be mended be repaired be rectified be adjusted be put in order درستی *dūrūs'tī* N.F. correction amendment reformation repair mending rectitude adjustment accuracy [P]

درشت *dūrūsh't* ADJ. harsh stern fierce coarse ; rough درشتی *durush'tī* N.F. harshness severity sternness fierceness [P]

درشن *dar'shan* N.M. (dial) look ; sight ; view درشنی *dar'shanī* ADJ. (of bill of exchange) payable at sight worthseeing specious درشنی ہنڈی *dar'shanī hūn'ḍī* N.F. bill of exchange payable at sight [S]

درفش *diraf'sh* N.M. flag ; ensign; banner درفش کاویانی *diraf'sh-e kāviyā'nī* N.M. legendary ensign of Iran [P]

درک *dar'k* N.M. understanding comprehension secret approach [A]

درکار *dar-kār'* ADJ. (see under در N.M. & SUF. ★)

درگاہ *dargāh'* N.F. shrine (saint's) mausoleum royal court درگاہ معلی *dargā'h-e mo'al'lā* N.F. elevated court [P]

درگت *dūr'gat* N.F. ill-treatment maltreatment rough handling unfavourable response درگت کرنا *dūr'gat kar'nā* V.T. maltreat درگت ہونا *dūr'gat ho'nā* V.I. be maltreated [~ گت]

درگزر *dar-gū'zar* N.F. (see under N.M. & SUF.★)

درم *d'iram* N.M. (same as درہم N.M. ★)

درماں *darmāṅ'* (col. درمن *dar'man*) N.M. cure ; remedy درد بے درماں *dar'd-e be-darmāṅ'* N.M. incurable malady [P]

درماندہ *dar-māṅ'dah* ADJ. helpless distressed miserable درماندگی *dar-māṅ'dagī* N.F. helplessness distress misery [P ~ در + ماندن]

درماہہ *dar-mā'hah* N.M. monthly payment ; (monthly) salary [P ~ در + ماہ]

درمتی *dūr'matī* N.M. &. ADJ. fool

درمٹ *dūr'mūṭ* N.M. hand implement levelling macadamized roads درمٹ چلانا *dūr'mūṭ chalā'nā* V I level (road) with that implement.

درمن *darman* N.M. (same as درماں N.M. ★)

درمیان *dar-mayāṅ'* (lit. also *dar-mayāṅ'*) N.M. درمیانہ *darmuyā'nah* ADJ., درمیانی *darmayā'nī* ADJ. (see under در N.M. & SUF. ★)

درندہ *dariṅ'dah,* درند *darīrd* N.M. (PL. درندگاں *dariṅ'dagāṅ*) beast of prey ADJ. rapacious ; ravenous ferocious beastly inhuman درندگی *dariṅ'dagī* N.F. rapacity beastliness ferocity [P ~ دریدن]

درنگ *dirang'* N.M. delay hesitation درنگ کرنا *dirang' kar'nā* V.I. delay hesitate dilly-dally [P]

دروازہ *darvā'zah* N.M. door gate دروازہ بند کرنا یا بھیڑنا *darvā'zah band' kar'nā* (or *bheṛ'nā*) V.I. close or shut the door دروازہ کھٹکھٹانا *darvā'zah khaṭkhṭa'nā* V.I. knock at the door دروازہ کھولنا *darvā'zah khol'nā* V.I. open the door دروازے کی مٹی لے ڈالنا *darvā'ze kī maṭ'ṭī le ḍāl'nā* V.T.&I. pay frequent visits (to)

دروبست *da'r-o bas't* ADJ. whole ; entire دروبست حقوق *da'r-o bas't ḥuqooq'* PH. all right and title whatsoever

درود *darood'* N.M. blessing ; benediction salutation prayer درود بھیجنا یا پڑھنا *darood' bhej'nā* (or *paṛh'nā*) V.I. invoke God's blessings on the Holy Prophet [P]

دروغ *darogh'* N.M. lie ; falsehood دروغ برگردن راوی *darogh' bar gar'dan-e rā'vī* PH. I accept no responsibility for the report دروغ حلفی *darogh'-hal'fī* N.F. perjury swearing falsely دروغ حلفی کرنا *darogh'-hal'fī kar'nā* V.I. perjure swear falsely دروغگو *darogh'-go* N.M. liar دروغگو را حافظہ نباشد *darogh'-go rā ḥa'fizah na bā'shad* PROV. falsehood has no legs to stand upon دروغگوئی *darogh'-go'ī* N.F. lying ; falsehood [P]

دروں *darooṅ'* ADV. in within N.M. inside heart conscience [P]

درویش *darvesh'* N.M. mendicant , dervish , 'calender' saint student undergoing a course of Islamic education درویشانہ *darveshā'nah* ADJ. dervishlike poor unassuming saintly درویشی *darve'shī* N.F. poverty mendicancy saintliness disgust of lay life

دره *da'rah* (or *dar'rah*) N.M. pass ; mountain pass ; glen ; lane valley

دره¹ *dūr'rah* (ped. *dir'rah*) N.M. whip ; scourge [P]

دره² *dūr'rah* N.M. (same as در *dūr* N.M. ★)

درہم dir'ham, درم di'ram N.M. drachm small silver coin ; drachm ; drachme money درہم و دینار dir'ham-o dīnār' N.M. PL. money [A ~ G]

درہم dar'-ham ADJ. jumbled confused ; confounded upset درہم برہم dar'-ham bar'-ham ADJ. topsy-turny jumbled confused ; confounded disarranged upset lying in a state of mess درہم برہم کرنا dar'-ham bar'-ham kar'nā V.T. upset درہم برہم ہونا dar'-ham bar'-ham ho'nā V.I. be upset lie in a state of a mess [P]

دری[1] da'rī N.F. cotton carpet ; 'durrie' bed cover

دری[2] da'rī N.F. name of an old Persian dialect name of the chaste Persian spoken in Tajikistan [P]

دریا daryā' N.M. river (lit. & rare) sea ; waters دریا اترنا daryā' ū'tarnā V.I. (of river) recede دریا برد daryā'-būr'd ADJ. (of land) diluvial; washed away by the river N.F. diluvium inundated دریا برد ہو جانا daryā'-būr'd ho jā'nā V.I. (of land) be washed away by river دریا چڑھنا daryā'-chaṛh'nā V.I. (of river) be in spate ; inundate دریا دل daryā'-dil ADJ. large-hearted generous; liberal municificent magnanimous دریا دلی daryā'-dilī N.F. largeheartedness generosity ; liberality ; munificence magnanimity دریا کوزے میں بند کرنا daryā' koo'ze meṅ band' kar nā V.I. say much in a few words attempt the impossible نیکی کر دریا میں ڈال ne'kī kar daryā' meṅ ḍāl' PROV. accept no return for the good you have done دریا میں رہنا مگرمچھ سے بیر daryā' meṅ raihnā ma'gar-machh' se bair PROV. it is hard to reside in Rome and quarrel with the Pope دریائے شور daryā'-e shor' N.M. sea ; ocean عبور دریائے شور 'ūboo'r-e daryā'-e shor' ADV. overseas N.M. transportation (for life) دریائی daryā''ī ADJ. aquatic marine riverain ; riverine ; riparian دریائی گھوڑا daryā''ī gho'ṛā N.M. hippopotamus ; hippo [P]

دریافت dar-yāf't N.F. discovery inquiry investigation detection discernment دریافت کرنا dar-yāf't kar'nā V.T. discover find out inquire investigate detect to discern ascertain دریافت ہونا dar-yāf't ho'nā V.I. be discovered be detected be ascertained be found out [~ در + یافتن]

دریائی daryā''ī N.F. starting pull given to kite a kind of silk cloth now out of fashion ADJ. (see under دریا N.M. ★)

دریبہ darībah N.M. betel-market

دریچہ darī'chah N.M. window casement [P]

دریز darīz' N.F. printed muslin

دریدہ darī'dah ADJ. torn rent دریدہ دہن darī'da-da'han ADJ. impudent ; pert ; saucy [P ~]

دریڑا dare'ṛā N.M. (dial.) forceful current (of river) downpour

دریس darais' ADJ. fallen in line alert دریسی کرنا darai'sī kar'nā V.T. & I. line , dress level ground [~E dress]

دریغ daregh N.M. regret grudge denial; refusal hesitation INT. ah ; alas دریغ آنا daregh' ā'nā V.I. rue; regret دریغ رکھنا daregh' rakh'nā V.T. be grudging in with hold from; refuse hesitate دریغ کرنا daregh' kar'nā V.T. be grudging in withhold from sigh regret doing ; refuse [P]

دریوزہ daryoo'zah N.M. beggary ; begging دریوزہ گر daryoo'za-gar N.M. beggar medicant دریوزہ گری daryoo'za-garī N.F. beggary ; begging mendican [P]

دڑبا darbā, دڑبہ dar'bah N.M. pigeon-house (dove-)cote (hen-) coop

دربڑانا darbaṛa'nā V.T. give the lie to

دڑنگا daṛań'gā N.M. long step baste دڑنگے لگانا daṛange lagā'nā V.I. leap rove baste

دزد dūz'd N.M. thief ; burglar robber ; highwayman ; footpad دزد حنا dūz'd-e ḥinā' N.M. spot missed by henna in dying hands, etc. دزدی dūz'dī N.F. theft burglary robbery دزدیدہ dūzdī'dah ADJ. stolen pilfered sly دزدیدہ نظر (نگاہ) duzdī'da-na'zar (or -nigāh') N.F. sly look side glance ADJ. looking askance at دزدیدہ نگاہی dūzdīda-nigā'hī N.F. sly looks looking askance [P]

دس das ADJ. ten دس گز کی زبان das' gaz kī zabān' N.F. pertness ; sauciness دسوں انگلیاں دسوں چراغ da'soṅ ūṅgliyāṅ da'soṅ chirāgh PH. accomplished (young lady)

دساتیر dasātīr' N.M. constitutions (of countries) (rare) modes ; methods [A ~ SING. دستور]

دساور disā'var N.M. foreign country foreign market دساوری disā'varī foreign imported N.M a superior quality of betel-leaf دساوری مال disa'varī māl' N.M. imported stuff [~ دیس]

دسپنا das'panā, دست پناہ dast-panāh' N.M. pair of tongs [P + دست + پناہ]

دست dast N.M. watery motion animal's foreleg دست آور das't-ā'var ADJ. purgative ; cathartic

دست dast N.M. hand cubit power دست آموز das't āmoz' trained (bird) مرغ دست آموز mūr'gh-e das't-āmoz' N.M. (fig.) stooge decay دستاویز N.F. ★ دست آنا dast ā'nā V.I. have a watery motion دست اندازی das't-andā'zī N.F. interference exercise of authority cognizance قابل دست اندازی پولیس qābi'l-e das't-āndā'zī-e pūlis' ADJ. cognizable (offence) دست اندازی کرنا dast-andā'zī kar'nā V.T. interfere exercise the authority دست بدست das't ba-das't ADJ. hand-to-hand (fight etc.) دست بدعا ہونا das't ba-do'ā' ho'nā V.I. pray دستبرد das't-būr'd N.F. usurpation exploitation extortion encroachment کی دستبرد سے بچنا (یا محفوظ رہنا) kī das't-būr'd se bach'nā (or mahfooz raih'nā) V.I. escape being exploited by دستبردار ہونا das't-bar-dār' ho'nā V.I. quit ; give up reliquish retire abstain (from) wash one's hand withdraw (from) renounce دستبرداری das't-bar-dā'rī N.F. withdrawl renunciation دست بستہ das't-bas'tah ADV. humbly respectfully with folded hands دست بوسی کرنا das't bo'sī kar'nā, دست بوس ہونا das't-bos' ho'nā V.T. kiss the hands (of) ; to salute دست پناہ das't-panāh' N.M. (same as دسپنا ★) دستخط das't-khat N.M. signature دستخط کرنا das't-khat kar'nā V.T. sign endorse دستخطی das't-khā'tī ADJ. signed endorsed زیر دستخطی zer-das't-khā'tī N.M. the undersigned دست خود دہان خود das't-e khūd dahā'n-e khūd PH. help yourself (or yourselves) to it دست دراز das't-darāz' ADJ. indulging invidence oppressive violating دست درازی das't-darā'zī N.M. violence oppression violation (of honour etc.) دست درازی کرنا das't-darā'zī kar'nā V.T. indulge in violence oppress violate (the chastity of) دسترس dast'-ras N.F. reach power دست شفا das't-e shifā' N.M. kill in medicine دست غیب das't-e ghaib' N.M. supernatural financial help to saints (usu. in form of money found under prayer-mat etc.) دست قدرت das't-e qūd'rat N.F. providence nature's work ability دستکار das't-kār N.M. handicraftsman artisan دستکاری das't-kā'rī N.F. handicraft needlework دستگاہ das't-gāh' N.F. skill ; ability دست گردان das't-gar'dān N.M. current loan ; loan for a very short term دستگیر das't-gīr' N.M. helper also پیر دستگیر pī'r-e das't-gīr' appellation of the well known saint Hazrat Abdul Qadir Jilani دستگیری das't-gī'rī N.F. help دست نگر das't-ni'gar ADJ. dependant (on) in need; needy دست وگریباں ہونا das't-o gire'bān ho'nā V.T. fight be engaged in combat دستیاب das't-yāb' ADJ. available دستیاب ہونا das't yāb ho'nā V.I. be available (with) be procured دستیابی das't-yā'bī N.F. availability procurement دستیاری das't-yā'rī N.F help ; support [P]

دستار dastār' N.F. turban دستار بندی dastār'-ban'dī N.F. convocation function for honouring (learned man, student, etc.) by tying turban round his head giving academic robes (to student) on qualify final examination such function for formalizing succession دستار فضیلت dastā'r-e fazī'lat N.F. turban of honour a diploma at Convocation) [P]

دستانہ dastā'nah N.M. glove gauntlet [P ~ دست]

دستاویز das't-āvez' N.F. document deed bond certificate note دستاویز انتقال das't-āve'z-e intiqāl' N.F. transfer deed mutation certificate دستاویز بیع بالوفا das't āve'z-e bai bil-vafā' N.F. deed of conditional sale دستاویز ضمانت das't-āve'z-e zamā'nat N.F. bail-bond دستاویز لادعویٰ das't-āve'z-e lā da''vā N.F. deed of renunciation جعلی دستاویز ja''lī das't-āvez' N.F. forged document [P ~ دست hand + آویختن hang]

دسترخوان das'tarkhān' N.M. table cloth piece of cloth spread on ground for serving dishes on meals thus served dishes دسترخوان بچھانا das'tarkhān bichhā'na V.T. lay the table دسترخوان بڑھانا dastarkhān baṛhā'na V.T. clear the table کا دسترخوان کھلا ہونا kā das'tarkhān khū'lā ho'nā V.I. keep open house ; be liberal in entertaining [P]

دستک das'tak N.M. knock (at the door) دستک دینا das'tak de'nā V.T. knock at the door دستکی das'takı N.F. note-book falconer's glove handle (of trunk, etc.) [P + دست]

دستور dastoor' (or dūstoor') N.M. (PL. دساتیر dasātīr') constitution custom ; manner; mode fashion procedure usage practice rule; regulation code; manual دستور اساسی dastoo'r-e asā'sī N.M. constitution rules and regulations دستور العمل dāstoo'r-ūl 'a'mal N.M. rules of procedure 'modus operandi' rules and regulations code ; manual دستور ساز dastoor'-sāz ADJ. constituent (assembly) مجلس دستور ساز maj'lis-e dastoor'-sāz N.F. Constituent Assembly دستوری dastoo'rī ADJ. constitutional customary N.F. (broker's or servants) commission fees perquisites [A ~ P]

دستہ das'tah N.M. handle sheat of twent, four hilt quire (of paper) (arrow) bouquet or nosegay (of flowers) detachment (of army) squadron (of aircraft) (police)

posseor contingent pestle دستہ گل das't -e gŭl, گلدستہ gŭl das'-tah N.M. bunch of flowers nosegay bouquet [P]

دستی das'tī ADJ. by hand manual hand-prepelled stand N.F. portable torch portable pen-case handled vessel name of wrestling trick physical exercise with hands pressed each against the other handkerchief [P ~ دست hand]

دسمبر disam'bar N.M. December [E]

دسہرہ dasaihrah, دسہرا dasaih'ra N.M. Hindu festival of tenth Ranvar' at which Ceylonese ruler Ravana's effigies are burnt in public [S]

دسیسہ کاری dasī'sa-kā'rī N.F. intrigue fraud [P ~ A]

دشت dash't N.M. desert arid plain wood ; forest ; jungle دشت پیما dash't-paimā,' دشت گرد dash't-gar'd, دشت نورد dash't-navar'd N.M. wanderer traveller دشت گردی، دشت پیمائی dash't-paimā'ī dash't-gar'dī دشت نوردی dasht-navar'dī N.F. wandering travelling across the desert ; desert-travel دشتی dash'tī ADJ. wild savage forest ; of the forest [P]

دشمن dūsh'man N.M. enemy; foe adversary; antagonist دشمن زیر پا dūsh'man zer-'e pā' INT. (on wearing new pairs of shoes) may your foes be tramplled by your foes دشمن سوئے نہ سونے دے dush'-man so''e na so'ne de PROV. an enemy is a constent spy جانی دشمن jā'nī dūsh'man N.M. deadly enemy ; mortal foe دلی دشمن di'lī dūsh'man N.M. an enemy at heart ; a hidden enemy دشمنی dūsh'manī N.F. enmity hostility malice ; hatred ; rancour دشمنی پڑنا dūsh'manī paṛ'na V.I. (of enmity) be bred (between) دشمنی ڈالنا dūsh'manī ḍāl'na V.T. sow seeds of enmity [P]

دشنام dūshnām' N.F. abuse ; invective swear word دشنام طراز dūshnām' tirāz' ADJ. foul-mouthed دشنام طرازی dūsh'nām-tirā'zī N.F. burling abuses of swearing at resort to abusive language [P]

دشنہ dash'nah N.M. dagger [P]

دشوار dūshvār' ADJ. difficult hard arduous دشوار تو یہ ہے dūshvār' to yeh' hai PH. the difficulty is; the trouble is دشواری dūshvā'rī N.F. difficulty hardship [P]

دعا do'ā' N.F. (PL. ادعیہ ad''iyah) prayer invocation wish blessing ; benediction compliments regard's دعائے خیر do'ā'-e khair' N.F. blessing ; benediction bless دعا دینا do'ā' de'nā V.I. give a blessing دعا سلام do'ā' salām salutations regards ; compliments دعا سلام کہنا do'ā' salām' kaih'nā V.I. send one's compliments (to دعا مانگنا do'ā' māng'nā V.I. pray ; invoke blessing دعا گو do'ā'-go N.M. well-wisher one who prays for دعائیہ do'ā'iy'yah ADJ. benedictory comprising prayer دعائیہ کلمات do'āiy'yah kalimāt' N.M. PL. benedictory words بد دعا bad do'ā' imprecation curse ; anathema [A]

دعاوی da'ā'vī N.M. PL. law-suits demands claims [A ~ SING. دعوی]

دعوت da''vat N.F. treat ; feast banquet repast entertainment invitation convocation call دعوت جنگ da''vat-e jang N.F. proclamation of war دعوت شیراز da''vat-e shīrāz' N.F. homely repast دعوت صلح da''vat-e sŭl'ḥ N.F. call for peace دعوت کرنا da''vat kar'nā V.T. invite give a feast ; throw a party دعوت ولیمہ da''vat-e valī'mah N.F. post-marital feast at groom's house [A]

دعوی da''vā N.M. law-suit charge ; accusation pretension claim ; demand assertion reiteration دعوی بیدخلی da''vā-e be-dakh'lī N.M. action for dispossession ; ejectment suit دعوی بلا دلیل da''vā bi-lā dalīl' N.M. unsupported claim دعوی جمانا da''vā jamā'na V.T. assert one's claim دعوی خارج کرنا da''vā khā'rij kar'na V.T. dismiss a suit دعویدار da''ve-dār' (arch. دعوی دار da''va-dār') N.M. claimant plaintiff pretender (to some office) دعوی شفعہ da''vā-e sh f''ah N.M. pre-emption claim دعوی مہر da''va-e maih'r (ped. mah'r) N.M. claim to dower دعوی وراثت da''vā-e virā'sat N.M, claim to inheritance بیجا دعوی be-jā da''va N.M. baseless assertion ; unfounded claim زائد المیعاد دعوی za''id-ŭl-mī'ād da'vā N.M. time-barred claim [A]

دغا da'ghā N.M. fraud ; deception ; deceit delusion treachery betrayal treason desertion دغا باز da'ghā-bāz' ADJ. deceitful ; fraudulent betraying treacherous betrayer traitor imposter دغا بازی da'ghā-bā'zī N.F. trickery deceitfulness ; fraud treachery betrayal imposture دغا دینا (یا کرنا) da'ghā de'nā (or kar'nā) V.T. deceive ; defraud to cheat act treacherously betray [P]

دغدغانا daghdaghā'nā V.I. glitter flush دغدغاہٹ daghdaghā'hat N.F. glitter flush

دغدغہ dagh'dagha (col. دگدگا dag'dagā) N.M. fear; dread ; danger ; apprehension tumult N.F. a kind of small candle

دغل da'ghal N.M. hypocrisy ruining the party from inside اہل دغل aih'l-e da'ghal N.M. PL. false adherents to cause [A]

دغنا dagh'nā V.I. (of gun) be fired [~ داغنا]

دغیلا daghī'lā ADJ. rotten spotted [~ داغ]

دف daf N.M. 'daf' ; a small tambourine دف بجانا daf' bajā'nā V.I. play on the small tambourine ; play on the 'daf' دفالی dafā'lī N.M. 'daf' player

دفاتر dafā'tir N.M. PL. offices departments [A ~ SING دفتر]

دفاع difā'' N.M. defence دفاعی difā''ī ADJ. defence [A ~ دفع]

دفان dafān', دفع دفان da'fā dafān', دور دفان door dafān', دفان دور dafān' door' ADV. & INT. (dial.) be off دفان ہونا dafān' ho'nā V.I. (dial.) be off make (oneself) scarce [~ A دفع CORR.]

دفائن dafā''in N.F. PL. buried treasures [A ~ SING. دفن ~ دفینہ]

دفتر daf'tar N.M. (PL. دفاتر dafā'tir) office department establishment volume tome long letter register record دفتری daf'tarī ADJ. official beaurocratic N.M. book binder stationery keeper ; official in charge of stationery دفتری حکومت daf'tarī hukoo'mat N.F. bureaucracy دفتری کارروائی daf'tarī karravā''ī N.F. real-tape ; action in line with official procedure

دفتی daf'tī N.M. straw board boards for using the two sides of book's binding

دفع daf'' N.M. warding off prevention repulsion دفع الوقتی daf''-ul-vaq'tī N.F. beguiling the time دفع دفان da'fā dafān' ADV. & INT. (see under دفان ADV. & INF. ★) دفع کرنا daf'' kar'nā V.T. avert repel ward off prevent dispel turn back rout send away دفع ہونا daf'' ho'nā V.T. turn back be driven away be roured be recalled [A]

دفعہ daf''ah N.F. section ; clause ; article turn time ; moment detachment دفعتہً daf'a'tan ADV. suddenly ; all of a sudden دفعدار daf''a-dār' (col. da'fe-dār) N.M. cavalry N.C.O. 'Daffadar' کئی دفعہ ka''ī daf''ah, کتنی دفعہ kit'nī daf'ah ADV. repeatedly on several occasions [A]

دفعیہ daf'iy'yah N.M. remedy prevention repulsion end ADJ. curative preventive [A ~ دفع]

دفن daf'n ADJ. buried ; interred N.M. (rare) burial ; interment دفن کرنا daf'n kar'nā V.T. bury ; دفن ہونا daf'n ho'nā V.I. be buried ; be interred دفنانا dafnā'nā V.T. bury ; inter [A]

دفینہ dafī'nah N.M. (PL. دفائن dafā''in) buried treasure ; treasure-trove

دق diq N.F. pulmonary ; tuberculosis ; consumption ; hectic fever ADJ. vexed pestered teased ; termented دق کا مریض diq' ka marīz' N.M. tuberculous ; tubercular patient دق کرنا diq' kar'nā V.T. tease ; torment to vex . annoy دق ہونا diq' ho'nā V.T. be vexel ; be annoyed ; be irritated be teased ; be termented

دقائق daqā''iq N.M. PL. minutes points subtleties [A ~ SING. دقیقہ]

دقت diq'qut N.F. difficulty ; trouble intricacy ; abstruseness minute point ; delicate point nicety ; subtlety دقت میں پڑنا diq'qat men par'nā V. to get into trouble ; to be involved in difficulty دقت نظر diq'qat-e na'zar N.F. minuteness perspicacity [A]

دقیانوسی daqyānoo'sī ADJ. outmoded ; obsolete [~ A دقیانوس ~ G Diogenes]

دقیق daqīq' ADJ. subtle minute delicate fine obstruse [A ~ PREC.]

دقیقہ daqī'qah N.M. (PL. دقائق daqā''iq) minute particle triffling matter delicate question nicety دقیقہ فروگزاشت نہ کرنا daqī'qah firo'-gūzāsh't na kar'nā V.T. leave no stone unturned

دقیقہ رس daqī'qa-ras ADJ. quick-witted; intelligent subtle ; shrewd دقیقہ رسی daqī'qa-ra'sī N.F. subtlety shrewdness ; quick-wittedness [A ~ دقت ~ دقیق]

دکان dūkān' (ped. dūkkān') N.F. (PL. دکاکین dakākīn) shop دکان بڑھانا (یا بند کرنا) dūkān' barhā'na (or band kar'nā) V.T. close the shop دکان چلانا dūkān chalā'na V.I. run a shop دکان چلنا dūkān' chal'nā V.I. have a good sale ; have thriving business ; have good custom دکاندار dūkān'-dār' (or dū'kan-) N.M. shopkeeper دکانداری dūkān'-dā'rī (or kan-) shopkeeping business دکان کرنا dūkān' kar'nā V.I. run a shop ; open a shop دکان کھولنا dūkān' khol'nā V.T. run a shop open (one's) shop دکان لگانا dūkān' lagā'nā V. open (one's) shop [A]

دکڑی dūk'rī N.F. two-horse carriage same as . ڈکی N.F. ★

دکھ dūkh N.M. suffering ; affliction misery distress trouble دکھ اٹھانا dukh ūthā'na V.I. bear pain be afflicted undergo suffering دکھ بٹانا dūkh batā'na V.I. sympathise (with) share (someone's) sorrow دکھ بھرنا (یا بھوگنا) dūkh bhar'nā (or bhog'nā) V.I. suffer misfortune labour دکھ دینا dūkh de'na V.T. tornment bring suffering دکھ سکھ dūkh sūkh N.M. pains and pleasures ups and downs of life , vicissitude of fortune دکھ کا مارا dūkh' ka ma ra ADJ miserable ; wretched afflicted unfortunate unlucky دکھانا dūkhā'na V.T. hurt grieve دکھنا dūkh'na V.I. pain ache smart دکھڑا dūkh'ra N.M. suffering ; affliction grievance

دکھڑا (یا دکھڑے) رونا *dūkh'ṛā* (or *dūkh're*) *ro'nā* V.I. vent one's grievance(s); tell one's tale of woe دکھی *dūkhī* ADJ. & N.M. (F. دکھیا *dūkh'yā*) ADJ. & N.M. دکھیارا *dūkhyā'ra*) ADJ. & N.M. (F. دکھیاری ADJ. & N.F. afflicted; in distress or pain sorrowful; sad

دکھانا *dikhā'nā* V.T. show exhibit display evince دکھاوا *dikhāvā*, دکھاوٹ *dikhā'vaṭ* N.F. show ostentation دکھائی *dikhā''ī* N.F. (rare) sight دکھائی دینا *dikhā''ī de'nā* V.I. appear be seen be sighted be able to see دکھائی نہ دینا *dikhā''ī na de'nā* V.I. not to be seen not to be sighted be unable to see be blind دکھلانا *dikhlā'nā* V.T. cause to show دکھلاوا *dikh'lā'vā* N.M. (same as دکھاوا N.M. ★)

دکھڑا *dūkh'ṛa* N.M. misfortunes; calamities; troubles دکھڑا رونا *dūkh'ṛa ro'nā* V. relate (one's) tale of woes [~ دکھ]

دکھلانا *dikhla'nā* V.T. (see under دکھانا V.T. ★)

دکن *da'kan* N.M. the Deccan south دکنی *da'kanī* ADJ. southern of the Deccan N.F. Old Urdu [~FOLL.]

دکھن *dak'khan* N.M. south دکھنی *dak'khanī* ADJ. southern دکھنا *dak'khinā* N.F. southern wind; south wind

دکی *dūk'kī* دکڑی، *dūk'ṛī* N.F. two (at cards) [~دو]

دگانہ *dūgā'nah* N.M. same as دوگانہ N.M. (see under دو ★)

دگدا *dug'dā* N.F (same as دبدھا N.M. ★)

دگدگا *dag'daga* N.M. (CORR. دغدغہ N.M. ★)

دگدگی *dug'dūgī* N.F. throat دگدگی میں دم ہونا *dug'dūgī meṅ dam ho'nā* V.T. be on the verge of death

دگر *di'gar* ADJ. other another second time ADJ. again دگرگوں *di'gar-goon* ADJ. altered; changed deteriorated miserable (of condition) likely to end in death [P]

دگلہ *dag'lah*, دگلا *dag'lā* N.M. loose quilted coat

دگنا *dūg'nā* ADJ. double twofold [~دو+ گن *gūna*]

دل *dil* N.M. heart courage mind wish soul conscience generosity; liberality magnanimity دل آرا *dil-ārā'* ADJ. heart adorner beloved N.M. sweetheart دل آرام *dil-ārām'* ADJ. beloved heart soother N.M. sweetheart دل آزار *dil-āzār'* ADJ. heart breaking tormenting vexing cruel دل آزاری *dil-āzā'rī* N.F. heart-breaking torent vexations cruel دل آزردگی *dil-āzūr'dgī* N.F. heart breaking sorrow دل آزردہ *dil-āzūr'dah* (ADJ. & N.M. PL. دل آزردگان *dil-āzūr'dagān*) sad broken heartec دل آنا *dil' ā'nā* V.I. fall in love (with) دل آویز *dil-āvez'* ADJ. attractive; captivating, pleasing دل آویزی *dil-āve'zī* N.F. attractiveness; attraction; allurement دل اٹکنا *dil a'ṭaknā* V.I. fallen in love (with) be captivated (by) دلاسا *dil-ā'sa* N.M. consolation encouragement دلاسا دینا *dilā'sa de'nā* V.T. console encourage دل اچاٹ ہونا *dil ūchāṭ ho'nā*, دل اچٹنا *dil ū'chaṭnā* V.I. be disgusted (with) grow weary (of) دل امنڈنا *dil' ū'manḍnā* V.I. feel like crying دلاور *dil ā'var* ADJ. & N.M. (PL. دلاوراں *dilā'varāṅ*) brave courageous valiant bold; intrepid دلاوری *dil-ā'varī* N.F. bravery courage valour boldness interpidity دل باغ باغ ہونا *dil bāgh' bāgh' ho'nā* V.I. be highly pleased دل باندھنا *dil bāndh'nā* V.T. encourage دل بیٹھنا *dil' baiṭh'nā* V.I. be dispirited be disgusted دلبر *dil'-bar* N.M. heart-ravisher beloved; sweetheart ADJ. heart-ravishing lovely دلبری *dil'-ba'rī* N.F. loveliness being a beloved دل برا کرنا *dil bu'ra kar'nā* V.I. be displeased be disperited take (something) ill; take offence دل برا ہونا *dil bu'ra ho'nā* V.I. be displeased take offence; take umbrage be dispirited feel sick; feel like vomiting دل برداشتہ ہونا *dil-bar-dash'tah ho'na* V.T. be disgusted (with) be fed up with; have one's heart in one's boots دل بڑھانا *dil baṛhā'na* V.T. encourage دلبستگی *dil-bas'tgī* N.F. attachment love affection ADJ. affectionate دلبند *dil band'* N.M. son فرزند دلبند *farzan'd-e dil-band'* N.M. affectionate son دل بھر آنا *dil bhar ā'nā* V.I. be on the verge of weeping; feel like crying دل بھر جانا *dil' bha'r jā'nā* V.I. feel satiated be sick of دل بہلانا *dil' baihlā'nā* V.T. amuse divert entertain دل بہلنا *dil' bai'halnā* V.I. be amused be diverted دل بیٹھ جانا *dil baiṭh' jā'nā* V.I. (of heart) sink have (one's) heart in one's mouth دلپسند *dil pasand'* ADJ. after (one's) heart دلپذیر *dil pazīr* ADJ. agreeable pleasant دلپذیری *dil-pazī'rī* N.F. agreeableness دل پھٹنا *dil phaṭ'nā* V.I. be grieved be shocked دل پھرنا *dil phir'nā* V.I. be disgusted feel sick (of) دل پھنسنا *dil phans'nā* V.T. fall in love (with) be captivated by دل پھیرنا *dil pher'nā* V.T. disgust effect a change of heart دل تڑپنا *dil ta'ṛapnā* V.I. be dying (for) be anxious (for) دلتنگ *dil-tang* ADJ. niggardly; miserly; close-fisted sad distressed disgusted دلتنگی *dil-tan'gī* N.F. miserliness distrust disgust دل توڑنا *dil toṛ'nā* V.T. break 'someone's) heart ; dishearten discourage disappoint mortify دل ٹوٹنا *dil ṭooṭ'nā* V.I. be heartbroken دل ٹھکنا *dil ṭhuk'nā* V.T. be inclined (to) دل جلا *dil ja'lā* ADJ. & N.M. afflicted (lover) bold ; courageous lover دلجمعی *dil-jam''ī* N.F. peace of mind ease of mind self-confidence satisfaction ; consolation دلجمعی سے *dil-jam''ī se* ADV. with confidence reassured with all (one's) heart دلجمعی کرنا *dil-jam''ī kar'nā* V.T. satisfy console دل جمنا *dil jam'nā* V.I. (of one's heart) be set upon get used (to) دلجوئی *dil-jo''ī* N.F. bid to please consolation دلجوئی کرنا *dil-jo''ī kar'nā* V.T. console try to please دل چرانا *dil chūrā'nā* . steal the heart abstain (from enterprise) show the white feather evade ; avoid ; shirk steal the heart (of) دلچسپ *dil-chas'p* ADJ. interesting pleasant; entertaining delightful charming دلچسپی *dil-chas'pī* N.F. interest entertainment دلچسپی لینا *dil-chas'pī le'nā* V.I. take or evince interest (in) دلخراش *dil-kharāsh'* ADJ. heart-rending دلخواہ *dil-khāh'* ADJ. desirable حسب دلخواہ *has'b-e dil khāh* ADV. as desired after one's heart دل خوش کرنا *dil khūsh' kar'nā* V.T. & I. please gladden the heart (of) enjoy (oneself) دلدادہ *dil-dā'dah* N.M. lover ADJ. loving ADV. enamoured (of) in love (with) دلدار *dil-dār'* N.M. beloved ; sweetheart ADJ. charming ; captivating دلداری *dil-dā'rī* N.F. solace friendship kindness encouragement دلداری کرنا *dil-dā'rī kar'nā* V.T. console encourage show kindness دل دکھانا *dil dūkhā'nā* V.T. hurt (someone's) feelings دلدوز *dil-doz'* ADJ. heartrending piercing دلدوزی *dil-do'zī* N.F. heart-rending misery دل دہلنا *dil-dai'halnā* V.T. be frightened ; have (one's) heart in one's mouth دلدہی *dil'-dehī* N.F. solace encouragement دلدہی کرنا *dil'-dehī kar'nā* V.T. solace console comfort دل دینا *dil' de'nā* V.I. lose one's heart (to) ; fall in love (with) دل ڈوبنا *dil ḍoob'nā* V.I. (of heart) sink feel enervated be grieved (by recollection of some misfortune) دلربا *dil-rūbā'* N.M. beloved ; sweetheart a kind of guitar ADJ. alluring ; fascinating ; bewitching ; ravishing دلربائی *dil-rūbā''ī* N.F. allurement ; charm دل رکنا *dil rūk'nā* V.I. be disgusted not to feel a liking (for) دل رکھنا *dil rakh'nā* V.I. console encourage دلزدہ *dil'-adah* ADJ. sad دل سنبھالنا *dil sambhāl'nā* V.I. control one's feelings دلسوختہ *dil sokh'tah* ADJ. suffering grieved ; afflicted دلسوختگی *dil-sokh'tagī* N.F. sorrow ; grief دلسوز *dil-soz'* ADJ. pathetic ; touching heart-burning دلسوزی *dil-so'zī* N.F. heart burning sorrow ; grief دل سے *dil' se* ADV. heart and soul دل سے اترنا *dil' se ū'larnā* V.I. be banished (from one's) heart دلشاد *dil-shād'* ADJ. happy glad cheerful دلشکستہ *dil-shikas'tah* ADJ. broken-hearted ; comfortless دلشکن *dil'-shi'kan* ADJ. heartbreaking grievous دلشکنی *dil-shi'kanī* N.F heart-break دلفریب *dil-fareb'* ADJ. charming , fascinating alluring ; enticing lovely ; beautiful دلفریبی *dil-fare'bī* N.F. charm ; allurement fascination دلفگار *dil-figar'* ADJ. mournful grief-stricken دل کا بخار نکالنا *dil kā būkhār' nikāl'nā* V.I. vent one's rage or feelings دل کڑا کرنا *dil' ka'ṛā kar'nā* V.I. harden the heart muster (one's) courage دلکش *dil'-kash'* ADJ. attractive ; charming alluring ; fascinating winning (ways) دلکشا *dil'-kūshā'* ADJ. pleasing ; delightful ; دلکشی *dil'-ka'shī* N.M. charm ; attraction fascination دل کو دل سے راہ ہونا *dil' ko dil' se rāh' ho'nā* V.I. reciprocate (love, etc.) دل کو قرار ہونا *dil' ko qarār' ho'nā* V.I. (of heart) be at ease (بات) دل کو لگنا *(bāt) dil' ko lag'nā* V.I. (of matter) be convincing; appeal to the heart دل کھٹا ہونا *dil khaṭ'ṭā ho'nā* V.I. feel disgusted دل کھٹا میٹھا ہونا *dil khaṭ'ṭā mī'ṭhā ho'nā* V.I. feel a longing for دل کھلنا *dil khil'nā* V.I. feel happy دل کھلنا *dil khūl'nā* V.I. no longer have any reservation دل کی دل میں رہنا *dil' kī dil' meṅ raih'nā* V.I. not to be able give expression to one's feelings دل کی لاگ (یا لگی) *dil kī lāg'* (or *la'gī*) N.F. love دل کے پھپھولے پھوڑنا *dil ke phapho'le phoṛ'nā* V.I. rip up old sores دلگداز *dil-gūdāz'* ADJ. touching; moving ; pathetic دل گردہ *dil gūr'dah* N.M. courage ; guts دلگیر *dil-gīr'* ADJ. sad ; melancholy ; mournful دلگیری *dil-gī'rī* N.F. sorrow دل لگانا *dil lāgā'nā* V.T. be amused (with) fall in love (with) دل لگنا *dil lag'nā* V.I. be amused (with) fall in love (with) دل لگی *dil-la'gī* N.F. amusement jest دل لگی باز *dil-la'gī bāz'* ADJ. & N.M. jocose (person) دل لگی کرنا *dil-la'gī kar'nā* V.I. jest دل لینا *dil-le'nā* V.T. captivate throw a feeler (to) دل مارنا *dil mār'nā* V.T. curb one's passions دل مر جانا *dil mar' jā'nā* V.I. (of passions) be curled for ever دل مسوس کر رہ جانا *dil masos' kar raih jā'nā* V.I. bear patiently ; suffer in silence دل ملنا *dil mil'nā* V.I. have mutual love find (someone) congenial دل موہ لینا *dil moh' le'nā* V.T. charm ; captivate دل میلا کرنا *dil mai'lā kar'nā* V.I. be grieved دل میں آنا *dil' meṅ ā'nā* V.I. be thought دل میں اترنا *dil' meṅ ū'tarnā* V.I. find a response in the heart ; effect دل میں جگہ کرنا *dil' meṅ ja'gah kar'nā* V T. win the heart of دل میں چٹکیاں لینا *dil' meṅ chūṭ'kiyāṅ le'nā* V.I. rouse interest in the heart دل میں چور بیٹھنا *dil' meṅ chor' baiṭh'nā* V.I. have misgivings (about) دل میں ڈالنا *dil meṅ ḍāl'nā* v.t. suggest put it in someone's heart دل میں رکھنا dil' meṅ rakh'nā v.t. keep something secret bear malice about دل میں کانٹا سا کھٹکنا dil meṅ kāṅ'ṭā sā kha'ṭaknā v.i. rankle in the heart دل میں کھلنا dil' meṅ khul'nā v.i. charm ; captivate دل میں گرہ پڑنا dil meṅ gi'reh paṛ'nā v.i. have had blood between دل میں گڑ جانا dil meṅ gaṛ' jā'nā v.i. charm دل میں گھر (یا راہ) کرنا dil meṅ ghar' (or rāh') kar'nā v.t. & i. charm become intimate دلنشین dil-nashīn' adj. impressive دلنشین کرنا dil-nashīn' kar'nā v.t. impress upon the mind دلنواز dil-navāz' adj. kind دلنوازی dil-navā'zī n.f. kindness دل والا dil' vā'lā adj. generous ; brave دل و جان سے di'l-o jān' se adv. willingly heartily دلوں میں فرق آنا di'loṅ meṅ far'q ā'nā v.i. be no longer mutually friendly دل ہاتھ میں لینا dil hāth' meṅ le'nā v.i. win the heart (of) دل ہٹ جانا dil haṭ' jā'nā v.t. no longer like دل ہلانا dil' hilā'nā v.t. move ; affect دل ہلنا dil hil'nā v.i. be moved ; be affected دل ہی دل میں dil' hī dil meṅ adv. in ones heart of hearts secretly ایک دل ہو کر ek' dil' ho kar adv. with one heart like one man unitedly دلی di'lī adj. hearty cordial[P]

دل dal n.m. army crowd thickness دل بادل dal' bā'dal n.m. thick clouds (of)

دلار dūlār' n.m. fondling; caress (usu. as) پیار دلار payār' dūlār' n.m. fondling دلارا dūlā'rā, dūlā'rī adj. darling apple of (one's) eye راج دلارا rāj dūlā'rā n.m. darling son راج دلاری rāj dūlā'rī n.f. darling daughter

دلاسا dilā'sā n.m. solace consolation encouragement دلاسا دینا dilā'sā de'nā v.t. solace console encourage [P ~ آسائیدن + دل]

دلاک dal'lāk n.m. masseur [A ~ دلک]

دلال dal'lāl n.m. broker comission agent pimp ; pander دلالہ dallā'lah n.f. procuress دلالی dallā'lī n.f. brokerage being broker being a pimp ; procuring [A ~ foll.]

دلالت dalā'lat n.f. pointing out guidance indication evidence دلالت کرنا dalā'lat kar'nā v.t. point out denote ; indicate guide be evidence (of) [A ~ دلیل]

دلانا dilā'nā v.t. to cause to give ; to cause to pay ; to assign ; to cause to yield ; to put in possession assign cause to pay cause to give [~ دینا]

دلائی dūlā''ī n.f. light quilt

دلائی لامہ dalā''ī lā'mah n.m. Dalai Lama [Tib.]

دلائل dalā''il n.m. arguments reasons proofs [A ~ sing. دلیل]

دلبا dal'bā n.m. trained bird decoy

دلتی dūlat'tī n.f. (same as دولتی do-lat'tī n.f. ★)

دلدر dalid'dar n.m. penury misfortune ominousness دلدر دور کرنا dalid'dar door kar'nā v.t. end penury or misfortune (of)

دلدل dūl'dūl n.m. (rare) hedgehog name of the Holy Prophet's mule received as gift from Byzantine governor of Egypt and given away to Hazrat Ali

دلدل dal'dal n.f. marsh ; swamp ; bog; quagmire دلدلی dal'dalī adj. marshy ; swampy ; boggy دلدلی زمین dal'dalī zamīn' n.f. marsh swamp

دلق dal'q n.f patched garment sackcloth as mendicant's dress دلق پوش dal'q-posh adj. clothed in rags ; ragged n.m. mendicant [P]

دلکنا dūl'aknā, دلکھنا dūlakhnā v.t. cross (someone) in speech take exception (to) ; object دلکی dūl'kī n.f. trot دلکی جانا (یا چلنا) dūl'kī jā'nā (or chal'nā) v.i. trot

دلنا dal'nā v.t. split (pulse) grind coarsely دلوانا dalvā'nā v.t. cause (pulse) to be split cause to be ground coarsily دلوائی dalvā''ī n.f. remuneration for coarse grinding

دلو dal'v n.m. (rare) bucket Aquarius [A]

دلوانا dilvā'nā v.t. cause to be paid or given [~ دینا double caus.]

دلہن dūl'han n.f. bride newly wedded women [~ دولہا n.m. ★]

دلی dil'ī adj. (see under دل dil n.m. ★)

دلیا dal'yā n.m. half-ground cereal porridge واہ فقیر علیا پکائی تھی کھیر ہو گیا دلیا vāh' faqīr' 'al'yā pakā''ī thī khīr ho' ga'yā dal'yā prov. misfortunes do no come singly

دلیر daler' adj. daring courageous brave valiant intrepid دلیرانہ dalerā'nah adj. hold adv. boldly ; bravely ; intrepidly دلیرانہ اقدام کرنا dalerā'nah iqdām' kar'nā v.i. take a bold step دلیری dale'rī n.m. daring ; courage bravery ; valour boldness [P]

دلیل dalīl' n.f. (pl. دلائل dalā''il) argument reason proof (lit.) guide زوردار دلیل zor'-dār dalīl' n.f. cogent reason بودی دلیل bo'dī dalīl' n.f. flimsy argument دلیل راہ dalī'l-e rāh n.m. guide دلیل پیش کرنا dalīl' pesh' kar'nā v.t. argued adduce argument give reasons (of) bring forward proof دلیل لانا dalīl' lā'nā v. argue adduce argument پر (یا کی) دلیل ہونا par (or kī) dalīl' ho'nā v.i. be a proof (of) [A ~ دلالت]

دلیل dalel' N.F. soldier's penalty parade with full kit on دلیل دینا dalel' de'na V.T. penalize thus

دم ۱ dam N.M. blood دموی da'mavi plethoric [A]

دم ۲ dam N.M. breath gasp puff; pull air leakage life vitality moment edge (of sword, etc.) trick; fraud; coaxing; wheedling existence; sake blowing over (someone) after incantation دما دم da'ma-dam' ADV. continuously; unceasingly دم الٹنا dam' ūlaṭnā V.T. be suffocated be on the last gasp دم باز dam-baz' ADJ. artful; fraudulent, treacherous N.M. deceiver; tricky person دم بخود dam' ba-khūd' ADJ. dubile-founded struck dumb aghast دم بخود رہ جانا (یا ہونا) dam' ba-khūd raih jā'nā (or ho'nā) V.I. be dumbfounded be pertified دم بدم dam' ba-dam ADV. every moment continuously; unceasingly دم بڑھانا dam barhā'nā V.I. practice holding one's breath دم بند کرنا dam band' kar'nā V.T. & I. silence (someone) hold one's breath دم بند ہونا dam band' ho'nā V.I. be suffocated, be choked be unable to speak دم بھرانا dum bharā'nā V.T. (of wrestling instructor) give practice (to trainees) exercise دم بھر dam' bhar N.M. & ADV. a little while دم بھر کو dam' bhar ko ADV. for a moment; for a while دم بھر میں dam' bhar meṅ ADV. in a moment دم بھرنا dam bhar'nā V.T. take sides (with) land; sing praises (of) profess love (for) be fatigu d with exercise, etc. دم پخت dam-pūkh't N.M. stew cooking in pressure cooker دم پھولنا dam phool'nā V.I. gasp; pant be out of breath be exhausted دم توڑنا dam tor'na V.I. breathe one's last; die دم ٹوٹنا dam ṭooṭ'nā V.I. be out of breath دم جھانسا dam jhāṅ'sā N.M. trick; fraud دم چرانا dam churā'nā V.I. feign collapse or death دم چڑھنا dam charh'nā V.I. pant; gasp دم چھوڑنا dam chhoṛ'nā V.I. die show the white feather throw up the sponge دم خشک ہونا dam khūsh'k ho'nā V.I. be afraid دم خفا ہونا dam khafā ho'nā V.I. be choked find it hard to breathe دم خم dam' kham N.M. guts stamina strength; vigour کے دم خم دیکھنا ke dam' kham dekh'nā V.T. see what guts (the adversary) has دم دلاسا dam dil-ā'sā N.M. solace soothing encouragement vain hopes make-believe دم دینا dam de'nā V.T. & I. die be ready to lay down one's life (for) deceive; inveigle stew cook in steam دم رکنا dam rūk'nā V.I. be choked; be suffocated find it difficult to breath دم سادھنا dam sādh'nā V.T. (of ascetic, etc.) hold (his) breath keep mum over دم زدن dam'-za'dan N.M. boasting speaking دمساز dam-sāz' N.M. ADJ. intimate concordant; harmonious supporting assenting N.M. companion friend supporting singer yes-man دم سوکھنا dam sookh'nā V.I. have no courage left be afraid (of) دم تیغ da'm-e tegh, دم شمشیر da'm-e shamshīr' N.M. edge of a sword دم عیسیٰ da'm-e 'ī'sā N.M. quickening or animating influence دم غنیمت ہونا dam' ghanī'mat ho'nā V.I. (of someone's existence) lessing دم فنا ہونا dam fanā' ho'nā V.I. be afraid of (expense, etc.) دم قدم dam' qa'dam N.M. presence existence دم کرنا dam' kar'nā V.T. blow over (someone) after incantation دم کشی dam'-ka'shī ADJ. asthma دم کھانا dam' khā'nā V.I. be duped keep quite pester, badger cooked over light fire دم کھینچنا dam' khench'nā V.I. suspend breath keep main smoke; puff دم لگانا dam' lagā'nā V.T. smoke; have a puff or pull at دم کے دم میں dam' ke dam' meṅ ADV. in a moment; in a jiffy دم گھٹنا dam' ghūṭ'nā V.I. be choked find it difficult to breath دم لینا dam' le'nā V.T. take breath halt rest oneself دم مارنا dam' mar'nā V.I. speak object boast claim دم میں آنا dam' meṅ ā'nā V.I. be duped (by) دم میں دم آنا dam' meṅ dam' ā'nā V.I. feel reassured be relieved come to دم ناک میں آنا dam nāk' meṅ ā'nā, ناک میں دم آنا nak' meṅ dam ā'nā V.I. be harassed be driven to straits دم نکالنا dam ni'kalnā V.T. & I. die grudge (doing something) be dying in love (for) دم نہ مارنا dam' na mār'nā V.I. be unable to protest دم ہونا dam' ho'nā V.I. be cooked in steam دم واپسیں dam-e vā'-pasīṅ N.M. the last gasp [P]

دم dūm N.F. tail end دم چنور dūm chan'var kar'nā V.I. lift the tail moveabout with a raised tail دم چھلا dūm chhal'lā N.M. tail of paper-kite hanger-on stooge دمدار تارا dūm'-dār tā'rā N.M. comet ADJ. دم دبا کر بھاگنا dūm dabā' kar bhāg'nā V.I. turn tail flee; run away sneak away دم گزا d.m' gaz'ā N.M. root of tail ump دم میں گھسنا dūm meṅ ghus'nā V.T. fawn (on) دم ہلانا dūm hilā'nā V.T. wag the tail to be faithful دمچی dūm'chī N.F. tail piece of harness [P]

دمار damār' N.M. death ruin [A]

دماغ dimāgh' N.M. brain gray-matter mind pride vanity wisdom; intellect mental faculty (rare) nose; organ of smell دماغ آسمان (یا عرش) پر ہونا dimāgh āsmān' (or 'arsh) par ho'na V.I. be excessively proud ; suffer from overweening pride دماغ پریشان کرنا dimāgh' pireshān' kar'nā V.I. vex paster bother confuse دماغ چاٹنا dimāgh' chāṭ'nā V.T. bore with prattle دماغ چٹ dimāgh'-chaṭ N.M. & ADJ. talkative (person) . prettier bore دماغ چل جانا dimāgh' chal jā'nā V.I. become crazy دماغ رکھنا dimāgh' rakh'nā V.I. have a good brain be proud دماغ سوزی کرنا dimāgh'-so'zī kar'nā V.T. & I. cudgel one's brains work hard try hard to drive something home to a dance دماغ خالی کرنا dimāgh' khā'lī kar'nā V.I. beat brain to no purpose دماغ دار dimāgh' dār ADJ. proud ; arrogant ; vain دماغ کرنا dimāgh' kar'nā V.I. be vain ; be proud دماغ میں خلل ہونا dimāgh' men kha'lal ho'nā V.I. be insane be mentally deranged . be deranged in mind دماغ ہونا dimāgh' ho'nā V.I. be proud ; be vain خر دماغ khar'-dimāgh ADJ. & N.M. blockhead روشن دماغ rau'shan-dimāgh' عالی دماغ 'ā'lī dimāgh' ADJ. high-minded noble having an open mind intelligent

دماغی dimā'ghī ADJ. mental دماغی پریشانی dimā'ghī pire-pire shā'nī N.F. mental worry خر دماغی khar-dimā'-ghī N.F. blockheadedness ; being a duffer روشن دماغی rau'shan-dimā'ghī, عالی دماغی 'ā'lī-dimā'ghī intelligence nobility open-mindedness [P]

دمامہ damā'mah N.M. kettle-drum (fig.) pomp and glory

دماں damān ADJ. fierce ; truculent [P]

دمانا damā'nā V.T. bend (sword) [~ دمنا]

دماوند damāvand', کوہ دماوند ko'h-e damā vand' N.M. (peak of) the Demavand (a mountain of the Alburz range in Persia) where the mythical tyrant Zahhak was later imprisoned

دمچی dum'chī N.F. (see under دم dum N.F. ★)

دمدمہ dam'damah N.M. parapet ; mound sand-bag shelter entrenchment raised battery beat of drum boom of cannon

دمرک dam'rak N.F. leather piece holding spindle washer

دمڑی dam'ṛī N.F. eighth part of old paisa . a small coin, now long out of use sois دمڑی کے تین تین ہونا dam'ṛī ke tīn' tīn' ho'nā V.I. to sell dirt cheap ; to be reduced to abject poverty go very cheap دمڑی کی گڑیا ٹکا سر منڈائی dam'ṛī kī gūṛ'ya ṭa'kā sir munḍā''ī PROV it is easier to build a new house then to patch and old one what an unfair deal ; how unfair دمڑی کی ہانڈی گئی مگر کتے کی ذات پہچانی گئی dam'ṛī kī hān'ḍī ga''ī ma'gar kut'te kī zāt pahchā'nī ga''ī PROV. little loss resulting in much gain دمڑی کی ہنڈیا لیتے ہیں تو ٹھونک بجا کر لیتے ہیں dam'ṛī kī hanḍ'yā le'te hain to ṭhonk bajā' kar le'te hain PROV. even ordinary take of work needs untelligence [~ دام DIM.]

دمکلا dam'-kalā N.F. pump (arch.) fire engine crane jack sling catapult

دمکنا da'maknā V.I. glitter ; glisten دمک da'mak N.F. glitter ; glisten

دمل dūm'mal N.M. (same as دنبل N.M. ★)

دمن diman' N.F. litter ; rubbish dung heap خضراء الدمن khazrā'-'ud-diman' grass growing on dunghill (of person) mean though outwardly pretty [A]

دمنا dam'nā V.I. (of sword) bend

دموی da'mavī ADJ. (see under دم dam N.M. ★)

دمہ da'mah N.M. asthma [~ P دم]

دمی da'mī N.F. small 'hookah' [~ P دم]

دمیدہ damī'dah ADJ. sprouting blosoming dawned (of wind) blown دمیدگی damī'dagī N.F. blossoming forth blowing [P ~ دمیدن]

دن din N.M. day day-time festival (PL.) age ; period of life (PL.) circumstances (PL.) lot ; fate دن آنا din ā'nā V.I. the time of be the season (for) (of one's day's) be numbered menstruate دن بھاری ہونا din bhā'rī ho'nā V.I. fall on evil days . be in straitened circumstances دن بھر din' bhar ADV. the whole day , all the day long دن پورے کرنا din' poo're kar'nā V.I. pass one's days as best as one can eke out one's existence دن پھرنا din' phir'nā V.I. (of one's circumstances) take a favourable turn دن چڑھنا din' chaṛh'nā V.T. (of sun) rise (of day) break . dawn دن چڑھے din' cha'ṛhe ADV late in the day دن چھپنا din' chhup'nā V.I. (of sun) set دن چھپے din' chhu'pe ADV. at dusk ; aftersunset , at sundown دن دونی رات چوگنی ترقی کرنا din doo'nī rāt chau'-gunī taraq'qī kar'nā V.I. prosper by leaps and bounds دن دہاڑے din dehā'ṛe ADV. in broad daylight دن ڈھلنا din' ḍhal'nā V.I. be late in the day دن ڈھلے din' ḍhā'le ADV. in the afternoon دن عید رات شب برات din 'īd' rāt shab-barāt' PROV. rejoicing by day and night palmy days دن عیش کے گھڑیوں میں گزر جاتے ہیں din 'aish ke ghaṛ'yon men guzar ja'te hain PROV. pleasant hours fly fast دن کاٹنا din kāṭ'nā V.I. pass one's days willy-nilly have a hard time دن کٹنا din kaṭ'nā V.I. (of days) pass دن کو دن اور رات کو رات نہ جاننا (یا سمجھنا) din ko din' aur rāt ko rāt' na jān'nā (or sa'majhnā) V.I. work hard day and night وہ دن (لد) گئے voh din (lad) ga''e PH. these are things of the past دن لگنا din' lag'nā V.I. take time (of mean person) get rich boast brag دن نکلنا din' ni'kalnā V.I. dawn (of sun) rise بڑا دن ba'ṛā din N.M. (dial.) Christmas longer day بڑے دن ba'ṛe din N.M. PL. longer days

دن dan N.F. thud دن سے dan' se ADV. with a thud دنادن da'nā dan N.F. consecutive firing or volley of guns

دنانیر danānīr' N.M. PL. of دینار N.M. ★)

دنایت dana'yat N.F. meanness ; baseness [A]

دنبالہ dumba'lah N.M. tail stern outer corner (of eye) دنبالہ دار dumba'la-dār ADJ. tailed [P]

دنبل dun'bal, دمل dum'mal N.M. boil ; abscess ; bube

دنبہ dum'bah N.M. fat-tailed ram [P]

دنتیلا dan'ti'lā ADJ. one with large teeth [~ دانت]

دندان dan'dān N.M. tooth دندان آز تیز کرنا dandā'n-e āz' tez' kar'na V.I. be very greedy دندان ساز dan'dān sāz N.M. dentist دندان سازی dandān-sā'zī N.F. dentistry دنداں شکن جواب dan'dāṅ-shi'kan javāb N.M. crushing reply [P]

دندانہ dandā'nah N.M. tooth (of saw) cog (of wheel) dent دندانے پڑنا dandā'ne paṛ'nā V.I. become dented [~ P PREC.]

دندنانا dandanā'nā V.I. be in high spirits enjoy full powers move about without let or hindrance

دنکا dun'kā N.M. (see under دانہ ★)

دنگ daṅg ADJ. astonished, wonderstruck دنگ رہ جانا daṅg' raih jā'nā V.I. be astonished

دنگا dan'gā N.M. tumult , riot disturbance breach of the peace melee row ; wrangle دنگا کرنا dan'gā kar'nā V.I. run a riot commit a breach of the peace wrangle دنگئی daṅgā''ī N.M. one who breaks the peach [A ~ ادنی]

دنگل dan'gal N.M. arena ; amphitheatre دنگل لڑنا dan'gal laṛ'nā V.I. have a wrestling bout wrestle

دنگل

دنی da'nī ADJ. mean ; base vile ignoble ; ignominious دنیائے دنی dun'yā-e da'nī N.F. the vile world [A ~]

دنیا dūn'yā N.F. world people mundane life worldly goods pelf ADJ. (rare) lower nether دنیا آنکھوں میں اندھیر ہونا dun'yā āṅ'khoṅ meṅ andher' ho'nā V.I. be rudely shocked suffer great loss have no hope left for the future دنیا بامید قائم dun'yā ba-ummīd' qā''im PH. people live by hope alone دنیادار dun'yā-dār ADJ. worldly N.M. man of the world دنیاداری dun'yā-dā'rī N.F. worldliness concern for matters of the world show of politeness married life one's family دنیا ساز dun'yā-sāz ADJ. crafty showy دنیا کی ہوا لگنا dūn'yā kī havā' lag'nā V.I. come under corrupting influences دنیا کے پردے سے اٹھ جانا dun'yā ke par'de se uṭh jā'nā V.I. die disappear become extincts دنیا و مافیہا dun'yā-o mā' fī-hā N.F. the world and all that is in it دنیاوی dunyā'vī, دنیوی dun'yavī ADJ. world ; worldly [A ~ M. ادنی]

دو do ADJ. TWO PREF. two double دوآبہ do-āb'ah N.M. area bordered lying by two rivers دوآتشہ do ā'tashah ADJ. doubled-stilled wine liquour دو آنسو بہانا do āṅ'soo bahā'nā V.I. weep a little express some sorrow over دواسپہ do-as'pah N.F. two horsed (carriage) دوبارہ do-bā'rah ADV. again twice دوبدو doo-ba-doo' ADV. confronting face to face 'vis-a-vis' دوپایہ do-pā'yah ADJ. two-legged N.M. man liped دوپٹا dūpaṭ'ṭā, دوپٹہ dūpaṭ'ṭah N.M. stole دوپرتا do-par'tā دوپرتہ do par'tah ADJ. two-ply (wood) دوپلڑی do-pal'ṛī N.F. light folding cap دوپہر do-pai'har N.F. noon ; midday بعد دوپہر ba''d do-paihar, دوپہر ڈھلے do-pāi'hār ḍha'le ADJ. 'post meridian' ; p.m. قبل از دوپہر qab'l az do-pāi'har ADJ. antimeridia a m. دوپیازہ do-payā'zah N.M. onioned stew ملا دوپیازہ mul'lā do-payā'zah N.M. appellation of one of the Great Moghul Akbar's courtier famous for repartee etc. دوچھتی do-chat'tī inner gallery ; improvised garret under-flat roof دوتا do-tā ADJ. bent doubled sagging دوتارا do-tā'rā N.M. two-stringed guitar دوتہی do-te'hī N.F. two-folded coverlet دوٹوک do-ṭook' (or ṭok') ADJ. decisive court (reply) flat (refusal) دوٹوک جواب دینا do ṭook' javāb' de'nā V.T. flatly refuse give a curt reply دوجیا do-ji'yā N.F. & ADJ. pregnant (woman) دوجی سے ہونا do-jī se ho'nā V.I be in the family way دوچار do'-chār ADJ & N.M. a few (persons) دوچار duchār' ADV. face to face دوچار ہونا duchār' ho'nā V.T. reply come across دوچند do chand' ADJ. twofold double دودانے کو پھرنا do' dā'ne ko phir'nā V.I. beg from door to door for a crust of bread دو دن کا مہمان do' din kā mehmān' ADJ. short lived transient ; transitory , ephemeral دودھاری do dhā'rī ADJ. double-edged (sword) دوراہہ do rā'hah N.M. bifurcation (of road, etc.) converging or parting of the ways دوراہۂ امید و بیم do rā'ha-e ummī'd-o-bīm N.M. meeting place of hope and fear دورخہ do-rū'khah ADJ. facing both ways same on both sides double faced دورخی do-rū'khī ADJ. 'double-faced (policy) N.F. duplicity دورنگا do-rań'ga ADJ. two-coloured piebald double-dealer ; hypocrite (one) with two different aspects of life دورنگی do'rań'gī ADJ. having two colours with two divers aspects of life N.F. duplicity ; double-dealing ; hypocrisy two divers aspects of life دوروزہ do-ro'zah ADJ. short-lived ; transient ; transitory ephemeral دورویہ do-ro'yah ADJ. two-sided ADV. on both sides right and left دوزانو بیٹھنا do-zā'noo baiṭh'nā V.I. sit on the hams ; sit with folded legs دوسار do-sār' ADV. transfixed دوساکھی do-sākhī دوساہی do-sā'hī N.M. & ADJ. (land) yielding two crops in a year دوسرا dū-sarā' N.F. the world and the hereafter دوسالہ do-sā'lah ADJ. biennial - two-year-old دوسوتی do-soo'tī N.F. cloth with double thread warp and weft ; coarse linen دوسیری do-se'rī N.F. two-seer weigh دوشاخہ do shā'khah N.M. rake two-fork pronged candle stick دوشالہ do-shā'lah N.M. (usu. embroidered) shawl ; double-folded shawl دوشنبہ dū sham'bah N.M. Monday دوطرفہ do-ta'rafah (col. tar'fah) ADJ. two sided mutual reciprocal دوعملی do 'a'malī N.F. dyarchy دوغزلہ do-ghaz'lah (ped. -gha'zalah) N.M two odes in same metre and rhyme دوفصلی do-fas'lī ADJ. & N.F. (land) yielding two crops a year دوکرنا do kar'nā V.T. bisect cut into two دوگاڑا do gā'rā, دوگاڑا dugā'rā N.M. double barrelled gun دوگامہ do-gā'mah N.M. slow paced horse ADV. slowly دوگانہ do-gā'nah, دگانہ dū-gā'nah, دگانا dugā'nā N.M. prayers with two genuflexions supererogatory prayers duet (dial.) copulation ADJ. double دوگانہ ادا کرنا do-gā'nah adā' kar'nā V.I. say supererogatory prayers, (as thanks giving, etc.) دوگونہ do goo'nah ADJ. double دولتی do-lat'tī N.M. (same as دلتی dūlat'tī N.F. ★) دولڑا do la'ṛā' N.M. دولڑی do-la'ṛī N.F. double-stringed necklace دوملاؤں میں مرغی حرام do mūllā''oń meń mūr'ghī ḥarām' PROV. too many cooks spoil the broth دومنزلہ do-man'zila ADJ. (arch. دومحلہ do maiḥ'lā) double-storeyed ; two storeyed double decker دومونہی do mooń'hī (or dūmoo''ī N.F. serpent with a fat tail; two-mouthed serpent دو میں تیسرا آنکھوں میں ٹھیکرا do' meń tīs'rā āń'khoń meń ṭhīk'rā PROV. intruders are always unwelcome دونالی dū-nā'lī ADJ. double barelled (gun) دونوں do'noń ADJ. both; both of ; both the the two ; the two of the twain دونوں وقت ملنا do'noń vaq't mil'nā V.I. be twilight تالی دونوں ہاتھوں سے بجتی ہے tā'lī do'noń hā'thoń se baj'tī hai PROV. it takes two to quarrel دونی dūvan'nī N.F. (old coin worth) one-eighth of rupee · two-anna bit دونیم dū-nīm' ADJ. cut into two ; sundered دوورقی do-va'raqī N.F. booklet ; brochure دوہاجن dohā'jan N.F. دوہاجو dohā'joo N.M. remarried widow(er) دوہتڑ dū-hat'taṛ N.M. slap or stroke with both hands together دوہتڑ مارنا dū-hat'taṛ mār'nā V.T. slap thus express grief by beating one's breast thus دوہتھا do-hat'thā ADJ. (F. دوہتھی do-hat'thī) two-handled

دو dau SUF. running [P ~ دویدن]

دوا doo''ā N.M. (at dice) deuce (in weighing) two (rare) two (at cards) [~ دو]

دوا davā' N.F. (PL. ادویہ ad'viyah) medicine cure ; remedy دوا پینا یا کھانا davā' pī'nā (or khā'nah) V.I. take a medicine دواخانہ davā'-khā'nah N.M. dispensary apothecary's shop ; the druggist's pharmacy دوا دارو davā' dā'roo, دوا درمن davā' dar'man N.F. medical treatment cure ; remedy دوا دارو کرنا davā' dā'roo kar'nā V.T. treat (patient), arrange medical treatment (for) دواساز davā'-sāz N.M. dispenser ; compounder chemist ; druggist pharmacist دواسازی davā'-sā'zī N.F. pharmacy pharmaceutical دوافروش davā'-firosh' N.M. druggist ; chemist دوا کرنا davā' kar'nā V.T. give or undergo medical treatment cure heel find some remedy (for) دوا کو نہ ملنا davā' ko na mil'nā PH. not at all to be available

دواب davāb' N.M. PL. beasts of earth ; quadrupeds [A ~ SING. دابہ]

دوات davāt' N.F. inkpot ; ink قلم دوات qaa'lm davāt N.F. pen and ink

دوادوی da'va'da'vī N.F. bustle [P]

دوار davvār' ADJ. revolving rotating circling moving. [A ~ دور]

دوارا davā'rā, دوار davār' N.M. (dial.) gate place [S]

دوال davāl' N.M. leather srtap lower strap of brassiers

دوال divāl' N.M. one likely to make payment

دوازدہ davāz'dah ADJ. & N.M. (rare) twelve دوازدہم davāz'dahūm ADJ. twelfth [P]

دوالا divā'lā N.M. same as دیوالہ dīvā'lah N.M. ★)

دوام davām' N.M. permanence perpetuity eternity ADV. always perpetually eternally perennially علی الدوام 'alad-davām' ADV. always ; permanently دوامی davā'mī ADJ. lasting permanent constant continual continuous , incessant perennial perpetual eternal [A]

دوان davāń' ADJ. running current ADV running (rare) [~ P دویدن]

دوائر *davā''ir* N.M. PL. circles groups fields [A ~ SING. دائرہ]

دوب *doob* N.F. thickly grown soft grass

دوبھر *doo'bhar* ADJ. burdensome irksome boring

دوج *dooj* N.F. (dial.) second day of lunar fortnight evening of new moon's appearance [~ دو]

دوجا *doo'jā* ADJ. (dial.) second secondary [~ دو]

دوختہ *dokh'tah* SUF. sewn ; stitched fixed (at)

دود *dood* N.M. smoke (fig.) sigh دودِ دل *doo'd-e dil* N.M. sigh دودکش *dood'-kash* N.M. chimney [P]

دودمان *dood'mān* N.M. house ; family ; dynasty دودمانِ عالی (یا عالیہ) *dood' mān-e 'ā'lī* (or *'ā'liyah*) N.M. noble family great dynasty [P]

دودھ *doodh* N.M. milk milky juice (of plant) دودھ بڑھانا (یا چھڑانا) *doodh' baṛhā'nā* (or *chhuṛā'-nā*) V.T wean (baby) دودھ بھائی (یا بہن) *doodh' bhā''i* (or *bai'han*) N.M. (F.) foster-brother (or sister) دودھ بھر آنا *doodh bhar' ā'nā* V.I. feel affection (for) دودھ پلانا *doodh pilā'nā* V.T. suckle دودھ پلائی *doodh-pilā''ī* N.F. wet nurse ; foster-mother دودھ پیتا بچہ *doodh-pī'tā bach'chah* N.M. infant inexperienced person ; green born دودھ دوہنا *doodh doh'nā* V.T. milk دودھ کا دودھ پانی کا پانی *doodh' kā doodh' pā'ni kā pā'ni kar'nā* PH. separate chalk from cheese despense justice expose falsehood دودھ کا رشتہ *doodh' kā rish'tah* N.M. foster-relation دودھوں نہاؤ پوتوں پھلو *dood'hon nahā''o poo'ton phalo* INT. (to woman) may God bless you with progany and health to rear it دودھار *doodhār*, دودھل *doo'dhal* ADJ. (same as دودھیا ADJ. ★) دودھیا *doo-dhiyā* ADJ. milky milk-white unripe ; raw دودھیا پتھر *doo'dhiyā pat'thar* N.M. pumice a kind of soft milkwhite stone

دور *door* ADJ. distant remote ADV. at a distance; for away INT. be off to hell with it PREF. far fore unrelated un- ; in دور از کار *door'az kār'* ADJ. irrelevant concerned دور افتادہ *door-'ftā'dah* ADJ. distant remote ; for off separate دور اندیش *door-andesh'* ADJ. far sighted provident sagacious ; prudent cautious دور اندیشی *door ande'shī* N.F. farsightedness prudence cautiousness دور باد *door'-bād* INT. God forbid May God protect you دور باش *door bāsh* INT. be off , make yourself scarce دور بلا *door' balā'* INT. (dial.) may God protect you دور بھاگنا *door' bhāg'nā* V.I. run away avoid ; shun abhor abstain (from) دوربین *door'-bīn'* N.M. telescope ; binoculars دوربیں *door-bīn'* ADJ. farsighted prudent able to see in the distance دوربینی *door'-bī'nī* N.F. foresight prudence دور پار *door'-pār* INT. (dial.) God forbid may God keep you safe دور تک پہنچنا *door' tak pahūṅch'nā* V.I. go far contact the higher authorities be a far reaching affair دور دراز *door' darāz'* ADJ. distant دور دست *door'-das't* ADJ. far-flung دور دور *door' door* ADJ. at a great distance maintaining respectable distance دور رہنا *door' raih'nā* V.I. keep at an arm's length stay away from remain aloof دور کا مضمون *door' kā mazmoon'* N.M. far-fetched idea nice idea conceit دور کا *door kā* ADJ. distant دور کرنا *door' kar'nā* V.T turn out remove dismiss avert dispel دور کی بات *door' kī bāt'* N.F. deep thought far-off matter دور کی سوجھنا (یا کوڑی لانا) *door kī soojh'nā* (or *kauṛī lā'nā*) V.T. (of someone) hit upon a novel idea دور کی کہنا *door' kī kaih'nā* V.I. speak with foresight دور کے ڈھول سہانے (یا سہاؤنے) *door' ke dhol' sohā'ne* (or *sohā''one*) PROV. distant drums are gratifying دور ہونا *door' ho'nā* V.I. get away make oneself scarce be removed be dispelled دوری *doo'rī* N.F distance . remoteness absence separation [P]

دور *daur* N.M. age ; period , time , era cycle course orbit circuit circular motion revolution rotation circulation vicissitude round of wine-cup reasoning in a circle mutual recitation of the Holy Quran دور دورہ *daur' dau'rah* N.M. sway reign ; rule rage , craze دور کرنا *daur kar'nā* V I (of two persons) recite the Holy Quran to each other [A]

دوراں *dau'rān* ADJ. time گردشِ دوراں *gar'dish-e dau'rān* PH. vicissitudes of fortune [~ A PREC.]

دوران *daurān'* (ped. *davarān'*) N.M. circulation duration pendency دورانِ خون *daurā'n-e khoon'* N.M. circulation of blood دورانِ سر *daurā'n-e sar'* N.M. dizziness . giddiness vertigo headache اس دوران میں *is' daurān (meṅ)* PH. meanwhile in the meantime کے دوران میں *ke daurān' (meṅ)* ADV in the course of ; during [A ~ دور]

دورہ *dau'rah* N.M. tour turn sway ; reign fit دورہ پڑنا *dau'rah par'nā* V.I. have a fit دورہ کرنا *dau'rah kar'nā* V.T. & I. go on a tour review [A]

دوری *dau'rī* N F. trough irrigating basket [~ A دور *daur*]

دوری *doorī* N.F (see under دور *door* ADV ★)

دوڑ *daur'* N.F. race running scramble (for) effort دوڑ دھوپ *daur' dhoop'* N.F. effort endeavour running about hue and cry دوڑ دھوپ کرنا *daur' dhoop kar'nā* V.T. run hither and thither (for) toil hard (for) make hue and cry (about) leave no stone unturned [~ FOLL]

دوڑنا *daur'nā* V.I. run to gallop circulate permeate make an effort (for) دوڑانا *daurā'nā* V.T. cause to run cause to gallop drive fast despatch hurriedly give wings (to) cause to circulate cause to try hard send in pursuit

دوز *doz* SUF. sewing ; stitching piercing fixing maker دوزی *do'zī* N.F. sewing piercing fixing making [P دوختن]

دوزخ *do'zakh* N.M. (dial. F.) hell stomach misery دوزخ کا کندہ *do'zakh kā kun'dah* N.M. arrant sinner damned person دوزخ بھرنا *do'zakh bhar'nā* V.I. eat fill the stomach دوزخی *do'zakhī* ADJ. hellish ; infernal ; damned N.M. condemned sinner damned creature greedy person glutton [P]

دوست *dos't* N.M. male friend, friend lover beloved ; sweetheart دوستانہ *dostā'nah* N.M. friendship ADJ. friendly ADV. amicably cordially دوستانہ تعلقات (یا مراسم) *dostā'nah ta'allūqāt'* (or *marā'sim*) N.M. PL. friendly contacts friendly relations دوستانے میں *dostā'ne meṅ* ADV. as a friend in a friendly manner دوست بنانا *dos't banā'nā* V.T. make friends be on friendly terms (with) develop intimacy (with) دوستداری *dost'-dā'rī* N.F. love friendliness good whishes دوست رکھنا *dos't rakh'nā* V.T. hold dear دوست نما دشمن *dost'-nūmā' dūsh'man* N.M. hidden enemy ; enemy in disguise ; a snake in the grass دوست نواز *dost'-navāz'* ADJ. & N.M. friendly person friends' friend دوستی *dos'tī* N.F. amity , friendship intimacy attachment دوستی کا دم بھرنا *dos'tī kā dam' bhar'nā* V.I. assert friendship claim privileges of friendship [P ~ دوسیدن cling to]

دوسرا *doos'rā,* ADJ. (F. دوسری *doos'rī*) second other next following match , equal duplicate outside (pers.n) step (mother etc) N.M. (F.) outsider دوسرے *doos're* ADV. secondly ; in the second place on the other hand again · furthermore ; moreover

دوش *dosh* N.M. shoulder last night past دوش بدوش *dosh ba dosh'* ADV. shoulder to shoulder محو غم دوش *mah'v-e gham-e-dosh'* N.M. ruing the past meditating on that has been and is no more وبال دوش *vabā'l-e dosh'* N.M. cursed responsibility دوشینہ *doshī'nā* ADJ. last night's; of last night [P]

دوش *dosh,* دوس *dos* N.M. (dial.) blame دوش دینا (یا لگانا) *dosh de'nā* (or *lagā'nā*) V.T. blame ; accuse ; lay blame at the door (of) [S]

دوشیزہ *doshī'zah* N.F. virgin spinster دوشیزگی *doshī'zagī* N.F virginity maidenhood [P]

دوغ *dogh* N.F. (dial. M.) curds buttermilk

دوغلا *dogh'lā,* ADJ. (F. دوغلی *dogh'lī*) cross-breed ; of mixed breed mongrel hybrid mullatto off-spring of parents of different races دوغلی نسل *dogh'lī nas'l* N.F. cross breed

دول *dū'val* (or rare *di'val*) N.M. PL. (see under دولت N.F. ★)

دولاب *doolāb* N.M. persian wheel pulley [P]

دولت *dau'lat* N.F. wealth ; riches money State Power kingdom empire (rare) government دولتخانہ *dau'lat-khā'nah* N.M. your house دولت مشترکہ *dau'lat-e mushta'rakah* N.F. Commonwealth the British Commonwealth دولتمند *dau'lat-mand* N.M. wealthy person ADJ. rich wealthy ; opulent دولتمندی *dau'lat-man'dī* N.F. riches ; wealth wealthness opulence دولتی *dau'lati* ADJ. State ; of State imperial government ; governmental بدولت *ba-dau'lat* ADV. by favour (of) through the good offices (of) through by means of owing (to) ; because (of) در دولت *da'r-e dau'lat* N.M. gateway to (superior's) house نودولت *nau-dau'lat* N.M. upstart ; one who has become rich overnight [A]

دولتی *do-lat'tī,* دلتی *dūlat'tī* N.F. animal's kick with hind legs ; kick دولتی (یا دولتیاں) مارنا (یا جھاڑنا) *dolat'tī* (or *dolat'liyaṅ*) *mār'nā* (or *jhāṛ'nā*) PH. (of animal) kick show disapproval intermittently

دولہا *doo'lhā* N.M. bridegroom; groom دولہا بھائی *doo'lhā bhā''ī* N.M. sister's husband ; brother-in-law

دوم *dū'vām* ADJ. second دوومیں *dūv'vāmīṅ* ADJ. second ADV. secondly [P]

دون *doon* N.F. boast ; brag دون کی لینا *doon' kī le'nā* V.T. boast ; brag

دوں *dooṅ* ADJ. low , mean base ; vile ignoble lacking دوں ہمت *dooṅ-him'mat* ADJ mean no guts دوں ہمتی *dooṅ'-him'matī* N.F. meanness petty mindedness lack of courage [P]

دون *daun* N.F. scorching beat great thirst دون لگنا *daun' lag'nā* V.T. feel very thirsty

دونا *dau'nā* N.M. leaves folded to form a cup ; leaf-cup

دونا *doo'nā*, ADJ. (F. دونی *doo'nī*) دگنا *dūg'nā* (F. دگنی *dūg'nī*) twice as much ; twofold double

دول دول *doon doon* N.F. beat (of drum)

دونگڑا *daung'ṛā* N.M. heavy short-lived shower دونگڑا برس جانا *daung'ṛā ba'ras jā'nā* V.I. (of heavy shower) fall for a while and end تعریف (یا واہ واہ) کے دونگڑے برسنا *ta'rīf'* (or *vāh' vāh ke daung'ṛe ba'rasnā* V.I. be profusely applauded be praised

دونوں *do'noṅ* ADJ. (see under دو ADJ. & N.M. ★)

دوونی *dūvan'nī* N.F. (see under دو ADJ. & N. ★)

دوہا *do'hā* N.M. couplet of Hindi poetry

دوہائی *dohā''ī* N.F. (same as دہائی *dūhā''ī* N.F. ★)

دوہنا *doh'nā* V.I. milk دوہنی *doh'nī* N.F. milk pail

دوئی *dū''ī* (or *doo''ī*,) N.F. being two quality polytheism lack of intimacy not being own [~ دو

دہ *deh* N.M. (PL. دیہات *dehāt'*, دہات *dehāt'*) village دہ بندی *deh-ban'dī* N.F. detailed revenue statement of village's دہ خدا *deh khū'dā* N.M. landlord

دہ *dah* ADJ. ten دہ چند *dah'-chand* ADJ. tenfold ; ten times دہ دنیا ستر آخرت *dah'-dūn'yā sat'tar ā'khirat*, دہ در دنیا صد در آخرت *dah'-dar dūn'yā sad' dar ā'khirat* PROV. charity here well get you manifold reward hereafter

دھابا *dhā'ba* N.M. thatched roof thatched house

دھاپڑ *dhā'par* N.M. (usu. PL.) eruptions on skin

دیہات *dehāt'*, دیہات *dehāt'* N.M. (PL.) دہاتی دیہاتی *dehā'tī* N.M. & ADJ. (see under دیہات N.M. ★)

دھات *dhāt*. (VUL. دھانت *dhānt*) N.F. metal mineral ore ; gun metal bronze (VUL.) aluminium (VUL.) semen

دھا *dhā* N.M. sixth note of national gamut, sol N.F. wet nurse

دھار *dhār* N.F. edge (of knife, etc.) sharpness strain (of milk, etc.) current flow line streak دھاردار *dhār'-dār* ADJ. sharp-edge دھار مارنا *dhār mār'nā* V.I. urinate دھار نکالنا *dhār nikāl'nā* V.T. milk, cause strain (of milk) to come out whet

دھارا *dhā'rā* N.M. water course, current ; stream source (of river)

دھارنا *dhār'nā* V.T. & I. foment with hot jet ; pour (water) rear adopt think without expressing

دھاری *dhā'rī* N.F. stripe streak دھاری دار *dhā'rī-dār* ADJ. striped streaked

دھاڑ *dhāṛ* N.F. group ; bevy crowd loud cry دھاڑ کی دھاڑ *dhāṛ kī dhāṛ* N.F. a whole army (of) دھاڑ (یں) مار کر رونا *dhāṛ'(eṅ) mār' kar ro'nā* V.I. cry aloud

دھاڑنا *dahāṛ'nā* V.I. (of lion or tiger) roar (fig.) thunder دھاڑ *dahāṛ'* N.F. roar (of lion or tiger)

دہاڑی *dehā'ṛī* N.F. (rare) daily wages

دھاڑی *dhā'ṛī* N.M. notorious thief or dacoit

دھاک *dhāk'* N.F. prestige awe دھاک باندھنا (یا بٹھانا) *dhāk' bāndh'nā* (or *biṭhā'nā*) V.T. establish the fame (of) make (someone's) name a terror دھاک بندھنا *dhāk bandh'nā* V.I. come to be known as a terror achieve fame

دہاکا *dahā'kā* N.M. ten tens ; fear ; shock ; terror [~ دس]

دھاگا *dhā'gā*, تاگا *tā'gā* N.M. thread دھاگا پرونا *dhā'gā piro'nā*, دھاگا ڈالنا *dhā'gā ḍāl'nā* V.T. thread (a needle) put stiches (in quilt)

دہان *dahān'* دہن *dahan'* N.M. mouth orifice opening [P]

دھان *dhān* N.M. paddy دھان پان *dhān pān'* ADJ. sleak slender دھانی *dhā'nī* ADJ. light green

دھاندلی *dhānd'lī*, دھاندل *dhān'dal* N.F unfair means row ; wrangle دھاندلی باز *dhānd'lī-bāz* ADJ. & M.M. cheat wrangler دھاندلی کرنا *dhānd'lī kar'nā* V.T. use unfair means ; cheat play false wrangle دھمکی دھونس اور دھاندلی *dham'kī dhauns aur dhānd'lī* N.F threats, bullying and cheating (as recipes for progress in rotten society)

دھانس *dhāṅs* N.F. tang pungent odour cough caused by it دھانسنا *dhāṅs'nā* V.I. (of horse) cough

دہانہ *dahā'nah* N.M. mouth mouth (of river) opening orifice mouth cover bit (of bridle) [P ~ دہان]

دھانی *dhā'nī* ADJ. (see under دھان N.M. ★)

دھاوا *dhā'vā* N.M. attack, assault raid inroad ; incursion دھاوا بولنا (یا کرنا یا مارنا) *dhā'vā bol'nā* (or *kar'nā* or *mār'nā*) V.T attack, assault raid

دہائی *dahā''ī* N.F tens ten ; the tenth part; the tens [~ دس]

دہائی *dohā''ī*, دوہائی *dūhā''ī* N.F. cry for help cry for mercy complaint دہائی دینا *dohā''ī de'nā* V.I. cry for mercy complain against injustice

دھبہ *dhab'bah*, دھبا *dhab'bā* N.M. spot speck stain blot dap ; blotch stigma دھبا ڈالنا *dhab'bā ḍāl'nā* V.T. blot; stain دھبا لگانا *dhab'bā lagā'nā* V.T. sully stigmatized stain دھبا لگنا *dhab'bā lag'nā* V.I. be sullied be stigmatized be stained

دھپ *dhap* N.F. sound ; clock ; noise slap thump thud دھپ جمانا *dhap' jamā'nā* V.T. slap

دھپا *dhap'pā* N.M. slap thump thud loss دھول دھپا *dhaul' dhap'pā* N.M. slap fight , brawl

دھت *dhat* N.F. bad habit addiction دھتیا *dhat'yā* N.M. addict fond (of) ; habituated (to)

دھت *dhut* INT. be off ADJ. dead drunk ADV. deeply (drunk)

دھتا *dhattā* N.F. dodging , evasion ; putting (something) off driving out ; turning (someone) out دھتا بتانا (یا دینا) *dhat'tā batā'nā* (or *de'nā*) V.F. put (something) off turn (someone) away

دھت دھت بری بری *dhat' dhat ba'rī ba'rī* INT. (for urging elephant) on

دھتکارنا *dhutkār'nā* V.T. drive (dogs, etc.) out revile ; reprove

دھتورا *dhatoo'rā* N.M. stramonium

دھج *dhaj* N.F. appearance ; shape ; form air ; mien grace سج دھج *saj' dhaj* N.F. air gracefulness

دھجی *dhaj'jī* N.F. shred strip (of cloth) rag ; tatter دھجیاں اڑانا (یا بکھیرنا یا لینا) *dhaj'jiyāṅ uṛā'nā* (or *bakher'nā* or *le'nā*) V.T. tear into pieces expose ; pull to pieces دھجیاں لگنا *dhaj'jiyāṅ lag'nā* V.I. be in tatters

دھچکا *dhach'kā* N.M. jolt jerk shock دھچکا لگنا *dhach'kā lag'nā* V.I. be jerked be jolted be shocked ; have a shock [ONO.]

دہر *dah'r* N.M. (PL. دہور *dūhoor'*) time age world دہریت *dahriy'yat* N.F. atheism materialism دہریہ *dahriy'yah* N.M. atheist materialist [A]

دھرا *dhū'rā* N.M. axle axle-tree axis دھرا دھر *dhū'rā dhūr'* ADV. right through ; from one end to another to the end

دہرا *doh'rā* ADJ. double ; twofold twice sagged ; sagging دہرا ہو جانا *doh'ra ho ja'nā* V.I. sag be bent دہرانا *dohrā'nā* V.T. repeat say or do over again revise (lesson)

دھرپد *dhūr'pad*, دھرپت *dhūr'pat* N.F. chief highbrow mode of classical music دھرپد الاپنا *dhūr'pad alāp'nā* V.I. sing in this mode

دھرتی *dhar'tī* N.F. (dial.) soil ; land earth دھرتی کا پھول *dhar'tī kā phool* N.M. mushroom دھرتی ماتا *dhar'tī mā'tā* N.F. (dial.) mother earth [S] دہر دہر جلنا *da'har da'har jal'nā* V.I. burn furiously

دھرم *dhar'm* (or *dha'ram*) N.M. (dial.) Hindu faith religion دھرماتما *dharmāt'mā* N.M. (dial.) Hindu saint دھرم بگاڑنا (یا بھرشٹ کرنا) *dhar'm bigāṛ'nā* (or *bharish't kar'nā*) V.T. (dial.) defile and outcaste دھرم پتنی *dhar'm pat'nī* N.F. (dail.) (man's) duly married spouse دھرم سالہ *dhar'm-sālah*, دھرم شالہ *dhar'm-shā'lah* N.F. (dial.) Hindu community centre Hindu poor house Hindu charitable rest house دھرم شاستر *dhar'm-shās'tar* N.M. (dial.) code of Hindu religious law Hindu scriptures [S]

دھرن *dha'ran* N.F. (dial.) navel ovary colic pain ; pain in the navel

دھرنا *dhar'nā* V.T. place ; lay ; put down set up lay (blame) at the door (of) grasp take possession of N.M. dun , dunning sit down strike دھرا کیا ہے *dha'ra kyā hai* PH. there is nothing in it دھرا ہونا *dha'rā ho'nā* V.T. be placed lie unused دھرا رہ جانا *dha'rā raih jā'nā* V.I. lie unused go to waste be totally ignored دھر رکھنا *dhar rakh'nā* V.T. set apart دھرنا دے (یا مار) کر بیٹھنا *dhar'nā de'* (or *mār'*) *kar bai'ṭh'nā* V.I. dun ; sit doggedly at the door of debtor stage a sit down strike

دھروانا *dharvā'nā* V.T. cause to placed cause to be paid have arrested

دھرے اڑانا *dhū're ūṛā'nā* V.T. give a good hiding spoil pull to pieces

دھری *dhū'rī* N.F. axle axis [F. of دھرا used as its DIM.]

دہریت *dahriy'yat* N.F. دہریہ *dahriy'yah* N.M. (see under دہر ★)

دھریل *dharel'* N.F. conclusive junior wife fully accepted at member of family

دھڑ *dhaṛ* N.M. trunk ; torso body دھڑ رہ جانا *dhaṛ raih jā'nā* V.I. be paralysed ; be palsied

دھڑا *dha'ṛā* N.M. party ; faction clique balancing weight دھڑا کرنا *dha'ṛa kar'nā* balance (scale) balance (receptacle, etc.) in scale دھڑے بندی *dha'ṛe-ban'dī* N.F. splitting up into opposed parties party spirit factions feelings دھڑا دھڑ *dha'ṛā dhaṛ* ADV. rapidly in rapid succession دھڑا دھڑ *dha'ṛā dhaṛ bik'nā* V.I (of something) sell like hot cakes have a buying spree

دھڑاکا *dhara'ka* N.M. thud sport (of gun, etc.) along shower loud report of farting دھڑاکے سے *dhara'ke se* ADV with a crash swiftly

دھڑام *dharam* N.F. thud دھڑام سے *dharam se* ADV with a thud

دھڑکنا *dha'raknā* V.I. (of heart) beat, palpitate feel uneasy دھڑکا *dhar'ka* N.M. fear doubt suspens دھڑکن *dhar'kan* N.F. palpitation

دھڑلا *dharal'la* N.M. bravery boldness; guts intrepidity دھڑلے سے *dharal'le se* ADV. fearlessly; intrepidity openly without fear or favour

دھڑی *dha'rī* N.F. five seers five-seer weight layer (of lipstick, etc.) مسی کی دھڑی جمانا *mis'sī kī dha'rī jamā'nā* paint (the lips) دھڑیوں *dhar'yon* ADV. in abundance

دھسا *dhūs'sā* N.M. heavy woollen shawl; twofold shawl

دھسکنا *dha'saknā* V.I. sag (of wall) collapse

دھسنا *dhasnā*, دھنسنا *dhañ'sanā* V.I. sink (into) be thrust (into) elbow one's way (into crowd, etc.) go deep into sag دھسان *dha'sān* N.F. marshy ground bog: quagmire slough دھسانا *dhasā'nā*, دھنسانا *dhañsā'nā* V.T. cause to sink

دہش *de'hish* N.F. (usu. as داد و دہش *dā'd-o dehish*) bounty munificence charity [P ~ دادن give]

دہشت *daih'shat* (ped. *dah'-*) N.F fear: terror: dread awe scare alarm threat; menace horror دہشت انگیز *daih'shat-añgez'* ADJ. alarming scaring terrifying awe-inspiring horrid; horrible دہشت زدہ *dah'shat-za'dah* ADJ. scared alarmed panicky panic-striken terrified; terror-striken دہشت کھانا *dah'shat khā'nā* V.I. be panicky be alarmed be terrified be terror struck دہشتناک *daih'shat-nāk* ADJ. dreadful horrid; horrible alarming terrifying [A]

دہقان *dehqān'* N.M. villager; boor; rustic peasant, tiller of the soil (rare) landlord دہقانی *dehqā'nī* N.M. villager peasant ADJ. rustic boorish دہقانیت *dehqāniy'yat* N.F. rustic manners [P ~ دہ deh]

دھک *dhak* N.F shock thud young one of louse دھک سے رہ جانا *dhak se raih' jā'nā* V.I. stand aghast be paralysed through fear دھک دھک کرنا *dhak' dhak' kar'nā* V.T (of heart) beat, palpitate

دھکا *dhak'kā* N.M. shove, push; jostle shock loss, damage stroke (of ill-luck) دھکا پیل *dhak'kā pel*, دھکم دھکا *dhak'kam dhak'kā* N.F. jostling دھکا دینا *dhak'kā de'nā* V.T. jostle push elbow shove turn out bring misfortune (on) دھکے کھانا *dhak'ke khā'nā* V.I. be kicked from door to door be forced to wander about aimlessly suffer reverses of fortune be pushed be shoved be jostled دھکا لگنا *dhak-kā lag'nā* V.I. be jostled suffer a shock sustain loss suffer reverses of fortune

دہکنا *dai'haknā* V.I. glow burn be ablaze be consumed (with grief rage, etc.) دہکانا *daihkā'nā* V.I. light or kindle (fire)

دھکدھکی *dhūk'dūkī*, دھگدگی *dhūg'd'gī* N.F palpitation anxiety: worry outer part of throat towards end of neck دھکدکی میں دم ہونا *dhūk'-dhū'kī meñ dam' ho'nā* V.I. be on the last gasp

دھکڑ پکڑ *dhū'kar pū'kar* N.F. palpitation; agitation. suspense

دھکیلنا *dhakel'nā* (dial. ڈھکیلنا *dhakel'nā*) V.T jostle push shove دھکیل دینا *dhakel' de'nā* (dial. *dha'-*) V.T. jostle push shove down

دھگدگی *dhūg'dūgī* N.F. (same as دھکدھکی N.F ★)

دھگڑا *dhag'rā* N.M. paramour

دہل *do'hūl* N.M. drum tabor بہ بانگ دہل *ba-bāñ'g-e do'hūl* ADV with the beat of drum openly [P]

دہلا *daih'la* N.M. (at cards) ten [~ دس]

دہلنا *dai'halnā*, دہل جانا *dai'hal jā'nā* V.I. be scared shiver in one's shoes shocked دہلانا *daihlā'nā*, be دہلا دینا *daihlā' de'nā* V.T. scare frighten

دھلنا *dhūl'nā* V.I. be washed, be laundered دھلائی *dhūlā'ī* N.F. washing laundry remuneration for laundering دھلوانا *dhūlvā'nā* V.T get (someone) launder cause (something) to be washed دھلیا ملیا کرنا *dhūlyā mil'yā kar'nā* V.T hush up (dispute)

دہلی *deh'lī* (Persianized and commoner form of دلی *dil'lī*) N.F. Dehli دہلوی *deh'lavī* N.M. one from Delhi ADJ. of Delhi

دہلیز *dehlīz'* N.F. threshold porch, portico دہلیز کا کتا *dehlīz' kā kut'tā* N.M. hanger-on parasite (of) دہلیز کی مٹی لے ڈالنا *dehlīz' kī maṭ'ṭī le ḍāl'nā* V.I. sits

دہم *da'hum*, دہمیں *da'humīñ* ADJ. tenth [P ~ دہ]

دھم *dham* N.F. thud دھم سے *dham' se* ADV. with a thud (come) unexpectedly ; all of a sudden

دھماچوکڑی *dha'mā chau'kaṛī* N.F. roistering [ONO.]

دھمادھم *dha'mā dham'* N.F. & ADV. (with) the sound of jumpings about [ONO.]

دھماکا *dhamā'kā* N.M. sound of explosion report (of gun) crash thud thump [ONO.]

دھمال *dhamāl'* N.F. mendicants' group dance their jumping into fire دھمال کھیلنا (یا کرنا) *dhamal' khel'nā* (or *kar'nā*) V.I. play thus دھمالیہ *dhamā'liya* N.M. one who plays thus

دھمک *dha'mak* N.F. footfall thud thump pulsation shooting pain (in head)

دھمکی *dham'kī* N.F. threat threatening snub bluff دھمکی دینا *dham'kī de'nā* V T. threaten snub bluff دھمکی میں *dham'kī meṅ* ADV. just with a threat دھمکی میں آنا *dham'kī meṅ ā'nā* V.I. be coerced by threats be frightened be scared be bluffed دھمکنا *dha'maknā* V.I. throb shoot with pain make a thud آ دھمکنا *ā' dha'maknā* V.I. come unexpectedly be unwelcome arrival دھمکانا *dhamkā'nā* V.I. threaten; hold out a threat snub

دھن *dhun* N.F. keynote tune assiduity perseverance fad craze دھن کا پکا *dhun ka pak'kā* ADJ. persevering دھن میں مگن *dhun' meṅ ma'gan* ADJ. obsessed with the idea absorbed in the thought

دھن *dhan* N.M. (dial.) riches ; wealth fortune دھن دولت *dhan dau'lat* N.F. riches ; wealth ; fortune [S]

دہن *da'han*, دہاں *dahān'* N.M. mouth [P]

دہن *doh'n* N M. (rare) oil دہنیت *dohniy'yat* N.F. oil content

دہنا *dah'nā* ADJ. (same as داہنا ADJ. ★)

دھناسری *dhanā'sirī* N.F. name of a musical mode

دھننا *dhun'nā* V.T. comb ; card cotton beat rack سر دھننا *sir dhun'nā* V.I. rue rack one's brains fret and fume دھنیا *dhun'ya* N.M. carder

دھند *dhund* N.F. fog mist ; haze dim-sightedness dim ; lack of charity دھندلا *dhund'lā* ADJ. foggy misty ; hazy dim دھندلاپن *dhund'la-pan* N.M. dimness fogginess dullness دھندلکا *dhu'ndalkā* N.M. twilight early hours of the morning

دھندا *dhan'dā* N.M. means of livelihood avocation business work occupation

دھندلا *dhun'dlā* ADJ دھندلکا *dhun'dalkā* N.M. (see under دھند ★)

دھنک *dha'nak* N.F. narrow gold lace (dial.) rainbow

دھنکنا *dhunak'nā* V.T. card ; comb دھنکنی *dhunak'nī* N.F. carding bow

دھنوان *dhan-vān'* ADJ. (dial.) rich ; wealthy [S ~ دھن *dhan*]

دھنی *dha'nī* ADJ. (dial.) rich expert (at something) [~ دھن]

دھنیا *dhan'yā* N.M coriander seed quality rice

دھنیا *dhun'yā* N.M. (see under دھننا V.T. ★)

دھو *dhau* N.M. steel rim for wheel ; tyre

دھواں *dhū'āṅ* N.M. smoke دھواں دھار *dhū'āṅ-dhār* ADJ. smoky dark torrential (rain) fiery; impassioned (speech, etc.) دھواں سا *dhu'āṅ'sā* N.M. soot ADJ. soo دھواں سا جانا *dhū'āṅ'sā jā'nā* V.I. be covered with soot

دھوبن *dho'ban* N.F. (see under دھوبی N.M. ★)

دھوبی *dho'bī* N.V. washerman ; launderer دھوبی پاٹ (یا پٹڑا) *dho'bī-pāṭ* (or *paṭ'ra*) N.M. wash-board wrestling trick (in which one throws adversary right over ones shoulders) دھوبی گھاٹ *dho'bī ghāṭ'* N.F. washing wharf wash-house دھوبی کا کتا نہ گھر کا نہ گھاٹ کا *dho'bī kā kut'tā na ghar' kā na ghāṭ' kā* PROV. dog who running after two bones would catch neither دھوبن *dho'ban* N.F. laundress wagtail

دھوپ *dhoop* N.F. sun ; shining; sunshine incense دھوپ پڑنا *dhoop par'nā* V.I. be sunny ; have the sun shining (on) دھوپ چڑھنا (یا نکلنا) *dhoop chaṛh'nā* (or *nikal'nā*) V.I. be broad day-light (of sun) rise high دھوپ چھاؤں *dhoop' chhāoṅ* N.F. sunshine and shade shot silk sun-proof (gaberdine) دھوپ دینا *dhoop' de'nā* V.T. air ; put in the sun دھوپ کھانا (یا لینا) *dhoop' khā'nā* (or *le'nā*) V.I. bask in the sun دھوپ گھڑی *dhoop' gha'ṛī* N.F. sundial دھوپ میں *dhoop' meṅ* ADV. in the sun دھوپ میں بال (یا سر یا چونڈا) سفید ہونا *dhoop' meṅ bāl'* (or *sir* or *choon'ḍā*) *sifed' ho'nā* V.I. be green despite age دھوپ نکلنا *dhoop' ni'kalnā* V.I. (of sun) shine

دھوتر *dho'tar* N.F. flimsy linen

دھوتی *dho'tī* N.F. waiste piece (passing between legs and fastened behind) sheet used as cover for lower part of body

دھورا *dhoo'rā* N.M. dusting powder

دھوکا *dho'ka* N.M. deception imposture delusion make-believe betrayal treachery scarecrow دھوکا بازی *dho'kā-bā'zī* N.F. fraud ; imposture دھوکا دینا *dho'kā de'nā* V.T. defraud betray the confidence (of) دھوکا کھانا *dho'kā khā'nā*, دھوکے میں آنا *dho'ke meṅ ā'na* V.I be taken in be defrauded take a false step make a mistake دھوکے کی ٹٹی *dho'ke kī ṭaṭ'ṭī* N.F. false screen smoke screen (of) دھوکے باز *dho'ke-bāz'* N.M. & ADJ. (coll.) fraudulent (person) دھوکے بازی *dho'ke-bā'zī* N.F. fraud دھوکے میں رکھنا *dho'ke meṅ rakh'nā* V.I. feed with false hopes دھوکے میں رہنا *dho'ke meṅ raih'nā* V.I. be in the dark

دھول *dhool* N.F. dust دھول اڑانا *dhool uṛā'nā* V.T. raise dust slander دھول اڑنا *dhool uṛ'nā* V.I. (of dust) be raised be defamed be ruined دھول جھاڑنا *dhool jhāṛ'nā* V.T. dust , beat

دھول *dhaul* N.M. slap thump دھول جڑنا (لگانا یا مارنا) *dhaul jaṛ'nā* (or *lagā'nā* or *mār'nā*) slap thump دھول دھپا *dhaul dhap'pā* N.M. slapping fisticuffs

دھولا *dhau'la* ADJ. milkwhite snowwhite (hair)

دھوم *dhoom* N.F. fame pomp; parade دھوم دھام *dhoom' dhām'*, دھوم دھڑکا *dhoom' dhaṛak'kā* N.F. pomp and show parade ; splendid display دھومک دھیا *dhoo'mak dhay'ya* N.F. noise uproar دھوم مچانا *dhoom' machā'nā* V.T & I make an uproar publicize make famous دھوم مچنا (یا ہونا) *dhoom' mach'nā* (or *ho'nā*) V.I become famous or notorious

دھون *dhaun* N.M. half maund (weight)

دھونا *dho'na* V.T wash cleanse rinse دھوون *dho'van* N.F water in which something has been washed

دھونتال *dhauntāl'* ADJ. skilful quick brave

دھوں دھوں *dhauṅ' dhauṅ* N.F (sound of) constant coughing [ONO.]

دھوں دھوں *dhooṅ' dhooṅ* N.F (sound of) constant gunshots [ONO.]

دھونس *dhauns* N.F. bluff bullying دھونس دینا (یا جمانا) *dhauns' de'nā* (or *jamā'nā*) V.T. bluff bully دھونس میں آنا *dhauns' meṅ ā'na* V.I. be bluffed be bullied دھونسیا *dhauṅ'siya* N.M. bully

دھونسا *dhauṅ'sa* N.M. large drum

دھونکنا *dhauṅk'nā* V.I. blow air into (something) with the bellows دھونکنی *dhauṅk'nī* N.F bellows ; pair of bellows

دھونی *dhoo'nī* N.F fumigation incense smoke دھونی دینا *dhoo'nī de'nā* V.T. burn incense fumigate smoke دھونی رمانا (یا لگانا) *dhoo'nī ramā'na* (or *lagā'na*) V.I (dial.) burn incense like a Hindu ascetic (of Hindu) become an ascetic دھونی لینا *dhoo'nī le'nā* V.I. inhale smoke or undergo fumigation

دہی *da'hī* N.M. (dial. F.) curds , yogurt

دھیان *dhyān* N.M. attention contemplation (dial.) meditation دھیان بٹانا *dhyān baṭā'nā* V.I. divide attention , distract دھیان دینا (یا لگانا) *dhyān de'nā* (or *lagā'na*) V.I. (dial.) contemplate meditate دھیان رکھنا *dhyān' rakh'nā* V.I. bear in mind keep in view attend (to) look (after) دھیان کرنا *dhyān' kar'na* V.I. pay attention (to) take notice (of) دھیان میں نہ لانا *dhyan' meṅ na la'nā* V. ignore ; disregard ; pay no attention (to) , pay no heed (to)

دھیرج *dhī'raj* N.F. composure fortitude perseverance firmness دھیرج رکھنا (یا سے کام لینا) *dhī'raj rakh'nā* (or *se kām le'nā*) V.I. be composed show fortitude be firm perseverance

دھیرے دھیرے *dhī're dhī're* ADV. slowly softly noiselessly ; without noise gradually ; step by step gently

دھیلا *dhe'la* N.M. (old coin) half-pice (equivalent to 132nd of a rupee) دھیلی *dhe'lī* N.F. half-rupee , 50-paisa coin

دھیما *dhī'mā*, ADJ. (F. دھیمی *dhī'mī*) not severe mild soft (sound) calm subdued mitigated temperate dim slow lacking vehemence دھیما پڑنا *dhī'ma paṛ'na* V.I. be calm become less severe lose vehemence be mitigated دھیما دھیما *dhī'ma dhī ma* ADJ. gentle mild ADV. gently mildly

دھینگا *dhīṅ'ga* ADJ. stout fat

دھینگا مشتی *dhīṅ'ga mush'tī* N.F. fisticuffs melee

دیا *di'ya* N.M. lamp earthen lamp without any glass to cover flame دیا بتی کرنا *di'ya bat'tī kar'na* V.T. light a lamp دیا بڑھانا *di'ya barhā'na* V.I put out a lamp دیا سلائی *di'ya-salā''ī* N.F. match; match-stick match-box دیا سلائی کی ڈبیہ *di'ya'-salā''ī kī ḍib'ya'* N.F. match-box

دیا *da ya* N.F. (dial.) mercy benevolence favour دیالو *dayā'loo* N.M. (dial.) merciful charitable [S]

دیار *diyār* N.M. country region territory; soil ; land N.M. PL. (rare) houses دیارِ غیر *diyā'r-e ghair'* N.M. alien soil foreign land [A ~ SING دار house]

دیالو *diyā'loo* ADJ. (dial.) generous [~ دینا]

دیانت *diyā'nat* N.F. honesty , probity ; integrity faith fidelity دیانتدار *diyā'nat-dār*

ADJ. honest faithful conscientious دیانتداری *diyā'nat-dā'rī* N.F. honesty ; probity ; integrity fidelity faithfulness [A ~ دین]

دیبا *dī'bā* N.M. tissue brocade [P]

دیباچہ *dība'chah* N.M. preface ; foreword ; introduction [P]

دیپ *dīp* N.M. (dial.) lamp [S]

دیپک *dī'pak* N.M. name of a major mode of classical Indo-Pakistan music pertaining to summer (dial.) lamp [S]

دیت *de'yat* N.F. blood money [A ~ ادا]

دیجور *daijoor'* N.F. long dark night ADJ. dark ; pitch-dark شب دیجور *sha'b-e daijoor'* N.F. very dark night [P]

دید *dīd* N.F. seeing watching دیدہ شنید *dīd' na shunīd'* PH. strange preposterous no information دیدار *dīdār'* N.M. sight view interview or meeting (with beloved) دیدارباز *dīdār'-bāz* N.M. & ADJ. ogling (person) دیدارو *didā'roo* ADJ. (col.) pretty ; handsome ; comely دیدنی *dī'danī* ADJ. worth seeing دیدہ *dī'dah* ADV. having seen SUF. seen دیدہ دانستہ *dī'dah dānis'tah* *dī'da-o dānis'tah* ADV. knowingly deliberately [P ~ دیدن to see]

دیدار *dīdār'* N.M. (see under دیدن V.T.)

دیدہ *dī'dah* N.M. eye دیدہ ریزی *dī'da-re'zī* N.F. hard work work calling for great effort minute work دیدہ ریزی کا کام *dī'da-re'zī kā kām* N.M. minute tope of work دیدوں کا پانی ڈھلنا *dī'don kā pā'nī ḍhal'nā* V.T. become impudent lose modesty be shameless دیدے پھاڑنا *dī'de phāṛ'na* V.T. ogle gaze stare دیدے پھٹنا *dī'de phaṭ'na* ADJ. shamefaced impudent دیدے مٹکانا *dī'de maṭka'na* V.T. ogle ; make eyes at ; to wanton with the eyes دیدے نکالنا *dī'de nikal'na* V.T. glare at شوخ دیدہ *shokh-dī'dah* ADJ. impudent shamefaced [P]

دیر *dair* N.M. monastry temple [A]

دیر *der* N.F. delay tardiness passage of time دیر آید درست آید *de'r ā'yad duru'st a'yad* PROV. better late than never better because late دیرپا *der'-pā* ADJ. lasting durable دیر تک *der' tak* ADV. for a long time till late (in the evening, etc.) دیر سے *der' se* ADV. since long late دیر سے آنا *der' se ā'na* V.I. be late; come late دیر لگانا *der' lagā'na* V.T. delay be late waist time take a lot of time (over or in) دیر ہونا *der' ho'na* V.I. be late دیری *de'rī* N.F. (col.) delay tardiness [P]

دیرینہ *derī'nah* ADJ. old ; ancient veteran seasoned stale [P]

دیروز *dīroz'* N.M. yesterday the past *dīro'zah* ADJ. yesterday's past stale [P]

دیس *des.* (dial. دیش *desh*) N.M. country ; land دیس بدیس یا دیس دیس پھرنا *des' ba-des'* (or *des' des'*) *phir'na* V.I. wander from country to country travel about دیس نکالا *des-nikā'la* N.M. exile ; banishment ; ostracism extradition دیس نکالا دینا *des'-nikā'lā de'nā* V.T. exile ; banish دیس نکالا ملنا *des-nikā'lā mil'nā* V.I. be exiled ; be banished be extradited دیسی *de'sī* ADJ. indigenous home-made native real (stuff) vernacular N.M. native

دیکھنا *dekh'na* V.I. see look at behold observe inspect search weigh well take care feel (pulse) دیکھ بھال *dekh' bhāl* N.F. looking after ; care check-up scrutiny reconnaissance دیکھا بھالا *de'khā bhā'la* ADJ. tried دیکھا دیکھی *de'khā de'khī* ADV. emulating in imitation دیکھا کرنا *de'khā kar'na* V.I. keep looking be waiting دیکھا ہوا *de'khā hū''ā* ADJ. tried known seen دیکھتے دیکھتے *dekh'te dekh'te* ADV. in the presence of before one's very eyes through looking continuously or for long دیکھتے رہ جانا *dekh'te raih jā'na* V.I. gaze in vain stand gazing in wonder or dismay دیکھتے رہنا *dekh'te raih'nā* V.I. look after keep an eye (on) keep a watch go on looking دیکھنا بھالنا *dekh'nā bhāl'nā* V.T. try examine inspect reconnoitre دیکھنے میں آنا *dekh'ne meṅ ā'nā* V.I. appear ; come into sight be visible be found دیکھ پانا *dekh pā'na* V.T. get a chance to see ascertain دیکھنا *dekh'na* V.I. (col.) be seen appear come in sight be found be able to see not to be blind

دیگ *deg* N.F. big pot cauldron wrought iron دیگچہ *deg'chah* N.M. large saucepan دیگچی *deg'chī* N.F. saucepan دیگدان *deg'-dān* N.M. (rare) fireplace [P]

دیگر *dī'gar* ADJ. (also دگر *di'gar*) other another again N.M. afternoon prayers [P]

دیگی *de'gī* ADJ. wrought (iron) [~ دیگ]

دیمک *dī'mak* N.F. white-ant ; termite دیمک خوردہ *dī'mak-khūr'dah* ADJ. eaten by termite دیمک لگنا *dī'mak lag'nā* V.I. be eaten by termite [P]

دین *dīn* N.M. (PL. ادیان *adyān'*) religion ; faith دین پناہ *dīn'-panāh'* ADJ. defender of the faith

دینِ حق *dī'n-e haq* N.M. Islam (as the true faith) دیندار *dīn'-dār* ADJ. & N.M. religious (person) the faithful pious دینداری *dīn'-dā'rī* N.F. religiousness piety دین کی لڑائی *dīn' kī laṛā''ī* N F. religious war دین میں ملانا *dīn' meṅ milā'nā* V.T. convert ; proselytize دینی *dī'nī* ADJ. religious [A]

دین *dain* N.M. debt liability [A]

دین *den* N.F. (see under دینا V.T. ★)

دینا *de'nā* V.T. give pay grant confer offer yield produce emite allot lay (egg) دے دینا *de de'nā* V.I. give away make over (to) دین *den* N.F. gift bestowal giving لین دین *len' den* N.M. dealings monetary transactions traffic (in) give and take

دینار *dīnār'* N.M. dinar [A ~ L]

دیو ¹ *dev'* (col. *de'o'*) N.M. giant ogre (lit.) devil دیوپیکر *dev-pai'kar* ADJ. gigantic huge

دیو ² *dev'* N.M. (dial.) deity , God دیوتا *deyo''tā* (or Persianized *dev'tā*) N.M. (dial.) deity God دیوبانی *dev'-bā'nī* N.F (dial.) Sanskrit (as the language of Gods') دیومالا *dev'-mā'lā* N.F. mythology دیوناگری *dev-nāg'rī* N.F. Sanskrit script دیوی *de'vī* N.F. (dial.) goddess noble lady pious woman دیوی دیوتا *de'vī dev'tā* N.M. PL. (dial.) gods and goddesses pantheon

دیوار *dīvār'* N.F. wall دیوار اٹھانا (یا بنانا یا چننا یا کھینچنا) *dīvār' uṭhā'nā* (or *banā'nā* or *chūn'nā* or *khench'nā*) V.T. raise build or rear دیوار بیچ گھر *dīvār' bīch' ghar* PH. adjacent house دیوارِ چین *dīvā'r-e chīn'* N.F. the great wall of China bighavier دیوارِ قہقہہ *dīvā'r-e qaih'qahah* N.F. the great wall of China (as inducing its scalers to laugh) hearty laugh دیوار کے بھی کان ہیں *dīvār' ke bhī kān' haiṅ*, دیوار ہم گوش دارد *dīvār' ham gosh' dā'rad* PROV. walls have ears دیوارگیری *dīvār'-gī'rī* N.F. bracket wall-lamp arras ADJ. wall (lamps, etc.) [P]

دیوالہ *dīvā'lah*, دوالہ *divā'lah* N.M. bankruptcy ; insolvency دیوالہ نکالنا *dīvā'lah nikāl nā* V.T. declare one's insolvency bring to verge of financial collapse دیوالہ نکلنا *dīvā'lah nikal'nā* N.F. become insolvent collapse financially be absolutely lacking (in) دیوالیہ *dīvā'liyah* N.M. bankrupt ; insolvent lacking دیوالیہ پن *dīvā'liyah-pan* N.M. bankruptcy ; insolvency lack (of)

دیوالی *dīvā'lī* N.F. (Hindu) festival of illuminations (celebrating Ramas resumption of power) [S]

دیوان *dīvān'* N.M. collected odes of single poet with all pieces alphabetically arranged according last letter of couplets divan , courts ; cushioned platform (arch.) royal court (arch.) Prime Minister (arch.) secretary, revenue or financial secretary; minister (arch.) tribunal (arch.) revenue department ; secretariat دیوانِ خاص *dīvā'n-e khās'* N.M. Cabinet; Privy Council Privy Council Chamber دیوان خانہ *dīvān'-khā'nah* N.M. drawing room lounge hall prival hall of audience ; court دیوانِ عام *dīvā'n-e 'ām'* N.M. public hall of audience [A ~ P]

دیوانہ *dīvā'nah* N.M. madman ; lunatic frenzied lover ADJ. mad ; insane ; lunatic frenzied (lover) fanatical crezy دیوانہ بکارِ خویش ہشیار *dīvā'nah ba-kār-e khesh' hushiyār'* PROV. even a madman is save enough to look after own interests دیوانہ پن *dīvā'na-pan* N.M. دیوانگی *dīvā'nagī* N.F. insanity ; madness , lunacy frenzy craze, fanatacism دیوانی *dīvā'nī* N.F .mad woman ADJ. mad (woman) [P]

دیوانی *dīvā'nī* N.F civil court (see under دیوانہ ★) ADJ. civil (court, law, procedure, etc.) (see under دیوانہ ★) [P]

دیوتا *dev'ta* N.M. (see under دیو ² N.M.)

دیوٹ *dīvaṭ* N.M. lamp-stand candle stick [~ دیا]

دیوث *dayyoos'* N.M. cuckold دیوثی *dayyoo'sī* N.F. cuckoldry [A]

دیودار *deodār'* N.M. cedar

دیور *de'var* N.M. husband's younger brother ; brother-in-law دیورانی *deyorā'nī* N.F. wife of husband's younger brother ; sister-in-law

دیولا *deyo'lā* N.M. large lamp دیولی *deyo'lī* N.F. small lamp [~ دیا]

دیون *d·yoon'* N.M. PL. debts [A ~ SING. دین *dain*]

دیوی *de'vī* N.F. (see under دیو ² N.M. ★)

دہ *deh* N.M. village دیہی *de'hī* ADJ. rural ; rustic دیہات *dehāt'*, دہات *dehāt'* N.M. village N.M. PL. villages دیہاتِ خالصہ *dehāt-e khā'lisah* N.M. PL. villages comprising Crown lands ; State villages دیہاتی *dehā'tī*, دہاتی *dehā'tī* ADJ. rural rustic; bonish N.M. rustic ; boor [P doublet of دہ *deh*]

دہیم *daihīm'* N.M. crown [P]

ڈ

ڈ *ḍal* twelfth letter of Urdu alphabet (equivalent to English *d*) (in jummal reckoning (equivalent to د *dāl*) four

ڈاب *ḍāb* N.M. unripe cocoanut sword-belt a kind of grass twined to form bed-strings

ڈابر *ḍā'bur* N.M. pond, pool (dish.) wash-stand; basin

ڈابک *ḍā'bak* N.M. (dial.) fresh water from well

ڈاٹ *ḍāṭ* N.F. arch arched doorway vault stopper cork ڈاٹ لگانا *ḍāṭ lagā'nā* V.T. close (doorway, arch, etc.) with brick-work arch vault cork; put a stopper (on) ڈاٹ لگنا *ḍāṭ' lag'nā* V.I. be arched be vaulted (of arch, etc.) be closed with brick-work be corked; have a stopper put on

ڈار *ḍār* N.F. swarm; flock branch; bough

ڈاڑھ *ḍāṛh* N.F. (usu. variant of دھاڑ *dohāṛ'*, roar) loud cry (dial. for داڑھ N.F. ★) ڈاڑھیں مار کر رونا *ḍāṛheṅ mār' kar ro'nā* V.I weep bitterly

ڈاڑھا *ḍā'ṛhā* N.M. (dial. for داڑھا N.M. ★)

ڈاڑھی *ḍā'ṛhī* N.F. (dial. for داڑھی N.F ★)

ڈاک *ḍāk* N.F. post, mail (arch.) postal relays of men or horses for continual communications series of; spasms of ADJ. post; postal ڈاک بٹھانا (یا لگانا) *ḍāk' biṭhā'nā* (or *lagā'nā*) V.T. send out postal relays communicate rapidly and for long ڈاک بیٹھنا *ḍāk' baiṭh'nā* V.I. (of communications) take place rapidly and for long ڈاک بنگلہ *ḍāk'-bang'lah* N.F. dak bunglow; rest house ڈاک چوکی *ḍāk'-chau'kī* N.F. (arch.) postal relay stage ڈاک خانہ *ḍāk'-khā'nah* N.M. post office postal department ڈاک گاڑی *ḍāk' gā'ṛī* N.F. mail train mail van ڈاک لگنا *ḍāk lag'nā* V.I. (of communications) take place rapidly and for long have frequent spasms (of vomiting or hiccup) ڈاکیہ *ḍā'kiyah*, ڈاکیا *ḍā'kiya* N.M. postman courier

ڈاکو *ḍā'koo* N.M. dacoit; robber; brigand; bandit; highwayman; footpad بحری (یا سمندری) ڈاکو *baih'rī* (or *samun'darī*) *ḍākoo* N.M. pirate ڈاکہ *ḍā'kah* ڈاکا *ḍā'kā* N.M. dacoity banditry; robbery; highway robbery; brigandage ڈاکا پڑنا *ḍā'kā paṛ'nā* V.I. be attacked by dacoits be robbed ڈاکا ڈالنا *ḍā'kā ḍāl'nā* V.T. commit a dacoity rob ڈاکا زنی *ḍā'ka-za'nī* N.F dacoity; robbery; highway; banditry; brigandage

ڈاکیہ *ḍā'kiyah* N.M. (see under ڈاک N F ★)

ڈال *ḍāl* N.F. branch, bough twig; spray irrigation basket ڈال کا پکا *ḍāl' kā pak'kā* ADJ. ripened on the branch ڈال کا ٹوٹا *ḍāl' kā too'ṭā* ADJ. plucked from the branch fresh تو ڈال ڈال میں پات پات *too ḍāl' ḍāl' maiṅ pāt' pāt'* PROV over-reaching; I can outwit you at your game you can't get me I know how to harass you

ڈالر *ḍā'lar* N M. dollar ADJ. dollar ڈالری *ḍā'larī* ADJ. dollar U.S. financial ڈالری سیاست *ḍā'larī siyā'sat* N.F. U.S. financial strategy; dollar diplomacy [E]

ڈالنا *ḍāl'nā* V.T. pour lay wear; put on sow; broadcast; scatter vomit throw down post take (woman) as mistress ڈال دینا *ḍāl' de'nā* V.T. lay down throw away; cast away quit; abandon

ڈالی *ḍā'lī* N.F. branch; bough bribe present of fruits, etc. spread on tray and partially covered with flowers

ڈامچا *ḍām'chā* N.M. field watchman's elevated platform

ڈانٹنا *ḍāṅṭ'nā* V.T. chide; scold rebuke reprove browbeat ڈانٹ، ڈپٹ *ḍāṅṭ*, *ḍāṅṭ ḍapaṭ* N.F. chiding; scolding rebuke reproof

ڈانڈ *ḍāṅḍ* N.M. oar staff ڈانڈی *ḍāṅ'ḍī* N.M. oarsman boatman

ڈانڈا *ḍāṅ'ḍā* N.M. boundry line کے ڈانڈے ملنا *ke ḍāṅ'de mil'nā* V I. (of two or twain) meet; become adjacent to each other converge merge into one another

ڈانڈی *ḍāṅ'ḍī* N.F. sedan-chair N.M. (see unde ڈانڈ ★)

ڈانگ *ḍāṅg* N.F. hilltop (dial.) jump

ڈانواں ڈول *ḍāṅ'vāṅ ḍol* ADJ. unsteady unsettled homeless ڈانواں ڈول پھرنا *ḍāṅ'vāṅ ḍol phir'nā* V.I. tramp be unsettled

ڈاہ *ḍāh* N.F. spite jealousy malice

ڈائرکٹر *ḍā'eraik'ṭar* N.M. director ڈائرکٹری *ḍā'eraik'ṭarī* N.F. directory [E]

ڈائری *ḍā''irī* N.F. diary [E]

ڈائل ḍa''il, ḍa-yal N.M. dial [E]

ڈائمنڈجوبلی ḍa'yamaṇḍ joob'lı N.F. Diamond Jubilee [E]

ڈائن ḍā''in N.F. witch hag malicious woman ڈائن بھی دس گھر چھوڑ کر کھاتی ہے ḍā''in bhi das' ghar' chhoṛ' kar khā'li hai

ڈائنامیٹ ḍā''inamaiṭ N.M. dynamite [E]

ڈائنمو ḍā''inamo, ḍainmo N.M. dynamo [E]

ڈب ḍab N.F. leather going into oil-pot manufacture fastening end of waist-piece (also used as purse)

ڈبا dib'ba N.M. (same as N.M. ڈبہ ★)

ڈباؤ ḍubā''oo ADJ. (see under ڈوبنا V.I. ★)

ڈبڈبانا ḍubḍubā'na, ڈبڈبا آنا (یا جانا) ḍub'ḍubā ā'na (or jā'na) V.I. (of eyes) be filled with tears

ڈبرا dab'rā N.M. pool

ڈبکا ḍab'kā N.M. also ڈبکے کا پانی ḍab'ke kā pa'nī PH. freshly drawn water from well

ڈبل روٹی ḍa'bal ro'ṭi N.F. bread ; Western-style leavened loaf

ڈبونا ḍubo'nā V.T. drown sink dip ; immerse inundiate waste ruin disgrace ; humiliate ڈباؤ ḍubā''oo ADJ. out of man's depth ; drowning quite deep

ڈبکی ḍub'ki N.F. dip plunge ڈبکی لگانا ḍūb'kī lagā'nā V.T. dive

ڈبہ ḍib'bah N.M. box packet carton (also ڈبہ اطفال ḍib'bā atfāl') infantile pleurisy

ڈبیہ ḍib'yah N.F. small box packet carton

ڈپٹ ḍa'paṭ' N.F. ڈپٹانا ḍapṭā'nā V.T. (see under ڈپٹنا V.I. ★)

ڈپٹنا ḍa'paṭ'nā V.T. rebuke chide browbeat (of horse) gallop ; canter ڈپٹ ḍa'paṭ N.F. rebuke menace challenge threat (usu. with ڈانٹ ḍaṇṭ) ڈپٹانا ḍapṭā'nā V.T. gallop (a horse)

ڈپٹی ḍip'ṭī N.M. Deputy ڈپٹی کلکٹر dip'ṭī kalak'tar (col. ڈپٹی کلٹر ḍipṭī kalaṭ'ṭar) N.M. Deputy Collector ڈپٹی کمشنر dip'ṭī kamish'nar N.M. Deputy Commissioner ڈپٹی سپرنٹنڈنٹ ḍip'ṭī sūp'raṇṭanḍaṇṭ N.M. Deputy Superintendent Deputy Superintendent of Police ; D.S.P. [E]

ڈپلوما ḍiplo'mā N.M. diploma ڈپلوما یافتہ ḍiplo'mā-yāf'tah ADJ. diplomaed ; diplomad ; diploma-holder [E]

ڈپو ḍi'poo N.M. depot ration depot [E]

ڈپوٹیشن ḍepoote'shan N.M. deputation [E]

ڈٹنا ḍaṭ'nā, ڈٹ جانا ḍaṭ jā'na V.I. take a form stand ; put up a bold front be pitted (against)

ڈر ḍar N.M. fear dread awe scare danger ڈرپوک ḍar'pok ADJ. coward dastardly timid ڈرنا ḍar'nā V. be afraid of fear be frightened be terrified be scarred ڈرانا ḍarā'nā V.T. frighten terrify ڈراؤنا ḍarā''ona ADJ. frightful terrifying dreadful horrid horrible

ڈرافٹسمین ḍrāf'smain N.M. draftsman [E]

ڈرامہ ḍarā'mah, ڈراما ḍarā'mā N.M. drama [E]

ڈرائنگ روم ḍarā''ing room N.M. drawing room

ڈرائیور ḍarā''ivar N.M. driver [E]

ڈرل ḍaril' N.F. drill [E] .

ڈرھیل ḍaṛh'yal N.M. & ADJ. (derog.) bearded (person) [~ ڈاڑھی]

ڈسپنسری ḍispain'sarī N.F. dispensary [E]

ڈسٹرکٹ dis'ṭik N.M. district ڈسٹرکٹ بورڈ dis'tik bor'ḍ N.M. District Board ڈسٹرکٹ کونسل ḍis'tik kauṅ'sal N.F. District Council ڈسٹرکٹ مجسٹریٹ ḍis'ṭik majis'ṭareṭ N.M. District Magistrate [E]

ڈسمس ḍis'mis ADV. dismiss ADJ. dismissed ڈسمسل ḍis'misal N.F. dismiscal [E]

ڈسنا ḍūs'nā V.T. (of snake) bite

ڈف ḍaf N.M. tabor ; small drum

ڈفلی ḍaf'lī N.F. tambourine اپنی اپنی ڈفلی اپنا اپنا راگ ap'nī ap'nī ḍaf'lī ap'nā ap'nā rāg' PROV. each one striking a different note ڈفالی ḍafā'lı ڈفالچی ḍafal'chī N.M. drumbeater [~ A دف CORR.]

ڈکار ḍakār' N.F. belch ; eructation ڈکار جانا ḍakār' jā'nā V.T. (fig.) embezzle ; defalcate ڈکار لینا ḍakār' le'nā V.I. belch ڈکار نہ لینا ḍakār' na le'nā V.T. & I. not to belch eat voraciously (fig.) embezzle (fig.) keep one's counsel ڈکارنا ḍakār'na V.T. & I. belch embezzle

ڈکٹیٹر ḍikṭe'ṭar N.M. dictator ڈکٹیٹری ḍikṭe'ṭarī N.F. dictatorship [E]

ڈکرانا ḍakrā'nā V.I. low bellow

ڈکشنری ḍiksh'narī N.F. dictionary [E]

ڈکوسنا ḍakos'nā, ڈھکوسنا ḍhakos'nā V.T. gulp down greedily

ڈکیت dakait' N.M. dacoit, robber, bandit, brigand, highwayman footpad ڈکیتی dakai'tī N.F. dacoity; robbery highway; robbery banditry, brigandage [doublet of ڈاکو]

ڈگ ḍag N.M. stride step pace ڈگ بھرنا ḍag bhar'na V.I. step out stride take (long) steps

ڈگانا digā'na V.T. cause to stagger [~ ڈگنا CAUS.]

ڈگڈگی ḍūg'ḍūgī N.F drum, juggler's drum

ڈگر ḍa'gar N.F path track پرانی ڈگر پر چلنا pūrā'nī ḍa'gar par chal'nā V.I. tread a beaten path

ڈگری ḍig'rī N.F decree degree استقراریہ ڈگری istiqrā'riyyah ḍig'rī N.F. declaratory decree ڈگری پانا (یا حاصل کرنا) ḍig'rī pā'nā (or ḥā'sil kar'nā) V.I get or obtain a decree obtain a decree (from court) ڈگری جاری کرنا ḍig'rī jā'rī kar'na V.T. enforce or execute a decree ڈگری دار ḍig'rī-dār N.M. decree-holder ADJ. judgment ڈگری دینا ḍig'rī de'nā V T decree, adjudge admit to the degree (of) ڈگری یافتہ ḍig'rī-yāf'tah ADV. degree-holder; diploma'd اقبالی ڈگری iqbā'lī ḍig'rī N.F. judgment by cognovit یکطرفہ ڈگری yak-tar'afah ḍig'rī N.F. ex parte decree

ڈگمگانا ḍagmagā'nā V.I. stagger real tottor ڈگمگ ḍag'mag ADV staggering realing ڈگمگاہٹ ḍagmagā'hat N.F stagger reel

ڈگنا ḍig'nā V.I stagger

ڈگی ḍūg'gī N.F beat of drum for some announcement such announcement

ڈلا ḍa'la N.M. lump clod ڈلی ḍa'lī N.F lump piece clod betel-nut loaf, lump or cubic (of sugar) مصری کی ڈلی mis'rī kī ḍa'lī N.F sugar loaf

ڈلاؤ ḍalā''o N.M. heap of rubbish

ڈلکنا ḍa'laknā V.I. glitter ڈلک ḍa'lak glitter

ڈلنا ḍal'nā V.I. (coll.) be put

ڈلوانا ḍalvā'nā V.T. cause to be put cause to be shoved in ~ ڈالنا CAUS.]

ڈلی ḍa'lī N.F (see under ڈلا N.M. ★)

ڈلہ ḍal'lah, مائی ڈلہ mā''ī ḍal'lah N.F (fig.) seductive hag

ڈلیا ḍal'ya N.F. basket wicker-work tray

ڈمرو ḍam'roo N.M. hour glass-like drum

ڈنٹھل ḍan'ṭhal N.M. stalk; stem of plant chaff; straw petiole

ڈنڈ ḍand N.M. damages; compensation indemnity penalty (less usu. variant ڈنٹر ★) ڈنڈ بھرنا ḍand bhar'na V.I. pay the damages: indemnify ڈنڈ پڑنا ḍand' par'na V.I. be penalized have to indemnify be held responsible for damages ڈنڈ ڈالنا ḍand' ḍāl'na V.T. panalize charge damages hold responsible for damages

ڈنڈا ḍan'ḍa N.M. rod stick staff club flag-pole ڈنڈا ڈولی کرنا ḍan'ḍa ḍo'lī kar'na V.T. lift some one up by his arms and legs ڈنڈے بجاتے پھرنا ḍan'ḍe bajā'te phir'na V.I. loaf about without earning one's livelihood

ڈنڈوت ḍanḍaut N.F. (dial.) prostration (before idol.) ڈنڈوت کرنا ḍanḍaut' kar'na V.I. (dial.) prostrate oneself (before idol) [S]

ڈنڈی ḍan'ḍī N.F beam (of scales) lever path stem petiole ڈنڈی وار ḍan'ḍī dar N.M. weighman ڈنڈی مارنا ḍan'ḍī mār'na V.T. give short weight

ڈنر ḍi'nar N.M. dinner [E]

ڈنڑ ḍanr' N.M. crossbar-like gymnastic exercise performed on the ground ڈنڑ پیلنا ḍanr' pel'na V.I perform this exercise

ڈنک ḍank N.M. sting (of wasp or scorpion) (fig.) malicious step ڈنک لگانا (یا مارنا) ḍank lagā'na (or mār'nā) V.T. sting (fig.) damage

ڈنکا ḍan'ka N.M. kettle-drum (fig.) fame (fig.) notoriety ڈنکا بجانا ḍan'kā bajā'na V.T. & I. beat a drum make a name (for) rule, reign ڈنکا بجنا ḍan'kā baj'na V.I. (of drum) be beaten be famous ڈنکے کی چوٹ کہنا ḍan'ke kī choṭ kaih'na V.I. proclaim by beat of drum declare assert boldly

ڈنگر ḍan'gar N.M (usu. in PH. ڈھور ڈنگر ḍhor ḍan'gar) cattleherd

ڈنگیا ḍūng'ya N.F. small mug [DIM. ~ ڈونگا]

ڈوب *ḍob.* ڈوبا *ḍo'bā* N.M (see under ڈوبنا ۱. ★)

ڈوبنا *ḍoob na.* ڈوب جانا *ḍoob' jā'na* V.I. drown : be drowned sink ; be sunk be dipped; be immersed be flooded : be inundated be absorbed or engrossed (in) (of heart or pulse) grow weak ; collapse (of money, etc.) go to waste (of debt) the irresoverable ڈوب *ḍob* N.M dip (of pen ink) immersion (of cloth in dye dive plunge ڈوب دینا *ḍob' de'nā* V.T. immerse for dyeing ڈوبا *ḍo'bā* N.M. dipping of pen in inkpot to draw ink ; dip ڈوبا لینا *ḍo'ba le'nā* V.I. dip pen in inkpot ڈوبتے کو تنکے کا سہارا *ḍoob'te ko tin'ke kā sahā'ra* PROV. a drowning man catches at a straw ڈوب مرنا *ḍoob' mar'nā* V.I. drown oneself ; die by drowning be much disgraced take a disgrace to heart ڈوب مرنے کا مقام ہونا *ḍoob' mar'ne kā maqām' ho'nā* V.I. be very shameful ; be a shame

ڈوڈا *ḍo'ḍā* N.M. (cotton or poppy) pod ; seed-vessel

ڈور *ḍor* N.F. starched thread ; kite string string ; cord ڈور پر لگانا *ḍor' par lagā'nā* V.T. tame (a child) ڈور ڈھیلی چھوڑنا *ḍor ḍhī'lī chhoṛ'nā* let kite drift give a long rope ڈور کو سلجھانا *ḍor ko sūljhā'nā* V.T. unravel ڈور کو مانجھا لگانا *ḍor ko mān'jhā lagā'nā,* ڈور کو سوتنا *ḍor' soot'nā* V.T. starch kite-string for dyeing

ڈورا *ḍo'rā* N.M. cord line baste ; stitch graceful motion (of neck) redness (of ophalmveins) streak (of collyrium) آنکھ کا ڈورا *ānkh' kā ḍo'rā* N.M. blood shot eye ڈورے ڈالنا *ḍo're ḍāl'nā* V.I. wheedle ; coax seduce stitch (quilt) ڈوری *ḍo'rī* N.F. string cord ڈوریا *ḍo'riyā* N.M. striped muslin

ڈورو *ḍau'roo* N.M. a simple kind of musical instrument

ڈول *ḍaul* N.M. mode ; manner ; fashion device pattern ; form ; figure constitution foundation appraisal path separating fields ڈول پر لانا *ḍaul' par lā'nā* V.T. bring into shape systematize in order ڈول ڈالنا *ḍaul' ḍāln'a* V.T. lay the foundation (of) ڈول ڈول جانا *ḍaul' ḍaul jā'na* V.I. go or walk along the path in the fields ڈول سے لگانا *ḍaul' se lagā'nā* V.T. put in order بیڈول *be-ḍaul'* ADJ. deformed ungainly

ڈول *ḍol* N.M. bucket ڈولچی *ḍol'chī* N.F. small bucket

ڈولا *ḍo'lā* N.M. cradle hung from tree lady's sedan chair (fig.) bride ڈولا اچھالنا *ḍo'la uchhal'nā* V.I. make love to the husband (of) ڈولا دینا *ḍo'la de'nā* V.T. & I. give away in marriage (esp. to a rich suitor) ڈولی *ḍo'lī* N.F. ★

ڈولا *ḍau'lā* N.M. assessment raised boundary line of field

ڈولنا *ḍol'nā* V.I. reel shake ; be shaken stagger swing deviate feel shaky

ڈولی *ḍo'lī* N.F. (esp. bride's) sedan chair

ڈوم *ḍom* N.F. hereditory singer ; one of a caste of singers ڈوم ڈھاری *ḍom' ḍhā'rī* N.M. PL. singers and musicians low-caste entertainers ڈومنی *ḍom'nī* N.F. a woman belonging to this caste dancing girl singing and dancing in women gatherings only a kind of chattering bird

ڈونڈی *ḍauṅ'ḍī* N.F. proclamation by beat of drum ڈونڈی پٹنا *ḍauṅ'ḍī piṭ'na* V.I. be proclaimed by beat of drum be bruited ڈونڈی پیٹنا *ḍauṅ ḍī piṭ'na* V.T. proclaim by beat of drum make (something) a town talk

ڈونگا *ḍoṅ'gā* N.M. dish mug small boat canoe ڈونگی *ḍo'ngī* N.F. very small boat

ڈونگرے *ḍoṅg're* N.M. heavy showers تعریف کے ڈونگرے برسانا *tā'rīf' ke ḍoṅg re barsā'nā* V.I. lovish praises (on) give great ovation (to)

ڈوئی *ḍo''ī* N.F. wooden ladle

ڈویژن *ḍavī'zhan* (col. *ḍavī'zan*) N.M. division [E]

ڈھاٹا *ḍhā'ṭā* N.M. cloth band tied over beard to turn hair upwards : whisker-band ڈھاٹا باندھنا *ḍhā'ṭā bāndh'nā* V.I. tie whisker-band ڈھاٹی *ḍhā'ṭī* N.F. piece of cloth used as bridle ڈھاٹی چڑھانا (یا دینا یا لگانا) *ḍhā'ṭī chaṛhā'nā* (or *de'nā* or *lagā'nā*) bridle (horse) with cloth piece

ڈھارس *ḍhā'ras* N.F. encouragement reassurance solace : comfort ڈھارس بندھنا *ḍhā'ras bandh'na* V.I. b reassured be encouraged keep the spirits be solaced ڈھارس بندھانا (یا دینا) *ḍhā'ras bandhā'na* (or *de'nā*) V.T. solace ; comfort encourage reassure ڈھاڑیں (یا ڈھاریں) مار کر رونا *ḍhā'ṛeṅ* (or *ḍhā'reṅ*) *mār kar ro'nā* V.I. weep bitterly

ڈھاک *ḍhāk* N.M. butia frondesa (وہی) ڈھاک کے تین پات (*vo'hī*) *ḍhāk' ke tīn' pāt* PROV. be obstinate be unswarving be unyielding always be penurious : ever be short of money

ڈھاک

ڈھال *ḍhāl* N.F. shield slope ; declivity

ڈھالنا *ḍhāl'na* V.T. cast : mould forge form ; shape

ڈھالو *ḍhā'loo* ADJ. (same as ڈھلوان ADJ. ★)

ڈھانا *ḍhā'nā* V.T. raze ; demolish ; pull down knock down subject to (tyranny, etc.) قیامت ڈھانا *qiyā'mat ḍhā'nā* V.T. & I. let loose a reign of tyranny do some enormity

ڈھاپنا *ḍhāṅp'nā*, ڈھانکنا *ḍhāṅk'nā* V.T. hide ; conceal cover ; put lid, etc. over

ڈھانچ *ḍhāṅch*, ڈھانچہ *ḍhāṅ'chah* N.M. skeleton skinny person draft plan outline

ڈھانکنا *ḍhāṅk'nā* V.T. (same as ڈھاپنا V.T. ★)

ڈھانگر *ḍhāṅ gar* N.M. bank of stream

ڈھائی *ḍhā''ī* اڑھائی *aṛhā''ī* ADJ. two-and-a-half (fig.) short lived ; ephameral sudden ; swift ڈھائی چلو پانی پینا *ḍhā''ī chul'loo la'hoo pī'nā* V.I. murder (someone) to appease one's anger ڈھائی دن کی بادشاہت *ḍhā''ī din kī bādshā'hat* PH. ephemeral glory ڈھائی گھڑی کی آنا *ḍhā''ī gha'ṛī kī ā'nā* V.I (as imprecation) come to sudden death

ڈھب *ḍhab* N.M. fashion ; style ; mode manner (ones) liking use profit benefit control ڈھب پر چڑھانا (یا لگانا) *ḍhab' par chaṛhā'nā* (or *lagā'nā*) V.T. mould (someone) after one's heart ڈھب پر چڑھنا *ḍhab' par chaṛh'nā* V.I. come under the control (of) be wheedled by ڈھب کا *ḍhab' kā* ADJ. reasonable useful timely ڈھبیلا *ḍhabī lā* ADJ. well proportioned body N.M. person with such body ڈھب ڈھب *ḍhab ḍhab* ADJ. watery and tasteless (stew)

ڈھبری *ḍhib'rī* N.F. nut

ڈھبس *ḍhab'bas*, ڈھبوس *ḍhaboos* ADJ. fat and ungainly ڈھبیلا *ḍhabī'lā* ADJ. comely ; well proportioned

ڈھپ *ḍhap* N.F. tambourine ڈھپ ڈھپ *ḍhap ḍhap* V.I. drum-beat

ڈھپو *ḍhap'poo* ADJ. N.M. tall and fat (person)

ڈھٹائی *ḍhiṭā''ī* N.F. shamelessness impudence audacity [~ ڈھیٹ]

ڈھٹینگر *ḍhaṭiṅ'gar*, ڈھٹینگڑا *ḍhaṭiṅg'ṛā* N.M. ڈھٹینگڑی *ḍhaṭiṅg'ṛī* N.F. stout (person) : well-built (person)

ڈھچر *ḍha'char* ADJ. old and emaciated N.M. fuss skeleton [~ ڈھانچ]

ڈھڈو *ḍhaḍ'ḍo* N.F. hag

ڈھڈہا *ḍah'ḍahā* ADJ. blooming ; blossoming bright red or yellow ڈھڈہانا *ḍahḍahā'nā* V.I. bloom flourish

ڈھہر *ḍaih'r* N.M. pool pit

ڈھرا *ḍhar'rā* N.M. path ; way line

ڈھکنا *ḍhak'nā* V.T. hide ; conceal cover N.M. lid ; cover

ڈھکوسلا *ḍhakos'lā* N.M. babble silly talk deception ; fraud

ڈھکوسنا *ḍhakos'nā* V.T. & I. eat greedily gulp down

ڈھلان *ḍhalān'* N.M. slope ; declivity [~ ڈھلنا]

ڈھلانا *ḍhalā'nā*, ڈھلوانا *ḍhalvā'nā* have moulded ; get forged ڈھلائی *ḍhalā''ī* N.F. forging remuneration for it

ڈھلائی *ḍhulā''ī* N.F. carriage ; transportation charges for it ; carriage

ڈھلکنا *ḍha'lak'nā* V.I. roll down drip slip down ڈھلکا *ḍhal'kā* N.M. watering of eyes

ڈھلکانا *ḍhalkā'nā* V.T. roll down cause to spill cause to slip down ڈھلمل یقین *ḍhil -mil yaqīn'* ADJ. wavering ; vacillating credulous

ڈھلنا *ḍhal'nā* V.I. be cast ; be moulded be forged (of youth beauty, etc.) pass away decline دن ڈھلنا *dīn' ḍhal'nā* V. of day decline) دن ڈھلے *dīn' ḍha'le* ADV. towards the evening ڈھلتی پھرتی چھاؤں *ḍhal'tī phir'tī chhā''oṅ* ADJ. changeableness of worldly things ; vicissitudes of life or fortune

ڈھلوان *ḍhalvān'*, ڈھالو *ḍhā'loo* ADJ. sloping ; slanting

ڈھلوانا *ḍhalvā'nā* V.T. (same as ڈھلانا V.T ★

ڈھلوانا *ḍhulvā'nā* V.T. to cause to carry cause to be transported cause to be carried on shoulders or back [~ ڈھونا CAUS.]

ڈھنڈنا *ḍhūnd'nā* V.I. be searched ڈھنڈوانا *ḍhūndvā'nā* V.T. cause to be searched [~ ڈھونڈنا]

ڈھنڈورا *ḍhando'rā* N.M. proclamation by beat of drum ڈھنڈورا پٹنا *ḍhando'rā piṭ nā* be proclaimed thus ڈھنڈورا پیٹنا *ḍhando'rā pīṭ'nā* V.T. proclaim thus give wide currency to لڑکا بغل میں ڈھنڈورا شہر میں *laṛ'kā ba'ghal meṅ ḍhando'rā shaih'r meṅ* PROV. much ado about nothing ڈھنڈورچی *ḍhandor'chī* N.M. town crier one who proclaims by beat of drum

ڈھنڈیا *ḍhūnd'yā* N.F. search ڈھنڈیا پڑنا *ḍhūnd'yā par'nā* V.I. be much sought for be searched everywhere [~ ڈھونڈنا]

ڈھنگ *ḍhang* N.M. manner ; made device ; method ڈھنگ ڈالنا *ḍhang' ḍāl'nā* V.T. begin

ڈھوانا *ḍhavā'nā* V.T. cause to be pulled down ; be demolished [~ ڈھانا CAUS.]

ڈھور *ḍhor* N.M. cattle (usu. as) ڈھور ڈنگر *ḍhor' ḍan'gar* N.M. PL. cattle

ڈھورا *ḍho'rā* ڈھوڈھا *ḍho'ḍhā* N.M gram weevil

ڈھول *ḍhol* N.M. large drum, tomtom ڈھول کا پول *ḍhol' kā pol* N.M. hollowness being exposed ڈھول کا پول کھلنا *ḍhol' kā pol khul'nā* V.I. be exposed ڈھولک *ḍhol'lak* N.F. small drum; tomtom

ڈھولی *ḍho'lī* N.F. bundle of two hundred (betel-leaves)

ڈھونا *ḍho'nā* V.T bear carry transport remove

ڈھونچا *ḍhaun'chā* ADJ. & N.M. four-and-a-half

ڈھونڈنا *ḍhoonḍ'nā*, ڈھونڈ لینا *ḍhoonḍ' le'nā* V.T search for; look for seek track out track down ڈھونڈ ڈھانڈ کر *ḍhoonḍ' ḍhaonḍ' kar* ADV after some search

ڈھونگ *ḍhong* N.M. hoax feint imposture fraud false excuse ڈھونگ رچانا *ḍhong rachā'na* V.T. & I. put up a hox feign ڈھونگیا *ḍhon'giyā* ADJ. impostor trickster

ڈھئی *ḍhai''ī* N.F. hanging on; stay as an unwanted guest ڈھئی دینا *ḍhai''ī de'nā* stay thus; hang on ڈھینا *ḍhai'nā*, ڈھے پڑنا (یا جانا) *ḍhai paṛ'nā* (or *jā'nā*) V.I. collapse fall down

ڈھیٹ *ḍhīṭ* ADJ. shameless; shamefaced, brazen-faced lacking sense of honour

ڈھٹائی *ḍhiṭā''ī* N.F. ★

ڈھیڈ *ḍhīd* N.F. discharge from eye corner

ڈھیر *ḍher'* N.M. heap stack; accumulation ADJ. much abundant; ample ڈھیر کرنا *ḍher kar'nā* V.T. heap up accumulate kell; murder ڈھیر ہو جانا *ḍher' ho jā'nā* V.I. collapse be slain; be killed, be murdered become a heap ڈھیری *ḍhe'rī* N.F. small heap lot

ڈھیل *ḍhīl* N.F. loosening slackness relaxation ڈھیل دینا *ḍhīl' de'nā* V.T. & I. give a long rope relax loosen release more of kite's string ڈھیل کرنا *ḍhīl' kar'nā* V.I. delay dawdle ڈھیلا *ḍhī'la*, ADJ. (F. ڈھیلی *ḍhī'lī*) loose not tight slack inattentive courageless ڈھیلا پڑ جانا *ḍhī'la paṛ jā'nā* V. to become loose; to skulk ڈھیلا پن *ḍhī'la-pan* N.M. looseness slackness ڈھیلی زنا *ḍhī'lī za'nā* PH. N.F. slut, loose woman [~ ڈھیلا + P زن woman]

ڈھیلا *ḍhe'la* N.M. clod eyeball ڈھیلا لینا *ḍhe'la le'nā* V.I. use clod for toilet

ڈھینچوں ڈھینچوں *ḍhen' choon ḍhen' choon* N.F bray (of ass)

ڈھینکلی *ḍhenk'lī* N.F sweep someself

ڈھینگر *ḍhin'gar*, ڈھینگڑا *ḍhing'ra* ADJ & N.M. stout person lout ڈھینگڑی *ḍhing'ṛī*

ADJ. & N.F. well build (girl, etc)

ڈپارٹمنٹ *ḍīpart'manṭ* N.M department ڈپارٹمنٹل *ḍīpart'manṭal* ADJ. departmental [E]

ڈیٹھ *ḍīṭh* N.F. evil eye ڈیٹھ بندی *ḍīṭh ban'dī* N.F charm, etc. to offset influence of evil eye

ڈیرہ *ḍe'rāh* N.M. (temporary) dwelling male apartment ڈیرہ ڈالنا (یا کرنا) *ḍe'rah ḍāl'nā* (or *kar'nā*) V.I. encamp pitch a tent hang on

ڈیری *ḍe''arī* N.F dairy ڈیری فارم *ḍe''arī fa'rm* [E]

ڈیزائن *ḍīzā''in* N.M. design [E]

ڈیفنس *ḍifains'* N.M. defence [E]

ڈیڑھ *ḍeṛh* ADJ. & N.M. one-and-a-half اپنی ڈیڑھ اینٹ کی مسجد الگ بنانا *ap'nī ḍeṛh' īnṭ' kī mas'jid alag' banā'nā* V.I. withdraw from the majority and form a small party of one's own; be too opinionate to side with others; withdraw from the society of other through overweaning pride

ڈیل *ḍīl* N.M. bulk stature corn ڈیل ڈول *ḍīl ḍaul'* N.M. bulk stature

ڈیلیگیٹ *ḍai'ligeṭ* N.M. delegate ڈیلیگیشن *ḍai'ligeshan* N.M. delegation [E]

ڈینگ *ḍīng* N.F. boasting; vaunting; pride ڈینگ مارنا (یا ہانکنا) *ḍīng' mār'nā* (or *hāṅk'nā*) V.I. brag; boast

ڈیوٹی *ḍoo'ṭī* N.F duty [E]

ڈیوڑھا *ḍeyo'ṛhā* ADJ one-and-a-half; half again ڈیوڑھا درجہ *ḍeyo'ṛhā dar'jah* (ped. *da'rajah*) N.M. inter class (compartment, etc.)

ڈیوڑھی *ḍeyo'ṛhī* N.F. entrance threshold porch; portico

ڈیوک *ḍiyook'* N.M. duke [E]

ڈیئر *ḍī''ar* ADJ. & N.M. dear [E]

ذ

ذ *zāl* thirteenth letter of Urdu alphabet (also called *zāl-e mo''jamah* (equivalent to English *th* soft) (in jummal reckoning) 700

ذات *zāt* N.F. (PL. ذوات *zavāt'*) personality entity existence self person body caste PREF. partaining to possessor of possessed of ذات الجنب *zā't-ul-janb'* N.M. pleurisy ذات الریہ *zā't-ul-ri'yah*, ذات الصدر *zā't-us-sud'r* N.M. pneumonia ذات باہر *zāt' bā'hir* ADJ. outcaste ذات باہر کرنا

zat' ba'hir kar'na declare an outcaste ; excommunicate ذات پات *zat' pat'* N.F. caste caste system ذات شریف *za't-e sharif'* N.M. (iron.) arrant or consummate knave ذات میں بٹہ لگانا *zat' meṅ baṭ'ṭah laga'na* V.T. bring bad name (to) ذات میں بٹہ لگنا *zat' meṅ baṭ'ṭah lag'na* V.I. get a bad name ذاتی *za'ti* ADJ. personal intrinsic inborn ; innate private ذاتی تعلقات *za'ti ta'alluqat* N.M. PL. personal relations ; personal contacts ذاتی حیثیت *za'ti ḥaisiy'yat* N.F. personal status ذاتی لیاقت *zati liya'qat* N.F. intrinisic value real merit ذاتی معاملات *za'ti mo'amalat'* N.M. PL. personal affairs [A]

ذاکر *za'kir* N.M. (PL. ذاکرین *zakirin'*) professional reciter of Shi'ite varses ADJ. (one) who remembers ذاکری *za'kiri* N.F. profession of reciting such elegies [A ~ ذکر]

ذاہل *za'hil* N.M. & ADJ. careless [A]

ذائقہ *za''iqah* N.M. taste relish sense of taste ذائقہ دار *za''iqa-dar'* ADJ. tasty savoury [A ~ ذوق]

ذبح *zib'ḥ* N.M. slaughtered animal, etc. ; victim [A ~ FOLL.]

ذبح *zab'ḥ* N.M. sacrifice slaughter according to Islamic tenets ذبح کرنا *zab'ḥ kar'na* V.T. kill sacrifice slaughter (according to Islamic tenets) ذبح ہونا *zab'ḥ ho'na* V.I. be killed be slaughtered be sacrified ذبیح *zabiḥ'* N.M. victim sacrificial animal ذبیح اللہ *zabi'ḥ ullah'* N.M. appellation of Ishmael ذبیحہ *zabi'ḥah* N.M. animal slaughtered for food according to Islamic tenets [A]

ذوتنا *zatvan'ta* N.M. ذوتنی *zatvan'ti* N.F. scion of a noble family [~ A ذات]

ذخائر *zakha''ir* N.M. (see under ذخیرہ ★)

ذخیرہ *zakhi'rah* N.M. stock store hoard treasure ذخیرہ کرنا *zakhi'rah kar'na* V.I. stock store ذخائر *zakha''ir* N.M. PL. stocks stores hoards [A]

ذرا *zara'* ADJ. (dial ذری *za'ri*) a little while; little while INT. please would you ذرا ذرا *za'ra za'ra* ADJ. little by little ; bit by bit every bit the whole of ذرا ذرا کرکے *za'ra za'ra kar'-ke* ADV. little by little bit by bit by degrees ذرا سا *za'ra sa* ADJ. a little trivial ذرا سا منہ نکل آنا *za'ra sa muṅh' ni'kal a'na* V.I. grow very weak ذرا کی ذرا *za'ra ki za'ra* ADV. just for a while [~ A ذرہ *zar'rah*]

ذرات *zarrat'* N.M. particles specks molecules atoms [A ~ SING. ذرہ]

ذراع *zira''* N.M. cubit fore-arm yard [A]

ذرائع *zara''e'* N.M. means resources agencies media [A ~ SING. ذریعہ]

ذرہ *zarrah* N.M. (PL. ذرات *zarrat'*) particle speck mote molecule atom [A]

ذری *za'ri* ADJ. (dial. for ذرا ★)

ذریت *zurriy'yat* N.F. (PL. ذریات *zurriyyat'*) offspring: progeny [A]

ذریعہ *zari''ah* N.M. (PL. ذرائع *zara''e'*) means medium agency source intervention influence help recourse ذریعہ پیدا کرنا *zari''ah pai'da kar'na* V.I. find means have recourse to بذریعہ *ba-zari''ah*, کے ذریعے (سے) *ke zari''e (se)* ADV. by means of with the help of by virtue of through the intervention of by having recourse to [A]

ذقن *za'qan* N F. chin چاہ ذقن *cha'h-e za'qan* N.M. dimple of chin [A]

ذکا *zaka'* N.M. sagacity acumen perspicacity discernment ذکاوت *zaka'vat* N.F. acumen shrewdness ; sagacity perspicacity ذکاوت حس *zaka'vat-e his'* N.F. super-sensitiveness of sexual organs (as disease) ذکاوت طبع *zakavat-e tab''* N.F. penetration of mind

ذکر *zik'r* N.M. mention remembrance account fame statement narration reference repeated invocation of God's name ذکر کرنا *zik'r kar'na* V.T. mention state ; express relate narrate repeatedly invoke God's name ذکر مذکور *zik'r mazkoor'* N.M. mention talk reference ; allusion ذکر ہونا *zik'r ho'na* V.I. be mentioned (of a group) be invoking God's name [A]

ذکر *za'kar* N.M. penis [A]

ذکور *zukoor'* N.M. PL. men males ; male sex ذکور و اناث *zukoo'r-o inas'* N.M. PL. men and women males and females both the sexes the two sexes

ذکی *za'ki* ADJ. acute ingenius shrewd fiery ; flaring [A ~ ذکاوت]

ذل *zul* N.M. gentleness mercy docility [A]

ذلت *zil'lat*, ذلالت *zala'lat* ذل *zil* N.F. dishonour; disgrace indignity insult; affront ignominy baseness ; meanness ذلت اٹھانا (یا پانا) *zil'lat uṭha'na* (or *pa'na*) V.I. suffer disgrace (at the hands of) ذلت دینا V.T. disgrace ; dishonour abase ; debase [A]

ذلیل *zalil'* ADJ. means ; base contemptible dishonoured ; disgraced ذلیل کرنا *zalil' kar'na* V.T. base ; debase dishonour ; disgrace put to shame ذلیل النفس zalī'l-ūn-naf's ADJ. mean, abject ذلیل ہونا zalīl' ho'na V.I. be dishonoured, be disgraced be brought low suffer ignominy be put to shame [A ~ ذلت]

ذم zam N.F. censure obloquy, opprobrium ذم کا پہلو نکالنا zam kā paih'loo nik'kalna V.I. be opprobrious ذمیمہ zamī'mah N.F. (PL. ذمائم zamā''im) something earning opprobrium ADJ. opprobrious ذمائم zamā''im N.M.PL. opprobrious acts or traits of character [A]

ذمہ zim'ma N.M. (PL. ذمم) charge responsibility duty trust onus or burden (of proof) obligation ذمہ دار zi'm'ma-dār' ADJ. responsible answerable N.M. assignee trustee ذمہ داری zim'ma-dā'rī N F. responsiblity charge obligation duty trust ذمہ لینا zim'ma le'nā V.I. take responsibility (for) take charge take care (of) stand surety (for) [A]

ذمی zim'mī, اہل الذمہ ah'l-ūz-zim'mah N.M. non-Muslim citizens of Islamic State (as people held in trust [A ~ PREC.]

ذنب za'nab N.M. (PL. ذنوب zānoob') sin crime ذنب za'nab N.F. (PL. اذناب aznab') tail [A]

ذو zoo, ذی zī PREF. (PL. ذوی zavi' or ذوو zavoo') PREF. having; possessing with -er ذوار بعۃ الاضلاع zoo arba''at-il-azlā' ADJ. & N.M. quadrilateral (figure) ذواضعاف zoo-az'ā'f' N.M. common multiple ذواضعاف اقل zoo-az'ā'f-e aqal' N.M. (Math.) least common multiple (L.C.M.) ذوالجلال zūl-jalal' ADJ. glorious; splendid. ذوالجناح zūl-janah' N.M. the winged horse (as the name of Imam Husain's horse) the horse taken out in procession during Muharram to commemorate the Imam's martyrdom ذوالحجہ zūl-hij'jah N.M. last month of the Hijri year ذوزنقہ zoo-zan'qah N F. quadrilateral with only two sides parallel ذوالفقار zūl-faqār' N.F spined sword (as name of Hazrat Ali's sword given him by the Holy Prophet as one of the spoils of the Battle of Badr) ذوالقرنین zūl--qarnain' N.M. (arch. use) lord of the two horns *i.e.* East and West (as epithet of Alexander) the sovereign with a double horned crown (as epithet of Cyprus the Great) ذوالقعدہ zūl-qa''dah N.M. eleventh month of Hijri year ذوالنورین zūn-noorain' N.M. the possessor of two lights (as the appellation) of Hazrat Usman's who married two of the Holy Prophets daughters in succession ذوفنون zoo-fūnoon' N.M. man of many parts trickster fraudulent person ذوالمنن zūl-mi'nan ADJ. & N.M. the Bountiful (as an epithet of God) ذومعنی zoo ma'nī (or ped. nā) ذومعنیین zoo ma'nayain') ADJ. with double meaning N.F. double entendre ذومعنی بات zoo-ma'nī bat' N.F pun double entendre [A]

ذوق zauq N.M. taste relish liking pleasure literary or artistic taste fervour ذوق سلیم zau q-e salīm' N.M. right type of (literary, etc.) taste ذوق و شوق zau'q-o shauq' N.M fervour [A]

ذوی zavi' PREF. having, possessing endowed with with -er ذوی الارحام zavi-l-arhām' N.M uterine relations ذوی الاقتدار zavī-l iqtidār' N.M those in authoriry ADJ. powerful [A]

ذہاب zahāb' N.M. going departure مجی و ذہاب majī'-o zahāb' N.M. comings and goings [A]

ذہانت zihā'nat N.F (see under ذہن N.M. ★)

ذہب za'hab N.M. gold [A]

ذہن zeh'n (rare zah'n, col. zaih'n) N.M mind mental faculty memory understanding ability acumen ذہن کھلنا zeh'n khūl-na V.I. (of mental faculties) come into play be no longer a blockhead ذہن سے نکل جانا zeh'n se ni'kal jā'na V.I. slip out of the mind be forgotten ذہن لڑانا zeh'n larā'na V.T. think, exercise one's mental faculties ذہن لڑنا zeh'n lar'na V.I. (of something) strike the mind ذہن میں آنا zeh'n meṅ ā'na V.I. strike in mind be understood ذہن میں بیٹھنا zeh'n meṅ baiṭh'na V.I. be instilled into the mind ذہن نشین کرنا zeh'n-nashīn' kar'na V.T. instil: impress on the mind drive (something) home to ذہن نشین ہونا zeh'n-nashīn' ho'na V.I. be instilled ذہنیت zehniy'yat N.F. mentality ذہین zahīn ADJ. intelligent [A]

ذہول zūhool N.M. forgetfulness bad memory [A]

ذی zī PROV (same as ذو zoo PROF. ★) ذی اختیار zī-ikhtiyar ADJ. in authority, weilding authority authorized ذی استعداد zī-iste'dād' ADJ. capable, acute ذی اقتدار zī-iqtidār' ADJ. in authority; wielding authority having competent powers ذی الحج zil-hij' N.M. (col. for ذوالحجہ N.M. ★) ذی حیات zī-hayat' ADJ. living, animate N.M. living being ذی خرد zī-khi'rad ADJ. wise, sensible ذی رتبہ، ذی مرتبہ zī-rūt'bah, zī-mar'tabah ADJ. of rank enjoying a high status ذی روح zī-rooh' ADJ. living beings ذی شعور zī-sho'oor' ADJ. sensible ذی عزت zī-'iz'zat ADJ. respectable honourable venerable ذی قعد zī-qa''d N.M. (col for ذوالقعدہ N.M. ★) ذی ہوش zī-hosh' ADJ. wise sensible wide-awake غیر ذی روح ghair zī-rooh' ADJ & N.M. inanimate (object) [A]

ذیابیطس *zayābī'tas* N.M. diabetes ذیابیطس کا مریض *zayābī'tas kā marīz'* N.M. dibetic [A]

ذیل *zail* N.M. (of garment); skirt minor revenue sub-division; 'zail' what follows; under-mentioned details ذیلدار *zaildār'* N.M. honorary or part-time official in change of a 'zail': 'Zaildar' ذیل کا (یا کے) *zail kā* (or *ke*) ADJ. the following; the undermentioned ذیل میں *zail meṉ'* ADV. as follows; as below; as under حسب ذیل *ḥas'b-e zail* ADV. as follows; as below; as under; following مفصلہ ذیل *mūfas'sala-e zail'* ADV. as per detail; as below; as under ذیلی *zai'lī* ADJ. subsidiary minor ذیلی صنعت *zai'lī san''at* N.F. subsidiary industry [A]

ر

ر *re* (or in construction *rā'*) fourteenth letter of Urdu alphabet (equivalent to English *r*) (also called *rā'-e moh'malah* or *ra-e ghair manqoo'tah* (in jummal reckoning) 200

راب *rāb* N.F. treacle; molasses golden syrup

رابطہ *rā'bitah* N.M. (PL. روابط *ravā'bit*) connexion; relation liaison contact touch communication bond familiarity knowledge رابطہ پیدا کرنا *rā'bitah pai'dah kar'nā* V.I. get into contact (with) رابطہ توڑنا *rā'bitah toṛ'nā* V.I. snap (with) رابطہ قائم رکھنا *rā'bitah (qā''im) rakh'nā* V.I. maintain contacts with افسر رابطہ *af'sar-e rā'bitah* N.M. liaison officer [A ~ ربط]

رابع *rā'be''* ADJ. fourth رابعاً *rā'be'an* ADV. fourthly رابعہ *rābe'ah* ADJ. (F.) fourth

راپی *rā'pī* N.F. (same as رانپی N.F. ★)

رات *rāt'* N.F. night رات آنکھوں میں کاٹنا (یا کٹنا) *rāt' aṉ'khoṉ meṉ kāṭ'nā* (or *kaṭ'nā*) V.I. have a sleepless night; have a restless night رات بھاری ہونا *rāt' bhā'rī ho'nā* V.I. have a long and wearisome night رات بھیگنا *rāt' bhīg'nā* V.I. be late in the night (of night) grow cooler رات تھوڑی اور سانگ بہت *rāt' tho'ṛī aur sāṉg' bahūt'* PROV. art is long and time is fleeting رات دن *rāt' din* ADV. day and night رات کا پیٹ بھاری ہے *rāt' kā peṭ' bhā'rī hai* PROV. night's time is pregnant with possibilities رات کی رات *rāt' kī rāt'* ADV. just for a night رات کی رانی *rāt' kī rā'nī* N.M. a kind of lily emitting fragrance at night; champak (fig.) prostitute رات گئے *rāt' ga''e* ADV late in the evening راتوں رات *rā'toṉ rāt'* ADV. within one night رات والا *rāt' vā'lā* N.M. (dial.) owl moon آدھی رات *ā'dhī rāt* V.F. midnight بڑی رات *ba'ṛī rāt'* the dead of the night پچھلی رات *pichh'lī rāt* N.F. early hours of the morning پہلی رات *paih'lī rāt* N.F. late evening (hours)

راتب *rātib*, (col. *rā'tab*) N.M. (arch.) rations daily allowance for food D.A. stipend feed [A]

راج *rāj* N.M. brick-layer; mason (dial.) reign (dial.) dominion; principality ADJ. (dial.) large PREF. kingly راج بہا *rāj'-ba'hā* N.M. (same as رجباہا N.M. ★) راج پاٹ *rāj' pāṭ* N.M. (dial.) dominion راجپوت *rāj'poot* N.M. (one of) a martial Indo-Pakistan tribe راج پھوڑا *raj pho'ṛā* N.M. carbuncle راج دربار *rāj' dar'bār* N.M. (dial.) royal court راج دلاری *rāj' dūlā'rī* N.F. (dial.) princess ADJ. darling راجدھانی *rāj'-dhā'nī* N.F. (dial.) capital راج رانی *rāj'-rā'nī* N.F. (dial.) queen راج سبھا *rāj'-sa'bhā* N.F. (dial) king's council راج کرنا (یا رجنا) *rāj' kar'nā* (or rare *raj nā*) V.T. reign be in authority live a comfortable life راجکمار *rāj'-kūmār'* N.M. Hindu prince راجکماری *rāj'-kūmā'rī* N.F. Hindu princess راجکوی *rāj'-ka'vī* N.M (dial.) poet laureate راج گدی *rāj'-gad'dī* N.F. (dial) throne راج گیری *rāj'-gī'rī* N.F. masonry; bricklaying راج مزدور *rāj'-maz'door* (ped. *-mūz-*) N.M. bricklayers راج نیتی *rāj'-nī'tī* N.F. (dial.) political science diplomacy راجواڑہ *rāj'-vā'ṛa* N.M. (same as رجواڑہ N.M. ★) راج ہٹ *rāj'-haṭ* N.F. sovereign's stub bornness راج ہنس *rāj'-han's* N.M. goose

راجا *raja*, راجہ *rā'jah* N.M. sovereign Rajah petty prince (euphem.) barber [~ PREC.]

راجح *rā'jeḥ* ADJ. better; superior stronger (idea, etc.) inclined [A ~ رجحان]

راجع *rā'je'* ADJ. returning concerning [A ~ رجوع]

راجی *rā'jī* ADJ. & N.M. hopeful (person) [A ~ رجا]

راچھس *rā'chhas* N.M. (same as راکشس N.M. ★)

راحت *rā'ḥat* N.F. comfort; ease joy; pleasure relief rest; repose راحت افزا *rā'ḥat-afzā'* ADJ. comforting delightful; delectable راحت جان *rā'ḥat-e jāṉ'* ADJ. comforting N.M. be love; sweet heart one's children one's family

راحلہ *rā'ḥilah* N.M. caravan riding animal carriage [A ~ رحلت]

راحم *rā'ḥim* ADJ. merciful; compassionate [A ~ رحم]

رادھا *rā'dhā* N.F. (Hindu myth.) Krishna's chief beloved نہ نو من تیل ہوگا نہ رادھا ناچے گی *na nau' man tel' ho' gā na rā'dhā nā'chegī* PROV. put impossible preconditions

راڑ *rāṛ* N.F. quarrel fuss راڑ مچانا *rāṛ machā'nā* V.I. create a fuss راڑیا *rā'ṛiya* N.M. fussy person

راز *rāz* N.M. (lit. PL. رازہا *rāz'hā*) secret confidence mystery راز بتانا *rāz batā'nā* V.T. & I. repose one's confidence (in) betray someone's confidence disclose a secret رازدار *rāz'-dār* ADJ. faithful ; trusted ; trusty ; confident N.M. confident confidant رازداری *rāz'-dā'rī* N.F. secrecy confidence keeping a secret رازدان *rāz'-dān'* (or *dāṅ*) ADJ. friend confident confidant ; one in the know of secrets رازِ درونِ پردہ *rā'z-e daroo'n-e par'dah* N.M. inside story (of) رازِ سربستہ *rā'z-e sarbas'tah*, رازِ نہانی *rā'z-e nehā'nī*, رازِ نہفتہ *rā'z-e nehuf'tah* N.M. close secret ; closely guarded secret راز فاش (یا افشا) کرنا *rāz fāsh'* (or *ifshā'*) *kar'nā* V.I. disclose a secret betray someone's confidence راز کھولنا *rāz' khol'nā* V.I. disclose a secret راز کی بات *rāz kī bāt'* N.F. secret confidence راز و نیاز *rā'z-o niyāz'* N.M. loving prattle ; tete-a-tete secret-talk humble prayer (to God) [P]

رازق *rā'ziq* N.M. cherisher, sustainer, as an attribute of God) [A ~ رزق]

راس *rās*, (ped. etc. *rā''s*) N.M. head head (of cattle) cape top ; peak ; summit angle ; edge of angle راس الجدی *rā''s-ul-jady* N.M. winter solstice راس السرطان *rās''-us-sartān'* N.M. summer solstice راس المال *rā''s-ul-māl'* N.M. capital stock-in-trade [A]

راس *rās* N.F. suitability adaptability (arch.) street drama circular dance in honour of Krishna ; Hindu religious ballet ADV. suitable agreeable profitable راس آنا *rās' ā'nā* V.I. be agreeable be suitable be profitable راس دھاری *rās-dhā'rī* N.M. actor in Hindu religious ballet boy-actor doing woman's part

راست *rās't* ADJ. right . (OPP. left) straight true ; right ADV. to the right ; on the right side راستباز *rāst'-bāz* ADJ. honest ; upright righteous truthful راستبازی *rāst'-bā'zī* N.F. honesty ; uprightness ; integrity plain dealing ; fair play truthfulness راست گفتار *rāst-guftār'*, راستگو *rāst'-go* ADJ. truthful راست گفتاری *rāst' guftā'rī*, راست گوئی *rāst-go'ī* N.F. truthfulness راست معاملگی *rāst'-mo'ā'malagī* N.F. fair deal راست معاملہ *rās't mo'ā'malah* ADJ fair in dealing راستی *rās'tī* N.F. ★

راستہ *rās'tah* N.M. way path road manner ; mode way out راستہ بتانا *rās'tah batā'nā* V.I. show the way (to) guide send away ; dismiss راستہ دیکھنا *rās'tah dekh'nā* V.T. wait (for)

راستی *rās'tī* N.F. truth , veracity rectitude honesty ; uprightness truthfulness [P ~ راست]

راسخ *rā'sikh* ADJ. established; well-established firm constant thorough [A ~ رسوخ]

راشد *rā'shid* ADJ. (PL. راشدین *rāshidīn'*) follower of right path , following the right path , orthodox [A ~ رشد]

راشن *rā'shan* N.M. ration راشن بندی *rā'shan-bandī* N.F rationing راشن ڈپو *rā'shan-ḍi'poo* N.M. ration depot راشن شدہ *rā'shan-shūdah* ADJ. rationed راشن کارڈ *rā'shan kārḍ* N.M. ration-card [E]

راشی *rā'shī* N.M. one who gives bribe (wrong but col.) one who accepts bribe corrupt [A ~ رشوت]

راضی *rā'zī* ADJ. pleased agreeable (to) contented satisfied consenting resigned to the will (of) راضی برضا ہونا *rā'zī ba-rizā' ho'nā* V.I. be resigned to the will of God راضی خوشی *rā'zī khu'shī* ADJ. well and happy ADV. happily راضی کرنا *rā'zī kar'nā* V.T. appease conciliate; satisfy reconcile bring round راضی نامہ *rā'zī-nā'mah* N.M. compromise deed of compromise راضی ہونا *rā'zī ho'nā* V.I. agree (to) assent (to) accede (to) acquiesce (in) be willing (to) be satisfied (with) راضی نامہ کر لینا *rā'zī-nā'mah kar le'nā* V.I. compromise ; have a compromise compound (a case) [A ~ رضا]

راعی *rā''ī* N.M. shepherd pastor ruler [A]

راغ *rāgh* N.M. meadow valley submontane region [P]

راغب *rā'ghib* ADJ. inclined (to) willing (to) having a leaving (towards) راغب کرنا *rā'ghib kar'nā* V.T. make (someone) agree to cause to be inclined (to) [A ~ رغبت]

رافت *rā'fat* (ped. *ra''fat*) N.F. pity , compassion tenderness [A]

رافضی *rā'fizī* N.M. (PL. روافض *ravā'fiz*) dissenter (one of) a Shi'ite dissenting sect

رافع *rā'fe'* N.M. & ADJ. (one) who elevates , elevator [A ~ رفعت]

راقب *rā'qib* N.M. one who watches (over) [A ~ رقیب]

راقم *rā'qim* N.M. writer I ; writer (of this letter, etc.) راقم الحروف *rā'qim-ul huroof'* N.M.

I : the writer (of this letter, etc.) the undersigned [A ~ رقم]

راکب ra'kib N.M. (PL. رکاب rūkkab') a rider (rare) camel-rider ADJ. mounted-riding [A]

راکٹ ra'kiț N.M. rocket [E]

راکشس rak'shas, راچھس ra chhas N.M. (dial.) demon [S]

راکھ rakh N.M. ashes راکھ کر ڈالنا (جلاکر) (jalā kar) rakh kar ḍāl'nā V.T. reduce to ashes راکھ ہونا rakh ho'nā V.I. be reduced to ashes

راکھی ra khī N.F. string tied round someone's wrist by a Hindu women on a festival of that name to set up brotherly relations with him راکھی باندھنا ra'khī baṅdh'nā V.I. tie such string [S]

راگ rāg N.M musical mode tune ; air song one of the six (or more) modes of classical Indo-Pakistan music (viz. bhai'roṅ, māl'-kaus, sri rāg, megh, haṅdol' & dī'pak) (iron.) quarrel ; row راگ الاپنا rāg' alāp'nā V.I. sing harp on the (same) tune ; beat (one's own) drum راگ بدیا rāg' bid'diyā N.F. music ; science of music راگ رنگ rāg' raṅg N.M. dance and song ; music and merriment festivals ; merrymaking carefree life راگ گانا rāg' gā'nā V.I. sing a song ; to tell one's own story ; to sing راگ لانا rāg' lā'nā V.I. kick up a row راگ مالا rāg' mā'lā N.M. principles of music guide book comprising these travellers tale ; old wives tale ; yarn راگنی rāg'nī N.F. musical mode ; minor ; one of the thirty-six ramifications of the major modes of classical Indo-Pakistan music راگی ra'gī N.M. expert in classical music (dial.) singer

رال rāl N.F. saliva pitch رال ٹپکنا (منہ سے) (muṅh se) rāl' ṭa'paknā V.T. (of mouth) water evince keen desire for slubber

رام[1] rām ADJ. tame domesticated submissive tractable obedient رام کرنا rām' kar'nā V.T. subdue bring round tame ; domesticate رام ہونا rām' ho'nā V.I. be tamed

رام[2] rām N.M. Hindu god Rama رام دہائی rām dohā'ī N.F. & INT. (dial.) God forbid رام رام rām' rām N.M. form of Hindu salutation رام رام جپنا پرایا مال اپنا rām' rām jap'nā parā'yā māl ap'nā PROV. hypocrisy رام کہانی rām kahā'nī N.M. Rama's legend ; the Ramayan traveller's tale اپنی رام کہانی ap'nī rām kahā'nī PH. one s tale of woe رام لیلا rām-lī'lā N.F. Hindu religious play based on the legend of Rama رام نومی rām' nau'mī N.M. Rama's birthday celebrations

رامائن rāmā'yan N.F. Hindu epic based on the legend of Rama in Valmik's Sanskrit or Tulsi Das's Hindi [~ PREC.]

رامش rā'mish N.F. harmony ; melody ; music رامشگر rāmish'gar N.M. musician رامش ورنگ rā'mish-o raṅg N.F. music and festivity [P]

ران[1] rān, ران rāṅ SUF. driver wielder [P ~ راندن]

ران[2] rān N.F. thigh ران پٹڑی جمانا rān' paṭ'rī jamā'nā V.I. ride like a horseman ران تلے آنا rān' ta le ā'nā V.I. be subdued ران تلے کرنا rān' ta'le kar'nā V.T. control ; subdue rids ; mount

رانا ra'nā N.M. Rajput's (princely) title king ; petty ruler

رانپی rāṅ'pī, راپی ra'pī N.F. cobbler's knife

رانده rāṅ'dah ADJ. cursed driven out ; expelled rejected; spurned رانده درگاه rāṅ'da-e dargāh' N.M. accursed by heaven spurned driven out [P ~ رانده]

رانڈ rāṅḍ N.F. widow رانڈ کا سانڈ rāṅḍ' kā sāṅḍ N.M. spoilt child

رانگ rāṅg N.F. pewter tin رنگ بھریا (یا رنگ) rāṅg' (or raṅg) bhar'yā N.M. tinman

رانگھڑ rāṅ'ghaṛ N.M. (one of) a clan of Rajputs

رانی[1] ra'nī N.F (dial.) queen ; petty ; princess consort رانی خاں کا سالا ra'nī khāṅ kā sā'lā PH (derog.) self-conceited person

رانی[2] ra'nī SUF. driving wielding [P ~ راندن]

راول ra'val N.M. warrior chieftain hereditary astrologer

راوی ra'vī N.M. narrator name of a West Pakistan river راوی چین ہی چین لکھتا ہے ra'vī chain' (hī chain') likhtā hai PH. peace reigned thereafter what a wonderful life the brave new world [A ~ روایت]

راه rāh, ره rah N.F. way path passage means of access method ; manner mode ; fashion راه بتانا rāh' baṭā'nā V.T. show the way guide deceive prevaricate راہبر rāh'-bar, رہبر rah'-bar (or raih'-) N.M. guide leader mentor راہبری rāh'-ba'rī. رہبری rah'-ba'rī (or raih'-) N.F. guidance leadership راه پر آنا rah' par ā'nā V.I. mend one's ways be brought round راه پر لانا (یا لگانا) rah' par lā'nā (or lagā'-nā) V.I. bring (someone) round reform bring on the right path راه (ورسم) پیدا کرنا ra'h(-o-ras'm) pai'dā kar'nā V.T. form an acquaintance with establish relations (with) راه تکنا (یا دیکھنا) rāh' tak'nā (or dekh'nā) V.T. wait expect look forward to a meeting (with) راہ چلتا *rāh chal'ta* N.M. passer-by way-farer راہ چلتوں کا پلہ پکڑنا *rāh' chal'toṅ kā pal'lah pakaṛ'nā* V.T. pick up a row with every. one راہ چھوڑنا *rāh' chhoṛ'nā* V.I. clear the road get out of the way راہ خرچ *rāh'-khar'ch* N.M. travel expenses travelling allowance راہ دار *rāh'-dār* N.M. road patrol ; toll collector راہداری *rāh'-dā'rī*, رہداری *rah-dā'rī* (or *raih'-*) N.F. transit duties ; toll پروانۂ راہداری *parvā'na-e rāh'-dā'rī* N.F. passport راہ دکھانا (یا دکھلانا) *rāh' dikhā'nā* (or *dikhlā'nā*) V.T. show the way cause (someone) to wait (for) راہ دیکھنا *rāh' dekh'nā* V.I. wait (for) expect راہ دینا *rāh' de'nā* V.T. admit make room (for) راہ ڈالنا *rāh ḍāl'nā* V.T. establish a custom put on the right path راہِ راست *rā'h-e rās't* N.F. straight path good conduct راہرو *rāh'-rau*, رہرو *rah-rau'* N.M. way farer traveller راہ ریت *rāh rīt* N.F. custom راہزن *rāh'-zan*, رہزن *rah'-zan* (or *raih'-*) N.M. robber ; brigand ; bandit footpad راہزنی *rāh'-za'nī*, رہزنی *rah'-za'nī* N.F. highway robbery راہ سے بے راہ ہونا *rāh' se be-rāh' ho'nā* V.I. go astray راہ کھوٹی کرنا *rāh kho'ṭī kar'nā* V.I. longer in the way راہگیر *rāh' gīr* N.M. way farer traveller راہگزر *rāh'-gū'zar*, رہگزر *rah'-gū'zar* N.F. (dial M.) way path اپنی راہ لگنا *ap'nī rāh lag'nā* V.I. pursue one's own course ; not to poke one's nose into other people's affair راہ لینا *rāh' le'nā* V.I. start ; set out go one's way راہ میں *rāh' meṅ* ADV. on the way (to) in the path (of) for the sake (of) راہ نکالنا *rāh' nikal'nā* V.T. open a new road hit upon a device find a way out راہنما *rāh-nūmā*, رہنما *rah'-nūmā'*, رہنمون *rah'-nūmoon'* N.M. leader guide راہنمائی *rāh'-nūmā''ī* رہنمائی *rah'-nūmā''ī* N.F. leadership guidance رہ نورد *rah'-navar'd* N.M. wayfarer رہ نوردی *rāh'-navar'dī* رہ نوردی *rah'-navar'dī* N.F. travel ; wayfaring راہوار *rāh-vār'* N.M. ambling horse steed راہ و رسم *rāh'-o-ras'm* راہ و ربط *rā'h-o-rab'l* N.F. friendly relations ; intercourse راہ ہونا *rā'h ho'nā* V.I. be in love (with) be on friendly terms (with) راہی *rā'hī* N.M. ★ [P]

راہب *rā'hib* N.M. monk [A]

راہن *rā'hin* N.M. pledger mortgager ; pawner [A ~ رہن]

راہنا *rāh'nā* V.I. roughen (mill-stone, etc.)

راہو *rā'hoo* N.M. (Hindu myth.) demon supposed to cause eclipse by seizing the sun or the moon (dial.) name of a star [S]

راہی *rā'hī* N.M. traveller wayfarer passer-by [P ~ راہ]

رائتہ *rā''etah*, رائتا *rā''eta* N.M. salt dish made with pumpkin and curds

رائٹر *rā''iṭar* N.M. name of a British news agency, Reuter [E]

رائج *rā''ij* ADJ. current in vogue fashionable customary in force رائج الوقت *rā''ij-ūl-vaq't* ADJ. current in vogue in force رائج کرنا *rā''ij kar'nā* V.T. introduce give currency to set the fashion [A ~ رواج]

رائحہ *rā''ehah* N.F. sweet smell [A]

رائفل *rā''efal*, رفل *ra'fal* N.F. rifle [E]

رائگاں *rā''egāh* ADJ. vain useless ; fruitless bootless ADV. in vain . waste [P]

رائلٹی *rā''ilṭī* N.F. royalty [E]

راؤ *rā''o* N.M. (dial.) prince ; chief ; warrior

راؤٹی *rā' oṭī* N.F. small pyramidical tent

راؤنڈ ٹیبل کانفرنس *rā'ūnḍ ṭe'bal kān'farans* N.F. round-table conference ; all-party talks between members on an equal status [E]

رائی *rā''ī* N.F. a kind of mustard ; mustard seed رائی بھر *rā'ī bhar* ADJ. very little as much as a mustard seed رائی کا پہاڑ (یا پربت) بنانا *rā''ī kā pahāṛ'* (or *par'bat*) *banā'nā* PH. make a mountain out of a mole-hill

رائے¹ *rā''e* N.M. (dial.) king ; petty a Hindu title PREF. large رائے بیل *rā''e bel* N.F. species of jessamine رائے جامن *rā''e jā'man* N.F. large 'jambolana'

رائے² *rā''e* N.F. (PL. آرا *ārā'*) opinion view advice judgment verdict رائے زنی *rā''e-za'nī* N.F. criticism رائے زنی کرنا *rā''-e za'nī kar'nā* V.T. express one's opinion criticism رائے عامہ *rā''e 'ām'mah* N.F. public opinion رائے لینا (یا پوچھنا) *rā''e le'nā* (or *poochh'nā*) V.I. invite the opinion (of) اظہارِ رائے *izhā'r-e rā'e* N.F. expression (of) [A]

رایت *rā'yat* N.F. flag ; banner ; standard [A]

رب *rab* N.M. (PL. ارباب *arbāb'*) God god ; deity preserver cherisher ; sustainer master ; lord رب العالمین *rabb-ūl-'alamīn'* N.M. God (as Lord of the universe) ربانی *rabbā'nī*, ربی *rab'bī* ADJ. of God divine

رب *rūb* N.M. extract رب السوس *rūb'b-ūs-soos* extract of liquorice [A]

ربا *rūbā'* SUF. robbing ravishing ربائی *rūba''ī* SUF robbing ravishing [P ~ ربودن]

ربا *ribā'* (more correctly ربو) N.M. interest usury [A]

رباب *rabāb* N.M. a kind of stringed musical instrument ربابی *rabā'bī* N.M. musician fiddler [A]

رباط *ribāt'* N.M. camp ; contonment inn ligament [A]

رباعی *rūbā''ī* N.F. (PL. رباعیات *rūbā'iyyāt'* col. *rūbā'-iyāt'*) quatrain [A ~ اربعہ]

ربانی *rabbā'nī* ADJ. (see under رب *rab* N.M. ★)

ربڑ *ra'baṛ*, ربر *ra'bar* N.M. rubber ; eraser decisive of three games in a set [E]

ربڑ *ra'baṛ* N.F. hardships of travel N.M. same as ربر N.M.) ★

ربڑی *rab'ṛī* N.F. sweet condensed cream

ربط *rab't* N.M. nexus ; relation ; connexion coherance relevance intimacy knowledge; familiarity ربط بڑھانا *rab't baṛhā'nā* V.T. develop intimacy ربط و ضبط *rab't (-o-) zab't* N.M. intimacy organization coherence بے ربط *be-rab't* ADJ. incoherent unrelated ; irrelevant disjointed بے ربطی *be-rab'tī* N.F. incoherent irrelevant disjointed

ربع *rūb''* ADJ. quarter ; one-fourth ربع مسکون *rūb''-e maskoon'* N.M. inhabited quarter of earth [A ~ اربعہ]

ربوبیت *rūboobiy'yat* ADJ. providence [رب]

ربیب *rabīb'* N.M. man's step-son ربیبہ *rabī'bah* N.F. (PL. ربائب *rabā''b*) man's step-daughter

ربیع *rabī''* N.F. spring harvest ربیع الاول *rabī''-ul-av'val* N.M. third month of Hijri calendar ربیع الثانی *rabī''us-sā'nī* N.M. fourth month of Hijri calendar [A]

رپٹ *ra'paṭ* N.F. (police slang for رپورٹ N.F. ★)

رپٹنا *ra'paṭnā* V. slip slides glide رپٹ *ra'paṭ* N.F. slipperiness (same as رپورٹ N.F. ★) *rapṭā'nā* V.T. cause to slip, slide or glide

رپلی *rūpal'lī* N.F. (derog.) rupee [DIM. of روپیہ]

رپورتاژ *rapor'tāzh* N.M. rapportage [E]

رپورٹ *ripoṛṭ*, رپٹ *ra'paṭ* N.F. report رپورٹر *repor'ṭar* N.M. Press reporter [E]

رت *rūt* N.F. season weather رت بدلنا (یا پلٹنا یا پھرنا) *rūt ba'dalnā* (or *pa'laṭ nā* or *phir'nā*) V.I. (of weather or season) change

رت *rat* PREF. night رت جگا *rat-ja'gā* N.M. night spent in prayer , vigils festive night ; vigils رت جگا کرنا *rat-ja'gā kar'nā* V.I. keep the vigils

رتالو *ratā'loo* N.M. yam

رتبہ *rūt'bah* N.M. rank ; status designation distinction , eminence کم رتبہ *kam-rūt'bah* ADJ. of low rank کم رتبہ لوگ *kam-rūt'bah log* N.M. PL. the small fry

رتق و فتق *rat'q-o-fat'q* N.M. control management [A]

رتن *ra'tan* (ped. *rat'n*) N.M. (dial.) gem ; jewel pearl رتناولی *ratnā'valī* N.F. (dial.) pearl-necklace رتن جوت *ra'tan jot* N.F. a kind of drug used as a colouring condiment رتن مالا *ra'tan-mālā* N.F. (dial.) pearl-necklace نورتن *nau'-ra'tan* N.M. PL. nine different gems in a necklace company of nine wise men Moghul Emperor Akbar's nine famous courtiers

رتنا *rit'nā* V.I. be filed ; be smoothed with file [~ ریتی]

رتناولی *ratnā'valī* N.F. (dial.) (see under رتن N.M. ★)

رتوا *rat'vā* N.M. boring insect ; borer

رتوندھا *rataun'dhā* N.M. night-blindness ; nyctalopia رتوندھیا *rataun'dhyā* N.M. night-blind person ; nyctalopic [~ اندھا + رات]

رتھ *rath* N.F. (dial. M.) four-wheeled carriage (arch.) chariot رتھ بان *rath'-bān'* N.M. carter charioteer

رتی *rat'tī* N.F. 'arbus precatorius' its seed used as weight equivalent to eight barley-corns ; 'ratti' رتی بھر *rat'tī bhar* ADJ. weighing as much as a 'ratti' a little ; wee-bit رتی رتی *rat'tī ra'tī* ADV. to a farthing ADJ. each and every (word)

رٹنا *raṭ'nā* V.I. mug up repeat persistently reiterate رٹ *raṭ* N.F. persistent ; repetition reiteration رٹ لگا رکھنا *raṭ' lagā' akh'nā* V.I. repeat 'ad nauseum'

رجا *rajā'* N.M. hope رجائیت *rajā'iy'yat* N.F optimism hopefulness رجائیت پسند *rajā'iyat-pasand'* N.M. optimist ADJ. optimistic ADJ. optimistic رجائیت پسندانہ *rajā'iy'yat-pasandā'nah* ADJ. optimistic ADV. optimistically رجائیت پسندی *rajā'iy'yat-pasan'dī* N.F. optimism بیم و رجا *bī'm-o rajā* N.M. hopes and fecls [A]

رجا پجا *ra'jā pū'jā* ADJ. not hungry satisfied ; not greedy

رجال *rijāl'* N.M. men (also اسماء الرجال *asmā'-ur-rijāl'*) biographical literature of Hadith narrators رجال الغیب *rijā'l-ūl-ghaib'* invisible beings supposed to orbit round world whom it is regarded inauspicious for travellers to face [A ~ SING. رجل]

رجائیت *raja'iy'yat* N.F. (see under رجا N.F. ★)

رجب *ra'jab* N.M. Rajab : seventh month of Hijri calendar رجب المرجب *ra'jab-ul muraj'jab* N.M. the sacred month of Rajab (so called because of Holy Prophet Accension in it) [A]

رجحان *r'jhan'* N.M. tendency inclination leanings [A]

رجز *ra'jaz* N.F. (Arab) martial song rajaz ; metre used for it : martial metre رجز پڑھنا *ra'jaz parh'na* V.I. recite a martial song رجز خواں *ra'jaz-khan'* N.M. martial minstrel رجز خوانی *ra'jaz-kha'ni* N.F. recitation of martial song incitement to war [A]

رجز *rij'z* N.M. profanity blasphemy unholiness [A]

رجسٹر *rajis'tar* N.M. registar رجسٹر پیدائش *rajis'tar paima''ish* N.M. survey register رجسٹر ترسیل *rajis'tar tarsil'* N.M. despatch register رجسٹر جائداد *rajis'tar ja'edad'* N.M. property register رجسٹر جرائم *rajis'tar jara''im* N.M. crime register رجسٹر رسید (یا وصولی) *rajis'tar rasid'* (or *vusoo'li*) N.M. stock register رجسٹر محصلی *rajis'tar mohas'sali* N.M. daily collection register رجسٹرار *ragis'tarar* N.M. registrar, رجسٹری *rajis'tari* N.F. registry registration رجسٹری کرنا *rajis'tari kar'na* V.T. & I. register send by registered post رجسٹری کرنا *rajis'tari kar'na* V.T. get registered [E]

رجعت *raj''at* N.F. return retracing retraction retrogression resurrection remarriage one's conditionally divorced wife رجعت پسند *raj''at pasand'* N.M. one opposed to progressive dishard ; conservative ADJ. conservative retrogressive not progressive رجعت پسندانہ *raj''at-pasanda'nah* ADJ. retrogressive not progressive رجعت پسندی *raj''at-pasan'di* N.F. conservation not being progressive رجعت قہقری *raj''at-e qah'qari* (ped-ra) N.F. retracing one's steps retrogression [A doublet of رجوع]

رجم *raj'm* N.M. stoning to death driving away رجم بالغیب *raj'm bil ghaib'* N.M. hazarding a guess [A]

رجمنٹ *raj'mant* N.F. regiment [E]

رجنا *raj'na* V.I. (dial.) be satiated

رجنی *raj'ni* N.F. (dial.) night [S]

رجواڑا *rajva'ra* N.M. principality : Raja's territory [~ راجہ]

رجوع *rujoo'* N.M. return inclination ; bent appeal reference recourse re marriage with own conditionally divorced wife رجوع کرنا *r'joo'' kar'na* V. refer to ; have course (to) (in or to) remarriage with own conditionally divorced wife [A]

رجولیت *rujooliy'yat* N.F. virility [A ~ رجل]

رجھانا *rijha'na* V.T. seduce please ravish incite

رجیم *rajim'* ADJ. rejected spurned [A ~ رجم]

رچنا *rach'na* V.I. (of wedding, etc.) be held ; be celebrated (of henna) become red scent be connected رچانا *racha'na* V.T. celebrate (marriage, etc.) henna add (perfume, etc.) scent with رچاوٹ *racha'vat* N.F. celebration dye ; paint colouring scenting رچتا پچتا *rach'ta pach'ta* tasty ; savoury رچنی *rach'ni* ADJ. (of henna) leaving good colour

رحل *rah'l* (col. *raih'l*) N.F. folding stand for the Holy Quran ; lectern

رحلت *reh'lat* N.F. death ; demise departure (rare) travels (rare) travelogue رحلت کرنا *reh'lat kar'na* V.T. die ; pass away [A]

رحم *reh'm* N.M. (ped. *rahim'*) womb ; uterus صلہ رحمی *sila'-e reh'mi* N.M. uterine relationship tenderness towards one's relations [A]

رحم *ra'ham* N.M. uncooked rice ; pudding

رحم *raihm* (ped. *rah'm*) N.M. mercy pity ; compassion kindness tenderness رحم دل *raih'm-dil* ADJ. merciful: kind hearted رحم دلی *raih'm-di'li* N.F. tenderness compassion mercy رحم کرنا (یا کھانا) *raih'm kar'na* (or *kha'na*) V.T. show mercy (to) take pity (on) [A]

رحمان *raihman'* N.M. God ADJ. most merciful ; Beneficent (as attribute of God) رحمانی *raihma'ni* ADJ. divine [A ~ رحم]

رحمت *rah'mat* (col. *raih'-*) N.F. blessing; grace bounty ; divinefavour mercy compassion [A ~ رحم]

رحیق *rahiq'* N.M. pure wine [A]

رحیل *rahil'* N.M. departure [A ~ رحلت]

رحیم *rahim'* ADJ. (PL. رحما *rohama'*) merciful (as attribute of God) compassionate رحیمی *rahi'mi* N.F. mercifulness grace [A ~ رحم]

رخ *rukh* N.M. face ; countenance cheek facade direction ; side (in chess) castle rook attention favour رخ بدلنا (یا پھیرنا) *rukh' ba'dalna* (or *pher'na*) V.T. & I. turn in another direction change the course of ignore ; little heed (to) be offended ; take offence ; take umbrage رُخ دے کر بات نہ کرنا *rūkh' de' kar bāt' na kar'nā* V.I. talk attentively رُخ (نہ) کرنا *rukh' na) kar'nā* V.T. (never) to go (to) (not) to turn the face (towards) [P]

رخام *rukhām'* N.M. marble [A]

رخت *rakh't* N.M. clothes ; garments goods and chattles رختِ سفر *rakh't-e sa'far* N.F. baggage رختِ سفر باندھنا *rakht-e sa'far bāndh'nā* V.I. get ready to go pack up ; quit ; depart [P]

رخسار *rukhsār'*, رخسارہ *rukhsār'rah* N.M. the cheek, face ; countenance ; complexion ; aspect [P]

رخش *rakh'sh* N.M. name of Rustam's horse steed رخشاں *rakh'shān* ADJ. dazzling resplendent refulgent رخشانی *rakhsha'nī*, رخشندگی *rakhshin'dagī* N.F. brightness refulgence رخشندہ *rakhshindah* ADJ. right resplendent refulgent رخشندہ و تابندہ *rakhshin'da-o-tābin'dak* ADJ. refulgent resplendent [P ~ رخشیدن]

رخصت *rūkh'sat* N.F. leave permission indulgence (rare) discharge ; dismissal sending out (daughter, etc.) as bride اتفاقی رخصت *ittifā'qī rūkh'sat* N.F. casual leave رخصت استحقاقی *rukh'sat isteḥqā'qī* N.F. privilege leave رخصت بلا تنخواہ *rukh'sāt bi-lā' tankhāh'* N.F. leave without pay طبّی رخصت *tib'bī rukh'sat* N.F. medical leave غیر معمولی رخصت *ghair-ma'moo'lī rukh'sat* N.F. extraordinary leave رخصت دینا *rūkh'sat de'nā* V.I. permit give (someone) leave (rare) dismiss ; sack رخصت کرنا *rūkh'sat kar'nā* V.T. bid farewell (to) permit discharge ; dismiss ; sack send out (daughter) as bride رخصت مانگنا *rūkh'sat māng'nā* V.T. apply for leave crave (someone's) indulgence رخصت ہونا *rūkh'sat ho'nā* V. take leave (of) depart (of girl) set out as bride رخصتانہ *rūkhsatā'nah* N.M. parting present from patron, etc. gratuity رخصتی *rūkh'satī* ADJ. on leave N.F. sending out (daughter, etc.) as bride departure [A]

رخنہ *rakh'nah* N.M. crack fissure obstacle obstruction hindrance defeet ; fault رخنہ انداز *rakh'na-andāz'* ADJ. obstrusive N.M. obstructionist رخنہ اندازی *rakh'na-andā'zī* N.F. رخنہ ڈالنا *rakh'nah ḍāl'nā* V.T. obstruct; hinder رخنہ نکالنا *rakh'-nah nikal'nā* V.T. carp ; cavil ; pick holes in) [P]

رد *rad* N.M. refutation rebuttal turning down ردّ کرنا *rad' kar'nā* V.T. refute turn down رد و بدل *rad'd-o ba'dal* N.F. change ; alteration رد و قدح *rad'd-o-qad'ḥ*, رد و کد *rad d-o-kad* N.F. expostulation رد ہونا *rad' ho'nā* V.I. be rejected [A]

ردا *ridā'* (PL. اردیہ *ar'diyah*) sheet stole robe [A]

ردہ *rad'dah*, ردا *rad'dā* N.M. layer (of bricks) in a wall ردا جمانا (یا رکھنا یا لگانا) *rad'dā jama'nā* (or *rakh'nā* or *lagā'nā*) V.T. lay down a layer of bricks

ردی *rad'dī* (ped. *ra'dī*) refuse waste worthless N.F. waste paper ردی دان *rad'dī dān'* N.M. waste-paper basket ; W.P.B. ردی کاغذ *rad'dī kā'ghaz* N.M. waste paper ردی کرنا *rad'dī kar'nā* V.T. reject waste [A]

ردیف *radīf'* N.F. word(s) repeated towards end of each couplet throughout a poem or stanza ; post-rhyme word ردیف وار *rad f -var* ADV. alphabetically ; according to the last letter of the post-rhyme word

رذالت *razā'lat* N.F. meanness ; baseness رذیل *razīl'* ADJ. & N.M. mean ; base ; mean fellow ; vile person رذالہ *razā'lah* N.M. (col.) mean fellow [A]

رز *raz* N.F. vine دخترِ رز *dukh't-e raz'*, *dukh'-tar-e raz'* N.F. wine [P]

رزاق *razzāq'* N.M. providence sustainer (as attribute of God) رزاقی *razza'qī* N.F. providence sustainer (as attribute of God) [A ~ FOLL.]

رزق *riz'q* N.M. daily bread subsistence [A]

رزم *raz'm* N.M. battle war رزم گاہ *raz'm-gah* N.F. battle-field رزمی *raz'mī* ADJ. relating to war warlike truculant N.M. warlike person رزمیہ *razmiy'yah* ADJ. & N.M. epic [P]

رس *ras* N.M. juice sugarcane juice essence relish taste sweetness lusciousness melody love رس بھرا *ras'-bhara* ADJ. juicy luscious sweet رس بھری *ras'-bha'rī* N.F. raspberry ADJ. juicy luscious sweet رس ٹپکنا *ras' ṭa'paknā* V.I. be luscious (of juice) trickle be sweet کانوں میں رس گھولنا *ka'noṅ meṅ ras' ghol'na* V.I. be cry melodious ; melodious رسیلا *rasī'la* ADJ. ★)

رس *ras* SUF. arriving ; reaching dispensing ; administering رسی *rasī* SUF. arriving ; reaching dispensation; administration [P ~ رسیدن]

رسا *rasā* ADJ. penetrating (mind) effective رسائی *rasā'ī* N.F. & SUF. ★ [P ~ PREC.]

رسا *ras'sā* N.M. (same as رسہ N.M. ★)

رسالت *risā'lat* N.F. apostleship ; prophethood ; رسالت پناہ *risā'lat-panāh'*, رسالت مآب *risā'lat ma'āb'*

ADJ. & N.M. the Holy Prophet (as focus of divine mission)

رساله risā'lah N.M. (PL. رسائل rasā''il) magazine, tract; pamphlet, brochure booklet (rare) letter cavalry troop of horse رسالدار risāl'-dār N.M. cavalry officer, squadron leader رسالداری risāl'-dā'rī N.F command of squadron [A doublet of prec.]

رساول rasāv'al N.M. rice pudding prepared in cane juice [~ رس]

رسان rasāṅ' SUF. bearer delivery رسانی rasā'nī SUF. bearing; delivering [P ~ رسانیدن ~ رسیدن]

رسائل rasā''il N.M. magazines pamphlets [A ~ SING. رسالہ]

رسائی rasā''ī N.F access approach penetration (of mind) effectiveness [P ~ رسیدن]

رسائن rasā'yan N.M. (dial.) alchemy metallic drug [S]

رسپانڈنٹ raspāṅ'daṅṭ N.M respondent [E]

رستاخیز rūstākhez', رستخیز rūstakhez' N.M doomsday resurrection [P]

رستگاری rūstagā'rī N.F liberation deliverance; salvation [P ~ رستن rūs'tan]

رستم rūs'tam N.M. name of a legendary Persian hero; Persian Hercules hero brave man رستمی rūs'tamī N.F bravery, valour [P]

رستہ[1] rastah N.M (same as راستہ rās'tah N.M ★)

رستہ[2] ras'tah ADJ. blossoming; blossomed [P ~ رستن ras'tan]

رسد ra'sad N.F. supplies, provisions rations رسد پہنچانا ra'sad pahuṅchā'na V.T. sending the supplies رسد رسانی ra'sad-rasā'nī N.F supplies provisioning رسدی ra'sadī ADJ. proportionate حصّہ رسدی his'sa-e-ra'sadī N.M proportionate share [P ~ رسیدن]

رسکپور ras'-kapoor N.M. a poisonous mercury compound

رسل و رسائل ras'l-o rasā''il (CORR. of رسل و رسائل rū'sūl-o rasā''il) N.M. PL. communications (ped.) exchange of envoys and epistles سلسلہ رسل و رسائل sil'sila-e ras'l-o rasā''il N.M. communications system [A ~ رسالت]

رسل rū'sūl N.M. PL. prophets messengers envoys رسل و رسائل N.M PL ★ [A ~ SING. رسول]

رسم ras'm N.F. (PL. رسوم rūsoom') rite custom, established usage practice mode manner formality ceremony (rare) marking writing رسم پر چلنا ras'm par chal'na V.I. observe a custom رسم الخط ras'm-ūl-khat N.M. alphabet writing, orhography رسم ڈالنا rasm ḍal'nā V.I. introduce a custom set up a practice رسم و رواج ras'm-o-rivāj' N.M. custom and usage ways and manners رسماً ras'man ADV by way of formality رسمی ras'mī ADJ. customary formal superficial [A]

رسمسا ras'masa ADJ. (F. رسمسی ras'masī) wet thick (soup)

رسن ra'san N.F. rope, cord رسن باز ra'san-baz N.M. rope-dancer juggler رسن بازی ra'san-bā'zī N.F. rope trick [P]

رسنا ris'nā V.I. leak ooze drip trickle exude

رسنا بسنا ras'na bas'nā V.I. have a happy home-life

رسوا rūsvā' ADJ. notorious scandalized رسوا کرنا rūsvā kar'na V.T scandalize disgrace رسوا ہونا rūsvā' ho'nā V.I. become notorious be scandalized be disgraced رسوائے زمانہ (یا عالم) rūsvā''-e zamā'nah (or 'ālam) ADJ. very notorious infamous everywhere رسوائی rūsvā''ī N.F notoriety infamy opprobrium disgrace [P]

رسوت rasaut N.F. 'amomum anthorhizum' extract, name of a bitter drug

رسوخ rūsookh' N.M. access influence flavour (rare) firmness اثر و رسوخ a'sar-o-rūsookh' N.M influence اثر و رسوخ ہونا a'sar rūsookh' ho'nā V.I be an influential person

رسول rasool' N.M. (PL. رسل rū'sūl) prophet messenger رسول اکرم (یا پاک یا کریم) rasoo'l-e ak'ram (or -pāk' or -karīm') N.M. the Holy Prophet [A ~ رسالت]

رسولی rasau'lī N.F tumour

رسوم rūsoom N.F PL. rites customs formalities N.F. free, duty رسوم سرکار rūsoo'm-e sarkār N.F stamp duty رسوم عدالت rūsoo'm-e 'adā'lat N.F court-fee [A ~ SING. رسم]

رسوئی raso''ī N.F (dial.) kitchen meals

رسہ ras'sah رسا ras'sa N.M. rope رسی ras'sī N.F rope cord string رسی بٹنا ras'sī baṭ'nā V.I. twist or twine a rope رسی جل گئی پر بل نہیں گیا ras'sī jal ga''ī par bal na'hīṅ ga'yā PROV habits take long to depart his arrogance survives his financial ruin (برے کی) رسی دراز ہونا (bū're kī) ras'sī darāz ho'nā V.I. (of evil-doer) get a long rope رسی ڈھیلی چھوڑنا ras'sī ḍhī'lī chhor'na V.T. give a long rope (to) let the reins drops رسی کا سانپ بنانا ras'sī ka sāṅp *bana'na* V.I. exaggerate ; draw the long bow spread a panic

رسیا *ras'ya* ADJ. fond addict [~ رس]

رسید *rasīd'* N.F. receipt acknowledgement arrival رسید جاری کرنا *rasīd' ja'rī kar'na* V.I. issue receipt رسید دینا *rasīd' de'nā* V.T. give receipt issue acknowledgement رسید نقد *rasīd' naq'dī.* رسید نقد *rasī'd-e naq'd* N.F. cash memo رسیدگی *rasī'dagī* N.F. arrival maturity ripeness ; mellowness SUF. personal knowledge ; intimacy رسیدہ *rasī'dah* SUF. arrived received ripe ; mellow advanced (in years) intimate (with God) [P]

رسیلا *rasī'lā* ADJ. juicy luscious sweet (music) [~ رس]

رسیور *risī'var* N.M. receiver [E]

رشتہ *rish'tah* N.M. relationship ; kinship connexion affinity (lit.) thread ; string رشتہ دار *rish'te-dar* (ped. *-ta-*) N.M. relation; relative kinsman kith and kin عزیز رشتہ دار *azīz' rish'te-dar'* N.M. PL. kith and kin ; kinsfolk ; relations رشتہ داری *rish'te-dā'rī* (ped. *-ta-*) N.F. relationship kinship [P]

رشحات *rashhāt'* N.M. PL. drops رشحات قلم *rash'ha't-e-qa'lam* N.M. PL. (met.) writings (of)

رشد *rāsh'd* N.M. reetitude discernment سن رشد *sin'n-e rāsh'd* N.M. majority ; maturity سن رشد کو پہنچنا *sin'n-e rāsh'd ko pahuṅch'na* V.I. attain majority [P]

رشک *rash'k* N.M. envy رشک کرنا (یا ہونا) *rash'k kar'na* (or *ho'na*) V.I. be envious ; envy [A]

رشوت *rish'vat* N.F. bribe illegal gratification graft رشوت خور (یا خوار یا ستاں) *rish'vat-khor* (or *-khar* or *sitāṅ'*) N.M. & ADJ. (one) who takes bribes; corrupt (person) رشوت خوری (یا خواری یا ستانی) *rish'vat-kho'rī* (or *khā'rī* or *sitā'nī*) N.F. acceptance of bribe or illegal gratification رشوت دینا (یا کھلانا) *rish'vat de'na* (or *khilā'na*) V.T. bribe ; offer illegal gratification رشوت لینا (یا کھانا) *rish'vat le'na* (or *khā'nā*) V.I. take bribe : accept illegal gratification .

رشی *ri'shī* N.M. Hindu saint رشی منی *ri'shī mūṅ'nī* N.M. PH. saints and ascetics [S]

رشید *rashīd'* ADJ. pious ; righteous rightly-guided ; orthodox [A ~ رشید]

رضہ *ra'ziya* N.M. (ABB. for رضی اللہ عنہ PH. ★)

رضا *riza'* N.F. leave ; permission pleasure approval good office wish ; desire رضاجوئی *rizā'-jo'ī* N.F. seeking the good offices (of) asking (someone) about his wish bid to fulfil the wish (of) رضاکار *rizā'-kar* N.M. volunteer رضاکارانہ *rizā'-kāra'nah* ADV. voluntarily رضامند *rizā-mand* ADJ. willing agreeable (to) رضامندی *rizā'-man'dī* N.F. willingness consent approval condescension رضا و رغبت *rizā'-o ragh'bat* N.F. free consent and pleasure ; willingness and inclination رضا و رغبت سے *rizā'-o-ragh'bat se*, بہ رضا و رغبت *ba-rizā'-o ragh'bat* ADV. willingly with pleasure of own accord [A]

رضاعت *rizā''at* N.F. suckling ; foster ; affinity; fosterage foster رضاعی *rizā''ī* ADJ. foster رضاعی بھائی *rizā''ī bhā'ī* foster-brother رضاعی بہن *rizā''ī bai'han* N.F. foster-sister [A]

رضائی *razā''ī* N.F. quilt coverlet ; counterpane

رضوان *rizvān'* N.M. (name of angel who is) Paradise janitor God's pleasure good offices condescension [A doublet of رضا]

رضوی *ri'zavī* N.M. (F. رضویہ *rizaviy'yah*) descendent of Imam Musa Riza [A]

رطب *rū'tab* N.M. PL. ripe dates [A]

رطب *rat'b* ADJ. moist ; damp verdant supple رطب اللسان *rat'b-ūl-lisān'* ADJ. facile رطب و یابس *rat'b-o yā'bis* N.M. padding , worthless stuff [A]

رطل *rat'l* N.M. (arch.) weight equivalent to about one pound wineglass رطل گراں *rat'l-e garāṅ'* N.M. large measure of wine [A]

رطوبت *rūtoo'bat* N.F. moisture damp humidity sap [A]

رعایا *ra'ā'yā* N.F. subjects populace public tenants [A ~ SING. رعیت]

رعایت *re'ā'yat* N.F. regard , favour partiality bias indulgence kindness remission rebate grace privilege *re'ā'yat kar'nā* V.I. show favour be particle to remit allow a rebate رعایت ہونا *re'ā'yat ho'nā* V.I. be shown special or undue favour be remitted be allowed a rebate رعایتی *re'ā'yatī* ADJ. grace (marks, etc.) complimentary privilege reduced (rare, etc.) [A]

رعب *ro''b* N.M. awe commanding personality fear terror bullying ; bluff display of rank or dignity pomp and show رعب بٹھانا (یا جمانا یا ڈالنا یا گانٹھنا) *ro''b bi ṭhānā* (or *jamā'na* or *dāl'nā* or *gāṅth'nā*). inspire with awe over-awe frighten terrify bluff ; bully رعب دار *ro''b-dar* ADJ. awesome ; awe-inspiring commanding domineering (personality) stentorian (voice) رعب میں آنا *ro''b meṅ ā'na* V.I be overawed (by) be bluffed (by) رعب داب

ro''b(-o) dāb' N.M. awe display of rank and dignity commanding personality [A]

رعد ra''d N.M. thunder [A]

رعشہ ra''shah N.M. shaking palsy رعشہ دار یا زدہ ra''sha-dar (or -za'dah) ADJ. palsied; suffering from the shaking palsy [A]

رعنا ra'nā' ADJ. graceful exquisitely beautiful cute two coloured and bright (eye, flower, etc.) رعنائی ra'nā''ī N.F. grace exquisite ; beauty cuteness colourfulness رعنائی خیال ra'nā''ī-e khayāl' N.F. exquisite ideas flights of fancy [A]

رعونت ro'oo'nat N.F. arrogance ; haughtiness pride ; vanity ; conceit [A]

رعیت ra'iy'yat N.F. (PL. رعایا ra'ā'yā) subjects people populace public tenants رعیت پرور ra'iy'yat par'var, رعیت نواز ra'iy'yat-navāz' ADJ. protector of subjects benevolent رعیت پروری ra'iy'yat-par'varī, رعیت نوازی ra'iy'yat-navā'zī N.F. protection of subjects benevolence [A]

رغبت ragh'bat N.F. inclination wish : esteem ; predilection desire keenness رغبت ظاہر کرنا ragh'bat za'hir kar'na V.I. show inclination for [A]

رغم ragh'm N.M. touching the ground (only in PH.) علی الرغم 'al-ar-ragh'm ADV. in spite of ; despite contrary to the wishes (of) [A]

رف raf ADJ. rough N.M. rough work ; rough copy

رفاقت rifā'qat N.F. companion ; comradeship friendship loyalty association society ; company رفاقت کرنا rifā'qat kar'na V.T. accompany ; keep (someone) company be friendly (with) حق رفاقت ادا کرنا haq' q-e rifā'qat adā' kar'nā V.I. be loyal [A ~ رفیق]

رفاہ rafāh' N.M., رفاہیت rafā'hiyat N.F. long and comfortable life رفاہ عام (یا عامہ) کے کام rafā'h-e 'ām' (or 'ām'mah) (ke kām') N.M. public welfare [A]

رفت raf't V.I. went AFFIX. going آمدورفت ā'mad-o-raf't N.F. coming and going traffic continued movement of people ingress and egress رفت گزشت raf't gūzash't ADV. settled ; forgiven and forgotten matter of the past ; dead had gone رفتنی raf'tanī ADJ. mortal likely to go [P ~ رفتن]

رفتار raftār' N.F. speed pace conduct ; disport رفتار و گفتار raftār-o-goftār' N.F. manners conduct behaviour demeanour disport [P ~ رفتن]

رفتہ raf'tah ADJ. deceased gone ; departed lost رفتہ رفتہ raf'tah raf'tah ADV. step by step ; by degrees gradually in due course رفتگاں raf'tagān N.M. the departed ones ; the dead and gone [P ~ رفتن]

رفرف raf'raf N.M. Holy Prophet's conveyance during ascension from Jerusalem upwards fine printed silk carpet large pillow [A]

رفض raf'z N.M. schism dissention رافضی rā'fizī N.M. ★ [A]

رفع raf'' N.M. nominative case vowel point indicative of it removal eradication lifting ; elevation exallation رفع دفع raf''-daf'' (col. ra'fa' da'fa') N.M. settlement رفع شر raf''-e shar N.M. settlement of dispute eradication of evil رفع کرنا ra'fa' kar'na V.T. set at rest eradicate (evil, etc.) remove (cause for complaint) رفع یدین raf''-e yadain' N.M. lifting of hands with post-preliminary 'takbirs' [A]

رفعت rif''at N.F. height; altitude eminence nobility exaltation [A]

رفقا rfaqa N.M. companions ; comrades friends [A ~ SING. رفیق]

رفل ra'fal N.F. fine muslin fine woollen stole

رفو ra foo (ped. rfoo') N.M. darn daring stitching (of wound) رفو کرنا ra'foo kar'na V.T. darn رفوگر ra'foo-gar N.M. darner رفوگری ra'foo ga'rī N.F. darning (as profession) [P]

رفو چکر ہو جانا ra'foo-chak'kar ho jā'na V.I. sneak away ; slink away

رفیدہ rafī'dah N.M. pad on which baker puts bread in oven ; baker's pad

رفیع rafī'' ADJ. high ; sublime ; exalted ; elevated رفیع الشان rafī''-ush-shān' (rare رفیع الدرجات rafī''-ūd-darajāt', رفیع القدر rafī''-ūl-qad'r, رفیع المرتبت rafī''-ūl-mar'tabat ADJ. of high status dignified ; exalted [A]

رفیق rafīq' N.M. (PL. رفقا rfaqā') comrade ; companion confederate رفیق جرم rafī'q-e jūr'm N.M. accomplice رفیق راہ rafī'q-e rāh' N.M. fellow traveller رفیقہ rafī'qah N.F. partner (in life) ; wife رفیقۂ حیات (یا زندگی یا زیست) rafī'qa-e hayāt' (or zin'dagī or zīs't) N.M. (one's) wife ; spouse [A]

رقابت raqā'bat N.M. rivalry ; in love antagonism رقیب raqīb' N.M. ★ [A]

رقاص raqqās' N.M. pendulum dancer raqqā'sah N.F. dancing girl prostitute ; whore ; strumpet [A ~ رقص]

رقبہ raq'bah N.M. area رقبۂ اراضی raq'ba-e ara'zī N.M. area of land land رقبہ نکالنا raq'bah nikal-nā V.T. find out the area (of) [A]

رقبہ *ra'qabah* N.M. (PL. رقاب *riqab'*) neck slave [A]

رقت *riq'qat* N.F. tenderness weeping thinness رقت آمیز (یا انگیز) *riq'qat-āmez'* (or *-angez'*) ADJ. touching رقت قلب *riq'qat-e qal'b* N.F. kindness, tenderness of heart رقیق *raqīq'* ADJ. ★ [A]

رقص *raq's* N.M. dance رقص بسمل *raq's-e bis'mil* N.M. writhing of slaughtered (animals, etc.) رقص و سرود *raq's-o sūrod'* N.M. dance and music concomitants of gay world [A]

رقعات *rūq'āt'* N.M. PL. (see under رقعہ N.M. ★)

رقعہ *rūq''ah* N.M. letter ; epistle note invitation prospective groom's particulars sent over as marriage proposal in form of note to girl's family patch رقعات *rūq'āt'* N.M. letters ; epistles collection of (someone's) epistles [A]

رقم *raq'm* N.M. (PL. رقوم *rūqoom'*) numeral figure item sum total amount writing stole [A]

رقم *ra'qam* رقم طراز *ra'qam-tarāz'* N M. writer (of) رقم طراز ہونا *ra'qam-tarāz' ho'nā* V I. write رقم کرنا *ra'qam kar'nā* V.T. write ; indite put down رقم وار *ra'qam-vār* ADV. item by item رقم ہونا *ra'qam ho'nā* V.I. be written [A]

رقیب *raqīb'* N.M. rival one who keeps guard (over) as attribute of God [A]

رقیق *raqīq'* ADJ. (of fluid) thing not dense رقیق القلب *raqī'q-ūl-qal'b* ADJ. kind hearted [A ~ رقت]

رقیمہ *raqī'mah* N.M. letter [A ~ رقم *raq'm*]

رکاب *rikāb'* (col. *rakāb'*) stirrup (rare) dish رکابدار *rikāb'-dār* N.M. footman accompanying rider ; rider's attendant chef; expert cook

رکابی *rakā'bī* N.F. small dish plate رکابی مذہب *rakā'bī maz'hab* N.M. parasite ; one who joins every feast uninvited پا بہ رکاب *pa ba-rikāb'* ADJ. & ADV. ready to start (old man) expecting death any moment ہم رکاب *ham rikāb'* ADV. in attendance riding in company with ; accompanying [A]

رکاکت *rakā'kat* N.F. indecency (of words, etc.) [A]

رکان *rakān'* N.F manner

رکاو *rukā''o* N.M., رکاوٹ *rukā'vat* N.F. (see under رکنا V.I. ★)

رکشا *rak'shā* N.M. rickshaw [E]

رکعت *rak''at* N.F. (PL. رکعات *rak'āt'*) one set of standing, genuflexion and prostration in prayers [A doublet of رکوع]

رکن *rūk'n* N.M. member essential foot metre one of the fundamentals of faith (rare) pillar [A]

رکنا *rūk'nā* V.I. stop stay (at or with) refrain (from) ; desist from stammer ; falter (in speech) come to a stop ; cease to flow cease to have inspiration hesitate رکاو *rūkā''o* N.M. رکاوٹ *rūkā vaṭ* N.F. obstacle obstruction delay رک رک کر *rūk' rūk' kar* ADV. falteringly

رکوع *rūkoo''* N.M. bow ; bowing in prayer ; (Muslim form of) genuflexion [A]

رکھ *rūkh* N.M. (same as روکھ N.M. ★)

رکھ رکھاو *rakh rakkhā'o* N.M. (see under رکھنا ★)

رکھائی *rūkhā''ī* N.F. curtness indifference [~ روکھا]

رکھشا *rakh'shā* N.F. (dial.) protection رکھشا بندھن *rakh'shā-ban'dhan* N.F. a Hindu festival also called 'rakhī ★ راکھی [S]

رکھنا *rakh'na* V.I. put place keep passes hold keep back reserve bury, inter mortgage ; pledge ; pawn save, lay by رکھا *rakh'hā* (rare. *ra'khā*) PAST PARTICIPLE kept placed employed mortgaged رکھا رکھایا *rakh'khā rakhā'ya* ADJ. kept back laid by, saved رکھ چھوڑنا *rakh' chhor'nā* V.T. keep back laid by ; saved رکھ رکھاو *rakh rakhā''o* N.M. formalities ceremonial behaviour, ceremony رکھ لینا *rakh lenā* V.T. accept ; take engage keep back رکھوال *rakh'vāl'* N M. guard ; used only in PROV. چھوٹی بلی جلیبیوں کی رکھوال *chot'ī bil'lī jale'biyon kī rakhvāl'* PH. thief guarding a treasure set a wolf to watch the fold رکھوالا *rakhvā'la* N.M. watchman keeper guard رکھوالی *rakhvā'lī* N.F. care custody watch رکھوالی کرنا *rakhvā'lī kar'na* V.T. keep watch over safeguard رکھوانا *rakhvā'na* V.T. cause to put cause to keep give in charge arrange burial ; perform funeral rites deposit

رکیک *rakīk'* ADJ. indecent (words, remarks, attack, etc.) [A ~ رکاکت]

رکین *rakīn'* ADJ. strong ; stable ; resolute رکن رکین *rūk'n-e rakīn'* PH. strong pillar ; prominent member force of strength [A ~ رکن]

رگ *rag* N.F vein artery vein (of plant, etc.) strain controls رگ اترنا *rag' ū'tarnā* V.I. be appeased have a rapture رگ پٹھا rag' paṭ'ṭha N.M. PL. veins and sinews live of descent رگ پھڑکنا rag' pha'rakna V.I. have a premonition have an itch to (do some mischief or say something witty) رگ دار rag'-dār ADJ. veined رگ زن rag'-zan N.M. phlebotomist surgeon رگ وپے ra'g-o pai' N.M. veins and muscles every vein رگ وپے (یا ریشہ) میں سرایت کرنا ra'g-o pai' (or re'sha) meṅ sirā'yat kar'na N.F. affect the whole body رگ و ریشہ ra'g-o re'shah N.M. every vein ; veins and fibres ; nature ; constitution رگ جاں ra'g-e jān, شاہ رگ shāh'-rag, شہ رگ shah'-rag N.M. jugular vein [P]

رگڑ ra'gaṛ N.M. رگڑا rag'ṛā N.M. (see under رگڑنا V.T.) ★

رگڑنا ra'garnā V.T. rub chafe scour grate grind reprove ; chastise excruciate رگڑ ra'gaṛ N.F. friction attrition abrasion رگڑ کھانا ra'gaṛ khā'nā V.I. be rubbed be grazed رگڑا rag'ṛā N.M. rubbing harsh treatment dispute رگڑا جھگڑا rag'ṛā jhag'ṛā N.M. dispute argument altercation trouble

رگیدنا raged'nā V.T. inflict a crushing defeat (in wrestling or fighting) handle adversary harshly manhandle chastise use roughly

رلانا rūla'nā V.T. cause to weep tease vex excruciate [~ رونا CAUS]

رلنا ral'nā V.I. get mix up (with) get lost (in crowd, etc.) رل مل کر ral' mil' kar ADV. together رلا ملا ra'lā mi'lā ADJ. mixed adultrated get lost in crowd رلانا rala'nā V T. mix up shuffle adulterate

رلنا rūl'nā V.I. be rolled be tidied up be taken from top [~ رولنا]

رم ram N.M. flight scramble stampede scare رم کرنا ram' kar'nā take to one's heels fly away رمیدگی ramī dagī N.F. flight scare [P ~ رمیدن]

رمال rammāl' N.M. geomancer fortune-teller [A ~ رمل]

رمان rāmmān' N.M. pomegranate [A]

رمانا ramā'nā V.T., رمتا ram'tā ADJ (see under رمنا ★)

رم جھم rim' jhim N.F. pattering sound (of rain) رم جھم برسنا rim' jhim' ba'rasnā V.I. rain with a pattering sound

رمد ra'mad N.M. redness of eyes [A]

رمز ram'z N.F. hint symbol secret secret (of) controlling power (of) رمز شناس ram'z-shinās' ADJ. one who takes a hint conversant with in and outs (of) [A]

رمضان ramazān' (col. ramzān') ninth month of Hijri calendar ; fasting month ; Ramazan رمضان المبارک ramaẓā'n-ul-mubā'rak N.M. the blessed Ramadan (so called because of being the month of fasting and the one in which the revelation of the Holy Quran began) [A]

رمق ra'maq N.F. the last gasp a little tincture (of) ; spark (of) [A]

رمل ram'l N.M. divination ; geomancy (rare) sand [A]

رمل ra'mal (also بحر رمل bah'r-e ra'mal) N.F. a kind of verse metre [A]

رمنا ram'nā V.I. tramp wander ; be absorbed (in) N.M. (also رمنہ ram'nah) game preserve park رمانا ramā'na V.T. cause to wander adopt entice wheedle blandish رمتا ramtā ADJ. roaming ; wandering رمتا جوگی ram'tā jo'gī N.M. wandering Hindu ascetic tramp رمتا فقیر ram'tā faqīr' N.M. wandering mendicant

رموز rūmooz' N.M. PL. (see under رمز N.F. ★)

رمہ ra'mah N.M. herd ; flock [P]

رمیدگی ramidagī N.F. (see under رم N M. ★)

رمیم ramīm' ADJ. decayed [A]

رن[1] ran N.M. battle ; war ; combat ; conflict wood ; waste ; desert گھمسان کا رن پڑنا ghamsān' kā ran paṛ'nā V.I. (of battle) ensue ; break out

رن[2] ran N.M. (or dial. F.) (in cricket) run رن بنانا ran banā'nā V.I. make a run [A]

رنج rañj N.M. grief ; distress anguish agony (rare) toil رنج و غم rañ'j-o gham N.M. distress sufferings رنج اٹھانا (یا سہنا) rañj uṭhā'nā (or saih'nā) V.I. undergo sufferings aggrieve رنج دینا rañj de'nā V.I. bring sufferings to vex offend رنج کرنا rañj kar'nā V.I. grieve be vexed ; fret and fume take offence (at) take umbrage (at) رنج مول لینا rañ'j mol' le'nā V.I. court trouble

رنجش rañ'jish N.F. unpleasantness between (persons) strained relations رنجش ہونا rañ'jish ho'nā V.I. have unpleasantness have strained relations

رنجک rañ'jak N.M. (arch.) touchhole ; match (of gun) priming powder رنجک اڑانا rañ'jak uṛā'nā V.T. flash in the pan رنجک پلانا rañ'jak pilā'na V.T. prime رنجک چاٹ جانا rañ'jak chāṭ' jā'nā V.T. (of musket) fail to go off رنجک دان ranjak-dan' N.M. priming pan [P]

رنجور ranjoor' ADJ. grieved ; distressed ill ; afflicted رنجوری ranjoo'ri N.F. illness ; affliction grief ; anguish [P ~ رنج]

رنجیدہ ranji'dah ADJ. sad ; grieved displeased ; offended chagrined رنجیدہ خاطر ranji'da-khatir ADJ. afflicted in mind ; grieved ; displeased رنجیدہ کرنا ranji'dah kar'na V.T. displease grieve رنجیدہ ہونا ranji'dah ho'na V.I. be grieved be displeased رنجیدگی ranji'dagi N.F. sadness displeasure [P ~ رنج]

رند rind N.M. (PL. rare رنود ranood') libertine boozer sceptic ; free-thinker trickster ADJ. licentious (person) bold رندانہ rinda'nah ADJ. licentious ; bold dissolute ADV. like a reprobate boldly رندمشرب rind'-mash'rab ADJ. licentious bold رندی rin'di N.F. licentionsness boozing boldness free thinking trickery [P]

رند rand N.M. holes in rampart through which to fire outside

رندنا rand'na V.T. (see under رندہ N.M. ★)

رندہ ran'dah N.M. (carpenter's) plane رندہ پھیرنا ran'dah pher'na, رندنا rand'na V.T. plane [P]

رندھنا randh'na V.T. (of throat) be choked be crushed

رنڈ rund N.M. torso branchless trunk of tree رنڈ منڈ rund mund ADJ. branchless clean shaven (etc.)

رنڈاپا randa'pa N.M. widowhood رنڈسالا rand-sa'la N.M. (dial.) widow's weeds رنڈوا rand'va N.M. widower رانڈ rand N.F. ★

رنڈی ran'di N.F. prostitute ; whore ; harlot (rare) woman رنڈی باز ran'di-baz N.M. whoremonger rake رنڈی بازی ran'di-ba'zi N.F. licentiousness whoremongering [doublet of رانڈ N.F. ★]

رنگ rang N.M. colour ; hue pigment paint dye (in cards) suit merriment ; revelry sort manner ; mode condition pomp and show رنگ آمیزی rang-ame'zi N.F. colouring painting colouring (of facts); misrepresentation ; tainting رنگ آمیزی کرنا rang-ame'zi kar'na V.T. & I. colour paint taint ; misrepresent رنگ اڑنا (یا اترجانا) rang ur'na (or u'tar jana V.T. fade ; lose colour become pale have the blue funks رنگا رنگ ran'ga rang ADJ. variegated colourful رنگ افشانی rang-afsha'ni N.F. colouring sprinkling colour رنگ اکھڑنا rang u'khaṛna V.I. lose splendour (of colour ; pomp, etc.) vanish (of effect) be no longer strong رنگ باندھنا rang bandh'na V.I. create much effect رنگ بدلنا rang ba'dalna V.I. change colour be changed be fickle ; be capricious رنگ برنگ rang' ba-rang', ADJ. variegated of various types colourful رنگ بگڑنا rang bi'garna V.I. lose colour ; fade suffer a change for the worse رنگ بھرنا rang' bhar'na V.T. colour ; paint رنگ پاشی rang-pa'shi N.F. sprinkling of colour رنگ پر آنا rang par a'na become prosferous become effective رنگ پکڑنا rang' pa'karna V.I be coloured adopt (someone's) ways fresh up رنگ پھیکا (یا مندا) پڑجانا rang phi'ka (or man'da) par ja'na V.I. lose colour lose lustre be no longer effective رنگ پیدا کرنا rang' pai'da kar'na V.I. adopt (someone's) ways رنگ جمانا rang jama'na V.I. make effective رنگ جمنا rang jam'na V.I. be effective رنگ چڑھانا rang charha'na V.T. paint dye teach (own) ways intoxicate رنگ چڑھنا rang charh'na V.I. be painted be dyed adopt (someone's) ways be intoxicated رنگدار rang'-dar ADJ. coloured painted lawdry رنگ دکھانا rang dikha'na V.T. & I. display bring into play produce a result رنگ دیکھنا rang' dekh'na V.I. examine the state (of) see the result (of) see or suffer through the vicissitudes (of) witness the splendour (of) رنگ ڈھنگ rang' dhang N.M. style ; fashion manners appearance رنگ رس rang' ras N.F. gay life dance and music رنگ رنگیلا rang' rangi'la ADJ. coloured رنگ رلیاں rang ral'yan N.F. revels ; revelry gaiety like of luxury رنگ رلیاں منانا rang ral'yan mana'na V.I. lead a gay life live in luxury رنگ روپ rang' roop N.M. complexion form ; character رنگ روغن rang' rau'ghan N.M. colour lustre رنگریز rang-rez' N.M. a dyer رنگریزی rang re'zi N.F. dying رنگ زرد ہونا rang zar'd ho'na V.I. grow pale have the blue funks رنگساز rang'-saz N.M. painter رنگ فق ہونا rang' faq ho'na V.I. have the blue funks رنگ کاٹنا rang kat'na V.T. bleach رنگ کٹ rang'-kat N.M. bleaching powder رنگ کٹنا rang kat'na V.I. be bleached (of colour) be washed off رنگ کرنا rang' kar'na V.T. paint رنگ کھلنا (یا کھلنا) rang' khil'na (or khul'na) V.I. (of colour) grow lovelier رنگ کھیلنا rang' khel'na V.I. (dial.) sprinkle colour (esp. during Hindu festival Holi) رنگ لانا rang la'na V. bloom fresh up bring about a change produce a result succeed cause trouble رنگ محل rang'-ma'hal N.M. festive palace banquet hall رنگ میں بھنگ ڈالنا rang' men bhang' dal'na V.T. spoil a sport رنگ میں بھنگ پڑنا rang' men bhang' par'na V.I. (of sport, gaiety, etc.)

be spoilt (اپنے رنگ میں رنگنا (ap'ne) rang men rang'nā v.t. make (someone) like oneself رنگ میں ڈوبنا rang' men doob'nā v.i. become a hopeless reprobate رنگ نکلنا rang ni'kalnā v.i. look bright radiate with health (or colour) appear رنگنا rang'nā, رنگوانا rangvā'nā v.t. get coloured get dyed get painted رنگائی rangā''ī, رنگوائی ra gvā''i n.f. painting colouring dying remuneration for these رنگت ran'gat n.f. colour ; hue complexion condition ; state رنگنا rang'nā v.t. paint colour dye make (someone) like (oneself, etc.) رنگے سیار ran'g-e siy'ar n.m. (sing. with pl. v.) fraudulent person رنگیلا rangī'lā, adj. (f. رنگیلی rangi'lī) colourful gaudy lively ; lovial given to a life of pleasure depraved ; lewd رنگین rangin' adj. coloured dyed painted gaudy lively ; jovial elegant given to a life of pleasure florid; ornate ; euphuistic رنگین ادا ran'gīn-ada' adj. of elegant manners رنگین عبارت rangīn' 'ibā'rat n.f. passage in euphuistic style ; ornate writing رنگین مزاج rangin'-mizāj' adj. given to a life of pleasure lewd jovial ; lively رنگینی rangī'ni n.m. colourfulness ornateness lewdness رنگینیِ عبارت rangī'ni-e 'ibā'rat n.f florid style ornate writing [P]

رنگترہ rang'tarah n.m. (arch.) orange [pseudo P]

رنگروٹ rangroot' n.m. recruit رنگروٹی rangroo'ṭī n.f. recruits training its period

رنگنا rang'nā v.t. رنگیلا rangī'lā adj. رنگین rangīn' adj. (see under رنگ n.m. ★)

رو rau n.m. current stream flux inertia line of thinking fervour suf. going moving [P ~ رفتن go]

رو ro (or roo) (mispronounced rau) suf. growing ; germinating خودرو khūd ro growing adj. wild (plant) [P ~ روئیدن]

رو roo n.m. face countenance surface reason ; cause روبراہ roo ba-rāh' adv. ready to set out adj. ready reformed (کے) روبرو (ke) roo' ba-roo' adv. before face to face (with) روبصحت roo ba-seh'hat adv. convalescing on way to recovery روبکار roo ba-kār' n.m. (col. rob'-kār) court proceedings warrant adj. ready a foot روبکاری roo bā-kā'rī n.f court proceedings ; hearing in a law-court روپوش roo-posh' adj. absconding adv. at large روپوش ہونا roo-posh ho'nā v.i. abscond ; be at large go underground روپوشی roo-po'shī n.f absconding ; going underground رودار roo-dār adj. (person) of rank and dignity رورعایت roo' re'ā yat n.f favour . partiality (کی) رو سے (ki) roo' se adv. by way (of) according (to) روسیاہ rōo-siyāh' n.m. criminal sinner adj. notorious int. may (I) be disgraced روسیاہی roo-siyā'hī n.f. disgrace criminal conduct sinfulness روشناس roo-shinās' n.m. casual acquaintance ; one known by face only adj. knowing ; acquainted روشناسی roo-shinā'si n.f. casual acquaintance acquaintance (with something) روکش roo'-kash n.m. opponent adversary contender (old use) cover of mirror adj. resembling disaffiliated contesting contending روکشی rooka'shi n.f. contest abandoning ; deserting disobedience turning or revolting (against) disaffiliated روگردانی roo-gardā'nī n.f. disaffiliation ; disaffection disobedience رومال roomāl' n.m. handkerchief kerchief رومالی roo-mā'lī n.f. loincloth adj. fine (vermicilli) رونما ہونا roo nūmā' ho'nā v.i. transpire رونمائی roo-nūmā''ī n.f. brigle's first unveiled appearance before in-laws monetary gift to be on the occasion روئے سخن roo'-e sā'khan n.m hint [P]

روا ravā' adj. right proper justified permissible lawful upheld روادار rav'-dār' adj. tolerant indulgent liberal-minded condescending رواداری ravā'-dā'rī n.f. tolerance toleration liberalmindedness condescension روا رکھنا ravā' rakh'nā v.t. justify deem lawful uphold [P]

روا ra'vā n.m. coarsely ground wheat ; 'rava' grains (of sand) filings (of metal) crystals

روابط ravā'bit n.m. relations connections ties . bonds [A ~ sing. رابطہ]

رواج rivāj' (ped. ravāj') n.m. custom usage practice fashion ; vague ; craze currency customary law رواج پانا (یا پکڑنا) rivāj' pa'nā (or pa'kaṛ'nā) v.i. be current be in vogue رواج پڑنا rivāj' paṛ'nā v.i. become customary be in vogue رواج دینا rivāj' de'nā v.t. introduce give currency (to) popularize رواجی rivā'jī adj. customary [A]

رواروی ra'vā ra'vī n.f. hurry haste رواروی میں ra'vā ra'vi men adv. hurriedly in passing [P]

رواسا ro'ā'sā, روانسا ro'āṅsā adj. (same as روہانسا rohāṅ'sa adj. ★

رواق rūvāq' n.m. patio canopy رواقی rūvā'qī n.m. (pl. رواقیین rūvāqiyyin') stoic adj. stoical [A]

رواں *ravāṅ'* ADJ. moving flowing fleeting going on viable current ADV. (read) fluently ; without spelling out رواں پڑھنا *ravāṅ' paṛh'nā* V.I. read fluently without spelling out رواں کرنا *ravāṅ' kar'nā* V.T. get going set right رواں ہونا *ravāṅ' ho'nā* V.I. be current be a going concern be in progress سالِ رواں *sā'l-e ravāṅ'* N.M. current year عمرِ رواں *um'r-e ravāṅ* N.M. fleeting life روانی *ravā'nī* N.F. flux fluency working طبیعت کی روانی *tabī''at kī ravā'nī* N.F. readiness of mind felicity of phrase or fancy [P ~ رفتن go]

رواں *ruvāṅ'* N.F. soul روح و رواں *roo'ḥ-o-rūvāṅ'* N.F. soul the soul (of) [P]

رواں *roo''āṅ* N.M. down small hair (of body) nap رواں رواں دعا دیتا ہے *roo''āṅ roo''āṅ du'ā' de'tā hai* PH. I pray for you from the core of my heart رواں رواں کانپنا *roo''āṅ roo''āṅ kāṅp'nā* V.I. be jittery; tremble all over رویں دار *roo''eṅ-dār'* ADJ. downy with raised nap

روانہ *ravānah* (dial. *ravā'nā*) ADV. proceeding despatched روانہ کرنا *ravā'nah kar'nā* V.T. despatch send روانہ ہونا *ravā'nah ho'nā* V.I. set out ; depart روانگی *ravāṅ'gī* N.F. (ped. *ravā'nagī*) departure despatch روانی *ravā'nī* N.F. (see under ADJ. ★) [P ~ رفتن]

روایات *rivā'yāt* N.F. PL. (see under روایت N.F ★)

روایت *rivā'yat* N.F. (PL. روایات *rivāyāt'*) narration narrative tradition legend story statevent ; version [A]

روباہ *robāh'*, روبہ *ro'bah* N.F. fox روباہ بازی *robah-bā'zī*, روباہی *robā'hī* N.F. cunning [P]

روبکار *robkār'* N.F. (see under رو *roo* N.M. ★)

روبل *roo'bal* N.M. rouble [R]

روپ *roop* N.M. (dial.) beauty elegance form disguise ; guise روپ بدلنا *roop ba'dalnā* V.T. change form روپ بگاڑنا *roop bigāṛ'nā* V.T. mar deface ; disfigure روپ بنانا (یا دھارنا) *roop banā'nā* (or *dhār'nā*) V.T. personate روپ دکھانا *roop dikhā'nā* V.T. show one's lovely face روپ سنگار *roop singār'* N.M. beauty and make-up پَیل روپ *pai'hal-roop* N.M. chrysalis (of insect)

روپہلا *rūpaih'lā* ADJ. (F. روپہلی *rūpaih'lī*) silver ; silvery [S ~ روپا silver]

روپیہ *rūpa'yah* N.M. rupee money wealth; riches روپیہ اٹھانا *rupa'yah uṭhā'nā* V.T. spend (so much) money روپیہ اٹھنا *rūpa'yah uṭh'nā* V.I. (of so much) be spend روپیہ بھنانا (یا تڑوانا) *rūpa'yah bhūnā'nā* or *tuṛā'nā*) V.I. get a change روپیہ ٹھیکری کرنا *rūpa'yah ṭhīk'rī kar'nā* V.I spend lavishly . waste money [S ~ روپا silver]

روٹ *roṭ* N.M. (see under روٹی ★)

روٹ *rooṭ* N.M. route روٹ پرمٹ *rooṭ' par'miṭ* N.F route permit [E]

روٹھنا *rooṭh'nā* V.I. cool down (towards friend, etc.) owing to be misunderstanding displeased not to be on speaking terms (with friend, etc.)

روٹی *ro'ṭī* N.F. loaf ; bread meals board livelihood ; means of livelihood روٹی پکانا *ro'ṭī pakā'nā* V.I. bake bread روٹی دینا *ro'ṭī de'nā* V.I. support روٹی چپڑنا *ro'ṭī chū'paṛnā* V.T butter the bread روٹی کپڑا *ro'ṭī kap'ṛā* N.M. maintenance maintenance allowance روٹیاں توڑنا *ro'ṭiyāṅ toṛ'nā*, روٹیوں پر پلنا *roṭiyoṅ par pal'nā* V. be a hanger on روٹیوں کا مارا *ro'ṭiyoṅ kā mā'rā* ADJ. starved روٹی والا *ro'ṭī vā'lā* N.M. baker روٹ *roṭ* N.M. thick large loaf

روح *rooḥ'* N.F. (PL. ارواح *arvāḥ'*) soul essence quintessence the reality (behind) heart life spirit روح افزا *roo'ḥ-afzā'*, روح فزا *rooḥ'-fizā'* ADJ. exhilarating روح الامین *roo'ḥ-ūl-amīn'*, روح القدس *roo'ḥ-ūl-qūd's* N.M. Gabrial the Holy Ghost روح اللہ *roo'ḥ ullāh'* N.M. Jesus (as the Holy Ghost) روح بھٹکنا *rooḥ' bha'ṭaknā* V.I. (of soul) be uneasy ; having frequent recourse to the world owing to some uneaniness روح پرواز کرنا (یا نکلنا) *rooḥ' parvāz' kar'nā* (or *ni'kalnā*) V.I. die , pass away ; give up the ghost be frightened to death ; have the blue funks روح و رواں *roo ḥ-o rūvāṅ'* N.F. heart and soul جیسی روح ویسے فرشتے *jai'sī rooḥ' vai'se firish'te* PROV. like priest like people روحانی *roohā'nī* ADJ. spiritual روحانیت *roohāniy'yat* N F spirituality روحی *roo'ḥī* ADJ. (rare spiritual [A]

رود *rod* N.M. river stream (rare) a guitar like musical instrument رودبار *rod bār'* N.F. gulf ; strait area abounding in srreams [P]

روداد *roodād'*, روئداد *roo''edād*, روئیداد *roo''edād* N.F. account report proceedings state روداد جلسہ *roodā'd-e jal'sah* N.F. proceedings of a meeting روداد مقدمہ *roodā'de mūqad'damah* N.F. proceedings of a case روداد نویس *roodād'-navīs'* N.M. (arch.) reporter [P ~ رو + دادن take place]

رودہ *ro'dah* N.M. gut string of musical instrument [P]

روڈ *roḍ* N.F. road [E]

روڑا *ro'ṛā* N.M. brickbat small piece of stone or brick old resident (of) روڑا اٹکانا (یا روڑا اٹکانا) *ro'ṛā aṭkā'nā* V T put obstacles in the way (*kā*) *ro'ṛā hona* V.I. be a part and parcel of روڑی *ro'ṛī* N.F. broken stones or bricks

روز *roz* N.M. day daytime ADV. daily per day always day in and day out روزافزوں *roz-afzoon'* ADJ. ever-increasing ADV. increasing day by day روز بروز *roz' ba-roz'* ADV. day by day constantly روز جزا *ro'z-e jazā'* N.M. day of Judgement ; doomsday روز حساب *ro'z-e ḥisāb'* N.M. day of reckoning روز حشر *ro'z-e ḥash'r* N.M. Day of Resurrection روز روز *roz' roz* ADV. every day always روز روشن میں *ro'z-e rau'shan meṅ* ADV. in broad daylight روز سیاہ *roz-e siyāh'* N.M. calamity روز قیامت *roz-e qiyā'mat* N.M. Doomsday روزمرہ *roz mar'rah* N.M. spoken language ADJ. customary usual ADV. daily ; everyday روزنامچہ *roz-nām'chah* N.M. diary day book (of accounts) روزنامچہ نویس *roz'nām'-cha-navīs'* V.I. literary diarist police clerk روزنامچہ نویسی *roz-nām'cha navī'sī* N.F. diary writing روزنامہ *roz-nā'mah* N.M. newspaper ; daily شبانہ روز *shabā'nā-roz*, روز و شب *ro'z-o-shab'* ADV. round the clock روزانہ *rozā'nah* ADV. daily روزگار *roz-gār'* N.M. livelihood employment world age time روزگار چھوٹنا *roz'-gār chhooṭ'nā* V.I. be sacked be out of job ; be unemployed روزگار لگنا (یا ملنا) *roz-gār' lag'nā* (or *mil'nā*) V.I. get a job , be fix up روزہ *rozah* N.M. fast lent روزہ افطار کرنا (یا کھولنا) *ro'zah iftār kar'nā* (or *khol'nā*) V.I. break one's fast روزہ توڑنا *ro'zah toṛ'nā* V. break one's fast before time روزہ خور *ro'za-khor* N.M. & ADJ. (one) who does not fast روزہ دار *ro'zah-dār* N.M. & ADJ. fasting (person) روزہ رکھنا *ro'zah rakh'nā* V.I. fast روزہ کھانا *ro'zah khā'nā* V.I. not to fast روزی *ro'zī* N.F. daily bread livelihood wages pay ; salary job روزی دہ *ro'zī-deh*, روزی رساں *ro'zī-rasāṅ'* N.M. providence ; God (as the Giver of daily bread) روزینہ *rozī'nah* N.M. stipend daily allowance daily wages روزینہ دار *rozī'nā dār* N.M. stipendiary one granted a daily allowance [P]

روزگار *roz-gār'* N.M. (see under روز N.M. ★)

روزن *rau'zan* N.M. inlet for fresh air ; ventilator hole (in wall) [P]

روزہ *ro'zah* N.M. روزی *ro'zī* N.F. روزینہ *rozī'nah* N.M. (see under روز N.M. ★)

روستا *ros'tā* (or *roos'tā*) N.M. village روستازادہ *'tā-zā'dah* N.M. villager ; rustic روستائی *rostā''ī* N.M. villager ; rustic سلام روستائی *salā'm-e rostā''ī* N.M. greetings or meeting with a motive [P]

روسلی *roos'lī* ADJ. (of land) not quite fertil

روش *ra'vish* N.F. avenue walk made manner fashion ; style behaviour [P ~ رفتن go]

روشن *rau'shan* ADJ. bright shining lighted manifest evident ; obvious روشندان *rau'shan-dān* N.M. ventilator (arch.) skylight روشن دماغ *rau'shan-dimāgh'* ADJ. broad-minded intelligent روشن ضمیر (یا دل) *rau'shan-zamīr'* (or *dil*) ADJ. godly pure of heart روشنائی *roshnā''ī* (ped. *raushnā''i*) N.F. ink (rare) light روشنک *rau'shanak* N.F. torch-bearer روشنی *raush'ni* (ped. *raushā'ni*) N.F. light روشنی ڈالنا *raush'nī dāl'nā* V.T. throw light (on) روشنیٔ طبع *rau'shanī-e tab'* N.F. intelligence sagacity ; shrewdness روشنی کرنا *raush'ni kar'nā* V.I. light light (a lamp) illuminate روشنی ہونا *raush'ni ho'nā* V.I. be illuminated dawn [P]

روضہ *rau'zah* N.M. (PL. ریاض *riyāz'*) mausoleum shrine (rare) garden (also روضۃ الشہدا *rau'zat-ush-shuhadā'*) name of a Shi'ite book recited at mourning assemblies روضہ خواں *rau'za khān* N.M. reciter of this book reciter of elegies روضہ خوانی *rau'za-khā'ni* N.F. recitation of elegies, etc. روضۂ رضوان *rau'za-e riz'vān* N.M. paradise [P]

روغن *rau'ghan* N.M. paint polish oil allow روغن بلسان *rau'ghan-e balsān'* N.M. balsam روغن زرد *rau'ghan-e zar'd* N.M. (arch.) butter oil ; clarified butter ; ghee روغن سیاہ *rau'ghan-e siyāh* N.M. (arch.) mustard oil روغن قاز ملنا *rau'ghan-e qāz' mal'nā* V.T. pull (someone's) leg روغن نفت *rau'ghan-e naf't* N.M. (rare) kerosene oil ; petroleum روغنی *raughā'nī* ADJ. (of bread) with butter mixed in dough ; cake-like oily [P]

روکڑ *ro'kaṛ* N.M. (slang) cash , ready money روکڑ بکری *ro'kaṛ bik'rī* N.F. cash sale روکڑ بہی *ro'kaṛ ba'hī* N.F. cash book

روکن *roo'kan* N.F. extra quantity or additional article given in the bargain to please the customer ; extra quantity ; additional attraction

روکنا *rok'nā* V.T. stop withhold detain restrain prohibit hinder check impede interrupt block avert prevent bar challenge stay *rok* N.M. bar barrier snag obstacle obstruction hindrance restraint limitation restriction interruption prevention prohibition check stay support brake روک تھام *rok' thām* N.F. check restraint stay prevention remedy eradication stoppage روک ٹوک *rok'-ṭok* N.F. let or hindrance obstruction prohibition opposition بے روک ٹوک *be-rok'-ṭok*, (col. بلا روک ٹوک *bi-lā'-rok'-ṭok* ADV without let or hindrance freely

روکھ *rookh*, (dial. *rokh*) N.M. tree

روکھا *roo'khā* ADJ. (F. روکھی *roo'khī*) without stew, etc. plain dry unbuttered unseasoned poor indifferent curt uncivil روکھا جواب *roo'khā javāb'* N.M. curt reply روکھا سا *roo'khā sā* ADJ. curt indifferent uncivil insipid روکھا پھیکا *roo'khā phī'kā* روکھا سوکھا *roo'khā soo'khā* ADJ. plain curt blunt N.M. poor meal ; plain food روکھا پن *roo'khā-pan*, روکھائی *rūkhā''ī* N.F. coldness ; indifference incivility curtness

روگ *rog* N.M. illness ; disease روگ پالنا (یا لگا لینا) *rog' pāl''nā* (or *lagā' le'nā*) V.I. be masochistic hug trouble nurse some illness روگی *ro'gī* N.M. sick man ADJ. sick سدا روگی *sa'dā-ro'gī* N.M. invalid

رولا *rau'lā* N.M. noise riot ; disturbance hue and cry رولا مچانا *rau'lā machā'nā* V.I. make a noise create a disturbance raise a hue and cry

رولنا *rol'nā* V.T. roll gather up thus make much money

روم[1] *rom* N.M. small hair of body down

روم[2] *rom*, روما *ro'mā* N.M. Rome رومن *ro'man* N.M. Roman N.F. Roman script Urdu written in Roman script رومن کیتھولک *ro'man kai'thūlik* ADJ. & N.M. Roman Catholic [E]

روم *room* N.M. Asia Minor Byzantine Empire Ottoman Caliphate (arch.) Turkey رومی *roo'mī* ADJ. & N.M. Roman Turk Turkish [A ~ E Rome]

رومان *roomān'* N.M. Romance رومانی *rooma'nī* ADJ. romantic رومانیت *roomaniy'yat* (or *roomā'nīyat*) N.F. Romanticism رومانیت پسند *roomaniy'yat-pasand'* N.M. & ADJ. Romantic رومانیت پسندی *roomaniy'yat-pasan'dī* N.F. romanticism [E]

رونا *ro'nā* V.T. & I. weep cry mourn grieve رو دینا *ro de'nā* V.I. burst into tears رو رو (پیٹ یا دھو یا رو) کر *ro pīṭ'* (or *dho'* or *ro'*) *kar* ADV. with great difficult after weeping رونی صورت *ro'nī soo'rat* N.M. (person with) sad countenance kill-joy رونا پیٹنا *ro'nā pīṭ'nā*, رونا دھونا *ro'nā dho'nā* V. cry weep bitterly mourn N.M. fuss رونا رونا *ro'nā ro'nā* V.I. relate (one's) tale of woe رونی صورت *ronī sūrat* ADJ. of a sad countenance . about to weep روہانسا *rohāṅ'sā* (dial. رواسا *ro'a'sā* روانسا *ro'āṅ'sā*) ADJ. (F. روہانسی *rohāṅ'sī* dial روانسی ، رواسی) feeling like crying

روند *raund* N.F. patrol round [~ E round CORR.]

روندنا *raund'nā* V.T. trample tread under foot روندن *rauṅ'dan* trample روندن میں آنا *rauṅ'dan meṅ ā'nā* V.I. be trampled

رونده *raviṅ'dah* N.M. (PL. روندگان *raviṅ'dagān*) one who goes [P ~ رفتن go]

رونق *rau'naq* N.F. flourishing state being crowded (of market) being busy being in full swing freshness bloom splendour pomp and show رونق افروز ہونا *rau'naq afroz' ho'nā* V.I. (euph.) grace the occasion arrive sit رونق والا *rau'naq-vā'lā*, پر رونق *pūr-rau'naq* ADJ. busy well-attended full of activity flourishing blooming fresh splendid successful [P]

رونگٹا *roṅg'ṭā* N.M. small hair of body fine wool رونگٹے کھڑے ہونا *roṅg'ṭe khaṛe ho'nā* V.I (of hair) stand on end (from fear or cold) ; feel jittrey

رونہ *ravan'nah*. رونا *ravan'nā* N.M. errand boy pass octroi permit [P ~ روانہ CORR.]

روہانسا *rohāṅ'sā* ADJ. (F. روہانسی *rohāṅ'sī*) (see under رونا ★)

روہت *roo'hat* N.F. freshness

روہو *ro'hoo* N.F. a kind of fish corners of eyelids

روئداد *roo''edād*, روئیداد *roo'edād'* N.F. (same as روداد N.F ★)

روئی *roo''ī* N.F. cotton cotton wool روئی تومنا *roo''ī tom'nā* V.I. comb cotton with the hand روئی دار *roo''ī-dār'* ADJ stuffed with cotton روئی دھنکنا (یا دھننا) *roo''ī dhūnak'nā* (or *dhūn'nā*) V.I. card cotton روئی کا گالا *roo''ī kā gā'lā* N.M. cotton flake something while and soft روئی کانوں میں ٹھونسنا *roo''ī kā noṅ meṅ ṭhoṅs'nā* V.I. turn a deaf ear (to)

روئے *roo''e* N.M. (construct form of رو *roo* N.M. ★)

روئیدگی *ro'ī'dagī* N.M. vegetation plant growth [P ~ روئیدن grow]

رویا *ro'yā* (or *ro''-*) N.M dream vision رویائے صادقہ *royā'-e sā'diqah* N.M. true dream تعبیر الرویا *ta'bīr-ūr-ro''yā* N.F. interpretation of dreams [A ~ FOLL.]

رویت *ro'yat* (or *ro''-*) N.M. sighting observation رویت ہلال *ro'yat-e-hilāl'* N.M. sighting of new moon

رویت *raviy'yat* N.F consideration thought [A doublet of FOLL]

روبیہ *raviy'yah* N.M. conduct behaviour [A]

رہ *rah* N.F. (same as راہ N.F. ★) رہبر *rah'-bar* N.M. رہزن *rah'-zan* N.M. رہگزر *rah'-gū'zar* N.F. رہنما *rah'-nūmā'* N.M. رہنموں *rah'-nūmoon'* N.M. رہ نورد *rah'-navar'd* N.M. رہوار *rah-var'* N.M. (see under راہ N.F. ★)

رہا *rahā'* ADJ. released liberated freed disengaged رہا کرنا *rehā' kar'nā* V.T. release free set at liberty ; liberate disengage رہا ہونا *rehā' ho'nā* V.I. be relbased be set at liberty be liberated be disengaged رہائی *rehā''ī* N.F. ★)

رہا سہا *ra'hā sa'hā* ADJ. (see under رہنا V.I. ★)

رہانا *rahā'nā* V.T. have (millstone, etc.) roughened

رہائش *rehā''ish* N.F. residence stay abode رہائش اختیار کرنا *rehā''ish ikhti'yār kar'nā* V.I. take up abode رہائش رکھنا *rehā''ish rakh'nā* V.I. stay [pseudo- P ~ رہنا]

رہائی *rehā''ī* N.F. release liberation discharge acquittal رہائی پانا *rehā''ī pa'nā* V.I. be released be set free ; be set at liberty be discharged ; be acquitted رہائی دینا (یا عطا کرنا) *rehā''ī de'nā* (or *'atā' kar'nā*) V.T. release ; set free P رہا *rehā*]

رہبانیت *rahbā'niyat* N.F. monkey ; monastic life as an institution [A]

رہبان *roh'ban'* N.M. PL. (see under راہب N.M. ★)

رہٹ *ra'haṭ* N.M. Persian wheel (rare) continuity (usu in) رہٹ لگانا *ra'haṭ lagā na* V.I. pay frequent visits رہٹی *raih'ṭī* N.F. small Persian wheel routine instalment رہٹی باندھنا *raih'ṭī bandh'nā* V.I. set up a routine settle instalment رہٹی چلانا *raih'ṭī chalā'nā* V.I. sell on instalments

رہس *raih's* N.F (same as راس *rās* N.F. ★)

رہکلا *ra'hakla* N.M. a kind of small cannon

رہن *reh'n* (ped. *rah'n*) N.M. mortgage; pledge رہن اراضی *reh'n-e arā'zī* N.M. land mortage رہن انتفاعی *reh'n-e intif'ā'ī* N.M. a profitable mortgage رہن باقبضہ *reh'n bā-qab'zah*, رہن بالقبض *reh'n bil-qab'z* N.M. mortgage with possession رہن بلا قبضہ *reh'n bi-la' qab'zah* N.M. mortgage without possession رہن دار *reh'n-dār* N.M. mortgage رہن (سے) چھڑانا *reh'n (se) chhūṛā'nā* V.T. redeem رہن رکھنا *reh'n rakh'nā* V.I. mortgage pledge رہن نامہ *reh'n-nā'mah* N.M. mortgage deed فک رہن *fak'k-e reh'n*, فک الرہن *fak'k-ūr-reh'n* N.M. redemption mortgage رہن در رہن *reh'n dar reh'n* N.M. mortgagee's repledging of property [A]

رہن سہن *raih'n saih'n* N.M. (see under رہنا V.I. ★)

رہنا *raih'nā* V.I. live reside dwell stay remain last fare ADV. continue (to do or doing) ; go on (doing) (for emphasis) do رہتے *raih'te* ADV. in the presence of during his life-time under his very nose رہتے رہتے *raih'te raih'te* ADV. through continued stay through unchecked deterioration رہتی دنیا تک *raih'ti dūn'ya tak* ADV. for ever ; ever and anon رہ جانا *raih' jā'nā* V.I. stay behind be left undone be omitted miss be fatigued ; be tired be exhausted become useless grow too old and weak رہ رہ کر (یا کے) *raih' raih' kar* (or *ke*) ADV. repeatedly time and again رہنے دینا *raih'ne de'nā* V.I. leave aside ; leave alone let remain permit to stay رہن سہن *raih'n saih'n* N.M. mode of life (ہمیشہ) رہے نام اللہ کا *(hame'shah ra'he nām' allāh' ka* PH. vanity of vanties all is vanity

رہوار *rahvār'*, راہوار *rah'var* N.M. (see under راہ N.F. ★)

رہین *rahīn'* N.M. (rare) mortgaged PREF. under رہین منت *raihī'n-e min'nat* ADJ. under obligation (to) ; obliged (to) indebted (to) [A ~ رہن]

رؤسا *ro'asā'* N.M. (PL. ~ SING. رئیس ★)

رؤف *ra'oof'* (occ. spelt as رءوف) ADJ. very kind N.M. the Merciful (as attribute of God) [A ~ رأفت]

رئی *ra'ī* N.F. churning staff رئی چلانا *ra''ī chala'nā* V.I. churn

رئیس *ra'is'* N.M. (PL. رؤسا *ro'asā'*) rich person landlord magnate chief ; head (of department) [A]

رے *re* N.M. second note of national gamut ; INT oh hallo dear dear what you (etc.)

ریا *riyā'* N.M. hyprocrisy pretence dissimulation show ریاکار *riyā'-kār'* N.M. & ADJ. hypocrite pretender dissembler decitful (person) ریاکارانہ *riyā'-kāra'nah* ADJ. & ADV. hypocritical (by) ریاکاری *riyā'-kārī* N.F. hypocricy pretence dissimulation show ریائی *riyā''ī* ADJ. hypocritical [A]

ریاح *riyāḥ'* N.M. PL. (~ SING. ریح N.F ★)

ریاست *riyā'sat* N.F. State princely State being a big landlord being very rich ways of the rich ریاست بے سیاست نہیں چلتی *riyā'sat be siyā'sat na'hīn chal'tī* PROV. policy (or penalization) is the mainstay of the ship of State

ریاض *riyāz'* N.M. (PL. of روضہ *rau'zah*); gardens (SING.) (in music) practice (esp. as a professional) ریاضت *riyāzat* N.F. physical exercies austerity drill mystic exercise ریاضت کرنا *riyā'zat kar'nā* V.I. perform mystic exercise ریاضتی *riyā'zatī* ADJ. devoting much attention to mystic exercises [A]

ریاضی *riyā'zī* N.M. mathematics science of numbers, etc. including music ریاضی دان *riyā'zī-dān* N.M. mathematician [A]

ریب *raib* N.M. (rare) doubt لاریب *lā-raib'* ADV. doubtless ; certainly [A]

ریپبلک *ripab'lik* N.F. republic [E]

ریت *rīt* N.F. custom rite observance fashion manners habit ریت رسم *rīt' ras'm* N.F. manners and customs

ریت *ret* N.F. ریتا *re'tā*, ریتہ *re'tah* N.M. sand ریتلا *ret'lā* ADJ. (F. ریتلی *ret'lī*) sandy ریتنا *ret'na* V.T. rasp ; file ریتی *re'tī* N.F. file sandy beach sand stretch (usu. along river)

ریٹ *reṭ* N.M. rate [E]

ریٹھا *rīṭhā* N.M. soap-wort ; soapnut ; soappod

ریجھنا *rījh'nā* V.I. have a desire to possess fall (for) incline (to) find oneself in love (with)

ریچھ *richh* N.M. bear

ریح *rīḥ* N.F. (PL. ریاح *riyāh'*) air wind flatulence fart ریح کا درد *rīḥ' kā dar'd* N.M. gout; rheumatism ریحی *rī'hī* ADJ. windy of wind ریاح *riyāḥ'* N.F. flatulence N.F. PL. winds [A]

ریحان *raiḥān'* N.M. sweet basil تخم ریحان *tukh'm-e raiḥān'* N.M. its seed used as drug ; 'ocimum pelosum' seed

ریخ *rekh* N.F. fissure part of gums within teeth

ریختہ *rekh'tah* N.M. (arch.) Urdu (arch.) 'pucca wall or house (arch.) plaster ADJ. scattered fallen apart ریختہ گو *rekh'ta-go* N.M. (PL. ریختہ گویاں *rekh'tā-go'yān*) urdu poet ریختی *rekh'tī* N.F. (arch.) women's idiom in Urdu verse composed in it [P]

ریڈ انڈین *red in'diyan* N.M. & ADJ. Red Indian [E]

ریڈ کراس *red'-karās'* N.M. Red Cross [E]

ریڈیم *re'diyam* N.M. radium [E]

ریڈیو *re'diyo* N.M. radio ADJ. radio ریڈیائی *rediyā'ī* ADJ. radio [E]

ریڑھ *rīṛh*, ریڑھ کی ہڈی *rīṛh kī had'ḍī* N.F. backbone backbone (of)

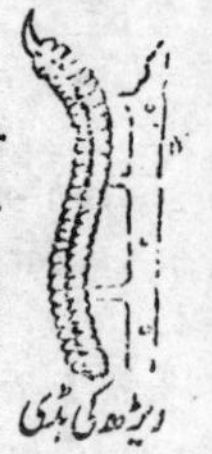

ریز *rez* SUF. shedding pouring scattering N.F. chirp a kind of land ریز کرنا *rez' kar'nā* V.I. chirp together blandish ریزش *re'zish* N.F. cold catarrh scattering flowing in small quantities ریزش ہونا *re'zish ho'na* V.I. run at the nose ریزگاری *rez-gā'rī* N.F. change ; small coins [P ~ ریختن]

ریزر *re'zar* N.M. razor سیفٹی ریزر *sef'ṭī re'zar* N.M. safety razor [E]

ریزہ *re'zah* N.M. crumb bit piece scrap ADJ. skilful minute ریزہ چینی *re'za-chī'nī* N.F. picking up of crumbs plagiarize draw inspiration (from) ریزہ ریزہ *re'za re'zah* ADJ. in piece broken to pieces battered [P ~ ریختن]

ریس *ris* N.F. emulation ریس کرنا *ris' kar'nā* V.I. emulate vie (with)

ریس *res* N.F. race ریس کا گھوڑا *res' ka gho'ṛā* N.M. race horse ریس کا میدان *res' kā maidan'* ریس کورس *res kor's* N.M. race course [E]

ریسٹورنٹ *raistoraint'* ریستوران *rais'torān* N.M. restaurant [E]

ریسماں *ris'mān* N.F. rope cord thread [P]

ریش *rīsh* N.F. beard ریشائیل *rī'shā'īl'* N.M. (joc.) long bearded (person) ریشخند *rīsh'khand* N.M. ridicule laughter for ridicule [P]

ریشم *re'sham* N.M. silk ریشمی *resh'mī* (or ued. *re'shamī*) (arch. ریشمیں *re'shamīn*) ADJ. silk ; silken [P]

ریشہ *re'shah* (or *rī-*) N.M. fibre string (of mango, etc.) vein (of leaf, etc.) ریشہ خطمی ہونا *re'shah khat'mī ho'nā* V.I. (vul.) fall for be pleased ریشہ دار *re'sha-dār* ADJ. fibrous stringy بے ریشہ *be-re'shah* ADJ. fibreless stringless ریشہ دوانی *re'sha-davā'nī* N.F. intrigue mischief-making [P]

ریعان *rai'ān'* (ped. *raya'ān'*) N.M. beginning (of) [A]

ریف *rīf* N.F. sub-montane region (esp. of North Africa) [A]

ریفارم *rifār'm* N.F. reform ریفارمر *rifār'mar* N.M. reformer ریفارمز *rifār'mz* N.M. PL. reforms [E]

ریفریجریٹر *rifrijre'ṭar* N.M. refrigerator fridge [E]

ریکارڈ *rikār'd* N.M. record ریکارڈ توڑنا *rikār'd toṛ'nā* V.T. break the record ; better the record [E]

ریکٹ *rai'kaṭ* N.M. racket [E]

ریکھا *re'khā* N.F. (dial.) lines on palm of hand

ریگ *reg* N.F. (lit.) sand ریگِ رواں *re'g-e ravāh'* N.F. shifting sands ریگمال *reg'māl* N.M. sandpaper ریگماہی *re'g-mā'hī* N.F. skink dried skink (used as drug) ریگزار *reg'-zār* N.M. desert ; sandy tract ریگستان *re'gistān* N.M. desert lage sandy tratt [P]

ریل *rel* N.F. railway train railway ریل گاڑی *rel'-gā'ṛī* N.F. railway train ریلوائی *rel'-vā'ī* N.M. (dial.) railwayman ; railway employee ریلوے *rel've* N.M. railway ; railroad railway department [E]

ریل *rīl* N.F. real spool bobbin [E]

ریلنا *rel'nā* V.I. (of crowd) ruch push forward sally forth ریلا *re'la* N.M. push (of crowd) rush sally sortie torrent flood (of people) ریل پیل *rel' pel* N.F. crowd large numbers plenty (of) ; abundance (of)

ریم[1] *rīm* N.F. pus ; matter [P]

ریم[2] *rīm* N.F. ream [E]

ریمارک *rimār'k* N.M. remark ریمارک پاس کرنا *rimār'k pās' kar nā* pass a remark quip [E]

ریمانڈ *rimānḍ'* N.M. remand ریمانڈ لینا *rimānḍ' le'nā* V.I. (of police) get (accused) remanded to police custody) [E]

رین *rain* N.F. (dial.) night رین بسیرا *rain' base'rā* N.M. night's halt night lodge رینی *rai'nī* ADJ. pet (bird) chirping at night [S]

رینٹھ *renṭh* N.F. snot ; snivel

ریں ریں *reṅ' reṅ* (or *rīṅ' rīṅ*) N.F. (child's) whining ریں ریں کرنا *reṅ' reṅ kar'na* V.I. whine

ریندھنا *rīndh'nā* V.I. cook (used only with پکانا as) پکانا ریندھنا *pakā'nā rīndh'nā* V.T. & I. do the cooking

رینڈیر *ren'ḍiyar* N.M. reindeer [E]

رینکنا *renk'nā* V. . (of ass) bray

رینگنا *rīng'nā* V.I. creep ; crawl

ریوڑ *re'vaṛ* N.M flock of (goats)

ریوڑی *re'vaṛī* (or *reyo'ṛī*) N.F. sweet cracker ریوڑی کے پھیر میں آنا *reyo'ṛī ke pher' meṅ ā'nā* V.I. land (oneself) in trouble ; be involved in difficulties

ریوند *re'vand* N.M. rhubarb ریوند چینی *re'vand-e chīnī* N.M. the Chinese rhubarb

ریونیو *rai'veniyoo* N.M. revenue ریونیو افسر *rai'veniyoo af'sar* N.M. Revenue Assistant [E]

ریویو *rīviyoo'* N.M. review periodical [E]

ریہ *riyah'* N.M. lung [A]

ریہہ *reh* N.F. Fuller's earth

ڑ *re* fifteenth letter of Urdu alphabet (also called *rā'-e hin'dī*) never used as an initial sound in any word in Urdu or any other known language of the world (in jummal reckoning) (equivalent to) 200

ز *ze* sixteenth letter of Urdu alphabet (also called *za'-e mo jamah* or *sa'-e manqoo'tah*) equivalent to English z) (in jummal reckoning) seven

زا *zā* SUF. born of ; offspring of ; scion of giving birth to giving rise to [P ~ زادن]

زاج *zāj* N.M copper sulphate ; vitriol زاجِ سفید *zā'j-e sifed'* N.M. alum [P]

زاد[1] *zād* N.M. provisions victuals زادِ راہ *za'd-e rāh'*, زادِ سفر *za'd-e sa'far* N.M. provisions for journey [A

زاد[2] *zād* N.M. birth SUF. born of ; offspring of زاد بوم *zād-boom* N.M. birthplace native land زادہ *zā'dah* SUF. born of son of زادی *zā'dī* SUF. born of daughter of [P ~ زادن]

زار[1] *zār* N.M. Czar [E ~ R ~ L]

زار[2] *zār* ADJ. afflicted aggrieved wounded ADV. (weeping) bitterly SUF. place abounding in (something) زار زار *zār' zār*, زار و قطار *zā'r-o-qatār'* ADV. (weep) bitterly زار و نزار *zā'r-o-*

nizar' ADJ. weak emaciated زار حال *ha'l-e zar'* N.M. miserable condition ; pitiable plight زاری *za'ri* N.F. crying wailing lamentation [P]

زار[2] *zar* SUF. place abounding in سبزہ زار *sab'za-zar'*. N.M. lawn meadow ; pasture park گلزار *gul-zar'* N.M. garden لالہ زار *la'la-zar* N.M. bed of tulips مرغزار *mar'gh-zar'* N.M. meadow ; pasture [P]

زاغ *zagh'* N.M. crow vitriol a mode of song [P]

زال *zal* N.M. name of Rustam's father ADJ. snowhite silver-haired very old پیر زال *pir' zal'* N.F. old hag (fig.) world [P]

زانو *za'noo* N.M. knee زانو بدلنا *za'noo ba'dalna* V.I. change knees for rest in sitting دو زانو بیٹھنا *du-za'noo baiṭh'na* V. squat زانوئے ادب تہ (یا طے) کرنا *za'noo-e a'dab taih'* (or *tai'*) *kar'na* V.I. sit respectfully show respect (to) be the disciple (of) زانوئے تلمذ تہ (یا طے) کرنا *za'noo-e talam'muz taih'* (or *tai'*) *kar'na* V.I. be or become the pupil (of) [P]

زانی *za'ni* N.M. adulterer fornicator whore-monger ADJ. lax in morals ; lewd زانیہ *za'niyah* N.F. adultress fornicatress ADJ. loose (woman) [A ~ زنا]

زاویہ *za'viyah'* N.M. (PL. زوایا *zava'ya*) angle corner hermit's abode زاویہ حادہ *za'viya-e had'dah* N.M. acute angle زاویہ قائمہ *za'viyah-e qa''imah* N.M. right angle زاویہ متبادلہ *za'viya-e mutaba'dalah* N.M. alternate angle زاویہ متناظرہ *za'viya-e mutana'zarah* N.M. corresponding angle زاویہ منفرجہ *za'viya-e mun'farijah* N.M. obtuse angle زاویہ نشین (یا گزین) *za'viya-nashin'* (or *guzin'*) N.M. & ADJ. person leading a secluded life hermit زاویہ نظر (نگاہ) *za'viya-e na'zar* (or *nigah'*) N.M. viewpoint ; point of view ; angle of vision اندرونی (یا بیرونی) زاویہ *andaroo'ni* (or *beroo'ni*) *za'viah* N.M. inner (or outer) circle [A]

زاویے

زاہد *za'hid* N.M. (PL. زہاد *zohhad'*) ascetic mystic hermit ADJ. devout abstinent ascetic [A ~ زہد]

زائچہ *za''echah* N.M. horoscope زائچہ کھینچنا (یا بنانا) *za''echah khench'na* (or *bana'na*) V.I. cast a horoscope [P]

زائد *za''id* ADJ. surplus excess extra redundant ; superfluous ADV. above over and above more than زائد از ضرورت *za''id az zaroo'rat* ADJ. surplus excessive زائد المیعاد *za''id ul-mi'ad'* ADJ. time-barred [A ~ زیادہ]

زائر *za''ir* N.M (PL. زوار *zuvvar'*) pilgrim [A ~ زیارت]

زائل *za''il* ADJ. vanishing declining waning ADV. vanished declined waning come to nought زائل کرنا *za''il kar'na* V.T end زائل ہونا *za''il ho'na* V.T. end [A]

زبان *zuban'* (or *zaban'*) N.F. tongue language dialect speech flame (of candle, etc.) point (of pen) زبان آب کوثر سے دھلی ہونا *zuban' a'b-e kau'sar se dhu'li ho'na* V.I. speak very chaste language زبان آور *zuba'n-a'var* ADJ. eloquent fluent voluble glib facile زبان آوری *zuba'n-a'vari* N.F. eloquence fluency volubility glibness facility زبان الٹنا (یا بدلنا) *zuban' u'laṭna* (or *ba'dalna*) N.F. go back on (one's) word ; retract from one's stand زبان بگاڑنا *zuban' bigaṛ'na* V.I. spoil one's tongue ; use foul language use idiomatic language زبان بگڑنا *zuban' bi'gaṛna* V.I. (of someone's language) become idiomatic (of someone) be using foul language زبان بند کرنا *zuban' band kar'na* V.T. & I. silence keep quiet زبان بند ہونا *zuban' band' ho'na* V.I. be tongue-tied be unable to speak زبان بندی *zuban' ban'di* N.F. holding of the tongue enforced silence curbs on freedom of speech زبان بندی کرنا *zuban'-ban'di kar'na* V.T. curb freedom of speech restrain from making statements زبان پر چڑھنا *zuban' par chaṛh'na* V.I. be frequently uttered (by) become able to promounce with ease زبان پر رکھنا *zuban' par rakh'na* V.T. taste put (live coal, etc.) on the tongue زبان پر لانا *zuban' par la'na*, V.I. utter ; mention زبان پکڑنا *zuban' pa'kaṛna* V.T. stop from talking slanderously زبان تتلانا *zuban' tutla'na* V.I. lisp زبان تڑاق پڑاق چلنا *zuban' taṛaq' taṛaq' chal'na* V.I. talk fast be facile زبان پلٹنا *zuban' pa'laṭ'na* V.T. go back on (one's) word ; retract from one's stand زبان تالو سے نہ لگنا *zuban' ta'loo se na lag'na* V.I. keep on chattering زبان تلے زبان ہونا *zuban' ta'le zuban' ho'na* V.I. be fickle ; not to stick to one's word زبان چار ہاتھ کی ہونا *zuban' char' hath ki ho'na* V.I. be impudent speak irresponsibly زبان چلانا *zuban' chala'na* V.I. talk too much ; be loquacious abuse ; swear at زبان چلنا *zuban' chal'na* V.I. be able to speak fluently speak with a glib tongue زبان حال *zuban'-e hal'* N.M. self-evident ; state of affairs زبان حال سے کہنا *zuba'n-e hal' se kaih'na* V.I. be self-evident زبان خلق کو نقارۂ خدا سمجھو *zuba'n-e khal'q ko naqqa'ra-e khuda' sam'jho* PROV. what all men say is always true زبان داب کے کہنا *zuban' dab' ke kaih'na* V.I. speak with bated breath say with one's tongue in one's cheek زباندان *zuban'-dan'* N.M & ADV (one) havi g a command of the language

زباندانی *zūbān'-dānī* N.F. command of the language زبان دراز *zūbān'-darāz'* (col. -*bān*-) ADJ. impudent abusive زبان درازی *zūbān'-darā'zī* N.F. impudence use of abusive language ; abusing زبان درازی کرنا *zūbān'-darāzī kar'nā* (col. -*bān*-) V.I. be impudent abuse; swear at زبان دینا *zūbān' de'nā* V.T. promise ; give one's word زبان زد خلائق *zūbān'-za'd-e khalā''iq* ADJ. talk of the town open secret scandal زبان زد ہونا *zūbān'-zad ho'nā* V.I. be the talk of the town be an open secret زبان سنبھال کر *zūbān' sambhāl' kar* V.I. carefully not irresponsibly زبان سنبھالنا *zūbān' sambhāl'nā* V.I. hold one's tongue not to talk irresponsibly

زبان سے نکالنا *zūbān' se nikāl'nā* V.T. speak utter pronounce زبان سے نکلنا *zūbān' se ni'kalnā* V.I. escape one's lips be blurted out زبان سے خندق پار *zūbān' se khan'daq pār* PH. brag lip service زبان سینا *zūbān' sī'nā* V.T. & I. be tongue-tied keep silent زبان شمع *zūbā'n-e sham''* N.F. flame زبان قینچی سی چلنا *zūbān' qainchī sī chal'nā* V.I. talk fast be talkative زبان کا پھوڑا *zūbān' kā pho'ṛā* N.M foul-mouthed (person) زبان کاٹنا *zūbān' kāṭ'nā* V.T. interrupt (someone's) speech زبان کا چسکا *zūbān' kā chas'ka* N.M. sweet tooth childish fondness for tasty things waste of money on tasty foods زبان کا میٹھا *zūbān' kā mī'ṭhā* N.M. honey-tongued ; soft-spoken زبان کٹنا *zūbān' kaṭ'nā* V.I. be penalized for speaking out زبان کرنا *zūbān' kar'nā* V.T. promise ; give one's word of honour زبان کو لگام دینا *zūbān' ko lagām' de'nā* V.T & I. hold one's tongue retrain from talking irresponsibly زبان کو لگام نہ ہونا *zūbān' ko lagām' na ho'nā* V.I. talk irresponsibly زبان کھلوانا *zūbān' khulvā'nā* V.I. force to do some plain speaking زبان کھولنا *zūbān' khol'nā* V.I. speak out give tit for tat زبان (گدی سے) کھینچنا *zūbān' (gūd'dī se) khench'na* V T. penalize by extirpating the tongue زبان کے چٹخارے لینا *zūbān' ke chaṭ-khāre le'nā* V.I. smack the lips relish enjoy (someone's command of idiomatic language زبان گھس جانا *zūbān' ghis' jā'nā* V.I. (iron.) be fatigued with speaking زبان لال ہونا *zūbān' lal' ho'na* V.I. be tonguetied زبان لڑکھڑانا *zūbān' laṛkhaṛā'nā* V.I. falter; speak in a faltering voice زبان ملانا *zūbān' milā'nā* V.I. give rejoinder زبان منہ میں رکھنا *zūbān' mūṉh meṉ rakh'nā* V.I. be able to speak زبان میں کانٹے پڑنا *zūbān' meṉ kāṉ'ṭe paṛ'nā* V.I. be very thirsty (of tongue) be furred زبان نکالنا *zūbān' nikāl'nā* V.T & I pull out (someone's) tongue be impudent زبان نکل پڑنا *zūbān' ni'kal paṛ'nā* V.I. be very thirsty زبان ہارنا *zūbān' hār'nā* V.I. promise give one's word of honour زبان ہلانا *zūbān' hilā'nā* V.I say at least a few words speak open one's mouth زبان ہی ہاتھی پر چڑھائے زبان ہی سر کٹائے *zūbān' hī hā'thī par chaṛhā''e, zābān' hī sir kaṭā''e* PROV the tongue talks at the cost of the head one's speech determines one's weed زبان شیریں ملک گیری *zūbān shī'rīṉ mūl'k-gī'rī* PROV. soft words have victor's reward زبانہ *zūbā'nah* (or *zabā'nah*) N.M. tongue of flame زبانۂ شمع *zūbān'na-e sham''* N.M. flame of candle زبانی *zūbā'nī* (or *zabā'nī*) ADJ. verbal ; oral traditional ADV. by word of mouth : verbally زبانی امتحان *zūbā'nī imtehān'* N.M. oral examination ; oral test 'viva voce' زبانی جمع خرچ *zūbān'ī jam'' khar'ch* N.M. mere words ; all talk and no substance زبانی حساب *zūbā'nī ḥisāb'* N.M. mental arithmetic [P]

زبدہ • *zūb'dah* N.M. cream ; butter cream (of) ; best (of) زبدۃ الحکما *zūb'dat-ūl-ḥukamā'* N.M. choicest practitioner of indigenous medical system this as a diploma [A]

زبر *za'bar* N.M. the vowel point 'zabar' point PREF. high top victorious زبردست *za'bar-das't* ADJ. strong powerful vigorous oppressive; tyrannical N.M. superior strong man tyrant زبردست کا ٹھینگا سر پر *za'bar-das't kā ṭhīṉ'gā sir' par* PROV. everyone feels the strong man's thumb زبردست مارے اور رونے نہ دے *za'bar-das't mā're aur ro'ne na de* PROV. the tyrant won't even let you cry زبردستی *za bar-das'tī* N.F. tyranny ; oppression violence ADV. forcefully زبردستی سے *za'bar-das'tī se* ADV. forcefully violently highhandedly زبردستی کرنا *za'bar-das'tī kar'nā* V.I. show high-handedness [A]

زبرجد • *zabar'jad* N.M. topaz , jasper ; beryl chrysolite ; olivine [A]

زبس • *zi-bas* ADV. (same as ازبس) (see under از PREF. ★) [P]

زبور • *zaboor'* N.F. (PL. زبر *zū'būr*) Psalms of David ; Psalms [A]

زبوں • *zaboon'* ADJ. weak helpless bad evil disgraced bad (condition) زبونی *zaboo'nī* N.F. weakness helplessness evil disgrace ; bad condition ruin [P]

زٹل *zaṭal'* N.F nonsense quibble ADJ. nonsense . silly زٹل باز *zaṭal'-bāz* ADJ. (one) who talks nonsense quibbler زٹل مارنا (یا ہانکنا) *zaṭal' mār'nā* (or *hāṉk'nā*) V.T. talk nonsense quibble زٹلی *zaṭal'lī* N.M. & ADJ. (one) who tells false and idle stories ; idle talker

زجاج *zūjāj'* N.M. glass glass splinter glass flask glassware [A]

زجاج *zajjāj'* N.M. manufacturer of or dealer in glassware [A ~ PREC.]

زجر *zaj'r* N.F. scolding reproof **زجر و توبیخ** *zaj'r-o taubīkh'* N.M. scolding reproof [A]

زچ *zich* ADJ (at chess) mate driven to the straits, driven to the wall **زچ کرنا** *zich kar'na* V.T. (at chess) mate harass drive to the straits **زچ ہونا** *zich' ho'na* V.I. (at chess) be mated be harassed be vexed

زچہ *zach'chah* N.F. woman with a recent delivery: lying-in woman **زچہ خانہ** *zach'cha-khā'-nah* N.M. maternity home; maternity centre **زچگی** *zach'chagī* N.F. maternity **زچہ و بچہ** *zach'cha-o bach'-chah* N.M. PL. mother and baby **زچہ گیریاں** *zach'cha-gī'riyañ* N.F. songs sung before lying-in woman [P]

زحاف *zehāf'* N.M. (PL **زحافات** *zehāfāt'*) metrical variation [A]

زحل *zo'hal* N.M. Saturn [A]

زحمت *zah'mat* (or *zaih'-*) N.F. trouble; inconvenience hardship **زحمت اٹھانا** *zah'mat uṭhā'na* V.I. take the trouble (of) undergo hardship **زحمت ہونا** *zah'mat ho'na* V.I. be put to inconvenience have to undergo hardship [A]

زخار *zakhkhār'* ADJ. (of sea) raging; tumultous overflowing full to the brim [A]

زخم *zakh'm* N.M. wound gash; sore loss harm; damage **زخم آنا** *zakh'm ā'na* V.I. be wounded **زخم بھر جانا** *zakh'm bhar'. jā'na* V.I. (of wound) heal up **زخم (یا زخموں) پر نمک چھڑکنا** *zakh'm* (or *zakh'moñ*) *par na'mak chhiṛak'na* V.I. touch (someone) on a sore place **زخم پکنا** *zakh'm pak'na* V.T. suppurate **زخم دینا** *zakh'm de'na* V.T. injure cause grievous loss **زخم کاری، کاری زخم** *zakh'm-e kārī, kā'rī zakh'm* N.M. mortal wound fatal blow **زخم کرنا** *zakh'm kar'na* V.T. injure; wound **زخم کھانا** *zakh'm khā'na* V.I. sustain an injury: be wounded **زخم ہرا ہونا** *zakh'm ha'ra ho'na* V.I. (of wound, memory of loss) recrudesce **زخمی** *zakh'mī* N.M. wounded person casualty ADJ. injured wounded hurt **زخمی کرنا** *zakh'mī kar'na* V.T. injure: wound **زخمی ہونا** *zakh'mī ho'na* V.I. be wounded [P]

زخمہ *zakh'mah* N.M. plectrum **زخمہ ور** *zakh'ma-var* N.M. musician [P]

زد • *zad* N.F. range target attack blow: hit: stroke loss effect SUFF. beating **زد پر ہونا** *zad par ho'na* V.I. be within range (of) **زد پڑنا** *zad' paṛ'na* V.I. suffer a loss be adversely affected (by) **کی زد میں** *kī zad' meñ* ADV. within range of **زد و کوب** *za'd-o-kob'* N.F. beating thrashing manhandling **زد و کوب کرنا** *za'd-o-kob' kar'nā* V.T. manhandle ADJ. wornout weak wretched [P ~ **زدن** beat]

زر • *zar* N.M gold money wealth; riches pollen **زر اصل** *za'r-e as'l*, **اصل زر** *as'l zar* N.M. principal; basic amount on which interest is leviable **زر افشاں** *za'r-afshāñ'* **زر فشاں** *zar'-fishāñ* ADJ. golden polliniferous **زر امانت** *za'r-e amā'nat* N.M. deposit money **زر باف** *zar-bāf* N.M. (col. **زری باف** *za'rī bāf*) gold-lace worker tissue-weaver **زر بافی** *zar-bā'fī* N.F. (col. **زری بافی** *za'rī-bā'fī*) gold-lace work tissue-weaving **زر بفت** *zar-baf't* N.M. brocade **زر بل نہ زور بل** *zar' bal na zor' bal* PH. neither pelf nor power **زر بیعانہ** *za'r-e bai'ā'nah* N.M earnest money **زر پیشگی** *za'r-e pesh'gī* (ped. *-pe'sha-*) N.M. advance money **زر خرید** *zar'-kharīd'* ADJ. self-purchased **زر خیز** *zar-khez'* ADJ. fertile **زر خیزی** *zar-khe'zī* N.F. fertility **زر دار** *zar'-dār'* ADJ. rich; wealthy; opulent **زرداری** *zar-dā'rī* N.F. opulence **زر دوز** *zar-doz'* N.M. gold embroiderer **زر دوزی** *zar-do'zī* N.F. gold embroidery **زر ضمانتی** *za'r-e za'mini*, **زر ضمانت** *zar'-e zamā'nat* N.F. surety money **زر کش** *zar'-kash* ADJ. excessively fond of money-making N.M. brocade **زر کشی** *zar' ka'shī* N.F. excessive fondness for money making N.M. brocade-work **زر کنار** *zar-kanār'* ADJ. gilt-edged **زر کوب** *zar-kob'* N.M. gold beater **زر کوبی** *zar-ko'bī* N.F. gold-beating **زر گر** *zar'-gar* N.F. goldsmith **زر گری** *zar'-garī* N.F. goldsmith's trade **زر گل** *za'r-e gul* N.M. pollen **زر لگان** *za'r-e lagān'* N.M. land revenue **زر مبادلہ** *za'r-e mubā'dalah* N.M. exchange discount **زر مطالبہ** *za'r-e mutā'labah* N.M. claims dues debts demands **زر معاوضہ** *za'r-e mo'ā'vazah* N.M. compensation; indemnity **زر منافع** *za'r-e munā'fa'* N.M. profits; net income **زر نقد** *za'r-e naq'd* N.M. cash; ready money **زر نگار** *zar-nigār'* ADJ. gilt; guilded **زر نگاری** *zar-nigā'rī* N.F. gilding; gold plating **زری** *za'rī* N.F. gold lace tissue; brocade **زر یافتنی** *za'r-e yāf'tanī* N.F. outstanding amounts(s) **زریں** *zar'rīñ* ADJ. gold; golden **مرغ زریں** *mur'gh-e zar'rīñ*, **زریں مرغ** *zar'rīñ murgh* ADJ. (fig.) sun **زریں موقع (یا موقعہ)** *zar'rīñ mau'qe'* (or usu. but wrongly *-mau'qa*) N.M. golden opportunity **زرینہ** *zarī'nah* (wrong col. F. of **زریں**) ADJ. golden [P]

زراعت • *zirā'at* N.M. agricultural tillage cultivation **زراعت پیشہ** *zirā''at-pe'shah* N.M. agriculturist cultivator; peasant **زراعتی** *zirā''atī*, **زرعی** *zar''ī* agricultural [A]

زرافہ • *zarā'fah* N.M. giraffe [A]

زراقی • *zarrā'qī* N.F hypocrisy [A ~ **زرق**]

زرتشت zartush't (or zara-) زردشت zardush't N.M. Zoroaster زرتشتی zartush'tī زردشتی zar-dush'tī N.M. & Zoroastrian [P]

زرد zar'd ADJ. yellow pale : wan dull discoloured زرد آلو zar'd-a'loo N.M. apricot زرد پڑنا (یا ہو جانا) zar'd paṛ'na (or ho ja'na) V.I. be discoloured be enfeebled ; become weak turn pale ; grow pallid زرد چوب zar'd chob N.F. (arch.) turmeric زرد رنگ zar'd rang' N.M. yellow colour ADJ. pale ; wan weak terror-stricken زرد رو zar'd-roo' ADJ. pale ; wan weak terror-tricken زردک zar'dak N.F. (lit.) carrot زردہ zar'dah N.M. yellow dish of sweet rice chewing tobacco زردی zar dī N.M. yellowness paleness yolk pollen زردی چھانا zar'dī chha'na V.I. look pale [P]

زرع zar'' N.M. (rare) agricultural tilling sowing زرعی zar''ī N.M. agricultural : agrarian زرعی آلات zar''ī a'lat' N.M. PL. agricultural implements زرعی اصلاحات zar''ī islahat' N.M. PL. aparian reforms زرعی انقلاب zar''ī inqilab' N.M. agricultural revolution زرعی معیشت zar''ī ma'ī'shat N.F. agricultural economy agronomy [A]

زرغل zar'ghal ADJ. worthless.

زرق برق zar'q bar'q ADJ. splendid glittering gaudy tawdry [A]

زرنیخ zarnīkh' N.F. arsenic sulphurate : a poisonous drug [A ~ P]

زرہ zi'reh (col. zi'rah) N.F. chain armour زرہ بکتر zi'reh-bak'tar N.M. armour زرہ پوش zi'reh-posh N.M. & ADJ. (one) clad in armour [P]

زڑ ziṛ N.F. persistent repetition obsession زڑ لگنا (یا ہونا) ziṛ' lag'na (or ho'na) V.I. insist repeat persistently have an obsession

زشت zish't ADJ. ugly hideous repulsive; revolting زشت خو zish't-khoo ADJ. of repulsive ill-disposed harsh malicious زشت خوی zish't-khoo''ī N.F. repulsive habits harshness malice زشت رو zish't-roo' ADJ. ugly; ungainly repulsive to sight ; hideous زشت روئی zish't-roo''ī N.F. ugliness hideousness زشتی zish'tī N.F. ugliness repulsiveness evil malice [P]

زعفران za'faran' N.F. saffron زعفران زار za''faran-zar' زعفران کا کھیت za'faran' ka khet' N.M. saffron field (fig.) place where one instinctively laughs زعفرانی za'farā'nī ADJ. saffron-coloured yellow N.M. yellow colour [A]

زعم zo''m (or za''m) N.M. over-weening pride; vanity ; conceit over confidence presumption conjecture [A]

زعیم za'īm' N.M. prominent personality leader chief زعما zo'ama' N.M. PL. prominent personalities leaders chief [A]

زغال zughal'. N.M. (lit.) coal [A]

زغن za'ghan N.F. (lit.) kite (the bird) [P]

زقند zaqand' N.F. leap ; bound زقند بھرنا zaqand' bhar'na V.I. leap; bound الٹی زقند ul'ṭī zaqand' N.F. a leap backwards retrogression [P]

زفاف zifaf' N.M. bride's personal presentation of herself to groom consummation of marriage شب زفاف sha'b-e zifaf' N.F. night of the consummation of marriage [A]

زفیر zafīr' N.F. warning signal [A]

زفیل zafīl' N.F. whistle signal for pigeons (given by with fingers in mouth) زفیل بجانا (یا دینا) zafīl' baja'na (or de'na) V.I. signal thus [~ A PREC. CORR.]

زقوم zaqqoom' N.M. cactus [A]

زک zak N.F. discomfiture reverse زک اٹھانا zak' uṭha'na V.I. suffer a reverse be discomfited زک دینا (یا پہنچانا) zak' de'na (or pahuncha'na) V.T.. discomfit defeat ; put to rout upset the applecart (of) disgrace

زکا zaka' N.F. piety زکاوت zaka'vat N.F. probity piety [A]

زکام zukam' N.M. cold ; catarrh [A]

زکوٰۃ (or زکات) zakat' N.F. religious tax as a basic in function of Islam [A ~ زکا]

زکی za'kī N.M. (PL. ازکیا azkiya'). pious person ADJ. pure ; pious ; virtuous زکیہ zakiy'-yah N.F. pious woman ADJ. pious [A ~ زکا]

زلال zulal' ADJ. (of water) clear and sweet, wholesome ; limped N.M. (also آب زلال a'b-e zulal') clear and sweet water [A]

زلزلہ zal'zalah N.M. (PL. زلازل zala'zil) earth quake; earth tremor; quake زلزلہ پیما zal'zala-paima' N.M. seismometer seismograph seismoscope [A]

زلف zul'f N.F. (PL. زلفیں zul'f-ha) lock ; tress curl ; ringlet زلف پریشاں zul'f-e pire'shan N.F. dishevelled locks ; flowing hair زلف تابدار zul'f-e tab-dar' N.F. ringlets ; curls ; glossy locks زلف دراز zul'f-e daraz' N.F. long locks زلف عنبریں (یا معنبر) zul'f-e 'am'barīn (or mo'am'bar) N.F. perfumed locks, tresses scented with ambergris [P]

زلفی zul'fī N.M. (arch.) door-fastening chain sword knot [~ P PREC]

زلہ *zal'lah* N.M. leavings of food crumbs زلّہ رُبا (یا بردار) *zal'la-rūbā'* (or *-bar-dār'*) N.M. & ADJ. (one) who eats crumbs from (someone's) table plagiarist stooge (of) one indebted (to) زلہ ربائی *zal'la-rūbā''ī* N.F. eating crumbs from the table (of) being indebted (to) [A]

زمام *zamām'* N.F. (PL. ازمّہ *azim'mah*) rein bridle زمامِ اقتدار *zamā'm-e iqtidār'* N.F. reins of power [A]

زمان *zamān'* N.M. (PL. ازمنہ *az'minah*) time زمان و مکان *zamā'n-o-makān'* (or *-makān'*) N.M. time and space [A]

زمانہ *zamā'nah* N.M. (PL. *az'minah*) age; period; epoch ; era time; times world زمانہ دیکھنا *zamā'nah dekh'nā* V.I. have experience see the way of the world زمانہ دیکھا ہوا *zamā'nah de'khā hū''ā'* ADJ. very experienced (person) veteran زمانہ ساز *zamā'na-sāz* ADJ. & N.M. time server turn-coat unprincipled (person) زمانہ سازی *zamā'na-sā'zī* N.F. turning with the tide ; trimming one's sails according to the prevailing wind ; trimming حالاتِ زمانہ موافق (یا سازگار) ہونا *ḥālā't-e zamā'nah mo'ā'fiq* (or *sāz gār'*) *ho'nā* V.I. have favourable circumstances

زمرد *zamūr'rad* (rare. *zamūr'rūd*) N.M. emerald زمردیں *zamūr'radīṅ* ADJ. emerald ; of emerald colour studded with emeralds [P]

زمرہ *zūm'rah* N.M. (PL. زمر *zū'mar*) group class ; category concourse [A]

زمزم *zam'zam* N.M. sacred well in Mecca آبِ زمزم *ā'b-e zam'zam* N.M. zamzam water زمزمی *zam'zamī* N.F. small sealed container for zamzam water [A]

زمزمہ *zam'zamah* N.M. singing chanting song chant زمزمہ پرداز *zam'zama-pardāz'* N.M. singer ; songster ; songstress chanter ADJ. & ADV. singing chanting زمزمہ پرداز ہونا *zam'-zama-parāz' ho'nā* V.I. sing chant [A]

زمستان *zamis'tān* N.M. winter [P]

زمن *za'man* N.M. (PL. ازمنہ *az'minah*) time age [A]

زمہریر *zamharīr'* N.M. intense cold (also کرۂ زمہریر *kū'ra-e zamharīr'*) atmospheric region ; intense cold [A]

زمین *zamīn'* N.F. earth land ground soil floor ; a region ; country زمین آسمان کا فرق *zamīn' āsmān' kā far'q* PH. world of difference ; radicals difference زمین آسمان کے قلابے ملانا *zamīn' āsmān' ke qūlā'be milā'nā* V.I. highly exaggerate زمین بوس ہونا *zamīn'-bos' ho'nā* V.I. kiss the ground ; make a profound bow; (of building collapse زمین بیٹھنا *zamīn baiṭh'nā* V.I. (of ground) have a fault sag زمین پاؤں (یا پیروں) تلے سے نکل جانا *zamīn' pā''oṅ* (or *pai'roṅ*) *ta'le se ni'kal jā'nā* V.I. jitter ; feel jittery ; be in a blue funk زمین پر پاؤں نہ رکھنا (یا نہ ٹکنا) *zamīn' par pā''oṅ na rakh'nā* (or *na ṭik'nā*) V.I. be greatly elated strut about proudly or joyfully زمین پکڑنا *zamīn pa'karnā* V.I. not to get up after fall زمین پھٹے اور سما جاؤں *zamīn' pha'ṭe aur samā' jā''ooṅ* PH. I am (or was) feeling much humiliated زمین پیمائی *zamīn' paimā''ī* N.F. land survey زمین (پر) چڑھنا *za'mīn (par) chaṛh'nā* V.I. (of horse, etc.) increasingly gain skill زمینِ خالصہ *zamī'n-e khā'lisah* N.M. Crown land زمیندار *zamīn'-dār* N.M. landlord ; owner of large tracts of agrarian property زمینداری *zamīn'-dār'nī* N.F. landlord's wife زمینداری *zamīn'-dā'rī* N.F estate being a landlord زمین دوز *zamīn'-doz'* N.F. underground subterranean زمین دکھنا (یا دکھلانا) *zamīn' dikh'nā* (or *dikhlā'nā*) V.T. humiliate throw (adversary) down زمین دیکھنا *zamīn' dekh'nā* V.I. eat the humble pie vomit زمین سخت آسمان دور *zamīn' sakh't hai āsmān' door* INT. alas, I find myself helpless زمینِ غیر مزروعہ *zamī'n-e ghair-mazroo''ah* N.F uncommanded land زمین کا گز *zamīn' kā gaz* N.M. traveller زمین کھا گئی یا آسمان *zamīn' khā ga''ī yā āsmān'* INT. it is strange how it has disappeared , where gone زمین کی پوچھنا آسمان کی کہنا *zamīn' kī poochh'nā āsmān' kī kaih'nā* V.I. talk irrelevantly dodge or fail to understand the question زمینِ مرہونہ *zamī'n-e marhoo'nah* N.F mortgaged land زمینِ مزروعہ *zamī'n-e mazroo''ah* N.F. cultivated land ; land under the plough شرم سے زمین میں گڑ جانا *shar'm se zamīn' meṅ gaṛ' jānā* مارے شرم کے زمین میں گڑ جانا *mā're shar'm ke zamīn' meṅ gaṛ' jā'nā* V.I. feel ashamed ; be greatly humiliated پیوندِ زمین ہو جانا *paivaṅ'd-e zamīn' ho' jā'nā* V.I. die come to dust be buried (of building) lie in ruins زمینی *zamī'nī* ADJ. earthly; terrestrial ground [P]

زن *zan* N.F. (PL. زناں *za'nāṅ*) woman wife SUF. beater striker doer player زنِ مدخولہ *zan-e madkhoo'lah* N.F. concubine زن مرید *zan-murīd'* N.M. & ADJ hen-pecked (husband) زنِ منکوحہ *za'n-e mankoo'ḥah* N.F. lawful wife زن بچہ *zan bach'chah* زن و فرزند *za'n-o-farzand'* N.M. (one's) family the entire family زناشوئی *zanā'-sho''ī* N.F marital relations ADJ. marital [P]

زنا *zinā'* N.M. adultery fornication extra-marital sexual relations زنا بالجبر *zinā' bil-jabr'* N.M. rape ; ravishment ; violation زناکار *zinā'-kār* N.M. adulterer fornicator adultress fornicatres زناکاری *zinā'-kā'rī* N.F. adultery fornication illicit intercourse , extra-marital relations [A]

زناٹا zannā'ṭā N.M. zoom زن سے، زناٹے سے zan' se, zannā ṭe se. ADV. with a zoom swiftly like an arrow) [ONO.]

زنادقہ zanā'diqah N.M. PL. (see under زندق N.M. ★)

زنار zūnnār' N.M. cross thread ; sacred thread worn by crosswise round body by Hindus زنار بند zūnnār'-band زناردار zūnnār'-dār ADJ. & N.M. (one) wearing cross thread

زناشوئی zanā'-sho''ī N.F. (see under زن N.F. ★)

زنانہ zanā'nah ADJ. feminine ; female women's N.M. female apartment harem ; seraglio eunuch hermaphrodite زنانی zanā'nī ADJ. female woman [~P زن]

زنبور zamboor' (ped. zūm-) N.M. wasp ; hornet pincers ; pliers also زنبورہ zamboo'rah) a kind of small cannon [A]

زنبور

زنبیل zambīl' N.F. bag ; haversack [E]

زنجبیل zanjabīl' N.F. dry ginger [A]

زنبیل

زنجیر zanjīr' N.F. chain door chain shackles (gold) necklace زنجیر کرنا zanjīr' kar'nā V.T chain; shackle; fatter زنجیر کھٹکھٹانا zanjīr khaṭkhaṭā'na V.I. jerk the doorchain ; knock at the door زنجیرہ zanjī'rah N.M. chain-like embroidery chain-like necklace زنجیری zanjī'rī ADJ. chain-like N.M. prisoner [P]

زنخا zankhā, زنخہ zan'khah N.M. effiminate person one fond of make-up like women eunuch ; emasculate person minion [~P زن]

زنخدان za'nakhdān (rare زنخ za'nakh) N.F. chin [P]

زند zand N.M. (same as ژند N.M. ★)

زندان zin'dān N.M. prison : jail : goal زندانی zinda'nī N.M. prisoner . captive [P

زندقہ zan'daqah N.M. hypocrisy in profession of Islam (esp by some Zoroastrian converts) lip service to religion false profession of Islam heresy زندیق zindīq' N.M religious hypocrite heretic false Zoroastrian professor of Islam زندیقی zindī'qī N.F. heresy infidelity religious hypocrisy زنادقہ zana diqah N.M PL religious hypocrites heretics false Zoroastrian professors of Islam [A ~ P زند]

زندگانی zin'dagā'nī N.F. زندگی zin'dagī N.F. (see under زندہ ADJ. ★)

زندہ zin'dah ADJ. living alive extent existing ; gay زندہ دل zin'da-dil' ADJ. cheerful ; lively ; mergy زندہ دلی zin'da-di'lī N.F. mirth ; cheerfulness ; gaiety : liveliness زندہ درگور zin''da dar gor' ADJ. leading an unhappy life half-dead as good as dead زندہ کرنا zin'dah kar'nā V.T. quicken ; bring to life ; revive ; rèsussinate ; restore to life زندہ ہونا zin'dah ho'nā V.I. be alive exist be refreshed be revived زندگانی zin'dagā'nī N.F. life existence زندگی zin'dagī N.F. life existence زندگی تلخ ہونا zin'dagī tal'kh ho'na V.I. sick of life زندگی سے تنگ آنا zin'dagī se tang' ā'na V.I. be fed up with life [P]

زندیق zindīq' N.M. (see under زندقہ N.M. ★)

زن سے zan' se ADV. (see under زناٹا N.M. ★)

زنگ zang N.M. rust (rare) bell زنگ آلود(ہ) zang aloo'd(ah) ADJ. rusty زنگ لگنا zang lag'na V.I. become rusty زنگار zangār N.M. verdigris paint on mirror's reverse foil (to) زنگاری zangā'rī ADJ. green of verdigris مرہم زنگاری zangā'rī mar'ham, مرہمِ زنگاری mar'ham-e zangā'rī V. copper-ointment [P]

زنگولہ zangoo'lah N.M. bell ; small bell [P]

زنگی zan'gī N.M. Hamite ebon Negro [P ~ زنگ]

زنہار zinhār', زینہار zīn'hār INT. beware watch ADV. on no account ; by no means , never [P]

زوال zavāl' N.M. decline wane setting (of sun) decay fall misery زوال پذیر zavāl'-pazīr' ADJ. declining decaying [A]

زوائد zavā''d N.M. PL. surpluses superfluities additions accretion [A ~ SING. زائد]

زوج zauj N.M. (PL. ازواج azvāj') couple pair (rare) consors ; spouse زوجہ zau'jah N.F. wife زوجیت zaujiy'yat N.F. wifehood حقوق زوجیت hūqoo'q-e zaujiy'yat N.M. conjugal rights زوجین zaujain' N.M. husband and wife [A]

زود zood ADV. soon ; quickly ; swiftly زود آشنا zoo'd-ashna' ADJ. quick in developing friendship زود پشیمان zood-pishe'man ADJ. (iron.) repenting too soon زود رنج zood'-ranj' ADJ. touchy ; testy sensitive irascible زود فہم zood'-faih'm (or -fah'm) ADJ. sharp witted intelligent easy to understand زود نویس zood'-navīs' N.M. stenographer زود نویسی zood'-navī'sī N.F. stenography زودی zoo'dī N.F. quickness swiftness زودی سے zoo'dī se, بزودی ba-zoo'dī ADV. quickly ; swiftly [P]

زور *zoor* N.M. falsehood ; untruth dissimulation hypocrisy [A]

زور *zor* N.M. vigour power strength force violence coercion stress influence authority ADJ. (arch.) strange ; wondrous زور آزمانا *zo'r āzmā'nā* V.T. try one's strength ; have a trial of strength (with) زور آزمائی *zo'r-azmā''ī* N.F. trial of strength زور آزمائی کرنا *zo'r-āzmā''ī kar'nā* V.I. have a trial of strength (with) زور آور *zo'r-ā'var* ADJ. strong ; powerful vigorous زور آوری *zo'r-ā'varī* (or -ā-) N.F. power ; force (اپنے) زور بازو سے (*ap'ne*) *zo'r-e ba'zoo* N.M. power *zo'r-e bā'zoo se* ADV. by the (one) strength of arms by dint of hard work زور پکڑنا *zo'r pa'karnā* V.I. grow powerful زور چلنا *zo'r chal'nā* V.I. have influence over زوردار *zor-dār'* ADJ. strong ; powerful; vigorous زور دینا *zor' de'nā* V.T. stress press زور ڈالنا *zor dāl'nā* V.T. force ; bring pressure to bear (upon) زور سے *zor' se* ADV. loudly forcefully with force زور شور *zor' shor* N.F. force زور لگانا *zor' lagā'nā* V.I. to do one's best to use influence زور مارنا *zor' mār'nā* V.I. endeavour ; try hard to strive; to toil بڑا زور مارنا *ba'ṛā zor' mār'nā* V.I. try one's level best زوروں پر ہونا *zo'roṅ par ho'nā* V.I. be in full force (of river) be in spate [P]

زورق *zau'raq* N.M. small boat [A]

زوف *zoof'* INT. fie زوف زاف کرنا *zoof' zāf kar'nā* V.T. chastise

زوفہ *zoofah* N.M. hyssop [P]

زہ *zeh* N.F. bow-string navel دردِ زہ *dar'd-e zeh'* N.M. pangs of birth

زہار *zehār'* N.M. private parts موئے زہار *moo'-e zehār'* N.M. PL. pubic hair

زہاد *zohhād'* N.M. PLU. pious persons ascetics mystics [A ~ SING زاہد]

زہد *zoh'd* N.M. asceticism abstinence ; continence mysticism [A]

زہر *zaih'r* N.M. poison venom baneful thing or influence زہر آب *zaihr-āb'* N.M. dilute poison زہر آلودہ *zaihr-āloo'd(ah)* ADJ. poisoned baneful زہر اگلنا *zaih'r ū'galnā* V.I. spit venom زہر باد *zaih'r-bād'* N.M. quinsy زہر خند *zaih'r-khand* N.M. sardonic laughter forced laugh زہردار *zaih'r-dār* ADJ. poisonous venomous baneful زہر قاتل *zaih'r-e qā'til,* زہر ہلاہل *zaih'r-e halā'hil* N.M. deadly poison زہر کھانا *zaih'r khā'nā* V.I. take poison commit or attempt sound زہر کے (سے) گھونٹ پینا یا پی کر رہ جانا *zaih'r ke (se) ghooṅṭ' pī'nā* (or *pī' kar raih jā'nā*) V.I. have to put up with have to bear patiently زہر لگنا *zaih'r lag'nā* V.I. be hateful to زہر مار کرنا *zaih'r mār' kar'nā* V.I. swallow reluctantly زہر مہرہ *zaih'r-moh'rah* N.M. bezoar (used as antidote to venom) زہر میں بجھا ہوا تیر *zaih'r meṅ bu'jhā hu''ā tīr'* N.M. poisonous arrow زہریلا *zaihrī'lā* ADJ. (F. زہریلی *zaihrī'lī*) poisonous venomous baneful spiteful malicious [P]

زہرا *zahrā'* ADJ. bright ; luminous white blonde N.F. appellation of Hazrat Fatimah [A ~ M. زہر ~ زہرۃ]

زہرہ *zoh'rah* N.M. gall-bladder courage ; pluck زہرہ آب ہونا *zoh'rah āb ho'nā* V.I. feel jittery ; be terrified زہرہ گداز *zoh'ra-gudāz'* ADJ. terrifying زہرہ *zoh'rah* N F. Venus Aphrodite زہرہ جبیں *zoh'ra-jabīn',* زہرہ وش *zoh'ra-vash* ADJ. exquisitely beautiful ; handsome [A]

زہرہ *zah'rah* N.M. freshness beauty sweetness of voice ; melodiousness

زہریلا *zaihrī'lā* ADJ. (F. زہریلی *zaihri'lī*) (see under زہر N.M. ★)

زہے *ze'he* INT. excellent ; wonderful زہے قسمت *ze'he qis'mat,* زہے نصیب *zeh'e nasīb'* INT. lucky

زی *zī* N.M. (rare) social status [~ A]

زیادتی *ziyā'datī* (col. *-yād'tī*) N.F. increase excess high-handedness transgression of limits زیادتی کرنا *ziyā'datī kar'nā* V.I. show high-handedness exceed limits [~ A FOLL.]

زیادہ *ziyā'dah* ADJ. more much excessive additional ADV. more much excessively in addition زیاد *ziyād'* ADJ. & ADV. (lit. (same as زیادہ ADJ. ★) زیادت *ziyā'dat* N.F. addition

زیارت *ziyā'rat* N.F. pilgrimage visit (to superior, etc.) privilege of seeing (someone) shi'ite shrine visit to it زیارت کرنا *ziyā'rat kar'nā* V.I. perform a pilgrimage visit (a superior, etc.) زیارت گاہ *ziyā'rat-gāh* N.M. pilgrim centre shrine زیارت ہونا *ziyā'rat ho'nā* V.I. have the privilege of seeing someone [A]

زیاں *ziyāṅ'* N.M. loss detriment زیاں کار *ziyāṅ'-kār'* N.M. one incurring a loss loss-sustainer ; ADJ. loss-sustaining زیاں کاری *ziyāṅ'-kā'rī* N.F. sustaining a loss damaging trades [P]

زیب *zeb* N.F. elegance adornment SUF adorning looking زیبِ تن کرنا *ze'b-e tan' kar'nā* V.T. wear ; put on ; down زیب دینا *zeb' de'nā* V.T. suit adorn set off behave become be proper زیبندہ *zebin'dah* ADJ. becoming lovely beautiful زیبندگی *zebin'dagī* N.F. loveliness ; beauty grase propriety زیب و زینت *ze'b-o zī'nat* N.F. adornment elegance زیبا *ze'bā*

ADJ. graceful pretty , lovely ; beautiful proper becoming زیبائش zebā''ish N.F. elegance beauty adornment decoration زیبائشی zebā''ishī ADJ. decorative ornament زیبائی zebā''ī N.F. elegance beauty adornment [P ~ زیبیدن]

زیبرا zaib'rā N.M. zebra [E]

زیبق zi'baq N.M. mercury [A]

زیتون zaitoon' N.M. olive [A].

زیٹ zīṭ N.F. nonsense baseless story زیٹ اڑانا zīṭ ūṛā'nā V.I. talk nonsense

زید zaid N.M. common Arabic name used as a fictitious name زید عمر و بکر zaid' 'am'r bak'r N.M. Tom, Dick and Harry [A]

زیر zer N.M. vowel point (ـِ) transliterated as i ADV. below PREF. under زیر بار کرنا ze'r-e bar' kar'nā V.T. put (someone) under obligation make (some-one) foot the bill over burden put (someone) in financial difficulty زیر بار ہونا ze'r-e bār' ho'nā V.I. be overburdened be in debt come under obligation زیر بار احسان ہونا ze r-e bā'r-e ehsān' ho'nā N.F. come under obligation زیر باری zer-bā'rī N.F. overburdening expenses indebtedness obligation زیر بند zer'-band N.M. martingale زیر پائی zer'-pā''ī N.F. (arch.) slippers زیر تجویز ze'r-e tajvīz' ADJ. under consideration زیر تحقیقات ze'r-e tahqīqāt' ADJ. under enquiry زیر تفتیش ze'r-e taftīsh' ADJ. under investigation زیر جامہ zer-jā'mah N.M. drawers ; underwear زیر حراست ze'r-e hirā'sat ADJ. under custody زیر دست zer'-dast N.M. & ADJ. subordinate week or powerless (person) زیر کرنا zer' kar'nā V.T. overpower subdue defeat vanquish زیر لب ze'r-e lab ADV. numbling in undertones furtively زیر لب کہنا ze'r-e lab kaih'nā V.I. mumble mutter talk in undertones زیر لب مسکرانا ze'r-e lab mūskurā'nā V.I. smile furtively زیر مشق ze'r-e-mash'q N.M. pad to support paper in writing ADJ. understudy زیر نظر ze'r-e na'zar ADJ. ADV. under reference under survenilanec under observation زیر نگیں ze'r-e nagīn ADJ. & ADV. subjugated under control under the influence (of) زیر و زبر ze'r-o-za'bar ADJ. topsy-turvy upside down disintegrated ruined زیر و زبر کرنا ze'r-o-za'bar kar'nā V.T. turn topsy-turvy overturn disintegrate ruin زیر و زبر ہونا ze'r-o-za'bar ho'nā V.I. be upset topsy-turvy be ruined [P]

زیر zīr N.F. treble ; sharpest note of a musical instrument lowest note زیر و بم zī'r-o bam N.M. treble and bass low and high notes ups and down (of) [P]

زیرک zī'rak ADJ. wise intelligent shrewd perspicacious زیرکی zī'rakī N.F. wisdom intelligence shrewdness perspicacity [P]

زیرہ zī'rah N.M. cuminseed carraway seed pollen زیرہ سیاہ zī'rah siyah N.M. carraway seed زیرہ سفید zī'rah sifed' N.M. cuminseed [P]

زیریں ze'rīn ADJ. (see under زیر zer ADV. ★)

زیست zīs't N.M. life existence تا زیست tā-zīs't ADV. the whole life ever ; always [P ~ زیستن]

زین zīn N.F. saddle زین پوش zīn -posh N.M. saddlecloth housing زین ساز zīn'-sāz N.M. saddler [P]

زین zain N.M. grace elegance beauty adornment زین خان zain' khān N.M. name of a bogey [A]

زینت zī'nat N.F. grace elegance beauty adornment زینت پانا zī'nat pā'nā V.I. be adorned be graced by زینت دینا zī'nat de'nā V.T. adorn grace [A ~ PREC.]

زینہ zī'nah N.M. staircase ; stairs ladder step of ladder, etc. [P]

زینہار zīn'hār ADV. (same as زنہار ADV ★)

زیور ze'var N.M. ornament decoration جڑاؤ زیور jaṛa'oo ze'var N.M. gold (or silver) ornaments studded with jewels زیورات ze'varāt' N.M. (usu. but ungram) PL. jewellery ; ornaments [P]

ژ

ژ zhē seventeenth letter of Urdu alphabet (also called zā'-e fā'risī or zā'-e 'a'jamī) ; (equivalent to English zh) used basically in words of Persian extraction (in jummal reckoning held equivalent to 7)

ژاژ zhāzh' N.M. nonsense obscenity (rare) ژاژ خا zhāzh'-khā ADJ. & N.M. (one) talking nonsense (one) talking obscenity idle-talken ژاژ خائی zhāzh-khā''ī N.F. idle talk obscene talk [P] •

ژالہ zhā'lah N.M. hail ژالہ باری zhā'la-bā'rī N.F. hailstorm ژالہ باری ہونا zhā'la-bā'rī ho'nā V.I. hail [P]

ژرف zhar'f ADJ. deep penetrating ژرف نگاہ zhar'f-nigāh' ADJ. &

N.M. perspicacious ژرف نگاہی zhar'f-nigā'hī N.F. denth of vision penetrating perspicacity [P]

ژند zhand, زند zand N.F. Old Persian (also ژندواوستا zhan'd-avis'tā) Zoroastrian scriptures with their official exegesis ژندہ zhandah, ژند zhand N.M. rags ADJ. old ; wornout mumoth ; huge ژندہ پیل zhan'da-pīl' N.M. huge elephant appellation of a mystic ژندگی zhan'dagī N.F. oldness ; being worn out [P]

ژنگ zhang N.M. (same as ازژنگ N.M. ★)

ژولیدہ zholī'dah (or zhoo'-) ADJ. dishevelled unkempt mathed entangled confused miserable ژولیدہ بیان zholī'da-bayan' N.M. & ADJ. confused (speaker) ژولیدہ بیانی zholī'da-baya'nī N.F. confused talk ژولیدہ حال zholī' da-hal ADJ. wretched ; miserable in a bad way ژولیدہ مو zholīda-moo ADJ. & N.M. with dishevelled unkempt or matted hair ژولیدگی zholī'dagī N.F distress ; perplexity ; entanglement [P]

ژیاں zhiyañ ADJ. fierce ; ferocious ; truculent شیر ژیاں she'r-e zhiyañ' N.M. truculent tiger [P]

س

س sin (colloquially called chho'ṭā sin) eighteenth letter of Urdu alphabet (equivalent to English s) also written as س (in jummal reckoning) 60

سا sā (PL. سے se ; F. SING. & PL. سی sī) ADV. somewhat a little SUF. -ish ; somewhat -ever ; any ADJ. (also کا سا kā' sā) like looking like resembling N.M. (in musical scale) first note of national gamut ; gamma

ساباط sabāt' N.F. upper storey pavilion rare gallery connecting houses on opposite sides of street, etc. suspension gallery [A]

ساباط

سابر sā'bar N.M. elk imitation chamois leather

سابق sā'biq ADJ. former prior foregoing ; preceding سابق الذکر sā'biq-uz-zik'r ADJ. abovementioned ; aforesaid سابق میں sā'biq men ADV. in the past previously heretofore formerly سابقاً sā'biqan ADV. easlier above formerly ; previously سابقہ sa'biqah N.M. (PL. سوابق sava'biq rare) contact dealing ADJ. past previous transaction prefix earlier ; preceding سابقہ پڑنا sa'biqah par'na V.I. come into contact (with) have to deal (with) have dealings (with) سابقہ ڈالنا sā'biqah ḍāl'na V.T. (deprec.) put in touch (with) سابقین sābiqīn' N.M. earlier people ; earlier generations ; people in ages gone by the pious those rewarded most by God [A ~ سبقت]

سابودانہ sā'boo da'nah N.M. (same as ساگودانہ N.M. ★

سات sāt' ADJ. seven ساتا روہن sa'ta roo'han N.M. group attack by wolves mischievous clique against someone سات پانچ sāt' pānch N.F. wrangle fraud reluctance سات پانچ کرنا sāt' pānch' kar'na V.T & I. wrangle defraud hesitate سات پانچ نہ جاننا sāt' pānch na jān'na V.I. be straightforward be simple سات پردوں میں چھپا کر رکھنا sāt' par'don men chhūpā' kar rakh'nā V.T. keep with good care keep closely guard سات پشت sāt' pūsh't N.F. seven generations family with a long tradition (of evil, etc.) سات پشت سے sāt' pūsht' se ADV for ages سات دھار ہو کر نکلنا sāt' dhār ho kar ni'kalna V.I. (of food) pass through stools without being fully digested سات سمندر پار sāt' samūn'dar pār' ADV. overseas abroad سات سنگار sāt' singār' N.M. PL. make-up (old use) full make-up of Muslim ladies (comprising henna, well سات سہیلیوں کا جھمکا sāt' sahe'liyon kā jhūm'ka N.M. Pleiades سات ماموؤں کا بھانجا sāt' ma'ma'oñ ka bhāñ'ja N.M. darling of the whole family ساتواں sāt'vañ ADJ. seventh

ساتگین sāt'gīn N.M. wine cup ; goblet [P]

ساتھ sāth company ADV. along (with) together کے ساتھ ke sāth ADV. with ; along with ایک ساتھ ek' sāth' ADV. togethers ساتھ چھوٹنا sāth chhooṭ'na V.I. be separated (from) ساتھ چھوڑنا sāth' chhoṛ'na V.T. desert ساتھ دینا sāth de'na V.T. co-operate (with) side (with) stand by the side of ساتھ رہنا sāth' raih'na V.I. live together ساتھ ساتھ چلنا sāth' sāth chal'na V.I. walk side by side walk beside follow lose at heels ساتھ کھیلا sāth kā khe'la N.M. childhood's playmate ساتھ لگے پھرنا sāth' la'ge phir'na V.I. follow (someone) about walk along ساتھ والا sāth' vā'lā N.M. companion ; comrade partner neighbour ADJ. adjoining ; adjacent ; neighbouring next door ساتھ ہو لینا sāth' ho le'nā V.I. join join the company (of) ساتھ ہی sāth' hī CONJ. along with it ; together with it ADV. close by simultaneously ; at the same time there and then ساتھن sā'than N.F. (usu. lady's) female companion ساتھی sā'thī N.M. supporter ally comrade ; companion زندگی کا ساتھی zin'dagī kā sā'thī (dial جیون ساتھی jī'van sā'thī) N.M. spouse husband wife

ساٹا sā'ṭā N.M. transaction in bill of exchange return two marital deals one in exchange for the other ; matrimonial barter ساٹے میں دینا sa'ṭe meṅ de'nā V.T. (agree to) marry a girls of one's family into a family whose girl has been married into one's family

ساٹن sā'ṭan N.F. satin [E]

ساٹھ sāṭh ADJ. & N.M. sixty ساٹھا sā'ṭhā N.M. sexagenarian ساٹھا پاٹھا sā'ṭhā pā'ṭhā N.M. & ADJ. stout sexagenarian ساٹھواں sāṭh'vāṅ ADJ. sixtieth

ساج sāj N.M. teak [A]

ساجد sā'jid N.M. & ADJ. (PL. ساجدین sājidīn', F. ساجدہ sā'jidah F. PL. ساجدات sājidāt') prostrating in prayer adorer prostrating in adoration [A ~ سجدہ]

ساجن sā'jan N.M. (dial. سجنوا sājan'vā F. سجنی saj'nī dial. سجنیا sajan'yā) beloved ; sweetheart

ساجھا sā'jhā N.M. partnership association ساجھے کا کام sā'jhe kā kām N.M. something done in association (with) ساجھے کی ہنڈیا چوراہے میں پھوٹتی ہے sā'jhe kī hanḍ'yā chaurā'he meṅ phooṭ'tī hai PROV. partnership always ends in fiasco ساجھے میں sā'jhe meṅ ADV. jointly in partnership (with) in association (with) ساجھی sā'jhī N.M. partner shareholder associate ساجھی بننا (یا ہونا) sā'jhī ban'nā (or ho'nā) V.T. become a partner ; enter into partnership (with)

ساچق sā'chaq N.F. (correctly but less usu. for ساچق N.F. ★)

ساحت sā'hat N.M. expanse [A]

ساحر sā'hir N.M. (PL. سحرہ sa'harah) magician wizard sorceher charmer ساحرہ sā'hirah N.F. enchantress exquisitely beautiful woman ; cavishing beauty witch ساحری sā'hirī N.F. magic sorcery necromancy enchantment [A ~ سحر seh'r]

ساحل sā'hil N.M. (PL. سواحل savā'hil] shore ; seashore ; coast sea-board beach [A]

ساخت sākh't N.F. structure manufacture make PREF. (sākh't-e) made in ساخت پاکستان sākh't-e pā'kistān PL. made in Pakistan ساختہ sākh'tah ADJ. made faked ; trumped up ساختہ پرداختہ sākh'tah pardākh'tah N.M. & ADJ. trumped up ; faked ; made up patronized (by) بیساختہ be-sākh'tah ADJ. extempore ; impromptu unpremeditated ADV. spontaneously extempore ; impromptu [P ~ ساختن]

سادات sādāt' N.M. holy prophet's descendents through his daughter Hazrat Fatimah [A ~SING. سادات ~ سید]

سادس sā'dis ADJ. sixth سادساً sā'disan ADV. sixthly [A]

سادہ sā'dah ADJ. simple plain unadorned artless blank beardless (face, etc.) simpleminded سادہ پن sā'da-pan N.M. (same as سادگی N.F. ★)

سادہ دل sā'da-dil ADJ. artless guileless simple ; stupid سادہ دلی sā'da-di'lī N.F. artlessness simplemindedness سادہ کار sā'da-kār' N.M. goldsmith silversmith سادہ لوح sā'da-lauh' ADJ. & N.M. simpleton سادہ لوحی sā'da-lauhī N.F. simple-mindedness ; stupidity سادی sā'dī N.F. stupid woman ADJ. uuadorned unembellished سادگی sā'dagī N.F. simplicity plainness artlessness simplemindedness stupidity childlike behaviour rankness [P]

سادھنا sādh'nā V.T. hold (breath) regulate exercise ; train ; practise سادھ sādh N.M. (dial.) ascetic simple سادھو sā'dhoo N.M. Hindu ascetic [S]

سادی sā'dī ADJ. (see under سادہ ADJ. ★)

سار sār SUF. abounding in like having suffering from head [P]

سارا[1] sā'rā SUF. pure undefiled

سارا[2] sā'rā (PL. سارے sā're F. ساری sā'rī) ADJ. entire whole ; complete ADV. entirely in entirety ; completely سارا دھن جاتا دیکھیے تو آدھا دیجیے بانٹ sā'rā dhan jā'tā de'khiye to ā'dhā dī'jiye bānṭ' PROV: better lose half than lose all

ساربان sār'bān N.M. camel-driver [P]

سارجنٹ sār'janṭ N.M. sergeant [E]

سارس sā'ras N.M. crane ; a kind of heron سارس کی سی جوڑی sā'ras kī sī jo'ṛī PH. (fig.) constant companions

سارق sā'riq N.M. thief pilferer [A ~ سرقہ]

سارنگ sārang' N.M. name of a musical mode peacock its cry

سارنگی sārañ'gī N.F. a kind of fiddle or violin سارنگیا sārañ'giyā N.M. fiddler ; violinist [~ PREC.]

ساری[1] sā'rī ADJ. percolating penetrating pervading جاری و ساری jā'rī-o- sā'rī ADJ. penetrating flowing [A ~ سرایت]

ساری[2] sā'rī N.F. (same as ساڑھی sā'ṛhī N.F. ★)

ساری *sā'rī* ADJ. (see under سارا ADJ. ★)

ساڑھی[1] *sā'ṛhī*, ساری *sā'rī* N.F. woman's outer garment comprising single piece of cloth

ساڑھی[2] *sā'ṛhī*, اساڑھی *asā'ṛhī* N.F. spring harvest [~ اساڑھ]

ساڑھے *sā'ṛhe* ADJ. half again

ساز *sāz* N.M. musical instrument harness accountrements concord good relations ADV. agreeable SUF. making preparing ساز باز *sāz'-bāz* N.F. (dial. N.M.) intrigue ; conspiracy connections ; good relations ساز باز رکھنا *sāz'-bāz rakh'nā* V.I. have good relations (with) ساز باز کرنا *sāz'-bāz kar'nā* V.T. plot ; intrigue ; conspire ساز گار *sāz-gār'* ADJ. agreeable favourable ساز و برگ *sā'z-o bar'g* N.M. (lit.) belongings سازو سامان *sā'z-o-sāmān'* N.M. equipment furniture [P]

سازش *sā'zish* N.F. plot ; intrigue ; conspiracy collusion سازش کرنا *sā'zish kar'nā* V.I. plot ; intrigue ; conspire سازشی *sā'zishī* N.M. plotter ; intriguer ; conspirator ADJ. plotting collusive [P ~ ساختن make]

سازندہ *sāzin'dah* N.M. instrumentalist accompanist [~ ساز]

ساس *sās* N.F. mother-in-law ساس بہو کی لڑائی *sās' ba'hoo kī laṛā''ī* PH. differences between someone's wife and mother

ساطع *sā'te'* ADJ. bright enlightening [A]

ساعت *sā''at* N.M. hour time moment [A]

ساعد *sā''id* N.M. wrist fore-arm ساعد سیمیں *sā''id-e sī'mīṅ* N.M. lovely wrist [A]

ساعی *sā''ī* N.M. endeavourer backbiter ساعی و نمام *sā''ī-o nammām'* N.M. backbiter

ساغر *sā'ghar* N.M. (also ساغر مے *sā'ghar-e mai*) winecup ; cup ; bowl ; goblet ساغر چلنا *sā'ghar chal'nā* V.I. have a round of drink ; drink (usu.) in company ساغری *sā'gharī* N.F. (dial.) space between horses tail and anus ADJ. pertaining goblet-like ; bowl- shaped [P]

سافل *sā'fil* N.M. mean fellow ADJ. lower nether [A]

ساق *sāq* N.F. shank stem (of plant) ساق سیمیں *sā'q-e sī'mīṅ* N.F. lovely leg(s) [A]

ساقط *sā'qit* ADJ. annulled eliminated lapsed out of use dropped (of foetus) miscarried ساقط کرنا *sā'qit kar'nā* V.T. eliminate annull render null and void cause to lapse drop ساقط ہونا *sā'qit ho'nā* V.I. be eliminated be annulled lapse lose value drop miscarry [A ~ سقوط]

ساقن *sā'qan* N.F. (see under ساقی N.M. ★)

ساقی *sā'qī* N.M. cup-bearer Ganymede potboy steward beloved sweetheart one offering drink to the thirsty ساقی کوثر *sā'qī-e kau'sar* N.M. Holy Prophet (as steward of the heavenly spring 'Kausar') ساقی گری *sā'qī-ga'rī* N.F. being a cup bearer steward ship [A]

ساکت *sā'kit* ADJ. silent ; quiet reticent immobile ساکت ہونا *sā'kit ho'nā* V.I. keep quiet be reticent be immobile [A ~ سکوت]

ساکن *sā'kin* ADJ. resident (of) quiescent quiet calm ; tranquil peaceful ; undisturbed immobile at rest N.M. (PL. سکنہ *sa'kanah*) resident quiescent letter [A ~ سکون]

ساکھ *sākh* N.F. good-will credit ساکھ بنانا *sākh banā'nā* V.T. create goodwill ساکھ بننا *sākh ban'nā* V.I. build up goodwill ساکھ جاتی رہنا *sākh jā'tī raih'nā* V.I. lose credit ; lose good-will ساکھ گنوانا *sākh' ganvā'nā* V.I. lose credit ساکھ ہونا *sākh' ho'nā* V.I. have good credit گئی ساکھ پھر نہیں آتی *ga''ī sākh phir' na'hīṅ ā'tī* PROV. a lost reputation is seldom redeemed

ساکھا[1] *sā'khā* N.M. (dial.) heroism Hindu chivalrous story [S]

ساکھا[2] *sā'khā* N.M. bough [CORR. of P شاخ]

ساگ *sāg* N.M. potherb ساگ پات *sāg' pāt* N.M. potherbs ; greens ساگا *sā'ga* N.M. (dial.) green stalk of onion

ساگر *sā'gar* N.M. (dial.) sea ; ocean

ساگوان *sāg'vān* N.M. teak-wood ; teak

ساگودانہ *sā'goo-dā'nah*, سابودانہ *sā'boo-dā'nah* N.M. sago [E ~ Malay]

سال[1] *sāl* N.M. (PL. سالہا *sāl-hā'*) year سال آئندہ *sāl-e āin'dah* N.M. next year سالانہ *sālā'nah* ADJ. annual سالانہ نقشہ جات *sālā'nah naqsha jāt'* N.M. PL. annual returns سال بسال (or سال بہ سال) *sāl' ba-sāl* ADV. year by year سالخوردہ *sāl-khūr'dah* ADJ. old aged experienced ; veteran worn-out سال رواں *sā'l-e ravāṅ'* N.M. current year سال شمسی *sā'l-e sham'sī*, شمسی سال *sham'sī sāl* N.M. solar year سال قمری *sā'l-e qa'marī*, قمری سال *qa'marī sāl*, سال ہجری *sāl-e hij'rī*, ہجری سال *hij'rī sāl* N.M. lunar year ; Hij'ri year سال عیسوی *sā'l-e 'ī'savī* N.M. Christian year ; 'Anno Christie' ; A.C. 'Anno Domini'; A.D. سال کبیسہ *sā'l-e kabī'sah*

N.M. leap year (in solar calendar with an extraday to February every fourth year) (arch.) leap lunar year (with an extra month every third year) سالگرہ sal'-gi'rah N.F. birthday ; birth anniversary (col. -rah) سالِ مہاجنی sa l-e maha'-janī N.M. (dial.) commercial year سالنامہ sāl-na'mah N.M. annual issue (of periodical) year book almanac سالوار sal'-vār ADJ. yearly ; annual ADV. yearly ; annually سالہاسال sal'-hā-sāl N.M. ADV. a long time years on end several years سالہاسال سے sal'-ha sal se ADV. for many year now for a long like ; since تدریسی (یا تعلیمی) سال tadrī'sī (or ta'lī'mī) sāl N.M. academic year تقویمی سال taqvī'mī sāl N.M. calendar year مالی سال ma'lī sāl N.M. financial year [P]

سال ۲ sal N.F. a kind of timber

سال ۳ sal N.F. (see under سالنا V.T. ★)

سالا sa'la N.M. wife's brother; brother-in-law (as mild swear-word) mean fellow ADJ. (F: سالی sa'lī vul.) mean good-for-nothing

سالار salar' N.M. commander chief leader سالارِ جنگ salā'r-e jang' (col. sālar' jang') N.M. Field-Marshal this as honorofic title (joc.) wife's brother سالارِ قافلہ salā'r-e qa'filah, قافلہ سالار qa'fila-salar' N.M. caravan leader سالارِ قوم salā'r-e qaum' N.M. national leader [P]

سالانہ sala'nah ADJ. (see under سال N.M. ★)

سالک sa'lik N.M. (PL. سالکان salikan') mystic initiate devotee traveller سالکِ رہ sa'lik-e rah' N.M. mystic initiate [A ~ سلوک]

سالم salim ADJ. whole complete perfect صحیح و سالم sahi'h-o-sa'lim ADJ. safe and sound سالمہ sa'limah N.M. atom molecule سالماتی salima'tī ADJ. atomic سالماتی بم salima'tī bam N.M. atom bomb سالماتی توانائی salima'tī tāvana''ī N.F. atomic energy [A]

سالن sa'lan N.M. curry stew salt dish

سالنا sal'na, سال دینا sal' de'na, سال ڈالنا sal' ḍal'na V.T. cut a mortise in سال sal N.F. mortice ; mortise

سالوس saloos' N.F. hypocrisy fraud خرقۂ سالوس khir'qa-e saloos' N. cloak put to desiaud others ; subterfuge [P]

سالی sa'lī N.F. wife's sister ; sister-in-law (as mild swear-word) mean women ADJ. (vul.) mean good-for-nothing

سامان sāmān' N.M. necessaries good and chattels wares tools implements arrangements : preparations custom wealth equipment material provisions سامانِ آخرت sāma'n-e ā'khirat N.M. good deads ; preparations for hereafter سامانِ جنگ sāma'n-e jang' N.M. war material (کا) سامان کرنا (kā) sāman kar'na V.T. arrange make preparation (for) (کا) سامان ہونا (ka) sāma'n ho'na V.I. take place be arranged سر و سامان sa'r-o sāman' N.M. arrangements (for) preparations (for) provisions (for) بے سر و سامان be'-sa'r-o saman' ADJ. unprovided helpless بے سر و سامانی be'-sa'r-o sāmā nī N.F. helplessness [P]

سامراج sām'raj N.M. (dial.) imperialism سامراجی samra'jī ADJ. (dial) imperialist [S]

سامری sa'mirī N.M. Samaritan who made a golden calf for worship by Israelites magician [A]

سامع sa'me' N.M. (PL. سامعین same'īn') listener prompter (in prayers) سامعہ sa'me'ah' N.M. audition ; hearing sense of hearing سامعہ نواز sa'me'a-nabaz' ADJ. melodious سامعہ نوازی same'a-nava'zī N.F. melodiousness [A ~ سماعت]

سامنا sām'na N.F. front facade meeting encounter confrontation سامنا کرنا sām'na kar'na V.I. encounter confront سامنا ہونا sām'na ho'na V.I. come across meet stand face to face (with) سامنے sām'ne ADV. before in front (of) in presence (of) opposite سامنے آنا sām'ne ā'na V.T. face appear before oppose challenge سامنے ہونا sām'ne ho'na V.T. oppose race stand face to face (with) appear before oppose challenge

سامی sa'mī ADJ. exalted [A ~ سمو]

سان ۱ san N.F. whetstone ; grindstone سان چڑھانا san' charha'na V.T. whet ; sharpen سان چڑھنا san' chaṛh'na V.I. be whetted ; be sharpened سان دھرنا san' dhar'na V.T. whet ; sharpen

سان ۲ san N.M. (col. for شان only as) سان گمان san' gumān' N.M. trace sign idea ; expectation سان نہ گمان san' na gumān' ADV. unawares all of a sudden [~ A شان]

سانپ sānp' N.M. serpent ; snake سانپ سونگھ جانا sānp' soongh ja'na V.I. be struck dumb when it is imperative to speak سانپ بھی مرے لاٹھی بھی نہ ٹوٹے sāṇp' bhī ma're la'ṭhī bhī na ṭoo'ṭe PH. achieve the object without sustaining any loss سانپ کا کاٹا رسی سے ڈرتا ہے sānp ka kaṭa ras'sī se ḍar'tā hai PROV. a burnt child dreads the fire سانپ کا بچہ سنپولیا sānp' ka bach'chah sanpo'liya PROV. enemy's progeny is no less dangerous گیا ہے سانپ نکل اب لکیر پیٹا کر *gayā' hai sāṅp ni'kal ab lakīr' pī'ṭa kar* PROV. it is no use crying over spilt milk سانپن *sāṅ'pan* N.F. female snake سپولیا *sapo'liya*, سنپولیا *sāṅpo'liya* N.M. young snake سپیرا *sape'ra*, سنپیرا *saṅpe'ra* N.M. snake-charmer

سانٹ *sāṅṭ*, سانٹھ *sāṅṭh* N.F. union confederacy سانٹھ لگانا (یا ملانا) *sāṅṭh lagā'na* (or *milā'nā*) V.I plot together ; conspire with سانٹھنا، سانٹھ لینا *sāṅṭh'nā*, *sāṅṭh le'na* V.T, cause (someone) to agree with one آنٹ سانٹ *āṅṭ' sāṅṭ* (dial. سانٹھ گانٹھ) (*sāṅṭh'gāṅṭh*) N.F. plot

سانٹا *sāṅ'ṭa* N.M. lash sprig used as such

سانجھ *sāṅjh* N.F. dusk evening سانجھ سویرے (یا سویر) *sāṅjh' save're* (or rare. *saver'*) ADV. night and day ; all the time ; ever ; always

سانچ *sāṅch* N.F. (dial.) truth (only in) سانچ کو آنچ نہیں *sāṅch' ko āṅch' na'hīṅ* PROV. truth ultimately prevails [doublet of سچ]

سانچا *sāṅ'chā* N.M. mould matrice (dial.) ovary (dial.) truthful person) سانچے میں ڈھالنا *sāṅ'che meṅ ḍhāl'na* V.T. mould سانچے میں ڈھلنا *sāṅ'che meṅ ḍhal'na* V.I. (fig.) (of human figure) be very lovely

سانچق *sāṅ'chaq*, (correctly but less usu. ساچق *sā'chaq*) N.F. dowry sent by husband's parents to bride's house the day before marriage [~T]

سانحہ *sā'neḥah* (PL. سانحات *sāneḥāt'*) accidents occurrances [A]

ساندہ *sāṅ'dah* N.M. leg-band (for cows, etc.)

سانڈ *sāṅḍ* N.M. bull stallion lewd youth رانڈ کا سانڈ *rāṅḍ' kā sāṅḍ* N.M. lewd youth brought up as cherished orphan سانڈنی *sāṅḍ'nī* N.F. dromedary سانڈنی سوار *sāṅḍ'nī-savār'* N.M. camel-rider سانڈیا *sāṅ'ḍiya* N.M. young male camel lace-making wheel

سانڈا *sāṅ'ḍa* N.M. sand lizard سانڈے کا تیل *sāṅ'ḍe kā tel* N.M. sand-lizard fat (used as aphrodisiac, etc.)

سانڈا

سانس *sāṅs* N.F. (dial. M.) breath sigh سانس اکھڑنا *sāṅs ū'khaṛnā* V.I. be out of breath pant be on the last gasp لمبی سانس بھرنا (*lam'bī*) *sāṅs bhar'nā* V.I heave a (deep) sigh سانس پھولنا (یا چڑھنا) *sāṅs' phool'na* (or *chaṛh'na*) V.I. pant be out of breath سانس ٹوٹنا *sāṅs' ṭooṭ'na* V.I. be out of breath breath in unsuccessful bid to hold breath سانس رکنا *sāṅs' rūk'na* V.I. be stifled ; be suffocated be choked سانس روکنا *sāṅs' rok'nā* V.I. hold one's breath سانس لینا *sāṅs' le'na* V.I. breathe inhale have a rest

سانسا *sāṅ'sā* N.M. care ; worry سانسا چڑھنا *sāṅ'sa chaṛh'na* V.I. have a worry

سانسی *sāṅ'sī* N.M. name of a nomadic people (declared criminal by the British) ; Romany

سانکھ *sāṅkh* N.F. (us. PL.) fried macaroni

ساننا *sān'nā* V.T. knead stain smear ; soil

سانوٹا *sāṅ'oṭa* ADJ. alert

سانولا *sāṅv'lā* (dial. سانورا *sāṅ''ora*) ADJ. (F. سانولی *sāṅv'lī* dial. سانوری *sāṅ'orī*) sallow nut-brown charming lovely; comely سانولا سلونا *sāṅv'lā silo'nā* ADJ. (F. سانولی سلونی *sāṅv lī silo'nī*) charming lovely ; comely

سانی *sā'nī* N.F. forage ; mixture of straw, grain and oil cake used as such

ساون *sā'van* N.M. fifth month of Hindu calendar (corresponding to July) ساون کا اندھا *sā'van kā aṅ'dhā* ADJ. one blinded with self-interest ساون بھادوں *sā'van bhā'doṅ* N.M. the two months of the rainy season a kind of fireworks counterparts of a set ساون کی جھڑی *sā'van kī jha'ṛī* N.F. incessant downpour (of the rainy season) ساون کے اندھے کو ہرا ہی (ہرا) سوجھتا ہے *sā'van ke aṅ'dhe ko ha'rā hī* (*ha'ra*) *soojh'tā hai* PROV. to a jaundiced eye everything is yellow ساون ہرے نہ بھادوں سوکھے *sā'van ha're na bhā'doṅ soo'khe* PROV. always in the same condition indifferent ساونی *sā'vanī* N.F. autumn harvest

ساہا *sā'ha* N.M. (dial.) opportune moment for marriage ساہا چمکنا (یا کھلنا) *sā'ha cha'makna* (or *khul'nā*) V.I. (dial.) (of wedding opportunity) come

ساہوکار *sā'hookār* N.M. money-lender Hindu banker rich man ساہوکارہ *sāhookā'rah* N.M. money-lending money-market ساہوکاری *sāhookā'rī* N.F. money-lending banking business

ساہول *sāhool'*, سہول *sa'hūl* N.F. plumb-line [~A ساقول T ~ شاقول CORR.]

ساہی *sā'hī* N.F. (same as سیہہ N.F. ★)

سائبان *sā'ebān'* N.M. housetop shed (esp. one with roof of corrugated iron sheets) canopy

سائر *sā''ir* ADJ. moving wandering current prevelant contingent whole all سائر خرچ *sā''ir khar'ch* N.M. contingent expenses [A ~ سیر]

سائن بورڈ *sā''in bord* N.M. signboard , sign [E]

سائنس *sā''ins* N.F. science سائنٹیفک *sa'intifik* ADJ. scientific [E]

1 **سائی** *sā''ī* N.F. earnest money

2 **سائی** *sā''ī* SUF. rubbing [P ~ سائیدن]

سائیس *sā'īs'* N.M. horse-keeper ; groom سائیسی *sā''īsī* N.F. stable-keeping; groom's work سائیسی علم دریاؤ ہے *sā''īsī 'il'm daryā''o hai* PROV. each knows the intricacies of his own trade each one regards his own field as the best [~ A سائس CORR.]

سائل *sā''il* N.M. petitioner applicant beggar [A ~ سوال]

سائیں *sā''īṅ* N.M. mendicant beggar (dial.) master (dial.) master

سائیں سائیں *sā''eṅ sā''eṅ* N.F. rustle (of wind) [ONO.]

1 **سایہ** *sa yah* N.M. shadow shade apparition ; spectre obsession protection influence سایہ پڑنا *sā'yah par'nā* V.I. be obsessed (by) came under (someone's) influence (of) be under the shadow (of) سایہ دار *sā'ya-dār* ADJ. shady سایہ ڈالنا *sā'yah dāl'nā* V.T. cast a shadow (over) show favour (to) give protection (to) سایہ ڈھلنا *sā'yah ḍhal'nā* V.I. be dasky be the afternoon سایہ ہونا (یا ہو جانا) *sā'yah ho'nā* (or *ho jā'nā*) V.I. be possessed : be obsessed (by) [P]

2 **سایہ** *sā'yah* N.M. dress ; woman's gown [Por]

1 **سب** *sab* ADJ. all whole entire total every سب ایک ہی تھیلی کے چٹے بٹے ہیں *sab ek' hī thai'lī ke chaṭ'ṭe baṭ'ṭe haiṅ* PROV. they are chips of the same block سب سے بھلی چپ *sab' se bha'lī chūp'* PROV. silence is gold سب کا سب *sab' kā sab* ADV. altogether the whole completely entirely سب (یا سبھی) کچھ *sab'* (or *sa'bhī*) *kūchh* N.M. everything ADV. entire complete

2 **سب** *sab* N.F. filthy language abuse ; swear-word سب و شتم *sab'b-o shat'm* N.F. (use of) abusive language ; swearing [A]

سبا *sabā'* (ped. *sa'ba*) N.M. Sheba a part of S. Arabia [A]

سبابہ *sabbā'bah* N.F. (ped.) forefinger [A]

سب انسپکٹر *sab-inspaik'ṭar* N.M. sub-inspector [E]

سباع *sibā''* N.M. PL. beasts of prey [A]

سبب *sabab'* N.M. (PL. اسباب *asbāb'*) cause reason ; ground means motive بسبب *ba-sabab'* ADV. by means of on account of owing to [A]

سبت *sab't* N.M. sabbath; Lord's day (ped.) Saturday [A]

سبحان *sūbḥān'* ADJ. holy ADV. be glorified ; praised سبحان اللہ *sub'ḥa'n-allāh'* INT. God be praised سبحان تیری قدرت *sūbḥān' te'rī qūd'rat* PH. (as words supposedly heards in parrots cry) inscrutable are the ways of ; providence ; wonderful are the ways of God [A]

سبحہ *sub'ḥah* N.F. rosary سبحہ گردانی *sub'ḥa-gardā'nī* N.F. telling one's beads [A ~ PREC.]

سبد *sa'bad* N.F. baskset سبد گل *sa'bad-e gūl* basket of flowers گل سر سبد *gū'l-e. sar sa'bad* top flower in the basket choicest thing [P]

سبز *sab'z* ADJ. green fresh سبز باغ *sab'z bāgh* N.M. PL. سبز باغ دکھانا *sab'z bāgh dikhā'nā* V.I. raise false hopes seduce tempt سبز پوش *sab'z-posh* ADJ. dressed in green green liveried سبز قدم *sab'z qa'dam* ADJ. inauspicious oil-omened ominous unlucky سبزہ *sab'zah* N.M. verdure bloom insipient beard iron-grey horse a kind of ear-ring a kind of green gem سبزہ آغاز *sab'za-āghāz'* ADJ. one with insipient beard سبزہ زار *sa'bza-zār* N.M. lawn meadow ; pasture سبزہ لہلہانا *sab'zah laihlahā'nā* V.I. have verdure all over (of green plants) move with wind سبزۂ بیگانہ *sab'za-e begā'nah* N.M. weed [P]

سبزی *sab zī* N.F. verdure greens , potherbs hemp preparation سبزی پینا (یا اڑانا) *sab'zī pī na* (or *ūṛā'nā*) V.I. drink hemp preparation سبزی فروش *sab'zī firosh'* N.M. green-grocer سبزی منڈی *sab'zī man'ḍī* N.F. vegetable market [~ P PREC.]

سبط *sib't* N.M. (PL. اسباط *asbāt'*) (esp naternal) grandchild jewish tribe the Tribe *sibtain'* N.M. grandsons of the Holy Prophet (viz. Imam Hasan and Imam Husain)

سبع *sab''* سبعہ *sab''ah* ADJ. seven سبع سیارہ *sab'' sayyā'rah* N.M PL. the seven planets سبعہ معلقہ *sab''ah mo'al'laqah* N.M. the seven Golden Odes of ancient Arabia [A]

سبق *sa'baq* N.M. (PL. اسباق *asbāq'*) lesson academic lecture سبق پڑھنا (یا لینا) *sa'baq paṛh'nā* (or *lenā*) V.I. study have a lesson learn a (good) lesson سبق دینا (یا پڑھانا) *sa'baq de'nā* (or *paṛhā'nā*) V.T. instruct ; lecture teach a lesson . give a lesson [A]

سبقت *sab'qat* N.F. lead initiative precedence surpassing excellence **سبقت کرنا** *sab'qat kar'nā* V.I. advance precede ; take the lead **سبقت لے جانا** *sab'qat le jā'nā* V.I. take the lead outstrip surpass excel

سبک *sū'būk, sa'būk* ADJ. delicate light trivial ; trifling swift ; nimble low ; degraded ; debased worthless **سبکبار** *sū'būk-bār* ADJ. light ; unencumbered **سبک پا** *sū'būk-pā'* ADJ. nimble . swift-footed **سبک پائی** *sū'būk-pā''ī* N.F. nimbleness **سبک پرواز** *sū'būk-parvāz'* ADJ. swift in flight **سبک خیز** *sū'būk khez'* ADJ. swift nimble rising ; swiftly **سبکدوش** *sū'būk-dosh'* ADJ. retired discharged absolved of responsibility unburdened **سبکدوشی** *sū'būk-do'shī'* N.F. retirement relieved of responsibility **ملازمت سے سبکدوش کرنا** *mūlā'zamat se sū'būk-dosh' kar'nā* V.T. retire (someone) from service ; retire **ملازمت سے سبکدوش ہونا** *mūlā'zamat se sū'būk-dosh ho'nā* V.I. retire from service; retire ; be retired **سبک رو** *sū'būk-rau,* **سبک رفتار** *sū'būk-raftār'* ADJ. light footed fast ; swift **سبکسار** *sū'būk-sār* ADJ. & N.M. (one) living in comfort **سبک سر** *sū'būk-sar* ADJ. debased ADV. with head hanging down in shame **سبک گام** *sū'būk-gām* ADJ. light-footed fast ; swift **سبک مزاج** *sū'būk-mizāj'* ADJ. fickle minded mean **سبک ہونا** *sū'būk ho'nā* V.I. be put to shame be debased **سبکی** *sūb'kī* N.F. slight ; dishonour ; disgrace ; indignity lightness [P]

سبک *sab'k* N.M. style [A]

سبکی[1] *sūb'kī* N.F. sob **سبکیاں لینا (یا بھرنا)** *sūbkiyāṅ le'nā* (or *bhar'nā*) V.I. sob

سبکی[2] *sūb'kī* N.F. (see under **سبک** ★)

سبل *sūb'bal* N.M. iron rod for digging hole through wall

سبل *su'bul* N.M. (PL. of **سبیل** N.M. ★)

سبو *suboo'* (or *saboo'*) N.M. ewer pitcher **سبو بدوش** *suboo'-ba dosh'* N.M. & ADV. (one) bearing a pitcher boozer **سبوچہ** *suboo'chah* N.M. small ewer [P]

سبوتاژ *sabotāzh'* N.M. sabotage **سبوتاژ کرنا** *sabotāzh' kar'nā* V.T. sabotage [E]

سبوس *sāboos'* N.M. pollard bran [P]

سبھ *subh,* **شبھ** *shūbh* ADJ. (dial.) propitious [S]

سبھا *sa'bhā* N.F. (dial.) assembly [S]

سبھاگ *sūbhāg'* ADJ lucky propitious [S]

سبھاؤ *subhā''o* N.M manners ; behaviour good nature

سبھیتا *sabhe'tā* N.F. riddance **اپنا سبھیتا کرنا** *ap'nā sabhe'tā kar'nā* V.I. get rid (of)

سبیل *sabīl'* N.F. (PL. **سبل** *su'būl*) way out means course free wayside stall for drinking water (esp. as improvised during 'Muharram') **سبیل لگانا** *sabīl' lagā'nā* V. keep such stall **سبیل نکالنا (یا کرنا)** *sabīl' nikāl'nā* (or *kar'nā*) V.I. devise (some) way out **فی سبیل اللہ** *fī sabī'l-illāh'* ADV. in God's way free as a charity charitably **ابن السبیل** *ib'n-ūs-sabīl'* N.M. traveller [A]

سپا *sip'pā* N.M. aim track mode **سپا بیٹھنا** *sip'pā bai'ṭh'nā* V.I. be successful **سپا لگانا (یا مارنا)** *sip'pā lagā'nā* (or *mār'nā*) V.T. hit the nail on the head be not wide of the mark

سپاٹ *sapāṭ* ADJ. flat inspid (style) in need of re-roughening

سپاٹا *sapā'ṭā* N.M. leap long jump **سپاٹا بھرنا** *sapā'ṭā bhar'nā* V.I. take a long jump **سیر سپاٹا** *sair' sapā'ṭā* N.M. walk ; stroll

سپارہ *sipā'rah* (lit. & ped. **سیپارہ** *sī-pā'rah*) N.M. one of the 30 chapters of Holy Quran [P ~ **سی** thirty + **پارہ** piece]

سپاری *sūpā'rī* N.F. betel-nut 'glans penis'

سپاس *sipās'* N.M. thanks giving gratitude **سپاس گزاری** *sipās'-gūzā'rī* N.F. thanksgiving **سپاسنامہ** *sipās'-nā'mah* N.M. address of welcome ; address [P]

سپاہ *sipāh',* **سپہ** *sipah'* N.M. arm troops [P]

سپاہی *sipā'hī* N.M. (police) constable sentry (arch.) soldier **سپاہیانہ** *sipāhiyā'nah* ADJ. soldierly brave [P ~ PREC.]

سپر *si'par* N.F. shield **سپر انداز** *si'par-andāz'* ADJ surrendering **سپر اندازی** *si'par andā'zī* N.F. surrender ; throwing up the sponge **سپر ڈالنا (یا پھینکنا)** *si'par ḍāl'nā* (or *phenk'nā*) V.I surrender ; throw up the sponge **(سینہ) سپر ہونا** *(sī'na-) si'par ho'nā* V.I put up a bold front defend boldy come to the rescue take the brunt of assault [P]

سپرد *sipūr'd* N.F. custody ; charge ; care delivery entrusting ; trust **سپرد کرنا** *sipūr'd kar'nā* V.T entrust (to) consign put in charge (of) **سپردگی** *sipūr'dagī* N.F. commitment delivery entrusting surrender yielding [P]

سپردائی *saparda''i* N.M. dancing girl's accompanist

سپستان *sapistan'* (or *sapis'tan*) N.M. a kind of glutinous berry used as drug [P]

سپنا *sūp'nā* (or *sap'nā*) N.M. (dial.) dream [E]

سپنج *sapanj'* N.M. (same as سنج N.M. ★)

سپند *sipand* N.M. wild rule [P]

سپوت *sapool'* (ped. *sū-*) dutiful son praiseworthy scion (of) [S ~ پوت]

سپولیا *sapo'liya*, سنپولیا *sanpo'liya* N.M. see under سانپ N.M. ★)

سپہ *sipah'* (CONTR. of سپاہ N.F.★) سپہ سالار *si'pah-salar'* N.M. Commander-in-Chief ; C-in C سپہ سالاری *si'pah-sala'ri* N.F. command (of troops) سپہگری *si'pah-ga'ri* N.F. soldiering tactics [P]

سپہر *sipeh'r* N.M. sky ; firmament ; celestial sphere گردش سپہر *gar'dish-e sipeh'r* N.F. vicissitudes of fortune [P]

سپید *siped'* ADJ. (same as سفید ADJ. ★)

سپیدہ *sipe'dah* N.M. dawn eucalyptus tree white paint powder سپیدہ سحر *sipe'da-e sahar'* N.M. break of day سپیدی *sipe'di* N.M. same as سفیدی N.F. (see under سفید ADJ. ★) [P ~ PREC.]

سپیرا *sape'ra* سنپیرا *sanpe'ra* see under سانپ ★]

سپیکر *sapi'kar* N.M. speaker Speaker (of Legislature) [E]

ست[1] *sat* PREF. seven ; hepta ست بجھڑا *sat b jh'ra* ADJ. hybrid mixed N.M. salmagundi medley ست پوتی *sat-poo'ti* N.F. mother of seven sons ADJ. (woman) having seven sons fortunate (woman) ست خصمی *sat khas'mi* N.F. & ADJ. (wife) of seven successive husbands lascivious (woman) ست کونا *sat-ko'na* ADJ. heptagonal ست کھنڈا *sat-khan'da* ADJ. seven storeyed ست لڑا *sat-la'ra* N.M. & ADJ. seven-stringed (necklace) ست ماسا *sat-ma'sa*, ستوانسا *sat-van'sa* N.M. & ADJ. prematurely born (baby) make-up articles sent to expectant mother by her parents during seventh month of pregnancy ست نجا *sat-na'ja*, ست ناجا *sat-na'ja* N.M. mixture of seven different cereals medley [~ سات CONTR.]

ست[2] *sat* N.M. essence stamina spirit of defince ست چھوڑ (یا ہار) دینا *sat chhor* (or *har'*) *de'na* V.I. lose heart

ست[3] *SAT* N.M. (dial.) truth ADJ. (dial.) true [S]

ستار *sitar'* N.M. three-stringed guitar ستار بجانا (یا چھیڑنا) *sitar' baja'na* (or *chher'na*) V.I. play on a guitar ستار نواز *sitar'-navaz'* N.M. guitarist [P ~ سہ + تار]

ستار *sattar'* N.M. coverer of human fallings (a attribute of God) ستار العیوب *satta'r-ul-'uyoob* N.M. God (as Coverer of human fallings) [A ستر *sat'r*]

ستارہ *sita'rah* N.M. star spangle ستارہ اوج پر ہونا *sita'rah auj par ho'na* V.I. have one's star in the ascendant ستارہ اچھا (یا نیک) ہونا *sita rah achchha* (or *nek'*) *ho'na* V.I. have lucky stars ستارہ بلند ہونا *sita'rah buland' ho'na* V.I. have one's star in the ascendant (کی قسمت کا) ستارہ چمکنا (*ki qismat ka*) *sita'rah cha'makna* V.I. have one's star in the ascendant have a sudden stroke of luck ستارہ شناس *sita'rah-shinas'* N.M. astrologer ستارہ شناسی *sita'ra-shina'si* N.F. astrology ستارہ صبح *sita.ra-e sub'h* N.M. Venus ; the Morning Star ستارہ گردش میں ہونا *sita'rah gar'dish men ho'na* V.I. be in bad luck ; suffer from the vicissitudes of fortune ستارہ قطبی *sita'ra-e qut'bi*, قطبی تارہ *qut'bi ta'rah* N.F. the Pole-star ستاروں بھرا *sita'ron bha'ra* ADJ. (F. ستاروں بھری *sita'ron bha'ri*) starry ; star-spangled ستاروں کا جھرمٹ *sita'ron ka jhur'mat* N.M. galaxy ٹوٹنے والا ستارہ *toot'ne va'la sita'rah*, N.M. shooting star دنبالہ دار ستارہ *dum'-aar sita'rah* دمدار ستارہ *dumba'la-dar sita'rah* طالع کا ستارہ *ta'le' ka sita'rah* N.M. star governing (one's) fortune [P]

ستاسی *sata'si* (or *satta'si*) ADJ. & N.M. eighty-seven ستاسیواں *sata'sivan* ADJ. eighty-seventh

ستان[1] *sitan'* SUF. taking seizing snatching usurping ستانی *sita'ni* SUF taking seizing ; seizure [P ~ ستاندن]

ستان[2] *sitan'* (or *sitan* or *is'tan*) SUF. place ; station

ستانا *sata'na* V.T. annoy ; vex harass hackle tease trouble

ستانوے *satan've* (or *sattan've*) ADJ. ninety-seven ستانوے واں *sattan'vevan* ADJ. ninety-seventh

ستاون *sata'van* (or *satta'van*) ADJ. & N.M. fifty-seventh ستاوواں *satta'vanvan* ADJ. fifty-seventh

ستائش *sita''ish* N.F. praise [P ~ ستودن]

ستائیس *satta''is* ADJ. twenty-seven ستائیسواں *satta'isvan* ADJ. twenty-seventh

ستتر *satat'tar* ADJ. & N.M. seventy-seven ستترواں *satat'tarvan* ADJ. seventy-seventh

ستر *sat'r* N.M. (PL. استار *astar'*) covering veil concealment ; hiding not exposing ستر عورت *sat'r-e 'au'rat* N.M. not exposing the private parts (by men and slave-girls) covering from navel to knee covering entire body (save face, hands and feet) [A]

ستر sat'tar ADJ. & N.M. seventy ستر ابہترا sat'tarā bahat'tarā ADJ. (F. ستری بہتری sat'tarī bahat'tarī) dotard ستروان sat'tarvāṅ ADJ. seventieth

سترہ sat'rah ADJ. & N.M. seventeen سترھواں sat'rahvāṅ ADJ. seventeenth

سترہ sut'rah N.M. stick, etc. put up as cover by person saying prayers ; prayer-hedge [A ~ ستر sat'r]

ستلی sut'lī N.F. coarse twine

ستم si'tam N.M. injustice oppression ; tyranny ستم اٹھانا (یا سہنا) si'tam uṭhā'nā (or saih'nā) V.I. suffer injustice be oppressed ستم اٹھنا si'tam uṭh'nā V.I. undergo sufferings ستم ایجاد si'tam-ījād' N.M. & ADJ. tyrant ستم ایجاد کرنا si'tam ījād' kar'nā V.T. do injustice tyrannize ; oppress ستم دیدہ (یا رسیدہ یا زدہ یا کش) si'tam-dīdah (or -rasī'dah or -za'dah or -kash) ADJ. & N.M. oppressed ستم ظریف si'tam-ẓarīf' N.M. & ADJ. ironical (person) ingenious in tyranny ستم ظریفی si'tam-ẓarī'fī N.F. irony ingeniousness in tyranny قدرت کی ستم ظریفی qūd'rat' kī si'tam-ẓarī'fī PH. irony of fate ستم کرنا (یا توڑنا یا ڈھانا) si'tam kar'nā (or toṛ'nā or ḍhā'nā) V.T. do injustice (to) ; be unjust (to) oppress tyrannize ستم گر (یا کار یا شعار) si'tam-gar (or -kār' or -she'ār') ADJ. & N.M. tyrant ; oppressive N.F. tyranny ; oppression injustice ستم ہونا (یا ٹوٹنا) si'tam ho'nā (or ṭooṭ'nā) V.I. be oppressed [P]

ستمبر sitam'bar N.M. September [E]

ستنا sūt'nā V.I. be tightened (of nose) be pointed ; be thin ستواں sut'vāṅ ADJ. delicate (nose) [~ سونتنا]

ستو sat'too N.M. parched barley meal sweet beverage prepared from it ; barley beverage ستو کھا کے شکر کرنا sat'too khā ke shuk'r kar'nā V.I. lead a simple life be thankful even for a minor favour

ستواں sūt'vāṅ ADJ. (see under ستنا ★)

ستودہ sitoo'dah ADJ. laudable ستودہ خصائل (یا صفت) sitoo'da-khaṣā''il (or sifat') ADJ. of laudable qualities ; praiseworthy [P ~ ستودن]

ستور sutor' N.M. animal beast of burden [P]

ستون sūtoon', satoon', sitoon' N.M. pillar ; column [P]

ستہ sit'tah ADJ. six [A]

ستھرا suth'rā ADJ. neat ; clean : tidy N.M. clean shaven mendicant minstrel ستھراؤ sūthrā''o N.M. collapse of buildings in entire area massacre heaps of casualties ستھراؤ پڑنا sūthrā''o par'nā V.I. (of place) be strewn with corpses ستھراؤ کرنا sūthrā''o kar'nā V.T. strew (place) with corpses give a blood bath ; massacre ستھرائی sūthrā''ī N.F. neatness skill

ستی sa'tī N.F. (dial.) women burning herself to death on husband's funeral pyre ADJ. (dial.) chaste or virtuous (woman) [S]

ستیاناس sat'tiyānās N.M. spoiling ruin annihilation INT. to hell with it ستیاناس کرنا sat'tiyānās kar'nā V.T. spoil destroy ; ruin ستیاناس ہونا sat'tiyānās ho'nā V.I. be spoiled be ruined ; be destroyed

ستیز satez' SUF. fighting N.M. (rare.) fight battle ستیزہ sate'zah N.M. fight battle contention ستیزہ کار sate'za-kār ADJ. contending ; fighting ستیزہ کار رہنا se sate'za-kār raih'nā V.T. take up the challenge against [P]

ستیہ گرہ sat'tiyah ga'rah N.M. (dial.) passive resistance [S]

سٹ saṭ N.F. plot league confederacy clandestine relations سٹ لڑانا saṭ' laṛā'nā V.T. plot ; intrigue ; conspire have clandestine relations (with)

سٹا siṭ'ṭā N.M. ear of corn ; cob

سٹا saṭ'ṭā, سٹہ saṭ'ṭah N.M. speculation forwards ; forward trading in cereals سٹا بٹا saṭ'ṭā baṭ'ṭā N.M. clandestine relations leage ; confederacy سٹے باز saṭ'ṭe-bāz N.M. speculator forwards trader سٹے بازی saṭ'ṭe-bā'zī N.F. speculation forward trading

سٹاپ siṭāp', اسٹاپ isṭāp' stop bus stop [E]

سٹا سٹ sa'ṭā saṭ ADV. (of thrashing) in quick succession pat swiftly

سٹاف siṭāf', اسٹاف isṭāf' N.M. staff [E]

سٹاک saṭāk' N.M. & ADV. crack (of whip, etc.) ; whack ; thwack سٹاک سے saṭāk' se ADV. with a whack [ONO.]

سٹاک siṭāk', اسٹاک isṭāk' N.M. stock [E]

سٹال siṭāl', اسٹال isṭāl' N.M. stall [E]

سٹپٹانا saṭpaṭā'nā V.I. fret and fume be confounded

سٹرابری saṭrab'rī (or seṭab'rī) N.F. strawberry [A]

ستڑپٹڑ *sa'ṭar pa'ṭar* N.F. routine duties minor engagements

سٹرلنگ *siṭar'ling*, سٹرلنگ | *isṭar'ling* N.M. sterling [E]

سٹک *siṭik'*, اسٹک | *isṭik'* N.F. stick [E]

سٹک *saṭik'* N.F. small hubble-bubble delicate woman

سٹکنا *sa'ṭakna*, سٹک جانا *sa'ṭak ja'nā* V.I. slink away ; sneak away

سٹلا *saṭal'lā* N.M. slovenly person سٹلو *saṭal'lo* N.F. slut ; slattern

سٹور *siṭor'*, اسٹور | *isṭor'* N.M. store stores [E]

سٹھانی *siṭhā'nī* N.F. (see under سیٹھ N.M. ★)

سٹھنی *siṭh'nī* N.F. (usu. in PL.) abuses cordially bandied between in-laws at wedding سٹھنیاں دینا *siṭh'niyāṅ de'nā* V.T. hurl abuses thus

سٹھورا *sūṭho'rā* N.M. sweet gingered meal used as candie

سٹھیانا *saṭhyā'nā* V.I. dote ; be in dotage [~ ساٹھ]

سٹی *siṭ'ṭī* N.F. senses ; wisdom سٹی بھول جانا (یا گم ہو جانا) *siṭ'ṭī bhool jā'nā* (or *gūm' ho jā'nā*) be confounded be unnerved

سٹیج *saṭej'* N.M. (same as اسٹیج ★)

سٹیشن *isṭe'shan* N.M. (same as سٹیشن N.M. ★)

سٹیشنری *siṭesh'narī*, سٹیشنری | *isṭesh'narī* N.F. stationary [E]

سٹیمر *siṭī'mar*, اسٹیمر | *isṭī'mar* N.M. steamer ; steamship [E]

سجاد *sajjād'* ADJ., سجادہ *sajjā'dah* N.M. (see under سجدہ ★)

سجانا *sūjā'nā* V.T. cause to swell منہ سجانا *mūṅh' sūjā'nā* V.I. pull a long face grow angry

سجانا *sajā'nā* V.T. arrange adorn decorate سجاوٹ *sajā'vaṭ* N.M. decoration adornment gracefulness arrangement سج دھج *saj'dhaj* N.F. grace elegance decoration [~ CAUS.]

سجدہ *saj'dah* (ped. *sij'dah*) N.M. (PL. سجدات *sajdāt'*) prostration prostration on knees and forehead adoration (of God) سجدہ سہو *saj'da-e sah'v* N.M. (see under سہو ★) سجدہ کرنا *saj'dah kar'nā* V.T. adore (God) prostrate oneself سجدہ گاہ *saj'da-gāh* N.M. prayer mat mosque ; temple place of adoration سجاد *sajjād'* N.M. adorer سجادہ *sajjā'dah* N.M. prayer-mat سجادہ نشین *sajjā'da-nashīn'* (or *nashīn'*) N.M. Shrine Superior successor to saint سجادہ نشینی *sajjā'dah-nashī'nī* N.F. succession to saint [A]

سجع *saj'* N.M. rhymed prose double entendre about someone's name in verse [A]

سجل *si'jil* ADJ. nice ; fine well-arranged orderly tidy

سجل *sijil'* N.M. scroll [A]

سجن *sij'n* N.M. prison [A]

سجن *sa'jan*, ساجن *sā'jan* (dial. سجنوا *sajan'vā*) N.M lover beloved ; sweetheart friend سجنی *saj'nī* (dial. سجنیا *sa'jan'yā*) N.F. beloved ; sweetheart mistress

سجنا *saj'nā* V.I. fit well adorn oneself look pretty سجانا *sajā'nā* V.T. سجاوٹ *sajā'vaṭ* N.M

سج دھج *saj'dhaj* N.F. (see under سجانا V.T. ★) سجوانا *sajvā'nā* V.T. cause (someone) to adorn get arranged well get tidied up سجیلا *sajī'lā* ADJ. lovely ; handsome graceful elegant

سجھانا *sūjhā'nā* V.T. point out hint at drive (something) home (to) cause to understand make (someone) see the point in (something) سجھائی دینا *sūjhā''ī de'nā* V.I. be visible [~ سوجھنا CAUS.]

سجود *sūjood'* N.M. prostration [A]

سجی *saj'jī* N.F. impure carbonate of soda

سجیلا *sajī'lā* ADJ. (see under سجنا ★)

سچ *sach* N.M. truth ; veracity ADJ. true ; veritable ADV. truly actually indeed in earnest سچ سچ *sach' sach* ADV. truly سچ ماننا *sach' mān'nā* V.I. believe to be true trust in the accuracy (of) سچ مچ *sach' mūch* ADV. truly really in fact INT indeed really

سچا *sach'chā*, ADJ. (F. سچی *sach'chī*) true ; real genuine sincere faithful bona fide (transaction) full (weight) unallowed untouched by hand (of meals) not left over سچائی *sachchā''ī* N.F. truth verity genuineness purity

سحاب *sahāb* N.M. cloud سحابہ *sahā'bah* N.M. nebula سحابی *sahā'bī* ADJ. nebulous [A]

سحر *seh'r* N.M. magic black art ; necromancy ; socery bewitching charm enchantment سحر بیان *seh'r-bayān'* (or *-bayān'*) ADJ. convincing speaker سحر حلال *seh'r-e halāl'* N.M. fine-speech bewitching talk charm of beauty سحر چل جانا *seh'r chal jā'nā* V.I. come under the spell (of) be charmed (by) سحر سامری *seh'r-e sā'mirī* N.M. influence leading astray [A]

سحر *sa'har* N.M. (PL. سحور *suhoor'*, اسحار *ashar'*) dawn daybreak morning سحرخیز *sa'har-khez* ADV. early riser سحر دم *sa'har-dam*, سحرگاہ *sa'har-gah'* ADV. in the early hours of the morning سحرگاہی *sa'har-ga'hi* ADJ. early morning (prayers, etc.) سحری *sa'hari* ADJ. early morning N.F. (ped. سحور *sahoor'*) pre-dawn meals during fasting month سحری کھائے سو روزہ رکھے *sa'hari kha''e so ro'zah rak'khe* PROV. he who claims right must also perform duty [A]

سخاوت *sakha'vat*, سخا *sakha'* N.F. generosity munificence ; liberality [A]

سخت *sakh't* ADJ. hard rigid ; stiff cruel obdurate harsh strict , severe difficult austere strong ; vigorous vehement extreme ; drastic ; radical ADV. very extremely severely intensely violently سخت بات *sakh't bat* N.F. (usu. in PL.) cruel words pinching word سخت جان *sakh't-jan'* (or *-jan*) ADJ. tough ; diehard سخت جانی *sakh't-ja'ni* N.F. toughness سخت دل *sakh't-dil* ADJ. hard-hearted; adamant سخت دلی *sakh't-di'li* N.F. hard-heartedness سخت دن *sakh't din* N.M. PL. hard times سخت زمین *sakh't-zamin'* N.M. pebbly soil verse in difficult metre and rhyme سخت زمین میں کہنا *sakh't zamin' men kaih'na* V.I. versify thus سخت سست کہنا *sakh't sus't kaih'na* V.T. chide ; scold ; reproach سخت گیر *sakh't-gir* ADJ. strict cruel ; oppressive N.M. hard taskmaster سخت گیری *sakh't-gi'ri* N.F. strictness cruelty سخت گیری کرنا *sakh't-giri kar'na* V.I. be strict show cruelty سختی *sakh'ti* N.F. hardness rigidity stuffness obstinacy harshness ; strictness ; severity . cruelty oppression difficulty poverty distress misfortune austerity strength vigorousness ; vehemence force ; violence سختی کرنا *sakh'ti kar'na* V.T. treat harshly ; be severe use force ; use violence سختی ہونا *sakh'ti ho'na* V.I. be shown severity be subjected to vic nce [P]

سخن *su'khan* (also *sa'khun*, *su'khun*) N.M. speech talk words language poetry matter ; affair سخن پرداز *su'khan-pardaz'* ADJ. & N.M. eloquent elegant poet garrulous سخن پردازی *sukhan-parda'zi* N.F. eloquence garrulity سخن پرور *su'khan-par'var* ADJ. & N.M. bigoted or opinionated (person) (person) fulfilling his promise سخن پروری *su'khan-par'vari* N.F. bigotry being true to one's word سخن چیں *su'khan chin* ADJ. & N.M. back-biter ; tale-bearer critic سخن چینی *su'khan-chi'ni* N.F. tale-bearing ; back biting cavilling سخندان *sukhan-dan* (or *-dan'*) ADJ. & N.M. eloquent elegent poet shrewd intelligent critic سخندانی *su'khan-da'ni* N.F. eloquence elegance as a poet shrewdness critical acumen سخن دینا *su'khan de'na* V.I. pledge one's word سخن رانی *su'khan-ra'ni* N.F. eloquence garrulity سخن ساز *su'khan-saz'* ADJ. & N.M. eloquent (person) facile ; glib ; (one) with a facile tongue سخن سازی *su'khan-sa'zi* N.F. eloquence glibness سخن سنج *sukhan-sanj'*, سخن شناس *su'khan-shinas'* ADJ. & N.M. shrewd intelligent critic poet سخن شناس نہ دلبرا خطا اینجاست *su'khan-shinas na-'i' dil'-bara khata' in-jast* PH. the trouble is you do not see the point سخن سنجی *su'khan san'ji*, سخن شناسی *su'khan-shina'si* ADJ. shrewdness critical acumen elegance as poet سخن طرازی *su'khan-tira'zi* N.F eloquence skill in versification سخن فہم *su'khan-faih'm* ADJ. & N.M. shrewd perspicacious intelligent critic سخن فہمی *su'khan-faih'mi* N.F. shrewdness perspicacity critical acumen سخن فہمی عالم بالا معلوم شد *su'khan-faihmi-e 'a'lam-e ba'la ma'loom' shud* PROV. poetical elegance has poor reward (to a lit. pretender) I have seen your depths سخنگو *su'khan-go* ADJ. & N.M. poet eloquent (person) سخن گوئی *su'khan-go''i* N.F elegance as poet eloquence سخن نشنو *su'khan-nash'nau* ADJ. heedless سخنور *su'khan-var* N.M. & ADJ. eloquent elegant poet سخنوری *su'khan-va'ri* N.F. eloquence elegance as poet کم سخن *kam'-sukhan* ADJ. & N.M. reserved (person) : reticent (person) [P]

سخی *sa'khi* N.M. & ADJ. generous, liberal ; bountiful or munificent (person) سخی سے سوم بھلا جو ترت دے جواب *sa'khi se soom' bha'la jo tur't de javab'* PROV. the niggard who gives a curt refusal is preferable to the benevolent who procrastinates [A ~ سخاوت]

سخیف *sakhif'* ADJ. nonsense stupid [A]

سد *sad* N.M. wall barrier obstruction سد باب *sad'd-e bab'* N.M. end control remedy سد باب کرنا *sad'd-e bab' kar'na* V.T. end control remedy سد راہ *sad'd-e rah'* N.M. obstruction stumbling block سد راہ ہونا *sad'd-e rah' ho'na* V.I. impede ; obstruct stand in the way (of) سد رمق *sad'd-e ra'maq* N.M. just enough to subsist سد سکندری *sad'd-e sikan'dari* N.M. the Great Wall of China [A]

سدا *sa'da* ADV. always ; ever ; perpetually سدا ایک رخ ناؤ چلتی نہیں *sa'da ek' rukh na''o chal'ti na'hin* PROV. times incessantly change سدابہار *sa'da-bahar'* ADJ. evergreen سدابرت *sa'da-bar't* N.M. (dial.) poor house free mess سدا رہے نام اللہ کا

sa'dā ra'he nām' allāh' kā PH. all perish save God سدا سہاگن *sa'dā sohā'gan* N.F. whore ; prostitute mendicant dressing himself as woman INT. may you never become a widow سدا ناؤ کاغذ کی بہتی نہیں *sa'dā nā''o kā'ghaz kī baih'tī nahīṅ'* PROV. flimsy things soon fall apart falsehood will not one day

سدرشن *sūdar'shan* ADJ. (dial.) handsome; comely [S]

سدرہ *sid'rah* N.M. berry; plum tree سدرۃ المنتہیٰ *sid'rat-ul-mūntahā'* N.M. the heavenly tree beyond which even the Holy Ghost cannot advance

سدھ *sūdh*, سدھ بدھ *sūdh' būdh* N.M. common-sense intelligence care attention consciousness presence of mind سدھ رکھنا *sūdh' rakh'nā* V.I. bear in mind سدھ لینا *sūdh' le'nā* V.I. look after take care (of) بے سدھ *be sūdh'* ADJ. senseless ; unconscious careless

سدھارنا *sidhār'nā* V.I. go ; depart set out die ; pass away

سدھارنا *sūdhār'nā* V.T. better ; improve correct ; act as a corrective (to) set right ; mend (matters) سدھرنا *sūdhar'nā* V.I. be improved be corrected ; be set right

سدھانا *sidhā'nā* V.T. tame (animal) train (animals for performance) discipline سدھنا *sidh'nā* V.I. be tamed (of animal) be trained for performance be disciplined سدھوانا *sidhvā'nā* V.T. cause to be tamed get trained

سدے *sad'de* N.M. PL. banners taken out in procession during Muharram سدے نکلنا *sad'de ni'kalnā* V.I. (of Muharram banners) be taken out in procession

سڈول *siḍaul'* (ped. *sūḍaul'*) ADJ. well-shaped ; graceful (body) [~ ڈول *ḍaul*]

سر ۱ *sar* N.M. sir ; Sir [E]

سر ۲ *sar* N.F. hand (at cards)

سر ۳ *sar* N.M. (dial.) pool ; pond a kind of grass with stout stalks

سر ۴ *sar* N.M. (ped. or in P. construction) head top pinnacle tip point end beginning commencement chief main ; major ; principal سرآمد *sar-ā'mad* N.M. & ADJ. chief salient most prominent chosen سرآمد روزگار *sar-ā'mad-e roz'gār'* ADJ. & N.M. the most prominent person of the times سراپا *sar-ā'-pā* N.M. organwise description of human figure (usu. as verse encomium) ADJ. entire incarnate ADV. all over the body entirely; wholly; fully سراسر *sar-ā-sar'* ADV. wholly; entirely; completely سراسیمہ *sar-āsī'mah* ADJ. perplexed confounded سراسیمگی *sar-āsī'magī* N.F. perplexity confusion سر اجلاس *sa'r-e ijlās'* ADV. in court in public openly publicly سرافراز *sar-afrāz'* ADJ. exalted elevated successful سرافگندہ *sar-afgan'dah* ADJ. hanging down one's head in shame downcast brought low سرانجام *sar-anjām'* end result ; consequence arrangement سرانجام کرنا (یا دینا) *sar-anjām' kar'nā* (or *de'nā*) انجام دینا *anjām' de'nā'* V.I. accomplish bring to a successful conclusion سرانگشت *sar-e angūsh't* N.M. finger tip سرباز *sar-bāz* ADJ. reckless ; ready to lay down intrepid ready to lay down one's life N.M. (rare) soldier سربازار *sar-e bāzār'* ADV. publicly ; in public ; openly سربام *sar-e bām'* ADV. on top of the house from housetops سربراہ *sar ba-rāh'* N.M. chief ; head (of) سربراہ کار *sar ba-rā'h-e kār'* N.M. (col.) agent, representative manager سربراہی کرنا *sar ba-ra'hī kar'nā* V.I. be at the head manage conduct سربستہ *sar-bas'tah* ADJ. hidden (secret) ; closed ; shut سربسر *sar ba-sar'* ADV. wholly ; entirely from end to end ; from top to bottom سربلند *sar-būland'* ADJ. exalted eminent سربلندی *sar-būlan'dī* N.F. exaltation eminence سربلندی حاصل کرنا *sar-būlan'dī ha'sil kar'nā* V.I. achieve eminence سربمہر *sar ba-moh'r* ADJ. sealed سرپرست *sar-paras't* N.M. guardian patron سرپرستی *sar-paras'tī* N.F. guardianship patronage سرپستان *sar-e pistān* N.M. nipple teat; dug یاران سرپل *yārā'n-e sar-e pūl* N.M. PL. wayside companions faithless friends سرپنچ *sar-panch'* N.M. (arch.) president (joc.) chief سرپوش *sar-posh'* N.M. lid ; cover سرپیچ *sar pech'* N.M. turban ornament worn on it سرتاب ہونا *sar-tāb' ho'nā* V.I. disobey (orders of) سرتابی *sar tā'bī* N.F. refraction سرتابی کرنا *sar-tā'bī kar'nā* V.T disobey (orders of) سرتاپا *sar-tā-pā'* ADV. wholly entirely ; totally from top to toe from top to bottom سرتاج *sar-tāj* N.M. husband (rare.) chief (rare.) crown سرتسلیم خم کرنا (یا ہونا) *sar-e taslīm' kham' kar'nā* (or *ho'nā*) V. obey ; submit سرچشمہ *sar-chash'mah* N.F. fountain head سرحد *sar-had'* N.M. border ; frontier bounds; limits ; bourne former North-West Frontier Province of West Pakistan سرخط *sar'-khat* N.M. lease (of house) receipt (to tenant) deed of agreement سرخوش *sar-khūsh'* ADJ. tipsy ; inebriate سرخوشی *sar-khū'shī* N.F. intoxication سرخیل *sar-khail'* N.M. chief ; leader head of family (old use) troop commander سردار *sardār* N.M. chief leader commander ruler Junior commissioned officer ; J.O.C. سردارنی *sardār'nī* N.F.

chief's consort سرداری sarda'ri N.F. supremacy rule leadership command J.C.O's rank سردست sa'r-e das't ADV. at present right now سردفتر sar-daf'tar N.M. Section Officer office superintendent سردھڑکی بازی لگانا sar' dhar' ke ba'zi laga'na V.I. burn one's boats سرراہ sar-e rah' ADV. on the road by the way سرراہے sar-e ra'he N.M. periodical's humorous column ; by the way ; by the by ADV. by the way in passing سررشتہ sar-rish'tah (col. سرشتہ sarish'tah) department سررشتہ دار sar-rish'ta-dar (col. sarish'-) N.M. (magistrate's) reader سرزد ہونا sar'-zad ho'na V.I. (of crime, mistake, etc.) be committed سرزمین sar-zamin' N.F. country land ; region; territory سرزمین بے آئین sar-zami'n-e be-a'in' N.F. lawless state state of lawlessness سرزنش sar'-za'nish' N.F. snubbing rebuke reproof ; reprimand سرزوری sar-zo'ri N.F. waywardness ; restiveness headstrongness سرسبز sar-sabz' ADJ. verdant fresh flourishing ; prosperous ; thriving سرسبزی sar-sab'zi N.F. verdure freshness ; flourishing state ; prosperity سرشار sar-shar' ADJ. dead-drunk ; inebriate سرشاری sar-sha'ri N.F. intoxication سرشام sa'r-e sham' N.F. early evening سرشام (ہی سے) sa'r-e sham' (hi se) ADV. (from) early in the evening سرقلم کرنا sar qa'lam kar'na V.T. behead سرقلم ہونا sor qa'lam ho'na V.I. be beheaded سرکردہ sar-kar'dah ADJ. prominent سرکردگی sar-kar'dagi N.F. prominence; eminence سرکرنا sar' kar'na V.T. conquer subdue fire (gun, etc.) سرکش sar'-kash ADJ. headstrong refractory wayward ; restive rebellions سرکشی sar'-ka'shi N.F. headstrongness refraction waywardness ; restiveness rebellion سرکشی کرنا sar'-ka'shi kar'na V.T. rebel ; revolt be headstrong be restive سرکوبی sar'-ko'bi N.F. punishment nipping in the bed سرگراں sar'-garan' ADJ. displeased ; angry سرگرانی sar'-gara'ni N.F. irritation ; anger ; displeasure سرگرداں sar'-gardan' ADJ. straying wandering (in search of) perplexed سرگردانی sar'-garda'ni N.F. perplexity amazement confusion wandering (in search of) سرگرم sar-gar'm ADJ. active earnest eager ; zealous ; ardent diligent سرگرمی sar-gar'mi N.F. activity earnestness eagerness ; zeal ; ardour diligence سرگروہ sar-garoh' N.M. ringleader chief سرگذشت sar guzash't N.F. account ; narrative details سرگشتہ sar-gash'tah ADJ. & N.M. bewildered perplexed at (one's) wit's end سرگشتگی sar-gash'-tagi N.F. perplexity bewilderment عالم سرگشتگی میں 'a'lam-e sar-gash'tagi men ADV. bewildered ; in a state of bewilderment سرگوشی sar-go'shi N.F whisper سرگوشیاں کرنا sar-go'shiyan kar'na V.I. whisper speaks in whispers سرمست sar-mas't ADJ. dead-drunk ; inebriate سرمستی sar-mas'ti N.F. intoxication ; being dead drunk سرمشق sar-mash'q N.F original line written by teacher for giving pupils practice in calligraphy سرمغزی sar-magh'zi N.F. deep thought vain bid to drive something home (to) سرمو sa'r-e moo' N.M. & ADV a hair's breadth سرنامہ sar-na'mah N.M. superscription address (on letter) سرنگوں sar-nigoon' ADJ. vanguished (of flag) flying at half-mast with head hanging down in shame سرنوشت sar-navish't N.F. destiny ; fate سرورق sar-var'aq N.M. title (of book) سروسامان sar-o saman' V.I. be a preparation(s) arrangements necessaries سروسامان ہونا sar-o-saman' ho'na V.I. be a preparation (for) سروکار sa'r-o-kar' N.M. concern connection relation سروکار رکھنا sa'r-o-kar' rakh'na V.T. be concerned with سرہونا sar' ho'na V.I. be conquered ; be vanquished be subdued ; be subjugated fall (to) (of gun) be fired pester (someone) with dun impertune ایک سر ہزار سودا ek' sar hazar' sauda' PROV. individual facing a thousand troubles [P]

سر sir', sar N.M. head top pinnacle highest part tip point end سرآنکھوں پر sir' an'khon par INT. certainly ; means ; with pleasure ADV. cordially respectfully سرآنکھوں پر بٹھانا sir' an'khon' par bitha'na V.T. receive ; cordially extend a warm welcome (to) سراٹھاکے چلنا sir' utha' ke chal'na V.I. strut about ; conceitedly have nothing to fear or feel ashamed of سراٹھانا sir' utha'na V.I. rebel سراڑانا (یا اڑادینا) sir' ura'na (or ura' de'na) V.T. behead سراونچا کرنا sir' ooh'cha kar'na V.T. & I. hold one's head high exalt سربھاری ہونا sir' bha'ri ho'na V.I. have a headache feel giddy سربیچنا sir' bech na V.I. jeopardize one's life سرپاؤں پر رکھنا (یا دھرنا) sir' pa''on par rakh'na (or dhar'na) V.I. fall at the feet of سرپاؤں پر رکھ کر بھاگنا sir' pa''on par rakh' kar bhag'na V.I. flee سرپاؤں نہ ہونا sir' pa''on na ho'na V.I. be baseless be unable to make head or tail (of) سرپٹخنا (یا پٹکنا) sir pa'takhna (or pa'takna) V.I. try in vain سرپر sir' par ADV. close at hand سرپرآبننا sir' par (a') ban'na ADV. be in trouble سرپرآرے چلنا sir' par a're chal'na V.I. be in great trouble سرپرآنکھیں نہ ہونا sir' par an'kheh na ho'na V.I. be stupid سرپراجل (یا قضا) کھیلنا sir' par a'jal (or qaza') khel'na V.I. (of death) approach court (death) سرپراٹھالینا sir' par utha' lena V.I. make much noise ; to cause a tumult سرپر(آ) پڑنا sir' par (a') parna V.I. find oneself in trouble be entrusted to سر پر بولنا sir' par bol'na v.i. (of apparition) speak through possessed person سر پر جن چڑھنا (یا سوار ہونا) sir' par jin' charh'nā (or savār' ho'nā) v.i. be possessed fly into a passion سر پر چڑھانا sir' par charhā'na v.t. spoil by over indulgence سر پر چڑھنا sir' par charh'na v.i. be spoilt by kindness behave rudely سر پر چھپر رکھنا sir' par chhap'par rakh'nā v.i. put under debt of gratitude سر پر خاک ڈالنا sir' par khāk' dal'na v.i. mourn ; lamant سر پر خون سوار ہونا sir' par khoon' savār' ho'nā v.i. be mad with murder سر پر خون لینا sir' par khoon' le'na v.i. murder سر پر رکھنا (یا اٹھانا) sir par rakh'na (or uthā'na) v.t. treat with great respect سر پر سوار رہنا (یا ہونا) sir par savar' raih'na (or ho'na) v.t. & i. boom large before pester with سر پر کھڑا ہونا sir par khaṛa ho'nā v.i. be close at hand سر پر گھر (یا زمین) اٹھا لینا sir' par ghar (or zamīn') uṭhā le'nā v.i make much noise make a fuss about سر پر ہاتھ پھیرنا sir' par hath' pher'na v.t. fondle console patronize سر پر ہاتھ رکھنا (یا دھرنا) sir par hath' rakh'nā (or dhar'nā) v.t. foster patronize take under one's protection سر پڑے کا سودا sir pa'ṛe kā sau dā PH. something that cannot be helped سر پکڑ کر رہ جانا sir' pa'kar kar raih' ja'na v.i. be downcast سر پھٹنا sir' phaṭ'nā v.i. have a splitting headache (of head be smashed injure one's head سر پھٹول sir phuṭav'val N.F. quarrell fight wrangle mutual differences سر پھوٹنا sir phooṭ'na v.i. injure one's head (of head) be smashed سر پھرا sir-phi'rā ADJ. mad fanatic سر پھرنا sir' phir'na v.i. go mad be crazy سر پھوڑنا sir phoṛ'na v.t. & i. strike one's head (against) smash (someone's) head سر پیٹنا (یا پیٹ لینا) sir' pīṭ'nā (or pīṭ le'nā) v.i. mourn ; lament give up as lost vent one's rage on oneself سر پیر نہ ہونا sir' pair na ho'nā v.i. be unable to make hear or tail (of) سر پھیرنا sir' pher'nā v.t. disobey (God's orders) سر توڑ sir' toṛ' ADJ. extreme (effort) سر تھام لینا sir' tham le'na v.i. rue ; repine lament سر تھوپنا (یا چپکنا) sir thop'na (or chapak'nā) v.t. lay blame at (other person's) door shift one's responsibility (to) سر جوڑ کر بیٹھنا sir' joṛ' kar baiṭh'nā v.i. (of people join their head together سر جھاڑ منہ پہاڑ sir' jhāṛ munh' pahāṛ' ADV. savagely lamenting untidily with unkempt hair سر جھکانا sir' jhukā'na v.t. bow submit سر چڑھا sir' charhā ADJ. rude audacious spoiled by over-indulgence سر چڑھ کر بولنا sir' charh' kar bol'na v.i. (of apparition) speak through possessed (person) become self-apparent سر چڑھ کر مارنا sir' charh kar mar'na v.i. commit suicide as a protest against سر چکٹنا sir' chi'kaṭ'na v.i. (of head) become sticky سر چوٹ sir choṭ' N.F. (dial.) teasing ADV (dial.) against one's will سر دکھانا sir dikhā'na v.t. get lice picked from (one's) head سر دکھنا sir' dukh'na v.i. have a mild headache سر دھرا sir' dha'rā ADJ. patron سر دھننا sir dhun'na v.i. repine lament grieve over one's trouble enjoy grow ecstatic over سر دھونا sir dho'nā v.i. have a shampoo سر دے دے مارنا sir de' de mar'na v.i. try to kill oneself in desperation سر دینا sir' de'na v.t. die (for the sake of) ; jeopardize one's life (for) سر ڈوب sir'-doob' ADJ. (of water) just deeper than man's stature سر سفید ہونا sir sifed' ho'nā v.i. grow grey ; grow old سر سہرا ہونا sir seh'ra ho'na v.i. be the cause of success سر سہلانا sir saihla'na v.t. pat one's head in shame sawn on سر سے بلا ٹالنا sir se balā' ṭal'na v.i. (of some difficulty) end unexpectedly سر سے بوجھ اتارنا sir se bojh ūtār'na (of responsibility) end سر سے پاؤں تک sir se pā''on tak ADV. from top to bottom ; entirely سر سے پانی گزر جانا sir' se pā'nī gu'zar ja'na v.i. behead over ears (in trouble, etc.) سر سے کفن باندھنا sir se ka'fan bāndh'na v.i. engage in a desperate endeavour سر سے تنکا اتارنے کا احسان ماننا sir' se tin'ka ūtār'ne kā ehsān' mān'nā v.i. be thankful for minor or favour سر سے کھیلنا sir' se khel'nā v.i. of possessed person) shake one's head under the influence of evil spirit die (for) do a brave deed سر سے گزرنا sir' se gu'zarna v.i. despair of one's life سر سینگ ہونا sir sīng' ho'nā v.i (iron.) have a distinctive feature be easy to recognize سر کالا منہ بالا sir kā'lā mūnh bā'la PH. be still young سر کٹا sir' ka'ṭā ADJ. beheaded سر کرنا sir' kar'na v.t. & i. (of women) do her hair entrust (to) سر کھانا sir' khā'na v.i. bother make much noise سر کھپانا sir khapā'nā v.t. & i. rack one's brain bother (someone) سر کھپ جانا sir kh' jā'na v.i. be non-plussed invite trouble try to think سر کھجانے کی فرصت نہ ہونا sir' kh' jā'ne kī fūr'sat na ho'nā v.i. be very busy ; have one's hand full سر کے بل sir' ke bal ADV. headlong; with head foremost; head over heals voluntarily debasing oneself سر گنجا کرنا sir' gan'jā kar'na v.t. beat severely on the head سر گوندھنا sir' goondh'nā v.i. plait one's hair سر گھومنا sir' ghoom'nā v. to suffer from vertigo ; to be of unsound mind سر لگنا sir' lag'nā v.i. be blamed سر (پر) لینا sir' (par) le'na v.t. take (something) upon oneself سر مارنا sir' mar'na v.i. make a strenuous effort take great pains سر منڈاتے ہی اولے پڑنا sir' mūndvā'te hī o'le par'na PROV. misfortune befalling the very first venture سر منڈانا sir' mūndā'nā v.t. get one's head tonsured be duped become a mendicant سر مونڈنا sir' moond'nā v.t. tonsure (someone's) head cheat ; defraud; dupe سر میلا ہونا sir *mai'la ho'nā* V.I. be menstruating سر نہ پیر *sir' na pair'* PH. baseless ; unfounded awkward سر نہوڑانا *sir nahūṛā'na*, سر نیچا کرنا *sir nī'chā kar'nā* V.I. hang down one's head in shame سر ہتھیلی پر لیے پھرنا *sir hathe'lī par li'ye phir'nā* V.I. be ready to lay down one's life

سر *sūr* N.M. tune note music ; melody start of game (at cards) سر ملانا *sūr milā'na* V.T. & I. sing in tune tune attune اونچا سر *ooñ'chā sūr* N.M. major key ; alto بے سر *be-sūr*, بے سرا *be-sū'rā* ADJ. out of tune discordant unmusical دھیما سر *dhī'mā sūr* N.M. tenor ; contralto نیچا سر *nī'chā sūr* N.M. low tone ; bass

سر *sir* (PL. اسرار *asrār'*) secret mystery sacrament [A]

سرا *si'ra* N.M. tip point end beginning top سرے سے *si're se* ADV. at all 'ab initio' : from the beginning [~ سر *sir*]

سرا¹ *sarā* N.F. (same as سرائے N.F. ★)

سرا² *sarā'* SUF. singing singer سرائی *sarā''ī* N.F. singing

سراب *sarāb'* N.M. mirage (fig.) illusion [A]

سراپ *sarāp'* N.M. (dial.) curse [S]

سراپا *sarā'pa* N.M. (see under سر *sar* ★)

سراٹا *sarrā'ṭa* N.M. sound of strong wind

سراج *sirāj'* N.M. lamp [A]

سرادھ *saradh'* N.M. (dial.) funeral obsequies [S]

سراسر *sarā'sar* ADV. (see under ³سر *sar* N.M. ★)

سراسیمگی *sar-āsī'magī* N.F., سراسیمہ *sar-āsī'mah* ADJ. (see under ³سر *sar* ★)

سراغ *surāgh'* N.M. trace track sign سراغرسان *surāgh'-rasāñ'* N.M. detective سراغرسانی *surāgh'-rasā'nī* N.F. detective's job tracing ; tracking search detection سراغ لگانا (یا ڈھونڈنا) *surāgh' lagā'na* (or *ḍhooñḍ'nā*) V.T. detect track trace out search out seek ; discover get a clue (to) سراغ لینا *surāgh' le'nā* V.T. search سراغ ملنا (یا پانا) *surāgh' mil'nā* (or *pā'na*) V. get a clue (to) get an inkling (of) سراغی *surā'ghī* N.M. who tracks detective [P]

سراہنا *sarāh'na* V.T. approve commend praise

سرائے *sarā''e* (also سرا *sarā'*) N.F. inn ; caravanserai temporary abode (fig.) world [P]

سرایت *sirā'yat* N.F. penetration seeping running through سرایت کرنا *sirā'yat kar'nā* V.T. penetrate [A]

سرپٹ *sar'paṭ* N.F. gallop سرپٹ دوڑانا (یا اڑانا) *sar'paṭ dauṛā'nā* (or *ūṛā'nā*) V.T. gallop (one's horse) سرپٹ دوڑنا *sar'paṭ dauṛ'nā* V.I. gallop run at full speed

سرت *sūr't* N.F. consciousness care : attention (to) سرت نہ ہونا (یا رہنا) *sūr't na ho'nā* (or *rajh'nā*) be unconscious be utterly unmindful of

سرجری *sar'jarī* N.F. surgery سرجن *sar'jan* N.M. surgeon [E]

سرخ *sūr'kh* ADJ. red N.M. 'arbus precatorius' seed used as weight سرخباد *sūr'kh-bād'* N.M. erisypelas سرخرو *surkh-roo'* ADJ. successful triumphant honoured fulfilling mission سرخرو ہونا *sur'kh-roo' ho'nā* V.I. succeed سرخروئی *sur'kh-roo''ī* N.F. success triumph honour ; fulfilling a mission سرخ وسفید *sūr'kh-o-sifed'* ADJ. red and white in perfect health blooming with youthful vigour سرخ ہونا *sūr'kh ho'nā* V.I. be red flush with anger سرخہ *sūr'khah*, سرخا *sūr'khā* N.M. roan or bay horse red pigeon (joc.) communist ; red سرخی *sūr'khī* N.F. brick-dust rouge newspaper heading شہ سرخی *shah'-sūr'khī* N.F. banner headline سرخی جمانا (یا قائم کرنا) *sūr'khī jamā'na* (or *qā''m kar'nā*) V.T. give a heading (to) سرخی مائل *sūr'khī mā''il* ADJ. reddish [P]

سرخاب *surkhāb'* N.M. ruddy goose سرخاب کا (کے) پر لگنا *sūrkhāb' kā* (or *ke*) *par' lag'nā* V.I. be exalted win a distinction [P ~ PREC.]

سرد *sar'd* ADJ. cool cold chilled dead listless indifferent ; apathetic dull market lifeless سرد آب *sard-āb'* سرد آبہ *sard-ā'bah* N.M. (arch.) cold cellar cold both cold storage سرد بازاری *sar'd-bāzā'rī* ADJ. slump ; dullness of market سرد جنگ *sar'd jang* N.F. cold war سرد خانہ *sar'd-khā'nah* N.M. cold storage سرد کرنا *sar'd kar'na* V.T. cool chill refrigerate سرد مزاج *sar'd-mizāj'* ADJ. unambitious cold ; apathetic ; indifferent سرد مہر *sar'd-meh'r* ADJ. cold; apathetic; indifferent سرد مہری *sar'd-meh'rī* N.F. coldness, apathy ; indifference سرد ہونا (یا ہو جانا) *sar'd ho'nā* (or *ho jā'nā*) V.I. become cold chilled become apathetic or indifferent die دل سرد ہو جانا *dil-sar'd ho jā'nā* V.I. become apathetic be disgusted [P]

سردہ *sar'dah*, سردا *sar'dā* N.M. musk melon سردئی *sardai'ī* N.M. & ADJ. light green colour

سردی *sar'dī* N.F. colds coolness (slang) cold ; catarrh سردی پڑنا *sar'dī par'nā* V.I. get cold be chilly (of temperature) fall سردی لگنا *sar'dī lag'nā* V.I. feel cold shiver with cold (slang) suffer from cold [P]

سردل *sar'dal* N.M. door lintel

سرسام *sarsām* N.M. delirium ; frenzy

سرسرانا *sursūrā'nā* V.I. shiver with cold

سرسرانا *sarsarā'nā* (of lice, etc.) creep (of leaves, etc.) rustle (of sound) trill produce low trilling sound سرسراہٹ *sarsarā'haṭ* N.F. rustle hiss

سرسری *sar'sarī* ADJ. cursory by the way careless ; displaying lack of attention skipping superficial [~سر]

سرسری *sūr'sūrī* N.F. veewil corn-veewil titillation by creeping of small insects ; creeping sensation

سرسوں *sar'soṅ* N.F. a species of mustard mustard-seed سرسوں کا تیل *sar soṅ kā tel'* N.M. mustard-seed oil سرسوں کی کھلی *sar'soṅ kī khal'lī* N.F. mustard-seed oil cake سرسوں آنکھوں میں پھولنا *sar'soṅ āṅ'khoṅ meṅ phool'nā* V.I. be enraptured be very happy be jaundiced سرسوں پھولنا *sar'soṅ phool'nā* V.I. (of mustard) bloosom سرسوں ہتھیلی پر جمانا *par jamā'nā* V.I. accomplish immediately

سرشار *sar-shar'* ADJ. (see under سر³ *sar* ★)

سرشت *sirish't* N.F. nature ; disposition ; temperament SUF. tempered; disposed سرشتہ *sirish'tah* ADJ. & PREF. kneaded mixed [P ~ سرشتن]

سرشک *sirish'k* N.M. tear [P]

سرطان *sarṭān'* N.M. cancer Cancer (as a sign of Zodiac) (rare) crab خط سرطان *khal't-e sarṭān'* N.M. Tropic of Cancer [A]

سرعت *sūr''at* N.F. swiftness haste ; speed lack of retentive power [A]

سرغنہ *sar'ghanah* N.M. ringleader [P ~ سر]

سرفہ *sūr'fah* N.M. cough [P]

سرقہ *sarqah* (or ped. *sa'riqah*) N.M. plagiarism theft ; larceny

سرقفلی *sar-quf'lī* N.F. advance partial payment of rent [P]

سرکار¹ *sarkār'* N.F. government authority سرکار دربار چڑھنا *sarkār' darbār' chaṛh'nā* V.I. sue go to a court of law سرکاری *sarkā'rī* ADJ. official government State سرکاری درباری *sarkā'rī darbārī* ADJ. official belonging to the government party سرکاری اہلکار (یا ملازم) *sarkā'rī aihl'-kār* (or *mūlā'zim* N.M. government servant [P]

سرکار² *sarkār'* N.F. (title of respect) sir madam miss

سرکس *sar'kas* N.M. circus [E]

سرکل *sar'kal* N.M. circle سرکلر *sar'kūlar* N.M. circular ; instructions circulated [E]

سرکنا *sa'rakna* V.I. slide glide out of the way سرکانا *sarkā'na* V.T. push aside shift remove cause to slide

سرکنڈا *sarkaṅ'dā* N.M. reed

سرکہ *sir kah* N.M. vinegar [P]

سرکی *sir'kī* N.F. reed-screen (used as roofing, etc.) سرکی کا چھپر *sir'kī kā chhap' par* N.F make-shift roof made with it

سرگ *sūr'g* N.M. سرگباشی *sūrgbā'shī* (see under سورگ N.M. ★)

سرگشتگی *sargash'tagī* N.F., سرگشتہ *sargash'tah* ADJ. (see under سر² *sar* N.M.)

سرگم *sar'gam* N.F. gamut nation scale of music

سرگیں *sūr'giṅ* N.M. cowdung [P]

سرما *sar'mā* N.M. winter سرمائی *sarmā''ī* ADJ. winter (clothing, headquarters, etc.) [P]

سرمایہ *sarmā'yah* N.M. capital stock-in-trade funds means سرمایہ دار *sarma'ya-dār'* N.M. & ADJ. capitalist rich (person) سرمایہ دارانہ *sarmā'ya-dāra'nah* ADJ. & ADV. capitalistic سرمایہ داری *sarmā'ya-dā'rī* N.F. capitalism سرمایہ کاری *sarmā ya-kārī* N.F. investment سرمایہ کار *sarmā'ya-kār* ADJ. one who invests ; enterpreneur سرمایہ لگانا *sarmā'ya lagā'nā* V.T. invest capital make an investment [P]

سرمد *sar'mad'* N.M. & ADJ. eternal , everlasting perpetual سرمدی *sar'madī* ADJ. eternal ; perpetual [A]

سرمہ *sūr'mah* N.M. antimony collyrium سرمہ آلود *sūr'ma-ālood'*, سرمہ آلودہ *sūr'ma-āloo'dah*, سرمگیں *sūrmagīṅ'* ADJ. (eyes) stained with antimony or collyrium سرمہ دانی *sūr'me dā'nī* N.F. antimony (or collyrium) container سرمہ ڈھلکنا *sūr'ma dha'laknā* V.I. (of antimony stains) spread (owing to tears, etc.) سرمہ لگانا *sūr'ma lagā'nā* V.T. stain (eyes) with antimony (or collyrium) سرمہ ہو جانا *sūr'ma ho jā'nā* V.I. be reduced to very fine power سرمئی *sūrm''ī* antimony-coloured ; greyish ; ash-coloured [P]

سرنگ *su'rang* N.F. subterranean passage : mine (explosive) mine passage in wall made by burglar N.M. roan or bay horse ADJ. pretty coloured سرنگ اڑانا *su'rang uṛa na* V.I. explode a mine سرنگ لگانا *sū'rang lagā'na* V.I. break into a house mine سرنگیا *su'rangyā* N.M. miner : one who lays down mines

سرو *sar'v* N.M. cypress سروِ آزاد *sar'v-e azād'* N.M. tall cypress سرو اندام *sar'v-andām'* ADJ. with a cypress-like graceful body سروِ چراغاں *sar'v-e chirā'ghāñ* N.M., a kind of cypress سروِ رواں *sar'v-e ravāñ'* ADJ. a kind of cypress sweet heart with a graceful gait سروِ سہی *sar'v-e sehi'* N.M. branched cypress tall and graceful sweetheart سرو قامت *sar'v-qā'mat*, سرو قد *sar'v-qad'* ADJ. tall and graceful [P]

سروپ *saroop'* (ped. *suroop'*) N.F. (dial.) beauty : comeliness دیوتا سروپ *dev'tā-saroop'* ADJ. (dial) beautiful like a deity [S]

سروتا *sarau'tā* N.M. betel-nut cracker nut-cracker

سرود *sarod'* (or *sūrod'*) N.M. music melody song anthem lyre رقص و سرود *raq's-o sūrod'* N.M. dance and music gay life [P]

سرور *suroor'* N.M. joy , delight pleasure : exhilaration slight intoxication سرور آنے لگنا *suroor' ā'ne lag'nā* V.I. begin to grow rapturous begin to feel effect of drink [A]

سرور *sar'var* N.M. sovereign lord master chief سرورِ کائنات *sar'var-e kā'ināt'* N.M. (the Holy Prophet) (as the chief of God's Creation) سروری *sar'varī* N.F. sovereignty. sway overlordship a female name [P]

سروس *sar'vis* N.F. service سروس بک *sar'vis-būk* N.F. service-book [E]

سروش *surosh'* N.M. angel voice (from heaven سروشِ غیب *sūro'sh-e ghaib'* N.M. voice of prophecy [P]

سرون *sar'van* N.M. name of a folk song

سروہی *saro'hī* N.F. a kind of dagger

سرہانا *sirhā'nā, sarhā'nā* N.M. head of the bed head part (of) سرہانے *sirhā'ne* ADV. at the head of the bed N.M. (PL. of سرہانا ★) [~ سر *sir*]

سری *si'rī* N.F. head (of slaughtered animal) as food سری پائے *si'rī pā''e* N.M. PL. head and feet (of slaughtered animal) as food their stew

سری *si'rī* (ped. *srī*) N.M. (same as سری N.M. ★)

سری راگ *si'rī rāg'* (or *srī'-*) N.M. one of the major modes of classical of Indo-Pakistan music connected with midwinter [S]

سریانی *suryā'nī* N.F. Syriac.; Syriac language ADJ. Syriac [A]

سریر *sarīr'* N.M. throne (rare) bad سریر آرائے سلطنت ہونا *sarī'r-ārā'e sal'tanat ho'nā* V.I. ascend the throne سریرِ سلطنت *sarī'r-e sal'tanat* N.M. throne [A]

سریر *sarīr'* N.M. (dial.) body [S]

سریش *saresh'* N.M. glue [P]

سریع *sarī'* ADJ. fast ; quick ; swift nimble سریع التاثیر *sarī'' ūl-tāsīr'* ADJ. (of drug prayer, etc.) quick to produce desired effect سریع الفہم *sarī''-ūl-fah'm* (col. *-faih'm*) ADJ. quick-witted perspicacious سریع الہضم *sarī''-ūl-haz'm* ADJ. easy to digest [A]

سریلا *sūrī'lā*, ADJ. (F. سریلی *sūrī'lī*) melodious musical

سرین *sūrīn'* N.F. buttocks [P]

سڑ *siṛ* N.F. madness craze سڑن *si'ṛan* N.F. & ADJ. mad woman crazy (woman) سڑی *si'ṛī* N.M. & ADJ. mad crazy سڑی سودائی *siṛī saudā''ī* N.M. & ADJ. mad man crazy (person)

سڑا *sa'ṛā* ADJ., سڑانا *saṛā'nā* V.T., سڑاند *sarāñd* N.F. (see under سڑنا V.I. ★)

سڑا سڑ *sa'ṛā saṛ'* ADV. (of whip, blows, etc.) continuously raining

سڑاپا *saṛap'pā* N.M. large sip سڑاپا لگانا *saṛap' pā lagā'nā* V.T. take a very large sip finish off at a draught

سڑسٹھ *saṛ'saṭh*, سرسٹھ *sar'saṭh* ADJ. & N.M. sixty-seven سڑسٹھواں *saṛ'saṭhvāñ* سرسٹھواں *sar' saṭhvāñ* ADJ. sixty-seven

سڑسڑ *sūṛ'sūṛ* N.F. sound of hookah'

سڑک *sa'ṛak* N.F. road سڑک بنانا *sa'ṛak banā'nā* V.T. build a road سڑک کاٹنا *sa'ṛak kāṭ'nā* V.I. build a road (through)

سڑکنا *su'ṛaknā* V.I. gulp down with a splash

سڑکی *suṛ'kī* N.F. large sip sudden slackening of kite string

سڑن *si'ṛan* N.F. & ADJ. (see under سڑ *siṛ* N.F. ★

سڑنا *saṛ'nā* V.I. rot putrefy decompose سڑا *sa'ṛā* ADJ. (F. سڑی *sa'ṛī*) rotten putrefied decomposed گلا سڑا ga'la sa'ṛa ADJ. (F. گلی سڑی ga'lī sa'ṛī) rotten putrefied decomposed سڑانا saṛa'na V.T. cause to rot cause to decompose سڑاند saṛand' N.F. stench of rotting thing سڑیل saṛ'yal ADJ. peevish rotten

سڑی siṛī N.M. & ADJ. (see under سڑ siṛ N.F. ★)

سڑی sa'ṛī ADJ., سڑیل saṛ'yal ADJ. (see under سڑنا V.I. ★)

سزا sazā' N.F. punishment penalty retribution ; requital chastisement سزا پانا sazā' pā'nā V.I. be punished سزا دینا sazā' de'na V.T. 1 punish penalize chastise سزایاب sazā'-yāb' سزا یافتہ sazā'-yāf tah ADJ. & N.M. punished or penalized (person) سزایاب ہونا sazā'-yāb' ho'nā V.I. be punished

سزاوار sazāvar' ADJ. worthy (of) deserving; meriting سزاوار ہونا sazā var' ho'nā V.I. deserve ; merit [P]

سزاول sazā'-val N.M. (arch.) rent-collector tax-collector سزاولی sazā'valī N.F. (arch.) tax-collection tax-collector's job [T]

سست sūs't ADJ. slow tardy slothful dull ; sluggish inactive lazy ; idle ; indolent feeble (rare) loose ; lax (rare) infirm ; weak سست اعتقاد sūs't-e-'tiqād' ADJ. incredulous sceptical سست بنیاد sūs't-būnyād' ADJ. infirm unstable shaky سست پیماں sūs't-paimān' N.M. & ADJ. fickle ; capricious سست رفتار sūs't-raftār' ADJ. slow beggard سست کرنا sūs't kar'nā V.I. slow down make lazy make sluggish سست ہونا sūs't ho'nā V.I. be lazy be somewhat unwell سستی sūs'tī N.F. laziness ; idleness ; indolence slowness سستی کرنا یا سے کام لینا sūs'tī kar'nā (or se kām' le'nā) N.M. delay ; procrastinate be tardy be lazy [P]

سستا sas'tā ADJ. (F. سستی sas'tī) cheap inexpensive worthless سستا چھوٹنا sas'tā chhooṭ'-na V.I. be rid (rare) sell at a cheap rate ; be sold for a pittance سستا روئے بار بار مہنگا روئے ایک بار sas'ta ro''e bār' bār maihn'gā ro''e ek bār' PROV. expensive things may be difficult to buy but cheap stuff is a permanent unisance سستی بھیڑ کی ٹانگ بار بار اٹھا کر دیکھتے ہیں sa'stī bher kī ṭāng' bār bār' ūṭhā' kar dekh'te hain PROV. cheapness makes worth suspicious look a gift horse in the mouth

سستانا sastā'nā V.I. rest have a respite repose lie down a while

سسر sūs'ar (dial. sa'sūr) N.M. father-in-law سسرا sūs'rā (dial. sa'sūrā) N.M. (rare) father-in-law (mild abuse) the devilish person سسرال sūsrāl' (dial. sasūrāl') N.F. in-laws' family in-laws' house سسرال کا کتا sūsrāl' kā kūt'tā N M one who sponges on his in-laws سسرالیا sūsrā'lıyā ADJ. of in-laws سسری sus'rī) (dial. sa'sūrī) N.F. (rare) mother-in-law (mild abuse) the devilish person [~ ساس sās N.F. ★]

سسکارنا sūskār'na V.T. & I. sibilate do so to help sleeping child make water (of snake) hiss urge (dog) to fly (at someone) سسکاری sūskā'rī N.F. sole sound emitted for letting dog fly at someone hiss to urge sleeping child to urinate

سسکنا si'saknā V.I. sob be at the last gasp lead a miserable life سسک سسک کر si'sak si'sak kar ADV. with great difficulty in much trouble very miserably سسکی si'skī N.F. sob سسکیاں بھرنا si'skiyān bhar'nā V.I. sob

سشن si'shan سشن کورٹ si'shan-kor'ṭ N.F. Session Court سشن جج si'shan jaj N.M. Sessions Judge [E]

سطح sat'ḥ N.F. surface plane سطح مرتفع sat'h-e mūr'tafa' N.F. plateau سطح مستوی sat'ḥ-e mūs'tavī N.M. level ground flat plane سطحی sat'ḥī ADJ. superficial trivial سطحی بات sat'ḥī bāt' N.F. (usu. PL.) triviality superficial comment [A]

سطر sat'r (col. sa'tar) N.F. (PL. سطور sūtoor') line ruling lineament row rank سطر بندی sat'r-ban'dī N.F. ruling [A]

سطوت sat'vat N.F. majesty (rare) assault شاہانہ سطوت shāhā'na sat'vat N.F. royal majesty [A]

سطور sūtoor' N.F. (PL. of سطر N.F. ★)

سعادت sa'ā'dat N.F. good fortune felicity auspiciousness سعادتمند sa'ā'dat-mand ADJ. dutiful fortunate obedient سعادتمندی sa'ā'dat-man'dī N.F. dutifulness obedience good fortune [A]

سعایت se'ā'yot N.F. backbiting [A]

سعد sa''d ADJ. auspicious fortunate N.M. félicity good fortune سعد اکبر sa''d-e ak'bar N.M. Jupiter سعدین sa'dain' N.M. PL. Jupiter and Venus سعد ونحس sa''d-o nah's N.M. PL. the auspious and the ominous قران السعدین qira'n-ūs-sa'dain' N.M. conjunction of Jupiter and Venus meeting of two auspicious persons سعید sa'īd ADJ. & N.M. fortunate folicitous auspicious [A]

سعی sa''y (col. sa''ī) N.F. effort attempt ; endeavour enterprise (rare) running سعی کرنا sa''y kar'nā V.T. try attempt deavour strive سعی لاحاصل sa''y-e lā-ḥa'sil N.F. vain attempt ; futile endeavour سعی وسفارش sa''y-o sifā'rish N.F. recommendation great effort سعی ہونا sa''y ho'na V.I. be endeavoured (of attempt); be made [A]

سعید sa'īd' ADJ. (see under سعد N.M. ★)

سعیر sa'īr' N.F. name of one of the seven parts of hell hell fire [A]

سفارت sifā'rat N.M. diplomatic mission . embassy ; embassadorial assignment representation ; going about as a representative سفارت خانہ sifā'rat-khā'nah N.M. Embassy [A]

سفارش sifā'rish N.F. recommendation intercession influence سفارش کرنا sifā'rish kar'na V.T. recommend (someone or someone's case) سفارشی چٹھی sifā'rishi chiṭ'ṭhī N.F. letter of recommendation سفارشی ٹٹو sifā'ri'shi ṭaṭ'too N.M. undeserving person ; getting a job through an influential person's interest [P]

سفاک saffāk' N.M. & ADJ. blood-shedder tyrant cruel (ruler) butcher [A ~ سفک]

سفال sifāl' N.M. potsherd earthenware سفالیں sifā'līn ADJ. earthen جامِ سفال (یا سفالیں) jā'm-e sifāl' (or sifālīn) N.M. earthen goblet [P]

سفاہت sifā'hat N.F. foolishness stupidity folly [A]

سفتہ saf'tah N.M. (rare.) bill of exchange [P]

سفتہ sūf'tah ADJ. pierced (pearl) perforated bored ناسفتہ nā-suf'tah unpierced (pearl) dur'(r)e nā-suf'tah N.M. unpierced pearl (fig.) virgin [P ~ سفتن]

سفر sa'far N.M. (PL. اسفار asfār', سفرہا sa'far-hā) journey voyage travel air travel ; flight departure سفر ہونا sa'far ho'na V.I. have to undertake a journey سفر خرچ sa'far-khar'ch N.M. travelling allowance T.A. سفر کا خرچ sa'far kā khar'ch N.M. travelling expenses سفر کرنا sa'far kar'na V.I. travel journey ; go on a journey undertake a voyage fly (from or to) depart سفرنامہ sa'far-nā'mah N.M. account of (one's) travels travelogue سفری sa'farī ADJ. travel portable N.M. traveller [A]

سفرجل safar'jal N.M. quince [A]

سفرمینا sa'far mai'nā N.M. sappers and miners [corr. of E]

سفلہ sif'lah ADJ. mean ; base ; low ignoble contemptible ; despicable envious petty-minded سفلہ پرور sif'la-par'var ADJ. & N.M. one patronizing mean persons سفلہ پروری sif'la par'varī N.F. patronage extended to mean persons سفلہ پن sif'la-pan N.M. meanness . baseness سفلہ خو sif'la-khoo ADJ. of mean disposition puny hearted petty-minded

سفلی sif'lī ADJ. inferior infernal سفلی عمل sif'lī 'a'mal N.M. occult influence supposedly wrought through evil spirits [A]

سفوف soof' N.M. powder [A]

سفید sifed, (col. s'faid), سپید siped' ADJ. white snow white grey (hair) blank or unwritten (paper, etc.) سفید پوش sufaid-posh N.M. & ADJ. white-collared (worker) cleanly dressed person (person) with a sense of respectability officially-recognized respectable person from among the masses gentleman from the lower middle classes ; gentleman سفید پوشی sifed'-po'shī N.F. respectability (lower) middle class standard of living سفید پوشی قائم رکھنا sifed'-po'shī qā''im rakh'nā V.I. try to look respectable ; try to maintain middle class living standards سیاہ و سفید siyā'h-o-sifed' N.M. everything good points (of) ADJ. red and white سیاہ و سفید کا مالک ہونا siyā'h-o sifed' kā mālik ho'nā V.I. enjoy full power (over) لہو سفید ہونا la'hoo sifed ho'na V.I. be ungrateful سفیدہ sufai'dah, (or sife'dah) N.M. white poplar white lead dish of) sweet boiled rice a species of buff-skinned mango سفیدہ صبح sife'da-e sūb'h N.M. streak of dawn سفیدی sufe'dī (or sife'dī) N.F. whiteness white-washing light ; day-light white (of egg) سفیدی پھیرنا (یا کرنا) sufai'dī pher'nā (or kar'nā) V.T. white-wash [P]

سفیر safīr' N.M. ambassador envoy touring agent or representative [A ~ سفارت]

سفینہ safī'nah N.M. (PL. سفن sū'fūn, سفائن safā''in) ship ; vessel ; boat commonplace-book ; a notice ; summons

سفیہ safīh' ADJ. & N.M. (PL. سفہا s'fahā') foolish ; stupid dunce [A ~ سفاہت]

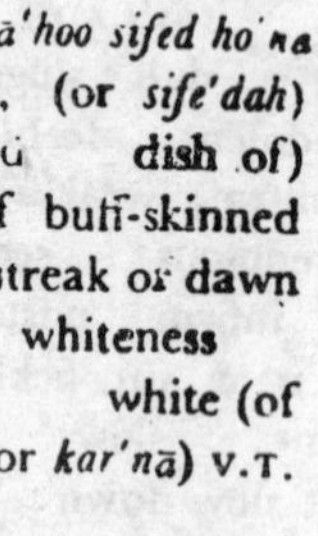

سقا saqqā' (col. سقہ saq'qah) N.M. wate-carrier [A ~ سقایت]

سقاوہ saqā'vah N.M. small public bath [A]

سقاوہ

سقر sa'qar N.M. severest part of hell hell-fire [A]

سقف saqf N.F. roof ceiling canopy sky platform [A]

سقم sūq'm N.M. (PL. اسقام asqām') flaw defect (rare.) disease سقم نکالنا sūq'm nikāl'na V.T. find fault with سقیم saqīm' N.M. & ADJ sick ailing (person) diseased infirm faulty worthless [A]

سقمونیا *saqmoo'nyā* N.M. scammony ; dried juice of 'convolvulus skammonia, [A ~ G]

سقنقور *saqanqoor'* N.M. skink [A]

سقوط *suqoot'* N.M. fall; capitulation defeat falling off [A]

سقیم *saqīm'* ADJ. & N.M. (see under N.M. ★)

سکارنا *sakār'nā* V.T. accept (bill of exchange) undertake responsibility سکار *sakār'* N.F. acceptance (of bill of exchange)

سکال *sūkāl'* N.M. good times times of economic prosperity times of cheapness

سکان *sūkkān'* N.M. PL. residents ; inhabitants N.M. rudder ; helm [A ~ SING. ساکن]

سکاؤٹ *sakā''ūṭ* N.M. scout سکاؤٹنگ *sakā''ūṭing* N.M. scouting [E]

سکت *sa'kat* N.F. strength stamina power of resistance

سکتر *sikat'tar* N.M. (col.) secretary سکتری *sikat'tarī* N.F. secretary's office [~ E CORR.]

سکتہ *sak'tah* N.M. a kind of swoon hardly distinguishable from death ; deathswoon consternation unmetrical سکتہ پڑنا *sak'tah paṛ'nā* V.I. have unmetrical caesura ; be unmetrical سکتہ ہونا *sak'tah ho'nā* V.I. fall into deathswoon سکتہ طاری ہونا *sak'tah tā'rī ho'nā* V.I. be struck with consternation سکتے کا عالم *sak'te kā 'ālam* N.M. consternation [A ~ سکون]

سکر *sūk'r* N.M. intoxication liquor ; alcoholic drink [A]

سکرات *sakarāt'* N.F. agony (of death) strong fit (of fainting) سکرات موت *sakarā't-e maut'* N.F. last gasps agony of death [A ~ سکر]

سکڑدادا *sa'kaṛ-dā'dā* N.M. paternal great grandfather's father

سکڑنا *sū'kaṛnā* V.I. shrink contract tighten up shrival dwindle feel chilly سکڑا ہوا *sūk'ṛā (hu'ā)* (F.) سکڑی ہوئی *sūk'ṛī (hū''ī)* ADJ. shrink shrivelled contracted thin ; lean

سکنا *sak'nā* AUX. V. can be able to

سکنا *sik'nā* V.I be toasted [~ سینکنا]

سکنجبین *sikanjabīn'* N.F. ❶ freshly prepared lime juice cordial ❷ acid syrup [P]

سکندر *sikan'dar*, اسکندر *iskan'dar* N.M. Alexander سکندری *sikan'darī* ADJ. pertaining to Alexander N.F. ❶ tripping up ❷ stumbling (of horse) سکندری کھانا *sikan'darī khā'nā* V.I. trip up (of horse) trimble [P ~ G]

سکنہ *sa'kanah* N.M. PL. residents ; inhabitants N.M. (col.) (usu. *sak'nah*) resident of [A ~ SING. ساکن]

سکوت *sukoot'* N.M. reticence quietness ; silence peace calm ; tranquillity [A]

سکورہ *sakọ'rah* N.M. earthen cup

سکوڑنا *sakoṛ'nā* V.T. (same as سکیڑنا V.T. ★)

سکول *sakool'*, اسکول *iskool'* N.M. school سکول ماسٹر *sakool' mās'ṭar* N.M. schoolmaster [E]

سکون *sūkoon'* N.M. state of rest respite motionlessness peace calm ; tranquility allevation ; end of restlessness [A]

سکونت *sūkoo'nat* N.F. residence dwelling سکونت پذیر ہونا *sūkoo'nat-pazīr' ho'nā* V.I. reside ; take up residence (at or with) [A]

سکہ *sik'kah* N.M. coin coining die lead سکہ بٹھانا *sik'kah biṭhā'nā* V.T. establish (one's) prestige overawe bring (a people or country) under one's rule سکہ بنانا *sik'kah banā'nā* V.T. coin money mint coins سکہ جمانا *sik'kah jamā'nā* V.I. establish (one's) prestige سکہ زن *sik'ka-zan* N.M. coiner; mint master جعلی سکہ *ja''lī sik'kah* N.M. base, spurious or counterfeit coin رائج الوقت سکہ *rā''ij-ul-vaq't sik'kah* N.M. current coin [A]

سکھ *sikh* N.M. Sikh سکھنی *sikh'nī* N.F. Sikh woman [~ سیکھنا]

سکھ *sūkh* N.M. comfort ease easy circumstances solace relief happiness affluence leisure peace of mind tranquillity سکھ پال *sūkh-pāl'* N.F. (arch.) sedan chair سکھ پانا *sūkh' pā'nā* V.I. know comfort get relief سکھ تلا *sūkh-ta'lā* N.M. inner soul سکھ چین *sūkh'-chain* N.M. easy circumstances life of ease leisure and pleasure سکھ کی نیند *sūkh kī nīnd'* N.F. sound sleep carefree sleep سکھ کی نیند سونا *sūkh' kī nīnd' so'nā* V.I. have a carefree sleep

سکھی *sū'khī* ADJ. & N.M. (one) living in easy circumstances (one) enjoying good relations سکھی رہنا *sū'khī raih'nā* V.I. live in easy circumstances enjoy good relations سکھ میں ADV. in peace in comfort comfortably

سکھانا *sukhā'nā* V.T. dry up dehydrate evaporate [~ سوکھنا CAUS.]

سکھانا *sikhā'nā*, سکھلانا *sikhlā'nā* V.T. teach instruct tutor (witness) سکھلائی *sikhlā''ī* N.F. training teaching instruction ; for schooling instructional charges [~ سیکھنا CAUS.]

سکھی *sa'khī* N.F. (arch.) woman's female friend ,

companion

سکیڑنا *sūkeṛ'na* V.T. shrink shrivel contract gather up tighten [~ سکڑنا CAUS.]

سگ *sag* N.M. (lit.) dog سگِ بازاری *sag-e baza'rī* N.M. stray dog سگ باش برادرِ خرد مباش *sag' bash' bira'dar-e khūr'd ma-bā'sh* PROV better be a dog than a younger brother [P]

سگا *sa'ga*, ADJ. (F. سگی *sa'gī*) born of the same parents full uterine sincere

سگار *sigar'* N.M. cigar سگار کش (یا نوش) *sigar'-kash* (or *nosh'*) N.M. & ADJ. (one) who puffs at or smokes a cigar سگارکشی (یا نوشی) *sigar'-kashī* (or *no'shī*) puffing at or smoking a cigar [E]

سگائی *saga''ī* N.F. betrothal سگائی کرنا *saga''ī kar'na* V.T. betroth affiance سگائی ہونا *saga''ī ho'na* V.T. be betrothed ; be affianced

سگرئی *sūgra''ī* N.F. name of a musical mode timed for forenoon [S]

سگند *sūgand'* N.F. (arch.) perfume ; fragrance [~ گندھ]

سگھڑ *sū'ghaṛ* ADJ. accomplished (girl) well-versed in housekeeping سگھڑاپا *sūghṛa'pa*, سگھڑپن *sū'ghaṛ-pan* N.M. accomplishment expertness in housekeeping

سِل[1] *sil* N.F. slab this used for grinding سینے پر سل رکھنا *sī'ne par sil rakh'na* V.I. endure patiently

سِل[2] *sil* N.F. consumption ; pulmonary tuberculosis [A]

سلاجیت *salajīt'* N.F. storax

سلاح *silaḥ'* N.F. (PL. اسلحہ *as'leḥah*) weapon; implement of war سلاح بند *silaḥ-band* ADJ. armed سلاح خانہ *silaḥ'-kha'nah*, اسلحہ خانہ *as'leḥah kha'nah* N.M. arsenal ; armoury سلاح دار *silaḥ-dar* N.M. armourer

سلاخ *salakh'* N.M. iron bar spit

سلاست *sala'sat* N.F. plain words simple style ; simplicity of style سلیس *salīs'* ADJ. ★ [A]

سلاسل *sala'sil* N.F. PL. chains [A ~ SING. سلسلہ]

سلاطین *salatīn* N.M. PL. sovereigns monarchs; kings emperors [A ~ SING. سلطان]

سلام *salam* N.M. salutation greeting wishes regards compliments good (etc.) peace blessings ; benediction concluding act of prayers INT. farewell (to) ; better be rid (of) سلام پھیرنا *salam' pher'na* V.I. finish (one's) prayers سلام پیام *salam payam'* N.M. discourse talk , conversation سلام دینا (یا کہنا) *salam de'na* (or *kaih'na*) V.I. wish , send one's compliments (to) (of officer) send for (assistant) سلام وعلیکم *sala'mo 'alai'kūm* (or -*ma*-) (col. for *sala'mūn 'alai'kūm*) N.M. good morning (etc.) PL. peace be with you سلام کرنا *salam' kar'na* V.T. salute wish ; greet quit , get rid of سلام لینا *salam' le'na* V.I. return salutation (of) سلام ہونا *salam ho'na* V.I. be better rid of سلام ہے *salam' hai* INT. I am better rid of you (etc.) (iron.) what a wonderful person [A]

سلامت *sala'mat* ADJ. & ADV. safe surviving سلامت روی *sala'mat-ra'vī* N.F. good conduct moderate way of life صحیح سلامت *saḥīḥ' sala'mat* ADJ. & ADV. safe and sound سلامتی *sala'matī* N.F. safety security well-being health good health سلامتی کا جام پینا *sala'matī ka jam' pī'na* V.I. drink to the health (of) ; drink a health ; toast [A]

سلامی *sala'mī* N.F. guard of honour presentation of arms salute of guns present made to bride, etc. present made to landlord for lease (in construction work) slope [~ A]

سلائی[1] *sila''ī* N.F. seam stitching stitching charges needlework [~ سینا ~ سلانا]

سلائی[2] *sala''ī* N.F. knitting needle appliance for the staining eyes with collyrium ; staining needle (آنکھوں میں) سلائی پھیر دینا (*āṅ'khoṅ meṅ*) *sala''ī pher' de'na* V.T. blind (the eyes)

سلانا[1] *sila'na* V.T. cause to sew get stitched [~ سینا CAUS.]

سلانا[2] *sūla'na* V.T. put to sleep lull to sleep kill ; murder [~ سونا CAUS.]

سلب *sal'b* N.M. seizure taking away divesting ; taking away negation (logic) negative argument سلب کر لینا *sal'b kar le'na* V.T. divest (someone) of power, etc. [A]

سلپچی *si'lapchī* N.F. (same as سلفچی N.F. ★)

سلجھانا *sūljha'na* V.I. solve (problem) settle (dispute, etc.) unrevel disentangle teach manners make cultured سلجھاؤ *sūljha''o* N.M. unravelling disentanglement solution (of problem) settlement (of dispute) manners culture سلجھنا *sū'lajhna* V.I. learn manners become cultured be unravelled be disentangled (of problem) be solved (of dispute) be settled

سلح *si'laḥ* N.M. weapon of war ? armour سلح پوش *si'laḥ-posh'*, سلح شور *si'laḥ-shor'* ADJ. armoured N.M. soldier [A]

سلخ *sal'kh* N.M. last day of lunar month [A]

سلس البول *sa'las-ul-baul'* N.M. morbid copiousness of urine [A]

سلسبیل *salsabil'* N.F name of a heavenly spring or stream [A]

سلسلانا *salsala'na* V.T. & I. have a creeping sensation tingle itch titillation سلسلاہٹ *salsala'hat* N.F. creeping sensation tingle itch titillation

سلسلہ *si'lsilah* N.M. (PL. سلسلہ ہا *si'lsila-ha'*) series link succession arrangement class ; category connexion saintly line (PL. سلاسل *sala'sil*) chains سلسلہ جنبانی *si'lsila-jumba'ni* N.F. setting the ball rolling cutting the ice سلسلہ نکالنا *si'lsilah nikal'na* V.I. begin be the means of سلسلہ وار *si'lsila-var* ADJ. consecutive serial ; serially arranged serialized linked together [A]

سلطان *sultan'* N.M. (PL. سلاطین *salatin'*) sovereign, monarch ; ruler emperor (rare) authority سلطانہ *sulta'nah* N.F. queen empress سلطانی *sulta'ni* ADJ. princely royal , regal N.F sovereignty empire dominion authority سلطانی جمہور *sulta'ni-e jumhoor'* N.F. people's government sovereignty of the peoples سلطانی گواہ *sulta ni gavah'* N.M. crown witness , approver سلطنت *sal'tanat* N.F. realm dominion kingdom empire [A]

سلف *sa'laf* N.M. (PL. اسلاف *aslaf''*) ancient people predecessors ancestors , ADJ. old ; ancient former ; poet ; preceding [A]

سلف *sul'f* N.M. (adjunct for سودا *sau'da* N.M. ★)

سیلف گورنمنٹ *sail'f-gaurmint* N.F. selfgovernment local selfgovernment [E]

سلفہ *sul'fah*, سلفا *sul'fa* N.M. hemp extract (smoked as drug) tobacco enough for one smoke in 'hookah' سلفہ پینا *sul'fah pi'na* V.I smoke hemp extract سلفہ ہونا *sul'fah ho'na* V.I. be destroyed come to nought

¹سلک *sil'k* N.F. silk [E]

²سلک *sil'k* N.F. (rare) thread لاسلکی *la-sil'ki* N.M. & ADJ. wireless [A]

سلگنا *su'lagna* V.I. burn without smoke or flame kindle سلگانا *sulga'na* V.T. light (a fire) kindle stir (trouble)

سلم *sa'lam* N.M. advance payment بیع سلم *bai''-e sa'lam* N.F. sale agreement by advance payment [A]

سلمہ *sal'mah* N.M. tiny embroidery spring سلمہ ستارہ *salmah sita'rah* N.M. tiny springs and spangles embroidery with it

¹سلمیٰ *sal'ma* N.F. a female name this as a token name for beloved in verse, etc.

سلنا *sal'na* V.I. be pierced be bored [~ سالنا]

سلنا *sil'na*, سل جانا *sil ja'na* V.I. be sewn be stitched سلوانا *silva'na* V.T cause to sew get stitched سلوائی *silva''i* N.F. remuneration for sewing ; stitching charges [~ سینا]

سلوتری *salo'tari* N.M. veterinary surgeon

سلوٹ *sil'vat* N.F. crease fold سلوٹ پڑنا *sil'vat par'na* V.I. not to be smooth crease سلوٹ ڈالنا *sil'vat dal'na* V.I. cause to crease

سلوک *sulook'* N.M. behaviour treatment kindness civility good terms good turn mystic initiation سلوک سے رہنا *sulook' se raih'na* V.I. have cordial relations be at peace with be on good terms سلوک کرنا *sulook' kar'na* V.T treat kindly do good turn (to) [A]

سلولائیڈ *sa'lola-id* N.M. celluloid [E]

سلونا *salo'na* ADJ. salted dark complexioned but attractive charming (beauty) N.M. savoury salt dish سلونی *salo'ni* ADJ. seasoned complexioned but attractive N.F brunette

سلوا *sal'va* N.M quail (only in) من و سلویٰ *man'n-o sal'va* N.M. manna and quail heavenly gift easily obtained food [A]

سلہج *sal'haj*, *sa'laj* N.F. brother-in-law's wife sister-in-law [~ سالا]

سلی *sil'li* N.F. hone grain and chaff on threshing floor before winnowing

سلیپر *sali'par* N.M. slipper [E]

سلیٹ *salet'* N.F. slate [E]

سلیس *salis'* ADJ. easy to understand plain (words) simple (style)

سلیقہ *sali'qah* N.M. house-keeping skill observance of rules of etiquette good manners dexterity nice arrangement good taste سلیقہ شعار *sali'qa-she'ar'*, سلیقہ مند *sali'qa-mand* (rare سلیقہ دار *sali'qa-dar'*) ADJ. good house-keeper well mannered skilful cultured سلیقہ شعاری *sali'qa-she'a'ri*, سلیقہ مندی *sali'qa-man'di*, سلیقہ داری *sali'qa-da'ri* N.F. (same as سلیقہ N.M. ★)

سلیم *salim'* ADJ. perfect healthy right سلیم الطبع *sali'm-ut-tab'* ADJ. right-minded affable سلیم شاہی جوتا *salim'shahi joo'ta* N.M. old type embroidered shoe with painted toe [A ~ سلامت]

سم *sum* N.M. poison ; venom ; bane سم الفار *sam'm-ul-far'* N.M. arsenic سمیت *sammiy'yat* N.F. poison poisonous nature banefulness [A]

سم sam N.M. tune of music سم تال sam'-tāl' time of music سم تال سے دور ست sam'-tāl' se dūras't PH. not out of gear

سم sum N.M. hoof

سما sa'ma N.M. (same as سماں N.M. ★)

سما samā' N.M. (PL. سماوات samāvāt') sky ; the heavens , firmament سماوی samā'vī ADJ. celestial heavenly آفات سماوی āfā't-e samā'vī N.F. PL. calamities acts of God [A]

سماج samāj N.M. (dial F.) society سماجی samā'jī ADJ. social سماجی برائیاں samā'jī būrā''iyāñ N.F. social evils [S]

سماجت samā'jat N.F. adulation منت سماجت min'nat samā'jat N.F. imploration and adulation (منت) سماجت کرنا (min'nat) samā'jat kar'na V.T. (entreat and) adulate [A]

سماحت samā'hat N.F. generosity [A]

سمادھ samādh', سمادھی samā'dhī N.F tomb where (someone's) ashes are buried tomb of a Hindu saint buried alive at own request [S]

سمادھی samā'dhī N.F. (dial.) mystic contemplation (same as سمادھ ★) سمادھی لگانا samā'dhī lagā'na V.I. (dial.) (of Hindu ascetic) be absorbed in contemplation [S]

سماع samā'' N.M. music listening to music , audition وجد سماع vaj'd-e samā'' N.M. ecstacy caused by music سماعت samā''at N.F sense of hearing ; audition listening hearing (of a case) date of hearing سماعت کرنا samā''at kar'na V.I. hear a case ; try a suit سماعی samā''ī ADJ. (gram.) irregular (formation) traditional based on hearsay

سماق samāq N.M. porphyry [A]

سماں sa'māñ, سما sa'ma, (dial سمے sa'me N.M. weather conditions ; weather atmosphere ecstatic state سماں باندھنا sa'māñ bāndh'nā V.I. create a delectable atmosphere enrapture

سمانا samā'na, سماجانا samā' jā'na V.I. be accomodated (in) disappear (in) become a part (of) possess ; obsess die سمائی samā''ī N.F. accommodation (for). access (to)

سماوات samāvāt' N.M. (PL. of سما N.M. ★)

سماوار samāvār' N.M. samovar P . R]

سماوی samā'vī ADJ. (see under سما N.M. ★)

سمائی samā''ī N.F. (see under سمانا V.I ★)

سمت sam't (coll. sim't, N.F. direction سمت الراس sam't-ūr-rās' N.F. Zenith [A]

سمت sam'mat, سمبت sam'bat N F. (dial.) Hindu era [S]

سمٹنا si'maṭna V.I. draw close together contract gather rejoin concentrate (of work) end ; get finished

سمجھ sa'majh N.F. commonsense understanding comprehension discernment (one's) lights discretion سمجھ آنا sa'majh ā'na V.I. grow to years of direction become sensible سمجھ بوجھ sa'majh boojh' N.F. commonsense understanding سمجھ پر پتھر پڑنا sa'majh par pat'thar paṛ'na V I. be an arrant fool be too stubborn to realize the exigency of the situation سمجھ جانا sa majh jā'na V.I. understand mend one's ways سمجھدار sa'majh-dār' ADJ sensible intelligent سمجھ کا پھیر sa'majh ka pher' N.M. folly stupidity perverse understanding سمجھ کے sa'majh ke ADV sensibly ; intelligently سمجھ لینا sa'majh le'na V.I. understand well سمجھ میں آنا sa'majh meñ ā'na V.I. (of someone) understand become clear (to) سمجھنا sa'majhnā V.I. understand comprehend think ; consider deem believe . suppose take a lesson from others or something (سے سمجھنا se samajh'nā) take a revenge from ; teach (someone) a lesson سمجھے sam'jhe INT. do you see the point or game ? have you learnt a lesson now سمجھانا samjhā'na V.I. make (something) clear (to) advise explain teach ; instruct drive home (to) convince account for ; satisfy warn admonish tutor (witness) سمجھانا بجھانا samjhā'na b-jhā'na V.T. advise admonish appease سمجھوتا samjhau'tā, سمجھوتہ samjhau'tah N.M. compromise understanding (between) pact alliance

سمدھی sam'dhī N.M. father-in-law (of someone's) child سمدھیانہ samdhiyā'nah N.M. family or house of parents-in-law (of someone's child) سمدھن sam'dhan N.F. mother-in-law (of someone's child

سمرتی sam'ratī N.F. (dial.) meditation this as a genre of Hindu literature [S]

سمرن sum'ran N.F. (dial.) rosary [S]

سم سم sim sim N.M. (rare) sesame ; sesamum charm word کھل سم سم khul' sim' sim PH. open sesame [A]

سمع sam'' N.M. hearing ear سمع خراش sam''-kharāsh' ADJ. boring N.M. bore سمع خراشی sam''-

khara'sht N.F. jarring on the ear boring سمع نوازی sam' nava'zi N.F. conveying sweet sounds

سمک sa'mak N.F. (sign of Zodiac) Pisces (PL. اسماک asmak') fish [A]

سمن 1 sa'man N.M. corpulence [A]

سمن 2 sa'man N.F. Jassamine سمن آباد sa'man-abad', سمن زار sa'man-zar N.M. Jassamine garden سمن بر sa'manbar ADJ. & N.M. (sweetheart) with a lovely figure [P]

سمن 3 sa'man N.M. Summon [E]

سمند samand' N.M. steed ; courser thoroughbred horse سمند ناز کو تازیانہ ہونا saman'd-e naz' ko taziya'nah ho'na PH. be an occasion for further diligence

سمندر samań'dar N.M. salamander

سمندر samun'dar (dial. samań'dar) N.M. sea ocean سمندر پھل samun'dar-phal N.M. a medicine سمندر جھاگ samun'dar jhag N.M. cuttle-bone ; cuttle-fish bone سمندر کھار samun'dar-khar N.M. arsenic

سموچا samo'cha ADV. (gulp down) the whole of

سمنک samank' N.F. wheat pith starch

سمور samoor' (ped. sammoor') N.M. sableskin sable ; marten [A]

سموسا samo'sa, سموسہ samo'sah, (arch. سمبوسہ sambo'sah) N.M. saltish triangular pie hemmed triangular piece of cloth

سموم samoom' N.F. simoom [A ~ سم]

سمونا samo'na V.T. (used as میں سمونا men samo'na) mix hot water with cold water make (water) luke warm moderate mix adulterate

سمیت samet', (or samait) ADV. along with ; together with including ; inclusive of

سمیت sammiy'yat N.F. (see under سم sam ★)

سمیٹنا samet'na V.T. roll up wrap up gather finish (work) amass (wealth) سمیٹ سمٹ کر samet' samat' kar ADV. having gathered having amassed [~ سمیٹنا]

سن 1 san (also پٹ سن pat'-san) N.M. jute

سن 2 san N.M. year سن وار san'-var ADJ. & ADV year-wise [~ A سنہ CORR.]

سن san' N.F. whiz rustle crack (of whip) سن سے san' se ADV. with a whiz سن سے جی ہو جانا san' se ji ho ja'na V.I. be struck dumb سن سے نکل جانا san' se ni'kal ja'na V.I. pass quickly [ONO.]

سن sin N.M. (PL. سنین sinin) age (rare) tooth سن بلوغ sin'n-e bulooghʹ, سن بلوغت sin'n-e baloo'ghat N.M. maturity ; puberty سن تمیز sin'n-e tamiz', سن شعور sin'n-e shoʻoor' N.M. years of discretion ; maturity سن رسیدہ sin-rasi'dah ADJ. advanced in years ; elderly ; سن وسال sin'(n)-o-sal' N.M. age ; years کم سن kam'-sin ADJ. young ; juvenile raw ; inexperienced [A]

سن sun' ADJ. & ADV. numb ; benumbed struck dumb سن ہو جانا sun' ho ja'na V.I. be benumbed

سنا sana' N.F. senna ; 'cassia senn'

سناتن دھرم sana'tan dhar'm ADJ. (dial.) eternal religion (as name of orthodox Hindu faith) [S]

سناٹا sanna'ta N.M. pindrop silence awesome stillness howling wilderness consternation shock ; stunning blow howling (of storm) violent gust ; blast (of wind) سناٹے سے برسنا sanna'te se ba'rasna V.I. rain cats and dogs سناٹے میں آ (یا رہ) جانا sanna'te men a' (or raih') ja'na V. be struck with consteration

سنار sunar' N.M. goldsmith this as a caste سنار کی کھٹالی اور درزی کے بند sunar' ki kutha'li aur dar'zi ke band' PROV. excuses put up for delay سنارن suna'ran N.F. goldsmith's wife any woman of this caste

سنان sinan' سنال sinah' N.F. (PL. اسنہ asin'nah) spearhead [A]

سنانا suna'na V.T. tell relate inform. read out (to) say or repeat (lesson) announce ; proclaim cause (someone) to hear rail at carpet speak sternly (to) give a curtain lecture (to) ایک کی دس سنانا ek' ki das' suna'na PH. give tit for tat سناونی suna'oni N.F. news of (someone's) death سناونی سنانا suna'oni suna'na V.T. give news of (someone's) death (to)

سنبل sum'bul N.M. hyacinth ; spikenard ; valerian سنبل خطائی sum'bul-e khata''i N.M. angelica سنبل ہندی sum'bul-e hin'di N.M. hyacinth ; spikenard; valerian [P]

سنبلہ sum'bulah N.M. (sign of the Zodiac) Virgo ear of corn) [A]

سنبوسہ sambo'sah (same as سموسا ★)

سنبھ sum'bah N.M. spike iron bar

سنبھل sam'bhal N.M. (same as سمل N.M. ★)

سنبھلنا san'bhalna V.I. steady ; befirm recover from a fall recover no longer go astray سنبھالنا san'bhal'na V.T. support hold up control keep safe سنبھل کر (یا سنبھال کر) ADV. carefully ; cautiously سنبھالا *sanbha'la* N.M. support apparent recovery from illness on eve of death سنبھالا لینا *sanbha'la le'na* v.i. recover thus recoup سنبھالے نہ سنبھلنا *sanbha'le na san'bhalna* v.i. be out of control ; be in a miserable condition

سنپولیا *sanpo'liya* N.M. (same as سپولیا N.M. see under سانپ N.M. ★)

سنت *sant* N.M. (dial.) saint ; Hindu ascetic [E]

سنّت *sun'nat* N.F. (PL. سنن *su'nan*) tradition(s) practice of the Holy Prophet religious rite ordained by the Holy Prophet practice (of) ; way (of) circcumcision سنت ابراہیمی *sun'nat-e ibrahi'mi* N.F. Abrahams practice سنت رسول *sun'nat-e rasool'*, سنت نبوی *sun-nat-e na'bavi* N.F. the Holy Prophet's practice اہل السنہ *ah'l-us sunnah*, اہل السنہ والجماعۃ *ah'l-us sun'nat-e val-jama''ah*, اہل سنت *ah'l-e sun'nat* N.M. PL. (col. SING.) orthodox Muslim(s) (as people following of the Holy Prophet's practice and commanding a majority) سنت کرانا *sun'nat kara'na* v.i. get circumcised سنت کرنا *sun'nat kar'na* v.t. circumcise سنت پر عمل کرانا *sun'nat par 'a'mal' kar'na* v.i. act according to the Holy Prophet's practice [A]

سنترہ *san'tarah*, سنگترہ *sang'tarah* N.M. tangerine

سنتری *san'tari* N.M. sentinel ; sentry [E]

سنٹر *sain'tar* N.M. centre سنٹرل *sain'tral* ADJ. central سنٹرل جیل *sain'tral jel'* N.M. F. central jail [E]

سنجاب *sanjab'* N.F. ermine its fur ; ermine [A]

سنجاف *sinjaf'* N.F. hem border broad lace fringe سنجاف لگانا *sinjaf' laga'na* v.t. tack lace on (to)

سنجوگ *sanjog'* N.M. good chance matrimonial match suitable connexion union meeting ; association سنجوگ کرنا *sanjog' kar'na* v.t. join or unite (with) سنجوگ ملانا *sanjog' mila'na* v.t. unite (friends, etc.) سنجوگی *sanjo'gi* N.M. non-celibate Hindu ascetic [A]

سنجھلا *sanjh'la* ADJ. & N.M. the third of four brothers سنجھلی *sanjh'li* ADJ. & N.F. the third of four sisters

سنجیدہ *sanji'dah* ADJ. cultured serious weighty grave ; solemn سنجیدگی *sanji'dagi* N.F. solemnity seriousness gravity [P]

سنچائی *sinchaa''i* N.F. act of irrigating remuneration for it [~ سینچنا]

سند *sa'nad* N.F. (PL. اسناد *asnad'*) degree ; diploma certificate testimonial credential proof reason authority grant deed سند کارگزاری *sa'nad-e kar-guza'ri* N.F. certificate of meritorious services سند معافی *sa'nad-e mo'a'fi* N.F. rent free grant سند یافتہ *sa'nad-yaf'tah* ADJ. qualified certified accerdited [A]

سندان *sindan'* سنداں *sindan* N.F. anvil [P]

سندباد *sand'-bad* N.F. Sinbad the sailor [A ~ P]

سندر *sun'dar* ADJ. (dial.) beautiful سندرتا *sun'darta* N.F. beauty سندری *sun'dari* N.F. pretty woman [S]

سندس *sun'dus* N.M. broeade [A]

سندلا *sand'la* N.M. a kind of masonic plaster سندلا پھیرنا (یا کرنا) *sand'la pher'na* (or *kar'na*) v.t. plaster (wall, etc.)

سندور *sindoor* N.M. (same as سیندور N.M. ★)

سندھ *sindh* N.M. Sind Indus سندھی *sin'dhi* ADJ. & N.M. of Sind N.F. Sindhi language

سندھیا *san'dhiya* N.M. (dial.) evening Hindu vaspers

سندیسا *sande'sa*, سندیس *sandes'*, سندیسہ *sande'sah* N.M. (dial.) message

سنڈا *sanda* ADJ. stout سنڈا مسٹنڈا *san'da mustan'da*, سنڈ مسٹنڈ *sand' mustand'* ADJ. well-developed ; fat ; plump ; stout

سنڈاس *sandas'* N.M. upper-storey latrine with excrement falling on ground-floor excrement sink

سنڈاسی *sanda'si* N.F. pincers (for holding hot vessel)

سنڈیکیٹ *sin'diket* N.F. syndicate [E]

سنسار *sansar'* N.M. (dial.) world [S]

سنسان *sunsan'* ADJ. uninhabited desolate dreary and quiet howling (wilderness)

سنسر *sain'sar* N.M censor سنسر شپ *sain'sar-ship* N.F. censorship [E]

سنسکرت *sans'krit* ADJ. Sanskrit N.F. the sacred and classical language of the Hindus سنسکرتی *sans'kriti* N.F. (dial.) culture ; civilization [S]

سنسنانا *sansana'na* v.i. feel a tingling sensation when is about to faint ; tingle collapse simmer سنسناہٹ *sansana'hat* N.F tingle tingling sensation rustle simmer hiss سنسنی *san'sani* N.F. stir ; sensation tingle ; tingling sensation سنسنی پھیلانا *san'sani phaila'na* v.t. create a stir; cause a sensation سنسنی خیز *san'sani-khez* ADJ. (col.) sensational

سنسی san'sī N.F. pincers

سنسنی san'sanī N.F. (see under سنسنانا V.I. ★)

سنک sa'nak N.F. eccentricity craze سنکی sa'nakī ADJ. crazy eccentric (rare) tipsy

سنکنا si'nakna V.T blow (one's nose)

سنکنا sa'nakna V.I. (of breeze) begin to blow

سنکو sūnak'ko N.F woman in the habit of eaves-dropping

سنکھ sankh N.M conch-shell ADJ. one trillion سنکھ بجانا sankh baja'na V.I. blow a shell

سنکھنی san'khnī N.F (dial.) tall sexy blonde

سنکھیا san'khiya N.F. arsenic

سنگ[1] sang N.M. stone سنگ آمد و سخت آمد san'g ā'mad-o-sakh't ā'mad PH. calamitous indeed سنگ آستان san'g-e āstān' N.M. doorsill سنگ آہن ربا san'g-e ā'han-rūbā' N.M. magnet سنگ اسود san'g-e as'vad N.M. the Holy Black Stone (of Ka'aba) سنگباری sang-bā'rī N.F. pelting with stones ; brick-batting سنگ بنیاد san'g-e būnyad' N.F. foundation-stone سنگ بنیاد رکھنا san'g-e būnyād' rakh'na V.I. lay the foundation-stone (of) سنگ پشت sang'-pūsht' N.M. turtle ; turtoise سنگتراش sang-tarāsh' N.M. sculptor lapidary سنگتراشی sang-tarā'shī N.F. sculpture stone cutting سنگ جراحت san'g-e jirā'hat N.M. soap-stone سنگ خارا san'g-e khā'ra N.M. flint سنگ خوار sang'-khār' N.M a falcon-like bird of prey سنگدانہ sang-dā'nah N.F. gizzard سنگدل sang'-dil ADJ. callous ; hard hearted cruel ; merciless سنگدلی sang-di'lī N.F. callousness; hard-heartedness cruelty سنگ راہ san'g-e rāh' N.F. snag ; hindrance , obstruction سنگریزہ sang-re'zah N.M. pebble سنگسار sang-sār' ADJ. stoned to death سنگسار کرنا sang-sār' kar'na V.T. stone to death ; lapidate سنگساز sang-sāz' N.M. one who corrections on the lithographic stone سنگ سرخ san'g-e sūr'kh N.M. red stone , granite سنگ سرمہ san'g-e sūr'mah N.M. antimony سنگ سلیمانی san'g-e sulaimā'nī N.M. onyx سنگ سماق san'g-e samaq' N.M. porphyry سنگلاخ sang-lākh' ADJ rocky (land) سنگ گردہ san'g-e gūr'dah N.M. kidney stone سنگ لرزاں san'g-e lar'zāṅ N.M. tremulous stone سنگ لوح san'g-e lauh' N.M tomb stone سنگ مثانہ san'g-e masā'nah N.M. calculus سنگ مرمر san'g-e mar'mar N.M. marble سنگ میل san'g-e mīl' N.M. mile stone (fig.) landmark سنگ مقناطیس san'g-e maqnatīs N.M loadstone سنگ نشان san'g-e nishān N.M. road sign landmark سنگ موسیٰ san'g-e moo'sā N.M. blackstone سنگ یشب san'g-e ya'shab N.M. jasper سنگین sangīn' N.F. bayonet ADJ. of stone ; stone heavy (punishment) heinous (crime) hard سنگینی sangī'nī N.F. heaviness heinousness hardness solidity [P]

سنگ[2] sang ADV. the company (of) N.M. company (also سنگھ) (dial.) party جن سنگھ jan' sangh N.M. (name of a strongly anti-Muslim) Hindu people's party (of India) سنگت san'gat N.F company accompanists سنگت کرنا san'gat kar'na V.I. bear (someone) company go along with سنگی san'gī (rare سنگتی san'gatī) N.M friend companion سنگی ساتھی san'gī sā'thī N.M. companion(s) comrade(s) سنگار ، سنگھار singār , singhār' N.M. make-up , toilet decoration سنگاردان singār'-dān N.M. toilet , dressing case سنگار کرنا singār' kar'na V.I. do one's make-up سنگار میز singār'-mez N.F. dressing table ست سنگار sat'-singār N.M. PL. (see under ست ADJ. & N.M ★) سولہ سنگار so'lah singār' N.M. PL. sixteen appliances of Hindu woman's toilet

سنگت san'gat N.F (see under سنگ[2] ADV. ★)

سنگترہ sang'tarah N.M. (same as سنترہ N.M. ★)

سنگتی san'gatī N.M. (see under سنگ[2] ★)

سنگرنا sin'garna V.I. be adorned

سنگرہنی sangraih'nī, سنگرینی sangrī'nī N.F. chronic dysentry

سنگم san'gam, سنگھم san'gham N.M. confluence (of rivers) (dial.) junction (of planets) meeting ; union [~ سنگ]

سنگھ singh N.M. (sign of Zodiac) Leo lion (as appendage to Sikh or rare. Hindu male names)

سنگھاڑا singhā'ra N.M. water chestnut water plant yielding this and water lily anything triangular name of a species of fish

سنگھاسن singhā'san N.M (dial.) throne

سنگھانا sūnghā'na V.T. cause to smell administer olifactorily [~ سونگھنا CAUS.]

سنگوانا sangva'na V.T get (things) properly arranged get sorted take possesion of

سنگی sangī N.M (see under سنگ[2] ADV. ★)

سنگیت sangīt' N.M. dance to the accompaniment of song and music this as art concert

سنگین *saṅgīn'* ADJ., سنگینی *saṅgī'nī* N.F. (see under سنگ N.M. ★)

سنن *sū'nan* N.F. PL. (SING. سنت *sun'nat* N.F. ★)

سننا *sūn'nā* V.T. & I. hear listen (to) listen in attend (to) be carpeted ; be taken to task ; face the music learn ; come to know hear pupil repeat lesson ; give oral test (to pupil) on earlier lesson provide relief or redress (to) listen to (someone's) word of advice سن گن *sūn' gin* N.F. inkling سن گن پانا *sun' gin pā'nā* V.I. get on inkling (of) سنا *sū'nā* ADJ. & N.M. (F. سنی *sū'nī*) (something) heard سنی ان سنی کر دینا *sū'nī an-sū'nī kar de'nā* V.I. turn a deaf ear to سنی سنائی *sū'nī sunā''ī* N.F. hearsay ایک کہنا نہ دس سننا *ek' kaih'nā na das' sūn'nā* V.I. not to provoke into harsh rejoinder

سنورنا *saṅvar'nā* V.I do one's make-up adorn oneself be adorned be set right be streamlined بننا سنورنا *ban'nā saṅ'var'nā* V.I. do one's make-up adorn oneself سنوار *saṅvār'* N.F. (dial.) curse; chastisement تجھے خدا کی سنوار *tu'jhe khu'dā ki saṅ'vār'* INT. May God chastise you سنوارنا *saṅ'var'nā* V.T. adorn , decorates embellish arrange adjust set right streamline chastise

سنہ *san* N.M. year era سنہ بکرمی *san'n-e bik'ramī* N.M. Hindu era (beginning Bikramajit's accession in 52 B C.) , Bik'rami era سنہ جلوس *san'n-e jiloos'* N.M. year of (someone's) accession to throne سنہ عیسوی *san'n-e 'isavī* N.M. Christian era ; A.C. سنہ ہجری *san-e hij'rī* N.M. Hijri era ; the Muslim lunar era beginning the Holy Prophet's exodus to Medina in 622 A.C. [A]

سنہرا *sūnaih'rā*, ADJ. (F. سنہری *sūnaih'rī*) golden gilded ; gilt

سنی *sū'nī* ADJ. & N.M. (see under سننا ★)

سنی *sūn'nī* N.M. orthodox Muslim ADJ. orthodox (Muslim) سنی نہ شیعہ جو جی میں آیا کیا *sūn'nī na shī''ah jo jī' meṅ ā'yā kī'yā* PROV. neither a Catholic nor a Protestant, he is an eclectic to his own advantage

سنیاس *sanyās'* (ped. *sann' yās*) N.M. (dial.) Hindu asceticism سنیاسی *sanyāsī* N.M. (dial.) Hindu ascetic [S]

سنیچر *sanī'char* N.M. (dial.) Saturn (also سنیچر وار *sanī'char-vār'*) Saturday [S]

سنیما *sine'mā* (or *si'namā*) N.M. cinema ; picture-house [E]

سنین *sinīn'* N.M. PL. year eras ; epochs [A ~ SING. سنہ]

سو *soo* ADJ. evil ; vicious علمائے سو *ulamā'-e soo* N.M. PL. vicious savants ; scholars with an axe to grind سوئے اتفاق سے *soo'-e ittifāq' se* ADV. unfortunately سوئے ادب *soo-e o'dab* N.M. impudence سوئے ظن *soo'-e zan'* N.M. unwarranted suspicion سوئے ہضم *soo'-e haz'm* N.M. indigestion [A]

سو *soo* N.F. direction side سو بسو *soo ba-soo'* ADV. all round ; on every side ; in all directions سوئے *soo''e* ADV. towards ; in the direction of [P]

سو *sau* ADJ. hundred ADV. howevermuch سو نکٹوں میں ایک ناک والا نکو *sau nak'toṅ meṅ ek nāk vā'lā nak'koo* PROV. fools would ridicule a wise individual in their company ; evil companions bring much woe سواں *sa'vāṅ* ADJ. hundredth سو باتوں کی ایک بات *sau' bā'toṅ kī ek' bāt'* PH. very reasonable point (or proposition) سو بسوے *sau' bis've* ADJ. surely ; certainly ; in all probability سو جان سے *sau jān' se* ADV. with all one's heart سو دن چور کے ایک دن سادھ کا *sau' din chor' ke ek' din sādh' ha* PROV. the thief is ultimately caught سو سو بل کھانا *sau' sau bal' khā'nā* V.I. fret and fume سو سنار کی ایک لہار کی *sau' sūnār' kī ek lohār' kī* PROV mighty person's is something to be afraid of سو سو کوس *sau' sau kos'* ADV. far and wide out of the reach (of) سو سیانے اور ایک مت *sau siyā'ne aur ek mat'* PH. wise man always agree سو علاج ایک پرہیز *sau 'ilāj' ek parhez'* PROV. prevention is better than cure سو کے سوائے *sau ke savā''e* ADJ. a hundred and twenty-five per cent سو مارے اور ایک نہ گنے *sau mā're aur ek na gi'ne* PH. beating harshly

سو *so* CONJ. so ; hence ; therefore ADV. accordingly thereupon PROV. that ; he (or she or it) thy ; they

سوا *sa'vā* ADJ. one-and-a quarter quarter again سوا گز کی زبان ہونا *sa'vā gaz kī zabān' ho'nā* V.I. be foul-mouthed be rude سوا نیزے پر آفتاب آجانا *sa'vā nai'ze par āftāb' ā jā'nā* PH. be very hot (of doomsday) arrive سوایا *savā'yā* ADJ. (F. سوائی *savā'ī*) quarter again

سوا *sivā'* ADJ. & ADV. more کے سوا(ئے) *ke sivā'(e')* PREP. except ; save besides without CONJ. in addition to [A]

سوا *su''ā* N.M. large needle ; packing needle [~ F. سوئی]

سوا *so''ā* N.M. fennel

سوابق *savā'biq* N.M. PL. precedents the preceding ones (rare) prefixes ADJ. (with PL. N.) earlier ancient [A ~ SING سابقہ]

سواحل *savā'ḥil* N.M. PL shores ; coasts [A ~ SING. ساحل]

سواد *savād'* N.M. blackness blackspot (on heart) outskirts (of town) environs (of a place) intelligence skill aptitude knowledge سوادِ اعظم *savā'd-e a''zam* N.M. the majority (of) بے سواد *be-savād'* ADJ. ignorant unintelligent بے سوادی *be-savād'ī* N.F. ignorance کم سواد *kam-savād'* ADJ. not well-educated کم سوادی *kam-savā'dī* N.F. lack of deep knowledge [A]

سوار *savār'* (col. اسوار *asvār'*) ADJ. (one) riding anywhere mounted on (horse-back) in train, bus, car, etc.) N.M. one riding anywhere trooper ; cavalry man horseman سوار ہونا *savār ho'nā* V.T. ride mount get (into) travel (by) پانچوں سواروں میں ہونا *panch'veṅ savā'roṅ meṅ ho'nā* PH. be a braggart be a fool among knights سواری *savā'rī* N.F. (col. اسواری *asvā'rī*) conveyance one travelling by a conveyance riding سواری کرنا *savā'rī kar'nā* V.T. ride practise [P]

سوال *so'āl'* (col. *savāl'*) question issue problem query arithmetical sum request purpose سوال از آسمان جواب از ریسماں *so'ā'l az ās'mān javā'b az rīs'man* PH. inapt reply سوال پیدا ہونا *savāl' pai'dā ho'nā* V.I. (of question) arise سوال جواب *savāl' javāb'* N.M. question and answer سوالاً جواباً *so'ā'lan javā'ban* ADV. in question-and-answer form سوال جواب کرنا *savāl' javāb' kar'nā* V.I. discuss remonstrate سوال حل کرنا *savāl' ḥal' kar'nā* V.I. do a sum solve a problem سوال کرنا *savāl' kar'nā* V.T. question ask a question ask; request ; beg سوال دیگر جواب دیگر *so'ā'l-e dī'gar javā'b-e dī'gar,* سوال کچھ جواب کچھ *savāl' kuchh javāb' kuchh* PH. inapt reply evasive reply سوالی *savā'lī* NM. beggar [A]

سوامی *savā'mī* (or *so'ā'mī*) N.M. (dial.) husband lord head of Hindu religious order [S]

سوانح *savā'neḥ* N.M. biography (life) story PL. incidents accidents سوانح حیات *savā'neḥ-e ḥayāt'* N.M. PL. life history (of) N.F. biography سوانح نگار *savā'neḥ-nigār'* N.M. biographer سوانح عمری *savā'neḥ 'um'rī* N.F. biography [A ~ SING. سانحہ]

سوانگ *sāṅg* (ped. *so'āṅg'*) N.M. (same as سانگ N.M. ★)

سوانہ *sivā'nah* N.M. village or field boundary ; bourne

سوایا *savā'yā* ADJ. (F. سوائی *savā''ī*) (see under سوا *sa'vā* ADJ. ★)

سوپ *soop* N.M. soup [E]

سوپ *sop* N.M soap [E]

سوکن **سوت** *saut* (rare سوتن *sau'tan*), (سوک *sauk*), *sau'kan* N.F. co-wife second (etc.) wife سوت پر سوت اور جلاپا *saut' pur saut' aur' jalā'pā* PROV. a third co-wife is worse than the second for the first one سوت کا لانا جیتے جی کا جلانا *saut' kā lā'nā jī'te jī kā jalā'nā* PROV. husband's remarriage is most heart-rending to the first wife سوتیاڈہ *sautyā'-ḍah*, سوتیاڈاہ *sau'tiyā'ḍāh'*, سوتاپا *sautā'pā* N.M. heart-burning caused by co-wife

سوت *soot* N.M. yarn walk on foot plumb-line one small rule one-sixteenth of 'tas'soo' سوت نہ کپاس جولاہے (یا کولی) سے لٹھم لٹھا *soot' na kapās' jaulā'he* (or *ko'lī*) *se laṭ'ṭham laṭ'ṭhā* PROV. unjustified dispute سوتی *soo'tī* ADJ. cotton سوتی کپڑا *soo'tī kap'ṛā* N.M. cotton cloth ; cotton

سوتا *so'tā* N.M., سوت *sot* N.F. spring fountainhead سوتے پھوٹنا *so'te phooṭ'nā* V.I. well up (of fountain heads) appear

سوتنا *soot'nā* V.T. (same as سونتنا V.T. ★)

سوتی *soo'tī* ADJ. (see under سوت *soot* N.M. ★)

سوتیلا *saute'lā* (rare. سوکیلا *sauke'lā*), سوتیلی *saute'lī* (rare. سوکیلی *sauke'lī*) ADJ. step (mother, etc.) half (brother, etc.) سوتیلا باپ *saute'lā bāp* N.F. stepfather سوتیلا بھائی *saute'lā bhā''ī* N.M. step-brother سوتیلی بہن *saute'lī bai'han* N M. step-sister سوتیلی ماں *saute'lī māṅ* N.F. stepmother

سوٹ *sooṭ* N.M, suit [E]

سوجنا *sooj'nā* V.I. be swollen ; be inflamed منہ سوجنا *mūṅh sooj'nā* look sulky سوجن *soo'jan* N.F swelling ; inflammation

سوجھنا *soojh'nā* V.I. be seen ; be visible be endowed with sense of sight be perceive strike (someone) ; come to (someone's) mind سوجھ *soojh* N.F. understanding perception سوجھ بوجھ *soojh' boojh* N.F. common-sense understanding intelligence

سوجی *soo'jī* N.F. granulated wheat flour ; butter of wheat ; fines ; wheat fine

سوچ *soch* N.F. (see under سوچنا V.I. ★)

سوچ *savich'* N.M. switch [E]

سوچنا *soch'nā* V.I. think reflect mediate believe consider ponder conceive imagine opine ; be of opinion (that) muse سوچ *soch* N.F. thought ; reflection ; attention ; regard ; anxiety ; consideration ; meditation ; reverie ; imagination ; idea ; notice سوچ بچار *soch'-bichār'* N.M. consideration thought; thinking care worry سوچ میں رہنا soch' meh raih'na V.I. buried in thought be worried

سوچنا sooch'na V.T. lave (private parts after stools)

سوخت sokht N.F. burning ; incineration (rare) revoke (at cards) سوختگی sokh'tagi N.F. burning ; incineration سوختنی sokh'tani ADJ. deserving to be burnt fit for burning ; fire (wood) سوختہ sokh'tah ADJ. burnt scorched consumed (with love, grief, etc.) سوختہ جاں sokh'ta-jan, سوختہ دل sokh'ta-dil' ADJ. love-sick grieved [P]

سود sood N.M. interest usury gain ; profit benefit ; advantage سود بٹا sood' baṭ'ṭa N.M. profit and loss سود پر دینا sood' par de'na V.I. lend (money) at interest سود پر لینا sood' par le'na V.I. borrow (money) at interest سود خور sood'-khor سود خوار sood'-khur, N.M. & ADJ. usurer ; usurious (person) سود خوری sood-khori, سود خواری sood'-khā'ri N.F. usury سود در سود sood' dar sood N.M. compound interest سود کھانا sood' khā'na V.I. take interest be a usurer سود لگانا sood' lagā'na V.I. charge interest calculate interest سود مرکب soo'd-e murak'-'ab N.M. compound interest سود مفرد soo'd-e m'f rad N.M. simple interest سود مند sood'-man'd ADJ. gainful profitable beneficial advantageous useful ; of use سود مندی sood'-man'di N.F. usefulness ; use advantage benefit profit سود مساوی الاصل sood' musā'vi-l-as'l N.M. interest equal to principal بے سود be-sood' ADJ. useless fruitless ; vain ADV. in vain سودی soo'di ADJ. interest bearing [P]

سودا saudā' N.M. madness ; insanity ; lunacy love strong passion ambition frenzy craze ; melancholy; black bile سودا اچھلنا saudā' u'chhalna V.I. go mad سودا ہو جانا saudā' ho jā'na V.I. go mad ; a fit of madness be crazy (after) be passionately in love (with) have one's heart set (upon) سوداوی saudā'vi ADJ. melancholic سوداوی مزاج saudavi mizaj' ADJ. melancholic temperament سودائی saudā''i ADJ & N.M. mad ; insane ; lunatic (one passionately in love (with) [A]

سودا sau'da N.M. bargain goods ; wares سودا کرنا (یا پٹانا) sau'da kar'na (or paṭ'āna) V.I. buy strike a bargain settle the rate سودا ہونا (یا پٹنا) sau'da ho'nā (or paṭ'na) V.I. be bought (of bargain) be struck (of rate) be settled سودا نہ ہونا sau'da na ho'na V.I. (of rate) not to be settled سودا خریدنا (یا لینا) sau'da kharid'na (or. le'na) V.I. buy ; make a purchase do shopping سودا خریدنے جانا sau'da kharid'ne jā'na V.I. go for a shopping سودا سلف sau'da sul'f N.M. goods ; things bought سوداگر sauda'-gar N.M. merchant سوداگری saudā'gari N.F. commerce trade سوداگری مال saudā'gari māl N.M. merchandise [P]

سواداوی saudā'vi ADJ., سودائی saudā''i N.M. (see under سودا saudā' N.M. ★)

سودی soo'di ADJ. (see under سود N.M. ★)

سودیشی saude'shi ADJ. (dial.) national indigenous [S]

سوڈا so'da N.M. (bi)carbonate of soda سوڈا واٹر so'da-vā'ṭar N.M. aerated water سوڈیم so'ḍiyam N.M. sodium [E]

سور soor N.M. (dial.) hero سور بیر soor' bir N.M. (PL.) (dial.) hero(es) [S]

سؤر su''ar N.M. swine ; pig ; hog ; boar (as swear-word) swine سؤر کا بچہ su''ar ka bach'chah N.M. pig young (as swear-word) swine سؤر کا گوشت su''ar ka gosh't N.M. pork ; bacon; ham something forbidden سؤرنی su''arni N.F. sow

سوراج savaraj' N.M. (dial.) self-government ; home-rule [S]

سوراخ soorākh' N.M. hole burrow orifice perforation سوراخ دار soorakh'-dar ADJ. having hole(s) perforated [P]

سورت soo'rat N.F. سورہ soo'rah N.M. chapter (of the Holy Quran) [A]

سورج soo'raj N.M. sun سورج بنسی soo'raj ban'si N.M. of solar descent (as name of a Rajput clan) سورج ڈوبنا (یا چھپنا یا غروب ہونا) soo'raj doob'na (or chhip'na or ghuroob' ho'nā) V.I. (of sun) set ; god own سورج گرہن soo'raj girah'n (rare سورج گہن soo'raj gai'han) N.M. solar eclipse سورج مکھی soo'raj mu'khi N.M. sunflower سورج نکلنا (یا طلوع ہونا) soo'raj ni'kalna (or tuloo'' ho'na) V.I. (of sun) rise

سورداس soor'-das N.M. (dial.) (euphemism for a) blind man

سورگ so'arg' (occ. سرگ sur'g) N.M. (dial.) paradise سورگ باشی so'arg'-bashi, (سرگ باشی surg'-bā'shi) (dial.) the late ; deceased [S]

سورما soor'ma ADJ. brave ; valiant ; bold

سورنجان soo'ranjān N.M. meadow-saffron [P]

سورہ soo'rah N.M. (same as سورت N.F. ★) سورۂ اخلاص soo'ra-e ikhlas' N.F. the chapter entitled Ikhlas سورۂ فاتحہ soo'ra-e fa'tchah N.F. the Opening Chapter سورۂ یٰسین soo'ra-e yasin' N.M. the Chapter entitled Ya-sin' generally recited at people's deathbed [A]

سوز soz N.M. passion depth of feeling hurt-burning grief elegiac stanza

SUF. burning inflamming rending سوزخوان soz'-khan N M. dirge-chanter سوزخوانی soz'-kha'nī N.F. dirge-chanting in commemoration of Karbala martyrs سوز و گداز so'z-o-gūdaz' N.M. depth of feeling ardour سوزاک sozak' N.M. gonorrhoea سوزاں so'zan ADJ. & SUF. burning ; kindling سوزش so'zish inflammation burning sensation ardour سوزناک soz-nak' ADJ. heart-rending سوزندہ sozin'dah N.M. & ADJ. burning consuming سوزی so'zī SUF. burning consuming [P ~ سوختن]

سوزن so'zan N.F. needle ; sewing needle سوزن کاری so'zan ka'rī N.F. tambour work سوزنی soz'nī (ped. so'zani) N.F. (arch.) quilted coverlet tamboured coverlet [P]

سوس soos N.M. (rare) liquorice رب السوس rūb'h-ūs-soos N.M. liquorice extract [A]

سوسائٹی sosa''itī N.F. society [E]

سوسمار soosmar' N.M. porpoise [P]

سوسن so'san N.F. iris سوسنی so'sanī N.M. bluish colour ADJ. iris-coloured ; bluish [P]

سوسن

سوسی soo'sī N.F. coarse striped silk cloth [P ~ سوس]

سوشلسٹ so'shalist N.M. & ADJ. socialist سوشلزم so'shalizm N.M. socialism [E]

سوغات saughat' N.F. present (brought from a far-off land) ; rare gift rarity [P ~ T]

سوفار soofar' N.M. notch of arrow [P]

سوفسطائی soofista''ī N.M. sophist [A ~ G]

سوق sooq N.M. street (rare) market سوقیانہ sooqiya'nah ADJ. vulgar (words, manners, etc.) سوقیانہ پن sooqiya'na-pan N.M. vulgarity [A]

سوک sauk, سوکن sau'kan N.F. (same as سوت saut N.F. ★)

سوکھنا sookh'na V.I. dry evaporate shrivel wither be parched be emaciated pine away become thin or lean سوکھا soo'kha ADJ. (F. سوکھی soo'khī) dry juiceless parched withered shrivelled thin ; lean without anything extra mere flat ; utter N.M. dry land 'terra firma' dry tobacco rickets سوکھا ٹرخانا soo'kha tarkha'na V.T. dismiss (someone) without asceding to his request ; send away سوکھ کر کانٹا ہونا sookh kar kan'ṭa ho'na V.I. become gaunt سوکھی الفن soo'khī al'fan N.F. very lean woman سوکھی چنائی soo'khī chūna'ī N.F. dry paving ; paving the floor with brick without laying mortar سوکھے دھانوں پانی پڑنا soo'khe dha'noṅ pa'nī paṛ'na V.I. have revived hopes سوکھے گھاٹ اتارنا soo'khe ghaṭ ūtar'na V.I. disappoint dismiss (someone) without acceding to his request ; send away سوکھا جواب soo'kha javab' N.M. flat refusal سوکھا لگنا soo'kha lag'na V.I. have rickets

سوگ sog N.M. mourning سوگ کرنا (یا منانا) sog' kar'na (or mana'na) V.I. mourn grieve سوگوار sog-var' ADJ. mourning aggrieved ; afflicted ; sorrowful سوگواری sog'-va'rī N.F. mourning grief; affliction سوگن so'gan ADJ. & N.F. afflicted سوگی so'gī ADJ. & N.M. afflicted

سوگند saugan'd. N.M. oath سوگند دینا saugan'd de'na V.T. administer an oath (to) سوگند کھانا saugan'd kha'na V.I. say on oath take an oath ; swear [P]

سول si'val ADJ. civil سول جج si'val jaj N.M. civil judge سول سرجن si'val sar'jan N.M. civil surgeon سول سروس si'val sar'vis N.F. civil service سول سوٹ si'val sooṭ N.M. civil suit سول کورٹ si'val korṭ N.F. civil court سول نافرمانی si'val na-farma'nī N.F. civil disobedience سول وار si'val var' N.F. civil war [E]

سول sool N.M. thorn ; a spike ; a dart colic acute pain pin pricks sting سول چبھنا sool' chūbh'na, سول سی لگنا sool' sī lag'na V.I. cut to the quick

سولہ so'lah ADJ. & N.M. sixteen سولہ سنگار so'lah singar' (see under سنگار N.M. ★) سولہواں so'lhavan ADJ. sixteenth

سولی soo'lī N.F. cross gibbet (fig.) continued torture سولی دینا soo'lī de'na V.T. execute crucify سولی پر بھی نیند آ جاتی ہے soo'lī par bhī nīnd a ja'tī hai V.I. sleep can overtake one even on the cross سولی پہ جان ہونا soo'lī par jan' ho'na V.I. suffer continuous torture live in constant fear of one's life سولی (پر) چڑھانا soo'lī par chaṛha'na V.T. execute crucify torture

سوم soom N.M. miser ; niggard [~ A شوم CORR.]

سوم sivūm ADJ. third N.M. (col. سیم so'yam) third-day funeral rites [P]

سوموار som-var' ADJ. Monday [S]

سوں sauṅ N.F. oath (arch. except in) اللہ سوں al'la sauṅ INT. by God

سون soon N.F. reticence numbness سون کھینچنا soon' khenchh'na V.I. keep mum

سونا soo'na ADJ. (F. سونی soo'nī) deserted سونا پڑا ہونا soo'na pa'ṛa ho'na V.I. lie deserted سونا کر جانا soo'na kar ja'na V.I. desert (a place) ; depart leaving a place ; deserted سونا گھر بھڑوں کا راج soo'na ghar bhi'ṛoṅ ka raj' PROV. fools assume power where there is a scarcity of statesmen

سونا[1] *so'nā* V.I. sleep repose take a siesta cohabit (with) lie dead ابدی نیند سونا *a'badī nīnd' so'nā* V.T. die سوتے فتنے جگانا *so'te fit'ne jagā'nā* V.I. fan dying embers سوتے جاگتے منہ دیکھنا *so'te jāg'te mūṉh' dekh'nā* V.I. ever anticipate

سونا[2] *so'nā* N.M. gold riches ; wealth (thing) of real and unalterable value (of person) gem ; jewel سونا اچھالتے جانا *so'nā ūchhāl'te jā'nā* V.I. (of conditions in a country) be very peaceful سونا جانے کسے آدمی جانے بسے *so'nā jā'ne ka'se ā'damī jā'ne ba'se* PROV. title is known only after first hand experience سونا سگند *so'nā sūgand'* ADJ. good quality of good descent سونا چھوئے مٹی ہوتا ہے *so'nā choo''e maṭ'ṭī ho'tā hai* V.I. be always unlucky سونے پر سہاگہ *so'ne par sohā'gah* ADJ. adding to beauty or elegance سونے سے گھڑواں مہنگی *so'ne se ghaṛ-vāṉ' maiṉh'gī* . PROV. the incidental charges are much more than the basic ones سونے کا *so'ne kā* ADJ. golden ; gold exquisite سونے کا پانی *so'ne kā pā'nī* N.M. gilding سونے کا پترا *so'ne kā pat'rā* N.M. gold plate سونے کی چڑیا *so'ne kī chirya* N.F. 1 golden bird wealthy person سونے کا نوالہ *so'ne kā nivā'lah* N.M. nice food given to one's child سونے کا ورق *so'ne kā va'raq* N.M. gold leaf

سونپنا *sauṉp'nā* V.T. entrust delivered خدا کو سونپنا *khudā ko sauṉp'nā* leave to God the affair of entrust to God

سونتنا *soonl'nā*, سوتنا *sool'nā* V.T. draw (sword) message by rubbing down strip (vegetable etc.) of leaves starch (kite-string)

سونٹا *soṉ'ṭā* N.M. staff ; club سونٹا سے ہاتھ *soṉ'ṭā se hāth'* N.M. PL. (of woman) have no bangles in her hands

سونٹھ *soṉṭh* N.F. dry ginger cherished trifle سونٹھ کی ناس لینا *soṉṭh kī nas le'nā* V.I. bear ; brook

سون چڑیا *son'-chiṛ'yā* N.F. see under سونا[2] N.M. ★

سوندھا *soṉ'dhā* ADJ. (F. سوندھی *soṉ'dhī*) (usu. سوندھا سوندھا *soṉ'dhā soṉ'dhā* (F. سوندھی سوندھی *soṉ'dhī soṉ'dhī*) sweet smelling (like freshly moistened earth)

سوندھنا *saundh'nā* V.T. mix into a dough mix rub (cloth) in cowdung, etc., before washing

سونڈ *sooṉḍ* N.M. (elephant's) trunk

سونڈی *sooṉḍī* N.F. weevil

سوں سوں *sooṉ' sooṉ* N.F. sound of breath ; sniff sizzle سوں سوں کرنا *sooṉ' sooṉ kar'nā* V.I. sniff ; snuff sizzle

سونف *sauṉf* N.F. anise seed ; aniseed sweet fennel سونف کا عرق *sauṉf' kā 'a'raq* N.M. anise water

سونگھنا *sooṉgh'nā* V.I. smell get the scent (of) N.M. hound one who tracks

سونگھنی *sooṉgh'nī* N.F. (rare) snuff

سوویٹ *so'vi'eṭ* N.M. & ADJ. Soviet سوویٹ روس *so'vi'eṭ roos'* N.M. Soviet Russia; U.S.S R [E ~ R]

سوہا *soo'hā* ADJ. crimson ADV. deep (red) N.M name of a musical mode

سوہان *sohān'* N.M. file ; rasp سوہان روح *sohā'n-e rooh'* ADJ. & N.M. vexatious (person or affair) سوہان روح بنا ہونا *sohā'n-e rooh' ba'nā ho'nā* V.T. be a constant source of vexation [P]

سوہن *so'han* ADJ. (dial.) beautiful N.M. (dial.) sweetheart سوہن حلوہ *so'han hal'vā* N.M. kind of crisp sweetmeat ; wheat toffee

سوہنی *so'hanī* N.F. سوہنا *so'hanā* ADJ. (dial.) nick-name of a musical mode

سوئی *soo''ī* N.F. needle pin indicator hand (of clock, etc.) tongue (of scales) pointer on compass سوئی پرونا *soo''ī piro'nā* V.I. thread a needle سوئی کا بھالا ہو جانا *soo''ī kā bhā'lā ho' jā'nā* V.I. be grossly exaggerated سوئی کا کام *soo''ī kā kām'* N.M. needlework سوئی کا ناکہ *soo''ī kā na'kah* N.M eye of a needle سوئی کے ناکے سے اونٹ گزارنا (یا نکالنا) *soo''ī ke nā'ke se ooṉṭ' gūzār'nā* (or *nikāl'na*) V.T. make a camel pass through the eye of a needle ; achieve the impossible

سوئی گیس *soo''ī gais* N.F. fuel gas from Sui in Baluchistan ; Sui gas

سویا[1] *so'yā* (P.T. of سونا V.I. ★)

سویا[2] *so'yā* N.M. (usu. PL. as سوئے *so''e*) fennel; a kind of potherb

سویابین *so'yā-bīn'* N.M. Soya bean(s)

سویاں *sivay'yāṉ* N.F. vermicelli macaroni sweet vermicelli dish with milk

سویدا *sūvai'dā* N.M. black spot (on heart) ADJ. black

سویرا *save'rā* N.M. dawn daybreak early morning سویرا ہونا *save'ra ho'nā* V.I. be daybreak سویرے *save're* ADV. at dawn early : early enough too early ذرا سویرے *zā'rā save're* ADV. a bit earlier

سویمبر *so'em'bar* N.M. ancient Hindu custom of public selection of husband from among assembled suitors سویمبر رچانا *so'em'bar rachā'nā* V.I. assemble suitors for such selection [S]

سہ *sek* ADJ. three PREF. (*se-*) سہ پہر *se-pai'har* N.M. afternoon ADV in the afternoon سہ چند *se-chand'* ADJ. triple, treble threefold سہ حرفی *se-har'fi* ADJ. triliteral سہ درہ *se-da'rah* N.M. & ADJ. three-doored (portico) سہ سالہ *se-sā'lah* ADJ. tri-annual ; three-yearly سہ شنبہ *se-sham'bah* N.M. Tuesday سہ فصلہ *se-fas'lah* ADJ. yielding three crops a year ; triple-cropped سہ کرر *se-kar'rar* ADJ. (col.) three times as much ADV. (col.) the third time سہ گوشہ *se-go'shah* (col. سہ گوشیہ *se-goshiyah*) ADJ. three cornered سہ ماہی *se-ma'hi* ADJ. quarterly سہ منزلہ *se-man'zilah* ADJ. three-storeyed N.M. (dial.) second floor [P]

سہا *soha'* N.M. name of a far-off star in the constellation of the Greater Bear

سہارنا *sahār'nā* V.T. bear support (the weight of) brook tolerate endure سہار *sahar* N.F. patience; endurance سہارا *sahā'rā* N.M. supporter earning member (of family) support help; aid prop سہارا ٹوٹنا *sahā'rā toot'nā* V.I. lose all hope lose support of سہارا دینا *sahā'rā de'nā* V.I. support help ; aid سہارا ڈھونڈنا *sahā'ra dhoond'nā* V.I. seek ; support be on the lookout for some aid سہارا لینا *sahā'rā le'nā* V.I. depend (on) seek the help (of) be helped by

سہاگ *sohāg'* N.M. wifehood as married woman's auspicious state marriage song سہاگ اترنا (یا اجڑنا یا لٹنا) *sohāg' ū'tarna* (or *ū'jarna* or *lūt'nā*) V.I. widowed سہاگ بھری *sohāg'-bha'rī* ADJ. (dial.) beloved wife سہاگ پڑا *sohāg'-pū'ra* N.M. cosmetics bag presented to bride by groom's family on eve of wedding سہاگ رات *sohāg-rāt'* N.M. nuptials سہاگ سیج *sūhāg' sej'* N.F nuptial bed (سہاگ) گھوڑیاں *(sohāg'-) gho'rīyān* N.F PL. songs sung on eve wedding ; nuptial songs سہاگن *soha'gan* N.F. woman whose husband is alive favourite wife بوڑھ سہاگن *boorh'-sohā'gan* N.F. woman enjoying happy marital state till late in life سات سہاگنوں کے ہاتھ لگوانا *sat' sohā'ganon ke hath' lagvā'na* V.T. get the blessings of seven happy wifes (as a premarital rite)

سہاگہ *soha'gah*, سہاگا *sohā'ga* N.M. boric acid ; borax harrow

سہام *sehām'* N.M. (PL. of سہم N.M. ★)

سہانا *sohā'nā*, سہاونا *sohā''onā* ADJ (F. سہانی *sohā'nī*, سہاونی *sohā''onī*) pleasant delectable

سہج *sai'haj* ADJ. easy ; simple ADV. (also سہج سہج *sai'haj sai'haj*) slowly cautiously carefully سہج سبھاؤ *sai'haj-subhā''o* N.M. natural ease suave disposition سہج سے *sai'haj se* ADV. slowly gradully carefully in a low voice; soft ; softly

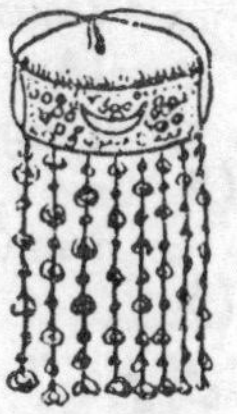

سہرا *seh'rā* N.M. groom's adornment groom's chaplet encomium to on this occasion credit سہرا باندھنا *seh'rā bāndh'nā* V.T. & I. garland the groom (of groom) garland himself ; be garlanded put on the floral chaplet سہرا گوندھنا *seh'rā-gaondh'nā* V.I. string flowers into a garland کے سر سہرا ہونا *ke sir seh'rā ho'nā* V.I. get the credit for ; (of credit) redound (to) سہرے سہاگ *seh're sohāg'* N.M. PL. marital melodies ; nuptial songs

سہل *sah'l* (col. *saih'l*) ADJ. easy; simple سہل انگاری *sah'l-angā'rī* N.F. easygoing attitude carelessness سہل بنانا (یا کرنا) *sah'l banā'nā* (or *kar'nā*) facilitate simplify سہل ممتنع *sah'l-e mūmtane''* N.M. inimitably easy style

سہل *sa'hūl* N.F. (same as ساہول N.F. ★)

سہلانا *saihlā'nā* V.I. stroke rub gently titillate سر سہلانا *sir saih'lā'nā* V.I. (fig.) invite punishment

سہم *sah'm* N.M. (PL. سہام *sehām'*) arrow share ; lot [A]

سہم *saih'm* N.M fear ; terror سہمنا *saihm'nā*, سہم جانا *saih'm jā'nā* V.I. be afraid be alarmed سہما سہما *saih'mā saih'mā* ADV. (F. سہمی سہمی *saih'mī saih'mī*) afraid

سہنا *saih'nā* V.I. bear ; endure ; suffer سہتا سہتا *saih'tā saih'tā* ADJ. bearable

سہو *sah'v* N.F. omission oversight سہو قلم *sah'v-e qalam* N.M. slip of the pen oversight سہو کتابت *sah'v-e kitā'bat* N.M. clerical error slip of the pan سجدۂ سہو *saj'da-e sah'v* N.M. compensatory prostration (in prayers for some missed obligation of it) سہواً *sah'van* ADV. through oversight inadvertently by mistake ; mistakenly [A]

سہولت *sohoo'lat* N.F facility ease [A ~ سہل]

سہی *sehī'* ADJ. proposed (cypress) ADJ. (used in PH. سرو سہی *sar'v-e sehī'*) (see under سرو N.M. ★)

سہی *sa'hī* ADV. (used predicatively) all right let it be so who cares well granted however ; though this if nothing more at least

سہیل *sohail'* N.M. Canopus ; the dog star [A]

سہیلی *saheli* N.F. woman's friend of own sex, girl's girl friend

سہیم *sahim'* N.M. partner equal, peer [A ~ سہم]

سی *si* ADJ. thirty [P]

سی *si* ADV. (see under سا ADV. ★)

سی سی *si' si* N.F. hiss hissing sound denoting effect of sting, pongency or cold

سے *se* PREP. from with by than (see under سا ★) میں سے *men se* ADV. through out of اس وجہ سے *is vaj'h se* CONJ. therefore because of سے کہنا *se kaih'na* ask ; tell speak to

سیاح *sayyah'* N.M. traveller itinerant globe-trotter سیاحت *siya'hat,* سیاحی *sayya'hi* N.F. travel globe troting journey voyage

سیادت *siya'dat* N.F. leadership hegemoney suprencey seniority being a Sayyid ★ ; descent from the Holy Prophet [A]

سیار *siyar'* N.M. jackal رنگے سیار *rah'ge siyar'* N.M. (iron used as honorific) swindler criminal posing as pious person

سیارہ *sayya'rah* N.M. planet ADJ. (usu. سیار *sayyar'*) wandering [A ~ سیر]

سیاست *siyasat* N.F. politics strategy diplomacy management administration chastisement سیاستدان *siya'sat-dan'* N.M. & ADJ. statesman politician (derof.) diplomat, diplomatic سیاستدانی *siya'sat-da'ni* N.F. statesmanship سیاست مدن *siya'sat mu'dun* N.M. civics (old use) political science سیاسی *siya'si* ADJ. political diplomatic سیاسی جماعت *siya'si jama'at* political party سیاسی گفتگو *siya'si g'ftugoo'* N.F. diplomatic (way of) talk سیاسیات *siyasiy'yat'* N.F. political scinice ماہر سیاسیات *ma'hir-e siyasiyyat'* N.M. political scientist [A]

سیاق *siyaq'* (usu. سیاق و سباق *siya'q-o-sibaq'*) N.M. context اس سیاق و سباق میں *is siya'q-o-sibaq' men* CONJ. in this context [A]

سیال *sayyal'* N.M. & ADJ. fluid [A ~ سیل]

سیاں *say'yan* N.M. woman's sweetheart lover husband friend سیاں بھئے کوتوال اب ڈر کاہے کا *say'yan bha''e kot'val ab dar' ka'he ka* PROV. a friend in court makes the process short

سیانا *sya'na* ADJ. grown up ; mature wise hrewd ; sazacious clever thrifty N.M. exorciser قاضی جی کے گھر کے چوہے بھی سیانے *qa' zi ji ke ghar ke choo'he bhi sya'ne* PROV even the servant of a wise man is not a fools سیانا کوا گوہ کھاتا ہے *sya'na kav'va gooh kha'ta hai* PROV person who are too clever have to eat the humble pie ; some persons overreach themselves سیانا پن *sya'na-pan,* سیان پن *syan-pan* N.M. سیان پت *syan'-pat* N.F. sagacity shrewdness cleverness maturity thrift

سیاہ *siyah'* (CONTR. سیہ *siyah'*) ADJ. black dark ominous sombre سیاہ (یا سیہ) باطن *siyah'* (or *siyah'*)-*ba'tin* ADJ. malicious (person) سیاہ (یا سیہ) باطنی *siyah'* (or *siyah'*)-*ba'tini* N.F. malice; maliciousness hypocrisy سیاہ (یا سیہ) بخت *siyah* (or *siyah'*)-*bakh't* ADJ. unlucky; unfortunate سیاہ (یا سیہ) بختی *siyah'* (or *siyah'*)-*bakh'ti* N.F. misfortune سیاہ (یا سیہ) پوش *siyah'* (or *siyah'*)-*posh* ADJ. dressed in black (as sign of mourning) N.M man in black N.F. one in widow's weeds سیاہ (یا سیہ) چشم *siyah'* (or *siyah'*)-*chash'm* ADJ. black-eyed سیاہ (یا سیہ) فام *siyah'* (or *siyah'*)-*fam* ADJ. park complexioned black jet black dark سیاہ (یا سیہ) کار *siyah'* (or *siyah'*)-*kar'* ADJ. sinful lewd ; debanched wicked N.M. sinner سیاہ (یا سیہ) کاری *siyah'* (or *siyah'*)-*ka'ri* N.F. lewdness ; debanchery sinfulness wickedness سیاہ گوش *siyah'-gosh* N.M. lynx سیاہ (یا سیہ) مست *siyah'* (or *siyah'*)-*mast'* ADJ. dead drunk سیاہ و سفید *siya'h-o-sifed'* N.M. full powers everything good or bad سیاہ و سفید کا مالک ہونا *siya'h-o-sifed' ka ma'lik ho'na* V.I. evield full powers be in control سیاہ کرو چاہے سفید *siyah' ka'ro cha'he sifed'* PH. do whatever you like the discretion lies with you you are invested with full powers

سیاہہ *siya'hah* N.M. (arch.) account book. register سیاہہ کرنا *siya'hah kar'na* V.T. (arch.) enter into a register سیاہہ ہونا *siya'hah ho'na* V.I. be entered thus سیاہہ نویس *siya'ha-navis'* N.M. accountant

سیاہی *siya'hi* N.F. ink blackness ignominy lamp black [P]

سیب *seb* N.M. apple سیب زنخدان *se'b-e za'nakh-dan* N.M. (fig.) small lovely chin [P]

سیپ *sip,* سیپی *si'pi* N.F. oyster shell سیپ سا منہ نکل آنا *sip' sa munh ni'kal a'na* V.I. grow very weak

سیت *sit* N.F. exudation (esp. from limb ends)

سیتا *si'ta* N.M. Hindu deity Rama's consort ; Sita سیتا پھل *si'ta phal* N.M a kind of sweet pumpkin [S]

سیتلا *sit'la* N.F (dial.) smallpox [S]

سیٹھ *seth* N.M. business magnate capitalist (title of respect for) tycoon

سیٹھا *si'tha* ADJ. insipid ; vapid tasteless سیٹھا پن *sitha-pan* N.M. insipidity ; vapidity tastelessness

سیٹی *sī'ṭī* N.M. whistle سیٹی بجانا *sī'ṭī baja'na* V.T. blow a whistle ; whistle سیٹی بجنا *sī'ṭī baj'na* V.I. whistle

سیج *sej* N.F. bed ; couch سیج بچھانا (یا لگانا) *sej bichha'na* (or *laga'na*) V.I. make the bed پھولوں کی سیج *phoo'loṅ kī sej* N.F. floral wreath for bed (fig.) bed of roses کانٹوں کی سیج *kāṅ'ṭoṅ kī sej* N.F. bed of thorns

سیحوں *se'hoon* (ped. *saihoon'*) N.M. Jexartes [A ~ T]

سینچنا *sīṅch'na* (or *seṅch'na*) V.T. irrigate water (a plant) feed (with one's blood) سنچائی *siṅchā'ī* N.F. irrigation remuneration for it

سیخ *sīkh* N.F. spit skewer سیخ پا ہونا *sīkh'-pa ho'na* V.I. (of horse) rear fly into a passion be incensed سیخ پر لگانا *sīkh' par laga'na* V.I. put (meat) on a spit ; roast سیخنا *sīkh'na* ADJ. (of grilled meat) prepared on spit [P]

سید *say'yid* N.M. descendant of the Holy Prophet ; Syed (rare) lord سیدزادہ *say'yid-zā'dah* N.M. one born of a Syed ; descendant of the Holy Prophet سیدانی *saidā'nī* N.F. descendant of the Holy Prophet [A ~ سیادت]

سیدھ *sīdh* N.F. direction being straight سیدھ باندھنا *sīdh' bāndh'na* V.I. take aim gain a direct line کی سیدھ میں *kī sīdh' meṅ* ADV. in the direction of ناک کی سیدھ میں *nāk' kī sīdh' meṅ* ADV. straight on

سیدھا *sīdha*, ADJ. (F. سیدھی *sī'dhī*) upright erect straight direct straight forward simple right correct سیدھاپن *sī'dhā-pan* N.M. simplicity being straight سیدھاسادہ *sī'dha sā'dah* ADJ. simple homely unpretentions unembellished سیدھا کرنا (یا بنانا) *sī'dhā kar'na* (or *bana'na*) V.T. straighten poise (gun, etc.) to take aim correct chastise سیدھا ہاتھ *sī'dha hāth'* N.M. right hand سیدھا ہونا *sī'dhā ho'na* N.M. be set right سیدھی راہ چلنا *sī'dhī rāh' chal'na* V.I. take the right path سیدھی طرح *sī'dhī tar'h* ADV. unhesitatingly properly سیدھے *sī'dhe* ADV. direct straight on سیدھے ہاتھ *sī'dhe hāth* ADV. to the right سیدھے منہ بات نہ کرنا *sī'dhe mūṅh bāt na kar'na* V.I. be too proud be curt [above]

سیدی *sī'dī* N.M. (coll. شیدی *shī'dī*) N.M. (title for) Negro [~ A سید CORR.]

سیر *sair* N.F. walk ; stroll ; perambulation excursion picnic sight seeing amusement ; recreation travel tour delectable experience سیربین *sair' bīn'* N.F. panorama سیرسپاٹا *sair' sapā'ṭa* N.M. walk or travel for amusement سیر دیکھنا *sair dekh'na* V.I. see a lot of fun ; enjoy سیر کرنا *sair' kar'na* V.I. take a walk, stroll ; to take the air, perambulate travel see a place round (a place) go out sight-seeing enjoy سیرگاہ *sair'-gah* N.F. beauty spot ; recreation centre amusement park garden walk سیرو تفریح *sair' (-o-) tafrīh'* N.F recreation سیرو شکار *sair'(-o-)shikar'* N.M. shooting and hunting ; shikar [A]

سیر[1] *ser* ADJ. satiated satisfied content filled ; saturated fed up [P]

سیر[2] *ser* N.M. weight equivalent to about 2 lb, seer سیر کو سوا سیر *ser' ko sa'vā ser'* PH. tit for tat ; one better سیر کی ہانڈی میں سوا سیر پڑا اور ابل گیا *ser' kī hāṅ'ḍī meṅ sa'va ser pa'ṛa aur ū'bal ga'ya* PROV. the upstart has his head turned سیروں لہو بڑھنا *se'roṅ la'hoo baṛh'na* V.I. grow very happy

سیر *si'yar* N.F. (PL. of سیرت N.F ★)

سیراب *serāb'* ADJ. well-watered satisfied fresh ; blooming سیراب کرنا *serāb' kar'na* V.T. irrigate saturate سیراب ہونا *serāb ho'na* V.I. be irrigated be saturated be happy be fresh سیرابی *serā'bī* N.F. irrigation saturation content سیرچشم *ser'-chash'm* ADJ. satisfied; content not greedy سیرچشمی *ser-chashmī* N.F. satisfaction, content lack of greed ; not being greed سیرحاصل *ser'-hā'sil* ADJ. comprehensive detailed productive سیری *se'rī* N.F. satiety being fed up [P]

سیرت *sī'rat* N.F. (PL. سیر *si'yar*) biography the Holy Prophet's life or biography character [A]

سیروا *ser'va* N.M. head (or foot) piece of bed

سیڑھی *sī'ṛhī* N.F. ladder staircase step سیڑھی سیڑھی چڑھنا *sī'ṛhī sī'ṛhī chaṛh'na* V.I. climb step by step ; make gradual progress

سیزدہ *sez'dah* ADJ. thirteen سیزدہم *sez'-dahūm* ADJ. thirteenth [P]

سیس *sīs* N.M. (dial.) head سیس ناگ *sīs'-nāg* شیش ناگ *shīsh'-nāg* N.M. king cobra (Hindu myth.) serpent-god سیس نوانا *sīs' nivā'na* V.I. (dial.) bow yield ; submit [S]

سیسہ *sī'sah* N.M. lead سیسہ پلائی دیوار *sī'sāh pilā'ī divar* PH. leaden wall fully united, standing like one man

سیف *sef* N.M. safe ADJ. safe [E]

سیف *saif* N.M. (PL. سیوف *suyoof'*, اسیاف *asyāf'*, *as'yāf*) sword سیف الملوک *saif-ūl-mūlook'* N.M. name of a legandary prince سیف زبان *saif'-zabān'* (or *zubān'*) ADJ. & N.M. (pious person) whose pronouncements prove to be true [A]

سیکنڈ *sakint, saikand* N.M. & ADJ. second سیکنڈری *sai'kandrī* ADJ. secondary سیکنڈری بورڈ *sai'kand'rī-bor'd* N.M. Board of Intermediate and Secondary Education [E]

سیفہ *sai'fah* N.M book-binder's knife ; guillotine سیفہ کرنا *sai'fah kar'nā* V.T. cut book edges smooth [~A سیف]

سیفی *saī'fī* ADJ. & N.F. imprecation prayer meant to harm someone rosary سیفیاں پڑھنا *saifiyān paṛh'nā* V.I. say imprecatory prayers

سیکرٹری *saik'reṭarī* N.M. secretary [E]

سینکڑا *saink'ṛā*, سیکڑا *saik'ṛā* N.M. hundred hundred(s) ADV. percent ; per hundred سینکڑوں *saink'ṛoṅ* ADJ. hundreds

سیکھنا *sīkh'nā* V.I. learn study acquire knowledge get instructions from be an understudy سیکھ *sīkh* N.F. (dial.) instruction advice سیکھ دینا *sīkh de'nā* V.T (dial.) advise ; tender or offer advice to سیکھ لینا *sīkh' le'nā* V.T. learn acquire proficiency in

سیگون *segaun'* N.M. mixture of sand and clay

سیل *sīl* N.F. moisture ; damp humidity respect bashfulness سیلا *sī'lā* ADJ. (F. سیلی *sī'lī*) moist damp cool سیل جانا *sīl' jā'nā* V.I. become damp

سیل *sīl* N.M. seal سیلڈ *sīl'd* ADJ. sealed [E]

سیل *sail* N.M. (same as سیلاب N.M. ✱)

سیلا *se'lā* N.M. a kind of rice a kind of mantle a kind of silk turban

سیلاب *sailāb'*, سیل *sail* N.M. flood , spate inundation سیلابی *sailā'bī* ADJ. inundated (land ; (land) dependent (for crops) on inundation inundation سیلابی نہر *sailā'bī naih'r* N.F inundation canal [A سیل + P آب]

سیلان *sailān'* N.M. (rare) flow (also سیلان الرحم *sailā'n-ūr-rahm'*) N.F. leucorrhoea سیلانی *sailā'nī* N.M. & ADJ wanderer tramp hedonist one of the gay world [A]

سیلکھڑی *sīlakh'ṛī* N.F. a species of steatite , soapstone

سیلی[1] *se'lī* N.F slap ; cuff (fig.) rebuff [P]

سیلی[2] *se'lī* N.F necklace of black thread silk or hair worn by mendicants

سیم *sīm* N.F. silver (rare) card; wire سیم تن *sīm'-tan*, سیمیں تن *sī'mīn-tan* ADJ fair , blonde

سیم و زر *sī'm-o-zar'* N.M. riches ; wealth سیمیں *sī'mīn* ADJ. silver ; silvery white fair ; blonde [P]

سیم *sem* N.F. broad bean ; flat bean (dial.) water logging سیم اور تھور *sem' aur thoor'* N.F. (dial.) water-logging and salinity سیم زدہ *sem'-za'dah* ADJ. (dial.) water-logged (land or area)

سیما *sīmā'* N.M. face ; countenance ; aspect ; visage SUF. visaged [P]

سیماب *sīmāb'* N.M. mercury ; quicksilver سیماب وش *sīmāb'-vash* ADJ. restless سیمابی *sīma'bī* ADJ. tinctable rest [P ~ سیم + آب]

سیمرغ *sīmūr'gh* N.M. phoenix ; a legendary bird [P ~ سی + مرغ]

سیمنٹ *sī'mant* N.F. cement [E]

سیمیا *sīmiyā* N.M. occult art supposedly enabling practitioner to cause an migration of souls illusion magic سیمیائی *simiyā''ī* ADJ. illusory [P]

سین *sīn* N.F. scene [E]

سیمل *se'mal*, سنبھل *sam'bhal* N.M. plant with fruit yielding a kind of down ; 'semal'

سیمیں *sī'mīn* ADJ. (see under سیم *sīm* N.F. ✱)

سیمینار *sai'mīnar* N.M. seminar [E]

سینا *sī'nā*, *sai'nā* N.M. Sinai طور سینا *too'r-e sai'nā* N.M. Mount Sinai [A]

سینا[1] *se'nā* V.I. hatch (eggs) ; sit on (eggs)

سینا[2] *se'nā* N.F. (dial.) army ; force سیناپتی *se'nā-pa'tī* N.M. (dial.) Commander-in-Chief ; C-in-C [S]

سینا *sī'nā* V.T. sew stitch

سینات *sīnat'* N.F. senate [~E]

سینتالیس *saintā'lis* ADJ. & N.M. forty-seven سینتالیسواں *saintā'līsvāṅ* ADJ. forty-seventh

سینتنا *sent'nā*, *saint'nā* V.I. save ; put by keep carefully سینت سینت کر رکھنا *sent' sent kar rakh'nā* V.I. save ; put by

سینتیس *saintīs'* ADJ & N.M. thirty-seven سینتیسواں *saintīs'vāṅ* ADJ. thirty-seventh

سینٹ *saint* N.M. scent [E]

سینٹ *saināt* N.F Senate سینیٹر *sai'neṭar* N.M

سیندور *sendoor'* N.M. vermillion , minium , cinnabar سیندوری *sendoo'rī* ADJ. vermillion سیندوریا

sendoo'riyā ADJ. & N.M. a species of mango ; red-spotted mango

سینده sendh N.F. hole made in wall by burglar house-breaking سینده لگانا sendh' lagā'nā V.T. break into a house N.M. house-breaking

سیندھی sen'dhī N.F. date-liquor ; date-palm juice used also polic drink

سینک sīnk N.F. stick ; small thin stick small piece of straw, etc. toothpick

سینکنا senk'nā V.I. warm (oneself before fire) آنکھیں سینکنا āṅ'kheṅ senk'nā V.I. enjoying looking at pretty woman or women سینک senk N.M. warmth induced (by fire)

سینگ sīng N.M. horn سینگ کٹا کر بچھڑوں میں شامل ہونا sīng' kaṭā' kar bachh'ṛoṅ meṅ sha'mil ho'nā V.I. try to look young in old age سینگ مارنا sīng' mār'nā V. butt gore سینگ نکلنا sīng' ni'kalnā V.I. (of animals) grow get horns attain majority go mad (with) جہاں سینگ سمائیں نکل جائیں ja'hāṅ' sīng' samā'eṅ ni'kal jā'nā PH. go (one's) way shift for oneself not to be subject to discipline

سینگڑا sīng'ṛā N.M. (musical) horn powder-horn سینگی sīṅ'gī N.F. cupping horn سینگی (یا سینگیاں) لگانا sīṅ'gī (or sīṅ'giyāṅ) lagā'nā V.T. cup

سینگیاں

سینہ sī'nah N.M. breast chest bosom (fig.) heart سینہ افگار (یا فگار) sī'na afgār' (or figār') سینہ چاک sī'na-chāk ADJ. & N.M afflicted (person سینہ ابھار کر چلنا sī'na ūbhār' kar chal'nā V.I. strut سینہ بند sī'na-band N.M. bodice ; stays ; brassiers (or سینہ بہ سینہ ، سینہ بسینہ sī'na ba-sī'nah ADV. secret unwritten whishered ADV. secretly (transmitted) in strict confidence سینہ بیں sī'na-bīn N.F. stethoscope سینہ زنی sī'na-zanī', سینہ کوبی sī'na-ko'bī N.F. beating the breast سینہ زور sī'na-zor' ADJ. headstrong ; wayward proud of one's strength cruel ; oppressive ; tyrannical سینہ زوری sī'na-zo'rī N.F. waywardness strength cruelty; oppression سینہ سپر sī'na-si'par ADJ. defending ; shielding سینہ سپر ہو جانا sī'na-si'par ho jā'nā V.I. defend ; shield take a firm stand سینہ سوزی sī'na-so'zī N.F. anguish ; torment سینہ کاوی sī'na-kā'vī N.F. great eff... very hard work سینے سے لگانا sī'ne se lagā'nā V.T. embrace (lovingly or patronisingly) سینے کا ابھار sī'ne kā ūbhār' N.M. smelling of breasts (as sign of puberty) contour(s) of female figure [P]

سینی sīnī N.F. tray salver

سینیئر sī'niyar ADJ. senior سینیارٹی sīniyār'ṭī N.F. seniority [E]

سیو seyo' N.M. thick fried macaroni seyo' sāṅ'kheṅ N.F. PL. fried macaroni (thick or otherwise)

سیوا se'vā N.F. (dial.) service سیوادار se'vā-dār' N.M. (dial.) attendant at Sikh shrine سیوا کرنا se'vā kar'nā V.T. (dial.) serve سیوک se'vāk (dial.) N.M. attendant [S]

سیوتی siyo'tī N.F. dogrose

سیوف suyoof' N.M. (PL. of سیف saif N.F. ★)

سیوک se'vak N.M. (see under سیوا N.F. ★)

سیون sī'van N.F. seam suture urinary duct [~ سینا]

سیونگ se'ving N.F. سیونگ بنک se'ving-bank N.M. savings bank سیونگ بنک اکاؤنٹ se'ving-baink' aikā'-uṅṭ N.M. Savings Bank account [E]

سیہ (or سیہ) seh N.F. porcupine

سیئہ sayye'ah N.F. evil ; evil deed ADJ. evil سیئات sayye'āt' N.F. PL. evils [A]

ش

ش shīn (colloquially called ba'ṛā sīn) nineteenth letter of Urdu alphabet (equivalent to English sh) (in jummal recoking) 300 شین قاف سے درست ہونا shīn' qāf se dūrus't ho'nā V.I. have a faultless pronunciation be cultured

شاب shab N.M. (PL. شبان shūbbān') youth شیخ و شاب shaikh-o shab' N.M. the old and the young

شاباش shābāsh' INT. bravo ; well done ; excellent buck up N.M. praise appreciation pat شاباش دینا shābāsh' de'nā V.I. praise buck up pat شاباشی shābā'shī N.F. (col.) (same as شاباش INT. ★) [P ~ شا + باش]

شاخ shākh N.F. branch bough sprig ; spray scion (of plant) branch (of establishment piece (of) objection ; cavil (dial.) a kind of wheat sweet rolled like a sprig ; sprig-sweet (rare) horn شاخ آہو shā'kh-e ā'hoo N.M. horn of deer bow crescent برات عاشقاں بر شاخ آہو barā't-e 'āshiqāṅ bar shā'kh-e ā'hoo PROV. the unfortunate are always tantalized by nature vain hopes شاخدار shākh'-dār ADJ. branched bifurcating horned شاخ در شاخ shākh' dar shākh

ADJ. intricate with one point leading to another شاخ زعفران *shā'kh-e za'farān'* N.M. one with too high an opinion of oneself strange matter شاخ طوبیٰ *shā'kh-e too'bā* N.M. a branch of the heavenly tree blessed sign شاخ لگانا *shākh' lagā'nā* V.T. plant sapling (of) set someone extra work شاخ نبات *shā'kh-e nabāt'* N.F. crystallizing stick very sweet thing lovely maiden شاخ نکالنا *shākh nikāl'nā* V.T. cavil find (another) cause for quarrel شاخسار *shākh-sār* bower garden place abounding in trees ADJ. (rare) having many branches شاخسانہ *shākhsā'nah* N.M. cavil suspicion calumny dilemma new point شاخسانہ پیدا (یا کھڑا) کرنا *shākhsā'nah pai'dā* (or *khā'ṛā*) *kar'nā* *shā'khah* ADJ. pronged [P]

شاد *shād* ADJ. happy, glad joyful, cheerful pleased ; delighted شاد باید زیستن ناشاد باید زیستن *shād' bā'yad zīs'tan nā-shād' bā'yad zīs'tan* PROV. one has the put up with all sorts of conditions شاداں *shā'dāṅ*, شادماں *shād'māṅ* ADJ happy delighted شادکام *shād'-kām'* ADJ. successful happy delighted شاد کرنا *shād'-kar'nā* V.T. delight, gladden شادکامی *shād kā'mī* N.F. elation with success شادمانی *shād-mā'nī* N.F. happiness rejoicing [P]

شاداب *shādāb'* ADJ. well-watered green, verdant lush (of face) radiant with health شادابی *shādā'bī* N.F. verdure fertility being well-irrigated (of face) radiating with health شادی *shā'dī* N.F. ★ [P ~ شاد + آب]

شادی *shā'dī* N.F. marriage wedding pleasure ; delight rejoicing ; festivity شادی رچانا *shā'dī rachā'nā* V.T. & I. celebrate marriage شادی کرنا *shā'dī kar'nā* V.T. marry شادی مرگ *shā'dī-mar'g* N.F. death from sudden joy کی شادی مرگ ہو جانا *kī shā'dī mar'g ho jā'nā* V.I. (of someone) die thus شادی و غم *shā'dī-o-gham* N.M. PL. غم و شادی *gha'm-o shā'dī* N.M. joy and grief شادی غمی *shā'dī gha'mī* N.F. (COL.) joy and grief (on) festive occasions or (at) funeral gatherings شادی ہونا *shā'dī ho'nā* V.I. be married شادیانہ *shādiyā'nah* N.M. festive music (usu. PL.) festive song(s) شادیانے بجانا *shādiyā'ne bajā'nā* V.I. play festive music rejoice [P]

شاذ *shāz* ADJ. rare ADV. rarely seldom few and far between شاذ و نادر *shā'z-o nā'dir* ADJ. ADV. rare(ly) [A]

شارح *shā'reh* N.M. exegesist commentator annotator expositer [A ~ شرح]

شارع *shā're'* N.M. the Holy Prophet as the law giver law-giver legislator road; highway شارعِ عام *shā're'-e 'ām* N.M. thoroughfare [~ شریعت]

شاستر *shās'tar* (ped. *shās'tr*) N.M. (dial.) Hindu code of law having religious sanction شاستری *shās'tarī* (ped. *shāstrī*) N.M. one skilled in Hindu law [S]

شاشہ *shā'shah* N.M. urine ; piss [P ~ شاشیدن]

شاطر *shā'tir* N.M. (rare) chess-player ADJ. cunning ; sly clever shrewd smart یارِ شاطر *yā'r-e shā'tir* N.M. shrewd friend یارِ شاطر ہوں نہ بارِ خاطر *yā'r-e shā'tir hooṅ' na bār-e khā'tir* PL. I am a shrewd friend not a bore [A]

شاعر *shā''ir* N.M. (PL. شعرا *sho'arā'*) poet bard minstrel شاعرانہ *shā'irā'nah* ADJ. poetical exaggerated fantastic rhapsodic شاعرہ *shā''irah* N.F. (PL. شاعرات *shā'irāt'* ped PL. شواعر *shavā''ir*) poetess شاعری *shā''irī* N.F. poety; art of poetry verse, poetic composition exaggeration ; hyperbole rhapsody fantasy fancy highfalutin' language [A ~ شعر]

شاغل *shā'ghil* ADJ. busy ; occupied [A ~ شغل]

شافع *shā'fe'* N.M. intercessor شافعِ (روزِ) محشر *shāfe'-e (ro'z-e) mah'shar* N.M the Holy Prophet (as his followers' intercess or with God on the Day of Reckoning) شافعی *shā fe''ī* N.M. Shaafiite follower of Imam Sh'fi'is school of Islam jurisdiction [A]

شافہ *shā'fah* N.M. suppository pessary cotton wool soaked in liquid medicine and applied to wound dressing lint [P]

شافی *shā'fī* ADJ. healing sanative curative efficacious (fig.) convincing (reply) N.M. healer شافیِ مطلق *shā'fī-e mut'laq* N.M. God (as the Healer) ; the Absolute Healer [A ~ شفا]

شاق *shāq* ADJ. hard ; trying disliked unsavoury ; unpalatable (پر) شاق گزرنا (*par*) *shāq gu'zarnā* V.I. be very trying (for) be disagreeable (to) شاقہ *shāq'qah* ADJ. very hard (work): tiring محنتِ شاقہ *meh'nat-e shāq'qah* N.F. very hard work burning the midnight oil [A ~ مشقت]

شاقول *shāqool'* N.M. plumb-line [A ~ T ساقول]

شاکر *shā'kir* ADJ. thankful or grateful (to God) content (with one's lot) [~ شکر *shuk'r*]

شاکی *shā'kī* ADJ. complaining querulous discontented (with one's lot, etc.) N.M. complainant murmerer aggrieved (party) [A ~ شکایت]

شاگرد *shāgir'd* N.M. pupil student ; scholar disciple apprentice (rare) servant شاگرد بننا (یا ہونا) *shagir'd ban'nā* (or *ho'nā*) V.I. become student or apprentice (لوگ) شاگرد پیشہ *shāgird'-pe'sha (log')* N.M. PL. servants ; retainers شاگردی *shāgir'di* N.F. studentship pupilage apprenticeship [P]

شال *shāl* N.M. shawl ; stole شالباف *shāl'-bāf* N.M. shawl-weaver ; shawl-maker شالبافی *shāl-bā'fi* N.M. shawl-weaver's trade shawl-making شال دوز *shāl'-doz* N.M. shawl-embroiderer شالدوزی *shāl-do'zī* N.F. shawl-embroidery [P]

شالیمار *shāli'mār* (col. شالامار *shā'lāmār'*) N.M. Shalimar Gardens ; either of the two gardens of that name built under the Moghuls

شام[1] *shām* N.F. evening شام اودھ *shā'm-e a'vadh* N.F. lovely evening scene of Lucknow in pre-British days ; the Lucknow evening (OPP. صبح بنارس see under صبح N.M. ★) شام غریباں *shā'm-e gharī'bāṅ* N.F. hapless traveller's evening the evening finalizing Muharram mourning شام کلیان *shām kalyān'* N.M. name of a musical mode set for evening شام و سحر *shā'm-o-sa'ḥar* N.M. morning and evening all the time (PL.) days and nights (of) [P]

شام[2] *shām* N.F. ferrule (of stick, etc.) [~ P سم *sum* CORR.]

شام[3] *shām* N.M. Syria شامی ADJ. & N.M. ★)

شام[4] *shām*, شیام *shyām'* N.M. tawny (as appellation of Hindu apostle Krishna) [S]

شاما *shā'ma*, شیاما *shyā'ma* N.F. native cuckoo [S ~ PREC.]

شامت *shā'mat* N.F. misfortune ; ill-luck evil days punishment شامت اعمال *shā'mat-e a'māl'* N.F. punishment for evil deeds misfortune شامت آنا *shā'mat ā'na* V.I. face bad-luck fall upon evil days شامت کا مارا *shā'mat ka mā'ra* ADJ. & N.M. unfortunate (person) miserable (person) [P]

شامل *shā'mil* ADJ. PREP. (used alone or with *meṅ* or ped. *ko* or *ke*) comprising including included (in) mingled or blended (with) ; going along (with) شامل حال *shā'mil-e hāl'* ADJ. connected with accompanied by ADV. accompanying given ; granted شاملات *shāmilāt'*, شاملات دہ *shā'milā't-e deh* N.F. village common شاملاتی *shāmila'tī* ADJ. joint co-parcenary [A ~ شامل]

شامہ *shām'mah* N.M. sense of smell ; olfaction [A ~ شم]

شامی *shā'mī* ADJ. & N.M. Syrian شامی کباب *shā'mī kabāb'* N.M. fried mince cake ; mince pie [~ شام[3]]

شامیانہ *shāmiyā'nah* N.M. awning pavilion canopy [P]

شان *shān* N.F. dignity splendour (rare) state ; condition (rare) circumstances (of) شان چوٹا *shān' choṭ'ṭā* N.M. one trying to emulate another شاندار *shān-dār'* ADJ. splendid stately dignified شان دکھانا *shān' dikhā'na* V.T. make a display (of) show off شان گھٹانا *shān' ghaṭā'na* V.T. be derogatory (to) شان میں بٹہ لگنا *shān' meṅ baṭ'ṭah lag'na*, شان گھٹنا *shān' ghaṭ'na* V.I. be lowered in dignity شان نزول *shā'n-e nūzool'* N.M. circumstances of revelation (of Quranic verse) (joc.) cause or account of arrival شان و شوکت *shān-o-shau'kat* N.F. pomp and show glory splendour [A]

شانتی *shānt* ADJ. (dial.) calm peaceful شانت *shān'tī* N.F. (dial.) peace tranquillity calm [S]

شانہ *shā'nah* N.M. shoulder comb شانہ پھڑکنا *shā'nah pha'ṛakna* V.I. have a good omen of someone arriving شانہ کرنا *shā'nah kar'na* V I. comb شانے ہلانا *shā'ne hilā'na* V.T. shake (someone) by the shoulder to rouse him from sleep [P]

شاہ *shāh*, شہ *shah* N.N. king ; monarch king (at chess) title of Syed or Muslim mendicant PREF. chief large royal شاہانہ *shāha'nah* ADJ. royal ; regal splendid شہباز *shah'bāz'* شاہباز *shāh'bāz* gowshak falcon شہبالا *shah-bā'lā* N.M. bestman ; groom's young attendant شاہ بلوط *shāh'-balloot'* (col. *-baloot'*) N.M. oak شہتیر *shaihtīr'* (ped. *shahtīr'*, arch. شاہ تیر *shāh-tīr'*) N.M. beam شاہ خاور *shā'h-e khā'var* N.M. (rare) sun شہپر *shah'-par*, شاہ پر *shāh-par* N.M. principal feather in bird's wing شاہترہ *shāh-tarah*, شہترہ *shah'tarah* N.M. fumitory شاہ توت *shāh-toot'*, شہتوت *shaihtoot'* N.M. mulberry شاہ خانم *shāh'-khā'nūm* N.M. (iron.) proud woman شاہدرہ *shāh-da'rah* N.M. gateway (to) شاہ دولہ کا چوہا *shāh' dau'lah kā choo'hā* N.M. (dial.) small-headed imbecile (known) after Shah Daulah of Gujrat W. Pakistan in whose sanctuary they found asylum شاہراہ *shāh'rāh'* N.F. thoroughfare highway شہ رگ *shah'-rag* شاہ رگ *shāh'-rag* N.F jugular vein شہزادہ *shah-zā'dah*, شاہزادہ *shāh'-zā'dah* N.M. prince شہزادی *shah-zā'dī*, شاہزادی *shāh'-zā'dī* N.F. princess شہزادگی *shah-zā'dagī* شاہزادگی *shāh-zā'dagī* N.F. state of being a prince ; princehood شہسوار *shah-savār'*, شاہ سوار *shāh'-savār'* N.M. horseman jockey شاہکار *shāh'-kār*, شہکار *shahkār'* N.M. masterpiece شاہ گام *shāh gām'* N.F. (animal's) nice gait شاہ مرداں *shā'h-e mar'dāṅ*, شہ مرداں *sha'h-e mar'dāṅ* N.M. master-chevalier (as appellation of Hazrat Ali) شہ نشین

shah-nashin, شاہ نشیں shah'-nashin' N.M. balcony dais royal seat شہوار شاہوار shah-var' shah-var' ADJ. worthy of a sovereign royal شہنشاہ shahin-shah', شاہنشاہ sha'hin-shah' N.M. shahinshah ; emperor شاہی sha'hi ADJ. royal ; regal N.F. sovereignty dominion reign name of a small coin [P]

شاہد sha'hid N.M. (PL. شواہد shava'hid) witness deponent sweetheart [A]

شاہیں sha'hin (or -hin') N.M. falcon this as Iqbal's symbol for Muslim youth [P]

شائبہ sha''ibah N.M. (PL. شوائب shava''ib) doubt ; suspicion trace (of) (rare) adulteration [A ~ شوب]

شائستہ sha''is'tah ADJ. polite ; courteous cultured ; well-bred proper ; suitable decent شائستگی sha''istagi N.F. courtesy ; politeness good manners affability propriety decency [P ~ شائستن]

شائع sha''e' ADJ. published propagated broadcast patent (fast) شائع کرنا sha''e' kar'na V.T. publish ; bring out propagate شائع ہونا sha''e' ho'na V.I. be published ; be brought out be propagated [A]

شائق sha''iq ADJ. fond (of) ardent; zealous [A ~ شوق]

شائگان sha''e-gan N.M. name of an ancient royal Persian treasure wealth defective rhyme ADJ. royal ; regal [P]

شایان sha'yan ADJ. fit (for) ; suitable (for) worthy (of) ; worth [P]

شاید sha'yad ADV. perhaps possibly probably [P ~ شائستن]

شب shab N.F. night شبانہ روز shaba'na-roz ADJ. unceasing round-the-clock ADV. night and day all the time round the clock شب باز shab-baz' N.M. (arch.) puppet showman شب بازی shab-ba'zi N.F. puppet show شب باش shab-ba'sh' N.M. night lodger شب باش ہونا shab-bash' ho'na V.I. stay for the night (with or at) شب باشی shab-ba'shi N.F. staying for the night cohabiting (with) شب بخیر shab-ba-khair' INT. goodnight شب برات shab-e bara''at (col. شب برات shab'-barat') N.F. fifteenth night of Sha'ban (bringing salvation and fulfilment of wishes to those who pray for these شب برات کی آتشبازی shab'-barat' ki a'tash-ba'zi N F. fire work display on his festival shab'bo N.M. a kind of lily emitting fragrance at night ; champak شب بیدار shab-bedar' ADJ. & N.M. (one) waking all night in worship شب بیداری shab-beda'ri N.F. waking all night in worship vigil شب تاب shab-tab' N.F. (usu. کرمک شب تاب kir'mak-e shab-tab') glow-worm ; firefly ADJ. incandescent شب تابی shab-ta'bi N.F. incandescence شب تار (یک) shab-e tar' (ik') N.F dark night : moonless night شب چراغ shab-chiragh' N.M. (also گوہر شب چراغ gau'har-e shab-chiragh') N.M. a kind of jewel carbuncle شب خوابی کا لباس shab-kha'bi ka libas' N.M. night clothes ; the pyjamas شبخون shab-khoon' N.M. night attack ; sniping شبخون مارنا shab khoon' mar'na V.T. snipe شب خیزی shab-khe'zi N.F. rising at night (for prayer) شب دیجور shab-e daijoor' N.M. very dark night شبدیز shab-dez' N.M. dark horse شب دیگ shab-deg' N.F. meat and turnip stew cooked all night شب رنگ shab-rang' ADJ. dark-coloured شب زفاف shab-e zifaf' N.F. (see under زفاف ★) شب زندہ دار shab zin'da-dar ADJ. & N.M. (one) waking all night (for worship) شب زندہ داری shab zin'da-da'ri N.F. waking all night thus شبستان shabis'tan N M bed chamber harem ; seraglio شب قدر sha'b-e qad'r (col. shab'qad'r) N.F. night during which the Holy Quran's revelation began (occurring the last ten nights of Ramazan usu. regarded as 27th) شب کور shab-kor' ADJ. night blind شب کوری shab-ko'ri N.F. night blindness شبگوں shab-goon' ADJ. jet black darksome شبگیر shab-gir' ADJ. of early hours of morning شب ماہ sha'b-e mah'. شب ماہتاب sha'b-e mahtab' N.F. moonlit night شب یلدا sha'b-e yalda' N.F. longest and darkest night of the year شبینہ shabi'nah ADJ. left over from the previous night overnight N.M. Ramazan night (or three nights towards the end of that month) in which the whole of the Holy Quran is recited in prayers such recital شب و روز sha'b-o roz, روز و شب ro'z-o shab' ADV. night and day, always ; all the time N.M. PL. nights and days (of) ; all the time (of) [P]

شباب shabab' N.M. youth ; prime of life [A]

شبان shub'ban N.M. (PL. of شاب N M. ★)

شبان shuban' N.M. shepherd ; pastor [P]

شباہت shaba'hat N.F likeness , similarity resemblance figure شکل و شباہت shak'l-o shaba'hat N.F. features [A]

شبد shab'd N.M. (dial.) word Hindu hymn [S]

شبر shab'bar N.M. appellation of Imam Hasan [A ~ Syriac]

شبستان shabistan' N.M. (see under شب N.M. ★)

شبنم shab'nam N.F. dew a kind of fine linen ; lawn شبنمی shab'nami ADJ. dewy N.M canopy for bed [P]

شبہ *shib'h* N.M. likeness similitude image (of) وجہ شبہ *vaj'h-e shib'h* N.F. point of similitude [A]

شبہ *shub'h* (col. *shu'ba*) N.M. doubt ; suspicion uncertainty شبہ دور کرنا *shub'h door kar'na* شبہ مٹانا *shub'h miṭa'na* V.T. dispel a doubt شبہ (ظاہر) کرنا *shub'h (za'hir) kar'na* V T. suspect شبہ ہونا *shub'h ho'na* V.I. be a doubt (about) have a suspicion [A]

شبھ *shubh'* ADJ. (dial.) suspicious [A]

شبیر *shabbir'* N.M. an appellation of Imam Husain [A ~ Syriac]

شبینہ *shabi'nah* ADJ. (see under شب N.F. ★)

شبیہ *shabih'* N.F. picture ; portrait image figure ADJ. like ; resembling [A ~ شبہ]

شپا *ship'pa* N.M. relation شپا لڑانا *ship'pa lara'na* V.T. concoct relationship (with)

شپاشپ *sha'pa-shap* N.F. splash ADV. rapidly [ONO.]

شپر *shap'par*, شپرہ *shap'parah* N.M. bat شپرہ چشم *shap'para-chash'm* ADJ. day-blind [P ~ شب + پریدن]

شتا *shi'ta* N.M. winter [A]

شتاب *shitab'* ADV. soon swiftly PREF. quick haste ; quickness شتابی *shita'bi* N.F. swiftness haste despatch ADV. (also شتابی سے *shita'bi se*) soon swiftly

شتر *shu'tur*, اشتر *ush'tur* N.M. camel شتربان *shu'tur-ban* N.M. camel driver شتر بے مہار *shu'tur-e be-mohar'* (fig.) ADJ. & N.M. wayward ; refractory incorrigible (person) out of control شتر خانہ *shu'tur-kha'nah* N.M. camel shed شتر غمزہ *shu'tur-gham'zah* N M. uncalled for coquetry fraud ; deceit شتر کینہ *shu'tur-ki'nah* N M. unending malice ADJ. & N.M. very malicious (person) شتر گربہ *shu'tur-gur'bah* N.M. unmatched pair change of pronoun with reference some noun شتر مرغ *shu'tur-mur'gh* N.M. ostrich شتر نال *shu'tur-nal* N.F. (arch.) a kind of small gun carried on camel's back [P]

شتری *shu'tri* N.F. large kettle-drum (for carrying on camel back) camel colour ADJ. camel coloured camel hair camel skin [P]

شتم *shat'm* N.F. villifying swearing at سب و شتم *sab'b-o-shat'm* N.F. (see under سب ★) [A]

شجاع *shuja'* ADJ. brave bold ; courageous شجاعت *shaja''at* N.F. bravery; valour [A]

شجر *sha'jar* N.M. (PL. اشجار *ashjar'*) tree plant شجرہ *sha'jarah* (col *shaj'rah*) N.M. (PL. شجرات *shajarat'*) (rare) tree genealogical table ; family tree list of a saintly line agrarian field-map [A]

شحم *shaḥ'm* N.F. fat شحیم *shaḥim'* ADJ. fat لحیم شحیم *laḥi'm-o-shaḥim'* ADJ. plump ; fat [A]

شحنہ *sheḥ'nah* N.M. metropolitan police chief اترا شحنہ مردک نام *ut'ra sheh'nah mar'dak nam* PROV. a fallen angel is dubbed a devil [P]

شخص *shakh's* N.M. (PL. اشخاص *ashkhas'*) person individual body ; human body شخصی *shakh'si* ADJ. personal private individual شخصی حکومت *shakh'si ḥukoo'mat* N.F. one-man rube ; individual's rule absolute monarchy شخصیت *shakhsiy'yat* N.F. personality (rare) prestige شخصیت بگاڑنا *shakhsiy'yat bighar'na* V.I. talk tall be vain [A]

شد *shad* N.M. stress ; emphasis intensification (gram.) doubling (of letter) شد و مد *shad'd-o mad* N.F. force ; invigour intensity severity stress ; emphasis شداد *shaddad'* N.M. name of an Adermite ruler claiming divinity ; Shaddad [A]

شدائد *shada''id* N.M. PL. hardships ; tribulations [A ~ SING. شدیدہ ~ شدید]

شدبد *shud' bud* N.F. sight knowledge (of) nodding acquaintance (with language), etc.) [P شد + بد ~ بود was]

شدت *shid'dat* N.F. intensity vehemence severity rigours (of) شدت کا *shid'dat ka* ADJ. severe [A]

شدنی *shu'dani* ADJ. destined inexorable N.F. inexorable matter ناشدنی *na-shu'dani* ADJ. & N.F. undesirable

شدھ *shudh* ADJ. (dial.) purified (development) شدھی *shud'dhi* N.F Hindu proselytism (esp. as an early 20th century political movement [S]

شدہ شدہ *shu'da-shu'dah* ADV. gradually in course of time

شدید *shadid'* ADJ. intense severe rigorous violent acute (pain) heinous (crime) [A ~ شدت]

شذرہ *shaz'rah* N.M. (PL. شذرات *shazarat'*) editorial note ; leaderette [A]

شر *shar* N.M. evil ; wickedness turmoil unrest شر اٹھانا *shar' uṭha'na* V.I. create unrest ; cause a breach of the peace raise malicious objection [A]

شری (or شرا) *shara'* (or *shira'*) N.M. purchase بیع و شری *bai'-o-shara* N.F. (see under بیع N.F. ★)

شراب **sharāb'** N.F. liquor wine (rare.) beverage شراب دوآتشہ **shara'b-e do-ā'tashah** N.M. double-distilled wine. strong drink شراب خانہ **sharāb'-khā'nah** N.M. public house ; pub ; bar ; tavern شراب طہور **sharā'b-e tahoor'** N.F. nonalcoholic beverage ; non-intoxicating drink (as heavenly beverage) شرابی **sharā'bī** N.M. drunkard boozer [A]

شرابور **sharābor'** (col. شور بور **shor-bor'**) ADJ. dripping ; drenched; wet through پسینے میں شرابور **pasī'ne meṅ sharā'bor** PH. perspiring dipping with sweat

شراٹا **sharrā'ṭā** N.M. spurt beating sound (of rain, etc.) [ONO.]

شرادھ **sharādh'** N.M. PL. (dial.) food given their priests by Hindus for the dead this as festival [S]

شرار **sharār'**, شرارہ **sharā'rah** N.M. spark [P]

شرارت **sharā'rat** N.F. naughtiness mischief wickedness ; villainy شرارتی **sharā'ratī** ADJ. naughty villainous N.M. mischievous child varmint شریر **sharīr'** ADJ. ★ [A]

شرافت **sharā'fat** N.F. virtue ; virtuous character good manners politeness ; courtesy; civility nobility شریف **sharīf'** ADJ. ★ [A]

شراکت **sharā'kat** N.F. partnership شراکت کرنا **sharā'kat kar'nā** V.I. enter into partnership شراکت نامہ **sharā'kat-nāmah** N.M. dead of partnership شرکت N.F. ★ شریک ADJ. & N.M. ★)

شرائط **sharā''it** N.M. (PL. of شرط N.F. ★)

شرائین **shar'īn** N.F. (PL. of شریان N.F. ★)

شرب **shūr'b** N.M. drinking اکل و شرب **ak'l-o-shūr'b** N.M. eating and drinking [A]

شربت **shar'bat** N.M. syrup شربت پلائی **shar'bat pilā''ī** N.F. money given to barber of bride's family) for offering drink to groom at marriage ; drink-reward شربت کے پیالے پر نکاح پڑھانا **shar'bat ke piyā'le par nikāḥ' parhā'nā** V.T. give away a girl in marriage with little expenditure شربتی **shar'batī** ADJ. & N.M. light orange reddish N.M. this colour a kind of fine muslin kind of small sweat berry [A ~ PREC.]

شرح **shar'ḥ** (col. **sharaḥ**) N.F. explanation commentary exegesis rate charge ratio details exposition شرح بندی **shar'ḥ-bań'dī** N.F. fixation of rates rate schedule شرح صدر **shar'ḥ-e sad'r** N.M. conviction ; inner light lack of reservations شرح صدر کے ساتھ **shar'ḥ-e sad'r ke sāth** ADV. with an open mind without reservations شرح کرنا **shar'ḥ kar'nā** V.I. explain write a commentary (on) ; write an exegesis (of) شرح مقرر کرنا **shar'ḥ mūqar'rar kar'nā** V.I. fix the rate of [A]

شرر **sha'rar** N.M. spark شرر بار **sha'rar-bār**, شرر فشاں **sha'rar-fishāṅ'** ADJ. fiery sore (heart) sparkling ; scintillating ; coruscating [P]

شرط **shar't** N.F. (PL. شرائط **sharā''it** rare شروط **shūroot'**) term condition stipulation proviso provision rider bet ; stake ; wager شرط باندھنا (یا بدنا یا لگانا) **shar't bāndh'nā** (or **bad'nā** or **lagā'nā**) V.I. bet ; lay a wager شرطیہ **shartiy'yah** ADJ. sure guaranteed ; warranted ADJ. certainly ; undoubtedly definitely (gram conditional (clause) بشرطیکہ **ba-shar'te-keh** ADV. if provided in case بلا شرط **bi-lā-shar't** ADJ. unconditional مردوں سے شرط باندھ کر سونا **mūr'doṅ se shar't bāndh ke so'nā** V.I.

شرع **shar''** (col. **sha'ra'**) N.M. divine law religious dogma Islamic law (as such) شرعاً **shar''an** ADV. legally ; in point of law ; according to the law ; juridically according to Islamic law شرعاً و عرفاً **shar''an-o-'ūr'fan** ADV. according religious and customary law شرع میں کیا شرم **shar'' meṅ kyā' shar'm** PH. why be ashamed of a divinely sanctioned act why be ashamed of an inquiry on a point of religious law شرعی **shar''ī** ADJ. lawful religious dogmatic [A]

شرف **sha'raf** N.M. honour rank dignity glory nobility eminence excellence شرف حاصل ہونا **sha'raf ḥā'sil ho'nā** V.I. be honoured (by) شرف لے جانا **sha'raf le jā'nā** V.T. excel شرف یاب **sha'raf-yāb'** ADJ. honoured ; exalted شرف یاب ہونا **sha'raf-yāb' ho'nā** V.I. be honoured شرف یابی **sha'raf-yā'bī** N.F. honour audience شرف یابی بخشنا **sha'raf-yā'bī bakhsh'nā** V.T. grant audience [A]

شرفا **shūrafā'** N.M. (PL. of شریف N.M & ADJ. ★)

شرق **shar'q** N.M. east شرقاً غرباً **shar'qan ghar'ban** ADV. ADJ. laterally East West شرق سے غرب تک **shar'q se ghar'b tak** ADV. from East to West throughout the world شرقی **shar'qī** ADJ. Eastern oriental [A]

شرک **shir'k** N.M. polytheism pasanism شرک جلی **shir'k-e ja'lī** N.M. idolatry شرک خفی **shir'k-e khā'fī** N.M. infidelity [A]

شرکا **shūrakā'** N.M. (PL. of شریک ★)

شرکت shir'kat N.F. (ped. sha'rikat) participation (rare) firm ; company شراکت N.F. ★ شریک ADJ. & N.M. ✯) [A]

شرم shar'm N.F. shame bashfulness modesty disgrace ; indignity honour ; prestige sense of honour شرما شرمی shar'ma shar'mī ADV. out of shame driven by a sense of prestige شرم دلانا shar'm dilā'na V.T put to shame disgrace challenge (someone's) sense of honour شرم رکھنا shar'm rakh'nā' V.T. protect (someone) from being put to shame شرم رہ جانا shar'm raih jā'nā V.I. have one's prestige or honour undamaged شرم کرنا shar'm kar'nā V.I. feel ashamed شرمسار shar'm-sār ADJ. ashamed repentant sorry (for) شرمسار ہونا shar'm-sār ho'nā V.I. regret; be sorry (for) شرمساری shar'm-sā'rī N.F. shame disgrace sorrow ; regret repentance شرم سے پانی پانی ہونا shar'm se pānī pā'nī ho'nā V.I. feel much ashamed شرمگاہ shar'm gāh' N.F. private parts (of one's body) شرمگیں shar'm-gīn' ADJ. ashamed bashful modest blushing شرمناک shar'm-nāk' ADJ. shameful disgraceful discreditable شرم و حیا shar'm-o-ḥayā' N.F. modesty بے شرم be-shar'm ADJ. shameless devoid of a sense of shame بے شرم بے غیرت be-shar'm be-ghai'rat INT. (as a swear-word) devoid of all sense of shame شرمندہ sharmin'dah ADJ. ashamed regretting ; sorry (for) repentant simpering شرمندۂ احسان sharmin'da-e ehsān' (or -sāh') ADJ. under obligation (to) شرمندۂ معنی sharmin'da-e ma''nī (or -nā) ADJ. meaningful شرمندہ ہونا sharmin'dah ho'nā V.I. feel ashamed ; be ashamed be sorry (for) : regret شرمندگی sharmin'dagī N.F. shame disgrace bashfulness regret , sorrow شرمندگی اٹھانا sharmin'dagī uṭhā'na V.I. suffer shame be disgrace شرمانا sharmā'na V I feel ashamed be bashful fight shy (of) شرمیلا sharmī'lā (F. شرمیلی sharmī'lī) ADJ. modest bashful shy [P]

شروا shūr'vā N.M. (col.) stew ; broth [~P شوربہ CORR.]

شروط shūroot' N.M. (PL. of شرط N.F. ✯)

شروع shū'roo' N.M. start , beginning; commencement شروع سے آخر تک shū'roo' se ā'khır tak ADV. from beginning to end شروع کرنا shū'roo' kar'nā V.T. begin , start , commence set up institute take the lead شروع ہونا shū'roo' ho'nā V I be begun get going شروعات shūroo'āt' N F (col.) beginning ; start [A]

شری shi'rī (ped shrī). سری si'rī ADJ. (dial) (Indian title equivalent to) Mr. شریمتی shi'rīmatī ADJ. (Indian title equivalent to) Mrs. Madam [S]

شریان shiryān' N.F. (PL. شرائین sharā'īn') artery [A]

شریر sharīr' ADJ. mischievous naughty wicked evil bad N.M. mischief-monger ; mischief maker [A ~ شرارت]

شریعت sharī''at N.F. (PL. شرائع sharā''e') Islamic jurisprudence divine law [A ~ شرع]

شریف sharīf' ADJ. (PL. شرفا shūrafa') virtuous gentle polite ; courteous noble honourable N.M. gentleman (ped.) syed , descendent of the Holy Prophet (rare.) chieftain , chief شریفانہ sharīfā'nāh ADJ. gentlemanly (conduct, etc.) شریف النفس sharī'f-ūn-naf's ADJ. noble N.M. a noble soul شریف خاندان sharīf khān'dān N.M. good family شریف زادہ sharīf'-zā'dah (N.M. scion of a gentlemanly family) ADJ. of good family [A ~ شرافت]

شریفہ sharī'fah N.M. custard apple

شریک sharīk' N.M. (PL شرکا shūrakā') participant accomplice comrade associate confederate partner peer ADV included شریک کرنا sharīk' kar'nā V.I. join include make a partner شریک ہونا sharīk' ho'nā V.T join participate [A ~ شراکت]

شست shas't (col. shis't) N.F. aim (rare) pinch (ped.) fishing-hook شست باندھنا یا لگانا shas't bāndh'nā (or lagā'nā) V T take aim (at) [P]

شستہ shūs'tah ADJ. cultured chaste (language, etc.) شستگی shūs'tagī N F good manners chastity of language [P]

شش shūsh N.M. lung [P]

شش shash ADJ. SIX PREF hexa , six شش پہلو shash-paih'loo ADJ. hexagonal شش جہت shash-je'hat N.M. the six directions شش جہت میں shash-je'hat meṅ ADV. all over everywhere شش دانگ shash-dāng' ADJ. all over the world ششدر shash'dar ADJ astonished perplexed stunned agape, six-doored N.M. (arch.) dice ششدر ہونا یا رہ جانا shash'dar ho'nā (or raih' jā'nā) V.I. be astonished be left wondering be agape ششماہی shash-mā'hī ADJ. half-yearly ; biennial N.F half year , six-month period شش و پنج sha'sh-o-panj' N.M. perplexity confusion hesitation

ششم sha'shūm ADJ sixth [P]

شصت shas't ADJ sixty [P]

ششکارنا shūshkār'nā V.T. urge (hound) on to quarry ششکار shūshkār' , ششکاری shūshkā'rī

N.F. sound emitted for urging thus

شط shat N.M. river bank شط العرب shat' t-ul-'a'rab N.M. Tigris and Euphrates after their conflux [A]

شطاح shattah' N.M. pert ; saucy [A ~ foll.]

شطحیات shathiyyat' N.M. & F. blasphemous writings irreverent criticism of Islamic dogma profane talk by insane mystics [A]

شطرنج shatranj N.F chess شاطر (یا شطرنج باز) shatir N.M. chess-player شطرنجی shatran'ji N.M. chequered carpet loaf made of assorted cereals' flour شطرنجی باف shatran'ji-baf' N.M. carpet weaver [A ~ S]

شعار she'ar' N.M. (PL. شعائر sha'a''ir) sign habit ; custom manner (rare) undergarment PREF. in the habit (of) accustomed (to) شعاری she'a'ri SUF. being in the habit (of) [A]

شعاع sho'a'' N.M. (PL. اشعہ ashe''ah) ray ; beam [A]

شعائر sha'a''ir N.M. PL. signs (of God) (pilgrimage) rites [A ~ SING. شعار or شعیرہ]

شعبان sha'ban' N.M. eighth month of Hijri year [A]

شعبدہ sha''badah N.M. sleight of hand ; juggling ; conjuring deceit ; fraud شعبدہ باز sha''bada-baz' N.M. juggler ; conjurer ADJ. fraudulent ; deceitful شعبدہ بازی sha''bada-ba'zi N.F. sleight of hand duping deceitfulness [A]

شعبہ sho''bah N.M. (PL. شعبہ جات sho'ba-jat') department branch ramification field (of knowledge. etc.) [A]

شعر sha''r N.M. (PL. شعار she'ar' or اشعار ash'ar') hair [A]

شعر she''r N.M. (PL. اشعار ash'ar') couplet verse poetry شعر خوانی she''r-kha'ni N.F. recitation of poetry fondness for poetry

شعر کہنا she''r kaih'na V.I. compose verses ; versify she''r-go''i N.F. versification fondness for poetry شعرا sho'ara' N.M. (PL. of شاعر N.M. ★) شعریت she'riy yat N.F. poetical beauty poetic element [A]

شعشعہ sha''sha'ah N.M. flash [A]

شعلہ sho''lah N.M. flame , blaze شعلہ افشاں sho''la-afshan, شعلہ فشاں sho''la-fishan', شعلہ بار sho''la-bar' ADJ. flaming blazing raining fire and brimstone firebrand شعلہ بھبوکا ہونا sho''lah bhaboo'-ka ho'na V.I. fly into a passion ; flush with anger شعلہ جوالہ sho''la-e javva'lah N.M pirouetting flame (fig.) beloved ; sweatheart شعلہ خو sho''la-khoo' ADJ. fiery-tempered شعلہ رخ sho''lah-rukh, شعلہ رو sho''la-roo' N.M. & ADJ. blazing beauty شعلہ زن sho''la-zan' ADJ. blazing flashing شعلہ زنی sho''la-za'ni N.F. blaze ; blazing شعلہ فشاں sho''la-fishan' ADJ. flame-scattering ; fire-spitting fiery شعلہ فشانی sho''la-fisha'ni N.F. blaze ; blazing fire-spitting [A]

شعور sho'oor' N.M. consciousness ego intellect wisdom شعوری sho'oo'ri ADJ conscious تحت الشعور tah't-ush-sho'oor' N.M. sub-conscious mind ; the sub-conscious تحت الشعوری tah't-ush-sho'oo'ri N.M. sub-conscious لاشعور la sho'oor' N.M. the unconscious mind sub-conscious mind ; the sub-conscious Id لاشعوری la-sho'oo'ri ADJ. sub-conscious [A]

شغال shaghal' N.M. jackal سگ زرد برادر شغال sa'g-e zar'd bira'dar-e shaghal' PROV. the two are equally bad [P]

شغب sha'ghab N.M. tumult (usu. as) شور و شغب shor-o-sha'ghab N.M. noise and tumult [A]

شغف sha'ghaf N.M. interest in [A]

شغف shagh'f N.M. deep love [A]

شغل shugh'l (or shagh'l) N.M. (PL. اشغال ashghal') occupation business vocation avocation engagement [A]

شفا shifa' N.F. cure healing recovery شفاخانہ shifa'-kha'nah N.M. (PL. شفاخانجات shifa'-kha'najat') hospital [A]

شفاعت shafa''at N.F. intercession شافع sha'fe' N.M ★ [A]

شفاف shaffaf' ADJ. transparent pellucid clear [A]

شفتالو shafta'loo N.M. peach [P]

شفتل shaf'tal N.F. (dial.) slut

شفعہ sh'f'ah N.M. pre-emption حق شفعہ haq q-e sh'f'ah N.M. right of pre-emption [A]

شفق sha'faq N.F. evening twilight ; redness in the horizon at evening شفق پھولنا sha'faq phool'na V.I. (of redness) appear in the horizon [A]

شفقت shaf'qat (ped. sha'faqat) N.F. affection favour kindness شفیق N.M. ★ [A]

شفیع shafi' N.M. intercessor شافع sha'fe' N.M & ADJ. ★ [A ~ شفاعت]

شفیق shafiq' ADJ. affectionate kind N.M. kind friend [A ~ شفقت]

شق shaq N.M. rent; cleavage split ; fissure شق القمر shaq' q-ul-qa'mar N.M lunar fissure ; split the moon (as a miracle of the Holy Prophet) شق ہونا shaq' ho'nā V.I be rent, be split [A]

شق shiq N F item [A]

شقاق shiqāq' N.M enmity rift schism [A]

شقاوت shaqā'vat N.F. misfortune wretchedness villainy callousness [A]

شقائق shaqā''iq N.M (also PL.) tulip [A]

شقہ shūq qah N.M edict letter from a superior flag, piece of cloth hoisted on Shi'ite mourning flag [A]

شقی sha'qī N.M. & ADJ. (PL اشقیا ashqiyā') unfortunate wretched; miserable villainous; vicious callous شقی القلب shaqiy'y-ul-qal'b ADJ. callous [A ~ شقاوت]

شقیق shaqiq' N.M. (PL. اشقا ashqqā') brother [A]

شقیقہ shaqī'qah N.M temple, side of head (properly درد شقیقہ dar'd-e shaqī'qah)

شک shak N.M. (PL. شکوک shukook') doubt suspicion uncertain incredulity شک پڑنا shak' par'nā V.I. suspect, have a doubt شک ڈالنا shak' dāl'nā V.T make suspicious cast a doubt upon شک رفع کرنا shak' raf'' kar'nā V.T. dispel a doubt remove a doubt شک کرنا shak' kar'nā V.I. doubt, suspect شکی shuk'kī ADJ. suspicious sceptical شکی مزاج shuk'kī-mizāj ADJ. incredulous suspicious sceptical [A]

شکار shikār' N.M. game, hunting, shikar chase prey quarry شکار بند shikār'-band N.M saddle straps near horses tail for tying game in شکارپور shikār'-poor N.M (fig.) Gotham شکار پور کا چوتیا shikār'-poor kā choo'tiyā N.M. wise man of Gotham شکار کرنا shikār' kar'nā V.T. hunt, prey upon catch shoot (game) ensnare bag make (someone) one's victim; capture شکار کھیلنا shikār' khel'nā V.I. go on a hunting expedition; go out for shikar chase (quarry) hunt شکار کے وقت کتیا ہگائی shikār' ke vaq't kut'yā hagā''ī, بوقت شکار کتیا ہگائی ba-vaq't-e shikār kut'yā hagā''ī PROV false excuses put up at critical juncture شکارگاہ shikār'-gāh N.F. game preserve hunting ground شکار ہونا shikār' ho'nā V.I. fall a prey (to) become a victim (of) be ensnared (by) شکاری shikā'rī N.M. shikaree; sportsman; hunter follower angler ADJ. of the chase: hunting شکاری کتا shikā'rī kut'tā N.M. hound a species of large lean dogs kept for hunting [P]

شکارا shikā'rā N M light pleasure boat water taxi

شکایت shikā'yat N.F complaint plaint accusation grievance illness شکایت رفع کرنا shikā'yat raf'' kar'nā V.I redress a grievance [A]

شکتی shak'tī N.F (dial.) strength [S]

شکر shūk'r N.M. thanks gratitude thanks giving شکر کرنا (یا بجا لانا) shūk'r kar'nā (or ba-jā' lā'nā) V T. & I. thank return thanks rest content شکرگزار shūk'r-güzār' ADJ. thankful grateful: obliged شکرگزار ہونا shūk'r-guzār' ho'nā V.I شکرگزاری shūk'r-güzā'rī N.F. thankfulness; gratitude; thanksgiving شکرانہ shukrā'nah N.M. thanksgiving, gratitude شکرانے کے نفل shūkrā'ne ke naf'l N.M. PL. thanksgiving; prayers شکریہ shūkriy'yah (or shūk'ri'yah) N.M thanks INT. thank you, 'k you [A]

شکر sha'kar N.F sugar شکر پارہ sha'kar-pā'rah N.M sugar-coated vermicelli شکرتری sha'kar-ta'rī N.F. (arch.) white sugar شکرخند sha'kar-khand N.M. smile joyful smile شکرخورہ sha'kar-kho'rah N.M. one having a sweet tooth شکررنجی sha'kar-ran'jī N.F tiff usu. temporary estrangement between friends, estrangement خدا شکرخورے کو شکر ہی دیتا ہے khūdā' sha'kar-kho're ko sha'kar hī de'tā hai PROV. he that eats good meal shall have a good meal شکر سے منہ بھرنا sha'kar se muṅh bhar'nā V.T reward (someone) for conveying good news شکرریز sha'kar-rez ADJ. sweet tongued mellifluous شکرقندی sha'kar-qan'dī (ped. شکر قند sha'kar-qand) N.F. sweet potato شکرلب sha'kar-lab ADJ. having sweet speech N.M. (fig.) sweetheart شکری sha'karī N.M. a kind of small sweet berry شکرین sha'karīn ADJ. sugary sugar; of sugar شکرین shakarīn N.F saccharin [P]

شکرم shik'ram N.M. phaeton

شکرہ shik'rah N.M. hawk; falcon

شکست shikas't N.F. defeat rout failure breakage dilapidation depreciation شکست خوردہ shikas't-khur'dah ADJ. defeated, routed defeatist شکست خوردہ ذہنیت shikas't-khur'dah zehniy'yat N.F. defeatist mentality شکست خوردگی shikas't-khur'dagī N.F. defeatism شکست وریخت shikas't-o-rekh't N.F dilapidation خط شکست khat'-e shikas't N.M. running hand (as a form of Urdu script) شکستہ shikas'tah ADJ broken snapped ruined; lying in ruins dilapidated in a state of ill repair N.M. running hand this as a form of Urdu script شکستہ بال shikas'ta-bāl' شکستہ پر shikas'ta-par' ADJ. wretched, miserable afflicted helpless شکستہ پا shikas'ta-pa' ADJ. helpless unable to move شکستہ پائی shikas'ta pa''ī N.F. inability to move helplessness شکستہ حال shikas'ta ḥāl' ADJ. miserable; wretched down-trodden broken down ADV. in straitened circumstances شکستہ حالی shikas'ta-ḥā'lī N.F. being broken down wretchedness; misery شکستہ خاطر shikas'ta-khā'tir ADJ. depressed grieved شکستہ دل shikas'ta-dil' ADJ. broken hearted شکستہ دلی shikas'ta-di'lī N.F. state of being broken hearted شکستگی shikas'tagī N.F. breaking being broken breakage fracture dilapidation dejection ruin [P ~ شکستن]

شکل shak'l (col. sha'kal) N.F. (PL. اشکال ashkāl') shape form figure image diagram condition; state fashion; style means kind ADJ. like شکل بگاڑنا shak'l bigāṛ'na V.T. mar disfigure شکل بنانا shakl-banā'nā V.T. & I. draw a diagram make a likeness (of) give shape (to) شکل تو دیکھو shak'l to de'kho INT. look fool (etc.) posing as sage (etc.) شکل چڑیلوں کی ناز پریوں کا shak'l chuṛe'loṅ kī nāz' par'yoṅ kā PROV. ugly witch strutting about as beauty شکل نکالنا shak'l nikāl'nā V.I. find (some) way out; give (oneself or something) a form شکل و شمائل shak'l-o shamā'il N.F. appearance and character ہم شکل ham-shak'l ADJ. similar (to) looking like looking alike [A]

شکم shi'kam N.M. stomach; belly شکم پرور shi'kam-par'var ADJ. & N.M. glutton شکم پروری shikam-par'varī N.M. gluttony شکم سیر shi'kam ser' ADJ. & ADV. satiated well-to-do; well-off شکم سیر ہو کر کھانا shi'kam-ser' ho kar khā'nā V.I. eat to one's fill شکم سیری shi'kam-se'rī N.F. satiaty شکمی shi'kamī ADJ. of or relating to the belly private; secret inherent dependent; subordinate شکمی کرایہ دار shi'kamī kirā'ya-dār' N.M. subtenant [P]

شکن shi'kan N.F. crease wrinkle fold SUF. breaking شکن پڑنا shi'kan par'nā V.I. be creased ماتھے (یا ابرو میں) شکن پڑنا mā'the (or ab'roo meṅ) shi'kan par'nā V.I. frown; show signs of displeasure شکن ڈالنا shi'kan ḍāl'nā V.T. crease fold ماتھے (یا ابرو میں) شکن ڈالنا mā'the par (or ab'roo meṅ) shi'kan ḍāl'nā V.T. show sign of displeasure [P]

شکنجہ shikan'jah N.M. clamp book-binder's press stocks torture straitened circumstances شکنجے میں کھینچنا shikan'je meṅ khench'nā V.I. put on the stocks torture; put in straitened circumstances [P]

شکوک shukook' N.M. (PL. of شک N.M. ★)

شکور shakoor' N.M. thankful person deserving thanks [A ~ شکر shuk'r]

شکوہ shukoh' (col. shikoh') N.M. pomp grandeur splendour state; majesty شان و شکوہ shā'n-o-shukoh' N.M. pomp and show grandeur [P]

شکوہ shik'vah N.M. complaint; plaint lamentation جواب شکوہ javā'b-e shik'vah N.M. answer to the complaint شکوہ و جواب شکوہ shik'va-o-javā'b-e shik'vah N.M complaint and answer [A ~ شکایت]

شکوئی shak'vā N.M. complaint; plaint lamentation [A ~ doublet of PREC.]

شکی shak'kī ADJ. (see under شک N.M. ★)

شکیب shikeb' N.F. patience endurance صبر و شکیب sab'r-o-shikeb' N.M. patience and endurance شکیبا shike'bā ADJ. patient شکیبائی shikebā''ī N.M. patience endurance [P]

شکیل shakīl' ADJ. handsome; comely [A ~ شکل

شگاف shigaf' N M. split (in pen or nib) crevice crack cleft rent slit fissure chasm شگاف پڑ جانا shigaf' paṛ jā'nā V.I. have a slit شگاف دینا (یا لگانا) shigaf' de'nā (or lagā'nā) V.T. split (a pen) cleave [P]

شگرف shigar'f ADJ. strange curious [P]

شگفتہ shig f'tah N.M. blooming happy شگفتہ خاطر shigūf'ta-khā'tir, شگفتہ مزاج shigūf'ta-mizāj' N.M. & ADJ. cheerful humorous (person) شگفتہ رو shigūf'ta-roo' ADJ. & N.M. (one) with a cheerful countenance شگفتگی shigūf'tagī N.F. blooming cheerfulness happy countenance streak of humour شگفتن shigūf'tan N.M. blossoming شگوفہ shigoo'fah N.M. bud blossom (fig.) fib; squib شگوفہ پھوٹنا (یا کھلنا) shigoo'fah phooṭ'nā (or khil'nā) V.I. blossom bud spread شگوفہ چھوڑنا shigoo'fah chhoṛ'nā V. fib let off a squib شگوفہ لانا shigoo'fah lā'nā V.I. bud blossom sprout [P]

شگوفہ shigoo'fah N.M. (see under شگفتہ ADJ. ★)

شگون shugoon' N.M. omen; augury شگون لینا shugoon' le'nā V.T. practise augury consider as an omen شگون ہونا shugoon' ho'nā V.I. be an omen of پرائے شگون کے لیے اپنی ناک کٹوانا parā'e shugoon' ke li'ye ap'nī nāk' kaṭvā'na PROV. cut one's nose to spite one's face [P]

شل shal ADJ. (usu. of hands or feet) benumbed palsied crippled greatly fatigued [P]

شلجم shal'jam, شلغم shal'gham N.M. turnip شلجمی shal'jamī ADJ. large (eyes)

شلاق shalāq' N.M. box ضرب شلاق کرنا zarb-e shalāq' kar'nā V.T. box

شلک shal'lak N.F. volley of guns volley

شلنگ shaling' N.M. shilling [E]

شلنگ shalang' N.F. leap ; bound شلنگ بھرنا shalang' bhar'nā V.I. leap [P]

شلنگا shilan'ga N.M. tack شلنگے بھرنا shilan'ge bhar'na V.T. & I. tack ; baste

شلوار shalvār' N.F. a kind of loose cover for lower limbs ; trousers ; breeches ; pantaloon [P]

شلوک shalok, اشلوک ashlok' N.M. (dial.) hymn [S]

شلوکا shaloo'kā N.M. half-sleeved waistcoat with pockets

شلہ shal'lah, شولہ sho'lah N.M. rice cooked in mince, potherb and pulse [P]

شلیتہ shalī'tah N.M. canvas sack tent, etc. stuffed in such sack

شماتت shamā'tat N F. rejoicing at (another's) distress [A]

شمار shumār' N.M. counting ; enumeration estimation account (usu. نمبر شمار nam'bar shumār') number شمار کرنا shumār' kar'nā V.I. count compute reckon consider شمار میں آنا یا ہونا shumār' meṇ ā'nā (or ho'nā) V.I. be worth consideration شمارہ shumā'rah N.M. issue (of periodical) number شماری shumā'rī SUF. counting ; enumeration census مردم شماری mar'-dūm-shumā'rī N.F. census ; population census شماریات shumāriyyāt' N.F. statistics شماریاتی shumā-riyyā'tī ADJ. statistical [P]

شمال shimāl' N.M. north شمال رویہ shimāl'-roo'yah ADJ. opening on the north شمال مشرق shimāl'-mash'riq N.M. north-east شمال مشرقی shimāl'-mash'riqī ADJ. north-eastern north-easterly شمال مغرب shimāl'-magh'rib N.M. north-west شمال مغربی shimāl' magh'ribī ADJ. north-western north-westerly شمالی shimā'lī ADJ. northern شمالی ہوا shimā'lī havā', باد شمال ba'd-e shimāl' N.F. north wind ; Boreas [A]

شمال shamāl' (or shi-) N.F. north wind : Boreas [A]

شمامہ shamā'mah N.M. fragrance [A]

شمائل shamā''il N.M. PL. nature , disposition qualities ; excellences [A]

شمر shi'mar N.M. name of one of Yazid's generals who killed Imam Husain (hence as abusive term) inhuman [A]

شمس sham's N M. (PL. شموس shumoos') sun شمس العلما sham's-ūlama' N.M. sun of the savants (as title conferred on Muslim religious scholars of British India) شمسہ sham'sa N.M. thread circlet in rosary gold disc on tomb, etc. شمسی sham'sī ADJ. solar شمسی سال sham'sī sal' ADJ. solar year [A]

شمشاد shamshād' N.M. box-tree قد شمشاد qad'(d)-e shamshād' N.M tall and graceful stature like that of pyx [P]

شمشو کرنا sham'shoo kar'nā V.T. separate gravel, etc. from cereal soaked in water

شمشیر shamshīr' (or shamsher') N.F. scimitar ; sword شمشیر باز shamshīr'-baz ADJ. swordman, master of fence شمشیر بازی shamshīr'-ba'zī N.F. sword-play ; fencing شمشیر زن shamshīr'-zan N.M. swordsman شمشیر زنی shamshīr'-za'nī N.F. sword-play ; fencing [P ~ شم]

شمع sham'' (col. sha'ma') N.F. candle (extend sense) lamp شمع دان sham''-dān' N.M. candlestick شمع رو sham''-roo' ADJ. lovely شمع سامنے آنا sham'' sām'ne ā'nā V.I. (in a poetical symposium) be one's turn to recite شمع ساں sham''-sāṇ' bright like the candle شمع مردہ یا کشتہ sham''-e mūr'dah (or kūsh'tah) N.F. extinguished lamp [P]

شملہ sham'lah N.M. loose end of turban شملہ بمقدار علم sham'lah ba-miqdā'r-e 'il'm PROV. style of dress bespeaks the man

شمول shūmool' N.M. شمولیت shūmooliy'yat participation inclusion [A ~ شامل]

شمہ sham'mah N.M. (rare) white of fragrance a little شمہ بھر sham'mah bhar ADJ. little [A]

شمیم shamīm' N.F fragrance fragrant breeze [A]

شناخت shinā'kht (ped. shanākh't) N.F. recognition identification acquaintance knowledge being conversant (with letters of the alphabet) identify شناخت پریڈ shinākh't-pared' N.F. identification parade شناخت کرنا shinākh't kar'nā V.T recognise identify know be able to decipher (letters of alphabet) [F]

شناس shinās' (ped. shanās') PREF. knowing acquainted with understanding able to read (something) شناسی shinā'sī (ped shanā'sī) PREF knowing acquaintance with understanding ability to read (something) [P ~ شناختن]

شناسا **shina'sa'** (ped. **shana'sa**) N.M acquaintance شناسائی **shinasa''i** (ped. **shana'sa**) N.F acquintance, knowledge [P ~ شناختن]

شناور **shina'var** N.M. swimmer شناوری **shina'vari** N.F. swimming [P]

شنبہ **sham'bah** N.M. Saturday یکشنبہ **yak-sham'bah** N.M. Sunday دوشنبہ **do-sham'bah** N.M. Monday سہ شنبہ **se-sham'bah** N.M. Tuesday چہار شنبہ **chahar'-sham'bah** N.M. Wednesday پنج شنبہ **panj-sham'bah** N.M. Thursday [P]

شنگ **shang** ADJ amorously playful (usu. as شوخ و شنگ (see under شوخ ADJ. ★)

شنگرف **shang'raf**, شنجرف **shanj'raf** N.M. cinnabar; vermillion شنگرفی **shang'rafi** ADJ. vermillion [P]

شنوا **shunva'** (ped. **shunuva'**) ADJ. & N.M. hearer; listener شنوائی **shunva''i** (ped. **shunuva''i**) N.F. giving a hearing, response to (someone's) call, etc. شنوائی ہونا **shunva''i ho'na** V.I obtain a hearing; be attended to; have a response (to) [P ~ شنودن]

شنید **shunid'** N.M. act of hearing شنیدنی **shuni'dani** ADJ. worth hearing شنیدہ **shuni'dah** ADJ. heard N.M. rumour that which is heard شنیدہ کے بود مانند دیدہ **shuni'dah kai' bavad' manan'd-e di'dah** PROV. seeing is believing reports are no substitute for first-hand knowledge [P ~ شنیدن]

شنیع **shani'**, (PL. شنیعہ **shani''ah**) ADJ. bad, evil abaminable افعال شنیعہ **af'a'l-e shani''ah** N.M. PL. evil deeds [A]

شو **shau** N.M. husband [P ~ شوہر CONT.]

شو **shiv** N.M. (Hindu deity) Shiva شوالہ **shiva'lah**, شوالا **shiva'la** N.M. Shiva's temple any Hindu temple; temple [S]

شوال **shavval'** N.M. tenth month of Hijri year (heralding 'Id-ul-Fitr') [A]

شوالا **shiva'la**, شوالہ **shiva'lah** N.M. (see under شو **shiv** N.M. ★)

شواہد **shava'hid** N.M. (PL. of شاہد N.M. ★)

شوب **shob** N.M. washing; wash ink sticking on to nib شوب پڑنا **shob' par'na** V.I. (of clothes) be washed [P]

شوخ **shokh** ADJ. sprightly wanton naughty saucy; pert bold; daring bright (colour) fast (colour) شوخ چشم **shokh'-chash'm** ADJ. insolent, impudent wanton-eyed شوخ چشمی **shokh'-chash'mi** N.F. insolence; impudence wantonness شوخ مزاج **shokh'-mizaj'** ADJ. gay naughty شوخ و شنگ **sho'kh-o-shang'** ADJ. gay and amorously playful شوخی **sho'khi** N.M. humour playfulness wantonness coquetry sauciness mischief, naughtiness [P]

شودر **shoo'dar** (ped **shood'r**) untouchable fourth and servile caste among the Hindus [S]

شور **shor** N.M. noise uproar; tumult clamour outcry; agitation fame; renown salimity, soil salimity ADJ. salt, brackish PREF evil; ill شوربخت **shor'-bakht'** ADJ. unlucky شور اٹھنا **shor' uth'na** V.I. (of noise; be (of uproar) be raised شور زمین **shor'-zamin'**, زمین شور **zami'n-e shor'**, N.F. saline soil unculturable land شور شرابا **shor' shara'ba** N.M. noise disturbance شور کرنا (یا مچانا) **shor' kar'na** (or **macha'na**) V.I make a noise disturb hoot kick up a row agitate (against) clamour (for) شور و شر **sho'r-o-shar'**, شور و شغب **sho'r-o-sha'ghab** N.M. uproar clamour tumult bustle شور و شین **sho'r-o-shain'** N.M. outcry wailing **sho'r-o-ghul**, شور و غوغا **sho'r-o-ghau'gha** N.M. noise disturbance شورش **sho'rish** N.F. tumult commotion agitation disruption breach of the peace شورش پسند **sho'rish-pasand'** N.M disruptionist شورش پسندی **sho'rish pasan'di** N.F disruption شورہ **sho'rah** N.M. nitre; saltpetre ADJ. & PREF. mad شورے کا تیزاب **sho're ka tezab'** N.M. nitric acid شورہ پشت **sho'ra-push't** ADJ. unruly; refractory N.M. disruptionist شورہ پشتی **sho'ra-push'ti** N.F disruption شورہ زار **sho'ra-zar'** N.M saline soil, unculturable land شوریت **shoriy'yat** N.F. salinity brackishness شوریدہ **shori'dah** ADJ. & N.M. disturbed mad lunatic wretched or miserable (person) شوریدہ سر **shori'da-sar** ADJ. mad refractory desperately in love شوریدہ سری **shori'da sa'ri**, شوریدگی **shori'dagi** N.F. madness refractoriness passionate love [P]

شوریٰ **shoo'ra** N F. Privy Council consultative body council consultation; deliberation [A ~ شورہ]

شوربا **shor'ba**, شوربہ **shor'bah** (col. شروا **shur'va**) N.M. stew broth [P]

شوربو **shor'bor** ADJ. (same as شرابور ADJ. ★)

شورش **sho'rish** N.F شورہ **sho'rah** N.M. شوریت **shoriy-yat** N.F شوریدگی **shori'dagi** N.F. شوریدہ **shori'dah** ADJ. (see under شور N.M. ★)

شوشہ **sho'shah** N.M. flourish (of pen, etc.) mischief (rare) particle شوشہ چھوڑنا **sho'shah chhor'na** V.I. start mischief; stir trouble نیا شوشہ **naya sho'shah** N.M. mischievous hint or act [P]

شوفر *shau'far* N.M. chauffer [E]

شوق *shauq* N.M. desire longing passion fondness eagerness avidity interest pleasure شوق چرانا *shauq chirrā'nā* (dial. *chirrā'nā*) V.I. have a desire for (ابڑے) شوق سے (*ba're*) *shauq' se* ADV. with (great) pleasure certainly شوق و ذوق *shauq-o-zauq'* N.M. شوقین *shauqīn'* ADJ. fond (of) eager (for) lustful N.M. one leading a gay life, rake شوقیہ *shauqiy'yah* ADV. lovingly just for fun [A]

شوکت *shau'kat* N.F power might pomp grandeur magnificence splendour state dignity شان و شوکت *shā'n-o-shau'kat* N.F. state and dignity power and might splendour grandeur [A]

شوم *shoom* ADJ. & N.M. miser ; niggardly (person) unlucky شومی *shoo'mī* N.F. miserliness ; niggardliness ; stinginess misfortune شومئ بخت (یا تقدیر) *shoo'mī-e bakh't* (or *taqdīr* or *ta'le'*) N.F. illuck ; misfortune [P]

شوں شاں *shooṅ' shāṅ'* N.F. vanity

شوہارن *shoo'-hārn* (or *-ha'ran*) N.M. shoe horn [E]

شوہر *shau'har* N.M. husband زن و شوہر *za'n-o shau'-har* N.M. PL. man and wife [P]

شہ *shah* N.M. (CONTR. of شاہ N.M. ★)

شہاب *shihāb'* N.M. (PL. شہب *sho'hūb*) flame spark live coal meteor شہاب ثاقب *shihā'b-e sā'qib* N.M. meteor bright flame [A]

شہادت *shahā'dat* N.F. martyrdom witness ; evidence testimony شہادت (کا مرتبہ) پانا *shahā'dat* (*kā mar'tabah*) *pā'nā* V.I. be martyred شہادت دینا *shahā'dat de'nā* V.I. give testimony or evidence bear witness (to) testify شہید *shahīd* N.M. ★ شہادت کی انگلی *shahā'dat kī ūng'lī* انگشت شہادت *angūsh't-e shahā'dat* N.F. fore-finger شہادت گاہ (یا گہ) *shahā'dat-gāh* (or *-gah*) N.F. place of martyrdon [A]

شہامت *shahā'mat* N.F. prowess bravery heroism [A]

شہانہ *shahā'nah* N.M. name of a musical mode marital song bridal dress time for wedding procession lovely weather [~P شاہ]

شہد *shaih'd* (ped. *shah'd*, col. *shai'had*) N.M honey شہد کی مکھی *shaih'd kī mak'khī* N.M. bee شہد لگا کر چاٹنا *shaih'd lagā' kar chāṭ'nā* V.I. (iron) keep (trifle) as souvenir [A]

شاہباز *shah'baz* N.M. (falcon (also see under شاہ) [P]

شہپر *shah'par* N.M. principal feather in bird's wring (also see under شاہ ★)

شاہترہ *shah'tarah* N.M. fumitory (also see under شاہ ★) [P] (see under شاہ ★)

شہتوت *shaihtoot'* N.M. mulberry (also see under شاہ ★) [P]

شہتیر *shaihtīr'* N.M. beam (also see under شاہ ★) [P]

شہدا *shoh'dā* N.M. rake ; debauchee rascal, scoundrel tramp ; loafer (dial) buffoon لچا شہدا *luch' chā shoh'dā* N.M. شہدا پن *shoh'dā-pan*, شہد پن *shoh'd-pan* N.M. debauchery rascality

شہدا *shohadā'* N.M. (PL. of شہید N.M. ★)

شہر *shah'r* N.M. (PL. شہور *shohoor'* ا شہر *ash'hur*) month [A]

شہر *shaih'r* (col. *shai'har*) N.M. city شہر آشوب *shaih'r-āshob'* N.M. poem describing a ruined city social satire شہر بدر *shaih'r ba-dar'* ADJ. banished شہر بدر کرنا *shaih'r ba-dar' kar'nā* V.T. banish شہر بسانا *shaihr' basā'nā* V.I. found a city set up a new colony شہر پناہ *shaih'r-panāh'* N.F. city walls fortifications of a town شہر خبرا *shai'har khab'rā* N.M. one who could tell you all the scandals of the town شہر خموشاں *shaih'r-s khamo'-shāṅ* N.M. graveyard ; cemetery شہر داری *shai'har-dā'rī* N.F. (col.) citizenship شہر گرد *shaih'r-gar'd*, شہر گشت *shaih'r-gash't*, شہر پیما *shaih'r-paimā'* N.M. (arch.) city patrol (arch.) tramp ADJ. moving all over the town ; city-wide شہر میں اونٹ بدنام *shaih'r meṅ ooṅ'ṭ bad'-nām'* PROV. notorious person a bad wound heals but a bad name kills شہر یار *shaih'r-yār'* N.M. king ; sovereign شہر یاری *shaih'r-yā'rī* N.F. sovereignty شہری *shaih'rī* ADJ. urban N.M. townsman citizen national of a State شہریت *shaih'riy'yat* N.F. civics citizenship nationality [P]

شہرت *shoh'rat* N.F. fame ; reputation known celebrity report (of) شہرت پیدا کرنا *shoh'rat pai'dā kar'nā* V.I. become famous build up a reputation [A]

شہرہ *shoh'rah* N.M. fame ; reputation renown ; calabrity report publicity, propaganda شہرہ آفاق *shoh'ra-e āfāq'* ADJ famous ; renowned ; of world fame [A doublet of PREC.]

شہانی *shaha'nī* ADJ. bridal bright red [~P شاہ]

شہرگ *shah'rag* N.F. jugular vein (also see under شاہ N.M. ★)

شہری *shaih'rī* ADJ. & N.M. شہریت *shaihriy'yat* N.F (see under شہر *shaih'r* N.M ★)

شہزادہ shaihza'dah (ped. shah'-) N.M. prince شہزادی shaihza'di (ped. shah') N.F. princess شہزادگی shaihza'dagi (ped. shah'-) N.F. state of being prince; princehood (also under شاہ N.M.★) [P]

شہسوار shahsavar' N.M. horseman jockey (also see under شاہ ★) [P]

شہکار shah'kar N.M. masterpiece (also see under شاہ N.M. ★) [P]

شہلا shah'la ADJ. dark (narcissus) dark grey (eyes) (eyes) betraying signs of intoxication N.F. blonde نرگس شہلا nar'gis-e shah'la N.F. dark narcissus (fig.) lovely inebriated eyes [A]

شہنائی shahna''i N.F. flageolet ; flute [P ~ شاہ + نائے]

شہنشاہ shahan-shah' N.M. emperor (also see under شاہ ★) [P]

شہوار shahvar' ADJ. worthy of a sovereign royal (also see under شاہ N.M. ★) [P]

شہ نشین shah nashin' N.F. balcony dais royal seat (also see under شاہ ★) [P]

شہوانی shahva'ni ADJ. (see under شہوت N.F. ★)

شہوت shah'vat (col. shaih'vat) N.F. lust; lechery; lasciviousness شہوت انگیز shah'vat-angez' ADJ. lascivious aphsodisiac شہوت پرست shah'vat paras't ADJ & N.M. lustful (person) ; lascivious (person) ; rake ; debauchee شہوت پرستی shah'vat-paras'ti N.F. lustfulness ; lasciviousness شہوانی shah'vani ADJ. carnal [A]

شہود shohood' N.M. omnipresence of God (as a mystical experience) [A ~ شہادت]

شہ shaih N.F. incitement undue support شہ دینا shaih de'na V.T. incite give undue support (to)

شہید shahid' N M. (PL. شہدا shohada') martyr شہید کرنا shahid' kar'na V.T. martyr شہید ہونا shahid' ho'na V.I. be martyred ; become a martyr لہو لگا کر شہیدوں میں شامل ہونا la'hoo laga' kar shahi'don men sha'mil ho'na PROV. claim a reward without making a sacrifice شہیدی shahi'di ADJ. (dial.) martyr ; comprising (would-be) martyrs (of water-melon) red through and through [A ~ شہادت]

شہیر shahir' ADJ. famous ; well-known , renowned [A ~ شہرت]

شئون sho'oon' N M. PL. conditions affairs [A ~ SING. شان]

شے sha'i (PL. اشیا ashya') N.F. thing object matter ; affair something extraordinary شئے لطیف sha'-e-latif' N F. shrewdness brains

شیاطین shayatin' N.M. (PL. of شیطان N.M. ★)

شیام sh yam' ADJ. (same as شام ADJ. & N.M. ★)

شیب shaib N.M. old age senility greyness of hair شیب و شباب shai'b-o-shab' N.M. PL youth and age [A]

شیخ shaikh (col. shekh) N.M. (PL. شیوخ shu yookh') Azad tribal chief ; sheik venerable old man saint one's saintly guide (as title for convert to Islam) venerable name of a Muslim business community title of one of its members (member of) a respectable Muslim family (courtesy title for) weaver شیخ جی shaikh' ji N.M. courtesy title for shaikh (iron.) prude شیخانی shekha'ni or (shai-) N.F. woman belonging to a shaikh family wife of a shaikh شیخوخیت shekhookhiy'yat N.F. old age شیخ چلی shekh chil'li N.M. name of a legendary fool idle schemer ; one building castles in the air visionary شیخ چنڈال shekh chandal' N.M. (sat.) glutton شیخ ڈونڈو shekh dondo N.F. traveller's small effigy with sack on bag for causing rain to cease شیخڑا shekh'ra N.M. derogatory title for a shaikh شیخ سدو shekh sad'do N.M. legendary evil spirit supposed to possess woman or bless them with children [A]

شیخی she'khi N.F. boast ; brag شیخی باز she'khi-baz' , شیخی خورا she'khi-kho'ra N.M. boaster ; braggart شیخی بگھارنا she'khi baghar'na (or mar'-na) V.I boast ; to brag شیخی کرکری کرنا she'khi kir'-kiri kar'na, شیخی نکالنا she'khi nikal'na V.T. have one's pride humbled شیخی کرکری ہونا she'khi kir'kiri ho'na, شیخی نکلنا she'khi ni'kalna V.I. (of bluff) be called (of one's pride) be humbled

شیدا shaida' ADJ. loving doting (on) N.M. lover شیدائی shaida''i N.F. lover [P]

شیدی shi'di شیدی si'di N.M. (title for) Negro [P]

شیر sher' N.M. tiger (fig.) lion-heart. ADJ. brave lion-heart ADJ. brave lion hearted شیر افگن she'r-af'gan ADJ. & N M. brave (person) شیر ببر she'r-e ba'bar (col. ببر شیر ba'bar sher N.M. lion شیر بچہ sher'-bach'hah N.M. (arch.) brave person tiger (or lion) cub a kind of small musket شیر بکری ایک گھاٹ پانی پیتے ہیں sher' bak'ri ek' ghat pa'ni pi'te hain PROV. perfect peace prevails (under) high and low get equal justice the reign of شیر خدا she'r-e khuda' N.M. Lion of God (as appellation of Hazrat Ali) شیر قالین

she'r-e qālīn' N.M. a carpet lion ; a figure head ; a braggart شیر کا بچہ sher' kā bach'chah N.M. tiger (or lion) cub شیر کی خالہ sher' kī khā'lah N.F. (euphemism for) cat شیر مرد sher'-mard N.M. lion-heart ; brave man ADJ. brave ; valorous lion-hearted شیر مردی sher'-mar'dī N.F. bravery ; valour شیر ہونا (یا ہو جانا) sher' ho'nā (or ho jā'na) V.I. get encouragement شیرنی sher'nī N.F. tigress lioness شیرانہ sherā'nah ADJ. & ADV. like a lion brave(ly) [P]

شیر shīr N.M. milk شیر پیما shīr'-paimā' N.M. lactometer شیر خوار shīr'-khār' N.M. infant; babe suckling شیر گرم shīr' gar'm ADJ. lukewarm شیر مادر shī'r-e mā'dar ADJ. lawful ; permissible N.M. mother's milk شیر مال shīr'-māl N.M. bread made from leaven kneaded in milk ; milk-bread ; bun شیر و شکر shī'r-o-sha'kar ADJ. hand in glove شیر و شکر ہونا shī'r-o sha'kar ho'nā V.I. be intimate friends be hand in glove (with) [P]

شیرازہ shīrā'zah N.M. stiching (in book binding) organisation (fig.) شیرازہ بکھرنا shīrā'zah bi'kharnā V.I. be disorganised ; be in a mess شیرازہ بندی shīrā'za-ban'dī N.F. stitching (in book binding) (fig.) organisation ; control شیرازی shīrā'zī N.M. a kind of pigeon (inhabitant) or Shiraz (in Iran) [P]

شیرنی sher'nī N.F. (see under شیر N.M. sher ★)

شیرہ shī'rah N.M. syrup treacle ; molasses golden syrup (fruit) juice sap [P]

شیریں shī'rīn ADJ. sweet mellow mellifluous gentle ; suave N.M. name of Khusro Parvez of Persia's queen passionately loved by a quarryman-artist Farhad شیریں ادا shīr'īn-adā' ADJ. snave شیریں بیان (یا زبان یا کلام یا مقال) shīr'īn bayān' (or zabān' or kalām' or maqāl') ADJ. eloquent soft-spoken شیرینی shīrī'nī N.F. sweetmeat sweets sweetness malliflu-ence [P]

شیشم shī'sham N.F. a kind of tree prized for its hards wood ; 'shishum' its wood

شیش shīsh N.M. (same as سیس N.M. ★)

شیش shīsh PREF. (see under شیشہ N.M ★)

شیشہ shī'shah N.M. glass looking glass glass pane bottle ; flask شیشہ باز shī'sha-bāz N.M. acrobat dancing with flasks balanced on head juggler fraudulent person شیشہ بازی shī'sha-bā'zī N.F. feats of such acrobats jugglery fraud شیشہ باشہ shī'sha-bā'shā ADJ. fragile شیشہ گر shī'sha-gar N.M. glazier fraudulent person شیشہ گری shī'sha-ga'rī N.F. glazier's trade fraud شیشہ دکھانا shī'shah dikhā'nā V.T. show a looking glass (to) let (some one) see his misdeeds شیشے میں اتارنا shī'she meṅ ūtār'nā V.T. tame a spirit شیشی shī'shī N.F. bottle phial شیش shīsh PREF. glass glassy شیش محل shīsh'-mahal' (col. shīsh'-mai'haal) N.M. glass house mirror hall [P]

شیطان shaitān' N.M. (PL. شیاطین shayātīn) satan devil ; demon (fig.) mischievous person (fig.) evil genius (fig.) imp شیطان سے زیادہ (یا زادہ) مشہور shaitān' se ziyā'dah (or zā'de) mashhoor' ADJ. notorious شیطان سر پر چڑھنا (یا سوار ہونا) shaitān' sir par chaṛh'na (or savār' ho'nā) V.I. be possessed by the devil became devilish شیطان کی آنت shaitān' kī ānt' ADJ. & N.F. tedious (matter) very long (object) long and intricate شیطان کی خالہ shaitān' kī khā'lah N.F. mischievous woman شیطان کے کان بہرے shaitān' ke kān baih're INT. God forbid may none hear it شیطان نے کان میں پھونک دیا ہے shaitān' ne kān' meṅ phoonk' di'ya hai PH. has been beguiled by the devil شیطانی shaitā'nī ADJ. devilish; diabolical N.F. mischief ; wickedness شیطانی حرکت shaitā'nī ḥar'kat (ped. -ḥa'ra-) N.F. mischief wickedness diabolical act شیطانی (یا شیطان کا) لشکر shaitā'nī (or shaitān' kā) lash'kar N.M. imps impish crowd شیطانی وسوسہ shaitā'nī vas'vasah N.M. atheistic doubt evil trend شیطنت shai'tanat N.F. wickedness devilishness unchief mailce [A]

شیعہ shī''ah N.M. sect regarding Hazrat Ali as direct lawful successor to the Holy Prophet rejecting the other orthodox caliphs follower of this sect ; Shi'ite ; Shiah (rare) group ; coterie شیعی shī''ī N.M. & ADJ. (PL. شیعیان shī''iyyān') Shi'ite [A ~ شیعہ علی]

شیفتہ shef'tah ADJ. enamoured infatuated with love شیفتگی shef'tagī N.F. love fondness madness [P ~]

شیکسپیئر shek'spi'yar N.M. Shakespeare the greatest playwright (of) [E]

شیم shiyam' N.M. PL. habits manners [A ~ SING. شیمہ]

شین shīn N.M. name of the letter شین قاف سے درست ہونا shīn' qāf' se dūrūst' ho'nā V.I. have a good pronunciation not to boor [A]

شیوا she'vā ADJ eloquent شیوا بیان she'vā-bayān' (or -zabān) eloquent شیوا بیانی she'vā-bayā'nī N.F. eloquence [P]

شیوخ shuyookh' N.M. (of PL. شیخ N.M ★)

شیوع shūyoo'' N.M. (giving or gaining) currency (to something) spread issue (of periodical [A ~ شائع]

شیون *she'van* N.M. lamentation · plaint نالہ و شیون *na'la-o she'van* N.M. crying and lamentation [P]

شیوہ *she'vah* N.M. manner peculiar habit coquetry ; blandishment [A]

ص

ص *sād*, (col. *swād*) twentieth letter of Urdu alphabet (also called *sā'd-e moh'malah*) ; (equivalent to *s* in English) ; (used only in words of Arabic extraction) (according to jummal recoking) 90

ص *sād* (ABB. of *sahīh'*) O.K. ; okay (ABB. of sallallahu 'alai-he va-sallam) (written after the Holy Prophet's name) peace be on him [A]

صابر *sā'bir* ADJ. patient enduring forbearing [A ~ صبر]

صابن *sā'bun*, صابون *sabooh'* N.M. soap

صابی *sā'bī* N.M. Sabaean [A]

صاحب *sā'hib* (col. *sab*) N.M. (PL. اصحاب *ashāb*, صاحبان *sāhibān'*) courtesy title put at end of name) Mr. (F. میم *mem*, میم صاحبہ *mem' sā'hibah*) Englishman (F. صاحبہ *sā'hibah*) Westernized Oriental Anglophile courtesy title appended to masculine or feminine names master (rare) companion ADJ. having ; possessing possessed of endowed with صاحب اختیار *sā'hib-e ikhtiyar'* ADJ. & N.M. (one) vested with authority powerful (person) authority صاحب اخلاق *sā'hib-e akhlaq'* ADJ. polite ; well behaved صاحب اقبال *sā'hib-e iqbāl'* ADJ. lucky ; fortunate صاحب تاج و تخت *sā'hib-e tā'j-o-takh't* N.M sovereign صاحب تدبیر *sā'hib-e tadbīr'* N.M. & ADJ. actful (person) prudent person diplomatist صاحب تمیز *sā'hib-e tamīz'* ADJ. intelligent صاحب جائداد *sā'hib-e jā'idād'* N.M. landlord man of propert ADJ. propertied (person, class, etc.) صاحب جمال *sā'hib(-e) jamāl'* ADJ. pretty ; beautiful ; handsome ; lovely صاحب حال *sā'hib-e hāl* N.M & ADJ. mystic(al) صاحب حال و قال *sā'hib-e hā'l-o-qāl'* ADJ. scholarly mystic صاحب خانہ *sā'hib(-e) khā'nah* N.M. master of the house hostel صاحب دل (or صاحبدل) (*sā'hib(-e) dil'* ADJ. & N.M. God-fearing (person) mystic صاحب ذوق *sā'hib(-e) zauq'* ADJ. & N.M. cultured person a man) of taste صاحبزادہ *sā'hib-zā'dah* N.M. son (of a respectable person young gentleman صاحب سلامت *sā'hib salā'mat* N.F. nodding acquaintance exchange of greatings being on speaking terms with) صاحب سلیقہ *sā'hib-e salī'qah* ADJ. skilled in managemed ; well-organzing صاحب عدالت *sā'hib(-e) 'adā'lat* N.M. just or equitable person صاحب عقل *sā'hib-e 'aq'l* N.M. & ADJ. wise intelligent shrewd صاحب فراش *sā'hib-e farāsh'* ADJ. bed ridden صاحبقران *sā'hib-qirān'* ADJ. & N.M. fortunate (person) ; one born with Venus and Mercury in one sign of Zodiac صاحب قلم *sā'hib-e qa'lam* N.M. writer; penman صاحب کتاب *sā'hib-e kitāb'* N M. prophet having a book revealed to him صاحب کرامت *sā'hib-e karā'mat* ADJ. & N.M. (saint) able to do marvels صاحب کمال *sā'hib(-e) kamāl'* ADJ. perfect ; accomplished having consumate ability صاحب نظر *sā'hib(-e) nazar* ADJ. & N.M. intelligent perspicacious mystic(al) صاحبان *sāhibān'* N.M. PL. gentlemen (arch.) Englishmen صاحبہ *sā'hibah* N.F. lady ; a woman of rank ADJ. having possessing possessed of endowed (with) بیگم صاحبہ *be'gūm sā'hibah* (col. بیگم صاحب *be'gam sāb*) N.M. lady mistress of the house میم صاحب *mem' sā'hib* (col. *mem' sā'b*) N.M. English woman any Western woman صاحب اور میم صاحب *sā'hib aur mem sā'hib* میم صاحب صاحب *mem' sāb sāb'* N.M. PL. Western(ized) couple صاحبی *sā'hibī* N.F. Westernivation (arch.) being a master [A]

صاد *sād* N.M. name of letter ص O.K. ; okay صاد کرنا *sād' kar'na* V.T. okay [A]

صادر *sā'dir* ADJ. issued passed arrived proceeding (from) ; emanating (from) صادر کرنا *sā'dir kar'na* V.T. issue (order) pass (order) enact (law) صادر ہونا *sā'dir ho'na* V.I. be issued be passed be enacted (of crime, etc.) be committed ; be perpetrated emante (from) be received (from) [A ~ صدور]

صادق *sā'diq* ADJ. true sincere just faithful veracious act صادق آنا *sā'diq ā'na* V.T. & I. apply ; be applicable (to) be apt suit come true صادق القول *sā'diq-ul-qaul'* ADJ. true to one's word N.M. a man of his word [A ~ صدق]

صارف *sā'rif* N.M. (PL. صارفین *sarifīn'*) consumer [A ~ صرف]

صاعقہ *sā''iqah* N.F. lightning ; thunderbolt [A]

صاف *sāf* ADJ. clean clear pellucid bright (sky) smooth legible plain distinct simple plain precise open frank innocent pure entire ADJ. cleanly clearly entirely صاف انکار کرنا *sāf' inkar' kar'na* V.I. refuse pointblank صاف بات *sāf' bāt* N.F. fact of the matter frank talk something said without reserve صاف باتیں saf'-ba'tin ADJ. with a clear conscience صاف چھوٹ جانا saf' chhoot ja'na V.I. escape unpunished be let off without punishment صاف دل saf'-dil' ADJ. frank ; candid open hearted guileless صاف شفاف saf shaffaf' ADJ. transparent pellucid صاف صاف saf' saf ADV. plainly openly flatly without reserve صاف صاف سنانا saf' saf suna'na V.I. give (someone) a piece of one's mind ; do some plain peaking صاف صاف کہنا saf' saf kaih'na V.I. say openly say plainly blurt out speak without reserve صاف کرنا saf' kar'na V.T. clean wash cleanse wipe tidy up clarify make a fair copy (of) purify effect a catharsis purge comb out صاف کر جانا saf' kar ja'na V.T. make a clean sweep (of) eat everything up finish off صاف نکل جانا saf' ni'kal ja'na V.I. get off scot-free make off with all speed steer clear (of) صاف ہونا saf' ho'na V.I. be clean be tidy be tidied up (of sky) be clear ; be cloudless (of copy) be made fair (of account) be settled ; be cleared

صافہ sa'fah N.M. small turban ; cloth wrapped round head صافی safi N.F. duster dish clout piece of cloth for straining ADJ. (rare) clean clear pure صفائی safa''i N.F. ★ [~A صفا ~صافی]

صالح sa leh (PL. صلحا sulaha') ADJ. (F. صالحہ sa'lehah PL. صالحات salehat') pious virtuous righteous orthodox صالحیت salihiy'yat N.F. piety virtue righteousness صالحات sa'lehat' N.M. PL. chaste women [A ~ صلاح]

صامت sa'mit ADJ. silent quiet reticent ساکت و صامت sa'kit-o-sa'mit ADJ. mum tongue-tied stunned [A]

صانع sa'ne' pl. صناع sunna') N.M. the Creator (as an attribute) of God maker صانع حقیقی sa'ne'-e haqi'qi God ; the real Creator صانع قدرت sa'ne'-e qud'rat N.M. (God as) the Author of Nature [A ~ صنعت]

صائب sa'ib ADJ. right well aimed sound (in judgment) صائب الرائے sa''ib-ur-ra''e ADJ. judicious ; sound judgement [A ~ صواب]

صائم sa''im N.M. & ADJ. fasting ; one who fasts صائم الدہر sa''im-ud-dah'r N.M. & ADJ. (person) fasting all days of this life [A ~ صوم]

صبا saba' N.F. zephyr morning breeze spring breeze easterly breeze [A]

صباح sabah' N.F. morning dawn ; daybreak علی الصباح 'al-as-sabah' ADV. early in the morning at dawn [~ doublet of صبح]

صباحت saba'hat N.F. fair complexion being a blonde [~ PREC.]

صبح sub'h (col. su'bah dial. suboh) N.F. morning daybreak ; dawn صبح بنارس sub'h-e bana'ras N.F. ravishing morning scene at Benaras with beautiful semi-nude female devotees bathing in the Ganges صبح خیز sub'h-khez' ADJ. rising early in the morning N.M. early riser صبح خیزا sub'h-khe'za N.M. (col.) (euphemism for) burglar looting people in the early hours of the morning صبحدم sub'h-dam ADV. early in the morning at dawn ; at daybreak صبح شام کرنا sub'h sham' kar'na V.T. put off time and again prevaricate صبح صادق sub'h-e sa'diq N.F. dawn صبح صبح sub'h sub'h ADV. early in the morning صبح کا تارا sub'h ka ta'ra N.M. Morning Star ; Venus صبح کاذب sub'h-e ka'zib N.F. evanescant light before daybreak صبح کا بھولا شام کو گھر آ جائے تو اسے بھولا نہ کہنا چاہیے sub'h ka bhoo'la sham' ko ghar a ja''e to u'se bhoo'la na kaih'na cha'hiye PROV. it is not lost that comes at last the Prodigal deserves no reproach after his return صبح کرنا sub'h kar'na V.I. keep awake till in the morning pass the night صبح کس کا منہ دیکھا تھا sub'h kis' ka munh de'kha tha PL. what an inauspicious person you come across this morning صبح و مسا sub'h-o-masa' N.F. PL. morning and evenings ADV. all the time at the two ends of the day [A]

صبر sab'r N.M. patience endurance suffering forbearance ; self-restraint submission to the will of God ; resignation to one's fate (helpless person's) curse صبر آزما sab'r-azma' ADJ. trying صبر آزمائی sab'r-azma''i N.F. being such as to try one's patience difficult صبر آنا sab'r a'na V.T. & I. endure patiently get over one's grief صبر بٹورنا (یا لینا) sab'r bator'na (or le'na) V.I. reap the reward of one's misdeeds be under the curse (of helpless persons) صبر پڑنا sab'r par'na V.I. be under curse (of a helpless person) صبر کا پھل میٹھا sab'r ka phal mi'tha PROV. patience has its reward صبر کرنا sab'r kar'na V.I. be patient keep patience exercise self-restraint resign oneself to one's fate [A]

صبغہ sib'ghah N.M. colour baptism صبغۃ اللہ sib'ghat-ullah' N.M. true faith colour given by God Himself

صبوح sabooh', صبوحی saboo'hi N.F. morning draught of liquor صبوحی کش saboo'hi-kash N.M& ADJ. drunkard ; boozer (one) in the habit of taking a morning draught of wine [A ~ صبح]

صبوری *saboo'rī* N.F. patience enduranced forbearance ناصبوری *nā-saboo'rī* N.F. impatience restlessness [A ~ صبر]

صبی *sabī'* N.M. (PL. صبیان *sibyān'*) infant boy صبیہ *sabiy'yah* N.F. female infant girl [A]

صبیح *sabīh'* ADJ. blond ; fair-complexioned صبیحہ *sabī'hah* ADJ. & N.F. blonde [A ~ صباحت]

صحابہ *sahā'bah* N.M. PL. Companions of the Holy Prophet ; Muslims who had the felicity to see the Holy Prophet during his life-time (usu. as) صحابۂ کرام *sahā'ba-e kirām'* N.M. PL. Venerable Companions of the Holy Prophet صحابی *sahā'bī* N.M. one of the Companions of the Holy Prophet [A ~ صاحب]

صحاح ستہ *sehā'h-e sit'tah* N.F. the six famous sunni collections of the Holy Prophet's traditions made by Bukhari, Muslim, Tirmidhi, Abu Dawood. Nasa'i and Ibn Majjah

صحافت *sahā'fat* N.M. journalism آزاد صحافت *āzād'-sahā'fat* N.F. a free Press پابندیٔ صحافت *pāban'dī-e sahā'fat* N.F. Press curbs صحافی *sahā'fī* N.M. journalist ADJ. journalist's Press ; journalistic کارکن صحافی *kār'-kūn sah'fī* N.M. working journalist صحافی آزادی *sahā'fī āzā'dī* N.F. freedom of the Press [A ~ صحیفہ]

صحائف *sahā'if* N.M. (PL. of صحیفہ ★)

صحبت *soh'bat* N.F. meeting company (euphemism for) sexual intercourse صحبت اٹھانا (یا برتنا) *soh'bat uṭhā'nā* (or *baret'nā*) V.I. (arch.) enjoy the company (of cultured of saintly person) صحبت داری *soh'bat-dā'rī* N.F. (arch.) keeping company (with) صحبت کرنا *soh'bat kar'nā* V.T. cohabit ; have sexual intercourse (with a woman) صحبت گرم ہونا *soh'bat gar'm ho'nā* V.I. (of meeting) warm up صحبت نہ رہنا *soh'bat na raih'nā* V.I. (of joyous company come to an end *soh'batī* N.M. friend companion صحبت یافتہ *soh'bat-yāf'tah* ADJ. having enjoyed the company of [A]

صحت *seh'hat* N.F. health ; soundness of body correction correctness accuracy validity صحت افزا *seh'hat afzā'* ADJ. salubrious health giving صحت افزا مقام *seh'hat-afzā' maqām'* N.M. health resort صحت بخش *seh'hat-bakh'sh* ADJ. health ful health-giving ; salubrious bracing curative صحت بخش مقام *seh'hat-bakh'sh maqām'* N.M. health resort صحت نامہ *seh'hat-nā'mah* N.M. corrigendum [A]

صحرا *sahrā'* N.M. (PL. صحاری *sahā'rī, sahā'ra*) desert صحرا گرد *sahrā'gar'd* صحرا نورد *sahrā'-navar'd* N.M & ADJ. (one) wandering about in the desert traveller tramp صحرا گردی *sahrā-gar'dī*, صحرا نوردی *sahrā-navar'dī* N.F. wandering about in the desert صحرا نشین *sahrā'nashīn* N.M. & ADJ. (one) living the desert bedonin صحرا نشینی *sahrā'-nashī'nī* N.F. desert life leading a bedonin's life صحرائے اعظم *sahrā-e a'zam* N.M. the Sahara صحرائے لق و دق *sahrā'-e la'q-o-daq'* N.M. lonely wilderness صحرائی *sahrā''ī* ADJ. of the desert wild uncivilized N.M. Bedouin desert-dweller [A]

صحف *so'haf* N.M. (PL. of صحیفہ N.M. ★)

صحن *seh'n* (or *saih'n* ; ped. *sah'n*) N.M. courtyard صحن چمن *saihn-e cha'man* N.M. lawn [A]

صحنک *saih'nak* N.F. trough devotional dish prepared in a trough and distributed in the name of Hazrat Fatimah صحنک کھلانا *saihnak khilā'nā* V.T. prepare and distribute such devotional dish [A ~ PREC.]

صحیح *sahīh'* ADJ. right correct accurate bring sure ; certain proper ; appropriate genuine ; authentic (usu. as صحیح سالم *sahīh' sā'lim*, صحیح سلامت *sahīh' salā'mat*) safe and sound صحیح البدن *sahī'h-ul-ba'dan* ADJ. able-bodied صحیح العقل *sahī'h-ul-'aq'l* ADJ. of sound mind صحیح النسب *sahī'h-un-na'sab* ADJ. legitimate of a noble family صحیح کرنا *sahīh' kar'nā* V.T. correct (dial.) sign صحیح ہونا *sahīh' ho'nā* V.I. be correct [A ~ صحت]

صحیفہ *sahī'fah* N.M. (PL. صحائف *sahā''if*, صحف *so'haf*) revealed book magazine ; periodical صحیفۂ آسمانی *sahī'fa-e āsmā'nī* N.M. a revealed book (iron.) supposedly authoritative statement, etc. صحف سماوی *so'haf-e samā'vī* N.M. PL. revealed books

صد *sad* ADJ. & N.M. hundred cent صد آفریں *sad āfarīn'* INT. well done (گل) صد برگ *(gū'l-e) sad-bar'g* N.M. marigold صدہا *sad-hā'* ADJ hundreds (of) a great many فی صد (or فیصد) *fī'-sad* ADV. per cent *sa'dī* N.F. century فیصدی *fī'-sa'dī* ADV. per cent ; per hundred [P]

صدا *sadā'* N.F. voice sound call صدا بصحرا *sadā' ba-sahrā'* N.M. cry in the wilderness *sadā'-ban'dī* N.F. recording (of voice) صدا دینا *sadā' de'nā* V.I. call about out beg صدا کرنا (یا لگانا) *sadā' kar'nā* (or *lagā'nā*) V.I. beg alms beg from door to door صدائے احتجاج *sadā'-e ehtijāj'* N.F. protest صدائے احتجاج بلند کرنا *sadā'-e ehtijā'j' būland' kar'nā* protest raise one's voice in protest صدائے بازگشت *sadā'-e bāz'-gash't*, گنبد کی صدا *gūm'bad kī sada'* N.M. echo retaliatory remark صدائے برنخاست *sada''e bar na-khast'* PL. no respons [P]

صدارت *sada'rat* N.F. chairmanship presidentship presidency کرسی صدارت *kūr'si-e sada'rat* N.F. the Chair chairmanship صدارتی *sada'ratī* ADJ. Presidential صدارتی نظام (حکومت) *sadā ratī niza'm-e (ḥūkoo'mat)* N.M. Presidential system of Government [P ~ صدر].

صداع *sūda''* N.M. headache ; vertigo [A]

صداقت *sada'qat* N.F. truth sincerity friendship fidelity صداقت شعار *sadā'qat-she'ār'* ADJ. true [A doublet of صدق]

صدر *sad'r* N.M. (PL. صدور *sūdoor'*) President chairman ; the Chair (arch.) district headquarters (arch.) seat of Government cantonment business centre in cantonment area chest facade ADJ. chief main major head (office) صدر اعظم *sad'r-e a''zam* N.M. (arch.) Premier ; Prime Minister صدر الصدور *sad'r-ūs-sūdoor'* N.M. (arch.) Chief Justice صدر بازار *sad'r bazar'* N.M. cantonment business area ; Saddar صدر دیوان *sad'r dīvān'* N.M. (arch.) Finance Minister صدر مجلس *sad'r-e-maj'lis*, صدر نشین *sad'r-nashīn'* N.M. president ; chairman صدر نشین محفل *sad'r-nashī'n-e mah'fil* N.M. President , chairman صدر مدرس *sad'r-mūdar'ris* N.M. headmaster (arch.) Principal (of academy) صدر مقام *sad'r maqam'* N.M. headquarter (of) Headquarters ; H.O capital (of a country) صدارت *sada rat* N.F. ★ صدری *sadr'ī* ADJ. relating to chest secretly transmitted secret unwrite N.F. waistcoat [A]

صدف *sa'daf* N.F. oyster shell [A]

صدق *sid'q* N.M. truth verity ; veracity sincerity honesty صدق دل سے *sid' q-e dil se* صدق نیت سے *sid' q-e niy'yat se* ADV. sincerely ; honestly [A]

صدقہ *sad'qah* (ped. *sa'daqah*) N.M. (PL. صدقات *sadaqat'*) propitiatory offerings such alms or sacrifice charity صدقہ اتارنا (یا دینا) *sad'qah ūtar'na* or *de'na*) V.I. give charity (for ending misfortune) صدقہ سلا *sad' qa sil'la* N.M. (col.) propitiatory صدقے *sad' qe* ADV. sacrificed for averting ill-luck (from someone) صدقے جانا *sad' qe ja'na* V.I. become a sacrifice for (someone's) welfare صدقے کرنا *sad' qe kar'na* V.T. sacrifice for (someone's) curse someone welfare صدقے واری *sad' qe va'rī* ADV. sacrificed for averting ill-luck (from someone) [A]

صدمہ *sad'mah* N.M. (PL. صدمات *sa'damat* col. *sadmat'*) shock blow hust reverse صدمہ اٹھانا *sad'mah ūṭha'na* V.I. meet with misfortune صدمہ پہنچانا *sad'mah pahūṅcha'na* V.T. give (someone) a shock injure the feelings (of) hurt صدمہ جانکاہ *sad'ma-e jāṅ-kah'* N.M. fatal blow grievous injury صدمہ گزارنا *sad'mah gū'zarna* V.T. (of calamity) befall صدمہ ہونا *sad'mah ho'na* V.I. be shocked

صدور *sūdoor'* N.M. issuing emanation (PL. of صدر N.F. ★) صادر *sa'dir* ADJ. & ADV. ★ [A]

صدی *sa'dī* N.F. (see under صد ADJ. & N.M ★)

صدیق *sadīq'* N.M. friend صدیق *siddīq'* ADJ. ever-truthful N.M. faithful witness of the truth (as appellation of Hazrat Abu Bakr) صدیقہ *siddī'qah* ADJ. ever-truthful N.M. this as appellation of Hazrat Aeshah [A ~ صدق]

صراحت *sara'ḥat* N.F. clarity specific mention; specification elucidation صراحت کرنا *sara'ḥat kar'na* V.T. clarify specify elucidate صراحتاً *sara'ḥatan* ADV. clearly expressly explicitly صریح *sarīḥ'* ADJ. ★ [A]

صراح *sūrāḥ* N.M. unadulterated stuff [A صریح]

صراحی *sūra'ḥī* N.F. long necked flask ; goblet small triangular piece of cloth صراحی دار *sūra'ḥī-dār* ADJ. gobletshaped · long and lovely (neck) [P]

صراط *sirāt'* N.F. path ; way صراط مستقیم *sirā't-e mūstaqīm'* N.F. the right way پل صراط *pūl-sirāt'* N.M. narrow passage leading to paradise [A]

صراف *sarraf'* N.M. bullion dealer jeweller (arch.) banker صرافہ *sarrā'fah* N.M. bullion market jewellery mart (arch.) money-market jellewer's trade صرافی *sarrā'fī* N.F. jeweller's trade (arch.) bullion trade (arch.) banking [A ~ صرف]

صرصر *sar'sar*, باد صرصر *ba'd-e sar'sar* N.F boistrous cold wind [A]

صرع *sar''* N.F. falling sickness . epilepsy knocking down. [A]

صرف *sar'f* N.M expense ; expenditure use consumption (gram.) etimology accidence (rare) conjugation turning away diversion صرف کرنا *sar'f kar'nā* V.T. spend use consume صرف و نحو *sar'f-o-nah'v* N.F. accidence and syntax grammar صرف ہونا *sar'f ho'na* V. be spent be disturbed be used be consumed صرفی *sar'fī* ADJ. pertaining to accidence etymological N.M. etymologist grammarian صرفہ *sar'fah* N.M. expense economy profit interest benefit صرفہ کرنا

sar'fah kar'nā v.i. be thrifty economise صرفہ ہونا sar'fah ho'nā v.i. be spent be in the interest (of) [A]

صرف sir'f ADJ. & ADV. only more(ly) sheer exclusive(ly) ; pure(ly) unmixed unadulterated [A]

صرہ sur'rah N.F. purse [A]

صریح sarīḥ' ADJ. evident ; obvious ADV. flatly ; point blank ; outright صریح انکار کرنا sarīḥ' inkar' kar'nā v.i. refuse point blank deny outright صریحاً sarī'ḥan ADV. openly plainly explicitly clearly evidently ; obviously flatly ; outright صریحی sarī'ḥī ADJ. (col. for صریح ★) [A ~ صراحت]

صریر sarīr' N.F. scratching sound (of pen) صریر خامہ (یا قلم) sarī'r-e khā'mah (or qa'lam) N.F. scratching sound of pen [A]

صعب sa''b ADJ. difficult herd troublesome arduous صعوبت so'oo'bat N.F. difficulty hardship trouble [A]

صعود so'ood' N.M. ascent climbing involution sublimation [A]

صعوہ sa''vah N.M. wagtail [A]

صغار sighar' N.M. (PL. of صغیر) صغائر saghā''ir N.M. (PL. of صغیرہ) (see under صغر N.M. ★)

صغر sigh'r N.M. smallness minuteness tenderness (of age) صغر سنی si'ghar-sinī N.F. (col.) tender age minority صغار sighār' ADJ. small young inferior صغار و کبار sighā'r-o-kibār' N.M. young and old small and great [A]

صغریٰ sūgh'ra N.F. minor term of a syllogism ; minor premises ADJ. smallest [A ~ PREC.]

صغیر saghīr' ADJ. small minute young inferior صغیرہ saghī'rah ADJ. small minute young venial N.M. venial sins صغائر saghā'ir N.N. PL. venial sins صغائر و کبائر sighā'ir-o-kabā''ir N.M. PL. sins venial and mortal [A]

صف saf N.F. (PL. صفوف sūfoof') rank row prayer mat for one row of congregation ; pew pat صف آرا saf-ārā' ADJ. (of army) arrayed ; marshalled ; ranged صف آرا ہونا saf-ārā' ho'nā v.i. be arrayed or ranged (against) be set for battle صف آرائی saf-ārā'ī, صف بندی saf-ban'dī N.F. battle-array ; battle formation fight (against) صف (یا صفیں) الٹنا saf' (or sa'feṅ) ūlaṭ'nā v.T. rout the enemy صف (یا صفیں) باندھنا saf (or sa'feṅ) bāndh'nā v.i. draw up in ranks draw up in a line صف بستہ saf-bas'tah ADJ. drawn up in ranks ready to give battle ; arrayed (against) ready ; in all readiness صف جنگ sa'f-e jang' N.F. (arch.) battle-field ranks of war صفدر saf'-dar ADJ. & N.M. routing ; (warrior) breaking enemy ranks this as appellation of Hazrat Ali صف شکن saf'-shi'kan ADJ. routing صف در صف saf'-dar-saf ADJ. in ranks and file (of soldiers) in one formation after another teaming صف ماتم sa'f-e ma'tam N.F. carpet spread for mourners and condolers to sit on ; mourners mat صف ماتم بچھنا sa'f-e ma'tam bichh'nā v.i. have an occasion for mourning be struck with grief صف نعال sa'f-e ne'āl' N.F. place near door (where the company's shoes are placed) low place in company [A]

صفا safā' N.F. name of hill near Mecca (lit.) (same as صفائی N.F. ★) ADJ. (rare) clean (usu. only in) صفا چٹ sa'fā chaṭ ADJ. clean clean-shaven صفا چٹ کرنا sa'fā chaṭ kar'nā v.T. shave clean lick (plate) clean devour everything [A]

صفات sifāt' N.F. (PL. of صفت ★)

صفائی safā''ī N.F. clean ; cleanliness ; clearness hygiene hygienic conditions sanitation conservancy purification piety settlement ; rapproachment frankness sleight (of hand) being level smoothness lustre defence (in law-suit) honesty destruction annihilation صفائی دینا safā''ī batanā v.T. refuse POINT blank صفائی کرنا safā''ī kar'nā v.i. clean tidy up cleanse bring about a rapproachement (between) effect a compromise destroy squander make short work (of) [A ~ صفا]

صفت si'fat N.F. attribute quality ; epithet praise (properly اسم صفت is'm-e si'fat) adjective صفت موصوف si'fat mausoof' N.M. adjective with its substantive صفات sifāt' N.F. (dial. M.) (PL. of صفت ★) صفاتی sifā'tī ADJ. attributive [A doublet of وصف]

صفحہ saf'ḥah N.M. page (rare) face (fig.) surface صفحۂ ہستی saf'ḥa-e has'tī N.M. face of the earth world صفحۂ ہستی سے مٹانا saf'ḥa-e has'tī se miṭa'nā v.T. obliterated [A]

صفر sa'far N.M. second month of Hijri year [A]

صفر sif'r N.M. cypher , zero ; naught [A]

صفرا safrā' N.M. bile gall choler صفراوی safrā'vī ADJ. bilious (person) biliary [A ~ صفر]

صفو *saf'foo* N.M. (col.) without any cards صفو کر دینا *saf'foo kar de'nā* V.T. win all cards from [~ A CORR.]

صفوت *saf'vat* ADJ. select ; choicest [A]

صفوف *safoof'* N.F. (PL. of صف ★)

صفه *sāf'fah* N.M. platform platform in the Holy Prophet's Mosque which served as the first Islamia university (rare) sofa اصحاب صفہ *ashā'b-e sāf'fah* N.M. PL. Fellows of this university who were Companions of the Holy Prophet [A]

صفی *sa'fī* N.M. & (PL. اصفیا *asfiyā'*) pure righteous elect saint صفی اللہ *safiy'y-ullāh'* N.M. God's elect (as appellation of Adam) [A ~ صفا]

صفیر *safīr'* N.F. chirping whistling [A]

صل *sal'le* (or *-li*) INT. may God bless صلی اللہ علیہ وسلم *sallallā'hū 'alai'hi va sal'lam* (ABB. as صلعم or ص) may God bless the Holy Prophet and send his peace to him

صلا *salā'* N.F. invitation call ; challenge of a foe ; cry of a salesman صلائے عام *salā'-e 'ām'* N.F. open invitation [A]

صلابت *salā'bat* N.F. hardness (fig.) firmness [A ~ صلب]

صلاح *salāh'* N.F. opinion advice ; counsel welfare prosperity goodness (of state) rectitude صلاح دینا *salāh' de'nā* V.T. advise ; counsel صلاح کار N.M. (*salāh'-kar*) adviser ; counsellor N.F. (*salāh'-e kār'*) exigency of situation right course صلاح کرنا *salāh' kar'nā* V.T. consult صلاح لینا *salāh' le'nā* V.I. consult ; take advice صلاح مشورہ *salāh' mash'varah* N.M. mutual consultation deliberations صلاحیت *salāhiy'yat* N.F. suitability ability capacity [A doublet of صلح]

صلب *sūl'b* N.M. (PL. اصلاب *aslāb'*) spine ; backbone loins (fig.) offspring صلبی *sūl'bī* ADJ. descended from (male progenitor) (some male progenitor's) own (offspring) [A]

صلح *sūl'h* N.F. peace treaty truce concord rapprochement patch-up صلح شکنی *sūl'h-shi'kanī* N.F. breach of the peace صلح کرنا *sūl'h kar'nā* V.T. be reconciled make a truce make peace with صلح کل *sūl'h-e kūl'* ADJ. & N.M. peace-loving (person) صلحنامہ *sūl'h-nā'mah* N.M. piece ; treaty compromise deed [A]

صلحا *sūlahā'* N.M. (PL. of صالح ★)

صلعم *sal'am* ABB. for صلی اللہ علیہ وسلم (see under صل INT.)

صلوٰة *salāt'* N.F. ritual prayer benediction for the Holy Prophet [A]

صلوات *salavāt'* N.F. (PL. of صلوٰة ★)

صلوات N.F. (*salavāt'*) (PL. of صلوٰة ★) N.F. (*salvāt'*) (usu. PL.) curse(s)

صلہ *si'lah* N.M. reward ; prize remuneration gift ; present (gram.) relative pronoun صلۂ رحم *si'la-e rahim'* صلۂ رحمی *si'la-e ra'himī* N.M. kindness towards one's (esp. uterine) relations maintenance of ties with them [A doublet of وصل]

صلیب *salīb'* N.F. cross crucifix the Cross (as symbol of Christianity) صلیب و ہلال *salī'b-o hilāl'* N.M. the Cross and the Crescent صلیبی *salī'bī* ADJ. pertaining to the Cross Christian صلیبی جنگ *salī'bī jang'* N.F. Crusade : Christian fanatic war on Muslims صلیبی جنگیں *salī'bī jah'geh* N.F. PL. the Crusades [A]

صم *sūm* ADJ. deaf صم بکم *sūm'mūn* ADJ. deaf and dumb unresponsive [A ~ SING. اصم]

صمد *samad'* ADJ. eternal ; perpetual sublime (one) who can go without food or drink in battle N.M. the sublime the Eternal as attribute of God) صمدانی *samadā'nī* ADJ. divine godly صمدیت *samadiy'yat* N.F. sublimity [A]

صمصام *samsām'* N.F. sharp sword

صمغ *sam'gh* N.M. gum صمغ عربی *sam'gh-e 'a'rabī* N.M. gum Arabic [A]

صمیم *samīm'* ADJ. pure sincere N.M. best part (of) (fig.) core ; bottom صمیم قلب *samī'm-e qal'b se* ADV. from the core of my heart [A]

صنادید *sanādīd'* N.M. PL. brave chiefs noblemen celebrities صنادید عجم *sanādī'd e a'jam* N.M. PL. Persian celebrities آثار الصنادید *āsā'r-ūs sanādīd'* N.F. PL. relics of celebrities [A ~ SING صندید *sindīd'*]

صناع *sannā''* ADJ. N.M. skilful artist skilled workman artisan صناعی *sannā'ī*, صنع *sūn'* N.F. craftsmanship skill creative powder

sūnnā'' N.M. (PL. of صانع ★)

صنائع *sanā'e''* N.M. (PL. of N.F. ★)

صندل *san'dal* N.M. sandal ; sandalwood صندلی *san'dalī* ADJ. sandalwood light brown [A ~ S ~ Malay]

صندوق sandooq' (pcd. sŭn'dooq') N.M. (PL. صنادیق sanādīq') trunk box chest cabinet coffin coffer case صندوقچہ sandooq'chah N.M., صندوقچی sandooq'chī N.F. small box ; casket [A]

صنع sŭn'' N.F. (same as صناعی)(see under صناع N.M. ★)

صنعت san''at N.F. industry manufacture handicraft craftmanship miracle figure of speech صنعتگر san''at-gar N.M. artisan craftsman صنعتگری san''at-ga'rī N.F. mechanical skill manufacture صنعتی san''atī ADJ. industrial artistic صنائع sanā''e' N.F. PL. figures of speech crafts (rare) صنائع بدائع sanā''e' badā''e' N.M. figures of speech ; rhetorical devices [A]

صنف sin'f N.F. (PL. اصناف asnāf') sex gender category صنف نازک sin'f-e nā'zŭk N.F. fair sex صنفی sin'fī ADJ. pertaining to sex ; (change, etc.) of sex [A]

صنم sa'nam N.M. (PL. اصنام asnām') idol mistress beloved ; sweetheart (arch.) a kind of word-building game in which each participant has to name a plue beginning with a particular letter in turn صنم خانہ sa'nam-khā'nah, صنم کدہ sa'nam-ka'dah N.M. idol temple (fig.) place with a vevy of beauties [A]

صنوبر sanau'bar N.M. any cone-bearing tree fir pine [P]

صواب savab' N.M. correctness rectitude صوابدید savab'-dīd N.F. advisability expediency opinion discretion اپنی صوابدید کے مطابق ap'nī savab'-dīd ke mŭta'biq PH. according to one's discretion [A]

صوب saub N.M. direction [A]

صوبائی sooba''ī ADJ., صوبجات soobajat' N.M. PL. (see under صوبہ ★)

صوبہ soo'bah N.M. (PL. صوبجات soo'bajāt') province صوبیدار soo'ba'-dār (col. soo'be-dār) N.M. governor a Junior Commissioned Officer (of army); subahdar صوبہ داری soo'ba-dā'rī (col. -be-) N.F. governship subahdar's rank صوبائی sooba''ī ADJ. provincial [~A]

صوت saut N.F. (PL. اصوات asvāt') sound voice [A]

صور soor N.M. (also صور اسرافیل soor'e isrāfīl') horn (to be blown on doomsday) clarion ; trumpet [A]

صور sŭ'var N.F. (PL. of صورت ★)

صورت soo'rat N.F. (PL. صور sŭ'var) figure form ; shape appearance face ountenance aspect state ; condition plight ; circumstance (gram.) mood manner means way out plan صورت آشنا soo'rat-āsh'nā ADJ. slight acquaintance ; known by sight صورت آشنائی soo'rat-āshnā''ī N.F. slight acquaintance صورت بدلنا soo'rat ba'dalnā V.I. change transform metamorphose صورت بگاڑنا soo'rat bigāṛ'nā V.T. mar ; deform , disfigure صورت بنانا soo'rat banā'nā V.T. & I. give shape (to) plan find a way out put up a (false, etc.) appearance صورت پذیر ہونا soo'rat-pazīr' ho'nā V.I. happen ; occur ; come to pass come into existence take shape صورت تو دیکھو soo'rat to de'kho INT. (iron.) how brave look up your face in the mirror what a man صورت حال soo'rat-e ḥal' N.F. state of affairs صورت دکھانا soo'rat dikhā'nā V.T. turn up appear ; make one's appearance صورت کرنا soo'rat kar'nā V.T. plan devise (some) way صورتگر soo'rat-gar N.M. artist sculptor صورتگری soo'rat-ga'rī N.F. artist's work painting sculpture صور sŭvar' N.F. (PL. of صورت ★) صوری sŭ'varī ADJ. outward ; eternal bodily physical extrinsic صوری و معنوی sŭ'varī-o-ma''navī ADJ. extrinsic and intrinsic (qualities) [A]

صوف soof N.M. (rare) wool (old use) a kind of thick silk cotton waste piece of it placed in inkpot [A]

صوفی soo'fī N.M. (PL. صوفیا soofiyā') mystic صوفیانہ soofiyā'nah ADJ. mystic ; mystical (of dress) simple (of colour) dall [A ~ صوف or صفا]

صولت sau'lat N.F. commanding personality awe (rare) assaulting lug lion, etc.) دبدبہ و صولت dab'daba-o-sau'lat N.M. awe obedience commanded (by) [A]

صوم saum N.M. (PL. صیام siyām') fast fasting [A]

صومعہ sau'ma'ah N.M. (PL. صوامع savā'me') church hermitage ; monastery [A]

صہبا sahbā' N.F. claret wine liquor [A]

صہیل suhīl' N.F. neigh neighing صہیل فرس sahī'l-e fa'ras N.F. neighing of a horse [A]

صیاد sayyād' N.M. (see under صید N.M. ★)

صیام siyām' N.M. (PL. of صوم ★)

صیانت siyā'nat N.F defence support preservation صیانت نفس siyā'nat-e naf's N.F. self preservation [A]

صید *said* N.M. (PL. صیود *suyood'*) game prey quarry hunting chase shikar (fig.) lover صید افگن *sai'd-af'gan* N.M. one who kills game hunter ; shilkaree صید زبوں *sai'd-e zaboon'* N.M. weak quarry injured quarry صیدگاہ *said'-gah* N.F. hunting ground ; park صیاد *sayyad'* N.M. hunter fowler shikaree (fig.) beloved ; sweetheart صیادِ اجل *sayya'd-e a'jal* N.M. death [A]

صیغہ *sighah* N.M. grammatical form showing tense (of verb) or case (of noun) along with number, gender and person ; grammatical pattern declined or inflected form department branch side (of judiciary) (rare) fixed-time matrimony صیغۂ دیوانی *si'gha-e diva'ni* N.M. the Civil side صیغۂ فوجداری *sigha-e fauj-da'ri* N.M. the Criminal side صیغہ گردانا *sighah gardan'na* V.I. (arch.) conjugate [A]

صیف *saif* N.F. (rare) summer [A]

صیقل *sai'qal* N.F. burnish nickel plating metal polish صیقل کرنا *sai'qal kar'na* V.T. burnisher [A]

صیہون *saihoon'* N.M. Zion صیہونی *saihoo'ni* ADJ. & N.M. Zionist صیہونیت *saihooniy'yat* N.F. Zionism [A]

ض *zad* (col. *zwad*) N.M. twenty-first letter of Urdu alphabet (also called *za'd-e mo''jamah* or *za'd-e manqoo'tah*) ; (used in words of purely Arabic extraction) (according to jummal reckoning) 300

ضابط *za'bit* ADJ. (see under ضبط ★)

ضابطہ *za'bitah* N.M. (PL. ضوابط *zava'bit*) code (of law) rule regulation law by law control ; discipline ضابطہ برتنا *za'bitah ba'ratna* V.I. act according to law the rules follow the procedure ضابطۂ تعزیری *za'bita-e ta'zi'ri* N.M. Penal Code ضابطۂ تعلیم *za'bita-e ta'lim'* N.M Education Code ضابطۂ دیوانی *za'bita-e diva'ni* N.M. Civil Procedur Code ضابطۂ فوجداری *za'bita-e fauj-da'ri* N.M. Criminal Procedure Code ضابطے کی کارروائی *za'bit-e ki kar-rava''i* N.F. procedural measures ضابطے کی کارروائی کرنا *za'bite ki kar-rava''i kar'na* V.I. take procedural measures act according to rules باضابطہ *ba-za'-bitah* ADJ. regular formal according to law بےضابطہ *be-za'bitah* ADJ. irregular unusual ; out of the way خلافِ ضابطہ *khila'f-e za'bitah* ADJ. irregular contrary to rules unlawful ; illegal ضابطگی *za'bitagi* N.F. regularity (used only in NEG. form as) بےضابطگی *be-za'bitagi* N.F. irregularity ; contravention of rules and regulations قواعد و ضوابط *qava''id-o-zava'bit* N.M. PL. rules and regulations [A]

ضامن *za'min* N.M. surety ; security sponsor ضامن بنانا (یا ہونا) (*za'min ban'na* or *ho'na*) V.I. stand surety (for) ضامن در ضامن *za'min dar za'min* N.M. a collateral security ضامن دینا *za'min de'na* V.T. give security ضامن لینا *za'min le'na* V.T. ask for security ضامنی *za'mini* N.F. surety ; security bail guarantee pledge ضامنی منظور کرنا *za'mini manzoor' kar'na* V.I. admit as bail ﷲ فعل ضامنی *l'e'fe'l za'mini* N.F. security for good conduct [A ~ ضمانت]

ضائع *za''e'* ADJ. wasted lost misapplied squandered destroyed fruitless ضائع کرنا *za''e' kar'na* V.T. waste lose misapply squander ضائع ہونا *za''e' ho'na* V.T. be wasted ; go waste ; go to waste be vain ; prove fruitless be lost be squandered [A]

ضبط *zab't* N.M. discipline ; order control check restraint (rare) confiscation seizure; proscription ; distraint ضبط کرنا *zab't kar'na* V.T. confiscate proscribe forfeit sieze distrain ضبط ہونا *zab't ho'na* V.I. be confiscated be proscribed be forfeited be seized be distrained ضبطی *zab'ti* N.F. confiscation proscription forfeiture seizure distraint ضبطی کا حکم *zab'ti ka hük'm* N.M. confiscation order ضبطی کے لائق *zab'ti ke la''iq*, لائقِ ضبطی *la''iq-e zab'ti* N.F. liable to seizure contraband ضابط *za'bit* N.M. & ADJ. disciplinarian strict exercising self-restraint [A]

ضحی *zoha'* N.F. breakfast time supererogatory prayers at breakfast time [A]

ضخامت *zakha'mat* N.F. bulk volume thickness (of book, etc.) ضخیم *zakhim'* ADJ. bulky voluminous thick [A]

ضد *zid* N.F. stubbornness persisant ; solicitation importunity opposition contrariety ADJ. opposite (of) ; contrary (to) ضد باندھنا *zid' bandh'na*, ضد پر آنا *zid' par a'na*, ضد کرنا *zid' kar'na* V.I. show stubbornness importune ; persistently insist (upon) ضد ہونا *zid' ho'na* V.I. be opposed to ; be antagonistic to be possessed of a spirit of opposition (to) ضدی *zid'di* ADJ. stubborn obdurate contrary wilful ; wayword unmanageable ; intractable ضدین *ziddain'* N.F. PL the two opposites the two contraries اجتماعِ ضدین *ijtima''-e ziddain'* N.M combination of two contraries [A]

ضراب *zarrāb'* N.M. mint master coiner (A ~ ضرب)

ضرار *zirār'* N.M. reciprocal injury quarrel مسجدِ ضرار *mas'jid-e zirār'* N.F. name of a Medina mosque built by hypocrites which was later demolished under the Holy Prophet's orders [A ~ ضرر]

ضرب *zar'b* N.F. (PL. ضربات *zarabāt'* col. *zarbāt*) multiplication blow hurt ; injury stamping (of coin) emphatic recital of God's name so as to cause a minor concussion of one's heart ضرب آنا *zar'b ā'nā* V.I. suffer injury be injured hurt oneself (in a part of body) ضرب المثل *zar'b-ūl-ma'sal* N.F. proverb saying ; saw ; aphorism ضرب المثل ہونا *zar'b-ūl-ma'sal ho'nā* V.I. become proverbial ضرب دینا *zar'b de'nā* V.T. multiply ضرب شدید *zar'b-e shadīd'* N.F. grievous hurt ; grievous injury ضرب لگانا *zar'b lagā'nā* V.T. beat strike give a blow stamp (a coin) recite (God's name) emphatically ضرب مرکب *zar'b-e mūrak'kab* N.F. compound multiplication compound injury ضرب مفرد *zar'b-e mū frad* N.F. simple multiplication simple injury ضرب مہلک *zar'b-e moh'lik* N.F. fatal injury حاصلِ ضرب *hā'sil-e zar'b* N.M. (multiplication) product دار الضرب *dā'r-ūz-zar'b* N.F. (arch.) mint [A]

ضرر *za'rar* N.M. harm damage loss detriment disadvantage baneful effect hurt injury ضرر اٹھانا *za'rar ūṭhā'nā* V.I. incur a loss suffer ضرر پہنچانا *za'rar pahūṅchā'nā* V.T. harm damage hurt injure ضرر رساں *za'rar-rasāṅ'* ADJ. harmful injurious baneful damaging ضرر رسانی *za'rar-rasā'nī* N.F. causing injury damaging doing harm (to) [A]

ضرور *zaroor'* ADV. surely ; certainly definitely perforce absolutely without fail of course ADJ. (lit.) same as (ضروری)

ضرورت *zaroo'rat* N.F. need want necessity exigency occasion (for) desire (of) ضرورت ایجاد کی ماں ہے *zaroo'rat ījād' kī māṅ' hai* PROV. necessity is the mother of invention ضرورت پڑنا *zaroo'rat par'nā* V.I. have the need of have occasion for ضرورتمند *zaroo'rat-mah'd* ADJ. needy poor indigent ضرورت کے وقت گدھے کو بھی باپ بنا لیتے ہیں *zaroo'rat ke vaq't ga'dhe ko bhī bāp banā' le'te haiṅ* PROV. many kiss the child for nurse's sake ضرورتاً *zaroo'ratan* ADV. out of necessity (ped.) necessarily ; of necessity ضروری *zaroo'rī* ADJ. necessarily ; of necessary expedient indispensable ; unavoidable obligatory essential requisite needful urgent essential ضروریات *zaroo'riyyāt'* N.F. PL. necessities necessaries requisites ضروریاتِ زندگی *zaroo'riyyā't-e zin'dagī* N.F. necessities of life ; necessities [A]

ضریح *zarīh'* N.F. sarcaphogus tomb likeness of Imam Husain's tomb [A]

ضریح

ضعف *ze''f* N.M. (PL. اضعاف *az'āf'*) double equal [A]

ضعف *zo''f* N.M. weakness feebleness infirmity fainting fit ضعف آنا *zo''f ā'nā* V.I. faint swoon ضعفِ باہ *zo''f-e bāh'* N.M. loss of virility sexual weakness ضعفِ بصارت *zo''f-e basā'rat* N.M. weakness of eyesight ; weak eyesight ضعفِ معدہ *zo''f-e me''dah* N.M. dyspepsia [A]

ضعیف *za'īf* N.M. (PL. ضعفا *zo'afā'*) old man ADJ. old weak feeble frail infirm ضعیف الاعتقاد *za'ī' f-ūl-e'tiqād'* ADJ. credulous ضعیف البیان *za'īf-ūl-bayan'* ADJ. of frail foundation ضعیف العقل *za'īf-ūl-'aq'l* ADJ. weak-minded imbecile ضعیف ہونا *za'īf ho'nā* V.I. be advanced in years ; be old ضعیف ہو جانا *za'īf' ho' jā'nā* V.I. grow old ضعیفہ *za'ī'fah* N.F. old woman ضعیفی *za'ī'fī* N.F. old age weakness infirmity [A]

ضعیف آدمی

ضغطہ *zagh'tah* (ped. *zūgh'tah*) N.M. difficulty worry (caused by someone's dodging tactics) pull ; jerk [A]

ضلال *zalāl'* N.M. ضلالت *zalā'lat* N.F. (rare) ضل *zal* N.M. deviation from the right path going astray walking ungodly ways [A]

ضلع *zil''* (col. *zi'la'*) N.M. (PL. اضلاع *azlā''*) district side (of rectilinear figure) rib stretched double-entendre-stretched metaphor ضلع بولنا *zil'' bol'nā* V.I. used stretched-metaphor ضلع جگت *zil'' jū'gat* N.F. stretch metaphor wit ضلعدار *zil''-dār'* N.M. a minor office of Canal Department a minor revenue official [A]

ضم *zam* N.M. merger (same as ضمہ *zam'mah* N.M. vowel-point [A]

ضماد *zimād'* N.M. embrocation paste ; plaster ضماد کرنا *zimād' kar'nā* V.T. apply paste (to a part of body) [A]

ضمانت *zamā'nat* N.F. surety security bail guarantee ضمانت دینا (یا داخل کرنا) *zamā'nat de'nā* (or *dā'khil kar'nā*) V.I. give bail furnish security ضمانت کے قابل *zamā'nat ke qā'bil* ADJ. bailable ضمانت منظور کرنا *zamā'nat manzoor' kar'nā* V.T.

grant bail admit to bail ضمانت نامہ zamā'nat-nā'mah N.M. security bond surety deed ضمانتی zamā'natī ADJ. security N.M. (col.). (same as ضمانت N.M. ★) [A]

ضمائر zamā''ir N.F. (PL. of ضمیر ★)

ضمن zim'n N.M. inside ; inner part (usu. as ضمن میں zim'n meṅ ADV. in the course (of) in (this) connection ضمناً zim'nan ADV. incidentally by the way ; by the by by implication ضمنی zim'nī ADJ. incidental implicit collateral or corroborative (evidence) N.F. (police investigation report [A]

ضمیر zamīr' N.F. (PL. ضمائر zamā''ir) conscience (gram.) personal pronoun ضمیر فاعلی (یا مفعولی یا اضافی) zamī'r-e fā''ilī (or maf'ōō'lī or izā'fī) N.F. personal pronoun in nominative (or accusative or possessive) case [A]

ضمیمہ zamī'mah N.M. supplement (of newspaper) ; its special small issue for some important piece of news appendix

ضو zau N.F. light lustre ضو فشاں zau-fishāṅ' ADJ shining ; lustrous shedding light [A]

ضو فشانی zau-fishā'nī ADJ. shedding of light [A]

ضوابط zavā'bit N.M. (PL. of ضابطہ ★)

ضیا ziyā' N.F. light brilliance ضیا بار ziyā'-bār', ضیا پاش ziyā'-pāsh' ADJ. shinning; lustrous shedding light ضیا باری ziyā'-bā'rī, ضیا پاشی ziyā'-pāshī N.F. shedding of light [A]

ضیاع zayā'' N.M. waste loss ضائع za''e' ADJ & ADV. ★ [A]

ضیافت ziyā'fat N.F. feast banquet treat entertainment ضیافت طبع ziyā'fat-e tab'' N.F. entertainment (by jokes, etc.) ضیافت کرنا ziyā'fat kar'nā V.T. feast banquet treat entertain [A ~ ضیف]

ضیغم zai'gham N.M. lion [A]

ضیف zaif N.M. (PL. اضیاف azyāf') guest [A]

ضیق zīq N.F. difficulty جان ضیق میں آنا (یا ہونا) jān' zīq' meṅ ā'nā (or ho'nā) V.I. be fed up (with) be vexed ضیق النفس zī'q-ūn-naf's N.M. asthma [A]

ضیق zay'yiq ADJ. narrow [A]

ط

ط to''e N.F. twenty-second letter of Urdu alphabet called ta in Arabic (also known as tā-e moh'malah or tā'-e ghair-manqoo'tah) (according to jummal reckoning) 9

طاب tāb ADJ. be purified be fragrant (used in) طاب ثراہ tā'ba sarā'hū may his grave become fragrant طاب اللہ ثراہ tā'b allā'hū sarā'hū PH. may God purify his grave [A]

طابع tā'bi' N.M. printer [A ~ طباعت]

طابق النعل بالنعل tā'baq-an-na''l-ū bin-na''l-e PH. one exactly alike the other [A ~ مطابقت]

طارق tā'riq N.M. (rare) Morning Star night traveller جبل الطارق ja'bal-ūt-tā'riq N.M. Gibralter Spanish promontory name after its Muslim conqueror, Tariq [A]

طارم tā'rūm N.M. wooden bulbous pavilion (fig.) firmament [A]

طاری tā'rī ADJ. spreading occurring ; overtaking طاری ہونا tā'rī ho'nā V.I. spread overshadow overtake

طاس tās N.M. basin (of river) [A ~ P]

طاسہ tā'sah (col. تاشہ tā'shah) N.M. kettledrum [~ PREC.]

طاعت tā''at (PL. طاعات tā'āt') N.F. obedience submission devotion act of devotion [A]

طاعن tā''in N.M. ADJ. & N.M. (one) who taunts (rare) one who snacks with a spear [A ~ طعن]

طاعون tā'oon' N.M. bubonic plague [A]

طاغوت tāghhoot' N.M. (PL. طواغیت tavāghīt') devil idol (arch) name of Arab deities 'Lat' and 'Uzza' falsehood [A]

طاغی tā'ghī ADJ. rebellious refractory [A ~ طغیان]

طاق tāq N.M. recess in wall niche arch odd number ADJ. odd (number) arched clever skilled expert (in) طاق ابرو tā'q-e ab'roo N.M. arch of the brow طاق بھرنا tāq bhar'nā V.I. make a votive offering (at shrine mosque) by lightning a lamp there طاق جفت tāq' juf't N.M. odd or even game of guessing this طاق کرنا (یا کر دینا) tāq' kar'nā (or kar de'nā) V.T. make (someone) an expert (in) طاق ہونا (یا ہو جانا) tāq' ho'nā (or ho jā'nā) V.I. become an expert V.I. be an expert (in) be proficient (in) طاق نسیاں پر رکھنا tā'q-e nis'yān par rakh'nā V.T. put (something) forget ignore altogether

طاقچہ tāq'chah N.M. small recess in wall طاقی tā'qī ADJ. squint-eyed wild-eyed [A]

طاقت tā'qat N.F. strength might power force endurance energy capacity; ability vitality virility potency طاقت آزمائی tā'qat-azmā''ī N.F. trial of strength طاقت طاق ہونا tā'qat taq ho'na V.I. have no strength left طاقتور tā'qatvar ADJ. strong powerful might طاقت مہمان نداشت خانہ بہ مہمان گزاشت tā'qat-e meh'mān na-dāsh't khā'na ba-meh'mān guzāsh't PROV. (person who) leaves the house to get rid of the guest [A]

طالب tā'lib, (PL. طلاب tullāb') N.M. seeker candidate lover suitor طالب خدا tā'lib-e khudā' N.M. & ADJ. one who seeks God طالب دنیا tā'lib-e dun'yā N.M. & ADJ. man of the world worldly minded worldly person طالب دیدار tā'lib-e dīdār' N.M. one who longs for the sight (of) a lovers suitor طالب زر tā'lib-e zar N.M. lover of wealth طالب علم tā'lib-e 'il'm (col. tā'lib 'il'm (ped. طالب العلم tā'lib-ul-'il'm) N.M. (PL. طلبہ ta'labah col. طلبا talabā') student (arch.) Traditionist طالب علمی tā'lib-e 'il'mī N.F. studentship طالب و مطلوب tā'lib-o matloob' N.M. PL. lover and beloved طالبہ tā'libah (ped. طالبہ علم tā'liba-e 'il'm) (PL. طالبات tālibāt') N.F. girl student [A]

طالح tā'leh ADJ. bad evil [A]

طالع tā'le' N.M. luck; fortune lot destiny rising star; controlling star ADJ. rising ascending طالع آزما tā'le' āzmā' ADJ. adventurer soldier of fortune طالع آزمائی tā'l-e' azmā''ī N.F. trying one's luck being a soldier of fortune طالع شناس tā'le'-shinās' N.M. astrologer fortune teller طالعمند tā'le'man'd, طالع ور ta'le'-var ADJ. lucky; fortunate rich; wealthy طالع مندی tā'le'man'dī, طالع وری tā'le'-va'rī N.F. good fortune being wealthy [A ~ طلوع]

طالوت tāloot' N.M. Saul [A ~ Heb.]

طامات tām'māt' N.M. PL. vainful talk of pseudo-mystics; tall talk [A]

طامع tā'me' ADJ. greedy; covetous (rare) avid [A ~ طمع]

طاؤس tā'oos' N.M. peacock a kind of large guitar; peacock-guitar طاؤس ورباب tā'oo's-o-rabāb' N.M. (fig.) song and music gay life [A]

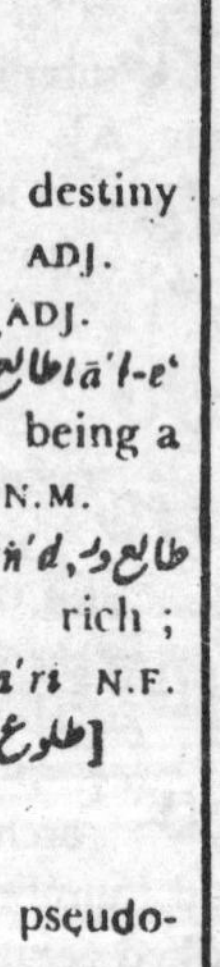

طاہر tā'hir ADJ. pure; chaste [A ~ طہارت]

طاہری tā'hirī N.F. (same as تہری N.F ★)

طائر tā''ir N.M. (PL. طیور tuyoor') bird طائر روح tā''ir-e rooh' N.M. soul life طائر قدس tā''ir-e qūd's N.M. Gabriel, the Holy Ghost (as heavenly bird) [A]

طائف tā''if N.M. circumambulator name of a town near Mecca [A]

طائفہ tā''ifah N.M. troupe (rare) group band طائفہ نچانا tā''ifah nachā'nā V.T. arrange an entertainment by a troup (of dancers or street-actors) [A]

طائی tā''ī ADJ. (of the tribe) of Tai حاتم طائی hā'tim tā''ī N.M. a pre-Islamic Arab chieftain renowned for generosity generous person (iron.) miser [A ~ طے ★]

طب tib N.F. science of medicine indigenous system of medicine طب یونانی tib'b-e yoonā'nī N.F indigenous system of medicine; Unani طبی tib'bī ADJ. medical pertaining indigenous system of medicine طبیب tabib' N.M. physician one practicing indigenous system of medicine [A]

طبابت tibā'bat N.F. practice of indigenous medicine medical practitce [A ~ doublet of PREC.]

طباخ tabbākh' N.M. cook [A]

طباشیر tabāshīr' N.F. bamboo-sugar [A]

طباع tabbā'' ADJ. very intelligent quick-witted perspicacious طباعی tabbā''ī N.F. keen intelligence quick comprehension perspicacity [A ~ طبع]

طباعت tabā''at N.F. printing [A]

طباق tabāq' N.M. large dish basin طباق سا منہ tabāq' sā mūnh PH. wide mouth طباقی کتا tabā'qī kūt'tā N.M. (fig.) sponger [A]

طبائع tabā''e' N.F. (PL. of طبیعت ★)

طبع tab'' N.F. (PL. طباع tibā'') temperament disposition nature print or impression (of book) طبع آزمائی tab''-āzmā''ī N.F. trial of skill versification (on particular theme or pattern) طبعزاد tab''-zād' ADJ. original (composition) طبع رسا tab''-e rasā N.F. perspicacity ability to versify well طبع کرنا tab''-kar'nā V.T. print طبع ہونا tab' ho'na V.I. be printed طبعی tab''ī ADJ. natural by nature (col. for طبیعی see under طبیعت N.F. A)

طبق ta'baq N.M. layer; stratum tray lid; cover طبق زنی ta'baq-za'nī N.F. female homosexuality [A]

طبقات tabaqāt' N.M. (PL. of طبقہ ★)

طبقہ *tab'qah* (ped. *ta'baqah*) N.M. (PL. طبقات *tabaqat'*) class (of people or society category layer stratum طبقہ الٹ جانا *tab'qah u'lat ja'na* V.I. be upset be topsy turvy طبقہ بندی *ta'baqa-ban'di* N.F. classification categorization طبقات الارض *tabaqā't-ul-ar'z* geological strata (also علم طبقات الارض *'il'm-e tabaqā't-ul-ar'z*) geology طبقات الارضی *tabaqā't-ul-ar'zi* ADJ. geological survey طبقات الارضی جائزہ *tabaqā't-ul-ar'zi jā''izah* N.M. geological survey طبقاتی *tabaqā'ti* ADJ. class طبقاتی جنگ (یا کشمکش) *tabaqā'ti jang'* (or *kashmakash'*) N.F. class war (or struggle [A]

طبل *tab'l* (col *tabal'*) N.M. drum طبل جنگ *tab'l-e jang'* N.M war-cry طبلچی *ta'balchi* one who plays on tabla طبلہ *tab'lah* N.M tambourines (usu. played in a set of two) casket طبلہ نواز *tab'la-navāz'* N.M. (dignified name for طبلچی ★) [A]

طبی *tib'bi* ADJ. طبیب *tabib'* N.M. (see under طب N.F. ★)

طبیعت *tabi''at* N.F. (PL. طبائع *tabā''e'*) temperament ; disposition habits طبیعت آنا *tabi''at ā'nā* V.T. fall in love (with) be attached (to) have a liking (for) طبیعت الجھنا *tabi''at u'lajhnā* V.I. be puzzled طبیعت بحال ہونا *tabi''at ba-hāl' ho'nā* V.I. recover from illness , recover طبیعت بگڑنا *tabi''at bi'garnā* V.I be upset طبیعت بھر جانا *tabi''at bhar' jā'nā* V.I. be satiated feel nausea be fed up (with) طبیعت بہلنا *tabi''at bah'halnā* V.I. be amused be diverted طبیعت بیزار ہونا *tabi''at bezār' ho'nā* V.T. & I be disgusted (with) طبیعت ٹھہرنا *tabi''at thai'har'nā* V.I. find solace ; be comforted recover get over the shock طبیعت پر زور دینا (یا ڈالنا) *tabi''at par zor' de'nā* (or *dāl'nā*) V.I exert one's mind طبیعت ثانیہ *tabi''at-e sā'niyah* N.F second nature habit طبیعت علیل ہونا *tabi''at 'alil' ho'nā* V.I. fall ill be indisposed طبیعت لگنا *tabi''at lag'nā* V.T. & I. be attached (to) take interest (in) get used (to) feel at home (in) طبیعت نہ لگنا *tabi''at na lag'nā* V.T. & I. have no attachment (with) be disinclined (towards) feel uncomfortable , not to feel at home (in) طبیعت لڑانا *tabi''at larā'nā* V.T grapple mentally (with) طبیعت لڑنا *tabi''at lar'nā* V.T. hit upon fall in love (with) grapple mentally (with) طبیعی *tabi''i* ADJ. (F. or PL. طبیعیہ *tabi'iy'yah*) natural physical innate , intrinsic علوم طبیعی (یا طبیعیہ) *'uloo'm-e tabi''i* (or *tabi'iy'yah*) N.M. PL. physical sciences طبیعیات *tabi'iyyāt'* N.M physics طبیعیاتی *tabi'iyyā'ti* ADJ pertaining to physics N.M physicist [A ~ طبع]

طپاں *tapān'*, طپیدہ *tapi'dah* ADJ. restless , uneasy agitated distressed [P ~ طپیدن]

طپش *ta'pish* N.F restless uneasiness distress [P ~ طپیدن]

طپنچہ *tapan'chah*, طمانچہ *tamān'chah* N.M. pistol revolver (slang) mistress [T]

طحال *tchāl'* N spleen [A]

طرار *tarrār'* ADJ. cute facile طرار تیز (o-) *tez-* *tarrār'* ADJ. cute , clever and sharp-tongued طراری *tarrā'ri* N.F. cuteness facile tongue [A]

طرارہ *tarā'rah* N.M. leap , bound run at full speed طرارے بھرنا *tarā're bhar'nā* V.I run at full speed leap , bound ; frisk

طراز *tirāz'* N.M. embroidery cloth print , print printed cloth print SUF embroiderer adorner طرازی *tirā'zi* SUF adorning embroidery making

طراوت *tarā'vat* N.F freshness verdure [A]

طرب *ta'rab* N.F. joy mirth ; merriment hilarity طرب انگیز *ta'rab-angez* ADJ. joyful mirthful mirth exciting طرب انگیزی *ta'rab-ange'zi* N.F mirthfulness طربیہ *tarabiy'yah* N.M. comedy ADJ comic [A]

طرح *tar'h* (col. *ta'rah*) N.F. manner ; mode way kind grace ; beauty cuteness disregard , overlooking foundation line of verse set versification pattern ADV in the manner (of) طرح اڑانا *ta'rah ūṛā'nā* V.T. copy imitate emulate طرح بطرح *ta'rah ba-ta'rah* ADV. in various manners طرحدار *ta'rah-dār* ADJ. pretty, handsome graceful ; elegant stylish cute طرحداری *ta'rah-dā'ri* N.F. cuteness طرح دینا *ta'rah de'nā* V.I dodge disregard turn a deaf ear (to) set a verse pattern طرح ڈالنا *ta'rah dāl'nā* V.T. lay the foundation (of) plan out devise طرح طرح کا *tarah tarah kā* ADJ. of various types [A]

طرز *tar'z* N.F. (or M. style way , fashion mode طرز اڑانا *tar'z urā'nā* V.I. copy a fashion طرز تحریر *tar'z-e tah'rir* N.F. (or M.) style ; of writing طرز عمل *tar'z-e 'a'mal* N.M. course of action conduct طرز کلام *tar'z-e kalām'* N.M. manner of speech mode of address phraseology [A]

طرف *ta'raf* N.F. (PL اطراف *atrāf'*) direction side quarter corner PREP towards, in the direction of طرفدار *ta'raf-dār* N.M supporter partisan ADJ. partial prejudiced طرفداری *ta'raf-dā'ri* N.F. support partiality partisanship طرفداری کرنا *ta'raf-dā'ri kar'nā* V.T.

support be partial (to) طرف ہونا ta raf he na v.i. quarrel (with) ایک طرف ek' ta'raf ADJ. apart separate ایک طرف... دوسری طرف ek' ta'raf......doos'ri ta raf CONJ. on the one hand...on the other برطرف bar'-ta'raf ADJ. dismissed ADV apart برطرف کرنا bar'-ta raf kar'na V.T. dismiss; sack برطرف ہونا bar'-ta'raf ho'na V.I. be dismissed; be sacked برطرفی bar'-ta'rafi (col. bar'-tar'fi) N.F. dismissal طرفین tarafain' N.M. PL. both parties; parties concerned [A]

طرفہ tar'fah N.F. wink; blink twinkling of an eye طرفۃ العین میں tar'fat-ul'ain men V.I. in the twinkling of an eye in a jiffy [A]

طرفہ tur'fah ADJ. strange wonderful rare طرفہ تماشا turfa tama'sha N.M. someting strange طرفہ عالم tur'fa 'a'lam N.M. wonderful state طرفہ ماجرا tur'fah ma'jara N.M. wonderful thing strange affair طرفہ معجون tur'fah ma joon' N.F. strange person mixture of opposites طرفگی tur'fagi N.F. strangeness wonderfulness [A]

طرق ta'ruq N.M. (PL. of طریق ★)

طرہ tur'rah N.M. crest (of turban) forelock curl; ringlet strange thing wonder addition (rare) lines on forehead draught of hemp ADJ. strange unfair extra طرہ چڑھانا tur'rah charha'na V.T. & I. exaggerate be strange طرہ دار tur'ra-dar ADJ. rested طرہ لگانا tur'rah laga'na V.I. be vain طرہ ہونا tur'rah ho'na V.I. be strange be unfair [A]

طریق tariq N.M. path; way; road course custom rite manner procedure [A]

طریقت tari'qat N.F. mystic way of life شریعت، طریقت، حقیقت، معرفت shari'at tari'qat, haqi'qat, ma''rifat N.F. PL. observance of outward law, mystic way of life, knowledge of reality, intimate knowledge of God (as four stages of religious devotion اہل طریقت ah'l-e tari'qat (or aih-) N.M. mystics [A doublet of FOLL.]

طریقہ tari'qah N.M. manner method manner procedure custom rite course way; path road طریقہ بتانا tari qah bata'na V.T. show the way point out the proper course explain the method (of) طریقہ برتنا tari'qah be'ratna V.I. employ the method (of) [A]

طس ta'sin' N.M. one of a set of code letters in the Holy Quran (this interpreted as) an appellation of the Holy Prophet (used by Iqbal in PL. as طواسین tavasin to mean) the spirit of a Prophet's teaching [Ab+ س]

طشت tash't N.M. tray large basin; trough طشت از بام ہونا tash't az bam' ho'na V.I. (of secret) leak out come to be known طشتری tash'tari N.F. plate saucer اڑن طشتری u'ran tash'tari N.F. flying saucer [P]

طعام ta'am' N.M. (PL. اطعمہ at'imah) meals food victuals طعمہ to''mah N.M. food morsel [A]

طعن ta''n, طعنہ ta''nah N.M. taunt blame; reproach censure childing (rare) assault with spear طعن و تشنیع ta''n-o tashni'' N.F. (col. طعنہ تشنہ ta''nah-tish'nah) N.M. taunting remarks زبان طعن دراز کرنا zaba'n-e ta''n daraz kar'na V.T. taunt طعنہ تشنہ ta''na tish'nah N.M. (col. same as طعن و تشنیع N.F. ★) طعنے تشنے دینا ta''ne tish'ne de'na V.T. taunt طعنہ دینا ta''nah de'na V.T. taunt reproach chide طعنہ زن ta''na-zan N.M. & ADJ one who taunts طعنہ زن ہونا ta''na-zan ho'na V.I. taunt طعنہ زنی ta''na-za'ni N.F. taunt taunting طعنہ زنی کرنا ta''na-za'ni kar'na V.T. taunt reproach chide [A]

طغرا tugh'ra N.M. monogram (arch.) imperial signature (arch. خط طغرا kha't-e tugh'ra) a kind of intricate handwriting (used for inscriptions, etc.)

طغیان tugh'yan' N.M transgression [A]

طغیانی tughya'ni N.F overflowing; deluge flood spate inundation طغیانی پر ہونا tughya'ni par ho'na V.I. be flooded be in spate be on the rampage طغیانی کی نہریں tughya'ni ki naih'ren N.F. PL. inundation canals [~ A طغیان]

طفل tif'l N.M. (PL. اطفال atfal') boy child (rare) infant طفل تسلی tif'l tasal'li N.F. (usu. PL.) false promise vain hope طفل تسلیاں دینا tif'l tasal'liyan de'na V.T. raise false hopes طفل شیرخوار tif'l-e shir-khar N.M. infant; baby suckling child طفل مکتب tif'l-e mak'tab N.M. school boy raw and inexperienced person طفلانہ tifla nah ADJ. childish child like طفلی tif'li طفولیت tafooliy yat N.F. childhood (rare) infancy عالم طفلی (یا طفولیت) 'a'lam-e tif'li (or tafooliy'yat) N.M childhood early years of (one's) life [A]

طفیل tufail' N.M intervention; mediation means ADJ. by means (of); through the agency (of) طفیلی tufai'li. (col. طفیلیا tufai'liya) N.M. hanger-on; parasite sponger [A~ طفل]

طلا tila' N.M. gold aphrodisiac طلائی tila''i ADJ. gold; golden [P]

طلا *til'la*, تلہ *til'lah* N.M. gold thread

طلاب *tullāb'* N.M. (PL. of طالب★)

طلاق *talāq'* N.F. divorce طلاق پانا (یا لینا) *talaq' pā'nā* (or *le'nā*) V.I. be divorced get a divorce طلاق دینا *talāq' de'nā* V.T. divorce طلاق نامہ *talāq'-na'mah* deed of divorce طلاق یافتہ *talāq-yāf'tah* ADJ. divorced (woman) طلاقن *talā'qan* N.F. (sat.) divorced woman [A]

طلاقت *talā'qat* N.M. eloquence fluency طلاقت لسانی *talā'qat-e lisā'nī* N.F facile tongue [A]

طلائی *tilā''ī* ADJ. (see under طلا *tilā'* ★)

طلب *ta'lab* N.F. demand process summons seek solicitation pay; salary craving desire طلب بجھانا *ta'lab bujhā'nā* V.I. satisfy one's craving طلب کرنا *ta'lab kar'nā* V.I. demand call for send for summon seek طلبگار *ta'lab-gār* N.M. seeker (one) desirous (of) suitor ADJ. seeking desirous طلب نامہ *ta'lab-nā'mah* N.M. (arch.) summons طلبانہ *talabā'nah* N.M. process serving fees طلبی *ta'tabī* N.F summons audience, sending for طلبی ہونا *ta'labī ho'nā* V.I. be given audience [A]

طلبا *tūlabā*, طلبہ *ta'labah* N.M. (PL. of طالبعلم) (see under طالب N.M.★)

طلبی *ta'labī* N.F (see under طلب N.F ★)

طلسم *tilis'm* N.M. magic spell talisman wonder wonderland طلسم باندھنا *tilis'm bāndh'nā* V.I. cast a spell perform a miracle work wonders طلسمات *tilismāt'* N.M. talisman wonderland spell magic طلسمی *tilis'mī*, طلسماتی *tilismā'tī* ADJ. magic magical [A]

طلعت *tal'at* N.F. face; aspect; visage, countenance ماہ طلعت *māh'-tal''at* ADJ. having a lovely face [A ~ FOLL.]

طلوع *tūloo'* N.M. rising (of sun or other heavenly body) طلوع ہونا *tūloo'' ho'nā* V.I. (of sun, etc.) rise

طماع *tammā'* ADJ. very greedy covetous, avaricious [A ~ طمع]

طمانچہ *tamān'chah* N.M. slap buffet طمانچہ مارنا (یا جڑنا یا لگانا) *tamān'chah mār'nā* (or *jar'nā* or *lagā'nā*) V.I. slap (someone in the face, etc.)

طمانیت *tamāniy'yat*, (or *tamānīyat*) (ped. طمانیت *tamānī'nat*) N.F. peace (of mind) tranquillity reassurance طمانیت قلب *tamāniy'yat-e qal'b* N.F. peace of mind confidence [A ~ اطمینان]

طمطراق *tūmtūrāq'* N.M. pomp and show (rare) fanfare [P]

طمع *ta'ma'* N.F. greed; avarice; covetousness avidity allurement temptation طمع خام *ta'ma'-e khām'* N.F. vain hope طمع دینا *tama'' de'nā* V.T. tempt bere allure طمع راسہ حرف است وہر سہ تہی *ta'ma' rā se har'f as't-o har se tehī'* PROV. greed is alurred greedy person is never satisfied طمع کرنا *ta'ma' kar'nā* V.I. covet be tempted; be lured [A]

طناب *tanāb'* N.M. (PL. طنب *tū'nūb* اطناب *atnāb'*) tent-rope fastening card [A]

طناز *tannāz'* ADJ. coquetish playful facetious N.M. (rare) satirist بت طناز *bū't-e tannāz'* N.M. coquetish beloved طنازی *tānnā'zī* N.F coquetish playfulness facetiousness being a satirist [A ~ طنز]

طنب *tū'nūb* N.F. (PL. of طناب★)

طنبور *tūmboor'* N.M. tambour tambourin tambourine six-stringed guitar, lutes طنبورہ *tamboo'rah* N.M. long six-stringed guitar; lute [A]

طنز *tan'z* N.M. taunt; jeer sarcasm wit witticism satire طنز کرنا *tan'z kar'nā* V.T. taunt jeer طنزاً *tan'zan* ADV. tauntingly, jeeringly sarcastically ironically [A]

طنطنہ *tan'tanah* N.M. show of authority awesome dignity [A]

طواسین *tavāsīn'* N.M. PL. spirit of a prophet's teaching [A ~ SING. طٰس]

طواف *tavāf'*, *tauf* N.M. circumambulation (of the Holy Ka'aba as a religious rite) frequent visits (to) or calls (at) طواف حرم *tavāf-e ha'ram* N.M. circumambulation of the Holy Ka'aba طواف کوئے جاناں *tavāf-e koo''-e jā'nān* N.M frequent visits to the beloved's area [A]

طوالت *tavā'lat* N.F length prolong [A ~ طول]

طوائف *tavā''if* N.F. prostitute, whore strumpet singstress dancing girl N.M. PL. (rare) bands طوائف الملوکی *tavā''if-ul-mūlookī* N.F. political disorder disorderly decentralization of a State anarchy [A ~ SING. طائفہ]

طوبیٰ *too'bā* N.M. name of a heavenly tree yielding very delicious fruit joy; happiness good news [A]

طور *taur* N.M. (اطوار *atvār'*) manner, mode fashion; style; way conduct practice state; condition طور طریق *taur' tarīq*, طور طریقہ *taur'tarī'qah* N.M. (usu PL.) ways and manners etiquette behaviour conduct طور بے طور ہونا taur' be-taur' hona V.I. (of condition) be critical بطور ba-taur', بہ طور ba-taur' ADV. as by way of [A]

طور toor N.M. (rare) hill; mount extended to (denote) Sinai; Mount Sinai کوہ طور ko'h-e toor' N.M. Mount Sinai طور سینا too'r-e sai'nā (or -sī'nā) N.M. (see under سینا sai'nā ★) (A)

طوس toos N.M. (arch.) a kind of soft woolen fabric name of a Persian city; Tus طوسی too'sī N.M. (arch.) pale purple colour a native of Tus [P]

طوطا to'tā N.M. (usu. but less favoured spelling of توتا N.M.★)

طوطی too'tī, too'tī N.M. parakeet; paroquet parrot eloquent person (fig.) fame; renown (کا) طوطی بولنا (kā) too'tī bol'nā V.I. (of someone) have his fame spread far and wide wield great influence or authority طوطی شکر مقال too'tī-e shak'(k)ar-maqāl, طوطی شیوا بیان too'tī-e she'vā bayān' N.M. eloquent person forceful orator [P]

طوطیا too'tiya N.M. copper sulphate, blue vitriol [P]

طوع tau' N.M. voluntary obedience طوعاً و کرہاً tau''an-o karhan ADV. willy-nilly; willingly or unwillingly [A]

طوف tauf N.M. (same as طواف N.M.★)

طوفان toofān' N.M. storm wind storm hurricane tempest typhoon rainstorm flood indulge inundation onrush (of) host or sea (of troubles) commotion; upheaval calamity great injustice calumny; slander طوفان آنا toofān' ā'na V.I. of storm) blow be a hue and cry (over) طوفان اٹھانا toofān' uṭhā'na V.T. cause a commotion make a great noise be rowdy calumniate; slander طوفان برپا یا کھڑا کرنا toofān' bar-pā' (or khā'ṛa) kar'nā V.T. agitate furiously cause an upheaval rowd cause serious repercussions طوفان باندھنا یا جوڑنا too'fān' bāndh'nā (or joṛ'nā) V.T. slander; calumniate scandalize accuse falsely طوفان ہونا toofān' ho'nā V.I. be very quarrelsome or rowdy be intractable طوفان نوح toofā'n-e nooh N.M. Noah's Deluge; the Deluge طوفانی toofā'nī ADJ. stormy tempestuous slanderous; calumniating whirlwind; swift طوفانی دورہ toofā'nī daurah N.M. whirlwind tour [A]

طوق tauq N.M. collar; (for animals chain) a kind of necklace; neckbrace iron collar for slave's neck symbol of servility طوق غلامی tau'q-e ghulā'mī N.M. collar of slavery servility; throldom طوق غلامی پہننا tau'q-e ghulā'mī pai'hannā V.I. become the slave (of) dote (on)

طول tool' N.M. length prolixity طول البلد tool-ul-ba'lad (col. طول بلد tool' ba'lad) N.M. longitude طول امل too'l-e amal' N.M. distant hopes corratousness طول پکڑنا (یا کھینچنا) tool' pa'karnā (or khench'nā V.I. be prolonged become complicated طول دینا tool' dena V.T. lengthen elongate spin a long yarn make matters complicated طول طویل tool' tavīl' ADJ. very long diffuse prolix طول سخن too'l-e sū'khan, طول کلام too'l-e kalam' N.M. verbosity circumlocution طول عمرہٗ tūv'-vila 'ūm'rūhoo PH. may he have a long life طولیٰ too'lā ADJ. long (only in) ید طولیٰ ya'd-e too'lā N.M. see under ید N.M.★) طولاً too'lan ADV. lengthwise طولانی toolā'nī ADJ. lengthy prolix طویل tavīl' ADJ. ★

طومار toomār N.M. roll of papers; scroll heap pack of lies طومار باندھنا toomār' bāndh'nā V.I. fabricate lies (against) exaggerate [P]

طویل tavīl' ADJ. (see under طول ADJ. ★)

طویلہ tave'lah N.M. stable; stall بندر کی بلا طویلے کے سر ban'dar kī balā' tave'le ke sar' PROV. the innocent fool suffering for the guilty knave justice misplaced [~A طویلہ tave'lah]

طٰہٰ tā'hā N.M. one of a set of code letters in the Holy Quran (this interpreted as) an appellation of the Holy Prophet the name of a chapter of the Holy Quran [A ط + ہ]

طہارت tahā'rat N.F. cleanliness; ablution purity; sanctity [A]

طہر tohr' N.M. purification (after menses) [A doublet of PREC.]

طہور tahoor' ADJ. pure purifying [A]

طے tai N.M. travessing; covering (a distance) folding settling deciding ADJ. traversed; travelled folded settled decided طے شدہ tai' shū'dah ADJ. settled decided closed (affair) طے کرنا tai' kar'nā V.T. traverse cover; travel fold settle decide طے ہونا tai' ho'nā V.I. be traversed; be covered; be travelled be folded be settled be decided [A]

طیار tay'yar ADJ. flying (usu. تیار tayyār') ADJ. ★)

طیارہ *tayyā'rah* N.M. aeroplane aircraft airship

طیاری *tayyā'rī* N.F. (usu. تیاری) see under تیار *tayyār* ADJ. ★)

طیب *tīb* N.F. perfume willingness; pleasure طیب خاطر *tī'be khā'tir* N.F. willingness (with) pleasure بہ طیب خاطر *ba-tī'b-e khā'tir* ADV. willingly gladly with pleasure [A]

طیب *tay'yib* ADJ. good pure chaste طیبہ ADJ. (F. & PL.) good pure chaste N.F. chaste woman N.M. name of Madina کلمہ طیبہ *ka'lima-e tay'yibah* N.M. (see under کلمہ N.M.) طیبات *tayyibāt'* N.F. (PL. joys chaste women طیبین *tayyibīn'* N.M. PL. pious men [A]

طیبہ *tai'bah* N.M. a name of Medina [A]

طیر *tair,* *tā''ir* N.M. (PL. طیور *tuyoor'*) bird [A]

طیش *taish'* N.M. levity ; folly ; anger. rage fit of passion طیش (میں) آنا *taish'* (*meṅ*) *ā'na* V.I. be enraged طیش دلانا *taish'dilā'nā* V.I. enrage ; incense [A]

طیلسان *tailasān'* N.M. (PL. طیالسہ *tayāli'sah*) academic robe ; gown (arch.) mantle worn over turban طیلسانی *tailasā'nī* N.M. graduate (of a university) [A]

طینت *tī'nat* N.F. nature disposition بدطینت *bad-tī'nat* ADJ. malicious ill-disposed نیک طینت *nek-tī'nat* ADJ. good-natured [A]

طیور *tūyoor'* N.M. (PL of طیر ★)

ظ

ظ *zo''e* N.F. twenty-third letter of Urdu alphabet (pronounced *zā* in Arabic) (also called *zā-e mo''jamah* or *zā'-e manqoo'tah*) (according to jummal reckoning) 900

ظالم *zā'lim* ADJ. cruel unjust tyranical N.M. cruel person unjust person oppressor tyrant ظالم کی رسی دراز ہے *zā'lim ki ras'si darāz' hai* PROV. Nemesis is slow, even though sure, to overtake ظالمانہ *zālimā'nah* ADJ. cruel unjust oppressive tyranical ADV. cruelty unjustly oppressively tyranically [A ~ ظلم]

ظاہر *zā'hir* ADJ. (PL. ظواہر *zavā'hir*) obvious; evident clear plain manifest visible apparent explicit N.M. the out side outward condition apparent meaning ظاہر بیں *zā'hir-bīn,* ظاہر پرست *zā'hir paras't* N.M. & ADJ. (one) looking at superficial things , one who takes (one) having superficial values (one) influenced by outward show ظاہر دار *zā'hir-dār* ADJ. showy plausible ; hypocritical N.M. hypocrite one pretending friendship ظاہرداری *zā'hir-dā'rī* N.F. show ceremony plausibility pretence of friendship ظاہرداری برتنا *zā'hir-dā'rī ba'ratnā* V.T. pretend or make a show (of on 's friendship) ظاہر کچھ باطن کچھ *zā'hir kuchh bā'tin kuchh* V.I. (of someone) be a hypocrite ظاہر کرنا *zā'hir kar'nā* V.T reveal ; disclose pretend; make a show of ظاہر میں *zā'hir' meṅ* ADV. apparently seemingly on the face of it ظاہر و باطن *zā'hir-o-bā'tin* N.M. the inside and outside (of someone) ظاہر ہونا *zā'hir ho'nā* V.I. appear be seen come into sight come to light be revealed ; be disclosed become manifest ظاہرا *zā'hirā,* (ped. ظاہراً *zā'hiran*) ADV. outwardly ظاہری *zā'hirī* ADJ. apparent outward external not real [A ~ ظہور]

ظرافت *zarā'fat* N.F. wit irony jest ; humour ; pleasantry jocundity (rare) sagacity , wisdom ظرافۃً *zarā'fatan* ADV. facetiously ; by way of jest ظریف *zarī'f'* N.M. & ADJ. witty (person) jocund (person) (rare) wise (man) ظریفانہ *zarīfā'nah* ADJ. witty ironic jocose jocular ; jocund [A]

ظرف *zar'f* N.M. (PL. ظروف *zūroof'*) vessel capacity ability (good or bad) qualities of heast (gram.) adverb (of time or place) ظرف زمان *zar'f-e zamān'* N.M. adverb (of place) ظرف مکان *zar'f-e makān'* N.M. adverb (of place) تنگ (یا تنک) ظرف *tang'* (or *tū'nūk*)-*zar'f* ADJ. pretty minded تنگ (یا تنک) ظرفی *tang* (or *tū'nūk*)-*zar'fī* N.F. petty-mindedness عالی ظرف *'ā'lī-zar'f* ADJ. large-hearted ; magnanimous عالی ظرفی *'ā'lī-zar'fī* N.F. large heartedness ; magnanimity [A]

ظریف *zarīf',* ظریفانہ *zarīfā'nah* ADJ. (see under ظرافت N.F. ★)

ظفر *za'far* N.F. victory triumph conquest ظفر موج *za'far-mauj* ADJ. conquering (army) ظفریاب *za'far-yāb* ADJ. victorious (person)

ظل *zil* N.M. (PL. اظلال *azlāl'*) shadow protection projection ظل اللہ *zil'l-ūllāh* ظل الٰہی *zil'l-e ilā'hī* N.M. (sovereign as) the shadow of God ظل خیال *zil'l-e khayāl',* خیال الظلی *khayā'l-ūz'zil'* N.M. shadow-play [A]

ظلم *zūl'm* N.M. cruelty oppression tyranny harm ; wrong ; injury injustice hardship ظلم کرنا (توڑنا یا ڈھانا) *zūl'm kar'nā* (or toṛ'nā or ḍhā'na) V.T. oppress tyrannise do wrong (to) ظلم ہونا (یا ٹوٹنا) zūl'm ho'na (or ṭooṭ'nā) V.I. be oppressed be tyrannized suffer injustice be subjected to hardships [A]

ظلمت zūl'mat N.F. (PL. ظلمات zūlūmāt' or col. zūlmāt') darkness region of darkness بحر ظلمات bah'r-e zūlūmāt' N.M. (arch.) Atlantic Ocean ظلماتی zūlūmā'tī ADJ. dark [A]

ظلوم zaloom' ADJ. oppressive tyrannical highly unjust ظلوم و جہول zaloo'm-o jahool' ADJ. unjust and ignorant [A ~ PREC.]

ظن zan N.M. (PL. ظنون zūnoon') presumption conjecture surmise supposition suspicion ظن غالب zan'n-e ghā'lib N.M. strong presumption ظن فاسد zan'n-e fā'sid N.M. wrong presumption ظن کرنا zan kar'nā V.T. suppose surmise suspect conjecture ظن و تخمین zan'n-o takh'mīn' N.M. more conjecture ; guesswork حسن ظن hūs'n-e zan N.M. gracious presumption سوئے ظن soo''-e zan N.M. wrong suspicion ظنی zan'nī ADJ. conjectural unreal ; unsubstantial [A]

ظہار zehār' N.M. devoice effective elevation of one's wife to the supposed status of one's mother or sister [A]

ظہر zah'r N.F. back ظہری zah'rī ADJ. obverse ADV. on the reverse written on the back of a document ADV. on the reverse [A]

ظہر zoh'r N.M. early afternoon ; time immediately following midday

ظہور zohoor' N.M. manifestation becoming visible appearance rise ; arising occurance ; coming to pass ظہور میں آنا zohoor' meṅ ā'na V.I. occur ; come to pass ; come into being rise ; arise be manifest ظہور میں لانا zohoor' meṅ lā'na V.T. bring into being make manifest [A]

ظہیر zahīr' N.M. supporter ally ظہیرہ zahī'rah N.F. (rare) summer midday

ع 'ain twenty-fourth letter of Urdu alphabet (also called 'ain-e moh'malah or 'ain-e ghair'-manqoo'tah) (used in words of pure Arabic extraction) (according to Jummal reckoning) 70

عابد 'ā'bid N.M. (F. عابدہ 'ā'bidah) worshipper adorer devotee votary ADJ. godly pious devout [A ~ عبادت]

عاج 'āj N.M. ivory [A]

عاجز 'ā'jiz ADJ. helpless powerless unable ; incapable frustrated meek ; humble عاجز آنا (یا ہونا) 'ā'jiz ā'na (or ho'na) V.I. be helpless fall short (of) be frustrated عاجزانہ 'ājiza'nah ADV. helpless humble ; meek ADV. helplessly humbly ; meekly عاجزی 'ā'jizī N.F. helplessness humbleness; submissiveness humility lutreaty ; supplication inability ; incapacity عاجزی کرنا 'ā'jizī kar'nā V.I. show humility (to) make a humble entreaty entreat ; beseech ; implore [A ~ عجز]

عاجل 'ā'jil ADJ. hasty short-lived عاجلانہ 'ājilā'nah ADJ. hasty speedy [A ~ عجلت]

عاد 'ād, عاد ارم 'ā'd-e i'ram N.M. Adermites [A]

عاد 'ād N.M. (Math.) factor عاد اعظم 'ad'd-e a''zam N.M. (Math.) highest common factor H.C.F. عاد مشترک 'ad'd-e mūsh'tarak N.M. (Math.) common factor [~ A عدد]

عادت 'ā'dat N.F (PL. عادات 'ādāt') habit (rare) custom (rare) practice عادت پڑنا 'ā'dat paṛ'nā V.I. become a habit form the habit (of) get into the habit (of) get or be used (to) عادت ڈالنا 'ā'dat ḍāl'nā V.T. & I. form a habit make or get used (to) adopt the practice (of) set a craze (for) عادت کرنا 'ā'dat kar'nā V.I. (arch.) get used to عادۃً 'ā'datan ADV. habitually by habit عادی 'ā'dī ADJ. habitual used (to) accustomed (to) addicted (to) عادی کرنا 'ā'dī kar'nā V.T. habituate make used (to) accustom عادی مجرم 'ā'dī mūj'rim N.M. habitual offender عادی ہونا 'ā'dī ho'nā V.I. be addicted (to) be or get used (to) be accustomed (to) form the habit (of) [A ~ PREC.]

عادل 'ā'dil ADJ. just upright equitable عادلانہ 'ādilā'nah ADJ. just equitable based on justice ADV. justly equitably [A ~ عدل]

عادی 'ā'dī ADJ. (see under عادت N.F. ★)

عار 'ār N.F. shame disgrace modesty عار آنا 'ār ā'nā V.I. feel ashamed find (something) disgraceful عار کرنا 'ār kar'nā V.T. & I. shun as below one's dignity عار ہونا 'ār' ho'nā V.I. & I. feel ashamed ; have a feeling of shame regard (something) as disgraceful or below one's dignity [A]

عارض 'ā'riz N.M. cheek (rare) cloud ADJ. happening occurring befalling عارض سیمیں 'ā'riz-e sī'mīn N.M. bright cheek عارض گلگوں 'ā'riz-e gul-goon' N.M. rosy cheek عارض ہونا 'ā'riz ho'nā V.I. befall (someone) happen (to) عارضہ 'ā'rizah N.M. (PL. عوارض 'avā'riz) sickness ; disease disorder ; trouble complaint عارضہ لاحق ہونا 'ā'rizah lā'hiq ho'nā V.I. catch a sickness fall a prey (to) عارضی 'ā'rizī ADJ. temporary transitory ephemeral accidental casual [A ~ عرض]

عارف 'ā'rif N.M. (PL. عرفا 'urafā', F عارفہ 'ā'rifah F. (PL. عارفات 'ā'rifāt') mystic one having an intimate knowledge of God ADJ. knowing wise pious devout عارفانہ 'ārifā'nah ADJ. wise devout ADV. wisely devoutly [A ~ عرفان]

عاری 'ā'rī ADJ. free (from) void (of) [A]

عاریت 'ā'riyat N.F. something got on loan ; borrowed article something loaned out ADJ. borrowed loaned عاریتاً 'ā'riyatan ADV. on loan عاریتاً لینا 'ā'riyatan le'nā V.T. borrow for use عاریتی 'ā'riyatī ADJ. borrowed lent [A]

عازم 'ā'zim(e) ADJ. 'en route' (to), bound (for) resolved (on) determined [A ~ عزم]

عاشر 'ā'shir ADJ. tenth [A ~ عشر]

عاشق 'ā'shiq N.M. (PL. عشاق 'ushshāq') lover suitor paramour عاشق مزاج 'ā'shiq-mizāj' ADJ. amorous gay عاشق مزاجی 'ā'shiq-mizā'jī N.F. being amorous leading a gay life عاشق ہونا 'ā'shiq ho'nā V.I fall in love (with) fall (for) عاشقانہ 'āshiqā'nah ADJ. loving amorous like that of a lover عاشق معشوق 'ā'shiq ma'shooq' N.M. (as PL.) lover and beloved , devoted couple embroidered button and button hole gems of mount colours (set in a ring) عاشقی 'a'shiqī N.F love amour gallantry courtship [A ~ عشق]

عاشورا 'āshoo'rā (usu. but wrongly spelt as عاشورہ 'āshoo'rah) sacred N M. day of the tenth of Muharram doubly sanctified by Imam Husain's martyrdom [A ~ عشر]

عاصم 'ā'sim ADJ. safe virtuous chaste saviour عاصمہ 'ā'simah N.M capital (of state, etc.) ADJ chaste (woman) [A ~ عصمت]

عاصی 'ā'sī ADJ. & N.M (F عاصیہ 'ā'siyah) sinful (person)

عاطفت 'ā'tifat N.F. affection kindness favour اپنے سایۂ عاطفت میں لینا ap'ne sā'ya-e 'ā'tifat meṅ le'nā V.T. take (someone) under one's protection [A]

عافیت 'ā'fiyat N.M. safety peace خیروعافیت khai'r-o-'ā'fiyat N.F. health and safety (of) welfare (of) خیروعافیت کی خبر khai'r-o-'ā'fiyat kī kha'bar PH. good tidings (about) [A]

عاق 'āq ADJ. (rare) undutiful (extended sense) disinherited , disowned عاق کرنا 'āq' kar'nā V.T. disinherit cut off from inheritance [A ~ عقوق]

عاقبت 'ā'qibat N.F. Hereafter future life consequence ADV. at last after all عاقبت اندیش 'ā'qibat-andesh' ADJ. provident prudent far-seeing discreet عاقبت اندیشانہ 'ā'qibat-andeshā'nah ADJ. wise عاقبت اندیشی 'ā'qibat-ande'shī N.F. foresight prudence provision for the future عاقبت بگاڑنا (یا خراب کرنا) 'ā'qibat bigāṛ'nā (or kharāb kar'nā) V.I. mar one's future state of bliss invite damnation by (one's) sinful conduct عاقبت کے بوریے سمیٹنا 'ā'qibat ke bo'riye samet'nā V.I live a very long life (usu. full of greed for worldly things عاقبت نا اندیش 'ā'qibat nā-andesh' (col. ناعاقبت اندیش nā-'ā'qibat-andesh') ADJ. indiscreet imprudent عاقبت نا اندیشی 'ā'qibat nā ande'shī, (col ناعاقبت اندیشی nā 'ā'qibat ande'shī) N.F. indiscretion imprudence [A]

عاقرقرحا 'ā'qarqarha N.M pellitory [A]

عاقل 'ā'qil ADJ. & N.M. (PL. عقلا 'uqalā) (F. عاقلہ 'ā'qilah) wise (person) sensible (being) intelligent (person) عاقلانہ 'āqilā'nah ADJ. wise prudent [A ~ عقل]

عالم 'ā'lam N.M (PL. عوالم 'avā'lim) world universe state ; condition grace time creatures people ; public عالم آرا 'ā'lam ārā' ADJ world-adorning عالم ارواح 'ā'lam-e arvāh' N M spirites egile spiritual world عالم اسباب 'ā'lam-e asbāb' N.M. the world ; the world of cause and effect عالم افروز 'ā'lam-afroz' ADJ. world-illuminating عالم بالا 'ā'lam-e bā'lā N.M. heavenly world heavenly people عالم برزخ 'ā'lam-e bar'zakh N.M. period or state between death resurrection عالم پناہ 'ā'lam-panāh' N.M. (sovereign as) asylum of the world عالمتاب 'ā'lam-tāb ADJ. world-illuminating عالم خیال 'ā'lam-e khayāl' N.M. fancy pensive mood عالم رویا 'ā'lam-e ro'yā N M dream world state of dreaming عالم سفلی

'ā'lam-e si'flī N.M. earth world عالم صغیر 'ā'lam-e saghīr' N.M. microcosm عالم عالم 'ā'lam 'ā'lam ADV. very much عالم علوی 'ā'lam-e 'ūl'vī N.M. heaven عالم غیب 'ā'lam-e ghaib' N.M. the invisible world extra-sensary world عالم فانی 'ā'lam-a fā'nī N.M. world the mortal world عالم کبیر 'ā'lam-e kabīr' N.M. macrocosm عالمگیر 'ā'lam-gīr' ADJ. worldwide universal world-conquering N.M. world conqueror (as appellation of a Moghul ruler عالم لاہوت 'ā'lam-e lāhoot' N.M. world (or state) of creature's oneness with God عالم مثال 'ā'lam-e misāl' N.M. (Platonic) world of ideas عالم مستی 'ā'lam-e mas'tī N.M. state of intoxication heat period lasciviousness عالم ملکوت 'ā'lam-e malakooot' N.M. angalic world ; the world of angels عالم ناسوت 'ā'lam-e nāsoot' N.M. world ; the mortal world عالمی 'ā'lamī ADJ. international world world wide global universal [A]

عالم 'ā'lim N.M. (PL. علما 'ūlamā' F. عالمہ 'ā'limah) learned man sage savant Muslim theoligean ADJ. learned knowing عالم الغیب 'ā'lim-ūl-ghaib' N.M. God (one knowing the invisible as well) عالمانہ 'ā'lima'nah ADJ. learned (disconise, etc.) sage-like [A ~ علم 'ilm]

عالمی 'ā'lamī ADJ. (see under عالم 'ā'lam N.M ★)

عالی 'ā'lī ADJ. (F. عالیہ 'ā'liyah) high lofty elevated ; exalted eminent noble grand ; magnificant عالی تبار 'ā'lī-tabār' ADJ. of noble descent عالی جاہ 'ā'lī-jāh ADJ. highly placed ; high-ranking INT. (PL. عالیجاہا 'ā'lī-jā'hā) your honour your excellency عالیجناب 'ā'lī-janāb'. ADJ. esteemed high-ranking INT. your honour your excellency عالی خاندان 'ā'lī-khāndān' ADJ. of noble birth N.M. noble family ; well to-do family عالی دماغ 'ā'lī-dimāgh' ADJ. intelligent (one) with high notions proud ; vain عالیشان 'ā'lī-shān ADJ. grand splendid magnificent عالی ظرف 'ā'lī-zar'f ADJ. magnanimous عالی ظرفی 'ā'lī-zar'fī N.F. magnanimity عالی فطرت 'ā'lī fit'rat ADJ. noble عالی مرتبت 'ā'lī-mar'tabat ADJ. noble high ranking عالی ہمت 'ā'lī-him'mat ADJ. ambitious daring عالی ہمتی 'ā'lī-him'matī N.F. daring ; courage ambition ; ambitiousness [A]

عام[1] 'ām ADJ. common ordinary general all customary usual widely known mass عام فہم 'ām-fah'm ADJ. intelligible to the common man ; simple and easy خاص و عام khā's-o 'ām (or ped. khāss-) high and low عامہ 'ām'mah ADJ. public of the masses عامۃ الناس 'ām'mat-ūn-nās' N.M. PL common people عامی 'ā'mī N.M. commoner ADJ. common (man) عامیانہ 'ā'miyānah ADJ. vulgar عوام 'avām N.M. PL ★ [A ~ عموم]

عام[2] 'ām N.M. (PL. اعوام a'vām') (rare) year [A]

عامرہ ā'mirah ADJ. replete well-in-habited (fig.) royal خزانۂ عامرہ khizā'na-e 'ā'mirah N.M. royal exchequer [A]

عامل 'ā'mil N.M. labourer worker agent spiritualist revenue collector ; ruler [A ~ عمل]

عامہ 'ām'mah ADJ. عامی 'ā'mī N.M. & ADJ. عامیانہ 'amiya'nah ADJ. (see under عام عام ADJ. ★)

عائد 'ā''id ADJ. incumbent devolving عاید ہونا 'ā''id ho'nā V.I. (of duty) devolve (upon) incumbent (on)

عائلہ 'ā''ilah N.M (PL. عیال 'iyāl) family عائلی 'ā''ilī ADJ. family عائلی قوانین 'ā'ilī qavānīn' N.M. N.M. PL. family laws ; special laws governing marriage, divorce, etc. [A]

عبا 'abā' N.F. cloak [A]

عباد 'ibād' N.M. (PL. of عبد ★)

عبادت 'ibā'dat N.F. worship prayers church service devotion عبادت کرنا 'ibā'dat kar'na V.T. worship ; عبادت گاہ 'ibā'dat-gāh N.F. place of worship temple mosque church عبادت گزار 'ibā'dat gūzār' ADJ. worshipping N.M. worshipper votary عبادت گزاری 'ibā'dat-gūzā'rī N.F. worship devotion [A ~ عبد]

عبارت 'ibā'rat N.F. passage (of writing) diction phraseology expression consist عبارت آرائی 'ibā'rat-ārā''ī N.F. ornamentation of style (usu. overmuch) ; attention to style [A]

عباس 'abbās' N.M. (rare) lion name of one of the Holy Prophet's uncle's who was the progenitor of the Abbasids عباسی 'abbā'sī, گل عباسی gū'l-e 'abbā'sī N.M. a species of red flower Marvel of Peru [A]

عبث 'ā'bas ADJ. useless ; unavailing ; of no avail vain bootless ADV. uselessly vain to no purpose [A]

عبد 'ab'd N.M. (PL. عباد 'ibād') slave (fig.) devotee عبداللہ 'abdūllāh N.M. God's slave (fig.) Muslim عباداللہ 'ibā'dūl'lāh N.M. PL. slaves of God people masses Muslims عبودیت 'ūboodiy'yat N.F. servitude (fig.) devotion being God slave [A]

عبرانی *'ibra'ni*, (rare عبری *'ib'ri*) ADJ. Hebrew [A]

عبرت *'ib'rat* N.F. example ; lesson warning; admonition عبرت انگیز *'ib'rat-angez'* ADJ. exemplary ; serving as a warning ; admonitory عبرت انگیزی *'ib'rat-ange'zi* N.F. serving as a warning عبرت پذیر *'ib'rat pazir'* ADJ. taking a warning عبرت پذیری *'ib'rat pazi'ri* N.F. taking a warning عبرت پکڑنا *'ib'rat pa'karna* V.I. be warned ; take a warning (from) عبرت دلانا *'ib'rat dila'na* V.T. teach a lesson (to) ; make an example of عبرت ہونا *'ib'rat ho'na* V.T. & I. be warned prove a warning (to) [A]

عبقری *'ab'qari* N.M. paragon of beauty ADJ. the best [A]

عبور *'uboor'* N.M. crossing (river, etc.) passing transportation perfect knowledge (of) عبور دریائے شور *'uboo'r-e darya'-e shor* N.M. transportation beyond the seas (as form of life imprisonment عبور حاصل کرنا *'uboor' ha'sil kar'na* V.T. be (come) fully conversant with عبور کرنا *'uboor' kar'na* V.T. cross ; go across pass [A]

عبوس *'aboos'* ADJ. testy عبوساً قمطریرا *'aboo'san qamtari'ra* ADJ. (joc.) strict and testy [A]

عبہر *'ab'har* N.M. yellow narcissus [A]

عبید *'ubaid'* N.M. small slave [A ~ عبد]

عبیر *'abir'* (corr. ابیر *abir'*) N.M. talc powder mixed powder of rose, sandal saffron and cut mica (esp. for sprinkling during Holi) [A]

عتاب *'itab'* N.M. displeasure reproof reprimand عتاب زدہ *'itab'-za'dah* ADJ. (someone) who has incurred another's displeasure عتاب کرنا *'itab' kar'na* V.T. reprimand عتاب (نازل) ہونا *'itab' (na'zil) ho'na* V.I. be reprimanded incur displeasure (of) [A]

عترت *'it'rat* N.F. progeny [A]

عثمان *'usman'* N.M. young ruddy goose young dragon name of the Orthodox Caliph name of the founder of Ottoman Caliphate عثمانی *'usma'ni* ADJ. Ottoman N.M. descandent of the third Orthodox Caliph [A]

عتیق *'atiq'* ADJ. (F. or PL. عتیقہ *'ati'qah*) ancient antique آثار عتیقہ *asa -e 'atiqah* N.M. ancient monuments relics of the part archeological finds [A]

عجائب *'aja''ib* N.M. PL. (double PL. عجائبات *aja'ibat'*) curios curiosities wonders ; wonderful things marvels عجائب خانہ *'aja''ib-kha'nah*, عجائب گھر *'aja''ib-ghar* N.M. museum

عجائب وغرائب *'aja''ib-o-ghara''ib* N.M. PL curios and rarities wonders [A ~ SING. عجیبہ ~ عجیب]

عجب *'a'jab* N.M. wonder surprise ADJ. strange wonderful marvellous rage [A]

عجب *'uj'b* N.M. pride ; vanity ; conceit arrogance hauteur عجب و نخوت *'aj'b-o-nakh'vat* N.M. hauteur and self-panperedness [A]

عجز *'aj'z* (col. *'ij'z*) N.M. helplessness powerlessness humility submission عجز و انکسار *'aj'z-o-inkisar'* N.M. humility and lowliness [A]

عجلت *'uj'lat* (ped. *ujalat*) N.F haste hurry عجلت میں *'ujlat men* ADV. in haste hurriedly [A]

عجم *'a'jam* N.M. non-Arab peoples as dumb tongue-tied or barbarian races) Persia عجمی *'a'jami* (ped. اعجمی *a''jami*) N.M. (PL. عجم *'a'jam*, اعاجم *a'a'jum*) Persian non-Arab dumb ; mute [A]

عجوبہ *'ajoo'bah* N.M. (col. for اعجوبہ *'o'joo'bah* ★)

عجوز *'ajooz'* (or usu. but wrong عجوزہ *'ajoo'zah*) N.F. old woman hag [A ~ عجز]

عجیب *'ajib'* ADJ. strange wonderful admirable surprising ; astonishing marvellous عجیب وغریب *'aji'b-o-gharib'* ADJ. strange marvellous curious عجائب *'aja''ib* N.M. PL.★ [A ~ عجب]

عدالت *'ada'lat* N.F. court of law ; lawcourt ; court tribunal judge equity ; justice عدالت خفیفہ *'ada'lat-e khafi'fah* N.F. Small Causes Court عدالت عالیہ *ada'lat-e 'a'liyah* N.F. High Court ; Chief Court عدالت علیا *ada'lat-e 'ul'ya* N.F. Supreme Court عدالت کرنا *'ada'lat kar'na* V.T. & I. sat as court give judicial verdict (rare) do justice عدالت لگانا *'ada'lat laga'na* V.T. hold the court عدالت لگنا *'ada'lat lag'na* V.I. (of court, be held) عدالت دیوانی ,دیوانی عدالت *diva'ni 'ada'lat*, *'ada'lat-e diva'ni* N.F. civil court فوجداری عدالت *fauj-da'ri 'ada'lat*, عدالت فوجداری *'ada'lat-e fauj-da'ri* N.F. criminal court عدالتی *'ada'lati* ADJ. judicial court عدالتی کارروائی *'ada'lati kar-rava''i* N.F. judicial proceedings court proceedings عدالتی مسائل *'ada'lati masa''il* N.M. PL. (arch.) maxims of equity [A ~ عدل]

عداوت *'ada'vat* N.F. enmity hostility animosity malice feud عداوت رکھنا *'ada'vat rakh'na* V.I. bear malice (towards) be inimical (to) عداوت نکالنا *'ada'vat nikal'na* V.T gratify (one's) malice [A ~ عدو]

عدت 'id'dat N.F. probationary period (of three months for divorced woman or of four months ten days for widow) (rare) number (of) عدت پوری کرنا (یا گزرنا) 'id'dat poo'rī kar'nā (or guzar'nā) V.I. complete the probationary period عدت میں بیٹھنا 'id'dat meṅ baiṭh'nā V.I. wait (before remarriage, etc.) for probationary period [A]

عدد 'a'dad N.M. (PL. اعداد a'dād') number numeral figure number of packages, etc. with traveller total of jummal reckoning (of word, etc.) عدد صحیح 'a'dad-e saḥīḥ' N.M. integer ; whole number عدد وصفی 'a'dad-e vas'fī N.M. cardinal number عدد ترتیبی 'a'dad-e tartī'bī N.M. ordinal number عددی 'a'dadī ADJ. numeral numerical عددی فوقیت 'a'dadī fauqiy'yat N.F. numerical superiority صفت عددی si'fat-e 'a'dadī N.F. numeral adjective [A]

عدل 'ad'l N.M. justice ; equity division into halves عدل پرور 'ad'l-par'var ADJ. just عدل پروری 'ad'l-par'varī N.F. justice عدل کرنا 'ad'l karnā V.T. do justice عدل گستری 'ad'l-gūs'tarī N.F. administration of justice عدل ہونا 'ad'l ho'nā V.I. (of justice) be administered [A]

عدم 'a'dam N.M. nothingness non-existence Hereafter default (ped.) lack (of) PREF. (col.) non-existence عدم ادائیگی 'a'dam adā''igī N.F non-payment عدم استطاعت 'a'dam(e) istitā''at N.F inability ; incapacity insolvency poverty عدم اندراج 'a'dam(-e) indirāj' N.M. non-entry عدم پیروری 'a'dam pai'ravī N.F. non-appearance (in court) ; default of prosecution عدم تعاون 'a'dam(-e) ta'ā'vūn N.M. non-co-operation عدم تعمیل 'a'dam(-e) ta'mīl N.F. non-compliance non-service ; non-execution عدم تشدد 'a'dam-e tashad'dūd N.M. non-violence عدم توجہ 'a'dam-e tavaj'joh, عدم توجہی 'a'dam tavaj'johī N.F. lack of attention عدم ثبوت 'a'dam(-e) sūboot' N.M. lack want or absence of proof عدم جواز 'a'dam(-e) javāz N.M. unlawfulness ; illegality lack of authority عدم حاضری 'a'dam ḥā'zirī N.F. non-attendance عدم فرصت 'a'dam-e fūr'sat (col. عدم فرصتی a'dam fūr'satī, عدیم الفرصتی 'adī'm-ūl-fūr'satī) N.F. want of leisure عدم مداخلت 'a'dam(-e) mūdā'khalat N.F. non-intervention عدم موجودگی 'a'dam maujoo'dagī N.F. absence non-existence عدم واقفیت 'a'dam vaqifiy'yat N.F. want of information عدم (و) وجود 'a'dam(-o-) vūjood' N.M. existence and non-existence عدم (و) وجود برابر ہونا 'adam(-o-) vūjood bara'bar ho'nā V.I. (of someone) be a non-entity be of no significance کالعدم kal-'a'dam ADJ. null and void annulled quashed کالعدم کرنا kal-'a'dam kar'nā V.T. quash annul rescind کالعدم ہونا kal-'a'dam ho'na V.I. be quashed be annulled become extinct ملک عدم mūl'k-e 'a'dam N.M. next world Hereafter [A]

عدن 'ad'n N.F. Paradise Eden (rare) perpetuity [A]

عدن 'a'dan N.M. Aden (A)

عدو 'adoo' N.M. (PL. اعدا a'dā' enemy ; foe [A ~ عداوت]

عدوان 'ūdvān' N.M. transgression cruelty [A]

عدول 'ūdool' N.M. non-compliance aberration عدولِ حکمی 'udoo'l-e ḥūk'm, (col. حکم عدولی ḥūk'm 'ūdao'lī) N.M. disobedience insubordination حکم عدولی کرنا ḥūk'm 'ūdoo'lī kar'nā V.T. disobey ; refuse to obey ; refuse to comply with orders be refractory be guilty of insubordination [A ~ عدل]

عدیل 'adīl' N.M. equivalent equal ; peer ; of the some status (as) [A ~ عدل]

عدیم 'adīm' ADJ. extinct lacking عدیم الفرصت 'adī'm-ūl-fūr'sat ADJ. having no leisure very busy with ones hands full عدیم المثال 'adī'm-ul-misal' ADJ. unparalleled incomparable peerless عدیم النظیر 'adī'm-ūn-nazīr' ADJ. unprecedented [A ~ عدم]

عذاب 'azāb' N.M. punishment torment ; torture misfortune trouble troublesome person عذاب ہونا 'azāb' ban'nā V.T. prove to be a nuisance (for) عذاب بنانا 'azāb' banā'nā V.T. make a nuisance (for) عذاب دینا 'azāb' de'nā V.T. punish torture ; torment عذاب مول لینا 'azāb' mol' le'nā V.I. invite trouble land oneself in trouble عذاب میں پھنسنا (یا گرفتار ہونا) 'azāb' meṅ phaṅs'nā (or giriftār' ho'nā) V.I. be involved in difficulties [A]

عذار 'azār' N.M. cheek گلعذار gūl-'azār' ADJ. & N.M. rosy-cheeked (sweetheart) [A]

عذب 'az'b ADJ. sweet ; mellifluous عذب البیان 'az'būl-bayān' ADJ. sweet-tongued ; eloquent [A]

عذر 'ūz'r N.M. excuse pretext plea apology (legal) objection counter-claim ; cross demand عذر بیجا 'ūz'r-e be-jā' N.M. improper plea عذرخواہ 'ūz'r-khāh ADJ. apologising N.M. apologist عذرخواہ ہونا 'ūz'r-khāh ho'nā V.I. raise an objection عذرخواہی 'uz'r-khā'hī N.F. excuse apology عذرخواہی کرنا 'ūz'r-khā'hī kar'nā V.I. apologize put up an excuse عذردار 'ūz'r-dār N.M. objector عذرداری 'ūz'r-dā'rī N.F. legal statement of objections cross demand ; counter-claim عذر قانونی 'ūz'r-e qānoo'nī N.M. legal objection عذر کے قابل 'ūz'r ke qā'bil ADJ. excusable objectionable عذر لنگ 'ūz'r-e lang' N.M. lame excuse

(نا) قابل سماعت عذر (*na*) *qa'bil e sama''at ūz'r* ADJ. (un-) tenable plea [A]

عذرا *'az'ra* N.F. virgin (sign of Zodiac) Virgo [A]

عراق *'iraq'* N.M. Iraq name of a musical mode عراقی *'ira'qi* ADJ. Iraqi [A]

عرائض *'ara''iz* N.F. PL. petitions عرائض نویس *ara''iz-navis'* N.M. petition-writer [A ~ SING. عریضہ or عرضی]

عرب *'a'rab* N.M. Arab Arabia (correctly only) Arabs بلاد عرب *bila'd-e 'a'rab* جزیرۃ العرب *jazi'rat-'a'rab* N.M. Arabia عربی *'a'rabi* N.F. ADJ. Arab ; Arabian [A]

عربدہ *'ar'badah* N.M. quarrelsomeness عربدہ جو *'ar'bada-joo* ADJ. quarrelsome touchy testy [A]

عربی *'a'rabi* N.F. & ADJ. (see under عرب N.M. ★)

عرس *'ūr's* N.M. death anniversary (of saint) [~A]

عرش *'ar'sh* N.M. the empyrean (as throne of God) (fig.) throne high seat عرش بریں *'ar'sh-e barin'*, عرش معلیٰ *'ar'sh-e mo'al'lā* N.M. the empyrean throne of God عرش پر جھولنا *'ar'sh par jhool'na* V.I. be exalted be very high be very lofty عرش پر چڑھانا *'ar'sh par charka'na* V.I. exalt ; elevate the highest states lavish indue praises (on) عرش پر دماغ ہونا *'ar'sh par dimagh' ho'na*, دماغ عرش پر ہونا *dimagh' 'ar'sh par ho'na* V.I. be very proud عرش سے فرش تک *'ar'sh se far'sh tak* ADV. everywhere all over the universe عرش کے تارے توڑنا *'ar'sh ke ta're tor'na* V.I. work wonders عرشہ *'arshah* N.M. deck (of ship) [A]

عرصہ *'ar'sah* N.M. period ; time ; space of time interval duration place field space scope (of) عرصۂ حیات *'ar'sa-e hayat'* N.M. span of life عرصہ لگانا *'ar'sah laga'na* V.I. delay take a long time; take long (over) عرصۂ حیات تنگ کرنا *'ar'sa-e hayat' tang' kar'na* V.T. give hell (to) make things difficult (for) عرصۂ حیات تنگ ہونا *'ar'sa-e hayat' tang' ho'na* V.I. find things difficult (for one) عرصۂ محشر *'ar'sa-e mah'shar* N.M. resurrection plain ایک عرصہ تک *ek 'ar'se tak* ADV. long ; for a long time ایک عرصہ سے *ek 'ar'se se* ADV. since long اس عرصہ میں *is ar'se men* ADV. during this time in the meantime ; meanwhile [A]

عرض *'ar'z* N.F. (PL. اعراض *a'raz'*) request ; entreaty petition representation (arch.) repart review (of parade) width ; breadth عرض ارسال *'ar'z irsal'* N.F. (arch.) report return invain عرض بیگی *'ar'z-be'gi* N.M. (arch.) officer presenting representations to the sovereign عرض حال *'ar'z-e hal'* N.M. submission statement of facts عرضداشت *'arz-dash't* N.F. memorial memorandum petition عرض کنندہ *'ar'z-kunin'dah* N.M. petitioner عرض معروض *'ar'z-ma'rooz'* N.F. petition entreaty purport of request عرضاً *'ar'zan* ADJ. breadthwise عرضی *'ar-zi* N.F. application petition representation عرضی دینا *'ar-zi de'na* V.T. submit a petition apply عرضی دعویٰ *'ar'zi da'va* N.M. petition of plaint عرضی لکھنا *'ar'zi likh'na* V.I. write an application draft a petition عرضی نویس *'ar'zi-navis'* N.M. petition-writer notary ; notary public [A]

عرض *'ir'z* N.F. (PL. اعراض *a'raz'*) honour [A]

عرض *'a'raz* N.M. (PL. اعراض *a''raz*) attribute [A]

عرضہ *'ur'zah* N.M. butt ; target [A]

عرف *'ūr'f* N.M. alias (rare) common law law of the land ADJ. known (by the name of) ; commonly called ; alias عرفاً *'ūr'fan* ADV. (rare) according to common law عرفی *'ūr'fi* ADJ. well known formal [A]

عرفا *'ūrafa'* N.M. (PL. of عارف★)

عرفات *'arafat'* N.M. vaste expanse twelve miles from Mecca, where major Haj rite is performed میدان عرفات *maida'n-e 'arafat'* N.M. the Arafat expanse [A]

عرفان *'irfan'* N.M. intimate knowledge of God highest form of mystical experience discernment [A]

عرفہ *'ar'fah* N.M. major Haj day ; day before sacrificial Eid day preceding either Eid [A]

عرفی *'ūr'fi* ADJ. (see under عرف N.M. ★)

عرق *'a'raq* N.M. (PL. عروق *'urooq'*) distilled concoction ; water (of) perspiration ; sweat عرق آجانا *'a'raqa ja'na* V.I. sweat ; perspire عرق آلود(ہ) *'a'raq-aloo'd(ah)* ADJ. sweaty ; perspiring عرق ریزی *'a'raq-rezi* N.F. hard work doing something by the sweat of one's brow عرق ریزی کرنا *'a'raq-re'zi kar'na* V.I. work hard عرق عرق ہو جانا *'a'raq a'raq ho ja'na* V.I. perspire through shame عرق کھینچنا (یا کشید کرنا) *'a'raq khench'na* (or *kashid' kar'na*) V.T. distil عرق گلاب *'a'raq-e gulab'* N.M. rose-water عرق گیر *'a'raq-gir'* N.M. saddle cloth ; sweat-cloth [A]

عرق *'ir'q* N.M. (PL. عرقات *'irqat*, عروق *'urooq'*) vein عرق النسا *'ir'q-un-nasa'* N.M. sciatica [A]

عروج *'urooj'* N.M. rise success elevation exaltation height نقطۂ عروج *nuq'ta-e* '*ūrooj*' N.M. height (of) highest point (of) acme [A]

عروس '*aroos*' N.F. bride عروسی '*aroo'sī*' ADJ. bridal nuptial N.F. marriage ; wedding تقریب عروسی *taqrī'b-e 'aroo'sī* N.F. wedding ceremony حجلۂ عروسی *haj'la-e 'aroo'sī* N.M. bridal apartment (rare) nuptial bed [A]

عروض '*ūrooz*' N.M. prosody (rare) second quarter of couplet علم عروض '*il'm-e ūrooz*', علم العروض '*il'm-ul''ūrooz*' N.M. science of prosody عروضی '*ūroo'zī* ADJ. prosodic [A]

عروق '*ūrooq*' N.F. (PL. of عرق '*a'raq* N M. ★ or عرق '*irq* N.F. ★)

عریاں '*ūr'yān* ADJ. nude ; nacked bare devoid (of) divested obscene عریاں نگار (یا نویس) '*ūr'yān-nigār*' (or *navīs*') N.M. & ADJ. obscene (writer) عریاں نگاری (یا نویسی) '*ūr'yān-nigā'rī* (or *navī'sī*) N.F. obscene writing obscenity in writing عریانی '*ūryā'nī* N.F. nudity nakedness obscenity [A]

عریض '*arīz*' ADJ. wide ; broad وسیع و عریض *vasī''-o-'arīz*' ADJ. wide and expansive [A ~ عرض]

عریضہ '*arī'zah* N.M. (PL. عرائض '*arā''iz*) (polite word for) letter (rare) petition [A ~ عرض]

عز '*iz* N.M. glory عز '*az'za* INT. glorified (be) glorious (be) عز و جل '*az'za va jal'la* INT. glorified and exalted be the name of (God) [A]

عزا '*azā*' N.F. mourning condolence عزادار '*azā'-dār*' N.M. mourner (esp. of Imam Hussain) عزاداری '*azā'-dā'rī* N.F. mourning (esp. of Imam Hussain)

عزازیل '*azāzīl*' N.M. Satan [A]

عزائم '*azā''im* N.M. (PL. of عزیمت '*azī'mat* or عزم '*az'm* ★)

عزیٰ '*ūz'zā* N.F. the most honoured women (as the name of a pre-Islamic Arab idol) [A ~ عزت]

عزت '*iz'zat* N.F. respect honour dignity esteem reputation izzat عزت اتارنا '*iz'zat ūtār'na* V.T. insult disgrace; dishonour abuse rape عزت بگاڑنا '*iz'zat bigar'nā* V.T. & I. disgrace (someone or oneself) عزت دار '*iz'zat-dār*, عزت والا '*iz'zat-vā'la* ADJ. respectable عزت دارانہ '*iz'zat-dārā'nah* ADJ. respectable عزت داری '*iz'zat-dā'rī* N.F. respectability عزت دینا '*iz'zat-de'na* V. exalt confer honour or dignity (upon) dignify عزت رکھنا '*iz'zat rakh'na* V.T. & I. preserve (one's or someone's) honour or good name achieve or give success (in endeavour) عزت رہنا '*iz'zat raih'nā* V.T. & I. preserve (one's or someone's) honour or good name achieve or give success (in endeavour) عزت کا لاگو ہونا '*iz'zat ka la'goo ho'na*, عزت کے پیچھے پڑنا '*iz'zat ke pī'chhe par'nā* V.T. he bent upon ruining the honour or reputation (of) try to give a bad name (to) sully (someone's) name kill a character عزت کرنا '*iz'zat kar'nā* V. honour dignify pay respect (to) عزت لینا '*iz'zat le'nā* V.T. insult disgrace ; dishonour put to shame destroy the reputation (of) abuse rape عزت میں فرق آنا '*iz'zat meṅ far'q ā'nā* V.I. (of one's name) be sullied عزت مآب '*iz'zat ma'āb*' ADJ. honourable ; hon'ble عزت میں بٹہ لگنا (یا فرق آنا) '*iz'zat meṅ bat'tah lag'nā* (or *far'q ā'nā*) V.I. have one's reputation, character or name sullied بے عزت *be-'iz'zat* ADJ. disgraced ; dishonoured disreputable defamed notorious بے عزتی *be 'iz'zatī* N.F. disgrace insult [A]

عزرائیل '*izrā'īl* N.M. name of the angel of death ; Izra''il [A ~ H]

عزل '*az'l* N.M. dismissal removal (from office) (rare) exterior ejection a method of birth control عزل ونصب '*az'l-o-nas'b* N.M. dismissal and appointment [A]

عزلت '*ūz'lat* N.F. retirement solitude گوشۂ عزلت *go'shā-e 'ūz'lat* N.M. solitary corner عزلت گزیں '*ūz'lat-gūzīṅ*' N.M. recluse ADJ. (one) leading a life of retirement [A ~ عزل]

عزم '*az'm* N.M. (PL. عزائم '*azā''im*) resolve determination aim ; purpose ; intention عزم بالجزم '*az'm bil-jaz'm*, عزم مصمم '*az'm-e mūsam'mam* N.M. firm resolve [A]

عزیز '*azīz*' ADJ. dear (rare) mighty N.M. (PL. اعزہ *a'iz'zah*) relative friend (arch.) potentate the omnipotent (as an attribute of God) عزیز جاننا (یا رکھنا) '*azīz*' *jān'nā* (or *rakh'nā*) V.T. hold dear [A ~ عزت]

عزیمت '*azī'mat* N.F. (PL. عزائم '*azā''im*) resolve ; determination intention design aim ambitious plan باعزیمت *bā 'azī'mat*, صاحب عزیمت *sā'hib-e 'azī'mat* ADJ. ambitious (one) with lofty aims [A]

عساکر '*asā'kir* N.M. (PL. of عسکر ★)

عسرت '*ūs'rat* N.F. difficulty distress, hardship ; poverty عسر '*ūs'r* N.M. hard times عسیر '*asīr*' ADJ. difficult poor [A]

عسکر '*as'kar* N.M. (PL. عساکر '*asā'kir*) army , armed force عسکری '*as'karī* ADJ. army ; military N.M. (rare) soldier [A]

عسس *'a'sas* N.M. nightwatch metropolitan police chief [A]

عسل *'a'sal* N.M. honey [A]

عسیر *'asīr'* ADJ. (see under عسرت ★)

عشاق *'ushshāq'* N.M. PL. lovers name of a Persian musical mode [A ~ SING. عاشق]

عشا *'ishā'* N.F. night prayers (rare) first watch of night عشا کی نماز *'ishā' kī namāz'* N.F. night prayers عشائیہ *'ishā'iy'yah* N.M. supper ; dinner [A]

عشا *'ashā'* N.M. supper عشائے ربانی *'ashā'-e rabbā'nī* N.F. (dial.) Lord's sacrament sacrament of Lord's supper

عشبہ *'ush'bah* N.M. sarsaparilla [A]

عشر *'ash'r*, عشیر, *'asharah* ADJ. & N.M. ten عشر *'ush'r* ADJ. one-tenth N.M. tithe عشر عشیر *'ush'r-e 'ashīr'* N.M. very minute part (of) عشر عشیر بھی نہ ہونا *'ush'r-e 'ashīr' bhī na ho'nā* V.I. be no match (for) not to be even a minute part (of) عشرہ *'ash'rah* ADJ. ten N.M. ten-day opening period (of Muharram as period of mourning over Imam Husain's martyrdom عشرۂ مبشرہ *'ash'ra-e mubash'sharah* N.M. PL. the blessed ten , the ten companions of the Holy Prophet blessed with salvation even during their lifetime عشرہ محرم *'ash'ra-e mohar'ram* N.M. Muharram mourning period [A]

عشرت *'ish'rat* N.F. gaiety happy social life pleasure عشرت کدہ *'ish'rat-ka'dah* N.M. house of pleasure عیش و عشرت *'ai'sh-o-'ish'rat* N.F. gaiety debauchery [A]

عش عش *'ash 'ash'* INT. (expressive of approving astonishment) (used only in) عش عش کرنا *'ash 'ash' kar'na* V.I. admire greatly [ONO.]

عشق *'ish'q* N.M. love passion عشق باز *'ish'q-baz'* N.M. gallant lover عشق بازانہ *'ish'q-bāzā'nah* ADJ. amorous عشق بازی *'ish'q-ba'zī* N.F. love-making amour gallantry عشق پیچاں *'ish'q-pechāṅ'* N.M. American jasmine ivy عشق حقیقی *'ish'q-e haqī'qī* N.M. divine love , spiritual love عشق مجازی *'ish'q-e majā'zī* N.M. mundane love , carnal love عشقیہ *'ishqiy'yah* ADJ. love , of love amatory erotic [A]

عشوہ *'ish'vah* N.M. ogle coquetry blandishment عشوہ گر *'ish'va-gar* ADJ. coquettish N.M. coquette amorously playful ogler عشوہ گری *'ish'va-garī* N.F. coquetry blandishment [A]

عشیر *'ashīr'* ADJ. one-tenth عشر عشیر *'ush'r-e 'ashīr'* ADJ. (see under عشر ADJ. & N.M. ★)

عصا *'a'sā'* N.M. stick ; staff ; club sceptre mace عصا بردار *'asā'-bar-dār'* N.M. mace-bearer عصائے پیری *'asā'-e pī'rī* N.M. old man's staff (fig.) old man's son عصائے شاہی *'asā-e shā'hī* N.M. royal sceptre عصائے موسوی *'asā'-e moo'savī*, عصائے کلیم *'asā'-e kalīm'*, N.M. miraculous rod of shoes [A]

عصارہ *'asā'rah* N.M. extract juice [A ~ عصر]

عصب *'a'sab* N.M. (PL. اعصاب *a'sāb'*) muscle , sinew tendon ligament nerve عصبانی *'asabā'nī* (col. عصباتی *'asbā'tī*) ADJ. nervous restless , uneasy عصبہ *'asabah* (PL. عصب *'a'sab* double PL. اعصاب *a'sāb'*) N.M. muscle , sinew tendon ligament nerve distant relations on paternal side dentitle inheritance in certain cases) one's people whom one is honour-bound to support and defend the elite عصبیت *'asabiy'yat* N.M. bigotry ; prejudice support or defence of one's people [A]

عصر *'as'r* N.M. time age ; epoch , era late afternoon prayers extract juice عصر حاضر *'as'r-e hā'zir* N.M. modern world ; present-day world ; modern age عصر کی نماز *'as'r kī namāz'* N.F. late afternoon prayers ہم عصر *ham 'as'r* N.M. & ADJ. contemporary عصرانہ *'asrā'nah* N.M. tea party garden party afternoon tea عصری *'as'rī* ADJ. modern [A]

عصفور *'usfoor'* N.M. (PL. عصافیر *asāfīr*) sparrow [A]

عصمت *'is'mat* N.F. chastity عصمت و عفت *is'mat-o-'if'fat* N.F. chastity باعصمت *bā-'is'mat* ADJ. chaste (woman) جوہر عصمت *jau'har-e 'is'mat* N.M. quality of chastity [A]

عصیاں *'is'yān* N.M. sin disobedience [A ~ عصی]

عضلہ *'a'zalah* N.M. (PL. عضلات *'azalāt'*) muscle tissue [A]

عضو *'uz'v* N.M. (PL. اعضا *a'zā'*) limb organ (rare) member (of) عضو تناسل *'uz'v-e tanā'sul* N.M. penis عضو معطل *'uz'v-e mo'at'tal* N.M. derelict organ ineffectual person or institution [A]

عطا *'atā'* N.F. gift , present endowment bounty favour bestowal grant عطا کرنا *'atā' kar'nā* V.T. confer bestow grant accord , give عطا ہونا *'atā' ho'nā* V.I. be conferred be bestowed be granted be accorded be given عطائے تو بہ لقائے تو *'atā'-e to ba-liqā'-e to* PROV. you are another I have the honour to return the gift to you [A]

عطار 'attar' N.M. chemist, druggist, apothecary perfumer عطاری 'atta'ri N.F. druggist's business perfumer's trade [A ~ عطر]

عطارد 'uta'rid N.M. (planet) mercury penman calligraphist عطارد رقم 'utarid raqam N.M. calligraphist [A]

عطائی 'ata''i, اتائی ata''i N.M. quack charlatan [A ~ عطا]

عطر 'it'r N.M. scent ; perfume ; 'can-de-cologne' otto ; attar عطر بیز 'it'r-bez' ADJ. scent-bearing perfume-spreading عطر بیزی 'it'r-be'zi N.F. spread of fray عطر دان 'it'r-dan N.M. perfume box عطر کا پھویا 'it'r ka pho'ya N.M. cotton flock of scent عطر کھینچنا (یا کشید کرنا) 'it'r khench'na (or kashid' kar'na) V.T. extract essence (of) عطر لگانا (یا ملنا) 'it'r laga'na (or mal'na) V.T. & I. apply perfume ; scent عطر میں بسانا 'it'r men basa'na V.T. scent [A]

عطسہ 'at'sah N.M. sneeze [A]

عطش 'a'tash N.F. thirst العطش al-'a'tash INT thirst ; I am thirsty عطشان 'at'shan' ADJ. thirsty [A]

عطف 'at'f N.M. co-ordinating two words phrases or clauses with a conjunction turning ; diverting kindness, favour حرف عطف har'f-e 'at'f conjunction [A]

عطیہ 'ati'yah N.M. (PL. عطایا 'ata'ya) gift, present grant assignment endowment [عطا]

عظم 'az'm N.M. (PL. عظام 'izam') bones [A]

عظام 'izam ADJ. (PL. of عظیم 'azim) (see under N.F. ★)

عظمت 'azmat (ped. 'azamat) N.F. عظام 'izam N.M. greatness magnificence grandeur عظمیٰ 'uz'ma ADJ. greatest of great magnitude عظیم 'azim' ADJ. (PL. عظام 'izam') great grand magnficent عظیم الشان 'azi'm-ush-shan' ADJ. grand magnificent [A]

عفت 'if'fat N.F., عفاف 'afaf' N.M chastity continence [A]

عفریت 'ifrit' N.M. (PL. عفاریت 'afarit') giant, ogre, demon [A]

عف عف 'af 'af N.M. bow vow, cry of dog [ONO.]

عفو 'af'v N.M. pardon ; forgiveness عفو کرنا 'af'v kar'na V.T. pardon عفو و در گزر 'af'v-o-dar-gu'zar N.F pardoning and over-looking [A]

عفونت 'ufoo'nat N.F. stink bad smell [A]

عفی عنہ 'u'fiya 'an'hu, عفی اللہ عنہ 'afal'lahu 'an'hu PH may God grant him remission of sins [A ~ عفو]

عفیفہ 'afi'fah N.F. & ADJ. chaste (woman) [A ★ عفت]

عقاب 'uqab' N.M. eagle [A]

عقاب 'iqab' N.M. punishment [A]

عقاب

عقائد 'aqa''id N.M. (PL. of عقیدہ N.M ★)

عقب 'aq'b N.M. (rare) coming after ADJ. slow کے عقب میں ke 'aq'b men ADV. behind after at the back of [A]

عقبیٰ 'u'qba N.F. the next world ; hereafter [A ~ عقب]

عقد 'aq'd N.M. (PL. 'uqood' marriage ; matrimony ; wedding (rare) knot ; bond ; tie 'aq'd kar'na V.T. & I. marry ; wed عقد نامہ 'aq'd-na'mah N.M. marriage contract عقد نکاح 'aq'd-e nikah' N.M. bond of marriage عقد ہونا 'aq'd ho'na V.I. be married [A]

عقد 'iq'd N.M. (PL. عقود 'uqood') necklace garland [A]

عقدہ 'uq'dah N.M. problem, difficulty ; trouble mystery enigma perplexity عقدہ حل کرنا 'uq'dah hal kar'na V.T. solve a pressing problem عقدہ حل ہونا 'uq'dah hal ho'na V.I. (of problem) be solved عقدہ کشا 'uq'da-kusha' ADJ. & N.M. (one) who removes (anothers) difficulties عقدہ کشائی 'uq'da-kusha''i N.F. removal of difficulties ; solution of problem عقدہ کھلنا 'uq'dah khul'na V.I. (of mystery) come to light [A]

عقرب 'aq'rab N.M. (PL. عقارب 'aqa'rib) scorpion (sign of Zodiac) Scorpion [A]

عقل 'aq'l N.M' (PL. عقول 'uqool') wisdom sense commonsense understanding reason intelligence intellect عقل انسانی 'aq'l-e insa'ni N.F. reason human intellect عقل بڑی یا بھینس 'aq'l bari ya bhains INT how silly of you why don't you use commonsense عقل پر پردہ (یا پتھر) پڑنا 'aq'l par par'dah (or pat'thar) par'na V.I do something foolish take a wrong decision عقل (گھاس) چرنے جانا 'aq'l (ghas') char'ne ja'na V.I display stupidly عقل چکرانا (یا چکر میں آنا) 'aq'l chakra'na (or chak'kar men a'na) V.I. be confused be at one's wits end عقل حیوانی aq'l-e haiva'ni (ped (-hayava'-) N F animal instinct عقل داڑھ 'aq'l darh N.F wisdom tooth عقل خرچ کرنا 'aq'l khar ch kar'na V.T use one's sense عقل دنگ ہونا 'aq'l dang ho'na V.I. be astonished عقل (کے گھوڑے) دوڑانا 'aq'l (ke gho'ri) daura'na V.T. think guess reason use one's sense عقل دینا 'aq'l de'na V.T advise عقل سلیم 'aq'l-e salim' N.F. sound mind عقل سے باہر 'aq'l se ba'hir ADJ. ineonceivable beyond compre hension unreasonable nonsense عقل کا اندھا گانٹھ کا پورا *'aq'l ka an'dha ganth' ka poo'ra* PH. foolish rich man greedy simpleton عقل کا پورا *'aq'l ka poo'ra* ADJ. (iron.) silly (person) عقل کا دشمن *'aq'l ka dush'man* N.M. fool ; a blockhead عقل کام نہیں کرتی *'aq'l kam' na'hin kar'ti* PH. I (etc.) fail to understand عقل کل *'aq'l-e kul'* N.M. prime intellect Gabriel in this capacity very intelligent person عقل کی مار *'aq'l ki mar'* PH. cursed (in) intellect عقل کے پیچھے ڈنڈا (یا لٹھ) لیے پھرنا *'aq'l ke pich'he dan'da (or lath) li'ye phir'na* V.I. be too silly عقل کے ناخن لینا *'aq'l ke na'khun le'na* V.I. not to be silly عقل ماری جانا *'aq'l ma'ri ja'na* V.I. lose one's wits عقل میں آنا *'aq'l men a'na* V.I. understand عقل میں فتور آنا *'aq'l men futoor' a'na* V.I. lose (one's) head go mad be demented عقلا *'uqala'* ADJ. & N.M. (PL. of عاقل ★) عقلاً *'aq'lan* ADV. by inference ; by guess through intellect through ordinary senses عقلمند *'aq'l-mand* ADJ. wise sensible sane intelligent shrewd sagacious عقلمند کی دور بلا *'aq'l-mand ki door' bala* PROV. wisdom will soon get you out of trouble عقلی *'aq'li* ADJ. rational intellectual reasonable ; credible [A]

عقوبت *'uqoo'bat* N.F. persecution [A]

عقیدت *'aqi'dat* N.F. great respect (for saint, etc.) devotion firm belief (in someone) عقیدتمند *'aqi'dat-mand* N.M. & ADJ. devoted (person) ; devotee عقیدتمندی *'aqi'dat-man'di* N.F. devotion (to) belief (in) [A doublet of FOLL.]

عقیدہ *'aqi'dah* N.M. faith belief creed tenet article of faith doctrine dogma [A]

عقیق *'aqiq'* N.M. cornelian [A]

عقیقہ *'aqi'qah* N.M. party thrown on seventh day after new birth in family tonsuring of baby on this occasion بچے کا عقیقہ کرنا *bach'che ka 'aqi'qah kar'na* V.I. throw out a party on seventh day of the birth of one's child [A]

عقیل *'aqil'* N.M. wise or sensible (man) عقیلہ *'aqi'lah* N.F. wise women chaste lady [A ~]

عقیم *'aqim'* ADJ. barren (woman)

عکاس *'akkas'* N.M. عکاسی *'akka'si* N.F. (see under FOLL.)

عکس *'ak's* N.M. reflection photograph image shadow converse opposition ; contrariety antonym ADJ. برعکس *bar 'ak's* ADV. on the other hand ; on the contrary ; contrary (to) عکسی *'ak'si* ADJ. (printed) from photo-blocks photographic illustrated عکسی تصویر *'ak'si tasvir'* N.F. photograph عکاس *'akkas'* N.M. photographer عکاسی *'akka'si* N.F photography portrayal کی عکاسی کرنا *ki 'akka'si kar'na* V.T. portray [A]

علا *'ala,* علی *'ula'* N.M. height of status glory [A]

علاتی *'alla'ti* ADJ. half (brother or sister) step-(brother or sister) from the mother's side [A]

علاج *'ilaj'* N.M. cure treatment ; medical treatment remedy علاج بالضد *'ilaj'-biz-zid'* N.M. allopathy علاج بالمثل *'ilaj'-bil mis'l* homoeopathy علاج کرنا *'ilaj' kar'na* V.T. curse treat ; treat medically remedy لاعلاج *la 'ilaj'* ADJ. incurable irremediable [A]

علاقہ *'ila'qah* (ped. *'ala'qah*) N.M. area region ; circle ; division ; jurisdiction estate territory relation ; connection interest concern علاقہ بند *'ila'qa-band* N.M. gold lace worker [A]

علالت *'ala'lat* N.F. illness ; ailment malady علیل *'alil'* ADJ. ★ [A]

علام *'allam'* ADJ. Omniscient (as an attribute of God) علام الغیوب *'alla'm-ul'ghuyoob'* ADJ. knowing the unknown (as an epithet of God) *'alla'mah* ADJ. very learned person ; savant . Allama [A ~ علم]

علامت *'ala'mat* N.F. (PL. علامات *'alamat'*) symbol sign mark emblem symptom علامت استفہام *'ala'mat-e istifham'* N.F. mark (or sign) of interrogation [A]

علانیہ *'alaniy'yah* (or *'alainiyah*) ADV. openly publicly [A ~ اعلان]

علاوہ *'ila'vah* ADV. in addition (to) علاوہ ازیں (یا بریں) *'ila'vah az-in* (or *bar-in*) CONJ. besides کے علاوہ *ke 'ila'vah* ADV. besides ; in addition (to) [A]

علائق *'ala''iq* N.M. PL. (worldly) worries connections ; relations [A ~ SING. علاقہ]

علت *'il'lat* N.F. (PL. علل *'i'lal*) cause pretence ground (of accusation, etc.) defect ; fault disease ; malady علت صوری *'il'lat-e su'vari* N.F. formal cause علت غائی *'il'lat-e gha''i* N.F. ultimate final cause علت مادی *'il'lat-e mad'di* N.F. material cause علت و معلول *'il'lat-o-ma'lool'* N.M. cause and effect علت لگا لینا *'il'lat laga' le'na* V.I. become an addict (to) become slave of a bad habit علتی *'il'lati* ADJ. having a bad habit N.M. addict [A]

علف *'a'laf* N.M. alfalfa ; lucerne [A]

علل 'i'lal N.F. (PL. of علت ★)

علم 'il'm N.M. (PL. علوم 'ulooṁ') knowledge learing (arch.) science (of) علم اخلاق 'il'm-e akhlaq' N.M. ethics (arch.) branch of knowledge dealing with ethics, domestic economy and political scienee علم ادب 'il'm-e a'dab N.M. literature علم الیقین 'l'm-ul-yaqin' N.M. convincing knowledge (of) علم بلاغت 'il'm-e bala'ghat N.M. figure of speech علم بیان 'il'm-e bayan' N.M. metaphor and simile ; rules of metaphorical language علم دین 'il'm-e din N.M. divinity acquaintance with religious precepts علم غیب 'il'm-e ghaib' N.M. foreknowledge knowledge of the invisible علم قیافہ 'il'm-e qaya'fah N.M. physiognomy علم کلام ''m-e kalam' N.M. scholastic philosophy علم کیمیا 'il'm-e ki'miya N.M. chemistry علم لدنی 'il'm-e ladūn'nī N.M. inspired knowledge علم مباحثہ 'i''m-e mūba'ḥasah N.M. dialectics علم مثلث 'il'm-e mūsal'las N.M. trigonometry علم معانی 'il'm-e ma'a'nī N.M. rhetoric علم مناظرہ 'il'm-e mūnazarah N.M. polamics: apologetics علم موجودات 'il'm-e maujoodat' N.M. natural science علم نجوم 'il'm-e n'joom'. علم ہیئت 'il'm-e hai'at N.M. astronomy علم وفضل 'il'm-o-faz'l N.M. learning and exeellency علم ہندسہ 'il'm-e handa'sah (col. hind'sah N.M. geometry علما 'ulama' N.M. (PL. of عالم 'a'lim★) علمی 'il'mī ADJ. scholarly inllectually scientific علمیت 'ilmiy'yat N.F. learning ; scholarship pedantry علوم 'ulooṁ' N.M. fields or branches of knowledge sciences علوم جدیدہ 'uloo'm-e-jadi'dah N.M. PL. modern knowledge ; modern science ; modern fields of learing علوم شرقیہ 'uloo'm-e sharqiy'yah, مشرقی علوم mash'riqi 'ulooṁ' N.M. PL. Oriental learing علوم قدیمہ 'uloo'm-e qadi'mah N.M. PL. ancient sciences , old fields of learing علوم مروجہ 'uloo'm-e-mūrav'vajah N.M. current branches of learning علوم وفنون 'uloo'm-o-fūnoon' N.M. PL. arts and sciences [A]

علم 'a'lam N.M. (PL. اعلام a'lam') proper noun standard ; banner علمبردار 'a'lam-bar-dar' N.M. supporter or protagonist (of cause, etc.) standard-bearer علم ٹوٹنا 'a'lam ṭooṭ'na V.I. be cursed علمدار 'a'lam-dar N.M. standard-bearer علم کرنا 'a'lam kar'na V.T. draw (sword, etc.) علم ہونا 'a'lam ho'na V.I. be notorious [A]

علو 'ulūv' N.M. height sublimity [A]

علوی 'ul'vi ADJ. celestial (of incantations) with a religious sanction [A ~ علی 'ula']

علوی 'a'lavī ADJ (see under FOLL.)

علی 'alī N.M. Ali ; name of fourth Orthodox Caliph the Sublime (as attribute of God) ADJ. (rare) high sublime علوی 'a'lavī N.M. one descended from Hazrat Ali [A]

علیٰ 'ala' PREF. on ; upon ; at (never used sane in PH.) علی الاتصال 'alal-ittisal' ADV. (arch.) continuously ; consecutively علی الاطلاق 'alal-itlaq' ADJ. & ADV. (ped.) absolute(ly) علی التوکل 'alat-tavak'-kul ADV. on trust without apparent surety علی الٹپ , ال ٹپ 'alal'-ṭap', alal'-ṭap' ADV. (col.) thoughtlessly علی الحساب 'alal ḥisab' N.M. suspense account علی الحساب دینا 'alal-ḥisab' de'na V.T. advance (money to) علی الحساب لینا alal-ḥisab' le'na V.I. take on advance علی الخصوص 'alal-khusoos' ADV. especially particularly علی الدوام 'alad-davam' AD permanently for ever علی الرغم 'alar-ragh'm ADV. against in the teeth of علی الصباح 'alas-sabaḥ' ADV. early in the morning علی العموم 'alal-ūmoom' ADV. generally usually in general علی ہذا القیاس 'ala' ha'z-al-qiyas' PH. and so on علی قدر مراتب 'ala' qadr-e mara'lib (PH.) each according to his status

علیحدہ 'ala'hidah (also spelt علیحدہ) ADJ. seperate distinct ADV. part asunder distinct disconnected separately علیحدہ رکھنا 'ala'hidah rakh'na V.T. set apart separate keep away علیحدگی 'ala'hidagi (or -ḥa-) N.F. separation dismissal [A]

علیک 'alaik ADJ. on you (one person) علیکم 'alai kūm ADV. on you (all) 'alai'kūma ADV. on you (two) علیک سلیک 'alaik' salaik' N.F. nodding acquaintance علیک سلیک ہونا 'alaik' salaik' ho'na V.T. exchange greetings have nodding acquaintance (with) [A ~ علی + ک]

علیہ 'alai'hi ADV. on him علیہا 'alai'ha ADV. on her علیہ الرحمۃ 'alai'h-ir-raḥ'mah INT. (with names of dead saints, etc.) mercy on him علیہ السلام 'alaih-is-salam' INT. (with name of prophets) peace be upon him علیہم 'alai'him ADV. on them علیہما 'alai'hima ADV. on the two of them [A ~ علی]

علیا 'ul'ya ADJ. nighest (woman, etc.) علیا حضرت 'ul'ya-haz'rat PH. Her Highness ; Her Fxcellency ; Her Majesty [A ~ M. اعلیٰ]

علیل 'alīl ADJ. ill ; sick ; indisposed [A ~ علت]

علیم 'alīm' ADJ. wise (one) who knows everything N.M. All-knowing ; Omniscient (as attribute of God) [A ~ علم 'il'm]

عم 'am' N.M. uncle ; father's brother عمزاد 'am-zad' ADJ. & N.M. (son or daughter) of one's uncle , cousin بنت عم bin't-e 'am' N.M. cousin;

esp. beloved female cousin [A]

عماد 'imād' N.M. (PL. عمد 'ū'mūd) pillar [A]

عمارت 'imā'rat N.F. (PL. عمارات 'imārat') building structure (rare) construction [A]

عماری 'amā'rī N.F. canopied seat on back of elephant or camel

عمال 'ummāl N.M. PL. revenue collectors governors workers agents عمال حکومت 'ūmmā'l-e hukoo'mat N.M. PL. government officials [A ~ SING. عامل]

عمامہ 'imā'mah N.M. turban [A]

عمائد 'amā''id N.M. (PL. of عمید ★)

عمد 'am'd (col. 'a'mad) ADJ. deliberate ; intentional N.M. (rare) intension; resolve عمداً 'am'dan (col. 'a'madan) ADV. proposely ; deliberately ; intentionally [A]

عمدہ 'ūm'dah ADJ. nice ; fine excellent grand class ; posh N.M. pillar ; prop ; stay trusted person ; trustee عمدۃ الملک 'ūm'dat-ūl-mūl'k N.M. national trustee عمدگی 'ūm'dagī N.F. nicety ; fineness excellence [A]

عمر 'ūmr 'ūmr (col. 'ū.mar) N.F. age life life-time عمر بھر 'ūm'r bhar (or 'ūmar') ADV. life-long ever عمر پٹہ لکھانا 'ū'mar pat'tah likha'nā V.I. get a deed for immortality عمر خضر 'ūm'r-e kha'zir, عمر نوح 'ūm'r-e nooh' N.F. a very long life عمر دراز 'ūm'r-darāz' INT. may you live long ADJ. long-lived عمر رسیدہ 'ūm'r-rasī'dah (or 'ū'mar-) ADJ. one advanced in years عمر طبعی (یا طبیعی) 'um'r-e tab''ī (or tab''ī) N.F. normal span of life عمر کاٹنا (یا تیر کرنا) 'ūm'r kat'nā (or tīr' kar'nā) V.I. pass the life عمر کٹنا (یا تیر ہونا) 'ūm'r kat'nā (or tīr' ho'nā) V.I. (of life) pass [A]

عمر 'ū'mar N.M. Umar ; name of second Orthodox Caliph

عمرو 'am'r N.M. Amr ; a fictitious name (used for drill in grammatical patterns) عمرو عیار کی زنبیل 'am'r-e 'ayyār' kī zambīl' PH. something that can contain a lot

عمران 'ūmrān' N.M. society ; population عمرانی 'ūmrā'nī ADJ. sociological عمرانیات 'ūmrāniyyāt' N.F. sociology [A]

عمرہ 'ū'm'rah N.M. off-seasonal pilgrimage to Mecca [A]

عمق 'ū'muq N.M. (PL. اعماق a'māq') depth profoundity عمیق 'amīq' ADJ. deep intense profound [A]

عمل 'a'mal N.M. (PL. اعمال a'māl') action deed practice work operation process administration ; jurisdiction time (of) spell ; charm ; incantation effect sway rule عمل پڑھنا 'a'mal parh'nā V.I. mutter a spell or charm ; to practice a spell عمل پیرا ہونا 'a'mal-pairā' ho'nā V.I. act (upon) عمل جراحی 'a'mal-e jarrā'hī N.M. surgery ; surgical operation عملداری 'a'mal-dā'rī N.F. reign government sway authority عمل دخل 'a'mal dakh'l N.M. say sway ; authority عملدرآمد 'a'mal dar-ā'mad N.F. implementation acting (upon) عملدرآمد کرنا 'a'mal dar-ā'mad kar'nā V. act (upon) enforce ; implement عملدرآمد ہونا 'a'mal dar-ā'mad ho'nā V.I. be acted (upon) be enforced ; be implemented عمل کرنا 'a'mal kar'nā V.I. act (upon) عمل ہونا 'a'mal ho'nā V.I. be implemented عملاً 'amalan ADV. practically ; for all practical purposes [A]

عملہ 'a'malah (col. 'am'lah) N.M. staff ; establishment عملہ فعلہ 'am'lah fe''lah N.M. (col.) office establishment ; members of staff عملی 'a'malī ADJ. practical عملی جامہ پہنانا 'a'malī jā'mah pahnā'nā V.T. implement [A]

عمود 'ūmood' N.M. perpendicular pillar عمودی 'ūmoo'dī ADJ. perpendicular [A]

عموم 'ūmoom' N.M. commonness generality عموماً 'ūmoo'man, بالعموم bil-'ūmoom' ADV. usually ; commonly ; generally عمومیت 'ūmoomiy'-yat N.F. generalization [A ~ عام]

عمید 'amīd' N.M. (PL. عمائد 'amā''id) pillar important personality dignitary عمائد سلطنت 'amā''d-e sal'tanat N.M. dignitaries of the state [A]

عمیق 'amīq' ADJ. (see under عمق N.M. ★)

عمیم 'amīm' ADJ. comprehensive all-embracing [A ~ عام]

عنا 'anā' N.F. trouble ; distress [A]

عناب 'ūnāb' (ped. 'unnāb') N.M. jujube عنابی 'ūnā'bī (ped. 'ūnnābī) ADJ. dark red [A]

عناد 'inād' N.M. enmity ; hostility [A]

عنادل 'anā'dil N.F. PL. (~ SING. عندلیب ★)

عناصر 'anā'sir N.M. PL. (~ SING. عنصر ★)

عنان 'inān' N.F. bridle ; rein عنان حکومت 'inā'n-e hukoo'mat N.F. reins of government [A]

عنانت 'anā'nat N.F. impotence [A]

عنایت *'inā'yat* N.F. (PL. عنایات *'ina yat'*) favour; kindness gift ; present attention [A]

عنب *'i'nah* N.M. grapes [A]

عنبر *'am'bar* N.M. ambergris عنبر اشہب *am'bar-e ash'hab* N.M. black ambergris عنبریں *'am'barīn* ADJ. smellings of ambergris ; sweet-smelling jet black [A]

عند *'ind* PREF. at on ; upon near during in time of عندالاستفسار *'in'd-al-istifsar'* ADV. on inquiry عندالضرورت *'in'd-az-zaroo'rat* ADV. in case of need when required عندالطلب *in'd-at-ta'lab* ADV. on demand عنداللہ *'in'd-allah'* ADV. before God ; in the eye's of God عندالملاقات *'in'd-al-mulāqat'* ADV. when we meet ; at our meeting عندالاصول *'in'd-al-vusool* ADV. on receipt on arrival عندالوقوع *'in'd-al-vūqoo'* ADV. in that event at its occurrence عندیہ *'indiy'yah* N.M. view ; opinion intention plan ; design عندیہ پانا (یا لینا یا معلوم کرنا) *'indiy'yah pā'na* (or *le'nā* or *ma'loom' kar'nā*) V.T. ascertain the view (of) [A]

عندلیب *'andalīb'* N.F. (dial. M.) (PL. عنادل *'anā'dil*) nightingale [A]

عندیہ *indiy'yah* N.M. (see under عند ★)

عنصر *'ūn'sar* (or *'ūnsūr*) N.M. (PL. عناصر *'anā'sir*) element part factor عنصری *'ūn'sarī* ADJ. elemental [A]

عنفوان *ūnf'van'* N.M. bloom, flower or prime (of youth) [A]

عنق *'ū'nūq* N.F. (PL. اعناق *a'nāq'*) neck [A]

عنقا *'anqā'* N.M. phoenix (fig.) ra'ra a'vis' ADJ. rare ; curious hard to find عنقا ہونا *'anqā' ho'na* V.I. be rare not to be available vanish [A ~ PREC.]

عنکبوت *'ankaboot'* N.F. spider تارِ عنکبوت *ta'r-e 'ankaboot'* N.M. spider's web something flimsy [A]

عنوان *'ūnvan'* N.M. (PL. عناوین *'anavīn'*) title heading headline manner ; mode something serving as an indication [A]

عنین *'anīn'* ADJ. & N.M. impotent (person) [A]

عوارض *'avā'riz* N.M. PL. disease attributes things happening (to) [A ~ SING. عارضہ]

عواطف *'avā'tif* N.M. PL. affection ; feelings [A ~ SING. عاطفہ]

عواقب *'avā'qib* N.M. PL. consequences [A ~ SING. عاقبت]

عوام *'avām'* N.M. PL. public masses common people ; commonalty lower strata of society عوام الناس *'avam-ūn-nas'* (ped. *'avam'm-*) N.M. common run of mankind lower strata of society [A ~ SING. عام]

عوامل *'avā'mil* N.M. PL. agents factors (gram.) governing words [A ~ SING. عامل]

عوج بن عنق *'ooj ūb'n-ū 'ooq'*, (col. عوج بن عنق *'auj' bin 'ū'naq*) N.M. name of a very tall legendary figure (joc.) very tall person [A]

عود *'ood* N.M. aloeswood harp; lute عودِ ہندی *'oo'd-e hin'dī* N.F. aloeswood عود سوز *'ood'-soz* N.M. censer [A]

عود *'aud* N.M. return ralapse ; man of abilities, experience and prudence عود کر آنا *'aud' kar ā'na* V.I. return relapse [A]

عورت *'au'rat* N.F. woman female wife nakedness ; nordity parts of body that should go covered عورت ذات *'au'rat zat'* N.F. woman female sex weaker vessel [A]

عوض *'i'vaz* N.M. exchange substitution recompense reward ADV. in turn (for) instead (of) عوض معاوضہ *'i'vaz mo'ā'vazah* N.M. (col.) exchange عوض معاوضہ گلہ ندارد *'i'vaz mo'ā'vazah gi'lah nadā'rad* PROV. tit for tat let us call quits عوضانہ *'ivza'nah* (ped. *'ivazā'nah*) N.M. exchange ; compensation عوضی *'iv'zī* (ped. *'i'vazī*) ADJ. officiating N.M. substitute عوضی دینا *'iv'zī de'nā* V.T. supply a substitute عوضی کرنا *'iv'zī kar'nā* V.I. officiate [A]

عون *'aun* N.M. (PL. اعوان *a'vān'*) helper [A]

عہد *'aih'd* (or *'aihad* ; ped. *'ah'd*) N.M. vow oath promise covenant ; agreement ; testament reign era ; epoch ; age time ; reason عہد باندھنا *'aih'd bāndh'nā* V.I. vow (to) promise (to) عہد توڑنا *'aih'd toṛ'nā* V. break (one's) promise back out of one's comment) عہدِ حکومت *'aih'd-e hūkoo'mat* N.M. reign (of) کے عہدِ حکومت میں *ke 'aih'd-e ḥūkoo'mat meṅ* PH. during the reign of ; while (someone) sat on the throne عہد شکن *'aih'd-shi'kan* ADJ. not true to one's word faithless; false ; treacherous عہد شکنی *'aih'd-shi'kanī* N.F. breach of contract breach of faith infidelity عہد کرنا *'aih'd kar'nā* V.I. promise ; give one's word vow عہد نامہ *'aih'd-nā'mah* N.M. treaty agreement covenant testament پرانا عہد نامہ *purā'na 'aih'd-nā'mah* N.M. Old Testament نیا عہد نامہ *na'ya 'aih'd-nā'mah* New Testament عہد و پیمان *'aih'd-o-paiman'* (or *pai'mān*) N.M. pledges and assurances secret understanding alliances agreement [A]

عہدہ *'oh'dah* N.M. post ; rank duty ; obligation ; resposibility عہدہ برآ ہونا *'oh'dah* *bar-a' ho'na* V.I. achieve the object come out successful do (one's) duty discharge the responsibility (of) عہدہ برائی *'oh'dah bar-a''i* N.F. accomplishment performance success discharge of responsibility عہدہ دار *'oh'da-dar* (col. *-de-*) N.M. officer official non-commissioned officer in army ; N.C.O. officer-holder office-bearer [A]

عیادت *'iya'dat* N.F. visiting (of the sick) inquiring (after ailing person) [A]

عیاذ *'iyaz'* N.M. seeking protection عیاذ باللہ *'iya'zan-billah'* INT. God forbid ; may God protect العیاذ *al-'iyaz'* INT. God forbid [A]

عیار *'iyar'* N.M. touchstone کامل عیار *ka'mil 'iyar* ADJ. pure (gold, etc.) کم عیار *kam-'iyar* ADJ. base [A]

عیار *'ayyar'* N.M. impostor swindler knave ADJ. crafty artful sly ; cunning عیاری *'ayya'ri* N.F. cunning slyness craftiness artfulness swindling imposture knavery [A]

عیاش *'ayyash'* ADJ. rakish ; voluptuous leading a gay life عیاشی *'ayya'shi* N.F. voluptuousness luxury [A ~ عیش]

عیال *'iyal'* N.M. family children عیالدار *'iyal-dar'* N.M. & ADJ. family man ; (one) shouldering the responsibility of maintaining a family عیالداری *'ayal'-da'ri* N.F. family worldly affairs [A ~ SING. عائلہ]

عیاں *'iyan'* ADJ. obvious ; evident clear manifest apparent visible عیاں را چہ بیاں *'iyan' ra che bayan'* PROV. self evident needs no exposition عیاں کرنا *'iyan' kar'na* V.T. make clear lay bare make manifest عیاں ہونا *'iyan' ho'na* V.I. be clear become evident be manifest appear [P]

عیب *'aib* N.M. (PL. عیوب *'u yoob'*) sin blemish vice fault defect imperfaction عیب بیں *'aib'-bin*, عیب چیں *'aib'-chin'* ADJ. fault-finding; critical N.M. caviller fault-finder عیب بینی *'aib'-bi'ni*, عیب چینی *'aib'-chi'ni* N.F. cavil fault-finding عیب پوش *'aib'-posh'* ADJ. & N.M. (one) conniving at others faults forgiving عیب پوشی *'aib'-po'shi* N.F. conniving overlooking عیب جو *aib'-joo'* N.M. fault-finder caviller ; carper malignant critic ADJ. fault-finding carping ; cavilling picking holes (in) عیب جوئی *'aib'-joo''i* N.F. fault-finding cavil malignant criticism picking holes (in) عیب دار *'aib'-dar* ADJ. defective faulty damaged soiled sullied عیب گو *'aib'-go* N.M. slanderer calumniater عیب گوئی *'aib'-go''i* N.F. slander ; calumny slandering عیب لگانا *'aib laga'na* V.T. defame malign cast aspersious on slander stigmatize عیب نکالنا *'aib' nikal'na* V.T. find fault with pick holes (in) پانچوں عیب شرعی *pan' chon 'aib shar''i* PH. all the deadly sins عیبی *'ai'bi* ADJ. vicious ; sinful faulty defective [A]

عید *'id* N.F. (PL. عیاد *ayad'*) Eid festival عید الفطر *'i'd-ul-fit'r* N.F. Eid-ul-Fitr ; festivities marking the end of Ramzan ; Lesser Bairam عید الاضحیٰ *'i'd-ul-az'la*, عید اضحیٰ *'i'd-e az'ha* (col. عید الضحیٰ *'id-uz-zoha'*) N.F. Eid-ul-Azha ; Greater Bairam saerificial festival ; festival marking the completion of Haj rites festival commemorating Abraham's sacrifice of his son عید پیچھے ٹر *'id' pi'chhe tar'* PH. untimely festivity belated arrangements [A]

عیسیٰ *'i'sa* N.M. Jesus عیسیٰ مسیح *'i'sa masi'h* N.M. Jesus Christ عیسائی *'isa''i* N.M. & ADJ. Christian عیسوی *'i'savi* ADJ. Christian سن عیسوی *san'n-e 'i'savi* N.M. Christian era ; 'anno Christi'; A C ; 'anno domini' ; A.D. [A ~ H]

عیش *'aish* N.M. gay life ; a life of pleasure and enjoyment luxury عیش اڑانا (یا کرنا) *'aish' ura'na* (or *kar'na*) V.I. enjoy oneself live in luxury lead a gay life عیش منغص کرنا *'aish' munagh'-ghas kar'na* V.T. mar the pleasure (of) عیش و عشرت *'ai'sh o-'ish'rat* N.F. عیش و نشاط *'ai'sh-o nashat'* N.M. luxury gaiety and happy social life [A]

عین *'ain* ADV. exactly precisely positively N.M. (PL. عیون *'u yoon'*) spring ; fountain N.F. (PL. عیون / اعیُن *a'yun*) eye عین الیقین *'ai'n-ul-yaqin'* N.M. positive knowledge عین غین *'ain' ghain* ADJ. almost alike squint-eyed عین مین *'ain' main* ADV. exactly exactly alike بعینہٖ *be-'ai'ni-hi* (col. *ba*) ADV. exactly ; precisely عینی *'aini* ADJ. eye-(witness) [A]

عین *'in* ADJ. & N.M. PL. large-eyed حور عین *hoo'r-e 'in'* N.M. PL. larged-eyed houries [A ~ PREC.]

عینک *'ai'nak* N.F. glasses, spectacles goggles [P ~ A عین]

عیوب *'uyyoob'* N.M. (PL. of عیب ★)

عیون *'u yoon'* N.M. (PL. of عین ★)

غ

غ *ghain* N.F. twenty-fourth letter of Urdu alphabet ; (also called *ghai'n-e mo''jamah* or *ghai'n-e manqoo'tah*) (according to Jummal reckoning) 1,000

غاٹیا **gha'ṭiya**, غاٹیر **ghaṭiyar** ADJ. (dial.) stocky ; stuggy

غاذیہ **gha'ziyah** N.M. قوت غاذیہ qav'vat-e gha'ziyah N.F. the faculty assimiliating food; assimilating faculty [A ~ غذا]

غار **ghar** N.M. cave ; cavern pit lair ; den یار غار ya'r-e ghar' (col. yar' ghar) N.M. intimate friend(s) [A]

غارت **gha'rat** N.F. devastation ; destruction plunder ; pilage ravage raid waste ; ruin غارت غول ہونا gha'rat ghol' ho'na V.I. go to waste غارت کرنا gha'rat kar'na V.T. plunder pillage ravage waste ; ruin غارتگر gha'rat-gar N.M. raider plunderer he who lays waste غارتگری gha'rat-ga'ri N.F. destruction plunder ; pillage غارت ہونا یا جانا gha'rat ho'na (or ja'na) V.I. be destroyed be ruined be cursed ; be damned [A]

غازہ **gha'zah** N.M. powder ; performed powder : face-powder غازہ و گلگونہ gha'za-o gulgoo'nah N.M. powder and rouge [P]

غازی **gha'zi** N.M. Muslim soldier hero conqueror (col.) rake magician غازی مرد gha'zi mard hero (col.) horse [A ~ غزا]

غاشیہ **gha'shiyah** N.M. saddle-cloth غاشیہ بردار gha'-shiya-bar-dar' N.M. obedient servant lackey ; flunkey [A]

غاصب **gha'sib** N.M. usuper plunderer [A ~ غصب]

غافل **gha'fil** ADJ. inattentive ; unmindful thoughtful negligent ; remiss [A]

غالب **gha'lib** ADJ. overpowering domineering predominant larger probable having the upper hand victorious غالب آنا یا ہونا gha'lib a'na (or ho'na) V.T. win ; overcome beat ; gain the upper hand gha'liban ADV. probably ; in all probability [A ~ غلبہ]

غالی **gha'li** ADJ. extremist ; fanatic ; fanatical (rare) dear ; expensive [P]

غالیچہ **ghali'chah** N.M. carpet [P]

غالیہ **gha'liyah** N.M. perfume made from comphor, ambergris, etc. غالیہ مو (یا مو) gha'liya-moo (or -mo) ADJ. with perfumed tresses [A]

غامض **gha''miz** ADJ. abstruse (point) [A]

غائب **gha''ib** ADJ. absent invisible concealed vanished N.M. (gram.) third person غائب غلہ ہونا gha''ib ghallah ho'na V.I. غائب کرنا gha''ib kar'na V.T. make away with remove stealthily غائب ہونا gha''ib ho'na V.I. vanish disappear غائبانہ gha'iba'nah ADV. 'in absentia' without actually coming across [A ~ غیب]

غائر **gha''ir** ADJ. deep ; penetrating (vision) [~ غور]

غائی **gha''i** ADJ. (see under FOLL.)

غایت **gha'yat** N.F. (PL. غایات ghayat') and purpose ADJ. extreme excessive ADV. extremely excessively غایت درجے کا gha'yat dar je ka ADJ. extreme utmost غائی gha''i ADJ. final ultimate علت غائی 'il'lat-e gha''i N.F. ultimate cause [A]

غبار **ghubar'** N.M. dust cloud of dust ill-feeling estrangement (also خط غبار khat't-e ghubar') style of Urdu writing in minute characters غبار آلود (ہ) ghubar'-alood'(ah) ADJ. dusty dustcovered foggy not clear غبار آنا ghubar' a'na grow suspicious about غبار اٹھنا ghubar' uṭh'na V.I. (of a cloud of dust) rise غبار خاطر khuba'r-e kha'tir N.M. mental agony heart-burning fit of spleen غبار نکالنا ghubar nikal'na V.T. take one's revenge vent one's spleen غبار نکلنا ghubar' nikal-na V.I. (of heart burning) end (of anger) subside [A]

غبارہ **ghuba'rah** N.M. balloon

غباوت **ghaba'vat** N.F. (see under غبی ADJ. & N.M. ★)

غبغب **ghab'ghab** N.M. double chin چاہ غبغب cha'h-e ghab'ghab N.M. dimple in the chin [A]

غبن **gha'ban** N.M. misappropriation ; embezzlement ; defalcation غبن کرنا gha'ban kar'na V.T. misappropriate ; embezzle ; defalcate [A]

غبی **gha'bi** ADJ. stupid; thick-skulled N.M. dunce غباوت ghaba'vat N.F. stupidity [A]

غپ **ghap** N.F. (same as گپ N.F. ★)

غپا **ghap'pa** N.M. same as گپا N.M. ★)

غٹ **ghaṭ** N.M. sound made in gulping down crowd

غت ربود **ghat rabood'** ADV. & ADJ. jumbled misconstrued (of sense) confused [~ P ironically or foolishly misconstrued from ذکر گو گئے بلا غت ربود]

غٹاغٹ **gha'ṭa-ghaṭ**, غٹ غٹ ghaṭ ghaṭ ADV at a gulp غٹ کے غٹ ghaṭ' ke ghaṭ' N.M. PL. crowd (of) [ONO.]

غٹرغوں **ghu'ṭar ghoon'** N.F. cooing [ONO.]

غچ **ghach** N.F. sound of walking in mud sound of sword, etc. moving in flesh [ONO.]

غچا **ghach'chā** (dial. غپا ghap'pā) N.M. fraud ; deceit غچا دینا ghach'chā de'nā V.T. gull; dupe غچا کھانا ghach'chā kha'nā V.I. be gulled ; be duped

غدر **ghad'r** N.M. prefidy ; treachery mutiny (as name given to 1857 Freedom Fight by British rulers)

غدار **ghaddār'** N.M. & ADJ. perfidious ; treacherous (person) غداری ghaddā'rī N.F. treachery; perfidy [A ~ FOLL.]

غدود **ghūdood'** N.M. gland غدہ ghūd'dah N.M. (PL. غدد ghū'dad) gland

غدیر **ghadīr'** N.F. pool small lake عید غدیر 'ī'd-e ghadīr' N.F. (see under عید N.F. ★)

غذا **ghizā'** N.F. (PL. اغذیہ agh'ziyah) food. diet nourishment aliment غذائے ثقیل ghizā'-e saqīl N.F. rich food غذائے لطیف ghizā'-e latīf' N.F. light food غذائی ghizā''ī ADJ. nutritious alimental dietery غذائیت ghizā'iy'yat N.F. nourishment nutritive value ; food value [A]

غرا **gharrā'** ADJ. lustrous ; refulgent illustrious [A]

غراب **ghūrab'** N.M. crow ; raven [A]

غرابت **gharā'bat** N.F. uncommonness ; unfamiliarity غریب ADJ. ★ [A]

غرارہ **gharā'rah** N.M. gargle long parted skirt (arch.) large sack غرارہ دار پاجامہ gharā'ra-dār pajā'mah N.M. (old name for غرارہ N.M. ★)

غرانا **ghūrrā'nā** V.I. growl غراں ghur'rāh ADJ. growling [~ P]

غرائب **gharā''ib** N.M. PL. strange things rarities عجائب غرائب 'ajā''ib-o-gharā''ib N.M. PL. (see under عجائب N.M. PL. ★) A ~ SING غریبہ]

غرب **gharb'** N.M. west غربی ghar'bī ADJ. & N.M. western ; occidental مشرق و غرب shar'q-o ghar'b N.M. PL. the East and the West [A]

غربال **ghirbāl'** N.F. sieve riddle [A]

غربا **ghurabā'** N.M. (PL. غریب ADJ. & N.M. ★)

غربت **ghūr'bat** N.F. poverty penury being away from home being an alien being in foreign land غربت زدہ ghūr'bat-za'dah ADJ. poverty-stricken impoverished doomed to stay away from home [A]

غربی **ghar'bī** ADJ. (see under غرب N.M. ★)

غرض **gha'raz** N.F. selfishness interest motive aim ; object purpose; intention design wish end use concern; business necessity target CONJ. in short غرض آشنا gha'raz-ash'nā ADJ. selfish غرض باؤلی ہوتی ہے gha'raz ba''olī ho'tī hai, غرض بری بلا ہے gha'raz bu'rī balā hai PROV. necssity makes man mad غرض کا باؤلا (یا دیوانہ) gha'raz kā ba''olā (or divā'nah) N.M. slave to one's passions extremely selfish person غرض کا یار gha'raz kā yar' N.M. one who has an axe to grind غرض مند gha'raz-mand ADJ. needy interested selfish غرض مندی gha'raz-man'dī N.F. self-aggrandizement need غرض نکالنا gha'raz nikāl'nā V.I. have one's end served غرض نکلی آنکھ بدلی gha'raz nik'lī āṅkh bad'lī PROV. selfish person is never true to anyone الغرض al-gha'raz CONJ. in short بے غرض be gha'raz ADJ. disinterested بے غرضانہ be-gharazā'nah ADJ. & ADV. disinterested(ly) بے غرضی be-gha'razī N.F. altruistic attitude ; altruism [A]

غرغرہ **ghar'gharah** N.M. gargle [A]

غرفش **ghur'-fish** N.F. bullying growl [ONO.]

غرفہ **ghūr'fah** N.M. (PL. غرفات ghur fat') window attic [A]

غرق **ghar'q** N.M. drowning sinking immersion absorption ADJ. drowned sunk immersed absorbed غرق کرنا ghar'q kar'nā V.I. drown submerge ruin غرق ہونا ghar'q ho'nā V.I. be drowned be submerged be ruined غرقاب gharq-āb' ADJ. drowned N.M. (also غرقابہ ghar-qā'bah) whirlpool deep water [A]

غروب **ghūroob'** N.M. sunset setting (of sun, moon, etc.) [A]

غرور **ghūroor'** N.M. pride ; haughtiness vanity ; vainglory haughtiness ; 'hauteur' boast brag غرور کا سر نیچا gh ūroor' kā sir' nī'chā PROV. pride goeth before a fall غرور کرنا ghūroor' kar'nā V.I. be proud boast ; brag [A]

غرہ **ghar'rah** N.M. pride vanity haughtiness ; 'hauteur' [A]

غرہ **ghūr'rah** N.M. appearance of crescent first of a lunar month white spot on horses forehead off-day going about without meals ; inforced fasting [A]

غریب **gharīb'** N.M. stranger foreigner traveller poor person miserable person ADJ. poor destitute indigent penurious wretched miserable غریب الوطن gharī'b-ūl va'tan N.M. alien one away from home غریب الوطنی gharī'b-ūl-va'tanī N.F. being a foreigner being away from home غریب پرور gharīb'-par'var

ADJ. & N.M. gracious (person) غریب پروری gharīb'-par'varī N.F. graciousness غریب خانہ gharīb'-khā'nah N.M. humble above (as euphemism for 'my house') غریب الدیار gharī'b-ud-diyār' غریب الوطن gharī'b-ul-va'tan ADJ. & N.M. foreigner ; alien (one) away from home غریب غربا gharīb' ghu'rabā' N.M. poor people ; paupers غریب کی جورو سب کی بھابی gharīb' kī jo'roo sab' kī bhā'bī PROV. the weakest the poor are taken lightly غریب مار gharīb'-mār N.F. oppression of the poor ; troubling the poor غریب نے روزے رکھے دن بڑے آئے gharīb' ne ro'ze rak'khe din ba'ṛe ā''e PROV. the weak always suffers the very first attempt causing misery غریب نواز gharīb'-navāz' ADJ. & N.M. gracious hospitable courteous to strangers kind to the poor غریب نوازی gharīb'-navā'zī N.F. graciousness courtesy to strangers kindness to the poor غریبانہ gharībā'nah ADJ. poor bumble ADV. like (or befitting) a poor person humble ; in a humble way like a foreigner غریبی gharī'bī N.F. poverty ; penury indigence humility misery being a traveller غریبی آنا gharī'bī ā'nā V.I. be reduced to poverty have a hard time ; fall on evil days [A ~ غربت]

غریزی gharī'zī ADJ. natural invate حرارت غریزی ḥarā'rat-e gharī'zī N.F. natural heat of body [A]

غریق gharīq' N.M. drowning person ADJ. drowned sunk immersed submerged overwhelmed غریق رحمت gharī'q-e raḥ'mat (or raih-) ADJ. whelmed with divine mercy خدا غریق رحمت کرے khudā' gharī'q-e raḥ'mat ka're PH. May God overwhelm (him) with mercy (he) who is dead [A ~ غرق]

غریو gharev' N.M. noise [P]

غڑاپ ghaṛap', ghaṛap' N.F. sound of fall or plunge into the water غڑاپ سے ghaṛap' se ADV. in a jiffy [ONO.]

غزا ghaza' N.M. fighting 'jehad' [A ~ doublet of غزوہ]

غزالہ ghazā'lah N.F. gazelle ; fawn (rare) sun delicate beloved [A]

غزل gha'zal N.F. ode amatory verse غزل پڑھنا gha'zal paṛh'nā V.I. read or recite a verse غزل خواں gha'zal-khān, غزل سرا gha'zalsarā ADJ. reciting verse N.M. poet غزل خوانی gha'zal-khā'nī, غزل سرائی gha'zal-sarā''ī N.F. reading or reciting an ode poet غزل کہنا gha'zal kaih'nā V.I. compose an ode [A]

غزوہ ghaz'vah N.M. (PL. غزوات ghazavāt') war against infidels, in which the Holy Prophet himself participated (as against سریہ sariy'yah in which he did not [A]

غسال ghassāl' N.M. (see under غسل N.M. ★)

غسل ghus'l N.M. bath ablution laving غسل آفتابی ghus'l-e āftā'bī N.M sun bath غسل خانہ ghus'l-khā'nah N.M. bath room ; bath غسل صحت ghus'l-e seh'hat N.M. bathing after recovery ; convalescence bath غسل میت ghus'l-e may'yit N.M. washing the dead body ; corpse-laving غسال ghassāl' N.M. (F. غسالہ ghassā'lah) undertaker whose work is restricted to washing the dead corpse; laver [A]

غش ghash N.M. swoon; fainting fit غش آنا یا پڑنا یا کرنا یا کھانا یا ہونا ghash ā'nā (or paṛnā or kar'nā or khā'nā or ho'nā, V.I. faint ; swoon غشی gha'shī N.F. (col.) swoon ; fainting غشی کا دورہ gha'shī kā dau'rah N.M. fainting fit [A]

غصب ghas'b N.M. usurpation taking by force غصب کرنا ghas'b kar'nā V.T. take by force usurp غصب و نہب ghas'b-o-nah'b N.M. usurpation and pillage [A]

غصہ ghus'sah N.M. anger rage ; passion (rare) suffocation (with) grief غصہ اتارنا یا نکالنا ghus'sah utār'nā (or nikāl'nā) V.I. vent one's spleen retaliate غصہ پینا یا مارنا ghus'sah pī'nā (or mār'nā) V.I. suppress one's anger غصہ دلانا ghus'sah dilā'nā V.T. enrage irritate offend ; give offence ; incense غصہ کرنا ghus'sah kar'nā V.I. be angry be enraged; fly into a passion غصہ ناک پر ہونا ghus'sah nāk' par-ho'nā V.I. be very irritable wear one's heart upon one's sleeve be easily offended غصے میں بھر جانا ghus'se men bhar' jā'nā V.I. fly into a passion غصیلا ghusī'lā, غصیل ghusail' ADJ. touchy; testy irritable ; irascible wrathful [A]

غضب gha'zab N.M. (God's) wrath anger ; rage calamity ADJ. exquisite extraordinary strange unexpected غضب آلود(ہ) gha'zab-ālood'(ah) ADJ. furius indignant ; wrathful غضب ٹوٹنا gha'zab ṭooṭ'nā V.I. be visited by wrath (of God) be overtaken by calamity غضب توڑنا gha'zab-toṛ'nā V.I. be cruel do or say something strange غضب خدا کا gha'zab-khu'dā kā INT. how strange to hell with غضب ڈھانا gha'zab-dhā'nā V.T. be cruel be guilty of impropiety look exquisitely beautiful غضب کا gha'zab kā ADJ. & ADV. extreme(ly) exquisite(ly) غضب کرنا gha'zab kar'nā V.I. be cruel do something strange or unexpected غضبناک gha'zab-nāk ADJ. furious wrathful indignant irate غضب ہونا gha'zab-ho'nā V.I. be very bad غضبی ghaz'bī, ADJ. & N.M. (F. غضبیٰ ghaz'bān) (col.) touchy ; testy irritable ; irascible [A]

غضروف ghuzroof' N.M. cartilage ; glistle

غضنفر ghazan'far N.M. lion [A]

غف ghaf ADJ. thick (cloth)

غفار ghaffar' ADJ. very forgiving (as an attribute of God) [A ~ FOLL.]

غفران ghufran' N.M. remission of sins; absolution deliverance salvation [A]

غفرلہ ghu'fira la'hoo' (or -lah) غفراللہ لہ gha'far-alla'hu la-hoo' (or -lah') INT. may be have salvation [A ~ PREC.]

غفور ghafoor' ADJ. forgiving (as an attribute of God) [A ~ غفران]

غفیر ghafir' ADJ. milling (crowd) جم غفیر jam'm-e ghafir' N.M. milling crowd [A ~ PREC.]

غفلت ghaf'lat N.F. negligence remissness thoughtlessness carelessness [A]

غل ghil N.M. rancour malice بے غل وغش be ghil'l-o-ghish' ADJ. & ADV. unreserved(ly) unadulterated [A]

غل ghul N.M. noise clamour tumult غل غپاڑا ghul' ghapa'ra N.M. disturbance clamour tumult غل کرنا (یا مچانا) ghul' kar'na (or macha'na) V.I. make a noise shout raise a tumult hoot [A]

غلاظت ghila'zat N.F. filth night-soil litter (rare) roughness (rare) hardness [A]

غلاف ghilaf' (PL. غلف ghul'f) N.F. cover (pillow) sheath تکیے کا غلاف tak'ye ka ghilaf' N.M. pillow-case ; pillow-slip غلافی آنکھ ghila'fi ankh N.F. large pretty with conspirous eyelid [A]

غلام ghulam' N.M. slave knave (at cards) (rare) boy غلام بنانا (یا کرنا) ghulam' bana'na (or kar'na) V.T. enslave ; enthral captivate غلام گردش ghulam'-gar'dish N.F. servants walk corridor round the house for household servants بے دام غلام be-dam' ghulam' N.M. very fond (of) very obedient (to) زرخرید غلام zar'-kharid' ghulam' N.M. very obedient person self-purchased slave غلامی ghula'mi N.F. slavery servitude غلامی میں دینا ghula'mi meh de'na V.I. marry (someone) to the daughter (of) [A]

غلبہ ghal'bah (ped. gha'labah) N.M mastery overcoming excess prevalence overwhelming غلبہ پانا ghal'bah pa'na V.T. obtain mastery (over) ; get the better (of) gain the upper hand [A]

غلط gha'lat ADJ. incorrect wrong mistaken erroneous inaccurate fallacious N.M. (rare) mistake غلط العام gha'lat-ul-'am' N.M. common linguistic error (as being idiomatic) غلط العوام ghalat-ul 'avam' N.M. vulgarism غلط انداز gha'lat-andaz' ADJ. deceptive (glances of beloved) chance (looks) غلط ٹھہرانا (یا قرار دینا) gha'lat thaihra'na (or qarar' de'na) V.T. prove to be wrong expose the hollowness of show the fallacy of غلط سلط gha'lat sa'lat ADJ. wrong right or wrong غلط فہمی gha'lat-faih'mi N.F. misunderstanding ; misconception ; misapprehension غلط کار gha'lat-kar' N.M. & ADJ. wrongdoer غلط کاری gha'lat-ka'ri N.F. wrongdoing (sexual) excess (usu. PL.) masturbation غلط گو gha'lat-go ADJ. & N.M. liar (one) spreading false reports غلط گوئی gha'lat-go''i N.F. falsehood lie غلط نامہ gha'lat-na'mah N.M. errate غلطی gha'lati (col. ghal'ti) N.F. PL. اغلاط aghlat') mistake : error inaccuracy oversight a slip (of the pen, etc.) miscalculation fault of omission fallacy wrong step غلطی کرنا gha'lati kar'na V.T. make a mistake take a wrong step غلطی ہونا gha'lati ho'na V.I. be wrong (of mistake) be made (of wrong step) be taken [A]

غلطاں ghal'tan ADJ. rolling wallowing غلطاں و پیچاں ghal'tan(-o) pe'chan ADJ. (fig.) confused ; confounded absorbed in thought [P]

غلطی gha'lati (col. ghal'ti) N.F. (see under غلط ADJ.)

غلظت ghil'zat N.F. density thickness [A]

غلغلہ ghul'ghulah N.M. tumult uproar clamour غلغلہ برپا کرنا ghul'ghulah bar-pa' kar'na V.T. raise a hue and cry غلغلہ برپا ہونا ghul'ghulah bar-pa' ho'na V.I. (of tumult) be or be raised [P]

غلک ghul'lak, گلک gul'lak, گولک go'lak N.F. till cash-box safe [~A غلہ]

غلمان ghilman' N.M. lovely young male servants in paradise [A ~ SING. غلام]

غلو ghuluv' N.F. excessive exaggeration hyperbole غلو سے کام لینا ghuluv' se kam' le'na V.I. highly exaggerate

غلہ ghal'lah N.M. corn grain ; cereal (same as غلک N.F. ★)

غلہ بھرنا ghal'lah bhar'na V.T. store up grain غلہ فروش ghal'la-firosh' N.M. (rare) grain merchant [P]

غلہ ghul'lah, غلیلہ ghule'lah N.M. pellet [P]

غلیان ghalyan' N.M. ebullition [A]

غلیظ ghaliz' ADJ. dirty filthy (fig.) coarse ; broad ; obscene ; smutty (rare) thick [A ~ غلاظت]

غلیل ghulel' N.F. pellet bow ; catapult غلیلچی ghule'l'chi N.M. pellet-bow shooter [P]

غم gham (PL. غموم ghumoom') N.M. sorrow ; grief sadness woe mourning bereavement concern ; worry غمخوار gham-khar' N.M. & ADJ. sympathising (friend) ; comforter afflicted (person) غمخواری gham-kha'ri N.F. sympathy ; commiseration affliction غمخواری کرنا gham-kha'ri kar'na V.T. commiserate ; sympathise (with) غمزدہ gham'-za'dah, غم دیدہ gham-di'dah, غم رسیدہ gham-rasi'dah ADJ. afflicted grieved ; aggrieved غمزدگی gham-za'dagi N.F. affliction sorrow غم غلط کرنا gham gha'lat kar'na V.T. divert one's mind to get over grief comfort solace غمکدہ gham'-ka'dah N.M. house of grief unfortunate person's residence غم کرنا gham' kar'na V.T. & I. grieve lament غم کھانا gham' kha'na V.T. & I. suffer endure grief feel sympathy (for) غمگسار gham-gusar' ADJ. sympathising (friend) ; comforter غمگساری gham-gusa'ri N.F. sympathy ; commiseration غمگین gham-gin' (or gham'-gin) ADJ. sad griefstriken غمگینی gham-gi'ni N.F. sorrow ; sadness غمناک gham-nak' ADJ. sad; sorrowful woeful ; pathetic غمناکی gham-na'ki N.F. sorrowfulness pathos غم والم gha'm-o-a'lam N.M. sorrow ; affliction غمی gha'mi N.F. sorrow ; (rare) grief mourning غمیں ghamin' ADJ. dejected [A]

غماز ghammaz' N.M. backbiter an informer ; tale-bearer (rare) winking غمازی ghamma'zi N.F. backbiting tale-bearing (rare) winking [A ~ غمزہ]

غمزہ gham'zah N.M. ogling ; amorous glance ; glad eye غمزہ دکھانا gham'zah dikha'na V.T. ogle شتر غمزہ shu'tur-gham'zah N.M. (see under شتر N.M. ★)

غمی gha mi N.F. (see under غم N.M. ★)

غنا ghina' N.M. singing ; vocal music (also ghana) riches ; wealth [A]

غنائم ghana''im N.M. (PL. of غنیمت N.F.) ★

غنچہ ghun'chah N.M. bud ADJ. rosebud غنچہ دہن ghun'cha-da'han ADJ. having with a rose-bud mouth N.M. sweetheart ; beloved [P]

غنج ghanj (or ghunj) N.M. coquetry [P]

غنڈہ ghun'dah, گنڈا gun'da N.M. hooligan ; hoodlum ; bad character ; 'goonda' rowdy tough ; rough غنڈہ گردی ghunda-gar'di N.F hooliganism ; 'goondaism'

غنغنانا ghunghuna'na V.I. speak through the nose ; speak with nasal overtones غنغنا ghun'ghuna ADJ. & N.M. (F. غنغنی ghun'ghuni) (one) speaking through the nose [ONO.]

غنودگی ghunoo'dagi N.F. drowsiness غنودگی آنا ghunoo'dagi a'na V.I. feel drowsy doze off [P ~ غنودن]

غنہ ghun'nah ADJ. nasal N.M. sound produced through nose نون غنہ noo'n-e ghun'nah N.M. nasal n (joc.) nonentity

غنی gha'ni N.M. (PL. اغنیا aghniya') rich [A ~ غنا]

غنیم ghanim' N.M. enemy ; foe [A]

غنیمت ghani'mat N.F. (PL. غنائم ghana''im) plunder ; prize boon ; blessing [A]

غواص ghavvas' N.M. diver pearl diver غواصی ghavva'si N.F. diving pearl diving [A]

غوامض ghava'miz N.F. PL. abstruse points subtleties (of) [A ~ SING. غامض ~ غامضہ]

غوث ghaus N.M. one who redresses another's grievance ; one who comes to another's rescue (one of) an upper category of mystics غوث اعظم ghau's-e a'zam, غوث الاعظم ghau's-ul a''zam N.M appellation of famous Sunnite saint Abdul Qadir Jilani [A]

غور ghaur N.M. consideration deliberation (rare) depth غور سے ghaur' se, بغور ba-ghaur' ADV. attentively carefully غور طلب ghaur'-ta'lab ADJ. worth consideration ADV. under consideration غور کرنا ghaur' kar'na V.T. & I. consider reflect deliberate غور و پرداخت ghau'r-o-pardakht N.F. attention (to) maintenance (of) غور و خوض ghau'r-o-khauz' N.M. deliberation consideration غور ہونا ghaur' ho'na V.I. be considered be under consideration [A]

غوطہ gho'tah (ped. ghau'tah) N.M. plunge ; dip dive غوطہ خور gho'ta-khor, غوطہ زن gho'ta-zan' N.M. diver frogman غوطہ خوری gho'ta-kho'ri, غوطہ زنی gho'ta za'ni N.F. diving (usu. as a profession) غوطہ دینا gho'tah de'na V.I. plunge ; dip غوطہ کھانا gho'tah kha'na V.I. plunge ; dip ; dive miss ; leave out ; forget غوطہ لگانا (یا مارنا) gho'tah laga'na (or mar'na) V.T. plunge ; dip ; dive be absorbed in thought fail to turn up [A]

غوغا ghau'gha N.M. noise uproar ; clamour; tumult شور و غوغا sho'r-o-ghau'gha N.M. noise and clamour غوغائی ghaugha''i N.M. & ADJ. turbulent (person) [P]

غول ghol N.M. swarm band ; crowd ; throng; mob ; gang غول کے غول ghol' (ke) ghol N.M. crowds ; whole crowds

غول ghool, (PL. غیلان ghilan') غول بیابانی ghoo'l-e bayaba'ni N.M. will-o'-the-wisp ; jack-o'-lantern ; 'ignis fatuus' [A]

غوں غاں ghoon' ghāṅ N.F. infant's cry غوں غاں کرنا ghoon' ghāṅ kar'na V.I. (of infant) cry ; utter sound [ONO.]

غیاب ghiyāb' N.M. absence disappearance غیاب و حضور ghiyā'b-o-ḥuzoor' N.M. absence and presence [A]

غیاث ghiyās' N.F. plaint seeking redress N.M. one who redresses [A ~ غوث]

غیب ghaib N.M. the hidden the invisible ADJ. hidden ; concealed invisible غیب دان ghaib'-dāṅ' (or-dāṅ) ADJ. & N.M. (one) knowing hidden things ; a prophet ; a seer ; diviner ; the omniscient being غیب دانی ghaib'-dā'nī N.F. knowledge of hidden things عالم غیب 'ā'lam-e ghaib' N.M. the invisible world غیبت ghai'bat N.F. absence کی غیبت میں kī ghai'bat meṅ ADV. in the absence (of) behind (someone's) back غیبی ghai'bī ADJ. unseen invisible heavenly [A]

غیبت ghī'bat N.F. backbiting غیبت کرنا ghī'bat kar'na V.T. backbite [A]

غیبی ghai'bī ADJ. (see under غیب N.M. ★)

غیر ghair N.M. outsider unrelated person stranger ADJ. strange different ADV. (of condition) serious ; grave PREP. not ; un- ; in- غیر آباد ghair-ābād' ADJ. uninhabited deserted uncommanded (land) غیر اختیاری ghair-ikhtiyā'rī ADJ. involuntary unintentional غیر تربیت یافتہ ghair'-tar'biyat-yāf'tah ADJ. unskilled untrained غیر جانبدار ghair'-jā'nib-dār' ADJ. & N.M. neutral غیر جانبداری ghair'-jā'nib-dā'rī N.F. neutrality غیر حاضر ghair'-ḥā'zir ADJ. absent غیر حاضری ghair'-ḥā'zirī N.F. absence غیر سمجھنا ghair' sa'majhnā V.T. not to regard as one's own غیر شخص ghair' shakh's N.M. stranger ; a third person غیر متاثر ghair'-mūta'as'sar ADJ. unaffected ; unimpressed غیر مترقبہ ghair'-mūtaraq'qabah ADJ. unexpected (blessing) غیر متناسب ghair'-mūtanā'sib ADJ. disproportionate غیر متناہی ghair'-mūtanā'hī ADJ. unending ; limitless ; unlimited غیر محدود ghair'-maḥdood' ADJ. unlimited boundless endless غیر مزروعہ ghair'-mazroo''ah ADJ. uncultivated غیر مستعملہ ghair-mūsta''malah (rare غیر مستعمل ghair'-mūsta''mal) ADJ. unused new غیر مشروط ghair'-mashroot' ADJ. unconditional غیر مصافی ghair'-masā'fī ADJ. non-combatant non-belligerent (of area) lying outside war zone غیر مطلوب ghair-matloob' ADJ. unwanted ; undesirable غیر معتبر ghair'-mo''tabar' ADJ. untrustworthy unreliable incredible غیر معمولی ghair-ma'moo'lī ADJ. unusual ; extraordinary غیر معمولی طور پر ghair-ma'moo'lī taur' par ADV. unusually غیر معین ghair-mo'ay'yan ADJ. indefinit غیر مکمل ghair-mūkam'mal ADJ. incomplete imperfect غیر ملکی ghair'-mūl'kī ADJ. foreign exotic غیر ممکن ghair-mūm'kin ADJ. impossible uncultivable ; unculturable غیر ممکن الوصول ghair'-mūm'kin-ūl-vūsool' ADJ. irrecoverable غیر مناسب ghair'-mūnā'sib ADJ. unsuitable unbecoming undesirable improper غیر منقولہ ghair-manqoo'lah ADJ. immovable غیر منقولہ جائداد ghair-manqoo'lah jā'edād' N.F. immovable property ; real estate غیر منکوحہ ghair-mankoo'ḥah ADJ. unmarried living (as someone's wife) out of wedlock غیر واجب ghair'-vā'jib ADJ. improper not due غیریت ghairiy'yat N.F. not being one's own strangeness [A]

غیرت ghai'rat N.F. sense of honour shame bashfulness modesty envy one exciting the envy of غیرت چمن (یا حور یا ماہ) ghai'rat-e cha man (or -ḥoor' or -māh') N M. & ADJ. one exciting envy of garden or 'houri' or 'moon') غیرت سے مر جانا ghai'rat se mar' jā'na, غیرت کھا کے ڈوب مرنا ghai'rat khā ke ḍoob mar'nā V.I. be put to great shame غیرت کھانا ghai'rat khā'nā V.I. experience shame get ready to retaliate غیرت مند ghai'rat-mand ADJ. & N.M. (one) with a keen sense of honour modest envious بے غیرت be-ghai'rat ADJ. shameless brazen-faced بے غیرتی be-ghai'ratī N.F. shamelessness [A]

غیریت ghairiy'yat N.F. (see under غیر N.M. & ADJ. ★)

غیظ ghaiz N.M. anger ; rage ; ire غیظ و غضب ghai'z-o-gha'zab N.M. ire and fury [A]

غین ghain N.F. name of the letter غ (ghain) غین ہونا ghain ho'nā V.I. be dead drunk ; be tipsy [A]

غیں پیں ghīṅ' pīṅ N.F. brawl cry of child's wailing [ONO.]

غیور ghayoor' ADJ. high-minded with a keen sense of honour N.M. Honour guarding (as an attribute of God) [A ~ غیرت]

ف fe twenty-sixth letter of Urdu alphabet (pronounced fā in Arabic) ; (equivalent to English f) (according to jummal reckoning) 80

فاتح fā'teḥ N.M. conqueror ADJ. conquering (rare) opening [A ~ فتح]

فاتحہ fā'teḥah N.F. (dial. M.) opening chapter of the Holy Quran this recited as prayers for the dead فاتحہ پڑھنا fā'teḥah parh'na V.T. pray thus for the dead despond (of) فاتحہ دینا fā'teḥah de'nā V.T. make offerings to God with such prayers for dead مر گئے مردود فاتحہ نہ درود mar' ga''e mardood' fā'tehah na darood' PROV. he dies unmourned the devil is dead [A ~ فتح]

فاتر fā'tir ADJ. unsound (used only in) فاتر العقل fā'tir-ul-'aq'l ADJ. crack ; of unsound mind [A ~ فتور]

فاجر fā'jir ADJ. & N.M. (PL. فجار fujjār') sinful (person) rake ; libertine ; debauchee فاجرہ fā'jirah N.F. & ADJ. sinful (woman) unchaste or loose (woman) [A ~ فجور]

فاجعہ fā'je'ah ADJ. (of event). tragic painful ; grievous [A ~ فجع]

فاحش fā'hish ADJ. obscene ; indecent ; smutty egregious (mistake) فاحشہ fā'hishah N.F. loose woman prostitute ; harlot ADJ. unchaste (woman) immodest [A ~ فحش]

فاختہ fākh'tah N.F. dove ringed turtle-dove وہ دن گئے جب خلیل خاں فاختہ اڑایا کرتے تھے voh' din ga''e jab khalīl' khān fākh'tah urā'yā kar'te the PROV. gone is the goose that lay the golden eggs the days of prosperity are at as end فاختئی fākhta'ī ADJ. fawn ; ashen (colour) [P]

فاخرہ fā'khirah ADJ. (M. فاخر fā'khir) ADJ. splendid ; elegant (rare) bragging [A ~ فخر]

فاران fārān' N.M. Faran ; name of a hill near Mecca [A]

فارس[1] fā'ris N.M. (PL. فوارس favā'ris) horseman cavalier [A ~ فرس]

فارس[2] fā'ris N.M. Iran ; Persia فارسی fā'risī (col. fār'sī) N.F. the Persian language ; persian ADJ. Persian ; Iranian فارسی بگھارنا fār'sī baghār'na (arch.) V.T. try to impress people with one's linguistic knowledge boast of one's culture [A ~ P پارس]

فارغ fā'righ ADJ. free ; not busy at leisure unoccupied discharged ; dismissed (rare) empty فارغ البال fā'righ-ul-bāl' ADJ. & ADV. at case free from care in easy circumstances having no (or no more any) responsibilities to discharge فارغ البالی fārigh-ul-bā'lī N.F. freedom from care and worries easy circumstances فارغ التحصیل fā'righ-ul-tahsīl' ADJ. graduate ; having graduated (from) فارغ خطی fār'khatī, (ped. fā'righ-khat'tī) N.F. written acquittance deed of divorce فارغ خطی لکھنا (یا دینا) fār'khatī likh'nā (or de'nā) V.T. divorce write a deed of acquittance فارغ کرنا fā'righ kar'nā V.T. spare discharge make carefree فارغ ہونا fā'righ ho'nā V.I. be discharge be free be spared be carefree [A ~ فراغ]

فارق fā'riq N.M. distinctive feature [A ~ فرق]

فارقلیط fār'qalīt N.M. Paraclete (as an appellation of the Holy Prophet) [A ~ G]

فارم[1] fā'ram, fār'm N.M. farm [E]

فارم[2] fā'ram, fār'm N.M. form فارم بھرنا fā'ram bhar'nā V.I. fill up a form [E]

فارمولا fārmoo'lā N.M. formala [E]

فارن fā'ran ADJ. foreign فارن آفس fā'ran āfis N.M. foreign office فارن ایکس چینج fā'ran aikschej' N.F. foreign exchange فارن سروس fā'ran sar'vis N.F. foregin service [E]

فاروق fā'rooq' ADJ. & N.M. (one) distinguishing between right and wrong (as appellation of second Orthodox caliph, Hazrat Umar [~ فرق]

فاسخ fā'sikh ADJ. that puts an end (to) ; breaking فاسد fā'sid ADJ. (F. & PL. فاسدہ fā'sidah) vitiated depraved perverse corrupt sinister evil (ideas) [A ~ فساد]

فاسق fā'siq N.M. & ADJ. (PL. فساق fāssāq') sinful (person) ; sinner transgressor rake فاسد و فاجر fā'sid-o-fā'jir N.M. & ADJ. sinful and debauched (person) فاسقہ fā'siqah N.F. & ADJ. sinful (woman) lewd, unchaste loose or wanton (woman) [A ~ فسق]

فاش fāsh ADJ. revealed ; divulged (of mistake) obvious (of mistake) serious ; gross egregious فاش کرنا fash' kar'na V.T. let out, disclose, reveal or divulge (a secret) فاش ہونا fash' ho'nā V.I. be divulged [A]

فاصل fā'sil ADJ. separating ; dividing حد فاصل had'd-e fā'sil N.F. dividing line (between) [A ~ فصل]

فاصلہ fā'silah N.M. distance ADJ. dividing فاصلے پر fā'sile par ADV. at a distance (of) distant far-off فاصلہ طے کرنا fā'silah tai' kar'nā V.I. traverse (some) distance [A ~ فصل]

فاضل fā'zil N.M. (PL. فضلا fuzalā') scholar accomplished person balance ; remainder Honours (in) name of oriental titles exam. ADJ. surplus remaining accomplished talented scholarly فاضل اجل fā'zil-e ajal' N.M. great scholar فاضل باقی fā'zil-bā'qī N.F. (arch.) balance فاضل باقی نکالنا fā'zil-bā'qī nikāl'nā V.I. (arch.) strike the balance فاضل ہونا fā'zil ho'nā V.I. exceed ; be فاضل باقی نویس fa'zil-bā'qī-navīs' N.M. (arch.) accountant more than be scholarly be accomplished [A ~ فضل]

فاطمہ fāti'mah ADJ. weaned (baby) N.F. name of Holy Prophet's youngest daughter ; Fatimah فاطمی fā'timī ADJ. descendant of Hazrat Fatimah Fatimid (dynasty) [A]

فاعل *fā''il* N.M. (gram.) subject; nominative active agent; doer ; maker ; performer sodomist ; pederast فاعل حقیقی *fā''il-e ḥaqī'qī* N.M. God (as the real performer) فاعل مختار *fā''il-e mukh-tār'* N.M. free agent فاعل و مفعول *fā''il-o-maf'ool'* N.M. (gram.) subject and object sodomist and his minion فاعلی *fā''ilī* ADJ. active efficient ; effective operative nominative فاعلی حالت *fā''ilī ḥā'lat*, حالتِ فاعلی *ḥā'lat-e fā''ilī* N.F. nominative case فاعلیت *fā'iliy'yat* N.F. being in the nominative case subjectivity agency [A ~ فعل]

فاقد *fā'qid* ADJ. (one) having lost (something) [A ~ فقدان]

فاقہ *fā'qah* N.M. starvation fasting (rare) poverty ; penury فاقہ زدہ *fā'qa-za'dah* ADJ. starved فاقہ زدگی *fā'qa-za'dagī* N.F starvation فاقہ کرنا *fā'qah kar'nā* V.T. go without food ; fast ; have to fast ; starve فاقہ گزرنا *fā'qah gu'zarnā* V.I. starve N.M. have to go without food فاقہ کش *fā'qa-kash* ADJ. & N.M. starved or famished (person) فاقہ کشی *fā'qa-ka'shī* N.F. starvation فاقہ مست *fā'qa-mas't* ADJ. cheerful even in adversity N.M. starveling affecting airs of affluence فاقہ مستی *fā'qa-mas'tī* N.F. cheerfulness in adversity فاقوں مرنا *fā'qoṅ mar'nā* V.I. starve ; be famished be penurious فاقوں کا مارا *fā'qoṅ kā mā'ra* N.M. & ADJ. starveling ; famished (person) ; starved (for so many days [A]

فال *fāl'* N.F. prediction omen augury presage with the help of some occult, etc. book فال دیکھنا یا کھولنا یا لینا یا نکالنا *fāl' dekh'nā* (or *khol'nā* or *le'nā* or *nikāl'nā*) V.I. foretell take an omen from فال کھلوانا *fāl' khulvā'nā* V.T. get prediction thus فال گو *fāl'-go* N.M. soothsayer one foretelling thus فالِ گوش *fā'l-e gosh'* N.F. omen taken from words overheard فالنامہ *fāl-nā'mah* N.M. book of omens بری فال *bū'rī fāl'*, فالِ بد *fāl-e bad'* N.F. ill omen نیک فال *nek' fāl'*, فالِ نیک *fāl-e nek'* N.F. good omen [A]

فالتو *fāl'too* ADJ. extra spare surplus additional ADV. in addition

فالج *fā'lij* N.M. hemiplegia palsy paralysis فالج زدہ *fālij-za'dah* ADJ. palsied ; paralysed فالج زدگی *fālij-za'dagī* palsy ; paralysis فالج گرنا *fā'lij gir'nā* V.I. be palsied ; be paralysed ; be stricken with paralysis [A]

فالسہ *fāl'sah* N.M. a kind of small, purple edible berry فالسئی *fāl'sa'ī* ADJ. purple (colour) [P]

فالودہ *fāloo'dah* N.M. sieved flummery cold drink prepared from it ; flummery drink [P]

فالیز *fālez'* پالیز *pālez'* N.F. melon field [P]

فام *fām* SUF. complexioned coloured [P]

فانوس *fānoos'* N.F. chandelier lampshade فانوس خیال *fānoo's-e-khayāl'* N.M. lantern projecting on its shade shadows of pictures revolving round its flame ; shadow-play lantern [A]

فانہ *fa'nah* N.M. wedge

فانی *fā'nī* ADJ. mortal transitory (world) [A ~ فنا]

فائدہ *fā''idah* N.M. advantage benefit profit gain use ; utility efficacy cure فائدہ اٹھانا *fā''idah uṭhā'nā* V.I. gain profit benefit ; reap benefit use ; utilize take advantage (of) فائدہ مند *fā''ida-mand* ADJ. useful advantageous beneficial profitable ; gainful efficacious [A]

فائر *fā'yar* N.M. fire firing فائر انجن *fā'yar in'jan* N.M. fire engine فائر بریگیڈ *fā'yar barigeḍ'* N.M. fire brigade فائرنگ *fā'yariṅg* N.F. firing [E]

فائز *fā''iz* ADJ. fixed up ; holding (a job) (rare) successful فائز المرام *fā''iz-ul-maram'* ADJ. successful in achieving the object [A ~ فوز]

فائق *fā'iq* ADJ. surpassing excellent لائق (و) فائق *lā''iq(-o-) fa''iq* ADJ. surpassingly efficient [A ~ فوق]

فائل *fā''il* N.M. file فائل کرنا *fā''il kar'nā* V.T. file [E]

فبہا *fa' be-hā'* ADV. all right (then) [A ~ ف then + ب with + ہا it]

فتا (or فتیٰ) *fatā'* N.M. youth young ; man chivalrous person [A]

فتاح *fattāḥ'* N.M. (see under فتح N.F. ★)

فتان *fat'tān* ADJ. seductive (eye) [A ~ فتنہ]

فتاوی *fatā'vā*, (rare *fatā'vī*) N.M. (PL. of فتویٰ★)

فتح *fat'ḥ* (col. *fa'taḥ*) N.F. (PL. فتوحات *fātooḥāt'* rare. فتوح *fūtooḥ'*) victory conquest (rare) opening. فتح پانا *fat'ḥ pā'nā* V.I. conquor ; obtain a victory. be victorious فتح کا ڈنکا یا نقارہ بجانا *fat'ḥ kā daṅ'kā* (or *naqqā'rah*) *bajā'nā* V.I. declare victory with fanfare beat of victorious drum فتحمند *fat'ḥ-mand*, فتح کرنا *fat'ḥ-kar'nā* V.T. conquor subdue فتحیاب *fat'ḥ-yāb* ADJ. victorious triumphant فتحمندی *fat'ḥ-mand dī*, فتحیابی *fat'ḥ-yā'bī* N.F. victory trumph success فتحہ *fat'ḥah* N.M. vowel point فتاح *fattāḥ'* N.M. opener (God as) one who awards victory فتوح *fūtooḥ'* N.F. extra income (PL. of فتح ★) [A]

فتراک *fitrāk'* N.M. saddle-straps [P]

فتق *fat'q* N.M. hernia ; rupture [A]

فتن *fi'tan* N.M. (PL. of فتنہ ★)

فتنہ *fit'nah* N.M. (PL. فتن *fi'tan*) mischief revolt temptation trial ; tribulation a kind of scent very naughty person ADJ. naughty ; mischievous فتنہ اٹھانا (یا برپا کرنا) *fit'nah uṭhā'na* (or *barpā' kar'nā*) V.T. create disturbance raise a hue and cry فتنہ انگیز *fit'na-angez'*, فتنہ پرداز *fit'na-pardāz'* ADJ. & N.M. mischievous (person) mischief-mong فتنہ انگیزی *fit'na-ange'zi*, فتنہ پردازی *fit'na-pardā'zi* N.F. mischief-making فتنہ خوابیدہ *fit'na-e khābī'dah* N.M. dormant trouble سوتے فتنے جگانا *so'te fit'ne jagā'nā* V.T. stir up trouble فتنی *fit'nī* N.F. (col.) mischief-maker [A]

فتوح *fūtooḥ'* فتوحات *fūtooḥāt'* N.M. (PL. of فتح N.F. ★)

فتوحی *fatoo''ī* (ped. *fatoo'ḥī*) N.F. (arch.) (usu. sleeveles) waistcoat

فتور *fūtoor'* N.M. defect derangement unsoundness disorder disturbance فتور برپا کرنا *fūtoor' bar-pā' kar'nā* V.T. create disturbance raise a hue and cry فتور عقل *fūtoo'r-e 'aq'l*, عقل کا فتور *'aq'l kā fūtoor'* N.M. unsoundness of mind فتوریا *fūtoo'riya*, فتوری *fūtoo'rī* N.M. & ADJ. (col.) mischievous person factious person [A]

فتویٰ *fat'vā* N.M. legal opinion judicial verdict فتویٰ دینا *fat'vā de'nā* V.I. give a legal opinion give a verdict فتاویٰ *fatā'vā* (rare. *fatā'vī*) N.M. PL. legal opinions verdicts ; case-law [A]

فتیلہ *fatī'lah* N.M. wick فتیلہ سوز *fatī'la-soz* N.M. metallic bowl for wicks ; lamp [A ~ فتل twist]

فٹ *fūṭ* N.M. foot فٹ بال *fūṭ'-bāl* N.M. football [E]

فٹ *fit* ADJ. fit tight-fitting فٹ ہونا *fit' ho'nā* V.I. fit be suitable فٹ کرنا *fit kar'nā* V.T. prepare or adjust so as to fit [E]

فٹر *fi'ṭar* N.M. fitter [E ~ PREC.]

فٹن *fi'ṭan* N.F. phaeton [E]

فجار *fūj'jār* N.M. (PL. of فاجر ★)

فجر *faj'r* N.F. daybreak dawn morning فجر کے وقت *faj'r ke vaq't* ADV. in the morning فجر ہی فجر *faj'r hī faj'r* ADV. early in the morning so early [A]

فجور *fujoor'* N.M. debauchery wickedness فسق و فجور *fis'q-o-fujoor'* N.M. sinfulness and debauchery [A]

فحش *foḥ'sh* N.M. obscenity grossgess ; indecency foul language فحش بکنا *foḥ'sh bak'nā* V.I. abuse ; use foul language فحش کلامی *foḥ'sh-kalā'mī*, فحش گوئی *foḥ'sh-go''ī* N.F. foul language , obscenity فحش نویس *foḥ'sh-navīs'* N.F. writer of obscene stuff فحاشی *faḥḥā'shī* N.F. obscene writing obscenity [A]

فحویٰ *faḥvā'* N.M. drift or tenor (of speech), import style فحوائے کلام *fahvā'-e kalām'* N.M. tenor of speech [A]

فخر *fakh'r* N.M. just pride boast glory , ostentation , pride ; something to be proud of ; pride (of) فخر خاندان *fakh'r-e khāndān'* N.M. & ADJ. pride of one's family فخر سمجھنا *fakh'r sa'majhnā* V.T. take pride in فخر کرنا *fakh'r kar'nā* V.I. boast (of) ; be proud (of) pride oneself on or upon فخریہ *fakhriy'yah* ADV. proudly , with just pride boastfully [A]

فدا *fidā'* ADJ. devoted (to) dying (for) sacrificed (rare) ransomed فدا کرنا *fidā' kar'nā* V.I. devote (something to) sacrifice (one's life for) فدا ہونا *fidā' ho'nā* V. love passionately be devoted (to) be a sacrifice (for) ; lay down one's life (for) فدائی *fidā''ī* N.M. (person) hazarding his life (for) pledged devotee lover (arch.) Assassin فدائیان *fidā''iyān* N.M. PL pledged devotees فدائیین *fidā'iy'yīn* N.M. PL. (arch.) Assassins [A]

فدک *fa'dak* (usu. باغ فدک *bā'gh-e fa'dak*) N.M. name of a Khyber orchard in Arabia [A]

فدوی *fid'vī* (ped. *fi'davī*) N.M. devoted servant (as formula opening subscription to application) Yours obediently ; the humble applicant [P ~ A فدا]

فدیہ *fid'yah* N.M. ransom [A ~ فدا]

فر ۱ *far* N.F. splendour pomp [P]

فر ۲ *far* N.M. flight [A]

فر ۳ *far* N.F. fur [E]

فرات *fūrāt'* N.M. Euphrates [A]

فراٹا *farrā'ṭa* N.M. sound of swift movement or flight فراٹے بھرنا *farrā'ṭe bhar'nā* V.I. run fast ; move at a swift pace فراٹے کا *farrā'ṭe kā* ADJ. quick ; swift

فراخ *farākh* ADJ. large , spacious ; expansive wide ; broad فراخ چشم *farākh'-chash'm* ADJ. satisfied ; contented فراخ حوصلہ *farākh'-ḥau'salah* ADJ. hearted ; magnanimous فراخ حوصلگی *farākh-ḥau'salagī* large-heartedness ; magnanimity فراخ دستی *farākh' das'li* N.F. wealth ; easy circumstances فراخدل *farakh'-dil* ADJ. generous broad-minded فراخدلی *farakh'-di'li* N.F. generosity broad mindedness فراخی *fara'khi* N.F largeness roominess sopaciousness easy circumstances [P]

فرار *firar'* N.M. flight ; running away فرار ہونا *firar' ho'na* V.I. flee ; run away abscond elope راہ فرار اختیار کرنا *ra'h-e firar' ikhtiyar' kar'na* V.I. flee make oneself scarce فراری *fira'ri* ADJ. escaped absconding runaway ; fugitive N.F. (col.) (same as فرار N.M. ★ فراری مجرم *fira'ri mujrim* N.M. absconder escaped convict [A]

فراز *faraz'* N.M. top height SUF. exalted holding high فرازی *fara'zi* SUF. exaltation [A]

فراست *fira'sat* N.F. sagacity shrewdness discernment perspicacity intuition [A]

فراش *farash'* N.M. bedding صاحب فراش *sa'hib(-e) firash* ADJ. bed-ridden N.M. ill [A doublet of فرش]

فراش *farrash'* N.M. (arch.) carpet spreader (arch.) tent-pitcher servant فراش خانہ *farrash'-kha'nah* N.M. servant's room فراشی *farra'shi* ADJ. (arch.) (of fan) pulled by a servant فراشی پنکھا *farra'shi pan'kha* N.M. ceiling fan large hand fan [A ~ فرش]

فراشبین *farash'-bin* N.F. French beans [E]

فراغ *faragh'* N.N. leisure freedom from worries [A]

فراغت *faraghat* N.F. leisure respite easy circumstances فراغت پانا *fara'ghat pa'na* V.I. be free (from) have leisure فراغت سے بیٹھنا *fara'ghat se baith'na* V.I. sit at case be free from worries فراغت ہونا *fara'ghat ho'na* V.I. have leisure be free [A]

فراق *firaq'* N.M. separation فراق زدہ *firaq'-za'dah* ADJ. separated from one's sweetheart [A ~ فرق]

فراک *firak'* N.M. frock [E]

فراموش *faramosh'* ADJ. forgotten neglected ignored فراموش کار *faramosh'-kar* N.M. & ADJ. forgetful person (one) ignoring others فراموشی *faramo'shi* N.F. forgetfulness oblivion [A]

فرامین *faramin'* N.M. (PL. of فرمان ★)

فرانسیسی *fransi'si* N F French N.M Frenchman ADJ. French [F Francaise]

فراواں *fira'van* ADJ. ample abundant plenty copious فراوانی *firava'ni* N F plenty abundance [P]

فراہم *fara'ham* ADJ. collected , gathered , obtained فراہم کرنا *fara'ham kar'na* V.I obtain supply manage فراہمی *fara'hami* N.F collecting ; gathering obtaining [P ~ فرا before ہم together]

فرائض *fara''iz* N.M. PL. duties obligations inheritance shares (also علم الفرائض *'il'm-ul-fara''iz*) inheritance law فرائض منصبی *fara''iz-e man'sabi* N.M. official duties حقوق و فرائض *huqoo'q-o-fara''iz* N.M. PL. rights and duties فرائضی *fara''izi* N.M. name of anti-British Bengali Muslim movement of early days [A ~ فریضہ]

فربہ *far'bah* ADJ. fat ; corpulent , plump فربہ اندام *far'ba-andam'* ADJ. fat , corpulent; plump فربہی *far'bahi* N.F. fatness ; corpulence flesh [P]

فرتوت *fartoot'* ADJ. very old ; decrepit پیر فرتوت *pi'r-e fartoot'* N.M. decrepit old man [P]

فرج *far'j* N.F. (rare) ease (col. *fur'j*) vagina [A]

فرجام *farjam'* N.M. end , consequence نیک فرجام *nek'-farjam'* ADJ. something with happy consequence [P]

فرح *fa'rah* N.F. cheerfulness joy , happiness فرحاں *farhan'* ADJ. glad ; happy cheerful شاداں و فرحاں *sha'dan-o-farhan* ADJ. happy and cheerful [A]

فرحت *far'hat* N.M. pleasure delight cheerfulness ; amusement ; recreation ; diversion فرحت افزا *far'hat-afza'* ADJ. pleasant delightful entertaining فرحت انجام *far'hat-atjam'* ADJ. with a cheerful ending فرحت بخش *far'hat bakh'sh* ADJ pleasant refreshing [A ~ فرح]

فرخ *far'rukh* ADJ. auspicious [P ~ فر + رخ]

فرخندہ *farkhan'dah* (ped. *farkhun'dah*) ADJ. auspicious فرخندہ بخت *farkhan'da-bakht'* ADJ. lucky , fortunate [P]

فرد *far'd* N.M (PL. افراد *afrad'*) individual couplet N.F. sheet , list , roll ; register outer fold of quiet ADJ. one single incomparable فرداً فرداً *far'dan far'dan* ADV. one by one individual فرد بشر *far'd-e ba'shar* N M. human being فرد باقیات *far'd-e baqiyat'* N.F. (arch) balance sheet فرد جرم *far'd-e jur'm* N.M. charge-sheet فرد جرم عائد کرنا *far'd-e jur'm 'a''id kar'na* V.T. charge sheet فرد جمعبندی *far'd jam'' ban'di* N.F. rent roll (of land) فرد فرد *far'd far d* ADV separate [A]

فردا *far'da* N.M tomorrow doomsday فردائے قیامت *farda'-e qiya'mat* N.M day of resurrection فردا و دی *farda-o-di* N.M yesterday and tomorrow future and past [P]

فرداً فردا *far'dan far'dan* ADV. (see under فرد N.M. ★)

فردوس *firdaus'* N.M. (PL. فراویس *faradīs*) paradise فردوس گوش *firdau's-e gosh'* N.M. & ADJ. enrapturing sound فردوس مکانی (یا آشیانی) *firdaus'-makā'nī* (or *ashiyā'nī*) ADJ. the late [A]

فرزانہ *farzā'nah* ADJ. & N.M. (PL. فرزانگاں *farzā'nagāṅ*) wise (person) فرزانگی *farzā'nagī* N.F. wisdom [P]

فرزند *farzand'* N.M. son (rare) child; offspring فرزندِ رشید *farzan'd-e rashīd'* N.M. dutiful son فرزندِ ناخلف *farzan'd-e nā-kha'laf* N.M. undutiful son فرزندی *farzan'dī* N.F. filial relations فرزندی میں لینا *farzan'dī meṅ le'nā* V.T. accept as son-in-law [P]

فرزیں *far'zīṅ* N.F. (at chess) queen [P]

فرس *fa'ras* N.M. (PL. افراس *afrās'* فروس *fūroos'*) horse mare (at chess) knight [A]

فرسا *farsā'* SUF. chafing rubbing wearing away فرسائی *farsā''ī* SUF. rubbing wearing away [P ~ فرسودن]

فرستادہ *firistā'dah* N.M. & ADJ. (one) sent (by) envoy (of) ; messenger (of) [P ~ فرستادن]

فرسٹ *fars'ṭ* ADJ. first فرسٹ ایڈ *fars'ṭ-ed'* N.F. first فرسٹ ڈویژن *fars'ṭ' davi'zan* N.F. first division فرسٹ کلاس *fars'ṭ kalās'* N.M. first class [E]

فرسخ *far'sakh*, فرسنگ *farsang'* N.M. league parasang [P]

فرسودہ *farsoo'dah* ADJ. outmoded trite worn-out فرسودگی *farsoo'dagī* N.F. being worn-out . being outmoded triteness depreciation (of machinery) اخراجاتِ فرسودگی *akh'rājāt-e farsoo'dagī* N.M. PL. depreciation charges [P ~ فرسودن]

فرش *far'sh* (PL. فروش *fūroosh*) N.M. floor pavement carpet ; mat bedding فرش بچھانا (یا کرنا) *far'sh bichhā'nā* (or *kar'nā*) V.I. carpet فرش باندھنا (یا لگانا) *far'sh banā'nā* (or *lagā'nā*) V.T. pave فرش بننا (یا لگنا) *far'sh ban'nā* (or *lag'nā*) V.I. paved فرش فروش *far'sh fūroosh'* N.M carpetting فرشی *far'shī* ADJ. pedestal (lamp, fan, etc.) low فرشی سلام *far'shī salām'* N.M. low bow [A]

فرشتہ *firish'tah* N.M. (PL. فرشتگاں *firish'tagāṅ*) angel فرشتہ خصلت *firish'ta-khas'lat'* فرشتہ سیرت *firishta-sī'rat*, فرشتہ صفات *firish'ta-si'fat* ADJ. angelic virtuous فرشتوں کو خبر نہ ہونا *firish'toṅ ko kha'bar na ho'nā* PH. (of someone) be totally unaware فرشتوں کے پر جلنا *firish'toṅ ke par' jal'nā* PH. (of place, etc.) he inaccessible فرشتے دکھائی دینا *firish'te dikhā''ī de'nā* فرشتے نظر آنا *firish'te na'zar-ā'nā* PH. find one's death approaching [P]

فرصت *fūr'sat* N.F. leisure opare time opportunity فرصت پانا *fūr'sat pā'nā* V.I. find the opportunity (to) have time (for) have leisure فرصت ملنا (یا ہونا) *fūr'sat mil'nā* (or *ho'nā*) V.I. have a respite have some leisure get an opportunity (to) [A]

فرض *far'z* N.M. duty obligation responsibility supposition فرض ادا کرنا *far'z adā' kar'nā* V.I. do (one's) duty فرضِ عین *far'z-e 'ain'* N.M. strict obligation ADJ. obligatory فرض کرنا *far'z kar'nā* V. suppose speak hypothetically assume presume ; take for granted make (something) obligatory (for) فرض کرو *far'z ka'ro* PH. suppose hypothetically speaking فرضِ کفایہ *far'z-e kifā'yah* N.M. general obligation whose performance by an adequate number absolves all ; adequate obligation بفرضِ محال *ba-far'z-e mohāl'* ADV. if worst come to worst فرض ہونا *far'z ho'nā* V.I. be obligatory (for) بالفرض *bil-far'z* ADV. supposing فرضاً *far'zan* ADV (arch.) granting supposing فرضی *far'zī* ADJ. assumed fictitious supposed hypothetical insubstantial unreal فرضی نام *far'zī nām* N.M. pseudonym ; assumed name ; fictitious name [A]

فرط *far't* N.F. abundance ; excess ; depth فرطِ شوق *far't-e shauq'* N.F. great longing depth of passion فرطِ محبت *far't-e mahab'bat* N.F. great affection excessive love [A]

فرع *far''* N.F. (PL. فروع *fūroo''*) bough branch ramification ; subsidiary development اصل و فرع *as'l-o-far''* N.F. root and branch [A]

فرعون *fir'aun'* (PL. فراعنہ *farā''inah*) N.M. pharoah arrogant person فرعونِ بے ساماں *fir'au'n-e be-sāmāṅ'* N.M. one proud despite povert فرعونیت *fir'auniy'yat* N.F. overweennig pride [A ~ Egyp.]

فرغل *far'ghul* N.M. quilted cloak [P]

فرفر *far'far* ADJ. fluently فرفر پڑھنا *far'far paṛh'nā* V.I. read fluently

فرفری *far'farī* N.F. (esp. unmarried) women's cant (particulary by the addition of *fa.foo* or *fī* to every syllable of ordinary speech)

فرق *far'q* N.M. difference distinction distance intervening space change estrangement deterioration parting of the hair brow forehead فرق آجانا *far'q ā jā'nā* V.I. undergo a change deteriorate be estranged فرق آنا (یا پڑنا) *far'q ā'nā* (or *paṛ'nā*) V.I. show a difference (of) undergo change be estranged فرق کرنا *far'q kar'nā* V.I. differentiate show partially فرق نکالنا *far'q nikāl'nā* V.T. show a difference remove a difference دلوں میں فرق آنا *di'loṅ meṅ far'q ā'nā* PH. be estranged [A]

فرق *fi'raq* N.M. (PL. of فرقہ ★)

فرقان *fūrqān'* N.M. the Holy Quran (as distinguishing truth from falsehood (rare) such distinction [A ~ فرق]

فرقت *fūr'qat* N.F. separation فرقت زدہ *fūr'qat-za'dah*, فرقت کا مارا *fūr'qat kā mā'rā* ADJ. (of lover) afflicted with separation [A]

فرقدان *farqadān'*, فرقدین *farqadain'* N.M. name of two brilliant stars near the pole-stars [A]

فرقہ *fir'qah* N.M. (PL. فرق *fi'raq*) sect فرقہ بندی *fir'qa-bañ'dī* N.F. organization into various sects فرقہ پرست *fir'qa-parast'* N.M. sectarian communalist ADJ. sectarian communalistic فرقہ پرستانہ *fir'qa-parastā'nah* ADJ. sectarian communal فرقہ پرستی *fir'qa-paras'tī* N.F. sectarianism communalism [A]

فرلانگ *farlāng'* N.F. furlong [E]

فرلو *far'lo* N.F. furlough [E]

فرما[1] *far'm* N.M. & ADJ. firm [E]

فرما[2] *farmā'* SUF. (one) who says, does or orders something فرمائی *farmā''ī* SUF. saying, doing or ordering something [P ~ فرمودن]

فرما[3] *far'mā*, فرمہ *far'mah* N.M. forme [E]

فرمان *farmān'* N.M. edict command charter فرمانبردار *far'mān-bar-dār'* ADJ. obedient dutiful فرمانبرداری *far'mān-bar-dā'rī* N.F. obedience فرماں پزیر *far'mān pazīr'* ADJ. obedience فرماں پزیری *far'mān-pazī'rī* N.F. obedience فرمانروا *far'mān-ravā'* N.M. sovereign فرمانروائی *far'mān-ravā''ī* N.F. sovereignty ; suzerainty [P ~ فرمودن]

فرمانا *farma'nā* V.I. (of superior) say V.T. order ; command [~ P فرمودن]

فرمائش *farmā''ish* N.F. request or order (for something) a kind of buttered pencake فرمائش پوری کرنا *farmā''ish poo'rī kar'nā* V.I. supply (someone's) order present (something) requested (by someone) فرمائش کرنا *farmā''ish kar'nā* V.T. place an order (with) make request (for a present from) فرمائشی *farmā''ishī* ADJ. request ; requested as ordered strong ; vigorous فرمائشی پڑنا یا کھانا *farmā''ishī paṛ'nā* (or *khā'nā*) V.I. have a good hiding get a sound shoe beating فرمائشی قہقہہ *farmā''ishī qaih'qahah* N.M. horse laugh loud laugh [P ~ فرمودن]

فرنٹ *farañṭ'* N.F. front opposed (to) فرنٹ ہو جانا *farañṭ' ho' jā'nā* V.I. become inimical to [E]

فرنٹیر *farañ'ṭiyar* N.M. frontier فرنٹیر میل *farañ'ṭiyar mel* N.M. Frontier Mail [E]

فرنچ *farañch* ADJ French فرنچ ٹوسٹ *farañch tost* N.M. egg-soaked toast ; French toast [E]

فرنگ *farang* فرنگستان *farañ'gistān* N.M. the West Western countries فرنگی *farañ'gī* N.M. & ADJ. Weternized (person) European [~ E Frank]

فرنی *fir'nī*, فیرینی *fīrī'nī* N.F. hasty pudding فرنی فالودہ ایک بھاؤ نہیں ہوتا *fir'nī fāloo'dah ek' bhā''o na'hīñ ho'tā* PROV. everything has a value of its own [P]

فرنیچر *farnī'chār* N.M. furniture [E]

فرو *firo'* ADJ. put out ; extinguished ADV. low below down فروتن *firo'-tan'* ADJ. humble ; lowly فروتنی *firo'-ta'nī* N.F. humility ; lowliness فرو کرنا *firo' kar'nā* V.T. extinguished curb ; quell فروکش ہونا *firo'-kash ho'nā* V.I. stay put up (at or with) فروگزاشت *firo'-gūzāsht'* N.F. omission sin of omission فروگزاشت کرنا *firo-gūzāsht' kar'nā* V.I. be guilty of an omission فرومانده *firo'-māñ'dah* ADJ. weak helpless weary . tired ; fatigued فروماندگی *firo'-māñ'dagī* N.F. weakness helplessness weariness ; fatigue فرومایہ *firo'-mā'yah* ADJ. mean ; object poor فرومائیگی *firo'-mā'yagī* N.F. meanness poverty فرو ہونا *firo' ho'nā* V.I. be put out ; be extinguished be curled ; be quelled [A]

فروٹ *far'vaṭ* ADV. at a gallop

فروخت *firokh't* N.F. sale ; disposal فروخت کرنا *firokh't kar'nā* V.T. sell ; dispose of فروخت شدہ *firokh't shūdah* ADJ. sold ; disposed of خرید و فروخت *kharī'd-o-firokh't* N.F. (see under خرید ★) [P ~ فروختن]

فرود *firod'* ADV. (rare.) down ; beneath PREF. alighting soujourning فرودگاہ *firod'-gāh* N.F. camping ground rest house [P]

فروردین *far'vardīn* N.M. first month of Persian calendar [P]

فروری *far'varī* N.M. February [E]

فروز *fūroz'*, افروز *afroz'* SUF. illuminating فروزاں *fūro'zāñ* ADJ. lit ; lighted refulgent فروزندہ *fūrozin'dah* N.M. one who illuminates [P ~ افروختن]

فروش *firosh'* selling seller ; vendor فروشندہ *firoshin'dah* ADJ. seller ; vendor فروشی *firo'shī* SUF. selling [P ~ افروختن]

فروع *fūroo''* N.M. PL. off-shoots ; branches ramification subsidiary developments minor points (rare) distant relatives practical tenets فروعی *fūroo''ī* ADJ. minor subsidiary extra ; additional [A ~ SING. فرع]

فروغ *fūrogh'* N.M. rise to fame or power honour popularity prosperity glory ; splendour فروغ پانا یا حاصل کرنا *fūrogh' pa'nā* (or *ḥa'sil kar'nā*) V.I. thrive ; prosper fame or power become popular achieve glory [P]

فرہنگ *farhang'* N.F. dictionary glossary ; vocabulary ; meanings and explanations wisdom [P]

فریاد *faryād'* N.F. crying out for assistance complaint plaint petition فریادرس *faryād'-ras* N.M. & ADJ. (one) who redresses grievances فریادرسی *faryad'-ra'.ī* N.F. redress *faryād' kar'nā* V.I. cry out for assistance complain sue ; file a suit (against) *farya'dī* N.M. plaintiff complaining

فریب • *fareb'* (ped. فریب *fireb'*) N.M. fraud cheating ; deceit ; deception seduction SUF. captivating deluding فریب آمیز *fare'b-āmez* ADJ. cunning ; deceitful فریب خوردہ *fareb'-khur'dah* ADJ. gulled ; duped defrauded ; swindled beguiled فریب دہی *fareb'-de'hī* N.F. swindling cheating ; defrauding beguiling (کو) فریب دینا (*ko*) *fareb' de'nā*, (سے) فریب کرنا (*se*) *fareb' karna* V.T. cheat ; deceive defraud dupe swindle (کا) فریب کھانا (*kā*) *fareb kha'nā*, (کے) فریب میں آنا (*ke*) *fareb' men ā'nā* V.I. be cheated (by) be deceived (by) be beguiled (by) ; be deluded (by) be seduced (by) فریبندہ *farebin'dah* N.M. deceiver فریبی *fare'bī* N.M. cheat fraud fraudulent [P]

فرید *farīd'* ADJ. singular ; peerless فریدہ *farī'dah* ADJ. matchless N.M. matchless pearl [A ~ فرد]

فریضہ *farī'zah* N.M. (PL. فرائض *farā''iz*) obligation duty obligatory prayer فریضہ ادا کرنا *farī'zah adā' kar'nā* V.I. do one's duty offer obligatory prayer perform (Haj. etc.) obligation [A ~ فرض]

فریفتہ *faref'tah* ADJ. infatuated (with) fascinated (by) N.M. lover فریفتہ کرنا *faref'tah' kar'nā* V.T. infatuate fascinate فریفتہ ہونا *faref'tah ho'nā* V.I. infatuated (with) ; fall in love (with) be fascinated (by) فریفتگی *faref'tagī* N.F. infatuation [P ~ فریفتن]

فریق *farīq'* N.M. party to a lawsuit section (of class) division فریق اول *farī'q-e av'val* N.M. first party ; principal party plaintiff فریق ثانی *farī'q-e sā'nī* N.M. opposite party defendant فریقین *farīqain'* N.M. both parties the two parties to a lawsuit ; plaintiff and defendant [A ~ فرق]

فریم *farem'* N.M. frame فریم شدہ *farem'-shū'dah* ADJ. framed ; mounted on a frame فریم کرنا *farem' kar'nā* V.T. frame فریم میں لگانا *frrem' men lagā'nā* V.T. frame [E]

فزا *fizā'*, افزا *afzā'* SUF. increasing ; reinforcing [P ~ فزودن]

فزع *fa'za'* cry for helps bewailing (rare) fear [A]

فزوں *fizooṅ'*, افزوں *af'zooṅ* ADJ. more increase فزوں از *fizooṅ' az* ADJ. more than [P ~ فزودن]

فساد *fasād'* N.M. disturbance ; trouble outbreak rebellion dissension mischief brawl ; melee tumult disorder ; upsetting فساد برپا کرنا *fasād' bar-pā' kar'na* V.T. create disturbance فساد اٹھانا (یا کرنا یا مچانا) *fasād' ūṭhā'nā* (or *kar'nā* or *machā'nā*) V.T. raise a tumult create trouble فساد کی جڑ *fasād kī jaṛ* N.F. bone of contention one lying at the root of all trouble mischief-monger فسادی *fasā'di* ADJ. mischievous tumultous factious N.M. mischief-monger tumultous (person) [A]

فساں *fisāṅ'*, افساں *afsāṅ'*, سنگِ فساں *saṅ'g-e fisaṅ* N.M. whetstone [P]

فسانہ *fasā'nah* N.M. (same as افسانہ N.M. ★)

فسخ *fas'kh* N.M. cancellation (of programme) giving up (of idea) annulment (of marriage, etc.) breaking off فسخ کرنا *fas'kh kar'nā* V.T. cancel annul give up break off [A]

فسردہ *fisūr'dah* ADJ. فسردگی *fisūr'dagī* N.F. (see under افسردہ ADJ. ★)

فسطائی *fastā''ī* N.M. fascist فسطائیت *fastā'iyyat* N.F. fascism [E ~ It]

فسق *fis'q*, فسوق *fūsooq'* N.M. disobedience sinfulness debauchery فسق و فجور *fis'q-o-fūjoor'* N.M. sinfulness and impiety [A]

فسوں *fūsooṅ'*, افسوں *afsooṅ'* N.M. spell incantation sorcery ; black art ; magic فسوں ساز *fūsooṅ'-sāz*, فسوں گر *fūsooṅ'-gar* N.M. ravisher ; enchanter magician ; sorcerer ; charming ; ravishing فسوں سازی *fūsooṅ-sā'zī*, فسوں گری *fūsooṅ'-garī* N.F. enchantment [P]

فش *fish* INT. bosh ; trash [ONO.]

فشار *fashār'* N.M. pressure squeezing *fashā'r-ūd-dam'*, فشارِ خون *fashā'r-e khoon'* N.M. blood pressure [P]

فشاں *fishāṅ'* SUF. diffusing strewing spitting (fire) shedding tears فشانی *fishā'nī* SUF. diffusing strewing spreading shedding [P ~ فشاندن]

فشردہ *fashūr'dah* N.M. juice (of) ADJ. pressed squeezed فشردہ انگور *fashūr'da-e aṅgoor'* N.M. wine [P ~ فشردن]

فصاحت *fasā'hat* N.F. eloquence فصیح *fasīh'* ADJ. ★ [A]

فصاد *fassād'* N.M. (see under فصد N.F. ★)

فصحا *fūsahā'* N.M. (PL. of فصیح ★)

فصد *fas'd* N.F. phlebotomy ; bleeding ; opening a vein فصد کھلوانا *fas'd khūlvā'nā* V.I. have one's vein opened be bled فصد کھولنا (یا لینا) *fas'd khol'nā* (or *le'nā*) V.T. bleed · open a vein فصاد *fassād'* N.N. phlebotomist [A]

فصل *fas'l* N.F. (PL. فصول *fūsool'*) crop harvest produce season section (of book) separation ; segregation فصل استادہ ,استادہ فصل *fas'l-e istā'dah, istā'dah fas'l* N.F. standing crop فصل بہار (یا بہاراں یا بہاری) *fas'l-e bahār'* (or *bahā'rān* or *bahā'rī*) N.F. spring ; spring season · spring-time ; spring-tide فصل خریف *fas'l-e kharīf'* N.F. autumnal harvest فصل ربیع *fas'l-e rabī''* N.F. spring harvest فصل کاٹنا *fas'l kāt'nā* V.T. to cut a crop to harvest فصل گل *fas'l-e gūl* N.F. spring; blossoming season فصلی *fas'lī* ADJ. seasonal pertaining to the harvest فصلی سال *fas'lī sāl* N.M. revenue (as instituted by Emperor Akbar from 1555 A.C.) [A]

فصیح *fasīh'* N.M. & ADJ. eloquent (person) [A ~ فصاحت]

فصیل *fasīl'* N.F. city-wall [A]

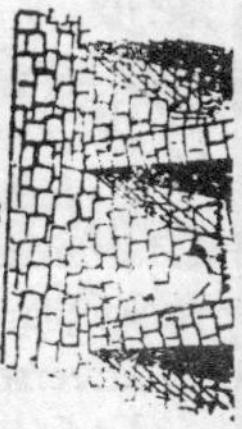

فضا *fazā'* (col. *fizā'*) N.F. atmosphere mental environment bloom (rare) expanse [A]

فضائل *fazā''il* N.M. (PL. of فضیلت N.F. ★)

فضل *faz'l* N.M. (PL. افضال *afzāl'*) excellence grace bounty mercy فضل کرنا *faz'l kar'nā* V.T. be gracious show mercy (پر) فضل ہونا *(par) faz'l ho'nā* V.I. prosper خدا کا فضل *khū'dā kā faz'l* N.M. God's grace (iron.) graft [A]

فضلا *fūzalā'* N.M. (PL. of فاضل ★)

فضلہ *fūz'lah* N.M. (PL. فضلات *fūzlāt'*) excrement ; refuse [A]

فضول *fūzool'* ADJ. useless needless worthless silly (talk, person, etc.) فضول خرچ *fūzool'-khar'ch* ADJ. & N.M. extravagant (person); spendthrift ; prodigal فضول خرچی *fūzool'-khar'chī* N.F. extravagance ; prodigality فضول گو *fūzool'-go* ADJ. & N.M. talkative (person) babbler فضول گوئی *fūzool' go''ī* N.F. babbling silly talk بوالفضول *būl-fūzool'* N.M. babbler uncultured person [A doublet of فضل]

فضہ *fiz'zah* N.F. silver [A]

فضیتا *fazī'tā* N.M. (col.), فضیتی *fazī'tī* N.F. (col.) brawl ignominy [~A FOLL.]

فضیحت *fazī'hat* N.F. infamy ; ignominy disgrace scandal (col.) brawl ; quarrel فضیحت کرنا *fazī'hat kar'nā* V.T. defame disgrace scandalize فضیحت ہونا *fazī'hat ho'nā* V.T. be disgraced be scandalized فضیحتی *fazī'hatī* (col. فضیتی *fazī'tī*) N.F. brawl ignominy [A]

فضیلت *fazī'lat* N.F. (PL. فضائل *fazā''l*) excellence learning preference proficiency , mastery master's degree دستار فضیلت *dastā'r-e fazī'lat* N.F. diploma robe of honour فضیلت رکھنا *fazī'lat rakh'nā* V.I. excel surpass be preferable (to) [A ~ فضل]

فطانت *fitā'nat* N.F. intelligence ; shrewdness wisdom فطین *fatīn'* ADJ. ★ [A]

فطر *fit'r* N.F. breaking a fast صدقۂ فطر *sa'daqa-e fit'r*, فطرانہ *fitrā'nah* N.M., فطرہ *fit'rah* N.M. charity prescribed for Eid-ul-Fitr عیدالفطر *ī'd-ūl-fit'r* N.F. (see under عید N.F. ★) [A]

فطرت *fit'rat* N.F. nature disposition inherent quality فطری *fit'rī* ADJ. natural inherent فطرتی *fit'ratī* ADJ. cunning ; crafty mischievous [A]

فطرہ *fit'rah* N.M. (see under فطر N.F. ★)

فطری *fit'rī* ADJ. (see under فطرت N.F. ★)

فطیر *fatīr'* N.M. unleavened dough فطیری *fatī'rī* ADJ & N.M. unleavened (bread) [A]

فعال *fa''al* N.M. Accomplisher (as an attribute of God) ADJ. active (ingredient) dynamic personality [A ~ فعل]

فعل *fe''l* N.M. (PL. افعال *af'āl'*) verb work ; act ; deed action ; operation (unlawful) sexual intercourse فعل عبث *fe''l-e 'a'bas* N lost labour فعل کرنا *fe''l kar'nā* V.I. do something do ; act فعل لازم *fe''l-e la'zim* N.M. intransitive verb فعل متعدی *fe''l-e mūta'ad'dī* N.M. transitive verb فعل مجہول *fe''l-e majhool'* N.M. a verb in the passive voice فعل معروف *fi''l ma'roof'* N.M. a verb in the active voice فعل ناشائستہ *fe''l-e nā-shā'is'tah* N.M. impropriety فعل ناقص *fe''l-e nā'qis* N.M. a verb of incomplete predication بالفعل *bil-fe''l* CONJ. actually at present فعلاً *fe''lan* ADV. (arch) indeed قولاً و فعلاً *qau'lan va fe''lan* ADV. in word and deed فعلی *fe''lī* (of Holy Prophet's tradition) expounded through action [A]

فغاں *fūghān', fighān'* (rare افغاں *afghān'*) N.M. cry of pain lament; lamentation plaint [P]

فغفور *faghfoor'* N.M. (arch.) emperor (of China sovereign فغفوری *faghfoo'rī* N.F. sovereignty [P]

ففروہونا *fa-fir'roo ho'nā* V.T. flee ; run away [~A ف + فرار]

فق *faq* ADJ. (of colour from face) lost رنگ فق ہو جانا *rang' faq' ho ja'na* V.I. turn pale do so owing to guilty conscience

فقاہت *faqa'hat* N.F juridical acumen [A ~ doublet of فقہ]

فقدان *fūqdān'* (or *fiqdān'*) N.M. lack (of) ; want (of) loss (of) [A]

فقر *faq'r* N.M. poverty ; penury ; indigence mendicancy; mendicity piety فقر و فاقہ *faq'r-o-fā'qah* N.M. poverty and hunger . straitened circumstances فقرا *fūqarā'* N.M. (PL. of ★) [A]

فقرہ *fiq'rah* N.M. (PL. فقرات *fiqarāt'*) sentence : period (rare) passage; paragraph witticism witty remark deception ; glib talk vertebra فقرہ باز *fiq'ra-bāz'* ADJ. & N.M. trickster witty (person) فقرہ بازی *fiq'ra-bā'zī* N.F. deception witticism فقرہ بازی کرنا *fiq'ra-bā'zī kar'nā*, (پر) فقرہ چست کرنا *(par) fiq'ra chūs't kar'nā*, فقرے گھڑنا *fiq're ghaṛ'nā* V.I. indulge in witticisms pass witty remarks (کے) فقروں میں آنا *(ke) fiq'roṅ meṅ ā'nā* V.I. be duped by [A]

فقط *faqat'* N.M. end ; finis ADV. just ; only ; merely [A]

فقہ *fiq'h* (col. *fi'qah*) Islamic law (rare) understanding اصول فقہ *ūsool'l-e fiq'h* N.M. PL. Islamic jurisprudence فقیہ *faqīh'* N.M. (PL. فقہا *fuqahā*) Muslim jurist [A]

فقید *faqīd'* ADJ. missing lost absent فقید المثال *faqī'd-ūl-misāl'* ADJ. unparallelled ; unprecedent [A ~ فقدان]

فقیر *faqīr'* N.M. (PL. فقرا *fūqarā'*) beggar mendicant calendar dervish fakir saint poor man pauper poor ; penniless indigent : penurious فقیرانہ *faqīrā'nah* beggarly poor unpretentions ADV. like a beggar فقیرنی *faqīr'nī* V.I. beggar-maid beggar woman فقیری *faqī'rī* N.F. poverty ; penury ; indigence mendicity begging (as a trade) saintliness ADJ. poor beggarly [A ~ فقر]

فقیہ *faqīh'* N.M. (see under فقہ N.F. ★)

فک *fak* N.M. dropping or omission (of vowel-point) redemption فک اضافت *fak'k-e izā'fat* N.M. omission (of sign of genitive) فک الرہن *fak'-k-ūr-raih'n*. فک رہن *fak'k-e raih'n* N.M. redemption of mortgage [A]

فکاہات *fūkahāt'* N.F. tit bits jokes [A ~ SING. فکاہت]

فکر *fik'r* N.M. (dial. F. PL. افکار *afkār'*) worry ; anxiety thought ; thinking idea imagination فکر کرنا *fik'r kar'nā* V.I. be worried be anxious (about) : be concerned (over) think (upon) provide (for or against) do some .inking bring one's imagination into play for composing (verse) فکرمند *fik'r-mand'* ADJ. worried anxious thoughtful فکرمندی *fik'r-man'dī* N.F. worry anxiety thoughtfulness فکر معاش *fik'r-e ma'ā'sh* N.F. concerned for earning one's livelihood فکر میں رہنا *fik'r meṅ raih'nā* V.T. & I. be worried be thinking of be after [A]

فگار *figār'* ADJ. sore ; wounded ; lacerated SUF. wounded ; lacerated [P]

فلاح *falāḥ'* N.F. success victory prosperity فلاح و بہبود *falā'ḥ-o-behbood'* N.F. welfare and prosperity [A]

فلاح *fallāḥ'* N.M. cultivator ; tiller ; peasant fellah فلاحت *falā'hat* N.F. cultivation [A]

فلاخن *falā'khūn* N.M. sling ; catapult [P]

فلاسفر *filās'far* N.M. philosopher [E]

فلاسفہ *falā'sifah* N.M. (PL. of فلسفی ★)

فلاسفی *filās'fī* N.F. philosophy [E]

فلاکت *falā'kat* N.F. adversity misfortune misery فلاکت زدہ *falā'kat-za'dah* ADJ. unlucky ; unfortnnate miserable ; wretched ADV. in adverse circumstances [A ~ فلک]

فلالین *fa'lālain* N.F. flannel [E]

فلاں *fūlāṅ'* N.M. so-and-so ADJ. such (person or thing) فلان *falān'* N.M. (as swear word) male or female sexual organ فلانا *fūlā'nā* ADJ. & N.M. (F. فلانی *fūlā'nī* so-and so such (person) [A]

فلٹر *fil'ṭar* N.M. filter [E]

فلز *filiz'* N.F. metal فلزات *filizzāt'* N.F. PL. metals فلزاتی *filizzā'tī*. ADJ. metallic (currency) [A]

فلس *fal's*, N.M. (PL. فلوس *fūloos'*) pice scale (of fish) [A]

فلسفہ *fal'safah* N.M. philosophy wisdom 'raison d"etre' فلسفی *fal'safī* N.M. (PL. فلاسفہ *falā'sifah*) philosopher wise man فلسفیانہ *falsafiya'nah* ADJ. philosophical [A ~ G]

فلفل *fil'fil* N.F. pepper [A]

فلک *fa'lak* N.M. (PL. افلاک *aflāk'*) sky ; the heaven ; firmament sphere (of moon, etc.) fate فلک الافلاک *fa'lak-ūl-aflāk'* N.M. the empyrean فلک بوس *fa'lak-bos'* ADJ. sky-high فلک بوس عمارت *fa'lak-bos' 'ima'rat* N.F. very tall structure sky-scrape (کے) فلک کو خبر نہ ہونا *(ke) fa'lak ko kha'bar na ho'nā* V be totally unaware of فلکی *fa'lakī*

ADJ. heavenly celestial [A]

فلم *fil'm* N.M. (dial. F.) film فلمی *fil'mī* ADJ film [E

فلوس *fūloos'* N.M. money (PL. of فلس★) [A]

فلیتہ *falī'tah* N.M wick fuse or match (of (gun) فلیتہ دار *falī'ta-dār* ADJ. matchlock (gun) فلیتہ دینا (یا دکھانا) *falī'tah de'nā* (or *dikkā'nā*) V.T. ignite [~ A فتیلہ CORR.]

فم *fam* N.M. mouth opening orifice فم معدہ *fa'm-e me''dah* N.F. orifice of stomach [A]

فن *fan* N.M. (فنون *fūnoon'*) art skill art (of) craft فنون لطیفہ *fūnoo'n-e latī'fah* N.M. PL. fine arts فنکار *fan'kār* N.M artist فنکارانہ *fan-kārā'nah* ADJ. artistic فنکاری *fan-kā'rī* N.F art فنی *fan'nī* ADJ. teachical [A]

فنا *fanā* N.F. death mortality destruction squandering فنا پذیر *fanā'-pazīr'* ADJ. mortal perishable فنا پذیری *fanā'-pazī'rī* mortality being perishable فنا فی اللہ *fanā' fil'lāh* ADJ. contemplation at one with God dead فنا کرنا *fanā kar'nā* V.T. annihilate فنا ہو جانا *fanā' ho' jā'nā* V.I die perish [A]

فنانس *finans'* N.M finance فنانشل *finān'shal* ADJ. financial [E]

فنجان *finjān'* N.F tea-cup ; cup [A]

فند *fand* N.M trick deceit [P]

فندق *fun'dūq* N.F. filbert ; hazel-nut (fig.) stained finger or toe (of one's sweetheart) [A]

فنڈ *fand* N.M. fund [E]

فنس *fi'nas* N.F (same as پنس N.F. ★)

فنون *fūnoon'* N.M. PL. فنی *fan'nī* ADJ. (see under فن★)

فواحش *favā'hish* N.M. PL. immodesties obvious sins [A ~ SING. فاحشہ]

فواد *fo'ād'* N.M. (PL. افئدہ *af''idah*) heart [A]

فوارہ *favvā'rah* N.M. fountain jet فوارہ چھوٹنا *favvā'rah chhooṭ'nā* V.I. spout (of fountain) play [A ~ فور]

فواکہ *favā'keh* N.M PL. fruits [A ~ SING. فاکہہ]

فوائد *favā''id* N.M. (PL. of فائدہ★)

فوت *faut* N.F. loss (of) omission ADJ. dead lost فوت ہو جانا *faut ho jā'nā* die : pass away be lost فوتی *fau'tī* ADJ. (arch.) dead: deceased فوتی فراری *fau'tī farā'rī* ADJ. (arch.) dead or absconded killed or missing فوتیدگی *fautī'dagī* N.F. ped.) death [A]

فوٹو *fo'ṭo*, فوٹوگراف *fo'ṭo grāf* N.M (photograph) فوٹوگرافر *fo'ṭo-garāfar* N.M photographer فوٹوگرافی *fo'ṭo-garā'fī* N.F. photography [E]

فوج *fauj* N.F. (PL. افواج *afvāj'*) army crowd (of) host (of) فوج بھرتی کرنا *fauj' bhar'tī kar'nā* V.I. levy army فوجدار *fauj'-dār* N.M. (arch.) district military commandant فوجداری *fauj-dā'rī* ADJ. criminal (side, etc.) N.F. criminal criminal case عدالت فوجداری *'adā'lat-e fauj-dā'rī* N.F. criminal court فوج کشی *fauj' ka'shī* N.F. invasion ; inroad ; incursion فوج کشی کرنا *fauj'-ka'shī kar'nā* V.I. march an army (against) attack ; invade بحری فوج *bah'rī fauj* N.F. army فضائی (یا ہوائی) فوج *fazā''ī* (or *havā''ī*) *fauj* N.F. air force فوجی *fau'jī* ADJ military N.M. soldier [A]

فور *faur* N.M. hurry ; haste ; celerity ; agility (only as) فوراً *fau'ran* or فی الفور *fil-faur'* ADV. at once ; immediately ; instantly without delay directly ; straightaway [A]

فوز *fauz* N.F. success victory [A]

فوطہ *fo'tah* N.M (PL.) scrotum testicle (arch.) purse (arch.) treasure فوطہ خانہ *fo'ta-khā'nah* N.M. treasure ; treasury فوطہ دار *fo'ta-dār'* N.M. (arch.) cashier ; treasurer revenue collector فوطہ داری *fo'ta-dā'rī* N.F. (arch.) treasureship revenue collector's office [P]

فوق *fauq* ADV. & PREP above فوق البشر *fau'q-ūl-ba'shar* N.M. superman فوق البھڑک *fau'q-ūl-bha'rak* ADJ. glittering tawdry فوق العادت *fau'q-ūl-'a'dat* ADJ. supernatural unusual ; extraordinary مافوق *ma-fauq'* PREF. above فوقانی *fauqā'nī* ADJ. upper ; superier supra-dotted (letter of the alphabet) فوقیت *fauqiy'yat* N.F. supremacy heremony superiority pre-eminence excellence فوقیت چاہنا *fauqiy'yat chāh'nā* V.T. strive to exbell want to have supremacy فوقیت لیجانا *fauqiy'yat le jā'nā* V.I. excel supercade [A]

فولاد *faulād'* (rare. پولاد *polād'*) N.M steel فولادی *faulā'dī* ADJ. steel strong or iron (man) [P]

فوں *foon'* N.F. hiss (of snake) [ONO.]

فہرست *fehris't* (rare ped. فہرس *fehris*) N.F. list catalogue table (of contents) فہرست مضامین *fehris't-e-mazā'mīn* N.F. contents ; table of contents [A]

فہم *faih'm* (ped. *fah'm*) N.M. understanding perception comprehension sense intelligence فہم و دانش *faih'm-o-dā'nish* N.F intelligence and wisdom فہیم *fahīm'* N.M. & ADJ intelligent (person) [A]

فہمائش *faihmā''ish* N.F. admonition warning (rare) causing to understand فہمائش کرنا *faihmā''ish kar'na* V.T. admonish warn (rare) cause to understand فہمیدہ *faihmī'dah* ADJ. wise intelligent (rare) understood فہمیدگی *faihmī'dagī* N.F. understanding [P ~ A]

فہوالمراد *fa-hūv-al'-mūrād'* that is this is what was meant [A ~ ف + ہو + مراد]

فہیم *fahīm'* N.M. & ADJ. (see under فہم N.M. ★)

فی *fī* PREP. per in ; to ; with ; for ; by N.F. objection ; observation فی البدیہہ *fil-badī'hah* ADJ. impromptu extempore فی الجملہ *fil-jūm'lah* ADV. in all in short فی الحال *fil-ḥal'* ADV. now ; present فی الحقیقت *fil-ḥaqī'qat* ADV. indeed ; in fact فی الواقع *fil-vā'qe'* ADV. in fact فی امان اللہ *fī amā'n-illāh'* PH. good-bye فی زمانہ *fī zamā'nah* (ped. فی زمانا *fī zamā'ninā*) ADV. nowadays ; these days فی سبیل اللہ *fī salī'l-illāh'* PH. in God's way free ; as a charity فی صدی *fī'-sadī* ADV., فی صد *fī'-sad* ADV. per cent ; per hundred فی کس *fī' kas* ADV. per head ; 'per capita' فی مابعد *fī' mā-ba''d* ADV. thereafter فی مابین *fī mā-bain'* ADV. between فی نکالنا *fī nikāl'na* V.I. cavil at فی یوم *fī' yaum'* ADV. per day ; daily per diem [A]

فیاض *fay'yāz'* ADJ. generous ; liberal munificent ; benevolent فیاضی *fayyā'zī* N.F. generosity ; liberality ; munificence benevolence فیاضی کرنا (یا سے کام لینا) *fayyā'zī kar'na* (or *se kām' le'nā*) V.I. be liberal [A ~ فیض]

فیتہ *fī'tah* N.M. ribbon tape lace فیتی *fī'tī* N.F. chevron ; stripe

فیروز *fīroz'* ADJ. vitorious successful فیروزبخت *fīroz'-bakh't*, فیروزمند *firoz'-mand* ADJ. vitorious successful lucky ; fortunate ; prosperous فیروزبختی *firoz'-bakh'tī*, فیروزمندی *firoz'-man'-dī* N.F. success good fortune prosperity

فیروزہ *fīro'zah* N.M. turquoise فیروزی *fīro'zī* ADJ. turquoise blue N.F. (see under فیروز ★)

فیرینی *fīrī'nī* N.F. (same as فرنی N.F. ★)

فیس *fīs* N.F. fee ; fees [E]

فیشن *fai'shan* N.M. fashion فیشن زدہ *fai'shan-za'dah* ADJ. foppish fashion addict فیشن ایبل *faish'-ne'bal* ADJ. fashionable [E]

فیصل *fai'sal* ADJ. decide N.M. final decision (rare) authority ; judge فیصل کرنا *fai'sal kar'nā* V.I. decide settle فیصل ہونا *fai'sal ho'nā* N.M. be decided be settled [A]

فیصلہ *fai'salah*, (col. *fais'lah*) N.M. decision verdict decree settlement decision فیصلہ عدالت *fai'sala-e 'adā'lat* N.M. judicial decision; decree فیصلہ کرنا *fai'sala kar'nā* V. decide settle فیصلہ ہونا *fai'sdla ho'nā* V.I. be decided be settled [A ~ فیصل]

فیض *faiz* N.M. (PL. فیوض *fūyooz'*) favour bounty beneficence good influence فیض پہنچانا *faiz pahūṅchā'na* V.T. do favour (to) فیض رساں *faiz'-rasāṅ'* ADJ. bountiful beneficent فیض رسانی *faiz'-rasā'nī* N.F. beneficence فیض عام *fai'z-e 'ām'* N.M. public good فیضیاب *faiz-yāb'* ADJ. benefited successful فیضیابی *faiz-yā'bī* N.F. being benefited فیضان *faizān'* N.M. favour bounty beneficence good influence [A]

فیکٹری *faik'ṭarī* N.F. factory فیکٹری ایریا *faikṭarī e'riyā* N.M. factory area [E]

فیل *fel* ADJ. failed فیل کرنا *fel' kar'na* V.T. fail (some-one) فیل ہونا *fel' ho'nā* V.I. fail the examination fail امتحان میں فیل ہونا *imteḥān' meṅ fel' ho'nā* V.I. fail the examination [E]

فیل *fail* N.M. (usu. PL.) craftiness ; cunning trickery obstinacy malingering فیل کرنا (یا مچانا) *fail' kar'nā* (or *machā'nā*) V.I. be obstinate feign a state as trick فیلیا *fai'liyā* N.M. trickster

فیل *fīl* N.M. elephant (also فیلہ *fī'lah*) piece of this name at chess فیلبان *fīl'bān'* N.M. elephant driver فیل پا *fīl'-pā* N.M. elephantiasis *fīl'-khā'nah* N.M. elephant house *fīl'-mūr'gh* N.M. turkey [A]

فیلڈ *fīld'* N.M. field فیلڈمارشل *fīl'd-mār'shal* N.M. field-Marshal [E]

فیلسوف *failsoof'* N.M. sophist ADJ. cunning . artful فیلسوفی *failsoo'fī* N.F. sophistry cunning ; artfulness [~ A ~ G]

فیلو *fai'lo* N.N. fellow [E]

فیلہ *fī'lah* N.M. (see under فیل N.M. ★)

فیوض *fūyooz'* N.M. (PL. of فیض)

ق *qaf* twenty-seventh letter of Urdu alphabet (transliterated as *q*); occurring (except rarely) in words of purely Arabic extraction only (according to Jummal reckoning) 100

قاب *qāb* N.F. large plate [P]

قاب ۲ *qāb* N.M. length space ; distance between (only in) قاب قوسین *qā'ba qausain'* N.M just two bow-lengths quite close [A]

قابض qā'biz N.M. possessor occupant possessing holding seizing astingent [A ~ قبض]

قابل qā'bil ADJ. able capable qualified competent worthy deserving worth -able قابل ادائیگی qā'bil-e adā''igī ADJ payable قابل اعتبار qā'bil-e e'tibār' ADJ. trustworthy credible : believeable قابل اعتراض qā'bil-e e'tirāz' ADJ. objectionable قابل انتقال qā'bil-e intiqāl' ADJ. transferable mutable قابل بنانا (یا کرنا) qā'bil banā'nā (or kar'nā) V.T. make competent enable قابل پذیرائی qā'bil-e pazīrā''ī ADJ. admissible قابل تعریف qā'bil-e ta'rīf' ADJ. praiseworthy قابل دست اندازی پولیس qā'bil-e das't-andā'zī-e (pūlis') ADJ. congnizable (offence) قابل سزا qā'bil-e sazā' ADJ. punishable قابل ضمانت qā'bil-e zamā'nat ADJ. bailable قابل غور qā'bil-e ghaur' ADJ. worthy-considering قابل فروخت qā'bil-e farokh't ADJ salable قابل معافی qā'bil-e mo'ā'fī ADJ. pardonable قابل مواخذہ qā'bil-e. mo'ā'khazah ADJ. falling under judicial notice ; culpable قابل وصول qā'bil-e vūsool' ADJ. recoverable قابل ہونا qā'bil ho'nā V.I. be competent be capable (of) ; be able (to) be fit (for) قابلیت qābiliy'yat N.F. ability capability qualification competence capacity accomplishment fitness worth [A]

قابلہ qā'bilah N.F. midwife ADJ. capable (woman) [A]

قابو qā'boo N.M. control hold قابو پانا (یا چلنا) qā'boo pā'nā (or chal'nā) V.T. control bring under control keep (someone) under someone's thumb قابو میں رکھنا qā'boo men rakh'nā V.T. restrain keep under one's control قابو میں کرنا (یا لینا) qā'boo men kar'nā (or le'nā) V.T. bring under one's control subdue restrain قابوچی qāboo'chī N.M. good-for nothing fellow mean person (arch.) door-keeper ; jointer [T]

قاتل qā'til N.M. murderer assassin homicide ADJ. deadly ; fatal ; mortal [A ~ قتل]

قادر qā'dir ADJ. having a command (of) capable (of) able (to) skilful (in) ; skilled (at) N.M. Almighty قادر انداز qā'dir-andāz' AD. sure shot قادر مطلق qā'dir-e mut'laq N.M. omnipotent (as an attribute of God) [A ~ قدرت]

قارورہ qāroo'rah N.M. urine urinal (for medical examination) (arch.) bottle قارورہ ملنا qāroo'rah mil'nā V.I. be in harmony (with) be of the same temperament be thick (with) [A]

قاری qā'rī N.M. (PL. قرا qarrā') reciter of the Holy Quran (PL. قارئین qāre'īn') reader A ~ قراءت]

قاز qāz N.F. goose روغن قاز ملنا rau'ghan-e qāz' mal'nā V.T. coax ; cajole ; wheedle [T]

قازق qā'ziq N.M. Cossack [T]

قاسم qā'sim N.M. distributor allotting official [A]

قاش qāsh N.F. slice piece (of) قاشیں کرنا qā'shen kar'nā V.T. slice cut into pieces [T]

قاصد qā'sid N.M. messenger courier envoy [A ~ قصد]

قاصر qā'sir ADJ. failing (in) deficient (in) unable (to) ; incapable (of) قاصر ہونا qā'sir ho'nā V.I. be deficient (in) be unable (to) ; be incapable (of) [A ~ قصور]

قاضی qā'zī N.M. (PL. قضاۃ qūzāt') judge ; justice magistrate supplier ; purveyor قاضی الحاجات qā'zil-hājāt' N.M. (God as Purveyor of all needs (joc.) money ; pelf قاضی القضاۃ qā'zil-qazāt' N.M. Chief Justice [A ~ قضا]

قاطبۃً qā'tibatan ADV. entirely [A]

قاطع qā'te' ADJ. cutting definite decisive rebutting incontrovertible ; irrefutable conclusive برہان قاطع burhā'n-e qā'te' N.F. incontrovertible argument rebuttal [A ~ قطع]

قاعدہ qā''idah N.M. rule regulation maxim formula system established order base (of geometrical figure) (rare) foundation plinth primer قاعدہ باندھنا qā''idah bāndh'nā V.T. establish a rule قاعدہ بنانا qā''idah banā'nā V.T. frame a rule [A]

قاف qāf N.M. name of letter Caucasus (usu. کوہ قاف ko'h-e qāf', col. koh' qāf') Caucasus as legendary abode of fairies قاف (سے) تا قاف qāf' (se) tā qāf' N M. the whole world ADV. all over the world [A ~ T]

قافلہ qā'filah N.M. caravan قافلہ سالار qā'fila-sālār', سالار قافلہ salā'r-e qā'filah N.M. leader of the caravan [A]

قافیہ qā'fiyah N.M. (PL. قوافی qavā'fī) rhyme قافیہ بندی (یا پیمائی) qā'fiyah-ban'dī (or paima''ī) N.F. rhyming writing doggerel verse قافیہ بندی (یا پیمائی) کرنا qā'fiya-ban'dī (or -pamā''ī) kar'nā V.I. versify compose doggerel verse قافیہ تنگ کرنا qā'fiyah tan'g kar'nā V.T. reduce to straits drive to the wall قافیہ تنگ ہونا qā'fiyah tang' ho'nā V.I. be hard pressed be driven to the wall قافیہ ملانا qā'fiyah milā'nā V.T. find a rhyme (for)

قاق qāq ADJ. lean ; gaunt N.M. dried meat [A]

قاقم qā'qum N.M. ermine [A]

قاقلہ *qā'qulah* N.M. large cardamom [P]

قال *qāl* N.M theoretical knowledge lacking intimacy of experience قیل وقال *qī'l-o-qāl'* N.F. alteration quibbling [A]

قالب *qā'lab* N.M. mould frame (shoemaker's) last centering (of structure) body قالب بدلنا *qā'lab badal'nā* V.I. be metamorphosed قالب خالی کرنا *qā'lab khā'lī kar'nā* V.I die ; give up the ghost یک جان دو قالب *yak' jān' do qā'lab* PH. hand in glove (with) [A]

قالین *qā'līn* N.M. carpet ; woollen carpet قالیچہ *qālī'chah*, غالیچہ *ghālī'chah* N.M. (arch.) small carpet [A]

قامت *qā'mat* N.F. stature قدّ وقامت *qad'(d)-o-qā'mat* N.M. build and stature دراز قامت *darāz qā'mat*, طویل القامت *tavīl-ūl-qā'mat* ADJ. tall [A]

قاموس *qāmoos'* N.M. dictionary (arch.) ocean [A]

قانت *qā'nit* ADJ. & N.M. (PL. قانتین *qānitīn'* ; F. قانتہ *qā'nitah* F. PL. قانتات *qānitāt'*) obedient to God [A ~ قنوت]

قانع *qā'ne'* ADJ. content ; contented [A ~ قناعت]

قانون *qānoon'* N.M. law act statute ordinance (arch.) dulcimer name of Avicenna's treatice; 'canon' قانون بنانا *qānoon' banā'nā* V.T. legislate قانون پر چلنا *qānoon' par chal'nā* V.I. act according to the law قانونچہ *qānoon'chah* N.M. name of medical treatise ; 'Canon's Digest' قانون چھانٹنا *qānoon' chhānṭ'nā* V.T. (iron pettifog قانون دان *qānoon'-dān'* N.M. lawyer jurist قانون دانی *qānoon'-dā'nī* N.F. legal acumen juridical knowledge قانونِ دیوانی *qānoo'n-e dīvā'nī*, دیوانی قانون *dīvā'nī qānoon'* N.M. civil law قانونِ فوجداری *qānoo'n-e fauj-dā'rī*, فوجداری قانون *fauj-dā'rī qānoon'* N.M. criminal law قانونگو *qānoon'-go* (col. *qā'noon-go*) N.M. petty revenue official of second last rank ; Qanoongo قانوناً *qānoo'nan* ADV. by law ; according to law under the rules قانونی *qānoo'nī* ADJ. legal statuary lawful legitimate قانونیا *qānoo'niyā* N.M. (iron.) pettifogger litigous person [A]

قاہر *qā'hir* ADJ. subduing قاہرہ *qā'hirah* N.M. Cairo ADJ. (F. OF PL.) subduing [A ~ قہر]

قائد *qā'id* N.M. leader (arch.) (rare) commander قائدِ اعظم *qā''id-e a'zam* the Great Leader (as the title of the founder of Pakistan, the late Muhammad Ali Jinnah) ; the Quaid-e-Azam قائدِ ملت *qā''id-e mil'lat* N.M. the Nation's leader (as the title of the Quaid-i-Azam's chief lieutenant, the late Liaqat Ali Khan) ; the Quaid-i-Millat [A ~ قیادت]

قائل *qā''il* ADJ. convinced (one) conceding point N.M. speaker another (of a saying) قائل کرنا *qā''il kar'nā*, قائل معقول کرنا *qā''il ma'qool' kar'nā* V.T. convince bring (someone) round to one's viewpoint confute (someone) قائل ہونا *qā''il ho'nā* V.I. be convinced acknowledge admit [A ~ قول]

قائم *qā''im* ADJ. firm constant unwavering standing established N.M. draw (at chess) قائم بالذات *qā''im-biz zāt'* ADJ. independent not depending on others for its existence قائم بالغیر *qā''im-bil-ghair'* ADJ. dependent , depending on others for its existence قائم رہنا *qā''im raih'nā* V.I. stick (to) stand firm keep one's footing قائم کرنا *qā''im kar'nā* V.T. set up ; establish قائم مزاج *qā''im-mizaj* ADJ. resolute unwavering قائم مقام *qā''im maqām'* ADJ. officiating N.M. viceroy vicegerent successor قائم مقام ہونا *qā''im-maqām' ho'nā* V.I. officiate قائم مقامی *qā''im-maqā'mī* N.F. officiating period of officiating قائم ہونا *qā''im ho'nā* V.I. be set up ; be established be firm stand (on) stand firmly قائمہ *qā''imah* N.M. perpendicular right angle ADJ. right (angle) قائمی *qā''imī* N.F. firmness durability existence بقائمی ہوش وحواس *ba-qā''imī-e ho'sh-o havās'* ADJ.. while in one's senses deliberately thoughtfully [A ~ قیام]

قبا *qabā'* N.F. tunic ; jacket quilted coat ADJ. torn ; tattered [A]

قباحت *qabā'hat* N.F. harm ; wrong defect قباحت لازم آنا *qabā'hat lā'zim ā'nā* V.I. (of harm lie [A ~ قبح]

قبالہ *qabā'lah* N.M. title deed sale-deed of real estate such certificate قبالہ لکھوانا (یا لینا) *qabā'lah likhvā'nā* (or *le'nā*) V.T. & I. become property owner get a title deed come into possession (of a property) قبالہ نویس *qābā'la-navīs'* N.M. deed writer [~A ~ قبل]

قبائح *qabā''ḥ* N.M. PL. evils bad habits ignoble traits of character [A ~ SING. قبیحہ]

قبائل *qabā''il* N.M. PL. tribes قبائلی *qabā''ilī* ADJ. tribal N.M. tribesman ; tribal قبائلی علاقہ *qabā''ilī 'ilā'qah* N.M. tribal area قبائلی نظام *qabā''ilī nizām'* N.M. tribal system [A ~ SING. قبیلہ ~ قبح]

قبح *qūb''eḥ* N.M. (PL. قبائح *babā''eḥ*) evil bad habit deformity ugliness حسن وقبح *ḥus'n-o qūb'ḥ* N.M. good and bad points (of) beauty and ugliness beauty and the beast [A]

قبر *qab'r* N.F. (PL. قبور *qūboor'*) grave tomb قبر بنانا (یا کھودنا) *qab'rbanā'nā* (or *khod'nā*) V.I. dig a grave

آنا (یا) قبر میں سے نکل کر from a very serious illness قبر میں پاؤں لٹکائے بیٹھنا qab'r meṅ pā''oṅ laṭkā''e baiṭh'nā V.I. have one foot in the grave قبرستان qabris'tān N.M. graveyard ; burial ground ; cemetry [A]

قبض qab'z N.M. constipation ; costiveness seizure (of soul) قبض الوصول qab'z-ūl-vūsool' N.M. acquittance roll قبض کرنا qab'z kar'nā V.T. constipate روح قبض کرنا rooḥ' qab'z kar'nā V.I. seize the soul (of) ; cause death (to) [A]

قبضہ qab'zah N.M. possession holding occupancy handle hilt hinge قبضہ اٹھانا qab'zah ūṭhā'nā V.T. dispossess قبضہ بحال کرنا qab'zah ba-ḥāl' kar'nā N.M. reinstate قبضہ پانا (یا لینا یا حاصل کرنا) qab'zah pā'nā (or le'nā or ḥā'sil kar'nā) V.T. obtain legal possession (of) قبضہ جمانا (یا کرنا) qab'zah jamā'nā (or kar'nā) V.T. take possession (of) grab قبضہ رکھنا qab'zah rakh'nā V.T. keep in possession hold fast قبضہ مخالفانہ qab'za-e mūkhālifā'nah N.M. adverse possession قبضے پر ہاتھ ڈالنا qab'ze par hāth ḍāl'nā V.T. be ready to draw the sword قبضے میں کرنا qab'ze meṅ kar'nā V.T. get hold of have a firm grasp (of) A ~ قبض]

قبل qab'l ADV. previous (to) ; before سے قبل se qab'l ADV. before قبل ازیں qab'l az-īṅ' قبل اس کے کہ qab'l is ke (keh) ADV. before (this) ما قبل mā qab'l ADJ. preceding ما قبل آخر mā qab'l-e ā'khir ADJ. second last , last but one ; penultimate [A]

قبلہ qib'lah N.M. 'qiblah' ; direction in which Muslims turn in prayer the Holy Ka'aba venerable person title of respect for elder ; etc. قبلہ حاجات qib'la-e ḥājāt' N.M. the centre of (one's) hopes قبلہ رو qib'la-roo ADJ. facing the Holy Ka'aba قبلہ عالم qib'la-e 'ā'lam INT. (fig.) your (of his) majesty قبلہ کونین qib'la-e kaunain' N.F. (fig.) father قبلہ گاہ qib'la-gāh' N.M. (fig.) father superior قبلہ نما qib'la-nūmā' N.M. compass ; mariner's compass قبلہ و کعبہ qib'la-o-ka''bah ADJ. & N.M. venerable (person INT. respected sir [A]

قبور qūboor' N.F. (PL. of قبر N.F. ★)

قبول qabool' N.M. acceptance consent ; concurrence (public) recognition قبول صورت qabool'-soo'rat ADJ. good looking handsome ; comely قبول عام qaboo'le-'ām' N.M. قبولیت عامہ qabooliy'yat-e 'ām'mah N.F. popularity public recognition قبول کرنا qabool' kar'nā V.T. accept قبولنا qabool'nā V.T. (col.) aceept confess قبول ہونا qabool' ho'nā V.I. be acceptable be accepted قبولی qaboo'lī N.F. rice boiled with whole gram قبولیت qabooliy'yat N.F. acceptance (public) recognition

(old use) written agreement [A]

قبہ qūb'bah N.M dome cupola (fig. (tomb (rare) alcove[A]

قبیح qabīḥ' ADJ. (F. قبیحہ qabī'ḥah PL. قبائح qabā''iḥ) ugly deformed vile ; base [A ~ قبح]

قبیل qabīl' N.M. kind ; sort type ; category اسی قبیل کا is'ī qabīl' kā PH. of the same sort ; similar [A ~ قبلی]

قبیلہ qabī'lah N.M (PL. قبائل qabā''il) tribe clan

قتال qitāl' N.M. قتالہ qattā'lah N F. (see under قتل N.M. ★)

قتل qat'l N.M. murder ; assassination killing slaughter execution قتل عام qat'l-e 'ām N.M. massacre قتل عمد qat'l-e 'am'd N.M wilful murder , homicide قتل کرنا qat'l kar'nā V T. kill murder ; slay قتل گاہ qat'l-gāh N.F place of execution قتل ہونا qāt'l ho'nā V.I. be killed ; be murdered قتال qitāl' N.M. fight battle قتالہ qattā'lah N.F ravishing beauty قتیل qatīl' ADJ killed ; murdered N.M. victim [A]

قتلہ qat'lah N.M. cutlet slice piece]~ A PREC.]

قحبہ qaḥ'bah N.F prostitute ; whore [A]

قحط qaiḥ't (ped qaḥ't) N.M. famine drought leck (of) , dearth of ; scarcity (of) قحط الرجال qaḥ't-ūr-rijāl' N.M. dearth of the right قحط پڑنا qaiḥ't par'nā V.I. (of area) (of famine) be (of erea) be struck with famine be in short supply be very dear قحط زدہ qaiḥ't-za'dah ADJ. famine-stricken قحط سالی qaiḥ't-sā'lī N.F. famine drought crop-failure [A]

قد qad N.M. stature height قد آدم qad'd-e ā'dam ADJ. of man's stature , as tall as a man قد آور qad'-ā'var ADJ. tall , of a commanding stature قد نکالنا qad nikāl'nā V.I. (of child, etc) grow tall قد و قامت qad'd-o-qā'mat N.M. personal appearance stature build (of person) [A]

قدامت qadā'mat N.F. oldness ancientness antiquity priority قدامت پرست qadā'mat-paras't ADJ. conservative traditionalist قدامت پرستی qadā'mat-paras'tī conservatism traditionalism قدامت پسند qadā'mat-pasand' ADJ. conservative dichard old fashioned قدامت پسندی qadā'mat pasan'dī N.F. conservatism being old fashioned [A]

قدح qa'daḥ N.M. large cup ; bowl wine cup (rare) empty glass قدح کش qa'daḥ-kash, قدح خوار qa'daḥ-khar, قدح نوش qa'daḥ-nosh N.M. & ADJ drunkard اپنے قدح کی خیر منانا ap'ne qa'daḥ kī khair' manā'nā V.I.

be motivated by self-interest ردّ قدح rad'd-e qa'daḥ N.M. refusal to drink [A]

قدح qad'ḥ N.F. قدح کرنا qad'ḥ kar'nā V.T. cavil at criticize ردّ و قدح rad'd-o-qad'ḥ N.M. heated argument [A]

قدر qad'r (rare qa'dar) N.F. (PL. اقدار aqdār') respect ; honour worth value brilliance (of star) قدردان qad'r-dān' (or qa'dar-) ADJ. & N.M. patron one knowing the worth (of) true judge one giving due appreciation قدردانی qad'r-dā'nī N.F. patronage true due regard (to) قدرشناس qad'r-shinās ADJ. & N.M. (one) knowing the worth (of) (one) showing due regard (to) true judge قدرشناسی qad'r-shinā'sī N.F. appreciation patronge قدر کھو دیتا ہے ہر روز کا آنا جانا qad'r kho de'tā hai har roz kā ā'nā jā'nā PROV. too much familiarity breeds contempt قدرِ مشترک qad'r-e mush'tarak N.F. common value قدر و منزلت qad'r-o-man'zilat N.F. respect ; honour بے قدر be-qad'r ADJ. debased بے قدری be-qad'rī, ناقدری nā-qad'rī N.F lack of appreciation بیش قدری besh-qad'rī N.F. appreciation (of money) کم قدر kam-qad'r ADJ. depreciated (money) not greatly respected کم قدری kam-qad'rī N.F. depreciation (of money) being unhonoured [A]

قدر qa'dar (rare. qad'r) N.F. lot divine decree quantity قدر انداز qa'dar-andāz N.M. marksman اس قدر is' qa'dar ADV. so much this much کس قدر kis' qa'dar CONJ. how much [A doublet of PREC.]

قدرت qud'rat N.F. nature universe divine power , omnipotence ability or power (to do) command (of language, etc.) قدرت رکھنا (یا ہونا) qud'rat rakh'nā (or ho'nā) V.T. be able (to) wield power (over) have command (of قدرتی qud'ratī ADJ. natural قدرتی اسباب qud'ratī asbāb' N.M. natural causes of God قدرتی وسائل qud'ratī vasā''il N.F. natural resources [A]

قدرے qad're ADV. a little somewhat [A ~ قدر]

قدس qud's, (or qu'dūs) N.M. sanctity ; holiness Jerusalem Gabriel قدسی qud'sī ADJ. (F. or PL. قدسیہ qud'siyah, (ped. qudsiy'yah) holy heavenly ; celestial N.M. (PL. قدسیاں qud'siyān) angle holy person قدسی الاصل qudsī-ul asl ADJ. heaven-born ; celestial نفوس قدسیہ nufoos-e qudsiy'yah N.M. PL. sacred persons [A]

قدغن qad'ghan N.F. ban ; prohibition ; forbidding (rare) urging قدغن کرنا (یا لگانا) qad'ghan kar'nā (or laga'nā) V.T. forbid ; prohibit (rare) urge [T]

قدم qa'dam N.M. (PL. اقدام aqdām') foot footstep ; step pace step ; measure قدم اٹھا کر چلنا qa'dam uṭhā' kar chal'nā V I. walk fast قدم اٹھانا qa'dam uṭhā'nā V I. make a move take a step go ahead (with) قدم اٹھنا qa'dam uṭh'nā V.I walk move قدم اکھڑنا qa'dam u'kharnā V I. (of army) retreat be no longer able to take a firm stand قدم بڑھانا (یا آگے رکھنا) qa'dam baṛhā'nā (or ā'ge rakh'nā) step forward overstep the limits قدم بقدم چلنا qa'dam ba-qa'dam chal'nā V.I. walk along side follow in (someone's) footsteps قدم بوس qa'dam-bos ADJ. doing obeisance showing respect قدم بوس ہونا qa'dam-bos ho'nā V.I. show respect قدم بوسی qa'dam-bo'sī N.F, obeisance respect ; homage قدم بوسی کرنا qa'dam-bo'sī kar'na V.T. show (کے) قدم بھاری ہونا (ke) qa'dam bhā'rī ho'nā V.I. be ominous قدم پھونک پھونک کر رکھنا qa'dam phoonk phoonk kar rakh'nā V.I. move very cautiously قدم چومنا qa'dam choom'nā, قدم چھونا qa'dam chhoo'nā, قدم کو ہاتھ لگانا qa'dam ko hāth' lagā'nā V.T. show great respect frostrate oneself (before) قدم رنجہ فرمانا (یا کرنا) qa'dam ran'jah farmā'nā (or kar'nā) take the trouble of coming قدم قدم qa'dam qa'dam ADV. ambling slowly قدم قدم پر qa'dam qa'dam par ADV. at every step قدم قدم جانا (یا چلنا) qa'dam qa'dam jā'nā (or chal'nā) V.I. amble move slowly (کا) قدم درمیان ہونا (kā) qa'dam darmiyān' ho'nā (of someone) have to do with قدم دھرنا (یا رکھنا) qa'dam dhar'nā (or rakh'nā) enter step on meddle (with) قدم لینا qa'dam le'nā V. acknowledge the superiority (of) ; show respect (to) ; keep pace قدم مارنا qa'dam mār'na V I. move a pace endeavour قدم نکالنا qa'dam nikāl'na V.I. train (horse) قدموں سے لگنا qad'mon se lag'na V.I. live under the tutelage of سبز قدم sab'z-qa'dam ADJ. inauspicious [A]

قدم qi'dam N.M. antiquity ; oldness [A]

قدما qudamā' N.M. PL. the ancients [A ~ SING. قدیم]

قدمچہ qa'damchah N.M. footboard seat on native commode ; footrest in latrine [~ P ~ A]

قدوس quddoos' ADJ. Holy (as attribute of God) [A ~ قدس]

قدوم qudoom' N.M. arrival approach قدوم میمنت لزوم qudoo'm-e mai'manat-luzoom' PH. (polite word for) coming auspicious arrival (of) [A ~ قدم]

قدوہ qud'vah (or qad'- or qid'-) V.I. model exemplar [A]

قدیر qadīr' ADJ. powerful (as an attribute of God) [A ~ قدرت]

قدیم *qadīm'*, (col. قدیمی *qadī'mī*) ADJ. old ; ancient former bygone antiquated outmoded [~ A قدم]

قرابادین *qarā'badīn* N.F. pharmacopoeia ; materia medica [A]

قرابت *qarā'bat* N.F. relationship ; kinship قرابتدار *qarā'bat'-dār* N.M. relation ; relative ; kinship قرابتداری *qarā'bat-dā'rī* N.F. relationship ; kinship قرابتی *qarā'batī* N.M. relation ; relative ADJ. related (to) ; akin (to) [A ~ قرب]

قرابہ *qarā'bah* N.M. flagon decanter [A]

قرابین *qarābīn'* N.F. carbine [T]

قرار *qarār'* N.M. rest tranquillity consistency stability firmness agreement قرار آنا *qarār' ā'nā* V.I. be no longer restless be set at rest قرار پانا *qarār' pā'nā* V.I. be resolved be agreed upon be decided be setted be established be set at rest (of sperm) settle in ovary قرارداد *qarār'-dād* N.F. resolution قرارداد پیش ہونا *qarār'-dād pesh ho'nā* V.I. (of resolution) be moved قرارداد مسترد ہونا *qarār-dād mūs'tarad ho'nā* V.I. of resolution) be rejected قرارداد مقاصد *qarār'dād-e maqā'sid* N.F. objectives resolution قرارداد منظور ہونا *qarār'-dād manzoor' ho'nā* V.I. (of resolution) be passed ; be carried قرار دینا *qarār' de'nā* V.T. fix settle قرار واقعی *qarār-e vā'qe'ī* ADV. truly positively fully rightly [A]

قراضہ *qūrā'zah* N.M. paring [A]

قراقر *qarā'qar* N.M. grumbling (of bowels) [~ A]

قرآن *qur'ān* N.M. Scriptures , the Holy Quran (rare) reader , reading-text قرآن اٹھانا *qur'ān ūṭhā'nā*, قرآن پر ہاتھ رکھنا *qur'ān' par hath rakh'nā* V.I. swear by the Holy Book قرآن شریف *qūr'ān sharīf*, قرآن کریم (یا) مجید *qūr''an-e karīm'* (or *-majīd'*) N.M. the Holy Quran قرآن ٹھنڈا کرنا *qūr'an thah'ḍa kar'nā* V.T. bury or sink tattered leaves of the Holy Quran قرآن درمیان ہونا *qūr'ān' dar'miyān' ho'nā* V.I. say while swearing by the Holy Quran قرآن کا جامہ پہننا (یا پہن کر آنا) *qūr'ān' kā ja'mah pai'han'nā* (or *pai'han kar ā'nā*) V.T swear by the Holy Book قرآن کا ہدیہ *qūr'ān' kā hadyah* N.M. (euph. for) price of a copy of the Holy Quran قرآن کی مار *qūr'ān' kī mār* N.F. & INT. curse by the Holy Book قرآن ہدیہ کرنا *qūr'ān' had'yah kar'nā* V.T. (euph. for) sell a copy of the Holy Quran (to) [A ~ قراءت]

قران *qirān'* N.M. conjunction (of planets) performance of Haj and out-of-season pilgrimage in same trip قران السعدین *qirā'n-ūs-sa'dain'* N.M. conjunction of two suspicious planets, VIZ., Jupiter and Venus meeting of two big personalities [A]

قراول *qarā'vūl* N.M. picket scout ; advanced guard (of army) gun man (fig.)-avant-guard [A]

قراءت *qirā'at* (preferably to be written as قرائت (col. but incorrect قرأت *qir''at*) N.F. recitation of the Holy Quran (col.) its musical recitation recension قاری N.M. ☆ [A]

قرہ *qūr'rat* N.F. coldness (used only in) قرۃ العین *qūr'rat-ūl-'ain'* N.F. comfort for eyes (fig.) cherished child [A]

قرائن *qarā''in* N.M. PL. circumstantial evidence conjectures; presumptions [A ~ SING. قرینہ]

قرب *qūr'b* N.M. nearness proximity propinquity (fig.) trust ; confidence قرب وجوار *qūr'b-o-javār'* N.M. vicinity environs قرب (کا) حاصل کرنا (*kā*) *qūr'b ḥā'sil kar'nā* V.T. gain the confidence (of) (کا) قرب حاصل ہونا (*kā*) *qūr'b ḥā'sil ho'nā* V.I. be very close to [A]

قربان *qūrbān'* N.M. offering INT. may I be a sacrifice for you etc. قربانگاہ *qūrbān'-gāh* (or *ḥān-gāh'*) N.F. alter قربان جانا *qūrbān' jā'nā* V.T. express love (for) lay down one's life (for) قربان کرنا *qūrbān' kar'nā* V.T. sacrifice (something for) قربان ہونا *qūrbān' ho'nā* V.I. be sacrificed (for) lay down one's life. (for) قربانی *qūrba'nī* N.F. sacrifice قربانی کا بکرا *qūrba'nī kā bak'rā* N.M. scapegoat قربانی کرنا *qūrba'nī kar'nā* V.T. sacrifice (animal) ; offer victim

قربت *qūr'bat* (ped. *qū'rūbat*) N.F. nearness relationship intercourse [A ~ قریب]

قربیٰ *qūr'bā* N.F. kinship ذوی القربیٰ *zavi-l'-qūr'bā* N.M. relations [A ~ قرب]

قرحہ *qar'ḥah* N.M. sore ; ulcer [A]

قریشی *qū'rashī* (col. *qar'shī* or قریشی *qurai'shī*) N.M. (descendant of) a member of the Prophet's tribe Quraish [A]

قرص *qūr's* N.M. (PL. قرص *qā'ras*, اقراص *aqrās*) tablet (rare) disc [A]

قرض *qar'z*, قرضہ *qar'zah* N.M. debt ; loan ; credit قرض اٹھانا (یا لینا) *qar'z ūṭhā'nā* (or *le'nā*) V.T. & I. borrow ; take a loan قرض ادا کرنا *qar'z adā kar'nā*, قرض چکانا *qar'z chūkā'nā* V.T. & O. pay off or repay a debt قرض حسنہ *qar'z-e ḥa'sanah* N.M. loan without interest قرضخواہ *qar'z-khāh* N.M. lender creditor قرضدار *qar'z-dār* N.M. borrower debtor ; one in debt قرضدار ہر جگہ سے پتھر کھاتا ہے qar'z-dār har ja'gah se pat'thar khā'tā hai PROV. a person in debt is rebuked by everybody قرض دہندہ qar'z-dehin'dah N.M. lender قومی قرضہ qau'mī qar'zah N.M. national debt [A]

قرطاجنہ qartā'jinah N.M. Carthage [A]

قرطاس qirtās' N.M. (PL. قراطیس qarātīs') (rare) paper قرطاس ابیض qirtā's-e ab'yaz N.M. white paper ; (British) government report (in some issue) [A]

قرعہ qūr''ah N.M. lot die anything used for drawing lots lottery raffle قرعہ اندازی qur''a-andā'zī N.F. drawing of lots lottery raffle قرعہ ڈالنا، قرعہ اندازی کرنا qur''a-andā'zī kar'nā, qur''ah ḍāl'nā V.T. (of lot) come to or fall upon (someone) [A]

قرق qūr'q ADJ. forfeited ; confiscated attached ; distrained contrehand (rare) seizure ; attachment embargo guard for attached properly قرق امین qūr'q amīn' N.M. bailiff قرقی qūr'qī N.F. forfeiture ; confication seizure ; attachment ; distraint قرقی بٹھانا qūr'qī biṭhā'nā V.T. & O. place a guard on attached property قرقی کا پروانہ qūr'qī kā parvā'nah N.M. warrant of attachment قرق کرنا، کی قرقی ہونا qūr'q kar'nā kī qūr'qī kar'nā V.T. seize attach ; distrain قرق ہونا qūr'q ho'nā, کی قرقی ہونا kī qūr'qī ho'nā V.I. be seized be attached ; be distrained [T]

قرمز qir'miz N.M. (rare) crimson قرمزی qir'mizī ADJ. crimson قرمزی رنگ qir'mizī rang N.M. crimson colour ; crimson

قرمساق qū'rumsāq N.M. cuckold [T]

قرن qar'n N.M. (PL. قرون qūroon') age ; epoch century period of thirty-eight years (rare) horn (rare) chief ; important personality [A]

قرنا qar'nā N.F. clarion horn قرنا پھنکنا qar'nā phu.nk'na V.I. (of horn) be belown قرنا پھونکنا qar'nā phoonk'na V.T. & O. sound the clarion [P]

قرنبیق qaranbīq' N.M. alembic ; retort still [A]

قرنفل qaran'fal N.M. clove [A ~ S]

قرنطینہ qarantī'nah N.M. quarantine [E]

قرولی qarau'lī N.F. hunting knife [T]

قرون qūroon' N.F. PL. ages ; epochs centures قرون اولی qūroo'n-e oo'lā N.F. PL. the earlier ages (of Islam) قرون خالیہ (یا ماضیہ) qūroo'n-e khā'liyah (or mā'ẓiyah) N.F. PL past centuries earlier times قرون مظلمہ qūroo'n-e muz'limah N.F. PL. (Europe's) Dark Ages قرون وسطی qūroo'n-e vūs'tā N.F. PL. (Europe's) Middle Ages ; Mediaeval times [A ~ SING. قرن]

قرات qir''at N.F. (usual but wrong spelling of قراءت ★)

قریب qarīb' ADJ. near neighbouring ADV. near about almost قریب الاختتام qarī'b-ul-ikhtitām' ADV. nearing the end قریب الفہم qarī'b-ul-faih'm ADJ. easy to understand قریب المرگ qarī'b-ul-marg' (ped. قریب مرگ qarī'b-e marg') ADJ. on the point of death قریب قریب qarīb' qarīb' (col. qarī'-ban) ADV almost about nearly; approximately عنقریب an-qarīb' ADV. shortly soon soon enough [A ~ قرب]

قریشی qūrai'shī ADJ. (same as قرشی ADJ. ★)

قریشیا qure'shiyā, کروشیا karo'shiyā N.M. crochet قریشیے کا کام qure'shiye kā kām N.M. crochet work [E]

قرین qarīn' (or -rin) ADJ. akin (to) closely connected with N.M. friend قرین قیاس qarī'n-e qiyās' ADJ. possible conceiveable credible قرین قیاس ہونا qarī'n-e qiyās' ho'nā V.I. be credible be possible قرین مصلحت qarī'n-e mas'lahat ADJ. expedient advisable [A]

قرینہ qarī'nah N.M. likelihood context order ; arrangement ; system style ; mode قرینے سے رکھنا (یا لگانا) qarī'ne se rakh'nā (or lagā'nā) V.T. put (things) in order ; to arrange ; tidy up قرینے سے کرنا qarī'ne se kar'na V.T. do (something) methodically [A ~ قرن]

قریہ qar'yah N.M. (PL. قری qurā') village town

قزاق qazzāq' N.M. robber footpad highaway (rare) cossach قزاق اجل qazzā'q-e a'jal N.M. (fig.) the angel of death بحری قزاق baih'rī qazzāq N.M. pirate ; freebooter قزاقی qazzā'qī N.F. robbery free-booting [T]

قزح qūzah'. N.M. PL. multi-coloured stripes N.M. (Myth.) name of deity controlling the clouds قوس قزح qau's-e qūzah' (or qau's-o-) N.M. rainbow ; spectrum [A]

قزلباش qi'zil-bāsh' N.M. (arch.) Red-cap (as a knight of Persian Safavid army) descendent of Red-caps Shi'ite knight-errant of Persian extraction [T ~ قزل red]

قسام qassām' N.M. apportioner قسام ازل qassā'm-e a'zal N.M. (God as) Eternal Apportioner [A ~ قسمت]

قساوت qasā'vat N.F. hard-heartedness ; callousness - cruelty قساوت قلب (یا قلبی) qasā'vat-e qal'b (or qal'bī) N.F. hardheartedness ; callousness [A]

قسائی qasā''ī N.M. (F. قسائن qasā''in) (same as قصائی N.M. ★)

قسط *qis't* N.F. (PL. اقساط *aqsāt'*) instalment (rare) justice قسط باندھنا *qist' bāndh'nā* V.I. settle payment by instalments قسط بندی *qis't-ban'dī* N.F. settling payment by instalment قسط دینا (یا ادا کرنا) *qis't de'nā* (or *adā' kar'nā*) V.T. & I. pay the instalment قسط کرنا *qist' kar'nā* V.T. agree to pay by instalments قسط وار *qis't-vār* ADJ. & ADV. by instalments [A]

قسطاس *qistās'* N.F. balance قسطاس مستقیم *qistā's-e mūstaqīm'* N.M. reliable balance [A]

قسم *qa'sam* N.M. (PL. اقسام *aqsām'*) oath قسم توڑنا *qa'sam tor'nā* V.T. & O. perjure oneself violate an oath abjure ; renounce an oath قسم تو کھانے ہی کے لیے ہوتی ہے *qa'sam to khā'ne hī ke liye ho'tī hai* PROV. promises, like piece crusts are made to be broken قسم دینا *qa'sam de'nā* V.T. administer an oath (to) put (someone) under an oath قسم دلانا (یا کھلانا) *qa'sam dilā'nā* (or *khilā'nā*) V.T. make (someone) swear قسم کھانا *qa'sam khā'nā* V.T. & O. swear ; take an oath قسم لینا (یا لے لینا) *qa'sam le'nā* (or *le le'nā*) V.T. administer an oath (to) put (someone) under an oath قسما قسمی *qas'mā qas'mī* N.F. swearing on both sides قسمیہ *qasamiy'yah* (col. *qasmiy'yah*) ADV. on oath [A]

قسم *qis'm* N.F. kind ; sort ; type division class ; category grade species nature part ; portion قسم وار *qis'm-vār* ADJ. classified categorized graded ADV. according to grade or quality [A]

قسمت *qis'mat* N.F. luck ; fortune fate ; destiny lot ; portion apportioning (Math.) divsion (administrative) division (departmental) section قسمت آزمائی *qis'mat-azmā'ī* N.F. trying one's luck قسمت آزمائی کرنا *qis'mat-azmā'ī kar'nā* V.I. try one's luck قسمت الٹ (یا پلٹ یا پھر) جانا *qis'mat ū'lat* (or *pa'lat* or *phir'*) *jā'nā*, قسمت پھوٹنا *qis'mat phoot'nā* come under an unlucky star fall on evil days قسمت پھرنا (یا کھلنا یا جاگ اٹھنا یا چمک اٹھنا) *qis'mat phir'nā* (or *khūl'nā* or *jāg' ūth'nā* or *cha'mak ūth'nā*) V.I. be in luck قسمت سے *qis'mat se* ADV. luckily ; fortunately by chance ; fortuitously قسمت کا پھیر *qis'mat kā pher'* N.M. ill-luck ; misfortune adversity قسمت کا دھنی *qis'mat kā dha'nī* ADJ. & N.M. lucky or fortunate (person (iron) unlucky (person) قسمت کا لکھا *qis'mat kā li(k)'khā* N.M. one's lot destiny قسمت کا لکھا پورا ہونا *qis'mat kā li(k)'khā poo'rā ho'nā* V.I. (of destiny) be fulfilled قسمت کا ہیٹا *qis'mat kā he'tā* ADJ. & N.M. unlucky or unfortunate (person) ; ill-starred (person) قسمت کرنا *qis'mat kar'nā* V.T. (arch.) apportion قسمت کو جھینکنا (یا رونا یا کوسنا) *qis'mat ko jhenk'nā* (or *ro'nā* or *kos'nā*) V.T. & O course one's fate bless one's stars قسمت لڑنا *qis'mat la*[illegible] run of luck قسمت والا *qis'mat vā'lā* ADJ. [illegible] fortunate (person) lucky guy قسمت ہر جگہ آن ملتی ہے *qis'mat har ja'gah par ān' mil'tī hai* PROV. fortune will make its way through stonewalls خارج قسمت *khā'rij-e qis'mat* N.M. quotient [A ~ قسم]

قسور *qas'var* N.M. lion [A]

قسیس *qissīs'* N.M. Christian priest deacon [A]

قسی القلب *qasiy'y-ūl-qal'b* ADJ. & N.M. hardhearted or callous (person) [A ~ قلب + قساوت]

قسیم *qasīm'* N.M. distributor portion handsome person [A ~ قسمت]

قشر *qish'r* N.M. (PL. قشور *qūshoor'*) crust shell busk skin قشر *qash'r* V.T. peel break the shell (of) [A]

قشقہ *qash'qah* N.M. mark forehead made by Hindus قشقہ کھینچنا *qash'qah khench'nā* V.I. paint this mark [P]

قشون *qūshoon'* N.M. army قشون قاہرہ *qūshoo'n-e-qā'hirah* N.M. conquering army [T]

قصاب *qassāb'* N.M. butcher beefvendor بکر قصاب *bak'r qassāb'* N.M. mutton vendor goat or sheep slaughterer [A]

قصابہ *qasā'bah* N.M. lady's scarf [A]

قصاص *qisās'* N.M. capital punishment like retaliation for physical injury retaliation law قصاص لینا *qisās' le'nā* V.T. punish with like retaliation kill for murder award capital punishment (to) [A]

قصائد *qasā''id* N.M. (PL. of قصیدہ N.M. ★)

قصائی *qasā''ī*, قسائی *qasā''ī* N.M. (F. قسائن *qasā''in*) butcher meat-vendor قصائی کے کھونٹے سے بندھنا *qasā''ī ke khoon'te se bandh'nā* V.I. have one's life jeopardized be married to a cruel husband [~ A قصاب CORR.]

قصباتی *qasbā'tī* ADJ. (see under قصبہ N.M ★)

قصبہ *qas'bah* N.M. (PL. قصبات *qasbāt'*) town قصباتی *qasbā'tī* ADJ. urdian mofussil' N.M. townsman [A]

قصد *qas'd* N.M. aim ; object resolve ; intention attempt design قصد کرنا *qas'd kar'nā* V.T. aim resolve intend design attempt set as one's goal undertake a journey (to) proceed (to) قصداً *qas'dan* ADV. purposely ; deliberately ; intentionally voluntraily [A]

قصر¹ *qas'r* N.M (PL. قصور *qusoor'*) palace [A]

قصر² *qas'r* N.M curtailment نماز میں قصر *namāz' men qas'r* N.M. curtailment of obligatory prayers

... ā V.T curtail

... N.M. ★)

... palaces [A ~ SING. قصر]

... failure omission قصور کرنا ... ā V.I. commit a fault fail ... ' ADJ. blameworthy ADV. at fault ... N.M. (PL. قصص qi'sas) tale story ... ion narration matter affair ... قصہ پاک کرنا qis'sah pāk' kar'nā V.T. & O. settle a dispute kill destory get rid (of) قصہ پاک ہونا qis'sah pāk' ho'nā V.I. be killed be destroyed be got rid of قصہ تمام کرنا qis'sah tamām' kar'nā V.T. conclude a story kill; destory قصہ جھونا qis'sah jho'nā V.T. air one's grievances قصہ چکانا qis'sah chukā'nā V.T. settle a dispute قصہ خوان qis'sah-khāñ N.M. story-teller ; قصہ خوانی qis'sa-khā'nī N.F. story-telling قصہ کوتاہ qis'sah kotāh' ADV. in short ; briefly قصہ کوتاہ کرنا qis'sah kotāh' kar'na V.T. cut the long story short قصہ خوانی qis'sah kahā'nī N.M. fiction قصہ مختصر qis'sah mukh'tasar ADV. in short INT. to cut the long story short [A]

قصیدہ qasī'dah N.M (PL. قصائد qasā''id) encomium ode ; genre of poetry couched usu. in high-flown language 16 to 90 couplets with even lines rhyming together ; it usu. comprises four parts, viz., tashbih' or amatory prelude, gurez' or change of mood, eulogy or other main subject and khātimah or conclusion قصیدہ خوانی qasī'dā-khā'nī N.F. sycophancy flattery [A ~ قصہ]

قضا qazā N.F. death fate fatality administration of justice judicature order ; decree lapse (of time of prayer) قضا پڑھنا qazā' park'nā V.T. say one's prayers late قضا بھی کبھی ٹلتی ہے qazā' bhī ka'bhi tal'tī hai PROV. death is inevitable قضارا qazā' rā ADV. by chance قضا سر پر کھیلنا (یا کھڑی ہونا) qazā' sir par khel'na (or kha'rī ho'nā) V.I. (of death) be impending; loom large قضا کا مارا qazā' ka mā'ra ADJ. & N.M. (one) driven by fate قضا کرنا qazā' kar'nā V.I. say one's prayers late pass away قضا و قدر qazā'-o-qad'r N.F. divine decree fate کارکنان قضا و قدر karkunā'n-e qazā-o qad'r N.M. the agents implementing the divine decree ; fate قضا ہونا qazā' ho'nā V.I. (of prayer) be late (of its time) lapse قضائے الٰہی سے مرنا qazā'-e ilā'hī se mar'nā V.I. predestination ; die a natural death قضائے حاجات qazā'-e hā'jat N.F. answering the call of nature قضائے کار qazā'-e kār ADV. by chance ; fortuitously قضائے عمری qazā'-e 'um'rī N.F. type of supererogatory prayers قضائے مبرم qazā'-e mub'ram N.F. inexorable fate inevitable death ناگہانی qazā'-e nā-gahā'nī N.F. sudden death [A]

قضات qūzāt' N.M. PL. judges قاضی القضاۃ qā'zi-l qāzāt' N.M. Chief Justice [A ~ SING. قاضی]

قضایا qazā'yā N.M. (PL. of قضیہ N.M. ★)

قضیب qazīb' N.M. penis (rare) sword (rare) slender branch [A]

قضیہ qaziy'yah N.M. (PL. قضایا qazā'yā) quarrel dispute case matter affair (logic) syllogism قضیہ کرنا qaziy'yah kar'nā V.T & O. kick up a row قضیہ مول لینا qaziy'yah mol le'nā V.T. meddle with or poke one's nose in to other's affairs get unnecessarily involved in some trouble [A]

قط qat N.M. cut at pen point قط لگانا qat legā'nā V.T. trim or mend pen-point قط زن qat'-zan, قط گیر qat-gīr' N.M. piece of bone, etc. on which pen-point is trimmed [A]

قطار qatār' N.F. queue line row ; rank range قطار باندھنا qatār' bāndh'na V.T. & I. queue up stand in aline put in a line set in a row make a bee-live for [A]

قطاع الطریق qūttā''-ūt-tarīq' N.M. PL. highwayman footpading [A ~ قاطع الطریق]

قطامہ qattā'mah N.F. whore ; strumpet ; loose woman [A]

قطب qūt'b N.M. (PL. اقطاب aqtāb') polestar pole highest cadre in spiritual pivot قطب جنوبی qūt'b-e jūnoo'bī N.M. South Pole Antarctic قطب سماوی qūt'b-e samā'vī N.M. Celestial Pole قطب شمالی qūt'b-e shimā'lī N.M. North Pole Arctic قطب نما qūt'b-nūmā N.M. mariner's compass قطبی qūt'bī ADJ. Polar قطبی تارا qūt'bī ta'rā N.M. Polestar قطبین qūtbain' N.M. PL. North and South Pole [A]

قطر qūt'r N.M. diameter [A]

قطرہ qat'rah N.M. (PL. قطرات qatarāt') drop minim قطرہ آنا qat'rah 'ā'nā V.I. suffer from Brights disease قطرہ قطرہ qat'rah qat'rah ADV drop by drop ; by drops قطرہ قطرہ بہم شود دریا qat'rah qat'rah ba-hām' shavad' daryā' PROV. light gains made a heavy purse [A]

قطع qat'' N.M. cut style ; fashion crossing covering (distance) interception intersection severence sundering snapping segment قطع تعلق qat''-e ta'al'lūq N.M. separation; severance of relations ; snapping of ties قطع تعلق کرنا (یا کر لینا) qat''-e ta'l'lūq kar'nā (or kar' le'nā) V.T.

break off all connections (with) ; sever relations (with) ; snap, ties (with) قطع کرنا *qat'' kar'nā* V.T. cut (cloth) cut (someone) short ; cut in traverse (distance) snap (ties) ; put an end (to love, etc.) قطع کلام کرنا *qat''-e kalām' kar'nā* V.T. cut in ; interrupt قطع نظر *qat''-e na'zar* N.M. (ignoring) turning (one's eyes) from ADV. irrespective (of) اس سے قطع نظر *is se qat''-e na'zar* PH. inrespect of the fact (that) despite قطع نظر کرنا *qat''-e na'zar kar'nā* V.I. ignore something قطع و برید *qat''-o-būrīd'* N.M. cutting change emendation قطع ہونا *qat'' ho'nā* V.I. be cut be deducted be cut short be severed be traversed وضع قطع *vaz'-(-o-)qat''* N.F. style ; fashion

قطعاً *qat''an* ADV. positively ; definitely entirely absolutely plot (of land) قطعی *qat''ī* ADJ. absolute categorical imperative decisive ; conclusive final ; ultimate binding قطعی گز *qat''ī gaz* N.M. tailor's tape قطعی طور پر *qat''ī taur par* ADV. absolutely categorically finally [A ~ قطع]

قطعہ *qit''ah* (dial. *qat''ah*) N.M. (PL. قطعات *qita''āt'*) stanza this as independent genre of poetry piece ; fragment section plot (of land) قطعہ بند *qit''a-band* N.M. more than one couplete read together to form complete sentence [A ~ قطع]

قطمیر *qitmīr'* N.M. name of dog accompanying the Seven Sleepers in the Catacomb (fig.) anything small [A]

قطن *qut'n* N.F. cotton قطنی *qūt'nī* ADJ. cotton [A]

قعدہ *qa''dah* N.M. final sitting in prayers ; sitting up in crouching position ; genuflexion [A]

قعود *qo'ood'* N.M. short sitting in prayers sitting down flexion [A ~ قعدہ]

قعر *qa''r* N.M. depth cavity bottom abyss gulf being concave قعر دریا *qa''r-e daryā'* N.M. depth of (a river) قعر مذلت *qa''r-e mazal'lat* N.M. depth of disgrace قعر مذلت میں گرانا *qa''r-e mazal'lat meṅ girā'nā* V.T. land (someone) into abysmal ignominy [A]

قفا *qafā'* N.F. nape [A]

قفس (rare قفص) *qa'fas* N.M. cage (fig.) world [P]

قفل *qūf'l* N.M. lock قفل ابجد *qūf'l-e ab'jad* N.M. keyless lock worked by special arrangement of letters (or figures) on it قفل توڑنا *qūf'l tor'nā* V.I. break open a lock burgle قفل چھوٹا ہونا *qūf'l jhoo'tā ho'nā* V.I. (of lock) be defective قفل لگانا *qūf'l lagā'nā* V.T. & O lock lock up قفل لگنا (یا پڑنا) *qūf'l lagā'nā* (or *par'nā*) V.I. be locked have locks (in) قفلی *qūf'lī* N.F. (ped. for قلفی N.F. ★)

ققنس *qūq'nūs* N.M. phoenix [A ~ G]

قل *qūl* N.M. one of the final chapters of the Holy Quran beginning with this word third day funeral rites ; 'soyem' end ; close قل آعوزی *qūl a'oo'zī*, قل آعوزیا *qūl ā'oo'ziyā* N.M. one living on alms (deprecatory term for) minor Muslim priest ; Mulla قل ہو جانا *qūl' ho jā'nā* V.I. come to a close ; be all over with [A ~ قول]

قلاب *qallāb'* N.M. one who makes fake coins ; counterfeiter swindler قلابی *qullā'bī* N.F. swindling counterfeiting [A ~ قلب]

قلابازی *qa'lā-bā'zī* (col. کلابازی *ka'lā-bā'zī*) N.F. somersault ; somerset قلابازی کھانا *qa'lā-bā'zī khā'nā* V.I. turn a somersault

قلابہ *qūllā'bah* N.M. (rare) fishing hook hasp زمین آسمان کے قلابے ملانا *zamīn asmān' ke qūllā'be milā'nā* PH. try one's utmost ; leave no stone unturned exaggerate very much (in praise of) [A]

قلادہ *qilā'dah* N.M. (PL. قلائد *qalā''id*) collar necklace cross-belt [A]

قلاش *qallāsh'*, قلانچ *qallānch'* ADJ. & N.M. poor, penurious or poverty-stricken (person) wretched (person) (rare) trickster ; rogue [P]

قلاع *qilā''* N.M. (PL. of قلعہ N.M. ★)

قلاع *qūlā'* N.M. soreness of mouth

قلاقنا *qalā'qinā* N.M. (slang) jeers

قلاقند *qa'lāqand* N.F. (dial. M.) (indigenous toffee ; taffy

قلانچ *qūlānch* (col. کلانچ *kūlānch*) N.F. (of horse, etc. caper قلانچ بھرنا (یا لگانا) *qūlānch' bhar'nā* (or *lagā'nā*) V.I. cut a caper [T]

قلب *qal'b* N.M. (PL. قلوب *qūloob'*) heart soul mind centre centre or main body (of army) inversion ADJ. inverse counterfeit قلب ساز *qal'b-sāz'* N.M. (rare) counterfeiter قلب کرنا *qal'b kar'nā* V.T. turn ; invert قلب ماہیت *qal'b-e mā'hiyat* N.M. basic chance metamorphosis

qal'bī ADJ. hearty cordial [A]

قلبہ *qūl'bah* N.M. (lit.) plough قلبہ ران *qūlba-rān* (lit.) N.M. cultivator قلبہ رانی *qūl'ba-rā'nī* N.F. (lit.) ploughing ; cultivation [P]

قلت *qil'lat* N.F. shortage ; scarcity paucity dearth want ; deficiency [A]

قلتبان *qaltabān'* N.M cuckold [T]

قلزم *qūl'zūm* N.M. clysma (name of an Egyptian city) (fig.) sea بحیرۂ قلزم *bŭhai'ra-e qūlzūm* N.M Red Sea [A]

قلع قمع *qal'' qam'* N.M. rooting out; extirpation destruction ending putting an end (to) [A قلع + قمع]

قلعہ *qil''ah* (ped. *qal''ah*) N.M. (PL. قلع *qilā'* قلعہ جات *qil''a-jāt'*) fort castle قلعہ دار *qil'a-dār'* N.M. garrison commander قلعۂ معلّی *qil'a-e mo'al'lā* N.M. (esp.) the Red Fort of Delhi as the seat of Moghul emperors Moghul court قلعے کی زبان *qil'e kī zabān'* v.i. chaste Urdu; Emperor's Urdu King's English [A]

قلعی *qal''ī* N.F. tin tinning; plating قلعی کرنا *qal''ī kar'nā* v.T. tin vessels, etc.) قلعی کھلنا (یا کھل جانا) *qal''ī khūl'nā* (or *khūl jā'nā*) v.i. be exposed be shown in one's true colours قلعی کھولنا (یا کھول دینا) *qal''ī khol'nā* (or *khol de'nā*) v.T. expose (someone) قلعی گر *qal''ī-gar* N.M. tinman one who tins vessels قلعی گری *qal''ī ga'rī* N.F. tinman's job job of tinning pots [A ~ قلع]

قلفی *qūl'fī* (ped. قفلی *qūf'lī*) N.F. icecream container or mould for it small 'hookah' movable joint in 'hookah' pipes hasp metal cup with adjustable lid tiffin-carrier قلفی جمنا *qūl'fī jam'nā* [A ~ قفل CORR.]

قلق *qa'laq* N.M. sorrow anxiety; disquietude قلق رہنا *qa'laq raih'nā* v.i. feel sad (about) be disturbed (at) قلق گزرنا (یا ہونا) *qa'laq gū'zarnā* (or *ho'nā*) v.i. regret feel sorrow be perturbed be concerned (over) [A]

قلقاری *qilqā'rī* N.F. (same as کلکاری N.F. ★)

قلقل *qūl'qūl* N.F. gurgling (of wine-bottle, etc.)

قلم *qa'lam* (PL. اقلام *aqlām'*) N.M. pen pen-holder fountain-pen reed-pen handwriting authority N.F. graft cutting crystal matric hair on temple; whisker; upper part of beard قلم اٹھا کر *qa'lam ūṭhā' kar* ADJ. (write) off hand قلم اٹھانا *qa'lam ūṭhā'nā* v.T. write (on a topic) قلم برداشتہ *qa'lam-bar-dāsh'tah* ADJ. & ADV. off-hand)writing) قلم بنانا *qa'lam banā'nā* v.T. & O. mend a pen (usu. pl.) set the whiskers a matrix قلمبند *qa'lam-band* ADJ. & ADV. reduced to writing in black and white قلمبند کرنا *qa'lam-band kar'nā* v.T. write; reduced to writing; put in black and white jot down; take down; down قلم پاک *qa'lam pāk'* N.M. pen-wiper قلم پھیرنا *qa'lam pher'nā* v.T. strike off قلمتراش *qa'lam-tarāsh* N.M. pen-knife قلم توڑ دینا *qa'lam toṛ' de'nā* PH. write exquisitely as a calligraphist produce a work of great literary merit قلمدان *qa'lam-dān* N.M. portfolio inkstand writing case قلمدان وزارت *qa'lam-dā'n-e vizā'rat* N.M. ministerial portfolio قلمرو *qa'lam rau* N.F. domininion territory قلمزن کرنا *qa'lam-zan kār'nā* v.T. delate strike off قلم زدہ *qa'lam-za'dah* ADJ. struck off قلمکار *qa'lam-kār'* N.M artist painter engraver; figured calico قلمکاری *qa'lam-kā'rī* N.F. painting engraving قلم کرنا *qa'lam kar'nā* v.T. cut (someone's head) off prune قلم لگانا *qa'lam lagā'nā* v.T. & O. graft plant cuttings قلم ہونا *qa'lam ho'nā* v.i. be cut off; be severed موقلم *moo'-qa'lam* N.M. brush; paint brush یک قلم *yak-qa'lam* ADV. altogether totally; entirely بیک جنبش قلم *ba-yak' jūm'bash-e qa'lam* ADV. with one stroke of pen قلمی *qa'lamī* ADJ. hand-written grafted crystal; crystallized قلمی نسخہ *qa'lamī nūs'khah* N.M. manuscript hand-written book قلمی آم *qa'lmī ām* N.M. grafted mangoes قلمی شورہ *qa'lamī sho'rah* N.M. crystallised saltpetre [A]

قلماقنی *qalmā'qinī* N.F. Amazonian harem guard [A]

قلندر *qalan'dar* N.M. calender cleanshaven and tousured vagabond professing to mysticism person not tied down by religious or worldly conventions dauntless person free-thinker livestime monkey-dancer قلندرانہ *qalan-darā'nah* ADJ. bold; dauntless; undaunted free thinking قلندری *qalan'darī* N.F. uncoventional mysticism dauntless spirit a kind of tent [P]

قلوب *qūloob'* N.M. PL. hearts souls minds [A ~ SING. قلب]

قلوپطرہ *qaloopat'rah* N.F. Cleopatra

قلہ *qūl'lah* N.M. peak; top; summit قلۂ کوہ *qūl'la-e koh* N.M. hilltop peak [A]

قلی *qū'lī* N.M. coolie porter (arch.) slave [T]

قلیا *qūl'yā* N.F. chapter of the Holy Quran entitled infidels (and opening with the words *qūl yā'...*) کی قلیا تمام کرنا *kī qūl'yā tamām' kar'nā* v.T. end (someone's) prestige (etc.) [~A قل]

قلیان *qalyān'* N.M. hookah قلیان کش *qal'yān'-kash* ADJ. & N.M. smoker

قلیل *qalīl'* ADJ. fex little small short [A ~ قلت]

قلیہ *qal'yah* N.M. stew stewed meat mince [A]

قم *qūm* INT rise قم باذن اللہ *qūm' bi-izn-illāh* INT (formula of Jesus for quickening the dead)

rise by the grace of God [A ~ قیام]

قمار qimār' N.M. gambling قمارباز qimār'-bāz N.M. gambler قماربازی qimār'-bā'zī N.F. gambling قمار خانہ qimār'-kha'nah N.M. gambling den [A]

قماش[1] qumāsh' N.M. (PL. اقمشہ aq'mishah) household goods quality cloth [A]

قماش[2] qūmā'sh N.M. manners وضع و قماش vaz''-o-qūmāsh' N.M. style and manners [T]

قمچی qam'chī N.F. whip ; horse-whip (rare) switch [T]

قمر qa'mar N.M. (PL. اقمار aqmār') moon قمری qa'marī ADJ. lunar قمری مہینہ qa'marī mahī'nah N.M. lunar month ; month [A]

قمری qūm'rī N.F. (PL. قماری qamā'rī) ringdove ; turtle-dove [A]

قمع qam'' N.M. pulverize قلع و قمع qal''-o-qam'' N.M. (see under قلع N.M. ★)

قمقمہ qūm'qūmah N.M. (electric) bulb lamp-shade ; globe [A]

قمیص qamīs' (col. qamīz') N.F. (PL قمص qū'mūs) shirt قمیص پہننا qamīs' paihan'nā V.I. put on one's shirt [A]

قنات qanā.' N.F tent-wall [A]

قنادیل qanādīl' N.F. (PL. of قندیل ★)

قناعت qanā''al N.F. content , contentment [A]

قند qand' N.M. sugar sugar candy [A ~ P]

قندیل qindīl' N.F. candle chandelier lamp [A ~ G]

قنوت qūnoot' N.F obedience to God (usu. دعائے قنوت do'ā''e qūnoot') prayer-words repeated while standing [A]

قنوط qūnoot' N.F despair , despondency قنوطی qūnoo'tī N.M. pessimist ADJ. pessimistic قنوطیت qūnootiy'yat N.F. pessimism [A]

قویٰ qūvā' N.M. PL. capacities powers potentialities قوائے جسمانی qūvā''-e jismā'nī N.M. PL. physical potentialities قوائے ذہنی qūvā'-e zeh'nī N.M PL. mental powers قوائے طبعی qūvā'-e tab''ī N.M. PL. natural faculties ; faculties supposedly emanating from liver, viz., jā'zibah, mā'sikah, mo'al'lidah, nā'miyah, hā'zimah قوائے نفسانی qūvā-e nafsā'ni N.M. PL. ten internal and external mental faculties, viz., bā'sirah, zā''iqah, sā'me'ah, shām'mah, lā'misah, hāfzah, his's-e mushtarak, mūtakhy'yilah, mūtafak'kirah, vā'himah

قواعد qavā''id N.F grammar N.M. drill parade N.M. PL. rules rules and regulations قواعد صرف و نحو qavā''id sar'f-o nah'v N.M. PL. rules of accidence and syntax قواعد سکھنا qavā''id sikhā'nā V.T. drill teach grammar [A SING. قاعدہ]

قوافی qavā'fī N.M. (PL. of قافیہ N.M. ★)

قواعددان qavā''id-dān N.M. grammarian one conversant with rules [A ~ SING. قاعدہ

قوال qavvāl'. N.M. chorister ; member of band singing light music stressing words qavvā'lī N.F. choral song of this type indigence chorus mystic chorus [A ~ قول]

قوام qivām' N.M. (thick) syrup stay A ~ قیام]

قوانین qavānīn' N.M. (PL. of قانون ★)

قوت qoot' N.F. (PL. اقوات aqvāt') food sustenance قوت لایموت qoo't-e lā yamoot' N.F just enough food to keep body and soul together ; bare sustenance [A]

قوّت qūv'vat N.F. (PL. قویٰ qūvā') strength vigour force power capacity potentiality virtue ; influence ; effect faculty قوت باصرہ qūv'vat-e bā'sirah N.F. sense of sight ; eyesight vision قوت باہ qūv'vat-e bāh' N.F. potency قوت پانا qūv'vat pā'nā V.T. be strengthened be reinforced قوت جاذبہ qūv'vat-e jā'zibah N.F. power of absorption ; power of attraction قوت حافظہ qūv'vat-e hā'fizah N.F memory قوت دافعہ qūv'vat-e dā'fe'ah N.F. power of expulsion قوت دینا qūv'vat de'nā V.T. strengthen قوت ذائقہ quv'vat-e zā''iqah N.F. sense of taste قوت سامعہ qūv'vat-e sā'me'ah N.F. sense of hearing قوت شامہ quv'vat-e shām'mah N.F. sense of smell قوت غضبیہ qūv'vat-e ghā'zabiy'yah N.M. passion ; fury قوت لامسہ qūv'vat-e lā'misah N.F. sense of touch قوت ماسکہ qūv'vat-e māsi'kah N.F. power of retention قوت متخیلہ qūv'vat-e mūtakhay'yilah N.F. fancy; faculty of imagination قوت مدرکہ qūv'vat-e mūd'rikah N.F. intellect; faculty of perception or apprehension قوت متفکرہ qūv'vat-e mūtafak'kirah N.F. faculty of thought قوت ممیزہ qūv'vat-e mūmay'yizah N.F. faculty of discrimination قوت نامیہ qūv'vat-e nā'miyah N.F. faculty of growth قوت ہاضمہ qūv'vat-e hā'zimah N.F. digestive power ; assimiliation قوت مولدہ qūv'vate mo'al'lidah N.F. generative faculty [A]

قور qor N.M. arms قورچی qor'chī soldier armourer قورخانہ qor'-khā'nah N.M. armoury ; arsenal [P]

قورمہ qor'mah N.M. seasoned spicy stew [T]

قوس qaus N.F. bow arc (of circle) (sign of Zodiac) Sagittarious قوس قزح qau's-e qūzah' (or qau's-o) N F (see under قزح) N.M. ★)

قوسی qau'sī ADJ. arched bow-shaped [A]

قول *qau'l* N.M. promise ; word saying utterance assertion ; affirmation name of a musical mode قول توڑنا (یا سے پھرنا) *qau'l tor'nā* (or *se phir'nā*) V.T. & O. go back on one's word قول دینا (یا کرنا) *qaul de'nā* (or *hār'nā*) V.T. give word ; to promise ; give (someone) one's word of honour قول (و) فعل *qau'l(-o-) fe''l* N.M. precept and practice word and deed قول فیصل *qau'l-e fai'sal* N.M. last word decisive pronouncement قول (و) قرار *qau'l(-o-) qarār'* N.M. mutual agreement compect ; covenant قول (و) قرار کرنا *qau'l(-o-) qarār' kar'nā* V.T. & O. give one's word to قول کا پورا *qau'l kā poo'rā* ADJ. true to one's word قولاً *qau'lan* ADV. by word of mouth verbally بقول *ba-qau'l* ADV according to as reported by [A]

قولنج *qoolanj'* (or *qaulanj'*) N.M. colic [A ~ G]

قوم *qaum* N.M. nation ; people rare group ; group of persons قومی *qau'mī* ADJ. national قومی اسمبلی *qau'mī asamb'li* N.F. National Assembly قومی حکومت *qau'mī ḥukoo'mat* N.F. national government قومی ملکیت *qau'mī milkiy'yat* N.F. state ownership قومی ملکیت میں لینا *qau'mī milkiy'yat meṅ le'nā* V.T. nationalize قومیانا *qaumiyā'nā* V.T. nationalize قومیت *qaumīy'yat* N.F. nationality [A]

قومہ *qau'mah* N.M. standing up in prayers after making the bow [A ~ قیام]

قونصل *qauṅ'sal* N.M. consul ; envoy قونصل خانہ *qauṅ'sal-khā'nah* N.M. consulate

قوی *qa'vī* ADJ. strong vigorous mighty powerful قوی الجثہ *qa'viy'y-ul-jus'sah* ADJ. able-bodied robust قوی ہیکل *qa'vī-hai'kal* ADJ. robust gigantic [A ~ قوت]

قہار *qahhār'* ADJ. (see under قہر N.M. ★)

قہر *qaih'r* (ped. *qah'r*) N.M. anger ; in dignation rage ; wrath ; fury calamity curse injustice cruelty (rare) overpowering قہر الٰہی *qaih'r-e ilā'hī* N.M. divine wrath قہر توڑنا (یا کرنا) *qaih'r tor'nā* (or *kar'nā*) V.T. & I. crack down upon mete out harsh treatment do something undesirable act in an irresponsible manner قہر ٹوٹنا *qaih'r ṭooṭ'nā* V.I. be cursed (of calamity descend) قہر درویش برجان درویش *qaih'r-e darvesh' bar jā'n-e darvesh* PROV. a poor man's rage hurts none but himself قہر کا *qaih'r kā* ADJ. exquisite ravishing قہر و غلبہ *qaih'r-e-ghal'bah* N.M. overpowering and control قہر ہونا *qaih'r ho'nā* V.I. be calamitous be very undersirable قہراً *qah'ran* ADV. by force perforce قہرمان *qaih'r-mān* N.M. tyrant hero قہار *qahhār'* N.M. vanquisher controller this as attribute of God [A]

قہقری *qaih'qarī* (ped. قہقریٰ *qah'qarā*) ADJ. retrograde , retrogressive رجعت قہقری *raj'at-e qaih'qarī* N.F. retrogression [A]

قہقہہ *qaih'qahah* N.M. laugh , laughter ; burst of laughter قہقہہ لگانا (یا مارنا) *qaih'qahah lagā'nā* (or *mār'nā* V.I. laugh loudly , burst into laughter roar with laughter

قہوہ *qah'vah* N.M. coffee tea without milk قہوہ خانہ *qah'va-khā'nah* N.M coffee house قہوہ فروش *qah'va-firosh'* N.M tea-vendor coffee-house kee[illegible] [A]

قے *qai* N.F. vomit ; puke قے آنا *qai ā'nā* V.I. feel sick ; feel nausea be disgusted (with the sight of) قے آور *qai'-ā'var* ADJ. emitic قے کرنا *qai kar'nā*, کو قے ہونا *ko qai' ho'nā* V.I. vomit ; puke; spew [A]

قیادت *qiyā'dat* N.F. leadership صحیح قیادت *saḥīḥ' qiyā'dat* N.F. right of leadership [A]

قیاس *qiyās'* N.M. analogy guess ; supposition conjecture presumption (gram.) regular formation (rare) syllogism قیاس سے باہر *qiyās' se bā'hir* ADJ. & ADV. incredible inconceivable قیاس کرنا *qiyās' kar'nā* V.T. think estimate قیاس لگانا *qiyās' lagā'nā* V.T. guess conjecture قیاس میں آنا *qiyās' meṅ ā'nā* V.I be credible be conceivable قیاساً *qiyā'san* ADV. presuming by conjecture by analogy قیاسی *qiyā'sī* ADJ. conjectural imaginary analogous (gram.) of regular formation [A]

قیاصرہ *qayāsirah* N.M. (PL. of قیصر N.M. ★)

قیافہ *qiyā'fah* N.M. conjecture features ; appearance قیافہ شناس *qiyā'fa-shinās'* N.M. physiognomist قیافہ شناسی *qiyā'fa-shinā'sī* N.M. physiognomy [A]

قیام *qiyām'* N.M. stay ; residence standing up establishment existence stability permanence قیام پزیر *qiyām'-pazīr'* ADJ. resident ADV. staying قیام پزیر ہونا *qiyām'-pazīr' ho'nā*, قیام کرنا *qiyām' kar'nā* V.I. reside stay (at or with) [A]

قیامت *qiyā'mat* N.F. Doomsday Day of Resurrection cruelty calamity scene of trouble or distress exquisiteness ADJ excessive ; excessively great exquisite ADV. extremely exquisitely INT. wonderful : exquisite قیامت آنا *qiyā'mat ā'nā* V.I. (of Doomsday come (of calamity) be قیامت اٹھانا (یا توڑنا یا برپا کرنا) *qiyā'mat uṭhā'nā* (or *tor'nā* or *bar-pā' kar'nā* V.I. raise a tumult be very cruel bring down calamity قیامت خیز *qiyā'mat-khez'* ADJ.

calamitous ravishing قیامت خیزی qiyā'mat-khe'zī N.F. calamitousness قیامت ڈھانا qiyā'mat ḍhā'nā V.I. act inadvisably oppress have ravishing beauty قیامت صغریٰ qiyā'mat-e sūgh'rā N.F. individual ; death قیامت کا qiyā'mat kā ADV. extreme exquisite ravishing قیامت کبریٰ qiyā'mat-e kūb'rā N.M Doomsday قیامت گزرنا qiyā'mat gūzar'nā V.I. (of calamity) be قیامت وسطیٰ qiyā'mat-e vūs'tā N.F. widespread calamity destruction of nation, etc. کیا قیامت ہے kyā qiyā'mat hai INT. what a pity how sad how miserable [A ~ قیام]

قید qaid N.F. imprisonment ; confinement ; incarceration restraint condition ; stipulation (rare) shackle قید بامشقت qai'd-e bā-mashaq'qat N.F. rigorous imprisonment ; R.I. penal servitude قید بھگتنا (یا کاٹنا) qaid' bhūg'gatnā (or kāṭ'nā) V.I. undergo a term of imprisonment قید تنہائی qai'd-e tanhā''ī N.F. solitary confinement قید خانہ qaid'-khā'nah N.M. prison ; jail ; gaol قید فرنگ qai'd-e farang' N.F. inprisonment for defining order of (former) British rulers of the Indo-Pakistan subcontinent قید لگانا qaid' lagā'nā V.T. stipulate make conditional upon restrict قید محض qai'd-e maḥ'z N.F. simple imprisonment قید ہونا qaid' ho'nā V.I be imprisoned be behind bars, be in prison be restrained be stipulated بلاقید bi-lā'-qaid' ADJ. unconditional unrestricted ADV. unconditionally unreservedly at large قیدی qai'dī N.M. prisoner captive convict [A]

قیر qīr' N.M. pitch · tar قیرگوں qīr'-goon ADJ. pitch-dark [A]

قیراط qīrāt' N.M. twenty-fourth part of an ounce ; carat [A]

قیس qais' N.M. legendary Arab lover of the dark-beauty, Laila or of the blond, Lubna [A]

قیصر qai'sar N.M. (PL. قیاصرہ qayā'sirah Caesar emperor sovereign potentate [A ~ L]

قیف qīf N.F. funnel [T]

قیل و قال qī'l-o-qāl' N.F. controversy objection ; criticism altercation passage-at-arms [A ~ قول]

قیلولہ qailoo'lah N.M. nap ; siesta قیلولہ کرنا qailoo'lah kar'nā V.I. take a nap ; take a siesta [A]

قیم qay'yim ADJ. true correct straight N.M. chief convener secretary [A ~ قیام]

قیمت qī'mat N.M. price value worth cost قیمت پانا qī'mat pā'nā V.I. be sold for fetch a high price قیمت ٹھہرانا (یا چکانا) qī'mat thaihrā'na (or chukā'nā) V.T. settle a price قیمت لگانا (یا چکانا) qī'mat lagā'nā (or māqar'rar kar'nā) VT. name the price fix the price evaluate put a price upon قیمتہً qī'matan ADV. on payment قیمتی qī'matī ADJ expensive costly precious valueable highly prized [A]

قیمہ qī'mah N.M. minced meat ; mince قیمہ کرنا qī'mah kar'nā V.T. mince back to pieces make mince-meat (of)

قینچی qaiṅ'chī N.M. scissors truss قینچی سی زبان چلانا qaiṅ'chī sī zabān chalā'nā V.I. talk very fast talk glibly قینچی سی زبان چلنا qaiṅ'chī zabān chal'nā V.I. talk very fast have facile tongue قینچی لگانا qaiṅ'chī lagā'nā V.T. with the scissors pared ; trim make a tru قینچی لگنا qaiṅ'chī lag'nā V.I. be cut be pared be trimmed

قیود qūyood' N.F PL. conditions ; stipulations limitations قیودات qūyoodāt' N.F. (rare.) (same as قیود ★) [A ~ SING. قید]

قیوم qayyoom' N.M. (as an attributive name of God) He who exists by himself Unparallelled [A ~ قیام]

ک

ک kāf twenty-eighth letter of Urdu alphabet (equivalent to English k) (according to jummal reckoning) 20 PARTICLE like

کا kā (inflected form & PL. کے ke ; F. کی kī) PREP. of

کابک kā'būk N.F. pigeon-house ; dove-cote

کابل kā'bul N.M. name of the capital of Afghanistan ; Kabul کابل میں کیا گدھے نہیں ہوتے kā'būl men kyā ga'dhe na'hīṅ ho'te PROV. every land has all sorts of persons fools are to be found everywhere کابلی kā'būlī ADJ. of Kabul unusually large N.M. Afghan robust person کابلی چنے kā'būlī cha'ne N.M PL. large white gram

کابلہ kāb'lah, کابلا kāb'lā N.M. bolt

کابوس kāboos' N.M. nightmare [A]

کابین kābīn' N.M. dower کابین نامہ kābīn'-na'mah N.M. dower deed [P]

کابینہ kābī'nah N.F. Cabinet [E]

کاپی kā'pī N.F. copy note-book for lithography کاپی رائٹ kā'pī-rā''iṭ N.F.

right E

کاتب *kā tib* N M. (Pl کتّاب *kuttāb'*) calligraphist (lit.) scribe (arch.) secretary کاتبِ تحریر *kā'tib-e tahrīr'* N.M the writer of a document, etc. کاتبِ تقدیر *kā-tib-e taqdīr'*, کاتبِ وحی *kā'tib-e vaḥ'y* N.M. the Holy Prophet's scribe taking dowry from him the revealed word [A ~ کتابت]

کاتک *kā'tak* N.M. name of seventh month of Hindu calendar (corresponding to October November) کاتک کی کتیا *kā'tak kī kut'ya* N.F. (fig.) bitch

کاتنا *kāt'nā* V.T spin N.M. spinning کاتا اور لے دوڑی *kā'tā aur le dau'ṛī* PROV very hasty person

کاتی *kā'tī* N.M. goldsmith's clipper

کاٹنا *kāṭ'nā* V.I. cut sever, sunder cleave dissect strike off : bite trim prune reap ; harvest mow deduct cut (someone) short pass (one's day, time, etc.) ; while away (one's time) clear (forest) (of acid, etc) corrode (of shoe) pinch traverse (distance) serve (term of imprisonment) divert (water) dig (canal) cross someone's (path) کاٹ پھانس *kāṭ-phāns* N.F. tampering with tale-bearing ; back-biting backing کاٹ *kāṭ* N.F. cut wound incision discount deduction کاٹ چھانٹ کرنا *kāṭ' chhānṭ kar'nā* V.I. deduct ; make deductions from prone کاٹ ڈالنا *kāṭ' ḍāl'nā* V.T. cut off strike off hew amputate کاٹ کرنا *kāṭ' kar'nā* V.T counter contradict corrode (of sword) cut make an incision کاٹ کھانا *kāṭ' khā'nā* V.T. bite (کاٹنے (یا کاٹ کھانے) کو دوڑنا *kāṭ'ne* (or *kāṭ' khā'ne*) *ko dauṛ'nā*, کاٹے کھانا *kāṭ'khā'nā* V.T. & I. be rude look daggers fly at (someone) try to bite or sting

کاٹھ *kāṭh* (rare کاٹ *kāṭ*) N.M. wood timber (arch.) the stock کاٹھ کا الو *kāṭh kā ul'loo* N.M. کاٹھ کا گھوڑا *kāṭh kā gho'ṛā* N.M. wooden horse (fig.) crutches کاٹ (یا کاٹھ) کباڑ *kāṭh* (or *kāṭh*) *kabāṛ'* N.M. bumber کاٹھ کی گھوڑی *kāṭh kī gho'ṛī* N.F. (dial.) bier کاٹھ کی ہنڈیا بار بار نہیں چڑھتی *kāṭh' kī hanḍ'yā bār' bār na'hīṅ chaṛhtī* PROV. once a traitor always a traitor once bitten twice careful کاٹھ کے گھوڑے دوڑانا *kāṭh ke gho're daurā'nā* V.T. spin yarns

کاٹھی *kā'ṭhī* N.F. saddle body ; physique اچھی کاٹھی پانا *achchhī kā'ṭhī pā'nā* V.I. have a good physique

کاج *kāj* N.M. buttonhole business ; work (usu. as) کام کاج *kām' kāj* N.M. (see under کام ★) کاج بنانا *kāj' banā'nā* V.T. & O. make a buttonhole

کاجل *kā'jal* N M. soot lamp-black collorium کاجل پاڑنا *kā'jal pāṛ'nā* V.T. & O. sublimate soot ; get lamp-black deposited on plate held above wick ; collect collorium on suffers کاجل لگانا *kā'jal lagā'nā* V.T. apply lamp-black (to the eye) کاجل کی کوٹھڑی *kā'jal kī koṭh'ṛī* N.M. coal-celler

کاجو *kājoo* N.M. cashew nut ADJ. fragile کاجو بھوجو *kā'joo bhoo'joo* ADJ. quite fragile

کاچھ *kāchh* N.F. (dial.) loin کاچھا *kā'chhā* N.M drawers

کاچھی *kā'chhī* N.M. (F. کاچھن *kā'chhan*) (dial.) greengrocer gardener cultivating vegetables

کاخ *kākh* N.M palace villa mansion [A]

کاذب *kā'zib* N.M. liar [A ~ کذب]

کار *kār* N.M. affair ; work ; labour ; action, operation ; profession ; business ; function, duty کار آزمودہ *kār-āzmoo'dah*, آزمودہ کار *āzmoo'da-kār* ADJ. veteran کار آگاہ *kār-āgāh'* ADJ. (one) possessing the know-how useful کار آمد *kār-ā'mad* ADJ. useful serviceable کار بار *kār'-bār* N.M. (col for کاروبار N.M. ★) کار براری *kār'-bar-ā'-rī* N.M. getting one's desire fulfilled wheedling کاربند *kār'-band* ADJ. complying (with) acting up to کاربند ہونا *kār'-band ho'nā* V.I. comply (with) act up to کارپرداز *kār-pardāz'* N.M. worker manager efficient (person) کارپردازی *kār-pardā'zī'* N.F. work efficiency management کارِ ثواب *kā'r-e savāb'* N.M. virtue good deed good turn کارِ ثواب کرنا *kā'r-e savāb' kar'nā* V.T. & O. do a good deed کارچوب *kār'-chob* N.M. embroiderer embroidery frame ADJ. embroidered کارچوبی *kār-cho'bī* N.F. embroidery ADJ. embroidered کارخانہ *kār-khā'nah* N.M. workshop factory mill system کارخانہ دار *kār-khā'na-dār* N.M. millowner manufacturer industrialist کارخانۂ قدرت *kār-khā'na-e qud'-rat* کارخانۂ خدائی *khudā''ī kār-khā'nah* N.M. nature کارِ خیر *kā'r-e khair'* N.M. good deed ; virtuous deed کاردار *kār-dār* N.M. manager officer in charge کارداں *kār'-dān* ADJ. & N.M. efficient (person) (one) possessing the know-how کاردانی *kār-dā'nī* N.F. efficiency know-how کارروائی *kār-ravā''ī* N.F. proceedings procedure action trial کارروائی کرنا *kār-ravā''ī kar'nā* V.T. take action deal according to procedure hold proceedings کارزار *kār'-zār'* N.M. battle war میدانِ کارزار *maidā'n-e kār'-zār'* N.M. battlefield ; field of battle کارساز *kār-sāz'* ADJ. helping skilful N.M. doer maker workshop (esp. کارسازِ حقیقی kar-sa'z-e haqi'qi) N.M. God (as True Accomplisher) کارسازی kar-sa'zi N.F. skill کارستانی karasta'ni N.F. mischief کارستانی کرنا karasta'ni kar'na V.T. make mischief کی کارستانی ہونا ki karasta'ni ho'na V.I. be the chief of کارفرما kar-farma' N.M. authority ; one wielding power controller کارفرمائی kar farma''i N.F. control exercise of authority کارکردگی kar-kar'dagi N.F. work performance out put efficiency کارکن kar'-kun N.M. worker ADJ. working کارکن صحافی kar-kun saha'fi N.M. working journalist کارگاہ kar'-gah N.F. workshop field of activity کارگر kar'-gar ADJ. effective efficacious active (ingredient) کارگر ہونا kar'-gar ho'na V.I. be effective کارگزار kar'-guzar' ADJ. effective N.M. worker کارگزاری kar'-guza'ri N.F. work performance output efficiency کارنامہ kar'-na'mah N.M. deed heroic deed memorable work زندگی کا کارنامہ zin'dagi ka kar'-namah N.M. life-work .. (of) کارندہ karin'dah N.M. worker agent ; representative کارِ نمایاں ka'r-e numa'yan N.M. memorable کاروبار ka'r-o-bar', (col. کاربار kar'-bar) N.M. business trade commerce کاروباری kar-o-ba'ri N.M. business کارے دارد ka'r-e da'rad PH. it is no easy task کارے نہ مسلے ka'r-e na mas'le PH. useless in vain SUF. (one) who does ; doing کاری ka'ri SUF. doing [P ~ کردن do]

کار² kar SUF. cultivator planter کاری ka'ri SUF. cultivating planting [P ~ کاشتن]

کار³ kar N.F. motor-car [E]

کاربالک karba'lik ADJ. & N.M. carbolic acid [E]

کاربانک ایسڈ گیس karba'nik e'sid gas N.F. carbonic acid gas [E]

کارپوریشن karpore'shan N.F. corporation [E]

کارتوس kartoos' N.M. cartridge [E]

کارڑائی kart'ara''i N.F. corduroy [E]

کارٹون kar'toon N.M. cartoon کارٹونسٹ kartoo'nist N.F. cartoonist [E]

کارڈ kar'd N.M. port-card کارڈ بورڈ kar'd-bord N.M. cardboard [E]

کارسپانڈنٹ ka'raspandant N.M. correspondent کارسپانڈنس ka'raspandans N.F. correspondence [E]

کارک kar'k N.M. cork [E]

کارن ka'ran N.M. cause (only as) کے کارن ke ka'ran PH. because of

کارنس kar'nas کانس ka'nis N.F cornice [E]

کارنیول kar'nival N.M. carnival [E]

کارواں kar'van [N.M.. company of travellers ; caravan کارواں سرائے kar'van-sara''e N.F. inn caravanserai [P]

کاروونیشن ka'roneshan N.F. coronation [E]

کاری ka'ri ADJ. fatal or mortal (wound, etc.) [P ~ کار]

کاریز karez' N.F. subterranean canal sewer [P]

کاریگر ka'ri-gar N.M. skilled labourrer workman artisan ADJ. skilful (person) ingenious کاریگری ka'ri-ga'ri N.F. skill workmanship ingenuity [P]

کاڑھنا karh'na V.T. embroider embroider (pattern on) draw (veil) boil

کاڑھا ka'rha N.M. decoction

کاسب ka'sib N.M. artisan doer perpetrator [A ~ کسب]

کاست kas't N.F. whittling down (only in) بےکم وکاست be-ka'm-o-kas't PH. complete(ly) [P ~ کاستن]

کاسد ka'sid ADJ. false ; base ; spurious ; counterfeit [A ~ کساد]

کاسر ka'sir ADJ. breaker کاسرِ ریاح ka'sir-e riyah' N.M. (of medicine) curing flatulence [A ~ کسر]

کاسنی kas'ni N.F. a kind of chicory ; endive , lilac ADJ. purple [P]

کاسہ ka'sah N.M. cup ; bowl cup shaped shell, etc. کاسہ زانو ka'sa-e za'noo N.M. kneecap کاسہ سر ka'sa-e sar N.M. skull کاسہ گدائی ka'sa-e gada''i N.M beggar's bowl کاسہ لیس ka'sa-les ADJ. flatterer; sycophant ; boot-licker ; toady کاسہ لیسی ka'sa-le'si N.F. flattery , sycophancy toadyism [A]

کاش kash, کاش کہ kash ke کاشکے kash-ke would that , how I wish [P]

کاشانہ kasha'nah N.M. abode [P]

کاشت kash't N.F. cultivation ; tillage ; bringing under the plough کاشتکار kash't-kar N.M. cultivator ; tiller ; farmer , agriculturist کاشتکاری kash't-ka'ri N.F. cultivation tillage ; agriculture بےکاشت be-kash't ADJ. untilled ; uncultivated fellow uncommanded خودکاشت khud-kash't ADJ. self-cultivated owner cultivated sponsored by (someone) himself کاشتہ kash'tah ADJ. cultivated , tilled [P ~ کاشتن]

کاشف ka'shif ADJ. one who discloses or reveals [A ~ کشف]

کاشی ¹ *kā'shī* N.M. old name for Hindu temple Town, Benares [S]

کاشی ² *kā'shī* N.F. glazed tile ADJ. of the Persian city Kashan کاشی کاری *kā'shī-kā'rī* N.F. glazed-tile work ; chips work

کاظم *kā'zim* N.M. one controlling one's rage appelation of a Shi'ite Imam [A]

کاغذ *kā'ghaz* N.M. (PL. کاغذات *kāghhzāt'*) paper document کاغذ سا *kā'ghaz sā* ADJ. very thin کاغذ سیاہ (یا کالا) کرنا *kā'ghaz siyah'* (or *kā'lā*) *kar'nā* V.T. scribble write at length write silly stuff کاغذ فروش *kā'ghaz-firosh'* N.M. paper merchant ; paper-dealer کاغذ کی ناؤ *kā'ghaz kī nā''o* N.F. paper boat frail thing کاغذ کی ناؤ ڈوبی کہ ڈوبی *kā'ghaz kī nā''o ḍoo'bī ke ḍoo'bī* PROV. baseless things are doomed to collapse کاغذ کی ناؤ بنانا *kā'ghaz kī nā''o banā'nā* V.I. be engaged in useless task کاغذ کے گھوڑے دوڑانا *kā'ghaz ke gho're dauṛā'nā* PH. keep up brisk corresponding send frequent letters کاغذی *kā'ghazī* ADJ. paper ; of paper delicate thin-shelled کاغذی بادام *kā'ghazī bādām'* N.M. thin-shelled almond کاغذی پیرہن (یا پیراہن) *kā'ghazī pairahan'* (or *pairā'han*) N.M. کاغذی کارروائی *kā'ghazī kār-ravā''ī* N.F. redtapism ; official correspondence [P]

کاف *kāf* N.M. name of the letter *kāf* چہل کاف *che'hal kāf* N.M. forty 'kafs' ; prayer poem with forty 'kafs' کاف لام *kāf' lām*, کاف لام *lām' kāf* N.M. beast lie کاف نون *kāf' noon* N.M. God's command *kūn* ; be

کافر *kā'fir* (col. *kā'far*) N.M. & ADJ. (PL. کفار *kaffār'*) infidel beloved.; sweetheart ungrateful (person) cruel (person) ; tyrant کافر ادا *kā'fir-adā'* ADJ. & N.M. coquet ; coquette کافر ماجرائی *kā'fir-mā-jarā''ī* N.F. cruelty کافر نعمت *kā'fir-e ne''mat* ADJ. & N.M. ungrateful person کافرانہ *kāfirā'nah* ADJ. like an infidel impious ADV. impiously کافری *kā'firī* N.F. infidelity ; disbelief [A ~ کفر]

کافور *kāfoor'* N.M. camphor کافور ہونا (یا ہو جانا) *kāfoor' ho'nā* (or *ho jā'nā*) V.I. evaporate vanish scamper کافوری *kāfoo'rī* ADJ camphor milk-white کافوری شمع *kāfoo'rī sham''* N.F incandescent camphor light [A ~ S]

کافہ *kāf'fah* N.M. all (only in) کافۃ الناس *kāf'fat-ün-nas'*, کافۂ انام *kāf'fa-e anām'* N.M. all persons whole mankind [A]

کافی ¹ *kā'fī* ADJ. enough ; sufficient; adequate ample ; abundant کافی و وافی *kā'fī-o-vā'fī* PH enough and too spare [A]

کافی ² *kā'fī* N.M. coffee کافی ہاؤس *kā'fī-hā''us* N.M. coffee-house [E]

کاکا ¹ *kā'kā* N.M. (dial.) paternal uncle

کاکا ² *kā'kā* N.M. (rare) elder brother a slave now grown old in master's home [P]

کاکاتوا *kā'kā tū''ā* N.M. cockatoo [E ~ Malay]

کاکل *kā'kūl* N.F. lock , curl ; ringlet forelock کاکل پیچاں *kā'kūl-e pe'chāṅ* N.F. curled locks [P]

کاکو *kā'koo* N.M. (dial.) maternal uncle

کاکی *kā'kī* N.F. (dial.) aunt

کاگ ¹ *kāg*, کاگا *kā'gā* N.M. crow , raven uvula کاگا رول *kā'gā rol* N.M. cawing of crows

کاگ ² *kāg* N.M. cork [~ E CORR.]

کال ¹ *kāl* N.M. famine dearth scarcity ; shortage (rare) death کال پڑنا *kāl' paṛ'nā* V.I. (of famine) be کال کا مارا *kāl' kā mā'rā* ADJ. famine-stricken ; starveling

کال ² *kāl* PREF. black کال کوٹھڑی *kāl' koṭhrī* N.F. black-hole ; dungeon [~ کالا ABB. of کالا]

کالا ¹ *kā'lā* ADJ. (F. کالی *kā'lī*) black dark N.M. black snake کالا آدمی *kā'la ād'mī* N.M. derogatory) an Africusian of a subject race کالا بھجنگ *kā'lā bh jang'* ADJ. jet black کالا پانی *kā'la pā'nī* N.M. transportation for life کالا پن *kā'la pan* N M. blackness کالا پہاڑ *kā'la pahāṛ'* N.M. black mountain (fig.) anything huge and dark , terrible thing کالا چور *kā'la chor* N.M. great thief (fig.) dark horse کالا دانہ *kā'la dā'nah* N.M. indigo seed this used as purgative کالا دیو *kā'la dev* N.M. black demon (fig.) huge dark person کالا زیرہ *kā'la zī'rah* N.M. nigella indica seeds کالا کرنا *kā'la kar'nā* V.T. blacken deface scribble on (paper) منہ کالا کرنا *mūnh kā'la kar'nā* V.T. & I. forcinate disgrace (someone) by blackening his face منہ کالا ہونا *muṅh kā'la ho'nā* V.I. be disgraced do something shameful کالا کلوٹا (یا کلونٹا) *kā'la kalo'ṭā* (or *kaloṅ'ṭā*) jet black کالا کوا *kā'la kav'vā* N.M. raven (fig.) dark person کالا کوا کھایا ہے *kā'lā kav'vā khā'yā hai* PH. is talkative کالا کوئلہ *kā'la ko''ela* ADJ. jet black کالا منہ نیلے ہاتھ پاؤں *kā'lā mūnh nī'le hāth pa''on* PH. may he be cursed to Hell with it کالا ناگ *kā'la nāg* N M. black cobra کالے صابن مل کر گورے نہیں ہوتے *kā'le sā'būn mal kar go're na'hīṅ ho'te* a crow cannot become whiter by washing itself with soap کالی آندھی *kā'lī āṅ'dhī* N.F. black storm کالی بلا *kā'lī balā'* N.F. great evil ugly dark woman کالی پیلی آنکھیں کرنا *kā'lī pī'lī aṅ'kheṅ kar'nā* V.I turn red with rage look threateningly کالی تلسی *kali tul'sī* N F basil ocymum sanctum کالی جمعرات *kali jum'e-rat* N.F. hypothetical day for fulfilment of promise کالی زبان *ka'li zaban'* ADJ. black-tongued ; inauspicious کالی زیری *ka'li zi'ri* N.F. black cummin seed 'verusnico' کالی کلونٹی (یا کلونٹی) *ka'li kalo'ṭi* (or *kaloṅṭi*) ADJ. very black woman کالی کھانسی *ka'li khan'si* N.F. whooping cough , hiccup کالی گھٹا *ka'li gha'ṭa* N.F. dark rain-bearing cloud ominous clouds کالی مٹی *ka'li maṭ'ṭi* N.F. clay slime (esp. one from dirty pool) کالی مرچ *ka'li mir'ch* N.F. black pepper کالی ہڑ *ka'li haṛ* N.F. black myrobalan کالی ہانڈی سر پر رکھنا *ka'li han'di sir par dhar'na* V.I. be put to shame کالے کا کاٹا پانی نہیں مانگتا *ka'le ka ka'ṭa pa'ni na'hin mang'ta* V.I. it is difficult to escape a treacherous person's guiles کالے کے آگے چراغ نہیں جلتا *ka'le ke age ch ragh' na'hin jal'ta* V.I. defiance of a dangerous person is very difficult کالے کوس *ka'le kos* N.M. long distance ADV. very far کالے کے کاٹے کا نہ جنتر نہ منتر *ka'le ke ka'ṭe ka na jan'tar na man'tar* PROV cobra's bite cannot be cured by charm or skill

کالا [2] *ka'la* N.M. property goods and chattles نے غم دزد نہ اندیشہ کالا *nai gha'me duz'd na ande'-sha e ka'la* PH. neither have nor fear loss [P]

کالانعام *kal-'an'am'* ADV. brutish [A ~ ک like + ال + انعام animals]

کالبد *kal'bud* N.M. (human) body کالبد خاکی *kal'bud-e-kha'ki* N.M. human body ; mortal coal [A]

کالبوت *kalboot'* N.M. last ; shoemaker's last boot-tree [~P PREC. CORR.]

کالج *ka'lij* N.M. college کالجیٹ *kal'ji'eṭ* ADJ. collegiate [E]

کالر *ka'lar* N.M. collar [E]

کالک *ka'lak* N.F. blackness lamp-black ; soot stigma ; stain ; blemish black spot disgrace mortification کالک کا ٹیکا *ka'lak ka ṭi'ka* N.M. stain ; stigma

کالم *ka'lam* N.M. column ففتھ کالم *fif'th ka'lam* N.M. fifth column fifth columnist [E]

کام [1] *kam* N.M. work task duty job vocation avocation feat craftsmanship workmanship deed interest concern کام آخیر ہونا *kam a'khir ho'na* V.I. end (of work) finish کام آنا *kam a'na* V.I. be killed prove to be of use be used be well spent be skilled in (some) work کام اٹکا رہنا *kam' aṭ'ka raih'na* V.I. (of some work) be hindered کام بگاڑنا *kam' bi'gaṛna* V.T. put a spoke in (someone's) wheel upset (someone's) applecart mar something spoil make a mess of کام بگڑنا *kam' bi'gaṛ'na* V.I., (of someone's applecart) be upset (of something) be spoilt کام بنانا *kam' bana'na* V.I. bring suc e. to) accomplish something کام بننا (یا بن جانا) *kam' ban'na* (or *ban ja'na*) V.I. succeed ; gain one s end (of something) be accomplished کام پر لگانا *kam' .. laga'na* V.T. engage ; get fixed up in some job کام پڑنا *kam' paṛ'na* V.T. come into contact (with) have business (with) کام پیارا کہ چام *kam pya'ra ke cham'* PROV. handsome is that handsome does کام تمام کرنا *kam' tamam' kar'na* V.T. kill finish ; accomplish کام تمام ہونا *kam' tamam ho'na* V.I. be killed be accomplished کام چلانا *kam' chala'na* . V.T. manage کام چلاؤ *kam' chala'oo* ADJ. enough for the purpose make shift temporary کام چلنا *kam' chal'na* V.I. be managed have something going on be a going concern کام چمکنا *kam' cha'mak'na* V.I. (of some business) flourish, prosper, thrive کام چوپٹ ہو جانا *kam' chau'paṭ ho ja'na* V.I. (of some business) collapse be upset کام چور *kam'-chor'* ADJ. & N.M. shirker ; skulker idler good for-nothing کام دار *kam'-dar* ADJ. embroidered کام دینا *kam' de'na* V.T. be serviceable render good service wear well provide (someone) work fix (someone) up in some job *kam se* ADV. on business کام سے کام آتا ہے *kam se kam a'ta hai* PROV practice makes a man perfect کام رواں ہونا *kam rava' ho'na* V.I. (of work) get going کام سے جاتا رہنا *kam' se ja'ta raih'na,* کام کا نہ رہنا *kam' ka na raih'na* V.I. be no longer of any use be injured or damaged : beyond repair کام سے کام رکھنا (یا ہونا) *kam' se kam rakh'na* (or *ho'na*) V.I. mind one's (own) business کام کا *kam' ka* ADJ. useful ADV. of use to کام کاج *kam' kaj* N.M. job means of livelihood business کام کرنا *kam' kar'na* V.T. do (someone's) work have effect کام لینا *kam' le'na* V.T. use ; make use (of) get work done (by) get contract (or assignment, etc. from) کام میں لانا *kam' men la'na* V.T. use , put to use کام نکالنا *kam' nikal'na* V.T. get (one's) work done accomplish one's desire make use (of) کام نکلنا *kam' ni'kal'na* V.I. (of someone's purpose) be served prove to be of use کام ہو جانا *kam' ho ja'na* V.I. (of someone's purpose) be served die collapse be done with have some work to do

کام [2] *kam'* N.M. (rare) passion کام دیو *kam' dev* N.M. Hindu cupid ; god of love and passion کام روپی *kam'-roo'pi* ADJ. & N.F. pruriant girl ; wanton woman ; lascivious lady [S]

کام [3] *kam* N.M. object ; intention , purpose desire (rare) palate [P]

کامران *kāmrān'* ADJ. successful achieving one's wish(es) کامرانی *kāmrā'nī* N.F. success achievement of one's wish(es) [P ~ PREC.]

کامگار *kām-gar'* ADJ. successful lucky ; fortunate achieving one's wish(es) کامگاری *kam-gā'rī* N.F. success good luck ; good fortune achievement of one's wish(es) [P ~ کام ۳]

کامیاب *kām-yab'* ADJ. successful achieving one's wish(es) passed ; qualifying (an examination) کامیاب کرنا *kām-yab' kar'nā* V.T. give success to کامیاب ہونا *kām-yab' ho'nā* V.I. succeed pass or qualify (an examination) کامیابی *kām-yabī* N.F. success achievement of one's wish(es) کامیابی انسان کے بس میں نہیں *kām-yā'bī insān' ke bas meṅ na'hīṅ* PROV: success cannot be commanded کامیابی کے لیے استقلال شرط ہے *kām-yā'bī ke liye istiqlāl' shar't hai* PROV. perseverence is the prerequisite of success کامیابی پانا (یا حاصل کرنا) *kām-yā'bī pā'nā* (or *ḥā'sil karnā*) V.I. succeed achieve one's object کامیابی دینا (یا عطا کرنا) *kām-yā'bī de'nā* (or *'atā' kar'nā*) V.T. give success (to) کامیابی ملنا (یا میسر آنا) *kām-yā'bī mil'nā* (or *mūyas'sar ā'nā*) V.I. succeed ; meet with success [P ~ کام ۳]

کامل *kā'mil* ADJ. (F. or PL. کاملہ *kā'milah*) full entire ; complete categorical decisive learned accomplished perfect انسان کامل *insā'n-e kā'mil* N.M (the Holy Prophet as) the Perfect Man N.M. (PL. کملا *kūmalā'*) perfect people [A ~ کمال]

کامنی *kām'nī* N.F. lovely delicate woman [S]

کامود *kāmod'* N.M. name of a nocturnal musical mode [S]

کان *kān* N.F. mine quarrry کانکن *kān'-kan* N.M. miner کانکنی *kān'-ka'nī* N.F. mining کان نمک *kā'n-e na'mak* N.M. salt mine ہر کہ در کان نمک رفت نمک شد *har' ke dar kā'n-e namak' raf't namak' shud* PROV. whoever goes to see becomes a part of it کان ملاحت *kā'n-e malā'hat* N.F. lovely brunette [P]

کان ۲ *kān* N.M. ear (fig.) attention ; heed (fig.) lesson کان آشنا ہونا *kān ash'nā ho'nā* V.I. be familiar (with voice, etc.) کانا باتی *kā'nā-ḥā'tī* N.F. whisper child's joke by whispering loudly into the ears کانا باتی کانا باتی کر *kā'nā-b'ātī kā'nā-ba'tī kūr'r* PH. formula whispered in this joke کاناپھوسی *kā'nā-phoo'sī* N.F. whispher کاناپھوسی کرنا *kā'nā-phoo'sī kar'nā* V.I. whisper کان اڑے (یا پھٹے) جانا *kān' ūṛe* (or *phaṭe*) *jā'na* V. be deafened by noise کان اینٹھنا (یا کسنا) *kān ainṭh'nā* (or *kas'nā*) V.T. twist (someone) ears reprove کان بجنا *kān' baj'nā* V.I. (of ears) sing ; (of someone) have a singing in the ears fancy کان بجیانا (یا دبانا) *kān' būchyā'na* (or *dabā'na*) V.T. (of horse) turn ears back when preparing to bite کان بندھوانا *kān bindhvā'na* V.T. & O. get ears bored کان بہرے کرنا *kān' baih're kar'nā* V.T. & I. turn a deaf dear (to) render unable to hear کان بھرنا *kān' bhar'na* V.T. poison the ears (of) کان بہنا *kān' baih'na* V.I. (of ear) suppurate کان پر جوں تک نہ چلنا (یا رینگنا) *kān' par jooṅ' tak na chal'na* (or *rīng'na*) be heedless not to take a lesson from be quite unaffected by کان پڑنا *kān' par'na* V.I. be heard کان پڑی آواز سنائی نہ دینا *kān' pa'ṛī āvāz' sūnā''ī na de'nā* PH. be in the midst of a deafening noise کان پکڑنا *kān' pa'kaṛ'na* V.T. & I. twist one's ears (fig) be penitent vow never to repeat the mistake admit someone's superiority be obedient be loyal ; be faithful کان پکڑی لونڈی *kān' pak'ṛī lauṅ'dī* PH. very faithful be obedient کان پھاڑنا *kan' phaṛ'nā* V.T. make a deafening pierce the ear-lobe کان پھٹے جانا *kān' pha'ṭe jā'na* V.I. (of noise) be deafening کان پھڑپھڑانا *kān pharphṛā'na* V.T. & I. (of dog) jerk the ears (fig). be alert کان تلے کی چھوڑنا *kān' ta'le kī chhoṛ'na* V.I. say something scarrilous or unpalable divulge a secret کان جھنانا *kan' jhanā'nā* V.I. be deafened by noise کان چھوڑ لے جانا *kān' chor' le jā'na* PH. turn a deaf ear to کان چھیدنا *kān' chhed'na* V.T. pierce the ear lobe کان دبانا *kān' dabā'na* V.I. keep mum کان دھرنا *kān' dhar'na* V.I. listen to ; give or lend one's ears to (someone's words) کان رکھنا *kān' rakh'na* V.I. listen کان کا پردہ *kān' ka par'dah* N.M. eardrum: tympanum کے کان کاٹنا (یا کترنا) *ke kān' kaṭ'na* (or *ka'tarna*) PH. outwit کان (یا کانوں) کا کچا *kān'* (or *kā'noṅ*) *kā kach'chā* ADJ. & N.M. too credulous (person) کان کا میل *kān' kā mail'* N.M. ear-wax ; cerumen کان کھانا *kān' khā'na* V.T. pester with too much noise or talk کان کھجانے کی فرصت نہ ہونا *kān' khūjā'ne kī fūr'sat na ho'nā* V.I. be extremely busy کان کھڑے کرنا *kān' khaṛe kar'nā* V.I. prick one's ears be on the alert کان کھڑے ہونا *kān' khaṛe ho'nā* V.I. be alarmed کان کھلنا *kān' khūl'nā* PH. be warned کان کھول دینا *kān' khol' de'nā* V.T. warn someone کان کھول کر *kān' khol' kar* ADV. attentively کان کھولنا *kān' khol'nā* V.I. open one's ears warn (someone) کان لگانا *kān' lagā'nā* V.T. listen attentively (to) overhear کان مروڑنا (یا ملنا) *kān' maroṛ'nā* (or *mal'nā*) V.T. twist the ear ; reprove (fig.) chastise کان میلیا *kān'-mai'liya* N.M. one whose profession it is to clean ears ; earclear کان میں آواز پڑنا *kān' meṅ āvāz' paṛ'nā* V.I. happen to catch the sound (of)

(یا لینا) کان میں انگلی دے رکھنا *kān' meṅ ūng'lī de rakh'nā* (or *le'nā*) V.T. turn a deaf ear (to) کان میں بات کہنا *kān' meṅ bāt kaih'nā* V.T. whisper into (someone's) ears کان میں بات مارنا *kān' meṅ bāt' mār'na* V.I. turn a deaf ear to a pretend not to hear کان میں بھنک پڑنا *kān' meṅ bhi'nak par'nā* V.I. get wind (of) کان میں پارہ بھر *kān' meṅ pā'rah bhar'nā* V.I. pretend not to hear کان میں پھونکنا *kān' meṅ phoonk'nā* V.T. whisper into the ears (of) (fig.) set (someone) against کان میں تیل ڈال کے سو رہ *kān' meṅ tel' dāl' ke so raih'nā* V.I. be attentive ; pay no heed at all کانوں میں جھنجھی کوڑی ڈال *kan' meṅ jhin'jhī kau'rī dāl'nā* become slave (of) کان میں ڈالنا *kān' meṅ dāl'nā* V.T. inform ; to warn کان میں ڈھول بجانا *kān' meṅ dhol' bajā'nā* V.T. din into the ears (of) کان (یا کانوں) میں رس پڑنا *kān'* (or *kā'noṅ*) *meṅ ras' par'nā* V.I. hear a musical voice have an ear for music کان (یا کانوں) میں رس گھول *kān'* (or *kā'noṅ*) *meṅ ras' ghol'nā* V.I. speak or sing in a very sweat voice کان (یا کانوں) میں روئی ٹھونسنا *kān'* (or *kā'noṅ*) *meṅ roo'ī thoṅs'nā* V.I. plug one's ears (fig.) pay no heed (to) disregard کان نہ ہلا *kan' na hilā'na* V.I. be docile (fig) not to raise one's little finger کان پر ہاتھ دھرنا (یا رکھنا) *kā'noṅ par hāth' dhar'na* (or *rakh'nā*) V T. refuse disclaim deny feign ignorance کانوں کے پردے پھٹے جا *kā'noṅ ke par'de pha'te jā'nā* V.I. (of noise) be deafening کانوں کان خبر نہ ہونا *kā'noṅ kan khabar na ho'na* V.I. not at all to leak out کانوں میں کھٹکنا *kānoṅ meṅ kha'taknā* V.I. (of word, etc.) sound unfamiliar be cocophanous کانوں میں انگلیاں *kā'noṅ meṅ ūng'liyāṅ de'nā* V.I. be inattentive ; turn a deaf ear to کان ہونا *kān' ho'nā* V.I take a lesson (from) be warned

کان *kān* N.F crookedness (in cloth, bed, etc.) کان نکالنا *kān' nikāl'na* V.T. straighten کان نکلوانا *kān' nikalvā'na* V.T. get straightened

کانا، کانڑا *kā'na*, *kāṅ'ṛa* (F. کانی *kā'nī*, کانڑی *kāṅ'ṛī*) ADJ. & N.M. one-eyed (person) having rotten kernel blemished defective کانا پردہ *kā'na pur'dah* N.M. 'purdah' not fully observed کانے کی ایک رگ *kā'ne kī ek' rag sivā'* PROV. one-eyed person is always mischievous

کانپ *kamp* N.M. rib (of umbrella) curved rib (of paper-kite)

کانپنا *kāmp'na*, کانپ اٹھنا *kāmp ūṭh'na* V.I tremble shiver shake rock quake

کانٹا *kāṅ'ṭā* N M thorn fork quill spur bone (of fish) fishinghook small balance tongue of balance fur (on tongue) hand (for pulling something out) unpalateable remark ADJ. lean , thin کانٹا چبھونا *kāṅ'ṭā chubho'nā* V.T. prick with a thorn کانٹا سا کھٹکنا *kāṅ'ṭā sā khaṭak'nā* V.I. rankle کانٹا لگنا *kāṅ'ṭā lag'nā* V I be pricked by a thorn کانٹا مارنا *kāṅ'ṭā mār'nā* V.I. strike with spur or wing کانٹا نکل جانا *kāṅ'ṭā ni'kal jā'nā* V I. be freed from pain no longer to rankle کانٹا ہونا *kāṅ'ṭā ho'nā* V I. be a thorn in the flesh of سوکھ کر کانٹا ہو جانا *sookh kar kāṅ'ṭā ho jā'nā* V.I. become lean کانٹوں پر لوٹنا *kāṅ'ṭoṅ par loṭ'nā* V.I. suffer pain lie on a bed of thorns کانٹوں پر کھینچنا *kāṅ'ṭoṅ par khench'nā*, کانٹوں میں گھسیٹنا *kāṅ'ṭoṅ meṅ ghasīṭ'na* V.T. pull (someone's) leg ; praise (someone) too much کسی کے حق میں کانٹے بونا *ki'sī ke ḥaq meṅ kāṅ'ṭe bo'nā* V.I. sow the seed of trouble for someone کانٹے میں تلنا (یا تل کر بکنا) *kāṅ'ṭe meṅ tūl'nā* (or *tūl' kar bik'nā*) V.I. sell at the price of gold ; be very valuable

کانجی *kāṅ'jī* N.F. pickled carrot gruel

کانجی ہوس *kāṅ'jī hauz* N.M. cattle look-up کانجی ہوس میں بند کرنا *kāṅ'jī kanz band kar'na* V.T. impound (cattle, etc.)

کانچ *kāṅch* N.F. glass protrusion of rectum کانچ نکلنا *kāṅch' ni'kalnā* V.I. (of rectum) protrude کانچ نکالنا *kāṅch nikāl'nā* V.T. give (someone) his gruel

کاندھا *kāndhā* N.M. (dial for کندھا ★)

کانڑا *kāṅ'ṛā* ADJ. (same as کانا ★)

کانڑا *kāṅ'ṛā* N.M. name of a musical mode 'kahura'

کانسٹیبل *kaṅs'tebal* N.M constable کانسٹیبلری *kaṅsteb'larī* N.F. constabulary [E]

کانسی *kāṅ'sī* N.F. bronze ; bell-metal

کانفرنس *kāṅ'farans* N.F conference کانفرنس کرنا *kān farans kar'nā* V T. hold a conference plot, intrigue [E]

کانکھنا *kaṅkh'nā* V.I groan while carrying load or evacuating bowels

کانگرس *kāng'ras* N F. Congress [E]

کانگڑی *kāng'ṛī* N F. (dial) portable Kashmir stove ; wicker-work covered chafing bowl

کانور *kāṅ'var* N.M. (with PL. V.) jaundice کو کانور ہونا *ko kāṅ'var ho'nā* V.I. suffer from jaundice

کانورا *kāṅv'rā* ADJ. non-plussed

کانون *kānoon'* N.M. stove [A]

کانوکیشن *kānvokē'shan* N.F. convocation [E]

کاو *kav, kāv' kāv* کاو، کاوش N.F. delving deep diligent search meditation [P ~ کاویدن dig]

کاوا *kā'va* N.M. lounging (a horse) کاوا دینا *kā'va de'nā* V.T. lounge (a horse)

کاواک *kā'vāk* ADJ. awkward hollow [P]

کاوش *kā'vish* N.F. inquiry research scratching one's head when puzzled animosity [P]

کاوہ *kā'vah* N.M. name of a legendary national hero of Persian کاویانی *kaviyānī* ADJ. of Kavah درفشِ کاویانی *daraf'sh-e kāviyā'nī* N.M. ancient Persia's liberation flag [P]

کاہ[1] *kāh* SUF. consuming [P]

کاہ[2] *kāh* N.M. (shortened as کہ *kah*) grass hay پرِ کاہ *pa'r-e kāh'* N.M. blade of grass پرِ کاہ کے برابر *pa'r-e kāh' ke barā'bar* ADV. least; in the least amount [P]

کاہش *kā'hish* N.F. waning decline pining wear and tear [P ~ کاستن]

کاہل *kā'hil* ADJ. lazy; indolent clothful slow; tardy N.M. (PL. کواہل *kavā'hil*) shoulders کاہل وجود *kā'hil vujood'*, کاہل الوجود *kā'hil-ul v jood'* ADJ. & N.M. lazy fellow کاہلی *kā'hilī* N.F. laziness; indolence sloth tardiness کاہلی کرنا (یا سے کام لینا) *kā'hilī kar'na* (or *se kām' le'nā*) V.I. be lazy; be indolent be slothful show tardiness [A]

کاہن *kā'hin* N.M. (PL. کہنہ *ka'hanah*) soothsayer wizard [A]

کاؤنٹ *kā''ūnṭ* N.M. Count کاؤنٹس *kā''ūnṭais* N.F. Countess [E]

کاہو *kā'hoo* N.M. lettuce [P]

کاہی *kā'hī* ADJ. grass-green

کاہیدہ *kāhī'dah* ADJ. waned gaunt کاہیدگی *kāhī'dagī* N.F. waning gauntness [P ~ کاہیدن]

کاہے کو *kā'he ko* ADV. why what for; wherefore

کائنات *kā'ināt'* N.F. universe creatures creation; possession stock; prestige worth [A ~ کون]

کائیں کائیں *kā''eṅ kā''eṅ* N.F. caw (of crow) confused noise کائیں کائیں کرنا *kā''eṅ kā''eṅ kar'na* V.I. caw

کائی *kā'ī* N.F. alga moss licken mould کائی سی پھٹ جانا *kā''ī sī phaṭ ja'nā* V.I. disperse scatter

کائیاں *kā''iyāṅ* ADJ. crafty

کایا *kā'yā* N.F. state; condition body کایا پلٹ جانا *kā'yā pa'laṭ ja'nā* V.I. undergo a radical change (use for the better) have a new look کایا کلپ *kā'yā ka'lap* N.F. rejuvenation [S]

کایستھ *kā'yasth* N.M. a Hindu caste wellknown for their knowledge of Persian during the Moghul rule; 'Kayasth'

کب *kūb* N.M. hump hunch (of plaster) stick out or up کب نکلنا *kūb' ni'kalnā* V.I. be hunch-backed (of plaster) stick up (from the wall, etc.)

کب *kab* ADV. when: at what time how in what manner کب تک *kab' tak*, (arch. کب تلک *kab' ta'lak*) ADV. how long; for how long till when کب سے *kab' se*, کب کا *kab' kā* ADV. since when since how long long enough; long since; since long

کباب *kabāb'* N.M. grilled mince ADJ. grilled burnt out کباب کرنا *kabāb' kar'nā* V.T. gril (fig.) burn (with rage, every or love) disconfit کباب ہونا *kabāb' ho'nā* V.I. be grilled burn; be consumed with rage, etc. be chagrined کباب چینی *kabāb' chī'nī* N.F. wild clave; cubeb; piper cubeb کبابی *kabā'bī* ADJ. grilled mince vendor [~ A]

کبار *kabār'* N.M. PL. high-ups very important personalities; V.T. & Ps. digrataries ADJ. great [A ~ SING. کبیر]

کباڑ *kibāṛ'* N.M. broken furniture second-hand stuff lumber کباڑ خانہ *kabā'ṛ-khā'nah* N.M. lumber-room کباڑی *kabā'ṛī*, کباڑیا *kabā'ṛiya* N.M. dealer in secondhand stuff

کبائر *kabā''ir* N.M. PL. deadly sins; mortal sins [A ~ SING. کبیرہ]

کبت *kabit'* N.M. eulogistic limmeric (improvised by minstrels) [~ S کویتا]

کبد *ka'bid* N.M. (PL. اکباد *akbad'*) liver [A]

کبڈی *kabaḍ'ḍī* N.F. a popular Pakistani game resembling prisoners' base or (bars); 'kabaddi' کبڈی کھیلنا *kabaḍ'ḍī khel'nā* V.I.

کبر *ki'bar* N.M. old age being advanced (age) کبیر السن *kabir-us-sin'* N.M. being advanced in years; old age [A]

کبر *kib'r* N.M. pride; consert; haughtiness dignity [A]

کبرا *kab'ra* ADJ. spotted; piebald چتکبرا *chitkab'ra* ADJ. piebald

کبرا *kubarā'* N.M. PL. high-ups; grandees; dignitaries; V.I.P's. [A ~ کبر]

کبریٰ kūb'ra N.M. major proposition of a syllogism ; major elder (or eldest) one ADJ. great elder or eldest صغریٰ کبریٰ مرتب کرنا sūgh'ra kūb'ra mūrai'tab kar'nā V.T. & O. form a syllogism

کبریا kibriyā' N.M. magnificence Magnificent (as an attribute of God) کبریائی kibriya''ī N.F. magnificence grandeur [A ~ کبر]

کبریت kibrīt' N.M. sulphur ; brimstone کبریت احمر kibrī't-e ah'mar N.F. red sulphur philosopher's stone [A]

کبڑا kūb'ṛa ADJ. & N.M. (F. کبڑی kūb'ṛī) hunch-backed or hump-backed (person) ; hunchback [A ~ کب kūb]

کبک kab'k N.M. a kind partridge ; pheasant کبک دری kab'k-e da'rī N.M. highland of partridge of lovely plumage ; snow pheasant کبک رفتار kab'k-raftār' ADJ. graceful in motion کبک رفتاری kab'k-raftā'rī N.F. graceful motion [A]

کبوتر kaboo'tar N.M. pigeon کبوتر باز kaboo'tar-bāz N.M. (dep.) pigeon-breeder one fond of pigeon-flying کبوتر بازی kaboo'tar-bā'zī N.F. (der.) pigeon-breeding pigeon-flying کبوتر بام حرم kaboo'tar-e bā'm-e ḥa'ram N.M. picture taking abode on Holy Ka'aba's rooftop (fig.) one unaware of others trouble کند ہم جنس با ہم جنس پرواز کبوتر با کبوتر باز با باز kūnad' ham-jin's bā ham-jin's parvāz' kaboo'tar bā kaboo'tar bāz' bā bāz' PROV. birds of the same feather flock together کبوتر خانہ kaboo'tar-khā'nah N.M. pigeon-house ; dove-cote کبوتری kaboo'tarī N.F. dove ; female pigeon (rare) village dancer [P]

کبود kabood' ADJ. & N.M. sky-blue ; blue ; azure cerulean چرخ کبود char'kh-e kabood' N.M. sky ; the heavens ; firmament (fig.) fate کبودی kaboo'dī ADJ. sky-blue; blue ; azure cerulean [P]

کبھو ka'bhoo ADV. (arch.) (same as کبھی ★)

کبھی ka'bhī ADV. sometimes seldom ; rarely کبھی تولہ کبھی ماشہ ka'bhī to'lah kabhī mā'shah PH. inconstant whimsical ; capricious کبھی کا ka'bhī kā ADV. sometimes ago long ago long since ; since long کبھی کبھار kabhī kabhār', کبھی کبھی ka'bhī ka'bhī ADV. at times now and then ; occasionally کبھی نہ کبھی ka'bhī na kabhī' ADV. sometime or other once in a while for once at least

کبیدہ kabī'dah ADJ. aggrieved ; afflicted (rare) folded , crumpled کبیدہ خاطر kabī'da-khā'tir ADJ. aggrieved ; grief-stricken کبیدہ خاطری kabī'da khā'tırī, کبیدگی kabī'dagī N.F. grief being grief stricken [P]

کبیر kabīr ADJ. (F. OF PL. کبیرہ) by large great immense N.M. (PL. کبرا kūbarā', kibār') important , personality کبیر پنتھ kabīr-panth N.M. name of a synthetic Indo-Pakistani creed founded by Kabir کبیر پنتھی kabīr-panthī N.M. follower of this creed [A ~]

کبیسہ kabī'sah ADJ. intercalary سال کبیسہ sā'l-e kabī'sah N.M. intercalary year [A]

کپ kūp N.M stack

کپا kūp'pa N.M. leathern oil-container ADJ. bloated پھول کر کپا ہو جانا phool' kar kūp'pā ho jā'nā V.I. grow very fat; put on flesh be bloated be swollen

کپاس kapās' N.F. cotton کپاس اوٹنا (یا بیلنا) kapās' oṭ'nā (or bel'nā) V.T. & O. given cotton کپاس (اوٹنے) کا کارخانہ kapās' (oṭ'ne) kā karkhā'nah N.M. cotton-ginning factory

کپتان kaptān' N.M. Captain Superintendent of Police ; S.P. کپتانی kaptā'nī N.F. captain's rank [E[

کپٹ ka'paṭ N.M. emnity ; animosity malice fraud کپٹ رکھنا ka'paṭ rakh'nā V.T. bear malice کپٹی kap'ṭī ADJ. false ; insincere; hypocritical malicious fraudulent (person)

کپڑ ka'paṛ PREF. (CONTR. of FOLL. ★)

کپڑا kap'ṛa N.M. cloth piece of cloth garment کپڑوں میں نہ سمانا kap'ṛoṅ meṅ na samā'nā V.T. be very happy ; not to contain oneself for joy کپڑوں سے ہونا kap'ṛoṅ se ho'nā, کپڑے آنا kap'ṛe ā'nā V.I. mensturate ; have the menses کپڑے kap'ṛe N.M. PL. clothes کپڑے اتارنا kap'ṛe ūtār'nā V.T. & O. take off one's clothes ; doff change clothes کپڑے پہننا kap'ṛe paihan'nā V.T. & O. put on clothes; don ; dress; change clothes کپڑاہند kapṛāhnd', کپڑگند ka'paṛ-gand N.F. smell of burning cloth کپڑچھن ka'paṛ-chhan ADJ. strain کپڑچھان ka'paṛ-chhān' kar'nā V.T. strain sift کپڑکوٹ ka'paṛ-goṭ N.M. (dial.) tent

کپکپانا kapkapā'nā V.I. shiver tremble shudder shake quake کپکپاہٹ kap-kapāhaṭ, کپکپی kap'kapī N.F. shiver trembling shudder کپکپی چڑھنا kap'kapī chaṛh'nā V.T. shiver with cold have a fit of ague

کپوت kapoot' N.M. prodigal disobedient son [~ ک + پوت]

کپور kapoor' N.M. (dial.) camphor کپوری kapoo'rī ADJ. milk-white ; white-like camphor also

N.M.) a kind of white betel leaf [S]

کپورا *kapoo'ra* N.M. testicle (as part of mutton)

کپی *kūp'pī* N.F. metallic bottle leathern bottle [~ کپا DIM]

کتا *kūt'ta* N.M. (F. کتیا *kūt'ya*) dog trigger spring of gun-lock mean person کتا بھی دم ہلا کر بیٹھتا ہے *kūt'ta bhī dūm hila'-kar baiṭh'ta hai* PROV. even animals like to keep then abade clean کتا گھاس *kūt'ta-ghas* N.F. a kind of fragrant but barbed grass کتے خانہ *kūt'te kha'nah* N.M. a kennel for dog کتے خسی (یا خصی) *kūt'te kha'si* (or *khas'mī*) N.M. useless boring work کتے کا کاٹا *kūt'te ka ka'ṭa* ADJ. bitten by dog dog-bite کتے کا کتا بیری *kūt'te ka kūt'ta bai'rī* PROV. colleagues tend to become rivals کتے کا کفن *kūt'te ka ka'fan* N.M. (W. dial.) (der.) coarse cloth کتے کو گھی ہضم نہیں ہوتا *kūt'te ko ghī haz'm nahīn ho'ta* PROV. a mean person will always give himself out کتے کی دم *kūt'te kī dūm* ADJ. mean malicious کتے کی دم کو بارہ برس نلکی میں رکھا پھر ٹیڑھی کی ٹیڑھی *kūt'te kī dūm ko ba'rah ba'ras nal'kī men rak'kha phir' ṭe'ṛhī kī ṭe'ṛhī* PROV. what is bred in the bone will never come out of the flesh کتے کی سی ہڑک اٹھنا *kūt'te kī sī hū'ṛak uṭh'na* PROV. have a sudden passion for some evil act کتے کی موت آتی ہے تو مسجد کی طرف دوڑتا ہے *kūt'te kī maut a'tī hai to mas'jid kī taraf daur'ta hai* PROV. destiny drives one to death کتے کی موت مرنا *kūt'te kī maut mar'na* V.I. die a dog's d eath be killed like a dog

کتاب *kitab'* N.M. (PL. کتب *kū'tūb*) book (rare) letter کتاب الٰہی *kita'b-e ila'hī*, آسمانی کتاب *asma'nī kitab* N.F. revealed book, holy book scriptures کتاب کا کیڑا *kitab' ka ki'ṛa* N.M. bookworm درسی کتاب *dar'sī kitab'* N.F. text-book کتابت *kita'bat* N.F. calligraphy copying کتابی *kita'bī* ADJ. theoretical (learning) book (lore, adjustment, etc.) (of face) oval, oblong کتابی چہرہ *kita'bī cheh'rah*, روئے کتابی *roo''e-kita'bī* N.M. lovely oblong face کتابی علم *kita'bī 'il'm* N.M. bookish knowledge (hence) lack of worldly experience

کتارہ *kata'ra* N.M. (dial. for کٹارا N.M. ★)

کتان *katan'* N.F. fine linen [A]

کتانا *kata'na* V.T. cause to spin کتائی *kata''ī* N.F. spinning remuneration for it [~ کاتنا CAUS.]

کتب *kū'tūb* N.F. PL. books کتب خانہ *kū'tūb-kha'nah* N.M. library (rare) bookshop کتب فروش *kū'tūb-firosh'* N.M. book seller کتب فروشی *kū'tūb'-firo'shī* N.F. book trade [A ~ SING. کتاب]

کتبہ *kat'bah* N.M. epitaph inscription plaque

کتخدا *kat-khū'da*, (rare کدخدا *kad-khūda*) ADJ. married bridegroom head of family کتخدائی *kat-khūda''ī*, کدخدائی *kad-khūda''ī* N.F. marriage [P]

کترانا *katra'na* V.I. dodge evade avoid leave the high road take to by-paths slink away (from) edge away کترا کر چلنا *katra' kar chal'na* V.I. cut the society (of) desert one's companion

کترنا *ka'tarna* V.T. cut pare prune trim کتر بیونت *ka'tar biyont'* N.F. cutting out (clothes) cuts emendations کترن *kat'ran* N.F. cutting clipping paring کترنی *ka'tarnī* N.F. scissors ; pair of scissors کتروان *ka'tarvan* ADJ. sidelong (walk, move, etc.) away

کترنا *kū'tarna* V.T. gnaw

کتف *ka'tif* N.M. (PL. اکتاف *aktaf'*) shoulder [A]

کتل *kat'tal* N.F. brickbat

کتکا *kūt'ka*, کھتکا *khūt'ka* N.M. baton

کتم *kat'm* N.M. veil concealment کتم عدم *kat'm-e 'a'dam* N.M. non-existence کتمان *kitman'* N.M. concealment keeping secret [A]

کتنا *kit'na* ADJ. (PL. کتنے *kit'ne* F. کتنی *kit'nī*) how much how many many ; several ADV. how ; how very very کتنا ہی *kit'na hī* ADV. a lot ; a great deal CONJ. howsoever, howevermuch کتنے پانی میں ہے *kit'ne pa'nī men hai* (etc.) PROV. how shallow he (etc.) is (I know) his depth

کتنا *kat'na* V.I. be spun کتوانا *katva'na* V.T. get spun cause to spin [~ کاتنا]

کتنا *kūt'na* V.I. be estimated

کتوانا *katva'na* V.T. cause to spin [~ کاتنا CAUS.]

کتھا *ka'tha* N.F. Hindu sermon traveller's tale someone's boring tale of woes کتھا بکھانا *ka'thā bakha'na* V.T. tell traveller's tale

کتھا *kat'tha*, کتھہ *kat'thah* N.M. catechu ; 'terra japonica'

کتھک *ka'thak* N.M. boy playing female dancer's role caste of dancers [S]

کتیا *kūt'ya* N.F. female dog bitch [~ M. کتا]

کتیرا *katī'ra* N.M. tragacanth clipper کتیرا گوند *katī'ra gond* N.F. tragacanth gum

کٹ *kūṭ* N.M. name of a vegetable yielding a die

کٹ¹ *kaṭ* N.F. cut deduction کٹ پیس *kaṭpres'* N.M. cut-piece [E]

کٹ² *kaṭ* N.M. black colour ADJ. black ADV. jet (black)

کٹ³ *kaṭ* V.I. IMP. of کٹنا ★ biting cutting being hacked کٹ کھانا *kaṭ kha'nā* ADJ. addicted to biting N.M. (usu. as PL.) broken letter (as copying pattern, etc.) (der.) help-books کٹ مستا *kaṭ mas'tā* ADJ. & N.M. fat (person) rough ; tough ; hoodlum [~ کٹنا]

کٹ⁴ *kaṭ* PREF. wood hard hidebound کٹ پتلی *kaṭ-pūt'lī*, کٹھ پتلی *kaṭh-pūt'lī* N.F. puppet (fig.) stooge ADJ. not enjoying real power کٹ حجتی *kaṭ-ḥuj'jatī* N.M. quibbling silly argument quibber کٹ ملا *kaṭ-mūl'lā* N.M. hedge-priest hide-bound religious man

کٹا *kūṭ'ṭā* N.M. pigeon with trimmed wings

کٹا *kaṭ'ṭā* ADJ. (same as کٹر *kaṭ'ṭar* ★)

کٹا چھنی *ka'ṭā-chha'nī*, کٹی چھنی *ka'ṭī chha'nī* N.F. clash; enmity کٹا چھنی رہنا *ka'ṭā chha'nī raih'nā* V.I. (of enmity) exist (between)

کٹار *kaṭār'* N.M. dagger

کٹارا *kaṭā'rā* N.M. tamarind seed thin sugarcane globe thistle large dagger کٹاری *kaṭā'rī* N.F. dagger

کٹانا *kaṭā'nā*, کٹوانا *kaṭvā'nā* V.T. cause to cut cause to bite کٹاؤ *kaṭā''o* N.M. cutting cut slash pattern floral pattern undulating pattern کٹائی *kaṭā''ī* N.F. harvest harvest time reaping harvesting remuneration for it [~ کٹنا]

کٹر *kaṭ'ṭar*, کٹا *kaṭ'ṭā* ADJ. bigoted hide-bound

کٹر کٹر *ka'ṭar ka'ṭar* N.F. munching ; munching [ONO]

کٹرا *kaṭ'rā* N.M. young male buffalo market; mart compound quadrangle کٹری *kaṭ'rī* N.F. young female buffalo small mart compound quadrangle

کٹکٹ *kaṭ'kaṭ* N.F. nibbling کٹ کٹ کرنا *kaṭ kaṭ kar'nā* V.I. nibble

کٹکٹانا *kiṭkiṭā'nā* V.T. grind (one's teeth) دانت کٹکٹانا *dant kiṭkiṭā'nā* V.T. & O. grind one's teeth (fig.) fret and fume کٹکی دینا (یا لگانا) *kuṭ'kī de nā* (or *lagā'nā*) V.T. biting edge of (sting, etc.) [ONO]

کٹلس *kaṭ'las* N.M. cutlet [~E CORR.]

کٹنا *kaṭ'nā* V.I. be cut be cut off be snapped be clipped be deducted (of time, etc.) pass (of kite) suffer defeat (of bank, etc.) be washed away (of canal) be taken out (of colour) fade out (of name) be struck off be abashed ; be put to shame

کٹنا¹ *kūṭ'nā* V.I. be pounded [~ کوٹنا]

کٹنا² *kūṭ'nā* N.M. pimp ; pander ; procurer کٹناپا *kūṭnā'pā* N.M. pandering کٹنائی *kūṭnā''ī* N.F. procurer's wages کٹنی *kūṭ'nī* N.F. bawd ; procures

کٹوتی *kaṭau'tī* N.F. discount deduction

کٹورا *kaṭo'rā* N.M. metallic bowl ADJ. (dial.) flourishing (town, etc.) کٹورا بجنا (یا کھنکنا) *kaṭo'rā baj'nā* (or *kha'naknā*) V.I. (arch.) (of water) be offered by water-carriers be a thriving town کٹورا پھرانا (یا دوڑانا) *kaṭo'rā phirā'nā* (or *daurā'nā*) V.T. guess criminals names (by occult means through rotating a bowl and drawing lots from it کٹوری *kaṭo'rī* N.F. small metallic bowl

کٹھ *kaṭh* PREF. wood کٹھ بندھن *kaṭh-ban'dhan*, کٹھ پتلی *kaṭh-pūt'lī* N.F. (same as کٹ پتلی N.F. (see under کٹ ★) کٹھ پھوڑا *kaṭh-pho'rā* N.M. wood-pecker [~ کاٹھ CONTR.]

کٹھالی *kūṭhā'lī* N.F. melting pot crucible

کٹہرا *kaṭaih'rā* N.M. railing raised piece at head (or foot) of bed

کٹھرا *kaṭh'rā* N.M. wooden trough

کٹھلا *kūṭh'lā* N.M. granary lime-kiln

کٹھن *ka'ṭhin* ADJ. hard ; difficult arduous

کٹھور *kaṭhor'* ADJ. callous relentless cruel کٹھورتا *kaṭhor'tā* N.F. (dial.) callousness

کٹی *kūṭ'ṭī* N.F. chapped fodder anything chopped to small pieces pickles snapping friendly ties کٹی کرنا *kūṭ'ṭī kar'nā* V.T. snap friendly ties (with) chop to small pieces

کٹیا *kūṭ'yā* (dial. کٹی *kū'ṭī*) N.F. cottage

کٹیا *kaṭ'yā* N.F. young female buffalo fishing hook a kind of hook-like ear-ring

کٹیا *kaṭay'yā* N.M. a kind of thistle (dial.) butcher [~ کاٹنا]

کٹیلا *kaṭī'lā* ADJ. (F. کٹیلی *kaṭī'lī*) piercing sharp-edged charming کٹیلے لگنا *kaṭ'ṭe lag'nā*

V.I. be misappropriated (by). [~ کاٹنا]

کثافت *kasā'fat* N.F. grossness impurity density opaqueness [A]

کثرت *kas'rat* N.F. plenty excess ; abundance majority bulk کثرت رائے *kas'rat-e rā''e* N.F. majority of votes majority opinion کثرت سے *kas'rat se* ADV. amply ; abundantly plentifully in a large measure بکثرت ہونا *ba-kas'rat ho'nā*, کثرت سے ہونا *kas'rat se ho'nā* V.I. abound ; be found in abundance [A]

کثیر *kasīr'* ADJ. many multifarious much ample copious abundant plentiful PREF. multi- poly کثیر الاستعمال *kasī'r-ūl-iste'māl'* ADJ. widely used کثیر الاضلاع *kasī'r-ūl-azlā''* N.F. polygon, کثیر الالسنہ *kasī'r-ūl-al'sinah* ADJ. polyglot کثیر ترین *kāsīr'-tarīn* ADJ. too much ; too many کثیر العیال *kasī'r-ūl-'iyāl'* ADJ. one having a family کثیر الوقوع *kasī'r-ūl vūqoo''* ADJ. frequent : of frequent occurrence [A ~ کثرت]

کثیف *kasīf* ADJ. dense ; impure ; opaque ; gross untidy dense opaque کثیف الطبع *kas'f-ūl tab''* ADJ. untidy (person) (one) with unclean habits [A ~ کثافت]

کج *kaj* ADJ. curved crooked awry oblique cross unfair fraudulent wrong perverse PREF. ill mal کج ادا *kaj-adā'* ADJ. ill-mannered cross perverse کج ادائی *kāj-adā''ī* N.F. perverseness ; perversity crossness in manners being ill-mannered کج بحث *kaj-baih's* ADJ. quibbler کج بحثی *kaj-baih'sī* N.F. quibble quibbling کج چشم *kaj-chash'm* ADJ. squint-eyed کج خلق *kaj-khūl'q* ADJ. surly ; ill-tempered rude کج دار و مریز *kaj dā'r-o-ma-rez'* PH. tantalizing tantalization کج رائے *kaj-rā''e* ADJ. pigheaded perverse کج رائی *kaj-rā''ī* N.F. perversity کج رفتار *kaj-raftār*, کج رو *kaj-rau'* ADJ. unprincipled perverse irregular motion کج رفتاری *kaj raftā'rī*, کج روی *kaj-ra'vī* N.F. being unprinciple of perversity irregular motion walking in ungodly ways کج فہم *kaj-faih'm* ADJ. wrong-headed person کج فہمی *kaj-faih'mī* N.F. wrong-headness کج کلاہ *kaj-kūlāh'* ADJ. (one) with hat acock ; foppish sovereign N.M. fop ; bean (fig.) sovereign کج کلاہی *kaj-kūlā'hī* N.F. wearing one's that acock ; foppery ; dandyism (fig.) sovereignty کج مج زبان *kaj'-maj zabān'*, کج مج بیانی *kaj'-maj bayān'* ADJ. & N.M. (one) lacking felicity of phrase ; (one) having no command of language کج نظر *kaj-na'zar* ADJ. envious malignant کج نظری *kaj-na'zarī* N.F. envy malice کج نہاد *kaj-nehād'* ADJ. ill-natured کج نہادی *kaj-nehā'dī* N.F. being ill-natured کجی *ka'jī* N.F. crookedness perversity کج نکالنا *kaj'-nikāl'nā* V.T. straighten set (someone) right [P]

کجا *kūjā'* ADV. where whither از کجا *az kūjā'* PH. whence [P]

کجات *kūjāt'* ADJ. (dial.) of low caste mean base-born [~ ک + جات]

کجاوہ *kajā'vah* N.M. (camel's saddle litter for camel's back [P]

کجکول *kajkol'* N.M. (same as کشکول N.M. ★)

کجل *ka'jal*, کجلا *kaj'lā* N.M. (rus. or dial.) (same as کاجل ★)

کجلانا *kajlā'nā* V.I. become tawny (of fire) be about to be extinguish (of coals) smoulder کجلوٹی *kajlau'tī* N.F. collyrium snuffers [~ کاجل]

کجلی بن *kajlī ban* N.M. elephant forest

کجی *ka'jī* N.F. (see under کج ADJ. ★)

کچ *kach* PREF. raw unripe immature کچ لوہا *kach-lo'hā* N.M. untempered iron کچ لہو *kach-la'hoo* N.M. mixture of blood and pus [~ کچا CONTR.]

کچا *kach'chā*, (F کچی *kach'chī*) ADJ. raw unripe half-done uncooked unbaked (flour or brick) (of colour) not fast fading away weak crude immature abortive inexperienced green undeveloped rough not finalized sub-standard allyed gross young کچا بانس *kach'chā bāns* N.M. green bamboo docile کچا پکا *kach'chā pak'kā* ADJ. half-cooked halfbaked half-done partially clay-built not finalized کچا تاگا (یا دھاگا) *kach'chā tā'gā* (or *dhā'gah*) N.M. weak thread (fig.) weak ties کچا چبا جانا *kach'chā chabā' jā'nā* V.T. eat raw be very harsh (on) کچا پڑ جانا *kach'chā par jā'nā* V.I. put to shame کچا پن *kach'chā-pan* N.M. unripeness inexperience کچا پیسہ *kach'chā pai'sah* N.M. (arch.) ingot used in place of pice کچا تخمینہ *kach'chā takhmī'nah* N.M. rough estimate کچا چٹھا *kach'chā chiṭ'ṭhā* N.M. (arch.) rough account (fig.) whole story (of) (fig.) evil designs (of) کچا چٹھا سنانا *kach'chā chiṭ'ṭhā su'nā'nā* N.M. disclose the evil designs (of) کچا دودھ *kach'chā doodh* N.M. unboiled milk کچا ساتھ *kach'chā sāth* N.M. company of ladies and children family comprising small children کچا سیر *kach'chā ser* N.M. a weight sub-standard 'seer' کچا کرنا *kach'chā kar'nā* V.T. baste put to shame کچی اسامی *kach'chī assā'mī* N.F.

temporary post none hereditary tenant کچی اینٹ *kach'chī īṅṭ* N.F. unbaked brick کچی پیشی *kach'chī pe'shī* prelminary hearing کچی سڑک *kach'chī sa'ṛak* N.F. unmettalled road ; 'kutcha' road کچی سلائی *kach'chī silā''ī* N.F. basting کچی عمر *kach'chī 'ūm'r* N.F. tender age کچی کلی *kach'chī ka'lī* N.F. new bud budding young girl کچی کلی توڑنا *kach'chī ka'lī ṭoot'nā* V.I. die at a tender age (of virginity) be lost at early age کچی گولیاں کھیلنا *kach'chī go'liyān khel'nā* V.I. (fig.) be inexperienced ہم کوئی کچی گولیاں نہیں کھیلے *ham ko''ī kach'chī go'liyāṅ na'hīṅ khe'le* PH. we are not inexperienced کچی گھڑی میں *kach'chī gha'ṛī meṅ* ADV. in a short while کچے پکے دن *kach'che pak'ke din,* کچے دن *kach'che din* N.M. PL. first half of pregnancy period rainy season (as making one more susceptible to disease) کچے بانس جدھر جھکاؤ جھک جاتے ہیں *kach'che bāns' ji'dhar jhukā''o jhuk ja'te haiṅ* PROV. bend a twig while it is young کچے تاگے (یا دھاگے) میں بندھے آنا *kach'che tā'ge* (or *dhā'ge*) *meṅ bandhe ā'nā* PH. come submissively کچے گھڑے پانی بھرنا *kach'che gha'ṛe pā'nī bhar'nā,* پانی کے کچے گھڑے بھرنا *pā'nī ke kach'che ghaṛe bhar'nā* PH. undertake a difficult task show servility (to) کچے گھڑے (میں) پانی بھروانا *kach'che gha'ṛe (meṅ) pā'nī bharvā'nā* PH. make (someone) undertake a difficult task force (someone) to servility کچے گھڑے کی چڑھنا *kach'che gha'ṛe kī chaṛh'nā* V.I. be tipsy کچاہند *kachāhnd* N.F. tang of unripeness

کچالو *kachā'loo* N.M. yam boiled potatoes mixed with citric juice

کچ پچ *kich'pich,* کھچ پچ *khich'pich* ADJ. milling (crowd, etc.) N.F. sound of walking in slush [ONO.]

کچرا *kach'rā* ADJ. (F. کچری *kach'rī*) (of musk-melon, etc.) not fully ripe

کچر کچر *ka'char ka'char* N.F. sound made in chewing raw food [~ PREC. ONO.]

کچرکھان *ka'char khān* N.M. numerous small children (esp. of same parents)

کچ کچ *kich kich* (or *kach kach*) N.F. chitchat noise altercation

کچک *ka'chak* N.F. stroke (of sword) (fig.) wound

کچکچانا *kichkichā'nā* V.T. grind (one's teeth) grind one's teeth ; fret and fume [ONO.]

کچکول *kach'kol* N.M. (same as کشکول N.M. ★)

کچلنا *ku'chal'nā,* کچل ڈالنا *ku'chal ḍāl'nā* V.T. trample crush کچل (یا کچلا) جانا *ku'chal* (or *kuch'lā*) *jā'nā* V.I. be trampled be crushed

کچلوہا *kach-lo'hā* N.M. (see under کچ PRFF. ★)

کچلہ *kūch'lah* N.M. nuxvomica

کچلہو *kach la'hoo* N.M. (see under کچ PREF. ★)

کچلی *kūch'lī* N.F. fang eye tooth ; canine tooth

کچنار *kach'nār* N.F. tree yielding buds used as vegetable buds

کچوری *kachau'rī* N.F. fried saltish cake کچوری سے گال *kachau'rī se gāl* N.M. PL. chubby cheeks

کچوکا *kacho'kā* N.M hit of sword) piercing thrust (fig.) wound (fig.) censure

کچومر *kachoo'mar* N.M. chopped mango pickle something chopped to bits کچومر کرنا *kachoo'mar kar'nā* V.T. chop to bits کچومر نکلنا *kachoo'mar nikāl'nā* V.T. (beat) black and blue

کچھ *kūchh* ADJ. any some whichever whatever N.M. something anything کچھ تو *kūchh' to* ADV. little N.M. something at least کچھ ٹھکانا ہے *kūchh ṭhikā'nā hai* PH. how wonderful to what length کچھ دال میں کالا کالا ہونا *kūchh dāl meṅ kā'lā ka la ho'nā* V.I. (of something) be fishy کچھ دور نہیں *kūchh door' na'hīṅ* PH. quite possibly it is not very far away کچھ سونا کھوٹا کچھ سنار کھوٹا *kūchh so'nā kho'ṭa kūchh sūnār' kho'ṭā* PROV. we stand to lose in any case کچھ سے کچھ ہونا *kūchh se kūchh' ho'nā,* کچھ کا کچھ ہونا *kūchh' ka kūchh' ho'nā* V.I. undergo a radical change کچھ کچھ *kūchh' kūchh* ADV. almost somewhat کچھ کر دینا *kūchh kar' de nā* V.T. do something cast a spell on کچھ کھا لینا *kūchh khā' le'nā* V.T & O. take something take poison کچھ کھو کے سیکھنا *kūchh kho' ke sīkh'nā* V.I. gain valuable experience through some loss کچھ نہ پوچھو *kūchh' na poo'chho* PH. it defies all description ; it is too good for words use your own imagination and do not ask me کچھ ہو *kūchh' ho* ADV. come what may whatever may happen کچھ ہو جانا *kūchh ho' jā'nā* V.I. become something be possessed کچھ ہو رہنا *kūchh ho' raih'nā* V.I. (of something) to pass (of something decisive) happen کچھ ہی کرو *kūchh hī ka'ro* PH. do what you may جو کچھ *jo' kūchh* PROV. whatever ; whatsoever سب کچھ *sab' kūchh* ADV. everything

کچھ *kachh* N.M. (same as کچھوا N.M. ★)

کچھار *kachhār'* N.M. moist low land by river side lair

کچہری *kachaih'rī* N.F. law-court ; court of law ضلع کچہری *zil'' kachaih'rī* N.M. District Courts ; Cutchery کچہری برخاست ہونا *kachaih'rī-bar'khast ho'nā* V.I. (of court) rise کچہری چڑھانا *kachaih'rī char̤'hā'nā* V.T. bring an action (someone) ; go to the court کچہری چڑھنا *kachaih'rī charh'nā* V.I. appear before the court کچہری کرنا (یا لگانا) *kachaih'rī kar'nā* (or *lagā'nā*) V.I. hold a court ; try cases in court

کچھنا *kach'nā* N.M. کچھنی *kach'nī* N.F. short drawers

کچھوا *kachh'vā* N.M. (F. کچھوی *kachh'vī*) tortoise ; turtle کچھوے کی چال *kachh've kī chāl* N.F. slow speed ADV. very slowly ; at snail's pace

کچیا *kach'yā* N.M. ear-lobe

کچیانا *kach yā'nā* V.T. feel shy lose heart be frightened کچیاہٹ *kach yā'haṭ* N.F. fear bashfulness

کحل *koḥ'l* N.M. antimony collyrium کحل الجواہر *koḥ'l-ul jawā'hir* N.M. collyrium prepared with pearls [A]

کحال *kaḥḥāl* N.M. eye-specialist ; opthalmologist [A]

کد *kad* PREF. house کدبانو *kad-bā'no* N.F. (lit.) mistress of the house کدخدا *kad-khūdā'* N.M. کدخدائی *kad-khūda''ī* N.F. (see under کتخدا ADJ. ★)

کد *kad* N.F. effort ; endeavour persistence importunity کد کرنا *kad kar'nā* V.T. try hard ; make an effort ; endeavour urge ; importune کدوکاوش *kad'd-o kā'vish* N.F. diligent search persistent effort [A]

کدارا *kidā'ra* N.M. name of a musical mode ; 'kidara'

کدال *kūdāl'* N.M. pickaxe کدالی *kūdā'lī* N.F. mattock

کدانا *kūdā'na* V.T. cause (horse, etc.) leap dance (child) on knee ; dandle کدائی *kūdā''ī* N.F. leaping (of horse) prize awarded for it [~ کودنا CAUS.]

کدر *ka'dir* ADJ. muddy ; turbid impure [A]

کدکنا *kū'daknā* V.I. leap ; jump frisk ; gambol کدکڑا *kūdak'ṛa* N.M. leap gambol کدکڑے مارتا پھرنا *kūdak're mar'tā phir'nā* V.I. leap about frisk about caper

کدم *kū'dam* N.M. a kind of tree

کدو *kad'doo* (lit. or ped. *ka'doo*) N.M. pumpkin gourd bottle کدو دانہ *kad'doo-dā'nah* N.M. intestinal worms کدوکش *kad'doo-kash* N.M. grater

کدورت *kūdoo'rat* N.F. ill-will bad-blood resentment (rare) muddiness

turbidness [A ~ کدر]

کدہ *ka'dah* SUF. house ; abode centre (of)

کدھر *ki'dhar* ADV. where ; whither کدھر جاؤں کیا کروں *ki'dhar jā''ooṅ kyā ka'rooṅ* INT. to be or not to be, that is the question کدھر کا چاند نکلا *ki'dhar kā chāṅd nik'lā* INT. O, it is a pleasant surprise to have you here کدھر کو *ki'dhar ko* ADV. whither

کڈھب *kūḍhab'* N.M. unmanageable intractable difficult dangerous unreasonable [~ ک + ڈھب]

کذب *kiz'b* N.M. lie lying کذاب *kazzāb'* N.M. confirmed liar [A]

کر ١ *kar* N.M. power ; strength ; grandeur ; pomp ADJ. deaf کروفر *kar'r-o-far'* N.F. splendour pomp and show (rare) attack and strategic retreat [A]

کر ٢ *kar* ADJ. deaf [A]

کر ٣ *kar* N.M. hand (elephants) trunk

کرات *karrāt'* N.M. number of times کرات و مرات *karrā't o-marrāt'* N.M. PL. number of times [A ~ SING. کر]

کرار *karrār'* ADJ. attacking time and again and again ; impetuous کرارا *karā'rā* ADJ. (F. کراری *karā'rī*) sevoury hot ; spicy crisp (fig.) curt (reply, etc.) کرارا پن *karā'rā-pan* N.M. being savoury being hot ; being spicy crispness curtness کرارے دم *karā're dam* ADV while fresh ; while yet untired

کراڑ *kiraṛ'* N.M. (dial.) (derog.) (petty) shopkeeper Hindu

کراکل *ka'rākūl* N.M. curlew ; heron ; hern

کرام *kirām'* ADJ. & N.M. PL. noble ; great کراماً کاتبین *kirā'man katibain'* N.M. twin recording angels ; guardian angels [A ~ SING. کریم]

کرامات *karāmat'* N.F. miracle کراماتی *karāmā'tī* N.M. (col.) one showing miracles ADJ. miraculous کرامت *karā'mat* N.F. (lit.) (PL. کرامات *karāmat'*) miracle (rare) magnanimity [A]

کراں *karāṅ'*, کرانہ *karā'nah* N.M. shore margin bounds بیکراں *be-karāṅ'* ADJ. unbounded ; boundless [P]

کرانا *karā'na* V.T. cause to be done get done [~ کرنا CAUS.]

کرانچی *karāṅ'chī* N.F. camel-cart (col.) (variant for name of Pakistan's first capital) Karachi

کرانی *kirā'nī* N.M. (as nickname) Christian (derog.) Westernized Muslim

کراہت *karā'hat*, کراہیت *karā'hiyat* N.F. abomination abhorrence aversion scorn disgust odium کراہت سے دیکھنا *karā'hat se dekh'nā* V.T. scorn look down upon abominate کراہتاً *karā'hatan* ADV. unwillingly scornfully [A]

کراہنا *karāh'nā* V.I. moan groan

کرایہ *kirā'yah* N.M. fare ; rent ; hire کرائے پر چلانا *kirā''e per chalā'nā* V.T. hire out run as a cab, etc. کرائے پر دینا (یا اٹھانا) *kirā''e par de'na* (or *ūṭhā'na*) V.T. let rent out کرائے کا ٹٹو *kirā''e kā ṭaṭ'ṭoo* N.M. کرایہ اگاہنا *kirā'yah ūgāh'nā* V.T. realize rent کرایہ دار *kirā'ya-dār*, کرائے دار *kirā''e-dār* N.M. tenant کرایہ کرنا *kirā'ya kar'nā* V.T. settle rent settle hire rates (USU. *kirā''e kar'nā*) take out on hire کرایہ نامہ *kirāya-nā'mah*, کرائے نامہ *kirā''e-nā'mah* N.M. deed of rent

کرب *kar'b*, کربت *kūr'bat* N.F. anguish ; agony affliction درد و کرب *dar'd-o-kar'b* N.M. pain and affliction کرب و بلا *kar'b-o-balā'* N.F. trials and tribulations [A]

کربڑا *kar'barā*, کرِبڑا *kar'barā* ADJ. (F. کربڑی *karbarī*, کرِبڑی *karba'ṛī*) grizzled (hair)

کربلا *karbalā'* N.F. Kerbala ; name of a place in Iraq where Imam Husain was martyred Imam Husain's sarcophagus this is Shi'ite shrine (fig.) Calvary [A]

کرپا *kir'pa* (ped. *kri'pā*) N.F. (dial.) favour [S]

کرتا *kūr'tā* N.M. (same as کرتہ N.M. ★)

کرتا دھرتا *kar'tā dhar'tā* N.M. head (of) one enjoying power person in charge emcee ; master of ceremonies [~ کرنا]

کرتار *kartār* N.M. (H. dial.) Creator [S]

کرتب *kar'tab* N.M. feat jugglery sleight of hand finesse کرتبی *kar'tabī* N.M. skilful person crafty person

کرتوت *kartoot'* N.M. PL. behaviour ; conduct

کرتہ *kūr'tah*, کرتا *kūr'tā* N.M. shirt collarless shirt; old-fashioned shirt کرتی *kūr'tī* N.F. loose waistcoat bodice tunic لال کرتی *lal' kūr'tī* N.F. British army

کرتیا *kar'tiyā* N.M. & ADJ. one who has practice in ; adept [~ کرنا]

کرچ *ki'rich* N.F. sword small splinter of glass ; splinter کرچھ *kir'chī* N.F. very small splinter کرچی کرچی ہوجانا *kir'chī kir'chī ho jā'nā* V.I. be broken to pieces

کرچھا *kar'chhā* N.M. frying pan (slang) ; sycophant ; toady کرچھی *kar'chhī* N.F. ladle

کرخت *karakh't* ADJ. harsh curt (reply, etc.) کرختگی *karakh'tagī* N.F. harshness curtness [P]

کردار *kirdār'* N.M. behaviour , conduct character (of play, etc.) کردار نگاری *kirdār'-nigā'rī* N.F. characterization [P]

کردگار *kūr'dgār* N.M. Creator : God [P]

کردنی *kar'danī* ADJ. & N.F. (something) worth doing کردنی خویش آمدنی پیش *kar'danī khesh' am'-dam pesh'* PROV. as you sow so shall you reap [کردن ~ P]

کردہ *ka'dah* ADJ. & SUF. done accomplished (of crime) committed ; perpetrated

کرسٹان *karistān'* N.M. Christian Christian convert ; neophyte Westernized person کرسچن *karis'chan* N.M. & ADJ. Christian کرسچینٹی *karischai'nitī* N.F. Christianty [E ~ Christian]

کرسمس *karis'mas* N.M. Christmas کرسمس ڈے *karis'mas de* N.M. Christmas Day [E]

کرسی *kur'sī* N.F. chair office of authority base (of pillar) plinth (of building) (rare) God's throne کرسی دینا *kūr'sī de'nā* V.T. show respect to offer some one a chair کرسیٔ صدارت *kur'sī-e sada'rat* N.F. chairmanship ; chair کرسی نامہ *kur'sī-nā'mah* N.M. genealogical tree کرسی نشین *kūr'sī-nashīn'* N.M. one entitled to a seat in a British officer's person [A]

کرشمہ *kirish'mah* N.M. marvel wonder phenomenon amorous glances blandishment کرشمہ دکھانا (یا دکھلانا) *kirish'mah dikhā'nā* (or *dikhlā'nā*) V.T. work wonders do a marvel perform a miracle cast an amorous glance [P]

کرشن *karish'n* N.M. Krishna ; Hindu religious black ; dark blue ; blue bader regarded as incarnation of Indian god Vishnu کرشن اور گوپیاں *karish'n aur go'piyāṅ* N.F. PL. Karishna and his female devotees [S]

کرفس *karaf's* N.F. parsley [P]

کرک *kar'rak* N.M. pain ; ache rankling

کرکٹ *kari'kaṭ* N.F. cricket [E]

کرکٹ *kar'kaṭ* N.M. sweepings (usu. as) کوڑا کرکٹ *koo'ṛā kar'kaṭ* N.M. litter ; rubbish

کرکرا *kūr'kūrā* (F. کرکری *kūr'kūrī*) ADJ. crisp brittle

کرکرا *kar'ka'rā* (F. کرکری *kar'karī*) ADJ. cruel

کرکرا *kir'kirā*, (F. کرکری *kir'kirī* ADJ. gritty spoilt ; insipid ; vapid کرکرانا *kirkirā'nā* V.T sound gritty کرکراہٹ *kirkirā'hat* N.F. grittiness

کرکری *kir'kirī* N.F. grittiness disgrace ; shame کرکری کردینا *kirkirī kar de'nā* V.T. put to shame ; disgrace کرکری ہو جانا *kir'kirī ho jā'nā* V.I. be disgraced ; be put to shame

کرکری *kūr'kūrī* ADJ. crisp N.F. cartilege dysantery a horse disease

کرکل *kir'kal* N.F. grit کرکل رہ جانا *kir'kal raih' jā'nā* V.I. be griety

کرگدن *kar'gadan* N.M. (lit.) rhinoceros [P]

کرگس *kar'gas* N.M. vulture [P]

کرگھا *kar'ghā*, کرگہ *kar'gah* N.M. loom weaver's pit [~ P کار + کہ]

کرم *kar'am* N.M. kindness favour grace graciousness bounty benignity generosity ; liberality کرم کرنا *ka'ram kar'na* V.T. do favour show favour treat generously [A]

کرم *ka'ram* (ped. *kar'm*) N.M. (usu. PL.) fate ; destiny کرم پھوٹنا *ka'ram phoot'nā* V.I. have bad luck جس نے کی شرم اس کے پھوٹے کرم *jis' ne kī shar'm us' ke phoo'te kar'm* PROV. hesitate and suffer

کرم *kir'm* N.M. worm moth کرم پیلہ *kir'm pī'lah* N.M. silkworm کرم خوردہ *kirm'-khūrdah* ADJ. moth-eaten ; vermicular [P]

کرم کلا *kar'm-kal'la* N.M. cabbage

کرمک *kir'mak* N.M. small worm کرمک شب تاب *kir'-mak-e shab-tāb'* N.M. firefly : glow-worm [P DIM of کرم *kirm*]

کرن *ki'ran* N.F. ray beam sunbeam moonbeam tasselled lace of gold or silver

کرن *ka'ran* N.M. (dial.) ear کرن پھول *ka'ran phool* N.M. ear tops

کرنا¹ *kar'nā* V.T. do perform execute effect implement act perform make (widely used to form transitive verbs from foreign nouns کر بیٹھنا *kar baiṭh'nā* V.T. have done کرجگ *kar jūg* N.M. (col.) times of action fruit of one's deeds کر دکھانا *kar dikhā'nā* V.T. accomplish successfully succeed in (doing)

کر گزرنا *kar' gū'zarnā* V.I. act stubbornly جیسا کرنا ویسا بھرنا *jai'sā kar'nā vaisā bhar'nā* PH. suffer for one's own doing کرے داڑھی والا پکڑا جائے مونچھوں والا *ka're dā'ṛhī vā'lā pak'ṛā jā''e mooṅ'chhoṅ vā'lā* PROV. one does the harm another gets the blame کرے کوئی بھرے کوئی *ka're ko''ī bha're ko''ī* PROV. the sins of parents visit their children کرے ایک پکڑے جائیں سب *ka're ek pak're jā'eṅ sab* PROV. misdeeds of a few and in trouble for all

کرنا² *kar'nā* N.M. citron bud a kind of citron used for pickling

کرنا *kar'nā*, کرنا *karranā'* N.M. (same as قرنا N.M. ★)

کرنا *kir'nā* V.I. (of edge) wear out (of crowd) thin

کرنٹا *karaṅ'ṭā* N.M. (derog.) Christian

کرنجا *karaṅ'ja*, کرنجی *karaṅ'jī* ADJ. (see کنجا ADJ.★)

کرنجوا *karaṅj'vā* N.M. a kind of brown medicinal plant its colour ADJ. brown

کرنڈ *kūraṅd'* N.M. hone corundum

کرنڈی *karaṅ'ḍī* N.M. a kind of cloth made of untwisted silk

کرنسی *karaṅ'sī* OI-*raṅ*-) N.F. currency [E]

کرنل *kar'nal* N.M. (same as کرنیل N.M. ★)

کرنی¹ *kar'nī* N.F. trowel

کرنی² *kar'nī* N.F. deed doing کوئی کرے تو کیوں بھرے *kar'nī ka're to kyoṅ' bha're* PROV. do what you deem proper and do not be afraid جیسی کرنی ویسی بھرنی *jai'sī kar'nī vai'sī bhar'nī* PROV. as you sow so shall you reap

کرنیل *karnail'*, کرنل *kar'nal* N.M. Colonel [~E colonel]

کروا *kar'vā* N.M. (dial.) spouted earthernware vessel

کروانا *karrā'nā* V.T. cause to make ; have made (vul.) submit to sexual act [~ کرنا CAUS.]

کروبی *karroo'bī* N.M. cherub کروبیاں *karroo'biyaṅ* N.M. PL. cherubs ; cherubim [A ~ H]

کروٹ *kar'vaṭ* N.F. side in sleeping , side کروٹ بدلنا (یا لینا) *kar'vaṭ ba'dalnā* (or *le'nā*) V.I. (also PL.) turn from side to side (in bed) (PL.) have a disturbed sleep ; feel uneasy in sleep خدا کروٹ کروٹ جنت نصیب کرے *khūdā' kar'vaṭ kar'vaṭ jan'nat nasīb' ka're* PH. may God bless his soul

کرودھ *karodh'* N.M. (dial.) rage , wrath [S]

کروڑ *karoṛ* N.M. & ADJ. ten million کروڑپتی *karoṛ'-pati* ADJ. millionaire very rich person

کروندا *karauṅ'dā* N.M. corinda gland close to ear

کروہ *karoh'* N.M. (arch.) league ; three-mile distance [P]

کروی *kū'ravī* ADJ. (see under کرہ N.M. ★)

کرہ *kū'rah* N.M. sphere ; orb globe region ; globe ; sphere ball (of eye, etc.) کرۂ آب *kū'ra-e āb'* N.M. hydrosphere کرۂ آتش *kūr-e ā'tash* N.M. empyrean empy real region کرۂ ارض *kū'ra-e ar'z* N.M. earth کرۂ باد *kūra-e bād'* N.M. atmosphere کرۂ خاک *kū'ra-e khāk'* N.M. terrestrial globe کرۂ فلک *kū'ra-e fa'lak* N.M. celestial globe کرۂ نار *kū'ra-e nār'* N.M. empyrean کروی *kūra'vī* ADJ. spherical ; globular [A]

کری *kūr'rī*, کرٹی ہڈی *kūr'rī had'dī* N.F. cartilege

کری کری *kū'rī kū'rī*, کرٹی کرٹی *kū'rī kū'rī* INT. call to poultry

کریا *kir'ya*, (ped. *kri'yā*), کریا کرم *kri'ya kar'm* N.M. (H. dial.) funeral rites [S]

کریال *kūryal'* N.F. preening کریال کرنا یا میں آنا *kūryal' kar'nā* (or *meṅ ā'nā*) V.I. feel very happy کریال میں غلہ لگنا *kūryal' meṅ ghūl'lah lag'nā* have one's pleasure spoilt

کریانہ *kiryā'nah* N.M. small change grocery کریانہ فروش *kiryā'na-firosh'* N.M. grocer

کریپ *karep'* N.M. crepe [E]

کریدنا *kūred'nā* V.T. scratch search; probe کریدنی *kūred'nī* N.F. poker کرید *kūred'* N.F. search ; probe کرید کرید کر پوچھنا *kūred' kūred' kar poochh'nā* V.I. conduct a thorough probe ; inquire searchingly

کریر *karīr'* N.M. (same as کریل N.M. ★)

کریز *kūrīz'* N.F. moulting (of birds) ugliness resulting from it کریز کرنا *kūrīz' kar'nā* V.T. moult lock-ugly owing to this

کریل *karīl'*, کریر *karīr'* N.M. a kind of thorny strub

کریلا *kare'lā* N.M. bitter gourd ایک کریلا دوسرے نیم چڑھا *ek kare'lā doos're nīm' cha'ṛhā* PROV. evil nature that has been further incited

کریم *karīm'* ADJ. merciful generous bountiful [A ~ کرم *ka'ram*]

کریہ *karīh* ADJ. abominable execrable odious ugly revolting کریہ الصوت *karī'h-ūs-saut'* ADJ. cacorphorous ; illsounding کریہ منظر *karīh'-man'zar* ADJ. abominable execrable ugly odious offensive disgusting revolting [A ~]

کڑا *ka'ṛā* N.M. bracelet large ring used do door-knob ; door-ring rim ; ring (dial.) dome ADJ. (F. کڑی *ka'ṛī*) strong unbending hard harsh rude curt ; sharp

کراڑا *kaṛā'ṛā* N.M. high and steep river bank ; precipice ; declivity

کڑاکا *kaṛā'kā* N.M. کڑک *ka'ṛak* N.F. clap or burst (of thunder) crack twang roor crash starvation intensity ; severity کڑاکا گزرنا *kaṛā'kā gū'zarnā* V.I. starve to pass days in extreme poverty کڑاکے کا *kaṛā'ke kā* ADJ. severe ; extreme کڑاکے کا جاڑا *kaṛā'ke kā jā'ṛā* N.M. severe cold ; very cold winter

کڑاکڑ *ka'ṛākaṛ* ADV. crackling [ONO.]

کڑاہ *kaṛāh'* N.M. (rare) cauldron کڑاہی *kaṛā'hī* N.F. small cauldron ; frying pan کڑاہی چاٹنا *kaṛā'hī chāṭ'nā* V.T. lick the pot this as reproachful habit in child as likely cause rain much later in his wedding day کڑاہی چڑھنا *kaṛā'hī chaṛh'nā* V.I. be fried (of arrangement) be made for preparing cookies

کڑبڑا *kaṛ'baṛā* ADJ. (same as کڑبڑا ADJ. ★)

کڑک *ka'ṛak* N.F. (same as کڑاکا N.M. ★)

کڑک *kūṛak* N.F. clucking (of hen) ; cackle کڑک ہونا *kū'ṛak ho'nā* V.I. (of hen) cluck ; cackle lay no more eggs

کڑکڑانا *kaṛkaṛā'nā* V.I. sizzle crackle be intense ; be rigorous کڑکڑ *kaṛ'kaṛ* N.F. sizzle crackle [ONO.]

کڑکڑانا *kiṛkiṛā'nā* V.I. (of teeth) gnash کڑکڑ *kiṛ kiṛ* N.F. gnashing [ONO.]

کڑکڑانا *kūṛkūṛā'nā* V.I. cluck ; cackle کڑکڑ *kūṛ'kūṛ* N.F. cluck ; cackle

کڑکنا *ka'ṛaknā* V.I. thunder ; burst roar

کڑوا *kaṛ'vā* ADJ. (F. کڑوی *kaṛ'vī*) bitter unpalatable touchy ; testy harsh ; curt کڑوا بول *kaṛ'vā bol* N.M. harsh words کڑواپن *kaṛ'vā-pan* N.M. bitterness کڑوا تیل *kaṛ'vā tel* N.M. mustard-seed oil کڑوا کسیلا *kaṛ'vā kasai'lā* ADJ. bitter unpalatable کڑوا لگنا *kaṛ'vā lag'nā* V.I. taste bitter leave a bitter taste in the mouth be offensive ; give offence (to) کڑوا ہونا *kaṛ'vā ho'nā* V.I. be bitter be enraged ; to be harsh کڑواہٹ *karvā'haṭ* N.F. bitterness کڑوی روٹی *kaṛ'vī ro'ṭī*

N.F. first funeral feast کڑوے کسیلے دن *kar've kasai'le din* N.M. PL. hard times کڑوے کسیلے گھونٹ *kar've kasai'le ghoont* N.M. PL. unpalatable words etc.

کڑھانا *kuṛhā'nā* V.T. vex جی کڑھانا *jī kuṛhā'nā* V.T. fret and fume کڑھن *kuṛ'han* N.F. vexation mortification jealousy کڑھنا *kuṛh'nā* V.I. fret and fume ; be vexed

کڑھنا *kaṛh'nā* V.I. (of milk) be boiled be embroidered کڑھا ہوا *ka'ṛhā hū'ā* ADJ. (of milk) be boiled embroidered کڑھائی *kaṛhā''ī* N.F. embroidery

کڑھی *ka'ṛhī* N.F. hot dish prepared by cooking gram flour in dilute curds; curry کڑھی کا سا ابال *ka'ṛhī ka sa ūbāl'* N.F. sudden but swiftly ending rage باسی کڑھی میں ابال آنا *bā'sī ka'ṛhī meṅ ūbāl' ā'nā*

کڑی *ka'ṛī* N.F. beam ; rafter link (of chain) anklet (usu. pl.) difficulty ; hardship ; trouble harsh words ADJ. strong unbending stiff hard strict hard vigilant wrathful strong intense (flame, sun, etc.) کڑیاں (یا کڑی) جھیلنا (یا اٹھانا) *kaṛ'yāṅ* (or *ka'ṛī*) *jhel'nā* (or *ūṭhā'nā*) V.I. undergo hardship کڑی سنانا *ka'ṛī sūnā'nā* V.I. address in harsh words کڑی کمان کا تیر *ka'ṛī kamān' kā tīr'* N.M. swift piercing arrow کڑی منزل *ka'ṛī man'zil* N.F. difficult stage (in)

کڑیل *kaṛ'yal* ADJ. strong muscular (youth) N.M. earthen

کژدم *kazh'dūm* N.M. (rare) scorpion [P ~ کژ ~ کج + دم *dūm*]

کس *kas* N.M. person individual ; one SUF. capita کس مپرسی *kas' ma-pūr'sī* N.F. helplessness ہر کس و ناکس *har-kas-o nā'-kas* N.M. all and sundry بیکس *be'-kas* ADJ. helpless فی کس *fī'-kas* ADJ. 'per capita' ; per head [P]

کس *kis* PRON. (interrog.) who whom which what کس طرح *kis'ta'raḥ* (or ped. *-tar'h*) ADV. how کس برتے پہ تتا پانی *kis bir'te pa tat'tā pā'nī* PROV. why this empty boast کس بلا کو پیچھے لگا لیا *kis balā' ko pī'chhe lagā' li'yā* PH. why did you invite trouble in the form of this person کس پر پھولے ہو *kis' par bhoo'le ho* PH. what misleads you to this confidence کس حساب میں ہے *kis ḥisab meṅ hai* PH. it (etc.) has no value کس دن کے لیے اٹھا رکھا ہے *kis' din' ke liye ūṭhā' rak'khā hai* PH. what for have you laid it by کس شمار قطار میں ہے *kis shūmar' qatār' meṅ hai* PH. it has no standing it is worthless کس قدر *kis' qa'dar* ADV. how much how many کس کام کا ہے *kis kām' kā (hai)* PH. it is worthless کس کتاب میں لکھا ہے *kis' kitāb' meṅ li(k)'khā hai* PH. on what authority کس کس دکھ کو روئیں *kis' kis' dūkh' ko ro''eṅ* PH. which of my numerous grievances can I air کس کھیت (یا باغ) کی مولی ہے *kis' khet'* (or *bāgh'*) *kī moo'lī hai* PH. he (etc.) has no standing کس لیے *kis liye* ADV. why ; wherefore کس مرض کی دوا ہے *kis' ma'raz kī davā'hai* PH. after all what for he (etc.) is کس منہ سے *kis' mūnh se* PH. how dare you (etc.) کس وقت *kis' vaq't* ADV. when ; at what time کس ہوا میں ہے *kis havā' meṅ hai* PH. why is he so presumptive

کس *kūs* N.F. vulva ; vagina

کساد *kasād'* N.M. (rare) slump کساد بازاری *kasād'-bāzā'rī* N.F. slump [A]

کسالا *kasā'lā* N.M. effort labour grief [CORR. ~ FOLL.]

کسالت *kasā'lat* N.F. laziness ; indolence indisposition [A doublet of کسل]

کسان *kisān'* N.M. peasant ; tiller کسان کمیٹی *kisān' kame'ṭī* N.F. communist party aiming at peasants uplift ; 'kissan' committee

کسانا *kasā'nā* V.T. get tightened get tested (of milk, etc.) become poisonous owning to chemical action of metallic container کساؤ *kasā''o* N.M. this poisonous effect tension

کسب *kas'b* N.M. trade ; profession acquisition ; attornment of skill wages of sin کسب کرنا *kas'ab kar'nā* V.I. acquire a skill follow a trade gate the wages of sin کسب کمال *kas'b-e kamāl'* N.M. کسب معاش *kas'b-e ma'āsh* N.M. earning of livelihood

کسبت *kis'bat* N.F. (same as کسوت N.F. ★)

کسبی *kas'bī* N.F. prostitute ADJ. acquired [~ A کسب]

کستورا *kastoo'rā* N.M. muskdeer blackbird, thrush oyster

کستوری *kastoo'rī* N.F. musk

کسٹم *kas'ṭam* N.M. custom

کسر *kas'r,* (PL. کسور *kūsoor'*) N.F. deficiency loss vowel mark corresponding to English (path) fraction کسر اٹھا رکھنا *kas'r ūṭhā'rakh'nā* V.I. leave a deficiency کسر اٹھا نہ رکھنا *kas'r ūṭhā' na rakh'nā* V.I. leave no stone unturned کسر اعشاریہ *kas'r-e a'shariy'yah* N.F. decimal fraction کسر اعشاریہ متوالی *kas'r-e a'shariy'ya-e mūtavā'lī* N.F. recurring decimal fraction کسر پڑنا (یا رہنا یا رہ جانا) *kas'r paṛ'nā* (or *raih'nā* or *raih jā'nā*) V.I. suffer a loss have a deficiency be deficient (in) be incomplete کسر شان *kas'r-e shān'* N.F. derogation ; something beneath one's dignity کسر عام *kas'r-e 'ām'* N.F. vulgar fraction کسر کرنا *kas'r kar'nā* V.T. fall short کسر مدور *kas'r-e mūdav'var* N.F. recurring fraction کسر مرکب *kas'r-e mūrak'kab* N.F. mixed number کسرمفرد kasr-e mūf'rad N.F. simple fraction کسرنفسی kas'r-e naf'sī N.F. humility over-much humility underrating oneself کسرنفسی سے کام لینا kas'r-e naf'sī se kām le'nā V.I. underrate oneself کسر نکالنا kas'r nikāl'nā V.T. make good a deficiency take revenge رہی سہی کسر ra'hī sa'hī kas'r PH. whatever else had to be done [A]

کسریٰ kis'rā N.M. Chosroes [A ~ P خسرو]

کسرت kas'rat N.F. exercise ; physical exercise کسرت کرنا kas'rat kar'nā V.I. take physical exercise کسرتی kas'ra'tī N.M. athlete (adj.) (of body) dveloped by exercise کسرتی بدن kas'ratī ba'dan N.M. well developed body

کسرہ kas'rah N.M. vowel-point corresponding to English i کسرۂ اضافت (یا اضافی) kas'ra-e izā'fat (or izā'fī) N.M. this vowel-point denoting genitive case ; genitive vowel [A ~ کسر]

کسک ka'sak N.F. pain کسک اٹھنا kas'ak ūṭh'nā V.I. feel sudden pain کسک مٹانا ka'sak miṭā'nā V.I. alleviate pain.

کسگر kas'-gar N.M. (F. کسگرن kas'-garan) potter plasterer

کسل ka'sal N.M. laziness ; indolence indisposition کسلمند ka'sal-mand ADJ. indisposed lazy ; indolent

کسم kū'sūm N.M. bastard saffron ; safflower red dye obtained from it (fig.) menses کسم کا آزار kū'sūm kā āzār' N.M. unceasing menstuṛation

کسمسانا kasmasā'nā V.I. writhe and wriggle fidget become restless کسمساہٹ kasmasā'haṭ N.F restlessness

کسنا kas'nā V.I. tighten brace tie ; bind test (gold, etc.) on touchstone fry (meat) in butter oil till it almost dries up hurl (shouts at) N.M. string for tightening bed string for tying bed cover for straw box کسوانا kasvā'nā V.I. get tightened up

کسوت kis'vat N.F. (rare) robe , dress (also کسبت kis'bat) barber's bag [~ A]

کسوٹی kasau'ṭī N.F. touchstone کسوٹی پر رکھنا (یا کسنا یا لگانا) kasau'ṭī par pa'rakhnā (or kas'nā or lagā'nā) V.T. test ; prove [~ کسنا]

کسو ki'soo PRON. (arch.) (same as کسی PRON. ★)

کسور kūsoor' N.F. (arch.) (PL. of کسر★)

کسوف kūsoof' N.M. solar eclipse [A]

کسی ki'sī PRON. anyone someone کسی ایک ki'sī ek PROV & ADV anyone certain کسی پر جان (یا دم) دینا ki'si par jān' (or dam') de'nā V.T. love someone کسی پہلو (یا کسی سے عنوان) ki'sī paih'loo (or 'ūnvān') in some way کسی سے سائی کسی سے بدھائی ki'sī se sā''ī ki'sī se badhā''ī PROV. make false promises with all کسی قدر ki'sī qad'r ADV. little ; to some extent کسی کا گھر جلے کوئی تاپے ki'sī kā ghar' ja'le ko''ī tā'pe PROV. banking on others misfortunes کسی کا ہاتھ چلے کسی کی زبان ki'sī kā hāth' cha'le ki'sī kī zabān' PROV. he who cannot left his little finger will wag his tongue کسی کا ہو رہنا ki'sī kā ho raih'nā PH. be deep in love with be subservient to کسی کی آئی آنا ki'sī kī ā'ī ā'nā PH. (dial.) (as curse) die an untimely death کسی کے ٹکڑوں پر پڑنا ki'sī ke ṭuk'ron par par'nā V.I. sponge on کسی لائق ہونا ki'sī lā''iq ho'nā V.I. establish oneself in life کسی نہ کسی ki'sī nā ki'sī PROV. & ADV. some someone or the other

کسی kas'sī N.F. hoe

کسے ki'se PRON. whom which what [~ کس kis)

کسے ka'se ADJ. (rare) anybody کسے باشد ka'se bā'shad PH. let it be anybody ; no matter ; what it is [P ~ کس kas]

کسیانا kasyā'nā V.I. (of milk, etc.) become poisonous owing to its metallic container

کسیرا kase'rā N.M. brazier pewterer کسیرہٹا kaser'-haṭ'ṭa N.N. pewterer's market [~ کانسی]

کسیس kasīs' N.M. iron sulphate ; ferrous sulphate; green vitriol

کسیلا kasai'lā ADJ. bitter tasting like milk spoilt by contact with bronze [~ کانسی]

کش kash N.M. pull at hookah SUF. (one) drawing ; (one) who pulls ; pulling drawing enduring suffering bearing ; carrying کش لگانا kash lagā'nā V.T. pull at hookah کشاکش kashā-kash, کشمکش kash'-ma-kash' N.F. struggle contention dilemma ; perplexity کشانہ kashā'nah SUF. pulling drawing enduring کشی ka'shī SUF. pulling drawing enduring ; suffering bearing ; carrying [P ~ کشیدن]

کش kūsh SUF. one who kills or destroys killing -cide کشانہ kūshā'nah SUF. cidal کشی kū'shī SUF. killing destruction -cide کشا kūsha SUF. opening revealing conquering exhilerating [P ~ کشتن]

کشاد kūshad N.F. opening revealing کشادگی kūshā'dagī N.F. spaciousness expansion exhilaration کشادہ kūshādah ADJ. wide , spacious; expansive capacious open uncovered PREF. open کشادہ ابرو kūshā'da ab'roo ADJ.

with eyebrows wide apart gay کشادہ پیشانی *kushā'dah peshā'nī* کشادہ جبین *kushā'da-jabīn'*, کشادہ دل *kushā'da-dil* ADJ. generous large-hearted ; magnanimous کشادہ رو *kushā'da-roo'* ADJ. (one) with a wide forehead cheerful; gay large-hearted کشادہ دلی *kūshā'da di'lī* N.F. generosity large-heartedness ; magnanimety کشادہ روئی *kushā'da-roo''ī* N.F. cheerfulness ; gaiety [P ~ کشادن open]

کشاکش *ka'shā kash* N.F. (see under کش *kash* N.M. & SUF. ★)

کشاں *kashāń* SUF. suffering ; bearing drawing [P]

کشائش *kūshā''ish* N.F. easing way out solution opening relief [P ~ کشادن]

کشت و خون *kush't-o-khoon'* N.M. killing carnage ; massacre [P ~ کشتن]

کشت *kish't* N.F. field sown-field (at chess) check کشت زار *kish't-zār'* N.F. field sown-field کشتہ *kish'tah* ADJ. & N.M. something sown [P ~]

کشتم کشت *kūsh'tam kūsh't* N.F. large-scale sword-fights [~ P کشتن]

کشتہ *kūsh'tah* ADJ. killed ; slain N.M. martyr lover one whose love is unrequited calx ; oxide کشتنی *kūsh'tanī* N.M. & ADJ. (one) deserving death کشتۂ ناز *kush'ta-e naz* N.M. & ADJ. (one) killed by blandishments ; lover [P ~ کشتن]

کشتی *kish'tī* (lit. کشتی *kash'tī*) N.F. boat; a tray کشتی بان *kash'tī-ban* N.M. boatman sailor ; marinar navigator کشتی چلانا (یا کھینا) *kish'tī chalā'na* (or *khe'na*) V.T. row a boat *kash'tī-ra'nī* N.F. rowing boating [~ P]

کشتی *kush'tī* N.F. wrestling wrestling-bout کشتی باز *kūsh'tī-baz* N.M. wrestler کشتی کرنا (یا لڑنا) *kūsh'tī kar'nā* (or *laṛ'nā*) V.I. wrestle

کشش *ka'shish* N.F. attraction allurement pull ; drawing affinity کشش ثقل *ka'shish-e siq'l* N.F. gravitational pull کشش کیمیائی *kashish-e kimiyā''ī* N.F. chemical affinity [P ~ کشیدن]

کشف *kash'f* N.M. revelation manifestation divination کشف و کرامات *kash'f-o-karamat'* N.F. miracle کشفی *kash'fī* ADJ. revealed ; manifest [A]

کشکول *kashkol'*, کجکول *kajkol'*, کچکول *kachkol'* N.M. beggar's bowl commonplace book [P]

کشمش *kish'mish* N.F. raisins; currants; کشمشی *kish'mishī* ADJ. reddish crown [P]

کشمیری *kashmī'rī* N.M. PL. کشامرہ *kashā'mirah*) Kashmiri ADJ. of Kashmiri

کشنیز *kishnīz'* N.M. coriander [P]

کشود *kūshood'* N.F. way out ; solution achievement success کشود کار *kūshoo'd-e kār* N.F. achievement of aim success [P ~ کشودن]

کشور *kish'var* N.F. territory country کشورستانی *kish'var-sitā'nī*, کشور کشائی *kish'var kūshā''ī* N.F. subjugation conquest [P]

کشید *kashīd'* N.F. brewing کشیدگی *kashī'dagī* N.F. tension کشیدنی *kashī'danī* ADJ. worth drawing کشیدہ *kashī'dah* ADJ. displeased annoyed having embittered relations brewed drawn; stretched tall کشیدہ خاطر *kashī'da-khā'tir* ADJ. displeased ; annoyed not on good terms (with) کشیدہ قامت *kashī'da-qā'mat* ADJ. tall having a commanding stature کشیدہ کاری *kashī'da-kā'rī* N.F. embroidery کشیدہ کاڑھنا *kashī'dah-kaṛh'na* V. embroider ; do needlework [P]

کعب *ka''b* N.M. lie (rare) ankle (rare) cube کعبتین *ka'batain'* N.M. PL. dice game of chance played with these gambling [A]

کعبہ *ka''bah* N.M. the Holy Ka'aba (lit.) cube [A]

کف ¹ *kaf* N.M. froth ; foam phleam palm (of hand) sole (of foot) کف افسوس ملنا *kaf-e afsos' mal'nā* V.I. be sorry (for) ; wring one's hands with regret کف آور *kaf ā'var* ADJ. expectoran کف پا *kaf-e pā'* N.M. sole of the foot کف پائی *kaf-pā''ī* N.F. low-heeled slipper کف دست *ka'f-e das't* N.M. palm of the hand ADJ. bleak (plain, etc.) کف لانا *kaf lā'nā* V.I. foam at the mouth ; be greatly enraged [P]

کف ² *kaf* N.F. cuff [E]

کفار *kūffār'* N.M. (PL. of کافر ★)

کفارہ *kaffā'rah* N.M. expiation (for sins) ; atonement کفارہ دینا *kaffā'rah de'na* V.T. expiate (for one's sins) ; atone (for these [A ~ کفر]

کفاف *kafāf'* N.M. daily bread starvation wages mere pittance livelihood just enough for subsistence ADJ. sufficient just equal وجہ کفاف *vaj'h-e kafāf'* N.F. means of subsistence [A]

کفالت *kafā'lat* N.F. security ; surety guarantee responsibility bail support ; maintenance کفالت نامہ *kafā'lat-nā'mah* N.M. bail-bond [A]

کفایت *kifā'yat* N.F. thrift ; economy ; frugality sufficiency answering a purpose کفایت شعار *kifā'yat-she'ar'* ADJ. thrifty , frugal کفایت شعاری *kifā'yat she'ā'rī* N.F. thrift ; frugality

کفایت کرنا *kifā'yat kar'nā* V.I. suffice answer a purpose (of food, etc.) last (for a period) کفایتی *kifā'yatī* ADJ. cheap inexpensive economical [A doublet of FOLL.]

کفایہ *kifā'yah* N.M. sufficiency فرض کفایہ *far' z-e kifā'yah* N.M. sufficiency obligation ; religious obligation of which the rest are all absolved of a sufficient number [A]

کفتار *kaftar'* N.M. badger

کفچہ *kaf'chah* N.M. hood (of a snake) skimmer [P]

کفر *kūf'r* N.M. infidelity heathenism pagamism blasphemy profanity ingratitude کفر بکنا *kūf'r bak'nā* V.I. talk blasphemously ; utter profane words کفر توڑنا *kūf'r toṛ'nā* PH. overcome obstinacy (of someone) کفر ٹوٹنا *kūf'r ṭooṭ'nā* PH. (of obstinacy) end کفر کا فتویٰ دینا *kūf'r kā fat'vā de'nā* V.T. condemn (someone) as an infide کفر کا کلمہ منہ سے نکالنا *kūf'r kā kal'mah mūnh' se nikāl'nā* V.I. talk blasphemously کفر کچہری *kūf'r kachaihrī* N.F. evil company کفر گو *kūfr-go* ADJ. blasphemous (person) [A]

کفران *kūfrān'* N.M. thanklessness ingratitude disbelief کفران نعمت *kūfrā'n-e ne''mat* N.M. thanklessness : ingratitude [A]

کفرستان *kūfris'tān* N.M. pagan territory ; heathen land [P ~ A کفر]

کفش *kaf'sh* N.F. shoe کفش بردار *kaf'sh-bardār'* N.M. menial servant sycophant کفش برداری *kaf'sh-bardā'rī* N.F. sycophency کفش دوز *kaf'sh-doz'* N.M. shoe-maker cobbler [P]

کفگیر *kafgīr'* N.M. cullander ; colander ; flat ladle ; skimmer (slang) sycophant ; today [P ~ کف + گیر]

کفن *ka'fan* N.M. shroud ; winding-sheet کفن پھاڑ کے بولنا *ka'fan phaṛ ke bol'nā* PH. exclaim speak unexpectedly کفن چور *ka'fan-chor,* کفن کھسوٹ *ka'fan-khasoṭ'* N.M. shroud-thief ruffian کفن دفن *ka'fan da'fan* N.M. burial funeral rites کفن سر سے باندھنا *ka'fan sar se bāndh'nā* PH. engage in a perilous undertaking ; jeopardize one's life be ready to lay down one's life for کفن میلا نہ ہونا *ka'fan mai'lā na ho'nā* V.I. have died only recently کفنانا *kafnā'nā* V.T. lay out a corpse ; shroud کفنی *kaf'nī* N.F. unstitched shirt as part of shroud this as mendicant's dress [A]

کفو *kafoo'* N.M. (PL. اکفا *akfā*) N.M. kith and kin ; kindred (rare) peer equal [A]

کفور *kafoor'* N.M. infidel ; disbeliever thankless , ungrateful [A ~ کفر]

کفیل *kafīl'* N.M. surety supporter ; کفیل ہونا *kafīl' ho'nā* V.I. stand surety ; give bail (for) خود کفیل *khūd-kafīl'* ADJ. self-sufficient خود کفیل ہونا *khūd-kafīl' ho'nā* V.I. be self-sufficient achieve self-sufficiency N.M. self-sufficiency

ککا *kak'kā* ADJ. (dial.) albino one of the five religious obligations of Sikhs

ککرالی *kakrā'lī* N.F. armpit tumour

ککرمتا *kū'kūrmūt'tā* N.M. mushroom ; toadstool

ککروندا *kakroṅ'dā* N.M. 'celsia'

ککڑ *kak'kaṛ* N.M. (dial.) hookah a kind of strong tobacco

ککڑ *kūk'kaṛ* N.M. (dial.) cock old man (Hindu dial.) (derog-term for) Muslim ککڑوں کوں *kūk'ṛooṅ kooṅ* N.F. crow (of cock) ککڑوں کوں کرنا *kūk'ṛooṅ kooṅ kar'nā* V.I. (of cock) crow

ککڑی *kūk'ṛī* N.F. corn cob skein (dial.) hen

ککڑی *kak'ṛī* N.F. cucumber ککڑی ہو جانا *kak'ṛī ho jā'nā* V.I. shrink from cold grow lean

کل[1] *kal* N.M. tomorrow near future yesterday near past doomsday N.F. machine ease ; comfort ; relief کل آنا *kal' ā'nā* V.I. be at ease ; set one's heart at rest کل بگڑنا *kal' bi'gaṛnā* V.I go out of order be out of gear be in a bad mood کل پانا *kal' pā'nā* V.I. have peace of mind کل پڑنا *kal' paṛ'nā* V.I. feel at ease کلدار *kal-dār'* ADJ. machine-made (of rupee) with milled rim (of gun) having a trigger کلدار بندوق *kal-dār' būndooq'* N.F. matchlock کل کا آدمی *kal' kā ā'dāmī* N.M. robot puppet upstart کل کا گھوڑا *kal' kā gho'ṛā* N.M. mechanical horse (euph. for) bicycle ; motor bicycle ; scooter کل کا لڑکا *kal' kā laṛ'kā* N.M. raw youth inexperienced person کل کلاں (کو) *kal' kalāṅ' (ko)* ADV. some day ; in future کل کل کرنا *kal kal kar'nā* V T. & I. dilly dally ; shilly shally ; employ delaying tactics کل کی بات *kal' kī bāt'* PH. only a recent matter کل کی بات ہونا *kal'kī bāt' ho'nā* V.I. be a recent happening only the other day کل مروڑنا *kal' maroṛ'nā* V.T. switch on a machine pull the stringe influence کل نہ پڑنا *kal' na paṛ'nā* V.I. feel uneasy ; have no peace of mind

کل[2] *kal* N.M. PREF. (CONTR. ~ کالا) black کل جبھا *kal jī'bhā* ADJ. (F. کل جبھی *kal jibhī*) malignant black-tongued کل جھواں *kal jhavāṅ* ADJ. tawny کل چڑی *kal'chiṛī* N.F. blackheaded sparrow کل سرا *kal sirā* ADJ. blackheaded کلموہا *kal-mooṅ'hā* ADJ. & N.M. (F. کلموہی *kal-mooṅ'hī*)

ill-omened (person) unwanted rogue

کل ۲ **kūl** ADJ. all whole entire aggregate PREF. whole کل وقتی *kūl-vaq'tī* ADJ. whole-time کلہم *kūllo-hūm* ADV. all of them بالکل *bil-kūl* ADV. completely wholly ; entirely [A]

کلا **kalā** N.M. (dial) fine art trick wrestling trick somersault کلابازی *ka'lā-bā'zī* N.F. (same as قلابازی N.F. ★) کلاجنگ *ka'lā jang* N.M. name of a wrestling trick کلا کھیلنا *ka'lā khel'nā* V.I. do wrestling tricks کلاکار *ka'lā-kār* dial.) N.M. artist ADJ. crafty

کلا ۱ **kal'la** N.M. (same as کلہ *kal'lah* N.M. ★)

کلا ۲ **kal'lā** INT. never [A]

کلاب **kilāb'** N.M. (PL. of کلب *kal'b* ★)

کلابہ **kalā'bah** N.M. (same as کلاوہ N.M. ★)

کلابتون **ka'lābatoon** (col. کلابتو *ka'lābat'too*) N.M. gold (or silver) thread [T]

کلال **kalāl'** N.M. tavern-keeper کلال خانہ *kalāl-khā'-nah* N.M. liquor-shop tavern ; pub

کلالہ **kalā'lah** N.M. childless person whose parents are also dead [A]

کلام **kalām'** N.M. talk ; conversation ; speech; discover (gram) sentence verse (of) works ; complete poetical works (of) objection; dout apologetics کلام اللہ *kalā'm-ūllāh'* N.M. the Holy Quran کلام اللہ اٹھانا *kalām'ūllāh ūṭhā'na* V.I. swear by the Holy Quran کلام مجید *kalām' majīd'* N.M. the Holy Quran کلام کرنا *kalām' kar'nā* V.I. speak (to) سے کلام ہونا *se kalām' ho'nā* V.T. have a word with میں کلام ہونا *men kalām' ho'nā* V. object to; doubt [A]

کلاں **kalāṅ'** ADJ. large elder

کلانچ **kūlāṅch'** N.F. (same as قلانچ N.F. ★)

کلاونت **kalāv'ant** N.M. virtuoso

کلاوہ **kalā'vah** (ped. کلابہ *kalā'bah*) N.M. roll of dyed yarn [~P]

کلاہ **kūlāh'** N.M. (ABB. کلہ *kūlah*) (lit.) cap ; head-gear کلاہ پوش *kūlāh'-posh'* ADJ. wearing a cap [P]

کلائی **kalā''ī** N.F. wrist کلائی مروڑنا *kalā''ī maroṛ'nā* V.T. twist (someone's) wrist twist wrists N.M. this as game

کلب **kal'b** N.M. (PL. کلاب *kilāb'*) dog [A]

کلب **kalab'** N.M. club [E]

کلبل **kil'bil** N.F. crawling of insects کلبل کلبل *kil'bil kil'bil* N.F. such crawling sensation

کلبلانا **kūlbūlā'nā** V.I. (of worms) wriggle ; writhe itch fidget be restless ; feel uneasy grumble کلبلاہٹ *kūlbūlā'haṭ* N.F. vermicular motion ; writhing ; wriggling itch ; fidget restlessness ; uneasiness

کلبہ **kūl'bah** N.M. cottage ; cell کلبۂ احزان *kūl'ba-e āhzāṅ'* N.M. cottage of sorrow [P]

کلپ **kalip** N.M. clip [E]

کلپ **ka'lap** N.M. (col. for کلف *ka'lāf* ★)

کلپانا **kalpā'nā** V.T. cause to fret afflict pain ; grieve کلپنا *ka'lapnā* V.I. fret and fume grieve ; be grieved be agonized

کلتھی **kūl'thi** N.F. a kind of pulse ; vetch

کلجگ **kal'-jūg** N.M. (dial.) evil times ; worst times [S ~ جگ + کل]

کلچر **kal'char** N.M. culture کلچرل *kal'charal* ADJ. cultural [E]

کلچہ **kūl'chah** N.M. a kind of bun

کلر **kal'lar** N.M. nitre barren land ; land impregnated nitre ADJ. barren ; sterile ; unproductive کلر لگنا *kal'lar lag'nā* V. be impregnated with nitre ; become barren

کلرک **kilar'k** (or ka-) N.M. clerk [E]

کلڑھ **kūl'laṛh** N.M. small earthen cup with gunpowder filled in it to make a kind of fireworks ; pyrotechnical pot

کلس **ka'las** N.M. spire pinnacle

کلسا **kal'sā** N.M. (dial.) narrow-mouthed spherical brass vessel, metallic waterpot

کلسی **kal'sī** N.F. small spire [~ کلس]

کلغی **kal'ghī** N.F. cockcomb crest plume ; decorative feather

کلف **ka'laf** (col. کلپ *ka'lap*) N.M. starch morbid tan of skin

کلفت **kūl'fat** N.F. affliction trouble ; distress کلفت دور ہونا *kūl'fat door' ho'nā* V.I. be relieved [A]

کلک *kil'k* N.F. (arch.) reed pen [P]

کلکاری *kilkā'rī*, قلقاری *qilqā'rī* N.F. joyful scream titter کلکاریاں مارنا *kilkā'riyāṅ mār'nā* V.I. shriek or scream with joy giggle ; titter

کلکل *kil'kil* N.M. wrangling tiff کلکل کرنا *kil'kil kar'nā* V.T. wrangle ; use bawdy words with

کلمہ *ka'limah* (col. *kal'mā*) N.M. (PL. کلمات *kalimāt*) word Islamic creed ; Muslim creed کلمۃ الحق *ka'lima-tūl-ḥaq* N.M. truth word of God کلمہ پڑھانا *ka'limah paṛhā'nā* V.T. convert (someone) to Islam teach (someone) the Islamic creed کلمہ پڑھنا *ka'limah paṛhnā* V.I. become a Muslim ; be converted to Islam be devoted (to) have unshakable faith (in someone) cherish کلمۂ خیر *ka'lima-e khair* N.M. a kind word (in favour of) کلمۂ شہادت *ka'lima-e shahā'dat* N.M. Muslim creed in form of testimony ; credal testimony ; credal declaration کلمۂ شہادت پڑھنا *ka'lima-e shahā'dat paṛh'nā* V. recite the Muslim creed declare belief in Muslim creed کلمۂ کفر *ka'lima-e k'f'r* N.M. profane words ; blasphemy brag ; boast کلمہ گو *ka'lima-go* N.M. Muslim کلمے کی انگلی *kal'me kī ūṅg'lī* N.F. forefinger ; index finger; first finger [A]

کلنج *kūlaṅj'* ADJ. knock-kneed (horse)

کلنک *kalaṅk'* N.M. stigma infamy کلنک کا ٹیکہ *kalaṅk' kā tī'kah* N.M. stigma ; brand of infamy کلنک کا ٹیکہ لگانا *kalaṅk' kā tī'kah lagā'nā* V.T. stigmatize ; calumniate ; give a bad name (to) کلنک کا ٹیکہ لگنا *kalaṅk' kā tī'kah lag'nā* V.I. be branded ; be stigmatized کلنکی *kalaṅ kī* N.M. & ADJ. (dial.) disreputable (person)

کلنگ *kūlaṅg'* N.M. heron (fig.) tall person

کلو *kal'loo* N.M. dark person ; black man کلو *kul'lo* N.F. dark woman

کلوٹا *kalo'ṭā*, کلونٹا *kaloṅ'ṭā* ADJ. (F. کلوٹی *kalo'ṭī*, کلونٹی *kaloṅ'ṭī*) jet (black) کالا کلونٹا *ka'lā kaloṅ'ṭā* ADJ. jet black (person) [~ کالا]

کلوخ *kūlookh'* N.M. clod brickbat کلوخ اندازی *kūloo'kh-aṅdā'zī* N.F. brickbatting stoning hurling abuses (at) [P]

کلوروفارم *kalo'rafā'ram* N.M. chloroform [E]

کلوگرام *ki'lo-garām'* N.M. kilogramme [E]

کلول *kilol'* N.F. sport ; gambol frisk ; frolie کلول کرنا *kilol' kar'nā* V.I. sport ; gambol ; frisk ; frolic

کلومیٹر *ki'lo-mī'ṭar* N.M. kilometer [E]

کلونٹا *kaloṅ'ṭā* ADJ. (same as کلوٹا ADJ. ★)

کلونجی *kalauṅ'ji* N.F. 'nigella indica' its seed

کلہ *kal'lah* (col. کلا *kal'lā*) N.M. jaw کلہ بہ کلہ لڑنا *kal'la ba-kal'lah laṛ'nā* V. to fight face to face ; to fight on equal footing کلہ توڑ جواب *kal'la-toṛ javāb'* N.M. crushing reply کلہ ٹھلہ *kal'lah ṭhal'lah* N.M. noise and bustle; pomp and splendour کلہ دراز *kal'la-darāz'* ADJ. rude ; imprudent [P]

کلہاڑا *kulhā'rā* N.M. axe کلہاڑی *kulhā'rī* N.F. hatchet اپنے پاؤں آپ کلہاڑا (یا کلہاڑی) مارنا *ap'ne pā'oṅ āp' kulhā'rā* (or *kūlhā'rī*) *mār'nā* PH. dig one's own grave

کلھڑ *kūl'lhar* N.M. large earthen tumbler unwieldy bumpkin

کلھیا *kūlh'yā* N.F. (PL. کلھیاں *kūlh'yāṅ*) small earthen cup this use as fireworks this used for cupping کلھیا میں گڑ پھوڑنا *kūlh'yā meṅ gūṛ' phoṛ'nā* PH. try to do something stealthily

کلی *ka'lī* N.F. bud triangular piece of cloth used in stitching ; transverse piece small hookah

کلی[1] *kūl'lī* N.F. rising of the mouth gargle کلی کرنا *kūl'lī kar'nā* V.I. rinse the mouth gargle

کلی[2] *kūl'lī* ADJ. universal general generic all ; entire N.F. universal truth generalization general rule principle formula کلیات *kūlliyyāt* N.M. ★)

کلیہ *kūlliy'yah* N.M. & ADJ. [A ~ کل *kūl*]

کلیات *kūlliyyāt'* N.M. poetical works ; complete works ; work's formulae [A ~ SING. کلی]

کلیان *kalyān'* N.M. name of a musical mode (dial.) prosperity (dial.) death

کلیانا *kalyā'nā* V.I. bloom ; blossom

کلیتہً *kūlliy'yatan* ADV. totally ; in toto' [A ~ کل *kūl*]

کلیجہ *kale'jah* N.M. liver heart magnanimity guts کلیجہ بلیوں (یا ہاتھوں) اچھلنا *kale'jah bal'liyoṅ* (or *hā'thoṅ*) *ūchhal'nā* V.I. (of heart) leap with joy کلیجہ الٹ (یا پلٹ) جانا *kale'jah ū'lat* (or *pa'lat*) *jā'nā* V.I. be exhausted with excessive vomiting have one's heart in one's mouth کلیجہ بڑھ جانا *kale'jah baṛh jā'nā* V.I. (of liver) enlarge take courage N.M. enlargement of liver کلیجہ بیٹھا جانا *kale ja baiṭhā jā'nā* V.I. be depressed in spirits کلیجہ پاش پاش ہو جانا *kale'jah pāsh pāsh' ho jā'nā* V.I. be heartbroken کلیجہ پک جانا *kale'jah pak jā'nā* V.I. be deeply grieved feel helpless کلیجہ پکڑ کر رہ جانا *kale'jah pa'kar kar raih' jā'nā* V.I. choke one's emotions کلیجہ پھٹنا *kale'jah phaṭ'nā* V.I. be shocked (to) feel great pity envy کلیجہ تر ہونا *kale'jah tar ho'nā* V.I. be at ease ; be well off کلیجہ تھام کر (یا کے) رہ جانا *kale'jah thām' kar* (or *ke*) *raih' jā'nā* V.I. be greatly shocked suppress one's grief bear patiently کلیجہ تھام تھام کر (یا کے) رونا *kale'jah thām' thām kar* (or *ke*) *ro'nā* V.I. weep bitterly کلیجہ ٹھنڈا کرنا *kale'jah ṭhan'ḍā kar'nā* V. to satisfy the heart's longings ; to obtain one's wish ; to get satisfaction کلیجہ ٹھنڈا ہونا *kale'jah ṭhan'ḍā ho'nā* V.I. کلیجہ جلنا *kale'jah jal'nā* V. to suffer sorrow ; to burn with envy ; to mourn; to be heart-sore کلیجہ چھلنی کر دینا *kale'jah chhal'nī kar de'nā* V.T. grieve deeply cause to suffer heavy shocks کلیجہ چھلنی ہو جانا *kale'jah chhal'nī ho jā'nā* V.I. be deeply grieved کلیجہ دھک دھک ہونا *kale'jah dhak' dhak' ho'nā* V I. have one's heart in one's mouth کلیجہ دھک سے رہ (یا ہو) جانا *kale'jah dhak' se raih* (or *ho*) *jā'nā* V.I. be utterly surprised have the shock of one's life کلیجہ کانپنا *kale'jah kāṅp'nā* V.I. have one's heart in one's mouth کلیجہ کٹنا *kale'jah kaṭ'nā* V.I. have one's liver cut to pieces by poison, etc. کلیجہ مسوس کر رہ جانا *kale'jah masos' kar raih jā'nā* V.I. repress one's grief کلیجہ ملنا *kale'jah mal'nā* V.I. regret کلیجہ منہ کو آنا *kale'jah mūṅh' ko ā'nā* V.I. have one's heart in one's mouth feel sick (of) be fatigued with excessive vomiting کلیجے پر ہاتھ دھرنا *kale'je par hāth' dhar'nā* V.I. try to control one's emotions کلیجے سے لگانا *kale'je se lagā'nā* V.T. cherish hold very dear caress embrace کلیجے کا ٹکڑا *kale'je kā ṭuk'ṛā* N.M. son own child one's deer child کلیجے میں آگ لگنا *kale'je men āg' lag'nā* V. be very thirsty have a buring sensation کلیجی *kale'jī* N.F. liver ; animal vitals used as food

کلید *kalīd'* N.F. (lit) key [P]

کلیسا *kalī'sā* N.M. church the Church ; field of religion کلیسیا *iklī'siya* N.F. church Christian community

کلیل *kūlel'* N.F. sport ; gambol ; frisk ; frolic کلیلیں کرنا *kūle'leṅ kar'nā* V.I. gambol ; frisk about

کلیم *kalīm'* N.M. interlocutor ; one who has a talk (with someone) also کلیم اللہ *kalī'm-ūllāh'* N.F. God's interlocutor (as title of Moses) کلیمی *kalī'mī* N.F. being like Moses [A ~ کلام]

کلیہ *kūl'yah* N.M. kidney [A]

کلیہ *kūlliy'yah* N.M. (PL. کلیات *kūlliyyāt'*) formula ADJ. generic general universal (principle etc.) [A ~ کل]

کم *kam* ADJ. little scanty less few rare seldom کم آزار *kam-āzār'* ADJ. not troublesome کم آزاری *kam-āzā'rī* N.F. not being troublesome کم اختلاط *kam-ikhtilāt'* ADJ. lacking intimacy not mixing up well کم اختلاطی *kam-ikhtilā'tī* N.F. not mixing up lack of intimacy کم اصل *kam-as'l* ADJ. base-born mean کم اصلی *kam-as'lī* N.F. being base-born meanness کمبخت *kam-bakh't* N.M. scoundrel ; villain ADJ. villainous cursed wretched unlucky ; unfortunate کمبختی *kam-bakh'tī* N.F. ill-luck ; misfortune adversity mishap calamity کمبختی آنا *kam-bakh'tī ā'nā* V.I. find oneself in trouble کمبختی جب آئے تو اونٹ چڑھے کو کتا کاٹے *kam-bakh'tī jab ā''e to ooṅṭ' cha'ṛhe ko kūt'tā kā'ṭe* PROV. there is no remedy against misfortune کمبختی کا مارا *kam-bakh'tī kā mā'rā* PH. as ill-luck would have it ADJ. unfortunate (person) کمبختی کے دن *kam-bakhtī ke din* N.M. evil days ; hard times کم پایہ *kam-pā'yah* ADJ. of low status sub-standard کم پڑنا *kam' paṛ'nā* V.I. be less ; be wanting کمتر *kam'-tar* ADJ. fewer ADV. seldom کمترین *kam-tarīn'* ADJ. least very humble کم توجہی *kam-tavaj'johī* N.F. lack of attention کم حوصلہ *kam-haus'lah* (or *-hau'salah*) ADJ. weak cowardly unaspiring ; unambitious mean ; narrow-minded کم حوصلگی *kam-haus'lagī* (or *-hau'salagī*) N.F. weakness cowardliness unambitiousness meanness ; narrow-mindedness کم حیثیت *kam-ḥaisiy'yat* ADJ. of low status of small means کم حیثیتی *kam-ḥaisiy'yatī* N.F. low status small means کم خرچ *kam-khar'ch* ADJ. thrifty frugal niggardly cheap; inexpensive کم خرچ بالا نشین *kam-khar'ch bā'lā nashīn'* PROV. good quality at low cost ; good but inexpensive ; cheap and best ; cheap and wonderful کم خرچی *kam-khar'chī* N.F. cheapness parsimony niggardliness کم خرد *kam-khi'rad* ADJ. unwise کمخواب *kam-khāb'* ADJ. sleepless one sleeping little one suffering from mild insomnia کم خوابی *kam-khā'bī* N.F. sleeplessness sleeping little mild insomnia کم خور *kam-khor'* ADJ. sparing in diet abstemious کم خوری *kam-kho'rī* N.F. being sparing in diet abstemiousness کم ذات *kam-zāt'* ADJ. base-born mean ; vile کم دماغی *kam-dimā'ghī* N.F. lack of imagination pride ; conceit کم راہ *kam-rāh'* ADJ. slow-paced (horse) کم رو *kam-roo'* ADJ. ugly low ;

base کمزور kam-zor' ADJ. weak ; feeble frail powerless کمزوری kam-zo'rī N.F. weakness ; feebleness frailty debility powerlessness کم سخن kam-su'khan ADJ. taciturn کم سخنی kam-su'khanī N.F. taciturnity کمسن kam-sin' ADJ. young ; minor ; of tender years کمسنی kam-si'nī N.F. tender age ; nonage ; minority کم سننا kam' sun'nā V.I. be hard of hearing کم سے کم kam' se kam ADV. at least the very least کم شوق kam-shauq' ADJ. indifferent کمیِ شوق kamī-e shauq' N.F. indifference کم ظرف kam-zar'f ADJ. mean narrow-minded malicious کم ظرفی kam-zar'fī N.F. meanness narrow-mindedness کم عقل kam-'aq'l ADJ. foolish ; silly ; stupid کم عقلی kam-'aq'lī N.F. foolishness stupidity کم عمر kam-'um'r ADJ. young ; minor ; of tender years کم عمری kam-'um'rī N.F. tender age ; nonage ; minority کم عیار kam-'ayār' ADJ. base (metal, coin, etc.) کم فرصت kam-fur'sat ADJ. busy with a tight programme کم فرصتی kam-fur'satī N.F. want of leisure کم فہم kam-faih'm ADJ. thick-skulled dull silly ; stupid کم فہمی kam faih'mī N.F. dullness stupidity کم قیمت kam-qī'mat ADJ. cheap low priced ; inexpensive کم قیمتی kam-qī'matī N.F. cheapness ; inexpensiveness کم کرنا kam' kar'nā V.T. decrease کم کم kam' kam ADV. somewhat little seldom rarely کم گو kam-go ADJ. reserved taciturn کم گوئی kam-go'ī N.F. being reserved taciturnity کم مایہ kam-māyah ADJ. poor having little capital کم مائگی kam-mā'igī N.F. poverty smallness of means کم نصیب kam-nasīb' ADJ. unlucky ; unfortunate کم نصیبی kam-nasī'bī N.F. ill luck ; misfortune کم نظر (یا نگاہ یا نگہ) kam-na'zar (or nigāh' or ni'gah) ADJ. short-sighted کم نظری (یا نگاہی یا نگہی) kam'-na'zarī (or nigā'hī or ni'gahī) N.F. short sightedness کم و بیش ka'm-o-besh' ADJ. more or less کم و کاست ka'm-o-kās't N.M. loss deficiency کم ہمت kam-him'mat ADJ. spiritless daunted ; cowardly کم ہمتی kam-him'matī N.F. lack of courage cowardliness کم ہونا kam' ho'nā V.I. کمیاب kam-yāb ADJ. scarce rare کمیابی kam-yā'bī N.F. scarcity rarity کمی ka'mī N.F. ★ [P]

۲کم kam ADV. how much how many N.M quantity کمیت kamiy'yat N.F. ★ [A]

کم kum N.F. (PL. اکمام akmām') (rare) cuff [A]

کما kamā ADV. (rare) just as کما حقہ kamā' haq'qo-hoo ADV. duly properly as it should be کما ہی kamā'hiya ADV as it is as is کما ینبغی kamā' yam'baghī ADV. as desired as ought to be [A ~ ک + ما]

کماچ kūmāch' N.F a kind of fat bread کماچ سا منہ kūmāch sā mūṅh PH. chubby cheeks [T]

کمار kūmār' N.M. (dial.) prince ; son of a Hindu ruler کماری kūmā'rī N.F princess (rare) maiden [S]

کمال kamāl' N.M. (PL. کمالات kamālāt') perfection excellence wonder ; marvel (rare) miracle ADJ. extreme utmost کمال حاصل کرنا kamāl' ḥā'sil kar'nā V.I. attain perfection reach utmost limits کمال (درجے) کا kamāl' (dar je) kā ADJ. extreme utmost of the highest order ADV. to the utmost کمال دکھانا kamāl' dikhā'nā V.I. work wonders perform a miracle show consummate skill کمال کرنا kamāl' kar'nā V.I. work wonders be guilty of an enormity do something unexpected or undesirable کمال کو پہنچانا kamāl' ko pahūṅchā'nā V.T. bring (something) to perfection ; make perfect کمال کو پہنچنا kamāl' ko pahūṅch'nā V.I. attain perfection ; be perfect ہر کمالے را زوالے har kamā'le rā zavāl' PROV every rise hath a fall [A]

کمالا kamā'lā N.M. sham fight

۱کمان kamān' N.F. bow rain-bow ; spectrum ADJ. bent arched (rare) flexible کمان ابرو kamā'n-e ab'roo ADJ. arched eyebrows کمان اتارنا kamān' utār'nā V. unbend or unstring a bow کمان تاننا (یا چڑھانا) kamān' tān'nā (or chaṛhā'nā) bend or string a bow کمان چڑھنا kamān' chaṛh'nā V.I. be victorious ; lord it over کماندار kamān'-dār N.M. bowman archer کمانگر kamān'-gar, kaman-gar, N.M. bow-maker (old use) bone-setter کمانِ گردوں kamā'n-e gar'doon N.F. (sign of the Zodiac) Sagittarius [P]

۲کمان kamān' N.F. command کمان افسر kamān' af'sar N.M. Officer Commanding ; O.C. [~E command CORR.]

کمانا kamā'nā V.T. earn do (good) commit (crime) build (body) with exercise dress or curry (leather) scavenge ; clean latrine of (house) beat (iron) into softness کماؤ kamā''oo ADJ. earning (member, person, etc.); breadwinning کماؤ آئے ڈرتا نکھٹو آئے لڑتا kamā''oo ā''e dar'tā nikhaṭ too ā''e laṛ'tā PROV. worthless person is foolishly proud کمائی kāmā''ī N.F. earnings profit work ; performance virtuous deeds کمائی کرنا kamā''ī kar nā V.I. earn have a profit do some virtuous deed

کمانچہ kamān'chah N.M. fiddlestick [P] ~ کمان DIM.]

کمانڈر *kamān'dar* N.M. commander کمانڈر انچیف *kamān'dar-in-chif'* N.M commander-in-chief ; c-in-c [E]

کمانی *kamā'nī* N.M. spring (of watch, etc.) hairspring ; mainspring spring for protecting jar in vehicle, etc. bow spring بال کمانی *bal' kamā'nī* N.F. hairspring [~P کمان]

کماؤ *kamā''oo* ADJ. کمائی *kamā'ī* N.F. (see under کمانا *kamā'nā* V.I. ★)

کمبل *kam'bal*, (rare کمل *kam'mal*) N.M. blanket کمبل پوش *kam'bal-posh* N.M. one leading a very simple life ; ascetic ; dervish کملی *kam'lī* N.F. ★

کمبھ *kūmbh'* N.M. (dial.) (sign of the Zodiac) Aquarius کمبھ کا میلہ *kūmbh' ka me'lah* N.M. Hindu religious festival held every twelfth year [S]

کمپا *kam'pā* N.M. fowler's stick with bird lime ; lime-stick کمپا لگانا (یا مارنا) *kam'pā lagā'nā* (or *mār'nā*) V.T. catch birds with lime-stick

کمپاس *kam'pās* N.F. compass [E]

کمپانا *kampā'nā*, کمپا دینا *kam'pā de'nā* V.T. shake ; cause to tremble doublet of کنپانا V.T.]

کمپاؤنڈ *kampā'ūnḍ* N.M. compound [E]

کمپنی *kam'panī* N.F. company ; India Company کمپنی بہادر *kam'panī bahā'dūr* N.F. (arch.) (term of respect for) East India Company [E]

کمپو *kam'poo* N.M. (arch.) camp ; cantonment British infantry [~E camp CORR.]

کمپوزنگ *kampo'zing* N.F. composing کمپوزیٹر *kampā'zitar* N.M. compositor [E]

کمتی *kam'tī* ADJ. little ; less ; scanty N.M. shortfall decrease کمتی بڑھتی *kam'tī baṛh'tī* ADJ. more or less N.F. shortfall or surplus error and omission [~P کم]

کمخاب *kamkhāb'* N.M. kincob ; brocade ; tissue [P]

کمر *ka'mar* N.F. waist loin belt ; girdle sash middle (of a mountain) flank (of army) کمر باندھنا *ka'mar bāndh'nā* V.T. gird up one's loins resolve to do something be on the alert کمر بستر سے نہ لگنا *ka'mar bis'tar se na lag'nā* V.I. pass a sleepless night ; be restless کمر بستہ *ka'mar-bas'tah* ADJ. ready ADV. in a state of readiness کمر بستہ ہونا *ka'mar-bas'tah ho'nā* V.I. get ready for کمر بند *ka'mar-band* N M. drawer-string ; waist band ready alert کمر پکڑ کے اٹھنا *ka'mar pa'kaṛ ke uṭh'nā* V.I. become weak ; put one's hand on one's waist in getting up owing to weakness کمر پیچ *ka'mar-pech'* N.M. (dial.) turn; turning کمر توڑنا *ka'mar toṛnā* V.T. break the back (of) make helpless disappoint discourage کمر ٹوٹ جانا *ka'mar ṭooṭ jā'nā* V.I. suffer a heavy loss be helpless lose spirit be disappointed be hump-backed کمر ٹھونکنا *ka'mar ṭhonk'nā* V.T. put (someone) on the back buck up encourage کمر جھکنا *ka'mar jhūk'nā* V.I. have one's back bent ; be old کمر رہ جانا *ka'mar-raih jā'nā* V.I. have a pain in the loins feel very weak کمر کرنا *ka'mar kar'nā* V.T. (of horse) twist its back to shake rider of it (of pigeon) take somersault flight (of wrestlers) do a trick like that کمر سیدھی کرنا *ka'mar sī'dhī kar'nā* V.I. rest a while ; lie down کمر کا ڈھیلا *ka'mar kā ḍhī'lā* ADJ. impotent کمر کا مضبوط *ka'mar kā maz'boot* ADJ. strong virile کمر کس *ka mar-kas* N.F indigenous drug used as cure for Bright's disease resinous compound containing it and used as caudle کمر کس کے باندھنا *ka'mar kas' ke bāndh'nā* V.I. resolve on an undertaking کمر کسنا *ka'mar kas'nā* V.I. resolve (on) get ready (for) کمر کمر *ka'mar ka'mar* ADJ. waist-deep ADV. up to the waist کمر کوٹ *ka'mar-koṭ* N.M. waist-high wall کمر کوٹھا *ka'mar ko'ṭhā* N.M. end of beam projecting from wall کمر کوہ *ka'mar-e koh'* N.F. middle part of hill slope کمر کھولنا *ka'mar khol'nā* V.I. take of the belt ungird one's loins sit at ease کمر لگنا *ka'mar lag'nā* V.I. have a sore-back have a back-ache کمر مارنا *ka'mar mār'nā* V. attack (army) in the flank strike sideways کمر مضبوط کرنا *ka'mar mazboot' kar'nā* V.T. give a strong support take courage in both hand

کمرک *kam'rak* N.F. cambric [E]

کمرکھ *kam'rakh* N.M. a kind of citron

کمرہ *kam rah* N.M. room apartment chamber

کمری *kam'rī* N.F. waist-coat [~P کمر]

کمشنر *kamish'nar* N.M. commissioner کمشنری *kamish'narī* N.F. administrative division comprising a few districts ; division [E]

کمک *kū'mak* N.F. succour reinforcement کمک بھیجنا (یا دینا یا پہنچانا) *kū'mak bhej'nā* (or *de'nā* or *pahūñchā'nā*) V.T. succour send reinforcements (to)

کمل *kam'mal* N.M. (same as کمبل N.M. ★)

کملا *kam'la* N.F. an appellation of Hindu goddess Lakshmi N.M. melon-worm

کملا kumala' N.M. (PL. of کامل ★)

کملانا kūmla'na, کمھلانا kūmhla'nā V.I. wither be blighted

کملی kam'lī N.F. small blanket ; robe کملی والا kam'lī-vā'lā ADJ. the Robed (as the Holy Prophet's appellation)

کمند kamand' N.F. scaling ladder ; cope-ladder lasso کمند پھینکنا (یا ڈالنا) kamand' pheṅk'na (or ḍāl'nā) V.T. throw up a scaling ladder

کمنگر kaman-gar N.M. (same as کمان گر) (see under کمان N.F. ★)

کموانا kamvā'na V.T. cause to earn get cleaned, curried, etc. cause to clean, every etc. [~ کمانا CAUS.]

کمون kammoon' N.M. cumminseed کمونی kammoo'nī ADJ. cumminseed

کمہار kumhār' N.M. potter کمہار کا چاک kumhār ka-chāk' N.M. potter's wheel کمہاری kumhā'rī N.F. potter's wife any female member ; potter's family ; insect building a clay-house for itself

کمی ka'mī N.F reduction decrease shortfall scarcity ; dearth paucity کمی بیشی ka'mī be'shī N.F. profit and loss change fluctuation کمی نہ کرنا ka'mī na kar'na V.T. leave no stone unturned [P ~ کم]

کمیت kūmait' ADJ., N.M. & ADJ. reddish-brown (horse) ; bay [P]

کمیت kamiy'yat N.F. quantity [A ~ کم]

کمیٹی kame'ṭī N.F. committee a meeting of elders municipality ; municipal committee saving through regular monthly deposits repaid in turn by drawing monthly lots کمیٹی پڑنا kame'ṭī paṛ'nā V.I. (of such deposits) be arranged کمیٹی ڈالنا kame'ṭī ḍāl'nā V.T. deposit for this purpose کمیٹی کرنا kame'ṭī kar'nā V.T. deliberate collectively

کمیدان kūmīdān' N.M. commander [T]

کمیرا kamī'ra N.M. gardener's assistant menial [~ کام]

کمیشن kāmī'shan N.M. commission count [E]

کمیلہ kame'lah N.M slaughter-house

کمیلہ kamī'lah N.M. a kind of red medicinal powder

١ کمین kamīn' (or -māṅ') N.F. ambush کمین گاہ kamīn-gāh' N.F ambush ; ambuscade کمین میں بیٹھنا kamīn' meṅ baiṭh'na V.I. lie in ambush ; take or lay an ambush ; lie in wait

٢ کمین kamīn' N.M. base-born person menial [~ P کمینہ CORR.]

کمینڈ kumainḍ' N.M. trick ; fraud کمینڈیا kumainḍ'-diyā N.M. trickster

کمینہ kamī'nah ADJ. mean ; low ; base ignoble vulgar wicked کمینہ پن kamī'na-pan N.M., کمینگی kamī'nagī N.F. meanness vulgarity wickedness [P]

کمیونسٹ kam'yoonist N.M. & ADJ. Communist کمیونزم kam'yoonizm N.M. Communism [E]

کمیونل kam'yoonal ADJ. communal کمیونلزم kam'yoonalism N.M. communalism [E]

کمیونٹی kamyoo'niṭī N.F. community [E]

١ کن kan N.M. mote bud ; blossom strength side half کنکھیاں kankhi'yāṅ, کن انکھیاں kan aṅkh'yāṅ N.F. PL. furtive look کنکھیوں (یا کن انکھیوں) سے دیکھنا kanakh'yoṅ (or kan aṅkh'yoṅ) se dekh'nā V.T. look with furtive glances

٢ کن kan PREF. ear aural (usu. PL. کنپٹی) kan-pa'ṭī N.F. temple (of head) کن پھیڑ kan-pher N.M. mumps کنٹوپ kanṭop' N.M. cap coming down to below ears کن چھدا kan-chhidā ADJ one whose ears are bored کن رس kan-ras N.M. ear for music کن رسیا kan-ras'yā N.M. one having an ear for music کن سلائی kan-salā''ī N.F. a centipede-like insect ; scolopendra کن سوئیاں لینا kan-soo''yāṅ le'na V.T. overhear ; eavesdrop کن کٹا kan-ka'ṭa ADJ. with a lopped ear کنکھجورا kan-khajoo'ra N.M. centipede [~ کان ABB.]

کن kan SUF. digger کنی ka'nī SUF. digging [P ~ کندن]

کن kin who whom which what [~ کس PL.]

١ کن kūn SUF. making ; doing کارکن kār'-kūn N.M. worker ADJ. working کارکن صحافی kār'-kūn sihā'fī N.M. working journalist [P]

٢ کن kūn INT. be کن فکاں kūn'-fa-kāṅ' PH. universe all the creation کن فیکون kūn'-fa-yakoon' PH. God said let there be, and it came into being immediate result [A]

کنا kanna N.M. base string (of kite) to which main string is tied lace notches in shoe upper

کنار kanār N.F. lap ; bosom bank shore ; coast margin edge brink بوس و کنار bo's-o-kanār' N.F. kissing and hugging ; fondling ; toying amorously درکنار dar-kanār' ADV. apart

کنارا kinā'rā (lit. کنارہ kanā'rah) N.M. bank shore ; coast margin edge brink

کنارا کرنا *kinā'rā kar'nā* V.I. withdraw retire refrain ; keep aloof ; abstain کنارہ کش *kanā'rā-kash* ADJ. withdrawing retiring کنارہ کش ہونا *kanā'rā-kash ho'nā* V.I. withdraw retire keep aloof abstain کنارہ کشی *kanā'rā-ka'shī* N.F. withdrawal retirement کنارے کنارے *kinā're kinā're* ADV. along کنارے کنارے لگنا *kinā're kinā're chal'nā* V.I. walk along the shore (etc.) کنارے لگانا *kinā're lagā'nā* V.T. run (boat) up on ashore beach (a boat) accomplish (someone's) task کنارے لگنا *kinā're lag'nā* V.I. (of boat) touch the shore come to an end ; be finished کنارے ہو جانا *kinā-re ho jā'na* V.I. keep aloof withdraw [P]

کناری *kinā'rī* N.F. lace border [~P کنارہ]

کنال *kanāl'* N.M. land measure equivalent to 20 'marlas'

کنایہ *kinā'yah* N.M. (PL. کنایات *kinā'yāt'*) allusion metaphor hint اشارہ کنایہ *ishā'rah kinā'yah* N.M., اشارے کنائے *ishā're kinā''e* N.M. PL. hints amorous glances کنایتہً *kinā'yatan* ADV. indirectly allusively metaphorically [A]

کنبہ *kūn'bah* N.M. family one's people کنبہ پرور *kūn'ba-par'var* ADJ. nepolist supporter of one's tamily کنبہ پروری *kūn'ba-par'varī* N F nepotism support of one's people

کنٹر *kan'ṭar* N-M. decanter [E ~ CORR.]

کنٹھ *kanṭh'* N.M. Adam's apple (rare) throat کنٹھ مالا *kanṭh ma'lā* N.F. scrofula pearl necklace کنٹھ نکلنا (یا پھوٹنا) *kanṭh ni'kalnā* (or *phooṭ'nā*) V. attain the age of puberty کنٹھا *kanṭhā* N.M. pearl necklace beaded necklace ; string of beads کنٹھی *kan'ṭhī* N.F. neck rosary beaded neckband pearl neckband (animal) collar a kind of measles

کنج *kūnj* N.M. bower ; grove ; arbour corner (arm, etc.) pit کنج تنہائی *kūn'je tanhā''ī* N.M. secluded corner [P]

کنجا *kan'jā*, کرنجا *karan'jā* ADJ. (F. کنجی *kan'jī*, کرنجی *karan'jī*) blued-eyed

کنجر *kan'jar* gipsy ; romany کنجری *kan'jarī* N.F. gipsy girl

کنجڑا *kunj'rā* N.M., کنجڑن *kunj'ran* green grocer

کنجشک *kunjish'k* (or *-jash'k*) N.M. sparrow

کنجوس *kanjoos'* N.M. miser ; niggard ADJ. miserly ; stingy کنجوس مکھی چوس *kanjoos' mak'khī choos'* N.M. (joc.) miser ; niggard ; skinflint کنجوسی *kanjoo'sī* N.F miserliness

کنجی *kūn'jī* N F. key solution (to)

کنچن *kan'chan* N.M. (dial.) gold wealth ; money میں کنچن برسنا *meṅ kan'chan ba'rasnā* V.I. (of society, etc.) be affluent [S]

کنچنی *kan'chanī* N.F. prostitute ; whore , woman who hires out her body for money dancing girl [~ کنچن]

کند *kūnd* ADJ. blunt dull obtuse کند ذہن *kund'-zeh'n* ADJ. stupid slow-witted block headed ; obtuse N.M. dunce ; dolt ; dullard [P]

کند *kū'nad* V.T. & I. does کند ہم جنس با ہم جنس پرواز *kū'nad ham-jin's bā ham-jin's parvāz'* PROV. birds of a feather flock together [P ~ کردن]

کندا *kūn'dā* N.M. (same as کندہ *kūn'dah* N.F. ✭)

کندلا *kūnd'lā* N.M. gold thread

کندن *kūn'dan* N.M. pure gold ADJ. lustrous exquisite having lovely qualities

کندوری *kandoo'rī* N.F. table-cloth piece of cloth for wrapping loaves in ; loaf wrapper

کندہ *kun'da*, کندا *kūn'da* N.M. stock (of gun) log or block (of wood) pinion end of kite rib dehydrated milk pillory کندا بھوننا (یا کسنا) *kūn'dā bhoon'nā* (or *kas'nā*) V.T. dehydrated milk کندہ چڑھانا *kūn'dah charhā'nā* V.T. equip a gun barrel with stock کندۂ ناتراش *kūn'dah-e nā-tarāsh'* N.M. lout undesciplined person ; unruly person کندے تولنا *kūn'de tol'nā* V.I. flutter one's wings get ready (to go, etc.)

کندہ *kan'dah* ADJ. engraved ; carved کندہ کار *kan'da-kār* N.M. engraver , carver کندہ کرانا *kan'dah karā'nā* V.T. get engraved ; have carved کندہ کاری *kan'da-kā'rī* N.F. engraver ; carving کندہ کرنا *kan'dah kar'nā* V.T. engrave; carve [P ~ کندن *kan'dan* dig]

کندھا *kan'dhā*, (dial. کاندھا *kān'dhā*) N.M. shoulder *kan'dhā ba'dalnā* V.I. change shoulder in carrying coffin کندھا پکڑ کے چلنا *kan'dhā pa'kaṛ ke chal'na* V I. walk by leaning on someone's shoulder , to walk with another's help کندھا دینا *kan'dhā de'na* V.T carry a dead body کندھا ڈالنا *kan'dhā ḍāl'nā* V.T & I. throw off the yoke lost spirit ; throw up the sponge کندھا لگ جانا *kan'dhā lag ja'nā* V.I. have a sore neck (owing to heaviness of yoke) کندھے چڑھانا *kan'dhe charhā'nā* V.T. life (child or champion) on shoulders کندھے لگانا *kan'dhe lagā'na* V.T. carry baby with its head resting on one's shoulder کندھے ہلانا *kan'dhe hilā'na* V.T. shrug one's shoulders

کندئی *kandai'i* N.F. door-mortice

کنڈی *kūn'di* N.F. calendering کنڈی کرانا *kūn'di kara'na* V.T. get calendered have (someone) thrashed کنڈی کرنا *kūn'di kar'na* V.T. calender beat ; thrash کنڈی گر *kūn'di-gar* N.M. calenderer one who launders expensive stuff ; laundry-man

کنڈ *kūnd* N.M. (dial.) sacred spring or pool fire-pit for hurrling ritual stuffin

کنڈا *kūn'da* N.M. hook hook for dogchain staple

کنڈل *kūn'dal* N.M. curl ; lock coil halo (Hindu ascetic's) large earring circle کنڈل مارنا (یا کرنا یا میں بیٹھنا) *kūn'dal mar'na* (or *kar'na* or *men baiṭh'na*) (of snake) coil up of moon, etc.) be in a halo کنڈلی *kūnd'li* N.F. curl coil (of snake) halo (dial.) horoscope کنڈلی بنانا *kūnd'li bana'na* V.T. curl cast a haroscope کنڈلی مار کر بیٹھنا *kūnd'li mar kar baiṭh'na* V.I. coil up

کنڈی *kūn'ḍi* N.F. door-chain کنڈی دینا (یا چڑھانا یا لگانا یا بند کرنا) *kūn'ḍi de'na* (or *charha'na* or *laga'na* or *band' kar'na*) V.T chain door ; fasten the door-chain کنڈی کھٹکھٹانا (یا کھڑکھڑانا) *kūn'ḍi khaṭ-khaṭa'na* (or *khar'-khara'na*) V.T rattle the door-chain knock at the door

کنز *kan'z* N.M. (PL. کنوز *kūnooz'*) treasure treasury [A ~ P گنج]

کنزرویٹر *kanzarveṭar* N.M. conservator of forests [E]

کنزرویٹو *kan'zarveṭiv* N.M. & ADJ. conservative [E]

کنستر *kanas'tar* N.M. canister [E]

کنشت *kūnish't* N.M. pagan temple church snynagogue [P]

کنفرم *kanfar'm* V.T. confirm کنفرمیشن *kan'-farmeshan* N.F. confirmation [E]

کنعان *kan'an'* (or '*'an*) N.M. Canaan پیر کنعان *pi'r-e kan''an* N.M. (appellation of) Jacob [A ~ H]

کنف *ka'naf* N.F. (PL. اکناف *akna'f'*) side direction اکناف عالم *akna'f-e 'alam* N.M. PL. all sides of the world [A]

کنک *ka'nak* N.M. (slang) wheat gold particle کنکی *kan'ki* ADJ. broken (rice, etc.)

کنکر *kan'kar* N.M. gravel small piece of stone, etc. grit کنکر پتھر *kan'kar pat'thar* N.M. PL. coarse pieces of stone کنکر سا *kan'kar sa* ADJ. cold (water) کنکری *kan'kari* N.F grit gravel very small piece of stone, etc. کنکریلا *kankari'la* ADJ. (F. کنکریلی *kankari'li* gravelly gritty

کنکنا *kūn'kūna* ADJ. tepid (water)

کنکوا *kankav'va* N.M. kite ; paper-kite کنکوا اڑانا (یا بڑھانا) *kankav'va ūṛa'na* (or *baṛha'na*) V.T. fly a kite کنکوا لڑانا *kankav'va laṛa'na* V.T. engage in a test to snap kitestrings

کنکی *kan'ki* ADJ. (see under کنک N.F. ★)

کنگ *king* N.M. king [E]

کنگال *kan'gal'*, کنگلا *kang'la* ADJ. & N.M. (F. *kang'li*) bankrupt poor ; penniless pauper کنگال کر دینا *kan'gal' kar de'na* V.T. reduce to bankruptcy impoverish ; make penniless کنگال ہو جانا *kan'gal' ho ja'na* V.I. become a bankruptcy be reduced to property ; be impoverished ; become panniless

کنگرو *kūng'roo* N.M. kangaroo [E]

کنگرہ *kan'gūrah* (col. *kūng'rah*), کنگورہ *kangoo'rah* N.M. parapet turrett کنگرہ دار *kan'gūra-dar'* ADJ. turreted [P]

کنگلا *kang'la* ADJ. & N.M. (F. کنگلی *kang'li*) (see کنگال ADJ. & N.M. ★)

کنگن *kan'gan* N.M. bangle ; thick bracelet *kang'na* N.M. died yarn tied round groom's right or bride's left wrist ; wrist-string

کنگنی *kang'ni* N.F. millet cornice bracelet ; light bangle

کنگھا *kan'gha* N.M. comb weaver's comb کنگھی *kan'ghi* N.F. comb کنگھی چوٹی *kan'ghi cho'ṭi* N.F. make-up hairdo کنگھی چوٹی کرنا *kan'ghi cho'ṭi kar'na* V.T. braid or plait the hair do one's make-up کنگھی کرنا *kan'ghi kar'na* V.T. comb do one's hair dress (the hair)

کنمنانا *kanmana'na* V.I. whine ; whimper moon grumble be uneasy

کن میلیا *kan-mai'liya* N.M. (see under کن PREF. ★)

کنوارا *kūnva'ra* N.M. bachelor ADJ. unmarried (man) کنوارپت *kūnvar'-pat*, کنوارپتا *kūnvar'-pa'ta*, کنوارپن *kūnvar'-pan*, کنوارپنا *kūnvar' pa'na* N.M. maidenhood کنوارپنے کے دن *kūnvar'-pate ke din'* N.M. PL. maidenhood کنواری *kūnva'ri* N.F. maiden virgin کنواری کو ارمان بیاہی پشیمان *kūnva'ri ko arman' baya'hi pisheman'* PROV. wistful before rueful after

کنوانسا *kūnva'sa* N.M. daughter's grandson

کنواں *kūṅ''aṅ* N.M. well کنواں بیچا ہے کنویں کا پانی نہیں بیچا *kūṅ''aṅ be'cha hai kūṅ''eṅ kā pa'nī na'hīṅ be'cha* PROV. quibbling کنواں پیاسے کے پاس نہیں جاتا پیاسا کنویں کے پاس جاتا ہے *kūṅ''aṅ payā''se ke pās na'hīṅ jā'tā payā'sā kūṅ''eṅ ke pās jā'tā hai* PROV. he who has need must take the initiative کنواں (یا کنویں) جھانکنا *kūṅ''aṅ* (or *kūṅ''eṅ*) *jhāṅk'nā* V.I. look into well as cure for hydrophobia search a lot be non-plussed کنواں (یا کنویں) جھنکانا (یا جھنکوانا) *kūṅ''aṅ* (or *kūṅ''eṅ*) *jhaṅkā'nā* (or *jhaṅkvā'nā*) cause (someone) to see his reflection in a well get this done as cause for hydrophobia perplex کنواں چلانا *kūṅ''aṅ chalā'nā* V.I. work a Persian wheel on the well کنواں کھودنا *kūṅ''aṅ khod'nā* V.T. dig a well dig a pit for (someone) کنویں بھانگ پڑنا *kūṅ''eṅ bhang par'nā* V.I. (of all) be dead-drunk کنویں پڑ گئے اور پیاسے آئے *kū''eṅ par ga''e aur payā'se ā''e* PROV an unlucky person knows nothing but deprivation کنویں کی مٹی کنویں میں لگنا *kūṅ''eṅ kī maṭ'ṭī kūṅ''eṅ meṅ lag'nā* PROV. ill-got ill-spent کنویں میں بانس ڈالنا *kūṅ''eṅ meṅ bāṅs' ḍāl'nā* V.T. make a thorough search کنویں میں بولنا *kūṅ''eṅ meṅ bol'nā* PH. mutter unintelligibly کھاری کنواں *khā'rī kūṅ''aṅ* N.M. well yielding brackish water میٹھا کنواں *mī'ṭhā kūṅ''aṅ* N.M. well yielding sweet water

کنوتی *kanau'tī* N.F. (horses) ear earring کنوتیاں کھڑی کرنا *kanau'tiyāṅ khaṛ'ī kar'nā* V.I. (of horse) become alert ; raise its ears [~ کان]

کنور *kūṅ'var* N.M. (dial.) prince

کنول *kaṅ'val* N.M. lotus کنول گٹا *kaṅ'val-gaṭ'ṭā* N.M. lotus nut دل کا کنول کھلنا *dil' kā kaṅ'val khil'nā* PH. (of heart) swell with pleasure

کنہ *kūṅ'h* N.F. essence (of) reality (about) [A]

کنونڈا *kanauṅ'ḍā* (F. کنونڈی *kanauṅ'ḍī*) ADJ. ashamed

کنھیا *kanhay'yā* N.M. (dial.) lovely lad this as appellation of Hindu deity, Krishna [S]

کنی *ka'nī* N.F. spark (of diamond, etc.) not fully boiled grains of rice ایک کنی رہ جانا *ek' ka'nī raih' jānā* V.I. (of rice) be almost but not fully boiled

کنی *kan'nī* N.F. kite-fillet ; make weight at its lighter end border کنی باندھنا *kan'nī bāndh'nā* V.T. fillet the lighter end of kite-rib کنی دینا *kan'nī de'nā* V.T. hold ribs of kite to help someone fly it کنی کترانا *kan'nī katrā'nā* V.I. avoid dodge evade کنی کھانا *kan'nī khā'nā* V.T. (of paper-kite) incline to one side

کنیا *kan'niyā* N.F. (dial.) maiden کنیا دان *kan'niyā-dān'* N.M. (dial.) giving away of a girl in marriage [S]

کنیانا *kanyā'nā* V.I. avoid ; evade, dodge (of paper-kite) incline to one side [~ کنی]

کنیت *kūn'yat* N.F. patronymic filial appellation [A]

کنیر *kaner'* N.F. oleander

کنیز *kanīz'* (dim. کنیزک *kanīz'zak*) N.F. girl (fig.) devotee [P]

کنیسہ *kanī'sah* N.M. church [P]

کو *ko* PARTICLE (follows the object as) sign of accusative (follows subject as) sign of nominative when predicate is an infinite PREP to towards upto about ; ready to in ; in terms of ; for the sake of

کو *koo* N.F. street ; a lane; a market place کو بکو *koo' ba-koo* ADV. from street to street where; all over the place کوچہ *koo'chah* N.M. ★[P]

کوا *kav'vā* N.M. crow raven uvula کوا اٹھانا *kav'vā ūṭhā'nā* V.T. raise (infant's) uvula کوا پری *kav'vā pa'rī* N.F. dark woman کوا چلا ہنس کی چال اپنی بھی بھول گیا *kav'vā cha'lā han's kī chāl ap'nī bhī bhool' ga'yā* PROV. one who tries to emulate others blindly stands to lose کوے اڑانا *kav've ūṛā'nā*, کوے ہکنی *kav've hak'nī* N.F. maid-servant Cinderella silly girl

کوآپریٹو *ko'āp'reṭiv* ADJ. Co-operative کوآپریٹو سوسائٹی *ko'āp'reṭiv sosā''iṭī* N.F. co-operative society کوآپریشن *ko'āp'reshan* N.F. co-operation [E]

کوار *ko'ār'* N.M. seventh month of Hindu calendar (same as اسوج N.M. ★)

کوارٹر *ko'ā'ṭar* N.M. quarter کوارٹر ماسٹر *ko'ā'ṭar-mās'ṭar* N.M. quarter-master کوارٹر ماسٹر جنرل *ko'ā'ṭar-mās'ṭar jan'ral* N.M. Quartermaster General [E]

کوارنٹین *ko'ā'ranṭīn* N.F. quarantine [E]

کواڑ *kivāṛ'* N.M. door کواڑ بند کرنا *kivāṛ' band' kar'nā*, کواڑ بھیڑنا (یا دینا یا لگانا) *kivāṛ' bheṛ'nā* (or *de'nā* or *lagā'nā*) V.T. close or shut the door کواڑ کھٹکھٹانا *kivāṛ' khaṭ-khaṭā'nā* V.T. knock the door

کواکب *kavā'kib* N.M. (PL. of کوکب)

کوالٹی *ko'ā'leṭī* N.F. quality [E]

کوانٹٹی *ko'āṅ'ṭeṭī* N.F. quantity [E]

کوائف *kava'if* N.M. particulars ; details [A ~ SING. کیفیت]

کوب *kob* SUF. beating one who beats کوبی *ko'bī* SUF. beating [P ~ کوبیدن]

کوبانس *kobāns'* INT. (used for) scaring away crows کوبانس کوبانس کرتے پھرنا *kobāns' kobāns' kar'te phir'nā* V.I. (fig.) loiter like an idle lout

کوبڑ *koo'bar* N.M. hump

کوبہ *kobah* N.M. clod-break کوبہ کاری *koba-kā'rī* N.F. (arch.) beating [P ~ کوبیدن]

کوت *koot'* N.F. estimate کوتنا *koot'nā* V.T. estimate

کوتاہ *kotāh'*, کوتہ *ko'tah* ADJ. small little short brief کوتہ اندیش *ko'ta-andesh'* ADJ. short-sighted indiscreet improvidence کوتہ اندیشی *ko'ta-ande'shī* N.F. short-sightedness indiscretion improvidence کوتہ بین *ko'ta-bīn'* ADJ. short-sighted indiscreet imprudence کوتہ بینی *ko'ta-bī'nī* N.F. short-sightedness indiscretion imprudence کوتہ دست *ko'ta-das't* ADJ. weak ; unable (to) کوتہی دست *ko'tahī-e dast'* N.F. inability (to) کوتہ عقل *ko'ta-'aq'l* ADJ. unwise کوتہی عقل *ko'tahī-e 'aq'l* N.F. lack of wisdom کوتہ عمر *ko'ta-'um'r* ADJ. short-lived کوتہ عمری *ko'ta-'um'rī* N.F. early death کوتہ قامت (یا قد) *ko'ta-qā'mat* (or *qad*) ADJ. short-statured dwarfish undersized کوتہ گردن *ko'ta-gar'dan* ADJ. short-necked wicked کوتہ نظر *ko'ta-na'zar* ADJ. short-sighted indiscreet improvident کوتہ نظری *ko'ta-na'zarī*, کوتاہی نظر *kotā'hī-e na'zar* N.F. shortsightedness indiscretion improvidence کوتاہی *kotā'hī*, کوتہی *ko'tahī* N.F. smallness shortness littleness narrowness brevity deficiency short fall کوتاہی کرنا *kotā'hī kar'nā* V.I. fail lack fall short (of) make a mistake ; err کوتاہی ہونا *kotā'hī ho'nā* V.I. (of mistake) be made lack fail (to) کوتک *ko'tak* N.M. (usu. PL.) (one's own) doings ; (own) misdeeds [P]

کوتل *ko'tal* N.M. led horse horse kept for show well-caparisoned horse [P]

کوتوال *kotvāl'* N.M. police chief (of a town) کوتوالی *kotvā'lī* N.F. town police headquarters [~ کوٹ fort + والا]

کوتہ *ko'tah* ADJ. (short for کوتاہ ADJ. ★) کوتہی *ko'tahī* N.F. (short for کوتاہی) (see under ADJ. ★)

کوٹ *kot* N.M. jacket ; coat coating [E]

کوٹ *koṭ* N.M. fort walled city کوٹلا *koṭ'lā* N.M. fortress walled town

کوٹنا *kooṭ'nā* V.T. beat ; pound powder ; pulverize کوٹ کوٹ کر بھرا ہونا *kooṭ' kooṭ' kar bhạ'rā ho'nā* V.I. be full (mischief, virtue, etc.)

کوٹھا *ko'ṭhā* N.M. upper storey brothel barn کوٹھے پر بیٹھنا *ko'ṭhe par baiṭh'nā* V.I. (esp.) be or become a prostitute کوٹھے والیاں *ko'ṭhe vā'liyāṅ* N.F. PL. prostitutes ; whores

کوٹھڑی *koṭh'rī* N.F. small room ; cabin ; closet [~ کوٹھا]

کوٹھی *ko'ṭhī* N.F. bungalow granary masonry house ; chamber (of gun wooden rim under wall of well ; curb (arch.) factory (arch.) warehouse (arch.) banking firm

کوٹیشن *koṭe'shan* N.F. quotation [E]

کوثر *kau'sar* N.M. name of a fool, fountain or river (rare) abundance [A ~ کثرت]

کوچ *kooch* N.M. march departure کوچ کرنا *kooch' kar'nā* V.I. march decamp depart die ; pass away [P]

کوچ[1] *kooch*, کونچ *koonch* N.M. weaver's brush

کوچ[2] *kooch* N.F. (same as کونچ N.F. ★)

کوچ *koch* N.F. coach کوچبان *koch'-bān*, کوچوان *koch'-van* N.M. coach-driver [E]

کوچ *kauch* N.M. sofa couch [E]

کوچا *koo'chā* N.M. green tamerind pod

کوچا *ko'chā* ADJ. (see under کوچنا V.T. ★)

کوچک *ko'chak* ADJ. small younger ایشیائے کوچک *eshiyā'-e ko'chak* N.M. Asia Minor [P]

کوچنا *koch'na*, کونچنا *konch'nā* V.T. prick pierce کوچا *ko'chā* ADJ. pricked N.M. prick کوچے دینا *ko'che de'nā* V.T. taunt

کوچوان *koch'vān* N.M. (usual form of کوچبان see under کوچ *koch* N.F. ★)

کوچہ *koo'chah* N.M. narrow street ; lane ; alley کوچہ بکوچہ *koo'cha ba-koo'chah* ADV. from street to street everywhere ; all over the place کوچہ بندی کرنا *koo'cha-ban'dī kar'nā* V.T. mark off the limits of a lane کوچہ گردی *koo'cha-gar'dī* N.F. wandering ; aimlessly ; roaming about [P ~ کو *koo*]

کوچی *koo'chī* کونچی *koon'chī* N.F. coarse rush brush for whitewashing ; mason's brush ; whitewashing brush کوچی پھیرنا (یا مارنا) *koo'chī pher'na* (or *mar'nā*) V.T. whitewash

کودپھاند *kood' phand'* N.F. see under کودنا V.I. ★)

کودک *ko'dak* N.M. baby boy stripling [P]

کودنا *ko'dan* ADJ. stupid thick-headed N.M. stupid person (rare) pack-horse [P]

کودنا *kood'nā* V.T. & I. jump leap ; bound ; frisk rejoice ; dance about کود پڑنا *kood' paṛ'nā* V.I. jump in کودپھاند *kood' phand* N.F. leap and jump skipping about capers ; gambols کودتے پھرنا *kood'te phir'nā* V.I. frisk about with joy, etc. کود مارنا *kood mar'nā* V.I. jump

کودو *ko'do*, کودوں *kodoṅ* N.M. a kind of small grain کودوں دے کر پڑھنا *ko'doṅ de ke paṛh'nā* PH. fail to pay the extra two pence for manners get cheap education

کور *kor* N.F. border ; edge edge of nail (سے) کور دبنا *(se) kor' dab'nā* V.I. find oneself helpless against کورکسر *kor' ka'sar* N.F. slight deficiency

کور *kor* ADJ. blind کورباطن *kor-bā'tin* ADJ. benighted کورباطنی *kor'-bā'tinī* N.F. being benighted کوربخت *kor'-bakh't* ADJ. unlucky ; unfortunate کوربختی *kor'-bakh'tī* N.F. ill-luck ; misfortune کورچشم *kor'-chash'm* ADJ. blind کورنمک *kor'-na'mak* ADJ. unthankful ; ungrateful disloyal N.M. ungrateful person کوری *ko'rī* N.F. blindness [P]

کورا *ko'rā* (F. کوری *ko'rī*) ADJ. unbleached (cloth) unused (earthenware) blank (paper) unlettered uneducated unscathed unmarried untouched thinly populated matter curt (reply) کورا بچنا *ko'ra bach'nā* V.I. escape unscathed کوراپن *ko'rā-pan* N.M. newness inexperience ignorance deprivation کوراپنڈا *ko'rā piṅ'ḍā* N.M. (fig.) virgin کورا رہنا *ko'rā raih'nā* V.I. be deprived be ignorant ; be unlettered be blank

کورٹ *kor'ṭ* N.F. court کورٹ آف وارڈز *kor'ṭ af var'dz* N.F. court of wards کورٹ انسپکٹر *kor'ṭ inspaik'ṭar* N.M. Court Inspector; Prosecuting Inspector کورٹ شپ *kor'ṭ'ship* N.F. courtship کورٹ فیس *kar'ṭ-fees*, فیس کورٹ *fees'-kor'ṭ* N.F. court fees judicial stamp کورٹ مارشل *kor'ṭ-mār'shal* N.M. court martial [E]

کورس *kor's* N.M. course [E]

کورم *ko'ram* N.M. quorum [E]

کورنش *kaur'nish* (ped. *kūr'nish*) N.F. (PL. کورنشات *kūrnishāt'*) salutation obeisance کورنش بجالانا *kaur'nish baja' la'nā* V.I salute do obeisance [T]

کوری *ko'rī* N.F. ADJ. see under کور ★ (ADJ. see under کورا ADJ. ★)

کوڑا *ko'ṛā* N.M. whip ; lash , scourge کوڑے (یا کوڑا) لگانا (یا مارنا) *ko're* (or *ko'ṛā*) *lagā'nā* (or *mār'nā*) V.T. whip ; lash ; scourge ; castigate

کوڑا *kau'ṛā* N.M. (rare) large cowrie

کوڑا *koo'ṛā* N.M. dirt sweepings refuse rubbish کوڑا کرکٹ *koo'ṛā kar'kaṭ* N.M. litter refuse rubbish lumber

کوڑمغز *kooṛ'-magh'z* ADJ. thick-skulled

کوڑھ *koṛh* N.M. leprosy کوڑھ ٹپکنا (یا چونا) *koṛh' ṭa'paknā* (or *choo'nā*) V.I. be afflicted with leprosy کوڑھ میں کھاج *koṛh' meṅ khāj'* PROV. one misfortune added to another کوڑھی *ko'ṛhī* N.M. leper ADJ. leprous

کوڑی *ko'ṛī* N.F. score ; twenty

کوڑی *koo'ṛī* N.F. dunghill

کوڑی *kau'ṛī* N.F. cowrie this used as coin son breat bone کوڑی بھر *kau'ṛī bhar* ADJ. very little کوڑی پاس نہ ہونا *kau'ṛī pas' na ho'nā* V.I. be hard up ; have no money کوڑی پھیرا کرنا *kau'ṛī phe'rā kar'nā* V.T. run to the market every now and then unnecessarily ; to be coming and going constantly without purpose کوڑی حرام لقمہ حلال *kau'ṛī ḥarām' lūq'mah ḥalāl'* PROV. strain at a gnat and swallow a camel کوڑی کا *kau'ṛī kā* ADJ. worthless ; good-for-nothing mean کوڑی کا آدمی *kau'ṛī kā ād'mī* N.M. mean or worthless fellow کوڑی کا مال *kau'ṛī kā māl'* N.F. worthless stuff کوڑی کا ہو جانا *kau'ṛī kā ho jā'nā* V.T. become worthless کوڑی کفن کو نہ ہونا *kau'ṛī ka'fan ko na ho'nā* V.I. be penniless ; have no money کوڑی کوڑی *kau'ṛī kau'ṛī* N.F. every farthing کوڑی کوڑی ادا کرنا *kau'ṛī kau'ṛī adā' kar'nā* V. pay every farthing کوڑی کوڑی جوڑنا *kau'ṛī kau'ṛī joṛ'nā* V.T. save up every farthing ; save every bit کوڑی کوڑی چکانا *kau'ṛī kau'ṛī chūkā'nā* V.T. pay in full کوڑی کوڑی کو تنگ ہونا *kau'ṛī kau'ṛī ko tang' ho'nā* V.T. be reduced to abjecs poverty کوڑی کوس دوڑنا *kau'ṛī kos' dauṛ'nā* V.I. be very greedy ; run up a mile for a penny کوڑی کو نہ پوچھنا *kau'ṛī ko na poochh'nā* V.I. regard as worthless کوڑی کے تین تین بکنا *kau'ṛī ke tīn' tīn bik'nā* V.I. sell very cheap have no value left be disgraced کوڑی کے کام کا نہ ہونا *kau'ṛī ke kām kā na ho'nā* V.T. be worthless ; be good for nothing کوڑیوں کے مول بکنا *kauṛī'yoṅ ke mol' bik'nā* V.I go very cheap پھوٹی کوڑی *phoo'ṭī kau'ṛī* N.F. (usu.

neg.) sou کوڑیا kau'ṛiyā ADJ. worthless (rare) damn cheap کوڑیا غلام kauṛi'yā ghulām' N.M. (fig.) devoted person کوڑیالا kauṛiyā'lā ADJ. & N.M. spotted (snake)

کوز kooz PREF. hump ; hunch کوزپشت kooz'-pūsh't ADJ. hump-backed ; N.M. hunch-back [P]

کوزہ koo'zah N.M. pitcher ; goblet small earthern pot کوزہ گر koo'za-gar N.M. potter کوزہ گری koo'za-ga'rī N.F. pottery کوزہ مصری koo'zah mis'rī N.M. crystallized sugar lump کوزے میں دریا بند کرنا koo'ze meṅ daryā' band kar'nā V.T. put something in a nutshell

کوس kos N.M. league unstandardized distance measure calculated variously from one-and-a-quarter to three miles کوسوں دور ko'soṅ door ADV. at a great distance ; far away کالے کوسوں پر kā'le ko'soṅ par ADV. far away کوسوں دور بھاگنا ko'soṅ door' bhāg'nā V.I. shun ; avoid

کوسا ko'sā N.M. (see under FOLL. ★)

کوسنا kos'nā V.T. curse ; imprecate N.M. curse imprecation کوسنے دینا kos'ne de'nā V.I. curse ; imprecate پانی پی پی کر کوسنا pā'nī pī pī' kar kos'nā V.I. curse greatly کوسا ko'sā N.M. curse; imprecation کوسا کاٹی ko'sā-kā'ṭī N.F. curse taunt

کوسہ koo'sah ADJ. (same as کھوسہ ADJ. ★)

کوش kosh SUF. attempting ; endeavouring labouring کوشاں ko'shāṅ ADJ. attempting ; endeavouring struggling کوشاں ہونا ko'shāṅ ho'nā V.I. make a bid کوشش ko'shish N.F. bid ; attempt effort ; endeavour exertion ; labour کوشش کرنا ko'shish kar'nā V.T. make an attempt have a go (at) [P ~ کوشیدن]

کوشک kau'shik N.M. (lit.) palace [P]

کوفت kof't N.F. vexation anguish fatigue [P ~ کوفتن]

کوفتہ kof'tah N.M. mince ball (PL.) dish prepared from it ; stewed mince ball ADJ. powdered ; pulverized beaten ; pounded کوفتہ و بیختہ kof'ta-o-bekh'tah ADV. pounded and sifted ADJ. sifted powder [P ~ PREC.]

کوک kook N.F. (see under کوکنا kook'nā V.T.★)

کوک kok N.F. (see under کوکنا kok'nā V.T. ★)

کوکا ko'kā N.M. small nail

کوکب kau'kab N.M. (PL. کواکب kavā'kib) small star [A]

کوکبہ kau'kabah N.M. (royal) procession کوکبۂ شاہی kau'kaba-e shā'hī N.M. royal procession [P]

کوک شاستر kok' shās'tar N.M. a popular sex-manual for males ; sex 'vade-mecum'

کوکنا kook'nā V.T. wind up (watch, etc.) shriek (of cuckoo) cry کوک kook N.F. winding cry (of cuckoo) ONO.

کوکنا kook'nā V.T. baste کوک kok N.F. tack

کوکنار kok'nār N.M. poppy poppyhead [P]

کوکنی kok'nī ADJ. short N.M. a kind of blue colour

کوکو koo' koo N.M. cooing (of dove) [ONO.]

کوکو ko'ko N.F. cocoa [E]

کوکہ ko'kah N.M. foster-brother child of one's wet-nurse [T]

کوکھ kokh N.F. abdomen ; belly womb (fig.) children ; offspring کوکھ اجڑ جانا kokh u'jaṛ jā'nā V.I. have lost all one's children کوکھ جلی kokh'-ja'lī ADJ. barren woman کوکھ کی آنچ kokh' kī āṅch' N.F. maternal love کوکھیں لگنا ko'kheṅ lag'nā V.I. feel very hungry کوکھ ماری جانا kokh' mā'rī jā'nā V.I. (of woman) become barren

کوکئی kokai''ī N.M. a kind of reddish blue colour

کوکین kokīn' N.F. cocaine [E]

کول kaul N.M. handful of grain put in mill at one time morsel canal distributory ; small canal

کول ka'val N.M. grain not fully cleaned

کولا ko'lā N.M. (arch. or dial. for کوئلہ N.M. ★)

کولا kau'lā N.M. doorway side side wall ;

کولتار kol'tār تارکول tār'kol N.M. tar ; coaltar [E]

کولنا kol'nā V.T. bore (with drill)

کولھا koo'lhā کولا koo'lā N.M. haunch ; hip کولھے مٹکانا koo'lhe maṭkā'nā V.T. walk with blandishing gait belly-dance

کولھو ko'lhoo N.M. oil-expeller oil press کولھو چلانا ko'lhoo chalā'nā V. set up or run an oil press کولھو کا بیل

ko'lhoo kā bail' N.M. ox driving an oil press person following killing routine کولھو میں پلوا دینا *ko'lhoo meṅ piḻvā' de'nā* V.T. crush in a mill torture to death ; annihilate

کولی *ko'lī* N.M. weaver dark tint caused by henna

کولی *kau'lī* embrace armful کولی بھرنا (یا میں لینا) *kau'lī bhar'nā* (or *meṅ le'nā*) V.I. embrace greedy

کومل *ko'mal* ADJ. tender soft downy کوملتا *ko'maltā* N.F. (dial) tenderness

کومل *koo'mal*, کومھل *koomhal* کونبھل *kooṅ'bhal* N.M. house-breaking hole made for the purpose کومھل لگانا *koo'mhal lagā'nā* V.T. break into a house

کون *kaun'* N.M. existence that which exists world universe کون و مکاں *kau'n-o-makāṅ'* N.M. universe عالمِ کون و فساد *'ālam-e kau'n-o-fasād'* N.M. the world of existence and destruction کونین *kau'nain'* N.M. PL. ★

کون[1] *kaun* PRON. who which what کون سا *kaun' sā*, کونسا *kauṇ'sā* ADV which which one what sort of

کون[2] *koon* N.F. anus کونی *koo'nī* N.F. catamite [P]

کونا *ko'nā*, کونہ *ko'nah* N.M. corner side کونہ کھدرا (یا کھترا) *ko'nā khūd'ra* (or *-khūt'ra*) N.M. some corner every nook and corner کونے کھدرے چھان مارنا *ko'ne khūd're chhān' mār'nā* V.I. search every nook and corner کونیدار *ko'ne-dar* ADJ. cornered ; angular

کونپل *koṅ'pal* N.F. shoot ; sprouting leaf کونپل پھوٹنا (یا نکلنا) *koṅ'pal phooṭ'nā* (or *ni'kalnā*) V.T. (of leaf) sprout

کونتھنا *koṅth'nā* V.I. put pressure on bowels for evacuation

کونج *kooṅj* N.M. heron

کونچ[1] *kooṅch*, کوچ *kooch* N.F. one of the five tendous at back of kee کونچیں کاٹنا *kooṅ'chen kaṭ'nā* V.T. hamstring

کونچ[2] *kooṅch*, کوچ *kooch* N.M. (same as کوچ *kooch* ★)

کونچا *kauṅ'chā* N.M. grain-parcher's handled pan

کونچنا *koṅch'nā* V.T. (same as کوچنا V.T. ★)

کونچلی *koṅch'lī* N.F new tooth lank tooth

کونچی *kooṅ'chī* N.F. (same as کوچی N.F. ★)

کوندنا *kauṅd'nā* V.I. (of lightning) flash کوندا *kauṅ'dā* N.M. flash (of lighting) thunderbolt کوندے کی لپک *kauṅ'de kī la'pak* N.F. flash of lightning. کوندا لپکنا *kauṅ'dā la'paknā* V.I. (of lightning) flash

کونڈا *kooṅ'ḍā* N.M. earthen trough (usu. kneeding flower), dough trough کونڈا کرنا *kooṅ'ḍā kar'nā* subject to mass criminal assault by turns ruin کونڈے بھرنا *kooṅ'de bhar'nā* N.M. ritual feast in commemoration of the Shi'ite Imam Jafar Sadiq

کونڈی *koaṅ'di* N.F mortar

کونرا *kauṅ'ra* ADJ. & N.M. (dial.) simple-minded person

کونسل *kauṅ'sal* N.F. council counsel کونسلر *kauṅs'lar* N.M. councillor [E]

کوں کوں *kooṅ' kooṅ* N.F. cry of puppies [ONO.]

کونی *koo'nī* N.M. (see under کون *koon* N.F ★)

کونین *koṅīn'* (or *kū-*) N.F. quinine [E]

کونین *kaunain'* N.M. PL. the world and the Hereafter the two worlds [A ~ کون dual]

کوہ *koh* N.M. mountain hill کوہِ آتش فشاں *ko'h-e ā'tash-fishāṅ'* N.M. volcano کوہِ الم (یا غم) ٹوٹنا *ko'h-e a'lam* (or *gham'*) *ṭooṭ'nā* V.I. be faced with a calamity کوہِ بیستوں *ko'h-e be-sūtoon'* N.M. Iranian mountain where the legendary lover, Farhad, cut out a canal to secure his mistress کوہ پیکر *koh'-pai'kar* ADJ. huge ; gigantic کہسار *koh-sār'*, *kohsār'* N.M. range of mountains کوہستان *kohistān'* N.M. mountainous country ; hilly tract ; highland کوہستانی *kohistā'nī* ADJ. hilly ; mountainous N.M. highlander کوہِ طور *ko'h-e toor'* N.M. (wrong but usual form) Mount Sinai کوہ کن *koh'-kan* N.M mountain-digger ; (as an epithet of Farhad) کوہ کندن وکاہ بر آوردن *kok'-kaṅ'dan-o kāh' bar-āvar'dan* PROV. the mountain was in travail to bear a mouse کوہِ نور *ko'h-e noor'* N.M. the Koh-i-Noor ; world's largest Diamond کوہی *ko'hī* ADJ. hilly ; mountainous [P]

کوہان *kohān'* N.M. hump (of camel) [P ~ PREC.]

کوئلہ *ko''elah* N.M. charcoal coal کوئلوں کی دلالی میں منہ کالا *ko''eloṅ kī dallā'lī meṅ muṅh' kā'la* PROV. he who handles peat is bound to defile his fingers کوئلے کی کان *ko''ele kī kān'* N.F. coalmine پتھر کا کوئلہ *pat'thar kā ko''elah* N.M. coal لکڑی کا کوئلہ *lak'ṛī kā ko''elah* N.M. charcoal

کوئی *ko''i* PRON. anybody somebody ADJ. any some کوئی بات نہیں *ko''i bat' nā'hin* PH. it matters little کوئی دم کا مہمان ہونا *ko''ī dam' kā mehmān' ho'nā* V.I. be about to die کوئی دن جاتا ہے کہ *ko''ī din jā'tā hai ke* PROV. soon enough کوئی دم میں *ko''ī dam men'* ADV. soon in a moment کوئی مال مست کوئی حال (یا کھال) مست *ko''ī māl' mas't ko''ī ḥal' (or khāl') mas't* PROV. one is content in poverty, another is happy in his riches کوئی کوئی *ko''ī ko''ī* ADJ. a few rare hardly any کوئی نہ کوئی *ko''ī na ko''ī* PROV. & ADJ. some one or the other somebody کوئی نہیں پوچھتا کہ تمہارے منہ میں کے دانت ہیں *ko''ī na'hin poochh'tā ke tūmha're mūnh' men kai' dānt hain* PROV nobody is solicitous for you everyone is free to do what he likes

کویہ *ko'yah,* کویا *ko'yā* N.M. corner (of the eye) cocoon (of silkworm)

کوی *ka'vī* N.M. (dial.) poet کویتا *ka'vitā* N F (dial.) poetry verse [S]

کوئل *ko'yal* (or *ko''il*) N.F Indian cuckoo کویلیا *koyalyā* N.F (dial or dim for) کویل N.F. ★)

۱ کہ *ke'* (or *keh*) PRON who which that what CONJ. that as ; use if , whether for when suddenly [P]

۲ کہ *keh* ADJ. mean small کہتر *keh'tar* ADJ. inferior junior smaller کہ و مہ *ke'h-o-meh'* N.M. PL. high and low [P]

کہ *kah* N.M. (short for کاہ N.F. ★)

کہہ *koh* N.M. (shortened form of کوہ N.M. ★)

کہہ *kaih* V.I. (imp. of کہنا V.I. ★)

کہا *ka'hā* N.M spoken word saying order ; command word of advice recommendation کہا بدا *ka'hā ba'dā* N.M کہی بدی *ka'hī ba'dī* N.F. pledge mutual agreement کہا سنا *ka'hā sū'nā* N.M. کہی سنی *ka'hī sū'nī* N.F advice instigation harsh reply ADJ well-known کہا کرنا *ka'hā kar'nā* V T carry out the instructions (of) obey orders (of) act upon the advice (of) کہا ماننا *ka'hā mān'nā* V.T obey act upon the advice

کھابڑ *khā'bar* ADJ. uneven

کھاتا پیتا *khā'tā pī'tā* ADJ. (see under V.T ★) *khat'rī* N.F riparian crop

کھاتی *khā'tī* N.M. carpenter

کھاتہ *khā'tah,* کھاتا *khā'tā* N.M. account ledger ; day book کھاتا کھولنا (یا ڈالنا) *khā'tah khol'nā* (or *dāl'nā*) V.T. open an account کھاتے پڑنا *khā'te par'nā* V.I. be entered into an account کھاتا واڑی *khā'tā-vā'ṛī* N.F. ledger entries بٹہ کھاتا *baṭ'ṭah-khā'tā* N.M. loss account bad debt بٹے کھاتے پڑنا *baṭ'ṭe-khā'te par'nā* V.I. prove a bad debt بہی کھاتا *ba'hī-khā'tā* N.M. account books

کھاٹ *khāṭ* N.F. (ABB. کھٹ *khaṭ*) cot , bed. bedstead bier کھاٹ بننا *khāṭ' būn'nā* V.T. plait with rush کھاٹ سے اتارنا *khāṭ' se ūtār'nā* V.T. (Hindu dial.) lay (dying person) on ground کھاٹ بنانا *khāṭ' būnā'nā* V.T. get cot plaited with rush down ; regard him as approaching کھاٹ سے لگ جانا *khāṭ se lag' jā'nā* V.I be bad-ridden کھاٹ کھٹولا *khāṭ' khaṭo'lā* N.M. goods and chattels کھاٹ نکلنا *khāṭ' ni'kal'nā* V.T. die مچھماچی کھاٹ نکلنا *machmachā'lī khāṭ' ni'kalnā* V.I. (as curse) die in one's youth کھاٹ بنا *khāṭ'-bū'nā* N.M. bed-weaver

کھاج *khāj* N.F itch [کھجانا ~ doublet of کھجلی]

کھاجا *khā'jā* N.M pie-crust food cherished food

کھاد *khād'* (rare کھات *khāt*) N.F. manure مصنوعی (یا کیمیاوی) کھاد *masnoo''ī* (or *kimyā'vī*) *khād* N.F artificial (or chemical) manure

کھادی *khā'dī* N.F home-spun cotton , 'Khaddar

کھادر *khā'dar* N.F. & ADJ low moist alluvial land ; lowland

کہار *kahār'* N.M. palanquin-bearer (dial.) water-carrier scullion کہاری *kahā'rī* N.F palanquin-bear's wife scullion female water-carrier wages of palanquin bearer

کھار *khār'* N.M. impure carbonate of potash or soda alkaline earth کھار لگنا *khār' lag'nā* V I be impregnated with alkalies

کھاروا *khār'vā* N.M coarse red cotton used as curtam-cloth or for wrapping

کھاری *khā'rī* ADJ brackish (water, well, etc.)

کھاڑی *khā'ṛī* N F creek straits bay gulf

کھانس *khās* N.F large net for carrying dung-cakes etc. in

کھاگ *khāg* N.M rhinoceros horn (used as stick handle, etc)

کھاکسی *khak'sī* N.F. streaks on belly, etc. resulting from (frequent) childbirth

کھال *khāl* N.F. skin hide bellows کھال اتارنا (یا کھینچنا) *khāl' ūtār'nā* (or *khench'nā*) V.T. skin;

flay ; beat blue and black charge an exorbitant rate (اپنی) کھال میں مست ہونا (ap'ni) khāl' meṅ mas't ho'nā V.I. be content with one's lot

کھالا khā'lā N.M. pit lowland abounding in streams

کھان khān N.F. (dial.) (same as کان N.F. ★)

کہاں ka'hāṅ ADV. where whither what a place why ; where fore nowhere کہاں پر ka'hāṅ par ADV. where ; at ; what place to what degree how far کہاں تک ka'hāṅ tak (arch کہاں تلک 'kahāṅ talak') ADV. how long ; how far to what degree ; to what extent کہاں راجہ بھوج کہاں گنگوا تیلی ka'hāṅ ra'jah bhoj' ka'hāṅ gang'vā te'lī PROV. stars not visible by sunshine کہاں رام رام کہاں ٹیں ٹیں ka'hāṅ rām' rām ka'hāṅ ṭaiṅ' ṭaiṅ PH. what a world of difference کہاں سے ka'hāṅ se ADV. whence where from ; from where کہاں سے ٹپک پڑا ka'hāṅ se ṭa'pak pa'ṛā PH. how does (he, etc.) happen to be here کہاں کا ka'hāṅ kā ADV. of what place what type کہاں ہو کہاں نہ ہو ka'hāṅ ho ka'hāṅ na ho' who knows where he (etc.) may be (etc.) کہاں (یہ) کہاں (وہ) ka'hāṅ (yeh) kahāṅ (voh) PH. what a difference between (this and that)

کھانا khā'nā V.T. eat sup dine eat up; devour swallow consume draw in breath ; inhale corrode embezzle ; defalcate accept bribe N.M. eating food ; meals supper dinner fare ; board feast کھانا اور غرانا khā'nā aur ghurrā'nā V.I. be ungrateful کھانا پینا khā'nā pī'nā V.T. eat and drink N.M. food ; meals board; fare entertainment کھاتا پیتا khā'tā pī'tā ADJ. well-to-do (person) کھانا کرنا (یا دینا) khā'nā kar'nā (or de'nā) V.T. give feast or banquet ; throw a party کھانا کھانا khā'nā khā'nā V.T. take food ; have one's meals lunch sup dine کھانا کھلانا khā'nā khilā'nā V.T. feed give food in charity to give feast to کھانے کا کمرہ khā'ne kā kam'rah N.M. dining-room کھانے کمانے کا ٹھیکرا khā'ne kamā'ne kā ṭhīk'rā PH. means of livelihood child adopted to grow up into a bread-winner کھانے کو دوڑنا khā'ne ko dauṛ'nā V.I. be surly pounce upon کھاؤ khā''oo N.M. & ADJ. glutton spendthrift defalcator کھاؤ اڑاؤ khā''oo uṛā''oo N.M. & ADJ. spendthrift کھائے پر کھایا وہ بھی گنوایا khā''e par khā'yā voh' bhī ganvā'yā PROV. greed causes double loss کھائیے من بھاتا پہنیے جگ بھاتا khā''iye man' bhā'tā pai'hanye jag' bhā'tā PROV. eat according to personal tastes dress according to public taste کھایا پیا انگ لگنا khā'yā pī'yā ang' lag'nā PH. assimilate food have a strong body thus کھایا پیا نکالنا khā'yā pī'yā nikāl'nā V.T. beat black and blue

کہانت kahā'nat N.F. soothsaying کاہن N.M. ★ [A]

کھانچا khāṅ'chā N.M. coop ; hen-coop کھانچی khāṅ'chī N.F. pannier basket with lid

کھانڈ khāṅḍ N.F. sugar unrefined sugar powdered sugar

کھانڈا khāṅ'ḍā N.M. double-edged sword (dial.) (same as کھنڈا N.M. ★) کھانڈا بجنا khāṅ'ḍā baj'nā V.I. (of swords) clash ; (of swordfight) occur

کھانسنا khāṅs'nā V.I. cough signify thus that one is awake or present کھانسی khāṅsī N.F. cough کھانسی آنا khāṅsī ā'nā V.I. cough suffer from cough

کہانی kahā'nī N.F. tale story ; fable (rare) plot made-up affair کہانی جوڑنا kahā'nī joṛ'nā V.T. make up or concoct a story (rare) prepare a plot کہانی کہنا kahā'nī kaih'nā V.T. tell a tale [~ کہنا]

کہاوت kahā'vat N.F. saying [~ کہنا]

کھاؤ khā''oo ADJ. (see under کھانا V.T. ★)

کھائی khā''ī N.F. ditch ; moat

کھبا khab'bā ADJ. left-hander

کھبنا khub'nā, کھب جانا khub' jā'nā V.T. & I. sink penetrate stick in fascinate ; charm

کھپاچ khappāch' N.F. (dial.) splinter (of piece of bamboo, etc.) lean person

کھپانا khapā'nā V.T. کھپت khā'pat N.F. (see under FOLL. ★)

کھپنا khap'nā V.I. be used up be consumed be dried up be disposed of be wasted pass muster کھپانا khapā'nā V.T. & I. use finish abs[orb] spend waste (one's life) جان کھپانا jān' khapā'nā V.T. peak and pine مغز کھپانا magh'z khapā'nā V.I. undergo mental strain try to drive something home (to)

کھپت khā'pat N.F. sale consumption

کھپچی khapach'chī N.F. splinter (of bamboo, etc.)

کھپرا khap'rā N.M. roofing tile pot sherd broad-pointed arrow scale کھپریل khaprail' N.F. tiling tiled house کھپریل چھانا khaprail' chhā'nā V.T. tile (a roof

کھپریل *khaprail'* N.F. (see under کھپرا N.M. ★)

کھپرانا *khaprā'na* V.T. grout

کھتا *khat'tā* N.M. کھتی *khat'tī* N.F. underground granary ; grain pit such store for anything

کہتر *keh'tar* ADJ. (see under کہ ★)

کھتونی *khatau'nī* N.F. annual land revenue record

کھتی *khat'tī* N.F. (same as کھتا N.M. ★)

کہتے ہیں *kaih'te hain* PH. (see under کہنا *kaih'na* ★)

کھتیانا *khatyā'nā* V.T. (see under کھاتہ ★)

کھٹ[1] *khaṭ* N.F. knock tap clatter کھٹ پٹ *khaṭ-paṭ* N.F. wrangle ; brawl clash (of weapons) clank کھٹ سے *khaṭ' se* ADV. at once with a clank کھٹ کھٹ *khaṭ' khaṭ* N.F. knocking repeated raps clank کھٹا پٹی *kha'ṭā pa'ṭī* N.F. wrangle ; brawl clash (of weapon) ; clank کھٹا پٹی ہونا *khaṭā-pa'ṭī ho'nā* V.I. wrangle

کھٹ[2] *khaṭ* N.F. (short for کھاٹ N.F. ★)

کھٹ *khaṭ* N.M. & PREF. (short for کھٹا ADJ. ★)

کھٹ *khūṭ* N.F. clash ; clank [ONO.]

کھٹا *khaṭ'ṭā* ADJ. sour acid N.M. citron کھٹا چوک *khaṭ'ṭā chook'* ADJ. very sour کھٹاس *khaṭās* N.F. acidity ; sourness کھٹا ساگ *khaṭ'ṭā sāg* N.M. sorrel (جی) کھٹا میٹھا ہونا *(jī) khaṭ'ṭā mī'ṭhā ho'nā* V.I. be tempted کھٹ مٹھا (یا میٹھا) *khaṭ mī'ṭhā* (or *miṭ'ṭhā*) ADJ. sour-sweet taste کھٹائی *khaṭā''ī* N.F. sauce acidity acid کھٹائی میں پڑنا *khaṭā''ī men par'nā* V.I. (of jewellery) be put into the acid put in cold storage ; be shelved کھٹائی میں ڈال رکھنا *khaṭā''ī men ḍāl' rakh'nā* V.T. put (jewellery) in acid for clean-sing put in cold storage ; shelve کھٹے میٹھے دن *khaṭ'ṭe mī'ṭhe din* N.M. PL. days of pregnancy جی (یا دل) کھٹا ہونا *jī* (or *dil*) *khaṭ'ṭā ho'nā* V.I. take offence be fed up

کھٹراگ *khaṭrag'* N.M. fuss ; ado wrangling

کھٹکنا *kha'ṭaknā* V.I. rample offend stick (the mind) کھٹک *kha'ṭak* N.F. pain کھٹکا *khaṭ'kā* N.M. scruple fear apprehension hitch in the mind presentiment کھٹکا لگنا *khaṭ'kā lag'nā* V.I. fear ; have an apprehension ; be apprehensive (of)

کھٹکنا *khū'ṭaknā* V.I. come out of egg by cracking its shell [ONO.]

کھٹکھٹانا *khaṭkhaṭā'nā* V.T. knock ; knock at [ONO.]

کھٹمل *khaṭ'mal* N.M. bug [~ کھاٹ]

کھٹو *khaṭ'too* N.M. & ADJ. bread-winner

کھٹولا *khaṭo'lā* N.M. کھٹولی *khaṭo'lī* N.F. small bed [~ کھاٹ]

کھٹیا *khaṭ'yā* N.F. small bed کھٹیا نکلنا *khaṭ'yā ni'kalnā* V.I. die (esp. in youth) [~ کھاٹ DIM.]

کھٹیک *khaṭīk'* N.M. tanner this as a caste کھٹیکنی *khaṭīk'nī* N.F. female member of a tanner's family tanners wife

کھجنا *khij'nā* V.I. be vexed be incensed . take umbrage at کھج *khij* N.F. vexation nickname کھجانا *khijā'nā*, کھج نکالنا *khij' nikāl'nā* V.T vex tease call names

کھجانا *khūjā'nā*, کھجلانا *khujla'nā* V.T. scratch tickle itch ; have the itch کھجلی *khuj'lī* N.F. itch (in animals) mange (fig.) prurience کھجلی اٹھنا (یا ہونا) *khūj'lī uṭh'nā* (or *ho'nā*) V.I. itch (fig.) have itch (to) ; have a temptation to beat ; be beaten, etc. (vul.) be prurient

کھجور *khajoor'* N.F. date date-palm a kind of sweetmeat looking like date-stone کھجوری *khajoo'rī* ADJ. of or like date well-plaited (hair)

کھچا کھچ *kha'chā khach'* ADV. closely (packed or stuffed) very much (crowded) کھچا کھچ بھرا ہونا *kha'chā khach' bha'rā ho'nā* V.I. be overcrowded be stuffed together

کھچڑی *khich'rī* N.F. rice boiled in split pulse berry flower plot mixture hotch-potch ; hodge-podge assortment (of) ADJ. grizzled (hair) assorted (stuff) کھچڑی پکانا *khich'rī pakā'nā* V.T. mix together ; jumble make a mess of

کھچنا *khich'nā*, کھنچنا *khinch'nā* V.I. be drawn be distended be attracted be estranged کھچا جانا (یا چلا آنا) *khichā ja'nā* (or *cha'la ā'nā*) V.I. be greatly attracted move fast towards کھچا رہنا *khi'chā raih'nā* V.I. be estranged avoid ; evade be glum کھچاؤ *khichā''o*, کھنچاؤ *khinchā''o*, کھچاوٹ *khichā'vaṭ* کھنچاوٹ *khinchā'vaṭ* N.M tension pull estrangement کھچائی *khichā''ī* کھنچائی N.F. dragging ; pulling ; price paid for drawing کھچوانا *khichvā'nā*, کھنچوانا *khinchvā'nā* V.T. cause to draw cause to pull cause to drag

کھدانا khudā'nā, کھدوانا khudvā'nā v.t. get engraved get tatooed cause to dig cause to sink (well) excavate کھدائی khudā''ī, کھدوائی khudvā''ī excavation carving, engraving tatooing digging sinking (of well, etc.) remuneration for any of these

کھدبدانا khadbadā'nā v.i. simmer کھدبد khad'bad N.F simmer [ONO.]

کھدر khad'dar N.M. homespun cotton cloth

کھدرا khud'rā ADJ. uneven N.M. corner (usu. as) کونا کھدرا ko'nā khud'ra PH. (see under کونا N.M. ★)

کھدنا khud'nā v.i. be carved be engraved be tatooed be dug out be excavated (of well, etc.) be sunk [~ کھودنا]

کھڈ khad N.M. valley gorge; chasm ravine کھڈا khad'dā N.M. pit cavity dimple

کھڈی khud'dī N.F seat or compartment in latrine; privy stool; privy seat

کھدیڑنا khuder'nā v.t pursue, chase کھدیڑ khūder N.F. pursuit

کہر koh'r N.F کہرا koh'rā N.M fog; mist کہر آلود دیا (کہر آلودہ) koh'r-ālood' (or āloo'dah) foggy

کھر khur N.M. cloven hoof; hoof cough sound of coughing کھربندی khūr-ban'dī N.F. shoeing (of horse, etc.) کھردار khūr'-dār ADJ. hoofed کھر کھوج مٹانا (یا کھونا) khūr' khoj miṭā'nā (or kho'nā) v.t. annihilate

کھرا khar'rā N.M. curry-comb draft (of letter, etc.) rough account کھرا کرنا khar'rā kar'nā v.t. curry

کھرا khūr'ra ADJ. (F. کھری khūr'rī) uncovered (bed or cot) curt (reply) harsh surly کھرا kha'rā ADJ. (F. کھری kha'rī) genuine unalloyed pure straightforward honest valid (bargain) standard (weight) true good; right کھراپن kha'rā-pan N.M. honesty frankness genuinness کھرا کھوٹا kha'rā kho'ṭā ADJ. genuine or spurious good or bad کھرا کھوٹا پرکھنا kha'rā kho'ṭā pa'rakhna v.t. judge people know one's friend and foe know right from wrong کھری سنانا kha'rī sūnā'na v.i. give a curt reply not to mince words کھری مزدوری چوکھا کام kha'rī mūzdoo'rī cho'khā kām PROV. a good servant must have good wages کھری اسامی kha'rī asā'mī N.F trustworthy person one fair in his dealings

کہرام kohrām' N.M. weeping; wailing; lamentation hue and cry fuss; ado کہرام مچانا kohrām' machā'nā v.t bewail raise a hue and cry make a fuss کہرام مچ جانا kohrām' mach jā'nā v.i. (of lamentation) occur

کھراند kharānd N.F. stench; offensive smell burnt taste

کھرب kha'rab ADJ. a hundred thousand million

کہربا kah-rūbā' (or kaih-) N.M. yellow amber clectricity کہربائی kahrūbā''ī N.F. electric [A ~ P کاہ kāh + ربا snatcher]

کھرپا khūr' pā N.M. hoe کھرپا جالی سنبھالنا khūr'pā jā'lī sanbhāl'nā v.i (have to) act as a grass-cutter کھرپی khūr'pī N.F weeding knife scraper

کھرتل khar'tal ADJ. straightforward outspoken

کھرج kha'raj N.F bass

کھرجا khūr'jā N.M. change, small coins [~ P خوردہ CORR.]

کھرچنا khū'rachnā v.t. scrape scratch کھرچن khūr'chan N.F. (pot or milk) scrapings

کھردرا khūr'dūrā ADJ. F. کھردری khūr'dūrī) rugged rough uneven shaggy unpolished کھردراپن khūr'dūrā-pan N.M. ruggedness unevenness

کھرسا khar'sā N.M dry summer کھرسا پڑنا khar'sa par'nā v.i. (of weather) be dry and hot

کھرل kha'ral N.F. mortar کھرل کرنا kha'ral kar'nā v.t. powder; pound; pulverise

کھرکھانسی khūr' khān'sī INT. (nurs.) away with this cursed cough [~ کھانسنا]

کھرلی khūr'lī N.F manger

کھرنجا kharan'jā, کھڑنجا kharan'jā N.M. pavement (with upright breaks)

کھرنڈ khū'rand N.M. scab; cicatrice کھرنڈ بندھنا khū'rand bandh'nā v.i. form a scab be about to heal

کھرنی khir'nī N.F. a kind of fruit like rawdate

کہروا kaiharvā N.M. name of a musical mode for morning a kind of lascivious dance and music associated with palanquin-bearers

کھری khū'rī N.F. shoe (for horse) iron heel [~ کھر N.M.★]

کھریا khar'ya N.F chalk, a piece of chalk کھریا مٹی khar'ya maṭ'ṭī N.F chalk

کھریرا kharai'rā N.M. curry comb کھریرا کرنا kharai'ra kar'na v curry (a horse)

کھڑا kha'ṛā ADJ. (F. کھڑی kha'ṛī) standing up right perpendicular vertical erect steep (of rice) not fully cooked elongated (vowel) کھڑا داؤں *kha'ṛā da''oṅ* N.M. stake laid half-heartedly when quitting ; last stake کھڑا رہنا *kha'ṛā raih'nā* V.I. stand keep standing stay wait کھڑا کرنا *kha'ṛā kar'nā* V.T. raise cause to stand set upright (vul.) make penis erect set on foot set up ; establish build institute (case) procure a fictitious person for some purpose کھڑا کھیت *kha'ṛā khet* N.M., کھڑی فصل *kha'ṛī fas'l* N.F. standing crop کھڑا کھیل *kha'ṛā khel* N.M. fair dealing swift work کھڑا ہونا *kha'ṛā ho'nā* V.I. stand stand up rise be set up be instituted be built کھڑے پانی نہ پینا *kha'ṛe pā'nī na pī'nā* V.I. stay not even for a moment کھڑے کھڑے *kha'ṛe kha'ṛe* ADV. standing all the while in or for a short while just now soon کھڑے گھاٹ دھلوانا *kha'ṛe ghāṭ dhūlvā'nā* V.T. get expressly washed

کھڑاؤں *kharā''oṅ* N.M. sandals

کھڑبڑانا *khaṛbaṛa'nā* V.I. clatter کھڑ بڑ *khaṛ'baṛ* کھڑبڑاہٹ *khaṛbaṛā'haṭ* N.F. clatter

کھڑکنا *kha'ṛaknā* V.T. rattle cling rustle be knocked clash ; clank کھڑکا *khaṛ'kā* N.M. knock foot-fall کھڑکھڑانا *khaṛkhaṛa'nā* V.T. knock rap rattle threaten کھڑکھڑاہٹ *khaṛ-khaṛā'haṭ* N.F. knock rattle clatter rustle

کھڑکی *khiṛ'kī* N.F. window casement

کھڑنجا *kharañ'ja* N.M. same as کھڑنچا N.M. ★)

کھڑنک *khaṛank'* ADJ. (of bread) very dry

کھڑینچ *khaṛaiñch* N.F. defect cavil کھڑینچ نکالنا *khaṛaiñch' ni'kal'nā* V.T. (at) کھڑینچیا *khaṛaiñchiya* N.M. caviller

کھسرپھسر *khū'sar phū'sar*, کھس پھس *khūs phūs* N.F. whisper; whispering کھسرپھسر (یا کھس پھس) کرنا *khū'sar phū'sar* (or *khūs' phūs*) *kar'nā* V.I. whisper

کھسرا *khas'rā* کھسرہ *khasrah* N.F. measles

کھسکنا *khi'saknā* V.I slip out slink away draw (oneself) away slide کھسکانا *khiskā'nā* V.T. slide draw or move away steal make away with spirit away کھسک جانا *khi'sak ja'nā* V.I. slip away slink away decamp (with)

کھسوٹنا *khasoṭ'nā* V.T. pluck tear at کھسوٹ *khasoṭ* N.F. tearing at snatching depredation

کھسیانا *khisyā'nā* ADJ. (F. کھسیانی *khisyā'nī*) humiliated mortified abashed confounded V.I. look blank feel mortified be confounded کھسیانا پن *khisyā'nā pan* N.M. humiliation mortification clashment being confounded کھسیانا ہو جانا *khisyā'nā ho jā'nā* V.I. feel humiliated be mortified be confounded be abashed

کہف *kah'f* N.M. catacomb cave اصحاب کہف *ashā'b-e kah'f* N.M. PL. companions of the catacomb [A]

کہکشاں *kah'-kashāṅ* (or *kaih'-*) N.F. Galaxy ; Milky Way [P ~ کاہ hay + کشاں drawing]

کھکھوڑنا *khakhoṛ'nā* V.T. scoop scrape search out

کھکھیڑ *khakheṛ'* N.F. vain or bootless labour quarrel کھکھیڑ اٹھانا *hkakheṛ' uṭhā'nā* V.I. undergo bootless labour

کہگل *kah'-gil* (or *kaih-'*) N.F. mud plaster [P ~ کاہ hay + گل mud]

کہل *kah'l* N.M. middle-aged person [A]

کھل *khal* N.F. (same as کھلی *khal'lī* N.F. ★)

کھل *khūl* IMP. کھلا *khūlā* ADJ. (see under کھلنا *khūl'nā* V.I. ★)

کھل *khil* (IMP. کھلا *khi'lā* ADJ. see under کھلنا *khil'nā* V.I. ★)

کھلاڑ *khilaṛ* ADJ. play frolicsome N.M. libertive N.F. loose or wanton کھلاڑ پن *khilaṛ'-pan* N.M. playfulness کھلاڑی *khilā'ṛī* N.M. player one expert at a game sportsman veteran ADJ. playful frolicsome funny کھلاڑیاں *khilā'ṛiyāṅ* N.F. PL. pranks frolics [~ کھیل]

کھلانا[1] *khilā'nā* V.T. feed feast cause to eat cause to take (oath) [~ کھانا CAUS.]

کھلانا[2] *khilā'na* V.T. cause to bloom [~ کھلنا CAUS.]

کھلانا[3] *khilā'na* V.T. cause to play allow to play (with) sport with amuse [~ کھیلنا CAUS.]

کہلانا *kaihlā'nā* V.T. be called cause to say cause to reprove or recommend کہلوانا *kaihalvā'nā* V.T. ★ [~ کہنا CAUS.]

کھلائی *khilā''ī* N.F. dry-nurse remuneration for nursing feeding support maintenance کھلائی پلائی *khilā''ī pilā''ī* N.F. maintenance maintenance charges [~ کھلانا]

کھلبلی *khal'balī* N.F. hurly-burly ; bustle confusion commotion ; agitation perturbation panic کھلبلی پڑنا *khal'balī par'nā*

V.I. be in a state of bustle be agitated ; be in a commotion be greatly perturbed feel panicky کھلبلی ڈالنا *khal'balī dāl'nā* V.T. throw into confusion cause a commotion create a panic

کھلکھلانا *khilkhilā nā* V.I. giggle کھلکھلاکے ہنسنا *khilkhilā ke hans'nā* V.I. have a hearty laugh ; burst into laughter کھل کھل *khil' khil* N.F. giggle

کھلنا *khil'nā* V.I. bloom blossom ; flower be parched (of paster) crack be delighted become happy کھلو *khil'lo* N.F. jocose woman woman fond of laughing without a cause

کھلنا *khul'nā* V.T. open be uncovered be laid bare be cut open open out be unfastened (of sky) clear (of appetite) come back (of tongue) become loose be manifest ; become clear be known become free (with)

کھلنڈرا *khilaṇḍ'ra* (F. کھلنڈری *khilaṇḍ'rī*) ADJ. playful ; sportive fond of playing ; inattentive to studies [~ کھیل]

کھلوانا *kaihalvā'na* V.T. cause to say give a message send a recommendation [~ کہنا]

کھلوانا[1] *khulvā'na* V.T. cause to open or be opened [~ کھولنا]

کھلوانا[2] *khilvāna* V.T. cause to eat cause to take (oath) [~ کھلانا[1]]

کھلوانا[3] *khilvā'na* V.T. cause to play permit to play [~ کھلانا[3]]

کھلونا *khilau'na* N.M. toy plaything

کھلی *kha'lī* (or *khal'lī*) N.F. کھل ، *khal* N.F. oilcake

کھلی *khil'lī* N.F. joke ; jest general laughter کھلی اڑانا *khil'lī ūṛa'na* V.T. ridicule کھلی اڑنا *khil'lī ūṛ'na* V.I. be ridiculed کھلی باز *khil'lī-bāz* ADJ. jocund or jocose (person) کھلی بازی *khil'lī-bā'zī* N.F. jocundity ; jocularity کھلی مچنا *khil'lī mach'na* V.I. (of general laughter) be provoked

کھلیان *khalyan'* N.M. rick ; stack

کھم *kham* N.M. (arch.) post کھم گڑا ہونا *kham' ga'ṛa ho'na* V.I. (of post) be driven (esp. for swings)

کھماچ *khammach'* N.F. name of a light musical mode

کھمبا *kham'ba* N.M. post pillar

کھمبی *khum'bī* N.F. mushroom

کہن *ko'han* (lit.), کہنہ *koh'nah* ADJ. ancient old worn out کہن سال *kohan-sāl'* ADJ. old ; aged ; advanced in years ancient کہن سالی *ko'han-sā'lī* N.F. old age کہنہ مشق *koh'na-mashq* ADJ. experienced veteran کہنگی *koh'nāgī* N.F. being worn-out being old [P]

کہنا *kaih'nā* V.T. & I. (used as کہنا say ; tell relate speak utter assert ; affirm avow recommend advise declare versify (کو کہنا) call ; describe as N.M. advice order word of mouth کہنا کرنا (یا ماننا) *kaih'na kar'nā* (or *man'na*) V.I. carry out the instructions (of) obey, the orders (of) act upon the advice of کہہ *kaih'* IMP. & PREF. say کہہ بیٹھنا (یا چکنا) *kaih' baiṭh'nā* (or *chuk'na*) V.T. have said blurt out کہہ (یا کہے) دینا *kaih'* (or *ka'he*) *de'nā* V.T. tell point out warn کہہ گزرنا *kaih' gu'zarnā* V.T. blurt out کہہ مکرنی (یا مکری) *kaih'-mū'karnī* (or *muk'rī*) N.F. limmeric based on double-entendre کہتے ہیں *kaih'te hain* PH. they say it is said کہنے کو *kaih'ne ko* ADV. only outwardly سب کہنے کی باتیں ہیں *sab kaih'ne kī ba'teṅ hain* PH. there is no substance in it کہے دینا *ka'he de'nā* V.T & I. warn make manifest کا کیا کہنا *ka kya' kaih'na* INT. how wonderful (it is)

کھنچاؤ *khincha''o* N.M. same as کھچاؤ *khicha''o* کھنچنا *khinch'na* V.I. same as کھچنا *khich'na* کھنچوانا *khinchvā'na* V.T, same as کھچوانا *khichva'na* کھنچوائی *khinchvā''ī* N.F. same as کھچوائی *khichva''ī* (see under کھچنا *khich'na* V.I. ★)

کھندلنا *khun'dalnā* V.T. trample

کھنجری *khan'jarī* N.F. same as خنجری N.F. ★)

کھنڈ *khaṇḍ'* N.M. (dial.) part ; portion chapter [S]

کھنڈا *khan'ḍa* N.M. cutlass bruised rice

کھنڈت *khan'ḍat* N.F. becoming topsy-turvy کھنڈت پڑنا (یا ہونا) *khan'ḍat paṛ'na* (or *ho'na*) V.I. be upset ; be topsy-turvy

کھنڈر *khan'ḍar* N.M. (col. PL. کھنڈرات *khanḍarat'*) ruins ADJ. ruined ; dilapidated

کھنڈسار *khaṇḍ-sār'*, کھنڈسال *khaṇḍ-sāl'* N.M. (arch) sugar-mill کھنڈساری *khaṇḍ-sa'rī* ADJ. indigenous (sugar)

کھنڈلا *khaṇḍ'la* (dial. کھانڈا *khān'ḍa* N.M. slice (esp.) fish slice

کھنڈلا *khūnḍ'la* N.M. cottage dilapidated house

کھنڈنا *khand'nā*, کھنڈ جانا *khinḍ jā'nā* V.I. scatter ; be scattered کھنڈانا *khinḍā'nā* V.T. scatter disperse [~ کھنڈ]

کھنسانا *khūnsā'nā* V.I. be jealous of be cross not to be on good terms with کھنس *khuns* N.F. rancour irritation

کھنکارنا *khankār'nā* V.T. cough ; expectorate clear the throat hem ; h'm کھنکار *khankār'* N.M. spittle ; expectoration

کھنکنا *kha'naknā* V.I. (of coin, glasses, etc. V.I. jingle کھنک *kha'nak* N.F. jingle کھنکانا *khankā'nā* V.T. jungle

کھنکھنا *khan'khanā* ADJ. cracked (earthenware)

کھنکھنانا *khinkhinā'nā* V.I. (of sickly child) wail with a nasal sound

کھنگالنا *khangāl'nā* V.T. (of cloth or utensil) rinse purify thus

کھنگر *khan'gar*, کھنگڑ *khan'gaṛ* N.M. over-burnt brick anything dry and hard dross کھنگر لگ جانا *khan'gaṛ lag' jā'nā* V.I. be reduced to a skeleton

کہنگی *koh'nagī* N.F., کہنہ *koh'nah* ADJ. (see under کہن ADJ. ★)

کہنی *koh'nī* N.F. elbow کہنی مارنا *koh'nī mār'nā* V.T. jostle signal thus

کھوا *khā'vā* N.M. shoulder (only in PH.) کھوے سے کھوا چھلنا *khā've se khā'vā chhil'nā* V.I. be overcrowded

کھوپرا *khop'rā* N.M. cocoanut its dried kernels ; copra

کھوپری *khop'rī*, کھوپڑی *khop'ṛī* N.F. skull (fig) brain ; understanding کھوپڑی کھا جانا *khop'rī khā jā'nā* V.I. plague ; (someone) کھوپڑی چٹخنا (یا چٹکنا) *khop'rī cha'takhnā* (or *cha'taknā*) کھوپڑی گنجی (یا پلپلی) کرنا *khop'rī gan'jī* (or *pil'pilī*) *kar'nā* V.T. beat severely ; thrash

کھوٹ *khoṭ* N.F. alloy adulteration impurity defect deceit; in sincerity کھوٹ ملانا *khoṭ' milā'nā* V.T. alloy کھوٹ نکالنا *khoṭ nikāl'nā* V.T. purify ; remove impurity (of) find fault (with) ; cavil (at) کھوٹا *kho'ṭā* ADJ. (F. کھوٹی *kho'ṭī*) base counterfeit spurious alloyed insincere ; perfidious fraudulent mischievous کھوٹا پیسہ بھی برے وقت میں کام آتا ہے *kho'ṭā paisah bhī bū're vaq't kām' ā'tā hai* PROV. even rejected things sometimes prove useful کھوٹا کھرا دیکھنا *kho'ṭā khā'rā dekh'nā* V.I. distinguish between good and bad کھوٹی بات *kho'ṭī bāt* N.F. foul language deception کھوٹی کھری سنانا *kho'ṭī khā rī sunā'nā* V.T. abuse ; revile

کھوج *khoj* M.M. track ; footprint sign ; trace search ; quest کھوج پانا *khoj' pā'nā* V.T. find a clue (to) کھوج کھاج *khoj' khāj* N.F. inquiry کھوج لگانا *khoj' lagā'nā* V.T. track trace look for a clue search کھوج لگنا (یا ملنا) *khoj' lag'nā* (or *mil'nā*) V.I. be traced کھوج مٹانا *khoj miṭā'nā* V.I. obliterate all trace (of) کھوج میں رہنا *khoj' meṅ raih'nā* V.T. pick a hole in another's coat be in search (for) کھوج نکالنا *khoj' nikāl'nā* V.T. track ; discover the track (of) find a clue (to) کھوجی *kho'jī* N.M. detective inquisitive person

کھوچڑ *khoo'chaṛ*, کھونچڑ *khooṅ'chaṛ* N.M. one who puts spoke in another's wheel

کھودنا *khod'nā* V.T. dig delve uproot scrape carve; engrave کھود کھود کر پوچھنا *khod khod' kar poochh'nā* V.I. inquire searchingly

کھور *khaur* N.F. manger

کھورو *khau'roo* N.M. (of ox) pawing the ground digging the earth with the hoofs (animal's) wickedness کھورو کرنا (یا لانا) *khau'roo kar'nā* (or *lā'nā*) V.T. paw the ground

کھوسا *kho'sā* (ped. کھوسہ *ko'sah*) ADJ. having little or no beard [~P کوسہ CORR.]

کھوسٹ *khoo'saṭ* ADJ. very old decrepit N.M. decrepit old man worthless fellow

کھوسنا *khos'nā* V.T. entangle stick (in)

کھوکھا *kho'khā* N.M. (dial.) stall ADJ. blank (rounds)

کھوکھلا *khokh'lā* ADJ. (کھوکھلی *khokh'lī*) hollow blank (round) lacking substance or meaning

کھولنا *khaul'nā* V.I. boil کھولانا *khaulā'nā* V.T. cause to boil کھولاؤ *khaulā''o* N.M. boiling boiling point درجۂ کھولاؤ *dar'jah khaulā''o* N.M. boiling point

کھولنا *khol'nā* V.T. open uncover ; lay bare unfold untie unravel losen disengage disclose ; reveal display explain ; clarify expose cut open ; rip open start expand spread out liberate ; set free unfasten cause to become free کھول کر کہنا (یا بتانا) *khol' kar kaih'nā* (or *batā'nā*) V.T. speak out elucidate

کھونا *kho'nā* V.T. lose waste squander not to be attentive ; be thinking of something else at the moment کھو بیٹھنا *kho' baiṭh'nā* V.T. lose fail to retain be deprived of کھو جانا *kho' ja'na* V.I. be lost be absorbed in deep thought کھو دینا *kho' de'na* V.T. lose waste کھویا کھویا سا رہنا *kho'ya kho'ya sa raih'na* V.I. be absorbed in some other thoughts not to be attentive کھو کر سیکھنا *kho' kar sikh'na* V.I. learn through loss learn from experience

کھونٹ *khoont* N.M. corner direction چاروں کھونٹ *cha'ron khoont* ADV. on all the four sides

کھونٹا *khoon'ta* N.M. peg (animal's) tether-pin tent-pin (fig.) protection : support کھونٹے سے باندھنا *khoon'te se bandh'na* V.T. tie (animal) (fig.) keep (someone) under control کھونٹے سے بندھنا *khoon'te se bandh'na* V.I. (of animal) be tied come under control کھونٹے کے بل کودنا *khoon'te ke bal kood'na* V.T. presume on (someone) protection کھونٹی *khoon'ti* N.F. peg central pin (of handmill) knob (of guitar) hair root کھونٹی نکلوانا *khoon'ti nikalva'na* V.T. have a close shave

کھونچ *khonch* N.F. کھونچا *khon'cha* N.M. rent in cloth ; rent کھونچ آنا (یا لگنا) *khonch' a'na* (or *lag'na*) V.I. (of cloth) be rent

کھونچا *khaun'cha* N.M. six-and-a-half times (table)

کھونچڑ *khoon'char* N.M. (same as کھوچڑ N.M. ★)

کھوندنا *khoond'na* V.T. work with feet trample dig

کھوہ *khoh* N.F. cave ; cavern پہاڑ کی کھوہ *pahar' ki khoh* N.F. cave in the hillside

کھوئی *kho''i* N.F. cane after extraction of juice ; sugar-cane refuse

کھویا *kho'ya* N.M. condensed milk ; ADJ. (from کھونا V.T. ★)

کھویا *khivay'ya*, کھیون ہار *khe'van-har'* N.M. rower boatman (fig.) guide [~ کھینا]

کھویا *khavay'ya* N.M. glutton [~ کھانا]

کھیپ *khep* N.F. trip with load or passenger ass load of cargo load or passenger as carried once کھیپ بھرنا *khep' bhar'na* V.T. load

کھیت *khet* N.M. field land crop expanse field of battle massacre shining or spread of moonlight کھیت پڑنا *khet' par'na* V.T. be massacred (of blood bath) be given کھیت جوتنا *khet' jot'na* V.T. till a field کھیت رہنا *khet' raih'na* V.T. be slain on the battlefield کھیت کاٹنا *khet kat'na* V.T. harvest a crop کھیت کرنا *khet kar'na* V.I. (of moonlight) shine کھیت کمانا *khet' kama'na* V.T. till a field well ; work hard on it کھیت ہاتھ ہونا *khet' hath' ho'na* V.I win succeed be victorious کھیتی *khe'ti* N.F. crop (usu. کھیتی باڑی *khe'ti ba'ri*) farming ; husbandry کھیتی باڑی کرنا *khe'ti ba'ri kar'na* V.T. till ; cultivate کھیتی خصم سیتی *khe'ti khas'm se'ti* PROV. he who ploughs himself reaps a good harvest self-done is best done you stand to lose when you leave work to others

کھیدا *khe'da* N.M. pit for catching elephants ; elephant trap

کھیر *khir* N.F. rice pudding (کی) کھیر دلیا ہو جانا (*ki*) *khir dal'ya ho ja'na* V.I. suffer a reverse of fortune

کھیرا *khi'ra* N.M. cucumber

کھیری *khi'ri* N.F. udder this as food

کھیڑا *khe'ra* N.M. village ; hamlet کھیڑی *khe'ri* N.F. small village membrane enveloping foetus a kind of steel

کھیس *khes'* N.M. twilled bedcover with patterns : damask

کھیس *khis* N.F. first milk after calving molar (used only in) کھیس (یا کھیسیں) نکالنا (یا نپوڑنا) *khis* (or *khi'sen*) *nikal'na* (or *nipor'na*) V.T. grin

کھیسا *khi'sa* N.M. message glove used in bath ; sponge

کھی کھی *khi' khi* N.F. suppressed silly laughter کھی کھی کرنا *khi khi kar'na* V.T. laugh in a silly manner

کھیل *khil* N.F. parched inflated rice کھیل تک اڑ کر منہ میں نہ جانا *khil tak ur kar munh men na ja'na* PH. get nothing to eat

کھیلنا *khel'na* V.I. play frish ; gambol ; frolic fondle copabit (of obsessed (person) move head violent کھیل *khel* N.M. game sport frolic play drama ; show entertainment pastime child play; easy affair skill کھیل بگاڑنا *khel' bi'gar'na* V.T. spoil someones game کھیل بگڑنا *khel' bi'gar'na* V.I. (of someone's game) be spoilt کھیل بنانا *khel bana'na* V.T. regard as a joke ridicule get something done (for) کھیل جانا *khel' ja'na* V.T. play out one's part جان پر کھیل جانا *jan' par khel ja'na* V.I. die lay down one's life for کھیل سمجھنا *khel' sa'majhna* V.I. regard as child's play کھیل کرنا *khel' kar'na* V.T. sport play-put on a show کھیل کود *kelh' kood* N.M. skipping and jumping frolic someones کھیل کود میں وقت (یا سارا دن) گزارنا *khel' kood men vaq't* (or *sa'ra din*) *gu'zar'na* کھیل کھلانا *khel khila'na* V.T. cause to put up a show کھیل کھیلنا

khel' khel'nā V.I. play sport treat as joke سرسے کھیلنا *sar' se khel'nā* V.I. (of obsessed person) move (head) violently do an act of great courage بچوں کا کھیل *bach'chon -kā khel'* N.M. child's play

کہیں *ka'hin* ADV. somewhere anywhere perhaps ; perchance lest ever a little would that کہیں سے *ka'hin se* ADV. from anywhere کہیں کا *ka'hin kā* ADV. of anywhere N.M. (col.) fellow ; bloke کہیں کا نہ رکھنا *ka'hin ka na rakh'nā* V.T. render useless make worthless spoil the future (of) کہیں کا نہ رہنا *ka'hin kā na raih'nā* V.I. be hemiliated have one's future turned کہیں کہیں *ka'hin ka'hin* ADV. here and there کہیں نہ کہیں *ka'hin na ka'hin* ADV. somewhere or other کہیں مُردے بھی زندہ ہوتے ہیں *ka'hin mūr'de bhī zin'dah ho'te hain* PROV. can the dry bones live کہیں ہتھیلی پر بھی سرسوں جمتی ہے *ka'hin hathe'lī par bhī sar'son jam'tī hai* PROV. Rome was not built in a day

کھینا *khe'nā* V.T. row ; paddle (boat)

کھینچنا *khench'nā* (or *khīnch'nā*) V.T. pull drag draw (thing, line, picture, etc.) elongate distil suck up draw out heave (a sigh) suffer (trouble etc.) give (oneself airs) کھینچا تانی *khen'chā tā'nī* N.F. tension stress and strain struggle ; contention کھینچا تانی کرنا *khen'chā tā'nī kar'na* V.T. struggle; contend کھینچ *khench* (or *khīnch*) N.F. pull کھینچ تان *khench' tān* N.F. struggle tension کھینچ تان کے *khench' tān' ke* ADV. with difficulty ; with great effort کھینچ دینا *khench' de'nā* V.T. pull draw scribble کھینچ ڈالنا *khench' ḍal'nā* V.T. scribble (few lines, etc.) write or compose quickly کھینچ لانا *khench' lā'nā* V.T. draw ; bring round کھینچ لینا *khench le'nā* V.T. to pull or draw out ; to extract ; to extort

کھیوا *khe'vā* N.M. ferry money ferry crossing a river passengers in a ferry boat [~ کھینا]

کھیوٹ *khe'vaṭ* N.F. share of revenue record of revenue share land mutation record کھیوٹ دار *khe'vaṭ-dār* N.M. holder of a village share holder کھیوٹ کھتونی *khe'vaṭ khatau'nī* N.F. land mutation record

کھیونہار *khe'van-hār'* N.M. (same as کھویا *khivay'ya* N.M. ★)

کھیّ *khe''ī* N.F. dry bush used in a hedge

1 کئی *ka''ī* ADJ. many several کئی ایک *ka''ī ek* ADJ. a few ; some کئی بار (یا دفعہ یا مرتبہ) *ka''ī bār* (or *daf''ah* or *mar'tabah*) ADV. several times ; many times ; many a time ; often repeatedly again and again ; time and again

2 کئی *ka''ī*, کیانی *kayā'nī* ADJ. (see under ★ کے 3 *kai* N.M.)

1 کے *kai* ADJ. how many

2 کے *kai* ADV. when [P]

3 کے *kai* N.M. (PL. کیاں *kayān*) of ancient Persian emperors royal شان کئی *shā'n-e ka''ī* N.F. royal glory [P]

کیا *kyā* PRON. what PARTICLE (sign of the interrogative has no English equivalent) کیا آئے کیا چلے *kyā' ā''e kyā chа'le* PH. going soon کیا بات ہے *kyā' bāt' hai* PH. what is the matter well-done it goes without saying ; there is no doubt about it کیا پدی کیا پدی کا شوربہ *kyā' pid'dī kyā' pid'dī kā shor'bā* PROV. the matter is not worth taking notice of کیا جاتی دنیا دیکھی ہے *kyā' jā'tī dun'ya de'khī hai* PH. is the change in your (etc.) attitude brought about by a thought of death کیا خبر (یا معلوم) *kyā' kha'bar* (or *ma'loom'*) PH. who knows کیا خوب (یا کہنا) *kyā' khoob'* (or *kaih'nā*) INT. beautiful ; wonderful ; well done ! کیا دھرا (یا رکھا) ہے *kyā' dha'rā* (or *rak'k a*) *hai* PH. there is nothing (in it) now کیا قیامت ہے *kya qiyā'mat hai* PH. how terrible ; how awful کیا (کہنا) ہے *kyā' kaih'na (hai)* INT. wonderful excellent کیا معنی *kyā' ma''nā* PH. why. how کیا یاد کروگے *kyā' yād' ka'roge* INT. you will remember me (etc.) for a long time after today

کیا *ki'ya* P.T. (~ کرنا V.T. ★ N.M.) doing deed کیا دھرا *kiyā dha'ra* N.M. doing کیا کرایا *ki'ya karā'yā* ADJ. & N.M. (work) already done اپنا کیا پانا *ap'na ki'ya pā'na* V.I. reap what one sows

کیاری *kiya'rī* N.F. flower bed part of tilled land

کیاست *kiya'sat* N.F. sagacity [A]

کیبنٹ *kaib'inaṭ* N.F. Cabinet [E]

کیتکی *kel'kī* N.F. name of a fragrant plant

کیتلی *kel'lī* N.F. kettle [E]

کیتھولک *kai'tholik* N.M. & ADJ. (also رومن کیتھولک *ro'man kai'tholik*) Roman Catholic [E]

کیٹ *kiṭ* N.F. hookah sediment oil dregs found in lamp

کیچڑ *ki'chaṛ* (dial. کیچ *kich*) N.F. dirt ; mud ; mire ; slime watery discharge collecting in eye corners کیچڑ اچھالنا kī'chaṛ ūchhāl'nā V.T. fling or throw mud (on) indulge in mud-slinging کیچڑ کی کوڑی دانتوں سے اٹھانا kī'chaṛ kī kau'ṛī dāṅtoṅ se ūṭhā'nā PH. be very niggardly

کیچوا kech'vā N.M. earthworm intestinal worm

کید kaid N.M. (lit.) stratagem fraud [A]

کیر ker N.M. penis [P]

کیرا kai'rā ADJ. & N.M. blue-eyed (man) کیری kai'rī ADJ. blue (eye) blue-eyed N.F. blue-eyed woman

کیری ke'rī N.F. unripe mango

کیڑا kī'ṛā N.M. insect worm maggot (rare) snake کیڑا لگنا kī'ṛā lag'nā V.I. be worm-eaten کیڑا مکوڑا kī'ṛā makau'ṛā N.M. (usu. PL.) any insect کیڑے پڑنا kī're par'nā V.I. rot (fig.) go to hell میں کیڑے ڈالنا men kī're ḍāl'nā V.T. & I. pick holes (in) depreciate

کیڑی kī'ṛī N.F. ant leech

کیس[1] kes N.M. (dial.) long hair on head (as worn by Sikhs)

کیس[2] kes N.M. case [E]

کیسا kai'sā ADJ. (F. کیسی kai'sī) how ; in what manner what sort of ; what type of کیسا زمانہ آگیا ہے kai'sā zamā'nah ā' gayā hai PH. how awful are the times

کیسر ke'sar N.M. saffron کیسری kes'rī ADJ. saffron-coloured N.M. (dial.) lion

کیسہ kī'sah N.M. (lit.) pocket bag کیسہ بر kī'sa-būr N.M. (lit.) pick-pocket [A]

کیش kesh N.M. faith way of life [P]

کیش kaish N.M. cash کیش بک kaish'-būk N.F. cash book [E]

کیف kaif N.M. intoxication exhilaration rapture ; ecstasy کیف و کم kai'f-o-kam N.M. quality and quantity particulars کیفی kai'fī N.M. drunkard ; boozer ADJ. tipsy کیفدان kaif'-dān N.M. (rare) drug casket

کیفر kai'far N.M. punishment (for evil) کیفر کردار kai'far-e kirdār' N.M. recompence for one's evil deeds کیفر کردار کو پہنچنا kai'far-e kirdār' ko pahūṅch'nā V.I. suffer for one's evil deeds [P]

کیفیت kaifiy'yat N.F. state ; condition situation particulars remarks schedule news details facts (of) exhileration rapture ; ecstasy [A ~ کیف]

کیک kek N.M. cake [E]

کیکر kī'kar N.M. acacia کیکر کا گوند kī'kar kā goṅd N.M. gum arabic

کیکڑا kek'ṛā N.M. crab

کیل kīl N.F. nail spike boss gold pin for nose pimple core of boil کیل کانٹا kīl' kāṅ'ṭā N.M. equipment ; accoutrements کیل کانٹے سے درست (یا لیس) kīl' kāṅ'ṭe se dūrūs't (or lais') ADJ. & ADV. well-equipped ; well-accoutred کیلنا kīl'nā V.T. nail exorcise thus prevent snake from by biting by playing 'been' incapacitate by breathing a spell (over)

کیلا kī'lā کیلہ kīlah N.M. peg fang (dial.) acre کیلی kī'lī N.F. peg pivot ; axis

کیلا ke'lā N.M. banana ; plaintain

کیلنڈر kailaṅ'dar N.M. calendar [E]

کیلو kī'lo PREF. thousand ; kilo کیلوگرام kī'lo-garām N.M. kilogramme کیلومیٹر kī'lo-mī'ṭar N.M. kilometre [E]

کیلوس kailoos' N.M. chile [A ~ G]

کیلی kī'lī N.F. (see under کیل N.F. ★)

کیمخت kīmūkh't N.M. shagreen [P]

کیمرا kaim'rā, کیمرہ kaim'rah N.M. camera [E]

کیمسٹری kaimis'ṭarī N.F. chemistry [E]

کیمیکل kai'mīkal ADJ. chemical [E]

کیموس kaimoos' N.M. chyme [A ~ G]

کیمیا kī'miyā N.F. chemistry (old use ; now rare) alchemy کیمیا بنانا kī'miyā banā'nā V.T. alchemize turn baser metals into gold make easy money کیمیادان kīmiyā-dān N.M. chemist کیمیادانی kī'miyā-dā'nī N.F. knowledge of chemistry کیمیاگر kī'miyā-gar N.M. alchemist deceiver کیمیاگری kī'mi-yā garī N.F. alchemy [A ~ G]

کین kīn N.M. (same as کینہ N.M. ★)

کینچلی keṅch'lī N.F. slough (of snake) (fig.) dress کینچلی بدلنا keṅch'lī ba'dalnā V.I. slough (fig.) change clothes کینچلی چھوڑنا keṅch'lī chhoṛ'nā V.T. cast off the (old) slough

کینڈا *kain'dā* N.M. rough estimate (fig.) calibre (within someone's) means اس کینڈے کا آدمی *is kain'de kā ād'mī* PH. man of such calibre کے کینڈے میں آنا *ke kain'de meṅ ā'nā* V.I. fall within the means (of)

کینہ *kī'nah* N.M. malice rancour کینہ توز *kīna'-toz*, کینہ ور *kī'na-var*, کینہ ورز *kī'na-var'z* ADJ. malicious کینہ توزی *kī'na-to'zī*, کینہ وری *kī'na-va'rī*, کینہ ورزی *kī'na-var'zī* N.F. malice; spite کینہ رکھنا *kī'nah rakh'nā* V.T. bear enmity [P]

کیواں *kaivāṅ* N.M. Saturn seventh heaven [P]

کیوٹی *kiyo'ṭī*, کیوکی *kiyo'kī* N.F. a mixture of different kinds of pulses

کیوڑا *kiyo'ṛā*, کیوڑہ *kiyo'ṛah* N.M. a kind of fragrant plant

کیوں *kyooṅ* (or *kyoṅ*) PROV. why wherefore how well کیونکر *kyooṅ'-kar*, کیونکہ *kyooṅ-ke* ADV. how why what for (L. dial.) since; because کیونکہ *kyooṅ-ke* CONJ. because since for inasmuch as کیوں ہم نہ کہتے تھے *kyooṅ ham' na kaih'te the* PH. didn't I tell (or warn) you beforehand کیوں نہ ہو *kyooṅ na ho* PH. why not there is no gainsaying the fact that; it cannot be gainsaid کیوں نہیں *kyooṅ' na'hīṅ* PH. why not

گ

گ *gaf* twenty-ninth letter of Urdu alphabet (also called *kā'f-e fā'risi*) (equivalent to English *g*) (in jummal reckoning held equivalent to) 20

گا[1] *gā* V.A. (PL. گے *ge* F. گی *gī*) (sign of future tense) shall; will

گا[2] *gā* N.M. third note of national gamut; re

گابھ *gābh* N.M. pregnancy (of cattle) گابھ ڈالنا *gābh ḍāl'nā* V.I. (of cattle) miscarry گابھن *gābhan* N.F. & ADJ. pregnant cattle گابھن گابھ ڈالتی ہے *gā'bhan gābh' ḍāl'tī hai* PROV. everyone is overawed

گابھا *gā'bhā* N.M. leaf in bud

گات *gāt* N.F. (usu. woman's) bosom or bust

گاتی *gā'tī* N.F. stole knotted in front after passing over one and under other shoulder; cross-belt-like stole گاتی باندھنا *gā'tī bāndh'nā* V.T. put on stole like cross-belt

گاج *gāj* N.F. foam thunderbolt glass bangla threat

گاجا *gā'jā* N.M. (meaningless adjunct to N.M. ★)

گاجر *gā'jar* N.F. carrot گاجر مولی *gā'jar moo'lī* N.F. carrot and radish (fig.) cheap stuff (fig.) rubbish

گاد *gād* N.F. sediment less; degs dense oil گاد بیٹھنا *gād' baiṭh'nā* V.I. (of sediment) settle down

گار *gār* SUF. agent doer matter گاری *gā'rī* SUF. doing making [P]

گارا *gā'rā* N.M. mud kneaded clay گارا بنانا (یا کرنا) *gā'rā banā'nā* (or *kar'nā*) V.T. knead clay

گارد *gā'rad* N.F. guard guard-room [~E guard CORR.]

گارڈ *gār'd* N.M. guard (on railway train) [E]

گارڈن *gāṛ'dan* N.M. garden گارڈن پارٹی *gāṛ'dan pāṛ'tī* N.F. garden party [E]

گارنٹی *gāraṅ'ṭī* N.F. guarantee گرنٹیڈ *garaṅ'ṭīḍ* ADJ. guaranteed [E]

گاڑنا *gāṛ'nā* bury; inter drive (nail etc.) fix pitch (tent, etc.)

گاڑھ *gāṛh* N.F. difficulty; fix weavers' pit handloom

گاڑھا *gā'ṛhā* ADJ. (F. گاڑھی *gāṛ'hī*) thick dense (rare) coarse intimate (friendship) powerful difficult (times) N.M. coarse cloth; khaddar ambush must; frenzied elephant (with) گاڑھے پسینے کی کمائی *gā'ṛhe pasī'ne kī kamā''ī* N.F. hard-earned penny

گاڑی *gā'ṛī* N.F. ox-cart conveyance coach phaeton motor car (also ریل گاڑی *rel'-gā'ṛī*) railway train گاڑیبان *gā'ṛī-bān* N.M. carter coachman گاڑی جوتنا *gā'ṛī jot'nā* V.T. harness horses or yoke bullocks to a conveyance گاڑی چلانا *gā'ṛī chalā'nā* V.T. drive a conveyance drive a train hire out a cab گاڑی چھوٹ جانا (یا چکنا) *gā'ṛī chhooṭ' jā'nā* (or *chūk'nā*) (of train) start (of train) be missed گاڑی خانہ *gā'ṛī-khā'nah* N.M. (rare) garage گاڑی کو دیکھ کر قدم پھولنا *gā'ṛī ko dekh kar qa'dam phool'nā* PH. become idle on getting help گاڑی ہانکنا *gā'ṛī hāṅk'nā* V.T. drive a cart چلتی گاڑی میں روڑا اٹکانا *chal'tī gā'ṛī meṅ ro'ṛā aṭkā'nā* V.T. put a spoke in (someone's) wheel

گاز[1] *gāz* N.F. wick-trimming scissors [P]

گاز[2] *gāz* N.F. dressing guaze [E]

گاف[1] *gāf* N.M. name of the letter گ

گاف[2] *gāf* N.F. (same as گالف N.F. ★)

گاگر *gā'gar* N.F. mettallic pitcher

گال *gāl* N.M. cheek گال بجانا *gāl' bajā'nā* V.I. boast ; brag talk nonsense گال پچکنا *gāl' pi'chaknā* V.I. have sunken cheeks گال پر گال چڑھنا *gāl' par gāl chaṛh'nā*, گال بھرنا *gāl bhar'nā* V.I. have chubby cheeks گال پھلانا *gāl phŭlā'nā* V.I. sulk گال کاٹنا *gāl' kāṭ'nā* V.T. bite cheeks in kissing cause loss (to) گالوں میں چاول بھرنا *gā'loṅ meṅ chā'val bhar'nā* PH. mince words

گالا *gā'lā* N.M. ball (of corded cotton) (snow) flake

گالی *gā'lī* N.F. swear word ; abuse abusive language گالی (یا گالیاں) بکنا (یا دینا یا سنانا) *gā'lī* (or *gā'liyāṅ*) *bak'nā* (or *de'nā* or *sunā'nā*) V.T. swear at ; abuse revile call (someone) names گالی (یا گالیاں) کھانا *gā'lī* (or *gā'liyāṅ*) *khā'nā* V.I. be abused گالی گلوچ *gā'lī galoch'* N.F. mutual abuse ; brawl گالیوں پر اتر آنا *gā'liyoṅ par ŭ'tar ā'nā* V.I. descend to the level of using abusive language گالیوں کی بوچھاڑ (یا بھرمار) کرنا *gā'liyoṅ kī bauchhāṛ'* (or *bharmār'*) *kar'nā* V.I. hurl abuses (at)

گام *gām* N.M. pace (of horse) (lit.) foot گام زن *gām'-zan* ADJ. moving ; treading گام زن ہونا *gām'-zan ho'nā* V.I. start ; commence (fig.) move (on the path of) [P]

گاں *gāṅ* SUF. befitting -ly [P]

گانا *gā'nā* V.I. sing chant (fig.) sing the praises (of) N.M. song singing vocal music گانا بجانا *gā'nā bajā'nā* N.M. singing and playing music song and music ; vocal and instrumental music this as one's profession ~ a life of luxury گاتے گاتے کلاونت ہو جانا *gā'te gā'te kalāṅ'ŭt ho jā'nā* V.I. become an expert with long practice

گانٹھنا *gāṅṭh'nā* V.T. tie knot fasten stitch cobble repair bring round ; bring over to one's side plot گانٹھ *gāṅṭh* N.F. knot hardened gland bulbous root piece (of) misunderstanding ill-feelings bundle (arch.) pocket گانٹھ باندھنا (یا دینا یا لگانا) *gāṅṭh bāndh'nā* (or *de'nā* or *lagā'nā*) V.T. tie a knot do so to bear in mind join together گانٹھ پڑنا *gāṅṭh paṛ'nā* V.I. be knotted (fig.) have ill-feelings گانٹھ سے جانا *gāṅṭh se jā'nā* V.I. incure a loss ; lose money (on a transaction, etc.) گانٹھ کا پورا *gāṅṭh kā poo'rā* ADJ. & N.M. (person) not allowing a penny to slip out of his hands عقل کا اندھا گانٹھ کا پورا *'aq'l kā aṅ'dhā gāṅṭh' kā poo'rā* ADJ. & N.M. silly rich (person) گانٹھ کا پیسہ بھی کام آتا ہے *gāṅṭh kā pai'sah bhī kām ā'tā hai* PROV. the penny in the pocket is the best companion گانٹھ کاٹنا (یا کترنا) *gāṅṭh kāṭ'nā* (or *ka'tarnā*) V.T. pick (someone's) pocket گانٹھ کھولنا *kāṅṭh khol'nā* V.T. untie a knot remove ill-feelings گانٹھ گٹھیلا *gāṅṭh goṭhī'lā* ADJ having many knots گانٹھ میں رکھنا *gāṅṭh meṅ rakh'nā* V.T. pocket گانٹھ گرہ میں کوڑی نہیں بانکے پور کی سیر *gāṅṭh' gi'reh meṅ kaṅ'ṛī na'hīṅ bāṅ'ke-poor kī sair'*, گانٹھ نہ مٹھی پھڑ پھڑاتی اٹھی *gāṅṭh na mŭṭ'ṭhī phaṛ phaṛā'tī ŭṭṭhī* PROV. building castles in the air silly brag گانٹھ لینا *gāṅṭh le'nā* V.T. bring over to one's side ; make friends (with)

گانجا *gāṅ'jā* N.M. smoking hemp

گاندھی گندھی *gāṅ'dhī gaṅ'dhī* N.M. perfumer [~ گندھ]

گانڈ گانڑ *gāṅḍ gāṅṛ* N.F. (vul.) anus bum bottom گانڑو *gāṅ'ḍoo* N.M. & ADJ. (vul.) catamite ; bum boy (fig.) coward

گائڈ *gā''iḍ* N.M. guide [E]

گائک *gā''ik* N.M. singer male ; virtuoso گائکی *gā''ikī* N.F. art of singing music گائن *gā''in* N.F. female singer

گانو *gāṅ''o* N.M. (arch. for گاؤں N.M. ★)

گاہ *gāh*, گہ *gah* N.F. time occasion place ADV. sometimes SUF. place of ; centre گاہ بہ گاہ *gāh' ba-gāh'* ADV. occasionally گاہ گاہ *gāh, gāh*, گاہے گاہے *gā'he gā'he* ADV. occasionally not very often ; rarely once in a blue moon [P]

گاہک *gā'hak* N.M. customer گاہکی *gā'hakī* N.F. sale custom

گاہنا *gāh'nā* V.T. thresh ; thrash

گاہے *gā'he* ADV (see under گاہ N.F. ★)

گاؤ *gā''o* N.M. cow CX bull PREF. large گاؤ آہن *gā''o ā'han* N.M. ploughshare گاؤ تکیہ *gā''o tak'yah* N.M. bolster large pillow گاؤ چشم *gā''o chash'm* ADJ. (derog.) large-eyed گاؤ خانہ *gā''o-khā'nah* N.M. cow-shed گاؤ خورد *gā''o-khurd* ADJ. destroyed گاؤ خورد ہو جانا *gā''o-khurd ho jā'nā* V.I. be lost گاؤ پچھاڑ *gā''o-pichhāṛ* N.M. name of a wrestling trick گاؤ دم *gā''o dūm* ADJ. tapering conical N.M. bugle گاؤ دم ہونا *gā''o-dūm ho'nā* V.I. taper گاؤ دیدہ *gā''o-dīdah* N.M. (dial.) oval bread گاؤ زبان *gā''o-zabān'* N.F.

primula : oxlip (dial.) fried bun گاؤ زمین *ga'v-e zamin'* N.M. legendary bull on whose horns the earth rests گاؤ زوری *ga''o-zo'ri* N.F. (usu. PL.) wrestling گاؤ زوریاں کرنا *ga''o-zo'riyan kar'na* V.I. wrestle to assert one's strength گاؤ شیر *ga''o-shir* N.M. gum-resin گاؤ شماری *ga''o-shuma'ri* N.F. cattle census cattle cess گاؤ فلک *ga''v-e falak'* N.M. (fig.) Taurus گاؤ کشی *ga''o-kushi* N.F. cow-slaughter گاؤ میش *ga''o-mesh'* N.M. buffalo [P]

گاؤدی *ga''odi* N.M. fool simpleton

گاؤں *ga'on* (arch. گانو *gan''o* or گانوں *gan''on*) N.M. (PL. same or گانوں *gan''on*) village ; hamlet گاؤں میں گھر نہ جنگل میں کھیتی *ga''on men ghar na jan'gal men khe'ti* PH. be a very poor person

گائے *ga''e* N.F. (PL. گائیں *ga''en* DATIVE PL. گایوں *ga'yon*) cow گائے کرنا *ga''e kar'na* V.T. slaughter a cow گائے کو اپنے سینگ بھاری نہیں ہوتے *ga''e ko ap'ne sing bha'ri nahin ho'te* PROV. one's own burden feels light

گایتری *gayat'ri* N.F. (dial.) name of sacred prayer-verse from the Vedas

گبدا *gab'da* ADJ. plump : fleshy

گبر *gab'r* N.M. fire-worshipper ; Zoroastrian; Magus 'giaour' [P]

گبرو *gab'roo,* گبھرو *gabh'roo* N.M. youth ADJ. well-built (youth)

گبرون *gabroon'* N.M. a kind of coarse cloth

گبریلا *gubri'la* N.M. dung-worn dung-beetle

گبھا *gab'bha* N.M. (dial.) Chitral carpet with patched patterns

گپ *gap* N.F. chat tattle gossip false report گپ بازی *gap'-ba'zi* N.F. chat gossip گپ شپ *gap'-shap* N.F. chit chat idle talk false report گپ شپ کرنا *gap'-shap kar'na* گپ مارنا (یا ہانکنا یا اڑانا) *gap mar'na* (or *hank'na* or *ura'na*) V.T. tattle gossip brag give currency false report گپی *gap'pi* N.M. & ADJ. idle talker prather liar

گپت *gup't* ADJ. (dial.) hidden invisible ADV. secretly ; privately گپت مار *gup't mar'* N.F. invisible hurts گپت مال *gup t mal'* N.M. hidden wealth گپتی *gup'ti* N.F. swordstick [S]

گپ چپ *gup' chup* ADJ. quiet N.F. silence easily soluble (sweet meat)

گپڑ چوتھ *ga'par chauth* N.F. confusion ; confused state underhand dealings

گپھا *gu'pha* N.F. (dial.) cave گپھا میں بیٹھنا *gu'pha men baith'na* V.I. lead a hermit's life

گپھا *gu'pha* N.M. tassel skein of silk or gold thread bunch (of flowers)

گپی *gap'pi* ADJ. & N.M. (see under گپ N.F.★)

گت *gat* N.F. plight ; predicament state; condition severe beating browbeating gait made of dancing tune ; air گت بجانا *gat' baja'na* V.T. play a tune ; play an air گت بنانا (یا کرنا) *gat' bana'na* (or *kar'na*) V.T. beat severely ; give a sound beating bear down ; browbeat گت بھرنا (یا ناچنا) *gat' bhar'na* (or *nach'na*) V.I. dance to music ; dance in a particular mode گت کا *gat' ka* ADJ. good serviceable گت ہونا (یا بننا) *gat' ho'na* (or *ban'na*) V.I. be given a sound beating be browbeaten

گتا *gat'la* N.M. cardboard

گتکا *gat'ka,* گدکا *gad'ka* N.M. foil (for fencing) blunt wooden sword (rare) fencing

گتھنا *guth'na* V.T. contend ; fall to be plaited be closely knit گتھم گتھا ہونا *gut'-tham gut'tha ho'na* V.T. contend physically fall to each other گتھواں *guth'van* ADJ. plaited close-knit

گتھی *gut'thi* N.F. tangle complication گتھی پڑنا *gut'thi par'na* V.I. be tangled گتھی (یا گتھیاں) سلجھانا *gut'thi* (or *gutthi yan*) *suljha'na* V.T. solve a problem disentangle (something) گتھی سلجھنا *gut'thi su'lajhna* V.I. (of problem) be solved

گٹا *gat'ta* N.M. corn (on skin) stopper knee-joint ankle-joint part of hookah pipe fitting into container a kind of crisp sweetmeat گٹا سا *gat'ta sa* ADJ. wee-bit گٹے پڑنا *gat'te par'na* V.I. have corns

گٹا *gut'ta* ADJ. dwarfish N.M. (also گول گٹا *gol' gut'ta*) marble ; pebble (گول) گٹے کھیلنا *(gol') gut'te khel'na* V.I. (of child) play with pebbles

گٹ پٹ *gat' pat* ADJ. mixed up ADV. wrestling jocosily or in a friendly manner گٹ پٹ ہو جانا *gat' pat ho ja'na* V.I. come to grips be mixed up

گٹ پٹ *git' pit* N.F. (joc. or derog.) speaking English گٹ پٹ کرنا *git' pit kar'na* V.I. (joc. or derog.) speak English [ONO.]

گٹکا *gut'ka* N.M. (dial.) small book ; pocket edition small ball magic ball chessman draughtsman betelnut and catcher mixture chawed implace of betel-leaves

گٹکری *git'kari* N.F. undulating voice in singing گٹکری لینا *git'kari le'na* V.I. cause one's voice to undulase

گٹکنا *gū'ṭaknā* V.I. coo [ONO.]

گٹھ *gaṭh* N.F. knot ; tie گٹھ بندھن *gaṭh ban'dhan* N.M. alliance گٹھ جوڑ *gaṭh-jor'* N.M. (dial.) nuptial tie alliance plot [~ گانٹھ CONTR.]

گٹھا *gaṭ'ṭhā* N.M. bundle three-yard knot in 'jarib' indicating its 20th part

گٹھانا *gaṭhā'nā*, گٹھوانا *gaṭhvā'nā* V.T. (of shoe, etc.) get mended

گٹھڑ *gaṭ'ṭhaṛ* N.M. large bundle گٹھڑی *gaṭh'ṛī* N.F. bag bundle گٹھڑی کر دینا *gaṭh'ṛī kar de'nā* V.T. bundle up ; tie someone's hand and feet گٹھلی *gūṭh'lī* N.F. stone (of fruit) unkneaded knot in dough گٹھلیاں پڑنا *gūṭh'liyān paṛ'nā* V.I. be brotted be uneven گٹھل *gūṭ'ṭhal* N.M. unusually large stone (of fruit)

گٹھنا *gaṭh'nā* be mended join look nice on (of someone) be raised in prestige (of body) be well-built گٹھا ہوا *ga'ṭhā hū''ā* ADJ. well-built (body) گٹھوائی *gaṭhvā''ī* N.F. mending charge

گٹھیا *gaṭh'yā*, گنٹھیا *ganṭh'yā* N.F. gout ; rheumatism [~ PREC.]

گٹھیلا *gaṭhī'lā* ADJ. knotty robust or well-built (body) [~ گٹھنا]

گٹی *gūṭ'ṭī* N.F. reel stopper for hookah bowl

گٹے *gūṭ'ṭe* N.M. PL. گول گٹے *gol gūṭ'ṭe* N.M. (see under گٹا *gūṭ'ṭā* N.M. ★)

گج *gaj* N.M. (dial.) elephant ADJ. elephant very large گج گاہ *gaj-gāh*, N.M. tasselled trappings for horse or elephant گجنال *gajnāl'* N.F. (arch.) cannon

گجر *ga'jar* N.M. four-hourly stroke of gong early morning گجر بجنا *ga'jar baj'nā* V.I. (of four-hourly gong) strike گجر دم *ga'jar dam* ADV. early in the morning

گجرا *gaj'rā* N.M. flower bracelet گجرا گوندھنا *gaj'rā goondh'nā* V.T. prepare a flower bracelet

گجر بھتا *ga'jar-bhat'tā* N.M. sweet rice cooked with carrot [~ گاجر + بھات]

گجگجانا *gijgijā'nā* V.I. be moist and flaccid (of worms) move incite ; egg on

گجگجا *gij'gijā* ADJ. (F. گجگجی *gij'gijī*) jelly-like moist and flaccid

گجھا *gūj'jhā* ADJ. (F گجھی *gūj'jhī*). hidden ; invisible گجھی مار *gūj'jhī mār* N.M. invisible hurt

گجئی *gūjaī'ī* N.F. a kind of centipede mixture of wheat and barley

گجیا *gūj'ya*, گجھیا *gūjh'ya* N.F. cookie

گچ *gach* N.M. mortar lime used as mortar cemented floor, etc. گچ کاری *gach-kā'rī* N.F. mortar work گچاکا *gachā'kā* N.F. going woman sudden blow sudden jolt

گچاگچ *ga'chā-gach* ADV. with sound as of knife in cutting meat

گچ پچ *gich' pich* ADV. crowded

گچھا *gūch'chhā* N.M. bunch cluster skein (of thread) tassel گچھے دار *gūch'chhe-dār* ADJ. tasselled گچھی *gūch'chhī* N.F. skein (of thread)

گچی *gūch'chī* N.F. small hole in earth used as goal in children's game ADJ. small گچی پالا *gūch'chī pā'lā* N.M. name of a children's game

گدا *gadā'* N.M. beggar ; mendicant گدائی *gadā''ī* N.F. begging beggary poverty گدایانہ *gadāyā'nah* ADJ. & ADV. beggarly ; beggar-like [P]

گدا *gad'dā* N.M. mattress

گدا *gūd'dā* N.M. thick bough

گداختہ *gūdākh'tah* ADJ. melted soft [P ~ گداختن]

گداز *gūdāz'* ADJ. melted soft N.M. effect pathos SUF. melting softening گدازی *gūdā'zī* SUF. melting [P ~ گداختن]

گداگر *gadā'-gar* N.M. (wrong but usual form) beggar ; mendicant گداگری *gadā'-garī* N.F. begging beggary poverty [~P گدا]

گدبد *gad' bad* ADV., گداگد *ga'dā gad* ADV. falling constantly N.F. such sound

گدائی *gadā''ī* N.F. گدایانہ *gadāyā'nah* ADV. (see under گدا N.M. ★)

گدرانا *gadrā'nā* V.I. (of fruit) be halfripe (of body) fill up owing to puberty گدرایا ہوا *gadrā'yā hū''ā* ADJ. fully developed (body) گدرا *gad'rā*, گدر *gad'dar* ADJ. گدراہٹ *gadrā'haṭ* N.F. (of fruit) being half-ripe (of female body) being freshly developed

گدڑی *gūd'ṛī*, گودڑی *goọd'ṛī* N.F. tattered quilt rags beggar's tattered gown گودڑی میں لال (یا لعل) *gūd'ṛī men lāl'* (or *la''l*) N.M. a jewel in rags گدڑیا *gū'daṛ yā* N.F. rags N.M. one in rags

گدکا *gad'kā* N.M. (same as گتکا N.M. ★)

گدگدا *gūd'gūdā* ADJ. plump and soft

گدگدانا **gŭdgŭda'na** V.T. tickle titillate try to humour incite ; egg on گدگداہٹ gŭdgŭda'haṭ, N.F. گدگدی gŭd'gŭdī N.F. tickling sensation titillation excitement; incitement گدگدی کرنا gŭd'gŭdī kar'na V.T. tickle ; titillate گدگدی ہونا gŭd'gŭdī ho'na V.I. be tickled have an urge (to)

گدلا **gad'la** ADJ. (F. گدلی gad'lī) muddy ; turbid گدلاپن gad'la-pan N.M. turbidness ; turbidity

گدنا **gŭd'na** V.I. be tatooed گدوانا gŭdva'na V.T. cause to tatoo get tatooed [~ گودنا]

گدھ **gidh** N.M. vulture

گدھا **ga'dha** N.M. donkey ; ass fool ass ADJ. foolish ; stupid گدھاپن ga'dha-pan N.M. foolishness ; stupidity گدھا برسات میں بھوکا مرے ga'dha barsat' meṅ bhoo'ka ma're PROV. a fool suffers owing to own mistake گدھا پیٹنے سے گھوڑا نہیں ہوتا ga'dha piṭ'ne se gho'ra na'hīṅ ho'ta PROV. nothing can make a born fool wise گدھا کیا جانے زعفران کا بھاؤ ga'dha kya ja'ne za'faran' ka bha''o PROV. be a caviare to the general a fool cannot relish good things گدھا گھوڑا ایک بھاؤ ga'dha gho'ra ek bha''o PROV. have no appreciation for talent گدھے پر سوار کرنا ga'dhe par savar' kar'na PH. bring public disgrace (to) گدھے پر کتابیں لادنا ga'dhe par kitabeṅ lad'na PROV. book-lore cannot make a fool wise ضرورت کے وقت گدھے کو باپ بنانا zaroo'rat ke vaq't ga'de ko bap' bana'na PH. pretend to honour a fool one's need گدھے کے ہل چلوانا ga'dhe ke hal' chalva'na PH. ruin ; destroy گدھے کی آنکھ میں نون دیا اس نے کہا میری آنکھیں پھوڑیں ga'dhe kī aṅkh' meṅ noon' diya ŭs' ne ka'ha me'rī a'ṅkheṅ pho'ṛīṅ PH. try to do good to a fool گدھی ga'dhī N.F. she ass ADJ. foll ; silly (woman)

گدی **gad'dī** N.F. cushion seat throne seat of honour office of saints ; successor گدی پر بٹھانا gad'dī par biṭha'na V.T. instal (king, religious leader, etc.) گدی پر بیٹھنا gad'dī par baiṭh'na V.I. ascend the throne succeed (someone) گدی سے اتارنا gad'dī se ŭtar'na V.T. dethrone گدی نشین gad'dī-nashīn' N.M. successor of a saint گدی نشینی gad'dī-nashī'nī N.F. accession to the throne succession to saint's office, etc.

گدی **gŭd'dī** N.F. nape of the neck گدی بھانا (یا ناپنا) gŭd'dī bhan'na (or napna) V.T. slap one on the neck گدی سے زبان کھینچنا gŭd'dī se zaban' khench'na V.T. punish by pulling the tongue from the nape گدی ناپنا gŭd'dī nap'na V.T. slap (someone) on the neck

گدیلا **gade'la** N.M. mattress quilted covering (for elephant) [doublet of گدا]

گڈا **gaḍ'ḍa** N.M bullock cart ; lump of clay

گڈا **gŭḍ'ḍa** N.M. male doll ; puppet effigy lovely male child گڈا بنانا gŭḍ'ḍa bana'na V.T. make an effigy (of) گڈا بنا کے جوتے مارنا gŭḍ'ḍa bana' ke joo'te mar'na V.T. raise (someone) to a position of honour and then disgrace disgrace (someone) in an effigy

گڈامی **gŭḍa'mī**, گڈامیر gŭḍa'mīr ADJ. mixed or impure (dialect)

گڈریا **gaḍar'ya** N.M. shepherd

گڈمڈ **gaḍ' maḍ** (dial. گڈبڈ gaḍ' baḍ) ADJ. jumbled muddled confused گڈمڈ کرنا gaḍ' maḍ kar'na V.T. jumble up confuse گڈمڈ ہونا gaḍ' maḍ ho'na V.I. be jumbled up be confused

گڈھ **gaḍh** N.M. (same as گڑھ N.M. ★) گڈھی ga'ḍhī N.F. same as گڑھی N.F. (see under گڑھ N.M. ★)

گڈی **gaḍ'ḍī** N.F. sheaf

گڈی **gŭḍ'ḍī** N.F. small paper-kite bone-joint pinion

گذارش **gŭza'rish** N.F. (same as گزارش N.F. ★)

گذشتہ **gŭzash'tah** ADJ. (same as گزشتہ ADJ. ★) گذشتنی guzash'tanī ADJ. same as گزشتنی ADJ. (see under گزشتہ ADJ. ★)

گر **gar** CONJ. (lit.) if ; in case in the event of [P ~ اگر CONTR.]

گر **gar** SUF. maker worker گری ga'rī SUF. making working

گر **gŭr** N.M. formula way ; trick

گرا **gar'ra** ADJ. (F. گری gar'rī) reddish

گراب **girab'** N.M. shower of small shots from cartridge

گراری **gara'rī** N.F. pulley cogged wheel reel

گرام **garam'** N.M. gram ; gramme [E]

گرام **giram'** N.M. (dial.) village ; hamlet [S]

گرامر **gara'mar**, گریمر garai'mar N.F. grammar [E]

گراموفون **gira'mofon** N.M. gramophone ; phonograph [E]

گرامی **gira'mī** ADJ. respectable ; venerable high (position) ADV. highly (placed)

greatly (valued) گرامی قدر *gira'mī-qad'r* ADJ. venerable مزاجِ گرامی *mizā'j-e gira'mī* INT. how do you do ; how are you [P]

گراں *girāṅ'* ADJ. dear ; costly ; expensive heavy undesirable ; unbearable گرانبار *girāṅ'-bār'* ADJ. heavily ; burdened laden with fruit گرانبہا *girāṅ'-baha'* ADJ. costly ; precious جنسِ گراں بہا *jin's-e girāṅ-bahā'* N.M. precious stuff گراں خاطر *girāṅ'-khā'tir* ADJ. sad ; dejected unbearable گراں سر *girāṅ'-sar*, سرگراں *sar-girāṅ'* ADJ. proud ; haughty گرانفروش *girāṅ'-firosh'* ADJ. one who sells dear ; one who sells at higher rates (پر) گراں گزرنا (یا ہونا) *(par) girāṅ' gū'zar'nā* (or *ho'nā*) V.I. be unpalatable (to) be unbearable (for) گراں مایہ *girāṅ'-mā'yah* ADJ. of great value ; valuable گراں ہونا *girāṅ' ho'nā* V. to rise in price ; to become more costly گرانی *girā'nī* N.F. dearness rise in price price spiral dearth ; scarcity heaviness indigestion being unpalatable ; being unbearable سرگرانی *sar'-girā'nī* N.F. (see under سر *sar* N.M. ★)

گرانا *girā'na* V.T. drop let fall fell shed (leaves, etc.) let flow raze to the ground lower rank, status, (price, etc.) قیمت گرانا *qī'mat girā'nā* V.T. devaluate ; devalue گرا دینا *girā' denā* V.T. drop let fall raze [~ گرنا CAUS.]

گراوٹ *girā'vaṭ* N.F., گراؤ *girā''o* ADJ. گراؤ *girā'o'o* ADJ. & ADV. (see under گرنا V.I. ★)

گرانٹ *girānṭ* N.F. grant-in-aid ; grant [E]

گرانڈیل *girāndīl* ADJ. hefty ; husky huge [~ گراں P + ڈیل]

گراؤنڈ *garā''ūnḍ* N.F. ground [E]

گربز *gūr'būz* ADJ. fraudulent person گربزی *gūr'bū'zī* N.F. fraudulence [P]

گربہ *gūr'bah* N.F. (lit.) cat گربہ کشتن روزِ اول *gūr'bah kāsh'tan ro'z-e av'val* PROV. as you train so you will bring up گربۂ مسکین *gūr'ba-e miskīn'* N.M. (fig.) meek but wicked person [P]

گربھ *gar'bh* N.M. (dial.) pregnancy [S]

گرج *ga'raj* N.F. thunder roar گرجنا *ga'rajnā* V.I. thunder roar (also گرج کر بولنا *ga'raj kar bol'nā*) V.I. thunder at speak with a stentorian voice گرجتے ہیں سو برستے نہیں *ga'rajte haiṅ so ba'raste na'hīṅ* PROV. barking dogs seldom bite

گرجا *gir'jā* N.M. church [Pg.]

گرجا *gar'jā* ADJ. cracked (pearl)

گرجی *gūr'jī* N.M. a small species of dog

گرد *gar'd* N.F. dust insignificant thing گرد آلود *gar'd-ālood'*, گرد آلودہ *gar'd-āloo'dah* ADJ. covered with dust ; dusty گرد اڑانا *gard' ūṛā'na* V.T. raise dust ruin گرد اڑنا *gard ūṛ'nā* V.I. to (of dust) fly about be ruined گرد بیٹھنا *gard' baiṭh'nā* V.I. (of dust) settle down گرد جھاڑنا *gard' jhāṛ'nā* V.T. dust گرد کو نہ پانا (یا پہنچ سکنا) *gard' ko na pā'nā* (or *pahūnch' sak'nā*) V.I. be unable to equal گرد ہونا *gard' ho'nā* V.I. come to nought

گرد *gir'd* ADV. about round about near in the environs (of) گرداگرد *gir'dā gird* ADV. all round (a place) گرداور *gird-ā'var* N.M. land revenue inspector گرداوری *gird-ā'varī* ADJ. touring (inspector) N.F. this office such official's rounds inspection tour گرد باد *gird'-bād* N.F. whirlwind گردگھما *gird'-ghūm'mā* N.M. tramp sycophant گرد و پیش *gir'd-o-pesh'* ADV. on all sides ; all round N.M. environs گرد و پیش کے حالات *gir'd-o-pesh' ke ḥālāt'* N.M. PL. conditions obtaining somewhere گرد و نواح *gir'd-o-navāḥ'* N.M. vicinity; environs ADJ. near round about گرد ہونا *gir'd ho'nā* V.T. surround begin to pester [P]

گرد *gūr'd* N.M. (PL. گرداں *gūr'dāṅ*) (lit.) brave fighter

گردا *gar'dā* N.M. dust [~ P]

گرداب *gird-āb'* N.M. whirlpool ; eddy ; vortex [P ~ گرد + آب]

گردان *gar'dān* N.F. paradigm conjugation گردان کرنا *gardān' kar'nā* V.T. conjugation repeat adnanscam' [P ~ گردیدن]

گرداں *gardāṅ* ADJ. & SUF. turning ; revolving گردانی *gardā'nī* SUF. turning ; revolving [P doublet of PREC.]

گردانک *gardā'nak* N.F. mortice [P ~ گردانیدن turn]

گردانا *gardān'nā* V.T. consider ; regard [~ P گردانیدن turn]

گردانی *gardā'nī* N.F. double turn of stole in prayer by women [~ P گردانیدن turn]

گردش *gar'dish* N.F. rotation revolution stroll misfortune vicissitudes of fortune گردشِ آسماں *gar'dish-e asmāṅ'*, گردشِ ایام *gar'dish-e ayyām'* N.F. (fig.) vicissitudes of fortune گردش کرنا *gar'dish kar'nā* V.I. rotate ; revolve ; turn round گردش میں آنا *gar'dish meṅ ā'nā* V.I. be unlucky ; be unfortunate ; fall on evil days [P ~ گردیدن]

گردگاں *gird'-gāṅ* N.M. (lit.) walnut [P]

گردن *gar'dan* N.F. neck گردن اڑانا (یا کاٹنا یا مارنا) *gar'dan ūṛā'nā* (or *kaṭ'nā*. or *mār'nā*) V.T. behead ; slay گردن پر بوجھ ہونا *gar'dan par bojh' ho'nā* V.I. be pressed down by (an obligation or sense of sin) گردن پر جوا رکھنا *gar'dan par joo''ā rakh'nā* V.T. & I. entrust with or accept heavy responsibility marry ; make or become a family man come or put under the yoke of گردن پر خون ہونا *gar'dan par khoon' ho'nā* V.I. be guilty of murder گردن پر سوار ہونا *gar'dan par savār' ho'nā* V.I. pester urge for redemption of debt گردن پھنسانا *gar'dan phaṅsā'nā* V.T. & I. entrust with or accept responsibility make or become a surety jeopardise گردن پھیرنا *gar'dan pher'nā* V.T. & I. disobey گردن جھکانا *gar'dan jhukā'nā* V.T. (bow one's) head shame etc.) feel ashamed submit make a bow گردن زدنی *gar'dan-za'danī* ADJ. deserving to be beheaded گردن سے جوا اتارنا *gar'dan se joo''ā ūtār'nā* V.T. throw off the yoke (of) گردن کا منکا ڈھلکنا *gar'dan kā man'kā ḍha'laknā* V.I. be about to die گردن فراز *gar'dan-farāz'* ADJ. exalted haughty گردن کٹنا *gar'dan kaṭ'nā* V.T. be beheaded be ruined گردن مروڑنا *gar'dan maroṛ'nā* V.T. throttle ; strangle ; strangulate گردن ناپنا *gar'dan nāp'nā* V.T. deal sternly with take (someone) by the scuff of گردن نہ اٹھانا *gar'dan na ūṭhā'nā* V.I. not hold one's head high گردن ہلانا *gar'dan hilā'nā* V.T. nod ; shake the head گردن ہلنے لگنا *gar'dan hil'ne lag'nā* V.I. become old گردنا *gar'danā* N.M. thick neck blow on the neck گردنہ *gar'danah* N.M. ridge گردنی *gar'danī* N.F. horse-cloth blow on the neck as a wrestling trick گردنی دینا *gar'danī de'nā* V.T take (someone) by the scruff of the neck [P]

گردوارہ *gūrdo'ā'rah* N.M. Sikh temple [~S گورو + دوارہ]

گردوں *gar'dooṅ* N.M. sky ; firmament ; the heavens [P ~ گردیدن]

گردہ *gūr'dah* N.M. kidney دل گردے کا کام *dil' gūr'de kā kām'* PH. something requiring great courage [P]

گردہ *gir'dah* N.M. circumference [~P گرد]

گردہ *gar'dah* N.M. painters' powder sketch [P ~ گرد]

گرز *gūr'z* N.M. mace گرز بردار *gūr'z-bar-dār'* N.M. macebearer البرزشکن گرز *albūr'z-shi'kan-gūrz* N.M. mountain-splitting mace [P]

گرس *gūr'z* N.M. & ADJ. gross [E]

گرسل *gūr'sal* N.F. a kind of small bird ; passerine

گرسنہ *gūr'sanah*, (or *gūras'nah*) ADJ. hungry avid گرسنگی *gūr'sanagī*, *gūras'nagī* N.F. hunger avidity [P]

گرفت *girif't* N.F. grasp hold possession objection گرفت کرنا *girif't kar'nā* V.T. find fault (with) گرفت میں آنا *girif't meṅ ā'nā* V.I. be caught ; be nabbed become actionable under law [P ~ گرفتن]

گرفتار *giriftār'* ADJ. held seized ; arrested captive prisoner involved entangled captivated گرفتار کرنا *giriftār' kar'nā* V.T. arrest ; apprehend ; nab take prisoner jail ; gaol گرفتار ہونا *giriftār' ho'nā* V.I. arrest take prisoner fall in love with گرفتاری *giriftā'rī* N.F. arrest ; apprehension imprisonment گرفتگی *girif'tagī* N.F. & SUF. dejection دل گرفتگی *dil-girif'tagī* N.F. dejection گرفتہ *girif'tah* ADJ. & AFFIX. afflicted sad ; dejected گرفتہ خاطر *girif'ta-khā'ṭir*, دل گرفتہ *dil-girif'tah* ADJ. afflicted in mind ; sad ; dejected [P ~ گرفتن]

گرگ *gūrg* N.M. wolf گرگ باراں دیدہ *gūr'g-e bā'rāṅ-dī'dah*, گرگ کہن *gūr'g-e kohan'* experienced person shrewd person گرگ بند *gūrg'-band*, گرگ زادہ *gūrg'-zā'dah* N.M. wolf's cub [P]

گرگا *gūr'gā* N.M. informer ; common informer scullion underling ADJ. very naughty [~P گرگ CORR.]

گرگابی *gūrgā'bī* N.F. ladies' laceless shoe; sandal [P]

گرگٹ *gir'gaṭ* N.M. chameleon گرگٹ کی طرح رنگ بدلنا *gir'gaṭ kī ṭar'ḥ rang' ba'dalnā* PH. be capricious be constantly changing fashions

گرل *gar'l* N.F. girl گرلز اسکول (یا سکول) *gar'lz iskool'* (or *sakool'*) N.M. girls school [E]

گرم *gar'm* ADJ. hot warm busy eager, zealous brisk (trade) گرم اختلاطی *gar'm-ikhtilā'ṭī* N.F. warmth of friendship گرما گرم *gar'mā gar'm* ADJ. hot heated hot and fresh گرما گرمی *gar'mā gar'mī* N.F. heat (of) گرم بازاری *gar'm-bāzā'rī* N.F. brisk trade ; great demand گرمجوشی *gar'm-jo'shī* N.F. zeal warmth of affection; cordiality گرم و سرد *gar'm-sar'd* N.M. ups and downs of life گرم و سرد چشیدہ *gar'm-o-sar'd chashī'dah* ADJ. seasoned ; experienced گرم و سرد زمانہ *gar'm-o-sar'd-e zamā'nah* N.M. vicissitudes of life گرم و سرد دیکھنا *gar'm-o- sar'd dekh'nā* be experienced گرم کرنا *gar'm kar'nā* V.T. warm heat enrage incide گرم مزاج *gar'm-mizāj'* ADJ. hot-tempered گرم مزاجی *gar'm-mizā'jī* N.F. being hot-tempered گرم مسالحہ *gar'm-masā'lah* N.M. condiments گرم ہونا *gar'm ho'nā* V.T become hot be enraged خبر گرم ہونا *khabar garm ho'na* V.I (of rumour) be current گرمی *gar'mi* N.F ★) [P]

گرما *gar'mā* N.M. summer heat [P ~ PREC.]

گرمابہ *garm-ā'bah* N.M. bath ; hot bath [P ~ گرم + آب]

گرمانا *garmā'nā* V.T. heat warm up enrage enliven

گرمکھی *gūrmū'khī* N.F. script used by Sikhs for Panjabi Sikh dialect of Punjabi [~ گورو + مکھ]

گرمہ *gar'mah*, گرما *gar'mā* N.M. sweeter variety of musk-melon , sweet musk-melon

گرمی *gar'mī* N.F. summer heat warmth venereal disease anger , rage cordiality love , passion feavour گرمی پڑنا *gar'mī par'nā* V.I. become hot (of summer) set in گرمیٔ سخن (یا کلام یا مضمون) *gar'mi-e sū'khan* (or *kalam* or *mazmoon'*), گرمی دینا *gar'mī dā'ne* N.M. PL. prickly heat گرمی کرنا *gar'mī kar'nā* V.T prove to be warm گرمیٔ محفل *gar'mi-e mah'fil* N.F. cause of warmth of a company گرمی نکالنا *gar'mī nikal'nā* V.T give vent to one's anger گرمی ہونا *gar'mī ho'nā* V.T (of season) become hot have syphills

گرنا *gir'nā* V.I fall ; tumble down drop collapse (of rain, price, etc.) fall (of health) deteriorate (of foetus) miscarry be disgraced گرا پڑا *gi'rā pa'rā* ADJ. fallen mean گراوٹ *girā'vaṭ* N.F. fall ; debasement گراؤ *girāoo''* ADJ. ready to fall precariously balanced گراؤ *gira''oo* ADJ. & ADV. about to fall unbalanced گر پڑنا (یا جانا) *gir' paṛ'nā* (or *jā'nā*) V.I. fall down

گرنتھ *garan'th* N.F (dial.) Sikh Scriptures گرنتھی *garan'thī* N.M. (dial.) reciter of Sikh Scriptures [S]

گرنڈ *garand'* N.M mud enclosure round handmill

گرو (or rare گورو *gū'roo* N.M. (dial.) spiritual guide (iron.) knave گرو گھنٹال *gu'roo ghantal'* N.M. consummate knave [S]

گرو *girau'* N.M. mortgage pawn ; pledge گرو رکھنا (یا کرنا) *girau' rakh'nā* (or *kar'nā*) V.T. pledge ; pawn (something) with گرونامہ *girau'-nā'mah* N.M mortgage deed [P]

گروانا *girvā'nā* V.T. cause to fall down get demolished have a miscarriage [~ گرنا ~ CAUS.]

گروہ *guroh'* N.M group party band troupe [P]

گروی *gir'vī* (ped. *gi'ravī*) ADJ. mortgaged pledged ; pawned N.F. mortgage pawn ; pledge گروی رکھنا *gir'vī rakh'na* V.T. mortgage ; pledge pawn [~ P گرو *girau'*]

گرویدہ *giravī'dah* ADJ. attached , enamoured , captivated گرویدگی *giravi'dagī* N.F. attachment (for) being enamoured (of) [P ~ گرویدن]

گرہ *gi'reh* (col. *gi'rah*) N.F. knot onesixteenth of a yard (fig.) dissention ; bad blood گرہ پڑنا *gi'reh paṛ'nā* V.I. (of dissention) arise , (of bad blood) be created have rancour (in heart) گرہ دار *gi'reh-dār* ADJ. knotted گرہ دینا *gi'reh de'nā* V.T. tie a knot . knot گرہ سے دینا *gi'reh se de'nā* V T give (someone) from one's own pocket گرہ سے کچھ جانا *gi'reh se kūchh jā'nā* V.I. spend something . incur an expenditure گرہ کشائی *gi'reh-kūshā''ī* N.F. untying a knot solution of difficulty گرہ کھلنا *gi'reh khul'nā* V.I. (of knot) be untied (of misunderstanding) end incur an (undesirable) expenditure گرہ کھولنا *gi'reh khol'nā* V.T. knotted گرہ گیر *gi'reh-gīr* ADJ untie a knot remove misunderstanding گرہ لگانا *gi'reh lagā'nā* V.T. tie a knot complete a couplet by adding a hynistick to another(s) گرہ میں باندھنا *gi'reh meṅ bāndh'nā* V.I. bear in mind tie a knot in handkerchief, etc. for this purpose گرہ میں پیسہ ہونا *gi'reh meṅ pai'sah ho'nā* V.I. be rich گرہ میں رکھنا *gi'reh meṅ rakh'nā* V.T keep in one's pocket [P]

گرہ *garah'* N.F. (dial.) planet پر گرہ آنا *par garah' ā'nā* V.T. have a reverse of fortune [S]

گرہست *gir'hast'* N.F. (dial.) showed life گرہستن *girhas'tan* N.F. house keeper homely woman گرہستی *girhas'tī* N.M. household goods ADJ. (affair, etc.) [S]

گرہن *garaih'n* N.M. (same as گہن *gaih'n* N.M. ★)

گری *gi'rī*, *ga'rī* N.F. (PL. گریاں *gir'yāṅ*) copra kernel (of fruit seed, etc.)

گریاں *gir'yāṅ* ADJ. weeping ; shedding tears [P ~ گریستن]

گریبان *gireban'* (lit. *girebāṅ'*) N.M. collar breast (of garment) گریبان پھاڑنا *gireban phāṛ'nā* V.T. tear one's garment to shreds became a lover گریبان پکڑنا (یا میں ہاتھ ڈالنا) *gireban' pa'kaṛ'nā* (or *meṅ hāth' ḍāl'nā*) V.T. collar (someone) , seize him by the collar گریبان چاک (یا تار تار) ہونا *gireban' chāk'* (or *tār tār'*) *kar'nā* V.T. tear one's garment to sheds (through madness, rage, grief etc.) گریبان گیر *girebān-gīr'* ADJ. & N.M. (one) seizing by the collar accuser گریباں گیر ہونا *gire'bāṅ-gīr ho'nā* V I seize someone by the collar گریباں میں منہ ڈالنا *gireban' meṅ muṅh ḍāl'nā* V.I. be ashamed of one's own misdeeds ; do a little heart searching [P]

گریجوایٹ *garai'jū'eṭ* N.M. graduate [E]

گریڈ *gareḍ'* N.M. grade [E]

گریز *gurez'* N.F. flight escape evasion digression turning to the real subject of the poem ; coming to the point گریز پا *gurez'-pā* ADJ. evanescent گریز کرنا *gurez' kar'nā* V.I. avoid evade ; dodge گریزاں *gure'zāṅ* ADJ escaping [P ~ گریختن run away]

گریمر *garāi'mar* N.F. (same as گرامر N.F. ★)

گریہ *gir'yah* N.M. weeping ; crying cries ; lamentation گریہ کناں *gir'ya-kūnāṅ'* ADJ. weeping ; crying گریہ وزاری *gir'ya-o-zā'rī* N.F. cries ; lamentation [P ~ گریستن weep]

گڑ *guṛ* N.M. raw sugar ; raw dehydrated sugar ; dried molasses گڑامبہ *gūṛ-am'bah* N.M. mangoes boiled in molasses گڑاکو *gūṛā'koo* N.M. tobacco kneaded in molasses گڑ دیئے مرے تو زہر کیوں دیجیے *guṛ' di'ye ma're to zaih'r kiyooṅ' dī'jiye* PROV. why resort to harsh words where sweet ones succeed گڑ کھائیں گلگلوں سے پرہیز *gūṛ' khā''eṅ gūl'gūloṅ se parhez'* PROV. lumps of sugar he devours but refrains from eating sweet cakes strain at a guat but swallow a camel گڑ کھانے سے منہ میٹھا نہیں ہوتا *gūṛ kaih'ne se muṅh' mī'ṭhā na'hīṅ ho'tā* PROV. fine words butter no parsnips گڑ کی بھیلی *guṛ kī bhe'lī* N.F. lump of raw sugar گڑ کی جوتی *gūṛ' kī joo'tī* PH. luxury denied to the poor

گڑبڑ گڑبڑی *gaṛ'baṛ* (col. گڑبڑاہٹ *gaṛbaṛā'haṭ* or *gaṛ'baṛī*) (iron. گڑبڑ جھالا *gaṛ'baṛ jhā'lā*) N.F. disorder ; confusion ; chaos ; mess گڑبڑ ہونا *gaṛ'baṛ ho'nā* V.I. lie confused be made a mess of گڑبڑانا *gaṛbaṛā'nā* V.I. get confused [ONO.]

گڑگج *gaṛ gaj'* N.M. bastion large turret

گڑگڑ *gūṛ gūṛ* N.M. gurgle rumble گڑگڑ کرنا *gūṛ gūṛ kar'nā* V.I. gurgle ; bubble rumble گڑگڑا *gūṛ' gūṛā* N.M. a kind of large hookah گڑگڑی *gūṛ' gūṛī* N.F. hubble-bubble [ONO.]

گڑگڑانا *gaṛgaṛā'nā* V.T. rumble thunder گڑگڑاہٹ *gaṛgaṛā'haṭ* N.F. rumble thunder [ONO.]

گڑگڑانا *giṛgiṛā'nā* V.I. implore ; beseech گڑگڑاہٹ *gaṛgaṛā'haṭ* N.F. (see under گڑگڑ N.F. ★)

گڑگڑی *gūṛgū'ṛī* N.F. (see under گڑگڑ *gūṛ gūṛ* N.F. ★)

گڑنا *gaṛ'nā* V.I. (of nail) be pitched penetrate be buried be ashamed ; feel disgraced گڑے مردے اکھیڑنا *ga'ṛe mūr'de ūkheṛ'nā* PROV. renew old grievances ; dig up old feuds

گڑوانا *gaṛvā'nā* V.T. cause to be driven in get pitched

گڑوا *gaṛ'vā* N.M. (see under گڑوی N.F. ★)

گڑوانا *gaṛvā'nā* N.M. go-cart

گڑونا *gaṛo'nā* V.T. pierce ; transfix stick into ; drive in fix (eyes) at bury گڑوتے کا پان *gaṛo'te kā pān* N.M. beetle-leaf mellowed by burial in sand

گڑھ *gaṛh* N.M. fort (fig.) hot bed (of) گڑھ جیتنا *gaṛh jīt'nā* V.I. (fig.) achieve the impossible

گڑھا *ga'ṛhā* N.M. pit hole cavity

گڑھی *ga'ṛhī* N.F. small fort گڑھیا *gaṛhay'yā* N.F. very small fort

گڑیا *gūṛ'yā* N.F. (PL. گڑیاں *gūṛ'yāṅ* DATIVE PL. گڑیوں *gūṛ'yoṅ*) doll گڑیا سنوار دینا *gūṛ'yā saṅvāṛ' de'nā* give one's daughter a dowry good enough for one's means گڑیاں کھیلنا *gūṛ yāṅ khel'nā* V.I. play with dolls be (like) a young girl گڑیوں کا کھیل *gūṛ' yoṅ kā khel* N.M. playing with dolls (fig.) child's play گڈے گڑیا کا بیاہ *gūḍ'de gūṛ'yā kā bayāh'* PH. wedding celebrated without pomp

گز *gaz* N.M. yard ramrod bow (for playing fiddle, etc.) گز بھر کی زبان *gaz' bhar kī zabān'* PH. sharp tongue

گزارا *guzā'rā*, گزارہ *guzā'rah* N.M. livelihood maintenance subsistence گزارا کرنا *guzā'rā kar'nā* V.I. subsist pass one's days get along with گزارہ ہونا *guzā'ra ho'nā* V.I. make both ends meet

گزارش *gūzā'rish* N.F. request submission گزارش کرنا *gūzā'rish kar'nā* V.T. request submit make a submission [P ~ گزاشتن]

گزارنا *gūzār'nā* V.T. pass life) bring to pass lay before state [~ گزرنا CAUS.]

گزاشتنی *gūzash'tanī* ADJ. worth quitting [P ~ گزاشتن]

گزاف *gizāf'* N.F. brag ; boast [P]

گزٹ *ga'zaṭ* N.M. gazette [E]

گزر *ga'zar* N.M. (lit.) carrot [P]

گزر *gū'zar* N.F. livelihood ; living ingress and egress loving together inference گزر بسر *gū'zar ba'sar* N.F. subsistence pulling together living گزر بسر ہونا *gū'zar ba'sar ho'nā* V.I. live subsist گزرگاہ *gū'zar-gāh'* N.F. passage

گزرگاہ عام gū'zar-gāh-e 'ām' N.F. thoroughfare گزراں gūzarāṅ' ADJ. transitory evanescent [P]

گزران gūzrān' N.F. livelihood living pulling together getting along گزران کرنا gūzrān' kar'nā V.T. pull together maintain oneself گزر گئی گزران کیا جھونپڑی کیا مکان gū'zar ga''ī gūzrān' kyā' jhoṅp'ṛī kyā' makān' PROV. good or bad, the days are past [~ گزرنا ~ P گزشتن]

گزرنا gū'zarnā V.I. go by ; pass by cross end die ; pass away happen ; occur (to) pull together feel ; experience [~ P گزشتن]

گزرانا gūzrān'nā V.T. submit ; put up گزری gūz'rī N.F. evening market گزری لگنا gūz'rī lag'nā V.I. (of evening market) be held [~ PREC.]

گزشتہ gūzash'tah ADJ. past elapsed ended bygone last late گزشتگان guzashtagāṅ N.M. PL. the dead گزشتہ راصلوٰۃ آئندہ را احتیاط gūzash'tah rā salāt' ā'iṅ'dah rā eḥtiyāt PROV. let bygones ; be bygones think of tomorrow for yesterday is no more [P ~ گزشتن]

گزشت guzash't INT. past ; ended گزشتنی gūzash'tanī ADJ. passing ; mortal [P ~ گزشتن]

گزک ga'zak N.F. a kind of crisp sweetmeat relish [P ~ گز]

گزند gazand' N.M. loss harm injury گزند پہنچنا gazand' pahāṅch'nā V.I. come to grief [P]

گزیدہ gazī'dah ADJ. bitten stung [P ~ گزیدن gazī'dan]

گزیدہ gūzī'dah ADJ. chosen selected [P ~ گزیدن gazī'dan]

گزیر gazīr' N.M. help ; remedy (only in) ناگزیر na-gūzīr' ADJ. indespensable [P]

گزیں gūziṅ' SUF. choosing ; selecting adopting گزینی gūzī'nī SUF. selection adoption [P ~ گزیدن]

گسار gūsar' SUF. consuming ; drinking گساری gūsa'rī SUF. consuming [P]

گسائیں gūsa''īṅ, گوسائیں gosā''īṅ N.M. (dial.) Hindu saint (arch.) cowherd (as appellation of Krishna) [S]

گستاخ gūstākh' ADJ. saucy audacious rude ; insolent; impudent گستاخانہ gustā'khā'nah ADJ. rude ; unsolent ADV. rudely ; insolently گستاخی gūstākhī N.F. rudeness ; insolence sauciness audacity گستاخی کرنا (یا سے پیش آنا) gustā'khī kar'nā (or se pesh ā'nā) V.T. & I. be rude ; be insolent ; behave impudently be saucy گستاخی معاف gūstā'khī mo'āf' INT. excuse me I crave your indulgence [P]

گستر gūs'tar SUF. spreading dispensing administring گسترده gūstar'dah ADJ. spread گستری gūsta'rī SUF. spreading dispensing administ [P ~ گستردن]

گستہ gūsas'tah ADJ. broken گسستگی gusas'tagī N.F. being broken [P ~ گسستن]

گسل gūsil' SUF. breaking ; ruining [P]

گشت gash't N.F. beat (of police, etc.) round touring walk ; stroll گشت کرنا (یا لگانا) gash't kar'nā (or lagā'nā) V.I. go one's rounds patrol tour walk ; stroll گشت ناچنا gash't nāch'nā V.T. (of dancing-girl) lead marriage procession dancing ahead of it گشتی gash'tī ADJ. circulating touring itinerant گشتی چٹھی gash'tī chiṭ'ṭhī N.F. گشتی مراسلہ gash'tī mūrā'salah N.M. circular letter ; circular [P ~ گشتن]

گف gaf ADJ. (of cloth) thick ; of close texture

گفتار gūftār' N.F. (lit.) speaking talk ; speech ; discourse [P ~ گفتن]

گفتگو gūftu'goo N.F. talk conversation ; dialogue chit-chat (rare) parleys ; negotiations گفت و شنید gūf't-o-shunīd' N.F. parleys negotiations talks discussion conversation گفتنی gūf'tanī ADV. & ADJ. worth mention [P ~ گفتن]

گگری gag'rī گگریا gagar'yā N.F. metal pitcher [گاگر DIM.]

گگن ga'gan N.M. (dial.) sky گگن کھیلنا ga'gan khel'na V.I. (of water) spurt high گگن ہونا ga'gan ho'nā V.I. rocket be sky-high [S]

گل gul N.M. flower rose (fig.) beloved ; sweetheart ; one's lady love گل اشرفی gu'l-e ash'rafī N.M. marigold گل افشاں gul-afshāṅ ADJ. strewn with flowers showering flower petals speaking sweetly گل افشانی gul afsha'nī N.F. showering of flower petals (lit.) sweet speech گل افشانی کرنا gul afshā'nī kar'na V.T. (polite or iron) speak گل اندام gūl-andām' ADJ. graceful N.M. exquisite beauty beloved گل اورنگ gul-e aurang' N.M. a species of marigold گلبانگ gul-bāng' N.F. shouts of joy nighting graceful N.M. exquisite beauty beloved gales cry good news گلبدن gūl-ba'dan ADJ. graceful N.M. exquisite beauty a kind of silk cloth گلبرگ gūl-bar'g N.M. rose leaf (fig.) beloved's lips گل بکاؤلی gul'-bakā''olī N.M. a species of white fragrant flower گلبن gūl'ban N.F. garden گل بوٹا gul boo'ṭā N.M. flower and its plant decoration گل بوٹے gul boo'ṭe flowers and plants vegetation floral patterns گل بیگانہ gul-e begā'nah N.M. wild flower گلپوش gūl'-posh ADJ. strewn with flowers with a prolific growth of flowers گل پھولنا gul phool'na v.i. (of something new or wonderful) happen be in trouble گل پیادہ gūl payā'dah N.M. wild rose گل پیراہن gūl-pairā'han, گل پیرہن gūl-pai'rahan ADJ. graceful N.M. exquisite beauty beloved گل تراش gūl-tarā'sh' N.M. gardner's scissors گل جھڑنا gūl jhaṛ'nā v.i. (of talk) sound sweet گل جعفری gū'l-e ja''farī N.M. 'tagetes patula' گل چاندنی N.M. moon flower گل چشم gū'l-chash'm ADJ. & N.M. albugo; albugineous (person) گلچہرہ gūl-cheh'rah ADJ. rosy cheeked N.M. exquisite beauty beloved گلچیں gūl-chīn' N.M. flower-gatherer; florist who enjoys the close company (of a beauty) successful lover گلچینی gul'-chī'nī N.F. plucking or gathering of flowers having a happy time (with) گلچینی کرنا gūl-chī'nī kar'nā v.i. pluck flower's have a happy time (with) گل خطمی gūl-e khat'mī N.M. marsh-mallow flower گل خیرا (یا خیرو) gūl-khai'rā (or khai'roo) N.M. gilly flower; Chinese hollyhock گلدان gūl-dān' N.M. flower pot vase گل داؤدی gūl-e dā''oodī N.M. chrysanthemum گلدستہ gūl-das'tah N.M. bouquet; nosegay گل دوپہر gūl-e do-paihar', گل دوپہریا gūl dopaih'riya N.M. the marvel of Peru گلدم gūl'-dūm N.F. a species of nightingale گلرخ gūl'-rūkh, گلرو gūl-roo' ADJ. rosy-cheeked N.M. exquisite beauty beloved گل رعنا gūl-e ra'nā' N.M. a species of red and pale rose beloved گلرنگ gūl-rang' ADJ. red, rosy گلریز gūl-rez' ADJ. shedding flowers petals N.F. a kind of fireworks گلریزی gūl-re'zī N.F. shedding of flowers گلزار gūlzār' N.M. garden گلزار ابراہیم (یا ابراہیمی) gūlzā'r-e ibrāhīm' (or ibrāhī'mī) N.M. pyre raised by Nimrod to burn Abraham alive but which was miraculously changed into a garden (fig.) unexpected relief گلستاں gū'is'tān, (rare gūl' sitān) N.M. rose garden گل سرسبد gūl-e sar sabad N.M. choicest flower گل سورنجان gūl-e sooranjān' N.M. hermodactyl flower گل سوسن gū-le sosan N.M. lily گل شبو gūl-e shab'bo N.M. a species of flower emitting fragrance at night گلشن gūl'shan N.M. garden گل صد برگ gūl-e sad-bar'g N.M. marigold گل عباسی gūl-e 'abbā'sī N.M. 'mitabilis jalopa' گلعذار gūl-'azār' ADJ. rosy cheeked N.M. exquisite beauty beloved گلفام gūlfām' ADJ. rosy-cheeked (beloved, etc.) cherry red (wine, etc.) گل فرنگ gūl-e farang' N.M. 'vinca rosea' گلفروش gūl-firosh' N.M. florist; flower-seller گلقند gūlqand' N.M. candied roses; conserve of rose گلکاری gūl-kā'rī N.M. embroidery painting of flowers گلکاری کرنا gūl-kā'rī kar'nā v.T. embroider گل کترنا gūl' ka'tarnā v.i. work wonders گل کھلانا gūl' khilā'nā v.i. stir up some trouble sow seeds of dissention bring down trouble upon do something unexpected come to blossom گل کھلنا gul' khil'nā v.i. (of something unexpected) happen (of flower) blossom گلگشت gūl-gash't N.M. walking in a garden; stroll گلگوں gūl-goon' ADJ. rosy; rose coloured; roseate گلگونہ gūlgoo'nah N.M. rouge; safflower powder گل لالہ gū'l-e lā'lah N.M. tulip; poppy flower گل مخمل gū'l-e makh'ma N.M. globe amaranth گل مہندی gūl-maihn'dī N.M. balsam گل میخ gūl-mekh' N.F. stud گلنار gūlna' N.M. pomegranate flower scarlet colour ADJ. scarlet گل ناشگفتہ gūl-e nā-shigū f'tah N.M. (fig.) virgin; maiden گل نسرین gūl-e nasrīn' N.M. jonquil گل ہزارہ gū'l-e hazā'rah N.M. double poppy [P]

گل ۲ gūl N.M. snuff (of wick) charred tobacco (in hookah bowl) stigma; brand live coal گل جھڑنا gūl jhaṛ'nā v.T. flick the ash (of cigerette) trim the wick squander money گل کرنا gūl' kar'nā v.T. put out (lamp) گل کھانا gūl' khā'nā v.T. & I. cauterize oneself (in proof of love) be cauterized گلگیر gūl'-gīr N.F. snuffer; pick wick گل ہونا gūl' ho'nā v.i. be put out; be extinguished

گل gil N.F. mud, clay earth گل ارمنی gil-e ar'manī N.F. Armenian bole گل حکمت gil ḥik'mat N.F heat in container mode airtight by mud plaster; heat in tight container گل حکمت کرنا gil ḥik'mat kar'nā v.T. heat thus bedraggle گلی gi'lī ADJ. earthen [P]

گل gal PREF. neck cheek throat گل بہنیاں (یا بیاں) ڈالنا gal-bahn'yān (or bay'yān) ḍal'nā v.T. embrace fondly گلپھڑا gal'-phaṛā N.M. gill گل پھولا gal-phoo'lā ADJ. chubby گل پھیڑ gal-pher' N.M mumps گل تکیہ gal-tak'yah N.M. small pillow for cheek گل تنی gal'-ta'nī N.F. harness fitting underneath a yoke گل جنڈرا gal-jand'rā N.M. sling (for injured arm, etc.) گل جوٹ gal jot' N.F rope for yoking two bullocks together (fig.) one who pesters others گلخور gal-khor' N.F. halter گل گوتھنا gal-gauth'nā ADJ. & N.M. chubby گل مچھے gal-mūch'chhe گلچھے galach'chhe N.M. PL. whiskers [~ FOLL. or ~ گال cheek CONT.]

گلا ga'lā N.M. throat neck collar; breast (of shirt, etc.) voice گلا آنا ga'lā ā'nā v have a sore throat گلا اٹھانا ga'lā ūṭhā'nā v.T. message (child's) uvula as a cure for cold گلا بندھنا ga'lā bandh'nā v.i. be heavily in debt گلا بند ہونا ga'lā band ho'nā v.T. lose voice be choked گلا بیٹھنا (یا پڑنا) ga'lā baiṭh'nā (or par'nā) v.i. be hoarse; have a sore throat گلا پکڑا جانا ga'lā pakṛā jā'nā v.i. have a burning in the throat گلا پکڑنا ga'lā pa'karnā v.T seize (someone) by the throat ; collar irritate the throat گلا پھاڑنا ga'lā phār'nā v.i. shriek گلا پھاڑ پھاڑ کر ga'lā phāṛ phāṛ' kar ADV. at the top of one's voice گلا پھیرنا ga'lā pher'nā v.i. modulate one's voice in singing گلا دبانا ga'lā dabā'nā v.t. strangle ; throttle press hard (for) oppress ; suppress گلا کاٹنا ga'la kaṭ'nā v.t. cut the throat oppress ; suppress defraud گلا گھوٹنا ga'lā ghoṭ'nā v.t. strangle ; throttle گلے باندھنا ga'le bandh'nā v.t. foist on گلے پڑنا (یا بندھنا) ga'le paṛ'nā (or bandh'nā) v.t. & i. be foisted on foist one's company (or someone) be entrusted گلے سے اتارنا ga'le se ūtār'nā v.t. gulp down ; swallow shake off گلے سے اترنا ga'le se ū'tarnā v.i. be swallowed be shaken off گلے کا ہار ga'le kā hār' N.M. unwanted companion گلے کا ہار ہو جانا ga'le kā hār' ho' jā'nā v.t. pester ; plague importune گلے کی رگیں پھولنا ga'le kī ra'geṅ phūlā'na v.t. be enraged گلے لگانا ga'le lagā'nā v.t. embrace (someone) گلے لگنا (یا ملنا) ga'le lag'nā (or mil'nā) v.t. embrace get reconciled to each other گلے منڈھنا (یا مڑھنا) ga'le maṅḍh'nā (or maṛh'ra) v.t. foist palm off (on) گلے میں اٹکنا ga'le meṅ a'ṭaknā v.t. & i. choke not to be swallowed down گلے میں کانٹے پڑنا ga'le meṅ kāṅ'ṭe paṛ'nā v.i. have a parched throat feel thirsty

گلا gal'la N.M. (same as گلہ gal'lah² ★)

گلاب gūlāb' N.M rose گلاب پاش gūlāb'-pāsh N.M. rosewater sprinkler گلاب پاشی gūlāb' pā'shī N.F. sprinkling of rose water گلاب پاشی کرنا gūlāb'-pā'shī kar'nā v.t. sprinkle rose-water گلاب جامن gūlāb'-jā'man N.F. luscious juicy ball ; a kind of sweetmeat گلابی gūlā'bī ADJ. rosy ; roseate ; pink . mild not fanatic N.F. flagon . wine cup wine گلابی آنکھیں gūlā'bī ankheṅ N.F. eyes red with inebriation گلابی جاڑا gūlā'bī jā'ṛā N.M. mild winter [P]

گلابہ gilā'bah N.M. plastering mud [~ P گل gil + آبہ]

گلاس gilās' N.M. glass ; tumbler [E]

گلال gūlāl' N.M. red powder thrown over one another during Holi گلال اڑانا gūlāl ūṛā'nā v. to throw red powder at one گلالی gūlā'lī ADJ. of red colour ; dyed with it لال گلال lāl' gūlāl ADJ. bright red

گلانا galā'nā v.t. (see under گلنا v.i. ★)

گلتھی gūlat'thī ADJ. (of boiled rice, etc.) softened overmuch and clotted

گلٹ gilṭ N.M. gilt nickel plating گلٹی gil'ṭī ADJ. gilt ; gilded nickel plated [E]

گلٹی gil'ṭī N.F. tumour gland

گلجھٹی gūljhūṭī N.F tangle ill-feeling . rancour

گلچھرے gūlchar're N.M. PL. life of pleasure گلچھرے اڑانا gūlchhar're ūṛā'nā v.i. lead a life of luxury

گلچھے galach'chhe N.M. PL. (same as گل چھے (see under گل gal N. ★)

گلخپ gal'khap N.F. struggle (fig.) quarrel گلخپ ہونا gal'khap ho'nā v.i. have a quarrel (with) [~ گلا]

گلخن gūl'khan N.M. furnace [P]

گلڈانگ gūldang' N.M. bull dog [~ E bull-dog COR.]

گلک gūl'lak N.F. (same as غلک N.F. ★)

گلگل gal'gal N.M. citron

گلگلا gūl'gūla N.M. fried cookie

گلگلانا galgalā'nā v.i. become jelly-like گلگلا gal'galā ADJ. jelly-like گلگلاہٹ galgalā'haṭ N.F. being jelly-like

گلنا gal'nā v.i. be cooked well soften thus melt dissolve be mortified rot گلا سڑا ga'la sa'ṛa ADJ. rotten putrid گلانا galā'nā v.t. cook well soften thus . melt dissolve mortify cause to rot گلاؤ galā''o N.M., گلاوٹ galā'vaṭ N.F. dissolving ; dissolution گلاؤ galā''oo ADJ. & N.M. melting (stuff) soluble or dissolving (stuff)

گلم gūl'am N.M. hardened swelling (resulting from injury)

گلو gūloo' N.M. (lit.) gullet , wind pipe throat neck گلوبند gū'loo-band N.M. scarf ; muffler ; cravet ; neckcloth jewellery for neck ; neckband گلوخلاصی gūloo'-khalā'sī N.F. escape گلوگیر gūloo'-gīr ADJ. irritating to the throat choking causing hoarseness . choked seizing by the neck ; collaring [A]

گلو gilaū' N.F. 'menropermum glabrum'

گلو gil'lo N.F. (same as گلہری N.F. ★)

گلوب galob' N.M. globe [E]

گلوری gilau'rī N.F. seasoned betel-leaf rolled a pyramid

گلہ *gi'lah* N.M. (usu. friendly) complaint گلہ کرنا *gi'lah kar'na* V.T. complaint (in a friendly manner) گلہ گزاری *gi'la-guza'ri* N.F. (usu. friendly) complaint [P]

گلّہ ¹ *gal'lah* N.M. flock herd drove گلہ بان *gal'la-ban'* N.M. shepherd herds man گلہ بانی *gal'la-ba'ni* N.F. flock-keeping

گلّہ ² *gal'lah*, گلا *gal'la* N.M. safe

گلہری *gilaih'ri* (nurs. گلو *gil'lo*) N.F. squirrel

گلھڑ *gil'lhar* N.M. glandular swelling on throat

گلی *ga'li* N.F. street ; lane ; alley گلی کوچہ *ga'li koo'chah* N.M. street ; lane every street گلی گلی *ga'li ga'li* ADJ. from street to street in every street گلیوں کی خاک چھاننا *gal'yon ki khak chhan'na* V.I. wander aimlessly; tramp

گلی *gi'li* ADJ. (see under گل *gil* N.F. ★)

گلی *gil'li*, *gul'li* N.F. cat (used in game tip-cat) corn cob گلی ڈنڈا *gil'li dan'da* N.M. tip-cat گلی ڈنڈا کھیلنا *gil'li-dan'da khel'na* V.I. play tip-cat

گلیر *gil'yer* ADJ. lazy ; idle slovenly

گلیم *galim'* N.F. rug [P]

گم *gum* ADJ. lost missing wanted گمراہ *gum-rah'*, گمرہ *gum'-rah* ADJ. misled ; misguided depraved wicked heretical ADV. astray گمراہ کرنا *gum'rah kar'na* V.T mislead ; misguide lead astray seduce گمراہ ہونا *gum-rah' ho'na* V.I. be misled be led astray apostatise be seduced گمراہی *gum-ra'hi* N.F. being misled seduction heresy apostasy گم سم *gum' sum* ADV. (ped. گم صم *gum'-sum*) struck dumb ADV. quiet glum گم صم بیٹھنا (یا ہونا) *gum' sum baith'na* (or *ho'na*) V.I. be struck dumb ; be dumb-founded be glum گمشدہ *gum'-shu'dah* ADJ. lost missing گمشدگی *gum'-shu'dagi* N.F. loss . being missing گم کرنا *gum' kar'na* ADJ. (one) having lost گم کردہ راہ *gum-kar'da-rah'* ADJ. & N.M. (one) led astray گم کرنا *gum' kar'na* V.T. lose hide ; conceal گم گشتہ *gum-gash'tah* ADJ. lost missing (one) having lost one's way گمنام *gum-nam'* ADJ. anonymous unknown obscure گم ہونا *gum' ho'na* V.I. be lost ; get lost be missing

گما *gum'ma* N.M. large thick brick

گماشتہ *gumash'tah* N.M. (PL. گماشتگان *gumash'tagan*) agent ; representative ; factor [P ~ گماشتن]

گمان *guman'* N.M. idea ; thought ; action supposition ; conjecture doubt ; suspicion (usu. prop. *guman*) pride ; vanity گمان غالب *guma'n-e gha'lib* N.M. likelihood گمان کرنا *guman' kar'na* V.I. think ; believe ; suppose doubt ; suspect show pride ; be conceited ; be vain [P]

گمبھیر *gambhir'* ADJ. serious ; grave deep ; profound thoughtful N.M. carbuncle

گمٹی ¹ *gum'ti* N.F. turret small minaret

گمٹی ² *gum'ti* (or *gim'ti*) N.F. dimity [~E CORR.]

گمک *gu'mak* N.F. echo in musical instrument [ONO.]

گملا *gam'la* N.M. flower pot evacuation pot in close stool ; pot chamber-pot

گن *gun* N.M. merit skill virtue quality گن اوگن *gun' au'gun* N.M. merits and merits گن گانا *gun' ga'na* V.I. extol ; sing the praises (of) گن ماننا *gun' man'na* V.T. be grateful (to) گن ونت *gun-vant'*, گنی *guni'* ADJ. & N.M. skilful

گنا *gu'na* ADJ. times SUF. fold دگنا *dug'na* ADJ. twofold تین گنا *tin' gu'na* ADJ. three fold

گنا *gan'na* N.M. sugar-cane گنے کا رس *gan'ne ka ras* N.M. cane juice گنے کی پھانڈی *gan'ne ki phan'di* N.F. bundle of sugar-cane

گنانا *gina'na* V.T. same as گنوانا (CAUS. ~ گننا V.T. ★)

گناہ *gunah'*, گنہ *gunah* N.M. (rare) fault گناہ بخشنا *gunah' bakh'shna* V.T. forgive sin pardon گناہ بے لذت *guna'h-e be-laz'zat* N.M. joyless sin (fig.) lie ; telling a lie گناہ صغیرہ *guna'h-e saghi'rah* N.M. venial sin گناہ کبیرہ *guna'h-e kabi'rah* N.M. mortal sin گناہ کرنا *gunah' kar'na* V.T. sin ; commit a sin do a wrong گنہگار (یا گنہگار) گناہگار N.M. & ADJ. sinful (person) guilty ; at fault گنہگار ٹھہرانا *gunah'-gar thaihra'na* V.T. condemn hold guilty گناہگاری *guna'-ga'ri*, گنہگاری *gunah'-ga'ri* N.F. sinfulness [P]

گنبد *gum'bad* N.M. dome ; cupola گنبد خضرا *gum'bad-e khazra'* N.M. Holy Prophet's mausoleum ; Green Dome گنبددار *gum'bad-dar* ADJ. domed گنبد کی آواز (یا صدا) *gum'bad ki avaz* (or *sada'*) N.F. echo fig. bomerang (fig.). recoiling of one's misdeeds on one گنبد گرداں *gum'bad-e gar'dan*, گنبد لاجوردی *gum'bad-e lajvar'di* N.M. heavenly dome

گنت *gin't* AFFIX. count (only in) ان گنت *an-gin't* ADJ. innumerable [~ گننا]

گنتی gin'tī N.F. count counting ; reckoning; computing number roll call گنتی کے gin'tī ke ADJ. a few گنتی میں آنا gin'tī meṅ ā'nā V.I. be taken into account be cared for گنتی میں لانا gin'tī meṅ lā'nā V I. take into account care for [~ گننا]

گنٹھیا gaṅ'ṭhiyā N.F. (same as گٹھیا N.F. ★)

گنج gaṅj' N.M. treasure heap market (esp.) grain market گنج بخش gaṅj'-bakh'sh ADJ. wealth-bestowing ; munificent appelation of Muslim Saint Ali Hujveri گنج شائگاں gaṅ'j-e shā''egāṅ' N.M. royal treasury ; treasure befitting a king گنج شہیداں gaṅ'j-e shahī'dāṅ N.M. joint grave of numerous dead martyrs' burial place گنج قارون gaṅ'j-e qāroon' N.M. the proverbial wealth of Croesus (fig.) countless riches [P]

گنج gaṅj N.M. (see under گنجا ADJ. ★)

گنجا gaṅ'jā ADJ. & N.M. (F. گنجی gaṅ'jī) bald person گنجے کو خدا ناخن نہ دے gaṅ'je ko khudā' nā'khun na de PROV. mean person becomes a nuisance if invested with power

گنجان gūṅ'jān' ADJ. thick ; dense گنجانی gūṅjā'nī N.F. thickness ; denseness [P]

گنجائش gūṅja''ish N.F. capacity room ability (to do something) [P]

گنجفہ gaṅ'jafah N.M. (game of) cards pack of cards گنجفہ باز gaṅ'jafa-bāz' N.M. card player sharper [P]

گنجلک gūṅ'jalak N.F. tangle complication

گنجور gaṅjoor' N.M. (rare gaṅj'-var) treasurer owner of a treasure فیض گنجور faiz-gaṅjoor' ADJ. munificent [P]

گنجی gaṅ'jī N.F. & ADJ. (see under گنجا N.F. & ADJ ★)

گنجیا gaṅjī'yā N.F. tool box

گنجینہ gaṅjī'nah N.M. treasure repository [P ~ گنج]

گند[1] gand' N.F. filth litter uncleanliness (fig.) trouble ; nuisance گند اچھالنا gand uchhāl'nā V.T. wash dirty linen in public گند کٹنا gand' kaṭ'nā V.T. get rid of trouble

گند[2] gand, گندھ gandh N.F. stench ; noxious smell [S]

گندا gaṅ'dā ADJ., گندگی gaṅ'dagī N.F. (see under گندہ gaṅ'dah ADJ. ★)

گندم gaṅ'dum N.M. wheat گندم از گندم بروید جو از جو gaṅ'dūm az gaṅ'dūm bi-ro'yad jau zi jau' PROV. as you sow so shall you reap گندم اگر بہم نہ رسد بھس غنیمت است gaṅ'dūm a'gar ba-ham' na rasad' bhus' ghanī'mat ast PROV. (joc.) deny not the little if much is not forthcoming گندم گوں gaṅ'dum-goon ADJ. wheaten ; brown گندم نما جو فروش gaṅ'dūm-nūmā' jau'-firosh' ADJ. hypocrite گندمی gaṅdū'mī ADJ. wheaten ; brown [P]

گندنا gand'nā N.M. leek

گندہ gaṅ'dah, گندا gaṅ'dā ADJ. (F. گندی gaṅ'dī) ADJ. dirty filthy untidy unclean گندہ بیروزہ gaṅ'dah biro'zah N.M. resin ; rosin گندا بغل gaṅ'dā-baghal ADJ. & N.M. (one) stinking in the armpits گندہ دہن gaṅ'da-da'han ADJ. & N.M. (one) with a stinking breath گندگی gaṅ'dagī N.F. filth refuse dirt untediness stench uncleanliness evil influence گندی بات gaṅ'dī bāt N.F indecent talk, etc. گندی باتیں gaṅ'dī bāteṅ N.F. PL. indecency smutty jokes ordure

گندھار gandhār' N.M. name of a musical mode

گندھارا gandhā'rā N.M. Gandhara ; region having Taxila in modern Pakistan as its centre which came under Hellenic influence after Alexander [S]

گندھرب gandhar'b N.M. (H. myth.) musician at Indra's court (dial.) virtuoso [S]

گندھک gaṅ'dhak N.F. sulphur گندھک کا تیزاب gaṅ'dhak kā tezāb N.M. sulphuric acid

گندھنا gūndh'nā V.I. be kneaded be headed; strung be plaited گندھانا gūndhā'nā, گندھوانا gūndhvā'nā V.T. cause to knead cause bead; cause to string cause to plait

گندھی gaṅ'dhī گاندھی gaṅ'dhī N.M. perfumer [~ گندھ]

گندی gaṅ'dī ADJ. (see under گندہ ADJ. ★)

گنڈا[1] gūṅ'ḍā, غنڈہ ghūṅ'ḍah N.M. hooligan ; hoodlum tough ; rough bad character

گنڈا gaṅ'ḍā N.M. old coin equivalent to four cowrie knotted string (used as charm) ring ; circlet (arch.) four گنڈے دار gaṅ'ḍe-dār ADJ. intermittent (prayers, colouring, etc.)

گنڈاسا gaṅḍā'sā N.M. chopper

گنڈیری gaṅḍe'rī N.F. sugar-cane bit

گنگ gūṅg' ADJ. dumb ; mute [P]

گنگ gaṅg N.F. (Persianized form of گنگا N.F ★)

گنگا *gaṅga* N.F. Ganges ; river regarded by Hindus as a sacred mother گنگا اشنان *gaṅ'ga-ashnān* N.M. (dial.) bathing in the Ganges (as a purifying act) کی گنگا بہنا *kī gaṅ'gā baih'nā* V.T. be profound (in) گنگا جل *gaṅ'ga jal* N.M. (dial.) water of the Ganges (as holy water) گنگا جلی *gaṅ'gā-ja'lī* N.M. small container for the Ganges water گنگا جلی اٹھانا *gaṅ'gā-ja'li uṭhā'na* V.T. (of Hindus) swear by the holy water of the Ganges گنگا جمنی *gaṅ'gā-jam'nī* ADJ. mixed metallic (vessel) engraved to show off a different metal گنگا نہانا *gaṅ'gā nahā'nā* V.I. be absolved of sin by bathing in the Ganges بہتی گنگا *baih'tī gaṅ'gā* N.M. (fig.) opportunity open to all بہتی گنگا میں ہاتھ دھونا *baih'tī gaṅ'gā meṅ hāth' dho'nā* V.T. avail oneself of general opportunity

گنگنا *gun'gunā* ADJ. (same as گنگنا ADJ. ★)

گنگنانا *gungunā'nā* V.I. snuffle hum گنگنا *gung'unā* ADJ. & N.M. snuffler گنگناہٹ *gungunā'haṭ* N.F. snuffle hum

گننا *gin'nā* V.T. count ; reckon count up regard (as) ; count upon (as) گنا گنایا *gi'nā ginā'yā* ADJ. reckoned already known گن گن کر *gin' gin kar* ADV. counting one by one in the exact amount with great difficulty گن گن کر دن کاٹنا *gin' gin kar din kaṭ'nā* PH. pass one's days with great difficulty ; to live a hard life گن گن کر قدم رکھنا *gin' gin kar qa'dam rakh'nā* V.T. move slowly stop cautiously گنی بوٹیاں نپا شوربا *gi'nī bo'ṭiyāṅ na'pā shor'bā* PH. parsimony be parsimonious گنتی *gin'tī* N.F. ★ گنوانا *ginvā'nā* V.T. cause to count help reckon

گنوار *gaṅvār'* N.M. villager ; countryman ; rustic churl ; boor ; clown ADJ. low-bred uncultured person unmannerly rude گنوار پن *gaṅvār'-pan* N.M. boorishness lack of manners rudeness گنوار کا لٹھ *gaṅvār' kā laṭh* N.M. arrant fool گنوارو *gaṅvā'roo* ADJ. rustic (taste, fashion, etc.) گنواری *gaṅvā'rī* N.F. country woman

گنوانا *gaṅvā'nā* V.T lose waste ; squander

گنوانا *ginvā'nā* V.T. (CAUS. ~ گننا V.T. ★)

گنہ *gunah'* N.M. (short for of گناہ N.M. ★)

گنی *gi'nī* ADJ. guinea [E]

گنیا *gun'ya* N.M. square ; mason's square ; L-square

گو *geo* N.M. (lit.) ball گوئے سبقت لے جانا *goo''e sab'qat le jā'nā* PH. steal a march (on) [P]

گو ۱ *go* CONJ. though ; although , even though thugh گو کہ *go keh* ADV. (arch.) although

گو ۲ *go* (or *goo*) V.T. IMP. (rare) say SUF. saying narrator گو مگو کی حالت *go ma-go' kī hā'lat* N.F. hesitation ; reluctance fix گوئی *go''ī* SUF. saying ; speaking ; uttering [P ~ گفتن]

گوار *gavār'* N.M. a species of corn

گوار *gūvār'* SUF. (see under گوارا ADJ. ★)

گوارا *gūvā'rā* ADJ. so-so ; indifferent tolerable pleasant ; agreeable گوارا کرنا *gūvā'ra kar'nā* V. brook ; tolerate ; endure گوار *gūvār'* SUF. (untoler)-able (pleas)-ant [P]

گوالا *gavā'lā* N.M. cowherd milkman گوالن *gavā'lan* N.F. milkmaid cowherd's wife [~ گئو or گانے + والا]

گوانا *gavā'nā* V.T. cause to sing [~ گانا CAUS.]

گواہ *gavah'* (ped. *gūvāh'*) N.M. witness گواہ بنانا *gavah' banā'nā* V.T. call to witness name a witness گواہ تعلیمی *gavā'h-e ta''līmī* N.M. tutored witness گواہ صفائی *gavā'h-e safā''ī* N.M. defence witness گواہ کرنا *gavāh' kar'nā* V.T. make (someone) a witness call to witness چشم دید گواہ *chash'm-dīd gavāh'* N.M. eye-witness گواہی *gavā'hī* (ped. *gūvā'hī*) N.F. evidence ; testimony گواہی دینا *gavā'hī de'nā* V.T. depose give evidence ; bear testimony bear witness [P]

گوبر *go'bar* N.M. dung cow-dung گوبری *gob'rī* N.F. cow-dung plaster گوبری کرنا *gob'rī kar'nā* V.T. (dial.) plaster with cowdung

گوبھی *go'bhī*, گوبھی کا پھول *go'bhī kā phool* N.F. cauliflower بند گوبھی *band go'bhī* N.F. cabbage

گوپال ۱ *gopāl'* N.M. (lit.) mace [P]

گوپال ۲ *gopāl'* N.M. (dial.) cowherd this as appellation of Hindu deity Krishna [S ~ گئو + پالنا]

گوپیا *go'piyā*, گوپھن *go'phan*, گوپھیا *go'phiyā* N.M. sling catapult

گوپی *go'pī* N.F. milkmaid as one of the girl friends of Hindu deity Krishna [S]

گوت *got* M.M. (dial.) sub-caste lineage [S]

گوتھنا *gooth'nā* V.T. (same as گونتھنا V.T. ★)

گوٹ *goṭ* N.F. counter ; draughtsman hem people ; population (also گاؤں گوٹ *gā'oṅ goṭ*) village

گوٹا *go'ṭa* N.M. brocade fillet ; gold (or silver) lace

گوجر *goo'jar* N.M. cowherd dairyman name of a martial caste of this subcontinent گوجری *gooj'rī*, گجری *gūj'rī* N.F. milkmaid ; dairy maid dairymans wife, etc. woman of a particular martial caste of this sub-continent

گوجرا *goj'ra* N.M. a mixture of wheat and barley

گوچنی *goch'nī* N.F. field of wheat and gram sown together mixed wheat and gram

گود *god* N.F. lap گود بھرنا *god' bhar'nā* V.T. & I. place seven types of fruit in pregnant woman's lap as a good omen be blessed with a child گود بھری *god'-bha'rī* ADJ. blessed with a child in arms گود (یا گودیوں) کھلانا *god* (or *go'diyoṅ*) *khilā'na* V.T. bring up (a child) dandle گود لینا *god' le'nā* V T. adopt (a child) گود میں بیٹھنا *god meṅ baiṭh'nā* V.I. leap into (someone's) arms sit in the lap of گود میں بیٹھ کر داڑھی نوچنا *god meṅ baiṭh' kar dā'ṛhī noch'nā* PH subtly abuse one's benefactor be rude to him گود میں لینا *god' meṅ le'nā* V.T. here (child) on one's lap dandle (child)

گودا *goo'da* N.M. pulp ; pap pith marrow گودے کی ہڈی *goo'de kī haḍ'dī* N.F. marrow bone

گودام *godām'* N.M. godown [E ~ Malay godong]

گودڑ *goo'daṛ* N.M. cotton wool taken out from old quilt worn-out quilt rag گودڑ میں لعل *goo'daṛ meṅ la''l* N.M. a jewel in rags گودڑی *go'daṛī* N.F. (same as گدڑی N.F. ★)

گودی *go'dī* N.F. lap pier , wharf ; jetty

گور *gor* N.F. grave tomb گور غریباں *go'r-e gharī'bāṅ* N.F. unattended grave yard ; burial-place of the poor گور کا منہ جھانک کر آنا (یا پھرنا) *gor kā mūnh' jhānk' kar ā'nā* (or *phir'nā*) PH. recover from serious illness گورکن *gor'kan* N.M. grave-digger گور کنارے *gor' kinā're* ADV. about to die decrepit گور و کفن *go'r-o ka'fan* N.M. funeral rites , obsequies ; burial بے گور و کفن *be-gor'-o-ka'fan* ADJ. unburied ; uninterred زندہ در گور *zin''dā-dar-gor'* ADJ. (see under زندہ ADJ. ★) گورستان *go'ristān* N.M. graveyard , burial ground [P]

گورا *go'ra* ADJ. (F. گوری *go'rī*) fair blond western English N.M Westerner Englishman British soldier گورا چٹا *go'ra chiṭ'ṭa* ADJ. fair , fair-complexioned گورا شاہی *go'ra-shā'hī* N.F. British rule ADJ of Britishers Army (boots) گوری *go'rī* N.F English woman Western lady

گورخر *gor'-khar* N.M zebra [P]

گورکھا *gor'khā* N.M. Gurkha

گورکھ دھندا *go'rakh-dhan'dā* N.M. puzzle lock puzzle-ring intricate problem

گورنر *gavar'nar* N.M. Governor گورنری *gavar'narī* N.F. gubernatorial office گورنر جنرل *govar'nar-jan'ral* N.M. Governor-General [E]

گورنمنٹ *ga'varnmeṅṭ* N.F. Government [E]

گورو *gū'roo* N.M. (same as گرو N.M. ★)

گوری *go'rī* ADJ. & N.F. (see under گورا ADJ. & N.M. ★)

گوری *gaurī* N.F. name of a musical mode

گورگان *gūr'gan* (or *gūrgān'*) ADJ. leading a life of luxury [T]

گوریا *gauray'ya* N.F. (dial.) sparrow

گوڑنا *gor'nā* V.T scrape (weeds) dig (earth)

گوز *goz* N.M. fart گوز شتر *go'z-e shū'tūr* N.M. (fig.) silly idea ; word carrying no weight گوز شتر سمجھنا *go'z-e shū'tūr sa'majhnā* PH. treat lightly disregard گوز مارنا *goz' mār'na* V.I. fart ; break wind [P]

گوزن *gavaz'n* N.M. stag ; deer [P]

گوسالہ *gosā'lah* N.M. calf گوسالہ پرست *gosā'la-paras't* ADJ. cow-worshipper گوسالہ پرستی *gosā'la paras'tī* N.F cow-worship (esp. of ancient Egypt) [P]

گوسائیں *gosā''īṅ* N.M. (same as گسائیں N.M. ★)

گوسپند *gospand'*, گوسفند *gosfand'* N.M. sheep goat [P]

گوش *gosh* N.M. ear گوش بر آواز ہونا *gosh-bar-āvāz ho'na* V.I. be in a state of expectency گوش زد ہونا *gosh-zad ho'na* V.I. be heard گوش زدہ *gosh'-za'dah* ADJ. heard گوش شنوا *go'sh-e shan'vā* N.M. an ear ready to listen گوش گزار کرنا *gosh'-gūzār' kar'na* V.T. submit bring to the notice (of) intimate گوش گزار ہونا *gosh'-gūzār' ho'na* V.I. be informed , be intimated گوشمالی *gosh-mā'lī* N.F. reproof گوشمالی کرنا *gosh-ma'lī kar'nā* V.T. scold , reprove , chide گراں گوش *giran'-gosh'* ADJ. hard of hearing , deaf [P]

گوشت *gosht* N.M. flesh meat گوشت پوست *gosh't-pos't* N.M. flesh and blood one's flesh گوشت خور *gosh't-khor* ADJ. flesh-eating ; carnivorous گوشت سے ناخن جدا ہونا *gosh't se nākhūn jūda' ho'na* PH. (of near relations) be permanently estranged گوشت کا لوتھڑا *gosh't ka loth'ra* N.M. lump of flesh [P]

گوشوارہ *goshvā'rah* N.M. schedule abstract (of account, etc.) return (arch.) earring [P]

گوشہ *go'shah* N.M. corner end (of) horn (of bow) گوشۂ تنہائی *go'sha-e tanhā''ī* N.M. secluded corner گوشہ دار *gosha'-dār* ADJ. angular گوشۂ چشم *go'sha-e chash'm* N.M. corner of the eye گوشۂ عافیت *go'sha-e 'ā'fiyat* N.M. refuge retreat گوشۂ کماں *go'sha-e kamān'* N.M. horn of the bow گوشہ نشین *go'sha-nashīn'*, گوشہ گزیں *go'sha-gūzīn'*, گوشہ گیر *go'sha'gīr* ADJ. leading a retired life N.M. recluse گوشہ نشینی *go'sha-nashī'nī*, گوشہ گزینی *go'sha-guzī'nī*, گوشہ گیری *go'sha-gī'rī* N.F. leading a retired life [P]

گوکھرو *gokhroo* N.M. thistle caltrop ; crow's-foot tinkle round wrist-band or anklet fretted gold lace

گوگا *go'gā* N.M. name of the legendary religious leader of Hindu untouchables

گوگرد *googir'd* N.M. sulphur ; brimstone گوگرد احمر *googir'd-e ah'mar* N.M. red sulphur, philosopher's stone [P]

گول *gol* ADJ. round circular globular vague or ambiguous (remarks, etc.) deceitful (reply, etc.) گول بات *gol' bat* N.F vague remarks ambiguous expression گول سا *gol' sā* ADJ roundish گول گول *gol' gol*, گول مول *gol' mol* ADJ. vague ambiguous, double-meaning round گول مال *gol'-māl* N.M. embezzlement mess گول مال کرنا *gol'-māl kar'nā* V.T. embezzle make a mess (of) گول مٹول *gol'-maṭol'* ADJ. fat, plump گول میز کانفرنس *gol'-mez kān'farans* N.F. roundtable conference گولائی *golā''ī* N.F. roundness curve curvature circumference round

گولہ *golah*, گولا *go'lā* N.M. cannon ball, shell shot large ball ball (of thread, etc.) whole copra round beam ring round something curb (round) well swelling flatus a species of pigeon metalled part of road گولا انداز *go'lā-andāz'* N.M. gunner گولا اندازی *go'lā andā'zī* N.F. bombardment گولا چلانا (یا مارنا) *go'lā chalā'nā* (or *mār'nā*) V.T bombard

گولائی *golā''ī* N.F. (see under گول ADJ. ★)

گولڈ *gol'd* N.M. gold گولڈن *gol'dan* ADJ. golden گولڈن جوبلی *gol'dan job'lī* N.F golden jubilee [E]

گولر *goolar* N.M. wild fig گولر کا پھول *goo'lar kā phool* N.M. (fig.) rare commodity گولر کا کیڑا *goo'lar kā kī'rā* N M. (fig.) one confined to home

N F. (same as غلک *ghallak* N.F. ★)

گولی *go'lī* N.F. bullet gunshot pill marble (for playing) ball (of) گولی چلانا *go'lī chalā'nā* V.T. fire ; fire a gun ; fire a shot گولی لگنا *go'lī lag'nā* V.I. be shot at be shot dead be injured by a bullet گولی لگے *go'lī la'ge* INT. to hell with it گولی مارنا (یا چلانا) *go'lī mār'nā* (or *chalā'nā*) V.T. shoot shoot (someone) down گولی مارو *go'lī mā'ro* INT. to hell with it (or you, etc.) گولیاں کھیلنا *go'liyān khel'nā* V.T. play with marbles میں کچی گولیاں نہیں کھیلا *main kach'chī go'liyān na'hīn khe'lā* PH. I am no fool

گومڑ *gom'r*, گومڑا *gom'rā* N.M. boil swelling dent or pit (in something) گومڑا پڑنا *gom'rā par'nā* V.I. have a swelling

گوں *goon* SUF. coloured ; hued of a kind ; of a style گونا گوں *goo'nā-goon* ADJ. diverse of various types [P]

گوں *gaun* N.F. strength benefit ; use want ; need گوں کا یار *gaun kā yār'* N.M. selfish person ; timeserver گوں نکلنا *gaun' nikal'nā* V.T. serve one's purpose کی گوں *kī gaun'* PH. strength enough to کی گوں کا *kī gaun' kā* PH. of any use to

گون ۱ *gaun* N.F. large double-chambered gunny bag for carrying grain, etc., on horseback

گون ۲ *gaun* N.M. dress gown academic robe ; gown [E]

گونا *gau'nā* N.M. bringing one's bride back home first time after marriage گونا کرنا *gau'nā kar'nā* V T. bring bride home thus

گونا گوں *goo'nā-goon* ADJ. (see under گوں *goon* ★)

گونتھنا *goonth'nā*, گوتھنا *gooth'nā* V.T. baste stitch clumsily or like a novice

گونجنا *goonj'nā* V.I. echo ; resound roar (of dove or pigeon) coo گونج *goonj* N.F. echo ; resounding hollow sound roar گونج اٹھنا *goonj' ūṭh'nā* V.I. echo, resound

گوند *gond* N.M. gum گوند پنجیری *gond' panjī'rī* N F., گوند مکھانا *gond' makhā'nā* N.M. kinds of dry or pudding-like caudle گونددانی *gond'-dā'nī* N.F. gum pot

گوندھنا *goondh'nā* V.T knead braid plait string

گوندنی *gond'nī*, گوندی *gon'dī* N.F a kind of tree bearing gummy berry

گونگا *gūn'gā*, ADJ. (F گونگی *gūn'gī*) dumb mute

گونہ *goo'nah* SUF. kind ; quality quantity times ; fold یک گونہ *yak-goo'nah* ADV. a little, somewhat دو گونہ *do-goo'nah* ADJ. double [P ~ گوں]

گوہ *goh* N.F. iguana

گوہ *gooh* N.M. excrement; filth ; ordure گوہ اچھالنا *gooh' uchhal'na* V.T. wash dirty linen in public گوہ کا کیڑا گوہ ہی میں خوش رہتا ہے *gooh' ka ki'ra gooh' hi men khush' raih'ta hai* PROV. people like the environment in which they are born گوہ کرنا *gooh' kar'na* V.T. evacuate bowels make a poor show گوہ کھانا *gooh' kha'na* V.T. commit a sin talk nonsense گوہا چھی چھی *goo'ha chhi chhi* N.F. (nurs.) filth (fig.) silly talk

گوہار (or گہار) *gohar'* N.F. cry for help bandying or abuses one's fight against many گوہار لڑنا *gohar' lar'na* V.I. fight single-handed against many

گوہانجنی *gohanja'ni* N.F. sty ; stye

گوہر *goh'r* N.M. passage for ox-cart

گوہر *gau'har*, گہر *go'har* N.M. pearl gem; jewel descent essence ; quintessence talent sharpness of sword گوہر افشاں *gau'har-afshan'* ADJ. (fig.) ADJ. eloquent ADV. (polite) speaking گوہر افشانی *gau'har'-afsha'ni* N.F (fig.) (polite or joc.) speaking utterance گوہر بار *gau'har-bar* ADJ. raining pearls coming in fine drops highly prized گوہر سنج *gau'har-sanj*, گوہر شناس *gau'har-shinas'* N.M. & ADJ. lapidary (fig.) critic [P]

گوئندہ *go''in'dah* N.M. informer (pl. گوئندگاں *go''indagan*) speakers ; utterers [P ~ گفتن say]

گوئی *go''i* SUF. (see under گو *go* ★)

گوئے *goo''e* N.M. (genitive form of گو *goo* ★)

گوئیاں *goo''iyan* N.F. female's friend or playmate of own sex ; friend

گویا *go'ya* N.M. & ADJ. speaking person , (one) able to talk CONJ. as if so to say in a way perhaps گویائی *goya''* N.F. utterance (power of) speech [P ~ گفتن say]

گویا *gavay'ya* N.M. singer vocalist

گہ *gah* N.M. (short for گاہ N.F ★)

گھات *ghat* N.F ambush , ambuscade opportune moment (for attack, etc.) (rare) trick گھات لگانا (میں بیٹھنا) *ghat laga'na* (or *men baith'na*) V.T ambush ; lie in ambush , lay or make ambush ; lie in wait (for) گھاتی *gha'ti*, گھاتیا *gha'tiya* N.M. & ADJ. lurking (one) lying in ambush

گھاتا *gha'ta* N.M. excess charged on paid price گھاتے میں *gha'te men* ADV. gratuitously

گھاٹ *ghat* N.M. wharf ; ferry riverside bathing place such place for drawing water or washing clothes brassiers brest point where sword blade curves گھاٹ گھاٹ کا پانی پینا *ghat ghat ka pa'ni pi'na* PH. be widely experienced گھاٹ مارنا *ghat' mar'na* V.T. smuggle dutiable goods گھاٹ مانجھی *ghat'-man'jhi* N.M. ferryman

گھاٹا *gha'ta* N.M. loss deficiency damages گھاٹا اٹھانا *gha'ta utha'na* V.T suffer a loss کو گھاٹا پڑنا *ko gha'ta par'na* V.I. incur a loss [~ گھٹنا]

گھاٹی *gha'ti* N.F. valley pass اوگھٹ گھاٹی *au'ghat gha'ti* N.F. difficult pass

گھاس *ghas* (vul. گھانس *ghans*) N.F grass hay گھاس پات *ghas' pat* N.F. greens گھاس پھوس *ghas' phoos* N.M. straw گھاس کاٹنا *ghas' kat'na* V.T. cut grass grub up grass do something haphazardly گھاس کھانا *ghas' kha'na* V.T. & I. graze lose one's wits ; go mad گھاس کھودنا *ghas' khod'na* V.T. grub up grass

گھاگ *ghag* ADJ. veteran wily (old man)

گھاگرا *ghagh'ra*, گھگرا *ghag'ra* N.M. long skirt petticoat (rare) kilt گھاگرا پلٹن *ghagh'ra pal'tan* N.F. (joc.) kilted soldiers ; Highland regiment bevy of ladies

گھال میل *ghal' mel* ADJ. mixed

گھالنا *ghal'na* N.T. ruin کا گھر گھالنا *ka ghal'na* PH. ruin ; reduce to straits

گھامڑ *gha'mar* N.M. & ADJ. fool ; blockhead

گھان *ghan* N.M. quantity cast once into frying pan, mill, etc. گھان اتارنا *ghan' utar'na* V.T. take out prepared quantity گھان ڈالنا *ghan' dal'na* V.T. cast a quantity (of something) for frying, etc. گھانی *gha'ni* N.F. quantity cast once in oil expeller, etc. کچی گھانی *kach'chi gha'ni* N.M. first round of such quantity

گھاؤ *gha''o* N.M. wound sore گھاؤ بھرنا *gh o bhar'na* V.I. (of wound or sort) heal گھاؤ کرنا *gha''o kar'na* V.T wound ; inflict a wound (fig.) injure (someone's) feelings گھاؤ کھانا *gha''o kha'na* V.I. be wounded گھائل *gha'yal* N.M. & ADJ ★

گھاؤ گھپ *gha''o-ghup* ADJ. embezzler گھاؤ گھپ کرنا *gha''o-ghup kar'na* V.T. embezzle

گھائی *gha''i* N F. angle formed between (two finder, branch and stem, etc.) fraud trick گھائیاں بتانا *gha''iyan bata'na*

اڑن گھائی بتانا *uran ghā''ī batā'nā*, V.T. defraud outwit

گھایل *ghā'yal* ADJ. injured ; wounded (fig.) smitten with love گھایل کرنا *ghā'yal kar'nā* V.T. wound , inflict a wound (fig.) smite with love گھایل ہونا *ghā'yal ho'nā* V.I. be wounded (fig.) be smitten with love

گھبرانا *ghabrā'nā* V.T. & I. feel nervous be unnerved , be embarrased be perplexed be confused unnerve confuse perplex گھبراہٹ *ghabrā'haṭ* N.F confusion bewilderment embarassment

گھپ *ghup'* ADJ. & ADV. very ; pitch (dark) گھپ اندھیرا *ghup' andhe'ra* N.M. pitch dark

گھپلا *ghap'lā* N.M. discrepancy (in accounts) mess , confusion گھپلا پڑنا (یا لگنا) *ghap'lā par'nā* (or *lag'nā*) V.I. be in a mess ; be thrown into confusion (of discrepancy) occur (in accounts) گھپلا ڈالنا *ghap'lā ḍāl'nā* V.T. make a mess (of) cause discrepancy (in accounts)

گھپنا *ghūp'nā* V.I. (of knife, etc.) pierce (into something) [~ گھونپنا]

گھٹا *ghaṭā* N.F. cloud gathering of clouds گھٹا آنا (یا اٹھنا یا امنڈنا یا ہونا) *gha'ṭā ā'nā* or *uṭh'nā* or *ūmaṇḍ'nā* or *ho'nā*) V.I. (of clouds) gather in the horizon (of sky) become cloudy; be overcast گھٹا جھوم (یا گھر) کر آنا *ghā'ṭa jhoom'* (or *ghir'*) *karā'nā* V.I. (of clouds) gather suddenly lour ; lower . گھٹا چھانا *gha'ṭā chhā'nā* V.I. (of clouds) lour ; lower گھٹا ٹوپ *gha'ṭā-ṭop* ADJ. & ADV. pitch (dark)

گھٹا *ghaṭ'ṭā*, گٹا *gaṭ'ṭā* N.M. corn (on skin)

گھٹانا *ghaṭā'nā* V.T. decrease; lessen ; reduce, diminish abate subtract lower ; degrade demote devalue ; devaluate cause to decline گھٹاؤ *ghaṭā''o* N.M. fall reduction lowering depreciation گھٹاؤ بڑھاؤ *ghaṭā''o-baṛhā''o* N.M. rise and fall decrease and increase گھٹنا *ghaṭ'nā* V.I. decrease ; lessen be substracted (of price) come down fall (of moon) wane subside dwindle be lowered be devalued گھٹتی کا پہرہ *ghaṭ'tī kā paih'rah* PH. time when something is on the wane old age گھٹیا *ghaṭ'yā* (rare گھٹیل *ghaṭ'yal*) ADJ. inferior cheap

گھٹنا *ghūṭ'nā* V.I. be well-rubbed be pounded ; be powdered (of head, etc.) be tonsured ; be close-shaven be chocked (of breath) be suffocated گھٹ کے *ghūṭ ke* ADV. (die) of suffocation گھٹوانا *ghuṭvā'nā* V.T. cause to pound get (head) tonsured گھٹاؤ *ghūṭā''o* N.M. close atmosphere گھٹس *ghūṭ'tas* N.F. close atmosphere suffocation pressure on space

گھٹنا *ghūṭ'nā* N.M. knee گھٹنوں میں سر دے لینا (کے بیٹھنا) *ghūṭ'non meṅ sir' de le.nā* (or *ke baiṭh'na*) V.T. hang down one's head with shame try to hide oneself be overwhelmed with grief گھٹنے سے لگا کر بٹھانا *ghūṭ'ne se lagā kar biṭhā'nā* PH. (of mother) not to set daughter apart from her گھٹنے سے لگے بیٹھے رہنا *ghūṭ'ne se la'ge bai'ṭhe raih'nā* PH. to be tied to another's apronstrings گھٹنیوں چلنا *ghūṭ'niyoṅ chal'nā* V.I. (of child) crawl on his knees

گھٹی *ghūṭ'tī* N.F. first-ever dose to new born infant گھٹی میں پڑنا (یا ہونا) *ghūṭ'tī meṅ par'nā* (or *ho'nā*) PH. become one's second nature

گھٹیا *ghaṭ'yā*. گھٹیل *ghaṭ'yal* ADJ. (see under گھٹنا *ghaṭ'nā* V.I. ★)

گھچ پچ *ghich'-pich* N.F crowd close writing ADJ. crowded closely written over

گہر *gohar'* N.M (short for گوہر *gau'har* N.M. ★)

گھر *ghar* N.M. house ; residence abade ; dwelling , habitation home family native place soure ; origin , spring place of production groove ; socket گھر آباد کرنا (یا بسانا) *ghar' ābād' kar'nā* (or *basā'nā*) V.T. & I. marry ; take a wife come to live with (someone) as his wife beget children کا گھر آباد ہونا *kā ghar ābād' ho'nā* V.I. (of man) get married marry گھر اجڑنا (یا برباد ہونا یا ویران ہونا) *ghar' ūjarnā* (or *barbād' ho'nā* or *vīrān' ho'nā*) V.I. (of home) be ruined suffer a loss of someone in family (of house) be burgled گھر صاف ہو جانا *ghar sāf' ho jā'nā* V.I. (of one's home) be ruined گھر بار *ghar'-bār* N.M. home family house household good کا گھر بسانا *kā ghar' bas'na* V.I. (of man) get married ; marry گھر بسی *ghar-ba'sī* N.F. (rare) wife گھر بگاڑنا *ghar'-bigāṛ'nā* V.T. ruin a family cause friction in family کا گھر بگڑنا *ka ghar' bi'garnā* V.I. lose one's consort (by death or otherwise) have frequest tiffs گھر بنانا *ghar' banā'nā* V.I. build a house keep house seen not to ludge from گھر بھائیں بھائیں کرنا *ghar bhā''en bhā''en kar'nā* V. (of house) look desolate be deserted گھر بھر *ghar' bhar* N.M. the whole family گھر بیٹھنا *ghar' baiṭh'nā* V.I. (of house) collapse (of woman) be practically divorced کے گھر بیٹھنا *ke ghar' baiṭh'nā* V.I. become the mistress of گھر بیٹھے *ghar' bai'ṭhe* ADV. without the least exertion کے گھر (میں) پڑنا *ke ghar' (meṅ) par'nā* V.I. (of woman) marry (someone) become the wife of (someone) گھر پھونک تماشا دیکھنا *ghar' phoonk' tamā'-shā dekh'nā* PH. waste one's substance in idle pleasure گھر تک پہنچانا *ghar' tak pahūñchā'nā* V.I. escort (someone) to his home گھر تک پہنچنا *ghar' tak pahūñch'nā* PH. abuse members of someone's family برے کے گھر تک پہنچنا *būre' ke ghar tak pahūñch'nā* V.T. pursue (wicked person, etc.) to the utmost (joc.) persue to the utmost گھر جنوائی *ghar janvā''ī* N.M. man living with his in laws گھر چڑھ کر لڑنے آنا *ghar' charh' ka lar'ne ā'nā* PH. go to (someone's) house in order to pick up a quarrel گھر چلانا *ghar' chalā'nā* V.T. run a house maintain one's family گھر چلنا *ghar' chal'nā* V.I. (of family) be maintained گھر دار *ghar'-dār'* ADJ. family man گھر داری *ghar'-dā'rī* N.F. being a family man گھر دیکھ لینا *ghar' dekh' le'nā* V.T. see a house visit a house frequently (of death, etc.) spot a house for visitation گھر ڈبونا (یا اجاڑنا یا برباد کرنا) *ghar' ḍūbo'nā* (or *ūjāṛ'nā* or *bar'bād kar'nā*) V.T. ruin a family گھر سر پر اٹھانا *ghar' sir' par ūṭhā'nā* V.T. make much noise raise a great hue and cry maintain a family گھر سے *ghar' se* ADV. from one's own pocket گھر سے بے گھر ہونا *ghar' se be-ghar' kar'nā* V.T. evict گھر سے پاؤں باہر نکالنا *ghar' se pā''oṅ bā'har nikāl'nā* V.T. come out of the house become vograd گھر سے دینا *ghar' se de'nā* V.T. pay out of one's pocket گھر سے لڑ کر تو نہیں آئے *ghar' se laṛ' kar to na'hīṅ ā''e* INT. why are you unnecessarily cross گھر سینا *ghar' se'nā* V.I. (fig.) idle away one's time at home گھر کا *ghar' kā*, ADJ. (F. گھر کی *ghar' kī*) own of one's family گھر کا آدمی *ghar' kā ād'mī* N.M. member of one's family trustworthy person گھر کا آنگن ہو جانا *ghar' kā āṅ'gan ho jā'nā* V.I. (of house or household) be ruined گھر کا اجالا *ghar' kā ūjā'la*, گھر کا چراغ *ghar' kā chirāgh'* N.M. son ; successor ; scion of a family گھر کا بوجھ اٹھانا *ghar' kā bojh' ūṭhā'nā* V. be responsible for the upkeep of the house ; maintain one's family گھر کا بھیدی *ghar' kā bhe'dī* N.M. confident confidant گھر کا بھیدی لنکا ڈھائے *ghar' kā bhe'dī lañ'kā ḍhā''e* PROV. an estranged friend is one's worst foe گھر کاٹنے (یا کاٹ کھانے) کو دوڑتا ہے *ghar' kāṭ'ne* (or *kāṭ khā'ne*) *ko dauṛ'tā hai* INT. I miss my people very much the home is desolate گھر کا راستہ بتانا *ghar' kā rās'tah batā'nā* PH. prevaricate گھر کا راستہ لینا *ghar' kā rās'tah le'nā* INT. make oneself scarce گھر کا گھر *ghar' kā ghar'* N.M. the whole family گھر کا گھروا ہو جانا *ghar' kā ghar'vā ho jā'nā* V.I. (of family) be ruined گھر کا مال *ghar' kā māl* N.M. one's own property گھر کا نہ گھاٹ کا *ghar' kā na ghāṭ' kā* PH. (one) rejected by both sides گھر کا نام ڈبونا *ghar kā nām' ḍūbo'nā* V.T. bring shame on one's family گھر کر ستر بلا سر *ghar' kar sat'tar balā' sar* PROV. being a family man means a lot of trouble گھر کرنا *ghar' kar'na* V.T. have a separate home for oneself marry capture make room for oneself influence گھر کمانا *ghar' kamā'nā* V.T. clean night-soil ; scavenge گھر کی آدھی نہ باہر کی ساری *ghar' kī ā'dhī na bā'har kī sā'rī* PROV. less income at home is preferable to more at both (dry bread at home is better than roast meat abroad گھر کی طرح رہنا *ghar' kī tar'h raih'nā* live as a member of a family feel at ease in a home گھر کی کھیتی *ghar' kī khe'tī* N.F. (fig.) something to be had without incurring any expenditure own possession گھر کی لونڈی *ghar' kī lauṅ'ḍī* N.F. handmaiden گھر کی مرغی دال برابر *ghar' kī mūr'ghī dāl' barā'bar* PROV. no one is a hero to his own valet ; a prophet is not valued in his own country گھر کے جالے لیتے پھرنا *ghar' ke jā'le le'te phir'nā* V.T. search every nook and corner of the house roam about all over گھر کے لوگ *ghar' ke log* N.M. one's family گھر گھاٹ *ghar' ghāṭ'* N.M. address ways and manner secrets (of) گھر گھالنا *ghar' ghāl'nā* V.T. ruin a household گھر گھر *ghar' ghar'* N.M. every house ADV. in every house گھر گھر مانگتے پھرنا *ghar' ghar' maṅg'te phir'nā* V.T. beg from door to door گھر گھسو *ghar' ghūs'roo* N.M. & ADJ. (one) who always keeps at home گھر گھوڑا نخاس مول *ghar' gho'ṛā nakhkhās' mol* PROV. who will buy a pig in a poke گھر گرہست *ghar' gareh'st* N.F. household virtuous housewife گھر لٹانا *ghar' lūṭā'nā* V.T. squander one's wealth گھر لینا *ghar' le'nā* V.T. buy a house rent a house گھر موسنا *ghar' moos'nā* V.T. impoverish a household by continuous demands or filching گھر میں بھونی بھانگ تک نہ ہونا *ghar' meṅ bhoo'nī bhāṅg' tak na ho'nā* PH. have nothing at home ; be extremely poor گھر میں خاک اڑانا *ghar' meṅ khāk' ūṛ'nā*, گھر میں چوہے دوڑنا *ghar' meṅ choo'he dauṛ'nā* PH. have nothing in the house to eat ; be extremely poor گھر میں ڈالنا *ghar' meṅ ḍāl'nā* V.T. make one's mistress one's wedded wife گھر نہ بار میاں محلے دار *ghar' na bār' mīyāṅ mahal'le dār* PROV. feel proud without possession گھر والا *ghar'-vā'lā* N.M. master of the house husband landlord گھر والی *ghar'-vā'lī* N.F. housewife wife landlady اونچا گھر *ooñchā ghar'* N.M. high family بھرا گھر *bha'rā ghar* N.M. rich family with many members ڈاک گھر *ḍāk' ghar'* N.M. (rare) post office تار گھر *tā'r-ghar*

N.M. telegraph office گھروا *ghar'vā* N.M. (dial.) small house گھریلو *ghare'loo* ADJ. ★)

گھرا *ghar'rā* N.M. death rattle گھرا لگنا *ghar'rā lag'nā* V.I. be at the last gasp

گہرا *gaih'rā* ADJ. (F. گہری *gaih'rī*) deep sharp (colour) intimate (friend) strong, in dissoluble (link, etc.) well-observed profound (thought) deep or cunning (person) dense گہرا پردہ *gaih'rā par'dah* N.M. well-observed purdah; total seclusion (of women) گہری بات *gaih'rī bāt* N.F. profound truth sly matter گہری چھاننا *gaih'rī chhān'nā* V.T. prepare a dense solution of hamp be intoxicated with it میں گہری چھننا *men gaih'rī chhan'nā* V.T be close friends. to have a great fight گہری نیند سونا *gaih'rī nīnd so nā* N.F. sleep soundly; have a sound sleep گہرے چلنا *gaih're chal'nā* V.I. (highwaymen's slang) walk swiftly and kill the patient کے گہرے ہونا *ke gaih're ho'nā* V.I. (of someone) earn a lot; have good business گہری *gaih'rī* N.F. intimate friendship dense solution of hemp گہرائی *gaihrā''ī* N.F. depth deepness profundity

گھر آنا *ghir ā'nā* V.I. (see under گھرنا V.I. ★)

گھرانا *gharā'nā*, گھرانہ *gharā'nah* N.M. household family dynasty [~ گھر]

گہرائی *gaihrā''ī* N.F. (see under گہرا ADJ. ★)

گھرر گھرر *gha'rar gha'rar* N.F. whirr گھرر گھرر چلنا (یا کرنا) *gha'rar gha'rar chal'nā* (or *kar'nā*) V.I. whirr [ONO.]

گھرکنا *ghū'raknā* V.T rebuke browbeat گھرکی *ghūr'kī* N.F. rebuke browbeating

گھرگھر *ghar ghar* N.M. whirr [ONO.]

گھرنا *ghir'nā* V.I. (of clouds) gather be surrounded (by) be besieged be busy (with work, etc.)

گھرنی *ghir'nī* N.F pulley handle rope twisting wheel vertigo گھرنی کھانا *ghir'nī khā'nā* V.I. fall down owing to vertigo

گھروندا *gharaun'dā* (or *ghi-*). N.M. toy-house; sand or clay house made and unmade by children [~ گھر]

گھریلو *ghare'loo* ADJ. home homely simple, unsophisticated domesticated tame private گھریلو زندگی *ghare'loo zin'dagī* N.F. private life گھریلو معاملہ *ghare'loo mo'ā'malah* N.M. internal affair [~ گھر]

گھڑ *ghūr* N.M. horse گھڑ سوار *ghūr-savār'*, گھڑ چڑھا *ghūr'-char'hā* N.M. horseman cavalier گھڑ دوڑ *ghūr-daur'* N.F. horse race گھڑسال *ghu.-sāl'* N F (arch.) stable گھڑنال *ghūr-nāl'* N.F. a kind of small gun گھڑ نعل *ghūr-na''l* N.F. & ADJ. horse-shoe [~ گھوڑا CONTR.]

گھڑا *gha'rā* N.M. earthen water pot; jar; pitcher گھڑوں پانی پڑ جانا *gha'ron pā'nī par jā'nā* V.T be greatly ashamed گھڑونچی *gharaun'chī* N.F. pitcher stand

گھڑانا *gharā'nā* V.T. گھڑائی *gharā''ī* N.F. گھڑت *gha'rat* N.F گھڑنت *gharant'* N.F. see FOLL. ★)

گھڑنا *ghar'nā*, (dial. گڑھنا *garh'nā*) V.T. beat, etc. into shape forge invent or fabricate (lie, story, etc.) گھڑانا *gharā'nā*, گھڑوانا *gharvā'nā* V T. cause to forge get (ornament) made گھڑائی *gharā''ī* N.F. remuneration price workmanship گھڑت *gha'rat*, گھڑنت *gharant* N.F. faked story make-believe

گھڑی *gha'rī* N.F. chronometer watch (arch. space of 24 minutes (this, that; etc.) moment occasion time گھڑی بنانا *gha'rī banā'nā* V.T. repair a watch گھڑی بھاری ہونا *gha'rī bhā'rī ko'nā* PH. (of time) hang heavy گھڑی بھر میں *gha'rī bhar men* ADV. in a moment; in a trice in a jiffy in a short while گھڑی پل کی آس نہیں *gha'rī pal kī ās na'hīn* PH. who can be sure next moment گھڑی ساز *gha'rī-sāz* N.M. watch maker گھڑی گھڑی *gha'rī gha'rī* ADV time and again گھڑی میں تولہ گھڑی میں ماشہ *gharī men to'lah gha'rī men ma'shah* PH. fickle; capricious گھڑیاں گننا *ghar'yān gin'nā* V.T wait impatiently

گھڑیال *ghaṛyāl'* N.M. crocodile gong grandfather clock گھڑیالی *ghaṛ'ya'lī* N.M one striking the hours at a gong

گھڑیا *ghūr'yā* N.F. pony [~ گھوڑی DIM.]

گھسانا *ghisā'nā* V.T. rub cause to wear out گھسا *ghis'sā* N.M. rubbing; abrasion shoving in push stroke trick fraud گھسامیری *ghis'sā-mī'rī* N.F. game in which contenders try to snap each other's string گھساوٹ *ghisā'vat* N.F. گھساؤ *ghisā''o* N.M. rubbing abrasion friction گھسائی *ghisā''ī* N.F. friction rubbing rubbing charges گھسنا *ghis'nā* V.T. rule گھس جانا *ghis jā'nā* V.I. wear out wear out; be worn out گھسن پٹی *ghi'san-piṭ'ṭī* N.F. brawl fight گھسوانا *ghisvā'nā* V.T. cause to rub cause to wear out گھس پس کر *ghis' pis kar* ADV. (of clothes) after a long and happy use گھس کر لگانے کو نہیں *ghis' kar lagā'ne ko na'hīn* PH. is not at all there

گھسٹنا ghi'saṭnā V.I. trail be dragged

گھس کھدا ghas-khud'dā N.M. grass cutter novice [~ گھاس + کھودنا]

گھسنا ghus'nā V.I. enter by force penetrate rush in telescope meddle گھس آنا ghus ā'nā V.I. enter by force rush in گھس پڑنا (یا جانا) ghus' par'nā (or jā'nā) V.I. rush in penetrate گھس پیٹھ کے ghus' paiṭh' ke ADV with effort elbowing one's way somehow or other by hook or by crook گھسوانا ghusvā'nā V.T. cause to thrust (into) ; cause to shove (in)

گھسیارا ghasyā'rah N.M گھسیارن ghasyā'ran N.F. grass cutter [~ گھاس]

گھسیٹنا ghasīṭ'nā V.T. drag pull trail bedraggle scribble گھسیٹا گھسائی ghasī'ṭā-ghasā'ī N.F pulling and resisting dragging گھسیٹن ghasī'ṭan N.F mark of pulling

گھسیڑنا ghuser'nā V.T shove (in) thrust (into) cram foist telescope

گھگرا ghag'rā N.M. same as گاگرا ghāg'rā ★ گھگری ghag'rī N.F small petticoat long skirt comparatively less loose

گھگی ghig'gī N.F hiccup temporary loss of power of speech (through fear or sobbing) گھگی بندھ جانا ghig'gī bandh jā'nā V.I. loss power of speech be struck dumb founded گھگیانا ghig'yānā V.I. beseech falter in speaking be dumbfounded

گھلنا ghul'nā, گھل جانا ghul' jā'nā V.I. dissolve: to be dissolved be mellowed waste away , pine away : peak and pine گھل مل جانا ghul' mil jā'nā V.I. mix up گھل مل کے ghul' mil ke ADV. together گھلو ملو ہو جانا ghul'loo mil'loo ho jā'nā V.I. become intimate soon گھلانا ghulā'nā V.T dissolve soften mellow cause to waste away گھلاوٹ ghulā'vaṭ N.F. softness mellowness گھلا ہوا ghu'lā hū'ā ADJ. dissolved soft mellow گھل گھل کے ghul' ghul ke ADV. washing

گہما گہمی gaih'ma gaih'mī N.F cheer hustle and bustle

گھمانا ghūma'nā V.T. whirl round wheel turn round brandish take out for a stroll show (someone) round a place

گھمر گھمر ghū'mar ghū'mar N.F. whirr (of handmill) گھمری ghum'rī, گھمیر ghūmer', گھمیری ghume'rī N.F. vertigo گھمریاں لینا ghum'riyāṅ le'nā, گھمیر آنا ghumer' ā'nā V.I. feel giddy

گھمسان ghamsān' N.M. heavy fight گھمسان کا رن gham'sān kā ran' N.M. furious fight گھمسان کا رن پڑنا ghamsān' ka ran' paṛ'na V.I. (of furious fight) occur

گھمنڈ ghūmanḍ' N.M. pride ; arrogance گھمنڈ کرنا ghūmanḍ' kar'nā V.I. be vain be proud (of) گھمنڈی ghūman'ḍī ADJ. proud; arrogant

گھمیر ghūmer, گھمیری ghume'rī N.F. (same as گھمری ghūm'rī N.F. ★)

گہن gai'han, گرہن garai'han N.M. eclipse گہنا gaih'nā gaihnā'nā, گہنا جانا gaihnā' jā'nā V.I. be eclipsed گہن چھٹنا gai'han chhūṭ'nā V.I. come out of eclipse گہن لگنا gai'han lag'nā V.I. eclipse گہن میں آنا gai'han meṅ ā'nā V.I. be eclipsed have a physical deformity owing to occurence of eclipse in prenatal stage

گھن ghan N.M. sledge-hammer (rare) cloud-gathering (rare) cloud گھن کی چوٹ ghan kī choṭ N.F. heavy blow گھن چکر ghan-chak'kar N.M. a kind of rotating fire-works (fig.) fool آدمی ہے یا گھن چکر ād'mī hai yā ghan-chak'kar PH. he is an arrant fool گھن دار ghan-dār گھن کا ghan kā ADJ. thick (forest) گھنگھور گھٹا ghanghor' ghaṭā N.F. dark louring clouds

گھن ghin N.F. nausea (fig.) aversion گھن آنا ghin ā'nā V.I. feel nausea (fig.) have an aversion (for)

گھن کھانا ghin khā'nā V.T. have an aversion (for) گھناؤنا ghinā'ōnā ADJ. (F. گھناؤنی ghinā'ōnī) nauseating disgusting

گھن ghūn N.M. weevil rancour ; grief گھن لگنا ghun' lag'nā V.T. be eaten up by weevil (fig.) be the victim of a wasting disease

گہنا gaih'nā N.M. ornament گہنا پاتا gaih'nā pā'tā N.M. jewellery گہنے رکھنا gaih'ne rakh'nā V.T. pawn pledge ; mortgage

گھنا ghā'nā (F. گھنی ghā'nī) ADJ. thick ; dense deep (shadow) گھنیرا ghane'rā ADJ. ★

گھنا ghun'nā (F. گھنی ghun'nī) ADJ. designedly silent ; cunning گھنی سادھنا ghun'nī sādh'nā V.I. be designedly silent ; keep mum

گہنانا gaihnā'nā V.I. (see under گہن N.M. ★)

گھناؤنا ghinā'ōnā ADJ. (see under گھن ghin N.F. ★)

گھنٹہ ghan'ṭah, گھنٹا ghan'ṭā N.M. hour clock (joc) penis گھنٹہ بجنا ghan'ṭah baj'nā (of clock) chime ; strike the hour گھنٹہ گھر ghan'ṭa-ghar N.M. clock-tower

گھنٹی ghan'ṭī N.F. bell gong گھنٹی بجانا ghan'ṭī bajā'nā V.T. ring a bell گھنٹی بجنا ghan'ṭī baj'nā V.I. (of bell) ring خطرے کی گھنٹی khaṭ're kī ghan'ṭī N.F. alarm

گھنڈی ghun'ḍī N.F. cloth button topknot (of mango) گھنڈی لگانا ghun'ḍī lagā'nā V.T. button ; stitch a cloth button گھنڈی کھولنا ghun'ḍī khol'nā V.T. unbutton (fig.) unravel

گھنگچی *ghung'chī* N.F. 'arbus precatorious' seed

گھنگر *ghun'gar* N.M. curl گھنگر والا *ghūngarā'lā* گھنگرالا *ghun'gar-vā'lā*, گھنگریالہ *ghūngaryā'lā* ADJ. curly (hair)

گھنگرو *ghun'roo* N.M. tinkle ; small bell protected on all sides tinkling anklet ; band containing these bells death-rattle گھنگرو باندھنا *ghung'roo bāndh'nā* V.T. tie tinkling anklet (in preparation for dance) گھنگرو بولنا *ghūng'roo bol'nā* V.I. have the death-rattle

گھنگنی *ghung'nī* N.F. boiled corn منہ میں گھنگنیاں ڈالے (یا ڈال کر) بیٹھنا *munh meṅ ghung'niyāṅ ḍā'le* (or *ḍāl kar*) *baiṭh'nā* PH. keep mum despite the need to speak

گھنگولنا *ghangol'nā* V.T. stir up (liquid) with one's hand make it turbid pierce with (something)

گہوارہ *gahvā'rah* N.M. cradle

گھوٹا *gho'ṭā* N.M. polishing stone wooden pestle

گھوٹنا *ghoṭ'nā*, گھونٹنا *ghonṭ'nā* V.T grind pound pulverize (arch.) glaze (paper) by rubbing cram

گھور *ghor* ADJ. terrible dark گھنگھور *ghanghor'* ADJ. (see under گھن *ghan* ★)

گھورا *ghoo'rā* N.M. dung-hill گھورا گھاری *ghoo'rā ghā'rī* N.F. (see under گھورنا V.T. ★)

گھورا *ghau'rā* N.M. shady pen (for animals)

گھورنا *ghoor'nā* V.T. scowl, glower stare (at) gaze intently (on) ogle, cast amorous glances گھورا گھاری *ghoo'rā ghā'rī* ogling گھور گھور کر دیکھنا *ghoor ghoor kar dekh'nā* V.T. stare at scowl ogle

گھوڑا *gho'ṛā* N.M. horse trigger ; cock (at chess) knight گھوڑا بڑھانا *gho'ṛā baṛhā'nā* V.T. urge a horse گھوڑا چڑھانا *gho'ṛā chaṛhā'nā* V.T. cock a gun گھوڑا چھوڑنا *gho'ṛā chhoṛ'nā* V.T. unharness a horse gallop a horse get a mare covered گھوڑا دبانا *gho'ṛā dabā'nā* V.T. pull trigger گھوڑا دوڑانا *gho'ṛā dauṛā'nā* V.T. gallop a horse گھوڑا ڈالنا (یا پھینکنا) *gho'ṛā ḍāl'nā* (or *phenk'nā*) V.T. race a horse at full speed set one's horse on گھوڑا نکالنا *gho'ṛā nikāl'nā* V.T. take out symbol of Imam Husain's horse during Muharram گھوڑے بیچ کر سونا *gho'ṛe bech kar so'nā* V.I. sleep too soundly گھوڑے پر آسن جمانا *gho'ṛe par ā'san jamā'nā* V.T. sit firmly on horse back گھوڑے جوڑے کی خیر *gho'ṛe jo'ṛe kī khair'* INT. may be continue to enjoy the happy marital life and his high status گھوڑی *gho'ṛī* N.F. mare crude machine for making macaroni lace-maker s stand wooden strip used as clip in circumcision (USU. PL.) song sung at گھوڑیا *gho'ṛiyā* ... گھوڑی چڑھانا *gho'ṛī chaṛhā'nā* ... *gho'ṛī tap'pā* N.M. leap frog ... *chaṛhā'na* V.T. get boy circumcised make a bridegroom

گھوس *ghoos* گھونس *ghoons* N.F. bribe

گھوسی *gho'sī* N.M. milkman cowherd گھوسن *gho'san* N.F. milkmaid cowherd's wife

گھولنا *ghol'nā* V.T. dissolve put in رس گھولنا *ras ghol'nā* V.I. pour dulcet tune's (into ears) گھول پینا *ghol pī'nā* V.T. (fig.) care a hang for have no shame گھول میل *ghol' mel* N.M. intimacy

گھولا [1] *gho'lā*, گھولوا *ghol'vā* N.M. opium solution opiate [~ PREC.]

گھولا [2] *gho'lā* N.M. perplexity difficulty

گھومنا *ghoom'nā* V.I. turn round rotate revolve whirl take a stroll feel giddy گھومتا گھامتا (یا پھرتا) *ghoom'tā ghām'tā* (or *phir'tā*) ADV. walking around just by the way گھوم گھوم کے *ghoom' ghoom ke* ADV after a walk after all

گھونٹ *ghoonṭ* N.M. draught pull (at) hookah, etc.) گھونٹ پینا (یا لینا) *ghoonṭ pī'nā* (or *le'nā*) V.T. take a draught have a pull (at hookah etc.)

گھونپنا *ghoṅp'nā* V.T. pierce with (knife, etc.)

گھونٹنا *ghoonṭ'nā* (or *ghoṭ'nā*) V.T. press, grind گلا گھونٹنا *ga'lā ghoonṭ'nā* V.T throttle, strangle ; strangulate دم گھونٹنا *dam' ghoonṭ'nā* V.I make it hard to breathe

گھونسا *ghooṅ'sā* N.M. blow with the fist shock گھونسا لگانا (یا رسید کرنا یا مارنا) *ghooṅ'sā lagā'nā* (or *rasīd' kar'nā* or *mār'nā*) V.T. give a blow گھونسم گھونسہ *ghooṅ'sam ghāṅ'sah* N.M. fisticuffs گھونسے بازی *ghooṅ'se-bā'zī* N.F fisticuffs (rare) boxing

گھونسلا *ghoṅs'lā* N.M. nest گھونسلا بنانا *ghoṅs'lā banā'nā* V.T. make a nest

گھونگا *ghoṅ'gā* N.M. conch-shell

گھونگٹ *ghooṅ'gaṭ* N.M. veil corner of mantle drawn over face screening wall against door skin protruding over penis (of army) retreat گھونگٹ اٹھانا (یا الٹانا یا کھولنا) *ghooṅ'gaṭ uṭhā'nā* (or *ulṭā'nā* or *khol'nā*) V.T. unveil draw away the mantle from the face گھونگٹ کھانا *ghooṅ'gaṭ khā'nā* V.I. (of army) retreat گھونگٹ کرنا (یا کاڑھنا) *ghooṅ'gaṭ kar'nā* (or *karh'nā*) V.T. draw mantle over the face گھونگٹ والی *ghoon'gaṭ vā'lī* N.F. veiled woman

گھی *ghī* N.M. clarified butter ; butter-oil ; ghee گھی چپڑنا *ghī' chū'paṛnā* V.T. rub with butter-oil گھی سنوارے سالن بڑی بہو کا نام *ghī' sanvā're sāl'nā ba'ṛī ba'hoo kā nām'* PROV. get credit for nothing or for another's work گھی کھچڑی *ghī' khich'ṛī* N.F. close friendship گھی کھچڑی ہونا *ghī' khichṛī ho'nā* V.I. have close friendship گھی کے چراغ جلانا *ghī ke chirāgh' jalā'nā* V.T. rejoice گھی کے چراغ جلنا *ghī ke chirāgh' jal'nā* V.T. prosper evince happiness

گہے *ga'he* ADV. & CONJ. occasionally ; at times [P ~ گاہ]

گھیا *ghīy'yā* N.M. pumpkin ; gourd

گھیپنا *ghep'nā* V.T. (dial.) mix well make into a paste

گھیتلی *ghet'lī* ADJ. heelless upturned (slipper) for ladies

گھیرنا *gher'nā* V.T. encircle ; surround enclose hem in hedge blockade invest , by seige to press paster گھیر *gher* N.M. width fulness (of dress) circuit ; boundary گھیردار *gher-dār* ADJ. ample ; loose گھیر گھار کے (یا کر) *gher' ghār ke* (or *kar*) ADV. surrounding with great difficulty گھیرا *ghe'rā* N.M. circumference boundary circle blockade siege cordon گھیرا ڈالنا *ghe'rā dāl'nā* V.T. blockade lay siege (to) throw a cordon round گھیراؤ *gherā''o* N.M. industrial blockade ; gherao گھیراؤ کرنا *gherā''o kar'nā* V.T. blockade , gherao

گھیکوار *ghī-ka'vār*, گھیگوار *ghī'-ga'vār* N.M. name of a medicinal plant with pulpy leaves

گیا *ga'yā* (P.T. of V.I. ★) گیا گزرا *ga'yā gūz'rā* ADJ. (F. گئی گزری *ga''ī gūz'rī*) (DATIVE & PL. گئے گزرے *ga''e gūz're*) worthless (person) cowardly (of times, etc.) dead and gone گئی گزری باتیں جانے دو *ga''ī gūz'rī bā'teṅ jā'ne do* PH. let bygones , be bygones گیا وقت پھر ہاتھ آتا نہیں *ga'yā vaq't phir hāth' ā'tā nahīṅ'* PROV. time past is gone for ever گیا ہے سانپ نکل اب لکیر پیٹا کر *ga'yā hai sāṅp' ni'kal ab lakīr' pī'ṭā kar* PH. what- ever has been done cannot be undone

گیارہ *gyā'rah* ADJ. & N.M. eleven گیارھواں *gyā'r-havāṅ* ADJ. eleventh گیارھویں *gyā'rhavīṅ* N.F. eleventh of a month offering on this day for Sunnite saint Abdul Qadir Jilani

گیان *gayān'* (ped. *gyān'*) N.M. (dial.) knowledge wisdom گیان دھیان *gayān' dhayān'* N.F. (dial.) meditation گیان ہونا *gayān' ho'nā* V.T (dial.) acquire spiritual knowledge گیانی *gayā'nī* N.M. (dial.) sage [S]

گیاہ *gayāh'* N.F. grass [P]

گیت *gīt* N.M. song lyric

گیتا *gī'tā* N.F. song of Krishna : a Hindu scripture (dial.) song [S cognate of PREC.]

گیتی *gī'tī* N.F. world گیتی آرا *gī'tī-ā'rā* ADJ. world adorning گیتی افروز *gī'tī-afroz'* ADJ. world-illuminating گیتی نورد *gī'tī-navar'd* N.M. globe-trotter [P]

گیٹ *geṭ* N.M. gate گیٹ کیپر *geṭ'-kīper* N.M. gate-keeper [E]

گیدڑ *gī'daṛ* N.M. (F. گیدڑی *gīd'ṛī*) jackal گیدڑ بھبکی *gī'dar bhab'kī* N.F. (usu. PL.) bullying bluff گیدڑ بھبکیاں دینا *gī'daṛ bhab'- kiyāṅ de'na* V.T. bully

گیدی *gī'dī* N.M. dolt shameless person ADJ. stupid shameless

گیر *gīr* SUF. holding conquering گیری *gī'rī* SUF. holding conquest دار و گیر *dār'o gīr'*, گیر و دار *gī'r-o dār'* N.F. roundup (of culprits etc.) fighting and killing (rare) melle ہنگامۂ دار و گیر *hangā'ma-e dā'r-o gīr'* N.M. fighting and killing (rare) melee گیرائی *gīrā''ī* N.F. hold strength گہرائی و گیرائی *gaihrā''ī-o-gīrā''ī* N.F. depth and hold [P]

گیرو *ge'roo* N.M. red ochre گیروا *ge'ro'ā* ADJ. reddish ; like red ochre

گیڑی *ge'ṛī* N.F. one of several small pieces of wood with which children play 'geriyan'

گیسو *ge'soo* N.M. lock ; tress گیسو بریدہ *ge'soo būrī'-dah* N.F. one with bobbed hair (arch.) shameless woman [P]

گیس[1] *gais'* N.F. gas [E]

گیس[2] *gais* N.M. guess گیس پیپر *gais' pe'par* N.M. guess paper [E]

گیگلا *geg'lā* ADJ. (F. گیگلی *geg'lī*) simple-minded silly , stupid گیگلا پن *geg'lā-pan* N.M. simple mindedness stupidity

کے گیل *(ke) gail'* ADV. (dial.) along with

گیلا *gī'lā* ADJ. (F. گیلی *gī'lī*) wet moist damp گیلا پن *gī'lā pan* N.M. moisture dampness گیلا کرنا *gī'la kar'na* V.T. damp moisten گیلا ہونا *gī'lā ho'na* V.T. be moist گیلی لکڑی *gī'lī lak'ṛī* N.F (fig.) person of impressionable age

گیلری *gail'rī* N.F. gallery [E]

گیلن *gai'lan* N.M. gallon [E]

گیلڑ gai'laṛ N.M. child by the former husband of one's wife

گیں gīn SUF. having ful گینی gī'nī SUF. having fulness [P]

گینا gai'nā ADJ. (F. گینی gai'nī) (of cow, etc.) short and thick (usu. through non-breeding)

گینتی geṅ'tī N.F. pickaxe

گینجنا geṅj'nā N.F. crumple : mash with one's hands

گیند gend N.F. ball گیند بلا gend' bal'lā N.M. ball and bat (rare) cricket گیند دینا gend' de'nā V.T. bowl

گیندا geṅ'dā N.M. marigold

گینڈا gaiṅ'ḍā N.M. rhinoceros

گیہاں gai'hāṅ N.M. world universe [P doublet of جہاں]

گیہوں ge'hooṅ N.M. wheat گیہوں کے ساتھ گھن بھی پس جاتا ہے ge'hooṅ ke sāth ghun bhī pis' jā'tā hai PROV the innocent suffering along with the wicked گیہواں ge'ho'āṅ ADJ. wheaten

ل lām thirtieth letter of Urdu alphabet (equivalent to English l) (in jummal reckoning) 30

لآلی la'ā'lī N.M. (PL. of لولو ★)

لا lā PREF. not un un-;in- less لاابالی lā-ūbā'lī ADJ. careless reckless devil-may-care (attitude) N.M. dare devil careless person لاابالی پن lā-ūbā'lī-pan N.M. carelessness recklessness devil may-care attitude لاالٰہ lā'-ilāh PH. there is no God لاالٰہ الااللہ lā' ilā'ha il'lallāh' PH. there is no God save Allah لاالٰہ الااللہ محمد رسول اللہ lā' ilā'ha il'lallā'ho moḥam'mad ūr rasoo'lūllāh PH. there is no God save Allah and Muhammad is His messenger لابد lā būd ADV. inevitably indispensably لابدی lā bū'dī ADJ. necessary essential inevitable indispensable لاتعداد lā-ta'dād' ADJ. countless ; innumerable لاثانی lā-sā'nī ADJ. unparalleled ; matchless ; incomparable لاجرم lā-ja'ram ADV. definitely : undoubtedly CONJ. doubtless لاجواب lā-javab' ADJ. silenced (by apt reply) لاجواب کر دینا lā-javab' kar de'nā V.T. silence lā-javab' ho jā'nā V.I. silence

لاچار lā-c̲h̲ār' (usual but less correct variant of ناچار nā-c̲h̲ār) ADJ. helpless destitute ADV. of necessity ; perforce inevitably لاچار کرنا lā-c̲h̲ār' kar'nā V.T. render helpless reduce to straits force (to) لاچار ہونا lā-c̲h̲ār' ho'nā V.I. become helpless be disabled forced (to) ; constrained (to) لاچارگی N.F. PL. lā-c̲h̲ār'gī, لاچاری lā-c̲h̲ā'rī N.F. helplessness inability poverty لاحاصل lā-ḥā'sil ADJ. useless ; bootless fruitless unprofitable unavailing unproductive not carried forward : leaving no balance سعی لاحاصل sa''y-e lā ḥā'sil N.M. vain attempt abortive attempt لاحاصلی lā-ḥā'silī N.F. لاحول ولاقوۃ lā-ḥau'la va lā qūv'vah, لاحول lā ḥaul', لاحول ولاقوۃ الا باللہ lā ḥau'la va lā qūv'vatā il'lā-billāh' PH. there is no sway or strength save that of God INT. God forbid to hell with it لاحول بھیجنا (یا پڑھنا) lā-ḥaul' bhej'nā (or paṛh-nā) V.T. curse imprecate spurn لادعویٰ lā-da''vā N.M. relinquishment of claim لادعویٰ لکھنا lā-da''vā likh'nā V.T. relinquish one's claim لادوا lā-davā' ADJ. incurable irremediable لادینی lā-dī'nī ADJ. secular لادینیت lā dīniy'yat N.F. irreligiousness secularism لاریب lā-raib' ADV. (lit.) doubtless ; undoubtedly لازوال lā-zavāl' ADJ everlasting ; eternal لاسلکی lā-sil'kī N.F. & ADJ. wireless لاشعور lā-s̲h̲o'oor' N.M. the subconscious لاشعوری lā-s̲h̲o'oo'rī ADJ. subconscious لاطائل lā-tā''il ADJ. useless ; bootless unprofitable vain (attempt) لاعلاج lā-'ilāj' ADJ. incurable irremediable لاعلم lā-il'm ADJ ignorant unaware لاعلمی lā-il'mī N.F. ignorance unawareness لاعلمی ظاہر کرنا lā-'il'mī zā'hir kar'nā V.T. pretend or plead ignorance لاکلام lā-kalām' ADV. (lit.) doubtless ; undoubtedly positively لامحالہ lā-maḥā'lah ADV. surely ; certainly assuredly ; definitely لامذہب lā-maz'hab ADJ. irreligious secular لامذہبی lā-maz'habī ADJ. irreligious secular لامذہبیت la-maz'habiy'yat N.F. irreligiousness secularism لامکاں lā-makān' ADJ. homeless omnipresent N.M. nowhere utopia Throne of God لاوارث lā-vā'ris N.M. waif ADJ. stray unclaimed (goods or property) (ped.) hairless لاوارثی lā-vā'risī ADJ. unclaimed (property) N.F. being unclaimed لاولد lā va'lad ADJ. is issueless ; childless لاولدی lā va'ladī N.F. (ped. لاولدیت lā-valadiy'yat) being issueless لایزال lā-yazāl' ADJ eternal لایعنی *lā-ya'nī* ADJ. absurd obscene irrelevant لایموت *lā-yamoot'* ADJ. immortal لاینحل *lā-yan'ḥal* ADJ. insoluble abstruse عقدۂ لاینحل *'uq'da-e lā-yan'ḥal* N.M. insoluble difficulty لاینفک *lā-yan'fak* ADJ. inseparable ; indivisible جزوِ لاینفک *juz'v-e lā-yan'fak* N.M. inseparable part [A]

²لا *lā* N.M. stratum ; layer لا بر لا *lā'-bar-lā'* ADV. layer upon layer [P]

لابھ *lābh* N.M. (dial.) gain ; profit لابھ اٹھانا *lābh uṭhā'nā* V.T. (dial.) gain

¹لات *lāt* N.F. leg kick لات مارنا *lāt' mār'nā* V.T. kick ; spurn

²لات *lāt'* N.F. name of an ancient Arab goddess لات و عزیٰ *lāt-o-'uz'zā* names of two goddesses of pagan, Arabs, 'Laat' and 'Uzza'

¹لاٹ *lāṭ* N.F. lord governor chief لاٹ پادری *lāṭ' pād'rī* N.F. bishop [E ~ lord CORR.]

²لاٹ *lāṭ* N.M. lot [E]

³لاٹ *lāṭ*, لاٹھ *lā'ṭh* N.F. pillar tower

لاٹری *lāṭ'rī* N.F. lottery [E]

لاٹھی *lā'ṭhī* N.F. stick club ; cudgel لاٹھی پونگا کرنا *lā'ṭhī pon'gā kar'nā* V.T. fight with clubs لاٹھی ٹیک کے چلنا *lā'ṭhī ṭek' ke chal'nā* V.T. walk with the aid of a stick لاٹھی چلانا *lā'ṭhī chalā'nā* V.T. cudgel سانپ بھی مر جائے لاٹھی بھی نہ ٹوٹے *sānp' bhī mar jā''e lā'ṭhī bhī na too'ṭe* PROV. kill two birds with one stone

لاج *lāj* N.F. modesty bashfulness good name sense of honour لاج آنا (یا لگنا) *lāj' ā'nā* (or *lag'nā*) V.T. be abashed be provoked by the sense of (family, etc.) honour لاج رکھنا *lāj' rakh'nā* V.T. protect the honour (of) live up to the traditions (of) لاج سے مرنا *lāj' se mar'nā*, لاجوں مرنا *lā'jon mar'nā* V.T. feel greatly ashamed لاج کھونا (یا گنوانا) *lāj khonā* (or *ganvā'nā*) V.I. lose all sense of shame

لاجورد *lāj'vard* N.M. armenian stone ; lapis-lazuli azure لاجوردی *lāj'vardī* ADJ. sky-blue , azure [P]

لاجونتی *lāj'vantī* N.F. (dial.) sensitive plant ADJ. (dial.) bashful (woman)

لاحق *lā'ḥiq* ADJ. (usu. of illness) adhering affecting کو لاحق ہونا *ko lā'ḥiq ho'nā* V.I. suffer from ; be ailing from catch (an illness)

لاحقہ *lā'ḥiqah* N.M. suffix [A]

لادنا *lād'nā* V.T load heap (upon) burden (with) لاد چلنا *lād chal'nā* V.I pack up (fig.) die لادی *lā'dī* N.F. washerman's load of clothes لادیا *lā'diyā* N.M. one who loads

لاڈ *lāḍ* N.M. fondling caress affection لاڈ پیار *lāḍ' payār* N.M. fondling caress لاڈ کرنا *lāḍ' kar'nā* V.T. fondle لاڈلا *lāḍ'lā* ADJ. & N.M dear darling pet spoilt child لاڈلی *lāḍ'lī* ADJ. & N.F. dear pet darling spoilt child لاڈو *lāḍ'do* N.F. darling ; favourite (child or wife) spoilt child

لارا لیری *lā'rā lī'rī* N.F. prevarication لارا لیری لگانا *lā'rā lī'rī lagā'nā* V.T. prevaricate

لاروا *lār'vā* N.M. larva [E]

لاری *lā'rī* N.F. bus ; omnibus [~E lorry]

لازم *lā'zim* ADJ. necessary incumbent essential indispensable obligatory intransitive (verb) لازم آنا *lāzim ā'nā* V.I. become necessary be incumbent (on) follow out of necessity لازم جاننا *lā zim jān'nā* V.T. regard as essential consider to be obligatory لازم کرنا *lāzim kar'nā* V.T. make (something) incumbent or obligatory (on) لازم (و) ملزوم *lā'zim(-o-) malzoom'* ADJ. inseparable closely related to each other لازمہ *lā'zimah* N.M. something going along with (another) لازمی *lā'zimī* ADJ. (col.) necessary inevitable [A]

لاسا *lā'sā*, لاسہ *lā'sah* N.M. bird-lime لاسا لگانا *lā'sā lagā'nā* V.T. catch with bird-lime catch kick up a row لاسے پر لگانا *lā' se par lagā'nā* V.T. bring (someone) round

لاش *lāsh* N.F. (lit. also لاشہ *lā'shah* N.M.) dead body corpse کی لاش نکالنا *kī lāsh nikal'nā* V.I. be carried away for burial جوان لاشہ *javān' lā'shah* N.M. مچھمچاتی لاش *machmachā'tī lāsh* N.F. dead body of a youthful person [P]

لاطینی (rare لاتینی) *lātī'nī* N F. & ADJ. Latin

لاغر *lā'ghar* ADJ. thin ; lean , slander لاغری *lā'gharī* N.F. thinless ; leanness ; slenderness [P]

لاف *lāf* N.F. boast ; brag ; bluster لاف زن *lāf'-zan* ADJ. braggart : boastful person لاف زنی *lāf'-za'nī* N.F boasting ; bragging ; blustering لاف زنی کرنا *lāf-za'nī kar'nā*, لاف مارنا *lāf' mār'nā* V.T. boast ; brag ; bluster draw the long bow لاف و گزاف *lā'f-o-gizāf'* N.F. boast ; brag; bluster [P]

¹لاکھ *lākh* N.M. & ADJ. lakh ; lac , hundred thousand ADV. howevermuch لاکھ بسوے *lākh' bis've* ADV. surely ; definitely لاکھ (یا لاکھوں) پر بھاری ہونا *lākh* (or *lākhon par bhā'rī ho'nā* PH.

be very strong be very brave لاکھ جی سے lākh jī se ADV. with all one's heart لاکھ کا گھر خاک کر دینا lākh' kā ghar khāk' kar de'nā PH. reduce (someone) to abject poverty ; ruin a family play drucks and drakes with one s money لاکھوں lā'khoṅ ADJ. lakhs many لاکھ (یا لاکھوں) میں lākh (or lā'khoṅ) meṅ N.M. one in lakh(s) publicly لاکھ پتی lākh'-pa'tī لکھ پتی lakh-pa'tī N.M. & ADJ. millionaire

لاکھ lākh N.F. lac ; sealing-wax لاکھا lā'khā N.M. paint for lips lac, etc. used as lipstick لاکھا جمانا lā'khā jamā'nā V.T. paint the lips red (with lipstick or betel-leaf) لاکھی lā'khī N.F. red colour prepared from lac ADJ. made of lac of the colour of lac

لاگ lāg N.F. rancour grudge enmity connection ; relation love لاگ ڈانٹ lāg' ḍāṅṭ N.F. enmity rancour لاگ رکھنا lāg' rakh'nā V.T. harbour ill-will (against) ; have a grudge (against) لاگ لگنا lāg' lag'nā V.T. fall for بے لاگ be-lāg' ADJ. & N.F. impartial (comment)

لاگت lā'gat N.F. cost expenses , expenditure outlay لاگت آنا lā'gat ā'nā V.I. cost لاگت لگانا lā'gat lagā'nā V.T. spend money (on) ; lay out money [~ لگنا]

لاگو lā'goo N.M. enemy friend ADJ. inimical friendly , attached لاگو ہونا lā'goo ho'nā V.T. be intent (on) love ; like کی جان کا لاگو ہونا kī jān' kā lā'goo ho'nā V.I. resolved on killing or pestering (someone)

لال lāl ADJ red لال انگارہ lāl angā'rah ADJ. red hot flushed with rage لال بجھکڑ lāl-bhujak'kar N.M wiseacre لال بھبوکا lāl bhaboo'kā ADJ. blushed (with rage) لال بیگ lāl'-beg N.M. name of a saint of sweepers لال بیگی lāl'-be'gī, لال بیگیا lāl'-be'giyā N.M. sweeper لال پری lāl'-pa'rī N.F fairy dressed in red (fig.) wine لال پلکا lāl -pal'kā N.M. white-tailed red pigeon لال پیلا ہونا lāl'-pī'lā ho'nā PH. لال پیلی آنکھیں نکالنا lāl'-pī'lī āṅkheṅ nikāl'nā PH. fly into a passion لال خاں کا لکڑا lāl'-khāṅ kā lak'ṛā N.M. a kind of pillory لال ڈورا lāl' ḍo'rā N.M. red tape (usu. PL) red streak (in the eye) لال سوداگر lāl' saudā'gar N.M. petty merchant quickly selling out wares at low profits لال کتاب lāl' kitāb' N.F. (joc.) supposed memoirs of the wiseacre Lal Bujhakkar (joc.) repository of answer to every question (joc.) any red book لال کرتی lāl' kur'tī N.F. British infantry (owing to its red jackets) cantonment لال مرچ lāl' mir'ch N.F chilly لال ہونا lāl' ho'nā V.I. redden fly into a passion لالی lā'lī N.F redness

لال lāl N.M. ruby son favourite child لالوں کا لال lāloṅ kā lāl PH. very dear child لالڑی lāl'ṛī N.F. small ruby small favourite child

لالا lālā ADJ. lustrous , refulgent لولوئے لالا loo' lū''e lālā' N.M. lustrous pearl [A]

لالا lā'lā N.M. slave [P]

لالٹین lāl'ṭain N.F. lantern [~E CORR.]

لالچ lā'lach N.M greed avarice covetousness avidity temptation لالچ دینا lā'lach de'nā V.T. tempt لالچ ہونا lā'lach kar'nā V.I. covet لالچ میں آنا lā'lach meṅ ā'nā V.T. be moved by covetousness لالچی lāl'chī ADJ. greedy ; avaricious covetous

۱ لالہ lā'lah N.M. tulip , poppyflower لالہ رخ lā'lah-rūkh, لالہ رو lā'la roo, لالہ عذار lā'la-'azār ADJ. tulip-cheeked N.M. (fig.) beloved ; sweetheart لالہ زار lā'la zār' N.M. bed of tulip [P]

۲ لالہ lā'lah N.M. Hindu gentleman ADJ. (H. dial.) Mr. لالائن lalā''in N.F. Hindu lad. ADJ. (H. dial.) Mrs.

لآلی la'ā'lī N.M. pearls [A ~ SING لولو]

لالی la'lī N.F. (see under لال ADJ. ★)

لالے پڑنا lā'le paṛ'nā V.I. be hopeless (of) جان کے لالے پڑنا jān' ke lā'le paṛ'nā V.I. (of one's life) be jeopardized

۱ لام lām N.M. name of letter ل lām (fig.) ringlet لام کاف lām' kāf N.F. abusive language لام کاف بکنا (یا پر اترنا) lām' kāf bak'nā (or par u'tarnā) V.T. abuse revile

۲ لام lām N.M. army , armed force لام باندھنا lām bāndh'nā V.I. mobilize line up crowd gather together لام بندی lām'-ban'dī N.F. mobilization ; recruitment

لاما lā'mā N.M. Lama [Tibetan]

لامسہ lā'misah N.F. sense of touch ; sense of feeling tactile sense [A ~ لمس]

لامع lā'me' ADJ. bright ; shining [A ~ لمع]

لان lān N.M. lawn [E]

لانا lā'nā V.T bring produce introduce persuade , win over buy , purchase

لانبا lāṅ'bā ADJ. (dial) (same as لمبا ADJ. ★)

لانڈری *lāṅḍ'rī* N.F. laundry [E]

لانک *lāṅk* N.F. a cereal cut in the straw

لانگنا *lāṅg'nā*, لانگھنا *lāṅgh'nā* V.T. take (something) in a stride لانگاگیر *laṅ'gāgair* N.F. bee-line line of two-way traffic لانگن *laṅ'gan*, لانگھن *lāṅ'ghan* N.F. stride لانگھن میں آنا *lāṅ'ghan meṅ ā'nā* V.I. be in the course of someone's stride

لاوا *lā'vā* N.M. lava [E]

لاون *lā'van* N.M. (dial.) stewed vegetable, etc.

لاہن *lā'han* N.M. brewed stuff

لاہوت *lāhoot'* N.M. world lying beyond space and time mystic stage in which human existence passes into God's [A]

لائبریری *lā'ibre'rī* N.F. library لائبریرین *lā''ibre'-riyan* N.M. librarean [E]

لائحہ *lā''iḥah* N.M. (rare) guide line programme لائحہ عمل *lā''eḥa-e 'a'mal* N.M. programme 'modus operandi' rules of procedure [A ~ لائح illumined]

لائسنس *lā'isans* N.M. licence لائسنسڈ *lā''isansd* لائسنس یافتہ *lā'isans yāf'tah* ADJ. licenced [E]

لائق *lā''iq* ADJ. able ; capable competent qualified worthy suitable کے لائق *ke lā''iq* ADV worth لائق ہونا *lā''iq ho'nā* V.I. be able ; be capable be competent

لائم *lā''im* N.M. reproachful person بلاخوفِ لومتہ لائم *bi-lā' khauf-e lau'mat-e lā''im* ADV. without fearing anyone's reproach [A ~ ملامت]

لائن *lā'in* N.F. line rail track لائن بلاک *lā''in-balak'* N.M. line-block [E]

لاؤ *lā''o* N.M. thick rope

لاوڈ سپیکر *lā''ūḍ sepī'kar* N.M. loud speaker [E]

لاؤلشکر *lā''o lash'kar* N.M. army with camp follower

لاؤنی *lā''onī* N.F. minstrel's song ; song telling a story

لب *lūb*. N.M. (PL. البات *albab*) wisdom (PL. لبوب *lāboob'*) essence لب لباب *lūb'b-e lūbab'* N.M. crux of the question quintessence [A]

لب[1] *lab* N.M. lip edge brime bank ; shore ; coast brow (of hill) لبالب *la'ba-lab* ADV. (fall) to the brim لب بام *lab-e bam'* N.M. & ADV. (at) the roof's corner لب بند ہونا *lab band ho'nā* V.T. be silent لب بستہ *lab-bas'tah* ADJ. with lips sealed ; quiet لب دریا *lab-e daryā'* N.M. & ADV. (on or along) the rever bank or sea-shore لب دوز *lab-doz'* ADJ. sealing the lips very sweet لبریز *lab-rez'* ADJ. brimful ; overflowing لب سوز *lab-soz'* ADJ. piping hot لب شیریں *lab-e shī'rīṅ* N.M. honeyed lips لب کھولنا *lab' khol'nā* V. speak open the mouth لب گور *la'b-e gor'* ADJ. with one foot in the grave لب ہلانا *lab' hilā'nā* V.I. speak ; open the mouth لب و لہجہ *lab-o-laih'jah* N.M. pronunciation intonation tone of voice لبوں پہ جان ہونا *laboṅ pa* (or *pe*) *jān' ho'nā* V.I. be dying [P]

لب[2] *lab* N.M. saliva لب لگانا *lab lagā'nā* V.T. apply saliva [~ PREC.]

لب[3] *lab* N.F. moustache لبیں بڑھنا *la'beṅ baṛh'na* V.I. (of moustache) grow لبیں لینا *labeṅ le'nā* V.T. clip the moustache [~ لب]

لبادہ *labā'dah* N.M. warm cloak [P]

لباڑی *labā'rī*, لباڑیا *labā'riyā* N.M. babbler liar

لباس *libās'* N.M. (PL. البسہ *al'bisah*) clothes : dress ; apparet [A]

لبرل *lib'ral* ADJ. liberal (E)

لبر سبڑ *la'bar sa'baṛ* N.M. silly talk ; nonsense

لبلبا *lab'labā* ADJ. (F. لبلبی *lab'labī*) sticky

لبلبی *lab'labī* N.F. sere ; sear

لبن *la'ban* N.M. (rare) milk [A]

لبنی *lab'nī* N.F. small earthen pot

لبوب *lūboob'* N.M. a kind of sweet medicinal preparation N.M. PL. essences [A ~ SING. لب *lūb*]

لبون *laboon'* (F. OR PL. لبونہ *laboo'nah* milk-yielding حیوانات لبونہ *ḥaivānā't-e laboo'nah*(ped. *ḥaya-*) N.M. PL. mammals [A ~ لبن]

لبھانا *lūbhā'na* V.T. allure charm fascinate لبھاؤ *lūbhā''o* N.M. allurement ; attraction

لبیب *labīb'* ADJ. wise [A ~ لب *lūb*]

لبیرا *labe'ra* N.M., لبیری *labe'rī* N.F. rag لبیریاں لگانا *labe'riyaṅ lagā'nā* V.T. go about in rags

لبیک *labbaik'* INT. (pilgrims' declaration during the Haj) at Thy beck and call N.F. being at someone's service

لپ *lap* N.M. a handful ; as much as both palms joined together will hold لپ بھر *lap' bhar* ADJ. handful

لپا *lap'pa* N.M. brocade lace slap

لپا پتا *li'pa pū'ta* ADJ. plastered with mud لپائی *lipā''ī* N.F. plastering remuneration for it

لپاٹی *lapā'ṭī*, لپاٹیا *lapā'ṭiyā* N.M. babbler liar

لپالپ *la'pa lap'* ADV. full quickly continuously

لپاڈگی *lap'pa dūg'gī* N.F. fight with blows

لپٹ *la'paṭ* N.F. (PL. لپٹیں *lap ṭeṅ* sweet smell flame

لپٹنا *li'paṭnā* V.T. embrace cling (to) stick (to) coil (round) fight ; wrestle pester لپٹ پڑنا (یا جانا) *li'paṭ paṛ'nā* (or *ja'nā*) V.T. embrace wrestle لپٹانا *lipṭa'nā* V.T. embrace enwrap, enfold لپٹنٹ *lipṭaṇṭ* N.F. embrace

لپ جھپ *lap' jhap* N.F. agility

لپ چخنی *lap chakh'nī* N.F. babbler flatterer

لپڑ *lap'par* N.M. slap

لپڑ شپڑ *la'paṛ sha'paṛ* N.F. chatter confused talk mess prevarication

لپڑ لپڑ کرنا *la'paṛ la'paṛ kar'nā* V.T. babble [ONO.]

لپڑی *lūp'ṛī* N.F. poultice (derog.) turban

لپک *la'pak* N.F. (see under لپکنا V.I. ★)

لپسی *lap'sī* ADJ. (of boiled rice) softened overmuch

لپکا *lap'kā* N.M. bad habit excessive fondness for some dish etc., vitiated taste لپکا پڑنا *lap'kā paṛ'nā* V.I. be addicted (to)

لپکنا *la'paknā* V.T. & I. move quickly rush forth ; dart forth (of dog) snap at leap (on) throb (of lightning) flash across لپک *la'pak* N.F. flash leap, bound ; bounce swiftness ; nimbleness لپک جھپک *la'pak jha'pak* N.F. swiftness ; nimbleness ADV. with leaps and bounds ; swiftly ; nimbly لپک کر *la'pak kar* ADV. quickly hurriedly

لپکی *lap'kī* N.F. tacks لپکی بھرنا (یا مارنا) *lap'kī bhar'nā* (or *mār'nā*) V.T. baste

لپنا *lip'nā* V.I. be smeared (with mud) be plastered لپوانا *lipvā'nā* V.T. get smeared with mud get plastered [~ لیپنا]

لپیٹنا *lapeṭ'nā* V.T. fold roll wrap envelope bind ; pack involve ; entangle ; implicate لپیٹ *lapeṭ'* N.F. revolution ; rotation entanglement deception ; fraud لپیٹ جھپیٹ *lapeṭ' jhapeṭ'* N.F. entanglement deception لپیٹ لینا *lapeṭ' le'nā* V.T. roll fold wrap envolve ; entangle لپیٹ میں آنا *lapeṭ meṅ ā'nā* V.I. be involved be entangled .be weaver roll for rolling cloth on [A ~ لپٹنا CAUS.]

لت *lat* N.F. bad habit لت پڑنا *lat' paṛ'nā* V.I. have a bad habit لتیا *lat'yā* N.M. one having a bad habit

لتاڑنا *latāṛ'nā* V.T. rail at reproach take to task trample massage (someone) with one's feet لتاڑ *latāṛ* N.F. rebuke reproach trampling [~ لات]

لت پت *lat' pat* ADJ. besmeared with mud ; bedrabbled

لترا *lūt'rā* N.M. لتری *lūt'rī* N.F. tell-tale back-biter mischief-monger babbler لترا پن *lūt'rā-pan* N.M. backbiting mischief making babbling لتر لتر کرنا *lū'tar kū'tar kar'nā* V.I. babble

لتہ *lūt'tah* N.M. rag cloth (usu. as) کپڑا لتہ *kap'rā lot'tah* N.M. clothes لتے لینا *lat'te le'nā* V.T. take to task revite ; rail at

لتھڑنا *li'thaṛnā* V.I. be bedraggled be besmeared (with mud, etc.) be bedrabbled لتھیڑنا *latheṛ'nā* V.I. bedraggle besmear (with mud, etc.)

لتھوگرافی *li'thogarāfī* N.F. lithorgraphy [E]

لتیا *lat'yā* ADJ. (see under لت N.F.)

لتیانا *latyā'nā* V.T. kick [~ لات]

لٹ *laṭ* N.F. lock ; curl matted hair لٹ دبانا *laṭ' dabā'nā* V.T. capture ; seize لٹورا *laṭoo'rā* N.M. tangled lock لٹوریا *laṭoo'riyā* N.M. man with long locks

لٹاپٹا لٹاؤ لٹس *lū'ṭā pi'ṭā* ADJ. لٹانا *lūṭā'nā* V.T. لٹاؤ *lūṭā''oo* ADJ. لٹس *lūṭ'pas* N.F. (see under ★)

لٹانا *liṭā'nā*, لٹا دینا *liṭā' de'nā* V.T. lay (someone or something) down [~ لیٹنا CAUS.]

لٹ پٹ *laṭ' paṭ* ADJ. topsy-turvy N.M. dandy drunkard

لپٹانا *laṭpaṭā'na* V.I. have a temptation be tempted (to)

لٹائی *lūṭā''i* N.F. roller for kite string

لٹریچر *liṭre'char* N.M. literature لٹریری *liṭre'rī* ADJ. literary [E]

لٹس *lūṭ'ṭas* N.F. (see under لٹنا V.I.)

لٹکنا *la'ṭakna* V.I. hang swing dangle be pending ; hang fire لٹک *la'ṭak* N.F. coquetry coquetish or affected gait fall (of clothes jewellery, etc.) ADJ. coquetish (gait) لٹک کر چلنا *la'ṭak kar chal'na* V.I. coquetishly لٹکا *laṭ'kā* N.M. trick charm incantation magic way out simple remedy ; quack's remedy لٹکانا *laṭkā'nā* V.T. hang keep pending لٹکاو *laṭkā''o* N.M. fall (of clothes, etc.) لٹکن *laṭ'kan* N.M. nose-ring eardrop pendant (rare) pendulum anything handing down

لٹنا *lūṭ'na* V.I. be robbed : be plundered be robbed of be squandered be ruined , be undone لٹا پٹا *lu'ṭā pi'ṭā* ADJ. robbed and beaten undone لٹانا *luṭā'nā*, لٹوانا *luṭvā'na* V.T. spend lavishly squander ; waste لٹاؤ *lūṭā''oo* N.M. prodigal : spendthrift لٹ جانا *lūṭ' jā'nā* V.I. be robbed be plundered be undone لٹس *lūṭ'ṭas* N.F. plunder embezzlement ; misappropriation لٹس مچانا *luṭ ṭas machā'nā* V.T. plunder; rob لٹس مچنا *lūṭ'ṭas mach'na* V.I. be robbed ; be plundered be misappropriated

لٹو *laṭ'ṭoo* N.M. top plummet ADJ. enamoured (only in) پر لٹو ہو جانا *par laṭ'ṭoo ho jā'nā* V.T. fall in love with ; be enamoured (of)

لٹوانا *luṭvā'nā* V.T. (see under لٹنا V.I. ★)

لٹھ *laṭh* N.M. stick , club cudgel لٹھ باز *laṭh-bāz'* N.M. & ADJ. (one) fighting لٹھ بازی *laṭh'-bā'zī* N.F. cudgelling لٹھ مار *laṭh'-mār'* N.M. & ADJ. speak tactlessly لٹھ مارنا *laṭh' mār'nā* V.T. club (also لٹھ سا مار دینا *laṭh' sā mār de'nā*) speak tactlessly گنوار کا لٹھ *ganvār' kā laṭh* N.M. (fig.) dangerous fool. لٹھا *laṭ'ṭhā* N.M. beam (rare) railway sleeper لٹھم لٹھا *laṭ ṭham laṭ'ṭhā* N.M. & ADV. fight with sticks لٹھیا *laṭh'yā* N.F. short stick ; cudgel لٹھیت *laṭhait'* N.M. one skilled in cudgelling or clubbing لٹھیتی *laṭhe'tī* N.F. fight with sticks this as an art with a cudge)

لٹھا *laṭ'ṭhā* N.M. longcloth (see under PREC. ★)

لٹیا *lūṭ'yā* N.M. child's spouted metallic feeder spoutless metallic vessel لٹیا ڈبونا *lūṭ'yā ḍubo'nā* V.T. ruin (oneself, etc.) wreck (one's, etc.) plans cut a sorry figure لٹیا ڈوبنا *lūṭ'yā doob'nā* V.I. be ruined be wrecked come to nought [~ لوٹا DIM.]

لٹیرا *luṭe'rā* N.M. robber : plunderer gangster highwayman footpad swindler one selling his wares at much higher than market rates ; trader who overcharges [~ لوٹنا]

لجاجت *lajā'jat* N.F. entreaty importunity adulation لجاجت کرنا *lajā'jat kar'nā* V.I. entreat

لجانا *lajā'nā* V.T. be modest be bashful [~ لاج]

لجلجا *lij'lijā* ADJ. (F. لجلجی *lij'lijī*) clammy

لجہ *lujjah* N.M. (PL. لجج *lū'jaj*) midstream vast expanse of water [A]

لچا *luch'chā* N.M. rake ; libertine vagabond hooligan wicked person ADJ. profligate wicked لچی *luch'chī* N.F. harlot ; prostitute wanton woman ADJ. loose (woman) لچاپن *luch'chā-pan*, لچپن *lūch'-pan* N.M. wantoness ; profligacy wickedness hooliganism

لچر *la'char* ADJ. foolish ; silly

لچک *lachak* N.F. elasticity flexibility resilience buoyancy adaptability لچکا *lach'kā* N.M. light brocade lace twist لچک آنا *la'chak ā'nā* V.I. bend لچک دار *la'chak-dār* ADJ. elastic flexible resilient buoyant adaptable لچکیلا *lachkī'la* ADJ. elastic flexible resilient buoyant لچکنا *la'chakna* V.I. bend be elastic لچکانا *lachkā'nā* VT. bend strain move

لچھا *lach'chhā* N.M. skein long thin pieces of onion, etc.) spiralling anklet set of glass banlges لچھے دار *lach'chhe-dār* ADJ. long and involved (talk, etc.)

لچھمی *lachh'mī*, لکشمی *laksh'mī* N.F (dial.) Hindu goddess of wealth wealth prosperity daughter daughter-in-law لچھمی گھر میں آنا *lachh'mī ghar' meṅ ā'nā* V.I. live in prosperity be blessed with a fortunate daughter-in-law

لچھن *lach'chhan* N.M. PL, signs (of depravity) لچھن پکڑنا (یا سیکھنا) *lach'chhan pa'karnā* (or *sikh'nā*) V.I. learn (depraved) manners degenerate (into)

لچئی *lŭchai''ī* N.F. soft thin fried loaf

لچی *lŭch'chī* N.F. & ADJ. (see under لچا *lŭch'cha* N.M. & ADJ. ★)

لحاظ *lehāz'* N.M. regard deference respect honour modesty shame لحاظ اٹھا دینا *lehāz' uṭhā de'na* V.I. abandon shame ; fling all modesty to the winds لحاظ کرنا *lehāz' kar'na* V.T. consider have regard (for) pay respect (to) لحاظ نہ کرنا *lehāz' na kar'nā* V.I. pay no attention (to) ; disregard lose all sense of shame [A cognate with لحظہ]

لحاف *lehāf'* N.M. quilt [A]

لحد *lai'had* (ped. *lah'd*) N.F. niche in side of grave wherein the corpse is placed (fig.) grave [A]

لحظہ *laihzah* (ped. *lah-*) N.M. moment twinkling of an eye لحظہ بہ لحظہ *laih'za ba-laih'zah* ADV. every moment : minute by minute لحظہ بھر *laih'zah bhar* ADV. for a moment [A cognate with لحاظ]

لحم *lah'm* N.M. PL. لحوم *lŭhoom'* (rare) flesh meat لحیم *lahīm'* ADJ. plump ; corpulent [A]

لحن *laih'n* (or ped. *lah'n*) N.M. (PL. الحان *al'hān'*) melody modulation لحن داؤدی *laih'n-e dā''oo'dī* N.M. (fig.) very sweet voice [A]

لخت *lakh't* N.M. piece ; bit لخت جگر *lakh't-e ji'gar* N.M. (one's) own child لخت لخت *lakh't lakh't* ADJ. torn to pieces لختے *lakh'te* ADV. a little ; somewhat [P]

لخ لخ *lakh' lakh* ADJ. weak , feeble thin : lean لخ لخ کرنا *lakh' lakh kar'nā* لخلخانا *lakh-lakhā'nā* V.I. pant from thirst or hunger be emaciated

لخلخہ *lakh'lakhah* N.M. burning incense used for medicinal purposes

لدنا *lad'na*, لد جانا *lad' ja'nā* V.I. be loaded ; be laden (of days) pass وہ دن لد گئے جب خلیل خاں فاختہ اڑایا کرتے تھے *voh din lad' ga''e jab khalīl' khān fākh'tah uṛā'ya kar'te the* PROV. gone is the goose that lay the golden eggs لدا پھندا *la'dā phan'dā*, ADJ. (F. لدی پھندی *la'dī phan'dī*) packed and loaded لدا لد *la'da-lad* N.F. thud of fruit falling or cargo being loaded لدانا *ladā'na*, لدوانا *ladvā'na* V.T. cause to load لداڑا *ladā'ṛā*, لداؤ *ladā''o* N.M. load , burden cargo لداؤ کی چھت *ladā''o kī chhat* N.F. vaulted roof لدو *lad'doo* ADJ. fit to carry a burden pack animal ; beast of burden

لدنی *ladŭn'nī* ADJ inspired : God-given علم لدنی *'il'm-e ladŭn'nī* N.M. inspired knowledge [A ~ لدن from ; near]

لدھڑ *lad'dhar* ADJ heavy unseemly ; ungainly

لڈو *lad'doo* N.M. well-known sweetmeat , sweet ball ; 'laddu' any sweet thing rolled into a ball لڈو کھانا *lad'doo khā'nā* V.I. be feasted thus (on an occasion) لڈو کھلانا *lad'doo khilā'nā* V.I. feast (someone) usu. with 'laddus' at one's success or as a bribe)

لذت *laz'zat* N.F. (PL. لذائذ *lazā''iz*, لذات *laz'zāt*) pleasure joy taste flavour deliciousness لذت اٹھانا *laz'zat uṭhā'nā* V.I. enjoy لذت پرست *laz'zat paras't* N.M. hedonist لذت پرستانہ *laz'zat parastā'nah* ADJ. hedonistic لذت پرستی *laz'zat-paras'tī* N.F. hedonism لذت پسند *laz'-zat pasand'* ADJ. & N.M. epicurean لذت پسندانہ *laz'zat pasandā'nah* ADJ. epicurean لذت پسندی *laz'zat pasan'dī* N.F. epicureanism لذت نفسانی *laz'zat-e nafsā'nī* N.F. sensualism carnal pleasure لذت یاب *laz'zat yāb* ADJ. enjoying delighted لذت یاب ہونا *laz'zat-yāb ho'nā* V.I. enjoy taste

لذیذ *lazīz'* ADJ. tasteful ; delicious [A ~ PREC.]

لر *lur* N.M. fool bumpkin [P]

لرزنا *la'raznā*, لرز جانا *la'raz jā'nā* V.I. shake shiver ; tremble لرزاں *lar'zāṅ* ADJ. shaking ; shivering trembling ; tremulous fearing لرزانا *larzā'na* V.T. cause to quiver [~ P لرزیدن]

لرزش *lar'zish* N.F. tremble tremulousness tremour [~ P لرزیدن]

لرزہ *lar'zah* N.M. tremor quake shivering تپ لرزہ *ta'p-e lar'zah* N.F. ague [~ P لرزیدن]

لڑ *laṛ* N.F strand (of rope) لڑا *la'ṛa* SUF. stringed

لڑاکا *laṛā'kā* ADJ. (always uninflected) quarrelsome

لڑانا *laṛā'nā* V.T cause to fight lead to battle [~ لڑنا CAUS.]

لڑائی *laṛā''ī* N.F battle war fight ; fighting quarrel strained relations لڑائی بڑھانا ، لڑائی باندھنا *laṛā''ī bāndh'nā* V.T. make a quarrel *laṛā''ī baṛhā'nā* V.T. fan a fire put a stop to fighting لڑائی بھڑائی *laṛā''ī bhiṛā''ī* N.F. quarrel لڑائی بھڑائی پر خاک ڈالنا *laṛā''ī bhiṛā''ī par khāk ḍāl'nā* V.T bury the hatchet لڑائی بھڑائی پلے باندھنا *laṛā''ī bhiṛā''ī pal'le bāndh'nā* V.T. stir up frequent tiffs لڑائی ٹھاننا *laṛā''ī ṭhān'na* V.T. declare war (on or upon) fight (it) out لڑائی کا سامان *laṛā''ī kā sāmān'* N.M. arms and ammunition cause of quarrel لڑائی کا گھر *laṛā''ī ka ghar* N.M. hotbed of quarrels quarrel-provoking (person, etc.) لڑائی کا نعرہ ، لڑائی کا گیت *laṛā''ī kā gīt'* N.M. war-song lara''i ka na''rah N.M. war cry war slogan لڑائی کرنا lara''i kar'na V.T. quarrel wrangle fight give battle (to) لڑائی لڑنا lara''i lar'na V.T. fight it out (with) wage a war لڑائی لینا lara''i le'na V.I. provoke quarrel invite war لڑائی مول لینا lara''i mol' le'na V.I. pick up a quarrel ; involve oneself in trouble لڑائی ہونا lara''i ho'na V.I. have a quarrel be at war (of war) be waged

لڑبڑانا lar bara'na V.I. stutter speak falteringly [ONO.]

لڑھانا lurha'na V.T. (same as لنڈھانا V.T. ★)

لڑکا lar'ka N.M. boy lad son ; child ADJ. inexperienced : green لڑکا بالا lar'ka ba'la N.M. a mere child لڑکے بالے lar'ke ba'le N.M. PL. children boys (one's family) لڑکے والے lar'ke-va'le N.M. PL. bridegroom's people لڑکپن larak'pan N.M. boyhood childishness لڑکورا larko'ra N.M., لڑکوری larko ri N.F. one blessed with a son لڑکوں کا کھیل lar'kon ka khel' N.M. child's play heartless pursuit لڑکی lar'ki N.F. girl; lass daughter لڑکی والے lar'ki va'le N.M. PL bride's people

لڑکھڑانا larkhara'na V.I. stagger reel زبان لڑکھڑانا zaban larkhara'na V.I. falter in speech

لڑکی lar'ki N.F. (see under لڑکا N.M. ★)

لڑنا lar'na V.I. fight give battle (to) go to war wrangle clash (with) contend (with) struggle against wrestle (with) لڑ پڑنا lar par'na V.I. fall out with لڑ مرنا lar mar'na V.I. fight to death fight it out between themselves لڑنا بھڑنا lar'na bhir'na, لڑنا جھگڑنا lar'na jha'garna V.I. fight wrangle quarrel لڑنے مرنے پر اتر آنا lar'ne mar'ne par utar' a'na V.I. decide to fight it out لڑنے مرنے والا lar'ne mar'ne va'la N.M. desperate fighter لڑنت laran't' N.F. fighting wrestling لڑنتیا laran'tiya wrestling fighting N.M. wrestler

لڑھکنا lu'rhakna V.I. roll down slip slide fall down turn turtle die لڑھکنی lurh'kani N.F. somersault لڑھکنی کھانا lurh'kani kha'na V.I. turn a somersault لڑھکانا lurh'kana V.T. cause to roll down ,

لڑی la'ri N.F. string

لزوجت luzoojat N.F. glutinosity ; viscosity [A]

لزوم luzoom' N.M. necessity ; compulsion adherence transitideness

لس las N.M. being sticky ; viscosity لس دار las'-dar ADJ. sticky ; viscous لسلسا las'lasa ADJ. (F. لسلسی las'lasi) viscous ; adhesive لسلسانا laslasa'na V.T. be viscous : be sticky

لسان lisan N.F. (PL. السنہ al'sinah) tongue language voice لسان العصر lisa'n-ul-'as'r N.M. voice of the times honorific title of the Urdu poet Akbar لسان الغیب lisa'n-ul-ghaib' N.F. oracle ; voice of prophecy honorific title of the Persian poet Hafiz لسان lassan' N.M. & ADJ. eloquent (person) facile (person) لسانی lisa'ni ADJ. lingual لسانی lassani, لسانیت lassaniy'yat N.F. eloquence felicity of phrase [A]

لسانیات lisaniyyat' N.F. linguistics لسانیاتی lisaniyya'ti ADJ. linguistic [A ~ PREC.]

لسلسا las'lasa ADJ. (see under لس N.M. ★)

لسن las'san N.M. (same as لہسن N.M. ★)

لسوڑا lisoora N.M. glutinous berry used medicinally

لسی las'si N.F. diluted curds curds or milk . 'lassi'

لشتم پشتم lash'tam pash'tam, لشٹم پشٹم lash'tam pash'tam ADV. somehow or other

لشکارنا lashkar'na V.T. tallyho لشکار lash'kar N.F. tallyho

لشکر lash'kar N.M. army armed force crowd ; throng لشکر جرار lash'kar-e jarrar' N.M. strong army لشکر کشی lash'kar-ka'shi N.F. invasion, inroad ; incursion پر لشکر کشی کرنا par lash'kar-ka'shi kar'na V.I. invade لشکرگاہ lash'kar-gah' N.M. camp ; camping ground لشکری lash'kari N.M. (arch.) soldier ADJ. of the army military [P]

لطافت lata'fat N.F. fineness softness pleasantness elegance exquisiteness subtlety [A]

لطائف lata''if N.M. jokes amedotes لطائف الحیل lata''if-ul hi'yal N.M. PL. subtle excuses لطائف و ظرائف lata''if-o-zara''if N.M. PL. jokes and witticisms [A ~ SING. لطیفہ]

لطف lut'f N.M. (PL. الطاف altaf') kindness favour benignity grace pleasure enjoyment taste ; relish لطف آنا lu'f a'na V.I. enjoy find (something) pleasant لطف اٹھانا lut'f utha'na V.I. enjoy لطف و کرم lut'f-o-ka'ram N.M favour and grace لطف یہ ہے کہ lut'f yeh hai (ke) PH. it is strange that ; what is interesting is that [A]

لطمہ lat'mah N.M. (PL. لطمات latamat') slap buffet (of billows, etc.) لطمہ موج lat'ma-e mauj' N.M. buffet (of a billow)

لطیف latif' ADJ. fine rarified light delicate elegant exquisite cheerful ; pleasant kind gentle tender لطیف طبع *latīf'-tab'* ADJ. of gentle disposition of cheerful spirit لطیف غذا *latīf'-ghiza* N.F. light food [A ~ لطافت]

لطیفہ *latī'fah* N.M. (PL. لطائف *latā''if*) joke ; jest pleasantry witticism 'bon mot' anecdote لطیفہ چھوڑنا *latī'fah chhor'nā* V.T. tell a new tale لطیفہ گو *latī'fah-go* N.M. wit, witty person factious person لطیفہ گوئی *latī'fa-go''ī* N.F. indulging in witticisms telling anecdotes [A]

لعاب *lo'āb* N.M. saliva viscous extraction لعابدار *lo'āb-dār* ADJ. viscous [A]

لعان *le'an'* N.M. mutual cursing (by a couple in a law-court in a case of adultery) [A ~ لعنت]

لعب *la''ib* N.M. play sport لہو ولعب *lah'v-o la''ib* N.M. play playfulness

لعبت *lo''bat* N.F. doll puppet لعبت بازی *lo''bat-bā'zī* N.F. puppet show playing with dolls [A ~ PREC.]

لعل *la''l* N.M. ruby لعل اگلنا *la''l u'galnā* V.I. cast up rubies (fig.) peak well (iron.) use abusive language لعل بدخشاں (یا یمن) *la''l badakhshāň'* (or *ya'man*) N.M. high-quality ruby from Badakhshan (or Yemen) لعل لب *la''l-e lab* N.M. ruby lips ; lips red like ruby لعل لگے ہونا *men la''l la'ge ho'nā* V.I. (iron.) be of valuably characteristics لعلیں *la''līn* ADJ. ruby-red red [P]

لعن *la''n* N.F. imprecation curse لعن طعن *la''n ta''n* N.F. taunts and curses reproof لعن طعن کرنا *la''n ta''n kar'nā* V.T. reprove ; rebuke لعن طعن ہونا *la'n ta'n ho'na* V.T. be taunted [P]

لعنت *la''nat* N.F. curse ; anathema execration imprecation reproach ; rebuke disgrace لعنت بھیجنا (یا کرنا) *la''nat bhej'nā* (or *kar'nā*) V.T. curse imprecate renounce abjure ; renounce لعنت کا طوق *la''nat kā lauq* N.M. ignominy لعنت کا مارا *la''nat kā mā'ra* ADJ. accursed لعنت کی روٹی *la''nat kī ro'ṭī* N.F. disgraceful life of a hanger on لعنت ملامت *la''nat malā'mat* N.F. reproach admonition لعنت ملامت کرنا *la''nat malā'mat kar'na* V. reproach ; rebuke لعنتی *la''natī* لعین *la'īn'* ADJ. excerable accursed; cursed cussed [A ~ لعن]

لعوق *la'ooq'* N.M. electuary [A]

لعین *la'īn'* ADJ. (see under لعنت N.F. ★)

لغات *lughāt* N.M. dictionary ; lexicon N.M PL. (ped.) words (rare) dialects [A ~ SING. لغت]

لغایت *li-ghā'yat* ADV. up to ; to the end of [A - ل to + غایت end]

لغت *lu'ghat* N.M. dictionary ; lexicon (pec.) word (rare) dialect لغت تراشنا *lu'ghat tarash'na* V.I. coin a word لغت جھاڑنا (یا چھانٹنا) *lu'ghat jhār'na* (or *chhāṅṭ'na*) V.T. use high-falutin language لغت شناس *lu'ghat-shinās'* N.M. philologist لغوی *lugh'vī* (ped. *lu'gha'vī*) ADJ. literal ; verbal لغوی معنی *lugh'vī ma''nī* N.M. literal meaning ; verbal sense [A]

لغز *lugh'z* N.F. riddle [P]

لغزش *lagh'zish* N.F. slip faux pas . false step going astray لغزش آنا *lagh'zish ā'na* V.I. slip لغزش کھانا (یا ہونا) *lagh'zish khā'nā* (or *ho'nā*) V.I. slip take false step [P ~ لغزیدن]

لغو *lagh'v* ADJ. absurd INT. nonsense لغویت *laghv-yat* N.F. (PL. لغویات *laghviyyat'*) absurdity, foolishness

لف *laf* ADJ. enclosed لف ونشر *laf'f-o-nash'r* N.M. involution and evolution ; figure of speech in which a series of epithets or predicates follows a series of subjects لف ونشر مرتب *laf'f-o-nash'r-e murat'tab* N.M. such parallel series لف ونشر غیر مرتب *laf'f-o-nash'r-e ghair'-murat'tab* N.M. such disjointed series [A]

لفاظ *laffāz'* ADJ. loquacious prolix, verbose voluble facile eloquent لفاظی *laffā'zī* N.F. loquacity prolixity verbosity volubility eloquence [A ~ لفظ]

لفافہ *lifā'fah* N M. envelope cover wrapper outward show لفافہ بنا کر رکھنا *lifā'fah banā' kar rakh'nā* V.I. put up a false show لفافہ بنانا *lifā'fah banā'nā* V.T. make an envelope لفافہ کھل جانا *lifā'fah khul' jā'nā* V.I. be exposed ; be unmasked (of secret) be let out [A ~ لف]

لفافیا *lifā'fiyā* ADJ. slender fragil insubstantial [~ PREC.]

لفٹ *lif'ṭ* N.F. lift لفٹی *lif'ṭī* N.F. lifty, women's shoe with sole on level (rather than below heel [E]

لیفٹ *laif'ṭ* (or *lef'ṭ*) N.M., ADJ. & ADV. left [E]

لفظ *laf'z* N.M. word لفظ بہ لفظ *laf'z ba-laf'z* ADV. word by word, verbatim) لفظاً *laf'zan* ADJ. literal literally لفظی *laf'zī* ADJ. verbal ; literal لفظی بحث *laf'zī bah's* N.F. a wordy discussion لفظی ترجمہ *laf'zī tar'jamah* N.M. literal translation or rendering لفظی معنی *laf'zī ma''nī* N.M. literal meaning

لفنگا *lafan'gā* N.M. hoo ligan ; hoodlum bad character لفنگاپن *lafan'gā-pan* N.M. hooliganism

لقا *liqa'* N.F. meeting ; seeing someone ; encountering some one [A]

لقا *laqā'* N.F. face ; countenance مہ (یا ماہ) لقا *mah'* (or *māh'*)-*la'qā* ADJ. & N.M. with a face as lovely as the moon (fig.) beloved ; sweetheart [P]

لقا *laqā'* N.M. name of a lengendary character with his beard stringed with pearls لقا کی ڈاڑھی *laqā' kī ḍā'ṛhī* N.F. such pearly beard [P]

لقا *laq qā* N.M. fan-tailed pigeon

لقات *laq'qāt* ADJ. (dial.) gaunt

لقب *la'qab* N.M. (PL. القاب *alqāb'*) appellation [A]

لقطہ *lūq'tah* N.M. unclaimed stuff [A]

لقلق (or لق لق) *laq' laq* N.M. stork لقلقہ *laq'-laqah* N.F. female stork N.M. stork's cry

لقمان *lūqmān* N.M. name of a wise godly Semite sometime identified with Aesop ; he is supposed to have been a great physician Aesop very wise man وہم کی دوا لقمان کے پاس بھی نہیں *vaih'm kī dava' lūqmān' ke pās' bhī na'hīn* PROV. nobody can cure a fool's worries [A ~ H]

لقمہ *lūq'mah* N.M. morsel mouthful (of) لقمہ اجل ہونا *lūq'ma-e a'jal ho'nā* V.I. die ; go into the jaws of death لقمۂ تر *lūq'ma-e tar* تر لقمہ *tar' lūq'mah* N.M. choice morsel morsel of rich food (fig.) bribe لقمہ دینا *lūq'mah de'nā* V.T prompt ایک ہی لقمہ کرنا *ek' hī lūq'mah kar'nā* V.T. make a mouthful of swallow ; gulp down [A]

لقندرا *lūqand'rā* لقہ *lūq'qah* N.M. rogue ; scoundrel rake

لق و دق *la'q-o-daq'* (ped. *laq'q-o-daq'*) ADJ. desolate (land) ; howling (wilderness [A]

لقوہ *laq'vah* N.M. facial paralysis [A]

لقہ *lūq'qah* N.M. (same as لقندرا N.M. ★)

لک *lūk'* N.M. coaltar paint

لکاعہ *lakā''ah* N.F. wanton woman [A]

لکچر *laik'char* N.M. lecture لکچرار *laikcharār'* N.M. lecturer لکچراری *laikchara'rī* N.F. lectureship [E]

لکد *la'kad* N.F. kick لکد زنی *la'kad-za'nī*, لکد کوب *la'kad-kob* N.F. kicking [P]

لکڑی *lak'rī* N.F. wood timber fuel stick ; staff club ; cudgel cudgelling as an art لکڑی پھینکنا *lak'rī phenk'nā* V.T. cudgelling لکڑی لگانا *lak'rī lagā'nā* V.T. (vul.) (of male) perform the sexual act ; fuck لکڑ *lak'kar*, لکڑا *lak'ṛa* N.M. log PREF. wood لکڑہارا *lak'kar ha'rā* N.M. wood-cutter

لکشمی *lak'shmī* N.F. (same as لچھمی N.F. ★)

لکنا *lūk'nā* V.I. hide (of woman) not to appear (before) لکونا *luko'na* V.T. hide a girl thus

لکنت *lūk'nat* N.F. stammer ; lisp زبان میں لکنت ہونا *zabān' men lūk'nat ho'nā* V.I. stammer ; stutter ; lisp [A]

لکہ *lūk'kah* N.M. speck (of cloud) لکۂ ابر *lūk'ka-e ab'r* N.M. a speck of a cloud

لکھ *lakh* PREF. a hundred thousand لکھ پتی *lakh'-pa'tī* ADJ. millionaire لکھپیڑا *lakh-pe'ṛā* ADJ. orchard with a very large number of trees لکھ لٹ *lakh-lūṭ* ADJ. prodigal لکھوکھا *lakhookh'hā* N.M. PL. lakhs [~ لاکھ]

لکھنا *likh'nā* V.T. write draft compose register record enter ; make an entry copy take down لکھنا پڑھنا *likh'nā paṛh'nā* V.I. read and write rective education N.M. education لکھا (یا لکھنا) *likhā'* (or *lik'khnā*) N.M. fate lot لکھا پڑھا *lik'khā pa'ṛhā* ADJ. educated (person) لکھا پڑھی *lik'khā par'hī* N.F. written agreemnt قسمت کا لکھا *qis'mat kā lik'khā* PH. one's destined portion (قسمت کا) لکھا پورا کرنا (*qis'mat kā*) *lik'khā poo'rā kar'nā* PH. pass one's days in hardship ; suffer what fate has ordained لکھانا *likhā'nā*, لکھوانا *likhvā'na* V.T. cause to write have something recorded dictate لکھائی *likhā''ī*, لکھاوٹ *likhā'vaṭ* N.F. writing hand writing for writing remuneration لکھائی پڑھائی *likhā''ī parhā''ī* N.F. education لکھت *li'khat* N.F. (arch.) inditing لکھت پڑھت *li'khat pa'ṛhat* N.F. (arch.) inditing لکھت پڑھت ہونا *li'khat pa'ṛhat ho'nā* V.I. be indited ; be reduced to writing لکھے موسیٰ پڑھے خدا *lik'khe moo'sā pa'ṛhe khūdā'* PH. illegible hand لکھے نہ پڑھے نام محمد فاضل *lik'khe na pa'ṛhe nām muham'mad fā'zil* PH. a fool parading as a learned man

لکیر *lakīr'* N.F. line lineament streak لکیر پیٹنا *lakīr' pīṭ'nā*, لکیر کا فقیر *lakīr' kā faqīr ho'nā* PH. follow the beaten path لکیر کھینچنا *lakīr' khench'nā* V.T. rule draw a line fix a boundary strike out put a mark (under a word) ; underline لکیرنا *lakīr'nā* V.T. draw a line rule underline

لگ *lag* ADV. (arch. or dial.) till

لگا *lag'ga* N.M. similarity equality attachment pole for impelling a boat long bamboo **لگا سگا** *lag'gā sag'gā* N.M. attachment; intimacy **لگا کھانا** *lag'ga khā'nā* V.T. be comparable (with)

لگام *lagām* N.F bridle rein **لگام دینا (یا چڑھانا)** *lagām' de'na* (or *charhā'nā*) V.T. bridle check ; control **لگام ڈھیلی چھوڑنا** *lagām' dhī'li chhor'nā* V.T.

لگان *lagān'* N.M. land revenue (economic) rent

لگانا *lagā'nā* V.T. join attach put set arrange ; put in order apply engage employ busy fix (price) spend (on) include shoves in scandalize ; bring (accusation against) plant **لگانا بجھانا** *lagā'nā b jhn'nā* V.T. to sow dissension ; to excite quarrels **لگا بندھا** *la'gā ban'dhā* ADJ. appointed fixed obedient **لگاتار** *la'gā-tār'* continuous incessant successive ADV. constantly continuously incessantly ; uninterruptedly successively **لگا تو تیر نہیں تو تکا** *la'ga to tīr' na'hīn to tuk'kā* PROV. if it hits the mark, well and good; it not, we do not spand to lose **لگا دینا** *lagā' de'nā* V.T. fix (someone) up put set instal **لگا رہنا** *la'gā raih'nā* V.I. continue (doing) be engaged (in) persevere (in) stick (to) lie (in ambush) **لگا لگایا** *la'ga lagā'yā* ADJ. settled fixed in stalled **لگا لینا، راہ پر لگا لینا** *la'gā le'nā, rāh' par lagā' lā'nā* V.T. bring (someone) round **لگانا بجھانا** *lagā'nā b jhā'nā* V.T. sow seeds of dissension **لگاوٹ** *lagā'vaṭ* N.F. connection inclination attachment affection coquetry **لگاوٹ دکھانا (یا کرنا)** *lagā'vaṭ dikhā'nā* (or *kar'nā*) V.I. show love **لگاوٹ کی باتیں** *lagā'vaṭ kī bā'ten* N.M. coquetry seductive ways **لگاوٹ کی باتیں کرنا** *lagā'vaṭ kī bā'ten kar'nā* V.I. speak or act coquetishly **لگاؤ** *lagā''o* N.M. connection inclination attachment affection *la'ga hū''ā* ADJ. fixed appointed ADV. busy ; engaged near ; close-by **لگائی بجھائی** *lagā''ī b jhā''ī* N.F. (dial **لگائی لتری** *lagā''ī lut'rī*) backbiting mischief-making **لگائی بجھائی کرنا** *lagā''ī bujhā''ī kar'nā* V.I. backbite mischief making **لگائے رکھنا** *lagā''e rakh'nā* V.T. keep (someone) employed keep (someone) busy or occupied keep (someone) close to **لگتا ہوا** *lag'tā hū''ā* ADJ. continuous piercing or trenchant **لگتی کہنا** *lag'tī kaih'nā* V.I. say acceptable words speak trenchant words **لگ چلنا** *lag' chal'nā* V.T go along with **لگے ہاتھوں** *la'ge hā'thon* ADV. in passing by the way **لگنت** *lagant'* N.F. copulation **لگو بندھو** *lag'goo ban'dhoo* N.M. PH. (col.) friends **لگوا** *lag'vā*, **لگواڑ** *lagvār'* ADJ. selfish person **لگن** *la'gan* N.F. love enthusiasm ; devotion N.M. (dial.) moment (of) rising of a sign of the zodiac **لگن دھرنا** *la'gan dhar'nā* V.T. (H. dial.) fix a date for marriage **لگن لگنا** *la'gan lag'nā* V.T. fall in love (with) be enthusiastic (about) **لگنا** *lag'nā* V.T. & I. be affixed (to) be appended (to) be attached (to) be connected (with) be applied (to) be consumed (in) be caught (by disease) be hurt ; be hit come into contact (with) take root come into contact (with) fixed up have effect be soiled (by) be contiguous (to) fuck : (of male) copulate (of tree) be planted bear (fruit) (of money be spent on be invested (in) be a relation (of) (of eye) be closed with sleep (of boat) touch the shore (of door, etc.) be closed (of things) be set (of hunger or cold) be felt (of mind) feel interest (in) rot be staked incur (blame) V. AUX. begin to do, etc.) **لگوانا** *lagvā'nā* V.T. cause to be applied ; cause to apply submit to sexual act **لگی** *la'gī* N.F. love ; passion **لگی بری ہوتی ہے** *la'gī bū'rī ho'tī hai* PH. love is blind passions are irrestible **لگی کو بجھانا** *la'gī ko bujhā'nā* V.T. bring one's love to a successful conclusion **لگی لپٹی** *la'gī lip'ṭī* ADJ. partiality **لگی لپٹی رکھے بغیر کہہ دینا** *la'gī lip'ṭī rak'khe ba-ghair' kaih de'nā* PH. say (something) without mincing matters **لگی نہ رکھنا** *la'gī na rakh'nā* V.I. show no partiality snap all ties (with)

لگائی *lūgā''ī* N.F. (dial.) wife woman

لگ بھگ *lag' bhag'* ADV. near resembling (usu. as) **کے لگ بھگ** *ke lag' bhag'* ADV. about ; approximately

لگدی *lūg'dī* N.F lump of moistened powder

لگڑ بگڑ *la'gar ba'gar*, **لگڑ بھگا** *la'gar bhag'gā* N.M. hyena

1 **لگن** *la'gan* N.M. basin ; trough **لگنی** *lag'nī* N.F. small trough [P]

2 **لگن** *la'gan* N.F. & N.M. (see under **لگنا** V.T. ★)

للا *la'lā* N.M. (dial.) son dear one little one [S]

للت *la'lit* N.F. name of a musical mode ADJ. (dial.) cute [S]

للچانا *lalchā'nā* V.I. long for ; covet be tentalized be tempted **للچا دینا** *lalchā' de'nā* V.T. tempt tantalize **للچا کے رہ جانا** *lalchā' ke raih' jā'nā* V.I. be tantalized [~ **لالچ**]

للک *la'lak* N.F enthusism

للکارنا *lalkār'nā* V.T. call out bawl (at) challenge للکار *lalkār'* N.F. shout : cry challenge

للو *lal'loo* N.F. (is dial.) tongue للونہ رہنا *lal'loo na raih'nā* PH. (dial.) be unable to keep mum

للوپتو *lal'loo pat'too* N.F. flattery ; adulation ; sycophancy للوپتو کرنا *lal'loo pat'too kar'nā* V.I. flatter ; fawn on

للّٰہ *lillah* INT. for God's sake للّٰہ الحمد *lil'lāh'il ḥam'd* INT. thank God thank goodness [A]

لم *lim* N.F. reason ; cause charge blemish لم لگانا (یا دھرنا یا رکھنا) *lim lagā'nā* (or *dhar'nā* or *rakh'nā*) V.T. accuse point out a blemish in [A ~ ل + م]

لم ¹ *lam* PREF. in an (only in) لم یزل *lam ya'zal* ADJ. immortal [A]

لم ² *lam* PREF tall long لم ترنگا *lam-tarań'gā*, ADJ. tall and stout لم ٹنگا *lam'tań'gā*, لم ٹنگو *lam-tań'goo* ADJ. long-legged لم چھڑ *lam'chhar* ADJ. tall لم دڑھیا *lam'darh'yā* ADJ. long-beared لم ڈھینگ *lam-dhīng* ADJ. tall N.M. heron لم کنا *lam-kan'nā* ADJ long-eared N.M. rabbit hare [CONTR ~ FOLL.]

لمبا *lam'bā* ADJ. (F. *lam'bī*) (dial. *lāń'bā* F. لانبی *lāń'bī*) long tall distant (journey) لمبا ترنگا *lam'bā tarań'gā* ADJ. tall and stout لمبا چوڑا *lam'bā-chau'ṛā* ADJ. spacious extensive tall and stout لمبا ہونا *lam'bā ho'nā* V I. be long be tall be distant depart لمبان *lambān'*, لمبائی *lambā''i* N.F. length ; tallness لمبانا *lambā'nā* V.T. lengthen elongate لمبائی چوڑائی *lambā''i chaurā''i* N.F. size length and breadth dimensions لمبڑ *lam'baṛ*, لمبو *lam'boo* ADJ. tall and foolish لمبوترا *lamboot'rā* ADJ. oblong لمبی *lam'bī* N.F. a long stride in a horse ADJ long لمبی تاننا (یا تان کرسونا) *lam'bī tān'nā* (or *tān' kar so'nā*) V.I. sleep at ease لمبی چوڑی ہانکنا *lam'bī chau'ṛī hāńk'nā* V. boast ; brag لمبی (یا لمبا) سانس بھرنا *lam'bī* (or *lam'bā*) *sāńs bhar'nā* V.I. heave a deep sigh

لمبر *lam'bar* N.M. (arch.) number لمبردار *lambar'-dar* N.M. (arch.) lambardar ; village headman [~ E number CORR.]

لمحہ *lam'ḥah* N.M. (PL لمحات *lamḥāt'*) minute moment twinkling of an eye لمحہ بھر *lam'ḥah bhar* ADV. for a minute for a while N M. hardly a moment [A]

لمڈا *lam'ḍā* N M (same as لونڈا N.M. ★)

لمس *lam's* N M touch sense of touch [A]

لمعہ *lam''ah* N.M. (PL. لمعات *lam'āt*) brightness

لن *lan* PREF never , certainly not [A]

لن ترانی *lan-tarā'ni* N.F. boast . brag tall talk لن ترانی کرنا (یا کی لینا) *lan-tarā'nī kar'nā* (or *kī le-nā*) V.I. brag ; boast indulge in tall talk [A ~ God's reply to Moses in these words meaning : thou shall not see Me (the Holy Quran 7 : 143)].

لنجا *lūń'jā* ADJ. (F. لنجی *lūń'jī*) lame of hand(s) ; crippled لنجاپن *lūń'jā-pan* N.M. such lameness

لنجھاڑا *lūnjhā'ṛā*, لنجھیڑا *lūnjhe'ṛā* N.M. problem(s) of lay life

لنچ *lanch* N.M. lunch [E]

لنڈ *lanḍ* N.M. penis

لنڈا *lūń'ḍā* ADJ. (F. لنڈی *lūń'ḍī*) tail-cropped *lūń'ḍī* N.F. (derog.) woman

لنڈ منڈ *lūnḍ' mūnḍ* ADJ. leafless (tree) tail-less one with all to has shaven

لنڈکری *lūnḍak'rī* N.F. somersault لنڈکریاں کھیلنا *lunḍak'-riyāń khel'nā* V.I. turn a somersault.

لنڈورا *lanḍoo'rā* ADJ. (F. لنڈوری *lanḍoo'rī*) tail-cropped. with no relatives with no children

لنڈھانا *lūnḍhā'nā* ا لڑھانا *lūṛhā'nā* V.T. spill ; let flow لنڈھنا *lanḍh'nā* V.I. be spilt

لنک *lank* N.M. heap

لنکا *lań'kā* N.M. Ceylon لنکا میں جسے دیکھا سو باون گز کا *lankā meń ji'se de'khā so bā'van gaz kā* PH everyone here more wicked (or naughty) than others

لنگ *ling* N.M. phallus [S]

لنگ *lūng* N.M. loincloth [~ P]

لنگ *lang* N.M. lameness ; limping ADJ. lame لنگ کرنا *lang kar'nā* V.I. (of animals) limp

لنگارا *langā'rā*, لنگاڑا *langā'ṛā* N.M. rake wicked person لنگاراپن *langā'rā-pan*, لنگاڑاپن *langā'ṛā-pan* N.M. profligacy wickedness

لنگر ¹ *lań'gar* N.M. anchor free public kitchen ; alms house victuals distributed to the poor لنگر اٹھانا *lań'gar ūṭhā'nā* V.T. & .. weigh anchor لنگر جاری کرنا *lań'gar jā'rī kar'nā* V.T. to set up a free public kitchen لنگر خانہ *lań'gar-khā'nah* N.M. free public kitchen لنگر ڈالنا *lań'gar ḍāl'nā* V.T. cast anchor

لنگر ² *lań'gar* N.M. pendulum thick rope wrestler's لنگر لنگوٹ (یا لنگوٹا) *lań'gar langoṭ'* (or *lango'ṭa)* N.M. underwear wrestlers' loincloth لنگرلنگوٹ باندھنا *lan'gar langoṭ' bandh'na* V.I. enter the lists

لنگری *lang'rī* N.F. kind of tray

لنگڑا *lang'ra* N.M. a kind of mango لنگڑا *lang'ra* ADJ. & N.M. (F. لنگڑی *lang'rī*) lame; lumping (person) cripple لنگڑانا *langṛa'na* V.I. limp

لنگوٹ *langoṭ'* N.M., لنگوٹا *lango'ṭa* N.M., لنگوٹی *lango'ṭī* N.F. loincloth لنگوٹ باندھنا *langoṭ bandh'na* V.I. gird up one's loins be ready to fight لنگوٹ بند *langoṭ'-band* ADJ. & N.M. one wearing a long-cloth confirmed bachelor لنگوٹ دار *langoṭ'-dar* ADJ. (of kite) with a coloured piece of paper at its tail لنگوٹ کا سچا *langoṭ ka sach'cha* ADJ. &. N.M. one not guilty of unwedded love لنگوٹی میں پھاگ کھیلنا *lango'ṭī men phag' khel'na* V.I. be happy despite poverty لنگوٹیا *lango'ṭiya* N.M. crony chum childhood playmate ADJ. intimate (friend) لنگوٹیا یار *lango'ṭiya yar* N.M. crony

لنگوچا *langoo'cha* N.M. sausage: entrails in which sausage meat is filled

لنگور *langoor'* N.M. black-faced a species monkey with a very long tail

لنگی *lun'gi* N.F. coloured sheet meant to cover lower part of body thick coloured turban

لو *lo* INT. lo look لو اور سنو *lo aur' su'no* INT. how strange [~ لینا]

لو *loo* N.F. hot wind لو لگنا *loo lag'na* V.I. have a heat stroke

لو *lau'* N.F. flame (of candle, etc.) lobe of ear attention meditation devotion لو لگانا *lau' laga'na* V.T. devoted (oneselfs to) لو لگنا *lau' lag'na* V.I. devoted (to)

لوا *la'va* N.M. lark

لوا *liva'* N.M. (PL. الویہ *al'viyah*) banner; standard [A]

لواحق *lava'hiq* (col. لواحقین *lavahiqin'*) N.M. PL. dependants [A ~ SING. لاحق]

لوازم *lava'zim* (col. لوازمات *lavazimat'*) N.M. PL. necessaries. ingredient things going along with another [A ~ SING. لازم]

لواطت *liva'tat* N.F. sodomy; paederasty [A ~ H لوط Lot]

لوانا *liva'na*, لوا لانا *liva' lana* V.I. fetch (someone)

لوبان *looban'* N.M. frankincense لوبان جلانا *looban' jala'na* V.T. burn incence لوبان دانی *looban'-da'nī* N.F. censer

لوبھ *lobh* N.M. (dial.) greed, avarice: covetousness لوبھی *lo'bhī* ADJ. (dial.) covetous [S]

لوبیا *lo'biya* N.M. a kind of bean

لوتھ *loth* N.F. dead body لوتھ پوتھ *loth poth* ADV. dead tired

لوتھڑا *loth'ra* N.M. lump of flesh

لوٹا *lo'ṭa* N.M. spouted jug (fig.) fickle-minded person لوٹے ڈالنا *lo'ṭe ḍal'na* V.I. (dial.) take a bath بے پیندی کا لوٹا *be pen'dī ka lo'ṭa* PH. fickle-minded (person); capricious (person) unreliable (person)

لوٹنا *lauṭ'na* V.I. come back; return (rus.) return; send back (rus.) turn over (page) لوٹ آنا *laut' a'na* V come back: return لوٹ جانا *laut ja'na* V.I. go back: return لوٹانا *lauṭa'na* V.T. send back, return turn over

لوٹنا *loṭ'na* roll toss about be restless love لوٹ *loṭ* ADJ. loving. devoted لوٹ پوٹ *loṭ' poṭ* ADJ. restless (in love) having a side-splitting laughter. printed from same plate on both sides لوٹ پوٹ ہونا *loṭ' poṭ ho'na* be restless (in love) have a side-splitting laughter لوٹ پوٹ چھاپنا *loṭ' poṭ chhap'na* V.T. print from same plate on both sides لوٹ جانا *loṭ ja'na*. لوٹ ہو جانا *loṭ ho ja'na* V.I. be greatly attracted by لوٹن *lo'ṭan* ADJ tumbling (pigeon) N.M. ground-tumbler (pigeon) لوٹنی *loṭ'nī* N.F. somerset; somersault lossing لوٹنیاں کھانا *loṭ'niyan kha'na* V.I. turn a somersault be restless (owing to pain, etc.)

لوٹنا *looṭ'na* N.F rob loot; plunder charge an exorbitantly high price لوٹ *looṭ'* N.F. highway robbery plunder; booty, spoil لوٹ پڑنا *looṭ par'na* V.I. be robbed. be pillaged be plundered لوٹ کا مال *looṭ' ka mal'* N.M. plunder booty good stuff going very cheap لوٹ کھانا *looṭ kha'na* V.I. sponge لوٹ کھسوٹ *looṭ' khasooṭ'* N.F. exploitation لوٹ کھسوٹ کرنا *looṭ' khasooṭ' kar'na* V.T. exploit لوٹ مار *looṭ' mar* N.F plunder; pillage sacking exorbitant charges لوٹ مچانا *looṭ' macha'na* V.T. under; pillage sack charge exorbitant rates لوٹم لاٹ *loo'ṭam laṭ* (or لوٹ یا *looṭ*) bid to rob each other

لوٹن *lo'ṭan* ADJ. لوٹنی *loṭ nī* N;F. (see under لوٹنا *loṭ'na* V.I. ★)

لوٹھا *lauṭha* ADJ. (F. لوٹھی *lau'ṭhī*) well-developed (youth)

لوث *laus*. N.M. contamination (only as) بے لوث *be-laus'* ADJ. unselfish ADV. without ulterior motives (much) [A]

لوچ *loch* N.M. sweetness (of voice) suppleness viscocity or storchiness (of dough)

لوچدار **loch'-dār** ADJ. sweet (voice, etc. supple (body viscous ; starchy

لوح **lauh** N.F. tablet plague ; stone titel page لوح تربت **lau'h-e tur'bat**, لوح مزار **lau'h-e mazār'** N.F. tombstone لوح طلسم **lau'h-e tilis'm** N.F. (arch.) tablet on which method of undoing a charm is detailed ; talismanic tablet لوح محفوظ **lau'h-e mah'fooz'** N.F. divine tablet recording all mankind's doings divine knowledge لوح مشق **lau'h-e mash'q** N.F. practising tablet ; tablet for calligraphia exercises لوح نویس **lauh'-navis** N.M. title page designer لوح و قلم **lau'h-o qa'lam** N.M. divine decree tablet and pen recording it [A]

لوحش اللہ **lau'hash-al'lah** INT. wonderful [A ~ لوحش + اللہ + لا]

لوری **lo'rī** N.F. lullaby لوری دینا **lo'rī de'nā** V.T. sing a lullaby ; lull a child to sleep

لوڑھی **lor'hi** N.F. mid winter Hindu festival on which bonfires are made ; bonfire festival

لوز **lauz** N.M. lozenge (rare) almond لوزینہ **lauzi'nah** N.M. almond pudding [A]

لوطی **loo'ti** N.M. sodomite ; paederast [A ~ H لوط Lot]

لوک **lok** N.M. (dial.) people world PREF. folk لوک دھن **lok'-dhun** N.F. folk-tone لوک گیت **lok'-gīt** N.M. folk-song لوک ناچ **lok'-nāch** N.M. folk-dance

لوکا **loo'kā** N.M. flame pieces of burning matter thrown out from a torch, etc. لوکا لگانا (یا دینا) **loo'kā lagā'nā** (or **de'nā**) V.T. set fire to incite passions لوکا لگے **loo'kā la'ge** INT. (dial.) to hell with it

لوکاٹ **lokāt'** N.M. loquat [E ~ Ch. **luh kwat** rush orange]

لوکٹ **lau'kat** N.F. partly charred wood ; brand

لوکل **lo'kal** ADJ. local لوکل سیلف گورنمنٹ **lo'kal sail'f-ga'varnmint** N.F. local self-government [E]

لوکی **lau'ki** N.F. (dial.) bottle gourd

لوگ **log'** N.M. people mankind family folk لوگ باگ **log'bāg** N.M. people ; various types of people ; people of all walks of life

لولا **loo'lā** ADJ. & N.M. (F. لولی **loo'li**) (one) with hands cropped لولا لنگڑا **loo'lā lang'rā** ADJ. & N.M. (F. لولی لنگڑی **loo'lī lang'rī**) cripple

لولاسی **laulā'sī** N.F. spray with which groom is first greated by his sisters-in-law

لولاک **laulāk'** PH. raison 'detre' of whole creation صاحب لولاک **sā'hib-e laulāk'** PH. (the Holy Prophet as) the raison 'detre of creation [A ~ لو + لا + ک ~ Tradition recording divine words "But for thee, I would not have created the universe"]

لولو **lo''lo''** (or **loo'loo**) (PL. لآلی **la'ā'lī**) pearl N.M. لولوے لالا **loo'lū'e lā'lā** N.M. pearl of the first water [A]

لولی **loo'li** N.F. dancing-girl prostitute ADJ. lovely (woman) لولی فلک **loo'li-e fa'lak** N.M. planet Venus [P]

لومڑ **lom'r** N.M. fox لومڑی **lom'rī** N.F. fox vixen

لوم **laum**, لومہ **lau'mah** N.M. reproach [A]

لون **loon'** N.M. salt : common salt لون مرچ لگانا **loon' mir'ch lagā'nā** V.T. exaggerate

لون[1] **lon** N.M. loan [E] لونی **loo'nī** N.F. salt efflorescing from wall لونی لگنا **loo'nī lag'nā** V.I. (of building, etc.) decay thus لونیا **loo'niya** N.F salt-maker a kind of brackish potherb [E]

لون[2] **lon** N.F. lawn a kind of muslin [E ~ CORR.]

لون **laun** N.M. (PL. الوان **alvān'**) colour [A]

لوند **laund** N.M. intercalary month , an extra month

لونڈا **laun'dā** (col. لمڈا **lam'dā**) N.M. boy , lad minion ; catamite لونڈاپن **laun'dā-pan** N.M. boyishness لونڈے باز **laun'de bāz** N.M sodomite . paederast N.F. woman going in for youthful men لونڈے بازی **laun'de-bā'zī** N.F. sodomy ; paederasty ; homosexuality لونڈے لاڑے (یا لاڑیے یا پہاڑیے) **laun'de lā're** (or **lā'riye** or **pahā'riye**) N.M. young inexperienced persons unfaithful minions لونڈی **laun'dī** N.F. maid ; slave-girl لونڈی بچہ **laun'di bach'chah** N.M. (derog.) freeman's son by a slave-girl slave-born لونڈیا **laun'd ya** (col. **lam'diya** N.F. girl . lass daughter

لونڈر **lavin'dar** N.M. lavinder [E]

لونکنا **launk'nā** (of lightning) flash

لونگ **laung** N.F. clover nose-pin

لوہا **lo'hā** N.M. iron لوہا بجانا **lo'hā bajā'nā** V.T. fight with the sword لوہا برسنا **lo'hā ba'rasnā** V.I. have a free use of swords have a general massacre کا لوہا تیز ہونا **kā lo'hā tez ho'nā** V.I. be harsh (on) لوہا دینا (یا کرنا) **lo'hā de'nā** (or **kar'nā**) V.T. iron (a cloth) لوہا لاٹھ **lo'hā lāth'** N.M. iron-bound club verse with difficult rhymes ADJ. strong لوہا ٹوٹ جانا **lo'hā toot jā nā**

V.I. (of sword) break or bend (of an affair) get spoiled لوہا ماننا lo'hā mān' jā'na V.T. acknowledge the superiority (of) لوہے کی چھاتی کر لینا lo'he ki chhā'tī kar le'na V.I. be adamant put up a bold front لوہے ٹھنڈے ہو جانا lo'he ṭhan'ḍe ho jā'na V.I. lose all enthusiasm لوہے کے چنے چبانا lo'he ke cha'ne chabā'na V.I. work very hard face great odds لوہار (or لہار) lohār' N.M. blacksmith ; ironmaster ; smith (rare) ironmonger لوہار خانہ lohār'-khānah N.M. smithy لوہار خانے میں سوئیاں بیچنا lohār'-khā'ne men soo''iyāṅ be'ch'nā V.I. bring coals to Newcastle لوہار کی بھٹی lohār' kī bhaṭ'ṭī N.F. forge , furnace لوہارن (or لہارن) lohā'ran, لوہاری (or لہاری) lohā'rī N.F. female member of a smith's family لوہ loh PRFF. iron لوہ چون loh' choon N.F. iron filings لوہیا lo'hiyā N.M. iron monger

لوہار lohār' N.M., لوہیا lo'hiyā N.M. (see under لو N.M. ★)

لوئر lo''ar ADJ. lower

لوئی lo''ī N.F. coarse woollen shawl

لہار lohār', لہارن lohā'ran, لہاری lohā'rī under لوہ N.M. ★)

لہات lohāt' N.M. uvula [A]

لہاڑا lahā'ṛā N.M. not good at repaying debts

لہان lohān' ADJ. blood-stained (only in) لہولہان la'hoo lohān' ADJ. blood stained

لہجہ laih'jah (ped. lah'jah) N.M. PL. لہجات laih'jāt') tone accent [A]

لہذا li-hā'zā ADV. therefore ; for this reason consequently , with the result that [A ~ ل for + ہذا this]

لہر laih'r (col. lai'har N.F. wave ; undulation waving pattern fluctuation physical reaction to venour from snake-bite intoxication ; inebriation frenzy fancy whim caprice لہر آنا (یا اٹھنا) laih'r ā'nā (or uṭh'nā) V.I. undulate fluctuate feel enthusias feel enrapture feel the effect of veno... لہرا laih'rā N.M. lively tune لہر بہر laih'r baih'r N.F. prosperity لہر چڑھنا laih'r chaṛh'nā V.I. be an influx (of) have a fit (of) feel the effect of drug or venom لہریں لینا laih'ren le'nā V.I. (of river, etc.) be wavy لہرانا laih'ra'nā V.I. wave ; flutter fluctuate لہری laih'rī ADJ. emotional capricious لہریا laih'riya ADJ. wavy ; undulating dyed or painted thus

لہسن laih'san N.M. garlic blotch

لہف lah'f N.M. grief [A]

لہکا laih'kā N.M. thin brocade lace

لہکارنا laihkār'nā V.T. pat or encourage (horse)

لہکنا lai'hak'nā V.T. glow ; kindle up ; rise up into a flame flash chirp ; warble raise one's voice be filled with passion get excited لہک lai'hak N.F. glitter ; flash ; blaze لہک لہک کر (یا کے) lai'hak lai'hak kar (or ke) ADV. enthusiastically excitedly loudly لہکانا lai'hka'na V.T. kindle (fire) , stir (fire) shine or glitter excite cause cause to to chrip or warble cause to speak up

لہلہانا laihlaha'na V.I. wave ; flourish bloom by verdant لہلہا laih'lahā ADJ. (arch.) blossoming لہلہاہٹ laihlahā haṭ N.F. waving (of corn, etc.) before the wind blooming verdure

لہلوٹ laihloṭ' ADV. restless

لہنگا laihn'gā N.M. long skirt

لہو la'hoo, (rare lohoo') N.M. blood لہو آنا la'hoo ā'nā V.I. pass blood (by stool) (آنکھوں میں) لہو اترنا (ah'khon men) la'hoo u'tarnā V.T. (of eyes) be bloodshot لہو برسنا la'hoo ba'ras'na V.I. bleed لہو بگڑنا la'hoo bigaṛ'nā V.I. (of blood) become infections lack fraternal (etc.) sympahies لہو پانی ایک کرنا la'hoo pā'nī ek kar'na V.I. work very hard ; sweet and toil لہو پینا la'hoo pi'nā V.T. wory a great deal be very angry لہو تھوکنا (یا ڈالنا) la'hoo thook'na (or dal'nā) V.T. spit blood suffering from phthisis لہو ٹپکنا la'hoo ṭa'pak'nā V.I. (of blood) ooze لہو خشک کرنا la'hoo khush'k kar'na V.T. terrorize be very harsh on لہو خشک ہونا la'hoo khush'k ho'nā V.I. be terrorized لہو رونا la'hoo ro'na V.I. weep bitterly لہو کا پیاسا la'hoo kā piyā'sā ADJ. blood thirsty N.M. bitter enemy (of) لہو کے گھونٹ پینا (یا پی کر رہ جانا) la'hoo ke ghoonṭ pi'nā (or pī kar raih' jā'nā) V.I. suffer patiently لہو لگا کے شہیدوں میں ملنا (یا شامل ہونا) la'hoo lagā' ke shahī'doṅ men mil'nā (or shā'mil ho'nā) PH. much credit for little لہو لہان la'hoo lohān' ADJ. blood-stained

لہو lah'v N.M. pastime ; fun ; amusement لہو و لعب lah'v-o-la''ib N.M. fun and sport [A]

لہینڈی lahen'ḍī N.F. basket for drawing water

la''iq ADJ. able capable [A ~]

لہیب *lahīb'* ADJ. flaming ; blazing [A]

لئیم *la''īm* ADJ. reproached (person) mean ; base ; sordid niggardly [A ~ ملامت]

لے *lai* N.F. air ; tune keeping time

لے *le* V.T. (imp. of لینا V.T. ★)

لیاقت *liyā'qat* N.F. ability capabiltiy proficiency suitability worth merit [A]

لیبارٹری *'laibar'tarī* N.F. laboratory [E]

لیبر *le'bar* N.M. labour لیبر پارٹی *le'bar par'tī* N.F. Labour Party [E]

لیپ کا سال *līp' kā sāl'* N.M. leap year [E]

لیبر *lī'bar* N.M. morbid water discharge from eye

لیپنا *lep'nā* V.T. plaster bedaub besmear with لیپ *lep* N.M. plaster ointment لیپ پوت *lep' pot* N.F. plastering and mad-washing لیپ کرنا (یا لگانا) *lep' kar'nā* (or *lagā'nā*) V.T. plaster apply a plaster or ointment لیپا پوتا *le'pā po'tā* ADJ. plastered and mud washed clean لیپا پوتی *le'pā po'tī* N.F. plastering (fig.) window-dressing لیپنا پوتنا *lep'nā pot'nā* V.T. plastering and mud washing

لے پالک *le'-pā'lak* ADJ. & N.M. adopted (child) [~ لینا + پالنا]

لیتڑا *līt'ṛā* N.M. worn-out shoe لیتڑے پڑنا *līt're paṛ'nā* V.I. get a shoe-beating

لیت و لعل *lai't-o-la'al'* N.F. evasion prevarication لیت و لعل کرنا *lai't-o la'al' kar nā* V.T. evade prevaricate [~ A لیت *lai'ta* + و + لعل *la'al'la*]

لیٹنا *leṭ'nā* V.I. lie down rest ; repose (of crop be no longer standing)

لیجسلیٹو *laijisle'ṭiv* ADJ. legislative لیجسلیٹو اسمبلی *laijisle'ṭiv asaimb'lī* N.F. Legislative Assembly لیجسلیچر *laijisle'char* N.M. Legislature [E]

لیجھی *le'jhī* N.F. refuse of chewed betel-leaf worthless stuff

لیچڑ *lī'chaṛ* ADJ. & N.M. stingy (fellow) niggardly (person) لیچڑپن *lī'chaṛ-pan'* N.M. stinginess ; niggardliness

لیچی *lī'chī* N.F. litchi [E ~ Ch.]

لید *līd* N.F. dung (of horse, ass, etc.)

لیدر *laidar* N.M. leather [E]

لیڈر *lī'ḍar* N.M. leader editorial لیڈرانی *līḍarā'nī* (joc.) female leader لیڈری *lī'ḍarī* N.F leadership [E]

لیڈی *le'ḍī* N.F. lady لیڈی ڈاکٹر *le'ḍī ḍāk'ṭar* N.F lady doctor [E]

لیر *līr* N.F. strip or slip of cloth rag

لیس 1 *lais* ADJ. accoutred ready لیس ہونا *lais ho'nā* V.I. be ready be accoutred

لیس 2 *lais* N.F. lace [E]

لیس 1 *les* N.F. stickiness ; glutinosity لیسدار *les'-dār* ADJ. sticky ; glutinous ; jelly like

لیس 2 *les* SUF. licking لیسی *le sī* SUF. licking

لیک *līk* N.F. rut track ; beaten path mark left by snake, ete. (derog.) old order, custom blemish لیک پر چلنا *līk' par chal'nā* لیک لیک چلنا *līk' līk chal'nā* V.I. follow the rut follow the beaten path

لیک *lek* ADJ. (arch. or poet) but still however ; nevertheless [P ~ FOLL.]

لیکن *le'kin* CONJ. but still however ; nevertheless [P ~ A لاکن]

لیکھ *līkh* N.F. small louse nit

لیکھا *le'khā* N.M. (dial) account [~ لکھنا]

لیگ *līg* N.F. league مسلم لیگ *mus'lim līg* N.F. Muslim League لیگ آف نیشنز *līg' af ne'shanz* N.F. League of Nations [E]

لیل *lail* (rare لیلہ *lai'lah*) N.F. (PL. لیالی *layā'lī*) night لیل و نہار *lail-o-nahār'* N.M. night and day times; position; circumstances لیلۃ القدر *lai'lat-ul-qad'r* N.F. the Ramazan night (generally regarded as 27th) on which the Holy Quran's revelation commenced ; anniversary of Quranic revelation الف لیلہ *al'f lai'lah* N.M The Arabian Nights [A]

لیلا *le'la* N.M lamb kid

لیلا *lī'lā* N.F. (dial.) theatrical performance sport amorous sport marvel لیلا دھاری *lī'lā-dhā'rī* N.M. لیلاوتی *lī'lavatī* N.F (dial.) wanton ; playful woman [S]

لیلیٰ *lai'la* (CORR لیلی *lai'lī*) ADJ. dark-complexioned N F beloved of legendary Arab lover Qais whose madness in love won him the name Majnoon [A ~ لیل]

لیمن *lai'man* N.M. lemon لیمونیڈ lemonade [E ~ A ~ P]

لیمو *li'moo*, لیموں *li'mooñ* (ped لیموں *laimooñ'*) N.M. lemon; lime لیموں نچوڑ *li' ooñ-nichor'* N.F. uninvited guest sponger لیموں نچوڑنا *li'mooñ nichor'nā* V.T. crush lemon [~P]

لینا *le'nā* V.T. take take over ; assume buy ; purchase accept borrow receive usurp win ; conquer لے *le* INT. come well take لے آنا *le ā'na* V.T. bring fetch ; go and get produce لیا دیا *li'yā di'yā* N.M. (fig.) act of charity good deed لیا دیا آڑے (یا آگے یا کام) آنا *li'yā di'yā ā're* (or *ā'ge* or *kām*) *ā'nā* V.I. escape owing to some good deed done earlier لے اڑنا *le' ūr'nā* V.T. run away with carry tales لے بھاگنا *le' bhāg'nā* V.T. & I. abduct run away (with) abduct لے بیٹھنا *le' baiṭh'nā* V.T. ruin others along with oneself cause other parts to collapse with it force (someone) to become concubine لے پڑنا *le' par'nā* V.T. lie down with a child lie down with a woman forcibly لیتا بھولے نہ دیتا *le'tā bhoole na de'tā* PH. cash deeling as involving no trouble لے جانا *le' jā'nā* V.T. take away run away with win convey لیجیے *lī'ji''e* INT. lo please take it لے دے *le' de* N.F. objections effort لے دے کر (یا کے) *le' de kar* (or *ke*) ADV. merely altogether لے دے کرنا *le' de kar'nā* VT.. take a strong exception to لے دے ہونا *le' de ho'nā* V.I. be strongly objected (to) لے ڈوبنا *le' doob'nā* V.T. ruin another person along with oneself لے لینا *le' le'nā* V.T. take ; take power take by force ; extort take back accept receive force to yield لے مرنا *le' mar'na* V.T. & I. try hard and succeed ruin others along with oneself لین دین *len' den* N.M. business dealings لین دین کا کھرا *len' den kā kha'rā* ADJ. fair in one's dealings لینا ایک نہ دینا دو *le'nā ek' na de'nā do'* PH. have nothing to do (with) : have no connection whatsoever (with) ; have no truck (with) لین دین *len' den* N.M. business dealing لینا نہ دینا کارے نہ مسلے *le'nā na de'nā kā're na mas'le* PH. useless لینی *le'nī* N.F. ceremony on taking back child from wet nurse ; weaning لینے کے دینے پڑ جانا *le'ne ke de'ne par' jā'nā* V.T. have tables turned on one لینے میں نہ دینے میں *le'ne meñ na de'ne meñ* PH. having nothing to do ; have one's hand clean

لینڈ *lend* N.F. one separate part of excrement لینڈی *len'dī* N.F. one separate part of excrement ADJ. coward لینڈی تر کرنا *len'dī tar'kar'nā* V.T. humour ; cajole لینڈی کتا *len'dī kūt'ta* N.M. small underdeveloped dog

لین ڈوری *lain' do'rī* N.F. bee-line unbroken traffic لین ڈوری بندھی (یا لگی) ہونا *lain do'rī bañ'dhī* (or *la'gī*) *ho'nā* V.I. have unbroken traffic

لینڈ لارڈ *laind'lārd* N.M. landlord لینڈ لیڈی *laind' le'dī* N.F. landlady [E]

لیو *lev* N.M. layer plaster لیو اترنا *lev ū'tarnā* V.I. (of plaster) come down لیو چڑھانا *lev' charhā'nā* V.T. plaster لیو چڑھنا *lev' charh'nā* V.I. be plastered grow fat

لیوا *le'vā* N.M. mud-plastering on vessel bottom SUF. taking جان لیوا *jān'-le'vā* ADJ. killing

لئی *le'ī* N.F. paste

لیے *li'ye* ADV. because (of) ; on account (of) کے لیے *ke li'ye* PREF. for

م

م *mīm* thirty-first letter of Urdu alphabet (equivalent to English *m*) according to jummal reckoning) 40

مآب *ma'āb'* N.M. recourse SUF. focus (of) centre (of) repository (of) able -ible

مآثر *ma'ā'sir* N.M. PL. memorable deeds (of person, family, etc.) glorious traditions (rare) celebrities [A ~ SING. مأثرت]

مآخذ *ma'ā'khiz* N.M. (PL. of ماخذ N.M. ★)

مآل *ma'āl'* N.M. consequence end ; termination مآل اندیش *ma'āl-andesh'* ADJ. prudent faresighted مآل اندیشی *ma'āl ande'shī* N.F. prudence farsight مآل کار *ma'āl-e kar'* N.M. consequence ADV. at last ; at length ultimately [A]

ما¹ *mā* N.F. (same as ماں *māñ* N.F. ★)

ما² *mā* N.M. fourth note of national gamut

ما³ *mā* PROV. we ما بدولت *mā ba-dau'lat* PROV. (of sovereign) we ما و شما *mā'-o-shumā* N.M. PL. all and sundry ما و من *mā'-o-man'* N.F. (rare) egotism [P]

ما⁴ *mā* SUF whatever ; whatsoever that which while ; whilst as long as مابعد

... ADJ. following ; that follows ADV. later PREF. meta, مابعدالطبیعات *mā ba''d-ūt-tabi'iyyat'* N.M. metaphysics مابقا (or مابقی) *mā-baqā'* (col. *mā-baqī'*) N.M. the rest, remainder remnant ; balance ; arrears مابہ الاحتیاج *mā-bih-il-ehtiyāj'* N.M. whatever is necessary requisites مابہ الامتیاز *mā-bih-il-imtiyāz'* N.M. distinctive feature مابہ النزاع *mā-bih-in-nizā''* N.M. point at issue bone of contention مابین *mā-bain'* ADV. during between among ماتحت *mā-taiht* (or ped. *-taht*) N.M. subordinate ADJ. subordinate inferior ADV. under ماتقدم *mā-taqad-dam* ADJ. earlier bygone afore-said ; above-mentioned ماجرا *mā'jarā* (col. *māj'rā*) N.M. event circumstances happening ; occurrence state ; condition predicament matter ماحصل *mā-ḥā'sal* N.M. produce profit sum and substance (of) outcome ماحضر *mā-ḥa'zar* N.M. pot-luck ماحضر تناول فرمائیے *mā-ḥa'zar tanā'ūl farmā''-iye* PH. come and take pot-back with us ماحول *mā-ḥaul'* N.M. environment surroundings 'milieu' ماسبق *mā-sa'baq* ADJ. preceding ماسلف *mā-sa'laf* ADJ. bygone ; what has gone before ماسوا *mā-sivā'* ADV. moreover besides in addition (to) N.M. universe ruinous God ماشاءاللہ *mā-shā''allāh'* INT. (rare) what God may God preserve it from evil eye wonderful gosh مافات *mā-fāt'* ADJ. what is dead and gone missing mitted مافوق *mā-fauq'* ADJ. higher upper PREF. ultra meta مافوق الفطرت *mā-fau'q-ul-fit'rat* ADJ. supernatural مافی الضمیر *mā fiz-zamīr'* N.M. motive intention design مافیہا *mā-fī'-hā* PH. what it contains ; its contents دنیا و مافیہا *dūn'yā-o-mā-fī'hā* PH. the world and whatever it contains ماقبل *mā-qab'l* ADJ. preceding previous ماقبل آخر *mā-qab'l-e ā'khir* ADJ. penultimate ماقل و دل *mā-qal'la-va-dal'* PH. to the point مالاکلام *mā-lā kalām* ADJ. ineffable indescribable مالایطاق *mā-lā-yutāq'* ADJ. unbearable تکلیف مالایطاق *takli'f-e mā-lā-yutāq'* PH. unbearable responsibility (col.) great trouble مالاینحل *mā-lā-yan'ḥal* ADJ. insoluble that cannot be resolved مالہ و ماعلیہ *mā-la-hoo'vā-mā-'alaih'* N.M. pros and cons ماضی *mā-mazā'* ADJ. & ADV. by gone مضیٰ مامضیٰ *mazā' mā-mazā'* PH. let bygones by bygones ماوجب *mā va'jab* N.M. & ADJ. necessary ; whatever is necessary ماورا *mā-varā'* ADJ. beyond besides over and above PREF. ultra N.M. that lies beyond ماورائی *mā-varā''i* ADJ. transcendental ماورائیت *mā-varā''iy'yat* N.F. transcendentalism مایحتاج *mā-yaḥtāj'* ADJ. necessary [A]

ما۵ *mā* PREF. no ; not مازاغ *mā-zāgh'* PH. (rare) did not go astray N.M. (fig.) beatific vision [A]

ما۶ *mā* N.M. water ماءاللحم *mā'ūl-lah'm* N.M. distilled or strong soup مائی *mā''i* ADJ. watery liquid hydro مائیت *mā''iy'yat* N.F. liquidity wateriness liquid content [A]

ماپنا *māp'nā* V.T. (same as ناپنا V.T. ★) ماپ *māp* N.M. same as ناپ (see under ناپنا V.T. ★

مات *māt* N.F. checkmate defeat being cutdone مات دینا (یا کرنا) *māt de'nā* (or *kar'nā*) V.T. mate : checkmate defeat : beat (at) outdo confound مات کھانا (یا ہونا) *māt' khā'nā* (or *ho'nā*) V.I. be mated : be checkmated be defeated ; be beaten (at) be outdone be confounded شہ مات *shah-māt'* N.M. checkmate [P ~ A died]

ماتا۱ *mā'tā* N.F. small-pox (dial.) mother ماتا پتا *mā'tā pi'tā* N.M. (dial.) parents ماتا نکلنا *mā'tā ni'kalnā* V.I. (of someone) have small pox

ماتا۲ *mā'tā* ADJ. (F. ماتی *mā'tī*) intoxicated نیند کا ماتا *nīnd' kā mā'tā* N.M. one given to too much sleep one in deep sleep one not conscientious

ماتم *mā'tam* N.M. mourning obsequies grief ritual mourning (for Imam Hussain's martyrdom) ماتم پرسی *mā'tam pūr'si* N.F. condolence ماتم پرسی کرنا *mā'tam pūr'si kar'nā* V.T., condole ماتم خانہ *mā'tam-khā'nah*, ماتم سرا(ے) *mātam-sarā('e)*, ماتم کدہ *mā'tam-ka'dah* N.M. house of mourning (fig.) world as this ماتم دار *mā'tam-dār* ADJ. mourning N.M. mourner ماتم داری *mā'tam-dā'rī* N.F. mourning ماتم زدہ *mā'tam-za'dah* ADJ. bereaved ماتم کرنا *mā'tam-kar'nā* V.T. mourn grieve ; lament perform ritual mourning ماتمی *mā'tamī* N.M. mourner ADJ. mourning mournful funeral ماتمی لباس *mā'tamī libās'* N.M. (usu. black) mourning dress (widow's) weeds [A]

ماتھا *mā'thā* N.M. forehead facade brow front (of) ماتھا پیٹنا *mā'thā pīṭ'nā* V.T. (fig.) grieve over one's misfortune ماتھا ٹھنکنا *mā'thā ṭha'nakna* V.I. (fig.) have a presentiment of the coming evil ; have ill-forebodings ماتھا رگڑنا *mā'thā ra'gaṛnā* V.T. (fig.) prostrate oneself (before) beseach ; supplicate متھے مارنا *mat'the mār'nā* (rare ماتھے مارنا *mā'the mār'nā*) V.T. throw back (at) ; return (with bad grace)

ماٹ *māṭ* N.M. large earthen receptacle for food grains, etc. vat indigo pal

ماٹ کا ماٹ ہی بگڑا ہے *māṭ ka māṭ hī big'ṛa hai* PROV the whole group is spoiled

ماٹھو *mā'ṭhoo* N.M. harlequin, merryandrew audacious fool

ماٹی *mā'ṭī* N.F. (dial.) same as مٹی N.F ★)

ماثورہ *māsoo'rah* ADJ. mentioned in the Holy Prophet's traditions دعائے ماثورہ *do'a-e māsoo'rah* N.F. a prayer thus transmitted, the Holy Prophet's prayer [A ~ اثر]

ماجایا *mā-jā'yā* N.M. (see under ماں N.F ★)

ماجد *mā'jid* ADJ. (F. & PL. ماجدہ *mā'jidah*) glorious [A ~ مجد glory]

ماجو *mā'joo*, ماجو پھل *mā'joo-phal*, مازو *mā'zoo* N.M. gall-nut

ماجور *mājoor'* ADJ. rewarded عنداللہ ماجور ہونا *in'd-allah' mājoor' ho'na* V.I be rewarded by God [A ~ اجر]

ماچا *mā'chā* N.M. large bed (gardner's) scaffolding

ماچس *mā'chis* N.F. match-box match-stick [E]

ماچی *mā'chī* N.F. dicky, dickey small bed

ماچین *māchīn'* N.M. (arch.) Indo-china

ماخذ *mā'khaz* N.M. (PL. مآخذ *ma'ā'khiz*) source [~ اخذ take]

ماخوذ *mākhooz'* ADJ. taken arrested, apprehended called to account involved adopted (of article) lifted (from some paper, etc.) [A ~ اخذ take]

مادر *mā'dar* N.F. mother مادر بخطا *mā'dar ba'khaṭā'* ADJ. illegitimate; bastard mischievous مادر خواہی کرنا *mā'dar-khā'hī kar'nā* PH. abuse someone by making indecent remarks about his mother مادرزاد *mā'dar-zād'* ADJ. born (blind) stark (naked) مادرزاد برہنہ *mā'dar-zād baraih'nah* ADJ. stark naked; nude مادرزاد اندھا (یا نابینا) *mā'dar-zād an'dhā* (or *nābī'nā*) ADJ. & N.M. born blind مادرانہ *mādarā'nah* ADJ. motherly (affection, etc.) مادری *mā'darī* ADJ. maternal matriarchal mother مادری زبان *mā'darī zabān'* N.F. mother tongue [P]

مادہ *mā'dah* N.F. female نر (و) مادہ *nar(-o-)mā'dah* N.M. male and female [P]

مادہ *mād'dah* N.M. matter body root (of word): radical letters capacity to understand (also مادۂ تاریخ *mād'da-e tārikh'*) chronogram مادۂ تاریخ نکالنا *mād'da-e tārikh' nikal'na* V.T compose a chronogram (of) مادہ پرست *mād'da paras't* N.M. materialist ADJ. materialistic مادہ پرستانہ *mād'da parastā'nah* ADJ. materialistic مادہ پرستی *mād'da-paras'tī* ADJ. materialism مادی *mād'dī* ADJ. material materialistic مادیت *māddiy'yat* N.F. materiality substance materialism [A]

مادیاں *mā'diyān* N.F. mare [P]

مادیت *māddiy'yat* N.F. (see under مادہ N.M. ★)

ماڈل *mā'ḍal* N.M. & ADJ. model [E]

مار *mār* N.M. (lit.) snake; serpent مار آستین *mār-āstīn'* N.M. foe in friendly guise مارگزیدہ *mār'-gazī'dah* ADJ. & N.M. snake bitten (person) مارمہرہ *mār'-moh'rah* N.M. jewel supposedly found in serpent's head and used as antidote for snake poison; toadstone [P]

مارنا *mār'nā* V.T. beat; drub; give a beating; give a hiding; thrash use third degree methods hit; strike hurt at strike at shoot (gun) kill win defeat rain; destroy mar mortify embezzle; usurp; withhold (something) wrongfully sting (of male) copulate; fuck oxidize (metal) مار *mār* N.F beating striking hit; stroke range (of missile) severity curse soil; a rich black loam مار بھگانا *mār' bhagā'nā* V.T. put to rout put to flight مار بیٹھنا *mār' baiṭh'nā* V.T. beat hit; strike embezzle, withold wrongfully مار پڑنا *mār' paṛ'na* V.I. be beaten be under cause مار پیٹ *mār' pīṭ* مار دھاڑ *mār' dhāṛ'* N.F drubbing fighting affray مار پیچھے سنوار *mār' pī'chhe sanvār'* PH. patch-up مار دینا *mār' de'nā* V.T. kill beat to death مار ڈالنا *mār' ḍāl'nā* V.T. kill murder (of woman) ravish someone with one's beauty; make someone mashed on (oneself) مار رکھنا *mār' rakh'nā* V.T. withhold wrongfully usurp مار کھانا *mār' khā'nā* V. be beaten مار گرانا *mār' girā'nā* V. knock down مار لانا *mār' lā'nā* V.T. kill and bring obtain by plunder مار لینا *mār' le'nā* V.T. withhold wrongfully; usurp (of male) copulate مارا *mā'rā* ADJ. & ADV. beaten struck down smitten killed ruined; undone lost spoilt N.M. loamy soil مارا جانا *mā'rā jā'nā* V.I. be killed be lost be ruined be undone مارا مار *mā'rā-mār* N.F ado bustle varied and toilsome efforts ADV. with much ado with a burried effort مارا مارا پھرنا *mā'rā mā'rā phir'nā* V.I knock about aimlessly مارا مار کرنا *mā'rā mār kar'nā* V.T. & I. bustle about try one's best مارُوں گھٹنا پھوٹے آنکھ *ma'roon ghuṭ'nā phoo'ṭe āṅkh* PH. irrelevant reply; etc.

مارتول *mar'tol* N.M. mortello, turn-screw [Pg.]

مارچ *mār'ch* N.M. March march مارچ پاسٹ *mār'ch past* N.M. march past مارچ کرنا *mār'ch kar'nā* V.I. march [E]

مارشل لا *mār'shal-lā* N.M. martial law مارشل لاحکومت *mār'shal lā ḥukoo'mat* N.F. martial law regime or administration [E]

مارکہ *mār'kah* N.M. brand trade mark

مارو *mā'roo* N.F. name of a musical mode N.M. kettledrum warlike musical instrument N.F. name of a musical mode ADJ. large (brinjal, etc.)

ماروت *māroot'* N.M. name of legendary angel

مارے *mā're* ADV. for; for the sake (of) on account (of) owing (to) بھوک کے مارے *bhook* (etc.) *ke mā're*, مارے بھوک کے *mā're bhook'* (etc.) *ke* ADV. owing to hunger (etc.) [~ مارنا]

ماڑا *mā'ṛā* ADJ. (F. ماڑی *mā'ṛī*) weak; lean languid

ماڑی *mā'ṛī* N.F. gruel starch

مازو *mā'zoo* N.M. (same as ماجو N.M. ★)

ماس *mās* مانس *māṅs* N.M. (dial.) flesh meat ماس نوچنا *mās' noch'na* V.T. claw; mangle

ماسٹر *mās'ṭar* N.M. (usu. as ماسٹرجی *mās'ṭar ji*) master; teacher [E]

ماسکہ *mā'sikah* N.F. focus power of retaining food in body نقطۂ ماسکہ *nuq'ta-e mā'sikah* N.M. focal point [A]

ماسی *mā'sī* N.F. (dial.) aunt; mother's sister

ماش *māsh* N.M. kind of vetch ماش کی دال *māsh' kī dal* N.F. pulse made from it ماش مارنا *māsh' mār'na* V.T. cast vetch (on someone) with a malignant charm

ماشہ *mā'shah* N.M. weight equivalent to 16 grains گھڑی میں تولہ گھڑی میں ماشہ ہونا *gha'ṛī meṅ to'lah gha'ṛī meṅ mā'shah ho'na* V.I. be fickle; be capricious

ماضی *mā'zī* N.F. & ADJ. past ماضی احتمالی *mā'zī eḥtimā'lī*, ماضی شکیہ *mā'zī shak'kiy'yah* N.F. past conditional ماضی استمراری *mā'zī(-e) istimrā'rī* N.F. past imperfect; past continuous ماضی بعید *mā'zī(-e) ba'īd'* N.F. past perfect ماضی تمنائی *mā'zī(-e) tam annā''ī* N.F. past optative ماضی قریب *mā'zī(-e) qarīb'* N.F. present perfect ماضی مطلق *mā'zī(-e) mut'laq* N.F. past indefinite ماضیہ *mā'ziyah* ADJ. (F. & PL.) past [A ~ مضی went]

ماکول *mākool'* N.M. eatable dish (for meal); victual ماکولات *makoolat'* N.M PL. eatables; victuals ماکولات ومشروبات *ma'koolat-o-mashroobāt'* N.M. PL. dishes and drinks

ماکیاں *mā'kiyāṅ* N.F. hen [P]

ماگھ *māgh* N.M. eleventh month of Hindu calender equivalent to January ماگھ ننگی بیساکھ بھوکی *māgh' naṅ'gī baisākh bhoo'kī* PROV. always poor

مال ۱ *māl* N.F. (also چرخے کی مال *char'khe kī māl*) distaff string

مال ۲ *māl* SUF. rubbed trodden مالی *mā'lī* SUF. rubbing trampling [P ~ مالیدن]

مال ۳ *māl* N.M. (PL. اموال *amvāl'*) stock wares goods cargo riches; wealth property dainty; dainties lovely person revenue; land revenue مال اڑانا *māl' uṛā'na* V.T. squander wealth feed on dainties مال بردار جہاز *māl' bar-dār' jahāz'* N.M. cargo vessel مال حرام *mā'l-e ḥarām'* N.M. unlawful acquisitions مال خانہ *māl'-khā'nah* N.M. treasury مالدار *māl'-dār* ADJ. rich; wealthy moneyed مالداری *māl'-dā'rī* N.F. riches wealth wealthiness مالزادی *māl'-zā'dī* N.F. whore; bawd مال حلال *mā'l-e ḥalāl'* N.M. legitimate earnings مال عرب پیش عرب *mā'l-e 'a'rab pe'sh-e 'a'rab* PROV. the best custodian of one's property is one'e own self مال غنیمت *māl-e ghanī'mat* N.M. booty مال غیر منقولہ *māl-e ghair manqoo'lah* N.M. real estate; immovable property مال کا بندوبست *māl' kā band-o-bas't* N.M. revenue settlement مال گاڑی *māl-gā'ṛī* N.F. goods train مالگزار *māl-guzār'* N.M. landholder مالگزاری *māl-guzā'rī* N.F. land revenue revenue assessment مال مارنا *māl-mār'na* V.T. swindle embezzle مال مست *māl'-mas't* ADJ. & N.M. (one) proud of one's wealth مال مسروقہ *mā'l-e masroo'qah* N.M. stolen property مال مفت *mā'l-e muf't* N.M. something got without effort مال مفت دل بے رحم *mā'l-e muf't di'l-e be-raiḥ'm* PROV. money got without effort is swiftly squandered مال منقولہ *māl-e manqoo'lah* N.M. movable property مال وقف *māl-e vaq'f* N.M. endowment مال ومتاع *mā'l-o-matā''* N.M. money and effects riches; wealth لاوارث مال *lā-vā'ris māl'* N.M. unclaimed property escheat متروکہ مال *matroo'kah māl* N.M. evacuee property legacy; bequest مالا مال *mā'lā-māl* ADJ. rich ADV replete (with) abounding (in) مالا مال کرنا *mā'lā-*

mal kar'nā V.T. enrich مالی *mā'lī* ADJ. financial pecuniary مالی سال *mā'lī sāl* N.M. financial year مالیہ *mā'liyah* (ped. *māliy'yah*) N.M. land revenue مالیت *māliy'yat* N.F. cost value

مالیتی *māliy'yatī* ADJ. costly ADV. costing [A]

مال *māl* مال روڈ *māl'-roḍ* N.F. the Mall [E]

مالا *mā'lā* N.F. (dial. M.) rosary ; string of beads garland necklace مالا پھیرنا *mā'lā pher'nā* V.T. tell one's beads

مالتی *māl'tī* N.F. a kind of jasmine

مالٹا *māl'ṭā* N.M. orange [E]

مالسری *māl'sirī* N.F. name of a musical mode

مالش *mā'lish* N.F. massage nausea مالش کرنا *mā'lish kar'nā* V.T. & I. massage feel nausea [P ~ مالیدن]

مالک *mā'lik* N.M. owner proprietor master lord husband God مالک بنانا (یا کرنا) *mā'lik banā'nā* (or *kar'nā*) V.T. empower make someone the owner (of) مالکانہ *mālikā'nah* ADJ. proprietary ADV. like an owner N.M. allowance paid by tenant annuity or allowance paid to onsted tenant مالکانہ رسوم *mālikā'nah rūsoom'* N.F. proprietary dues [A ~ ملک]

مالکوس *mālkaus* N.M. one of the major modes of national music connected with late winter

مالن *mā'lan* N.F. (see under مالی N.M. ★)

مالوف *māloof'* ADJ. loved (native country) [A ~ الفت]

مالی¹ *mā'lī* N.M. gardener مالن *mā'lan* N.F. woman gardener female member of gardener's family

مالی² *mā'lī* N.M. مالیہ *mā'liyah* N.M. مالیت *māliy'yat* N.F. مالیتی *māliy'yatī* ADJ. (see under مال² ★)

مالیخولیا *mālīkhoo'liyā* N.M. (arch.) melancholy [A ~ G]

مالیدہ *mālī'dah* N.M. bread mashed in butter and sugar ; mashed bread softened piece of woollen stuff [~ P مالیدن]

ماما¹ *mā'mā* N.M. (col.) mamma ; mummy ; mom [E]

ماما² *mā'mā* N.M. (dial.), مامی *mā'mī* N.F. (dial.) (see under ماموں *mā'mooṅ* N.M. ★)

ماما³ *mā'mā* N.F. maid-servant ماما پخت ریاں کھانا *mā'mā pukh'tariyāṅ khā'nā* PH. be attended by servants ; lead a comfortable life ماماگری *mā'mā-ga'rī* N.F. maidservant's job

مامتا *mam'tā* N.F. motherly love , maternal affection مامتا ٹھنڈی رہنا *mam'tā ṭhaṅ'ḍī raih'nā* V.I. of mother be happy in the sight of her children مامتا ٹھنڈی کرنا *mam'tā ṭhaṅ'ḍī kar'nā* V.I. (of mother) look affectionately on her child مامتا کی ماری *mam'tā kī mā'rī* ADJ. driven by love for her child

مامن *mā'man* (or *ma''man*) N.M. place of safety ; haven [A ~ امن]

مامور *māmoor'* ADJ. appointed commanded ; commissioned detailed for duty مامور من اللہ *māmoor' min-allāh'* N.M. one commissioned by God ; prophet مامور ہونا *māmoor' ho'nā* V.T. be appointed be entrusted (with a duty) [A ~ امر]

مامون *māmoon'* ADJ. safe ; secure [A ~ امن]

ماموں *mā'mooṅ* N.M. maternal uncle مامی *mā'mī*, ممانی *mamā'nī* N.F. maternal aunt maternal uncles's wife

ماں *māṅ* (rare ما *mā*) N.F. mother ماں باپ *māṅ' bāp* N.M. PL. father and mother parents patron ماں بہن کرنا *māṅ' bai'han kar'nā* V.T. abuse (someone) by casting aspersions on his mother and sister ماں جایا *māṅ'-jā'yā* N.M. uterine brother own brother ماں جائی *māṅ-jā''ī* ماجائی *mā-jā''* N.F. uterine sister own sister ماں سے زیادہ چاہے پھاپھا کٹنی کہلائے *māṅ' se ziyū'dah chā'he phā'phā kuṭ'nī kaihlā''e* PROV. a show of too much affection is a cause of suspicion ماں کا دودھ سمجھنا *māṅ' kā doodh sa'majhnā* V.T. usurp something ماں مر جانا *māṅ mar' jā'nā* V.I. have a shock for one's vanity ماں مرے ماسی جیے *māṅ' ma're mā'sī ji'ye* PROV. an aunt is no less affectionate than the mother

مان *mān* N.M. pride arrogance : conceit ; vanity confidence ; faith (dial.) respect مان رکھنا *mān' rakh'nā* V.T. have confidence (in) مان کرنا *mān kar'nā* V.I. be vain ; give oneself the airs

مانجھا *māṅ'jhā* N.M. paste mixed with ground glass and applied to kite string wearing of marital kit مانجھے بیٹھنا *māṅ'jhe baiṭh'nā* V.I. don on untidy dress worn on the eve of marriage مانجھے کا جوڑا *mā'ṅjhe kā jo'ṛā* N.M. marital dress

مانجھنا *māṅjh'nā* V,T. cleanse

مانجھی *māṅ'jhī* N.M. boatman مانجھن *māṅ'jhan* N.F. female member of boatman's wife

ماند **mand** ADJ. dull dim faint tarnished eclipsed ماند پڑ جانا mand' par' ja'na V.I. fade be tarnished be eclipsed

ماندہ **mań'dah** ADJ. left ; weary ; remaining tired , weary left ; remaining (F ماندی mań'dī) ill ; indisposed SUF. tired left ماندگی mań'dagī N.F. fatigue ; weariness illness , indisposition SUF. being left over [~ P ماندن]

مانڈ **mańd** N.M rice-water

مانڈا **mań'ḍa** N.M. a kind of pancake speck (on eyeball)

مانس **ma'nas** (ped. manus) N.M. (dial.) human being بھلا مانس bha'la-ma'nas N.M. gentleman bloke ; guy

مانع **ma'ne'** N.M. hinderance impediment obstacle مانع آنا (یا ہونا) ma'ne' a'na (or ho'na) V.T hinder obstruct be an obstacle (in the way of)

مانگ **mang** N.F. a line on head where hair is parted مانگ اجڑنا mang' u'jarna V.I. be widowed مانگ بنانا (یا نکالنا) mang' bana'na (or nikal'na V.T. part the hair (old use) do one's hair مانگ بھرنا mang' bhar'na V.T. fill parting live of hair with red-lead or pearls (fig.) give (a going woman) away in marriage مانگ بھری mang'-bha'rī N.F. married woman favourite wife مانگ پٹی mang' paṭ'ṭī N.F. braiding doing one's hair make up مانگ پٹی میں لگا رہنا mang' paṭ'ṭī men la'ga raih'na V. take a long time in make-up مانگ جلی mang'-ja'lī N.F. widow مانگ سنوارنا mang' sanvar'na V. braid the hair مانگ کوکھ سے ٹھنڈی رہنا mang' kookh' se ṭhań'ḍī raih'na V.I. (of woman) enjoy a happy married life and be blessed with children مانگ کھلنا mang' khul'na V.I. (of girl) have her fiance dead

مانگنا **mang'na** V.T. beg borrow demand pray seek girl's hand in marriage (for one's son, etc.) مانگ mang N.F. demand betrothal (rare) fiance مانگ تانگ کر کام چلانا mang' tang' kar kam chala'na V. to beg, borrow or steal ; to tide over a difficult period somehow مانگ تانگ کر کھانا mang' tang' kar kha'na V.I. live by begging be forced to beg or borrow مانگ لینا mang' le'na V.T. borrow مانگ ہونا mang' ho'na V.I. be in demand مانگے تانگے پر گزارا ہونا mań'ge tań'ge par guza'ra ho'na V.I. be forced to borrow ; have no regular source of income مانگے کا mań'ge ka ADJ. (F. مانگے کی mań'ge kī) borrowed

مانمت **mań'mat** N.F. hullabaloo ado; find مانمت کرنا (یا مچانا) mań'mat kar'na (or macha'na) V.I. make much hullabaloo

ماننا **mań'na** V.T. accept confess acknowledge agree (to) , assent (to) concede; grant suppose believe obey comply with (instructions, etc.) مانا کہ ma'na ke INT. granted ; I concede ; I admit مان نہ مان میں تیرا مہمان mań' na mań' main te'ra mehmań' N.F. fousting oneself upon another مانو ma'no INT. (arch.) believe me

مانند **manand'** (col. manind') ADJ. like [P ~ مامدن]

مانو **ma'no** N.F. (nurs.) pussy مانو بلی ma'no bil'lī N.F. (nurs.) pussy-cat

مانوس **manoos'** ADJ. friendly ; intimate attached ; familiar (with) used (to) [A ~ انس]

مانی **ma'nī**, مانی جی ma'nī jī N.F. (dial.) governess [A ~ انس ūn's]

ماوا **ma'va** N.M. condensed milk substance

ماوا **(or** ماویٰ) ma'va, N.M. shelter ; asylum resort ملجا و ماویٰ ma'lja-o-ma'va N.M. shelter and asylum (fig.) patron [A]

ماہ **mah** N.M. (cont. as مہ mah) moon month ماہ بماہ mah' ba mah' ADV. monthly ماہ پارہ mah'-pa'rah, مہ پارہ mah'-pa'rah ADJ. handsome (person) N.M. beloved ; sweetheart ماہتاب mah-tab', مہتاب mahtab' N.M. moon moonlight ماہتابی mah-ta'bī, مہتابی mahta'bī N.F. kind of firework cloth embroidered with starry pathern fenced terraced ماہ (یا مہ) جبیں mah' (or mah)-jabīn, ماہ (یا مہ) رخ mah' (or mah')-rukh ماہ رو، مہ رو mah'-roo, mah-roo' ماہ (یا مہ) سیما mah (or mah)-sī'ma, ماہ (یا مہ) طلعت mah (or mah)-tal''at, ماہ (یا مہ) لقا mah' (or mah)-laqa', ماہ (یا مہ) وش mah' (or mah)-vash ADJ. exquisitely beautiful N.M. beloved ; sweetheart ماہچہ mah'chah N.M. ensign metallic moon on top of ensign ماہ رواں ma'h-e ravań' N.M. current month ماہ (یا مہ) کامل ma'h (or ma'h)-e ka'mil N.M. full moon ماہ (یا مہ) کنعان ma'h (or ma'h)-e kan'an' N.M. (fig.) Joseph ماہ (یا مہ) نخشب ma'h (or ma'h)-e nakh'shab N.M. artificial moon made by political wizard, Muqan'na' who lived at Nakhshab ماہوار mah'-var' ADJ. & N.M. monthly ماہواری mah'-va'rī ADV. per mensem N.F. menses ; menstral cycle ماہانہ maha'nah ADJ. & ADV. monthly ماہیانہ mahiya'nah N.M. (arch.) monthly salary [P]

ماہر māhir ADJ & N.M., (PL ماہرین māhirīn' ped. PL. مہرہ ma'harah) expert master (of) adept ; skilful skilled (in) PREF -ist ماہر ہونا mā'hir ho'nā V. I. be an expert (in) ماہر ارضیات mā'hir-e arẓiyyāt' N.M. geologist ماہر السنہ māh'ir-e al'sinah N.M master of languages ماہر لسانیات mā'hir-e lisāniyyāt' N.M. linguist ماہر تعلیمات mā'hir-e ta'līmāt' N.M. educationist ; educationalist ماہر حشریات mā'hir-e hashriyyāt' N.M entomologist ماہر خصوصی mā'hir-e khusoo'sī N.M specialist ماہر طبیعیات mā'hir-e tabī'iyyāt' N.M physicist ماہر اشعاعیات mā'hir-e ish'ā'iyyāt' N.M radiologist ماہر حیوانیات mā'hir-e haivaniyyāt' N.M. zoologist ماہر علم کیمیا mā'hir-e 'il'm-e kīmiyā' N.M. chemist ماہر نباتیات mā'hir-e nabātiyyāt' N.M. botanist ماہر معاشیات mā'hir-e mā'āshiyyāt' N.M. economist ماہر نفسیات mā'hir-e nafsiyyāt' N.M psychologist [A ~ مہارت]

ماہی mā'hī N.F fish ماہیِ بے آب mā'hī-e be ā̀b' ADJ. (fig.) restless ; uneasy ماہی پشت mā'hī-pūsh't N.M a kind of embroidery looking like fish-bone ماہی توا mā'hī-ta'vā N.M. fish-frying pan ماہی خوار mā'hī-khār N.M. cormorant ماہی گیر mā'hī-gīr N.M. fisherman ماہی گیری mā'hī-gī'rī N.F. fishing ماہی مراتب mā'hī marā'tib N.M. insignia of honour carried before princes, etc. [P]

ماہیت mā'hiyat N.F. nature intrinsic value real worth essence [A ~ ما what + ہی it]

مائع mā''e' N.M. & ADJ fluid , liquid [A]

مائل mā''il ADJ. fond (of) towards مائل کرنا mā''il kar'nā V.T persuade [A]

ماؤف mā'oof' ADJ. afflicted (of bodily organ faculting, etc.) not functioning [A]

مائی[1] mā'ī N.F maid-servant old woman mother

مائی[2] mā''ī ADJ see under ما

مایا mā'yā N.F (dial.) wealth illusion [S]

مایوس māyoos' ADJ. disappointed despondent frustrated chagrined مایوس کرنا māyoos' kar'nā V.T disappoint ; frustrate مایوس کن māyoos'-kun ADJ hopeless مایوس کن انداز māyoos'-kun andāz N.M. hopeless manner مایوس ہونا māyoos' ho'nā V.I. despair (of) , be disappointed (with) be frustrated be chagrined مایوسی māyoo'sī N.F disappointment despair despondence ; air of despondence frustration chagrin [A ~ یاس]

مایہ mā'yah N.M. stock ; capital cause (of) مایہ ناز mā'ya-e nāz' cause of pride (to) فرومایہ firo-mā'yah ADJ. base mean [P]

مباح mūbāh' ADJ. permissible lawful مباح رکھنا (یا سمجھنا) mūbāh' rakh'nā (or sa'majhnā) V.T. permit . allow , regard as lawful مباح کرنا mūbāh' kar'nā V.T make lawful , legalise [A ~ اباحت]

مباحث mabā'his N.M (PL. of بحث N.M ★)

مباحثہ mūbā'hasah N.M debate discussion مباحثہ کرنا mūbā'hasah kar'nā V.T debate ; hold debate discuss [A ~ بحث]

مبادا ma-bā'dā, مبادا کہ ma-bā'dā ke ADV [P ~ ما not + بودن be]

مبادرت mūbā'darat N.F expedition vieing with hastening (towards) [A]

مبادلہ mūbā'dalah N.M. exchange barter مبادلہ کرنا mūbā'dalah kar'nā V.T. exchange زرِ مبادلہ za'r-e mūbā'dalah N.M. foreign exchange [A ~ بدل]

مبادی mabā'dī مبادیات mabādiyyāt' N.M. PL fundamentals first principles elements rudiments [A ~ بدایت]

مبارز mūbā'riz N.M. warrior challenger مبارزت mūbā'razat N.F. single combat (rare) challenge دعوتِ مبارزت دینا da''vat-e mūbā'razat de'na V.T. challenge someone to single combat [A]

مبارک mūbā'rak N.F congratulation; felicitation ADJ. lucky ; fortunate auspicious blessed INT. (also مبارک ہو mūbā'rak ho) congratulations bless you مبارک دینا mūbā'rak de'nā V.T. congratulate مبارک لینا mūbā'rak mil'nā V.I be congratulated مبارک ہونا mūbā'rak ho'nā V.I. be lucky (for) مبارک باد mūbā'rak bād N.F congratulation ; felicitation INT. congratulations مبارکباد کہنا mūbā'rak-bād kaih'nā V.T. congratulate مبارک بادی mūbā'rak-bā'dī N.F. congratulation marital song مبارکبادیاں گانا mūbā'rak-bā'diyān gā'nā V.T sing مبارکی mūbā'rakī N.F. (col.) same as مبارک N.F. ★ [A ~ برکت blessing]

مباشرت mūbā'sharat N.F. sexual intercourse copulation (rare) (of stripped couple) fondling مباشرتِ فاحشہ mūbā'sharat-e fā'hishah N.F. copulation مباشرت کرنا mūbā'sharat kar'nā V.T. have sexual intercourse (with) ; (of male) copulate (with) [A]

مبالغ mabā'ligh N.M. (PL. of مبلغ mab'lagh ★)

مبالغہ mūbā'laghah N.M. exaggeration hyberbole مبالغہ آرائی mūbā'lagha-ārā''ī N.F exaggeration (مبالغہ کرنا (یا سے کام لینا) mūbā'laghah kar'na (or se kam' le'nā) V.T. exaggerate use hyperboles [A]

مباني mabā'nī N.M. PL. buildings ; structures [A ~ SING. مبنی]

مباہات mūbāhat' N.F. pride contenting for glory فخر و مباہات fakh'r-o-mūbāhat' N.M. price and glory

مباہلہ mūbā'halah N.M. mutual imprecation to prove truth of one's point [A]

مبتدا mūb'tadā N.M. subject (of predicate or proposition) مبتدا و خبر mūb'tadā-o-kha'bar N.M. subject and predicate [A ~ ابتدا]

مبتدی mūb'tad N.M. beginner novice ; tyro young scholar; beginning student [A ~ ابتدا]

مبتذل mūb'tazal ADJ. trite (idea or expression); (phrase) worn threadbare [A ~ ابتذال]

مبتلا mūbtalā' ADJ. suffering (from) afflicted (with) involved (in) distressed ; distracted ; unfortunate ; enamoured captivated ; enthralled [A ~ ابتلا]

مبحث mab'has N.M. (PL. مباحث mabā'his) point at issue topic [A ~ بحث]

مبدا mab'dā N.M. source ; origin ; fountainhead مبدا فیض mab'da-e faiz' fountainhead of bounty ; God's grace [A ~ ہدایت]

مبدل mūbad'dal ADJ. changed مبدل بہ mūbad'dal ba ADJ. changed into مبدل منہ mūbad'dal min'-hū PH. case in apposition

مبذر mūbaz'zir N.M. (PL. مبذرین mūbazzirīn') spendthrift [A ~ تبذیر]

مبذول mabzool' ADJ. given devoted ; bestowed توجہ مبذول کرنا (یا کرانا) tavaj'joh mabzool' karnā (or karā'nā) V.T. call attention to devote attention (to) ; attend (to)

مبرا mūbar'rā ADJ. free (of or from) exempted (from) innocent (of) [A ~ بری]

مبرز mab'raz N.M. anus [A ~ براز]

مبرم mūb'ram ADJ. inevitable ; inexorable قضائے مبرم qazā'-e mūb'ram N.F. inevitable calamity trouble some person [A ~ ابرام]

مبرور mabroor' ADJ. the late ; one who has found salvation (of pilgrimage) accepted by God [A ~ بر]

مبسوط mabsoot' ADJ. detailed [A ~ بسط]

مبشر mūbash'shir N.M. evangelist ; one who brings glad tidings مبشر mūbash'shar N.M. one who has been brought glad tidings [A ~ بشارت]

مبصر mūbas'sir N.M. observer ADJ. perspicacious [A ~ بصارت]

مبعوث mab'oos' ADJ. sent ; commissioned [A ~ بعث]

مبغوض mabghooz' ADJ. object of God's wrath in (someone's) bad (or black) books [A ~ بغض]

مبلغ mab'lagh N.M. destination limit quantity ; number coin مبلغ علیہ السلام mab'lagh 'alai'h is-salam' N.M. Mammon مبلغ علم mab'lagh-e 'il'm N.M. limits of one's knowledge مبلغات mablaghat' N.M. PL. money ; coins [A ~ بلاغ]

مبنی mab'nī ADJ. based on ; founded on N.M. word which is never inflected

مبہم mū'bham ADJ. ambiguous ; equivocal [A ~ ابہام]

مبہوت mabhoot' dumb-founded ; struck dumb with amazement [A]

مبہی mūbah'hī ADJ. aphrodisiac [A ~ باہ]

مبین mūbīn' ADJ. clear : manifest [A ~ بیان]

مبینہ mūbay'yanah ADJ. alleged [A ~ بیان]

مت¹ mat' ADV. do not ; don't

مت² mat N.F. sense ; commonsense wit مت دینا mat' de'nā V.T. advise ; counsel مت ماری جانا mat mā'rī jā'nā V.I. lose one's senses ; act as a fool become a dotard

متابعت mūtā'ba'at N.F. doing something in the manner of ; following [A]

متاثر mūta'as'sir ADJ. (F. or PL. متاثرہ mūta'as'sarah) affected impressed afflicted [A ~ اثر]

متاخر mūta'a'kh'khir ADJ. following ; coming later متاخرین mūtā'akhkhirīn' N.M. PL. the modern ; modern writers ; later [A ~ آخر]

متاسف mūta'as'sif ADJ. grieved regretful repentant متاسفانہ mūta'assifā'nah ADV. regretfully ; ADJ. regretful [A ~ اسف]

متاع matā'' N.F. (PL. امتعہ am'te'ah) stock ; merchandise goods ; effects property possessions [A]

متاعی mūtā''ī N.F. temporary wife [~A متعہ]

متامل muta'am'mil ADJ. hesitant [A ~ تامل]

متانا *mūta'na* V.T. cause to make water [~ موت *moot*]

متانت *mata'nat* N.F. gravity [A]

متاہل *mūta' ah'hil* ADJ. married N.M. family man [A ~ اہل]

متبادر *mūtaba'dir* ADJ. easily ; comprehensible [A]

متبادل *mūtaba'dil* ADJ. (F. & PL. متبادلہ *mūtabā'-dilah*) alternate alternatives متبادلہ زاویے *mūtabā'dilah zā'viye* N.M. alternate angles [A ~ بدل]

متبائن *mūtabā'yin* ADJ. different [A ~ تباین]

متبحر *mūtabaḥ'ḥir* ADJ. deeply (read) ; great scholar [A ~ بحر sea]

متبرک *mutabar'rak* ADJ. holy ; sacred blessed [A ~ برکت]

متبسم *mutabas'sim* ADJ. smiling (face, etc.) [A ~ تبسم]

متبع *mūt'tabe'* N.M. follower disciple [A ~ اتباع]

متبنیٰ *mutaban'nā* ADJ. & N.M. adopted (son) متبنیٰ کرنا *mutaban'nā kar'nā* V.T. adopt (some-some) [A ~ ابن]

متجاوز *mūtaja'viz* ADJ. (one) exceeding (one's) limits ADV. more than (is necessary [A ~ تجاوز]

متجسس *mūtajas'sis* ADJ. searching (eyes, etc.) [A ~ تجسس]

متحد *mūt'taḥid* ADJ. (F. & PL. متحدہ *mūt'taḥidah*) united [A ~ اتحاد]

متحرک *mūtaḥar'rik* ADJ. moving mobile movable vowelized متحرک تصاویر *mūtaḥar'rik tasā'vir* N.F. PL. movie ; pictures غیر متحرک *ghair-mūtaḥar'rik* ADV. inmovable not having a vowel [A ~ حرکت]

متحقق *mūtaḥaq'qaq* ADJ. proved [A ~ حقیقت]

متحمل *mūtaḥam'mil* ADJ. patient considerate [A ~ تحمل]

متحیر *mūtaḥay'yir* ADJ. amazed ; astonished [A ~ تحیر]

متخاصم *mūtakhās'sim* ADJ. contending متخاصمین *mūtakhāsimain'* N.M. plaintiff and defendant متخاصمین *mūtakhasimīn'* N.M. PL. contenders [A ~ خصومت]

متخلص *mūtakhal'lis* ADJ. surname ; having the poetical surname المتخلص *al-mūtakhal'lis ba* ADJ. surnamed [A ~ تخلص]

متخیلہ *mūtakhay'yilah* N.F. (also قوت متخیلہ *qūvvat-e mūtakhay'yilah*) fancy ; imagination [A ~ خیال]

متدارک *mūtadā'rik* ADJ. one who finds a lost thing N.M. this as name of a prosodic metre [A ~ درک]

متداول *mūtadā'val* ADJ. (F. & PL. متداولہ *mūtada'-valah*) current [A]

متدین *mūtday'yin* ADJ. religious-minded [A ~ تدین]

متذبذب *mūtazab'zib* ADJ. hesitant [A ~ تذبذب]

متذکرہ *mūtazak'karah* ADJ. stated متذکرہ بالا (صدر) *mūtazak'kara-e bā'lā* (or *sad'r*) ADJ. aforesaid ; above-mentioned

متر *mit'tar* (ped. *mit'r*) N.M. (dial.) friend مترائی *mitra''ī* N.F., مترتا *mit'rtā* N.F. (dial.) friendship [S]

مترادف *mūtarādif* ADJ. synonymous N.M. (PL. مترادفات *mūtarādifāt'*) synonym [A ~ ردف]

مترتب *mūtarat'tab* ADJ. arranged [A]

مترجم *mutar'jim* N.M. translator مترجم *mutar'jam* ADJ. translated ; rendered into other language published along with translation [A ~ ترجمہ]

متردد *mūtarad'did* ADJ. hesitant [A ~ تردد]

مترشح *mūtarash'sheḥ* ADJ. apparent ; evident drizzling [A ~ ترشح]

مترصد *mūtaras'sid* ADJ. one looking forward (to) [A ~ ترصد]

مترقبہ *mūtaraq'qabah* ADJ. expected غیر مترقبہ *ghair-mūtbraq'qabah* ADJ. unexpected [A ~ رقابت]

مترنم *mutaran'nim* ADJ. singing melodious [A ~ ترنم]

متروک *matrook'* (F. & PL. متروکہ *matroo'-kah*) forsaken ; abandoned archaic ; obsolete N.M. (PL. متروکات *matrookāt'*), متروک الاستعمال *matrook-ūl-iste'māl'* ADJ. no longer in use; obsolete *matroo'kah jā''edad* N.F. evacuee property A ~ ترک]

متزائد *mūtazā''īd* ADJ. increasing ; multiplying [A ~ تزائد ~ زیادت]

متزلزل *mūtazal'zil* ADJ. shaken made to tottering ; shaky ; rickety [A ~ تزلزل]

متساوی *mūtasā'vī* ADJ. equal PREF. equi- متساوی الاضلاع *mūtasā'vi-l-azlā'* (col. -vi-ūl-) ADJ. equilateral [A ~ مساوات]

متشابہ *mūtashā'beh* ADJ. like ; similar resembling ambiguous N.M. (PL. متشابہات

mūtasha'behāt') ambiguous verse Holy Quran
متشابہ لگنا *mūtasha'beh lag'nā* V.I. (in recitation of the Holy Quran) be misled from one place to another by similarity of verses [A ~ تشابہ]

متشاعر *mūtashā''ir* N.M. pseudo-poet [A ~ شعر]

متشدد *mūtashad'did* ADJ. violent strict متشددانہ *mūtashad'didā'nah* ADJ. strict violent ADV. strictly violently using third degree methods

متشرع *mūtashar're'* ADJ. religious strict in observance of religious [A ~ شریعت]

متشکک *mūtashak'kik* ADJ. & N.M. agnostic [A ~ شک]

متشکل *mūtashak'kil* ADJ. taking shape [A ~ شکل]

متصادم *mūtasā'dim* ADJ. colliding clashing [A ~ تصادم]

متصدع *mūtasad'de* ADJ. causing inconvenience ; hardache (for) [A ~ تصدع]

متصدی *mūtasad'dī* N.M. clerk (arch.) private secretary منشی متصدی *mūn'shī mūtasad'dī* N.M. PL. clerks and private secretaries [A ~ تصدی]

متصرف *mūtasar'rif* ADJ. (one) who usurps [A ~ تصرف]

متصف *mūt'tasif* ADJ. described [A ~ وصف]

متصل *mūt'tasil* (F. & PL. متصلہ *mūt'tasilah*) ADJ. adjoining ; contiguous ; ADV. continuously near ; close by [A ~ اتصال]

متصور *mūtasav'var* ADJ. imaginable considered ; deemed متصور ہونا *mūtasav'var ho'nā* V.I. be considered ; be deemed [A ~ تصور]

متضاد *mūtazād'* ADJ. opposite contrary N.M. (PL. متضادات *mūtazaddāt'*) antonym [A ~ تضاد]

متضمن *mūtazam'min* ADJ. inclusive [A ~ ضمن]

متعارض *mūta'ā'riz* ADJ. clashing ; conflicting reports, etc.) [A ~ تعارض]

متعارف *mūta'ā'raf* ADJ. (F. & PL. متعارفہ *mūta'ā'rafah*) ADJ. widelyknown self-evident axiomatic already introduced اصول متعارفہ *usoo'l-e mūta'ā'rafah* N.M. self-evident truths ; axioms [A ~ تعارف]

متعاقب *mūta'ā'qib* ADJ. pursuing subsequent [A ~ تعاقب]

متعالی *mūta'āl'* ADJ. exalted sublime [A ~ علو]

مشاہد *mūshā'hid* ADJ. allied ; confederate [A ~ اشاہدہ]

متعجب *mūta'aj'jib* ADJ. surprised astonished ; amazed ; wonderstruck [A ~ تعجب]

متعدد *mūta'ad'dad* ADJ. numerous many ; many a a number of متعدد بار *mūta'ad'dad bār* ADV. many a time ; on many occasions [A ~ تعدد]

متعدی *mūta'ad'dī* ADJ. transitive (verb) infectious (disease) متعدی المتعدی *mūta'addi-l-mūta'ad'dī* N.M. causative متعدی امراض *mūta'ad'dī amraz* N.M. PL. infectious diseases ; epidemics [A ~ تعدی]

متعرض *mūta'ar'riz* ADJ. resisting ; standing in the way (of) [A ~ تعرض]

متعصب *mūta'as'sib* ADJ. prejudiced bigotted N.M. bigot [A ~ تعصب]

متعفن *mūta'af'fin* ADJ. stinking [A ~ تعفن]

متعلق *mūta'al'liq* ADJ. connected with ; relating (to) ; appropriate attached (to) dependent (on) relevant (to) متعلق فعل *mūta'al'liq-e fe''l* N.M. adverb متعلق کرنا *mūta'alliq kar'nā* V.T. attach entrust (to) متعلقات *mūta'alliqāt'* N.M. relevant matters adjuncts متعلقات فعل *mūta'alliqāt-e fe''l* N.M. adverbial adjuncts متعلقین *mūta'alliqīn'* N.M. dependents [A ~ تعلق]

متعلم *mūta'al'lim* N.M. pupil ; student [A ~ تعلم]

متعہ *mūt''ah* N.M. marriage valid for stipulated period only ; usu. functionary marriage [A ~ متاع]

متعہد *mūta'ah'hid* N.M. & ADJ. (one) who enters into a covenant : (one) who accepts a responsibility [A ~ تعہد]

متعین *mūta'ay'yan* (F. & PL. متعینہ *mūta'ay'yanah* ADJ. appointed fixed determined متعین کرنا *mūta'ay'yan kar'nā* V. appoint determine متعین ہونا *mūta'ay'yan ho'nā* V.I. be appointed be dertermined [A ~ تعین]

متغزل *mūtaghaz'zil* N.M. (PL. متغزلین *mūtaghazzilīn'*) composer of odes [A ~ تغزل]

متغیر *mūtaghay'yar* (F. & PL. متغیرہ *mūtaghay'yarah* ADJ. changed inconsistant [A ~ تغیر]

متفاوت *mūtafā'vit* ADJ. different [A ~ تفاوت]

متفحص *mūtafah'his* ADJ. searching seeking N.M. researcher [A ~ تفحص]

متفرع *mūtafar're'* ADJ. branching out [A ~ فرع]

متفرق mūtafar'raq ADJ. various miscellaneous scattered ; dispersed متفرق ہونا mūtafar'raq ho'nā be dispersed ; be scattered متفرقات mūtafarraqāt' N.F. miscellaneous items various things sundries [A ~ تفرق]

متفق mūt'tafiq ADJ. agreeing agreeable متفق الرائے mut'tafiq-ur-rā'e ADJ. (of persons) unanimous متفق ہو جانا mut'tafiq ho jā'nā V. agree together unite سے متفق ہونا se mut'tafiq ho'nā V.T. agree (to) see eye to eye (with) متفق mut'tafaq ADJ. agreed متفق علیہ mut'tafaq 'alaih' ADJ. unanimous decision, etc.) [A ~ اتفاق]

متفکر mutafak'kir ADJ. concerned (over) [A ~ تفکر]

متفنی mūtafan'ni ADJ. mischievous crafty [A]

متقابل mūtaqā'bil N.M. 'per contra' opposite ADV. lying opposite [A ~ تقابل]

متقارب mūtaqā'rib ADJ. convergent ; close N.M. this as name of a prosodic metre [A ~ قرب]

متقاضی mūtaqā'zī ADJ. demanding wiging [A ~ تقاضا]

متقدم mūtaqad'dim ADJ. ancient preceding متقدمین mūtaqaddimīn' N.M. PL. the ancients [A ~ تقدم]

متقشف mūtaqash'shif ADJ. ascetical (one) living on bare subsistence level [A ~ تقشف]

متقی mūt'taqī N.M. & ADJ. (PL. متقین mūttaqīn') pious (person) [A ~ اتقا]

متکبر mūtakab'bir ADJ. proud ; haughty ; arrogant متکبرانہ mūtakabbirā'nah ADJ. proud; arrogant ; haughty ADV. proudly; arrogantly ; haughtily [A ~ تکبر]

متکفل mūtakaf'fil N.M. bail ; surety [A ~ تکفل]

متکلف mūtakal'lif N.M. & ADJ. (person) putting someone to inconvenience [A ~ تکلف]

متکلم mūtakal'lim N.M. (gram.) first person schoolman ; scholastic philosopher A ~ تکلم]

متلاشی mūtalā'shī ADJ. seeking enquiring [pseudo- A ~ P تلاش]

متلاطم mūtalā'tim ADJ. stormy (sea) dashing (waves) [A ~ تلاطم]

متلانا matlā'nā V.I. be sick ; feel nausea متلی mat'lī N.F. nausea متلی ہونا mat'lī ho'nā V.I. sick

متلذذ mūtalaz'ziz ADJ. enjoying [A ~ تلذذ]

متلون mūtalav'vin ADJ. whimsical fickle ; capricious متلون مزاج mūtalav'vin-mizāj ADJ. fickle-minded [A ~ تلون]

متلی mat'lī N.F. (see under متلانا ★)

متماثل mūtamā'sil ADJ. similar : identical [A ~ مثل]

متمتع mūtamat'te' ADJ. enjoying; availing oneself (of) متمتع ہونا mūtamat'te' ho'na V.I. enjoy ; avail oneself (of) [A ~ تمتع]

متمدن mūtamad'din ADJ. civilised cultured [A ~ تمدن]

متمرد mūtamar'rid ADJ. proud ; haughty refractory ; wayward [A ~ تمرد]

متمکن mūtamak'kin ADJ. occupying ; seated strong ; powerful [A ~ تمکن]

متمم mutam'mim N.M. one who completes complement [A ~ تمام]

متمنی mutaman'ni desirous (of) [A ~ تمنا]

متموج mutamav'vij ADJ. (of waters) surging ; billowing [A ~ تموج]

متمول mūtamav'vil ADJ. rich ; wealthy ; affluent [A ~ تمول]

متمیز mutamay'yiz ADJ. distinct [A]

متن mat'n N.M. (PL. متون mūtoon') text [A]

متنا mūt'nā متوڑا muto'ṛā N.M. child who wets bed [~ موت moot]

متنازع mūtanā'za' ADJ. (F. & PL. متنازعہ mūtanā'za'ah) disputed ; controversial متنازعہ فیہ mūtanā'za'ah fīh' ADJ. (wrong but current form for متنازع فیہ mūtanā'zā' fīh') controversial ; disputed (point) at issue [A ~ تنازع]

متناسب mutanā'sib ADJ. proportionate [A ~ تناسب]

متناقض mūtanā'qiz ADJ. opposite ; contrary [A ~ تناقض]

متناہی mūtanā'hī ADJ. extreme terminated [A ~ تناہی]

متنبی mūtanab'bī N.M. pseudo-prophet [A ~ نبی]

متنبہ mūtanab'bah ADJ. warned cautious متنبہ کرنا mūtanab'bah kar'nā V.T. warn caution متنبہ ہونا mūtanab'bah ho'nā V.I. be warned wake up to danger, etc. [A ~ تنبہ]

متنجن mūtan'jan N.M. sour-sweet rice dish

متنفر mūtanaf'fir ADJ. disgusted with repugnant [A ~ تنفر]

متنفس **mutanaf'fis** N.M. individual [A ~ نفس]

متواتر **mutavā'tir** ADV. repeatedly ; continually continuously [A ~ تواتر]

متوازی **mūtavā'zī** ADJ. parallel متوازی الاضلاع **mūtavā'zi-l-azlā''** ADJ. & N.M. quarilateral (figure) متوازی الساقین **mūtavā'zi-s-sāqain'** ADJ. & N.M. isosceles (triangle) [A]

متواضع **mūtavā'ze'** ADJ. hospitable (rare) modest [A ~ تواضع]

متوالا **matvā'lā** ADJ. (F. متوالی **matvā'lī**) drunk; intoxicated fond (of) ; in love (with) متوالا ہونا **matvā'la ho'nā** V.I. be drunk ; be intoxicated be fond (of)

متوالی **mutavā'lī** ADJ. continuous ; successive , recurring [A ~

متوجہ **mūtavaj'jeh** ADJ. Attentive turning towards متوجہ کرنا (یا کرانا) **mūtavaj'jeh kar'nā** (or **kara'nā**) V.T. call or draw (someone's) attention متوجہ ہونا **mūtavaj'jeh ho'nā** V.I. attend to ; to turn the attention to address (someone) turn one's face (towards) ; attention to proceed (to-wards) [A ~ توجہ]

متوحش **mūtavah'hish** ADJ. desolate (place) terrified person scared away unfriendly [A ~ توحش]

متورع **mūtavar're'** ADJ. pious [A ~ تورع]

متورم **mūtavar'ram** ADJ. swollen [A ~ ورم]

متوسط **mūtavas'sit** ADJ. middle medium ; medium sized middling mediocre متوسط الحال **mūtvas'sit-ūl-hal'** ADJ. (member) of middle class [A ~ توسط]

متوسل **mūtavas'sil** ADJ. (person) who regards someone as his intercessor with God [A ~ توسل]

متوطن **mūtavat'tin** ADJ. & N.M. native inhabitant [~ توطن]

متوفی **mūtavaf'fī** ADJ. (ped. متوفیٰ **mutavaf'fā**) deceased [A ~ وفات]

متوقع **mūtavaq'qe'** AD. expectant ; anticipating متوقع ہونا **mūtavaq'qe' ho'nā** V.I. expect anticipate متوقع **mūtavaq'qa'** ADJ. expected anticipated متوقع ہونا **mutavaq'qa' ho'nā** V.I. be expected be anticipated

متوکل **mūtavak'kil** ADJ. resigned to the will of God resigned to fate ; resigned [A ~ توکل]

متوڑا **muto'ṛa** N.M. & ADJ. (same as متنا N.M. & ADJ. ★)

متولد **mūtaval'lid** ADJ. born [A ~ تولد]

متولی **mūtaval'lī** N.M. trustee [A]

متوہم **mūtavah'him** ADJ. doubtful ; distracting ; apprehensive ; scrupulous [A ~ توہم]

متھا **mat'thā** N.M. (sae as ماتھا N.M. ★) متھا پھٹول **mat'thā-phūtav'val** N.F. nodding acquaintance

متھانی **mathā'nī** N.F. same as متھنی N.F. (see under متھنا V.T. ★)

متہم **mūt'taham** ADJ. accused [A ~ اتہام]

متھنا **math'nā** V.T. ground (something) saucepan knead cover (fish, etc.) with dough or paste N.M. crusher متھنی **math'nī**, **mathā'nī** N.F. crushing rod ; crusher

متی **mi'tī** N.F. (dial.) day of maturity (of bill of exchange, etc.) متی کاٹا **mi'tī kā'ṭa** N.M. discount (on bill of exchange

متیقن **mutqyaq'qan** ADJ. certain , ascertained [A ~ تیقن]

متین **matīn'** ADJ. grave ; serious (rare) solid حبل متین **hab'l-e matīn'** N.F. strong rope (fig.) true faith [A ~ متانت]

مٹاپا **mūṭā'pā** N.M. fatness ; plumpness , corpulence مٹاپا چڑھنا **mūṭā'pa charh'nā** V.I. grow fat [~ موٹا]

مٹانا **miṭā'nā** V.T. destroy obliterate efface bring to an end rub off ; erase حرف غلط کی طرح مٹانا **har'f-e gh'alat kī tar'h miṭā'nā** PH. obliterate نام و نشان مٹانا **nā'm-o-nishān' miṭā'nā** V.T. obliterate

مٹائی **mūṭā''ī** N.F. thickness [~ موٹا]

مٹ بھیڑ **mūṭ bhīṛ** N.F. (same as مٹھ بھیڑ **mūṭh bheṛ** N.F. ★)

مٹر **ma'ṭar** N.F. pea ; peas مٹر سی **ma'ṭar sī** ADJ. small (eyes)

مٹرگشت **ma'ṭar-gasht** N.F. ramble مٹرگشت کرنا **ma'ṭar-gasht kar'nā** V.T. ramble

مٹرمٹر **mū'ṭar mū'ṭar** ADV. (look) with astonished eyes ; with amazement

مٹک **ma'ṭak** N.F. (see under مٹکنا V.I. ★)

مٹکا **maṭ'kā** N.M. large earthen jar مٹکی **maṭ'kī** N.M. earthen jar

مٹکنا **ma'ṭaknā** V.I. move with dalliance مٹک **ma'ṭak** N.F. mincing gait ; dalliance مٹک کر **ma'ṭak kar** with dalliance ADV. مٹکو **maṭak' ko** N.F. (col. woman who walks with dalliance مٹکانا *maṭkā'nā* V.T. wink move (part of body) with dalliance

مٹنا *miṭ'nā* V.I. be destroyed become extinct be obliterated be effaced be rubbed off, be erased come to an end

مٹھ *maṭh* N.M. (H dial.) convent ; monastery indigo vat

مٹھ بھیڑ *mŭṭh-bher'* N.F (same as مڈ بھیڑ N.F. ★)

مٹھا *maṭ'ṭhā* N.M. dense butter milk ADJ. (of person) slow

مٹھا *mŭṭ'ṭhā* N.M. sheaf handle hilt carder's cudgel

مٹھارنا *mŭṭhar'nā* V T knead well press with fists give a round shape (to) talk with a relish مٹھار مٹھار کر *mŭṭhār' mŭṭhār' kar* ADV. (talk) with a relish

مٹھاس *miṭhās'* N.F. sweetness [~ میٹھا]

مٹھائی *miṭhā''ī* N.F. sweets sweetmeat ; confection [~ میٹھا]

مٹھری *miṭh'rī* N.F. sweet-saltish biscuit مٹھریاں *miṭhriyāṅ* N.F. PL. infants hiccups

مٹھلونا *miṭhloo'nā* ADJ. with little salt [~ میٹھا + لون]

مٹھو *miṭ'ṭhoo* N.M. (nurs.) poll; parrot talkative child

مٹھی *miṭ'ṭhī* N.F. (nurs.) kiss مٹھی دینا *miṭ'ṭhī de'nā* V.I (of child) let someone kiss (kind) مٹھی لینا *miṭ'ṭhī le'nā* V.T. (nurs) kiss

مٹھولا *mŭṭho'lā* N.M. (vul.) masturbation مٹھولے مارنا *mŭṭho'le mār'nā* V.I. (vul.) masturbate

مٹھی *mŭṭ'ṭhī* N.F. fist handful مٹھی بھرنا *mŭṭ'ṭhī bhar'nā* V.T. massage ; press body with hands for massage مٹھی گرم کرنا *mŭṭ'ṭhī gar'm kar'nā* V.T. bribe ; grease the palm (of) مٹھی میں ہونا *mŭṭ'ṭhī meṅ ho'nā* V I. be under (someone's) influence ; be under the thum (of) مٹھیا *mŭṭh'yā* N.F. handle hilt thick end of stick carder's cudgel

مٹی *maṭ'ṭī*. (or *miṭ'ṭī*) N.F earth soil clay dirt (fig) dead body مٹی اڑانا *maṭ'ṭī ŭṛā'nā* V. raise dust مٹی برباد (یا پلید یا خراب یا خوار) کرنا *maṭ'ṭī barbād'* (or *palīd'* or *kharāb'* or *khār'*) *kar'nā* V.T. disgrace scandalize make a fool (of) ; make a butt of ridicule مٹی برباد (یا پلید یا خراب یا خوار) ہونا *maṭ'ṭī barbād* (or *palīd'* or *kharāb'* or *khār'*) *ho'nā* V I be disgraced be scandalized مٹی ٹھکانے لگانا *maṭ'ṭī ṭhikā'ne lagā'nā* V.T. perform funeral rites (of someone) properly مٹی ٹھکانے لگنا *maṭ'ṭī ṭhikā'ne lag'nā* V.I receive proper burial مٹی دینا *maṭ'ṭī de'nā* V.T. cast dust (into someone's grave) during burial مٹی ڈالنا *maṭ'ṭī ḍāl'na* V.T. forgive and forget hush up let go with a curse مٹی ڈھونا *maṭ'ṭī ḍho'nā* V.T. carry loads of earth مٹی عزیز کرنا *maṭ'ṭī azīz' kar'nā* V.T. give proper burial مٹی کا پتلا (یا پنجر) *maṭ'ṭī kā pŭt'lā* (or *pin'jar*) N.M. (fig.) mortal coil human being مٹی کا تیل *maṭ'ṭī kā tel'* N.M. kerosine oil ; petroleum مٹی کا عطر *maṭ'ṭī kā 'iṭ'r* N.M. essence of clay مٹی کا گھڑا بھی ٹھونک بجا کر لیتے ہیں *maṭ'ṭī ka gha'ṛā bhī ṭhonk' bajā' kar le'te haiṅ* PROV. a buyer thoroughly examines the wares before purchase مٹی کا مادھو *maṭ'ṭī kā mā'dho* N.M. fool ; dunce dummy ; non entity مٹی کرنا *maṭ'ṭī kar'nā* V.T. ruin squander ; fool away (one's money) spoil مٹی کی مورت *maṭ'ṭī kī moo'rat* N.F. clay figure (fig.) mortal coil مٹی کے مول *maṭ'ṭī ke mol* ADV. very cheap مٹی لے ڈالنا *maṭ'ṭī le ḍāl'nā* V.T. pay frequent visits (to the house of) مٹی میں لوٹنا *maṭ'ṭī meṅ loṭ'nā* V. roll in dust مٹی میں ملانا *maṭ'ṭī meṅ milā'nā* V. spoil mar disgrace ruin bring to nought bring about the death (of) مٹی میں مل جانا *maṭ'ṭī meṅ mil jā'nā* V.I. to be spoiled be marred be ruined be disgraced die مٹی ہو جانا *maṭ'ṭī ho jā'nā* V.I. labour under hard conditions come to dust grow weak become worthless مٹیا *maṭ'yā* N.F. small pitcher ADJ. clay earthen earthwork dust-coloured مٹیا برج *maṭ'yā-bŭr'j* N.M. clay tower مٹیا پھونس *maṭ'yā-phoons* ADJ. decrepit N.M. very old person مٹیا ٹھس *maṭ'yā-ṭhŭs* ADJ. lazy ; indolent مٹیا محل *maṭ'yā-mahal'* N.M. habitation مٹیار *maṭyār'* N.F. clayey soil young woman ADJ. dust-coloured مٹیالا *maṭ yā'lā* ADJ. dust-coloured مٹیانا *maṭ yā'nā* V.I. come to dust be rubbed with dust (of lamp) be extinguished turn a deaf ear

مثاب *masāb'* N.M. resort SUF. resorting (to) [A]

مثال *misāl'* N.F. example ; instance solved exercise parable saying ; proverb (platonic world of) ideas ideal مثال دینا (یا پیش کرنا) *misāl de'nā* (or *pesh kar'nā*) V.T give an example quote instance cite a precedent relate a parable عالم مثال *'ālam-e misāl'* N.M. plotonic world of ideas مثالی *misā'lī* ADJ. ideal model [A]

مثانہ *masā'nah* N M. bladder [A]

مثبت *mŭs'bat* ADJ positive affirmative proved endorsed written [A ~ اثبات]

مثقال *misqāl'* N.M. weight equivalent to four-and-half 'mashes' [A ~ ثقل]

¹مثل mis'l N.F. (usu. but wrong spelling of مسل N.F. ★)

²مثل mis'l ADJ. as ; like ; resembling [A]

مثل ma'sal N.F. (PL. امثال amsal') saying proverb مثلاً ma'salan ADJ. for example ; for instance [A]

مثلث mūsal'las N.F. triangle poem with three lined stanzas ADJ. triangular مثلث حاد الزاویہ mūsal'las had'd-ūz-zā'viyah N.F. acute-angled triangle مثلث قائم الزاویہ mūsal'las qā''im ūz-zā'viyah N.F. right-angled triangle مثلث متساوی الاضلاع mūsal'las(-e) mūtasā'vi-l-azlā' N.F. equilateral triangle مثلث متساوی الساقین mūsal'las(-e) mūtasā'vi-s-sāqain' N.F. isosceles triangle مثلث مختلف الاضلاع mūsal'las(-e) mūkh'talif-ūl-azlā'' N.F. scalene triangle مثلث منفرج الزاویہ mūsala'las(-e) mūn'farij-ūz-zā'viyah N.F. obtuse angled triangle [A ~ ثلثة three]

مثمر mūs'mir ADJ. fruit-bearing productive; fruitful [A ~ ثمر]

مثمن mūsam'man N.M. octagon poem with eight lined stanzas ADJ. octagonal [A ~ ثمانیہ eight]

مثنوی mas'navī N.F. verse comprising couplets this as verse genre used for narrative poetry [A ~ اثنان or اثنین]

مثنیٰ mūsan'nā N.M. & ADJ. duplicate counter-foil مثنیٰ بہ mūsan'nā beh N.M. original (of a copy [A ~ تثنیہ]

مجادل mūjā'dil ADJ. contentious مجادلہ mūjā'dalah N.M. contention struggle dispute [A ~ جدل]

مجاز mūjāz' ADJ. competent authorised licenced مجاز سماعت mūjā'z-e samā''at, سننے کا مجاز sūn'ne kā mūjāz' ADJ. competent to hear law-suit, etc. کا مجاز ہونا ka mujāz' ho'na V.I. be authorized to; be empowered to [A ~ اجازت]

مجاز majāz' N.F. metaphorical language outward appearance ; shadow (as opposed to reality) مجاز مرسل majā'z-e mūr'sal N.M. metonymy حقیقت و مجاز haqī'qat-o-majāz' N.M. مجازاً majā'zan ADV metaphorically ; metaphorically speaking مجازی majā'zī ADJ. metaphorical ; figurative mundane ; worldly [A]

مجازات mūjazāt' reward and punishment [A ~ جزا]

مجال majāl' N.F. power ; ability ; authority room ; opportunity مجال رکھنا یا ہونا majāl' rakh'nā (or ho'nā) V. to have the power ; to have the ability (to) کیا مجال (ہے) جو kyā' majāl' (hai) jo PH. who dares how can it [A doublet of جولان]

مجالس majā'lis N.F. (PL. of مجلس N.F. ★)

مجالست mūjā'lasat N.F. sitting together company سے مجالست رکھنا se mūjā'lasat rakh'nā V.I. often be in the company of [A ~ جلوس]

مجاملت mūjā'malat N.F. kind treatment [A جمال]

مجامعت mūjā'ma'at N.F. sexual intercourse ; copulation ; coition سے مجامعت کرنا se mūjā'ma'at kar'nā V.F. copulate (with) [A doublet of جماع]

مجانبت mūjā'nabat N.F. keeping away (from) [A ~ جانب]

مجانست mūjā'nasat N.F. being of the same stock [A ~ جنس]

مجاور mūjā'vir N.M. attendant (of mosque, shrine, etc.) مجاوری mūjā'virī N.F. job of mosque (or shrine) attendance [A ~ جوار]

مجاہد mūjā'hid N.M. Muslim soldier warrior in defence of faith crusador endeavourer [A ~ جہاد]

مجاہدہ mūjā'hadah N.M. effort ; struggle ; endeavour [A doublet of جہاد]

مجبور majboor' ADJ. forced compelled ; constrained helpless مجبور کرنا majboor' kar'na V.T. force ; compel ; constrain render helpless مجبور ہونا majboor' ho'nā V.I. be forced ; be compelled ; be constrained be helpless مجبوراً majboo'ran ADV. by force ; under compulsion helplessly مجبوری majboo'rī N.F. helplessness ; powerlessness compulsion ; constraint مجبوری کی بات majboo'rī kī bāt something in which one is helpless مجبوری کی بات اور ہے majboo'rī kī bāt' aur hai PH. it is quite different if there is no other way out [A ~ جبر]

مجتبیٰ mūj'tabā ADJ. chosen ; elect this as an epithet of the Holy Prophet [A اجتبا]

مجتمع mūj'tama' ADJ. united accumulated [A ~ اجتماع]

مجتنب mūj'tanib ADJ. keeping oneself aloof avoiding ; shunning shirking ; hesitating سے مجتنب رہنا se mūjtan'ib raih'nā V.T. avoid evade keep aloof from [~ اجتناب]

مجتہد mūj'tahid N.M. jurist entitled to independent opinion vicar of Shi'ite Imam [A ~ اجتہاد]

مجد maj'd N.M. honour glory [A]

مجدد mūjad'did ADJ. revivalist مجدد الف ثانی mūjad'did-e al'f-e sā'nī N.M. revivalist of the second millennium this as appellation of an Indo-Pakistan saint [~ تجدید]

مجذوب *majzoob'* N.M. one lost in divine meditation mad man ; lunatic مجذوب کی بڑ *majzoob' kī bar* N.F. lunatic's ravings [A ~ جذب]

مجذور *majzoor'* N.M. square (of a number) [A ~ جزر]

مجذوم *majzoom* ADJ. leprous N.M. (rare) leper [A ~ جذام]

مجرا *mūj'rā* N.M. deduction rebate salutation obeisance audience (with sovereign) dirge ; elegy ; usu. small elegiac piece beginning with salutation dance number مجرا پانا *mūj'rā pā'na* V.I. receive credit (for) be granted audience مجرا دینا *mūj'ra de'na* V.T. allow rebate مجرا کرنا *mūj'rā kar'nā* V.I. dance ; perform a dance number مجرا عرض کرنا *mū j'rā 'ar'z kar'na*, مجرا بجا لانا *mūj'ra ba'ja lā'na* V.I. make obeisance مجرا ہونا *mūj'ra ho'nā* V.I. be deducted مجرائی *mūjrā''ī* N.M. servant one who makes obeisance composer or reciter of such dirge N.F. deduction rebate [~A]

مجریٰ *maj'ra* N.M. PL. مجاری *maja'rī* channel [A]

مجرب *mujar'rab* ADJ. (of remedy, etc.) proved ; tried ; pecific مجربات *m'jarrabāt'* N.M. specifics ; proved remedies [A ~ تجربہ]

مجرد *m jar'rad* N.M. bachelor calibate ADJ. alone bare incorporeal مجردات *mujarradat'* N.F. incorporeal beings [A ~ تجرید]

مجرم *muj'rim* N.M. criminal culprit ; offender ADJ. guilty مجرم اشتہاری *mūj'rim-e ishtehā'rī* N.M. a notified criminal مجرم ٹھیرانا (یا قرار دینا) *muj'rim thaihrā'nā (or qarār' de'na)* V.T. find (someone) guilty convict an offender اشتہاری مجرم *ishtehā'rī muj'rim* N.M. proclaimed offender عادی مجرم *'ā'dī muj'rim* N.M. habitual offender مجرمانہ *mūjrimā'nah* ADJ. criminal ; culpable مجرمانہ حملہ *mujrimā'nah ham'lah* N.M. criminal assault [A ~ جرم]

مجروح *majrooh'* ADJ. hurt wounded ; injured N.M. (PL. مجروحین *majroo-hīn'*) casualty مجروح کرنا (یا کر دینا) *majrooh' kar'nā (or kar de'nā)* V.T. hurt wound ; injure مجروح ہونا (یا ہو جانا) *majrooh' ho'nā (or ho jā'nā)* V.I. be hurt be wounded be injured be a casualty [A ~ جراحت]

مجریہ *maj'riyah* ADV. issued on (a date) [A]

مجسٹریٹ *majis'taret* N.M. magistrate [E]

مجسطی *majis'tī* N.F. Almagest [A ~ G]

مجسم *mūjas'sam* ADJ. incarnate ; incorporate مجسم کرنا *mūjas'sam kar'na* V.T. give a corporeal form ; incarnate مجسمہ *mūjas'samah* N.M. statue ; graven image [A ~ جسم ~ تجسیم]

مجلد *mujal'lad* N.M. (PL. مجلدات *mujalladāt'*) (of book) bound [A ~ جلد ~ تجلید]

مجلس *maj'lis* (PL. مجالس *māja'lis*) party company body ; organization group ; society ; association board committee assembly institute meeting meeting held to commemorate Imam Husain's martyrdom مجلس (برپا) کرنا *maj'lis (bar-pa') kar'na* V.I. hold a meeting to commemorate Imam Husain's martyrdom مجلس برخاست کرنا *maj'lis bar-khāst' kar'nā* V.T. conclude a meeting مجلس برخاست ہونا *maj'lis bar-khāst' ho na* V.I. (of meeting) come to an end ; conclude مجلس دستور ساز *maj'lis-e dustoor'-saz* N.F. constituent assembly مجلس شوریٰ *maj'lis-e shoo'ra* N.M. legislature ; legislative assembly or council advisory body ; consultative committee مجلس عاملہ *maj'lis-e 'ā'milah* N.F. working committee مجلس علمی *maj'lis-e 'il'mī* N.F. literary society مجلس عمل *maj'lis-e 'a'mal* N.M. action committee مجلس قانون ساز *maj'lis-e qānoon'-sāz*, مجلس مقننہ *maj'lis-e muqan'ninah* N.F. legislature ; legislature council or assembly مجلس قائمہ *maj'lis-e qa''imah* N.F. standing committee مجلس منتظمہ *maj'lis-e muntazimah* N.F. managing body (or committee) مجلس منعقد کرنا *maj'lis mun''aqid kar'nā* V.T. convene a meeting hold a meeting مجلسی *maj'lisī* ADJ. social مجلسی آداب *maj'lisī ādāb'* N.M. PL. مجلسی زندگی *maj'lisī zin'dagī* N.F. social [A ~ جلوس]

مجلہ *mujal'lah* N.M. (PL. مجلات *mūjallāt'*) periodical [~A]

مجلیٰ *mujal'lā* ADJ. bright burnished [A ~ جلا]

مجمع *maj'ma'* N.M. crowd ; throng meeting assembly ; gathering confluence PREF archi مجمع البحرین *maj'ma'-ūl-bahrain'* N.M. confluence (fig.) person (or thing) in whom (in which) two streams of thought meet مجمع الجزائر *maj'ma' ūl-jaza''ir* N.M archipelago مجمع خلاف قانون *maj'ma'-e khilā'f-e qānoon'* N.M unlawful assembly مجمع عام *maj'ma'-e 'ām'* N.M. public gathering [A ~ جمع]

مجمل *mūj'mal* ADJ. brief abridged N.M. abridgment ; compendium abstract مجمل حساب *mūj'mal hisab* N.M. abstract account مجملاً *mūj'malan* ADV. in short ; in brief [A ~ اجمال]

مجموعہ *majmoo''ah* N.M. sum ; total collection , anthology compendium ADJ. all ; whole مجموعہ تعزیرات *majmoo''-e ta'zīrāt'* N.M. penal code مجموعہ قوانین *majmoo''-e qavānīn* N.M. code of law statute book مجموعی *majmoo''ī* ADJ total aggregate مجموعی قیمت majmoo'ī qī'mat N.F. total value [A ~ جمع]

مجنوں maj'noon, مجنوں majnoon' ADJ. mad ; insane desperately in love N.M. appellation of the celebrated Arab pat-lover Qais of the Amir tribe' very loan person [A ~ جنون]

مجوز mūjav'viz N.M. proposer (of a motion) مجوزہ mūjav'va zah ADJ. proposed prescribed [A ~ تجویز]

مجوسی majoo'sī N.M. fire-worshipper ; Zoroasterian ; guebre ; Magus مجوس majoos N.M. PL. Magi [P]

مجوف mūjav'vaf ADJ. concave hollow vaulted [A ~ جوف]

مجھ mūjh PRON. me مجھ کو m jhī ko, مجھے mū'jhe PRON. me ; to me مجھی mujhī PRON. only me

مجہول majhool' ADJ. passive (voice, etc.) (of vowel or having an open sound ; open unknown littleknown مجہول النسب majhoo'l-ūn-na'sab ADJ. of unknown parentage or lineage [A ~ جہل]

مجھولا majho'lā (F. مجھولی majho'lī) ADJ. middling N.M. medium-sized utensil for community cooking

مجھے mū'jhe PRON. same as مجھ کو PRON. (see under مجھ PRON. ★)

مجیب mājīb' N.M. one who responds one who grants مجیب الدعوات mūjīb-ud-da'vāt' ADJ. ne who grants prayers ; this as attribute of God [A ~ جواب]

مجیٹھ majīṭh' N.F. name of a root used red dye

مجید mājīd' ADJ. glorious قرآن مجید qūr'ā'ne mājīd' N.M. the Glorious Quran کلام مجید kalā'm-e majīd' the Glorious word for God [A ~ مجد]

مجیرا majī'rā, N.M. cymbals

مچان machān' N.M. scaffolding

مچانا machā'nā V.T. make (noise) create (trouble)

مچرب mūchar'rab ADJ. fatty (of dish) having a lot of butter content [pseudo A ~ چربی]

مچکا mach'kā N.M. break ; interruption looseness cheapness مچکا پڑنا mach'kā par'nā have a break loosen become cheap

مچکانا michkā'nā V.T. shut and open (eyes) repeatedly and quickly آنکھ مچکانا ānkh michā'nā V.T. wink

مچکنا ma'chak'nā V.I. creak quake be rickety

مچلا mach'lā ADJ. (F. مچلی mach'lī) (person) feigning ignorance designedly silent مچلاپن mach'lā-pan N.M. being designedly silent

مچلکہ mūchal'kah N.M. bond recognizance مچلکہ حفظ امن mūchal'kah hif'z-e am'n M.M. bond to keep the peace مچلکہ نیک چلنی mūchal'kah nek chal'nī N.M. bond for good behaviour [T]

مچلنا machal'nā V.I. be obstinate (of wayward child) roll on the ground cry (for) persist in

مچمچانا machmachā'nā V.I. be frenzied with sexual urge be excited be in full-blooded (youth) مچمچاتی ہوئی لاش machmachā'tī hu'ī lāsh N.F. youthful corpse مچمچاہٹ machmachā'hat N.F. closing one's jaws with force owing to strong passion

مچنا mach'nā V.I. (of flames) rage of noise report, etc.) spread مچوانا mach'vānā V.T. (of noise) cause to be made

مچنا mich'nā V.I. (of eye) close مچوانا michvā'nā V.T. (of eye) cause to be closed [~ میچنا]

مچھ machh N.M. large fish مگر مچھ ma'gar-machh N.M. crocodile

مچھر mach'chhar N.M. mosquito مچھر دانی mach'chhar-dā'nī N.F. (wrong but usu. mosquito net

مچھلی machh'lī N.F. fish Pisces (as sign of Zodiac) flesh of arm or foreleg ear-drop looking like fish nose-ring like it مچھلی ابھرنا machh'li ū'bhar'nā V.I. have a well developed muscle مچھلی پکڑنا machh'lī pa'kar'nā, مچھلی کا شکار کرنا machh'li kā shikār' kar'nā V.T. fish, angle مچھلی کا پر machh'li kā par N.M. fin مچھلی کا تیل machh'lī kā tel N.M. cod liver oil fish oil مچھلی کا سریش machh'lī kā saresh' N.M. fish gluc مچھلی کا کانٹا machh'lī kā kān'ṭā N.M. fish bone (also مچھلی پکڑنے کا کانٹا machh'lī pa'kar'ne kā kān'ṭā) fish hook مچھلی کی طرح تڑپنا machh'lī kī tarh ta'rapnā PH. feel like a fish out of water writhe with agony مچھلی والا machh'lī vā'lā N.M fish monger اڑن مچھلی ū'ran machh'lī N.F skip-jack fish تارا مچھلی tā'rā machh'lī N.F star fish مچھوا machh'vā N.M. fisherman (dial.) fish-monger [~ مونچھ]

مچھندر mūchhan'dar N.M. clown ; buffoon merry-andrew person with large moustaches

مچھی mach'chhī N.F. (dial.) kiss مچھیاں لینا machhiyān le'nā V.T. kiss

مچھیل machhail N.M one with big moustache [~ مونچھ]

محابا mohā bā N.M. leaning (towards) partiality (for) scruple help aid

بے محابا *be-moha'ba* ADJ. careless ADV without scruples [~A محابات]

محاذ *mohaz'* N.M. (war) front محاذ جنگ *moha'z-e jang* N.M. war front محاذی *moha'zi* ADV. opposite (to) [A]

محارب *moha'rib* ADJ. fighting N.M. fighter محاربہ *moha'rabah* N.M. fight battle war محاربین *mohāribīn'* N.M PL nations (etc.) at war [~ حرب]

محاسب *maha'sib* N.M. accountant auditor محاسب اعلیٰ *moha'sib-e a''la* N.M accountant-general auditor-general محاسبہ *moha'sabah* N.M. settlement of accounts checking of accounts; auditing محاسبہ کرنا *moha'sabah kar'na* V.T. check accounts; audit call to account محاسبی *moha'sibi* N.M. auditing ADJ. audit [A ~ حساب

محاسن *moha'sin* N.M. PL good qualities [A ~ حسن]

محاصرہ *moha'sarah* N.M siege محاصرہ اٹھانا *moha'sarah uṭha'na* V T raise a siege محاصرہ کرنا *moha'sarah kar'na* V besiege, lay a siege (to); beleaguer محاصرے میں آ جانا *moha'sare meṅ ā' ja'na* V.I. be besieged; be beleagured [A ~ حصار fort]

محاصل *moha'sil* N.M (PL. of محصول N.M ★)

محافظ *moha'fiz* N.M protector guardian keeper guard محافظ حقیقی *moha'fiz-e haqī'qi* N.M. (God as) the protector محافظ خانہ *moha'fiz-kha'nah* N.M record room محافظ دفتر *moha'fiz-e daf'tar* N.M record keeper محافظ ذاتی *moha'fiz-e za'tī* N.M. body guard محافظت *moha'fazat* N.F. protection guardianship custody preservation [A ~ حفاظت]

محافل *maha'fil* N.F. (PL. محفل N.F ★)

محافہ *maha'fah* N M. litter; palanquine [~A محفہ]

محاق *mohaq* N.M. waning of the moon last days of lunar month [A]

محاکات *mohakat'* N.F reproduction or imitation (as literary device) account of loving couple's talk [A ~ حکایت]

محاکمہ *mohakamah* N.M. evaluation, decision based on comparative study [A]

محال *mohal'* ADJ. absurd impossible impracticable difficult محالات *mohalat'* N.F PL absurdities impossibilities impracticable things [A]

[1] محال *mahal'* N.M. PL smallest unit of revenue assessment, village [~A SING. محل]

[2] محال *mahal'* N.M bee-hive large bee

محامد *maha'mid* N.M. PL. laudable qualities [A ~ SING. محمدت ~ حمد]

محاورہ *moha'varah* N.M. idiom usage (rare) dialogue skill habit محاورہ پڑنا *moha'varah par'na* V.I. form the habit (of) محاورہ ڈالنا *moha'varah dal'na* V.T habituate (someone to) محاورات *moha'varat* N.M. PL. idioms [A]

محب *mohib'* N.M. friend محب وطن *mohib'b-e va'tan* N.M. patriot محبانہ *mohibba'nah* ADV. friendly [A ~ حب]

محبت *mahab'bat* (col. *mohab'bat*) N.F love affection محبت آمیز *mahab'bat-āmez'* ADJ. loving affectionate محبت رکھنا *mahab'bat rakh'na* V.T love show affection; feel affection (for) محبت کا دم بھرنا *mahab'bat ka dam' bhar'na* V.T. profess love محبت کرنا *mahab'bat kar'na* V.T. love دلی محبت *di'li mahab'bat* N.F. true love [A doublet of حب]

محبس *mah'bas* N.M. (PL. محابس *maha'bis*) prison jail; gaol [A ~ حبس]

محبوب *mahboob'* N.M beloved, sweetheart ADJ. beloved liked favourite (pursuit, etc.) محبوبانہ *mahbooba'nah* ADJ. like that of a sweetheart in the manner of a sweetheart محبوبہ *mahboo'bah* N.F. mistress beloved sweetheart darling ADJ. beloved محبوبی *mahboo'bi*, محبوبیت *mahboobiy'yat* N.F being a beloved loveliness [A ~ حب]

محبوس *mahboos'* N.M. prisoner captive ADJ. imprisoned; jailed; shut up: confined; incarcerated [A ~ حبس]

محتاج *mohtaj'* N.M. poor person pauper ADJ. poor; indigent needy ADV. standing in need (of) محتاج خانہ *mohtaj'-kha'nah* N.M poor house; alms-house محتاج ہونا *mohtaj' ho'na* V.I. be poor, be indigent; be needy stand in need of محتاجی *mohta'ji* N.F. poverty, indigence need want [A ~ احتیاج]

محتاط *mohtat'* ADJ. cautious; careful wary circumspect [A ~ احتیاط]

محتال *mohtal'* N.M. & ADJ. cunning (person) [A ~ حیلہ]

محترز *moh'tariz* ADJ. refraining from shunning [A ~ احتراز]

محترم *moh'taram* ADJ. honourable respectable [A ~ احترام]

محتسب *moh'tasib* N.M. censor (arch.) inspector of weights measures police official محتسب را درون خانہ چہ کار *moh' tasib ra-daroo'n-e kha'nah chekar* PROV none has a right to meddle with people's private affairs [A احتساب]

محتشم *moh'tashim* ADJ. respectable (rare) person having a large retinue [A ~ احتشام]

محتوی *moh'tavī* ADV. consisting (of) [A ~ احتوا]

محجوب *mahjoob'* N.M. ashamed bashful veiled محجوبی *mahjoo'bī* N.F. shame bashfulness [A ~ حجاب]

محدب *mohad'dab* ADJ. convex محدب شیشہ *mohad'dab shi'shah* N.M. convex mirror (col.) magnifying glass محدب عدسہ *mohad'dab 'ad'sah* N.M. convex lens [A]

محدث *moh'dis* N.M. creator innovator [A ~ احداث]

محدث *mohad'dis* (PL. محدثین *mohaddisīn'*) N.M. one well-verse in the Holy Prophet's Traditions ; scholar of Tradition

محدود *mahdood'* (or *maih-*) ADJ. limited restricted محدود کرنا *mahdood' kar'nā* V.T. limit restrict [A ~ حد]

محذوف *mahzoof'* ADJ (of word, letter, etc.) understood , elided ; omitted ; dropped [A ~ حذف]

محراب *mehrab'* N.F. arch niche priests niche in mosque curve محراب دار *mehrab' dār* ADJ arched محرابی *mehrā'bī* ADJ. arched [A]

محرر *mohar'rir* N.M. clerk , scribe ; amanuensis محرر ترسیل *mohar'rir-e tarsīl'* N.M. despatcher محرر تقسیم *mohar'rir-e taqsīm'* N.M. diary clerk ; diarist محرر متعلقہ *mohar'rir-e mūtā'al'liqah* N.M. dealing clerk محرری *mohar'rirī* N.F. clerical job clerical work محررہ *mohar'rarah* ADJ. written inscribed [A ~ تحریر]

محرف *mohar'raf* ADJ. clerical work (of text) tampered with interpolated [A ~ تحریف]

محرق *moh'riq* (F. & PL. محرقہ *moh'riqah*) ADJ. burning تپ محرقہ *ta'p-e moh'riqah* N.M. tpphoid fever [A ~ احرق]

محرک *mohar'rik* N.M. proposer or mover (of motion) stimulant ADJ. moving bringing into motion stimulating [A ~ تحریک]

محرم *mah'ram* N.M. close relation from when women need not go into hiding intimate friends confidant N.F. bodice ; gussets , brassiere محرم اسرار (یاراز) *mah'ram-e asrār'* (or *rāz'*) N.M. confidant bosom friend محرمی *mah'ramī* N.F. intimacy محرمانہ *mahramā'nah* ADJ. private ADV in private [A]

محرم *mohar'ram* N.M. first month of Hijri year (also محرم الحرام *mohar'ram-ūl-harām*) N.M. (the sacred month of) Muharram ADJ. sacred ; venerable forbidden ; tabooed [A ~ تحریم]

محرمات *moharramāt'* N.F. unlawful things ; borbidden things [A ~ PREC.]

محروسہ *mahroo'sah* ADJ. protected fortified; garrisoned ممالک محروسہ *mamā'lik-e mahroo'sah* N.M. PL. protectorates [A ~ حراست]

محروم *mahroom'* ADJ. deprived (of) debarred refused (something) unlucky ; unfortunate محروم الارث *mahroom'-ūl-ir's* ADJ. deprived of heredity محروم رکھنا *mahroom' rakh'nā* V. disappoint محروم کرنا *mahroom' kar'nā* V.T. deprive (of) disappoint محرومی *mahroo'mī*, محرومیت *mahroomiy'yat* N.F. deprivation [A]

محزون *mahzoon'* (or *-zoon'*) ADJ. sad , grieved [A ~ حزن]

محسن *moh'sin* N.M. benefactor patron ADJ. beneficent محسن کش *moh'sinkush* ADJ & N.M. ungrateful person [A ~ احسان]

محسنات *mohsanāt'* N.F. virtues good deeds [A ~ SING. محسنہ *moh'sanah* virtue]

محسوب *mahsoob'* ADJ. calculated deducted محسوب کرنا *mahsoob' kar'nā* V.T. take into account deduct محسوب ہونا *mahsoob' ho'nā* V.I. be taken into account be deducted [A ~ حساب]

محسود *mahsood'* ADJ. envied , looked upon with jealously [A ~ حسد]

محسوس *mahsoos'* ADJ. felt perceived perceptible محسوس کرنا *mahsoos' kar'nā* V.T. feel perceive محسوس ہونا *mahsoos' ho'nā* V.I be felt محسوسات *mahsoosāt'* N.M. things felt or perceived sensations [A ~ حس]

محشر *mah'shar* (or *maih'-*) N.M. day of resurrection tumultuous place commotion by the elegance of a sweetheart's gait [A ~ حشر]

محشی *mohash'shī* ADJ. annotator محشی *mohash'shā* ADJ. having marginal notes annotated [A ~ حاشیہ]

محصل *mohas'sil* N.M. tax-gatherer revenue collector dun [A ~ تحصیل]

محصن *moh'san* ADJ continent محصنہ *mah'sanah* N.F. (PL. محصنات *mohsanāt'*) chaste woman [A ~ حصن ~ احصان]

محصور *mahsoor'* ADJ besieged , beleagued N.M. (PL. محصورین *mahsoorīn'*) besieged person محصور کرنا *mahsoor' kar'nā* V.T besiege , lay a siege (to) محصور ہونا *mahsoor' ho'nā* V.I be besieged [A ~ حصار]

محصول mahsool' N.M. (PL. محاصل mahā'sil or محصولات mahsoolāt') duty tax revenue cess toll محصول آبکاری mahsool-e abkā'rī N.M. excise duty محصول ادا کرنا (یا چکانا) mahool' adā kar'nā (or chūkā'nā) V.T. pay duty محصول چور mahsool'-chor N.M. (rare) smuggler محصول ڈاک mahsool'-dāk N.M. postage محصول فروخت mahsoo'l-e farokh't N.M. sales tax محصول لگانا (یا عائد کرنا) mahsool' lagā'nā (or 'ā'id kar'nā) V.T. levy tax, duty, etc. assess بے محصول be-mahsool' ADJ. tax free duty-free فرد محصول far'd-e mahsool' N.F. tariff محصولی mahsoolī ADJ. taxable dutiable (of land) paying revenue bearing, unpaid to pay [A]

محض mah'z ADJ. mere (rare) pure; unalloyed [A]

محضر mah'zar N.M. statement of a case or suit laid before a judge along with affidavits, depositions, etc. public attestation (also محضر نامہ mah'zar-na'mah) public representation with remuneration signatures محضر نامہ mahzar-na'mah N.M. (wrong but usu. form of محضر sense 3 ★) [A]

محظوظ mahzooz' ADJ. pleased, delighted [A ~ حظ]

محفل maih'fil (ped. mah-) N.F. gathering meeting; assembly party society dance and song party محفل برخاست کرنا maih'fil bar'-khāst' kar'nā V.T conclude a meeting محفل برخاست ہونا maih'fil barkhāst' ho'nā V.I. (of meeting) conclude محفل جمنا maih'fil jam'nā V.I. (of party) be well-set; reaching an interesting stage محفل کرنا maih'fil kar'nā V.T. hold a meeting have a dance party [A]

محفوظ maihfooz ADJ. safe, secure protected guarded sheltered immune [A ~ حفاظت]

محقر mohaq'qar ADJ. poor; mean contemptible [A ~ تحقیر]

محقق mohaq'qiq N.M. (PL. محققین mohaqqiqin') research scholar, research worker; researcher first-rate scholar philosopher محققانہ mohaqqiqā'nah ADJ scholarly research worker's (manner) ADV. in a well established manner from a scholarly view point محقق mohaq'qaq ADJ. certain, positive confirmed; established; proved [A ~ تحقیق]

محک mehak' N.M. touchstone [A ~ حک]

محکم moh'kam ADJ. strong firm unshakable lasting [A ~ احکام ehkā'm']

محکمہ maih'kamah (ped. mah'-) N.M. department, bureau; office (arch.) court) محکمہ آبادکاری (یا بحالیات) maih'kama-e ābād-kā'rī or bahāliyāt' N.M. rehabilitation department settlement محکمہ آبکاری maih'kama-e āb'kā'rī N.M. excise department محکمہ اطلاعات maih'kama-e ittelā'āt' N.M information department محکمہ امداد باہمی maih'kama-e imdā'd-e bāhamī N.M. co-operative department محکمہ انہار maih'kama-e anhā'r N.M. irrigation department محکمہ بحالی اراضی maih'kama-e bahā'lī-e arā'zī N.M. land reclamation department محکمہ بھرتی maih'kamah bhar'tī N.M. recruiting department محکمہ پولیس maih'kamah polis' N.M. police department محکمہ تار maih'kamah tār N.M. telegraph department محکمہ تجارت maih'kamah-e tijā'rat N.M. commerce department محکمہ تعلقات عامہ maih'kama-e ta'alloqā't-e-'ām'mah N.M. public relations department محکمہ تعلیم maih'kama-e ta'līm' N.M. education department of public instruction محکمہ جنگلات maih'kamah jangalāt' N.M. forest department, conservation department محکمہ چونگی maih'kamah chūn'gī N.M. octroi department محکمہ خوراک maih'-kama-e khoorāk' N.M. food department محکمہ ڈاک maih'kamah dāk' N.M. postal department محکمہ ریل maih'kamah rel' N.M. railway department محکمہ زراعت maih'kama-e zirā''at N.M. agriculture department محکمہ صنعت و حرفت maih'kamk-e san''at-o-hir'fat N.M. industries department محکمہ قانون maih'kama-e qānoon N.M. law department محکمہ مساحت maih'kama-e masā'hat N.M. survey department محکمہ مواصلات maih'kama-e mo'āsalāt N.M. communications department [A ~ وصل]

محکوم mahkoom' (col. maih-) ADJ. & N.M. subject governed (person); subjugated (person) محکومی mahkoo'mī, محکومیت mahkoomiy'yat N.F. state of subjugation [A ~ حکومت]

محل mahal' (col. mai'hal) N.M. (PL. محلات maha-lāt' (col. maihalāt palace mansion) palatial building place time occasion N.F. (arch.) (sovereign's) consort; queen محل خاص mahal'-e khās' N.F. (arch.) chief queen particular place or juncture محل دار mahal-dār N.M. harem steward محل داری mahal-dar'ī N.F. harem stewarders محل سرا mahal-sarā' N.F. harem; seraglio محل نظر mahal'l-e na'zar ADJ. doubtful برمحل bar-mahal' ADJ. apt appropriate ADV. fitting the occasion بے محل be-mahal' ADJ. inappropriate inopportune ADV. out of place uncalled for محلی mahal'lī N.M. emasculate steward of harem [A]

محلات mahal'lāt N.M. (PL. of محل PL. of محلہ N.M. ★)

محلل mohal'lil ADJ. causing to dissolve [A ~ تحلیل]

محلول *mahlool'* N.M. solution ADJ. dissolved [A ~ حل]

محلہ *mahal'lah* (PED. PL محلات *mahallāt'*) street, lane; alley (rare) quarter (of town) محلہ دار *mahal'la-dār* N.M. resident of the same quarter headman of a quarter محلے داری *mahal'le-dā'rī* N.F. good-neighbourly relations neighbourliness [A]

محمد *moham'mad* ADJ. highly praised N.M. the Praised One (as the name of the Holy Prophet). Muhammad, Mohammed محمدی *moham'madī* ADJ. pertaining to or walking in the ways of the Holy Prophet, Mohammedan [A ~ حمد]

محمل *maḥ'mil* (or *maiḥ-*) N.M litter carried on camel back camel's saddle [A ~ حمل]

محمود *maḥ'mood* (or *maiḥ-*) ADJ. (F or PL. محمودہ *mahmoo'dah* or *maiḥ-*) praised laudable praiseworthy

محمول *maḥ'mool* (or *maiḥ-*) N.M. (logic) object ADJ. attributed پر محمول کرنا *par maḥ'mool kar'nā* V.T. attribute (something to) regard (something) as resulting from محمولہ *mahmoo'lah* (or *maiḥ-*) ADJ. attributed [A ~ حمل]

محن *mehan'* N.M. PL. sufferings, trials and tribulations [A ~ SING. FOLL.]

محنت *meḥ'nat* N.F. (PL. محن *me'ḥan*) hard-work; industry; diligence labour toil trouble محنت اٹھانا *meḥ'nat ūṭhā'nā* V.T. undergo trouble take pains محنت ٹھکانے لگنا *meḥ'nat ṭhikā'ne lag'nā* V.I. be reward of one's labour succeed محنت شاقہ *meḥ'nat-e shāq'qah* N.F. consistant hard work great toil محنت کرنا *meḥ'nat kar'nā* V.I. work hard toil be industrious محنت کش *meḥ'nat-kash* N.M. labourer ADJ. consistantly doing hard work working (man) محنت کش طبقہ *meḥ'nat-kash tab'qah* N.M. working class محنت مزدوری *meḥ'nat mūzdoo'rī* N.F hard work محنت مزدوری کرنا *meḥ'nat mūzdoo'rī kar'nā* V.I work as a labourer earn by the sweat of one's brow محنتانہ *mehnlā'nah* N.M. wages fees (of lawyer, etc.) محنتی *meḥ'natī* ADJ hard working; industrious [A]

محو *maḥ'v* ADJ. engrossed, absorbed effaced, obliterated erased; rubbed off محو کرنا *maḥ'v kar'nā* V.T. erase efface; obliterate fascinate; engross محو ہونا *maḥ'v ho'nā* V.I. be absorbed; be engrossed be effaced; be obliterated محویت *mahviy'yat* N.F fascination engrossment; absorption

محوری *meḥ'varī* ADJ. axis axial محوری طاقتیں *meḥ'va'rī tā'qateṅ* N.M. PL. axis powers

محولہ *moḥav'valah* ADJ. stated referred to: stated, mentioned محولہ بالا *moḥav'vala(-e) bā'lā* ADJ. abovementioned [A ~ تحویل]

محیر *moḥay'yir* ADJ. amazing محیر العقول *moḥay'yir-*

محیط *muḥīṭ* (A) *adj.* Encircling; surrounding; comprehending; circumambient; containing; guarding; knowing. *n.m.* Circumference; the ocean.

muḥīṭ honā, *v.* To circumscribe; محیط ہونا to surround; to encircle.

مخارج *makhā'rij* N.M. expenditure outlets outlets for sounds (of letters) [A ~ SING. مخرج]

مخاصمت *mūkhā'samat* N.F enmity; hostility [A ~ خصم]

مخاطب *mūkhā'tib* N.M. person addressing another, speaker مخاطب *mūkhā'tab* N.M. person addressed (gram) second person [A ~ خطاب]

مخالف *mūkhā'lif* N.M. opponent; adversary enemy; foe ADJ. opposite adverse unfavourable repugnant contrary [A ~ خلاف]

مخالفت *mokhā'lafat* N.F. opposition discord disagreement dissidence enmity, hostility مخالفت کرنا *mūkhā'lafat kar'nā* V.T. oppose go against dissent resist [A doublet of اختلاف]

مخبر *mūkh'bir* N.M. informer; informant one who brings news or intelligence مخبر صادق *mūkh'bir-e sā'diq* ADJ. bringer of vertiable intelligence (as the Holy Prophet's appellation) مخبری *mūkh'birī* N.F. informer's job report; information مخبری کرنا *mūkh'birī kar'nā* V.T. inform against inform; act as a spy [A ~ خبر]

مخبوط *makhboot'* ADJ. foolish confused مخبوط الحواس *makhboo't-ūl-ḥavas'* ADJ. foolish (one) who has lost his head confused; confounded [A ~ خبط]

مختار *mūkhtār'* N.M. attorney; agent; representative (arch.) attorney ADJ. authorized empowered having free will مختار خاص *mūkhtā'r-e khās* N.M. special attorney مختار عام *mūkhtā'r-e 'ām* N.M. general attorney مختار کار *mūkh'tār-e kār'* N.M. authorized manager attorney مختارکاری mūkhta'r-kari N.F attorneyship مختار نامہ mūkhtar-na'mah N.M. power of attorney مختار ہونا mūkhtar' ho'na V.I. be authorized represent (someone) مختاری mūkhtari N.F attorneyship authority free will [A ~ اختیار]

مخترع mūkh'tare' N.M. innovator مخترعات mūkhtara'at N.F PL. innovations contraptions [P ~ اختراع]

مختص mūkhtas' ADJ. peculiar (to) specific appropriated [A ~ خاص]

مختصر mūkh'tasar ADJ. short concise succinct abbreviated abridge epitemized مختصر کرنا mūkh'tasar kar'na V.T shorten abridge curtail epitomize مختصر نویس mūkh'tasar navis' (arch اختصار نویس ikhtisar' navis') N.M. stenographer, shorthand writer مختصر نویسی mūkh'tasar-navi'si (arch. اختصار نویسی ikhtisar navi'si) N.F shorthand ; stenography مختصراً mūkh'tasaran ADV briefly in short [A ~ اختصار]

مختل mūkhtal' ADJ. confused ; confounded [A ~ خال]

مختلف mukh'talif ADJ. different various divers unlike; dissimilar مختلف الاضلاع mukh'talif-ul-azla' ADJ. of unequal sides ; scalene مختلف النوع mūkh'talif-ūn-nau'' ADJ. of various kinds of different species or kind مختلف mūkh'talaf ADJ. differed (only in) مختلف فیہ mūkh'talaf-fih' ADJ. about which there is difference of opinion [A ~ اختلاف]

مختوم makhtoom' ADJ. sealed signed [A ~ خاتم]

مختون makhtoon' ADJ circumcised [A ~ ختنہ]

مخدر mūkhad'dir ADJ benumbing narcotic [A ~ خدر kha'dar]

مخدرات mūkhaddarat' N.F. harem secluded women ladies [A ~ خدر khid'r partitioning screen].

مخدوش makhdoosh' ADJ doubtful (position) serious (condition) [A ~ خدشہ]

مخدوم makhdoom' ADJ. (F مخدومہ makhdoo'mah) served, waited on N.M. master respected person [A ~ خدمت]

مخرب makhar'rib ADJ. ruin spoiling مخرب اخلاق makhar'rib-e akhlaq' N.M. ruinous to character [A ~ تخریب]

مخرج makh'raj N.M. (PL. مخارج makha'rij) outlet denominator outlet for sound (of letter [A ~ خارج]

مخروطی makhroo'ti ADJ. conical tapering [A]

مخزن makh'zan N.M. store-house treasury مخزن الادویہ makh'zan-ūl-ad'viyah N.M. materia medica مخزن العلوم makh'zan-ūl-'uloom' N.M. encyclopedia, cyclopaedia [A ~ خزانہ]

مخصوص makhsoos' ADJ. special particular peculiar private مخصوص مقام مقام مخصوص makhsoos' maqam' N.M. peculiar position maqa'm-e makhsoos' N.M. private parts ; genitals [A ~ خصوص]

مخطوبہ makhtoo'bah ADJ. betrothed ; affianced, fiance [A ~ خطبہ khit'bah]

مخطی mūkh'ti ADJ. & N.M. sinning or wrong doing (person) [A ~ خطا]

مخفف mūkhaf'faf ADJ. abbreviated ; shortened N.M. contraction [A ~ تخفیف]

مخفی makh'fi ADJ. secret hidden, concealed private [A ~ خفا]

مخل mūkhil' ADJ. interfering intruding meddling ; intermeddling N.M. intruder intermeddler مخل ہونا makhil' ho'na V T interfere intrude meddle; intermeddle [A ~ خلل]

مخللہ mūkhal'la ADJ. free مخلا بالطبع mokhal'la bil-tab'' ADV. (ped.) with mind unoccupied with other things at perfect ease [A ~ خلو]

مخلص mūkh'lis ADJ. sincere ; true (to) ADV. sincerely, truly N.M. a sincere friend آپ کا مخلص āp' ka mūkh'lis PH. Yours sincerely; Sincerely yours مخلصانہ mūkh-lisa'nah ADJ sincere ; friendly ADV. in a friendly manner مخلصی mūkh'lisi N.F. sincerity [A ~ اخلاص]

مخلصی mūkh'lisi N.F. deliverance ; salvation riddance [A ~ خلاص]

مخلوط makhloot ADJ. mixed promiscuous heterogeneous مخلوط النسل makhloo't-un-nas'l N M. cross breed مخلوط تعلیم makhloot' ta'lim' N F. coeducation [A ~ خلط khal't]

مخلوق makhlooq' N.F. creature creation ADJ. created مخلوقات makhlooqat' N F. creatures, created things [A ~ خلق]

مخمر mokham'mir ADJ. leavening مخمر mokham'mar ADJ. leavened [A ~ مخمور]

مخمس mokham'mas N.M. pentagon verse written in five-lined stanzas ADJ. pentagular [A ~ خمسہ]

مخمصہ makh'masah N.M. perplexity dilemma مخمصے میں پڑنا makh'mase men par'na V.I. get into a difficulty be on the horns of a dilemma [~A hunger]

مخمل makh'mal N.M. velvet مخملی makh'mali ADJ. velvety soft [P]

مخمور makhmoor' ADJ. drunk ; intoxicated ; inebriated

مخنث mukhan'nas N.M. eunuch [A]

مخول makhaul' N.M. joke ; jest nonserious thing مخولیا makhaul'liya N.M. jester ADV. non serious (person)

مخیر mūkhay'yir N.M. philanthropist liberal or charitable person [A ~ خیرات]

مخیلہ mokhay'yilah N.M. imagination [A ~ تخیل]

مد 1 mad N.F. (same as مدہ N.F. ★)

مد 2 mad N.M. prolongation mark over long vowel tide ; flood-tide lengthening stretch ; extension N.F. (PL. مدات maddāt') head ; head of account ; head of expenditure entry item article مدامانت mad'd-e amā'nat N.F. head of deposits مدبندی mad-bań'dī N.F. appropriation (of accounts) مدحساب mad'd-e hisāb' N.F. head of account مدمقابل mad'd-e mūqā'bil N.M. opponent antagonist مدنظر mad'd-e na'zar ADV. in view (of) مدنظر رکھنا mad'd-e na'zar rakh'nā V.T. keep in view مدوجزر mad'd-o-jaz'r N.M. tide ; the flux and reflux of the sea ; neaptide and ebb-tide مدے mad'de ADV. in the account (of) [A]

مدظلہ mad'da zil'lo-hoo (F. مدظلہا mad'da zil'lo-hā, مدظلہ العالی mad'd zillo-h-ūl-'ā'lī PH. may he live long [A ~ PREC.]

مداح maddāh' N.M. eulogist ; an encomiast ; panegyrist مداحی maddā'hī N.F. eulogizing [A ~ مدح]

مداخل madākhil' N.F. income revenue receipts entrances مداخل ومخارج madā'khil-o-makhā'rij N.F. income and expenditure [A ~ SING. مدخل]

مداخلت mūdā'khalat N.F. interference interruption intrusion meddling entry trespass مداخلت بیجا mūdā'khalat-e be-jā' N.F. trespass undue interference مداخلت کرنا mūdā'khalat kar'nā V. interfere intrude trespass ; force entry [A ~ دخل]

مداد midād' N.F. ink [A]

مدار 1 madar' N.M. swallow-wort ; milk-weed ; celadine مدار کی بڑھیا madar' kī būṛh'yā N.F. swallow-wort

مدار 2 madar' N.M. axis orbit dependence basis ; ground مدار ارضی madā'r-e ar'zī N.M. earth's axis مدار دعوی madār-e da''vā N.M. grounds of the claim مدار کار madā'r-e kār' N.M. what something depends upon [A ~ دور]

مدار mūdār' N.M. person in charge (of) مدارالمہام mūdā'r-ūl-mohām' N.M. the prime minister someone's deputy for important jobs [A ~ ادارہ]

مدارات mūdārāt' N.F., خاطر مدارات khā'tir mūdārāt' N.F. (col.) مدارا mūdā'rā N.M. (poet.) politeness ; courtesy hospitality entertainment (خاطر) مدارات کرنا (khā'tir) mūdārāt' kar'nā V.T. treat hospitality ; be a goodly host

مدارج madā'rij N.M. (PL. of درجہ N.M. ★)

مدارس madā'ris N.M. (PL. of مدرسہ N.M. ★)

مداری madā'rī N.M. juggler conjurer مداری کا کھیل (یا تماشہ) madā'rī kā khel' (or tamā'shah)

مدافعت modā'fa'at N.F. self-defence مدافع modā'fe ADJ. repellant defening N.M. defender [A doublet of دفاع]

مدام mūdām' ADV. always perpetually [A ~ دوام]

مداومت mūdā'vamat N.F. continual use , continuance [A ~ دوام]

مداوا modā'vā N.M. cure ; remedy [~ A مداوت ~]

مداہنت mūdā'hanat N.F being facile hypocristy [A]

مدائح madā''eh N.M. (PL. of مدیحہ N.F. ★) دوا

مدائن madā''in N.M. (PL. of مدینہ N.M. ★ name of an ancient Persian capitale ; Ctesiphon

مدبر modab'bir N.M. & ADJ. statesman مدبری modab'birī N.F. statesmanship [A ~ تدبیر]

مدت mūd'dat N.F. time length of time space of time duration interval age ; period مدت العمر mūd'dat-ūl-'ūm'r N.F. lifetime ADV. throughout his life as long as he (etc.) lived (or lives) for keeps مدت مدید mūd'dat-e madīd' N.F. a long time مدت مقررہ mūd'dat-e moqar'-rarah N.F. fixed time ; specified period ایک مدت ek mūd'dat N.F. a long period ADV. for a very long period مدتوں mūd'daton ADV. for quite a long period [A]

مدح mad'h, مدحت mid'hat N.F. praise eulogy ; encomium ; panegyric مدح خواں mad'h-khān N.M. euloist ; encomiast ; panegyrist [A]

مدخل madkhal N.F. PL. مداخل madā'khil entrance (arch.) income ; revenue [A ~ دخل]

مدخولہ madkhoo'lah N.F. concubine ; kept mistress [A ~ دخول]

مدد madad (A) n.f. Help; assistance; reinforcement; succour; aid; labourers; masons; wages.

(کرنا *ma'dad pahunchā'nā* (or *de'nā* or *kar'nā*) V.T. help; assist aid succour; reinforce مدد گار *ma'dad-gār'* N.M. assistant helper auxiliary ally (یا مانگنا) مدد لینا *ma'dad le'nā* (or *māng'nā*) V.T. seek help or assistance [A]

مدر *mūdir'* ADJ. diuretic [A ~ ادرار]

مدرس *mūdar'ris* N.M. (PL. مدرسین *mūdari-sīn'*) teacher schoolmaster اول مدرس *av'val mūdar'-ris* N.M. headmaster مدرسی *mūdar'risī* N.F. teacher's job [A ~ تدریس]

مدرسہ *mad'rasah* N.M. school academy seminary academic مدرسۃ العلوم *mad'rasat-ūl-'ūloom'* N.M. (arch.) college; university مدرسہ شبینہ *mad'rasa-e shabī'nah* N.M. night school مدرسہ بالغاں *madrasah-e ba'lighān* N.M. an adult school ابتدائی مدرسہ *ibtidā''ī mad'rasah* N.M. primary school مدرسہ ثانوی *mad'rasa-e sā'navī* N.M. secondary school خیراتی مدرسہ *khairā'tī mad'rasah* N.M. free school زنانہ مدرسہ *zanā'nā mad'rasah* N.M. girls' school سرکاری مدرسہ *sarkā'rī mad'rasah* N.M. government school غیر سرکاری مدرسہ *ghair'-sarkā'rī mad'rasah* N.M. private school صنعتی مدرسہ *san''atī mad'rasah* N.M. industrial school فوقانی مدرسہ *fau'qa'nī mad'rasah* N.M. (ped.) high school ہم مدرسہ *ham-mad'rasah* N.M. schoolfellow, school-mate [A ~ درس]

مدرک *mūd'rik* ADJ. perceptive مدرکہ *mūd'rikah* N.F. parception intellect comprehension ADJ. perceptive [A ~ ادراک]

مدعا *mudda'ā'* N.M. aim; object objective wish; desire; intent; intention scope (rare) stolen property (rare) object claimed or sued for ADJ. sued مدعا علیہ *mūdda'ā-'alaih'* N.M. respondent; defendant (یا حاصل کرنا) مدعا پانا *mūdda'ā' pā'nā* (or *hā'sil kar'nā*) V.T. achieve one's object (یا نکلنا) مدعا ملنا *mūdda'ā' mil'nā* (or *ni'kalnā*) V.I. (of stolen property) be recovered

مدعو *mad'oo'* ADJ. invited مدعوین *mad'ūvvīn'* N.M. invites [A ~ دعوت]

مدعی *mūd'da'ī* N.M. plaintiff claimant adversary rival مدعیہ *mūd'da'iyah* N.F. plaintiff claimant [A ~ ادعا]

مدغم *mud'gham* ADJ. merged (of letter) doubled [A ~ ادغام]

مدفن *mad'fan* N.M. burial place; grave [A ~ دفن]

مدفون *madfoon'* ADJ. buried interred (of treasure) hidden underground [A ~ دفن]

مدقق *mūdaq'qiq* ADJ. & N.M. (one) going into minute details [A ~ تدقیق]

مدقوق *madqooq'* N.M. & ADJ. consumptive (person) [A ~ دق]

مدک *ma'dak* N.F. mixture of opium and bran smoked as sedative مدکی *ma'dakī* N.M. opium-smoker

مدلل *mūdal'lal* ADJ. reasonable; wellgrounded [A ~ دلیل]

مدمغ *mūdam'migh* ADJ. proud; haughty; conceited [A ~ دماغ]

مدن *mū'dan* N.M. (H. myth.) god of love (dial.) love (dial.) lust [S]

مدن *mū'dan* N.M. PL. مدنی *ma'danī* ADJ. مدنیت *madaniy'-yat* N.F. (see under مدینہ N.M. ★).

مدور *mudav'var* ADJ. round circular spherical; globular [A]

مدھ *madh*, مد *mad* N.F. wine honey lust مدھ بھرا *madh'-bha'rā* (F. مدھ بھری *madh'-bha'rī*), مدھ ماتا *madh-mā'tā* (F. مدھ ماتی *madh'-mā'tī*) ADJ. drunk; intoxicated مدھ پر آنا *madh' par ā'nā* V.I. be in the prime of one's youth مدھر *ma'dhūr* ADJ. sweet مدھرتا *ma'dhūrtā* N.F. sweetness [S]

مدھم *mad'dham* ADJ. low moderate; light dim مدھم روشنی *mad'dham rau'shanī* N.F. dim-light مدھم سر *mad'dham sūr* N.M. low note مدھم کرنا *mad'dham kar'nā* V.T. lower (sound) dim or dip (light) مدھم ہونا *mad'dham ho'nā* V.I. be low be lowered grow dim

مدہوش *madhosh'* ADJ. astonished, drunk; intoxicated senseless; unconscious stunned مدہوشی *madho'shī* N.F. intoxication unconsciousness being stunned [A ~ مدہوش *madhoosh'* mixed up with P ہوش *hosh*]

مدید *madīd'* ADJ. (F. or PL. مدیدہ *madī'dah*) (rare) long; extensive [A]

مدیر *mudīr'* N.M. editor مدیر معاون *mūdī'r-e mo'ā'vin* N.M. assistant editor مدیر اخبارات *mūdī'r-e mūkhā'-barāt'* N.M. newseditor

مدینہ *madī'nah'* N.M. (PL. مدن *mū'dan*) city Islam's first capital city (of); centre (of) [A]

مدیون *madyoon'* ADJ. debtor [A ~ دین *dhin*]

مدبھیڑ *mūdbheṛ'*, مٹ بھیڑ *mūṭ bheṛ'*, مٹھ بھیڑ *mūṭhbheṛ'* N.F. encounter meeting مڈبھیڑ ہونا *mūḍ bheṛ' ho'nā* V.I. encounter have a confrontation (with)

مڈل *mid'al* ADJ. middle N.M. middle standard [E]

مذاق *mazāq'* N.M. taste; relish; nice joke; plesantry relish taste (for) مذاقاً *mazā'qan* ADV. humorously; wittily; in jest; by way of joke; jocosely; jocularly مذاقیہ *mazaqiy'yah* ADJ. humorous; witty ADV. homorously jocularly [A doublet of ذوق]

مذاکرہ *mūzā'karah* N.M. symposium conference discussion مذاکرات *mūzākarāt'* N.M. PL. parleys , talks [A ~ ذکر *zik'r*]

مذاہب *mazā'hib* N.M. (PL of مذہب N.M. ★)

مذبح *maz'bah* N.M (PL مذبح *mazā'beh*) slaughter house , shambles [A ~ ذبح]

مذبذب • *mūzab'zab* ADJ. wavering hesitating ; reluctant [A]

مذبوح *mazbooh'* ADJ. slaughtered . killed مذبوحی *mazboo'hi* ADJ. of slaughtered animal suicidal مذبوحی حرکت *mazboo'hi harakat'* N.F. suicidal acts

مذکر *mūzak'kar* ADJ. masculine male N.M. masculine gender [A ~ ذکر *za'kar*]

مذکور *mazkoor'* N.M. mention ADJ. (F. & PL. مذکورہ *mazkoo'rah*) related ; mentioned مذکورہ بالا *mazkoo'ra(-e) bā'lā*, مذکورہ صدر *mazkoo'ra-e sad'r* ADJ. above mentioned ; aforesaid مذکوری *mazkoo'ri* N.M. (arch.) process-serving process-server [A ~ ذکر *zikr*]

مذلت *mazal'lat* N.F abjectness disgrace [A doublet of ذلت]

مذمت *mazam'mat* N.F. derogatory remarks contempt censure impeachment قرار داد مذمت *qarār-dā'd-e mazam'mat* N F. censure motion [A doublet of ذم]

مذموم *mazmoom'* (F. & PL. مذمومہ *mazmoo'mah*) ADJ. blame worthy ; contemptible mean ; base [A ~ PREC.]

مذنب *mūz'nib* N.M. & ADJ. (PL. مذنبین *mūz'nibīn'*) sinner ; sinful (person) [A ~ ذنب *za'hab*]

مذہب •*mūzah'hab* ADJ. gilded goldplated [A ~ ذہب *za'hab* gold]

مذہب • *maz'hab* N.M. religion ; faith way of living ; mode of life creed doctrine school of thought مذہب میں لانا *maz'hab meṅ lā'nā* V.T. convert to a faith مذہب بدلنا *maz'hab ba'dalnā* V.T & I. convent ; be convert مذہبی *maz'habī* ADJ. religious religious minded (person) N.M. (Sikh) sweeper مذہبیت *mazhabiy'yat* N.F. religiousness religiosity religious -mindedness [A ~ ذہاب go]

مذی *ma'zi* N.F. minor involuntary seminal discharge [A]

مر *mūr* N.M. myrrh [A]

مرآۃ *mir'āt'* N.M. mirror مرآۃ العروس *mir'ā't-ūl-'ūs* N.M. bride's mirror [A ~ رویت]

مراتب *marā'tib* N.M. (PL. of مرتبہ N.M. ★)

مراثی *marā'sī* N.M. (PL. of مرثیہ N.M. ★)

مراجعت *mūrā'ja'at* N.F return recourse doing over and over again مراجعت کرنا (یا فرما ہونا) *mūrā'ja'at kar'nā* (or *farmā' ho'nā*) V.T. return [A ~ رجوع]

مراحل *marā'hil* N.M. (PL. of مرحلہ N.M. ★)

مراحم *marā'him* N.M. PL. favours مراحم خسروانہ *marā'him-e khūsrūvā'nah* N.M PL. royal favours [A ~ SING. مرحمت]

مراد *mūrād'* N.F. intention object; objective meaning ; purport wish (کی) مراد بر آنا (*kī*) *mūrād' bar ā'nā* V.I. gain one's wish مراد پانا (یا پوری ہونا یا حاصل ہونا) *mūrād' pā'nā* (or *poo'rī ho'nā* or *hā'sil ho'nā*) V.I gain one's wish مراد پوری کرنا *mūrād' poo'rī kar'nā* V.T. someone's- wish مراد لینا *mūrād' le'nā* V.T mean (by) understand (by) ; infer (from) مراد مانگنا *mūrād māṅg'nā* V. ask for a favour pray for a boon مراد ماننا *mūrād' mān'nā* V.T. & I. vow . make a vow مراد مند *mūrād'-mand* ADJ. desirous ; needy مرادوں کے دن *mūrā'doṅ ke din* N.M. longed-for happiness youthful days مرادی *mūrā'dī* ADJ. [i]mplied (meaning) secondary (sense) [A ~ ارادہ]

مرادف *mūrā'dif* ADJ. synonymous N M. (rare) hind rider [A ~ ردیف]

مراری *mūrā'rī* N.M. (H. dail.) enemy of devils [E]

مراسلت *mūrā'salat'* N.F. correspondence exchange of letters مراسلتی نصاب *mūrā'salati nisāb'* N.M. correspondence course [A ~ رسالہ]

مراسلہ *mūrā'salah* N.M. (PL. مراسلات *mūrā'salāt'*) N.M. letter ; epistle [A doublet of PREC.]

مراسم *marā'sim* N.M. PL relations customs سے دوستانہ مراسم ہونا *se dostā'nah marā'sim ho'nā* V.I. have friendly relations with [A ~ SING.]

مراعات *mūrā'āt'* N.F. PL. privileges concessions N.F. consideration privilege ; concession مراعات النظیر *morā'ā't-ūn-nazīr'* N.F. use of related words to form a prolonged metaphor [A ~ رعایت]

مرافعہ *mūrā'fa'ah* N.M. appeal مرافعہ کرنا *mūrā'fa'ah kar'nā* V.T. appeal (to a higher-court A ~ رفع lift]

مرافقت *mūrā'faqat* N.F. kindly treatment travelling in the company (of) [A ~ رفق]

مراق *mirāq'* N.M. a kind of madness ; melancholia مراقی *mirā'qī* ADJ. mad ; melancholic crazy mad N.M. mad man [A]

مراقبہ *mūrā'qabah* N.M. observation ; meditation ; [con]templation مراقبہ کرنا *mūrā'qabah karnā* V.T. meditate مراقبے میں جانا *mūrā'qabe meṅ jā'nā* V.I.

be absorbed in meditation.; be lost in contemplation [A ~ ارتقاب]

مرام *marām* N.M. aim, object. goal بے نیلِ مرام *be-nai l-e marām'* ADV. unsuccessfully [A]

مربہ *mū'ra'bah* (ped. مربّیٰ *mūrab'bā*) N.M. jam preserved fruit [A ~ مربّیٰ]

مربع *murab'ba'* N.M. square quadrangle verse comprising fou-lined stanza quartan ague. piece of land equivalent to twenty-five acres; square; rectangle ADJ. square foursided; quadrangular ADV. cross-legged مربع بیٹھنا *mūrab'ba' baiṭh'nā* V.I. sit cross-legged [A ~ مربعہ]

مربوط *marboot'* ADJ. consistent concordant well-knit [A ~ ربط]

مربی *mūrab'bī* N.M. patron مربیانہ *murabbiyā'nah* patronising ADV. patronisingly [A ~ تربیت]

مرتاض *murtāz'* ADJ. disciplined ascetical زاہدِ مرتاض *zā'hid-e-mūrtaz'* N.M. disciplined ascetic [A ~ ریاضت]

مرتب *marat'tib* N.M. editor compiler one who draws up مرتب *murat'tab* ADJ. & ADV. edited compiled arranged مرتب کرنا *mūrat'tab kar'na* V.T. edit compile arrange draw up marshal مرتبہ *morat'tabah* ADJ. edited (by) compiled (by) arranged drawn up [A ~ ترتیب]

مرتبان *mar'tabān'* N.M. earthern or porcelain jar (for jams, etc.) [P]

مرتبت *mar'tabat* N.F. rank SUF. ranked [A ~ FOLL.]

مرتبہ *mar'tabah* N.M. (PL. مراتب *marā''tib*) rank; office time, turn ایک مرتبہ *ek' mar'tabah* ADV. once ایک مرتبہ کا ذکر ہے *ek' mar'tabah kā zik'r hai* PH.. once upon a time [A ~ رتبہ]

مرت بیائی *mar't-biy'ā''i* N.F. & ADJ. woman whose children die at an early age

مرتد *mūrtad'* N.M. apostate مرتد ہونا *mūrtad' ho'nā* V.I. apostatize [A ~ ارتداد]

مرتسم *murtasam* ADJ. impressed; engraved [A ~ ارتسام]

مرتضیٰ *mur'tazā* ADJ. approved chosen this as appellation of Hazrat Ali مرتضوی *murta'zavī* ADJ. Alid [A ~ ارتضا]

مرتعش *mūr'ta'ish* ADJ. shaking; quaking palsied [A ~ ارتعاش]

مرتفع *mūr'tafa'* ADJ. high; ofty; elevated [A ~ ارتفاع]

مرتکب *mūr'takib* ADJ. guilty (of) (one) who perpetrating (crime); (one) who commits (sin, etc.) مرتکب ہونا *mūr'takib ho'nā* V.I. commit.; perpetrate be guilty (of) [A ~ ارتکاب]

مرتہن *mūr'tahin* N.M. mortgage مرتہن قابض *mūr'tahin-e qā biz* N.M mortgagee in possession [A ~ ارہن]

مرثیہ *marsi'yah* N.M. elegy: dirge: epicedium elegy (as a genre of literature commemorating Imam Husain's martyrdom) مرثیہ خواں *mar'siya-khan'* N.M. chanter of dirge lamenter مرثیہ خوانی *mar'siya-khā'nī* N.F. chanting of dirges lamentation مرثیہ نگار, مرثیہ گو *mar'siya-go, mar'siya-nigar* N.M. elegiac poet مرثیہ گوئی *mar'siya-go''i*, مرثیہ نگاری *mar'siya-nigā'rī* N.F. writing of elegiac verse [A]

مرج *mar'j* N.M. worry (only in) ہرج مرج *har'j mar'j* N.M. (see under ہرج N.M. ★)

مرجان *marjān'* N.M. coral [A]

مرجح *muraj'jah* ADJ. preferable

مرجع *mar'ja'* N.M. (gram.) antecedent asylum; resort مرجعِ خلائق *mar'ja'-e khalā''iq* مرجعِ عام *mar'ja'-e 'ām'* N.M. the resort of all [A ~ رجوع]

مرجھانا *murjhā'nā* V.T. wither droop fade be dispirited

مرچ *mir'ch* N.F. pepper chillies دکنی مرچ *dak'kanī mir'ch* N.F. white pepper کالی مرچ N.F. black pepper لال مرچ *lāl mir'ch* N.F. chillies مرچیں (رسی) لگنا *mir'chīn (sī) lag'na* V.I. take amiss smart be offended.; take offence be incensed find (something) pungent find (something) hot

مرچنٹ *mar'chanṭ* N.M. merchant جنرل مرچنٹ *jan'ral mar'chanṭ* N.M. general merchant [E]

مرچنگ *mūrchang'* N.M. Jews' harp [P ~ مور + چنگ]

مرحبا *mar'ḥaba* INT. luck up bravo well-done welcome [A]

مرحلہ *mar'ḥalah* N.M. (PL. مراحل *marāhil*) stage (in journey) difficult stage; difficulty; crisis مرحلہ طے کرنا *mar'ḥalah tai kar'na* V.T. pass through a stage successfully remove a difficulty; tide over a cry مرحلہ طے ہونا *mar'halah tai ho'nā* V.T. (of some stage) be traversed (of crisis) be tided over [A]

مرحمت *mar'ḥamat* N.F. (PL. مراحم *mara'-ḥim*) favour mercy مرحمت فرمانا (یا کرنا) *mar'ḥamat farmā'nā* (or *kar'nā*) V.T bestow confer [A ~ رحم]

مرحوم *marḥoom'* ADJ. (F. مرحومہ *marḥoo'mah*) dead deceased the late one who has had divine mercy [A ~ رحم]

مرخص *mūrakh'khas* ADJ. permitted to depart مرخص ہونا *mūrakh'khas ho'nā* V.I. take leave (of) [A ~ رخصت]

مرد *mar'd* N.M. man male husband hero fellow مرد آدمی *mar'd ā'damī* N.M. tall well-built man brave man gentleman INT. my good sir مرد بچہ *mar'd bach'chah* N.M. brave man's son ; brave child ; brave boy مرد بننا *mar'd ban'nā* V.I. be a man ; show courage مرد خدا *mar'd-e khūdā'* N.M. a pious man INT. my good sir (مرد کی ذات (یا صورت *mar'd kī zāt* (or *soo'rat*) N.F. man ; male مرد کی صورت نہ دیکھنا *mar'd kī soo'rat nā dekh'nā* PH. be still a virgin مرد میدان *mar'd-e maidān'* N.M. brave man ; man of action مردا مردی *mar'dā mar'dī* ADV. forcibly مردانگی *mardā'nagī* N.F. manliness ; bravery ; heroism مردانگی کا کام *mardā'nagī ke kām'* N.M. brave deeds ; heroic deeds مردانہ *mardā'nah* ADJ. of or for men male masculine manly ; brave mens' lounge ; apartment for male members of house مردانہ وار *mardā'na-vār'* ADJ. manly heroic ADV. bravely ; courageously heroically مردانی *mardā'nī* ADJ. of or for men N.F. tomboy brave woman

مردک *mar'dak* N.M. manikin mean fellow اترا شحنک مردک نام *ūtrā shaih'nah mar'dak nām* PROV. (see under شحنہ N.M. ★)

مردار *mūrdār'* N.M. carrion ADJ. unclean ill-gotten (wealth) INT. (W. dial.) wretch ; hussy مردار خور *mūrdār'-khor* N.M. carrion-eater مردار سنگ *mūrdār'-sang,* مردہ سنگ *mūr'da-sang* N.M. red lead ; litharge مرداری *murdā'rī* N.F. lizard [P]

مردم *mar'dūm* N.M. pupil (of eyes) (PL. مردمان *mardūmān*) N.M. PL. people مردم آزار *mar'dūm-azār'* N.M. oppressor ; tyrant tormentor مردم آزاری *mar'dūm azā'rī* N.F. oppression مردم خور *mar'dūm khor,* مردم خوار *mar'dūm-khār* ADJ. man-eater cannibal مردم خوری *mar'dūm kho'rī,* مردم خواری *mar'dūm-khā'rī* N.F. counilialism مردم خیز *mar'dūm-khez* ADJ. (or area) producing famous men مردم خیزی *mar'dūm-khe-zī* N.F. being productive of famous men مردم دوست *mar'dūm dos't* N.M. philanthropist مردم دوستی *mar'dūm-dos'tī* N.F. philanthrophy مردم دیدہ *mar-dūm-e dī'dah* N.M. pupil of the eye most precious thing the people who have been seen مردم شماری *mar-dūm-shūmā'rī* N.F. census مردم شناس *mar'dūm-shinās'* ADJ. having knowledge of men مردم شناسی *mar'dūm-shinā'sī* N.F. knowledge of men مردم کش *mar'dūm-kush* ADJ. murderous مردم کشی *mar'dūm-ku'shī* N.F. murder ; homicide مردمی *mar'dūmī* N.F. manliness bravery (also قوت مردمی *qūvvat-e mar'dūmī* V.T. virility [P]

مردمک *mar'dūmak* N.F. pupil of the eye [P ~ PREC.]

مردنگ *mirdang'* N.F. a kind of long tom-tom ; 'mirdang' مردنگی *mirdan'gī* N.M. one who plays on 'mirdang'

مردنی *mūr'danī* N F. dismalness death-like paleness death-like stillness ADJ. fit to die deserving death مردنی چھانا *mūr'danī chhā'nā* V. become deadly pale [~ P مردن die]

مردوا *mar'dū'ā* N.M. (see under مرد N.M. ★)

مردود *mardood'* ADJ. reprobate [A ~ رد]

مردہ *mūr'dah* N.M. corpse ; dead body ADJ. dead weak مردہ اٹھانا *mūr'dah ūṭhā'nā* V.T. give a proper burial (to) perform the funeral rites (of) مردہ بدست زندہ *mūr'da ba-das't-e zin'dah* PH. one to weak to move about for himself مردہ بھاری ہونا *mūr'dah bhā'rī ho'nā* V.I. (of dead body) be heavy (supposedly owing to sins) مردہ پرست *mūr'da-paras't* ADJ. (of society or person) idiolizing the dead ; acknowledging great men's services after their death مردہ خراب ہونا *mūr'dah kharab' ho'nā* V.I. not to get a proper burial مردہ دل *mūr'da-dil* ADJ. dispirited dejected مردہ دلی *mūr'da-di'lī* N.F. dispiritedness dejection مردہ شو *mūr'da-sho* N.M. washing the dead مردوں سے شرط باندھ کر سونا *mūr'doṅ se shar't bāndh' kar so'nā* V.I. sleep very soundly مردوں کی ہڈیاں اکھیڑنا *mūr'doṅ kī haḍ'diyāṅ ūkher'nā* PH. talk evil of the dead express trite ideas مردوں کی ہڈیاں چچھوڑنا *mūr'doṅ kī haḍ'diyāṅ chichoṛ'nā* V.T. (of worhless persons) feel pride in the deeds of one's ancestors [P]

مردی *mar'dī* N.F. (see under مرد N.M. ★)

مرزبوم *mar'z boom* N.M. native land [P]

مرزا *mir'zā,* (ped. or arch.) میرزا *mīr'za* title of respect for descendants of Moghuls chieftain مرزا پھویا *mir'zā pho'yā* N.M. a very (nickname for) a delicate and inactive person مرزا منش *mir'zā ma'nish* ADJ. of princely disposition مرزائی *mirzā''ī* N.F. (arch.) princedom ; gentility (arch.) arrogance ; pride (also *mirzai''ī* loose-sleeved quilted waist coat مرزئی N.M. (member) of Ahmadiyyah community

مرسل *mūr'sal* N.M. (PL. مرسلین *mūrsalīn*) apostle ADJ. (Tradition) with second top link in chain of narrators missing مرسل الیہ *mūr'sal-ilaih'* N.M. addressee مرسلہ *mūr'salah* ADJ. sent ; despatched مرسل *mūr'sil* N.M. sender ; despatcher [A ~ ارسال]

مرسوم *marsoom'* N.M. allowance; dole [A ~ رسم]

مرشد *mur'shed* N.M. spiritual guide mentor [A ~ ارشاد]

مرصع *muras'sa'* ADJ. set or studded with jewels (of verse, etc.) comprising balanced words or phrases مرصع ساز *muras'sa'-saz,* مرصع کار *muras'sa'-kar* N.M. stone-setter ; lapidary مرصع سازی *muras'sa'-sa'zi,* مرصع کاری *muras'sa'-ka'ri* N.F. stonesetting [~ ترصیع]

مرصوص *marsoos'* ADJ (F. & PL. مرصوصہ *marsoo'-sah*) very strong (structure) reinforced [A]

مرض *ma'raz* N.M (PL. امراض *amraz'*) illness; sickness : disease مرض الموت *maraz ul-maut'* N.M. mortal disease متعدی مرض *muta'ad'di ma'raz* N.M infectious disease مہلک مرض *moh'lik mar az* N.M fatal disease کس مرض کی دوا ہو *kis' ma'raz ki dava' ho* PH. of what use are you (etc)

مرضع *mur'ze',* مرضعہ *murze'ah* N.M. mother foster-mother ; wet nurse

مرضی *mar'zi* N.F. pleasure choice will consent مرضی کے موافق *mar'zi ke mo'a'fiq* ADV according to the will or pleasure (of) to the entire satisfaction (of) اپنی مرضی *ap'ni mar'zi* ADV willingly ; voluntarily of one's own free will [A ~ رضا]

مرطوب *martoob'* ADJ. wet ; moist ; humid [A ~ رطوبت]

مرعوب *mar'oob'* ADJ. awe-struck brow-beaten frightened ; terrified [A ~ رعب]

مرغ *mur'gh* N.M. cock bird; fowl مرغ بادنما *mur'gh-e bad'-numa'* N.M. weather-cock مرغ باز *mur'gh-baz* N.M. cock-fighter مرغ بازی *mur gh-ba'zi* N.F cock-fighting مرغبان *mur'gh-ban'* N.M. poulterer مرغبانی *mur'gh-ba'ni* N.F. poultry farming مرغ چمن *mur'gh-e cha'man* N.M. garden bird chirping bird nightingale مرغ دست آموز *mur'gh-e das't-amoz* N.M. stooge (of) مرغ سحر *mur'gh-e sa'har* N.M. morning bird ; harbinger of day chanticlear nightingale مرغ قبلہ نما *mur'gh-e qib'la-numa'* N.M. compass needle [P]

مرغ *mar'gh* N.M. kind of grass (only in) مرغزار *margh'-zar* N.M. pasture ; meadow [P]

مرغا *mur'gha* N.M. cock ; chanticlear مرغا بانگ نہ دے گا تو کیا صبح نہ ہوگی *mur'gha bang na de'ga to kya' sub'h na ho'gi* PROV non-co-operation by one cannot upset the whole show (وہی) مرغے کی ایک ٹانگ *(vo'hi) mur'ghe ki ek' tang'* PH. silly insistence

مرغی *mur'ghi* N.F. hen مرغی انڈے کی بحث *mur'ghi an'de ki baih's* PH. reasoning in a circle pointless discussion (*e.g.*, which came first be created, the egg or the hen) مرغی جان سے گئی کھانے والے کو مزا نہ آیا *mur'ghi jan' se ga'i kha'ne va'le ko ma'za na a'ya* PROV. the sacrifice goes unrewarded مرغی خانہ *mur'ghi kha'nah* N.M. poultry farm مرغی میجر *mur'ghi-me'jor* N.M. (iron) poulterer مرغی والا *mur'ghi-va'la* N.M. fowl vender [~ P مرغ *mur'gh*]

مرغابی *mur'gha'bi* N.F. wild-duck مرغابی کا شکار *murgha'bi ka shikar'* N.M. wild-duck shooting [~ P مرغ + آب]

مرغوب *marghoob'* ADJ. desired ; desirable agreeable pleasant . lovely [A ~ رغبت]

مرغولہ *margho'lah* N.M. spiral (of) [P]

مرفوع *marfoo''* ADJ. letter having a pesh (') over it raised مرفوع القلم *marfoo''-ul-qa'lam* ADJ. mad ; not answerable for his crime [A ~ رفع]

مرفہ *muraf'fah* ADJ. well-off مرفہ الحال *muraf'fah-ul-hal'* ADJ. well-off ; prosperous ; in easy circumstances [A ~ رفاہ]

مرقد *mar'qad* N.M. grave . tomb ; sepulchre [A ~ رقود]

مرقع *moraq'qa'* N.M. (PL. مرقعے *moraq'qe'*) album collection of paintings rags ; tatters ADJ. patched حیرت کا مرقع بن جانا *hai'rat ka muraq'qa' ban ja'na* V.I. be perplexed ; be amazed [A ~ رقعہ]

مرقوم *marqoom'* ADJ. (F. & PL. مرقومہ *marqoo'-mah*) ADJ. written ; inscribed recorded مرقومہ بالا *marqoo-ma(-e) ba'la* ADJ. aforesaid; above-mentioned [A ~ رقم]

مرکانا *murka'na* V.T. twist snap [~ مرکنا CAUS.]

مرکب *mar'kab* N.M. conveyance pack-horse [A ~ رکوب]

مرکب *murak'kab* ADJ. compound not simple N.M. compound ink مرکب کیمیائی (یا کیمیاوی) *kimiya''i* (or *kimiya'vi*) *marak'kab* N.M. chemical compound مرکبات *murakkabat* N.M. PL. compounds medicinal preparations [A ~ ترکیب]

مرکز *mar'kaz* N.M. (PL. مراکز *mara'kiz*) centre headquarters ; Centre upper flourish (of letters گ and ک) مرکز ثقل *mar'kaz-e siq'l* N.M. centre of gravity مرکز بنیادی *mar'kaz-e bunya'di* N.M. radical centre مرکز گریز *mar'kaz-gurez'* ADJ. centrifugal (force) بنیادی مرکز *bunya'di mar'kaz* N.M. chief centre pivotal point

ہم مرکز *ham-mar'kaz* ADJ. concentric مرکزی *mar'kazī* ADJ. central مرکزی اسمبلی *mar'kazī asaimb'lī* N.F. Central Assembly مرکزی حکومت *mar'kazī hukoo'mat* N.F. Central Government مرکزی مقننہ دیا مرکزی مجلس قانون ساز *mar'kazī-mūqan'ninah* (or *maj'lis-e qānoon-saz*) N.F. Central Legislature [A]

مرکنا *mū'rakna* V.T. be twisted, get sprained be snapped

مرکوز *markooz'* ADJ. focussed impressed مرکوز خاطر *markoo'z-e khā'tir* ADJ. impressed upon the mind [A ~ مرکز]

مرکھنا *mar'khana* ADJ. (F. مرکھنی *mar'khanī*) goring

مرکی *mūr'kī* N.F. ear-ring

مرگ *mar'g* N.F. death مرگ انبوہ جشنے دارد *mar'g-e amboh jash'ne dā'rad* PROV. general calamity is a festival by itself مرگ مفاجات *mar'g-e mūfajāt'*, مرگ ناگہاں *mar'g-e nā-gahāṅ'* N.F. sudden death [P]

مرگ *mir'g* N.M. (dial.) deer مرگ چھالا *mir'g-chhā'lā* N.M. dear-skin مرگ سالا *mir'g-sā'lā* N.M. (dial.) deer preserve مرگ نینا *mir'g nainā* ADJ. (dial.) gazelle-eyed

مرگل *mar'gal* N.M. fried fish its slice

مرگھٹ *mar'ghaṭ* N.M. (dial.) cremation ground [S]

مرگی *mir'gī* N.F. epilepsy مرگی کا دورہ پڑنا *mir'gī kā dau'rah paṛ'na* V.T. have an epileptic fit مرگیا *mir'giya* ADJ. & N.M. epileptic

مرلہ *mar'lah* N.M. (dial.) land measure equivalent to 5½ square yards

مرلی *mūr'lī* N.F. flute مرلیا *mūralī'ya* N.F. small flute

مرمت *maram'mat* N.F. repairs; repair mending مرمت طلب *maram'mat-talab* ADJ. broken out of order; out of gear out of repair; not in good repair مرمت کرنا *maram'mat kar'nā* V.T. repair mend set right; put right beat; give a hiding punish [A]

مرمر *mar'mar* N.M. marble مرمریں *mar'marīṅ* ADJ. marble beautiful like marble [P]

مرمرا *mūr'mūrā* N.M. swollen parched rice

مرمم *mūram'mam* ADJ. (F. & PL. مرممہ *mūram'-mamah*) (rare.) repaired amended [A ~ ترمیم]

مرن *ma'ran* N.M. (dial) death. جیون مرن *jī'van ma'ran* N.M. (dial.) living and dying life and death مرن برت *mar'n-bar't* N.M. fast unto death مرن ہار *mar'n-hār* ADJ. doomed to die [S]

مرنا *mar'nā* V.I. die; expire; breath one's last cease fade lose strength work hard; sweat and toil suffer hardship; be in great trouble long for fall for; be desperately in love with مرنا جینا *mar'nā jī'nā* N.M. life and death living and dying مرنا جینا ساتھ ہونا *mar'nā jī'nā sāth ho'nā* V.I. (of possibility of death) life مرنے جوگا *mar'ne jo'gā* ADJ. fit or deserving to die مرنے کی فرصت نہ ہونا *mar'ne kī fūr'sat na ho'nā* V.T. be overwhelmed with have no leisure مرا جانا *ma'rā jā'nā* V.I. be very anxious or impatient مربھکا *mar'-bhūk'kā* ADJ. glutton مرپیٹ کر *mar' piṭ kar* ADV. with great difficulty مرتا کیا نہ کرتا *mar'tā kyā' na kar'tā* PH. I (etc.) was reduced to the straits; perforce I (etc.) had to do مرتے دم تک *mar'te dam tak* ADV. till death; till the last gasp مرتے مرتے *mar'te mar'te* ADV. while at the point of (one's) death مرتے مرگیا (پر) *mar'te mar' ga'ya (par)* PH. never at all did he (etc.) مرجانا *mar jā'nā* V.I. die مرچلنا *mar' chal'nā* V.I. be on the point of death مر رہنا *mar' raih'nā* V.I. delay sweat and toil مرکر (یا کے) *mar' kar* (or *ke*) ADV. hardly great difficulty مرکھپ جانا *mar' khap jā'nā* V.T. have did long ago مر مر کے *mar' mar ke* V T. with great difficulty مر مٹنا *mar miṭ'nā* V.T. come to dust be ruined fall for toil hard مری بھیڑ خواجہ خضر کے نام *ma'rī bheṛ khā'ja kha'zir ke nām'* PROV. the worst stiff goes in fulfilment of vow مرے کو مارے شاہ مدار *ma're ko mā'ren shāh' madār'* PROV. misfortunes never come singly a bully would beat the weak

مرنڈا *mūran'ḍā* N.M. sweetmeat prepared from parched wheat and 'gur'

مروا *mar'vā* N.M. name of a scented plant

مروارید *mar'vārīd* N.M. pearl مروارید ناسفتہ *mar'vārīd-e na-sūf'tah* N.M. unbored pearl (fig.) virgin [P]

مروانا *marvā'nā* V.T. get killed cause to be beaten be subjected to sexual act [~ مارنا]

مروت *mūrūv'vat* (col. *mūrav'vat*) N.F. favour; kindness benevolence politeness regard (rare) chivalry مروت کرنا (یا برتنا یا سے کام لینا) *mūrūv'vat kar'nā* (or *ba'ratnā* or *se kām' le'nā*) V.T. show regard for treat kindly [A ~ man]

مروج *mūrav'vaj* ADJ. (F. & PL. مروجہ *marav'-vajah*) current customary; usual ADV. in force in vogue [A ~ رواج]

مرور *mūroor'* N.M. passage (of time, etc.) [A]

مروڑنا *maroṛ'nā* V.T. twist contort مروڑ *maroṛ'* N.F. affectation vanity N.M. PL. (dial. F.) gripes ; colic کے پیٹ میں مروڑ اٹھنا *ke peṭ' meṅ maroṛ' ūṭh'nā* V.I. have gripes or colic feel jealous مروڑ پھلی *maroṛ'-phā'lī* N.F. a drug used at cure for colic ; gripe-cure beans مروڑا *maro'ṛā* N.M. twist ; strain مروڑا تروڑی *maro'ṛā taro'ṛī* N.F. struggle internal commotion مروڑی *maro'ṛī* N.F. knot screw twist ; contortion small roll of grime, dough, etc. rubbed off palm مروڑی دینا *maro'ṛī de'nā* V.T. twist مروڑی کھانا *maro'ṛī khā'nā* V.I. be twisted

مروی *mar'vī* ADJ. related ; stated ; narrated [A ~ روایت]

مرہ *mar'rah* N.M. time ; turn SUF. (sign of adverb)-ly [A]

مرہٹہ *mar'haṭah* N.M. Mahratta مرہٹی *mar'haṭī* N.F. language of Maharattas; Mahratti (arch.) maladministration under the Mahrattas (rare) misrule

مرہم *mar'ham* N.M. ointment unguent salve مرہم پٹی کرنا *mar'ham paṭ'ṭī kar'nā* V.T. dress a wound (joc.) set right [P]

مرہن *mūrhan* N.M. dry powdered tobacco

مرہون *marhoon'* ADJ. (F. مرہونہ *marhoo'nah*) pledged; mortgaged مرہون منت *marhoon-e min'nat* ADJ. indebted (to) ; under obligation (to)

مرئی *mar''ī* ADJ. visible [A ~ رؤیت]

مری *me'rī* PRON. (short for میری PRON. ★)

مری *ma'rī* N.F. animal pestilence مری پڑنا *ma'rī paṛ'nā* V. breaking out of animal plague or pestilence

مری *mū'rī* N.F. alimentary canal

مری *mūr'rī* N.F. upper end of men's toga among Hindus مری پھندا *mūr'rī phan'dā* N.M. a kind of stitch in embroidery

مریخ *mirrikh'* N.M. Mars [A]

مرید *mūrīd'* N.M. religious or mystic disciple مرید کرنا *mūrīd' kar'nā* V.T. make disciple (of) مرید ہونا *mūrīd' ho'nā* V.I. become a disciple مریدی *mūrī'dī* N.F. being a disciple [A ~ ارادت]

مریض *marīz'* N.M. (F. مریضہ *marī'zah*) patient [A ~ مرض]

مریل *mar'yal* ADJ. weak; feeble emaciated lean lazy مریل ٹٹو *mar'yal ṭaṭṭoo* PH. weakling [~ مرنا]

مریم *mar'yam* N.F. Mary ; the Virgin مریم کا پنجہ *mar'yam kā panjah* N.M. Mary's hand ; a sweet-scented grass supposed to facilitate delivery [A ~ H]

مرینہ *marī'nah* N.M. merino [E]

مڑنا *mūṛ'nā* V.I. turn turn back bend be twisted مڑ آنا *mūṛ' ā'nā* V.I. come back مڑ جانا *mūṛ' jā'nā* V.I. turn back bend be twisted مڑ کر نہ دیکھنا *mūṛ' kar na dekh'nā* V.T. not to look back (upon) have no regard (for) مڑ مڑ کر دیکھنا *mūṛ' mūṛ kar dekh'nā* V.T. turn round and look time and again

مڑکنا *mū'ṛaknā* V.I. be sprained get fractured

مڑھنا *maṛh'na,* منڈھنا *manḍh'nā* V.T. cover with (leather) impute

مڑھی *maṛhī* N.F. (dial.) Hindu hermit's cell

مزا *ma'zā* N.M. (same as مزہ N.M. ★)

مزاج *mizāj'* N.M. temperament disposition temper ; mood vanity SUF. temper مزاج آسمان پر ہونا *mizāj' asmān' par ho'nā* V.I. be vain مزاج برہم ہونا *mizāj' bar'-ham ho'nā* V.I. be upset مزاج بگڑنا *mizāj' bigaṛ'nā* V.T. spoil (someone's) temper (by sycophancy, etc.) مزاج بگڑنا *mizāj' bi'gaṛnā* V.I. get out of temper مزاج پانا *mizāj' pā'nā* V.T. feel the temperamental pulse (of) ; be familiar with (someone's) disposition مزاج پوچھنا (یا مزاج پرسی کرنا) *mizāj' poochh'nā* (or *pūr'sī kar'nā*) V.T. enquire after (someone) health مزاج پیٹی *mizāj'-pī'ṭī* ADJ. conceited (woman) مزاجدار *mizāj'-dār* ADJ. conceited ; haughty مزاج دان *mizāj'-dān'*, مزاج شناس *mizāj'-shinās'* ADJ. familiar with the disposition (of) مزاج شریف *mizā'j-e sharīf' mizā'j-e 'ā'lī,* مزاج مبارک *mizā j-e mūbā'rak* PH. how do you do ; how are you مزاج کرنا *mizāj' kar'nā* V.I. put on airs مزاج نہ ملنا *mizāj' na mil'nā* V.I. give oneself airs بد مزاج *bad-mizāj'* ADJ. ill-tempered تنک مزاج *tū'nūk-mizāj'* ADJ. testy ; touchy ; irritable تیز مزاج *tez'-mizāj'* ADJ. hot-headed خوش مزاج *khūsh-mizāj'* ADJ. jolly ; jovial مزاجن *mizā'jan,* مزاجو *mizā'jo* N.F. proud woman مزاج والا *mizāj' vā'lā* ADJ. (F. مزاج والی *mizāj' vā'lī*) conceited مزاجی *mizā'jī* SUF. temper [A]

مزاح *mūzāḥ'* N.M. humour مزاح نگار *mūzāḥ'-nigār'* ADJ. & N.M. humorist مزاح نگاری *mūzāḥ'-nigā'rī* N.F. humour طنز و مزاح *tan'z-o mūzāḥ'* N.M. wit and humour مزاحیہ *mūzāḥiy'yah* ADJ. humorous [A]

مزاحم *mūzā'ḥim* ADJ. hindering ; obstructing ; impeding N.M. hindrance ; obstruction ; impediment مزاحم ہونا *mūzā'ḥim' ho'nā* V.I. hinder; obstruct ; impede مزاحمت *mūzā'ḥamat* N.F. hindrance; obstruction impediment opposition resistance مزاحمت کرنا *mūzā'ḥamat kar'nā* V.I. hinder ; obstruct ; impede oppose resist بلا مزاحمت *bi-lā'-mūzā'ḥamat* ADJ unopposed unhindered ; unchecked [A]

مزار *mazār'* N.M. (PL. مزارات *mazārāt'*) shrine grave ; tomb [A ~ زیارت]

مزارع *mūzā're'* N.M. cultivator ; tiller ; peasant [A ~ زراعت]

مزامیر *mazāmīr'* N.M. (PL. of مزمار N.M. ★)

مزاوجت *mūzāva'jat* N.F. marriage [A ~ زوج]

مزاولت *mozā'volat* N.F. regular practice [A]

مزبور *mazboor'* ADJ. written ; recorded [A]

مزجات *mūzjāt'* ADJ. petty ; little [A]

مزخرفات *mūzakhrafāt'* N.M. PL. nonsense [A ~ SING. مزخرف]

مزد *mūz'd* N.F. wages [P]

مزدور *mazdoor'* (ped. *mūzdoor'*) N.M. labourer porter مزدور یونین (یا انجمن) *mazdoor'-yoo'niyan* (or *an'jūman*) trade union مزدور تحریک *mazdoor' taiḥrīk'* N.F. labour movement مزدوری *mazdoo'rī* (ped. *mūzdoo'rī*) N.F. wages labour work [P]

مزرع *maz'ra'*, مزرعہ *maz'ra'ah* N.F. (PL. مزارع *mazā're'*) farm ; field مزرعۂ ہستی *mazra'a-e-has'tī* N.F. (fig.) world [A ~ زراعت]

مزروعہ *mazroo''ah* ADJ. cultivated ; tilled culturable [A ~ زراعت]

مزعفر *mūza''far* N.M. sweet saffron-coloured dish of rice ADJ. saffron-coloured [A ~ زعفران]

مزعومہ *maz'oo'mah* ADJ. supposed ; presumed مزعومہ بات *maz'oo'mah bāt* N.F. presumption [A ~ زعم]

مزمہ *mūzam'mā* N.M. tether مزمے لینا *mūzam'me le'nā* V.T. (fig.) harass [A]

مزور *mūzav'var* ADJ. base ; counterfeit [A ~ زور]

مزمار *mizmār'* N.F. (PL. مزامیر *mazāmīr'*) musical instrument flute [A]

مزمن *mūz'min* ADJ. chronic (disease) [A ~ زمانہ]

مزہ *ma'zah*, مزا *ma'zā* N.M. taste flavour relish deficiousness pleasure enjoyment fun مزہ آنا *ma'zah ā'nā* V. relish ; enjoy مزہ اٹھانا (یا اڑانا یا پانا) *ma'zah ūṭhā'nā* (or *ūṛā'nā* or *pā'nā*) V.T. enjoy revel مزہ پڑنا *ma'zah paṛ'nā* V.I. acquire a taste (for) fall into the habit (of) مزہ چکھانا *ma'zah chakhā'nā* V.T. teach (someone) lesson مزہ چکھنا *ma'zah chakh'nā* V.I. learn a lesson face the music مزہ کرکرا ہونا *ma'zah kir'kirā ho'nā* V.T. (of someone's game) get spoiled مزہ (یا مزے) کرنا (یا لوٹنا) *ma'zah* (or *ma'ze*) *kar'nā* (or *looṭ'nā*) enjoy oneself مزیدار *ma'ze-dār* ADJ. tasteful delicious interesting مزیداری *maze-dā'rī* N.F. taste deliciousness interest ; being interesting مزے کا *ma'ze kā* ADJ. (F. مزے کی *ma'ze kī*) interesting مزے کی بات *ma'ze kī bāt'* N.F. interesting thing [P]

مزید *mazīd'* ADJ. more greater increased ADV. more further مزید برآں *mazīd'-bar-āṅ'* CONJ. moreover [A ~ زیادہ]

مزین *mūzay'yan* ADJ. bedecked ; decorated ; adorned [A ~ زینت]

مژدہ *mūzh'dah* N.M. good news ; glad tidings مژدہ سنانا *mūzh'dah sūnā'nā* V. to announce good news (to) [P]

مژہ *mi'zhah* N.F. (PL. مژگان *mi'zhagāṅ*) eyelash [P]

مس ¹ *mis* N.F. Miss [E]

مس ² *mis* N.M. copper مسی *mi'sī* ADJ. copper [P]

مس ¹ *mas* N.F. (usu. PL.) down on lips مسیں بھیگنا (یا پھوٹنا یا آغاز ہونا) *ma'seṅ bhīg'nā* (or *phooṭ'nā* or *āghāz' ho nā*) (of down on lips) appear grow up

مس ² *mas* N.M. louch taste (for something) مس کرنا *mas' kar'nā* V.T. touch feel مس ہونا *mas' ho'nā* V.I have a taste for feel [A]

مسا *masā'* N.F. evening صبح و مسا *sūb'ḥ-o-masā'* N.F. day and night [A]

مسا *ma'sā* N.F. difficulty (only in) مسا کر کے *ma'sā kar ke* ADV. hardly

مسا *mas'sā* N.M. wart

مسا *mis'sā*, مسا کسا *mis'sā kūs'sā* N.M. cheap flour ground from mixed grain

مسابقت *mūsā'baqat* N.F. مسابقہ *mūsā'baqah* N.M. race ; competition [A ~ سبقت]

مساجد *masājid* N.F. (PL. of مسجد N.F. ★)

مساحت *masā'hat* N.F survey mensuration **مساحت پاکستان** *masā'hat-e pākistān'* N.M. survey of Pakistan **مساح** *massāh'* N.M. surveyor [A]

مساس *misās'* N.M. massage contact of naked organs of sex [A ~ مس]

مساعد *mūsā''id* ADJ. favourable N.M. helper ; supporter **مساعدت** *mūsā''adat* N.F. help ; support aid ; assistance [A ~ مساعد]

مساعی *masā''ī* N.F. efforts ; endeavours **مساعیِ جمیلہ** *masā''i-e jamī'lah* N.F praiseworthy endeavours [A ~ سعی]

مسافت *masā'fat* N.F. (PL. **مسافات** *masāfāt'*) distance **مسافت طے (یا قطع) کرنا** *masā'fat tai* (or *qat'*) *kar'nā* V.I. cover on traverse a distance ; travel [A]

مسافر *mūsā'fir* N.M. traveller passenger stranger alien **مسافر پروری** *mosā'fir-par'varī*, **مسافر نوازی** *mūsā'fir-nova'zī* N.F. hospitality **مسافر خانہ** *mūsā'fir-khā'nah* N.M. waiting-room (at railway station, etc.) **مسافرانہ** *masāfirā'nah* ADJ. traveller-like as a stranger ADV. as a traveller **مسافرت** *mūsā'farat* N.F. travel journey **مسافری** *mūsā'firī* N.F. travel journey [A ~ سفر]

مساکن *masā'kin* N.M (PL. of **مسکن** N.M. ★)

مساکین *masākīn'* N.M. poor ; indigent [A ~ SING. مسکین] [A]

مسالا *masā'lā*, **مسالہ** *masā'lah* N.M. (usu but wrought **مصالحہ** or **مصالح** *masā'lah*) condiments ; materials spices ingredients material **مسالا بنانا** *masā'lā banā'na* V T mix condiments **مسالا ٹانکنا** *masā'lā tānk'nā* V T. lace ; stitch a cloth (with trinkets, etc.) **مسالا ڈالنا** *masā'lā dāl'nā* V. season **مسالےدار** *masā'le-dār* ADJ. seasoned with spices ; spiced ; hot

مسالک *masā'lik* N.M. (PL. of **مسلک** N.M. ★)

مسام *masām'* N.M. (PL. **مسامات** *masāmāt'*) pore **مسام دار** *masām'-dār* ADJ. porous [A]

مسامحت *mūsā'mahat* N.F. pardon connivance [A]

مسان *masān'* N.M. (dial.) crematory [S]

مساوات *mūsāvāt'* N.F equality (Math.) equation **مساواتِ درجۂ اول** *musāv'āt(-e) da'raja-e av'val* N.F. simple equation **مساواتِ درجۂ دوم** *mosāvā't(-e) da'raja-e dūvum* N.F. quadratic equation ; simultaneous equation **مساوی** *mūsā'vī* ADJ. equal (to) ; equivalent (to) **مساوی الاضلاع** *mūsā'vi-l-azlā''* (col. -*ūl*-) N.F equilateral figure [A]

مسائل *masā''il* N.M. (PL. of **مسئلہ** N.M. ★)

مسبب *mūsab'bib* N.M. cause ; causer **مسبب الاسباب** *mūsab'bib-ūl-asbāb'* N.M. (God as) the causer of causes **مسبب حقیقی** *mūsab'bib-e haqī'qī* N.M. the real doer of things . God [A ~ سبب]

مسبوق *masbooq'* ADJ. past ; former [A ~ سبقت]

مست *mas't* ADJ. drunk ; intoxicated one devoid of senses must ; run amuck lustful ; lascivious ; frenzied with sex impulse drunk with divine love N.M. mad-saint **مستِ الست (یا ازلی)** *mas't-e alas't* (or *a'zalī*) N.M. mad saint **بدمست** *bad-mas't*, **سیہ مست** *siyah'-mas't* ADJ. dead drunk **حال مست** *hal'-mas't* ADJ. intoxicated with divine love **کھال مست** *khāl'-mas't* ADJ. (joc.) happy despite poverty **مال مست** *māl'-mas't* ADJ. purseproud **مستان (شاہ)** *mastān'* (*shāh*) N.M. (nick-name for a) mad saint **مستانا** *mastā'na* V.I get frenzied **مستانہ** *mastā'nah* ADJ. & ADV. like an intoxicated person charming staggering (motion) **مستانی** *mastā'nī* N.F. mad saintly woman **مستی** *mas'tī* N.F. intoxication frenzy **مستی آنا (یا چڑھنا)** *mas'tī ā'na* (or *charh'nā*) V.I. have sexual frenzy [P]

مستاجر *mustā'jir* N.M. lessee of agricultural land revenue farmer **مستاجری** *mustā'jiri* N.F lease of land revenue farming [A ~ اجر]

مستاصل *mūsta'sal* ADJ. uprooted [A ~ اصل]

مستبد *mustabid'* ADJ. despotic [A ~ استبداد]

مستبعد *mustab''ad* ADJ. unlikely far-fetched [A ~ استبعاد]

مستانہ *mastā'nah* ADJ. **مستانی** *mastā'nī* N.F. (see under **مست** ADJ. ★)

مستتر *mus'tatar* ADJ. hidden; concealed [A ~ ستر]

مستثنیٰ *mustas'na* ADJ. excepted exempted **مستثنیٰ کرنا** *mustas'nā kar'nā* V T. except exempt **مستثنیات** *mustasnayāt'* N.F. PL. exceptions [A ~ استثنا]

مستجاب *mūstajāb'* ADJ. responded (to) granted ; accepted **مستجاب الدعوات** *mustaja'b ūd-da'avāt'* ADJ. (person) whose prayers are accepted by God [A ~ جواب]

مستجمع الصفات *mūstaj'me'-us-sifāt'* ADJ. (man) of many parts repository of attributes [A ~ صفت + استجماع]

مستجیب *mustajīb'* N.M. one who grants prayer [A ~ استجاب]

مستحب *mus'tahab* ADJ. desirable [A ~ استحباب]

مستحسن *mūstaḥ'san* (or *-taiḥ-*) ADJ. commendable [A ~ استحسان]

مستحضر *mūstaḥ'zar* ADJ. present remembered [A ~ حضور]

مستحق *mūstaḥiq'* ADJ. deserving entitled مستحق ٹھہرانا *mūs'taḥiq ṭhaihrā'nā* V.T. consider deserving مستحق ہونا *mūs'taḥiq ho'na* V.I. deserve be entitled (to) [A ~ استحقاق]

مستحکم *mūstaḥ'kam* (or *-taih-*) ADJ. strong firm established [A ~ استحکام]

مستحیل *mūstaḥīl'* ADJ. difficult baseless [A ~ استحالہ]

مستخرج *mūstakhraj* ADJ. derived taken out [A ~ استخراج]

مستدعی *mūstad''ī* ADJ. beseeching ; imploring [A ~ استدعا]

مستدیر *mūstadīr'* ADJ round spherical, globular [A ~ دور *daur*]

مسترد *mūs'tarad* ADJ. rejected thrown out مسترد کرنا *mūs'tarad kar'nā* V.T. reject throw out [A ~ استرداد]

مستری *mis'tarī* N.M. mechanic mason ; brick-layer artificer skilled worker

مستزاد *mūstazād'* ADJ. extra additional ADV. over and above N.F. verse form with an extra foot or two appended to each line [A ~ استزادہ]

مستشار *mūstashār'* N.M. one whose council is sought ; counsellor

مستشرق *mūstash'riq* N.M. (PL. مستشرقین *mūstashriqīn'*) Orientalist [A ~ مشرق]

مستطاب *mūstatāb'* ADJ. good delectable [A طیب]

مستطیع *mūstatī''* ADJ. (one) enjoying the means of accomplishing something [A ~ استطاعت]

مستطیل *mūstatīl'* N.F. rectangle ADJ. rectangular [A ~ طول]

مستظہر *mūstaz'hir* ADJ. (one) seeking help N.M petitioner [A ~ استظہار]

مستعار *mūsta'ār'* ADJ. borrowed ; got on loan [A ~ استعارہ]

مستعان *mūsta'ān'* ADJ. one whose help is sought [A ~ عون]

مستعجل *mūsta''jil* ADJ. short-lived [A ~ عجلت]

مستغاث *mūstaghās'* ADJ. (one) to whom complaints are made for redress [A ~ استغاثہ]

مستعد *mūsta'id'* ADJ ready, prepared prompt showing alacrity مستعدی *mūsta'id'dī* N.F readiness promptness promptitude alacrity [A ~ استعداد]

مستعفی *mūsta''fī* ADJ. resigned مستعفی ہونا *mūsta''fī ho'nā* V.I. resign

مستعمرہ *mūsta''marah* N.F (PL. مستعمرات *mūsta'marāt'*) colony [A ~ عمران]

مستعمل *mūsta''mal* ADJ. current in use in vogue used ; secondhand مستعملہ *mūsta''malah* ADJ. used (stuff) ; second-hand goods [A ~ استعمال]

مستغرق *mūstagh'raq* ADJ. absorbed ; engrossed [A ~ استغراق]

مستغفر *mūstagh'fir* ADJ. penitent ; repentant [A ~ استغفار]

مستغنی *mūstagh'nī* ADJ. rich contented content [A ~ استغنا]

مستغیث *mūstaghīs'* N M plaintiff [A ~ استغاثہ]

مستفاد *mūstafād'* ADJ. meant gained benefited [A ~ استفادہ]

مستفتی *mūstaf'tī* ADJ seeking legal opinion [A ~ استفتا]

مستفسر *mūsta'fsir* ADJ. seeking interpretation [A ~ استفسار]

مستفید *mūstafīd'* ADJ. profiting gaining acquiring [A ~ استفادہ]

مستفیض *mūstafīz'* ADJ. (one) seeking favour [A ~ فیض]

مستقبل *mūstaq'bil* N.M. future future tense فعل مستقبل *fe''l-e mūstaq'bil* N M. future tense [A ~ استقبال]

مستقر *mūs'taqar* N.M. halting place فضائی مستقر *fazā''ī mūs'taqar* N.M. airport ; aerodrome [A]

مستقل *mūs'taqil* ADJ. permanent confirmed unshaken unshakable firm (rare) separate ; independent مستقل ارادہ *mūs'taqil irā'dah* ADJ. fixed resolve . determination مستقل اسامی *mūs'taqil asā'mī* N.F. permanent post permanent vacancy مستقل مزاج *mūs'taqil-mizāj'* ADJ resolute , of unshakable resolve مستقلی *mūstaqil'lī* N.F. confirmation [A ~ استقلال]

مستقیم *mūstaqīm'* ADJ. straight صراط مستقیم *sirā'te-mūstaqīm'* N.M. straight path (fig.) Islam [A ~ استقامت]

مستک *mas'tak* N.M. elephant's forehead (dial.) head

مستلزم *mūstal'zam* ADJ. necessitating کو مستلزم ہونا *ko mustal'zam ho'nā* V.T. necessitate [A ~ لازم]

مستمر *mūs'tamir* ADJ. permanent [A ~ استمرار]

مستمند *mūst'mand* ADJ. poor needy [A]

مستند *mūs'tanad* ADJ. authoritative authentic ; reliable [A ~ مسند]

مستنبط *mūstam'bat* ADJ. derived extracted [A ~ استنباط]

مستوجب *mūstau'jib* ADJ. liable (to punishment, etc.) [A ~ وجوب]

مستور *mastoor'* ADJ. veiled covered hidden ; concealed مستورات *mastoorāt'* N.F. PL. (~ SING. مستورہ) ladies purdah observing women مستوری *mastoo'rī* N.F. concealment retirement [A ~ ستر]

مستوفی *mūstau'fī* N.M. one who realises in full chief collector [A ~ استیفا]

مستول *mastaul'* (or *mastool'*) N.M. mast [~ Por]

مستولی *mūstau'lī* ADJ. possessing (someone's) mind [A ~ استیلا]

مستوی *mūs'tavī* ADJ. level plane straight [A ~ استوا]

مستی *mas'tī* N.F. (see under مست ADJ. ★)

مسٹنڈا *mūsṭan'ḍa* ADJ. & N.M. (F مسٹنڈی *mūsṭan'ḍa* stout person hooligan tough سنڈا مسٹنڈا *san'ḍu mūstan'ḍa*, ہٹا کٹا مسٹنڈا *haṭ'ṭa kaṭ'ṭa mūstan'ḍa* N.M. stout tough ; hoodlum

مسٹر *mis'ṭar* N.M. Mr. ; Mister مسٹریس *mis'ṭarais* N.F. & SUF. mistress

مسجد *mas'jid* N.F. mosque مسجد اقصیٰ *masjid-e aq'sā* N.F. Dome of the Rock مسجد الحرام *mas'jid-ūl-ḥarām'* N.F. the Holy Ka'aba جامع مسجد *jā'me' mas'jid* N.F. chief mosque (of city, etc.) large mosque [A ~ سجدہ]

مسجع *mūsaj'ja'* ADJ. rhymed (prose) [A ~ سجع]

مسجود *masjood* N.M. object of worship [A ~ سجدہ]

مسح *mas'ḥ* N.M. wiping anointing [A]

مسحور *mashoor'* ADJ. fascinated bewitched; enchanted [A ~ سحر *seḥr*]

مسخ *mas'kh*, مسخ شدہ *ma'skh-shū'dah* ADJ. mutilated metamorphosed into a lower species مسخ ہونا *mas'kh ho'nā* V.I. be multilated be metamorphosed thus [A]

مسخر *mūsakh'khar* ADJ. overcome ; subdued [A ~ تسخیر]

مسخرہ *mas'kharah* N.M. jester , fool ; buffoon wag مسخرہ پن *mas'khara-pan* N.M. مسخرگی *mas'kharagī* N.F jesting foolery ; buffoonery [A]

مسدس *mūsad'das* N.M. hexagon verseform comprising six-lined stanzas ADJ. hexagonal [A ~ سادس]

مسدود *masdood'* ADJ. shut ; closed [A ~ سد]

مسرت *masar'rat* (col. *mūsar'rat*) N.F. joy ; delight ; pleasure ; happiness [A]

مسرف *mūs'rif* ADJ. & N.M. (PL. مسرفین *mūsrifīn'*) extravagant ; prodigal [A ~ اسراف]

مسرور *masroor'* ADJ. happy ; glad ; pleased ; delighted ; cheerful [A ~ سرور]

مسروقہ *masroo'qah* ADJ. stolen [A ~ سرقہ]

مسطح *mūsal'taḥ* ADJ. plane ; level ; even [A ~ سطح]

مسطر *mis'tar* N.M. ruler (arch.) threaded paper (used as a ruler for unruled sheets of paper) such ruled paper calligraphist's ruled sheet [A ~ سطر]

مسطور *mastoor'* ADJ. written [A ~ سطر]

مسعود *mas'ood'* ADJ. (F. & PL. مسعودہ *mas'oo'dah*) lucky ; fortunate [A ~ سعد]

مسقف *mūsaq'qaf* ADJ. roofed [A ~ سقف]

مسک *mis'k* N.F. (same as مشک *mūsh'k* N.F. ★)

مسکا *mūsak'kā* N.M. muzzle (for animal)

مسکانا *mūskā'na* V.I. (dial.) (same as V.I. ★)

مسکت *mūs'kit* ADJ. silencing (reply) A ~ سکوت

مسکرات *mūskirāt'* N.F. intoxicants [A ~ سکر *sūk'r*]

مسکرانا *mūskūrā'na* V.I. (dial مسکانا *mūskā'na*) smile simper ; smirk grin *mūskūrā'haṭ* N.F. smile simper smirk grin

مسکن *mas'kan* N.M. (PL. مساکین *masā'kin*) residence ; abode , habitation [A ~ سکونت]

مسکن *mūsak'kin* ADJ. sedative N.M. anodyne [A ~ تسکین]

مسکنا *ma'saknā*, مسک جانا *ma'sak ja'nā* V.I. be torn at the seams

مسکنت *mas'kanat* N.F. indigence humility

مسکون *maskoon'* ADJ. inhabited ; habitable

مسکہ *mas'kah* N.M. butter مسکہ لگانا *mas'kah lagā'nā* V.T. cajole flatter [A]

مسکین *miskīn'* ADJ. poor meek N.M. (PL. مساکین *masākīn'*) poor person meek person مسکینی *miskī'nī* N.F. poverty ; indigence meekness [A]

مسل *mis'l* (col. *mi'sal*) N.F. file record (of case); file file cover مسل خواں *mis'l-khān* N.M. reader مسل مرتب کرنا *mis'l murat'tab kar'nā* V.T. prepare record (of case)

مسلح *mūsal'lah* ADJ. armed ; equipped armoured [A ~ سلاح]

مسلسل *mūsal'sal* ADJ. coherent ; linked together consecutive ; successive ADV. consecutively [A ~ سلسلہ]

مسلط *mūsal'lat* ADJ. conquered ; subdued appointed; set over ruling [A ~ سلطان]

مسلک *mas'lak* N.M. (PL. مسالک *masā'lik*) way conduct school of thought [A]

مسلم *mūs'lim* N.M. (PL. مسلمین *mūslimīn'*) one who professes Islam ; Muslim one who surrenders himself to Allah's will [A ~ اسلام]

مسلم *mūsal'lam* ADJ. admitted ; granted ; conceded (of fowl, etc.) cooked whole مرغ مسلم *mur'gh-e mūsal'lam* N.M. roast fowl [A ~ تسلیم]

مسلمان *mū'salman* N.M. (ped. PL. مسلمانان *mūsalmānān'* or -*aṅ*) Muslim مسلمانی *mūsalmā'nī* N.F. Islamic faith (a ch.) circumcision ADJ. Islamic [P ~ A مسلم]

مسلمہ *mūsal'lamah* ADJ. universally admitted accepted (truth, etc.) [A ~ تسلیم]

مسلنا *ma'salnā* V.T. crush

مسلوب *masloob'* ADJ. (of thing) snatched away (of person) deprived of مسلوب الحواس *masloo'b-ūl-havās'*, مسلوب العقل *masloo'b-ul-'aq'l* ADJ. deprived of senses (one) in his dotage [A ~ سلب]

مسلول *masool'* ADJ. drawn (sword) [A ~ سل]

مسمات (ped. مسماة) *mūsammat'* N.F. legal title used before woman's name to point out the sex ; Mrs. Miss ; Lady ADJ. named [A ~ M. مسمی]

مسمار *mismar'* (of building) razed ; demolished [A]

مسمریزم *mismare'zam* N.M. mesmerism مسمریزم کرنا *mismare'zam kar'nā* V.T. mesmerize مسمریزم کرنے والا *mismare'zam kar'ne vā'lā* N.M. mesmerist [E]

مسمسا *mūs'mūsā* ADJ. (F. مسمسی *mūs'mūsī*) having an air of humbleness (one) with an air of innocence مسمسی شکل (یا صورت) بنا *mūs'mūsī shak'l* (or *soo'rat*) *banā''e* ADJ. with an air of humbleness or innocence

مسموع *masmoo'* ADJ. heard [A ~ سماعت]

مسموم *masmoom'* ADJ. poisoned ; venomous [A ~ سم *sam*]

مسمی *mosam'mā* ADJ. named ; called [A ~ اسم]

مسمی ¹ *mūsam'mī* N.M. (PL. مسمیان *mūsam'miyān*) legal title used before man's name to point out the sex [~ A مسمیٰ *mosam'ma* CORR.]

مسمی ² *mūsam'mī* N.F. sweet tangerine [CORR. of A ~ موسمی seasonal]

مسن *mūsin'* ADJ. old ; aged ; advanced in years grown up [A ~ سن *sin* age]

مسند *mas'nad* N.F. throne exalted مسند آرا *mas'nad-ārā'*, مسند نشین *mas'nad-nashīn'* ADJ. adorning a throne enthroned N.M. reigning prince مسند آرائی *mas'nad-ārā''ī*, مسند نشینی *mas'nad nashī'nī* N.F. accession to the throne [A ~ سند]

مسند *mūs'nad* N.M. predicate مسند الیہ *mūs'nadilaih* N.M. subject [A ~ اسناد *isnād'*]

مسنون *masnoon'* ADJ. as practiced by the Holy Prophet ; Traditional [A ~ سنت]

مسواک *misvāk'* N.F. tooth-brush [A]

مسودہ *mūsav'vadah* N.M. (col. *mūsvad'dah*) draft manuscript [A ~ تسوید]

مسور *masoor* N.F. lentils ; a kind of pulse یہ منہ اور مسور کی دال *yeh mūṅh aur masoor' kī dāl'* PROV. how can he (etc.) deserve it ?

مسوڑھا *masoo'ṛhā* N.M. gum (holding one's set of teeth) مسوڑھے پھولنا *masoo'ṛhe phool'nā* V.I. have revollen gums

مسوسنا *masos'nā* V.T. twist (heart, etc.) owing to grief: کلیجہ مسوس کر رہ جانا *kale'jā masos' kar raih jā'nā* V.I. suffer grief patiently

مسہری *masaih'rī* N.F. canopied bed mosquito net

مسہل *mus'hil* ADJ. aperient N.M. aperient looseness of bowels [A ~ اسہال]

مسئلہ *mas''alah* N.M. (PL. مسائل *masā''il*) issue; question theorem proposition [A doublet of سوال]

مسئول *mas''ool* ADJ. responsible ; answerable [A ~ سؤال]

مسی *mis'sī* N.F. red lead used as toothpowder and lipstick for its darknessing effect مسی کاجل کرنا *mis'sī kā'jal kar'nā* V.T. do one's make-up مسی کی دھڑی ہونٹوں پر جمانا *mis'sī kī dha'ṛī hon'ṭoṅ par jamā'nā* V.T. paint one's lips dark

مسیح *masīh'* N.M. Christ ; Messiah anointed مسیحی *masī'hī* N.M. & ADJ. Christian مسیحا masī'hā N.M. Messiah healer beloved مسیحائی masīhā''ī N.F. healing power power to restore to life, suspire مسیحائی کرنا masīhā''ī kar'nā V.T heal quicken

مشابہت mūshā'bahat N.F. resemblance similarity; likeness similitude مشابہ mūshābeh ADJ. like resembling analogous [A ~ شبہ shib'h]

مشار mūshār' ADJ. indicated; signified مشارٌ الیہ mūshā'r ūn ilaih' ADJ. aforesaid; the said (person) abovementioned [A ~ اشارہ]

مشارب mashā'rib N.M. (PL. of مشرب N.M. ★)

مشارق mashā'riq N.F. (PL of مشرق N F. ★)

مشارکت mūshār akat N F partnership [A ~ شرکت ★]

مشاطہ mashshā'tah N.F waiting maid make-up expert; tire-woman woman acting as marriage-agent مشاطگی mashshā'tagī N.F. make-up acting as marriage agent [A ~ مشط mush't comb]

مشاعرہ mūshā''arah N.M. meeting at which poets recste their verse in turn; 'musha'ira' [A ~ شعر]

مشاغل mashā'ghil N.M. (PL. of مشغلہ N.M. ★)

مشافہہ mūshā'fahah N.M. facing one another (only in) بالمشافہہ bil-mūshā'fahah ADJ. private (talk) ADV. face-to-face بالمشافہہ گفتگو bil-moshā'fahah g'ft-ū-goo' tete-a-tete face-to-face talk confrontation [A ~ شفتہ lip]

مشاق mashshāq' ADJ. practised; expert مشاقی mashshā'qi N.F. practice; expertness [A ~ مشق]

مشام mashām' N.F. smell sense of smell organ of smell [A ~ شامہ]

مشاورت mūshā'varat N.F. mutual consultation [A ~ مشورہ]

مشاہدہ mūshā'hadah N.M. observation witnessing the divinity; contemplation مشاہدہ کرنا mūshā'hadah kar'nā V.T. & I. observe contemplate مشاہد mūshā'hid N.M. observer [A ~ شہادت]

مشاہرہ mūsh'hārah N.M. monthly pay; salary [A ~ شہر month]

مشاہیر mashāhīr' N.M. famous persons celebrities the elite [A ~ SING. مشہور]

مشائخ mashā'ikh N.M. (PL. of شیخ N.M. ★)

مشائی mashā''ī N.M. (PL. مشائیین mashā'iyyin') peripatetic [A ~ مشی]

مشایعت mūshā'ya'at N.F. going along (someone) to see him off [A]

مشبہ mūshab'bah N.M. object for which a smile is used ADJ. likened (object) مشبہ بہ moshab'bah be-hi' N.M that to which anything is likened [A ~ شبہ]

مشت mūsh't N.F. fist blow handful مشت استخوان mūsh't-e ustukhān' N.F. mere skeleton; very weak body مشت خاک (یا غبار) mūsh't-e khāk' (or ghūbār') N.F. handful of dust (fig.) man مشت زنی mūsh't-zanī N.F. masturbation (joc.) boxing مشتالی کرنا mūsht-mā'lī kar'na V.T. massage مشتے نمونہ از خروارے mūsh'te nūmoo'nā(-e) az kharvā're PH. specimen; a handful out of a heap [P]

مشتاق mūshtāq' ADJ. found; ardent wistful; longing مشتاق ہونا mūshtāq ho'nā V.T be fond of long for مشتاقانہ mūshtāqā'nah ADJ. fond longing ADV. fondly longingly مشتاقی mūshtā'qī N.F. fondness longing [A ~ اشتیاق]

مشتبہ mūshtabah' ADJ. doubtful; dubious suspect N.M. suspect [A ~ اشتباہ]

مشترک mūsh'tarak, (F. & PL. مشترکہ mūshta'rakah) ADJ. joint common shared ADV. jointly in partnership (with) مشترکہ طور پر mūshtar'akah taur' par PH. jointly [A ~ اشتراک]

مشتری mūsh'tarī N.M. Jupiter N.M. buyer [A]

مشتعل mūsh'ta'il ADJ. enraged kindled مشتعل ہونا mūsh'ta'il ho'nā V.I. be enraged be kindled مشتعل ہوکر mūsh'ta'il ho kar ADV under provocation [A ~ شعلہ]

مشتق mūsh'taq N.M. derivative ADJ. drived from [A ~ اشتقاق]

مشتمل mūsh'tamil ADJ. inclusive (of); including; containing comprehending consisting (of); comprising مشتمل ہونا mūsh'tamil ho'nā V.I. consist of; comprise [A ~ اشتمال]

مشتہر mūsh'tahar ADJ. advertised made public مشتہر کرنا mūsh'tahar kar'nā V T. advertise make publie مشتہر mūsh'tahir N.M. (PL. مشتہرین mūshtahirīn') advertiser [A ~ اشتہار]

مشتہی mūsh'tahī ADJ. appetizing N.M. appetizer [A ~ اشتہا]

مشجر mūshaj'jar ADJ. silk with arboreal patterns tapestry [A ~ اشجار]

مشخص mūshakh'khas ADJ. defined; specified individualized مشخص ہونا mūshakh'khas kar'nā V T. defoul; specify individualize نامشخص nā-mūshakh'khas ADJ. unspecified نامشخص خرنا kha'r-e nā-mshakh'khas (ped.) unspecified ass, arrant fool [A ~ تشخیص]

مشدد *mushad'dad* ADJ. doubled (letter) (this) bearing tashdid (ّ) [A ~ شد]

مشرب *mash'rab* N.M. (PL. مشارب *mashā'rib*) way of life (rare) place of drinking [A]

مشرح *mushar'rah* ADJ. detailed annotated with a commentary having an exegesis [A ~ تشریح]

مشرف *mushar'raf* ADJ. honoured exalted مشرف بہ اسلام کرنا *mushar'raf ba-islām' kar'nā* V.T. convert to Islam [A ~ شرف]

مشرق *mash'riq* N.F. (PL. مشارق *mashā'riq*) east place of sunrise مشرق بعید (یا اقصیٰ) *mash'riq-e ba'īd'* (or *aq'sā*) N.F. Far East مشرق قریب (یا ادنیٰ) *mash'riq-e qarīb'* (or *ad'nā*) N.F. Near East مشرق وسطیٰ *mash'riq-e vūs'tā* N.F. (wrong but usu. form for مشرق اوسط *mash'riq-e au'sat*, شرق اوسط *shar'q-e au'sat*) N.M. Middle East ; Mid-East مشرقی *mash'riqī* ADJ. Eastern , oriental مشرقین *mashriqain'* N.M. PL. the two Easts ; extremely points of sunrise during summer and winter بعد المشرقین *bo''d-ūl-mashriqain'* N.M. a world of difference [A ~ شرق]

مشرک *mūsh'rik* N.M. polytheist [A ~ شرک]

مشروب *mashroob'* N.M. (PL. مشروبات *mashroobāt'*) drink beverage

مشروط *mashroot'* ADJ. conditional سے مشروط ہونا *se mashroot' ho'nā* V.I. be conditional on [A ~ شرط]

مشروع *mashroo'* ADJ. lawful legitimate permissible (rare) programme *na-mashroo'* ADJ unlawful [A ~ شرع]

مشعل *mash''al* (or wrong but ped. *mish''al*) N.F. torch مشعلچی *mash''alchī* N.M. torch-bearer [A ~ شعلہ]

مشغلہ *mash'ghalah* N.M. (PL. مشاغل *moshā'ghil*) avocation hobby amusement ; pastime job , vocation [A doublet of شغل]

مشغول *mashghool'* ADJ. busy ; occupied ; engaged مشغولی *mashghoo'lī*, مشغولیت *mashghooliy'yat* N.F. preoccupation ; being occupied (with) [A ~ شغل]

مشفق *mūsh'fiq* N.M. friend ADJ. kind ; considerate affectionate مشفقانہ *mūsh'fiqa'nāh* ADJ. kind affectionate ADV. kindly affectionately [A ~ شفقت]

مشق *mash'q* N.F. exercise practice model lettering its copy ; repeated copies of it ; copy مشق کرنا *mash'q kar'nā* V.T. exercise practise copy مشق ہونا *mash'q ho'na* V.I. have practice be skilled (in) مشقی *mash'qī* ADJ. exercise (book) practice (work) practical (lesson)

مشقت *mashaq'qat* (col. *mū-*) N.F. hard work toil labour مشقت شدید *mashaq'qat-e shadīd'* N.F. hard labour بے مشقت *bā-mashaq'qat* ADJ. rigorous (imprisonment) بلا مشقت *bi-lā-mashaq'qat* ADJ. simple (imprisonment) [A]

مشک *mūsh'k* N.F. water-skin مشکیزہ *mashkīzah* N.M. small water-skin [P]

مشک *mūsh'k* N.M. musk مشک آنست کہ خود ببوید نہ کہ عطار بگوید *mūsh'k ā'n-ast ke khūd' bi-bo'yad na ke 'attār' bi-go'yad* PROV. selfpraise is no recommendation مشکبار *mūsh'k-bār* ADJ. diffusing musk fragrant مشکباری *mūsh'k-bā'rī* N.F fragrance مشک بو *mūsh'k-boo* ADJ. muskscented fragrant مشک فام *mūsh'k-fām* ADJ. jet black مشک نافہ *mūsh'k-nā'fah* N.M. musk bag مشکی *mūsh'kī* ADJ. (of horse) black N.M. black-horse مشکیں *mūsh'kīn* ADJ. musk of or like musk black [P]

مشکک *mūshak'kik* ADJ. sceptical Pyrrhonic N.M. sceptic Pyrrhonian [A ~ تشکیک]

مشکل *mūsh'kil* ADJ. difficult ; hard N.F. (PL. مشکلات *mūshkilāt'*) difficulty ; hardship مشکل آسان کرنا *mūsh'kil āsān' kar'nā* V.T. remove a difficulty solve (someone's) problem مشکل آسان ہونا *mūsh'kil āsān' ho'nā* V.I. (of difficulty) be removed of a hardship مشکل پسند *mūsh'kil-pasand'* ADJ. (one.) given to using difficult language (one) enjoying difficulties مشکل پسندی *mūsh'kil-pasan'dī* N.F. fondness for difficult styles (or situations) مشکل سے *mūsh'kil se* ADV. with difficulty hardly مشکل کشا *mūsh'kil-kūshā* N.M. one who removes difficulties مشکل کشائی *mūsh'kil-kūshā''ī* N.F. removal of difficulty مشکل میں پڑنا (یا گرفتار ہونا) *mūsh'kil meṅ paṛ'nā* (or *giriftār' ho'nā*) V.T. land oneself into trouble [A ~ اشکال]

مشکوٰۃ *mishkāt'* N.F. niche (for lamp) مشکوٰۃ المصابیح *mishkā't-ūl-masābīh'* N.M. niche for lamps [A]

مشکور *mashkoor'* ADJ. (col. though wrong) thankful ; grateful [A ~ شکر]

مشکوک *mashkook'* ADJ. doubtful ; dubious ; uncertain [A ~ شک]

مشکی *mūsh'kī* ADJ., مشکیں *mūsh'kīn* (see under مشک *mushk* N.M. ★)

مشکیزہ *mashkī'zah* N.M. (see under مشک *mash'k* N.F ★)

مشکیں *mūsh'keṅ* N.F. both the arms or the shoulders tied behind as punishment مشکیں باندھنا (یا کسنا) *mūsh'keṅ bāndh'na* (or *kas'na*) V.T. pinion

مشمول *mashmool'* (F. & PL. مشمولہ *mashmoo'lah*) ADJ included (in) ; incorporated (with) [A ~ شمول]

مشن *mi'shan* N.F. mission ADJ. serving the ends of a Christian mission مشنری *mish'narī* N.M. missionary N.F. (col.) Christian mission [E]

مشورہ *mash'varah*, N.M. (rare) مشورت *mash'varat*) N.F. consultation counsel (usu. PL.) plot, conspiracy مشورہ کرنا *mashvarah kar'nā* V.T. consult take advice deliberate مشورہ ہونا *mash'varah ho'nā* V.I. be consulted come to the conclusion [A]

مشوش *mūshav'vash* ADJ. perplexed uneasy ; disturbed [A ~ تشویش]

مشہد *mash'had* N.M. place of (someone's) martyrdom mausoleum of a martyr [A ~ تشہید]

مشہود *mashhood'* ADJ. clear ; manifest witnessed [A ~ شہادت]

مشہور *mashhoor'* ADJ. well-known famous celebrated reputed notable مشہور و معروف *mash'hoor-o-ma'roof'* ADJ. well-known famous reputed مشہوری *mashhoo'rī* N.F. fame reputation [A ~ شہرت]

مشی *mash'y* N.F. walking مشی فی النوم *mash'y fin-naum'* N.F somnambulism [A]

مشیت *mashiy'yat* N.F. will pleasure (also مشیت ایزدی *mashiy'yat-e ē'zadī*) the will of God ; fate [A ~ شا]

مشیخت *mashī'khat* N.F. ptide ; vanity مشیخت کرکری ہونا *mashī'khat kir'kirī ho'nā* V.I. (of some one's pride) humbled مشیخت مآب *mashī'khat ma'āb'* ADJ. vainglorious [A ~ شیخ]

مشید *mūshay'yad* (F. & PL. مشیدہ *mūshay'yadah*) ADJ. rainforced cemented [A]

مشیر *mūshīr'* N.M. adviser ; counsellor consultant مشیر خاص *mūshī'r-e khās* N.M. privy counsellor special consultant مشیر الدولہ *mūshī'r-ud-dau'lah* N.M. State adviser مشیر مال *mūshīr-e māl* N.M. financial adviser قانونی مشیر *qānoo'nī mūshīr'* N.M. legal adviser [A ~ اشارہ]

مشین *mashīn'* N.F. machine sewing machine مشین گن *mashīn'-gan* N.F. machine-gun مشینی *mashī'nī* ADJ. mechanical machine مشینی دور *mashī'nī daur* N.M. machine age [E]

مصابیح *masābīh'* N.M. (PL. of مصباح N.M. ★)

مصاحب *mūsā'hib* N.M. companion 'aid-de-camp' ; A.D.C. مصاحبت *mūsā'habat* N.F. companionship ; company ; society [A ~ صحبت]

مصاحف *masā'hif* N.M. (PL. of مصحف N.M. ★)

مصادر *masā'dir* N.M. (PL. of مصدر N.M. ★)

مصارف *masā'rif* N.M. (PL. of مصرف N.M. ★)

مصافحہ *mūsā'fahah* N.M. handshake مصافحہ کرنا *mūsā'fahah kar'nā* V.T. shake hands ; shake (someone) by the hand [A]

مصالح *masā'leh* N.M. (PL. of مصلحت N.F. ★)

مصالح[2] *masā'la* N.M. (same as مسالہ N.M. ★)

مصالحت *mūsā'lahat* N.F. reconciliation composition ; compounding ; adjustment specification cessation of hostilities مصالحت کرانا *mūsā'lahat karā'nā* V.T. reconcile bring about an end of hostilties (between) مصالحت کرنا *mūsā'lahat kar'nā* V. become reconciled (to) make peace (with) adjust ; compound [A ~ صلح]

مصائب *masā''ib* N.M. (PL. of مصیبت N.F. ★)

مصباح *misbāh'* N.M. (PL. مصابیح *masābīh'*) lamp [A ~ صبح]

مصحح *mūsah'heh* N.M. emendator (rare) proof-reader one who

مصحف *mūs'haf* N.M. (PL. مصاحف *masā'hif*) the Holy Quran page beloved's (usu. sleek) face [A]

مصداق *misdāq'* N.M. proof ; evidence ; (only in) *ke misdāq'* PH. according to [A]

مصدر *mas'dar* N.M. (PL. مصادر *masā'dir*) infinitive ; infinitive mood noun of action source origin مصدر لازم *mas'dar-e lā'zim* N.M. intransitive verb مصدر متعدی *mas'dar-e mūta'ad'dī* N.M. transitive verb [A ~ صدور]

مصدق *mūsad'dīq* ADJ. verifier [A ~ تصدیق]

مصدقہ *musad'daqah* ADJ. true attested authenticated مصدقہ نقل *mūsad'daqah naq'l* N.M. true eopy [A ~ تصدیق]

مصر *mis'r* N.M. Egypt (PL. امصار *amsār'*) garrison town ; city مصری *mis'rī* N.M. & ADJ. Egyptian [A]

مصر *mūsir'* ADJ. insistent [A ~ اصرار]

مصرح *mūsar'rah* ADJ. clarified ; elaborated elucidated [A ~ تصریح]

مصرع *mis'ra'*, مصرعہ *mis'ra'ah* N.M. hemistitch , line of a verse (rare) leaf (of door) مصرع اٹھانا *mis'ra' ūthā'nā* V.T. (of audience) repeat reciting) poet' line as sign of appreciation مصرع طرح *mis'ra'-e tar'h* N.M. line set for completion of verse مصرع لگانا *mis'ra' lagā'nā* V.T. complete a couplet by adding a line to given hemistich [A]

مصرف *mas'raf* N.M. (PL. مصارف *masā'rif*) expenditure use ; utility [A ~ صرف]

مصروع *masroo''* ADJ. epileptic [A ~ صرع]

مصروف *masroof'* ADJ. busy ; occupied ; engaged ; having one's hand full مصروف ہونا *masroof' ho'na* V.I. be busy مصروفیت *masroofiy'yat* N.F. engagement ; preoccupation [A ~ صرف *sar'f*]

مصری¹ *mis'rī* N.F. sugar-candy مصری کا کوزہ *mis'rī ka koo'zah* N.M. cup of sugar-candy ADJ. very sweet مصری کی ڈلی *mis'rī kī da'lī* N.F. lump of sugar ADJ. very sweet sugar-cake

مصری² *mis'rī* ADJ. (see under مصر N.M. ★)

مصطفیٰ *mūs' tafā* ADJ. chosen ; selected N.M. this as the Holy Prophet's appellation [A ~ اصطفا]

مصطگی *mas'tagī* N.F. mastic ; gum-mastic [P ~ A مَصطکی ~ G]

مصطلحات *mūstalahāt'* N.F. (dial. M.) technical terms terminology [A ~ اِصطلاح]

مصفیٰ (or مصفا *mūsaf'fa* ADJ. clean clarified pure [A ~ تصفیہ]

مصفی *mūsaf'fī* ADJ. cleaning ; purifying ADJ. cleaner ; purifier مصفی خون *mūsaf'fi-e khoon'* ADJ. blood purified [A ~ تصفیہ]

مصلیٰ (or مصلا *mūsal'la* N.M. prayer-carpet [A ~ صلوٰۃ]

مصلح *mūs'leh* N.M. (PL. مصلحین *mūslehīn*) reformer corrective [A ~ اِصلاح]

مصلحت *mas'lahat* N.F. (PL. M. مصالح *masā'leh*) expedience ; expediency advisability prudence considerations مصلحت بین *mas'lahat-bīn* ADJ. prudent ; wise ; farseeing مصلحت دیکھنا *mas'lahat dekh'na* V.T. regard as advisable مصلحت وقت *mas'lahat-e vaq't* N.F. expediency opportune moment seasonable caution مصلحتاً *mas'lahatan* ADV. as a measure of expediency [A ~ صلح]

مصلوب *masloob'* ADJ. crucified [A ~ صلیب]

مصلی *mūsal'lī* N.M. one who says prayers sweeper converted to Islam [A ~ صلوٰۃ]

مصمم *mūsam'mam* ADJ. firm (resolve) مصمم ارادہ *mūsam'mam ira'dah* N.M. firm resolve; determination [A ~ تصمیم]

مصنف *mūsan'nif* N.M. (PL. مصنفین *mūsannifīn'*) writer ; author مصنفہ *mūsan'ni-fah* N.F. (PL. مصنفات *mūsannifāt'*) writer ; authoress [A ~ تصنیف]

مصنف *mūsan'naf* N.M. (PL. مصنفات *mūsan'nafāt*) volume comprising the Holy Prophet's Traditions arranged subjectwise مصنفہ *mūsan'nafah* ADV. by ; written by [A ~ تصنیف]

مصنوعہ *masnoo''ah* ADJ. made; prepared ; manufactured made up مصنوعات *masnoo'āt'* N.F. PL. manufactures مصنوعی *masnoo''ī* ADJ. artificial fabricated false unnatural [A ~ صنعت]

مصوّر *mūsav'vir* N.M. (PL. مصورین *mūsavvirīn'*) painter artist مصوری *mūsav'virī* N.F. painting drawing graphic art [~ تصویر]

مصوّر *mūsav'var* ADJ. pictorial illustrated [A ~ تصویر]

مصئون *masoon'* ADJ. safe ; protected ; guarded [A ~ صیانت]

مصیبت *mūsī'bat* N.F. trouble affliction disaster misfortune calamity مصیبت اٹھانا (یا بھرنا یا بھگتنا یا جھیلنا) *mūsī'bat ūṭhā'nā* (or *bhar'nā* or *bhū'gatnā* or *jhel'nā*) V.I. undergo trouble مصیبت زدہ *mūsī'bat-zadah* ADJ. unfortunate miserable afflicted مصیبت زدگان *mūsī'bat-zadagān* N.M. PL. the afflicted مصیبت کے دن کاٹنا *mūsī'bat ke din' kaṭ'nā* V.T. pass one's days in trouble مصیبت میں پڑنا *mūsī'bat men par'nā* V.I. be overtaken by misery ناگہانی مصیبت *nā-gahā'nī mūsī'bat* N.F. unexpected trouble ; a bolt from the blue [A]

مضار *mazār'* N.M. (PL. of مضرت N.F. ★)

مضارع *mūzā're'* N.M. (gram.) aorist tense aorist name of a common prosodic metre [A]

مضاعف *mūzā''af* ADJ. doubled multiplied ; increased N.M. stem (of word) repeating one or more letters [A ~ ضعف *ze''f*]

مضاف *mūzāf'* N.M. noun in the possessive case , possessor ADJ. related or appended to مضاف الیہ *mūzāf'-elaih'* N.M. possessed noun or pronoun [A ~ اضافت]

مضافات *mūzāfāt'* N.F. (also مضافات شہر *mūzā'fā't-e shaih'r*) suburbs [A ~ اضافہ]

مضامین *mazāmīn'* N.M. (PL. of مضمون N.M. ★)

مضایقہ *mūzā'yaqah* N.M. harm (in doing something) کچھ مضایقہ نہیں *kūchh mūzā'yaqah na'hīn* PH. don't you worry · it is of no consequence [~ A straitening]

مضبوط *mazboot'* ADJ. strong ; fixed ; fast firm (resolve) cogent ; (reasoning) durable ; lasting مضبوطی *mazboo'tī* N.F. strength firmness cogency durability ; long wear [A ~ ضبط]

مضحک *mūz'hik* ADJ. ridiculous ludicrous droll facetious [A ~ FOLL.]

مضحکہ *mūz'hakah* N.M. fun ridicule drollery facetiousness مضحکہ اڑانا *māz'hakah ūṛā'nā* V.T. ridicule مضحکہ خیز *maz'haka-khez'* ADJ. ridiculous ludicrous laughter-provoking [A]

مضر *muzir'* ADJ. injurious hurtful pernicious deleterious noxious baneful detrimental [A ~ ضرر]

مضراب *mizrāb'* N.F. plectrum [A ~ ضرب]

مضرت *mazar'rat* N.F. (PL. مضرات *mazarrāt'*) harm; damage detriment مضرت رساں *mazar'rat-rasāṅ'* ADJ. harmful damaging detrimental مضرت رسانی *mazar'rat rasā'nī* N.F. harm ; damage damaging capacity mischievousness ; mischief [A ~ ضرر]

مضروب *mazroob'* ADJ. hurt ; wounded injured N.M. (math.) multiplicant مضروب فیہ *mazroob'-fīh'* N.M. (Math). multiplier [A ~ ضرب]

مضطر *mūz'tar* ADJ. afflicted desperate ; chagrined powerless ; left with no choice [A ~ اضطرار]

مضطرب *mūz'tarib'* ADJ. disturbed uneasy troubled ; agitated مضطرب الحال *mūz'-tarib-ul-ḥāl'* ADJ. in straitened circumstances مضطرب ہونا *mūz'tarib ho'nā* V.I. be restless be uneasy ; be disturbed be agitated ; be in a state of commotion مضطربانہ *mūztaribā'nah* ADJ. disturbed uneasy agitated ADV. uneasily in a agitated state of mind [A ~ اضطراب]

مضمحل *mūz'maḥil* ADJ. fatigued ; exhausted weak ; infirm [A ~ اضمحلال]

مضمر *mūz'mar* ADJ. hidden ; latent N.M. (gram.) antecedent [A ~ اضمار]

مضموم *mazmoom'* ADJ. (of some letter) having a pesh' (ـُـ) over it [A ~ ضمہ]

مضمون *mazmoon'* N.M. (PL. مضامین *mazāmīn'*) composition ; essay ; article subject topic subject-matter ; contents meaning ; sense ; purport مضمون نگار *mazmoon'-nigār'* N.M. contributor to a periodical writer of essay , article, etc. مضمون نگاری *mazmoon'-nigā'rī* N.F. article-writing essay-writing contribution to a periodical مضمون نویس *mazmoon'-navis'* N.M. writer of an article essayist مضمون نویسی *mazmoon'-navī'sī* N.F. article-writing essay-writing composition [A]

مضیٰ ما مضیٰ *mazā' mā-mazā'* PL. let bygones be bygones ; forgive and forget [A ~ مضیٰ went]

مطابع *matā'be'* N.M. (PL. of مطبع N.M. ★)

مطابق *mūtā'biq* ADV. like ; alike corresponding (to) ; conforming (to) in accordance (with) ; according (to) مطابق کرنا *mūtā'biq kar'nā* V.T. make alike مطابق ہونا *mūtā'biq ho'nā* V.T. conform (to) ; correspond (to) be like be alike مطابقت *mūtā'baqat* N.F. similarity conformity [A]

مطاع *mūtā''* N.M. & ADJ. one who is obeyed [A ~ اطاعت]

مطالب *matā'lib* N.M. (PL. of مطلب *mat'lab* ★)

مطالبہ *mūtā'labah* N.M. (PL. مطالبات *mūtālabāt'*) demand requisition [A ~ طلب]

مطالع *matā'le'* N.M. (PL. of مطلع N.M. ★)

مطالعہ *mūtā'la'ah* N.M. study ; reading ; perusal مطالعہ کرنا *mūtā'la'ah kar'nā* V.T. study ; read ; peruse [A]

مطایبہ *mūtā'yabah* N.M. (PL. مطایبات *mūtāyabāt'*) jest ; joke [A ~ طیب]

مطب *matab'* N.M. clinic [A ~ طب]

مطبخ *mat'bakh* N.M. kitchen [A ~ طبخ]

مطبع *mat'ba'* N.M. (PL. مطابع *matā'be'*) press ; printing press [A ~ طبع]

مطبوع *matboo''* ADJ. agreeable delectable liked by born (poet) مطبوع خلائق *matboo''-e khalā''iq* ADJ. according to the public taste [A ~ طبع]

مطبوعہ *matboo''ah* ADJ. printed مطبوعات *matboo'āt'* N.F. books publications [A ~ طباعت]

مطر *ma'tar* N.M. (rare) rain [A]

مطرب *mūt'rib* N.M. singer ; songster singing-man (rare) entertainer مطربہ *mūt'ribah* N.F. (PL. مطربات *mūtribāt'*) female singer ; songstress female artiste [A ~ طرب]

مطعون *mat'oon'* ADJ. reproached ; child blameworthy [A ~ طعن]

مطلا *mūtal'lā* ADJ. gilded ; gilt [P ~ A]

مطلب *mat'lab* N.M. (PL. مطالب *matā'lib*) meaning purport wish ; desire object ; aim; purpose motive concern مطلب براری *mat'lab-bar-ā'rī* N.F. selfishness achieving one's object مطلب رکھنا *mat'lab rakh'nā* V.I. have an interest (in) be motivated by something مطلب سعدی دگر است *mat'lab-e sa''di di'gar-as't* PH. the real purpose is different مطلب کا یار *mat'lab kā yār'* N.M. selfish person time-server one having ulterior motives مطلب نکالنا *mat'lab nikāl'nā* V. gain one's object to serve the purpose مطلب نکلنا *mat'lab nikal'nā* V.I. have one's object served مطلب ہونا *mat'lab ho'nā* V.T. & I. mean have a concern مطلبی *mat'labī* ADJ. selfish ; self-seeking ; one driven by ulterior motives [A ~ طلب]

مطلع *mat'la'* N.M. place of rising east (of sun, etc.) sky exordium (of ode, etc.) مطلع صاف ہونا *mat'la' sāf' ho'nā* V.I. (of weather) be clear [A ~ طلوع]

مطلع *mūl'tala'* ADJ. notified ; informed ; intimated aware (of) مطلع کرنا *mūl'tala kar'na* V.T. notify ; inform ; intimate مطلع ہونا *mūl'tala' ho'na* V.I. be informed ; become aware (of) [A ~ اطلاع]

مطلق *mūl'laq* ADJ. absolute (rare) free independent ADV. entirely altogether (not) at all ; (not) in the least مطلق العنان *mūl'laq-ūl-'inān'* ADJ. absolute (authority) despotic (ruler) مطلقاً *mūl'laqan* ADV. absolutely entirely altogether (not) at all ; (not) in the least [A ~ اطلاق]

مطلقہ *mūtal'laqah* ADJ. & N.F. (PL. مطلقات *mūtallaqāt'*) divorced (woman) [A ~ طلاق]

مطلوب *matloob'* N.M. object of one's love ; beloved ADJ. desired فہوالمطلوب *fa-hū'v val-matloob'* PH. Q E D [A ~ طلب]

مطمحِ نظر *mat'mah-e nazar* N.M. goal ; aim ; object ; objective [P ~ A place where one casts one glance]

مطمئن *mūt'ma'in* ADJ. satisfied [A ~ اطمینان]

مطول *mūtav'val* ADJ. lengthy ; prolonged [A ~ طول]

مطہر *mūtah'har* (F. & PL. مطہرہ *mūtah'harah*) ADJ. purified cleansed مطہر *mūtah'hir* ADJ. purifying cleansing [A ~ تطہیر]

مطیر *matīr'* ADJ. raining ; coming down in drops [A ~ مطر]

مطیع *mūtī''* ADJ. submissive obedient [A ~ اطاعت]

مظالم *mazā'lim* N.M. (PL. of ظالم N.M. ★)

مظاہر *mazā'hir* N.M. (PL. of مظہر N.M. ★)

مظاہرہ *mūzā'harah* N.M. demonstration [A ~ ظہور]

مظفر *mūzaf'far* ADJ. victorious successful مظفر و منصور *mūzaf'far-o-mansoor'* ADJ. & ADV. triumphant(ly) [A ~ ظفر]

مظلوم *mazloom'* ADJ. wronged aggrieved oppressed N.M. (PL. مظلومین *mazloomīn*) wronged party oppressed (person) مظلومی *mazloo'mī* N.F. being the victim of oppression [A ~ ظلم]

مظہر *maz'har* N.M. phenomenon مظاہر *mazā'hir* N.M. PL. phenomena مظاہرِ قدرت *mazā'hir-e qūd'rat* N.M. PL. natural phenomena [A ~ ظہور]

مظہر *mūz'hir* N.M. (PL. مظہران *mūzhirān'*) witness ADJ. communicating ; revealing ایک خبر مظہر ہے *ek' kha'bar mūz'hir hai* V.T. a news-item reveals [A ~ اظہار]

مع *ma'* PREP. with along with مع الخیر *ma'-al-khair'* ADV. safely ; safe and secure معہذا *ma''a-hā'zā* ADJ. in addition to in spite of despite معاً *ma'an'* ADV. all of a sudden instantaneously معیت *ma'iy'yat* N.M. ★) [A]

معابد *ma'ā'bid* N.M. (PL. of معبد N.M. ★)

معاتب *mo'ā'tib* N.M. (PL. معاتبین *mo'ātibīn'*) reprover expostulator معاتب *mo'ā'tab* N.M. blameworthy person [A ~ عتاب]

معاد *ma'ād'* N.F. the next world ; hereafter معاش و معاد *ma'ā'sh-o-ma'ād'* N.F. this world and the next temporal and spiritual needs [A ~ عود place of return]

معادن *ma'ā'din* N.F. (PL. of معدن N.M. ★)

معاذ *ma'ā'z* N.F. refuge ; shelter معاذاللہ *ma'ā'z-allah'* INT. God forbid [A]

معارج *ma'ā'rij* N.M. (PL. of معراج N.F. ★)

معارض *mo'ā'riz* ADJ. contending ; opposing N.M. contender معارضہ *mo'ā'razah* N.M. contention comparison of manuscripts (rare) evasion [A]

معارف *ma'ārif* N.M. fields of knowledge دائرۃ المعارف *dā''irat-ūl-ma'ā'rif* N.M. encyclopaedia [A ~ معرفت]

معارک *ma'ā'rik* N.M. (PL. of معرکہ N.M. ★)

معاش *ma'āsh* N.F. (ped. PL. معایش *ma'ā'yish*) means of livelihood (rare) worldly life معاش و معاد *ma'ā'sh-o-ma'ād* N.F. (see under معاد N.F. ★) معاشی *ma'ā'shī* ADJ. economic معاشیات *ma'āshiyyāt'* N.M. economics [A doublet of عیش life]

معاشرت *mo'ā'sharat* N.F. way of living ; mode of life معاشرتی *mū'ā'sharatī* ADJ. (ungrammatical but usu. form for) معاشری *mo'ā'sharī* ADJ. social معاشرہ *mo'ā'sharah* N.M. society [A]

معاشی *ma'ā'shī* ADJ., معاشیات *ma'ā'shiyyāt'* (see under معاش ★)

معاصر *mo'ā'sir* ADJ. & N.M. (PL. معاصرین *mo'ā'sirīn'*) contemporary [E]

معاصی *ma'ā'sī* N.M. (PL. of معصیت N.F.)

معاطفت *mo'ā'tafat* N.M. kindness [A ~ عطوفت]

معاف *mo'āf* ADJ. forgiven ; pardoned ; absolved (of fine, etc.) معاف کرنا *mo'āf kar'nā* V.T. forgive ; pardon excuse remit reprieve معاف کیجیے *mo'āf kī'jiye* INT. excuse me pardon ; I beg your pardon معافی *mo'ā'fī* N.F.

forgiveness ; pardon remission reprieve salvation ; deliverance معافی چاہنا (یا طلب کرنا یا مانگنا) *mo'ā'fī chah'nā* (or *ta'lab kar'nā* or *mang'nā*) V.T. apologize ; ask for pardon ; seek forgiveness معافی دار *mo'ā'fī-dār* N.M. holder of rent-free grant ; grantee معافی نامہ *mo'ā'fī-nā'mah* N.M. deed of immunity written pardon

معالج *mo'ā'lij* N.M. physician ; doctor معالجہ *mo'ā'lajah* N.M. treatment معالجہ کرنا *mo'ā'lajah kar'nā* V.T. treat hail ; cure attend (as physician) [A ~ علاج]

معالی *ma'ā'lī* N.M. PL. eminent heights [A ~ علو]

معاملہ *mo'ā'malah* N.M. (PL. معاملات *mo'āmalāt'*) matter ; affair deal dealing business behaviour concern land revenue account of loving couple's meeting معاملہ باندھنا *mo'ā'malah bāndh'nā* V.T. describe loving couple's meeting معاملہ بندی *mo'ā'mala-bań'dī* N.F. this as literary device معاملہ بندی کرنا *mo'ā'mala-bań'dī kar'nā* V.T. use this litetary device معاملہ پڑنا *mo'ā'malah paṛ'nā* V.T. have to deal (with) have anything to do (with) معاملہ شناس *mo'ā'mala-shinās'* معاملہ فہم *mo'ā'mala-faih'm* ADJ. well-acquainted with shrewd معاملہ شناسی معاملہ فہمی *mo'ā'malah shinā's*ī *mo'ā'mala-faih'mī* N.M. shrewdness معاملہ کرنا *mo'ā'malah kar'nā* V.T. contract bargain strike a bargain . a business deal معاملہ ہونا *mo'ā'malah ho'nā* V.I. (of bargain) be struck معاملے کا سچا *mo'ā'male kā sach'chā* ADJ. honest in one dealings معاملے کا کھوٹا *mo'ā'male kā kho'ṭā* ADJ. dishonest in dealing سنگین معاملہ *sańgīn' mo'ā'malah* N.M. something serious معاملت *mo'ā'malat* N.F. (rare) same معاملہ N.M. ★ [A ~ عمل]

معاند *mo'ā'nid* N.M. enemy antagonist (rare) one who wrangles (rare) one who evades ADJ. hostile معاندانہ *mo'ā'nidā'nah* ADJ. hostile معاندت *mo'ā'nadat* N.F. enmity wrangling conflict (rare) evasion [A ~ عناد]

معانقہ *mo'ā'naqah* N.M. embrace [A ~ عنق]

معانی *ma'ā'nī* N.M. rhetoric N.M. PL. meaning [A ~ SING. معنی]

معاودت *mo'ā'vadat* N.M. return [A ~ عود]

معاوضہ *mo'ā'vazah* N.M. compensation recompense consideration [A ~ عوض]

معاون *mo'ā'vin* N.M. assistant abetter tributary ADJ. assistant assisting ; helping auxiliary معاون جرم *mo'ā'vin-e jūr'm* N.M. accomplice معاونت *mo'ā'vanat* N.F. help ; assistance [A ~ عون]

معاہدہ *mo'ā'hadah* N.M. contract agreement pack ; treaty confederacy معاہد *mo'ā'hid* N.M. (PL. معاہدین *mo'āhidīn'*) confederate [A ~ عہد]

معائب *mo'ā'ib* N.M. vices ; faults blemishes [A ~ عیب]

معاینہ *mo'ā'enah* (ped. *mo'ā'yanah*) N.M. inspection معاینہ کرنا *mo'ā''inah kar'nā* inspect V.T. [A ~ عین eye]

معبد *ma''bad* N.M. (PL. معابد *mā'ā'bid*) temple place of worship [A ~ عبادت]

معبر *ma''bar* N.M. bridge ferry-boat [A ~ عبور]

معبر *mo'ab'bir* N.M. (PL. معبرین *mo'abbirīn'*) interpreter of dreams [A ~ تعبیر]

معبود *ma'bood'* N.M. god ; diety ADJ. worshipped ; adored [A ~ عبادت]

معتاد *mo'tād'* ADJ. habituated , accustomed customary [A ~ اعتاد]

معتبر *mo''tabar* ADJ. reliable ; trustworthy credible respectable معتبری *mo''tabarī* N.F. reliability ; trustworthiness respectability minor social standing [A ~ اعتبار]

معتد *mo'tad'* ADJ. computed معتد بہ *mo'tad' beh* ADJ. enough ; sufficient substantial (amount, etc.) [A ~ عدد]

معتدل *mo''tadil* ADJ. temperate (climate) mild moderate معتدل آب و ہوا *mo''tadil ā'b-o-havā'* N.F. temperate climate [A ~ اعتدال]

معترض *mo''tariz* N.M. (PL. معترضین *mo'tarizīn'*) objector fault finder ADJ. objecting fault-finding معترض ہونا *mo''tariz ho'nā* V.T. object find fault (with) [A ~ اعتراض]

معترف *mo''tarif* N.M. one who owns or acknowledges confessor one who pleads guilty [A ~ اعتراف]

معتزلہ *mo'ta'zilah* N.M. a rationalistic sect of Muslims dissenters ; non-conformists معتزلی *mo'ta'zilī* N.M. & ADJ. non-formist [A ~ اعتزال]

معتصم *mo''tasim* N.M. (one) holding fast (to God) abstemious person [A ~ اعتصام]

معتقد *mo''taqid* (PL. معتقدین *mo'taqidīn'*) N.M. believer follower of a faith devotee [A ~ اعتقاد]

معتقدات *mo''taqadāt'* N.M. PL. beliefs [A ~ اعتقاد]

معتکف *mo''takif* N.M. & ADJ. (one) secluding oneself for prayers [A ~ اعتکاف]

معتمد *mo''tamad* N.M. secretary ADJ. reliable , trustworthy معتمد علیہ *mo''tamad-'alaih'* N.M. & ADJ. reliable person ; trustworthy person confidant معتمد عمومی *mo''tamad-e ūmoo'mī* N.M. general secretary , secretary general معتمدی *mo''tamadī* N.F. Secretariat [A ~ اعتماد]

معتوب *ma''loob'* ADJ. & N.M. object of (someone's) displeasure [A ~ عتاب]

معجزہ *mo''jizah* N.M. (PL. معجزات *mo'jizat'*) miracle معجز *mo''jiz*, معجزانہ *mo'jiza'nah* معجز نما *mo''jiz-nūma'* ADJ. miraculous [A ~ اعجاز]

معجل *mo'aj'jal* ADJ. immediate ; promptly done مہر معجل *maih're mo'aj'jal* N.M. prompt dower ; part of dower paid in cash, etc., right at the time of marriage [A ~ تعجیل]

معجم *mo''jam* ADJ. (F. & PL. معجمہ *mo''jamah*) dotted (letter) [A ~ اعجام]

معجون *ma'joon'* N.F. (PL. معاجین *ma'ā'jīn*) electuary hashish electuary

معدل *mo'ad'dil* N.M. equalizer [A ~ تعدیل]

معدلت *ma''dalat* N.F. justice ; equity معدلت گستر *ma''dalat-gūs'tar* ADJ. just معدلت گستری *ma''dalat-gūs'tarī* N.F. justice ; equity [A ~ عدل]

معدن *ma''dan* (ped. *ma''din*) N.F. (PL. معادن *ma'ā'din*) mine quarry معدنی *ma''danī* (ped. *-di-*) ADJ. mineral معدنیات *ma'daniy'yāt'*) (ped. *-di-*) N.F. PL. minerals [A]

معدولہ *ma'doo'lah* ADJ. (of) quiescent ; written but not pronounced [A ~ عدل]

معدود *ma'dood'* ADJ. numbered (only in) معدودے چند *ma'doo'de chan'd* ADJ. very few [A ~ عدد]

معدوم *ma'doom'* ADJ. non-existent ; extinct annihilated ; put to the sword معدوم کرنا *ma'doom' kar'na* V.T. annihilate معدوم ہونا *ma'doom' ho'nā* V.T become extinct معدومی *ma'doo'mī* N.F extinction [A ~ عدم]

معدہ *me''dah* N.M. stomach معدے کا *me''de kā*, معدی *me''dī* ADJ. stomach ; stomachic [A]

معذرت *ma''zirat* N.F. an excuse ; a plea apology excuse معذرت چاہنا (یا کرنا) *ma''zirat chāh'na* (or *kar'na*) V.T. apologize معذرت خواہ *ma''zirat-khah'* ADJ. معذرت خواہی *ma''zirat-khā'hī* N.F. apology apologizing [A doublet of عذر]

معذور *ma'zoor'* ADJ. excused ; excusable disabled N.M. (PL. معذورین *ma'zoorīn'*) disabled persons معذور رکھنا *ma'zoor' rakh'na* V.T. excuse معذوری *ma'zoo'rī* N.F. excuse disability [A ~ عذر]

معرا *mo'ar'ra* ADJ. plain (text) ; one without notes ; translation [A ~ عاری]

معراج *me'raj'* N.F. معالج *ma'ā'rij*) the Holy Prophet' Accession acme ; height (rare) ladder [A ~ عروج]

معرب *mo'ar'rab* ADJ. Arabicized (word, etc.) [A ~ تعریب]

معرض *ma''riz* N.M. field معرض التوا میں پڑنا *ma''riz-e iltiva' men par'nā* V.I. be put off ; be postponed معرض خطر میں پڑنا *ma''riz-e kha'tar men par'na* V.I. be endangered ; be jeopardized [A]

معرفت *ma''rifat* N.F. knowledge of God ; mystic knowledge recognition ADV. through the medium of [A ~ عرف]

معرفہ *ma''rifah* ADJ. proper (noun) [A ~ doublet of PREC.]

معرف *mo'arrif* N.M. (arch.) usher معرف *mo'ar'raf* ADJ. defined ; changed into proper (noun) [A ~ تعریف]

معرکہ *ma''rikah* N.M. (ped. PL. معارک *ma'ā'-rik*) bottle ; engagement معرکہ آرا *ma''rika-ārā'* ADJ. with troops marshalled معرکہ آرا ہونا *ma''rika-ārā' ho'nā* V.T. fight have troops marshalled معرکۃ الآرا *ma''rikat-ūl-ārā'* ADJ. causing great diversity opinion معرکے کا *ma''rike kā* ADJ. important (person) mentous (decision, etc.) [A]

معروض *ma'rooz'* N.F. object (rare) submission ; petition ADJ. submitted معروضہ *ma'roo'zah* N.M. submission ; petition letter to superior [A ~ عرض]

معروف *ma'roof'* ADJ. well-known ; celebrated (gram.) active (voice of verb) (of و) long ; preceded by 'pesh' (of ی) long , preceded by 'zer'

معزز *mo'az'zaz* ADJ. honourable ; respectable ; esteemed ; revered [A عزت]

معزول *ma'zool'* ADJ. deposed ; dethroned معزول کرنا *ma'zool' kar'na* V.T. depose ; dethrone معزول ہونا *ma zool' ho'nā* V.I. be deposed ; be dethroned معزولی *ma'zoo'lī* N.F. deposition ; dethronement [A ~ عزل]

معشر *ma''shar* N.M. group ; party معشر جن وانس *ma''shar-e jin'n-o-ins* V.T. the group of spirit and human being. [A]

معشوق *ma'shooq'* N.M. beloved ; a sweetheart معشوقانہ *ma'shooqa'nah* ADJ. lovely ; facinating coquetish like a beloved معشوقہ *ma'shoo'qah* N.F. beloved ; mistress معشوقی *ma'shoo'qī* N.F. state of being beloved loveliness coquetry [A ~ عشق]

معصوم *ma'soom'* ADJ. innocent sinless N.M. infant (PL. معصومین *ma'soomīn'*) sinless persons معصومیت *ma'soomiy'yat* N.F. innocence infancy child's simplicity معصیت *ma''siyat* N.F. sin [A ~ عصیان]

معطر *mo'at'tar* ADJ. perfumed ; scented [A ~ عطر]

معطل *mo'at'tal* ADJ. suspend effects ADV. held in abeyance rendered ineffective

معطل کرنا *mo'at'tal kar'nā* V.T. suspend ren... ineffective hold in abeyance معطل ہونا *mo'a...* *ho'nā* V.I. be suspended be ineffective ... *mo'āt'talī* N.F. suspension ineffectiveness abeyance [A]

معطوف *ma'toof'* N.M. first of two words or claus... joined together with a conjunction AD... turned معطوف علیہ *ma'toof' 'alaih'* N.M. second o... two words or clauses joined together with ... conjunction

معطی *mo''tī* ADJ. & N.M. (PL. معطیان *mo'tiy'ān'*) donor donating (person) [A ~ اعطا]

معظم *mo'az'zam* (F. & PL. معظمہ *mo'az'zamah*) ADJ. great ; exalted [A ~ تعظیم]

معقول *ma'qool'* ADJ. reasonable plausible fair ; just substantial (amount, salary, etc.) sensible (person) intellectual part of knowledge ; field of extra-religious knowledge ; معقولات *ma'qoo'lāt'* N.M. PL. works of philosophy and logic extra-religious fields of knowledge معقولیت *ma'qooliy'yat* N.F. reasonableness plausibility fairness sense [A ~ عقل]

معکوس *ma'koos'* ADJ. inverted reversed ترقیِ معکوس *taraq'qi-e ma'koos'* N.F. retrogression [A ~ عکس]

معلق *mo'al'laq* ADJ. suspended pending ; hanging fire معلق پڑا ہونا *mo'al'laq pa'ṛā ho'nā* V.I. be pending معلق رکھنا *mo'al'laq rakh'nā* V.T. keep pending معلق ہونا *mo'al'laq ho'nā* V.T. be suspended [A ~ تعلیق]

معلم *mo'al'lim* N.M. (PL. معلمین *mo'allimīn'*) teacher ; instructor pedagogue معلم ثانی *mo'al'lim-e sā'nī* N.M. the second teacher ; Farabi معلم ثالث *mo'al'lim-e sā'lis* N.M. the teacher ; Aivicenna معلم الملکوت *mo'al'lim-ūl-malakoot'* N.M. the teacher of angels ; Satan معلمانہ *mo'allimā'nah* ADJ. pedagogic ADV. pedagogically معلمہ *mo'al'limah* N.F. school mistress ; teacher معلمی *mo'al'limī* N.F. teacher's job ; teaching profession pedagogy [A ~ تعلیم]

معلن *mo''lin* N.M. announcer ; advertiser المعلن *almo''lin* N.M. (as subscript) the advertiser ; the notifier [A ~ اعلان]

معلوم *ma'loom'* ADJ. known obvious ; evident ADV. (iron.) none ; nonexistent معلوم کرنا *ma'loom' kar'nā* V.T. learn find out discover معلوم ہوتا ہے *ma'loom' ho'tā hai* PH. it appears it seems معلوم ہونا *ma'loom' ho'nā* V.I. appear seem look like become known be found out come to light نہیں معلوم *na'hīn ma'loom'*, معلوم نہیں *ma'loom' nahīn* ADV. it is not known; God knows; who knows معلومات *ma'loomāt'*

...mal N.M. laboratory [A ~ عمل]

معمور *ma'moor'* ADJ. inhabited populous prosperous ; flourishing full (of); replete (with) ; abounding (in) معمورہ *ma'moo'rah* N.M populated place ; town معمورۂ ہستی *ma'moo'ra-e has'tī* N.F. (fig.) world معموری *ma'moo'rī* N.F. population flourishing state [A ~ عمران]

معمول *ma'mool'* N.M. (PL. معمولات) practice ; custom hypnotic subject معمول باندھنا *ma'mool' bāndh'nā* V.I. do something regularly ; make it a regular practice (to do) معمول کے دن *ma'mool' ke din* N.M. PL. monthly course ; menstural period معمول کے دن ٹل جانا *ma'mool ke din ṭal' jā'nā* V.I. be pregnant معمولی *ma'moo'lī* ADJ. ordinary ; usual customary common [A ~ عمل]

معنبر *mo'am'bar* ADJ. perfumed with ambergris perfumed ; scented [A ~ عنبر]

معنون *mo'an'van* ADJ. dedicated معنون کرنا *mo'an'van kar'nā* V.T. dedicate [A ~ عنوان]

معنی *ma''nī* (ped. *ma''nā*) N.M. meaning senses purport import intent significance intrinsic quality ; spirituality ; substance ; essence ; reality ; hidden or interior part of anything معنی بیان کرنا *ma''nī bayān' kar'nā* V.T. explain interpret معنیِ بیگانہ *ma''ni-e begā'nah* N.M. a new ideal (in some literary composition معنی دینا *ma''nī de'nā* V.I. mean give the sense (of) معنی رکھنا *ma''nī rakh'nā* V. have the meaning of have the sense (of) imply معنوی *ma''navī* ADJ. pertaining to meaning or sense intrinsic real intllectual ; spiritual معنویت *ma'naviy'yat* N.F. meaningfulness [A]

... عون]

... promised ; ... -e ma'hood' N.M. ... عہد]

... d. PL. معایر ma'āyeer') ... e) touchstone [A ~ عیار]

... F. company (of) ; association

... shat N.F. livelihood subsistence way of life ; mode of living علم المعیشت ...-ūl-ma'i'shat N.F. economics معیشی ma'i'shī ADJ. economic [A doublet of عیش]

معین mo'īn N.M. helper ; assistant promoter [A ~ اعانت]

معین mo'ay'yan (F. & PL. معینہ mo'ay'yanah) ADJ. fixed settled established appointed معین کرنا mo'ay'yan kar'nā V.T. fix settle establish appoint [A ~ تعین]

معیوب ma'yoob' ADJ. bad improper indecent opprobrious معیوب بات ma'yoob' bāt N.F. something against etiquette ; improper [A ~ عیب]

مغ mūgh N.M. (PL. مغان mū'ghān) magus tavern-keeper ; publican مغبچہ mūgh-ba'chah N.M. pot-boy ; pot-man lovely lad پیر مغاں pī'r-e mūghāṅ' N.M. religious leader of the Magi [P]

مغالطہ mūghā'latah N.M. (PL. مغالطات mūghālatāt') fallacy delusion misunderstanding مغالطہ دینا mūghā'latah de'nā V.T. mislead delude lead into fallacy مغالطہ ڈالنا mūghā'lata ḍāl'nā V.I. lead into fallacy cause to make mistake [A ~ غلط]

مغائرت mughā'yarat N.F. estrangement repugnance مغائر mūghā'yar ADJ. contrary (to) ; repugnant (to) [A ~ غیر]

مغتنم mugh'tanam ADJ. prized مغتنمات mūghtanamāt' N.M. PL. prized things ; treasures [A ~ غنیمت]

مغرب magh'rib N.M. west accident the West sunset ; sundown evening مغرب کی نماز magh'rib kī namāz' N.F. evening prayer مغرب زدہ magh'rib-za'dah ADJ. (derog.) Wertenized مغرب زدگی magh'rib-za'dagī N.F. (derog.) Westernization المغرب al-magh'rib N.M. North-West Africa مغربی magh'ribī ADJ. Western ; accidental مغربیت maghribiy'yat N.F. (derog.) Westernization [A ~ غروب]

مغرق mūghar'raq ADJ. ornamented سونے میں مغرق so'ne meṅ mūghar'raq N.M. bedecked with a large number of gold ornaments [A ~ غرق]

مغرور maghroor' ADJ. proud ; vain ; arrogant naughty ; conceited مغروری maghroo'rī N.F. pride ; arrogance ; vanity haughtiness ; conceit [A ~ غرور]

مغز magh'z N.M. kernel marrow pith brain intellect essence مغز اڑا جانا magh'z ū'ṛā jā'nā V.I. upset مغز اڑانا magh'z ūṛā'nā V.T. upset (someone) مغز پچی (یا خالی) کرنا magh'z-pich'chī (or khā'lī) kar'nā V.T. try to drive home (to) مغز چاٹنا magh'z chāṭ'nā V.I. bother someone) pester (someone) with silly talk مغز چٹ magh'z-chaṭ N.M. idler talker ; garrulous person مغز چلنا magh'z chal'nā V.I. be proud go mad مغز کو چڑھ جانا magh'z ko chaṛh' jā'nā V.T. affect the head (of) ; magh'z khā'nā V.T. tease worry ; tax the brain مغز کے کیڑے اڑانا magh'z ke kī'ṛe ūṛā'nā V.I. chatter ; brag bother a great deal مغز کے کیڑے جھڑنا magh'z ke kī'ṛe jhaṛ'nā, مغز کی کیل نکالنا magh'z kī kīl ni'kalnā V.I. be humbled face the music be set right ; come to one's senses بے مغز be-magh'z ADJ. emptyheaded ; dullard پر مغز pūr-magh'z ADJ. profound مغزی magh'zī N.F. hem ; thin border مغزی لگانا magh'zī lagā'nā V.T. hem [P]

مغضوب maghzoob' ADJ. (one) who has incurred (God's) displeasure [A ~ غضب]

مغفر migh'far N.M. helmet [A]

مغفرت magh'firat N.F. absolution ; salvation deliverance خدا مغفرت کرے khudā' magh'firat ka're PH. may God bless his soul [A doublet of غفران]

مغفور magh foor' ADJ. forgiven ; pardoned dead ; deceased مرحوم و مغفور marḥoo'm-o-maghfoor' ADJ. deceased

مغل mū'ghal N.M. Mongols Moghul ; a racial mixture of Turks and Mongols a descendent of these مغلا mūgh'lā N.M. (derog.) Moghul مغلانی mūghlā'nī N.F. Moghal woman attendant in harem needle-woman female governess مغلئی mūghlai''ī ADJ. Moghul (style, etc.) مغلئی پھوڑا mūghlai''ī pho'ṛā N.M. Lahore sore مغلیہ mūghaliy'yah ADJ. Moghul [P]

مغلظ mūghal'laz ADJ. foul dense thick مغلظات mūghallazāt' N.F. PL. abusive language swear-words ; curses مغلظات سنانا mūghallazāt' sūnā'nā V.T. use abusive language ; hurl abuses (at)

مغلق mūgh'laq ADJ. (PL. مغلقات mūghlaqāt') difficult (word) obscure (passage) A ~ اغلاق]

مغلم mūgh'lim N.M. sodomite ; paederast [A ~ اغلام]

مغلوب maghloob' ADJ. conquered ; subdued overcome brought low مغلوب الغضب maghloo'b ul-gha'zab ADJ. short tempered ; irascible مغلوب کرنا maghloob' kar'na V.T. subdue overcome مغلوب ہونا maghloob' ho'na V.I. be brought low be subdued [A ~ غلبہ]

مغموم maghmoom' ADJ. sad ; sorrowful grieved mournful [A ~ غم]

مغنی mugh'ni N.M. one making free from want this an attribute of God A ~ اغنا]

مغنی mughan'ni N.M. singer ; songster مغنیہ mughan'niyah N.F. female singer ; songstress [A ~ غنا]

مغویہ mugh'vayah ADJ. & N.F. abducted woman [A ~ اغوا]

مغیلاں mughi'lan N.M. acacia خار مغیلاں kha'r-e mughi'lan N.M. acacia thorn [P]

مفاتیح mafat'ih' N.F. (PL. of مفتاح N.F. ★

مفاجات mufajat' N.F. suddenness ; unexpectedness مرگ مفاجات mar'g-e mufajat' N.F. sudden death [A]

مفاخرت mufa'kharat N.F. boast contention for dignity مفاخر mafakhir N.M. PL. glories; causes of just pride [A ~ فخر]

مفاد mafad' N.M. (PL. مفادات mafadat') interest مفادات کی حفاظت mafadat' ki hifa'zat V.T. safeguarding of (one's or someone's) interests [A]

مفارقت mufa'raqat N.F. separation forsaking; desertion [A ~ فراق]

مفاسد mafa'sid N.M. PL. evils [A ~ SING. مفسدہ]

مفاصل mafa'sil N.M. PL. joints (of body) [A ~ SING. مفصل]

مفت muf't ADJ. free ; gratis gratuitous ADV. free ; without payment gratuitous causelessly ; without any rhyme or reason مفت خور muf't-khor' N.M. parasite ; sponger ; hanger-on ADJ. who sponges on ; who hangs on مفت خورا muf't-kho'ra N.M., مفت را چہ گفت muf't ra che guf't PROV. do not look a gift horse in the mouth مفت کی شراب قاضی کو بھی حلال ہے muf't ki sharab' qa'zi ko bhi halal' hai PROV. a free offer is welcome to every body مفت میں muf't men ADV. free ; gratis ; for nothing ; for a song gratuitously مفت ہاتھ لگنا muf't hath' lag'na V.I. get free of cost get for a song [P]

مفتاح miftah' N.F. (PL. مفاتیح mafatih') key A ~ فتح]

مفتخر muf'takhar ADJ. honoured ; dignified [A ~ افتخار]

مفتری muf'tari ADJ. N.M. slanderer ; calumniator mischief-monger ; ADJ. mischievous (person) slanderous (person) [A ~ افترا]

مفتوح maftooh' ADJ. conquered ; subdued taken ; captured (of letter) having zabar (ـَ) over it [A ~ فتح]

مفتون maftoon' (or -toon') ADJ. fascinated ; enamoured dotard mad مفتون ہونا maftoon' ho'na V.I. be enamour (of) ; be fascinated with date (upon) [A ~ فتنہ]

مفتی muf'ti N.M. (PL. مفتیان muftiyan') Muslim jurist ; Muslim counsel مفتیان شرح متین mufti'ya'n-e shar''-e matin' N.M. PL. expounders of the irrevocable code of Muslim law [A ~ افتا]

مفتخر mufakh'khar ADJ. honoured ; esteemed dignified [A ~ فخر]

مفر mafar' N.M. asylum [A ~ فرار]

مفرح mufar'reh ADJ. reviving N.M. cordial مفرحات mufarrehat' N.F. PL. cordials [A ~ تفریح]

مفرد muf'rad ADJ. simple (medicine) uncompounded, single singular ADV. alone مفردات mufradat' N.F. uncompounded medicines single (drugs) [A ~ افراد]

مفرس mufar'ras ADJ. Persianized (word, etc.) [A ~ تفریس]

مفرط muf'rit ADJ. excessive [A ~ افراط]

مفرور mafroor ADJ. & N.M. escaped (prisoner, etc.) fugitive N.M. fugitive runaway [A ~ فرار]

مفروش mafroosh' ADJ. spread ; carpetted N.M. article of furniture مفروشات mafrooshat' N.M. PL. furniture [A ~ فرش]

مفروضہ mafroo'zah N.M. hypothesis ADJ. supposed hypothetical [A ~ فرض]

مفسد muf'sid ADJ. mischievous (person) seditious (person) N.M. (PL. مفسدین mufsidin') mischief-monger seditious person مفسدانہ mufsida'nah ADJ. riotous (assembly) mischievous (manner) ; seditious (speech etc.) ADV. mischievously seditiously riotously [A ~ فساد]

مفسدہ maf'sadah N.M. (PL. مفاسد mafa'sid) riot ; tumult ; disturbance mischief مفسدہ پرداز maf'sadu-pardaz' N.M. mischief-monger ; mischief-maker ; rioter مفسدہ پردازی maf'sada-parda'zi N.F. mischief-making rioting [A ~ فساد]

مفسر mufas'sir N.M. (PL. مفسرین mufassirin') exegetical writer ; writer of Quranic exegesis [A ~ تفسیر]

مفصل *mūfas'sal* ADJ. detailed ADV at length ; in detail N.M. concluding portion of the Holy Quran (usu. مفصلات *m'fassalāt'*) countryside; rural area outlying area of district (as distinct from its headquarters or cities مفصلہ ذیل (یا صدر) *m'fas'sala-e zail'* (or *sad'r*) ADJ. following ADV. as follows [A ~ تفصیل]

مفعول *maf'ool'* N.M. object ; catemite , minion مفعول بہ *maf'ool' be-hi'* N.M. direct object مفعول ثانی *maf'ool-e sā'nī* N.M. indirect object مفعول فیہ *maf'ool fih'* N.M. locative case مفعول لہٗ *maf'ool' la-hoo'* N.M. oblative case مفعول معہٗ *maf'ool' ma'a-hoo* N.M. accusative case in opposition with a noun in nominative ; object telling of something that accompanies another [A ~ فعل]

مفقود *mafqood'* ADJ. missing مفقود الخبر *mafqoo'd-ūl-kha'bar* ADJ. (one) untraceable (person) [A ~ فقدان]

مفکر *m'fak'kir* N.M. (PL. مفکرین *m'fak'kirīn'*) [A ~ فکر]

مفلس *m'f'lis* ADJ. poor ; indigent beggarly penniless N.M. pauper penniless person مفلسا بیگ *m'f'lisā beg* N.M (iron.) pauper مفلسی *m'f'lisī* N.F. poverty , indigence pauperism , pauperdom مفلسی میں آٹا گیلا *mūf'lisī meṅ ā'ṭā gī'lā* PROV. misfortunes never come alone [A ~ افلاس]

مفلوج *maflooj'* ADJ. paralytic , palsied [A ~ فالج]

مفلوک الحال *maflooʼk-ūl-ḥāl'* ADJ. destitute ADV. in straitened circumstances [A ~ فلاکت + حال]

مفوضہ *m'fav'vazah* ADJ. assigned , entrusted [A ~ تفویض]

مفہوم *mafhoom'* N.M. (PL. مفاہیم *mafāhīm'*) sense meaning connotation مفہوم لینا *mafhoom' le'nā* V.T. interpret مفہوم ہونا *mafhoom' ho'nā* V.I. mean be understood [A ~ فہم]

مفید *mūfīd'* ADJ. useful profitable ; beneficial advantageous officacious that has utility مفید پڑنا *mūfīd' par'nā* V.I. (something) agree (with) مفید معلوم ہونا *mūfīd ma'loom' ho'nā* V.T (appear to) be useful [A ~ افادہ]

مقابر *muqā'bir* N.M. (PL. of مقبرہ N.M. ★)

مقابلہ *mūqā'balah* N.M. comprison contrast competition contast confrontation opposition ; contention مقابلے پر آنا *mūqā'bale par ā'nā* V.I. oppose challenge the authority (of) مقابل *mūqā'bil* ADJ. opposite against compared opposed opposing confronting [A]

مقابہ *mūqā'bah* N.M. toilet-box

مقاتلہ *mūqā'talah* N.M. slaughter , carnage ; battle conflict [A doublet of قتال]

مقادیر *maqādīr'* N.F. (PL. of مقدار N.F ★)

مقاربت *mūqā'rabat* N.M. approximation affinity sexual intercourse [A ~ قرب]

مقارنت *mūqā'ranat* N.F. companionship conjunction propinquity مقارن *mūqā'rin* ADJ. near ; close [A doublet of قران]

مقاصد *maqā'sid* N.M. (PL. of مقصد N.M. ★)

مقاطعہ *mūqā'ta'ah* N.M. boycott [A ~ قطع]

مقال *maqāl'* N.M. word , talk , speech شیریں مقال *shī'rīn-maqāl'* ADJ softspoken sweet-tongued [A ~ قول]

مقالہ *maqā'lah* N.M. (PL. مقالات *maqālāt'*) treatise dissertation ; thesis discourse ; disquisition article مقالہ افتتاحیہ *maqā'la-e iftitāhiy'yah* N.M. leading article ; editorial [A ~ قول]

مقام *maqām'* N.M. (PL. مقامات *maqāmāt'*) place site situation encampment position station status ; dignity tune bases occasion ; opportunity مقام ابراہیم *maqā'm-e ibrāhīm'* N.M. name of a place in precincts of the Holy Ka'aba where lies the stone on which Abraham rests his feet while building the sanctuary مقام کرنا *maqām' kar'nā* V.T. halt مقام محمود *maqā'm-e maḥmood* (or *-maih-*) N.M. desired status lofty station where the Holy Prophet's Ascension took him مقامی *maqā'mī* ADJ. local N.M. native ; local (as distinct from refugee [A ~ قیام]

مقاومت *mūqā'vamat* N.F. resistance [A ~ قیام]

مقامرت *mūqā'marat* N.F. gambling مقامر *mūqā'mir* N.M. (PL. مقامرین *mūqā'mirīn'*) gambler [A ~ قمار]

مقبرہ *maq'barah* N.M. (PL. مقابر *maqā'bir*) tomb , sepulchre , mausoleum [A ~ قبر]

مقبوضہ *maqboo'zah* ADJ. seized ; captured ; occupied taken possession of مقبوضات *maqboozāt'* N.M. PL possessions , conquered territories [A ~ قبضہ]

مقبول *maqbool'* ADJ. popular acceptable مقبولیت *maqbooliy'yat* N.F. popularity acceptance [A ~ قبول]

مقتبس *mūq'tabas* ADJ. culled (from) excerpt (of) ; extract (from) [A ~ اقتباس]

مقتدا *mūq'tadā* N.M. leader مقتدی *mūq'tadī* N.M. follower (prayers) [A ~ اقتدا]

مقتدر *mŭq'tadir* ADJ. powerful (one wilding authority [A ~ اقتدار]
مقتضا *mŭqtazā'* N.M. demands (of justice) inclination (of mind) exigency (of situation) مقتضی *mŭq'tazī* ADJ. desirous demanding ; wiging requiring ; calling for exacting [A ~ اقتضا]
مقتل *maq'tal* N.M. place of execution [A ~ قتل]
مقتول *maqtool'* N.M. (PL. مقتولین *maqtoolīn'*) one who is killed victim ADJ. killed ; slain [A ~ قتل]
مقدار *miqdār'* N.F. (PL. مقادیر *maqādīr'*) quantity amount measure size ; magnitude length ; term ; span expression مقدار غیر متماثل *miqdā'r-e ghair-mŭtamā'sil* N.F. one of the heterogenous expressions مقدار متغیرہ *miqdā'r-e mŭtaghay'yirah* N.F. variable quantity or expression مقدار متماثل *miqdā'r-e mŭtamā'sil* N.F. one of the homogeneous expressions مقدار مجہول *miqdā'r-e majhool'* N.M. unknown quantity or expression مقدار مرکب *miqdā'r-e mŭrak'kab* N.F. compound quantity or expression مقدار معروف *miqdā'r-e ma'roof'* N.F. known quantity or expression مقدار منفی *miqdā'r-e man'fī* N.M. negative quantity or expression مقررہ مقدار *mŭqar'rarah miqdār'* PH. fixed amount constant quantity or expression [A ~ قدر]
مقدر *mŭqad'dar* N.M. fate ; destiny ADJ. destined ; predestined ; ordained by God ; preordained (of word or expression) understood مقدر آزمانا *mŭqad'dar azmā'na* V.T. try one's luck مقدر آزمائی *mŭqad'dar-azmā''ī* N.F. trying one's luck مقدر برگشتہ ہو جانا *mŭqad'dar bar-gash'tah ho jā'nā* V.T. be unluck ; have an adverse fortune مقدر چمکنا *mŭqad'dar cha'makna* V.I. thrive ; prosper have a sudden stroke of good fortune [A ~ تقدیر]
مقدرت *maq'dirat* (or-da-) N.F. power ; ability [A doublet of قدرت]
مقدس *mŭqad'das* ADJ. (F. & PL. مقدسہ *mŭqad'dasah*) holy ; sacred sanctified consecrated hallowed مقدس کتاب *mŭqad'das kitāb'* N.F. holy book or scriptures (of کتاب مقدس *kitā'b-e moqad'das* N.F. (dial.) Bible مقامات مقدسہ *maqamā't-e mŭqad'dasah* N.M. PL. holy places ; sanctuaries مقدس *maq'dis* N.M. sacred place بیت المقدس *bai't-ul-mŭqad'das* (or -*maq'dis*) N.M. Jerusalem [A]
مقدم *maq'dam* N.M. arrival onrush; flux [A ~ قدوم]
مقدم *mŭqad'dam* ADJ. chief superior prior more important N.M. antecedent major premise village headman a minor official of agriculture department مقدم جاننا (یا سمجھنا) *mŭqad'dam jān'nā* (or *sa'majhnā*) V. give priority (to) prefer regard as more important مقدم رکھنا *mŭqad'dam rakh'nā* V.T. give priority (to) place the first on the list give precedence (to) مقدم ہونا *mŭqad'dam ho'nā* V.T. receive priority be the first on the list مقدمہ *mŭqad'damah* N.M. (PL. مقدمات *mŭqaddamāt'*) indroduction ; preface preamble ; prolegomena advance-guard case; law-suit مقدمۃ الجیش *mŭqad'damat-ŭl-jaish'* N.M advance-guard مقدمے باز *mŭqad'dame-bāz* N.M. & ADJ. litigous (person) مقدمے بازی *mŭqad'dame-bā'zī* N.F. litigation litigiousness [A ~ تقدیم]
مقدور *maqdoor'* N.M. authority power ability capacity guts ; courage wealth means; resources مقدور بھر (یا تک) *maqdoor' bhar* (or *tak*), تا بہ مقدور *ta-ba-maqdoor'*, حتی المقدور *hat'ta-l-maqdoor'* ADV. the best of one's ability مقدور کی بات *maqdoor' kī bat'* N.F. aquestion of one's resources مقدور نہ رکھنا (یا ہونا) *maqdoor' na rakh'nā* (or *ho'nā*) V.I. be unable (to do) not to be in a position to مقدور والا *maqdoor'-vā'la* N.M. man of means مقدور ہونا *maqdoor' ho'nā* V.T. have power or ability be in a position (to do) [A ~ قدرت]
مقر *maqar'* N.M. (lit.) abode station [A ~ قرار]
مقر *mŭqir'* N.M. (PL. مقران *mŭqirran'*) confessor affirmer one who pleads guilty one who executes a deal ADJ. confessing professing ; acknowledging affirming undertaking; assuring مقر ہونا *muqir' ho'nā* V.I. confess admit avow plead guilty execute a deed
مقراض *miqrāz'* N.F. (lit.) scissors a wrestling-trick ; trouncing by trampling upon adversary's neck [A]
مقرب *mŭqar'rab* N.M. (PL. مقربین *mŭqarrabīn'*) trusted person close friend favourite person confident ADJ trusted favourite close ; intimate مقرب الخدمت *muqar'rab-ul-khid'mat* مقرب بارگاہ *mŭqar'rab-e bārgāh'* N.M. (arch.) personal assistant favourite trusted servant [A ~ تقریب]
مقرر *mŭqar'rar* ADJ. & ADV. appointed employed fixed ; settled agreed upon prescribed established defined regarded مقرر کرنا *mŭqar'rar kar'nā* V.T. appoint settle prescribe regard مقرر ہونا *mŭqar'rar ho'nā* V.I. be appointed be settled be prescribed مقررہ *mŭqar'rarah* ADJ. appointed fixed settled prescribed established defined settled agreed upon مقرری *mŭqar'rarī* N.F. (arch.)

fixed tenure in perpetuity tenure at fixed rate of interest [A]

مقرر **mūqar'rir** N.M. (PL. مقررین **mūqarririn'**) lecturer; orator [A ~ تقریر]

مقرض **mūqar'raz'** ADJ. sheared مقراض **miqraz'** N.F. ★ [A]

مقروض **maqrooz'** N.M. debtor ADJ. indebted [A ~ قرض]

مقرنس **mūqar'nas** ADJ. spiralled roof or building N.M. spiralled building [A]

مقروقہ **maqroo'qah** ADJ. (of property) attached; confiscated [A ~ قرق]

مقرون **maqroon'** ADV. near connected [A]

مقسط **mūq'sit** ADJ. just N.M. this as an attribute of God [~ قسط]

مقسوم **maqsoom'** N.M. fate; destiny dividend ADJ. divided apportioned مقسوم جاگنا (یا چمکنا) **maqsoom' jāg'nā** (or **cha'maknā** V.T. have good fortune مقسوم علیہ **maqsoom' 'alaih'** N.M. (Math.) divisor مقسوم کا لکھا **maqsoom' kā lik'khā** (or **likhā**) N.M. fate [~ قسمت]

مقشر **mūqash'shar** ADJ. peeled; skinned [A ~ قشر]

مقصد **maq'sad** (ped. **-sid**) N.M. (PL. مقاصد **maqā'sid**) purpose; aim; object intent; intention design wish; desire meaning; purport مقصد بر آنا **maq'sad bar-ā'nā** V.I. (of someone's object) be achieved [A ~ قصد]

مقصر **mūqas'sir** ADJ. deficient; falling short of [A ~ تقصیر]

مقصود **maqsood'** N.M. aim; object intent design [A ~ قصد]

مقصورہ **maqsoo'rah** ADJ. shortened (alif) closely-guarded N.M. niche in mosque for leader of congregation house owner's private apartment [A ~ قصر]

مقطر **mūqat'tar** ADJ. distilled (water, etc.) [A ~ تقطیر]

مقط **miqat'** N.M. rest for pen in trimming [P ~ A قط]

مقطع **maq'ta'** N.M. concluding couplet (of poem) [A ~ قطع]

مقطع **mūqat'ta'** ADJ. (of beard) properly trimmed reserve; serious; solemn cultured مقطعات **mūqatta'at'** N.M. PL. small pieces of cloth verse in short metre [A ~ قطع ~ تقطیع]

مقعد **maq''ad** N.M. anus (rare) seat [A]

مقفی **mūqaf'fā** ADJ. rhymed [A ~ قافیہ]

مقفل **mūqaf'fal** ADJ. locked [~ قفل]

مقلب **mūqal'lib** ADJ. & N.M. (one) who brings about a change مقلب القلوب **mūqal'lib-ūl-qūloob'** ADJ. & N.M. who brings about a change of heart God as such; converter of hearts [A ~ قلب]

مقلد **mūqal'lid** N.M. conformist disciple, follower غیر مقلد **ghair'-mūqal'lid** N.M. non-conformist [A ~ تقلید]

مقلوب **maqloob'** ADJ. inverted reversed مقلوب مستوی **maqloo'b-e mūs'tavī** N.M. palindrome [A ~ قلب]

مقناطیس **maq'nā'tīs** N.M. magnet مقناطیسی **maqnāṭī'sī** ADJ. magnetic مقناطیسیت **maqnātīsiy'yat** N.F magnetism [A ~ G]

مقنع **mūqan'na'** ADJ. veiled N.M. veiled prophet of Khorasan [A]

مقنن **mūqan'nin** N.M. law-maker; legislator مقننہ **mūqan'ninah** N.M. legislature ADJ. legislative مجلس مقننہ **maj'lis-e mūqan'ninah** legislative assembly or council [A ~ قانون]

مقوا (or مقوی) **mūqav'vā** N.M. cardboard, pasteboard [A reinforced ~ تقویت]

مقولہ **maqoo'lah** N.M. sayiug quotation maxim; adage; aphorism [A ~ قول]

مقوی **mūqav'vī** ADJ. strengthening; invigorating مقوی باہ **mūqav'vī-e bāh'** N.M. & ADJ. aphordisiac مقوی جگر (یا کبد) **mūqav'vi-e ji'gar** (or **ka'bid**) N.M. & ADJ. hepatic (drug) مقوی دل (یا قلب) **mūqav'vi-e dil'** (or **qal'b**) N.M. & ADJ. cardiac; cordial مقوی دماغ **mūqav'vi-e dimāgh'** N.M. & ADJ. cephalic (drug) مقوی معدہ **moqav'vi-e me''dah** N.M. & ADJ. stomachic (drug) [A ~ تقویت]

مقہور **maqhoor'** ADJ. oppressed (one) in the bad books (of) [A ~ قہر]

مقیاس **miqyās'** N.M. gauge; meter PREF. meter مقیاس الحرارت **miqyā's-ūl-ḥarā'rat** N.M. thermometer مقیاس اللبن **miqyā's-ūl-la'ban** N.M. lactometer مقیاس الما **miqya's-ūl-mā'** N.M. hydrometer water-guage مقیاس الموسم **miqyā's-ūl-mau'sim** N.M. meteorograph مقیاس الہوا **miqya's-ūl-havā'** N.M. (rare) barometer [A ~ قیاس]

مقیت **mūqit'** N.M. one who gives everyone his or her livelihood this as attribute of God [A ~ قوت **qoot**]

مقید **mūqay'yad** ADJ. imprisoned incarcerated confined bound in chains fettered shackled bound down (to something) [A ~ قید]

مقیش **muqqaish'** N.F. gold (or silver) thread brocade مقیشی **mūqqai'shī** ADJ. brocaded embroidered in gold or silver thread

مقیم **mūqim'** ADJ. residing; stationed مقیم رہنا (یا ہونا) **mūqim' raih'nā** (or **ho'nā**) V.I. stay [A ~ اقامت]

مکا **mak'kā** N.F maize [doublet of مکی]

مکا *mŭk'ka*, مکہ *mŭk'kah* N.M. blow with the fist مکا لگانا (یا مارنا) *mŭk'ka laga'na* (or *mar'na*) V.T. give a blow with the fist مکے باز *mŭk'ke-baz* N.M. boxer مکے بازی *mŭk'ke-ba'zi* N.F boxing fisticuffs

مکاتب *maka'tib* N.M. (PL. of مکتب N.M. ★)

مکاتیب *makatib'* N.M. (PL. of مکتوب N.M. ★)

مکار *makkar'* ADJ. cunning ; crafty ; deceitful N.M. (F. مکارہ *makka'rah*) cheat deceitful person pretender impostor rogue knave مکاری *makka'ri* N.F. cunning ; artifice cheating deceitfulness imposture knavery roguery [A ~ مکر]

مکارم *maka'rim* N.M. (PL. of مکرمت N.F. ★)

مکاشفہ *mŭka'shafah* N.M. revelation ; apocalypse [A ~ کشف]

مکافات *mŭkafat'* N.F. retribution مکافات ملنا (یا کو پہنچنا) *mŭkafat' mil'na* (or *ko pahunch'na*) V.I. suffer for one's misdeed [A]

مکالمہ *mŭka'lamah* N.M. (PL. مکالمات *mŭkalamat'*) conversation ; dialogue [A ~ کلام]

مکان *makan'* N.M. (PL. مکانات *makanat'*) house ; abode lodging ; dwelling lodge flat apartment (rare) place ; space مکان بیٹھنا *makan' baiṭh'na* V.I. (of house) collapse (owing to rain, etc.) مکاندار *makan'-dar* N.M. owner of rented house ; landlord مکان کرائے (پر) دینا *makan' kira''e (par) de'na* V.T. let a house مکان کرائے (پر) لینا *makan' kira''e (par) le'na* V.T. rent a house [A]

مکائد *maka''id* N.M. PL. tricks ; frauds [A ~ کید]

مکبر *mŭkab'bir* N.M. enlarger one of the congregation repeating the leader of prayers cautions [A ~ تکبیر]

مکتب *mak'tab* N.M. (PL. مکاتب *maka'tib*) elementary religious school school (of thought, etc.) (arch.) school ; academy مکتب خیال (یا فکر) *mak'tab-e khayal'* (or *fik'r*) N.M. school of thought [A ~ کتابت]

مکتبہ *mak'tabah* N.M. bookshop ; bookstall (rare) library [A ~ کتاب].

مکتفی *mŭk'tafi* ADJ. sufficient (rare) content [A ~ اکتفا]

مکتوب *maktoob'* N.M. (PL. مکاتیب *makatib'*) letter ; epistle مکتوب الیہ *maktoob' elaih'* N.M. addressee [A ~ کتاب]

مکتوم *mak'toom* ADJ. hidden ; concealed [A ~ کتم]

مکتی *mŭk'ti* N.F. (dial.) salvation ; exemption of soul from further transmigration مکتی فوج *mŭk'ti fauj* N.F. Salvation Army [S]

مکٹ *mŭ'kaṭ* N.M. coronet tiara ; ornamental coronet for groom, etc.

مکدر *mŭkad'dar* ADJ. turbid (water) uneasy disturbed or troubled ; (atmosphere) displeared [A ~ کدر]

مکر *mak'r* (col. *ma'kar*) N.M. cunning ; wile ; artifice ; craftiness deceit ; cheating pretence unposture fraud (rare) strategem مکر کرنا *mak'r kar'na* V.T. cheat deceiv defraud feign ; pretend resert to strategem مکر چاندنی *mak'r chand'ni* N.F. moonlight in early hours of morning which has the false effect of down مکر چکر *ma'kar cha'kar* N.M. (col) fraud [A]

مکرر *mukar'rar* ADV. encore again ; a second time مکرر آنکہ *mŭkar'rar aṅ-ke* ADV. 'post scriptum' P.S. مکرر سہ کرر *mŭkar'rar se-kar'rar* ADV. (col.) twice, thrice ; repeatedly [A ~ کر]

مکرم *mŭkar'ram* ADJ. respectable ; honourable مکرمی *mŭkar'rami* PH. (superscription to letters) dear sir مکرم بندہ *mŭkar'ram(-e) ban'dah* PH. (arch.) dear sir [A ~ تکریم]

مکرمت *mak'romat* N.F. (PL. مکارم *maka'rim*) grace ; nobility of character [A]

مکرنا *mŭkar'na* V.I. refuse to own up go back on one's words ; retract one's confussion صاف مکر جانا *saf' mŭ'kar ja'na* V.I. deny altogether مکرنی *mŭ'karni*, مکری *mŭk'ri* N.F. (also کہہ مکرنی *kaih'-mŭ'karni*) (usu. PL. as کہہ مکرنیاں *kaih' mŭ'karniaṅ*) assertion denial riddle based on double-entendre

مکروہ *makrooh'* ADJ. unbecoming bad disgusting loathsome ; abominable odious (in law) though not unlawful disapproved مکروہ تحریمی *makroo'h-e taḥ'rimi* N.M. disapproved to the point of being for bidden مکروہات *makroohat'* N.F. PL. unbecoming things disapproved though not unlawful things

مکڑا *mak'ṛa*, مکڑ *mak'kar* N.M. large spider مکڑی *mak'ṛi* N.F. spider مکڑی کا جالا *mak'ṛi ka ja'la* N.M. cobweb

مکسر *mŭkas'sar* ADJ. broken جمع مکسر *jam''-e mŭkas'sar* N.M. broken plural ; irregular plural of Arabic noun [A ~ کسر]

مکسور *maksoor'* N.M. (Math) fraction ADJ. (F. & PL. مکسورہ *maksoo'rah*) (letter) having 'zer' (ـِ) under it مکسور اعشاریہ *maksoo'r-e a'shariy'yah* N.M. decimal fraction مکسور عام *maksoo'r-e 'am* N.M. vulgar fraction [A ~ کسر]

مکشوف *makshoof'* ADJ. open ; manifest disclosed ; revealed brought to light [A ~ کشف]

مکعب *mŭka''ab* N.M. cube ADJ. cubic ; cubical مکعب نما *mŭka''ab-nŭma'* N.M. cuboid [A]

مکفول *makfool'* N.M. pledged ; mortgaged [A ~ کفالت]

مکلاوہ *mŭkla'vah* N.M. (H. dial.) (same as گونا N.M. ★)

مکلف *mukal'laf* ADJ. & N.M. (one) entrusted (with) duty ; responsibility مکلف *mūkal'lif* ADJ. & N.M. (one) entrusting (duty or responsibility (as subscription to invitation letter, etc. esp. as المکلف *almukal'lif* one putting (someone) to inconvenience [A ~ تکلیف]

مکلل *mūkal'lal* ADJ. burnished (rare) crowned [A ~ اکلیل *iklīl'*]

مکمل *mūkam'mal* ADJ. complete ADV. finished ; completed [A ~ تکمیل]

مکنون *maknoon'* ADJ. hidden ; concealed (fig.) yet undercovered (fig. precious در مکنون *dūr'(r-e) maknoon'* PH. hidden pearl ; precious pearl [A]

مکو *mako'* N.F. cape gooseberry ; brazil cherry; 'solamum rubrum'

مکوڑا *makau'ṛā* N.M. large ant کیڑے مکوڑے *kī'ṛe* : *makau'ṛe* N.M. PL. insects

مکوکب *mūkau'kab* ADJ. speckled [A ~ کوکب ★]

مکہ *mak'kah* N.M. Mecca مکی *mak'kī* ADJ. Meccan [A]

مکھ *mūkh* N.M. (dial.) face month مکھڑا *mūkh'ṛa* N.M. face چاند سا مکھڑا *chand' sa mūkh'ṛa* N.M. lovely face

مکھانا *makhā'nā* N.M. dry water-lily seed

مکھن *mak'khan* N.M. butter مکھن توس *mak'khan tos* N.M. bread and butter

مکھنا *makh'nā* N.M. a kind of large elephant with small tusks ADJ. such (elephant)

مکھی *mak'khī* N.F. fly sight (of gun) مکھی پر مکھی مارنا *mak'khī par mak'khī mār'nā* V.I. copy blindly مکھی چوس *mak'khī choos'* N.M. miser; a niggard; stingy person مکھی چھوڑنا اور ہاتھی نگلنا *mak'khī chhoṛ'nā aur hā'thī ni'galnā* PROV. swallow the camel and strain at a gnat مکھی نگلنا *mak'khī ni'galnā* V.T. court trouble land oneself in trouble مکھیاں بھنکنا *mak'khiyān bhi'naknā* V.I. be sordid مکھیاں مارنا *mak'khiyān mār'nā* V.I. sit idle have nothing to do (of shopkeeper) have slump in trade مکھیوں کے چھتے کو چھیڑنا *mak'khiyon ke chhat'te ko chheṛ'nā* V.T. stir up a hornet's nest دودھ سے مکھی کی طرح نکال پھینکنا *doodh se mak'khī ki tar'ḥ nikāl' phenk'nā* V.I. get rid of without compunction ناک پر مکھی نہ بیٹھنے دینا *nāk' par mak'khī na baiṭh'ne de'ne* V.I. avoid incurring even the least obligation

مکھیا *mūkh'ya* N.M. village headman

مکئی *makai'* مکی *mak'kī* N.F. maize, Indian corn

مکی *mūk'kī* N.F. pressure with the fist آٹے کو مکی دینا *ā'ṭe ko mūk'kī de'nā* N.M. knead flour with fist ; press dough with fist مکیانا *mūkyā'nā* V.T give a blow with the fist

مکین *makīn'* N.M. resident inhabitant مکین ہونا *makīn' ho'nā* V.T. live [A ~ مکان]

مگدر *mūg'dar* N.M. club for exercising muscles like dumb-bells ; exercising club مگدر ہلانا *mūg'dar hilā'nā* V.T. exercise muscles with clubs

مگدمبر *magdam'bar* N.M. a kind of high tent large wooden palanquin

مگر *ma'gar* CONJ. but (lit.) perhaps اگر مگر *a'gar ma'gar* PH. if and but اگر مگر کرنا *a'gar ma'gar kar'nā* V.T. prevaricate [~P]

مگر ۲ *ma'gar* N.M. crocodile ; alligator eardrop

مگرا *mag'rā* ADJ. (F مگری *mag'rī*) cunning ; crafty one who feigns ignorance, etc. to shirk work مگراپن *mag'ra-pan* N.M. cunning ; craftiness ; artifice

مگس *ma'gas* N.F. (lit.) fly bee مگس ران *ma'gas-rān* N.M. fly-flap مگس رانی *ma'gas-rā'nī* N.F. driving away flies inactivity perform servile office [P]

مگن *ma'gan* ADJ. absorbed ; engrossed self-satisfied ; self-contented overjoyed مگن ہونا *ma'gan ho'nā* V.I. be overjoyed transported with joy be engrossed

مگھم *mūg'gham* N.M. abtruse remark secrecy draw [~A مبہم CORR.]

مل *mūl* N.F. (rare) ; wine گل و مل *gū'l-o-mūl* N.M. (fig.) woman and wine [P]

مل *mal* N.M. (H. dial.) stout warrior dregs excrement [S]

مل *mil* N.F. (or M.) mill [E]

ملا *mūl'la* N.M. (derog.) priest (derog.) one knowing only religious lore teacher in a mosque (arch.) learned person ملا کی دوڑ مسجد تک *mūl'la kī daur' mas'jid tak* PH. none can go beyond his resources this is my resort ملانہ *mullā'nah* N.M. (F. ملانی *mūllā'nī*) (derog.) religious sounded person priest

ملاء اعلیٰ *ma'la'-e a''la* N.M. angels unmates of Heaven [A ~ ملاء + اعلیٰ]

ملاپ *milāp'* N.M. meeting reconciliation agreement concord union ; unity combination ملاپ کرنا *milāp' kar'nā* V.T. get reconciled ملاپ ہونا *milāp' ho'nā* V.I. be reconciled

ملا جلا *mi'lā jū'lā* ADJ. مل جل *mil' jūl* IMP. (see under ملنا *mil'nā* V.T. ★)

ملاح mallah' N.M. boatman sailor ; mariner ; seaman ملاح کا لنگوٹا ہی بھیگتا ہے mallah' kā lango'ṭa hī bhīg'tā hai PROV. a poor man stands to lose little ; a poor person has little at stake ملاحی malā'ḥī N.F. seamanship see separate entry ★) ADJ. long ملاحی ہاتھ mallā'hī hath N.M. long stroke in swimming [A]

ملاحت malā'ḥat N.F. nut brown complexion brunethe's complexion as source of attraction brackishness elegance ; beauty ; charm [A doublet of ملح mil'h]

ملاحدہ malā'ḥidah N.M. (PL. of ملحد N.M. ★)

ملاحظہ mūlā'ḥazah N.M. inspection review close examination regard ; consideration ملاحظہ کرنا mūlā'ḥazah kar'na V.T. inspect review examine closely ; look attentively show regard or consideration (for) [A doublet of لحاظ]

ملاحی mallā'ḥī N.F. (usu PL.) curse without naming any names ملاحیاں سنانا mallā'ḥiyāṅ sunā'na V.T. abuse thus ; curse

ملادلا ma'lā da'lā ADJ. see under ملنا mal'nā V.T. ★)

ملاذ malāz' N.M. refuge ; shelter [A]

ملار malār' N.F. (same as ملہار N.F. ★)

ملازم mūlā'zim N.M. (PL. mūlāzimīn') servant (rare) attendant خانگی (یا گھریلو) ملازم khān'gī (or ghare'loo) mlūā'zim N.M. domestic servant سرکاری ملازم sarkā'rī mūlā'zim N.M. government servant ملازمت mūlā'zamat N.F. service employment (arch.) paying respects to a superior (rare) attendance (on) ملازمت اختیار کرنا mūlā'zamat ikhtiyār' kar'nā V.T. take up service (with) ; enter the service (of) ملازمت پیشہ mūlā'zamat-pe'shah ADJ. (one) who adopts (govt.) service as his profession [A ~ لزوم]

ملاطفت mūlā'tafat N.F. kindness ; favour ; consideration [A ~ لطف]

ملاعین malā'in' N.M. (PL. of ملعون N.M. ★)

ملاقات mūlāqat' N.F. meeting call visit interview introduction ملاقات پیدا کرنا mūlāqat' pai'dā kar'nā V.I. obtain an introduction ملاقات کرنا mūlāqat' kar nā V.T. arrange a meeting (between) introduce (someone to) ملاقات کرنا mūlāqat' kar'na V.T. meet visit call on interview ملاقات ہونا mūlāqat' ho'nā V.I meet be known (to) ملاقاتی mūlāqa'tī N.M visitor caller acquaintance ملاقی mūlā'qī ADJ. meeting ; visiting ملاقی ہونا mūlā'qī ho'na V.T. call on ; meet ; visit [A]

ملاگیری malāgī'rī ADJ. of sandal-wood colour nut-brown

ملال malāl' N.M. displeasure grief dejection (rare) fatigue , weariness tiredness ملال آنا malāl' ā'nā V.I. be displeased to be seized with be grieved be dejected چہرے پر ملال آنا cheh're par malāl' ā'nā V.I. show signs of displeasure [A]

ملامت malā'mat N.F. censure reproach reprehension reproof obloguy ملامت کرنا malā'mat kar'nā V.T. censure reproach ملامتی malā'matī ADJ. & N.M. censured (person) reprehensible (person) [A]

ملانا milā'nā V.T. join unite mixblend harmonize compare ; tall introduce ; present bring together reconcile ملا لینا milā' le'nā V.T. win (someone) over ملاؤ milā''o N.M. ملاوٹ milā'vaṭ N.F. adulteration غذائی ملاوٹ ghizā''ī milā'vaṭ N.F. food adulteration ; adulteration of foodstuffs [~ ملنا CAUS.]

ملائک malā''ik, ملائکہ malā''ikah N.M. (PL. of ملک malak N.M. ★)

ملائم mūlā''im ADJ. soft tender mollified mild gentle ملائم کرنا mūlā''im kar'nā V.T. soften mallify appease ملائمت mūlā''imat, ملایمت mūlā''yamat N.F. softness tenderness mildness ; gentleness [A]

ملائی malā''ī N.F. cream (see under ملنا mal'nā V.T. ★)

ملبا mal'bā, ملبہ mal'bah N.M. debris ملبا خرچ mal'ba-khar'ch N.M. money realized by headman from peasant for officer's enterainment

ملبب mūlab'bab ADJ. wrong but approved brinful [pseudo- A ~ P لب]

ملبوس malboos' N.M. (PL. ملبوسات malboosat') clothes ; garment ; apparel suit dress ADV. clothed (in) [A ~ لباس]

ملت ma'lat N.F. worn-out coin

ملت[1] mil'lat N.F. society ; friendship ملت کا آدمی mil'lat ka ād'mī ADJ. friendly ; affable sociable [~ ملنا]

ملت[2] mil'lat N.F. (PL. ملل mi'lal) followers of a faith following (of) Muslim nation ملی mil'lī ADJ. national of Muslim nation [A]

ملتانی mūlta'nī N.F. name of a musical mode ADJ. of or as of Multan (a town in West Pakistan) ملتانی مٹی mūlta'nī maṭ'ṭī N.F.

armenian bole [~ ملتان a city name]

ملتا جلتا *mil'tā jūl'tā* ADJ (see under ملنا *mil'nā* V.T. ★)

ملتجی *mūl'tajī* N.M. applicant petitioner, suppliant ADJ. applying requesting imploring ; supplicating ملتجی ہونا *mūl'tajī ho'nā* V.T request ; implore ; beseen [A ~ التجا]

ملتزم *mūl'tazam* N.M. place for prayer near southern corner of the Holy Ka'aba [A ~ التزام]

ملتفت *mūl'tafit* ADJ. attentive ADV. inclined (towards) looking (towards) [A ~ التفات]

ملتمس *mūl'tamis* ADJ. requesting, beseeching ; imploring [A ~ التماس]

ملتوی *mūl'tavī* ADJ. put off ; postponed adjourned ملتوی کرنا (یا رکھنا) *mūl'tavī kar'nā* (or *rakh'nā*) V.T. put off ; postpone [A ~ التوا]

ملٹھی *mūlaṭ'ṭhī* N.F. (same as ملہٹی *mūlaih'ṭī* N.F. ★)

ملجا *mal'jā* N.M. refuge; asylum ملجا و ماویٰ *mal'jā-o-mā'vā* N.M. refuge ; asylum (fig.) retreat [A]

ملتہب *mūl'tahib* ADJ. flaming ملتہب ہونا *mūl'tahib ho'nā* V.I. be in flames [A ~ التہاب]

ملٹ *ma'laṭ* N.M. mallet [E]

ملٹری *mil'ṭarī* ADV. & N.M. military [E]

ملح *mil'ḥ* N.M. (rare) salt brackishness [A]

ملحد *mūl'ḥid* N.M. (PL. ملاحدہ *malā'ḥidah*) atheist heretic infidel [A ~ الحاد]

ملحق *mūl'ḥaq* (F. & PL. ملحقہ *mūl'ḥaqah*) ADJ. adjoining contiguous subjoined ملحق کرنا *mūl'ḥaq kar'nā* V.T. include ملحق ہونا *mūl'ḥaq ho'nā* V.I. be adjoining ; be contiguous ملحقات *mūlḥaqāt'* N.M. PL. subjoined remarks, etc. [A ~ الحاق]

ملحوظ *malḥooz'* ADJ. regarded considered ملحوظ خاطر *malḥoo'z-e khā'tir* ADV. borne in mind ملحوظ رکھنا *malḥooz' rakh'nā* V.T. bear in mind take into consideration ملحوظ رہنا *malḥooz raih'nā* V.T. be taken into consideration [A ~ لحظہ]

ملخ *ma'lakh* N.M. locust مور و ملخ *mo'r-o-ma'lakh* N.M. PL. ant and locust ; insects [P]

ملخص *mūlakh'khas* N.M. gist summary ; abstract ; epitome [A ~ تلخیص]

ملذذ *mūlaz'ziz* ADJ. & N.M. aphrodisiac ملذذ *mūlaz'ziz* ADJ. delicious [A ~ لذت]

ملر ملر *mū'lūr mū'lūr* ADV aghast helplessly ملر ملر تکنا *mū'lūr mū'lūr tak'nā* V.I look aghast look helplessly

ملزم *mūl'zam* N.M. (PL. ملزمین *mūlzamīn'*) the ADJ. accused [A ~ الزام]

ملزوم *malzoom'* ADJ. necessitated لازم و ملزوم *lā'zim-o-malzoom'* N.M. PL. inseparable persons (or things, etc.) [A ~ لزوم]

ملعون *mal'oon'* ADJ. & N.M. cursed (person) execrated being [A ~ لعنت]

ملغوبا *malgho'bā* ملغوبہ *malgho'bah* N.M. any mashed food ; mash thick soup fulsome liquid mixture of food [T]

ملفوظ *malfooz'* ADJ. (of letter) that is sounded ملفوظات *malfoozāt'* N.M. PL. sayings (of saint, etc.) [A ~ لفظ]

ملفوف *malfoof'* ADJ. enclosed put in the envelope [A]

ملقب *mūlaq'qab* ADJ. entitled nicknamed الملقب بہ *al-mūlaq'qab-ba* PH. entitled nicknamed [A ~ لقب]

ملک *ma'lak* N.M. (PL. ملائک *malā''ik*, ملائکہ *malā''ikah*) angel ملک الموت *ma'lak-ūl-maut'* N.M. the angel of death ملکوت *mal'koot'* N.F. dominion (also عالم ملکوت *'ā'lam-e malakoot'* N.F world of angels ملکوتی *malakoo'tī* ADJ. angel, angelic ملکوتی صفات *malakoo'tī sifāt'* N.M. PL. angelic qualities [A]

ملک *ma'lik* N.M. (PL. ملوک *mūlook'* F. ملکہ *ma'likah*) king, monarch ; sovereign chief (of) ; prince (of) ; magnate ; king ملک التجار *ma'lik-ūt-tūjjār'* N.M. merchant prince business magnate ملک الشعرا *ma'lik-ūsh-sho'arā'* N.M. laureate ; poet-laureate جلالۃ الملک *jalā'lat-ūl-ma'lik* PH. His Majesty ملکہ *ma'likah* N.F. ★ [A]

ملک *mūl'k* N.M. (PL. ممالک *mamā'lik*) country dominion ; realm territory ملک بدر *mūl'k-ba-dar* ADJ. exiled ; banished ; ostracised N.M. exile ملک بدر کرنا *mūl'k-ba-dar' kar'nā* V.T. exile ملک خدا تنگ نیست پائے گدا لنگ نیست *mūl'k-e khūdā' tang' nes't pā''e gadā' lang' nes't* PH. one can try one's fortune elsewhere there is no end to resources ملک گیری *mūl'k-gī'rī* N.F. territorial aggrandizement of ہوس ملک گیری *ha'vas-e mūl'k-gī'rī* N.F. lust for territorial aggrandizement ملکی *mūl'kī* ADJ. & N.M. indigeneous national [A] نواب بے ملک *navvā'b-e be mūl'k* PH. pretender proud person [A]

ملک *mil'k* N.F. (PL. املاک *amlāk'*) property possession ملکی *mil'kī* N.M. propertied person landlord ملکی کہے نہ دل کی *mil'kī ka'he na dil' kī* PH. a rich person would never open out his heart to others, how can the opulent wear their heart on the sleeve ملکیت *milkiyat*

N.F ★ [A]

ملکات *malakāt'* N.M. (PL of ملکہ *ma'lakah* N.M. ★)

ملکانا *malkā'nā* V.I. speak with an affected tone ملکنا *ma'laknā* V.I. walk with an affected gait

ملکوت *malakoot'* N.M. ملکوتی *malakoo'tī* ADJ. (see under ملک *ma'lak* N.M. ★)

ملکہ *ma'likah* N.F. (PL. ملکائیں *malikā''eń*) queen ADJ. (rare) large ملکہ مسور *ma'likah masoor'* N F a large species of lentil [A F. ~ ملک *malik*]

ملکہ *ma'lakah* N.M. (PL. ملکات *malakāt'*) ability proficiency skill ملکہ (حاصل) ہونا *ma'lakah (ḥa'sil) ho'nā* V.T. be able to be proficient (in)

ملکیت *milkiy'yat* N.F. property possesson [A ~ ملک *mil'k*]

ملگجا *mal'gajā* ADJ. (F. ملگجی *mal'gajī*) dirty; soiled faded discoloured dusty

ملل *mi'lal* N.M. (PL. of ملت *mil'lat* ★)

ملمع *mulam'mā'* N.M. gilt plating electroplating ADJ. gilt electroplated tawdry ملمع ساز *mulam'mā'-sāz* N.M. gilder plater dissembler ملمع سازی *mulam'mā'-sā'zī* N.F. gilding plating dissembling ملمع کرنا *mūlam'ma' kar'nā* V.T. gild plate electroplate [A ~ لمع lustre]

ململ *mal'mal* N.F. muslin

ململا *mal'malā* ADJ glum; dejected ململاہٹ *malmalā'haṭ* N.F. dejection ruiny

ملما *mūlam'mā,* ملمہ *mūlam'mah* N.M. (arch.) provisions stored in house to last a whole month or season

ملنا *mil'nā* V.T. & I. meet come across have and interview embrace be reconciled get together get ; obtain ; find join touch mix ; mingle ; commingle blend resemble tolly مل بانٹ کے *mil' bānṭ ke* ADV. conjointly مل بیٹھنا *mil' baiṭh'nā* V.I. come together get reconciled مل جانا *mil' ja'na* V.T. & I. be found ; be recovered ; be received get mixed up join together be reconciled مل جل کر *mil' jūl kar* ADV. together with a united effort ملنا جلنا *mil'nā jūl'nā* V.T. meet frequently have friendly relations (with) N.M. friendly relations ملا جلا *mil'tā jul'ta* ADJ. resembling ملن *mi'lan* N.M. (dial.) meeting ملنسار *mi'lan-sār* ADJ. sociabli ; affable ملنساری *mi'lan-sā'rī* N.F. sociability , affability ملنی *mil'nī* N.F. (dial.) meeting on wedding day between elders of two families wedding procession's reception

ملنا *mal'nā* V.T. rub message aniont scrub ملائی *malā''ī* N.F. remuneration for scrubbing

ملنگ *malang'* N.M. one of a category of mendicants ; unorthodox mendicant ; drug-addict calender [P]

ملنی *mil'nī* N.F. (see under ملنا *mil'nā* V.T. & I. ★)

ملونی *milau'nī* N.F. (arch.) adulteration [~ ملانا]

ملوانا *milvā'nā* V.T. get joined [~ ملنا *mil'nā* CAUS.]

ملوانا *malvā'nā* V.T. cause to rub, anoint or scrub [~ ملنا *mal'nā* .CAUS.]

ملوث *mūlav'vas* ADJ. tainted گناہ سے ملوث *gunah' se mūlav'vas* PH. tainted with sin [A ~ لوث]

ملوک *mūlook'* N.M. PL. kings ملوکانہ *mūlookā nah* ADJ. kingly ; royal ; regal ملوکیت *mulookiy'yat* N.F. monarchy ; monarchical system [A ~ ملک *ma'lik*]

ملول *malool'* ADJ. sad ; dejected (rare) weary [A ~ ملال]

ملولا *malo'lā* N.M. yearning , wish grief

ملہار *malhār'*, ملار *malār'* N.F. name of a musical mode sung during rains ملہار گانا *malhār' gā'nā* V I. sing in this mode be in a happy mood

ملہٹی *mūlaih'ṭī*, مُلٹھی *mūlaṭ'ṭhī* N F liquorice

ملہم *mūlham* N M. inspired person one to whom something is revealed prophet ملہم بالغیب *mūl'ham bil-ghaib'* N.M. one to whom something is revealed ملہم *mūl'him* N M. inspirer [A ~ الہام]

ملی *mi'lī* ADJ. (see under ملت *mil'lat* N F. ★)

ملیامیٹ *mal'yā-meṭ* ADV. ruined effaced ملیامیٹ کرنا *mal'yā-meṭ kar'nā* V.T. ruin efface ملیامیٹ ہونا *ma'lyā-meṭ ho'nā* V.I. come to nought be ruined be effaced

ملی بھگت *mi'lī bha'gat* N.F plot ; conspiracy plot to defraud others [~ ملنا]

ملیچھ *malīchh'* N.M. (H dial.) pagan unclean person [S]

ملیح *malīḥ'* ADJ. nut brown beautiful charming ملیحہ *malī'ḥah* N F nut-brown maid (etc.) [A ~ ملاحت ★]

مليده *mali'dah* N.M. bread mashed in butter-oil and sugar woollen cloth washed and rubbed into fineness [~P مالیدن rub CORR.]

مليريا *male'riyā* N.M. malaria [E]

ملی میٹر *mil'īmiṭar* N.M. millimetre [E]

مم *mam* N.M. (nurs.) water

ملین *mil'yan* N.M. million [E]

ملین *mūlay'yin* ADJ. & N.M. aperient ; laxative [A ~ لین]

ممات *mamāt'* N.F. (rare) death حیات وممات *hayāt-o-mamāt'* N.F. life and death [A doublet of موت]

مماثلت *mūmā'salat* N.F. likeness ; similarity resemblance مماثل *mūmā'sil* ADJ. similar ; alike [A ~ مثل]

ممارست *mūmā'rasat* N.F. practice ; exercise [A]

مماس *mamās'* N.M. (Math.) tangent [A ~ مس]

ممالک *mamā'lik* N.M. PL. countries states kingdoms ; realms territories ممالک غیر *mamā'lik-e ghair'* N.M. foreign countries ممالک محروسہ *mamā'lik-e maḥroo'sah* N M. protectorates ممالک مفوضہ *mamā'lik-e mūfav'vazah* N.M. ceded territories [A ~ SING. مملکت]

ممالیک *mamālik'* N.M. PL. slaves slave dynasty [A ~ SING. مملوک]

ممانعت *mūmā'na'at* N.F. prevention prohibition ممانعت کرنا *mūmā'na'at kar'nā* V.T. ban forbid prohibit ممانعت ہونا *mūmā'na'at ho'nā* V.I. be refused be prohibited [A ~ منع]

ممانی *mamā'nī* N.F. wife of the mother's brother; maternal aunt ; aunt [~ ماموں]

ممبر *mim'bar* N.M. member ممبرانی *mimbarā'nī* (care or joc.) female member ممبری *mim'barī* N.F. membership [E]

ممتاز *mūmtāz'* ADJ. distinguished honoured illustrious ; eminent ; pre-eminent ممتاز کرنا (یا فرمانا) *mūmtāz' kar'nā* (or *farmā'nā*) V.T. distinguish honour [A ~ امتیاز]

ممتحن *mūm'taḥin* N.M. (PL. ممتحنین *mūmtaḥinīn'*) examiner [A ~ امتحان]

ممتد *mūmtad'* ADJ. extended stretched [A ~ امتداد]

ممتلی *mūm'talī* ADJ. brimful [A ~ امتلا]

ممتنع *mūm'tana'* ADJ. prohibited ; forbidden impossible سہل ممتنع *sah'l-e mūm'tana'* N.M. easy style that is nevertheless impossible to emulate [A ~ امتناع]

ممثل *mūmas'sil* N.M. (PL. ممثلین *mūmas'silīn'*) actor ممثلہ *mūmas'silah* N.F. actress [A ~ تمثیل]

ممد *mūmid'* N.M. & ADJ. helper ; protector ممد و معاون *mūmid'd-o-mo'ā'vin* N.M. & ADJ. helper ممد و معاون بننا (یا ہونا) *mūmid'd-o-mo'ā'vin ban'nā* (or *ho'nā*) V.T. become (or be) helper [A ~ امداد]

ممدوح *mam'dooḥ* ADJ. (F. ممدوحہ *mamdoo'ḥah*) praiseworthy ; landable venerable aforesaid ; above-mentioned N.M. patron laudable personality [A ~ مدح]

ممدودہ *mamdoo'dah* ADJ. elongated ('alif', etc.) [A ~ مد]

ممر *mamar'* N.M. course channel passage [A ~ مرور]

ممریز *mamrez'* N.F. rowel

ممزوج *mamzooj'* ADJ. mixed ; blended [A ~ مزاج]

ممسک *mūm'sik* ADJ. miserly niggardly retentive (medicine) N.M. miser [A ~ امساک]

ممکن *mūm'kin* ADJ. possible practicable; feasible plausible ; credible ; conceivable likely liable PREF. -able ; -ible ممکن الحصول *mūm'kin-ul-ḥusool'* ADJ. obtainable ; procurable ممکن الدخول *mūm'kin-ud-dūkhool'* ADJ. accessible ممکن الوجود *mūm'kin-ul-vūjood'* ADJ. liable to exist distinct from one necessary to exist ممکن الوقوع *mūm'kin-ul-vuqoo'* ADJ. liable to happen ممکنات *mūmkināt'* N.F. PL. possibilities ممکنات میں سے نہ ہونا *mūmkināt' meṅ se na ho'nā* V.I. be utterly impossible

مملکت *mam'lūkat* (or *mam'lakat*) N.F. (PL. ممالک *mamā'lik*) kingdom realm country territory [A doublet of ملک *mul'k*]

مملو *mamloo'* ADJ. full (of) filled with [A]

مملوک *mamlook'* N.M. (PL. ممالک *mamā'lik* slave captive مملوکہ *mamloo'kah* ADJ. owned مملوکہ و مقبوضہ *mamloo'ka-o-maqboo'zah* ADJ. owned and possessed (by) [A ~ ملک *mil'k*]

ممنوعہ *mamnoo''ah* ADJ. prohibited forbidden contraband ممنوع *mamnoo'* ADJ. & ADV. porhibited out of bounds embargoed ممنوعات *mamnoo'āt'* N.M. PL. prohibited things [A ~ منع]

ممنون *mamnoon'* ADJ. obliged thankful grateful ممنون کرنا *mamnoon' kar'nā* V.T. oblige ممنون ہونا *mamnoon' ho'nā* V.I. be obliged

ممنونیت mamnooniy'yat N.F. being obliged [A ~ من]

ممولا mamo'lā N.M. wagtail

ممی[1] ma'mī N.F. mummy [E]

ممی[2] ma'mī N.F. mummy ; mummified corpse [E ~ A مومیا]

ممیا mam'yā PREF. maternal ; of maternal uncle ممیا ساس mam'yā-sās N.F. maternal aunt (of husband or, wife) ممیا سسر (یا خسر) mam'yā-sū'sar (or khū'sar) N.M. maternal uncle (of husband or wife) [~ ماموں]

ممیانا mamyā'nā V.T. (of goat or sheep) bleat [ONO.]

ممیت mūmīt' N.M. He who causes death (as attribute of God) [A ~ موت]

ممیرا mame'rā ADJ. (F. ممیری mame'rī) descended from maternal uncle [A ~ ماموں]

ممیرا mamī'rā (ped. ممیراں mamī'rāṅ) a medicinal root useful for eyesight [~ P مامیراں]

ممیزہ mūmay'yizah ADJ. discriminating (power) قوتِ ممیزہ qūv'vat-e mūmay'yizah N.M. discrimination ممیز mūmay'yaz ADJ. distinct distinguished [A ~ تمیز]

من[1] man' N.M. mind heart soul spirit inclination conscience attention maund gem (supposed to be) in snake's head ; serpentine gem من اٹکنا man' a'ṭak'nā V.T. fall in love (with) ; have an attachment من اٹھنا man' ūṭh'nā V.I. be satiated (with) من اکتانا man' ūktā'nā (or ūktā' jā'nā) V.I. be sick and tired (of) ; be fed up (with) من اگلنا man' ū'gal'nā (of snake) disgorge its stone من بھاتا man-bhā'tā ADJ. liked ; loved ; cherished ; favourite (dish) من بھاتا کھاجا man-bhā'ta khā'jā N.M. favourite dish من برا (یا بھاری کرنا) man' bū'rā (or bhā'rī kar'nā) V.I. be dejected من بھاؤنا man'-bhā''onā ADJ. liked by one من بھائے منڈیا ہلائے man' bhā''e mūṇḍ'yā hilā''e V.I. apparent refusal despite desire من بھر man'-bhar ADJ. to one's satisfaction about one maund من بھر جانا man' bhar' jā'nā be sated be satisfied ; to be sated من بھر کا سر ہلانا ٹکے کی زبان نہ ہلانا man' bhar kā sir' hilā'nā ta'ke kī zūbān' na hilā'nā V.I. nod rather than talk من بہلانا man' baihlā'nā V.I. amuse oneself (with) ; divert oneself من چلا man'-chā'la ADJ. (F. من چلی man'-chā'lī bold ; brave ; courageous من سمجھوتی man'-samjhau'tī N.F. resignation من کا کپٹی (یا کھوٹا یا میلا) man' kā kap'ṭī (or kho'ṭa or mai'la) ADJ. & N.M. malicious (person) من کچا کرنا man' kach'cha kar'nā V.I. lose heart من کرنا man', kar'nā V.T. desire من کھٹا ہونا man khaṭ'ṭā ho'nā V.I. be fed up (with) من کے لڈو پھوڑنا man'.ke laḍ-doo phoṛ'nā V.T. build castles in the air من کی من میں رہنا man' kī man' meṅ raih'nā V.I. (of desire) remain unfulfilled من کی موج man' kī mauj PH. whim ; caprice sudden desire من لگنا man' lag'nā V.T. have the heart set (upon) من لچانا man' lalchā'nā V.T. yearn long for hanker after من مار رہنا man' mār' raih'nā, من مار کے بیٹھ رہنا man' mār' ke baiṭh' raih'nā V.I. suffer patiently suppress one's desire من مارنا man' mār'nā V.T. suppress one's desire من مانی man'-mā'nī N.F. wilfulness ADV. according to one's wishes من مانی کرنا man'-mā'nī kar'nā V.I. be wilful; be head-strong do as one likes; act according to one's wishes من ملنا man' mil'nā V.I. be of the same mind (as another) من موجی man' mau'jī ADJ. whimsical ; capricious من موہ لینا man' moh' le'nā V.T. charm ; fascinate ; captivate من موہن man'-mo'han N.M. (dial.) beloved ; sweetheart من میں man' meṅ ADV. in the mind (of) into the heart (of) من میں آنا man' meṅ ā'nā V.T. & I. occur (to) ; strike fill (someone's) heart with one's love من ہی من میں man' hī man' meṅ ADV. in one's heart of hearts منوا man'vā N.M. (endearingly or as dim.) heart

من[2] man' N.M. hole in the middle of weighing-balance beam

من[3] man' PRON. I (to) me من آنم کہ من دانم man' ā'nam ke man' dā'nam PH. I know my limitations do not pull my leg من ترا حاجی بگویم تو مرا حاجی بگو man' tūrā' ḥā'jī bi-go'yam to mara' ḥā'jī bigo' PH. mutual admiration من چہ مے سرایم و طنبورہ من چہ مے سراید man' che me sarā'yam-o-tamboo'ra-e man' cheh me sarā'yad PH. contradictory reports from the same end من خوب می شناسم پیران پارسا را man' khoob' me shinā'sam pīrā'ne parsā' rā PH. (iron.) the veneer of false virtue is too thin for my eyes [P]

من[4] man' N.M. manna من و سلویٰ mann-o-sal'vā N.M. manna and quails (with which the Israelites were fed during the Exodus wonderful victuals [A ~]

من min PREF. (rare) from منجانب min-jā'nib ADV. from ; by منجانب اللہ min-jānib-illāh' ADV. from God منجملہ min-jūmlah ADV. from among ; out of all من حیث المجموع min-ḥai's-ūl-majmoo'' PH. on the whole من کل الوجوہ min kūl'l-il-vūjooh' PH. in every respect من وجہ min-vajoh PH. in one way for one reason من و عن mi'n-o-'an ADV. exactly ; as it was ; to the very letter منہا minhā' ADJ. & ADV. ★ [A]

منی *minā'* N.M. sacrificial centre on the outskirt of Mecca [A]

منا *mūn'nā* N.M. (F. منی *mun'nī*) small child ADJ. small ; little ننھا منا *nan'nhā mūn'nā* ADJ. (F. ننھی منی *nan'nhī mūn'nī*) small ; little

منابر *manā'bir* N.M. (PL. of منبر N.M. ★)

منات *manāt'* N.F. name of a pre-Islamic Arabian goddess [A]

مناجات *nūnājāt'* N.F. hymn supplication to God ; imploration مناجات پڑھنا *munajāt' parh'nā* V.T. sing a hymn implore God [A]

منادیٰ *munā'da* N.M. vocative case [A ~ ندا]

منادی *mūnā'dī* N.F. proclamation public announcement to the beat of drum N.M (ped.) proclaimer town-crier منادی کرنا *munā'dī kar'nā* V.T. proclaim to the beat of drum [A ~ PREC.]

منار *manār'*, منارہ *manā'rah* (pop. though ungrammatical مینار *mīnār'*) N.M. tower minaret light-house [A ~ نور]

منازعت *mūnā'za'at* N.F. quarrel contention [A ~ نزاع]

منازل *manā'zil* N.F. PL. stages storeys phases منازل قمر *manā'zil-e qa'mar* N.F. PL. phases of the moon [A ~ منزل]

مناسب *mūnā'sib* ADJ. proper meet ; becoming fit ; appropriate expedient suitable ; opposite ; pertinent corresponding مناسبت *munā'sabat* N.F. fitness ; suitability connection ; relation relevancy ; consistency [A ~ نسبت]

مناسک *manā'sik* N.M. PL. rites of pilgrimage rites prayers مناسک حج *manā'sik-e haj'* N.M. PL. Haj rites [A ~ منسک]

مناصب *manā'sib* N.M. (PL. of منصب N.M. ★)

مناظر *manā'zir'* N.M. (see under مناظرہ N.M. ★)

مناظر *manā'zir* N.M. PL. views ; scenes مناظر قدرت *manā'zir-e qūd'rat* N.M. natural scene [A ~ SING. منظر]

مناظرہ *mūnā'zarah* N.M. dialectic ; polemical writing or speech controversary ; dialogue مناظر *mūnā'zir* N.M. (PL. مناظرین *mūnāzirīn'*) dialectic ; dialectician ; polemical writer or speaker [A ~ نظر]

منافرت *mūnā'farat* N.F. hatred [A ~ نفرت]

منافست *munā'fasat* N.F. bid to out do another be one better strife [A]

منافذ *manā'fiz* N.M. (PL. of منفذ N.M ★)

منافع *manā'fe'* N.M. (PL. of منفعت N.F. ★)

منافع *mūnā'fa'* (or منافعہ) N.M. profit خالص منافع *khā'lis mūnā'fa'* N.M. net profit خام منافع *khām mūnā'fa'* N.M. gross profit

منافق *mūnā'fiq* N.M. (PL. منافقین *mānāfiqīn'*) hypocrite dissembler pretender to Islam منافقت *mūnā'faqat* N.F. hypocrisy dissimulation show ; pretence pretensions to Islam [A نفاق]

منافی *mūnā'fī* ADJ. contrary (to) ; negating [A ~ نفی]

مناقب *manā'qib* N.F praises qualities eulogy of Imams مناقبت *munā'qabat* N.F. composing encomium to Imams [A ~ منقبت]

مناقشت *mūnā'qashat* N.F., مناقشہ *mūnā'qashah* N.M. dispute contention [A]

مناکحت *mūnā'kahat* N.F. marriage [A doublet of نکاح]

منال *manāl'* N.M. what comes to hand (only in) مال و منال *mal-o-ma..l* N.M. wealth ; riches [A]

منان *mannān'* N.M. great benefactory this as attribute of God [A ~ منت]

منانا *manā'nā* V.T. coax ; cajole bring round persuade prevail upon wheedle conciliate appease ; propitiate celebrate (festival) [A ~ ماننا CAUS.]

مناہج *manā'hij* N.M. (PL. of منہج N.M. ★) highways ; roads ; routes [A ~ نہج]

مناہی *manā'hī* N.F. prohibition N.F. PL. prohibitions N.F. PL. prohibitions [~ A SING. منہی]

منبت *munab'bat* ADJ. (rare) embossed منبت کاری *munab'bat-kā'rī* N.F. embossing raised floral pattern [A]

منبر *mim'bar* N.M. (PL. منابر *manā'bir*) pulpit [A]

منبع *mam'ba'* N.M. (PL. منابع *manā'be'*) fountainhead source ; origin [A]

منت *man'nat* N.F. vow منت پوری کرنا *man'nat poo'rī kar'nā* V.T. fulfil a vow منت پوری ہونا *man'nat poo'rī ho'nā* V.T. (of vow) be fulfilled منت کا *man'nat kā* PH. got or kept as a result of vow منت کا طوق *man'nat kā tauq'* PH. neckband worn in fulfilment of vow منت کی بیڑی *man'nat kī be'rī* PH. such shackle on child's foot منت کے بال *man'nat ke bāl'* PH. hair worn thus منت ماننا *man'nat mān'nā* V.I. to make a vow [A ~ ماننا]

منت *min'nat* N.F. (PL. منن *mi'nan*) humble request , entreaty ; supplication (rare)

obligation منت اٹھانا *min'nat uṭhā'nā* V. come under obligation منت پذیر *min'nat-pazīr'* ADJ. acknowledging of (someone's) favour منت پذیری *min'nat-pazī'rī* N.F. acknowledgement of favour منت سماجت *min'nat samā'jat* N.F. entreaty ; supplication coaxing ; cajolery منت (یا منتیں) کرنا *min'nat* (or *min'nateṅ*) *kar'nā* V.T. beg ; earnestly ; implore ; entreat ; beseech منت کش *min'nat-kash* ADJ. obliged ADV. under obligation منت کشی *min'nat-ka'shī* N.F. come under obligation [A]

منتج *mūn'taj* ADV. leading (upto) ADJ. deduced پر منتج ہونا *par mūn'taj ho'nā* V.I. lead up to [A ~ نتیجہ]

منتخب *mūn'takhab* ADJ. chosen selected elected منتخب کرنا *mūn'takhab kar'nā* V.T. choose select elect ; return (someone) منتخب ہونا *mūn'takhab ho'nā* V.I. be chosen. be selected be selected [A ~ انتخاب]

منتر *man'tar* N.M. charm ; spell ; incantation (dial.) verse of Hindu scriptures منتر پڑھنا *man'tar paṛh'nā* V.T. & I. enchant recite incantation (dial.) recite verse of Hindu scriptures منتر پھونکنا *man'tar phoonk'nā* V.T. cast a spell منتر جنتر *man'tar jan'tar* جنتر منتر *jan'tar man'tar* N.M. charm incantation exorcism socery منتری *man'tarī* N.M. sorceror ; magician (dial.) minister پردھان منتری *pardhān' man'tarī* N.M. (dial.) prime minister ; premier منتری منڈل *man'tarī man'ḍal* N.M. (dial.) cabinet [S]

منتشر *mūn'tashir* ADJ. dispersed (crowd) distracted (ideas) منتشر کرنا *mūn'tashir kar'nā* V.T. disperse (crowd) distract (mind, ideas, etc.) منتشر ہونا *mūn'tashir ho'nā* V.I. (of crowd) be dispersed (of mind, ideas, etc.) be distracted [A ~ انتشار]

منتظر *mūn'tazir* ADJ. waiting ; awaiting ADV. on the look-out ; (for) منتظر *mūn'tazar* ADJ. awaited ; expected [A ~ انتظار]

منتظم *mūn'tazim* N.M. manager master of ceremonies ; emcee ADJ. one good at management [A ~ انتظام]

منتفع *mūn'tafe'* ADJ. profiting enjoying [A ~ انتفاع]

منتقل *mūn'taqil* ADJ. moved; shifted carried; transported منتقل کرنا *mūn'taqil kar'nā* V.T. shift carry ; transport منتقل ہونا *mūn'taqil ho'nā* V.I. be shifted be transported [A ~ انتقال]

منتقم *mūn'taqim* ADJ. taking revenge ; avenging ; avenger this as attribute of God منتقم حقیقی *mūn'taqim-e ḥaqī'qī* N.M. (God as) the Avenger منتقم مزاج *mūn'taqim-mizāj'* ADJ vindictive منتقم مزاجی *mūn'taqim-mizā'jī* N.F. vindictiveness ful [A ~ انتقام]

منتہا (ped. منتہیٰ) *mūntahā'* N.M. goal extremity منتہائے مقصود *mūntahā'-e maqsood'* N.M. goal ; ultimate aim منتہی *mūn'tahī* ADJ proficent learned N.M. one in his final years [A ~ انتہا]

منٹ *min't* N.F. mint [E]

منٹ *mi'naṭ* N.M. minute [E]

منثور *man'soor* ADJ. unbored (pearl) prose (writing) کلام منثور *kalā'm-e mansoor'* N.M. prose [A ~ نثر]

منجذب *mūn'jazib* ADJ. that can be absorbed [A ~ انجذاب]

منجلی *mūn'jalī* ADJ. clear ; lucid [A جلی]

منجم *mūnaj'jim* N.M. (PL. منجمین *mūnajjimīn'*) astrologer [A ~ تنجیم ~ نجم star]

منجمد *mūn'jamid.* ADJ. frozen congealed [A ~ انجماد]

منجملہ *min'jūm'lah* ADJ. (see under من *min* PREP.)

منجن *man'jan* N.M. tooth-powder ; dentifrice

منجھنا *mañjh'nā* V.I. be cleansed be polished ; become cultured (of language) become chaste منجھی ہوئی زبان *mañj'hī hū''ī zabān'* PH. chaste language

منجنیق *manjanīq'* N.M. (PL. مجانیق *majā'nīq*) catapult [A]

منجھ *mañjh* PREF. middle منجھدھار *mañjh-dhār* N.F. midstream منجھدھار میں پڑنا *mañjh-dhār' meṅ paṛ'nā* V.I. be in midstream be in great difficulty ; be in the midst of a crisis منجھلا *mañjh'lā* (F. منجھلی *mañjh'lī*) ADJ. between the eldest and the youngest ; middle منجھولا *mañjho'lā* ADJ. middling N.M. half-sized cauldron منجھیلا *mañjhe'lā* N.M. delay منجھیلا پڑنا *mañjhe'lā paṛ'nā* V.I. (of delay) occur منجھیلا ڈالنا *mañjhe'lā ḍāl'nā* V.T. delay منجھیلی *mañjhe'lī* N.F. midday ADJ. (of night) quiet fearful

منجیرا *mañjī'rā* N.M. (same as مجیرا N.M ★)

منحرف *mūn'ḥarif* ADJ. disaffected deviating declining deflecting منحرف ہونا *mūn'ḥarif ho'nā* V.I. rebel ; revolt be disaffected deviate deflect [A ~ انحراف]

منحصر *mūn'ḥasir* ADJ. dependent (on) resting (on) [A ~ انحصار]

منحنی *mūn'ḥanī* ADJ. weak lean bent ; curved [A ~ انحنا]

منحوس *manhoos'* ADJ. unlucky ; unfortunate; ill-starred inauspicious abominable ; execrable damned ; d—d [A ~ نحس]

مند *mand* SUF. able -ible -ful having مندی *man'di* SUF. -ability ; -ibility fulness having

مندا *man'dā* N.M. slump ADJ. dull cheap مندا بیچنا *man'dā bech'nā* V.T. sell cheap مندا پڑنا (یا ہونا) *man'dā par'nā* (or *ho'nā*) V.I. (of market) be dull of price fall ; slump

مندر *man'dar* (dial. -*dir*) N.M. (PL. منادر *manādir*) temple pagoda Hindu temple

مندرا *mūnd'rā* N.M. large ring ; a collar

مندرجہ *mūnda'rajah* ADJ. entered; inserted مندرجہ بالا *mūnda'raja-e bā'lā* ADJ. & ADV. abovementioned مندرجہ ذیل *mūndara'ja-e zail'* ADJ. & ADV following ; as follows ; as under ; as given below مندرج *mūn'daraj* ADV. entered ; inserted [A ~ اندراج]

مندمل *mun'damil* ADJ. healed up [A ~ اندمال]

مندنا *mūnd'nā* V.I. (of eyes, etc.) be shut ; be shut ; be closed [A ~ موندنا]

مندوب *mandoob'* N.M. (PL. مندوبین *mandoobīn'*) delegate [A ~ ندبہ]

مندیل *mindīl* N.F. a kind of brocade turban table cloth napkin [A]

منڈا *mūn'dā* ADJ. shaven ; tonsured a kind of shoe having no pointed toe [~ مونڈنا ~ منڈنا]

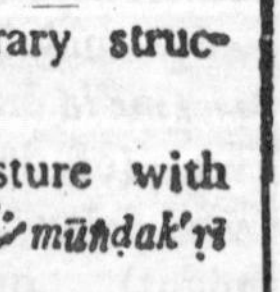

منڈاسا *mūndā'sā* N.M. a kind of small turban

منڈانا *mūndā'nā*, منڈوانا *mūndvā'nā* V.T. get (one's head, bread, etc.) shaved cause to be swindled منڈائی *mūndā''ī* N.F. remuneration for shaving or hair-cut [~ مونڈنا CAUS.]

منڈپ *man'dap* N.M. (dial.) temporary structure [S]

منڈکری *mūndak'rī* N.F. sitting posture with head resting on knees منڈکری مارنا *mūndak'rī mar'nā* V.I. sit thus

منڈل *man'dal* N.M. (dial.) circle circumference sphere sky [S]

منڈلانا *manlā'nā* V.T hover

منڈلی *mand'lī* N.F. group assembly [~ منڈل]

منڈنا *mūnd'nā* V.T. be shaved be tonsured be duped ; be swindled منڈن *mūndan* N.M. (H. dial.) the first shaving ceremony (of child) [~ مونڈنا

منڈوا *mand'vā* N.M. theatre a kind of coarse cereal

منڈوانا *mūndvā'nā* V.T. (same as منڈانا V.T. ★)

منڈھا *mand'dhā* N.M. pavilion bedecked with shoots and sprays prothalamion منڈھا گانا *mand'dhā gā'nā* V.T. sing a prothalamion [~ منڈنا]

منڈھنا *mandh'nā* V.T. cover drum, etc.) with parchment put parchment (over) encase impose ; palm (something) off (on منڈھوانا *mandhvā'nā* V.T. get (drum, etc.) covered with parchment

منڈی *mūn'dī* N.F. name of a medicinal plant hairless houseless (of mosque, with no minarets [~ منڈنا]

منڈیر *mūnder* N.F. parapet

منزل *man'zil* N.F. (PL منازل *manā'zil*) storey (of house) goal ; destination stage (of) journey one of the seven stages into which the Holy Quran is sub-divided ; Quranic stage منزل بہ منزل *man'zil ba man'zil* ADV. by stages منزل پر پہنچانا *man'zil par pahunchā'nā* V.T. take to destination perform the obsequies (of) منزل پر پہنچنا *man'zil par pahunch'nā* V.I. reach (one's) destination منزل دینا *man'zil de'nā* V.T place the coffin on ground for respite while on way to graveyard منزل طے کرنا *man'zil tai' kar'na* V.T. reach the journey's end get over a stage منزل کاٹنا *man'zil kaṭ'nā* V.I. act over a stage *man'zil kaṭ'nā* V.I. complete the journey منزل کرنا *man'zil kar'nā* V.I. halt ; go one stage in journey منزل کو پہنچنا *man'zil ko pahunch'nā* V.I. achieve (one's) object arrive at (one's) destination منزل کھوٹی ہونا *man'zil kho'ṭī ho'nā* V.I. be getting late for one's destination منزل (یا منزلیں) مارنا *man'zil* (or *man'zilen*) *mar'nā* V.I. journey finish a difficult task منزل مقصود *man'zil-e maqsood'* N.F. goal; destination منزل گاہ *man'zil gah* N.F (rare) destination منزلہ *man'zilah* ADJ. storied decker [A ~ نزول]

منزل *mūnaz'zal* ADJ. sent down منزل من اللہ *mūnaz'zal min-allāh'* PH. God's revelation [A ~ تنزیل]

منزلت *man'zilat* N.F. dignity status قدر و منزلت *qad'r-o-man'zilat* N.F. esteem قدر و منزلت کرنا *qad'r-o-manzi'lat kar'na* V.T. hold in high esteem [A ~ نزول]

منزلہ *man'zilah* N.M. place ; rank (only in) بمنزلہ ADJ. (see under ب PREF.)

منزہ *mūnaz'zah* ADJ. pure; free (from) [A ~ تنزیہ]

منزوی *mūn'zavī* ADJ. secluded (corner) [A ~ انزوا]

منسلکہ *mūn'salikah* ADJ. attached strung together منسلک *mūs'salik* ADJ. attached [A ~ سلک]

منسوب *mansoob'* ADJ. attributed imputed betrothed ; fiance منسوبہ *mansoo'bah* N.F. fiancee [A ~ نسبت]

منسوخ *mansookh'* ADJ. cancelled abolished abrogated; annulled منسوخی *mansoo'khī* N.F. cancellation. abolition abrogation ; annulment [A ~ نسخ]

منش *ma'nish* N.F. temperament SUF. minded [P ~ من]

منشا *man'shā* N.M. tenor ; purpert motive ; intention place of origin ; birth place حسب منشا *has'b-e man'shā* PH. as desired (by) مولد و منشا *mau'lid-o-man'shā* N.M. birth-place [A ~ نشو]

منشور *manshoor'* N.M. manifesto (arch.) proclamation prism [A ~ نشر]

منشی *mūnshī* N.M. clerk ; vernacular clerk (lawyer's) clerk (army officers) larguage teacher Persian teacher (rare) writer (arch.) amanuensis (arch.) secretary منشی خانہ *mūn'shī-khā'nah* N.M. vernacular office منشی فلک *mūn'shī-e fa'lak* N.M. (planet) Mercury منشی گری *mūn'shī-ga'rī* N.F. clerkship میر منشی *mīr-mūn'shī* N.M. superintendent of vernacular office منشیانہ *munshiyā'nah* ADJ. clerical N.M. clerk's fee [A ~ انشا]

منشی *mūnash'shī* ADJ. intoxicating منشیات *mūnashshiyāt'* N.M. PL. intoxicating drugs [pseudo A ~ P نشہ]

منصب *man'sab* (ped. -*sib*) N.M. (PL. مناصب *manā'sib*) office ; post منصبدار *man'sab-dār* N.M. (arch.) officer magistrate سرکاری منصب *sarkā'rī man'sab* N.M. government post official position

منصرف *mūn'sarif* ADJ. (gram.) inflected declined deviating (from) [A ~ انصراف]

منصرم *mun'sarim* N.M. administrator clerk of court manager one skilled in management [A ~ انصرام]

منصف *mūn'sif* N.M. (PL. منصفین *mūnsifīn'* sub-judge ; subordinate judge ADJ. (also منصف مزاج *mūn'sif-mizāj'*) ADJ. just ; fair-minded ; given to justice منصفانہ *mūnsifā'nah* ADJ. just ; fair ; equitable ADV. justly ; fairly ; equitably منصفی *mūn'sifī* N.F. court of a sub-judge justice ; equity judgment ; decision ; verdict arbitration منصف مزاجی *mūn'sif-mizā'ji* N.F. justice fairplay [A ~ انصاف]

منصوب *mansoob'* ADJ. in accusative case bearing the vowel-point zabar [A ~ نصب]

منصوبہ *mansoo'bah* N.M. preject plan ; scheme design ; plot ; conspiracy contrivance intention aspiration منصوبہ باز *mansoo'ba-bāz* ADJ. scheming منصوبہ باندھنا *mansoo'bah bāndh'na* V.T. plan resolve منصوبہ بندی *mansoo'ba-bah'dī* N.F. planning خاندانی منصوبہ بندی *khāndā'nī mansoo'ba-bah'dī* N.F. family planning قومی منصوبہ بندی *qau'mī mausoo'ba-bahdī* national planning معاشی (یا اقتصادی) منصوبہ بندی *ma'āshī* (or *iqtisādī*) *man'sooba-bah'dī* N.F. economic planning [A ~ نصب]

منصور *mansoor'* ADJ. victorious ; triumphant succoured ; aided N.M. (correctly ابن منصور *ibn-e mansoor'* though seldom used as such) name of a famous martyred mystic [A ~ نصرت]

منصوص *mansoos'* ADJ. definite and unequivocal order of the Holy ADV. such order [A ~ نص]

منصہ *manas'sah*. N.M. bridal chamber منصۂ شہود *manas'sa-e shohood'* N.M. place of appearance

منضج *mūn'zij* ADJ. & N.M. (PL. منضجات *mūnzijāt'*) suppurative [A ~ نضج]

منطبق *mūn'tabiq* ADJ. applicable conforming (to) coinciding (with) منطبق کرنا *mūn'tabiq kar'na* V.T. apply (to)

منطق *man'tiq* N.F. logic منطق چھانٹنا (یا بگھارنا) *man'tiq chhānt'na* (or *baghār'nā*) V.T. chop logic منطقی *man'tiqī* N.M. logician ADJ. logical [A ~ نطق]

منطقہ *min'taqah* N.M. (PL. مناطق *manā'tiq*) zone (rare) belt منطقۃ البروج *min'taqat-ūl-būrooj'* N.M. zodiac منطقۂ باردہ *min'taqa-e bā'ridah* N.M. frigid zone منطقۂ حارہ *min'taqa-e hār'rah* N.M. torrid zone منطقۂ معتدلہ *min'taqa-e mo''tadilah* N.M. temperate zone [A ~ نطاق]

منطوق *mantooq'* N.M. utterance [A ~ نطق]

منطوی *mūn'tavī* ADJ. rolled complicated [A ~ طے]

منظر *man'zar* N.M. (PL. مناظر *manā'zir*) scene sight spectacle view ; scape . scenery منظر عام *man'zar-e 'ām'* N.M. public view منظر عام پر لانا *man'zar-e 'ām' par la'na* bring into public view make public disclose divulge [A ~ نظر]

منظم *mūnaz'zam* ADJ. organized منظم کرنا *mūnaz'zam kar'nā* V.T. organize منظم ہونا *mūnaz'zam ho'nā* V.I. be organized [A ~ تنظیم]

منظور *manzoor'* ADJ. sanctioned ; granted accepted approved liked intended منظور خاطر *manzoo'r-e khā'tir* ADV. desired منظور نظر *manzoo'r-e na'zar* N.M. favourite ADJ. favourite beloved ADV. in the good books (of) منظوری *manzoo'rī* N.F. sanction permission approval منظوری دینا *manzoo'rī de'nā* V.T. sanction ; accord sanction (to) approve [A ~ نظر]

منظوم *manzoom'* ADJ. metrical ; versified ; in verse form (rare) strung together کلام منظوم *kalā'm-e manzoom'* N.M. verse ; poem منظومات *manzoomāt'* N.M. poems [A]

منع *man'* N.M. prevention dissuasion prohibition ADV. forbidden , prohibited منع کرنا *man'' kar'nā* V.T. prevent forbid dissuade prohibit منع ہونا *man'' ho'nā* V.I. be prevented be forbidden be dissuade be prohibited [A]

منعطف *mūn''atif* ADJ. diverted توجہ منعطف کرانا *tavaj'joh mūn''atif kar'nā* V.T. call (someone's) attention (to) توجہ منعطف کرنا *tavaj'joh mūn''atif kar'nā* V.T. pay attention (to) [A ~ انعطاف]

منعقد *mūn''aqid* ADJ. held convened celebrated منعقد کرنا *mūn'aqid kar'nā* V.T. hold; call; convene celebrate منعقد ہونا *mūn'aqid ho'nā* V.I. take place be held ; be convened be celebrated [A ~ انعقاد]

منعکس *mūn''akis* ADJ. & ADV. reflected منعکس ہونا *mūn'akis ho'nā* V.I. be reflected [A ~ انعکاس]

منعم *mūn''im* N.M. benefactor rich person منعم حقیقی *mūn''im-e haqī'qī* N.M. (God as) True Benefactor [A ~ انعام]

منغض *mūnagh'ghas* ADV. (of someone's) pleasure be disturbed [A]

منفذ *man'faz* N.M. (PL. منافذ *manā'fiz*) orifice passage exit [A ~ نفوذ]

منفرجہ *mūnfa'rijah* ADJ. obtuse (angle) [A ~ فرج]

منفرد *mūn'farid* ADJ. unique issolated solitary ; lonely [A ~ انفراد]

منفصل *mūn'fasil* ADJ. separated [A ~ انفصال]

منفعت *man'fa'at* N.F. (PL. منافع) gain ; profit advantage ; benefit منفعت اٹھانا *man'fa'at uthā'na* V.I. derive benefit (from) profit (by) [A ~ نفع]

منفعل *mūn'fa'il* ADJ. ashamed penitant passive [A ~ انفعال]

منفی *man'fī* ADJ. minus subtracted ; deducted deprived (of) ; without negative [A ~ نفی]

منفک *mūn'fak* ADJ. separated [A ~ انفکاک]

منقاد *mūnqād'* ADJ docile submissive [A ~ انقیاد]

منقار *minqār'* N.F. bill ; beak [A]

منقبت *man'qabat* N.F. dignity praise eulogy (of the Holy Prophet's Companions or relations [A]

منقسم *mūnqasim* ADJ. divided classified ; categorized [A ~ انقسام]

منقح *mūndq'qah* ADJ. elucidated [A ~ تنقیح]

منقبض *mūn'qabiz* ADJ. not feeling happy ; dejected [A ~ انقباض]

منقش *mūnaq'qash* ADJ. painted printed (cloth, etc.) impressed (upon) [A نقش]

منقضی *mūn'qazī* ADJ. past elapsed expired ended ; finished [A ~ انقضا]

منقطع *mūn'qate'* ADJ. snapped finished ; terminated exterminated [A ~ انقطاع]

منقلب *mūn'qalib* ADJ. altogether changed inverted ; upside down حالات منقلب ہونا *halat' mūn'qalib ho'nā* V.I. (of circumstances) be changed [A ~ انقلاب]

منقوش *manqoosh'* ADJ. printed carved ; engraved impressed [A ~ نقش]

منقوط *manqoot'* ADJ. (F. منقوطہ *manqoo'tah*) (of lether) dotted (of writing)

منقول *manqool'* ADJ. copied reported ; related ; narrated ; recounted traditionally reported (sciences, etc.) منقولات *manqoolāt'* N.M. traditionally; reported sciences; religious branches of knowledge منقولہ *mūnqoo'lah* ADJ. movable (property) reported [A ~ نقل]

منقیٰ *mūnaq'qa* N.M. large raisin ADJ. (rare) purged [A ~ تنقیہ]

منکا *man'ka* N.M. bead vertebrae (of neck) منکا ڈھلکنا *man'kā dha'laknā* V.I. be dying ; to be at the point of death

منکر *mūn'kir* N.M. (PL. منکرین *mūnkirīn'*) atheist منکر *mūn'kar* ADJ. strange disapproved منکر نکیر *mūn'kar nakīr'* N.M. names of two angels cross-questioning the dead in the grave [A ~ انکار]

منکسر *mūn'kasir,* منکسر المزاج *mūn'kasir-ul-mizāj'* ADJ. humble [A ~ انکسار]

منکشف **mūn'kashif** ADJ. revealed ; disclosed dawning (upon) : clear (to) [A ~ انکشاف]

منکوحہ **mankoo'ḥah** N.F. lawful wife ADJ. married (woman) [A ~ نکاح]

منگانا **mañgā'nā**, منگوانا **mañgvā'nā** V.T. cause to bring get an order placed

منگتا **mañg'tā** N.M. beggar mendicant ; borrower ADJ. (one) given to begging

منگتی **mañg'tī** N.F. beggar woman ; beggar ; maid borrower ADJ. (woman) given to begging or borrowing [A ~ مانگنا]

منگسر **mañg'sar** N.M. ninth Hindu month (corresponding to November-December)

منگل **mañ'gal** N.M. Tuesday (dial.) Mars bustle festivity pleasure song of pleasure منگل گانا **mañ'gal gā'nā** V.I. sing a song of joy or congratulation ; sing in praise or honour (of) منگل ہونا **mañ'gal ho'nā** V.I. be a lot of bustle or festivity منگلی **mañg'lī** N.F. irritable girl [S]

منگنی **mañg'nī** N.F. betrothal [~ مانگنا]

منگوانا **mañgvā'nā** V.T. (same as منگانا N.F ★)

منگوچی **mañgoo'chī** N.F. (same as مونگچی N.F. ★)

منگورا **mañgo'rā** N.M. seasoned gram meal roll منگوری **mañgo'rī** N.F. such vetch roll

منگیتر **mañge'tar** N.M. fiance N.F. fiancee [~ منگنی]

من من **min'-min** N.F. numble nasal tone slow working من من کرنا **min'-min kar'nā** منمنانا **minminā'nā** V.T. mumble speak through the nose go slow in work ; work slowly [ONO.]

منّنا **man'nā** V.T. be reconciled be soothed من من کر بگڑنا **man' man kar bi'gaṛnā** V.I. become estranged even after repeated reconciliations منوانا **manvā'nā** V.T. cause to agree cause to admit cause to recognize منوتی **manau'tī** N.F. reconciliation [~ ماننا]

منور **mūnav'var** ADJ. illuminated lustrous [A ~ تنور]

منون **mūnav'van** ADJ. nunated [A ~ تنوین]

منوہر **mano'har** ADJ. lovely bewitching [S]

منہ **mūñh'** (also written as مونہہ or مونھ) N.M. mouth face, countenance figure tongue opening, orifice guts regard direction منہ آنا **mūñh' ā'nā** V.T speak rudely or insolently have the thrush منہ آجانا **mūñh' ā jā'nā** V.I. have the thrush (اپنا سا) منہ لے کر رہ جانا **(ap'nā sā) mūñh' le' kar raih' jā'nā** V.I. lose hope feel ashamed منہ اترنا **mūñh' ūtar'nā** منہ اتنا سا نکل آنا **mūñh' it'nā sa ni'kal ā'nā** V.I. have the face thinned by weakness ; grow weak منہ اٹھا کر چلنا **mūñh' ū'ṭha kar chal'nā** V.I. walk carelessly منہ اٹھانا **mūñh' ūṭhā'nā** V.T. hold up one's head undertake a journey منہ اٹھائے **mūñh' ūṭhā''e** ADV. carelessly dauntlessly منہ اٹھائے چلے جانا **mūñh ūṭhā''e cha'le jā'nā** move ahead carelessly or fearlessly منہ اجلا ہو جانا **mūñh' ūj'lā ho jā'nā** V.I. succeed ; win success ; come off with flying colours منہ اس قابل ہونا **mūñh' is qā'bil ho'nā** V.I. be able to be able to face منہ اشکوں سے دھونا **mūñh' ash'koñ se dho'nā** V.I. weep bitterly منہ اندھیرے **mūñh' añdhe're** ADV. at dawn ; early in the morning منہ باندھ کے بیٹھنا **mūñh' bāndh' ke baiṭh'nā** V.I. hold one's tongue ; keep mum منہ برا بنانا **mūñh' bū'rā banā'nā** V express displeasure ; show dislike display effects of bad taste منہ بسورنا **mūñh' bisoor'nā** V.I. sulk ; left in the mouth ; pull a long face منہ بگاڑنا **mūñh' bigāṛ'nā** V.I. make faces make a way face منہ بگڑ جانا **mūñh' bi'gaṛ jā'nā** V.I. (of bad taste) be left in the mouth منہ بنا لینا **mūñh' banā' le'nā** V.I. sulk ; pull a long face منہ بنانا **mūñh' banā'nā** V.I. make faces pull a long face منہ بند کرنا **mūñh' bañd' kar'nā** V. cork put a stopper close the mouth worst (someone) in argument منہ بند کلی **mūñh'-bañd ka'lī** N.F. bud (fig.) virgin منہ بنوانا **mūñh' banvā'nā** V.T. (iron.) prove one's fitness for a task منہ بولا **mūñh'-bo'lā** ADJ. (F. منہ بولی **mūñh-bo'lī** adopted (child) sworn (brother, sister, etc.) منہ بولتی **mūñh'-bol'tī** ADJ. life-like (picture) منہ بھر آنا **mūñh' bha'r ā'nā** V.I. be cloyed منہ بھرائی (یا بھری) **mūñh bharā''ī** (or **bha'rī**) N.F bribe ; a sop منہ بھر دینا **mūñh' bhar' de'nā** V.T. bribe منہ بھر کے **mūñh' bhar ke** ADV. fully; much منہ بھر کوسنا **mūñh' bhar ke kos'nā** V.T. to heap curses (on) منہ پانا **mūñh' pā'nā** V.I. be heard find agreeable منہ پر **mūñh' par** ADV. to the face (of) منہ پر آئی بات **mūñh' par ā''ī bāt'** PH. on the point of being uttered منہ پر بات لانا **mūñh' par bāt' lā'na** V.T. & I. be on the point of uttering disclose a secret منہ پر بسنت پھولنا (یا پھلنا) **mūñh' par basañt' phool'nā** (or **phal'nā**) V.I. (dial.) grow pale منہ پر تھوک دینا **mūñh' par thook' de'na** V.T. spit on the face (of) منہ پر ٹھیکری رکھ لینا **mūñh' par ṭhīk'rī rakh le'na** V.I. refuse to have any regard for منہ پر پانی پھر جانا **mūñh' par pā'nī phir jā'nā** V.I. look healthier منہ پر پھینک مارنا **mūñh' par pheñk' mār'nā** V.I. return irritably منہ پر چڑھنا **mūñh' par chaṛh'nā** V.I. (of word, phrase, etc.) come easy or natural become an expletive منہ پر زردی کھنڈ جانا *mŭnh' par zar'dī khiṅd' jā'nā* v.i. grow pale منہ پر شفق پھولنا *mŭnh' par sha'faq phool'nā* v.i. (of face) be flushed with joy منہ پر فاختہ اڑ جانا *mŭnh' par fākh'tah ŭr' jā'nā* v.i. feel jittery منہ پر قفل (یا مہر) لگنا *mŭnh' par qŭf'l (or moh'r) lag'nā* v. be dumb-founded منہ پر کہنا *mŭnh' par kaih'nā* v.t. say to the face (of) منہ پر لانا *mŭnh' par lā'nā* v.i. say ; utter منہ پر لکھا ہونا *mŭnh' par li(k)'khā ho'nā* v.i. have visible proof منہ پر مارنا *mŭnh' par mār'nā* v.t. & i. return irritably tell to (someone's) face منہ پر مردنی چھانا (یا پھرنا) *mŭnh par mŭr'danī chā'nā (or phir'nā)* v.i. look ill have cadaverous looks منہ پر ناک نہ ہونا *mŭnh' par nāk' na ho'nā* v.i. be shameless منہ پر نمک ہونا *mŭnh' par na'mak ho'nā* v.i. be charming owing to nut-brown colour منہ پر نور نہ ہونا *mŭnh' par noor' na ho'nā* v.i. lack the appearance of piety be very weak منہ پر ہاتھ پھیرنا *mŭnh' par hāth' pher'nā* rub face with hand (do so) to threaten reprisal (do so) to vouch for truth of one's prediction منہ پر ہاتھ رکھنا *mŭnh' par hāth' rakh'nā* shut (one's or someone's) mouth with one's palm (do so) to enforce quietness منہ پر ہوائیاں اڑنا (یا چھوٹنا) *mŭnh par havā''iyāṅ ŭṛnā (or chhooṭ'nā)* v.i. change colour be confused have the blue funks منہ پڑنا *mŭnh' paṛ'nā* v.i. be eaten be talked about have the courage (to) منہ پڑی *mŭnh'-pa'ṛī* n.f. & adj. town-talk منہ پسار کر رہ جانا *mŭnh' pasār' kar raih jā'nā* v.i. look aghast be wonder-struck منہ پھٹ *mŭnh'-phaṭ* adj. & n.m. babbler abusive (person) منہ پھلانا *mŭnh' phŭlā'nā* v.t. be annoyed pull a long faee منہ پھیر دینا *mŭnh' pher' de'nā* v.t. cloy منہ پھیر لینا *mŭnh' pher le'nā* v.t. turn one's face (from) disown ; refuse to acknowledge منہ پھیلانا *mŭnh' phailā'nā* v.i. gape منہ پھیلائے *mŭnh' phailā''e* adv. agape منہ پیٹنا *mŭnh' piṭ'nā* v.t. slap oneself in the face منہ تک آنا *mŭnh' tak ā'nā* v.i. come close to the mouth be on the point of being uttered منہ تکنا *mŭnh' tak'nā* v.t. look blank ; have a blank look on the face gaze (at) look up to منہ تو دیکھو *mŭnh to de'kho* ph. (iron.) just look at it ; it (etc.) dare not منہ توڑ کے *mŭnh' toṛ' ke* ph. (reply) curtly ; bluntly منہ توڑنا *mŭnh' toṛ'nā* v.t. break (someone's) jaw-bone منہ ٹھتھانا (یا سجانا) *mŭnh' thŭthā'nā (or s' jā'nā)* v.i. show signs of annoyance or unhappiness منہ جوڑنا *mŭnh' joṛ'nā* v.t. backbite talk in whispering tones منہ جھٹالنا *mŭnh' jhŭṭāl'nā* v.t. eat just a little منہ چاٹنا *mŭnh' chāṭ'nā* v.t. lick the face kiss منہ چٹول *mŭnh' chaṭav'val* n.f. caress ; caressing منہ چڑانا *mŭnh chiṛā'nā* v.t. & i. make face ; mouth ; grimace منہ چڑھا *mŭnh' chaṛhā* adj. (f. منہ چڑھی *mŭnh' chaṛhī*) favourite منہ چڑھانا *mŭnh' chaṛhā'nā* v.t. show too much favour (to) cause to become saucy thus make a wry mouth منہ چڑھنا *mŭnh' chaṛh'nā* v.i. become the favourite (of) منہ چلانا *mŭnh' chalā'nā* v.i. go on eating dainties abuse منہ چلنا *mŭnh' chal'nā* v.i. move the tongue eat abuse talk irreverently منہ چور *mŭnh'-chor* adj. & adv. not facing others owing to shame or shyness منہ چوم کے چھوڑ دینا *mŭnh' choom' ke chhoṛ' de'nā* v.t. desert after achievement of own object منہ چومنا (یا چوم لینا) *mŭnh' choom'nā (or choom' le'na)* v.t. kiss ; caress منہ چھپانا *mŭnh chhŭpā'nā* v.i. hide one's face (from) ; observe 'purdah' from منہ چھوانا *mŭnh chho'ā'nā* v.t. treat with great but outward respect منہ خراب کرنا *mŭnh' kharāb' kar'nā* v.i. leave a bad taste in the mouth use foul language منہ سوکھ (یا خشک ہو) جانا *mŭnh' sookh' (or khŭsh'k ho) jā'nā* v.i. have a parched throat منہ در منہ *mŭnh' dar mŭnh'* adv. (col.) face to face منہ دکھانا *mŭnh' dikhā'nā* v.t. appear ; show one's face منہ دکھائی *mŭnh' dikhā''ī* n.f. present made to bride by groom's family on first meeting after marriage when she unveils before them منہ دھو رکھنا *mŭnh' dho' rakh'nā* v.i. give up all hope of منہ دے کر بات کرنا *mŭnh' de' kar bāt' kar'nā* v.i. talk with full attention منہ دیکھتے رہ جانا *mŭnh' dekh'te raih' jā'nā* v.i. stare (someone) in the face in amazement منہ دیکھنا *mŭnh' dekh'na* v.t. see the face (of) look up to (someone) look up to show regard (for) منہ دیکھے کی محبت *mŭnh' de'khe kī mahab'bat* n.f. mere show of friendship or love منہ دینا (یا ڈالنا) *mŭnh' de'na (or ḍāl'nā)* v.t. & i. attend (of animal) put its mouth to its feed bite منہ ڈھانپ کر رونا *mŭnh' ḍhāṅp ḍhāṅp' kar ro'nā* v.i. weep bitterly منہ ذرا سا نکل آنا *mŭnh' za'ra sā ni'kal ā'nā* v.i. grow week منہ رکھنا *mŭnh' rakh'nā* v.i. show regard (for) منہ زبانی *mŭnh'-zabā'nī* adv. from memory adv. verbal منہ زور *mŭnh'-zor*, منہ کا کڑا *mŭnh, kā ka'ṛā* adj. headstrong given to using harsh words hard mouthed منہ زوری *mŭnh'-zo'rī* n.f. headstrongness habit of منہ سنبھالنا *mŭnh' saṅ'bhal'nā* v.t. hold one's tongue منہ سی دینا *mŭnh' sī' de'nā* v.t. force to keep quiet silence to give hush-money منہ سی لینا *mŭnh' sī' le'nā* v.i. keep quiet ; keep mum منہ سے *mŭnh' se* adv. by word of mouth منہ سے بات نہ نکلنا *mŭnh' se bāt' na ni'kalnā* v.t. be unable to speak keep mum منہ سے بولو سر سے کھیلو *mŭnh' se bo'lo sir se khe'lo* ph. speak out don't keep quiet منہ سے پھوٹنا *mŭnh' se phooṭ'nā* v.i. (joc.) speak out منہ سے پھول جھڑنا *mŭnh' se phool' jhaṛ'nā* v.i speak lovely language speak sweetly منہ سے دودھ ٹپکنا *mūnh' se doodh' ṭa'pakna* V.I. be yet a child have little or no sense منہ سے رال ٹپکنا *mūnh se rāl' ṭa'pakna* V.I. (of mouth) water منہ سے نکلی کوٹھوں پر چڑھی *mūnh' se nik'li ko'ṭhon par charhi* PROV. secret once devulged becomes town talk منہ فق ہونا *mūnh' faq' ho'nā* V.I. change colour from fear منہ کا پھوڑا *mūnh' kā pho'ṛā* N.M. foul-mouthed person منہ کالا کرنا *mūnh' kā'la kar'na* V. incur dishonour bring disgrace (on) have unlawful sex relations منہ کا میٹھا پیٹ (یا دل) کا کھوٹا *mūnh' kā mi'ṭhā peṭ (or dil) kā kho'ṭā* PH. hypocrite fair without منہ کا کچا *mūnh ka kach'chā* ADJ. unreliable tender-mouthed (horse) منہ کا نوالہ *mūnh kā nivā'lah* ADJ. mouthful easily attained منہ کرنا *mūnh' kar'na* V.I. to confront ; to turn one's move (towards) attend burst open منہ کلنا *mūnh' kil'nā* V.I. keep mum refrain from opposition منہ کھلوانا *mūnh' khulva'na* V.T. provoke into saying unpleasant things make saucy منہ کھولنا *mūnh' khol'nā* V.T. open the mouth disclose abuse منہ کو خون (یا لہو) لگنا *mūnh' ko khoon (or la'hoo) lag'na* V.I. become carnivorous become cruel or rapacious منہ کو کالک لگانا *mūnh' ko kā'lak lagā'na* V.T. slander منہ کو لگام دو *mūnh' ko lagām' do* PH. shut up talk sense منہ کو لگنا *mūnh' ko lag'nā* V.I. know the good taste develop a relish for منہ کھائے آنکھ لجائے *mūnh' khā''e ānkh' lijā''e* PROV. one has to yield to one's benefactor منہ کھلنا *mūnh' khul'na* V.I. be about to say something become foul-mouthed منہ کے بل گرنا *mūnh' ke bal gir'na* V.I. fall face foremost ; fall flat منہ کے (یا سے) بات چھیننا (یا اچک لینا) *mūnh' ki (or se) bāt' chhin'na (or u'chak le'na)* V.I. say what (someone) was about to say منہ کی کھانا *mūnh' ki khā'na* V.I. suffer disgrace منہ کیلنا *mūnh' kil'nā* V.T. strike dumb force to keep quiet through charm منہ لال کرنا *mūnh' lāl' kar'nā* redden (one's) lips cause cheeks to flush (with slap) منہ لال ہونا *mūnh' lāl' ho'nā* V.I. (of face) flush with anger منہ لپیٹ کر پڑ رہنا *mūnh' lapeṭ' kar paṛ' raih'na* V.I. lie down in corner in low spirits or in protest منہ لٹکانا *mūnh' laṭkā'nā* V.I. pull a long face منہ لگانا *mūnh' lagā'nā* V.I. show undue favour to منہ لگنا *mūnh' lag'nā* V. suit the palate become used to اپنا سا منہ لے کر رہ جانا *ap'nā sā mūnh' le ke raih' ja'na* V.I. remain silent through shame منہ مارنا *mūnh' mār'nā* V. (of animal) bite put mouth in feed منہ مانگا *mūnh'-mān'ga* ADJ. (F. منہ مانگی *mūnh'-mān'gi*) asked for prayed for منہ مانگی مراد پانا *mūnh' mān'gi murād' pā'na* V.I. attain one's prayed for wish منہ مانگی موت بھی نہیں آتی *mūnh'-mān'gi maut' bhi nahīn ā'ti* PH. you cannot have every thing you wish منہ مانگے دام *mūnh'-mān'ge dām'* N.M. PL. price demanded fancy price منہ موڑنا *mūnh' moṛ'na* V. turn away once face (from) abstain from, desist (from) shun avoid منہ میٹھا کرانا *mūnh' mī'ṭha karā'nā* V.T. give a treat bribe منہ میٹھا کرنا *mūnh' mī'ṭhā kar'na* V.T. give (someone) a treat bribe sweaten the mouth (of) منہ میں آنا *mūnh' men ā'na* V.I. come to one's lips ; be about to be uttered منہ میں بولنا *mūnh men bol'nā* N.M. mumble منہ میں پانی بھر آنا *mūnh' men pā'nī bhar ā'na* V.I. (of mouth) water منہ میں پانی چوانا *mūnh men pā'nī chu'āna* V.T. trickle water into dying person's mouth منہ میں پڑنا *mūnh' men paṛ'nā* V.I. be eaten become talk of the town منہ میں پڑھنا *mūnh' men paṛh'na* V.T. read or pronounce inaudibly منہ (یا دانتوں) میں تنکا لینا *mūnh' (or dān'ton) men tin'ka le'na* V.I. acknowledge defeat show servility منہ میں خاک *mūnh' men khāk'* V.T. never to Hell with it منہ میں دانت نہ پیٹ میں آنت *mūnh' men dānt' na peṭ' men ānt'* PH. very old ; decrepit old person منہ میں گھنگھنیاں ڈال کر بیٹھنا *mūnh' men ghūngh'niyān ḍal' kar baiṭh'na* V.I. keep quiet when it is essential to speak (کے) منہ میں گھی شکر *(ke) mūnh' men ghī' shak'kar* PH. thank you for this wonderful piece of news come out with the happy news منہ نوچ لینا *mūnh' noch' le'na* V.T. scratch one's face (in intense grief) منہ نہ دیکھنا *mūnh' na dekh'na* V.T. disdain to look at منہ نہ کرنا (کی طرف) *(kī ta'raf) mūnh' na kar'nā* V.T. not to go (towards) have no truck (with) منہ نہ کھلواؤ *mūnh' na khul'vā''o* PH. do not force to disclose your secrets or weak points منہ نہ لگانا *mūnh' na lagā'na* V.T. not to encourage someone to become familiar منہ ہونا *mūnh' ho'na* V.I. have regard (for) dare کیا منہ ہے *kyā' mūnh' hai* PH. dare he منہ ہی منہ میں *mūnh' hi mūnh men* ADV. to one's self mumbling

منہا *minhā'* ADJ. & ADV. subtracted deducted منہا کرنا *minhā' kar'na* V.T. subtract منہائی *minhā''ī* N.F. subtraction deduction [A ~ من from + ہا]

منہاج *minhāj'* N.M. programme (rare) path [A ~ نہج]

منہار *manhār'*, منہیار *manhiyār'* N.M. maker or vendor of glass bangles منہاری *manhā'rī*, منہیاری *manhiyā'rī* N.F. female bangle-vendor

منہدم *mūn'hadim* ADJ. demolished [A ~ انہدام]

منہدی *meh'dī* N.F. (more favoured but less used form of مہندی ★

منہزم *mūn'hazim* ADJ. routed [A ~ انہزام]

منہضم *mūn'hazim* ADJ. digestible [A ~ انہضام]

منہمک *mūn'hamak* ADJ. absorbed ; engrossed [A ~ انہماک]

منہی *man'hī* ADJ. forbidden ; prohibited ; banned منہیات *manhiyyāt'* N.F. PL. forbidden things ; unlawful things [A ~ نہی]

منی *mū'nī* N.M. Hindu recluse with a vow of silence [S]

منی[1] *ma'nī* N.F. money منی آرڈر *ma'nī ār'ḍar* N.M. money order ; M.O. [E]

منی[2] *ma'nī* N.F. semen ; sperm [A]

منی[3] *ma'nī* N.F. egotism [P ~ من]

منیب *mūnīb'* N.M. penitent (rare) representative [A ~ انابت]

مینیجر *mai'nejar* (or *mane'jar*) N.M. manager [E]

منیر *mūnīr'* ADJ. illuminating [A ~ نور]

منیم *mūnīm'* N.M. (dial.) manager accountant منیمی *mūnī'mī* N.F. office of manager-cum-accountant [A ~ منیب CORR.]

مو *mau* N.F. bloom of youth مو پر آنا *mau par ā'nā* V.I. be in the prime of youth

مو *moo* N.M. (lit.) hair موباف *moo-bāf'* N.M. tassled strings for plaiting hair مو بہ مو *moo ba-moo'* ADV. exactly entirely ; in every part موشگافی *moo-shigā'fī* N.F. hairsplitting موشگافی کرنا *moo-shigā'fī kar'nā* V.I. split hairs موقلم *moo'-qa'lam* N.M. painters brush موئے زہار *moo-e zehār'* N.M. pubes ; pubic hair [P]

موا *mū''ā* ADJ. (F. موئی *mū''ī*) dead cursed ; damned ; d—d موا بادل *mū''ā bā'dal* N.M. sponge [مرنا ~]

مواثیق *mavā'sīq* N.M. (PL. of میثاق N.M. ★)

مواج *mavvāj'* ADJ. billowy stormy [A ~ موج]

مواجب *mavā'jib* N.M. salary dues [A ~ ما whatever + وجب was due]

مواجہہ *mūvā'jahah* N.M. confrontation بالمواجہ *bil-mūvā'jahah* PH. face-to-face [A ~ وجہ]

مواخات *mo'ākhāt'* N.F. brotherhood fraternization [A ~ اخ brother]

مواخذہ *mo'ā'khazah* N.M. accountability; calling to account arrest penalization مواخذہ کرنا *mo'ā'khazah kar'nā* V.T. call to account penalize [A ~ اخذ]

مواد *mavād'* N.M. matter raw material pus (arch.) humour مواد گندہ (یا فاسد) *gan'dah* (or *fā'sid*) *mavād'* N.M. matter bad humour [A ~ SING. مادہ *mād'dah*]

موازنہ *mo'ā'zanah* N.M. comparison [A ~ وزن]

موازی *mo'ā'zī* N.M. account of (annas, pice, paisa, etc.) ADJ. (rare) opposite [A]

مواشی *mavā'shī* N.M. (PL. same as مویشی N.M. PL. ★)

مواصلات *mo'āsalāt'* N.M. PL. communications نظام مواصلات *nizā'm-e mo'āsalāt* N.M. communications system [A ~ SING. مواصلت ~ وصل]

مواضع *mavā'ze'* N.M. (PL. of موضع N.M. ★)

مواطن *mavā'tin* N.M. (PL. of موطن or وطن N.M. ★)

مواظبت *mo'ā'zabat* N.F. regularity ; doing some thing regularly assiduity مواظبت کرنا *mo'ā'zabat kar'nā* V. do something regularly [A]

مواعظ *mavā''iz* N.M. (PL. of موعظت N.F. ★)

مواعید *mavā'īd'* N.M. promises [A ~ SING. میعاد]

موافق *mo'ā'fiq* ADJ. agreeable suitable conformable consonant ADV. for ; in favour (of) in accordance (with) موافق آنا *mo'ā'fiq ā'nā* V.I. agree (with) موافقت *mo'ā'faqat* N.F. agreement ; accord suitability conformity consonance accordance موافقت کرنا *mo'ā'faqat kar'nā* V.T. agree (with) [A]

مواقع *mavā'qe* N.M. (PL. of موقع N.M. ★)

موالات *mo'ālāt'* N.F. co-operation ترک موالات *tar'k-e mo'ālāt'* N.M. non-co-operation [A ~ ولی]

موالی *mavā'lī* N.M. slaves servants (rare) clients [A ~ SING. مولیٰ]

موالید *mavālīd'* N.M. PL. types of creation kingdoms (rare) progeny موالید ثلاثہ *mavālī'd-e salā'sah* N.M. PL. three kingdoms of nature ; animal, vegetable and mineral ; kingdoms [A ~ SING. مولود]

موانست *mo'ā'nasat* N.F. familiarity mutual love [A ~ انس]

موانع *mavā'ne* N.M. PL. obstacles impediments [A ~ مانع]

مواہب *mavā'hib* N.M. (PL. of موہبت N.F. ★)

موبد *moo'bid* N.M. Zoroastrian priest

موت *maut* N.F. death decease mortality موت آنا *maut ā'nā* V.T. die موت آنکھوں تلے پھرنا *maut āṅ'khoṅ ta'le phir'nā* V.I. feel approach of death موت پڑنا *maut paṛ'nā* V.I. (fig.) shun fear موت چاہنا (یا مانگنا) *maut' chāh'nā* (or *māṅg'nā*) V.T. & I. pray (for someone's) death be disgusted with life موت کا بازار گرم ہونا maut kā bāzār' gar'm ho'nā V.T. (of mortality) be widespread موت سر پر کھیلنا (یا سوار ہونا) maut'. sir par khel'nā (or savār' ho'nā) V.I. (of death) approach موت کے دن پورے کرنا maut ke din poo're kar'nā V.I. live in very poor circumstances موت کے گھاٹ اتارنا maut ke ghāṭ' ūtār'nā V.T. kill ; murder موت نے گھر دیکھ لیا ہے maut ne ghar' dekh' li'yā hai PH. death has singled out this house for visitations اپنی موت مرنا ap'nī maut' mar'nā V.I. die a natural death موتا mau'tā N.F. (dial.) death [A]

موت moot' N.M. (vul.) urine ; piss موتنا moot'nā V.I. (vul.) make water ; urinate ; pass urine

موتمر mo''tamar N.M. conference consultative committee [A ~ امر]

موتھا mo'thā N.M. a kind of grass its root medicinally

موتی mau'tā N.M. PL. the dead [A ~ موت maut]

موتی mo'tī N.M. pearl ADJ. pearls موتی پرونا mo'tī piro'nā V.I. string pearls speak eloquently write a lovely hand موتی چور mo'tī-choor N.M. tiny sweet drops N.F. sparking eyes (of Kabul pigeon) موتی چور کے لڈو mo'tī-choor ke lad'doo N.M. PL. balls rolled frout these drops موتی خاک میں رولنا mo'tī khāk' men rol'nā V.I. waste a treasure موتی رولنا mo'tī rol'nā V.T. collect pearls accumulate wealth موتی کوٹ کوٹ کر بھرے ہونا mo'tī kooṭ kooṭ kar bha're ho'nā V.I. (of eyes) be very lovely موتی کی آب mo'tī kī āb' N.F. lustre of a pearl موتی کی سی آب mo'tī kī sī āb' N.F. lustre like that of a pearl موتی کی سیپی mo'tī kī sī'pī N.F. shell موتیوں سے مانگ بھرنا mo'tiyon se māng bhar'nā V.I. string pearls in hair موتیوں کا جھالا mo'tiyon kā jhā'lā N.M. pearly ear-drops موتیوں کی لڑی mo'tiyon kī la'ṛī N.F., موتیوں کا ہار mo'tiyon kā hār' N.M. pearl necklace موتیوں میں تولنا mo'tiyon men tol'nā V.T. weigh (someone) with pearls do (someone) great honour

موتیا mo'tiyā N.F. a species of jasmine; jasmine ADJ. cream-colour موتیا بند mo'tiyā-band N.M. cataract

موٹا mo'ṭā ADJ. (F. موٹی mo'ṭī) fat ; plump ; corpulent bulky thick coarse large bold (type, etc.) major gross low type موٹا اناج mo'ṭā anāj' N.M. coarse grain; inferior kind of cereals موٹا تازہ mo'ṭā tā'zah ADJ. stout موٹا جھوٹا mo'ṭā jho'ṭā ADJ inferior ; low quality coarse موٹی اسامی mo'ṭī asā'mī N.F. rich person wealthy client موٹی بات mo'ṭī bāt N.F. straight talk plain-speaking موٹی گالی mo'ṭī gā'lī N.F. gross abuse

موٹر mo'ṭar N.F. motor-car motor موٹر ڈرائیور mo'ṭar ḍarā''ivar N.M. driver ; chauffer موٹر کار mo'ṭar-kar N.F. motor-car [E]

موٹھ moṭh N.M. kind of vetchling موٹھ چلانا mo'ṭh chalā'nā V.T. charm ; cast a spell (over)

موٹھ mooṭh N.F. fist handle ; grip موٹھ کرنا mooṭh kar'nā V.T. hold (quail, etc.) in hand and press it to make it ready for fight موٹھ مارنا mooṭh mār'nā V.I. masturbate

موٹھڑا moṭh'ṛā N.M. gold (etc.) chain on grip of sword (etc.)

موثر mo''as'sir ADJ. effective touching efficacious موثر ہونا mo''as'sir ho'nā V.I. be effective ; have effect prove efficacious [A ~ تاثیر]

موج mauj N.F. (PL. امواج amwāj') wave surge, billow whim; caprice ecstasy; rapture موج آنا mauj ā'nā V.I. (of wave) wave (of) rise or advance have a whim موج خیز mauj'-khez ADJ. billowy stormy موج زن mauj'-zan ADJ. billowy stormy ; tumultous raging موج زن ہونا mauj'-zan ho'nā V.I. (of storm or passion) rage موج زنی mauj-za'nī N.F. raging (of storm, passion, etc.) موج کرنا mauj'kar'nā V.I. enjoy oneself ; have a good time موج مارنا mauj'mār'nā V.I. billow enjoy oneself ; have a good time موج میں آنا mauj' men ā'nā V.I. be overjoyed . be in a fit of emotion feel enraptured موج نسیم mau'j-e-nasīm' N.F. waft of breeze موجہ mau'jah N.M. (lit.) billow موجی mau'jī N.M. & ADJ. cheerful (person) capricious (person) من موجی man-mau'jī N.M. & ADJ. whimsical or capricious (person) [A]

موجب moo'jib N.M. reason (of); cause (of) کے بموجب ke ba-moo'jib N.M. according to ; in accordance with pursuant to consequent upon [A ~ وجوب]

موجد moo'jid N.M. (PL. موجدین moojidīn') inventor (rare) cause (of) [A ~ ایجاد]

موجز moo'jaz N.M. compendium [A ~ ایجاز]

موجل mo'aj'jal ADJ. payable at a later date (of money settled on wife) payable on demand [A ~ اجل]

موجود maujood' N.M. that which is or exists ADJ. present ; existing existent extant ready at hand available موجودہ maujoo'dah ADJ. present present-day current موجودات maujoodāt' N.F. PL. beings existing things موجودگی maujood'gī (ped. -da-) N.F. presence ; existence موجودگی میں maujood'gī men ADV. in the presence (of) ; during the existence (of) during the currency (of) [A ~ وجود]

موجہ *mau'jah* N.M. موجی *mau'ji* N.M. & ADJ. (see under موج N.F. ★)

موجہ *müvaj'jah* ADJ. valid ; plausible (of reason) بدونِ عذرِ موجہ *bi-doo'n-e 'üz'r-e müvaj'jah* PH. without any valid reason [A ~ توجیہہ]

موچ *moch'* N.F. sprain موچ آنا *moch' a'na* V.I sprain (one's foot, etc.)

موچرس *moch'ras* N.M. gum yielded by 'semal' ; 'semal' gum

موچنا *moch'na* N.M. tweezers [~ P موچینہ]

موچھ *moochh* N.F. (same as مونچھ N.F. ★) موچھل *mooch'chhal* ADJ. & N.M. one having large moustaches

موچی *mo'chi* N.M. shoe-maker ; cobbler موچن *mo'chan* N.F. cobbler's wife female member of cobbler's family

موحد *mo''ah'hid* ADJ. & N.M. unitarian ; person believing in the unity of God موحدانہ *mo'ah-hida'nah* ADJ. unitarian [A ~ توحید]

موحش *movah'hish* ADJ. bewildering shocking [A ~ وحشت]

موخر *mo'akh'khar* ADJ. posterior put at the end موخر الذکر *mo'kh'khar-üzzik'r* ADJ. the latter last-mentioned

مودب *mo'ad'dab* ADJ. respectful disciplined well mannered polite , civil ; courteous ; مودبانہ *mo'addaba'nah* ADV. respectfully courteously [A ~ ادب]

مودت *mavad'dat* N.F. friendship affection love [A ~ ود]

مودھو *mo'dhoo* N.M. simpletion

مودی *mo'di* N.M. shopkeeper grocer keeper of provision stores مودی خانہ *mo'di-kha'nah* N.M. pantry

موذن *mo'az'zin* N.M. one who shouts the call to prayer [A ~ اذان]

موذی *moo'zi* N.M. tormentor miser ADJ. obnoxious pernicious tyrannical wicked miserly ; niggardly موذی کا مال *moo'zi ka mal'* N.M. miser's property or belongings [A ~ ایذا]

مور *mor'* N.M. peacock مورپنکھی *mor'-pan'khi* N.F. hand-fan opening out like peacock feathers peacock barge مورچال *mor'-chal* N.F peacock dance ; dancing on arms with feet in the air مورچھل *mor'-chhal* N.M. fan made of peacock feathers horse-hair fly-whisk مور کی سی گردن *mor ki si gar'dan* N.F. long and be

مور

مورنی *mor'ni* N.F. pea-hen

مور *mor* N.F. ant مور و ملخ *mo'r-o-ma'lakh* N.M. ants and locust [P]

مور *maur* N.M. blossom (of mango tree) پر مور آنا *par maur' a'na* V. (of mango tree) blossom

مورت *moo'rat* N.F. image figure figurine statuette مورتی *moo'ti* N.F. (dial.) idol مورتی پوجا *moor'ti-poo'ja* N.F. idol-worship ; idolatry

مورث *moo'ris* N.M. legator ancestor , progenitor مورثِ اعلیٰ *moo'ris-e a''la* N.M. remote ancestor [A ورثہ]

مورچہ[1] *mor'chah* N.M. trench entrenchment مورچہ بندی کرنا *mor'cha-ban'di kar'na* V. entrench dig trenches مورچہ جیتنا (یا لینا یا مارنا) *mor'chah jit'na* (or *le'na* or *mar'na*) V.T. capture enemy's trenches

مورچہ[2] *mor'chah* N.M. rust مورچہ کھانا (یا لگنا) *mor'chah kha'na* (or *lag'na*) V.T. rust [P]

مورخ *mo'ar'rikh* N.M. (PL. مورخین *mo'arrikhin'*) historian annalist مورخانہ *mo'arrikha'nah* ADJ. like a historian [~ تاریخ]

مورخہ *mo'ar'rakhah* ADV. dated [A ~ PREC.]

مورد *mau'rid* N.M. place of descent butt (of) object (of) موردِ الزام *mau'rid-e ilzam'* ADJ butt of accusation , object of indictment موردِ الطاف *mau'rid-e altaf'* ADJ. object or focus of favour [A ~ ورود]

مورکھ *moo'rakh* ADJ. & N.M. foolish (person)

موروثی *mauroo'si* ADJ. hereditary patrimonial ancestral موروثی اسامی *mauroo'si asa'mi* N.M hereditary tenant [A ~ ورثہ]

موری *mo'ri* N.F. drain drainpipe orifice

موڑ *mor* N.M. bend , turning meander موڑنا *mor'na* V.T. bend turn twist drive back restrain

موڑھا *moo'rha* N.M. (same as مونڈھا *moon'dha* N.M. ★)

موزوں *mauzoon'* ADJ. apt proper ; appropriate fit suitable metrical symmatrical rythmical well-balanced well-adjusted well-measured agreeable شعر موزوں کرنا *she''r mauzoon' kar'na* V.T. versify , compose verse) موزوں ہونا *mauzoon' ho'na* N.M. (of verse) be composed be suitable موزونیت *mauzooniy'yat* N.F aptness suitability [A ~ وزن]

موزہ *mau'zah* N.M. sock kid sock موزے کا گھاؤ میاں جانے یا پاؤں *mau'ze ka gha''o miyan ja'ne ya* PROV. the wearer best knows where

موسیٰ *moo'sā* N.M. Moses (rare) razor موسائی *moosā'ī*, موسوی *moo'savī* ADJ. Mosaic Jewish Hebraic [A ~ H]

مؤسس *mo'as'sis* N.M. (PL. مؤسسین *mo'assisīn'*) founder [A ~ تاسیس]

موسل *moo'sal* N.M. threshing pestle

موسلادھار *moos'lā-dhār* ADJ. heavey (rain) موسلادھار برسنا (یا بارش ہونا) *moos'lā-dhār ba'rasnā* (or *bā'rish ho'nā*) V.I. rain cats and dogs موسلی *moos'li* N.F. root of (plant)

موسم *mau'sam* (ped. *mau'sim*) N.M. (PL. مواسم *mavā'sim*) season time موسم برشگال *mau'sam-e barshagāl'* N.M. rainy season ; the rains ; monsoon season موسم بہار *mau'sam-e bahār'* N.M. spring season ; spring موسم حج *mausim-e haj'* N.M. pilgrimage season موسم خزاں *mau'sam-e khizāñ'* N.M. autumn season ; autumn ; fall موسم سرما *mau'sam-e sar'mā* N.M. winter season ; winter موسم گرما *mau'sam-e gar'mā* N.M. summer season ; summer موسم گل *mau'sam-e gul'* N.M. spring موسمی *mau'samī* ADJ. seasonal season's malarial موسمی بخار *mau'samī bukhār'* N.M. malaria [A ~ موسم *mau'sim* fair; gathering]

موسنا *moos'nā* V.T. wheedle defraud

موسوم *mausoom'* ADJ. called ; named کے نام سے موسوم کرنا *ke nam se mausoom' kar'nā* V.T. name (someone something) [A ~ اسم]

موسی *mau'sī* N.F. (dial.) mother's sister ; aunt

موسیقار *moosī'kar'* N.M. singer ; musician (arch.) legendary song bird with numerous holes in beak [~ A ~ G ~ FOLL.]

موسیقی *mausī'qī* N.F. music [~ A موسیقی *moo'sīqā* CORR. ~ G]

موش *moosh* N.M. mouse موش کور *moo'sh-e kor'* N.M. mole [P]

موصوف *mausoof'* N.M. qualified noun ADJ. (F. موصوفہ *mausoo'fah*) above-mentioned (person) celebrated اسم موصوف *is'm-e mausoof'* N.M. qualified noun [A ~ وصف]

موصول *mausool'* N.M. (gram.) relative pronoun ADJ. joined ; connected ; related اسم موصول *is'm-e mausool'* N.M. relative pronoun [A ~ وصل]

موصی *moo'sī* N.M. testator testate موصیہ *moo'siyah* N.F. testatrix موصیٰ الیہ *moo'sā-ilaih'* ADJ. one is whose favour a will is drawn legatee ; devisee موصیٰ بہ *moo'sa be-hī* ADJ. bequest موصیٰ لہ *moo'sā-la-hoo* ADJ. legatee ; devisce [A ~ وصیت]

موضح *moo'zeh* N.M. that which explains ADJ. explanatory , expositary [A ~ ایضاح]

موضع *mauza'* (ped. *mau'ze'*) N.M. village [A ~ وضع]

موضوع *mauzoo'* N.M. subject topic postulate ADJ. placed, manufactured unauthentic ; fake [A ~ وضع]

موطن *mau'tin* N.M. (PL. مواطن *mavā'tin*) native land [A ~ وطن]

موعدت *mau'idat* N.F. promise [A ~ وعدہ]

موعود *mau'ood'* ADJ. (F. موعودہ *mau'oo'dah*) promised [A ~ وعدہ]

موعظت *mau''izat* N.F. advice exhortation [A doublet of وعظ]

موفور *maufoor'* ADJ. abundant plentiful ; copious [A ~ وفور]

موقت *mo'aq'qat* ADJ. periodic temporary provisional موقت الیشوع *mo'aq'qit-ushū yoo''* ADJ. periodically published ; periodical [A ~ وقت]

موقر *mo'aq'qar* ADJ. esteemed [A ~ توقیر]

موقع *mau'qā'* (ped. *mau'qe'*) N.M. (PL. مواقع *mavā'qe'*) time ; occasion opportunity place where anything happens ; spot site ; situation place موقع بہ موقع *mau'qa' ba-mau'qa'* ADV. as and when needed ; whenever the need arose موقع پر *mau'qa' par* ADV. on the spot at the proper time موقع نکل جانا *mau'qa' ni'kal jā'nā* V. let slip an opportunity موقع واردات *mau'qa'-e vār'dāt'* (or *-ri-*) N.M. place of occurrence موقع ہاتھ سے نہ دینا *mau'qa' hāth' se na de'nā* V.T. not to let slip an opportunity ; take time by the forelook [A ~ وقوع]

موقف *mau'qif* N.M. stand ; position [A ~ وقوف]

موقوف *mauqoof'* ADJ. dismissed abolished suspended dependent (on) (rare) endowed موقوف رکھنا *mauqoof' rakh'nā* V.T. put off ; postpone موقوف کرنا *mauqoof' kar'nā* V.T. dismiss abolish موقوف ہونا *mauqoof' ho'nā* V.T. & I. be dismissed be abolished depend (on) موقوفی *mauqoo'fī* N.F. dismissal abolition suspension ; postponement [A ~ PREC.]

موکد *mo'ak'kad* ADJ. (F. موکدہ *mo'ak'kadah*) stressed emphasized [A ~ تاکید]

موکل *mo'ak'kil* N.M. (lawyer's) client موکل *mo'ak'kal* N.M. deputy trustee guardian angel supernatural being entrusted with some duty [A ~ وکیل]

موکھا *mo'khā* N.M. aperture small hole in wall for talk with neighbour (dial.) pigeon-hole

موگرا *mog'rā* N.M. double jasmine mallet

موگری mog'ri N.F. club for physical exercise mallet battledore

مول mool' N.M. (dial.) principal مول سے بیاج پیارا mool' se bayaj' paya'ra PROV. children's children are dear than children themselves

مول mol' N.M. price ; purchase money مول تول mol' tol N.M. haggling مول دینا mol' de'na pay the price purchase for a consideration مول لینا mol' le'na V.I. buy on payment invite trouble, etc.

مولی (or مولا) mau'la N.M. master lord God (rare) freed slave ; client مولا بخش mau'la-bakh'sh N.M. (fig.) rod ; cane ; baton مولینا (or مولانا) maula'na N.M. title of respect for Muslim religious scholars ; revered person (rare) my lord مولوی N.M. ★ [A]

مولد mau'lid N.M. birthplace native land (rare) nativity

مولسری maul'sari N.F. (tree bearing) jasmine-like flower

مولف mo'al'lif N.M. (مولفہ mo'al'lifah N.F. compiler مولفہ mo'al'lafah ADJ. compiled by [A ~ تالیف]

مولود maulood' N.M. baby (usu. مولود شریف maulood' sharif') meeting celebrating the Holy Prophet's nativity [A ~ ولادت]

مولوی maul'vi (ped. mau'lavi) Muslim priest ; Muslim divine [A ~ مولیٰ] [A]

مولی moo'li N.F. radish مولی گاجر کی طرح moo'li ga'jar ki tar'h PH. indiscriminately

موم mom N.M. wax موم بتی mom'-bat'ti N.F. candle موم جامہ mom'-ja'mah N.M. cere-cloth ; oil-cloth موم دل mom'-dil ADJ. tender-hearted موم کی گڑیا (یا مریم) mom' ki gur'ya (or mar'yam) N.F. delicate woman موم کی ناک mom' ki nak ADJ. fickle-minded docile ; amenable موم ہونا mom' ho'na V.I. soften be appeased ; be mollified مومی mo'mi ADJ. wax waxen soft like wax مومی کاغذ mo'mi ka'ghaz N.M. wax-paper مومی موتی mo'mi mo'ti N.M. glass bead filled with wax ; imitation pearl [P]

مومن mo'min N.M. believer ; faithful Shiete Muslim weaver ADJ. having full faith مرد مومن mar'd-e mo'min N.M. a Muslim having perfect faith in God [A ~ ایمان]

مومیا momiya N.F. mummy مومیانہ momiya'na ADV. mummify مومیائی momiya''i N.F. medicine supposedly extracted from rocks or human body and regarded as a cure for broken bones مومیائی نکالنا momiya''i nikal'na V.I. extract this juice drive like a slave [~ A moomi'ya

مؤنت ma'oo'nat N.F. provisions : daily food [A]

مونث mo'an'nas ADJ. feminine N.M. feminine gender [A ~ تانیث]

مونج moonj N.F. rush twisted into strings or ropes

مونچھ moonchh موچھ moochh N.F. moustache(s) ; mustachis(s) مونچھ کا بال moonchh' ka bal N.M. (fig.) one very close (to) outspoken person مونچھ مروڑا روٹی توڑا moonchh' maro'ra ro'ti to'ra PH. bragging idler مونچھکڑے moonchhak're N.M. PL. large moustaches مونچھوں کو تاؤ دینا moonch'hon ko ta''o de'na V.T. twirl one's moustaches مونچھیں نیچی کرنا moon'chhen ni'chi kar'na V.T. accept defeat

مونڈنا moond'na V.T. (arch.) shut ; close cover

مونڈنا moond'na V.T. shave cheat ; impose upon مونڈن moon'dan N.M. (dial.) first shaving of Hindu baby's head مونڈی کاٹا moon'di-ka'ta ADJ. (dial.) accursed ; cussed

مونڈھا mon'dha N.M. shoulder shoulder gusset مونڈھوں کے فرشتے mon'dhon ke firish'te N.M. PL. shoulder-angels (deputed to record one's actions)

مونڈھا moon'dha, موڑھا moo'rha N.M. reed stool reed chain

مونس moo'nis N.M. companion consoler ; sympathetic friend مونس تنہائی moo'nis-e tanha''i N.M. (fig.) book (as friend in solitude) [A ~ انس]

مون سون maun'soon N.M. monsoon [E ~ A موسم]

مونگ moong N.M. a kind of vetchling مونگ پھلی moong'-pha'li N.F. groundnut ; peanut مونگچی moong'chi, منگوچی mango'chi N.F. vetch ball seasoned and dehydrated مونگیا moon'giya ADJ. dark green

مونگا moon'ga N.M. coral مونگے کا جزیرہ moon'ge ka jazi'rah N.M. coral island

مونھ munh, مونہہ munh N.M. (same as منہ munh N.M. ★)

موون mo'van موَن mon N.M. dough kneaded in butter-oil

موہبت mau'hibat N.F. مواہب mava'hib) grant; bestowal munificence [A]

موہنا moh'na V.T. fascinate ; captivate charm allure موہ moh N.F. fascination; captivation charm ; allurement موہ لینا moh' le'na V.T. fascinate ; captivate charm ; allure موہن mo'han ADJ. (dial.) captivating N.M. (dial.) sweetheart appellation of Krishna موہنی mo'hani N.F. (dial.) charm beauty

ADJ (dial.) fascinating, captivating charming; alluring

موہوم *mauhoom'* ADJ. unreal imaginary fancied [A ~ وہم]

مؤید *mo'ay'yid* N.M. helper one who seconds ADJ. helping reinforcing

مؤید *mo'ay'yad* ADJ. aided strengthened reinforced [A ~ تائید]

مویز *mavez'* N.M. raisin مویز منقیٰ *mave'z-e mūnaq'qā* N.M. seedless raisin [P]

مویشی *mave'shī* (ped. مواشی *mavā'shī*) N.M. PL. cattle quadrupeds [~ A CORR. of ماشیہ ~ SING. مواشی]

مہ *mah* N.M. moon month مہ پارہ *mah-pārah* N.M. beauty مہ جبیں *mah-jabīn'*, مہ طلعت *mah-tal''at*, مہ لقا *mah-liqā'*, مہ وش *mah'-vash* ADJ & N.F. exquisite beauty [~ A ماہ CONT.]

مہ *meh* ADJ. chief big; great [P]

مہا *ma'hā* ADJ. (dial.) big; great, arrant; egregious ADV. greatly exceedingly مہا اوت *ma'hā-oot* ADJ. arrant fool مہا بلی *ma'hā-ba'lī* ADJ. (dial.) very powerful N.M. this as Moghal emperor Akbar's title مہا بھارت *ma'hā-bhā'rat* N.F. great war name of famous Sanskrit epic مہا پاپ *ma'hā-pāp'* N.M. (dial.) great crime cardinal sin مہاتما *mahāt'mā* ADJ. & N.M. (dial.) pious man مہاجن *mahā'jan* N.M. Hindu banker (dial.) big gun مہاجنی *mahā'janī* N.F. Hindu banker's business banking مہاراج *mahārāj'* N.M. sovereign; maharajah INT. (as polite form of address) my lord, sir مہاراجہ *mahārā'jah* N.M. sovereign chief prince مہاراج ادھیراج *mahārāj' adhirāj'* N.M. & INT. mighty sovereign مہارانی *mahārā'nī* N.F. chief consort of a 'maharajah' مہا سبھا *ma'hā-sa'bhā* N.F. (dial.) major organization of Hindus Mahasabha مہا سبھائی *ma'hā-sabhā''ī* N.M. & ADJ. Mahasabhite مہا شیر *ma'hā-sher'* N.M. a kind of fish; mahseer

مہابت *mahā'bat* N.F. fear dread awe [A ~ ہیبت]

مہاجر *mohājir* N.M. refugee immigrant emigrant evacuee (rare) one who abandon's something مہاجرت *mohā'jarat* N.F. abandoning migration flight [A ~ ہجرت]

مہار *mohār'* N.F (camel's) nose-string بے مہار *be-mohār'* ADJ. unbridled; unrestrained intractable شتر بے مہار *shū'tūr-e be-mohār'* N.M way ward person intractable person maverick

مہارت *mahā'rat* N.F. skill experience proficiency expertness [A ~ ماہر]

مہارنی *mohār'nī* N.F. cacophonous chorus (as by children memorizing tables)

مہاسا *mohā'sā* N.M. pimple مہاسے نکلنا *mohā'se ni'kalnā* V.I. have pimples

مہال *mohāl'* N.F. beehive, hive large kind of bee

مہالک *mahā'lik* N.M. PL. dangers [A ~ SING مہلک]

مہام *mohām'* N.F. PL. ventures, enterprises important matters [A ~ SING. مہم]

مہانا *mohā'nā* N.M. mouth of river [~ مونہہ]

مہاوت *mahā'vat* N.M. elephant-driver; mahout

مہاوٹ *mahā'vaṭ* N.F. winter rain

مہب *mahab'* N.M. place where wind blows [A ~ ہبوب]

مہبط *mah'bit* N.M. place of descent birth-place [A ~ ہبط]

مہتاب *mahtāb'* (col. *maih-*) moon moonlight مہتاب نے کھیت کیا *mahtāb' ne khet ki'yā* PH. the moon rose at moonrise مہتابی *mahtā'bī* N.F a kind of firework open terrace brocade ADJ. lunar moonlike [A ~ ماہ + تاب]

مہتدی *moh'tadī* N.F. guide مہتدی *moh'tadī* ADJ rightly guided [A ~ ہدایت]

مہتر *meh'tar* N.M. prince (euphemism for) sweeper ADJ. superior, greater مہترانی *mehtarā'nī* N.F. sweepress [~ P مہ *meh* + تر]

مہتمم *moh'tamim* N.M. manager superintendent administrator emcee مہتمم بندوبست *moh'tamim(-e) band-o-bast'* N.M. Settlement Officer [A ~ اہتمام]

مہجور *mahjoor'* ADJ. forsaken (lover) forlorn deserted مہجوری *mahjoo'rī* N.F forsaken state [A ~ ہجر]

مہد *maih'd* (ped. *mah'd*) N.M. cradle از مہد تا لحد *as maihd tā laih'd* مہد علیا *maih'd-e ūl'yā* N.F dowager-queen [A]

مہدی *maih'dī* (ped *mah'dī*) ADJ. guided N.M. appellation of twelfth Shi'ite Imam, awaited 'Imam' [A ~ ہدایت]

مہذب *mohaz'zab* ADJ. civilized well-mannered; well behaved cultured polite; civil [A ~ تہذیب]

مہر *maih'r* (ped. *mah'r*) N.M. money settled upon the wife; dower jointure alimony مہر باندھنا *maih'r bāndh'nā* V.T settle a dower on wife مہربخشنا maih'r bakh'shna v.t. give up a jointure مہرشرعی maih'r-e shar''i n.m. dower approved by Muslim law مہرمثل maih'r-e mis'l n.m. dower in force in the family ; proper dower ; customary dower مہر معجل maih'r-e mo'aj'jal n.m. prompt dower مہر موجل maih'r-e mo'aj'jal n.m. ferred dower مہر کا دعویٰ maih'r ka dā''va n.m. claim for dower [A]

مہر moh'r n.f. seal stamp gold coin ; guinea مہر اٹھنا moh'r ūṭh'na v.i. (of seal) give good unpression مہر بردار moh'r-bar-dār' n.m. seal-bearer مہربلب moh'r ba-lab' adj. silent mum taciturn مہر دستی moh'r-e das'tī n.f. signet مہر کرنا (یا لگانا) moh'r kar'nā (or lagā'nā) v.t. seal; put a seal (on) stamp rubber stamp مہرکن moh'r-kan n.m. engraver seal-engraver stamp-maker [P]

مہر meh'r n.m. sun n.f. kindness ; favour love; affection مہر انگیز meh'r-e angez' adj. exciting love ; loveable مہربان meh'r-bān' (or -bān) adj. kind considerate affectionate friendly loving مہربان ہونا meh'r-bān' ho'na v.t. be kind ; show favour مہربانی meh'r-ba'nī n.f. kindness favour regard ; consideration love ; affection مہر گیاہ meh'r-gayāh, مہر گیا meh'r-gayā' n.f. mandrake [P]

مہرا maih'ra n.m. sedan-bearer مہری maih'rī n.f. Hindu maid-servant

مہرہ moh'rah n.m. vertebra (neck) joint piece chessman draughtman , counter shell or piece of stone for polishing paper stooge; cat's paw مہرہ باز moh'ra bāz adj. sharper ; swindler ; cheat مہرہ بازی moh'rā-bā'zi n.f. cheating , swindling fraud مہرہ پشت moh'rā-e pūsh't n.m. spinal vertebra مہرہ کرنا moh'rah kar'na v.t. polish (paper) thus مہرہ نماز moh'ra-e namāz' n.m. piece of kerbala clay placed under forehead in prostration by Shi'ites [A]

مہری moh'rī n.f. end of trousers' leg

مہکنا mai'hakna v.i. emit sweet smell; perfume; be fragrant مہک mai'hak n.f. fragrance, weet smell مہکیلا maihkī'la adj. fragrant spicy aromatic مہکانا maihkā'nā v.t. perfume ; fill with sweet smell

مہلت moh'lat n.f. respite time grace deferment reprieve مہلت دینا moh'lat de'nā v t. give respite allow time defer reprieve [A]

مہلک moh'lik adj. (f. or pl. مہلکہ moh'likah) fatal mortal destructive ruinous [. ~ ہلاکت]

مہم mohim' n.f. (pl. مہمات mohimmāt') ex. pedition raid venture , enterprise exploit important affair مہم سر کرنا mohim' sar kar'nā v.t. overcome an obstacle succeed in a difficult affair [A]

مہمان mehmān', مہماں mehmāṅ (poet. میہماں meh'-māṅ) n.m. guest مہمان خانہ meh'mān-khānah n.m. guest-house , guest-room مہمان جانا mehman' jā'nā v.t. go as an invited guest مہماندار mehmān'-dār n.m. host مہمانداری mehmān'-dā'rī n.f. hospitality مہمان رکھنا (یا کرنا) mehmān' rakh'na (or kar'nā) v.t. keep (someone) as a guest مہمانسرائے mehmān'-sarā''e n.f. place of sojourn مہمان نواز meh'māṅ-navāz' adj. hospitable مہمان نوازی mehmān' navā'zī n.f. hospitality مہمان ہونا mehmān' ho'nā v.i stay as a guest مہمانی mehmā'nī n.f. feast , banquet hospitality مہمانی کرنا mehmā'nī kar'nā v t. entertain [P]

مہمل moh'mal adj. (f. مہملہ moh'malah) meaningless silly ; absurd dotless without any diacritical mark تابع مہمل tā'be'-e moh'mal meaningless adjunct مہملات mohmalāt' n.f. pl. nonsense absurdities [A]

مہموز mahmooz' adj hamzaeted [A ~ ہمزہ]

مہمیز maihmez' n.f. spur کو مہمیز کرنا ko maihmez' kar'na v.t. spur on [P]

مہنا meh'nā n.m. sneer; taunt مہنا دینا meh'na de'nā v.t. sneer ; taunt

مہنامت meh'nāmat n.f. (W. dial.) hue and cry مہنامت مچانا meh'nāmat machā na v.t (dial.) raise a hue and cry

مہنت mahan't n.m. presiding head of a Hindu religious order Hindu monk [S]

مہند mohan'nad adj Hindiized (word) [A ~ تہنید]

مہندس mohan'dis n.m. (pl. مہندسین mohan'disīn') engineer mathematician [A ~ ہندسہ]

مہندی maihn'dī (or مہنڈی) n.f. henna myrtle seventh day of Muharram celebrations

مہنگا maihn'gā (f مہنگی maihn'gī) adj. dear, expensive; highly-priced مہنگا سماں maihn'gā sa'māṅ n.m. inflationary times مہنگائی maihngā''ī n.f dearness مہنگائی الاؤنس maihngā''ī ailā''ūṅs n.m. dearness allowance

مہوا mahvā n.m. a kind of tree with fruit yielding liquour and seeds yielding oil

مہورت mahoo'rat n.f. (dial.) [illegible] auspicious moment inaugural ceremony [S]

مہوس *mohav'vis* N.M. alchemist greedy مہوسی *mohav'visi* N.F. alchemy greed

مہیا *mohay'yā* ADJ. available provided ready مہیا کرنا *mohay'yā kar'nā* V.T. supply provide مہیا ہونا *mohay'yā ho'nā* V.I. be available [A]

مہیب *mohīb'* ADJ. grim formidable [A ~ ہیبت]

مہین *mahīn'* ADJ. fine or thin (texture) feeble (voice)

مہینہ *mahī'nah,* مہینا *mahī'nā* N.M. month monthly salary مہینے سے ہونا *mahī'ne se ho'nā* V.I. menstruate مہینے کے مہینے *mahī'ne ke mahī'ne* ADJ. monthly ADV. a month ; permensum N.M. everymonth [~P ماہ]

مے *mai* N.F. liquor liquour wine مے آشام *mai-āshām',* مے پرست *mai-paras't,* مے خوار *mai-khār',* میکش *mai-kash',* میگسار *mai-gūsār',* مے نوش *mai-nosh'* N.M. drunkard sot ; boozy ADJ. wine-addict مے آشامی *mai-āshā'mī,* مے پرستی *mai-paras'tī,* میخواری *mai-khā'rī,* میکشی *mai-ka'shī,* میگساری *mai-gūsā'rī,* مینوشی *mai-no'shī* N.F. drinking drinking bout ; carousal میخانہ *mai-khā'nah,* میکدہ *maika'dah* N.M. liquor shop tavern public house ; pub مے فروش *mai'-firosh'* N.M. wine-merchant tavern-keeper ; publican مے فروشی *mai'-firo'shī* keeping a public house میگوں *mai'-goon* ADJ. reddish ; auburn flushed مئے ناب *mai-e nāb'* N.F. pure wine [P]

میا *may'yā* N.F. (dial.) mummy ; mom mother [~ ماں]

میاں *mi'yān* N.M. husband master ; lord (as formal title) Mr. (as vocative) میاں آدمی *mi'yān ād'mī* N.M. gentleman ; nice man میاں بیوی *mi'yān bī'vī* N.M. man and wife ; husband and wife میاں جی *mi'yān jī* N.M. elementary teacher in mosque school میاں مٹھو *mi'yan miṭ'ṭhoo* N.M. Poll ; parrot simpleton

میاں *miyān'* N.M. sheath ; scabbord waist centre ; middle ADV. between among in the midst of ; amidst میاں بستہ *miyān'-bas'tah* ADV. ready ; prepared تلوار میان سے کھینچنا *talvār' miyan' se khench'nā* V.T. whip out or unsheathe (one's sword) be ready to fight (تلوار) میان میں کرنا *(talvār') 'miyan' men kar'nā* V.T. sheathe (one's sword) stop quarrelling [P]

میانہ *miyā'nah* N.M. centre middle ADJ. midding medium moderate ADV. (*miyā'na-e*) between ; among میانہ روی *miyā'na-ra'vī* N.F. moderation میانہ قد *miyā'na-qad* ADJ. of medium stature [P doublet of PREC.]

میانی *miyā'nī* N.F. gusset ; transverse piece stitched between legs of pair of trousers [~P PREC.]

میاؤں *miyā''oṅ* N.F. cry of a cat ; mew ; miaow; miaul [ONO.]

میت *mīt* N.M. (dial.) friend [S]

میت *may'yit* N.F. dead body [A ~ موت]

میتھی *me'thī* N.F. fenugreek میتھی کا ساگ *me'thī kā sāg'* N.M. this used as potherb

میٹ *meṭ* N.M. mate [E]

میٹر *mī'ṭar* N.M. metre SUF. meter [E]

میٹرک *maiṭ'rik,* میٹریکولیشن *maiṭrikūle'shan* N.M. matriculation ; matrice

میٹنا *meṭ'nā* V.T. (col.) erase eradicate wipe out [~ مٹانا]

میٹنگ *mī'ṭing* N.F. meeting [E]

میٹھا *mī'ṭhā* ADJ. (F. میٹھی *mī'ṭhī*) sweet loving (of sleep) sound mild internal ; not visible ; not apparent N.M. sweetening substance sweet lemon میٹھا برس *mīṭhā' ba'ras* N.M. eighteenth year of life میٹھا بول *mī'ṭhā bol* N.M. sweet words میٹھا تیل *mī'ṭhā tel* N.M. sesamum oil میٹھا تیلیا *mī'ṭhā te'liya* N.M. aconite میٹھا ٹھگ *mī'ṭhā ṭhag* N.M. wheedler میٹھا درد *mī'ṭhā dar'd* N.M. mild pain میٹھا منہ کرانا *mī'ṭhā mūnh karā'nā* V.T. entertain with sweets to celebrate some joy میٹھا میٹھا *mī'ṭhā mī'ṭhā* ADJ. sweet mild میٹھا میٹھا ہپ اور کڑوا کڑوا تھو *mī'ṭhā mī'ṭhā hap' aur kar'vā kar'vā thoo'* PROV. selfishly grabbing good things to the exclusion of bad one's میٹھا کرنا *mī'ṭhā kar'nā* V.T. sweeten میٹھا ہونا *mī'ṭhā ho'nā* V.I. be sweet میٹھی بات (یا باتیں) *mī'ṭhī bāt* (or *bā'teṅ*) N.F. (PL.) sweet words میٹھی بولی *mī'ṭhī bo'lī* N.F. sweet words sweet tongue میٹھی چھری *mī'ṭhī chhū'rī* N.F. snake in the grass ; foe in friendly guise میٹھی عید *mī'ṭhī 'īd'* N.F. Eid-ul-Fitr میٹھی گالی *mī'ṭhī gā'lī* N.F. curse by beloved, etc.) giving no offence میٹھی مار *mī'ṭhī mār* N.F. contusion میٹھی مراد *mī'ṭhī mūrad'* N.F. sweet wish میٹھی نظر *mī'ṭhī nazar* N.F. affectionate look amorous glance میٹھی نیند *mī'ṭhī nīnd* N.F. sound sleep میٹھے میں سلونا ملانا *mī'ṭhe men salo'nā milā'nā* V.T. make the whole thing distasteful

میٹھی *mī'ṭhī* N.F. (nurs.) kiss ; repeated kiss

میثاق *mīsāq'* N.M. (PL. مواثیق *mavāsīq'*) agreement ; pact compact ; covenant alliance co-operation promise ; assurance میثاقِ ثلاثہ *mīsā'q-e salā'sah* N.M. triple entente میثاقِ ملی *mīsā'q-e mil'lī* N.M. national covenant [A ~ وثوق]

میجر *me'jar* N.M. major [E]

میجک *mai'jik* N.M. & ADJ. magic میجک لینٹرن *mai'jik lain'ṭarn* N.F. magic lantern [E]

میچ *maich* N.M. match [E]

میچنا *mīch'nā* V.I. shut or close (one's eyes)

میخ *mekh* N.F. peg tent-peg nail میخ اکھاڑنا *mekh' ūkhaṛ'nā* V.T. take out the nail (or peg) میخ ٹھونکنا *mekh' ṭhoṅk'nā* V.T. nail ; drive a nail میخچو *mekh'choo* N.M. mallet [P]

میدان *maidan'* N.M. (PL. میادین *mayādīn'*) plain ; level tract of land ground parade ground field (of battle) 'maidan' میدانِ جنگ *maid'n-e jang'*, میدانِ کارزار *maidā'n-e kārzār'* N.M. battlefield میدان چھوڑنا *maidān' chhoṛ'nā* V.I. retreat ; beat retreat میدان دینا *maidān de'nā* V.T. yield ground make room for میدان مارنا *maidān' mār'nā* V.T. win be victorious win the battle میدان میں آنا یا اترنا *maidān' meṅ ā'nā* (or *ū'tarnā*) V.I. enter the list come out and fight come out in the open میدان ہاتھ میں آنا یا رہنا *maidān' hāth meṅ ā'nā* (or *raih'nā*) V.I. win suffer a reverse be defeated میدان ہاتھ ہونا *maidān' hāth' ho'nā* V.I. come off with flying colours میدان ہونا *maidān' ho'nā* V.I. (of battle) take place میدانی *maidā'nī* ADJ. level of or coming from plains N.F. lamp installed in courtyard N.M. paste from which to prepare sweets (arch.) herald [P]

میدنی *mai'danī*, میندنی *maiṅ'danī* N.F. party of visitors to fair (dial.) party of Hindu pilgrims going on foot

میدہ *mai'dah* N.M. superfine flour ; 'maidah' fine powder میدہ کرنا *mai'dah kar'nā* V.T. grind very fine [P]

میڈ *maid* ADJ. mad [E]

میڈ *meḍ* ADJ. made میڈان *meḍ'-in* ADV made in [E]

میڈل *mai'dal* N.M., میڈلسٹ *maida'list* N.M. medallist [E]

میڈم *mai'dam* N.F. madam [E]

میڈیسن *mai'disan* N.F. medicine میڈیکل *mai'dikal* ADJ medical [E]

میر *mīr* N.M. title used for Syeds head ; chief leader professional singer میرِ آتش *mī'r-e ā'tash* N.M. (arch.) master-general of ordnance میرِ آخور *mī'r-e ākhoor'* N.M. (arch.) master of the stable میرِ بحر *mī'r-e bah'r* N.M. (arch.) admiral collector of port duty میر بخشی *mīr' bakh'shī* N.M. (arch.) paymaster-general میر بھجڑی *mīr bhūj'rī* N.M. prototype and saint of eunuchs میر جی *mīr' jī* PH. from of address to a Syed form of address to a professional singer میرِ حاج *mī'r-e haj'* N.M. leader of pilgrim party میرِ دیہہ *mī'r-e deh'* N.M. village headman میرِ ساماں *mī'r-e sāmān'* (or *sā'mañ*) N.M. (arch.) chief steward chef میرِ شکار *mī'r-e shikār'* N.M. game warden , a huntsman میرِ عرض *mī'r-e 'ar'z* N.M. (arch.) court official presenting people's petitions میرِ فرش *mī'r-e far'sh* N.M. pawn-like piece of stone put on corner of carpet to keep it in place میرِ قافلہ *mī'r-e qā'filah*, میرِ کارواں *mī'r-e kār'vān* N.M. caravan-leader میرِ کلام *mī'r-e kalām'* N.M. eloquent speaker میرِ مجلس *mī'r-e maj'lis* N.M. master of ceremonies ; emcee chairman ; president میرِ محلہ *mī'r-e mahal'lah* N.M. headman of a 'mohallah' میر محرر *mīr' mohar'rir* N.M. head clerk میرِ محکمہ *mī'r-e maih'kamah* N.M. head of department ; departmental head میرِ مشاعرہ *mī'r-e mushā''arah* N.M. president of the meeting of poets میرِ مطبخ *mī'r-e mat'bakh* N.M. chef میر منشی *mīr' mūn'shī* N.M. a head clerk person in charge of Urdu office senior language teacher to British officers of Indian army میری *mī'rī* ADJ. first (in kabaddi) chief; topmost ; unparallelled N.F. leadership being a Syed being a professional singer being a man of means میری کہ پھسڈی *mī'rī ke phisad'dī* PH. first or the last میری و فقیری *mī'rī-o faqī'rī* PH. wealth and penury [P]

میرا *me'rā* PROV. (F. میری *me'rī*) my mine میرا بس چلے تو تجھے کچا ہی چبا ڈالوں *me'rā bas' cha'le to tūj'he kach'chā'hī khā ja''ooṅ* INT. I would kill you if I could میرا تیرا *me'rā te'rā* N.M. stress on difference of ownership میرا حلوا کھائے *me'rā hal'va khā''e* PH. (fig.) find me dead میرا کیا گیا *me'rā kyā' ga'yā* PH. how do I stand to lose میری آنکھوں سے دیکھو *me'rī āṅ'khoṅ se de'kho* INT. see it with my eyes میری بلی اور مجھی سے میاؤں *me'rī bil'lī aur mū'jhī se miyā''oṅ* PH. my man challenging me میری بیزار ریا جوتی سے *me'rī paizār'* (or *joo'tī*) *se* PH. I care a hang for it who cares میری جوتی میرے ہی سر *me'rī joo'tī me're hī sir'* PH. (iron.) so that is the return for my favour میرے پوت کی لمبی لمبی باہیں *me're poot' kī lam'bī lam'bī bāṅ'heṅ* PH. every mother praises her own child میرے ملا کی الٹی ریت *me're mul'lā kī ūl'ṭī rīt*

PH. how perverse is my man's wit میرے منہ پر *me're mūnh par* PH. to my face میرے منہ پر میری تیرے منہ پر تیری *me're mūnh' par me'rī te're mūnh' par te'rī* PROV. hold with the hare and hunt with the hound میرے منہ سے *me're mūnh se* PH. for my sake

میراث *mīras'* N.F. legacy ancestral property hereditary estate [A ~ ارث]

میراثی (usu. but wrong spelling of) میراسی *mīra'sī* N.M. singer by hereditary profession میراثن (or میراسن *mīra'san* N.F. singing girl ; singing only in women's parties female member of hereditary singer's family میراں جی *mī'rāṅ-jī* N.M. (dial.) title of saint Hazrat Abdul Qadir Jilani or Muinuddin Ajmeri (also میراں جی کا چاند *mī'rāṅ-jī ka chānd'*) fourth month of Muslim calender as the death anniversary of Hazrat Abdul Qadir Jilani

میرزا *mīr'za* N.M. (same as مرزا N.M. ★)

میری *mī'rī* N.F. (see under میر N.M ★)

میز *mez* N.F. table میزبان *mīz'bān* (or *mez'-*) N.M. host میزبانی *mīzbā'nī* (or *mez-*) N.F. hospitality [P]

میزان *mīzān'* N.F. total (lit.) balance ; pair of scales (sign of the Zodiac) میزان پٹنا *mīzān' paṭ'na* V.I. pull logethu have an equation with میزان کل *mīzā'n-e kūl'* N.F. grand total میزان کرنا (یا لگانا) *mīzān' kar'na* (or *lagā'na*) V.I. total میزانیہ *mīzāniy'yah* N.M. budget ; budgetary ; estimate [A ~ وزن]

میسر *m*ᵉ*yas'sar* ADJ. available [A ~ تیسیر]

میسرہ *mai'sarah* N.M left wing of an army [A ~ یسار]

میش *mesh* N.M. sheep ewe ram میش چشم *mesh'-chash'm* ADJ. sheep-eyed ; shy میشا *me'shā*, میشہ *me'shah* N.M. tanned skin ; kid [P]

میعاد *mī'ād'* N.F. time-limit period ; duration term میعاد پوری ہونا *mī'ād' poo'rī ho'nā* V.I. (of term, period or time-limit) expire میعادی *mī'ā'dī* ADJ. lasting till the end of its term میعادی بخار *mī'ā'dī būkhār'* N.M. typhoid ; enteric fever میعادی ہنڈی *mī'ā'dī hūn'dī* N.F. bill payable at a fixed time [A ~ وعدہ]

میغ *megh'* N.M. (lit.) cloud [P]

میقات *mīqāt'* N.M. (PL. مواقیت *mavāqīt'*) one the four places in Arabic where pilgrims done prescribed robe cadamic term , semester [A ~ وقت]

میکائیل *mī'kā'īl* N.M Michael [A ~ H]

میکروب *maik'rob* N.M. bacterium میکروب شناسی *maik'rob-shinā'sī* N.F. bacteriology [E]

میکہ *mai'kah* N.M. (woman's) paternal home میکہ بسانا *mai'kah basā'na* V.I. (of wife) live with own parents [~ ماں]

میگھ *megh* N.M. one of the modes connected with rainsy season

میگزین *meg'zīn* N.F magazine [E ~ A مخزن]

میل[1] *mīl* N.M. appliance for staining eye; antimony, etc. ; staining needle [A]

میل[2] *mīl* N.M. (PL. امیال *amyāl'*) mile سنگ میل *sang-e mīl'* N.M. milestone [~ A & E]

میل *mel* N.M. association concord kind variety ; quality میل جول *mel' jol*, میل ملاپ *mel-milap'* N.M. familiarity friendly relations میل رکھنا *mel' rakh'na* V.T. be on good terms (with) میل کھانا *mel' khā'na* V.T. be in harmony (with) میلنا *mel'nā* V.T. (col.) join [~ ملنا]

میل[1] *mail* N.M. grime dirt filth scum sign of sorrow or anger دل میں میل لانا *di'l men mail' lā'na* V.I. show signs of sorrow or displeasure میلا *mai'lā* ADJ. (F. میلی *mai'lī*) dirty filthy grimy N.M. night soil میلا پن *mai'lā-pan* dirtiness untidiness میلا کچیلا *mai'lā kūchai'la* ADJ. dirty grimy میل چھٹنا *mail' chhūṭ'na* V.I. (of dirt) be washed away میل خورا *mail'-kho'ra* N.M. colour (of cloth) which will not show off dirt میل کا بیل بنانا *mail kā bail' banā'na* PROV. make a mountain out of a mole-hill میل کاٹنا *mail' kāt'na* V.T. remove dirt or scum

میل[2] *mail* N.M. aptitude bent inclination [A doublet of میلان]

میل[3] *mail* INT (usu. میل میل *mail' mail*) cry to make elephant walk

میلا *mai'la* ADJ. (F. میلی see under میل *mail* N.F ★)

میلہ *me'lah* N.M. fair concourse میلہ تماشہ *me'lah tamā'shah*, میلہ ٹھیلہ *me'lah ṭhe'lah* N.M fair concourse [~ میل *mel*]

میلاد *mīlād'* N.M. nativity meeting held to celebrate the Holy Prophet's nativity عید میلاد النبی *ī'd-e milā'd (-ūnn'bī)* the Holy Prophet's nativity as celebrated on twelfth day of third month of Islamic calender Eid-i-Milad (un-Nabi [A]

میلان *mailān* N.M bent ; inclination میلان طبع (یا خاطر) *mailan-e tab'* (or *khā'tir*) N.M. bend of mind [A ~]

میم *mem* N.F Western(ized) woman [~ E madam CORR.]

میمنا *mem'na* N.M kid [ONO.]

میمنت *maima'nat* N.F. good fortune قدوم میمنت لزوم *qūdoo'm-e mai'manat lūzoom'* N.M. propitious arrival [A ~ یمن]
میمنہ *mai'manah* N.M. right wing of the army A ~ یمین]
میمون *maimoon'* ADJ. lucky, fortunate; auspicious; propitious [A ~ یمن]
میمول *maimoon'* N.M. monkey baboon [P]
میں *main* PROV. I egotism میں بھی رانی تو بھی رانی کون بھرے گا پانی *main' bhī rā'nī too' bhī rā'nī kaun bha'regā pā'nī* PROV. this army has all generals and no soldier میں جانوں *main jā'noon* PH. I believe I suspect میں خوش میرا خدا خوش *main' khūsh' me'rā khūdā' khūsh'* PROV. it is (or will be) a real pleasure to me میں کون تو کون *main' kaun' too' kaun'* PROV. as soon the interest is served, we become strangers to each other میں نہ مانوں *main' na mā'noon* PH. disbelieve; despite obvious proof میں نے کیا تیری گدھی چرائی ہے *main' ne kyā tūmhā'rī ga'dhī chūrā''ī hai* PH. how have I harmed you
میں[1] *men* ADV. in within inside
میں[2] *men* N.M. (usu. میں میں *men' men*) cry of goat; bleat [ONO.]
مینا *mai'nā* N.F starling sweet-tongued child
مینڈ *mend* N.F. mound along field boundary parapet
مینڈک *men'dak* N.M. frog toad مینڈکی *mend'kī* N.F. female of frog or toad مینڈکی کو زکام ہونا *mend'kī ko zūkām' ho'nā* V.I. assume consequential airs
مینڈھا *men'dhā* N.M ram billow مینڈھے اچھلنا *men'dhe ū'chhalnā* V.I. (of water) be billowing مینڈھی *mīn'dhī*, میڈھی *mī'dhī* N.F (usu. PL.) small plaits of hair مینڈھیاں گوندھنا *mendhī'yān goondh'na* V.T. make small plaits of hair
مینگنی *meng'nī* N.F. the dung of sheep, goats and camels; droppings
مینو *mī'noo*, منو *minoo'* N.M paradise; heaven مینو سواد *mī'noo-savād'* ADJ heavenly in appearance
مینہ *meh'h* N.M. rain مینہ برسنا *meh'h ba'rasnā* V.I. rain
مینیجر *mane'jar* N-M. (same as منیجر N.M. ★)
میونسپل *miyoonis'pal* ADJ municipal میونسپلٹی *miyoonis-pail'ṭī* میونسپل کمیٹی *miyoonis'pal kame'ṭī* N.F. municipality میونسپل کمشنر *miyoonis'pal kamish'nar* N.M municipal commissioner [E]

میوہ *me'vah* N.M. fruit میوہ دار *me'va-dār* ADJ fruit bearing; fruitful, fructiferous میوہ فروش *me'va-firosh'* N.M. fruiterer [P]

ن

ن *noon* thirty-second letter of Urdu alphabet representing a dental (or as نون غنہ *noo'n-e ghūn'nah* purely nasal sound equivalent to English *n*) (according to jummal reckoning) 50
ں *noon'(-e) ghūn'nah* N.M this letter with a purely nasal sound
ن *nī* PREF un-; in-, -less
نا[1] *nā* PARTICLE (used for emphasis) do (come, etc.)
نا[2] *nā* PARTICLE no; never, in no case (used for stressing the negative that follows) نانکڑ کرنا *nonā' nūk'kaṛ kar'nā* V.T say "No", refuse
نا[3] *nā* PREF un- in-, im, il نا آزمودہ *nā āzmoo'dah* ADJ. untried unproved نا آزمودہ کار *nā-āzmoo'dah-kār'* ADJ. raw, green inexperienced نا آشنا *nā-āshnā'* ADJ. unknown unfamiliar; unacquainted N.M. stranger نا آشنائی *nā-āshnā''ī* N.F. unfamiliarity ناآگاہ *nā-āgāh'* ADJ. unaware ADV in the dark unawares نا آمیزگار *nā-āmezgār'* ADJ. unsocial نااتفاقی *nā-ittifā'qī* N.F disagreement; discord ناالتفاتی *nā-iltifā'tī* N.F indifference ناامیدی *nā-ūmmī'dī* (arch *nā-ūme'dī*) N F hopelessness, despondency نااندیش *nā-andesh'* SUF. careless (of), thoughtless (of) نااندیشی *nā-ande'shī* SUF. carelessless (of) ناانصاف *nā-insāf'* ADJ. unjust ناانصافی *nā-insā'fī* N.F injustice نااہل *nā-aih'l* ADJ. unefficient undeserving نااہلی *nā-aih'lī*, نااہلیت *nā-aihliy'yat* N F efficiency not being a deserving case نابالغ *nā-bā'ligh* ADJ not yet of age N.M minor نابالغی *nā-bā'ilghī* N.F minority, nonage نابکار *nā-ba-kār'* ADJ. wicked (rare) good for-nothing نابکاری *nā-ba-kā'rī* N.F. wickedness worthlessness نابلد *nā-ba'lad* ADJ. ignorant (of), unaware (of) N.M. novice نابود *..ā-bood* ADJ. non-existence annihilated نیست و نابود کرنا *(nes't-o-) nā-bood' kar'na* V.T annihilate نابینا *nā-bī'nā* ADJ. blind ناپاک *nā-pāk'* ADJ. polluted unclean defiled dirty ناپاکی *nā-pā'kī* N.F. uncleanliness defilement lewdness swint ناپائدار *nā-pā''e-dār'* ADJ. frail durable passing; transitory, transient unstable;

inconstant ناپائداری *nā-pā'e-dā'rī* N.F. frailty not being durable transitoriness instability; inconstancy ناپدید *nā-padīd'* ADJ. invisible vanished evanescent unavailable ناپسند *nā-pasand'* N.F. dislike disapproval ADJ. disliked rejected پسند ناپسند *pasand' nā-pasand'* N.F. likes and dislike (of) ناپسندیدہ *nā-pasandī'dah* ADJ. disliked ; disapproved unwholesome offensive rejected ناپسندیدگی *nā-pasandī'dagī* N.F. dislike ; disapproval being offensive ناپید *nā-paid'* ADJ. extinct non-existent unavilable ; invisible ناپید کرنا *nā-paid' kar'na* V.T. cause to vanish remove from the scene ناپید ہونا *nā-paid' ho'nā* V.I. vanish be removed from the scene ناپیدا کنار *nā-pai'dā-kanār'* ADJ. boundless ; unbounded expansive ناتجربہ کار *nā-taj'riba-kār'* ADJ. rew ; inexperienced ناتجربہ کاری *nā-tajri'ba-kā'rī* N.F. inexperienced ناتراش *nā-tarāsh'*, ناتراشیدہ *nā-tarāshī'dah* ADJ. not smoothed unpolished ; uncultured کندۂ ناتراش *kūn'da-e nā-tarāsh'* N.M. uncultured person ناتربیت یافتہ *nā-tar'biyat-yā f'tah* ADJ. untrained raw uncultured ناتربیت یافتگی *nā-tarbiyat-yā f'-tagī* N.F. lack of training lack of culture ناترس *nā-tar's* ADJ. fearless merciless SUF. unfearing ناترسی *nā-tar'sī* N.F. being unfearing ناتمام *nā-tamām'* ADJ. complete imperfect deficient ناتمامی *nā-tamā'mī* N.F. incompleteness imperfection deficiency ناتواں *nā-to'āṅ* (col. *nā-tavāṅ'*) ADJ. weak powerless infirm feeble frail ناتوانی *nā-to'ā'nī* (col. *nā-tavā'nī*) weakness powerlessness infirmity frailty ناجائز *nā-jā''iz* ADJ. unlawful contraband not permissible ناجنس *nā-jin's* ADJ. heterogeneous strange ignoble ناچار *nā-chār'* ADV. perforce ; of necessity ADJ. helpless constrained disabled cripple ناچاری *nā-chā'rī* N.F. helplessness constraint disability being crippled ناچاقی *nā-chā'qī* N.F discord strained relations ناچیز *nā-chīz'* ADJ. worthless ; good-for-nothing insignificant trifling of no account ; of no consequence بندۂ ناچیز *ban'da-e nā-chīz'* N.M. (this) worthless slave ناحق *nā-ḥaq'* ADV unjustly falsely in vain ناخدا ترس *nā-khuda-tar's* خدا ناترس *khūdā' nā-tar's* ADJ. ungodly ; hard-heartedly ناخلف *nā-kha'laf* ADJ. undutiful (son) degenerate (progeny) ناخواندہ *nā-khāṅ'dah* ADJ. illiterate uninvited (guest) ناخواندگی *nā-khāṅ'-dagī* N.F illiteracy ناخوش *nā-khūsh'* ADJ displeased . unhappy indisposed ناخوشی *nā-khū'shī* N F. displeasure ; unhappiness indisposition ناخوشگوار *nā-khūsh'-gūvār'* ADJ. unpleasant undesirable ناخوشگواری *nā-khūsh'-gūvā'rī* N.F. unpleasantness disagreeableness نادار *nā-dar* ADJ. poor ; indigent pauper insolven نادار ی *nā-dā'rī* N.F. poverty ; indigence pauperism insolvency ناداری سب سے بڑا گناہ ہے *nā-dā'rī sab se ba'ṛā gūnāh' hai* PROV. poverty is a great sin نادان *nā-dān'* ADJ. ignorant foolish innocent N.M. fool child نادانی *nā-dā'nī* N.F. ignorance folly innocence نادان دوست سے دانا دشمن بھلا *nā-dān' dos't se dānā' dūsh'man bha'lā* PROV. a wise foe is better than a foolish friend نادان کی دوستی جی کا زیاں *nā-dān' kī dos'tī jī ka zayāṅ'* PROV. even the friendship of a fool (or child) is dangerous نادانستہ *nā-dānis'tah* ADV. unknowingly ; unwittingly ; inadvertantly نادانستگی *nā-dānista'gī* N.F. inadvertance نادرست *nā-dūrūs't* ADJ. incorrect wrong نادرستی *nā-dūrūs'tī* N.F. incorrectness wrongness نادہندہ *nā-dehiṅ'dah* ADJ. close-fisted N.M. bad pay-master نادہندگی *nā-dehiṅ' dagī* (col. نادہندی *nā-dehiṅ'dī*) N.F. non-payment نادیدہ *nā-dī'dah* ADJ. unseen نادیدنی *nā-dīdanī* ADJ. too pitiable a sight ناراست *nā-rāst'* ADJ. crooked not straightforward dishonest unfair ناراستی *nā-rās'tī* N.F. crookedness dishonestly unfairness ناراض *nā-raz'* ADJ. displeased offended angry ; rage نارس *nā-ras'*, نارسیدہ *nā-rasī'dah* ADJ. unripe immature (fig.) young نارسا *nā-rasā'* ADJ. incapable of reaching ; falling short (of) نارسائی *nā-rasā''ī* N.F incapacity falling short (of) ; shortfall نارستہ *nā-rūs'tah* ADJ. unblossomed immature ناروا *nā-ravā'* ADJ. unlawful not permissible inadmissible prohibited (of money) not current نازیب *nā-zeb'*, نازیبا *nā-ze'bā* ADJ. unsuitable unseemly unbecoming ungainly ; ugly ناساز *nā-sāz'* ADJ. indisposed ; out of sorts ناسازی *nā-sā'zī* N.F indisposition ناسازیٔ طبع *nā-sā'zī-e tab''* N.F. indisposition ناسازگار *nā-sāz-gār'* ADJ. unfavourable unfortunate ناسازگاری *nā-sāz-gā'rī* N.F. unfavourable nature (of circumstances) ناسپاس *nā-sipās'* ADJ. unthankful ; ungrateful ناسپاسی *nā-sipā'sī* N.F thanklessness ; ingratitude ناسزاوار *nā-sazā'-vār'* ADJ. improper undeserving ; unworthy unmerited indecent silly ناسفتہ *nā-suf'tah* ADJ. unbored unstrung ناسمجھ *nā-sa'ma'jh* ADJ. silly ; foolish dull ; unintelligent raw ; inexperienced ناسمجھی *nā-sam'jhī* N.F folly dullness ; unintelligence inexperience ignorance ناشاد *nā-shād'* ADJ. unhappy cheerless unlucky ; unfortunate ناشائستہ *nā-shā'is'tah* ADJ. uncultured unmannerly ; ill-mannered ; indecorous unbecoming improper indecent ناشائستگی *nā-shā''is'tagī* N.F being uncultured unmannerliness impropriety indecency ناشُدنی *nā-shū'danī* ADJ. impossible ill-fated, unfortunate worthless ; good-for-nothing ناشُکرا *nā-shūk'rā* ADJ. & N.M thankless ; ungrateful ; ناشُکری *nā-shūk'rī* N.F. thanklessness, ungratefulness ; ingratitude ناشکیب *nā-shakeb'*, ناشکیبا *nā-shake'bā* ADJ. restless impatient ناشکیبائی *nā-shakebā''ī* N.F. impatience restlessness ناشناس *nā-shinās'* SUF. unrecognizing ; ignorant (of) ناشنو *nā-shinau'* ADJ. inattentive refusing to listen ناصاف *nā-sāf'* ADJ. unclean ; impure ناصواب *nā-savāb'* ADJ. wrong ; incorrect ناصبور *nā-saboor'* ADJ. impatient restless ناصبوری *nā-saboo'rī* N.F. impatience restlessness ناطاقت *nā-tā'qat* ADJ. weak ; feeble frail infirm ناطاقتی *nā-tā'qatī* N.F. weakness feebleness frailty infirmity ناعاقبت اندیش *nā-'āqibat-andesh'*, عاقبت نااندیش *'ā'qibat nā-andesh'* ADJ. shortsighted ناعاقبت اندیشی *nā-'ā'qibat ande'shī* N.F. shortsightedness recklessness indiscretion نافرجام *nā-farjām'* ADJ. that comes to grief that has an evil end نافرمان *nā-farmān'* ADJ. disobedient نافرمانی *nā-farmā'nī* N.F. disobedience نافہم *nā-faih'm* ADJ. dull ; stupid نافہمی *nā-faih'mī* N.F. dullness stupidity ناقابل *nā-qā'bil* ADJ. inefficient incapable unqualified unfit unworthy unable (to) AFFIX. un—able ; im—ible ناقابلِ استعمال *nā-qā'bil-e iste'māl'* ADJ. unserviceable ناقابلِ اصلاح *nā-qā'bil-e islāh'* ADJ. incorrigible irreclaimable ناقابلِ اعتبار *nā-qā'bil-e e'tibār'* ADJ. untrustworthy ; undependable ; unreliable ناقابلِ انتقال *nā-qā'bil-e intiqāl'* ADJ. inalienable ناقابلِ برداشت *nā-qā'bil-e bar-dāsh't* ADJ. intolerable unbearable ناقابلِ تردید *nā-qā'bil-e tardīd'* ADJ. incontrovertible; irrefutable unassailable ناقابلِ ترمیم *nā-qā'bil-e tarmīm* ADJ. unamendedable immutable ناقابلِ تسخیر *nā-qā'bil-e taskhīr'* ADJ. unconquerable impregnable indomitable ناقابلِ تلافی *nā-qā'bil-e talā'fī* ADJ. irremediable irretrievable ناقابلِ عمل *nā-qā'bil-e 'amal'* ADJ. impracticable ; not workable ناقابلِ فہم *nā-qā'bil-e faih'm* ADJ. unintelligible ناقابلِ قبول *nā-qā'bil-e qabool* ADJ. unacceptable inadmissible ناقابلِ کاشت *nā-qā'bil-e kāsh't* ADJ. unculturable, uncultivable ناقابلیت *nā-qābiliy'yat* N.F. inefficiency incapability inability lack of qualification unworthiness powerlessness ناقدرا *nā-qad'rā* ADJ. unappreciate ungrateful ناقدرشناس *nā-qad'r-shinās* قدرناشناس *qad'r nā-shinās* ADJ. unable or uuwilling to recognize someone's merit not giving the devil his due ناقدری *nā-qad'rī* N.F. disgrace ناقدرشناسی *nā-qad'r shinā'sī*, قدرناشناسی *qad'r nā-shinā'sī* N.F non-recognition of merit low estimation ناکارہ *nā-kā'rah* ADJ. useless worthless unserviceable otiose ناکام *nā-kām'* ADJ. failed unsuccessful disappointed ناکامی *nā-kā'mī* N.F failure; disappointment ناکتخدا *nā-katkhūdā'* ناکدخدا *nā-kadkhūdā'* ADJ. virgin unmarried spinster ناکتخدائی *nā-katkhūdā''ī*, ناکدخدائی *nā-kadkhūdā''ī* N.F. virginity unmarried state spinsterhood ناکردنی *nā-kar'danī* ADJ. not worth doing too bad to be done ناکردہ *nā-kar'dah* ADJ. not yet done ; uncommitted ناکردہ کار *nā-kar'da-kār'* ADJ. inexperienced unknowing ناکردہ گناہ *nā-kar'da-gūnah'* ADJ. innocent, ADV. faultlessly ناکس *nā-kas'* ADJ. worthless ; mean N.M. mere nobody ہرکس وناکس *har' ka's-o nā'-kas* N.M. high and low ; everyone irrespective of his status ناکسی *nā-ka'sī* N.F. worthlessness ناگاہ *nā'-gāh'* ناگہ *nā'-gah*, ناگہاں *nā-gahāṅ'* ADV. suddenly all of a sudden unexpected accidental ناگزیر *nā-gūzīr'* ADJ inevitable indispensable ناگفتنی *nā-gūf'tanī* ADJ. deplorable ; too bad to be described ناگفتہ *nā-gūf'tah* ADJ. unsaid untold ناگفتہ بہ *nā-gūf'ta beh* ADJ better left unsaid ناگوار *nā-gūvār'*, ناگوارا *nā-gūvā'rā* ADJ. unpalatable unpleasant awkward (question) offensive ناگوار گزرنا (یا ہونا) *nā-gūvā'rā gū'zarnā* (or *ho'nā*) V.I. be offensive, be unpalatable ناگواری *nā-gūvā'rī* N.F being unpalatable being offensive نالائق *nā-lā''iq* ADJ inefficient incapable unqualified unintelligent نالائقی *nā-lā''iqī* N.F inefficiency incapability stupidity lack of qualification نامانوس *nā-mānoos'* ADJ. unfamiliar (words etc.) نامبارک *nā-mūba'rak* ADJ. inauspicious نامحرم *nā-mah'ram* (col. *-maih'-*) N.M. & ADJ. (one) other than a close relative one from whom a Muslim woman has to observe purdah نامراد *nā-mūrād'* ADJ. chagrined, disappointed unlucky, unfortunate نامرادی *nā-mūrā'dī* N.F chagrin, disappointment ill-luck ; misfortune نامربوط *nā-marboot'* ADJ. unconnected dispointed ungrammatical construction, etc.) نامرد *nā-mar'd* ADJ. impotent coward ; unmanly N.M. impotent person coward نامرد کر دینا *nā-mar'd kar' de'nā* V.T emasculate نامردی *nā-mar'dī* N.F. impotency unmanliness; cowardice نامساعد *nā-mūsā''id* ADJ. unfavourable (circumstances etc.) نامشخص *nā-mūshak'khas* ADJ. undefined, unclassified خرِنامشخص *khā'r-e nāmūshakhkhas* N.M. (fig.) arrant fool نامشروع *nā-mashroo'* ADJ. unlawful inadmissible bad نامطابق *nā-mūtā'biq* ADJ. inconsistent (with) نامطبوع

na-malboo'' ADJ diasagreeable unpleasant contrary to nature نامعتبر nā-mo''tabar ADJ. unreliable undependable ; untrustworthy نامعقول nā-ma'qool' ADJ unreasonable improper indecent absurd silly (rare) irrational نامعقولیت nā- ma'qooliy'yat N.F silliness نامعلوم nā-ma'loom' ADJ. unknown ناملائم nā-mulā''im ADJ. rough harsh or uncivil (words, etc) ناممکن nā-mum'kin ADJ & INT impossible نامناسب nā-munā sib ADJ improper unbecoming indecorous نامنظور nā-manzoor ADJ. & ADV rejected refused turned down disallowed disapproved inadmissibility ناموافق nā-mo'ā fiq ADJ adverse (opinion, circumstances, etc) disagreeable or unwholesome (food, etc) unsuited unsuitable uncongenial ناموافقت nā-mo'ā faqat N.F. disagreement unsuitability unwholesomeness ناموزوں nā-mauzooń' ADJ. unsuitable unmetrical نامہربان nā-meh'rbāń ADJ. unkind , unsympathetic نامیسری nā-müyas'sarī N F. poverty ; peunry ناواجب nā-vā jib ADJ improper ناواقف nā vā'qif ADJ. ignorant unacquainted ; unaware inexperienced; unskilled , unknowing N.M stranger ناواقفی nā-vā'qifī, ناواقفیت nā-vāqifiy'yat N.F ignorance unawareness inexperience being a stranger ناوقت nā-vaq't ADV. out of time , at the wrong hour ADJ unseasonable ناہموار nā-hamvār ADJ uneven irregular (rare) uncouth ناہمواری nā-hamvā ri N F unevenness (rare) lack of manners ناہنجار nā-hańjār ADJ mean worthless , good-for-nothing wicked N.M. rogue , rascal نایاب nā-yāb' ADJ unprocurable rare scarce نایافت nā-yāf't N F unprocurability [P]

ناب nāb ADJ pure unadulterated clear [P]

نابغہ nā'bighah N.M (PL نوابغ navā'bigh) genius [A]

ناپنا nāp'nā V.T measure رستہ ناپنا ras'tah nāp'nā V.I. walk without any purpose walk just for the fun of it گردن ناپنا gar'dan nāp'nā V.T take someone by the scruff of the neck ناپ nāp N.M measure, measurement ناپ تول nāp' tol N.M. weighing and measuring

ناتا nā'tā N.M. relationship ties ; relations ناتا توڑنا nā'ta tor'nā V.T sever relations (with) sever ties (with) ناتا جوڑنا nā'ta jor'nā V.T form an alliance (with) establish relations (with) describe something as related (to)

ناتھ nāth (H.) N.M. nose-string (for) draught oxen (dial) husband ناتھنا nāth'nā V T pass a string in animal's nose-ring bring (someone) under control

ناتی nā'tī N.M. grandson, son of one's daughter ناتن nā'tin N F grand-daughter, daughter of one's daughter

ناٹا nā'ṭā ADJ. (F. ناٹی nā'ṭī) short , dwarfish

ناٹک nā'ṭak N.M. (arch.) drama , play dramatic performance ناٹکیا nā'ṭakyā (rare) actor

ناجی nā'ji ADJ. & N.M (one) delivered of sins [A ~ نجات]

ناچنا nāch'nā V.I dance ناچ nāch N.M. dance ball ballet ناچ دکھانا (یا کرنا) nāch dikhā'nā (or kar'nā) V.I. dance ناچ رنگ nāch'-rang N.M dance and music ناچ گھر nāch'-ghar N.M. dancing hall ball room ناچ نچانا nāch' nachā'nā V.T cause to dance تگنی کا ناچ نچانا tig'nī ka nāch' nachā'nā V T make (someone) dance to the tune (of) ناچ نہ جانے آنگن ٹیڑھا nāch na jā'ne āń'gan ṭe'ṛhā PROV a bad workman fights with his tools ناچنے لگی تو گھونگھٹ کیسا nāch'ne la'gī to ghūń'ghaṭ kai'sā PROV. strain at the guat after swallowing the camel

ناحیہ nā'hiyah N M. (PL. نواحی navā'hī) vicinity bourne [A]

ناخدا nākhudā' N.M seaman , sailor , captain skipper [P]

ناخن nā'khun, (rare ناخون nākhoon') N.M nail ناخن بندی nā'khun-bań'di N F (dial) service ناخن تدبیر nā'khun-e tadbir N.M. (fig.) device strategy ناخن تراش nā'khun-tarash N.M. nail-clipper nail-parer ناخن سے گوشت (یا گوشت سے ناخن) جدا ہونا nā'khun se gosh't (or gosh't se nā'khun) jü'dā ho'nā V.I (of separation) occur between near and dear ones ناخن شمشیر nā'khun-e shamshir' N.M. (fig.) edge of a sword ناخن شمشیر سے nā'khun shamshir se PH. with the help of the sword , by dint of force ناخن گرنا nā'khun gar'nā V.I. have control (of) ناخن گڑونا nā'khun garo'nā V.T dig one's nails (into) ناخن گیر nā'khun gir N.M nail-clipper , nail-parer ناخن لینا nā'khun le'nā V.T. pare the nails (of horse) trip ; stumble [P]

ناخنہ nā'khunah N.M. plectrum , guitar quill haw or web (in the eye) [PREC.]

ناخون nākhoon' N.M. (same as ناخن N M. ★)

نادر nā'dir ADJ. (F. نادرہ nā'dirah PL نوادر navā'dir) rare curious wonderful نادر (نادرۂ) روزگار nā'dir-e (or nā'dirā-e) rozgār N.M wonder of the world نادرشاہی nā' dir-shā'hī N.F tyrannical rule ADJ. tyrannical categorical of Nadir Shah, the 18th century conqueror of India and Persia نادرہ کار nā'dira-kār ADJ. & N.M.

(one) working wonder نادری na'dirī N.F. (at cards) ace or picture-card ADJ. of Nadir Shah tyrannical categorical نادری حکم na'dirī hūk'm N.M. tyrannical or categorical order [A ~ ندرت]

نادعلی na'd-e 'alī' N.F. opening words of a well-known prayer stone amulet on which it is carved [A invoke God]

نادم na'dim ADJ. sorry regretful ashamed repenting ; penitent نادم کرنا na'dim kar'na V.T. put to shame اپنے کیے پر نادم ہونا ap'ne ki'ye par na'dim ho'na PH. be sorry for one's doings

نادھنا nadh'na V.T. yoke (ox, etc.)

نادیا na'diya N.M. ox (or F. cow) with extra limb, horn, etc. taken round by Brahmins for begging alms

نار[1] nar N.F. fire hell ناری na'rī ADJ fiery cursed ; condemned be lash

نار[2] nar, ناری na'rī N.F. (dial.) woman نرناری nar' na'rī N.M. PL. man and woman [S]

نارائن nara''in N.M. (H. dial.) (God as) the Eternal

نارجیل narjīl' N.M. cocoanut [A ~ U ناریل]

نارمل nar'mal ADJ. normal نارمل سکول nar'mal sakool N.M. normal school

نارنج naranj' N.M orange نارنجی naran'jī ADJ. orange-coloured ; orange

نارنگی naran'gī N.F. tangerine

ناری na'rī ADJ. (see under نار N.F. see under نار[2] N.F. ☆)

ناریل na'riyal N.M. co-coanut cocoanut-tree small hookah made of cocoanut ناریل کا تیل na'riyal ka tel' N.M. cocoanut-oil

ناڑا na'ṛa N.M. trouser-string ناڑا باندھنا na'ṛa bāndh'na V.T. tie the trouser-string ناڑا کھولنا na'ṛa khol'na V.T. untie the trouser-string

ناز naz N.M. coquetry blandishment dalliance ; amorous playfulness whims and caprices ناز اٹھانا (یا کھینچنا) naz ūṭhā'na (or khench'na) V.I. bear with (someone's) whims and caprices نازبرداری naz-bar-dā'rī N.F. praising the coquetry ways (of) نازبرداری کرنا naz-bar-dā'ri kar'na V.I. bear with the نازپرورده naz-parvar'dah ADJ. tenderly nurtured spoil (child) ناز کرنا naz' kar'na V.I. take airs ; be full of pride نازنخره naz' nakh'rah N.M. coquetry ; blandishment ; dalliance نازونیاز na'z-o-nayaz' N.M. PL. coquetry and gallantry · loving couple's mutual relations نازونعمت na'z-o-ne''mat N.M. worldly comforts نازونعمت میں پلنا na'z-o-ne''mat meṅ pal'na, فخروناز fakh'r-o-naz' N.M. pride conceit پرفخروناز کرنا par fakh'r-o-naz' kar'na V.T be proud (of) take pride (in) V.T. be born with a silver spoon in the mouth be bred in نازاں na'zāṅ ADJ. proud (of) conceited [P]

نازش nāzish' N.F. pride conceit [P]

نازبو nāz'bo N.M. wild rue ; basil [P]

نازک na'zūk ADJ. delicate tender elegant ; graceful slim nice sensative subtle critical dangerous fragile نازک اندام na'zūk-andam' . نازک بدن na'zūk-ba'dan ADJ. delicate N.M. sweet-heart نازک خیال nā'zūk-khayāl' ADJ. fanciful; imaginative نازک خیالی nā'zūk-khaya'lī N.F imagination ; fancy subtlety of expression نازک دماغ na'zūk-dimagh' ADJ. touchy ; testy نازک زمانہ na'zūk zamā'nah, نازک وقت na'zūk vaq't N.M. critical moment dangerous times نازک مزاج na'zūk mizaj' ADJ touchy ; testy نازک معاملہ na'zūk mo'ā'malah N.M delicate matter نازکی na'zūkī N.F. delicacy tenderness [P]

نازل na'zil ADJ. descended alighting dismounting coming down arriving at arriving unexpected revealed (scriptures) نازل ہونا na'zil ho'na V.I. descend alight dismount come down arrive at unexpectedly be revealed نازل کرنا na'zil kar'na V.T. reveal (scriptures) نازلہ na'zilah N.M. (lit.) calamity ADJ. descended revealed [A ~ نزول]

نازنین nāz'nīn N.F. delicate person belle sweetheart . ADJ delicate lovely [P]

ناس[1] nās N.M. (rare) people [A]

ناس[2] nas N.F. snuff ناس کی چٹکی nās' kī chūṭ'kī N.F a pinch of snuff ناس لینا nās le'na V.T. take snuff sniff (something)

ناس[3] nas N.M. ruin · destruction ناس کردینا nas kar de'na V.I. spoil ruin ; destroy ناس ہوجانا nās' ho jā'na V.I. be spoilt be ruined go to rack and ruin ناستک nās' tik N.M. & ADJ. (dial.) atheist [S]

ناسخ na'sikh ADJ. annulling cancelling N.M. amanuensis scribe [A ~ نسخ]

ناسک na'sik N.M. (PL. نساک nūssak') worshipper ; devotee one who makes a sacrifice [A]

ناسوت *nāsoot'* N.M. physical universe mankind : humanity [A]

ناسور *nāsoor'* N.M. (PL. نواسیر *navāsīr'*) running sore ; ulcer; fistula ناسور بھرنا *nāsoor' bhar'nā* V.I. (of ulcer) heal ناسور پڑنا *nāsoor' paṛ'nā* V.I. become a running sore ; ulcerate [A]

ناشپاتی *nāshpā'tī* N.F. pear

ناشتہ *nāsh'tah* N.M. breakfast ناشتہ کرنا *nāsh'tah kar'nā* V.I. breakfast [~P ناشتا]

ناشر *nā'shir* N.M. (PL. ناشرین *nāshirīn'*) publisher [A ~ نشر]

ناصب *nā'sib* N.M. one setting something up particle putting a word in accusative case [A ~ نصب]

ناصح *nā'seh* ADJ. & N.M. (PL. *nūsahā'*) adviser ; counsellor ; monitor ; mentor [A ~ نصیحت]

ناصر *nā'sir* ADJ. (PL. انصار *ansār'*) N.M. helper ally [A ~ نصر]

ناصیہ *nā'siyah* N.F. (PL. نواصی *navā'sī*) forehead forelock over the head ناصیہ سا *nā'siya-sā*, ناصیہ فرسا *nā'siya-farsā'* N.M. & ADJ. (one) imploring humbly ناصیہ فرسائی *nā'siya-sā''ī*, ناصیہ سائی *nā'sia-farsā''ī* N.F. humble imploration [A]

ناطق *nā'tiq* ADJ. categorical (decision) rational (quality) talking (creature, etc.) ناطقہ *nā'tiqah* N.M. faculty of speech ناطقہ بند کرنا *nā'tiqah band' kar'nā* V.T. silence [A ~ نطق]

ناظر *nā'zir* N.M. beholder . spectator supervisor inspector a petty court official reader ناظر تعلیم *nā'zir-e ta'līmī'* N.M. Inspector of Schools ناظرین *nāzirīn'* N.M. PL. spectators ناظرہ *nā'zirah* N.F. (PL. ناظرات *nāzirāt'*) inspectress ; lady superintendent (rare) eye reading by sight ADV (reading) by sight ناظرہ پڑھنا *nā'zirah paṛh'nā* V.T. read (by sight) ناظرہ خواں *nā'zira-khāṅ* N.M. one who is able to recite the Holy Quran but is unable to understand its meaning ناظرین *nazirīn'* N.M. beholders; spectators onlookers [A ~ نظر]

ناظم *nāzim* N.M. (PL. نظما *nūzamā'*) administrator manager (rare) poet ; composer of verse (arch.) governor (of province, etc) [A ~ نظم]

ناغہ *nā'ghah* N.M. close day leave ناغہ کرنا *nā'ghah kar'nā* V.I. stay away from work [P]

ناف *nāf* N.F. navel ; umbilicus centre (of) ناف ٹلنا *nāf' ṭal'nā* V. (of navel muscle) be displaced ناف زمین *nā'f-e zamīn'* N.F. centre of the earth (fig.) the Holy Ka'bah [P]

نافذ *nā'fiz* ADJ. operative ; effective issued ADV. in force نافذ کرنا *nā'fiz kar'nā* V.T. issue (orders) enforce ; give effect to ; implement نافذ ہونا *nā'fiz ho'nā* V.T. (of orders, etc.) be issued be enforced ; be put into effect ; be implemented [A ~ نفوذ]

نافر *nā'fir* ADJ. & N.M. (one) who disdains [A ~ نفرت]

نافع *nā'fe'* ADJ. profitable ; beneficial useful ; advantageous [A ~ نفع]

نافلہ *nā'filah* N.F. & ADJ. supererogatory (devotion) [A ~ نفل]

نافہ *nā'fah* N.M. muskpod نافۂ آہو *nā'fa-e ā'hoo* N.M. musk deer's pod [P ~ ناف]

نافی *nā'fī*, نافیہ *nā'fiyah* ADJ. negative [A ~ نفی]

ناقد *nā'qid* ADJ. & N.M. (PL. ناقدین *nāqidīn'*) fault-finder (rare) critic ناقدانہ *nāqidā'nah* ADJ. & ADV. critical fault-finding [A ~ نقد]

ناقص *nā'qis* ADJ. defective deficient imperfect unsound wanting (in) worthless finite (verb) ناقص الخلقت *nā' qis-ul-khil' qat* ADJ. deformed defective by birth ناقص العقل *nā' qis-ul-'aq'l* ADJ. of unsound mind deficient in understanding [A ~ نقص]

ناقل *nā'qil* N.M. narrator [A ~ نقل]

ناقوس *nāqoos'* N.M. conch (ped.) wooden gong ناقوس بجانا *nāqoos' bajā'nā* V.T. strike the wooden gong ناقوس پھونکنا *nāqoos' phoonk'nā* V.T blow the conch [A]

ناقوس

ناقہ *nā'qah* N.M. she- camel ; dromedary ناقہ سوار *nā'qa-savār'* N.M. camel driver dromedary rider [A]

ناک *nāk* N.F. nose caspicuous person prominent thing honour (of) ناک آنا *nāk ā'nā* V.I. feel like blowing one's nose ناک اونچی ہونا *nāk' oonchī ho'nā* V.T. enjoy a respectable status (among) win greater honour ناک ادھر کہ ناک ادھر *nāk' i'dhar ke nak ū'dhar* PROV. a change either way would make little difference ناک بند *nāk'-band* N.M. nose-band (for horse) ناک بند ہونا *nāk' band ho'nā* V.I. have rasal passage choked owing to cold ناک بھوں چڑھانا *nāk' bhauṅ chaṛhā'nā* V.T. knit the brows frown ; scowl express one's disgust (with) ناک بہنا *nāk' baih'nā* V.I. (of someone) run at the nose ناک بیٹھنا (یا پچکنا) *nak baiṭh'nā* (or *pichaknā*) V.I. (of nose) flatten ناک بندھنا *nāk' bīndh'nā* V.T. bore the nose ناک پر انگلی رکھ کر بات کرنا *nāk' par ūng'lī rakh kar bāt' kar'nā* V.I. place one's finger on one's nose while talking be effeminate ; talk like woman کی ناک پر دیا جلا کر آنا *kī nāk' par di'ya jalā' kar ā'na* PH. (dial.) achieve success in the teeth of (someone) opposition ناک پر رکھ دینا *nāk' par rakh de'nā* PH. make prompt payment کی ناک پر غصہ ہونا *kī nāk' par ghus'sah ho'nā* V.T. (someone) be irritable ناک پر کی مکھی تک نہ اڑانا *nāk par kī mak'khī tak na ūṛa'nā* PH. be slothful ناک پر مکھی نہ بیٹھنے دینا *nāk' par mak'-khī na baiṭh'ne de'nā* PH. not be come under the least obligation ناک توڑنا *nāk' toṛ'nā* V.T. smash (someone's) nose disfigure ناک چڑھانا (یا سکوڑنا یا سکیڑنا) *nāk' chaṛhā'na* (or *sūkoṛ'na* or *sūkeṛ'nā*) V.I. frown (upon) express one's disgust ناک چڑھا *nāk' cha'ṛha* ADJ. (F. ناک چڑھی *nāk'-cha'ṛhī*) proud vain ; conceited ناک چڑھی رہنا *nāk' chaṛhī raih'na* V.I. be surly ناک چنے چبوانا *nāk' chane chabvā'na* V.T. torment harass ناک چوٹی کاٹنا (یا کاٹ کر ہاتھ دینا) *nāk' cho'ṭī kāṭ'nā* (or *kāṭ' kar hath' de'na*) V.T. disgrace (a woman) ناک چوٹی میں گرفتار رہنا *nāk' cho'ṭī men girif'tar' raih'na* V.I. be proud be initable be preoccupied with own worries ناک بجھی جانا *nāk' chhī' ja'na* V.I. (of nose) have its bore ناک رکھ لینا *nāk' rakh' le'na* V.T. preserve (someone's) honour ناک رگڑنا (یا گھسنا) *nāk' ra'gaṛna* (or *ghis'nā*) V.T. express regrets very humbly implore deplore oneself for the purpose ناک سے لکیریں کھینچنا *nāk' se lakī'ren khench'na* V.T. humbly assure not to repeat a mistake ناک کا بال *nāk' kā bal'* N.M. person having influence over (someone) confidant ناک کا بانسا (یا بانسہ) *nāk' ka bān'sa* (or *bān'sah*) N.M. bridge of the nose ناک کا بانسا پھر جانا *nāk' ka bān'sa phir' ja'nā* V.T. be at the point of death ناک کا تنکا *nāk' kā tin'ka* N.M. small ornamental nail for nose ناک کاٹ کر چوتڑوں میں رکھنا *nāk' kāṭ' choo'taroṅ men rakh'na*, ناک کاٹی مبارک کان کاٹے سلامت *nāk' ka'ṭī mūba'rak kān' ka'ṭe salā'mat* PH. be impervious to all sense of shame ناک (یا کان) کاٹنا *nāk' (kān') kaṭ'na* V.T. disgrace or debase (someone) ناک کٹنا *nāk' kaṭa'nā* V.I. be disgraced ناک کاٹنا *nāk' kaṭ'na* V.I. be disgraced (in family, etc.) ناک کی سیدھ میں *nāk' kī sīdh' men* ADV. straight ahead ناک کی پھنگی *nāk' kī phungī* N.F. tip of the nose ناک کے پھیرے بیان کرنا *nāk' ke phe're bayān' kar'na* PH. complicate some statement unnecessarily ناک مرنا *nāk' mar'nā* V.T. spurn ; dislike ناک میں بولنا *nāk' men bol'na* V.I. snuffle ناک میں تیر دینا (یا کرنا) *nāk' men tīr' de'na* (or *kar'nā*) V.T. harass ناک میں دم آنا *nāk' men dam' ā'na* V.I be harassed ناک میں دم کرنا *nāk' men dam' kar'na* V.T. harass ناک نہ دی جانا *nāk' na dī jā'na* PH. stink ناک نہ رہنا *nāk' na raih'nā* V.I. lose prestige ناک والا *nāk' va'la* ADJ. (F. ناک والی *nāk'-va'lī*) respectable (person)

ناکوں ناک بھر دینا *na'koṅ nāk bhar' de'na* V.T. fill to the brim ناکڑا *nāk'ṛa* N.M. thick nose

ناک ۲ *nak* SUF. -ful ناکی *na'kī* SUF. -fulness [P]

ناکہ *na'kah*, ناکا *na'ka* N.M. end of road check-post there eye (of needle) ناکہ بندی *na'ka-bandī* N.F. blockade ناکہ بندی کرنا *na'ka-ban'dī kar'na* V.T. blockade place a picket at the end (of street, etc.) ناکہ سنبھالنا *na'kah sambhāl'na* V.T. picket ناکے میں سے نکالنا *nake men se nikal'na* V.T. bring under one's yoke coerce make things difficult (for); put (someone) into a corner [doublet of ناک]

ناکح *na'keh* N.M. one who marries [A ~ نکاح]

ناگ *nāg* N.M. dangerous snake cobra (regarded by Hindus as a diety) ناگن *na'gan* (dial. *na'gin*) ناگنی *nāg'nī* N.F. dangerous female snake ناگ پھنی *nāg-pha'nī* N.F. a kind of cactus

ناگر بیل *na'gar-bel'* N.F. betel-leaf creeper ناگر موتھا *na'gar-mo'tha* N.M. a kind of fragrant grass

ناگری *nāg'rī*, دیو ناگری *dev-nāg'rī* N.F. Hindi script ; Devanagari

ناگل *na'gal* N.M. strap under yoke

ناگن *na'gan*, ناگنی *nag'nī* N.F. (see under ناگ N.M. ★)

نال *nal* N.F. pipe tube barrel (of gun) stalk stem (weaver's) shuttle pith (inside reed) navel string drencher نال گڑنا (یا دفن ہونا) *nal gaṛ'na* (or *daf'n ho'nā*) PH. have hereditary connections (with a place)

نالا *na'la*, نالہ *na'lah* N.M. ravine brook drain gutter

نالاں *na'lān* ADJ. (see under نالہ N.M. ★)

نالش *na'lish* N.F. suit ; law-suit ; legal action ; plaint نالش دیوانی *na'lish-e dīva'nī* N.F. civil suit نالش (دائر) کرنا *na'lish (dā''ir) kar'na* V.T. file a suit نالشی *na'lishī* N.M. plaintiff

نالکی *nal'kī* N.F. open palanquin for the rich

نالہ *na'lah* N.M. lamentation نالاں *na'lān* ADJ. lamenting complaining نالہ سر کرنا *na'lah sar kar'na* V.T. layment sigh ; heave a sigh نالۂ شبگیر *na'la-e shab-gīr'* N.M. lementation at night نالہ کش *na'la-kash* ADJ. & N.M. lamenter نالہ کشی *na'la-ka'shī* N.F. lamentation نالہ کرنا *na'lah kar'na* V.I. lament نالہ و فریاد *na'la-o-faryad*, نالہ و زاری *na'la-o-za'rī* N.F. lamentation moan نالی na'li SUF lamenting crying [P ~ نالیدن]

نالی na'li N.F drain pipe gutter vein tubulated tile

نام nam N.M. name appellation good name ; character ; fame نام آور na'm-a'var ADJ. famous ; renowned نام آوری na'm-a'vari N.F. fame ; renown نام اٹھنا nam' uṭh'na V.I. (of someone's name) be stamped well نام اچھالنا nam' uchhal'na V.T. defame make famous نام اچھلنا nam' u'chhal'na V.I. be defamed win fame نام باقی رہنا nam' ba'qi raih'na V.I. be immortalized نام بدنام کرنا nam bad-nam' kar'na V.T. defame نام بدنام ہونا nam bad-nam' ho'na V.I. be defamed نام بردہ nam'-bur'dah ADJ. above named نام بڑا درشن چھوٹے nam' ba'ṛa dar'shan chho'ṭe V.I. be famous beyond deserts نام بڑا ہونا nam' ba'ṛa ho'na V.I. a (of person or family) have great prestige نام بکتا ہے nam' bik'ta hai PH. the name sells نام بکنا nam' bik'na V.I. have a good market ; have a name (for) نام بگاڑنا nam' bigaṛ'na V.T. nickname defame نام بگڑنا nam' bi'gaṛ'na V.I. be nicknamed نام بنام nam' ba-nam' ADV. individually by name نام پانا nam' pa'na V.T. win a name for oneself ; become famous نام پر nam' par ADV. in the name (of) نام پر جان دینا nam' par jan' de'na V.T. be ready to lay down one's life for one's prestige نام پر حرف آنا nam' par ḥar'f a'na V.T. be defamed ; earn a bad name (for oneself) نام پر مٹنا nam' par miṭ'na V.T. be deep in love (with) نام پڑ جانا nam' par ja'na V.T. have an appellation نام پکارنا nam' pukar'na V.T. call out the name (of) نام پیدا کرنا nam' pai'da kar'na V.T. make a name ; become famous نام جاگنا nam' jag'na V.I. (of someone's fame) be rehabilitated نام جپنا nam' jap'na V.T. repeat the name of be devoted to ناموجو nam'-joo ADJ. fame-hunter نام چڑھنا nam chaṛh'na V.T. (of name) be entered نام چلنا nam' chal'na V.I. have a name (for) نام خاک میں مل جانا nam' khak' men mil' ja'na V.I. lose one's reputation نام خدا na'm-e khuda' INT. good heavens ; goodness gracious may God preserve him (etc.) from all harm نام خراب کرنا nam' kharab' kar'na V.T. defame , bring a bad name (to) نامدار nam'-dar ADJ. famous ; renowned ; celebrated نامداری nam'-da'ri N.F. fame ; renown , celebrity پر (یا پہ) نام دھرنا par (or pa) nam' dhar'na V.T blame ; accuse نام ڈبونا nam' dubo'na V.T lose one's (etc.) reputation نام ڈوبنا nam doob'na V.I (of reputation) be lost کو نام رکھنا ko nam' rakh'na V.T. name نام رکھنا nam' rakh'na V.T. blame , accuse نام روشن کرنا nam' rau'shan kar'na V.T make (someone) famous نام روشن ہونا nam' rau'shan ho'na V.I win fame نام زبان پر پھرنا nam' zaban' par phir'na V I. become famous (of name) not to be recalled fully نامزد nam'-zad ADJ. nominated (arch.) betrothed (to) (rare) earmarked (for) نام رہ جانا nam' raih' ja'na V.I. be remembered ever afterwards نامزد کرنا nam'-zad kar'na V.T. nominate (arch.) betroth (rare) earmark (for) نامزدگی nam'-za'dagi N.F. nomination (arch.) betrothal نام زندہ کرنا nam' zin'dah kar'na V.T. revive the name (of) نام سے nam se ADV. by the name (of) نام سے بیزار ہونا nam' se bezar' ho'na V.I. be fed up (with) ; be sick (of) نام سے تپ چڑھنا nam' se tap' chaṛh'na, نام سے دم نکلنا nam' se dam ni'kalna V.I. be afraid (of) نام سے واقف ہونا nam' se va'qif ho'na V.T. know (someone) by name نام کا سکہ جاری ہونا nam' ka sik'kah ja'ri ho'na V.I. rule be famous نام کا nam ka ADJ. nominal ADV. just in name نام کر جانا nam' kar ja'na V.I. leave a good name behind نام کرنا nam kar'na V.I. aehieve fame نام کو nam' ko ADV. nominally in name only ; just in name worth the name (not) at all نام کو دھبہ لگانا nam' ko dhab'bah laga'na V.T. & I. defame earn a bad name for oneself, etc.) نام لگانا nam' laga'na V.T. blame accuse (of) نام لگنا nam' lag'na V.T. be blamed be accused (of) نام لے کر nam' le kar ADV. in the name of نام لے لے کر nam' le le' kar ADV. openly by name نام لینا nam le'na V.T invoke the name (of) name call by name accuse falsely praise نام لیوا nam'-le'va N.M. heir descendent follower نام مٹنا nam' miṭ'na V.I. be forgotten for ever. نام نامی na'm-e na'mi N.M. famous name نام نکالنا nam' nikal'na V.T. & I. win fame hit upon name (for child from Scriptures, etc.) نام نکلنا nam' ni'kalna V.I. become famous be notorious become a by-word (for) (of name of culprit, etc.) be found out نام نہاد nam'-nehad ADJ. so-called نام نہ لینا nam na le'na V.T. forget all about be disgusted with نامور nam'-var ADJ. famous ; renowned N.M. celebrity ناموری nam'-va'ri N.F. fame ; renown ; celebrity نام و نشان na'm-o-nishan' (or -shan') (col. نام نشان nam' nishan') N.M. sign trace particulars نام و نمود na'm-o-numood' N.M. (col. نام نمود nam'-numood') mere show نام و ننگ na'm-o-nang' N.M. honour prestige نام ہونا nam ho'na V.I. win fame ; be renowned be entrusted to نامی na'mi ADJ. famous ; celebrated illustrious well-known نامی گرامی na'mi gira'mi ADJ. well-known [P]

ناموس namoos' N.F. (PL. نوامیس navamis') honour chastity female members of a family seraglio angel rule; law ناموسِ اکبر *nāmoo's-e ak'bar* N.M. gabriel the chief law ناموسی *nāmoo'sī* N.M. (col.) disgrace [A]

نامہ *nā'mah* N.M. letter record (of) نامۂ عمل *nā'ma-e a'māl'* N.M. record of (someone's) deeds نامہ بر *nā'ma-bar* N.M. messenger bearer of a note نامہ نگار *nā'ma-nigār'* N.M. correspondent (of periodical) نامہ و پیام *nā'ma-o-payām'* نامہ و پیغام *nā'ma-o-paighām'* N.M. correspondence exchange of latters messages [P]

نامی ۱ *nā'mī* ADJ. (see under نام N.M. ★)

نامی ۲ *nā'mī* ADJ. vegetal جسمِ نامی *jism-e nā'mī* N.M. living or vegetal body نامیاتی *nāmiyā'tī* ADJ. organic نامیاتی کیمیا *nāmiyā'tī kīmiyā'* N.F. organic chemistry نامیہ *nā'miyah* N.F. vegetal function ; vegetation [A ~ نمو]

نان *nān* N.F. loaf of breed نانبائی *nān-bā''ī* N.M. baker نان پاؤ *nān'-pā''o* N.F. (arch.) bread نانِ جویں *nā'n-e javīn'* N.F. barley bread (fig.) coarse diet نان خطائی *nān'-khatā''ī* N.F. cooky نانخواہ *nān'-khāh* N.M. seed of a plant of dill kind نان و نفقہ *nā'n-o-naf'qah* (col. نان نفقہ *nān' naf'qah*) N.M. maintenance allowance for one's family نان و نمک *nā'n-o-na'mak* N.M. simple food [P]

نانا *nā'nā* N.M. maternal grandfather نانی *nā'nī* N.F. maternal grandmother نانی کے آگے ننھیال کی باتیں *nā'nī ke ā'ge nanhyāl' kī bā'teṅ* PROV. complain to someone against his kith and kin نانی نے خصم کیا برا کیا کر کے چھوڑ دیا اور بھی برا کیا *nā'nī ne khas'm ki'yā bū'ra ki'yā kar' ke chhoṛ di'yā aur' bhī bū'ra kiyā* PROV. silly step followed by naive amends نانی یاد آنا *nānī yād' ā'nā* PROV. be reminded of one's palmy days

نانٹھا *nān'thā* ADJ. having no heir

ناند *nānd* N.F. vat trough

نادھنا *nāndh'na* V.T. begin (embroidery, etc.)

نانگا *nāṅ'gā* N.M. nude Hindu saint ADJ. nude [doublet of ننگا]

نانگھنا *nāngh'na* V.T. (dial.) jump over ; take in a stride

نانو *nāṅ''o*- ناؤں *nā''oṅ* N.M. (arch.) for (N.M. ★) ناواں *nāṅ'vaṅ* N.M. money debt ناواں چکانا *nāṅ'vāṅ chukā'nā* V.T. repay debt

ناوک *nā'vak* N.M. arrow ناوک انداز *nā'vak-aṅdāz'*, ناوک فگن *nā'vak-fi'gan* N.M. archer sagittrius; critical person ناوک اندازی *nā'vak-aṅdā'zī* ناوک فگنی *nā'vak-fi'ganī* N.F. archery harsh criticism [P]

ناول *nā'vil* N.M. novel ; fiction ناول نگار (یا نویس) *nā'vil-nigār'* (or *navīs'*) N.M. novelist ناول نگاری (یا نویسی) *nā'vil-nigā'rī* (or *navī'sī*) N.F. fiction-writer [P]

ناؤ و نوش *nā'-o-nosh'* N.M. carousing [P ~ نائے flute + نوش drinking]

ناہار *nahār'* N.M. breakfast [P]

ناہرو *nāh'roo* N.M. (same as نہروا N.M. ★)

ناہید *nāhīd'* N.M. Venus [P]

ناہیں *nā'hīṅ* ADV. (dial. for نہیں) no

نائب *nā''ib* N.M. deputy ; assistant attorney vicegerent locum tenens نائب السلطنت *nā''ib-ūs-saltanat* N.M. viceroy نائب مناب *nā''ib manāb'* N.M. vicegerent [A ~ نیابت]

نائرہ *nā''irah* N.M. fire flame (of) [A ~ نار]

نائزہ *nā''izah* N.M. penis [P]

نائک *nā''ik* N.M. corporal (rare) virtuoso نائکہ *nā''ikah* N.F. bawd ; mistress of brothel

ناؤ *nā''o* N.F. boat ناؤ خشکی میں نہیں چلتی *nā''o khūsh'kī meṅ nā'hīṅ chal'tī* PROV. one must spend to win honour ناؤ کھینا *nā''o khe nā* V.T. row a boat ناؤ میں خاک اڑانا *nā''o meṅ khāk ūṛā'nā* PROV. trump up a false charge

نائی *nā''ī* N.M. barber نائن *nā''in* N.M. barber's wife

نائے *nā''e*, نا *nā* AFFIX. flute gulf

نبات *nabāt'* N.F. sugar-candy [P]

نب *nib* N.M. nib [E]

نباتات *nabātāt'* N.F. vegetables نباتاتی *nabātā'tī* ADJ. botanical نباتیات *nabātiyyāt'* N.F. botany [A ~ SING. نبات]

نباض *nabbāz'* N.M. expert at feeling the pulse ; specialist in diagnosis shrewd person نباضی *nabbā'zī* N.F. such expertness shrewdness

نباہنا *nibāh'nā*, نبھانا *nibhā'nā* V.I. be faithful be constant in relations (with) live (happily, etc. with) for a long period accommodate نباہ *nibāh'*, نبھاؤ *nibhā''o* N.M. faithfulness constancy spirit of accommodation نباہ کرنا *nibāh' kar'na* V.I. be constant in relations (with) accommodate; have an accommodating spirit

نبٹانا nibṭā'nā, نپٹانا nipṭā'nā, نمٹانا nimṭā'na V.T. settle bring to a conclusion نبٹنا ni'baṭnā, نپٹنا ni'paṭnā, نمٹنا ni'maṭnā V.I. be settled be concluded ; be brought to a conclusion settle bring to a conclusion

نبرد nabar'd N.F. battle war fight نبرد آزمائی nabar'd-āzmā' N.M. warrior fighter

نبرد گاہ nabard'-gah N.F. battlefield [P]

نبڑنا ni'baṛnā V.I. be finished ; be completed come to an end be expended نبیڑنا nabeṛ'nā V.T. complete expend do ; perform ; execute

نبض nab'z N.F. pulse نبض دیکھنا nab'z dekh'nā V.T. feel the pulse (of) نبضیں چھوٹنا nab'zeṅ chhooṭ'nā V.I. (of pulse) cease beating be dying [A]

نبوت nūbūv'vat N.F. (see under نبی N.M. ★)

نبولی nibo'lī N.F. margose fruit [~ نیم]

نبوی na'bavī ADJ. (see under نبی N.M. ★)

نبھانا nibhā'nā V.T. (same as نباہنا V.T. ★) نبھاؤ nibhā''o N.M. (same as N.M.) (see under نباہنا V.T. ★)

نبھنا nibh'nā V.I. be faithful be constant live together pull together

نبی na'bī N.M. prophet نبی کریم nabiy'y-e karīm' N.M. the Holy Prophet نبی مرسل nabiy'y-e mūr'sal N.M. Prophet to whom scriptures are revealed نبوت nūbūv'at N.F. prophethood prophecy نبوی na'bavī ADJ. prophet; prophetical [A ~ نبا news]

نبیذ nabīz' N.F. 'nabiz' a non-alcoholic formented beverage prepared from malt

نبیرہ nabī'rah N.M. grandson [P]

نبیڑنا nabeṛ'nā V.T. (see under نبڑنا V.I. ★) cute

نپا تلا na'pa tūlā ADJ. measured limited [تولنا + ناپنا]

نپٹ ni'pāṭ N.F. (arch.) quite

نپٹانا nipṭā'nā V.T. (same as نبٹانا V.T. ★) نپٹنا ni'paṭnā V.T. & I. (same as نبٹنا V.T. & I. ★) (see under نبٹانا)

نپنا nap'nā V.I. be measured [~ ناپنا]

نت nit' ADV. always; ever نت کنواں کھودنا نت پانی پینا nit' kū''aṅ khod'nā nit' pā'nī pī'na PROV. live from hand to mouth نت نیا nit' na'ya ADJ. & ADV. (F. نت نئی nit' na''ī) ever new

نپوتا nipoo'tā N.M. نپوتی nipoo'tī N.F. (dial.) issueless [~ نہ + پوت]

نتائج natā''ij N.M. (PL. of نتیجہ N.M

نتھ nath N.F. large nose ring نتھ اتارنا nath ūtār'nā V.T. deflower نتھ بڑھانا nath baṛhā'na V.T. take nose-ring off نتھ چوڑی nath choo'ṛī چوڑی نتھ choo'ṛī nath N.F. nose-ring and bangles (as symbols of happy married (life) نتھنی nath'nī N.F. animal's nose-ring small nose-ring نتھیا nath'ya N.F. small nose-ring [~ نتھنا]

نتھارنا nithar'na V.T. (of liquid) draw or pour (of the sediment) نتھرنا ni'tharnā V.I. purified thus ; be drawn off ; be poured off

نتھنا nath'nā N.M. nostril نتھنے پھلانا (یا چڑھانا) nath'ne phūlā'na (or charhā'nā) PH. be angry ; be furious

نتھی nat'thī ADJ. tagged ; strung together enclosed N.F. (rare) tag file theread for filing نتھی شدہ nat'thī-shū'dah ADJ. tagged strung together enclosed placed on file نتھی کرنا nat'thī kar'na V.T. tag ; strung together enclose place on file

نتیجہ natī'jah N.M. (PL. نتائج natā''ij) result consequence conclusion inference; deduction issue نتیجہ نکالنا natī'jah nikal'na V.T. deduce infer declare the result نتیجہ نکلنا natī'jah ni'kalnā V.I. be deduced ; be inferred (of result (be declared)

نٹ naṭ N.M. rope-dancer juggler name of musical mode نٹنی nat'nī N.F. juggler's wife female rope-dancer

نٹ کھٹ naṭ'-khaṭ ADJ: naughty ; roguish N.M. knave نٹ کھٹی naṭ -kha'ṭī N.F. naughtiness ; roguery ; roguishness

نثار nisār' ADJ. sacrificed نثار کرنا nisār kar'na V.T. be sacrificed at the altar (of) ; be immalated (of money, etc.) throw over someone's head (fig.) devote (to) نثار ہونا nisār' ho'na V.I. be sacrificed at the altar (of) (fig.) be devoted (to) [A]

نثار nassār N.M. (see under FOLL. ★)

نثر nas'r N.F. prose نثر نگار nas'r-nigar' N.M. prose-writer نثار nassār' N.M. prose-writer [A]

نج nij' N.F. of private ownership (used only as) نج کا nij' kā (or) نجی ni'jī ADJ. own personal private unofficial

نجابت najā'bat N.F nobility ; gentility نجیب ADJ. & N.M. ★ [A]

نجات *najāt'* N.F. deliverance ; salvation absolution ; freedom , liberation escape [A]

نجاح *najāh* N.M. success [A]

نجار *najjār'* N.M. (lit.) carpenter نجاری *najjā'rī* N.F. carpentry [A]

نجاست *najā'sat* N.F. (see under نجس ADJ. ★)

نجاشی *najā'shī* N.M. Negus [A ~ Aetheopian]

نجبا *nūjabā'* N.M (PL. of نجیب A.M ★)

نجد *naj'd* N.M. Highland Arabian [A]

نجس *naj's, na'jis* ADJ. & N.M. filthy (thing or person) ; impure ; unclean (thing or person) نجس العین *na'jis-ūl-'ain*, ADJ. & N.M. inherently unclean (thing or person) [A ~ نجاست]

نجف *na'jaf* N.M. site of Hazrat Ali's tomb in Iraq (rate) waterless mound [A]

نجم *naj'm* N M. PL. انجم *anj'ūm*, نجوم *nūjoom'*) star planet نجم ثاقب *najm-ūs-sā'qib* N.M. (wrong but) popular variant of النجم الثاقب *an-naj'm-ūs-sā'qib* N M shining star

نجوم *nūjoom'* N M astrology N.M. PL stars نجومی *nujoo'mī* N M. astrologer [A ~ SING. نجم]

نجی *ni'jī* ADJ (see under نج N F ★)

نجیب *najīb'* N.M (PL. نجبا *nūjabā'*) person of noble birth ADJ. noble نجیب الطرفین *najī'b-ūt-tarafain'* ADJ having noble parents [A ~ نجابت]

نچا کھچا *nū'chā khū'chā* ADJ (see under نچنا V I. ★)

نچان *nichān'* N F slope ; declevity [A ~ نیچا]

نچانا *nachā'nā* V.T. cause to dance pester ; harass تگنی کا ناچ نچانا *tig'nī kā nāch nachā'nā* V.T. harass cause (someone) to dance to ones trone نچا مارنا *nachā' mār'nā* V.T. harass pester by demanding too much obedience tire (someone) out نچوانا *nachvā'nā* V.T. make (someone) dance نچویا *nachvay'ya* N.M. (derog.) dancer [~ نچنا CAUS.]

نچڑنا *ni'chūṛnā* V.I. (see under نچوڑنا V.T ★)

نچلا[1] *nich'lā* ADJ. نچلی *nich'lī*) motionless inactive quiet نچلا نہ بیٹھنا *nich'lā na baith'nā* V.I. not to sit quietly fidget

نچلا[2] *nich'la* (dial. *nichal'lā*) ADJ (F. نچلی *nich'lī*, dial. *nichal'lī*) lower (storey, etc.)

نچنا *nuch na* V I. be plucked be pinched be worn out نچا کھچا *nū'cha khū'cha* (or *khūs'ṭa*) ADJ. plucked pinched (fig) be crest-fallen نچوانا *nūchvā'na* V T. cause to be plucked [~ نوچنا]

نچنت *ni'chant* ADJ. free from care unconcerned leisurely careless ADV carelessly at leisure [S ~ چنتا]

نچوانا *nachvā'nā* V T (see under نچانا V.T. ★)

نچوانا *nūchvā'na* V.T (see under نچنا V I. ★)

نچوڑنا *nichoṛ'nā* V.T. rinse, rinse out squeeze wring strain exact ; extort drain the life blood (of) نچوڑ *nichoṛ'* N.M. essence summary the long and short (of)

نچویا *nachvay'ya* N.M. (see under نچانا *nachā'na* V.I. ★)

نچھاور *nichhā'var* ADJ. sacrificed at the altar (of money etc.) of scattered (over someone) a propitiatory offering نچھاور کرنا *nichhā'var kar'nā*, V.T. sacrifice at the altar of scatter money, etc., thus نچھاور ہونا *nachhā'var ho'nā* V.I be sacrificed at the altar of be scattered thus

نچھتر *nachhat'tar* N.M. (dial.) constellation in path of moon [S]

نحافت *nahā'fat* N F (see under نحیف ADJ. ★)

نحر *nah'r* N M. slaughter (of camel) sacrifice [A]

نحس *naihs* (ped. *na'hs*) ADJ ill-fated , inauspicious; ominous; portentous نحوست *nahoo'sat* N.F. misfortune portent ominousness evil influence laziness [A]

نحل *nah'l* N.F bee [A]

نحو *nah'v* N.F. syntax mode صرف و نحو *sar'f-o-nah'v* N.M. accidence and syntax grammar ADJ. syntactical grammatical نحوی *nah'vī* N.M expert in syntax Grammarian [A]

نخ *nakh* N.F. thread thin lacquer bangle [P]

نحیف *nahīf* ADJ. lean ; thin slender weak نحافت *nahā'fat* N.F leanness weakness [A]

نخاس *nakhkhās'* N.M. (arch) slave market cattle market market نخاس چڑھنا *nakhkhās' charh'nā* V.I. be put for sale in the market be ill-famed نخاس کی گھوڑی *nakhkhās' kī gho'ṛī* N.F. pony whore نخاس والی *nakhkhās'-vā'lī* N.F. whore [A]

نخالص *ni-khā'lis* ADJ. (col.) pure ; unadulterated [~P ن + A خالص used in exactly opposite meaning to literal sense]

نخچیر *nakhchīr'* N.M. prey ; game نخچیر گاہ *nakh-chīr'-gāh* N.F. game preserve hunting ground [P]

نخرا *nakh'rā*, نخرہ *nakh'rah* N.M. coquetry blandishment disdainful airs ; affectation نخرے باز *nakh're-bāz* N.M. & ADJ. coquetish; pretender ; an (person) affected (person) نخرے پیٹی *nakh're-pī'tī* N.F. & ADJ. (iron.) coquetish woman

نخست *nakhūs't*, نخستیں *nakhūs'tīn* ADJ. first [P]

نخشب *nakh'shab* N.M. name of a central Asian town ماہ نخشب *mā'h-e nakh'shab* N.M. (see under ماہ N.M. ★)

نخصمی *nikhas'mī* ADJ. divorced (woman) loose (woman) [~ خصم]

نخل *nakh'l* N.M. date palm نخل ایمن (یا طور) *nakh'l-e e'man* (or *toor'*) N.M. Sinai tree where God made Himself manifest نخل بند *nakh'l-band* N.M. gardeners market for artificial fruits نخلستان *nakh'-listān* N.M. (ped. نخلہ *nakh'lah*) oasis نخیل *nakhīl'* N.M. date grove [A]

نخوت *nakh'vat* N.M. pride ; haughtiness ; conceit [A]

نخود *nakhūd'* N.M. gram [P]

نخیل *nakhīl'* N.M. (see under نخل N.M. ★)

ند *nad* N.M. (rare) river stream [~ ندی]

ند *nid* N.F. like ; parallel [A]

ندا *nidā'* N.F. call voice حرف ندا *ḥar'f-e nidā'* N.M. vocative [A]

ندارد *na-dā'rad* ADV. missing ; gone [P + نہ + دارد]

ندامت *nadā'mat*, ندم *na'dam* N.F. regret repentance [A]

ندرت *nūd'rat* N.F. rareness singularity uniqueness ندرت خیال *nūd'rat-e khayāl'* N.F. rareness of vision unique idea [A]

ندما *nūda'mā* N.M. (PL. of ندیم N.M. ★)

ندولا *nado'la* N.M. trough ; large earthen pan [~ ناند ABB.]

ندوہ *nad'vah* N.M. group ; association (also ندوۃ العلما *nad'vat-ul 'ūlamā*) Muslim religious scholars' association as the name of academy founded by the Urdu writer Shibli No'mani ندوی *na'davī* ADJ. belonging to Nadvah

ندی *na'dī* (or *nad'dī*) N.F. stream ; rivulet ندی ناؤ سنجوگ *na'dī nā''o sanjog'* N.M. chance meeting

ندیدہ *nadī'dah* ADJ. & N.M. (F. ندیدی *nadī'dī*) covetous (one) looking covetously at eatables, etc. [~ P نہ + دیدن]

ندیم *nadīm'* N.M. (PL. ندما *nūdamā'*) boon companion courtier [A]

نڈر *nidar'* ADJ. fearless intrepid dauntless ; undaunted N.M. daring person dare-devil [~ ن + ڈر]

نڈھال *nidhāl* ADJ. & ADV. weak enervated tired run-down

نذر *naz'r* N.F. vow offering oblation gift ; present نذر چڑھانا *naz'r charhā'nā* V.T. make offerings at a shrine, etc. نذر دکھانا *naz'r dikhā'nā* V.T. make a present to authority نذر دینا (یا گزراننا) *naz'r de'nā* (or *gūzrān'nā*) V.T. make a present (to king) etc. کی نذر ہونا *kī naz'r kar'nā* V.T. present to نذر ماننا *naz'r mān'nā* V.I. make a vow (کی) نذر ہونا (*kī*) *naz'r ho'nā* V.I. be presented (to) be a present for someone نذر و نیاز *naz'r-o-niyāz* (col. نذر نیاز *naz'r niyāz*) N.M. gifts and oblations نذرانہ *nazrā'nah* N.M. present (to superior, etc.) (euphuism for) price (euphuism for) bribemoney [A]

نذیر *nazīr'* N.F. one who terrorizes [A]

نر *nar* N.M. & ADJ. male نرمادگی *nar mā'dagī* N.M. نر مادہ *nar-mā'dah* N.M (also نرمادین *nar-mā'dīn*) male and female pair of drums forming 'tabla' نرناری *nar-nā'rī* M.M. (dial.) man and woman نرینہ *narī'nah* ADJ. male (issue) [P]

نر *nir* PREF. without ; lacking un- ; in- -less [S]

نراس *nirās'* N.F. despondence ADJ. (dial.) (also نراسا *nirā'sā*) despondent [S]

نرا *ni'rā* ADJ. & ADV. (F. نری *ni'rī*) merely pure and simple through and through arrant

نرالا *nirā'la* ADJ. (F. نرالی *nirā'lī*) strange odd rare incomparable

نرانا *nirā'nā* V.T. weed نرائی *nirā''ī* N.F. weeding

نربسی *nir'basī* N.F. Zedoary

نربل *nir'bal* ADJ. (dial.) weak powerless [~ نر + بل]

نرت *ni'rat* N.F. [illegible] signs (also نرتکاری *ni'rat-kā'rī*) use of [illegible] signs

نرخ *nir'kh* N.M. rate price نرخ بندی *nir'kh-ban'dī* N.F. (arch.) fixation of rates price control نرخنامہ *nir'kh-nā'mah* N.M. price-list [P]

نرخرا *nar'kharā* N.M. windpipe نرخرا بولنا *nar'kharā bol'nā* V.I. have the death-rattle

نرد nar'd N.F. draughtsman ; counter [P]

نردبان nar'd-bān N.M. ladder [P]

نردوش nirdosh' ADJ. (dial.) innocent ; not guilty [S ~ نر + دوش blame]

نردهن nir'dhan ADJ. (dial.) poor [S ~ نر + دهن wealth]

نرس nar's N.F. nurse نرسنگ nar'sing N.F. nursing [E]

نرسل nar'sal, نرکل nar'kal N.M. reed ; matting-rush

نرسنگھا nar-sin'ghā N.M. horn (used as wind instrument) [~ نر + سینگ]

نرغہ nar'ghah N.M. cordon crowd (surrounding culprit, etc.) press نرغہ کرنا nar'ghah kar'nā V.T. throw a cordon (round) press ; crowd (round) نرغے میں آجانا nar'ghe meṅ ā jā'nā V.T. be surrounded (by) be pressed (by) [P]

نرک nar'k N.M. (H. dial) hell [S]

نرگس nar'gis N.F. narcissus نرگس بیمار (یا مخمور) nar'gis-e bīmār' (or makhmoor') N.F. (fig.) beloved's eye نرگس شہلا nar'gis-e shahlā' N.F. narcissus with black spot (fig.) beloved's eye نرگسی nar gisī ADJ. like narcissus نرگسی پلاؤ nar'gisī pulā''o N.M. egg-pie 'pulao' نرگسی کباب nar'gisī kabāb' N.M. boiled egg covered with cooked mince and cut lengthwise , egg-pie [P]

نرم nar'm ADJ. soft smooth mild gentle tender easy slow slack dull (market) نرم دل nar'm-dil ADJ gentle ; kind-hearted نرم رو nar'm-rau' ADJ. easy going considerate نرم کرنا nar'm kar'nā N.F. soften appease نرم گرم nar'm-gar'm N.M. harsh words نرم گرم سننا (یا سہنا) nar'm gar'm sūn'nā (or saih'nā) V.I. endure ; put up (with) ; brook نرم نرم nar'm nar'm ADJ. quite softy نرم ہونا nar'm ho'nā V.I. soften yield ; give in take pity be appeased نرمانا narmā'nā V.T. soften appease نرماہٹ nar'mā'hat, نرمائی narmā''ī N.F. (col.) softness نرمی nar'mī N.F. softness smoothness mildness gentleness ; tenderness slackness dullness (of market) [P]

نرمہ ¹ nar'mah, نرما nar'mā N.M. long-staple cotton [~ P نرم]

نرمہ ² nar'mah N.M. (ear.) lobe نرمۂ گوش nar'ma-e gosh' N.M. ear-lobe [P ~ نرم]

نروان nirvān' N.M. (F. dial.) salvation [S]

نروپ niroop' N.M. amorphism [S ~ ن + روپ]

نری na'rī N.F. kind ; tanned sheep-skin

نرینہ narī'nah ADJ. (see under نر ~ ADJ. ★)

نزار nazār' ADJ. thin ; lean ; gaunt weak نحیف ونزار nahī'f-o-nazār' ADJ. thin lean weak [P]

نزاع ni'zā' N.F. dispute altercation contention litigation point at issue [A]

نزاکت nazā'kat N.F. delicacy blindishment coquetry [P ~ نازک]

نزد niz'd (or naz'd) ADJ. (rare) near نزدیک naz-dīk' ADJ. ★ [P]

نزدیک nazdīk' ADJ. close (to) near in the opinion (of) ; according (to) کے نزدیک نہ جانا ke nazdīk' na jā'nā V.I. not to go near (fig.) keep away from ; fly away (from) نزدیکی nazdī'kī N.F. AD; near (relation) N.M. near relation N.F. nearness [P]

نزع nāz'' N.F. last breath ; last gasp agonies of death [A]

نزلہ naz'lah N.M. catarrh ; rheum نزلہ برعضو ضعیف naz'la bar 'ūz'v-e za'īf' PROV. the weaker always gets it in the neck نزلہ گرنا naz'lah gir'nā V.I. (of rage) be vented (on) [A ~ نزول]

نزول nūzool' N.M. revelation descent arrival sojourn state lands نزول اجلال nūzoo'l-e ijlāl' N.M. arrival (of some personage) نزول الما nūzoo'l-ūl-mā' N.M. cataract hydrocele نزول وحی nūzoo'l-e vah'y N.M. revelation divine revelation [A]

نزہت nūz'hat N.F. (rare) being away (from) [A]

نژاد nazhād' N.F. generation descent ; extraction نژاد نو nazhā'd-e nau' N.F. new generation [P]

نس nas N.F. sinew ; a tendon ; muscle (dial.), penis نس دار nas'-dār ADJ. sinewy mascular نس کٹا nas-ka'tā N.M. eunuch ADJ. emasculate effeminate

نس nis N.F. night (only in) نسدن nis'-din N.M. & ADV. night and day ; always

نسا nisā' N.F. women نسائی nisā''ī ADJ. female womanish نسائیت nisā'iy'yat N.F. effeminacy traits of women's character [A]

نسا nasā' N.F. (same as عرق النسا ir'q-ūn-nasā' N.F. (see under عرق 'ir'q N.F. ★)

نسب na'sab N.M. lineage Geneology family نسب نامہ na'sab-nā'mah N.M. pedigree ; geneological tree نسب نما na'sab-nūmā' N.M. (Math.) denominator نسبی na'sabī ADJ. family of good family حسب نسب ha'sab na'sab N.M. (see under حسب N.M. ★)

نسبت nis'bat N.F. connection ; relation reference comparison ratio betrothal ADV. (col.) in proportion (to) comparison (with) نسبت آنا nis'bat ā'nā V.I. (of girl) have an offer of marriage ; have an offer نسبت تناسب nis'bat-e tanā'sūb' N.F. ratio proportion نسبت ٹھہرنا nis'bat ṭhai'harnā V.I. be betrothed نسبت دینا nis'bat de'nā V.T. compare (with) relate (to) نسبت رکھنا nis'bat rakh'nā V.I. be related (to) be connected (with) نسبت کرنا nis'bat kar'nā V.T. betroth نسبت ہونا nis'bat ho'nā V.I. be betrothed be related to ; be connected with نسبتی nis'batī ADJ. in-law نسبتی بھائی nis'batī bhā''ī, برادر نسبتی birā'-dar-e nis'batī N.M. brother-in-law [A]

نسترن nas'taran N.F. dog-rose [P]

نستعلیق nasta'līq' N.M. fine round hand (as usual Urdu script) 'nastaliq' ADJ. cultured soft-spoken facile

نسخ nas'kh N.M. cancellation abolition repeal ; abrogation commonest Arabic script [A]

نسخہ nūs'khah N.M. (PL. نسخ nū'sakh) prescription copy (of book) edition [A doublet of PREF.]

نسر nas'r N.M. vulture نسر طائر nas'r-e tā''ir N.M. constellation of the Eagle نسر واقع nas'r-e vā'qe'' N.M. constellation of the Lyre

نسرین nas'rīn (or nasrīn') N.M. dog-rose [P]

نسق nas'q (or na'saq) N.M. order (rare) arrangement نظم و نسق naz'm-o nas'q (or nasaq') N.M. discipline [A]

نسرین

نسل nas'l N.F. race generation نسل بڑھانا nas'l barhā'nā V.T. breed نسل کشی nas'l-ka'shī N.F. breeding rearing نسل کشی کرنا nas'l-qa'shī kar'nā V.T. breed نسل کشی nas'l-kū'shī N.F. genocide نسل کشی کرنا nas'l-kū'shī kar'nā V.T. guilty of genocide نسلاً nas'lan ADV. by descent racially نسلاً بعد نسلٍ nas'lan ba''da nas'lin ADV. generation after generation نسلی nas'lī ADJ. racial نسلی امتیاز nas'lī imti'yāz' N.M. racial discrimination [A]

نسوار nasvār' N.F. snuff [~ ناس]

نسواں nis'vān N.F. women نسوانی nisvā'nī ADJ. effaminate female نسوانیت nisvāniy'yat N.F. effeminacy traits of women's character [A doublet of نسا]

نسیان nisyān' N.M. forgetfulness ; oblivion نسیاً منسیا nas'yan mansiy'yā ADV. forgotten obliterated [A]

نسیم nasīm' N.F. zephyr breeze نسیم سحر nasī'm-e sa'har N.F. morning breeze [A]

نسیہ nis'yah N.M. credit loan [A]

نشاۃ nash''at, نشاۃ nash''at N.F. creation نشاۃ اولیٰ nash''at-e oo'lā N.F. gensis نشاۃ ثانیہ nash'-'at-e sā'niyah, N.F. renascence ; renaissance [A]

نشاستہ nishās'tah N.M. starch [P]

نشاط nashāt' N.F. delight ارباب نشاط arbā'b-e nashāt' N.M. & PL. gay-girls [A]

نشان nishān' (or nishāṅ') N.M. mark sign trace Scar emblem ; betrothal ring, etc. flag ; ensign ; standard نشان بردار nishān-bar-dār' N.M. standard-bearer نشان پڑنا nishān'-par'nā V.I. have mark of (beeting, etc.) نشاندہی nishān'-de'hī N.F. pointing out identification نشاندہی کرنا nishān'-de'hī kar'nā locating V.T. point out locate نشانی nishā'nī V.T. ★ [P]

نشانہ nishā'nah N.M. aim target نشانہ باز ni'shā'na-bāz' نشانچی nishān'chī N.M. markman ; good shot نشانہ بازی nishā'na-bā'zī N.F. marksmanship نشانہ باندھنا ni'shā'nah bāndh'nā, V.T. & I. aim (at) take aim نشانہ خطا ہونا nishā'nah khatā' ho'nā V.I. be wide of the mark نشانہ کرنا یا لگانا n'shā'nah kar'nā (or lagā'nā) V.T. hit the mark [P]

نشانی nishā'nī N.F. mark sign token book mark keepsake ; souvenir نشانی دے جانا nishā'nī de' jā'nā V.T. give (something as) a souvenir leave a mark نشانی کا چھلا nishā'nī ka chhal'lā N.M. souvenir ring نشاں nishā'n N.M. ★ [~P نشان]

نشتر nish'tar N.M. lancet نشتر لگانا nish'tar lagā'nā V.T. rip (body, etc.) open [P]

نشٹ nash'ṭ ADJ. (dial.) annihilated [S]

نشر nash'r N.M. broadcasting spreading (of rumour) (rare) resuscitation نشرگاہ nash'r-gāh N.F. broadcasting house نشرواشاعت nash'r-o-ishā''at N.F. publication نشریات nashriyyāt' N.F. broadcasts نشریاتی nashriyyā'tī ADJ. broadcasting [A]

نشست nishas't (dial. nashis't) N.F. seat sitting posture fitting نشست برخاست nishas't barkhās't N.F. company manner ; etiquette نشستگاہ nishas't-gāh N.F. sitting room parlour lounge [P ~ نشستن]

نشو nash'v (rare نشوء nash'') N.M. growth ; vegetation nash'v-o-namā', نشوونما nash''-o-namā N.F. development [A]

نشور nūshoor' N.M. resurrection یوم النشور yau'm-ūn-nūshoor' N.M. Day of Resurrection [A]

نشہ *nash'shah* (or *na'shah*) N.M. intoxication نشہ اترنا *na(sh)'shah ū'tar'nā* V.I. come to one's senses نشہ پانی *na'sha-pā'nī* N.M. (col.) liquours drugs نشہ پانی کرنا *na'sha-pā'nī kar'nā* V.I. be a drunkard be a drug addict نشہ چڑھنا *na(sh)'shah chaṛh'nā* V.I. become intoxicated ; be inebriated نشہ کرکرا کرنا *na(sh)'shah kir'kirā kar'nā* V.T. (fig.) upset a feast disturb (someone's) pleasure) نشہ کرنا *na(sh)'shah kar'nā* V.I. be a drunkard be a drug-addict نشہ ہرن ہونا *na(sh)'shah ha'ran ho'nā* V.I. be no longer intoxicated (fig.) come to one senses نشے باز *na(sh)'she-bāz* N.M. drunkard drug-addict نشے میں چور ہونا *na(sh)'she meṅ choor' ho'nā* V.I. be dead drunk نشیلا *nashī'la* ADJ. (F. نشیلی *nashī'lī*) intoxicating toxicated

نشیب *nisheb'* (col. *nasheb'*) N.M. slope declivity low land نشیب و فراز *nishe'b-o-farāz'* N.M. declivity and acclivity (fig.) ups and downs (of life) ; vicissitudes (of life) (fig.) inuricacies (of) نشیبی *nishe'bī* ADJ. low-lying (land, area, etc.) [P]

نشید *nashīd'* N.M. (PL. انشاد *anshād'*) song [A]

نشیلا *nashī'la* ADJ. (F. نشیلی) *nashī'lī* (see under نشہ N.M. ★)

نشیمن *nashe'man* N.M. nest (fig.) residence [P]

نشین *nashīn'* SUF. sitting نشینی *nashī'nī* SUF. sitting [P ~ نشستن]

نص *nas* N.F. (PL. نصوص *nūsoos'*) categorical order of statement, etc. نص قرآنی *nas's-e qūr'ā'nī* N.F. definitive verse of the Holy Quran categorical Quranic injunction [A]

نصاب *nisāb'* N.M. course syllabus curriculum minimum taxable income (for purposes of 'zakat') نصابی *nisā'bī* ADJ. curricular prescribed (books, etc.) [A]

نصاریٰ *nasā'rā* N.M. (PL. نصرانی N.M & ADJ. ★)

نصائح *nasā''eh* N.F. (PL. of نصیحت N.F ★)

نصب *nas'b* N.M. fixation setting up establishment vowel-point 'zabar' accusative case نصب العین *nas'b-ul-'ain'* N.M. ideal goal نصب کرنا *nas'b kar'nā* V.T. fix ; set up ; establish [A]

نصر *nas'r* N.F. aid ; help succour (rare) victory [A]

نصرانی *nasrā'nī* N.M (PL نصاریٰ *nasā'rā* Christian, Nazarene نصرانیت *nasrānīy'yat* N.F Christianity [A ~ ناصرہ - H]

نصرت *nus'rat* N.F victory aid help succour [A]

نصف *nis'f* ADJ. & N.M. half; mid semi- نصف النہار *nis'f-ūn-nahār'* N.M. meridian midday; noon نصف دائرہ *nis'f dā''irah* N.M. semicircle نصف قطر *nis'f-qūt'r* N.M. radius (of circle) نصفا نصف *nis'fa-nis'f*, نصفا نصفی *nis'fā-nis'fī* N.M., ADJ. & ADV. half and half [A]

نصفت *nis'fat* N.F. justice ; equity [A doublet of PREC.]

نصوح *nasooh'* ADJ. honest or sincere (repenttance [A ~ نصیحت]

نصوص *nūsoos'* N.F. (PL. of نص N.F. ★)

نصیب *nasīb'* N.M. lot ; luck ; fate ; fortune (rare) portion نصیب آزمانا (یا لڑانا) *nasīb' āzmā'nā* (or *laṛā'nā*) V.T. try one's luck نصیب اعدا *nasī'b-e a'dā'*, نصیب دشمناں *nasī'b-e dūsh'manāṅ* INT. be it the lot of your enemies نصیب بگڑنا *nasīb' bigaṛ'nā*, نصیب پھوٹنا *nasīb' phooṭ'nā* V.I. be unlucky نصیب پھرنا (یا جاگنا یا چمکنا یا کھل جانا) *nasīb' phir'nā* (or *jāg'nā*, or *cha'maknā* or *khūl' jā'nā*) V.I. (of one's stars) be in the ascendent have a stroke of good fortune نصیب سونا *nasīb' so'nā* V.I. unlucky نصیب کا لکھا *nasīb' kā likh'khā* N.M. fate ; destiny ; that which is destined نصیب لڑنا *nasīb' laṛ'nā* V.I. have a stroke of good fortune نصیب ہونا *nasīb' ho'nā* V.T. get , obtain ; gain fall to the lot (of) نصیبہ *nasī'bah*, نصیبا *nasī'bā* N.M. lot ; fortune نصیبہ ور *nasī'ba-var* ADJ. lucky ; fortunate نصیبوں جلا *nasī'boṅ ja'lā* ADJ. (F. نصیبوں جلی *nasī'boṅ ja'lī*) unlucky ; unfortunate نصیبوں کو رونا *nasī'boṅ ko ro'nā* V.I. curse one's fate نصیبوں کی خوبی *nasī'boṅ kī khoo'bī* N.F. (iron.) misfortune نصیبوں کی شامت *nasī'boṅ kī shā'mat* N.F. misfortune نصیبے میں *nasī'be meṅ* ADV. destined [A]

نصیحت *nasī'hat* N.F. (PL. نصائح *nasā''eh*). advice ; counsel precept نصیحت آموز *nasī'hat-āmoz* ADJ. teaching good counsel نصیحت آمیز *nasī'-hat-āmez'* ADJ. full of counsel advice نصیحت پذیر *nasī'hat-pazīr'* ADJ. amenable to good counsel نصیحت دینا (یا کرنا) *nasī'hat de'nā* (or *kar'nā*) V.T advice counsel ; say a word of advice admonish exhort نصیحت گر *nasī'hat-gar* N.M. counsellor mentor نصیحت ہونا *nasī'hat ho'nā* V.I. learn a lesson be warned by experience [A]

نصیر *nasīr'* N.M. helper , ally [A ~ نصر]

نضارت *nazā'rat* N.F. verdure freshness [A]

نضج *naz'j* N.M. (lit.) ripening (arch.) maturing (of some humour) نضیج *nazī'j* ADJ. ripe نضیج الرائے *nazī'j-ūr-rā''e* ADJ. of mature judgment [A]

نطفہ nūt'fah N.M. semen sperm نطفہ بے تحقیق nūt'fa-e be-taḥqīq', نطفۂ حرام nūt'fah-e ḥarām' N.M. bastard (fig.) scoundrel نطفہ ٹھہرنا (یا قرار پانا) nūt'fah ṭhaihar'nā (or qarār' pā'nā) V.I. be pregnant (with) [A]

نطق nut'q N.M. speech ; power of speech

نظارت nazā'rat N.F. supervision office of Directorate نظارت تعلیم nazā'rat-e ta'līm' N.F. Directorate of Public Instruction [A]

نظارہ nazzā'rah (col. nazā'rah) N.M. sight view vista نظارہ بازی nazzā'ra-bā'zī N.F. ogling ; amorous glances نظارہ کرنا nazzā'rah kar'na V.T. view enjoy looking (at) cast amorous (glances at) نظارگی nazzā'ragī N.F. ogling viewing N.M. spectator one who casts amorous glances [A ~ نظر]

نظافت nazā'fat N.F. neatness ; cleanliness purity نظیف ADJ. ★ [A]

نظام nizām' N.M. system set-up order arrangement نظام الاوقات nizām-ul-auqāt' N.M. timetable نظام بطلیموسی nizā'm-e batlīmoo'sī N.M. Ptolemaic system astronomical theory regarding earth as the stationary centre of universe نظام تعلیم nizā'm-e ta'līm' N.M. educational set up نظام شمسی nizā'm-e sham'sī N.M. solar system نظام فیثاغورثی nizā'm-e fīsāghō'rasī N.M. Pythagorean system of astronomy regarding the sun as the stationary centre of the universe نظامت nizā'mat N.F. (arch.) office of 'Nazim' ; provincial administration [A ~ نظم]

نظائر nazā''ir N.F. (dial. M.) (PL. of نظیر N.F. ★)

نظر na'zar N.F. look ; glance sight ; vision view care ; supervision influence of evil eyes favour careful thought observation dialectics نظر آنا na'zar ā'nā V.I. be seen نظر اتارنا na'zar ūtār'nā V.T. counter influence of evil نظر اٹھانا na'zar ūṭhā'nā V.T. look up نظر اٹھا کر دیکھنا na'zar ūṭhā kar dekh'nā V.T. look up at نظر التفات na'zar-e iltifāt' N.F. kind attention نظر انداز na'zar-andāz' ADJ. rejected disregarded thrown out of favour نظر انداز کرنا na'zar-andāz' kar'nā V.T. disregard cast off from favour نظر باز na'zar-bāz' ADJ. & N.M. ogler licentious (person) gallant نظر بازی na'zar-bā'zī N.F. ogling gallantry نظر بانیکہ na'zar-ba-īñ'-ke ADV. in view, of the fact that نظر بچانا na'zar bachā'nā V.T. avoid the sight (of) evade, dodge نظر بد na'zar-e bad N.F. evil eye نظر (یا نظریں) بدلنا na'zar (or naz'reṅ) ba'dalnā V.I. with draw one's favour نظر بند na'zar-band N.M. detenu نظر بندی na'zar-ban'dī N.F. detention نظر بھر کر دیکھنا na'zar bhar' kar dekh'nā V.I. look to one's fill نظر پر چڑھنا na'zar (par) chaṛh'nā V.I. be specially noted (as good, bad, etc.) be taken a fancy (to) نظر پڑنا na'zar paṛ'nā V.I. come into view, be seen نظر پھر جانا na'zar phir jā'nā V.I. be no longer favoured by نظر پھسلنا na'zar phis'salna V.I. (of something) be very sleek نظر ٹھہرنا na'zar ṭhai'harnā V.I. be able to stare نظر ثانی na'zar-e sā'nī N.F. revision review نظر ثانی کرنا na'zar-e sā'nī kar'nā V.T. revise نظر جلانا na'zar jalā'nā V.T. counter influence of evil eye نظر جمنا na'zar jam'nā V.I. be able stare ; look with fixed eyes نظر (یا نظریں) چرانا na'zar (or naz'reṅ) chūrā'nā V.I. evade ; dodge look furtively نظر دوڑانا na'zar dauṛā'nā V.T. look all around look on all four sides نظر چڑھنا na'zar chaṛh'na V.T. take a fancy (to) نظر ڈالنا na'zar ḍāl'na V.T. cast a look at نظر رکھنا na'zar rakh'nā V.T. keep an eye (on) cast a wistful eye (on) نظر (یا نظروں) سے گرا دینا na'zar (or naz'roṅ) se girā' de'nā V.T. disgrace with draw one's favour from نظر (یا نظروں) سے گرنا (یا اترنا) na'zar (or naz'roṅ) se gir'nā (or ū'tarnā) V.T. be disgraced fall in the estimation (of) نظر سیدھی ہونا na'zar sī'dhī ho'nā V.T. (of someone) look with favour upon نظر سے گزرنا na'zar se gū'zarnā V.I. be ; seen have been read نظر فریب na'zar-fareb' ADJ. attractive ; charming ; enamouring enticing (rare) unreal نظر فریبی na'zar-fare'bī N.F. charm attraction unreality نظر کرنا na'zar kar'nā V.T. look at نظر گزر na'zar-gū'zar N.F (col.) influence of evil eye نظر گزر ہونا na'zar-gū'zar ho'nā V.I. come under such influence نظر گزر کی چیز na'zar-gū'zar kī chīz le'nā V.I. take the little given away to counter influence of evil eye نظر لڑنا na'zar laṛ'nā V.I. come across exchange amorous glances (with) be pitted (against) نظر لگانا na'zar lagā'nā V.T. cast a malignant look (upon) regard (someone) with evil intent نظر لگنا (یا کھا جانا) na'zar lag'nā (or khā' jā'nā) V.I. (of someone) come under influence of evil eye (of) come to harm thus نظر (یا نظریں) ملانا na'zar (or naz'reṅ) milā'nā V.T meet the gaze (of) look (at) نظر میں آنا na'zar meṅ ā'nā V.I. be seen come under the influence of an evil eye نظر (یا نظروں) میں پھرنا na'zar (or naz'roṅ) meṅ phir'nā, نظر میں جچنا (یا کھبنا) na'zar meṅ jach'nā (or khūb'nā) V.I. be liked ; look lovely نظر میں خار ہونا na'zar meṅ khār ho'nā V.I be an eye-sore be disliked (by) be not to one's mind نظر میں رکھنا na'zar meṅ rakh'nā V.T. keep in sight keep in view keep under control نظر (یا نظروں) میں سمانا na'zar (or na'zroṅ) meṅ samā'na v.i. be taken a fancy to win (someone's) respect نظر میں ہونا na'zar meṅ ho'nā v.i be in front of be aware of نظر ہائی na'zar hā''ī n.f., نظر ہایا na'zar-hā'ya n.m. one casting malignant looks or evil eye نظر ہو جانا na'zar ho ja'nā v.i. come under the influence of an evil eye نظر ہونا na'zar ho'nā v.i. come under the influence of an evil eye be attentive (to) have an expert's eye نظروں نظروں میں naz'roṅ naz'roṅ meṅ adv. through one's looks openly نظرے خوش گزرے na'zare khush'-gūz'are ph. cursory glance نظری na'zarī adj. 'a posteriori' theoretical نظریہ nazariy'yah n.m. (pl. نظریات nazariyyāt') theory نظریاتی nazariyyā'tī adj. theoretical [A]

نظم naz'm n.f. poetry ; verse (lit.) string n.m. order ; arrangement discipline نظم کرنا naz'm kar'nā v.t. versify compose a poem on نظم ونسق naz'm-o-nas'q n.m. (see under نسق n.m. ★) نظم ہونا naz'm ho'nā v.i. versified [A]

نظیر nazīr' n.f. (pl. نظائر nazā''ir) precedent adj. alike ; resembling ; equal to نظیر دینا (یا پیش کرنا) nazīr' de'nā (or pesh' kar'nā) v.t. quote a precedent [A ~ نظر]

نظیف nazīf' adj. clean ; neat pure [A ~ نظافت]

نعت na''t n.f. encomium (on the Holy Prophet) (rare) epithet [A]

نعرہ na''rah n.m. slogan cry ; shout نعرہ زن na''ra-zan adj. & n.m. slogan mongerer (one) who shouts or cries out نعرہ زن ہونا na''ra-zan ho'nā v.i. shout ; cry نعرہ لگانا (یا مارنا) na''rah lagā'nā (or mār'nā) v.i. rise a slogan cry ; shout [P]

نعش na''sh n.m. corpse (ped.) bier [A]

نعل na'l n.m. (pl. نعال ne'āl') horse shoe (rare) shoe نعل بند na''l-band n.m. farrier نعل بندی na''l-ban'dī n.f. shoeing of horse) (rare) light tribute نعل بہا na''l-bahā' n.m. tribute نعل در آتش na''l dar ā'tash ph. (fig.) worried نعلین na'lain' n.m. pair of shoes نعلین تحت العین na'lain' taht-ūl-'aiṅ' ph. keep your shoes belongings in sight [A]

نعم ne''m adj. very good ; nice نعم البدل ne''m-ūl-ba'dal n.m. change for the better better substitute [A]

نعم ne'am' n.f. (pl. of نعمت n.f. ★)

نعمت ne''mat n.f. (pl. نعم ne'am') grace divine blessings delicacy good things of life نعمت خانہ ne''mat-khā'nah n.m. locker protected with wire-gauze نعمت عظمیٰ ne''mat-e 'ūz'mā n.f. a great blessing نعمت غیر مترقبہ ne'mat-e ghair-mūtaraq'qabah n.m. windfall [A]

نعوذ na'ooz' ph. we flee for refuge (to God) (only in) نعوذ باللہ na'oo'z-ū bil'lāh int. we seek refuge in God Heaven preserve us God forbid [A]

نعوظ no'ooz' n.m. erection (of sex organ) [A]

نعیم na'īm' n.f. blessing delight comfort [A ~ نعمت]

نغز nagh'z adj. exquisite نغز گو nagh'z-go' adj. & n.m. one enjoying felicity of phrase نغز گوئی nagh'z-go''ī, نغز بیانی nagh'z-bayā'nī n.f. felicity of phrase lovely style [P]

نغزک nagh'zak n.m. (fig.) mango [P ~ prec.]

نغمہ nagh'mah n.m. (pl. نغمات naghmāt') song melody sweet voice نغمہ پرداز (یا ریز یا زن یا سرا یا سنج یا طراز) nagh'ma-pardāz' (or rez', zan' sanā', saṅ'j, tarāz' n.m. singer adj. singing warbling نغمہ پردازی (یا ریزی یا زنی یا سرائی یا سنجی یا طرازی) nagh'ma-pardā'zī (or rezī', zanī', sarā''ī, saṅ'jī, tarā'zī) n.f. song singing warbling [P]

نفاخ naf'f akh adj. (see under نفخ n.m. ★)

نفاذ nifāz' n.m. enforcement promulgation نافذ nā'fiz n.m. ★ [A]

نفاس nifās' n.m. puerperal haemorrhage [A]

نفاست nafāsat n.f. nicety refinement exquisiteness نفیس nafīs' adj. ★ [A]

نفاق nifāq' n.m. hypocrisy double-dealing differences enmity نفاق پڑھنا nifāq' par'nā v.i. have differences نفاق رکھنا nifāq' rakh'nā v.i. inwardly bear (someone) malice [A ~ doublet of منافقت]

نفاقنا nifāq'tā n.m. (f. نفاقتی nifāq'tī) (dial.) hypocrite [~ prec. corr.]

نفت naf''t n.m. petroleum [A]

نفتہ naf'tah n.m. white mottled pigeon

نفحہ naf'ḥah n.f. (pl. نفحات nafaḥāt') perfume [A]

نفخ naf'kh n.m. flatulence نفاخ naf'fakh adj. flatulent [A]

نفر na'far n.m. (arch.) servant individual نفرا naf'rā, نفرہ naf'rah n.m. (arch.) menial نفری na'farī n.f. staff persons employed on daily wages wages نفری میں نخرہ کیا na'farī meṅ nakh'rā kyā prov. v.i. it is no favour to pay the dues [~ A]

نفرت naf'rat n.f. dislike ; abomination ; aversion ; detestation نفرت انگیز naf'rat-aṅ'gez'

ADJ. loathsome ; abominable causing ill will نفرت کرنا (یا کھانا) naf'rat kar'nā (or khā'nā) V.T. dislike ; detest نفرت ہونا naf'rat ho'nā V.I. detested disgusted

نفرین nafrīn' (or -īn') (ped. nifrīn' or -īn') N.F. reproach , opprobrium نفرین کرنا naf'rīn kar'nā V.T. reproach curse

نفس na'fas N.M. (PL. انفاس anfās') breath ; gasp (PL. انفس an'fūs) moment نفس واپسیں (یا باز پسیں) na'fas-e vā-pasīn (or bāz'-pasīn) PH. last gasp [A]

نفس naf's N.M. (PL. نفوس nūfoos') mind ; psyche soul self person body ; flesh ; carnal life ; sensual appetites concupiscence (col.) penis substance ; essence (of) نفس الامر naf's-ūl-am'r N.M. the fact of the matter نفس امارہ naf's-e ammā'rah N.M. one's baser self inordinate appetites ; evil genius نفس بہیمی naf's-e bahī'mī نفس پرست (یا پرور) naf's-paras't (or par'var) ADJ. selfish sensual voluptuous N.M. sensualist selfish person نفس پرستی (یا پروری) naf's-paras'tī (or par'varī) N.F. selfishness sensuality voluptuousness نفس کشی naf's-kū'shī N.F. self-denial ; mortification selfabnegation ; نفس لوامہ naf's-e lavv'mah N.M. conscience ; one's accusing self نفس مارنا naf's mār'nā V.T. mortify the sensual appetites; restrain one's passions N,M. self-denial ; mortification نفس مطلب naf's-e mat'lab N.M. point of issue long and short of the matter نفس مطمئنہ naf's-e mūtma'in'nah N.M. one's satisfied self ; soul نفس ملہمہ naf's-e mūl'himah N.M. one's inspiring self ; intellect نفس ناطقہ naf's-e na'tiqah N.M. one's rational self ; reason mouth piece ; spokesman نفسا نفسی naf'sā-naf'sī (ped. نفسی نفسی naf'sī-naf'sī) ADV. each for himself بنفس نفیس ba-naf's-e nafīs' ADJ. euphuism for) by himself (etc.) نفسانی nafsā'nī ADV. sensual carnal نفسانیت nafsāniyyat' N.F. sensuality ; carnality voluptuousness luxury selfishness نفسی naf'sī ADJ. (rare) psychic PH. myself نفسیات nafsiy'yat N.F. psychology نفسیاتی nafsiyyā'tī ADJ. psychological نفوس قدسیہ nūfoo's-e qūdsiy'yah (or -si'yah) N.M. PL. prophets and angels [A]

نفع naf'' N.M. profits gain advantage ; benefit نفع اٹھانا naf'' ūṭhā'nā V.T. a profit profit (by) نفع رساں naf''-rasāṅ, نفع بخش naf''-bakh'sh ADJ. profitable gainful advantageous ; beneficial نفع میں دو جوتیاں naf'' meṅ do joo'tiyāṅ PH. foolish bargain نفع ونقصان naf''-o-nūq'sān N.M. profit and loss [A]

نفقہ naf'qah (ped. na'faqah) N.M. maintenance allowance alimony نان نفقہ nān'-naf'qah N.M maintenance alimony [A]

نفل naf'l N.M. (dial. N.F.) (PL. نوافل navā'fil supererogation supererogatory prayers [A]

نفوذ nūfooz' N.M. penetration influence اثر و نفوذ a'sar-o-nūfooz', نفوذ و اثر nūfoo'z-o-a'sar N.M. influence

نفور nafoor' ADJ. fleeing from abhorring N.M abhorrence detestation [A ~ نفرت]

نفوس nūfoos' N.M. (PL. of نفس naf's N.M. ★)

نفی naf'ī (ped. naf'y) N.F. negative negation نفی و اثبات naf'y-o-isbāt' N.M. negative and affirmative (fig.) Islamic creed as comprising negation of all deities save God [A]

نفیر nafīr, نفیری nafī'rī N.F. small trumpet

نفیس nafīs' ADJ. nice refined ; exquisite [A ~ نفاست]

نقاب niqāb' N.M./F. veil نقاب الٹنا niqāb' ūlaṭnā V.T. lift the veil نقاب پوش niqāb'-posh' ADJ. & N.M. veiled (person) نقاب ڈالنا (یا چھوڑنا) niqāb' ḍal'nā (or chhoṛ'nā) V.I. lift the veil let down the veil [A]

نقاد naqqād' N.M. critic reviewer [A ~ نقد]

نقارہ naqqā'rah N.M. drum نقارے کی چوٹ naqqā're kī choṭ PH. to the beat of the drum openly نقارچی naqqār'chī N.M. drummer نقارخانہ naqqār'-khā'nah N.M. place where drums are beaten to announce time نقارخانے میں طوطی کی آواز کون سنتا ہے naqqār'-khā'ne meṅ too'tī kī āvāz' kaun sūn'tā hai PROV. who listens to a poor man against his rich opponent who would listen to counsel of sanity in this insane world [A]

نقاش naqqāsh' N.M. painter draughtmanship نقاشی naqqāsh'shī N.F. painting decoration [~A نقش]

نقاط niqāt' N.M. (PL. of نقطہ N.M. ★)

نقال naqqāl' N.M. mimic clown imitator نقالی naqqā'lī N.F. mimicry clownishness imitation [A ~ نقل]

نقاہت naqā'hat N.F. weakness; debility convalescence نقیہ naqīh' ADJ. ★ [A]

نقائص naqā''is N.M. (PL. of نقص N.M. ★)

نقب naq'b N.F. house breaking ; burglary hole made by a burglar نقب زن naq'b-zan N.M. burglary , house-breaker نقب زنی naq'b-za'nī N.F burglary [A]

نقد naq'd N.M. (PL. نقود nūqood') cash criticism (rare) assay ADJ. cash (payment)

ready (money) نقدا نقد naq'dā naq'd ADV. promptly cash in cash نقد جان naq'd-e jān N.M. life نقد مال naq'd māl N.M. ready (money) نقد و تبصرہ naq'd-o-tab'sirah, نقد و نظر naq'd-o-na'zar N.M. review criticism نقد و جنس naq'd-o-jin's N.M. cash and kind نقدی naq'dī N.F. cash ; ready money [A]

نقرس niq'ris N.M. gout [A]

نقرہ nūq'rah N.M. silver white horse نقرئی nūq'ra'ī ADJ. silver (of horse) white [P]

نقش naq'sh N.M. (PL. نقوش nūqoosh) impression; mark ; print ; stamp drawing ; painting picture engraving ; carving charm influence idea ; imagination نقش اول naq'sh-e av'val N.M. rough sketch, etc. first draft نقش بٹھانا naq'sh biṭhā'nā V.T. make a strong impression ; impress (upon someone) strongly نقش بدیوار naq'sh ba-dīvār' ADJ. like a picture on the wall (fig.) dumbfounded نقش برآب naq'sh bar-āb' PH. evanescent نقشبند naq'sh-band N.M. painter designer name of founder of a mystic fraternity ; 'Naqshband' نقشبندی naq'sh-ban'dī N.F. painting designing ADJ. member of this mystic fraternity نقش پا naq'sh-e pā' N.M., نقش قدم naq'sh-e qa'dam N.M. footprint track نقش ثانی naq'sh-e sā'nī N.M. fair copy revised version نقش سویدا naq'sh-e suvai'dā N.M. care of heart black spot on heart نقش کرنا naq'sh kar'nā V.T. impress strongly upon stamp adorn with designs engrave ; carve نقش و نگار naq'sh-o-nigār' floral pattern embellishment designs decorations pictures ; paintings نقش ہونا naq'sh ho'nā V.I. be strongly impressed be carved be engraved leave strong impressions کالنقش فی الحجر kan-naq'sh-fil hajar' PH. indelible naq'shī, نقشین naq'shīn ADJ. engraved carved having coloured patterns [A]

نقشہ naq'shah N.M. map features outline design picture (of) ; pattern (of) condition ; state of affairs stance نقشہ اتارنا naq'shah ūtār'nā V.T. copy a design نقشہ بنانا naq'shah banā'nā V.T. draw a map reduce to a condition نقشہ بگاڑنا naq'shah bigāṛ'nā V.T. upset a plan نقشہ بگڑنا naq'shah bi'gaṛnā V.I. (of plan) be upset be put out of countenance نقشہ تیز ہونا naq'shah tez' ho'nā V.I. be lucky be influential نقشہ جمانا naq'shah jamā'nā V.I. establish (one's) authority influence imagine نقشہ جمنا naq'shah jam'nā V.I. be influential have (one's) authority established be imagined نقشہ حدبست naq'shah-e had'-bast N.M. boundary map (of agricultural lands) نقشہ کشی naq'sha-ka'shī N.M. cartography نقشہ نویس naq'sha-navīs' N.M. draughtsman نقشہ نویسی naq'sha-navī'sī N.F. draughtsmanship نقشہ (آنکھوں میں) کھنچ جانا naq'shah (āṅ'khoṅ meṅ) khinch jā'nā V.I. be conjured up [A ~ PREC.]

نقص naq's N.M. (PL. نقائص naqā''is) defect fault flaw deficiency blemish نقص جسمانی naq's-e jismā'nī N.M. physical deformity نقص نکالنا naq's nikāl'nā V.T. pick holes (in) cavil (at) ; criticize condemn [A]

نقصان nūqsān' N.M. loss detriment harm ; damage ; injury نقصان اٹھانا nūqsān' ūṭhā'nā V.I. incur a loss suffer a reverse نقصان پہنچانا nūqsān' pahūṅchā'nā V. harm ; injure ; damage نقصان دہ nūqsān'-deh, نقصان رساں nūqsān'-rasāṅ' ADJ. harmful; injurious detrimental نقصان کرنا nūqsān' kar'nā V.I. harm cause ; inflict loss do mischief نقصان ہونا nūqsān' ho'nā V.I. be harmed be lost [A doublet of PREC.]

نقض naq'z N.M. breach (of the peace) back out (of one's words) نقض امن naq'z-e am'n N.M. breach of the peace نقض عہد naq'z-e 'aih'd N.M. breach of contract [A]

نقط nū'qat N.M. (PL. of نقطہ N.M. ★)

نقطہ nūq'tah N.M. (PL. نقاط niqāt', نقط nū'qat) point ; dot name of a diacritical mark ; dot نقطۂ آغاز nūq'ta-e āghāz' N.M. starting point نقطۂ موہوم nūq'ta-e mauhoom' N.M. hypothetical point (fig.) beloved's mouth نقطۂ نظر nūq'ta-e na'zar N.M. view point ; point of view [A]

نقل nūq'l N.M. dessert with liquor snack [A]

نقل naq'l N.F. (PL. نقول nūqool') copy crib imitation mimickery narration narrative anecdote moving ; shifting (lit.) tradition نقل اڑانا naq'l ūṛā'nā V.T. crib ; copy by unfair means نقل در نقل naq'l dar naq'l N.F. copy of a copy (fig.) something for removed from the original نقل کرنا naq'l kar'nā V.T. copy relate ; imitate ; mimic shift نقل کفر کفر نہ باشد naq'l-e kuf'r kuf'r na-bā'shad PH. the responsibility is the original narrator's نقل لینا naq'l le'nā V.I. get a copy (of) نقل مطابق اصل naq'l mūtā'biq(-e) as'l N.F. true copy نقل مکانی naq'l-e makā'nī N.F. shifting of premises moving from a place نقل نویس naq'l navīs' N.M. copyist نقل نویسی naq'l-navī'sī N.F. copyist's job نقل و حرکت naq'l-o- har'kat (or -ha'ra) N.F. movement نقل وطن naq'l-e va'tan N.F. migration [A]

نقلی naq'lī ADJ. artificial counterfeit spurious fictitious assumed not real traditional [~A PREC.]

نقوش **nūqoosh'** N.M. PL. of نقش N.M. ★)

نقول **nūqool'** N.M. (PL. of نقل N.F. ★)

نقی **na'qī** ADJ. clean pure N.M. name of Shi'ite Imam نقوی **na'qavī** ADJ. descended from Imam Naqi

نقیب **naqīb'** N.M. herald proclaimer [A]

نقیض **naqīz'** N.F. opposite ; contrary [A ~ نقض]

نقیہ **naqīh** ADJ. weak ; feeble [A ~ نقاہت]

نک **nak** SUF. nose· نک بال **nak-bal'** N.M. favourite person exercising influence (over another) نک بہنا **nak-baih'nā** ADJ. & N.M. (F. نک بہنی **nak baih'nī**) (one) running at the nose نکتوڑا **nakto'ṛā** N.M. (dial.) ironical remark ; taunt نکتوڑے اٹھانا **nakto'ṛe ūṭhā'nā** V.T. humour نک چڑھا **nak-cha'ṛhā** ADJ. (F. نک چڑھی **nak-cha'ṛhī**) proud surly fastidious نک چھکنی **nak-chhik'nī** N.F. sneeze-wort ; tip top نک کٹا **nak'-ka'ṭā** ADJ. (same as نکٹا **nak'ṭā** ★) نک کٹی **nak-ka'ṭī** N.F. disgrace ; infamy نک کٹی ہونا **nak-ka'ṭī ho'nā** V.I. be disgraced نک گھسی **nak'-ghis'sī** N.F. rubbing the nose on the around by way of humiliation imploration نک گھسی کرنا **nak-ghis'sī kar'nā** V.I. implore ; beseach [~ ناک CONT.]

نکا **nūk'ka** N.M. point ; pointed part of anything

نکات **nikat'** N.M. (PL. of نکتہ N.M. ★)

نکاح **nikāḥ'** N.M. marriage ; matrimony نکاح پڑھانا (یا کرنا) **nikāḥ paṛhā'nā** (or **kar'nā**) V.T. marry perform matrimonial rites نکاح پڑھائی **nikāḥ-paṛhā''ī** N.F. remuneration for performance of matrimontal rites نکاح کی سی شرطیں باندھنا **nikāḥ' kī sī shar'teṅ bāndh'nā** V.T. put forth harsh conditions prevaricate نکاح نامہ **nikāḥ-nā'mah** N.M. matrimonial deed ; marriage deed نکاح ہونا **nikāḥ-ho'nā** V.I. (of matrimonial rites) be performed be married نکاحتا، نکاحی **nikāḥ'ta, nikā'ḥī** N.F. & ADJ. (woman) whose marital rites have been performed [A]

نکاس **nikas'** N.M., نکاسی **nika'sī** N.F. outlet out-turn ; turn over sale

نکالنا **nikāl'nā** V.T. turn out ; expel ; drive out dismiss ; sack take out pull out ; draw out extract distil subtract; deduct solve (sum) out work (problem) embroider (pattern) issue ; publish achieve (desire) eject hit upon (idea) devise (plan) نکالا **nikā'la** N.M. extradition نکالا ملنا **nikā'la mil'nā** V.I. be extradited be turned out دیس نکالا **des'-nikā'lā** N.M. banishment extradition دیس نکالا ملنا **des'-nikā'lā mil'nā** be banished be extradited نکال دینا **nikāl' de'nā** V.T. expel drive out take out extract subtract deduct eject ; to discard ; exclude banish ; extradite نکال لانا **nikāl' lā'nā** V.T. seduce elope with bring off

نکانا **nikā'nā** V.T. weed نکائی **nikā''ī** N.M. weeding remuneration for weeding

نکبت **nak'bat** N.F. (PL. نکبات **nakabat'**) adversity misfortune [A]

نکتہ **nūk'tah** N.M. (PL. نکات **nikāt'**) subtle point significance point (of joke, etc.) نکتہ آفرین **nūk'ta-āfrīn'** ADJ. (one) using conceits نکتہ آفرینی **nūk'ta-āfrī'nī** N.F. use of conceits نکتہ پرداز **nūk'ta-pardāz'** ADJ. subtle ingenius نکتہ پردازی **nūk'ta-pardā'zī** N.F. subtlety conceit نکتہ چیں **nūk'ta-chīn'** N.F. critical ; captious نکتہ چینی **nūk'ta-chī'nī** N.F. criticism ; cavilling ; captiousness نکتہ دان (یا رس یا شناس) **nūk'ta-dān'** (or **ras'** or **shinās'**), نکتہ دانی (یا رسی یا شناسی) **nūk'ta-dā'nī** (or **ra'sī** or **shina'sī**) N.M. sagacity discernment نکتہ شناس **nūk'ta-shinās'**, نکتہ سنج **nūk'ta-sanj'** ADJ. discriminating ; having critical ability نکتہ سنجی **nūk'ta-san'jī** N.F. discrimination; critical ability نکتہ گیر **nūk'ta-gīr'** ADJ. critical ; captious نکتہ گیری **nūktā-gī'rī** N.F. criticise cavil a نکتے نکالنا **nūk'te nikāl'nā** V.T. cavil (at) ; criticize

نکتی **nūk'tī** N.F a kind of sweetmeat

نکٹا **nak'ṭā** ADJ. & N.M. (F. نکٹی **nak'ṭī**) (one) having a cut nose shameless (person) نکٹا بوچا سب سے اونچا **nak'ṭā boo'chā sab se ooṅ'chā** PROV. a shameless person would stop at nothing [~ ناک + کٹنا]

نکرہ **na'kirah** N.M. & ADJ. common (noun)

نکڑ **nūk'kaṛ** N.M. (street) corner ; turning (of the street)

نک سک **nik'-sūk** (dial. **nik'-sik** or **nak'-sak**) N.F. appearance ; features (only in) نک سک سے ٹھیک (یا درست) **nik'-sūk se ṭhīk'** (or **dūrūst'**) PH. tip-top

نکسیر **naksīr'** N.F. vein of nose نکسیر پھوٹنا **nak.sīr phooṭ'nā** V. bleed at the nose [~ ناک]

نکلنا **ni'kalnā** V.I. come out go forth be taken out be pulled out ; drawn out distilled be hatched be produced sprout (of sun, etc.) rise flow set out depart secede elope be lost balance get lost overtake exceed (desire) be achieved appear issue be ejects نکل آنا **ni'kal** a'nā V. come out come forth appear (of sun, etc.) rise نکل بھاگنا nik'kal bhāg'nā V.I. run away elope with نکل پڑنا ni'kal paṛ'nā V.I. come out from ; to be drawn forth نکل جانا ni'kal jā'nā V.I. go away disappear escape نکلوانا nikalvā'nā V.T. cause to expel get sacked cause to come out ; cause to issue

نکما nikam'mā ADJ. (F. نکمی nikam'mī) worthless ; good-for-nothing N.M. idler ; slothful person [~ ن + کام]

نکو niko' PREF. good نکوکار niko'-kār' ADJ. & N.M. pious (person) ; beneficent persons نکوکاری niko'-kā'rī N.F. piety beneficence نکومحضر niko-mah'zar ADJ. & N.M. good (person) نکونام niko' nām' ADJ. & N.M. one having a good reputation نکونامی niko'-nā'mī N.F. good name ; reputation نکوئی niko''ī N.F. benevolence ; beneficence [P ~ نیکو CONT.]

نکو nak'koo ADJ. & N.M. big nosed (person) disgraced (person) laughing-stock self-righteous نکو بنانا (یا کرنا) nak'koo banā'nā (or kar'nā) disgrace make (someone) laughing stock [~ ناک]

نکوہش niko'hish N.F. threat rebuke ; reproach [P]

نکھرنا ni'kharnā V.I. be washed well ; be bleached look elegent نکھار nikhār' N.M. cleanliness elegance نکھارنا nikhār'nā V.T. wash (something) white ; make elegant

نکہت nak'hat (col. نگہت nig'hat) N.F. fragrance [~ A oral odour]

نکھٹو nikhaṭ'too ADJ. & N.M. idler worthless ; good-for-nothing (person) [~ ن + کھٹو]

نکھد nikhad' ADJ. worst worthless

نکھنڈ ni'khand' ADJ. half ; mid(night) ADV. exact

نکی nak'kī ADJ. & N.M. (one) speaking with a nasal accent [~ ناک]

نکیر nakīr N.M. angel questioning dead body about his faith نکیرین nakīrain, منکر نکیر mūn'kar nakīr' N.M. the two angels questioning man in his grave about his faith [A]

نکیل nakel' N.F. camel's bridle or halter نکیل ہاتھ میں ہونا nakel' haiṫh men ho'nā V.T. lead (someone) by the nose-string [~ ناک]

نکیلا nokī'lā ADJ. (F. نکیلی nokī'lī) pointed sharp نکیلاپن nokī'lā-pan N.M. sharpness [~ نوک]

نگ nag N.M. gem ; jewel ; precious stone نگ جڑنا nag' jaṛ'nā V.T. set a gem [~ P نگیں]

نگار nigar' N.M. beloved ; sweetheart painting lovely pattern decoration SUF. writer of stories, etc.) ; -ist نگار ارمنی nigar-e ar'manī N.M. Arminian beloved appellation of Farhad's beloved Shirin نگاربندی nigār'-ban'dī N.F. dying one's palms, etc. with henna in exquisite patterns نگارخانہ nigar'khā'nah N.M. studio picture gallery نگارستان nigaristān N.M. picture gallery نگاری nigā'rī SUF. painting writing نگارین nigā'rīn ADJ. beautiful ; lovely beautified (of hand) having lovely 'henna' patterns [P]

نگارش nigā'rish N.F. (wrong but usu. PL. نگارشات nigārishāt') writings

نگاہ nigāh' N.F. (or CONT. نگہ nigah') look, glance sight ; care custody ; surveillance attention favour نگاہ اٹھا کر نہ دیکھنا nigāh' uṭhā' kar na dekh'nā V.T. not to care to look at not to be attracted by show indifference نگاہ بان nigāh'-bān', نگہبان nigah'-bān' N.M. watchman custodian نگاہ بانی nigāh'-bā'nī, نگہبانی nigah'-bā'nī N.F. watching ; guarding custody نگاہ بد nigā'h-e bad' N.F. evil eye نگاہ (یا نگہ) بدلنا (یا پھیرنا) nigāh (or nigah') badal'na (or pher'na) V.T. give a cold shoulder (to) نگاہ بھر کے دیکھنا nigāh' bhar' ke dekh'nā V.T. look one's fill نگاہ پڑنا nigāh' paṛ'na V.I. be seen نگاہ ٹیڑھی ہونا nigāh' te'ṛhī ho'na V.I. be enraged نگاہ چرانا nigāh' chūrā'na V.T. evade ; dodge be unable to confront look furtively at نگاہ دار nigāh'-dār, نگہدار nigah'-dār ADJ. & N.M. guardian نگاہ داشت nigāh'-dāsht', نگہداشت nigah-dāsht' N.F. care custody نگاہ (یا نگہ) رکھنا nigāh' (or nigahi) rakh'na V.I. keep in view keep under one's eye cast amorous glances at نگاہ غلط انداز nigā'h-e gh'alat andāz' N.F. cursory glance deceptive glance beloved's amorous glance نگاہ کرنا nigāh' kar'na V.T. look at view observe نگاہ لڑانا nigāh' laṛā'na V.T. cast amorous glances نگاہ (یا نگاہیں) ملانا nigāh' (or nigā'hen) milā'na V.T. look (someone) full in the face نگاہ (یا نگاہوں) میں رکھنا nigāh' (or nigā'hon) men rakh'na V.I. keep in view keep an eye on کی نگاہ (یا نگاہیں) ہونا ki nigāh' (or nigā'hen) ho'na V.I. be earmarked by (for evil or good) نگاہ ناز nigā'h-e nāz' N.F. coquetry ; blendishment پر نگاہ نہ ٹھہرنا par nigah na ṭhai'harna V.I. be dazzling نگاہ نیچی کرنا nigāh' nī'chī kar'na V.T. hang down one's head in shame not to look up be abashed

نگر na'gar N.M., نگری nag'rī N.F. city town suburb colony

نگر nig'gar ADJ. solid heavy ; weighty

نگر *ni'gar* SUF. seeing ; beholding نگری *ni'garī* SUF. seeing beholding [P ~ نگریستن]

نگران *nigarāṅ'* (col. *nigrān'*) N.M. overseer superior protector ADJ. overseeing guarding نگران حال *nigarā'n-e ḥāl'* N.M. & ADJ. watchful (person) (one) looking after supervising نگرانی *nigarā'nī* N.F. care ; custody revision نگرانی کرنا *nigarā'nī kar'nā* V.T. look-after supervise درخواست نگرانی *darkhās't-e nigarā'nī* N.F. revision petition [P ~ نگریستن]

نگلنا *ni'galnā* V.T. swallow gulp down اگلے چین نہ نگلے چین *ūg'le chain' na nig'le chain'* PROV. peace neither way

نگندنا *nigand'nā* V.T. sew (quilt) with long stitches نگندا *nigan'dā* N.M. long ornamental stitching

نگوڑا *nigo'ṛā* ADJ. & N.M. (F. نگوڑی *nigo'ṛī*) (dial.) wretched (person) ; miserable (person) develish (person) نگوڑا ناٹھا *nigo'ṛā nā'ṭhā* ADJ. & N.M. (F. نگوڑی ناٹھی *nigo'ṛī nā'ṭhī*) (one) having no relative

نگون *nigooṅ'* AFF. hanging down adverse نگونی *nigoo'nī* SUF. hanging down adversity [P]

نگھرا *nigha'rā* ADJ. homeless N.M. waif [~ ن + گھر]

نگہ *nigah* N.F. (short for نگاہ N.F. ★]

نگہت *nig'hat* N.F. (col. for) نکہت N.F. ★

نگین *nagīṅ*, نگینہ *nagī'nah* N.M. gem ; jewel ; a precious stone something that sits well نگینہ جڑنا *nagī'nah jaṛ'nā* V.T. set a stone نگینہ ساز *nagī'na-sāz* N.M. lapidary

نل *nal* N.M. pipe hydrant tap water pump urinary duct پانی کا نل *pānī kā nal* N.M. water-pipe spout hydrant

نلانا *nalā'nā* V.T. weed out نلائی *nalā''ī* N.F. weedling remuneration for it

نلوا *nal'vā* N.M. tube for administering drug to animals [~ نال]

نلوہ *nil'vah* ADV. without resistance gratuitously unaffected

نلی *na'lī* N.F. tube pipe marrow bone shim-bone (weaver s) shuttle

نم *nam* ADJ. damp : moist humid N.M. (rare) dampness ; moisture humidity نم خوردہ *nam-khūr'dah*, نم دیدہ *nam-dīdah*, نم رسیدہ *nam-rasī'dah* ADJ. moist destroyed by moisture نم روک *nam-rok'* ADJ. & N.M. damp proof (substance) نم گیرہ *nam-gī'rah* N.M. awning canopy نمناک *nam-nāk'* ADJ. moist : damp wet with tears ; tearful نمناکی *nam-nā'kī* N.F. dampness tearfulness نمی *na'mī* N.F. dampness moisture humidity [P]

نما *nūmā'* SUF. like ; resembling appear-ing showing ; exhibiting نمائی *nūmā''ī* SUF. likeness ; resemblance show display [P ~ نمودن show]

نماز *namāz'* N.F. divine service ; Muslim prayers نماز استسقا *namā'z-e istisqā'* N.F. late afternoon prayers نماز عید *namā'z-e 'īd* N.F. Eid prayers نماز قصر *namā'z-e qas'r* N.F. reduced prayers (in travels) نماز کسوف *namā'z-e kasoof'* N.M. special congregational prayers during solar eclipse ; ecliptic congregation گئے تھے نماز بخشوانے روزے گلے پڑ گئے *ga''e the namāz' bakhsh'vā'ne ro'ze ga'le paṛ ga''e* PROV. bid to seek redress brought further trouble نمازی *namā'zī* ADJ. & N.M. one who prays (one) who says his prayers regularly نمازی کا ٹکا *namā'zī kā ṭa'kā* N.M. trap false hope [P]

نمائش *nūmā''ish* N.F. exhibition show display affectation smobbery نمائش گاہ *nūmā''ish-gāh* N.F. exhibition hall نمائشی *nūmā''ishī* ADJ. just for show ostensible showy [P ~ نمودن]

نمام *nammām'* ADJ. backbiter نمامی *nammā'mī* N.F. backbiting [A ~ نمیمہ]

نمائندہ *nūmā'in'dah* N.M. representative نمائندگی *nūmā'in'dagī* N.F. representation [P ~ نمودن show]

نمایاں *nūmā'yāṅ* ADJ. prominent ; conspicuous ; salient [P ~ نمودن show]

نمبر *nam'bar* N.M. number marks ; award نمبر پانا *nam'bar pā'nā* V.I. secure marks نمبر چھیننا *nam'bar chhīn'nā* V.T. exceed steal the march over نمبردار *nam'bar-dār* N.M. Lambardar ; village headman [E]

نمٹانا *nimṭa'nā* V.T. (same as نبٹانا V.T. ★)

نمٹنا *ni'maṭnā* V.T. (same as نبٹنا V.T. ★)

نمدہ *nam'dah* N.M. felt felt carpet rug saddle-cloth housing. نمد *namad* PREF. felt نمد پوش *na'mad-posh* ADJ. & N.M. (lit.) (one) clothed in felt mendicant [P]

نمستے *namas'te*, نمسکار *namaskār'* N.M. (H. dial.) salutation ; wishing [S]

نمش *na'mish* N.F. cool milk froth

نمط *na'mat* N.F. manner (only in) کی نمط *kī na'mat* ADV. like ; in the manner of

نمک *na'mak*, (lit.) *namak* N.M. salt saltish taste attraction ; charm grace ;

elegance نمک پاش *na'mak-pāsh'* ADJ. & N.M. (one) who taunts نمک پاشی *na'mak-pa'shī* N.F. pouring salt (fig.) taunt ; taunting نمک پروردہ *na'mak-parvar'dah*, نمک خور *na'mak-khār'* ADJ. & N.M. faithful (servant) (one) bred at another's money نمک پھوٹ پھوٹ کر نکلنا *na'mak phoot phoot' kar ni'kal'na* PH. suffer for ingratitude نمک چشی *na'mak-cha'shī* N.F. first feeding (of child) نمک چکھنا *na'mak chakh'na* V.T. taste (food) eat at the table (of) نمک حرام *na'mak-ḥarām'* ADJ. treachnous ; perfidious ungrateful unfaithful نمک حرامی *na'mak-ḥarā'mī* N.F. treachery ; perfidy ingratitude disloyalty نمک حلال *na'mak-ḥalāl'* ADJ. grateful ; true loyal ; faithful نمک حلالی *na'mak-ḥalā'lī* N.F. loyalty ; fidelity نمکدان *na'mak-dān'* N.M. salt-cellar نمک کا تیزاب *na'mak kā tezāb'* N.M. hydrochloric acid نمک کا حق ادا کرنا *na'mak kā ḥaq' adā' kar'nā*, حق نمک ادا کرنا *ḥaq' q-e na'mak adā' kar'na* V.T. discharge one's obligation نمک کی کان *na'mak kī kān'*, کان نمک *kā'n-e na'mak* N.F. salt mine ہر کہ در کان نمک رفت نمک شد *har' ke dar kā'n-e na'mak raf't na'mak shūd* PROV. none can escape the influence of environment نمک کی مار پڑنا *na'mak kī mār' paṛ'na* V.I. be cursed for ingratitude نمک لگانا *na'mak lagana* V.T. salt pickle with salt نمک مرچ لگانا *na'mak mir'ch lagā'na* V.T. give relish ; make tasteful garble ; give a garbled version colour-highly ; give a coloured version exaggerate harass taunt نمکین *namkīn'* ADJ. saltish saline brackish of brownish complexion ; nut-brown attractive ; charming نمکینی *namkī'nī* N.F. saltishness salmity brackishness agreeableness brown complexion charm ; attraction [P]

نمو *nūmoo'* N.M. growth increase [A]

نمود *nūmood'* N.F. show ; showness pomp and show fame ; celebrity known egotism appearance existence نمود بے بود *nūmoo'd-e be bood'* N.F. vanity ; outword show نمود کرنا *nūmood' kar'na* V.T. boast ; brag appear نمود کھونا *nūmood' kho'na* V.T. lose prestige نمود کی لینا *nūmood' kī le'na* V.I. brast ; brag نمودیا *nūmoo'diya* N.M. & ADJ. showy (person) نمودار *nūmoodār'* ADJ. visible apparent ; manifest نمودار کرنا *nūmoodār' kar'na* V.T. make visible نمودار ہونا *nūmoodār' ho'na* V.I. become visible appear (of sun, etc.) rise [P ~ نمودن]

نمونہ *nūmoo'nah* N.M. specimen type model pattern نمونہ دان *nūmoo'nah dān* N.M. (rare) show case [P ~ نمودن]

نمونیہ *nimon'iya* N.M. pneumonia [E]

نموہا *nimoo'hā* ADJ. (F. نموہی *nimoo'hī*) quiet ; taciturn helpless [~ منہ + ن]

نن *nan* N.F. nun [E]

نمیمہ *namī'mah* N.F. backbiting [A]

ننا *nan'nā* N.M. & ADJ. (F. ننی *nan'nī*) same as ننھا N.M. & ADJ. ★)

نناواں *ninain'vān* ADJ. & N.M. (dial.) ominous (person) [~ نہ + نام]

ننانوے *ninnān've* N.M. & ADJ. ninety-nine ننانویواں *ninnān'vevān* ADJ. ninety-ninth ننانوے کا پھیر *ninnān've kā pher'* PH. bid to increase one's wealth greed ننانوے کے پھیر میں آنا (یا پڑنا) *ninnān'ven ke pher' men ā'nā* (or *paṛ'nā*) PH. be after increasing one's wealth

نند *nand* (dial. *na'nad*) N.F. sister-in-law ; husband's sister نندوئی *nando''ī* N.M. brother-in-law husband of husband's sister

نندا *nin'dā* N.F. (dial.) disaparaging remarks کی نندا کرنا *kī nin'dā kar'na* V.T. (dial.) utter disparaging remarks against

ننگ[1] *nang* N.M. shame disgrace honour reputation ننگ خاندان *nan'g-e khāndān'* ADJ. & N.M. one who is a disgrace to one's family ننگ خلائق *nang-e khala''iq* ADJ. & N.M. one who is a disgrace to mankind ننگ و نام *nan'g-o-nām'*, ننگ و ناموس *nan'g-o-nāmoos'* N.M. honour prestige [P]

ننگ[2] *nang* N.M. nakedness shamelessness ADJ. nakedness penniless ننگ دھڑنگ *nang' dhaṛang'* ADJ. stark naked

ننگا *nan'ga* ADJ. (F. ننگی *nan'gī*) naked denuded bare shameless ; unashamed exposed ننگاپن *nanga'-pan* N.M. nakedness ننگا جھوری *nan'ga jho'rī* N.F. search of labour on coming out of factory ننگا دھڑنگا *nan'ga dhaṛan'ga* ADJ. quite naked stark naked مادر زاد ننگا *ma'dar-zad nan'gā* N.M. stark naked ننگی بچی *nan'gī buch'chī* ADJ. unadorned (woman) ننگا کرنا *nan'ga kar'nā* V.T. strip (someone) naked expose lay bare ننگی تلوار *nan'gī talvār'* N.F. drawn sword (fig.) fearless person outspoken person ; one who wears his heart on his sleeve ننگے پاؤں *nan'ge pa''on* ADJ. bare-footed ننگے پاؤں ننگے سر *nan'ge pa''on nan'ge sir* ADJ. bare-footed and bare-headed perplexed ننگے سر *nan'ge sir* ADV. bare-headed ننگی نہائے گی کیا اور نچوڑے گی کیا *nan'gī nahā''e gī kyā' aur nicho'ṛe gī kyā'* PROV. a poor person can never have enough and to spare

ننھا *nan'nhā*, ننا *nan'nā* ADJ. & N.M. (F. ننھی *nan'nhī*.

(نتی nan'nī) small tiny wee-bit small child ; child نھا کاتنا nan'nhā kāt'nā V.T. & I. spin fine yarn be niggardly

نھیال nankiyāl N.F. maternal grandfather's house or family [~ نانا]

نو nau ADJ. & N.M. nine نو تیرہ باتیں بنانا nau' te'rah bā'teṅ banā'nā V.I. prevaricate نو دو گیارہ ہونا nau'-do-gyā'rah ho'nā V.I. run away ; slip away نو رتن nau' ra'tan N.M. nine jewels (fig.) nine celebrities نو سو چوہے کھا کر بلی حج کو چلی nau' sau choo'he khā' kar bil'lī haj' ko cha'lī PROV. having sinned for six days he goes to church on the seventh نولکھا nau-lak'khā ADJ. valued at nine lakh rupees نو میں نہ تیرہ میں nau' meṅ na te'rah meṅ PH. worthless نو نقد نہ تیرہ ادھار nau' naq'd na te'rah ūdhār', نو نگا nau'-na'gā N.M. nine jewelled bracelet نواں na'vāṅ ADJ. ninth

نو ۲ nau ADJ. new fresh PREF. new fresh نوآباد nau-ābād' ADJ. newly settled (rare) newly commanded (land) colonized نوآباد کار nau-ābād'-kār N.M. colonizer نوآباد کاری nau-ābād'-kā'rī N.F. colonization نوآبادی nau-ābā'dī N.F. colony settlement نوآبادیات nau-ābādiyāt' N.F. colonies نوآموز nau-āmoz' ADJ. & N.M. beginner novice ; tyro raw hand inexperienced (person) نوآموزی nau-āmo'zī N.F. inexperience نو بہ نو nau' ba-nau' ADJ. ever new up-to-date نوبہار nau-bahār' N.F. early spring full bloom ADJ. in full bloom youth ; young man نوجوان nau-javān' N.M. (PL. نوجوانان nau-javā'nāṅ or -javānān') ADJ. (one) in the prime of (one's) life نوجوانی nau-javā'nī N.F. youth youthfulness ; prime of (one's) life نوچندی nau-chan'dī ADJ. of the new moon ; first (Thursday, etc.) of the lunar month نوخاستہ nau'khās'tah ADJ. & N.M. newly (rich) ; upstart نوخیز nau-khez' N.M. & ADJ. adolescent youthful beauty نوخیزی nau-khe'zī N.F. adolescence youthful beauty نودولت nau-dau'lat ADJ. & N.M. newly rich upstart نورس nau-ras' ADJ. & N.M. newly-mellowed نورستہ nau-rūs'tah ADJ. newly (fruit) sprung up نوروز nau-roz' N.M. new year's day this as a persian festival نوشہ nau'-shah N.M. bridegroom ; groom نو عمر nau-'ūm'r ADJ. young inexperienced N.M. beginner minor نو عمری nau-'ūm'rī N.F. minority ; childhood نو گرفتار nau-giriftār' ADJ. & N.M. newly captured (person) نومسلم nau-mūs'lim N.M. & ADJ. convert to Islam; neophyte نو مشق nau-mash'q ADJ. inexperienced ; novice نونہال nau-nehāl' N.M. (rare) sapling young man ; young man ; youth نووارد nau-vā'rid ADJ. & N.M. newcomer fresh arrival [P]

نوا navā' N.F. song tune voice sound subsistence belongings نوا پرداز navā' pardāz', navā'-sanj' ADJ. & N.M. singing one emitting a sound نوا پردازی navā'-pardā'zī, نوا سنجی navā'-san'jī N.F. singing emitting a sound بے برگ و نوا be bar'g-o-navā' N.M. belongings برگ و نوا bar'g-o-navā' ADJ. empty-headed [P]

نواب nav'vāb (col. navāb') N.M. lord (arch.) governor (arch.) petty ruler ; prince ; nabob بے ملک نواب be-mūl'k navvāb' N.M. haughty person نوابی navvā'bī N.F. lordship (arch.) princedom (arch.) governorship vanity ; pride misrule ADJ. lordly نوابی ٹھاٹھ navvā'bī ṭhāṭh N.M. PL. lordly ways [A ~ نیابت]

نواب nūvvab' N.M. (rare PL. of نائب N.M. ★)

نواح navāh' N.M. environs نواحی navā'hī ADJ. surrounding [~ A نواحی ~ SING. ناحیہ N.M. ★]

نوادر navā'dir N.M. PL. curios rarities curiosities نوادر روزگار navā'dir-e rozgār' N.M. wonders of the world [A ~ SING. نادرہ]

نوار nivār', (dial. نواڑ nivāṛ') N.F. tape (of the coarse kind)

نواز navāz' SUF. favouring; cherishing player (on musical instrument)

نوازش navā'zish N.F. (PL. نوازشات navāzishāt') favour ; courtesy نوازش نامہ navā'zish-nā'mah N.M. (euphuism for) letter ; kind letter [P ~ نواختن]

نوازنا navāz'nā V.T. favour ; show kindness (to) [~ P نواختن]

نواس nivās' N.M. (dial.) house ; residence [S]

نواسہ navā'sah N.M. grandson ; daughter's son نواسی navā'sī N.F. grand-daughter ; daughter's daughter

نواسی navā'sī ADJ. eighty-nine N.F. (see under نواسہ N.M. ★)

نواسیر navāsīr' N.F. (PL. of ناسور N.M. ★)

نوافل navā'fil N.M. (PL. of نفل N.M. ★)

نوال navāl' N.F. (lit.) beneficence [A]

نوالہ nivā'lah N.M. morsel ; mouthful نوالہ اٹھانا navā'lah ūṭhā'nā V.T. take a morsel ایک ہی نوالہ کرنا ek' hī nivā'lah kar'nā V.I. gulp down consume at once نوالہ نہ توڑنا nivā'lah na toṛ'nā N.M. not to eat تر نوالہ tar' nivā'lah N.M. choice morsel دیکھے شیر کی آنکھ کھلائے سونے کا نوالہ de'khe sher' kī āṅkh' khilā''e so'ne kā nivā'lah PROV. provide all amenities but be a strict disciplinarian

نواہی navā'hī N.F. PL. prohibitions interdicts injunctions اوامر و نواہی avā'mir-onava''hī N.M. PL. exhortations and injunctions ; orders and prohibitions [A ~ SING. نہی]

نوائب nava''ib N.M. PL. calamities ; unfortunate occurrences ; adversities [A ~ SING. نائبہ]

نوبت ۱ nau'bat N.F. turn period time ; occasion ; opportunity stage condition نوبت آنا nau'bat ā'nā V.T. (of somethings turn) come ; be the turn (of) نوبت بہ نوبت nau'bat ba-nau'bat ADV. turn by turn نوبت پہنچنا nau'bat pahūṅch'nā V.I. be reduced نوبت کو پہنچنا nau'bat ko pahūṅch'na V. reach a (certain) stage be reduced to the condition نوبتی nau'batī ADJ. intermittant (fever, etc.) [A]

نوبت ۲ nau'bat N.F. kettle-drum drum for announcing passage of time, etc. نوبت بجانا nau'bat bajā'na V.T. beat the drum announce the hour with beat of drum نوبت بجنا nau'bat baj'nā V.I. (of drum) be beaten (of hour) be announced with beat of drum نوبت خانہ nau'bat-khā'nah N.M place from where time is announced with beat of drum guard house to the condition (of stage) come [~PREC.]

نوبل پرائز no'bal-parā''īz N.M. Nobel Prize [E]

نوتہ nau'tah, نیوتہ nayo'tah N.M. monetary gift made at wedding نوتنا naut'nā V.I. invite as wedding guest نوتنی naut'nī N.F. wedding party نوتھاری nauthārī N.M. (dial.) wedding guest who has to give a gift

نوٹ noṭ N.F. currency note note نوٹ بک noṭ-bŭk N.F. note-book نوٹ کرنا noṭ'-kar'nā V.T. note ; make a note of [E]

نوٹس no'ṭis N.M. notice نوٹس دینا (یا بھیجنا) noṭis de'nā (or bhej'na) V.T. give notice [E]

نوج nauj INT. (dial.) God forbid [CORR. of A نعوذ we seek asylum (of God]

نوچنا noch'nā V.T. pinch claw tear at نوچا نوچی no'chā-nā'chī N.F. tearing at each other نوچ کھسوٹ noch'-khasoṭ' N.F. plunder exploitation

نوچی nau'chī N.F. bawd's girl young prostitute

نوح nooḥ N.M. Noah طوفان نوح toofā'n-e nooḥ' N.M. deluge عمر نوح ūm'r-e nooḥ' N.M. very long life [A ~ H]

نوحہ nau'ḥah N.M. lamentation dirge a kind of elegiac verse نوحہ خواں nau'ḥa-khāṅ N.M. & ADJ. mourner ; (one) who laments writer or reciter of elegiac verse نوحہ خوانی nau'ḥa-khā'nī N.F. lamentation writer or reciter of elegiac verse نوحہ گر nau'ḥa-gar' ADJ. & N.M. lamenting (person) ; mourner نوحہ گری nau'ḥa-ga'rī N.F. lamentation [A]

نور noor' N.M. (PL. انوار anvār') light luminosity refulgence splendour نور افزا noor'-afzā' ADJ. illuminating نور افشاں noor'-afshāṅ' ADJ. diffusing light نور باف noor'bā f N.M. (arch.) weaver نور بافی noor'-bā'fī N.F. (arch.) weaving نور جہاں noo'r-e jahāṅ' N.M. light of the world N.F. (noor'-jahāṅ') this as female name نور چشم noo'r-e chash'm. نور دیدہ noo'r-e dī'dah نور نظر noo'r-e na'zar N.M. (fig.) son نور چھانا noor' chhā'na V.T. be light all around نور ظہور کا وقت noor' zahoor' kā vaq't N.M. dawn : daybreak نور علیٰ نور noo'rŭn 'alā' noor' INT. wonderful نور کا تڑکا noor' kā taṛ'ka N.M. early hours of morning نور کے تڑکے noor' ke taṛ'ke ADV. in the early hours of the morning نور کے سانچے میں ڈھالنا noor' ke sāṅ'che meṅ ḍhal'na V.I. be exquisitely beautiful نور کا گلا noor' kā ga'lā N.M. melodious voice نور کا گلا پانا noor' kā ga'lā pā'na V.I. have a melodious voice نورانی noorā'nī ADJ. bright luminous brilliant refulgent resplendent saintly نورانیت nooraniy'yat N.F. brilliance saintliness نوری noo'rī ADJ. composed of light heavenly angel N.M. angel [A]

نورد navar'd SUF. traveller ; wanderer نوردی navar'dī N.F. travel ; wandering [P نوردن]

نوری noo'rī ADJ. & N.M. (see under نور N.M. ★)

نورہ nau'rah N.M. depilatory made of lime

نوش ۱ nosh N.M. honey نوشابہ noshā'bah N.M. elixir نوشدارو nosh'dā'roo N.M. name of medicine used as cordial or antidote نوشیں no'shīṅ ADJ. honey-like ; sweet [P]

نوش ۲ nosh N.M. eating drinking نوش (جاں) فرمانا (یا کرنا) nosh(-e jāṅ') farmā'nā (or kar'nā) V.T. eat drink [P ~ نوشیدن]

نوشادر naushā'dar N.M. ammonium chloride ; sal-ammoniac [P]

نوشت navisht'. SUF. writing N.F. writing (only in) نوشت و خواند navish't-o-khānd' N.F. writing and reading being reduced to writing نوشتہ navish'tah N.M. writing ADJ. written نوشتۂ تقدیر navish'ta-e taqdīr' N.M. fate ; destiny نوشتنی navish'tanī ADJ. worth-writing [P ~ نوشتن]

نوشہ nau'shah N.M. (see under نو ۲ ADJ. & PREF. ★

نوشیں no'shīṅ ADJ. (see under نوش ۱ N.M. ★)

نوع nau' N.F. (PL. انواع an'vā') species kind ; sort manner نوع انسان nau''-e in'sāṅ' N.F. mankind بہر نوع ba-har nau'' ADV. anyhow at any rate ; at all events somehow or other نوعیت

nau'iy'yat N.F. kind quality particular nature [A]

نوک nok N.F. point tip end نوک پلک nok' pa'lak N.F. beauty of features nicety of calligraphist نوک جھونک nok' jhonk N.F. passage-at-arms نوکدار nok'-dar ADJ. pointed نوک دم بھاگنا nok'-dam bhag'na V.T. run away ; show a clean pair of heels نوک زباں nok-e zuban' ADV. by heart ; on the tip of one's tongue (بر) نوک زباں ہونا (bar) no'k-e zuban' ho'na V.I. be on the tip of one's tongue [P]

نوکر nau'kar N.M. servant employer نوکر آگے چاکر nau'kar a'ge cha'kar PROV. one entrusting one's work to another نوکر چاکر nau'kar cha'kar N.M. servants domestic servants نوکر رکھنا nau'kar rakh'na V.T. engage or take up as a servant نوکر ہونا nau'kar ho'na V.I. be a servant take up service (with) نوکرانی nau'kara'ni N.F. maid-servant نوکری nau'kari service employment post ; job نوکری پیشہ nau'kari-pe'shah N.M. one defending on service as his means of livelihood ; salaried person نوکری پیشہ لوگ nau'kari-pe-'shah log' N.M. PL. salaried classes نوکری کرنا nau'kari kar'na V.T. take up service [P]

نوم naum N.F. sleep [A]

نومبر navam'bar N.M. November [E]

نومید naumid' (arch. naumed') ADJ. hopeless نومیدی naumi'di, (arch. naume'di) N.F. disappointment hopelessness ; despair ; despondency [P ~ نا + امید]

نون[1] noon N.M. name of the 'noon' (rare) fish نون غنہ noo'n-e ghun'nah N.M. nasal 'n' نون قطنی noo'n-e qut'ni N.M. superior (or inferior) 'noon' written at various places for nunation

نون[2] non (or noon) N.M. salt نون تیل (لکڑی) non' tel (lak'ri) N.M. (F.) minor necessities of life نون مرچ لگانا non' mir'ch laga'na V.T. exaggerate

نونی noo'ni N.F. infant's penis butteroil salinity on walls, etc. نونی لگنا noo'ni lag'na V.I. (of wall plaster) come off owing to salinity

نوے nav've ADJ. & N.M. ninety نویاں nau'veran ADJ. ninetieth

نوید nuvid' N.F. good news glad tidings [P]

نویس navis' SUF. writer (of) نویسندہ navisin'dah N.M. writer scribe نویسی navi'si SUF. writing [P ~ نوشتن navish'tan]

نویلا nave'la ADJ. (F. نویلی nave'li) new singular نیا نویلا na'ya nave'la ADJ. (F. نئی نویلی na''i nave'li) brand new

نہ[1] nah ADJ. no not neither nor نہ پوچھو na' poo'chho INT. it is indescribable نہ تھوکنا na' thook'na V.I. (also fig.) not to care a hang for نہ جانے (or نہ جانے) na-ja'ne ADV. who knows نہ رہے بانس نہ بجے بانسری na ra'he bans' na ba'je bans'ri PROV. let us strike at the root of the trouble نہ منہ میں دانت نہ پیٹ میں آنت na munh' men dant' na pet' men ant' PH. (fig.) very old (person) ; decrepit نہ لینا نہ دینا (na) le'na na de'na PH. of no use having no connection نہ نو من تیل ہوگا نہ رادھا ناچے گی na nau man tel' ho'ga na ra'dha na'chengi PROV. puttingforth impossible conditions نہ بڑ بڑ نہ کھڑ کھڑ na bar' bar na khar khar PH. with no quarrel

نہ[2] nah SUF. like ; -ish [P]

نہ noh N.M. nine نہم na'hum (ped. nohum') ADJ. ninth [P]

نہاد nehad' N.F. nature disposition [P ~ نہادن place]

نہار nahar' N.M. day لیل و نہار lai'l-o-nahar' N.M. PL. night(s) and day(s) ways ; habits [A]

نہار nahar' ADJ. without food since morning without breakfast نہار منہ nahar' munh ADV. on an empty stomach [P]

نہاری naha'ri (or ne-) N.F. skin of beef stew this used for breakfast horsefeed comprising condiments and raw sugar [~ نہارا]

نہال nehal' ADJ. (dial.) happy prosperous نہال کرنا nehal' kar'na V.T. please make prosperous نہال ہونا nehal' ho'na V.I. be happy prosper ; thrive

نہال nehal N.M. sapling lovely newgrown tree نہالی neha'li N.F. mattress ADJ. of or like a new-grown plant نہالچہ nehal'chah N.M. small mattress [P]

نہاں nihan' ADJ. hidden ; concealed latent clandestine نہاں خانہ nihan' kha'nah N.M. private room نہانی niha'ni ADJ. hidden ; concealed latent اندام نہانی anda'm-e niha'ni N.F. private parts of female body [P]

نہانا naha'na V.I. wash oneself ; bathe نہانا دھونا naha'na dho'na V.T. wash oneself ; bathe نہان nahan' N.M. (dial.) bath

نہانا neha'na N.M. tie milch-cattle's kind legs for milking

نہائی naha''i N.F. anvil

نہایت neha'yat N.F. limit ; end ; extremity boundary excess extreme ADV. very ; very much extremely exceedingly remarkably exquisitely [A]

نہتا nehat'ta, (F. نہتی nehat'ti) ADJ. unarmed empty-handed [~ ن + ہاتھ]

نہٹا nahut'ta N.M. nail-scratch نہٹا لگنا nahut'ta lag'na V.I. have a nail scratch نہٹا مارنا nahut'ta *mar'na* V.T. scratch hard with nails

نہج *naih'j* (ped. *nah'j*) N.M. mode manner [A]

نہر *naih'r* (ped. *nah'r*) N.F. (PL. انہار *anhar'*) canal نہر کاٹنا (یا نکالنا) *naih'r kaṭ'na* (or *nikal'na*) V.T. take out a canal from نہری *naih'rī* ADJ. canal-irrigated land [A ~ river]

نہرنا *nahūr'na* N.M. (col. نہننا *nahūn'na* N.F. نہرنی *nahūr'nī* N.F. nail-parer

نہروا *nahar'va*, ناہرو *nah'roo* N.M. long threadlike worm coming out of skin this as disease

نہضت *noh'zat* N.F. marching movement [A]

نہفتہ *nehuf'tah* ADJ. hidden ; concealed [P]

نہلا *naih'la* N.M. nine (at cards) نہلے پر (یا پہ) دہلا مارنا *naih'le par* (or *pa*) *daih'la mar'na* PH. go one better [~ نو]

نہلانا *naihla'na* V.T. wash or bathe (someone) نہلائی *naihla''ī* N.F. remuneration for giving a bath نہلوانا *naihlva'na* V.T. cause (someone) to be washed or bathed [~ نہانا CAUS.]

نہم *na'hum* (ped. *no'hum*) ADJ. (see under نہ *noh* ADJ. & N.M. ★)

نہمت *noh'mat* N.F. courage desire [A]

نہنگ *nahang'* N.M. crocodile alligator نہنگ اجل *nahan'g-e ajal'* N.M. (fig.) death [P]

نہنگ *nihang* ADJ. naked unconcerned shameless [P]

نہوت *nahot'* N.F. straitened circumstances penury ; pennilessness [~ نہ + ہونا]

نہورا *naho'ra*, نہوڑا *naho'ṛa* N.M. · coquetry vaunted favour ; obligation

نہوڑانا *nahūṛa'na* V.T. bow down (one's head)

نہی *nah'y* ADJ. prohibitory (tense) N.F. prohibitory tense interdict [A]

نہیں *na'hīn* ADJ. no ; not; nay نہیں تو *na'hīn to* INT no ; not at all ADV. otherwise

نئی *na''ī*, نئے *na''e* ADJ. inflected forms of نیا ADJ. ★)

نی *nī* N.M. seventh note of national gamut

نے *nai* N.F. flute ; pipe read نیستان *nayas'tan*, (or *nai'sitan*) N.M. place where reeds grow نے نواز *nai-navaz'* N.M. piper نے نوازی *nai-nava'zī* N.F. piping [P]

نے *nai* ADV. (lit.) no ; not ; nay نے ... نے *nai... nai* ADV neither...nor [P]

نے *ne* PARTICLE. (It follows subject of transitive verb used in past tense ; not translated into English)

نیا *na'ya* ADJ. (F. نئی *na''ī*, نئے *na''e*) new ; fresh recent modern نیا پھل *na'ya phal* N.M. new species of fruit new fruit (of the season) نیا جنم *na'ya ja'nam* (ped. *-jan'm*) N.M. new life complete recovery rebirth نیا راگ الاپنا *na'ya rag' alap'na* V.T. strike a new note create new problem نیا رنگ لانا *na'ya rang' la'na* V. (of events, etc.) take a new turn نیا فتنہ اٹھانا *na'ya fit'nah uṭha'na*, نیا گل کھلانا *na'ya gul khila'na* V.T. create new problem نیا کرنا *na'ya kar'na* V.T. eat new fruit of season (W. dial.) burn نیا نو دن پرانا سو دن *na'ya nau' din pura'na sau din* PH. old things outlast new one's نیا نوکر ہرن مارتا ہے *na'ya nau'kar hi'ran mar'ta hai* PROV. new broom sweeps well نیا نویلا *na'ya nave'la*, ADJ. (F. نئی نویلی *na''ī nave'lī*) new young beautiful untouched unused نئی جوانی *na''ī java'nī* N.F. budding youth نئی جوانی چڑھنا *na''ī java'nī chaṛh'na* V.I. become young again نئی روشنی *na''ī rau'shanī* N.F. new light; modern civilization نئے سرے سے *na''e si're se* ADV. anew ; afresh all over again نئے نواب آسمان پر دماغ *na''e navab asman' par dimagh'* PROV. an upstart is always arrogant نئے نئے حاکم نئی نئی باتیں *na''e na''e ha'kim na''ī na''ī ba'teṅ* PROV. new master, new laws

نیا *nay'ya* N.F. boat نیا کا کھویا *nay'ya ka khivay'ya* N.M. boats'n (fig.) breadwinner of family [~ ناؤ]

نیابت *niya'bat* N.F. vicegerancy deputizing (for) ; becoming an agent (of) نیابتاً *niyabatan* ADJ. as an agent نائب *na'ib* ADJ. ★ [A]

نیار *niyar'* N.M. fodder

نیارا *niya'ra*, ADJ. (F. نیاری *niya'rī*) (dial.) uncommon ; extraordinary separate N.M. scoria left after refining gold, etc. نیاریا *niya'riya* N.M. one who washes metal grains from scoria ADJ. clever

نیاز *niyaz'* N.M. humility meekness need meeting acquaintance N.F. offering ; libation نیاز چڑھانا *niyaz' chaṛha'na* V. make an offering نیاز حاصل کرنا *niyaz' ha'sil kar'na* V.T. pay one's respects (to) نیاز حاصل ہونا *niyaz' ha'sil ho'na* V.T. meet know be acquainted with نیاز دلوانا *niyaz dilva'na* V.T. make an offering in the name (of) give alms (to) نیاز رسول *niya'z-e rasool'* N.F. alms given in the Holy Prophet's name نیاز کیش *niyaz'-kesh'* ADJ. humble ; obedient نیاز مند *niyaz'-mand'* ADJ. humble ; obedient indigent ; needy supplicating نیاز مندی *niyaz'-man'dī* N.F. humble prayer ; supplication [P]

نیازا *niyā'za* N.M. penis [~P نیزه CORR.]

نیام *niyām'* N.F. sheath; a scabbard بے نیام *be-niyām'* ADJ. (of sword) uncovered ; unsheathed [P]

نیانا *niyā'nā*, نینا *nai'nā* N.M. piece of rope with which milch animal's hind knees are tied during milking

نیاؤ *niyā''o* N.M. justice ; just decision نیاؤ کرنا *niy''a''o kar'nā*, نیائے *niay''e* N.M. (dial.) justice dialectics logic نیایک *niyā'yak* N.M. judge dialectician logician

نیبو *nī'boo* N.M. lemon ; lime نیبو نچوڑ *nī'boo-ni chor'* N.M. lemon-crusher

نیت *niy'yat* N.F. intention intent ; purpose design wish ; will نیت باندھنا (یا کرنا) *niy'yat bāndh'nā* (or *kar'nā*) V.T. & I. resolve repeat formula for opening the prayer نیت بھرنا *niy'yat bhar'nā* V.I. be satiated ; have no more any desire to eat نیت بگڑنا (یا بدل جانا یا بد ہونا) *niy'yat bi'garnā* (or *ba'dal jā'nā* or *bad' ho'nā*) V.I. change one's mind suddenly have an evil intention نیت ثابت رکھنا *niy'yat sā'bit rakh'nā* V.T. stick to one's resolve نیت شب حرام *niy'yat-e shab ḥarām'* PH. I (etc.) have no intent to go to sleep نیت لگی رہنا *niy''yat la'gī raih'nā* V.I. bear in mind نیت میں فرق آنا *niy'yat meñ far'q ā'nā* V.I. suddenly have an evil intention [A]

نیتی *nī'tī* N.F. (dial.) conduct راج نیتی *raj-nī'tī* N.F. (dial.) conduct of state ; politics ; diplomacy [S]

نیچ *nīch* ADJ. low ; mean N.F. descent ; declivity نیچ ذات *nīch'-zāt* N.F. & ADJ. low caste ; depressed class اونچ نیچ *oonch'nīch* N.F. inequality of social status vicissitudes (of life) unevenness [~FOOL]

نیچا *nī'chā* ADJ. (F. نیچی *nī'chī*) low less mean ; base sloping lowlying نیچا دکھانا *nī'chā dikhā'nā* V.T bring (someone) low نیچا کرنا *nī'chā kar'nā* V.T. lower bend نیچی نظر کرنا *nī'chī na'zar kar'nā* V. look downward out of respect or shame نیچی نظر ہونا *nī'chī na'zar ho'nā* V.T. be ashamed نیچی نظروں سے دیکھنا *nī'chī naz'roñ se dekh'nā* V.T. look ashame look with downcaste eyes نیچے *nī'che* ADV. below ; beneath down under نیچے آنا *nī'che ā'nā* V.I. be thrown down نیچے سے اوپر تک *nī'che se oo'par tak* PH. all over; from top to bottom نیچے کا پاٹ بھاری ہونا *nī'che kā pāṭ bhā'rī ho'nā* PH. have petticoat government ; (of wife) wear the breeches نیچے کی سانس نیچے اور اوپر کی سانس اوپر رہ جانا *nī'che kī sāns' nī'che aur oo'par kī sāns' oo'par raih' jā'nā* V.I. be struck dumb be greatly shocked ; have the shock of one's life نیچے لانا *nī'che lā'nā* V.T. trounce

نیچر *ne'char* N.F. nature نیچرل *naich'ral* natural نیچری *nech'rī* N.M. materialist ; atheist [E]

نیچہ *nai'chah* N.M. hookah tubes نیچہ بند *nai'cha band* N.M. hookah tube binder [P ~ نے DIM]

نیچے *nī'che* ADV. (see under نیچا ADJ. ★)

نیر *nīr* N.M. (dial.) water

نیر *nay'yir* N.M. & ADJ. luminary نیر اصغر *nay'yir-e as'ghar* N.M. moon ; the lesser luminary نیر اعظم (یا تاباں یا درخشاں) *nay'yir-e a'zam* (or *tā'bāñ*) or *rakh'-shāñ* N.M. the sun; the greater luminary [A ~ نور]

نیرنگ *nairang'* N.M. sorcery ; magic miracle trick wonder نیرنگی *nairañ'gī* N.F. sorcery ; magic miracle trickery wonder نیرنگی روزگار (یا زمانہ یا عالم) *nairañ'gi-e rozgār'* (or *zamā'nah* or *'ā'lam*) N.F. the vicissitudes of fortune [P]

نیرو *ne'roo* N.M. strength ; power ; might [P]

نیز *nīz* CONJ. also again even [P]

نیزہ *ne'zah* (ped. *nai'zah*) N.M. spear ; lance javelin reed from which pens are made نیزہ باز *ne'za-bāz* N.M. spearman ; a lancer نیزہ بازی *ne'za-bā'zī* N.F. tilting jousting [P ~ نے *nai*]

نیساں *nai'sāñ* N.M. name of Iranian Spring month (corresponding to April-May ابر نیساں *ab're nai'sāñ* N.M. spring cloud ; spring shower

نیست *nes't* N.M. non-existence ADJ. non-existant ADV. no نیست و نابود کرنا *nes't-o nā-bood' kar'nā* V.T. ruin ; destroy annihilate obliterate نیستی *nes'tī* N.F. non-existence annihilation ruin ; destruction ill-luck indolence ; lethargy نیستی چھانا *nes'tī chhā'na* V.I. have ill-luck brought about by indolence نیستی کا مارا *nes'tī kā mā'ra* N.M. indolent ; lethargic wretched [P ~ نہ + است]

نیش *nesh* N.M. sting نیش دار *nesh'-dār* ADJ. stinging mordant نیش زنی *nesh'-za'nī* N.F. stinging taunts taunting [P]

نیفہ *ne'fah* N M. part of trousers through which string runs نیفے میں اڑسنا *ne'fe meñ ū'rasnā* V.T. hold (something) in purse improvised by upturning a part of trousers from under the belt

نیک *nek* ADJ. good , virtuous ; pious mannerly lucky ; fortunate نیک اختر *ne'k-akh'tar* ADJ. lucky ; fortunate نیک انجام *nek-anjām'* ADJ. having a happy end نیک اندیش *nek andesh'* ADJ. well-meaning well-disposed نیک اندیشی *nek-*

ande'shī N.F. good intention نیک بخت nek'-bakh't ADJ. lucky ; fortunate true ; dutiful ; well-behaved نیک بختی nek'-bakh'tī N.F. good luck ; good fortune being well-behaved نیک چلن nek-cha'lan ADJ. of good conduct ; having a good character. نیک چلنی nek'-chal'nī N.F. good conduct ; good character نیک خصال nek'-khisal' نیک خصلت nek'-khas'lat, نیک خو nek'-khoo ADJ. good-natured نیک خواہ nek'-khāh ADJ. well-wisher ; friend نیک خواہی nek'-khā'hī N.F. being a well-wisher ; friendliness نیک ساعت nek' sā''at N.F. auspicious moment نیک سیرت (یا طینت) nek'-sī'rat (or tī'nat) ADJ. well-behaved of good disposition نیک سیرتی nek-sī'ratī N.F. good behaviour نیک صلاح کا پوچھنا کیا nek' salāh' ka poochh'na kyā' PROV. implementation of good council should not be delayed نیک فال nek' fal N.F. good omen نیک فرجام nek'-farjam' ADJ. with a happy end نیک قدم nek'-qa'dam ADJ. welcome نیک کردار nek'-kirdār' ADJ. of good character نیک گھڑی nek' gha'rī N.F. auspicious moment نیک محضر nek'-mah'zar ADJ. well-behaved of good disposition نیک مزاج nek'-mizāj' ADJ. well-mannered; well-behaved نیک مزاجی nek'-mizā'jī N.F. being well-behaved good disposition نیک منش nek'-ma'nish ADJ. good-natured نیک منظر nek'-man'zar ADJ. lovely نیکنام nek'-nām' ADJ. reputed having a good character نیکنامی nek'-nā'mī N.F. repute good character نیک نہاد nek'-nehād' ADJ. good-natured نیک نیت nek'-niy'yat ADJ. well-meaning; well-intentioned نیک نیتی nek'-niy'yatī N.F. being well-intentioned نیک و بد ne'k-o-bad' N.M. good and evil pros and cous (of) نکو ne'ko PREF. (same as PREF. ★) نیکی ne'kī N.F. good goodness virtue piety beauty نیکی اور پوچھ پوچھ ne'kī aur poochh' poochh PROV. do not delay doing good نیکی بدی ne'kī ba'dī N.F. good and evil weal or woe نیکی برباد گناہ لازم ne'kī bar-bād' gūnah' lā'zim PROV. a good turn repaid by evil نیکی کر دریا میں ڈال ne'kī kar darya' men dāl' PROV. if you confer a favour do not boast

نیگ neg N.M. cash presents made by marrying couple to relatives ; menials or entertainers نیگ جوگ neg' jog N.M. (same as نیگ N.M. ★) نیگ دینا neg' de'nā V.T. make such presents نیگ لینا neg' le'nā V.T. accept such presents نیگ لگنا neg' lag'nā V.I. be well spent نیگی جوگی ne'gī jo'gī N.M. menials deserving such presents

نیل ¹ nīl N.M. & ADJ. ten billion

نیل ² nīl N.M. indigo dark bruise carried by blow, hurt, etc.) PREF. blue نیل بگڑنا nīl' bi'garnā V.T & I. (of false report) get round tell a white lie suffer reverse be unfortunate go mad (of indigo vat) be spoilt نیل پڑ جانا nīl' paṛ jā'nā V.I. be beaten black and blue نیل ڈھلنا nīl' dhul'nā V.I. lose all sense of shame (of dying man's eyes) run ; slime نیل کا ٹیکہ nīl' kā ṭī'kah N.M. slur ; stigma نیل کا ماٹ nīl' kā māṭ N.M. indigo vat نیل کنٹھ nīl'-kanṭh N.M. blue-necked jay نیل کی سلائیاں آنکھوں میں پھیرنا nīl' kī salā''i-yān ān'khon men pher'nā V.T. blind نیل کوٹھی nīl' kī ko'ṭhī N.F. indigo factory نیل گائے nīl'-gā'e N.F. white antelope نیلگوں nīl'goon ADJ. blue azure [P]

نیل nail N.M. achievement ; attainment ; acquisition نیل مرام nai'l-e marām' N.M. success , achievement of one's object بے نیل مرام be-nail-e marām' ADV. unsuccessfully ; without achieving one's object

نیلا nī'lā ADJ. (F. نیلی nī'lī) blue azure livid نیلا پیلا ہونا nī'la pī'lā ho'na V.I. be enraged , fly into a passion نیلا تھوتھا nī'la tho'tha N.M. blue vitriol , copper sulphate نیلا ڈورا باندھنا nī'lā ḍo'ra bāndh'na V.I. tie a blue string to offset of evil eye نیلاہٹ nilā'haṭ N.M. blueness azureness lividness

نیلام nīlām' N.M., نیلامی nīlā'mī N.F. auction نیلام کرنا nīlām' kar'nā V.T. auction نیلام گھر nīlām'-ghar N.M. auction house [Por]

نیلم nī'lam N.M. sapphire نیلم پری nī'lam-pa'rī N.F (legend) blue fair ; sapphire fairy [P]

نیلوفر nī'lofar N.M. water-lily ; lotus ; nenuphar نیلوفری nī'lofa'rī ADJ. blue گنبد نیلوفری gūm'bad-e nī'lofarī N.F. blue sky نیلی nī' lī ADJ. blue نیلی رواق nī'lī rūvāq' N.M. blue museum [P]

نیم ¹ nīm N.M. margosa ; ' metla azedirachta' نیم کی نبولی nīm kī nibo'lī N.F fruit of the margosa tree

نیم ² nīm ADJ. half middle SUF. half semi-quasi نیم باز nīm'-bāz ADJ. half-open (of eyes) drunk , intoxicated نیم برشت nīm' birisht' ADJ. (of meat) not fully roasted (of egg) purboiled ; soft-boiled half-fried poached soft-boiled نیم پخت nīm' pūkht, نیم پز nīm'paz ADJ. half-baked not well-cooked (of egg) parboiled; half-boiled نیم بسمل nīm'-bis'mil ADJ. mortally wounded نیم پختہ nīm'-pūkh'tah ADJ. half-ripe نیم تر nīm'-ṭar ADJ. (joc.) semi-literate نیم جان nīm'-jān ADJ. half-dead N.M. (fig.) lover نیم جوش nīm'-josh ADJ. half-boiled نیم حکیم nīm'-hakīm' N.M. quack ; charlaton mountebank نیم حکیم خطرۂ جان نیم ملا خطرۂ ایمان nīm'-hakīm' khat'ra-e jān' nīm'-mul'lā khat'ra-e īmān' PROV. half-knowledge is dangerous نیم خواب nīm'-khāb ADJ. half-asleep نیم خوابی

nīm'-khā'bī N.F. doze drowsiness نیم خوابیدہ *nīm'-khābī'dah* ADJ. half-asleep نیم خوردہ *nīm' khūr'-dah* N.M. remainder of victuals crusts and crumbs ADJ. half-eaten نیم راضی *nīm'-rā'zī* ADJ. somewhat agreeable half-satisfied نیم رسمی *nīm'-ras'mī* ADJ. demi official (letter) ; D.O. نیم روز *nīm'-roz'* N.M. midday ; noontide مہر نیمروز *meh'r-e nīm-roz'* N.M. noontide sun نیم سوختہ *nīm'-sokh'tah* ADJ. half-burnt نیم شب *nīm'-shab* N.F. mid-night نیمکار *nīm'-kār* N.M. worker working with hired implements, etc. and paying part wages to owner نیم کش *nīm'-kash* ADJ. half-drawn agonizing نیم کشتہ *nīm'-kūsh'tah* ADJ. half-killed نیم گرم *nīm'-gar'm* ADJ. lukewarm نیم مردہ *nīm'-mūr'dah* ADJ. emaciated tired ; jaded نیم ملا *nīm'-mūl'lā* ADJ. half-educated N.M. priest with a smattering knowledge [P]

نیمچہ *nīm'chah* N.M. dagger ; small sword نیمچہ تاننا (یا تولنا) *nīm'chah tān'nā* (or *tol'nā*) brandish the dagger whip out one's dagger [P ~ نیم]

نیمہ *nī'mah* PREF. half; semi- نیمہ آستین *nī'ma-ās'tīn* N.F. half-sleeved jacket [P ~ نیم]

نینا *nai'nā* N.M. (same as نیا ADJ. ★) (dim. of نین N.F.)

نین *nain*, N.M., نینا *nai'nā* N.F. eye نین سکھ *nain'-sūkh* N.M. (dial.) a kind of fine longcloth نین گنوانا *nain' ganvā'nā* V.T. lose one's sight by constant نین متنا *nain-mut'nā* ADJ. weeping at the smallest excuse

نیند *nīnd* N.F. sleep نیند آنا (یا پڑنا) *nīnd' ā'nā* (or *par'nā*) V.I. sleep feel sleep نیند اچٹ (یا اڑ) جانا *nīnd' ū'chaṭ* (or *ūṛ'*) *jā'nā* V.I. have one's sleep driven off نیند بھر سونا *nīnd' bhar' so'nā* V.I. have a sound sleep نیند حرام کرنا *nīnd' harām' kar'nā* V.T. disturbed someone's sleep نیند حرام ہونا *nīnd' harām' ho'nā* V.I. be unable to sleep نیند کا ماتا *nīnd' kā mā'tā*, (F. نیند کی ماتی *nīnd' kī mā'tī*) ADJ. sleepy ADJ. one who is fond of too much sleep نینڈریاں *nīn'daryān* N.M. PL. (nurs.) sleep نیندو *nīn'doo* N.M. one fond of too much sleep

نینو *nai'noo* N.M. a kind of embroidered cloth ; sprigged muslin

نیو *niyo'* N.F. (rare نیوا *nī'vā* N.M.) foundation نیو ڈالنا *niyo' ḍāl'nā* V.T. lay the foundation-stone (of)

نیوتا *niyo'tā* N.M. invitation

نیور *ne'var* N.M. wound on horse's knees

نیوز *niyooz'* N.F. news نیوز ایجنٹ *niyooz'-ejanṭ'* N.M. news agent نیوز ایجنسی *niyooz'-ejan'sī* N.F. news agency نیوز پیپر *niyooz'-pe'par* N.M. newspaper [E]

نیوش *niyosh'* SUF. (used in comp.) hearing ; listening [P ~ نیوشیدن]

نیولا *niyo'lā* N.M. mangoose ; ferret ; weasel

نیولی *niyo'lī* N.F. purse fastened to waist [~ PREC.]

نیوگ *nayog'* N.M. (Hindu dialect getting inseminated by a high-caste man with permission of impotent husband

نیہہ *neh'*, نیہا *ne'hā* N.M. love نیہہ لگانا *neh lagā'nā* V.T. become a lover نیہی *ne'hī* N.M. lover

و

و *vā''o* thirty-third letter of Urdu alphabet (equivalent to English *v*) in according to jummal reckoning) 6 VOWEL representing the sounds *ū*, *oo* or *au* CONJ. and PREP. by (God)

وا *vā'* ADJ. open PREF. & ADV. back ; behind re- ; again separate وابستہ *vā'bas'tah* N.M. (PL. وابستگان *vā'bastagān'*) dependent adherent ADJ. connected ; related bound together depending on وابستہ ہونا *vā-bas'tah ho'nā* V.I. be dependent (on) be attached (to) be connected (with) وابستگی *vā-bas'tagī* N.F. dependence connection واپس *vā'pas* ADJ. back behind واپسی *vā'pasī* N.F. return withdrawn واپسیں *vā'pasīn* ADJ. last دم واپسیں *da'm-e vā'pasīn* N.M. last gasp وارستہ *vā-ras'tah* ADJ. free escaped unconcerned وارستگی *vā'ras'tagī* N.F. freedom ; liberation unconcern وارفتہ *vā-raf'tah* ADJ. not in (one's) senses unconcerned infatuated distracted mad وارفتہ مزاج *vā-raf'ta-mizāj'* ADJ. infatuated with love mad careless وارفتگی *vā-raf'tagī* N.F. not being in one's sense unconcern infatuation distraction ; madness واژگوں *vā-zhagoon'* واژوں *vā-zhoon'* واژونہ *vā-zhoo'nah* ADJ. inverted ; upturned perverse واژگونی *vā-zhagoo'nī* واژونی *vā-zhoo'nī* N.F. inversion perversity واسوخت *vā-sokh't* N.M. disgust genre of poetry expressing chagrined lover's disgust with beloved ; lover's revolt واسوختہ *vā-sokh'tah* ADJ. burnt واسوختگی *vā sokh'tagī* N.F. being burnt down ; incineration واشگاف *vā-shigāf'* ADJ. open ADV. openly without mincing matters واکرنا *vā' kar'nā* V.T. open واگذار *vā-guzār'* ADJ. restored واگزار کرنا *vā-guzār' kar'nā* V.T. restore واگزاشتہ *vā-guzash'tah* ADJ. left behind restored واماندہ vā-mān'dah ADJ. & N.M. (PL. واماندگان vā-mān'dagān) tired ; fatigued ; persons those lagging behind un واماندگی vā-mān'dagī N.F fatigue lagging behind وا ہونا vā' ho'nā V.I. open be opened [P]

وا vā INT ah ; O ; alas واحسرتا vā'-has'rata INT. (lit.) the unfulfilment of wishes ; how unfortunate وامصیبتا vā-mūsī'bata INT. (lit.) what a misfortune [A]

واٹر پروف vā'ṭar-paroof' N.M. raincoat ; mackintosh ADJ. waterproof [E]

واثق vā'siq ADJ. firm (belief) strong (hope) [A ~ وثوق]

واجب vā'jib ADJ. expedient right proper necessary fit ; meet deserving ; worthy of pref-able; -ible N.M. (PL. واجبات vā'jibāt') obligation, duty due amount independent entity واجب الادا vā'jib-ūl-adā' ADJ. due payable واجب الاتباع vā'jib-ūl-ittibā' ADJ. binding worth following واجب الاذعان vā'jib-ūl-iz'ān' ADJ. obligatory واجب الاظہار vā'jib-ūl-izhār' ADJ. necessary to be disclosed واجب التسلیم vā'jib-ūl-taslīm' ADJ. acceptable plausible obligatory واجب التعزیر vā'jib-ūl-ta'zīr' ADJ. punishable ; culpable واجب التعظیم vā'jib-ūl-ta'zīm' ADJ. respectable ; venerable واجب الرحم vā'jib-ūr-raih'm ADJ. pitiable واجب الرعایت vā'jib-ūr-re'ā'yat ADJ. remissable deserving concession or leniency واجب الزیارت vā'jib-īz-ziyā'rat ADJ. worthseeing worth-paying a visit to واجب العرض vā'jib-ūl-'ar'z ADJ. worth-submission N.F. petition administration paper ; statement of 'mahal' constitution واجب العمل vā'jib-ūl-'amal' ADJ. obligatory worth following واجب القتل vā'jib-ūl-qat'l ADJ. deserving death واجب الوجود vā'jib-ul-vūjood' ADJ. self-existent N.M. this as attribute of God واجب الوصول vā'jib-ūl-vūsool' ADJ. recoverable واجب تھا سو عرض کیا vā'jib thā so 'ar'z kiyā PH. (used as conclusion to petitions) I have submitted it because it was expedient to do so واجب جاننا (یا سمجھنا) vā'jib jān'nā (or sa'majhnā) V.T. regard as obligatory واجبات vā'jibāt' N.M. PL. dues duties واجبی vā'jibī ADJ. a little, not much workable admissible necessary reasonable just واجبی بات vājibī bāt N.M. reasonable point واجبی سا vājī'bī sā ADV. so so a little [A ~ وجوب]

واجد vā'jid ADJ. finder this as an attribute of God [A ~ وجود]

واچ vāch N.F watch واچ میکر vāch me'kar N.M watch maker [E]

واحد vā'hid ADJ. once single (gram.) singular N.M. (gram.) singular number one (as attributive name of God) واحد العین vā'hid-ūl-'ain ADJ. & N.M. (Euphuism for) one-eyed (person)

وادی vā'dī N.F. valley vale ; dell pass channel (of river) (rare) desert وادیٔ ایمن vā'dī-e e'man N.F. the Sinai Peninsula وادیٔ خاموشاں (یا خموشاں) vā'dī-e khāmo'shāṅ (or khamo'shāṅ) N.F. grave-yard

وار¹ vār N.M. attack, assault stroke knock blow aim opportunity وار اوچھا پڑنا vār' o'chhā par'nā, وار خالی جانا vār khā'lī jā'nā V.I. miss the aim وار بچانا (یا خالی دینا) vār bachā'nā (or khā'lī de'nā) V.T. parry وار چلنا vār' chal'nā V.I. get an opportunity (to) وار کرنا vār' kar'nā V.T. attack assault وار ہونا vār' ho'nā V.T. be attacked

وار² vār ADV. this side

وار³ vār PREF. (sun, etc.) day

وار⁴ vār SUF having full deserving like -wise [P]

وار⁵ vār N.F war [E]

وارا vā'rā N.M. saving gain ; benefit وارے نیارے vā're nıyā're N.M. great benefit وارے نیارے ہونا vā're nıyā're ho'nā V.I. flourish, prosper thrive earn great profit have a stroke of fortune

وارث vā'ris N.M. (PL. ورثہ va'rasah) heir ; successor وارث تخت و تاج vār'ris-e takh't-o-tāj N.M. heir to the throne وارث حقیقی vā'ris-e haqī'qī N.M heir-apparent وارث قیاسی vā'ris-e qiyā'sī N.M. heir-presumptive وارث ہونا vā'ris ho'nā V.I. inherit [~ وراثت]

وارد vā'rid ADJ. arriving coming entering befalling وارد ہونا vā'rid ho'nā V.I. arrive come upon enter befall واردات vāridāt' N.F. accident crime occurrence (someone's) experience [A ~ ورود]

وارنٹ vā'ranṭ N.M. warrant (of arrest or search) وارنٹ جاری کرنا vā'ranṭ jā'rī kar'nā V.T. issue a warrant وارنٹ ناقابل ضمانت vā'ranṭ na-qā'bil-e zamā'nat N.M. (non-) bailable warrant وارنٹ گرفتاری vā'ranṭ giriftā'rī N.F. warrant of arrest واقعات vā'qe'āt' N.M PL. events, incidents happenings, occurrence circumstances واقعاتی vā'qe'ā'tī ADJ. circumstantial (evidence) [E]

وارنش vār'nish N.M. varnish وارنش کرنا vār'nish kar'nā V.T varnish [E]

وارنا vār'nā V.T wave (something) over (someone) at votive offering offer (something) as sacrifice واری vā'rī ADJ. sacrificed INT may God accept me as a votive offering and protect you

وارڈ *vār'ḍ* N.M. ward (of city or hospital) (someone's) ward **کورٹ آف وارڈ** *kor't af vār'd* N.F. court of wards [E]

وارڑا *vā'ṛā* N.M. quarter (of city)

واڑی *vā'ṛī* N.F. & SUF. enclosure

واسطہ *vās'tah* (ped. *vā'sitah*) N.M. medium intermediary agent go between connection concern **واسطہ پڑنا** *vās'tah paṛ'nā* V.I. come into contact (with) **واسطہ پیدا کرنا** *vās'tah pai'dā kar'nā* V.I find means of approach establish contact (with) learn **واسطہ دینا** *vās'tah de'nā* V.T. quote (someone) as intermediary cry for mercy **واسطہ رکھنا** *vās'tah rakh'nā* V.T. have concern (with) **واسطہ ہونا** *vās'tah ho'nā* V.T. have anything to do (with) ; have concern (with) be related (to) ; be connected (with) **بالواسطہ** *bil-vās'tah* (ped. *bil vās'itah*) ADJ. indirect **بلا واسطہ** *bi-lā-vās'tah* (ped. *vā'sitah*) ADJ. direct (elections) **کے واسطے** *ke vās'te* PREP. for ; for the sake of because of ; on account (of) ; owing (to) in order (to) ; to the end (that) [A ~ **وساطت**]

واسکٹ *vās'kaṭ* N.F. waistcoat [E]

واسع *vā'se'* ADJ. ample this as an attribute of God [A ~ **وسعت**]

واصف *vā'sif* N.M. one who sings praises (of) [A ~ **وصف**]

واصل *vā'sil* ADJ. joined to N.M. realization ; realized amount of revenue **واصل باقی** *vā'sil-bā'qī* N.F. revenue account ; revenue receipts and arrears **واصل باقی نویس** *vā'sil-bā'qī-navīs'* N.M. revenue official minor keeping an account of receipts and arrears; revenue accountant **واصل بحق ہونا** *vā'sil ba-ḥaq' ho'nā* V.T. die ; enter the kingdom of heaven **واصلات** *vāsilat'* N.F. proceeds (of estate, etc.) ; mesne-profits revenue receipts (from an area) [A ~ **وصول**]

واضح *vā'zeḥ* ADJ. evident ; clear ; apparent evident ; obvious manifest **واضح رہے (یا ہو)** *vā'zeḥ ra'he* (or *ho*) be it known that whereas now (that) **واضح کرنا** *vā'zeḥ kar'nā* V.T. clarify point out [A ~ **وضاحت**]

واضع *vā'ze'* N.M. one who lays down (law) maker ; giver ; establisher **واضع قانون** *vā'ze'-e qānoon'* N.M. law-giver law-maker ; legislator [A ~ **وضع**]

واعظ *vā''iz* N.M. (PL. **واعظین** *vā'izīn'*) preacher ; sermonizer [A ~ **وعظ**]

وافر *vā'fir* ADJ. ample ; copious plentiful ; abundent [A ~ **وفور**]

وافی *vā'fī* ADJ. enough ; sufficient ; adequate entire ; complete [A ~ **وفی**]

واقع *vā'qe'* ADJ. happening ; occurring befalling ADV. situated ; situate **واقع میں** *vā'qe' meṅ* **فی الواقع** *fil-vā'qe'* ADV. actually really ; in reality ; in fact **واقع میں بات یہی ہے** *vā'qe' meṅ bāt' yeh' hai* PH. the fact of the matter is **واقع ہونا** *vā'qe' ho'nā* V.T. happen ; occur befall **واقعی** *vā'qe'ī* ADJ. real actual factual ADJ. really ; in reality ; in fact ; truly ; certainly INT. really [A ~ **وقوع**]

واقعہ *vā'qe'ah* N.M. event ; incident happening ; occurrence (arch.) news , intelligence fact of the matter **واقعہ نویس** *vā'qe'a-navīs'* N.M. (arch.) newswriter **واقعات** *vā'qe'āt'* N.M. PL. events ; incidents happenings ; occurrences circumstances **واقعاتی** *vā'qe'ā'tī* ADJ. circumstantial (evidence) [A ~ PREC.]

واقف *vā'qif* ADJ. acquainted (with) ; aware (of) knowing ; conversant (with) well-informed well-posted sensible experienced N.M. one who makes an endowment ; donor of trust appropriator **واقف حال** *vā'qif-e ḥal'* ADJ. & N.M. (well-informed person) (one) who stands seized of the situation **واقف کار** *vā'qif-kār'* ADJ. experienced , skilled ; expert well-informed **واقفیت** *vāqifiy'yat* N.F. acquaintance knowledge information experience skill **واقفیت پیدا کرنا** *vāqifiy'yat pai'dā kar'nā* N. form acquaintance (with) acquire knowledge (of) [A]

والا ١ *vā'lā* ADJ. (F. **والی** *vā'li*) belonging to; hailing from doer ; maker keeper ; owner seller ; vendor **وال** *val* SUF. (col.) hailing from in the style current in

والا ٢ *vā'lā* ADJ. (of rank) high ; eminent ; exalted; sublime **والا جاہ** *jāh'*, **والا مرتبت** *vā'lā mar'-tabat* ADJ. exalted (in rank) **والا شان** *vā'la-shān'* ADJ. eminent ; dignified **والا قدر** *vā'la-qad'r* ADJ. highly esteemed **والا نامہ** *vā la-nā'mah* N.M. superior person's letter **والا نژاد** *vā'la-nazhād'* ADJ. of noble birth **والا ہمت** *vā'lā-him'mat* ADJ. courageous [P]

والد *vā'lid* N.M. father *va'lidah* N.F. mother **والدین** *vā'lidain'* N.M. father and mother , parents [A ~ **ولادت**]

والنٹیر *vā'lanṭiyar'* N.F. volunteer **والنٹیر کور** *vā'lanṭiyar-kor'* N.F. volunteer corps [E]

واللہ *val'lāh* INT. by God **واللہ اعلم بالصواب** *va'llah-u-a''lam bis-savāb'* PH. God knows (the real facts) [A]

والہ *vā'leh* ADJ. distracted with love ; madly in love **والہانہ** *valeha'nah* ADJ. & ADV mad with love والہانہ عقیدت valeha'nah 'aqi'dat N.F. great devotion [A]

والی va'li N.M. prince governor والی وارث va'li va'ris N.M. supporter guardian [A ~ ولایت]

وام vam N.M. loan debt وام لینا vam le'na V.T. V.T. borrow قرض وام کرنا qar'z vam kar'na V.I. borrow [P]

وامق va'miq N.M. lover name of legendary Arab heroine Azra's lover [A]

وان[1] van ADV. (poet.) there thither at that place [A ~ وہاں CONT.]

وان[2] van SUF. (dial.) processor (of) [S]

واؤ va''o N.F. name of letter واؤ عاطفہ va''ve-a'tifah N.F. conjunctive واؤ مجہول va've majhool' N.F. sounding like o واؤ معدولہ va'o-e ma'doo'lah N.F. quiescent واؤ معروف va've ma'roof' N.F. preceded by pesh (ـُـ)

واویلا vave'la (ped. va-vai'la) N.M. lamentation ; be wailling INT. alas ; ah [A ~ وا + ویل]

واہ vah INT. excellent ; exquisite bravo ; well done N.M. praise joyful واہ رے vah' re INT. strange ah واہ کیا بات ہے vah' kya' bat' hai PH. (praise or irony) wonderful واہ کیا کہنا vah' kya' kaih'na PH wonderful ; excellent واہ واہ vah' vah' (col. vah'va) INT. bravo ; excellent N.M. praise ovation

واہب va'hib ADJ. generous ; munificent [A]

واہمہ va'himah N.M. hallucination [A ~ وہم]

واہی va'hi ADJ. silly ; nonsense crazy vagrant واہی تباہی va'hi taba'hi ADJ. silly ; nonsensical واہی تباہی بکنا va'hi taba'hi bak'na V.T. talk nonsense ; to use foul language واہی تباہی پھرنا va'hi taba'hi phir'na V.I. tramp ; move about aimlessly

واہیات vahiyat' ADJ. silly ; nonsense [A ~ SING. واہیہ]

وائے va''e INT. (lit.) alas fie [A]

وبا vaba' N.F. epidemic ; plague ; pestilence وبا آنا (یا پھیلنا) vaba a'na (or phail'na) V.I. (of epidemic) spread وبائی vaba''i ADJ. epidemic ; pestilential وبائی امراض vaba''i amraz' N.M. epidemic; diseases [A]

وبال vabal' N.M. visitation burden nuisance vexation وبال جان vaba'l-e jan' (or jan') ADJ. nuisance [A]

وائرلیس va'yar-lais N.M. & ADJ. wireless [E]

وائسرائے va'isra'e N.M. viceroy [E]

وائلن va''elin N.M. vioilin [E]

وتد va'tad N.M. (PL. اوتاد autad') ped. (in prosody) three-lettered word [A]

وتر va'tar N.M. string (of bow) chord hypotenuse of right-angled triangle diagonal (of a quadrilaterel) [A]

وتیرہ vati'rah N.M. manner ; behaviour [A]

وٹامن vi'tamin N.M. vitamin [E]

وثائق vasa''iq N.M. (PL. of وثیقہ vasi'qah) bonds: written agreements ; pronote

وثوق vusooq' N.M. confidence reliance پورے وثوق سے poo're vusooq' se PH. with full confidence وثیقہ vasi'qah N.M. (PL. وثائق vasa''iq deed bound written agreement وثیقہ دار vasi'qa-dar' N.M. bond holder government pensioner وثیقہ نویس vasi'qa-navis' N.M. deed writer وثیقہ نویسی vasi'qa-navi'si N.F. deed-writing [A]

وجاہت vaja'hat N.F. commanding (male) personality dignity importance [A ~ وجہ]

وجب va'jab N.F. (rare) span [A]

وجد vaj'd N.M. ecstacy ; rapture ; transport fit of religious frenzy وجد کرنا (یا میں آنا) vaj'd kar'na (or meh a'na) V.T. be enraptured dance in a fit of religious frenzy وجد میں لانا vaj'd meh la'na V.T. enrapture [A]

وجدان vijdan' N.M. intuition وجدانی vijda'ni ADJ. intuitive [A]

وجع vaj'' N.M. pain ; ache وجع المفاصل vaj''-ul-mafa'sil N.M. gout ; rheumatism [A]

وجوب vujoob' N.M. necessity , obligation واجب ADJ. ★ [A]

وجود vujood' N.M. existence essence , being body وجود پانا (یا میں آنا) vujood' pa'na (or meh a'na) V.I. be born come into existence وجود میں لانا vujood' meh la'na V.T. create procreate bring into existence وجودی vujoo'di ADJ. existenialist وجودیت vujoodiy'yat N.F. existentialism [A]

وجہ vaj'h N.F. (PL. وجوہ vujooh' double PL. وجوہات vujoohat') reason , cause basis means N.M. (PL. وجوہ vujooh', اوجہ aujoh) face وجہ تسمیہ vaj'h-e tas'miyah N.F. basis of nomenclature وجہ معاش vaj'h-e ma'ash' N.M. means of livelihood وجہ موجہ vaj'h-e muvaj'jah N.F. cogent reason or argument [A]

وجیہ vajih' ADJ. man with a commanding personality [A ~ وجاہت]

وحدانی *vaḥdā'nī* ADJ. unitary showing oneness خطوط وحدانی *khūtoo't-e vaḥdā'nī* N.M. parenthesis وحدانیت *vaḥdāniy'yat* N.F. unity (of god-head) the belief in the unity of God [A ~ واحد]

وحدت *vaḥ'dat* (or *vaiḥ'*-) N.F. oneness; unity unit one-unit وحدت الوجود *vaḥ'dat-ūl-vūjood'*, وحدت وجود *vaiḥ'dat-e vūjood'* N.F. unity of existence ; pantheism وحدت شهود *vaiḥ'dat-e shohood'* N.F. unity of divine manifestation ; patheism وحدت فکر (یا خیال) *vaiḥ'dat-e fik'r* (or *khayāl'*) N.M. community of ideas community of interests [A]

وحدہٗ لاشریک (لہٗ) *vaḥ'da-hoo lā sharī'k(a la-hoo')* PH. He is alone and has no partner; God

وحش *vaḥ'sh* N.M. (PL. وحوش *voḥoosh'*) wild beast وحوش وطیور *vaḥ'sh-o-tair'* N.M. beasts and birds [A]

وحشت *vaiḥ'shat* N.F. (or ped. *vaḥ*-) N.F. wildness savageness ferocity fear ; dread; horror وحشت اثر ,وحشت انگیز *vaiḥ'shat-a'sar*, *vaiḥ'shat-angez'*, وحشت آلود (ہ) *vaiḥ'shat aloo'd(ah)* وحشتناک *vaiḥ'shatnāk'* ADJ. shocking frightful ; horrible ; horrid dreary desolate وحشت برسنا (یا ٹپکنا) *vaiḥ'shat ba'rasnā* (or *ṭa'paknā*) V.I. be dreary وحشت زدہ *vaiḥ'shat-za'dah* ADJ. aghast horrified وحشت ہونا *vaiḥ'shat ho'nā* V.I. be shocked be bewildered be horrified ; owing to loveliness [A ~ وحش]

وحشی *vaiḥ'shī* (ped. *vaḥ*-) N.M. wild beasts brute savage ADJ. wild untamed ferocious cruel uncivilised وحوش *voḥoosh'* N.M. (PL. of وحشی N.M. ★) [A ~ وحش]

وحی *vaḥ'y* (or col. *va'ḥī*) N.F. revelation [A]

وحید *vaḥīd'* ADJ. alone singular incomparable unique nonpareil وحید العصر *vaḥī'd-ūl-'as'r* N.M. non-pareil [A ~ واحد]

وداد *vadād'* N.F. friendship love ودود *vadood'* ADJ. friendly loving N.M. this as an attribute of God [A]

وداع *vadā'* N.M. farewell; adieu الوداع *al-vadā'* INT. & N.M. good-bye ; farewell ; adieu [A]

ودھوا *vidh'va* N.F. (dial.) widow [S]

ودیا *vid'diyā* N.F. (dial.) (same as بدیا N.F. ★)

ودیعت *vadī''at* N.F. deposit ; trust ودیعت کرنا *vadī''at kar'nā* V.T. entrust bestow ودیعت ہونا *vadī''at ho'nā* V.I. be given ; be entrusted [A]

ور *var* PREF. having ; possessing [P]

ورا *varā'* ADV. behind beyond besides [A]

وراثت *virā'sat* N.F. inheritance heritage ; legacy وراثت نامہ *virā'sat nā'mah* N.M. deed of inheritance وراثۃً *virā'satan* ADV. by inheritance ورثا *vorasā'* (wrong but usual form for ورثہ *varasah* N.M. heirs successors legatees ورثہ *vir'sah* N.M. bequest ; heritage ; legacy [A]

ورد *var'd* N.M. (rare) rose [A]

ورد *vir'd* N.M. daily round of prayer or recital daily recital daily practices ; something repeated daily وردِ زبان *vir'd-e zabān'* ADJ. known by heart وردِ زبان ہونا *vir'd-e zabān' ho'nā* V.T. have by heart ورد کرنا *vir'd kar'nā* V.T repeat (prayers, etc.) [A]

وردی *var'dī* N.F. uniform ; liver (arch.) reveille (arch.) retreat (arch.) report (by army scout or spy) وردی بجانا *var'dī bajā'nā* V.T. sound reveille or retreat وردی بولنا *var'dī bol'nā* V.T. (of spy or scout) report

ورزش *var'zish* N.F. physical exercise athletics gymnastics ورزش کرنا *var'zish kar'nā* V.I. do physical exercise ورزش گاہ *var'zish-gāh* N.F. gymnasium ورزشی *var'zishī* ADJ. athletic (body) N.M. athlete [P ~ ورزیدن practice ; exercise]

ورطہ *var'tah* N.M. whirlpool ورطۂ حیرت میں پڑنا *var'ta-e ḥai'rat meṅ paṛ'nā* V.I. be bewildered be at one's wit's end [A]

ورع *va'ra'* N.F. abstinence ; continence [A]

ورغلانا *varghalā'nā* V.T. entice ; seduce ; inveigle coax ; cajole ; wheedle provoke or incite (against)

ورق *va'raq* N.M. (PL. اوراق *aurāq'*) leaf leaf (of book) foil (gold or silver) leaf ورق الٹنا (یا پلٹنا) *va'raq ū'laṭnā* (or *pa'laṭnā*) V.T. turn a (new leaf) ورق الٹیے (یا پلٹیے) *va'raq ū'laṭye* (or *pa'laṭye*) please turn over ; P.T.O. ورق ساز *va'raq-sāz'* N.M. one who beats gold or silver leaf ; leaf-beater ورق سازی *va'raq-sā'zī* N.F. leaf-beating ورق کوٹنا *va'raq kooṭ'nā* V.T. beat (metal) into leaves ورق گردانی کرنا *va'raq-gardā'nī kar'nā* V.T. skip over (a book) turn leaves (of a book) ورقِ گل *va'raq-e gūl* N.M. petal ورقہ *vara'qah* N.M. a leaf ورقی *va'raqi* (col. *var'qī*) ADJ. leaf-like leaved [A]

ورک *var'k* N.M. work ورکس *varks'* N.M. works

ورکشاپ *vark'-shāp* N.F. workshop [E]

ورکنگ کمیٹی *var'king kame'ṭī* N.F. working committee [E]

ورم *va'ram* N.M. (PL. اورام *aurām'*) swelling ; inflammation ورم کرنا *va'ram kar'nā* V.T. swell ; cause an inflammation [A]

ورنہ *var'nah* ADV. otherwise [P ~ و + اگر + نہ]

ورود *vūrood'* N.M. coming arrival ورودِ مسعود *vūroo'd-e mas'ood'* N.M. auspicious arrival (fig.) birth [A]

ورا *varā'* ADV. beyond save ; except [A]

وریٰ (or ورا) *varā'* N.F. people ; creation [A]

ورے *va're* ADV. on this side (of) at this end (of) ورلا *var'la* ADJ. this ; this one the one on this side or at the near end

ورید *varīd'* N.F. (PL. اورده *au'ridah*) vein [A]

وزارت *vizā'rat* N.F. ministry وزارتِ اطلاعات *vizā'rat-e ittelā'āt'* N.F. ministry of information وزارت (امورِ) خارجہ *vizā'rat-e (ūmoo'r-e) khā'rijah* N.F. ministry of external affairs ; foreign ministry وزارتِ تجارت *vizā'rat-e tijā'rat* N.F. ministry of trade and commerce ; commerce وزارتِ تعلیم *vizā'rat-e ta'līm'* N.F. ministry of education وزارتِ خزانہ (یا مالیات) *vizā'rat-e khiza'nah* (or *maliyyāt'*) N.F. ministry of finance ; finance ministry وزارتِ داخلہ *vizā'rat-e dā'khilah* N.F. ministry of internal affairs ; home ministry وزارتِ دفاع *vizā'rat-e difā'* N.F. ministry of defence وزارتِ زراعت *vizā'rat-e zirā''at* N.F. ministry of agriculture وزارتِ صنعت *vizā'rat-e san''at* N.F. ministry of industry ; industries ministry وزارتِ قانون *vizā'rat-e qānoon'* law ministry وزارتِ مال *vizā'rat-e māl'* N.M. revenue ministry وزارتِ مواصلات *vizā'rat-e mo'āsalāt'* N.F. ministry of communications ; communications ministry [A]

وزرا *vūzarā'* N.M. (PL. of وزیر N.M. ★)

وزن *vaz'n* N.M. (PL. اوزان *auzān'*) weight weighing (of verse) metre وزن کرنا *vaz'n kar'nā* V.T weigh وزن ہونا *vaz'n ho'nā* V.I. be weighed be heavy be weighty وزن دار *vaz'n-dār*, وزنی *vaz'nī* ADJ. heavy weighty [A]

وزیر *vazīr'* N.M. (PL وزرا *vūzarā'*) minister وزیرِ اعظم *vazī'r-e a''zam* N.M. prime minister; premier وزیرِ اعلیٰ *vazī'r-e a''lā* N.M. chief minister

وزیرے چنیں شہریارے چناں *vazī're chūnīn' shaih'r-yā're chūnāh'* PROV. like man like master وزارت *vizā'rat* N.F. ★ [A]

وسادہ *visā'dah* N.M. (rare) bolster [A]

وساطت *vasā'tat* N.F. means mediation medium کی وساطت سے *kī vasā'tat se* PH. through [A ~ وسط]

وسامت *vasā'mat* N.F. beauty وسیم ADJ. & N.M. ★ [A]

وساوس *vasā'vis* N.M. (PL. of وسوسہ N.M. ★)

وسائل *vasā''il* N.M. PL. resources means قومی وسائل *qau'mī vasā''il* PH. national resources [A ~ SING. وسیلہ]

وسط *vas't* (rare *va'sat*) N.M. middle کے وسط میں *ke vas't men* ADV. in the middle of among ; amongst وسطی *vas'tī* ADJ. middle central intermediate وسطیٰ *vūs'tā* ADJ. middle; mid [A]

وسع *vūs'* N.F. (rare) expanse [A]

وسعت *vūs''at* N.F. extent expanse range amplitude breadth dimensions area span means ; wealth [A]

وسکی *vis'kī* N.F. whisky [E]

وسل *vi'sal* N.F. whistle [E]

وسمہ *vas'mah* N.M. hair-dye hair darkener indigo leaves as such وسمہ لگانا (یا کرنا) *vas'mah lagā'nā* (or *kar'nā*) V.T. dye hair (of one's head or beard) black [A]

وسواس *vasvās'* N.M. apprehension ; lurking fead superstition distraction evil suggestion tempter ; devil وسواسی *vasvā'sī* ADJ. apprehensive ; superstition وسوسہ *vas'vasah* N.M. lurking fear evil suggestion temptation [A]

وسیع *vasī'* ADJ. spacious ; extensive وسیع الاختیار *vasī''-ūl-ikhtiyār'* ADJ. enjoying extensive powers high powered وسیع النظر *vasī''ūn-na'zar* ADJ. broadminded ; magnanimous breath of vision وسیع النظری *vasī-ūn-na'zarī* N.F. breadth of vision broadmindedness; magnanimity [A ~ وسعت]

وسیلہ *vasī'lah* N.M. (PL. وسائل *vasā''il*) mediation support ; intercessor (one) who recommends or will speak in favour of means of approach to ; means resource وسیلہ پیدا کرنا *vasī'lah pai'dā kar'nā* V.T find out means of approach (to) [A]

وسیم vasīm' ADJ. handsome [A ~ وسامت]

وش vash SUF. resembling ; like ; -ic وشی va'shī SUF. ness ; likeness [P]

وشنو vish'noo N.M. (H. dial.) God the creator Vishnu ویشنو vaish'noo N.M. Vishnoo's worshipper vegetarian [S]

وشواش vishvāsh N.M. (H. dial.) trust ; faith belief [S]

وصال visāl' N.M. meeting ; interview sexual intercourse death (usu. of a saint) union (with God) وصال ہو جانا visāl' ho jā'nā V.T. die ; pass away unite with God meet ; have a meeting [A ~ وصل]

وصایا vasā'yā N.M. (PL. of وصیت N.F. ★)

وصف vas'f N.M. (PL. اوصاف ausāf') quality virtue ; merit attribute ; epithet description praise ; encomium; eulogy [A]

وصل vas'l N.M. (rare وصلت vas'lat) intercourse union joining meeting; interview وصل ہونا vas'l ho'nā V.I. (of sexual intercourse) take place be joined (to) [A]

وصلی vas'lī N.F. pasteboard (used) as support for paper while writing thick paper for practising calligraphy on it وصلی سیاہ کرنا vas'lī siyah' kar'nā V.T. write and over write on the same sheet to practise calligraphy [PREC.]

وصول vūsool' ADJ. & ADV. receiver N.M. receipt (ped.) realization collection ; recovery (rare) arrival وصولی vūsoo'lī N.F. receipt realization ; collection ; recovery [A]

وصی va'sī N.M. (see under وصیت N.F. ★)

وصیت vasiy'yat N.F. (PL. وصایا vasā'yā) will ; testament (rare) advice ; word of advice ; counsel وصیت کرنا vasiy'yat kar'nā V.T. draw up one's will leave by will ; bequeath (rare) advice counsel وصیت نامہ vasiy'yat-nā'mah N.M. will ; testament وصی va'sī N.M. (PL. اوصیا ausiyā') executor lagatee [A]

وضاحت vazā'hat N.F. clarification clarity; lucidity وضاحت کرنا vazā'hat kar'nā V.T. clarify ; explain واضح vā'zeh ADJ. ★ [A]

وضع vaz'' N.F. (PL. اوضاع auzā'') style fashion behaviour manner; procedure attitude deduction delivery laying down coming وضع بدلنا vaz'' ba'dalnā V.T. change one's mode attitude or behaviour وضع حمل vaz''-e ham'l N.M. delivery وضعدار vaz''-dār' ADJ. formalist stylish elegant (one) sticking to one's mode, attitude or behaviour وضع داری vaz''-dā'rī N.F. style formalism elegance sticking to the last one's mode, attitude or behaviour وضع قطع waza qat'' N.F. style mode وضع کرنا vaz'' karnā, V.T. deduct ; subtract coin (word, etc.) پاس وضع pā's-e vaz'' formalism خوش وضع khūsh-vaz'' ADJ. stylish fashionable elegant [A]

وضو vū'zoo N.M. ablution وضو تازہ کرنا vū'zoo ta'zah kar'nā V.T. perform ablution before there is need for its renewal وضو توڑنا vū'zoo tor'nā V.T. do something necessitating renewal of ablution وضو ٹوٹنا vū'zoo ṭooṭ'nā V.I. be need for renewal of ablution وضو ٹھنڈا (یا ڈھیلا) ہونا vū'zoo ṭhan'ḍā (or ḍhī'lā) ho'nā V.I. lose one's enthusiasm

آدمی وضو کر رہا ہے

وضوح vūzooh' N.M. clearness ; lucidity clarification [A doublet of وضاحت]

وضیع vazī'' ADJ. mean ; low ; base ignoble شریف و وضیع sharī'f-o-vazī'' N.M. PL. high and low ; noble and ignoble [A]

وطن va'tan N.M. motherland ; fatherland country native country ; native land land of birth وطن پرست va'tan-paras't N.M. patriot وطن پرستی va'tan paras'tī N.F. patriotism وطن دشمن va'tan-dūsh'man N.M. traitor وطن دشمنی va'tan-dūsh'manī N.F. treason ہموطن ham-va'tan N.M. compatriot ہموطنی ham-va'tani N.F. belonging to same country وطنی va'tanī ADJ. country-made [A]

وظائف vazā''if N.M. (PL. of وظیفہ N.M. ★)

وطی vat'y N.F. copulation (by male) [A]

وظیفہ vazī'fah N.M. (PL. وظائف vazā''if) scholarship fellowship stipend (lit.) pension function daily round of practice or recital incantation وظیفہ دار vazī'fa-dār N.M. scholarship-holder stipendiary pensioner وظیفہ کرنا (یا پڑھنا) vazī'fah kar'nā (or paṛh'nā) V.T. repeat incantation [A]

وعدہ va''dah N.M. promise assurance وعدہ آپہنچنا va''dah ā' pa'hūnch'nā V.I. (of time of death) approach وعدہ ٹالنا va''dah ṭāl'nā V.T. evade ; procrastinate ; dilly-dally ; shilly-shally وعدہ خلاف va''da-khilāf', وعدہ شکن va''da-shi'kan ADJ. & N.M. (one) who goes back on his word وعدہ خلافی va''da-khilā'fī, وعدہ شکنی va''da-shi'kanī N.F. going back on one's word وعدہ فراموش va''da-farāmosh' ADJ. & N.M. (one) who fails to keep one's word وعدہ فراموشی va''da-farāmo'shī N.F. failure to keep one's word وعدہ معاف گواہ va''da-mo'āf' gavāh' N.M. approver وعدہ وعید va''dah va'īd'

N.M. promise prevarication وعدہ وفا va'da-vafā ADJ. true to one's words وعدہ وفا کرنا va'da vafā kar'nā V.T. make good one's word [A]

وعظ va'z N.M. (PL. مواعظ mava''iz) sermon ; homily. وعظ کرنا va'z kar'nā V.T. deliver a sermon وعظ و نصیحت va''z-o nasī'hat N.M. wise wise counsel sermonizing [A]

وعلیکم السّلام va 'alai'kūm-ūs-salām' N.M. and peace be on you ; formula in reply to greeting [A ~ و + علی + کم + ال + سلام]

وعید va'īd' N.M. threat [A]

وغا vaghā' N.F. war ; battle ; enagement [A]

وغیرہ vaghai'rah ADV. etcetera ; etc., and so forth ; and others [A ~ و + غیر + ہ]

وفا vafā' N.F. faithfulness ; fidelity fulfilment sufficiency وفا پرست vafā'-paras't, وفا پیشہ vafā'-pe'shah, وفا شعار vafā'-she'ar', وفا پیش vafā'-pesh' ADJ. faithful ; sincere ; loyal وفا پرستی vafā'-paras'tī, وفا پیشگی vafā'-pe'shagī وفا شعاری vafā'-she'ārī وفا کیشی vafa'-ke'shī N.F. faithfulness ; fidelity loyalty constancy وفادار vafā'-dār' ADJ. faithful constant loyal وفاداری vafā'-da'rī N.F. faithfulness constancy loyalty وفا کرنا vafā'-kar'nā V.T. be true or faithful (to) be loyal (to) fulfil (promise) (rare) suffice [A]

وفات vafāt' N.F. death ; demise تاریخ وفات tārī'kh-e vafāt' N.F. date of death death chronogram وفات پانا vafāt' pā'nā V.I. die ; pass away [A]

وفاق vifāq' N.M. federation (rare) agreement ; concord بالا وفاق ba'la vifāq' N.M. confederation ذیلی وفاق zai'lī vifāq' N.M. sub-federation علاقائی وفاق 'ilāqā''ī vifāq' N.M. zonal federation وفاقی vifā'qī ADJ. federal بالا وفاقی bala-vifā'qī ADJ. confederal وفاقی حکومت vifā'qī ḥukoo'mat N.F. وفاقیہ vifāqiy'yah N.M. federal government وفاقیت vifāqiy'yat N.F. federalism موافقت N.F. ★ [A]

وفد vaf'd N.M. (PL. وفود vūfood') delegation deputation [A]

وفق vaf'q N.M. accordance بروفق bar vaf'q PH. in accordance (with)

وفور vufoor' N.M. plenty ; abundance ; plenitude وافر ADJ. ★ [A]

وقار vaqār' N.M. prestige dignity (rare) gravity (of manner, etc.) باوقار bā-vaqār', پُر وقار pūr-vaqār' ADJ. dignified [A]

وقائع vaqā''e' N.M. annals events ; occurrences (arch.) news ; intelligence وقائع نگار (یا نویس) vaqā''e'-nigār' (or navīs') N.M. annalist despatch writer correspondent واقعہ N.M. ★ [A ~ SING. وقیعہ]

وقت vaq't N.M. (PL. اوقات auqāt') time hour opportunity respite season adversity ; hard times وقت بے وقت vaq't be-vaq't ADV. at all times ; in season or out of season وقت پر vaq't par ADV. on time ; in time on time of need ; when there is need for it وقت پر کام آنا vaq't par kām ā'nā V.T. stand by in time of need وقت پر گدھے کو بھی باپ بنا لیتے ہیں vaq't par ga'dhe ko bhī bāp' banā' lete hain PROV. bow down before the fox in season وقت پڑنا vaq't paṛ'nā V.T. be faced with adversing stand in need وقت پڑے پر جانیے کو بیری کو میت vaq't paṛe par jā'niye ko bai'rī ko mīt' PROV. adversity is the best judge of friend and foe وقت تنگ ہونا vaq't tang' ho'nā V.I. for (something) be very short وقت کا پابند vaq't kā pāband' ADJ. punctual وقت کاٹنا vaq't kāṭ'nā V.T. pass one's days in trouble pass away the time وقت کھونا vaq't kho'nā V.T. waste time وقت کو غنیمت جاننا vaq't ko ghanī'mat jān'nā PH. make hay while the sun shine make the best of an opportunity وقت کے وقت vaq't ke vaq't ADV. in the nick of time at the eleventh hour نازک وقت na'zūk vaq't PH. critical time or moment وقت نکالنا vaq't nikāl'nā V.T. find time (for) ; take time (for something) off one's duties وقت نکل جاتا ہے بات رہ جاتی ہے vaq't ni'kal jā'tā hai bāt' raih jā'tī' hai PROV. difficulties get resolved with time, but people's harsh treatment is never forgotten وقت وقت کی راگنی vaq't vaq't kī rāg'nī, وقت وقت کا راگ vaq't vaq't kā rāg' PROV. modes of life suited to one stage are out of tune with another وقتاً فوقتاً vaq'tan fa-vaq'tan ADV. from time to time ; occasionally وقتی vaq'tī ADJ. provisional transitory ephemeral وقتی طور پر vaq'tī taur par ADV. for the time being [A]

وقر vaq'r N.M. dignity ; prestige وقر پانا vaq'r pā'nā V.I. honour وقر کھونا va'qr kho'nā V.T. suffer a blow to one's prestige [A doublet of وقار]

وقس علیٰ ہٰذا va qis' 'alā hazā PH. and so on

وقعت vaq''at N.F. honour; respect prestige وقعت رکھنا vaq''at rakh'na V.I. command respect ; enjoy prestige وقعت کھونا vaq''at kho'nā V. lose respect or prestige

وقیع vaqī'' ADJ. weighty (remark, problem etc.) [A]

وقف vaqf N.M. (PL. اوقاف auqāf') trust endowment foundation for public charity devoting (one's life, etc. to) stop punctuation mark وقف کرنا vaqf kar'nā V.T. make an endowment endow (property, etc.) وقف لازم vaq'f-e lā'zim N.M. compulsory stop وقف نامہ vaq'f-nā'mah N.M. trust deed deed of endowment [A]

وقفہ vaq'fah N.M. interval pause [A ~ وقف]

وقوع vuqoo'' N.M. occurrence (of something) being ; existence situation وقوع جرم vūqoo''-e jūr'm N.M. commission of a crime وقوع میں آنا vūqoo'' meń ā'na V.I. happen ; occur جائے وقوع jā''e vūqoo'' N.F. محل وقوع mahal'l-e vūqoo'' N.M. situation (of a place) وقوعہ vūqoo''ah N.M. accident criminal act ; crime [A]

وقوف vūqoof' N.M. sense understanding discernment wisdom (lit.) standing بیوقوف be-vūqoof' ADJ. fool senseless person [A]

وقیع vaqe'' ADJ. (see under وقعت N.F. ★)

وکالت vakā'lat, (or vikā'lat) N.F. legal practice advocacy proxy وکالت کرنا vakā'lat kar'na V.T. be or become a legal practitioner ; practise at the bar plead ; advocate [A] وکالت نامہ vakā'lat-nā'mah N.M. power of attorney وکالتاً vakā'latan ADV. by proxy وکیل vakīl' N.M. (PL. وکلا vūkalā') lawyer counsel pleader ; advocate attorney (rare) proxy وکیل کرنا vakīl' kar'na V.T. engage (as) a lawyer

وکٹ vi'kaṭ N.F. wicket stumps وکٹ کیپر vi'kaṭ-ki'par N.M. wicket-keeper وکٹ کیپری vi'kaṭ-ki'parī N.F. wicket-keeping [E]

وکٹوریہ vikṭo'riyā N.F. victoria ; a kind of carriage وکٹوریہ کراس vikṭo'riyā karās' N.M. Victoria Cross

وگر va'gar CONJ. and if وگرنہ va'gar-nah CONJ. otherwise [P ~ و + گر + نہ]

ولا vilā' N.F. friendship ; amity [A]

ولادت vilā'dat N.F. birth ; nativity ولد N.M. ★ [A]

ولایت vilā'yat N.F. ruler's country foreign land England ; Blighty the West; Western lands dominion Kabul as this government ; control ownership guardianship (rare) friendship saintliness ولایت پانا vilā'yat pā'na V.T. become a saint ; be canonized ولایتی vilā'yatī ADJ. foreign ; imported N.M. (F. ولایتن vilā'yatan) Briton foreigner ولی N.M. ★ [A]

ولد va'lad (col. vald) N.M. son; offspring ولد الحرام va'lad-ūl-ḥarām', ولد الزنا va'lad-ūz-zinā N.M. bastard ولد الحلال va'lad-ūl-ḥalāl' N.M. legitimate son ولد الحیض va'lad-ūl-ḥaiz' N.M. offspring of sexy parents فلاں ولد فلاں fūlāń va'lad fūlāń PH. so-and-so, the son of so-and-so ولدیت valdiy'yat (ped. valadiy'yat) N.F. parentage [A]

ولولہ val'valah N.M. (PL. ولولہا val'vala-hā) enthusiasm ; zeal ; fervour ; ardour

ولی va'lī N.M. (PL. اولیا auliyā) saint friend guardian owner (of) ولی اللہ valiy'yūlah N.M. (PL. اولیاءاللہ auliyā-ūllāh) saint ولی عہد va'lī-ai'hd (ped. valiy'y-e 'ah'd) N.M. heir-apparent ; crown prince ولی کھنگر (یا کھنگڑ) va'lī khangar (or khań'gaṛ) N.M. pseudo-saint ولی نعمت va'lī ne''mat (ped. valiy'y-e ne''mat) N.M.. (PL. اولیائے نعمت auliyā-e ne''mat) patron ; benefactor ولایت N.F. ★ [A]

ولے va'le ولیک valek', ولیکن va-le'kin CONJ. (poet.) but [P ~ A و + لکن]

ولیمہ valī'mah N.M. wedding party thrown by groom's family [A]

ووٹ voṭ N.M.. vote ووٹر vo'ṭar N.M. voter ووٹنگ vo'ṭing N.F. voting [E]

وولٹ vol'ṭ N.M. volt وولٹیج vol'ṭej N.F. voltage [E]

ووں vooń ADV. in that manner in that state

ووئی voo''ī, vū''i INT. (dial.) oh ; ah

وہ vah INT. bravo wonderful [~ واہ]

وہ voh PRON. he she it they that those وہ آنکھیں نہیں رہیں voh āṅkheń na'hīń ra'hīń PROV. the times are changed no longer is that earlier love evinced وہ تو (یہ) کہیے voh to (yeh) kaihiye PH. it is well that وہ دن اور آج کا دن voh' din aur āj' kā din PH. never since then ; never after وہ دن گئے جب خلیل خاں فاختہ اڑایا کرتے تھے voh' din ga'e jab khalīl' khān fākh'tah ūṛā'yā kar'te the PROV. gone is the goose that lay the golden eggs

وہاب vahhāb' ADJ. & N.M. bestower this as attribute of God وہابی vahābī (ped. vahhā'bī) N.M. & ADJ. purist in religion follower of the Holy Prophet's Traditions unorthodox Muslim with a revolutionary political creed [A ~ nicknamed after 19th century Arab religious leader Abdul Wahhab]

وہاں va'hāń ADV. there thither yon, yonder وہاں گردن ماریے جہاں پانی نہ ملے va'hāń gar'dan mā'riye jahāń pā'nī na mi'le PH. be (etc.) deserves no sympathy

وہب vah'b N.F. giving ; bestowing وہبی vah'bī ADJ. born (poet.) inherent ; innate وہبی و کسبی vah'bī-o-kas'bī PH. inherent and acquired [A]

وہم vaih'm (ped. vah'm) N.M. (PL. اوہام auhām) vision superstition fear ; apprehens ; anxiety doubt ; misgiving وہمی vaih'mī ADJ. visionary superstitious fearful ;

apprehensive [A]

واہن *vah'n* N.F. sluggishness ; indolence

وہی *vo'hī* PRON. the same ; that very he himself (etc.)

وہیل *vhel* N.F. (same as ویل *vel* N.F. ★)

وہیں *va'hīn* ADV. there and then immediately

وی۔پی *vī' pī* N.F. V.P.P. ; value payable post

وے *vai* PRON. (dial.) they those

وید *ved* N.F. Hindu scripture(s) ویدانت *vedānt'* N.M. Hindu metaphysics Vedanta [S]

وید *vaid* N.M. physician practising Hindu system of medicine

ویدک *vai'dak* N.M. Hindu system of medicine ADJ. of this system [S]

ویر *vīr* N.M. (dial.) hero [S]

ویرا *vai'ra* N.M. government goods sold to public at high rates

ویراگ *vairag'* N.M. renunciation of the world leading the life of a recluse ویراگی *vairā'gī* N.M. recluse [S]

ویران *vīrān'* ADJ. deserted depopulated desolate waste laid waste ruined; lying in ruins disconsolate (mind, etc.) ویران کرنا *vīrān' kar'nā* V.T. ruin lay waste depopulate ویرانہ *vīrā'nah* N.M. deserted place desolate place ruins ; ruined place wasteland ویرانی *vīrā'nī* N.F. desolation ruin depopulation (of mind) being disconsolate ; wretchedness ; misery

ویزا *vī'zā* N.M. visa ویزا دینا *vī'za de'nā* V.T. give a visa (for) ویزا ملنا *vī'za mil'nā* V.I. get a visa (for) [E]

ویرنا *vair'na* N.M. ploughshare

ویسا *vai'sa* ADJ. (F. ویسی *vai'si*) such similar ADV. so in that manner like that of that kind ویسا ہی *vai'sa hī* PH. similar in the same manner or state in 'status quo' ; in 'status quoante' ویسے *vai'se* ADV. thus ; in that manner ویسے کا ویسا *vai'se kā vai'sa* ADV. same as before ADJ. unchanged ویسے تو *vai'se to* PH. short of that otherwise though ویسے ہی *vai'se hī* ADV. in the same manner just by chance without any particular object in view free ; free of cost

ویش *vaish* N.M. (dial.) one of the mercantile class (seconed last in the heirarchy of Hindu caste system

وشنو *vaish'noo* N.M. (see under وشنو N.M. ★)

ویکیشن *vike'shan* N.F. vacation سمر ویکیشن *sam'ar vike'shan* N.F. summer vacation [E]

ویل *vail* N.M. woe (only in) واویلا N.M. ★ [A]

ویل *vel*, وہیل *vhel*, ویل مچھلی *vel machh'lī* N.F. whale [E]

ویل

ویلکم *vail'kam* N.M. & INT. welcome ویلکم کرنا *vail'kam kar'nā* V.T. welcome [E]

ہ

ہ *he* thirty-fourth letter of Urdu alphabet (also called ہائے ہوز *hā'-e hav'vaz*) (in *nasta'līq*) written as ہ or as or or if pronounced alone or as ھ (called ہائے دوچشمی *hā'-e do chash'mī* or ہائے مخلوط التلفظ *hā'-e makhloo't-ūt-talaf'fūz*) when sounded as part of another consonant (in *jūmmal* reckoning) 5.

ہا[1] *ha* N.F. Arabic name for letter ہ ہائے دوچشمی *hā'-e do chash'mī* ہائے مخلوط التلفظ *hā'-e makhloo't-ūt-talaffūz* N.F. (see under ہ ★) ہائے مختفی *hā'-e mūkhta'fī* N.F. quiescent inserted just to indicate that the preceding letter bears a vowel sign ہائے ملفوظی *hā'-e malfoo'zī* N.F. aspirate

ہا[2] *ha* SUF. (sign of PL.)-s ; -en; -ren

ہا[3] *ha* INT. (W. dial.) oh ; O

ہابوڑا *haboo'ṛa* N.M. (dial.) highwayman bugaboo

ہات *hat* N.M. (same as ہاتھ N.M. ★)

ہاتف *ha'tif* N.M. voice of the unseen oracle angel ہاتف غیبی *hā'tif-e ghai'bī* N.M. voice from heaven angel [A]

ہاتھ *hath'* (poet. ہات *hat*) N.M. hand cubit slap blow stroke (of sword) hand (in) trick authority ہاتھ آنا *hath' ā'nā* V.I. come by ; come to hand be got ; be gained ; be obtained ہاتھ اٹھا بیٹھنا *hath' ūṭhā' baiṭh'nā* V.T. beat get ready to beat ہاتھ اٹھا لینا *hath' ūṭha le'nā* V.I. reabandon ; keep one's hands off ہاتھ اٹھانا *hath' ūṭhā'nā* V.T. raise (one's) hand or hands do so (to greet, pray or course) beat give up ; despair (of) ہاتھ اٹھنا *hath' ūṭh'nā* V.I. (of hand) be raised be attacked or beaten (by) ہاتھ اوچھا پڑنا *hath' o'chhā paṛ'nā* V.I. (of stroke in fighting) go awry; graze along ہاتھ اونچا رہنا *hath' oon'chā raih'nā* V.I.

have the upper hand give (alms, etc. rather than receive) ہاتھ باندھنا *hath' bandh'na* V.T. tie (someone's) hands fold one's hands (to show respect, etc.) beg with folded hands ہاتھ باندھے *hath' ban'dhe* ADV. respectfully with folded hands ہاتھ باندھے کھڑا رہنا *hath' ban'dhe kha're rah'na* PH. wait upon ہاتھ بٹانا *hath' baṭa'na* V.T. help ; lend (someone) any hand or helping hand ہاتھ بڑھانا *hath' baṛha'na* V.T. stretch (one's) hand do so to get or lift something (کے) ہاتھ بکنا *(ke) hath' bik'na* V.I be sold out (to) be under the thumb (of) be subservient (to) ہاتھ بند ہونا *hath' band' ho'na* V.I. be poor be helpless have one's hands full ہاتھ بھر پور پڑنا *hath' bhar poor' paṛ'na* V.I. receive blow etc. in full force ہاتھ بھر جانا *hath' bhar' ja'na* V.I. (of hands) be stained or smeared ہاتھ بھر کا *hath' bhar ka* ADJ. a cubit long (of tongue) uncontrolled (of heart) brave ہاتھ بھر کی زبان ہونا *hath' bhar ki zaban' ho'na* V.I. be cheeky ; be insolent ہاتھ بہکنا *hath' bai'hakna* V.I. miss the aim ; (of hand) falter (کے) ہاتھ بھیجنا *(ke) hath' bhej'na* V.T send (through someone) send (per bearer) (پر) ہاتھ بیٹھنا *(par) hath' baiṭh'na* V.I. become deft or dextrous ; acquire skill (in some manual work) ہاتھ بیچے ہیں ذات نہیں بیچی *hath' be'che hain zat' na'hin be'chi* PROV. though a servant, I (etc.) shall not be abuse ہاتھ پانی لینا *hath' pa'ni le'na* V.T. wash anus after evacuation lave ہاتھ پاؤں *hath' pa''on* N.M hands and feet (fig.) helping hand ہاتھ پاؤں بچانا *hath' pa''on bacha'na* V.T. protect oneself ; protect one's life and limb ہاتھ پاؤں پھول جانا *hath' pa''on phool' ja'na* V.T be unnerved have blue funks ; be jittery be tired ; be fatigued ہاتھ پاؤں پھیلانا *hath' pa''on phaila'na* V.I. extend one's plans or business begin to show oneself in one's true colours ہاتھ پاؤں توڑ کر بیٹھنا *hath' pa''on toṛ' kar baiṭh'na* V.I. do nothing to earn one's livelihood ہاتھ پاؤں توڑنا *hath' pa''on toṛ'na* V.T. fracture (someone's) limbs ہاتھ پاؤں ٹوٹنا *hath' pa''on ṭooṭ'na* V.I. feel feverish ہاتھ پاؤں ٹھنڈے ہونا *hath' pa''on ṭhan'ḍe ho'na* V.I. (of limbs) grow cold swoon be diging ہاتھ پاؤں چلنا *hath' pa''on chal'na* V.I. be still strong enough to work be fidgety ہاتھ پاؤں دابنا *hath' pa''on dab'na* V.T. massage by pressing (someone's) limbs ہاتھ پاؤں رہ جانا *hath' pa''on raih' ja'na* V.I become decrepit (of limbs) be paralysed ہاتھ پاؤں سنبھالنا *hath' pa''on sanbhal'na* V.I. begin to show off become well-developed ہاتھ پاؤں سے چھوٹ *hath' pa''on se chhooṭ'na* V.I. be endelivered of child ہاتھ پاؤں مارنا *hath' pa''on mar'na* strive ; struggle hard endeavour ; make an all out bid to ہاتھ پاؤں نکالنا *hath' pa''on nikal'na* V.I. grow into a strong body become saucy or too independent ہاتھ پاؤں ہارنا *hath' pa''on har'na* V.I. (of limbs) be enfeebled ہاتھ پاؤں ہلانا *hath' pa''on hila'na* V.T. do something to earn one's livelihood work hard ہاتھ پتھر تلے آنا (یا دبنا) *hath pat'thar ta'le a'na (or dab'na)* V.I. find oneself helpless ہاتھ پٹھے پر نہ رکھنے دینا *hath' puṭ'ṭhe par na rakh'ne de'na* V.T. (of horse) sky (fig.) be too clever ہاتھ پر توتا پالنا *hath' par to'ta pal'na* V.I. have the hand wounded have a boil on the hand ہاتھ پر دھرا ہونا *hath' par dha'ra ho'na* V.I (of something) be ready (کے) ہاتھ پر قرآن رکھنا *(ke) hath' par quran' rakh'na* V.T. make (someone) swear by the Scriptures ہاتھ پر گنگا جلی دھرنا *hath' par gan'ga-ja'li dhar'na* V.I. (dial.) swear solemnly ہاتھ پر ہاتھ دھر کر بیٹھنا *hath' par hath dhar' kar baiṭh'na* V.T. sit idle do nothing to earn one's livelihood have a slump in business ہاتھ پر ہاتھ رکھنا *hath' par hath' rakh'na* V.T. promise ; assure ہاتھ پر ہاتھ مارنا *hath' par hath mar'na* V.T. put one's hand into that of another bet thus assure thus ہاتھ پڑنا *hath' paṛ'na* V.I. come to hand ; come by be hit by hand be robbed ہاتھ پسارنا *hath pasar'na* V.T. beg; beg alms ہاتھ پکڑنا *hath' pa'kaṛ'na* V. help support cause to desist ; withhold ہاتھ پورا پڑنا *hath' poo'ra paṛ'na* V.T. assault with full force ہاتھ پہنچنا *hath' pahunch'na* V.T. have access (to) ہاتھ پھیرنا *hath' pher'na* V.T. fondle ; caress cheat rob ہاتھ پھیلانا *hath' phaila'na* V.T. beg ; beg for alms ہاتھ پھینکنا *hath' phenk'na* V.T. wield sword (etc.) ہاتھ پیلے کرنا *hath' pi'le kar'na* V.T. get (a girl) married ہاتھ تکنا *hath' tak'na* V.T. depend on (someone) for subsistence look up to (someone) for support ہاتھ تنگ ہونا *hath' tang ho'na* V.I. be poor ; be hard up ہاتھ ٹوٹیں *hath' tooṭen* INT. ہاتھ جوڑنا *hath' joṛ'na* V.T. fold (one's) hand entreat ; emplore ہاتھ جوڑ کر کہنا *hath' joṛ' kar kaih'na* V.T. say with folded hands ; say humbly ہاتھ جھاڑنا *hath' jhaṛ'na* V.T. give a jerk one's hand give a blow give bestow empty (one's) hands of money be disappointed ہاتھ جھٹکنا *hath' jha'ṭakna* V.T. give a jerk to one's hand free one's hand ہاتھ جھلانا *hath' jhula'na* V.T. wave the hands sideways in walking ہاتھ جھلائی *hath' jhulai''i* N.F. safe passage money realized by government , landlord or highwaymen ہاتھ جھوٹا پڑنا *hath' jhoo'ṭa paṛ'na* V.I. (of blow) not to be struck in full force ہاتھ جھوٹا کرنا *hath' jhoo'ṭa kar'na* V.I. east just a little ہاتھ چالاکی *hath' chala'ki* N.F. thievishness (of child) strong fighting ہاتھ چالاکی کرنا *hath chala'ki kar'na*

V.T. fight thus strike steal ہاتھ چڑھنا hāth'-chaṛh'nā V.T. & I. gaim ; come into the hands (of) be overpowered (by) ہاتھ چلانا hāth-chalā'nā V.I. strike move (one's) hand's swiftly flourish (one's) hands ہاتھ چلنا hāth' chal'nā V.T. (of hands) flourish in talking strike (in talking, etc.) ہاتھ چومنا hāth' choom'nā V.T. kiss the hand to show respect ہاتھ چھڑانا hāth' chhuṛā'nā V.T. free one's hand ہاتھ دانتوں سے کاٹنا hāth' dantoṅ se kaṭ'nā V.T. rue ; bitterly feel the consequences of ہاتھ دکھانا hāth' dikhā'nā V. show the hand to a fortune-teller let the physician feel the pulse display one's swordsmanship, etc. trick (someone) ہاتھ دھرنا hāth dhar'nā V.T. touch with the hand swear by support select ہاتھ دھونا hāth' dho'nā V.T. & I. wash one's hands wash one's anus and hands after evacuation despair (of) ہاتھ دھو بیٹھنا (یا رکھنا) hāth' dho' baiṭh'nā (or rakh'nā) V.T. despair (of) ; give up as lost lose all hope (of) ہاتھ دھو کر (یا کے) پیچھے پڑنا hāth' dho kar (or ke) pī'chhe paṛ'nā V.T. make an all-out bid for pursue despite of stiff opposition persecute ہاتھ دے دے مارنا hāth' de de mār'nā V.T. continually beat ہاتھ دیکھنا hāth' dekh'nā V. feel the pulse (of) tell the fortune (of) depend on (someone) for subsistence look up to (someone) for support ہاتھ دینا hāth' de'nā V.T. lend a hand or helping hand support pledge shake hands do so to praise (of lantern, etc.) put out (of pox boils) subside (of brokers) strike a bargain with finger under cover (of grain dealer) shuffle grain lying in heap ہاتھ ڈالنا hāth' ḍal'nā V.T. take upon oneself lay (one's) hand (on) arrest meddle (with) tinker (with) rape; ravish ہاتھ رکنا hāth rūk'nā V.I. be with held be economized ہاتھ رکھنا hāth' rakh'nā V.T. touch select support swear by ہاتھ رنگنا hāth' rang'nā V.T. dize one's hands (with henna) earn a lot take bribe earn by unfair means ہاتھ رواں کرنا hāth' ravāṅ' kar'nā V.T. gain or get skill (in) ہاتھ رواں ہونا hāth' ravāṅ ho'nā V.I. become skilful (at) ; attain skill in ہاتھ روکنا hāth' rok'nā V.T. & I. withhold keep back desist (from); refrain (from) ہاتھ سانا hāth' sām'nā V.T smear one's hands (with) ہاتھ سر پر رکھنا hāth' sir par rakh'nā V swear by the head (of) patronize caress ; fondle ہاتھ سکیڑنا (یا سمیٹنا) hāth' sūker'nā (or sameṭ'nā) V.T. exercise a keep on expenditure ہاتھ سن ہو جانا hāth' sūn' ho jā'nā, ہاتھ سو جانا hāth' so' jā'nā V.T (of hand) become stiff ہاتھ سے hāth' se ADV by hand کے ہاتھ سے ke hāth' se PH. through ہاتھ سے جاتا رہنا hāth' se jā'tā raih'nā V.I. get out of one's hand or control lose an opportunity , to be helpless ہاتھ سے دینا hāth' se de'nā V.T. give bestow give up ہاتھ سے کام نکالنا hāth' se kām' nikāl'nā V.T. gain a practical experience of something get it done through get out of (someone's) hands ہاتھ سے ہاتھ ملانا hāth' se hāth milā'nā V.I. shake hands ہاتھ سے ہاتھ ملنا hāth' se hāth' mal'nā V.T. wring one's hands rue ہاتھ شل ہو جانا hāth' shal' ho jā'nā V.I. (of hand) become senseless through cold (of hand) be paralized ہاتھ صاف کرنا hāth' sāf kar'nā V.T play fraud upon steal (something or someone's belongings) plunder murder practise doing gain skill ہاتھ قبضے پر ڈالنا hāth' qabze par ḍal'nā V.T. be about to draw sword ہاتھ کا جھوٹا hāth' kā jhoo'ṭā PH. one who does not repay debts dishonest ہاتھ کا دیا hāth' kā di'yā N.M. alms ; charity ہاتھ کا دیا آڑے آنا hāth' kā di'yā ā'ṛe ā'nā PROV. (of charity given earlier) stand in good stem ہاتھ کا سچا hāth' kā sach'chā PH. one who repays debts on time honest ہاتھ کا میل hāth' kā mail' N.M. (disparagingly) money ; pelf ہاتھ کان سے ننگی hāth' kān' se nan'gī PH. (dial.) (of woman) without jewellery ہاتھ کانوں پر رکھنا hāth' kānoṅ par rakh'nā V.T. wash one's hands of ; deny out right ہاتھ کٹ جانا hāth' kaṭ jā'nā V.I. (of one's) hands be cut off have signed document curtailing one's powers, etc. ہاتھ کرنا (یا دکھانا) hāth' kar'nā (or dikhā'nā) V.I. perform a valorous feat make (sword, etc.) thrust cheat ہاتھ کنگن کو آرسی کیا hāth' kan'gan ko ār'sī kyā PROV. as plain as the pikestaff obvious truths need no proof ہاتھ کو ہاتھ پہچانتا ہے hāth' ko hāth' paihchān'tā hai PH. one repays him from whom one borrows ہاتھ کو ہاتھ سجھائی نہ دینا hāth' ko hāth' sūjhā''ī na de'nā PH. be pitch dark ہاتھ کھانا hāth khā'nā V.I. be hit by (sword thurst, etc.) ہاتھ کھلنا hāth' khul'nā V.I. become a bully attain skill in manual work become rich ہاتھ کھینچنا hāth' khenčh'nā V.T. withhold (from) ہاتھ کی لکیریں hāth' kī lakī'reṅ N.F. PL. lines on the palm ہاتھ کی لکیریں نہیں مٹتیں hāth' kī lakī'reṅ na'hīṅ miṭ'tīṅ PROV. fate cannot be changed ہاتھ (یا ہاتھوں) کے طوطے اڑ جانا hāth' (or ha'thoṅ ke to'te ūṛ jā'nā PH. be unnerved be flabbergasted be nonplussed ہاتھ گاڑی hāth'-gā'ṛī N.F. pram ; perambulator hand-driven cart ہاتھ گلے میں ڈالنا hāth' ga'le meṅ ḍal'nā V.T. embrace ہاتھ گھسانا hāth' ghisā'nā V.I. make useless effort , waste time and energy ہاتھ گھسائی hāth'-ghisā''ī N.F. useless effort ہاتھ گھنگولنا hāth' ghangol'nā V.T stir up (water) shake up (water) thus and make it turbid ہاتھ لا استاد کیسی کہی hāth' lā ūstād' kai'sī ka'hī PH. come tell me how much did you like the remarks ہاتھ لپک hāth'-lapak ADJ. light-fingured knave pilferer ہاتھ لگانا hāth' lagā'nā V.T. touch lay hands (on) lend (someone) a hand meddle (with) tinker (with) ہاتھ لگائے کمھلانا hāth' lagā''e kūmhlā'nā V.I. be very delicate ہاتھ لگائے میلا ہونا hāth' lagā''e mai'lā ho'nā V.I. be very fair ; be exquisitely beautiful be very clean ہاتھ لگنا hāth' lag'nā V.I. be touched come to hand fall into the hands (of) (of something) be begin ہاتھ مارنا hāth mār'nā V.T. acquire ; illegally pilfer plunder usurp strike with sword slay eat gluttonously ہاتھ ملانا hāth' milā'nā V.T. shake hands (with) do so to express agreement ; close a bargain or begin a wrestling bout ہاتھ ملنا hāth' mal'nā V.I. wring one's hands repent; rue ہاتھ (میں) آنا hāth' (men) ā'nā V.I. come to hand (کے) ہاتھ میں ٹھیکرا دینا (ke) hāth' men ṭhīk'rā de'nā V.T. reduce (someone) to extreme poverty ہاتھ میں دے روٹی اور سر پر مارے جوتی hāth' men de ro'ṭī aur sir' par mā're joo'tī PROV. give alms and curses ہاتھ میں رکھنا hāth' men rakh'nā V.T possess be able to influence (someone) ہاتھ میں سمرنی بغل میں کترنی hāth' men sa'marnī ba'ghal men ka'tarnī PROV. foul within fair without ہاتھ میں لینا پات میں (دھر) کھانا hāth' men le'nā pāt' men (dhar') khā'nā PROV. live from hand to mouth ہاتھ میں لینا hāth men le'nā V.T. take up (fig.) undertake ہاتھ میں ہاتھ دینا hāth' men hāth' de'nā V.T. shake hands (with) give into the charge of ; entrust give away in marriage (to) ; give (woman's) hand (to) ہاتھ میں ہنر ہونا hāth' men hū'nar ho'nā V.I. be a skilled workman ہاتھ نہ آنا hāth' na ā'nā V.T & I. not to fall into hands (of) slip out of the hands (of) dodge ; evade ہاتھ نہ پڑنا hāth' na paṛ'nā V.I. be out of one's reach ہاتھ نہ لگنا hāth' na lag'nā V.T. not to touch not to beat not to treat harshly ہاتھ نہ مٹھی بلبلاتی اٹھی hāth' na mūṭ'ṭhī bilbilā'tī ūṭ'ṭhī PROV. burning with rage without power to avenge ہاتھوں hā'thon N.M. PL. hands ADV. with hands cubits high very high greatly کے ہاتھوں ke hā'thon ADV. at the hands of through owing to ہاتھوں ہاتھ hā'thon hāth' ADV. from one person to another swiftly stealthily , furtively ہاتھوں ہاتھ اڑ (یا بک) جانا hāthon hāth ūṛ' (or bik') jā'nā V.T. find a ready sale ; sell like hot cakes ہاتھوں ہاتھ اڑا لینا hā'thon hāth' ūṛā' le'nā V.T take away stealthily ہاتھوں ہاتھ لینا hā'thon hāth' le'nā V.T. receive (someone) respectfully ; show due deference to ہاتھا پائی hā'thā-pā''ī N.F. fight ; scuffle ہاتھا پائی کرنا hā'thā pā''ī kar'nā V.T. fight ہاتھا چھانٹی hā'thā-chhānṭ'ī N.F. embezzlement ہاتھا ہاتھی hā'thā-hā'thī ADV. from one person to another quickly ; swiftly

ہاتھی hā'thī N.M. (F. ہتھنی hath'nī) elephant ہاتھی پاؤں hathī pā''on N.M. elephantiasis ہاتھی پھرے گاؤں گاؤں جس کا ہاتھی اسی کا ناؤں hā'thī phi're gā''on gā''on jis kā' hā'thī ū'sī kā nā''on PROV. no matter in whose possession a property may temporarily rest, its title vests in the owner ہاتھی جھولنا hā'thī jhool'nā V. be very rich ہاتھی جھومنا hā'thī jhoom'nā V.I. (fig.) be very rich have a grown-up daughter who is yet to be married ہاتھی دانت hā'thī-dānt N.M ivory ہاتھی کا پاٹھا hāthī kā pā'ṭhā N.M. young male elephant ہاتھی کے پاؤں میں سب کا پاؤں hā'thī ke pā''on men sab ke pā''on PROV. rich persons contribution covers that of all everybody is subservient to a big personality ہاتھی کے دانت کھانے کے اور دکھانے کے اور hā'thī ke dānt' khā'ne ke aur dikhā'ne ke aur PROV all that glitters is not gold ہاتھی نال hāthī-nāl' N.F. (arch.) cannon ہاتھی نکل گیا ہے دم رہ گئی ہے hā'thī ni'kal ga'yā hai dūm' raih ga''ī hai PROV. we are at the tail-end of the work ہاتھی وان hā'thī-vān N.M. elephant-keeper , mahout ہاتھی ہزار لٹے تو بھی سوا لاکھ ٹکے کا hā'thī hazār' lū'ṭe to bhī sa'vā lākh ṭa'ke kā PROV a rich man, even if ruined, has his prestige

ہاتھی چوک hā'thī chok N.M. artichoke [~E CORR.]

ہاٹ hāṭ N.F. market

ہاجی hā'jī N.M satirist [A ~ ہجو]

ہادم hā'dim N.M. one who pulls down a building, etc. ہادم لذات، ہادم اللذات hā'di'm-e lazzāt', hā'dim-ūl-lazzāt' N.M. (fig.) death [A ~ ہدم]

ہادی hā'dī N.M. mentor spiritual guide ہادیٔ برحق hādī-e bar-haq ADJ true guide N.M. the Holy Prophet as such [A ~ ہدایت]

ہار 1 hār N.M. necklace garland chaplet ہار سنگار hār' singār' N.M. make-up weeping nyctanthes ہار گوندھنا hār goondh'nā V.T string a garland

ہار 2 hār N.F (see under ہارنا V.I. ★)

ہارا hā'rā, ہار hār SUF. doer one dealing or working in material

ہارج hā'rij ADJ obstructing [A ~ حرج]

ہارمونیم *hārmo'niyam* N.M. harmonium [E]

ہارنا *hār'nā* V.I. be defeated be worsted be routed ; be overcome lose be unsuccessful ہار بیٹھنا *hār' baiṭh'nā*, ہار جانا *hār' jā'nā* V.I. be defeated lose (a game) ہار *hār'* N.F. defeat rout ہار جیت *hār' jīt* N.F. victory and defeat hazard ہار کے جھک مار کے *hār' ke jhak mār' ke* PH. (disparagingly) ultimately ہار دینا *hār' de'nā* V.T. lose in gambling ہار ماننا *hār' mān'nā* V.I. accept defeat bow ; submit ہارو *hā'roo* N.M. (col.) one who often gets defeated

ہاروت ماروت *hāroot' māroot'* N.M. PL. name of two angels from whom Babylonians are stated to have learned black art [A ~ H]

ہاڑ *hāṛ* N.M. bodily frame

ہاڑنا *hāṛ'nā* V.T. balance one weight against another examine the correctness of a pair of scales guess weight (of)

ہاضمہ *hā'zimah* N.M. digestion ; digestive system ADJ. digestive ہاضم *hā'zim* ADJ. digestive

ہاکی *hā'kī* N.F hockey hockey-stick [E]

ہال ¹ *hāl* N.F. steel tyre (of wheel) movement jerk

ہال ² *hāl* N.M. hall [E]

ہالنا *hāl'nā* V.I. move ہالا ڈولا *hā'lā ḍo'lā* N.M. (col.) earthquake

ہالہ *hālah* N.M. halo (round the moon) halo ; nimbus [A]

ہالی *hā'lī* N.M. ploughman ; tiller [~ ہل *hal'*]

ہاموں *hā'moon* (or *hāmoon'*) N.M. plain desert [P]

ہامی *hā'mī* N.F. assent consent assurance ; promise (کی) ہامی بھرنا (*kī*) *hā'mī bhar'nā* V.I. give consent promise [~ ہاں]

ہاں ¹ *hāṅ'* INT. yes verily ; indeed okay ; O.K. aye well N.F. assurance assent permission ہاں جی *hāṅ' jī*, جی ہاں *jī hāṅ'* INT. yes sir (or madam or miss) be true why not N.F. second assent ہاں جی کا نوکر ہونا *hāṅ' jī kā nau'kar ho'nā* V.I. be a yesman ہاں کرنا (یا کہنا) *hāṅ' kar'nā* (or *kaih'nā*) V.T. & I. assent; 'yes' accept approve; okay; O.K. submit yield ہاں میں ہاں ملانا *hāṅ meṅ hāṅ' milā'nā* V.I. agree with another's opinion thoughtless ہاں نا *hāṅ' nā* N.F. yes or no categorical reply ہاں نا کا جواب دینا *hāṅ'-nā kā javāb' de'nā* V.I. say yes or no ; give a categorical reply

ہاں ہاں INT. (*hāṅ-hāṅ'*) yes ; certainly (*hāṅ'-hāṅ*) don't ہاں ہوں *hāṅ'-hooṅ* N.F. acceptance confession prevarication ہاں ہوں کرنا *hāṅ'-hooṅ kar'nā* V.I. acceptance confess (guilt) prevaricate

ہاں ² *hāṅ'* N.M. place (used only as) کے ہاں *ke hāṅ'* ADV. at (someone's) place at the house of at [~ یہاں CONTR.]

ہانپنا *hāṅp'nā* V.I. pant ; gasp ; be out of breath

ہانڈی *hāṅ'ḍī* N.F. pot ; saucepan cooker hanging lamp shade (vul.) strumpetan ہانڈی پکانا *hāṅ'ḍī pakā'nā* V.I. stew prepare curry, etc. ہانڈی چڑھانا *hāṅ'ḍī chaṛhā'nā* V.T. put cooker on stove

ہانکنا *hāṅk'nā* V.T. drive ; urge on bawl blurt out بڑ ہانکنا *baṛ' hāṅk'nā* V.I. boast ; brag ہانک *hāṅk* N.F. cry ; shout ; bawl ہانک پکار *hāṅk'-pūkār'* N.F. uproar ; hue and cry ہانک لگانا *hāṅk' lagā'nā* V.I. cry out ; shout ; bawl ہانکے پکارے *hāṅ'ke pūkā're* ADV. openly ہانکے پکارے کہنا *hāṅ'ke pūkā're kaih'nā* V.T. say openly

ہانگا *hāṅ'gā* N.M. pep ; strength

ہانگی *hāṅ,gī* N.F. large sieve piece of cloth for sifting flour

ہاون *hā'van* N.M. mortar ہاون دستہ *hā'van das'tah* (col. ہمام دستہ *hamām' das'tah*) N.M. pestle and mortar

ہاون دستہ

ہاؤ ہو *hā'-o-hoo* N.F. uproar ; tumult hue and cry ہاؤ ہو کرنا *hā'-o-hoo kar'na* V.T raise a hue and cry [P ~ ہا + ہو ONO.]

ہاویہ *hā'viyah* N.M. lowest region of hell

ہاہا *hā'-hā* N.F. ہاہا ٹھی ٹھی *hā'-ha ṭhī-ṭhī*, ہاہا ہی ہی *hā'-ha hī'-hī* N.F. boisterous laugh ہاہا ہی ہی کرنا *hā'-ha hī'-hī kar'na* V.I. laugh boisteriously [ONO.]

ہائل *hā''il* ADJ. (F. ہائلہ *hā''ilah*) terrible [A ~ ہول]

ہاؤس *haus* (ped. *hā''ūs*) N.M. house ہاؤس بوٹ *haus'-bot* N.F. house-boat

ہائی ¹ *hā''ī* N.F. (dial.) plight

ہائی ² *hā''ī* ADJ. high ہائی سکول *hā''ī sakool'* N.M. high school ہائی کورٹ *hā''ī kor'ṭ* N.F. (dial. M.) High Court [E]

ہائے *hā''e* INT. ah ! alas ! N.F. sigh moan cry of pain ہائے ہائے *hā''e hā''e* ہائے وائے *hā''e vā''e* N.F. sighing cry of pain ہائے ہائے کرنا *hā''e hā''e kar'na* V.I. sigh moan with pain [ONO.]

ہائڈروجن *ha''idro'jan* N.F. hydrogen [E]

ہبڑا *hab'ṛa* N.M. ugly person one with large teeth

ہبنق *haban'naq,* ہونق *havan'naq* ADJ fool; simpleton [A]

ہبوب *hūboob'* N.M. blowing (of wind) [A]

ہبوط *hūboot'* N.M. descent downfall fall ہبوطِ آدم *hūboot'-e ā'dam* N.M. fall of man [A]

ہبہ *hi'bah* N.M. gift ; present ہبہ کرنا *hi'bah kar'nā* V.T. execute a deed of gift ہبہ نامہ *hi'ba-nā'mah* N.M. deed of gift [A ~ وہب]

ہبہ ڈبہ *hab'bah ḍab'bah* N.M. rickets

ہپ *hap'* ہپ ہپ *hap'-hap* N.F. gulp sound of toothless person's voices ہپ جھپ *hap' jhap* ADV. greedily ہپڑ ہپڑ *ha'paṛ ha'paṛ* ADV. (gobble up) gluttonously ہپ کر جانا *hap' kar jā'nā* V.T gulp down ; gobble up ہپ ہپ کرنا *hap' hap kar'nā* V.I. speak or eat like a toothless person

ہپا *hap'pā* N.M. soft rice ہپو *hap'po* N.F. toothless old woman

ہپناٹزم *hip'naṭizm* N.F. hypnotism ہپناٹائز کرنا *hip'naṭa''iz kar'nā* V.T. hypnotize [E]

ہپو *hap'poo* N.M. (nurs.) opium

ہپہپانا *haphapā'na* V.I. pant ; gasp

ہت *hat'* INT. be off ہت تیرے کی *hat' te're kī* INT be off ; begone ; away ; avaunt mind you [ONO.]

ہتک *ha'tak* (ped. *hat'k*) N.F. libel; demafation disgrace affront ہتک آمیز *hat'k-āmez'* ADJ. libellous ; defamatory disgraceful deragatory ہتکِ عزت کا دعوےٰ *hat'k-e iz'zat kā-da''va* N.M. libel suit , defamation case ہتکِ عزت کرنا *hat'k-e 'iz'zat kar'nā* V. defame disgrace

ہتھ *hath'*, ہت *hat'* PREF. hand ہتھ ادھار *hath'-ūdhār'* N.M. loan advanced or taken without any security or IOU ہتھ باندھا غلام *hath-bān'dhā ghūlām'* N.M. devoted servant ہتھ پھول *hath-phool'* N.M. a kind of firework ہتھ پھیری *hath phe'rī* N.F. trickery sleight of hand caress; fondling ہتھ پھیری کرنا *hath' phe'rī kar'na* V.T. defraud caress ; fondle ہتھ چکی *hath' chak'kī* N.F. hand-mill ہتھ چھٹ *hath-chhūt'* ADJ. given to belabouring at the slightest provocation ہتھ چھٹ منہ پھٹ *hath chhūṭ munh'-phaṭ* ADJ. short-tempered ; given to cursing and beating ہتھ رسی *hath'ra'sī* N F self-abuse ; self-pollution ہتھ کٹی *hath'-ka'ṭī* N.F. fencing or cudgelling trick aiming at adversary's hand ہتھکڑی *hath'ka'ṛī,* ہتکڑی *hat'ka'ṛī* N.F. handcuffs; manacles ہتھکڑی لگانا *hath'-ka'ṛī lagā'na* V.T. handcuff ہتھکڑی لگنا *hath'-ka'ṛī lag'na* V.T. be hand cuffed ہتھ کل *hath'-kal* N.F. doorknob latch ہتھکنڈا *hath-kaṅ'ḍa* N.M. (usu. in PH.) trickery ہتھوٹی *hathau'ṭī,* ہتوٹی *hatau'ṭī* N.F. sleight of hand trickery handicraft [~ ہاتھ CONTR.]

ہتھا *hat'thā,* ہتا *hat'ta* N.M. handle hand ہتھا مارنا *hat'thā mār'na* V.T. pilfer acquire illegally ہتھے چڑھنا *hat'the chaṛh'na* V.I. fall into the hands (of) ہتھے پر ٹھوکنا *hat'the par ṭhok'-na* V.T. object to something right at the start ہتھے سے اکھڑنا *hat'the se ū'khaṛ'na* V.I. be uprooted be separated (of kite) have its string snapped be out of joint [~ PREC.]

ہتھنی *hath'nī* N.F. female elephant

ہتھی *hat'thī* N.F. handle rest for hand ہتھیا *hath'ya* N.F. small handle [~ ہاتھ]

ہتھیار *hathyār'* N.M. weapon tool implement instrument equipment accoutrement ہتھیار بند *hathyar'-band* ADJ. armed equipped accoutred ہتھیار باندھنا (یا سجنا یا لگانا) *hathyar' bāndh'na* (or *saj'na* or *lagā'na*) V.I. arm oneself ہتھیار ڈالنا *hathyar' ḍāl'na* V.I. surrender ; lay dawn one's arms

ہتھیانا *hathya'na* ہتیانا *hatya'na* V.T obtain by fraud [~ ہاتھ]

ہتھیلی *hathe'lī,* ہتیلی *hate'lī* N.F. palm ہتھیلی پر سر رکھنا *hrthe'lī par sir rakh'na* V.I. play with one's life ہتھیلی پر سرسوں جمانا *hāthe'lī par sar'son jamā'na* V.T. work wonders do something swiftly ہتھیلی پر سر لیے پھرنا *hathe'lī par sir' li'ye phir'na* V.I. be ready to lay down one's life ہتھیلی کا پھپھولا (یا پھوڑا) *hathe'lī ka phapho'la* (or *pho'ṛā*) PH. cherished grievance ہتھیلی کھجانا (یا سلسلانا) *hathe'lī khujā'na* (or *salsalā'nā*) V.I. (of one's palm) itch (as augury of one's coming by some money) ہتھیلی میں چور پڑنا *hathe'lī men chor' par'nā* V.I. (of henna) leave some white patches ; fail to dye whole palm [~ ہاتھ]

ہتیا *hatti'ya.* جیو ہتیا *jiyoo' hattiya* N.F. (dial.) killing ہتیارا *hattiya'rā* ADJ. & N.M. (dial.) blood-thirsty (person) [I]

ہٹ *haṭ* N.F. stubbornness ; obstinacy (اپنی) ہٹ پر آنا (*ap'nī*) *haṭ' par ā'na* V.I. show obstinacy be peevish ہٹ دھرم *haṭ' dhar'm* ADJ. stubborn , obstinate unreasonable ہٹ دھرمی *haṭ-dhar'mī* N.F stubbornness ; obstinacy unreasonable show ہٹ کرنا *hat' kar'nā* V.I. obstinacy be peevish ہٹیلا *haṭī'lā* (dial. ہٹی *haṭī*) ADJ. (F. ہٹیلی *haṭī'lī*) stubborn ; obstinate

ہٹاکٹا *haṭ'ṭā kaṭ'ṭā* ADJ. (F. ہٹی کٹی *haṭ'ṭī kaṭ'ṭī*) robust ; stout ablebodied

ہٹانا *haṭā'nā* V.T. remove push back ; drive back clear away repel repulse cause to retreat cause to recede cause to flinch [~ FOLL. CAUS.]

ہٹنا *haṭ'nā* V.I. get back be driven back ; be repulsed stop recede flinch (of milch animal) dry up

ہٹیلا *haṭī'lā* ADJ. (see under ہٹ N.F. ★)

ہجا *hijā'* N.M. (also علم الہجا *'ilm-ul-hijā*) orthography ہجے *hi'je* (col. *hij'je*) N.M. PL. spelling (کے) ہجے کرنا *(ke) hi'je* (or *hij'je*) *kar'nā* V.T. spell out (a word) [A]

ہجا *hijā'* N.F. satire lampoon [A doublet of ہجو]

ہجر *hij'r* (ped. *haj'r*) N.M. separation from beloved ; separation ہجراں *hij'rān* N.M. (lit.) separation [A]

ہجرت *hij'rat* N.F. migration fleeing ; flight exodus flight of the Holy Prophet from Mecca to Medina (in 622 A.C. the year from which Muslim era begins) ; Hegira ہجری *hij'rī* ADJ. of the Hegira سن ہجری *sann-e hij'rī* N.M. Muslim era ; Hegira era [A ~ PREC.]

ہجو *haj'v* N.F. satire lampoon speaking ill (of) ہجو کرنا *haj'v kar'nā* V.T. speak ill (of) ہجو کہنا *haj'v kaih'nā* V.T. satirize lampoon ہجو گو *haj'v-go'* N.M. satirist ہجو گوئی *haj'v-go''ī* N.F. satire (as a literary genre) satirizing ہجو ملیح *haj'v-e malīḥ* N.F. irony sugar-coated satire [A]

ہجوم *hujoom'* N.M. crowd ; concourse mob (rare) assault ہجوم کرنا *hujoom' kar'na* V. rush upon ہجوم ہونا *hujoom' ho'nā* V.I. (of crowd) be

ہجے *hi'je* N.M. PL. (see under ہجا N.M. ★)

ہچر مچر *hi'char-mi'char* N.F. quibbling prevarication ہچر مچر کرنا *hi'char-mi'char kar'nā* V.I. quibble prevaricate

ہچک *hi'chak* N.F., ہچکا *hich'kā* N.M. jerk jolt ہچکنا *hi'chaknā* V.I. (dial.) be jolted boggle ; hesitate draw back

ہچکا *hūch'kā* N.M. kite-string bobbin ; spool

ہچکچانا *hichkichā'nā* (dial. ہچمچانا *hichmichā'nā*) V.I. falter waver shrink (from) ; recoil shy ہچکچاہٹ *hichkichāhaṭ* N.F. hesitation ; suspense boggling faltering wavering

ہچکولا *hichko'lā* N.M. jerk jolt ہچکولے کھانا *hichko'le khā'nā* V.I. jolt

ہچکی *hich'kī* N.F. (usu. in PL.) hiccup; hiccough convulsive sobbing breathing spasm ہچکی (یا ہچکیاں) آنا *hich'kī* (or *hich'kiyān*) *ā'nā* V.I. hiccup (fig.) be remembered by someone ہچکی (یا ہچکیاں) بندھ جانا *hich'kī* (or *hichkī'yān*) *bandh jā'nā* V.T. hiccup ہچکی لگنا *hich'kī lag'nā* V.I. suffer from hiccup have the last gasp [ONO.]

ہدیٰ *(or* ہدا*) hūdā'* N.M. correct guidance [A doublet of ہدایت]

ہدایا *hadā'yā* N.M. (PL. of ہدیہ N.M. ★)

ہدایت *hidā'yat* N.F. correct guidance counsel of sanity righteous ہدایت پانا *hidā'yat pā'nā* V.I. be rightly guided become righteous ہدایت دینا (یا کرنا) *hidā'yat de'nā* (or *kar'nā*) V.T. show the path of righteousness ہدایت نامہ *hidā'yat-nā'mah* N.M. guide [A]

ہدر *ha'dar* N.M. exculpating (someone who sheds blood of) [A]

ہدف *ha'daf* N.M. butt target bull's eye object ; objective [A]

ہدم *had'm* N.M. razing ; pulling down [A]

ہدڑا *had'ṛā*, ہیدڑا *haid'ṛā* N.M. (dial.) plight

ہدہد *hūd'hūd* N.M. woodpecker hoopoe [A]

ہُدہُد

ہدی *had'y* N.F. sacrificial animal taken to Mecca for sacrifice during Haj ; pilgrimage victim [A]

ہدیہ *had'yah* (ped. *hadiy'yah*) N.M. (PL. ہدایا *hadā'yā*) gift ; present price (of a copy of the Holy Quran) ہدیہ کرنا *had'yah kar'nā* V.T. present make a present (of) sell (a copy of the Holy Quran) [A]

ہڈ *haḍ* PREF. bone N.M. (also ہڈا *haḍ'ḍā*) big bone spavin ہڈ حرام *haḍ' ḥarām* N.M. & ADJ. lazy (person) good-for-nothing [~ FOLL.]

ہڈی *haḍ'ḍī* N.F. bone hard inner part or core (of carrot) ہڈی پسلی توڑنا *haḍ'ḍī pas'lī toṛ'nā*, ہڈیاں توڑنا *haḍ'ḍiyān toṛ'nā* V.T. beat black and blue give a sound beating ہڈیوں کی مالا ہو جانا *haḍ'ḍiyon kī mā'lā ho jā'nā* PH. emaciated

ہذا *hā'zā* PRON. (rare) this [A]

ہذیان *hazyān'* (ped. *hazayān'*) N.M. delirium

1 ہر har ADJ. every each any ہرآن har ān' ADV. every moment constantly whenever ہرآئینہ har ā'ī'nah ADV. certainly ; indeed ہرایک har' ek ADJ. each every N.M. everyone everybody ہربار har' bār ADV. every time ہرجائی har-jā''ī ADV. (of beloved) ; inconstant ہرجائی پن har-jā''ī-pan N.M. faithlessness ; inconstancy ; infidility ہرچند har' chand ADV. although ; though ; even though howevermuch ہرچند کہ har' chand ke ADV. although ; though ; even though har' che ADV. whatever ہرچہ بادا باد har' che bā'dā bād' come what may ; whatever the consequences ہرچہ در کان نمک رفت نمک شد har' che dar kā'n-e na'mak raft' na'mak shud PROV. one soon gets absorbed in the milieu ہردلعزیز har'-dil-'azīz' ADJ. popular ہردلعزیزی har'-dil-'azī'zī N.F. popularity ہردم har' dam ADV. every moment any moment ہردو har' do ADJ. both ہردے گی چمچہ har-de'gī-cham'chah N.M. hanger-on one with no fixed principles ہرروز har' roz ADJ. every day ہرروز عید نیست کہ حلوہ خورد کسے har' roz 'īd' nest keh hal'va khā'rad ka'se PROV. one cannot nope to have a stroke of good luck every time ہرشب شب برات ہے ہرروز روز عید har' shab shab-e barāt' hai har' roz ro'z-e 'īd PH. happy times ; palmy days ; halagon days ہرفن مولا har' fan mau'lā N.M. jack of all trades ہرکس بخیال خویش خبطے دارد har' kas ba-khayāl-e khesh' khab'te dā'rad PROV everyone has a fad ہرکس وناکس har' ka's-o-nā-kas N.M. everyone high and low ; all and sundry ہرکہ آمد عمارت نوساخت har' ke ā'mad 'imā'rat-e nau' sākh't PROV. everyone implements own fad ہرملکے ہررسمے har' mūl'ke har' ras'me PROV. every place has its own traditions ہرکہیں har' ka'hīṅ ADV. everywhere ہرگاہ har' gah' CONJ. whereas ; since ہرہفت har-haf't N.M. (woman's) full make-up ADV. with full make-up

2 ہر har, ہری ha'rī N.M. name of Hindu god Vishnu or Mahadev ; God ; Har ہرکو بھجے سو ہرکا ہوئے har' ko bha'je so har' kā ho''e PH. he who worships God becomes his devotee ہرہرمہادیو har' har mahā-dev N.M. god of gods Har (as Hindu war cry) ہری بولنا ha'rī bol'nā V.I. (of Hindu) die ; pass away [S]

ہرا ha'rā ADJ. (F. ہری ha'rī) green verdant fresh unripe (fruit) raw (wound) (of debt or value) realised ہرا ہونا ha'rā ho'nā V.I. be green be verdant (of wound) become raw (of debt or value) be realized (of fruit) be unripe ہرا بھرا ha'rā bha'rā ADJ. (F. ہری بھری ha'rī bha'rī) lush or luxuriant (vegatation) prosperous ; thrieving کی گود ہری بھری ہونا ki god' ha'rī bha'rī raih'nā V.I. (of woman) be blessed with children ہری چگ ha'rī-chūg ADJ. & N.M. selfi time-server

ہراس hirās' N.M. fear ; terror ہراس زدہ hirās'-za'dah ADJ. terror-stricken ہراساں hirā'sāṅ ADJ. terror-stricken [P]

ہرانا harā'nā V.T. defeat worst overcome cause to lose [~ ہارنا CAUS.]

ہراند hirānd' N.F. tang of termeric tang of half-cooked stew

ہراول harā'val N.M. & ADJ. vanguard ; advance-guard

ہرہر نہ جاننا har' har na jān'nā V.I. not to know the difference between two things

ہرپھر کے hir' phir ke ADV. at last ; at length after all in the final analysis

ہرج har'j N.M. harm ; damage trouble wastage ہرج کرنا har'j kar nā V.T. harm ; damage waste ہرج ہونا har'j ho'nā V.I. suffer loss ; face trouble ہرج مرج har'j-mar'j N.M. trouble disorder ہرجہ har'jah N.M. damages compensation demurrage ہرجہ تشخیص کرنا har'jah tashkhīs' kar'nā V.T. assess damages

ہرجانہ harjā'nah N.M. indemnity damages compensation demurrage [~ PREC.]

ہردا hir'dā (dial. ہردے ha'ridai) N.M. heart ہردا کھلنا hir'dā khul'nā V.I. (of mind) become enlighted [S]

ہرزہ har'zah ADJ. absurd ; silly , nonsensical idle vain purposeless ہرزہ سرا har'za-sarā', ہرزہ گو har'za-go' ADJ. N.M. idler talker ; foolish prater ہرزہ سرائی har'za-sarā''ī ہرزہ گوئی har'za-go''ī N.F. silly talk ; prate ramble ہرزہ گرد har'za-gar'd ADJ. roving ; rambling N.M. tramp ہرزہ گردی har'za-gar'dī N.F. ramble ; roving [P]

ہرس har's N.F. ploughshare

ہرسا har'sā N.M. sandalwood abrading stone

ہرکارہ harkā'rah N.M. courier [P ~ ہر + کار]

ہرگز har'giz ADV. (emphasizing negative) (not) on any account [P]

ہرمچی hūrm'chī (ped. ہرمزی hir'mizī) N.F. red earth [P]

ہرن hi'ran (dial. ha'ran) N.M. dear ; antelope hart; buck roe ہرن کا چوکڑی بھرنا hi'ran kā chau'karī bhar'nā V.I. (of deer) leap ہرن کا چوکڑی بھول جانا hi'ran kā chau'karī bhool jā'nā P.H. be confounded be flabbergasted ہرن ہوجانا hi'ran ho jā'nā V.I. flee ; run away نشہ ہرن ہوجانا nash'shah hi'ran ho

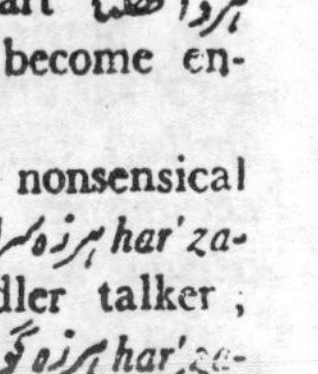

ہرن

ja'nā PH. come to one's senses be no longer under effect of drink ہرنا *hir'nā* N.M. buck pommel (of saddle) ہرنوٹا *hirnau'ṭā* N.M. roe

ہرنی *hir'nī* N.F. doe ; hind

ہرنا[2] *har'nā* V.I. lose (at gambling)

ہرنا[3] *har'nā* V.T. seize hold

ہری *ha'rī* N.M. (same as ہر[2] N.M. ★)

ہریا *har'yā* ADJ. green wild INT cry to drive away parrots, etc. ہریالا *haryā'lā* ADJ. green ; verdant young ; youthful N.M. a kind of nuptial song ہریالی *haryā'lī*, ہریاول *haryā'val* N.F. greenery ; verdure [~ ہرا]

ہریسہ *harī'sah* N.M. mashed pottage made of wheat and minced (fig.) pap [A]

ہریل *har'yal* N.M. green pigeon [~ ہرا]

ہڑ *haṛ* N.F. a myrobalan-like nut plaited tossel (rare) bone ہڑجوڑا *haṛ jo'ṛā* N.M. bone-setter name of a drug used for the purpose

ہڑبڑانا *haṛbaṛā'nā*, اڑبڑانا *arbaṛā'nā* V.I. start up be flurried ہڑبڑا کر *haṛbaṛā' kar* ADV. hurriedly ; in hot haste ہڑبڑا کر اٹھنا *ha'ṛ baṛā' kar uṭh'nā* V.I. start up from sleep ہڑبڑی *haṛ'baṛī* N.F. flurry scurry confusion nervousness ہڑبڑیا *haṛbaṛay'yā* N.M. nervous persons irascible (person)

ہڑبونگ *haṛbong'* N.F. uproat, tumult mess ; confusion commotion ہڑبونگ مچانا *haṛbong' machā'nā* V.T. & I. make n uproar create a commotion cause confusion

ہڑپ *haṛap'* N.F. sound of gobbling ADJ. gobbled up misappropriate ہڑپ کرنا *haṛap' kar'nā* V.T. gulp down ; gobble up embezzle usurp grab ہڑپا *haṛap'pā* N.M. gulp ; embezzlement usurpation

ہڑتال *haṛtāl'* N.F. strike closure of business centres as protest ; protest standstill sulphurate of arsenic ہڑتال کرنا *haṛtāl' kar'nā* V.T. strike ہڑتال ہونا *haṛtal' ho'nā* V.I. (of business centres, etc.) be closed in protest

ہڑدنگا *hūṛdaṅ'gā* N.M. children's noisy play ADJ. (F. ہڑدنگی *hūṛdaṅ'gī*) tumultous rowdy quarrelsome unskilful

ہڑکنا *hūṛak'nā* V.I. pine (of baby) miss someone

ہڑک *hū'ṛak* N.F. hydrophobia its effect pining haukering ہڑکا *hūṛ'kā* N.M. pining (of baby separated from parents) latch ہڑکانا *hūṛkā'nā* V.T cause to pine thus cause hydrophobia ہڑکایا *hūṛkā'yā* ADJ (F. ہڑکائی *hūṛkā''ī*) rabid

ہزار *hazār'* ADJ. thousand many innumerable however much N.M. nightingale ہزار پا *hazār'-pā* N.M. centipede ہزار جان سے فدا ہونا *hazār' jān se fidā' ho'nā* V.T. be deep in love (with) ہزار داستان *hazār'-dās'tān* N.M. nightingale ADJ. melodious ہزار علاج اور ایک پرہیز *hazār' 'ilāj' aur ek' parhez'* PROV. prevention is better than cure ہزاروں گھڑے پانی پڑ جانا *hazā'roṅ ghaṛe pā'nī paṛ jā'nā* PH. feel greatly ashamed ہزاروں میں *hazā'roṅ meṅ* ADJ. openly ; publicly ہزاروں میں ایک *hazā'roṅ meṅ ek* PH. pick ; choicest of the lot ہزارواں *hazār'vāṅ* ADJ. thousandth ہزارہا *hazārhā'* ADJ. thousands ہزاری *hazā'rī* N.F. command of a thousand soldiers ADJ. holding a fief for a thousand soldiers (fast) in commemoration of the Holy Prophet's Ascension ہزاری بزاری *hazā'rī bazā'rī* ADJ. (one) who meets both high and low unreliable [P]

ہزبر *hizab'r* N.M lion [P]

ہزج *ha'zaj* N.E. name of a verse metre [A]

ہزل *haz'l* N.M. jest ; joke drollery buffoonery (PL ہزلیات *hazliyyāt'*) this is a literary genre ; nonsense verse ہزل گو *haz'l-go* N.M. one who writes nonsense verse ہزل گوئی *haz'l-go''ī* N.F nonsense verse [A]

ہزیمت *hazī'mat* N.F. flight ; defeat ; rout ہزیمت اٹھانا *hazī'mat uṭhā'nā* V.I. be defeated ; be put to rout ہزیمت خوردہ *hazī'mat-khūr'dah* ADJ. defeated ; routed

ہست *has't* N.F. being ; existence present ہست و بود *has't-o-bood* PH all that is or has been [P ~ ہستن be]

ہستنی *has'tinī* N.F. the lowest of the four categories of women according to Hindu writers on sex [~S female elephant]

ہستی *has'tī* N.F being ; existence entity life world worth ; value [P ~ ہستن]

ہسکا *his'kā* N.M. (dial.) emulation ; bid to emulate

ہش *hūsh*, ہشت *hūsh't* INT cry for driving away birds and animals or set them ہشکارنا *hūshkār'nā* V.T. halloo [ONO.]

ہشاش بشاش *hashshāsh' bashshāsh'* ADJ. jolly ; jovial [A]

ہشت *hish't* INT fie ; for shame [ONO.]

ہشت hash'ṯ ADJ., N.M. & PREF. eight ہشت بہشت hash'ṯ behish'ṯ PH. eight parts of paradise called khul'd, dar-us-salam', da'rul qarar', jan'nat-e 'ad n, jan'natul l-ma'va ja'nat-un-na'im', illiy'yin and firdaus' ہشت پہلو hash'ṯ-paih'loo ADJ. octagonal ہشتم hash'tum ADJ eighth ہشتاد hashtad' ADJ. & N.M. eighty [P]

ہشیار hushyar' ہوشیار hoshyar' ADJ. clever shrewd intelligent awake ; alert skilled learned grown up ہشیار کرنا hushyar' kar'na V.T. caution ; warn rear unpart skill or knowledge wake up ; rouse ہشیاری hushya'ri, ہوشیاری hoshya'ri N.F. cleverness shrewdness alertness awareness being skilled or learned being grown up [P]

ہضم haz'm N.M. digestion assimilation misappropriation ہضم کرنا haz'm kar'na V.T. digest assimilate misappropriate ہضم ہونا ham'z ho'na V.I. be digested assimilated be misappropriated [A]

ہفت haf't ADJ. & N.M. seven ہفت اقلیم haf'tiqlim', ہفت کشور haf't-kish'var N.F. the seven climes; world [P] ہفت اندام haf't-andam' N.F. great vein running through arm N.M. seven outer portions of body VIZ. head, chest, belly and four limbs ہفت پشت haf't-push't N.F. seven generations ہفت پہلو haf't-paih'loo ADJ. seven-sided N.M. septagon ہفت خوان رستم haf't-kha'n-e rus'tam N.M. PL. seven difficult stages traversed by Rustum ; Herculean tasks ہفت رنگی haf't-ran'gi ADJ. capricious ; cunning ; artful versatile ہفت زبان haf't-zaban' N.M. master of many languages ; linguist ADJ. polyglot ہفت عجائب haf't-'aja''ib N.M. PL. seven wonders of the (ancient) world, according to Western nations ہفت قلم haf't-qa'lam N.M. seven calligraphic styles VIZ. sulus, mohaq'qaq', tauqi'', raihan, riqa'', nas'kh and ta'liq' master of these ہفت ہزاری haf't-haza'ri N.M. one holding a fief for seven thousand soldiers ہفت ہیکل haf't-hai'kal N.F. set of seven prayers repeated for personal safety ہفتم haf'tum ADJ. seventh ہفتاد haftad' ADJ. & N.M. seventy ہفتاد و دو ملت haf'ta'd-o-do mil'lat N.F seventy-two (Muslim) sects

ہفتہ haf'tah N.M. week Saturday name of a wrestling trick by which adversary's neck and are locked ہفتہ مختتمہ haf'ta e mukhtati'mah N.M. week ending (such and such date) ہفتہ وار haf'ta-var ADJ. weekly [P ~ PREC.]

ہفت نظر haf' na'zar INT. (dial.) may he (etc.) escape the effect the evil eye

ہفوات hafavat' N.F. PL. nonsense silly utterances [A]

ہفعی haf''i N.M. adder ADJ. crafty gluttonous [~A افعی CORR.]

ہک huk N.M. hook [E]

ہکا بکا hak'ka bak'ka ADJ. (never inflected) aghast ; dumb founded ہکا بکا رہ جانا hak'ka bak'ka raih'-ja'na V.I. be struck dumb

ہکذا ha'-kaza ADJ. thus similarly [A ~ ہا + کذا]

ہکلانا hakla'na V.I. stutter ; stammer ہکلا hak'la N.M. & ADJ. (F. ہکلی hak'li) stammerer ہکلا پن hak'la-pan ہکلاہٹ hakla'hat N.M. stutter ; stammer

ہگنا hag'na V.I. evacuate bowels ; go to stools ہگاس hagas' N.F. need to go to stools ہگاسا ha'gasa ADJ. (F. ہگاسی haga'si) (one) feeling that need cowardly ہگاسی بطخ haga'si bat'takh N.F. (fig.) coward ہگانا haga'na V.T. cause (child, etc.) to evacuate bowels ہگوڑا hagau'ra N.M. & ADJ. (F. ہگوڑی hagau'ri) (one) going to stools very often coward dastardly

ہل hal N.M. plough ہل جوتا hal-jo'ta N.M. ploughman ; tiller ہل جوتنا (یا چلانا یا پھیرنا) hal jot'na (or chala'na or pher'na) V.T. plough raze (struture) to ground thus ہل چلنا (یا پھرنا) hal'chal'na (or phir'na) V.I. be ploughed be razed thus

ہلاپتی ha'la-pa'ti, ہلاچلی ha'la-chali N.F. (same as ہلچلی N.F. ★)

ہلاس hulas' N.F. snuff ہلاس دانی hulas'da'ni N.F. snuff-box ہلاس لینا hulas' le'na V.I. snuff ; take snuff

ہلاک halak' ADJ. dead killed perished overwhelmed with grief N.M. (rare) pardition run ; destruction ہلاک کرنا halak' kar'na V.T. kill destroy overwhelm (with grief) ہلاک ہونا halak' ho'na V.T. be killed ; lose (one's) life perish be ruined be overwhelmed (with grief) ہلاکت hala'kat N.F. death destruction perdition extinction ; extermination

ہلاکو hilakoo' (ped. ہلاگو hula'goo) N.M. Hulagoo (fig.) tyrant (fig.) killer [T]

ہلال hilal' N.M. (PL. اہلہ ahil'lah) crescent ; new moon borned moon ہلال احمر hila'l-e-ah'mar N.M. Red Crescent انجمن ہلال احمر an'juman-e hila'l-e ah'mar N.F. Red Crescent Society ہلالی hila'li ADJ. of, pertaining to or having a crescent horned horseshoe

ہلالی پرچم *hilā'lī par'cham* N.M. flag with a crescent Muslim (country's) flag ہلال وصلیب *hilā'l-o-salib'* صلیب و ہلال *sali'b-o-hilal* N.M. PL. Crescent and Cross (fig.) Muslims and Christians [A]

ہلانا *hilā'nā* V.T. move jerk ; jolt shake agitate tame familiarize کا دل ہلانا *kā' dil hilā'nā* V.T. move (someone) to passion strike with terror

ہلاہل *halāhil* ADJ. deadly (only in) زہر ہلاہل *zaih'r-e halā'hil* N.M. deadly poison [A]

ہلبلانا *halbalā'nā* V.I. scurry be confused ہل بل *hal'bal* ہلبلاہٹ *halbalā'hat*. N.F. hurry ; scurry confusion

ہلچل *hal'-chal*, ہلا پتی *ha'lā-patī*, ہلاچلی *ha'lā-chalī* N.F. tumult ; commotion confusion fright ; alarm ; panic stampede ہلچل پڑنا (یا مچنا یا ہونا) *hal'-chal par'nā* (or *mach'nā* or *ho'nā*) V.I. panic stricken (of commotion) be caused

ہلدی *hal'dī* N.F. turmeric ہلدی کی گرہ لے کر پنساری بن بیٹھنا *hal'dī kī gireh le' kar pansā'rī ban baith'nā* PROV. boast despite meagre resources ; presume a great-deal ہلدی لگے نہ پھٹکری *hal'dī la'ge na phit'karī* V.I. without incurring any expenditure or undergoing much labour early grabs ہلدوا *hal'davā* N.M. a kind of yellow timber ہلدیا *hal'diya* ADJ. yellow N.M. jaundice a poisonous element of turmeric

ہلڑ *hūl'lar* N.M. rowdysm riot row tumult uproar ہلڑ مچانا *hūl'lar machā'nā* V.I. riot cause tumult cause uproar be rowdy

ہلسانا *hūlsā'nā* V.T. coax incite (thus) to quarrel

ہلکا *hal'kā* ADJ. (F. ہلکی *hal'kī*) light (in weight decree colour or character) mild soft cheap ; inexpensive easy of digestion soft (water) mean disgraced ashamed delicate ہلکا پھلکا *hal'kā phūl'kā* ADJ. (F. ہلکی پھلکی *hal'kī phūl'kī*) light lean ہلکا جاننا *hal'kā jān'nā* V.T. disdain look down upon regard as mild ہلکا کرنا *hal'kā kar'nā* V.T. lighten abate assuage ease refresh debase ہلکا ہونا *hal'kā ho'nā* V.I. be or become light grow mild be refreshed be relieved of burden (of fever, etc.) abate feel ashamed ہلکے ہلکے *hal'ke hal'ke* ADV. mildly soft lightly ہلکا پن *hal'kā pan* N.M. lightness softness (of water) levity despicableness

ہلکارنا *hūlkār'nā*, ہشکارنا *hūshkār'nā* V.T halloo (hound) [ONO.]

ہلکان *halkān'* ADJ. exhausted (with work) overwhelmed (with grief) جان ہلکان کرنا *jān halkān' kar'nā* V.T exhaust overwhelm with grief exercise mind ہلکان ہونا *halkān' ho'nā* V.I. be overwhelmed (with grief) be exercised in mind [~ A ہلاک]

ہلکم *hal'kam* N.F. (dial.) uproar

ہلکورا *hilko'rā* (dial. ہلورا *hilo'rā*) N.M. (usu. in PL. wane ; billow ; surge ripple ہلکورے لینا *hilko're le'nā* ہلورے لینا *hilo're le'nā*, ہلوریں لینا *hilo'reṅ le'nā* V.I. ripple billow

ہلگانا *hilgā'nā* V.T. hang ; suspend

ہل من مزید *hal'-mim' mazīd'* PH. is there more of it more still more [A ~ ہل + من + مزید]

ہلنا *hil'nā* V.I. move jolt shake tremble be tamed familiarize (of heart) be moved to passion

ہلہ *hal'lah* N.M. attack ; assault battery sally ; sortie uproar tumult rowdyism ہلہ کرنا (یا بولنا) *hal'lah kar'nā* (or *bol'nā*) V.T. attack ; assault

ہلہلا *hūl'hūla* N.M sudden desire spurt ہلہلانا *hūlhūlā'nā*, ہلہلا اٹھنا *hūlhūlā' uth'nā* V.I. have a sudden passion for

ہلہلانا *halhalā'nā* V.I. shake ; shiver

ہلیلہ *hale'lah* N.M. a myrobalan-like nut

¹ہم *ham* PRON. we (used) by him editor or wonder ہم کو *ham' ko*, ہمیں *ha'meṅ* PRON. us ہمارا *hamā'rā* PRON. our ہم بھی ہیں پانچوں سواروں میں *ham' bhī haiṅ pāṅch'veṅ savā'roṅ meṅ* PROV. We hounds killed the hare, quoth the lap dog.

²ہم *ham* ADV. also ; even too PREF. each other together mutually equal similar have ہم آغوش *ham-āghosh'* ADJ. embracing ; locked in each other's arms ہم آغوش ہونا *ham-āghosh' ho'nā* V.I. embrace each other ہم آواز *ham-āvāz'*, ہم آہنگ *ham-āhang'* ADJ. harmonious concordant (fig.) agreeing ; consenting , united ; (with) one voice ہم آہنگی *ham āhaṅ'gī* N.F. harmony agreement ہم اصل *ham-as'l* ADJ. of common origin or ancestry ہم بستر *ham-bis'tar* N.M. bedfellow ADJ. sharing the same bed ; cohabiting ; copulating ہم بستر ہونا *ham-bis'tar ho'nā* V.T. sleep together cohabit ; copulate ہم بستری *ham-bis'tarī* N.F. cohabitation copulation coition ہم بستری کرنا *ham-bis'tarī kar'-nā* V.T (col.) copulate (with) ہم پایہ *ham-pā'yah*, ہم پلہ *ham-pal'lah* ADJ. of the same status , equal in rank or dignity ہم پہلو *ham-paih'loo* ADJ. adjacent ہم پیالہ *ham-piyā'lah*, ہم پیالہ وہم نوالہ *ham-piyā'la-o-*

ham-nivā'lah ADJ. boon-companion chum ; intimated friend ہم پیشہ *ham-pe'shah* N.M. colleague ADJ. engaged in the same trade بود ہم پیشہ با ہم پیشہ دشمن *buvad' ham-pe'shah bā ham-pe'shah dush'man* PROV two of a trade never agree ہمتا *ham-tā'* N.M. equal ; peer ہمتائی *ham-tā''ī* N.F. equality , similarity of status ہم جلیس *ham-jalīs'* N.M. constant companion ہم جماعت *ham-jamā''at* N.M. classfellow ; classmate ADJ. studying in the same class ہم جنس *ham-jin's* ADJ. homogeneous of the same species having similar mental horizon ہم چشم *ham-chash'm* N.M. equal ; peer ہم چشمی *ham-chash'mī* N.F. equality of status being of the same status ہمدرد *ham-dar'd* ADJ. sympathetic N.M. sympathiser condoler ہمدردی *ham-dar'dī* N.F. sympathy condolence ہمدردی کرنا *ham-dar'dī kar'nā* V.T. sympathize condole ہمدرس *ham-dar's*, ہم سبق *ham-sa'baq* N.M. classfellow ہمدگر *ham-di'gar* ADV. (arch.) together ہمدم *ham'dam* N.M. friend ہم دوش *ham-dosh'* ADJ. equal ; peer ADV. shoulder to shoulder ہمذات *ham-zāt'* ADJ. of the same caste ہمراز *ham-rāz'* ADJ. confident ہمراہ *ham-rāh'* ADV. with ; along with N.M. (rare) fellow-traveller ہمراہی *ham-rā'hī* N.M. (col.) fellow-traveller N.F. company (in travelling) ہم مرتبہ *ham-rut'bah*, ہم مرتبہ *ham-mar'tabah* ADJ. equal in status ہمرکاب *ham-rikāb'* N.M. fellow-rider ADV. attending ; along with ہمرنگ *ham-rang'* ADJ. of the same colour of similar disposition دام ہمرنگ زمین *dā'm-e ham-rang'-e zamīn* N.M. camouflaged snares ہمزاد *ham-zād'* N.M. one's familiar spirit ; familiar (rare) twin ہمزبان *ham-zabān'* , ہمزبان *ham-zabān'* ADJ. speaking the same language unanimous ہمزباں ہو کر *ham-zabān' ho' kar* ADV. with one voice ہم زلف *ham-zūl'f* N.M. brother-in-law ; husband of wife's sister ہمسایہ *ham-sā'yah* N.M. neighbour کے ہمسایہ میں رہنا *ke hamsā''e meṅ raih'nā* PH. live in the neighbourhood of be the next door neighbour of ہمسائیگی *ham-sā''igī* (ped. ہمسایگی *ham-sā'yagī*) N.F. neighbourliness or neighbourhood ہمسائی *hamsā''ī* N.F neighbour ہم سخن *ham-su'khan* N.M. interlocutor ہمسر *ham'-sar* N.M. equal ; peer ہمسری *ham-sa'rī* N.F. equality . similarity of status ہمسفر *ham-sa'far* N.M fellow-traveller this as Communist sympathiser ہم سن *ham'-sin* ADJ. of the same age coevel ہم شکل *ham-shak'l* ADJ. like-shaped : appearing , alike , resembling homomorphic (fig.) like ; similar ; analogous ہمشیرہ *ham-shī'rah* (ped. ہمشیر *ham-shīr'*) N.F. sister ہم صحبت *ham-soh'bat* ADJ. associate moving in same society ہم صفیر *ham-safīr'* N.M. (of birds) fellow-songster (fig.) comrade ہم عصر *ham-'as'* ADJ. & N.M. contemporary ہم عمر *ham-'ūm'r* ADJ of the same age ; coeval ہم عناں *ham-'inān'* , ہم قدم *ham-qa'dam* ADJ. attendant ADV. attending ہم عہد *ham-'aih'd* (ped. -'*ah'd*) ADJ. of the same are contemporary ہم قوم *ham-qaum'* N M. fellow country man ; compatriot ہم قیمت *ham-qī'mat* ADJ. equivalent in value similarly-priced ہم کار *ham-kār'* N.M. colleague ہمکاری *ham-kā'rī* N.F. being a colleague ہم کفو *ham-kū'f'v* ADJ. enjoying similar social status ; belonging to the same social class of the same family ہمکلام *ham-kalām'* ADJ. & ADV. conversing together N.M. interlocutor ہم کلام ہونا *ham-kalām ho'nā* V.T. talk converse (with) ہم کلامی *ham-kalā'mī* N.F. mutual talk ; conversation dialogue ; intercourse ; interlocution ہمکنار *ham-kanār'* ADJ, embracing ہمکنار کرنا *ham-kanār' kar'nā* V.T. embrace (someone) ہمکنار ہونا *ham-kanār' ho'nā* V.I. embrace ہم مجلس *ham majlis,* N.M. companion ADJ. (one) keeping compaion (of) ہم مذہب *ham-maz'hab* ADJ. coreligionist ہم مرکز *ham-mar'kaz* ADJ. concentric (circles) ہم مشرب *ham, mash'rab* ADJ. having similar outlook on life sharing the same views ہم معنی *ham-ma''nī* (or ped. -nā) ADJ. synonymous ہم مکتب *ham-mak'tab* N.M. school-fellow ; school mate ADJ. studying or having studied at the same school ہمنام *ham-nām'* N.M. namesake ADJ. having the same name ہم نسل *ham-nas'l* ADJ. of the same race ; derived of the same racial stock ہم نشیں *ham-nashīn'* (or -*shīn'*) N.M companion ADJ. (one) bearing (someone) company ہم نشینی *ham-nashī'nī* N.F. companionship bearing (someone) company ہم نفس *ham-na'fas* N.M. friend comrade ہم نفسی *ham-na'fasī* N.F. comradeship ہمنوا *ham-navā'* ADJ. & N.M. (one) raising the same voice (as another) ; (one) expressing agreement one singing in harmony (with another) ہمنوائی *ham-navā''ī* N.F. singing in harmony (with) expression of agreement ہموار *ham-vār'* ADJ. level ; even smooth flat equable consistent ہموارہ *ham-vā'rah* ADV. (rare) always ; ever constantly ہمواری *ham-vā'rī* N.F. evenness smoothness flatness uniformity . equability consistency ہم وزن *ham-vaz'n* ADJ. of same weight ہم وطن *ham-va'tan* N.M. fellow-country man ; compatriot ہم وطنی *ham-va'tanī* N F. belonging to or hailing from the same country ; being compatriot(s) [P]

ہم *ham* N.M. (PL. ہموم *hūmoom'*) worry ; care ; anxiety ہم و غم *ham'm-o-gham* N.M. worry and grief [A]

ہما *humā* N.M. phoenix; a fabulous bird supposed to raise to throne anyone coming under shadow of its wing بالِ ہما *bā'l-e hūmā'*, شہپرِ ہما *shah'par-e hūmā'* N.M. wing of phoenix [P]

ہمارا *hamā'ra* PRON. (F. ہماری *hamā'rī*) our ہمارا کیا ہے *hamā'ra kyā' hai* PH. who cares, why should I worry تو ہمارا ذمہ *to hamā'ra zim'mah* PH. I vouch for it تو ہمارا سلام ہے *to hamā'rā salām' hai* PH. I wash my hands of the whole affair ہماری بلی ہمیں سے میاؤں *hāma'rī bil'lī ha'miṅ se miyā''oṅ* PH. challenging one's own benefactor ہماری بھتی کھائے *hamā'rī bhā'tī khā''e* PH. (dial.) may he find me dead

ہما شما *ha'mā shū'ma* ADJ. everybody ; all and sundry [~ P ہما we + شما you CORR.]

ہمالیہ *himā'li'yah*, ہمالہ *himā'lah* N.M. abode of snow ; the Himalayas [S]

ہمام دستہ *hamām das'tah* N.M. (same as ہاون دستہ N.M. ★)

ہماہمی *ha'mā ha'mī* N.F. boast brag ; tall talk

ہمایوں *hūmā'yoon* ADJ. lucky ; fortunate ; auspicious [P]

ہمت *him'mat* N.F. (PL. ہمم *hi'mam*) courage ; br very boldness gues ; spirit daring adventure ; enterprise ہمت باندھنا (یا کرنا) *him'mat bāndh'na* (or *kar'nā*) V.T. be bold; to take courage; muster courage ہمت بندھانا *him'mat bandh'nā* V.T. encourage ہمت پڑنا *him'mat paṛ'nā* V.I. take courage; to dare ہمت کا حامی خدا ہے *him'mat kā ḥā'mī khūdā hai*, ہمت مرداں مددِ خدا *him'mat-e mar'dāṅ ma dad-e khūdā'* PROV. God helps those who help themselves ہمت ہارنا *him'mat har'nā* V.I. have no courage left ; lose heart ہمتی *him'matī*, ہمت والا *him'mat vā'lā* ADJ. (F. ہمت والی *him'mat vā'lī*) bold, courageous daring ; spirited enterprising adventurous

ہمجولی *ham-jo'lī* N.M. & F. friend playmate

ہمزہ *ham'zah* N.M. hamzah ; name of penultimate latter of Urdu alphabet [A]

ہمزہ *ha'mazah* N.M. (PL. ہمزات *hamazāt'*) fear ; doubt ; suspicion [A]

ہمساواں *hamsā'vaṅ* N.M. (W. dial.) (name for) sixth month of Hijri calendar

ہمسنا *hū'masnā* V.T. move leave or place

ہمکنا *hu'maknā* V.I. (of infant) jump to go into another's lap

ہمم *hi'mam* N.F. (PL. of ہمت N.F. ★)

ہموم *hūmoom'* N.M. (PL. of ہم N.M. ★)

ہمہ *ha'ma* ADJ. all whole everyone PREF all omni- pan- ہمہ اوست *ha'ma os't* PH. pantheism ہمہ تن *ha'ma-tan* ADV. wholly ; entirely ADJ. whole ; entire ہمہ داں *ha'ma-dān'* ADJ. omniscient having a wild field of knowledge ہمہ دانی *ha'ma-dā'nī* N.F. omniscience wild field of knowledge ہمہ صفت موصوف *ha'ma si'fat mausoof'* ADJ. endowed with all good qualities ہمگی *ha'magī* ADJ. all, entirely *ha'ma-gīr* ADJ. all-embracing ہمہ گیری *ha'ma-gī'rī* N.F. all embracing nature ہمہ وقتی *ha'ma-vaq'tī* ADJ. wholetime (employee, etc.) بایں ہمہ *ba-īṅ' ha'mah* PH. nevertheless despite [P doublet of ~ ہم]

ہمیانی *hamyā'nī* N.F. purse [~ P ہمیان]

ہمیشہ *hame'shah* (dial. ہمیش *hamesh'*) ADV. always; ever continually perpetually ; incessantly [P]

ہمیں *ha'meṅ* PRON. us to us [~ ہم]

ہمیں *ha'miṅ*, ہمی *ha'mī* PRON. we ourselves, only we [~ ہم + ہی]

ہمیں *ha'mīṅ* ADJ. this very [P]

ہن *hūn* N.M. (fig.) gold, wealth (arch.) name of Deccan gold coin ہن برسنا *hūn ba'rasnā* V.I. (of wealth) be abundant

ہنٹر *haṅ'ṭar* N.M. whip [E]

ہنجار *haṅ'jār* N.M. right way (only in) ناہنجار *nā-haṅjār'* ADJ. wicked [P]

ہند *hind* N.M. India ; Indo-Pakistan subcontinent ہندنی *hind'nī* N.F. Hindu woman ہندو *hiṅ'doo* N.M. (PL. ہنود *hūnood'*) Hindu slave thief ADJ. black ہندوستان *hindūstān'* N.M. India ; Indo-Pakistan sub-continent Urdu-speaking area of the sub-continent ہندوستانی *hindūstā'nī* ADJ. Indian N.M. Indian N.F. Hindustani ; basic Urdu ہندی *hin'dī* ADJ. Indian pertaining to this subcontinent N.F. bastard form of Urdu written for Sanskrit script N.M. Hindu ہندی کی چندی کرنا (یا بنانا یا نکالنا) *hiṅ'dī kī chin'dī kar'nā* (or *batā'nā* or *nikāl'nā*) PH. do hair-splitting [~ A ~ Indus]

ہندسہ *haṅ'dasah* (col. *hin'sā*) N.M (usu. **hindsa(h)**, numeral (rare) engineering [A]

ہندوانہ *hindo'ā'nah* N.M. water-melon [P]

ہنڈا *haṅ'dā* N.M. earthernware pot hanging lampshade [~ ہانڈی]

ہنڈکلھیا *hand-kūlkyā* N.F. children's pastime of cooking dish thus cooked [~ ہانڈی]

ہنڈول **hańdol'** N.M. a major mode of classical Indo-Pakistan music connected with spring

ہنڈولا **hańdo'la** N.M. swing monsoon song sung on a swing ہنڈولا جھولنا **hańdo'lā jhool'nā** V.I. swing in cradle ہنڈولا گانا **hańdo'lā gā'nā** V.T. sing such monsoon song

ہنڈولا

ہنڈی **hūń'di** (arch. ہنڈوی **hūńd'vi**) V.T. bill of exchange bank draft ہنڈی بھیجنا **hūń'di bhej'nā** V.T. send a bill of exchange or bank draft ہنڈی پٹنا **huń'di paṭ'nā** V.I. (of bill) lie honoured ہنڈی سکارنا **hūń'di sakār'nā** V.T. honour a bill ہنڈی کرنا **hūń'di kar'nā** V.T. send money by draft ہنڈی کھڑی کرنا **hūń'di khaṛ'ri rakh'nā** V.T. let bill stand uncashed درشنی ہنڈی **darshani hūń'di** N.F. bill payable at sight

ہنڈیا **hańd'ya** N.F. (PL. ہنڈیاں **hańd'yań**) ہنڈیا **hańd'ya pakā'nā** V.T. cook ; stew (fig.) plot ; conspire ہنڈیا پکنا **hańd'yā pakā'nā** V.I. be stewed be cooked (of plot) be hatched ہنڈیا چڑھنا **hańd'yā chaṛh'nā** V.T. start cooking

ہنر **hu'nar** N.M. skill attainment art ; accomplishment cleverness ہنر فروش **hū'nar-firosh** N.M. pedant ADJ. pedantic ہنرمند **hū'nar-mańd**, ہنرور **hū'nar-var** ADJ. skilful clever ہنرمندی **hū'nar-mań'di** ہنروری **hū'nar-va'ri** N.F. skill cleverness

ہنس **hań's** N.M. goose راج ہنس **rāj'-hań's**

ہنسانا **hańsā'nā** V.T. ہنسائی **hańsā''i** N.F. ہنس مکھ **hań's-mūkh** ADJ. (see under ہنسنا V.I. ★)

ہنسلی **hań'sli** N.F. clavicle silver (or gold) band worn round collar as an ornament ; collar-band

ہنسنا **hańs'nā** V.I. laugh be merry bloom blossom laugh (at) ; ridicule ہنس بول کر **hańs' bol' kar** ADV. happily ہنستا چغل **hańs'tā chū'ghal** N.M. foe in friendly guise ہنستے بولتے **hańs'te bol'te** ADV. marrily ; cheerfully ہنستے ہنستے پیٹ میں بل پڑ جانا **hańs'te hańs'te peṭ meń bal' paṛ jā'nā**, ہنستے ہنستے لوٹ جانا **hańs'te hańs'te loṭ' jā'nā** V.I. have side-splitting laughter ہنس مکھ **hańs'-mūkh** ADJ. cheerful merry jocose ہنسنا بولنا **hańs'nā bol'nā** V.T. indulge in jokes be cheerful ہنسوڑ **hańsoṛ'** ADJ. cheerful murry jocose facetious ہنسوڑپن **hańsoṛ'-pan** N.M. cheerfulness jocularity facetiousness ہنسی **hań'si** N.F. laugh; laughter cheerfulness ; mirth joke; jest fun easy talk ; fun ; sport ridicule public ridicule ہنسی اڑانا **hań'si ūṛā'nā** V.I. ridicule ہنسی اڑنا **hań'si ūṛ'nā** V.I. be ridiculed ; be exposed to public ridicule ہنسی ٹھٹھا **hań'si** N.M. laughter joking ہنسی خوشی (سے) **hań'sī khū'shi (se)** ADV. gladly ; happily ہنسی سمجھنا **hań'sī sa'majhnā** V.I. consider a joke regard easy ہنسی سو پھنسی **hań'sī so phań'sī** PROV. a maid that responds to overtures with laughter is often half taken ہنسی کھیل **hań'sī khel** N.M. jesting easy task ; fun ; joke; sport ہنسی کی بات **hań'sī kī bāt** N.F. something to laugh ہنسی میں اڑا دینا **hań'sī meń ūṛā' de'nā** V.T. turn off with a joke ; dismiss jestingly ہنسی میں پھنسی ہو جانا **hań'sī meń phań sī ho jā'nā** V.I. (of bitterness) be caused in joke ہنسی ہنسی میں **hań'sī hań'sī meń** ADV. in jest ; humorously ہنسانا **hańsā'nā** V.T. cause to laugh ; rouse to laughter ہنسائی **hańsā''ī** SUF. ridicule

ہنسیا **hańs'ya** N.F. sickle

ہنکارنا **hūnkār'na** V.I. say yes ہنکار **hūnkar'** N.F. sound of 'yes' being uttered ہنکارا **hūnkā'rā** N.M. ہنکاری **hūnkā'ri** N.M., ہنکارا (یا ہنکاری) بھرنا **hūnkā'ra** (or **hūnkā'rī**) **bhar'nā** V.I. say 'yes' in listening ; hum [~ ہوں ONO.]

ہنکانا **hańkā'na** V.T. drive away (animals)

ہنگام **hańgām'** N.M. time ; occasion ہنگامی **hańgā'mi** ADJ. accidental extraordinary ; abnormal

ہنگامہ **hańgā'mah** N.M. uproar riot disturbance tumult ہنگامہ آرا **hańgā'mah ā'rā'**, ہنگامہ پرداز **hańgā'mah-pardāz'** riotous tumultous ہنگامہ آرائی **hańgā'mah-ārā''ī**, ہنگامہ پردازی **hańgāma pardā'zi** N.F. rioting causing tumult ہنگامہ برپا (یا گرم) کرنا **hańgā'mah bar-pā (or gar'm) kar'nā** V.T. cause uproar create trouble ہنگامہ خیز **hańgā'-mah-khez** ADJ. uproarious troublelesome discorderly ہنگامہ خیزی **hańgā'mah-khe'zi** N.F. causing uproar or disorder بڑا ہنگامہ کرنا **ba'ṛā hańgā'mah kar'nā** V.T. raise a hue and cry make muck ado ہنگامہ ہونا **hańgā'mah ho'na** V.I. (of riot, disorder or trouble) be created

ہنود **hūnood'** N.M. (PL. of ہنود ~ ہندو N.M. ★)

ہنوز **hanooz'** ADV. yet ; still ہنوز دہلی (یا دلی) دور است **hānooz' deh'lī (or dil'lī) door' ast** PROV. there is many a slip between the cup and the lip [P]

ہنومان **ha'nooman** N.M. monkey (as Hindu god) ہنومان جی مہاراج **ha'nooman jī mahārāj'** PH. (H. dial.) the venerable lord Monkey [S]

ہنہنانا **hinhinā'nā** V.I. neigh N.M. neighing

ہنی مون **ha'nī moon** N.M. honeymoon [E]

1 ہو ho V.I. (IMP. of ہونا V.I ★)

2 ہو ho. ہوت hot INT ho , hallo ; hello [ONO.]

1 ہو hoo N.F. groan noise [ONO.]

2 ہو hoo' INT. God N.M. nothingness save God ADJ. & ADV. annihilated ہو حق hoo' haq INT. God is true (as mystic's cry in ecstasy) ہو حق کرنا hoo' haq kar nā V.I. raise this cry remember God revel make a noise ہو (حق) ہو جانا hoo' (haq) ho jā'nā V.I. be ruined be annihilated (اک) ہو کا عالم (ik) hoo' kā 'ā'lam N.M. wilderness ; desert [~ اللّٰہ al'lā'hoo CONT.]

3 ہو hoo' PRON. he that He God ہو بہو (or ہو بہ ہو) hoo' ba-hoo ADV. exact (copy) ADV. exactly [A]

ہوا havā' N.F. air wind breeze atmosphere desire love lust good name ; reputation rumour PREF. air ہوا اڑانا havā' ūṛā'na V.T. & I. give out spread rumour cause (someone) to lose credit ہوا اڑنا havā' ūṛ' ja na V.I. lose credit (of secret) be given out be rumoured ہوا اکھڑنا havā' ū'khaṛnā V.I. lose credit ہوا باز havā'-bāz' N.M. pilot ; airman ; aeronaut ہوا بازی havā'-bā'zī N.F. airmanship aeronautics ہوا باندھنا havā' bāndh'na V.I. build (usu. false) reputation (of) brag bruit abroad ہوا بتانا havā' lag'nā V.I. dodge prevaricate get rid of (someone) by curt reply or false promise ہوا بدلنا havā' ba'dalnā V.T. & I. change climate ; go to a hill resort for the purpose (of circumstances) change; (of times) be changed ہوا بستہ havā'bas'tah ADJ. airtight ہوا بگڑنا havā' bi'gar'-nā V.I. lose credit (of circumstances or environment) ہوا بندھنا havā' bandh'na V.I. become famous ہوا بھر جانا havā' bhar' ja'nā V.I. be puffed up with pride پیٹ میں ہوا بھر جانا peṭ meṅ havā' bhar' jā'na V.I. have flatulence ; suffer from wind ہوا بھرنا havā' bhar'na V.T. inflate (tyre) ہوا بھی نہ دینا havā' bhī na de'nā V.T. keep hidden ; not to expose in the least not to leak out ہوا پر دماغ ہونا havā' par dimāgh ho'nā V.I. give oneself the air ہوا پرست havā-paras't ADJ. (one) seeking wordly pleasures fickle vain ہوا (کے گھوڑے) پر سوار ہونا havā' (ke gho're) par sovār' ho'na V. be in a hurry (زمانے کی) ہوا پلٹنا (zama'ne kī) havā pa'laṭnā V.I. (of times) be changed ہوا پھانکنا havā' phank'nā V.I. eat sparsely pretend to go without food ہوا پھر جانا havā' phir' ja'nā V.I. (of circumstances) change (usu. for the better) ہوا چلنا havā' chal'nā V.I. (of wind) (of breeze) waft become the vogue ; be in style ; be the fashion ہوا چھوڑنا havā' chhoṛ'nā V.I. fart , break wind ہوا خلاف ہونا havā' khilāf ho nā V.I. be faced with adverse circumstances ہوا خواہ havā'khāh' N.M. well-wisher sympathisers friend ہوا خواہی havā'-khā'hī N.F. good will friendship sympathy ہوادار havā'-dār' ADJ. open airy ; well-ventilated N.M. sympathiser well-wisher lover portable throne for a side ہواداری havā'-dā'rī N.F. airiness love sympathy ہوا دینا havā' de'na V.T. fan (flare) incite trouble ; foment quarrel air (clothes, etc.) ہوا زدگی havā'-za'dagī N.F. cold ہوا سا havā' sa ADV. a little ; wee bit ہوا سے اڑ جانا havā' se ūṛ' jā'na V.I. be so light as to be blown away by the least wind ہوا سے باتیں کرنا havā' se bā'teṅ kar'na V.I. be very fast rival the wind in speed کی ہوا سے بچ کر نکلنا kī havā' se bach' kar ni'kalnā V.T. avoid , shun ہوا سے لڑنا havā' se lar'na V.I. seek occasion for quarrel be peevish; be testy ; be touchy ہوا کا تھپیڑا havā' ka thape'ra N.M. gust or blast of wind ہوا کا رخ بدلنا havā' kā rukh batā'na V.T. indicate direction of wind show blows evade dismiss with a curt or subtle reply ہوا کا رخ دیکھنا havā' ka rukh dekh'na, دنیا (یا زمانے) کی ہوا دیکھنا dūn'ya (or zamā'ne) kī havā' dekh'na V.I. see which way the wind is blowing trim one's sails according to the prevailing ہوا کرنا havā' kar'na V.T. fan despatch ; send (someone) away swiftly ہوا کھانا havā' khā'na V. stroll ; go out for an airing have a taste or existence of live , remain alive ہوا کھاؤ havā' khā''o PH. quit ہوا کھونا havā' kho'na V.I. lose credit ہوا کے دوش پر havā' ke dosh' par ADV. on the air ہوا کی روٹی havā' kī ro'ṭī N.F very thin bread ہوا کے گھوڑے پر سوار ہونا havā' ke gho're par savār' ho'nā V.I. be in a great hurry be very proud ; be vain ہوا لگ جانا havā' lag jā'na V.I. catch cold have rheumatic pains have one's head turned become naughty come under outside influence ہوا لینا havā' le'na V.I. stroll go out for an airing ہوا مٹھی میں بند کرنا havā' muṭ'ṭhī meṅ band' kar'nā, ہوا میں گرہ دینا havā' meṅ gi'rah de'nā V.I. attempt the impossible make a vain effort ہوا نکلنا havā' nikal'nā V.I. lose credit be deflated have a flat tyre die ; breathe one's last be no longer puffed up with pride ہوا لگنے نہ دینا havā' lag'ne de nā V T. keep hidden ; not to expose in the least not to leak out ہوا و ہوس havā'-o-ha'vas N.F. greed lust ambition human wishes vanity ہوا ہو جانا havā' ho jā'na V.I. run away swiftly , scamper disappear ; vanish end become a matter of the past evaporate ہوائی

havā''ī ADJ. air wind airy swift light stray clever blue, azure incourtant N F rocket rumour parings (of nuts, etc.) ہوائی آنکھ havā''ī āṅkh N.F fickle lover ہوائی اڈہ havā''ī ad'dah, ہوائی مستقر havā''ī mus'taqar N.M. airport, aerodrome ہوائی اڑانا havā''ī ura nā V.T spread (usu. false) rumours ہوائی اڑنا (یا چھوٹنا) havā''ī ūr'nā (or chhoot'nā) V.I. (of false rumour) spread چہرے (یا منہ) پر ہوائی (یا ہوائیاں) اڑنا (یا چھوٹنا) cheh're (or mūṅh) par havā''ī (or havā''iyāṅ) ūr'nā (or chhoot'nā) V.I. lose colour; become suddenly pale through fear ہوائی بندوق havā''ī bandooq' N.F. airgun; pop-gun ہوائی تیر havā''ī tīr N.M. arrow shot in the direction of wind a kind of firework sent high up in the sky ہوائی جہاز havā''ī jahāz' N.M. aircraft, aeroplane; airplane ہوائی جہاز چلانا havā''ī jahāz' chalā'nā V.T. fly an aircraft ہوائی چھوڑنا havā''ī chhor'nā V.T. let off a pyrotechnic rocket ہوائی حملہ havā''ī ḥam'lah N.M. air-raid ہوائی حملہ سے بچاؤ کی تدبیر havā''ī ḥam'lah se bachā''o kī tadābīr' PH. air raid precautions; A.R.P. ہوائی خبر havā''ī kha'bar N.F. rumour ہوائی دیدہ havā''ī dī'dah ADJ. instant in love saucy ہوائی صدری havā''ī sad'rī N.F. air-jacket ہوائی قلعہ havā''ī qil''ah N.M. castle in the air ہوائی قلعے بنانا havā''ī qil''e banā'nā PH. build castles in the air

ہوا hū''ā V.I. (P.T. of ہونا V.I. ★)

ہوا hav vā N.M. bugbear, hobgoblin

ہواو havā''o N.M. courage, guts 'purdah', modesty ہواؤ کھلنا havā''o khūl'nā V.I. grow bold become less modest

ہوت 1 hot INT. (same as ہو INT ★)

ہوت 2 hot N.F. ہوتا ho'tā (or ہوتی ho'tī or ہوتے ho'te) PR.T (see under ہونا V.I. ★)

ہوٹل ho'ṭal N.M. hotel [E]

ہودہ hau'dah, (rare ہودج hau'daj) N.M. howdah litter (of camel) [~A]

ہوس ha'vas N F. lust lasciviousness sensuality pseudo-passion; false love desire greed, covetousnesss ہوس بجھنا ha'vas bujh'nā V.I. (of wish) be fulfilled ہوس پیشہ ha'vas-pe'shah ADJ greedy, covetous lusty sensual; lascivious ہوس پرور ha'vas-par'var ADJ. lustful lascivious ہوس پروری ha'vas-par'varī N F lasciviousness ہوس کرنا ha'vas kar'nā V T. covet ہوس کیش ha'vas-kesh ADJ lustful lascivious ہوسناک ha'vas-nāk ADJ lascivious covetous ہوسناکی ha'vās-nākī N F lasciviousness ہوس نکالنا ha'vas nikal'na V T satisfy one's desire

ہوش hoosh' ADJ uncultured

ہوش hosh' N.M senses sense understanding discretion ہوش آنا (یا پکڑنا یا سنبھالنا) hosh ā'nā (or pa'karnā or sanbhal'nā) V.T. & I. come to understand recollect reach the age of discretion ہوش اڑنا (یا اڑ جانا یا باختہ ہونا یا پراگندہ ہونا یا جاتے رہنا یا گم ہو جانا) hosh ūr'nā (or ūr jā'nā or bākh'tah ho'nā or paragan'dah ho'nā or jā'te raih'nā or gūm ho' jā'nā) V.I. lose one's senses become confounded ہوشمند hosh-mand' ADJ. sensible intelligent grown-up ہوشمندی hosh-man'dī N.F. sense wisdom intelligence being grown-up ہوش میں آنا hosh meṅ ā'nā V.I. come to come to one's senses ہوش و حواس hosh-o-ḥavās N.M. sense and understanding [P]

ہوشیار hosh yār', ہشیار hūsh yār' ADJ. clever careful watchful; cautious alert awake attentive sensible wise; intelligent grown-up INT. (also ہوشیار باش hosh yār' bāsh') be cautious take care watch it, (etc.) ہوشیار کرنا hosh yār' kar'nā V.T warn, caution train up make clever ہوشیار ہو جانا hosh yār' ho jā'nā V.I. be careful become cautious become clever ہوشیاری hosh yā'rī N.F cleverness carefulness accuracy watchfulness alertness wisdom prudence intelligence

ہوک hook N.F. deep sigh of helplessness, heaved by a lovely person; excruciating sigh ہوک اٹھنا hook'ūṭh'nā V.I. heave an excruciating sigh

ہوکا hau'kā N.F. greed; covetousness voracity ہوکا کرنا hau'kā kar'nā V.I. be greedy; be covetous be voracious

ہول haul N.M. fright; horror, terror restlessness; uneasiness ہول آنا haul ā'na V.I. be frightened ہول بیٹھ جانا haul baiṭh jā'nā V.I. be obsessed by a terror ہول دل hau'l-e dil N.M. fright ہول دلا haul'-di'lā ADJ. coward ہول دلی haul'-di'lī N.F. cowardice ہول زدہ haul'-za'dah ADJ. frightened, terrified aghast nervous ہول کھانا haul' khā'nā V.I. be afraid; to be frightened grow restless ہولناک haul'nak ADJ. fearful; frightful terrible terrific; dreadful; horrible; horrid dangerous risky ہولناکی haul-'nā'kī N.F. fearfulness; frightfulness, terror, direness, dreadfulness dangerousness [A]

ہولا hau'la ADJ. restless nervous terror stricken ہولا جولی hau'lā jau'lī N F restlessness nervousness [A]

ہولا holā N.M. chick-pea parched in the pod a Sikh festival following 'Holi'

ہولنا *haul'nā* V.T. goad ; urge an elephant thrust

ہولو *hau'loo* ADJ. (dial.) whimsical , capricious

ہولی *ho'lī* N.F. festival of Hindus celebrated by spilling dyes as one another song sung on the occasion ہولی کھیلنا (یا منانا) *ho'lī khel'nā* (or *manā'nā*) V.I. celebrate the Holi festival thus

ہولے *hau'le* ADV. showly gently ; softly gradually ہولے ہولے *hau'le hau'le* ADV. slowly gently ; softly gradually ; by and by ; step by step

ہوم ڈیپارٹمنٹ *hom dipār'tmant* N.M. home department ہوم رول *hom' rool'* N.M. Home rule ہوم سیکرٹری *hom' saik'reṭarī* N.M. Home secretary ہوم منسٹر *hom' minis'ṭar* N.M. Home minister [E]

ہومیوپیتھی *ho'miyopaithī* N.F. homoeopathy ہومیوپیتھ *ho'miyopaith* N.M. homoeopath ہومیوپیتھک *ho'miyopaithik*, ہومیو *ho'miyo* ADJ. homeopathic [E]

ہوں *hoon* INT. well yes may be ہوں ہاں کرنا *hoon' hān kar'nā* V.I. dilly-dally ; prevaricate assent half-heartedly ہوں ہوں *hoon' hoon'* INT. don't beware keep quiet yes and no ہونا *ho'nā* V.I. be exist become happen be born come into existence transpire existence *ho'* IMP. be SUBJUNCTIVE may be ہو آنا *ho' ā'na* V.I. return after a visit to ہو جانا *ho' jā'na* V.I. become ہو چکنا *ho' chuk'nā* PH. become fall for ; be devoted to (iron.) be impossible of achievement ہوجیو *ho'jiyo* SUBJUNCTIVE may it (etc.) be ہو رہنا *ho' raih'na* V.I. be devoted (to) become come into being ; talk place stay on somewhere ہو کے (یا کر) رہنا *ho' ke* (or *kar*) *raih'nā* V.I. definitely become ہوگا *ho'gā* V.I. might be shall or will be ہو گزرنا *ho' guzar'na* V.I. (of dead personality) have (once) lived ہو لینا *ho le'nā* V.I. be accomplished go along (with) ہو نہ ہو *ho' na ho* PH. definitely , of course whatever might happen ہوا *hū'a* PAST T. was became ہوا چاہتا ہے *hū'a chāh'tā hai* PH. is about to take place ہوا سو ہوا *hū'ā so hū'a* PH. let by gones be bygones ہوا کرے *hū'a ka're* PH. who cares ہوت *hot* N.F. (one's) power (one's) means (one's) resources ہوت جوت والا *hot' jot va'la* N.M. rich person resourceful man ہوت کی جوت ہے *hot' kī jot' hai* PH. splendour is bred by pelf ہوتا *ho'tā* PR. P. become P.T. were ADJ. (one) who is N.M. relation ہوتا ساتا *ho'tā sā'tā* N.M. (PL. ہوتے سوتے *ho'te sā'te* (dial.) supporter relation alive ہوتی آئی ہے *ho'tī ā'ī hai* PH. it is customary that ہوتے *ho'te* ADV. in the presence (of) ہوتے ہوتے *ho'te ho'te* ADV. gradually ; by and by ہوتے ہی *ho'te hī* ADV. soon after coming into being as soon at it happened ہوتے ہی ہوگا *ho'te hī ho'gā* PH. (it) will its own time ہوجیو *ho jiyo* INT. (arch.) wish to God that (it) may ہونی *ho'nī* N.F something that is going to occur the inevitable ہونے دو *ho'ne do* PH. let it go on come what may ہونے والا *ho'ne vā'lā* ADJ. & N.M. that is going to be what will be ہونے والا ہو کر رہے گا *ho'ne vā'la ho' kar ra'he ga* PH. what will be will be ہے *hai* PR. T. is ADV. present ہیں *hain* PR. T. are

ہونٹ *honṭ* N.M. lip ہونٹ چاٹنا *honṭ chāt'nā* V.I. relish ہونٹ چاٹتے رہ جانا *honṭ chāṭ'te raih ja'nā* be able to forget the relish of some dish ہونٹ سی دینا *honṭ sī' de'nā* V.T. force to keep quiet ہونٹ سی لینا *ho'nṭ sī' le'nā* V.I. keep mum ہونٹ کاٹنا *ho'nṭ' kāṭ'nā* V.I. bite one's lip ہونٹ کٹا *honṭ'-ka'ṭā* ADJ. & N.M. one whose lips are cut ہونٹ ہلانا *honṭ hilā'nā* V.I. speak ہونٹوں پر پپڑیاں جمنا *hon'ṭon par paparyāṅ jam'nā* V.T. (of lips) be parched ہونٹل *hon'ṭal* N.M. & ADJ. thick-lipped

ہونس *hoons* N.F. jealousy evil eye ہونسنا *hoons'nā* V.T. cost an evil eye on

ہونق *havan'naq* N.M. fool , simpleton

ہونکنا *haunk'nā* V.I. pant huff and puff

ہونہار *hon'hār* ADJ. budding (youth) ; promising that must happen ہونہار بروا کے چکنے چکنے پات *hon'hār bir'vā ke chik'ne chik'ne pāt'* PROV. a precocious child shows the man inside him greatness is visible even at a tender age [~ ہونا]

ہوہا *hoo'ha* N.F. hullahallo

ہویدا *hūvai'da* ADJ. obvious evident clear; manifest

ہئی[1] *ha''ī* N.F. hue and cry wonder cry ; noise

ہئی[2] *ha''ī* is there all right is very much there there is no doubt about it [CONTR. of ہے ہی]

ہی *hī* ADV. (not used with NEG.) only immediately on (doing)

ہے *hai* INT. alas strange wonderful ہے ہے *hai' hai* INT. alas ہے ہے نہ کھے *hai' hai na khai' khai* PH. no trouble after that no problem

ہیا *hi'yā* N.M. , hearth courage

ہیاو *hiyā''o* N.M. courage modesty ہیاو کھلنا *hiya''o khul'nā* V.I. become saucy

ہیبت *hai'bat* N.F. awe fear, dread ; horror ہیبت زدہ *hai'bat-za'dah* ADJ. aghast appalled ہیبت زدگی *hai'bat-za'dagi* N.F. being terror-stricken ہیبت ناک *hai'bat-nak* ADJ. awful fearful ; frightful; terrible tremendous ; appalling ہیبتناکی *hai'bat-na'ki* N.F. terror [A]

ہیبیس کارپس *he'biyas kar'pus* N.M. habeas corpus (also ہیبیس کارپس درخواست *hebiyas kar'pas darkhas't*) habeas corpus petition [E]

ہیٹا *heta* ADJ. inferior ہیٹی *heti* N.F. insult disgrace ADJ. inferior ہیٹی کرنا *heti kar'na* V.T. insult بڑی ہیٹی ہونا *ba'ri he'ti ho'na* V.T disgrace

ہیجا *haija'* N.F. battle [A]

ہیجان *haijan'*, ہیجان *hai'jan* N.M. tumult excitement ; commotion ہیجان پیدا ہونا *haijan' paida ho'na* V.I. (of commotion) be

ہیجڑا *hij'ra* N.M. eunuch

ہیچ *hech* ADJ. nothing insignificant ہیچ پوچ *hech poch'* ADJ. insignificant ہیچ مدان *hech'-madan'* ADJ. ignorant ہیچمدانی *hech'-mada'ni* N.F. ignorance ہیچ میرز *hech'-ma-yarz* ADJ. worthless (person) ہیچ میرزی *hech'-ma-yar'zi* N.F. worthlessness [P]

ہیڈ *haid* (col. *hed*) N.M. head this as a body of water kept at a height for taking off canals from it PREF head ; chief ہیڈکلرک *haid'-kilark* N.M. head clerk ہیڈ کوارٹر *haid-ko'ar'tar* N.M. headquarter H.Q. ہیڈ ماسٹر *haid-mas'tar* N.M. headmaster ہیڈ مسٹرس *haid-mis'tarais* N.F. headmistress [E]

ہیرا *hi'ra* N.M. diamond gem; jewel ہیرا آدمی *hi'ra a'dami* N.M. gem ; jewel of a man ہیرامن *hi'ra man* N.M. (legendary name for) parrot ہیرے کی کنی *hi're ki ka'ni* N.F. diamond particle

ہیرا پھیری *he'ra phe'ri* N.F. returning something after buying or fetching it wangling trick ہیر پھیر *her' pher* N.F. change trick wangling ہیر پھیر کرنا *her' pher kar'na* V.I. wangle defraud ہیر پھیر کی بات *her' pher ki bat'* N.F. something said with the tongue in the cheek fraud deceit

ہیرو *hi'ro* N.M. hero ہیروئن *hirau'in* (ped. *hi'ro'in*) N.F. heroin [E]

ہیرو *hi'roo* ہیرو *he'roo* N.M. a kind of song sung in 'Diwali' festival

ہیروا *her'va* N.M. (dial.) baby's impatience or pining while missing someone ہیروا کرنا *her'va kar'na* V.I. (of baby) be impatient or pine on missing (someone)

ہیز *hez* N.M eunuch [P]

ہیزم *he'zam* N.F. firewood faggot ہیزم فروش *he'zam-firosh'* N.M. firewood dealer ہیزم کش *he'zam-kash* N.M. wood-cutter [P]

ہیضہ *hai'zah* N.M. cholera ہیضہ پھیلنا *hai'zah phail'na* V.I. (of cholera) break out ہیضہ کرنا *hai'zah kar'na* V.I. suffer from cholera ہیضہ ہونا *hai'zah ho'na* V.I. suffer from cholera ہیضے کا ٹیکہ *hai'ze ka ti'kah* N.M. cholera inoculation ہیضے کا ٹیکہ لگانا *hai'ze ka ti'kah laga'na* V.T. inoculate against cholera [A]

ہیکڑ *hai'kar* ADJ. strong ; robust ہیکڑ مستامن *hai'kar musta'man* hector ; bully ہیکڑی *haika'ri* N.F. oppression bullying ہیکڑی جتانا (یا کرنا یا کی لینا) *hai'kari jata'na* (or *kar'na* or *ki le'na*) V.I. oppress bully

ہیکل *hai'kal* N.F. temple oracle body shape of body ; figure neckband necklace made of coins

ہیلا *hi'la* N.M. push work ہیلا دینا (یا مارنا) *hi'la de'na* (or *mar'na*) V.T. push

ہیلتھ *hail'th* (col. *hel'th*) health ہیلتھ افسر *hail'th af'sar* N.M. Health Officer ہیلتھ ڈیپارٹمنٹ *hailth di'part'-mant* N.M. Health department پبلک ہیلتھ *pub'lik hail'th* N.F. public health [E]

ہیمیا *hi'miya* N.F. magic a branch of black art

ہیں *hain'* INT. what why oh ہیں ہیں *hain'* *hain'* INT. oh oh no

ہینا *hi'na* ADJ. weak inferior worthless

ہینڈ *haind* N.M. hand ہینڈی *hain'di* ADJ. handy ہینڈل *haindal* N.M. handle ہینڈل کرنا *hain'dal kar'na* V.T handle tackle [E]

ہینگ *hing* N.F. assafoetida ہینگ لگا کر رکھنا *hing laga kar rakh'na* (iron.) V.T. keep safe ; set apart ہینگ ہگنا *hing hag'na* V.I. suffer from dysentery peak and pine

ہیولیٰ (or ہیولا) *hayoo'la* N.M. amorphous substance shapeless substance ; object devoid of form [A]

ہیہات *haihat'* INT. (poet.) alas (rare) away [A]

ہی ہی *hi'-hi* N.F. silly laughter sound of laughter ہی ہی ٹھی ٹھی *hi'-hi thi'-thi* N.F. silly laughter joyous but purposeless life ہی ہی ٹھی ٹھی کرنا *hi'-hi thi'-thi kar'na* V.I. lead such life laugh in a silly manner [ONO.]

ہیئت *hai''at* N.F. astronomy form figure appearance body organization ہیئت الافلاک *hai''at-ul-aflak'* N.F. form of heavens (rare) astronomy ہیئت اصلی *hai''at-e as'li* N.F. original form ہیئت پکڑنا *hai''at pa'karna* V.I. take shape ہیئت حاکمہ *hai''at-e ha'kimah* N.F. governing body authority form of government ہیئت داں hai''at-dān (or dāṅ) N.M. astronomer ہیئت کذائی hai''at-e kazā''ī (col. hai''at kazā''ī) N.F present form or state despicable looks ludicrous appearance [A]

ء

ء ham'za thirty-fifth letter of Urdu alphabet used either for giving a jerk to the tongue in pronunciation or just as a carrier for a short vowel ; n this letter case, it is equivalent to the carrier ا In Urdu it never occupies the initial position; instead the initial is termed *hamza* by Arab grammarians and their followers. No Urdu word begins with this letter [A]

ی

ی *ye* thirty-sixth letter of Urdu alphabet having a consonantal value equivalent to English y as a vowel it is usually written as ی when standing alone or in final position and is called *chho'ṭī ye* as a diphthing or open vowel it is written as ے in such positions and is called *ba'ṛī ye* omega (in *jummal* reckoning) 10 : [A]

یا *yā* N.F. Arabic name for یائے مجہول *yā'-e majhool* N.F. this representing the *ay* sound in the English word *'day'* یائے معروف *yā'-e ma'roof'* N.F this representing the *ee* sound

یا[2] *yā* CONJ. or either یا ... یا *yā...yā* CONJ. either...or [P]

یا[3] *yā* INT. oh ; O you یا اللہ *yā allāh'* INT. good God my God

یاب *yāb* SUF. finding ; discovering receiving getting gaining یابندہ *yābin'dah* N.M. payee recipient one who finds یابی *yā'bī* SUF. finding ; discovering receiving ; getting gaining [A ~ یافتن find]

یابس *yā'bis* ADJ. dry [A ~ یبس]

یابو *yā'boo* N.M. (rare.) pony ; nag

یاترا *yāt'rā* N.F. (dial.) pilgrimage to Hindu shrine [S]

یاجوج ماجوج *yājooj' majooj'* N.M. Gog and Magog [A ~ H]

یاد *yād* N.F. memory remembrance recollection reminiscence retrospect commemoration یاد آنا *yād' ā'nā* V.I come to mind be recollected ; be recalled یاد آوری *yād'-ā'varī* N.F remembrance یاد اللہ *yād' al'lāh* N.F. form of salutation between mendicants, etc acquaintance (long-standing) relations یاد ایام *yā'd-e ayyām'* N.M. old memories memory of days gone by INT. welladay یادداشت *yād'-dāsh't* N.F. memory memorandum note ; aide-memoire یاد دلانا *yād' dilā'nā* V.T. remind refresh someone's memory یاد دہانی *yād-dehā'nī* N.F. remindering reminder یاد رکھنا *yād' rakh'nā* V.T keep in mind remember یاد رہنا *yād' rah'na* V.I. be remembered be borne in mind یاد پڑنا *yād' paṛ'nā* V.I. come to mind be recalled یادش بخیر *yā'dash ba-khair'* PH. (for a cherished object recalled) may be (etc.) live in peace یاد فرمانا *yād' farmā'na* V.T. remember think (of) send (for) یاد کرنا *yād' kar'na* V.T. learn by heart ; learn by rote ; memorize ; commit to memory remember think (of) send (for) یادگار *yād-gār'* N.F. memorial monument keepsake souvenir ADJ. worth remembering یادگار زمانہ *yād-gā'r-e zamā'nah* ADJ. memorable peerless یادگاری *yād-gā'rī* ADJ. memorable commemorative ; commemoration یادگاری ٹکٹ *yād-gā'rī ṭi'kaṭ* N.M. commemoration stamp یاد ہونا *yād' ho'nā* V.I. be remembered be committed to memory ; be memorized ; be learnt by heart be borne in mind تمہیں یاد ہو کہ نہ یاد ہو *tum'heṅ yād' ho ke na yād' ho* PH. perhaps you may able to recall it

یار *yār* N.M. (PL. یاراں *yā'rāṅ*) friend companion (rare) supporter (vul.) paramour یار آشنا *yār āsh'nā* N.M. acquaintance paramour N.M. PL. friends and acquaintances یار باش *yār' bāsh* ADJ. friendly sociable jolly ; cordial voluptious یار باشی *yār'-bā'shī* N.F. friendliness ; cordiality sociability jollity ; voluptiousness یار بنانا *yār' banā'nā* V. make friends with form a friendship یار جانی *yār-e jā'nī* N.M. fast friend bosom friend یار دوست *yār' dos't* N.M. PL. friends ; chums یار زندہ صحبت باقی *yār' zin'dah soh'bat bā'qī* PH. hope lasts with life we will meet again if death gives a respite یار شاطر *yā'r-e shā'tir* PH. clever friend wise friend یار شاطر نہ (کہ) بار خاطر *yā'r-e shā'tir na (ke) bā'r-e khā'tir* PH. a wise friend and no bore یار غار *yār'-e ghār'* N.M. Hazrat Abu Bakr as the Prophet's companion of the cave during the exodus from Mecca sincere friend fast friend یار لوگ *yār* log N.M. PL. friends people یار لوگ (بات) لے اُڑے yār' log (bāt') le ū'ṛe PH. people made it a town talk یار مار yār' mār ADJ. (one) who betrays a friend یار ماری yār-ma'rī N.F. betrayal of a friend یار ماری کرنا yār ma'rī kar'nā V.T. betray one's friend یار وہ جو وقت پر کام آئے yār' vo jo vaq't par kām a''e PROV. a friend in need is a friend indeed یاران سرِ پل yārā'n-e sa'r-e pūl N.M. PL. chance acquaintance people who happen to meet on the way یاروں کا یار ya'roṅ kā yār N.M. a friend to friends very good friends companionable person یارانہ yārā'nah N.M. friendship ADJ. friendly ADJ. in a friendly manner یارانہ گانٹھنا yārā'nah gāṅṭh'nā V.T. form a friendship become friends with یاری yārī N.F. friendship help ; assistance ; support یاری دینا yārī de'nā V.T. help ; support یاری کٹ جانا yā'rī kuṭ' kar'nā V.T. (of children) snap friendly ties یاری کٹ ہونا yā'rī kuṭ' ho'nā V.I. (of children's friendship) end [P]

یارا ya'rā N.M. strength یارائے ضبط نہ ہونا yārā''e zabt' na ho'nā V.T. be unable to control or resist [P]

یازدہ yāz'dah ADJ. & N.M. eleven یازدہم yāz'dahum ADJ. eleventh [P]

یاس yās N.F. despair despondence frustration chagrin [A]

یاسمین yāsamīn', یاسمین yās'mīn, یاسمن yāsaman N.F. jasmine ; jessamine [A ~ P]

یاسین (also یٰسین yāsīn' N.M. name of a chapter of the Holy Quran recited especially at deathbed to facilitate someone's death appelation of the Holy Prophet ; chief یٰسین پڑھنا V.T recite this chapter at someone's deathbed [A]

یافت yāf't N.F. gain ; profit perquisite income earnings accessibility نایافت nā-yāf't N.F. lack of profit inaccessibility یافتہ yāf'tah N.F. got ; receive found discovered یافتنی yāf'tanī ADJ. due N.F dues [P ~ یافتن find]

یاقوت yāqoot' N.M. (PL. یواقیت yavāqīt') ruby یاقوت لب yāqoot'-lab ADJ. ruby-lipped یاقوت رُمّانی yāqoo't-e rūmmā'nī N.M. garnet یاقوتی yāqoo'tī ADJ. ruby-red N.M. garnet ; electuary [A]

یاک yak N.M. yak [Tibetan]

یال yal N.F. (same as ایال N.F. ★)

یاں yāṅ ADV (poet.) here [~ یہاں CONT.]

یانا yā'nā N.M. a mere child

یاور yā'var N.M. helping ADJ. helping یاوری yā'varī N.F. help ; support یاوری کرنا yā'varī kar'nā V T (of fate) help [P]

یاوہ yā'vah ADJ. silly ; absurd nonsense vain ; futile یاوہ گو yā'va-go ADJ. & N.M. (one) who talks nonsense ; babbler ; chatterer یاوہ گوئی yā'va-go''ī N.F. babble silly talk nonsense یاوہ گوئی کرنا yā'va-go''ī kar'nā V.T. babble talk nonsense

یبوست yūboo'sat N.F. dryness costiveness [A]

یتامیٰ yatā'ma N.M. (PL. of یتیم N.M. ★)

یتیم yatīm' N.M. (PL. یتامیٰ yatā'mā) orphan ADJ. fatherless (child) matchless ; peerless یتیم خانہ yatīm'-khā'nah N.M. orphanage دُرِّ یتیم du(r)'re yatīm' N.M. peerless pearl یتیمی yatī'mī N.F. orphanhood ; orphanage

یثرب yas'rab N.M. Medinah

یجروید ya'jur ved N.M. one of the four Hindu scriptures ; Yajur Veda [S]

یحییٰ yah'ya N.M. John ; John the baptist [A ~ H]

یخ yakh N.F. ice ADJ. very cold یخ بستہ yakh-bas'tah ADJ. frozen یخدان yakh'-dān N.M. ice-box leather box [P]

یخنی yakh'nī N.F. soup یخنی پکانا (یا تیار کرنا) yakh'nī pakā'nā (or tay'yār kar'nā) V.T prepare soup [P]

ید yad N.M. (PL. ایدی ai'dī, ایادی ayā'dī) hand یداللہ yad-ullah' N.M. the hand of God ; God's protection یدِ بیضا ya'd-e baizā' N.M. luminous hand (as the miracle of Moses) یدِ طولیٰ ya'd-e too'lā N.M. skill ; dexterity یدِ طولیٰ رکھنا ya'd-e too'lā rakh'nā V.I. have great skill (in) [A]

یدھ yūdh N.M. battle [S]

یراق yarāq' N.M. arms accoutrements سازو یراق sā'z-o-yarāq' N.M. equipment for horse and knight [A]

یرغمال yarghamal' N.M. hostage [P]

یرقان yarqān' N.M. jaundice یرقان زدہ yarqan'-za'dah

ADJ. jaundiced [A]

یزداں *yaz'dān* N.M. God (rare) Zoroastrian god of goodness and light (as opposed to N.M. ★) یزدانی *yazdā'nī* ADJ. divine godly (person) [P]

یزک *ya'zak* N.M. army scouts group [T]

یزید *yazīd'* N.M. the second Omayyad caliph during whose regime the tragedy of Kerbala took place ; Yezid ungodly tyrant یزیدیت *yazīdiy'yat* N.F. ungodliness and oppression [A]

یسار *yasār'* N.M. left hand left wing (of army) ADJ. left یمین و یسار *yamī'n-o-yasār'* N.M. (see under یمین N.M. ★) [A]

یساول *yasā'vūl* N.M. herald [T]

یسر *yūs'r* N.M. affluence ; easy circumstances ease یسیر *yasīr'* ADJ. little easy [A]

یسوع *yasoo'* N.M. Jesus یسوعی *yasoo''ī* N.M. & ADJ. Jesuit [A]

یشب *yash'b* N.M. agate jasper [P]

یعسوب *ya'soob'* N.M. queen bee [A]

یعقوب *ya'qoob'* N.M. Jacob گریۂ یعقوب *gir'ya-e ya'qoob'* PH. Jacob's wailing [A ~ H]

یعنی *ya'nī* ADJ. that is to say ; namely ; videlicet ; 'viz.' [A he means]

یغما *yagh'mā* booty; spoils plunder; pillage خوان یغما *khā'n-e yagh mā* N.M. feast at which booty is divided یغماگر *yagh'mā-gar* N.M. plunderer sweetheart یغمائی *yaghmā''ī* N.M. plunderer ADJ. plundered [T]

یقین *yaqīn'* N.M. belief faith confidence trust assurance certainty definiteness positiveness unequivocal terms یقیناً *yaqī'nan* ADV. indeed certainly verify as a matter of fact definitely positively یقینی *yaqī'nī* ADJ. certain definite positive convincing یقینی ثبوت *yaqī'nī subooť* N.M. convincing proof definite proof [A]

یک *yak* ADJ. one single a ; an یک انار و صد بیمار *yak anā'r-o-sad bīmār'* PROV. one post and lots of candidates یکایک *ya'kā-yak* ADV. suddenly ; all of a sudden یکبارگی *yak-bā'ragī* ADV. suddenly ; all of a sudden ; at once with one supreme effort all together یک بام و دو ہوا *yak' bā'm-o-do havā* PROV. application of different sets of rules to identical cases یک پشتہ *yak-pūsh'tah* ADJ. (paper) یک بیک *yak' ba-yak'* ADV. suddenly ; all of a sudden یکتا *yak-tā* ADJ. singular ; unique incomparable یکتائی *yak-tā''ī* N.F. uniqueness یکتارا *yak-tā'rā* N.M (arch.) single stringed gustar kind of fine muslin یکجا *yak-jā'* ADV. together in one place یکجائی *yak-jā''ī* N.F. being together intercourse یک جان *yak-jān'* ADJ. & ADV. well-mixed یک جان دو قالب *yak jān' do qa'lab* PH. intimate friends یک جدی *yak-jad'dī* ADJ. collateral یک جہتی *yak-je'hatī* N.F. unanimity accord ; agreement singleness of purpose یک چشم *yak-chash'm* ADJ. blind of one eye یک در گیر و محکم گیر *yak' dar gī'r-o-moh'kam gīr* PH. stick to one thing a rolling stone gathers, no moss یک دستی *yak-das'tī* N.F. name of a wrestling trick یکدگر *yak'-di'gar* PRON. one another ; each other یکدل *yak-dil'* ADJ. unanimous agreed (on) acting in union یکدلی *yak-di'lī* N.F. unanimity accords ; agreement acting in unison یکراں *yak-rāń'* ADJ. & N.M. (rare) thoroughbred (horse) یکرخہ *yak-rū'khah* onesided partial single-phased یکرخی *yak-rū'khī* N.F. partiality (arch.) kind of bow ADJ. (also یکرنگ *yak-rang'*) ADJ. of one colour uniform sincere devoted to one purpose یکرنگی *yak-rań'gī* N.F. being of one colour uniformity sincerity devoted to one purpose یکروزہ *yak-ro'zah* ADJ. just for a day ephemeral ; transitory transient یک زبان *yak-zūbān'* (or *zūbān'*) ADJ. unanimous یک زبان ہو کر *yak-zūbāń' ho kar* ADV. with one voice (speak) all together یکساں *yaksān'* ADJ. uniform like ; alike similar conformable even ; level ; plain ADV. alike in the same manner uniformity یکسانی *yak'sā'nī* PROP. though ungrammatical یکسانیت *yaksāniy'yat* N.F. uniformity sameness being level conformity یکسار *yak-sar'* ADV. entirely all together یکسو *yak-soo'* ADJ. lying on one side settled ; peaceful undisturbed attentive یکسوئی *yak-soo''ī* N.F. full attention peace of mind devotion یکشنبہ *yak-sham'bah* N.M Sunday یکصد *yak-sad* ADJ. one hundred یک طرفہ *yak-ta'rafah* (col. -tar'fah) ADJ. partial 'ex-parte' (decision, decree, etc.) یک قلم yak-qa'lam ADV. entirely all together ; all at once یک لخت yak-lakh't ADV. suddenly ; all of a sudden یک مشت yak-mush't ADV (of payment) in lump sum یک من علم را دہ من عقل باید yak' man 'il'm rā dah' man 'aq'l bā'yad PROV. knowledge needs a lot of wisdom for its application یک منزلہ yak-man'zilah ADJ. one-storeyed ; single-storied single-decker (bus, etc.) یک نہ شد دو شد yak' na shūd do' shūd PROV. one misfortune on the heels of another [P]

یکم ya'kum N.F. first of the month [~P PREC.]

یکہ yak'kah ADJ. one solitary unique N.M. ace (at cards) (same as اکہ N.F.) a kind of dog-cart ; one-horse shay یکہ تاز yak'ka-tāz ADJ. (one) who fights alone brave : valiant یکہ وتنہا yak'ka-o-tanhā' ADJ. & ADV. all alone یکے yake N.M. someone یکے بعد دیگرے ya'ke ba''d-e di'gare PH. one after the other in quick succession [~P یک]

یگانگت yagān'gat N.F. kindred [~P یگانہ]

یگانہ yagā'nah ADJ. peerless ; unmatched ; unparallelled ; incomparable singular unique (rare) kindred یگانگی yagā'nagī N.F. (rare) uniqueness peeslessness kindred [P]

یل yal N.M. (rare) hero [P]

یلدا yaldā' N.M. winter's longest night ADJ. dark (night) شب یلدا shab-e yaldā' N.F. long dark night [A]

یلدرم yil'dirim (or yal'daram) N.M. (rare) lightning [T]

یلغار yalghār N.F. inroad ; incursion forced march (of army) [P]

یم[1] yam N.M. sea; ocean یم بہ یم yam' ba-yam PH. from sea to sea all over the oceans [P]

یم[2] yam N.M. (H. myth.) God of Hades یمدوت yam. doot' N.M. (H. myth.) angel of death [S]

یمن ya'man N.M. the Yemen; south-western corner of Arabia famed for its shawls, ruby and cornelian عقیق یمن 'aqī'q-e ya'man N.M. Yemenite cornelian لعل یمن la''l-e yaman N.M. Yemenite ruby یمنی yama'nī, یمانی yamā'nī ADJ. Yemenite بردیمانی bar'd-e yamā'nī N.F. Yemenite shawl [A]

یمن yumn N.M. good luck; felicity یمن وبرکت yum n-o ba'rakat N.M. felicity and blessing [A]

یمین yamīn' N.M. oath right hand right wing (of army) ADJ. & ADV. right یمین ویسار yamī'n o-yasār' N.M. right and left wings (of army right and left hand ADJ. & ADV. right and left [A]

یورپ yoo'rap N.M. Europe یورپ زدہ yoo'rap za'dah ADJ. Europeanized یورپ زدگی yoo'rap-za'dagī N.F. Europeanization یورپی yoo'rapī ADJ. European یورپین yoo'rapīn (coll. yoor'pīn) ADJ. European N.M. European Europeanized person

یوراج yūvrāj (ped. yu'varāj) N.M. (dial.) crown prince [S]

یو-ایس-اے yoo'-ais-e N.M. U.S.A. ; the United States of America ; the States [E]

یو-این yoo'-ain, یو-این-او yoo'-ain-o N.M. U.N. ; U.N.O.; United Nations; United Nations Organization [E]

یو-کے yoo'-ke N.M. U.K. ; United Kingdom [E]

یورش yoorish (ped. yū'rish) N.F. invasion [T]

یوسف yoo'sūf N.M. Joseph یوسف ثانی yoo'sūf-e sā'nī N.M. very beautiful person; another Joseph [A ~ H]

یوم yaum N.M. (PL. ایام ayyām') day (rare) battle یوم الحساب yau'm-al-hisāb' N.M. the day of reckoning ; the day of judgment یوم الحشر yaum-ul-hash'r N.M. day of resurrection یوماً فیوماً yau'man fa-yau'man ADJ. day-to-day ADV. from day to day یومیہ yaumiy'yah ADJ. daily N.M. daily wages daily allowance [A]

یوں yooṅ ADV. thus ; in this manner یونہی yooṅ'-hī ADV. thus ; in this manner by chance ; accidentally ; casually unintentionally cursorily easily causelessly ; without rhyme or reason without yielding anything یونہی سہی yoon-hi sa'hi PH. well will be seen you will get a tit for tat

یونان yoonan' N.M. Greece ; Hellas یونانی yoona'ni N.M. Greek indigenous system of medicine based on ancient Greek science ADJ. Greek ; Hellenic indigenous (medicine, etc.) طب یونانی tib'b-e yoona'ni N.F. indigenous system of medicine یونانی طبیب yoona'ni tabib' N.M. physician practising indigenous system of medicine [A ~ G Gonia]

یونس yoonus N.M. Jonah

یونین yoo'niyan N.F. union یونین جیک yoo'niyan jaik N.M. Union Jack یونین کمیٹی yoo'niyan kame'ti N.F. union committee یونین کونسل yoo'niyan kaun'sal N.F. union council ٹرید یونین tared' yoo'niyan N.F. trade union ٹریڈ یونینسٹ tared' yoo'nianist N.M. trade unionist ٹریڈ یونین تحریک tared' yoo'niyan taihrik N.F. trade unionism trade union movement [E]

یونیورسٹی yoonivaras'ti (ped. yoo'ni var'siti) university [E]

یونیورسل yoo'nivarsal ADJ. universal ; working on both A.C. and D.C. currents

یہ yeh ADJ. this these PRON. he she it they N.M. my husband N.F. my wife یہ بھی کوئی بات ہے ye bhi ko''i bat hai PH. that is absurd it is unacceptable it is not plausible that is nothing یہ بھی کسی نے نہ پوچھا تمہارے منہ میں کے دانت ہیں ye bhi ki'si ne na poo'chha tumha're munh men ka dant' hain PH. nobody cared a hang for him (etc.) no one ever looked to his (etc.) interests or comforts یہ بیل منڈھے چڑھتی نظر نہیں آتی ye bel man'dh charh'ti na'zar na'hin a'ti PH. it appears difficult of achievement یہ جا وہ جا ye' ja vo' ja PH. he went away be disappeared he left everyone behind یہ منہ اور مسور کی دال ye' munh aur masoor' ki dal PROV. caviare to the general you (etc.) do not deserve it یہ وہ نشہ نہیں جسے ترشی اتار دے ye vo nashah' na'hin ji'se tur'shi utar' de PH. it is not easy to grow out of this habit this enthusiasm cannot abate یہی ye'hi ADJ. this very the very same this one in particular even this

یہاں ya'han ADV here hither at (our) place in (our) country etc. یہاں تک ya'han tak ADV. up to this place thus for hitherto to this degree یہاں سے ya'han se ADV hence ; from this place یہاں کہیں ya'han kahin ADV somewhere here hereabouts

یہودی yahoo'di N M. (PL. یہود yahood') Jew یہود و نصاریٰ yahoo'd-o-nasa'ra N.M. PL. Jews

یہی ye'hi ADJ (see under ADJ. یہ)

یہیں ya'hin ADV. here in this very place یہیں کہیں ya'hin ka'hin ADV. hereabouts in this place somewhere here

ییلاق yilaq' N.M. (PL. ییلاقات yilaqat) (arch.) summer resort [T]

THE END

ختم شد